The Heath Guide to Literature

The Heath Guide to Literature

THIRD EDITION

David Bergman
Towson State University

Daniel Mark Epstein
Towson State University

D. C. HEATH AND COMPANY
Lexington, Massachusetts   Toronto

Address editorial correspondence to:

D. C. Heath
125 Spring Street
Lexington, MA 02173

Cover: *Prayers of a Blue Corn Mother,* by Helen Hardin, 1974. Photo © Cradoc
Bagshaw.

About the cover: Corn is fundamental to the Hopi and Pueblo Indians, in that it
provides the basis for their physical and spiritual life. The traditional Hopi and Pueblo
Indians believed that the corn they ate "built its flesh into their own"; from this belief
followed the idea that the corn was a mother to them. For these tribes the Corn
Mother is a source of life, along with Mother Earth; both are accorded spiritual
reverence.

Helen Hardin (1943–1984), whose mother was Native American, felt a strong sense
of kinship with tribal culture, and all her paintings express its heritage. She painted
from a sense of being an individual in the mainstream culture, but always
incorporated elements that expressed aspects of her dual heritage. Of her own work,
she said, "I really like abstract painting, but I like the spiritual element too. I think all
my paintings have to have something alive in them."

What makes Hardin's paintings, such as *Prayers of a Blue Corn Mother,* so dynamic
is the tension created by combining elements of her Native American heritage with
her personal emotions—emotions of pain, exhilaration, and anger resulting from a life
of deep internal conflict about her place in the world. Painting offered Hardin a way
to integrate the incompatible aspects of her selfhood, reflecting her urgent need to
confine and control the disparate aspects of the world as she perceived it.

For permission to use copyrighted material, grateful acknowledgment is made to the
copyright holders listed on pages 1513–19, which are hereby considered an extension
of this copyright page.

Published simultaneously in Canada.

Printed in the United States of America.

International Standard Book Number: 0–669–20592–3

Library of Congress Catalog Number: 91–70286

10 9 8 7 6 5 4 3 2 1

Preface

To the Student

This book is a record of the bond between writers of literature and their readers. This is a special bond that stretches across time and space and unites people of very different cultures and experiences. But most writers have a sense of people somewhere out there taking pleasure in what they produce, people whom they can affect with nothing more direct than the written word. As writers, we have enjoyed hearing from our readers, knowing that we have connected with men and women whom we have not met, people who in many ways are so very different from us, but who share with us a delight in the imagination and a passion for language. Perhaps writers value their bond with readers because we all start out as readers.

Like most bonds, the one between writers and readers has its difficulties, disappointments, and frustrations as well as its delights and pleasures. An African proverb says: "It is difficult to make friends with an elephant." The proverb means that it is difficult to accommodate people or things of great power. An elephant that can be such a help to people—carrying them long distances and bearing great weights—can just as easily crush its keeper. Literature can be a great help as well—expressing emotions we could never articulate, teaching us lessons we would otherwise not learn, providing us with experiences too dangerous or unpleasant to get first hand. But it can also upset, confuse, bore, and disgust us. What we should not do is ignore literature, just as we should not ignore an elephant, especially if one is close at hand.

This book places in your hands a great variety of literature, some of which we hope you will enjoy. Because tastes and experiences vary, few will take pleasure equally from all the stories, poems, and plays in this volume, nor do we believe that all the works in the book are equally good. What we *do* believe is that they are all worth reading. To help you appreciate the literature in the book as much as you can we have provided notes to give you some background, questions to focus your thoughts, and in each chapter statements by writers about the art of writing.

Classics and Cultural Diversity

The word "classic" is used to describe a work that has been read and admired by many people for a long time. Many of the works in this book—the plays of Shakespeare and Sophocles, the poems of Milton and Dickinson, the stories of Eudora Welty and James Joyce—have achieved classic status. But there are works too new to have become classics and whose virtues may not be so widely accepted or so deeply admired. Yet these works can reward our attention because they speak to our experiences or provide access to experiences very different from our own. We have included a number of these works as well. Our literature is remarkably diverse, as diverse as the many peoples who inhabit this country and this planet. While this book cannot embody the staggering variety of cultural experience, it does try to provide a sense of the scope of our literary heritage. Thus to the more traditional offerings of European and Anglophone literature, we have added works from Asia, Africa, and South America, as well as works by Native American, Latino and Chicano, African-American, Asian-American, Jewish-American, and Irish-American writers.

We have also provided you with fairly detailed discussions of literary technique written so that you can understand these concepts on your own. We have tried to help you understand literary terminology, and at the close of the book there is a glossary of terms to help you.

Writing about Literature

Often this book is used in classes in which students are expected to write essays, exams, and reviews of these works or on productions based on these works. We have tried to help you in many ways to become better writers. First, we have developed for this edition a new introductory section that takes you step-by-step through the writing process, giving you pointers about how to read for a writing exercise, how to come up with ideas, how to organize those ideas once you get them, and how to express them so that they are clear and effective. The advice we give is based on our long experience as readers, writers, and teachers. We have also provided several student and professional writing samples for you to use as models. In addition, in the sections on fiction, poetry, and drama, there are individual chapters geared to the special critical demands of the genre. Moreover, we have sprinkled through the entire book hints to help you read and write better. Of course, no discussion of how to write can alone make you a good writer, but we believe that our approach will give you the basics and help you improve your skills.

We recommend that you look through the table of contents and then through the entire book and note all the features we have provided to help you. We have tried to anticipate your needs, questions, and uncertainties by providing a rich array of material to support you in the exciting, pleasurable, but often challenging job of reading and writing about literature.

To the Instructor

When we were undergraduates at Kenyon College, we were fortunate enough to study literature with several inspired teachers. The pedagogic atmosphere was still suffused with the New Criticism of John Crowe Ransom (who lived nearby), I. A. Richards, and William Empson. We learned to analyze syntax with reverent calculation and to sift stories and sonnets for metaphysical irony and ambiguity. We learned, in short, to read carefully, to pay attention to the text. But the text itself remained immortal and as aloof from the humble reader (and the author, strangely enough) as the *Book of Job* or the nearly anonymous plays of Shakespeare. Insofar as the study of literature might partake of the exactitude of the sciences, it should. Insofar as it seemed imprecise, this could only betray the inadequacy of our critical instruments.

Yet our teachers were inspired, and inspiration kept jamming those critical instruments. Analyzing a verse paragraph of *Paradise Lost,* our Milton scholar would begin ranting and railing along with Satan; the Donne scholar in reading a love poem showed subtle signs of rather unscholarly enthusiasm; the Conrad expert reciting Kurtz's lines, "the horror, the horror," became truly, unconcealably horrified. And so were we. The literature was obviously a living part of us, and would not lie still upon the examining table while we probed it.

It was then that we realized the study of literature is a passion rather than a discipline. The discipline, too, has its place: the reader must learn to read carefully and critically, must acquire certain tools—but only in the service of human curiosity and sympathy, the desire to hear what a writer has to say. Our teachers began and ended with the text, presuming its acknowledged greatness would compel our attention. We, as teachers, begin with ourselves as readers, passionate readers, and try to communicate our enthusiasms to our students. If we are successful, then our students are motivated, as we were, to obtain the tools of analysis this book has to offer.

Our teachers sometimes neglected the historical contexts of literary works, assuming quite sensibly that everyone who has lived for the past three thousand years is our contemporary. Yet one cannot explain Hamlet's delay without reference to the Renaissance education of noblemen. Nor can one know exactly how rash was Oedipus's murder of three travelers without referring to ancient Greek standards of aristocratic conduct and honor. Although this text does not pretend to be a thorough historical study of literature, we have an eye to history and try to locate works within a historical framework.

We have striven to present authors as human beings, for the most part with normal human concerns, rather than as gods or unworldly eccentrics. The numerous photographs should be helpful in establishing the intimacy between writers and readers we consider so important. Students who have become particularly interested in one author may find it fascinating to see how he or she uses different genres. So we have included both poems and stories by D. H. Lawrence, Stephen Crane, Herman Melville, James Joyce, and Alice Walker.

When students first begin reading serious literature, they often have difficulty because they have not learned how to experience certain literary conventions. They do not know what authors expect of them. For example, many inexperienced readers of stories approach fictional settings as mere filler-facts one may freely ignore. They do not realize that such passages usually have psychological, sociological, or symbolic significance. This book differs from other introductory texts in being explicit about author-reader conventions, helping students develop the reading conventions necessary to a full appreciation of literature.

In making our selections we have provided for a vast range of student abilities and classroom situations. In fact, any number of different courses may be taught with these materials, from advanced-placement high school literature to a high-powered college course, without leaving the students baffled or bored. Generally, each chapter begins with a selection that is classic in its simplicity and ends with several that are sophisticated, inexhaustible. The same pattern applies to the questions following a selection: the first questions concern factual information; the last are frequently open-ended. You should find more than enough material to engage and challenge students whatever their level of preparation, and we encourage you to experiment in choosing assignments.

This edition is about the same size as the previous one. We have taken out only what readers from all over the country told us was unnecessary or repetitious and have added what will broaden the literary and cultural perspectives of this collection. The selections are broader and more up-to-date, but still retain the balance between classic works students of literature should know and newer, exciting works that may become classics in the future. In this edition we have included for the first time

- short stories by Julio Cortázar, Hisaye Yamamoto, Estela Portillo Trambley, Ethan Canin, Ann Beattie, Louise Erdrich, Zora Neale Hurston, and Robert Stone;
- poems by Claude McKay, Charlotte Mew, Louis Omar Salinas, Kimiko Hahn, Fray Angelico Chavez, Emanuel di Pasquale, Margaret Danner, Mary TallMountain, Elizabeth Bishop, Gregory Corso, Aphra Behn, Elinor Wylie, James Welch, Alberto Ríos, Lisel Mueller, Jim Mitsui, Cathy Song, Gail N. Harada, and Gary Soto;
- plays by Luis M. Valdez, David Henry Hwang, Jane Bowles, and Ed Bullins. We hope we have included a few new surprises since the last edition, as well as a fuller representation of the many cultures contributing their voices to English-language literature.

The Instructor's Manual contains discussion of important thematic and technical aspects of each work, teaching suggestions, and selected bibliographies.

We are grateful to the many people who have helped us in the preparation of this book. It certainly would not have come to be written without the help of Gordon Lester-Massman, Paul Smith, Holt Johnson, and Linda Bieze. Linda Vlasak, Sylvia Mallory, and Janice Molloy helped us improve the style. We wish to thank Charles Haller, Jennifer Isaacs, Helen Jones, and Jane Rosenthal, who typed the manuscript and further advised us on style. Diskin Clay, Thomas Curley, Richard Howard, Hugh Kenner, David St. John, and Richard Wilbur graciously answered our questions. Elaine Hedges and Donald H. Craver shared their knowledge and experience, as did John E. Connolly and the research staffs of the Albert S. Cook Library and the Milton S. Eisenhower Library. We wish to thank John Irwin, Mary Camerer, and Dorothy De Witt for their many kindnesses during the preparation of the manuscript. We are also grateful to the Township of Heath, Massachusetts, for providing working space, to Johanna Ruth Epstein and Madeleine Irvine for help in organization and proofreading, and to Wendy Roberts for advice and support.

The following instructors provided detailed, indispensable advice: Lou-Ann Crouther, Western Kentucky University; Doug Garrison, College of the Desert; Frank Moon, Kellogg Community College; J. A. (Dermot) O'Dwyer, Hancock College; Arthrell Sanders, North Carolina Central University; and Emma Joahanne Thomas, Prairie View A&M University.

The following individuals also generously helped us with their suggestions: David Allen, Citadel Military College of South Carolina; Chris Antonides, Lansing Community College; Melinda Barth, El Camino College; Tom Barthel, Herkimer County Community College; John Bassett, North Carolina State University; Thomas Beverage, Coastal Carolina Community College; Alan Bickford, Macon Junior College; Peter Brier, California State–Los Angeles; Dorothy Brown, Macon Junior College; Jerald Butler, San Diego State University; Alice Carter, Ohio State University, Columbus; Robert Cosgrove, Saddleback College; Joan Doggrell, Clark County Community College; Richard Dowell, Indiana State University; Janice Edens, Macon Junior College; Alan Ehmann, University of Texas, El Paso; Gaye Elder, Abraham Baldwin Agricultural College; Toni Empringham, El Camino College; Adam Fischer, Coastal Carolina Community College; Patricia Lane Fountain, Coastal Carolina Community College; John Freeman, El Paso Community College; Leon Gatlin, University of North Carolina, Charlotte; Ernest Giordani, Broome Community College; Harriet Herlihy, Glendale Community College; David Hilton, Anne Arundel Community College; James Hines, Saddleback College; Eugene Hollahan, Georgia State University; Vicki Holmsten, San Juan College; Donald Holroyd, York College of Pennsylvania; Ralph D. Howell, Mississippi College, Clinton; Leon Jacobson, Lake City Community College; Ejner Jensen, University of Michigan, Ann Arbor; Gloria John, Catonsville Community College; Yvonne Jones, Shelby State Community College; Michael Joyce, Jackson Community College; Andrew Kelly, Shelby State Community College; Judy Kidd, North Carolina State University; Paulino Lim, California State University, Long

Beach; Amy Ling, University of Wisconsin–Madison; Joyce Lipkis, Santa Monica College; Steve Liu, Clark County Community College; Emery Maiden, Appalachian State University; Bill Martin, Armstrong State College; Robert McCoy, Kent State University; Tom McDermott, Southern Connecticut State University; Gayle Miller, University of Georgia; Terry Miller, Indian River Community College; Larry Mobley, Macon Junior College; Mariel Morison, University of California–Davis; Chadyeane Neuman, Prince George's Community College; Robin Olsen, University of California–Davis; Douglas A. Pearson, Jr., University of Wisconsin, Eau Claire; Les Perelman, Massachusetts Institute of Technology; William Pierce, Prince George's Community College; David Piwinski, Herkimer County Community College; Nancy Posselt, Midland Technical College; Richard Raymond, Armstrong State College; Phyllis Read, Bronx Community College–CUNY; Douglas Rose, SUNY A&T State University; Arthrell Sanders, North Carolina Central University; Virginia Schilt, Mt. San Antonio College; George Scott, Abraham Baldwin Agricultural College; Rebecca Sears, Okaloosa-Walton Community College; Jack Selzer, Pennsylvania State University; William Silver, Evergreen Valley College; Robert Tapply, Fitchburg State College; Ethel Taylor, North Carolina A&T State University; J. Chesley Taylor, Washington State University; Anne Thomas, San Jacinto College; Dennis Thompson, Macomb Community College; Jean Turner, Anne Arundel Community College; Gilbert Vaughan, Wayne State College; Thomas Waldrep, University of South Carolina; Michael Weiser, University of North Carolina–Charlotte; Barclay M. Wheeler, Evergreen Valley College; and Johnnie Williams, DeKalb College.

Finally we must acknowledge many students who, by their excitement, confusion, understanding, and impatience, have led us to improve ourselves as teachers and to grow as individuals.

David Bergman

Daniel Mark Epstein

Topical Contents

WRITING ABOUT LITERATURE

1 Writing and Interpretation   3

The Pleasures of Language • What Is an Interpretation? • Interpreting Language • Different Kinds of Criticism • How Do You Go about Interpreting a Text? • The Limits of Interpretation • Five Criteria for Acceptable Interpretations • Supporting an Interpretation • Conclusion

2 The Writing Process   14

Attitude and Experience • Fear of Writing • Step One: Getting the Assignment • Step Two: Reading • Step Three: Preliminary Thinking • Step Four: Research • Step Five: Mapping Your Way • Step Six: Writing the First Draft • Step Seven: Rewriting • Step Eight: The Final Version • Conclusions

3 Structure, Style, and Mechanics   26

Audience • Having a Point • Formulating a Thesis • Ways to Develop a Thesis • Developing the Comparison Thesis • Developing the Character Analysis • Developing a Historical Thesis • Choosing Supporting Material • Biographical Material • Organizing the Essay • Introductions • Conclusions • Body Paragraphs • Quotations • Documentation • Bibliographies

4 Nine Short Essays   50

FICTION

1 The Worlds of Fiction   75

Fictional Representation • The Fictional World and the Real World • Fictional Conventions • The Variety of Fictional Worlds • The Lessons of Fiction

2 Writing about Fiction: A Case Study   93

Talking to Your Teachers • Starting to Work • Narrowing Things Down • Re-readings • Talking with Friends • Starting Work in the Library • Freewriting—Getting Your Ideas Out • Outlines—The Map of the Paper • Writing the Essay • Reexamining Sally's Essay

3 Our Seat on the Action—Narration   116

Basic Narrative Types • An Omniscient Narration • The First-Person Narrative • Narrative Point-of-View • Limited Third-Person Narratives • Stories without Narrators

4 Unreliable Narrators—Don't Believe Everything You Hear   145

How to Determine a Narrator's Unreliability • Irony in Unreliable Narrations • Authors' and Narrators' Points-of-View

5 The Pattern of Action—Plot   167

Choosing Action to Narrate • The Ordering of Events • Surprise • Suspense • Flashbacks and Foreshadowing • Conflict • Narrative Stages • Twists and Frames • Stories with Frames • Reading the Frame Story • Stories with a Twist • Good and Bad Twist Endings • Reading the Twist Ending

6 Characters   228

Flat Characters • The Character as Literary Form • Round Characters • Motivation • Consistency of Actions • Reading for Character • Heroes and Villains

7 Setting the Scene   250

Reading for Setting • Setting as Social Indicator • Settings that Reveal Character • Symbolic Settings • Time Settings • Clothing • Summary

8 **Symbols**   282

Traditional Symbols • Representative Symbols • Levels of Symbolic Meaning • Reading Symbols

9 **What Happens between Stories**   303

Stories by a Single Author • Development, Maturity, and Decline • Theme • How to Discover the Theme • Influence • Nathaniel Hawthorne • Isaac Babel and Doris Lessing • Anne Tyler and John Updike

10 **The Novella**   349

Length • Expansion and Compression • Structure • Summary

11 **Good and Great Fiction**   381

Checklist of Questions for Evaluating Fiction • Personal Preference and Excellence • Narrative Conventions • Plot • Character • Setting • Style • Perfection • Sinclair Lewis and Anton Chekhov

12 **Stories for Further Reading**   405

POETRY

1 **The Definition of Poetry**   519

2 **Writing about Poetry: The In-Class Explication**   526

Read the Instructions • Reading the Poem • The Short Outline • Writing in Class

3 **Listening in on the Poem**   539

The Persona and the Poet • The Importance of Context • The Poet as Speaker

4 **Narrative Poetry: The Poet as Storyteller**   545

Formulae • Transitions in Narrative Poetry • Epic Poetry • Personal History in Narrative Poems • Use of Language in Narrative Poetry • Poems for Further Study

5 Lyric Poetry: The Solitary Singer   566

The Love Poem • Curses • Poems of Praise, Poems for the Dead • Elegy • The Meditative Poem • Poems for Further Study

6 Dramatic Poetry: The Poet as Actor   591

The Soliloquy • The Epistolary Monologue • Poetic Dialogues • The Posthumous Monologue • Poems for Further Study

7 Images: Seeing Is Feeling   614

Haiku • Combining Images • Synesthesia • Images and Commentary • Landscapes • Meanings of Words • Surrealistic Imagery • Poems for Further Study

8 The Dance of the Mind: Metaphor and Simile   635

The Metaphor • The Simile • The Conceit • Poems for Further Study

9 The Idea Dresses Up: Personification, Allegory, Symbol   654

Personification • Allegory • Fable • Symbol • Poems for Further Study

10 More Figures of Speech   675

Hyperbole • Understatement • Synecdoche, Metonymy, Allusion, and Paradox • Poems for Further Study

11 The Music of Poetry   692

Rhythm • Accent and Emphasis • Meter • The Line and Line Endings • Syllabic Verse • Rhyme • Alliteration and Assonance • Vowel Tones • Songs

12 Tones of Voice   723

The Range of Tones • Irony • Didactic Poetry • Toughness • The Comic Tone • Diction Levels • Dialects

13 The Poem's Shape   741

The Structure of Free Verse • Some Traditional English Forms • Italian Forms • French Forms • Classic Forms • Asian Forms • Comic Forms • Shaped Verses and Concrete Poetry

14 The Well-Made Poem   772

Overall Effectiveness • Economy • Coherence and Consistency • Naturalness • Tone: Sentimentality and Coldness • Completeness • The Good and the Great • Checklist of Questions for Evaluating Poetry

15 Poems for Further Reading   808

Poems about Death • Poems about Families

DRAMA

1 Literature Onstage   895

Dramatic Action • The Audience • The Playwright as Collaborator

2 The Script—How to Read a Play   899

Genre and Length • The Characters • The Scene • The Action

3 Writing about Drama: The Review   914

Why Review? • Preparations • Taking Notes • Beginning a Review • The Middle and Conclusion of a Review • Supporting Detail

4 Action   929

The Dramatic Situation • The Plot • Exposition • The Rising Action • The Climax • The Falling Action • Catastrophe and Denouement • Greek Drama and *Oedipus Rex*

5 Heroes and Heroines—Dramatic Character   976

Virtues and Flaws • Heroes, Heroines, Villains, and Others • Actions and Words • Dramatic Diction and Character • A Drama of Characters: *The Glass Menagerie*

6 Tragedy   1026

Fear and Pity • Recognition and Reversal • Catharsis • The Tragic Hero • Shakespeare and the Elizabethan Theater • *Desire Under the Elms*—An American Tragedy • Eugene O'Neill—The First American Tragedian

7 Comedy   1187

High and Low Comedy • Romantic Comedy • *The Importance of Being Earnest* • Satire • *Los Vendidos* (The Salesmen) • Tragicomedy • *Twelfth Night*

8 The Rise of Realism   1316

Social Realism • *A Doll's House* • The Drama of Catastrophe • Realism in America

9 New Directions   1427

Symbolist Drama • *The Sound of a Voice* • *A Quarreling Pair* • American Gothic—*Crimes of the Heart* • New Directions in Staging: *A Son, Come Home*

Glossary of Literary Terms 1501

Acknowledgments 1513

Index of First Lines 1521

Index of Authors and Titles 1531

Contents

WRITING ABOUT LITERATURE

1 Writing and Interpretation   3

THE PLEASURES OF LANGUAGE   3
WHAT IS AN INTERPRETATION?   5
INTERPRETING LANGUAGE   5
DIFFERENT KINDS OF CRITICISM   6
HOW DO YOU GO ABOUT INTERPRETING A TEXT?   7
THE LIMITS OF INTERPRETATION   8
FIVE CRITERIA FOR ACCEPTABLE INTERPRETATIONS   9
SUPPORTING AN INTERPRETATION   10
CONCLUSION   13

2 The Writing Process   14

ATTITUDE AND EXPERIENCE   14
FEAR OF WRITING   15
STEP ONE: GETTING THE ASSIGNMENT   17
STEP TWO: READING   18
STEP THREE: PRELIMINARY THINKING   20
STEP FOUR: RESEARCH   21
STEP FIVE: MAPPING YOUR WAY   22
STEP SIX: WRITING THE FIRST DRAFT   23
STEP SEVEN: REWRITING   24
STEP EIGHT: THE FINAL VERSION   25
CONCLUSIONS   25

3 Structure, Style, and Mechanics   26

AUDIENCE   26
HAVING A POINT   28

FORMULATING A THESIS   28
WAYS TO DEVELOP A THESIS   30
DEVELOPING THE COMPARISON THESIS   31
DEVELOPING THE CHARACTER ANALYSIS   32
DEVELOPING A HISTORICAL THESIS   34
CHOOSING SUPPORTING MATERIAL   34
BIOGRAPHICAL MATERIAL   36
ORGANIZING THE ESSAY   37
INTRODUCTIONS   38
CONCLUSIONS   39
BODY PARAGRAPHS   40
QUOTATIONS   40
DOCUMENTATION   42
BIBLIOGRAPHIES   44

4 Nine Short Essays   50

ALICE HALL PETRY, *Faulkner's "A Rose for Emily"*   51
ERNEST W. SULLIVAN, II, *The Cur in "The Chrysanthemums"*   53
DAVID MATTHEW ROSEN, *Time, Identity, and Context in Wyatt's Verse*   56
PETER B. CLARKE, *Frost's "Mending Wall"*   58
ELEANOR LESTER, *"Skunk Hour": An Explication*   60
ALLISON CHANG, *"Sadie and Maud"*   63
JOHN LESSNER, *Hamlet and the Gravedigger*   66
LESLIE MILLER, *O'Hara's Conversation with the Sun*   68
BRENDA PISKOR, *Jim O'Connor in Tennessee Williams's* The Glass Menagerie: *Seized by the Moment*   70

FICTION

1 The Worlds of Fiction   75

FICTIONAL REPRESENTATION   76
THE FICTIONAL WORLD AND THE REAL WORLD   77
FICTIONAL CONVENTIONS   78
THE VARIETY OF FICTIONAL WORLDS   79
THE LESSONS OF FICTION   79

ITALO CALVINO, *The Canary Prince*   81
Writers on Writing—Calvino   85
GIOVANNI BOCCACCIO, *A Dinner of Hens*   86
JEAN RHYS, *I Used to Live Here Once*   87
MAXINE HONG KINGSTON, *On Mortality*   88
JULIO CORTÁZAR, *Continuity of Parks*   91

2 Writing about Fiction: A Case Study   93

TALKING TO YOUR TEACHERS   93
STARTING TO WORK   95
NARROWING THINGS DOWN   95
RE-READINGS   96
TALKING WITH FRIENDS   97
STARTING WORK IN THE LIBRARY   99
FREEWRITING—GETTING YOUR IDEAS OUT   102
OUTLINES—THE MAP OF THE PAPER   103
WRITING THE ESSAY   105
REEXAMINING SALLY'S ESSAY   111

3 Our Seat on the Action—Narration   116

BASIC NARRATIVE TYPES   116
AN OMNISCIENT NARRATION   117
THE FIRST-PERSON NARRATIVE   117

RAYMOND QUENEAU, From *Exercises in Style*   118

NARRATIVE POINT-OF-VIEW   119
LIMITED THIRD-PERSON NARRATIVES   120
STORIES WITHOUT NARRATORS   121

TONI CADE BAMBARA, *My Man Bovanne*   121
Writers on Writing—Bambara   126
MARGARET ATWOOD, *Giving Birth*   126
V.S. NAIPAUL, *The Night Watchman's Occurrence Book*   137

4 Unreliable Narrators—Don't Believe Everything You Hear   145

HOW TO DETERMINE A NARRATOR'S UNRELIABILITY   145
IRONY IN UNRELIABLE NARRATIONS   146
AUTHORS' AND NARRATORS' POINTS-OF-VIEW   147

CHARLOTTE PERKINS GILMAN, *The Yellow Wall-Paper*   148
EDGAR ALLAN POE, *The Cask of Amontillado*   160
Writers on Writing—Poe   166

5 The Pattern of Action—Plot   167

CHOOSING ACTION TO NARRATE   167
THE ORDERING OF EVENTS   169
SURPRISE   169
SUSPENSE   170
FLASHBACKS AND FORESHADOWING   170
CONFLICT   171
NARRATIVE STAGES   171

TWISTS AND FRAMES 172
STORIES WITH FRAMES 172
READING THE FRAME STORY 172
STORIES WITH A TWIST 173
GOOD AND BAD TWIST ENDINGS 174
READING THE TWIST ENDING 174

ARTHUR CONAN DOYLE, *The Adventure of the Speckled Band* 175
HISAYE YAMAMOTO, *Seventeen Syllables* 193
D.H. LAWRENCE, *The Horse Dealer's Daughter* 203
GRACE PALEY, *A Conversation with My Father* 215
ALICE WALKER, *Everyday Use* 219
Writers on Writing—Walker 227

6 Characters 228

FLAT CHARACTERS 229
THE CHARACTER AS LITERARY FORM 229

ELIAS CANETTI, *The Earwitness* 230

ROUND CHARACTERS 231
MOTIVATION 231
CONSISTENCY OF ACTIONS 232
READING FOR CHARACTER 233
HEROES AND VILLAINS 234

KATHERINE ANNE PORTER, *The Jilting of Granny Weatherall* 235
Writers on Writing—Porter 242
ESTELA PORTILLO TRAMBLEY, *The Burning* 243

7 Setting the Scene 250

READING FOR SETTING 251
SETTING AS SOCIAL INDICATOR 252
SETTINGS THAT REVEAL CHARACTER 252
SYMBOLIC SETTINGS 253
TIME SETTINGS 254
CLOTHING 255
SUMMARY 255

BOBBIE ANNE MASON, *Shiloh* 255
JAMES JOYCE, *Araby* 267
Writers on Writing—Hemingway 272
ETHAN CANIN, *Emperor of the Air* 272

8 Symbols 282

TRADITIONAL SYMBOLS 283
REPRESENTATIVE SYMBOLS 283

LEVELS OF SYMBOLIC MEANING   283
READING SYMBOLS   284

BERNARD MALAMUD, *The Jewbird*   286
Writers on Writing—Malamud   293
GABRIEL GARCÍA MÁRQUEZ, *A Very Old Man with Enormous Wings*   293
ANN BEATTIE, *Janus*   299

9 What Happens between Stories   303

STORIES BY A SINGLE AUTHOR   303
DEVELOPMENT, MATURITY, AND DECLINE   304
THEME   304
HOW TO DISCOVER THE THEME   305
INFLUENCE   306
NATHANIEL HAWTHORNE   307
ISAAC BABEL AND DORIS LESSING   307
ANNE TYLER AND JOHN UPDIKE   308

NATHANIEL HAWTHORNE, *The Minister's Black Veil*   308
NATHANIEL HAWTHORNE, *Young Goodman Brown*   318
ISAAC BABEL, *My First Goose*   328
DORIS LESSING, *Homage for Isaac Babel*   331
Writers on Writing—Atwood   334
ANNE TYLER, *The Artificial Family*   334
JOHN UPDIKE, *Separating*   340

10 The Novella   349

LENGTH   350
EXPANSION AND COMPRESSION   350
STRUCTURE   351
SUMMARY   352

Writers on Writing—Melville   353
HERMAN MELVILLE, *Bartleby the Scrivener*   353

11 Good and Great Fiction   381

CHECKLIST OF QUESTIONS FOR EVALUATING FICTION   381
PERSONAL PREFERENCE AND EXCELLENCE   382
NARRATIVE CONVENTIONS   383
PLOT   384
CHARACTER   384
SETTING   385
STYLE   385
PERFECTION   386
Writers on Writing—Forster   386
Sinclair Lewis and Anton Chekhov   386

SINCLAIR LEWIS, *Virga Vay and Allan Cedar*   386
ANTON CHEKHOV, *Lady with Lapdog*   392

12 Stories for Further Reading   405

JAMES BALDWIN, *Sonny's Blues*   405
STEPHEN CRANE, *The Bride Comes to Yellow Sky*   429
LOUISE ERDRICH, *The Red Convertible*   437
WILLIAM FAULKNER, *A Rose for Emily*   445
Writers on Writing—Faulkner   451
ERNEST HEMINGWAY, *Hills Like White Elephants*   452
ZORA NEALE HURSTON, *Sweat*   455
FRANZ KAFKA, *A Hunger Artist*   464
FLANNERY O'CONNOR, *Everything That Rises Must Converge*   470
JOHN STEINBECK, *The Chrysanthemums*   481
ROBERT STONE, *Helping*   489
EUDORA WELTY, *A Worn Path*   510

POETRY

1 The Definition of Poetry   519

JAMES WRIGHT, *A Blessing*   520
EMILY DICKINSON, *I Felt a Funeral in My Brain*   521
CHRISTOPHER MARLOWE, *The Passionate Shepherd to His Love*   523
THEODORE ROETHKE, *The Lady and the Bear*   524
Writers on Writing—Dickinson   525

2 Writing about Poetry: The In-Class Explication   526

READ THE INSTRUCTIONS   526
READING THE POEM   527
THE SHORT OUTLINE   528
WRITING IN CLASS   529

3 Listening in on the Poem   539

WALTER SAVAGE LANDOR, *Mother, I Cannot Mind My Wheel*   539

THE PERSONA AND THE POET   540

LINDA PASTAN, *25th High School Reunion*   540

THE IMPORTANCE OF CONTEXT   542

W.H. AUDEN, *Musée des Beaux Arts*   542

THE POET AS SPEAKER 543

BEN JONSON, *On My First Son* 543
Writers on Writing—Spender 544

4 Narrative Poetry: The Poet as Storyteller 545

FORMULAE 545

ANONYMOUS, *Sir Patrick Spence* 546

TRANSITIONS IN NARRATIVE POETRY 547

LANGSTON HUGHES, *Sylvester's Dying Bed* 548

EPIC POETRY 549
PERSONAL HISTORY IN NARRATIVE POEMS 549

EDWARD FIELD, *My Polish Grandmother* 550

USE OF LANGUAGE IN NARRATIVE POETRY 551

DANIEL MARK EPSTEIN, *Madonna (with Child Missing)* 551

POEMS FOR FURTHER STUDY 552

DUDLEY RANDALL, *Ballad of Birmingham* 552
ROBERT FROST, *'Out, Out—'* 553
SHARON OLDS, *The Race* 554
EDGAR ALLAN POE, *The Raven* 555
Writers on Writing—Pound 558
HOMER, from the *Odyssey* 558
DANTE ALIGHIERI, *Ulysses' Speech* from *Inferno* (Canto XXVI) 564

5 Lyric Poetry: The Solitary Singer 566

CATULLUS, *LXXXV* 566

THE LOVE POEM 566

WILLIAM BUTLER YEATS, *He Wishes for the Cloths of Heaven* 566
H.D. (HILDA DOOLITTLE), *Never More Will the Wind* 568
WILLIAM SHAKESPEARE, *When, in Disgrace with Fortune and Men's Eyes* 568
ANDREW MARVELL, *To His Coy Mistress* 569

CURSES 570

ARCHILOCHUS, *May He Lose His Way on the Cold Sea* 570

POEMS OF PRAISE, POEMS FOR THE DEAD 571

WILLIAM WORDSWORTH, *The Solitary Reaper* 571
CLAUDE MCKAY, *The Harlem Dancer* 572
GERARD MANLEY HOPKINS, *Pied Beauty* 573
CHRISTOPHER SMART, *For I Will Consider My Cat Jeoffrey*, From *Jubilate Agno* 574

ELEGY   575

THEODORE ROETHKE, *Elegy for Jane*   575
MARGARET WALKER, *For Malcolm X*   576
ALFRED, LORD TENNYSON, *Dark House, by Which Once More I Stand*   576
A.E. HOUSMAN, *To an Athlete Dying Young*   577
W.H. AUDEN, *In Memory of W.B. Yeats*   578
Writers on Writing—Auden   580

THE MEDITATIVE POEM   580

OMAR KHAYYAM, *XXVI* and *XXVII*, the *Rubaiyat*   581
JOHN MILTON, *When I Consider How My Light Is Spent*   582
ROBERT FROST, *Fire and Ice*   582
JOHN KEATS, *Ode on a Grecian Urn*   583

POEMS FOR FURTHER STUDY   583

E.E. CUMMINGS, *somewhere i have never travelled, gladly beyond*   585
CESARE PAVESE, *Encounter*   586
SYLVIA PLATH, *Daddy*   587
JOHN CROWE RANSOM, *Here Lies a Lady*   589
WILLIAM BLAKE, *To See a World in a Grain of Sand*   589
IMAMU AMIRI BARAKA (LEROI JONES), *Preface to a Twenty Volume Suicide Note*   589

6   Dramatic Poetry: The Poet as Actor   591

THE SOLILOQUY   591

WILLIAM CARLOS WILLIAMS, *The Widow's Lament in Springtime*   591
ROBERT BROWNING, *Porphyria's Lover*   593
WILLIAM BLAKE, *The Little Vagabond*   594
ANNE SEXTON, *Unknown Girl in the Maternity Ward*   595
ALFRED, LORD TENNYSON, *Ulysses*   597

THE EPISTOLARY MONOLOGUE   599

RIHAKU (POUND), *The River Merchant's Wife, A Letter*   600
EDWARD HIRSCH, *The River Merchant: A Letter Home*   601

POETIC DIALOGUES   601

JOHN CROWE RANSOM, *Piazza Piece*   602
Writers on Writing—Jarrell   603

THE POSTHUMOUS MONOLOGUE   603

RANDALL JARRELL, *The Death of the Ball Turret Gunner*   604
EDGAR LEE MASTERS, *Fiddler Jones*   604

POEMS FOR FURTHER STUDY   605

WILLIAM BUTLER YEATS, *An Irish Airman Foresees His Death*   605
ROBERT BROWNING, *My Last Duchess*   606
MICHAEL HARPER, *A Mother Speaks: The Algiers Motel Incident, Detroit*   607

FRANK O'HARA, *A True Account of Talking to the Sun at Fire Island* 608
CHARLOTTE MEW, *The Farmer's Bride* 610
PETER KLAPPERT, *Mail at Your New Address* 611
LOUISE ERDRICH, *Windigo* 612
LOUIS OMAR SALINAS, *In a Farmhouse* 612

7 Images: Seeing Is Feeling 614

HAIKU 615

Haiku by KAWAHIGASHI KEKIGODO, MATSUO BASHO, OZAKI HOSAI 615
WILLIAM CARLOS WILLIAMS, *The Great Figure* 615
THEODORE ROETHKE, *Child on Top of a Greenhouse* 617

COMBINING IMAGES 617

EZRA POUND, *In a Station of the Metro* 617
ARTHUR SYMONS, *Pastel* 618
JIM HARRISON, *Sound* 618

SYNESTHESIA 619

ANN STANFORD, *Listening to Color* 619
KIMIKO HAHN, *When You Leave* 620

IMAGES AND COMMENTARY 620

JAMES WRIGHT, *Lying in a Hammock at William Duffy's Farm in Pine Island, Minnesota* 620
HENRY HOWARD, EARL OF SURREY, *The Soote Season* 622

LANDSCAPES 622

THOMAS HARDY, *Neutral Tones* 622
MATTHEW ARNOLD, *Dover Beach* 624

MEANINGS OF WORDS 625

HENRY DAVID THOREAU, *Pray to What Earth Does This Sweet Cold Belong* 626
GARY SNYDER, *Oil* 627

SURREALISTIC IMAGERY 627

WILLIAM BLAKE, *London* 628
PIERRE REVERDY, *Departure* 629

POEMS FOR FURTHER STUDY 630

SAMUEL TAYLOR COLERIDGE, *Kubla Khan* 630
ALFRED, LORD TENNYSON, *The Eagle: A Fragment* 631
AMY LOWELL, *Chinoiseries* 631
WILLIAM CARLOS WILLIAMS, *The Red Wheelbarrow* 632
ROBERT LOWELL, *Skunk Hour* 632
ETHERIDGE KNIGHT, *Haiku* 634
Writers on Writing—Browning 634

8 The Dance of the Mind: Metaphor and Simile 635

THE METAPHOR 635

CHARLES SIMIC, Watermelons 635
WALT WHITMAN, From Leaves of Grass 636
EMILY DICKINSON, "Hope" is the thing with feathers 637
H.D. (HILDA DOOLITTLE), Oread 638
HART CRANE, My Grandmother's Love Letters 638
BILL KNOTT, Hair Poem 639
CHARLES HENRI FORD, Somebody's Gone 640

THE SIMILE 641

T.E. HULME, Autumn 642
BILL KNOTT, Death 642
THOMAS MERTON, The Regret 643

THE CONCEIT 643

WILLIAM SHAKESPEARE, Shall I Compare Thee to a Summer's Day? 644
RICHARD CRASHAW, The Tear 644
JOHN DONNE, A Valediction: Forbidding Mourning 646

POEMS FOR FURTHER STUDY 647

FRAY ANGELICO CHAVEZ, Rattlesnake 647
THOMAS MERTON, Elegy for the Monastery Barn 648
N. SCOTT MOMADAY, The Delight Song of Tsoai-Talee 649
EZRA POUND, The Bath Tub 649
DYLAN THOMAS, Fern Hill 650
LOUISE GLÜCK, The Pond 651
WILLIAM SHAKESPEARE, Let Me Not to the Marriage of True Minds 651
PERCY BYSSHE SHELLEY, Fragment: Thoughts Come and Go in Solitude 652
JOHN DONNE, The Flea 652
FEDERICO GARCÍA LORCA, Half Moon 653
EMANUEL DI PASQUALE, Rain 653
Writers on Writing—Thomas 653

9 The Idea Dresses Up: Personification, Allegory, Symbol 654

PERSONIFICATION 654

SAPPHO, Then 654
MURIEL RUKEYSER, Song: Love in Whose Rich Honor 655

ALLEGORY 656

EMILY DICKINSON, Because I Could Not Stop for Death 656
GEORGE HERBERT, The Pilgrimage 657
AURELIAN TOWNSHEND, A Dialogue Betwixt Time and a Pilgrim 658

FABLE 659

JOHN GAY, The Lion, the Fox, and Geese 660

SYMBOL   661

D.H. LAWRENCE, *Sorrow*   661
WALT WHITMAN, *I Saw in Louisiana a Live-Oak Growing*   662
ROBERT FROST, *For Once, Then, Something*   663
Writers on Writing—Frost   664
EDMUND WALLER, *Go, Lovely Rose*   664
WILLIAM BUTLER YEATS, *The Rose of Peace*   665

POEMS FOR FURTHER STUDY   666

THOMAS HARDY, *The Subalterns*   666
MAY SARTON, *The Lady and the Unicorn*   667
ROBINSON JEFFERS, *Rock and Hawk*   668
DELMORE SCHWARTZ, *The Heavy Bear Who Goes with Me*   669
D.H. LAWRENCE, *Snake*   670
CHRISTOPHER SMART, *The Ant and the Caterpillar*   672
GEORGE HERBERT, *Love (III)*   673
ROBERT SOUTHWELL, *The Burning Babe*   673
EDMUND SPENSER, *One Day As I Unwarily Did Gaze*   674
MARGARET DANNER, *This Is an African Worm*   674

10 More Figures of Speech   675

HYPERBOLE   675

CARL SANDBURG, *They Have Yarns*   676
CECCO ANGIOLIERI, *In Absence from Becchina*   676
RANDALL JARRELL, *The Mockingbird*   677

UNDERSTATEMENT   678
SYNECDOCHE, METONYMY, ALLUSION, AND PARADOX   678

PO CHU-I, *Seeing Hsia Chan Off by River*   679
Writers on Writing—Brooks   679
RALPH WALDO EMERSON, *Letters*   679
WILLIAM BUTLER YEATS, *The Great Day*   680
DONALD HALL, *Ox Cart Man*   681
JAMES DICKEY, *Buckdancer's Choice*   682
ALEXANDER POPE, *Intended for Sir Isaac Newton*   683
BOB KAUFMAN, *Blues Note*   684
GEORGE HERBERT, *Bitter-Sweet*   685
WILLIAM SHAKESPEARE, *When Most I Wink, Then Do Mine Eyes Best See*   686
SIMONIDES, *For the Spartan Dead at Plataia (479 B.C.)*   686

POEMS FOR FURTHER STUDY   687

JAMES MERRILL, *Charles on Fire*   687
ANONYMOUS, *Grief of a Girl's Heart*   688
DYLAN THOMAS, *The Hand That Signed the Paper*   688
JOHN CROWE RANSOM, *Winter Remembered*   689
WELDON KEES, *Aspects of Robinson*   689

SAMUEL TAYLOR COLERIDGE, *Pity*   690

CHIDIOCK TICHBORNE, *Elegy, Written with His Own Hand in the Tower Before His Execution*   690

JOHN ASHBERY, *Paradoxes and Oxymorons*   691

11 The Music of Poetry   692

Writers on Writing—Poe   692
RHYTHM   692
ACCENT AND EMPHASIS   693
METER   694

ALFRED, LORD TENNYSON, *The Mermaid*   697

THE LINE AND LINE ENDINGS   699

ALGERNON CHARLES SWINBURNE, *Rococo*   700
EDNA ST. VINCENT MILLAY, *Recuerdo*   702

SYLLABIC VERSE   703

MARIANNE MOORE, *Nevertheless*   703
Writers on Writing—Moore   705

RHYME   705

ROBERT CREELEY, *If You*   705
W.H. AUDEN, *Fleet Visit*   707
ROBERT FROST, *The Road Not Taken*   708

ALLITERATION AND ASSONANCE   709

MARGARET WALKER, *Lineage*   710
EDGAR ALLAN POE, *The Bells*   711

VOWEL TONES   714

MARY TALLMOUNTAIN, *Peeling Pippins*   715
WILLIAM BUTLER YEATS, *The Lake Isle of Innisfree*   716
WILLIAM CARLOS WILLIAMS, *The Dance*   717

SONGS   718

ANONYMOUS, *Frankie and Albert*   719
BILLIE HOLIDAY, *God Bless the Child*   720
COLE PORTER, *My Heart Belongs to Daddy*   721

12 Tones of Voice   723

THE RANGE OF TONES   723

WILLIAM CARLOS WILLIAMS, *The Young Housewife*   723
D.H. LAWRENCE, *Gloire de Dijon*   725

IRONY   725

WALT WHITMAN, *A Boston Ballad*   726
ALAN DUGAN, *Morning Song*   727
DENISE LEVERTOV, *To the Snake*   728

DIDACTIC POETRY   728

EMILY DICKINSON, *Success is Counted Sweetest*   730
ALEXANDER POPE, From *An Essay on Man (Epistle IV)*   730

TOUGHNESS   731

PHILIP LEVINE, *To a Child Trapped in a Barber Shop*   731
CHARLES BUKOWSKI, *Yellow*   732

THE COMIC TONE   733

ANONYMOUS, *Miss Bailey's Ghost*   733
EDMUND CLERIHEW BENTLEY, *Lord Clive*   734
ANONYMOUS, *There Was a King*   734
HILAIRE BELLOC, *On His Books*   735

DICTION LEVELS   735

RICHARD WILBUR, *The Death of a Toad*   736
LANGSTON HUGHES, *Who but the Lord?*   736

DIALECTS   737

ROBERT BURNS, *John Anderson My Jo*   737
PAUL LAURENCE DUNBAR, *In the Morning*   738
Writers on Writing—Rich   740

13 The Poem's Shape   741

THE STRUCTURE OF FREE VERSE   741
Psalm 121: A Song of Degrees   742
DENISE LEVERTOV, *The Ache of Marriage*   742
Writers on Writing—Levertov   743

SOME TRADITIONAL ENGLISH FORMS   743
COUNTEE CULLEN, *Incident*   744
JOHN DRYDEN, *To the Memory of Mr. Oldham*   745
THOM GUNN, *Moly*   746

ITALIAN FORMS   747

JOHN KEATS, *On First Looking into Chapman's Homer*   747
WILLIAM SHAKESPEARE, *That Time of Year Thou Mayst in Me Behold*   748
EDNA ST. VINCENT MILLAY, *Pity Me Not Because the Light of Day*   749
CLAUDE MCKAY, *If We Must Die*   749
GEORGE MEREDITH, *In Our Old Shipwrecked Days There Was an Hour*   750
PERCY BYSSHE SHELLEY, *Ode to the West Wind*   752

FRENCH FORMS   754

DYLAN THOMAS, *Do Not Go Gentle into That Good Night*   755
ELIZABETH BISHOP, *One Art*   756

CLASSIC FORMS   757

PINDAR, *Olympian 11*   758
JOHN KEATS, *Ode to a Nightingale*   759
RICHARD WILBUR, *The Beautiful Changes*   761

ASIAN FORMS   762

MATSUO BASHO, *Nine Haiku*   762
LADY KASA, *Six Tanka*   763
WALLACE STEVENS, *Thirteen Ways of Looking at a Blackbird*   764

COMIC FORMS   766

OGDEN NASH, *Gervaise*   767
OGDEN NASH, *Edouard*   767
EDWARD GOREY, *There Was a Young Woman Named Plunnery*   767

SHAPED VERSES AND CONCRETE POETRY   767

GEORGE HERBERT, *Easter Wings*   768
MAY SWENSON, *Unconscious Came a Beauty*   769
JOHN HOLLANDER, *Swan and Shadow*   770
MARY ELLEN SOLT, *Forsythia*   771

14 The Well-Made Poem   772

OVERALL EFFECTIVENESS   773
ECONOMY   773

CLAUDE MACKAY, *Only a Thought*   774

COHERENCE AND CONSISTENCY   775

CHARLES KINGSLEY, *I Once Had a Sweet Little Doll, Dears*   775
ERASMUS DARWIN, *Eliza*   776

NATURALNESS   778

WILLIAM SHAKESPEARE, *My Mistress' Eyes Are Nothing like the Sun*   778
WILLIAM EMPSON, *Villanelle*   779
CORNELIUS WHUR, From *Village Musings*   780

TONE: SENTIMENTALITY AND COLDNESS   781

ELIZA COOK, *The Old Arm Chair*   782
THOMAS ASHE, *Old Jane*   783
ROBERT FROST, *Provide, Provide*   784
WILLIAM BUTLER YEATS, *Crazy Jane Talks with the Bishop*   785
PATRICK KAVANAGH, *Tinker's Wife*   785
GREGORY CORSO, *The Vestal Lady on Brattle*   786

ROBERT SERVICE, *Dylan*   787
THOMAS SPRAT, *On His Mistress Drowned*   788

COMPLETENESS   789

COVENTRY PATMORE, *If I Were Dead*   789

THE GOOD AND THE GREAT   790
Writers on Writing—Pound   791
JOHN MILTON, *Lycidas*   791
WILLIAM WORDSWORTH, *Lines*   796
MARIANNE MOORE, *The Steeple-Jack*   799
WILLIAM BUTLER YEATS, *Sailing to Byzantium*   801
T.S. ELIOT, *The Love Song of J. Alfred Prufrock*   802

CHECKLIST OF QUESTIONS FOR EVALUATING POETRY   806

15 Poems for Further Reading   808

GEOFFREY CHAUCER, *The Complaint of Chaucer to His Purse*   808
SIR THOMAS WYATT, *They Flee from Me*   809
SIR WALTER RALEIGH, *The Nymph's Reply to the Shepherd*   809
SIR PHILIP SIDNEY, From *Astrophel and Stella, Sonnet #71*   810
THOMAS CAMPION, *There Is a Garden in Her Face*   810
JOHN DONNE, *Death Be Not Proud*   811
ROBERT HERRICK, *Delight in Disorder*   811
ROBERT HERRICK, *Upon Julia's Clothes*   812
ANNE BRADSTREET, *To My Dear and Loving Husband*   812
APHRA BEHN, *A Thousand Martyrs I Have Made*   812
EDWARD TAYLOR, *Upon a Spider Catching a Fly*   813
JONATHAN SWIFT, *A Description of the Morning*   814
THOMAS GRAY, *Ode on the Death of a Favorite Cat*   815
WILLIAM BLAKE, *The Tyger*   816
ROBERT BURNS, *A Red, Red Rose*   817
WILLIAM WORDSWORTH, *I Wandered Lonely as a Cloud*   817
WILLIAM WORDSWORTH, *The World Is Too Much with Us*   818
WALTER SAVAGE LANDOR, *On His Seventy-fifth Birthday*   818
GEORGE GORDON, LORD BYRON, *She Walks in Beauty*   818
PERCY BYSSHE SHELLEY, *Ozymandias*   819
JOHN KEATS, *When I Have Fears*   819
JOHN KEATS, *To Autumn*   820
THOMAS LOVELL BEDDOES, *Song: How Many Times Do I Love Thee, Dear?*   821
HENRY WADSWORTH LONGFELLOW, *The Jewish Cemetery at Newport*   821
ELIZABETH BARRET BROWNING, *How Do I Love Thee?*   823
ROBERT BROWNING, *Meeting at Night*   823
ROBERT BROWNING, *Parting at Morning*   824
EMILY BRONTË, *The Sun Has Set*   824
HERMAN MELVILLE, *On the Photograph of a Corps Commander*   825
WALT WHITMAN, *A Noiseless Patient Spider*   825
FRANCES E.W. HARPER, *The Slave Auction*   826

EMILY DICKINSON, *My Life Had Stood, a Loaded Gun* 826

EMILY DICKINSON, *Apparently with No Surprise* 827

EMILY DICKINSON, *I Heard a Fly Buzz—When I Died* 827

EMILY DICKINSON, *After Great Pain, A Formal Feeling Comes* 828

CHRISTINA ROSSETTI, *After Death* 828

GERARD MANLEY HOPKINS, *Spring and Fall* 829

GERARD MANLEY HOPKINS, *The Windhover* 829

ALICE MEYNELL, *The Threshing-Machine* 830

OSCAR WILDE, *The Harlot's House* 830

A.E. HOUSMAN, *Loveliest of Trees* 831

A.E. HOUSMAN, *When I Was One-and-Twenty* 832

W.E.B. DUBOIS, *The Song of the Smoke* 832

EDWIN ARLINGTON ROBINSON, *Mr. Flood's Party* 833

STEPHEN CRANE, *A Man Adrift on a Slim Spar* 834

PAUL LAURENCE DUNBAR, *Compensation* 835

ROBERT FROST, *After Apple-Picking* 835

ROBERT FROST, *The Silken Tent* 836

JAMES JOYCE, *All Day I Hear the Noise of Waters* 837

ARCHIBALD MACLEISH, *Ars Poetica* 837

ELINOR WYLIE, *Prophecy* 838

WILFRED OWEN, *Anthem for Doomed Youth* 838

E.E. CUMMINGS, *in Just-* 839

E.E. CUMMINGS, *the Cambridge ladies who live in furnished souls* 840

LOUISE BOGAN, *Night* 840

ARNA BONTEMPS, *Southern Mansion* 841

W.H. AUDEN, *Lay Your Sleeping Head, My Love* 841

W.H. AUDEN, *As I Walked Out One Evening* 842

THEODORE ROETHKE, *My Papa's Waltz* 844

THEODORE ROETHKE, *I Knew a Woman* 844

RICHARD WRIGHT, *Four Haiku* 845

IRVING LAYTON, *Cain* 845

MAY SARTON, *Lady with a Falcon* 847

ROBERT HAYDEN, *Those Winter Sundays* 847

RANDALL JARRELL, *The Woman at the Washington Zoo* 848

HENRY REED, *Naming of Parts* 849

WILLIAM STAFFORD, *Traveling Through the Dark* 849

GWENDOLYN BROOKS, *Sadie and Maud* 850

ROBERT LOWELL, *Robert Frost* 850

ROBERT DUNCAN, *My Mother Would Be a Falconress* 851

LAWRENCE FERLINGHETTI, *[In Goya's Greatest Scenes We Seem to See]* 853

MONA VAN DUYN, *Open Letter from a Constant Reader* 854

RICHARD WILBUR, *Love Calls Us to the Things of This World* 855

PHILIP LARKIN, *Faith Healing* 855

AMY CLAMPETT, *The Sun Underfoot Among the Sundews* 856

ANTHONY HECHT, *The Dover Bitch, A Criticism of Life* 857

RICHARD HUGO, *Driving Montana* 858

A.R. AMMONS, *The Visit* 859

ALLEN GINSBERG, *A Supermarket in California* 859

ANNE SEXTON, *Pain for a Daughter* 860

RICHARD HOWARD, *Giovanni da Fiesole on the Sublime, or Fra Angelico's Last Judgement* 862

TED HUGHES, *Hawk Roosting* 863

DEREK WALCOTT, *Sea Grapes* 864

COLETTE INEZ, *Spanish Heaven* 865

SYLVIA PLATH, *Lady Lazarus* 865

WENDELL BERRY, *The Old Elm Tree by the River* 868

JIM BARNES, *A Season of Loss* 869

AUDRE LORDE, *Now That I Am Forever with Child* 869

N. SCOTT MOMADAY, *Earth and I Gave You Turquoise* 870

SONIA SANCHEZ, *summer words of a sistuh addict* 871

LUCILLE CLIFTON, *Good Times* 871

DARYL HINE, *The Survivors* 872

JUNE JORDAN, *My Sadness Sits Around Me* 872

DIANE WAKOSKI, *Backing Up, Or Tearing Up the Garden Next to the Driveway* 873

ISHMAEL REED, *beware: do not read this poem* 873

MARGARET ATWOOD, *You Are Happy* 874

SEAMUS HEANEY, *The Forge* 875

MARILYN HACKER, *Villanelle* 875

ERICA JONG, *How You Get Born* 876

JAMES WELCH, *The Man from Washington* 876

DAVE SMITH, *Picking Cherries* 877

ALFRED CORN, *Fifty-Seventh Street and Fifth* 877

NIKKI GIOVANNI, *Nikki-Rosa* 878

TOM WAYMAN, *Unemployment* 879

GREGORY ORR, *All Morning* 879

MOLLY PEACOCK, *Petting and Being a Pet* 879

LESLIE MARMON SILKO, *Love Poem* 880

JOHN YAU, *For Alexander Pope's Garden* 880

POEMS ABOUT DEATH 881

STEVIE SMITH, *Not Waving But Drowning* 881

STANLEY KUNITZ, *The Portrait* 881

MAXINE KUMIN, *For a Shetland Pony Brood Mare Who Died in Her Barren Year* 882

W.S. MERWIN, *For the Anniversary of My Death* 883

ADRIENNE RICH, *A Woman Mourned by Daughters* 883

POEMS ABOUT FAMILIES 884

JIM MITSUI, *When Father Came Home for Lunch* 884

ALBERTO RÍOS, *Nani* 884

LISEL MUELLER, *After Whistler* 886

CATHY SONG, *Lucky* 886

GAIL N. HARADA, *New Year* 887

ALICE WALKER, *My Daughter Is Coming!* 888

GARRETT HONGO, *The Hongo Store 29 Miles Volcano Hilo, Hawaii* 889

GARY SOTO, *History* 890

LORNA DEE CERVANTES, *Para un Revolucionario* 891

DRAMA

1 Literature Onstage   895

DRAMATIC ACTION   895
THE AUDIENCE   896
THE PLAYWRIGHT AS COLLABORATOR   897

2 The Script—How to Read a Play   899

GENRE AND LENGTH   899
THE CHARACTERS   900
THE SCENE   902
THE ACTION   903

Writers on Writing—Synge   904
JOHN MILLINGTON SYNGE, *Riders to the Sea*   904

3 Writing about Drama: The Review   914

WHY REVIEW?   914
PREPARATIONS   915
TAKING NOTES   916
BEGINNING A REVIEW   917
THE MIDDLE AND CONCLUSION OF A REVIEW   918
SUPPORTING DETAIL   919

JOHN MASON BROWN, *John Gielgud's Hamlet*   920
ROBERT BRUSTEIN, *Shakespeare with a Few Tears*   922
STARK YOUNG, The Glass Menagerie   923
ROBERT COLDHILL, A *Review of* A Raisin in the Sun   926

4 Action   929

THE DRAMATIC SITUATION   929
THE PLOT   930
EXPOSITION   930
THE RISING ACTION   931
THE CLIMAX   931
THE FALLING ACTION   932
CATASTROPHE AND DENOUEMENT   932
GREEK DRAMA AND *OEDIPUS REX*   933

SOPHOCLES, *Oedipus Rex*   935
Writers on Writing—Miller   975

5 Heroes and Heroines—Dramatic Character   976

VIRTUES AND FLAWS   977
HEROES, HEROINES, VILLAINS, AND OTHERS   977

ACTIONS AND WORDS   979
DRAMATIC DICTION AND CHARACTER   979
A DRAMA OF CHARACTERS: *THE GLASS MENAGERIE*   980

TENNESSEE WILLIAMS, *The Glass Menagerie*   981
Writers on Writing—Williams   1024

6 Tragedy   1026

FEAR AND PITY   1027
RECOGNITION AND REVERSAL   1027
CATHARSIS   1028
THE TRAGIC HERO   1028
SHAKESPEARE AND THE ELIZABETHAN THEATER   1029

WILLIAM SHAKESPEARE, *The Tragedy of Hamlet, Prince of Denmark*   1032

DESIRE UNDER THE ELMS—AN AMERICAN TRAGEDY   1148
EUGENE O'NEILL—THE FIRST AMERICAN TRAGEDIAN   1149

EUGENE O'NEILL, *Desire Under the Elms*   1150

7 Comedy   1187

HIGH AND LOW COMEDY   1188
ROMANTIC COMEDY   1189
THE IMPORTANCE OF BEING EARNEST   1189

OSCAR WILDE, *The Importance of Being Earnest*   1190

SATIRE   1229
LOS VENDIDOS (THE SALESMEN)   1230

LUIS M. VALDEZ, *Los Vendidos*   1231
Writers on Writing—Valdez   1238

TRAGICOMEDY   1239
TWELFTH NIGHT   1239

WILLIAM SHAKESPEARE, *Twelfth Night; or, What You Will*   1240

8 The Rise of Realism   1316

SOCIAL REALISM   1317
A DOLL'S HOUSE   1317
THE DRAMA OF CATASTROPHE   1318

HENRIK IBSEN, *A Doll's House*   1319
Writers on Writing—Ibsen   1368

REALISM IN AMERICA   1368

LORRAINE HANSBERRY, *A Raisin in the Sun*   1369

9 New Directions   1427

SYMBOLIST DRAMA   1427
THE SOUND OF A VOICE   1428

DAVID HWANG, *The Sound of a Voice*   1429
Writers on Writing—Hwang   1442

A QUARRELING PAIR   1443

JANE BOWLES, *A Quarreling Pair*   1443

AMERICAN GOTHIC—CRIMES OF THE HEART   1446

BETH HENLEY, *Crimes of the Heart*   1447

NEW DIRECTIONS IN STAGING: *A Son, Come Home*   1488

ED BULLINS, *A Son, Come Home*   1490

Glossary of Literary Terms 1501

Acknowledgments 1513

Index of First Lines 1521

Index of Authors and Titles 1531

Writing about Literature

1 🌿 Writing and Interpretation

The Pleasures of Language

Language is a source of enormous pleasure. We enjoy telling stories, jokes, and riddles. The most popular game shows on television are word games. But language isn't just an adult pleasure; it's open to all of us. If you listen to little children, you soon recognize that a great deal of their language isn't meant to "communicate ideas," but to give them pleasure as they sing and talk to themselves and invent long and fantastic stories for their own enjoyment. As children, we would sneak downstairs when our parents had friends or relatives over. We couldn't hear what they were saying, but we were comforted by the buzz of voices periodically bursting into laughter.

Language is not only a source of pleasure in itself, but it is a way of extending other pleasures. We are writing this chapter a week before the Super Bowl game. The airwaves are full of people discussing the upcoming event. No matter who wins, for at least a week afterward postgame analysts will dissect and evaluate each move of each play. Why all of this talk? Because through language we relive those pleasurable and exciting moments again; we participate in the experience and make it our own, and we get enormous pleasure out of such discussions, speculations, and analysis. Writing about literature is no different: it is a means of reliving, re-experiencing, and rejoicing in a pleasurable experience— the reading experience. Our first tip to students who are assigned to write about literature is, *whenever possible write about a work that you have enjoyed. You'll find such writing easier and more pleasurable than writing about a work you didn't particularly like.*

Of course, writing about writing did not become the central activity of higher education because it was pleasurable, but rather because the activity brings into play all the higher cognitive and intellectual functions. Writing about literature helps develop our abilities to analyze, to evaluate, to synthesize, and to imagine. A person who can write about literature is not merely literate, but educated.

Today's colleges and universities are the outgrowths of medieval seminaries that trained priests. In these seminaries, men studied the Bible as well as the writings of the Church Fathers and philosophical tracts. Those who made it through this rigorous training were celebrated people who exerted enormous power over their communities and even entire empires. They advised monarchs and taught princes. Thus, today's colleges and universities arose out of institutions that trained people to write and discuss written works.

The process of writing about literature involves six stages. In the first stage, we come to understand what a work is telling us or what an author is attempting to persuade us to believe. Many people stop at this first stage, and these people believe everything they read. But educated people step back and examine the work critically; they enter into a second stage—the analysis of the work. In this stage, they locate the methods by which the author attempts to persuade us of the truth of his or her position, in other words the work's "rhetoric"; they expose the unspoken assumptions and connections between the author's arguments; and they test the soundness of those arguments. In the third stage, educated readers evaluate the success of the author's rhetorical strategies and whether they believe the author's position to be sound, valuable, and worthy of acceptance. In the first part of the process, the reader comprehends, analyzes, and evaluates.

Then the reader becomes a writer and in many ways duplicates the process he or she has just been studying. The reader-turned-writer must decide which points to make, how to organize those points in the most effective manner, and how best to express those points in the way that will be most convincing. In the second part of the process, the reader-turned-writer develops material, organizes it, and renders it comprehensible and persuasive. In short, the reader-turned-writer is involved in synthesizing ideas and expressing them.

You can see now why writing about literature is emphasized in higher education: it requires mastery of the most important intellectual skills—comprehension of ideas, analysis of ideas, synthesizing of ideas, organization of ideas, evaluation of ideas, and presentation of ideas. These intellectual skills are needed in business, industry, and government. Indeed, as the American economy changes from a manufacturing base to a service base, these skills are in greater and greater demand and those who possess them are more and more valued. Consequently, law schools argue that the best undergraduate training is majoring in English or history, disciplines that put the greatest emphasis on writing about writing. At a business meeting we recently attended, the complaint we heard over and over again from executives was that recent college graduates could not give clear and persuasive presentations and that their memos were incomprehensible. "I don't want to have to call up someone to find out what he or she *meant* to say," one corporate president told us. "I need to be able to read it in black and white."

In fact, the electronic revolution is putting a greater strain on people to write clearly and effectively in shorter and shorter times. With electronic mail and FAX machines, executives don't have all day to come back with well-worded replies to detailed and complicated questions or requests for information. They must be able to shoot back responses that are coherently organized, comprehensibly expressed, and tactfully worded. Success and failure in business or in the professions is often based on the ability to analyze problems and communicate solutions swiftly, cogently, and forcefully. You can't develop those skills just on the job. You need to come to your job already practiced in analyzing, synthesizing, evaluating, and expressing complex notions and situations. Writing about literature is one of the best ways of developing those cognitive and communication skills.

What Is an Interpretation?

Most of your writing about literature will be involved in "interpretation" and "evaluation." These are very broad terms for understanding and judging a literary work. But it is not always clear what people mean by interpretation. Can't you interpret a work in any way that pleases you? And isn't beauty in the eye of the beholder? Who has the authority either to assert a particular meaning for a work of art or to judge it? These are important questions that any student of literature should ask, and although there is no absolute answer to these questions it is valuable to consider them at least briefly.

Interpreting Language

Ambiguity is a part of language, and no one can use language so clearly that his or her words cannot be misinterpreted. Consequently, everyone is interpreting language all the time without even being aware of it. In a cartoon we once saw, a mother asks her son to open a window, and the son throws a chair through it. He has, indeed, opened the window, but we can be pretty certain his mother did not envision his method of opening it. Her request, which seemed simple and clear enough, was not specific enough for a child who wished to misunderstand. But if we sometimes misinterpret language that seems on the face of it clear and straightforward, we more often correctly interpret language that is highly ambiguous. Take this classic interchange:

> "Do you have the time?" asked Mr. Smith.
> "Well, the letter carrier just came," Mrs. Smith answered.
> "Is it that late!" exclaimed Mr. Smith.

In the most literal sense, "the letter carrier just came" does not answer the question "Do you have the time?" but from Mr. Smith's exclamation we can see that he has successfully interpreted Mrs. Smith's statement. As readers, we can safely infer that the letter carrier comes at a certain time each day, and that this appearance is a good indication of the approximate hour. Thus, when Mrs. Smith says the letter carrier has already left, Mr. Smith knows he is late. Daily life is filled with such unconscious interpretations. And to those who ask, "Why must we interpret language?" we answer, "If we did not interpret language, there would be no reason to have it."

Language cannot exist without shared meaning, shared practices, and shared understandings. When the mother asks her son to open a window, she assumes correctly that he knows what the word *window* means. Similarly, the mother has a right to suppose that her son shares with her the understanding that there are appropriate ways as well as inappropriate ways to open windows under normal circumstances. If, let us suppose, the room were in flames and the only way out were the window, then the son's action of throwing the chair through the window would be an appropriate interpretation of her request. We can share understanding because we share a context.

What do we do when we interpret what people say? We supply the unspoken connections and contexts around what is said. We make explicit what would otherwise remain implicit. An interpreter is a go-between, a person who stands between the original communication and the person trying to understand that communication. And the interpreter acts by filling in what is not understood, either by supplying different language or by articulating the unspoken connections. Thus in your interpretations you will be stating the relationships that the author has left silent. An interpretation involves drawing connections that make the work more understandable.

Exercise

Pretend an extraterrestrial has come to Earth who has learned English only by studying a dictionary. Compare how the alien would interpret the following sentences to how you as an experienced speaker of English make sense of them. What kind of assumptions can you make about the speaker of these sentences that the alien could not make?

1. He thinks his car is the greatest thing since sliced bread.
2. Your old man is off his rocker!
3. I booted up the system, but the hard drive crashed.
4. I'm going to catch some Z's until the flick comes on the tube.
5. Let's do lunch tomorrow.
6. Man, he's a totally cool dude!
7. Our troops wasted the enemy with their superior fire.
8. He went out last night and came home wasted.
9. Waste not, want not.
10. You big turkey, you bought a car that's a lemon.

Different Kinds of Criticism

Every literary work is involved in a web of unstated connections. The various types of criticism are defined by the sorts of connections they make explicit. For example, criticism that explores the connection between the author's life and his or her work is called *biographical criticism*. Criticism that explores the relationship between the work and its historical context is called *historical criticism*. Criticism that explores the relationship between the parts of a work and its artistic totality is called *formal criticism*. Criticism that explores the text's relationship to its audience is called *reception criticism* or *reader-response criticism*. Finally, criticism that explores the relationship between the parts of the literary work and an overriding theme is, understandably enough, called *thematic criticism*. These are not the only critical types available, and each type can be broken down into smaller, more specific branches. For example, some historical critics use a Marxist technique and are, therefore, called *Marxist critics*, while some biographical critics are indebted to Freud's theories and are referred to as *Freudian critics*. But we may say that each text has at least six specific relationships: (1) to the author, (2) to history, (3) to the reader, (4) to other literature, (5) to itself, and (6) to the language, and you may explore one or all of these relationships in your writing.

How Do You Go About Interpreting a Text?

The uncritical reader passes his or her eyes across the page, line by line, and stops when the story, poem, or play comes to an end. The first step in becoming a critical reader is to stop this unimpeded forward motion. By making notes, by stopping at the end of a paragraph and reflecting about what it means or what has happened, one begins the long process of critical interpretation. Two propositions may help you in formulating your thoughts.

1. Nothing is in a work of art by accident. Even the smallest detail is an artistic decision made by the author. Consequently, you may ask of any detail, "Why has this been chosen to be a part of the work?"
2. Every element in a literary work ought to contribute to the effectiveness of the whole. We may therefore ask of any detail, "How does it contribute to the wholeness of the work?" and we may ask of any two details, "In what ways are they related?"

In short, there are three questions you may ask of any detail in a literary work: (1) Why was it chosen? (2) How does it contribute to the work as a whole? (3) How does it relate to the other details around it? Sometimes the answers to these questions will not be very revealing, especially if you begin with a rather unimportant detail. However, by asking these questions of the most important actions, phrases, or crucial details can generate surprising answers.

 Tips for Readers

People often shy away from the things they don't know or don't understand. The unknown is frightening. But all education begins with *not* knowing. After all, we don't have to learn or come to understand that which we already know. Thus, don't be afraid of those portions of a literary work that seem odd or fuzzy or don't seem to belong to the rest of the story. They are frequently the stress points where the literary work will open to interpretation, indeed, the very points where interpretation is necessary. So instead of ignoring those tough patches, you should note them and make a special effort to try to explain to yourself what they are doing.

Another point to remember is that since all questions of interpretation are based on the unstated relationship between the text and something else, all interpretation must begin with a close reading of the text. Almost all *bad* interpretations begin by imposing on the text something external. Thus some readers believe, for example, that if the author was an alcoholic the work must show signs of alcoholism. Such a method only creates forced, distorted, and unreliable interpretations. Similarly, some readers may think that any work written during World War II must be about the war. Again, that is to impose a historical fact on a text. However, if a work, such as W. H. Auden's "Musée des Beaux Arts," is about human suffering and we learn that it was written at the time of the outbreak of World War II, we are at liberty to draw a connection between the text and such events because our starting point was the text and its subject matter.

The Limits of Interpretation

Is there such a thing as a single "correct" interpretation of a work of art? No. Nor can one "prove" that an interpretation is "correct." Nevertheless, there are interpretations that are clearly wrong. Is this illogical?

Let's return to that silly scene that illustrated the ambiguity of even the simplest request. A mother asks her son to open a window, and he throws a chair through the glass. On the one hand we can say that the son has misinterpreted his mother, since no reasonable person would assume that the request to open a window gave a person under normal circumstances the permission to destroy the window. On the other hand, we might say that her statement was ambiguous enough that, though the son's interpretation is unreasonable, one can see its logic. But let us consider another scene: a mother asks her son to open a window, and her son opens a book. "Why haven't you opened a window?" the mother asks him. "Today, I have decided that the word *window* means 'book.' Therefore I am following your instructions." Even under the most permissive standards, the son's interpretation of his mother's request makes no sense at all. One cannot arbitrarily assign a different meaning to a word than the word is accepted to have. As farfetched as this example sounds, it is similar to many student "interpretations" of literary works in which alternative meanings are arbitrarily given to words.

It is important to understand that although there *may* be an infinite number of different interpretations of a complex literary work, not *all* interpretations are reasonable or acceptable—just as there are an infinite number of even numbers, but three isn't one of them. Again, though there may be an infinite number of shades of blue, orange is not one of them.

Five Criteria for Acceptable Interpretations

Interpreting language is a very difficult, even tedious process. Our judicial system is based on a complex network of interpretations, and within that system there is often disagreement. If the nine justices on the federal Supreme Court at times disagree with one another about the proper interpretation of the law, each does understand how the other justices came to those different decisions. Interpretations are usually judged by five broad criteria: their appropriateness, comprehensiveness, simplicity, depth, and reasonability. Let's look at each of these criteria briefly.

Appropriateness

Certain kinds of literary works have over the ages invited certain types of interpretive strategies that are appropriate to them. Here's a pretty obvious example of what we mean. Let us say that a boy is upset because he was dropped from his high school baseball team. His dad comes up to his room, where he's been moping, pats him on the back, and says "Son, let me tell you a story of when I couldn't play on the football team because my grades were too low. Well, that team had the worst record of any team our high school ever put on the field. The players could hardly show their faces in school, they did so poorly. The next year, with my grades up, I could have joined the team, but by then I was too interested in my academic work to have time for practice." How should the son interpret this little anecdote? Of course, we know that the father wants to cheer his son up, and this little tale has a moral: good things can emerge from what first looks like a bad situation, or, in metaphoric terms, every cloud has a silver lining. We know how to make an appropriate interpretation because we have seen this little scene played out in dozens of television comedies. There are other kinds of works that have appropriate types of interpretations. English metaphysical poetry often used erotic imagery to speak about one's relationship to God. It may be inappropriate to interpret a modern erotic poem in a religious manner, but it would be appropriate to interpret one of John Donne's or George Herbert's poems in this manner. Such an interpretation is historically appropriate.

Comprehensiveness

An interpretation is like a key that can unlock meaning. Would you prefer to have a key that unlocked only some doors or one that opened all of them? Clearly, you would want the key that opens all of them. Consequently, the best interpretations don't explain just one or two details; they make sense of many details in the literary work, and the most powerful interpretations help us understand the literary work in its entirety. Thus you should look for explanations that make sense of the whole and not merely of an arbitrary number of details.

Simplicity

The most convincing and most powerful interpretations are those that can explain a vast number of relationships in the simplest way. Yet, be careful of being overly simple. An overly simple, or *simplistic*, explanation imposes on complex material a very simple pattern which ignores details that contradict it. Don't confuse simplicity, which is a virtue, with being simplistic, which is a defect. For example, a student once argued in a paper that Edgar Allan Poe's "Cask of Amontillado" is about the ruins of drink because Poe himself destroyed his life by drinking. To be sure, Fortunato is persuaded to enter the narrator's trap because of "his connoisseurship of wine." But that does not mean that Fortunato was an alcoholic, nor does alcoholism explain the narrator's malevolence or the manner in which Fortunato is killed. The student's interpretation was too simplistic and insufficiently comprehensive.

Depth

The best readings go beneath the surface of the literary work to explain its most profound aesthetic achievements or its most important ideas. Depth is also a function of comprehensiveness, since the deeper one's analysis can go, the more completely it reveals the unspoken relationships that bind the work of art together. If one examines only the more superficial relationships, then one has ignored too much of what is going on. Shallow reading can be quite true. For example, it is true that Poe's "Cask of Amontillado" does show that the love of good wine can lead to ruin. But that does not tell a reader very much about what makes it a compelling story. Again, it is true to say that Poe's story can be read in one sitting, but it is more profound to argue that "Cask of Amontillado" reflects Poe's theories about the unity of effect, which require literary works to be readable in one sitting.

Reasonability

Ultimately, the final test of an interpretation is whether it seems to make reasonable sense of the work it is trying to interpret. Reasonability is a vague and probably undefinable quality. But we all know when explanations strike us as reasonable, and when they strike us as forced, strained, or loony. It is important to distinguish between a reasonable interpretation of a work whose ideas we think are unreasonable and an unreasonable interpretation. We may think a story has a very unreasonable theme, but we applaud the interpretation that elucidates that theme clearly, effectively, comprehensively, and subtly. Inexperienced readers often try to make a work agree with their beliefs. Your job is to understand what the work has to say whether you agree with it or not.

Supporting an Interpretation

Students often develop interpretations that are appropriate, comprehensive, and reasonable, but they do not support their interpretation in an effective and convincing manner. Your reading of a work of literature will not be convincing and effective unless you can back up your interpretation with good evidence. What sort of evidence do you need to make a good "case" for your interpretation?

Over the years, scholars have developed terms for different sources of evidence. They speak of primary and secondary materials. *Primary sources* are the principal work you are investigating, other works by the same author or authors, and works written at the same time. For example, sonnets by other Elizabethan sonneteers may help you defend a reading of a particular Shakespeare sonnet. *Secondary sources* are works by later scholars *about* the primary sources. But although these terms look like they are clearly different, it is not always easy, or useful, to distinguish between them. If an author is living, the criticism of his or her work is a secondary source now, but to scholars in the future, it may turn into primary material.

Primary Sources

The most important primary source is the literary work or works you have decided to write about. At first, it seems that identifying the primary source would be the easiest part of your work, but sometimes this is not true. *The Heath Guide to Literature,* for example, prints poems and stories individually when, in fact, they are frequently parts of larger works. You may discuss a single Shakespeare sonnet, but remember that it is one in a series of more than 150 sonnets. Other sonnets in the sequence may shed light on the meaning of the individual sonnets you are examining. Moreover, literary works often exist in more than one version. Shakespeare's *Hamlet* is a case in point. As with all of Shakespeare's plays, we do not have the original manuscript or even a version of the play that Shakespeare saw through the publishing process. In Shakespeare's time, unscrupulous printers would publish versions of plays faultily remembered by actors or by members of the audience. The first published version of *Hamlet* appears to be faulty. Thus, all the published versions of Shakespeare's plays are the editors' best guesses at what Shakespeare actually wrote, since no authorized version exists. But even in cases not so shrouded in the mysteries of the past, there are questions. Faulkner often reworked his stories between their first magazine publications and their final book publications. W. H. Auden rewrote many of his poems throughout his career so that poems exist in a variety of versions. Works in translation are especially slippery, because every translation is already an interpretation of what the original meant. Although as beginning students of literature you may not need to be so sensitive to these subtle issues of the text, you should be aware that establishing what is the literary text is not always a simple matter.

An author's commentary on his or her own work can be very helpful to the interpreter of literature. Writers leave behind a great deal of related material— letters, notebooks, diaries, interviews, and their own critical writing. Reading Eudora Welty's talks entitled *One Writer's Beginnings* can throw valuable light on her craft and attitudes. But you must *always* be careful when dealing with what a writer says about his or her own literary work. Like everyone else, what they say about themselves and their work is what they want others to believe and not necessarily fact. Samuel Taylor Coleridge published with his poem "Kubla Khan" a note saying that it was written in one draft after a dream and left unfinished because he was interrupted by a visitor from Porlock. Experts examining this account have had reason to doubt its accuracy. Although the story makes for interesting reading, it may be less than the complete truth. To avoid questions, writers often pretend that they don't understand their works at all or that their works have no meaning. Be suspicious of such accounts.

Sometimes the accounts of friends or of contemporary critics give us an idea of what a work meant to readers at the time of composition. Because Coleridge and Wordsworth were friends who worked closely with one another, Coleridge's comments about Wordsworth's poetry have a value and importance that later commentary does not have. But once again, we must not view Coleridge's comments uncritically. Personal issues cloud his understanding of Wordsworth's poems, and perhaps the distance of two hundred years gives today's readers a clearer perspective on these poems than those intimately involved.

Secondary Sources

Reading what other people have said about a writer's work can be very useful. However, students are often more confused by criticism than helped by it, and before you read any criticism you should realize what you might gain from other people's thoughts.

Most literary scholars write for other literary scholars; most criticism is not written for introductory students. Consequently, most criticism takes for granted a background that you may not possess and is written in a language you may have a great deal of difficulty understanding. Don't be intimidated, but also don't pretend you understand something when you really don't. Our best advice is to learn what you can from critics and scholars, but don't repeat phrases or ideas just because they sound good. Reserve what you don't understand for the time when you will be able to understand it.

Literary scholars often disagree among themselves. Don't accept an interpretation just because someone wrote it down. You have to ask yourself whether it makes sense to you and whether it advances your understanding of the text. However, you should not reject an interpretation just because you don't like what the writer is saying. Perhaps the critic has a point you haven't considered. Keep an open mind. Sometimes by trying to figure out why you feel some statement is wrong, you learn what you feel to be true.

✍ Tips for Writers

The best time to consult secondary sources is after you have become familiar with the work on your own, but before your ideas have hardened. When you read secondary works you must maintain a delicate balance between being open to new ideas and approaches and not being swayed by everything that you read in print. It's best to have a general idea of what you think is happening in a work before you read what others have written.

Finding Secondary Sources

Secondary sources are usually found either in books or in periodicals. Books usually take one of two forms: a work by a single critic, or a collection of essays by various authors. You can find these books by consulting your library's catalog or its data bank. Important authors frequently have bibliographies written about them which contain the titles of important books and articles about the author.

The Dictionary of Literary Biography is a multivolume resource that contains individual essays on authors, accompanied by a selected bibliography. Since these essays are written for the general reader, they are a good starting point for many students.

Yet another important resource is the MLA *International Bibliography*, which is published annually. This bibliography is the most complete listing of books and articles on writers. In addition, this bibliography breaks down entries into sections on individual works, so, for example, you can immediately see the articles on Poe's "Cask of Amontillado." This will prove to be a very helpful resource since some authors have been written about extensively and you will need to focus your secondary research on a particular work.

Conclusion

The best essays on literature that students write combine a number of different factors. Of course, they are clear, well-organized, and grammatical. Professors ought to be able to expect that of any paper. But they also present an interpretation of the work that is reasonable, convincing, well-supported, and of real depth. The best essays indicate that the student has read the work carefully, with comprehension and feeling. In addition, such papers usually show that the student is open to ideas, emotions, and experience.

2 ❧ The Writing Process

Attitude and Experience

Over the years we have discussed writing with hundreds of student and professional writers. Students tell us that the single most important factor that influences the outcome of their paper is attitude. Professional writers tell us that the only way to learn to write well is to write often. Attitude and experience make the difference between good writing and bad writing.

You won't be surprised to hear that many students dislike writing papers. The truth is that writing is a lot of work even when you enjoy it, get paid for it, and are reasonably good at it. Writing this book has meant spending countless hours with pen and paper, typewriter and word processor writing, reading, and rewriting. Many times we wished we were doing other things. If nothing else, writing requires intellectual discipline—a quality that many of us need to develop. Such intellectual discipline does not spring from thin air. It is built up over a long period as one learns to do more and more complicated and demanding intellectual tasks. The best students—as well as our most successful graduates—have developed intellectual discipline which allows them to push through tasks when they get boring, frustrating, and difficult.

Student attitudes about writing affect their writing in several familiar ways: they don't give themselves enough time to do a good job; they wait until the last possible minute to get to work; they look for easy ways of getting around the task rather than confronting the assignments head on. If you have held any of these attitudes—and we think that all of us have at one time or another—then you will understand how your attitude harms the quality of your work.

Students tell us that there are four reasons they don't get down to work on their papers: (1) They are afraid of writing. (2) They are not really sure how to get started. (3) They have difficulty budgeting their time. (4) They really don't care how well they do, and don't believe that working harder will make any difference to their lives.

We're not sure what to say to students who don't believe there is any point in learning to write better. We can all point to people who can't write well and who are reasonably successful at business or in conducting their lives. You may be lucky, too. But most of the people we know who succeeded in business or in conducting their own affairs are people who have excellent communication skills and are confident not only in speaking, but in putting their ideas down on paper where their notions can be studied and serve as the basis for long-term action. As the American economy becomes more service-oriented and global, your ability to feel comfortable as a writer will become more and more important. Writing papers on literature may not be *exactly* what you will do for the rest of your life—it's probably more difficult than the writing you'll have to do on the job—but if you learn to do it well, the kind of writing you'll have to do will be that much easier.

Talking to students, we've learned that they *always* think they are taking too long to write their papers. Both weak and strong students have somehow come to believe that *real* writers can just sit down and whip up a good paper in no time. We're here to tell you that is nonsense. To be sure, writers in a burst of inspiration can sometimes produce works of great length in a short time. But those periods of inspiration are rare. All of the writers we know—and we've come to know journalists and novelists, poets and publicists, essayists and editors—rely on slow, hard work to get them through. If you also think that you write too slowly, you're probably writing as quickly as you can. Writing takes time, so you had better prepare to give it the time it takes.

✎ Tips for Writers

When you're given an assignment, make a list of how long you think each stage will take you. For example, reading the story carefully several times may take you two hours, researching the criticism three hours, outlining the paper 30 minutes, writing the first draft five hours, etc. Then look at your calendar and start blocking out the time, working backward from your deadline. In such a way, you'll discover pretty clearly how soon you'll have to start working on the paper to get it done on time. The process will also supply you with a lot of little deadlines that should keep you on target.

Fear of Writing

Some people are afraid of writing. This fear takes two forms. Some people feel insecure about the mechanics of writing; they fear that they won't express themselves effectively and will expose their ignorance of the language. Others are afraid that by expressing their ideas they will say something stupid or meet disapproval. But in both cases, the writers are afraid of what other people will think; they don't have enough confidence in themselves to assert their beliefs in writing.

People who are afraid to write often view an assignment as a mountain they will have to climb without support, preparation, or the necessary tools for the ascent. You can reduce some of the fears you have by breaking the assignment up into smaller, more manageable steps and by taking the steps one at a time. Think of the assignment as a process you must go through and not as a final object that will be judged. By moving slowly, step by step, the frightening mountain will be turned into unremarkable hills. Follow the tip above, scheduling the essay by designating specific times when you will work on it. Try to break down the task into smaller pieces and reward yourself after completing each one. For example, you might allow yourself to get up and stretch after you've completed a small task or to eat a candy bar after you've finished a somewhat larger one.

Furthermore, don't think you have to do it alone. Your teacher is there to help. Viewed from a distance, teachers are frightening people, but by and large they are interested in helping students who want to learn. If you go to speak to your professor not to make excuses, but to learn better what to do, you will most likely find a willing helper.

✍️ Tips for Writers

Two things you should keep in mind when speaking to your teachers: be polite and be ready. A professor is not a servant to be ordered around, but a professional you have gone to for help. Treat your teachers as you would your boss, a medical doctor, or your minister, that is, with the respect due to someone in authority. Also try to organize your thoughts *before* you go to see your teacher. Try to be as specific as you can about the things you need to know. If possible, make a list of questions before you speak. By being organized you will save yourself time, get what you need, and make a good impression.

You can turn to people other than your professor for help. A librarian can help you with research. There are now so many different research sources available—indexes, data banks, CD ram units, catalogues—that librarians expect even the best-trained scholar to ask for help. Your librarian can help you cut through a great deal of unnecessary material and confusion. Many schools have writing labs or tutorial services available to students who need more intensive help. Your friends can be of assistance. Ask the better students in the class what they are doing or whether they can lend you help. You'll often be surprised by their helpfulness and their willingness to talk over what they are doing for the class. If doing well in college is important to you—and it seems an incredible waste of time, effort, and money if it's not—then your work ought to be an interesting topic of conversation.

Finally, some students get very frightened by tests and other important assignments. This is a real problem that will stay with people and affect their entire lives. It is a problem that should be taken seriously and affects not just poor students, but some of the very best ones, too. Many colleges and universities have counseling centers that can teach people how to minimize their anxieties and eventually overcome them. These short workshops can be extremely helpful.

Tips for Writers

Students get panicked when they seem to get stuck in one stage of the writing process. Students get blocked by making perfectionistic demands on themselves. Give yourself a reasonable amount of time to do research, and when you have exhausted that time, go on to organizing the material. You could research a paper indefinitely. You could rewrite a paper indefinitely. Therefore, give yourself deadlines and keep to them. Such deadlines will keep the assignment in perspective. Avoid setting impossible standards for yourself.

Exercise

Before you can improve your study and writing habits, you need to make an inventory of what your habits are. Write down as precisely as you can the various stages you go through between being given an assignment and handing one in. Then go back and analyze which stages you think are effective or ineffective, easy or difficult. Suggest how you might change your writing practices to make them more effective. Be practical. Would merely closing the door to your room help block out distractions, or would it be necessary to go to another room? Sometimes little changes can make writing much easier.

Step One: Getting the Assignment

We can't begin to count how many students have done poorly because they did not pay attention to the assignment and failed to do what was required. Listen carefully when your teachers give you assignments. If you don't hear something, ask the teacher to repeat it. Be careful to note the number of pages, the subject, and the deadline.

Some of your professors will give very detailed instructions about what they want or how they want papers to be prepared. Pay close attention. Teachers don't go to all that trouble unless they have reasons for giving such specific instructions. Other teachers give much broader assignments. Don't be fooled into thinking such assignments are easier. The open assignments give you more freedom, but they also give you more responsibility.

Step Two: Reading

Writing about literature requires you to read the literature you're writing about. Our students have told us that after attitude, the most important factor influencing the success of a paper is how well they have read.

Reading is a broad term, and as everyone knows there are different ways to read. You can read in a cursory manner to get the gist—or main point—of an article or plot. You can read for pleasure, allowing yourself to be tugged along by the adventure or story. You can read like a lawyer, looking for little loopholes and problems. Each of these kinds of reading has its value, and the good student—and the successful person—knows when to employ each of the various reading styles. For example, if you were checking to see if an article discussed a certain short story, you would quickly run your eyes down the page looking for the title. You wouldn't bother reading it carefully until you thought you found something that would be useful to you. However, if you were reading a contract, you might stop at the end of every paragraph and think about its ramifications.

In fact, literature is not really read until it is re-read. If you are going to write about a poem, a story, or a play, you must read it several times in several different ways before you are ready to write about it. Even when read for decades, the finest works of literature reveal something new on each reading, and the finest literary critics are people who have read and thought about works repeatedly over many years before setting down their observations.

Our first readings are usually very quick ones in which we become familiar with the plot and characters and try to derive some pleasure. We let the work affect us as unselfconsciously as possible. We don't resist the forward drive of the text, but allow ourselves to be swept along with it. We hope to retain some of the freshness and pleasure of this first reading in all our subsequent readings, even as we attend to other facets of the story.

On subsequent readings we try to break the forward momentum of the work and try to become more aware of what the text is doing to us as readers. We try to pay attention to everything that passes in front of us. In order to pay attention we must break certain habits.

American society has put a premium on speed. We want fast cars, fast food, and fast answers. We take speed reading and speed writing courses. We have been taught to move as quickly as possible through the material we are studying. If reading a story is like taking a trip, most readers try to barrel down the highway as fast as they can, hoping they aren't caught by radar or the police. At such high speeds you aren't very likely to take in the scenery or appreciate the architecture. To be sure, you've kept your eye on the highway, observing signs, checking the traffic, but you haven't really seen what was around you. We have sometimes been shocked by noticing, for the first time, on some frequently traveled route, a beautiful vista or a lovely house that has been there all the time. "How did we overlook such beauty?" we ask ourselves, and the answer is usually that we have been in such a rush to get to our destination that we haven't been paying attention to the things around us. Our speed has screened out these perceptions.

Reading well means developing at least two different sorts of attention: a narrowing in on specific details, and an opening up to the unexpected. The only way to pay the second type of attention is by going slowly and repeatedly through a text. By the way, this sort of open attention to what's around you doesn't pay off just in literary studies. The smart businessperson is one who can spot an opportunity that other, "nearsighted" businesspeople have overlooked, and life isn't very interesting or worthwhile without taking some time "to smell the roses." Sometimes standing back and taking a slow, long, open look at what's around you is not only the best way to solve problems, but the prelude to enjoyment and success.

✍ Tips for Writers

You can increase your comprehension and attention by reading aloud to yourself. If you come to a difficult or complicated passage, try reading it aloud. Speaking slows down your reading, and by getting both auditory and visual stimuli, your brain can better process the information. Many of the best readers are ones that hear a small, internal voice speaking to them—the narrator's voice. Listening to the narrator also slows down the reading process and heightens awareness.

When you write, you should also read your writing aloud. Not only will reading aloud help you find omitted words, but it will also teach you when you've become wordy and unclear. Better yet, get someone else to read your paper aloud to you. You'll be amazed at how many awkward, vague, and confusing sentences you will catch in that manner.

During your various readings of a text don't be afraid to notice little details that seem odd or unusual or that merely stand out from the rest. You may not know at first why these details stand out—in fact, you may never know why they have caught your attention—but as you review the story in your mind or on subsequent readings, you may become suddenly aware of the connection between these small observations.

Some students choose short poems and the shortest of stories in the mistaken belief that these works require less effort and less time to study and write about. On the contrary, the hardest works to understand are the most concentrated, and the shortest works tend to be just these highly concentrated works. A twelve-line poem will demand as much time and concentration as a twenty-page story. And because each word of a poem must perform so many different tasks simultaneously, students often find it harder to separate the various, tightly woven strands of meaning and purpose in a short poem than in the less concentrated short story.

✍ Tips for Readers

Always read with a pencil or pen in your hand. If you own the book, don't be afraid to mark it up. Every reader has his or her own style of making notes. Sometimes merely underlining interesting things is enough to remind you. Some people have a system of symbols. For example, one line in the margin indicates mild interest, two lines substantial interest, three or more lines great importance. Still others like to write questions and comments in the margins. While reading a long work such as a novel, we frequently put a key word at the top of the page to aid us in finding important passages quickly. In time, you will evolve your own method. If you don't own the book, carry around a strip of paper and mark key words and page numbers. Then, when you have finished a reading, you can go back and take more extensive notes. Highlighting pens are less useful. Students get in the habit of highlighting everything, a habit which defeats their purpose. If you use a highlighting pen, make certain that you have a clear reason for wanting to highlight the passages you deem important.

In short, what we are advising you to do is begin the reading process by being open to all sorts of possibilities in the text. Take your time with it. Don't be afraid of being confused, but indicate what exactly confuses you. Sometimes you won't be so much confused as a bit uneasy with a word choice or an action. Don't shy away from such uneasy moments, but try to find out what has made you uneasy, why a certain detail stands out as strange, odd, or wonderfully appropriate.

Finally, re-reading the poem, story, or play is not a stage which once completed doesn't have to be repeated. At every stage of writing, you will want to go back to the text to see if you have overlooked something that can help you make your point or strengthen your position—or which complicates matters.

Step Three: Preliminary Thinking

You have now read the work you wish to write about several times in different moods and in different ways. It is time to begin to formulate some ideas about the work. Your ideas shouldn't be too fixed as yet—you have a lot of thinking to do before you sit down and write—but you have come to a certain understanding of the story, an understanding which may need to be enlarged, altered, or even rejected, but one that should give you some direction.

Often students don't even realize they have begun to interpret works of literature because they take for granted that others would have seen the work just as they do. Or to put it another way, some of our best interpretations come so naturally to us that we don't recognize them as interpretations until we discover that others have viewed the work differently. Thus, we recommend that students talk to each other outside of class, where they will be more comfortable in exchanging their ideas, about what they are reading. You will find that these conversations can be interesting and helpful for several reasons. First, they will help you develop your own ideas. Second, your friends may suggest a notion that you've overlooked. Third, by just speaking about the work, you will be developing language which will help you when you sit down to write. Fourth, you will find that reading, which is a private act, can be the source of a good deal of interesting and lively socialization. As co-authors we have, of course, spent many hours talking about this book. But even before we came to write this book, when we were students attending the same college, we spent many enjoyable and exciting hours discussing literature and writing.

People who have studied brainstorming sessions have discussed ways that can make them more productive. The first rule is that no idea is ever stupid. By being negative, you will close down a conversation before it starts. If you don't like someone's idea, you should throw out a suggestion of your own or modify the idea so it will be better. You might also ask questions: Why did you say that? How did you come to that notion? Where did you get that idea? Questions can lead you from one idea to another, from a weak notion to a stronger notion. The purpose of brainstorming is to develop ideas, not shoot them down.

Another way to get started is by writing to a friend about what you're doing or by simply jotting down notes to yourself. By writing to a friend, you will give yourself the challenge of explaining the work to someone who has not read it. Consequently, you will need to be *very* clear as well as straight to the point. You will also find useful language for discussing the story as well as what are the most important things to say about the work. In fact, one of the ways to generate a thesis is by asking yourself: "If I had only one thing to say about this work of literature, what would it be?" Such *nutshelling* will help you keep the work in focus.

Step Four: Research

The best time to start research is when you've begun to form your own ideas, but have not yet settled definitely on a position. At that stage you can better evaluate when a critic has something to say that is sensible and valuable and when what the critic is saying doesn't help.

In chapter one, we discussed various ways to find material. Here we will only repeat the advice that the research librarians at your college or university library are there to help you. Tell them what you're trying to discover as specifically as you can, and don't hesitate to ask what you may think are stupid questions. The only stupid questions are the ones to which you already know the answers.

You will find that the important authors of the past have been written about extensively. You may find such a mountain of information that you may need to narrow your search to the specific work you wish to learn about. However, you may find that contemporary or living authors have virtually nothing written about them. With such authors you may need to cast your research net more widely.

At the introductory level, do not get bogged down with a critic whose work you don't understand *unless* your teacher has specifically referred you to that work. You should think of criticism as either helpful or not helpful. Criticism that doesn't help you understand the work is best passed over for the moment with the hope that someday you will be in a position to appreciate the commentary. Be grateful to those critics and scholars whose work has given you insight into literature. Refer to them in your paper, and quote phrases, sentences, or if necessary longer passages that you have found particularly well expressed.

Useful critics send you back to reread the work. Good criticism should reveal to you things about the literary works you did not notice, ways of seeing them that are either interesting, refreshing, or supportive of your own ideas. If a critic says something that seems very odd to you, you might wish to go back to the work again. Perhaps you really did miss the point.

Step Five: Mapping Your Way

By this time, we're usually a little anxious to get something down on paper because we see the deadline coming up fast. We must now face those two important questions: What do I have to say? And how can it be presented best?

Some people can think through their ideas in outline form. They can develop a good thesis then break that thesis down into various propositions that need support and identify the places in the text and in their research that support the various propositions. These people are very lucky, for they can think both logically and systematically.

Other people don't know what they have to say until they say it. These people—and they make up a majority of our students—usually need a freewriting exercise in which they get down their ideas without having to consider their logical development. Once they know what they want to say, they can go back and begin to organize their thoughts coherently.

One technique that works very well if you have access to a word processor is to write a page-length statement about what you want to say, what is often called an *abstract*. This basic statement of purpose can generate topic sentences, and by filling in the spaces between the sentences of the abstract you produce your essay. Normally abstracts are written *after* an essay is complete, and then they are also very helpful as a test to see if you have really said what you intended to say, and whether your ideas have been sufficiently and comprehensively focused.

Whatever technique you use to prepare for writing, be sure that your outline or abstract is flexible enough to change. We frequently find that as we write an essay we recognize opportunities for clarifying, supporting, or strengthening our position that we did not see at the beginning. Don't give up those opportunities. Accept the fact that your plan may need to be altered once you start writing. We have known students who in the middle of writing an essay have come to conclusions that are the opposite of what they had started out believing. As inconvenient as such discoveries are, the students were lucky to recognize their errors before they handed their papers in. They could then take the opportunity to revise what they had written to reflect their altered understanding of the work. Writing a paper should not be a mechanical process of following a blueprint, but a journey with its own opportunities for discovery.

Even after writing a first draft, you should go back to the original texts to see if you have missed supporting evidence that might be useful to you. We often don't recognize that certain passages could bolster our positions until we have finished a draft of the entire essay. These specific additions are frequently the best parts because they so clearly illustrate what we hoped to be showing.

Step Six: Writing the First Draft

In the next chapter we will discuss specific writing techniques, but now it is useful to look at the conditions that bring about your most successful papers.

Over the years we have noticed that some students write better in class than at home. When we've questioned students, we have discovered that the hour or so of uninterrupted class time is a longer stretch of writing time than they give themselves at home, or in their dormitories, or in the library. Although some people can write only if they get up and move around frequently, most people do their best work when they concentrate over a long stretch of time. Some people have found that they do best when they write their first draft in one sitting. Their papers, then, have one continual chain of thought. Afterward, they can return to the essay and make the necessary corrections and improvements. But the initial continuity is important for the success of their work.

Where you write and under what condition also affect the success of your essays. Studies have shown that by reserving a specific place and time for studying you can improve your psychological readiness. That place should be one in which you feel comfortable, with adequate light and air and an acceptable noise level. A room that is too warm will make you sleepy and sluggish. A room without enough light will make writing and reading unnecessarily tiring. Noise levels are a very personal affair. Some people prefer having some kind of noise—radio, television, stereo—playing in the background. We do not need absolute quiet, but distraction-free environments to work. We often turn on a fan or air conditioner—something with a steady hum—to screen out distracting noises.

Writing well demands a great deal of concentrated energy. You must find those times of the day when you have enough energy to do your best work, but not so much energy that you are restless and impatient. Having access to high-energy foods can help. The poet W. H. Auden drank cup after cup of tea when he was writing; a friend of ours takes a shower before writing so he feels refreshed and awake. You should find your own ways of increasing your energy and attention levels. But if you are one of the students who seem to write only in the middle of the night, you should examine yourself to see if that is the hour when you *really* are at your best, or if it is the only time you're free from distractions. If it's the latter, then consider changing where you write. Find a place where your friends can't disturb you and the outside world doesn't distract you. Your writing deserves the best part of your mind.

Step Seven: Rewriting

Rewriting should not be a single look through your paper to catch spelling and grammatical mistakes. It should also be a process that is undertaken over time. If you've started your paper well enough in advance, you should be able to put it away for a day or two before reading it over. The time will allow you to gain some distance from your writing and help you be more objective about it. It's hard to see your own mistakes, and you need ways of distancing your writing from yourself.

If you compose on a word processor, always print out your drafts and go over them on paper. The computer screen has a sneaky way of hiding errors that are apparent in black and white. We catch a great number of errors from our printed versions that we don't seem to catch when they are up on the screen.

Look for specific things on each reading. At the beginning your attention should be on clarity and organization. Have I said what I want to say in a way that others will understand? Remember that if something sounds even a little awkward to you, it will probably sound very awkward to someone else. At some point, we read our writing aloud to ourselves. By reading aloud, we slow down the checking process and catch many errors we would have left uncorrected. Only after we are satisfied that we have made good sense do we look for spelling errors, wordiness, and faulty punctuation. We usually reserve one reading just to check for overworking the passive voice. Unless you're very unusual and highly trained, you won't catch all your errors in one reading. Only after multiple readings will you give yourself a fairly good chance of finding most of your errors. Don't, however, become a perfectionist. We've never seen an essay that was error free—not even our own. Our best efforts could always be improved upon.

You may find it useful to have someone you trust read over your paper—not at the end of the writing process, but somewhere in the middle. This reader cannot be given the responsibility of correcting errors—that's your responsibility—but this reader can tell you where and when he or she had trouble understanding what you wrote. Have your reader put a check next to those sentences he or she read twice. The sentence may be in perfectly grammatical English, but if it has to be read twice it is a candidate for clarification. Sometimes, of course, an idea is difficult, and even the clearest expression will need to be re-read. But the fact that an intelligent person re-read the sentence indicates that you might need to formulate the notion more cogently.

Step Eight: The Final Version

When you go for an interview you know that you should be clean, properly attired, and punctual. Your writing is your personal representative to your teacher, and the same rules apply. Your papers should be neatly presented, in proper form, and handed in on time.

You should have your papers clearly typed. A faint copy is hard to read and looks rushed. Make sure your typewriter or printer has a fresh ribbon in it. Don't blame your typist for errors. You are responsible for giving typists clear instructions and making certain they do their job. It is your responsibility to make sure the work is done properly. If you find errors in the typed or printed version, correct them *neatly* in pen. It is usually better to correct your own mistakes than to have your professor correct them for you. If you need an extension for a legitimate reason, you should ask your instructor politely as far in advance of the deadline as you can. Make certain that your request is in the form of a question. Extensions are a privilege sometimes granted, not a right you can demand. It is best if you propose a time when you can hand in the work. That alternative deadline ought to be as close to the original one as possible.

Conclusions

Yes, the writing process that we have outlined in this chapter *will* take you a long time. Writing is not simple, and good writing usually requires enormous effort. But it is our experience that if you start out giving yourself enough time to work and proceed in an orderly way, your writing will get better and better, and you will find the experience more rewarding and less difficult as you get practice.

No one can tell you what processes and conditions are best for your individual case. You will have to find out for yourself how you perform best. But if you're open to changing the way you write, you will sooner or later find a way that's right for you. Then you will experience not only the pleasures of getting good grades, but the more profound satisfaction of expressing your thoughts effectively to others.

3  Structure, Style, and Mechanics

We have discussed the general reasons for writing papers on literature and the process by which you might go about writing such essays; now it is time to discuss the structure, style, and mechanics of the critical essay. But before exploring the nuts and bolts of writing papers of literary analysis, we should address the larger issues of audience and aim.

Audience

Before writing anything, an author should consider his or her audience, his or her readership. There are several questions that always need answering: (1) What do the readers know? (2) What do they expect? (3) What do they want or should want to know? Sometimes the answers to these questions are simple to ascertain; at other times they are impossible to anticipate.

As a student, your reader is fairly clear—it is your teacher or grader—but the answers to these questions are not necessarily as self-evident.

What does your teacher know? Probably a great deal more about literature and writing than you do, but that does not mean your professor knows everything or has experienced all perspectives. One of the most important things that your teacher does *not* know is what is in your mind. Over the years, he or she has become pretty good at guessing what students mean, but a guess is not the same as knowledge. Unless you write clearly and fully, your teacher will only be guessing about what you know, and you want him or her to have a clear and accurate knowledge of the extent of your thinking. Only when you have successfully communicated what you know, feel, and understand will you have earned the grade you deserve.

Many good students feel they can never say anything that is new to their teachers, and they feel discouraged by what they see as the unoriginal nature of their work. We have taught for many years now, and we are frequently surprised, delighted, and stimulated by what our students have to say about works that are quite familiar to us. Sometimes they take a startling new approach; more frequently they bring to our attention a word, phrase, or perspective we had never considered or reflected so fully upon. Because your experiences are *different* from your teacher's experience, you may be able to observe or appreciate details your teacher has overlooked. If you have done research about a particular poem, story, or play, you may well have more expert knowledge of the work than your teacher. We can claim extensive knowledge about very few works in this book, and we have learned a great deal from readers who have written us to make corrections, observations, and recommendations.

We have noticed that students have problems deciding what and how much information is appropriate to put in their essays. You can assume that your reader knows *literary* terminology and English fairly well. Your reader also should know the basic facts of literary history. You don't need to remind the teacher, "Shakespeare was the greatest playwright in the English language, who wrote his many works during the end of the sixteenth and beginning of the seventeenth centuries." You may assume your *teacher* knows such elementary information even if you don't. A student once wrote in a discussion of Robert Lowell's poem "Skunk Hour," which includes a reference to a "Tudor Ford," that "the Ford is a popular make of automobile." You may assume that your teacher knows at least as much as your fellow students about the various major automotive companies, but you may wish to explain why Lowell specified that his car was a *"Tudor* Ford" and not some other model. Using common sense may help you to distinguish between what needs and doesn't need explanation.

A more subtle problem is trying to decide how much needs to be summarized of a story's or a play's plot in order to explain a particular point. If your instructor has assigned a particular work, you may safely assume that the teacher has read it. If you bring in other works—even by the same author—you cannot so safely assume your teacher's familiarity. Your instructor may have read the unassigned work long ago, in which case even the broad outlines of the work may be quite fuzzy. Yet details of a work, and particularly the specific language, fade quickly from a reader's memory. Don't avoid quoting a passage because you feel your teacher knows it by heart. Similarly, don't retell the entire plot of a work the instructor has assigned. You may assume your teacher remembers the plot and characters, even as you note in your paper details and specific language.

If the answers to questions about what your reader knows are difficult to figure out, the answers to what you want your teacher to understand are even more varied. Simply put, you want your teacher to believe that your essay is meritorious, that it not only fulfills the requirements established, but has done so with intelligence, taste, energy, insight, sensitivity, care, sophistication, and grace. You wish to show that you can write well, think well, respond profoundly, and shape your insights into an effective and expressive whole. You want to show your teacher that you have insight into the subject, control of the language, and mastery over your presentation.

Having a Point

One common weakness of papers written even by good and intelligent students is that they are pointless. They wander around the subject, going from one topic to another, without any sense of direction or propulsion. Such papers don't begin; they merely start. They don't conclude; they merely end. You need to have more of a point to your papers than just the need to write something. Even before you begin framing a thesis, you need to have some point that you wish to make, depart from, or arrive at.

One of the traditional ways of thinking about a paper is that you want to persuade your reader about the validity of a certain position, defending that position against attack and question. The essay is conceived as a battle fought for the reader's mind against competing concepts. Some people find this a useful way to think of their papers. But not everyone wants to put on full battle gear in order to write.

Yet another way of giving your paper a central thread or controlling idea is by having it answer an important question or consider the consequences of certain conditions or artistic decisions. For example, one might explore the way that Tennessee Williams's decision to cast *The Glass Menagerie* as a memory play affects the way we view the action, or the way that Charlotte Perkins Gilman's treatment for depression affected her story "The Yellow Wall-Paper." In such cases a particular area of concern motivates the entire process and will give direction to the work as a whole.

Formulating a Thesis

One of the traditional ways of organizing a paper is to state your major point, controlling idea, or thesis as the conclusion of the introductory section of your paper. The introduction is usually the first paragraph in short papers, but it can be several paragraphs long in extended essays. It is useful to express your controlling idea in a single sentence because such economy will give you a handy way of testing whether you're drifting from your topic and give your reader an easy way of finding your central point. Moreover, such concision is a useful intellectual habit which will provide you with practice in summarizing or "boiling down" long arguments into manageable form.

What sort of statement is a thesis? *A thesis is a statement that needs to be proved.* Thus it is something controversial, questionable, or in need of substantiation. Facts rarely make good theses. For example, one hardly needs to prove this statement: "Lorraine Hansberry wrote *A Raisin in the Sun*." No one has questioned her authorship. A better thesis would read: "*A Raisin in the Sun* is based upon events in which Hansberry's family was personally involved." If you used this thesis, you would need to describe those family events—which are not common knowledge—and then indicate how those events were used in the play. An essayist using such a thesis has a clear point that needs substantiation.

Good theses also need to be *restrictive* and *precise*. An essay will be much more convincing if it has a clear, limited point it wishes to prove.

Here are three theses written for the same essay. Let us evaluate them to see which one would make the best paper.

1. "Young Goodman Brown" is a good story.
2. "Young Goodman Brown" clearly and powerfully shows the mind at work.
3. "Young Goodman Brown" vividly depicts the anxiety and suspicion of the Puritan mind.

The first thesis is very broad. By what standard is "Young Goodman Brown" a good story? Is it a good adventure story, psychological portrait, or social commentary? The second thesis is clearer. The story is praised for its psychological clarity and power. But the second thesis does not tell us what psychological conditions the story so "clearly and powerfully shows." Does the story show us a variety of different psychological types? The third thesis is far more precise and restrictive. The story is now praised for its depiction of the anxiety and suspicion of the Puritan mind. This last is a far easier point to prove than the vague statement that "Young Goodman Brown" is merely good.

Two other factors go into making a good thesis. A writer must choose a thesis that he or she can prove in the allotted space and time. Some theses demand so much research that they require years of study to accumulate the necessary proof. Some theses need pages of development before they can be convincingly demonstrated. A writer facing a specific deadline with specific page requirements must consider whether he or she can successfully and convincingly substantiate and defend the thesis. If not, it is better to choose a less difficult notion to write about. For example, in *Hamlet* Shakespeare investigates the manipulation of royal succession that fascinated the Elizabethan Court. While this thesis may be true, it demands a detailed knowledge of British history. Most writers choose a less specialized topic.

Exercise

Of the ten statements that follow, some are good thesis statements, some are poor, and some are not thesis statements at all. Indicate the thesis statements and improve those that seem weak.

1. Ray Bradbury wrote "There Will Come Soft Rains."
2. Bradbury's "There Will Come Soft Rains" reflects his anxiety of nuclear holocaust.
3. There are some striking similarities between Hawthorne's "The Haunted Mind" and "Young Goodman Brown."
4. Dylan Thomas's "Do Not Go Gentle into That Good Night" is a villanelle.
5. "Do Not Go Gentle into That Good Night" is a very moving poem.
6. *Oedipus Rex* ends tragically for the hero.
7. Although the couple in George Meredith's *Modern Love* is married, the sequence is typical of Elizabethan sonnet sequences because it traces the dissolution of their love.

8. The comparison between the beloved and nature in Shakespeare's sonnets underscores the supernatural quality of human beauty.
9. *The Importance of Being Earnest* made me laugh again and again.
10. Ibsen's A *Doll's House* depicts the suffocating conditions in which middle-class Victorian women lived.

Ways to Develop a Thesis

Writers often have difficulty formulating thesis statements. Where do you find a thesis? How do you come up with a good thesis? These are questions writers frequently ask. Here are some questions whose answers will help you formulate thesis statements.

1. Since the thesis is the most important statement in your essay, it should contain the most important idea you wish to share with your reader. Ask yourself, "If I had only one notion I wanted my reader to understand, what would it be?"
2. The endings of literary works frequently contain crucial actions or statements. Ask yourself, "Why does the literary work end in the way it does?"
3. Often a story, play, or poem contains a section we find particularly puzzling. Instead of ignoring the section, ask yourself, "Why is this section here?" or "What does this section mean?"
4. Stories and plays usually contain at least one important action before the work concludes. Ask yourself, "What is the significance of this action?" For example, critics have long debated why Hamlet refrains from killing Claudius when they are alone in the chapel. Answering such a question will generate an interesting paper.
5. Each work is said to express at least one basic theme. Show how that basic theme gets articulated through the literary techniques the author has employed. Such a thesis would have two parts. The first part is a theme, and the second part suggests a literary technique that brought out the theme. For example, "By presenting many scenes that involve strange coincidences, Shakespeare suggests the working out of divine fate in *Hamlet*." Such a thesis gives the reader both a clear sense of the central topic (namely, divine fate) and how the student will explore the topic (namely, by examining scenes that contain strange coincidences.)

In general, the most interesting essays are those that try to solve some literary problem. A good way to proceed is by exploring what you find problematic, and trying to solve that problem yourself.

In addition, there are specific types of papers that one could write. For example, one could write a character analysis, a comparison between two works, or an essay which relates historical information to a literary work. Each of these specific essay types is developed in a particular way.

Developing the Comparison Thesis

Many students like to compare two literary works. But it is never enough to say that two works are alike or different. A central idea that is so vague and general is sure to lead to a vague and general essay. The more specific your central idea, the more specific your essay will be.

Let us say you are intrigued by two of Shakespeare's sonnets, the ones beginning "Shall I compare thee to a summer's day," and "My mistress' eyes are nothing like the sun." You have read them carefully and have consulted the critics. You are now ready to formulate a thesis. To aid in the process, you may compare them point by point by dividing a piece of paper into two columns, one for each poem. At the end of the process, your paper looks like this:

Summer's day	*Nothing like the sun*
1. sonnet	1. sonnet
2. compares beloved to nature	2. compares beloved to nature
3. beloved is "fair" (l. 7) golden complexion (l. 6)	3. beloved is dark black hair (l. 4) skin "dun" (l. 3)
4. the beloved's eye is better than the sun (l. 5)	4. beloved's eye inferior to sun (l. 1)
5. the beloved will become the poem in the future (l. 12)	5. the beloved stands beyond the poem (l. 14)
6. beloved's beauty made eternal in poetry (l. 14)	6. beloved's beauty greater than poem can represent (l. 14)
7. beloved possesses more typical beauty	7. beloved has atypical beauty
8. tone: serious throughout, laudatory	8. tone: sometimes comic, insulting; laudatory at end
9. poem emphasizes the lasting condition of poetry and the mutable condition of nature	9. poem emphasizes the false condition of poetry and the indefinable beauty of human beings

This list does not exhaust the points of comparison, but it does give you enough material with which to begin formulating your thesis.

You notice that some of your points are facts about the poems. For example, Shakespeare is writing about two different people, one light, the other dark. Both poems speak of the sun as an eye. Could these facts be the basis of an essay? No. A thesis *must be a statement that needs proof, something controversial or uncertain.* Facts, unless they are revolutionary discoveries, are not sufficiently in need of support to be adequate statements for a thesis.

However, some of the statements are interpretive, and these might be useful in formulating a thesis. For example, the entry under "tone" indicates that both poems end by praising the beloved but that the second poem arrives at its praise in a more complicated manner. One might argue as follows: "Though both poems conclude by praising their subjects, 'My mistress' eyes are nothing like the sun,' approaches the subject in a richer, more complicated way." Because this thesis is both interpretive and evaluative, it needs to be supported. It would make a good thesis.

There are other statements one could use as the basis for a thesis. Entry 9 is interesting. One might argue: "In 'My mistress' eyes,' Shakespeare acknowledges a beauty so peculiarly human that it eludes the criteria of nature and poetry." Or, perhaps, one might wish to argue: "In these two poems Shakespeare suggests that nature is not an adequate measure by which to judge human beauty." Your list of comparisons could lead to a number of interesting theses. Critics and scholars have been studying Shakespeare's sonnets for centuries without exhausting their richness and variety. Clearly, you might formulate many different theses comparing these sonnets. You must decide which thesis most interests you and is within your capacity to support.

A good thesis, then, should incorporate a number of characteristics:

1. It should grow out of your understanding of the poem and should not be imposed on a work it may not fit.
2. It should be evaluative or interpretive. It cannot be a statement of fact, unless the fact is not yet accepted.
3. It should be precise. The reader must know what you are trying to prove. Imprecise or vague terms obscure your point and make it difficult to defend your position adequately.
4. It should be restrictive. Think of your thesis as a sort of fort under attack by the skeptical mind of your reader. If you try to protect too wide an area, your supporting forces will be too widely dispersed. A tight defense of a small territory is more likely to succeed. Never argue any point *you* do not thoroughly believe.
5. Finally, your thesis should contain one central idea. One good idea is hard enough to support and defend. More than one compels you to scatter your forces.

Developing the Character Analysis

As the chapters on characterization will show, there are two sorts of characters: round and flat. Flat characters are poor choices for literary analysis because their behavior can be summarized in a sentence or two. Flat characters do not leave one much to say or explore. Successful essays are usually written about rounded characters.

In developing a thesis about a character, you must decide whether the character changes over the course of the work or remains the same. If the character changes, one can compare the character's earlier personality to his or her later personality. As you did with the comparison essay, you can develop a worksheet. Here is one for Dimitry Dmitrich Gurov in Chekhov's "Lady with Lapdog."

Early Gurov	Later Gurov
1. contempt for women	1. love for a woman
2. thinks himself above life	2. sees difficulties ahead
3. careless of affection	3. careful of affection
4. lots of superficial friends	4. one love
5. alone in a resort	5. mostly alone in Moscow
6. confident	6. less confident
7. brags of sexual conquests	7. silent about love
8. works in bank	8. works in bank
9. dresses well	9. dresses well
10. concerned for social acceptance	10. still concerned about acceptance

We notice that Gurov has not changed in every respect. Both at the beginning and at the end of the story he works for a bank, dresses well, and wants social acceptance. Love does not entirely change him. But we note some clear differences. We notice at the beginning that he is contemptuous, careless, and self-important, while at the close of the story he is respectful, careful, and sympathetic. How can we word a thesis that might indicate this change? Let's look at three attempts:

1. Gurov changes during the course of the story.
2. The love of Anna has made Gurov a better person.
3. Through his love of Anna, Gurov has lost his unfeeling confidence and gained a richer appreciation of the difficulties of life.

Clearly the last of these is more precise and restrictive. Can you focus the thesis even more sharply?

Yet another strategy in developing a character analysis is to review the conflicts within a character's personality. Here, for example, is a worksheet on the conflicts in Hamlet's character:

1. avoids involvement in court	1. drawn into intrigue
2. wants to revenge father	2. afraid to kill uncle
3. wants to be close to mother	3. wants to hurt mother
4. wants to be close to Ophelia	4. drives Ophelia away
5. believes ghost	5. doubts ghost

Again from the worksheet, we can begin to formulate a thesis. At first we are general:

"Hamlet is in conflict with himself."

We try to make it more precise:

"Hamlet tries to be close to people but cannot be."

Last we try to be as precise as possible:

"Because of the 'rotten . . . state of Denmark,' Hamlet forces himself to keep at a distance the very people he would like to show affection to."

This thesis develops only one important conflict in Hamlet's personality. For example, one might argue that Hamlet is in conflict between the desire to revenge his father and his own tendency to do nothing. Or one might argue that Hamlet is in conflict between hating his uncle and being just to him. In restricting your thesis, you have moved from general conflicts to one specific conflict.

Developing a Historical Thesis

Among the more difficult theses to write is one that relates historical conditions to works of literature. No doubt writers, like other people, are affected by historical events. But since these effects are so subtle, various, and personal, their relation to a literary text is difficult to pin down unless the literary work specifically refers to some event. For example, Frances Harper's "The Slave Auction" refers to American slavery practices and was written at a time of Abolitionist agitation. But other works are more allusive. W.H. Auden's "Musée des Beaux Arts" never refers to the political events of 1939 or the beginnings of World War II, but the topic of suffering is made more urgent by those events. A student of the period might know that an important issue of the late thirties was how writers should respond to the approaching war. Should they become soldiers, propagandists, or stop writing completely? One might have as a thesis: "In 'Musée des Beaux Arts' Auden indicates that the artist's role is to put suffering in its proper perspective, an act necessary in the face of the rise of fascism."

Choosing Supporting Material

Although you have now formulated your thesis, you are not yet ready to start writing. First you must consider the best way to defend and support your thesis.

The best evidence for supporting your thesis is the text of the work itself. This may seem obvious, but it is surprising how easily writers overlook the source while writing about it. *Never make a statement about a work that cannot be corroborated by a passage in it.* You should quote frequently and extensively. Before stating any opinion, you should be aware of the word, line, or passage that led you to that opinion.

One of the chief complaints teachers make about student literary essays is that they are *impressionistic;* that is, they make general comments about a story, play, or poem without indicating what in the work gave rise to those ideas, feelings, or evaluations. No matter how true, well worded, or insightful such impressions are, they are nearly worthless if the writer does not connect them to the text. Students concerned about improving their writing should guard against impressionistic writing.

Your second source of support material comes from what other critics and scholars have said about the work. As we cautioned earlier, your essay should not be a collage of other people's thoughts. A critic's work should be used only when it furthers your own understanding. You should quote or paraphrase a critic or scholar only in three situations:

1. When the critic makes a point so well that it is worthy of repetition. Some critics are especially articulate and polished writers. Make use of their beautifully turned observations.

2. When the critic supplies you with an idea, a fact (not of common knowledge), a method of presentation, or an opinion that is not your own but whose truth you both recognize and need for your own essay. It is any scholar's duty to acknowledge the intellectual debt by quoting the critic and/or noting the source of the observation.

3. When you believe your own evaluation needs support. By quoting a critic, you are saying indirectly, "See, I'm not alone in this belief. X believes it, too!" Such support is especially needed when you are evaluating a piece's literary merit. It is good to have someone on your side when either praising or disparaging someone's work.

In the following paragraphs we can observe all three uses of quotation and paraphrase. The passage is part of an essay on John Milton's use of the sonnet. (You will find one of his sonnets on page 582.) The author, James G. Mengert, wishes to show that Milton effectively used traditional aspects of the sonnet in his own special way. Mengert's aim is threefold: it is factual, interpretive, and evaluative. First, Mengert must establish the facts of the sonnet tradition. Second, he must interpret Milton's use of the tradition. Third, he must evaluate Milton's use of the tradition. Mengert cannot do all this work in one paragraph, but this excerpt shows how he goes about supporting his thesis.

> It was not until J. S. Smart's edition of the sonnets in 1921 that Milton was fully allowed to have a conception of the sonnet that was in any sense traditional rather than merely or substantially idiosyncratic.[1] The roots of Milton's sonnet form in traditional, especially Italian, practice were further explored by F. T. Prince.[2] Although there have since been refinements or qualifications of the work of these men, their basic contentions still stand; and studies of individual sonnets can now take for granted Milton's firm grasp of the tradition and resources of the sonnet and go on to examine the interaction of his own powerful, reshaping genius with that tradition. Indeed, it is possible to see this very reshaping as itself a participation in a flexible sonnet tradition. Thus Taylor Stroehr introduces his own analysis of the sonnets with this comment: "He chose the form, one supposes, exactly because it was demanding, suited by its brevity to the expression of occasional thoughts and feelings, by its complexity and sinewy movement to the development of powerful emotion and tough logic." And he concludes his essay with the observation that "Milton plays the

---

[1] John S. Smart, ed., *The Sonnets of Milton* (Glasgow: Maclehose, Jackson, 1921).

[2] F. T. Prince, *The Italian Element in Milton's Verse* (Oxford: Clarendon Press, 1954), 89–107.

conventional elements of linguistic structure off against the less flexible conventions of the sonnet form itself, to produce a compelling expression of poetic feeling, beyond the reach of less self-conscious art."[3]

Mengert refers to the historical work of J. S. Smart and F. T. Prince and summarizes their findings. He then quotes Taylor Stroehr twice, first because Stroehr so beautifully articulates Mengert's position and later to support Mengert's evaluation that Milton's sonnets are great works of art. This passage is more scholarly than the writing you may be called on to produce, but it clearly indicates how the skillful use of quotation, reference, and paraphrase can support and advance an argument.

Here is an example written by a good, hardworking student:

> The title of Tennessee Williams's play *The Glass Menagerie* clearly refers to Laura's collection of blown glass animals, but the title also recalls Hart Crane's poem "The Wine Menagerie." Crane was one of Williams's favorite writers. In his *Memoirs*, Williams wrote that Hart Crane with Arthur Rimbaud were poets who "touched fire that burned them alive," and Williams wonders whether "it is only through self-immolation of such a nature that we living beings can offer you [readers] the entire truth of ourselves" (250). Also in his *Memoirs*, Williams writes that he wishes to be buried in the waters off of Cuba so that his bones may be near Hart Crane's (117). Clearly, Williams not only respected Crane as a writer, but wished to follow him as an example. Alluding to Crane's poem in his title is one way that Williams could show his respect.

Again notice that the student does not always quote from his source. The student summarizes Williams's account of wishing to be buried like Hart Crane rather than reproducing the account.

Biographical Material

Biographical information is perhaps the most difficult information to use properly in an essay. The student paragraph above, which establishes the connection between Crane and Tennessee Williams, is a good example of how biographical information can be effectively used to illuminate a text. Some professors, however, forbid the use of biographical information, going so far as to remove the author's name from literary works. They argue that the reader should be concerned only with the text and that biographical information is merely sophisticated gossip that has no place in serious literary discussion. Other teachers do recognize a place for biographical information. The rule of thumb to use is that *no biographical information should be included unless it illuminates the literature.* For example, it does help the reader to know that Sylvia Plath's father was a German professor in order to understand why there are German words in her poem "Daddy" and why he is associated with fascism. But the poem is not

---

[3] Taylor Stroehr, "Syntax and Poetic Form in Milton's Sonnets," *English Studies* 45 (1964), 289, 301.

illuminated by the fact that Plath went to Smith College on a scholarship. Thus one biographical fact may be relevant, another irrelevant. Considerate and interesting writers typically do not set aside a paragraph to give a biographical summary of the author. They do not wish to waste precious space or their reader's time with irrelevant information.

Organizing the Essay

The literary essay, like most essays, is generally divided into three basic parts: an introduction, a body, and a conclusion. Each part has its own structure and purpose.

The chief feature of the introduction is the thesis, which typically appears as the last sentence of the introductory paragraph. The rest of the paragraph sets the stage for the thesis by raising the issue the thesis attempts to answer. Indeed, one could say that the opening or introductory paragraph tries to answer the following questions: Why should a reader be interested in the thesis? Does it answer some unsolved problem? Does the thesis assert something unusual?

Like the introduction, the conclusion is usually a single paragraph in smaller essays. Conclusions generally contain no new material. They summarize what has been said in the essay. They can also project from the material discussed to the further issues it raises. But writers should be careful not to let the conclusion be too provocative. Too many threads left hanging leave the reader dissatisfied.

Most of the essay, then, is made up of body paragraphs. A body paragraph contains three parts. It usually begins with a topic sentence. The topic sentence is followed by supporting material. An optional concluding sentence either summarizes the paragraph or serves as a transition to the next paragraph.

Before writing an essay, you should first prepare an outline. Even a brief outline can be helpful. For example, let us outline a possible essay based on Tennyson's "Ulysses." The thesis we developed earlier was: "In 'Ulysses,' Tennyson explores the hero's obsessive search for knowledge." We might break this down in three ways:

1. Ulysses' earlier wanderings were a quest for new experiences.
2. Ulysses sees life as a constant quest for knowledge.
3. Ulysses' dissatisfaction with his Ithaca is derived from intellectual boredom.

If we go back through the poem, we can find textual evidence to support our contentions.

1. Ulysses' earlier wanderings were a quest for new experiences:
   a. ll. 11–12 speak of "roaming with a hungry heart."
   b. ll. 13–17 speak of the various experiences he has had on his travels.
   c. l. 64 speaks of Achilles, the hero whom he knew.
2. Ulysses sees life as a constant quest for knowledge:
   a. ll. 19–21 speak of "experience as an arch."

b. ll. 30–33 speak of the desire "to follow knowledge like a sinking star."

c. ll. 56–57 speak of the wish to "seek a newer world."

d. l. 70 speaks of wanting "to strive, to seek, to find."

3. Ulysses is dissatisfied with Ithaca because it is intellectually boring:

a. ll. 35–43 speak of the slow labor of civilizing people.

b. ll. 4–5 speak of people as crude and uninteresting.

c. ll. 22–24 speak of the boredom of a life that is not challenging.

d. l. 3 suggests that his wife does not interest him.

To this basic outline you could add references to critics and scholars who support your interpretation of "Ulysses."

Several things about this outline are noteworthy. Every point you make about the work is directly supported by several key phrases in the text. One could diagram the relationship between the thesis and the text as a pyramid whose footing is the poem.

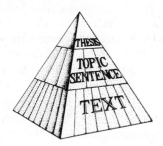

If the text were not there at every point, the entire structure would come crashing to the ground.

Another point you should notice about the outline is that we have chosen quotes from all over the text, but we have not necessarily followed the order of the poem. Under heading 3, we first begin with a quotation from the end of the poem; we then go to a quotation from the beginning, then to one from the middle, and finally to another reference to the opening lines. As a writer, you are busy proving your point. Your essay follows *your* organization, not Tennyson's.

Introductions

Even professional writers have difficulty deciding where to begin their discussions. Most often, students start the discussion far from their thesis statements and therefore never lead up to them clearly or adequately. Here, for example, is a typical opening of a student paper on "Ulysses."

Alfred, Lord Tennyson was one of the greatest English poets of the nineteenth century. He was fascinated by Greek epics and mythology. He wrote about the Greeks in such poems as "The Lotus-Eaters," "Tithonus," and "Ulysses." In "Ulysses," Tennyson explores the hero's obsessive search for knowledge.

Notice the jump between the thesis statement and the rest of the paragraph. The opening sentences are very general. They do not discuss Ulysses as either a man or a poem, nor do they mention his quest for knowledge. The key ideas of the thesis are not developed in this poor introductory paragraph.

Another error that students make in writing introductions is starting out with large claims about the human condition. For example, one student began a paper:

> Man has always had the desire to travel. The desire to wander is something we have all experienced. Sometimes the desire is to go no further than next door; at other times the desire takes us to the other side of the world. In "Ulysses," Tennyson explores the hero's obsessive desire for knowledge.

Again, the author has started too far away from the subject of the paper and thus must make large jumps to get to the thesis by the end of the paragraph. Let us rewrite the opening so that it more suitably prepares for the thesis.

> The Ulysses of Tennyson's poem has a problem understanding his own motives, for after struggling ten years to return to Ithaca, he is seized by the desire to go traveling again. He attempts to explain this desire in many ways. He feels useless in Ithaca; he is not a patient administrator; he is misunderstood by his people, who "hoard, and sleep, and feed, and know not me" (1. 5). But the heart of his dissatisfaction is a desire for knowledge. In "Ulysses," Tennyson explores the hero's obsessive desire for knowledge.

Notice how in this second version, the author has gotten straight down to business by eliminating any superfluous discussion of Tennyson in general and focusing immediately on the issue of Ulysses' motives for leaving Ithaca. The thesis, then, is a summary of the discussion in the introduction. Clear and to the point, this new introduction well prepares the reader for the discussion that follows.

Conclusions

Sophisticated writers will attempt to conclude an essay by suggesting the significance of the observations for a wider understanding of life or of the author's work. First, let us look at an adequate conclusion to our paper on "Ulysses."

> Ulysses is not a king satisfied with being an executive, a manager, a bureaucrat. In his past wanderings, Ulysses has accustomed himself to constantly-changing experience and ever-increasing knowledge. Ithaca has given him all of the experiences it contains, and now he feels compelled to "seek a newer world" (1. 57). With his band of aging mariners, he determinedly sets out "to strive, to seek, to find, and not to yield" (1. 70).

Here is another conclusion, one that extends the meaning of the poem while summarizing the argument.

> Through the poem, we come to understand Ulysses' needs better. For Ulysses, power is not enough, comfort is not enough; food, drink, shelter are insufficient for life. Ulysses has become aware of a great human emotion—curiosity, a

desire for new knowledge and experience. Once that appetite is developed, it is not forgotten or easily sated. Ulysses' curiosity elevates him above the swashbuckling heroism of his fellow warriors like Achilles, and makes him a new hero for an age yet to come.

Body Paragraphs

Body paragraphs are used to support the thesis. Topic sentences break down the thesis into smaller, defendable units. For example, in the following paragraph Michael Ferber discusses William Blake's poem "London" (the text of which is on page 628). Ferber's thesis is that "London" is basically a political poem, despite the claims of some critics. He hopes to show in part how political the poem is by explaining some of the political implications of the words used in the poem. Here is the paragraph that explains the phrase "charter'd street."

> We meet *charter'd street* right away. I have little to add to the discussions by David Erdman and E. P. Thompson of the connotations of *charter'd* which emerge when we set the poem in its historical context. London had a charter, granting it certain privileges or liberties, and so did many commercial associations in the City such as the East India Company, prominent along the banks of the Thames. Yet one man's charter is another's manacle; charters are exclusive. It was over just this two-sidedness of "charter" and its synonyms that Burke, Paine, and many others fought their pamphlet wars. In Part II of *Rights of Man*, published the year Blake probably wrote his poem (1792), Paine wrote, "It is a perversion of terms to say, that a charter gives rights. It operates by a contrary effect, that of taking rights away." The adjective "chartered" had as it still does the sense of "hired" or "leased," which combines with Paine's pejorative political nuance to suggest the monopolistic and exploitative practices of England's commercial empire. Under the regime of Pitt, as under every regime at least since the Conqueror, all Englishmen are "chartered," and the second half of the poem is a litany of typical cases: they are sold into slavery as chimney sweepers by their fathers, impressed into the army or navy for a few shillings, hired for a few hours as harlots, or bought and sold on the London marriage market.

Notice how full and yet economical the paragraph is. Ferber does not quote David Erdman and E. P. Thompson directly. He is content merely to refer to their work. His longest quotation is an elegant sentence from Thomas Paine, who perfectly exemplifies both Ferber's and Blake's position.

Quotations
Direct and Indirect Quotations

One difficulty in writing a body paragraph lies in integrating quotations into the flow of your own words. There are two general types of quotations: direct and indirect. An indirect quotation is a paraphrase of the author's words. For example, you might write:

Ulysses says *that* his wife is old.

The word *that* indicates you are not quoting Ulysses' precise words. However, you might have written:

> Ulysses complains of being "matched with an aged wife."

This second version is a direct quotation; consequently, the quoted phrase is enclosed by quotation marks. Indirect quotations save both space and explanation. Often one can more easily paraphrase an author than integrate direct quotations. However, indirect quotations are of limited use. Because the words are yours, they are less convincing than the poet's own words. You open yourself to the charge of altering the poet's meaning to suit your own purposes.

Long and Short Quotations

Direct quotations may be either short or extensive. Short quotations can be as brief as one word or as long as two lines, and they are placed within the text of the essay. For example, the sentence "Ulysses complains of being 'matched with an aged wife,' " represents a short quotation. Extensive quotations are any that are longer than two lines of poetry or two sentences in length. They are generally isolated from the main text and distinguished from it in some way, as in this example of an essay that discusses Robert Frost's "Out, Out—." (The text of "Out, Out—" can be found on pages 553–54.)

> The most painful of these encounters [with the physical world], of course, takes place in "Out, Out—," where a boy helping some adults work with a power saw loses his right hand to the saw and then, as a result, life itself. The implicit epigraph to this poem is contained in the passage in *Macbeth* that follows the words of the title:
>
> > Out, out, brief candle!
> > Life's . . . a tale
> > Told by an idiot, full of sound and fury,
> > Signifying nothing.
>
> These lines, as I have pointed out in another connection, express not Frost's cynical view of life, but his tacit condemnation of a world in which people make things go wrong, starting with the refusal of the unnamed "they" to allow the boy an extra half-hour at the end of the day to watch the sunset.

Notice that since the quotation begins in the middle of the poetic line, the quotation is placed in a way that indicates its position. Indeed, a writer is always expected to indicate where each line ends. In short quotations the slash is used to indicate line breaks, as in this discussion of Wordsworth's "The Solitary Reaper."

> The aloneness of the singer is intensified in the second stanza when she is compared to the lone nightingale singing in far-off Arabia and to the solitary cuckoo "Breaking the silence of the seas/Among the farthest Hebrides." The melancholy tone and rhythm established in the first stanza are developed in the third stanza.

The foregoing passage indicates several aspects of quoting. When you quote, you *must* quote the passage exactly as it is written, without making any alterations.

In the foregoing passage, the line break is indicated and Wordsworth's punctuation is preserved precisely as it was published.

Punctuating Quotations

Occasionally you will want to delete or add words to a quotation. Deletions must be indicated by an *ellipsis*, or three dots. Notice that in the quotation from Shakespeare, the author has deleted several words. The omission is indicated by an ellipsis. One should delete only unimportant words or phrases. You do not want to alter the meaning of the text by eliminating essential words. Additions are indicated by placing the inserted words in brackets. For example, note the addition in this sentence about "Out, Out—":

> The boy in Frost's poem has his life snuffed "out [like a] brief candle."

In quotations one may also replace pronouns with their antecedent nouns. One must be careful to preserve the original meaning, however. For example, in Tennyson's poem, Ulysses always speaks of himself in the first person. Such references may not be clear when quoted. In the following passage, note how a proper name has been substituted for the pronoun *me*.

> The people of Ithaca are lazy, stupid and barely civilized. They "hoard, and sleep, and feed, and know not [Ulysses]."

Deletions and additions are often necessary to integrate quotations into the text. Many writers prefer numerous short quotations over long ones. By quoting frequently, an essayist can constantly refer to the text and keep the poet's words in the reader's mind.

Not all quotations need to be preceded by a comma. A comma is not necessary if the quotation is part of the sentence's flow. Study the punctuation of the following two sentences.

1. Ulysses says, "I cannot rest from travel."
2. Ulysses is a man who "cannot rest from travel."

In the first sentence there is a grammatical break between the sentence and the quotation. In the second the quotation is part of the sentence's flow; thus no commas are needed in sentence 2. Examine how quotations are used in the passages we have studied. You will notice that careful writers try to integrate their quotations into the flow of their sentences.

Documentation

Writers should acknowledge the source of any ideas or quotations they have used by parenthetical notations in text and by a list of works cited at the end of the essay.

Why do authors document their sources? The practice may seem tedious, troublesome, and unnecessary, but it does serve important functions.

The first reason for documentation is to help the reader. Because most quotations are relatively short, the reader may wish to understand the context of the quotation or more of what the original author has to say. Without a citation, the reader would have no way to find the source of the quotation.

Second, documentation is a means of maintaining intellectual honesty. We are all indebted to others for ideas, skills, and knowledge, and it is only proper to acknowledge that debt. Without such acknowledgment we would be claiming other people's thoughts and language as our own. To the educated person, stealing people's ideas is as heinous as stealing their property. Indeed, copyright and patent laws make it a punishable offense to steal someone's words and ideas without compensation and permission.

Documentation must contain the author's name, the title of the work, and the page number citing where the quotation appears. In the case of an article, you must note the name of the journal in which it appeared and the volume and date of its appearance. For books, you must note the place of publication, the publisher, and the date of publication.

We cannot give a complete list of all the items you may need to document. For a complete list, consult the latest edition of the *MLA Handbook for Writers of Research Papers*.

PREPARING A LIST OF WORKS

On a separate page at the end of your essay or report, you must prepare a list of works cited. The page should be headed "Works Cited," and the list arranged in alphabetical order. Here are several of the commonest kinds of entries:

A book by a single author

> Huberman, Elizabeth. *The Poetry of Edwin Muir: The Field of Good and Ill*. New York: Oxford UP, 1971.

An article

> Mengert, James G. "The Resistance of Milton's Sonnets." *English Literary Renaissance* 11 (1981): 81–95.

A work in an anthology

> García Márquez, Gabriel. "A Very Old Man with Enormous Wings." *The Heath Guide to Literature*. Ed. David Bergman and Daniel Mark Epstein. 3rd ed. Lexington: Heath, 1991. 293–298.

Cross-references

Sometimes you will be using essays by several authors collected into one book. So that you do not have to repeat information unnecessarily, you should create entries patterned after the following:

> Brooks, Cleanth. "The Modern Poet and the Tradition." Hollander 105–139.
> Hollander, John, ed. *Modern Poetry: Essays in Criticism*. London: Oxford UP, 1968.
> Matthiessen, F. O. "Tradition and the Individual Talent." Hollander 176–200.

PREPARING PARENTHETICAL REFERENCES

When a list of works is cited at the end of the essay or report, you need only refer in parentheses to the name of the author followed by a page number to let the reader know where you obtained a specific idea or found a particular quotation. If the author's name is mentioned in the text, you only need to indicate the page number. The following examples illustrate the most common types of citation:

Parenthetical note when author is not mentioned in the text

> Latin American authors have developed out of folk traditions and popular culture a style called "magical realism." One story includes a molting angel and a woman transformed into a spider as punishment for disobeying her parents (García Márquez 186).

Parenthetical note when author is mentioned

> Latin American authors have developed out of folk traditions and popular culture a style called "magical realism." In one story of Gabriel García Márquez, a molting angel falls to earth and a woman who appears in a carnival is transformed into a spider for disobeying her parents (186).

Parenthetical note of direct quotation

> Latin American authors have developed out of folk traditions and popular culture a style called "magical realism." In Gabriel García Márquez's "A Very Old Man with Enormous Wings," a traveling carnival contains a "woman who had been changed into a spider for having disobeyed her parents" (186).

Parenthetical note of direct quotation without author's name

> Latin American authors have developed out of folk traditions and popular culture a style called "magical realism." In one instance, for example, a fallen angel competes for popularity with a "woman who had been changed into a spider for having disobeyed her parents" (García Márquez 186).

Bibliographies

Short essays do not need bibliographies. However, teachers may require bibliographies in order to give students practice in writing them. A bibliography lists alphabetically by the author's last name all the works consulted. Thus our list of books and articles would look like this.

> Huberman, Elizabeth. *The Poetry of Edwin Muir: The Field of Good and Evil.* New York: Oxford UP, 1971.
> Mengert, James G. "The Resistance of Milton's Sonnets," *English Literary Renaissance* 11 (1981). 81–95.
> Tennyson, Alfred Lord. "Ulysses," in *The Poems of Tennyson.* Ed. Christopher Ricks, London: Longman's, 1969. 560–566.

Exercise

Below is all the bibliographical information you will need for creating a "Works Cited" page for a paper on Sylvia Plath. Create such a page.

1. The checked article from *The Southern Review*

VOLUME IX, NEW SERIES   ★   JULY, 1973   ★   NUMBER 3

Contents

The Short, Short Poem, *Donald E. Stanford*   xix

ESSAYS

√ The Death Throes of Romanticism: The Poems of Sylvia Plath,
    Joyce Carol Oates   501

The Stratagems of Caroline Gordon; Or, The Art of the Novel
    and the Novelty of Myth, *Howard Baker*   523

2. This critical book

© 1979 *The University of North Carolina Press [Chapel Hill]*

All rights reserved
Manufactured in the United States of America
Library of Congress Catalog Card Number 78-14023
ISBN 0-8078-1338-9

Library of Congress Cataloging in Publication Data

Rosenblatt, Jon, 1947–
    Sylvia Plath: the poetry of initiation.

    Bibliography: p.
    Includes index.
    1. Plath, Sylvia—Criticism and interpretation.
    2. Initiations in literature.   I. Title.
PS3566.L27Z87   811'.54   78-14023
ISBN 0-8078-1338-9

3. The checked articles from this collection of critical essays

Copyright © 1984 by Linda W. Wagner
All Rights Reserved

Library of Congress Cataloging in Publication Data
Main entry under title:

Critical essays on Sylvia Plath

    (Critical essays on American literature)
    Includes index.
    1. Plath, Sylvia – Criticism and interpretation –
Collected works.   I. Wagner, Linda Welshimer.   II. Series.
PS3566.L27Z631984   811'.54   83-26562
ISBN 0-8161-8682-0

G. K. Hall & Company • Boston, Massachusetts

√ Marjorie Perloff. "Angst and Animism in the Poetry of
Sylvia Plath" 109

√ Guinevara A. Nance and Judith P. Jones. "Doing Away
with Daddy: Exorcism and Sympathetic Magic in
Plath's Poetry" 124

Pamela J. Annas. "The Sell in the World: The Social
Context of Sylvia Plath's Late Poems" 130

Frederick Buell. "Sylvia Plath's Traditionalism" 140

√ Susan R. Van Dyne. " 'More Terrible Than She Ever Was':
The Manuscripts of Sylvia Plath's Bee Poems" 154

Margaret Dickie. "Sylvia Plath's Narrative Strategies" 170

Melody Zajdel. "Apprenticed in a Bible of Dreams: Sylvia
Plath's Short Stories" 182

Roberta Mazzenti. "Plath in Italy" 193

√ Sandra M. Gilbert. "In Yeats' House: The Death and
Resurrection of Sylvia Plath" 204

4. This critical book published by the University of Illinois Press, Urbana, in 1979

Library of Congress Cataloging in Publication Data

Uroff, Margaret Dickie.
  Sylvia Plath and Ted Hughes.

  Includes index.
  1. Plath, Sylvia — Criticism and interpretation.
2. Hughes, Ted, 1930–   — Criticism and
interpretation. I. Title.
PS3566.L27Z94   821'.9'1409   79-74
ISBN 0-252-00734-4

5. This collection of Plath's poetry

FIRST U.S. EDITION

Library of Congress Cataloging in Publication Data

Plath, Sylvia.
  The collected poems.
  Includes index.
  1. Hughes, Ted, 1930-   II. Title.
PS3566.L27A17 1981   811'.54   75-25057
                              AACR2
ISBN 0-06-013369-4   82 83 84 85 10 9 8 7 6 5 4 3 2
ISBN 0-06-090900-5 (pbk.)   82 83 84 85 10 9 8 7 6 5 4 3 2

6. This edition of her journals

THE JOURNALS OF
Sylvia Plath

Foreword by Ted Hughes
Ted Hughes, Consulting Editor
and Frances McCullough, Editor

Published by The Dial Press • 1 Dag Hammarskjold Plaza •
New York, New York 10017

Text of the journals copyright © 1982 by Ted Hughes as the Executor of the
Estate of Sylvia Plath.

7. This bibliography

Library of Congress Cataloging in Publication Data

Northouse, Cameron.
   Sylvia Plath and Anne Sexton: a reference guide.

   (Reference guides in American literature, no. 1)
   1. Plath, Sylvia—Bibliography.   2. Sexton, Anne—
Bibliography.   I. Walsh, Thomas P., joint author.
II. Title.
Z8695.85.N67   016.811'5'4   74-14965
ISBN 0-8161-1146-4

G. K. HALL & CO., 70 LINCOLN STREET, BOSTON, MASS. 1974

8. The checked article from *Harper's*.

Harper's Magazine

FOUNDED IN 1850/VOL. 244 NO. 1460   JANUARY 1972

ARTICLES

Simone de Beauvoir	33	JOIE DE VIVRE
		An inquiry into the sexual dimensions of aging.
Russell Baker	64	THE SAYINGS OF POOR RUSSELL
		A celebrated observer's wit and wisdom.
Donald Hogan	73	THE CATHOLIC EDGE ON REVOLUTION
		Searching for articles of faith.
Orde Coombs	24	SOUL IN SUBURBIA
		The futility of black escape.
Robert Coover	82	BEGINNINGS

DEPARTMENTS

Lewis H. Lapham	10	THE EASY CHAIR
		Letter to a doctrinaire friend
Jeff Greenfield	16	PERFORMING ARTS
		Hockey fanatics
Fred Feldkamp	72	GAMES SOME PEOPLE PLAY
		The *Tiercé*
√ Irving Howe	88	BOOKS: Sylvia Plath
Garry Wills	92	BOOKS: LBJ
William C. Martin	95	MUSIC
		White gospel singers

Irving Howe

BOOKS

Sylvia Plath:
a partial disagreement

A GLAMOUR OF FATALITY hangs over the name of Sylvia Plath, the glamour that has made her a darling of our culture. Extremely gifted, her will clenched into a fist of ambition, several times driven to suicide by a suffering so absolute as to seem almost impersonal, yet in her last months composing poems in

Your page should look like this:

Works Cited

Gilbert, Sandra M. "In Yeats' House: The Death and Resurrection of Sylvia Plath." Wagner 204–231.

Howe, Irving. "Sylvia Plath: A Partial Agreement." *Harper's Magazine* Jan. 1972: 88+.

Nance, Guinevara A. and Judith P. Jones. "Doing Away with Daddy: Exorcism and Sympathetic Magic in Plath's Poetry." Wagner 124–39.

Northouse, Cameron. *Sylvia Plath and Anne Sexton: A Reference Guide*. Reference Guides in American Literature, No. 1. Boston: Hall, 1974.

Oates, Joyce Carol. "The Death Throes of Romanticism: The Poems of Sylvia Plath." *Southern Review* 9.3 (1973): 501–22.

Perloff, Marjorie. "Angst and Animism in the Poetry of Sylvia Plath." Wagner 109–23.

Plath, Sylvia. *The Collected Poems*. New York: Harper, 1981.

———. *The Journals of Sylvia Plath*. Ed. Ted Hughes and Frances McCullough. New York: Dial, 1982.

Rosenblatt, Jon. *Sylvia Plath: The Poetry of Initiation*. Chapel Hill: U of North Carolina P, 1979.

Uroff, Margaret Dickie. *Sylvia Plath and Ted Hughes*. Urbana: U of Illinois P, 1979.

Van Dyne, Susan R. "'More Terrible Than She Ever Was': The Manuscripts of Sylvia Plath's Bee Poems." Wagner 154–69.

Wagner, Linda W., ed. *Critical Essays on Sylvia Plath*. Critical Essays on American Literature. Boston: Hall, 1984.

4 ❧ Nine Short Essays

Here are nine short essays on stories, poems, and plays contained in this book. Many of the essays were written by students just like you, and they should provide you with examples that you should be able to equal or even surpass. We also have included several short professional examples. These will give you models at which to aim. None of these essays should be slavishly imitated. But they should provide you with ideas about how to go about the exciting, difficult, and always challenging task of writing about literature.

ALICE HALL PETRY

Faulkner's "A Rose for Emily"

In the more than fifty years since it was first published, "A Rose for Emily" has proved to be one of the most frequently anthologized and analyzed of Faulkner's short stories. The bulk of the criticism it has generated has tended to focus, understandably enough, on the two most salient features of the story: the disordered chronology and the shocking ending. Closely related to these two features is an element which has attracted significantly less interest: Faulkner's utilization of language. To suggest how complex and provocative is the language of "A Rose for Emily," I wish to focus on but one sentence of the story:

> Thus she passed from generation to generation—dear, inescapable,
> impervious, tranquil, and perverse. (128)

As Cleanth Brooks has remarked, it is "a fine sentence . . . well worth pondering," although regrettably he takes the matter no further (12). More probing, Austin McGiffert Wright argues that the passage is misleading: neither so authoritative nor complete as it may appear, the statement applies "only to the judgment of the town upon her before the secrets of Emily's private life are exposed" (334). But in fact the passage is not misleading. Since "A Rose for Emily" is essentially a series of flashbacks, the statement is offered by the narrator after the events in the story have transpired. With this in mind, one can see that the passage—strategically placed at the end of Part IV—serves both as an important unifying device for the story, as well as a subtle (but typically Faulknerian) element of foreshadowing.

The sentence in question offers a catalogue of five adjectives pertaining to Emily: "dear, inescapable, impervious, tranquil, and perverse." Terry Heller, in an excellent analysis of "A Rose for Emily" in *Arizona Quarterly*, comments that "only four" of the adjectives have been portrayed in the story by the time we encounter the passage (313); but Heller does not seem to recognize that the catalogue is sequential: that is to say, each of the five adjectives in the catalogue corresponds to one of the five parts of the story, in the order in which those parts are presented. Consider the adjectives themselves. The first one, "dear," can mean sweet or cherished; but as Heller notes, it can also mean "costly" (313)—and it is in Part I of the story that we see Emily refusing to pay her municipal taxes, despite a direct confrontation with the Board of Aldermen. The second adjective, "inescapable," refers to the incident of "the smell" in Part II: as the body of Homer Barron decomposes, the town cannot escape this graphic testimony to Emily's presence in the community. The third adjective, "impervious," would serve as an ideal title for Part III: Emily stonily refuses to concede to the law in regard to the purchase of poison ("Miss Emily just stared at [the druggist], her head tilted back in order to look him eye for eye, until he looked away and went and got the arsenic . . . (126); and, on a more ironic note, her sexual penetration in Part III confirms her imperviousness:

> She carried her head high enough—even when we believed that
> she was fallen. It was as if she demanded more than ever the

> recognition of her dignity as the last Grierson; as if it had wanted
> that touch of earthiness to reaffirm her imperviousness. (125)

The fourth adjective, "tranquil," refers to her post-murder life as portrayed in Part IV: she gives china-painting lessons for several years, sits passively in one of the downstairs windows "like the carven torso of an idol in a niche" (128) and, having fallen ill "in the house filled with dust and shadows," she quietly dies (128). The fifth adjective, "perverse," might be interpreted in a benign, general sense as meaning "stubborn" or "out of step with the community"; but, if one is sensitive to the fact that the four previous adjectives in the catalogue correspond successively (and in specific ways) to the first four parts of the story, then one should fully expect that Part V will illustrate Emily's "perverse" nature in the most specific sense of the word—moral and/or sexual perversity; and of course this is confirmed in the shocking final scene of the story.

Faulkner's placement of the adjective catalogue at the end of Part IV serves, then, as an important unifying device in this emotionally complex and chronologically confusing narrative. At a key moment in a story which is organized "by feeling rather than by logic," (Sullivan 168) the adjective catalogue affords the reader an opportunity to pause, to consider again the mass of information conveyed in the first four parts of the story, to anticipate the startling conclusion, to trace the narrator's protean emotional responses to Emily—in short, to seek the order which underlies the narrative. The organic five-adjective catalogue may be a more subtle unifying device than, say, the consistent focus on Emily, the recurrent eye imagery, or the symmetrical five-part format (Watkins 510), but its subtlety does not compromise its effectiveness.

It is not unreasonable to surmise that Faulkner consciously designed the adjective catalogue to function in this complex fashion. Warren Beck notes that Faulkner's oft-criticized tendency to "pile up words" has a viable place "in a style so minutely analytical" as his (35). And as Faulkner himself remarked in 1957, the short story as a genre demands precision of language: "In a short story that's next to the poem, almost every word has got to be almost exactly right. In the novel you can be careless but in the short story you can't" (Gwynn and Blotner 207). "A Rose for Emily" illustrates this precision of language admirably.

Works Cited

Beck, Warren. *Faulkner, Essays by Warren Beck*. Madison: U of Wisconsin P, 1976.
Brooks, Cleanth. *William Faulkner: First Encounters*. New Haven: Yale UP, 1983.
Faulkner, William. *Collected Stories*. New York: Random House, 1950.
Gwynn, Frederick I. and Joseph I. Blotner, eds. *Faulkner in the University: Class Conferences at The University of Virginia, 1957–1958*. Charlottesville: U of Virginia P, 1959.
Heller, Terry. "The Telltale Hair: A Critical Study of William Faulkner's 'A Rose for Emily.' " *Arizona Quarterly* 28 (1972):301–318.
Sullivan, Ruth. "The Narrator in 'A Rose for Emily.' " *Journal of Narrative Technique* 1 (1971):159–178.
Watkins, Floyd C. "The Structure of 'A Rose for Emily.' " *Modern Language Notes* 69 (1954):508–510.
Wright, Austin McGiffert. *The American Short Story in the Twenties*. Chicago: U of Chicago P, 1961.

ERNEST W. SULLIVAN, II

The Cur in "The Chrysanthemums"

Anyone reading John Steinbeck's "The Chrysanthemums" cannot help being struck by the repeated association of unpleasant canine characteristics with the otherwise attractive Elisa Allen. These associations identify her with the visiting tinker's mongrel dog, further suggesting a parallel between the Allens' two ranch shepherds and the tinker and Elisa's husband, Henry. The correspondences between people and dogs elucidate the social and sexual relationships of the three humans, as well as foreshadow and explain Elisa's failure at the end of the story to escape from her unproductive and sterile lifestyle.

The dog imagery related to Elisa is uncomplimentary. In her garden, she destroys unpleasant creatures such as "aphids," "bugs," "snails," "cutworms," and similar "pests" with her "terrier fingers."[1] When aroused by the tinker, she "crouched low like a fawning dog" (18). Finally, in response to the tinker's assertion that his life of freedom "ain't the right kind of life for a woman," she bares her teeth in hostile fashion: "Her upper lip raised a little, showing her teeth" (19). Burrowing in flower gardens, fawning, snarling—not a very pleasant picture of man's best friend.

The last two images directly link Elisa to the tinker's mongrel, and their physical descriptions clearly parallel these two unfortunates. She kneels before the tinker like a dog would to shake hands: "Kneeling there, her hand went out toward his legs in the greasy black trousers. Her hesitant fingers almost touched the cloth. Then her hand dropped to the ground. She crouched low like a fawning dog" (18). As Elisa bared her teeth in resistance to the tinker, so his mongrel resisted the two Allen ranch shepherds "with raised hackles and bared teeth" (13). Additionally, the cur is "lean and rangy" (13); Elisa is "lean and strong" (10). Finally, of course, the tinker's mongrel, unlike the ranch shepherds, contains a mixture of dog breeds, and Elisa's personality mixes masculine and feminine elements.[2]

Whereas Elisa shares several characteristics with the cur, the tinker and Henry resemble the two ranch shepherds. The two shepherds were born to their jobs, which they perform instinctively. Confident that "Pots, pans, knives, sisors, lawn mores" can all be "Fixed" (13), the tinker feels at home in his occupation and world: " 'I ain't in any hurry, ma'am. I go from Seattle to San Diego and back every year. Takes all my time. About six months each way. I aim to follow nice weather' " (14). Henry Allen is also successful at his job and derives satisfaction from it: "I sold those thirty head of three-year-old steers. Got nearly my own price, too" (11). On the other hand, Elisa, like the mongrel, does not participate in the main work on which her livelihood depends,

---

[1] John Steinbeck, *The Long Valley* (New York: Viking Press, 1956), 10–11. All quotations are from this text.

[2] The mixed elements of Elisa's personality are also suggested in the " 'good bitter smell' " (16) of the chrysanthemums with which she is usually identified.

even though her husband suggests that she should become useful: "I wish you'd work out in the orchard and raise some apples that big" (11). Both Elisa and the cur are merely companions for their respective breadwinners, their subservient position suggested by Elisa's kneeling before the tinker: "She was kneeling on the ground looking up at him" (18).

The interaction of the three dogs closely parallels that of the three people and foreshadows Elisa's eventual failure to escape her confined lifestyle. When the mongrel darts from its accustomed position beneath the tinker's wagon, the two ranch dogs shepherd it back. The mongrel considers fighting, but, aware that it could not overcome the two dogs secure on their home ground, retreats angrily back under the wagon and protection of its owner: "The rangy dog darted from between the wheels and ran ahead. Instantly the two ranch shepherds flew out at him. Then all three stopped, and with stiff and quivering tails, with taut straight legs, with ambassadorial dignity, they slowly circled, sniffing daintily. . . . The newcomer dog, feeling out-numbered, lowered his tail and retired under the wagon with raised hackles and bared teeth" (13).

Elisa, in the course of the story, moves out of her accustomed role to challenge Henry and the tinker on their home ground, their occupations and sexuality. In response to Henry's comment that she could put her skills to productive use in the orchards, "Elisa's eyes sharpened. 'Maybe I could do it, too'" (11). But she never does. Her challenge to his sexuality is equally unfulfilled; in response to her appearance in "the dress which was the symbol of her prettiness" (21), Henry observes that "You look strong enough to break a calf over your knee, happy enough to eat it like a watermelon" (21–22) and goes to turn on the car. Elisa directly expresses an urge to compete in the tinker's occupation: " 'You might be surprised to have a rival some time. I can sharpen scissors, too. And I can beat the dents out of little pots. I could show you what a woman might do' " (19). The tinker rebuts her challenge: " 'It ain't the right kind of a life for a woman' " (19), and her career as a tinker never gets started. The tinker's feigned interest in the chrysanthemums clearly arouses Elisa's sexual instincts: "Her breast swelled passionately" (18), and she does her unconscious best to arouse his: "Elisa's voice grew husky. . . . 'When the night is dark—why, the stars are sharp-pointed, and there's quiet. Why, you rise up and up! Every pointed star gets driven into your body. It's like that. Hot and sharp and—lovely' " (18). And, as had her husband, the tinker deflects the conversation to one involving a less carnal appetite: " 'It's nice, just like you say. Only when you don't have no dinner, it ain't' " (18).

In each case, when Elisa threatened to encroach upon male territory, she was rebuffed and shepherded back to the refuge of her submissive and unproductive place. Elisa, like the cur, might be " 'a bad dog in a fight when he gets started' " (13), but, like the cur, she rarely, if ever, gets started: " 'sometimes [he does] not [get started] for weeks and weeks' " (13). The positions of the dogs after the meeting between Elisa and the tinker foreshadow her final defeat. The cur "took his place between the back wheels" (20), and, with Elisa's occupational and sexual challenge to the tinker rebuffed, the ranch shepherds could cease their watchfulness: "Only the dogs had heard. They lifted their heads toward her from their sleeping in the dust, and then stretched out their chins and settled asleep again" (20).

Interestingly, neither the mongrel nor Elisa gives up until "out-numbered." Any previous challenges to her husband's role as breadwinner and sexual aggressor have apparently been frustrated; the story offers no evidence of her doing farm work; they have no children; and Henry responds unromantically to Elisa's effort to make herself sexually attractive. Yet her occupational and sexual challenges to the tinker show that she has not given up. After the tinker also rejects her by discarding the chrysanthemums that she had given him, Elisa, like the out-numbered cur baring his teeth at the two shepherds, vents her anger and frustration over her defeat through her description of the pain inflicted upon men in fights: " 'I've read how they break noses, and blood runs down their chests. I've read how the fighting gloves get heavy and soggy with blood' " (23). Overcome by the two men, Elisa never gets started in the fight to escape her role; she even decides against vicarious participation in the fight: " 'I don't want to go [to the fights]. I'm sure I don't' " (23). She retreats to the safety of her accustomed unproductive and sexless role, "crying weakly—like an old woman" (23).

DAVID MATTHEW ROSEN

Time, Identity, and Context in Wyatt's Verse

In reading Thomas Wyatt's poem "They Flee from Me," one is struck by the power of the human voice speaking in its lines. Though a lithe and simple lyric, "They Flee from Me" resonates with nuances of emotion that encompass not only the speaker's distress at the loss of love, but also his distress at the irrevocable passage of time.[1] How does Wyatt create this remarkable voice full of the evanescence of beautiful moments? It is through the layering of time, the juxtaposition of incident in a way that suggests the dissolution of one moment into the next, and so conveys impermanence, frustration, despair.

In "They Flee from Me" each stanza creates a context for the next. In the opening stanza, the poet relates his experience with some ambiguous creatures in an unclear past by juxtaposing their former tameness with their present return to a wilder state. The fragility of their momentary tameness is heightened by its distance in time and by our awareness of its extraordinary character. The preciousness of this experience and the poignancy of its loss serve as the context for our understanding of what follows.

The second stanza recreates a more particular time when unexpectedly the beloved kissed her lover. When the woman embraces the poet, the moment is sweet for being both unexpected and desired. Yet we are aware that, although longed for, the moment is disconnected from what appears to be the natural flow of things—the woman's usual behaviour, her distance. Like the creatures', it is the possibility of the woman's reversion to a wilder state, the sense of her underlying wildness that is brought to the moment, that, in fact, makes the moment precious. The woman and the creatures are so desirable because they can never be fully possessed.[2] They are, like creatures in much of Wyatt's verse, too complex to be contained by any person or any arbitrary set of rules.

The moment of the kiss, nonetheless, remains for the poet a sacred moment, fixed and transcendent, as he exclaims at the beginning of the second stanza. But this transcendent past, this luminous moment—that in religion would begin a new era and order different from the temporal one—remains unfulfilled expectation. In a world pressed forward by time, the kiss is inevitably juxtaposed with events as they actually turn out. Like the past changing to a present with which it is both connected and disconnected, the woman changes. Like time itself, she recognizes her relationship with her lover, but like time, she invites "newfangledness." Although to the poet's idealistic mind the woman's actions seem cruel and unexpected, they are no more cruel and unexpected than the creatures' actions with which they are linked. Only the poet's static position

---

[1] For an amusingly jaundiced review of critical background, see Richard L. Greene, "Wyatt's 'They Flee from Me' and the Busily Seeking Critics," *Bucknell Review* 12. 3 (1964): 17–30. Some have not been intimidated: Leonard E. Nathan, "Tradition and Newfangledness in Wyatt's 'They Flee from Me,'" *ELH* 32. 1 (1965): 1–16; Leigh Winser, "The Question of Love Tradition in Wyatt's 'They Flee from Me,'" *Essays in Literature (Western Illinois University)* 2. 1 (1975): 3–9; Carolyn Chiapelli, "A Late Gothic Vein in Wyatt's 'They Flee from Me,'" *Renaissance and Reformation* 1. 2 (1977): 95–102.

[2] Michael McCanles, "Love and Power in the Poetry of Sir Thomas Wyatt," *Modern Language Quarterly* 29. 2 (1968): 145–160.

makes them seem unexpected. In terms of the general lesson of the creatures and the poem's special logic, the poet should have anticipated what would happen.

This conflict of expectation and event is the crux of the poem, then. The poet, unlike the changing and complex world about him, remains rigid in his view of things. As a result things out of his control seem to happen to him. His sense of his own helplessness and our sense of it as well is heightened by the awareness that we develop and share as the poem develops, the awareness that time moves, that past and present do not form a pattern, that the world is complex and therefore its moments of simplicity are precious.

This sense of the distance of moments in a continuous time is intensified by the lover's static position, layering the final question of the poem with real emotion: "I would fain know what she has deserved." It is useless to answer, useless to ask. One might as properly inquire what "they" which flee deserve. There is no way for the speaker to ask for judgment, to assume control. By recourse to what system of rules? The question is heavy with emotion, vibrating sadness, cynicism, argumentativeness and more.

Thus when we examine the events of the poem, we find that they lead to complications that result in the poet's despair. And if we look again we will find that even the poet, though he won't admit it, has the same complexities and changeableness; he too is human and affected by time. We see this when he is taken in the woman's arms, for then it is he who is like the creatures who fed at his hand. However, when the woman gives him leave to fly, unlike the creatures and unlike her, he cannot. In spite of, or because of these various poses, the lover exposes his own complexity, a complexity he shares with all creatures. Although the speaker tries to maintain a steadfast position, we can see that his view continuously evolves as it copes with the contexts of past actions. This forced complexity of the lover's view grinds against his static faith and only serves to isolate him further in a world he cannot account for, control, or accept. In this way time past becomes more precious and more hopelessly lost. In the end, his final words are rather unconvincing as a call for justice, unconvincing to himself as well, it seems. Yet they are convincing as an expression of his mixed and authentic emotions. Our appreciation of the emotions that shape these simple words attests to the thickening of experience that the progress of the poem and Wyatt's handling of time have achieved.

From this poem we learn that the past acts like an after-image of a continuous action. The after-image continues to affect our view of the present moment from which it is now disjoined and which it can only partly explain. The progress of the poem is a process of accumulating detail, of accumulating these images that create a context for a present in which it becomes clear how time works and how complex things are. Reading becomes a process of changing or modifying our own viewpoints so that reading resembles the time which it often contemplates and in which it takes place. In other words, our sense of loss develops as the poem develops; as the reader must give up one beautiful word or image to go on to the next, so the poet has given up each moment of his life, savoring it and unwillingly losing it. Our sense of loss when the poem stops is like the poet's own sense of loss. Although the poet can never recover the beautiful moments that he has lost, luckily we may reread the poem and through it reexperience the beauty of Wyatt's own evanescent human voice expressing his poignant sense of loss, beauty and isolation.

PETER B. CLARKE

Frost's "Mending Wall"

The central problem of meaning in Frost's "Mending Wall" is the difficulty of deciding where ultimate wisdom lies: does it rest with the speaker of the poem who apparently would acquiesce to natural forces and let the wall crumble, or does it lie with the speaker's neighbor who offers the proverbial "Good fences make good neighbors" (33–34)? One solution to the problem is to decide that "the wall is both good and bad. The barrier serves both to separate the men and to bring them together. . . . The neighbor farmer simply sees that barriers are necessary without understanding why, while the speaker knows why they are and sees the defects of barriers, too" (Potter 49). Solving the problem by resorting to such a compromise is a tribute to the tension which Frost has created in the poem. But the compromise may underestimate the neighbor's position, for there is evidence to suggest that the neighbor's proverb carries the weight of ancient wisdom not readily apparent.

As George Monteiro has pointed out, Frost's ritual of walking the stone wall in spring to repair the boundary between neighboring farmers recalls an ancient Roman religious rite ("Unlinked" 11). Monteiro cites a description of the god Terminus from Edith Hamilton's *Mythology* and of the ritual from Oskar Seyffert's *A Dictionary of Classical Antiquities*. He then concludes that letting the allusion to myth and ritual remain "unlinked" (10) and implicit is characteristic of Frost and distinguishes him from Modernists such as Eliot and Pound. Monteiro is right as far as he goes; however, there are other conclusions to be drawn, and there are, in fact, descriptions of ancient boundary ritual and rule more pertinent to "Mending Wall" than are those cited by Monteiro.

For instance, H. J. Rose offers just such a pertinent description of the ritual of setting up and maintaining a boundary marker or *terminus*. Regarding such a marker, Rose observes,

> Care had indeed been taken to give it a sufficiency of that desirable quality [*numen* or supernatural power], by the farmers whose lands the mark bounded. . . . Nor were they content with doing all this once, for every year the proprietors between whose lands the holy objects lay used to meet at or near them and offer sacrifice again. When such precautions were duly observed, neighbors might hope that no quarrels would arise between them, and presumably that the mere ordinary and unconsecrated sticks or stones which were put where necessary to mark out the rest of the boundary line would be kept in order and at their posts of duty by their "numinous" fellows. (165)

Rose's description might depict the business of "Mending Wall" as well as that of Roman religious ritual. Indeed, his assertion that "When such precautions were duly observed, neighbors might hope that no quarrels would arise between them" seems to parallel rather closely the old proverb "Good fences make good neighbors" and, perhaps, to lend weight to the view that it is the neighbor's wisdom which we are to take more seriously.

In addition, the ritual seems to shed light on Frost's depiction of the neighbor as "an old-stone savage armed." The phrase reflects the speaker's view that his neighbor moves in the "darkness" or ignorance of earlier, less enlightened times, but it also suggests that Frost was aware that the neighbor was playing his part in an ancient—perhaps paleolithic, or "old-stone"—ritual (cf. Monteiro "Unlinked" *passim*). Indeed, Frost's identification of the proverb as the neighbor's "father's saying" may be an acknowledgement of its ancient wisdom if we understand the word "father" in the ancestral rather biological sense. And here again Rose provides a clue, for he connects the Roman ritual to "the Hebrew curse on him who removeth his neighbor's landmark . . ." (Deut. 19:14; 27:17; Rose 163).[1] Read literally, the injunctions in Deuteronomy are divine instructions, or God the "father's sayings." As such, the proverb must be taken more seriously than one might, at first, suppose.

Finally, then, although the speaker of "Mending Wall" might rather puckishly question this ritual, he must know that he had better participate in it: an "old statute laid down that if any man ploughed up a boundary-mark, both he and the oxen who drew his plough should be *sacri*, outlawed . . . if a man was *sacer* he had no human rights whatever, and anyone who chose to kill him might do so with impunity (Rose 164). It is no wonder that Frost's speaker not only takes part in, but also "initiates," this ritual each spring (Potter 49). Clearly, wisdom—ancient Roman and Hebrew religious wisdom at least—lies with the speaker's neighbor. Thus, Frost's employment of ancient boundary rule and rite sheds light, not only on Frost's method of allusion, but also on the question of the relative wisdom of the speaker of the poem and his neighbor.

Works Cited

Frost, Robert. *The Poetry of Robert Frost.* Ed. Edward Connery Lathem. New York: Holt, 1969.

Monteiro, George. "Unlinked Myth in Frost's 'Mending Wall.' " *Concerning Poetry* 7.2 [evidently misprinted as 7.1]: 10–14.

———. "Robert Frost's Linked Analogies." *New England Quarterly* 46 (1973): 463–468.

Potter, James L. *Robert Frost Handbook.* University Park: The Pennsylvania State UP, 1980.

Rose, H. J. *Religion in Greece and Rome.* New York: Harper, 1959.

---

[1] Monteiro traces the proverb to medieval Spain, but fails to pick up on the clue provided by the title of one of his sources ("Proverbes judéo-espanols") to pursue it back to ancient Hebrew tradition ("Linked" 463–468).

ELEANOR LESTER

Skunk Hour: An Explication

Robert Lowell's poem ''Skunk Hour'' is dedicated to
Elizabeth Bishop, whose poem ''The Armadillo'' Lowell
used as a model (On ''Skunk Hour'' 109). The poems do
indeed contain many similarities. But whereas Bishop
concludes her poem with the armadillo clenching ''a weak
mailed fist/ . . . ignorant against the sky'' (123), a
sign of impotent resistance against man's invasion,
Lowell's skunk ''jabs her wedge–head in a cup/of sour
cream'' (46–47) and will not be frightened away. The
skunk triumphs over both man and time not by resisting
them, but by adapting herself to them. For Richard Wilbur, ''they stand for stubborn, unabashed livingness,
and for [Lowell's] own refusal . . . to cease desiring a
world of vitality, freedom, and love,'' (87). The skunk
may not be the sweetest creature, but she survives.

The skunk's acceptance is in marked contrast to the
people who inhabit Nautilus Island. The ''heiress'' who
is '' in her dotage'' (6) fights the encroachment of civilization, and thus

> she buys up all
> the eyesores facing her shore
> and lets them fall. [10–12]

The result does not improve nature but increases the
number of ruins. Like the heiress, the decorator fights a
futile battle to improve the drab world by decorating
his shop. Nevertheless, ''there's no money in the
work,'' and ''he'd rather marry'' (23–24). The decorator's resistance achieves nothing.

The people of Nautilus Island are not regenerative.
The decorator is homosexual. The heiress has produced
one child, but he is a bishop with vows of celibacy.
''The summer millionaire/who seemed to leap from an
L. L. Bean/catalogue'' (14–16) is lost, either bankrupt
or dead. In either case, his holdings are not passed
down to his offspring, but sold off to the highest bid-
der. Lowell himself commented that in ''Skunk Hour,''
''Sterility howls through the scenery'' (On ''Skunk
Hour'' 107).

However, the most desperate character of all is the
speaker of the poem, Lowell himself. He admits that his

''mind's not right'' (30) and believes that like Milton's Satan, he himself is hell. A Puritan and a peeping
Tom, he prowls the local lovers' lane hoping to catch
some couple making love. Yet the locale of the lovers'
lane is not particularly auspicious; it tops the
''hill's skull'' (26) at the place ''where the graveyard
shelves in the town'' (29). In short it is a place not of
regeneration but of death, a location which Lowell
ghoulishly haunts.

Only the skunks thrive; in fact, they have taken over
the town:

> They march on their soles up Main Street,
> white stripes, moonstruck eyes' red fire
> under the chalk—dry and spar spire
> of the Trinitarian Church [39—42]

There may be something sinister in the ''red fire'' of
their eyes, but at least they show more life than the
''chalk—dry'' Trinitarian Church. Indeed, the skunk
does not march alone; she leads ''her column of kittens'' (45).

The skunks' triumph is not wholly laudable. They are
smelly. They are scavengers; they swill ''the garbage
pail'' (45). Their eyes are sinister. But they are not
merely bad. They have beautiful ostrich plume tails and
''moonstruck'' eyes. Yet, their survival rests not on
their beauty but on their adaptability to the world
around them. Unlike the humans, they are not caught up
in any of the outdated beliefs, fashions, or
hierarchies.

The choice Lowell seems to be giving us is not very attractive. We can either hold on to our cherished beliefs
and kill ourselves off, or we can become that somewhat
stinky and homely scavenger and flourish. Lowell is
trying to frighten us with this choice, but I for one
''will not scare'' (48) and hold out for a better
bargain.

Works Cited

Bishop, Elizabeth. *The Complete Poems.* New York:
    Farrar, 1969.
Lowell, Robert. ''On 'Skunk Hour.' '' *The Contemporary
    Poet as Artist and Critic.* Ed. Anthony Ostroff.
    Boston: Little, 1964.
———. *Life Studies.* New York: Noonday, 1964.
Wilbur, Richard. ''On Robert Lowell's 'Skunk Hour.' ''
    The Contemporary Poet as Artist and Critic. Ed.
    Anthony Ostroff. Boston: Little, 1964.

ALLISON CHANG

Sadie and Maud

The poem ''Sadie and Maud'' questions why society pays
much more respect to a person with a college degree than
to a person without a degree. In this poem, Sadie has not
gone to college, but she has lived a full and profitable
life. The poet praises Sadie but in a half-hearted way,
as if the poet is unsure if she should praise Sadie. Unlike her sister Sadie, Maud has gone to college, and she
has won the respect of her parents, but in comparison to
her sister, Maud has lived an empty life. By comparing
the two sisters, the poet shows the absurdity of basing
the worth of a person on a college degree. At the same
time, the poet admits that this value system is a hard
habit to break.

The poem begins with a very cold and distant introduction to the two women. The women are simply described as
''Maud went to college / Sadie stayed at home'' (1–2).
The two lines are the same length, as if the poet, an outsider, tries to hide her feelings of disrespect towards
Sadie. From an outsider's point of view, the fact that
Maud went to college is the most important difference between the two women. These lines imply that Maud has
done something with her life, she has left home to gain
knowledge; Sadie has wasted her life away. Yet the simplicity of the description of the sisters suggests that
this attitude is very childish.

The first two lines of this poem are a reminder of the
nursery rhyme, ''The Five Little Pigs,'' which goes,
''the first little pig went to market and the second little pig stayed home. . . .'' Children like songs like the
''Five Little Pigs'' because they are easy to understand. These songs have no deeper meaning behind them;
they are sung merely for entertainment. Like children,
adults make up simple categories that describe people.
These categories may have no real meaning, but they sim-
plify life. For instance, from the first impression,
Sadie can be placed in the category of those with unfulfilled lives. Yet such a category is untrue for Sadie.
Sadie's life is praiseworthy; she ''scraped life / With
a fine-tooth comb'' (3–4). Sadie's life was difficult but
she combed out her problems and straightened out her
life.

In this poem, life is the painful process of combing
through the problems of life; Sadie's life was so full
of tangles that she scraped her comb through her life.
Sadie combed out her family's disapproval of her, and

she managed to untangle the problem of her illegitimate children by herself. Her problems were painful, but
Sadie endured the pain. Sadie ''didn't leave a tangle
in'' her life (5); she dealt with her problems and made
her life smooth and beautiful to look at.

As Sadie deals with her problems, she becomes a
stronger person. By breaking away from her family, Sadie
lives her own life, free from the worries of conforming
to her family. She then deals with the biggest tangle in
her life, her illegitimate daughters. Sadie accepts her
daughters and raises them in the image of herself; thus,
when she dies, the girls carry on where Sadie left off.
The girls go a step beyond their mother; they leave home
completely because they are stronger than Sadie. All
they need is Sadie's fine-tooth comb to face life with.
The world does not lose anything when Sadie dies; instead, the world is strengthened by two young girls who
know how to deal with life.

Sadie's comb is her inner strength; her comb will not
allow a tangle or a strand of life to be left uncombed.
Sadie experiences all of life because ''her comb found
every strand'' (6). The problems in her life do not hold
her back; she overcomes her problems, and she experiences the happy side to life, as well.

As the poet comes to know Sadie, the tone of the poem
changes. Sadie is praised as being ''one of the livingest chits / In all the land'' (7–8). This sentence
doesn't fit; the rhythm has changed, and it is the longest sentence so far in this poem. Yet this sentence
sticks out for a purpose. The length of the sentence illustrates how full Sadie's life has been. The sentence
also emphasizes the fact that Sadie is someone different; she is someone special that people should take notice of. However, this sentence also carries a negative
meaning. Sadie is the exception to the rule; out of everyone else, only Sadie lived a full and profitable life
without a college degree. The poet seems to be overcome
by surprise that there could be such a person as Sadie.
The poet knows that Sadie should be praised because she
is a great woman, but to praise Sadie is difficult.

The next stanza, which says ''Sadie bore two babies /
Under her maiden name / Maud and Ma and Papa / Nearly
died of shame'' (9–12) brings up the point again that
Sadie is undeserving of praise. Sadie disgraces her family by her actions. Yet, for the first time the poet
admits that Maud is unworthy of praise. Maud may have
gone to college but even she does not know how to deal

with Sadie's problem, nor can she accept the children. College has not prepared Maud to face the problems of life. The only thing Maud has learned is to fear mistakes. Maud is deathly afraid of making horrible mistakes such as Sadie's; yet, since Maud won't allow herself to make mistakes, Maud does not experience life. Therefore, Maud never grows or changes.

From the beginning until the end of the poem, Maud is described as a person ''who went to college'' (17). The fact that Maud went to college is the only thing she accomplished her whole life. Maud is merely ''a thin brown mouse'' (18) hiding in her hole. For Maud, college was an escape from life; now that she is out of college, Maud again hides from life by ''living all alone / In this old house'' (19–20). The poet uses short, smooth sentences to describe Maud. The sentences illustrate how Maud has been cheated of life. Maud never enters life; thus, her life is empty of problems as well as accomplishments.

The fact that Maud is thin suggests that Maud hungers to join in life; yet she is too afraid to come out of her ''old house'' into a new life. In Maud's house, there is a sense of dying. Her house is old; there are no children and no chance of rebirth. In her house, Maud is cut off from society; there, her college degree means nothing because she is unable to add anything to society.

The poem is structured in such a way that it is impossible to compare Maud and Sadie evenly. Unlike Sadie, the poem says very little about Maud because she has done very little in her life. Maud's only mistake is not participating in life. Yet, because Maud went to college, it is obvious that the fault lies within herself. Maud does not have her sister's inner strength with which to face life. Though Maud is not worthy of respect, she is allowed to make mistakes. The person worthy of respect is Sadie because she faces life with courage. Sadie lives life fully, but because she is human, she makes mistakes. Yet the poet attributes Sadie's mistakes to the fact that she hasn't gone to college, not to the fact that Sadie is human. It is difficult to pay Sadie her due respect because when Sadie solves her problems, the poet is caught off guard. Sadie mixes up the simple categories in life when she solves her problems and rises above the category of the highly educated people.

JOHN LESSNER

Hamlet and the Gravedigger

Hamlet reveals his thoughts on death in Act V when he speaks to the gravedigger. This discussion is not the first time the Dane shows his fascination with death and decay. For example in the ''To be or not to be'' soliloquy, he speaks of his own death, and in the scene in which Claudius prays (III, iii), he contemplates killing his uncle. But in his conversation with the gravedigger, he most clearly shows the tension in his ideas. On the one hand, he wants to grow easy with death. On the other, he is afraid of and repulsed by it.

Hamlet is unusually concerned about the decaying process. He asks the gravedigger, ''How long will a man lie i' the earth ere he rot?'' (157). He also inquires why a tanner's body lasts longer than most people's. In fact Hamlet becomes so interested in the scientific questions of decay that he forgets his original question to the sexton—for whom is he digging the grave? This morbid curiosity is also revealed in Hamlet's question over the identity of Yorick's skull.

Hamlet's discussion leads him to the recognition that death is an equalizing force, affecting everyone and reducing all to the same level. Alexander the Great surely rotted as quickly as Yorick and smelled just as bad. A tanner's body would last longer than Alexander's, even though Alexander was a great conqueror. Death knows no social or political class. After his death, Hamlet will no longer be the Prince of Denmark. Like Caesar, he is likely to end up as a stopper in a beer barrel.

In strong contrast to Hamlet's obsession with death is the gravedigger's nonchalance. This country fellow has been sexton and gravedigger for thirty years. He is not at all intrigued or awed by or afraid of death and decay. It is part of his job and everyday life. He takes his task so lightly that he sings and jokes while digging. When he comes across a skull, he throws it aside and goes on digging.

The gravedigger is so comfortable with death that he can look beyond the foulness of decay and see in the corpses the lives they once contained. When Hamlet handles the skull, he says his ''gorge rises'' (181).

Hamlet is repulsed by and afraid of this all—too—real reminder of death. Hamlet tells the skull, ''get you to my lady's chamber, and tell her, let her paint an inch thick to this favour she must come.'' But death cannot be disguised or avoided. Death dressed up is still death.

We can also see Hamlet's uneasiness when he discusses the uses of the dead. Three times he alludes to the uses. He imagines them as stoppers or plugs: a bunghole for a cask, a stopper for a beer barrel, and a patch in the wall to keep the wind out. But it is important to note that the dead are merely parts of a larger whole and not Hamlet's primary object. The dead do not make up the cask, barrel, or wall; they are merely placed in them. The dead have no true value in themselves, but only as patches or plugs. This observation returns Hamlet to his central recognition that great and obscure alike are reduced to insignificance by death.

Through his encounter with the gravedigger Hamlet comes more to terms with death. His reconciliation with death is one of the major movements of the play. Death is an alien and powerful force for Hamlet, but in his conversation with the gravedigger he comes to grips with his fears.

LESLIE MILLER

O'Hara's Conversation with the Sun

Before his death in 1966, Frank O'Hara was known as a poet only to a small group of friends and to the few who occasionally stumbled upon him in periodicals. ''A True Account of Talking to the Sun at Fire Island'' is an affirmation of his importance as a poet. The Sun is Faith, the faith that someday the public will notice him and be convinced of his value.

The Sun is the faith that O'Hara seems to be lacking. According to the Sun, O'Hara is under attack from both conservative and avant-garde poets. He tells O'Hara:

> Now, I've heard some
> say you're crazy, they being excessively
> calm themselves to my mind, and other
> crazy poets think that you're a boring
> reactionary. (31–35)

But the Sun wishes to awaken O'Hara to his particular virtues and tells him not to pay attention to critics. ''Just keep right on,'' the Sun encourages him. ''I like it.'' (44)

The Sun also gives O'Hara faith in his subject matter. O'Hara wrote about his friends and the events happening right around him, but he could not believe that outsiders would recognize the value of those experiences. The Sun, however, urges O'Hara to make his poetry out of his common experiences. ''Always embrace things, people, earth / sky stars, as I do, freely and with / the appropriate sense of space,'' (65–67) the Sun advises.

Furthermore, The Sun advises O'Hara not to be worried about his poetic predecessors who wrote to philosophize. O'Hara must keep faith that he does not have to write like the famous poets of the past. The Sun has democratic taste, and tells O'Hara:

> And don't worry about your lineage
> poetic or natural. The Sun shines on
> the jungle, you know, on the tundra
> the sea, the ghetto. Wherever you were
> I knew it and saw you moving. (46–49)

Inspiration is not limited to only a few poets in a few places. The Sun's faith and inspiration can smile on O'Hara anywhere.

At the poem's conclusion, the Sun leaves because
''they're calling / me.'' (77–78) When O'Hara asks,
''Who are they?'' the Sun mysteriously answers,
''They're calling to you / too.'' (81–82) Destiny
speaks to both O'Hara and the Sun and through them as
well. The ''tiny poem'' (74) left in O'Hara's brain is
a colossal one that shows his importance not only to
himself and his friends, but to all of us who stumble
upon him and stay for a while.

BRENDA PISKOR

Jim O'Connor in Tennessee Williams's
The Glass Menagerie: Seized by the Moment

Jim O'Connor, the gentleman caller, has a lesser role in Tennessee Williams's *The Glass Menagerie* than the other characters; however, his character is no less important. In the cast of characters at the beginning of the play, Williams describes Jim as a ''nice, ordinary young man'' (968). At the start of Scene IV, Tom depicts Jim in a similar manner but includes details of his past glory. He tells us Jim was ''a star in basketball, captain of the debating club, president of the senior class and the glee club and he sang the male lead in the annual light operas'' (989). Tom also indicates that although Jim once was a high school hero, he now holds a job only slightly better than Tom's. Therefore, the image we have of Jim before he actually appears in the play is of a humbled high school hero. After the play has concluded, however, we are aware that Jim's character is far more complex; he is able to instill hope and confidence in Laura and destroy them again in one scene. What causes a ''nice, ordinary young man'' (968) to dash the hopes of a vulnerable young woman? In Jim's case it is the situation in which he finds himself which motivates him to act as he does.

We, the readers or viewers of the play, learn of Laura's infatuation for Jim in Scene II, when Amanda asks her if she has ever liked a boy. Laura replies, ''Yes. I liked one once. . . . His name was Jim'' (975). Tom does not know of his sister's fascination for his co-worker, but is aware that they had known each other: ''I knew that Jim and Laura had known each other at Solden, and I had heard Laura speak admiringly of his voice'' (989). When Jim finally appears in the play, he is naturally unaware of Laura's infatuation for him, but he also does not recognize her at all. It is not until Scene VII, when Laura and Jim are alone in the living room, that Jim discovers he knows Laura, and, in the same scene, Jim's complexities begin to become apparent to us.

Laura first gives Jim a clue that she knows him when she asks him if he kept up with his singing. When he acts surprised at her knowledge of his singing, Laura says, ''I remember what a beautiful voice you had'' (1000). Throughout the scene Laura continues to praise his

performances, his friendliness, and his popularity.
Jim, through Laura's flattery, escapes from present reality and relives the glory days of his past.

Laura's continual exaltation of Jim feeds his ego. At first he responds to her compliments with an ''Aw—'' or another noncommittal utterance, but after a time he becomes less modest and admits to his allure:

JIM   (with reflective relish) I was beleaguered by females in those days.
LAURA You were terribly popular!
JIM   Yeah—
LAURA You had such a—friendly way—
JIM   I was spoiled in high school. (1002)

Jim's confidence level increases as the scene progresses. He boasts not only of his past but also of the present; he says, ''Everybody excels in some one thing. Some in many! (Unconsciously glances at himself in the mirror.)'' (1003). The stage direction in this passage provides evidence for Jim's growing conceit.

Jim's boastfulness does not end with his past and present but continues into the future: ''I believe in the future of television, I wish to be ready to go up right along with it. . . . In fact, I've already made the right connections and all that remains is for the industry itself to get under way! Full steam—Knowledge—Zzzzzp! Money—Zzzzzzzp! Power!'' (1004). At this point, Jim is extremely enthusiastic; Laura, it seems, has instilled in him a newfound confidence and optimism.

Laura proves to be the ideal audience for Jim; she is perfectly content to listen quietly to him and allow him to manipulate the conversation. He abruptly changes the subject twice as Laura attempts to tell him about her favorite possessions in the world, her glass figurines. At another point in the play, Jim does not let Laura complete her sentences:

LAURA Yes, it sort of—stood between me—
JIM   You shouldn't have let it!
LAURA I know, but it did, and—
JIM   You were shy with people!
LAURA I tried not to be but never could—
JIM   Overcome it? . . .
LAURA (sorrowfully) Yes—I guess it—
JIM   Takes time! (1001)

Jim gains control of Laura's attention and her conversation, as well.

Although Laura is attentive when Jim speaks, he pays little attention to what she says. When the unicorn falls off the table and breaks, Jim says, ''I bet that was your favorite piece of glass'' (1005). Only a moment earlier in the play, however, Laura had told Jim, ''I shouldn't be partial, but he is my favorite one'' (1004). Jim is clearly too immersed in his own glorification to pay much attention to Laura.

Laura makes Jim feel better than he could ever have hoped; she has listened attentively and flattered him, thereby renewing his self-esteem. He tells her, ''You know—you're—well—very different! Surprisingly different from anyone else I know! . . . You make me feel sort of—I don't know how to put it!'' (1006) Laura has built up his confidence and, becoming caught up in the moment, he wants to do the same for her: ''Somebody needs to build your confidence up and make you proud instead of shy and turning away and—blushing—Somebody ought to—Ought to—kiss you, Laura!'' (1006) After he kisses her and sees the look in her eyes, Jim realizes he has made a mistake; instead of returning a favor, as he thought, he was breaking Laura's heart.

Laura, through her innocent, honest praise of Jim, builds up his confidence which in turn escalates her hopes of having a gentleman caller of her own. Jim immerses himself in his restored confidence, and, as he is oblivious to Laura's feelings, inadvertently hurts her. Jim is not a villain; he is simply a ''nice, ordinary young man'' who acts spontaneously, allowing himself to be led by his vanity.

Fiction

1 🌿 The Worlds of Fiction

Everyone loves stories. Children happily act out their fantasies; left alone, they will immerse themselves by the hour in cowboys and Indians, battles of the superheroes, or cops and robbers. Even before infants speak, they sit quietly and listen to grown-ups read them bedtime stories, following the pictures as the pages turn. As children, we sat spellbound around campfires listening to ghost stories that sent shivers up our spines and raised goose bumps along our legs and arms. As the cool evening breeze rattled the trees like the bars of a prison and the flames sizzled and popped above the glimmering logs, we strained to hear every word of the story, afraid we'd miss the next grisly detail. We didn't have to be persuaded to love stories then. We sought out the best storytellers we could find and hounded them until they unwound tale after tale. And although we came later to have a more adult appreciation for the art of fiction, we've never lost that elemental delight in the powers of a good story or our admiration for their tellers.

The autobiographies of writers are filled with early delight and enchantment in stories and books. Jean-Paul Sartre, the French novelist, playwright, and philosopher, recalls in his memoir, *The Words*, how his mother told him stories:

> While she spoke, we were alone and clandestine, far from men, gods and priests, two does in a wood, with those other does, the Fairies. I simply could not believe that someone had composed a whole book to tell episodes of our . . . life, which smelled of soap and eau de Cologne.

The magic of these stories colored his attitude toward books. Sartre had, he remembers, the irrational feeling that his "family's prosperity depended on them," and he prophesies, "I began my life as I shall no doubt end it: amidst books."

Why do children enjoy stories so much? As Sartre suggests, part of the enjoyment is the listener's physical closeness to the storyteller. But the psychologist

Bruno Bettleheim, who made a lengthy study of fairy tales, says there are other reasons. He contends that stories tell the child that life has its difficulties which can be met and overcome. The heroes of fairy tales "master all obstacles and emerge victorious." Bettleheim insists that fairy tales are not "escape" reading—stories read to avoid reality—rather they "confront the child squarely with the basic human predicaments."

Of course, as adults, we find in reading fiction something more than the thrills and chills of the ghost story: we gain some insight into ourselves and our world. In stories, we gain access to experiences that we ignore or deny, or that have been denied to us. Fiction is a controlled environment in which we can let ourselves experience emotions or confront ideas that we might find too dangerous or disturbing to encounter in reality. Fiction is a laboratory where we can go backwards and forwards in time and space without ever leaving the confines and comforts of our neighborhood.

But stories which provoke us, stretch us, or demand something unusual from us are more difficult to read or appreciate. Many people don't like to be tested in this way; they prefer to experience familiar things, because the *un*familiar is at best uncomfortable and at worst frightening. And people are lazy; doing something different demands more energy from us. Reading seriously demands energy, openness, and some bravery. It means losing some of our defenses, letting go of some of our prejudices and preconceptions, and pushing on into unknown territory. The best literature challenges us even as it pleases; it dares us while it delights.

Fictional Representation

All art is involved in what the ancient Greeks called *mimesis*. Mimesis means imitation or mimicry. The painting of a chair imitates a "real" chair. A character in a story or play mimics a real person. Thinking of art as mimesis is both helpful and problematic. It places a premium on how lifelike any representation is. The highest art, in this view, is the one closest to "real" life. No doubt, there is a rare delight to be found in those paintings that trick the eye into believing that the door painted on the wall is a real door one could open. What one should remember about even the most lifelike of representations is that the highly mimetic representation is *not* the same as real life. The most faithfully realistic account is never the same as reality. Indeed, for those who view art as only mimesis, art is always inferior, a poor substitute for the real thing. No matter how good a photograph you have of a loved one, you would prefer to have that loved one with you. If what you want is a real apple, the most photographic painting of an apple will be a poor, unsatisfactory substitute. You can't eat the painted apple, you can't juggle it, you can't smell it. The one advantage of the painted apple is that it will be bright and fresh long after the real apple has rotted away. Yet this "advantage" of the painted apple serves to show how different the "real" apple is from the mimetic one.

But viewing art as imitation can't explain how we can represent unicorns, to cite one example, since unicorns exist only in our imaginations and, therefore, we have no "real" unicorn to imitate. The depiction of a wholly imaginary being can't be said to be inferior since there is no real object against which to compare it. When we view art as an expression of our imagination, we free art from its subordinate status. Philosophers have called such a theory of art "ideal" since such an art grows out of imaginative *ideas* rather than an imitation of the "real." Art governed by a theory of the ideal gives us representations of how life should be, or how bad it might be, or how pleasant or horrible it could be.

Most art is a combination of ideal representation and realistic imitation. If science fiction represents places, creatures, universes never seen in real life, it nevertheless combines elements of places, creatures, and the planet we have experienced. The unicorn, for example, is a horse with a single horn on its forehead. We have seen horses, and we have seen horns, and thus we can imagine the unicorn. Moreover, the job of representing a unicorn is made easier because we have seen other representations of unicorns. In many circumstances art doesn't imitate life, it imitates other art.

Sometimes what we experience influences what we imagine. Just as frequently what we imagine influences what we experience. A friend of ours is an actor in a daytime serial. He often gets treated badly in restaurants or on the street because the character he represents is a villain. So powerful is the hold of this "fictional" representation on people's minds that they confuse the fictional character with the "real" person. In fact, we hear quite frequently of performers and politicians who wish to improve their images, that is, create a representation that is more likeable or agreeable than the one they have. Such image-building indicates that our notions of people are more strongly influenced by their representations on television or radio than by their actual being. In a classic psychological experiment, a "crime" is staged before a classroom full of students. Then the students are asked to describe what they saw. The students' accounts of what they saw differ enormously because what they see is determined to a large extent by what they imagine is true. By studying fiction, we can learn a lot about the belief systems we hold, the fictions out of which we make sense of the real world. By becoming more aware of the fictions around us, we can appreciate better both the power of fiction and the force of reality.

The Fictional World and the Real World

The world of fiction differs from the one we live in, and the study of fiction differs from the study of science. The sciences try to uncover the way things are or were: the facts and principles that govern our world and our lives. But fiction does not uncover facts. A story is a construction of language and a projection of the imagination. Although some writers restrict themselves to stories that conceivably could be true, their stories are still not "fact." Whether an author writes, "The cowboy rode into the sunset," or "The unicorn flew toward the sun," the sentences are still imaginative products, and it would be foolish to ask for proof of the cowboy's existence or the unicorn's present whereabouts.

Consequently, the storyteller has much greater freedom than the scientist. When scientists describe a chemical compound, a geologic formation, or the symptoms of a disease, they must describe things as faithfully and objectively as possible. A storyteller, however, can describe magic potions, enchanted islands, and fantastic diseases. The scientific report is an objective, rational survey of data. But for a storyteller, a book can contain all sorts of magical properties. In the folktale "The Canary Prince," retold by Italo Calvino, a witch gives a princess an enchanted book inscribed with the instructions: "Turn the pages forward, and the man becomes a bird; turn them back, and the bird becomes a man." A scientist would not explain events through magic.

Does it make any sense to complain that magic books are untrue? Italo Calvino would agree that no such books exist except in his imagination when he wrote about one and in our own minds when we read about it. But we would be naive to say that Calvino has lied to us or told us a falsehood. Because the work of fiction does not claim to be true, it cannot be said to be false. It exists in an imaginary space cut off from truth and falsity, fact and verification.

Fictional Conventions

Critics and students, however, sometimes say that stories contain improbable actions, inconsistent characters, or inappropriate material. Since a storyteller is free to narrate any action—flying carpets, life on stars, people the size of ants, ants the size of people—why are some stories improbable, inconsistent, or made with inappropriate materials?

The answer is that literature is governed by certain *conventions*. Conventions are agreed-upon rules, decisions, or practices. The Geneva Convention, for example, set up procedures for countries to handle prisoners-of-war. Literary conventions are practices that artists choose to follow in constructing their stories, plays, and poems. Just as athletes agree to certain rules of the game, so, too, do writers respect certain practices of their craft. Of course, there are many different games, each with its own conventions, and there are many different types of stories, each with its own particular set of expectations. Such restrictions do not, however, limit the pleasure of athletics or fiction. To the contrary, a game in which no one obeyed the rules would degenerate into chaotic action. So, too, a story that corresponds to no recognizable convention is impossible to follow or enjoy.

Thus, when we say a work is inconsistent, improbable, or inappropriate, we mean that the work has not followed its own chosen conventions, its own rules of procedure. For example, a *realistic* work—a story in which characters and action conform to natural laws and recognizable human behavior—cannot include magic books that turn men into canaries and canaries into men. Such a magical book would be inconsistent with the conventions of realistic fiction and inappropriate in a realistic story. Similarly, if an author creates an all-powerful character like Superman, the author would be breaking his own convention if the character were hurt in a car accident. Superman might pretend to be injured, but readers would assume from the conventions of the story that he is "really" well.

We might put it this way: each story has its own imaginative "facts" and "rules." As long as a story obeys its own conventions, it is consistent and appropriate. We get upset only when we notice that the imaginative rules are changed in mid-story.

The Variety of Fictional Worlds

So far we have mentioned "realistic" stories and supernatural stories such as folk stories and fairy tales. But these two sorts of fiction are merely extremes in a large range of possible fictions. For example, Jean Rhys's story "I Used to Live Here Once" is generally "realistic," except for a ghost who is surprised by its own existence. Maxine Hong Kingston's "On Mortality" begins as history but ends as fantasy. Because each story is governed by its own rules, readers must be attentive and flexible. Readers are like spectators who must figure out the rules of the game by watching it being played. Although other stories might help one figure out the basic principles of construction, each story must be judged on its own terms.

The Lessons of Fiction

If stories are not factual, why should we study them? What could we possibly learn from literature? After all, when we study history we gain a better sense of the past; we have a more accurate understanding of what happened. When we study biology, we learn how organisms function. But what do we gain by reading stories that are neither true nor possessed of facts? What benefit is derived from literary studies?

Philosophers since Aristotle have been asking these questions, and they have developed several answers. First, by showing how things *might* be, *could* be, or *ought* to be, writers indicate the consequences of actions. But authors can also show us examples of an ideal world. Boccaccio's tale from *The Decameron* depicts how an ideal wife rebuffs the amorous advances of a king and still remains a polite hostess. Stories are a helpful and enjoyable way to learn lessons in proper behavior. The moral tale instructs us how to be better people, and the political story can convey a potent message.

Literature can also show us how the mind works. Psychology and philosophy both concern themselves with mental processes. But students of literature have their own way of learning how the mind works: by observing one of its most fascinating products—stories and the fictional world they create.

For those of you who need a more practical justification for studying literature, consider this: American business and industry is known for its ingenuity, inventiveness, and imaginative use of resources. The wealth of America is based on its imagination. But the imagination is not a mental process that can be ignored until you need it. Like any bodily process, it must be exercised and cultivated to be in ready working condition. The person who comes up with a new product, method of production, marketing strategy, or design is using much the same type of imagination and inventive power as the writer. We have all heard stories of the poor, impractical artist. Such stories disguise the fact that many writers have also been successful business persons. Wallace Stevens is one outstanding example: a man who was simultaneously one of America's most celebrated poets and a successful insurance executive, as comfortable in the board room as in the literary salon. Hawthorne became in later life a fine diplomat; Chekhov was a physician. The successful professional or business person can look beyond present conditions and envision how things might be in the future. This demands imagination.

But perhaps the best reason for studying literature is that reading the best works is fun. Our horizons are widened; our capacity to understand and delight in life is greatly enhanced. Reading, of course, is not like the passive pleasure of watching television or listening to some sorts of "background" music. Reading is an activity. The enjoyment we get from literature is akin to the enjoyment we get from swimming, jogging, painting, or playing a musical instrument. All these activities demand time, concentration, patience, and knowledge. Reading demands more than passing your eyes across the page, just as playing the piano demands more than pressing down a few keys. The rewards of reading make up for the effort. A great story, poem, or play can leave an impression that lasts for life, an excitement that you can take with you, and thoughts always worth considering.

Suggestions for Essayists

1. We usually think of reality and fantasy as two distinct categories. Write an essay showing how in life that distinction is blurred.
2. Describe some of the benefits of studying literature.
3. Describe some of the social conventions that govern your life and discuss your thoughts about them.

Suggestions for Fiction Writers

1. Take a fairy tale and rewrite it to make it as realistic as possible. (For example, do away with the magic book in "The Canary Prince.") Observe just where the fantastic occurrences are necessary for the story to make sense.
2. Write down one of the stories you were told as a child. Make up any details you can't remember.
3. Narrate a dream as though it were reality.
4. Narrate an incident that really happened to you as though it were a fairy tale, using as many of the conventions of fairy tales as you can.

ITALO CALVINO (1923–1985)

The Canary Prince

There was a king who had a daughter. Her mother was dead, and the stepmother was jealous of the girl and always spoke badly of her to the king. The maiden defended herself as best she could, but the stepmother was so contrary and insistent that the king, though he loved his daughter, finally gave in. He told the queen to send the girl away, but to some place where she would be comfortable, for he would never allow her to be mistreated. "Have no fear of that," said the stepmother, who then had the girl shut up in a castle in the heart of the forest. To keep her company, the queen selected a group of ladies-in-waiting, ordering them never to let the girl go out of the house or even to look out the windows. Naturally they received a salary worthy of a royal household. The girl was given a beautiful room and all she wanted to eat and drink. The only thing she couldn't do was go outdoors. But the ladies, enjoying so much leisure time and money, thought only of themselves and paid no attention to her.

Every now and then the king would ask his wife, "And how is our daughter? What is she doing with herself these days?" To prove that she did take an interest in the girl, the queen called on her. The minute she stepped from her carriage, the ladies-in-waiting all rushed out and told her not to worry, the girl was well and happy. The queen went up to the girl's room for a moment. "So you're comfortable, are you? You need nothing, do you? You're looking well, I see; the country air is doing you good. Stay happy, now. Bye-bye, dear!" And off she went. She informed the king she had never seen his daugher so content.

On the contrary, always alone in that room, with ladies-in-waiting who didn't so much as look at her, the princess spent her days wistfully at the window. She sat there leaning on the windowsill, and had she not thought to put a pillow under them, she would have got calluses on her elbows. The window looked out on the forest, and all day long the princess saw nothing but treetops, clouds and, down below, the hunters' trail. Over that trail one day came the son of a king in pursuit of a wild boar. Nearing the castle known to have been unoccupied for no telling how many years, he was amazed to see washing spread out on the battlements, smoke rising from the chimneys, and open casements. As he looked about him, he noticed a beautiful maiden at one of the upper windows and smiled at her. The maiden saw the prince too, dressed in yellow, with hunter's leggings and gun, and smiling at her, so she smiled back at him. For a whole hour, they smiled, bowed, and curtsied, being too far apart too communicate in any other way.

The next day, under the pretext of going hunting, the king's son returned, dressed in yellow, and they stared at each other this time for two hours; in addition to smiles, bows, and curtsies, they put a hand over their hearts and waved handkerchiefs at great length. The third day the prince stopped for three hours, and they blew each other kisses. The fourth day he was there as usual, when from behind a tree a witch peeped and began to guffaw: "Ho, ho, ho, ho!"

"Who are you? What's so funny?" snapped the prince.

"What's so funny? Two lovers silly enough to stay so far apart!"

"Would you know how to get any closer to her, ninny?" asked the prince.

"I like you both," said the witch, "and I'll help you."

She knocked at the door and handed the ladies-in-waiting a big old book with yellow, smudgy pages, saying it was a gift to the princess so the young lady could pass the time reading. The ladies took it to the girl, who opened it at once and read: "This is a magic book. Turn the pages forward, and the man becomes a bird; turn them back, and the bird becomes a man once more."

The girl ran to the window, placed the book on the sill, and turned the pages in great haste while watching the youth in yellow standing in the path. Moving his arms, he was soon flapping wings and changed into a canary, dressed in yellow as he was. Up he soared above the treetops and headed straight for the window, coming to rest on the cushioned sill. The princess couldn't resist picking up the beautiful canary and kissing him; then remembering he was a young man, she blushed. But on second thought she wasn't ashamed at all and made haste to turn him back into a youth. She picked up the book and thumbed backward through it; the canary ruffled his yellow feathers, flapped his wings, then moved arms and was once more the youth dressed in yellow with the hunter's leggings who knelt before her, declaring, "I love you!"

By the time they finished confessing all their love for one another, it was evening. Slowly, the princess leafed through the book. Looking into her eyes the youth turned back into a canary, perched on the windowsill, then on the eaves, then trusting to the wind, flew down in wide arcs, lighting on the lower limb of a tree. At that, she turned the pages back in the book and the canary was a prince once more who jumped down, whistled for his dogs, threw a kiss toward the window, and continued along the trail out of sight.

So every day the pages were turned forward to bring the prince flying up to the window at the top of the tower, then turned backward to restore his human form, then forward again to enable him to fly away, and finally backward for him to get home. Never in their whole life had the two young people known such happiness.

One day the queen called on her stepdaughter. She walked about the room, saying, "You're all right, aren't you? I see you're a trifle slimmer, but that's certainly no cause for concern, is it? It's true, isn't it, you've never felt better?" As she talked, she checked to see that everything was in place. She opened the window and peered out. Here came the prince in yellow along the trail with his dogs. "If this silly girl thinks she is going to flirt at the window," said the stepmother to herself, "she has another thought coming to her." She sent the girl for a glass of water and some sugar, then hurriedly removed five or six hairpins from her own hair and concealed them in the pillow with the sharp points sticking straight up. "That will teach her to lean on the window!" The girl returned with the water and sugar, but the queen said, "Oh, I'm no longer thirsty; you drink it, my dear! I must be getting back to your father. You don't need anything, do you? Well, goodbye." And she was off.

As soon as the queen's carriage was out of sight, the girl hurriedly flipped over the pages of the book, the prince turned into a canary, flew to the window, and struck the pillow like an arrow. He instantly let out a shrill cry of pain. The yellow feathers were stained with blood; the canary had driven the pins into his breast. He rose with a convulsive flapping, trusted himself to the wind, descended in irregular arcs, and lit on the ground with outstretched wings. The frightened princess, not yet fully aware of what had happened, quickly turned the pages back in the hope there would be no wounds when he regained his human form. Alas, the prince reappeared dripping blood from the deep stabs that had rent the yellow garment on his chest, and lay back surrounded by his dogs.

At the howling of the dogs, the other hunters came to his aid and carried him off on a stretcher of branches, but he didn't so much as glance up at the window of his beloved, who was still overwhelmed with grief and fright.

Back at his palace, the prince showed no promise of recovery, nor did the doctors know what to do for him. The wounds refused to heal over, and constantly hurt. His father the king posted proclamations on every street corner promising a fortune to anyone who could cure him, but not a soul turned up to try.

The princess meanwhile was consumed with longing for her lover. She cut her sheets into thin strips which she tied one to the other in a long, long rope. Then one night she let herself down from the high tower and set on the hunters' trail. But because of the thick darkness and the howls of the wolves, she decided to wait for daylight. Finding an old oak with a hollow trunk, she nestled inside and, in her exhaustion, fell asleep at once. She woke up while it was still pitch-dark, under the impression she had heard a whistle. Listening closely, she heard another whistle, then a third and a fourth, after which she saw four candle flames advancing. They were four witches coming from the four corners of the earth to their appointed meeting under that tree. Through a crack in the trunk the princess, unseen by them, spied on the four crones carrying candles and sneering a welcome to one another: "Ah, ah, ah!"

They lit a bonfire under the tree and sat down to warm themselves and roast a couple of bats for dinner. When they had eaten their fill, they began asking one another what they had seen of interest out in the world.

"I saw the sultan of Turkey, who bought himself twenty new wives."

"I saw the emperor of China, who has let his pigtail grow three yards long."

"I saw the king of the cannibals, who ate his chamberlain by mistake."

"I saw the king of this region, who has the sick son nobody can cure, since I alone know the remedy."

"And what is it?" asked the other witches.

"In the floor of his room is a loose tile. All one need do is lift the tile, and there underneath is a phial containing an ointment that would heal every one of his wounds."

It was all the princess inside the tree could do not to scream for joy. By this time the witches had told one another all they had to say, so each went her own way. The princess jumped from the tree and set out in the dawn for the city. At the first secondhand dealer's she came to, she bought an old doctor's gown and a pair of spectacles, and knocked at the royal palace. Seeing the little doctor with such scant paraphernalia, the servants weren't going to let him in, but the king said, "What harm could he do my son who can't be any worse off than he is now? Let him see what he can do." The sham doctor asked to be left alone with the sick man, and the request was granted.

Finding her lover groaning and unconscious in his sickbed, the princess felt like weeping and smothering him with kisses. But she restrained herself because of the urgency of carrying out the witch's directions. She paced up and down the room until she stepped on a loose tile, which she raised and discovered a phial of ointment. With it she rubbed the prince's wounds, and no sooner had she touched each one with ointment than the wound disappeared completely. Overjoyed she called the king, who came in and saw his son sleeping peacefully, with the color back in his cheeks, and no trace of any of the wounds.

"Ask for whatever you like, doctor," said the king. "All the wealth in the kingdom is yours."

"I wish no money," replied the doctor, "Just give me the prince's shield bearing the family coat-of-arms, his standard, and his yellow vest that was rent and bloodied." Upon receiving the three items, she took her leave.

Three days later, the king's son was again out hunting. He passed the castle in the heart of the forest, but didn't deign to look up at the princess's window. She immediately picked up the book, leafed through it, and the prince had no choice but change into a canary. He flew into the room, and the princess turned him back into a man. "Let me go," he said. "Isn't it enough to have pierced me with those pins of yours and caused me so much agony?" The prince, in truth, no longer loved the girl, blaming her for his misfortune.

On the verge of fainting, she exclaimed, "But I saved your life! I am the one who cured you!"

"That's not so," said the prince. "My life was saved by a foreign doctor who asked for no recompense except my coat-of-arms, my standard, and my bloodied vest!"

"Here are your coat-of-arms, your standard, and your vest! The doctor was none other than myself! The pins were the cruel doing of my stepmother!"

The prince gazed into her eyes, dumbfounded. Never had she looked so beautiful. He fell at her feet asking her forgiveness and declaring his deep gratitude and love.

That very evening he informed his father he was going to marry the maiden in the castle in the forest.

"You may marry only the daughter of a king or an emperor," replied his father.

"I shall marry the woman who saved my life."

So they made preparations for the wedding, inviting all the kings and queens in the vicinity. Also present was the princess's royal father, who had been informed of nothing. When the bride came out, he looked at her and exclaimed, "My daughter!"

"What!" said the royal host. "My son's bride is your daughter? Why did she not tell us?"

"Because," explained the bride, "I no longer consider myself the daughter of a man who let my stepmother imprison me." And she pointed at the queen.

Learning of all his daughter's misfortune, the father was filled with pity for the girl and with loathing for his wicked wife. Nor did he wait until he was back home to have the woman seized. Thus the marriage was celebrated to the satisfaction and joy of all, with the exception of that wretch.

Translated by George Martin

Questions

1. What objects or actions in this story could not happen in real life?
2. What events in this story could conceivably happen in real life?
3. Do you recognize any features from other fairy tales in "The Canary Prince"?
4. In what sense do books turn men into canaries?
5. The king offers the princess disguised as a doctor whatever she likes, but she doesn't reveal her identity and ask for the prince's hand in marriage. Why not?
6. Is the princess's attitude toward her father justified? Does she act like a proper daughter?
7. Do you think Calvino believes in witches and magic books? Can you tell? Does it matter whether he does or not?

 Writers on Writing   *Italo Calvino*

In an age when other fantastically speedy, widespread media are triumphing, and running the risk of flattening all communication onto a single, homogeneous surface, the function of literature is communication between things that are different simply because they are different, not blunting but even sharpening the differences between them, following the true bent of written language.

The motor age has forced speed on us as a measurable quantity, the records of which are milestones in the history of the progress of both men and machines. But mental speed cannot be measured and does not allow comparisons or competitions; nor can it display its results in a historical perspective. Mental speed is valuable for its own sake, for the pleasure it gives to anyone who is sensitive to such a thing, and not for the practical use that can be made of it. A swift piece of reasoning is not necessarily better than a long-pondered one. Far from it. But it communicates something special that is derived simply from its very swiftness.

GIOVANNI BOCCACCIO (1313–1375)

A Dinner of Hens (*from* The Decameron)

The Marquess of Monferrato, Standard-bearer to the Church, was a man of great valour, and went overseas with the army of the Crusaders. There was talk of his bravery at the Court of Philip the One-eyed, who was preparing to leave France on the same Crusade. One of the knights said there was not another couple under the stars like the Marquess and his wife; for, just as the Marquess excelled all knights in courage, so did his wife exceed all other ladies in beauty and virtue.

These words entered the King of France's mind so deeply that, although he had never seen her, he fell violently in love with her, and made up his mind that he would sail from nowhere but Genoa. If he went to that port by land he would have a reasonable pretext for going to see the Marchioness; and, as the husband was away, he thought he would be able to get what he wanted from her.

He proceeded to carry out his plan. He sent his army on ahead, and started out himself with only a few gentlemen. When he was one day's march from the Marquess's lands, he sent to tell the lady that he meant to dine with her next day. The lady, who was prudent and wise, cheerfully answered that she considered it a very great honour, and that he would be welcome. Then she began to wonder why a King should come to visit her when her husband was away. Nor was she wrong when she concluded that he was attracted by the fame of her beauty.

However, as she was a great lady, she determined to show him all honour, and called together all the eminent men remaining with her to make all suitable arrangements with their advice. But she reserved to herself the banquet and the food. Without delay she got together all the fowls in the countryside, and ordered her cooks to use them only for the different courses at the royal banquet.

The King arrived at the time appointed, and the lady received him with all honour and rejoicing. When he observed her, he found that she was far more beautiful and virtuous and polite than the knight had said. He marvelled at her, and praised her highly; and, finding that the lady was so much more excellent than he had imagined, his desires increased proportionately. He then went to take his repose in apartments richly furnished with everything necessary for a King's reception. When dinner time came, the King and the Marchioness sat down together at one table, and the rest, according to their rank, were served at other tables.

Here the King was highly delighted, for he was served successively with many courses and the finest wines, while in addition he kept gazing at the beautiful Marchioness with the greatest pleasure. However, as one course succeeded another, the King began to wonder, for however differently they were served up, they were all made of chicken. He knew that the country round about must be filled with game, and, since he had warned the lady that he was coming, there had been plenty of time to hunt and shoot. He marvelled so much at this, that he wanted to make her talk about nothing but her fowls, and so turned to her gaily, saying:

"Why, Madam, are there only hens and no cocks born in this part of the country?"

The Marchioness perfectly understood what he meant, and felt that, just as she had wished, God had given her an opportunity to show the King her intentions. So, at the King's question, she turned bravely upon him and said:

"No, Sire, but the women are the same here as elsewhere, although they may differ in clothes and rank."

When the King heard her words, he understood the reason for the banquet of fowls and the virtue hidden in her words. He realised that words would be useless with such a woman, and he could not use force. And since he had so incautiously flamed up for her, the wisest thing to do for his own honour would be to extinguish this unlucky fire of passion. So he continued his dinner with no hope of success, and did not attempt to jest further with her, for he was afraid of her retorts. To cover up the cause of his unseemly visit by a swift departure, he thanked her immediately after dinner for the honour she had done him, commended her to God, and departed at once for Genoa.

Questions

1. Are there events in the story that could not happen? Does anything in the story contradict physical or natural laws?
2. Do the people in the story behave in typical human fashion?
3. In what sense is the Marchioness "too good to be true"? Does she act in any way that would contradict her reputation as one who surpassed "all other ladies in beauty and virtue"?
4. Why does she allow the King of France to visit her if she suspects that he will try to seduce her? Is it proper for her to serve him a meal?
5. Is the King evil? How would you judge his behavior?

JEAN RHYS (1894–1979)

I Used to Live Here Once

She was standing by the river looking at the stepping stones and remembering each one. There was the round unsteady stone, the pointed one, the flat one in the middle—the safe stone where you could stand and look round. The next wasn't so safe, for when the river was full the water flowed over it and even when it showed dry it was slippery. But after that it was easy and soon she was standing on the other side.

The road was much wider than it used to be but the work had been done carelessly. The felled trees had not been cleared away and the bushes looked trampled. Yet it was the same road and she walked along feeling extraordinarily happy.

It was a fine day, a blue day. The only thing was that the sky had a glassy look that she didn't remember. That was the only word she could think of. Glassy. She turned the corner, saw that what had been the old pavé had been taken up, and there too the road was much wider, but it had the same unfinished look.

She came to the worn stone steps that led up to the house and her heart began to beat. The screw pine was gone, so was the mock summer house called the ajoupa, but the clove tree was still there and at the top of the steps the rough lawn stretched away, just as she remembered it. She stopped and looked towards the house that had been added to and painted white. It was strange to see a car standing in front of it.

There were two children under the big mango tree, a boy and a little girl, and she waved to them and called "Hello" but they didn't answer her or turn their heads. Very fair children, as Europeans born in the West Indies so often are: as if the white blood is asserting itself against all odds.

The grass was yellow in the hot sunlight as she walked towards them. When she was quite close she called again, shyly: "Hello." Then, "I used to live here once," she said.

Still they didn't answer. When she said for the third time "Hello" she was quite near them. Her arms went out instinctively with the longing to touch them.

It was the boy who turned. His grey eyes looked straight into hers. His expression didn't change. He said: "Hasn't it gone cold all of a sudden. D'you notice? Let's go in." "Yes let's," said the girl.

Her arms fell to her sides as she watched them running across the grass to the house. That was the first time she knew.

Questions

1. What does the woman know for the first time?
2. Which details of the story are inconsistent with natural laws?
3. Do you think Rhys believes in ghosts? Can you tell? Does it matter?

MAXINE HONG KINGSTON (1940–)

On Mortality

As you know, any plain person you chance to meet can prove to be a powerful immortal in disguise come to test you.

Li Fu-yen told a story about Tu Tzu-chun, who lived from A.D. 558 to 618, during the Northern Chou and Sui dynasties. Tu's examiner was a Taoist monk, who made him rich twice, and twice Tu squandered his fortune though it took him two lifetimes to do so. The third time the Taoist gave him money, he bought a thousand li of good land, plowed it himself, seeded it, built houses, roads, and bridges, then welcomed widows and orphans to live on it. With the leftover money, he found a husband for each spinster and a wife for every bachelor in his family, and also paid for the weddings. When he met the Taoist again, he said, "I've used up all your money on the unfortunates I've come across."

"You'll have to repay me by working for me," said the Taoist monk. "I need your help on an important difficult task." He gave Tu three white pills. "Swallow these," he said, pouring him a cup of wine. "All that you'll see and feel will be illusions. No matter what happens, don't speak; don't scream. Remember the saying, 'Hide your broken arms in your sleeves.'"

"How easy," said Tu as he swallowed the pills in three gulps of wine. "Why should I scream if I know they're illusions?"

Level by level he descended into the nine hells. At first he saw oxheads, horsefaces, and the heads of generals decapitated in war. Illusions. Only illusions, harmless. He laughed at the heads. He had seen heads before. Soon fewer heads whizzed through the dark until he saw no more of them.

Suddenly his wife was being tortured. Demons were cutting her up into pieces, starting with her toes. He heard her scream; he heard her bones crack. He reminded himself that she was an illusion. *Illusion*, he thought. She was ground into bloodmeal.

Then the tortures on his own body began. Demons poured bronze down his throat and beat him with iron clubs and chains. They mortar-and-pestled and packed him into a pill.

He had to walk over mountains of knives and through fields of knives and forests of swords. He was killed, his head chopped off, rolling into other people's nightmares.

He heard gods and goddesses talking about him, "This man is too wicked to be reborn a man. Let him be born a woman." He saw the entrance of a black tunnel and felt tired. He would have to squeeze his head and shoulders down into the enclosure and travel a long distance. He pushed head first through the entrance, only the beginning. A god kicked him in the butt to give him a move on. (This kick is the reason many Chinese babies have a blue-gray spot on their butts or lower backs, the "Mongolian spot.") Sometimes stuck in the tunnel, sometimes shooting helplessly through it, he emerged again into light with many urgent things to do, many messages to deliver, but his hands were useless baby's hands, his legs wobbly baby's legs, his voice a wordless baby's cries. Years had to pass before he could regain adult powers; he howled as he began to forget the cosmos, his attention taken up with mastering how to crawl, how to stand, how to walk, how to control his bowel movements.

He discovered that he had been reborn a deaf-mute female named Tu. When she became a woman, her parents married her to a man named Lu, who at first did not mind. "Why does she need to talk," said Lu, "to be a good wife? Let her set an example for women." They had a child. But years later, Lu tired of Tu's dumbness. "You're just being stubborn," he said, and lifted their child by the feet. "Talk, or I'll dash its head against the rocks." The poor mother held her hand to her mouth. Lu swung the child, broke its head against the wall.

Maxine Hong Kingston (© *Franco Salmoiraghi*)

Tu shouted out, "Oh! Oh!"—and he was back with the Taoist, who sadly told him that at the moment when she said, "Oh! Oh!" the Taoist was about to complete the last step in making the elixir for immortality. Now that Tu had broken his silence, the formula was spoiled, no immortality for the human race. "You overcame joy and sorrow, anger, fear, and evil desire, but not love," said the Taoist, and went on his way.

Questions

1. How has Kingston suggested that her story is historical?
2. At what point is it clear that the story is fantasy?
3. After Tu takes the pills, is what he sees "real" or a hallucination? According to the conventions of the story, is the Taoist monk "real" or a hallucination?
4. How does Kingston's explanation of the "Mongolian spot" alter the notions of "hallucination" and "reality"?
5. Why is the human race mortal according to this story?
6. Does the Taoist feel that the loss of immortality is a serious loss? Is the Taoist angry at Tu?
7. Is Tu's failure to remain silent understandable? Is Tu able to remember the difference between fiction and reality? What does Tu's failure indicate about the strength of maternal affection?

JULIO CORTÁZAR (1914–1984)

Continuity of Parks

He had begun to read the novel a few days before. He had put it down because of some urgent business conferences, opened it again on his way back to the estate by train; he permitted himself a slowly growing interest in the plot, in the characterizations. That afternoon, after writing a letter giving his power of attorney and discussing a matter of joint ownership with the manager of his estate, he returned to the book in the tranquillity of his study which looked out upon the park with its oaks. Sprawled in his favorite armchair, its back toward the door—even the possibility of an intrusion would have irritated him, had he thought of it—he let his left hand caress repeatedly the green velvet upholstery and set to reading the final chapters. He remembered effortlessly the names and his mental image of the characters; the novel spread its glamor over him almost at once. He tasted the almost perverse pleasure of disengaging himself line by line from the things around him, and at the same time feeling his head rest comfortably on the green velvet of the chair with its high back, sensing that the cigarettes rested within reach of his hand, that beyond the great windows the air of afternoon danced under the oak trees in the park. Word by word, licked up by the sordid dilemma of the hero and heroine, letting himself be absorbed to the point where the images settled down and took on color and movement, he was witness to the final encounter in the mountain cabin. The woman arrived first, apprehensive; now the lover came in, his face cut by the backlash of a branch. Admirably, she stanched the blood with her kisses, but he rebuffed her caresses, he had not come to perform again the ceremonies of a secret passion, protected by a world of dry leaves and furtive paths through the forest. The dagger warmed itself against his chest, and underneath liberty pounded, hidden close. A lustful, panting dialogue raced down the pages like a rivulet of snakes, and one felt it had all been decided from eternity. Even to those caresses which writhed about the lover's body, as though wishing to keep him there, to dissuade him from it; they sketched abominably the frame of that other body it was necessary to destroy. Nothing had been forgotten: alibis, unforeseen hazards, possible mistakes. From this hour on, each instant had its use minutely assigned. The cold-blooded, twice-gone-over reexamination of the details was barely broken off so that a hand could caress a cheek. It was beginning to get dark.

Not looking at one another now, rigidly fixed upon the task which awaited them, they separated at the cabin door. She was to follow the trail that led north. On the path leading in the opposite direction, he turned for a moment to watch her running, her hair loosened and flying. He ran in turn, crouching among the trees and hedges until, in the yellowish fog of dusk, he could distinguish the avenue of trees which led up to the house. The dogs were not supposed to bark, they did not bark. The estate manager would not be there at this hour, and he was not there. He went up the three porch steps and entered. The woman's words reached him over the thudding of blood in his ears: first a blue chamber, then a hall, then a carpeted stairway. At the top, two doors. No one in the first room, no one in the second. The door of the salon, and then, the knife in hand, the light from the great windows, the high back of an armchair covered in green velvet, the head of the man in the chair reading a novel.

Questions

1. Did the ending of the story surprise you? Why did it surprise you (if it did)? Should you have been surprised by the ending?
2. You may have noticed that seemingly insignificant details in the early part of the story are essential for making sense of the ending. For example, the reference to the green velvet upholstery at the beginning of the story becomes a key to understanding the last sentence. What other details does Cortázar casually plant at the beginning of the story that become important at the end? What is the significance of these details? Are there any wasted details?
3. Does the novel that the man reads sound like a realistic story? Does "Continuity of Parks" strike you as a highly realistic story? What does this story illustrate about the relationship between life and fiction? What does the title mean?
4. Cortázar writes, "one felt it had all been decided from eternity." What does the *it* refer to? What does the line mean? Do such sentiments explain why the man reading the novel doesn't leave his chair?
5. Is the ending of the story a surprise to the man reading the novel? What is Cortázar's attitude toward surprises? Who could be the author of the novel read by the man in the story?

2 ❧ Writing about Fiction: A Case Study

Sally was a bit nervous as she left her Introduction to Literature class. Her teacher had assigned the students to "write an eight-page paper about a short story." Two things made her nervous about this assignment: the openness of the topic and the length of the paper. Her teachers in high school had been more specific. They told the class which stories to write about, or what sort of paper to write—character, plot, or thematic analysis—or sometimes, if the assignment were a character analysis, what specific character to write about. Now everything was up to her. Moreover, she had never written so long a paper, and she was worried about whether she had eight pages worth to say about any short story.

Talking to Your Teachers

Sally liked her teacher, Professor Brown, who had often invited his students to visit his office to discuss assignments, and this time Sally decided that she would take him up on the offer. She checked her professor's schedule to make certain of his office hours and then showed up at the scheduled time. Before meeting with Professor Brown, Sally thought through her questions so that she could get what she needed efficiently without wasting her teacher's time.

When she got to his office, she saw that Professor Brown was on the telephone. She remembered her parents' advice never to interrupt people when they were talking, and she waited patiently for him to put down the phone and then knocked. The last thing she wanted to do was show her teacher disrespect or rudeness.

"Excuse me, Professor Brown," she asked politely, "may I speak to you about the paper you assigned?"

"Of course, Sally. Come in."

Tentatively she walked in, and she was gladdened when he pointed to a chair for her to sit in.

"How can I help you?" he asked, "I'm afraid I have a meeting with the chairperson in fifteen minutes, so we can't talk for long."

Sally got the hint. She knew her teachers were busy people, so instead of beating about the bush she came right to the point. "Could you give me more direction about what sort of paper you want? An eight-page essay on a short story in our textbook is a very open topic."

"Well, that's what I intended. Up to now, I've given you much narrower topics to work on, but at this point in the semester I wanted to give you more freedom to explore the things you were interested in."

"Oh," she said, still unsure of what to do. "So we can write a character analysis, or a comparison of two stories, or a paper on a story's theme or symbolism."

"Yes. But remember that although we've discussed these things separately, this paper doesn't have to focus on just one issue or technique. In fact, one of the things I'm looking for is how well you can bring together these various aspects or elements of the short story into a clear and coherent paper."

"That raises my next question," Sally said. "Do you hold strictly to the eight-page limit? What if I write seven or nine pages. Will you reject the paper?"

Professor Brown laughed. "That's a question that always comes up, and I suppose I forgot to mention it in class. Some teachers are very strict about page length. It's a ticklish matter, but I'm more interested in the *quality* of work and the *intensity* of effort. Page length is a kind of shorthand that teachers have developed over the years to indicate what sort of effort they expect and how large a scope a paper should have. Obviously, a two-page paper indicates a fairly narrow topic written in fairly short order. A five-page paper indicates a somewhat greater effort, although the topic is still fairly narrow. A fifteen- or twenty-page paper usually suggests a major effort extended over the term. An eight- to ten-page paper means to me that a student should make a sizable effort over a couple of weeks. The grade on this paper will be a significant part of your final grade. But don't pad the paper or cut it short. Give me a clear, well-organized, well-developed paper. That's what I'm after. Does that help?"

Sally wasn't sure, and her face conveyed her lingering uncertainty.

"Do you have an idea yet what you want to write about?" he asked.

"Not yet."

"Do you know what story?"

"I'm thinking of several."

"When you've gotten a little further into the assignment, you can return if you still have questions or feel uncertain. There's a fine line teachers have to walk. On the one hand we want students to develop the confidence to do things on their own and to work and think independently. On the other hand, we want to give you the help you need to do well. Right now I want to encourage you to frame your ideas for yourself, but if you have genuine trouble we can talk again, and I can try to direct you a little more firmly."

Sally felt better. She still wasn't exactly sure what she would do, but she understood why her teacher wasn't more specific, and she was beginning to be excited about the freedom he had handed the students to explore their own interests within the framework of the course.

Starting to Work

As she got to her dorm room, Sally decided to start working that afternoon. She was by nature a procrastinator, and several times that semester already she had waited until the night before an assignment was due to start work on it. Sometimes she had been lucky, and the papers had turned out reasonably well. But at other times, things had gone badly. "From now on, I'm not going to chance it," thought Sally, "unless I have to." Her roommate Trina was already back from classes, and talking to Fran, who lived down the hall. They were talking excitedly about a band that was coming to play on campus. Sally joined in for a while, but she realized that she wouldn't study if she stayed in her room, so she took the one book she needed, a pen, and a pad of yellow paper, and excused herself.

"Where are you going?" Trina asked.

"To the library, to get a head start on this paper Professor Brown assigned today."

"If he assigned it today, then you have plenty of time. Don't you want to talk to us?"

"Of course, I do. That's exactly why I'm going to the library, so I can get some work done." She knew that Trina would be disappointed. She always wanted people around. But Sally also knew that she wanted to do better than she had done so far at college, and getting her grades up meant setting priorities and keeping to them. "I'll meet you at the dining hall at six, and we can play a challenge round of Tron-a-saurus." Tron-a-saurus was their favorite video game. Trina brightened. Sally was beginning to learn how to balance her academic and her social life and to set firm boundaries between them. She recognized that she could correct many of her writing problems simply by giving herself more time to work on her papers. Some people are fast writers, but she wasn't, and instead of fooling herself, she was willing now to accept reality.

Narrowing Things Down

Sally found a bright, comfortable seat in the library. She didn't want things to be too comfortable, however, because she was afraid she'd fall asleep.

She decided to reread some of her favorite stories with the idea of choosing one as the subject of her paper. Now that she had a purpose for reading the stories, she began to see them in a different light. She read one story and realized she had not understood it at all. "Scratch that one from the list," she thought. The second one she understood, but it was pretty dull, and besides she couldn't imagine what she would say about it. She read on and on, hoping one would catch her fancy or generate a working idea.

Between stories, she wondered why the school was making her write about stories. Why did it have such requirements? She didn't know what she was going to major in, but she didn't think it would be English. Part of the lesson, she supposed, was developing the discipline of studying a problem. Another part was sharpening her communication skills, and there was no doubt that this sort of assignment was going to tax her ability to read and write effectively. Her sports-minded friends would come back from a workout with sore legs and backs, and when she asked them why they did it, they would say, "No pain, no gain." Maybe education was like that—a mental workout.

Finally she got to D. H. Lawrence's "The Horse Dealer's Daughter." She liked the story. It was about falling in love or, rather, about discovering to one's surprise that one had been in love all along. It had a happy ending, or at least not a sad ending. (When she thought about it, she realized she didn't know how to describe the ending.) It was also kind of spooky—the doctor saves Mabel from suicide and then recognizes that he has been in love with her. She remembered summers when she swam in a lake near her grandparents' house, and the muddy feel of the bottom and the odor of vegetation. The story reminded her of that experience. "I think I'll try writing about 'The Horse Dealer's Daughter,' " she thought to herself, and then looked at the clock. It was already six, when she had promised Trina to meet her. Just choosing a story had taken more time than she had expected, but she was glad that she had spent the time picking it. She thought she had some feel for "The Horse Dealer's Daughter" even if she didn't understand it completely. She swiftly closed the book and ran to the Union where she beat Trina twice at Tron-a-saurus.

Re-readings

In the next couple of days Sally was too busy to go to the library to do more hard work on her English paper. She had a math exam and she also had to work part-time. Nevertheless, she didn't put the paper out of her mind. She kept reading "The Horse Dealer's Daughter" over and over. It was strange how something that seemed perfectly clear the first couple of times now seemed less clear and simple. For example, in the first paragraph, Mabel's brother Joe is twice described as feeling "quite safe himself." But three paragraphs later, Lawrence says that the brothers "were all frightened at the collapse of their lives." Here was a contradiction. Was Lawrence at fault, or did the contradiction signal something happening below the surface of the story? Something was going on that Sally hadn't noticed before. Perhaps Joe was trying to convince himself that he wasn't afraid when he really was—she knew her own brother liked to talk big when he was worried the most, trying to put on a brave face. But although she recognized that the story was more complicated than she had first imagined, Sally began to see things more clearly as she read the story over and over.

To write this paper, she also changed the way she took notes. She began to jot things down right in the margins of the story. In the past, teachers had told her not to write in her schoolbooks because the books were the school district's property, not hers, and the books had to be re-used year after year. But now the books were hers. At first she felt funny writing in them, but she saw that having her notes right beside the passages they referred to and not in a separate notebook saved her time and energy. Of course, some students don't write in their books because they plan to sell them back at the end of the semester, but Sally figured that her education was valuable and expensive, and the "savings" from selling her books was being "penny wise, pound foolish" if writing in them helped her learn more, do better, and save time. Besides, these books were the beginning of a library she would have all her life.

Each time she re-read the story, Sally tried to concentrate on something different. On one of her readings she underlined the words she didn't know or whose meanings she was uncertain of. She was surprised how long her list got, and she realized that this was one way to work on her limited vocabulary. In another reading she looked at recurring images. For example, the story was full of dog imagery. There was the Pervins' real dog, but Mabel is described as "the sulkiest bitch that ever trod"; Joe is said "to have his tail between his legs," and the entire family "was gone to the dogs." At this point, Sally didn't know quite what to make of these recurring images so at the top of one page she wrote a note to herself about it. It wasn't really a note so much as a question: "Why dogs?" Of course, no one would understand the note but Sally, but then she was writing the notes only for herself.

In fact, she wrote down a number of questions to herself, such as "Why is so much made of Dr. Fergusson having a cold?" "Why does Mabel put a chenille tablecloth on the table when everyone is leaving?" Sally didn't think that she would answer all these questions or even that all of them were really important, but asking these questions forced her to think. Sometimes a question she asked during one reading would be answered by a second reading. So below her question about the chenille tablecloth, Sally wrote: "Habit. Pride. Preparing for Funeral." Soon the pages were filled with questions, answers, and observations. She knew she had much more material than she could discuss in eight pages, but she still didn't have a central thread—a thesis—for her paper, and without a central thread she couldn't write the paper.

Talking with Friends

Trina and Sally were playing yet another game of Tron-a-saurus after dinner. "So have you finished your English paper yet?" Trina asked. She almost never asked about schoolwork, but perhaps even Trina was beginning to realize that they had come to college to learn.

"No, I'm stuck," Sally answered. "Have you started yours?"

"I've thought about it a little, but I haven't even picked out a story yet. What are you going to write about?"

"I'm going to do mine on 'The Horse Dealer's Daughter.' "

"Is that the one where the girl tries to kill herself?" Trina asked.

"Yeah."

"How could you write on that? It didn't make any sense to me."

Sally was used to Trina's way of putting things down, but she was curious about why Trina hadn't understood it. "Why didn't it make sense?" she asked.

"One second the doctor doesn't seem to know she's alive, and the next minute they're in love. What sense does that make? And they're so different. I mean, what do they have in common?"

Sally ignored the fact that Trina hadn't gotten the story exactly right. In point of fact Dr. Fergusson is "unsettled" by Mabel's "steady dangerous eyes" at the dining-room table. But Trina was right when she said Mabel and Fergusson were very different. Sally suggested, "Maybe opposites attract. Maybe the point is that they are so different that when they come together it's a sort of an explosion."

"Well, that's one way to think about it. Still, I wouldn't fall in love with anyone who was all covered with mud and dirty water," and Trina went back to the video game. But Sally stood still, thinking about the idea of how opposite Mabel and Fergusson were. Was this the thread she was looking for? Was this the thesis around which she could pull the rest of her observations? She tucked the idea away for safekeeping, and watched while the time traveller escaped through the herd of Tron-a-sauri.

She decided to talk to Brad, one of the best students in the class, about "The Horse Dealer's Daughter." The talk would give her a chance to get to know him, and even a short discussion might help clarify her ideas. She knew that many students shied away from discussing schoolwork because it wasn't supposed to be cool. Well, it might be a whole lot more interesting than discussing how bad the food at the dining hall was, the usual topic of mealtime conversation.

The next day at lunch, Sally talked to Brad about "The Horse Dealer's Daughter." What struck him was how quickly and with what certainty Mabel comes to believe that the doctor loves her. "It really took me by surprise," Brad said. "One second she asks who undressed her, and the next second she says he loves her. There's no logical progression, but it's absolutely right."

"Maybe it's female intuition?" suggested Sally.

"Whatever it is, it's not how Fergusson thinks. He has to see things before he can believe them. For example, he watches her walk into the pond, and he doesn't recognize she's committing suicide until she's completely underwater. Man, he's slow."

"But it's Mabel who's described as slow and Fergusson who's always running around in a hurry."

"Perhaps, physically," answered Brad, after a considerable pause, "but Fergusson's a doctor, a scientist, who doesn't make rash decisions easily. Mabel's the one who forces him into the realization that he's in love. She's the one who makes these leaps of logic."

"I wonder what the critics say about the story?" Sally said.

"It would be interesting to find out," answered Brad. "I'm going to the library this afternoon to research a business paper. Why don't we go together."

"How about now," suggested Sally, and without saying another word, Brad began to gather up his books.

Starting Work in the Library

The university had both a card catalog and a computerized listing. Sally looked under *Lawrence, D. H.* and was surprised to see a long list of holdings. She noticed that most of the books were given numbers around PR6023 (her library used the Library of Congress or LC cataloging system). She decided to start her search at PR6023.

When she got to the stacks—the shelves upon shelves where the books were kept—Sally got nervous. She had barely heard of D. H. Lawrence before, and now she discovered almost an entire bookcase taken up with his books and books about him. "I'll never get through all of this material," she thought to herself. For a second she was very discouraged, but then Sally remembered she didn't have to know all about D. H. Lawrence; she merely wished to see what people had said about "The Horse Dealer's Daughter."

She took up a collection of Lawrence's letters. "I wonder if he ever wrote anyone about the story," she thought to herself. The index contained one citation, and she flipped to the page the index had indicated. But, unfortunately, "The Horse Dealer's Daughter" appeared only as part of a list of short stories Lawrence was sending to his publisher. Nothing useful there. She returned the book to the exact place she had taken it from on the shelf.

She picked up another book, *Double Measure: A Study of the Novels and Stories of D. H. Lawrence* by George H. Ford. She turned to the back of the book to find the index.

> Holloway, John, 226n.
> Homer, 46–47, 134–35
> Honig, Edwin, 221, 236
> Hooker, Thomas, 153
> Hopkins, Gerard Manley, 49n., 50, 58, 158
> "Horse Dealer's Daughter, The," 27, 91–96, 99, 104, 107, 188
> Hough, Graham, 8, 51, 76, 82, 84, 118, 233n.
> Howard, Daniel, 228n.
> Hume, David, 125

There seemed to be a number of pages to consult, so she put the book aside and turned to another book, *D. H. Lawrence: The Critical Heritage*. She looked for an entry under "Horse Dealer's Daughter," and didn't find one. She was ready to put the book back when she saw that all the works of Lawrence were indexed together under his name.

> Lawrence, D. H. (*contd.*)
> 'Hibiscus and Salvia Flowers' (poem), 274
> *Him with His Tail in His Mouth*, 260
> 'History' (poem), 304
> *Horse Dealer's Daughter, The*, 190
> 'Hymn to Priapus' (poem), 139
> 'Intime' (poem), 134

Now she knew there were two ways of listing titles in an index. Some indexers list the titles of works under their own headings; other indexers group them together as subheadings under the author's name. She would have to look under both "Horse Dealer's Daughter" and "Lawrence, D. H., Works."

After Sally consulted the indexes of a number of other books, she took those that mentioned "The Horse Dealer's Daughter" to a table where she could examine them more closely. But before she started reading the books, she noted down *all* the bibliographical information she would need: author, title, place of publication, publisher, and publication date. She also copied the call number from the spine of the book, so that she could find the books again more easily. Only after she noted the preliminary information did Sally start reading.

Sally remembered several things her teachers had told her. Reading critics about literary works should help her make up her own mind. She didn't have to agree with everything a critic says. This is a hard lesson for anyone to put into practice, especially when, as in Sally's case, she doesn't feel very confident about her own opinions. Sally told herself, "I'm not going to believe everything I read. I'm going to put down only those things that seem interesting or correct to me. If it doesn't help me understand, it's not going to be useful." She also remembered two other pieces of advice her teachers gave her: (1) paraphrase whenever possible—but be certain to credit where you got an idea, (2) quote directly only those passages that seem particularly well expressed or whose specific language is important.

With these things in mind, Sally began to read George Ford's *Double Measure*. She tried to keep her notes short and to the point, and always wrote down the page reference for future citations. For example, Sally read this paragraph:

> The scene of the release from loneliness is preceded by the rescue itself in which the man undergoes a kind of deathly baptism—a total immersion in "the foul earthy water." The experience becomes for him, in Pauline terms, a stage of his dying into life. Knowing death he is ready to absorb life.

She wrote only this:

Fergusson experiences "a kind of deathly baptism" when he falls into the pond to save Mabel. Ford, 92

After reading two pages more, Sally wrote:

Mabel's feelings "are presented to us almost entirely by glances" (92) while Fergusson's feelings are carefully analyzed (93). Lawrence uses "a different technique" for presenting each of them. Ford

And then this:

> *Lawrence's work has been successfully translated to film, according to Ford, because "the storyteller seems to be operating a close-up camera."* 93

As you can see, she ignored a great deal. She tried to boil down what was important and put it as much as possible into her own words.

When she had finished the few pages in Ford's book devoted to "The Horse Dealer's Daughter," she opened up Janice Hubbard Harris's book. There she read this paragraph:

> In constructing this tale, Lawrence uses precisely the same principle he had employed in "The Thorn in the Flesh." We have a dual rescue here, a double vision of death and resurrection.[26] For example, Mabel finds joy and company in tending her mother's grave. Lawrence tells us that the life she followed in the world was less real than the death she inherited from her mother (CSS, 448). In her struggles, she has escaped humiliation only in her "subtle, intimate connection" with her mother. Sam Fergusson's experience is similar. Equally lonely and exhausted, he struggles along trying to treat an endless succession of illnesses in a community that he feels enslaves him. His escape is a similar subtle connection, in this case, with the working people he treats. Both compensatory connections are deathly. Lawrence implies that Fergusson's excitement in rubbing up against the lives of these "rough, strongly-feeling people" is voyeuristic. Like so many other characters in the middle tales, both Mabel and Sam physically exhibit their soul's malaise. Mabel's look is set, impassive, blank. Sam is pale, perpetually coughing, scarcely able to make his rounds.

Sally saw that Harris didn't so much disagree with Ford as extend the idea Ford had applied only in regard to Dr. Fergusson. Harris sees that both have been baptized, both rescued. Each in his or her way has saved the other. Sally saw that Harris's point might be very useful to her. If Sally wanted to show that opposites attract and that it was their differences that brought them together, then this idea of each saving the other fit in very nicely. She took careful notes about the various "parallels," as Harris called them, between "the pond and kitchen rescues."

Sally spent several hours reading and taking notes on the books she examined. When she was finished she realized just how much material she had gotten and how much she had to say. The problem wasn't filling eight pages, but keeping the length down to ten pages. Moreover, Sally hadn't looked at any of the periodical literature on "The Horse Dealer's Daughter."

Sally then went to the *MLA International Bibliography*, which is the most complete bibliography of criticism of literary works in English. *The MLA International Bibliography* comes out every year, so Sally first looked at the most recent one. The *MLA* bibliography also is on computer disk, but Sally's library only had the printed version. She was surprised to see just how many articles had been written about D. H. Lawrence. Under Lawrence's name the criticism was divided by subject: general studies and articles about his novels, his criticism, his poetry, and his short stories. The short stories were further broken down. By looking for articles about only "The Horse Dealer's Daughter," Sally soon discovered that not much had been written on it. Going back a decade, she found two articles: one in an obscure journal her library didn't have, and another which seemed to be on the subject of love and death. Sally jotted down all the bibliographical information on Jack F. Stewart's piece, "Eros and Thanatos in 'The Horse Dealer's Daughter,'" and then located the volume of *Studies in the Humanities* in which it appeared. By the end of the day, Sally felt that she had learned what she needed to know to write the essay, and now she had to sit down and figure out how to organize her ideas.

Freewriting—Getting Your Ideas Out

Sally found organizing her ideas to be the hardest part of writing. First, Sally didn't know what she thought until she said it, and second, her ideas seem to come out every which way when she started writing. Perhaps some people thought in an orderly way, but she found that her ideas seemed to scatter. She jumped one way and then another way.

Sally knew she wasn't alone with this style of thinking. Sometimes she regarded the scattershot style of her thinking as a problem, but usually she accepted it, like her hair color, as just another part of who she was. But she knew that for writing purposes she needed to get better control of her ideas. Consequently Sally added a step to the writing process that some of her more orderly thinking friends didn't need to go through. She sat down and for two hours wrote out all the ideas that were buzzing in her mind. During this "freewriting" period she wasn't worried about spelling, grammar, or style. Her only concern was to get down her thoughts in such a way that she could organize them later. Here, for example, is a portion of her freewriting:

Ferg. clearly helps M, but not so clear how M helps f. She gives him love? Perhaps. But she gets him into the muck of life by dragging him into the pond. He resists this, just as he resists saying he loves her. Just as he resists admitting he likes these strong-feeling working class people. Just as he resists showing too much emotion when he has to say good by to his friends. F. afraid to feel. Too educated. Too middleclass. Doctor in a town of ironworkers and coal workers. Yet he needs them. He is both attracted and repulsed by the grittiness of the town. He's like M in this way: She too resists the world around her. Stands back. Afraid to show her feelings.

By the time that Sally was done with her freewriting exercise she knew a great deal of what she wanted to say. Now she needed to organize it.

Outlines—The Map of the Paper

One of the more helpful tips her teachers told her was to think of a paper as a way to solve a problem or answer a question. By the time she finished her freewriting, Sally knew what that question was: Was Mabel's surprise announcement that Dr. Fergusson loves her a poor plot device, or was it carefully planned by D. H. Lawrence to reveal the psychological natures of the characters and the themes of the story? The question combined several different issues: narrative technique, theme and psychology. Sally found it an interesting question to ask, and she put it at the top of her paper.

Sally then saw that before she could answer the question, she needed to show why the question needed to be asked. Why was the announcement a surprise?

She remembered that Mabel and Fergusson hardly spoke in the opening scene. He didn't notice her at first. His questions were stiff and formal. Finally, they were very different. This last statement led to another question: In what way were Mabel and Fergusson different? What emerged was an outline that looked like a flow chart—one question resulting in a number of answers; the answers creating more questions. Sally's outline looked like this:

Is M's announcement prepared for or not?

Why is it a surprise?

M & F don't seem to speak
F doesn't notice M at first
Their contact in the breakfast scene is stiff/formal
They're so different

In what way are they different?

F. is: educated
a man
Scottish
on side of life
fast-moving

M is: a woman
not well educated
lower class
English
on side of death
slow moving

As she began to write this flow chart she began to see where some of her notes could fit in. For example, Jack Stewart talked about the fact that Fergusson was always rushing around and that Mabel was slow moving, "impassive" (she had looked up the word early on to make sure of its meaning). Now she wrote beside the terms *Stewart p. 12* to remind herself that she needed to cite Stewart. She also went back to the story to check whether Fergusson was in fact Scottish, and jotted down the reference to his slight Scottish accent.

When Sally was through, she had a pretty good idea of what she wanted to say, in what order things might be expressed, and the logical connection between the major statements she wished to make and the material which supported those statements. But she did not regard her outline as a blueprint she had to stick to no matter what happened during the writing process. Rather she saw it as a map that charted a number of different routes through the material. Only as she wrote would she know precisely how she would get through the subject.

Writing the Essay

Sally wrote her paper directly on a word processor. She liked writing on a computer because it gave her the greatest flexibility. Over the years she had developed a method that suited her temperament and style. She wrote a first draft very quickly, paying only a little more attention to style, spelling, and grammar than she had in the freewriting exercise. Her major aim in this first draft was getting down her ideas in a logical and convincing manner.

When she was finished with this first draft, she went back and worked on stating her ideas more clearly. Often, clarifying her ideas meant adding topic sentences, breaking down paragraphs into clearer units of thought, providing logical transitions from one idea to another, substituting nouns for pronouns.

On her third journey through the paper she began to check on grammar and style. She began to see places in which she had been very wordy and tried to get to the point more quickly. She looked for places where she could choose more precise terms for saying what she meant. She began to examine her use of punctuation. When she was done, she ran the spell-check program which spotted a number of typos and other spelling mistakes. Then she printed out a copy of her essay and saved the text on two different diskettes. She had learned through sad experience to save her text often and have back-up copies. Few things are more frustrating than losing hours of work because of an electrical failure or damaged diskettes.

Sally took her printout home and waited a few days. Then she read it over, making dozens of corrections of all sorts on the manuscript. Now was the time to check such small details as the punctuation of quotations and the different spellings of *its* and *to* and *their* (differences which the spell-check program wouldn't catch), and to examine questions of style (whether sentences would be better worded in the active voice). When she made all the corrections she could make, she showed the paper to Brad, who read it carefully and marked some places where he wasn't really sure what she meant. His reading gave her yet another chance to make herself clear. In the end, she took all her corrections back to the computer room, typed them into the diskette, and printed out a new version of her paper.

SALLY SCOTT
INTRODUCTION TO LITERATURE
PROFESSOR BROWN
12 NOVEMBER 1991

The Attraction of Opposites in "The Horse Dealer's Daughter"

"The Horse Dealer's Daughter" contains a number of surprises, such as Mabel's suicide attempt and Dr. Fergusson's marriage proposal. But no surprise is more startling than Mabel's sudden announcement that Fergusson
loves her. At first, the announcement seems crazy, a sign
of her disturbed mind. Dr. Fergusson has done nothing to
indicate that he loves her. He has, it is true, saved her
from drowning, but as a doctor and a human being, he is
morally obliged to save the lives of others, not just
those he loves. However, it soon becomes clear that she
is correct. How can we account for this rapid change? Is
Mabel's announcement a hollow narrative trick to create
a happy ending? Or has Lawrence carefully and subtlely
prepared this turn of events?

One reason that Mabel's announcement that Fergusson
loves her is so surprising is that they have had very little contact. When Fergusson arrives at Oldmeadow to say
goodbye to her brothers, he does not greet her, nor does
she greet him. In fact, only when Mabel rises to clear
the table do "they all . . . become aware of her existence" (123). When she returns to the dining room, Fergusson asks her a question, "What are you going to do,
then, Miss Pervin?" (124). The question, however,
doesn't seem very personal or friendly. They seem to
have a distant and formal relationship.

Yet, Mabel's distant and formal relationship to Fergusson is not all that different from the relationship
she has with her brothers. The first words used to describe Mabel are that "the girl was alone" (120). Fred
Henry calls her "the sulkiest bitch that ever trod"
(124). Mabel keeps the world at a great distance.

> No company came to the house, save dealers and
> coarse men. Mabel had no associates of her own sex,
> after her sister went away. But she did not mind.
> She went regularly to church, she attended her fa-
> ther. And she lived in the memory of her mother.
> (125)

So although Mabel is not close to Fergusson, he is the
one man outside of her family that she has any relation-

ship to. Moreover, Fergusson's question does suggest a certain level of concern.

Another reason that Mabel's announcement comes as such a surprise is that Mabel and Dr. Fergusson seem so different. Mabel is described as a kind of animal. She has a "bull-dog" face (121). She is a "bitch" (124). "Nothing," we are told "could shake the sullen, animal pride that dominated" her as well as the other members of her family (125). She is described as having "wild, bare, animal shoulders" (129). Like an animal, Mabel refuses to think. She asks herself, "Why should she think? Why should she answer anybody?" Her actions are "mindless and persistent," a kind of thoughtless instinct (125). Yet despite the animalistic qualities of her nature, Mabel is described as slow and unmoving. Her face has an "impassive fixity" (121). Two pages later, it is "impassive and unchanging" (123). A page after that, it is "perfectly impassive" (124). George H. Ford has commented that Mabel's "changes of feeling and her character . . . are presented to us almost entirely by glances" (92). Yet what Mabel conveys with her glances is mostly impassiveness, an unwillingness to express anything. Even her attempt at suicide is not a frantic, hysterical act. She performs it as though she were "something transmitted rather than stirring into voluntary activity" as she wades "slowly into the water" (127).

If Mabel is animal-like, unthinking, and slow, Dr. Fergusson is just the opposite. As Jack F. Stewart has pointed out, "while [Mabel's] rhythm is slowed down to the point of inertia, [Fergusson] is accelerated to the point of collapse" (12–13). His life is "nothing but work, drudgery, constant hastening from dwelling to dwelling among the colliers and the iron-workers" (126). He is in "perpetual haste," and he hurries all the more when he is feeling ill because "he fancied the motion restored him" (126). Whereas Mabel rejects thought, Fergusson's mind is always seeking out "stimulation." Unlike the uneducated laborers in the area, Fergusson is highly educated and constantly thinking and observing.

Yet as different as Fergusson and Mabel are, a number of things unite them. They are outsiders. Mabel, we are told, "did not share the same life as her brothers" (120–21). At the graveyard "she felt immune from the world . . . as in another country" (125). "For the life she followed here in the world," Lawrence tells us, "was far less real than the world of death she inherited from her mother" (126). Dr. Fergusson is also an outsider. He

speaks with "a slight Scotch accent" (123) indicating he
is not from England. He is an educated man who lives
among the laboring poor. He is a man of science in a
world of emotion. He regards the place where he lives as
an "alien, ugly little town" (126). Mabel and Jack are
also united by a sense of pride and reserve. She is described as "brutally proud, reserved" (125). He finds the
"introduction of the personal element was very distasteful to him, a violation of his professional honor"
(130). His pride is wounded when he finds himself vulnerable to the pain of love:

> That this was love! That he should be ripped open in
> this way! Him, a doctor! How they would all jeer if
> they knew! It was agony to him to think they might
> know. (131)

Neither Mabel nor Jack are people who allow themselves
to appear vulnerable. They protect themselves by displaying a certain distance and reserve. Yet both of them
seek contact with an energizing power that is greater
than either of them. Mabel seeks out the world of the
dead, and Jack Fergusson the powerful emotions of the laboring class.

Not only is Dr. Fergusson attracted to opposites, he
needs them in order to feel alive. Sometimes he grumbled
about his life of "drudgery, constant hastening from
dwelling to dwelling," but though it "wore him out," he
had "at the same time . . . a craving for it."

> It was a stimulant to him to be in the homes of the
> working people, moving as it were through the inner-
> most body of their life. His nerves were excited and
> gratified. He could come so near, into the very lives
> of the rough, inarticulate, powerfully emotional
> men and women. He grumbled, he said he hated the
> hellish hole. But as a matter of fact it excited
> him, the contact with the rough, strongly-feeling
> people was a stimulant applied directly to his
> nerves. (126)

Mabel—strong, instinctual, unintellectual, deeply
emotional—is just the sort of person whom Fergusson
would be attracted to. The differences that divide them
are part of the charm that brings them together.

Although Mabel and Jack do not exchange many words until he saves her from drowning, she does exert a strong
force over him even before her attempt at suicide. In
the opening breakfast scene, he is held by "her steady,
dangerous eyes, that always made him uncomfortable, un-

settling his superficial ease" (124). The word "always" tells us that Mabel has disturbed Dr. Fergusson many times before. Mabel's inexpressiveness, in fact, keeps "the young doctor watching her all the while" (124). While she tends her mother's grave, Fergusson watches "her as if spellbound" (126). Later, when he sees her walking to the pond, "His mind suddenly becomes alive and attentive" (127).

Not only is Jack fascinated by Mabel, but Mabel is aware of Jack's attention. In the graveyard, Mabel becomes aware that she is being observed.

> She lifted her eyes, feeling [Fergusson] looking. Their eyes met. And each looked away again at once, each feeling, in some way, found out by the other. (126)

Mabel might not at first recognize such attention as love, but she is aware that Fergusson is studying her with more than usual attention. On his part Fergusson is unaware that this fascination is part of love. Nevertheless, he finds himself mesmerized and excited by her. He feels "a heavy power in her eyes which laid hold of his whole being, as if he had drunk some powerful drug" (126). So even before Mabel's surprising announcement that Fergusson loves her, D. H. Lawrence has prepared the reader for this turn of events.

Yet if the hypnotic attraction between Mabel Pervin and Jack Fergusson has existed for a long time, why does Mabel recognize Fergusson's love for her only after he has pulled her from the pond? The simple answer, I suppose, is that this incident has brought them together more intimately than they have ever been before. As Mabel points out, Fergusson has seen her naked, and although such exposure is nothing unusual for a doctor, who must see many women naked as part of his professional duties, Mabel seems to feel that such a liberty derives from more than humanitarian interests. But as several commentators have brought out—particularly Jack Stewart and Janice Hubbard Harris—the rescue at the pond "symbolizes not only death, but transformation and rebirth" (Harris 15). Because Mabel and Jack have been transformed and reborn by the incident in the pond, she is aware that his actions signify his love for her.

Janice Hubbard Harris emphasizes that there are two rescues in "The Horse Dealer's Daughter" and that both Mabel and Jack are saved (127–8). Stewart explains that "in Lawrence's erotic rituals man is reborn from woman, as well as woman from man" (15). While it is obvious how

Jack saves Mabel, it is less clear how Mabel saves Jack. I think Mabel's surprising announcement that Jack loves her is a kind of shock treatment that teaches Jack, in Stewart's phrase, "to go beyond his inhibiting ego and give himself to the transforming energy of Eros" (13).

From the start of the story, Jack is sick, suffering from a bad cough. Joe Pervin jokes that "if a doctor goes round croaking with a cold [it] looks bad for the patients, doesn't it?" (123) His message is clear: a doctor should cure himself before trying to cure others. Jack is ill not so much with a cold, but with coldness. He is unable to become truly close to the lives of his patients. He still remains outside of the "innermost body of their lives" (126). In rescuing Mabel from the pond, however, Jack is completely submerged in the dirt and stink of those around him. Of course, Jack tries to keep his head above the water, reaching for Mabel's clothing without actually touching her. But the cloth "evaded his fingers" and in lunging after it, "he lost his balance and went under, horribly, suffocating in the foul earthy water, struggling madly for a few moments" (127). After Mabel regains consciousness, he immediately wants to change his clothes, free himself of the muck around him just as he held himself aloof from the people. Yet Mabel keeps him in his soiled clothes "as if she had the life of his body in her hands" (129) and doesn't allow him to change until she has gotten him to admit that he loves her. It is Mabel who finally finds dry clothes for Fergusson—presumably things her brothers had left behind—so that in the end Fergusson is dressed in the manner of the people whose existence he finds so life-giving and stimulating.

In the kitchen scene, according to Harris, "Lawrence traces Fergusson's mental struggle, he shows Fergusson's reluctance and pride, his impulse to remain apart, battling with his desire to yield to the love and intimacy Mabel offers" (128). Mabel has thrown Fergusson off balance both physically and mentally. She throws him off balance in the pond and by declaring that he loves her. But only by falling can Fergusson and Mabel rise again, better, happier, and more connected to the people and the life around them.

Mabel's surprise announcement is not, finally, a cheap narrative trick to provide "The Horse Dealer's Daughter" with a happy ending. It is well prepared psychologically, thematically, and symbolically. It is also one of the shocks needed to shake Fergusson out of the pride and reserve that keeps him from truly making contact

with the people he has dedicated his life to serving.
The very differences that keep Mabel and Jack apart are,
in fact, what finally bring them more closely together.
Each needs the other. In the end they rescue each other
from a world of isolation, death, and dissatisfaction.

Works Cited

Ford, George H. *Double Measure: A Study of the Novels
     and Stories of D. H. Lawrence*. New York: Holt, 1965.
Harris, Janice Hubbard. *The Short Fiction of D. H. Law-
     rence*. New Brunswick: Rutgers UP, 1984.
Lawrence, D. H. "The Horse Dealer's Daughter." *The Heath
     Guide to Literature*. Ed. David Bergman and Daniel Mark
     Epstein. 3rd ed. Lexington, MA: Heath, 1991. 203–215.
Stewart, Jack F. "Eros and Thanatos in 'The Horse
     Dealer's Daughter.'" *Studies in the Humanities* 12.1
     (1985): 11–19.

Reexamining Sally's Essay

On the following pages, we have reprinted Sally's essay, only this time we have added marginal glosses to point out how Sally has incorporated what she has learned into her essay. Sally learned that it is not enough to *know* how to do things correctly, one must *do* things correctly—put learning into action. The marginal comments may help alert you to the ways you could incorporate the lessons of this book into your own writing.

SALLY SCOTT
INTRODUCTION TO LITERATURE
PROFESSOR BROWN
12 NOVEMBER 1991

The Attraction of Opposites in "The Horse Dealer's Daughter"

"The Horse Dealer's Daughter" contains a number of surprises, such as Mabel's suicide attempt and Dr. Fergusson's marriage proposal. But no surprise is more startling than Mabel's sudden announcement that Fergusson loves her. At first, the announcement seems crazy, a sign of her disturbed mind. Dr. Fergusson has done nothing to indicate that he loves her. He has, it is true, saved her from drowning, but as a doctor and a human being, he is morally obliged to save the lives of others, not just those he loves. However, it soon becomes clear that she is correct. How can we account for this rapid change? Is Mabel's announcement a hollow narrative trick to create a happy ending? Or has Lawrence carefully and subtlely prepared this turn of events?

One reason that Mabel's announcement that Fergusson loves her is so surprising is that they have had very little contact. When Fergusson arrives at Oldmeadow to say goodbye to her brothers, he does not greet her, nor does she greet him. In fact, only when Mabel rises to clear the table do "they all . . . become aware of her existence" (123). When she returns to the dining room, Fergusson asks her a question, "What are you going to do, then, Miss Pervin?" (124). The question, however, doesn't seem very personal or friendly. They seem to have a distant and formal relationship.

Yet, Mabel's distant and formal relationship to Fergusson is not all that different from the relationship she has with her brothers. The first words used to describe Mabel are that "the girl was alone" (120). Fred Henry calls her "the sulkiest bitch that ever trod" (124). Mabel keeps the world at a great distance.

> No company came to the house, save dealers and
> coarse men. Mabel had no associates of her own sex,
> after her sister went away. But she did not mind.
> She went regularly to church, she attended her fa-
> ther. And she lived in the memory of her mother.
> (125)

So although Mabel is not close to Fergusson, he is the one man outside of her family that she has any relationship to. Moreover, Fergusson's question does suggest a certain level of concern.

Another reason that Mabel's announcement comes as such a surprise is that Mabel and Dr. Fergusson seem so different. Mabel is described as a kind of animal. She has a "bull-dog" face (121). She is a "bitch" (124). "Nothing," we are told "could shake the sullen, animal pride that dominated" her as well as the other members of her family (125). She is described as having "wild, bare, animal shoulders" (129). Like an animal, Mabel refuses to think. She asks herself, "Why should she think? Why should she answer anybody?" Her actions are "mindless and persistent," a kind of thoughtless instinct (125). Yet despite the animalistic qualities of her nature, Mabel is described as slow and unmoving. Her face has an "impassive fixity" (121). Two pages later, it is "impassive and unchanging" (123). A page after that, it

---

Marginal notes (left column):

These questions are the focus of her paper

Because Sally is clearly quoting from the story, she needs only to identify the page number in parentheses

Since the question mark is part of the quotation it goes inside the quotation marks.

Because this is a long quotation it is indented *without* quotation marks. Sally has correctly put the parenthetical page reference *after* the punctuation. In nonindented quotations she correctly puts them *before* the final piece of punctuation.

is "perfectly impassive" (124). George H. Ford has commented that Mabel's "changes of feeling and her character . . . are presented to us almost entirely by glances" (92). Yet what Mabel conveys with her glances is mostly impassiveness, an unwillingness to express anything. Even her attempt at suicide is not a frantic, hysterical act. She performs it as though she were "something transmitted rather than stirring into voluntary activity" as she wades "slowly into the water" (127).

If Mabel is animal-like, unthinking, and slow, Dr. Fergusson is just the opposite. As Jack F. Stewart has pointed out, "while [Mabel's] rhythm is slowed down to the point of inertia, [Fergusson] is accelerated to the point of collapse" (12–13). His life is "nothing but work, drudgery, constant hastening from dwelling to dwelling among the colliers and the iron-workers" (126). He is in "perpetual haste," and he hurries all the more when he is feeling ill because "he fancied the motion restored him" (126). Whereas Mabel rejects thought, Fergusson's mind is always seeking out "stimulation." Unlike the uneducated laborers in the area, Fergusson is highly educated and constantly thinking and observing.

Yet as different as Fergusson and Mabel are, a number of things unite them. They are outsiders. Mabel, we are told, "did not share the same life as her brothers" (120–21). At the graveyard "she felt immune from the world . . . as in another country" (125). "For the life she followed here in the world," Lawrence tells us, "was far less real than the world of death she inherited from her mother" (126). Dr. Fergusson is also an outsider. He speaks with "a slight Scotch accent" (123) indicating he is not from England. He is an educated man who lives among the laboring poor. He is a man of science in a world of emotion. He regards the place where he lives as an "alien, ugly little town" (126). Mabel and Jack are also united by a sense of pride and reserve. She is described as "brutally proud, reserved" (125). He finds the "introduction of the personal element was very distasteful to him, a violation of his professional honor" (130). His pride is wounded when he finds himself vulnerable to the pain of love:

> That this was love! That he should be ripped open in this way! Him, a doctor! How they would all jeer if they knew! It was agony to him to think they might know. (131)

Neither Mabel nor Jack are people who allow themselves to appear vulnerable. They protect themselves by displaying a certain distance and reserve. Yet both of them seek contact with an energizing power that is greater than either of them. Mabel seeks out the world of the dead, and Jack Fergusson the powerful emotions of the laboring class.

Not only is Dr. Fergusson attracted to opposites, he needs them in order to feel alive. Sometimes he grumbled about his life of "drudgery, constant hastening from dwelling to dwelling," but though it "wore him out," he had "at the same time . . . a craving for it."

> It was a stimulant to him to be in the homes of the working people, moving as it were through the innermost body of their life. His nerves were excited and gratified. He could come so near, into the very lives of the rough, inarticulate, powerfully emotional

men and women. He grumbled, he said he hated the
hellish hole. But as a matter of fact it excited
him, the contact with the rough, strongly-feeling
people was a stimulant applied directly to his
nerves. (126)

Mabel--strong, instinctual, unintellectual, deeply
emotional--is just the sort of person whom Fergusson
would be attracted to. The differences that divide them
are part of the charm that brings them together.

Although Mabel and Jack do not exchange many words until he saves her from drowning, she does exert a strong
force over him even before her attempt at suicide. In
the opening breakfast scene, he is held by "her steady,
dangerous eyes, that always made him uncomfortable, unsettling his superficial ease" (124). The word "always"
tells us that Mabel has disturbed Dr. Fergusson many
times before. Mabel's inexpressiveness, in fact, keeps
"the young doctor watching her all the while" (124).
While she tends her mother's grave, Fergusson watches
"her as if spellbound" (126). Later, when he sees her
walking to the pond, "His mind suddenly becomes alive
and attentive" (127).

Not only is Jack fascinated by Mabel, but Mabel is
aware of Jack's attention. In the graveyard, Mabel becomes aware that she is being observed.

> She lifted her eyes, feeling [Fergusson] looking.
> Their eyes met. And each looked away again at once,
> each feeling, in some way, found out by the other.
> (126)

Mabel might not at first recognize such attention as
love, but she is aware that Fergusson is studying her
with more than usual attention. On his part Fergusson is
unaware that this fascination is part of love. Nevertheless, he finds himself mesmerized and excited by her. He
feels "a heavy power in her eyes which laid hold of his
whole being, as if he had drunk some powerful drug"
(126). So even before Mabel's surprising announcement
that Fergusson loves her, D. H. Lawrence has prepared
the reader for this turn of events.

Yet if the hypnotic attraction between Mabel Pervin
and Jack Fergusson has existed for a long time, why does
Mabel recognize Fergusson's love for her only after he
has pulled her from the pond? The simple answer, I suppose, is that this incident has brought them together
more intimately than they have ever been before. As
Mabel points out, Fergusson has seen her naked, and although such exposure is nothing unusual for a doctor,
who must see many women naked as part of his professional duties, Mabel seems to feel that such a liberty
derives from more than humanitarian interests. But as
several commentators have brought out--particularly
Jack Stewart and Janice Hubbard Harris--the rescue at
the pond "symbolizes not only death, but transformation
and rebirth" (Harris 15). Because Mabel and Jack have
been transformed and reborn by the incident in the pond,
she is aware that his actions signify his love for her.

Janice Hubbard Harris emphasizes that there are two
rescues in "The Horse Dealer's Daughter" and that both
Mabel and Jack are saved (127-8). Stewart explains that
"in Lawrence's erotic rituals man is reborn from woman,
as well as woman from man" (15). While it is obvious how
Jack saves Mabel, it is less clear how Mabel saves Jack.
I think Mabel's surprising announcement that Jack loves

Sally uses a nice variety of long and short quotations. She supports all her generalizations with evidence.

Because it is not clear from the context, Sally names the source of the quotation in the parenthetical page reference.

Since Sally has given Stewart's full name earlier, she can refer to him simply as Stewart. Notice also that she gives page reference to an idea developed by Harris even though Sally has not quoted her.

her is a kind of shock treatment that teaches Jack, in Stewart's phrase, "to go beyond his inhibiting ego and give himself to the transforming energy of Eros" (13).

From the start of the story, Jack is sick, suffering from a bad cough. Joe Pervin jokes that "if a doctor goes round croaking with a cold [it] looks bad for the patients, doesn't it?" (123). His message is clear: a doctor should cure himself before trying to cure others. Jack is ill not so much with a cold, but with coldness. He is unable to become truly close to the lives of his patients. He still remains outside of the "innermost body of their lives" (126). In rescuing Mabel from the pond, however, Jack is completely submerged in the dirt and stink of those around him. Of course, Jack tries to keep his head above the water, reaching for Mabel's clothing without actually touching her. But the cloth "evaded his fingers" and in lunging after it, "he lost his balance and went under, horribly, suffocating in the foul earthy water, struggling madly for a few moments" (127). After Mabel regains consciousness, he immediately wants to change his clothes, free himself of the muck around him just as he held himself aloof from the people. Yet Mabel keeps him in his soiled clothes "as if she had the life of his body in her hands" (129) and doesn't allow him to change until she has gotten him to admit that he loves her. It is Mabel who finally finds dry clothes for Fergusson—presumably things her brothers had left behind—so that in the end Fergusson is dressed in the manner of the people whose existence he finds so life-giving and stimulating.

In the margin:

Notice Sally always refers to the author of a quotation in the text *before* she presents the quotation.

In the kitchen scene, according to Harris, "Lawrence traces Fergusson's mental struggle, he shows Fergusson's reluctance and pride, his impulse to remain apart, battling with his desire to yield to the love and intimacy Mabel offers" (128). Mabel has thrown Fergusson off balance both physically and mentally. She throws him off balance in the pond and by declaring that he loves her. But only by falling can Fergusson and Mabel rise again, better, happier, and more connected to the people and the life around them.

In the margin:

Sally effectively returns to the questions that began the paper

Mabel's surprise announcement is not, finally, a cheap narrative trick to provide "The Horse Dealer's Daughter" with a happy ending. It is well prepared psychologically, thematically, and symbolically. It is also one of the shocks needed to shake Fergusson out of the pride and reserve that keeps him from truly making contact with the people he has dedicated his life to serving. The very differences that keep Mabel and Jack apart are, in fact, what finally bring them more closely together. Each needs the other. In the end they rescue each other from a world of isolation, death, and dissatisfaction.

Works Cited

Ford, George H. *Double Measure: A Study of the Novels and Stories of D. H. Lawrence*. New York: Holt, 1965.
Harris, Janice Hubbard. *The Short Fiction of D. H. Lawrence*. New Brunswick: Rutgers UP, 1984.
Lawrence, D. H. "The Horse Dealer's Daughter." *The Heath Guide to Literature*. Ed. David Bergman and Daniel Mark Epstein. 3rd ed. Lexington, MA: Heath, 1991. 203–215.
Stewart, Jack F. "Eros and Thanatos in 'The Horse Dealer's Daughter.'" *Studies in the Humanities* 12.1 (1985): 11–19.

3 ❧ Our Seat on the Action— Narration

Picture for a moment two people sitting at a table with cups of coffee before them. One is telling a story, perhaps about a friend or a relative. You might say that they are gossiping, for like most gossipers they are less interested in the truth of the story than its ability to excite and delight. (In fact, one might say gossip becomes news when the speaker becomes concerned with conveying facts accurately.) The listener leans forward to catch each word. At various moments he or she interjects the question, "And what happened next?" or "And then what did they do?"

Such a scene conveys the essence of storytelling. We have a storyteller, an audience, and the story itself. In more formal situations, we have the writer, the reader, and the text. The question the listener asks is also part of the essence of storytelling. Stories are concerned with a sequence of actions. These actions can be hard and external—a battle, a murder, an escape from prison—or they can be subtle and internal. In Jean Rhys's "I Used to Live Here Once," the action consists of a woman crossing a stream and waving to two children and then recognizing that she is dead. In Rhys's story the act of recognition is the central and most important action. Quite often in fiction the most important changes and actions take place in the characters' minds. We will examine other aspects of fiction in Chapters 5 and 6. But now we are concerned with the narrator and with the ways by which a reader learns the story's "facts."

Basic Narrative Types

A story is typically told in two different ways: by someone involved in the action, or by someone wholly outside of the action. The voice that tells us the story is called the *narrator*. If someone involved in the action tells the story, he or she usually says, "*I* did this," or "*I* saw that." Because they use the first-person pronoun, these stories are called *first-person narratives*. In *third-person narratives*, the narrators generally do not refer to themselves. They remain outside of the story's action. The simplest sort of third-person narrator is called the *omniscient narrator*. Omniscient means "all knowing," and an omniscient narrator can tell the reader anything pertinent to the story no matter when it occurred, where it happened, or who did it. An omniscient narrator can enter the minds of all the characters and tell the reader what they saw, thought, and felt.

Each of these basic narrative types has its own advantages and disadvantages, and one of the hardest decisions an author must make is whether to cast a story as a first- or third-person narration.

An Omniscient Narration

One of the most interesting books exploring the various ways a story can be told is Raymond Queneau's *Exercises in Style*. In that book, Queneau tells the same everyday story in 99 different ways. Nor does Queneau exhaust the narrative possibilities, for he never tells the story in the manner of an omniscient narrator. If he had, he might have written this version:

> A young man with a long neck and funny hat, which was circled by string rather than by a hatband, entered a crowded bus one day. The man standing next to him did not like the young man's looks and decided to poke the young man in the ribs whenever a passenger moved through the aisle. Thinking that he was being deliberately poked, the young man shouted at his neighbor. When the first empty seat came vacant, the young man ran for it.
>
> Later that day, the young man met a friend who advised him to alter his ill-fitting coat.

Notice that the narrator never refers to him- or herself. Indeed, an omniscient narrator is more like a god than a person, a consciousness that can move wherever it pleases. In sentence 2, for example, the narrator tells us what the older man is thinking; he doesn't like the somewhat odd young man and decides to hurt him. In sentence 3, however, the narrator is in the mind of the young man, telling us the young man's thoughts. Finally, in the last sentence, the narrator has moved off the bus and witnesses the young man talking to a friend.

The First-Person Narrative

The author who adopts a first-person narration must follow certain conventions. Unlike omniscient narrators who can follow the actions and thoughts of all the characters, first-person narrators are limited to telling us what they themselves saw, heard, thought, felt. They can also make reasonable assumptions about what other characters see, think, or feel. In real life, we infer from people's actions and words what they think or feel. If people yell at us, we assume they are angry or upset. So, too, a first-person narrator can make assumptions about the thoughts and feelings of other characters. But as readers we must keep in mind that these assumptions are only the narrator's. They need not be our assumptions or the author's assumptions. In the next chapter, we will study the *unreliable narrator*—a narrator whose version of the story we, as readers, come to doubt—but for the moment it is enough to remember that first-person narratives are limited by the fictional perspective of a character involved in the action.

Here are three of Queneau's narratives. They are all first-person narratives, but because each narrator has a different relationship to the fictional action, the stories they tell are very different.

RAYMOND QUENEAU (1903-1976)

From Exercises in Style

Narrative

One day at about midday in the Parc Monceau[1] district, on the back platform of a more or less full S bus (now No. 84), I observed a person with a very long neck who was wearing a felt hat which had a plaited cord round it instead of a ribbon. This individual suddenly addressed the man standing next to him, accusing him of purposely treading on his toes every time any passengers got on or off. However he quickly abandoned the dispute and threw himself onto a seat which had become vacant.

Two hours later I saw him in front of the Gare Saint-Lazare[2] engaged in earnest conversation with a friend who was advising him to reduce the space between the lapels of his overcoat by getting a competent tailor to raise the top button.

The Subjective Side

I was not displeased with my attire this day. I was inaugurating a new, rather sprightly hat, and an overcoat of which I thought most highly. Met X in front of the Gare Saint-Lazare who tried to spoil my pleasure by trying to prove that this overcoat is cut too low at the lapels and that I ought to have an extra button on it. At least he didn't dare attack my headgear.

A bit earlier I had roundly told off a vulgar type who was purposely ill-treating me every time anyone went by getting off or on. This happened in one of those unspeakably foul omnibi which fill up with hoi polloi precisely at those times when I have to consent to use them.

Another Subjectivity

Next to me on the bus platform today there was one of those half-baked young fellows, you don't find so many of them these days, thank God, otherwise I should end up by killing one. This particular one, a brat of something like 26

---

[1] The Parc Monceau is a public garden in Paris.
[2] The Gare Saint-Lazare is one of the principal railway stations of Paris.

or 30, irritated me particularly not so much because of his great long featherless-turkey's neck as because of the nature of the ribbon round his hat, a ribbon which wasn't much more than a sort of maroon-coloured string. Dirty beast! He absolutely disgusted me! As there were a lot of people in our bus at that hour I took advantage of all the pushing and shoving there is every time anyone gets on or off to dig him in the ribs with my elbow. In the end he took to his heels, the milksop, before I could make up my mind to tread on his dogs to teach him a lesson. I could also have told him, just to annoy him, that he needed another button on his overcoat which was cut too low at the lapels.

Certain aspects of the story are quite clearly different in these three versions. For instance, the third narrator does not mention the young man's meeting with his friend in front of the Gare Saint-Lazare. The reason, of course, is that he wasn't there and had no way of knowing that it took place. Thus Queneau, following the conventions of first-person narratives, leaves out the meeting. Another clear difference is the way in which the young man orders the events. He tells about his meeting at the Gare Saint-Lazare first. The meeting is the more important event for him, because the meeting gave him the opportunity to show off his new clothes.

Perhaps of more interest is the way in which the bystander's account differs from the accounts of the more immediate participants. For example, the bystander says that the young man accused the older man of "purposely treading on his toes," whereas the older man claims he was poking the young man in the ribs. The first narrator also has a different version of the young man's conversation with his friend. According to the young man, the friend is advising adding a button—not having the top button raised. How do we account for such discrepancies? Usually we apply to a fictional situation the same sorts of explanations we apply to real life (unless, of course, the conventions of the story rule out such explanations). Here we might say that the bystander was just too far away to get all the details, though he correctly observes the basic events.

Of greatest interest is the way in which the characters' attitudes color their versions of the story. The young man sees his accoster as a "vulgar type," one of the "hoi polloi" whom he "roundly told off." In the older man's version, the young man is "a brat," a "dirty beast" and a "milksop." The older man seems to think he got the better of the argument. The bystander makes far fewer evaluations; he takes a matter-of-fact attitude toward what must be a frequent event on the crowded buses of Paris.

Narrative Point-of-View

These three narratives show us the consequences of *narrative point-of-view*. Narrative point-of-view has two aspects: physical point-of-view and psychological point-of-view. Physical point-of-view is the clearer. Where we are in relation to an event influences the way we experience it. If we are involved in a car accident, we will see the event from one perspective. If we are standing on the sidewalk, we will have another. If we are in a helicopter overhead, we will get a bird's-eye view.

Psychological point-of-view is far subtler. A person's preferences and prejudices shade descriptions. Often word choice will be a clue to the narrator's feelings. One narrator may describe a color as "lively," another narrator might describe it as "garish." The first hints of approval; the second shows disapproval. The bystander reveals his attitude toward the event. He writes that the young man "suddenly" accused the older man, then "quickly abandoned the dispute" and then "threw himself onto a seat." The combination of the words "suddenly," "quickly," and "threw" indicates the bystander's feeling that the young man behaved rashly and violently, and that the bystander disapproves.

Limited Third-Person Narratives

First-person narratives have certain advantages. They bring the reader closer to the action; they infuse the story with great psychological and narrative subtlety; they are a natural way to tell a story. But first-person narratives have limitations: they lack flexibility and objectivity. As readers, we can learn only what the narrator has learned, and the narrator's point-of-view colors the telling of events. Third-person narratives are far more flexible, but they seem colder and more distant. Writers have sought to combine the advantages of these two modes of narration by creating a variant: the *limited third-person narrator*. The limited third-person narrator speaks of the action from a point outside of the events— thus gaining distance and objectivity—but is limited to the perspective of one of the characters and tells the story through what that character experiences and thinks. Thus, we could write yet a fifth version of the bus incident:

> The young man was pleased with his attire as he stood in the crowded Paris bus that day. "What a nice hat I have on," he thought, "I like this cord instead of the usual hatband." Gradually he realized that the man next to him was poking him in the ribs whenever he had the opportunity. The young man began to argue with his fellow passenger, but then a seat became vacant. He hurried to sit down. "Such vulgar people ride the bus these days," the young man said to himself as he admired the cut of his coat.

Notice the advantages of this sort of narrative. We see the scene as though we were a participant, but we can step back and evaluate the principal character more objectively: though the young man is certainly vain, he isn't a troublemaker.

 Tips for Writers

Although the author's, the narrator's, and the main character's points-of-view often coincide, it is important to distinguish between them. Just because the authorial point-of-view and a character's point-of-view agree on many points, you should not assume that they agree on *all* points. In fact, good papers are often generated by carefully pointing out where an author's attitudes part company from his characters' attitudes and how the author indicates that parting of the ways.

Stories without Narrators

In the stories we have been discussing, the narrator is fully aware that he or she is telling a story. But some stories do not have such self-conscious narrators. Some stories are made up of documents which when pieced together give an attentive reader enough narrative information to construct a story. For example, some stories—including some novels—are collections of letters. By reading the exchange of letters, the reader can reconstruct the action. The *epistolary narrative*, one that consists of letters, is demanding both of the author and the reader. Samual Richardson's *Pamela* and *Clarissa* are well known examples of epistolary novels.

Narratives can also be constructed from pages of a fictional diary. Nicolai Gogol's "Diary of a Madman" is one of the more famous stories constructed in this manner. V. S. Naipaul's "The Nightwatchman's Occurrence Book" is another story without a single, self-conscious narrator. The story is a sequence of notes between the nightwatchman and two hotel managers. As you read it, pay close attention to the shifting narrative points-of-view, which result in a wonderfully comic conclusion.

Suggestions for Essayists

1. Discuss how point-of-view affects political debate. For example, discuss how coming from the Middle East might affect one's attitude toward oil prices.
2. Discuss whether men and women can share the same point-of-view or whether biology alters one's perspective.

Suggestions for Fiction Writers

1. Narrate the same event from at least three different first-person perspectives.
2. Narrate the same event from both omniscient and limited third-person perspectives.
3. Pretend you are a character in a story talking to a third-person narrator. What do you want the narrator to know? What arguments of interpretation would you have with the narrator? Why won't the narrator tell the story your way? Write the dialogue between the narrator and the character.

TONI CADE BAMBARA (1939–)

My Man Bovanne

Blind people got a hummin jones if you notice. Which is understandable completely once you been around one and notice what no eyes will force you into to see people, and you get past the first time, which seems to come out of nowhere, and it's like you in church again with fat-chest ladies and old gents gruntin a hum low in the throat to whatever the preacher be saying. Shakey Bee bottom lip all swole up with Sweet Peach and me explainin how come the sweet-potato bread was a dollar-quarter this time stead of dollar regular and he say uh hunh he understand, then he break into this *thizzin* kind of hum which is quiet, but fiercesome just the same, if you ain't ready for it. Which I wasn't. But I got used to it and the onliest time I had to say somethin bout it was when he was playin checkers on the stoop one time and he commenst to hummin quite churchy seem to me. So I says, "Look here Shakey Bee, I can't beat you and Jesus too." He stop.

So that's how come I asked My Man Bovanne to dance. He ain't my man mind you, just a nice ole gent from the block that we all know cause he fixes things and the kids like him. Or used to fore Black Power[1] got hold their minds and mess em around till they can't be civil to ole folks. So we at this benefit for my niece's cousin who's runnin for somethin with this Black party somethin or other behind her. And I press up close to dance with Bovanne who blind and I'm hummin and he hummin, chest to chest like talkin. Not jammin my breasts into the man. Wasn't bout tits. Was bout vibrations. And he dug it and asked me what color dress I had on and how my hair was fixed and how I was doin without a man, not nosy but nice-like, and who was at this affair and was the canapés dainty-stingy or healthy enough to get hold of proper. Comfy and cheery is what I'm tryin to get across. Touch talkin like the heel of the hand on the tambourine or on a drum.

But right away Joe Lee come up on us and frown for dancin so close to the man. My own son who knows what kind of warm I am about; and don't grown men call me long distance and in the middle of the night for a little Mama comfort? But he frown. Which ain't right since Bovanne can't see and defend himself. Just a nice old man who fixes toasters and busted irons and bicycles and things and changes the lock on my door when my men friends get messy. Nice man. Which is not why they invited him. Grass roots you see. Me and Sister Taylor and the woman who does heads[2] at Mamies and the man from the barber shop, we all there on account of we grass roots.[3] And I ain't never been souther than Brooklyn Battery[4] and no more country than the window box on my fire escape. And just yesterday my kids tellin me to take them countrified rags off my head and be cool. And now can't get Black enough to suit em. So everybody passin sayin My Man Bovanne. Big deal, keep steppin and don't even stop a minute to get the man a drink or one of them cute sandwiches or tell him what's goin on. And him standin there with a smile ready case someone do speak he want to be ready. So that's how come I pull him on the dance floor and we dance squeezin past the tables and chairs and all them coats and people

---

[1] Black Power was a slogan of certain Civil Rights groups during the 1960s and 70s.
[2] Hairdresser.
[3] "Grass roots" refers to the common people.
[4] Brooklyn Battery is a section of Brooklyn, New York.

standin round up in each other face talkin bout this and that but got no use for this blind man who mostly fixed skates and skooters for all these folks when they was just kids. So I'm pressed up close and we touch talkin with the hum. And here come my daughter cuttin her eye at me like she do when she tell me about my "apolitical" self like I got hoof and mouf disease and there ain't no hope at all. And I don't pay her no mind and just look up in Bovanne shadow face and tell him his stomach like a drum and he laugh. Laugh real loud. And here come my youngest, Task, with a tap on my elbow like he the third grade monitor and I'm cuttin up on the line to assembly.

"I was just talkin on the drums," I explained when they hauled me into the kitchen. I figured drums was my best defense. They can get ready for drums what with all this heritage business. And Bovanne stomach just like that drum Task give me when he come back from Africa. You just touch it and it hum thizzm, thizzm. So I stuck to the drum story. "Just drummin that's all."

"Mama, what are you talkin about?"

"She had too much to drink," say Elo to Task cause she don't hardly say nuthin to me direct no more since that ugly argument about my wigs.

"Look here Mama," say Task, the gentle one. "We just tryin to pull your coat. You were makin a spectacle of yourself out there dancing like that."

"Dancin like what?"

Task run a hand over his left ear like his father for the world and his father before that.

"Like a bitch in heat," say Elo.

"Well uhh, I was goin to say like one of them sex-starved ladies gettin on in years and not too discriminating. Know what I mean?"

I don't answer cause I'll cry. Terrible thing when your own children talk to you like that. Pullin me out the party and hustlin me into some stranger's kitchen in the back of a bar just like the damn police. And ain't like I'm old old. I can still wear me some sleeveless dresses without the meat hangin off my arm. And I keep up with some thangs through my kids. Who ain't kids no more. To hear them tell it. So I don't say nuthin.

"Dancin with that tom,"[5] say Elo to Joe Lee, who leanin on the folks' freezer. "His feet can smell a cracker a mile away and go into their shuffle number post haste. And them eyes. He could be a little considerate and put on some shades. Who wants to look into them blown-out fuses that—"

"Is this what they call the generation gap?" I say.

"Generation gap," spits Elo, like I suggested castor oil and fricassee possum in the milk-shakes or somethin. "That's a white concept for a white phenomenon. There's no generation gap among Black people We are a col—"

"Yeh, well never mind," says Joe Lee. "The point is Mama . . . well, it's pride. You embarrass yourself and us too dancin like that."

---

[5] "Tom" is short for "Uncle Tom," the central character in Harriet Beecher Stowe's novel *Uncle Tom's Cabin.* Uncle Tom is a term of derision used against blacks who act in a subservient manner to whites.

"I wasn't shame." Then nobody say nuthin. Them standin there in they pretty clothes with drinks in they hands and gangin up on me, and me in the third-degree chair and nary a olive to my name. Felt just like the police got hold to me.

"First of all," Task say, holdin up his hand and tickin off the offenses, "the dress. Now that dress is too short, Mama, and too low-cut for a woman your age. And Tamu's going to make a speech tonight to kick off the campaign and will be introducin you and expecting you to organize the council of elders—"

"Me? Didn nobody ask me nuthin. You mean Nisi? She change her name?"

"Well, Norton was supposed to tell you about it. Nisi wants to introduce you and then encourage the older folks to form a Council of the Elders to act as an advisory—"

"And you going to be standing there with your boobs out and that wig on your head and that hem up to your ass. And people'll say, 'Ain't that the horny bitch that was grindin with the blind dude?' "

"Elo, be cool a minute," say Task, gettin to the next finger. "And then there's the drinkin. Mama, you know you can't drink cause next thing you know you be laughin loud and carryin on," and he grab another finger for the loudness. "And then there's the dancin. You been tattooed on the man for four records straight and slow draggin even on the fast numbers. How you think that look for a woman your age?"

"What's my age?"

"What?"

"I'm axin you all a simple question. You keep talkin bout what's proper for a woman my age. How old am I anyhow?" And Joe Lee slams his eyes shut and squinches up his face to figure. And Task run a hand over his ear and stare into his glass like the ice cubes goin calculate for him. And Elo just starin at the top of my head like she goin rip the wig off any minute now.

"Is your hair braided up under that thing? If so, why don't you take it off? You always did do a neat cornroll."

"Uh huh," cause I'm thinkin how she couldn't undo her hair fast enough talking bout cornroll so countrified. None of which was the subject. "How old, I say?"

"Sixtee-one or—"

"You a damn lie Joe Lee Peoples."

"And that's another thing," say Task on the fingers.

"You know what you all can kiss," I say, gettin up and brushin the wrinkles out my lap.

"Oh, Mama," Elo say, puttin a hand on my shoulder like she hasn't done since she left home and the hand landin light and not sure it supposed to be there. Which hurt me to my heart. Cause this was the child in our happiness fore Mr. Peoples die. And I carried that child strapped to my chest till she was nearly two. We was close is what I'm trying to tell you. Cause it was more me in the child than the others. And even after Task it was the girlchild I covered in the night and wept over for no reason at all less it was she was a chub-chub like me and not very pretty, but a warm child. And how did things get to this, that she can't put a sure hand on me and say Mama we love you and care about you and you entitled to enjoy yourself cause you a good woman?

"And then there's Reverend Trent," say Task, glancin from left to right like they hatchin a plot and just now lettin me in on it. "You were suppose to be talkin with him tonight, Mama, about giving us his basement for campaign headquarters and—"

"Didn nobody tell me nuthin. If grass roots mean you kept in the dark I can't use it. I really can't. And Reven Trent a fool anyway the way he tore into the widow man up there on Edgecomb cause he wouldn't take in three of them foster children and the woman not even comfy in the ground yet and the man's mind messed up and—"

"Look here," say Task. "What we need is a family conference so we can get all this stuff cleared up and laid out on the table. In the meantime I think we better get back into the other room and tend to business. And in the meantime, Mama, see if you can't get to Reverend Trent and—"

"You want me to belly rub with the Reven, that it?"

"Oh damn," Elo say and go through the swingin door.

"We'll talk about all this at dinner. How's tomorrow night, Joe Lee?" While Joe Lee being self-important I'm wonderin who's doin the cookin and how come no body ax me if I'm free and do I get a corsage and things like that. Then Joe nod that it's O.K. and he go through the swingin door and just a little hubbub come through from the other room. Then Task smile his smile, lookin just like his daddy and he leave. And it just me in this stranger's kitchen, which was a mess I wouldn't never let my kitchen look like. Poison you just to look at the pots. Then the door swing the other way and it's My Man Bovanne standin there sayin Miss Hazel but lookin at the deep fry and then at the steam table, and most surprised when I come up on him from the other direction and take him on out of there. Pass the folks pushin up towards the stage where Nisi and some other people settin and ready to talk, and folks gettin to the last of the sandwiches and the booze fore they settle down in one spot and listen serious. And I'm thinkin bout tellin Bovanne what a lovely long dress Nisi got on and the earrings and her hair piled up in a cone and the people bout to hear how we all gettin screwed and gotta form our own party[6] and everybody there listenin and lookin. But instead I just haul the man on out of there, and Joe Lee and his wife look at me like I'm terrible, but they ain't said boo to the man yet. Cause he blind and old and don't nobody there need him since they grown up and don't need they skates fixed no more.

"Where we goin, Miss Hazel?" Him knowin all the time.

"First we gonna buy you some dark sunglasses. Then you comin with me to the supermarket so I can pick up tomorrow's dinner, which is goin to be a grand thing proper and you invited. Then we goin to my house."

"That be fine. I surely would like to rest my feet." Bein cute, but you got to

---

[6] Political party.

let men play out they little show, blind or not. So he chat on bout how tired he is and how he appreciate me takin him in hand this way. And I'm thinkin I'll have him change the lock on my door first thing. Then I'll give the man a nice warm bath with jasmine leaves in the water and a little Epsom salt on the sponge to do his back. And then a good rubdown with rose water and olive oil. Then a cup of lemon tea with a taste in it. And a little talcum, some of that fancy stuff Nisi mother sent over last Christmas. And then a massage, a good face massage round the forehead which is the worryin part. Cause you gots to take care of the older folks. And let them know they still needed to run the mimeo machine and keep the spark plugs clean and fix the mailboxes for folks who might help us get the breakfast program goin, and the school for the little kids and the campaign and all. Cause old folks is the nation. That what Nisi was sayin and I mean to do my part.

"I imagine you are a very pretty woman, Miss Hazel."

"I surely am," I say just like the hussy my daughter always say I was.

Questions

1. Is this a first- or third-person narrative?
2. Why do you suppose Bambara chose this sort of narration? Could an omniscient narrator have told the story as vividly or more vividly?
3. Why do the narrator's children object to her dancing with Bovanne?
4. Do the children think of themselves as being open-minded? Are they?
5. Nisi says, "old folks is the nation." What does she mean? Do you agree?
6. What sort of preconception do you have about the way older people should act?

❧ Writers on Writing   Toni Cade Bambara

All writers, musicians, artists, choreographers/dancers, etc., work with the stuff of their experiences. It's the translation of it, the conversion of it, the shaping of it that makes drama. I've never been convinced that experience is linear, circular, or even random. It just is. I try to put it in some kind of order to extract meaning from it, to bring meaning to it. . . . Ordering is the craft, the work, the wonder. It's the lifting up, the shaping, the pin-point presentation that matters.

MARGARET ATWOOD (1939–)

Giving Birth

But who gives it? And to whom is it given? Certainly it doesn't feel like giving, which implies a flow, a gentle handing over, no coercion. But there is scant gentleness here; it's too strenuous, the belly like a knotted fist, squeezing, the heavy trudge of the heart, every muscle in the body tight and moving, as in a slow-motion shot of a high-jump, the faceless body sailing up, turning, hanging for a moment in the air, and then—back to real time again—the plunge, the rush down, the result. Maybe the phrase was made by someone viewing the result only: in this case, the rows of babies to whom birth has occurred, lying like neat packages in their expertly wrapped blankets, pink or blue, with their labels Scotch Taped to their clear plastic cots, behind the plate-glass window.

No one ever says *giving death*, although they are in some ways the same, events, not things. And *delivering*, that act the doctor is generally believed to perform: who delivers what? Is it the mother who is delivered, like a prisoner being released? Surely not; nor is the child delivered to the mother like a letter through a slot. How can you be both the sender and the receiver at once? Was someone in bondage, is someone made free? Thus language, muttering in its archaic tongues of something, yet one more thing, that needs to be re-named.

It won't be by me, though. These are the only words I have, I'm stuck with them, stuck in them. (That image of the tar sands, old tableau in the Royal Ontario Museum, second floor north, how persistent it is. Will I break free, or will I be sucked down, fossilized, a sabre-toothed tiger or lumbering brontosaurus who ventured out too far? Words ripple at my feet, black, sluggish, lethal. Let me try once more, before the sun gets me, before I starve or drown, while I can. It's only a tableau after all, it's only a metaphor. See, I can speak, I am not trapped, and you on your part can understand. So we will go ahead as if there were no problem about language.)

This story about giving birth is not about me. In order to convince you of that I should tell you what I did this morning, before I sat down at this desk—a door on top of two filing cabinets, radio to the left, calendar to the right, these devices by which I place myself in time. I got up at twenty-to-seven, and, halfway down the stairs, met my daughter, who was ascending, autonomously she thought, actually in the arms of her father. We greeted each other with hugs and smiles; we then played with the alarm clock and the hot water bottle, a ritual we go through only on the days her father has to leave the house early to drive into the city. This ritual exists to give me the illusion that I am sleeping in. When she finally decided it was time for me to get up, she began pulling my hair. I got dressed while she explored the bathroom scales and the mysterious white altar of the toilet. I took her downstairs and we had the usual struggle over her clothes. Already she is wearing miniature jeans, miniature T-shirts. After this she fed herself: orange, banana, muffin, porridge.

We then went out to the sun porch, where we recognized anew, and by their names, the dog, the cats and the birds, blue jays and goldfinches at this time of year, which is winter. She puts her fingers on my lips as I pronounce these words; she hasn't yet learned the secret of making them. I am waiting for her first word: surely it will be miraculous, something that has never yet been said. But if so, perhaps she's already said it and I, in my entrapment, my addiction to the usual, have not heard it.

In her playpen I discovered the first alarming thing of the day. It was a small naked woman, made of that soft plastic from which jiggly spiders and lizards and the other things people hang in their car windows are also made. She was given to my daughter by a friend, a woman who does props for movies, she was supposed to have been a prop but she wasn't used. The baby loved her and would crawl around the floor holding her in her mouth like a dog carrying a bone, with the head sticking out one side and the feet out the other. She seemed chewy and harmless, but the other day I noticed that the baby had managed to make a tear in the body with her new teeth. I put the woman into the cardboard box I use for toy storage.

But this morning she was back in the playpen and the feet were gone. The baby must have eaten them, and I worried about whether or not the plastic would dissolve in her stomach, whether it was toxic. Sooner or later, in the contents of her diaper, which I examine with the usual amount of maternal brooding, I knew I would find two small pink plastic feet. I removed the doll and later, while she was still singing to the dog outside the window, dropped it into the garbage. I am not up to finding tiny female arms, breasts, a head, in my daughter's disposable diapers, partially covered by undigested carrots and the husks of raisins, like the relics of some gruesome and demented murder.

Now she's having her nap and I am writing this story. From what I have said, you can see that my life (despite these occasional surprises, reminders of another world) is calm and orderly, suffused with that warm, reddish light, those well-placed blue highlights and reflecting surfaces (mirrors, plates, oblong window-panes) you think of as belonging to Dutch genre[1] paintings; and like them it is realistic in detail and slightly sentimental. Or at least it has an aura of sentiment. (Already I'm having moments of muted grief over those of my daughter's baby clothes which are too small for her to wear any more. I will be a keeper of hair, I will store things in trunks, I will weep over photos.) But above all it's solid, everything here has solidity. No more of those washes of light, those shifts, nebulous effects of cloud, Turner sunsets,[2] vague fears, the impalpables Jeanie used to concern herself with.

I call this woman Jeanie after the song.[3] I can't remember any more of the song, only the title. The point (for in language there are always these "points," these reflections; this is what makes it so rich and sticky, this is why so many have disappeared beneath its dark and shining surface, why you should never try to see your own reflection in it; you will lean over too far, a strand of your hair will fall in and come out gold, and, thinking it is gold all the way down, you yourself will follow, sliding into those outstretched arms, towards the mouth

---

[1] Dutch genre paintings are extremely precise depictions of domestic life of nearly photographic exactness.

[2] J. M. W. Turner (1775–1851) was a British painter known for his enormous landscapes filled with light.

[3] "I Dream of Jeanie (with the Light Brown Hair)" is a song composed by the American songwriter Stephen Foster (1826–1864).

you think is opening to pronounce your name but instead, just before your ears fill with pure sound, will form a word you have never heard before. . . .)

The point, for me, is in the hair. My own hair is not light brown, but Jeanie's was. This is one difference between us. The other point is the dreaming; for Jeanie isn't real in the same way that I am real. But by now, and I mean your time, both of us will have the same degree of reality, we will be equal: wraiths, echoes, reverberations in your own brain. At the moment though Jeanie is to me as I will someday be to you. So she is real enough.

Jeanie is on her way to the hospital, to give birth, to be delivered. She is not quibbling over these terms. She's sitting in the back seat of the car, with her eyes closed and her coat spread over her like a blanket. She is doing her breathing exercises and timing her contractions with a stopwatch. She has been up since two-thirty in the morning, when she took a bath and ate some lime Jell-O, and it's now almost ten. She has learned to count, during the slow breathing, in numbers (from one to ten while breathing in, from ten to one while breathing out) which she can actually see while she is silently pronouncing them. Each number is a different colour and, if she's concentrating very hard, a different typeface. They range from plain roman to ornamented circus numbers, red with gold filigree and dots. This is a refinement not mentioned in any of the numerous books she's read on the subject. Jeanie is a devotee of handbooks. She has at least two shelves of books that cover everything from building kitchen cabinets to auto repairs to smoking your own hams. She doesn't do many of these things, but she does some of them, and in her suitcase, along with a washcloth, a package of lemon Life Savers, a pair of glasses, a hot water bottle, some talcum powder and a paper bag, is the book that suggested she take along all of these things.

(By this time you may be thinking that I've invented Jeanie in order to distance myself from these experiences. Nothing could be further from the truth. I am, in fact, trying to bring myself closer to something that time has already made distant. As for Jeanie, my intention is simple: I am bringing her back to life.)

There are two other people in the car with Jeanie. One is a man, whom I will call A., for convenience. A. is driving. When Jeanie opens her eyes, at the end of every contraction, she can see the back of his slightly balding head and his reassuring shoulders. A. drives well and not too quickly. From time to time he asks her how she is, and she tells him how long the contractions are lasting and how long there is between them. When they stop for gas he buys them each a Styrofoam container of coffee. For months he has helped her with the breathing exercises, pressing on her knee as recommended by the book, and he will be present at the delivery. (Perhaps it's to him that the birth will be given, in the same sense that one gives a performance.) Together they have toured the hospital maternity ward, in company with a small group of other pairs like them: one thin solicitous person, one slow bulbous person. They have been shown the rooms, shared and private, the sitz-baths, the delivery room itself, which gave the impression of being white. The nurse was light-brown, with limber hips and elbows; she laughed a lot as she answered questions.

"First they'll give you an enema. You know what it is? They take a tube of water and put it up your behind. Now, the gentlemen must put on this—and these, over your shoes. And these hats, this one for those with long hair, this for those with short hair."

"What about those with no hair?" says A.

The nurse looks up at his head and laughs. "Oh, you still have some," she says. "If you have a question, do not be afraid to ask."

They have also seen the film made by the hospital, a full-colour film of a woman giving birth to, can it be a baby? "Not all babies will be this large at birth," the Australian nurse who introduces the movie says. Still, the audience, half of which is pregnant, doesn't look very relaxed when the lights go on. ("If you don't like the visuals," a friend of Jeanie's has told her, "you can always close your eyes.") It isn't the blood so much as the brownish-red disinfectant that bothers her. "I've decided to call this whole thing off," she says to A., smiling to show it's a joke. He gives her a hug and says, "Everything's going to be fine."

And she knows it is. Everything will be fine. But there is another woman in the car. She's sitting in the front seat, and she hasn't turned or acknowledged Jeanie in any way. She, like Jeanie, is going to the hospital. She too is pregnant. She is not going to the hospital to give birth, however, because the words, the words, are too alien to her experience, the experience she is about to have, to be used about it at all. She's wearing a cloth coat with checks in maroon and brown, and she has a kerchief tied over her hair. Jeanie has seen her before, but she knows little about her except that she is a woman who did not wish to become pregnant, who did not choose to divide herself like this, who did not choose any of these ordeals, these initiations. It would be no use telling her that everything is going to be fine. The word in English for unwanted intercourse is rape. But there is no word in the language for what is about to happen to this woman.

Jeanie has seen this woman from time to time throughout her pregnancy, always in the same coat, always with the same kerchief. Naturally, being pregnant herself has made her more aware of other pregnant women, and she has watched them, examined them covertly, every time she has seen one. But not every other pregnant woman is this woman. She did not, for instance, attend Jeanie's pre-natal classes at the hospital, where the women were all young, younger than Jeanie.

"How many will be breast-feeding?" asks the Australian nurse with the hefty shoulders.

All hands but one shoot up. A modern group, the new generation, and the one lone bottle-feeder, who might have (who knows?) something wrong with her breasts, is ashamed of herself. The others look politely away from her. What they want most to discuss, it seems, are the differences between one kind of disposable diaper and another. Sometimes they lie on mats and squeeze each other's hands, simulating contractions and counting breaths. It's all very hopeful. The Australian nurse tells them not to get in and out of the bathtub by themselves. At the end of an hour they are each given a glass of apple juice.

There is only one woman in the class who has already given birth. She's there, she says, to make sure they give her a shot this time. They delayed it last time and she went through hell. The others look at her with mild disapproval. *They* are not clamouring for shots, they do not intend to go through hell. Hell comes from the wrong attitude, they feel. The books talk about *discomfort*.

"It's not discomfort, it's pain, baby," the woman says.

The others smile uneasily and the conversation slides back to disposable diapers.

Vitaminized, conscientious, well-read Jeanie, who has managed to avoid morning sickness, varicose veins, stretch marks, toxemia and depression, who has had no aberrations of appetite, no blurrings of vision—why is she followed, then, by this other? At first it was only a glimpse now and then, at the infants' clothing section in Simpson's Basement, in the supermarket lineup, on street corners as she herself slid by in A.'s car: the haggard face, the bloated torso, the kerchief holding back the too-sparse hair. In any case, it was Jeanie who saw her, not the other way around. If she knew she was following Jeanie she gave no sign.

As Jeanie has come closer and closer to this day, the unknown day on which she will give birth, as time has thickened around her so that it has become something she must propel herself through, a kind of slush, wet earth underfoot, she has seen this woman more and more often, though always from a distance. Depending on the light, she has appeared by turns as a young girl of perhaps twenty to an older woman of forty or forty-five, but there was never any doubt in Jeanie's mind that it was the same woman. In fact it did not occur to her that the woman was not real in the usual sense (and perhaps she was, originally, on the first or second sighting, as the voice that causes an echo is real), until A. stopped for a red light during this drive to the hospital and the woman, who had been standing on the corner with a brown paper bag in her arms, simply opened the front door of the car and got in. A. didn't react, and Jeanie knows better than to say anything to him. She is aware that the woman is not really there: Jeanie is not crazy. She could even make the woman disappear by opening her eyes wider, by staring, but it is only the shape that would go away, not the feeling. Jeanie isn't exactly afraid of this woman. She is afraid for her.

When they reach the hospital, the woman gets out of the car and is through the door by the time A. has come around to help Jeanie out of the back seat. In the lobby she is nowhere to be seen. Jeanie goes through Admission in the usual way, unshadowed.

There has been an epidemic of babies during the night and the maternity ward is overcrowded. Jeanie waits for her room behind a dividing screen. Nearby someone is screaming, screaming and mumbling between screams in what sounds like a foreign language. Portuguese, Jeanie thinks. She tells herself that for them it is different, you're supposed to scream, you're regarded as queer if you don't scream, it's a required part of giving birth. Nevertheless she knows that the woman screaming is the other woman and she is screaming from pain. Jeanie listens to the other voice, also a woman's, comforting, reassuring: her mother? A nurse?

A. arrives and they sit uneasily, listening to the screams. Finally Jeanie is sent for and she goes for her prep. Prep school, she thinks. She takes off her clothes—when will she see them again?—and puts on the hospital gown. She is examined, labelled around the wrist and given an enema. She tells the nurse she can't take Demerol[4] because she's allergic to it, and the nurse writes this down. Jeanie doesn't know whether this is true or not but she doesn't want Demerol, she has read the books. She intends to put up a struggle over her pubic hair—surely she will lose her strength if it is all shaved off—but it turns out the nurse doesn't have very strong feelings about it. She is told her contractions are not far enough along to be taken seriously, she can even have lunch. She puts on her dressing gown and rejoins A., in the freshly vacated room, eats some tomato soup and a veal cutlet, and decides to take a nap while A. goes out for supplies.

Jeanie wakes up when A. comes back. He has brought a paper, some detective novels for Jeanie and a bottle of Scotch for himself. A. reads the paper and drinks Scotch, and Jeanie reads *Poirot's Early Cases*.[5] There is no connection between Poirot and her labour, which is now intensifying, unless it is the egg-shape of Poirot's head and the vegetable marrows he is known to cultivate with strands of wet wool (placentae? umbilical cords?). She is glad the stories are short; she is walking around the room now, between contractions. Lunch was definitely a mistake.

"I think I have back labour," she says to A. They get out the handbook and look up the instructions for this. It's useful that everything has a name. Jeanie kneels on the bed and rests her forehead on her arms while A. rubs her back. A. pours himself another Scotch, in the hospital glass. The nurse, in pink, comes, looks, asks about the timing, and goes away again. Jeanie is beginning to sweat. She can only manage half a page or so of Poirot before she has to clamber back up on the bed again and begin breathing and running through the coloured numbers.

When the nurse comes back, she has a wheelchair. It's time to go down to the labour room, she says. Jeanie feels stupid sitting in the wheelchair. She tells herself about peasant women having babies in the fields, Indian women having them on portages with hardly a second thought. She feels effete.[6] But the hospital wants her to ride, and considering the fact that the nurse is tiny, perhaps it's just as well. What if Jeanie were to collapse, after all? After all her courageous talk. An image of the tiny pink nurse, antlike, trundling large Jeanie through the corridors, rolling her along like a heavy beach ball.

As they go by the check-in desk a woman is wheeled past on a table, covered by a sheet. Her eyes are closed and there's a bottle feeding into her arm through a tube. Something is wrong. Jeanie looks back—she thinks it was the other woman—but the sheeted table is hidden now behind the counter.

---

[4] Demerol is a potent painkiller.
[5] *Poirot's Early Cases* is a collection of stories about the fictional detective Hercule Poirot written by Agatha Christie (1891–1976).
[6] *Effete* is an adjective that means exhausted, incapable of efficient action.

In the dim labour room Jeanie takes off her dressing gown and is helped up onto the bed by the nurse. A. brings her suitcase, which is not a suitcase actually but a small flight bag, the significance of this has not been lost on Jeanie, and in fact she now has some of the apprehensive feelings she associates with planes, including the fear of a crash. She takes out her Life Savers, her glasses, her washcloth and the other things she thinks she will need. She removes her contact lenses and places them in their case, reminding A. that they must not be lost. Now she is purblind.

There is something else in her bag that she doesn't remove. It's a talisman, given to her several years ago as a souvenir by a travelling friend of hers. It's a rounded oblong of opaque blue glass, with four yellow-and-white eye shapes on it. In Turkey, her friend has told her, they hang them on mules to protect against the Evil Eye. Jeanie knows this talisman probably won't work for her, she is not Turkish and she isn't a mule, but it makes her feel safer to have it in the room with her. She had planned to hold it in her hand during the most difficult part of labour but somehow there is no longer any time for carrying out plans like this.

An old woman, a fat old woman dressed all in green, comes into the room and sits beside Jeanie. She says to A., who is sitting on the other side of Jeanie, "That is a good watch. They don't make watches like that any more." She is referring to his gold pocket watch, one of his few extravagances, which is on the night table. Then she places her hand on Jeanie's belly to feel the contraction. "This is good," she says, her accent is Swedish or German. "This, I call a contraction. Before, it was nothing." Jeanie can no longer remember having seen her before. "Good. Good."

"When will I have it?" Jeanie asks, when she can talk, when she is no longer counting.

The old woman laughs. Surely that laugh, those tribal hands, have presided over a thousand beds, a thousand kitchen tables . . . "A long time yet," she says. "Eight, ten hours."

"But I've been *doing* this for twelve hours already," Jeanie says.

"Not hard labour," the woman says. "Not good, like this."

Jeanie settles into herself for the long wait. At the moment she can't remember why she wanted to have a baby in the first place. That decision was made by someone else, whose motives are now unclear. She remembers the way women who had babies used to smile at one another, mysteriously, as if there was something they knew that she didn't, the way they would casually exclude her from their frame of reference. What was the knowledge, the mystery, or was having a baby really no more inexplicable than having a car accident or an orgasm? (But these too were indescribable, events of the body, all of them; why should the mind distress itself trying to find a language for them?) She has sworn she will never do that to any woman without children, engage in those passwords and exclusions. She's old enough, she's been put through enough years of it to find it tiresome and cruel.

But—and this is the part of Jeanie that goes with the talisman hidden in her

bag, not with the part that longs to build kitchen cabinets and smoke hams—
she is, secretly, hoping for a mystery. Something more than this, something
else, a vision. After all she is risking her life, though it's not too likely she will
die. Still, some women do. Internal bleeding, shock, heart failure, a mistake
on the part of someone, a nurse, a doctor. She deserves a vision, she deserves
to be allowed to bring something back with her from this dark place into which
she is now rapidly descending.

She thinks momentarily about the other woman. Her motives, too, are unclear. Why doesn't she want to have a baby? Has she been raped, does she have
ten other children, is she starving? Why hasn't she had an abortion? Jeanie
doesn't know, and in fact it no longer matters why. *Uncross your fingers*, Jeanie
thinks to her. Her face, distorted with pain and terror, floats briefly behind
Jeanie's eyes before it too drifts away.

Jeanie tries to reach down to the baby, as she has many times before, sending
waves of love, colour, music, down through her arteries to it, but she finds she
can no longer do this. She can no longer feel the baby as a baby, its arms and
legs poking, kicking, turning. It has collected itself together, it's a hard sphere,
it does not have time right now to listen to her. She's grateful for this because
she isn't sure anyway how good the message would be. She no longer has control
of the numbers either, she can no longer see them, although she continues
mechanically to count. She realizes she has practised for the wrong thing, A.
squeezing her knee was nothing, she should have practised for this, whatever it
is.

"Slow down," A. says. She's on her side now, he's holding her hand. "Slow
it right down."

"I can't, I can't do it, I can't do this."

"Yes, you can."

"Will I sound like that?"

"Like what?" A. says. Perhaps he can't hear it: it's the other woman, in the
room next door or the room next door to that. She's screaming and crying,
screaming and crying. While she cries she is saying, over and over, "It hurts.
It hurts."

"No, you won't," he says. So there is someone, after all.

A doctor comes in, not her own doctor. They want her to turn over on her
back.

"I can't," she says. "I don't like it that way." Sounds have receded, she has
trouble hearing them. She turns over and the doctor gropes with her rubber-
gloved hand. Something wet and hot flows over her thighs.

"It was just ready to break," the doctor says. "All I had to do was touch it.
Four centimetres," she says to A.

"Only *four*?" Jeanie says. She feels cheated; they must be wrong. The doctor
says her own doctor will be called in time. Jeanie is outraged at them. They
have not understood, but it's too late to say this and she slips back into the dark
place, which is not hell, which is more like being inside, trying to get out. *Out*,
she says or thinks. Then she is floating, the numbers are gone, if anyone told

her to get up, go out of the room, stand on her head, she would do it. From minute to minute she comes up again, grabs for air.

"You're hyperventilating,"[7] A. says. "Slow it down." He is rubbing her back now, hard, and she takes his hand and shoves it viciously further down, to the right place, which is not the right place as soon as his hand is there. She remembers a story she read once, about the Nazis tying the legs of Jewish women together during labor. She never really understood before how that could kill you.

A nurse appears with a needle. "I don't want it," Jeanie says.

"Don't be hard on yourself," the nurse says. "You don't have to go through pain like that." What pain? Jeanie thinks. When there is no pain she feels nothing, when there is pain, she feels nothing because there is no *she*. This, finally, is the disappearance of language. *You don't remember afterwards*, she has been told by almost everyone.

Jeanie comes out of a contraction, gropes for control. "Will it hurt the baby?" she says.

"It's a mild analgesic,"[8] the doctor says. "We wouldn't allow anything that would hurt the baby." Jeanie doesn't believe this. Nevertheless she is jabbed, and the doctor is right, it is very mild, because it doesn't seem to do a thing for Jeanie, though A. later tells her she has slept briefly between contractions.

Suddenly she sits bolt upright. She is wide awake and lucid. "You have to ring that bell right now," she says. "This baby is being born."

A. clearly doesn't believe her. "I can feel it, I can feel the head," she says. A. pushes the button for the call bell. A nurse appears and checks, and now everything is happening too soon, nobody is ready. They set off down the hall, the nurse wheeling. Jeanie feels fine. She watches the corridors, the edges of everything shadowy because she doesn't have her glasses on. She hopes A. will remember to bring them. They pass another doctor.

"Need me?" she asks.

"Oh no," the nurse answers breezily. "Natural childbirth."

Jeanie realizes that this woman must have been the anaesthetist. "What?" she says, but it's too late now, they are in the room itself, all those glossy surfaces, tubular strange apparatus like a science-fiction movie, and the nurse is telling her to get onto the delivery table. No one else is in the room.

"You must be crazy," Jeanie says.

"Don't push," the nurse says.

"What do you mean?" Jeanie says. This is absurd. Why should she wait, why should the baby wait for them because they're late?

"Breathe through your mouth," the nurse says. "Pant," and Jeanie finally remembers how. When the contraction is over she uses the nurse's arm as a lever and hauls herself across onto the table.

---

[7] Hyperventilation is a medical condition in which patients cannot stop their excessively rapid breathing.

[8] An analgesic is a pain reliever.

From somewhere her own doctor materializes, in her doctor suit already, looking even more like Mary Poppins than usual, and Jeanie says, "Bet you weren't expecting to see me so soon!" The baby is being born when Jeanie said it would, though just three days ago the doctor said it would be at least another week, and this makes Jeanie feel jubilant and smug. Not that she knew, she'd believed the doctor.

She's being covered with a green tablecloth, they are taking far too long, she feels like pushing the baby out now, before they are ready. A. is there by her head, swathed in robes, hats, masks. He has forgotten her glasses. "Push now," the doctor says. Jeanie grips with her hands, grits her teeth, face, her whole body together, a snarl, a fierce smile, the baby is enormous, a stone, a boulder, her bones unlock, and, once, twice, the third time, she opens like a birdcage turning slowly inside out.

A pause; a wet kitten slithers between her legs. "Why don't you look?" says the doctor, but Jeanie still has her eyes closed. No glasses, she couldn't have seen a thing anyway. "Why don't you look?" the doctor says again.

Jeanie opens her eyes. She can see the baby, who has been wheeled up beside her and is fading already from the alarming birth purple. A good baby, she thinks, meaning it as the old woman did: *a good watch*, well-made, substantial. The baby isn't crying; she squints in the new light. Birth isn't something that has been given to her, nor has she taken it. It was just something that has happened so they could greet each other like this. The nurse is stringing beads for her name. When the baby is bundled and tucked beside Jeanie, she goes to sleep.

As for the vision, there wasn't one. Jeanie is conscious of no special knowledge; already she's forgetting what it was like. She's tired and very cold; she is shaking, and asks for another blanket. A. comes back to the room with her; her clothes are still there. Everything is quiet, the other woman is no longer screaming. Something has happened to her, Jeanie knows. Is she dead? Is the baby dead? Perhaps she is one of those casualties (and how can Jeanie herself be sure, yet, that she will not be among them) who will go into postpartum depression⁹ and never come out. "You see, there was nothing to be afraid of," A. says before he leaves, but he was wrong.

The next morning Jeanie wakes up when it's light. She's been warned about getting out of bed the first time without the help of a nurse, but she decides to do it anyway (peasant in the field! Indian on the portage!). She's still running adrenaline, she's also weaker than she thought, but she wants very much to look out the window. She feels she's been inside too long, she wants to see the sun come up. Being awake this early always makes her feel a little unreal, a little insubstantial, as if she's partly transparent, partly dead.

(It was to me, after all, that the birth was given, Jeanie gave it, I am the result. What would she make of me? Would she be pleased?)

---

⁹ Postpartum depression is a psychological condition in which a mother feels dispirited after the birth of her child.

The window is two panes with a venetian blind sandwiched between them; it turns by a knob at the side. Jeanie has never seen a window like this before. She closes and opens the blind several times. Then she leaves it open and looks out.

All she can see from the window is a building. It's an old stone building, heavy and Victorian, with a copper roof oxidized to green. It's solid, hard, darkened by soot, dour, leaden. But as she looks at this building, so old and seemingly immutable, she sees that it's made of water. Water, and some tenuous jelly-like substance. Light flows through it from behind (the sun is coming up), the building is so thin, so fragile, that it quivers in the slight dawn wind. Jeanie sees that if the building is this way (a touch could destroy it, a ripple of the earth, why has no one noticed, guarded it against accidents?) then the rest of the world must be like this too, the entire earth, the rocks, people, trees, everything needs to be protected, cared for, tended. The enormity of this task defeats her; she will never be up to it, and what will happen then?

Jeanie hears footsteps in the hall outside her door. She thinks it must be the other woman, in her brown-and-maroon-checked coat, carrying her paper bag, leaving the hospital now that her job is done. She has seen Jeanie safely through, she must go now to hunt through the streets of the city for her next case. But the door opens, it's a nurse, who is just in time to catch Jeanie as she sinks to the floor, holding on to the edge of the air-conditioning unit. The nurse scolds her for getting up too soon.

After that the baby is carried in, solid, substantial, packed together like an apple, Jeanie examines her, she is complete, and in the days that follow Jeanie herself becomes drifted over with new words, her hair slowly darkens, she ceases to be what she was and is replaced, gradually, by someone else.

Questions

1. What kind of narration is "Giving Birth"?
2. What is the narrator's relationship to Jeanie?
3. Why does the narrator feel the need to prove she is *not* Jeanie? Does the evidence prove her point?
4. What is the relationship between Jeanie and the other woman who "did not wish to become pregnant"? Is there a reason the other woman is not given a name?
5. Who is A.? Is there a reason for his having no name?
6. Why does Jeanie think she deserves a vision? Does she get a vision?
7. In what ways has the other woman "seen Jeanie safely through [her delivery]"?
8. The narrator states that "giving birth" and "giving death . . . are in some ways the same." In what ways are they the same?

V. S. NAIPAUL (1932–)

The Night Watchman's Occurrence Book

November 21. 10.30 p.m. C. A. Cavander take over duty at C——Hotel all corrected. *Cesar Alwyn Cavander*

V. S. Naipaul (© *Thomas Victor*)

7 a.m. C. A. Cavander hand over duty to Mr Vignales at C——Hotel no report. *Cesar Alwyn Cavander*

November 22. 10.30 p.m. C. A. Cavander take over duty at C——Hotel no report. *Cesar Alwyn Cavander*

7 a.m. C. A. Cavander hand over duty to Mr Vignales at C——Hotel all corrected. *Cesar Alwyn Cavander*

> This is the third occasion on which I have found C. A. Cavander, Night Watchman, asleep on duty. Last night, at 12.45 a.m., I found him sound asleep in a rocking chair in the hotel lounge. Night Watchman Cavander has therefore been dismissed.
> Night Watchman Hillyard: This book is to be known in future as "The Night Watchman's Occurrence Book." In it I shall expect to find a detailed account of everything that happens in the hotel tonight. Be warned by the example of ex-Night Watchman Cavander, W. A. G. *Inskip, Manager*

Mr Manager, remarks noted. You have no worry where I am concern sir. *Charles Ethelbert Hillyard, Night Watchman*

November 23. 11 p.m. Night Watchman Hillyard take over duty at C——Hotel with one torch light 2 fridge keys and room keys 1, 3, 6, 10 and 13. Also 25 cartoons Carib Beer and 7 cartoons Heineken[1] and 2 cartoons American cigarettes. Beer cartoons intact Bar intact all corrected no report. *Charles Ethelbert Hillyard*

7 a.m. Night Watchman Hillyard hand over duty to Mr Vignales at C——Hotel with one torch light 2 fridge keys and room keys, 1, 3, 6, 10 and 13. 32 cartoons beer. Bar intact all corrected no report. *Charles Ethelbert Hillyard*

> Night Watchman Hillyard: Mr Wills complained bitterly to me this morning that last night he was denied entry to the bar by you. I wonder if you know exactly what the purpose of this hotel is. In future all hotel guests are to be allowed entry to the bar at whatever time they choose. It is your duty simply to note what they take. This is one reason why the hotel provides a certain number of beer cartons (please note the spelling of this word). *W. A. G. Inskip*

Mr Manager, remarks noted. I sorry I didnt get the chance to take some education sir. *Chas. Ethelbert Hillyard*

November 24. 11 p.m. N. W. Hillyard take over duty with one Torch, 1 Bar Key, 2 Fridge Keys, 32 cartoons Beer, all intact. 12 Midnight Bar close and Barman left leaving Mr Wills and others in Bar, and they left at 1 a.m. Mr Wills took 16 Carib Beer, Mr Wilson 8, Mr Percy 8. At 2 a.m. Mr Wills come back in the bar and take 4 Carib and some bread, he cut his hand trying to cut the bread, so please dont worry about the stains on the carpet sir. At 6 a.m. Mr Wills come back for some soda water. It didn't have any so he take a ginger beer instead. Sir you see it is my intention to do this job good sir, I cant see how Night Watchman Cavander could fall asleep on this job sir. *Chas. Ethelbert Hillyard*

> You always seems sure of the time, and guests appear to be in the habit of entering the bar on the hour. You will kindly note the exact time. The clock from the kitchen is left on the window near the switches. You can use this clock but you MUST replace it every morning before you go off duty. *W. A. G. Inskip*

Noted. *Chas. Ethelbert Hillyard*

November 25. Midnight Bar close and 12.23 a.m. Barman left leaving Mr Wills and others in Bar. Mr Owen take 5 bottles Carib, Mr Wilson 6 bottles Heineken, Mr Wills 18 Carib and they left at 2.52 a.m. Nothing unusual. Mr. Wills was helpless, I don't see how anybody could drink so much, eighteen one man alone, this work enough to turn anybody Seventh Day Adventist, and another man come in the bar, I dont know his name, I hear they call him Paul, he assist me

---

[1] Heineken is a Dutch beer.

because the others couldn't do much, and we take Mr Wills up to his room and take off his boots and slack his other clothes and then we left. Don't know sir if they did take more while I was away, nothing was mark on the Pepsi Cola board, but they was drinking still, it looks as if they come back and take some more, but with Mr Wills I want some extra assistance sir.

Mr Manager, the clock break I find it break when I come back from Mr Wills room sir. It stop 3.19 sir. *Chas. E. Hillyard*

More than 2 lbs of veal were removed from the Fridge last night, and a cake that was left in the press was cut. It is your duty, Night Watchman Hillyard, to keep an eye on these things. I ought to warn you that I have also asked the Police to check on all employees leaving the hotel, to prevent such occurrences in the future. W. A. G. *Inskip*

Mr Manager, I don't know why people so anxious to blame servants sir. About the cake, the press lock at night and I dont have the key sir, everything safe where I am concern sir. *Chas. Hillyard*

November 26. Midnight Bar close and Barman left. Mr Wills didn't come, I hear he at the American base tonight, all quiet, nothing unusual.

Mr Manager, I request one thing. Please inform the Barman to let me know sir when there is a female guest in the hotel sir. *C. E. Hillyard*

This morning I received a report from a guest that there were screams in the hotel during the night. You wrote All Quiet. Kindly explain in writing. W. A. G. *Inskip* Write Explanation here:

EXPLANATION. Not long after midnight the telephone ring and a woman ask for Mr Jimminez. I try to tell her where he was but she say she cant hear properly. Fifteen minutes later she came in a car, she was looking vex and sleepy, and I went up to call him. The door was not lock, I went in and touch his foot and call him very soft, and he jump up and begin to shout. When he come to himself he said he had Night Mere, and then he come down and went away with the woman, was not necessary to mention.

Mr Manager, I request you again, please inform the Barman to let me know sir when there is a female guest in the Hotel. *C. Hillyard*

November 27. 1 a.m. Bar close, Mr Wills and a American 19 Carib and 2.30 a.m. a Police come and ask for Mr Wills, he say the American report that he was robbed of $200.00¢, he was last drinking at the C——with Mr Wills and others. Mr Wills and the Police ask to open the Bar to search it, I told them I cannot open the Bar for you like that, the Police must come with the Manager. Then the American say it was only joke he was joking, and they try to get the Police to laugh, but the Police looking the way I feeling. Then laughing Mr Wills left in a garage car as he couldn't drive himself and the American was waiting outside and they both fall down as they was getting in the car, and Mr Wills saying any time you want a overdraft you just come to my bank kiddo. The Police left walking by himself. *C. Hillyard*

Night Watchman Hillyard: "Was not necessary to mention"!! You are not to decide what is necessary to mention in this night watchman's occurrence book. Since when have you become sole owner of the hotel as to determine what is necessary to mention? If the guest did not mention it I would never have known that there were screams in the hotel during the night. Also will you kindly tell me who Mr Jimminez is? And what rooms he occupied or occupies? And by what right? You have been told by me personally that the names of all hotel guests are on the slate next to the light switches. If you find Mr Jimminez's name on this slate, or could give me some information about him, I will be most warmly obliged to you. The lady you ask about is Mrs Roscoe, Room 12, as you very well know. It is your duty to see that guests are not pestered by unauthorized callers. You should give no information about guests to such people, and I would be glad if in future you could direct such callers straight to me. W. A. G. *Inskip*

Sir was what I ask you two times, I dont know what sort of work I take up, I always believe that nightwatchman work is a quiet work and I dont like meddling in white people business, but the gentleman occupy Room 12 also, was there that I went up to call him, I didn't think it necessary to mention because was none of my business sir. *C.E.H.*

November 28. 12 Midnight Bar close and Barman left at 12.20 a.m. leaving Mr Wills and others, and they all left at 1.25 a.m. Mr Wills 8 Carib, Mr Wilson 12, Mr Percy 8, and the man they call Paul 12. Mrs Roscoe join the gentlemen at 12.33 a.m., four gins, everybody calling her Minnie from Trinidad, and then they start singing that song, and some others. Nothing unusual. Afterwards there were mild singing and guitar music in Room 12. A man come in and ask to use the phone at 2.17 a.m. and while he was using it about 7 men come in and wanted to beat him up, so he put down the phone and they all ran away. At 3 a.m. I notice the padlock not on the press, I look inside, no cake, but the padlock was not put on in the first place sir. Mr Wills come down again at 6 a.m. to look for his sweet, he look in the Fridge and did not see any. He took a piece of pineapple. A plate was covered in the Fridge, but it didn't have anything in it. Mr Wills put it out, the cat jump on it and it fall down and break. The garage bulb not burning. *C.E.H.*

You will please sign your name at the bottom of your report. You are in the habit of writing Nothing Unusual. Please take note and think before making such a statement. I want to know what is meant by nothing unusual. I gather, not from you, needless to say, that the police have fallen into the habit of visiting the hotel at night. I would be most grateful to you if you could find the time to note the times of these visits. W. A. G. *Inskip*

Sir, nothing unusual means everything usual. I dont know, nothing I writing you liking. I dont know what sort of work this night watchman work getting to be, since when people have to start getting Cambridge certificate to get night watchman job, I ain't educated and because of this everybody think they could insult me. *Charles Ethelbert Hillyard*

November 29. Midnight Bar close and 12.15 Barman left leaving Mr Wills and Mrs Roscoe and others in the Bar. Mr Wills and Mrs Roscoe left at 12.30 a.m.

leaving Mr Wilson and the man they call Paul, and they all left at 1.00 a.m. Twenty minutes to 2 Mr Wills and party return and left again at 5 to 3. At 3.45 Mr Wills return and take bread and milk and olives and cherries, he ask for nutmeg too, I said we had none, he drink 2 Carib, and left ten minutes later. He also collect Mrs Roscoe bag. All the drinks, except the 2 Carib, was taken by the man they call Paul. I don't know sir I don't like this sort of work, you better hire a night barman. At 5.30 Mrs Roscoe and the man they call Paul come back to the bar, they was having a quarrel, Mr Paul saying you make me sick, Mrs Roscoe saying I feel sick, and then she vomit all over the floor, shouting I didn't want that damned milk. I was cleaning up when Mr Wills come down to ask for soda water, we got to lay in more soda for Mr Wills, but I need extra assistance with Mr Wills Paul and party sir.

The police come at 2, 3.48 and 4.52. They sit down in the bar a long time. Firearms discharge 2 times in the back yard. Detective making inquiries. I dont know sir, I thinking it would be better for me to go back to some other sort of job. At 3 I hear somebody shout Thief, and I see a man running out of the back, and Mr London, Room 9, say he miss 80 cents and a pack of cigarettes which was on his dressing case. I don't know when the people in this place does sleep. *Chas. Ethelbert Hillyard*

> Night Watchman Hillyard: A lot more than 80 cents was stolen. Several rooms were in fact entered during the night, including my own. You are employed to prevent such things occurring. Your interest in the morals of our guests seems to be distracting your attention from your duties. Save your preaching for your roadside prayer meetings. Mr Pick, Room 7, reports that in spite of the most pressing and repeated requests, you did not awaken him at 5. He has missed his plane to British Guiana as a result. No newspapers were delivered to the rooms this morning. I am again notifying you that papers must be handed personally to Doorman Vignales. And the messenger's bicycle, which I must remind you is the property of the hotel, has been damaged. What do you *do* at nights? *W. A. G. Inskip*

Please don't ask me sir.

Relating to the damaged bicycle: I left the bicycle the same place where I meet it, nothing took place so as to damage it. I always take care of all property sir. I don't know how you could think I have time to go out for bicycle rides. About the papers, sir, the police and them read it and leave them in such a state that I didn't think it would be nice to give them to guests. I wake up Mr Pick, room 7, at 4.50 a.m. 5 a.m. 5.15 a.m. and 5.30. He told me to keep off, he would not get up, and one time he pelt a box of matches at me, matches scatter all over the place. I always do everything to the best of my ability sir but God is my Witness I never find a night watchman work like this, so much writing I dont have time to do anything else, I dont have four hands and six eyes and I want this extra assistance with Mr Wills and party sir. I am a poor man and you could abuse me, but you must not abuse my religion sir because the good Lord sees All and will have His revenge sir, I don't know what sort of work and trouble I land myself in, all I want is a little quiet night work and all I getting is abuse. *Chas. E. Hillyard*

November 30. 12.25 a.m. Bar close and Barman left 1.00 a.m. leaving Mr Wills and party in Bar. Mr Wills take 12 Carib, Mr Wilson 6, Mr Percy 14. Mrs Roscoe five gins. At 1.30 a.m. Mrs Roscoe left and there were a little singing and mild guitar playing in Room 12. Nothing unusual. The police came at 1.35 and sit down in the bar for a time, not drinking, not talking, not doing anything except watching. At 1.45 the man they call Paul come in with Mr. McPherson of the SS Naparoni, they was both falling down and laughing whenever anything break and the man they call Paul say Fireworks about to begin tell Minnie Malcolm coming the ship just dock. Mr Wills and party scatter leaving one or two bottles half empty and then the man they call Paul tell me to go up to Room 12 and tell Minnie Roscoe that Malcolm coming. I don't know how people could behave so the thing enough to make anybody turn priest. I notice the padlock on the bar door break off it hanging on only by a little piece of wood. And when I went up to Room 12 and tell Mrs Roscoe that Malcolm coming the ship just dock the woman get sober straight away like she dont want to hear no more guitar music and she asking me where to hide where to go. I dont know, I feel the day of reckoning is at hand, but she not listening to what I saying, she busy straightening up the room one minute packing the next, and then she run out into the corridor and before I could stop she she run straight down the back stairs to the annexe. And then 5 past 2, still in the corridor, I see a big red man running up to me and he sober as a judge and he mad as a drunkard and he asking me where she is where she is. I ask whether he is a authorized caller, he say you don't give me any of that crap now, where she is, where she is. So remembering about the last time Mr Jimminez I direct him to the manager office in the annexe. He hear a little scuffling inside Mr Inskip room and I make out Mr Inskip sleepy voice and Mrs Roscoe voice and the red man run inside and all I hearing for the next five minutes is bam bam bodow bodow bow and this woman screaming. I dont know what sort of work this night watchman getting I want something quiet like the police. In time things quiet down and the red man drag Mrs Roscoe out of the annexe and they take a taxi, and the Police sitting down quiet in the bar. Then Mr Percy and the others come back one by one to the bar and they talking quiet and they not drinking and they left 3 a.m. 3.15 Mr Wills return and take one whisky and 2 Carib. He asked for pineapple or some sweet fruit but it had nothing.

6 a.m. Mr Wills come in the bar looking for soda but it aint have none. We have to get some soda for Mr Wills sir.

6.30 a.m. the papers come and I deliver them to Doorman Vignales at 7 a.m.
Chas. Hillyard

Mr Hillyard: In view of the unfortunate illness of Mr. Inskip, I am temporarily in charge of the hotel. I trust you will continue to make your nightly reports, but I would be glad if you could keep your entries as brief as possible. *Robt. Magnus, Acting Manager*

December 1. 10.30 p.m. C. E. Hillyard take over duty at C——Hotel all corrected 12 Midnight Bar close 2 a.m. Mr Wills 2 Carib, 1 bread 6 a.m. Mr Wills 1 soda 7 a.m. Night Watchman Hillyard hand over duty to Mr Vignales with one torch light 2 Fridge keys and Room Keys 1, 3, 6 and 12. Bar intact all corrected no report. *C.E.H.*

Questions

1. What sort of hotel is the C——Hotel?
2. Of what social class is Hillyard?
3. Of what race is Hillyard?
4. What is Inskip's attitude toward Hillyard?
5. What does Inskip think of himself?
6. How can you account for Inskip's attitude toward Hillyard?
7. What is Hillyard's attitude toward Inskip?
8. How does Hillyard bring about his own troubles?
9. What do you imagine is the source of Inskip's "unfortunate illness"?

4 ❧ Unreliable Narrators — Don't Believe Everything You Hear

In the last chapter we read about stories with omniscient narrators, limited third-person narrations, and first-person narrations. We discussed how a narrator's point-of-view determines a story's language, which events get narrated, and the way they are narrated. But though the narrators' attitudes may color the events in the stories in Chapter 3, those attitudes do not invalidate the narrators' conclusions or their accuracy. However, some narrators are "unreliable," that is, as readers we distrust their accounts as biased and their conclusions as twisted. We come to the conclusion that narrators are "unreliable" when and if they show us that they are insane, or highly prejudiced, or incapable of understanding events. At some point in the story, unreliable narrators tip their hands, and show us that they are not to be trusted.

✍ Tips for Writers

When writing about an unreliable narrator, you must distinguish between the narrator and the author, or between the *authorial point-of-view* and the *narrator's point-of-view*. In many stories these points-of-view are blurred, but in unreliable narratives the author's position and the narrator's diverge radically. The author forces the reader to try to penetrate to the fictional truth beneath the narrative surface.

How to Determine a Narrator's Unreliability

When a jury hears a case, it has to decide which witnesses to believe. The jury listens to the testimony, evaluates which accounts seem the most plausible, and sifts the evidence for contradictions. But it may base its decision on something less tangible—the credibility of the witness. Witnesses are judged as much on the manner of their testimony as on the substance of it.

What makes one witness credible and another less credible? First, no matter how well a witness speaks, the jury will be suspicious of a witness who might gain by lying. If someone might benefit from telling a lie, then clearly the person's testimony is suspect. Second, witnesses who seem confused or disoriented are less credible than those who speak with confidence and clarity. If one doesn't understand an event, one can hardly be a reliable witness of what happened. The confused witness often mixes up the sequence of actions and fails to recognize important but subtle signs and cues. Third, a witness who is emotionally unstable will not be a credible witness. The witness's feelings will so distort the nature of events that, without meaning to, he or she will give a false impression of what actually occurred.

We judge the reliability of speakers all the time. When people seem confused in giving street directions, we are likely to distrust them and go on to ask someone else. When salespersons seem too eager to make a sale or when they apply too much pressure, we tend to be suspicious of their motives. When people seem distraught or disturbed, we tend to distrust their accounts.

Writers are fascinated by the way in which good listeners can detect a speaker who is not credible and see through the speaker's distortions and lies. Consequently, many authors tell their stories with *unreliable narrators*—narrators whose accounts of events the reader recognizes as faulty, distorted, or untrustworthy.

Readers recognize the unreliability of narrators in the same manner that they recognize the lack of credibility in a witness. Unreliable narrators have something to gain by their falsehood, do not understand the stories they are asked to tell, or—and this is the most common cause—are too emotionally or psychologically disturbed to give a trustworthy account of events.

Irony in Unreliable Narrations

Part of the interest of unreliable narrations is the ironic relationship they create between the narrator's point-of-view and the reader's point-of-view. *Irony* is a complex phenomenon. Usually it involves a word, phrase, situation, or condition that comes to mean the opposite of what was intended. For example, it is ironic when a doctor sets out to help an injured person and ends up being sued for malpractice. Or when a student says, "I'm afraid of failing this course," and then earns an A.

Because the reader understands the situation better than the narrator, the reader perceives a number of ironies in what the narrator says. In "The Yellow Wall-Paper," for instance, the narrator repeatedly assures herself that her husband, a doctor, has her best interests at heart and that his medical advice will bring her back to health. The reader, however, comes to understand—as she does not—that the regimen her husband has prescribed is the cause of her illness. Unreliable narrators constantly make statements which mean something different than they realize. Thus such narratives always operate on at least two levels:

what the narrator wishes the reader to understand and what the reader ultimately realizes.

Authors' and Narrators' Points-of-View

The unreliable narrative is probably the clearest example of a story in which the narrator does not articulate the author's ideas, values, or attitudes. But one should never uncritically identify the narrator as the author or immediately assume that the narrator speaks for the author. Frequently the narrator's attitude—even in omniscient narrations—is more matter-of-fact, more neutral than is the author's. Usually authors avoid spelling out the values and attitudes that are contained in their stories, letting readers discover these values and attitudes for themselves. Authors avoid such explicit statements of intent in order to keep their stories from becoming sermons.

However, not all first-person narratives are unreliable. One must draw a distinction between the *limitations* of a narrator's point-of-view and the *distortions* of an unreliable narrator. If we examine Queneau's three versions of the bus argument, we see that all three narrators give fairly accurate accounts of the incidents. The older man is "vulgar," as the young man accuses him of being. And the young man is ridiculously vain, "a milksop," as the older man says. The difference between their stories is that neither narrator recognizes his own faults. Each is blind to his own failings. Their accounts are limited by their points-of-view. The unreliable narrator distorts what is happening, misrepresents people or things, misjudges experience. As readers, we must imaginatively reconstruct the fictional events to make them more reasonable, logical, and fair. Indeed, much of the fun and critical interest in unreliable narrators comes from ·trying to figure out how the narrator has distorted events.

Finally, unreliable narrations are not necessarily limited to realistic stories. Even an unrealistic tale can be narrated by an unreliable narrator, forcing the reader to reconstruct what "really" happened. Here, for example, is the Wolf's account of "Little Red Riding Hood."

> Listen, Woodman, I can explain everything. There's no need to kill me with your axe. You see, the little girl invited me in. She said, "You look so hungry, I'm sure my grandmother will feed you." She looked like a nice innocent kid, so I followed her to her grandmother's house. But as soon as I got inside, bam! She pulled out this butcher knife. She went wild, I tell you. Started screaming that if I didn't do what she told me to do she would cut me into little steak cubes. I was so frightened, I huddled next to the bed. But when she got near me, I tried to get the cleaver away from her. She was quick—boy, was she quick!—and cut me here and here. What else could I do? It was self-defense. If I hadn't eaten her up, she would have killed me.

Suggestions for Essayists

1. Discuss the morality of lying. Is it ever right to tell a lie? Can lies protect people, governments, a cause?

2. Write about the most notorious liar you know. What sorts of lies does this person tell? How can you tell that the person is lying?
3. Describe how you can tell when someone is distorting the truth. What signs do you look for? How do you verify your suspicions?

Suggestions for Fiction Writers

1. Rewrite a fairy tale from the point-of-view of the villain. What sorts of distortions occur when villains try to make their acts seem reasonable and sympathetic?
2. Newspapers are filled with the terrible acts of disturbed persons. Taking the basic events from a newspaper account, narrate what happened, using the disturbed person's voice.

CHARLOTTE PERKINS GILMAN (1860–1935)

The Yellow Wall-Paper

It is very seldom that mere ordinary people like John and myself secure ancestral halls for the summer.

A colonial mansion, a hereditary estate, I would say a haunted house, and reach the height of romantic felicity—but that would be asking too much of fate!

Still I will proudly declare that there is something queer about it.

Else, why should it be let so cheaply? And why have stood so long untenanted?

John laughs at me, of course, but one expects that in marriage.

John is practical in the extreme. He has no patience with faith, an intense horror of superstition, and he scoffs openly at any talk of things not to be felt and seen and put down in figures.

John is a physician, and *perhaps*—(I would not say it to a living soul, of course, but this is dead paper and a great relief to my mind)—*perhaps* that is one reason I do not get well faster.

You see he does not believe I am sick!

And what can one do?

If a physician of high standing, and one's own husband, assures friends and relatives that there is really nothing the matter with one but temporary nervous depression—a slight hysterical tendency—what is one to do?

My brother is also a physician, and also of high standing, and he says the same thing.

So I take phosphates or phosphites—whichever it is, and tonics, and journeys, and air, and exercise, and am absolutely forbidden to "work" until I am well again.

Personally, I disagree with their ideas.

Personally, I believe that congenial work, with excitement and change, would do me good.

But what is one to do?

I did write for a while in spite of them; but it *does* exhaust me a good deal—having to be so sly about it, or else meet with heavy opposition.

I sometimes fancy that in my condition if I had less opposition and more society and stimulus—but John says the very worst thing I can do is to think about my condition, and I confess it always makes me feel bad.

So I will let it alone and talk about the house.

The most beautiful place! It is quite alone, standing well back from the road, quite three miles from the village. It makes me think of English places that you read about, for there are hedges and walls and gates that lock, and lots of separate little houses for the gardeners and people.

There is a *delicious* garden! I never saw such a garden—large and shady, full of box-bordered paths, and lined with long grape-covered arbors with seats under them.

There were greenhouses, too, but they are all broken now.

There was some legal trouble, I believe, something about the heirs and coheirs; anyhow, the place has been empty for years.

That spoils my ghostliness, I am afraid, but I don't care—there is something strange about the house—I can feel it.

I even said so to John one moonlight evening, but he said what I felt was a *draught*, and shut the window.

I get unreasonably angry with John sometimes. I'm sure I never used to be sensitive. I think it is due to this nervous condition.

But John says if I feel so, I shall neglect proper self-control; so I take pains to control myself—before him, at least, and that makes me very tired.

I don't like our room a bit. I wanted one downstairs that opened on the piazza and had roses all over the window, and such pretty old-fashioned chintz hangings! but John would not hear of it.

He said there was only one window and not room for two beds, and no near room for him if he took another.

He is very careful and loving, and hardly lets me stir without special direction.

I have a schedule prescription for each hour in the day; he takes all care from me, and so I feel basely ungrateful not to value it more.

He said we came here solely on my account, that I was to have perfect rest and all the air I could get. "Your exercise depends on your strength, my dear," said he, "and your food somewhat on your appetite; but air you can absorb all the time." So we took the nursery at the top of the house.

It is a big, airy room, the whole floor nearly, with windows that look all ways, and air and sunshine galore. It was nursery first and then playroom and gymnasium, I should judge; for the windows are barred for little children, and there are rings and things in the walls.

The paint and paper look as if a boys' school had used it. It is stripped off—the paper—in great patches all around the head of my bed, about as far as I can reach, and in a great place on the other side of the room low down. I never saw a worse paper in my life.

One of those sprawling flamboyant patterns committing every artistic sin.

It is dull enough to confuse the eye in following, pronounced enough to constantly irritate and provoke study, and when you follow the lame uncertain curves for a little distance they suddenly commit suicide—plunge off at outrageous angles, destroy themselves in unheard of contradictions.

The color is repellent, almost revolting; a smouldering unclean yellow, strangely faded by the slow-turning sunlight.

It is a dull yet lurid orange in some places, a sickly sulphur tint in others.

No wonder the children hated it! I should hate it myself if I had to live in this room long.

There comes John, and I must put this away,—he hates to have me write a word.

We have been here two weeks, and I haven't felt like writing before, since that first day.

I am sitting by the window now, up in this atrocious nursery, and there is nothing to hinder my writing as much as I please, save lack of strength.

John is away all day, and even some nights when his cases are serious.

I am glad my case is not serious!

But these nervous troubles are dreadfully depressing.

John does not know how much I really suffer. He knows there is no *reason* to suffer, and that satisfies him.

Of course it is only nervousness. It does weigh on me so not to do my duty in any way!

I meant to be such a help to John, such a real rest and comfort, and here I am a comparative burden already!

Nobody would believe what an effort it is to do what little I am able,—to dress and entertain, and order things.

It is fortunate Mary is so good with the baby. Such a dear baby!

And yet I *cannot* be with him, it makes me so nervous.

I suppose John never was nervous in his life. He laughs at me so about this wall-paper!

At first he meant to repaper the room, but afterwards he said that I was letting it get the better of me, and that nothing was worse for a nervous patient than to give way to such fancies.

He said that after the wall-paper was changed it would be the heavy bedstead, and then the barred windows, and then that gate at the head of the stairs, and so on.

"You know the place is doing you good," he said, "and really, dear, I don't care to renovate the house just for a three months' rental."

"Then do let us go downstairs," I said, "there are such pretty rooms there."

Then he took me in his arms and called me a blessed little goose, and said he would go down to the cellar, if I wished, and have it whitewashed into the bargain.

But he is right enough about the beds and windows and things.

It is an airy and comfortable room as any one need wish, and, of course, I would not be so silly as to make him uncomfortable just for a whim.

I'm really getting quite fond of the big room, all but that horrid paper.

Out of one window I can see the garden, those mysterious deep-shaded arbors, the riotous old-fashioned flowers, and bushes and gnarly trees.

Out of another I get a lovely view of the bay and a little private wharf belonging to the estate. There is a beautiful shaded lane that runs down there from the house. I always fancy I see people walking in these numerous paths and arbors, but John has cautioned me not to give way to fancy in the least. He says that with my imaginative power and habit of story-making, a nervous weakness like mine is sure to lead to all manner of excited fancies, and that I ought to use my will and good sense to check the tendency. So I try.

I think sometimes that if I were only well enough to write a little it would relieve the press of ideas and rest me.

But I find I get pretty tired when I try.

It is so discouraging not to have any advice and companionship about my work. When I get really well, John says we will ask Cousin Henry and Julia down for a long visit; but he says he would as soon put fireworks in my pillow-case as to let me have those stimulating people about now.

I wish I could get well faster.

But I must not think about that. This paper looks to me as if it *knew* what a vicious influence it had!

There is a recurrent spot where the pattern lolls like a broken neck and two bulbous eyes stare at you upside down.

I get positively angry with the impertinence of it and the everlastingness. Up and down and sideways they crawl, and those absurd, unblinking eyes are everywhere. There is one place where two breadths didn't match, and the eyes go all up and down the line, one a little higher than the other.

I never saw so much expression in an inanimate thing before, and we all know how much expression they have! I used to lie awake as a child and get more entertainment and terror out of blank walls and plain furniture than most children could find in a toy-store.

I remember what a kindly wink the knobs of our big, old bureau used to have, and there was one chair that always seemed like a strong friend.

I used to feel that if any of the other things looked too fierce I could always hop into that chair and be safe.

The furniture in this room is no worse than inharmonious, however, for we had to bring it all from downstairs. I suppose when this was used as a playroom they had to take the nursery things out, and no wonder! I never saw such ravages as the children have made here.

The wall-paper, as I said before, is torn off in spots, and it sticketh closer than a brother—they must have had perseverance as well as hatred.

Then the floor is scratched and gouged and splintered, the plaster itself is dug out here and there, and this great heavy bed which is all we found in the room, looks as if it had been through the wars.

But I don't mind it a bit—only the paper.

There comes John's sister. Such a dear girl as she is, and so careful of me! I must not let her find me writing.

She is a perfect and enthusiastic housekeeper, and hopes for no better profession. I verily believe she thinks it is the writing which made me sick!

But I can write when she is out, and see her a long way off from these windows.

There is one that commands the road, a lovely shaded winding road, and one that just looks off over the country. A lovely country, too, full of great elms and velvet meadows.

This wall-paper has a kind of sub-pattern in a different shade, a particularly irritating one, for you can only see it in certain lights, and not clearly then.

But in the places where it isn't faded and where the sun is just so—I can see a strange, provoking, formless sort of figure, that seems to skulk about behind that silly and conspicuous front design.

There's sister on the stairs!

Well, the Fourth of July is over! The people are all gone and I am tired out. John thought it might do me good to see a little company, so we just had mother and Nellie and the children down for a week.

Of course I didn't do a thing. Jennie sees to everything now.

But it tired me all the same.

John says if I don't pick up faster he shall send me to Weir Mitchell in the fall.

But I don't want to go there at all. I had a friend who was in his hands once, and she says he is just like John and my brother, only more so!

Besides, it is such an undertaking to go so far.

I don't feel as if it was worth while to turn my hand over for anything, and I'm getting dreadfully fretful and querulous.

I cry at nothing, and cry most of the time.

Of course I don't when John is here, or anybody else, but when I am alone.

And I am alone a good deal just now. John is kept in town very often by serious cases, and Jennie is good and lets me alone when I want her to.

So I walk a little in the garden or down that lovely lane, sit on the porch under the roses, and lie down up here a good deal.

I'm getting really fond of the room in spite of the wall-paper. Perhaps *because* of the wall-paper.

It dwells in my mind so!

I lie here on this great immovable bed—it is nailed down, I believe—and follow that pattern about by the hour. It is as good as gymnastics, I assure you. I start, we'll say, at the bottom, down in the corner over there where it has not been touched, and I determine for the thousandth time that I *will* follow that pointless pattern to some sort of a conclusion.

I know a little of the principle of design, and I know this thing was not arranged on any laws of radiation, or alternation, or repetition, or symmetry, or anything else that I ever heard of.

It is repeated, of course, by the breadths, but not otherwise.

Looked at in one way each breadth stands alone, the bloated curves and flourishes—a kind of "debased Romanesque" with *delirium tremens*—go waddling up and down in isolated columns of fatuity.

But, on the other hand, they connect diagonally, and the sprawling outlines run off in great slanting waves of optic horror, like a lot of wallowing seaweeds in full chase.

The whole thing goes horizontally, too, at least it seems so, and I exhaust myself in trying to distinguish the order of its going in that direction.

They have used a horizontal breadth for a frieze, and that adds wonderfully to the confusion.

There is one end of the room where it is almost intact, and there, when the crosslights fade and the low sun shines directly upon it, I can almost fancy radiation after all,—the interminable grotesques seem to form around a common centre and rush off in headlong plunges of equal distraction.

It makes me tired to follow it. I will take a nap I guess.

I don't know why I should write this.

I don't want to.

I don't feel able.

And I know John would think it absurd. But I *must* say what I feel and think in some way—it is such a relief!

But the effort is getting to be greater than the relief.

Half the time now I am awfully lazy, and lie down ever so much.

John says I mustn't lose my strength, and has me take cod liver oil and lots of tonics and things, to say nothing of ale and wine and rare meat.

Dear John! He loves me very dearly, and hates to have me sick. I tried to have a real earnest reasonable talk with him the other day, and tell him how I wish he would let me go and make a visit to Cousin Henry and Julia.

But he said I wasn't able to go, nor able to stand it after I got there; and I did not make out a very good case for myself, for I was crying before I had finished.

It is getting to be a great effort for me to think straight. Just this nervous weakness I suppose.

And dear John gathered me up in his arms, and just carried me upstairs and laid me on the bed, and sat by me and read to me till it tired my head.

He said I was his darling and his comfort and all he had, and that I must take care of myself for his sake, and keep well.

He says no one but myself can help me out of it, that I must use my will and self-control and not let any silly fancies run away with me.

There's one comfort, the baby is well and happy, and does not have to occupy this nursery with the horrid wall-paper.

If we had not used it, that blessed child would have! What a fortunate escape! Why, I wouldn't have a child of mine, an impressionable little thing, live in such a room for worlds.

I never thought of it before, but it is lucky that John kept me here after all, I can stand it so much easier than a baby, you see.

Of course I never mention it to them any more—I am too wise,—but I keep watch of it all the same.

Charlotte Perkins Gilman   153

There are things in that paper that nobody knows but me, or ever will.

Behind that outside pattern the dim shapes get clearer every day.

It is always the same shape, only very numerous.

And it is like a woman stooping down and creeping about behind that pattern. I don't like it a bit. I wonder—I begin to think—I wish John would take me away from here!

It is so hard to talk with John about my case, because he is so wise, and because he loves me so.

But I tried it last night.

It was moonlight. The moon shines in all around just as the sun does.

I hate to see it sometimes, it creeps so slowly, and always comes in by one window or another.

John was asleep and I hated to waken him, so I kept still and watched the moonlight on that undulating wall-paper till I felt creepy.

The faint figure behind seemed to shake the pattern, just as if she wanted to get out.

I got up softly and went to feel and see if the paper *did* move, and when I came back John was awake.

"What is it, little girl?" he said. "Don't go walking about like that—you'll get cold."

I thought it was a good time to talk, so I told him that I really was not gaining here, and that I wished he would take me away.

"Why darling!" said he, "our lease will be up in three weeks, and I can't see how to leave before.

"The repairs are not done at home, and I cannot possibly leave town just now. Of course if you were in any danger, I could and would, but you really are better, dear, whether you can see it or not. I am a doctor, dear, and I know. You are gaining flesh and color, your appetite is better, I feel really much easier about you."

"I don't weigh a bit more," said I, "nor as much; and my appetite may be better in the evening when you are here, but it is worse in the morning when you are away!"

"Bless her little heart!" said he with a big hug, "she shall be as sick as she pleases! But now let's improve the shining hours by going to sleep, and talk about it in the morning!"

"And you won't go away?"I asked gloomily.

"Why, how can I, dear? It is only three weeks more and then we will take a nice little trip of a few days while Jennie is getting the house ready. Really dear you are better!"

"Better in body perhaps—" I began, and stopped short, for he sat up straight and looked at me with such a stern, reproachful look that I could not say another word.

"My darling," said he, "I beg of you, for my sake and for our child's sake, as well as for your own, that you will never for one instant let that idea enter your mind! There is nothing so dangerous, so fascinating, to a temperament like yours. It is a false and foolish fancy. Can you not trust me as a physician when I tell you so?"

So of course I said no more on that score, and we went to sleep before long. He thought I was asleep first, but I wasn't, and lay there for hours trying to decide whether that front pattern and the back pattern really did move together or separately.

On a pattern like this, by daylight, there is a lack of sequence, a defiance of law, that is a constant irritant to a normal mind.

The color is hideous enough, and unreliable enough, and infuriating enough, but the pattern is torturing.

You think you have mastered it, but just as you get well underway in following, it turns a back-somersault and there you are. It slaps you in the face, knocks you down, and tramples upon you. It is like a bad dream.

The outside pattern is a florid arabesque, reminding one of a fungus. If you can imagine a toadstool in joints, an interminable string of toadstools, budding and sprouting in endless convolutions—why, that is something like it.

That is, sometimes!

There is one marked peculiarity about this paper, a thing nobody seems to notice but myself, and that is that it changes as the light changes.

When the sun shoots in through the east window—I always watch for that first long, straight ray—it changes so quickly that I never can quite believe it.

That is why I watch it always.

By moonlight—the moon shines in all night when there is a moon—I wouldn't know it was the same paper.

At night in any kind of light, in twilight, candle light, lamplight, and worst of all by moonlight, it becomes bars! The outside pattern I mean, and the woman behind it is as plain as can be.

I didn't realize for a long time what the thing was that showed behind, that dim sub-pattern, but now I am quite sure it is a woman.

By daylight she is subdued, quiet. I fancy it is the pattern that keeps her so still. It is so puzzling. It keeps me quiet by the hour.

I lie down ever so much now. John says it is good for me, and to sleep all I can.

Indeed he started the habit by making me lie down for an hour after each meal.

It is a very bad habit I am convinced, for you see I don't sleep.

And that cultivates deceit, for I don't tell them I'm awake—O no!

The fact is I am getting a little afraid of John.

He seems very queer sometimes, and even Jennie has an inexplicable look.

It strikes me occasionally, just as a scientific hypothesis,—that perhaps it is the paper!

I have watched John when he did not know I was looking, and come into the room suddenly on the most innocent excuses, and I've caught him several times *looking at the paper!* And Jennie too. I caught Jennie with her hand on it once.

She didn't know I was in the room, and when I asked her in a quiet, a very quiet voice, with the most restrained manner possible, what she was doing with the paper—she turned around as if she had been caught stealing, and looked quite angry—asked me why I should frighten her so!

Then she said that the paper stained everything it touched, that she had found yellow smooches on all my clothes and John's, and she wished we would be more careful!

Did not that sound innocent? But I know she was studying that pattern, and I am determined that nobody shall find it out but myself!

Life is very much more exciting now than it used to be. You see I have something more to expect, to look forward to, to watch. I really do eat better, and am more quiet than I was.

John is so pleased to see me improve! He laughed a little the other day, and said I seemed to be flourishing in spite of my wall-paper.

I turned it off with a laugh. I had no intention of telling him it was *because* of the wall-paper—he would make fun of me. He might even want to take me away.

I don't want to leave now until I have found it out. There is a week more, and I think that will be enough.

I'm feeling ever so much better! I don't sleep much at night, for it is so interesting to watch developments; but I sleep a good deal in the daytime.

In the daytime it is tiresome and perplexing.

There are always new shoots on the fungus, and new shades of yellow all over it. I cannot keep count of them, though I have tried conscientiously.

It is the strangest yellow, that wall-paper! It makes me think of all the yellow things I ever saw—not beautiful ones like buttercups, but old foul, bad yellow things.

But there is something else about that paper—the smell! I noticed it the moment we came into the room, but with so much air and sun it was not bad. Now we have had a week of fog and rain, and whether the windows are open or not, the smell is here.

It creeps all over the house.

I find it hovering in the dining-room, skulking in the parlor, hiding in the hall, lying in wait for me on the stairs.

It gets into my hair.

Even when I go to ride, if I turn my head suddenly and surprise it—there is that smell!

Such a peculiar odor, too! I have spent hours in trying to analyze it, to find what it smelled like.

It is not bad—at first, and very gentle, but quite the subtlest, most enduring odor I ever met.

In this damp weather it is awful, I wake up in the night and find it hanging over me.

It used to disturb me at first. I thought seriously of burning the house—to reach the smell.

But now I am used to it. The only thing I can think of that it is like is the *color* of the paper! A yellow smell.

There is a very funny mark on this wall, low down, near the mopboard. A streak that runs round the room. It goes behind every piece of furniture, except the bed, a long, straight, even *smooch*, as if it had been rubbed over and over.

I wonder how it was done and who did it, and what they did it for. Round and round and round—round and round and round—it makes me dizzy!

I really have discovered something at last.

Through watching so much at night, when it changes so, I have finally found out.

The front pattern *does* move—and no wonder! The woman behind shakes it!

Sometimes I think there are a great many women behind, and sometimes only one, and she crawls around fast, and her crawling shakes it all over.

Then in the very bright spots she keeps still, and in the very shady spots she just takes hold of the bars and shakes them hard.

And she is all the time trying to climb through. But nobody could climb through that pattern—it strangles so; I think that is why it has so many heads.

They get through, and then the pattern strangles them off and turns them upside down, and makes their eyes white!

If those heads were covered or taken off it would not be half so bad.

I think that woman gets out in the daytime!

And I'll tell you why—privately—I've seen her!

I can see her out of every one of my windows!

It is the same woman, I know, for she is always creeping, and most women do not creep by daylight.

I see her on that long road under the trees, creeping along, and when a carriage comes she hides under the blackberry vines.

I don't blame her a bit. It must be very humiliating to be caught creeping by daylight!

I always lock the door when I creep by daylight. I can't do it at night, for I know John would suspect something at once.

And John is so queer now, that I don't want to irritate him. I wish he would take another room! Besides, I don't want anybody to get that woman out at night but myself.

I often wonder if I could see her out of all the windows at once.

But, turn as fast as I can, I can only see out of one at one time.

And though I always see her, she *may* be able to creep faster than I can turn!

I have watched her sometimes away off in the open country, creeping as fast as a cloud shadow in a high wind.

If only that top pattern could be gotten off from the under one! I mean to try it, little by little.

I have found out another funny thing, but I shan't tell it this time! It does not do to trust people too much.

There are only two more days to get this paper off, and I believe John is beginning to notice. I don't like the look in his eyes.

And I heard him ask Jennie a lot of professional questions about me. She had a very good report to give.

She said I slept a good deal in the daytime.

John knows I don't sleep very well at night, for all I'm so quiet!

He asked me all sorts of questions, too, and pretended to be very loving and kind.

As if I couldn't see through him!

Still, I don't wonder he acts so, sleeping under this paper for three months.

It only interests me, but I feel sure John and Jennie are secretly affected by it.

Hurrah! This is the last day, but it is enough. John is to stay in town over night, and won't be out until this evening.

Jennie wanted to sleep with me—the sly thing! but I told her I should undoubtedly rest better for a night all alone.

That was clever, for really I wasn't alone a bit! As soon as it was moonlight and that poor thing began to crawl and shake the pattern, I got up and ran to help her.

I pulled and she shook, I shook and she pulled, and before morning we had peeled off yards of that paper.

A strip about as high as my head and half around the room.

And then when the sun came and that awful pattern began to laugh at me, I declared I would finish it to-day!

We go away to-morrow, and they are moving all my furniture down again to leave things as they were before.

Jennie looked at the wall in amazement, but I told her merrily that I did it out of pure spite at the vicious thing.

She laughed and said she wouldn't mind doing it herself, but I must not get tired.

How she betrayed herself that time!

But I am here, and no person touches this paper but me,—not *alive!*

She tried to get me out of the room—it was too patent! But I said it was so quiet, and empty and clean now that I believed I would lie down again and sleep all I could; and not to wake me even for dinner—I would call when I woke.

So now she is gone, and the servants are gone, and the things are gone, and there is nothing left but that great bedstead nailed down, with the canvas mattress we found on it.

We shall sleep downstairs to-night, and take the boat home to-morrow.

I quite enjoy the room, now it is bare again.

How those children did tear about here!

This bedstead is fairly gnawed!

But I must get to work.

I have locked the door and thrown the key down into the front path.

I don't want to go out, and I don't want to have anybody come in, till John comes.

I want to astonish him.

I've got a rope up here that even Jennie did not find. If that woman does get out, and tries to get away, I can tie her!

But I forgot I could not reach far without anything to stand on!

This bed will *not* move!

I tried to lift and push it until I was lame, and then I got so angry I bit off a little piece at one corner—but it hurt my teeth.

Then I peeled off all the paper I could reach standing on the floor. It sticks horribly and the pattern just enjoys it! All those strangled heads and bulbous eyes and waddling fungus growths just shriek with derision!

I am getting angry enough to do something desperate. To jump out of the window would be admirable exercise, but the bars are too strong even to try.

Besides I wouldn't do it. Of course not. I know well enough that a step like that is improper and might be misconstrued.

I don't like to *look* out of the windows even—there are so many of those creeping women, and they creep so fast.

I wonder if they all come out of that wall-paper as I did?

But I am securely fastened now by my well-hidden rope—you don't get *me* out in the road there!

I suppose I shall have to get back behind the pattern when it comes night, and that is hard!

It is so pleasant to be out in this great room and creep around as I please!

I don't want to go outside. I won't, even if Jennie asks me to.

For outside you have to creep on the ground, and everything is green instead of yellow.

But here I can creep smoothly on the floor, and my shoulder just fits in that long smooch around the wall, so I cannot lose my way.

Why there's John at the door!

It is no use, young man, you can't open it!

How he does call and pound!

Now he's crying for an axe.

It would be a shame to break down that beautiful door!

"John dear!" said I in the gentlest voice, "the key is down by the front steps, under a plantain leaf!"

That silenced him for a few moments.

Then he said—very quietly indeed, "Open the door, my darling!"

"I can't," said I. "The key is down by the front door under a plantain leaf!"

And then I said it again, several times, very gently and slowly, and said it so often that he had to go and see, and he got it of course, and came in. He stopped short by the door.

"What is the matter?" he cried. "For God's sake, what are you doing!"

I kept on creeping just the same, but I looked at him over my shoulder.

"I've got out at last," said I, "in spite of you and Jane.[1] And I've pulled off most of the paper, so you can't put me back!"

Now why should that man have fainted? But he did, and right across my path by the wall, so that I had to creep over him every time!

Questions

1. At the story's beginning, John recommends idleness and isolation as remedies for the narrator's "nervous depression." She thinks a little work and company would do her some good. Who is right? What does this say about the medical treatment of the times?
2. Both of the narrator's doctors are men. What does their attitude say about the male view of the psychological needs of women?
3. How does her attitude toward the wallpaper change? What does she first think of it? What does it come to represent?
4. Why should she be fascinated by the wallpaper?
5. When does the narrator come to realize that she has difficulty in thinking straight?
6. Toward the middle of the story, John tells his wife that she is improving. Is he sincere? Why does he tell her of the improvement? Are his motives selfless?
7. Sigmund Freud believed that one's fantasies had meaning. Is there any reason the narrator should hallucinate the figures she sees?

EDGAR ALLAN POE (1809–1849)

The Cask of Amontillado

The thousand injuries of Fortunato I had borne as I best could, but when he ventured upon insult, I vowed revenge. You, who so well know the nature of my soul, will not suppose, however, that I gave utterance to a threat. *At length* I would be avenged; this was a point definitely settled—but the very definitiveness with which it was resolved precluded the idea of risk. I must not only punish, but punish with impunity. A wrong is unredressed when retribution overtakes its redresser. It is equally unredressed when the avenger fails to make himself felt as such to him who has done the wrong.

It must be understood that neither by word nor deed had I given Fortunato cause to doubt my good will. I continued, as was my wont, to smile in his face, and he did not perceive that my smile *now* was at the thought of his immolation.

He had a weak point—this Fortunato—although in other regards he was a man to be respected and even feared. He prided himself on his connoisseurship in wine. Few Italians have the true virtuoso spirit. For the most part their enthusiasm is adopted to suit the time and opportunity to practice imposture

---

[1] Jennie is a nickname for Jane. Jane and Jennie are the same character.

Edgar Allan Poe (*Culver Pictures, Inc.*)

upon the British and Austrian *millionaires*. In painting and gemmary[1] Fortunato, like his countrymen, was a quack, but in the matter of old wines he was sincere. In this respect I did not differ from him materially;—I was skillful in the Italian vintages myself, and bought largely whenever I could.

It was about dusk, one evening during the supreme madness of the carnival season, that I encountered my friend. He accosted me with excessive warmth, for he had been drinking much. The man wore motley. He had on a tight-fitting parti-striped dress, and his head was surmounted by the conical cap and bells.[2] I was so pleased to see him, that I thought I should never have done wringing his hand.

I said to him—"My dear Fortunato, you are luckily met. How remarkably well you are looking to-day! But I have received a pipe[3] of what passes for Amontillado,[4] and I have my doubts."

"How?" said he, "Amontillado? A pipe? Impossible! And in the middle of the carnival?"[5]

"I have my doubts," I replied; "and I was silly enough to pay the full Amontillado price without consulting you in the matter. You were not to be found, and I was fearful of losing a bargain."

---

[1] Gemmary is the art of gem cutting and gem engraving.
[2] In short, he is dressed like a clown.
[3] A pipe is a wine cask.
[4] Amontillado is a specific type of sherry made from grapes grown on the slopes of the Sierra de Montilla, south of Córdoba, Spain.
[5] The carnival or *Mardi Gras* is a yearly festival celebrated before Lent.

"Amontillado!"

"I have my doubts."

"Amontillado!"

"And I must satisfy them."

"Amontillado!"

"As you are engaged, I am on my way to Luchesi. If any one has a critical turn, it is he. He will tell me—"

"Luchesi cannot tell Amontillado from Sherry."

"And yet some fools will have it that his taste is a match for your own."

"Come, let us go."

"Whither?"

"To your vaults."

"My friend, no; I will not impose upon your good nature. I perceive you have an engagement. Luchesi—"

"I have no engagement; come."

"My friend, no. It is not the engagement, but the severe cold with which I perceive you are afflicted. The vaults are insufferably damp. They are encrusted with nitre."[6]

"Let us go, nevertheless. The cold is merely nothing. Amontillado! You have been imposed upon; and as for Luchesi, he cannot distinguish Sherry from Amontillado."

Thus speaking, Fortunato possessed himself of my arm. Putting on a mask of black silk, and drawing a *roquelaure*[7] closely about my person, I suffered him to hurry me to my palazzo.[8]

There were no attendants at home; they had absconded to make merry in honor of the time. I had told them that I should not return until the morning, and had given them explicit orders not to stir from the house. These orders were sufficient, I well knew, to insure their immediate disappearance, one and all, as soon as my back was turned.

I took from their sconces two flambeaux, and giving one to Fortunato, bowed him through several suites of rooms to the archway that led into the vaults. I passed down a long and winding staircase, requesting him to be cautious as he followed. We came at length to the foot of the descent, and stood together on the damp ground of the catacombs of the Montresors.

The gait of my friend was unsteady, and the bells upon his cap jingled as he strode.

"The pipe," said he.

"It is farther on," said I; "but observe the white web-work which gleams from these cavern walls."

He turned towards me, and looked into my eyes with two filmy orbs that distilled the rheum of intoxication.

---

[6] Nitre is a mineral of potassium nitrate, appearing as a saltlike crust on rocks and stone.

[7] A roquelaure is a short cape.

[8] A palatial residence; a mansion.

"Nitre?" he asked, at length.

"Nitre," I replied. "How long have you had that cough?"

"Ugh! ugh! ugh!—ugh! ugh! ugh!—ugh! ugh! ugh!—ugh! ugh! ugh!—ugh! ugh! ugh!"

My poor friend found it impossible to reply for many minutes.

"It is nothing," he said, at last.

"Come," I said, with decision, "we will go back; your health is precious. You are rich, respected, admired, beloved; you are happy, as once I was. You are a man to be missed. For me it is no matter. We will go back; you will be ill, and I cannot be responsible. Besides, there is Luchesi—"

"Enough," he said; "the cough is a mere nothing; it will not kill me. I shall not die of a cough."

"True—true," I replied; "and, indeed, I had no intention of alarming you unnecessarily—but you should use all proper caution. A draught of this Medoc[9] will defend us from the damps."

Here I knocked off the neck of a bottle which I drew from a long row of its fellows that lay upon the mould.

"Drink," I said, presenting him the wine.

He raised it to his lips with a leer. He paused and nodded to me familiarly, while his bells jingled.

"I drink," he said, "to the buried that repose around us."

"And I to your long life."

He again took my arm, and we proceeded.

"These vaults," he said, "are extensive."

"The Montresors," I replied, "were a great and numerous family."

"I forget your arms."

"A huge human foot d'or, in a field azure; the foot crushes a serpent rampant whose fangs are imbedded in the heel."

"And the motto?"

"*Nemo me impune lacessit.*"[10]

"Good!" he said.

The wine sparkled in his eyes and the bells jingled. My own fancy grew warm with the Medoc. We had passed through walls of piled bones, with casks and puncheons intermingling, into the inmost recesses of the catacombs. I paused again, and this time I made bold to seize Fortunato by an arm above the elbow.

"The nitre!" I said; "see, it increases. It hangs like moss upon the vaults. We are below the river's bed. The drops of moisture trickle among the bones. Come, we will go back ere it is too late. Your cough—"

"It is nothing," he said; "let us go on. But first, another draught of the Medoc."

I broke and reached him a flagon of De Grâve.[11] He emptied it at a breath.

---

[9] Medoc is a red Bordeaux wine made in the Medoc region of southwestern France.

[10] The motto "*Nemo me impune lacessit*" means "No one dare attack me with impunity."

[11] De Grâve is another French wine.

His eyes flashed with a fierce light. He laughed and threw the bottle upwards with a gesticulation I did not understand.

I looked at him in surprise. He repeated the movement—a grotesque one.

"You do not comprehend?" he said.

"Not I," I replied.

"Then you are not of the brotherhood."[12]

"How?"

"You are not of the masons."

"Yes, yes," I said, "yes, yes."

"You? Impossible! A mason?"

"A mason," I replied.

"A sign," he said.

"It is this," I answered, producing a trowel from beneath the folds of my *roquelaure*.

"You jest," he exclaimed, recoiling a few paces. "But let us proceed to the Amontillado."

"Be it so," I said, replacing the tool beneath the cloak, and again offering him my arm. He leaned upon it heavily. We continued our route in search of the Amontillado. We passed through a range of low arches, descended, passed on, and descending again, arrived at a deep crypt, in which the foulness of the air caused our flambeaux rather to glow than flame.

At the most remote end of the crypt there appeared another less spacious. Its walls had been lined with human remains piled to the vault overhead, in the fashion of the great catacombs of Paris. Three sides of this interior crypt were still ornamented in this manner. From the fourth the bones had been thrown down, and lay promiscuously upon the earth, forming at one point a mound of some size. Within the wall thus exposed by the displacing of the bones, we perceived a still interior recess, in depth about four feet, in width three, in height six or seven. It seemed to have been constructed for no especial use within itself, but formed merely the interval between two of the colossal supports of the roof of the catacombs, and was backed by one of their circumscribing walls of solid granite.

It was in vain that Fortunato, uplifting his dull torch, endeavored to pry into the depths of the recess. Its termination the feeble light did not enable us to see.

"Proceed," I said; "herein is the Amontillado. As for Luchesi—"

"He is an ignoramus," interrupted my friend, as he stepped unsteadily forward, while I followed immediately at his heels. In an instant he had reached the extremity of the niche, and finding his progress arrested by the rock, stood stupidly bewildered. A moment more and I had fettered him to the granite. In its surface were two iron staples, distant from each other about two feet, horizontally. From one of these depended a short chain, from the other a padlock. Throwing the links about his waist, it was but the work of a few seconds to secure it. He was

---

[12] The Freemasons are a secret sect of mystical persuasion whose origins go back at least to the 14th century. They were often hounded and imprisoned.

too much astounded to resist. Withdrawing the key I stepped back from the recess.

"Pass your hand," I said, "over the wall; you cannot help feeling the nitre. Indeed it is *very* damp. Once more let me *implore* you to return. No? Then I must positively leave you. But I must first render you all the little attentions in my power."

"The Amontillado!" ejaculated my friend, not yet recovered from his astonishment.

"True," I replied; "the Amontillado."

As I said these words I busied myself among the pile of bones of which I have before spoken. Throwing them aside, I soon uncovered a quantity of building-stone and mortar. With these materials and with the aid of my trowel, I began vigorously to wall up the entrance of the niche.

I had scarcely laid the first tier of masonry when I discovered that the intoxication of Fortunato had in a great measure worn off. The earliest indication I had of this was a low moaning cry from the depth of the recess. It was *not* the cry of a drunken man. There was then a long and obstinate silence. I laid the second tier, and the third, and the fourth; and then I heard the furious vibrations of the chain. The noise lasted for several minutes, during which, that I might hearken to it with the more satisfaction, I ceased my labors and sat down upon the bones. When at last the clanking subsided, I resumed the trowel, and finished without interruption the fifth, the sixth, and the seventh tier. The wall was now nearly upon a level with my breast. I again paused, and holding the flambeaux over the masonwork, threw a few feeble rays upon the figure within.

A succession of loud and shrill screams, bursting suddenly from the throat of the chained form, seemed to thrust me violently back. For a brief moment I hesitated—I trembled. Unsheathing my rapier, I began to grope with it about the recess; but the thought of an instant reassured me. I placed my hand upon the solid fabric of the catacombs, and felt satisfied. I reapproached the wall. I replied to the yells of him who clamored. I re-echoed—I aided—I surpassed them in volume and in strength. I did this, and the clamorer grew still.

It was now midnight, and my task was drawing to a close. I had completed the eighth, the ninth, and the tenth tier. I had finished a portion of the last and the eleventh; there remained but a single stone to be fitted and plastered in. I struggled with its weight; I placed it partially in its destined position. But now there came from out the niche a low laugh that erected the hairs upon my head. It was succeeded by a sad voice, which I had difficulty in recognizing as that of the noble Fortunato. The voice said—

"Ha! ha! ha!—he! he! he!—a very good joke indeed—an excellent jest. We will have many a rich laugh about it at the palazzo—he! he! he!—over our wine—he! he! he!"

"The Amontillado!" I said.

"He! he! he!—he! he! he!—yes, the Amontillado. But is it not getting late? Will not they be awaiting us at the palazzo, the Lady Fortunato and the rest? Let us be gone."

"Yes," I said, "let us be gone."

"*For the love of God, Montresor!*"

"Yes," I said, "for the love of God!"

But to these words I hearkened in vain for a reply. I grew impatient. I called aloud—

"Fortunato!"

No answer. I called again—

"Fortunato!"

No answer still, I thrust a torch through the remaining aperture and let it fall within. There came forth in return only a jingling of the bells. My heart grew sick—on account of the dampness of the catacombs. I hastened to make an end of my labor. I forced the last stone into its position; I plastered it up. Against the new masonry I reerected the old rampart of bones. For the half of a century no mortal has disturbed them. *In pace requiescat!*[13]

Questions

1. Does Montresor (the narrator) give any reasons for wanting to kill Fortunato? Are they very precise?
2. Why has Montresor chosen the night of the carnival for revenge?
3. What is the significance of Fortunato's costume?
4. What is the significance of Montresor's Masonic affiliation?
5. Why does Fortunato laugh?

 Writers on Writing   Edgar Allan Poe

A skillful literary artist has constructed a tale. If wise, he has not fashioned his thoughts to accommodate his incidents; but having conceived, with deliberate care, a certain unique effect to be wrought out, he then invents such incidents—he then combines such events as may best aid him in establishing this preconceived effect. . . . In the whole composition there should be no word written, of which the tendency, direct or indirect, is not to be the one pre-established design. And by such means, with such care and skill, a picture is at length painted which leaves in the mind of him who contemplates it with a kindred art, a sense of the fullest satisfaction. The idea of the tale has been presented, unblemished, because undisturbed; and this is an end unattainable by the novel. Undue brevity is just as exceptionable here as in the poem; but undue length is yet more to be avoided.

---

[13] The Latin "*in pace requiescat*" means "May he rest in peace."

5 ❧ The Pattern of Action—Plot

In casual conversation we often speak of plot as the summary of a story's major action. But plot is far more interesting and important. Plot, properly understood, is an author's choice and arrangement of events in a story. Consequently, it is one of the principal means by which writers give their fiction form, unity, and interest.

Plots don't have to contain violent or earthshaking events. Of course, some stories depict battles, murders, or daring escapes, but most deal with everyday happenings—visiting neighbors, buying a hat, or merely looking out a window. Some critics distinguish between physical and psychological action—what happens to the body and what happens to the mind. Many of the finest writers can invest the simplest actions with great psychological significance. Consequently, you shouldn't judge a plot by how much physical action it contains, but by how effectively the author has chosen events to narrate, how skillfully he or she has ordered those events within the story, and how well that order focuses on significant matters.

Choosing Action to Narrate

No storyteller can narrate everything. Consequently as readers, we constantly draw inferences about events the author has left unstated. For example, here is a detailed paragraph from "The Adventure of the Speckled Band," which at first glance may appear as though it left nothing out:

> It was early April in the year '83 that I awoke one morning to find Sherlock Holmes standing fully dressed, by the side of my bed. He was a late riser as a rule, and as the clock on the mantlepiece showed me that it was a quarter-past seven, I blinked up at him in some surprise, and perhaps just a little resentment, for I was myself regular in my habits.

To make sense of this paragraph, we need to assume that Sherlock Holmes had been asleep, and that he does not sleep fully dressed. If Holmes was in the habit of staying up all night or sleeping in his clothes, then Watson would not have been surprised to see him fully clothed in the morning. We also must assume that Watson considers 7:15 A.M. an early hour for Holmes to be up, but a late hour for himself to be still in bed. But why does Watson feel "a little resentment" at seeing Holmes by his bedside? We again must assume that Watson is proud of rising earlier than Holmes, and is angry that Holmes has discovered him still in bed. Watson might also "resent" having his sleep disturbed, especially by someone who usually stays in bed longer. Finally, we must guess that Holmes awoke Watson and stood there waiting until Watson woke up. Indeed, since Holmes is beside Watson's bed when Watson awakes, we might guess that Holmes shook Watson, rather than knocking at his door or calling to him from a distance. Notice how many inferences we draw from what appears at first to be a very straightforward passage. To be sure, some of these inferences are fairly unimportant. But the point is that when we read any story—no matter how simple it may seem—we are constantly making inferences, whether consciously or unconsciously. Some writers may try to narrow the narrative gaps so that readers don't have to make such large inferences. But no writer can tell a seamless story.

Authors must decide not only which events to narrate, but where the story should begin and end. Arthur Conan Doyle starts "The Adventure of the Speckled Band" by having Sherlock Holmes awaken Dr. Watson, but he could have started the story at any number of other points. For example, Watson might have started by narrating going to bed, or with first seeing Helen Stoner, or even with taking the train to Stoke Moran. Moreover, Doyle also must decide what events to leave out. We learn nothing, for example, about the train trip from Waterloo Station to Leatherhead, although Doyle could have imagined the details of the journey. As you can see, nothing in a story is there by accident, and consequently we may ask why any event or detail is included.

One of the major criteria for judging the quality of stories is the skill of their authors in choosing the best incidents to narrate. Well-written stories contain only those events that are necessary for or improve the effectiveness of the narrative. Good stories do *not* include extraneous or irrelevant material.

🖎 Tips for Writers and Readers

One way to generate ideas for a paper about a story is to explain why a seemingly unimportant or arbitrary event or detail has been placed in the story. Of course, some details serve limited functions, while others are central to the story. Notice how the discussion of the bell-pull becomes important in the Sherlock Holmes story. Don't ignore odd and seemingly insignificant details; you might be able to write a good paper about how they contribute to the overall effectiveness of the story.

The Ordering of Events

Let us look at just two sentences that recount virtually the same events but in different sequences.

1. Mr. Smith went walking and slipped on some ice on the sidewalk; the fall hurt his leg, and he entered his living room limping.
2. Mr. Smith entered his living room limping from a fall he had suffered during his walk when he slipped on some ice.

Sentence #1 orders the events chronologically. One event follows the other; each one is given about the same emphasis. Sentence #2, however, orders the material causally. We are thrust into a scene in which Mr. Smith enters his living room limping, a condition which is explained by recording the earlier events. Mr. Smith's slip on the ice is clearly subordinated to his entrance into the living room.

Though neither sentence is terribly exciting in itself, we can note that Sentence #1 is wordier, more plodding, and less interesting. In short, it lacks focus. A story has *narrative focus* when the less important events are subordinated to the more significant ones. Again we must not suppose that an event is significant merely because violent physical actions occur. A writer, for example, may find more significance in the events that lead up to a murder than in the murder itself. In a short story, focus is very important since the author's aim is maximum narrative efficiency.

Surprise

But focus is only one aspect of plot construction. Plots also arrange events to produce *suspense* and *surprise*. Surprise occurs when authors omit information and then spring events on the unsuspecting reader. As we did before, let us look at two passages that narrate the same central event but lead up to it in different ways.

1. The burglar waited until Mrs. Smith left her house before he entered it. But soon after he entered, he heard her car pull up in the driveway. Then he hid behind the front door and grabbed Mrs. Smith when she entered, holding his hand across her mouth so she could not scream.
2. Mrs. Smith went shopping, but before she arrived at the store, she remembered having left her wallet on her dresser. She drove back home, pulled the car into the drive, opened the door. Then before she knew it, she was grabbed from behind and a hand was placed across her mouth to keep her from screaming for help.

In Passage #2, we are surprised because the author keeps the burglar's presence a secret until it is suddenly thrust into the story. Passage #1 contains no surprises. The reader is allowed to know all of the relevant events as they occur. In fiction, too much knowledge can be very boring.

These two passages illustrate yet another point about fictional surprises. Frequently surprise is a function of point-of-view. In Passage #1 the narrator views the action primarily from the burglar's perspective. Passage #2, however, is narrated primarily from Mrs. Smith's perspective. In Passage #2 the reader is surprised because, like Mrs. Smith, the reader lacks important information. We can now see another advantage of the limited third-person narrator we discussed in Chapter 3. Such a limited narrator helps produce and control narrative surprise.

Suspense

Suspense is closely related to surprise. But in suspenseful situations the reader is allowed to know more of what is happening. We can see the difference by imagining two scenes in a movie. In the first, a person enters a house just as a bomb goes off. There is a great explosion, and the audience jumps in surprise. In the second scene, we see the time bomb ticking away and notice that it will go off in a few minutes. We then see the protagonist approaching the house where the bomb is planted. The time bomb ticks louder. The protagonist is climbing the front steps. The time bomb ticks still louder. The protagonist opens the front door. Will he see the bomb in time to defuse it? The audience is held in suspense.

From an author's perspective, suspense is a far more useful and powerful tool than surprise. The effect of most surprises is short-lived, while a skillful writer can use suspense in order to keep the reader turning pages throughout an entire book to learn what will happen next. Of course, suspense does not have to be so action-packed as the above example of the time bomb. It occurs whenever a reader is kept ignorant of the outcome of an action.

Flashbacks and Foreshadowing

Stories often don't follow simple chronological progressions; they skip around in time. We call a scene which interrupts another scene so that earlier events can be narrated a *flashback*.

It is important to distinguish between exposition and a flashback. Exposition gives the reader information about the character, scene, or action. For example, when Helen Stoner tells Sherlock Holmes that she is living with her stepfather, "who is the last survivor of one of the oldest Saxon families in England, the Roylotts of Stoke Moran, on the western border of Surrey," she is providing exposition. But her account of the night her sister died is a fully developed narrative that breaks the forward motion of the story and therefore could justly be called a flashback.

More subtle than the flashback is *foreshadowing*. A flashback is a jump *back* in time; foreshadowing is a veiled suggestion of what is *ahead* in the future. For example, in "Seventeen Syllables," Mr. Hayashi's angry departure from the Hayano household foreshadows his angry outburst later in the story. On our first reading, we might not clearly see precisely what his jealousy might lead to, but an attentive reader will feel that "something is up." Foreshadowing, if handled properly, is an important element in creating suspense. The reader or audience feels that some crisis is coming without knowing exactly what form the crisis will take. However, obvious foreshadowing, which makes the outcome of events easy to predict, weakens a story's suspense. Foreshadowing is, thus, a powerful narrative tool, but one that must be used with caution.

 Tips for Readers and Writers

When re-reading a story, look for events that foreshadow the conclusion of the story and carefully note them. Such events can help you write about character, narrative structure, or the thematic content of the story. For example, Sally Scott's essay in Chapter 2 is all about how a narrative twist in D. H. Lawrence's "The Horse Dealer's Daughter" is carefully foreshadowed in the earlier parts of the story. Many good papers have been written about the way seemingly "surprise" endings are carefully foreshadowed. Endings that "seem to come out of nowhere" are usually not good endings. Authors usually prepare the ending carefully from the outset of the story.

Conflict

One source of suspense is *conflict*. Conflict occurs when an obstacle blocks a character's pursuit of a goal or when the goals of two characters are opposed. If the forces are equally matched the reader cannot guess whether the character will succeed or fail in overcoming opposition. Traditionally critics have classified three types of conflict: people against nature, person against person, and people against themselves. But there are other possible conflicts. Stanislaw Lem, for example, has written several stories about people in conflict with computers, and in *Black Beauty*, a horse is in conflict with the humans around him.

A character's goals can be quite general and are often unstated. Happiness, comfort, youth, these may be what the character wants. In longer stories, a character's goals may change. In Lawrence's "The Horse Dealer's Daughter" Mabel first wishes to join her mother by committing suicide, but after she is saved she wishes to marry. A character may have a number of goals in conflict with each other. In Grace Paley's "A Conversation with My Father," the narrator wants to write a story that will please both her father and herself.

Narrative Stages

A narrative usually passes through several stages. Near the opening of a story, one usually finds the *exposition*, passages that give the reader basic information about who the characters are, where they are, and what they are doing. Conflict rises as the central character or *protagonist* encounters more and more obstacles in pursuit of his or her goal. The *climax* in fiction occurs at the point when the protagonist has either achieved or failed to achieve the goal. The climax is frequently followed by a *denouement* (which in French means "an untying"). The denouement narrates the consequences of the climax: how the characters respond to the success or failure of the protagonists. For example, in "The Adventure of the Speckled Band" the denouement recounts how Sherlock Holmes came to solve the mystery and tells us about the future of Helen Stoner, the young woman whose life Holmes had saved. Although the narrative stages in fiction are like those in drama, there are some differences. The most significant difference is that the climax in drama occurs when the hero's or protagonists's fortunes are reversed. (See pages 1027–28 for additional commentary.)

Twists and Frames

There are any number of ways that plots can be organized. Two of the most common ways that authors organize stories are by giving them surprise "twist" endings or by "framing" one story by placing it inside another. Stories with twist endings and frames invite particular kinds of reader responses and critical questions that are worth looking at on their own.

Stories with Frames

Stories with frames actually consist of two stories, one inside the other. Frequently the *frame,* or outer story, narrates how a group of people come together and exchange stories. Then one person from the group narrates the *inner story,* or the *tale-within-a-tale.* The work ends by returning to the group and recounting their reactions to the inner story. Occasionally several tales will be joined together by the same framing device. For example, "A Dinner of Hens," which appears in Chapter 1, is a tale-within-a-tale included in Boccaccio's *Decameron,* a collection of 100 stories. The frame of the *Decameron* concerns ten men and women who flee the plague-torn Italian city of Florence and gather in a country villa for safety. To pass the time, they swap stories. Chaucer's *Canterbury Tales* has a similar structure. Pilgrims on the road to Canterbury exchange stories to amuse each other on the long, tedious trip.

Reading the Frame Story

Choosing a frame for a story is much like choosing a frame for a picture. Authors, and art collectors, want their frames to fit properly and suit the subject. A small picture shouldn't be surrounded by something large and gaudy, and a large picture shouldn't have a frame that is thin and weak. Like a picture frame, the story frame exists to enhance the tale within it, to bring out its chief features.

Faced with a framed story, one should pay close attention to the relationship between the inner story and the framing device. The story and the frame are usually related in one or more of the following ways: (1) The theme of the story illustrates, disputes, or enlarges the discussion between the characters in the frame. (2) The inner story is told by a particularly fitting person. Typically, people tell stories about subjects they know and care about. Soldiers tell tales about war, widows about death and dying, sinners about sinning, and the virtuous about virtue. (3) The audience in the frame responds to the tale in a manner appropriate to their personalities. Thus, in the *Decameron* the noble women admonish some of the men for telling bawdy tales, and in *The Canterbury Tales* the drunken miller grows bored by the good knight's courtly tale of honor. (4) The situation in the frame may mirror the situation in the inner tale. For example, in "A Conversation with My Father" the frame shows a daughter trying to adjust herself to her father's values, while in the inner tale a mother adopts her son's values.

Be sure, even when the frame is brief, that you pay attention to it. Frames are an important artistic device, and readers should notice how the story has been clarified and enhanced by the addition of the frame.

 ## Tips for Writers

A question that should generate a good thesis is, "How does the frame of a story alter the story's meaning or effectiveness?" The answer to that question will come more easily if you try to imagine what would happen if the frame were taken away, or as in the case of Paley's "A Conversation with My Father," what is added by including the two drafts of the story-within-the-story.

Stories with a Twist

Stories, as we have mentioned, follow certain conventions—generally recognized rules of procedure. These conventions set up certain expectations. For example, the opening words "Once upon a time . . ." make the reader expect that the story will be a fairy tale. Experienced readers will immediately prepare themselves to hear about princes and princesses, talking animals, elves, fairies, wicked stepmothers, and all the other conventional elements of the fairy tale. Some works, such as TV situation comedies, are so conventional that the experienced viewer can guess what will happen in an entire episode by watching the first five minutes. Such expectations are not necessarily bad; there is a certain satisfaction in getting what you expected, and highly conventional works satisfy those highly predictable appetites.

But writers, on the whole, like a dash of spice in their writing lives. They especially like to play with conventions by giving them a little twist. Frequently, they like to prepare the reader to expect one sort of convention and then provide something else, a surprise that will more than compensate for the loss of the convention. Typically this twist—the unexpected turn of events—will come at the end of a story, but some stories have many twists arranged throughout. In detective fiction such a practice is called "keeping the reader guessing," and it makes for an exciting reading experience.

Good and Bad Twist Endings

Since twist endings are a technique of plotting, some readers have thought that they are manipulative, easy devices to gain attention. In short, they are sometimes regarded as a "cheap trick" of the storytelling trade.

Sometimes the charge is fair. The twist ending may be merely a clever ploy that gives an otherwise lifeless and uninspired story a bit of dash and sparkle. In such a story the surprise comes for no particular reason and illuminates very little of the prior action. The best twist endings, however, develop from possibilities always inherent in the story—possibilities that the reader has not fully recognized or entertained. The twist, thus, clarifies and enriches all that we have read. In "The Night Watchman's Occurrence Book," the surprising twist at the end makes us fully appreciate that behind Hillyard's mild, uneducated façade is a wily intelligence able to take advantage of the situation and gain revenge for the injustices committed against him.

Reading the Twist Ending

The reader should try to evaluate how the twist ending relates to the rest of the story and illuminates the events that precede it. If the twist is made possible by a new element in the plot—the appearance, for example, of a previously unknown letter or character—the result is less likely to suit the entire story, less able to please us after the first surprise. If, however, the twist derives from possibilities of character and situation present all along, the twist will generally delight us after many readings, continuing to shed light on the entire story.

Suggestions for Essayists

1. Discuss a goal that you have formulated for yourself, and the obstacles you must overcome to realize your goal.
2. Humans, it has been said, are in conflict with nature, with other humans, and with themselves. Discuss which is the most serious of those conflicts.
3. Have you ever planned a trip, a dinner, or a party that failed or succeeded because of unforeseen circumstances? Narrate that incident.

Suggestions for Fiction Writers

1. Write two versions of the same story by reversing the order in which you narrate the events.
2. Narrate a personal experience in which partial knowledge led you to be more anxious, worried, or frightened than you needed to be.

3. Place the same character in two different framing situations and have the character tell the same anecdote. What sorts of changes happen to the story depending on its fictional audience?

4. Take a well-known story or anecdote and give a twist to its ending. For example, imagine a version of Little Red Riding Hood in which grandmother rolls out from under the bed at the crucial moment.

ARTHUR CONAN DOYLE (1859–1930)

The Adventure of the Speckled Band

On glancing over my notes of the seventy odd cases in which I have during the last eight years studied the methods of my friend Sherlock Holmes, I find many tragic, some comic, a large number merely strange, but none commonplace; for, working as he did rather for the love of his art than for the acquirement of wealth, he refused to associate himself with any investigation which did not tend towards the unusual, and even the fantastic. Of all these varied cases, however, I cannot recall any which presented more singular features than that which was associated with the well-known Surrey family of the Roylotts of Stoke Moran. The events in question occurred in the early days of my association with Holmes, when we were sharing rooms as bachelors in Baker Street. It is possible that I might have placed them upon record before, but a promise of secrecy was made at the time, from which I have only been freed during the last month by the untimely death of the lady to whom the pledge was given. It is perhaps as well that the facts should now come to light, for I have reasons to know that there are widespread rumours as to the death of Dr. Grimesby Roylott which tend to make the matter even more terrible than the truth.

It was early in April in the year '83 that I woke one morning to find Sherlock Holmes standing, fully dressed, by the side of my bed. He was a late riser, as a rule, and as the clock on the mantelpiece showed me that it was only a quarter-past seven, I blinked up at him in some surprise, and perhaps just a little resentment, for I was myself regular in my habits.

"Very sorry to knock you up, Watson," said he, "but it's the common lot this morning. Mrs. Hudson has been knocked up, she retorted upon me, and I on you."

"What is it, then—a fire?"

"No; a client. It seems that a young lady has arrived in a considerable state of excitement, who insists upon seeing me. She is waiting now in the sitting-room. Now, when young ladies wander about the metropolis at this hour of the morning, and knock sleepy people up out of their beds, I presume that it is something very pressing which they have to communicate. Should it prove to be an interesting case, you would, I am sure, wish to follow it from the outset. I thought, at any rate, that I should call you and give you the chance."

"My dear fellow, I would not miss it for anything."

I had no keener pleasure than in following Holmes in his professional investigations, and in admiring the rapid deductions, as swift as intuitions, and yet always founded on a logical basis, with which he unravelled the problems which were submitted to him. I rapidly threw on my clothes and was ready in a few minutes to accompany my friend down to the sitting-room. A lady dressed in black and heavily veiled, who had been sitting in the window, rose as we entered.

"Good-morning, madam," said Holmes cheerily. "My name is Sherlock Holmes. This is my intimate friend and associate, Dr. Watson, before whom you can speak as freely as before myself. Ha! I am glad to see that Mrs. Hudson has had the good sense to light the fire. Pray draw up to it, and I shall order you a cup of hot coffee, for I observe that you are shivering."

"It is not cold which makes me shiver," said the woman in a low voice, changing her seat as requested.

"What, then?"

"It is fear, Mr. Holmes. It is terror." She raised her veil as she spoke, and we could see that she was indeed in a pitiable state of agitation, her face all drawn and gray, with restless, frightened eyes, like those of some hunted animal. Her features and figure were those of a woman of thirty, but her hair was shot with premature gray, and her expression was weary and haggard. Sherlock Holmes ran her over with one of his quick, all-comprehensive glances.

"You must not fear," said he soothingly, bending forward and patting her forearm. "We shall soon set matters right, I have no doubt. You have come in by train this morning, I see."

"You know me, then?"

"No, but I observe the second half of a return ticket in the palm of your left glove. You must have started early, and yet you had a good drive in a dogcart, along heavy roads, before you reached the station."

The lady gave a violent start and stared in bewilderment at my companion.

"There is no mystery, my dear madam," said he, smiling. "The left arm of your jacket is spattered with mud in no less than seven places. The marks are perfectly fresh. There is no vehicle save a dogcart which throws up mud in that way, and then only when you sit on the left-hand side of the driver."

"Whatever your reasons may be, you are perfectly correct," said she. "I started from home before six, reached Leatherhead at twenty past, and came in by the first train to Waterloo. Sir, I can stand this strain no longer; I shall go mad if it continues. I have no one to turn to—none, save only one, who cares for me, and he, poor fellow, can be of little aid. I have heard of you, Mr. Holmes; I have heard of you from Mrs. Farintosh, whom you helped in the hour of her sore need. It was from her that I had your address. Oh, sir, do you not think that you could help me, too, and at least throw a little light through the dense darkness which surrounds me? At present it is out of my power to reward you for your services, but in a month or six weeks I shall be married, with the control of my own income, and then at least you shall not find me ungrateful."

Holmes turned to his desk and, unlocking it, drew out a small casebook, which he consulted.

"Farintosh," said he. "Ah yes, I recall the case; it was concerned with an opal tiara. I think it was before your time, Watson. I can only say, madam, that I shall be happy to devote the same care to your case as I did to that of your friend. As to reward, my profession is its own reward; but you are at liberty to defray whatever expenses I may be put to, at the time which suits you best. And now I beg that you will lay before us everything that may help us in forming an opinion upon the matter."

"Alas!" replied our visitor, "the very horror of my situation lies in the fact that my fears are so vague, and my suspicions depend so entirely upon small points, which might seem trivial to another, that even he to whom of all others I have a right to look for help and advice looks upon all that I tell him about it as the fancies of a nervous woman. He does not say so, but I can read it from his soothing answers and averted eyes. But I have heard, Mr. Holmes, that you can see deeply into the manifold wickedness of the human heart. You may advise me how to walk amid the dangers which encompass me."

"I am all attention, madam."

"My name is Helen Stoner, and I am living with my stepfather, who is the last survivor of one of the oldest Saxon families in England, the Roylotts of Stoke Moran, on the western border of Surrey."

Holmes nodded his head. "The name is familiar to me," said he.

"The family was at one time among the richest in England, and the estates extended over the borders into Berkshire in the north, and Hampshire in the west. In the last century, however, four successive heirs were of a dissolute and wasteful disposition, and the family ruin was eventually completed by a gambler in the days of the Regency. Nothing was left save a few acres of ground, and the two-hundred-year-old house, which is itself crushed under a heavy mortgage. The last squire dragged out his existence there, living the horrible life of an aristocratic pauper; but his only son, my stepfather, seeing that he must adapt himself to the new conditions, obtained an advance from a relative, which enabled him to take a medical degree and went out to Calcutta, where, by his professional skill and his force of character, he established a large practice. In a fit of anger, however, caused by some robberies which had been perpetrated in the house, he beat his native butler to death and narrowly escaped a capital sentence. As it was, he suffered a long term of imprisonment and afterwards returned to England a morose and disappointed man.

"When Dr. Roylott was in India he married my mother, Mrs. Stoner, the young widow of Major-General Stoner, of the Bengal Artillery. My sister Julia and I were twins, and we were only two years old at the time of my mother's re-marriage. She had a considerable sum of money—not less than £1000 a year—and this she bequeathed to Dr. Roylott entirely while we resided with him, with a provision that a certain annual sum should be allowed to each of us in the event of our marriage. Shortly after our return to England my mother died—she was killed eight years ago in a railway accident near Crewe. Dr. Roylott then abandoned his attempts to establish himself in practice in London and took us to live with him in the old ancestral house at Stoke Moran. The money which my mother had left was enough for all our wants, and there seemed to be no obstacle to our happiness.

"But a terrible change came over our stepfather about this time. Instead of making friends and exchanging visits with our neighbours, who had at first been overjoyed to see a Roylott of Stoke Moran back in the old family seat, he shut himself up in his house and seldom came out save to indulge in ferocious quarrels with whoever might cross his path. Violence of temper approaching to mania has been hereditary in the men of the family, and in my stepfather's case it had, I believe, been intensified by his long residence in the tropics. A series of disgraceful brawls took place, two of which ended in the police-court, until at last he became the terror of the village, and the folks would fly at his approach, for he is a man of immense strength, and absolutely uncontrollable in his anger.

"Last week he hurled the local blacksmith over a parapet into a stream, and it was only by paying over all the money which I could gather together that I was able to avert another public exposure. He had no friends at all save the wandering gypsies, and he would give these vagabonds leave to encamp upon the few acres of bramble-covered land which represent the family estate, and would accept in return the hospitality of their tents, wandering away with them sometimes for weeks on end. He has a passion also for Indian animals, which are sent over to him by a correspondent, and he has at this moment a cheetah and a baboon, which wander freely over his grounds and are feared by the villagers almost as much as their master.

"You can imagine from what I say that my poor sister Julia and I had no great pleasure in our lives. No servant would stay with us, and for a long time we did all the work of the house. She was but thirty at the time of her death, and yet her hair had already begun to whiten, even as mine has."

"Your sister is dead, then?"

"She died just two years ago, and it is of her death that I wish to speak to you. You can understand that, living the life which I have described, we were little likely to see anyone of our own age and position. We had, however, an aunt, my mother's maiden sister, Miss Honoria Westphail, who lives near Harrow, and we were occasionally allowed to pay short visits at this lady's house. Julia went there at Christmas two years ago, and met there a half-pay major of marines, to whom she became engaged. My stepfather learned of the engagement when my sister returned and offered no objection to the marriage; but within a fortnight of the day which had been fixed for the wedding, the terrible event occurred which has deprived me of my only companion."

Sherlock Holmes had been leaning back in his chair with his eyes closed and his head sunk in a cushion but he half opened his lids now and glanced across at his visitor.

"Pray be precise as to details," said he.

"It is easy for me to be so, for every event of that dreadful time is seared into my memory. The manor-house is, as I have already said, very old, and only one wing is now inhabited. The bedrooms in this wing are on the ground floor, the sitting-rooms being in the central block of the buildings. Of these bedrooms the first is Dr. Roylott's, the second my sister's, and the third my own. There is no communication between them, but they all open out into the same corridor. Do I make myself plain?'

"Perfectly so."

"The windows of the three rooms open out upon the lawn. That fatal night Dr. Roylott had gone to his room early, though we knew that he had not retired to rest, for my sister was troubled by the smell of the strong Indian cigars which it was his custom to smoke. She left her room, therefore, and came into mine, where she sat for some time, chatting about her approaching wedding. At eleven o'clock she rose to leave me, but she paused at the door and looked back.

" 'Tell me, Helen,' said she, 'have you ever heard anyone whistle in the dead of the night?'

" 'Never,' said I.

" 'I suppose that you could not possibly whistle, yourself, in your sleep?'

" 'Certainly not. But why?'

" 'Because during the last few nights I have always, about three in the morning, heard a low, clear whistle. I am a light sleeper, and it has awakened me. I cannot tell where it came from—perhaps from the next room, perhaps from the lawn. I thought that I would just ask you whether you had heard it.'

" 'No, I have not. It must be those wretched gypsies in the plantation.'

" 'Very likely. And yet if it were on the lawn, I wonder that you did not hear it also.'

" 'Ah, but I sleep more heavily than you.'

" 'Well, it is of no great consequence, at any rate.' She smiled back at me, closed my door, and a few moments later I heard her key turn in the lock."

"Indeed," said Holmes. "Was it your custom always to lock yourselves in at night?"

"Always."

"And why?"

"I think that I mentioned to you that the doctor kept a cheetah and a baboon. We had no feeling of security unless our doors were locked."

"Quite so. Pray proceed with your statement."

"I could not sleep that night. A vague feeling of impending misfortune impressed me. My sister and I, you will recollect, were twins, and you know how subtle are the links which bind two souls which are so closely allied. It was a wild night. The wind was howling outside, and the rain was beating and splashing against the windows. Suddenly, amid all the hubbub of the gale, there burst forth the wild scream of a terrified woman. I knew that it was my sister's voice. I sprang from my bed, wrapped a shawl round me, and rushed into the corridor. As I opened my door I seemed to hear a low whistle, such as my sister described, and a few moments later a clanging sound, as if a mass of metal had fallen. As I ran down the passage, my sister's door was unlocked, and revolved slowly upon its hinges. I stared at it horror-stricken, not knowing what was about to issue from it. By the light of the corridor-lamp I saw my sister appear at the opening, her face blanched with terror, her hands groping for help, her whole figure swaying to and fro like that of a drunkard. I ran to her and threw my arms round her, but at that moment her knees seemed to give way and she fell to the ground. She writhed as one who is in terrible pain, and her limbs were dreadfully convulsed. At first I thought that she had not recognized me, but as I bent over her she suddenly shrieked out in a voice which I shall never forget, 'Oh, my God! Helen! It was the band! The speckled band!' There was something else which she would fain have said, and she stabbed with her finger into the air in the direction of the doctor's room, but a fresh convulsion seized her and choked her words. I rushed out, calling loudly for my stepfather, and I met him hastening from his room in his dressing–gown. When he reached my sister's side she was unconscious, and though he poured brandy down her throat and sent for medical aid from the village, all efforts were in vain, for she slowly sank and died without having recovered her consciousness. Such was the dreadful end of my beloved sister."

"One moment," said Holmes; "are you sure about this whistle and metallic sound? Could you swear to it?"

"That was what the county coroner asked me at the inquiry. It is my strong impression that I heard it, and yet, among the crash of the gale and the creaking of an old house, I may possibly have been deceived."

"Was your sister dressed?'

"No, she was in her night-dress. In her right hand was found the charred stump of a match, and in her left a match-box."

"Showing that she had struck a light and looked about her when the alarm took place. That is important. And what conclusions did the coroner come to?"

"He investigated the case with great care, for Dr. Roylott's conduct had long been notorious in the county, but he was unable to find any satisfactory cause of death. My evidence showed that the door had been fastened upon the inner side, and the windows were blocked by old-fashioned shutters with broad iron bars, which were secured every night. The walls were carefully sounded and were shown to be quite solid all round, and the flooring was also thoroughly examined, with the same result. The chimney is wide, but is barred up by four large staples. It is certain, therefore, that my sister was quite alone when she met her end. Besides, there were no marks of any violence upon her."

"How about poison?"

"The doctors examined her for it, but without success."

"What do you think that this unfortunate lady died of, then?"

"It is my belief that she died of pure fear and nervous shock, though what it was that frightened her I cannot imagine."

"Were there gypsies in the plantation at the time?"

"Yes, there are nearly always some there."

"Ah, and what did you gather from this allusion to a band—a speckled band?"

"Sometimes I have thought that it was merely the wild talk of delirium, sometimes that it may have referred to some band of people, perhaps to these very gypsies in the plantation. I do not know whether the spotted handkerchiefs which so many of them wear over their heads might have suggested the strange adjective which she used."

Holmes shook his head like a man who is far from being satisfied.

"These are very deep waters," said he; "pray go on with your narrative."

"Two years have passed since then, and my life has been until lately lonelier than ever. A month ago, however, a dear friend, whom I have known for many years, has done me the honour to ask my hand in marriage. His name is Armitage—Percy Armitage—the second son of Mr. Armitage, of Crane Water, near Reading. My stepfather has offered no opposition to the match, and we are to be married in the course of the spring. Two days ago some repairs were started in the west wing of the building, and my bedroom wall has been pierced, so that I have had to move into the chamber in which my sister died, and to sleep in the very bed in which she slept. Imagine, then, my thrill of terror when last night, as I lay awake, thinking over her terrible fate, I suddenly heard in the silence of the night the low whistle which had been the herald of her own death. I sprang up and lit the lamp, but nothing was to be seen in the room. I was too shaken to go to bed again, however, so I dressed, and as soon as it was daylight I slipped down, got a dogcart at the Crown Inn, which is opposite, and drove to Leatherhead, from whence I have come on this morning with the one object of seeing you and asking your advice."

"You have done wisely," said my friend. "But have you told me all?"

"Yes, all."

"Miss Stoner, you have not. You are screening your stepfather."

"Why, what do you mean?"

For answer Holmes pushed back the frill of black lace which fringed the hand that lay upon our visitor's knee. Five little livid spots, the marks of four fingers and a thumb, were printed upon the white wrist.

"You have been cruelly used," said Holmes.

The lady coloured deeply and covered over her injured wrist. "He is a hard man," she said, "and perhaps he hardly knows his own strength."

There was a long silence, during which Holmes leaned his chin upon his hands and stared into the crackling fire.

"This is a very deep business," he said at last. "There are a thousand details which I should desire to know before I decide upon our course of action. Yet we have not a moment to lose. If we were to come to Stoke Moran to-day, would it be possible for us to see over these rooms without the knowledge of your stepfather?"

"As it happens, he spoke of coming into town to-day upon some most important business. It is probable that he will be away all day, and that there would be nothing to disturb you. We have a housekeeper now, but she is old and foolish, and I could easily get her out of the way."

"Excellent. You are not averse to this trip, Watson?"

"By no means."

"Then we shall both come. What are you going to do yourself?"

"I have one or two things which I would wish to do now that I am in town. But I shall return by the twelve o'clock train, so as to be there in time for your coming."

"And you may expect us early in the afternoon. I have myself some small business matters to attend to. Will you not wait and breakfast?"

"No, I must go. My heart is lightened already since I have confided my trouble to you. I shall look forward to seeing you again this afternoon." She dropped her thick black veil over her face and glided from the room.

"And what do you think of it all, Watson?" asked Sherlock Holmes leaning back in his chair.

"It seems to me to be a most dark and sinister business."

"Dark enough and sinister enough."

"Yet if the lady is correct in saying that the flooring and walls are sound, and that the door, window, and chimney are impassable, then her sister must have been undoubtedly alone when she met her mysterious end."

"What becomes, then, of these nocturnal whistles, and what of the very peculiar words of the dying woman?"

"I cannot think."

"When you combine the ideas of whistles at night, the presence of a band of gypsies who are on intimate terms with this old doctor, the fact that we have every reason to believe that the doctor has an interest in preventing his step-daughter's marriage, the dying allusion to a band, and, finally, the fact that Miss Helen Stoner heard a metallic clang, which might have been caused by one of those metal bars that secured the shutters falling back into its place, I think that there is good ground to think that the mystery may be cleared along those lines."

"But what, then, did the gypsies do?"

"I cannot imagine."

"I see many objections to any such theory."

"And so do I. It is precisely for that reason that we are going to Stoke Moran this day. I want to see whether the objections are fatal, or if they may be explained away. But what in the name of the devil!"

The ejaculation had been drawn from my companion by the fact that our door had been suddenly dashed open, and that a huge man had framed himself in the aperture. His costume was a peculiar mixture of the professional and of the agricultural, having a black top-hat, a long frock-coat, and a pair of high gaiters, with a hunting-crop swinging in his hand. So tall was he that his hat actually brushed the cross bar of the doorway, and his breadth seemed to span it across from side to side. A large face, seared with a thousand wrinkles, burned yellow with the sun, and marked with every evil passion, was turned from one to the other of us, while his deep-set, bile-shot eyes, and his high, thin, fleshless nose, gave him somewhat the resemblance to a fierce old bird of prey.

"Which of you is Holmes?" asked this apparition.

"My name, sir; but you have the advantage of me," said my companion quietly.

"I am Dr. Grimesby Roylott, of Stoke Moran."

"Indeed, Doctor," said Holmes blandly. "Pray take a seat."

"I will do nothing of the kind. My stepdaughter has been here. I have traced her. What has she been saying to you?"

"It is a little cold for the time of the year," said Holmes.

"What has she been saying to you?" screamed the old man furiously.

"But I have heard that the crocuses promise well," continued my companion imperturbably.

"Ha! You put me off, do you?" said our new visitor, taking a step forward and shaking his hunting-crop. "I know you, you scoundrel! I have heard of you before. You are Holmes, the meddler."

My friend smiled.

"Holmes, the busybody!"

His smile broadened.

"Holmes, the Scotland Yard Jack-in-office!"

Holmes chuckled heartily. "Your conversation is most entertaining," said he. "When you go out close the door, for there is a decided draught."

"I will go when I have said my say. Don't you dare to meddle with my affairs. I know that Miss Stoner has been here. I traced her! I am a dangerous man to fall foul of! See here." He stepped swiftly forward, seized the poker, and bent it into a curve with his huge brown hands.

"See that you keep yourself out of my grip," he snarled, and hurling the twisted poker into the fireplace he strode out of the room.

"He seems a very amiable person," said Holmes, laughing. "I am not quite so bulky, but if he had remained I might have shown him that my grip was not much more feeble than his own." As he spoke he picked up the steel poker and, with a sudden effort, straightened it out again.

"Fancy his having the insolence to confound me with the official detective force! This incident gives zest to our investigation, however, and I only trust that our little friend will not suffer from her imprudence in allowing this brute to trace her. And now, Watson, we shall order breakfast, and afterwards I shall walk down to Doctors' Commons, where I hope to get some data which may help us in this matter."

It was nearly one o'clock when Sherlock Holmes returned from his excursion. He held in his hand a sheet of blue paper, scrawled over with notes and figures.

"I have seen the will of the deceased wife," said he. "To determine its exact meaning I have been obliged to work out the present prices of the investments with which it is concerned. The total income, which at the time of the wife's death was little short of £1100, is now through the fall in agricultural prices, not more than £750. Each daughter can claim an income of £250, in case of marriage. It is evident, therefore, that if both girls had married, this beauty would have had a mere pittance, while even one of them would cripple him to a very serious extent. My morning's work has not been wasted, since it has proved that he has the very strongest motives for standing in the way of anything of the sort. And now, Watson, this is too serious for dawdling, especially as the old man is aware that we are interesting ourselves in his affairs; so if you are ready, we shall call a cab and drive to Waterloo. I should be very much obliged if you would slip your revolver into your pocket. An Eley's No. 2 is an excellent argument with gentlemen who can twist steel pokers into knots. That and a tooth-brush are, I think, all that we need."

At Waterloo we were fortunate in catching a train for Leatherhead, where we hired a trap at the station inn and drove for four or five miles through the lovely Surrey lanes. It was a perfect day, with a bright sun and a few fleecy clouds in the heavens. The trees and wayside hedges were just throwing out their first green shoots, and the air was full of the pleasant smell of the moist earth. To me at least there was a strange contrast between the sweet promise of the spring and this sinister quest upon which we were engaged. My companion sat in the front of the trap, his arms folded, his hat pulled down over his eyes, and his chin sunk upon his breast, buried in the deepest thought. Suddenly, however, he started, tapped me on the shoulder, and pointed over the meadows.

"Look there!" said he.

A heavily timbered park stretched up in a gentle slope, thickening into a grove at the highest point. From amid the branches there jutted out the gray gables and high roof-tree of a very old mansion.

"Stoke Moran?" said he.

"Yes, sir, that be the house of Dr. Grimesby Roylott," remarked the driver.

"There is some building going on there," said Holmes; "that is where we are going."

"There's the village," said the driver, pointing to a cluster of roofs some distance to the left; "but if you want to get to the house, you'll find it shorter to get over this stile, and so by the foot-path over the fields. There it is, where the lady is walking."

"And the lady, I fancy, is Miss Stoner," observed Holmes, shading his eyes. "Yes, I think we had better do as you suggest."

We got off, paid our fare, and the trap rattled back on its way to Leatherhead.

"I thought it as well," said Holmes as we climbed the stile, "that this fellow should think we had come here as architects, or on some definite business. It may stop his gossip. Good-afternoon, Miss Stoner. You see that we have been as good as our word."

Our client of the morning had hurried forward to meet us with a face which spoke her joy. "I have been waiting so eagerly for you," she cried, shaking hands with us warmly. "All has turned out splendidly. Dr. Roylott has gone to town, and it is unlikely that he will be back before evening."

"We have had the pleasure of making the doctor's acquaintance," said Holmes, and in a few words he sketched out what had occurred. Miss Stoner turned white to the lips as she listened.

"Good heavens!" she cried, "he has followed me, then."

"So it appears."

"He is so cunning that I never know when I am safe from him. What will he say when he returns?"

"He must guard himself, for he may find that there is someone more cunning than himself upon his track. You must lock yourself up from him to-night. If he is violent, we shall take you away to your aunt's at Harrow. Now, we must make the best use of our time, so kindly take us at once to the rooms which we are to examine."

The building was of gray, lichen-blotched stone, with a high central portion and two curving wings, like the claws of a crab, thrown out on each side. In one of these wings the windows were broken and blocked with wooden boards, while the roof was partly caved in, a picture of ruin. The central portion was in little better repair, but the right-hand block was comparatively modern, and the blinds in the windows, with the blue smoke curling up from the chimneys, showed that this was where the family resided. Some scaffolding had been erected against the end wall, and the stone-work had been broken into, but there were no signs of any workmen at the moment of our visit. Holmes walked slowly up and down the ill-trimmed lawn and examined with deep attention the outsides of the windows.

"This, I take it, belongs to the room in which you used to sleep, the centre one to your sister's, and the one next to the main building to Dr. Roylott's chamber?"

"Exactly so. But I am now sleeping in the middle one."

"Pending the alterations, as I understand. By the way, there does not seem to be any very pressing need for repairs at that end wall."

"There were none. I believe that it was an excuse to move me from my room."

"Ah! That is suggestive. Now, on the other side of this narrow wing runs the corridor from which these three rooms open. There are windows in it, of course?"

"Yes, but very small ones. Too narrow for anyone to pass through."

"As you both locked your doors at night, your rooms were unapproachable from that side. Now, would you have the kindness to go into your room and bar your shutters?"

Miss Stoner did so, and Holmes, after a careful examination through the open window, endeavoured in every way to force the shutter open, but without success. There was no slit through which a knife could be passed to raise the bar. Then with his lens he tested the hinges, but they were of solid iron, built firmly into the massive masonry. "Hum!" said he, scratching his chin in some perplexity, "my theory certainly presents some difficulties. No one could pass these shutters if they were bolted. Well, we shall see if the inside throws any light upon the matter."

A small side door led into the whitewashed corridor from which the three bedrooms opened. Holmes refused to examine the third chamber, so we passed at once to the second, that in which Miss Stoner was now sleeping, and in which her sister had met with her fate. It was a homely little room with a low ceiling and a gaping fireplace, after the fashion of old country-houses. A brown chest of drawers stood in one corner, a narrow white-counterpaned bed in another, and a dressing-table on the left-hand side of the window. These articles, with two small wicker-work chairs, made up all the furniture in the room save for a square of Wilton carpet in the centre. The boards round and the panelling of the walls were of brown, worm-eaten oak, so old and discolored that it may have dated from the original building of the house. Holmes drew one of the chairs into a corner and sat silent, while his eyes travelled round and round and up and down, taking in every detail of the apartment.

"Where does that bell communicate with?" he asked at last, pointing to a thick bell-rope which hung down beside the bed, the tassel actually lying upon the pillow.

"It goes to the housekeeper's room."

"It looks newer than the other things?"

"Yes. it was only put there a couple of years ago."

"Your sister asked for it, I suppose?"

"No, I never heard of her using it. We used always to get what we wanted for ourselves."

"Indeed, it seemed unnecessary to put so nice a bell-pull there. You will excuse me for a few minutes while I satisfy myself as to this floor." He threw himself down upon his face with his lens in his hand and crawled swiftly backward and forward, examining minutely the cracks between the boards. Then he did the same with the wood-work with which the chamber was panelled. Finally he walked over to the bed and spent some time in staring at it and in running his eye up and down the wall. Finally he took the bell-rope in his hand and gave it a brisk tug.

"Why, it's a dummy," said he.

"Won't it ring?"

"No, it is not even attached to a wire. This is very interesting. You can see now that it is fastened to a hook just above where the little opening for the ventilator is."

"How very absurd! I never noticed that before."

"Very strange!" muttered Holmes, pulling at the rope. "There are one or two very singular points about this room. For example, what a fool a builder must be to open a ventilator into another room, when, with the same trouble, he might have communicated with the outside air!"

"That is also quite modern," said the lady.

"Done about the same time as the bell-rope?" remarked Holmes.

"Yes, there were several little changes carried out about that time."

"They seem to have been of a most interesting character—dummy bell-ropes, and ventilators which do not ventilate. With your permission, Miss Stoner, we shall now carry our researches into the inner apartment."

Dr. Grimesby Roylott's chamber was larger than that of his stepdaughter, but was as plainly furnished. A camp-bed, a small wooden shelf full of books, mostly of a technical character, an armchair beside the bed, a plain wooden chair against the wall, a round table, and a large iron safe were the principal things which met the eye. Holmes walked slowly round and examined each and all of them with the keenest interest.

"What's in here?" he asked, tapping the safe.

"My stepfather's business papers."

"Oh! you have seen inside, then?"

"Only once, some years ago. I remember that it was full of papers."

"There isn't a cat in it, for example?"

"No. What a strange idea!"

"Well, look at this!" He took up a small saucer of milk which stood on the top of it.

"No; we don't keep a cat. But there is a cheetah and a baboon."

"Ah, yes, of course! Well, a cheetah is just a big cat, and yet a saucer of milk does not go very far in satisfying its wants, I daresay. There is one point which I should wish to determine." He squatted down in front of the wooden chair and examined the seat of it with the greatest attention.

"Thank you. That is quite settled," said he, rising and putting his lens in his pocket. "Hello! Here is something interesting!"

The object which had caught his eye was a small dog lash hung on one corner of the bed. The lash, however, was curled upon itself and tied so as to make a loop of whipcord.

"What do you make of that, Watson?"

"It's a common enough lash. But I don't know why it should be tied."

"That is not quite so common, is it? Ah, me! it's a wicked world, and when a clever man turns his brains to crime it is the worst of all. I think that I have seen enough now, Miss Stoner, and with your permission we shall walk out upon the lawn."

I had never seen my friend's face so grim or his brow so dark as it was when we turned from the scene of his investigation. We had walked several times up and down the lawn, neither Miss Stoner nor myself liking to break in upon his thoughts before he roused himself from his reverie.

"It is very essential, Miss Stoner," said he, "that you should absolutely follow my advice in every respect."

"I shall most certainly do so."

"The matter is too serious for any hesitation. Your life may depend upon your compliance."

"I assure you that I am in your hands."

"In the first place, both my friend and I must spend the night in your room."

Both Miss Stoner and I gazed at him in astonishment.

"Yes, it must be so. Let me explain. I believe that that is the village inn over there?"

"Yes, that is the Crown."

"Very good, Your windows would be visible from there?"

"Certainly."

"You must confine yourself to your room, on pretence of a headache, when your stepfather comes back. Then when you hear him retire for the night, you must open the shutters of your window, undo the hasp, put your lamp there as a signal to us, and then withdraw quietly with everything which you are likely to want into the room which you used to occupy. I have no doubt that, in spite of the repairs, you could manage there for one night."

"Oh, yes, easily."

"The rest you will leave in our hands."

"But what will you do?"

"We shall spend the night in your room, and we shall investigate the cause of this noise which has disturbed you."

"I believe, Mr. Holmes, that you have already made up your mind," said Miss Stoner, laying her hand upon my companion's sleeve.

"Perhaps I have."

"Then, for pity's sake, tell me what was the cause of my sister's death."

"I should prefer to have clearer proofs before I speak."

"You can at least tell me whether my own thought is correct, and if she died from some sudden fright."

"No, I do not think so. I think that there was probably some more tangible cause. And now, Miss Stoner, we must leave you, for if Dr. Roylott returned and saw us our journey would be in vain. Good-bye, and be brave, for if you will do what I have told you you may rest assured that we shall soon drive away the dangers that threaten you."

Sherlock Holmes and I had no difficulty in engaging a bedroom and sitting-room at the Crown Inn. They were on the upper floor, and from our window we could command a view of the avenue gate, and of the inhabited wing of Stoke Moran Manor House. At dusk we saw Dr. Grimesby Roylott drive past, his huge form looming up beside the little figure of the lad who drove him. The boy had some slight difficulty in undoing the heavy iron gates, and we heard the hoarse roar of the doctor's voice and saw the fury with which he shook his clinched fists at him. The trap drove on, and a few minutes later we saw a sudden light spring up among the trees as the lamp was lit in one of the sitting-rooms.

"Do you know, Watson," said Holmes as we sat together in the gathering darkness, "I have really some scruples as to taking you to-night. There is a distinct element of danger."

"Can I be of assistance?"

"Your presence might be invaluable."

"Then I shall certainly come."

"It is very kind of you."

"You speak of danger. You have evidently seen more in these rooms than was visible to me."

"No, but I fancy that I may have deduced a little more. I imagine that you saw all that I did."

"I saw nothing remarkable save the bell-rope, and what purpose that could answer I confess is more than I can imagine."

"You saw the ventilator, too?"

"Yes, but I do not think that it is such a very unusual thing to have a small opening between two rooms. It was so small that a rat could hardly pass through."

"I knew that we should find a ventilator before ever we came to Stoke Moran."

"My dear Holmes!"

"Oh, yes, I did. You remember in her statement she said that her sister could smell Dr. Roylott's cigar. Now, of course that suggested at once that there must be a communication between the two rooms. It could only be a small one, or it would have been remarked upon at the coroner's inquiry. I deduced a ventilator."

"But what harm can there be in that?"

"Well, there is at least a curious coincidence of dates. A ventilator is made, a cord is hung, and a lady who sleeps in the bed dies. Does not that strike you?"

"I cannot as yet see any connection."

"Did you observe anything very peculiar about that bed?"

"No."

"It was clamped to the floor. Did you ever see a bed fastened like that before?"

"I cannot say that I have."

"The lady could not move her bed. It must always be in the same relative position to the ventilator and to the rope—or so we may call it, since it was clearly never meant for a bell-pull."

"Holmes," I cried, "I seem to see dimly what you are hinting at. We are only just in time to prevent some subtle and horrible crime."

"Subtle enough and horrible enough. When a doctor does go wrong he is the first of criminals. He has nerve and he has knowledge. Palmer and Pritchard were among the heads of their profession. This man strikes even deeper, but I think, Watson, that we shall be able to strike deeper still. But we shall have horrors enough before the night is over; for goodness' sake let us have a quiet pipe and turn our minds for a few hours to something more cheerful."

About nine o'clock the light among the trees was extinguished, and all was dark in the direction of the Manor House. Two hours passed slowly away, and then, suddenly, just at the stroke of eleven, a single bright light shone out right in front of us.

"That is our signal," said Holmes, springing to his feet; "it comes from the middle window."

As we passed out he exchanged a few words with the landlord, explaining that we were going on a late visit to an acquaintance, and that it was possible that we might spend the night there. A moment later we were out on the dark road, a chill wind blowing in our faces, and one yellow light twinkling in front of us through the gloom to guide us on our sombre errand.

There was little difficulty in entering the grounds, for unrepaired breaches gaped in the old park wall. Making our way among the trees, we reached the lawn, crossed it, and were about to enter through the window when out from a clump of laurel bushes there darted what seemed to be a hideous and distorted child, who threw itself upon the grass with writhing limbs and then ran swiftly across the lawn into the darkness.

"My God!" I whispered; "did you see it?"

Holmes was for the moment as startled as I. His hand closed like a vise upon my wrist in his agitation. Then he broke into a low laugh and put his lips to my ear.

"It is a nice household," he murmured. "That is the baboon."

I had forgotten the strange pets which the doctor affected. There was a cheetah, too; perhaps we might find it upon our shoulders at any moment. I confess that I felt easier in my mind when, after following Holmes's example and slipping off my shoes, I found myself inside the bedroom. My companion noiselessly closed the shutters, moved the lamp onto the table, and cast his eyes round the room. All was as we had seen it in the daytime. Then creeping up to me and making a trumpet of his hand, he whispered into my ear again so gently that it was all that I could do to distinguish the words:

"The least sound would be fatal to our plans."

I nodded to show that I had heard.

"We must sit without light. He would see it through the ventilator."

I nodded again.

"Do not go asleep; your very life may depend upon it. Have your pistol ready in case we should need it. I will sit on the side of the bed, and you in that chair."

I took out my revolver and laid it on the corner of the table.

Holmes had brought up a long thin cane, and this he placed upon the bed beside him. By it he laid the box of matches and the stump of a candle. Then he turned down the lamp, and we were left in darkness.

How shall I ever forget that dreadful vigil? I could not hear a sound, not even the drawing of a breath, and yet I knew that my companion sat open-eyed, within a few feet of me, in the same state of nervous tension in which I was myself. The shutters cut off the least ray of light, and we waited in absolute darkness. From outside came the occasional cry of a night-bird, and once at our very window a long drawn catlike whine, which told us that the cheetah was indeed at liberty. Far away we could hear the deep tones of the parish clock, which boomed out every quarter of an hour. How long they seemed, those quarters! Twelve struck, and one and two and three, and still we sat waiting silently for whatever might befall.

Suddenly there was the momentary gleam of a light up in the direction of the ventilator, which vanished immediately, but was succeeded by a strong smell of burning oil and heated metal. Someone in the next room had lit a dark-lantern. I heard a gentle sound of movement, and then all was silent once more, though the smell grew stronger. For half an hour I sat with straining ears. Then suddenly another sound became audible—a very gentle, soothing sound, like that of a small jet of steam escaping continually from a kettle. The instant that we heard it, Holmes sprang from the bed, struck a match, and lashed furiously with his cane at the bell-pull.

"You see it, Watson?" he yelled. "You see it?"

But I saw nothing. At the moment when Holmes struck the light I heard a low, clear whistle, but the sudden glare flashing into my weary eyes made it impossible for me to tell what it was at which my friend lashed so savagely. I could, however, see that his face was deadly pale and filled with horror and loathing.

He had ceased to strike and was gazing up at the ventilator when suddenly there broke from the silence of the night the most horrible cry to which I have ever listened. It swelled up louder and louder, a hoarse yell of pain and fear and anger all mingled in the one dreadful shriek. They say that away down in the village, and even in the distant parsonage, that cry raised the sleepers from their beds. It struck cold to our hearts, and I stood gazing at Holmes, and he at me, until the last echoes of it had died away into the silence from which it rose.

"What can it mean?" I gasped.

"It means that it is all over," Holmes answered. "And perhaps, after all, it is for the best. Take your pistol, and we will enter Dr. Roylott's room."

With a grave face he lit the lamp and led the way down the corridor. Twice he struck at the chamber door without any reply from within. Then he turned the handle and entered, I at his heels, with the cocked pistol in my hand.

It was a singular sight which met our eyes. On the table stood a dark-lantern with the shutter half open, throwing a brilliant beam of light upon the iron safe, the door of which was ajar. Beside this table, on the wooden chair, sat Dr. Grimesby Roylott, clad in a long gray dressing-gown, his bare ankles protruding beneath, and his feet thrust into red heelless Turkish slippers. Across his lap lay the short stock with the long lash which we had noticed during the day. His chin was cocked upward and his eyes were fixed in a dreadful, rigid stare at the corner of the ceiling. Round his brow he had a peculiar yellow band, with brownish speckles, which seemed to be bound tightly round his head. As we entered he made neither sound nor motion.

"The band! the speckled band!" whispered Holmes.

I took a step forward. In an instant his strange headgear began to move, and there reared itself from among his hair the squat diamond-shaped head and puffed neck of a loathsome serpent.

"It is a swamp adder!" cried Holmes; "the deadliest snake in India. He has died within ten seconds of being bitten. Violence does, in truth, recoil upon the violent, and the schemer falls into the pit which he digs for another. Let us thrust this creature back into its den, and we can then remove Miss Stoner to some place of shelter and let the county police know what has happened."

As he spoke he drew the dog-whip swiftly from the dead man's lap, and throwing the noose round the reptile's neck he drew it from its horrid perch and, carrying it at arm's length, threw it into the iron safe, which he closed upon it.

Such are the true facts of the death of Dr. Grimesby Roylott, of Stoke Moran. It is not necessary that I should prolong a narrative which has already run to too great a length by telling how we broke the sad news to the terrified girl, how we conveyed her by the morning train to the care of her good aunt at Harrow, of how the slow process of official inquiry came to the conclusion that the doctor met his fate while indiscreetly playing with a dangerous pet. The little which I had yet to learn of the case was told me by Sherlock Holmes as we travelled back next day.

"I had," said he, "come to an entirely erroneous conclusion which shows, my dear Watson, how dangerous it always is to reason from insufficient data. The presence of the gypsies, and the use of the word 'band,' which was used by the poor girl, no doubt to explain the appearance which she had caught a hurried glimpse of by the light of her match, were sufficient to put me upon an entirely wrong scent. I can only claim the merit that I instantly reconsidered my position when, however, it became clear to me that whatever danger threatened an occupant of the room could not come either from the window or the door. My attention was speedily drawn, as I have already remarked to you, to this ventilator, and to the bell-rope which hung down to the bed. The discovery that this was a dummy, and that the bed was clamped to the floor, instantly gave rise to the suspicion that the rope was there as bridge for something passing through the hole and coming to the bed. The idea of a snake instantly occurred to me, and when I coupled it with my knowledge that the doctor was furnished with a supply of creatures from India, I felt that I was probably on the right track. The idea of using a form of poison which could not possibly be discovered by any chemical test was just such a one as would occur to a clever and ruthless man who had had an Eastern training. The rapidity with which such a poison would take effect would also, from his point of view, be an advantage. It would be a sharp-eyed coroner, indeed, who could distinguish the two little dark punctures which would show where the poison fangs had done their work. Then I thought of the whistle. Of course he must recall the snake before the morning light revealed it to the victim. He had trained it, probably by use of the milk which we saw, to return to him when summoned. He would put it through this ventilator at the hour that he thought best, with the certainty that it would crawl down the rope and land on the bed. It might or might not bite the occupant, perhaps she might escape every night for a week, but sooner or later she must fall a victim.

"I had come to these conclusions before ever I had entered his room. An inspection of his chair showed me that he had been in the habit of standing on it, which of course would be necessary in order that he should reach the ventilator. The sight of the safe, the saucer of milk, and the loop of whipcord were enough to finally dispel any doubts which may have remained. The metallic clang heard by Miss Stoner was obviously caused by her stepfather hastily closing the door of his safe upon its terrible occupant. Having once made up my mind, you know the steps which I took in order to put the matter to the proof. I heard the creature hiss as I have no doubt that you did also, and I instantly lit the light and attacked it."

"With the result of driving it through the ventilator."

"And also with the result of causing it to turn upon its master at the other side. Some of the blows of my cane came home and roused its snakish temper, so that it flew upon the first person it saw. In this way I am no doubt indirectly responsible for Dr. Grimesby Roylott's death, and I cannot say that it is likely to weigh very heavily upon my conscience."

Questions

1. Where is the major section of the exposition?
2. How does the placement of the exposition contribute to narrative focus?
3. Where does Doyle place the death scene between the two sisters? How does that placement contribute to the narrative focus?
4. Doctor Roylott enters the story as a surprise. Why does Doyle choose that moment to present him? Could there have been a more appropriate time? Does his presence in Holmes's house alter events? Do we ever see him alive again?
5. Where is the climax of the story? Do we know all the narrative facts by the time of the climax? How does our knowledge or lack of it contribute to the effectiveness of the climax?
6. Why does Holmes refuse to tell Helen Stoner his suspicions about her stepfather? Why does he say only that he prefers to have "clearer proofs"?
7. Could this story have been told in chronological order? Would it have gained in clarity? In narrative focus? What would have happened to the character of Holmes?

HISAYE YAMAMOTO (1921–)

Seventeen Syllables

The first Rosie knew that her mother had taken to writing poems was one evening when she finished one and read it aloud for her daughter's approval. It was about cats, and Rosie pretended to understand it thoroughly and appreciate it no end, partly because she hesitated to disillusion her mother about the quantity and quality of Japanese she had learned in all the years now that she had been going to Japanese school every Saturday (and Wednesday, too, in the summer). Even so, her mother must have been skeptical about the depth of Rosie's understanding, because she explained afterwards about the kind of poem she was trying to write.

See, Rosie, she said, it was a *haiku*, a poem in which she must pack all her meaning into seventeen syllables only, which were divided into three lines of five, seven, and five syllables. In the one she had just read, she had tried to capture the charm of a kitten, as well as comment on the superstition that owning a cat of three colors meant good luck.

"Yes, yes, I understand. How utterly lovely," Rosie said, and her mother, either satisfied or seeing through the deception and resigned, went back to composing.

The truth was that Rosie was lazy; English lay ready on the tongue but Japanese had to be searched for and examined, and even then put forth tentatively (probably to meet with laughter). It was so much easier to say yes, yes, even when one meant no, no. Besides, this was what was in her mind to say:

I was looking through one of your magazines from Japan last night, Mother, and towards the back I found some *haiku* in English that delighted me. There was one that made me giggle off and on until I fell asleep—

It is morning, and lo!
I lie awake, comme il faut,
sighing for some dough.

Now, how to reach her mother, how to communicate the melancholy song? Rosie knew formal Japanese by fits and starts, her mother had even less English, no French. It was much more possible to say yes, yes.

It developed that her mother was writing the *haiku* for a daily newspaper, the *Mainichi Shimbun*, that was published in San Francisco. Los Angeles, to be sure, was closer to the farming community in which the Hayashi family lived and several Japanese vernaculars were printed there, but Rosie's parents said they preferred the tone of the northern paper. Once a week, the *Mainichi* would have a section devoted to *haiku*, and her mother became an extravagant contributor, taking for herself the blossoming pen name, Ume Hanazono.

So Rosie and her father lived for awhile with two women, her mother and Ume Hanazono. Her mother (Tome Hayashi by name) kept house, cooked, washed, and, along with her husband and the Carrascos, the Mexican family hired for the harvest, did her ample share of picking tomatoes out in the sweltering fields and boxing them in tidy strata in the cool packing shed. Ume Hanazono, who came to life after the dinner dishes were done, was an earnest, muttering stranger who often neglected speaking when spoken to and stayed busy at the parlor table as late as midnight scribbling with pencil on scratch paper or carefully copying characters on good paper with her fat, pale green Parker.

The new interest had some repercussions on the household routine. Before, Rosie had been accustomed to her parents and herself taking their hot baths early and going to bed almost immediately afterwards, unless her parents challenged each other to a game of flower cards or unless company dropped in. Now if her father wanted to play cards, he had to resort to solitaire (at which he always cheated fearlessly), and if a group of friends came over, it was bound to contain someone who was also writing *haiku*, and the small assemblage would be split in two, her father entertaining the non-literary members and her mother comparing ecstatic notes with the visiting poet.

If they went out, it was more of the same thing. But Ume Hanazono's life span, even for a poet's, was very brief—perhaps three months at most.

One night they went over to see the Hayano family in the neighboring town to the west, an adventure both painful and attractive to Rosie. It was attractive because there were four Hayano girls, all lovely and each one named after a season of the year (Haru, Hatsu, Aki, Fuyu), painful because something had been wrong with Mrs. Hayano ever since the birth of her first child. Rosie would sometimes watch Mrs. Hayano, reputed to have been the belle of her native village, making her way about a room, stooped, slowly shuffling, violently trembling (*always* trembling), and she would be reminded that this woman, in this same condition, had carried and given issue to three babies. She would look wonderingly at Mr. Hayano, handsome, tall, and strong, and she would look at her four pretty friends. But it was not a matter she could come to any decision about.

On this visit, however, Mrs. Hayano sat all evening in the rocker, as motionless and unobtrusive as it was possible for her to be, and Rosie found the greater part of the evening practically anaesthetic. Too, Rosie spent most of it in the girls' room, because Haru, the garrulous one, said almost as soon as the bows and other greetings were over, "Oh, you must see my new coat!"

It was a pale plaid of grey, sand, and blue, with an enormous collar, and Rosie, seeing nothing special in it, said, "Gee, how nice."

"Nice?" said Haru, indignantly. "Is that all you can say about it? It's gorgeous! And so cheap, too. Only seventeen-ninety-eight, because it was a sale. The saleslady said it was twenty-five dollars regular."

"Gee," said Rosie. Natsu, who never said much and when she said anything said it shyly, fingered the coat covetously and Haru pulled it away.

"Mine," she said, putting it on. She minced in the aisle between the two large beds and smiled happily. "Let's see how your mother likes it."

She broke into the front room and the adult conversation and went to stand in front of Rosie's mother, while the rest watched from the door. Rosie's mother was properly envious. "May I inherit it when you're through with it?"

Haru, pleased, giggled and said yes, she could, but Natsu reminded gravely from the door, "You promised me, Haru."

Everyone laughed but Natsu, who shamefacedly retreated into the bedroom. Haru came in laughing, taking off the coat. "We were only kidding, Natsu," she said. "Here, you try it on now."

After Natsu buttoned herself into the coat, inspected herself solemnly in the bureau mirror, and reluctantly shed it, Rosie, Aki, and Fuyu got their turns, and Fuyu, who was eight, drowned in it while her sisters and Rosie doubled up in amusement. They all went into the front room later, because Haru's mother quaveringly called to her to fix the tea and rice cakes and open a can of sliced peaches for everybody. Rosie noticed that her mother and Mr. Hayano were talking together at the little table—they were discussing a *haiku* that Mr. Hayano was planning to send to the *Mainichi*, while her father was sitting at one end of the sofa looking through a copy of *Life*, the new picture magazine. Occasionally, her father would comment on a photograph, holding it toward Mrs. Hayano and speaking to her as he always did—loudly, as though he thought someone such as she must surely be at least a trifle deaf also.

The five girls had their refreshments at the kitchen table, and it was while Rosie was showing the sisters her trick of swallowing peach slices without chewing (she chased each slippery crescent down with a swig of tea) that her father brought his empty teacup and untouched saucer to the sink and said, "Come on, Rosie, we're going home now."

"Already?" asked Rosie.

"Work tomorrow," he said.

He sounded irritated, and Rosie, puzzled, gulped one last yellow slice and stood up to go, while the sisters began protesting, as was their wont.

"We have to get up at five-thirty," he told them, going into the front room quickly, so that they did not have their usual chance to hang onto his hands and plead for an extension of time.

Rosie, following, saw that her mother and Mr. Hayano were sipping tea and still talking together, while Mrs. Hayano concentrated, quivering, on raising the handleless Japanese cup to her lips with both her hands and lowering it back to her lap. Her father, saying nothing, went out the door, onto the bright porch, and down the steps. Her mother looked up and asked, "Where is he going?"

"Where is he going?" Rosie said. "He said we were going home now."

"Going home?" Her mother looked with embarrassment at Mr. Hayano and his absorbed wife and then forced a smile. "He must be tired," she said.

Haru was not giving up yet. "May Rosie stay overnight?" she asked, and Natsu, Aki, and Fuyu came to reinforce their sister's plea by helping her make a circle around Rosie's mother. Rosie, for once having no desire to stay, was relieved when her mother, apologizing to the perturbed Mr. and Mrs. Hayano for her father's abruptness at the same time, managed to shake her head no at the quartet, kindly but adamant, so that they broke their circle and let her go.

Rosie's father looked ahead into the windshield as the two joined him. "I'm sorry," her mother said. "You must be tired." Her father, stepping on the starter, said nothing. "You know how I get when it's *haiku*," she continued, "I forget what time it is." He only grunted.

As they road homeward silently, Rosie, sitting between, felt a rush of hate for both—for her mother for begging, for her father for denying her mother. I wish this old Ford would crash, right now, she thought, then immediately, no, no, I wish my father would laugh, but it was too late: already the vision had passed through her mind of the green pick-up crumbled in the dark against one of the mighty eucalyptus trees they were just riding past, of the three contorted, bleeding bodies, one of them hers.

Rosie ran between two patches of tomatoes, her heart working more rambunctiously than she had ever known it to. How lucky it was that Aunt Taka and Uncle Gimpachi had come tonight, though, how very lucky. Otherwise she might not have really kept her half-promise to meet Jesus Carrasco. Jesus was going to be a senior in September at the same school she went to, and his parents were the ones helping with the tomatoes this year. She and Jesus, who hardly remembered seeing each other at Cleveland High where there were so many other people and two whole grades between them, had become great friends this summer—he always had a joke for her when he periodically drove the loaded pick-up up from the fields to the shed where she was usually sorting while her mother and father did the packing, and they laughed a great deal together over infinitesimal repartee during the afternoon break for chilled watermelon or ice cream in the shade of the shed.

What she enjoyed most was racing him to see which could finish picking a double row first. He, who could work faster, would tease her by slowing down until she thought she would surely pass him this time, then speeding up furiously to leave her several sprawling vines behind. Once he had made her screech hideously by crossing over, while her back was turned, to place atop the tomatoes in her green-stained bucket a truly monstrous, pale green worm (it had looked more like an infant snake). And it was when they had finished a contest this morning, after she had pantingly pointed a green finger at the immature tomatoes evident in the lugs at the end of his row and he had returned the accusation (with justice), that he had startlingly brought up the matter of their possibly meeting outside the range of both their parents' dubious eyes.

"What for?" she had asked.

"I've got a secret I want to tell you," he said.

"Tell me now," she demanded.

"It won't be ready till tonight," he said.

She laughed. "Tell me tomorrow then."

"It'll be gone tomorrow," he threatened.

"Well, for seven hakes, what is it?" she had asked, more than twice, and when he had suggested that the packing shed would be an appropriate place to find out, she had cautiously answered maybe. She had not been certain she was going to keep the appointment until the arrival of mother's sister and her husband. Their coming seemed a sort of signal of permission, of grace, and she had definitely made up her mind to lie and leave as she was bowing them welcome.

So as soon as everyone appeared settled back for the evening, she announced loudly that she was going to the privy outside, "I'm going to the *benjo!*" and slipped out the door. And now that she was actually on her way, her heart pumped in such an undisciplined way that she could hear it with her ears. It's because I'm running, she told herself, slowing to a walk. The shed was up ahead, one more patch away, in the middle of the fields. Its bulk, looming in the dimness, took on a sinisterness that was funny when Rosie reminded herself that it was only a wooden frame with a canvas roof and three canvas walls that made a slapping noise on breezy days.

Jesus was sitting on the narrow plank that was the sorting platform and she went around to the other side and jumped backwards to seat herself on the rim of a packing stand. "Well, tell me," she said without greeting, thinking her voice sounded reassuringly familiar.

"I saw you coming out the door," Jesus said. "I heard you running part of the way, too."

"Uh-huh," Rosie said. "Now tell me the secret."

"I was afraid you wouldn't come," he said.

Rosie delved around on the chicken-wire bottom of the stall for number two tomatoes, ripe, which she was sitting beside, and came up with a left-over that felt edible. She bit into it and began sucking out the pulp and seeds. "I'm here," she pointed out.

"Rosie, are you sorry you came?"

"Sorry? What for?" she said. "You said you were going to tell me something."

"I will, I will," Jesus said, but his voice contained disappointment, and Rosie fleetingly felt the older of the two, realizing a brand-new power which vanished without category under her recognition.

"I have to go back in a minute," she said. "My aunt and uncle are here from Wintersburg. I told them I was going to the privy."

Jesus laughed. "You funny thing," he said. "You slay me!"

"Just because you have a bathroom *inside*," Rosie said. "Come on, tell me."

Chuckling, Jesus came around to lean on the stand facing her. They still could not see each other very clearly, but Rosie noticed that Jesus became very sober again as he took the hollow tomato from her hand and dropped it back into the stall. When he took hold of her empty hand, she could find no words to protest; her vocabulary had become distressingly constricted and she thought desperately that all that remained intact now was yes and no and oh, and even these few sounds would not easily out. Thus, kissed by Jesus, Rosie fell for the first time entirely victim to a helplessness delectable beyond speech. But the terrible, beautiful sensation lasted no more than a second, and the reality of Jesus' lips and tongue and teeth and hands made her pull away with such strength that she nearly tumbled.

Rosie stopped running as she approached the lights from the windows of home. How long since she had left? She could not guess, but gasping yet, she went to the privy in back and locked herself in. Her own breathing deafened her in the dark, close space, and she sat and waited until she could hear at last the nightly calling of the frogs and crickets. Even then, all she could think to say was oh, my, and the pressure of Jesus' face against her face would not leave.

No one had missed her in the parlor, however, and Rosie walked in and through quickly, announcing that she was next going to take a bath. "Your father's in the bathhouse," her mother said, and Rosie, in her room, recalled that she had not seen him when she entered. There had been only Aunt Taka and Uncle Gimpachi with her mother at the table, drinking tea. She got her robe and straw sandals and crossed the parlor again to go outside. Her mother was telling them about the *haiku* competition in the *Mainichi* and the poem she had entered.

Rosie met her father coming out of the bathhouse. "Are you through Father?" she asked. "I was going to ask you to scrub my back."

"Scrub your own back," he said shortly, going toward the main house.

"What have I done now?" she yelled after him. She suddenly felt like doing a lot of yelling. But he did not answer, and she went into the bathhouse. Turning on the dangling light, she removed her denims and T-shirt and threw them in the big carton for dirty clothes standing next to the washing machine. Her other things she took with her into the bath compartment to wash after her bath. After she had scooped a basin of hot water from the square wooden tub, she sat on the grey cement of the floor and soaped herself at exaggerated leisure,

singing "Red Sails in the Sunset" at the top of her voice and using da-da-da
where she suspected her words. Then, standing up, still singing, for she was
possessed by the notion that any attempt now to analyze would result in spoilage
and she believed that the larger her volume the less she would be able to hear
herself think, she obtained more hot water and poured it on until she was free
of lather. Only then did she allow herself to step into the steaming vat, one leg
first, then the remainder of her body inch by inch until the water no longer
stung and she could move around at will.

She took a long time soaking, afterwards remembering to go around outside
to stoke the embers of the tin-lined fireplace beneath the tub and to throw on
a few more sticks so that the water might keep its heat for her mother, and when
she finally returned to the parlor, she found her mother still talking *haiku* with
her aunt and uncle, the three of them on another round of tea. Her father was
nowhere in sight.

At Japanese school the next day (Wednesday, it was), Rosie was grave and
giddy by turns. Preoccupied at her desk in the row for students on Book Eight,
she made up for it at recess by performing wild mimicry for the benefit of her
friend Chizuko. She held her nose and whined a witticism or two in what she
considered was the manner of Fred Allen; she assumed intoxication and a British
accent to go over the climax of the Rudy Vallee recording of the pub conversation about William Ewart Gladstone; she was the child Shirley Temple piping,
"On the Good Ship Lollipop"; she was the gentleman soprano of the Four
Inkspots trilling, "If I Didn't Care." And she felt reasonably satisfied when
Chizuko wept and gasped, "Oh, Rosie, you ought to be in the movies!"

Her father came after her at noon, bringing her sandwiches of minced ham
and two nectarines to eat while she rode, so that she could pitch right into the
sorting when they got home. The lugs were piling up, he said, and the ripe
tomatoes in them would probably have to be taken to the cannery tomorrow if
they were not ready for the produce haulers tonight. "This heat's not doing
them any good. And we've got no time for a break today."

It *was* hot, probably the hottest day of the year, and Rosie's blouse stuck
damply to her back even under the protection of the canvas. But she worked as
efficiently as a flawless machine and kept the stalls heaped, with one part of her
mind listening in to the parental murmuring about the heat and the tomatoes
and with another part planning the exact words she would say to Jesus when he
drove up with the first load of the afternoon. But when at last she saw that the
pick-up was coming, her hands went berserk and the tomatoes started falling in
the wrong stalls, and her father said, "Hey, hey! Rosie, watch what you're
doing!"

"Well, I have to go to the *benjo*," she said, hiding panic.

"Go in the weeds over there," he said, only half-joking.

"Oh, Father!" she protested.

"Oh, go on home," her mother said. "We'll make out for awhile."

In the privy Rosie peered through a knothole toward the fields, watching as
much as she could of Jesus. Happily she thought she saw him look in the

direction of the house from time to time before he finished unloading and went back toward the patch where his mother and father worked. As she was heading for the shed, a very presentable black car purred up the dirt driveway to the house and its driver motioned to her. Was this the Hayashi home, he wanted to know. She nodded. Was she a Hayashi? Yes, she said, thinking that he was a good-looking man. He got out of the car with a huge, flat package and she saw that he warmly wore a business suit. "I have something here for your mother then," he said, in a more elegant Japanese than she was used to.

She told him where her mother was and he came along with her, patting his face with an immaculate white handkerchief and saying something about the coolness of San Francisco. To her surprised mother and father, he bowed and introduced himself as, among other things, the *haiku* editor of the *Mainichi Shimbun*, saying that since he had been coming as far as Los Angeles anyway, he had decided to bring her the first prize she had won in the recent contest.

"First prize?" her mother echoed, believing and not believing, pleased and overwhelmed. Handed the package with a bow, she bobbed her head up and down numerous times to express her utter gratitude.

"It is nothing much," he added, "but I hope it will serve as a token of our great appreciation for your contributions and our great admiration of your considerable talent."

"I am not worthy," she said, falling easily into his style. "It is I who should make some sign of my humble thanks for being permitted to contribute."

"No, no, to the contrary," he said, bowing again.

But Rosie's mother insisted, and then saying that she knew she was being unorthodox, she asked if she might open the package because her curiosity was so great. Certainly she might. In fact, he would like her reaction to it, for personally, it was one of his favorite *Hiroshiges*.

Rosie thought it was a pleasant picture, which looked to have been sketched with delicate quickness. There were pink clouds, containing some graceful calligraphy, and a sea that was a pale blue except at the edges, containing four sampans with indications of people in them. Pines edged the water and on the far-off beach there was a cluster of thatched huts towered over by pine-dotted mountains of grey and blue. The frame was scalloped and gilt.

After Rosie's mother pronounced it without peer and somewhat prodded her father into nodding agreement, she said Mr. Kuroda must at least have a cup of tea after coming all this way, and although Mr. Kuroda did not want to impose, he soon agreed that a cup of tea would be refreshing and went along with her to the house, carrying the picture for her.

"Ha, your mother's crazy!" Rosie's father said, and Rosie laughed uneasily as she resumed judgment on the tomatoes. She had emptied six lugs when he broke into an imaginary conversation with Jesus to tell her to go and remind her mother of the tomatoes, and she went slowly.

Mr. Kuroda was in his shirtsleeves expounding some *haiku* theory as he munched a rice cake, and her mother was rapt. Abashed in the great man's presence, Rosie stood next to her mother's chair until her mother looked up inquiringly, and then she started to whisper the message, but her mother pushed her gently away and reproached, "You are not being very polite to our guest."

"Father says the tomatoes . . ." Rosie said aloud, smiling foolishly.

"Tell him I shall only be a minute," her mother said, speaking the language of Mr. Kuroda.

When Rosie carried the reply to her father, he did not seem to hear and she said again, "Mother says she'll be back in a minute."

"All right, all right," he nodded, and they worked again in silence. But suddenly, her father uttered an incredible noise, exactly like the cork of a bottle popping, and the next Rosie knew, he was stalking angrily toward the house, almost running in fact, and she chased after him crying, "Father! Father! What are you going to do?"

He stopped long enough to order her back to the shed. "Never mind!" he shouted, "Get on with the sorting!"

And from the place in the fields where she stood, frightened and vacillating, Rosie saw her father enter the house. Soon Mr. Kuroda came out alone, putting on his coat. Mr. Kuroda got into his car and backed out down the driveway onto the highway. Next her father emerged, also alone, something in his arms (it was the picture, she realized), and, going over to the bathhouse woodpile, he threw the picture on the ground and picked up the axe. Smashing the picture, glass and all (she heard the explosion faintly), he reached over for the kerosene that was used to encourage the bath fire and poured it over the wreckage. I am dreaming, Rosie said to herself, I am dreaming, but her father, having made sure that his act of cremation was irrevocable, was even then returning to the fields.

Rosie ran past him and toward the house. What had become of her mother? She burst into the parlor and found her mother at the back window watching the dying fire. They watched together until there remained only a feeble smoke under the blazing sun. Her mother was very calm.

"Do you know why I married your father?" she said without turning.

"No," said Rosie. It was the most frightening question she had ever been called upon to answer. Don't tell me now, she wanted to say, tell me tomorrow, tell me next week, don't tell me today. But she knew she would be told now, that the telling would combine with the other violence of the hot afternoon to level her life, her world to the very ground.

It was like a story out of the magazines illustrated in sepia, which she had consumed so greedily for a period until the information had somehow reached her that those wretchedly unhappy autobiographies, offered to her as the testimonials of living men and women, were largely inventions: Her mother, at nineteen, had come to America and married her father as an alternative to suicide.

At eighteen she had been in love with the first son of one of the well-to-do families in her village. The two had met whenever and wherever they could, secretly, because it would not have done for his family to see him favor her—her father had no money; he was a drunkard and a gambler besides. She had learned she was with child; an excellent match had already been arranged for her lover. Despised by her family, she had given premature birth to a stillborn son, who would be seventeen now. Her family did not turn her out, but she could no longer project herself in any direction without refreshing in them the memory of her indiscretion. She wrote to Aunt Taka, her favorite sister in America, threatening to kill herself if Aunt Taka would not send for her. Aunt Taka hastily arranged a marriage with a young man of whom she knew, but lately arrived from Japan, a young man of simple mind, it was said, but of kindly heart. The young man was never told why his unseen betrothed was so eager to hasten the day of meeting.

The story was told perfectly, with neither groping for words nor untoward passion. It was as though her mother had memorized it by heart, reciting it to herself so many times over that its nagging vileness had long since gone.

"I had a brother then?" Rosie asked, for this was what seemed to matter now; she would think about the other later, she assured herself, pushing back the illumination which threatened all that darkness that had hitherto been merely mysterious or even glamorous. "A half-brother?"

"Yes."

"I would have liked a brother," she said.

Suddenly, her mother knelt on the floor and took her by the wrists. "Rosie," she said urgently, "Promise me you will never marry!" Shocked more by the request than the revelation, Rosie stared at her mother's face. Jesus, Jesus, she called silently, not certain whether she was invoking the help of the son of the Carrascos or of God, until there returned sweetly the memory of Jesus' hand, how it had touched her and where. Still her mother waited for an answer, holding her wrists so tightly that her hands were going numb. She tried to pull free. Promise, her mother whispered fiercely, promise. Yes, yes, I promise, Rosie said. But for an instant she turned away, and her mother, hearing the familiar glib agreement, released her. Oh, you, you, you, her eyes and twisted mouth said, you fool. Rosie, covering her face, began at last to cry, and the embrace and consoling hand came much later than she expected.

Questions

1. Does this story contain any surprises? Did you expect Mr. Hayashi to destroy his wife's prize for the best *haiku?* Did you expect Jesus to kiss Rosie? Did you expect Mrs. Hayashi to ask Rosie to refrain from marrying?
2. Why does Mr. Hayashi destroy the picture? Is his action adequately motivated by the story?
3. Why does Mrs. Hayashi ask Rosie not to marry? Is the request adequately prepared for?
4. What are the similarities between Mrs. Hayashi's personal history and Rosie's relationship to Jesus? How are they different?

D. H. LAWRENCE (1885–1930)

The Horse Dealer's Daughter

"Well, Mabel, and what are you going to do with yourself?" asked Joe, with foolish flippancy. He felt quite safe himself. Without listening for an answer, he turned aside, worked a grain of tobacco to the tip of his tongue and spat it out. He did not care about anything, since he felt safe himself.

The three brothers and the sister sat round the desolate breakfast table, attempting some sort of desultory consultation. The morning's post had given the final tap to the family fortune, and all was over. The dreary dining room itself, with its heavy mahogany furniture, looked as if it were waiting to be done away with.

But the consultation amounted to nothing. There was a strange air of ineffectuality about the three men, as they sprawled at table, smoking and reflecting vaguely on their own condition. The girl was alone, a rather short, sullen-looking young woman of twenty-seven. She did not share the same life as her brothers. She would have been goodlooking, save for the impassive fixity of her face, "bull-dog," as her brothers called it.

There was a confused tramping of horses' feet outside. The three men all sprawled round in their chairs to watch. Beyond the dark holly bushes that separated the strip of lawn from the highroad, they could see a cavalcade of shire horses swinging out of their own yard, being taken for exercise. This was the last time. These were the last horses that would go through their hands. The young men watched with critical, callous look. They were all frightened at the collapse of their lives, and the sense of disaster in which they were involved left them no inner freedom.

Yet they were three fine, well-set fellows enough. Joe, the eldest, was a man of thirty-three, broad and handsome in a hot, flushed way. His face was red, he twisted his black moustache over a thick finger, his eyes were shallow and restless. He had a sensual way of uncovering his teeth when he laughed, and his bearing was stupid. Now he watched the horses with a glazed look of helplessness in his eyes, a certain stupor of downfall.

The great draught-horses swung past. They were tied head to tail, four of them, and they heaved along to where a lane branched off from the highroad, planting their great hoofs floutingly in the fine black mud, swinging their great rounded haunches sumptuously, and trotting a few sudden steps as they were led into the lane, round the corner. Every movement showed a massive, slumbrous strength, and a stupidity which held them in subjection. The groom at the head looked back, jerking the leading rope. And the cavalcade moved out of sight up the lane, the tail of the last horse, bobbed up tight and stiff, held out taut from the swinging great haunches as they rocked behind the hedges in a motion-like sleep.

Joe watched with glazed hopeless eyes. The horses were almost like his own body to him. He felt he was done for now. Luckily he was engaged to a woman as old as himself, and therefore her father, who was steward of a neighboring estate, would provide him with a job. He would marry and go into harness. His life was over, he would be a subject animal now.

He turned uneasily aside, the retreating steps of the horses echoing in his ears. Then, with foolish restlessness, he reached for the scraps of bacon rind from the plates, and making a faint whistling sound, flung them to the terrier that lay against the fender. He watched the dog swallow them, and waited till the creature looked into his eyes. Then a faint grin came on his face, and in a high, foolish voice he said:

"You won't get much more bacon, shall you, you little bitch?"

The dog faintly and dismally wagged its tail, then lowered its haunches, circled round, and lay down again.

There was another helpless silence at the table. Joe sprawled uneasily in his seat, not willing to go till the family conclave was dissolved. Fred Henry, the second brother, was erect, clean-limbed, alert. He had watched the passing of the horses with more sang-froid. If he was an animal, like Joe, he was an animal which controls, not one which is controlled. He was master of any horse, and he carried himself with a well-tempered air of mastery. But he was not master of the situations of life. He pushed his coarse brown moustache upwards, off his lip, and glanced irritably at his sister, who sat impassive and inscrutable.

"You'll go and stop with Lucy for a bit, shan't you?" he asked. The girl did not answer.

"I don't see what else you can do," persisted Fred Henry.

"Go as a skivvy," Joe interpolated laconically.

The girl did not move a muscle.

"If I was her, I should go in for training for a nurse," said Malcolm, the youngest of them all. He was the baby of the family, a young man of twenty-two, with a fresh, jaunty *museau*.[1]

But Mabel did not take any notice of him. They had talked at her and round her for so many years, that she hardly heard them at all.

The marble clock on the mantelpiece softly chimed the half-hour, the dog rose uneasily from the hearthrug and looked at the party at the breakfast table. But still they sat on in ineffectual conclave.

"Oh, all right," said Joe suddenly, apropos of nothing. "I'll get a move on."

He pushed back his chair, straddled his knees with a downward jerk, to get them free, in horsey fashion, and went to the fire. Still he did not go out of the room; he was curious to know what the others would do or say. He began to charge his pipe, looking down at the dog and saying, in a high, affected voice:

"Going wi' me? Going wi' me are ter? Tha'rt goin' further tha that counts on just now, dost hear?"

The dog faintly wagged its tail, the man stuck out his jaw and covered his pipe with his hands, and puffed intently, losing himself in the tobacco, looking down all the while at the dog with an absent brown eye. The dog looked at him in mournful distrust. Joe stood with his knees stuck out, in real horsey fashion.

---

[1] A *museau* is a kind of moustache.

"Have you had a letter from Lucy?" Fred Henry asked of his sister.

"Last week," came the neutral reply.

"And what does she say?"

There was no answer.

"Does she *ask* you to go and stop there?" persisted Fred Henry.

"She says I can if I like."

"Well, then, you'd better. Tell her you'll come on Monday."

This was received in silence.

"That's what you'll do then, is it?" said Fred Henry, in some exasperation.

But she made no answer. There was a silence of futility and irritation in the room. Malcolm grinned fatuously.

"You'll have to make up your mind between now and next Wednesday," said Joe loudly, "or else find yourself lodgings on the curbstone."

The face of the young woman darkened, but she sat on immutable.

"Here's Jack Fergusson!" exclaimed Malcolm, who was looking aimlessly out of the window.

"Where?" exclaimed Joe, loudly.

"Just gone past."

"Coming in?"

Malcolm craned his neck to see the gate.

"Yes," he said.

There was a silence. Mabel sat on like one condemned, at the head of the table. Then a whistle was heard from the kitchen. The dog got up and barked sharply. Joe opened the door and shouted:

"Come on."

After a moment a young man entered. He was muffled up in overcoat and a purple woolen scarf, and his tweed cap, which he did not remove, was pulled down on his head. He was of medium height, his face was rather long and pale, his eyes looked tired.

"Hello, Jack! Well, Jack!" exclaimed Malcolm and Joe. Fred Henry merely said, "Jack."

"What's doing?" asked the newcomer, evidently addressing Fred Henry.

"Same. We've got to be out by Wednesday. Got a cold?"

"I have—got it bad, too."

"Why don't you stop in?"

"*Me* stop in? When I can't stand on my legs, perhaps I shall have a chance." The young man spoke huskily. He had a slight Scotch accent.

"It's a knock-out, isn't it," said Joe, boisterously, "if a doctor goes round croaking with a cold. Looks bad for the patients, doesn't it?"

The young doctor looked at him slowly.

"Anything the matter with *you*, then?" he asked sarcastically.

"Not as I know of. Damn your eyes, I hope not. Why?"

"I thought you were very concerned about the patients, wondered if you might be one yourself."

"Damn it, no, I've never been patient to no flaming doctor, and hope I never shall be," returned Joe.

At this point Mabel rose from the table, and they all seemed to become aware of her existence. She began putting the dishes together. The young doctor looked at her, but did not address her. He had not greeted her. She went out of the room with the tray, her face impassive and unchanged.

"When are you off then, all of you?" asked the doctor.

"I'm catching the eleven-forty," replied Malcolm. "Are you goin' down wi' th' trap, Joe?"

"Yes, I've told you I'm going down wi' th' trap, haven't I?"

"We'd better be getting her in then. So long, Jack, if I don't see you before I go," said Malcolm, shaking hands.

He went out, followed by Joe, who seemed to have his tail between his legs.

"Well, this is the devil's own," exclaimed the doctor, when he was left alone with Fred Henry. "Going before Wednesday, are you?"

"That's the orders," replied the other.

"Where, to Northampton?"

"That's it."

"The devil!" exclaimed Fergusson, with quiet chagrin.

And there was silence between the two.

"All settled up, are you?" asked Fergusson.

"About."

There was another pause.

"Well, I shall miss yer, Freddy, boy," said the young doctor.

"And I shall miss thee, Jack," returned the other.

"Miss you like hell," mused the doctor.

Fred Henry turned aside. There was nothing to say. Mabel came in again, to finish clearing the table.

"What are *you* going to do, then, Miss Pervin?" asked Fergusson. "Going to your sister's, are you?"

Mabel looked at him with her steady, dangerous eyes, that always made him uncomfortable, unsettling his superficial ease.

"No," she said.

"Well, what in the name of fortune *are* you going to do? Say what you mean to do," cried Fred Henry, with futile intensity.

But she only averted her head, and continued her work. She folded the white table-cloth, and put on the chenille cloth.

"The sulkiest bitch that ever trod!" muttered her brother.

But she finished her task with perfectly impassive face, the young doctor watching her interestedly all the while. Then she went out.

Fred Henry stared after her, clenching his lips, his blue eyes fixing in sharp antagonism, as he made a grimace of sour exasperation.

"You could bray her into bits, and that's all you'd get out of her," he said in a small, narrowed tone.

The doctor smiled faintly.

"What's she *going* to do, then?" he asked.

"Strike me if *I* know!" returned the other.

There was a pause. Then the doctor stirred.

"I'll be seeing you to-night, shall I?" he said to his friend.

"Ay—where's it to be? Are we going over to Jessdale?"

"I don't know. I've got such a cold on me. I'll come round to the Moon and Stars, anyway."

"Let Lizzie and May miss their night for once, eh?"

"That's it—if I feel as I do now."

"All's one—"

The two young men went through the passage and down to the back door together. The house was large, but it was servantless now, and desolate. At the back was a small bricked house-yard, and beyond that a big square, graveled fine and red, and having stables on two sides. Sloping, dank, winter-dark fields stretched away on the open sides.

But the stables were empty. Joseph Pervin, the father of the family, had been a man of no education, who had become a fairly large horse dealer. The stables had been full of horses, there was a great turmoil and come-and-go of horses and of dealers and grooms. Then the kitchen was full of servants. But of late things had declined. The old man had married a second time, to retrieve his fortunes. Now he was dead and everything was gone to the dogs, there was nothing but debt and threatening.

For months, Mabel had been servantless in the big house, keeping the home together in penury for her ineffectual brothers. She had kept house for ten years. But previously it was with unstinted means. Then, however brutal and coarse everything was, the sense of money had kept her proud, confident. The men might be foul-mouthed, the women in the kitchen might have bad reputations, her brothers might have illegitimate children. But so long as there was money, the girl felt herself established, and brutally proud, reserved.

No company came to the house, save dealers and coarse men. Mabel had no associates of her own sex, after her sister went away. But she did not mind. She went regularly to church, she attended to her father. And she lived in the memory of her mother, who had died when she was fourteen, and whom she had loved. She had loved her father, too, in a different way, depending upon him, and feeling secure in him, until at the age of fifty-four he married again. And then she had set hard against him. Now he had died and left them all hopelessly in debt.

She had suffered badly during the period of poverty. Nothing, however, could shake the curious sullen, animal pride that dominated each member of the family. Now, for Mabel, the end had come. Still she would not cast about her. She would follow her own way just the same. She would always hold the keys of her own situation. Mindless and persistent, she endured from day to day. Why should she think? Why should she answer anybody? It was enough that this was the end, and there was no way out. She need not pass any more darkly along the main street of the small town, avoiding every eye. She need not demean herself any more, going into the shops and buying the cheapest food. This was at an end. She thought of nobody, not even of herself. Mindless and persistent, she seemed in a sort of ecstasy to be coming nearer to her fulfillment, her own glorification, approaching her dead mother, who was glorified.

In the afternoon she took a little bag, with shears and sponge and a small scrubbing brush, and went out. It was a gray, wintry day, with saddened, dark green fields and an atmosphere blackened by the smoke of foundries not far off. She went quickly, darkly along the causeway, heeding nobody, through the town to the churchyard.

There she always felt secure, as if no one could see her, although as a matter of fact she was exposed to the stare of every one who passed along under the churchyard wall. Nevertheless, once under the shadow of the great looming church, among the graves, she felt immune from the world, reserved within the thick churchyard wall as in another country.

Carefully she clipped the grass from the grave, and arranged the pinky white, small chrysanthemums in the tin cross. When this was done, she took an empty jar from a neighboring grave, brought water, and carefully, most scrupulously sponged the marble headstone and the coping-stone.

It gave her sincere satisfaction to do this. She felt in immediate contact with the world of her mother. She took minute pains, went through the park in a state bordering on pure happiness, as if in performing this task she came into a subtle, intimate connection with her mother. For the life she followed here in the world was far less real than the world of death she inherited from her mother.

The doctor's house was just by the church. Fergusson, being a mere hired assistant, was slave to the countryside. As he hurried now to attend to the outpatients in the surgery, glancing across the graveyard with his quick eyes, he saw the girl at her task at the grave. She seemed so intent and remote, it was like looking into another world. Some mystical element was touched in him. He slowed down as he walked, watching her as if spellbound.

She lifted her eyes, feeling him looking. Their eyes met. And each looked away again at once, each feeling, in some way, found out by the other. He lifted his cap and passed on down the road. There remained distinct in his consciousness, like a vision, the memory of her face, lifted from the tombstone in the churchyard, and looking at him with slow, large, portentous eyes. It *was* portentous, her face. It seemed to mesmerize him. There was a heavy power in her eyes which laid hold of his whole being, as if he had drunk some powerful drug. He had been feeling weak and done before. Now the life came back into him, he felt delivered from his own fretted, daily self.

He finished his duties at the surgery as quickly as might be, hastily filling up the bottle of the waiting people with cheap drugs. Then, in perpetual haste, he set off again to visit several cases in another part of his round, before teatime. At all times he preferred to walk if he could, but particularly when he was not well. He fancied the motion restored him.

The afternoon was falling. It was gray, deadened, and wintry, with a slow, moist, heavy coldness sinking in and deadening all the faculties. But why should he think or notice? He hastily climbed the hill and turned across the dark green fields, following the black cindertrack. In the distance, across a shallow dip in the country, the small town was clustered like smouldering ash, a tower, a spire, a heap of low, raw, extinct houses. And on the nearest fringe of the town, sloping into the dip, was Oldmeadow, the Pervins' house. He could see the stables and the outbuildings distinctly, as they lay towards him on the slope. Well, he would not go there many more times! Another resource would be lost to him, another place gone: the only company he cared for in the alien, ugly little town he was losing. Nothing but work, drudgery, constant hastening from dwelling to dwelling among the colliers and the iron-workers. It wore him out, but at the same time he had a craving for it. It was a stimulant to him to be in the homes of the working people, moving as it were through the innermost body of their life. His nerves were excited and gratified. He could come so near, into the very lives of the rough, inarticulate, powerfully emotional men and women. He grumbled, he said he hated the hellish hole. But as a matter of fact it excited him, the contact with the rough, strongly-feeling people was a stimulant applied direct to his nerves.

Below Oldmeadow, in the green, shallow, soddened hollow of fields, lay a square, deep pond. Roving across the landscape, the doctor's quick eye detected a figure in black passing through the gate of the field, down towards the pond. He looked again. It would be Mabel Pervin. His mind suddenly became alive and attentive.

Why was she going down there? He pulled up on the path on the slope above, and stood staring. He could just make sure of the small black figure moving in the hollow of the failing day. He seemed to see her in the midst of such obscurity, that he was like a clairvoyant, seeing rather with the mind's eye than with ordinary sight. Yet he could see her positively enough, while he kept his eye attentive. He felt, if he looked away from her, in the thick, ugly falling dusk, he would lose her altogether.

He followed her minutely as she moved, direct and intent, like something transmitted rather than stirring in voluntary activity, straight down the field towards the pond. There she stood on the bank for a moment. She never raised her head. Then she waded slowly into the water.

He stood motionless as the small black figure walked slowly and deliberately towards the center of the pond, very slowly, gradually moving deeper into the motionless water, and still moving forward as the water got up to her breast. Then he could see her no more in the dusk of the dead afternoon.

"There!" he exclaimed, "Would you believe it?"

And he hastened straight down, running over the wet, soddened fields, pushing through the hedges, down into the depression of callous wintry obscurity. It took him several minutes to come to the pond. He stood on the bank, breathing heavily. He could see nothing. His eyes seemed to penetrate the dead water. Yes, perhaps that was the dark shadow of her black clothing beneath the surface of the water.

He slowly ventured into the pond. The bottom was deep, soft clay, he sank in, and the water clasped dead cold round his legs. As he stirred he could smell the cold, rotten clay that fouled up into the water. It was objectionable in his lungs. Still, repelled and yet not heeding, he moved deeper into the pond. The cold water rose over his thighs, over his loins, upon his abdomen. The lower part of his body was all sunk in the hideous cold element. And the bottom was so deeply soft and uncertain he was afraid of pitching with his mouth underneath. He could not swim, and was afraid.

He crouched a little, spreading his hands under the water and moving them round, trying to feel for her. The dead cold pond swayed upon his chest. He moved again, a little deeper, and again, with his hands underneath, he felt all around under the water. And he touched her clothing. But it evaded his fingers. He made a desperate effort to grasp it.

And so doing he lost his balance and went under, horribly, suffocating in the foul earthy water, struggling madly for a few moments. At last, after what seemed an eternity, he got his footing, rose again into the air and looked around. He gasped, and knew he was in the world. Then he looked at the water. She had risen near him. He grasped her clothing, and drawing her nearer, turned to take his way to land again.

He went very slowly, carefully, absorbed in the slow progress. He rose higher, climbing out of the pond. The water was now only about his legs; he was thankful, full of relief to be out of the clutches of the pond. He lifted her and staggered on to the bank, out of the horror of wet, gray clay.

He laid her down on the bank. She was quite unconscious and running with water. He made the water come from her mouth, he worked to restore her. He did not have to work very long before he could feel the breathing begin again in her; she was breathing naturally. He worked a little longer. He could feel her live beneath his hands; she was coming back. He wiped her face, wrapped her in his overcoat, looked round into the dim, dark gray world, then lifted her and staggered down the bank and across the fields.

It seemed an unthinkably long way, and his burden so heavy he felt he would never get to the house. But at last he was in the stableyard, and then in the house-yard. He opened the door and went into the house. In the kitchen he laid her down on the hearthrug, and called. The house was empty. But the fire was burning in the grate.

Then again he kneeled to attend to her. She was breathing regularly, her eyes were wide open and as if conscious, but there seemed something missing in her look. She was conscious in herself, but unconscious of her surroundings.

He ran upstairs, took blankets from a bed, and put them before the fire to warm. Then he removed her saturated, earthy-smelling clothing, rubbed her dry with a towel, and wrapped her naked in the blankets. Then he went into the dining-room, to look for spirits. There was a little whisky. He drank a gulp himself, and put some into her mouth.

The effect was instantaneous. She looked full into his face, as if she had been seeing him for some time, and yet had only just become conscious of him.

"Dr. Fergusson?" she said.

"What?" he answered.

He was divesting himself of his coat, intending to find some dry clothing upstairs. He could not bear the smell of the dead, clayey water, and he was mortally afraid of his own health.

"What did I do?" she asked.

"Walked into the pond," he replied. He had begun to shudder like one sick, and could hardly attend to her. Her eyes remained full on him, he seemed to be going dark in his mind, looking back at her helplessly. The shuddering became quieter in him, his life came back in him, dark and unknowing, but strong again.

"Was I out of my mind?" she asked, while her eyes were fixed on him all the time.

"Maybe, for the moment," he replied. He felt quiet, because his strength came back. The strange fretful strain had left him.

"Am I out of my mind now?" she asked.

"Are you?" he reflected a moment. "No," he answered truthfully, "I don't see that you are." He turned his face aside. He was afraid now, because he felt dazed, and felt dimly that her power was stronger than his, in this issue. And she continued to look at him fixedly all the time. "Can you tell me where I shall find some dry things to put on?" he asked.

"Did you dive into the pond for me?" she asked.

"No," he answered. "I walked in. But I went in overhead as well."

There was silence for a moment. He hesitated. He very much wanted to go upstairs to get into dry clothing. But there was another desire in him. And she seemed to hold him. His will seemed to have gone to sleep, and left him, standing there slack before her. But he felt warm inside himself. He did not shudder at all, though his clothes were sodden on him.

"Why did you?" she asked.

"Because I didn't want you to do such a foolish thing," he said.

"It wasn't foolish," she said, still gazing at him as she lay on the floor, with a sofa cushion under her head. "It was the right thing to do. I knew best, then."

"I'll go and shift these wet things," he said. But still he had not the power to move out of her presence, until she sent him. It was as if she had the life of his body in her hands, and he could not extricate himself. Or perhaps he did not want to.

Suddenly she sat up. Then she became aware of her own immediate condition. She felt the blankets about her, she knew her own limbs. For a moment it seemed as if her reason were going. She looked round, with wild eye, as if seeking something. He stood still with fear. She saw her clothing lying scattered.

"Who undressed me?" she asked, her eyes resting full and inevitable on his face.

"I did," he replied, "to bring you round."

For some moments she sat and gazed at him awfully, her lips parted.

"Do you love me, then?" she asked.

He only stood and stared at her, fascinated. His soul seemed to melt.

She shuffled forward on her knees, and put her arms round him, round his legs, as he stood there, pressing her breasts against his knees and thighs, clutching him with strange, convulsive certainty, pressing his thighs against her, drawing him to her face, her throat, as she looked up at him with flaring, humble eyes of transfiguration, triumphant in first possession.

"You love me," she murmured, in strange transport, yearning and triumphant and confident. "You love me. I know you love me, I know."

And she was passionately kissing his knees, through the wet clothing, passionately and indiscriminately kissing his knees, his legs, as if unaware of everything.

He looked down at the tangled wet hair, the wild, bare, animal shoulders. He was amazed, bewildered, and afraid. He had never thought of loving her. He had never wanted to love her. When he rescued her and restored her, he was a doctor, and she was a patient. He had had no single personal thought of her. Nay, this introduction of the personal element was very distasteful to him, a violation of his professional honor. It was horrible to have her there embracing his knees. It was horrible. He revolted from it, violently. And yet—and yet— he had not the power to break away.

She looked at him again, with the same supplication of powerful love, and that same transcendent, frightening light of triumph. In view of the delicate flame which seemed to come from her face like a light, he was powerless. And yet he had never intended to love her. He had never intended. And something stubborn in him could not give way.

"You love me," she repeated, in a murmur of deep, rhapsodic assurance. "You love me."

Her hands were drawing him, drawing him down to her. He was afraid, even a little horrified. For he had, really, no intention of loving her. Yet her hands were drawing him towards her. He put out his hand quickly to steady himself, and grasped her bare shoulder. A flame seemed to burn the hand that grasped her soft shoulder. He had no intention of loving her: his whole will was against his yielding. It was horrible. And yet wonderful was the touch of her shoulders, beautiful the shining of her face. Was she perhaps mad? He had a horror of yielding to her. Yet something in him ached also.

He had been staring away at the door, away from her. But his hand remained on her shoulder. She had gone suddenly very still. He looked down at her. Her eyes were now wide with fear, with doubt, the light was dying from her face, a shadow of terrible grayness was returning. He could not bear the touch of her eyes' question upon him, and the look of death behind the question.

With an inward groan he gave way, and let his heart yield towards her. A sudden gentle smile came on his face. And her eyes, which never left his face, slowly, slowly filled with tears. He watched the strange water rise in her eyes, like some slow fountain coming up. And his heart seemed to burn and melt away in his breast.

He could not bear to look at her any more. He dropped on his knees and caught her head with his arms and pressed her face against his throat. She was very still. His heart, which seemed to have broken, was burning with a kind of agony in his breast. And he felt her slow, hot tears wetting his throat. But he could not move.

He felt the hot tears wet his neck and the hollows of his neck, and he remained motionless, suspended through one of man's eternities. Only now it had become indispensable to him to have her face pressed close to him; he could never let her go again. He could never let her head go away from the close clutch of his arm. He wanted to remain like that for ever, with his heart hurting him in a pain that was also life to him. Without knowing, he was looking down on her damp, soft brown hair.

Then, as it were suddenly, he smelt the horrid stagnant smell of that water. And at the same moment she drew away from him and looked at him. Her eyes were wistful and unfathomable. He was afraid of them, and he fell to kissing her, not knowing what he was doing. He wanted her eyes not to have that terrible, wistful, unfathomable look.

When she turned her face to him again, a faint delicate flush was glowing, and there was again dawning that terrible shining of joy in her eyes, which really terrified him, and yet which he now wanted to see, because he feared the look of doubt still more.

"You love me?" she said, rather faltering.

"Yes." The word cost him a painful effort. Not because it wasn't true. But because it was too newly true, the *saying* seemed to tear open again his newly torn heart. And he hardly wanted it to be true, even now.

She lifted her face to him, and he bent forward and kissed her on the mouth, gently, with the one kiss that is an eternal pledge. And as he kissed her his heart strained again in his breast. He never intended to love her. But now it was over. He had crossed over the gulf to her, and all that he had left behind had shriveled and become void.

After the kiss, her eyes again slowly filled with tears. She sat still, away from him, with her face drooped aside, and her hands folded in her lap. The tears fell very slowly. There was complete silence. He too sat there motionless and silent on the hearthrug. The strange pain of his heart that was broken seemed to consume him. That he should love her? That this was love! That he should be ripped open in this way! Him, a doctor! How they would all jeer if they knew! It was agony to him to think they might know.

In the curious naked pain of the thought he looked again to her. She was sitting there drooped into a muse. He saw a tear fall, and his heart flared hot. He saw for the first time that one of her shoulders was quite uncovered, one arm bare, he could see one of her small breasts; dimly, because it had become almost dark in the room.

"Why are you crying?" he asked, in an altered voice.

She looked up at him, and behind her tears the consciousness of her situation for the first time brought a dark look of shame to her eyes.

"I'm not crying, really," she said, watching him half frightened.

He reached his hand, and softly closed it on her bare arm.

"I love you! I love you!" he said in a soft, low vibrating voice, unlike himself.

She shrank, and dropped her head. The soft, penetrating grip of his hand on her arm distressed her. She looked up at him.

"I want to go," she said. "I want to go and get you some dry things."

"Why?" he said. "I'm all right."

"But I want to go," she said. "And I want you to change your things."

He released her arm, and she wrapped herself in the blanket, looking at him rather frightened. And still she did not rise.

"Kiss me," she said wistfully.

He kissed her, but briefly, half in anger.

Then, after a second, she rose nervously, all mixed up in the blanket. He watched her in her confusion, as she tried to extricate herself and wrap herself up so that she could walk. He watched her relentlessly, as she knew. And as she went, the blanket trailing, and as he saw a glimpse of her feet and her white leg, he tried to remember her as she was when he had wrapped her in the blanket. But then he didn't want to remember, because she had been nothing to him then, and his nature revolted from remembering her as she was when she was nothing to him.

A tumbling, muffled noise from within the dark house startled him. Then he heard her voice:—"There are clothes." He rose and went to the foot of the stairs, and gathered up the garments she had thrown down. Then he came back to the fire, to rub himself down and dress. He grinned at his own appearance when he had finished.

The fire was sinking, so he put on coal. The house was now quite dark, save for the light of a street-lamp that shone in faintly from beyond the holly trees. He lit the gas with matches he found on the mantelpiece. Then he emptied the pockets of his own clothes, and threw all his wet things in a heap into the scullery. After which he gathered up her sodden clothes, gently, and put them in a separate heap on the copper-top in the scullery.

It was six o'clock on the clock. His own watch had stopped. He ought to go back to the surgery. He waited, and still she did not come down. So he went to the foot of the stairs and called:

"I shall have to go."

Almost immediately he heard her coming down. She had on her best dress of black voile, and her hair was tidy, but still damp. She looked at him—and in spite of herself, smiled.

"I don't like you in those clothes," she said.

"Do I look a sight?" he answered.

They were shy of one another.

"I'll make you some tea," she said.

"No, I must go."

"Must you?" And she looked at him again with the wide, strained, doubtful eyes. And again, from the pain of his breast, he knew how he loved her. He went and bent to kiss her, gently, passionately, with his heart's painful kiss.

"And my hair smells so horrible," she murmured in distraction. "And I'm so awful, I'm so awful! Oh, no, I'm too awful." And she broke into bitter, heart-broken sobbing. "You can't want to love me, I'm horrible."

"Don't be silly, don't be silly," he said, trying to comfort her, kissing her, holding her in his arms. "I want you, I want to marry you, we're going to be married, quickly, quickly—tomorrow if I can."

But she only sobbed terribly, and cried:

"I feel awful. I feel awful. I feel I'm horrible to you."

"No, I want you, I want you," was all he answered, blindly, with that terrible intonation which frightened her almost more than her horror lest he should *not* want her.

Questions

1. How does Joe Pervin think of marriage? How do the other characters regard marriage?
2. At the beginning of the story what options does Mabel have for future employment now that Oldmeadow is sold?
3. How does Mabel show her "curious, sullen animal pride"?
4. How does Dr. Fergusson exhibit his "superficial ease"?
5. How do you explain Fergusson's attraction to Mabel?
6. Do Mabel and Fergusson change in the course of the story? If so, how?

GRACE PALEY (1922–)

A Conversation with My Father

My father is eighty-six years old and in bed. His heart, that bloody motor, is equally old and will not do certain jobs any more. It still floods his head with brainy light. But it won't let his legs carry the weight of his body around the house. Despite my metaphors, this muscle failure is not due to his old heart, he says, but to a potassium shortage. Sitting on one pillow, leaning on three, he offers last-minute advice and makes a request.

"I would like you to write a simple story just once more," he says, "the kind de Maupassant wrote, or Chekhov,[1] the kind you used to write. Just recognizable people and then write down what happened to them next."

I say, "Yes, why not? That's possible." I want to please him, though I don't remember writing that way. I *would* like to try to tell such a story, if he means the kind that begins: "There was a woman . . ." followed by plot, the absolute line between two points which I've always despised. Not for literary reasons, but because it takes all hope away. Everyone, real or invented, deserves the open destiny of life.

Finally I thought of a story that had been happening for a couple of years right across the street. I wrote it down, then read it aloud, "Pa," I said, "how about this? Do you mean something like this?"

Once in my time there was a woman and she had a son. They lived nicely, in a small apartment in Manhattan. This boy at about fifteen became a junkie,[2] which is not

---

[1] Guy de Maupassant (1850–1893) and Anton Chekhov (1860–1904) were two masters of short fiction whose works developed finely drawn psychological characters in realistic settings. One of Chekhov's stories, "Lady with Lapdog," appears on pp. 392–404.

[2] A junkie is a heroin user.

unusual in our neighborhood. In order to maintain her close friendship with him, she became a junkie too. She said it was part of the youth culture, with which she felt very much at home. After a while, for a number of reasons, the boy gave it all up and left the city and his mother in disgust. Hopeless and alone, she grieved. We all visit her.

"O.K., Pa, that's it," I said, "an unadorned and miserable tale."

"But that's not what I mean," my father said. "You misunderstood me on purpose. You know there's a lot more to it. You know that. You left everything out. Turgenev[3] wouldn't do that. Chekhov wouldn't do that. There are in fact Russian writers you never heard of, you don't have an inkling of, as good as anyone, who can write a plain ordinary story, who would not leave out what you have left out. I object not to facts but to people sitting in trees talking senselessly, voices from who knows where[4] . . ."

"Forget that one, Pa, what have I left out now? In this one?"

"Her looks, for instance."

"Oh. Quite handsome, I think. Yes."

"Her hair?"

"Dark, with heavy braids, as though she were a girl or a foreigner."

"What were her parents like, her stock? That she became such a person. It's interesting, you know."

"From out of town. Professional people. The first to be divorced in their county. How's that? Enough?" I asked.

"With you, it's all a joke," he said. "What about the boy's father? Why didn't you mention him? Who was he? Or was the boy born out of wedlock?"

"Yes," I said. "He was born out of wedlock."

"For Godsakes, doesn't anyone in your stories get married? Doesn't anyone have the time to run down to City Hall before they jump into bed?"

"No," I said. "In real life, yes. But in my stories, no."

"Why do you answer me like that?"

"Oh, Pa, this is a simple story about a smart woman who came to N.Y.C. full of interest love trust excitement very up to date, and about her son, what a hard time she had in this world. Married or not, it's of small consequence."

"It is of great consequence," he said.

"O.K.," I said.

"O.K. O.K. yourself," he said, "but listen. I believe you that she's good-looking, but I don't think she was so smart."

"That's true," I said. "Actually that's the trouble with stories. People start out fantastic. You think they're extraordinary, but it turns out as the work goes along, they're just average with a good education. Sometimes the other way around, the person's a kind of dumb innocent, but he outwits you and you can't even think of an ending good enough."

---

[3] Ivan Turgenev (1818–1883) is a precursor of the psychological-realist school of Chekhov and Maupassant.
[4] Paley is alluding to her story "Faith in a Tree."

"What do you do then?" he asked. He had been a doctor for a couple of decades and then an artist for a couple of decades and he's still interested in details, craft, technique.

"Well, you just have to let the story lie around till some agreement can be reached between you and the stubborn hero."

"Aren't you talking silly, now?" he asked. "Start again," he said. "It so happens I'm not going out this evening. Tell *the story* again. See what you can do this time."

"O.K.," I said. "But it's not a five-minute job." Second attempt:

Once, across the street from us, there was a fine handsome woman, our neighbor. She had a son whom she loved because she'd known him since birth (in helpless chubby infancy, and in the wrestling, hugging ages, seven to ten, as well as earlier and later). This boy, when he fell into the fist of adolescence, became a junkie. He was not a hopeless one. He was in fact hopeful, an ideologue and successful converter. With his busy brilliance, he wrote persuasive articles for his highschool newspaper. Seeking a wider audience, using important connections, he drummed into Lower Manhattan newsstand distribution a periodical called *Oh! Golden Horse!*[5]

In order to keep him from feeling guilty (because guilt is the stony heart of nine tenths of all clinically diagnosed cancers in America today, she said), and because she had always believed in giving bad habits room at home where one could keep an eye on them, she too became a junkie. Her kitchen was famous for a while—a center for intellectual addicts who knew what they were doing. A few felt artistic like Coleridge and others were scientific and revolutionary like Leary.[6] Although she was often high herself, certain good mothering reflexes remained, and she saw to it that there was lots of orange juice around and honey and milk and vitamin pills. However, she never cooked anything but chili, and that no more than once a week. She explained, when we talked to her, seriously, with neighborly concern, that it was her part in the youth culture and she would rather be with the young, it was an honor, than with her own generation.

One week, while nodding through an Antonioni[7] film, this boy was severely jabbed by the elbow of a stern and proselytizing girl, sitting beside him. She offered immediate apricots and nuts for his sugar level, spoke to him sharply, and took him home.

She had heard of him and his work and she herself published, edited, and wrote a competitive journal called *Man Does Live By Bread Alone*. In the organic heat of her continuous presence he could not help but become interested once more in his muscles, his arteries, and nerve connections. In fact he began to love them, treasure them, praise them with funny little songs in *Man Does Live* . . .

> the fingers of my flesh transcend
> my transcendental soul
> the tightness in my shoulders end
> my teeth have made me whole

---

[5] Horse is a slang term for heroin.

[6] Samuel Taylor Coleridge (1772–1834) was an English poet and essayist who suffered from opium addiction. Dr. Timothy Leary (1920–), former Harvard lecturer in psychology, became known during the 1960s for his experiments with psychedelic drugs.

[7] Michelangelo Antonioni (1912–) is an experimental Italian filmmaker; *Blow-up* (1966) made him famous in the United States.

To the mouth of his head (that glory of will and determination) he brought hard apples, nuts, wheat germ, and soybean oil. He said to his old friends, From now on, I guess I'll keep my wits about me. I'm going on the natch. He said he was about to begin a spiritual deep-breathing journey. How about you too, Mom? he asked kindly.

His conversion was so radiant, splendid, that neighborhood kids his age began to say that he had never been a real addict at all, only a journalist along for the smell of the story. The mother tried several times to give up what had become without her son and his friends a lonely habit. This effort only brought it to supportable levels. The boy and his girl took their electronic mimeograph and moved to the bushy edge of another borough. They were very strict. They said they would not see her again until she had been off drugs for sixty days.

At home alone in the evening, weeping, the mother read and reread the seven issues of *Oh! Golden Horse!* They seemed to her as truthful as ever. We often crossed the street to visit and console. But if we mentioned any of our children who were at college or in the hospital or dropouts at home, she would cry out, My baby! My baby! and burst into terrible, face-scarring, time-consuming tears. The End.

First my father was silent, then he said, "Number One: You have a nice sense of humor. Number Two: I see you can't tell a plain story. So don't waste time." Then he said sadly, "Number Three: I suppose that means she was alone, she was left like that, his mother. Alone. Probably sick?"

I said, "Yes."

"Poor woman. Poor girl, to be born in a time of fools, to live among fools. The end. The end. You were right to put that down. The end."

I didn't want to argue, but I had to say, "Well, it is not necessarily the end, Pa."

"Yes," he said, "what a tragedy. The end of a person."

"No, Pa," I begged him. "It doesn't have to be. She's only about forty. She could be a hundred different things in this world as time goes on. A teacher or a social worker. An ex-junkie! Sometimes it's better than having a master's in education."

"Jokes," he said. "As a writer that's your main trouble. You don't want to recognize it. Tragedy! Plain tragedy! Historical tragedy! No hope. The end."

"Oh, Pa," I said. "She could change."

"In your own life, too, you have to look it in the face." He took a couple of nitroglycerin.[8] "Turn to five," he said, pointing to the dial on the oxygen tank. He inserted the tubes into his nostrils and breathed deep. He closed his eyes and said, "No."

I had promised the family to always let him have the last word when arguing, but in this case I had a different responsibility. That woman lives across the street. She's my knowledge and my invention. I'm sorry for her. I'm not going to leave her there in that house crying. (Actually neither would Life, which unlike me has no pity.)

---

[8] Nitroglycerine is not only an explosive but also a drug for the treatment of some types of heart disease.

Therefore: She did change. Of course her son never came home again. But right now, she's the receptionist in a storefront community clinic in the East Village.[9] Most of the customers are young people, some old friends. The head doctor has said to her, "If we only had three people in this clinic with your experiences . . ."

"The doctor said that?" My father took the oxygen tubes out of his nostrils and said, "Jokes. Jokes again."

"No, Pa, it could really happen that way, it's a funny world nowadays."

"No," he said. "Truth first. She will slide back. A person must have character. She does not."

"No, Pa," I said. "That's it. She's got a job. Forget it. She's in that storefront working."

"How long will it be?" he asked. "Tragedy! You too. When will you look it in the face?"

Questions

1. In what ways does the frame mirror the story of the junkie?
2. In the inner story the mother wants to be a part of the son's world. Does anything in the frame mirror that desire?
3. In the inner story the mother becomes dependent on heroin. Is there a parallel in the frame?
4. Does the inner story depict the narrator's belief that "everyone, real or invented, deserves the open destiny of life"?
5. Does the narrator's belief in an "open destiny" relate to the conventions of character consistency, flat and round characters?
6. Has the narrator failed to look tragedy "in the face"? Does such a failure in the inner story relate to a similar "failure" in the frame?
7. Who are the realists in the story? In life?

ALICE WALKER (1944–)

Everyday Use

for your grandmama

I will wait for her in the yard that Maggie and I made so clean and wavy yesterday afternoon. A yard like this is more comfortable than most people know. It is not just a yard. It is like an extended living room. When the hard clay is swept clean as a floor and the fine sand around the edges lined with tiny, irregular grooves, anyone can come and sit and look up into the elm tree and wait for the breezes that never come inside the house.

Maggie will be nervous until after her sister goes: she will stand hopelessly in corners, homely and ashamed of the burn scars down her arms and legs, eying

---

[9] The East Village, a poor section of New York City, was one of the centers of the youth movement.

Alice Walker (*UPI/Bettmann Newsphotos*)

her sister with a mixture of envy and awe. She thinks her sister has held life always in the palm of one hand, that "no" is a word the world never learned to say to her.

You've no doubt seen those TV shows where the child who has "made it" is confronted, as a surprise, by her own mother and father, tottering in weakly from backstage. (A pleasant surprise, of course: What would they do if parent and child came on the show only to curse out and insult each other?) On TV mother and child embrace and smile into each other's faces. Sometimes the mother and father weep, the child wraps them in her arms and leans across the table to tell how she would not have made it without their help. I have seen these programs.

Sometimes I dream a dream in which Dee and I are suddenly brought to-gether on a TV program of this sort. Out of a dark and soft-seated limousine I am ushered into a bright room filled with many people. There I meet a smiling, gray, sporty man like Johnny Carson who shakes my hand and tells me what a fine girl I have. Then we are on the stage and Dee is embracing me with tears in her eyes. She pins on my dress a large orchid, even though she has told me once that she thinks orchids are tacky flowers.

In real life I am a large, big-boned woman with rough, man-working hands. In the winter I wear flannel nightgowns to bed and overalls during the day. I can kill and clean a hog as mercilessly as a man. My fat keeps me hot in zero weather. I can work outside all day, breaking ice to get water for washing; I can eat pork liver cooked over the open fire minutes after it comes steaming from the hog. One winter I knocked a bull calf straight in the brain between the eyes with a sledge hammer and had the meat hung up to chill before nightfall. But of course all this does not show on television. I am the way my daughter would want me to be: a hundred pounds lighter, my skin like an uncooked barley pancake. My hair glistens in the hot bright lights. Johnny Carson has much to do to keep up with my quick and witty tongue.

But that is a mistake. I know even before I wake up. Who ever knew a Johnson with a quick tongue? Who can even imagine me looking a strange white man in the eye? It seems to me I have talked to them always with one foot raised in flight, with my head turned in whichever way is farthest from them. Dee, though. She would always look anyone in the eye. Hesitation was no part of her nature.

"How do I look, Mama?" Maggie says, showing just enough of her thin body enveloped in pink skirt and red blouse for me to know she's there, almost hidden by the door.

"Come out into the yard," I say.

Have you ever seen a lame animal, perhaps a dog run over by some careless person rich enough to own a car, sidle up to someone who is ignorant enough to be kind to him? That is the way my Maggie walks. She has been like this, chin on chest, eyes on ground, feet in shuffle, ever since the fire that burned the other house to the ground.

Dee is lighter than Maggie, with nicer hair and a fuller figure. She's a woman now, though sometimes I forget. How long ago was it that the other house burned? Ten, twelve years? Sometimes I can still hear the flames and feel Maggie's arms sticking to me, her hair smoking and her dress falling off her in little black papery flakes. Her eyes seemed stretched open, blazed open by the flames reflected in them. And Dee. I see her standing off under the sweet gum tree she used to dig gum out of; a look of concentration on her face as she watched the last dingy gray board of the house fall in toward the red-hot brick chimney. Why don't you do a dance around the ashes? I'd wanted to ask her. She had hated the house that much.

I used to think she hated Maggie, too. But that was before we raised the money, the church and me, to send her to Augusta to school. She used to read to us without pity; forcing words, lies, other folks' habits, whole lives upon us two, sitting trapped and ignorant underneath her voice. She washed us in a river of make-believe, burned us with a lot of knowledge we didn't necessarily need to know. Pressed us to her with the serious way she read, to shove us away at just the moment, like dimwits, we seemed about to understand.

Dee wanted nice things. A yellow organdy dress to wear to her graduation from high school; black pumps to match a green suit she'd made from an old suit somebody gave me. She was determined to stare down any disaster in her efforts. Her eyelids would not flicker for minutes at a time. Often I fought off the temptation to shake her. At sixteen she had a style of her own, and knew what style was.

I never had an education myself. After second grade the school was closed down. Don't ask me why: in 1927 colored asked fewer questions than they do now. Sometimes Maggie reads to me. She stumbles along good-naturedly but can't see well. She knows she is not bright. Like good looks and money, quickness passed her by. She will marry John Thomas (who has mossy teeth in an earnest face) and then I'll be free to sit here and I guess just sing church songs to myself. Although I never was a good singer. Never could carry a tune. I was always better at a man's job. I used to love to milk till I was hooked in the side in '49. Cows are soothing and slow and don't bother you, unless you try to milk them the wrong way.

I have deliberately turned my back on the house. It is three rooms, just like the one that burned, except the roof is tin; they don't make shingle roofs any more. There are no real windows, just some holes cut in the sides, like the portholes in a ship, but not round and not square, with rawhide holding the shutters up on the outside. This house is in a pasture, too, like the other one. No doubt when Dee sees it she will want to tear it down. She wrote me once that no matter where we "choose" to live, she will manage to come see us. But she will never bring her friends. Maggie and I thought about this and Maggie asked me, "Mama, when did Dee ever *have* any friends?"

She had a few. Furtive boys in pink shirts hanging about on washday after school. Nervous girls who never laughed. Impressed with her they worshiped the well-turned phrase, the cute shape, the scalding humor that erupted like bubbles in lye. She read to them.

When she was courting Jimmy T she didn't have much time to pay to us, but turned all her faultfinding power on him. He *flew* to marry a cheap city girl from a family of ignorant flashy people. She hardly had time to recompose herself.

When she comes I will meet—but there they are!

Maggie attempts to make a dash for the house, in her shuffling way, but I stay her with my hand. "Come back here," I say. And she stops and tries to dig a well in the sand with her toe.

It is hard to see them clearly through the strong sun. But even the first glimpse of leg out of the car tells me it is Dee. Her feet were always neat-looking, as if God himself had shaped them with a certain style. From the other side of the car comes a short, stocky man. Hair is all over his head a foot long and hanging from his chin like a kinky mule tail. I hear Maggie suck in her breath. "Uhnnnh," is what it sounds like. Like when you see the wriggling end of a snake just in front of your foot on the road. "Uhnnnh."

Dee next. A dress down to the ground, in this hot weather. A dress so loud it hurts my eyes. There are yellows and oranges enough to throw back the light of the sun. I feel my whole face warming from the heat waves it throws out. Earrings gold, too, and hanging down to her shoulders. Bracelets dangling and making noises when she moves her arm up to shake the folds of the dress out of her armpits. The dress is loose and flows, and as she walks closer, I like it. I hear Maggie go "Uhnnnh" again. It is her sister's hair. It stands straight up like the wool on a sheep. It is black as night and around the edges are two long pigtails that rope about like small lizards disappearing behind her ears.

"Wa-su-zo-Tean-o!"[1] she says, coming on in that gliding way the dress makes her move. The short stocky fellow with the hair to his navel is all grinning and he follows up with "Asalamalakim,[2] my mother and sister!" He moves to hug Maggie but she falls back, right up against the back of my chair. I feel her trembling there and when I look up I see the perspiration falling off her chin.

"Don't get up," says Dee. Since I am stout it takes something of a push. You can see me trying to move a second or two before I make it. She turns, showing white heels through her sandals, and goes back to the car. Out she peeks next with a Polaroid. She stoops down quickly and lines up picture after picture of me sitting there in front of the house with Maggie cowering behind me. She never takes a shot without making sure the house is included. When a cow comes nibbling around the edge of the yard she snaps it and me and Maggie *and* the house. Then she puts the Polaroid in the back seat of the car, and comes up and kisses me on the forehead.

Meanwhile Asalamalakim is going through motions with Maggie's hand. Maggie's hand is as limp as a fish, and probably as cold, despite the sweat, and she keeps trying to pull it back. It looks like Asalamalakim wants to shake hands but wants to do it fancy. Or maybe he don't know how people shake hands. Anyhow, he soon gives up on Maggie.

"Well," I say. "Dee."

"No, Mama," she says. "Not 'Dee,' Wangero Leewanika Kemanjo!"

"What happened to 'Dee'?" I wanted to know.

"She's dead," Wangero said. "I couldn't bear it any longer, being named after the people who oppress me."

"You know as well as me you was named after your aunt Dicie," I said. Dicie is my sister. She named Dee. We called her "Big Dee" after Dee was born.

"But who was *she* named after?" asked Wangero.

"I guess after Grandma Dee," I said.

"And who was she named after?" asked Wangero.

"Her mother," I said, and saw Wangero was getting tired. "That's about as far back as I can trace it," I said. Though, in fact, I probably could have carried it back beyond the Civil War through the branches.

"Well," said Asalamalakim, "there you are."

"Uhnnnh," I heard Maggie say.

---

[1] *Wa-su-zo-Tean-o!* is a salutation in Swahili, an African language. Notice that Dee has to sound it out, syllable by syllable.

[2] *Asalamalakin* is a salutation in Arabic: "Peace be upon you."

"There I was not," I said, "before 'Dicie' cropped up in our family, so why should I try to trace it that far back?"

He just stood there grinning, looking down on me like somebody inspecting a Model A car.[3] Every once in a while he and Wangero sent eye signals over my head.

"How do you pronounce this name?" I asked.

"You don't have to call me by it if you don't want to," said Wangero.

"Why shouldn't I?" I asked. "If that's what you want us to call you, we'll call you."

"I know it might sound awkward at first," said Wangero.

"I'll get used to it," I said. "Ream it out again."

Well, soon we got the name out of the way. Asalamalakim had a name twice as long and three times as hard. After I tripped over it two or three times he told me to just call him Hakim-a-barber. I wanted to ask him was he a barber, but I didn't really think he was, so I didn't ask.

"You must belong to those beef-cattle peoples down the road," I said. They said "Asalamalakim" when they met you, too, but they didn't shake hands. Always too busy: feeding the cattle, fixing the fences, putting up salt-lick shelters, throwing down hay. When the white folks poisoned some of the herd the men stayed up all night with rifles in their hands. I walked a mile and a half just to see the sight.

Hakim-a-barber said, "I accept some of their doctrines, but farming and raising cattle is not my style." (They didn't tell me, and I didn't ask, whether Wangero (Dee) had really gone and married him.)

We sat down to eat and right away he said he didn't eat collards and pork was unclean. Wangero, though, went on through the chitlins and corn bread, the greens and everything else. She talked a blue streak over the sweet potatoes. Everything delighted her. Even the fact that we still used the benches her daddy made for the table when we couldn't afford to buy chairs.

"Oh, Mama!" she cried. Then turned to Hakim-a-barber. "I never knew how lovely these benches are. You can feel the rump prints," she said, running her hands underneath her and along the bench. Then she gave a sigh and her hand closed over Grandma Dee's butter dish. "That's it!" she said. "I knew there was something I wanted to ask you if I could have." She jumped up from the table and went over in the corner where the churn stood, the milk in it clabber[4] by now. She looked at the churn and looked at it.

"This churn top is what I need," she said. "Didn't Uncle Buddy whittle it out of a tree you all used to have?"

"Yes," I said.

"Uh huh," she said happily. "And I want the dasher, too."

"Uncle Buddy whittle that, too?" asked the barber.

Dee (Wangero) looked up at me.

---

[3] A Model A car is a popular low-priced automobile introduced by the Ford Motor Company in 1927.

[4] Clabber is sour milk or buttermilk.

"Aunt Dee's first husband whittled the dash," said Maggie so low you almost couldn't hear her. "His name was Henry, but they called him Stash."

"Maggie's brain is like an elephant's," Wangero said, laughing. "I can use the churn top as a centerpiece for the alcove table," she said, sliding a plate over the churn, "and I'll think of something artistic to do with the dasher."

When she finished wrapping the dasher the handle stuck out. I took it for a moment in my hands. You didn't even have to look close to see where hands pushing the dasher up and down to make butter had left a kind of sink in the wood. In fact, there were a lot of small sinks; you could see where thumbs and fingers had sunk into the wood. It was beautiful light yellow wood, from a tree that grew in the yard where Big Dee and Stash had lived.

After dinner Dee (Wangero) went to the trunk at the foot of my bed and started rifling through it. Maggie hung back in the kitchen over the dishpan. Out came Wangero with two quilts. They had been pieced by Grandma Dee and then Big Dee and me had hung them on the quilt frames on the front porch and quilted them. One was in the Lone Star pattern. The other was Walk Around the Mountain. In both of them were scraps of dresses Grandma Dee had worn fifty and more years ago. Bits and pieces of Grandpa Jarrell's Paisley shirts. And one teeny faded blue piece, about the size of a penny matchbox, that was from Great Grandpa Ezra's uniform that he wore in the Civil War.

"Mama," Wangero said sweet as a bird. "Can I have these old quilts?"

I heard something fall in the kitchen, and a minute later the kitchen door slammed.

"Why don't you take one or two of the others?" I asked. "These old things was just done by me and Big Dee from some tops your grandma pieced before she died."

"No," said Wangero. "I don't want those. They are stitched around the borders by machine."

"That'll make them last better," I said.

"That's not the point," said Wangero. "These are all pieces of dresses Grandma used to wear. She did all this stitching by hand. Imagine!" She held the quilts securely in her arms, stroking them.

"Some of the pieces, like those lavender ones, come from old clothes her mother handed down to her," I said, moving up to touch the quilts. Dee (Wangero) moved back just enough so that I couldn't reach the quilts. They already belonged to her.

"Imagine!" she breathed again, clutching them closely to her bosom.

"The truth is," I said, "I promised to give them quilts to Maggie, for when she marries John Thomas."

She gasped like a bee had stung her.

"Maggie can't appreciate these quilts!" she said. "She'd probably be backward enough to put them to everyday use."

"I reckon she would," I said. "God knows I been saving 'em for long enough with nobody using 'em. I hope she will!" I didn't want to bring up how I had offered Dee (Wangero) a quilt when she went away to college. Then she had told me they were old-fashioned, out of style.

Alice Walker 225

"But they're *priceless!*" she was saying now, furiously; for she has a temper. "Maggie would put them on the bed and in five years they'd be in rags. Less than that!"

"She can always make some more," I said. "Maggie knows how to quilt."

Dee (Wangero) looked at me with hatred. "You just will not understand. The point is these quilts, *these* quilts!"

"Well," I said, stumped. "What would *you* do with them?"

"Hang them," she said. As if that was the only thing you *could* do with quilts.

Maggie by now was standing in the door. I could almost hear the sound her feet made as they scraped over each other.

"She can have them, Mama," she said, like somebody used to never winning anything, or having anything reserved for her. "I can 'member Grandma Dee without the quilts."

I looked at her hard. She had filled her bottom lip with checkerberry snuff and it gave her face a kind of dopey, hangdog look. It was Grandma Dee and Big Dee who taught her how to quilt herself. She stood there with her scarred hands hidden in the folds of her skirt. She looked at her sister with something like fear but she wasn't mad at her. This was Maggie's portion. This was the way she knew God to work.

When I looked at her like that something hit me in the top of my head and ran down to the soles of my feet. Just like when I'm in church and the spirit of God touches me and I get happy and shout. I did something I never had done before: hugged Maggie to me, then dragged her on into the room, snatched the quilts out of Miss Wangero's hands and dumped them into Maggie's lap. Maggie just sat there on my bed with her mouth open.

"Take one or two of the others," I said to Dee.

But she turned without a word and went out to Hakim-a-barber.

"You just don't understand," she said, as Maggie and I came out to the car.

"What don't I understand?" I wanted to know.

"Your heritage," she said. And then she turned to Maggie, kissed her, and said, "You ought to try to make something of yourself, too, Maggie. It's really a new day for us. But from the way you and Mama still live you'd never know it."

She put on some sunglasses that hid everything above the tip of her nose and her chin.

Maggie smiled; maybe at the sunglasses. But a real smile, not scared. After we watched the car dust settle I asked Maggie to bring me a dip of snuff. And then the two of us sat there just enjoying, until it was time to go in the house and go to bed.

Questions

1. What is the narrator's attitude toward Dee at the beginning of the story? What is her attitude toward Maggie? Does her attitude toward her children change in the course of the story? How?

2. What is Dee's attitude to her mother and sister? Why does she have that attitude? Does it change in the course of the story?
3. What is Maggie's attitude toward her sister at the beginning of the story? Why does she have that attitude? Does it change?
4. What does Dee mean by "heritage"? In what ways does she honor her heritage? Are these ways profound or superficial? Are there other ways to honor one's heritage?
5. The story begins in the present tense and ends in the past tense. Is this a normal way to tell a story? Is it an appropriate way to tell *this* story? Why?

 ## *Writers on Writing*   Alice Walker

What the black Southern writer inherits as a natural right is a sense of community. Something simple but surprisingly hard, especially these days, to come by. . . .

No one could wish for a more advantageous heritage than that bequeathed to the black writer in the South: a compassion for the earth, a trust in humanity beyond our knowledge of evil, and an abiding love of justice. We inherit a great responsibility as well, for we must give voice to centuries not only of silent bitterness and hate but also of neighborly kindness and sustaining love.

6  Characters

Nothing fascinates human beings so much as other human beings. People-watching is one sport young and old, male and female enjoy playing. Sometimes people-watching is a solitary sport, but often it is a form of group entertainment, usually accompanied by language. Most conversations are about other people. They may take the form of idle gossip, or evaluations of corporate personnel. They may take the form of news items or private letters of recommendation. When we choose someone to marry, or to date, to hire as an employee, or to take on as a business partner, to talk to during business dealings or social gatherings, in short, in every phase of our public and private lives, we must evaluate people's character. Whether we like it or not, our success in life is measured by how well we understand the people around us. One way we can develop these skills is by studying literature, which presents to us characters from a wider range of classes, ethnic backgrounds, mental conditions, and geographical areas than we are likely to encounter in real life. We do *not* mean, however, that literary characters are *identical* to actual people. Far from it. But insofar as literary characters simulate properties of real human beings, we can learn something about ourselves as people by studying the characters in a story.

Not all stories emphasize characters, or dwell extensively on the psychology of a character. In fact, in many stories we learn very little about the people. Here, for example, is a German folktale in which we learn little about character.

Catching a Rabbit

Hans decided to catch rabbits, but he had nothing to make the usual trap. Instead he set out a cabbage leaf under a basket propped up by a weak twig. Hans covered the cabbage leaf with pepper. Finally, an unsuspecting rabbit came to nibble on the cabbage. The rabbit sniffed, sneezed, and knocked the basket on top of himself. That night, Hans ate his fill of fresh rabbit.

What do we know about Hans? Only that he is clever and has a good appetite. Do we know anything about his age, family, income, education? Do we know how he feels when he catches the rabbit? No. Hans is merely a name used by the author so that a series of actions can be narrated. If someone were to ask, "What is Hans really like?" we would shrug our shoulders and reply, "It doesn't matter."

Flat Characters

The novelist E. M. Forster would call Hans a *flat character*. Flat characters, according to Forster, "are constructed round a single idea or quality. . . . The really flat character can be expressed in one sentence." A flat character, then, has a single behavioral trait or a stereotyped group of behaviors. A stereotype is a simplified image of a class of people. Thus we have the stereotype that all professors are absent-minded, all athletes are slow-witted, and all good students are skinny, bespectacled, and friendless. Because stereotypes are so simplified, they never describe actual people. Hans, in the story, could be summed up as the clever sort of person who finds a solution to every mechanical problem. Beyond this single attribute Hans does not exist. But we must not assume that Hans is flat simply because of the brevity of this story. One could supply any number of additional anecdotes about Hans—how he built a fire that would never go out, or a device that would automatically let out the sheep to graze— and he would still be flat, because these additional tales are all based on the same behavioral trait.

Stories and novels frequently have flat characters. They serve important artistic functions. They are easy to identify. We easily recognize Hans's character because so many fictional characters have this trait. In a short story where economy is a virtue, such quickly drawn, easily recognizable characters help forward the action efficiently and smoothly. But even in the larger, roomier novel, flat characters are valuable. Just as in life, where we know some people better than others, so, too, in fiction all characters are not of equal importance. Some people we know as flat characters: the cheerful shopkeeper, the grumpy bankteller, the efficient librarian. These are people we might see frequently, but they are relatively uncomplicated figures compared to parents, relatives, and friends. If the novelist had to give a full biography each time his main character—or *protagonist*—met a minor character, no novel would ever end. Flat characters are necessary for the efficient functioning of a work.

The Character as Literary Form

But flat characters can be interesting in themselves. The Greek writer Theophrastus (371–287 B.C.) developed a literary form called *the character*, which is a short description of a figure with one dominant personality trait. This literary form continues today. Elias Canetti, winner of the 1981 Nobel Prize in literature, wrote an entire book of such characters.

ELIAS CANETTI (1905–)

The Earwitness

The earwitness makes no effort to look, but he hears all the better. He comes, halts, huddles unnoticed in a corner, peers into a book or a display, hears whatever is to be heard, and moves away untouched and absent. One would think he was not there for he is such an expert at vanishing. He is already somewhere else, he is already listening again, he knows all the places where there is something to be heard, stows it nicely away, and forgets nothing.

He forgets nothing, one has to watch the earwitness when it is time for him to come out with everything. At such a time, he is another man, he is twice as large and four inches taller. How does he do it, does he have special high shoes for blurting things out? Could he possibly pad himself with pillows to make his words seem heavier and weightier? He does nothing else, he says it very precisely, some people wish they had held their tongues. All those modern gadgets are superfluous: his ear is better and more faithful than any gadget, nothing is erased, nothing is blocked, no matter how bad it is, lies, curses, four-letter words, all kinds of indecencies, invectives from remote and little-known languages, he accurately registers even things he does not understand and delivers them unaltered if people wish him to do so.

The earwitness cannot be corrupted by anybody. When it comes to this useful gift, which he alone has, he would take no heed of wife, child, or brother. Whatever he has heard, he has heard, and even the Good Lord is helpless to change it. But he also has human sides, and just as others have their holidays, on which they rest from work, he sometimes, albeit seldom, claps blinders on his ears and refrains from storing up the hearable things. This happens quite simply, he makes himself noticeable, he looks people in the eye, the things they say in these circumstances are quite unimportant and do not suffice to spell their doom. When he has taken off his secret ears, he is a friendly person, everyone trusts him, everyone likes to have a drink with him, harmless phrases are exchanged. At such times, people have no inkling that they are speaking with the executioner himself. It is not to be believed how innocent people are when no one is eavesdropping.

Questions

1. What does the Earwitness do?
2. Why is the Earwitness invisible?
3. Is the Earwitness a good person or a bad person?
4. Does the Earwitness have a more realistic understanding of the people around him than others have?
5. Do you know any Earwitnesses? If so, what do you think of them?

The Earwitness is an interesting character, despite his "flatness," because his behavioral trait is an unusual one. Characters can be both flat and interesting if they are marked by an unusual or imaginative trait.

Write three short character studies of types you know in school. Avoid, however, the typical classification of students into athletes, preppies, or A students. Invent types of your own: the note-taker, the question-asker, the front-row-sleeper.

Round Characters

Yet as convenient and interesting as flat characters can be, they do not satisfy the need of most writers and serious readers for psychological depth. Because flat characters can be summarized so easily, they have little capacity to surprise us. Their energy, their action, and their single-mindedness may amuse us and temporarily hold our interest, but as psychological models they soon become repetitious and limited.

The round character, however, is a fictional creation that can sustain our interest long after we have finished reading. Round characters have a number of personality traits and seem as complex as actual people we know well. They seem to possess a life that extends beyond the action of the story. We can imagine them in different situations and places. In "The Horse Dealer's Daughter," Mabel Pervin has roundness of character. She cannot be summarized in a sentence. For although she is proud and cold, she is also vulnerable and full of fiery passion. Silent most of the time, she is not afraid to speak when occasion calls for speech. Strong-tempered, she is nevertheless gentle and submissive to Fergusson. In short, she is a mixture of various human traits. The fully drawn character is one of the great triumphs of imaginative art, one of the most satisfying and sustaining pleasures of reading.

Why does a fully realized character intrigue us? Forster's answer is, "we can know more about him than we can know about any of our fellow creatures." He goes on to explain the power of this greater understanding:

> We cannot understand each other, except in a rough and ready way; we cannot reveal ourselves, even when we want to; what we call intimacy is only a makeshift; perfect knowledge is an illusion. But in the novel we can know people perfectly, and, apart from the general pleasure of reading, we can find here a compensation for their dimness in life. [1]

People, according to Forster, are frustrated by their partial knowledge of other humans. Round characters satisfy that hunger for more knowledge; they are compensation for our imperfect understanding of the real world.

Motivation

When police investigate a crime, they must establish a suspect's *motives*, the person's reasons for performing the action. Like a police detective, the careful reader asks why characters do what they do. Frequently, motives are so obvious that the author doesn't bother to comment on them or readers to question them.

---

[1] E. M. Forster, *Aspects of the Novel* (New York: Harcourt, 1927), p. 98.

We understand that hunger is a very good reason to hunt rabbits, and so we don't ask for motivation for Hans's actions. Falling in love does not need to be motivated because we know from life that love is one of those inexplicable mysteries, and that the most unlikely people fall in love.

But motives are very slippery. As the French philosopher Blaise Pascal wrote: "the heart has reasons that the mind knows nothing of." We've all, at some point in our lives, done things without consciously knowing why we did them. Sometimes we don't want to admit even to ourselves our real reasons for certain actions because the hidden motives are so base, petty, embarrassing, or childish. In addition, actions and the reasons that motivated them often seem strangely unrelated. For example, we are angry at our parents, so we fight with a friend. When we take out our frustrations, we divert our emotions away from the person or thing which has evoked them, and direct them to people or things that are less threatening. Critics and psychologists speak about conscious and unconscious motives, and as readers we should be aware that characters need not be conscious of their motives. Dr. Fergusson does not seem to see at first that he saves Mabel Pervin's life because he loves her; indeed, he may not have loved her *until* he saved her life.

As readers we should also be aware that motivations can be very complex. Significant actions may have very different, even contradictory motives. If we asked the narrator's husband, John, in "The Yellow Wall-Paper," why he treats his wife as he does, he probably would say it is out of concern for her health. And yet, as readers we can see that his actions express a certain contempt for his wife, since he does not believe that she is seriously sick. We might even say he does not want her to get well if getting well means that she will assert her equality to him. Thus, John may be said to have many different motives for treating his wife as he does, not all of them as altruistic and loving as he thinks.

Consistency of Actions

If we look into our own hearts we know that at times we experience strange clashes of emotion. Simultaneously we can love and hate the same person, want something and fear it, be joyously happy and utterly sad. In fact, those stories that involve internal conflict focus their attention on just such problems of the human psyche, how we experience strange mixtures of often unrelated emotions.

Since our motives for acting are frequently mixed, our actions often seem inconsistent. We all have known (or at least heard about) the miser who is generous to a specific person, the bully who is gentle with children, the otherwise faithful wife who runs off with her hairdresser. Truth is often stranger than fiction, and although in life we accept a good deal of inconsistency, in fiction we often ask for coherence. Only in bad stories are misers suddenly transformed into philanthropists. In Charles Dickens's "A Christmas Carol," Scrooge is not made into a charitable Christian *until* he has gone through some devastating experiences that motivate his change, and even then, many people believe that the story is unrealistic, arguing that in life the Scrooges of the world never change.

When we read of a character acting in what seems to us to be an inconsistent manner, we should be careful before we judge the work as faulty. As readers, we must look to see if the character is motivated by conflicting emotions, which often lead to inconsistent behavior. We must also see whether unconscious motives have led to the seeming inconsistency. In fact, an author whose characters show *no* inconsistency may be faulted as well. Critics accuse such authors of creating stick figures, characters that are too good to be true or too evil to be real. Since we know that no one is entirely good or bad, we expect realistic characters to perform in a way consistent with human nature.

 Tips for Writers

A good strategy for generating papers is to find a character who appears to act inconsistently, but whose motives are sufficiently complex that the reader comes to understand the logic behind such inconsistencies. In the opening paragraphs, you generally present the *seeming* inconsistency, then in the body of the paper you develop the complexity of character and motive that explains such apparent contradictions.

Reading for Character

We understand characters in almost the same way that we understand real human beings. When we meet people for the first time, we listen to what they say and what is said about them, but most of all we watch what they do, how they behave. In reading a story, we perform almost the same act. We read what the narrator says (keeping in mind the limitations of the narrator's point of view), listen to what the characters say, and watch how they behave. As a reader, however, you may have another advantage: you may be allowed to know what the character is thinking. In real life we never have this advantage—access to someone else's unspoken thoughts. Indeed, writers have developed a special technique, called *stream-of-consciousness*, which reveals a character's innermost thoughts as they are formulated. In a stream-of-consciousness passage, trivial facts and important ones, memories and current experience, are seemingly jumbled together to form a rich, complex pattern. "The Jilting of Granny Weatherall" contains several *stream-of-consciousness* passages.

We should also watch for changes in the characters. Stories are usually organized in one of two ways: (1) The story reveals more and more traits of an essentially unchanging, *static character*. In such a story, the reader's understanding alters while the character remains the same. (2) The other type of narrative establishes the character's traits in the first part of the story and proceeds to show how events modify those traits. Such a character is said to be a *developing character*. Clearly, it is harder for an author to show a developing character than a static one, because the static character has only one set of traits while the developing character has two or more.

One should not confuse the length of time covered in a story with the character's development. In "The Horse Dealer's Daughter," both Mabel Pervin and Dr. Fergusson change in the course of an afternoon. In "The Jilting of Granny Weatherall," we watch a character who has stubbornly resisted change all her life.

Heroes and Villains

In Greek literature the term *hero* was reserved for the warrior noble who achieved great feats in battle. Since then, the term has been applied to any good central character. However, it may be best to reserve the word *hero* for the exceptionally brave and valiant character and refer to the usual run of central figures as protagonists. Similarly we will reserve the term *villain* for particularly evil scoundrels and refer to the person in conflict with the protagonist as the *antagonist*.

We make these distinctions because heroes and villains are special flat characters. They exist at the extremes of goodness and badness. Most central characters—especially of the round variety—are, like most people, neither very good nor very bad, very brave nor very cowardly. They are a mixture of these behavioral traits. Indeed, one of the ways we can tell a "realistic" character from a "fantastic" or "supernatural" character is that the realistic character has a mixture of good and bad traits, is neither an angel nor a devil. Such realistic characters often hold our interest longer because their actions are less predictable and because they are more like ourselves.

Suggestions for Essayists

1. Describe how you or someone you know has changed over the last few years.
2. Some people say that a particularly critical incident changed their lives; e.g., a brush with death, with the law, with love. Describe how such a critical incident changed you or someone you know.
3. Describe the man or woman of your dreams and explain why you value the qualities you describe.

Suggestions for Fiction Writers

1. Go through a newspaper or magazine and, without reading the copy, choose an anonymous face that interests you. Then write a fictional life of that person. When you are finished, compare your fictional life to the information in the newspaper or magazine.
2. Some people believe in reincarnation. Describe a life you might have led before your present existence.

KATHERINE ANNE PORTER (1890–1980)

The Jilting of Granny Weatherall

She flicked her wrist neatly out of Doctor Harry's pudgy careful fingers and pulled the sheet up to her chin. The brat ought to be in knee breeches. Doctoring around the country with spectacles on his nose! "Get along now, take your schoolbooks and go. There's nothing wrong with me."

Doctor Harry spread a warm paw like a cushion on her forehead where the forked green vein danced and made her eyelids twitch. "Now, now, be a good girl, and we'll have you up in no time."

"That's no way to speak to a woman nearly eighty years old just because she's down. I'd have you respect your elders, young man."

"Well, Missy, excuse me." Doctor Harry patted her cheek. "But I've got to warn you, haven't I? You're a marvel, but you must be careful or you're going to be good and sorry."

"Don't tell me what I'm going to be. I'm on my feet now, morally speaking. It's Cornelia. I had to go to bed to get rid of her."

Her bones felt loose, and floated around in her skin, and Doctor Harry floated like a balloon around the foot of the bed. He floated and pulled down his waistcoat and swung his glasses on a cord. "Well, stay where you are, it certainly can't hurt you."

"Get along and doctor your sick," said Granny Weatherall. "Leave a well woman alone. I'll call for you when I want you. . . . Where were you forty years ago when I pulled through milk-leg[1] and double pneumonia? You weren't even born. Don't let Cornelia lead you on," she shouted, because Doctor Harry appeared to float up the ceiling and out. "I pay my own bills, and I don't throw my money away on nonsense!"

She meant to wave good-by, but it was too much trouble. Her eyes closed of themselves, it was like a dark curtain drawn around the bed. The pillow rose and floated under her, pleasant as a hammock in a light wind. She listened to the leaves rustling outside the window. No, somebody was swishing newspapers: no, Cornelia and Doctor Harry were whispering together. She leaped broad awake, thinking they whispered in her ear.

"She was never like this, *never* like this!" "Well, what can we expect?" "Yes, eighty years old. . . . "

Well, and what if she was? She still had ears. It was like Cornelia to whisper around doors. She always kept things secret in such a public way. She was always being tactful and kind. Cornelia was dutiful; that was the trouble with her. Dutiful and good: "So good and dutiful," said Granny, "and I'd like to spank her." She saw herself spanking Cornelia and making a fine job of it.

"What'd you say, Mother?"

Granny felt her face tying up in hard knots.

"Can't a body think, I'd like to know?"

---

[1] Milk-leg is a swelling of the leg caused by childbirth.

Katherine Anne Porter (*Photograph© 1983 Jill Krementz*)

"I thought you might want something."

"I do. I want a lot of things. First off, go away and don't whisper."

She lay and drowsed, hoping in her sleep that the children would keep out and let her rest a minute. It had been a long day. Not that she was tired. It was always pleasant to snatch a minute now and then. There was always so much to be done, let me see: tomorrow.

Tomorrow was far away and there was nothing to trouble about. Things were finished somehow when the time came; thank God there was always a little margin over for peace: then a person could spread out the plan of life and tuck in the edges orderly. It was good to have everything clean and folded away, with the hair brushes and tonic bottles sitting straight on the white embroidered linen: the day started without fuss and the pantry shelves laid out with rows of jelly glasses and brown jugs and white stone-china jars with blue whirligigs and words painted on them: coffee, tea, sugar, ginger, cinnamon, allspice: and the bronze clock with the lion on top nicely dusted off. The dust that lion could collect in twenty-four hours! The box in the attic with all those letters tied up, well, she'd have to go through that tomorrow. All those letters—George's letters and John's letters and her letters to them both—lying around for the children to find afterwards made her uneasy. Yes, that would be tomorrow's business. No use to let them know how silly she had been once.

While she was rummaging around she found death in her mind and it felt clammy and unfamiliar. She had spent so much time preparing for death there was no need for bringing it up again. Let it take care of itself now. When she was sixty she had felt very old, finished, and went around making farewell trips to see her children and grandchildren, with a secret in her mind: This is the very last of your mother, children! Then she made her will and came down with a long fever. That was all just a notion like a lot of other things, but it was lucky too, for she had once for all got over the idea of dying for a long time. Now she couldn't be worried. She hoped she had better sense now. Her father had lived to be one hundred and two years old and had drunk a noggin of strong hot toddy on his last birthday. He told the reporters it was his daily habit, and he owed his long life to that. He had made quite a scandal and was very pleased about it. She believed she'd just plague Cornelia a little.

"Cornelia! Cornelia!" No footsteps, but a sudden hand on her cheek. "Bless you, where have you been?"

"Here, Mother."

"Well, Cornelia, I want a noggin of hot toddy."

"Are you cold, darling?"

"I'm chilly, Cornelia. Lying in bed stops the circulation. I must have told you that a thousand times."

Well, she could just hear Cornelia telling her husband that Mother was getting a little childish and they'd have to humor her. The thing that most annoyed her was that Cornelia thought she was deaf, dumb, and blind. Little hasty glances and tiny gestures tossed around her and over her head saying, "Don't cross her, let her have her way, she's eighty years old," and she sitting there as if she lived in a thin glass cage. Sometimes Granny almost made up her mind to pack up and move back to her own house where nobody could remind her every minute that she was old. Wait, wait, Cornelia, till your own children whisper behind your back!

In her day she had kept a better house and had got more work done. She wasn't too old yet for Lydia to be driving eighty miles for advice when one of the children jumped the track, and Jimmy still dropped in and talked things over: "Now, Mammy, you've a good business head, I want to know what you think of this? . . . " Old. Cornelia couldn't change the furniture around without asking. Little things, little things! They had been so sweet when they were little. Granny wished the old days were back again with the children young and everything to be done over. It had been a hard pull, but not too much for her. When she thought of all the food she had cooked, and all the clothes she had cut and sewed, and all the gardens she had made—well, the children showed it. There they were, made out of her, and they couldn't get away from that. Sometimes she wanted to see John again and point to them and say, Well, I didn't do so badly, did I? But that would have to wait. That was for tomorrow. She used to think of him as a man, but now all the children were older than their father, and he would be a child beside her if she saw him now. It seemed strange and there was something wrong in the idea. Why, he couldn't possibly recognize her. She had fenced in a hundred acres once, digging the post holes herself and clamping the wires with just a negro boy to help. That changed a woman. John would be looking for a young woman with the peaked Spanish comb in her hair and the painted fan. Digging post holes changed a woman. Riding country roads in the winter when women had their babies was another thing: sitting up nights with sick horses and sick negroes and sick children and hardly ever losing one. John, I hardly ever lost one of them! John would see that in a minute, that would be something he could understand, she wouldn't have to explain anything!

It made her feel like rolling up her sleeves and putting the whole place to rights again. No matter if Cornelia was determined to be everywhere at once, there were a great many things left undone on this place. She would start tomorrow and do them. It was good to be strong enough for everything, even if all you made melted and changed and slipped under your hands, so that by the time you finished you almost forgot what you were working for. What was it I set out to do? she asked herself intently, but she could not remember. A fog rose over the valley, she saw it marching across the creek swallowing the trees and moving up the hill like an army of ghosts. Soon it would be at the near edge of the orchard, and then it was time to go in and light the lamps. Come in, children, don't stay out in the night air.

Lighting the lamps had been beautiful. The children huddled up to her and breathed like little calves waiting at the bars in the twilight. Their eyes followed the match and watched the flame rise and settle in a blue curve, then they moved away from her. The lamp was lit, they didn't have to be scared and hang on to mother any more. Never, never, never more. God, for all my life I thank Thee. Without Thee, my God, I could never have done it. Hail, Mary, full of grace.

I want you to pick all the fruit this year and see that nothing is wasted. There's always someone who can use it. Don't let good things rot for want of using. You waste life when you waste good food. Don't let things get lost. It's bitter to lose things. Now, don't let me get to thinking, not when I am tired and taking a little nap before supper. . . .

The pillow rose about her shoulders and pressed against her heart and the memory was being squeezed out of it: oh, push down the pillow, somebody: it would smother her if she tried to hold it. Such a fresh breeze blowing and such a green day with no threats in it. But he had not come, just the same. What does a woman do when she has put on the white veil and set out the white cake for man and he doesn't come? She tried to remember. No, I swear he never harmed me but in that. He never harmed me but in that . . . and what if he did? There was the day, the day, but a whirl of dark smoke rose and covered it, crept up and over into the bright field where everything was planted so carefully in orderly rows. That was hell, she knew hell when she saw it. For sixty years she had prayed against remembering him and against losing her soul in the deep pit of hell, and now the two things were mingled in one and the thought of him was a smoky cloud from hell that moved and crept in her head when she had just got rid of Doctor Harry and was trying to rest a minute. Wounded vanity, Ellen, said a sharp voice in the top of her mind. Don't let your wounded vanity get the upper hand of you. Plenty of girls get jilted. You were jilted, weren't you? Then stand up to it. Her eyelids wavered and let in streamers of blue-gray light like tissue paper over her eyes. She must get up and pull the shades down or she'd never sleep. She was in bed again and the shades were not down. How could that happen? Better turn over, hide from the light, sleeping in the light gave you nightmares. "Mother, how do you feel now?" and a stinging wetness on her forehead. But I don't like having my face washed in cold water!

Hapsy? George? Lydia? Jimmy? No, Cornelia, and her features were swollen and full of little puddles. "They're coming, darling, they'll all be here soon." Go wash your face, child, you look funny.

Instead of obeying, Cornelia knelt down and put her head on the pillow. She seemed to be talking but there was no sound. "Well, are you tongue-tied? Whose birthday is it? Are you going to give a party?"

Cornelia's mouth moved urgently in strange shapes. "Don't do that, you bother me, daughter."

"Oh, no, Mother. Oh, no. . . . "

Nonsense. It was strange about children. They disputed your every word. "No what, Cornelia?"

"Here's Doctor Harry."

"I won't see that boy again. He just left five minutes ago."

"That was this morning, Mother. It's night now. Here's the nurse."

"This is Doctor Harry, Mrs. Weatherall. I never saw you look so young and happy!"

"Ah, I'll never be young again—but I'd be happy if they'd let me lie in peace and get rested."

She thought she spoke up loudly, but no one answered. A warm weight on her forehead, a warm bracelet on her wrist, and a breeze went on whispering, trying to tell her something. A shuffle of leaves in the everlasting hand of God. He blew on them and they danced and rattled. "Mother, don't mind, we're going to give you a little hypodermic." "Look here, daughter, how do ants get in this bed? I saw sugar ants yesterday." Did you send for Hapsy too?

It was Hapsy she really wanted. She had to go a long way back through a great many rooms to find Hapsy standing with a baby on her arm. She seemed to herself to be Hapsy also, and the baby on Hapsy's arm was Hapsy and himself and herself, all at once, and there was no surprise in the meeting. Then Hapsy melted from within and turned flimsy as gray gauze and the baby was a gauzy shadow, and Hapsy came up close and said, "I thought you'd never come," and looked at her very searchingly and said, "You haven't changed a bit!" They leaned forward to kiss, when Cornelia began whispering from a long way off, "Oh, is there anything you want to tell me? Is there anything I can do for you?"

Yes, she had changed her mind after sixty years and she would like to see George. I want you to find George. Find him and be sure to tell him I forgot him. I want him to know I had my husband just the same and my children and my house like any other woman. A good house too and a good husband that I loved and fine children out of him. Better than I hoped for even. Tell him I was given back everything he took away and more. Oh, no, oh, God, no, there was something else besides the house and the man and the children. Oh, surely they were not all? What was it? Something not given back. . . . Her breath crowded down under her ribs and grew into a monstrous frightening shape with cutting edges; it bored up into her head, and the agony was unbelievable: Yes, John, get the doctor now, no more talk, my time has come.

When this one was born it should be the last. The last. It should have been born first, for it was the one she had truly wanted. Everything came in good time. Nothing left out, left over. She was strong, in three days she would be as well as ever. Better. A woman needed milk in her to have her full health.

"Mother, do you hear me?"

"I've been telling you—"

"Mother, Father Connolly's here."

"I went to Holy Communion only last week. Tell him I'm not so sinful as all that."

"Father just wants to speak to you."

He could speak as much as he pleased. It was like him to drop in and inquire about her soul as if it were a teething baby, and then stay on for a cup of tea and a round of cards and gossip. He always had a funny story of some sort, usually about an Irishman who made his little mistakes and confessed them, and the point lay in some absurd thing he would blurt out in the confessional showing his struggles between native piety and original sin. Granny felt easy about her soul. Cornelia, where are your manners? Give Father Connolly a chair. She had her secret comfortable understanding with a few favorite saints who cleared a straight road to God for her. All as surely signed and sealed as the papers for the new Forty Acres. Forever . . . heirs and assigns forever. Since the day the wedding cake was not cut, but thrown out and wasted. The whole bottom dropped out of the world, and there she was blind and sweating with nothing under her feet and the walls falling away. His hand had caught her under the breast, she had not fallen, there was the freshly polished floor with the green rug on it, just as before. He had cursed like a sailor's parrot and said, "I'll kill him for you." Don't lay a hand on him, for my sake leave something to God. "Now, Ellen, you must believe what I tell you. . . ."

So there was nothing, nothing to worry about any more, except sometimes in the night one of the children screamed in a nightmare, and they both hustled out shaking and hunting for the matches and calling, "There, wait a minute, here we are!" John, get the doctor now, Hapsy's time has come. But there was Hapsy standing by the bed in a white cap. "Cornelia, tell Hapsy to take off her cap. I can't see her plain."

Her eyes opened very wide and the room stood out like a picture she had seen somewhere. Dark colors with the shadows rising towards the ceiling in long angles. The tall black dresser gleamed with nothing on it but John's picture, enlarged from a little one, with John's eyes very black when they should have been blue. You never saw him, so how do you know how he looked? But the man insisted the copy was perfect, it was very rich and handsome. For a picture, yes, but it's not my husband. The table by the bed had a linen cover and a candle and a crucifix. The light was blue from Cornelia's silk lampshades. No sort of light at all, just frippery. You had to live forty years with kerosene lamps to appreciate honest electricity. She felt very strong and she saw Doctor Harry with a rosy nimbus around him.

"You look like a saint, Doctor Harry, and I vow that's as near as you'll ever come to it."

"She's saying something."

"I heard you, Cornelia. What's all this carrying on?"

"Father Connolly's saying—"

Cornelia's voice staggered and bumped like a cart in a bad road. It rounded corners and turned back again and arrived nowhere. Granny stepped up in the cart very lightly and reached for the reins, but a man sat beside her and she knew him by his hands, driving the cart. She did not look in his face, for she knew without seeing, but looked instead down the road where the trees leaned over and bowed to each other and a thousand birds were singing a Mass. She felt like singing too, but she put her hand in the bosom of her dress and pulled out a rosary, and Father Connolly murmured Latin in a very solemn voice and tickled her feet. My God, will you stop that nonsense? I'm a married woman. What if he did run away and leave me to face the priest by myself? I found another a whole world better. I wouldn't have exchanged my husband for anybody except St. Michael himself, and you may tell him that for me with a thank you in the bargain.

Light flashed on her closed eyelids, and a deep roaring shook her. Cornelia, is that lightning? I hear thunder. There's going to be a storm. Close all the windows. Call the children in. . . . " Mother, here we are, all of us." "Is that you, Hapsy?" "Oh, no, I'm Lydia. We drove as fast as we could." Their faces drifted above her, drifted away. The rosary fell out of her hands and Lydia put it back. Jimmy tried to help, their hands fumbled together, and Granny closed two fingers around Jimmy's thumb. Beads wouldn't do, it must be something alive. She was so amazed her thoughts ran round and round. So, my dear Lord, this is my death and I wasn't even thinking about it. My children have come to see me die. But I can't, it's not time. Oh, I always hated surprises. I wanted to give Cornelia the amethyst set—Cornelia, you're to have the amethyst set, but Hapsy's to wear it when she wants, and, Doctor Harry, do shut up. Nobody sent for you. Oh my dear Lord, do wait a minute. I meant to do something about the Forty Acres, Jimmy doesn't need it and Lydia will later on, with that worthless husband of hers. I meant to finish the altar cloth and send six bottles of wine to Sister Borgia for her dyspepsia. I want to send six bottles of wine to Sister Borgia, Father Connolly, now don't let me forget.

Cornelia's voice made short turns and tilted over and crashed. "Oh, Mother, oh, Mother, oh, Mother. . . . "

"I'm not going, Cornelia. I'm taken by surprise. I can't go."

You'll see Hapsy again. What about her? "I thought you'd never come." Granny made a long journey outward, looking for Hapsy. What if I don't find her? What then? Her heart sank down and down, there was no bottom to death, she couldn't come to the end of it. The blue light from Cornelia's lampshade drew into a tiny point in the center of her brain, it flickered and winked like an eye, quietly it fluttered and dwindled. Granny lay curled down within herself, amazed and watchful, staring at the point of light that was herself; her body was now only a deeper mass of shadow in an endless darkness and this darkness would curl around the light and swallow it up. God, give a sign!

For the second time there was no sign. Again no bridegroom and the priest in the house. She could not remember any other sorrow because this grief wiped them all away. Oh, no, there's nothing more cruel than this—I'll never forgive it. She stretched herself with a deep breath and blew out the light.

Questions

1. Can you reconstruct from the fragments the story of the jilting of Granny? Who are John and George?
2. Who is Hapsy? Why isn't she there?
3. Does Granny have a "secret comfortable understanding with a few favorite saints"?
4. Granny asks God for a sign. Does one come? What is the significance of the bridegroom in the concluding paragraph?
5. Why have the memory of George and "losing her soul in the deep pit of hell" come to be mingled as one?
6. What is it that George did not give back to Granny?
7. Is Granny a developing or a static character? Has she changed over the long course of her married life?

 Writers on Writing   *Katherine Anne Porter*

One of the most disturbing habits of the human mind is its willful and destructive forgetting of whatever in its past does not flatter or confirm its present point of view. I must very often refer far back in time to seek the meaning or explanation of today's smallest event, and I have long since lost the power to be astonished at what I find there. This constant exercise of memory seems to be the chief occupation of my mind, and all my experience seems to be simply memory, with continuity, marginal notes, constant revision and comparison of one thing with another. Now and again thousands of memories converge, harmonize, arrange themselves around a central idea in a coherent form, and I write a story. I keep notes and journals only because I write a great deal, and the habit of writing helps me to arrange, annotate, stow away conveniently the references I may need later. Yet when I begin a story, I can never work in any of those promising paragraphs, those apt phrases, those small turns of anecdote I had believed would be so valuable. I must know a story "by heart" and I must write from memory.

The Burning

The women of the barrio, the ones pock-marked by life, sat in council. Existence in dark cubicles of wounds had withered the spirit. Now, all as one, had found a heath. One tired soul stood up to speak. "Many times I see the light she makes of darkness, and that light is a greater blackness, still."

There was some skepticism from the timid. "Are you sure?"

"In those caves outside the town, she lives for days away from everybody. At night, when she is in the caves, small blinking lights appear, like fireflies. Where do they come from? I say, the blackness of her drowns the life in me."

Another woman with a strange wildness in her eyes nodded her head in affirmation. "Yes, she drinks the bitterness of good and swallows, like the devil-wolf, the red honey milk of evil."

A cadaverous one looked up into a darkened sky. "I hear thunder; lightning is not far." In unison they agreed, "We could use some rain."

The oldest one among them, one with dirty claws, stood up with arms outstretched and stood menacingly against the first lightning bolt that cleaved the darkness. Her voice was harsh and came from ages past. "She must burn!"

The finality was a cloud, black and tortured. Each looked into another's eyes to find assent or protest. There was only frenzy, tight and straining. The thunder was riding the lightning now, directly over their heads. It was a blazing canopy that urged them on to deeds of fear. There was still no rain. They found blistering words to justify the deed to come. One woman, heavy with anger, crouched to pour out further accusations. "She is the devil's pawn. On nights like this, when the air is heavy like thick blood, she sings among the dead, preferring them to the living. You know why she does it . . . eh? I'll tell you! She chases the dead back to their graves."

"Yes, yes. She stays and stays when death comes. Never a whimper, nor a tear, but I sense she feels the death as life like one possessed. They say she catches the flitting souls of the dead and turns them into flies. That way the soul never finds heaven."

"Flies! Flies! She is a plague!"

A clap of thunder reaffirmed. The old one with nervous, clutching claws made the most grievous charge, the cause for this meeting of the judgment. She shaped with bony gestures the anger of the heart. "She is the enemy of God! She put obscenities on our doorsteps to make us her accomplices. Sacrilege against the holy church!"

There was a fervor now, rising like a tide. They were for her burning now. All the council howled that Lela must burn that night. The sentence belonged to night alone. The hurricane could feed in darkness. Fear could be disguised as outrage at night. There were currents now that wanted sacrifice. Sacrifice is the umbilical cord of superstition. It would devastate before finding a calm. Lela was the eye of the storm, the artery that must flow to make them whole when the earth turned to light. To catch an evil when it bounced as shadow in their lives, to find it trapped in human body, this was an effective stimulant to some; to others it was a natural depressant to cut the fear, the dam of frustration. This would be their method of revelation. The doubt of themselves would dissolve.

But women know mercy! Mercy? It was swallowed whole by chasms of desire and fear of the unknown. Tempests grow in narrow margins that want a freedom they don't understand. Slaves always punish the free.

But who was Lela? She had come across the mountain to their pueblo many years before. She had crossed la Barranca del Cobre alone. She had walked into the pueblo one day, a bloody, ragged, half-starved young girl. In an apron she carried some shining sand. She stood there, like a frightened fawn, at the edge of the village. As the people of the pueblo gathered around her strangeness, she smiled, putting out her hand for touch. They drew back and she fell to the ground in exhaustion.

They took her in, but she remained a stranger the rest of her life in the pueblo upon which she had stumbled. At the beginning, she seemed but a harmless child. But, as time passed and she resisted their pattern of life, she was left alone. The people knew she was a Tarahumara from Batopilas. Part of her strangeness was the rooted depth of her own religion. She did not convert to Christianity. People grew hostile and suspicious of her.

But she had also brought with her the miracle sand. It had strange curative powers. In no time, she began to cure those in the pueblo who suffered from skin disease, from sores, or open wounds.

"Is it the magic of her devil gods?" the people asked themselves. Still, they came for the miracle cure that was swift and clean. She became their *curandera* outside their Christian faith.

The people in her new home needed her, and she loved them in silence and from a distance. She forgave them for not accepting her strangeness and learned to find adventure in the Oneness of herself.

Many times she wanted to go back to Batopilas, but too many people needed her here. She learned the use of medicinal herbs and learned to set broken bones. This was what she was meant to do in life. This purpose would not let her return to Batopilas. Still, she did not convert to Christianity. The people, begrudgingly, believed in her curative powers, but did not believe in her. Many years had passed and Lela was now an old woman, and the council of women this night of impending storm had decided her fate.

Lela lay dying in her one room hut. There was a fire with teeth that consumed her body. She only knew that her time was near an end as she lay in her small cot. Above the bed was a long shelf she had built herself that held rows of clay figurines. These were painted in gay colors and the expressions on the tiny faces measured the seasons of the heart. They were live little faces showing the full circle of human joy and pain, doubt and fear, humor and sobriety. In all expressions there was a fierceness for life.

Lela had molded them through the years, and now they stood over her head like guardians over their maker. . . . Clay figurines, an act of love learned early in her childhood of long ago. In Batopilas, each home had its own rural god. He was a friend and a comforter. The little rural gods were like any other people. They did not rule or demand allegiance. The little rural gods of river, sky, fire, seed, birds, all were chosen members of each family. Because they sanctified all human acts, they were the actions of the living, like an aura. They were a shrine to creation.

Lela's mother had taught the little girl to mold the clay figures that represented the rural gods. This was her work and that of Lela's in the village, to provide clay little gods for each home and for festive occasions. This is why Lela never gave them up in her new home. She had molded them with her hands, but they dwelled boundless in the center of her being. The little gods had always been very real, very important, in her reverence for life.

There had been in Batopilas a stone image of the greater god, Tecuat. He was an impressive god of power that commanded silence and obedience. People did not get close to Tecuat except in ritual. As a girl, Lela would tiptoe respectfully around the figure of Tecuat, then she would breathe a sigh of relief and run off to find the little gods.

This was her game, god-hunting. One day, she had walked too far towards the pines, too far towards a roar that spoke of rushing life. She followed a yellow butterfly that also heard a command of dreams. She followed the butterfly that flitted towards a lake. As she followed, she looked for little gods in the glint of the sun, and in the open branches that pierced the absoluteness of the sky. The soft breath of wind was the breath of little gods, and the crystal shine of rocks close to the lake was a winking language that spoke of peace and the wildness of all joy.

When she had reached the lake, she stepped into the water without hesitation. She felt the cool wet mud against her open toes. She walked into the water, touching the ripple of its broken surface with her finger tips. After a while, there was no more bottom. She began to cut the water with smooth, clean strokes, swimming out towards the pearl-green rocks that hid the roar. She floated for a while looking up at the light filtering through eternal trees. The silence spoke of something other than itself. It spoke in colors born of water and sun. She began to swim more rapidly towards the turn that led to the cradle of the roar, the waterfall. . . .

This is what Lela, the old Lela dying on her bed, was remembering . . . the waterfall. It helped to ease the pain that came in waves that broke against her soul and blackened the world. Then, there was the calm, the calm into which the experience machine brought back the yesterdays that were now soft, kind memories. She opened her eyes and looked up at the row of clay figures. She was not alone. "The waterfall . . ." she whispered to herself. She remembered the grotto behind the waterfall. It had been her hermitage of dreams, of wonder. Here her Oneness had knitted all the little gods unto herself until she felt the whole of earth—things within her being. Suddenly, the pain cut her body in two. She gripped the edge of the cot. There were blurs of throbbing white that whirled into black, and all her body trembled until another interval of peace returned for a little while.

There was no thought; there was no dream in the quiet body. She was a simple calm that would not last. The calm was a gift from the little gods. She slept. It was a fitful, brief sleep that ended with the next crash of pain. The pain found gradual absorption. She could feel the bed sheet clinging to her body, wet with perspiration. She asked herself in a half-moan, "When will the body give way?" Give way . . . give way, for so long, Lela had given way and had found ways to open herself and the world she understood. It had been a vital force in her. She could have been content in Batopilas. The simple truths of Nature might have fulfilled her to the end of her days if she had remained in Batopilas. But there was always that reach in her for a larger self. Nature was a greatness, but she felt a different hunger and a different thirst.

There was a world beyond Batopilas; there were people beyond Batopilas. She was no longer a child. It was easy to find little gods in Nature, but as she grew older, it became a child's game. There was time to be a child, but there was now time for something more. That is why, one day, she had walked away from Batopilas.

Beyond the desert, she would find another pueblo. She knew there were many pueblos and many deserts. There was nothing to fear because her little gods were with her. On the first day of her journey, she walked all day. The piercing sun beat down on her and the world, as she scanned the horizon for signs of a way. Something at a distance would be a hope, would be a way to something new, a way to the larger self. At dusk, she felt great hunger and great thirst. Her body ached and her skin felt parched and dry. The night wind felt cold, so she looked for a shelter against the wind. She found a clump of mesquite behind some giant sahuaros. This was not the greenness she knew so well, but a garden of stars in the night sky comforted her until she fell asleep.

At first light she awakened refreshed and quickly resumed her journey. She knew she must make the best out of the early hours before the sun rose. By late morning, the desert yielded a mountain at a distance. She reached the mountain in time to rest from the sun and the physical effort of her journey. When the sun began to fall, she started up a path made narrow by a blanket of desert brush. It tore the flesh of her feet and legs as she made her way up the path. In a little while, it was hard to find sure footing. The path had lost itself in a cleavage of rocks. Night had fallen. She was not afraid, for the night sky, again, was full of blinking little gods.

Then it happened. She lost her footing and fell down, down over a crevice between two huge boulders. As she fell, her lungs filled with air. Her body hit soft sand, but the edge of her foot felt the sharpness of a stone. She lay there stunned for a few minutes until she felt a sharp pain at the side of her foot. Somewhat dizzy, she sat up and noticed that the side of her foot was bleeding profusely. She sat there and watched the blood-flow that found its way into the soft sand. She looked up at the boulders that silently rebuked her helplessness; then she began to cry softly. She had to stanch the blood. She wiped away her tears with the side of her sleeve and tore off a piece of skirt to use as a bandage. As she looked down at the wound again, she noticed that the sand where she had fallen was extremely crystalline and loose. It shone against a rising moon. She scooped up a handful and looked at it with fascination. "The sand of little gods," she whispered to herself. She took some sand and rubbed it on the wound before she applied the bandage. By now, she felt a burning fever. She wrapped the strip of skirt around the wound now covered with the fine, shining sand. Then she slept. But it was a fitful sleep, for her body burned with fever. Half awake and half in a dream, she saw the sands take the shapes of happy, little gods. Then, at other times, the pain told her she was going to die. After a long time, her exhausted body slept until the dawn passed over her head.

When she finally awakened, she felt extremely well. Her body was rested and her temperature, to her great surprise, was normal. She looked down at the wound. The blood was caked on the bandage. She took it off to look at the wound. She could hardly believe her eyes. There was no longer any open wound. There was a healthy scab, and the area around the wound had no infection. It was a healing that normally would have taken weeks. She stood on her foot and felt no pain. "My little gods!" she thought. She fell down on her knees and kissed the shining sand. After a while, she removed her apron and filled it with the shining sand. She secured it carefully before she set off on her climb. As she made her way out of the crevice, she marked the path leading to the shining sand to find her way to it again. It was hard making marks with a sharp stone, and it seemed to take forever. At last, she reached the top of the crevice and noticed, to her great joy, that it led down to a pueblo at a distance. She made her way to strangers that day. Now, at the end of a lifetime, Lela felt the pain roll, roll, roll, roll itself into a blindness. She struggled through the blackness until she gasped back the beginning of the calm. With the new calm came a ringing memory from her childhood. She saw the kindly face of the goddess, Ta Te. She who was born of the union of clean rock, she who was eternal. Yes, Ta Te understood all the verdant things . . . the verdant things.

And who were these women who sat in council? They were one full sweep of hate; they were one full wave of fear. Now these village women were outlined against a greyish sky where a storm refused to break. Spiderlike, apelike, toadlike was the ferocity of their deadness. These were creatures of the earth who mingled with mankind. But they were minions to torture because the twist of littleness bound them to condemn all things unknown, all things untried. The infernal army could not be stopped now. The scurrying creatures began to gather firewood in the gloom. With antlike obedience they hurried back and forth carrying wood to Lela's hut. They piled it in a circle around her little house. The rhythm of their feet sang, "We'll do! We'll do!"

"The circle of fire will drain her powers!" claimed the old one with claws.

"Show me! Show me! Show me!" Voices lost as one.

As the old one with claws ordered more wood, the parish priest came running from his church. With raised arms he shouted as he ran, "Stop! Do you hear? Stop this madness!"

It can be argued that evil is not the reversal of good, but the vacuum of good. Thus, the emptiness is a standing still, a being dead, an infinite pain . . . like dead wood. No one listened to him.

"Burn! Burn! Burn!"

Life? The wood? The emptiness? The labor pains were that of something already lost, something left to the indefinite in life. The priest went from one woman to another begging, pleading, taking the wood from their hands.

"Burn! Burn! Burn!"

The old priest reasoned. "All is forgiven, my children. She only made some figurines of clay!"

There was a hush. The one woman with the claws approached the priest and spit out the condemnation, "She took our holy saints, Mary, Joseph, and many others and made them obscene. How can you defend the right hand of the devil? Drinking saints! Winking saints! Who can forgive the hideous suggestions of her clay devils? Who?"

The priest said simply, "You."

But if there is only darkness in a narrow belief, who can believe beyond the belief, or even understand the belief itself? The women could not forgive because they did not believe beyond a belief that did not go beyond symbol and law. Somehow, symbol and law, without love, leaves no opening. The clay figures in the church with sweet, painted faces lifted to heaven were much more than figures of clay to these women. Their still postures with praying hands were a security. Now, the priest who had blessed them with holy water said they were not a sanctuary of God. Why did he contradict himself?

The old one with the claws felt triumphant. "She has made our saints into pagan gods!"

The priest shook his head sadly. "It is not a sin, what she did!"

No one listened. The piling of wood continued until the match was lit. Happy . . . Happy fire . . . it would burn the sin and the sinner.

Something in Lela told her this was the last struggle now. She looked up at her clay figurines one last time. Her eyes had lost their focus. The little gods had melted into one another; all colors were mixed. They grew into silver strands of light that crossed and mingled and found new forms that pulled away from one center. In half consciousness, she whispered, "Yes, yes, pull away. Find other ways, other selves, grow. . . ."

She smiled; the last calm had taken her back to the caves outside the pueblo. The caves were not like the grotto behind the waterfall, but they were a place for Oneness, where one could look for the larger self. Here the solitude of the heart was a bird in space. Here, in the silence of aloneness, she had looked for the little gods in the townspeople. In her mind, she had molded their smiles, their tears, their embraces, their seeking, their *just being*. Her larger self told her that the miracle of the living act was supreme, the giving, the receiving, the stumbling, and the getting up.

In the caves she had sadly thought of how she had failed to reach them as a friend. Her silences and her strangeness had kept them apart. But, she would find a way of communicating, a way of letting them know that she loved them. "If I give shape and form to their beauty," she thought. "If I cannot tell them I love them with words. . . ."

The light of the moving, mixing little gods was becoming a darkness. Her body would give in now. Yet, she still wished for Batopilas and the old ways with her last breath, "If only . . . if only I could be buried in the tradition of my fathers . . . a clean burning for new life . . . but here, here, there is a dark hole for the dead body. . . . Oh, little gods, take me back to my fathers. . . ."

The little gods were racing to the waterfall.

Questions

1. Why do the women wish to kill Lela? Do they understand Lela's character in the same way that the reader does?
2. Has Lela committed heresy, according to the priest? Do the women of the town maintain heretical beliefs? Who is the real heretic?
3. How does Lela view the women? Does she see them in the same way that the women see themselves? Does she view them in the same way that the narrator views them?
4. How do the women of the pueblo view Lela's death? How does Lela view her death? How does the narrator? How do you view her death?

7 ❧ Setting the Scene

For jewelers, a setting is the metal around a precious gem or stone that keeps the jewel in place and shows it off to its best advantage by letting the light catch the stone in the most attractive manner. In literature, settings serve a similar function. *Settings* place the events of the story in a particular time and location. This placement fixes the story in our imagination and shows off the action in its most meaningful and effective light. Often, in fact, the setting suggests the actions that take place within it. For example, an old abandoned house almost demands goblins or evil doings. Just as a fine gem needs a setting which is neither too flimsy nor too gaudy, so, too, a story must be carefully placed in an appropriate and effective time and location.

Settings vary tremendously. Some are realistic, some are fantastic. Some are highly detailed, some are vague. In the short tale "Catching a Rabbit," all we learn or need to learn is that the action occurred in the country. In the "Night Watchman's Occurrence Book," we learn the month, day, and time of each event. But the year of the action is not mentioned. *Peter Pan* takes place in Never-Never-Land, far from time and realistic geography. But the Queneau anecdotes take place "midday in the Parc Monceau district" aboard an "S bus (now No. 84)." In one section of James Joyce's novel *Ulysses*, the characters take rides on the Dublin trolleys. With the aid of a street map, timetables, and a stopwatch, Joyce tracked his characters from place to place so that the narrative details would be accurate. Joyce did not want to place a character at a location impossible to reach or have two characters meet at a time sooner than they could have arrived. In "Araby," one of Joyce's Dubliner stories, the place names are accurate. The Joyces, in fact, lived at 17 North Richmond, and James attended the Christian Brothers' School down the street. Few writers have Joyce's passion for accuracy.

But one must not judge the effectiveness of a setting by its realistic accuracy. The true test is whether the setting provides the information, mood, and context the story needs. Unnecessary detail—detail for its own sake—merely slows the action and blurs the narrative focus. A good setting is integrated into the whole structure and meaning of the story. It is not merely "background," but an active part in the telling of a tale. Thus, whenever one reads a passage of scenic description, one should be aware that the author is painting more than a backdrop; he or she is providing ways to illuminate and enhance the action.

Reading for Setting

We know in part how to "read" settings from actual experience. Walking into a stranger's house, we look around, noting details that might tell us something about the owner's social status and psychology. A room decorated in the latest style but with cheap furniture would alert us to the fact that the owners wanted to be trendy but did not have the money to be truly stylish. A room decorated with many fine old things might suggest that the owners have had money for a long time.

In "Araby," we enter a "wild garden behind the house that contained a central apple tree and a few straggling bushes" under one of which the narrator found "the late tenant's rusty bicycle pump." What do we learn from this setting? First, that the garden is "wild." No one has taken care of this backyard. The neglect has been going on for some time, because the bushes have become straggly and the bicycle pump, carelessly left out, has begun to rust. This last detail is somewhat ironic, for the bicycle pump, whose purpose is to help maintain the vehicle in good condition, is itself rusting away. We also learn that the garden is small; it has only enough room for "a central apple tree and a few straggling bushes." Putting these details together, we might assume that this is a small house inhabited by poor tenants who do not maintain their property very well. Not a happy place to live.

Our analysis of the garden in "Araby" yields three kinds of meaning: (1) sociological, (2) psychological, and (3) symbolic. Let us examine these three elements separately.

✍🏻 Tips for Readers and Writers

If you're one of those readers who rushes through stories, you may have developed the habit of skipping so-called descriptive paragraphs to get to the action. If you're going to be an effective reader, you'll have to break this habit.

Good writers choose details about setting with great care. Since part of the art of short-story writing is economy of language, they make sure that every word establishing the setting of a story pulls its weight of significance. Neither the setting—nor any other detail of the story—is there as "filler." Since the setting develops the context in which the action occurs, you should pay close attention to it. In fact, one effective way of generating a paper is by observing how details of description that might *seem* to be unimportant are, in fact, crucial to an understanding of the story.

Setting as Social Indicator

Setting is frequently used as an indicator of social status—to show whether characters are rich or poor and how long they have been rich or poor. In "Araby" the narrator suggests his social position—among other traits—by describing the house in which he lives:

> The former tenant of our house, a priest, had died in the back drawing-room. Air, musty from having been long enclosed, hung in all the rooms, and the waste room behind the kitchen was littered with old useless papers. . . . The wild garden behind the house contained a central apple tree and a few straggling bushes under one of which I found the late tenant's rusty bicycle pump.

What do we learn from this passage? First we learn that the narrator is a "tenant," not the owner of the house. This detail may indicate that they are too poor to be houseowners, especially since the house does not seem to be in very good condition. The rooms are stuffy and littered. The owner has not bothered to clean the property up. The garden is small and ill-kept—another sign of negligence. It has room enough for only an apple tree and a few straggling bushes. Taken all together, we might safely conclude that the narrator lives in a rented house that is small, messy, and uncared for and that his family is poor rather than rich.

Settings that Reveal Character

We often say that weather affects our moods. Sunny, clear days make us happy; dark, rainy days make us feel sad. Indications of weather usually mirror the mood of characters. We should note references to light and dark, rain and dryness, and see if they do not emphasize the moods of the characters.

We can observe how a character's mood and psychological state is reflected in setting by comparing two descriptions of the garden in Charlotte Perkins Gilman's "The Yellow Wall-Paper." The first time the narrator describes it, she is not very ill. She writes:

> There is a *delicious* garden! I never saw such a garden—large and shady, full of box-bordered paths, and lined with long grape-covered arbors with seats under them.

The second time she describes the garden, she is less well:

> Out of one window I can see the garden, those mysterious deep-shaded arbors, the riotous old-fashioned flowers, and bushes and gnarly trees.

We can detect the subtle change in her psychological condition by noting her choice of words. The garden that had been "delicious" is later "mysterious." What first appeared to be orderly is now "riotous." What seemed unique ("I never saw such a garden") is now "old-fashioned." The "gnarled tree" is a particularly revealing detail. The "delicious" garden has started to become twisted, stunted, and deformed. Everything that seemed so appealing has become ever so slightly threatening. Of course, the garden has not changed; the change has occurred in the narrator's mind. The "mystery," riotousness, and gnarling are signs of her growing insanity.

Symbolic Settings

We will discuss symbolism in more detail in chapter eight. For the moment, let us define a symbol as an object that signifies more than just itself. For example, a wedding ring is not just a decorative piece of metal: it signifies that the wearer is married and has formed an unbroken bond with his or her spouse. Again, the American flag is not merely a multicolored piece of cloth: it stands for this country, a democratic government, and the patriotic pride of the American people.

A person or object can become symbolic when it represents the whole group of things to which it belongs. At graduation, for example, one student is chosen to represent the class. That student symbolizes the class, and what the student does and says comes to symbolize the action of all the class members. Bearing these examples of symbolism in mind, let us look at a passage in Bobbie Ann Mason's "Shiloh." In this episode Leroy and his wife Norma Jean visit the Shiloh battlefield where the Confederate Army was defeated by the Union forces. Before traveling to Shiloh, Leroy offered to build his wife a log cabin in the new suburban subdivision, but Norma Jean has declared she wants a divorce.

> [Leroy and Norma Jean] sit in silence and stare at the cemetery for the Union dead and, beyond, at a tall cluster of trees. Campers are parked nearby, bumper to bumper, and small children in bright clothing are cavorting and squealing. . . .
> The cemetery, a green slope dotted with white markers, looks like a subdivision site. Leroy is trying to comprehend that his marriage is breaking up, but for some reason he is wondering about white slabs in a graveyard.

By stating that "for some reason" Leroy is wondering about the "white slabs in a graveyard," Mason invites us to supply a reason. Why is Leroy looking at gravestones when he wants to understand his marriage? We might recall that people often refer to "the battle of the sexes," and marriage as a "battleground." In some respects, then, Shiloh represents the battlefield of their marriage and the cemetery the death of their marriage. Leroy recognizes that the log cabin he wanted to build in the "subdivision," to save his marriage, is the symbolic equivalent of a grave marker. Such a reading does not exhaust the possible significance of the passage, but it helps explain Leroy's curious behavior.

Time Settings

Stories are set not just in a certain locale—Dublin, California, or Shiloh—but at a certain time. Some stories, like fairy tales, take place "once upon a time," that is, outside of any specific historical period. Others take place within a broad context. For example, the action in "The Yellow Wall-Paper" occurs some time in the latter half of the 19th century or in the early decades of the 20th. The largest number of stories occur vaguely in the present or recent past. Some stories are more precisely positioned within history. Isaac Babel's "My First Goose" takes place in the first years after the Russian Revolution, and "The Emperor of the Air" probably takes place in the 1980s since the main character tells us he's 68 years old and has lived in his house since the time "when a czar ruled Russia." You should be sensitive to these references to time.

How can you tell when a story takes place? Authors provide a number of different ways of indicating the time period, and usually it's not by giving you specific dates. Usually we can tell by the way people live. A story that has people driving cars and flying in airplanes is clearly set in the 20th century. A story that has characters watching television is set sometime after the 1940s. Another way a story is set in time is by the language the characters use. Archaic expressions will suggest that the action takes place in the distant past, while contemporary slang will tell us that the action is happening right now. Yet another way authors indicate the time frame is by references to historical events, figures, or concerns. The reference to reading Lenin's speech in the newspaper rather clearly defines the time frame in which "My First Goose" occurs, and in "The Emperor of the Air," Canin not only refers to czars in Russia but also to visiting the Great Wall of China. Since China wasn't opened to American tourists until the late 70s or early 80s, Canin gives us a pretty good way of fixing when the story takes place.

The more specific an author is in placing a story within a historical framework, the more important a factor time must be in a reader's comprehension of the story.

✍️ Tips for Readers and Writers

"Shiloh," like many stories, refers to a number of historical events. Authors do not casually incorporate such references. You might be able to generate a good paper by looking up these historical events in reference books and explaining their significance in the story.

"Shiloh" also refers to a number of songs, films, and other aspects of popular culture. In fact, "Shiloh" includes so many references to songs that were you making a film adaptation of the story, you'd find that Bobbie Ann Mason had already provided you with the musical setting or soundtrack for the movie. You might be able to generate a good paper by exploring why Mason has included references to these songs in particular and how they comment upon or advance the action.

Clothing

What a character wears can tell us as much as do the time and place of the story. People's clothes often indicate their economic class, as well as their psychological state. There is a great difference between a casually careless dresser and one who has dressed in distracted haste. The tilted hat, the pulled down tie, the shirttail coming out of pants are as much a sign of drunkenness as are a stumbly walk and slurred speech.

Summary

Writers locate their narratives in time and place, and these settings are not mere backdrops. They are important in interpreting the story's significance. The skillful reader of fiction watches the setting for subtle but important clues about the characters' social and psychological condition and for the symbolic significance of the action.

Suggestions for Essayists

1. Analyze what your room might tell a stranger about your personality and social background.
2. Classify the various clothing styles on campus. What do these styles tell us about the wearer?
3. Analyze the way you dress. What do you hope to communicate by what you wear? How do you wish you looked? What does this "look" tell us about your aspirations?

Suggestions for Fiction Writers

1. Describe what you think would be the ideal place to live.
2. Describe the home of a miser, a spendthrift, a loner, and a social butterfly. See if people can recognize who lived where.

BOBBIE ANN MASON (1940–)

Shiloh

Leroy Moffitt's wife, Norma Jean, is working on her pectorals. She lifts three-pound dumbbells to warm up, then progresses to a twenty-pound barbell. Standing with her legs apart, she reminds Leroy of Wonder Woman.[1]

"I'd give anything if I could just get these muscles to where they're real hard," says Norma Jean. "Feel this arm. It's not as hard as the other one."

"That's 'cause you're right-handed," says Leroy, dodging as she swings the barbell in an arc.

"Do you think so?"

---

[1] Wonder Woman, possessed of supernatural powers and strength, is a comic book character who later appeared in a television series.

"Sure."

Leroy is a truckdriver. He injured his leg in a highway accident four months ago, and his physical therapy, which involves weights and a pulley, prompted Norma Jean to try building herself up. Now she is attending a body-building class. Leroy has been collecting temporary disability since his tractor-trailer jackknifed in Missouri, badly twisting his left leg in its socket. He has a steel pin in his hip. He will probably not be able to drive his rig again. It sits in the backyard, like a gigantic bird that has flown home to roost. Leroy has been home in Kentucky for three months, and his leg is almost healed, but the accident frightened him and he does not want to drive any more long hauls. He is not sure what to do next. In the meantime, he makes things from craft kits. He started by building a miniature log cabin from notched Popsicle sticks. He varnished it and placed it on the TV set, where it remains. It reminds him of a rustic Nativity scene. Then he tried string art (sailing ships on black velvet), a macramé owl kit, a snap-together B-17 Flying Fortress,[2] and a lamp made out of a model truck, with a light fixture screwed in the top of the cab. At first the kits were diversions, something to kill time, but now he is thinking about building a full-scale log house from a kit. It would be considerably cheaper than building a regular house, and besides, Leroy has grown to appreciate how things are put together. He has begun to realize that in all the years he was on the road he never took time to examine anything. He was always flying past scenery.

"They won't let you build a log cabin in any of the new subdivisions," Norma Jean tells him.

"They will if I tell them it's for you," he says, teasing her. Ever since they were married, he has promised Norma Jean he would build her a new home one day. They have always rented, and the house they live in is small and nondescript. It does not even feel like a home, Leroy realizes now.

Norma Jean works at the Rexall drugstore, and she has acquired an amazing amount of information about cosmetics. When she explains to Leroy the three stages of complexion care, involving creams, toners, and moisturizers, he thinks happily of other petroleum products—axle grease, diesel fuel. This is a connection between him and Norma Jean. Since he has been home, he has felt unusually tender about his wife and guilty over his long absences. But he can't tell what she feels about him. Norma Jean has never complained about his traveling; she has never made hurt remarks, like calling his truck a "widow-maker." He is reasonably certain she has been faithful to him, but he wishes she would celebrate his permanent home-coming more happily. Norma Jean is often startled to find Leroy at home, and he thinks she seems a little disappointed about it. Perhaps he reminds her too much of the early days of their marriage, before he went on the road. They had a child who died as an infant, years ago. They never speak about their memories of Randy, which have almost faded, but now that Leroy is home all the time, they sometimes feel awkward around

---

[2] A B-17 Flying Fortress is a World War II bomber. At its time it was one of the largest airplanes in the American fleet.

each other, and Leroy wonders if one of them should mention the child. He has the feeling that they are waking up out of a dream together—that they must create a new marriage, start afresh. They are lucky they are still married. Leroy has read that for most people losing a child destroys the marriage—or else he heard this on *Donahue*. He can't always remember where he learns things anymore.

At Christmas, Leroy bought an electric organ for Norma Jean. She used to play the piano when she was in high school. "It don't leave you," she told him once. "It's like riding a bicycle."

The new instrument had so many keys and buttons that she was bewildered by it at first. She touched the keys tentatively, pushed some buttons, then pecked out "Chopsticks." It came out in an amplified fox-trot rhythm, with marimba sounds.

"It's an orchestra!" she cried.

The organ had a pecan-look finish and eighteen preset chords, with optional flute, violin, trumpet, clarinet, and banjo accompaniments. Norma Jean mastered the organ almost immediately. At first she played Christmas songs. Then she bought *The Sixties Songbook* and learned every tune in it, adding variations to each with the rows of brightly colored buttons.

"I didn't like these old songs back then," she said. "But I have this crazy feeling I missed something."

"You didn't miss a thing," said Leroy.

Leroy likes to lie on the couch and smoke a joint and listen to Norma Jean play "Can't Take My Eyes Off You" and "I'll Be Back."[3] He is back again. After fifteen years on the road, he is finally settling down with the woman he loves. She is still pretty. Her skin is flawless. Her frosted curls resemble pencil trimmings.

Now that Leroy has come home to stay, he notices how much the town has changed. Subdivisions are spreading across western Kentucky like an oil slick. The sign at the edge of town says "Pop: 11,500"—only seven hundred more than it said twenty years before. Leroy can't figure out who is living in all the new houses. The farmers who used to gather around the courthouse square on Saturday afternoons to play checkers and spit tobacco juice have gone. It has been years since Leroy has thought about the farmers, and they have disappeared without his noticing.

Leroy meets a kid named Stevie Hamilton in the parking lot at the new shopping center. While they pretend to be strangers meeting over a stalled car, Stevie tosses an ounce of marijuana under the front seat of Leroy's car. Stevie is wearing orange jogging shoes and a T-shirt that says CHATTAHOOCHEE SUPER-RAT. His father is a prominent doctor who lives in one of the expensive

---

[3] "Can't Take My Eyes Off You" is a song by Bob Crewe and Bob Guadio recorded by Frankie Valli in 1967 and by the Lettermen in 1968. "I'll Be Back" was composed by John Lennon and Paul McCartney and recorded by the Beatles in 1964. The song begins, "You know if you break my heart, I'll go,/But I'll be back again."

subdivisions in a new white-columned brick house that looks like a funeral parlor. In the phone book under his name there is a separate number, with the listing "Teenagers."

"Where do you get this stuff?" asks Leroy. "From your pappy?"

"That's for me to know and you to find out," Stevie says. He is slit-eyed and skinny.

"What else you got?"

"What you interested in?"

"Nothing special. Just wondered."

Leroy used to take speed[4] on the road. Now he has to go slowly. He needs to be mellow. He leans back against the car and says, "I'm aiming to build me a log house, soon as I get time. My wife, though, I don't think she likes the idea."

"Well, let me know when you want me again," Stevie says. He has a cigarette in his cupped palm, as though sheltering it from the wind. He takes a long drag, then stomps it on the asphalt and slouches away.

Stevie's father was two years ahead of Leroy in high school. Leroy is thirty-four. He married Norma Jean when they were both eighteen, and their child Randy was born a few months later, but he died at the age of four months and three days. He would be about Stevie's age now. Norma Jean and Leroy were at the drive-in, watching a double feature (*Dr. Strangelove* and *Lover Come Back*),[5] and the baby was sleeping in the back seat. When the first movie ended, the baby was dead. It was the sudden infant death syndrome. Leroy remembers handing Randy to a nurse at the emergency room, as though he were offering her a large doll as a present. A dead baby feels like a sack of flour. "It just happens sometimes," said the doctor, in what Leroy always recalls as a non-chalant tone. Leroy can hardly remember the child anymore, but he still sees vividly a scene from *Dr. Strangelove* in which the President of the United States was talking in a folksy voice on the hot line to the Soviet premier about the bomber accidentally headed toward Russia. He was in the War Room, and the world map was lit up. Leroy remembers Norma Jean standing catatonically beside him in the hospital and himself thinking: Who is this strange girl? He had forgotten who she was. Now scientists are saying that crib death is caused by a virus. Nobody knows anything, Leroy thinks. The answers are always changing.

When Leroy gets home from the shopping center, Norma Jean's mother, Mabel Beasley, is there. Until this year, Leroy has not realized how much time she spends with Norma Jean. When she visits, she inspects the closets and then the plants, informing Norma Jean when a plant is droopy or yellow. Mabel calls the plants "flowers," although there are never any blooms. She always notices if Norma Jean's laundry is piling up. Mabel is a short, overweight woman whose tight, brown-dyed curls look more like a wig than the actual wig she sometimes

---

[4] Speed is the slang term for amphetamines.

[5] *Dr. Strangelove* (1963) is a film by Stanley Kubrick satirizing the nuclear arms race. *Lover Come Back* (1961) is a light romantic comedy starring Doris Day and Rock Hudson. The two films are an unlikely double feature.

wears. Today she has brought Norma Jean an off-white dust ruffle she made for the bed; Mabel works in a custom-upholstery shop.

"This is the tenth one I made this year," Mabel says. "I got started and couldn't stop."

"It's real pretty," says Norma Jean.

"Now we can hide things under the bed," says Leroy, who gets along with his mother-in-law primarily by joking with her. Mabel has never really forgiven him for disgracing her by getting Norma Jean pregnant. When the baby died, she said that fate was mocking her.

"What's that thing?" Mabel says to Leroy in a loud voice, pointing to a tangle of yarn on a piece of canvas.

Leroy holds it up for Mabel to see. "It's my needlepoint," he explains. "This is a *Star Trek* pillow cover."

"That's what a woman would do," says Mabel. "Great day in the morning!"

"All the big football players on TV do it," he says.

"Why, Leroy, you're always trying to fool me. I don't believe you for one minute. You don't know what to do with yourself—that's the whole trouble. Sewing!"

"I'm aiming to build us a log house," says Leroy. "Soon as my plans come."

"Like *heck* you are," says Norma Jean. She takes Leroy's needlepoint and shoves it into a drawer. "You have to find a job first. Nobody can afford to build now anyway."

Mabel straightens her girdle and says, "I still think before you get tied down y'all ought to take a little run to Shiloh."

"One of these days, Mama," Norma Jean says impatiently.

Mabel is talking about Shiloh, Tennessee. For the past few years, she has been urging Leroy and Norma Jean to visit the Civil War battleground there. Mabel went there on her honeymoon—the only real trip she ever took. Her husband died of a perforated ulcer when Norma Jean was ten, but Mabel, who was accepted into the United Daughters of the Confederacy in 1975, is still preoccupied with going back to Shiloh.

"I've been to kingdom come and back in that truck out yonder," Leroy says to Mabel, "but we never yet set foot in that battleground. Ain't that something? How did I miss it?"

"It's not even that far," Mabel says.

After Mabel leaves, Norma Jean reads to Leroy from a list she has made. "Things you could do," she announces. "You could get a job as a guard at Union Carbide, where they'd let you set on a stool. You could get on at the lumberyard. You could do a little carpenter work, if you want to build so bad. You could—"

"I can't do something where I'd have to stand up all day."

"You ought to try standing up all day behind a cosmetics counter. It's amazing that I have strong feet, coming from two parents that never had strong feet at all." At the moment Norma Jean is holding on to the kitchen counter, raising her knees one at a time as she talks. She is wearing two-pound ankle weights.

"Don't worry," says Leroy. "I'll do something."

"You could truck calves to slaughter for somebody. You wouldn't have to drive any big old truck for that."

"I'm going to build you this house," says Leroy. "I want to make you a real home."

"I don't want to live in any log cabin."

"It's not a cabin. It's a house."

"I don't care. It looks like a cabin."

"You and me together could lift those logs. It's just like lifting weights."

Norma Jean doesn't answer. Under her breath, she is counting. Now she is marching through the kitchen. She is doing goose steps.

Before his accident, when Leroy came home he used to stay in the house with Norma Jean, watching TV in bed and playing cards. She would cook fried chicken, picnic ham, chocolate pie—all his favorites. Now he is home alone much of the time. In the mornings, Norma Jean disappears, leaving a cooling place in the bed. She eats a cereal called Body Buddies, and she leaves the bowl on the table, with the soggy tan balls floating in a milk puddle. He sees things about Norma Jean that he never realized before. When she chops onions, she stares off into a corner, as if she can't bear to look. She puts on her house slippers almost precisely at nine o'clock every evening and nudges her jogging shoes under the couch. She saves bread heels for the birds. Leroy watches the birds at the feeder. He notices the peculiar way goldfinches fly past the window. They close their wings, then fall, then spread their wings to catch and lift themselves. He wonders if they close their eyes when they fall. Norma Jean closes her eyes when they are in bed. She wants the lights turned out. Even then, he is sure she closes her eyes.

He goes for long drives around town. He tends to drive a car rather carelessly. Power steering and an automatic shift make a car feel so small and inconsequential that his body is hardly involved in the driving process. His injured leg stretches out comfortably. Once or twice he has almost hit something, but even the prospect of an accident seems minor in a car. He cruises the new subdivisions, feeling like a criminal rehearsing for a robbery. Norma Jean is probably right about a log house being inappropriate here in the new subdivisions. All the houses look grand and complicated. They depress him.

One day when Leroy comes home from a drive he finds Norma Jean in tears. She is in the kitchen making a potato and mushroom-soup casserole, with grated-cheese topping. She is crying because her mother caught her smoking.

"I didn't hear her coming. I was standing here puffing away pretty as you please," Norma Jean says, wiping her eyes.

"I knew it would happen sooner or later," says Leroy, putting his arm around her.

"She don't know the meaning of the word 'knock,' " says Norma Jean. "It's a wonder she hadn't caught me years ago."

"Think of it this way," Leroy says. "What if she caught me with a joint?"

"You better not let her!" Norma Jean shrieks. "I'm warning you, Leroy Moffitt!"

"I'm just kidding. Here, play me a tune. That'll help you relax."

Norma Jean puts the casserole in the oven and sets the timer. Then she plays a ragtime tune, with horns and banjo, as Leroy lights up a joint and lies on the couch, laughing to himself about Mabel's catching him at it. He thinks of Stevie Hamilton—a doctor's son pushing grass. Everything is funny. The whole town seems crazy and small. He is reminded of Virgil Mathis, a boastful policeman Leroy used to shoot pool with. Virgil recently led a drug bust in a back room at a bowling alley, where he seized ten thousand dollars' worth of marijuana. The newspaper had a picture of him holding up the bags of grass and grinning widely. Right now, Leroy can imagine Virgil breaking down the door and arresting him with a lungful of smoke. Virgil would probably have been alerted to the scene because of all the racket Norma Jean is making. Now she sounds like a hard-rock band. Norma Jean is terrific. When she switches to a Latin-rhythm version of "Sunshine Superman,"[6] Leroy hums along. Norma Jean's foot goes up and down, up and down.

"Well, what do you think?" Leroy says, when Norma Jean pauses to search through her music.

"What do I think about what?"

His mind had gone blank. Then he says, "I'll sell my rig and build us a house." That wasn't what he wanted to say. He wanted to know what she thought—what she *really* thought—about them.

"Don't start in on that again," says Norma Jean. She begins playing "Who'll Be the Next in Line?"[7]

Leroy used to tell hitchhikers his whole life story—about his travels, his hometown, the baby. He would end with a question: "Well, what do you think?" It was just a rhetorical question. In time, he had the feeling that he'd been telling the same story over and over to the same hitchhikers. He quit talking to hitchhikers when he realized how his voice sounded—whining and self-pitying, like some teenage-tragedy song. Now Leroy has the sudden impulse to tell Norma Jean about himself, as if he had just met her. They have known each other so long they have forgotten a lot about each other. They could become reacquainted. But when the oven timer goes off and she runs to the kitchen, he forgets why he wants to do this.

The next day, Mabel drops by. It is Saturday and Norma Jean is cleaning. Leroy is studying the plans of his log house, which have finally come in the mail. He has them spread out on the table—big sheets of stiff blue paper, with diagrams and numbers printed in white. While Norma Jean runs the vacuum, Mabel drinks coffee. She sets her coffee cup on a blueprint.

"I'm just waiting for time to pass," she says to Leroy, drumming her fingers on the table.

---

[6] "Sunshine Superman" is a song recorded by the British singer Donovan in 1966.
[7] "Who'll Be the Next in Line?" is a song by Ray Davies made popular in 1965 by the Kinks, a British musical group.

As soon as Norma Jean switches off the vacuum, Mabel says in a loud voice, "Did you hear about the datsun dog that killed the baby?"

Norma Jean says, "The word is 'dachshund.' "

"They put the dog on trial. It chewed the baby's legs off. The mother was in the next room all the time." She raises her voice. "They thought it was neglect."

Norma Jean is holding her ears. Leroy manages to open the refrigerator and get some Diet Pepsi to offer Mabel. Mabel still has some coffee and she waves away the Pepsi.

"Datsuns are like that," Mabel says. "They're jealous dogs. They'll tear a place to pieces if you don't keep an eye on them."

"You better watch out what you're saying, Mabel," says Leroy.

"Well, facts is facts."

Leroy looks out the window at his rig. It is like a huge piece of furniture gathering dust in the backyard. Pretty soon it will be an antique. He hears the vacuum cleaner. Norma Jean seems to be cleaning the living room rug again.

Later, she says to Leroy, "She just said that about the baby because she caught me smoking. She's trying to pay me back."

"What are you talking about?" Leroy says, nervously shuffling blueprints.

"You know good and well," Norma Jean says. She is sitting in a kitchen chair with her feet up and her arms wrapped around her knees. She looks small and helpless. She says, "The very idea, her bringing up a subject like that! Saying it was neglect."

"She didn't mean that," Leroy says.

"She might not have *thought* she meant it. She always says things like that. You don't know how she goes on."

"But she didn't really mean it. She was just talking."

Leroy opens a king-sized bottle of beer and pours it into two glasses, dividing it carefully. He hands a glass to Norma Jean and she takes it from him mechanically. For a long time, they sit by the kitchen window watching the birds at the feeder.

Something is happening. Norma Jean is going to night school. She has graduated from her six-week body-building course and now she is taking an adult-education course in composition at Paducah Community College. She spends her evenings outlining paragraphs.

"First you have a topic sentence," she explains to Leroy. "Then you divide it up. Your secondary topic has to be connected to your primary topic."

To Leroy, this sounds intimidating. "I never was any good in English," he says.

"It makes a lot of sense."

"What are you doing this for, anyhow?"

She shrugs. "It's something to do." She stands up and lifts her dumbbells a few times.

"Driving a rig, nobody cared about my English."

"I'm not criticizing your English."

Norma Jean used to say, "If I lose ten minutes' sleep, I just drag all day."

Now she stays up late, writing compositions. She got a B on her first paper—a how-to theme on soup-based casseroles. Recently Norma Jean has been cooking unusual foods—tacos, lasagna, Bombay chicken. She doesn't play the organ anymore, though her second paper was called "Why Music Is Important to Me." She sits at the kitchen table, concentrating on her outlines, while Leroy plays with his log house plans, practicing with a set of Lincoln Logs. The thought of getting a truckload of notched, numbered logs scares him, and he wants to be prepared. As he and Norma Jean work together at the kitchen table, Leroy has the hopeful thought that they are sharing something, but he knows he is a fool to think this. Norma Jean is miles away. He knows he is going to lose her. Like Mabel, he is just waiting for time to pass.

One day, Mabel is there before Norma Jean gets home from work, and Leroy finds himself confiding in her. Mabel, he realizes, must know Norma Jean better than he does.

"I don't know what's got into that girl," Mabel says. "She used to go to bed with the chickens. Now you say she's up all hours. Plus her a-smoking. I like to died."

"I want to make her this beautiful home," Leroy says, indicating the Lincoln Logs. "I don't think she even wants it. Maybe she was happier with me gone."

"She don't know what to make of you, coming home like this."

"Is that it?"

Mabel takes the roof off his Lincoln Log cabin. "You couldn't get *me* in a log cabin," she says. "I was raised in one. It's no picnic, let me tell you."

"They're different now," says Leroy.

"I tell you what," Mabel says, smiling oddly at Leroy.

"What?"

"Take her on down to Shiloh. Y'all need to get out together, stir a little. Her brain's all balled up over them books."

Leroy can see traces of Norma Jean's features in her mother's face. Mabel's worn face has the texture of crinkled cotton, but suddenly she looks pretty. It occurs to Leroy that Mabel has been hinting all along that she wants them to take her with them to Shiloh.

"Let's all go to Shiloh," he says. "You and me and her. Come Sunday."

Mabel throws up her hand in protest. "Oh, no, not me. Young folks want to be by theirselves."

When Norma Jean comes in with groceries, Leroy says excitedly, "Your mama here's been dying to go to Shiloh for thirty-five years. It's about time we went, don't you think?"

"I'm not going to butt in on anybody's second honeymoon," Mabel says.

"Who's going on a honeymoon, for Christ's sake?" Norma Jean says loudly.

"I never raised no daughter of mine to talk that-a-way," Mabel says.

"You ain't seen nothing yet," says Norma Jean. She starts putting away boxes and cans, slamming cabinet doors.

"There's a log cabin at Shiloh," Mabel says. "It was there during the battle. There's bullet holes in it."

"When are you going to *shut up* about Shiloh, Mama?" asks Norma Jean.

"I always thought Shiloh was the prettiest place, so full of history," Mabel goes on. "I just hoped y'all could see it once before I die, so you could tell me about it." Later, she whispers to Leroy, "You do what I said. A little change is what she needs."

"Your name means 'the king,' " Norma Jean says to Leroy that evening. He is trying to get her to go to Shiloh, and she is reading a book about another century.

"Well, I reckon I ought to be right proud."

"I guess so."

"Am I still king around here?"

Norma Jean flexes her biceps and feels them for hardness. "I'm not fooling around with anybody, if that's what you mean," she says.

"Would you tell me if you were?"

"I don't know."

"What does *your* name mean?"

"It was Marilyn Monroe's real name."[8]

"No kidding!"

"Norma comes from the Normans.[9] They were invaders," she says. She closes her book and looks hard at Leroy. "I'll go to Shiloh with you if you'll stop staring at me."

On Sunday, Norma Jean packs a picnic and they go to Shiloh. To Leroy's relief, Mabel says she does not want to come with them. Norma Jean drives, and Leroy, sitting beside her, feels like some boring hitchhiker she has picked up. He tries some conversation, but she answers him in monosyllables. At Shiloh, she drives aimlessly through the park, past bluffs and trails and steep ravines. Shiloh is an immense place, and Leroy cannot see it as a battleground. It is not what he expected. He thought it would look like a golf course. Monuments are everywhere, showing through the thick clusters of trees. Norma Jean passes the log cabin Mabel mentioned. It is surrounded by tourists looking for bullet holes.

"That's not the kind of log house I've got in mind," says Leroy apologetically.

"I know *that*."

"This is a pretty place. Your mama was right."

"It's O.K.," says Norma Jean. "Well, we've seen it. I hope she's satisfied."

They burst out laughing together.

At the park museum, a movie on Shiloh is shown every half hour, but they decide that they don't want to see it. They buy a souvenir Confederate flag for Mabel, and then they find a picnic spot near the cemetery. Norma Jean has brought a picnic cooler, with pimiento sandwiches, soft drinks, and Yodels.

---

[8] Marilyn Monroe (1926–1962) was born Norma Jean Mortenson (later) Baker. She became a film star in the 1950s, appearing in such films as *Some Like It Hot* and *The Seven Year Itch*.

[9] The Normans, a people of northwestern France, invaded England in 1066. Their leader, William the Conqueror, united England with Normandy. The Normans were the last foreign power to conquer England.

Leroy eats a sandwich and then smokes a joint, hiding it behind the picnic cooler. Norma Jean has quit smoking altogether. She is picking cake crumbs from the cellophane wrapper, like a fussy bird.

Leroy says, "So the boys in gray ended up in Corinth.[10] The Union soldiers zapped 'em finally. April 7, 1862."

They both know that he doesn't know any history. He is just talking about some of the historical plaques they have read. He feels awkward, like a boy on a date with an older girl. They are still just making conversation.

"Corinth is where Mama eloped to," says Norma Jean.

They sit in silence and stare at the cemetery for the Union dead and, beyond, at a tall cluster of trees. Campers are parked nearby, bumper to bumper, and small children in bright clothing are cavorting and squealing. Norma Jean wads up the cake wrapper and squeezes it tightly in her hand. Without looking at Leroy, she says, "I want to leave you."

Leroy takes a bottle of Coke out of the cooler and flips off the cap. He holds the bottle poised near his mouth but cannot remember to take a drink. Finally he says, "No, you don't."

"Yes, I do."

"I won't let you."

"You can't stop me."

"Don't do me that way."

Leroy knows Norma Jean will have her own way. "Didn't I promise to be home from now on?" he says.

"In some ways, a woman prefers a man who wanders," says Norma Jean. "That sounds crazy, I know."

"You're not crazy."

Leroy remembers to drink from his Coke. Then he says, "Yes, you *are* crazy. You and me could start all over again. Right back at the beginning."

"We *have* started all over again," says Norma Jean. "And this is how it turned out."

"What did I do wrong?"

"Nothing."

"Is this one of those women's lib things?" Leroy asks.

"Don't be funny."

The cemetery, a green slope dotted with white markers, looks like a subdivision site. Leroy is trying to comprehend that his marriage is breaking up, but for some reason he is wondering about white slabs in a graveyard.

"Everything was fine till Mama caught me smoking," says Norma Jean, standing up. "That set something off."

"What are you talking about?"

"She won't leave me alone—*you* won't leave me alone." Norma Jean seems

---

[10] Corinth is a city in extreme northeastern Mississippi near the Tennessee border. In the Civil War it was a strategic railroad center abandoned to the Union forces after the battle of Shiloh. The Mississippi city was named after the Greek city of Corinth, the site of numerous battles and of invasions by a succession of rulers.

to be crying, but she is looking away from him. "I feel eighteen again. I can't face that all over again." She starts walking away. "No, it *wasn't* fine. I don't know what I'm saying. Forget it."

Leroy takes a lungful of smoke and closes his eyes as Norma Jean's words sink in. He tries to focus on the fact that thirty-five hundred soldiers died on the grounds around him. He can only think of that war as a board game with plastic soldiers. Leroy almost smiles, as he compares the Confederates' daring attack on the Union camps and Virgil Mathis's raid on the bowling alley. General Grant, drunk and furious, shoved the Southerners back to Corinth, where Mabel and Jet Beasley were married years later, when Mabel was still thin and good-looking. The next day, Mabel and Jet visited the battleground, and then Norma Jean was born, and then she married Leroy and they had a baby, which they lost, and now Leroy and Norma Jean are here at the same battleground. Leroy knows he is leaving out a lot. He is leaving out the insides of history. History was always just names and dates to him. It occurs to him that building a house out of logs is similarly empty—too simple. And the real inner workings of a marriage, like most of history, have escaped him. Now he sees that building a log house is the dumbest idea he could have had. It was clumsy of him to think Norma Jean would want a log house. It was a crazy idea. He'll have to think of something else, quickly. He will wad the blueprints into tight balls and fling them into the lake. Then he'll get moving again. He opens his eyes. Norma Jean has moved away and is walking through the cemetery, following a serpentine brick path.

Leroy gets up to follow his wife, but his good leg is asleep and his bad leg still hurts him. Norma Jean is far away, walking rapidly toward the bluff by the river, and he tries to hobble toward her. Some children run past him, screaming noisily. Norma Jean has reached the bluff, and she is looking out over the Tennessee River. Now she turns toward Leroy and waves her arms. Is she beckoning to him? She seems to be doing an exercise for her chest muscles. The sky is unusually pale—the color of the dust ruffle Mabel made for their bed.

Questions

1. Why does Norma Jean take up body-building and start college?
2. Why does Leroy buy Norma Jean the electric organ? Why does she stop playing it?
3. What role does the death of their child play in the dissolution of their marriage?
4. Norma Jean says, "Everything was fine till Mama caught me smoking . . . That set something off." What did her mother's discovery "set off"? Why should the event have "set off" Norma Jean?
5. In the last paragraph Norma Jean waves her arms toward Leroy. Can Leroy tell what she is signaling? Can you as a reader tell what she is signaling? Does it matter?
6. Why does Leroy wish to build the log cabin? Should he build it?
7. Can their marriage be saved?

JAMES JOYCE (1882–1941)

Araby

North Richmond Street, being blind,[1] was a quiet street except at the hour when the Christian Brothers' School set the boys free. An uninhabited house of two stories stood at the blind end, detached from its neighbours in a square ground. The other houses of the street, conscious of decent lives within them, gazed at one another with brown imperturbable faces.

The former tenant of our house, a priest, had died in the back drawing-room. Air, musty from having been long enclosed, hung in all the rooms, and the waste room behind the kitchen was littered with old useless papers. Among these I found a few paper-covered books, the pages of which were curled and damp: *The Abbot,* by Walter Scott, *The Devout Communicant,* and *The Memoirs of Vidocq.*[2] I liked the last best because its leaves were yellow. The wild garden behind the house contained a central apple tree and a few straggling bushes under one of which I found the late tenant's rusty bicycle pump. He had been a very charitable priest; in his will he had left all his money to institutions and the furniture of his house to his sister.

When the short days of winter came dusk fell before we had well eaten our dinners. When we met in the street the houses had grown sombre. The space of sky above us was the colour of ever-changing violet and towards it the lamps of the street lifted their feeble lanterns. The cold air stung us and we played till our bodies glowed. Our shouts echoed in the silent street. The career of our play brought us through the dark muddy lanes behind the houses where we ran the gauntlet of the rough tribes from the cottages to the back doors of the dark dripping gardens where odours arose from the ash-pits, to the dark odorous stables where a coachman smoothed and combed the horse or shook music from the buckled harness. When we returned to the street, light from the kitchen windows had filled the areas. If my uncle was seen turning the corner we hid in the shadow until we had seen him safely housed. Or if Mangan's sister came out on the doorstep to call her brother in to his tea we watched her from our shadow peer up and down the street. We waited to see whether she would remain or go in and, if she remained, we left our shadow and walked up to Mangan's steps resignedly. She was waiting for us, her figure defined by the light from the half-opened door. Her brother always teased her before he obeyed and I stood by the railings looking at her. Her dress swung as she moved her body and the soft rope of her hair tossed from side to side.

Every morning I lay on the floor in the front parlour watching her door. The blind was pulled down to within an inch of the sash so that I could not be seen. When she came out on the doorstep my heart leaped. I ran to the hall, seized my books and followed her. I kept her brown figure always in my eye and, when

---

[1] A blind street is a dead-end street.

[2] François-Eugène Vidocq (1775–1857) helped create the French security police. *The Abbot* is one of Sir Walter Scott's Scottish historical romances. *The Devout Communicant* is a Catholic devotional manual.

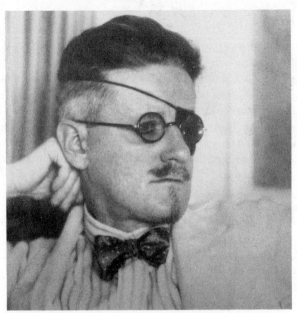

James Joyce (*The Bettmann Archive*)

we came near the point at which our ways diverged, I quickened my pace and passed her. This happened morning after morning. I had never spoken to her, except for a few casual words, and yet her name was like a summons to all my foolish blood.

Her image accompanied me even in places the most hostile to romance. On Saturday evenings when my aunt went marketing I had to go to carry some of the parcels. We walked through the flaring streets, jostled by drunken men and bargaining women, amid the curses of labourers, the shrill litanies of shop-boys who stood on guard by the barrels of pigs' cheeks, the nasal chanting of street-singers, who sang a *come-all-you* about O'Donovan Rossa,[3] or a ballad about the troubles in our native land. These noises converged in a single sensation of life for me: I imagined that I bore my chalice safely through a throng of foes. Her name sprang to my lips at moments in strange prayers and praises which I myself did not understand. My eyes were often full of tears (I could not tell why) and at times a flood from my heart seemed to pour itself out into my bosom. I thought little of the future. I did not know whether I would ever speak to her or not or, if I spoke to her, how I could tell her of my confused adoration. But my body was like a harp and her words and gestures were like fingers running upon the wires.

One evening I went into the back drawing-room in which the priest had died.

---

[3] Jeremiah Donovan (1831–1915), commonly called O'Donovan Rossa, was an Irish nationalist celebrated in street songs or *come-all-you*'s.

It was a dark rainy evening and there was no sound in the house. Through one of the broken panes I heard the rain impinge upon the earth, the fine incessant needles of water playing in the sodden beds. Some distant lamp or lighted window gleamed below me. I was thankful that I could see so little. All my senses seemed to desire to veil themselves and, feeling that I was about to slip from them, I pressed the palms of my hands together until they trembled, murmuring: "O love! O love!" many times.

At last she spoke to me. When she addressed the first words to me I was so confused that I did not know what to answer. She asked me was I going to *Araby*. I forgot whether I answered yes or no. It would be a splendid bazaar, she said she would love to go.

"And why can't you?" I asked.

While she spoke she turned a silver bracelet round and round her wrist. She could not go, she said, because there would be a retreat that week in her convent. Her brother and two other boys were fighting for their caps and I was alone at the railings. She held one of the spikes, bowing her head towards me. The light from the lamp opposite our door caught the white curve of her neck, lit up her hair that rested there and, falling, lit up the hand upon the railing. It fell over one side of her dress and caught the white border of a petticoat, just visible as she stood at ease.

"It's well for you," she said.

"If I go," I said, "I will bring you something."

What innumerable follies laid waste my waking and sleeping thoughts after the evening! I wished to annihilate the tedious intervening days. I chafed against the work of school. At night in my bedroom and by day in the classroom her image came between me and the page I strove to read. The syllables of the word *Araby* were called to me through the silence in which my soul luxuriated and cast an Eastern enchantment over me. I asked for leave to go to the bazaar on Saturday night. My aunt was surprised and hoped it was not some Freemason[4] affair. I answered few questions in class. I watched my master's face pass from amiability to sternness; he hoped I was not beginning to idle. I could not call my wandering thoughts together. I had hardly any patience with the serious work of life which, now that it stood between me and my desire, seemed to me child's play, ugly monotonous child's play.

On Saturday morning I reminded my uncle that I wished to go to the bazaar in the evening. He was fussing at the hall-stand, looking for the hat brush, and answered me curtly:

"Yes, boy, I know."

As he was in the hall I could not go into the front parlour and lie at the window. I left the house in bad humour and walked slowly towards the school. The air was pitilessly raw and already my heart misgave me.

When I came home to dinner my uncle had not yet been home. Still it was early. I sat staring at the clock for some time and, when its ticking began to

---

[4] Freemason societies, because they were secret, were frequently considered dangerous gatherings.

irritate me, I left the room. I mounted the staircase and gained the upper part of the house. The high cold empty gloomy rooms liberated me and I went from room to room singing. From the front window I saw my companions playing below in the street. Their cries reached me weakened and indistinct and, leaning my forehead against the cool glass, I looked over at the dark house where she lived. I may have stood there for an hour, seeing nothing but the brown-clad figure cast by my imagination, touched discreetly by the lamplight at the curved neck, at the hand upon the railings and at the border below the dress.

When I came downstairs again I found Mrs. Mercer sitting at the fire. She was an old garrulous woman, a pawnbroker's widow, who collected used stamps for some pious purpose. I had to endure the gossip of the tea-table. The meal was prolonged beyond an hour and still my uncle did not come. Mrs. Mercer stood up to go: she was sorry she couldn't wait any longer, but it was after eight o'clock and she did not like to be out late, as the night air was bad for her. When she had gone I began to walk up and down the room, clenching my fists. My aunt said:

"I'm afraid you may put off your bazaar for this night of Our Lord."

At nine o'clock I heard my uncle's latchkey in the hall-door. I heard him talking to himself and heard the hall-stand rocking when it had received the weight of his overcoat. I could interpret these signs. When he was midway through his dinner I asked him to give me the money to go to the bazaar. He had forgotten.

"The people are in bed and after their first sleep now," he said.

I did not smile. My aunt said to him energetically:

"Can't you give him the money and let him go? You've kept him late enough as it is."

My uncle said he was very sorry he had forgotten. He said he believed in the old saying: "All work and no play makes Jack a dull boy." He asked me where I was going and, when I had told him a second time, he asked me did I know *The Arab's Farewell to his Steed*.[5] When I left the kitchen he was about to recite the opening lines of the piece to my aunt.

I held a florin tightly in my hand as I strode down Buckingham Street towards the station. The sight of the streets thronged with buyers and glaring with gas recalled to me the purpose of my journey. I took my seat in a third-class carriage of a deserted train. After an intolerable delay the train moved out of the station slowly. It crept onward among ruinous houses and over the twinkling river. At Westland Row Station a crowd of people pressed to the carriage doors; but the porters moved them back, saying that it was a special train for the bazaar. I remained alone in the bare carriage. In a few minutes the train drew up beside an improvised wooden platform. I passed out on the road and saw by the lighted dial of a clock that it was ten minutes to ten. In front of me was a large building which displayed the magical name.

---

[5] A poem by Caroline Norton (1808–1877).

I could not find any sixpenny entrance and, fearing that the bazaar would be closed, I passed in quickly through a turnstile, handing a shilling to a weary-looking man. I found myself in a big hall girdled at half its height by a gallery. Nearly all the stalls were closed and the greater part of the hall was in darkness. I recognized a silence like that which pervades a church after a service. I walked into the center of the bazaar timidly. A few people were gathered about the stalls which were still open. Before a curtain, over which the words *Café Chantant* were written in coloured lamps, two men were counting money on a salver. I listened to the fall of the coins.

Remembering with difficulty why I had come I went over to one of the stalls and examined porcelain vases and flowered tea-sets. At the door of the stall a young lady was talking and laughing with two young gentlemen. I remarked their English accents and listened vaguely to their conversation.

"O, I never said such a thing!"

"O, but you did!"

"O, but I didn't!"

"Didn't she say that?"

"Yes. I heard her."

"O, there's a . . . fib!"

Observing me, the young lady came over and asked me did I wish to buy anything. The tone of her voice was not encouraging; she seemed to have spoken to me out of a sense of duty. I looked humbly at the great jars that stood like eastern guards at either side of the dark entrance to the stall and murmured:

"No, thank you."

The young lady changed the position of one of the vases and went back to the two young men. They began to talk of the same subject. Once or twice the young lady glanced at me over her shoulder.

I lingered before her stall, though I knew my stay was useless, to make my interest in her wares seem the more real. Then I turned away slowly and walked down the middle of the bazaar. I allowed the two pennies to fall against the sixpence in my pocket. I heard a voice call from one end of the gallery that the light was out. The upper part of the hall was now completely dark.

Gazing up into the darkness I saw myself as a creature driven and derided by vanity; and my eyes burned with anguish and anger.

Questions

1. In what ways is North Richmond Street blind?
2. How does the narrator regard Mangan's sister? Does she do or say anything to justify his attitude toward her?
3. How does Joyce contrast the beautiful and romantic with the ugly and banal? Which is closer to the truth?
4. Why does the narrator wait for his uncle in the room where the priest died? How does that setting emphasize his emotions?
5. How does Joyce contrast light and dark in "Araby"? What sort of feelings does this contrast evoke?
6. Is the narrator a creature "driven and derided by vanity"? Why?

Writers on Writing *Ernest Hemingway*

ETHAN CANIN (1961–)

Emperor of the Air

Let me tell you who I am. I'm sixty-nine years old, live in the same house I was raised in, and have been the high school biology and astronomy teacher in this town so long that I have taught the grandson of one of my former students. I wear my father's wristwatch, which tells me it is past four-thirty in the morning, and though I have thought otherwise, I now think hope is the essence of all good men.

My wife, Vera, and I have no children, and this has enabled us to do a great many things in our lives: we have stood on the Great Wall of China, toured the Pyramid of Cheops, sunned in Lapland at midnight. Vera, who is near my age, is off on the Appalachian Trail. She has been gone two weeks and expects to be gone one more, on a trip on which a group of men and women, some of them half her age, are walking all the way through three states. Age, it seems, has left my wife alone. She ice-skates and hikes and will swim nude in a mountain lake. She does these things without me, however, for now my life has slowed. Last fall, as I pushed a lawnmower around our yard, I felt a squeezing in my chest and a burst of pain in my shoulder, and I spent a week in a semi-private hospital room. A heart attack. Myocardial infarction, minor. I will no longer run for a train, and in my shirt pocket I keep a small vial of nitroglycerine pills. In slow supermarket lines or traffic snarls I tell myself that impatience is not worth dying over, and last week, as I stood at the window and watched my neighbor, Mr. Pike, cross the yard toward our front door carrying a chain saw, I told myself that he was nothing but a doomed and hopeless man.

I had found the insects in my elm a couple of days before, the slim red line running from the ground up the long trunk and vanishing into the lower boughs. I brought out a magnifying glass to examine them—their shiny arthroderms, torsos elongated like drops of red liquid; their tiny legs, jointed and wiry, climbing the fissured bark. The morning I found them, Mr. Pike came over from next door and stood on our porch. "There's vermin in your elm," he said.

"I know," I said. "Come in."

"It's a shame, but I'll be frank: there's other trees on this block. I've got my own three elms to think of."

Mr. Pike is a builder, a thick and unpleasant man with whom I have rarely spoken. Though I had seen him at high school athletic events, the judgmental tilt to his jaw always suggested to me that he was merely watching for the players' mistakes. He is short, with thick arms and a thick neck and a son, Kurt, in whose bellicose shouts I can already begin to hear the thickness of his father. Mr. Pike owns or partly owns a construction company that erected a line of low prefabricated houses on the outskirts of town, on a plot I remember from my youth as having been razed by fire. Once, a plumber who was working on our basement pipes told me that Mr. Pike was a poor craftsman, a man who valued money over quality. The plumber, a man my age who kept his tools in a wooden chest, shook his head when he told me that Mr. Pike used plastic pipes in the houses he had built. "They'll last ten years," the plumber told me. "Then the seams will go and the walls and ceilings will start to fill with water." I myself had had little to do with Mr. Pike until he told me he wanted my elm cut down to protect the three saplings in his yard. Our houses are separated by a tall stand of rhododendron and ivy, so we don't see each other's private lives as most neighbors do. When we talked on the street, we spoke only about a football score or the incessant rain, and I had not been on his property since shortly after he moved in, when I had gone over to introduce myself and he had shown me the spot where, underneath his rolling back lawn, he planned to build a bomb shelter.

Last week he stood on my porch with the chain saw in his hands. "I've got young elms," he said. "I can't let them be infested."

"My tree is over two hundred years old."

"It's a shame," he said, showing me the saw, "but I'll be frank. I just wanted you to know I could have it cut down as soon as you gave the word."

All week I had a hard time sleeping. I read Dickens in bed, heated cups of milk, but nothing worked. The elm was dying. Vera was gone, and I lay in bed thinking of the insects, of their miniature jaws carrying away heartwood. It was late summer, the nights were still warm, and sometimes I went outside in my nightclothes and looked up at the sky. I teach astronomy, as I have said, and though sometimes I try to see the stars as milky dots or pearls, they are forever arranged in my eye according to the astronomic charts. I stood by the elm and looked up at Ursa Minor and Lyra, at Cygnus and Corona Borealis. I went back inside, read, peeled an orange. I sat at the window and thought about the insects, and every morning at five a boy who had once taken my astronomy class rode by on his bicycle, whistling the national anthem, and threw the newspaper onto our porch.

Sometimes I heard them, chewing the heart of my splendid elm.

The day after I first found the insects I called a man at the tree nursery. He described them for me, the bodies like red droplets, the wiry legs; he told me their genus and species.

"Will they kill the tree?"

"They could."

"We can poison them, can't we?"

"Probably not," he said. He told me that once they were visible outside the bark they had already invaded the tree too thoroughly for pesticide. "To kill them," he said, "we would end up killing the tree."

"Does that mean the tree is dead?"

"No," he said. "It depends on the colony of insects. Sometimes they invade a tree but don't kill it, don't even weaken it. They eat the wood, but sometimes they eat it so slowly that the tree can replace it."

When Mr. Pike came over the next day, I told him this. "You're asking me to kill a two-hundred-and-fifty-year-old tree that otherwise wouldn't die for a long time."

"The tree's over eighty feet tall," he said.

"So?"

"It stands fifty-two feet from my house."

"Mr. Pike, it's older than the Liberty Bell."

"I don't want to be unpleasant," he said, "but a storm could blow twenty-eight feet of that tree through the wall of my house."

"How long have you lived in that house?"

He looked at me, picked at his tooth. "You know."

"Four years," I said. "I was living here when a czar ruled Russia. An elm grows one quarter inch in width each year, when it's still growing. That tree is four feet thick, and it has yet to chip the paint on either your house or mine."

"It's sick," he said. "It's a sick tree. It could fall."

"Could," I said. "It *could* fall."

"It very well *might* fall."

We looked at each other for a moment. Then he averted his eyes, and with his right hand adjusted something on his watch. I looked at his wrist. The watch had a shiny metal band, with the hours, minutes, seconds, blinking in the display.

The next day he was back on my porch.

"We can plant another one," he said.

"What?"

"We can plant another tree. After we cut the elm, we can plant a new one."

"Do you have any idea how long it would take to grow a tree like that one?"

"You can buy trees half-grown. They bring them in on a truck and replant them."

"Even a half-grown tree would take a century to reach the size of the elm. A century."

He looked at me. Then he shrugged, turned around, and went back down the steps. I sat down in the open doorway. A century. What would be left of the earth in a century? I didn't think I was a sentimental man, and I don't weep at plays or movies, but certain moments have always been peculiarly moving for me, and the mention of a century was one. There have been others. Standing out of the way on a fall evening, as couples and families converge on the concert hall from the radiating footpaths, has always filled me with a longing, though I don't know for what. I have taught the life of the simple hydra that is drawn, for no reasons it could ever understand, toward the bright surface of the water, and the spectacle of a thousand human beings organizing themselves into a single room to hear the quartets of Beethoven is as moving to me as birth or death. I feel the same way during the passage in an automobile across a cantilever span above the Mississippi, mother of rivers. These moments overwhelm me, and sitting on the porch that day as Mr. Pike retreated up the footpath, paused at the elm, and then went back into his house, I felt my life open up and present itself to me.

When he had gone back into his house I went out to the elm and studied the insects, which emerged from a spot in the grass and disappeared above my sight, in the lowest branches. Their line was dense and unbroken. I went inside and found yesterday's newspaper, which I rolled up and brought back out. With it I slapped up and down the trunk until the line was in chaos. I slapped until the newspaper was wet and tearing; with my fingernails I squashed stragglers between the narrow crags of bark. I stamped the sod where they emerged, dug my shoe tip into their underground tunnels. When my breathing became painful, I stopped and sat on the ground. I closed my eyes until the pulse in my neck was calm, and I sat there, mildly triumphant, master at last. After a while I looked up again at the tree and found the line perfectly restored.

That afternoon I mixed a strong insect poison, which I brought outside and painted around the bottom of the trunk. Mr. Pike came out onto his steps to watch. He walked down, stood on the sidewalk behind me, made little chuckling noises. "There's no poison that'll work," he whispered.

But that evening, when I came outside, the insects were gone. The trunk was bare. I ran my finger around the circumference. I rang Mr. Pike's doorbell and we went out and stood by the tree together. He felt in the notches of the bark, scratched bits of earth from the base. "I'll be damned," he said.

When I was a boy in this town, the summers were hot and the forest to the north and east often dried to the point where the undergrowth, not fit to compete with the deciduous trees for groundwater, turned crackling brown. The shrubbery became as fragile as straw, and the summer I was sixteen the forest ignited. A sheet of flame raced and bellowed day and night as loud as a fleet of propeller planes. Whole families gathered in the street and evacuation plans were made, street routes drawn out beneath the night sky, which, despite the ten miles' distance to the fire, shone with orange light. My father had a wireless with which he communicated to the fire lines. He stayed up all night and promised that he would wake the neighbors if the wind changed or the fire otherwise turned toward town. That night the wind held, and by morning a firebreak the width of a street had been cut. My father took me down to see it the next day, a ribbon of cleared land as bare as if it had been drawn with a razor. Trees had been felled, the underbrush sickled down and removed. We stood at the edge of the cleared land, the town behind us, and watched the fire. Then we got into my father's Plymouth and drove as close as we were allowed. A fireman near the flames had been asphyxiated, someone said, when the cone of fire had turned abruptly and sucked up all the oxygen in the air. My father explained to me how a flame breathed oxygen like a man. We got out of the car. The heat curled the hair on our arms and turned the ends of our eyelashes white.

My father was a pharmacist and had taken me to the fire out of curiosity. Anything scientific interested him. He kept tide tables, and collected the details of nature—butterflies and moths, seeds, wildflowers—and stored them in glass-fronted cases, which he leaned against the stone wall of our cellar. One summer he taught me the constellations of the Northern Hemisphere. We went outside at night, and as the summer progressed he showed me how to find Perseus and Arcturus and Andromeda, how some of the brightest stars illuminated Lyra and Aquila, how, though the constellations proceed with the seasons, Polaris remains most fixed and is thus the set point of a mariner's navigation. He taught me the night sky, and I find now that this is rare knowledge. Later, when I taught astronomy, my students rarely cared about the silicon or iron on the sun, but when I spoke of Cepheus or Lacerta, they were silent and attended my words. At a party now I can always find a drinking husband who will come outside with me and sip cognac while I point out the stars and say their names.

That day, as I stood and watched the fire, I thought the flames were as loud and powerful as the sea, and that evening, when we were home, I went out to the front yard and climbed the elm to watch the forest burn. Climbing the elm was forbidden me, because the lowest limbs even then were well above my reach and because my father believed that anybody lucky enough to make it up into the lower boughs would almost certainly fall on the way down. But I knew how to climb it anyway. I had done it before, when my parents were gone. I had never made it as far as the first limbs, but I had learned the knobs and handholds on which, with balance and strength, I could climb to within a single jump of the boughs. The jump frightened me, however, and I had never attempted it. To reach the boughs one had to gather strength and leap upward into the air, propelled only by the purchase of feet and hands on the small juttings of bark. It was a terrible risk. I could no more imagine myself making this leap than I could imagine diving headlong from a coastal cliff into the sea. I was an adventurous youth, as I was later an adventurous man, but all my adventures had a quality about them of safety and planned success. This is still true. In Ethiopia I have photographed a lioness with her cubs; along the Barrier Reef I have dived among barracuda and scorpion fish—but these things have never frightened me. In my life I have done few things that have frightened me.

That night, though, I made the leap into the lower boughs of the elm. My parents were inside the house, and I made my way upward until I crawled out of the leaves onto a narrow top branch and looked around me at a world that on two sides was entirely red and orange with flame. After a time I came back down and went inside to sleep, but that night the wind changed. My father woke us, and we gathered outside on the street with all the other families on our block. People carried blankets filled with the treasures of their lives. One woman wore a fur coat, though the air was suffused with ash and was as warm as an afternoon. My father stood on the hood of a car and spoke. He had heard through the radio that the fire had leaped the break, that a house on the eastern edge of town was in full flame, and, as we all could feel, that the wind was strong and blowing straight west. He told the families to finish loading their cars and leave as soon as possible. Though the fire was still across town, he said, the air was filling with smoke so rapidly that breathing would soon be difficult. He got down off the car and we went inside to gather things together. We had an RCA radio in our living room and a set of Swiss china in my mother's cupboard, but my father instead loaded a box with the *Encyclopaedia Britannica* and carried up from the basement the heavy glass cases that contained his species chart of the North American butterflies. We carried these things outside to the Plymouth. When we returned, my mother was standing in the doorway.

"This is my home," she said.

"We're in a hurry," my father said.

"This is my home, this is my children's home. I'm not leaving."

My father stood on the porch looking at her. "Stay here," he said to me. Then he took my mother's arm and they went into the house. I stood on the steps outside, and when my father came out again in a few minutes, he was alone, just as when we drove west that night and slept with the rest of our neighborhood on Army cots in the high school gym in the next town, we were alone. My mother had stayed behind.

Nothing important came of this. That night the wind calmed and the burning house was extinguished; the next day a heavy rain wet the fire and it was put out. Everybody came home, and the settled ash was swept from the houses and walkways into black piles in the street. I mention the incident now only because it points out, I think, what I have always lacked: I inherited none of my mother's moral stubbornness. In spite of my age, still, arriving on foot at a crosswalk where the light is red but no cars are in sight, I'm thrown into confusion. My decisions never seem to engage the certainty that I had hoped to enjoy late in my life. But I was adamant and angry when Mr. Pike came to my door. The elm was ancient and exquisite: we could not let it die.

Now, though, the tree was safe. I examined it in the morning, in the afternoon, in the evening, and with a lantern at night. The bark was clear. I slept.

The next morning Mr. Pike was at my door.

"Good morning, neighbor," I said.

"They're back."

"They can't be."

"They are. Look," he said, and walked out to the tree. He pointed up to the first bough.

"You probably can't see them," he said, "but I can. They're up there, a whole line of them.

"They couldn't be."

"They sure are. Listen," he said, "I don't want to be unpleasant, but I'll be frank."

That evening he left a note in our mail slot. It said that he had contacted the authorities, who had agreed to enforce the cutting of the tree if I didn't do it myself. I read the note in the kitchen. Vera had been cooking some Indian chicken before she left for the Appalachian Trail, and on the counter was a big jar filled with flour and spices that she shook pieces of chicken in. I read Mr. Pike's note again. Then I got a fishing knife and a flashlight from the closet, emptied Vera's jar, and went outside with these things to the elm. The street was quiet. I made a few calculations, and then with the knife cut the bark. Nothing. I had to do it only a couple more times, however, before I hit the mark and, sure enough, the tree sprouted insects. Tiny red bugs shot crazily from the slit in the bark. I touched my finger there and they spread in an instant all over my hand and up my arm. I had to shake them off. Then I opened the jar, laid the fishing knife out from the opening like a bridge, and touched the blade to the slit in the tree. They scrambled up the knife and began to fill the jar as fast as a trickling spring. After a few minutes I pulled out the knife, closed the lid, and went back into the house.

Mr. Pike is my neighbor, and so I felt a certain remorse. What I contemplated, however, was not going to kill the elms. It was going to save them. If Mr. Pike's trees were infested, they would still more than likely live, and he would no longer want mine chopped down. This is the nature of the world. In the dark house, feeling half like a criminal and half like a man of mercy, my heart arrhythmic in anticipation, I went upstairs to prepare. I put on black pants and a black shirt. I dabbed shoe polish on my cheeks, my neck, my wrists, the backs of my hands. Over my white hair I stretched a tight black cap. Then I walked downstairs. I picked up the jar and the flashlight and went outside into the night.

I have always enjoyed gestures—never failing to bow, for example, when I finished dancing with a woman—but one attribute I have acquired with age is the ability to predict when I am about to act foolishly. As I slid calmly into the shadowy cavern behind our side-yard rhododendron and paused to catch my breath, I thought that perhaps I had better go back inside and get into my bed. But then I decided to go through with it. As I stood there in the shadow of the swaying rhododendron, waiting to pass into the back yard of my neighbor, I thought of Hannibal and Napoleon and MacArthur. I tested my flashlight and shook the jar, which made a soft colliding sound as if it were filled with rice. A light was on in the Pikes' living room, but the alley between our houses was dark. I passed through.

The Pikes' yard is large, larger than ours, and slopes twice within its length, so that the lawn that night seemed like a dark, furrowed flag stretching back to the three elms. I paused at the border of the driveway, where the grass began, and looked out at the young trees outlined by the lighted houses behind them. In what strange ways, I thought, do our lives turn. Then I got down on my hands and knees. Staying along the fence that separates our yards, I crawled toward the back of the Pikes' lawn. In my life I have not crawled a lot. With Vera I have gone spelunking in the limestone caves of southern Minnesota, but there the crawling was obligate, and as we made our way along the narrow, wet channel into the heart of the rock, I felt a strange grace in my knees and elbows. The channel was hideously narrow, and my life depended on the sureness of my limbs. Now, in the Pikes' yard, my knees felt arthritic and torn. I made my way along the driveway toward the young elms against the back fence. The grass was wet and the water dampened my trousers. I was hurrying as best I could across the open lawn, the insect-filled jar in my hand, the flashlight in my pocket, when I put my palm on something cement. I stopped and looked down. In the dim light I saw what looked like the hatch door on a submarine. Round, the size of a manhole, marked with a fluorescent cross—oh, Mr. Pike, I didn't think you'd do it. I put down the jar and felt for the handle in the dark, and when I found it I braced myself and turned. I certainly didn't expect it to give, but it did, circling once, twice, around in my grasp and loosening like the lid of a bottle. I pulled the hatch and up it came. Then I picked up the insects, felt with my feet for the ladder inside, and went down, closing the hatch behind me.

I still planned to deposit the insects on his trees, but something about crime is contagious. I knew that what I was doing was foolish and that it increased the risk of being caught, but as I descended the ladder into Mr. Pike's bomb shelter, I could barely distinguish fear from elation. At the bottom of the ladder I switched on the flashlight. The room was round, the ceiling and floor were concrete, and against the wall stood a cabinet of metal shelves filled with canned foods. On one shelf were a dictionary and some magazines. Oh, Mr. Pike. I thought of his sapling elms, of the roots making their steady, blind way through the earth; I thought of his houses ten years from now, when the pipes cracked and the ceilings began to pool with water. What a hopeless man he seemed to me then, how small and afraid.

I stood thinking about him, and after a moment I heard a door close in the house. I climbed the ladder and peeked out under the hatch. There on the porch stood Kurt and Mr. Pike. As I watched, they came down off the steps and walked over and stood on the grass near me. I could see the watch blinking on Mr. Pike's wrist. I lowered my head. They were silent, and I wondered what Mr. Pike would do if he found me in his bomb shelter. He was thickly built, as I have said, but I didn't think he was a violent man. One afternoon I had watched as Kurt slammed the front door of their house and ran down the steps onto the lawn, where he stopped and threw an object—an ashtray, I think it was—right through the front window of the house. When the glass shattered, he ran, and Mr. Pike soon appeared on the front steps. The reason I say that he is not a violent man is that I saw something beyond anger, perhaps a certain doom, in his posture as he went back inside that afternoon and began cleaning up the glass with a broom. I watched him through the broken front window of their house.

How would I explain to him, though, the bottle of mad insects I now held? I could have run then, I suppose, made a break up and out of the shelter while their backs were turned. I could have been out the driveway and across the street without their recognizing me. But there was, of course, my heart. I moved back down the ladder. As I descended and began to think about a place to hide my insects, I heard Mr. Pike speak. I climbed back up the ladder. When I looked out under the hatch, I saw the two of them, backs toward me, pointing at the sky. Mr. Pike was sighting something with his finger, and Kurt followed. Then I realized that he was pointing out the constellations, but that he didn't know what they were and was making up their names as he spoke. His voice was not fanciful. It was direct and scientific, and he was lying to his son about what he knew. "These," he said, "these are the Mermaid's Tail, and south you can see the three peaks of Mount Olympus, and then the sword that belongs to the Emperor of the Air." I looked where he was pointing. It was late summer, near midnight, and what he had described was actually Cygnus's bright tail and the outstretched neck of Pegasus.

Presently he ceased speaking, and after a time they walked back across the lawn and went into the house. The light in the kitchen went on, then off. I stepped from my hiding place. I suppose I could have continued with my mission, but the air was calm, it was a perfect and still night, and my plan, I felt, had been interrupted. In my hand the jar felt large and dangerous. I crept back across the lawn, staying in the shadows of the ivy and rhododendron along the fence, until I was in the driveway between our two houses. In the side window of the Pikes' house a light was on. I paused at a point where the angle allowed me a view through the glass, down the hallway, and through an open door into the living room. Mr. Pike and Kurt were sitting together on a brown couch against the far wall of the room, watching television. I came up close to the window and peered through. Though I knew this was foolish, that any neighbor, any man walking his dog at night, would have thought me a burglar in my black clothing, I stayed and watched. The light was on inside, it was dark around me, and I knew I could look in without being seen. Mr. Pike had his hand on Kurt's shoulder. Every so often when they laughed at something on the screen, he moved his hand up and tousled Kurt's hair. The sight of this suddenly made me feel the way I do on the bridge across the Mississippi River. When he put his hand on Kurt's hair again, I moved out of the shadows and went back to my own house.

I wanted to run, or kick a ball, or shout a soliloquy into the night. I could have stepped up on a car hood then and lured the Pikes, the paper boy, all the neighbors, out into the night. I could have spoken about the laboratory of a biology teacher, about the rows of specimen jars. How could one not hope here? At three weeks the human embryo has gill arches on its neck, like a fish; at six weeks, amphibians' webs still connect its blunt fingers. Miracles. This is true everywhere in nature. The evolution of 500 million years is mimicked in each gestation: birds that in the egg look like fish; fish that emerge like their spineless, leaflike ancestors. What it is to study life! Anybody who had seen a cell divide could have invented religion.

I sat down on the porch steps and looked at the elm. After a while I stood up and went inside. With turpentine I cleaned the shoe polish from my face, and then I went upstairs. I got into bed. For an hour or two I lay there, sleepless, hot, my thoughts racing, before I gave up and went to the bedroom window. The jar, which I had brought up with me, stood on the sill, and I saw that the insects were either asleep or dead. I opened the window then and emptied them down onto the lawn, and at that moment, as they rained away into the night, glinting and cascading, I thought of asking Vera for a child. I knew it was not possible, but I considered it anyway. Standing there at the window, I thought of Vera, ageless, in forest boots and shorts, perspiring through a flannel blouse as she dipped drinking water from an Appalachian stream. What had we, she and I? The night was calm, dark. Above me Polaris blinked.

I tried going to sleep again. I lay in bed for a time, and then gave up and went downstairs. I ate some crackers. I drank two glasses of bourbon. I sat at the window and looked out at the front yard. Then I got up and went outside and looked up at the stars, and I tried to see them for their beauty and mystery. I thought of billions of tons of exploding gases, hydrogen and helium, red giants, supernovas. In places they were as dense as clouds. I thought of magnesium and silicon and iron. I tried to see them out of their constellatory order, but it was like trying to look at a word without reading it, and I stood there in the night unable to scramble the patterns. Some clouds had blown in and begun to cover Auriga and Taurus. I was watching them begin to spread and refract moonlight when I heard the paper boy whistling the national anthem. When he reached me, I was standing by the elm, still in my nightclothes, unshaven, a little drunk.

"I want you to do something for me," I said.

"Sir?"

"I'm an old man and I want you to do something for me. Put down your bicycle," I said. "Put down your bicycle and look up at the stars."

Questions

1. Why does Mr. Pike want the elm tree cut down? Why does the narrator want to keep it up? What does the tree symbolize for the narrator? Does it have the same (or any) symbolic meaning for Mr. Pike?
2. What is the narrator's initial attitude toward Mr. Pike? Does his attitude change during the course of the story? If so, how does it change? If not, why not?
3. In what ways does the narrator's fight to save the elm represent a clash of values? Why doesn't Mr. Pike value the tree in the same way that the narrator does?
4. Is there any symbolism to the insects eating the elm? Their color? Their shape? The way they eat?
5. Why does the narrator finally allow the elm to be cut down?

8  Symbols

The American essayist and poet Ralph Waldo Emerson once wrote, "We are symbols, and inhabit symbols." And, indeed, one difficulty in talking about symbolism is that all things soon turn into symbols. They dominate our lives. Consider for a moment how you are dressed. Out of many possible styles, you have chosen one that suits you. But your choice was not based merely on keeping your body warm. The shirt you wear may have an alligator or a number on it. These are symbols of a manufacturer and an athletic team. But they also symbolize social types: the preppy and the jock. Picture in your mind the clothing of a banker, a nun, a cook, and a judge. Is what they wear simply necessary for their work—like a construction worker's hard hat—or are their clothes chosen for their symbolic value? From a practical point of view, judges might be more comfortable in a T-shirt and shorts than in heavy, dark robes. Yet their attire is chosen out of respect for tradition and for the dignity of the judicial system. Their attire is a symbol of their high authority.

A *symbol*, then, is any object or action which refers to more than itself. The apple in your refrigerator is simply a fruit. Place it, however, with a snake, and it symbolizes forbidden knowledge and the source of man's first disobedience. Placed beside a piece of chalk and a stack of books, it becomes symbolic of the student's affection and respect for a teacher. The apple is, therefore, an ordinary object that can be charged with additional significance. And when it is charged with additional significance, it becomes a symbol.

The apple example makes several things clear about symbols.

1. It is the context in which objects and actions appear that usually lends them symbolic significance.
2. The same object can have different symbolic meanings depending upon its context.
3. Almost anything can be given symbolic meaning.

Traditional Symbols

Some objects and actions are so firmly established as symbols that they rarely, if ever, lose their symbolic significance. Religious symbols are among the most common traditional symbols. The cross, the dove, the olive branch, a crown of thorns—these objects seldom appear without religious significance. Conceivably, a dove might appear in a bird-watcher's manual as just another species. But such a context is the exception. Most often the dove will symbolize either peace or the Holy Spirit. It will not be merely a bird.

Representative Symbols

Frequently we choose one action or object to symbolize an entire group of similar or related objects and actions. For example, in Bobbie Ann Mason's story "Shiloh," Leroy's log cabin represents, at least in part, the pioneer past and his desire to return to it. A log cabin, of course, is only one of the many items associated with the American frontier, but in the story it comes to represent, or symbolize, the entire way of pioneer life. Such symbolic practices happen outside literature. Perhaps a teacher has picked one student from your class to represent the class at an assembly. That student symbolizes your class. Again, judges may sentence a particular individual to an unusually harsh punishment in order to use that person as "an example." The individual comes then to symbolize the court's concern, as a warning to similar offenders. In general, we may say that when something is set aside as an example, it also symbolizes the group from which it comes.

Levels of Symbolic Meaning

It is important to remember that symbols can have different meanings depending on their context and one's perspective. The apple, as we said, might symbolize forbidden knowledge in one context, respect for teachers in another context, and the importance of good diet for good health in quite another context. As a reader you must be sensitive to the context in which a symbol appears because context may determine how you should interpret the symbol.

But symbols can take on different meanings depending on your perspective. For one person a wedding ring may symbolize the infinite power of love; for another person it may symbolize emotional imprisonment. To a child a birthday cake comes to mean the joy of growing up; to an adult the same cake can mean the problems of growing old. Often writers play with the unstable nature of symbolic meaning, and as a reader, you should be sensitive to the ways that an object may shift symbolic meaning depending on the narrator's and the characters' points-of-view.

But a symbol may have many different meanings operating simultaneously.

In such cases, critics talk about "levels of symbolic meaning." The first level is the literal level—what the symbol actually is. Thus on the literal level Shiloh is a battlefield in northern Mississippi. However it has other levels of meaning and association. In the Bible, Shiloh was the place where the Ark of the Covenant was kept before the Philistines captured and removed it. Thus Shiloh symbolizes a sacred place related to a pact, such as the marriage pact. In the story Mabel associates Shiloh with her honeymoon; for her, Shiloh symbolizes love and the consummation of her marriage. Historically, Shiloh was a turning point in the Civil War. It thus can stand for any turning point of a battle, such as a turning point in the battle between Leroy and Norma Jean. As you can see, Shiloh is rich with symbolic associations, of which we have stated only a few possibilities. Though we talk of these symbolic levels separately, they appear simultaneously in the story and, consequently, with great force and economy. The concentrated force of symbols is, in fact, their greatest artistic attraction. Simply by setting the story in Shiloh, Mason has evoked an entire series of concepts, associations, and emotions simply, effectively, and powerfully.

Reading Symbols

Since symbols are everywhere, a natural tendency is to read everything symbolically. By drawing our attention even to the most mundane activities, authors charge those activities with added significance, and in that sense everything in a story *is* symbolic. But this symbol-making ability takes place outside of stories every time our attention is directed to someone or something. Remember in third grade, when your teacher ordered a student to open up a messy desk. The scene is repeated year after year in classroom after classroom. Out come books and wads of paper torn and mangled into balls, some chewing gum, a couple of broken pencils, a bent pair of scissors, and then—from deep inside the darkest reaches of the desk—the decayed remains of a sandwich or candy bar, long past the time when it should have been thrown away. Our teachers used to pick such things up with just the tips of their fingers, their faces screwed into a look of utter disgust. They would carry the moldy thing at arms length to the nearest garbage can and drop it in. By calling our attention to it, the teacher made it symbolize all the untidiness of our youth, all the things in our own desks that should have been thrown away, all our failures to impose order on the chaos of our lives. Our tendency is to generalize from a specific object or incident to similar incidents and objects. If we did not generalize, we could learn nothing from literature since whatever wisdom fiction teaches us comes from seeing in the fictional world conditions repeated in our own.

But though everything in a story is charged, not everything is charged with the same degree of added significance. We usually reserve the term "symbol" for those people, objects, or events that are especially charged with added significance.

✍️ Tips for Readers

Careful readers will refrain from reading something as a symbol until the story invites such a reading. How does a story make such an invitation? How do authors cue us about symbolic intents? Here are some useful hints:

1. Authors usually focus on their symbols by placing them in key locations in the narrative. The bridegroom fails to reappear at the end for Granny Weatherall. His absence is at a key moment in the story and suggests its significance.
2. Authors frequently repeat the symbolic action or object. Shiloh is mentioned throughout the story and gives the story its name.
3. Symbols are frequently odd or supernatural. In the two stories that follow, the talking bird and the fallen angel call attention to their symbolic nature by being "unrealistic." Indeed, fairy tales, science fiction, and fantasy stories usually have a great number of symbols, since the characters, actions, and objects function beyond the *literal level*. Dreamlike stories often employ a succession of symbolic figures and actions.
4. Descriptions of clothing and setting frequently contain symbolic significance.

In interpreting a symbol, one should never be arbitrary. Remember, the number of traditional symbols is small, and only traditional symbols carry their meaning wherever they go. All other symbols gain their meaning through their context. So one must never ascribe a symbolic meaning that is at variance with, or even unsupported by, the context of the story. Finally, one must remember that symbols usually have various levels of meaning. It is not enough to pin one single meaning to a symbol. One must be prepared to recognize the whole range of significance a symbol can have, to invite and entertain the wealth and power of meaning that fiction can give the simplest objects and gestures.

✍️ Tips for Writers

Symbols, as we said, are often repeated at key junctures in a story, and since symbols can have various meanings, the significance of a symbol may change between the beginning and end of a story. On re-reading the story, carefully note the appearance and reappearance of the symbol and its related forms, and then consider whether the symbol has a single and stable meaning or whether it shifts, develops, or takes on subtle differences of meaning.

Suggestions for Essayists

1. Discuss the traditional symbolic meanings of each of the following:
   1. an eagle   4. white
   2. a serpent   5. fire
   3. blue   6. the moon
2. Describe the objects to which you are most attached. What do they represent or symbolize for you?

Suggestions for Fiction Writers

1. Suggest a character by the sorts of things that character might keep in his or her car.
2. Place a traditional symbol in a scene in which it comes to represent just the opposite of its usual meaning. For example, place a rose in a scene in such a way that it represents ugliness and hate.

BERNARD MALAMUD (1914–1986)

The Jewbird

The window was open so the skinny bird flew in. Flappity-flap with its frazzled black wings. That's how it goes. It's open, you're in. Closed, you're out and that's your fate. The bird wearily flapped through the open kitchen window of Harry Cohen's top-floor apartment on First Avenue near the lower East River.[1] On a rod on the wall hung an escaped canary cage, its door wide open, but this black-type longbeaked bird—its ruffled head and small dull eyes, crossed a little, making it look like a dissipated crow—landed if not smack on Cohen's thick lamb chop, at least on the table, close by. The frozen foods salesman was sitting at supper with his wife and young son on a hot August evening a year ago. Cohen, a heavy man with hairy chest and beefy shorts; Edie, in skinny yellow shorts and red halter; and their ten-year-old Morris (after his father)—Maurie, they called him, a nice kid though not overly bright—were all in the city after two weeks out, because Cohen's mother was dying. They had been enjoying Kingston, New York, but drove back when Mama got sick in her flat in the Bronx.[2]

"Right on the table," said Cohen, putting down his beer glass and swatting at the bird. "Son of a bitch."

"Harry, take care with your language," Edie said, looking at Maurie, who watched every move.

The bird cawed hoarsely and with a flap of its bedraggled wings—feathers tufted this way and that—rose heavily to the top of the open kitchen door, where it perched staring down.

"Gevalt, a pogrom!"[3]

---

[1] A section of New York City called the Lower East Side. This was a poor Jewish neighborhood.
[2] Kingston is a resort town in the Catskill Mountains. The Bronx is the northernmost borough of New York City.
[3] A pogrom is an organized slaughter of a minority group, especially Jews. Gevalt is a Yiddish exclamation of woe.

"It's a talking bird," said Edie in astonishment.

"In Jewish," said Maurie.

"Wise guy," muttered Cohen. He gnawed on his chop, then put down the bone. "So if you can talk, say what's your business. What do you want here?"

"If you can't spare a lamb chop," said the bird, "I'll settle for a piece of herring with a crust of bread. You can't live on your nerve forever."

"This ain't a restaurant," Cohen replied. "All I'm asking is what brings you to this address?"

"The window was open," the bird sighed; adding after a moment, "I'm running. I'm flying but I'm also running."

"From whom?" asked Edie with interest.

"Anti-Semeets."

"Anti-Semites?" they all said.

"That's from who."

"What kind of anti-Semites bother a bird?" Edie asked.

"Any kind," said the bird, "also including eagles, vultures, and hawks. And once in a while some crows will take your eyes out."

"But aren't you a crow?"

"Me? I'm a Jewbird."

Cohen laughed heartily. "What do you mean by that?"

The bird began dovening. He prayed without Book or tallith,[4] but with passion. Edie bowed her head though not Cohen. And Maurie rocked back and forth with the prayer, looking up with one wide-open eye.

When the prayer was done Cohen remarked, "No hat, no phylacteries?"[5]

"I'm an old radical."

"You're sure you're not some kind of a ghost or dybbuk?"[6]

"Not a dybbuk," answered the bird, "though one of my relatives had such an experience once. It's all over now, thanks God. They freed her from a former lover, a crazy jealous man. She's now the mother of two wonderful children."

"Birds?" Cohen asked slyly.

"Why not?"

"What kind of birds?"

"Like me. Jewbirds."

Cohen tipped back in his chair and guffawed. "That's a big laugh. I've heard of a Jewfish but not a Jewbird."

"We're once removed." The bird rested on one skinny leg, then on the other. "Please, could you spare maybe a piece of herring with a small crust of bread?"

Edie got up from the table.

"What are you doing?" Cohen asked her.

"I'll clear the dishes."

Cohen turned to the bird. "So what's your name, if you don't mind saying?"

---

[4] Dovening is praying, especially softly and to oneself. A tallith is a prayer shawl.

[5] Phylacteries are leather-covered boxes containing scriptural passages that are worn on the left arm and forehead during prayers.

[6] A dybbuk is an evil spirit.

"Call me Schwartz."[7]

"He might be an old Jew changed into a bird by somebody," said Edie, removing a plate.

"Are you?" asked Harry, lighting a cigar.

"Who knows?" answered Schwartz. "Does God tell us everything?"

Maurie got up on his chair. "What kind of herring?" he asked the bird in excitement.

"Get down, Maurie, or you'll fall," ordered Cohen.

"If you haven't got matjes, I'll take schmaltz,"[8] said Schwartz.

"All we have is marinated, with slices of onion—in a jar," said Edie.

"If you'll open for me the jar I'll eat marinated. Do you have also, if you don't mind, a piece of rye bread—the spitz?"[9]

Edie thought she had.

"Feed him out on the balcony," Cohen said. He spoke to the bird. "After that take off."

Schwartz closed both bird eyes. "I'm tired and it's a long way."

"Which direction are you headed, north or south?"

Schwartz, barely lifting his wings, shrugged.

"You don't know where you're going?"

"Where there's charity I'll go."

"Let him stay, papa," said Maurie. "He's only a bird."

"So stay the night," Cohen said, "but no longer."

In the morning Cohen ordered the bird out of the house but Maurie cried, so Schwartz stayed for a while. Maurie was still on vacation from school and his friends were away. He was lonely and Edie enjoyed the fun he had, playing with the bird.

"He's no trouble at all," she told Cohen, "and besides his appetite is very small."

"What'll you do when he makes dirty?"

"He flies across the street in a tree when he makes dirty, and if nobody passes below, who notices?"

"So all right," said Cohen, "but I'm dead set against it. I warn you he ain't gonna stay here long."

"What have you got against the poor bird?"

"Poor bird, my ass. He's a foxy bastard. He thinks he's a Jew."

"What difference does it make what he thinks?"

"A Jewbird, what chutzpah.[10] One false move and he's out on his drumsticks."

At Cohen's insistence Schwartz lived out on the balcony in a new wooden birdhouse Edie had bought him.

"With many thanks," said Schwartz, "though I would rather have a human roof over my head. You know how it is at my age. I like the warm, the windows,

---

[7] Schwartz is German for "black," an appropriate name for a blackbird.

[8] Matjes is a better sort of herring; schmaltz herring is cheaper and greasier.

[9] The spitz is the heel of a bread loaf.

[10] Chutzpah is Yiddish for "pushiness."

the smell of cooking. I would also be glad to see once in a while the *Jewish Morning Journal* and have now and then a schnapps[11] because it helps my breathing, thanks God. But whatever you give me, you won't hear complaints."

However, when Cohen brought home a bird feeder full of dried corn, Schwartz said, "Impossible."

Cohen was annoyed. "What's the matter, crosseyes, is your life getting too good for you? Are you forgetting what it means to be migratory? I'll bet a helluva lot of crows you happen to be acquainted with, Jews or otherwise, would give their eyeteeth to eat this corn."

Schwartz did not answer. What can you say to a grubber yung?[12]

"Not for my digestion," he later explained to Edie. "Cramps. Herring is better even if it makes you thirsty. At least rainwater don't cost anything." He laughed sadly in breathy caws.

And herring, thanks to Edie, who knew where to shop, was what Schwartz got, with an occasional piece of potato pancake, and even a bit of soupmeat when Cohen wasn't looking.

When school began in September, before Cohen would once again suggest giving the bird the boot, Edie prevailed on him to wait a little while until Maurie adjusted.

"To deprive him right now might hurt his school work, and you know what trouble we had last year."

"So okay, but sooner or later the bird goes. That I promise you."

Schwartz, though nobody had asked him, took on full responsibility for Maurie's performance in school. In return for favors granted, when he was let in for an hour or two at night, he spent most of his time overseeing the boy's lessons. He sat on top of the dresser near Maurie's desk as he laboriously wrote out his homework. Maurie was a restless type and Schwartz gently kept him to his studies. He also listened to him practice his screechy violin, taking a few minutes off now and then to rest his ears in the bathroom. And they afterwards played dominoes. The boy was an indifferent checker player and it was impossible to teach him chess. When he was sick, Schwartz read him comic books though he personally disliked them. But Maurie's work improved in school and even his violin teacher admitted his playing was better. Edie gave Schwartz credit for these improvements though the bird pooh-poohed them.

Yet he was proud there was nothing lower than C minuses on Maurie's report card, and on Edie's insistence celebrated with a little schnapps.

"If he keeps up like this," Cohen said, "I'll get him in an Ivy League college for sure."

"Oh I hope so," sighed Edie.

But Schwartz shook his head. "He's a good boy—you don't have to worry. He won't be a shicker[13] or a wifebeater, God forbid, but a scholar he'll never be, if you know what I mean, although maybe a good mechanic. It's no disgrace in these times."

---

[11] Schnapps is a strong liquor.
[12] Grubber yung is Yiddish for "moocher."
[13] A shicker is a drunkard.

"If I were you," Cohen said, angered, "I'd keep my big snoot out of other people's private business."

"Harry, please," said Edie.

"My goddamn patience is wearing out. That crosseyes butts into everything."

Though he wasn't exactly a welcome guest in the house, Schwartz gained a few ounces although he did not improve in appearance. He looked bedraggled as ever, his feathers unkempt, as though he had just flown out of a snowstorm. He spent, he admitted, little time taking care of himself. Too much to think about. "Also outside plumbing," he told Edie. Still there was more glow to his eyes so that though Cohen went on calling him crosseyes he said it less emphatically.

Liking his situation, Schwartz tried tactfully to stay out of Cohen's way, but one night when Edie was at the movies and Maurie was taking a hot shower, the frozen foods salesman began a quarrel with the bird.

"For Christ sake, why don't you wash yourself sometimes? Why must you always stink like a dead fish?"

"Mr. Cohen, if you'll pardon me, if somebody eats garlic he will smell from garlic. I eat herring three times a day. Feed me flowers and I will smell like flowers."

"Who's obligated to feed you anything at all? You're lucky to get herring."

"Excuse me, I'm not complaining," said the bird. "You're complaining."

"What's more," said Cohen, "even from out on the balcony I can hear you snoring away like a pig. It keeps me awake at night."

"Snoring," said Schwartz, "isn't a crime, thanks God."

"All in all you are a goddamn pest and free loader. Next thing you'll want to sleep in bed next to my wife."

"Mr. Cohen," said Schwartz, "on this rest assured. A bird is a bird."

"So you say, but how do I know you're a bird and not some kind of a goddamn devil?"

"If I was a devil you would know already. And I don't mean because your son's good marks."

"Shut up, you bastard bird," shouted Cohen.

"Grubber yung," cawed Schwartz, rising to the tips of his talons, his long wings outstretched.

Cohen was about to lunge for the bird's scrawny neck but Maurie came out of the bathroom, and for the rest of the evening until Schwartz's bedtime on the balcony, there was pretended peace.

But the quarrel had deeply disturbed Schwartz and he slept badly. His snoring woke him, and awake, he was fearful of what would become of him. Wanting to stay out of Cohen's way, he kept to the birdhouse as much as possible. Cramped by it, he paced back and forth on the balcony ledge, or sat on the birdhouse roof, staring into space. In the evenings, while overseeing Maurie's lessons, he often fell asleep. Awakening, he nervously hopped around exploring the four corners of the room. He spent much time in Maurie's closet, and carefully examined his bureau drawers when they were left open. And once when he found a large paper bag on the floor, Schwartz poked his way into it to investigate what possibilities were. The boy was amused to see the bird in the paper bag.

"He wants to build a nest," he said to his mother.

Edie, sensing Schwartz's unhappiness, spoke to him quietly.

"Maybe if you did some of the things my husband wants you, you would get along better with him."

"Give me a for instance," Schwartz said.

"Like take a bath, for instance."

"I'm too old for baths," said the bird. "My feathers fall out without baths."

"He says you have a bad smell."

"Everybody smells. Some people smell because of their thoughts or because who they are. My bad smell comes from the food I eat. What does his come from?"

"I better not ask him or it might make him mad," said Edie.

In late November Schwartz froze on the balcony in the fog and cold, and especially on rainy days he woke with stiff joints and could barely move his wings. Already he felt twinges of rheumatism. He would have liked to spend more time in the warm house, particularly when Maurie was in school and Cohen at work. But though Edie was good-hearted and might have sneaked him in in the morning, just to thaw out, he was afraid to ask her. In the meantime Cohen, who had been reading articles about the migration of birds, came out on the balcony one night after work when Edie was in the kitchen preparing pot roast, and peeking into the birdhouse, warned Schwartz to be on his way soon if he knew what was good for him. "Time to hit the flyways."

"Mr. Cohen, why do you hate me so much?" asked the bird. "What did I do to you?"

"Because you're an A-number-one trouble maker, that's why. What's more, whoever heard of a Jewbird! Now scat or it's open war."

But Schwartz stubbornly refused to depart so Cohen embarked on a campaign of harassing him, meanwhile hiding it from Edie and Maurie. Maurie hated violence and Cohen didn't want to leave a bad impression. He thought maybe if he played dirty tricks on the bird he would fly off without being physically kicked out. The vacation was over, let him make his easy living off the fat of somebody else's land. Cohen worried about the effect of the bird's departure on Maurie's schooling but decided to take the chance, first, because the boy now seemed to have the knack of studying—give the black bird-bastard credit—and second, because Schwartz was driving him bats by being there always, even in his dreams.

The frozen foods salesman began his campaign against the bird by mixing watery cat food with the herring slices in Schwartz's dish. He also blew up and popped numerous paper bags outside the birdhouse as the bird slept, and when he had got Schwartz good and nervous, though not enough to leave, he brought a full-grown cat into the house, supposedly a gift for little Maurie, who had always wanted a pussy. The cat never stopped springing up at Schwartz whenever he saw him, one day managing to claw out several of his tailfeathers. And even at lesson time, when the cat was usually excluded from Maurie's room, though somehow or other he quickly found his way in at the end of the lesson, Schwartz was desperately fearful of his life and flew from pinnacle to pinnacle—light fixture to clothes-tree to door-top—in order to elude the beast's wet jaws.

Once when the bird complained to Edie how hazardous his existence was, she said, "Be patient, Mr. Schwartz. When the cat gets to know you better he won't try to catch you any more."

"When he stops trying we will both be in Paradise," Schwartz answered. "Do me a favor and get rid of him. He makes my whole life worry. I'm losing feathers like a tree loses leaves."

"I'm awfully sorry but Maurie likes the pussy and sleeps with it."

What could Schwartz do? He worried but came to no decision, being afraid to leave. So he ate the herring garnished with cat food, tried hard not to hear the paper bags bursting like fire crackers outside the birdhouse at night, and lived terror-stricken closer to the ceiling than the floor, as the cat, his tail flicking, endlessly watched him.

Weeks went by. Then on the day after Cohen's mother had died in her flat in the Bronx, when Maurie came home with a zero on an arithmetic test, Cohen, enraged, waited until Edie had taken the boy to his violin lesson, then openly attacked the bird. He chased him with a broom on the balcony and Schwartz frantically flew back and forth, finally escaping into his birdhouse. Cohen triumphantly reached in, and grabbing both skinny legs, dragged the bird out, cawing loudly, his wings wildly beating. He whirled the bird around and around his head. But Schwartz, as he moved in circles, managed to swoop down and catch Cohen's nose in his beak, and hung on for dear life. Cohen cried out in great pain, punched the bird with his fist, and tugging at his legs with all his might, pulled his nose free. Again he swung the yawking Schwartz around until the bird grew dizzy, then with a furious heave, flung him into the night. Schwartz sank like stone into the street. Cohen then tossed the birdhouse and feeder after him, listening at the ledge until they crashed on the sidewalk below. For a full hour, broom in hand, his heart palpitating and nose throbbing with pain, Cohen waited for Schwartz to return but the broken-hearted bird didn't.

That's the end of that dirty bastard, the salesman thought and went in. Edie and Maurie had come home.

"Look," said Cohen, pointing to his bloody nose swollen three times its normal size, "what that sonofabitchy bird did. It's a permanent scar."

"Where is he now?" Edie asked, frightened.

"I threw him out and he flew away. Good riddance."

Nobody said no, though Edie touched a handkerchief to her eyes and Maurie rapidly tried the nine times table and found he knew approximately half.

In the spring when the winter's snow had melted, the boy, moved by a memory, wandered in the neighborhood, looking for Schwartz. He found a dead black bird in a small lot near the river, his two wings broken, neck twisted, and both bird-eyes plucked clean.

"Who did it to you, Mr. Schwartz?" Maurie wept.

"Anti-Semeets," Edie said later.

Questions

1. What does the bird's color symbolize?
2. What are Cohen's reasons for hating the bird?
3. Is Edie right when she says that anti-Semites killed Schwartz?
4. What is the symbolic significance of Schwartz's refusal to migrate?
5. Jews have been called "the people of the book." In what ways does Schwartz fit that name?
6. Is there any significance to the location of the birdhouse on the balcony?
7. Is there symbolic significance to Cohen's job?

 Writers on Writing Bernard Malamud

> *As a writer I learned a lot from Charlie Chaplin. . . . the rhythm, the snap of comic presence—the beautiful distancing; the funny with sad; the surprise of surprise. . . . The funny bone is universal. I doubt humorists think of individual taste when they're enticing the laugh. With me humor comes unexpectedly, usually in defense of a character, sometimes because I need cheering up. When something starts funny I can feel my imagination eating and running.*

GABRIEL GARCÍA MÁRQUEZ (1928–)

A Very Old Man with Enormous Wings

On the third day of rain they had killed so many crabs inside the house that Pelayo had to cross his drenched courtyard and throw them into the sea, because the newborn child had a temperature all night and they thought it was due to the stench. The world had been sad since Tuesday. Sea and sky were a single ash-gray thing and the sands of the beach, which on March nights glimmered like powdered light, had become a stew of mud and rotten shellfish. The light was so weak at noon that when Pelayo was coming back to the house after throwing away the crabs, it was hard for him to see what it was that was moving and groaning in the rear of the courtyard. He had to go very close to see that it was an old man, a very old man, lying face down in the mud, who, in spite of his tremendous efforts, couldn't get up, impeded by his enormous wings.

Frightened by that nightmare, Pelayo ran to get Elisenda, his wife, who was putting compresses on the sick child, and he took her to the rear of the courtyard. They both looked at the fallen body with mute stupor. He was dressed like a ragpicker. There were only a few faded hairs left on his bald skull and very few teeth in his mouth, and his pitiful condition of a drenched great-grandfather

Gabriel García Márquez (*Wide World Photos, Inc.*)

had taken away any sense of grandeur he might have had. His huge buzzard wings, dirty and half-plucked, were forever entangled in the mud. They looked at him so long and so closely that Pelayo and Elisenda very soon overcame their surprise and in the end found him familiar. Then they dared speak to him, and he answered in an incomprehensible dialect with a strong sailor's voice. That was how they skipped over the inconvenience of the wings and quite intelligently concluded that he was a lonely castaway from some foreign ship wrecked by the storm. And yet, they called in a neighbor woman who knew everything about life and death to see him, and all she needed was one look to show them their mistake.

"He's an angel," she told them. "He must have been coming for the child, but the poor fellow is so old that the rain knocked him down."

On the following day everyone knew that a flesh-and-blood angel was held captive in Pelayo's house. Against the judgment of the wise neighbor woman, for whom angels in those times were the fugitive survivors of a celestial conspiracy, they did not have the heart to club him to death. Pelayo watched over him all afternoon from the kitchen, armed with his bailiff's club, and before going to bed he dragged him out of the mud and locked him up with the hens in the wire chicken coop. In the middle of the night, when the rain stopped, Pelayo and Elisenda were still killing crabs. A short time afterward the child woke up without a fever and with a desire to eat. Then they felt magnanimous and decided to put the angel on a raft with fresh water and provisions for three days and leave him to his fate on the high seas. But when they went out into the courtyard with the first light of dawn, they found the whole neighborhood in front of the chicken coop having fun with the angel, without the slightest reverence, tossing him things to eat through the openings in the wire as if he weren't a supernatural creature but a circus animal.

Father Gonzaga arrived before seven o'clock, alarmed at the strange news. By that time onlookers less frivolous than those at dawn had already arrived and they were making all kinds of conjectures concerning the captive's future. The simplest among them thought that he should be named mayor of the world. Others of sterner mind felt that he should be promoted to the rank of five-star general in order to win all wars. Some visionaries hoped that he could be put to stud in order to implant on earth a race of winged wise men who could take charge of the universe. But Father Gonzaga, before becoming a priest, had been a robust woodcutter. Standing by the wire, he reviewed his catechism in an instant and asked them to open the door so that he could take a close look at that pitiful man who looked more like a huge decrepit hen among the fascinated chickens. He was lying in a corner drying his open wings in the sunlight among the fruit peels and breakfast leftovers that the early risers had thrown him. Alien to the impertinences of the world, he only lifted his antiquarian eyes and murmered something in his dialect when Father Gonzaga went into the chicken coop and said good morning to him in Latin. The parish priest had his first suspicion of an imposter when he saw that he did not understand the language of God or know how to greet His ministers. Then he noticed that seen close up he was much too human: he had an unbearable smell of the outdoors, the back side of his wings was strewn with parasites and his main feathers had been mistreated by terrestrial winds, and nothing about him measured up to the proud dignity of angels. Then he came out of the chicken coop and in a brief sermon warned the curious against the risks of being ingenuous. He reminded them that the devil had the bad habit of making use of carnival tricks in order to confuse the unwary. He argued that if wings were not the essential element in determining the difference between a hawk and an airplane, they were even less so in the recognition of angels. Nevertheless, he promised to write a letter to his bishop so that the latter would write to his primate so that the latter would write to the Supreme Pontiff in order to get the final verdict from the highest courts.

His prudence fell on sterile hearts. The news of the captive angel spread with such rapidity that after a few hours the courtyard had the bustle of a marketplace and they had to call in troops with fixed bayonets to disperse the mob that was about to knock the house down. Elisenda, her spine all twisted from sweeping up so much marketplace trash, then got the idea of fencing in the yard and charging five cents admission to see the angel.

The curious came from far away. A traveling carnival arrived with a flying acrobat who buzzed over the crowd several times, but no one paid any attention to him because his wings were not those of an angel but, rather, those of a sidereal bat. The most unfortunate invalids on earth came in search of health: a poor woman who since childhood had been counting her heartbeats and had run out of numbers; a Portuguese man who couldn't sleep because the noise of the stars disturbed him; a sleepwalker who got up at night to undo the things he had done while awake; and many others with less serious ailments. In the midst of that shipwreck disorder that made the earth tremble, Pelayo and Elisenda were happy with fatigue, for in less than a week they had crammed their rooms with money and the line of pilgrims waiting their turn to enter still reached beyond the horizon.

The angel was the only one who took no part in his own act. He spent his time trying to get comfortable in his borrowed nest, befuddled by the hellish heat of the oil lamps and sacramental candles that had been placed along the wire. At first they tried to make him eat some mothballs, which, according to the wisdom of the wise neighbor woman, were the food prescribed for angels. But he turned them down, just as he turned down the papal lunches that the penitents brought him, and they never found out whether it was because he was an angel or because he was an old man that in the end he ate nothing but eggplant mush. His only supernatural virtue seemed to be patience. Especially during the first days, when the hens pecked at him, searching for the stellar parasites that proliferated in his wings, and the cripples pulled out feathers to touch their defective parts with, and even the most merciful threw stones at him, trying to get him to rise so they could see him standing. The only time they succeeded in arousing him was when they burned his side with an iron for branding steers, for he had been motionless for so many hours that they thought he was dead. He awoke with a start, ranting in his hermetic language and with tears in his eyes, and he flapped his wings a couple of times, which brought on a whirlwind of chicken dung and lunar dust and a gale of panic that did not seem to be of this world. Although many thought that his reaction had been one not of rage but of pain, from then on they were careful not to annoy him, because the majority understood that his passivity was not that of a hero taking his ease but that of a cataclysm in repose.

Father Gonzaga held back the crowd's frivolity with formulas of maidservant inspiration while awaiting the arrival of a final judgment on the nature of the captive. But the mail from Rome showed no sense of urgency. They spent their time finding out if the prisoner had a navel, if his dialect had any connection with Aramaic, how many times he could fit on the head of a pin, or whether he wasn't just a Norwegian with wings. Those meager letters might have come and gone until the end of time if a providential event had not put an end to the priest's tribulations.

It so happened that during those days, among so many other carnival attractions, there arrived in town the traveling show of the woman who had been changed into a spider for having disobeyed her parents. The admission to see her was not only less than the admission to see the angel, but people were permitted to ask her all manner of questions about her absurd state and to examine her up and down so that no one would ever doubt the truth of her horror. She was a frightful tarantula the size of a ram and with the head of a sad maiden. What was most heartrending, however, was not her outlandish shape but the sincere affliction with which she recounted the details of her misfortune. While still practically a child she had sneaked out of her parents' house to go to a dance, and while she was coming back through the woods after having danced all night without permission, a fearful thunderclap rent the sky in two and through the crack came the lightning bolt of brimstone that changed her into a spider. Her only nourishment came from the meatballs that charitable souls chose to toss into her mouth. A spectacle like that, full of so much human truth and with such a fearful lesson, was bound to defeat without even trying that of a haughty angel who scarcely deigned to look at mortals. Besides, the few miracles attributed to the angel showed a certain mental disorder, like the blind man who didn't recover his sight but grew three new teeth, or the paralytic who didn't get to walk but almost won the lottery, and the leper whose sores sprouted sunflowers. Those consolation miracles, which were more like mocking fun, had already ruined the angel's reputation when the woman who had been changed into a spider finally crushed him completely. That was how Father Gonzaga was cured forever of his insomnia and Pelayo's courtyard went back to being as empty as during the time it had rained for three days and crabs walked through the bedrooms.

The owners of the house had no reason to lament. With the money they saved they built a two-story mansion with balconies and gardens and high netting so that crabs wouldn't get in during the winter, and with iron bars on the windows so that angels wouldn't get in. Pelayo also set up a rabbit warren close to town and gave up his job as bailiff for good, and Elisenda bought some satin pumps with high heels and many dresses of iridescent silk, the kind worn on Sunday by the most desirable women in those times. The chicken coop was the only thing that didn't receive any attention. If they washed it down with creolin and burned tears of myrrh inside it every so often, it was not in homage to the angel but to drive away the dungheap stench that still hung everywhere like a ghost and was turning the new house into an old one. At first, when the child learned to walk, they were careful that he not get too close to the chicken coop. But then they began to lose their fears and got used to the smell, and before the child got his second teeth he'd gone inside the chicken coop to play, where the wires were falling apart. The angel was no less standoffish with him than with other mortals, but he tolerated the most ingenious infamies with the patience of a dog who had no illusions. They both came down with chicken pox at the same time. The doctor who took care of the child couldn't resist the temptation to listen to the angel's heart, and he found so much whistling in the heart and so many sounds in his kidneys that it seemed impossible for him to be alive. What surprised him most, however, was the logic of his wings. They seemed so natural on that completely human organism that he couldn't understand why other men didn't have them too.

When the child began school it had been some time since the sun and rain had caused the collapse of the chicken coop. The angel went dragging himself about here and there like a stray dying man. They would drive him out of the bedroom with a broom and a moment later find him in the kitchen. He seemed to be in so many places at the same time that they grew to think that he'd been duplicated, that he was reproducing himself all through the house, and the exasperated and unhinged Elisenda shouted that it was awful living in that hell full of angels. He could scarcely eat and his antiquarian eyes had also become so foggy that he went about bumping into posts. All he had left were the bare cannulae[1] of his last feathers. Pelayo threw a blanket over him and extended him the charity of letting him sleep in the shed, and only then did they notice that he had a temperature at night, and was delirious with the tongue twisters of an old Norwegian. That was one of the few times they became alarmed, for they thought he was going to die and not even the wise neighbor woman had been able to tell them what to do with dead angels.

And yet he not only survived his worst winter, but seemed improved with the first sunny days. He remained motionless for several days in the farthest corner of the courtyard, where no one would see him, and at the beginning of December some large, stiff feathers began to grow on his wings, the feathers of a scarecrow, which looked more like another misfortune of decrepitude. But he must have known the reason for those changes, for he was quite careful that no one should notice them, that no one should hear the sea chanteys that he sometimes sang under the stars. One morning Elisenda was cutting some bunches of onions for lunch when a wind that seemed to come from the high seas blew into the kitchen. Then she went to the window and caught the angel in his first attempts at flight. They were so clumsy that his fingernails opened a furrow in the vegetable patch and he was on the point of knocking the shed down with the ungainly flapping that slipped on the light and couldn't get a grip on the air. But he did manage to gain altitude. Elisenda let out a sigh of relief, for herself and for him, when she saw him pass over the last houses, holding himself up in some way with the risky flapping of a senile vulture. She kept watching him even when she was through cutting onions and she kept on watching until it was no longer possible for her to see him, because then he was no longer an annoyance in her life but an imaginary dot on the horizon of the sea.

Questions

1. The winged man represents a number of ideas, conditions, or qualities. What are they?
2. Is there any significance to the three days of rain?
3. How do people respond to the winged man? Is their response appropriate? How should one respond to a winged person?
4. What is the significance of the church's response to the man with wings?
5. Why does the spider woman lure the crowds away from the man with wings? What does her attraction say about human curiosity and attention?
6. Why does Elisenda lose her annoyance once the winged man becomes "an imaginary dot on the horizon of the sea"? What does her response say about the human capacity to respond to the unusual or miraculous?

---

[1] Cannulae are the reedlike shafts of feathers.

ANNE BEATTIE (1947–)

Janus

The bowl was perfect. Perhaps it was not what you'd select if you faced a shelf of bowls, and not the sort of thing that would inevitably attract a lot of attention at a crafts fair, yet it had real presence. It was as predictably admired as a mutt who has no reason to suspect he might be funny. Just such a dog, in fact, was often brought out (and in) along with the bowl.

Andrea was a real estate agent, and when she thought that some prospective buyers might be dog lovers, she would drop off her dog at the same time she placed the bowl in the house that was up for sale. She would put a dish of water in the kitchen for Mondo, take his squeaking plastic frog out of her purse and drop it on the floor. He would pounce delightedly, just as he did every day at home, batting around his favorite toy. The bowl usually sat on a coffee table, though recently she had displayed it on top of a pine blanket chest and on a lacquered table. It was once placed on a cherry table beneath a Bonnard still life, where it held its own.

Everyone who has purchased a house or who has wanted to sell a house must be familiar with some of the tricks used to convince a buyer that the house is quite special: a fire in the fireplace in early evening; jonquils in a pitcher on the kitchen counter, where no one ordinarily has space to put flowers; perhaps the slight aroma of spring, made by a single drop of scent vaporizing from a lamp bulb.

The wonderful thing about the bowl, Andrea thought, was that it was both subtle and noticeable—a paradox of a bowl. Its glaze was the color of cream and seemed to glow no matter what light it was placed in. There were a few bits of color in it—tiny geometric flashes—and some of these were tinged with flecks of silver. They were as mysterious as cells seen under a microscope; it was difficult not to study them, because they shimmered, flashing for a split second, and then resumed their shape. Something about the colors and their random placement suggested motion. People who liked country furniture always commented on the bowl, but then it turned out that people who felt comfortable with Biedermeier loved it just as much. But the bowl was not at all ostentatious, or even so noticeable that anyone would suspect that it had been put in place deliberately. They might notice the height of the ceiling on first entering a room, and only when their eye moved down from that, or away from the refraction of sunlight on a pale wall, would they see the bowl. Then they would go immediately to it and comment. Yet they always faltered when they tried to say something. Perhaps it was because they were in the house for a serious reason, not to notice some object.

Once, Andrea got a call from a woman who had not put in an offer on a house she had shown her. That bowl, she said—would it be possible to find out where the owners had bought that beautiful bowl? Andrea pretended that she did not know what the woman was referring to. A bowl, somewhere in the house? Oh, on a table under the window. Yes, she would ask, of course. She let a couple of days pass, then called back to say that the bowl had been a present and the people did not know where it had been purchased.

When the bowl was not being taken from house to house, it sat on Andrea's coffee table at home. She didn't keep it carefully wrapped (although she transported it that way, in a box); she kept it on the table, because she liked to see it. It was large enough so that it didn't seem fragile, or particularly vulnerable if anyone sideswiped the table or Mondo blundered into it at play. She had asked her husband to please not drop his house key in it. It was meant to be empty.

When her husband first noticed the bowl, he had peered into it and smiled briefly. He always urged her to buy things she liked. In recent years, both of them had acquired many things to make up for all the lean years when they were graduate students, but now that they had been comfortable for quite a while, the pleasure of new possessions dwindled. Her husband had pronounced the bowl "pretty," and he had turned away without picking it up to examine it. He had no more interest in the bowl than she had in his new Leica.

She was sure that the bowl brought her luck. Bids were often put in on houses where she had displayed the bowl. Sometimes the owners, who were always asked to be away or to step outside when the house was being shown, didn't even know that the bowl had been in their house. Once—she could not imagine how—she left it behind, and then she was so afraid that something might have happened to it that she rushed back to the house and sighed with relief when the woman owner opened the door. The bowl, Andrea explained—she had purchased a bowl and set it on the chest for safekeeping while she toured the house with the prospective buyers, and she . . . She felt like rushing past the frowning woman and seizing her bowl. The owner stepped aside, and it was only when Andrea ran to the chest that the lady glanced at her a little strangely. In the few seconds before Andrea picked up the bowl, she realized that the owner must have just seen that it had been perfectly placed, that the sunlight struck the bluer part of it. Her pitcher had been moved to the far side of the chest, and the bowl predominated. All the way home, Andrea wondered how she could have left the bowl behind. It was like leaving a friend at an outing—just walking off. Sometimes there were stories in the paper about families forgetting a child somewhere and driving to the next city. Andrea had only gone a mile down the road before she remembered.

In time, she dreamed of the bowl. Twice, in a waking dream—early in the morning, between sleep and a last nap before rising—she had a clear vision of it. It came into sharp focus and startled her for a moment—the same bowl she looked at every day.

She had a very profitable year selling real estate. Word spread, and she had more clients than she felt comfortable with. She had the foolish thought that if only the bowl were an animate object she could thank it. There were times when she wanted to talk to her husband about the bowl. He was a stockbroker, and sometimes told people that he was fortunate to be married to a woman who had such a fine aesthetic sense and yet could also function in the real world.

They were a lot alike, really—they had agreed on that. They were both quiet people—reflective, slow to make value judgments, but almost intractable once they had come to a conclusion. They both liked details, but while ironies attracted her, he was more impatient and dismissive when matters became many sided or unclear. But they both knew this; it was the kind of thing they could talk about when they were alone in the car together, coming home from a party or after a weekend with friends. But she never talked to him about the bowl. When they were at dinner, exchanging their news of the day, or while they lay in bed at night listening to the stereo and murmuring sleepy disconnections, she was often tempted to come right out and say that she thought that the bowl in the living room, the cream-colored bowl, was responsible for her success. But she didn't say it. She couldn't begin to explain it. Sometimes in the morning, she would look at him and feel guilty that she had such a constant secret.

Could it be that she had some deeper connection with the bowl—a relationship of some kind? She corrected her thinking: how could she imagine such a thing, when she was a human being and it was a bowl? It was ridiculous. Just think of how people lived together and loved each other . . . But was that always so clear, always a relationship? She was confused by these thoughts, but they remained in her mind. There was something within her now, something real, that she never talked about.

The bowl was a mystery, even to her. It was frustrating, because her involvement with the bowl contained a steady sense of unrequited good fortune; it would have been easier to respond if some sort of demand were made in return. But that only happened in fairy tales. The bowl was just a bowl. She did not believe that for one second. What she believed was that it was something she loved.

In the past, she had sometimes talked to her husband about a new property she was about to buy or sell—confiding some clever strategy she had devised to persuade owners who seemed ready to sell. Now she stopped doing that, for all her strategies involved the bowl. She became more deliberate with the bowl, and more possessive. She put it in houses only when no one was there, and removed it when she left the house. Instead of just moving a pitcher or a dish, she would remove all the other objects from a table. She had to force herself to handle them carefully, because she didn't really care about them. She just wanted them out of sight.

She wondered how the situation would end. As with a lover, there was no exact scenario of how matters would come to a close. Anxiety became the operative force. It would be irrelevant if the lover rushed into someone else's arms, or wrote her a note and departed to another city. The horror was the possibility of the disappearance. That was what mattered.

She would get up at night and look at the bowl. It never occurred to her that she might break it. She washed and dried it without anxiety, and she moved it often, from coffee table to mahogany corner table or wherever, without fearing an accident. It was clear that she would not be the one who would do anything to the bowl. The bowl was only handled by her, set safely on one surface or another; it was not very likely that anyone would break it. A bowl was a poor conductor of electricity: it would not be hit by lightning. Yet the idea of damage persisted. She did not think beyond that—to what her life would be without the bowl. She only continued to fear that some accident would happen. Why not, in a world where people set plants where they did not belong, so that visitors touring a house would be fooled into thinking that dark corners got sunlight—a world full of tricks?

She had first seen the bowl several years earlier, at a crafts fair she had visited half in secret, with her lover. He had urged her to buy the bowl. She didn't *need* any more things, she told him. But she had been drawn to the bowl, and they had lingered near it. Then she went on to the next booth, and he came up behind her, tapping the rim against her shoulder as she ran her fingers over a wood carving. "You're still insisting that I buy that?" she said. "No," he said. "I bought it for you." He had bought her other things before this—things she liked more, at first—the child's ebony-and-turquoise ring that fitted her little finger; the wooden box, long and thin, beautifully dovetailed, that she used to hold paper clips; the soft gray sweater with a pouch pocket. It was his idea that when he could not be there to hold her hand she could hold her own—clasp her hands inside the lone pocket that stretched across the front. But in time she became more attached to the bowl than to any of his other presents. She tried to talk herself out of it. She owned other things that were more striking or valuable. It wasn't an object whose beauty jumped out at you; a lot of people must have passed it by before the two of them saw it that day.

Her lover had said that she was always too slow to know what she really loved. Why continue with her life the way it was? Why be two-faced, he asked her. He had made the first move toward her. When she would not decide in his favor, would not change her life and come to him, he asked her what made her think she could have it both ways. And then he made the last move and left. It was a decision meant to break her will, to shatter her intransigent ideas about honoring previous commitments.

Time passed. Alone in the living room at night, she often looked at the bowl sitting on the table, still and safe, unilluminated. In its way, it was perfect: the world cut in half, deep and smoothly empty. Near the rim, even in dim light, the eye moved toward one small flash of blue, a vanishing point on the horizon.

Questions

1. In what ways is the bowl perfect?
2. Why does Andrea believe that the bowl "was meant to be empty"? How does it symbolize emptiness?
3. In what ways does the bowl represent Andrea's preference for "ironies," matters that become "many sided or unclear"?
4. In what ways does the bowl come to represent people in this story?
5. What is the significance of the fact that Andrea's husband is a stockbroker and she is a real-estate broker?
6. In what ways does the bowl come to represent Andrea's success?
7. Why is Andrea so afraid that the bowl will break? What does the breaking of the bowl symbolize?

9 ❧ What Happens between Stories

Thus far we have discussed stories one by one, noticing how they use certain fictional devices and exploit various conventions. But stories do not necessarily exist in isolation. Since writers read each other's works, the practices of one writer will "rub off" on another. One writer may particularly admire another writer and imitate some of that other author's manner as a sign of esteem and respect. Often authors will see their short stories as forming a series or collection, often linked by common elements. For example, Ernest Hemingway wrote a number of stories connected because the character Nick Adams appears in all of them. Sherwood Anderson wrote *Winesburg, Ohio* and James Joyce wrote *Dubliners*, collections in which the authors linked stories by setting, theme, and narrative technique. This chapter will examine some of the ways in which stories relate to one another.

Stories by a Single Author

We commonly think that stories written by any one author are related to one another just as children born of the same parents are related. But their connection is not always clear or simple. We all know of brothers or sisters who seem wholly different. Perhaps you have heard of twins one of whom became a doctor saving lives, the other a murderer taking them away. As varied as siblings can be, so, too, can be the stories of a single author. Yet even the most diverse family holds qualities in common, and the stories of a given author often seem to have a genetic relationship. Thus, we often speak of an author's work as forming a *corpus*, a single body. Discussion about an author's corpus is largely based on the analogy between it and the human body. For example, an author's work is said to develop, to mature, or to decline just as our bodies develop, mature, and decline into old age.

Development, Maturity, and Decline

A common technique of literary scholars and critics is to arrange the works of an author in as close to chronological order as possible and then to compare the stories. Scholars usually look for weak, rough, and unclear writing at the beginning of an author's career. They expect to find strong, polished, and well defined work as the author matures; and, typically, a falling-off of power—a decline—in the later stages of an author's life. But not all people follow this simple and common pattern. Indeed, some of the greatest authors seem to defy the laws of nature and write their most powerful, finished, and passionate works in their old age. And many begin their careers with works of surprising force, clarity, and depth.

Critics look for several elements to determine an author's progress. For example, they frequently examine characters to see if flat characters become rounded, complex, and believable. They scrutinize narratives to see if they become better focused and organized. But of special concern is the thematic relationship between stories.

Theme

The word *theme* is derived from a Greek word meaning "to set down." A theme, then, is the basic notion an author hopes to set down in the story, the idea or ideas illustrated by the story.

In talking about their fiction, writers express various attitudes toward the role themes play in the writing process. Some writers begin with a philosophy or belief they wish to express, and then fashion a story to illustrate their position. This sort of writing is usually *didactic*, that is, it is designed to teach a lesson.

But usually authors believe that their works "explore" a certain issue rather than "advance" a particular position or dogma. Such authors think of their themes as questions. For example, García Márquez may have asked himself, "How do people react when confronted with the miraculous or the divine?" His story "A Very Old Man with Enormous Wings" explores how two particular characters treat a fallen angel. But García Márquez might write another story in which the characters, rather than imprisoning or reducing the miraculous, are elevated and liberated by it. Most writers prefer to grapple with issues for which there are no simple or clear answers. Thus, two stories by the same author may seem to arrive at opposite conclusions. Does this mean that the author has changed his or her mind? Not necessarily. It may mean that the author is more concerned with exploring the issue than with coming to any hard and fast position.

✍️ Tips for Writers

One way of generating a paper is to compare works from different mediums that are connected by common themes. You might also wish to compare a film or video adaptation to the story on which it is based. How does the adaptation alter the themes of the story?

How to Discover the Theme

The way to find the theme of a story is to view the action in abstract terms. Stories are written about specific characters and specific situations. García Márquez's story is about a specific family who find a specific old man with enormous wings. But the theme concerns the ways in which people (of whom this family is one example) deal with the miraculous (the old man). The film "E. T." develops a similar theme, and W. H. Auden's poem "Musée des Beaux Arts" also concerns itself with this theme. All of these works develop the abstract theme in concrete terms.

Themes are frequently expressed as conflicts between two forces. In "Young Goodman Brown," we have a young man who wants to be good and live a moral life, yet he also wishes to understand evil. We might state the conflict of the story as the conflict between remaining good and recognizing evil. Does one remain good by being ignorant of the sources of evil, or does one need to know evil in order to stay clear of it? Grace Paley's "A Conversation with my Father" concerns the conflict between free will and determinism. Are people able to change themselves or are they destined to act as they do throughout their lives?

One should be aware that stories are not limited to a single theme. Indeed rich and complex stories can develop a number of different themes. Also, the same action can be seen as illustrating various notions. In Anne Tyler's "The Artificial Family," Mary's abandonment of her husband can be viewed as a search for independence, her inability to accept a conventional life style, or envy of her husband's affection for her daughter.

✍ Tips for Readers and Writers

Just as in sports, where the most exciting events involve competitors of similar abilities, so too in fiction the most exciting or interesting stories are those in which closely balanced thematic ideas compete. Stories in which the good guys are pitted against the bad guys usually are terribly lopsided and obvious, and critics often dismiss such stories as simplistic. But in stories such as "A Conversation with My Father," in which the arguments between determinism and free will are equally matched, there may not be a clear winner. Sometimes people dislike such stories because they have no clear solutions or because the stories' authors have not taken definitive stands. Others prefer such stories believing that in life there are no simple answers. In writing about stories whose themes are developed as conflicts between competing notions, you need not find a single victor. In fact, many of the most highly regarded stories have thematic conflicts that are never resolved. Do not impose a resolution of the thematic conflicts on a story, but try to see how the author has worked through these conflicts by the story's close.

Influence

People and experiences are said to exert an *influence* on us when they cause a change in our behavior or thinking. Parents, for example, are models whose behavior children imitate. But not all persons are positive models. A mean, violent neighbor may be a *negative model*—an example of a type we try to avoid becoming. And there are *bad influences*, persons or experiences that lead one into harmful or wasteful activity. Parents are particularly cautious that their offspring do not fall under bad influences. People or events at some distance can affect our lives. They can influence us in ways we may not realize. For example, American thought is influenced by the Founding Fathers, the group of individuals who wrote the Constitution. Although they lived long ago, they still influence the way you behave and think, even though you have not known them personally or perhaps have never taken time to read the Constitution.

Literary influences are as complex as personal influences. Authors are often friendly with other authors. These contacts may alter the way an author writes, either by providing positive models for emulation or negative models to be avoided. More important than these personal relations, perhaps, is the author's reading. Sometimes authors consciously model their works on other stories, novels, characters, and fictional incidents. At other times, the borrowings are unconscious. But authors can provoke strange reactions from their admirers. Frequently admiring writers rebel against their favorite authors just as children rebel against their parents. Consequently, the discussion of influence can be very tricky, and writers have been known to denounce the very works which have most affected their development.

A persistent problem of literary studies is whether writers can be influenced by authors they have not read. For example, scholars argue about the effects of Sigmund Freud's psychoanalytic work on Henry James's novels, even though James never read Freud. Scholars point out that Freud was read by Henry James's brother William, who was a psychologist. Thus, they argue an *indirect influence*, like the influence of the Founding Fathers upon many Americans. It is important to distinguish between direct influences, which are often quite specific, and indirect influences, which are usually broad in scope.

Writers are affected not only by people and books, but also by historical and social events. The First World War, for example, was said to produce "a lost generation" of writers, including Ernest Hemingway, F. Scott Fitzgerald, and William Faulkner. Critics do not mean that all writers reacted to the war in the same way. They do mean that the war had to affect all of the writers in one way or another. Similarly, contemporary writers have all gone through the experience of the Vietnam War and its aftermath. Whether or not they supported American involvement, they shared in its violence, social dislocation, and national cost.

Nathaniel Hawthorne

Nathaniel Hawthorne (1804–1864) is considered among the greatest writers of American literature. As one of the outstanding figures in the American literary renaissance, he was friendly with Herman Melville (whose *Moby Dick* is dedicated to Hawthorne), Ralph Waldo Emerson, Henry David Thoreau, and Henry Wadsworth Longfellow, with whom he attended Bowdoin College.

Recognition came slowly to Hawthorne, in part because he insisted on publishing his early work anonymously and in part because for the ten years after his graduation from college he remained a recluse in his uncle's house in Salem, Massachusetts, venturing out only late in the day on solitary walks. The two stories reprinted here, "The Minister's Black Veil" and "Young Goodman Brown," were written during this period of self-enforced isolation, which is one of the themes they share.

Salem, the setting of "Young Goodman Brown," is an important place for Hawthorne, and in American history. Hawthorne's ancestors were among the first settlers of Massachusetts, arriving between 1630 and 1633. Hawthorne's great-great-grandfather was Judge John Hathorne. (Nathaniel added the *w* to his name when he began to write.) The judge presided over the notorious Salem witch trials and, it was said, brought a curse upon the family by hanging an innocent girl. Hawthorne was fascinated by Salem, its Puritan past, and the dark mystery of the mind. Salem's history and Hawthorne's ancestral past greatly influenced his writing and its themes, settings, and plots.

Isaac Babel and Doris Lessing

At first glance, Isaac Babel (1894–1941) could not seem further removed from Doris Lessing (b. 1919). Doris Lessing was still an obscure clerical worker living in Zimbabwe (then Rhodesia) when Babel died in Siberia, a famous man imprisoned by Stalin for his political opinions. A Russian Jew living in Odessa, Babel was given an unusually fine education, graduating from Kiev University in 1915. Doris Lessing, however, after attending a Roman Catholic convent school and Girls' High School in Africa, dropped out when only fourteen. Lessing grew up on a farm in southern Africa, miles away from her nearest colonial neighbors. Babel was raised amidst the bustling port of Odessa, crowded with foreigners, where his father ran a warehouse. Finally, although Lessing has already written over a dozen novels, several collections of short stories, essays, reviews, plays, and memoirs, Babel's output in his abbreviated life was relatively small. A meticulous craftsman, his story "Lubka the Cossack" went through twenty-two versions before Babel was satisfied.

Yet there are distinct similarities. Both Lessing and Babel were outsiders. As a Jew in Russia, Babel's travel, work, and study were restricted. As part of the white minority in southern Africa, Lessing also felt isolated. Both Babel and Lessing involved themselves in social reform, Babel by participating in the Russian Revolution and Lessing by political organizing. And both grew weary of revolutionary change. Finally, both authors have engaged in what Lessing calls "a study of the individual conscience in its relation with the collective."

Doris Lessing wrote "Homage to Isaac Babel" well after his death. Like all homages, it attempts to acknowledge a debt, in this case the debt of one great writer to another.

Anne Tyler and John Updike

Anne Tyler and John Updike are two contemporary American writers born within a decade of one another. Updike has lived in and written about the Northeast. He was educated at Harvard and has written for *The New Yorker*. His characters are frequently wealthy citizens of New England or the mid-Atlantic states. The Maple family has appeared in a sequence of Updike stories. Tyler, however, was brought up in the South, although she was born in Minnesota. She was educated at Duke University and Columbia. She now makes her home in Baltimore, a city in which Northern and Southern traditions have mingled. Her characters frequently live in poor or reduced circumstances.

Both these stories deal with the break-up of marriages and the relationship between parents and their children. These two stories can indicate how roughly contemporary authors can take similar domestic events and shape them in their own way. Readers may wish to note how the two stories are different and what might account for their difference as well as what in the stories unites these two sensibilities.

Suggestions for Essayists

1. Discuss the ways in which someone you know has influenced your life.
2. Discuss how an event has influenced your development.
3. Discuss how a book has influenced your thinking.

Suggestions for Fiction Writers

1. Write a story borrowing characters from other works. For example, invent your own Sherlock Holmes mystery.
2. Imitate the style of an author you admire. For example, narrate a story in the style of Edgar Allan Poe. Then recast the story as you would tell it apart from his influence.

NATHANIEL HAWTHORNE (1804–1864)

The Minister's Black Veil

A PARABLE[1]

The sexton stood in the porch of Milford meeting-house, pulling busily at the bell-rope. The old people of the village came stooping along the street. Chil-

---

[1] Another clergyman in New England, Mr. Joseph Moody, of York, Maine, who died about eighty years since, made himself remarkable by the same eccentricity that is here related of the Reverend Mr. Hooper. In his case, however, the symbol had a different import. In early life he had accidentally killed a beloved friend; and from that day till the hour of his own death, he hid his face from men.

Nathaniel Hawthorne (*Courtesy Essex Institute, Salem, Massachusetts*)

dren, with bright faces, tripped merrily beside their parents, or mimicked a graver gait, in the conscious dignity of their Sunday clothes. Spruce bachelors looked sidelong at the pretty maidens, and fancied that the Sabbath sunshine made them prettier than on week days. When the throng had mostly streamed into the porch, the sexton began to toll the bell, keeping his eye on the Reverend Mr. Hooper's door. The first glimpse of the clergyman's figure was the signal for the bell to cease its summons.

"But what has good Parson Hooper got upon his face?" cried the sexton in astonishment.

All within hearing immediately turned about, and beheld the semblance of Mr. Hooper, pacing slowly his meditative way towards the meeting-house. With one accord they started, expressing more wonder than if some strange minister were coming to dust the cushions of Mr. Hooper's pulpit.

"Are you sure it is our parson?" inquired Goodman Gray of the sexton.

"Of a certainty it is good Mr. Hooper," replied the sexton. "He was to have exchanged pulpits with Parson Shute, of Westbury; but Parson Shute sent to excuse himself yesterday, being to preach a funeral sermon."

The cause of so much amazement may appear sufficiently slight. Mr. Hooper, a gentlemanly person, of about thirty, though still a bachelor, was dressed with due clerical neatness, as if a careful wife had starched his band, and brushed the weekly dust from his Sunday's garb. There was but one thing remarkable in his appearance. Swathed about his forehead, and hanging down over his face, so low as to be shaken by his breath, Mr. Hooper had on a black veil. On a nearer view it seemed to consist of two folds of crape, which entirely concealed his features, except the mouth and chin, but probably did not intercept his sight, further than to give a darkened aspect to all living and inanimate things. With this gloomy shade before him, good Mr. Hooper walked onward, at a slow and quiet pace, stooping somewhat, and looking on the ground, as is customary with abstracted men, yet nodding kindly to those of his parishioners who still waited on the meeting-house steps. But so wonder-struck were they that his greeting hardly met with a return.

"I can't really feel as if good Mr. Hooper's face was behind that piece of crape," said the sexton.

"I don't like it," muttered an old woman, as she hobbled into the meeting-house. "He has changed himself into something awful, only by hiding his face."

"Our parson has gone mad!" cried Goodman Gray, following him across the threshold.

A rumor of some unaccountable phenomenon had preceded Mr. Hooper into the meeting-house, and set all the congregation astir. Few could refrain from twisting their heads towards the door; many stood upright, and turned directly about; while several little boys clambered upon the seats, and came down again with a terrible racket. There was a general bustle, a rustling of the women's gowns and shuffling of the men's feet, greatly at variance with that hushed repose which should attend the entrance of the minister. But Mr. Hooper appeared not to notice the perturbation of his people. He entered with an almost noiseless step, bent his head mildly to the pews on each side, and bowed as he passed his oldest parishioner, a white-haired great grandsire, who occupied an arm-chair in the centre of the aisle. It was strange to observe how slowly this venerable man became conscious of something singular in the appearance of his pastor. He seemed not fully to partake of the prevailing wonder, till Mr. Hooper had ascended the stairs, and showed himself in the pulpit, face to face with his congregation, except for the black veil. That mysterious emblem was never once withdrawn. It shook with his measured breath, as he gave out the psalm; it threw its obscurity between him and the holy page, as he read the Scriptures; and while he prayed, the veil lay heavily on his uplifted countenance. Did he seek to hide it from the dread Being whom he was addressing?

Such was the effect of this simple piece of crape, that more than one woman of delicate nerves was forced to leave the meeting-house. Yet perhaps the pale-faced congregation was almost as fearful a sight to the minister, as his black veil to them.

Mr. Hooper had the reputation of a good preacher, but not an energetic one: he strove to win his people heavenward by mild, persuasive influences, rather than to drive them thither by the thunders of the Word. The sermon which he now delivered was marked by the same characteristics of style and manner as the general series of his pulpit oratory. But there was something, either in the sentiment of the discourse itself, or in the imagination of the auditors, which made it greatly the most powerful effort that they had ever heard from their pastor's lips. It was tinged, rather more darkly than usual, with the gentle gloom of Mr. Hooper's temperament. The subject had reference to secret sin, and those sad mysteries which we hide from our nearest and dearest, and would fain conceal from our own consciousness, even forgetting that the Omniscient can detect them. A subtle power was breathed into his words. Each member of the congregation, the most innocent girl, and the man of hardened breast, felt as if the preacher had crept upon them, behind his awful veil, and discovered their hoarded iniquity of deed or thought. Many spread their clasped hands on their bosoms. There was nothing terrible in what Mr. Hooper said, at least, no violence; and yet, with every tremor of his melancholy voice, the hearers quaked. An unsought pathos came hand in hand with awe. So sensible were the audience of some unwonted attribute in their minister, that they longed for a breath of wind to blow aside the veil, almost believing that a stranger's visage would be discovered, though the form, gesture, and voice were those of Mr. Hooper.

At the close of the services, the people hurried out with indecorous confusion, eager to communicate their pent-up amazement, and conscious of lighter spirits the moment they lost sight of the black veil. Some gathered in little circles, huddled closely together, with their mouths all whispering in the centre; some went homeward alone, wrapt in silent meditation; some talked loudly, and profaned the Sabbath day with ostentatious laughter. A few shook their sagacious heads, intimating that they could penetrate the mystery; while one or two affirmed that there was no mystery at all, but only that Mr. Hooper's eyes were so weakened by the midnight lamp, as to require a shade. After a brief interval, forth came good Mr. Hooper also, in the rear of his flock. Turning his veiled face from one group to another, he paid due reverence to the hoary heads, saluted the middle aged with kind dignity as their friend and spiritual guide, greeted the young with mingled authority and love, and laid his hands on the little children's heads to bless them. Such was always his custom on the Sabbath day. Strange and bewildered looks repaid him for his courtesy. None, as on former occasions, aspired to the honor of walking by their pastor's side. Old Squire Saunders, doubtless by an accidental lapse of memory, neglected to invite Mr. Hooper to his table, where the good clergyman had been wont to bless the food, almost every Sunday since his settlement. He returned, therefore, to the parsonage, and, at the moment of closing the door, was observed to look back upon the people, all of whom had their eyes fixed upon the minister. A sad smile gleamed faintly from beneath the black veil, and flickered about his mouth, glimmering as he disappeared.

"How strange," said a lady, "that a simple black veil, such as any woman might wear on her bonnet, should become such a terrible thing on Mr. Hooper's face!"

"Something must surely be amiss with Mr. Hooper's intellects," observed her husband, the physician of the village. "But the strangest part of the affair is the effect of this vagary, even on a sober-minded man like myself. The black veil, though it covers only our pastor's face, throws its influence over his whole person, and makes him ghostlike from head to foot. Do you not feel it so?"

"Truly do I," replied the lady; "and I would not be alone with him for the world. I wonder he is not afraid to be alone with himself!"

"Men sometimes are so," said her husband.

The afternoon service was attended with similar circumstances. At its conclusion, the bell tolled for the funeral of a young lady. The relatives and friends were assembled in the house, and the more distant acquaintances stood about the door, speaking of the good qualities of the deceased, when their talk was interrupted by the appearance of Mr. Hooper, still covered with his black veil. It was now an appropriate emblem. The clergyman stepped into the room where the corpse was laid, and bent over the coffin, to take a last farewell of his deceased parishioner. As he stooped, the veil hung straight down from his forehead, so that, if her eyelids had not been closed forever, the dead maiden might have seen his face. Could Mr. Hooper be fearful of her glance, that he so hastily caught back the black veil? A person who watched the interview between the dead and living, scrupled not to affirm, that, at the instant when the clergyman's features were disclosed, the corpse had slightly shuddered, rustling the shroud and muslin cap, though the countenance retained the composure of death. A superstitious old woman was the only witness of this prodigy. From the coffin Mr. Hooper passed into the chamber of the mourners, and thence to the head of the staircase, to make the funeral prayer. It was a tender and heart-dissolving prayer, full of sorrow, yet so imbued with celestial hopes, that the music of a heavenly harp, swept by the fingers of the dead, seemed faintly to be heard among the saddest accents of the minister. The people trembled, though they but darkly understood him when he prayed that they, and himself, and all of mortal race, might be ready, as he trusted this young maiden had been, for the dreadful hour that should snatch the veil from their faces. The bearers went heavily forth, and the mourners followed, saddening all the street, with the dead before them, and Mr. Hooper in his black veil behind.

"Why do you look back?" said one in the procession to his partner.

"I had a fancy," replied she, "that the minister and the maiden's spirit were walking hand in hand."

"And so had I, at the same moment," said the other.

That night, the handsomest couple in Milford village were to be joined in wedlock. Though reckoned a melancholy man, Mr. Hooper had a placid cheerfulness for such occasions, which often excited a sympathetic smile where livelier merriment would have been thrown away. There was no quality of his disposition which made him more beloved than this. The company at the wedding awaited his arrival with impatience, trusting that the strange awe, which had gathered over him throughout the day, would now be dispelled. But such was not the result. When Mr. Hooper came, the first thing that their eyes rested on was the same horrible black veil, which had added deeper gloom to the funeral, and could portend nothing but evil to the wedding. Such was its immediate effect on the guests that a cloud seemed to have rolled duskily from beneath the black crape, and dimmed the light of the candles. The bridal pair stood up before the minister. But the bride's cold fingers quivered in the tremulous hand of the bridegroom, and her deathlike paleness caused a whisper that the maiden who had been buried a few hours before was come from her grave to be married.

If ever another wedding were so dismal, it was that famous one where they tolled the wedding knell. After performing the ceremony, Mr. Hooper raised a glass of wine to his lips, wishing happiness to the new-married couple in a strain of mild pleasantry that ought to have brightened the features of the guests, like a cheerful gleam from the hearth. At that instant, catching a glimpse of his figure in the looking-glass, the black veil involved his own spirit in the horror with which it overwhelmed all others. His frame shuddered, his lips grew white, he spilt the untasted wine upon the carpet, and rushed forth into the darkness. For the Earth, too, had on her Black Veil.

The next day, the whole village of Milford talked of little else than Parson Hooper's black veil. That, and the mystery concealed behind it, supplied a topic for discussion between acquaintances meeting in the street, and good women gossiping at their open windows. It was the first item of news that the tavern-keeper told to his guests. The children babbled of it on their way to school. One imitative little imp covered his face with an old black handkerchief, thereby so affrighting his playmates that the panic seized himself, and he well-nigh lost his wits by his own waggery.

It was remarkable that of all the busybodies and impertinent people in the parish, not one ventured to put the plain question to Mr. Hooper, wherefore he did this thing. Hitherto, whenever there appeared the slightest call for such interference, he had never lacked advisers, nor shown himself averse to be guided by their judgment. If he erred at all, it was by so painful a degree of self-distrust, that even the mildest censure would lead him to consider an indifferent action as a crime. Yet, though so well acquainted with this amiable weakness, no individual among his parishioners chose to make the black veil a subject of friendly remonstrance. There was a feeling of dread, neither plainly confessed nor carefully concealed, which caused each to shift the responsibility upon another, till at length it was found expedient to send a deputation of the church, in order to deal with Mr. Hooper about the mystery, before it should grow into a scandal. Never did an embassy so ill discharge its duties. The minister received them with friendly courtesy, but became silent, after they were seated, leaving to his visitors the whole burden of introducing their important business. The topic, it might be supposed, was obvious enough. There was the black veil swathed round Mr. Hooper's forehead, and concealing every feature above his placid mouth, on which, at times, they could perceive the glimmering of a melancholy smile. But that piece of crape, to their imagination, seemed to hang down before his heart, the symbol of a fearful secret between him and them. Were the veil but cast aside, they might speak freely of it, but not till then. Thus they sat a considerable time, speechless, confused, and shrinking uneasily from Mr. Hooper's eye, which they felt to be fixed upon them with an invisible glance. Finally, the deputies returned abashed to their constituents, pronouncing the matter too weighty to be handled, except by a council of the churches, if, indeed, it might not require a general synod.

But there was one person in the village unappalled by the awe with which the black veil had impressed all beside herself. When the deputies returned without an explanation, or even venturing to demand one, she, with the calm energy of her character, determined to chase away the strange cloud that appeared to be settling round Mr. Hooper, every moment more darkly than before. As his plighted wife, it should be her privilege to know what the black veil concealed. At the minister's first visit, therefore, she entered upon the subject with a direct simplicity, which made the task easier both for him and her. After he had seated himself, she fixed her eyes steadfastly upon the veil, but could discern nothing of the dreadful gloom that had so overawed the multitude: it was but a double fold of crape, hanging down from his forehead to his mouth, and slightly stirring with his breath.

"No," said she aloud, and smiling, "there is nothing terrible in this piece of crape, except that it hides a face which I am always glad to look upon. Come, good sir, let the sun shine from behind the cloud. First lay aside your black veil: then tell me why you put it on."

Mr. Hooper's smile glimmered faintly.

"There is an hour to come," said he, "when all of us shall cast aside our veils. Take it not amiss, beloved friend, if I wear this piece of crape till then."

"Your words are a mystery, too," returned the young lady. "Take away the veil from them, at least."

"Elizabeth, I will," said he, "so far as my vow may suffer me. Know, then, this veil is a type and a symbol, and I am bound to wear it ever, both in light and darkness, in solitude and before the gaze of multitudes, and as with strangers, so with my familiar friends. No mortal eye will see it withdrawn. This dismal shade must separate me from the world: even you, Elizabeth, can never come behind it!"

"What grievous affliction hath befallen you," she earnestly inquired, "that you should thus darken your eyes forever?"

"If it be a sign of mourning," replied Mr. Hooper, "I, perhaps, like most other mortals, have sorrows dark enough to be typified by a black veil."

"But what if the world will not believe that it is the type of an innocent sorrow?" urged Elizabeth. "Beloved and respected as you are, there may be whispers that you hide your face under the consciousness of secret sin. For the sake of your holy office, do away this scandal!"

The color rose into her cheeks as she intimated the nature of the rumors that were already abroad in the village. But Mr. Hooper's mildness did not forsake him. He even smiled again—that same sad smile, which always appeared like a faint glimmering of light, proceeding from the obscurity beneath the veil.

"If I hide my face for sorrow, there is cause enough," he merely replied; "and if I cover it for secret sin, what mortal might not do the same?"

And with this gentle, but unconquerable obstinacy did he resist all her entreaties. At length Elizabeth sat silent. For a few moments she appeared lost in thought, considering, probably, what new methods might be tried to withdraw her lover from so dark a fantasy, which, if it had no other meaning, was perhaps a symptom of mental disease. Though of a firmer character than his own, the tears rolled down her cheeks. But, in an instant, as it were, a new feeling took the place of sorrow: her eyes were fixed insensibly on the black veil, when, like a sudden twilight in the air, its terrors fell around her. She arose, and stood trembling before him.

"And do you feel it then, at last?" said he mournfully.

She made no reply, but covered her eyes with her hand, and turned to leave the room. He rushed forward and caught her arm.

"Have patience with me, Elizabeth!" cried he, passionately. "Do not desert me, though this veil must be between us here on earth. Be mine, and hereafter there shall be no veil over my face, no darkness between our souls! It is but a mortal veil—it is not for eternity! O! you know not how lonely I am, and how frightened, to be alone behind my black veil. Do not leave me in this miserable obscurity forever!"

"Lift the veil but once, and look me in the face," said she.

"Never! It cannot be!" replied Mr. Hooper.

"Then farewell!" said Elizabeth.

She withdrew her arm from his grasp, and slowly departed, pausing at the door, to give one long shuddering gaze, that seemed almost to penetrate the mystery of the black veil. But, even amid his grief, Mr. Hooper smiled to think that only a material emblem had separated him from happiness, though the horrors, which it shadowed forth, must be drawn darkly between the fondest of lovers.

From that time no attempts were made to remove Mr. Hooper's black veil, or, by a direct appeal, to discover the secret which it was supposed to hide. By persons who claimed a superiority to popular prejudice, it was reckoned merely an eccentric whim, such as often mingles with the sober actions of men otherwise rational, and tinges them all with its own semblance of insanity. But with the multitude, good Mr. Hooper was irreparably a bugbear. He could not walk the street with any peace of mind, so conscious was he that the gentle and timid would turn aside to avoid him, and that others would make it a point of hardihood to throw themselves in his way. The impertinence of the latter class compelled him to give up his customary walk at sunset to the burial ground; for when he leaned pensively over the gate, there would always be faces behind the gravestones, peeping at his black veil. A fable went the rounds that the stare of the dead people drove him thence. It grieved him, to the very depth of his kind heart, to observe how the children fled from his approach, breaking up their merriest sports, while his melancholy figure was yet afar off. Their instinctive dread caused him to feel more strongly than aught else, that a preternatural horror was interwoven with the threads of the black crape. In truth, his own antipathy to the veil was known to be so great, that he never willingly passed before a mirror, nor stooped to drink at a still fountain, lest, in its peaceful bosom, he should be affrighted by himself. This was what gave plausibility to the whispers, that Mr. Hooper's conscience tortured him for some great crime too horrible to be entirely concealed, or otherwise than so obscurely intimated. Thus, from beneath the black veil, there rolled a cloud into the sunshine, an ambiguity of sin or sorrow, which enveloped the poor minister, so that love or sympathy could never reach him. It was said that ghost and fiend consorted with him there. With self-shudderings and outward terrors, he walked continually in its shadow, groping darkly within his own soul, or gazing through a medium that saddened the whole world. Even the lawless wind, it was believed, respected his dreadful secret, and never blew aside the veil. But still good Mr. Hooper sadly smiled at the pale visages of the worldly throng as he passed by.

Among all its bad influences, the black veil had the one desirable effect, of making its wearer a very efficient clergyman. By the aid of his mysterious emblem—for there was no other apparent cause—he became a man of awful power over souls that were in agony for sin. His converts always regarded him with a dread peculiar to themselves, affirming, though but figuratively, that, before he brought them to celestial light, they had been with him behind the black veil. Its gloom, indeed, enabled him to sympathize with all dark affections. Dying sinners cried aloud for Mr. Hooper, and would not yield their breath till he appeared; though ever, as he stooped to whisper consolation, they shuddered at the veiled face so near their own. Such were the terrors of the black veil, even when Death had bared his visage! Strangers came long distances to attend service at his church, with the mere idle purpose of gazing at his figure, because it was forbidden them to behold his face. But many were made to quake ere they departed! Once, during Governor Belcher's administration, Mr. Hooper was appointed to preach the election sermon. Covered with his black veil, he stood before the chief magistrate, the council, and the representatives, and wrought so deep an impression, that the legislative measures of that year were characterized by all the gloom and piety of our earliest ancestral sway.

In this manner Mr. Hooper spent a long life, irreproachable in outward act, yet shrouded in dismal suspicions; kind and loving, though unloved, and dimly feared; a man apart from men, shunned in their health and joy, but ever summoned to their aid in mortal anguish. As years wore on, shedding their snows above his sable veil, he acquired a name throughout the New England churches, and they called him Father Hooper. Nearly all his parishioners, who were of mature age when he was settled, had been borne away by many a funeral: he had one congregation in the church, and a more crowded one in the churchyard; and having wrought so late into the evening, and done his work so well, it was now good Father Hooper's turn to rest.

Several persons were visible by the shaded candlelight, in the death chamber of the old clergyman. Natural connections he had none. But there was the decorously grave, though unmoved physician, seeking only to mitigate the last pangs of the patient whom he could not save. There were the deacons, and other eminently pious members of his church. There, also, was the Reverend Mr. Clark, of Westbury, a young and zealous divine, who had ridden in haste to pray by the bedside of the expiring minister. There was the nurse, no hired handmaiden of death, but one whose calm affection had endured thus long in secrecy, in solitude, amid the chill of age, and would not perish, even at the dying hour. Who, but Elizabeth! And there lay the hoary head of good Father Hooper upon the death pillow, with the black veil still swathed about his brow, and reaching down over his face, so that each more difficult gasp of his faint breath caused it to stir. All through life that piece of crape had hung between him and the world: it had separated him from cheerful brotherhood and woman's love, and kept him in that saddest of all prisons, his own heart; and still it lay upon his face, as if to deepen the gloom of his darksome chamber, and shade him from the sunshine of eternity.

For some time previous, his mind had been confused, wavering doubtfully between the past and the present, and hovering forward, as it were, at intervals, into the indistinctness of the world to come. There had been feverish turns, which tossed him from side to side, and wore away what little strength he had. But in his most convulsive struggles, and in the wildest vagaries of his intellect, when no other thought retained its sober influence, he still showed an awful solicitude lest the black veil should slip aside. Even if his bewildered soul could have forgotten, there was a faithful woman at this pillow, who, with averted eyes, would have covered that aged face, which she had last beheld in the comeliness of manhood. At length the death-stricken old man lay quietly in the torpor of mental and bodily exhaustion, with an imperceptible pulse, and breath that grew fainter and fainter, except when a long, deep, and irregular inspiration seemed to prelude the flight of his spirit.

The minister of Westbury approached the bedside.

"Venerable Father Hooper," said he, "the moment of your release is at hand. Are you ready for the lifting of the veil that shuts in time from eternity?"

Father Hooper at first replied merely by a feeble motion of his head; then, apprehensive, perhaps, that his meaning might be doubted, he exerted himself to speak.

"Yea," said he, in faint accents, "my soul hath a patient weariness until that veil be lifted."

"And is it fitting," resumed the Reverend Mr. Clark, "that a man so given to prayer, of such a blameless example, holy in deed and thought, so far as mortal judgment may pronounce; is it fitting that a father in the church should leave a shadow on his memory, that may seem to blacken a life so pure? I pray you, my venerable brother, let not this thing be! Suffer us to be gladdened by your triumphant aspect as you go to your reward. Before the veil of eternity be lifted, let me cast aside this black veil from your face!"

And thus speaking, the Reverend Mr. Clark bent forward to reveal the mystery of so many years. But, exerting a sudden energy, that made all the beholders stand aghast, Father Hooper snatched both his hands from beneath the bed-clothes, and pressed them strongly on the black veil, resolute to struggle, if the minister of Westbury would contend with a dying man.

"Never!" cried the veiled clergyman. "On earth, never!"

"Dark old man!" exclaimed the affrighted minister, "with what horrible crime upon your soul are you now passing to the judgment?"

Father Hooper's breath heaved; it rattled in his throat; but, with a mighty effort, grasping forward with his hands, he caught hold of life, and held it back till he should speak. He even raised himself in bed; and there he sat, shivering with the arms of death around him, while the black veil hung down, awful, at that last moment, in the gathered terrors of a lifetime. And yet the faint, sad smile, so often there, now seemed to glimmer from its obscurity, and linger on Father Hooper's lips.

"Why do you tremble at me alone?" cried he, turning his veiled face round the circle of pale spectators. "Tremble also at each other! Have men avoided me, and women shown no pity, and children screamed and fled, only for my black veil? What, but the mystery which it obscurely typifies, has made this piece of crape so awful? When the friend shows his inmost heart to his friend; the lover to his best beloved; when man does not vainly shrink from the eye of his Creator, loathsomely treasuring up the secret of his sin; then deem me a monster, for the symbol beneath which I have lived, and die! I look around me, and, lo! on every visage a Black Veil!"

While his auditors shrank from one another, in mutual affright, Father Hooper fell back upon his pillow, a veiled corpse, with a faint smile lingering on the lips. Still veiled, they laid him in his coffin, and a veiled corpse they bore him to the grave. The grass of many years has sprung up and withered on that grave, the burial stone is moss-grown, and good Mr. Hooper's face is dust; but awful is still the thought that it mouldered beneath the Black Veil!

Questions

1. Why does Mr. Hooper wear a veil? Must his wearing of the veil be a sign of his having committed some terrible wrong?
2. What does Mr. Hooper mean when he says, "I, perhaps, like most other mortals, have sorrows dark enough to be typified by a black veil"?
3. Why doesn't Elizabeth marry him? Why does the veil separate him "from cheerful brotherhood and woman's love, and keep him in the saddest of all prisons, his own heart"?
4. What does Mr. Hooper mean when he says, "I look around me, and, lo! on every visage a Black Veil"?
5. Does Mr. Hooper exaggerate the evil in the world and in himself, or do the others minimize the evil around and within themselves?

NATHANIEL HAWTHORNE (1804–1864)

Young Goodman Brown

Young Goodman[1] Brown came forth at sunset into the street at Salem village; but put his head back, after crossing the threshold, to exchange a parting kiss with his young wife. And Faith, as the wife was aptly named, thrust her own pretty head into the street, letting the wind play with the pink ribbons of her cap while she called to Goodman Brown.

"Dearest heart," whispered she, softly and rather sadly, when her lips were

---

[1] Goodman is a title of respect for those otherwise untitled, especially farmers.

close to his ear, "prithee put off your journey until sunrise and sleep in your own bed to-night. A lone woman is troubled with such dreams and such thoughts that she's afeard of herself sometimes. Pray tarry with me this night, dear husband, of all nights in the year."

"My love and my Faith," replied young Goodman Brown, "of all nights in the year, this one night must I tarry away from thee. My journey, as thou callest it, forth and back again, must needs be done 'twixt now and sunrise. What, my sweet, pretty wife, dost thou doubt me already, and we but three months married?"

"Then God bless you!" said Faith, with the pink ribbons; "and may you find all well when you come back."

"Amen!" cried Goodman Brown. "Say thy prayers, dear Faith, and go to bed at dusk, and no harm will come to thee."

So they parted; and the young man pursued his way until, being about to turn the corner by the meeting-house, he looked back and saw the head of Faith still peeping after him with a melancholy air, in spite of her pink ribbons.

"Poor little Faith!" thought he, for his heart smote him. "What a wretch am I to leave her on such an errand! She talks of dreams, too. Methought as she spoke there was trouble in her face, as if a dream had warned her what work is to be done to-night. But no, no; 't would kill her to think of it. Well, she's a blessed angel on earth; and after this one night I'll cling to her skirts and follow her to heaven."

With this excellent resolve for the future, Goodman Brown felt himself justified in making more haste on his present evil purpose. He had taken a dreary road, darkened by all the gloomiest trees of the forest, which barely stood aside to let the narrow path creep through, and closed immediately behind. It was all as lonely as could be; and there is this peculiarity in such a solitude, that the traveller knows not who may be concealed by the innumerable trunks and the thick boughs overhead; so that with lonely footsteps he may yet be passing through an unseen multitude.

"There may be a devilish Indian behind every tree," said Goodman Brown to himself; and he glanced fearfully behind him as he added, "What if the devil himself should be at my very elbow!"

His head being turned back, he passed a crook of the road, and, looking forward again, beheld the figure of a man, in grave and decent attire, seated at the foot of an old tree. He arose at Goodman Brown's approach and walked onward side by side with him.

"You are late, Goodman Brown," said he. "The clock of the Old South was striking as I came through Boston, and that is full fifteen minutes agone."[2]

"Faith kept me back a while," replied the young man, with a tremor in his voice, caused by the sudden appearance of his companion, though not wholly unexpected.

It was now deep dusk in the forest, and deepest in that part of it where these

---

[2] Since Boston is fifteen miles from Salem, the man has traveled at superhuman speed.

two were journeying. As nearly as could be discerned, the second traveller was about fifty years old, apparently in the same rank of life as Goodman Brown, and bearing a considerable resemblance to him, though perhaps more in expression than features. Still they might have been taken for father and son. And yet, though the elder person was as simply clad as the younger, and as simple in manner too, he had an indescribable air of one who knew the world, and who would not have felt abashed at the governor's dinner table or in King William's[3] court, were it possible that his affairs should call him thither. But the only thing about him that could be fixed upon as remarkable was his staff, which bore the likeness of a great black snake, so curiously wrought that it might almost be seen to twist and wriggle itself like a living serpent. This, of course, must have been an ocular deception, assisted by the uncertain light.

"Come, Goodman Brown," cried his fellow-traveler, "this is a dull pace for the beginning of a journey. Take my staff, if you are so soon weary."

"Friend," said the other, exchanging his slow pace for a full stop, "having kept covenant by meeting thee here, it is my purpose now to return whence I came. I have scruples touching the matter thou wot'st[4] of."

"Sayest thou so?" replied he of the serpent, smiling apart. "Let us walk on, nevertheless, reasoning as we go; and if I convince thee not thou shalt turn back. We are but a little way in the forest yet."

"Too far! too far!" exclaimed the goodman, unconsciously resuming his walk. "My father never went into the woods on such an errand, nor his father before him. We have been a race of honest men and good Christians since the days of the martyrs; and shall I be the first of the name of Brown that ever took this path and kept"—

"Such company, thou wouldst say," observed the elder person, interpreting his pause. "Well said, Goodman Brown! I have been as well acquainted with your family as with ever a one among the Puritans; and that's no trifle to say. I helped your grandfather, the constable, when he lashed the Quaker woman so smartly through the streets of Salem; and it was I that brought your father a pitchpine knot, kindled at my own hearth, to set fire to an Indian village, in King Philip's war.[5] They were my good friends, both; and many a pleasant walk have we had along this path, and returned merrily after midnight. I would fain be friends with you for their sake."

"If it be as thou sayest," replied Goodman Brown, "I marvel they never spoke of these matters; or, verily, I marvel not, seeing that the least rumor of the sort would have driven them from New England. We are a people of prayer, and good works to boot, and abide no such wickedness."

"Wickedness or not," said the traveller with the twisted staff, "I have a very

---

[3] King William III ruled England from 1689 to 1702.

[4] *Wot'st* is the second person singular of the verb "to wit"; thus, the matter they know of.

[5] King Philip (Indian name Metacomet, c. 1639–1676) was the leader of the Wampanaug Indians, who were involved in the fiercest Indian war (1675–76) in American history as they tried to assert Indian sovereignty over appropriated lands.

general acquaintance here in New England. The deacons of many a church have drunk the communion wine with me; the selectmen of divers towns make me their chairman; and a majority of the Great and General Court are firm supporters of my interest. The governor and I, too—But these are state secrets."

"Can this be so?" cried Goodman Brown, with a stare of amazement at his undisturbed companion. "Howbeit, I have nothing to do with the governor and council; they have their own ways, and are no rule for a simple husbandman like me. But, were I to go on with thee, how should I meet the eye of that good old man, our minister, at Salem village? Oh, his voice would make me tremble both Sabbath day and lecture day."

Thus far the elder traveller had listened with due gravity; but now burst into a fit of irrepressible mirth, shaking himself so violently that his snake-like staff actually seemed to wriggle in sympathy.

"Ha! ha! ha!" shouted he again and again; then composing himself, "Well, go on, Goodman Brown, go on; but, prithee, don't kill me with laughing."

"Well, then, to end the matter at once," said Goodman Brown, considerably nettled, "there is my wife, Faith. It would break her dear little heart; and I'd rather break my own."

"Nay, if that be the case," answered the other, "e'en go thy ways, Goodman Brown. I would not for twenty old women like the one hobbling before us that Faith should come to any harm."

As he spoke he pointed his staff at a female figure on the path, in whom Goodman Brown recognized a very pious and exemplary dame, who had taught him his catechism in youth, and was still his moral and spiritual adviser, jointly with the minister and Deacon Gookin.

"A marvel, truly, that Goody[6] Cloyse should be so far in the wilderness at nightfall," said he. "But with your leave, friend, I shall take a cut through the woods until we have left this Christian woman behind. Being a stranger to you, she might ask whom I was consorting with and whither I was going."

"Be it so," said his fellow-traveller. "Betake you the woods, and let me keep the path."

Accordingly the young man turned aside, but took care to watch his companion, who advanced softly along the road until he had come within a staff's length of the old dame. She, meanwhile, was making the best of her way, with singular speed for so aged a woman, and mumbling some indistinct words—a prayer, doubtless—as she went. The traveller put forth his staff and touched her withered neck with what seemed the serpent's tail.

"The devil!" screamed the pious old lady.

"Then Goody Cloyse knows her old friend?" observed the traveller, confronting her and leaning on his writhing stick.

"Ah, forsooth, and is it your worship indeed?" cried the good dame. "Yea, truly is it, and in the very image of my old gossip, Goodman Brown, the

---

[6] Goody is a polite term applied to a woman of humble origin.

grandfather of the silly fellow that now is. But—would your worship believe it?—my broomstick hath strangely disappeared, stolen, as I suspect, by that unhanged witch, Goody Cory, and that, too, when I was all anointed with the juice of smallage, and cinquefoil, and wolf's bane"—[7]

"Mingled with fine wheat and the fat of a new-born babe," said the shape of old Goodman Brown.

"Ah, your worship knows the recipe," cried the old lady, cackling aloud. "So, as I was saying, being all ready for the meeting, and no horse to ride on, I made up my mind to foot it; for they tell me there is a nice young man to be taken into communion to-night. But now your good worship will lend me your arm, and we shall be there in a twinkling."

"That can hardly be," answered her friend. "I may not spare you my arm, Goody Cloyse; but here is my staff, if you will."

So saying, he threw it down at her feet, where, perhaps, it assumed life, being one of the rods which its owner had formerly lent to the Egyptian magi. Of this fact, however, Goodman Brown could not take cognizance. He had cast up his eyes in astonishment, and, looking down again, beheld neither Goody Cloyse nor the serpentine staff, but this fellow-traveller alone, who waited for him as calmly as if nothing had happened.

"That old woman taught me my catechism," said the young man; and there was a world of meaning in this simple comment.

They continued to walk onward, while the elder traveller exhorted his companion to make good speed and persevere in the path, discoursing so aptly that his arguments seemed rather to spring up in the bosom of his auditor than to be suggested by himself. As they went, he plucked a branch of maple to serve for a walking stick, and began to strip it of the twigs and little boughs, which were wet with evening dew. The moment his fingers touched them they became strangely withered and dried up as with a week's sunshine. Thus the pair proceeded, at a good free pace, until suddenly, in a gloomy hollow of the road, Goodman Brown sat himself down on the stump of a tree and refused to go any farther.

"Friend," said he, stubbornly, "my mind is made up. Not another step will I budge on this errand. What if a wretched old woman do choose to go to the devil when I thought she was going to heaven: is that any reason why I should quit my dear Faith and go after her?"

"You will think better of this by and by," said his acquaintance, composedly. "Sit here and rest yourself a while; and when you feel like moving again, there is my staff to help you along."

Without more words, he threw his companion the maple stick, and was as speedily out of sight as if he had vanished into the deepening gloom. The young man sat a few moments by the roadside, applauding himself greatly, and thinking with how clear a conscience he should meet the minister in his morning walk,

---

[7] Wolf's bane is a plant used in witchcraft.

nor shrink from the eye of good old Deacon Gookin. And what calm sleep would be his that very night, which was to have been spent so wickedly, but so purely and sweetly now, in the arms of Faith! Amidst these pleasant and praiseworthy meditations, Goodman Brown heard the tramp of horses along the road, and deemed it advisable to conceal himself within the verge of the forest, conscious of the guilty purpose that had brought him thither, though now so happily turned from it.

On came the hoof tramps and the voices of the riders, two grave old voices, conversing soberly as they drew near. These mingled sounds appeared to pass along the road, within a few yards of the young man's hiding-place; but, owing doubtless to the depth of the gloom at that particular spot, neither the travellers nor their steeds were visible. Though their figures brushed the small boughs by the wayside, it could not be seen that they intercepted, even for a moment, the faint gleam from the strip of bright sky athwart which they must have passed. Goodman Brown alternately crouched and stood on tiptoe, pulling aside the branches and thrusting forth his head as far as he durst without discerning so much as a shadow. It vexed him the more, because he could have sworn, were such a thing possible, that he recognized the voices of the minister and Deacon Gookin, jogging along quietly, as they were wont to do, when bound to some ordination of ecclesiastical council. While yet within hearing, one of the riders stopped to pluck a switch.

"Of the two, reverend sir," said the voice like the deacon's, "I had rather miss an ordination dinner than to-night's meeting. They tell me that some of our community are to be here from Falmouth[8] and beyond, and others from Connecticut and Rhode Island, besides several of the Indian powwows, who, after their fashion, know almost as much deviltry as the best of us. Moreover, there is a goodly young woman to be taken into communion."

"Mighty well, Deacon Gookin!" replied the solemn old tones of the minister. "Spur up, or we shall be late. Nothing can be done, you know, until I get on the ground."

The hoofs clattered again; and the voices, talking so strangely in the empty air, passed on through the forest, where no church had ever been gathered or solitary Christian prayed. Whither, then, could these holy men be journeying so deep into the heathen wilderness? Young Goodman Brown caught hold of a tree for support, being ready to sink down on the ground, faint and overburdened with the heavy sickness of his heart. He looked up to the sky, doubting whether there really was a heaven above him. Yet there was the blue arch, and the stars brightening in it.

"With heaven above and Faith below, I will yet stand firm against the devil!" cried Goodman Brown.

While he still gazed upward into the deep arch of the firmament and had lifted his hands to pray, a cloud, though no wind was stirring, hurried across the zenith and hid the brightening stars. The blue sky was still visible, except directly overhead, where this black mass of cloud was sweeping swiftly northward. Aloft in the air, as if from the depths of the cloud, came a confused and doubtful sound of voices. Once the listener fancied that he could distinguish the accents of towns-people of his own, men and women, both pious and ungodly, many of whom he had met at the communion table, and had seen others rioting at the tavern. The next moment, so indistinct were the sounds, he doubted whether he had heard aught but the murmur of the old forest, whispering without a wind. Then came a stronger swell of those familiar tones, heard daily in the sunshine at Salem village, but never until now from a cloud of night. There was one voice, of a young woman, uttering lamentations, yet with an uncertain sorrow, and entreating for some favor, which, perhaps, it would grieve her to obtain; and all the unseen multitude, both saints and sinners, seemed to encourage her onward.

"Faith!" shouted Goodman Brown, in a voice of agony and desperation; and the echoes of the forest mocked him, crying, "Faith! Faith!" as if bewildered wretches were seeking her all through the wilderness.

The cry of grief, rage, and terror was yet piercing the night, when the unhappy husband held his breath for a response. There was a scream, drowned immediately in a louder murmur of voices, fading into far-off laughter, as the dark cloud swept away, leaving the clear and silent sky above Goodman Brown. But something fluttered lightly down through the air and caught on the branch of a tree. The young man seized it, and beheld a pink ribbon.

"My Faith is gone!" cried he, after one stupefied moment. "There is no good on earth; and sin is but a name. Come, devil; for to thee is this world given."

And, maddened with despair, so that he laughed loud and long, did Goodman Brown grasp his staff and set forth again, at such a rate that he seemed to fly along the forest path rather than to walk or run. The road grew wilder and drearier and more faintly traced, and vanished at length, leaving him in the heart of the dark wilderness, still rushing onward with the instinct that guides mortal man to evil. The whole forest was peopled with frightful sounds—the creaking of the trees, the howling of wild beasts, and the yell of Indians; while sometimes the wind tolled like a distant church bell, and sometimes gave a broad roar around the traveller, as if all Nature were laughing him to scorn. But he was himself the chief horror of the scene, and shrank not from its other horrors.

"Ha! ha! ha!" roared Goodman Brown when the wind laughed at him. "Let us hear which will laugh loudest. Think not to frighten me with your deviltry. Come witch, come wizard, come Indian powwow, come devil himself, and here comes Goodman Brown. You may as well fear him as he fear you."

In truth, all through the haunted forest there could be nothing more frightful than the figure of Goodman Brown. On he flew among the black pines, brandishing his staff with frenzied gestures, now giving vent to an inspiration of horrid blasphemy, and now shouting forth such laughter as set all the echoes of the forest laughing like demons around him. The fiend in his own shape is less hideous than when he rages in the breast of man. Thus sped the demoniac on his course, until, quivering among the trees, he saw a red light before him, as when the felled trunks and branches of a clearing have been set on fire, and throw up their lurid blaze against the sky, at the hour of midnight. He paused, in a lull of the tempest that had driven him onward, and heard the swell of what seemed a hymn, rolling solemnly from a distance with the weight of many voices. He knew the tune; it was a familiar one in the choir of the village meeting-house. The verse died heavily away, and was lengthened by a chorus, not of human voices, but of all the sounds of the benighted wilderness pealing in awful harmony together. Goodman Brown cried out, and his cry was lost to his own ear by its unison with the cry of the desert.

In the interval of silence he stole forward until the light glared full upon his eyes. At one extremity of an open space, hemmed in by the dark wall of the forest, arose a rock, bearing some rude, natural resemblance either to an altar or a pulpit, and surrounded by four blazing pines, their tops aflame, their stems untouched, like candles at an evening meeting. The mass of foliage that had overgrown the summit of the rock was all on fire, blazing high into the night and fitfully illuminating the whole field. Each pendent twig and leafy festoon was in a blaze. As the red light arose and fell, a numerous congregation alternately shone forth, then disappeared in shadow, and again grew, as it were, out of the darkness, peopling the heart of the solitary woods at once.

"A grave and dark-clad company," quoth Goodman Brown.

In truth they were such. Among them, quivering to and fro between gloom and splendor, appeared faces that would be seen next day at the council board of the province, and others which, Sabbath after Sabbath, looked devoutly heavenward, and benignantly over the crowded pews, from the holiest pulpits in the land. Some affirm that the lady of the governor was there. At least there were high dames well known to her, and wives of honored husbands, and widows, a great multitude, and ancient maidens, all of excellent repute, and fair young girls, who trembled lest their mothers should espy them. Either the sudden gleams of light flashing over the obscure field bedazzled Goodman Brown, or he recognized a score of the church members of Salem village famous for their especial sanctity. Good old Deacon Gookin had arrived, and waited at the skirts of that venerable saint, his revered pastor. But, irreverently consorting with these grave, reputable, and pious people, these elders of the church, these chaste dames and dewy virgins, there were men of dissolute lives and women of spotted fame, wretches given over to all mean and filthy vice, and suspected even of horrid crimes. It was strange to see that the good shrank not from the wicked, nor were the sinners abashed by the saints. Scattered also among their pale-faced enemies were the Indian priests, or powwows, who had often scared their native forest with more hideous incantations than any known to English witchcraft.

"But where is Faith?" thought Goodman Brown; and, as hope came into his heart, he trembled.

Another verse of the hymn arose, a slow and mournful strain, such as the pious love, but joined to words which expressed all that our nature can conceive of sin, and darkly hinted at far more. Unfathomable to mere mortals is the lore of fiends. Verse after verse was sung; and still the chorus of the desert swelled between like the deepest tone of a mighty organ; and with the final peal of that dreadful anthem there came a sound, as if the roaring wind, the rushing streams, the howling beasts, and every other voice of the unconcerted wilderness were mingling and according with the voice of guilty man in homage to the prince of all. The four blazing pines threw up a loftier flame, and obscurely discovered shapes and visages of horror on the smoke wreaths above the impious assembly. At the same moment the fire on the rock shot redly forth and formed a glowing arch above its base, where now appeared a figure. With reverence be it spoken, the figure bore no slight similitude, both in garb and manner, to some grave divine of the New England churches.

"Bring forth the converts!" cried a voice that echoed through the field and rolled into the forest.

At the word, Goodman Brown stepped forth from the shadow of the trees and approached the congregation, with whom he felt a loathful brotherhood by the sympathy of all that was wicked in his heart. He could have well-nigh sworn that the shape of his own dead father beckoned him to advance, looking downward from a smoke wreath, while a woman, with dim features of despair, threw out her hand to warn him back. Was it his mother? But he had no power to retreat one step, nor to resist, even in thought, when the minister and good old Deacon Gookin seized his arms and led him to the blazing rock. Thither came also the slender form of a veiled female, led between Goody Cloyse, that pious teacher of the catechism, and Martha Carrier, who had received the devil's promise to be queen of hell. A rampant hag was she. And there stood the proselytes beneath the canopy of fire.

"Welcome, my children," said the dark figure, "to the communion of your race. Ye have found thus young your nature and your destiny. My children, look behind you!"

They turned; and flashing forth, as it were, in a sheet of flame, the fiend worshippers were seen; the smile of welcome gleamed darkly on every visage.

"There," resumed the sable form, "are all whom ye have reverenced from youth. Ye deemed them holier than yourselves, and shrank from your own sin, contrasting it with their lives of righteousness and prayerful aspirations heavenward. Yet here are they all in my worshipping assembly. This night it shall be granted you to know their secret deeds: how hoary-bearded elders of the church have whispered wanton words to the young maids of their households; how many a woman, eager for widows' weeds, has given her husband a drink at bedtime and let him sleep his last sleep in her bosom; how beardless youths have made haste to inherit their fathers' wealth; and how fair damsels—blush not, sweet ones—have dug little graves in the garden, and bidden me, the sole guest, to an infant's funeral. By the sympathy of your human hearts for sin ye shall scent out all the places—whether in church, bed-chamber, street, field, or forest—where crime has been committed, and shall exult to behold the whole earth one stain of guilt, one mighty blood spot. Far more than this. I shall be yours to penetrate, in every bosom, the deep mystery of sin, the fountain of all wicked arts, and which inexhaustibly supplies more evil impulses than human power—than my power at its utmost—can make manifest in deeds. And now, my children, look upon each other."

They did so; and, by the blaze of the hell-kindled torches, the wretched man beheld his Faith, and the wife her husband, trembling before that unhallowed altar.

"Lo, there ye stand, my children," said the figure, in a deep and solemn tone, almost sad with its despairing awfulness, as if his once angelic nature could yet mourn for our miserable race. "Depending upon one another's hearts, ye had still hoped that virtue were not all a dream. Now are ye undeceived. Evil is the nature of mankind. Evil must be your only happiness. Welcome again, my children, to the communion of your race."

"Welcome," repeated the fiend worshippers, in one cry of despair and triumph.

And there they stood, the only pair, as it seemed, who were yet hesitating on the verge of wickedness in this dark world. A basin was hollowed, naturally, in the rock. Did it contain water, reddened by the lurid light? or was it blood? or, perchance, a liquid flame? Herein did the shape of evil dip his hand and prepare to lay the mark of baptism upon their foreheads, that they might be partakers of the mystery of sin, more conscious of the secret guilt of others, both in deed and thought, than they could now be of their own. The husband cast one look at his pale wife, and Faith at him. What polluted wretches would the next glance show them to each other, shuddering alike at what they disclosed and what they saw!

"Faith! Faith!" cried the husband, "look up to heaven, and resist the wicked one."

Whether Faith obeyed he knew not. Hardly had he spoken when he found himself amid calm night and solitude, listening to a roar of the wind which died heavily away through the forest. He staggered against the rock, and felt it chill and damp; while a hanging twig, that had been all on fire, besprinkled his cheek with the coldest dew.

The next morning young Goodman Brown came slowly into the street of Salem village, staring around him like a bewildered man. The good old minister was taking a walk along the graveyard to get an appetite for breakfast and meditate his sermon, and bestowed a blessing, as he passed, on Goodman Brown. He shrank from the venerable saint as if to avoid an anathema. Old Deacon Gookin was at domestic worship, and the holy words of his prayer were heard through the open window. "What God doth the wizard pray to?" quoth Goodman Brown. Goody Cloyse, that excellent old Christian, stood in the early sunshine at her own lattice, catechizing a little girl who had brought her a pint of morning's milk. Goodman Brown snatched away the child as from the grasp of the fiend himself. Turning the corner by the meeting-house, he spied the head of Faith, with the pink ribbons, gazing anxiously forth, and bursting into such joy at sight of him that she skipped along the street and almost kissed her husband before the whole village. But Goodman Brown looked sternly and sadly into her face, and passed on without a greeting.

Had Goodman Brown fallen asleep in the forest and only dreamed a wild dream of a witch-meeting?

Be it so if you will; but, alas! it was a dream of evil omen for young Goodman Brown. A stern, a sad, a darkly meditative, a distrustful, if not a desperate man did he become from the night of that fearful dream. On the Sabbath day, when the congregation were singing a holy psalm, he could not listen because an anthem of sin rushed loudly upon his ear and drowned all the blessed strain. When the minister spoke from the pulpit with power and fervid eloquence, and, with his hand on the open Bible, of the sacred truths of our religion, and of saint-like lives and triumphant deaths, and of future bliss or misery unutterable, then did Goodman Brown turn pale, dreading lest the roof should thunder down upon the gray blasphemer and his hearers. Often, awaking suddenly at midnight, he shrank from the bosom of Faith; and at morning or eventide, when the family knelt down at prayer, he scowled and muttered to himself, and gazed sternly at his wife, and turned away. And when he had lived long, and was borne to his grave a hoary corpse, followed by Faith, an aged woman, and children and grandchildren, a goodly procession, besides neighbors not a few, they carved no hopeful verse upon his tombstone, for his dying hour was gloom.

Questions

1. Can we tell for certain whether Goodman Brown dreamt or actually had this vision? Does it matter for Goodman Brown?
2. Does the action arise out of a clear motive? Is Goodman a rounder or flatter character than the Minister?
3. Are the other characters rounder in "The Minister's Black Veil"?
4. Does Faith impart peacefulness to Goodman Brown's mind?
5. Is Brown saved at the end of the story?
6. Is anyone free from sin according to Brown? According to Hawthorne?
7. How would you state the theme of "Young Goodman Brown"? How different is it from the theme in "The Minister's Black Veil"?

ISAAC BABEL (1894–1939)

My First Goose

Savitsky, Commander of the VI Division, rose when he saw me, and I wondered at the beauty of his giant's body. He rose, the purple of his riding breeches and the crimson of his little tilted cap and the decorations stuck on his chest cleaving the hut as a standard cleaves the sky. A smell of scent and the sickly sweet freshness of soap emanated from him. His long legs were like girls sheathed to the neck in shining riding boots.

He smiled at me, struck his riding whip on the table, and drew toward him an order that the Chief of Staff had just finished dictating. It was an order for Ivan Chesnokov to advance on Chugunov-Dobryvodka with the regiment entrusted to him, to make contact with the enemy and destroy the same.

"For which destruction," the Commander began to write, smearing the whole sheet, "I make this same Chesnokov entirely responsible, up to and including the supreme penalty, and will if necessary strike him down on the spot; which you, Chesnokov, who have been working with me at the front for some months now, cannot doubt."

The Commander signed the order with a flourish, tossed it to his orderlies and turned upon me gray eyes that danced with merriment.

I handed him a paper with my appointment to the Staff of the Division.

"Put it down in the Order of the Day," said the Commander. "Put him down for every satisfaction save the front one. Can you read and write?"

"Yes, I can read and write," I replied, envying the flower and iron of that youthfulness. "I graduated in law from St. Petersburg University."

"Oh, are you one of those grinds?"[1] he laughed. "Specs on your nose, too! What a nasty little object! They've sent you along without making any enquiries; and this is a hot place for specs. Think you'll get on with us?"

"I'll get on all right," I answered, and went off to the village with the quartermaster to find a billet for the night.

The quartermaster carried my trunk on his shoulder. Before us stretched the village street. The dying sun, round and yellow as a pumpkin, was giving up its roseate ghost to the skies.

We went up to a hut painted over with garlands. The quartermaster stopped, and said suddenly, with a guilty smile:

"Nuisance with specs. Can't do anything to stop it, either. Not a life for the brainy type here. But you go and mess up a lady, and a good lady too, and you'll have the boys patting you on the back."

He hesitated, my little trunk on his shoulder; then he came quite close to me, only to dart away again despairingly and run to the nearest yard. Cossacks[2] were sitting there, shaving one another.

"Here, you soldiers," said the quartermaster, setting my little trunk down on the ground. "Comrade Savitsky's orders are that you're to take this chap in your billets, so no nonsense about it, because the chap's been through a lot in the learning line."

The quartermaster, purple in the face, left us without looking back. I raised my hand to my cap and saluted the Cossacks. A lad with long straight flaxen hair and the handsome face of the Ryazan Cossacks[3] went over to my little trunk

---

[1] A grind is a hard-working student.
[2] The Cossacks were warlike, in marked contrast to the narrator, a Jewish lawyer.
[3] Cossacks from Ryazan, a former principality in central Russia, southeast of Moscow.

and tossed it out at the gate. Then he turned his back on me and with remarkable skill emitted a series of shameful noises.

"To your guns—number double-zero!" an older Cossack shouted at him, and burst out laughing. "Running fire!"

His guileless art exhausted, the lad made off. Then, crawling over the ground, I began to gather together the manuscript and tattered garments that had fallen out of the trunk. I gathered them up and carried them to the other end of the yard. Near the hut, on a brick stove, stood a cauldron in which pork was cooking. The steam that rose from it was like the far-off smoke of home in the village, and it mingled hunger with desperate loneliness in my head. Then I covered my little broken trunk with hay, turning it into a pillow, and lay down on the ground to read in *Pravda* Lenin's speech at the Second Congress of the Comintern.[4] The sun fell upon me from behind the toothed hillocks, the Cossacks trod on my feet, the lad made fun of me untiringly, the beloved lines came toward me along a thorny path and could not reach me. Then I put aside the paper and went out to the landlady, who was spinning on the porch.

"Landlady," I said, "I've got to eat."

The old woman raised to me the diffused whites of her purblind eyes and lowered them again.

"Comrade," she said, after a pause, "what with all this going on, I want to go and hang myself."

"Christ!" I muttered, and pushed the old woman in the chest with my fist. "You don't suppose I'm going to go into explanations with you, do you?"

And turning around I saw somebody's sword lying within reach. A severe-looking goose was waddling about the yard, inoffensively preening its feathers. I overtook it and pressed it to the ground. Its head cracked beneath my boot, cracked and emptied itself. The white neck lay stretched out in the dung, the wings twitched.

"Christ!" I said, digging into the goose with my sword. "Go and cook it for me, landlady."

Her blind eyes and glasses glistening, the old woman picked up the slaughtered bird, wrapped it in her apron, and started to bear it off toward the kitchen.

"Comrade," she said to me, after a while, "I want to go and hang myself." And she closed the door behind her.

The Cossacks in the yard were already sitting around their cauldron. They sat motionless, stiff as heathen priests at a sacrifice, and had not looked at the goose.

"The lad's all right," one of them said, winking and scooping up the cabbage soup with his spoon.

The Cossacks commenced their supper with all the elegance and restraint of

---

[4] The Comintern is an abbreviation for the Communist International, a worldwide organization of Communist parties. The Comintern was under the direction of V. I. Lenin (1870–1924), one of the founders of the Communist Revolution and virtual dictator of the Soviet Union. He called the Second Congress of Comintern (1920) to wage a world communist revolution. *Pravda* is the official Communist Party newspaper.

peasants who respect one another. And I wiped the sword with sand, went out at the gate, and came in again, depressed. Already the moon hung above the yard like a cheap earring.

"Hey, you," suddenly said Surovkov, an older Cossack. "Sit down and feed with us till your goose is done."

He produced a spare spoon from his boot and handed it to me. We supped up the cabbage soup they had made, and ate the pork.

"What's in the newspaper?" asked the flaxen-haired lad, making room for me.

"Lenin writes in the paper," I said, pulling out *Pravda*. "Lenin writes that there's a shortage of everything."

And loudly, like a triumphant man hard of hearing, I read Lenin's speech out to the Cossacks.

Evening wrapped about me the quickening moisture of its twilight sheets; evening laid a mother's hand upon my burning forehead. I read on and rejoiced, spying out exultingly the secret curve of Lenin's straight line.

"Truth tickles everyone's nostrils," said Surovkov, when I had come to the end. "The question is, how's it to be pulled from the heap. But he goes and strikes at it straight off like a hen pecking at a grain!"

This remark about Lenin was made by Surovkov, platoon commander of the Staff Squadron; after which we lay down to sleep in the hayloft. We slept, all six of us, beneath a wooden roof that let in the stars, warming one another, our legs intermingled. I dreamed, and in my dreams saw women. But my heart, stained with bloodshed, grated and brimmed over.

Questions

1. What is the narrator's attitude toward Savitksy and the Cossacks?
2. Why does the Ryazan Cossack dump out the narrator's belongings?
3. Why does the landlady want to hang herself?
4. Why does the narrator kill the goose?
5. Why do the Cossacks then offer him soup?
6. How does the narrator feel about killing the goose?
7. Why do people respect senseless violence?

DORIS LESSING (1919–)

Homage for Isaac Babel

The day I had promised to take Catherine down to visit my young friend Philip at his school in the country, we were to leave at eleven, but she arrived at nine. Her blue dress was new, and so were her fashionable shoes. Her hair had just been done. She looked more than ever like a pink-and-gold Renoir[1] girl who expects everything from life.

---

[1] Pierre-Auguste Renoir (1841–1919) was a French impressionist painter known for his lovely pictures of French family life which included many rosy-cheeked young girls.

Catherine lives in a white house overlooking the sweeping brown tides of the river. She helped me clean up my flat with a devotion which said that she felt small flats were altogether more romantic than large houses. We drank tea, and talked mainly about Philip, who, being fifteen, has pure stern tastes in everything from food to music. Catherine looked at the books lying around his room, and asked if she might borrow the stories of Isaac Babel to read on the train. Catherine is thirteen. I suggested she might find them difficult, but she said: "Philip reads them, doesn't he?"

During the journey I read newspapers and watched her pretty frowning face as she turned the pages of Babel, for she was determined to let nothing get between her and her ambition to be worthy of Philip.

At the school, which is charming, civilised, and expensive, the two children walked together across green fields, and I followed, seeing how the sun gilded their bright friendly heads turned towards each other as they talked. In Catherine's left hand she carried the stories of Isaac Babel.

After lunch we went to the pictures. Philip allowed it to be seen that he thought going to the pictures just for the fun of it was not worthy of intelligent people, but he made the concession, for our sakes. For his sake we chose the more serious of the two films that were showing in the little town. It was about a good priest who helped criminals in New York. His goodness, however, was not enough to prevent one of them from being sent to the gas chamber; and Philip and I waited with Catherine in the dark until she had stopped crying and could face the light of a golden evening.

At the entrance of the cinema the doorman was lying in wait for anyone who had red eyes. Grasping Catherine by her suffering arm, he said bitterly: "Yes, why are you crying? He had to be punished for his crime, didn't he?" Catherine stared at him, incredulous. Philip rescued her by saying with disdain: "Some people don't know right from wrong even when it's *demonstrated* to them." The doorman turned his attention to the next red-eyed emerger from the dark; and we went on together to the station, the children silent because of the cruelty of the world.

Finally Catherine said, her eyes wet again: "I think it's all absolutely beastly, and I can't bear to think about it." And Philip said: "But we've got to think about it, don't you see, because if we don't it'll just go on and *on*, don't you see?"

In the train going back to London I sat beside Catherine. She had the stories open in front of her, but she said: "Philip's awfully lucky. I wish I went to that school. Did you notice that girl who said hullo to him in the garden? They must be great friends. I wish my mother would let me have a dress like that, it's *not* fair."

"I thought it was too old for her."

"Oh, *did* you?"

Soon she bent her head again over the book, but almost at once lifted it to say: "Is he a very famous writer?"

"He's a marvellous writer, brilliant, one of the very best."

"Why?"

"Well, for one thing he's so simple. Look how few words he uses, and how strong his stories are."

"I see. Do you know him? Does he live in London?"

"Oh no, he's dead."

"Oh. Then why did you—I thought he was alive, the way you talked."

"I'm sorry, I suppose I wasn't thinking of him as dead."

"When did he die?"

"He was murdered. About twenty years ago, I suppose."

"*Twenty years.*" Her hands began the movement of pushing the book over to me, but then relaxed. "I'll be fourteen in November," she stated, sounding threatened, while her eyes challenged me.

I found it hard to express my need to apologise, but before I could speak, she said, patiently attentive again: "You said he was murdered?"

"Yes."

"I expect the person who murdered him felt sorry when he discovered he had murdered a famous writer."

"Yes, I expect so."

"Was he old when he was murdered?"

"No, quite young really."

"Well, that was bad luck, wasn't it?"

"Yes, I suppose it was bad luck."

"Which do you think is the very best story here? I mean, in your honest opinion, the very very best one."

I chose the story about killing the goose. She read it slowly, while I sat waiting, wishing to take it from her, wishing to protect this charming little person from Isaac Babel.

When she had finished, she said: "Well, some if it I don't understand. He's got a funny way of looking at things. Why should a man's legs in boots look like *girls?*" She finally pushed the book over at me, and said: "I think it's all morbid."

"But you have to understand the kind of life he had. First, he was a Jew in Russia. That was bad enough. Then his experience was all revolution and civil war and . . . "

But I could see these words bouncing off the clear glass of her fiercely denying gaze; and I said: "Look, Catherine, why don't you try again when you're older? Perhaps you'll like him better then?"

She said gratefully: "Yes, perhaps that would be best. After all, Philip is two years older than me, isn't he?"

A week later I got a letter from Catherine.

Thank you very much for being kind enough to take me to visit Philip at his school. It was the most lovely day in my whole life. I am extremely grateful to you for taking me. I have been thinking about the Hoodlum Priest. That was a film which demonstrated to me beyond any shadow of doubt that Capital Punishment is a Wicked Thing, and I shall never forget what I learned that afternoon, and the lessons of it will be with me all my life. I have been meditating about what you said about Isaac Babel, the famed Russian short story writer, and I now see that the conscious simplicity of his style is what makes him, beyond the shadow of a doubt, the great writer that he is, and now in my school compositions I am endeavouring to emulate him so as to learn a conscious simplicity which is the only basis for a really brilliant writing style. Love, Catherine. P.S. Has Philip said anything about my party? I wrote but he hasn't answered. Please find out if he is coming or if he just forgot to answer my letter. I hope he comes, because sometimes I feel I shall die if he doesn't. P.P.S. Please don't tell him I said anything, because I should die if he knew. Love, Catherine.

Questions

1. How do the characters in Lessing's story compare to the ones in Babel's?
2. Why should the narrator wish "to protect [Catherine] from Isaac Babel"?
3. At the movie theatre, how does the doorman's attitude contrast with Catherine's? Does he express any of the sentiments in "My First Goose"?
4. Is Catherine too young to read Babel?
5. How would you describe her praise of Babel in her letter to the narrator?
6. Catherine desperately wants to be a part of Philip's social world. How does her desire compare with that of Babel's narrator?

 Writers on Writing   *Margaret Atwood*

> *There are two factors involved in the production of a "great art": the artist and the audience. The artist acts as vision or tongue, giving shape to patterns in which the audience may then recognize itself, for better or worse: "identify" itself. Take away the artist and the audience can never achieve self-knowledge. If we are to believe Shelley, the artist is both representative man and leader; in his work is made visible all that is best and worst in a society. He is us.*
>
> *But take away the audience, and the artist has part of himself cut off. He is blocked, he is like a man shouting to no one. Without a sense of his audience he can have no ultimate sense of purpose, no feeling that what he produces has any significance. He may also find himself with nothing to write about except himself. He might as well be living on the Moon. He is a man talking to himself, and talking to oneself is usually considered either a result of isolation or a symptom of insanity.*

ANNE TYLER (1941–)

The Artificial Family

The first full sentence that Mary ever said to him was, "Did you know I have a daughter?" Toby was asking her to dinner. He had just met her at a party—

a long-haired girl in a floor-length gingham dress—and the invitation was instant, offered out of desperation because she was already preparing to leave and he wasn't sure he could ever find her again. Now, how did her daughter enter into this? Was she telling him that she was married? Or that she couldn't go out in the evenings? "No," said Toby. "I didn't know."

"Well, now you do," she said. Then she wrote her address down for him and left, and Toby spent the rest of the evening clutching the scrap of paper in his pocket for fear of losing it.

The daughter was five years old. Her name was Samantha, and it suited her: she was an old-fashioned child with two thick braids and a solemn face. When she and her mother stood side by side, barefoot, wearing their long dresses, they might have been about to climb onto a covered wagon. They presented a solid front. Their eyes were a flat, matching blue. "Well!" Toby would say, after he and Samantha knew each other better. "Shall we all *three* go somewhere? Shall we take a picnic lunch? Visit the zoo?" Then the blue would break up into darker colors, and they would smile—but it was the mother who smiled first. The child was the older of the two. She took longer to think things over.

They would go to the Baltimore Zoo and ride the tiny passenger train. Sitting three abreast on the narrow seat—Toby's arm around Mary, Samantha scrunched between them—they rattled past dusty-looking deer fenced in among the woods, through a tunnel where the younger children screamed, alongside a parade of wooden cartoon animals which everyone tried to identify. "That's Bullmoose! There's Bugs Bunny!" Only Samantha said nothing. She had no television set. Bugs Bunny was a stranger to her. She sat very straight, with her hands clasped between her knees in her long skirt, and Toby looked down at her and tried to piece out her father from the curve of her cheek and the tilt of her nose. Her eyes were her mother's, but surely that rounded chin came from her father's side. Had her father had red hair? Was that what gave Samantha's brown braids that coppery sheen? He didn't feel that he could ask straight out because Mary had slammed a door on the subject. All she said was that she had run away with Samantha after two years of marriage. Then once, discussing some earlier stage in Samantha's life, she pulled out a wallet photo to show him: Samantha as a baby, in her mother's lap. "Look at you!" Toby said. "You had your hair up! You had lipstick on! You were wearing a sweater and skirt! Look at Samantha in her party dress!" The photo stunned him, but Mary hardly noticed. "Oh, yes," she said, closing her wallet, "I was very straight back then." And that was the last time she mentioned her marriage. Toby never saw the husband, or heard anything about him. There seemed to be no visiting arrangements for the child.

Mornings Mary worked in an art gallery. She had to leave Samantha with a teen-aged babysitter after kindergarten closed for the summer. "Summers! I hate them," she said. "All the time I'm at work I'm wondering how Samantha is." Toby said, "Why not let *me* stay with her. You know how Samantha and I get along." He was a graduate student with a flexible schedule; and besides, he seized on every excuse to entrench himself deeper into Mary's life. But Mary said, "No, I couldn't ask you to do that." And she went on paying Carol, and paying her again in the evenings when they went out somewhere. They went to dinner, or to movies, or to Toby's rambling apartment. They always came back early. "Carol's mother will kill me!" Mary would say, and she would gather up her belongings and run ahead of Toby to his car. When he returned from taking her home his apartment always smelled of her: a clean, straw smell, like burlap. Her bobby pins littered the bed and the crevices of the sofa. Strands of her long hairs tended to get wound around the rollers of his carpet sweeper. When he went to sleep the cracked bell of her voice threaded through all his dreams.

At the end of August, they were married in a civil ceremony. They had known each other five months. *Only* five months, Toby's parents said. They wrote him a letter pointing out all their objections. How would he support three on a university grant? How would he study? What did he want with someone else's child? The child: that was what they really minded. The ready-made grandchild. How could he love some other man's daughter? But Toby had never been sure he would know how to love his *own* children; so the question didn't bother him. He liked Samantha. And he liked the idea of her: the single, solitary treasure carried away from the disaster of the sweater-and-skirt marriage. If he himself ever ran away, what would he choose to take? His grandfather's watch, his favorite chamois shirt, eight cartons of books, some still unread, his cassette tape recorder—each object losing a little more worth as the list grew longer. Mary had taken Samantha, and nothing else. He envied both of them.

They lived in his apartment, which was more than big enough. Mary quit her job. Samantha started first grade. They were happy but guarded, still, working too hard at getting along. Mary turned the spare bedroom into a study for Toby, with a "Private" sign on the door. "Never go in there," she told Samantha. "That's Toby's place to be alone." "But I don't *want* to be alone," Toby said. "I'm alone all day at the lab." Nobody seemed to believe him. Samantha passed the doorway of his study on tiptoe, never even peeking inside. Mary scrupulously avoided littering the apartment with her own possessions. Toby was so conscientious a father that he might have written himself a timetable: At seven, play Old Maid. At seven-thirty, read a story. At eight o'clock, offer a piggyback ride to bed. Mary he treated like glass. He kept thinking of her first marriage; his greatest fear was that she would leave him.

Every evening, Samantha walked around to Toby's lab to call him for supper. In the midst of reaching for a beaker or making a notation he would look up to find her standing there, absolutely silent. Fellow students gave her curious looks. She ignored them. She concentrated on Toby, watching him with a steady blue gaze that gave all his actions a new importance. Would he feel this flattered if she were his own? He didn't think so. In their peculiar situation—nearly strangers, living in the same house, sharing Mary—they had not yet started to take each other for granted. Her coming for him each day was purely a matter of choice, which he imagined her spending some time over before deciding; and so were the sudden, rare smiles which lit her face when he glanced down at her during the walk home.

At Christmastime Toby's parents flew down for a visit. They stayed four days, each one longer than the day before. Toby's mother had a whole new manner which kept everyone at arm's length. She would look at Samantha and say, "My, she's thin! Is her father thin, Mary? Does her father have those long feet?" She would go out to the kitchen and say, "I see you've done something with Toby's little two-cup coffeepot. Is this *your* pot, Mary? May I use it?" Everything she said was meant to remind them of their artificiality: the wife was someone else's first, the child was not Toby's. But her effect was to draw them closer together. The three of them formed an alliance against Mrs. Scott and her silent husband, who lent her his support merely by not shutting her up. On the second evening Toby escaped to his study and Samantha and Mary joined him, one by one, sliding through the crack in his door to sit giggling silently with him over a game of dominoes. One afternoon they said they had to take Samantha to her art lesson and they snuck off to a Walt Disney movie instead, and stayed there in the dark for two hours eating popcorn and Baby Ruths and endless strings of licorice.

Toby's parents went home, but the alliance continued. The sense of effort had disappeared. Toby's study became the center of the apartment, and every evening while he read Mary sat with him and sewed and Samantha played with cut-outs at their feet. Mary's pottery began lining the mantel and the bookshelves. She pounded in nails all over the kitchen and hung up her saucepans. Samantha's formal bedtime ritual changed to roughhousing, and she and Toby pounded through the rooms and pelted each other with sofa cushions and ended up in a tangle on the hallway carpet.

Now Samantha was growing unruly with her mother. Talking back. Disobeying. Toby was relieved to see it. Before she had been so good that she seemed pathetic. But Mary said, "I don't know what I'm going to do with that child. She's getting out of hand."

"She seems all right to *me*," said Toby.

"I knew you'd say that. It's your fault she's changed like this, too. You've spoiled her."

"*Spoiled* her?"

"You dote on her, and she knows it," Mary said. She was folding the laundry, moving crisply around the bedroom with armloads of sheets and towels. Nowadays she wore sweaters and skirts—more practical for housework—and her loafers tapped across the floor with an efficient sound that made him feel she knew what she was talking about. "You give her everything she asks for," she said. "Now she doesn't listen to *me* any more."

"But there's nothing wrong with giving her things. Is there?"

"If you had to live with her all day long," Mary said, "eighteen hours a day, the way I do, you'd think twice before you said that."

But how could he refuse anything to Samantha? With him, she was never disobedient. She shrieked with him over pointless riddles, she asked him unanswerable questions on their walks home from the lab, she punched at him ineffectually, her thumbs tucked inside her fists, when he called her Sam. The only time he was ever angry with her was once when she stepped into the path of a car without looking. "Samantha!" he yelled, and he yanked her back and shook her until she cried. Inside he had felt his stomach lurch, his heart sent out a wave of heat and his knees shook. The purple marks of his fingers stayed on Samantha's arm for days afterward. Would he have been any more terrified if the child were his own? New opportunities for fear were everywhere, now that he was a family man. Samantha's walk from school seemed long and under-policed, and every time he called home without an answer he imagined that Mary had run away from him and he would have to get through life without her. "I think we should have another baby," he told Mary, although of course he knew that increasing the number of people he loved would not make any one of them more expendable. All Mary said was, "Do you?"

"I love that little girl. I really love her. I'd like to have a whole *armload* of little girls. Did you ever think I would be so good at loving people?"

"Yes," said Mary.

"I didn't. Not until I met you. I'd like to *give* you things. I'd like to sit you and Samantha down and pile things in your laps. Don't you ever feel that way?"

"Women don't," said Mary. She slid out of his hands and went to the sink, where she ran cold water over some potatoes. Lately she had started wearing her hair pinned up, out of the way. She looked carved, without a stray wisp or an extra line, smooth to the fingertips, but when Toby came up behind her again she ducked away and went to the stove. "Men are the only ones who have that much feeling left to spare," she said. "Women's love gets frittered away: every day a thousand little demands for milk and bandaids and swept floors and clean towels."

"I don't believe that," said Toby.

But Mary was busy regulating the flame under the potatoes now, and she didn't argue with him.

For Easter, Toby bought Samantha a giant prepacked Easter basket swaddled in pink cellophane. It was a spur-of-the-moment purchase—he had gone to the all-night drugstore for pipe tobacco, seen this basket and remembered suddenly that tomorrow was Easter Sunday. Wouldn't Samantha be expecting some sort of celebration? He hated to think of her returning to school empty-handed, when everyone else had chocolate eggs or stuffed rabbits. But when he brought the basket home—rang the doorbell and waited, obscured behind the masses of cellophane like some comical florist's-messenger—he saw that he had made a mistake. Mary didn't like the basket. "How come you bought a thing like that?" she asked him.

"Tomorrow's Easter."

"Easter? Why Easter? We don't even go to church."

"We celebrated Christmas, didn't we?"

"Yes, but—and Easter's not the question," Mary said. "It's this basket." She reached out and touched the cellophane, which shrank beneath her fingers. "We never *used* to buy baskets. Before I've always hidden eggs and let her hunt for them in the morning, and then she dyes them herself."

"Oh, I thought people had jellybeans and things," Toby said.

"*Other* people, maybe. Samantha and I do it differently."

"Wouldn't she like to have what her classmates have?"

"She isn't trying to keep up with the *Joneses,* Toby," Mary said. "And how about her teeth? How about her stomach? Do I always have to be the heavy, bringing these things up? Why is it you get to shower her with love and gifts, and then it's me that takes her to the dentist?"

"Oh, let's not go into *that* again," Toby said.

Then Mary, who could never be predicted, said, "All right," and stopped the argument. "It was nice of you to think of it, anyway," she said formally, taking the basket. "I know Samantha will like it."

Samantha did like it. She treasured every jellybean and marshmallow egg and plastic chick; she telephoned a friend at seven in the morning to tell her about it. But even when she threw her arms around Toby's neck, smelling of sugar and cellophane, all he felt was a sense of defeat. Mary's face was serene and beautiful, like a mask. She continued to move farther and farther away from him, with her lips perpetually curved in a smile and no explanations at all.

In June, when school closed, Mary left him for good. He came home one day to find a square of paper laid flat on a club sandwich. The sight of it thudded instantly against his chest, as if he had been expecting it all along. "I've gone," the note said. His name was nowhere on it. It might have been the same note she sent her first husband—retrieved, somehow, and saved in case she found another use for it. Toby sat down and read it again, analyzed each loop of handwriting for any sign of indecision or momentary, reversible anger. Then he ate the club sandwich, every last crumb, without realizing he was doing so, and after that he pushed his plate away and lowered his head into his hands. He sat that way for several minutes before he thought of Samantha.

It was Monday evening—the time when she would just be finishing with her art lesson. He ran all the way, jaywalking and dodging cars and waving blindly at the drivers who honked. When he arrived in the dingy building where the lessons were given he found he was too early. The teacher still murmured behind a closed door. Toby sat down, panting, on a bench beneath a row of coat hooks. Flashes of old TV programs passed through his head. He saw himself blurred and bluish on a round-cornered screen—one of those mysteriously partnerless television parents who rear their children with more grace and tact and unselfishness than any married couple could ever hope for. Then the classroom door opened. The teacher came out in her smock, ringed by six-year-olds. Toby stood up and said, "Mrs.—um. Is Samantha Glover here?"

The teacher turned. He knew what she was going to say as soon as she took a breath; he hated her so much he wanted to grab her by the neck and slam her head against the wall. "Samantha?" she said. "Why, no, Mr. Scott, Samantha didn't come today."

On the walk back, he kept his face stiff and his eyes unfocused. People stared at him. Women turned to look after him, frowning, curious to see the extent of the damage. He barely noticed them. He floundered up the stairs to his apartment, felt his way to the sofa and sat down heavily. There was no need to turn the lights on. He knew already what he would find: toys and saucepans, Mary's skirts and sweaters, Samantha's new short dresses. All they would have taken with them, he knew, was their long gingham gowns and each other.

Questions

1. How is Mary dressed in the snapshot of her first marriage? Does her dress change during her second marriage? If so, how does it compare to the snapshot?
2. What significance do the gingham dresses have for Samantha and Mary?
3. Why does Mary complain about Toby's purchase of the Easter basket?
4. Does Toby's sense of parental responsibility differ from Mary's?
5. Why does Mary leave Toby? Is her decision a sound one?
6. Is there anything that Toby could have done to preserve the marriage?
7. Are there any similarities between "The Artificial Family" and "Shiloh"?

JOHN UPDIKE (1932–)

Separating

The day was fair. Brilliant. All that June the weather had mocked the Maples' internal misery with solid sunlight—golden shafts and cascades of green in which their conversations had wormed unseeing, their sad murmuring selves the only stain in Nature. Usually by this time of the year they had acquired tans; but when they met their elder daughter's plane on her return from a year in England they were almost as pale as she, though Judith was too dazzled by the sunny opulent jumble of her native land to notice. They did not spoil her homecoming by telling her immediately. Wait a few days, let her recover from jet lag, had been one of their formulations, in that string of gray dialogues—over coffee, over cocktails, over Cointreau[1]—that had shaped the strategy of their dissolution, while the earth performed its annual stunt of renewal unnoticed beyond their closed windows. Richard had thought to leave at Easter; Joan had insisted they wait until the four children were at last assembled, with all exams passed and ceremonies attended, and the bauble of summer to console them. So he had drudged away, in love, in dread, repairing screens, getting the mowers sharpened, rolling and patching their new tennis court.

The court, clay, had come through its first winter pitted and windswept bare of redcoat. Years ago, the Maples had observed how often, among their friends, divorce followed a dramatic home improvement, as if the marriage were making one last twitchy effort to live; their own worst crisis had come amid the plaster dust and exposed plumbing of a kitchen renovation. Yet, a summer ago, as canary-yellow bulldozers gaily churned a grassy, daisy-dotted knoll into a muddy plateau, and a crew of pigtailed young men raked and tamped clay into a plane, this transformation did not strike them as ominous, but festive in its impudence; their marriage could rend the earth for fun. The next spring, waking each day at dawn to a sliding sensation as if the bed were being tipped, Richard found the barren tennis court, its net and tapes still rolled in the barn, an environment congruous with his mood of purposeful desolation, and the crumbling of handfuls of clay into cracks and holes (dogs had frolicked on the court in a thaw; rivulets

---

[1] Cointreau is an orange-flavored liqueur.

had evolved trenches) an activity suitably elemental and interminable. In his sealed heart he hoped the day would never come.

Now it was here. A Friday. Judith was reacclimated; all four children were assembled, before jobs and camps and visits again scattered them. Joan thought they should be told one by one. Richard was for making an announcement at the table. She said, "I think just making an announcement is a cop-out. They'll start quarrelling and playing to each other instead of focussing. They're each individuals, you know, not just some corporate obstacle to your freedom."

"O.K., O.K. I agree." Joan's plan was exact. That evening, they were giving Judith a belated welcome-home dinner, of lobster and champagne. Then, the party over, they, the two of them, who nineteen years before would push her in a baby carriage along Tenth Street to Washington Square,[2] were to walk her out of the house, to the bridge across the salt creek, and tell her, swearing her to secrecy. Then Richard Jr., who was going directly from work to a rock concert in Boston, would be told, either late when he returned on the train or early Saturday morning before he went off to his job; he was seventeen and employed as one of a golf-course maintenance crew. Then the two younger children, John and Margaret, could, as the morning wore on, be informed.

"Mopped up, as it were," Richard said.

"Do you have any better plan? That leaves you the rest of Saturday to answer any questions, pack, and make your wonderful departure."

"No," he said, meaning he had no better plan, and agreed to hers, though it had an edge of false order, a plea for control in the semblance of its achievement, like Joan's long chore lists and financial accountings and, in the days when he first knew her, her too copious lecture notes. Her plan turned one hurdle for him into four—four knife-sharp walls, each with a sheer blind drop on the other side.

All spring he had been morbidly conscious of insides and outsides, of barriers and partitions. He and Joan stood as a thin barrier between the children and the truth. Each moment was a partition, with the past on one side and the future on the other, a future containing this unthinkable *now*. Beyond four knifelike walls a new life for him waited vaguely. His skull cupped a secret, a white face, a face both frightened and soothing, both strange and known, that he wanted to shield from tears, which he felt all about him, solid as the sunlight. So haunted, he had become obsessed with battening down the house against his absence, replacing screens and sash cords, hinges and latches—a Houdini making things snug before his escape.[3]

The lock. He had still to replace a lock on one of the doors of the screened porch. The task, like most such, proved more difficult than he had imagined. The old lock, aluminum frozen by corrosion, had been deliberately rendered

<hr>

[2] The Maples' walk along Tenth Street to Washington Square took them through the northern part of the Greenwich Village area of New York City.

[3] Harry Houdini (1874–1926) was the American escape artist and magician. Several of his famous escapes have yet to be understood.

obsolete by manufacturers. Three hardware stores had nothing that even approximately matched the mortised hole its removal (surprisingly easy) left. Another hole had to be gouged, with bits too small and saws too big, and the old hole fitted with a block of wood—the chisels dull, the saw rusty, his fingers thick with lack of sleep. The sun poured down, beyond the porch, on a world of neglect. The bushes already needed pruning, the windward side of the house was shedding flakes of paint, rain would get in when he was gone, insects, rot, death. His family, all those he would lose, filtered through the edges of his awareness as he struggled with screw holes, splinters, opaque instructions, minutiae of metal.

Judith sat on the porch, a princess returned from exile. She regaled them with stories of fuel shortages, of bomb scares in the Underground,[4] of Pakistani workmen loudly lusting after her as she walked past on her way to dance school. Joan came and went, in and out of the house, calmer than she should have been, praising his struggles with the lock as if this were one more and not the last of their chain of shared chores. The younger of his sons, John, now at fifteen suddenly, unwittingly handsome, for a few minutes held the rickety screen door while his father clumsily hammered and chiselled, each blow a kind of sob in Richard's ears. His younger daughter, having been at a slumber party, slept on the porch hammock through all the noise—heavy and pink, trusting and forsaken. Time, like the sunlight, continued relentlessly; the sunlight slowly slanted. Today was one of the longest days. The lock clicked, worked. He was through. He had a drink; he drank it on the porch, listening to his daughter. "It was so sweet," she was saying, "during the worst of it, how all the butcher's and bakery shops kept open by candlelight. They're all so plucky and cute. From the papers, things sounded so much worse here—people shooting people in gas lines, and everybody freezing."

Richard asked her, "Do you still want to live in England forever?" *Forever:* the concept, now a reality upon him, pressed and scratched at the back of his throat.

"No," Judith confessed, turning her oval face to him, its eyes still childishly far apart, but the lips set as over something succulent and satisfactory. "I was anxious to come home. I'm an American." She was a woman. They had raised her; he and Joan had endured together to raise her, alone of the four. The others had still some raising left in them. Yet it was the thought of telling Judith—the image of her, their first baby, walking between them arm in arm to the bridge— that broke him. The partition between himself and the tears broke. Richard sat down to the celebratory meal with the back of his throat aching; the champagne, the lobster seemed phases of sunshine; he saw them and tasted them through tears. He blinked, swallowed, croakily joked about hay fever. The tears would not stop leaking through; they came not through a hole that could be plugged but through a permeable spot in a membrane, steadily, purely, endlessly, fruitfully. They became, his tears, a shield for himself against these others—their

---

[4] The Underground is the name for the London subway system.

faces, the fact of their assembly, a last time as innocents, at a table where he sat the last time as head. Tears dropped from his nose as he broke the lobster's back; salt flavored his champagne as he sipped it; the raw clench at the back of his throat was delicious. He could not help himself.

His children tried to ignore his tears. Judith, on his right, lit a cigarette, gazed upward in the direction of her too energetic, too sophisticated exhalation; on her other side, John earnestly bent his face to the extraction of the last morsels— legs, tail segments—from the scarlet corpse. Joan, at the opposite end of the table, glanced at him surprised, her reproach displaced by a quick grimace, of forgiveness, or of salute to his superior gift of strategy. Between them, Margaret, no longer called Bean, thirteen and large for her age, gazed from the other side of his pane of tears as if into a shopwindow at something she coveted—at her father, a crystalline heap of splinters and memories. It was not she, however, but John who, in the kitchen, as they cleared the plates and carapaces away, asked Joan the question: "Why is Daddy crying?"

Richard heard the question but not the murmured answer. Then he heard Bean cry, "Oh, no-oh!"—the faintly dramatized exclamation of one who had long expected it.

John returned to the table carrying a bowl of salad. He nodded tersely at his father and his lips shaped the conspiratorial words "She told."

"Told what?" Richard asked aloud, insanely.

The boy sat down as if to rebuke his father's distraction with the example of his own good manners and said quietly, "The separation."

Joan and Margaret returned; the child, in Richard's twisted vision, seemed diminished in size, and relieved, relieved to have the boogeyman at last proved real. He called out to her—the distances at the table had grown immense— "You knew, you always knew," but the clenching at the back of his throat prevented him from making sense of it. From afar he heard Joan talking, levelly, sensibly, reciting what they had prepared: it was a separation for the summer, an experiment. She and Daddy both agreed it would be good for them; they needed space and time to think; they liked each other but did not make each other happy enough, somehow.

Judith, imitating her mother's factual tone, but in her youth off-key, too cool, said, "I think it's silly. You should either live together or get divorced."

Richard's crying, like a wave that has crested and crashed, had become tumultuous; but it was overtopped by another tumult, for John, who had been so reserved, now grew larger and larger at the table. Perhaps his younger sister's being credited with knowing set him off. "Why didn't you *tell* us?" he asked, in a large round voice quite unlike his own. "You should have *told* us you weren't getting along."

Richard was startled into attempting to force words through his tears. "We *do* get along, that's the trouble, so it doesn't show even to us—" "That we do not love each other" was the rest of the sentence; he couldn't finish it.

Joan finished for him, in her style. "And we've always, *especially*, loved our children."

John was not mollified. "What do you care about *us?*" he boomed. "We're just little things you *had.*" His sisters' laughing forced a laugh from him, which he turned hard and parodistic: "Ha ha *ha.*" Richard and Joan realized simultaneously that the child was drunk, on Judith's homecoming champagne. Feeling bound to keep the center of the stage, John took a cigarette from Judith's pack, poked it into his mouth, let it hang from his lower lip, and squinted like a gangster.

"You're not little things we had," Richard called to him. "You're the whole point. But you're grown. Or almost."

The boy was lighting matches. Instead of holding them to his cigarette (for they had never seen him smoke; being "good" had been his way of setting himself apart), he held them to his mother's face, closer and closer, for her to blow out. Then he lit the whole folder—a hiss and then a torch, held against his mother's face. Prismed by his tears, the flame filled Richard's vision; he didn't know how it was extinguished. He heard Margaret say, "Oh stop showing off," and saw John, in response, break the cigarette in two and put the halves entirely into his mouth and chew, sticking out his tongue to display the shreds to his sister.

Joan talked to him, reasoning—a fountain of reason, unintelligible. "Talked about it for years . . . our children must help us . . . Daddy and I both want . . . ." As the boy listened, he carefully wadded a paper napkin into the leaves of his salad, fashioned a ball of paper and lettuce, and popped it into his mouth, looking around the table for the expected laughter. None came. Judith said, "Be mature," and dismissed a plume of smoke.

Richard got up from this stifling table and led the boy outside. Though the house was in twilight, the outdoors still brimmed with light, the long waste light of high summer. Both laughing, he supervised John's spitting out the lettuce and paper and tobacco into the pachysandra. He took him by the hand—a square gritty hand, but for its softness a man's. Yet, it held on. They ran together up into the field, past the tennis court. The raw banking left by the bulldozers was dotted with daisies. Past the court and a flat stretch where they used to play family baseball stood a soft green rise glorious in the sun, each weed and species of grass distinct as illumination on parchment. "I'm sorry, so sorry," Richard cried. "You were the only one who ever tried to help me with all the goddam jobs around this place."

Sobbing, safe within his tears and the champagne, John explained, "It's not just the separation, it's the whole crummy year, I *hate* that school, you can't make any friends, the history teacher's a scud."

They sat on the crest of the rise, shaking and warm from their tears but easier in their voices, and Richard tried to focus on the child's sad year—the weekdays long with homework, the weekends spent in his room with model airplanes, while his parents murmured down below, nursing their separation. How selfish, how blind, Richard thought; his eyes felt scoured. He told his son, "We'll think about getting you transferred. Life's too short to be miserable."

They had said what they could, but did not want the moment to heal, and talked on, about the school, about the tennis court, whether it would ever again be as good as it had been that first summer. They walked to inspect it and pressed a few more tapes more firmly down. A little stiltedly, perhaps trying to make too much of the moment, to prolong it. Richard led the boy to the spot in the field where the view was best, of the metallic blue river, the emerald marsh, the scattered islands velvet with shadow in the low light, the white bits of beach far away. "See," he said. "It goes on being beautiful. It'll be here tomorrow."

"I know," John answered, impatiently. The moment had closed.

Back in the house, the others had opened some white wine, the champagne being drunk, and still sat at the table, the three females, gossiping. Where Joan sat had become the head. She turned, showing him a tearless face, and asked, "All right?"

"We're fine," he said, resenting it, though relieved, that the party went on without him.

In bed she explained, "I couldn't cry I guess because I cried so much all spring. It really wasn't fair. It's your idea, and you make it look as though I was kicking you out."

"I'm sorry," he said. "I couldn't stop. I wanted to but couldn't."

"You *didn't* want to. You loved it. You were having your way, making a general announcement."

"I love having it over," he admitted. "God, those kids were great. So brave and funny." John, returned to the house, had settled to a model airplane in his room, and kept shouting down to them, "I'm O.K. No sweat." "And the way," Richard went on, cozy in his relief, "they never questioned the reasons we gave. No thought of a third person. Not even Judith."

"That *was* touching," Joan said.

He gave her a hug. "You were great too. Thank you." Guiltily, he realized he did not feel separated.

"You still have Dickie to do," she told him. These words set before him a black mountain in the darkness; its cold breath, its near weight affected his chest. Of the four children Dickie was most nearly his conscience. Joan did not need to add, "That's one piece of your dirty work I won't do for you."

"I know. I'll do it. You go to sleep."

Within minutes, her breathing slowed, became oblivious and deep. It was quarter to midnight. Dickie's train from the concert would come in at one-fourteen. Richard set the alarm for one. He had slept atrociously for weeks. But whenever he closed his lids some glimpse of the last hours scorched him— Judith exhaling toward the ceiling in a kind of aversion, Bean's mute staring, the sunstruck growth of the field where he and John had rested. The mountain before him moved closer, moved within him; he was huge, momentous. The ache at the back of his throat felt stale. His wife slept as if slain beside him. When, exasperated by his hot lids, his crowded heart, he rose from bed and dressed, she awoke enough to turn over. He told her then, "If I could undo it all, I would."

"Where would you begin?" she asked. There was no place. Giving him courage, she was always giving him courage. He put on shoes without socks in the dark. The children were breathing in their rooms, the downstairs was hollow. In their confusion they had left lights burning. He turned off all but one, the kitchen overhead. The car started. He had hoped it wouldn't. He met only moonlight on the road; it seemed a diaphanous companion, flickering in the leaves along the roadside, haunting his rearview mirror like a pursuer, melting under his headlights. The center of town, not quite deserted, was eerie at this hour. A young cop in uniform kept company with a gang of T-shirted kids on the steps of the bank. Across from the railroad station, several bars kept open. Customers, mostly young, passed in and out of the warm night, savoring summer's novelty. Voices shouted from cars as they passed; an immense conversation seemed in progress. Richard parked and in his weariness put his head on the passenger seat, out of the commotion and wheeling lights. It was as when, in the movies, an assassin grimly carries his mission through the jostle of a carnival—except the movies cannot show the precipitous, palpable slope you cling to within. You cannot climb back down; you can only fall. The synthetic fabric of the car seat, warmed by his cheek, confided to him an ancient, distant scene of vanilla.

A train whistle caused him to lift his head. It was on time; he had hoped it would be late. The slender drawgates descended. The bell of approach tingled happily. The great metal body, horizontally fluted, rocked to a stop, and sleepy teen-agers disembarked, his son among them. Dickie did not show surprise that his father was meeting him at this terrible hour. He sauntered to the car with two friends, both taller than he. He said "Hi" to his father and took the passenger's seat with an exhausted promptness that expressed gratitude. The friends got into the back, and Richard was grateful; a few more minutes' postponement would be won by driving them home.

He asked, "How was the concert?"

"Groovy," one boy said from the back seat.

"It bit," the other said.

"It was O.K.," Dickie said, moderate by nature, so reasonable that in his childhood the unreason of the world had given him headaches, stomach aches, nausea. When the second friend had been dropped off at his dark house, the boy blurted, "Dad, my eyes are killing me with hay fever! I'm out there cutting that mothering grass all day!"

"Do we still have those drops?"

"They didn't do any good last summer."

"They might this." Richard swung a U-turn on the empty street. The drive home took a few minutes. The mountain was here, in his throat. "Richard," he said, and felt the boy, slumped and rubbing his eyes, go tense at his tone, "I didn't come to meet you just to make your life easier. I came because your mother and I have some news for you, and you're a hard man to get ahold of these days. It's sad news."

"That's O.K." The reassurance came out soft, but quick, as if released from the tip of a spring.

Richard had feared that his tears would return and choke him, but the boy's manliness set an example, and his voice issued forth steady and dry. "It's sad news, but it needn't be tragic news, at least for you. It should have no practical effect on your life, though it's bound to have an emotional effect. You'll work at your job, and go back to school in September. Your mother and I are really proud of what you're making of your life; we don't want that to change at all."

"Yeah," the boy said lightly, on the intake of his breath, holding himself up. They turned the corner; the church they went to loomed like a gutted fort. The home of the woman Richard hoped to marry stood across the green. Her bedroom light burned.

"Your mother and I," he said, "have decided to separate. For the summer. Nothing legal, no divorce yet. We want to see how it feels. For some years now, we haven't been doing enough for each other, making each other as happy as we should be. Have you sensed that?"

"No," the boy said. It was an honest, unemotional answer: true or false in a quiz.

Glad for the factual basis, Richard pursued, even garrulously, the details. His apartment across town, his utter accessibility, the split vacation arrangements, the advantages to the children, the added mobility and variety of the summer. Dickie listened, absorbing. "Do the others know?"

Richard described how they had been told.

"How did they take it?"

"The girls pretty calmly. John flipped out; he shouted and ate a cigarette and made a salad out of his napkin and told us how much he hated school."

His brother chuckled. "He did?"

"Yeah. The school issue was more upsetting for him than Mom and me. He seemed to feel better for having exploded."

"He did?" The repetition was the first sign that he was stunned.

"Yes. Dickie, I want to tell you something. This last hour, waiting for your train to get in, has been about the worst in my life. I hate this. *Hate* it. My father would have died before doing it to me." He felt immensely lighter, saying this. He had dumped the mountain on the boy. They were home. Moving swiftly as a shadow, Dickie was out of the car, through the bright kitchen. Richard called after him, "Want a glass of milk or anything?"

"No thanks."

"Want us to call the course tomorrow and say you're too sick to work?"

"No, that's all right." The answer was faint, delivered at the door to his room; Richard listened for the slam of a tantrum. The door closed normally. The sound was sickening.

Joan had sunk into that first deep trough of sleep and was slow to awake. Richard had to repeat, "I told him."

"What did he say?"

"Nothing much. Could you go say good night to him? Please."

She left their room, without putting on a bathrobe. He sluggishly changed back into his pajamas and walked down the hall. Dickie was already in bed,

Joan was sitting beside him, and the boy's bedside clock radio was murmuring music. When she stood, an inexplicable light—the moon?—outlined her body through the nightie. Richard sat on the warm place she had indented on the child's narrow mattress. He asked him, "Do you want the radio on like that?"

"It always is."

"Doesn't it keep you awake? It would me."

"No."

"Are you sleepy?"

"Yeah."

"Good. Sure you want to get up and go to work? You've had a big night."

"I want to."

Away at school this winter he had learned for the first time that you can go short of sleep and live. As an infant he had slept with an immobile sweating intensity that had alarmed his babysitters. As the children aged, he became the first to go to bed, earlier for a time than his younger brother and sister. Even now, he would go slack in the middle of a television show, his sprawled legs hairy and brown. "O.K. Good boy. Dickie, listen. I love you so much, I never knew how much until now. No matter how this works out, I'll always be with you. Really."

Richard bent to kiss an averted face but his son, sinewy, turned and with wet cheeks embraced him and gave him a kiss, on the lips, passionate as a woman's. In his father's ear he moaned one word, the crucial, intelligent word: "Why?"

Why. It was a whistle of wind in a crack, a knife thrust, a window thrown open on emptiness. The white face was gone, the darkness was featureless. Richard had forgotten why.

Questions

1. What does the narrator mean when he calls Richard and Joan Maple "the only stain in Nature"?
2. How did Richard wish to tell the children the news of the separation? How did Joan? Whose plan was finally chosen? Whose plan was executed? Why?
3. Is there any difference between Joan's sense of responsibility to the family and Richard's? How is it manifested?
4. Why do you suppose Richard speaks privately to John and later to Dick and that Joan stays with the daughters in the house?
5. What does Richard mean when he tells Dick, "My father would have died before doing it to me"? What does this statement indicate about Richard? What does it indicate about changing social values?
6. Why is Richard leaving Joan?
7. Compare Richard's behavior with Mary's behavior in "The Artificial Family." Who seems to act more wisely? Who acts more typically? Do you feel sympathy for either Richard or Mary? Why?

10 🌿 The Novella

Today we speak of three major types of narrative fiction: the short story, the novella (or short novel), and the novel. But this was not always the case. In the long history of literature, these narrative types are very recent. In neither Homer's, Dante's, nor Shakespeare's time, did the novel as we know it exist. Instead there were two major forms of long, prose narrative fiction; the *romance,* which strung together a number of fantastic and supernatural episodes; and the *novella,* which—as in Boccaccio's *Decameron*—organized a number of anecdotes through a frame device. In sum, long prose works were made up of smaller works pieced together, and lacked the unity and coherence we associate with the modern novel.

The process by which these early forms evolved into the short story, novella, and novel took a long time, and is not entirely understood. But we can imagine its basic steps. Pretend that you wanted to write a long work of fiction because you had enjoyed and admired other long works of fiction and because you thought you could make some money from it. (Daniel Defoe and Aphra Behn, two early innovators of the novel, both tried to live off their writing.) How would you go about it? First you would see how others had gone about telling stories. You might copy the features you liked (or thought might make the work popular and profitable), ignoring those elements you thought less useful or pleasing. Then you might add some ideas of your own. The work would be a combination of the tried and the new, something like what had come before but a little different. You can see how a form would slowly evolve if such a process were repeated over several centuries.

Because the novel arose from a practical, trial-and-error process, there are no simple laws to define its shape or nature. Unlike some poetic forms, the novel, the modern novella, and the short story emerged without theory, rules, or clear procedures. Consequently, these forms are various, elusive, and hard to define.

349

In this chapter we will try to give you some rules of thumb by which you can distinguish among the various forms. But remember that there are numerous exceptions to these guidelines.

Length

One of the easiest ways of distinguishing these forms is by length. A short story, by definition, is relatively short. A novel is long, and a novella lies somewhere in between. Such distinctions are, of course, vague. How short is short? One page? Ten? A hundred?

Edgar Allan Poe, one of the earliest theorists of the short story, believed the short story should be read in one sitting. For a story to have its true and greatest impact, he felt that it should not be interrupted. Thus, for Poe, a short story was determined by the reader's span of attention. The outer limit was twenty pages.

There was another determining factor in the length of the short story—the newspapers and magazines in which it appeared. Until the second world war, short fiction was a common, indeed necessary part of magazines. In some journals the reading time appeared on the opening page to inform the busy reader how extensive an effort the story demanded. Because of the physical requirements of magazines, the short story took on a length of 6,000 to 8,000 words.

Similar practicalities determined the length of a novel. Hardbound books have always been expensive. Publishers realized that the public did not feel it had received its money's worth if a novel were short. A single volume novel should run at least three hundred pages or else it would look too skimpy to the money-conscious reader. Books, then as now, were often judged by their covers, or at least by the thickness of their binding.

The term *novella*, thus, came to describe a work between the two extremes of the ten-page short story and the three-hundred page novel. But there are other differences among these three types of fiction.

Expansion and Compression

Writers are torn between two basic and contrary impulses—either to expand their works, fully developing their fictive worlds, or to compress their stories into the shortest, most potent, most highly concentrated form. Classical rhetoric distinguished these impulses as *brevitas* or brevity and *amplificatio* or amplification. By following one or the other of these impulses, writers discover the form they wish to use.

The short story, clearly, is the most compressed of the forms. The short story writer wishes to cultivate *brevitas*. The short story usually limits the author to a few characters, a single setting, and a limited period of narrative time. The details of a short story are chosen for their imaginative resonance, for their suggestiveness. Short stories work *microcosmically*, that is, they present a world in miniature that has significance for a larger world or macrocosm. Thus the Salem of Hawthorne's "Young Goodman Brown" becomes a microcosm of Puritan society. The short story writer works in miniature, expecting the reader to see wider and deeper implications.

The novelist, in contrast, tries to develop and expand the material in his or her fiction. The novelist cultivates *amplificatio*. Instead of being limited to a few characters, a single setting, and a limited period of narrative time, the novel can trace families through several generations, continents, and cataclysmic events. George Eliot's *Middlemarch* is a panoramic study of an English town in the 1830s; Tolstoy's *War and Peace* tracks Napoleon's campaign through Russia. Of course, not all novels are so ambitious; nevertheless, the novelist has the option to develop any theme of the story as fully as possible.

The modern novella balances the tight restrictions of the short story and the limitless terrain of the novel. In the novella one typically finds more characters, more episodes, and a longer narrative time span than in the short story. Yet the total work is compact in comparison with the novel. In the typical novella one fictional element is fully developed. In Thomas Mann's "Death in Venice," the fully developed element is its psychological symbolism. In Joseph Conrad's "Heart of Darkness," the symbolic setting is fully developed. In "Bartleby the Scrivener," the story fully develops the psychological relationship between the narrator and Bartleby.

Structure

To achieve the degree of concentration necessary to keep a story short, the writers of short stories usually focus on one important event. For example, "The Horse Dealer's Daughter" is concerned with answering a single question: What's to become of Mabel? The entire action of the story takes place on the day the Pervins are vacating their home. "My Man Bovanne" concentrates on a neighborhood meeting. "The Jilting of Granny Weatherall" does narrate events that occurred throughout Granny's life, but it is important to note that the events are viewed from the perspective of her final illness and from the vantage point of her disoriented recollection. Because short story writers usually concentrate on one significant event, readers should ask themselves why the authors have chosen that particular event. For example, one should understand the significance of Mabel Pervin's departure from Oldmeadow or the importance of the neighborhood meeting in "My Man Bovanne."

The novel is far more complex. In most novels there is not just one significant event, but several. Moreover, many novels have several plots, narrated alternately. We usually refer to a *main plot* and *subplots* to distinguish between the central narrative and subordinate narratives. Short stories do not contain subplots.

The novella combines structural elements of both the novel and the short story. Although the novella usually has no subplots, it develops its narrative through a number of events. In "Bartleby the Scrivener," Melville concentrates on the end of Bartleby's life. What comes before is entirely mysterious.

Summary

A short story is distinguished by its concentration. It concentrates on a single event, a small number of characters, a single setting and short narrative time span.

A novel is distinguished by its expansiveness and inclusiveness. It contains numerous characters, events, and settings, and extends over a long narrative time span. Typically the novel includes subplots that further enlarge and complicate the structure.

The novella stands midway between the two. It fully develops one aspect of a narrative. While it generally contains no subplots, it does contain a number of different events, often emphasizing one sequence over the others. Though the novella expands one fictional element, it usually compresses the others as does the short story.

Henry James, one of America's greatest fiction writers, complained about "the general indifference" in distinguishing between these forms and the failure to appreciate the novella's special importance. James wrote:

> In that dull view [which did not distinguish the short story from the novella] a "short story" was a "short story," and that was the end of it. Shades and differences, varieties and styles, the value above all of the idea happily *developed*, [in the novella] languished, to extinction, under the hard-and-fast rule of the "from six to eight thousand words" . . . For myself, I delight in the shapely [novella].[1]

Suggestions for Essayists

1. Show how one entity is the microcosm of a larger entity. For example, show how your family is a microcosm of American society, how your growth is a microcosm of social maturity, or how your garden exhibits in microcosm ecological features of the entire planet.
2. Defend or attack the Shakespearean statement that "brevity is the soul of wit."
3. Discuss how economic and physical limitations affect films, television programs, or plays.

Suggestions for Fiction Writers

1. Take an anecdote and tell it in the shortest form you can. Then expand the anecdote as far as you can. (You might examine the two versions of the story in Grace Paley's "A Conversation with My Father.")
2. Write a story about how you go about writing a story. From what do you draw your inspiration?

---

[1] Henry James, *The Art of the Novel* (New York: Scribner's, 1934), p. 220.

> *Those whom books will hurt will not be proof against events. If some*
> *books are deemed more baneful and their sale forbid, how, then, with deadlier*
> *facts, not dreams of doting men? Events, not books, should be forbid.*

HERMAN MELVILLE (1819–1891)

Bartleby the Scrivener

I am a rather elderly man. The nature of my avocations, for the last thirty years, has brought me into more than ordinary contact with what would seem an interesting and somewhat singular set of men, of whom, as yet, nothing, that I know of, has ever been written—I mean, the law-copyists, or scriveners. I have known very many of them, professionally and privately, and, if I pleased, could relate divers histories, at which good-natured gentlemen might smile, and sentimental souls might weep. But I waive the biographies of all other scriveners, for a few passages in the life of Bartleby, who was a scrivener, the strangest I ever saw, or heard of. While, of other law-copyists, I might write the complete life, of Bartleby nothing of that sort can be done. I believe that no materials exist, for a full and satisfactory biography of this man. It is an irreparable loss to literature. Bartleby was one of those beings of whom nothing is ascertainable, except from the original sources, and, in his case, those are very small. What my own astonished eyes saw of Bartleby, *that* is all I know of him, except, indeed, one vague report, which will appear in the sequel.

Ere introducing the scrivener, as he first appeared to me, it is fit I make some mention of myself, my *employés*, my business, my chambers, and general surroundings; because some such description is indispensable to an adequate understanding of the chief character about to be presented. Imprimis:[1] I am a man who, from his youth upwards has been filled with a profound conviction that the easiest way of life is the best. Hence, though I belong to a profession proverbially energetic and nervous, even to turbulence, at times, yet nothing of that sort have I ever suffered to invade my peace. I am one of those unambitious lawyers who never addresses a jury, or in any way draws down public applause; but, in the cool tranquillity of a snug retreat, do a snug business among the rich men's bonds, and mortgages, and title-deeds. All who know me, consider me an eminently *safe* man. The late John Jacob Astor,[2] a personage little given to

---

[1] Imprimis is Latin for "in the first place." The word is used to begin a list.
[2] John Jacob Astor (1763–1848) was the founder of a family fortune based on fur trading and real estate.

Herman Melville (*The Bettmann Archive*)

poetic enthusiasm, had no hesitation in pronouncing my first grand point to be prudence; my next, method. I do not speak it in vanity, but simply record the fact, that I was not unemployed in my profession by the late John Jacob Astor, a name which, I admit, I love to repeat; for it hath a rounded and orbicular[3] sound to it, and rings like unto bullion.[4] I will freely add, that I was not insensible to the late John Jacob Astor's good opinion.

Some time prior to the period at which this little history begins, my avocations had been largely increased. The good old office, now extinct in the State of New York, of a Master in Chancery, had been conferred upon me. It was not a very arduous office, but very pleasantly remunerative. I seldom lose my temper; much more seldom indulge in dangerous indignation at wrongs and outrages;

---

[3] Orbicular means to be rounded like a sphere.
[4] Bullion is coined gold or silver in bars.

but, I must be permitted to be rash here, and declare, that I consider the sudden and violent abrogation of the office of Master in Chancery, by the new Constitution, as a——premature act; inasmuch as I had counted upon a life-lease of the profits, whereas I only received those of a few short years. But this is by the way.

My chambers were up stairs, at No.——Wall Street. At one end, they looked upon the white wall of the interior of a spacious sky-light shaft, penetrating the building from top to bottom.

This view might have been considered rather tame than otherwise, deficient in what landscape painters call "life." But, if so, the view from the other end of my chambers offered, at least, a contrast, if nothing more. In that direction, my windows commanded an unobstructed view of a lofty brick wall, black by age and everlasting shade; which wall required no spy-glass to bring out its lurking beauties, but, for the benefit of all near-sighted spectators, was pushed up to within ten feet of my window panes. Owing to the great height of the surrounding buildings, and my chambers being on the second floor, the interval between this wall and mine not a little resembled a huge square cistern.

At the period just preceding the advent of Bartleby, I had two persons as copyists in my employment, and a promising lad as an office-boy. First, Turkey; second, Nippers; third, Ginger Nut. These may seem names, the like of which are not usually found in the Directory. [5] In truth, they were nicknames, mutually conferred upon each other by my three clerks, and were deemed expressive of their respective persons or characters. Turkey was a short, pursy Englishman of about my own age—that is, somewhere not far from sixty. In the morning, one might say, his face was of a fine florid hue, but after twelve o'clock, meridian—his dinner hour—it blazed like a grate full of Christmas coals; and continued blazing—but, as it were, with a gradual wane—till six o'clock, P.M., or thereabouts; after which, I saw no more of the proprietor of the face, which, gaining its meridian with the sun, seemed to set with it, to rise, culminate, and decline the following day, with the like regularity and undiminished glory. There are many singular coincidences I have known in the course of my life, not the least among which was the fact, that, exactly when Turkey displayed his fullest beams from his red and radiant countenance, just then, too, at that critical moment, began the daily period when I considered his business capacities as seriously disturbed for the remainder of the twenty-four hours. Not that he was absolutely idle, or averse to business then; far from it. The difficulty was, he was apt to be altogether too energetic. There was a strange, inflamed, flurried, flightly recklessness of activity about him. He would be incautious in dipping his pen into his inkstand. All his blots upon my documents were dropped there after twelve o'clock, meridian. Indeed, not only would he be reckless, and sadly given to making blots in the afternoon, but, some days, he went further, and was rather

---

[5] The Directory is a listing of all the businesses and residences in the city.

noisy. At such times, too, his face flamed with augmented blazonry, as if cannel coal had been heaped on anthracite. He made an unpleasant racket with his chair; spilled his sand-box; in mending his pens, impatiently split them all to pieces, and threw them on the floor in a sudden passion; stood up, and leaned over his table, boxing his papers about in a most indecorous manner, very sad to behold in an elderly man like him. Nevertheless, as he was in many ways a most valuable person to me, and all the time before twelve o'clock, meridian, was the quickest, steadiest creature, too, accomplishing a great deal of work in a style not easily to be matched—for these reasons, I was willing to overlook his eccentricities, though, indeed, occasionally, I remonstrated with him. I did this very gently, however, because, though the civilest, nay, the blandest and most reverential of men in the morning, yet, in the afternoon, he was disposed, upon provocation, to be slightly rash with his tongue—in fact, insolent. Now, valuing his morning services as I did, and resolved not to lose them—yet, at the same time, made uncomfortable by his inflamed ways after twelve o'clock—and being a man of peace, unwilling by my admonitions to call forth unseemly retorts from him, I took upon me, one Saturday noon (he was always worse on Saturdays) to hint to him, very kindly, that, perhaps, now that he was growing old, it might be well to abridge his labors; in short, he need not come to my chambers after twelve o'clock, but, dinner over, had best go home to his lodgings, and rest himself till tea-time. But no; he insisted upon his afternoon devotions. His countenance became intolerably fervid, as he oratorically assured me—gesticulating with a long ruler at the other end of the room—that if his services in the morning were useful, how indispensable, then, in the afternoon?

"With submission, sir," said Turkey, on this occasion, "I consider myself your right-hand man. In the morning I but marshal and deploy my columns; but in the afternoon I put myself at their head, and gallantly charge the foe, thus"—and he made a violent thrust with the ruler.

"But the blots, Turkey," intimated I.

"True; but, with submission, sir, behold these hairs! I am getting old. Surely, sir, a blot or two of a warm afternoon is not to be severely urged against gray hairs. Old age—even if it blot the page—is honorable. With submission, sir, we *both* are getting old."

This appeal to my fellow-feeling was hardly to be resisted. At all events, I saw that go he would not. So, I made up my mind to let him stay, resolving, nevertheless, to see to it that, during the afternoon, he had to do with my less important papers.

Nippers, the second on my list, was a whiskered, sallow, and, upon the whole, rather piratical-looking young man, of about five and twenty. I always deemed him the victim of two evil powers—ambition and indigestion. The ambition was evinced by a certain impatience of the duties of a mere copyist, an unwarrantable usurpation of strictly professional affairs, such as the original drawing up of legal documents. The indigestion seemed betokened in an occasional nervous testiness and grinning irritability, causing the teeth to audibly grind together over mistakes committed in copying; unnecessary maledictions, hissed, rather than spoken, in the heat of business; and especially by a continual discontent with the height of the table where he worked. Though of a very ingenious mechanical turn, Nippers could never get this table to suit him. He put chips under it, blocks of various sorts, bits of pasteboard, and at last went so far as to attempt an exquisite adjustment, by final pieces of folded blotting-paper. But no invention would answer. If, for the sake of easing his back, he brought the table lid at a sharp angle well up towards his chin, and wrote there like a man using the steep roof of a Dutch house for his desk, then he declared that it stopped the circulation in his arms. If now he lowered the table to his waistbands, and stooped over it in writing, then there was a sore aching in his back. In short, the truth of the matter was, Nippers knew not what he wanted. Or, if he wanted anything, it was to be rid of a scrivener's table altogether. Among the manifestations of his diseased ambition was a fondness he had for receiving visits from certain ambiguous-looking fellows in seedy coats, whom he called his clients. Indeed, I was aware that not only was he, at times, considerable of a ward-politician, but he occasionally did a little business at the Justices' courts, and was not unknown on the steps of the Tombs.[6] I have good reason to believe, however, that one individual who called upon him at my chambers, and who, with a grand air, he insisted was his client, was no other than a dun, and the alleged title-deed, a bill. But, with all his failings, and the annoyances he caused me, Nippers, like his compatriot Turkey, was a very useful man to me; wrote a neat, swift hand; and, when he chose, was not deficient in a gentlemanly sort of deportment. Added to this, he always dressed in a gentlemanly sort of way; and so, incidentally, reflected credit upon my chambers. Whereas, with respect to Turkey, I had much ado to keep him from being a reproach to me. His clothes were apt to look oily, and smell of eating-houses. He wore his pantaloons very loose and baggy in summer. His coats were execrable; his hat not to be handled. But while the hat was a thing of indifference to me, inasmuch as his natural civility and deference, as a dependent Englishman, always led him to doff it the moment he entered the room, yet his coat was another matter. Concerning his coats, I reasoned with him; but with no effect. The truth was, I suppose, that a man with so small an income could not afford to sport such a lustrous face and a lustrous coat at one and the same time. As Nippers once observed, Turkey's money went chiefly for red ink. One winter day, I presented Turkey with a highly respectable-looking coat of my own—a padded gray coat, of a most comfortable warmth, and which buttoned straight up from the knee to the neck. I thought Turkey would appreciate the favor, and abate his rashness and obstreperousness of afternoons. But no; I verily believe that buttoning himself up in so downy and blanket-like a coat had a pernicious effect upon him—upon the same principle that too much oats are bad for horses. In fact, precisely as a rash, restive horse is said to feel his oats, so Turkey felt his coat. It made him insolent. He was a man whom prosperity harmed.

Though, concerning the self-indulgent habits of Turkey, I had my own private

---

[6] The Tombs is the name given to the New York City Jail located in lower Manhattan.

surmises, yet, touching Nippers, I was well persuaded that, whatever might be his faults in other respects, he was, at least, a temperate young man. But, indeed, nature herself seemed to have been his vintner, and, at his birth, charged him so thoroughly with an irritable, brandy-like disposition, that all subsequent potations were needless. When I consider how, amid the stillness of my chambers, Nippers would sometimes impatiently rise from his seat, and stooping over his table, spread his arms wide apart, seize the whole desk, and move it, and jerk it, with a grim, grinding motion on the floor, as if the table were a perverse voluntary agent, intent on thwarting and vexing him, I plainly perceive that, for Nippers, brandy-and-water were altogether superfluous.

It was fortunate for me that, owing to its peculiar cause—indigestion—the irritability and consequent nervousness of Nippers were mainly observable in the morning, while in the afternoon he was comparatively mild. So that, Turkey's paroxysms only coming on about twelve o'clock, I never had to do with their eccentricities at one time. Their fits relieved each other, like guards. When Nippers' was on, Turkey's was off; and *vice versa*. This was a good natural arrangement, under the circumstances.

Ginger Nut, the third on my list, was a lad, some twelve years old. His father was a car-man, ambitious of seeing his son on the bench instead of a cart, before he died. So he sent him to my office, as student at law, errand-boy, cleaner and sweeper, at the rate of one dollar a week. He had a little desk to himself, but he did not use it much. Upon inspection, the drawer exhibited a great array of the shells of various sorts of nuts. Indeed, to this quick-witted youth, the whole noble science of the law was contained in a nut-shell. Not the least among the employments of Ginger Nut, as well as one which he discharged with the most alacrity, was his duty as cake and apple purveyor for Turkey and Nippers. Copying law-papers being proverbially a dry, husky sort of business, my two scriveners were fain to moisten their mouths very often with Spitzenbergs,[7] to be had at the numerous stalls nigh the Custom House and the Post Office. Also, they sent Ginger Nut very frequently for that peculiar cake—small, flat, round, and very spicy—after which he had been named by them. Of a cold morning, when business was but dull, Turkey would gobble up scores of these cakes, as if they were mere wafers—indeed, they sell them at the rate of six or eight for a penny—the scrape of his pen blending with the crunching of the crisp particles in his mouth. Of all the fiery afternoon blunders and flurried rashnesses of Turkey, was his once moistening a ginger-cake between his lips, and clapping it on to a mortgage, for a seal. I came within an ace of dismissing him then. But he mollified me by making an oriental bow, and saying—

"With submission, sir, it was generous of me to find you in stationery on my own account."

Now my original business—that of a conveyancer and title hunter, and drawer-up of recondite documents of all sorts—was considerably increased by receiving

---

[7] Spitzenbergs are a variety of apple native to New York State.

the master's office. There was now great work for scriveners. Not only must I push the clerks already with me, but I must have additional help.

In answer to my advertisement, a motionless young man one morning stood upon my office threshold, the door being open, for it was summer. I can see that figure now—pallidly neat, pitiably respectable, incurably forlorn! It was Bartleby.

After a few words touching his qualifications, I engaged him, glad to have among my corps of copyists a man of so singularly sedate an aspect, which I thought might operate beneficially upon the flighty temper of Turkey, and the fiery one of Nippers.

I should have stated before that ground glass folding-doors divided my premises into two parts, one of which was occupied by my scriveners, the other by myself. According to my humor, I threw open these doors, or closed them. I resolved to assign Bartleby a corner by the folding-doors, but on my side of them, so as to have this quiet man within easy call, in case any trifling thing was to be done. I placed his desk close up to a small side-window in that part of the room, a window which originally had afforded a lateral view of certain grimy backyards and bricks, but which, owing to subsequent erections, commanded at present no view at all, though it gave some light. Within three feet of the panes was a wall, and the light came down from far above, between two lofty buildings, as from a very small opening in a dome. Still further to a satisfactory arrangement, I procured a high green folding screen, which might entirely isolate Bartleby from my sight, though not remove him from my voice. And thus, in a manner, privacy and society were conjoined.

At first, Bartleby did an extraordinary quantity of writing. As if long famishing for something to copy, he seemed to gorge himself on my documents. There was no pause for digestion. He ran a day and night line, copying by sun-light and by candle-light. I should have been quite delighted with his application, had he been cheerfully industrious. But he wrote on silently, palely, mechanically.

It is, of course, an indispensable part of a scrivener's business to verify the accuracy of his copy, word by word. Where there are two or more scriveners in an office, they assist each other in this examination, one reading from the copy, the other holding the original. It is a very dull, wearisome, and lethargic affair. I can readily imagine that, to some sanguine temperaments, it would be alto-gether intolerable. For example, I cannot credit that the mettlesome poet, Byron, would have contentedly sat down with Bartleby to examine a law document of, say five hundred pages, closely written in a crimpy hand.

Now and then, in the haste of business, it had been my habit to assist in comparing some brief document myself, calling Turkey or Nippers for this purpose. One object I had, in placing Bartleby so handy to me behind the screen, was, to avail myself of his services on such trivial occasions. It was on the third day, I think, of his being with me, and before any necessity had arisen for having his own writing examined, that, being much hurried to complete a small affair I had in hand, I abruptly called to Bartleby. In my haste and natural expectancy of instant compliance, I sat with my head bent over the original on my desk, and my right hand sideways, and somewhat nervously extended with the copy, so that, immediately upon emerging from his retreat, Bartleby might snatch it and proceed to business without the least delay.

In this very attitude did I sit when I called to him, rapidly stating what it was I wanted him to do—namely, to examine a small paper with me. Imagine my surprise, nay, my consternation, when, without moving from his privacy, Bartleby, in a singularly mild, firm voice, replied, "I would prefer not to."

I sat awhile in perfect silence, rallying my stunned faculties. Immediately it occurred to me that my ears had deceived me, or Bartleby had entirely misunderstood my meaning. I repeated my request in the clearest tone I could assume; but in quite as clear a one came the previous reply, "I would prefer not to."

"Prefer not to," echoed I, rising in high excitement, and crossing the room with a stride. "What do you mean? Are you moon-struck? I want you to help me compare this sheet here—take it," and I thrust it towards him.

"I would prefer not to," said he.

I looked at him steadfastly. His face was leanly composed; his gray eye dimly calm. Not a wrinkle of agitation rippled him. Had there been the least uneasiness, anger, impatience or impertinence in his manner; in other words, had there been any thing ordinarily human about him, doubtless I should have violently dismissed him from the premises. But as it was, I should have as soon thought of turning my pale plaster-of-paris bust of Cicero[8] out of doors. I stood gazing at him awhile, as he went on with his own writing, and then reseated myself at my desk. This is very strange, thought I. What had one best do? But my business hurried me. I concluded to forget the matter for the present, reserving it for my future leisure. So calling Nippers from the other room, the paper was speedily examined.

A few days after this, Bartleby concluded four lengthy documents, being quadruplicates of a week's testimony taken before me in my High Court of Chancery. It became necessary to examine them. It was an important suit, and great accuracy was imperative. Having all things arranged, I called Turkey, Nippers, and Ginger Nut, from the next room, meaning to place the four copies in the hands of my four clerks, while I should read from the original. Accordingly, Turkey, Nippers, and Ginger Nut had taken their seats in a row, each with his document in his hand, when I called to Bartleby to join this interesting group.

"Bartleby! quick, I am waiting."

I heard a slow scrape of his chairlegs on the uncarpeted floor, and soon he appeared standing at the entrance of his hermitage.

"What is wanted?" said he, mildly.

"The copies, the copies," said I, hurriedly. "We are going to examine them. There"—and I held towards him the fourth quadruplicate.

"I would prefer not to," he said, and gently disappeared behind the screen.

---

[8] Cicero (106–43 B.C.) was a Roman orator, statesman, and philosopher.

For a few moments I was turned into a pillar of salt, standing at the head of my seated column of clerks. Recovering myself, I advanced towards the screen, and demanded the reason for such extraordinary conduct.

"Why do you refuse?"

"I would prefer not to."

With any other man I should have flown outright into a dreadful passion, scorned all further words, and thrust him ignominiously from my presence. But there was something about Bartleby that not only strangely disarmed me, but, in a wonderful manner, touched and disconcerted me. I began to reason with him.

"These are your own copies we are about to examine. It is labor saving to you, because one examination will answer for your four papers. It is common usage. Every copyist is bound to help examine his copy. Is it not so? Will you not speak? Answer!"

"I prefer not to," he replied in a flutelike tone. It seemed to me that, while I had been addressing him, he carefully revolved every statement that I made; fully comprehended the meaning; could not gainsay the irresistible conclusion; but, at the same time, some paramount consideration prevailed with him to reply as he did.

"You are decided, then, not to comply with my request—a request made according to common usage and common sense?"

He briefly gave me to understand, that on that point my judgment was sound. Yes: his decision was irreversible.

It is not seldom the case that, when a man is browbeaten in some unprecedented and violently unreasonable way, he begins to stagger in his own plainest faith. He begins, as it were, vaguely to surmise that, wonderful as it may be, all the justice and all the reason is on the other side. Accordingly, if any disinterested persons are present, he turns to them for some reinforcement of his own faltering mind.

"Turkey," said I, "what do you think of this? Am I not right?"

"With submission, sir," said Turkey, in his blandest tone, "I think that you are."

"Nippers," said I, "what do you think of it?"

"I think I should kick him out of the office."

(The reader, of nice perceptions, will here perceive that, it being morning, Turkey's answer is couched in polite and tranquil terms, but Nippers' replies in ill-tempered ones. Or, to repeat a previous sentence, Nippers' ugly mood was on duty, and Turkey's off.)

"Ginger Nut," said I, willing to enlist the smallest suffrage in my behalf, "what do you think of it?"

"I think, sir, he's a little luny," replied Ginger Nut, with a grin.

"You hear what they say," said I, turning towards the screen, "come forth and do your duty."

But he vouchsafed no reply. I pondered a moment in sore perplexity. But once more business hurried me. I determined again to postpone the consideration of this dilemma to my future leisure. With a little trouble we made out to examine the papers without Bartleby, though at every page or two Turkey deferentially dropped his opinion, that this proceeding was quite out of the common; while Nippers, twitching in his chair with a dyspeptic[9] nervousness, ground out, between his set teeth, occasional hissing maledictions against the stubborn oaf behind the screen. And for his (Nippers') part, this was the first and the last time he would do another man's business without pay.

Meanwhile Bartleby sat in his hermitage, oblivious to everything but his own peculiar business there.

Some days passed, the scrivener being employed upon another lengthy work. His late remarkable conduct led me to regard his ways narrowly. I observed that he never went to dinner; indeed, that he never went anywhere. As yet I had never, of my personal knowledge, known him to be outside of my office. He was a perpetual sentry in the corner. At about eleven o'clock though, in the morning, I noticed that Ginger Nut would advance toward the opening in Bartleby's screen, as if silently beckoned thither by a gesture invisible to me where I sat. The boy would then leave the office, jingling a few pence, and reappear with a handful of ginger-nuts, which he delivered in the hermitage, receiving two of the cakes for his trouble.

He lives, then, on ginger-nuts, thought I; never eats a dinner, properly speaking; he must be a vegetarian, then; but no; he never eats even vegetables, he eats nothing but ginger-nuts. My mind then ran on in reveries concerning the probable effects upon the human constitution of living entirely on ginger-nuts. Ginger-nuts are so called, because they contain ginger as one of their peculiar constituents, and the final flavoring one. Now, what was ginger? A hot, spicy thing. Was Bartleby hot and spicy? Not at all. Ginger, then, had no effect upon Bartleby. Probably he preferred it should have none.

Nothing so aggravates an earnest person as a passive resistance. If the individual so resisted be of a not inhumane temper, and the resisting one perfectly harmless in his passivity, then, in the better moods of the former, he will endeavor charitably to construe to his imagination what proves impossible to be solved by his judgment. Even so, for the most part, I regarded Bartleby and his ways. Poor fellow! thought I, he means no mischief; it is plain he intends no insolence; his aspect sufficiently evinces that his eccentricities are involuntary. He is useful to me. I can get along with him. If I turn him away, the chances are he will fall in with some less-indulgent employer, and then he will be rudely treated, and perhaps driven forth miserably to starve. Yes. Here I can cheaply purchase a delicious self-approval. To befriend Bartleby; to humor him in his strange willfulness, will cost me little or nothing, while I lay up in my soul what will eventually prove a sweet morsel for my conscience. But this mood was not invariable with me. The passiveness of Bartleby sometimes irritated me. I felt strangely goaded on to encounter him in new opposition—to elicit some angry

---

[9] Dyspeptic refers to indigestion.

spark from him answerable to my own. But, indeed, I might as well have essayed to strike fire with my knuckles against a bit of Windsor soap. But one afternoon the evil impulse in me mastered me, and the following little scene ensued:

"Bartleby," said I, "when those papers are all copied, I will compare them with you."

"I would prefer not to."

"How? Surely you do not mean to persist in that mulish vagary?"

No answer.

I threw open the folding-doors near by, and, turning upon Turkey and Nippers, exclaimed:

"Bartleby a second time says, he won't examine his papers. What do you think of it, Turkey?"

It was afternoon, be it remembered. Turkey sat glowing like a brass boiler; his bald head steaming; his hands reeling among his blotted papers.

"Think if it?" roared Turkey; "I think I'll just step behind his screen, and black his eyes for him!"

So saying, Turkey rose to his feet and threw his arms into a pugilistic position. He was hurrying away to make good his promise, when I detained him, alarmed at the effect of incautiously rousing Turkey's combativeness after dinner.

"Sit down, Turkey," said I, "and hear what Nippers has to say. What do you think of it, Nippers? Would I not be justified in immediately dismissing Bartleby?"

"Excuse me, that is for you to decide, sir. I think his conduct quite unusual, and, indeed, unjust, as regards Turkey and myself. But it may only be a passing whim."

"Ah," exclaimed I, "you have strangely changed your mind, then—you speak very gently of him now."

"All beer," cried Turkey; "gentleness is effects of beer—Nippers and I dined together to-day. You see how gentle I am, sir. Shall I go and black his eyes?"

"You refer to Bartleby, I suppose. No, not to-day, Turkey," I replied; "pray, put up your fists."

I closed the doors, and again advanced towards Bartleby. I felt additional incentives tempting me to my fate. I burned to be rebelled against again. I remember that Bartleby never left the office.

"Bartleby," said I, "Ginger Nut is away; just step around to the Post Office, won't you? (it was but a three minutes' walk), and see if there is anything for me."

"I would prefer not to."

"You *will* not?"

"I *prefer* not."

I staggered to my desk, and sat there in a deep study. My blind inveteracy returned. Was there any other thing in which I could procure myself to be ignominiously repulsed by this lean, penniless wight?—my hired clerk? What added thing is there, perfectly reasonable, that he will be sure to refuse to do?

"Bartleby!"

No answer.

"Bartleby," in a louder tone.

No answer.

"Bartleby," I roared.

Like a very ghost, agreeably to the laws of magical invocation, at the third summons, he appeared at the entrance of his hermitage.

"Go to the next room, and tell Nippers to come to me."

"I prefer not to," he respectfully and slowly said, and mildly disappeared.

"Very good, Bartleby," said I, in a quiet sort of serenely-severe self-possessed tone, intimating the unalterable purpose of some terrible retribution very close at hand. But upon the whole, as it was drawing towards my dinner-hour, I thought it best to put on my hat and walk home for the day, suffering much from perplexity and distress of mind.

Shall I acknowledge it? The conclusion of this whole business was, that it soon became a fixed fact of my chambers, that a pale young scrivener, by the name of Bartleby, had a desk there; that he copied for me at the usual rate of four cents a folio (one hundred words); but he was permanently exempt from examining the work done by him, that duty being transferred to Turkey and Nippers, out of compliment, doubtless, to their superior acuteness; moreover, said Bartleby was never, on any account, to be dispatched on the most trivial errand of any sort; and that even if entreated to take upon him such a matter, it was generally understood that he would "prefer not to"—in other words, that he would refuse point-blank.

As days passed on, I became considerably reconciled to Bartleby. His steadiness, his freedom from all dissipation, his incessant industry (except when he chose to throw himself into a standing revery behind his screen), his great stillness, his unalterableness of demeanor under all circumstances, made him a valuable acquisition. One prime thing was this—*he was always there*—first in the morning, continually through the day, and the last at night. I had a singular confidence in his honesty. I felt my most precious papers perfectly safe in his hands. Sometimes, to be sure, I could not, for the very soul of me, avoid falling into sudden spasmodic passions with him. For it was exceeding difficult to bear in mind all the time those strange peculiarities, privileges, and unheard of exemptions, forming the tacit stipulations on Bartleby's part under which he remained in my office. Now and then, in the eagerness of dispatching pressing business, I would inadvertently summon Bartleby, in a short, rapid tone, to put his finger, say, on the incipient tie of a bit of red tape with which I was about compressing some papers. Of course, from behind the screen the usual answer, "I prefer not to," was sure to come; and then, how could a human creature, with the common infirmities of our nature, refrain from bitterly exclaiming upon such perverseness—such unreasonableness. However, every added repulse of this sort which I received only tended to lessen the probability of my repeating the inadvertence.

Here it must be said, that according to the custom of most legal gentlemen occupying chambers in densely-populated law buildings, there were several keys to my door. One was kept by a woman residing in the attic, which person weekly scrubbed and daily swept and dusted my apartments. Another was kept by Turkey for convenience sake. The third I sometimes carried in my own pocket. The fourth I knew not who had.

Now, one Sunday morning I happened to go to Trinity Church, to hear a celebrated preacher, and finding myself rather early on the ground I thought I would walk around to my chambers for a while. Luckily I had my key with me; but upon applying it to the lock, I found it resisted by something inserted from the inside. Quite surprised, I called out; when to my consternation a key was turned from within; and thrusting his lean visage at me, and holding the door ajar, the apparition of Bartleby appeared in his shirt sleeves, and otherwise in a strangely tattered deshabille,[10] saying quietly that he was sorry, but he was deeply engaged just then, and—preferred not admitting me at present. In a brief word or two, he moreover added, that perhaps I had better walk around the block two or three times, and by that time he would probably have concluded his affairs.

Now, the utterly unsurmised appearance of Bartleby, tenanting my law-chambers of a Sunday morning, with his cadaverously gentlemanly *nonchalance*, yet withal firm and self-possessed, had such a strange effect upon me, that incontinently I slunk away from my own door, and did as desired. But not without sundry twinges of impotent rebellion against the mild effrontery of this unaccountable scrivener. Indeed, it was his wonderful mildness chiefly, which not only disarmed me, but unmanned me as it were. For I consider that one, for the time, is somehow unmanned when he tranquilly permits his hired clerk to dictate to him, and order him away from his own premises. Furthermore, I was full of uneasiness as to what Bartleby could possibly be doing in my office in his shirt sleeves, and in an otherwise dismantled condition of a Sunday morning. Was anything amiss going on? Nay, that was out of the question. It was not to be thought of for a moment that Bartleby was an immoral person. But what could he be doing there?—copying? Nay again, whatever might be his eccentricities, Bartleby was an eminently decorous person. He would be the last man to sit down to his desk in any state approaching to nudity. Besides, it was Sunday; and there was something about Bartleby that forbade the supposition that he would by any secular occupation violate the proprieties of the day.

Nevertheless, my mind was not pacified; and full of a restless curiosity, at last I returned to the door. Without hindrance I inserted my key, opened it, and entered. Bartleby was not to be seen. I looked round anxiously, peeped behind his screen; but it was very plain that he was gone. Upon more closely examining the place, I surmised that for an indefinite period Bartleby must have ate, dressed, and slept in my office, and that, too, without plate, mirror, or bed. The cushioned seat of a rickety old sofa in one corner bore the faint impression of a lean, reclining form. Rolled away under his desk, I found a blanket; on a chair, a tin basin, with soap and a ragged towel; in a newspaper a few crumbs of ginger-nuts and a morsel of cheese. Yes, thought I, it is evident enough that Bartleby

---

[10] Deshabille (dishabille) is the state of being partially dressed.

has been making his home here, keeping bachelor's hall all by himself. Immediately then the thought came sweeping across me, what miserable friendlessness and loneliness are here revealed! His poverty is great; but his solitude, how horrible! Think of it. Of a Sunday, Wall Street is deserted as Petra;[11] and every night of every day it is an emptiness. This building, too, which of weekdays hums with industry and life, at nightfall echoes with sheer vacancy, and all through Sunday is forlorn. And here Bartleby makes his home; sole spectator of a solitude which he has seen all populous—a sort of innocent and transformed Marius[12] brooding among the ruins of Carthage!

For the first time in my life a feeling of over-powering stinging melancholy seized me. Before, I had never experienced aught but a not unpleasing sadness. The bond of a common humanity now drew me irresistibly to gloom. A fraternal melancholy! For both I and Bartleby were sons of Adam. I remembered the bright silks and sparkling faces I had seen that day, in gala trim, swan-like sailing down the Mississippi of Broadway; and I contrasted them with the pallid copyist, and thought to myself, Ah, happiness courts the light, so we deem the world is gay; but misery hides aloof, so we deem that misery there is none. These sad fancyings—chimeras, doubtless, of a sick and silly brain—led on to other and more special thoughts, concerning the eccentricities of Bartleby. Presentiments of strange discoveries hovered round me. The scrivener's pale form appeared to me laid out, among uncaring strangers, in its shivering winding sheet.

Suddenly I was attracted by Bartleby's closed desk, the key in open sight left in the lock.

I mean no mischief, seek the gratification of no heartless curiosity, thought I; besides, the desk is mine, and its contents, too, so I will make bold to look within. Everything was methodically arranged, the papers smoothly placed. The pigeon holes were deep, and removing the files of documents, I groped into their recesses. Presently I felt something there, and dragged it out. It was an old bandanna handkerchief, heavy and knotted. I opened it, and saw it was a saving's bank.

I now recalled all the quiet mysteries which I had noted in the man. I remembered that he never spoke but to answer; that, though at intervals he had considerable time to himself, yet I had never seen him reading—no, not even a newspaper; that for long periods he would stand looking out, at his pale window behind the screen, upon a dead brick wall; I was quite sure he never visited any refectory or eating house; while his pale face clearly indicated that he never drank beer like Turkey, or tea and coffee even, like other men; that he never went anywhere in particular that I could learn; never went out for a walk, unless, indeed, that was the case at present; that he had declined telling who he was, or whence he came, or whether he had any relatives in the world; that though

---

[11] Petra was a city in southwestern Jordan captured by the Muslims in the 7th century and the crusaders in the 12th. Johann Ludwig Burckhardt (1784–1817) discovered its ruins in 1812.

[12] Marius (155?–86 B.C.) was a Roman general driven from Rome during a civil war. Carthage was a city whose battles with Rome led to its total destruction in 146 B.C.

so thin and pale, he never complained of ill health. And more than all, I remembered a certain unconscious air of pallid—how shall I call it?—of pallid haughtiness, say, or rather an austere reserve about him, which had positively awed me into my tame compliance with his eccentricities, when I had feared to ask him to do the slightest incidental thing for me, even though I might know, from his long-continued motionlessness, that behind his screen he must be standing in one of those dead-wall reveries of his.

Revolving all these things, and coupling them with the recently discovered fact, that he made my office his constant abiding place and home, and not forgetful of his morbid moodiness; revolving all these things, a prudential feeling began to steal over me. My first emotions had been those of pure melancholy and sincerest pity; but just in proportion as the forlornness of Bartleby grew and grew to my imagination, did that same melancholy merge into fear, that pity into repulsion. So true it is, and so terrible, too, that up to a certain point the thought or sight of misery enlists our best affections; but, in certain special cases, beyond that point it does not. They err who would assert that invariably this is owing to the inherent selfishness of the human heart. It rather proceeds from a certain hopelessness of remedying excessive and organic ill. To a sensitive being, pity is not seldom pain. And when at last it is perceived that such pity cannot lead to effectual succor, common sense bids the soul be rid of it. What I saw that morning persuaded me that the scrivener was the victim of innate and incurable disorder. I might give alms to his body; but his body did not pain him; it was his soul that suffered, and his soul I could not reach.

I did not accomplish the purpose of going to Trinity Church that morning. Somehow, the things I had seen disqualified me for the time from church-going. I walked homeward, thinking what I would do with Bartleby. Finally, I resolved upon this—I would put certain calm questions to him the next morning, touching his history, etc., and if he declined to answer them openly and unreservedly (and I supposed he would prefer not), then to give him a twenty dollar bill over and above whatever I might owe him, and tell him his services were no longer required; but that if in any other way I could assist him, I would be happy to do so, especially if he desired to return to his native place, wherever that might be, I would willingly help to defray the expenses. Moreover, if, after reaching home, he found himself at any time in want of aid, a letter from him would be sure of a reply.

The next morning came.

"Bartleby," said I, gently calling to him behind his screen.

No reply.

"Bartleby," said I, in a still gentler tone, "come here; I am not going to ask you to do anything you would prefer not to do—I simply wish to speak to you."

Upon this he noiselessly slid into view.

"Will you tell me, Bartleby, where you were born?"

"I would prefer not to."

"Will you tell me *anything* about yourself?"

"I would prefer not to."

"But what reasonable objection can you have to speak to me? I feel friendly towards you."

He did not look at me while I spoke, but kept his glance fixed upon my bust of Cicero, which, as I then sat, was directly behind me, some six inches above my head.

"What is your answer, Bartleby," said I, after waiting a considerable time for a reply, during which his countenance remained immovable, only there was the faintest conceivable tremor of the white attenuated mouth.

"At present I prefer to give no answer," he said, and retired into his hermitage.

It was rather weak in me I confess, but his manner, on this occasion, nettled me. Not only did there seem to lurk in it a certain calm disdain, but his perverseness seemed ungrateful, considering the undeniable good usage and indulgence he had received from me.

Again I sat ruminating what I should do. Mortified as I was at his behavior, and resolved as I had been to dismiss him when I entered my office, nevertheless I strangely felt something superstitious knocking at my heart, and forbidding me to carry out my purpose, and denouncing me for a villain if I dared to breathe one bitter word against this forlornest of mankind. At last, familiarly drawing my chair behind his screen, I sat down and said: "Bartleby, never mind, then, about revealing your history; but let me entreat you, as a friend, to comply as far as may be with the usages of this office. Say now, you will help to examine papers to-morrow or next day: in short, say now, that in a day or two you will begin to be a little reasonable:—say so, Bartleby."

"At present I would prefer not to be a little reasonable," was his mildly cadaverous reply.

Just then the folding-doors opened, and Nippers approached. He seemed suffering from an unusually bad night's rest, induced by severer indigestion than common. He overheard those final words of Bartleby.

"*Prefer not*, eh?" gritted Nippers—"I'd *prefer* him, if I were you, sir," addressing me—"I'd *prefer* him; I'd give him preferences, the stubborn mule! What is it, sir, pray, that he *prefers* not to do now?"

Bartleby moved not a limb.

"Mr. Nippers," said I, "I'd prefer that you would withdraw for the present."

Somehow, of late, I had got into the way of involuntarily using this word "prefer" upon all sorts of not exactly suitable occasions. And I trembled to think that my contact with the scrivener had already and seriously affected me in a mental way. And what further and deeper aberration might it not yet produce? This apprehension had not been without efficacy in determining me to summary measures.

As Nippers, looking very sour and sulky, was departing, Turkey blandly and deferentially approached.

"With submission, sir," said he, "yesterday I was thinking abut Bartleby here, and I think that if he would but prefer to take a quart of good ale every day, it would do much towards mending him, and enabling him to assist in examining his papers."

"So you have got the word, too," said I, slightly excited.

"With submission, what word, sir," asked Turkey, respectfully crowding himself into the contracted space behind the screen, and by so doing, making me jostle the scrivener. "What word, sir?"

"I would prefer to be left alone here," said Bartleby, as if offended at being mobbed in his privacy.

"That's the word, Turkey," said I—*"that's* it."

"Oh, *prefer?* oh yes—queer word. I never use it myself. But, sir, as I was saying, if he would but prefer—"

"Turkey," interrupted I, "you will please withdraw."

"Oh, certainly, sir, if you prefer that I should."

As he opened the folding-door to retire, Nippers at his desk caught a glimpse of me, and asked whether I would prefer to have a certain paper copied on blue paper or white. He did not in the least roguishly accent the word prefer. It was plain that it involuntarily rolled from his tongue. I thought to myself, surely I must get rid of a demented man, who already has in some degree turned the tongues, if not the heads of myself and clerks. But I thought it prudent not to break the dismission at once.

The next day I noticed that Bartleby did nothing but stand at his window in his dead-wall revery. Upon asking him why he did not write, he said that he had decided upon doing no more writing.

"Why, how now? what next?" exclaimed I, "do no more writing?"

"No more."

"And what is the reason?"

"Do you not see the reason for yourself," he indifferently replied.

I looked steadfastly at him, and perceived that his eyes looked dull and glazed. Instantly it occurred to me, that his unexampled diligence in copying by his dim window for the first few weeks of his stay with me might have temporarily impaired his vision.

I was touched. I said something in condolence with him. I hinted that of course he did wisely in abstaining from writing for a while; and urged him to embrace that opportunity of taking wholesome exercise in the open air. This, however, he did not do. A few days after this, my other clerks being absent, and being in a great hurry to dispatch certain letters by the mail, I thought that, having nothing else earthly to do, Bartleby would surely be less inflexible than usual, and carry these letters to the post-office. But he blankly declined. So, much to my inconvenience, I went myself.

Still added days went by. Whether Bartleby's eyes improved or not, I could not say. To all appearance, I thought they did. But when I asked him if they did, he vouchsafed no answer. At all events, he would do no copying. At last, in reply to my urgings, he informed me that he had permanently given up copying.

"What!" exclaimed I; "suppose your eyes should get entirely well—better than ever before—would you not copy then?"

"I have given up copying," he answered, and slid aside.

He remained as ever, a fixture in my chamber. Nay—if that were possible—he became still more of a fixture than before. What was to be done? He would do nothing in the office; why should he stay there? In plain fact, he had now become a millstone to me, not only useless as a necklace, but afflictive to bear. Yet I was sorry for him. I speak less than truth when I say that, on his own account, he occasioned me uneasiness. If he would but have named a single relative or friend, I would instantly have written, and urged their taking the poor fellow away to some convenient retreat. But he seemed alone, absolutely alone in the universe. A bit of wreck in the mid Atlantic. At length, necessities connected with my business tyrannized over all other considerations. Decently as I could, I told Bartleby that in six days time he must unconditionally leave the office. I warned him to take measures, in the interval, for procuring some other abode. I offered to assist him in this endeavor, if he himself would but take the first step towards a removal. "And when you finally quit me, Bartleby," added I, "I shall see that you go not away entirely unprovided. Six days from this hour, remember."

At the expiration of that period, I peeped behind the screen, and lo! Bartleby was there.

I buttoned up my coat, balanced myself; advanced slowly towards him, touched his shoulder, and said, "The time has come; you must quit this place; I am sorry for you; here is money; but you must go."

"I would prefer not," he replied, with his back still towards me.

"You *must*."

He remained silent.

Now I had an unbounded confidence in this man's common honesty. He had frequently restored to me sixpences and shillings carelessly dropped upon the floor, for I am apt to be very reckless in such shirt-button affairs. The proceeding, then, which followed will not be deemed extraordinary.

"Bartleby," said I, "I owe you twelve dollars on account; here are thirty-two; the odd twenty are yours—Will you take it?" and I handed the bills towards him.

But he made no motion.

"I will leave them here, then," putting them under a weight on the table. Then taking my hat and cane and going to the door, I tranquilly turned and added—"After you have removed your things from these offices, Bartleby, you will of course lock the door—since every one is now gone for the day but you—and if you please, slip your key underneath the mat, so that I may have it in the morning. I shall not see you again; so good-by to you. If, hereafter, in your new place of abode, I can be of any service to you, do not fail to advise me by letter. Good-by, Bartleby, and fare you well."

But he answered not a word; like the last column of some ruined temple, he remained standing mute and solitary in the middle of the otherwise deserted room.

As I walked home in a pensive mood, my vanity got the better of my pity. I could not but highly plume myself on my masterly management in getting rid of Bartleby. Masterly I call it, and such it must appear to any dispassionate thinker. The beauty of my procedure seemed to consist in its perfect quietness. There was no vulgar bullying, no bravado of any sort, no choleric hectoring, and striding to and fro across the apartment, jerking out vehement commands for Bartleby to bundle himself off with his beggarly traps. Nothing of the kind. Without loudly bidding Bartleby depart—as an inferior genius might have done— I *assumed* the ground that depart he must; and upon that assumption built all I had to say. The more I thought over my procedure, the more I was charmed with it. Nevertheless, next morning, upon awakening, I had my doubts—I had somehow slept off the fumes of vanity. One of the coolest and wisest hours a man has, is just after he awakes in the morning. My procedure seemed as sagacious as ever—but only in theory. How it would prove in practice—there was the rub. It was truly a beautiful thought to have assumed Bartleby's departure; but, after all, that assumption was simply my own, and none of Bartleby's. The great point was, not whether I had assumed that he would quit me, but whether he would prefer so to do. He was more a man of preferences than assumptions.

After breakfast, I walked down town, arguing the probabilities *pro* and *con*. One moment I thought it would prove a miserable failure, and Bartleby would be found all alive at my office as usual; the next moment it seemed certain that I should find his chair empty. And so I kept veering about. At the corner of Broadway and Canal Street, I saw quite an excited group of people standing in earnest conversation.

"I'll take odds he doesn't," said a voice as I passed.

"Doesn't go?—done!" said I, "put up your money."

I was instinctively putting my hand in my pocket to produce my own, when I remembered that this was an election day. The words I had overheard bore no reference to Bartleby, but to the success or nonsuccess of some candidate for the mayoralty. In my intent frame of mind, I had, as it were, imagined that all Broadway shared in my excitement, and were debating the same question with me. I passed on, very thankful that the uproar of the street screened my momentary absent-mindedness.

As I had intended, I was earlier than usual at my office door. I stood listening for a moment. All was still. He must be gone. I tried the knob. The door was locked. Yes, my procedure had worked to a charm; he indeed must be vanished. Yet a certain melancholy mixed with this: I was almost sorry for my brilliant success. I was fumbling under the door mat for the key, which Bartleby was to have left there for me, when accidentally my knee knocked against a panel, producing a summoning sound, and in response a voice came to me from within—"Not yet; I am occupied."

It was Bartleby.

I was thunderstruck. For an instant I stood like the man who, pipe in mouth, was killed one cloudless afternoon long ago in Virginia, by summer lightning; at his own warm open window he was killed, and remained leaning out there upon the dreamy afternoon, till some one touched him, when he fell.

"Not gone!" I murmured at last. But again obeying that wondrous ascendancy which the inscrutable scrivener had over me, and from which ascendancy, for all my chafing, I could not completely escape, I slowly went down stairs and out into the street, and while walking round the block, considered what I should next do in this unheard-of perplexity. Turn the man out by an actual thrusting I could not; to drive him away by calling him hard names would not do; calling in the police was an unpleasant idea; and yet, permit him to enjoy his cadaverous triumph over me—this too, I could not think of. What was to be done? or, if nothing could be done, was there anything further that I could *assume* in the matter? Yes, as before I had prospectively assumed that Bartleby would depart, so now I might retrospectively assume that departed he was. In the legitimate carrying out of this assumption, I might enter my office in a great hurry, and pretending not to see Bartleby at all, walk straight against him as if he were air. Such a proceeding would in a singular degree have the appearance of home-thrust. It was hardly possible that Bartleby could withstand such an application of the doctrine of assumptions. But upon second thoughts the success of the plan seemed rather dubious. I resolved to argue the matter over with him again.

"Bartleby," said I, entering the office, with a quietly severe expression, "I am seriously displeased. I am pained, Bartleby. I had thought better of you. I had imagined you of such a gentlemanly organization, that in any delicate dilemma a slight hint would suffice—in short, an assumption. But it appears I am deceived. Why," I added, unaffectedly starting, "you have not even touched that money yet," pointing to it, just where I had left it the evening previous.

He answered nothing.

"Will you, or will you not, quit me?" I now demanded in a sudden passion, advancing close to him.

"I would prefer *not* to quit you," he replied, gently emphasizing the *not*.

"What earthly right have you to stay here? Do you pay any rent? Do you pay my taxes? Or is this property yours?"

He answered nothing.

"Are you ready to go on and write now? Are your eyes recovered? Could you copy a small paper for me this morning? or help examine a few lines? or step round to the post-office? In a word, will you do anything at all, to give a coloring to your refusal to depart the premises?"

He silently retired into his hermitage.

I was now in such a state of nervous resentment that I thought it but prudent to check myself at present from further demonstrations. Bartleby and I were alone. I remembered the tragedy of the unfortunate Adams and the still more unfortunate Colt in the solitary office of the latter; and how poor Colt, being dreadfully incensed by Adams, and imprudently permitting himself to get wildly excited, was at unawares hurried into his fatal act—an act which certainly no man could possibly deplore more than the actor himself. Often it had occurred to me in my ponderings upon the subject, that had that altercation taken place in the public street, or at a private residence, it would not have terminated as it did. It was the circumstance of being alone in a solitary office, up stairs, of a building entirely unhallowed by humanizing domestic associations—an uncarpeted office, doubtless, of a dusty, haggard sort of appearance—this it must have been, which greatly helped to enhance the irritable desperation of the hapless Colt. [13]

But when this old Adam of resentment rose in me and tempted me concerning Bartleby, I grappled him and threw him. How? Why, simply by recalling the divine injunction: "A new commandment give I unto you, that ye love one another." Yes, this it was that saved me. Aside from higher considerations, charity often operates as a vastly wise and prudent principle—a great safeguard to its possessor. Men have committed murder for jealousy's sake, and anger's sake, and hatred's sake, and selfishness' sake, and spiritual pride's sake; but no man, that ever I heard of, ever committed a diabolical murder for sweet charity's sake. Mere self-interest, then, if no better motive can be enlisted, should, especially with high-tempered men, prompt all beings to charity and philanthropy. At any rate, upon the occasion in question, I strove to drown my exasperated feelings towards the scrivener by benevolently construing his conduct. Poor fellow, poor fellow! thought I, he don't mean anything; and besides, he has seen hard times, and ought to be indulged.

I endeavored, also, immediately to occupy myself, and at the same time to comfort my despondency. I tried to fancy, that in the course of the morning, at such time as might prove agreeable to him, Bartleby, of his own free accord, would emerge from his hermitage and take up some decided line of march in the direction of the door. But no. Half-past twelve o'clock came; Turkey began to glow in the face, overturn his inkstand, and become generally obstreperous; Nippers abated down into quietude and courtesy; Ginger Nut munched his noon apple; and Bartleby remained standing at his window in one of his profoundest dead-wall reveries. Will it be credited? Ought I to acknowledge it? That afternoon I left the office without saying one further word to him.

Some days now passed, during which, at leisure intervals I looked a little into "Edwards on the Will," and "Priestley on Necessity." [14] Under the circumstances, those books induced a salutary feeling. Gradually I slid into the persuasion that these troubles of mine, touching the scrivener, had been all predestinated from eternity, and Bartleby was billeted upon me for some mysterious purpose of an allwise Providence, which it was not for a mere mortal like me to fathom. Yes, Bartleby, stay there behind your screen, thought I; I shall persecute you no more; you are harmless and noiseless as any of these old chairs; in short, I never feel so private as when I know you are here. At last I see it, I feel it; I penetrate to the predestinated purpose of my life. I am content. Others may have loftier parts

---

[13] In January, 1842, John C. Colt killed Samuel Adams in a notorious New York City murder case.

[14] These are two philosophic books. "Edwards on the Will" refers to *Freedom of the Will* (1754) by Jonathan Edwards (1703–1758), an American theologian. "Priestley on Necessity" refers to an essay by Joseph Priestley (1733–1804), the British clergyman and scientist.

to enact; but my mission in this world, Bartleby, is to furnish you with office-room for such period as you may see fit to remain.

I believe that this wise and blessed frame of mind would have continued with me, had it not been for the unsolicited and uncharitable remarks obtruded upon me by my professional friends who visited the rooms. But thus it often is, that the constant friction of illiberal minds wears out at last the best resolves of the more generous. Though to be sure, when I reflected upon it, it was not strange that people entering my office should be struck by the peculiar aspect of the unaccountable Bartleby, and so be tempted to throw out some sinister observations concerning him. Sometimes an attorney, having business with me, and calling at my office, and finding no one but the scrivener there, would undertake to obtain some sort of precise information from him touching my whereabouts; but without heeding his idle talk, Bartleby would remain standing immovable in the middle of the room. So after contemplating him in that position for a time, the attorney would depart, no wiser than he came.

Also, when a reference was going on, and the room full of lawyers and witnesses, and business driving fast, some deeply-occupied legal gentleman present, seeing Bartleby wholly unemployed, would request him to run round to his (the legal gentleman's) office and fetch some papers for him. Thereupon, Bartleby would tranquilly decline, and yet remain idle as before. Then the lawyer would give a great stare, and turn to me. And what could I say? At last I was made aware that all through the circle of my professional acquaintance, a whisper of wonder was running round, having reference to the strange creature I kept at my office. This worried me very much. And as the idea came upon me of his possibly turning out a long-lived man, and keep occupying my chambers, and denying my authority; and perplexing my visitors; and scandalizing my professional reputation; and casting a general gloom over the premises; keeping soul and body together to the last upon his savings (for doubtless he spent but half a dime a day), and in the end perhaps outlive me, and claim possession of my office by right of his perpetual occupancy: as all these dark anticipations crowded upon me more and more, and my friends continually intruded their relentless remarks upon the apparition in my room; a great change was wrought in me. I resolved to gather all my faculties together, and forever rid me of this intolerable incubus.

Ere revolving any complicated project, however, adapted to this end, I first simply suggested to Bartleby the propriety of his permanent departure. In a calm and serious tone, I commended the idea to his careful and mature consideration. But, having taken three days to meditate upon it, he apprised me, that his original determination remained the same; in short, that he still preferred to abide with me.

What shall I do? I now said to myself, buttoning up my coat to the last button. What shall I do? what ought I to do? what does conscience say I *should* do with this man, or, rather, ghost. Rid myself of him, I must; go, he shall. But how? You will not thrust him, the poor, pale, passive mortal—you will not thrust such a helpless creature out of your door? you will not dishonor yourself by such cruelty? No, I will not, I cannot do that. Rather would I let him live and die here, and then mason up his remains in the wall. What, then, will you do? For all your coaxing, he will not budge. Bribes he leaves under your own paper-weight on your table; in short, it is quite plain that he prefers to cling to you.

Then something severe, something unusual must be done. What! surely you will not have him collared by a constable, and commit his innocent pallor to the common jail? And upon what ground could you procure such a thing to be done?—a vagrant, is he? What! he a vagrant, a wanderer, who refuses to budge? It is because he will *not* be a vagrant, then, that you seek to count him *as* a vagrant. That is too absurd. No visible means of support: there I have him. Wrong again: for indubitably he *does* support himself, and that is the only unanswerable proof that any man can show of his possessing the means so to do. No more, then. Since he will not quit me, I must quit him. I will change my offices; I will move elsewhere, and give him fair notice, that if I find him on my new premises I will then proceed against him as a common trespasser.

Acting accordingly, next day I thus addressed him: "I find these chambers too far from the City Hall; the air is unwholesome. In a word, I propose to remove my offices next week, and shall no longer require your services. I tell you this now, in order that you may seek another place."

He made no reply, and nothing more was said.

On the appointed day I engaged carts and men, proceeded to my chambers, and, having but little furniture, everything was removed in a few hours. Throughout, the scrivener remained standing behind the screen, which I directed to be removed the last thing. It was withdrawn; and, being folded up like a huge folio, left him the motionless occupant of a naked room. I stood in the entry watching him a moment, while something from within me upbraided me.

I re-entered, with my hand in my pocket—and—and my heart in my mouth.

"Good-by, Bartleby; I am going—good-by, and God some way bless you; and take that," slipping something in his hand. But it dropped upon the floor, and then—strange to say—I tore myself from him whom I had so longed to be rid of.

Established in my new quarters, for a day or two I kept the door locked, and started at every footfall in the passages. When I returned to my rooms, after any little absence, I would pause at the threshold for an instant, and attentively listen, ere applying my key. But these fears were needless. Bartleby never came nigh me.

I thought all was going well, when a perturbed-looking stranger visited me, inquiring whether I was the person who had recently occupied rooms at No.——Wall Street.

Full of forebodings, I replied that I was.

"Then, sir," said the stranger, who proved a lawyer, "you are responsible for the man you left there. He refuses to do any copying; he refuses to do anything; he says he prefers not to; and he refuses to quit the premises."

"I am very sorry, sir," said I, with assumed tranquillity, but an inward tremor, "but, really, the man you allude to is nothing to me—he is no relation or apprentice of mine, that you should hold me responsible for him."

"In mercy's name, who is he?"

"I certainly cannot inform you. I know nothing about him. Formerly I employed him as a copyist; but he has done nothing for me now for some time past."

"I shall settle him, then—good morning, sir."

Several days passed, and I heard nothing more; and, though I often felt a charitable prompting to call at the place and see poor Bartleby, yet a certain squeamishness, of I know not what, withheld me.

All is over with him, by this time, thought I, at last, when, through another week, no further intelligence reached me. But, coming to my room the day after, I found several persons waiting at my door in a high state of nervous excitement.

"That's the man—here he comes," cried the foremost one, whom I recognized as the lawyer who had previously called upon me alone.

"You must take him away, sir, at once," cried a portly person among them, advancing upon me, and whom I knew to be the landlord of No.—Wall Street. "These gentlemen, my tenants, cannot stand it any longer; Mr. B—," pointing to the lawyer, "has turned him out of his room, and he now persists in haunting the building generally, sitting upon the banisters of the stairs by day, and sleeping in the entry by night. Everybody is concerned; clients are leaving the offices; some fears are entertained of a mob; something you must do, and that without delay."

Aghast at this torrent, I fell back before it, and would fain have locked myself in my new quarters. In vain I persisted that Bartleby was nothing to me—no more than to any one else. In vain—I was the last person known to have anything to do with him, and they held me to the terrible account. Fearful, then, of being exposed in the papers (as one person present obscurely threatened), I considered the matter, and, at length, said, that if the lawyer would give me a confidential interview with the scrivener, in his (the lawyer's) own room, I would, that afternoon, strive my best to rid them of the nuisance they complained of.

Going up stairs to my old haunt, there was Bartleby silently sitting upon the banister at the landing.

"What are you doing here, Bartleby?" said I.

"Sitting upon the banister," he mildly replied.

I motioned him into the lawyer's room, who then left us.

"Bartleby," said I, "are you aware that you are the cause of great tribulation to me, by persisting in occupying entry after being dismissed from the office?"

No answer.

"Now one of two things must take place. Either you must do something, or something must be done to you. Now what sort of business would you like to engage in? Would you like to re-engage in copying for some one?"

"No; I would prefer not to make any change."

"Would you like a clerkship in a dry-goods store?"

"There is too much confinement about that. No, I would not like a clerkship; but I am not particular."

"Too much confinement," I cried, "why you keep yourself confined all the time!"

"I would prefer not to take a clerkship," he rejoined, as if to settle that little item at once.

"How would a bar-tender's business suit you? There is no trying of the eye-sight in that."

"I would not like it at all; though, as I said before, I am not particular."

His unwonted wordiness inspirited me. I returned to the charge.

"Well, then, would you like to travel through the country collecting bills for the merchants? That would improve your health."

"No, I would prefer to be doing something else."

"How, then, would going as a companion to Europe, to entertain some young gentleman with your conversation—how would that suit you?"

"Not at all. It does not strike me that there is anything definite about that. I like to be stationary. But I am not particular."

"Stationary you shall be, then," I cried, now losing all patience, and, for the first time in all my exasperating connection with him, fairly flying into a passion. "If you do not go away from these premises before night, I shall feel bound—indeed, I *am* bound—to—to—to quit the premises myself!" I rather absurdly concluded, knowing not with what possible threat to try to frighten his immobility into compliance. Despairing of all further efforts, I was precipitately leaving him, when a final thought occurred to me—one which had not been wholly unindulged before.

"Bartleby," said I, in the kindest tone I could assume under such exciting circumstances, "will you go home with me now—not to my office, but my dwelling—and remain there till we can conclude upon some convenient arrangement for you at our leisure? Come, let us start now, right away."

"No: at present I would prefer not to make any change at all."

I answered nothing; but, effectually dodging every one by the suddenness and rapidity of my flight, rushed from the building, ran up Wall Street towards Broadway, and, jumping into the first omnibus, was soon removed from pursuit. As soon as tranquillity returned, I distinctly perceived that I had now done all that I possibly could, both in respect to the demands of the landlord and his tenants, and with regard to my own desire and sense of duty, to benefit Bartleby, and shield him from rude persecution. I now strove to be entirely care-free and quiescent; and my conscience justified me in the attempt; though, indeed, it was not so successful as I could have wished. So fearful was I of being again hunted out by the incensed landlord and his exasperated tenants, that, surrendering my business to Nippers, for a few days, I drove about the upper part of the town and through the suburbs, in my rockaway;[15] crossed over to Jersey City

---

[15] A rockaway is a four-wheeled, two-door carriage open only in the front.

and Hoboken, and paid fugitive visits to Manhattanville and Astoria. In fact, I almost lived in my rockaway for the time.

When again I entered my office, lo, a note from the landlord lay upon the desk. I opened it with trembling hands. It informed me that the writer had sent to the police, and had Bartleby removed to the Tombs as a vagrant. Moreover, since I knew more about him than any one else, he wished me to appear at that place, and make a suitable statement of the facts. These tidings had a conflicting effect upon me. At first I was indignant; but, at last, almost approved. The landlord's energetic, summary disposition, had led him to adopt a procedure which I do not think I would have decided upon myself; and yet, as a last resort, under such peculiar circumstances, it seemed the only plan.

As I afterwards learned, the poor scrivener, when told that he must be conducted to the Tombs, offered not the slightest obstacle, but, in his pale, unmoving way, silently acquiesced.

Some of the compassionate and curious bystanders joined the party; and headed by one of the constables arm in arm with Bartleby, the silent procession filed its way through all the noise, and heat, and joy of the roaring thoroughfares at noon.

The same day I received the note, I went to the Tombs, or, to speak more properly, the Hall of Justice. Seeking the right officer, I stated the purpose of my call, and was informed that the individual I described was, indeed, within. I then assured the functionary that Bartleby was a perfectly honest man, and greatly to be compassionated, however unaccountably eccentric. I narrated all I knew, and closed by suggesting the idea of letting him remain in as indulgent confinement as possible, till something less harsh might be done—though, indeed, I hardly knew what. At all events, if nothing else could be decided upon, the almshouse must receive him. I then begged to have an interview.

Being under no disgraceful charge, and quite serene and harmless in all his ways, they had permitted him freely to wander about the prison, and, especially, in the inclosed grass-platted yards thereof. And so I found him there, standing all alone in the quietest of the yards, his face towards a high wall, while all around, from the narrow slits of the jail windows, I thought I saw peering out upon him the eyes of murderers and thieves.

"Bartleby!"

"I know you," he said without looking round—"and I want nothing to say to you."

"It was not I that brought you here, Bartleby," said I, keenly pained at his implied suspicion. "And to you, this should not be so vile a place. Nothing reproachful attaches to you by being here. And see, it is not so sad a place as one might think. Look, there is the sky, and here is the grass."

"I know where I am," he replied, but would say nothing more, and so I left him.

As I entered the corridor again, a broad mean-like man, in an apron, accosted me, and, jerking his thumb over his shoulder, said—"Is that your friend?"

"Yes."

"Does he want to starve? If he does, let him live on the prison fare, that's all."

"Who are you?" asked I, not knowing what to make of such an unofficially speaking person in such a place.

"I am the grub-man. Such gentlemen as have friends here, hire me to provide them with something good to eat."

"Is this so?" said I, turning to the turnkey.

He said it was.

"Well, then," said I, slipping some silver into the grub-man's hands (for so they called him), "I want you to give particular attention to my friend there; let him have the best dinner you can get. And you must be as polite to him as possible."

"Introduce me, will you?" said the grub-man, looking at me with an expression which seemed to say he was all impatience for an opportunity to give a specimen of his breeding.

Thinking it would prove of benefit to the scrivener, I acquiesced; and, asking the grub-man his name, went up with him to Bartleby.

"Bartleby, this is a friend; you will find him very useful to you."

"Your sarvant, sir, your sarvant," said the grub-man, making a low salutation behind his apron. "Hope you find it pleasant here, sir; nice grounds—cool apartments—hope you'll stay with us sometime—try to make it agreeable. What will you have for dinner to-day?"

"I prefer not to dine to-day," said Bartleby, turning away. "It would disagree with me; I am unused to dinners." So saying, he slowly moved to the other side of the inclosure, and took up a position fronting the dead-wall.

"How's this?" said the grub-man, addressing me with a stare of astonishment, "He's odd, ain't he?"

"I think he is a little deranged," said I, sadly.

"Deranged? deranged is it? Well, now, upon my word, I thought that friend of yourn was a gentleman forger; they are always pale and genteel-like, them forgers. I can't help pity 'em—can't help it, sir. Did you know Monroe Edwards?" he added, touchingly, and paused. Then, laying his hand piteously on my shoulder, sighed, "he died of consumption at Sing-Sing.[16] So you weren't acquainted with Monroe?"

"No, I was never socially acquainted with any forgers. But I cannot stop longer. Look to my friend yonder. You will not lose by it. I will see you again."

Some few days after this, I again obtained admission to the Tombs, and went through the corridors in quest of Bartleby; but without finding him.

"I saw him coming from his cell not long ago," said a turnkey, "may be he's gone to loiter in the yards."

So I went in that direction.

"Are you looking for the silent man?" said another turnkey, passing me.

---

[16] Sing-Sing is now the State Prison at Ossining, New York.

"Yonder he lies—sleeping in the yard there. 'Tis not twenty minutes since I saw him lie down."

The yard was entirely quiet. It was not accessible to the common prisoners. The surrounding walls, of amazing thickness, kept off all sounds behind them. The Egyptian character of the masonry weighed upon me with its gloom. But a soft imprisoned turf grew under foot. The heart of the eternal pyramids, it seemed, wherein, by some strange magic, through the clefts, grass-seed, dropped by birds, had sprung.

Strangely huddled at the base of the wall, his knees drawn up, and lying on his side, his head touching the cold stones, I saw the wasted Bartleby. But nothing stirred. I paused; then went close up to him; stooped over, and saw that his dim eyes were open; otherwise he seemed profoundly sleeping. Something prompted me to touch him. I felt his hand, when a tingling shiver ran up my arm and down my spine to my feet.

The round face of the grub-man peered upon me now. "His dinner is ready. Won't he dine to-day, either? Or does he live without dining?"

"Lives without dining," said I, and closed the eyes.

"Eh!—He's asleep, ain't he?"

"With kings and counselors," murmured I.

There would seem little need for proceeding further in this history. Imagination will readily supply the meagre recital of poor Bartleby's interment. But, ere parting with the reader, let me say, that if this little narrative has sufficiently interested him, to awaken curiosity as to who Bartleby was, and what manner of life he led prior to the present narrator's making his acquaintance, I can only reply, that in such curiosity I fully share, but am wholly unable to gratify it. Yet here I hardly know whether I should divulge one little item of rumor, which came to my ear a few months after the scrivener's decease. Upon what basis it rested, I could never ascertain; and hence, how true it is I cannot now tell. But, inasmuch as this vague report has not been without a certain suggestive interest to me, however sad, it may prove the same with some others; and so I will briefly mention it. The report was this: that Bartleby had been a subordinate clerk in the Dead Letter Office at Washington, from which he had been suddenly removed by a change in the administration. When I think over this rumor, hardly can I express the emotions which seize me. Dead letters! does it not sound like dead men? Conceive a man by nature and misfortune prone to a pallid hopelessness, can any business seem more fitted to heighten it than that of continually handling these dead letters, and assorting them for the flames? For by the cartload they are annually burned. Sometimes from out the folded paper the pale clerk takes a ring—the finger it was meant for, perhaps, moulders in the grave; a banknote sent in swiftest charity—he whom it would relieve, nor eats nor hungers any more; pardon for those who died despairing; hope for those who died unhoping; good tidings for those who died stifled by unrelieved calamities. On errands of life, these letters speed to death.

Ah, Bartleby! Ah, humanity!

11 ❦ Good and Great Fiction

If we had time enough to read all the stories ever written, perhaps we would not need to make literary judgments. But our time for reading is short. And we must decide which stories are worthiest of our effort and energy, and which writers give us the greatest insight and pleasure. In literature there is no reason to read the slipshod, the ill-conceived, the poorly made, when works of excellence are as easily available. If we hope to cultivate what is best within ourselves, we must learn to appreciate the excellent things around us. Without an appreciation of the truly excellent, we will have no way to improve.

Throughout this book we have explored the basic elements of fiction. In a good story these elements work together to produce a work of expressive efficiency. In the best stories, however, this expressive efficiency is aimed at subjects that are profound and important. In short, great literature occurs when an author's skill matches an unusually deep and meaningful experience.

Checklist of Questions for Evaluating Fiction

Below is a checklist of questions to help you evaluate stories. This checklist does not contain all the criteria that may be used for making such an evaluation, but it will provide you with a starting point. Since each story is different, each story will demand different criteria for its evaluation. However, since all stories share common qualities, this checklist will help you see certain comparative virtues.

Narrative

1. Has the story maintained a consistent narrative perspective?
2. Does the narrator's voice fit the character?
3. Has the story maintained a consistent level of reality or made smooth transitions from one level to another?

Plot

1. Are the events arranged in the most effective manner?
2. Does the story maintain narrative focus?
3. Do any framing devices complement the stories?
4. Does the conclusion develop from the action which precedes it and cast light on the earlier events?

Character

1. Are the characters consistent?
2. Are their actions well motivated?
3. Are they appropriate types of characters for the story in which they are placed, or does the story need more rounded, more fully realized characters?
4. Are their changes motivated?

Setting

1. Is the setting appropriate to the story?
2. Does it fix the action socially, psychologically, or symbolically?
3. Is the setting recognizable?
4. Are there unnecessary or repetitious details?

Style

1. Does the dialogue fit the characters who are speaking?
2. Does the narrator's word choice fit the story?
3. Has the author avoided clichés?

Personal Preference and Excellence

We all have personal preferences. We prefer chocolate over vanilla ice cream. We prefer hot dogs over hamburgers. We prefer root beer to cola. Sometimes we are so passionate about what we like that we regard anyone who doesn't share our preferences as stupid, tasteless, stubborn, or insensitive. Yet we should understand that our personal preferences are just that—personal. We can be pleased when others share our preferences, but we should not become outraged when they don't. In fact, we know that we often prefer things that are not truly excellent. For example our love of peanut butter is out of all proportion to its nutritional and culinary value, yet not a day goes by in which we don't get a craving for it.

Coming to acknowledge one's personal likes and dislikes is an important part of individual development. As teachers, we do not want to take those preferences away. However, if you are to continue to develop further, you must go beyond your personal preferences before they become a wall between you and the rest of the world. Preferences turn into prejudices. If we merely hang on to what we like, we will never discover new pleasures, insights, or experience. We will become narrow, dull, and bigoted.

We do not expect you to like every story in this book. We would find it strange if you did, and to be truthful, we don't equally enjoy all the works we have included. However, we believe that all the works in this book are worth reading and studying. Part of the educational process—indeed the very nature of education itself—is to confront people with experiences that expand their understanding of the world. Of course there is value in reading works that deal with experiences you have had. Black readers may take a special pleasure in reading works about the experiences of black people. Midwestern readers may prefer stories set in the plains. Asian-American students may have particular insight into stories with an Asian background. But if *all* we like to do is look at ourselves in the mirror of literature, then our education is little more than a form of vanity. Thus, many critics regard the best literature as works that *defamiliarize* us; that is, those works that show us either familiar experiences in a new light or unfamiliar experiences in a comprehensible manner. The best works of art stretch us, expand us, demand things of us. Consequently, they may also make us uncomfortable. Sophisticated readers learn to tolerate the discomfort of the new and challenging.

Does this mean we want you to have "good taste," which usually means to share our preferences? No. Those readers who are interested only in "good taste," who approve only of things others have already approved of, are as locked into their prejudices as the most ignorant vulgarian. Our desire is for you to develop your own standards of judgment. The educated person must find a balance between the pursuit of what is acknowledged to be excellent and the willingness to explore the unfamiliar in hopes of finding excellence. We hope that the selections in this book have provided you with the opportunity to find that balance.

Narrative Conventions

One important feature of a good story is a consistent narrative perspective. Stories may be told in either the first person, the limited third person, or the omniscient voice. But once the author has chosen a perspective, he or she must be consistent in its application. An omniscient narrator cannot claim ignorance of certain details, and a first-person narrator cannot be certain of events the narrator did not witness. Another feature of narrative consistency extends to the narrator's voice. The narrator of "My Man Bovanne" is a black woman who is much wiser than her better-educated children. Toni Cade Bambara has caught the flavor of her narrator's direct, earthy language. The voice is consistent with the character. The voice would be inconsistent if it sounded like the English woman in "Homage for Isaac Babel."

Another mark of good stories is that they usually maintain a consistent level of reality. For example, "The Canary Prince" allows all sorts of supernatural or fantastic occurrences to happen. However, in a Sherlock Holmes story no unrealistic detail is allowed to enter the story. Indeed, part of the excitement of a Sherlock Holmes mystery is Holmes's ability to provide natural explanations for the seemingly inexplicable and supernatural. Doyle would destroy the credibility of his detective if he solved a mystery in which ghosts actually appeared or gypsies could truly walk through walls. To be sure, a story occasionally begins realistically and ends supernaturally or the other way around. But the authors of such stories are careful to make the transition graceful and smooth.

Among the questions you should ask about a story's narrator are: (1) Has the author maintained a consistent narrative perspective? (2) Does the narrator's voice fit the character? and (3) Has the author maintained a consistent level of reality or made a smooth transition from one level to another?

Plot

A good story, while it may not be action-packed, should not be dull. It is more difficult to evaluate a plot than to judge if the narrative voice is consistent.

In general, one should be able to follow the action of a story. Event should follow event in a clear, logical, and interesting manner. Information that is suppressed should be suppressed to develop suspense and surprise and not out of laziness or ineptitude. The events narrated should all contribute to the effectiveness of the story. Important action should not be left out and unimportant action should not be included. In short, the narrative should be focused, concentrating attention on the most significant events, subordinating less important events and eliminating superfluous ones.

If a frame surrounds the story, the frame should complement the story to which it is attached. If the story has a twist ending, then the ending should develop from the material in the first part of the story and cast light on the significance of the earlier action.

Among the questions you should ask concerning a story's plot are: (1) Are the events arranged in the most effective manner? (2) Does the story have narrative focus? (3) Do any framing devices complement the material? (4) Does the conclusion develop from the action leading up to it and cast light on the earlier events?

Character

Consistency is important in the creation of characters. Some characters are simple or flat. They have only a limited number of character traits. Once, however, those traits have been established, they should remain the same unless the author provides motivation for the character to change. A stingy character, for example, would not pick up the tab at a restaurant *unless* there is some special reason. Good authors either provide special motivation for uncharacteristic behavior or avoid the inconsistency.

Good comic, satiric, symbolic, and adventure stories often contain only flat, simple characters. Other stories seem thin and trite unless they present at least one round or full character. A psychological story requires at least one round character. Because such characters are more difficult to create, round characters give stories special merit. Like flat characters, round characters must act consistently. But because round characters are more complex, sometimes with many incompatible sets of traits, their actions are far less predictable. For example, a round character may be stingy, but also may have the desire to be a good friend. Faced with a bill for dinner, the character on one occasion may reach for the tab and on another hope he won't be asked to pay. The actions *are* consistent, consistent with the conflict in his personality. Indeed, quite often stories focus on the means by which round characters resolve conflicts between incompatible traits in their personalities.

Among the questions you should ask when evaluating an author's handling of character are: (1) Are the characters consistent? (2) Are their actions well motivated? (3) Are they appropriate types of character for the story in which they are placed, or are they too simple, too flat, to hold our interest? (4) Are their changes understandably motivated?

Setting

An author may place a story in any locality at any time, or even out of time and in a wholly fantastic place. Yet, whatever the setting, it should not only suit the story but also contribute to the effective functioning of the tale. Details should help us locate the character socially, psychologically, or symbolically. No detail should be superfluous, and all the important details should be present.

Among the questions one should ask in evaluating a story's setting are: (1) Is the setting appropriate to the story? (2) Does it fix the action socially, psychologically, or symbolically? (3) Is the setting recognizable? (4) Are there unnecessary or repetitious details in the description of the setting?

Style

The style of a work should be appropriate to the subject matter and the characters. For example, an illiterate should not speak like a professor and a professor should not ordinarily speak like an illiterate. What the characters *say* should be as consistent with their traits as what they do. Similarly, one would not narrate a comic story in the same way that one would narrate a sad tale. Good writers alter their language to fit the subjects they are treating or the mode of fiction they are writing.

Good writers avoid worn out or trite expressions. They try to make the language of the story fresh and interesting. When good writers use clichés, it is for a specific purpose. For example, the writer may want to show the commonplace thinking of a character, or to satirize the banality of society.

Among the questions about style you should ask are: (1) Does the dialogue fit the characters who are speaking? (2) Does the narrator's word choice fit the story? (3) Has the author avoided clichés?

Perfection

Judging a literary work is especially difficult because no story is ever "perfect." The literary critic must decide whether or not the faults of a work significantly mar it. Sometimes a lifeless, dull, and trivial story will be told with few faults. Another story will bristle with life and insight despite many imperfections. Such stories make the evaluation of literature an art rather than a science. Testing the excellence of a story is not like testing the gold content in a ring. There is no precise assay of a story's value. Yet, over time, the greatest works emerge and endure while trivial, ill-planned works are forgotten. We should remember that many works are great because they broke with convention and showed fictional possibilities people had not previously recognized. The great work is exceptional and may sometimes brilliantly depart from the common conventions of literary practice. As Alexander Pope wrote:

> Great minds may sometimes gloriously offend,
> And rise to faults true critics dare not mend.

 ## *Writers on Writing* E. M. Forster

> *What is so wonderful about great literature is that it transforms the man who reads it towards the condition of the man who wrote, and brings to birth in us also the creative impulse.*

Sinclair Lewis and Anton Chekhov

The two stories which follow can help you sharpen your critical skills. They concern similar situations—couples who fall in love despite being married to others. Both stories examine how illicit love affects the characters' lives.

Both Chekhov and Lewis were highly acclaimed in their day. Sinclair Lewis, an American, won the Nobel prize for literature in 1930. The Russian Anton Chekhov was as famous for his plays as for his short fiction. By most critical opinion, one of these stories is great, while the other is merely good. Evaluate the works on your own and support your reasons for preferring one story to the other.

SINCLAIR LEWIS (1885–1951)

Virga Vay and Allan Cedar

Orlo Vay, the Chippewa Avenue Optician, Smart-Art Harlequin Tinted-Tortus Frames Our Specialty, was a public figure, as public as a cemetery. He was resentful that his profession, like that of an undertaker, a professor of art, or a

Mormon missionary, was not appreciated for its patience and technical skill, as are the callings of wholesale grocer or mistress or radio-sports-commentator, and he tried to make up for the professional injustice by developing his personal glamor.

He wanted to Belong. He was a speaker. He was hearty and public about the local baseball and hockey teams, about the Kiwanis Club, about the Mayflower Congregational Church, and about all war drives.[1] At forty-five he was bald, but the nobly glistening egg of his face and forehead, whose arc was broken only by a pair of Vay Li-Hi-Bifocals, was an adornment to all fund-raising rallies.

He urged his wife, Virga, to co-operate in his spiritual efforts, but she was a small, scared, romantic woman, ten years his junior; an admirer of passion in technicolor, a clipper-out of newspaper lyrics about love and autumn smoke upon the hills. He vainly explained to her, "In these modern days, a woman can't fritter away her time daydreaming. She has to push her own weight, and not hide it under a bushel."

Her solace was in her lover, Dr. Allan Cedar, the dentist. Together, Virga and Allan would have been a most gentle pair, small, clinging, and credulous. But they could never be openly together. They were afraid of Mr. Vay and of Allan's fat and vicious wife, Bertha, and they met at soda counters in outlying drug stores and lovingly drank black-and-whites[2] together or Jumbo Malteds and, giggling, ate ferocious banana splits; or, till wartime gasoline-rationing prevented, they sped out in Allan's coupé by twilight, and made shy, eager love in mossy pastures or, by the weak dashlight of the car, read aloud surprisingly good recent poets: Wallace Stevens, Sandburg, Robert Frost, Jeffers, T. S. Eliot, Lindsay.[3]

Allan was one of the best actors in the Masquers, and though Virga could not act, she made costumes and hung about at rehearsals, and thus they were able to meet, and to stir the suspicions of Bertha Cedar.

Mrs. Cedar was a rare type of the vicious woman; she really hated her husband, though she did not so much scold him as mock him for his effeminate love of acting, for his verses, for his cherubic mustache, and even for his skill with golden bridgework. She jeered, in the soap-reeking presence of her seven sisters and sisters-in-law, all chewing gum and adjusting their plates, that as a lover "Ally" had no staying-powers. That's what *she* thought.

She said to her mother, "Ally is a bum dentist; he hasn't got a single rich patient," and when they were at an evening party, she communicated to the festal guests, "Ally can't even pick out a necktie without asking my help," and on everything her husband said she commented, "Oh, don't be silly!"

She demanded, and received, large sympathy from all the females she knew, and as he was fond of golf and backgammon, she refused to learn either of them.

Whenever she had irritated him into jumpiness, she said judiciously, "You seem to be in a very nervous state." She picked at him about his crossword

---

[1] War drives were events organized to sell savings bonds.
[2] Black-and-whites are ice cream sodas made with vanilla ice cream and chocolate syrup, or vice versa.
[3] These poets, except for Vachel Lindsay (1879–1931), are represented in this volume.

puzzles, about his stamp-collection, until he screamed, invariably, "Oh, let me *alone!*" and then she was able to say smugly, "I don't know what's the matter with you, so touchy about every little thing. You better go to a mind-doctor and have your head examined."

Then Bertha quite unexpectedly inherited seven thousand dollars and a house in San Jose, California, from a horrible aunt. She did not suggest to her husband but told him that they would move out to that paradise for chilled Minnesotans, and he would practise there.

It occurred to Allan to murder her, but not to refuse to go along. Many American males confuse their wives and the policeman on the beat.

But he knew that it would be death for him to leave Virga Vay, and that afternoon, when Virga slipped into his office at three o'clock in response to his code telephone call of "This is the Superba Market and we're sending you three bunches of asparagus," she begged, "Couldn't we elope some place together? Maybe we could get a little farm."

"She'd find us. She has a cousin who's a private detective in Duluth."

"Yes, I guess she would. Can't we *ever* be together always?"

"There is one way—if you wouldn't be afraid."

He explained the way.

"No, I wouldn't be afraid, if you stayed right with me," she said.

Dr. Allan Cedar was an excellent amateur machinist. On a Sunday afternoon when Bertha was visiting her mother, he cut a hole through the steel bottom of the luggage compartment of his small dark-gray coupé. This compartment opened into the body of the car. That same day he stole the hose of their vacuum-cleaner and concealed it up on the rafters of their galvanized-iron garage.

On Tuesday—this was in February—he bought a blue ready-made suit at Goldenkron Brothers', on Ignatius Street. He was easy to fit, and no alterations were needed. They wanted to deliver the suit that afternoon, but he insisted, "No, hold it here for me and I'll come in and put it on tomorrow morning. I want to surprise somebody."

"Your Missus will love it, Doc," said Monty Goldenkron.

"I hope she will—when she sees it!"

He also bought three white-linen shirts and a red bow-tie, and paid cash for the lot.

"Your credit is good here, Doc—none better," protested Monty.

Allan puzzled him by the triumphant way in which he answered, "I want to keep it good, just now!"

From Goldenkrons' he walked perkily to the Emporium, to the Golden Rule drug store, to the Co-operative Dairy, paying his bills in full at each. On his way he saw a distinguished fellow-townsman, Judge Timberlane, and his pretty wife. Allan had never said ten words to either of them, but he thought affectionately, "There's a couple who are intelligent enough and warm-hearted enough to know what love is worth."

That evening he said blandly to his wife, "Strangest thing happened today. The University school of dentistry telephoned me."

"Long distance?"

"Surely."

"Well!" Her tone was less of disbelief than of disgust.

"They're having a special brush-up session for dentists and they want me to come down to Minneapolis first thing tomorrow morning to stay for three days and give instruction in bridge-work. And of course you must come along. It's too bad I'll have to work from nine in the morning till midnight—they do rush those special courses so—but you can go to the movies by yourself, or just sit comfortably in the hotel."

"No—thank—*you!*" said Bertha. "I prefer to sit here at home. Why you couldn't have been an M.D. doctor and take out gallbladders and make some real money! And I'll thank you to be home not later than Sunday morning. You know we have Sunday dinner with Mother."

He knew.

"I hope that long before that I'll be home," he said.

He told her that he would be staying at the Flora Hotel, in Minneapolis. But on Wednesday morning, after putting on the new suit at Goldenkrons', he drove to St. Paul, through light snowflakes which he thought of as fairies. "But I haven't a bit of real poet in me. Just second-rate and banal," he sighed. He tried to make a poem, and got no farther than:

It is snowing,
The wind is blowing,
But I am happy to be going.

In St. Paul he went to the small, clean Hotel Orkness, registered as "Mr. A. M. Romeo & wife," asked for a room with a double bed, and explained to the clerk, "My wife is coming by train. She should be here in about seventeen minutes now, I figure it."

He went unenthusiastically to the palsied elevator, up to their room. It was tidy, and on the wall was an Adolph Dehn[4] lithograph instead of the fake English-hunting-print that he had dreaded. He kneaded the bed with his fist. He was pleased.

Virga Vay arrived nineteen minutes later, with a bellboy carrying her new imitation-leather bag.

"So you're here, husband. Not a bad room," she said indifferently.

The bellboy knew from her indifference and from her calling the man "husband" that she was not married to him, but unstintingly in love. Such paradoxes are so common in his subterranean business that he had forgotten about Virga by the time he reached his bench in the lobby. Six stories above him, Virga and Allan were lost and blind and quivering in their kiss.

Presently she said, "Oh, you have a new suit! Turn around. Why, it fits beautifully! And such a nice red tie. You do look so young and cute in a bow-tie. Did you get it for me?"

"Of course. And then—I kind of hate to speak of it now, but I want us to get

---

[4] Adolph Dehn (1895–1968) was an American painter and printmaker from Waterville, Minnesota.

so used to the idea that we can just forget it—I don't want us to look frowsy when they find us. As if we hadn't been happy. And we *will* be—we are!"

"Yes."

"You're still game for it?"

"With you? For anything."

He was taking off the new suit; she was tenderly lifting from her bag a nightgown which she had made and embroidered this past week.

They had all their meals in the room; they did not leave it till afternoon of the next day. The air became a little close, thick from perfume and cigarette smoke and the bubble baths they took together.

Late the next afternoon they dressed and packed their bags, completely. He laid on the bureau two ten-dollar bills. They left the luggage at the foot of their bed, which she had made up. She took nothing from the room, and he nothing except a paper bag containing a bottle of Bourbon whisky, with the cork loosened, and a pocket anthology of new poetry. At the door she looked back, and said to him, "I shall remember this dear room as long as we live."

"Yes. . . . as long as we live."

He took his dark-gray coupé out of the hotel garage, tipping an amazed attendant one dollar, and they drove to Indian Mounds Park, overlooking the erratic Mississippi. He stopped in the park, at dusk, and said, "Think of the Indians that came along here, and Pike and Lewis Cass!"[5]

"They were brave," she mused.

"Brave, *too!*" They nervously laughed. Indeed, after a moment of solemnity when they had left the hotel, they had been constantly gay, laughing at everything, even when she sneezed and he piped, "No more worry about catching pneumonia!"

He drove into a small street near by and parked the car, distant from any house. Working in the half-darkness, leaving the engine running, he pushed the vacuum-cleaner hose through the hole in the bottom of the luggage compartment, wired it to the exhaust pipe, and hastily got back into the car. The windows were closed. Already the air in the car was sick-sweet with carbon monoxide.

He slipped the whisky bottle out of the paper bag and tenderly urged, "Take a swig of this. Keep your courage up."

"Dearest, I don't need anything to keep it up."

"I do, by golly. I'm not a big he-man like you, Virg!"

They both laughed, and drank from the bottle, and kissed lingeringly.

"I wonder if I could smoke a cigarette. I don't *think* C_2O_2 is explosive," he speculated.

"Oh, sweet, be careful! It *might* explode!"

"Yes, it—" Then he shouted. "Listen at us! As if we cared if we got blown up now!"

---

[5] Lewis Cass (1782–1866) was an American statesman. As Secretary of War under Andrew Jackson, he favored the removal of Indians beyond the Mississippi. Zebulon Pike (1779–1813) was an American explorer who led expeditions to find the sources of the Mississippi, Arkansas, and Red Rivers.

"Oh, I am too brainless, Allan! I don't know if you'll be able to stand me much longer."

"As long as we live, my darling, my very dear, oh, my dear love!"

"As long as we live. Together now. Together."

His head aching, his throat sore, he forgot to light the cigarette. He switched on the tiny dashlight, he lifted up the book as though it were a bar of lead, and from Conrad Aiken's [6] "Sea Holly" he began to read to her:

> It was for this
> Barren beauty, barrenness of rock that aches
> On the seaward path, seeing the fruitful sea,
> Hearing the lark of rock that sings—

He was too drowsy to read more than just the ending:

> Stone pain in the stony heart,
> The rock loved and labored; and all is lost.

The book fell to the seat, his head drooped, and his arm groped drowsily about her. She rested contentedly, in vast dreams, her head secure upon his shoulder.

Harsh screaming snatched them back from paradise. The car windows were smashed, someone was dragging them out . . . and Bertha was slapping Virga's face, while Bertha's cousin, the detective, was beating Allan's shoulders with a blackjack, to bring him to. In doing so, he broke Allan's jaw.

Bertha drove him back to Grand Republic and nursed him while he was in bed, jeering to the harpies whom she had invited in, "Ally tried to—you know—with a woman, but he was no good, and he was so ashamed he tried to kill himself."

He kept muttering, "Please go away and don't torture me."

She laughed.

Later, Bertha was able to intercept every one of the letters that Virga sent to him from Des Moines, where she had gone to work in a five-and-ten-cent store after Orlo had virtuously divorced her.

"Love! Ally is learning what that kind of mush gets you," Bertha explained to her attentive women friends.

Questions

1. Are the events of the story logically organized? Are the settings appropriate?
2. Does the ending grow logically from earlier events? Does it throw additional light on what came before, or does it merely repeat your understanding of the characters?
3. Does Lewis summarize Virga and Allan in a sentence? Are they round or flat characters?
4. Is Bertha Cedar a round or flat character?
5. Do the characters develop during the course of the story?
6. How would you evaluate this story overall?

---

[6] Conrad Aiken (1889–1973) was an American poet.

ANTON CHEKHOV (1860–1904)

Lady with Lapdog

I

The appearance on the front of a new arrival—a lady with a lapdog—became the topic of general conversation. Dimitry Dmitrich Gurov, who had been a fortnight in Yalta[1] and got used to its ways, was also interested in new arrivals. One day, sitting on the terrace of Vernet's restaurant, he saw a young woman walking along the promenade; she was fair, not very tall, and wore a toque; behind her trotted a white pomeranian.

Later he came across her in the park and in the square several times a day. She was always alone, always wearing the same toque, followed by the white pomeranian. No one knew who she was, and she became known simply as the lady with the lapdog.

"If she's here without her husband and without any friends," thought Gurov, "it wouldn't be a bad idea to strike up an acquaintance with her."

He was not yet forty, but he had a twelve-year-old daughter and two schoolboy sons. He had been married off when he was still in his second year at the university, and his wife seemed to him now to be almost twice his age. She was a tall, black-browed woman, erect, dignified, austere, and, as she liked to describe herself, a "thinking person." She was a great reader, preferred the new "advanced" spelling, called her husband by the more formal "Dimitry" and not the familiar "Dmitry"; and though he secretly considered her not particularly intelligent, narrow-minded, and inelegant, he was afraid of her and disliked being at home. He had been unfaithful to her for a long time, he was often unfaithful to her, and that was why, perhaps, he almost always spoke ill of women, and when men discussed women in his presence, he described them as *the lower breed*.

He could not help feeling that he had had enough bitter experience to have the right to call them as he pleased, but all the same without *the lower breed* he could not have existed a couple of days. He was bored and ill at ease among men, with whom he was reticent and cold, but when he was among women he felt at ease, he knew what to talk about with them and how to behave; even when he was silent in their company he experienced no feeling of constraint. There was something attractive, something elusive in his appearance, in his character and his whole person, that women found interesting and irresistible; he was aware of it, and was himself drawn to them by some irresistible force.

Long and indeed bitter experience had taught him that every new affair, which at first relieved the monotony of life so pleasantly and appeared to be such a charming and light adventure, among decent people and especially among Muscovites, who are so irresolute and so hard to rouse, inevitably developed into an extremely complicated problem and finally the whole situation became rather

---

[1] Yalta is located on the Black Sea in southwestern Russia and is one of the biggest resort areas in the Soviet Union.

cumbersome. But at every new meeting with an attractive woman he forgot all about this experience, he wanted to enjoy life so badly and it all seemed so simple and amusing.

And so one afternoon, while he was having dinner at a restaurant in the park, the woman in the toque walked in unhurriedly and took a seat at the table next to him. The way she looked, walked, and dressed, wore her hair, told him that she was of good social standing, that she was married, that she was in Yalta for the first time, that she was alone and bored. . . . There was a great deal of exaggeration in the stories about the laxity of morals among the Yalta visitors, and he dismissed them with contempt, for he knew that such stories were mostly made up by people who would gladly have sinned themselves if they had had any idea how to go about it; but when the woman sat down at the table three yards away from him he remembered these stories of easy conquests and excursions to the mountains and the tempting thought of a quick and fleeting affair, an affair with a strange woman whose very name he did not know, suddenly took possession of him.

He tried to attract the attention of the dog by calling softly to it, and when the pomeranian came up to him he shook a finger at it. The pomeranian growled. Gurov again shook a finger at it.

The woman looked up at him and immediately lowered her eyes.

"He doesn't bite," she said and blushed.

"May I give him a bone?" he asked, and when she nodded, he said amiably: "Have you been long in Yalta?"

"About five days."

"And I am just finishing my second week here."

They said nothing for the next few minutes.

"Time flies," she said without looking at him, "and yet it's so boring here."

"That's what one usually hears people saying here. A man may be living in Belev and Zhizdra or some other God-forsaken hole and he isn't bored, but the moment he comes here all you hear from him is 'Oh, it's so boring! Oh, the dust!' You'd think he'd come from Granada!"

She laughed. Then both went on eating in silence, like complete strangers; but after dinner they strolled off together, and they embarked on the light playful conversation of free and contented people who do not care where they go or what they talk about. They walked, and talked about the strange light that fell on the sea; the water was of such a soft and warm lilac, and the moon threw a shaft of gold across it. They talked about how close it was after a hot day. Gurov told her that he lived in Moscow, that he was a graduate in philology but worked in a bank, that he had at one time thought of singing in a private opera company but had given up the idea, that he owned two houses in Moscow. . . . From her he learnt that she had grown up in Petersburg, but had got married in the town of S—, where she had been living for the past two years, that she would stay another month in Yalta, and that her husband, who also needed a rest, might join her. She was quite unable to tell him what her husband's job was, whether he served in the offices of the provincial governor or the rural council, and she found this rather amusing herself. Gurov also found out that her name and patronymic were Anna Sergeyevna.

Later, in his hotel room, he thought about her and felt sure that he would meet her again the next day. It had to be. As he went to bed he remembered that she had only recently left her boarding school, that she had been a schoolgirl like his own daughter; he recalled how much diffidence and angularity there was in her laughter and her conversation with a stranger—it was probably the first time in her life she had found herself alone, in a situation when men followed her, looked at her, and spoke to her with only one secret intention, an intention she could hardly fail to guess. He remembered her slender, weak neck, her beautiful grey eyes.

"There's something pathetic about her, all the same," he thought as he fell asleep.

II

A week had passed since their first meeting. It was a holiday. It was close indoors, while in the streets a strong wind raised clouds of dust and tore off people's hats. All day long one felt thirsty, and Gurov kept going to the terrace of the restaurant, offering Anna Sergeyevna fruit drinks and ices. There was nowhere to go.

In the evening, when the wind had dropped a little, they went to the pier to watch the arrival of the steamer. There were a great many people taking a walk on the landing pier; some were meeting friends, they had bunches of flowers in their hands. It was there that two peculiarities of the Yalta smart set at once arrested attention: the middle-aged women dressed as if they were still young girls and there was a great number of generals.

Because of the rough sea the steamer arrived late, after the sun had set, and she had to swing backwards and forwards several times before getting alongside the pier. Anna Sergeyevna looked at the steamer and the passengers through her lorgnette, as though trying to make out some friends, and when she turned to Gurov her eyes were sparkling. She talked a lot, asked many abrupt questions, and immediately forgot what it was she had wanted to know; then she lost her lorgnette in the crowd of people.

The smartly dressed crowd dispersed; soon they were all gone, the wind had dropped completely, but Gurov and Anna were still standing there as though waiting to see if someone else would come off the boat. Anna Sergeyevna was no longer talking. She was smelling her flowers without looking at Gurov.

"It's a nice evening," he said. "Where shall we go now? Shall we go for a drive?"

She made no answer.

Then he looked keenly at her and suddenly put his arms round her and kissed her on the mouth. He felt the fragrance and dampness of the flowers and immediately looked round him fearfully: had anyone seen them?

"Let's go to your room," he said softly.

And both walked off quickly.

It was very close in her hotel room, which was full of the smell of the scents she had bought in a Japanese shop. Looking at her now, Gurov thought: "Life is full of strange encounters!" From his past he preserved the memory of carefree, good-natured women, whom love had made gay and who were grateful to him for the happiness he gave them, however short-lived; and of women like his wife, who made love without sincerity, with unnecessary talk, affectedly, hysterically, with such an expression, as though it were not love or passion, but something much more significant; and of two or three very beautiful, frigid women, whose faces suddenly lit up with a predatory expression, an obstinate desire to take, to snatch from life more than it could give; these were women no longer in their first youth, capricious, unreasoning, despotic, unintelligent women, and when Gurov lost interest in them, their beauty merely aroused hatred in him and the lace trimmings on their négligés looked to him then like the scales of a snake.

But here there was still the same diffidence and angularity of inexperienced youth—an awkward feeling; and there was also the impression of embarrassment, as if someone had just knocked at the door. Anna Sergeyevna, this lady with the lapdog, apparently regarded what had happened in a peculiar sort of way, very seriously, as though she had become a fallen woman—so it seemed to him, and he found it odd and disconcerting. Her features lengthened and drooped, and her long hair hung mournfully on either side of her face; she sank into thought in a despondent pose, like a woman taken in adultery in an old painting.

"It's wrong," she said. "You'll be the first not to respect me now."

There was a water-melon on the table. Gurov cut himself a slice and began to eat it slowly. At least half an hour passed in silence.

Anna Sergeyevna was very touching; there was an air of a pure, decent, naïve woman about her, a woman who had very little experience of life; the solitary candle burning on the table scarcely lighted up her face, but it was obvious that she was unhappy.

"But, darling, why should I stop respecting you?" Gurov asked. "You don't know yourself what you're saying."

"May God forgive me," she said, and her eyes filled with tears. "It's terrible."

"You seem to wish to justify yourself."

"How can I justify myself? I am a bad, despicable creature. I despise myself and have no thought of justifying myself. I haven't deceived my husband, I've deceived myself. And not only now. I've been deceiving myself for a long time. My husband is, I'm sure, a good and honest man, but, you see, he is a flunkey. I don't know what he does at his office, all I know is that he is a flunkey. I was only twenty when I married him, I was eaten up by curiosity, I wanted something better. There surely must be a different kind of life, I said to myself. I wanted to live. To live, to live! I was burning with curiosity. I don't think you know what I am talking about, but I swear I could no longer control myself, something was happening to me, I could not be held back, I told my husband I was ill, and I came here. . . . Here too I was going about as though in a daze, as though I was mad, and now I've become a vulgar worthless woman whom everyone has a right to despise."

Gurov could not help feeling bored as he listened to her; he was irritated by her naïve tone of voice and her repentance, which was so unexpected and so out of place; but for the tears in her eyes, he might have thought that she was joking or play-acting.

"I don't understand," he said gently, "what it is you want."

She buried her face on his chest and clung close to him.

"Please, please believe me," she said. "I love a pure, honest life. I hate immorality. I don't know myself what I am doing. The common people say 'the devil led her astray.' I too can now say about myself that the devil has led me astray."

"There, there . . ." he murmured.

He gazed into her staring, frightened eyes, kissed her, spoke gently and affectionately to her, and gradually she calmed down and her cheerfulness returned; both of them were soon laughing.

Later, when they went out, there was not a soul on the promenade, the town with its cypresses looked quite dead, but the sea was still roaring and dashing itself against the shore; a single launch tossed on the waves, its lamp flickering sleepily.

They hailed a cab and drove to Oreanda.

"I've just found out your surname, downstairs in the lobby," said Gurov. "Von Diederitz. Is your husband a German?"

"No. I believe his grandfather was German. He is of the Orthodox faith himself."

In Oreanda they sat on a bench not far from the church, looked down on the sea, and were silent. Yalta could scarcely be seen through the morning mist. White clouds lay motionless on the mountain tops. Not a leaf stirred on the trees, the cicadas chirped, and the monotonous, hollow roar of the sea, coming up from below, spoke of rest, of eternal sleep awaiting us all. The sea had roared like that down below when there was no Yalta or Oreanda, it was roaring now, and it would go on roaring as indifferently and hollowly when we were here no more. And in this constancy, in this complete indifference to the life and death of each one of us, there is perhaps hidden the guarantee of our eternal salvation, the never-ceasing movement of life on earth, the never-ceasing movement towards perfection. Sitting beside a young woman who looked so beautiful at the break of day, soothed and enchanted by the sight of all that fairy-land scenery—the sea, the mountains, the clouds, the wide sky—Gurov reflected that, when you came to think of it, everything in the world was really beautiful, everything but our own thoughts and actions when we lose sight of the higher aims of existence and our dignity as human beings.

Someone walked up to them, a watchman probably, looked at them, and went away. And there seemed to be something mysterious and also beautiful in this fact, too. They could see the Theodosia boat coming towards the pier, lit up by the sunrise, and with no lights.

"There's dew on the grass," said Anna Sergeyevna, breaking the silence.

"Yes. Time to go home."

They went back to the town.

After that they met on the front every day at twelve o'clock, had lunch and dinner together, went for walks, admired the sea. She complained of sleeping badly and of her heart beating uneasily, asked the same questions, alternately worried by feelings of jealousy and by fear that he did not respect her sufficiently. And again and again in the park or in the square, when there was no one in sight, he would draw her to him and kiss her passionately. The complete idleness, these kisses in broad daylight, always having to look round for fear of someone watching them, the heat, the smell of the sea, and the constant looming into sight of idle, well-dressed, and well-fed people seemed to have made a new man of him; he told Anna Sergeyevna that she was beautiful, that she was desirable, made passionate love to her, never left her side, while she was often lost in thought and kept asking him to admit that he did not really respect her, that he was not in the least in love with her and only saw in her a vulgar woman. Almost every night they drove out of town, to Oreanda or to the waterfall; the excursion was always a success, and every time their impressions were invariably grand and beautiful.

They kept expecting her husband to arrive. But a letter came from him in which he wrote that he was having trouble with his eyes and implored his wife to return home as soon as possible. Anna Sergeyevna lost no time in getting ready for her journey home.

"It's a good thing I'm going," she said to Gurov. "It's fate."

She took a carriage to the railway station, and he saw her off. The drive took a whole day. When she got into the express train, after the second bell, she said:

"Let me have another look at you. . . . One last look. So."

She did not cry, but looked sad, just as if she were ill, and her face quivered.

"I'll be thinking of you, remembering you," she said. "Good-bye. You're staying, aren't you? Don't think badly of me. We are parting for ever. Yes, it must be so, for we should never have met. Well, good-bye. . . ."

The train moved rapidly out of the station; its lights soon disappeared, and a minute later it could not even be heard, just as though everything had conspired to put a quick end to this sweet trance, this madness. And standing alone on the platform gazing into the dark distance, Gurov listened to the churring of the grasshoppers and the humming of the telegraph wires with a feeling as though he had just woken up. He told himself that this had been just one more affair in his life, just one more adventure, and that it too was over, leaving nothing but a memory. He was moved and sad, and felt a little penitent that the young woman, whom he would never see again, had not been happy with him; he had been amiable and affectionate with her, but all the same in his behaviour to her, in the tone of his voice and in his caresses, there was a suspicion of light irony, the somewhat coarse arrogance of the successful male, who was, moreover, almost twice her age. All the time she called him good, wonderful, high-minded; evidently she must have taken him to be quite different from what he really was, which meant that he had involuntarily deceived her.

At the railway station there was already a whiff of autumn in the air; the evening was chilly.

"Time I went north too," thought Gurov, as he walked off the platform. "High time!"

III

At home in Moscow everything was already like winter: the stoves were heated, and it was still dark in the morning when the children were getting ready to go to school and having breakfast, so that the nurse had to light the lamp for a short time. The frosts had set in. When the first snow falls and the first day one goes out for a ride in a sleigh, one is glad to see the white ground, the white roofs, the air is so soft and wonderful to breathe, and one remembers the days of one's youth. The old lime trees and birches, white with rime, have such a benignant look, they are nearer to one's heart than cypresses and palms, and beside them one no longer wants to think of mountains and the sea.

Gurov had been born and bred in Moscow, and he returned to Moscow on a fine frosty day; and when he put on his fur coat and warm gloves and took a walk down Petrovka Street, and when on Saturday evening he heard the church bells ringing, his recent holiday trip and the places he had visited lost their charm for him. Gradually he became immersed in Moscow life, eagerly reading three newspapers a day and declaring that he never read Moscow papers on principle. Once more he could not resist the attraction of restaurants, clubs, banquets, and anniversary celebrations, and once more he felt flattered that well-known lawyers and actors came to see him and that in the Medical Club he played cards with a professor as his partner. Once again he was capable of eating a whole portion of the Moscow speciality of sour cabbage and meat served in a frying-pan.

Another month and, he thought, nothing but a memory would remain of Anna Sergeyevna; he would remember her as through a haze and only occasionally dream of her with a wistful smile, as he did of the others before her. But over a month passed, winter was at its height, and he remembered her as clearly as though he had only parted from her the day before. His memories haunted him more and more persistently. Every time the voices of his children doing their homework reached him in his study in the stillness of the evening, every time he heard a popular song or some music in a restaurant, every time the wind howled in the chimney—it all came back to him: their walks on the pier, early morning with the mist on the mountains, the Theodosia boat, and the kisses. He kept pacing the room for hours remembering it all and smiling, and then his memories turned into daydreams and the past mingled in his imagination with what was going to happen. He did not dream of Anna Sergeyevna, she accompanied him everywhere like his shadow and followed him wherever he went. Closing his eyes, he saw her as clearly as if she were before him, and she seemed to him lovelier, younger, and tenderer than she had been;

and he thought that he too was much better than he had been in Yalta. In the evenings she gazed at him from the bookcase, from the fireplace, from the corner—he heard her breathing, the sweet rustle of her dress. In the street he followed women with his eyes, looking for anyone who resembled her. . . .

He was beginning to be overcome by an overwhelming desire to share his memories with someone. But at home it was impossible to talk of his love, and outside his home there was no one he could talk to. Not the tenants who lived in his house, and certainly not his colleagues in the bank. And what was he to tell them? Had he been in love then? Had there been anything beautiful, poetic, edifying, or even anything interesting about his relations with Anna Sergeyevna? So he had to talk in general terms about love and women, and no one guessed what he was driving at, and his wife merely raised her black eyebrows and said:

"Really, Dimitry, the role of a coxcomb doesn't suit you at all!"

One evening, as he left the Medical Club with his partner, a civil servant, he could not restrain himself, and said:

"If you knew what a fascinating woman I met in Yalta!"

The civil servant got into his sleigh and was about to be driven off, but suddenly he turned round and called out:

"I say!"

"Yes?"

"You were quite right: the sturgeon *was* a bit off."

These words, so ordinary in themselves, for some reason hurt Gurov's feelings: they seemed to him humiliating and indecent. What savage manners! What faces! What stupid nights! What uninteresting, wasted days! Crazy gambling at cards, gluttony, drunkenness, endless talk about one and the same thing. Business that was of no use to anyone and talk about one and the same thing absorbed the greater part of one's time and energy, and what was left in the end was a sort of dock-tailed, barren life, a sort of nonsensical existence, and it was impossible to escape from it, just as though you were in a lunatic asylum or a convict chain-gang!

Gurov lay awake all night, fretting and fuming, and had a splitting headache the whole of the next day. The following nights too he slept badly, sitting up in bed thinking, or walking up and down his room. He was tired of his children, tired of the bank, he did not feel like going out anywhere or talking about anything.

In December, during the Christmas holidays, he packed his things, told his wife that he was going to Petersburg to get a job for a young man he knew, and set off for the town of S—. Why? He had no very clear idea himself. He wanted to see Anna Sergeyevna, to talk to her, to arrange a meeting, if possible.

He arrived in S—in the morning and took the best room in a hotel, with a fitted carpet of military grey cloth and an inkstand grey with dust on the table, surmounted by a horseman with raised hand and no head. The hall porter supplied him with all the necessary information: Von Diederitz lived in a house of his own in Old Potter's Street, not far from the hotel. He lived well, was rich, kept his own carriage horses, the whole town knew him. The hall-porter pronounced the name: Dridiritz.

Gurov took a leisurely walk down Old Potter's Street and found the house. In front of it was a long grey fence studded with upturned nails.

"A fence like that would make anyone wish to run away," thought Gurov, scanning the windows and the fence.

As it was a holiday, he thought, her husband was probably at home. It did not matter either way, though, for he could not very well embarrass her by calling at the house. If he were to send in a note it might fall into the hands of the husband and ruin everything. The best thing was to rely on chance. And he kept walking up and down the street and along the fence, waiting for his chance. He watched a beggar enter the gate and the dogs attack him; then, an hour later, he heard the faint indistinct sounds of a piano. That must have been Anna Sergeyevna playing. Suddenly the front door opened and an old woman came out, followed by the familiar white pomeranian. Gurov was about to call to the dog, but his heart began to beat violently and in his excitement he could not remember its name.

He went on walking up and down the street, hating the grey fence more and more, and he was already saying to himself that Anna Sergeyevna had forgotten him and had perhaps been having a good time with someone else, which was indeed quite natural for a young woman who had to look at that damned fence from morning till night. He went back to his hotel room and sat on the sofa for a long time, not knowing what to do, then he had dinner and after dinner a long sleep.

"How stupid and disturbing it all is," he thought, waking up and staring at the dark windows: it was already evening. "Well, I've had a good sleep, so what now? What am I going to do tonight?"

He sat on a bed covered by a cheap grey blanket looking exactly like a hospital blanket, and taunted himself in vexation:

"A *lady* with a lapdog! Some adventure, I must say! Serves you right!"

At the railway station that morning he had noticed a poster announcing in huge letters the first performance of *The Geisha Girl* at the local theatre. He recalled it now, and decided to go to the theatre.

"Quite possibly she goes to first nights," he thought.

The theatre was full. As in all provincial theatres, there was a mist over the chandeliers and the people in the gallery kept up a noisy and excited conversation; in the first row of the stalls stood the local dandies with their hands crossed behind their backs; here, too, in the front seat of the Governor's box, sat the Governor's daughter, wearing a feather boa, while the Governor himself hid modestly behind the portière so that only his hands were visible; the curtain stirred, the orchestra took a long time tuning up. Gurov scanned the audience eagerly as they filed in and occupied their seats.

Anna Sergeyevna came in too. She took her seat in the third row, and when Gurov glanced at her his heart missed a beat and he realized clearly that there was no one in the world nearer and dearer or more important to him than that little woman with the stupid lorgnette in her hand, who was in no way remarkable. That woman lost in a provincial crowd now filled his whole life, was his misfortune, his joy, and the only happiness that he wished for himself. Listening to the bad orchestra and the wretched violins played by second-rate musicians, he thought how beautiful she was. He thought and dreamed.

A very tall, round-shouldered young man with small whiskers had come in with Anna Sergeyevna and sat down beside her; he nodded at every step he took and seemed to be continually bowing to someone. This was probably her husband, whom in a fit of bitterness at Yalta she had called a flunkey. And indeed there was something of a lackey's obsequiousness in his lank figure, his whiskers, and the little bald spot on the top of his head. He smiled sweetly, and the gleaming insignia of some scientific society which he wore in his buttonhole looked like the number on a waiter's coat.

In the first interval the husband went out to smoke and she was left in her seat. Gurov, who also had a seat in the stalls, went up to her and said in a trembling voice and with a forced smile:

"Good evening!"

She looked up at him and turned pale, then looked at him again in panic, unable to believe her eyes, clenching her fan and lorgnette in her hand and apparently trying hard not to fall into a dead faint. Both were silent. She sat and he stood, frightened by her embarrassment and not daring to sit down beside her. The violinists and the flautist began tuning their instruments, and they suddenly felt terrified, as though they were being watched from all the boxes. But a moment later she got up and walked rapidly towards one of the exits; he followed her, and both of them walked aimlessly along corridors and up and down stairs. Figures in all sorts of uniforms—lawyers, teachers, civil servants, all wearing badges—flashed by them; ladies, fur coats hanging on pegs, the cold draught bringing with it the odour of cigarette-ends. Gurov, whose heart was beating violently, thought:

"Oh Lord, what are all these people, that orchestra, doing here?"

At that moment he suddenly remembered how after seeing Anna Sergeyevna off he had told himself that evening at the station that all was over and that they would never meet again. But how far they still were from the end!

She stopped on a dark, narrow staircase with a notice over it: "To the Upper Circle."

"How you frightened me!" she said, breathing heavily, still looking pale and stunned. "Oh dear, how you frightened me! I'm scarcely alive. Why did you come? Why?!"

"But, please, try to understand, Anna," he murmured hurriedly. "I beg you, please, try to understand. . . ."

She looked at him with fear, entreaty, love, looked at him intently, so as to fix his features firmly in her mind.

"I've suffered so much," she went on, without listening to him. "I've been thinking of you all the time. The thought of you kept me alive. And yet I tried so hard to forget you—why, oh why did you come?"

On the landing above two schoolboys were smoking and looking down, but Gurov did not care. He drew Anna Sergeyevna towards him and began kissing her face, her lips, her hands.

"What are you doing? What are you doing?" she said in horror, pushing him away. "We've both gone mad. You must go back tonight, this minute. I implore you, by all that's sacred . . . Somebody's coming!"

Somebody was coming up the stairs.

"You must go back," continued Anna Sergeyevna in a whisper. "Do you hear? I'll come to you in Moscow. I've never been happy, I'm unhappy now, and I shall never be happy, never! So please don't make me suffer still more. I swear I'll come to you in Moscow. But now you must part. Oh, my sweet, my darling, we must part!"

She pressed his hand and went quickly down the stairs, looking back at him all the time, and he could see from the expression in her eyes that she really was unhappy. Gurov stood listening for a short time, and when all was quiet he went to look for his coat and left the theatre.

IV

Anna Sergeyevna began going to Moscow to see him. Every two or three months she left the town of S—, telling her husband that she was going to consult a Moscow gynaecologist, and her husband believed and did not believe her. In Moscow she stayed at the Slav Bazaar and immediately sent a porter in a red cap to inform Gurov of her arrival. Gurov went to her hotel, and no one in Moscow knew about it.

One winter morning he went to her hotel as usual (the porter had called with his message at his house the evening before, but he had not been in). He had his daughter with him, and he was glad of the opportunity of taking her to school, which was on the way to the hotel. Snow was falling in thick wet flakes.

"It's three degrees above zero," Gurov was saying to his daughter, "and yet it's snowing. But then, you see, it's only warm on the earth's surface, in the upper layers of the atmosphere the temperature's quite different."

"Why isn't there any thunder in winter, Daddy?"

He explained that, too. As he was speaking, he kept thinking that he was going to meet his mistress and not a living soul knew about it. He led a double life: one for all who were interested to see, full of conventional truth and conventional deception, exactly like the lives of his friends and acquaintances; and another which went on in secret. And by a kind of strange concatenation of circumstances, possibly quite by accident, everything that was important, interesting, essential, everything about which he was sincere and did not deceive himself, everything that made up the quintessence of his life, went on in secret, while everything that was a lie, everything that was merely the husk in which he hid himself to conceal the truth, like his work at the bank, for instance, his discussions at the club, his ideas of the lower breed, his going to anniversary functions with his wife—all that happened in the sight of all. He judged others by himself, did not believe what he saw, and was always of the opinion that every man's real and most interesting life went on in secret, under cover of night. The personal, private life of an individual was kept a secret, and perhaps that was partly the reason why civilized man was so anxious that his personal secrets should be respected.

Having seen his daughter off to her school, Gurov went to the Slav Bazaar. He took off his fur coat in the cloakroom, went upstairs, and knocked softly on the door. Anna Sergeyevna, wearing the grey dress he liked most, tired out by her journey and by the suspense of waiting for him, had been expecting him since the evening before; she was pale, looked at him without smiling, but was in his arms the moment he went into the room. This kiss was long and lingering, as if they had not seen each other for two years.

"Well," he asked, "how are you getting on there? Anything new?"

"Wait, I'll tell you in a moment. . . . I can't . . ."

She could not speak because she was crying. She turned away from him and pressed her handkerchief to her eyes.

"Well, let her have her cry," he thought, sitting down in an armchair. "I'll wait."

Then he rang the bell and ordered tea; while he was having his tea, she was still standing there with her face to the window. She wept because she could not control her emotions, because she was bitterly conscious of the fact that their life was so sad: they could only meet in secret, they had to hide from people, like thieves! Was not their life ruined?

"Please, stop crying!" he said.

It was quite clear to him that their love would not come to an end for a long time, if ever. Anna Sergeyevna was getting attached to him more and more strongly, she worshipped him, and it would have been absurd to tell her that all this would have to come to an end one day. She would not have believed it, anyway.

He went up to her and took her by the shoulders, wishing to be nice to her, to make her smile; and at that moment he caught sight of himself in the looking glass.

His hair was already beginning to turn grey. It struck him as strange that he should have aged so much, that he should have lost his good looks in the last few years. The shoulders on which his hands lay were warm and quivering. He felt so sorry for this life, still so warm and beautiful, but probably soon to fade and wilt like his own. Why did she love him so? To women he always seemed different from what he was, and they loved in him not himself, but the man their imagination conjured up and whom they had eagerly been looking for all their lives; and when they discovered their mistake they still loved him. And not one of them had ever been happy with him. Time had passed, he had met women, made love to them, parted from them, but not once had he been in love; there had been everything between them, but no love.

It was only now, when his hair was beginning to turn grey, that he had fallen in love properly, in good earnest—for the first time in his life.

He and Anna Sergeyevna loved each other as people do who are very dear and near, as man and wife or close friends love each other; they could not help feeling that fate itself had intended them for one another, and they were unable to understand why he should have a wife and she a husband; they were like two migrating birds, male and female, who had been caught and forced to live in separate cages. They had forgiven each other what they had been ashamed of in the past, and forgave each other everything in their present, and felt that this love of theirs had changed them both.

Before, when he felt depressed, he had comforted himself by all sorts of arguments that happened to occur to him on the spur of the moment, but now he had more serious things to think of, he felt profound compassion, he longed to be sincere, tender. . . .

"Don't cry, my sweet," he said. "That'll do, you've had your cry. . . . Let's talk now, let's think of something."

Then they had a long talk. They tried to think how they could get rid of the necessity of hiding, telling lies, living in different towns, not seeing one another for so long. How were they to free themselves from their intolerable chains?

"How? How?" he asked himself, clutching at his head. "How?"

And it seemed to them that in only a few more minutes a solution would be found and a new, beautiful life would begin; but both of them knew very well that the end was still a long, long way away and that the most complicated and difficult part was only just beginning.

Questions

1. Does Chekhov summarize Gurov in a sentence? Can you?
2. Does Chekhov summarize Anna Sergeyevna in a sentence? Can you?
3. Does the conclusion grow out of the previous incidents? Does it throw a revealing light on what has come before?
4. Is Chekhov's implicit judgment of Anna and Gurov overly simple? Does he unquestioningly approve or disapprove of their relationship?
5. Are any incidents in the story superfluous?
6. Does Chekhov leave out any scene that would be helpful?
7. What is your overall appraisal of this story?

12 ❦ Stories for Further Reading

JAMES BALDWIN (1924–1987)

Sonny's Blues

I read about it in the paper, in the subway, on my way to work. I read it, and I couldn't believe it, and I read it again. Then perhaps I just stared at it, at the newsprint spelling out his name, spelling out the story. I stared at it in the swinging lights of the subway car, and in the faces and bodies of the people, and in my own face, trapped in the darkness which roared outside.

It was not to be believed and I kept telling myself that as I walked from the subway station to the high school. And at the same time I couldn't doubt it. I was scared, scared for Sonny. He became real to me again. A great block of ice got settled in my belly and kept melting there slowly all day long, while I taught my classes algebra. It was a special kind of ice. It kept melting, sending trickles of ice water all up and down my veins, but it never got less. Sometimes it hardened and seemed to expand until I felt my guts were going to come spilling out or that I was going to choke or scream. This would always be at a moment when I was remembering some specific thing Sonny had once said or done.

When he was about as old as the boys in my classes his face had been bright and open, there was a lot of copper in it; and he'd had wonderfully direct brown eyes, and great gentleness and privacy. I wondered what he looked like now. He had been picked up, the evening before, in a raid on an apartment downtown, for peddling and using heroin.

I couldn't believe it: but what I mean by that is that I couldn't find any room for it anywhere inside me. I had kept it outside me for a long time. I hadn't wanted to know. I had had suspicions, but I didn't name them, I kept putting them away. I told myself that Sonny was wild, but he wasn't crazy. And he'd always been a good boy, he hadn't ever turned hard or evil or disrespectful, the

James Baldwin (*Photograph* © 1983 *Jill Krementz*)

way kids can, so quick, so quick, especially in Harlem. I didn't want to believe that I'd ever see my brother going down, coming to nothing, all that light in his face gone out, in the condition I'd already seen so many others. Yet it had happened and here I was, talking about algebra to a lot of boys who might, every one of them for all I knew, be popping off needles every time they went to the head.[1] Maybe it did more for them than algebra could.

I was sure that the first time Sonny had ever had horse,[2] he couldn't have been much older than these boys were now. These boys, now, were living as we'd been living then, they were growing up with a rush and their heads bumped abruptly against the low ceiling of their actual possibilities. They were filled with rage. All they really knew were two darknesses, the darkness of their lives, which was now closing in on them, and the darkness of the movies, which had blinded them to that other darkness, and in which they now, vindictively, dreamed, at once more together than they were at any other time, and more alone.

When the last bell rang, the last class ended, I let out my breath. It seemed I'd been holding it for all that time. My clothes were wet—I may have looked as though I'd been sitting in a steam bath, all dressed up, all afternoon. I sat alone in the classroom a long time. I listened to the boys outside, downstairs, shouting and cursing and laughing. Their laughter struck me for perhaps the first time. It was not the joyous laughter which—God knows why—one associates with children. It was mocking and insular, its intent was to denigrate. It was disenchanted, and in this, also, lay the authority of their curses. Perhaps I was

---

[1] Head is slang for bathroom.
[2] Horse is slang for heroin.

listening to them because I was thinking about my brother and in them I heard my brother. And myself.

One boy was whistling a tune, at once very complicated and very simple, it seemed to be pouring out of him as though he were a bird, and it sounded very cool and moving through all that harsh, bright air, only just holding its own through all those other sounds.

I stood up and walked over to the window and looked down into the courtyard. It was the beginning of the spring and the sap was rising in the boys. A teacher passed through them every now and again, quickly, as though he or she couldn't wait to get out of that courtyard, to get those boys out of their sight and off their minds. I started collecting my stuff. I thought I'd better get home and talk to Isabel.

The courtyard was almost deserted by the time I got downstairs. I saw this boy standing in the shadow of a doorway, looking just like Sonny. I almost called his name. Then I saw that it wasn't Sonny, but somebody we used to know, a boy from around our block. He'd been Sonny's friend. He'd never been mine, having been too young for me, and, anyway, I'd never liked him. And now, even though he was a grown-up man, he still hung around that block, still spent hours on the street corner, was always high and raggy. I used to run into him from time to time and he'd often work around to asking me for a quarter or fifty cents. He always had some real good excuse, too, and I always gave it to him, I don't know why.

But now, abruptly, I hated him. I couldn't stand the way he looked at me, partly like a dog, partly like a cunning child. I wanted to ask him what the hell he was doing in the school courtyard.

He sort of shuffled over to me, and he said, "I see you got the papers. So you already know about it."

"You mean about Sonny? Yes, I already know about it. How come they didn't get you?"

He grinned. It made him repulsive and it also brought to mind what he'd looked like as a kid. "I wasn't there. I stay away from them people."

"Good for you." I offered him a cigarette and I watched him through the smoke. "You come all the way down here just to tell me about Sonny?"

"That's right." He was sort of shaking his head and his eyes looked strange, as though they were about to cross. The bright sun deadened his damp dark brown skin and it made his eyes look yellow and showed up the dirt in his conked hair.[3] He smelled funky. I moved a little away from him and I said, "Well, thanks. But I already know about it and I got to get home."

"I'll walk you a little ways," he said. We started walking. There were a couple of kids still loitering in the courtyard and one of them said good night to me and looked strangely at the boy beside me.

"What're you going to do?" he asked me. "I mean, about Sonny."

"Look. I haven't seen Sonny for over a year, I'm not sure I'm going to do anything. Anyway, what the hell *can* I do?"

---

[3] Conked hair is hair that has been straightened and greased.

"That's right," he said quickly, "ain't nothing you can do. Can't much help old Sonny no more, I guess."

It was what I was thinking and so it seemed to me he had no right to say it.

"I'm surprised at Sonny, though," he went on—he had a funny way of talking, he looked straight ahead as though he were talking to himself— "I thought Sonny was a smart boy, I thought he was too smart to get hung."

"I guess he thought so too," I said sharply, "and that's how he got hung. And how about you? You're pretty goddam smart, I bet."

Then he looked directly at me, just for a minute. "I ain't smart," he said. "If I was smart, I'd have reached for a pistol a long time ago."

"Look. Don't tell *me* your sad story, if it was up to me, I'd give you one." Then I felt guilty—guilty, probably, for never having supposed that the poor bastard *had* a story of his own, much less a sad one, and I asked, quickly, "What's going to happen to him now?"

He didn't answer this. He was off by himself some place. "Funny thing," he said, and from his tone we might have been discussing the quickest way to get to Brooklyn, "when I saw the papers this morning, the first thing I asked myself was if I had anything to do with it. I felt sort of responsible."

I began to listen more carefully. The subway station was on the corner, just before us, and I stopped. He stopped, too. We were in front of a bar and he ducked slightly, peering in, but whoever he was looking for didn't seem to be there. The juke box was blasting away with something black and bouncy and I half watched the barmaid as she danced her way from the juke box to her place behind the bar. And I watched her face as she laughingly responded to something someone said to her, still keeping time to the music. When she smiled one saw the little girl, one sensed the doomed, still-struggling woman beneath the battered face of the semi-whore.

"I never *give* Sonny nothing," the boy said finally, "but a long time ago I come to school high and Sonny asked me how it felt." He paused, I couldn't bear to watch him, I watched the barmaid, and I listened to the music which seemed to be causing the pavement to shake. "I told him it felt great." The music stopped, the barmaid paused, and watched the juke box until the music began again. "It did."

All this was carrying me some place I didn't want to go. I certainly didn't want to know how it felt. It filled everything, the people, the houses, the music, the dark, quicksilver barmaid, the menace; and this menace was their reality.

"What's going to happen to him now?" I asked again.

"They'll send him away some place and they'll try to cure him." He shook his head. "Maybe he'll even think he's kicked the habit. Then they'll turn him loose"—he gestured, throwing his cigarette into the gutter. "That's all."

"What do you mean, that's *all*?"

But I knew what he meant.

"I *mean*, that's *all*." He turned his head and looked at me, pulling down the corners of his mouth. "Don't you know what I mean?" he asked softly.

"How the hell *would* I know what you mean?" I almost whispered it, I don't know why.

"That's right," he said to the air, "how would *he* know what I mean?" He turned toward me again, patient and calm, and yet I somehow felt him shaking, shaking as though he were going to fall apart. I felt that ice in my guts again, the dread I'd felt all afternoon; and again I watched the barmaid, moving about the bar, washing glasses, and singing. "Listen. They'll let him out and then it'll just start all over again. That's what I mean."

"You mean—they'll let him out. And then he'll just start working his way back in again. You mean he'll never kick the habit. Is that what you mean?"

"That's right," he said, cheerfully. "*You* see what I mean."

"Tell me," I said at last, "why does he want to die? He must want to die, he's killing himself, why does he want to die?"

He looked at me in surprise. He licked his lips. "He don't want to die. He wants to live. Don't nobody want to die, ever."

Then I wanted to ask him—too many things. He could not have answered, or if he had, I could not have borne the answers. I started walking. "Well, I guess it's none of my business."

"It's going to be rough on old Sonny," he said. We reached the subway station. "This is your station?" he asked. I nodded. I took one step down. "Damn!" he said, suddenly. I looked up at him. He grinned again. "Damn if I didn't leave all my money home. You ain't got a dollar on you, have you? Just for a couple of days is all."

All at once something inside gave and threatened to come pouring out of me. I didn't hate him any more. I felt that in another moment I'd start crying like a child.

"Sure," I said. "Don't sweat." I looked in my wallet and didn't have a dollar, I only had a five. "Here," I said. "That hold you?"

He didn't look at it—he didn't want to look at it. A terrible, closed look came over his face, as though he were keeping the number on the bill a secret from him and me. "Thanks," he said, and now he was dying to see me go. "Don't worry about Sonny. Maybe I'll write him or something."

"Sure," I said. "You do that. So long."

"Be seeing you," he said. I went on down the steps.

And I didn't write Sonny or send him anything for a long time. When I finally did, it was just after my little girl died, he wrote me back a letter which made me feel like a bastard.

Here's what he said:

DEAR BROTHER,

You don't know how much I needed to hear from you. I wanted to write you many a time but I dug how much I must have hurt you and so I didn't write. But now I feel like a man who's been trying to climb up out of some deep, real deep and funky hole and just saw the sun up there, outside. I got to get outside.

I can't tell you much about how I got here. I mean I don't know how to tell you. I guess I was afraid of something or I was trying to escape from something and you know I have never been very strong in the head (smile). I'm glad Mama and Daddy are dead and can't see what's happened to their son and I swear if I'd known what I was doing I would never have hurt you so, you and a lot of other fine people who were nice to me and who believed in me.

I don't want you to think it had anything to do with me being a musician. It's more than that. Or maybe less than that. I can't get anything straight in my head down here and I try not to think about what's going to happen to me when I get outside again. Sometime I think I'm going to flip and *never* get outside and sometime I think I'll come straight back. I tell you one thing, though, I'd rather blow my brains out than go through this again. But that's what they all say, so they tell me. If I tell you when I'm coming to New York and if you could meet me, I sure would appreciate it. Give my love to Isabel and the kids and I was sorry to hear about little Gracie. I wish I could be like Mama and say the Lord's will be done, but I don't know it seems to me that trouble is the one thing that never does get stopped and I don't know what good it does to blame it on the Lord. But maybe it does some good if you believe it.

Your brother,

SONNY

Then I kept in constant touch with him and I sent him whatever I could and I went to meet him when he came back to New York. When I saw him many things I thought I had forgotten came flooding back to me. This was because I had begun, finally, to wonder about Sonny, about the life that Sonny lived inside. This life, whatever it was, had made him older and thinner and it had deepened the distant stillness in which he had always moved. He looked very unlike my baby brother. Yet, when he smiled, when we shook hands, the baby brother I'd never known looked out from the depths of his private life, like an animal waiting to be coaxed into the light.

"How you been keeping?" he asked me.

"All right. And you?"

"Just fine." He was smiling all over his face. "It's good to see you again."

"It's good to see you."

The seven years' difference in our ages lay between us like a chasm: I wondered if these years would ever operate between us as a bridge. I was remembering, and it made it hard to catch my breath, that I had been there when he was born; and I had heard the first words he had ever spoken. When he started to walk, he walked from our mother straight to me. I caught him just before he fell when he took the first steps he ever took in this world.

"How's Isabel?"

"Just fine. She's dying to see you."

"And the boys?"

"They're fine, too. They're anxious to see their uncle."

"Oh, come on. You know they don't remember me."

"Are you kidding? Of course they remember you."

He grinned again. We got into a taxi. We had a lot to say to each other, far too much to know how to begin.

As the taxi began to move, I asked, "You still want to go to India?"

He laughed. "You still remember that. Hell, no. This place is Indian enough for me."

"It used to belong to them," I said.

And he laughed again. "They damn sure knew what they were doing when they got rid of it."

Years ago, when he was around fourteen, he'd been all hipped on the idea of going to India. He read books about people sitting on rocks, naked, in all kinds of weather, but mostly bad, naturally, and walking barefoot through hot coals and arriving at wisdom. I used to say that it sounded to me as though they were getting away from wisdom as fast as they could. I think he sort of looked down on me for that.

"Do you mind," he asked, "if we have the driver drive alongside the park? On the west side—I haven't seen the city in so long."

"Of course not," I said. I was afraid that I might sound as though I were humoring him, but I hoped he wouldn't take it that way.

So we drove along, between the green of the park and the stony, lifeless elegance of hotels and apartment buildings, toward the vivid, killing streets of our childhood. These streets hadn't changed, though housing projects jutted up out of them now like rocks in the middle of a boiling sea. Most of the houses in which we had grown up had vanished, as had the stores from which we had stolen, the basements in which we had first tried sex, the rooftops from which we had hurled tin cans and bricks. But houses exactly like the houses of our past yet dominated the landscape, boys exactly like the boys we once had been found themselves smothering in these houses, came down into the streets for light and air and found themselves encircled by disaster. Some escaped the trap, most didn't. Those who got out always left something of themselves behind, as some animals amputate a leg and leave it in the trap. It might be said, perhaps, that I had escaped, after all, I was a school teacher; or that Sonny had, he hadn't lived in Harlem for years. Yet, as the cab moved uptown through streets which seemed, with a rush, to darken with dark people, and as I covertly studied Sonny's face, it came to me that what we both were seeking through out separate cab windows was that part of ourselves which had been left behind. It's always at the hour of trouble and confrontation that the missing member aches.

We hit 110th street and started rolling up Lenox Avenue. And I'd known this avenue all my life, but it seemed to me again, as it had seemed on the day I'd first heard about Sonny's trouble, filled with a hidden menace which was its very breath of life.

"We almost there," said Sonny.

"Almost." We were both too nervous to say anything more.

We live in a housing project. It hasn't been up long. A few days after it was up it seemed uninhabitably new, now, of course, it's already run-down. It looks like a parody of the good, clean, faceless life—God knows the people who live in it do their best to make it a parody. The beat-looking grass lying around isn't enough to make their lives green, the hedges will never hold out the streets, and they know it. The big windows fool no one, they aren't big enough to make space out of no space. They don't bother with the windows, they watch the TV screen instead. The playground is most popular with the children who don't play jacks, or skip rope, or roller skate, or swing, and they can be found in it after dark. We moved in partly because it's not too far from where I teach, and partly for the kids; but it's really just like the houses in which Sonny and I grew up. The same things happen, they'll have the same things to remember. The moment Sonny and I started into the house I had the feeling that I was simply bringing him back into the danger he had almost died trying to escape.

Sonny has never been talkative. So I don't know why I was sure he'd be dying to talk to me when supper was over the first night. Everything went fine, the oldest boy remembered him, and the youngest boy liked him, and Sonny had remembered to bring something for each of them; and Isabel, who is really much nicer than I am, more open and giving, had gone to a lot of trouble about dinner and was genuinely glad to see him. And she's always been able to tease Sonny in a way that I haven't. It was nice to see her face so vivid again and to hear her laugh and watch her make Sonny laugh. She wasn't, or, anyway, she didn't seem to be, at all uneasy or embarrassed. She chatted as though there were no subject which had to be avoided and she got Sonny past his first, faint stiffness. And thank God she was there, for I was filled with that icy dread again. Everything I did seemed awkward to me, and everything I said sounded freighted with hidden meaning. I was trying to remember everything I'd heard about dope addiction and I couldn't help watching Sonny for signs. I wasn't doing it out of malice. I was trying to find out something about my brother. I was dying to hear him tell me he was safe.

"Safe!" my father grunted, whenever Mama suggested trying to move to a neighborhood which might be safer for children. "Safe, hell! Ain't no place safe for kids, nor nobody."

He always went on like this, but he wasn't, ever, really as bad as he sounded, not even on weekends, when he got drunk. As a matter of fact, he was always on the lookout for "something a little better," but he died before he found it. He died suddenly, during a drunken weekend in the middle of the war, when Sonny was fifteen. He and Sonny hadn't ever got on too well. And this was partly because Sonny was the apple of his father's eye. It was because he loved Sonny so much and was frightened for him, that he was always fighting with him. It doesn't do any good to fight with Sonny. Sonny just moves back, inside himself, where he can't be reached. But the principal reason that they never hit it off is that they were so much alike. Daddy was big and rough and loud-talking, just the opposite of Sonny, but they both had—that same privacy.

Mama tried to tell me something about this, just after Daddy died. I was home on leave from the army.

This was the last time I ever saw my mother alive. Just the same, this picture gets all mixed up in my mind with pictures I had of her when she was younger. The way I always see her is the way she used to be on a Sunday afternoon, say, when the old folks were talking after the big Sunday dinner. I always see her wearing pale blue. She'd be sitting on the sofa. And my father would be sitting in the easy chair, not far from her. And the living room would be full of church folks and relatives. There they sit, in chairs all around the living room, and the night is creeping up outside, but nobody knows it yet. You can see the darkness growing against the window-panes and you hear the street noises every now and again, or maybe the jangling beat of a tambourine from one of the churches close by, but it's real quiet in the room. For a moment nobody's talking, but every face looks darkening, like the sky outside. And my mother rocks a little from the waist, and my father's eyes are closed. Everyone is looking at something a child can't see. For a minute they've forgotten the children. Maybe a kid is lying on the rug half asleep. Maybe somebody's got a kid on his lap and is absent-mindedly stroking the kid's head. Maybe there's a kid, quiet and big-eyed, curled up in a big chair in the corner. The silence, the darkness coming, and the darkness in the faces frightens the child obscurely. He hopes that the hand which strokes his forehead will never stop—will never die. He hopes that there will never come a time when the old folks won't be sitting around the living room, talking about where they've come from, and what they've seen, and what's happened to them and their kinfolk.

But something deep and watchful in the child knows that this is bound to end, is already ending. In a moment someone will get up and turn on the light. Then the old folks will remember the children and they won't talk any more that day. And when light fills the room, the child is filled with darkness. He knows that every time this happens he's moved just a little closer to that darkness outside. The darkness outside is what the old folks have been talking about. It's what they've come from. It's what they endure. The child knows that they won't talk any more because if he knows too much about what's happened to *them*, he'll know too much too soon, about what's going to happen to *him*.

The last time I talked to my mother, I remember I was restless. I wanted to get out and see Isabel. We weren't married then and we had a lot to straighten out between us.

There Mama sat, in black, by the window. She was humming an old church song, *Lord, you brought me from a long ways off*. Sonny was out somewhere. Mama kept watching the streets.

"I don't know," she said, "if I'll ever see you again, after you go off from here. But I hope you'll remember the things I tried to teach you."

"Don't talk like that," I said, and smiled. "You'll be here a long time yet."

She smiled, too, but she said nothing. She was quiet for a long time. And I said, "Mama, don't you worry about nothing. I'll be writing all the time, and you be getting the checks. . . ."

"I want to talk to you about your brother," she said, suddenly. "If anything happens to me he ain't going to have nobody to look out for him."

"Mama," I said, "ain't nothing going to happen to you *or* Sonny. Sonny's all right. He's a good boy and he's got good sense."

"It ain't a question of his being a good boy," Mama said, "nor of his having good sense. It ain't only the bad ones, nor yet the dumb ones that gets sucked under." She stopped, looking at me. "Your Daddy once had a brother," she said, and she smiled in a way that made me feel she was in pain. "You didn't never know that, did you?"

"No," I said, "I never knew that," and I watched her face.

"Oh, yes," she said, "your Daddy had a brother." She looked out of the window again. "I know you never saw your Daddy cry. But I did—many a time, through all these years."

I asked her, "What happened to his brother? How come nobody's ever talked about him?"

This was the first time I ever saw my mother look old.

"His brother got killed," she said, "when he was just a little younger than you are now. I knew him. He was a fine boy. He was maybe a little full of the devil, but he didn't mean nobody no harm."

Then she stopped and the room was silent, exactly as it had sometimes been on those Sunday afternoons. Mama kept looking out into the streets.

"He used to have a job in the mill," she said, "and, like all young folks, he just like to perform on Saturday nights. Saturday nights, him and your father would drift around to different places, go to dances and things like that, or just sit around with people they knew, and your father's brother would sing, he had a fine voice, and play along with himself on his guitar. Well, this particular Saturday night, him and your father was coming home from some place, and they were both a little drunk and there was a moon that night, it was bright like day. Your father's brother was feeling kind of good, and he was whistling to himself, and he had his guitar slung over his shoulder. They was coming down a hill and beneath them was a road that turned off from the highway. Well, your father's brother, being always kind of frisky, decided to run down this hill, and he did, with that guitar banging and clanging behind him, and he ran across the road, and he was making water behind a tree. And your father was sort of amused at him and he was still coming down the hill, kind of slow. Then he heard a car motor and that same minute his brother stepped from behind the tree, into the road, in the moonlight. And he started to cross the road. And your father started to run down the hill, he says he don't know why. This car was full of white men. They was all drunk, and when they seen your father's brother they let out a great whoop and holler and they aimed the car straight at him. They was having fun, they just wanted to scare him, the way they do sometimes, you know. But they was drunk. And I guess the boy, being drunk, too, and scared, kind of lost his head. By the time he jumped it was too late. Your father says he heard his brother scream when the car rolled over him, and he heard the wood of that guitar when it give, and he heard them strings go flying, and he heard them white men shouting, and the car kept on a-going and it ain't stopped till this day. And, time your father got down the hill, his brother weren't nothing but blood and pulp."

Tears were gleaming on my mother's face. There wasn't anything I could say.

"He never mentioned it," she said, "because I never let him mention it before you children. Your Daddy was like a crazy man that night and for many a night thereafter. He says he never in his life seen anything as dark as that road after the lights of that car had gone away. Weren't nothing, weren't nobody on that road, just your Daddy and his brother and that busted guitar. Oh, yes. Your Daddy never did really get right again. Till the day he died he weren't sure but that every white man he saw was the man that killed his brother."

She stopped and took out her handkerchief and dried her eyes and looked at me.

"I ain't telling you all this," she said, "to make you scared or bitter or to make you hate nobody. I'm telling you this because you got a brother. And the world ain't changed."

I guess I didn't want to believe this. I guess she saw this in my face. She turned away from me, toward the window again, searching those streets.

"But I praise my Redeemer," she said at last, "that He called your Daddy home before me. I ain't saying it to throw no flowers at myself, but, I declare, it keeps me from feeling too cast down to know I helped your father get safely through this world. Your father always acted like he was the roughest, strongest man on earth. And everybody took him to be like that. But if he hadn't had *me* there—to see his tears!"

She was crying again. Still, I couldn't move. I said, "Lord, Lord, Mama, I didn't know it was like that."

"Oh, honey," she said, "there's a lot that you don't know. But you are going to find it out." She stood up from the window and came over to me. "You got to hold on to your brother," she said, "and don't let him fall, no matter what it looks like is happening to him and no matter how evil you gets with him. You going to be evil with him many a time. But don't you forget what I told you, you hear?"

"I won't forget," I said. "Don't you worry, I won't forget. I won't let nothing happen to Sonny."

My mother smiled as though she were amused at something she saw in my face. Then, "You may not be able to stop nothing from happening. But you got to let him know you's *there*."

Two days later I was married, and then I was gone. And I had a lot of things on my mind and I pretty well forgot my promise to Mama until I got shipped home on a special furlough for her funeral.

And, after the funeral, with just Sonny and me alone in the empty kitchen, I tried to find out something about him.

"What do you want to do?" I asked him.

"I'm going to be a musician," he said.

For he had graduated, in the time I had been away, from dancing to the juke box to finding out who was playing what, and what they were doing with it, and he had bought himself a set of drums.

"You mean, you want to be a drummer?" I somehow had the feeling that being a drummer might be all right for other people but not for my brother Sonny.

"I don't think," he said, looking at me very gravely, "that I'll ever be a good drummer. But I think I can play a piano."

I frowned. I'd never played the role of the older brother quite so seriously

James Baldwin 415

before, had scarcely ever, in fact, *asked* Sonny a damn thing. I sensed myself in the presence of something I didn't really know how to handle, didn't understand. So I made my frown a little deeper as I asked: "What kind of musician do you want to be?"

He grinned. "How many kinds do you think there are?"

"Be *serious*," I said.

He laughed, throwing his head back, and then looked at me. "I *am* serious."

"Well, then, for Christ's sake, stop kidding around and answer a serious question. I mean, do you want to be a concert pianist, you want to play classical music and all that, or—or what?" Long before I finished he was laughing again. "For Christ's *sake*, Sonny!"

He sobered, but with difficulty. "I'm sorry. But you sound so—*scared!*" and he was off again.

"Well, you may think it's funny now, baby, but it's not going to be so funny when you have to make your living at it, let me tell you *that*." I was furious because I knew he was laughing at me and I didn't know why.

"No," he said, very sober now, and afraid, perhaps, that he'd hurt me, "I don't want to be a classical pianist. That isn't what interests me. I mean"—he paused, looking hard at me, as though his eyes would help me to understand, and then gestured helplessly, as though perhaps his hand would help—"I mean, I'll have a lot of studying to do, and I'll have to study *everything*, but I mean, I want to play *with*—jazz musicians." He stopped. "I want to play jazz," he said.

Well, the word had never before sounded as heavy, as real, as it sounded that afternoon in Sonny's mouth. I just looked at him and I was probably frowning a real frown by this time. I simply couldn't see why on earth he'd want to spend his time hanging around night clubs, clowning around on bandstands, while people pushed each other around a dance floor. It seemed—beneath him, somehow. I had never thought about it before, had never been forced to, but I suppose I had always put jazz musicians in a class with what Daddy called "good-time people."

"Are you *serious*?"

"Hell, *yes*, I'm serious."

He looked more helpless than ever, and annoyed, and deeply hurt.

I suggested, helpfully: "You mean—like Louis Armstrong?"

His face closed as though I'd struck him. "No. I'm not talking about none of that old-time, down home crap."

"Well, look, Sonny, I'm sorry, don't get mad. I just don't altogether get it, that's all. Name somebody—you know, a jazz musician you admire."

"Bird."

"Who?"

"Bird! Charlie Parker![4] Don't they teach you nothing in the goddamn army?"

---

[4] Charlie "Bird" Parker (1920–1955) was a jazz saxophonist who helped develop a style of jazz termed "bebop." Louis Armstrong represents a more conservative, old-fashioned jazz style.

I lit a cigarette. I was surprised and then a little amused to discover that I was trembling. "I've been out of touch," I said. "You'll have to be patient with me. Now. Who's this Parker character?"

"He's just one of the greatest jazz musicians alive," said Sonny, sullenly, his hands in his pockets, his back to me. "Maybe *the* greatest," he added, bitterly, "that's probably why *you* never heard of him."

"All right," I said, "I'm ignorant. I'm sorry. I'll go out and buy all the cat's records right away, all right?"

"It don't," said Sonny, with dignity, "make any difference to me. I don't care what you listen to. Don't do me no favors."

I was beginning to realize that I'd never seen him so upset before. With another part of my mind I was thinking that this would probably turn out to be one of those things kids go through and that I shouldn't make it seem important by pushing it too hard. Still, I didn't think it would do any harm to ask: "Doesn't all this take a lot of time? Can you make a living at it?"

He turned back to me and half leaned, half sat, on the kitchen table. "Everything takes time," he said, "and—well, yes, sure, I can make a living at it. But what I don't seem to be able to make you understand is that it's the only thing I want to do."

"Well Sonny," I said, gently, "you know people can't always do exactly what they *want* to do—"

"No, I don't know that," said Sonny, surprising me. "I think people *ought* to do what they want to do, what else are they alive for?"

"You getting to be a big boy," I said desperately, "it's time you started thinking about your future."

"I'm thinking about my future," said Sonny, grimly. "I think about it all the time."

I gave up. I decided, if he didn't change his mind, that we could always talk about it later. "In the meantime," I said, "you got to finish school." We had already decided that he'd have to move in with Isabel and her folks. I knew this wasn't the ideal arrangement because Isabel's folks are inclined to be dicty and they hadn't especially wanted Isabel to marry me. But I didn't know what else to do. "And we have to get you fixed up at Isabel's."

There was a long silence. He moved from the kitchen table to the window. "That's a terrible idea. You know it yourself."

"Do you have a *better* idea?"

He just walked up and down the kitchen for a minute. He was as tall as I was. He had started to shave. I suddenly had the feeling that I didn't know him at all.

He stopped at the kitchen table and picked up my cigarettes. Looking at me with a kind of mocking, amused defiance, he put one between his lips. "You mind?"

"You smoking already?"

He lit the cigarette and nodded, watching me through the smoke. "I just wanted to see if I'd have the courage to smoke in front of you." He grinned and blew a great cloud of smoke to the ceiling. "It was easy." He looked at my face. "Come on, now. I bet you was smoking at my age, tell the truth."

I didn't say anything but the truth was on my face, and he laughed. But now there was something very strained in his laugh. "Sure. And I bet that ain't all you was doing."

He was frightening me a little. "Cut the crap," I said. "We already decided that you was going to go and live at Isabel's. Now what's got into you all of a sudden?"

"*You* decided it," he pointed out. "*I* didn't decide nothing." He stopped in front of me, leaning against the stove, arms loosely folded. "Look, brother. I don't want to stay in Harlem no more, I really don't." He was very earnest. He looked at me, then over toward the kitchen window. There was something in his eyes I'd never seen before, some thoughtfulness, some worry all his own. He rubbed the muscle of one arm. It's time I was getting out of here."

"Where do you want to *go*, Sonny?"

"I want to join the army. Or the navy, I don't care. If I say I'm old enough they'll believe me."

Then I got mad. It was because I was so scared. "You must be crazy. You goddamn fool, what the hell do you want to go and join the *army* for?"

"I just told you. To get out of Harlem."

"Sonny, you haven't even finished *school*. And if you really want to be a musician, how do you expect to study if you're in the *army?*"

He looked at me, trapped, and in anguish. "There's ways. I might be able to work out some kind of deal. Anyway, I'll have the G.I. Bill when I come out."

"*If* you come out." We stared at each other. "Sonny, please. Be reasonable. I know the setup is far from perfect. But we got to do the best we can."

"I ain't learning nothing in school," he said. "Even when I go." He turned away from me and opened the window and threw his cigarette out into the narrow alley. I watched his back. "At least, I ain't learning nothing you'd want me to learn." He slammed the window so hard I thought the glass would fly out, and turned back to me. "And I'm sick of the stink of these garbage cans!"

"Sonny," I said, "I know how you feel. But if you don't finish school now, you're going to be sorry later that you didn't." I grabbed him by the shoulders. "And you only got another year. It ain't so bad. And I'll come back and I swear I'll help you do *whatever* you want to do. Just try to put up with it till I come back. Will you please do that? For me?"

He didn't answer and he wouldn't look at me.

"Sonny. You hear me?"

He pulled away. "I hear you. But you never hear anything *I* say."

I didn't know what to say to that. He looked out of the window and then back at me. "OK," he said, and sighed. "I'll try."

Then I said, trying to cheer him up a little, "They got a piano at Isabel's. You can practice on it."

And as a matter of fact, it did cheer him up for a minute. "That's right," he said to himself. "I forgot that." His face relaxed a little. But the worry, the thoughtfulness, played on it still, the way shadows play on a face which is staring into the fire.

But I thought I'd never hear the end of that piano. At first, Isabel would write me, saying how nice it was that Sonny was so serious about his music and how, as soon as he came in from school, or wherever he had been when he was supposed to be at school, he went straight to that piano and stayed there until suppertime. And, after supper, he went back to that piano and stayed there until everybody went to bed. He was at the piano all day Saturday and all day Sunday. Then he bought a record player and started playing records. He'd play one record over and over again, all day long sometimes, and he'd improvise along with it on the piano. Or he'd play one section of the record, one chord, one change, one progression, then he'd do it on the piano. Then back to the record. Then back to the piano.

Well, I really don't know how they stood it. Isabel finally confessed that it wasn't like living with a person at all, it was like living with sound. And the sound didn't make any sense to her, didn't make any sense to any of them— naturally. They began, in a way, to be afflicted by this presence that was living in their home. It was as though Sonny were some sort of god, or monster. He moved in an atmosphere which wasn't like theirs at all. They fed him and he ate, he washed himself, he walked in and out of their door; he certainly wasn't nasty or unpleasant or rude, Sonny isn't any of those things; but it was as though he were all wrapped up in some cloud, some fire, some vision all his own; and there wasn't any way to reach him.

At the same time, he wasn't really a man yet, he was still a child, and they had to watch out for him in all kinds of ways. They certainly couldn't throw him out. Neither did they dare to make a great scene about that piano because even they dimly sensed, as I sensed, from so many thousands of miles away, that Sonny was at that piano playing for his life.

But he hadn't been going to school. One day a letter came from the school board and Isabel's mother got it—there had, apparently, been other letters but Sonny had torn them up. This day, when Sonny came in, Isabel's mother showed him the letter and asked where he'd been spending his time. And she finally got it out of him that he'd been down in Greenwich Village, with musicians and other characters, in a white girl's apartment. And this scared her and she started to scream at him and what came up, once she began—though she denies it to this day—was what sacrifices they were making to give Sonny a decent home and how little he appreciated it.

Sonny didn't play the piano that day. By evening, Isabel's mother had calmed down but then there was the old man to deal with, and Isabel herself. Isabel says she did her best to be calm but she broke down and started crying. She says she just watched Sonny's face. She could tell, by watching him, what was happening with him. And what was happening was that they penetrated his cloud, they had reached him. Even if their fingers had been a thousand times more gentle than human fingers ever are, he could hardly help feeling that they had stripped him naked and were spitting on that nakedness. For he also had to see that his presence, that music, which was life or death to him, had been torture for them and that they had endured it, not at all for his sake, but only for mine. And Sonny couldn't take that. He can take it a little better today than he could then but he's still not very good at it and, frankly, I don't know anybody who is.

The silence of the next few days must have been louder than the sound of all the music ever played since time began. One morning, before she went to work, Isabel was in his room for something and she suddenly realized that all of his records were gone. And she knew for certain that he was gone. And he was. He went as far as the navy would carry him. He finally sent me a postcard from some place in Greece and that was the first I knew that Sonny was still alive. I didn't see him any more until we were both back in New York and the war had long been over.

He was a man by then, of course, but I wasn't willing to see it. He came by the house from time to time, but we fought almost every time we met. I didn't like the way he carried himself, loose and dreamlike all the time, and I didn't like his friends, and his music seemed to be merely an excuse for the life he led. It sounded just that weird and disordered.

Then we had a fight, a pretty awful fight, and I didn't see him for months. By and by I looked him up, where he was living, in a furnished room in the Village, and I tried to make it up. But there were lots of other people in the room and Sonny just lay on his bed, and he wouldn't come downstairs with me, and he treated these other people as though they were his family and I weren't. So I got mad and then he got mad, and then I told him that he might just as well be dead as live the way he was living. Then he stood up and he told me not to worry about him any more in life, that he *was* dead as far as I was concerned. Then he pushed me to the door and the other people looked on as though nothing were happening, and he slammed the door behind me. I stood in the hallway, staring at the door. I heard somebody laugh in the room and then the tears came to my eyes. I started down the steps, whistling to keep from crying, I kept whistling to myself, *You going to need me, baby, one of these cold, rainy days.*

I read about Sonny's trouble in the spring. Little Grace died in the fall. She was a beautiful little girl. But she only lived a little over two years. She died of polio and she suffered. She had a slight fever for a couple of days, but it didn't seem like anything and we just kept her in bed. And we would certainly have called the doctor, but the fever dropped, she seemed to be all right. So we thought it had just been a cold. Then, one day, she was up, playing, Isabel was in the kitchen fixing lunch for the two boys when they'd come in from school, and she heard Grace fall down in the living room. When you have a lot of children you don't always start running when one of them falls, unless they start screaming or something. And, this time, Grace was quiet. Yet, Isabel says that when she heard that *thump* and then that silence, something happened in her to make her afraid. And she ran to the living room and there was little Grace on the floor, all twisted up and the reason she hadn't screamed was that she couldn't get her breath. And when she did scream, it was the worst sound, Isabel says, that she'd ever heard in all her life, and she still hears it sometimes in her dreams. Isabel will sometimes wake me up with a low, moaning, strangled sound and I have to be quick to awaken her and hold her to me and where Isabel is weeping against me seems a mortal wound.

I think I may have written Sonny the very day that little Grace was buried. I was sitting in the living room in the dark, by myself, and I suddenly thought of Sonny. My trouble made his real.

One Saturday afternoon, when Sonny had been living with us, or, anyway, been in our house, for nearly two weeks, I found myself wandering aimlessly about the living room, drinking from a can of beer, and trying to work up the courage to search Sonny's room. He was out, he was usually out whenever I was home, and Isabel had taken the children to see their grandparents. Suddenly I was standing still in front of the living room window, watching Seventh Avenue. The idea of searching Sonny's room made me still. I scarcely dared to admit to myself what I'd be searching for. I didn't know what I'd do if I found it. Or if I didn't.

On the sidewalk across from me, near the entrance to a barbecue joint, some people were holding an old-fashioned revival meeting. The barbecue cook, wearing a dirty white apron, his conked hair reddish and metallic in the pale sun, and a cigarette between his lips, stood in the doorway, watching them. Kids and older people paused in their errands and stood there, along with some older men and a couple of very tough-looking women who watched everything that happened on the avenue, as though they owned it, or were maybe owned by it. Well, they were watching this, too. The revival was being carried on by three sisters in black, and a brother. All they had were their voices and their Bibles and a tambourine. The brother was testifying and while he testified two of the sisters stood together, seeming to say, Amen, and the third sister walked around with the tambourine outstretched and a couple of people dropped coins into it. Then the brother's testimony ended and the sister who had been taking up the collection dumped the coins into her palm and transferred them to the pocket of her long black robe. Then she raised both hands, striking the tambourine against the air, and then against one hand, and she started to sing. And the two other sisters and the brother joined in.

It was strange, suddenly, to watch, though I had been seeing these street meetings all my life. So, of course, had everybody else down there. Yet, they paused and watched and listened and I stood still at the window. *"Tis the old ship of Zion,"* they sang, and the sister with the tambourine kept a steady, jangling beat, *"It has rescued many a thousand!"* Not a soul under the sound of their voices was hearing this song for the first time, not one of them had been rescued. Nor had they seen much in the way of rescue work being done around them. Neither did they especially believe in the holiness of the three sisters and the brother, they knew too much about them, knew where they lived, and how. The woman with the tambourine, whose voice dominated the air, whose face was bright with joy, was divided by very little from the woman who stood watching her, a cigarette between her heavy, chapped lips, her hair a cuckoo's nest, her face scarred and swollen from many beatings, and her black eyes glittering like coal. Perhaps they both knew this, which was why, when, as rarely, they addressed each other, they addressed each other as Sister. As the singing filled the air the watching, listening faces underwent a change, the eyes focusing on something within; the music seemed to sooth a poison out of them; and time seemed, nearly, to fall away from the sullen, belligerent, battered faces, as though they were fleeing back to their first condition, while dreaming of their last. The barbecue cook half shook his head and smiled, and dropped his cigarette and disappeared into his joint. A man fumbled in his pockets for change and stood holding it in his hand impatiently, as though he had just remembered a pressing appointment further up the avenue. He looked furious. Then I saw Sonny, standing on the edge of the crowd. He was carrying a wide, flat notebook with a green cover, and it made him look, from where I was standing, almost like a schoolboy. The coppery sun brought out the copper in his skin, he was very faintly smiling, standing very still. Then the singing stopped, the tambourine turned into a collection plate again. The furious man dropped in his coins and vanished, so did a couple of the women, and Sonny dropped some change in the plate, looking directly at the woman with a little smile. He started across the avenue, toward the house. He has a slow, loping walk, something like the way Harlem hipsters walk, only he's imposed on this his own halfbeat. I had never really noticed it before.

I stayed at the window, both relieved and apprehensive. As Sonny disappeared from my sight, they began singing again. And they were still singing when his key turned in the lock.

"Hey," he said.

"Hey, yourself. You want some beer?"

"No. Well, maybe." But he came up to the window and stood beside me, looking out. "What a warm voice," he said.

They were singing *If I could only hear my mother pray again!*

"Yes," I said, "and she can sure beat that tambourine."

"But what a terrible song," he said, and laughed. He dropped his notebook on the sofa and disappeared into the kitchen. "Where's Isabel and the kids?"

"I think they went to see their grandparents. You hungry?"

"No." He came back into the living room with his can of beer. "You want to come some place with me tonight?"

I sensed, I don't know how, that I couldn't possibly say No. "Sure. Where?"

He sat down on the sofa and picked up his notebook and started leafing through it. "I'm going to sit in with some fellows in a joint in the Village."

"You mean, you're going to play, tonight?"

"That's right." He took a swallow of his beer and moved back to the window. He gave me a sidelong look. "If you can stand it."

"I'll try," I said.

He smiled to himself and we both watched as the meeting across the way broke up. The three sisters and the brother, heads bowed, were singing *God be with you till we meet again*. The faces around them were very quiet. Then the song ended. The small crowd dispersed. We watched the three women and the lone man walk slowly up the avenue.

"When she was singing before," said Sonny, abruptly, "her voice reminded me for a minute of what heroin feels like sometimes—when it's in your veins. It makes you feel sort of warm and cool at the same time. And distant. And—and sure." He sipped his beer, very deliberately not looking at me. I watched his face. "It makes you feel—in control. Sometimes you've got to have that feeling."

"Do you?" I sat down slowly in the easy chair.

"Sometimes." He went to the sofa and picked up his notebook again. "Some people do."

"In order," I asked, "to play?" And my voice was very ugly, full of contempt and anger.

"Well"—he looked at me with great, troubled eyes, as though, in fact, he hoped his eyes would tell me things he could never otherwise say—"they *think* so. And *if* they think so—!"

"And what do *you* think?" I asked.

He sat on the sofa and put his can of beer on the floor. "I don't know," he said, and I couldn't be sure if he were answering my question or pursuing his thoughts. His face didn't tell me. "It's not so much to *play*. It's to *stand* it, to be able to make it at all. On any level." He frowned and smiled: "In order to keep from shaking to pieces."

"But these friends of yours," I said, "they seem to shake themselves to pieces pretty goddamn fast."

"Maybe." He played with the notebook. And something told me that I should curb my tongue, that Sonny was doing his best to talk, that I should listen. "But of course you only know the ones that've gone to pieces. Some don't—or at least they haven't *yet* and that's just about all *any* of us can say." He paused. "And then there are some who just live, really, in hell, and they know it and they see what's happening and they go right on. I don't know." He sighed, dropped the notebook, folded his arms. "Some guys, you can tell from the way they play, they on something *all* the time. And you can see that, well, it makes something real for them. But of course," he picked up his beer from the floor and sipped it and put the can down again, "they *want* to, too, you've got to see that. Even some of them that say they don't—*some*, not all."

"And what about you?" I asked—I couldn't help it. "What about you? Do *you* want to?"

He stood up and walked to the window and remained silent for a long time. Then he sighed. "Me," he said. Then: "While I was downstairs before, on my way here, listening to that woman sing, it struck me all of a sudden how much suffering she must have had to go through—to sing like that. It's *repulsive* to think you have to suffer that much."

I said: "But there's no way not to suffer—is there, Sonny?"

"I believe not," he said, and smiled, "but that's never stopped anyone from trying." He looked at me. "Has it?" I realized, with this mocking look, that there stood between us, forever, beyond the power of time or forgiveness, the fact that I had held silence—so long!—when he had needed human speech to help him. He turned back to the window. "No, there's no way not to suffer. But you try all kinds of ways to keep from drowning in it, to keep on top of it, and to make it seem—well, like *you*. Like you did something, all right, and now you're suffering for it. You know?" I said nothing. "Well you know," he said, impatiently, "why *do* people suffer? Maybe it's better to do something to give it a reason, *any* reason."

"But we just agreed," I said, "that there's no way not to suffer. Isn't it better, then, just to—take it?"

"But nobody just takes it," Sonny cried, "that's what I'm telling you! *Everybody* tries not to. You're just hung up on the *way* some people try—it's not *your* way!"

The hair on my face began to itch, my face felt wet. "That's not true," I said, "that's not true. I don't give a damn what other people do, I don't even care how they suffer. I just care how *you* suffer." And he looked at me. "Please believe me," I said, "I don't want to see you—die—trying not to suffer."

"I won't," he said, flatly, "die trying not to suffer. At least, not any faster than anybody else."

"But there's no need," I said, trying to laugh, "is there? in killing yourself."

I wanted to say more, but I couldn't. I wanted to talk about will power and how life could be—well, beautiful. I wanted to say that it was all within; but was it? or, rather, wasn't that exactly the trouble? And I wanted to promise that I would never fail him again. But it would all have sounded—empty words and lies.

So I made the promise to myself and prayed that I would keep it.

"It's terrible sometimes, inside," he said, "that's what's the trouble. You walk these streets, black and funky and cold, and there's not really a living ass to talk to, and there's nothing shaking, and there's no way of getting it out—that storm inside. You can't talk it and you can't make love with it, and when you finally try to get with it and play it, you realize *nobody*'s listening. So *you've* got to listen. You got to find a way to listen."

And then he walked away from the window and sat on the sofa again, as though all the wind had suddenly been knocked out of him. "Sometimes you'll do *anything* to play, even cut your mother's throat." He laughed and looked at me. "Or your brother's." Then he sobered. "Or your own." Then: "Don't worry. I'm all right now and I think I'll *be* all right. But I can't forget—where I've been. I don't mean just the physical place I've been, I mean where I've *been*. And *what* I've been."

"What have you been, Sonny?" I asked.

He smiled—but sat sideways on the sofa, his elbow resting on the back, his fingers playing with his mouth and chin, not looking at me. "I've been something I didn't recognize, didn't know I could be. Didn't know anybody could be." He stopped, looking inward, looking helplessly young, looking old. "I'm not talking about it now because I feel *guilty* or anything like that—maybe it would be better if I did, I don't know. Anyway, I can't really talk about it. Not to you, not to anybody," and now he turned and faced me. "Sometimes, you know, and it was actually when I was most *out* of the world, I felt that I was in it, and that I was *with* it, really, and I could play or I didn't really have to *play*, it just came out of me, it was there. And I don't know how I played, thinking about it now, but I know I did awful things, those times, sometimes, to people. Or it wasn't that I *did* anything to them—it was that they weren't real." He picked up the beer can; it was empty; he rolled it between his palms: "And other times— well, I needed a fix, I needed to find a place to lean, I needed to clear a space to *listen*—and I couldn't find it, and I—went crazy, I did terrible things to *me*, I was terrible *for* me." He began pressing the beer can between his hands, I watched the metal begin to give. It glittered, as he played with it, like a knife, and I was afraid he would cut himself, but I said nothing. "Oh well. I can never tell you. I was all by myself at the bottom of something, stinking and sweating and crying and shaking, and I smelled it, you know? *my* stink, and I thought I'd die if I couldn't get away from it and yet, all the same, I knew that everything I was doing was just locking me in with it. And I didn't know," he paused, still flattening the beer can, "I didn't know, I still *don't* know, something kept telling me that maybe it was good to smell your own stink, but I didn't think that *that* was what I'd been trying to do—and—who can stand it?" and he abruptly dropped the ruined beer can, looking at me with a small, still smile, and then rose, walking to the window as though it were the lodestone rock. I watched his face, he watched the avenue. "I couldn't tell you when Mama died—but the reason I wanted to leave Harlem so bad was to get away from drugs. And then, when I ran away, that's what I was running from—really. When I came back, nothing had changed, *I* hadn't changed, I was just—older." And he stopped, drumming with his fingers on the windowpane. The sun had vanished, soon darkness would fall. I watched his face. "It can come again," he said, almost as though speaking to himself. Then he turned to me. "It can come again," he repeated. "I just want you to know that."

"All right," I said, at last. "So it can come again. All right."

He smiled, but the smile was sorrowful. "I had to try to tell you," he said.

"Yes," I said. "I understand that."

"You're my brother," he said, looking straight at me, and not smiling at all.

"Yes," I repeated, "yes. I understand that."

He turned back to the window, looking out. "All that hatred down there," he said, "all that hatred and misery and love. It's a wonder it doesn't blow the avenue apart."

We went to the only night club on a short, dark street, downtown. We squeezed through the narrow, chattering, jam-packed bar to the entrance of the big room, where the bandstand was. And we stood there for a moment, for the lights were very dim in this room and we couldn't see. Then, "Hello, boy," said a voice and an enormous black man, much older than Sonny or myself, erupted out of all that atmospheric lighting and put an arm around Sonny's shoulder. "I been sitting right here," he said, "waiting for you."

He had a big voice, too, and heads in the darkness turned toward us.

Sonny grinned and pulled a little away, and said, "Creole, this is my brother. I told you about him."

Creole shook my hand. "I'm glad to meet you, son," he said, and it was clear that he was glad to meet me *there*, for Sonny's sake. And he smiled, "You got a real musician in *your* family," and he took his arm from Sonny's shoulder and slapped him, lightly, affectionately, with the back of his hand.

"Well. Now I've heard it all," said a voice behind us. This was another musician, and a friend of Sonny's, a coal-black, cheerful-looking man, built close to the ground. He immediately began confiding to me, at the top of his lungs, the most terrible things about Sonny, his teeth gleaming like a lighthouse and his laugh coming up out of him like the beginning of an earthquake. And it turned out that everyone at the bar knew Sonny, or almost everyone; some were musicians, working there, or nearby, or not working, some were simply hangers-on, and some were there to hear Sonny play. I was introduced to all of them and they were all very polite to me. Yet, it was clear that, for them, I was only Sonny's brother. Here, I was in Sonny's world. Or, rather: his kingdom. Here, it was not even a question that his veins bore royal blood.

They were going to play soon and Creole installed me, by myself, at a table in a dark corner. Then I watched them, Creole, and the little black man, and Sonny, and the others, while they horsed around, standing just below the bandstand. The light from the bandstand spilled just a little short of them and, watching them laughing and gesturing and moving about, I had the feeling that they, nevertheless, were being most careful not to step into that circle of light too suddenly: that if they moved into the light too suddenly, without thinking, they would perish in flame. Then, while I watched, one of them, the small, black man, moved into the light and crossed the bandstand and started fooling around with his drums. Then—being funny and being, also, extremely cere-monious—Creole took Sonny by the arm and led him to the piano. A woman's voice called Sonny's name and a few hands started clapping. And Sonny, also being funny and being ceremonious, and so touched, I think, that he could have cried, but neither hiding it nor showing it, riding it like a man, grinned, and put both hands to his heart and bowed from the waist.

Creole then went to the bass fiddle and a lean, very bright-skinned brown man jumped up on the bandstand and picked up his horn. So there they were, and the atmosphere on the bandstand and in the room began to change and tighten. Someone stepped up to the microphone and announced them. Then there were all kinds of murmurs. Some people at the bar shushed others. The waitress ran around, frantically getting in the last orders, guys and chicks got closer to each other, and the lights on the bandstand, on the quartet, turned to a kind of indigo. Then they all looked different there. Creole looked about him for the last time, as though he were making certain that all his chickens were in the coop, and then he—jumped and struck the fiddle. And there they were.

All I know about music is that not many people ever really hear it. And even then, on the rare occasions when something opens within, and the music enters, what we mainly hear, or hear corroborated, are personal, private, vanishing evocations. But the man who creates the music is hearing something else, is dealing with the roar rising from the void and imposing order on it as it hits the air. What is evoked in him, then, is of another order, more terrible because it has no words, and triumphant, too, for that same reason. And his triumph, when he triumphs, is ours. I just watched Sonny's face. His face was troubled, he was working hard, but he wasn't with it. And I had the feeling that, in a way, everyone on the bandstand was waiting for him, both waiting for him and pushing him along. But as I began to watch Creole, I realized that it was Creole who held them all back. He had them on a short rein. Up there, keeping the beat with his whole body, wailing on the fiddle, with his eyes half closed, he was listening to everything, but he was listening to Sonny. He was having a dialogue with Sonny. He wanted Sonny to leave the shore line and strike out for the deep water. He was Sonny's witness that deep water and drowning were not the same thing—he had been there, and he knew. And he wanted Sonny to know. He was waiting for Sonny to do the things on the keys which would let Creole know that Sonny was in the water.

And, while Creole listened, Sonny moved, deep within, exactly like someone in torment. I had never before thought of how awful the relationship must be between the musician and his instrument. He has to fill it, this instrument, with the breath of life, his own. He has to make it do what he wants it to do. And a piano is just a piano. It's made out of so much wood and wires and little hammers and big ones, and ivory. While there's only so much you can do with it, the only way to find this out is to try and make it do everything.

And Sonny hadn't been near a piano for over a year. And he wasn't on much better terms with his life, not the life that stretched before him now. He and the piano stammered, started one way, got scared, stopped; started another way, panicked, marked time, started again; then seemed to have found a direction, panicked again, got stuck. And the face I saw on Sonny I'd never seen before. Everything had been burned out of it, and, at the same time, things usually hidden were being burned in, by the fire and fury of the battle which was occurring in him up there.

Yet, watching Creole's face as they neared the end of the first set, I had the feeling that something had happened, something I hadn't heard. Then they finished, there was scattered applause, and then, without an instant's warning, Creole started into something else, it was almost sardonic, it was *Am I Blue*.[5] And, as though he commanded, Sonny began to play. Something began to happen. And Creole let out the reins. The dry, low, black man said something awful on the drums, Creole answered, and the drums talked back. Then the horn insisted, sweet and high, slightly detached perhaps, and Creole listened, commenting now and then, dry, and driving, beautiful and calm and old. Then they all came together again, and Sonny was part of the family again. I could tell this from his face. He seemed to have found, right there beneath his fingers, a damn brand-new piano. It seemed that he couldn't get over it. Then, for awhile, just being happy with Sonny, they seemed to be agreeing with him that brand-new pianos certainly were a gas.

Then Creole stepped forward to remind them that what they were playing was the blues. He hit something in all of them, he hit something in me, myself, and the music tightened and deepened, apprehension began to beat the air. Creole began to tell us what the blues were all about. They were not about anything very new. He and his boys up there were keeping it new, at the risk of ruin, destruction, madness, and death, in order to find new ways to make us listen. For, while the tale of how we suffer, and how we are delighted, and how we may triumph is never new, it always must be heard. There isn't any other tale to tell, it's the only light we've got in all this darkness.

And this tale, according to that face, that body, those strong hands on those strings, has another aspect in every country, and a new depth in every generation. Listen, Creole seemed to be saying, listen. Now these are Sonny's blues. He made the little black man on the drums know it, and the bright, brown man on the horn. Creole wasn't trying any longer to get Sonny in the water. He was wishing him Godspeed. Then he stepped back, very slowly, filling the air with the immense suggestion that Sonny speak for himself.

Then they all gathered around Sonny and Sonny played. Every now and again one of them seemed to say, Amen. Sonny's fingers filled the air with life, his life. But that life contained so many others. And Sonny went all the way back, he really began with the spare, flat statement of the opening phrase of the song. Then he began to make it his. It was very beautiful because it wasn't hurried and it was no longer a lament. I seemed to hear with what burning he had made it his, with what burning we had yet to make it ours, how we could cease lamenting. Freedom lurked around us and I understood, at last, that he could help us to be free if we would listen, that he would never be free until we did. Yet, there was no battle in his face now. I heard what he had gone through, and would continue to go through until he came to rest in earth. He had made

---

[5] "Am I Blue" is a blues song by Grant Clark and Harry Akst from the 1920s.

it his: that long line, of which we knew only Mama and Daddy. And he was giving it back, as everything must be given back, so that, passing through death, it can live forever. I saw my mother's face again, and felt, for the first time, how the stones of the road she had walked on must have bruised her feet. I saw the moonlit road where my father's brother died. And it brought something else back to me, and carried me past it, I saw my little girl again and felt Isabel's tears again, and I felt my own tears begin to rise. And I was yet aware that this was only a moment, that the world waited outside, as hungry as a tiger, and that trouble stretched above us, longer than the sky.

Then it was over. Creole and Sonny let out their breath, both soaking wet, and grinning. There was a lot of applause and some of it was real. In the dark, the girl came by and I asked her to take drinks to the bandstand. There was a long pause, while they talked up there in the indigo light and after awhile I saw the girl put a Scotch and milk on top of the piano for Sonny. He didn't seem to notice it, but just before they started playing again, he sipped from it and looked toward me, and nodded. Then he put it back on top of the piano. For me, then, as they began to play again, it glowed and shook above my brother's head like the very cup of trembling.

STEPHEN CRANE (1871–1900)

The Bride Comes to Yellow Sky

I

The great Pullman was whirling onward with such dignity of motion that a glance from the window seemed simply to prove that the plains of Texas were pouring eastward. Vast flats of green grass, dull-hued spaces of mesquit and cactus, little groups of frame houses, woods of light and tender trees, all were sweeping into the east, sweeping over the horizon, a precipice.

A newly married pair had boarded this coach at San Antonio. The man's face was reddened from many days in the wind and sun, and a direct result of his new black clothes was that his brick-colored hands were constantly performing in a most conscious fashion. From time to time he looked down respectfully at his attire. He sat with a hand on each knee, like a man waiting in a barber's shop. The glances he devoted to other passengers were furtive and shy.

The bride was not pretty, nor was she very young. She wore a dress of blue cashmere, with small reservations of velvet here and there, and with steel buttons abounding. She continually twisted her head to regard her puff sleeves, very stiff, straight, and high. They embarrassed her. It was quite apparent that she had cooked, and that she expected to cook, dutifully. The blushes caused by the careless scrutiny of some passengers as she had entered the car were strange to see upon this plain, under-class countenance, which was drawn in placid, almost emotionless lines.

They were evidently very happy. "Ever been in a parlor-car before?" he asked, smiling with delight.

"No," she answered; "I never was. It's fine, ain't it?"

"Great! And then after a while we'll go forward to the diner, and get a big lay-out. Finest meal in the world. Charge a dollar."

"Oh, do they?" cried the bride. "Charge a dollar? Why, that's too much—for us—ain't it, Jack?"

"Not this trip, anyhow," he answered bravely. "We're going to go the whole thing."

Later he explained to her about the trains. "You see, it's a thousand miles from one end of Texas to the other; and this train runs right across it, and never stops but for four times." He had the pride of an owner. He pointed out to her the dazzling fittings of the coach; and in truth her eyes opened wider as she contemplated the sea-green figured velvet, the shining brass, silver, and glass, the wood that gleamed as darkly brilliant as the surface of a pool of oil. At one end a bronze figure sturdily held a support for a separated chamber, and at convenient places on the ceiling were frescos in olive and silver.

To the minds of the pair, their surroundings reflected the glory of their marriage that morning in San Antonio; this was the environment of their new estate; and the man's face in particular beamed with an elation that made him appear ridiculous to the negro porter. This individual at times surveyed them from afar with an amused and superior grin. On other occasions he bullied them with skill in ways that did not make it exactly plain to them that they were being bullied. He subtly used all the manners of the most unconquerable kind of snobbery. He oppressed them; but of this oppression they had small knowledge, and they speedily forgot that infrequently a number of travellers covered them with stares of derisive enjoyment. Historically there was supposed to be something infinitely humorous in their situation.

"We are due in Yellow Sky at 3:42," he said, looking tenderly into her eyes.

"Oh, are we?" she said, as if she had not been aware of it. To evince surprise at her husband's statement was part of her wifely amiability. She took from a pocket a little silver watch; and as she held it before her, and stared at it with a frown of attention, the new husband's face shone.

"I bought it in San Anton' from a friend of mine," he told her gleefully.

"It's seventeen minutes past twelve," she said, looking up at him with a kind of shy and clumsy coquetry. A passenger, noting this play, grew excessively sardonic, and winked at himself in one of the numerous mirrors.

At last they went to the dining-car. Two rows of negro waiters, in glowing white suits, surveyed their entrance with the interest, and also the equanimity, of men who had been forewarned. The pair fell to the lot of a waiter who happened to feel pleasure in steering them through their meal. He viewed them with the manner of a fatherly pilot, his countenance radiant with benevolence. The patronage, entwined with the ordinary deference, was not plain to them. And yet, as they returned to their coach, they showed in their faces a sense of escape.

To the left, miles down a long purple slope, was a little ribbon of mist where moved the keening Rio Grande. The train was approaching it at an angle, and the apex was Yellow Sky. Presently it was apparent that, as the distance from Yellow Sky grew shorter, the husband became commensurately restless. His brick-red hands were more insistent in their prominence. Occasionally he was even rather absent-minded and far-away when the bride leaned forward and addressed him.

As a matter of truth, Jack Potter was beginning to find the shadow of a deed weigh upon him like a leaden slab. He, the town marshal of Yellow Sky, a man known, liked, and feared in his corner, a prominent person, had gone to San Antonio to meet a girl he believed he loved, and there, after the usual prayers, had actually induced her to marry him, without consulting Yellow Sky for any part of the transaction. He was now bringing his bride before an innocent and unsuspecting community.

Of course people in Yellow Sky married as it pleased them, in accordance with a general custom; but such was Potter's thought of his duty to his friends, or of their idea of his duty, or of an unspoken form which does not control men in these matters, that he felt he was heinous. He had committed an extraordinary crime. Face to face with this girl in San Antonio, and spurred by his sharp impulse, he had gone headlong over all the social hedges. At San Antonio he was like a man hidden in the dark. A knife to sever any friendly duty, any form, was easy to his hand in that remote city. But the hour of Yellow Sky—the hour of daylight—was approaching.

He knew full well that his marriage was an important thing to his town. It could only be exceeded by the burning of the new hotel. His friends could not forgive him. Frequently he had reflected on the advisability of telling them by telegraph, but a new cowardice had been upon him. He feared to do it. And now the train was hurrying him toward a scene of amazement, glee, and reproach. He glanced out of the window at the line of haze swinging slowly in toward the train.

Yellow Sky had a kind of brass band, which played painfully, to the delight of the populace. He laughed without heart as he thought of it. It the citizens could dream of his prospective arrival with his bride, they would parade the band at the station and escort them, amid cheers and laughing congratulations, to his adobe home.

He resolved that he would use all the devices of speed and plainscraft in making the journey from the station to his house. Once within that safe citadel, he could issue some sort of vocal bulletin, and then not go among the citizens until they had time to wear off a little of their enthusiasm.

The bride looked anxiously at him. "What's worrying you, Jack?"

He laughed again. "I'm not worrying, girl; I'm only thinking of Yellow Sky."

She flushed in comprehension.

A sense of mutual guilt invaded their minds and developed a finer tenderness. They looked at each other with eyes softly aglow. But Potter often laughed the same nervous laugh; the flush upon the bride's face seemed quite permanent.

The traitor to the feelings of Yellow Sky narrowly watched the speeding landscape. "We're nearly there," he said.

Presently the porter came and announced the proximity of Potter's home. He held a brush in his hand, and, with all his airy superiority gone, he brushed Potter's new clothes as the latter slowly turned this way and that way. Potter fumbled out a coin and gave it to the porter, as he had seen others do. It was a heavy and muscle-bound business, as that of a man shoeing his first horse.

The porter took their bag, and as the train began to slow they moved forward to the hooded platform of the car. Presently the two engines and their long string of coaches rushed into the station of Yellow Sky.

"They have to take water here," said Potter, from a constricted throat and in mournful cadence, as one announcing death. Before the train stopped his eye had swept the length of the platform, and he was glad and astonished to see there was none upon it but the station-agent, who, with a slightly hurried and anxious air, was walking toward the water-tanks. When the train had halted, the porter alighted first, and placed in position a little temporary step.

"Come on, girl," said Potter, hoarsely. As he helped her down they each laughed on a false note. He took the bag from the negro, and bade his wife cling to his arm. As they slunk rapidly away, his hangdog glance perceived that they were unloading the two trunks, and also that the station-agent, far ahead near the baggage car, had turned and was running towards him, making gestures. He laughed, and groaned as he laughed, when he noted the first effect of his marital bliss upon Yellow Sky. He gripped his wife's arm firmly to his side, and they fled. Behind them the porter stood, chuckling fatuously.

II

The California express on the Southern Railway was due at Yellow Sky in twenty-one minutes. There were six men at the bar of the Weary Gentleman Saloon. One was a drummer who talked a great deal and rapidly; three were Texans who did not care to talk at that time; and two were Mexican sheep-herders, who did not talk as a general practice in the Weary Gentleman Saloon. The barkeeper's dog lay on the board walk that crossed in front of the door. His head was on his paws, and he glanced drowsily here and there with the constant vigilance of a dog that is kicked on occasion. Across the sandy street were some vivid green grass-plots, so wonderful in appearance, amid the sands that burned near them in a blazing sun, that they caused a doubt in the mind. They exactly resembled the grass mats used to represent lawns on the stage. At the cooler end of the railway station, a man without a coat sat in a tilted chair and smoked his pipe. The fresh-cut bank of the Rio Grande circled near the town, and there could be seen beyond it a great plum-colored plain of mesquit.

Save for the busy drummer and his companions in the saloon, Yellow Sky was dozing. The newcomer leaned gracefully upon the bar, and recited many tales with the confidence of a bard who has come upon a new field.

"—and at the moment that the old man fell downstairs with the bureau in his arms, the old woman was coming up with two scuttles of coal, and of course—"

The drummer's tale was interrupted by a young man who suddenly appeared in the open door. He cried: "Scratchy Wilson's drunk, and has turned loose with both hands." The two Mexicans at once set down their glasses and faded out of the rear entrance of the saloon.

The drummer, innocent and jocular, answered: "All right, old man. S'pose he has? Come in and have a drink, anyhow."

But the information had made such an obvious cleft in every skull in the room that the drummer was obliged to see its importance. All had become instantly solemn. "Say," said he, mystified, "what is this?" His three companions made the introductory gesture of eloquent speech; but the young man at the door forestalled them.

"It means, my friend," he answered, as he came into the saloon, "that for the next two hours this town won't be a health resort."

The barkeeper went to the door, and locked and barred it; reaching out of the window, he pulled in heavy wooden shutters, and barred them. Immediately a solemn, chapel-like gloom was upon the place. The drummer was looking from one to another.

"But say," he cried, "what is this anyhow? You don't mean there is going to be a gun-fight?"

"Don't know whether there'll be a fight or not," answered one man, grimly; "but there'll be some shootin'—some good shootin'."

The young man who had warned them waved his hand. "Oh, there'll be a fight fast enough, if any one wants it. Anybody can get a fight out there in the street. There's a fight just waiting."

The drummer seemed to be swayed between the interest of a foreigner and a perception of personal danger.

"What did you say his name was?" he asked.

"Scratchy Wilson," they answered in chorus.

"And will he kill anybody? What are you going to do? Does this happen often? Does he rampage around like this once a week or so? Can he break in that door?"

"No; he can't break down that door," replied the barkeeper. "He's tried it three times. But when he comes you'd better lay down on the floor, stranger. He's dead sure to shoot at it, and a bullet may come through."

Thereafter the drummer kept a strict eye upon the door. The time had not yet been called for him to hug the floor, but, as a minor precaution, he sidled near to the wall. "Will he kill anybody?" he said again.

The men laughed low and scornfully at the question.

"He's out to shoot, and he's out for trouble. Don't see any good in experimentin' with him."

"But what do you do in a case like this? What do you do?"

A man responded: "Why, he and Jack Potter—"

"But," in chorus the other men interrupted, "Jack Potter's in San Anton'."

"Well, who is he? What's he got to do with it?"

"Oh, he's the town marshal. He goes out and fights Scratchy when he gets on one of these tears."

"Wow!" said the drummer, mopping his brow. "Nice job he's got."

The voices had toned away to mere whisperings. The drummer wished to ask further questions, which were born of an increasing anxiety and bewilderment; but when he attempted them, the men merely looked at him in irritation and motioned him to remain silent. A tense waiting hush was upon them. In the deep shadows of the room their eyes shone as they listened for sounds from the street. One man made three gestures at the barkeeper; and the latter moving like a ghost, handed him a glass and a bottle. The man poured a full glass of whiskey, and set down the bottle noiselessly. He gulped the whiskey in a swallow, and turned again toward the door in immovable silence. The drummer saw that the barkeeper, without a sound, had taken a Winchester from beneath the bar. Later he saw this individual beckoning to him, so he tiptoed across the room.

"You better come with me back of the bar."

"No, thanks," said the drummer, perspiring; "I'd rather be where I can make a break for the back door."

Whereupon the man of bottles made a kindly but peremptory gesture. The drummer obeyed it, and, finding himself seated on a box with his head below the level of the bar, balm was laid upon his soul at sight of various zinc and copper fittings that bore a resemblance to armor-plate. The barkeeper took a seat comfortably upon an adjacent box.

"You see," he whispered, "this here Scratchy Wilson is a wonder with a gun—a perfect wonder; and when he goes on the war-trail, we hunt our holes—naturally. He's about the last one of the old gang that used to hang out along the river here. He's a terror when he's drunk. When he's sober he's all right—kind of simple—wouldn't hurt a fly—nicest fellow in town. But when he's drunk—whoo!"

There were periods of stillness. "I wish Jack Potter was back from San Anton'," said the barkeeper. "He shot Wilson up once—in the leg—and he would sail in and pull out the kinks in this thing."

Presently they heard from a distance the sound of a shot, followed by three wild yowls. It instantly removed a bond from the men in the darkened saloon. There was a shuffling of feet. They looked at each other. "Here he comes," they said.

III

A man in a maroon-colored flannel shirt, which had been purchased for purposes of decoration, and made principally by some Jewish women on the East Side of New York, rounded a corner and walked into the middle of the main street of Yellow Sky. In either hand the man held a long, heavy, blue-black revolver. Often he yelled, and these cries rang through a semblance of a deserted village, shrilly flying over the roofs in a volume that seemed to have no relation to the ordinary vocal strength of a man. It was as if the surrounding stillness formed the arch of a tomb over him. These cries of ferocious challenge rang against walls of silence. And his boots had red tops with gilded imprints, of the kind beloved in winter by little sledding boys on the hillsides of New England.

The man's face flamed in a rage begot of whiskey. His eyes, rolling, and yet keen for ambush, hunted the still doorways and windows. He walked with the creeping movement of the midnight cat. As it occurred to him, he roared menacing information. The long revolvers in his hands were as easy as straws; they were moved with an electric swiftness. The little fingers of each hand played sometimes in a musician's way. Plain from the low collar of the shirt, the cords of his neck straightened and sank, straightened and sank as passion moved him. The only sounds were his terrible invitations. The calm adobes preserved their demeanor at the passing of this small thing in the middle of the street.

There was no offer of fight—no offer of fight. The man called to the sky. There were no attractions. He bellowed and fumed and swayed his revolvers here and everywhere.

The dog of the barkeeper of the Weary Gentleman Saloon had not appreciated the advance of events. He yet lay dozing in front of his master's door. At sight of the dog, the man paused and raised his revolver humorously. At sight of the man, the dog sprang up and walked diagonally away, with a sullen head, and growling. The man yelled, and the dog broke into a gallop. As it was about to enter an alley, there was a loud noise, a whistling, and something spat the ground directly before it. The dog screamed, and, wheeling in terror, galloped headlong in a new direction. Again there was a noise, a whistling, and sand was kicked viciously before it. Fear-stricken, the dog turned and flurried like an animal in a pen. The man stood laughing, his weapons at his hips.

Ultimately the man was attracted by the closed door of the Weary Gentleman Saloon. He went to it and, hammering with a revolver, demanded drink.

The door remaining imperturbable, he picked a bit of paper from the walk, and nailed it to the framework with a knife. He then turned his back contemptuously upon this popular resort, and, walking to the opposite side of the street and spinning there on his heel quickly and lithely, fired at the bit of paper. He missed it by a half-inch. He swore at himself, and went away. Later he comfortably fusilladed the windows of his most intimate friend. The man was playing with this town; it was a toy for him.

But still there was no offer of fight. The name of Jack Potter, his ancient antagonist, entered his mind, and he concluded that it would be a glad thing if he should go to Potter's house, and by bombardment induce him to come out and fight. He moved in the direction of his desire, chanting Apache scalp-music.

When he arrived at it, Potter's house presented the same still front as had the other adobes. Taking up a strategic position, the man howled a challenge. But this house regarded him as might a great stone god. It gave no sign. After a decent wait, the man howled further challenges, mingling with them wonderful epithets.

Presently there came the spectacle of a man churning himself into deepest rage over the immobility of a house. He fumed at it as the winter wind attacks a prairie cabin in the North. To the distance there should have gone the sound of a tumult like the fighting of two hundred Mexicans. As necessity bade him, he paused for breath or to reload his revolvers.

Potter and his bride walked sheepishly and with speed. Sometimes they laughed together shamefacedly and low.

"Next corner, dear," he said finally.

They put forth the efforts of a pair walking bowed against a strong wind. Potter was about to raise a finger to point the first appearance of the new home when, as they circled the corner, they came face to face with a man in a maroon-colored shirt, who was feverishly pushing cartridges into a large revolver. Upon the instant the man dropped his revolver to the ground, and, like lightning, whipped another from its holster. The second weapon was aimed at the bridegroom's chest.

There was a silence. Potter's mouth seemed to be merely a grave for his tongue. He exhibited an instinct to at once loosen his arm from the woman's grip, and he dropped the bag to the sand. As for the bride, her face had gone as yellow as old cloth. She was a slave to hideous rites, gazing at the apparitional snake.

The two men faced each other at a distance of three paces. He of the revolver smiled with a new and quiet ferocity.

"Tried to sneak up on me," he said. "Tried to sneak up on me!" His eyes grew more baleful. As Potter made a slight movement, the man thrust his revolver venomously forward. "No; don't you do it, Jack Potter. Don't you move a finger toward a gun just yet. Don't you move an eyelash. The time has come for me to settle with you, and I'm goin' to do it my own way, and loaf along with no interferin'. So if you don't want a gun bent on you, just mind what I tell you."

Potter looked at his enemy. "I ain't got a gun on me, Scratchy," he said. "Honest, I ain't." He was stiffening and steadying, but yet somewhere at the back of his mind a vision of the Pullman floated: the sea-green figured velvet, the shining brass, silver, and glass, the wood that gleamed as darkly brilliant as the surface of a pool of oil—all the glory of the marriage, the environment of the new estate. "You know I fight when it comes to fighting, Scratchy Wilson; but I ain't got a gun on me. You'll have to do all the shootin' yourself."

His enemy's face went livid. He stepped forward, and lashed his weapon to and fro before Potter's chest. "Don't you tell me you ain't got no gun on you, you whelp. Don't tell me no lie like that. There ain't a man in Texas ever seen you without no gun. Don't take me for no kid." His eyes blazed with light, and his throat worked like a pump.

"I ain't takin' you for no kid," answered Potter. His heels had not moved an inch backward. "I'm takin' you for a—fool. I tell you I ain't got a gun, and I ain't. If you're goin' to shoot me up, you better begin now; you'll never get a chance like this again."

So much enforced reasoning had told on Wilson's rage; he was calmer. "If you ain't got a gun, why ain't you got a gun?" he sneered. "Been to Sunday school?"

"I ain't got a gun because I've just come from San Anton' with my wife. I'm married," said Potter. "And if I'd thought there was going to be any galoots like you prowling around when I brought my wife home, I'd had a gun, and don't you forget it."

"Married!" said Scratchy, not at all comprehending.

"Yes, married. I'm married," said Potter, distinctly.

"Married?" said Scratchy. Seemingly for the first time, he saw the drooping, drowning woman at the other man's side. "No!" he said. He was like a creature allowed a glimpse of another world. He moved a pace backward, and his arm, with the revolver, dropped to his side. "Is this the lady?" he asked.

"Yes; this is the lady," answered Potter.

There was another period of silence.

"Well," said Wilson at last, slowly, "I s'pose it's all off now."

"It's all off if you say so, Scratchy. You know I didn't make the trouble." Potter lifted his valise.

"Well, I 'low it's off, Jack," said Wilson. He was looking at the ground. "Married!" He was not a student of chivalry; it was merely that in the presence of this foreign condition he was a simple child of the earlier plains. He picked up his starboard revolver, and, placing both weapons in their holsters, he went away. His feet made funnel-shaped tracks in the heavy sand.

LOUISE ERDRICH (1954–)

The Red Convertible

I was the first one to drive a convertible on my reservation. And of course it was red, a red Olds. I owned that car along with my brother Henry Junior. We owned it together until his boots filled with water on a windy night and he bought out my share. Now Henry owns the whole car, and his younger brother Lyman (that's myself), Lyman walks everywhere he goes.

How did I earn enough money to buy my share in the first place? My one talent was I could always make money. I had a touch for it, unusual in a Chippewa. From the first I was different that way, and everyone recognized it. I was the only kid they let in the American Legion Hall to shine shoes, for example, and one Christmas I sold spiritual bouquets for the mission door to door. The nuns let me keep a percentage. Once I started, it seemed the more money I made the easier the money came. Everyone encouraged it. When I was fifteen I got a job washing dishes at the Joliet Café, and that was where my first big break happened.

It wasn't long before I was promoted to bussing tables, and then the short-order cook quit and I was hired to take her place. No sooner than you know it I was managing the Joliet. The rest is history. I went on managing. I soon become part owner, and of course there was no stopping me then. It wasn't long before the whole thing was mine.

After I'd owned the Joliet for one year, it blew over in the worst tornado ever seen around here. The whole operation was smashed to bits. A total loss. The

Louise Erdrich (*Michael Dorris*)

fryalator was up in a tree, the grill torn in half like it was paper. I was only sixteen. I had it all in my mother's name, and I lost it quick, but before I lost it I had every one of my relatives, and their relatives, to dinner, and I also bought that red Olds I mentioned, along with Henry.

The first time we saw it! I'll tell you when we first saw it. We had gotten a ride up to Winnipeg, and both of us had money. Don't ask me why, because we never mentioned a car or anything, we just had all our money. Mine was cash, a big bankroll from the Joliet's insurance. Henry had two checks—a week's extra pay for being laid off, and his regular check from the Jewel Bearing Plant.

We were walking down Portage anyway, seeing the sights, when we saw it. There it was, parked, large as life. Really as *if* it was alive. I thought of the word *repose*, because the car wasn't simply stopped, parked, or whatever. That car reposed, calm and gleaming, a FOR SALE sign in its left front window. Then, before we had thought it over at all, the car belonged to us and our pockets were empty. We had just enough money for gas back home.

We went places in that car, me and Henry. We took off driving all one whole summer. We started off toward the Little Knife River and Mandaree in Fort Berthold and then we found ourselves down in Wakpala somehow, and then suddenly we were over in Montana on the Rocky Boys, and yet the summer was not even half over. Some people hang on to details when they travel, but we didn't let them bother us and just lived our everyday lives here to there.

I do remember this one place with willows. I remember I laid under those trees and it was comfortable. So comfortable. The branches bent down all around me like a tent or a stable. And quiet, it was quiet, even though there was a powwow close enough so I could see it going on. The air was not too still, not too windy either. When the dust rises up and hangs in the air around the dancers like that, I feel good. Henry was asleep with his arms thrown wide. Later on, he woke up and we started driving again. We were somewhere in Montana, or maybe on the Blood Reserve—it could have been anywhere. Anyway it was where we met the girl.

All her hair was in buns around her ears, that's the first thing I noticed about her. She was posed alongside the road with her arm out, so we stopped. That girl was short, so short her lumber shirt looked comical on her, like a nightgown. She had jeans on and fancy moccasins and she carried a little suitcase.

"Hop on in," says Henry. So she climbs in between us.

"We'll take you home," I says. "Where do you live?"

"Chicken," she says.

"Where the hell's that?" I ask her.

"Alaska."

"Okay," says Henry, and we drive.

We got up there and never wanted to leave. The sun doesn't truly set there in summer, and the night is more a soft dusk. You might doze off, sometimes, but before you know it you're up again, like an animal in nature. You never feel like you have to sleep hard or put away the world. And things would grow up there. One day just dirt or moss, the next day flowers and long grass. The girl's name was Susy. Her family really took to us. They fed us and put us up. We had our own tent to live in by their house, and the kids would be in and out of there all day and night. They couldn't get over me and Henry being brothers, we looked so different. We told them we knew we had the same mother, anyway.

One night Susy came in to visit us. We sat around in the tent talking of this thing and that. The season was changing. It was getting darker by that time, and the cold was even getting just a little mean. I told her it was time for us to go. She stood up on a chair.

"You never seen my hair," Susy said.

That was true. She was standing on a chair, but still, when she unclipped her buns the hair reached all the way to the ground. Our eyes opened. You couldn't tell how much hair she had when it was rolled up so neatly. Then my brother Henry did something funny. He went up to the chair and said, "Jump on my shoulders." So she did that, and her hair reached down past his waist, and he started twirling, this way and that, so her hair was flung out from side to side.

"I always wondered what it was like to have long pretty hair," Henry says. Well we laughed. It was a funny sight, the way he did it. The next morning we got up and took leave of those people.

On to greener pastures, as they say. It was down through Spokane and across Idaho then Montana and very soon we were racing the weather right along under the Canadian border through Columbus, Des Lacs, and then we were in Bottineau County and soon home. We'd made most of the trip, that summer, without putting up the car hood at all. We got home just in time, it turned out, for the army to remember Henry had signed up to join it.

I don't wonder that the army was so glad to get my brother that they turned him into a Marine. He was built like a brick outhouse anyway. We liked to tease him that they really wanted him for his Indian nose. He had a nose big and sharp as a hatchet, like the nose on Red Tomahawk, the Indian who killed Sitting Bull, whose profile is on signs all along the North Dakota highways. Henry went off to training camp, came home once during Christmas, then the next thing you know we got an overseas letter from him. It was 1970, and he said he was stationed up in the northern hill country. Whereabouts I did not know. He wasn't such a hot letter writer, and only got off two before the enemy caught him. I could never keep it straight, which direction those good Vietnam soldiers were from.

I wrote him back several times, even though I didn't know if those letters would get through. I kept him informed all about the car. Most of the time I had it up on blocks in the yard or half taken apart, because that long trip did a hard job on it under the hood.

I always had good luck with numbers, and never worried about the draft myself. I never even had to think about what my number was. But Henry was never lucky in the same way as me. It was at least three years before Henry came home. By then I guess the whole war was solved in the government's mind, but for him it would keep on going. In those years I'd put his car into almost perfect shape. I always thought of it as his car while he was gone, even though when he left he said, "Now it's yours," and threw me his key.

"Thanks for the extra key," I'd said. "I'll put it up in your drawer just in case I need it." He laughed.

When he came home, though, Henry was very different, and I'll say this: the change was no good. You could hardly expect him to change for the better, I know. But he was quiet, so quiet, and never comfortable sitting still anywhere but always up and moving around. I thought back to times we'd sat still for whole afternoons, never moving a muscle, just shifting our weight along the ground, talking to whoever sat with us, watching things. He'd always had a joke, then, too, and now you couldn't get him to laugh, or when he did it was more the sound of a man choking, a sound that stopped up the throats of other people around him. They got to leaving him alone most of the time, and I didn't blame them. It was a fact: Henry was jumpy and mean.

I'd bought a color TV set for my mom and the rest of us while Henry was away. Money still came very easy. I was sorry I'd ever bought it though, because of Henry. I was also sorry I'd bought color, because with black-and-white the pictures seem older and farther away. But what are you going to do? He sat in front of it, watching it, and that was the only time he was completely still. But it was the kind of stillness that you see in a rabbit when it freezes and before it will bolt. He was not easy. He sat in his chair gripping the armrests with all his might, as if the chair itself was moving at a high speed and if he let go at all he would rocket forward and maybe crash right through the set.

Once I was in the room watching TV with Henry and I heard his teeth click at something. I looked over, and he'd bitten through his lip. Blood was going down his chin. I tell you right then I wanted to smash that tube to pieces. I went over to it but Henry must have known what I was up to. He rushed from his chair and shoved me out of the way, against the wall. I told myself he didn't know what he was doing.

My mom came in, turned the set off real quiet, and told us she had made something for supper. So we went and sat down. There was still blood going down Henry's chin, but he didn't notice it and no one said anything, even though every time he took a bite of his bread his blood fell onto it until he was eating his own blood mixed in with the food.

While Henry was not around we talked about what was going to happen to him. There were no Indian doctors on the reservation, and my mom was afraid of trusting Old Man Pillager because he courted her long ago and was jealous of her husbands. He might take revenge through her son. We were afraid that if we brought Henry to a regular hospital they would keep him.

"They don't fix them in those places," Mom said; "they just give them drugs."

"We wouldn't get him there in the first place," I agreed, "so let's just forget about it."

Then I thought about the car.

Henry had not even looked at the car since he'd gotten home, though like I said, it was in tip-top condition and ready to drive. I thought the car might bring the old Henry back somehow. So I bided my time and waited for my chance to interest him in the vehicle.

One night Henry was off somewhere. I took myself a hammer. I went out to that car and I did a number on its underside. Whacked it up. Bent the tail pipe double. Ripped the muffler loose. By the time I was done with the car it looked worse than any typical Indian car that has been driven all its life on reservation roads, which they always say are like government promises—full of holes. It just about hurt me, I'll tell you that! I threw dirt in the carburetor and I ripped all the electric tape off the seats. I made it look just as beat up as I could. Then I sat back and waited for Henry to find it.

Still, it took him over a month. That was all right, because it was just getting warm enough, not melting, but warm enough to work outside.

"Lyman," he says, walking in one day, "that red car looks like shit."

"Well it's old," I says. "You got to expect that."

"No way!" says Henry. "That car's a classic! But you went and ran the piss right out of it, Lyman, and you know it don't deserve that. I kept that car in A-one shape. You don't remember. You're too young. But when I left, that car was running like a watch. Now I don't even know if I can get it to start again, let alone get it anywhere near its old condition."

"Well you try," I said, like I was getting mad, "but I say it's a piece of junk."

Then I walked out before he could realize I knew he'd strung together more than six words at once.

After that I thought he'd freeze himself to death working on that car. He was out there all day, and at night he rigged up a little lamp, ran a cord out the window, and had himself some light to see by while he worked. He was better than he had been before, but that's still not saying much. It was easier for him to do the things the rest of us did. He ate more slowly and didn't jump up and down during the meal to get this or that or look out the window. I put my hand in the back of the TV set, I admit, and fiddled around with it good, so that it was almost impossible now to get a clear picture. He didn't look at it very often anyway. He was always out with that car or going off to get parts for it. By the time it was really melting outside, he had it fixed.

I had been feeling down in the dumps about Henry around this time. We had always been together before. Henry and Lyman. But he was such a loner now that I didn't know how to take it. So I jumped at the chance one day when Henry seemed friendly. It's not that he smiled or anything. He just said, "Let's take that old shitbox for a spin." Just the way he said it made me think he could be coming around.

We went out to the car. It was spring. The sun was shining very bright. My only sister, Bonita, who was just eleven years old, came out and made us stand together for a picture. Henry leaned his elbow on the red car's windshield, and he took his other arm and put it over my shoulder, very carefully, as though it was heavy for him to lift and he didn't want to bring the weight down all at once.

"Smile," Bonita said, and he did.

That picture. I never look at it anymore. A few months ago, I don't know why, I got his picture out and tacked it on the wall. I felt good about Henry at the time, close to him. I felt good having his picture on the wall, until one night when I was looking at television. I was a little drunk and stoned. I looked up at the wall and Henry was staring at me. I don't know what it was, but his smile had changed, or maybe it was gone. All I know is I couldn't stay in the same room with that picture. I was shaking. I got up, closed the door, and went into the kitchen. A little later my friend Ray came over and we both went back into that room. We put the picture in a brown bag, folded the bag over and over tightly, then put it way back in a closet.

I still see that picture now, as if it tugs at me, whenever I pass that closet door. The picture is very clear in my mind. It was so sunny that day Henry had to squint against the glare. Or maybe the camera Bonita held flashed like a mirror, blinding him, before she snapped the picture. My face is right out in the sun, big and round. But he might have drawn back, because the shadows on his face are deep as holes. There are two shadows curved like little hooks around the ends of his smile, as if to frame it and try to keep it there—that one, first smile that looked like it might have hurt his face. He has his field jacket on and the worn-in clothes he'd come back in and kept wearing ever since. After Bonita took the picture, she went into the house and we got into the car. There was a full cooler in the trunk. We started off, east, toward Pembina and the Red River because Henry said he wanted to see the high water.

The trip over there was beautiful. When everything starts changing, drying up, clearing off, you feel like your whole life is starting. Henry felt it, too. The top was down and the car hummed like a top. He'd really put it back in shape, even the tape on the seats was very carefully put down and glued back in layers. It's not that he smiled again or even joked, but his face looked to me as if it was clear, more peaceful. It looked as though he wasn't thinking of anything in particular except the bare fields and windbreaks and houses we were passing.

The river was high and full of winter trash when we got there. The sun was still out, but it was colder by the river. There were still little clumps of dirty snow here and there on the banks. The water hadn't gone over the banks yet, but it would, you could tell. It was just at its limit, hard swollen, glossy like an old gray scar. We made ourselves a fire, and we sat down and watched the current go. As I watched it I felt something squeezing inside me and tightening and trying to let go all at the same time. I knew I was not just feeling it myself; I knew I was feeling what Henry was going through at that moment. Except that I couldn't stand it, the closing and opening. I jumped to my feet. I took Henry by the shoulders and I started shaking him. "Wake up," I says, "wake up, wake up, wake up!" I didn't know what had come over me. I sat down beside him again.

His face was totally white and hard. Then it broke, like stones break all of a sudden when water boils up inside them.

"I know it," he says. "I know it. I can't help it. It's no use."

We start talking. He said he knew what I'd done with the car. It was obvious it had been whacked out of shape and not just neglected. He said he wanted to give the car to me for good now, it was no use. He said he'd fixed it just to give it back and I should take it.

"No way," I says, "I don't want it."

"That's okay," he says, "you take it."

"I don't want it, though," I says back to him, and then to emphasize, just to emphasize, you understand, I touch his shoulder. He slaps my hand off.

"Take that car," he says.

"No," I say, "make me," I say, and then he grabs my jacket and rips the arm loose. That jacket is a class act, suede with tags and zippers. I push Henry backwards, off the log. He jumps up and bowls me over. We go down in a clinch and come up swinging hard, for all we're worth, with our fists. He socks my jaw so hard I feel like it swings loose. Then I'm at his ribcage and land a good one under his chin so his head snaps back. He's dazzled. He looks at me and I look at him and then his eyes are full of tears and blood and at first I think he's crying. But no, he's laughing. "Ha! Ha!" he says. "Ha! Ha! Take good care of it."

"Okay," I says, "okay, no problem. Ha! Ha!"

I can't help it, and I start laughing, too. My face feels fat and strange, and after a while I get a beer from the cooler in the trunk, and when I hand it to Henry he takes his shirt and wipes my germs off. "Hoof-and-mouth disease," he says. For some reason this cracks me up, and so we're really laughing for a while, and then we drink all the rest of the beers one by one and throw them in the river and see how far, how fast, the current takes them before they fill up and sink.

"You want to go on back?" I ask after a while. "Maybe we could snag a couple nice Kashpaw girls."

He says nothing. But I can tell his mood is turning again.

"They're all crazy, the girls up here, every damn one of them."

"You're crazy too," I say, to jolly him up. "Crazy Lamartine boys!"

He looks as though he will take this wrong at first. His face twists, then clears, and he jumps up on his feet. "That's right!" he says. "Crazier 'n hell. Crazy Indians!"

I think it's the old Henry again. He throws off his jacket and starts swinging his legs out from the knees like a fancy dancer. He's down doing something between a grouse dance and a bunny hop, no kind of dance I ever saw before, but neither has anyone else on all this green growing earth. He's wild. He wants to pitch whoopee! He's up and at me and all over. All this time I'm laughing so hard, so hard my belly is getting tied up in a knot.

"Got to cool me off!" he shouts all of a sudden. Then he runs over to the river and jumps in.

There's boards and other things in the current. It's so high. No sound comes from the river after the splash he makes, so I run right over. I look around. It's getting dark. I see he's halfway across the water already, and I know he didn't swim there but the current took him. It's far. I hear his voice, though, very clearly across it.

"My boots are filling," he says.

He says this in a normal voice, like he just noticed and he doesn't know what to think of it. Then he's gone. A branch comes by. Another branch. And I go in.

By the time I get out of the river, off the snag I pulled myself onto, the sun is down. I walk back to the car, turn on the high beams, and drive it up the bank. I put it in first gear and then I take my foot off the clutch. I get out, close the door, and watch it plow softly into the water. The headlights reach in as they go down, searching, still lighted even after the water swirls over the back end. I wait. The wires short out. It is all finally dark. And then there is only the water, the sound of it going and running and going and running and running.

WILLIAM FAULKNER (1897–1962)

A Rose for Emily

I

When Miss Emily Grierson died, our whole town went to her funeral: the men through a sort of respectful affection for a fallen monument, the women mostly out of curiosity to see the inside of her house, which no one save an old manservant—a combined gardener and cook—had seen in at least ten years.

It was a big, squarish frame house that had once been white, decorated with cupolas and spires and scrolled balconies in the heavily lightsome style of the seventies, set on what had once been our most select street. But garages and cotton gins had encroached and obliterated even the august names of that neighborhood; only Miss Emily's house was left, lifting its stubborn and coquettish decay above the cotton wagons and the gasoline pumps—an eyesore among eyesores. And now Miss Emily had gone to join the representatives of those august names where they lay in the cedar-bemused cemetery among the ranked and anonymous graves of Union and Confederate soldiers who fell at the battle of Jefferson.

Alive, Miss Emily had been a tradition, a duty, and a care; a sort of hereditary obligation upon the town, dating from that day in 1894 when Colonel Sartoris, the mayor—he who fathered the edict that no Negro woman should appear on the streets without an apron—remitted her taxes, the dispensation dating from the death of her father on into perpetuity. Not that Miss Emily would have accepted charity. Colonel Sartoris invented an involved tale to the effect that Miss Emily's father had loaned money to the town, which the town, as a matter of business, preferred this way of repaying. Only a man of Colonel Sartoris' generation and thought could have invented it, and only a woman could have believed it.

When the next generation, with its more modern ideas, became mayors and aldermen, this arrangement created some little dissatisfaction. On the first of the year they mailed her a tax notice. February came, and there was no reply. They wrote her a formal letter, asking her to call at the sheriff's office at her convenience. A week later the mayor wrote her himself, offering to call or to send his car for her, and received in reply a note on paper of an archaic shape, in a thin, flowing calligraphy in faded ink, to the effect that she no longer went out at all. The tax notice was also enclosed, without comment.

They called a special meeting of the Board of Aldermen. A deputation waited upon her, knocked at the door through which no visitor had passed since she ceased giving china-painting lessons eight or ten years earlier. They were admitted by the old Negro into a dim hall from which a stairway mounted into still more shadow. It smelled of dust and disuse—a close, dank smell. The Negro led them into the parlor. It was furnished in heavy, leather-covered furniture. When the Negro opened the blinds of one window, they could see that the leather was cracked; and when they sat down, a faint dust rose sluggishly about their thighs, spinning with slow motions in the single sun-ray. On a tarnished gilt easel before the fireplace stood a crayon portrait of Miss Emily's father.

They rose when she entered—a small, fat woman in black, with a thin gold chain descending to her waist and vanishing into her belt, leaning on an ebony cane with a tarnished gold head. Her skeleton was small and spare; perhaps that was why what would have been merely plumpness in another was obesity in her. She looked bloated, like a body long submerged in motionless water, and of that pallid hue. Her eyes, lost in the fatty ridges of her face, looked like two small pieces of coal pressed into a lump of dough as they moved from one face to another while the visitors stated their errand.

She did not ask them to sit. She just stood in the door and listened quietly until the spokesman came to a stumbling halt. Then they could hear the invisible watch ticking at the end of the gold chain.

Her voice was dry and cold. "I have no taxes in Jefferson. Colonel Sartoris explained it to me. Perhaps one of you can gain access to the city records and satisfy yourselves."

"But we have. We are the city authorities, Miss Emily. Didn't you get a notice from the sheriff, signed by him?"

"I received a paper, yes," Miss Emily said. "Perhaps he considers himself the sheriff . . . I have no taxes in Jefferson."

"But there is nothing on the books to show that, you see. We must go by the—"

"See Colonel Sartoris." (Colonel Sartoris had been dead almost ten years.) "I have no taxes in Jefferson. Tobe!" The Negro appeared. "Show these gentlemen out."

II

So she vanquished them, horse and foot, just as she had vanquished their fathers thirty years before about the smell. That was two years after her father's death and a short time after her sweetheart—the one we believed would marry her— had deserted her. After her father's death she went out very little; after her sweetheart went away, people hardly saw her at all. A few of the ladies had the temerity to call, but were not received, and the only sign of life about the place was the Negro man—a young man then—going in and out with a market basket.

"Just as if a man—any man—could keep a kitchen properly," the ladies said; so they were not surprised when the smell developed. It was another link between the gross, teeming world and the high and mighty Griersons.

A neighbor, a woman, complained to the mayor, Judge Stevens, eighty years old.

"But what will you have me do about it, madam?" he said.

"Why, send her word to stop it," the woman said. "Isn't there a law?"

"I'm sure that won't be necessary," Judge Stevens said. "It's probably just a snake or a rat that nigger of hers killed in the yard. I'll speak to him about it."

The next day he received two more complaints, one from a man who came in diffident deprecation. "We really must do something about it, Judge. I'd be the last one in the world to bother Miss Emily, but we've got to do something." That night the Board of Aldermen met—three graybeards and one younger man, a member of the rising generation.

"It's simple enough," he said. "Send her word to have her place cleaned up. Give her a certain time to do it in, and if she don't . . ."

"Dammit, sir," Judge Stevens said, "will you accuse a lady to her face of smelling bad?"

So the next night, after midnight, four men crossed Miss Emily's lawn and slunk about the house like burglars, sniffing along the base of the brickwork and at the cellar openings while one of them performed a regular sowing motion with his hand out of a sack slung from his shoulder. They broke open the cellar door and sprinkled lime there, and in all the outbuildings. As they recrossed the lawn, a window that had been dark was lighted and Miss Emily sat in it, the light behind her, and her upright torso motionless as that of an idol. They crept quietly across the lawn and into the shadow of the locusts that lined the street. After a week or two the smell went away.

That was when people had begun to feel really sorry for her. People in our town, remembering how old lady Wyatt, her great-aunt, had gone completely crazy at last, believed that the Griersons held themselves a little too high for what they really were. None of the young men were quite good enough for Miss Emily and such. We had long thought of them as a tableau, Miss Emily a slender figure in white in the background, her father a spraddled silhouette in the foreground, his back to her and clutching a horsewhip, the two of them framed by the back-flung front door. So when she got to be thirty and was still single, we were not pleased exactly, but vindicated; even with insanity in the family she wouldn't have turned down all of her chances if they had really materialized.

When her father died, it got about that the house was all that was left to her; and in a way, people were glad. At last they could pity Miss Emily. Being left alone, and a pauper, she had become humanized. Now she too would know the old thrill and the old despair of a penny more or less.

The day after his death all the ladies prepared to call at the house and offer condolence and aid, as is our custom. Miss Emily met them at the door, dressed as usual and with no trace of grief on her face. She told them that her father was not dead. She did that for three days, with the ministers calling on her, and the doctors, trying to persuade her to let them dispose of the body. Just as they were about to resort to law and force, she broke down, and they buried her father quickly.

We did not say she was crazy then. We believed she had to do that. We remembered all the young men her father had driven away, and we knew that with nothing left, she would have to cling to that which had robbed her, as people will.

III

She was sick for a long time. When we saw her again, her hair was cut short, making her look like a girl, with a vague resemblance to those angels in colored church windows—sort of tragic and serene.

The town had just let the contracts for paving the sidewalks, and in the summer after her father's death they began the work. The construction company came with niggers and mules and machinery, and a foreman named Homer Barron, a Yankee—a big, dark, ready man, with a big voice and eyes lighter than his face. The little boys would follow in groups to hear him cuss the niggers, and the niggers singing in time to the rise and fall of picks. Pretty soon he knew everybody in town. Whenever you heard a lot of laughing anywhere about the square, Homer Barron would be in the center of the group. Presently we began to see him and Miss Emily on Sunday afternoons driving in the yellow-wheeled buggy and the matched team of bays from the livery stable.

At first we were glad that Miss Emily would have an interest, because the ladies all said, "Of course a Grierson would not think seriously of a Northerner, a day laborer." But there were still others, older people, who said that even grief could not cause a real lady to forget *noblesse oblige*—without calling it *noblesse oblige*. They just said, "Poor Emily. Her kinsfolk should come to her." She had some kin in Alabama; but years ago her father had fallen out with them over the estate of old lady Wyatt, the crazy woman, and there was no communication between the two families. They had not even been represented at the funeral.

And as soon as the old people said, "Poor Emily," the whispering began. "Do you suppose it's really so?" they said to one another. "Of course it is. What else could . . ." This behind their hands; rustling of craned silk and satin behind jalousies closed upon the sun of Sunday afternoon as the thin, swift clop-clop-clop of the matched team passed: "Poor Emily."

She carried her head high enough—even when we believed that she was fallen. It was as if she demanded more than ever the recognition of her dignity as the last Grierson; as if it had wanted that touch of earthiness to reaffirm her imperviousness. Like when she bought the rat poison, the arsenic. That was over a year after they had begun to say "Poor Emily," and while the two female cousins were visiting her.

"I want some poison," she said to the druggist. She was over thirty then, still a slight woman, though thinner than usual, with cold, haughty black eyes in a face the flesh of which was strained across the temples and about the eye-sockets as you imagine a lighthouse-keeper's face ought to look. "I want some poison," she said.

"Yes, Miss Emily. What kind? For rats and such? I'd recom—"

"I want the best you have. I don't care what kind."

The druggist named several. "They'll kill anything up to an elephant. But what you want is—"

"Arsenic," Miss Emily said. "Is that a good one?"

"Is . . . arsenic? Yes, ma'am. But what you want—"

"I want arsenic."

The druggist looked down at her. She looked back at him, erect, her face like a strained flag. "Why, of course," the druggist said. "If that's what you want. But the law requires you to tell what you are going to use it for."

Miss Emily just stared at him, her head tilted back in order to look him eye for eye, until he looked away and went and got the arsenic and wrapped it up. The Negro delivery boy brought her the package; the druggist didn't come back. When she opened the package at home there was written on the box, under the skull and bones: "For rats."

IV

So the next day we all said, "She will kill herself"; and we said it would be the best thing. When she had first begun to be seen with Homer Barron, we had said, "She will marry him." Then we said, "She will persuade him yet," because Homer himself had remarked—he liked men, and it was known that he drank with the younger men in the Elks' Club—that he was not a marrying man. Later we said, "Poor Emily" behind the jalousies as they passed on Sunday afternoon in the glittering buggy, Miss Emily with her head high and Homer Barron with his hat cocked and a cigar in his teeth, reins and whip in a yellow glove.

Then some of the ladies began to say that it was a disgrace to the town and a bad example to the young people. The men did not want to interfere, but at last the ladies forced the Baptist minister—Miss Emily's people were Episcopal—to call upon her. He would never divulge what happened during that interview, but he refused to go back again. The next Sunday they again drove about the streets, and the following day the minister's wife wrote to Miss Emily's relations in Alabama.

So she had blood-kin under her roof again and we sat back to watch developments. At first nothing happened. Then we were sure that they were to be married. We learned that Miss Emily had been to the jeweler's and ordered a man's toilet set in silver, with the letters H.B. on each piece. Two days later we learned that she had bought a complete outfit of men's clothing, including a nightshirt, and we said, "They are married." We were really glad. We were glad because the two female cousins were even more Grierson than Miss Emily had ever been.

So we were not surprised when Homer Barron—the streets had been finished some time since—was gone. We were a little disappointed that there was not a public blowing-off, but we believed that he had gone on to prepare for Miss Emily's coming, or to give her a chance to get rid of the cousins. (By that time it was a cabal, and we were all Miss Emily's allies to help circumvent the cousins.) Sure enough, after another week they departed. And, as we had expected all along, within three days Homer Barron was back in town. A neighbor saw the Negro man admit him at the kitchen door at dusk one evening.

And that was the last we saw of Homer Barron. And of Miss Emily for some time. The Negro man went in and out with the market basket, but the front door remained closed. Now and then we would see her at a window for a moment, as the men did that night when they sprinkled the lime, but for almost six months she did not appear on the streets. Then we knew that this was to be expected too; as if that quality of her father which had thwarted her woman's life so many times had been too virulent and too furious to die.

When we next saw Miss Emily, she had grown fat and her hair was turning gray. During the next few years it grew grayer and grayer until it attained an even pepper-and-salt iron-gray, when it ceased turning. Up to the day of her death at seventy-four it was still that vigorous iron-gray, like the hair of an active man.

From that time on her front door remained closed, save for a period of six or seven years, when she was about forty, during which she gave lessons in china-painting. She fitted up a studio in one of the downstairs rooms, where the daughters and granddaughters of Colonel Sartoris' contemporaries were sent to her with the same regularity and in the same spirit that they were sent to church on Sundays with a twenty-five-cent piece for the collection plate. Meanwhile her taxes had been remitted.

Then the newer generation became the backbone and the spirit of the town, and the painting pupils grew up and fell away and did not send their children to her with boxes of color and tedious brushes and pictures cut from the ladies' magazines. The front door closed upon the last one and remained closed for good. When the town got free postal delivery, Miss Emily alone refused to let them fasten the metal numbers above her door and attach a mailbox to it. She would not listen to them.

Daily, monthly, yearly we watched the Negro grow grayer and more stooped, going in and out with the market basket. Each December we sent her a tax notice, which would be returned by the post office a week later, unclaimed. Now and then we would see her in one of the downstairs windows—she had evidently shut up the top floor of the house—like the carven torso of an idol in a niche, looking or not looking at us, we could never tell which. Thus she passed from generation to generation—dear, inescapable, impervious, tranquil, and perverse.

And so she died. Fell ill in the house filled with dust and shadows, with only a doddering Negro man to wait on her. We did not even know she was sick; we had long since given up trying to get any information from the Negro. He talked to no one, probably not even to her, for his voice had grown harsh and rusty, as if from disuse.

She died in one of the downstairs rooms, in a heavy walnut bed with a curtain, her gray head propped on a pillow yellow and moldy with age and lack of sunlight.

V

The Negro met the first of the ladies at the front door and let them in, with their hushed, sibilant voices and their quick, curious glances, and then he disappeared. He walked right through the house and out the back and was not seen again.

The two female cousins came at once. They held the funeral on the second day, with the town coming to look at Miss Emily beneath a mass of bought flowers, with the crayon face of her father musing profoundly above the bier and the ladies sibilant and macabre; and the very old men—some in their brushed Confederate uniforms—on the porch and the lawn, talking of Miss Emily as if she had been a contemporary of theirs, believing that they had danced with her and courted her perhaps, confusing time with its mathematical progression, as the old do, to whom all the past is not a diminishing road but, instead, a huge meadow which no winter ever quite touches, divided from them now by the narrow bottle-neck of the most recent decade of years.

Already we knew that there was one room in that region above stairs which no one had seen in forty years, and which would have to be forced. They waited until Miss Emily was decently in the ground before they opened it.

The violence of breaking down the door seemed to fill this room with pervading dust. A thin, acrid pall as of the tomb seemed to lie everywhere upon this room decked and furnished as for a bridal: upon the valance curtains of faded rose color, upon the rose-shaded lights, upon the dressing table, upon the delicate array of crystal and the man's toilet things backed with tarnished silver, silver so tarnished that the monogram was obscured. Among them lay a collar and tie, as if they had just been removed, which, lifted, left upon the surface a pale crescent in the dust. Upon a chair hung the suit, carefully folded; beneath it the two mute shoes and the discarded socks.

The man himself lay in the bed.

For a long while we just stood there, looking down at the profound and fleshless grin. The body had apparently once lain in the attitude of an embrace, but now the long sleep that outlasts love, that conquers even the grimace of love, had cuckolded him. What was left of him, rotted beneath what was left of the nightshirt, had become inextricable from the bed in which he lay; and upon him and upon the pillow beside him lay that even coating of the patient and biding dust.

Then we noticed that in the second pillow was the indentation of a head. One of us lifted something from it, and leaning forward, that faint and invisible dust dry and acrid in the nostrils, we saw a long strand of iron-gray hair.

 Writers on Writing *William Faulkner*

> *The young man or woman writing today has forgotten the problems of the human heart in conflict with itself which alone can make good writing because only that is worth writing about, worth the agony and the sweat.*
>
> *He must learn them again. He must teach himself that the basest of all things is to be afraid; and, teaching himself that, forget it forever, leaving no room in his workshop for anything but the old verities and truths of the heart, the old universal truths lacking which any story is ephemeral and doomed—love and honor and pity and pride and compassion and sacrifice.*

ERNEST HEMINGWAY (1898–1961)

Hills Like White Elephants

The hills across the valley of the Ebro were long and white. On this side there was no shade and no trees and the station was between two lines of rails in the sun. Close against the side of the station there was the warm shadow of the building and a curtain, made of strings of bamboo beads, hung across the open door into the bar, to keep out flies. The American and the girl with him sat at a table in the shade, outside the building. It was very hot and the express from Barcelona would come in forty minutes. It stopped at this junction for two minutes and went on to Madrid.

"What should we drink?" the girl asked. She had taken off her hat and put it on the table.

"It's pretty hot," the man said.

"Let's drink beer."

"Dos cervezas," the man said into the curtain.

"Big ones?" a woman asked from the doorway.

"Yes. Two big ones."

The woman brought two glasses of beer and two felt pads. She put the felt pads and the beer glasses on the table and looked at the man and the girl. The girl was looking off at the line of hills. They were white in the sun and the country was brown and dry.

"They look like white elephants," she said.

"I've never seen one," the man drank his beer.

"No, you wouldn't have."

"I might have," the man said. "Just because you say I wouldn't have doesn't prove anything."

The girl looked at the bead curtain. "They've painted something on it," she said. "What does it say?"

"Anis del Toro. It's a drink."

"Could we try it?"

The man called "Listen" through the curtain. The woman came out from the bar.

"Four reales."

"We want two Anis del Toro."

"With water?"

"Do you want it with water?"

"I don't know," the girl said. "Is it good with water?"

"It's all right."

"You want them with water?" asked the woman.

"Yes, with water."

"It tastes like licorice," the girl said and put the glass down.

"That's the way with everything."

"Yes," said the girl. "Everything tastes of licorice. Especially all the things you've waited so long for, like absinthe."

"Oh, cut it out."

"You started it," the girl said. "I was being amused. I was having a fine time."

"Well, let's try and have a fine time."

"All right. I was trying. I said the mountains looked like white elephants. Wasn't that bright?"

"That was bright."

"I wanted to try this new drink. That's all we do, isn't it—look at things and try new drinks?"

"I guess so."

The girl looked across at the hills.

"They're lovely hills," she said. "They don't really look like white elephants. I just meant the coloring of their skin through the trees."

"Should we have another drink?"

"All right."

The warm wind blew the bead curtain against the table.

"The beer's nice and cool," the man said.

"It's lovely," the girl said.

"It's really an awfully simple operation, Jig," the man said. "It's not really an operation at all."

The girl looked at the ground the table legs rested on.

"I know you wouldn't mind it, Jig. It's really not anything. It's just to let the air in."

The girl did not say anything.

"I'll go with you and I'll stay with you all the time. They just let the air in and then it's all perfectly natural."

"Then what will we do afterward?"

"We'll be fine afterward. Just like we were before."

"What makes you think so?"

"That's the only thing that bothers us. It's the only thing that's made us unhappy."

The girl looked at the bead curtain, put her hand out and took hold of two of the strings of beads.

"And you think then we'll be all right and be happy."

"I know we will. You don't have to be afraid. I've known lots of people that have done it."

"So have I," said the girl. "And afterward they were all so happy."

"Well," the man said, "if you don't want to you don't have to. I wouldn't have you do it if you didn't want to. But I know it's perfectly simple."

"And you really want to?"

"I think it's the best thing to do. But I don't want you to do it if you don't really want to."

"And if I do it you'll be happy and things will be like they were and you'll love me?"

"I love you now. You know I love you."

"I know. But if I do it, then it will be nice again if I say things are like white elephants, and you'll like it?"

"I'll love it. I love it now but I just can't think about it. You know how I get when I worry."

"If I do it you won't ever worry?"

"I won't worry about that because it's perfectly simple."

"Then I'll do it. Because I don't care about me."

"What do you mean?"

"I don't care about me."

"Well, I care about you."

"Oh, yes. But I don't care about me. And I'll do it and then everything will be fine."

"I don't want you to do it if you feel that way."

The girl stood up and walked to the end of the station. Across, on the other side, were fields of grain and trees along the banks of the Ebro. Far away, beyond the river, were mountains. The shadow of a cloud moved across the field of grain and she saw the river through the trees.

"And we could have all this," she said. "And we could have everything and every day we make it more impossible."

"What did you say?"

"I said we could have everything."

"We can have everything."

"No, we can't."

"We can have the whole world."

"No, we can't."

"We can go everywhere."

"No, we can't. It isn't ours any more."

"It's ours."

"No, it isn't. And once they take it away, you never get it back."

"But they haven't taken it away."

"We'll wait and see."

"Come on back in the shade," he said. "You mustn't feel that way."

"I don't feel any way," the girl said. "I just know things."

"I don't want you to do anything that you don't want to do—"

"Nor that isn't good for me," she said. "I know. Could we have another beer?"

"All right. But you've got to realize—"

"I realize," the girl said. "Can't we maybe stop talking?"

They sat down at the table and the girl looked across at the hills on the dry side of the valley and the man looked at her and at the table.

"You've got to realize," he said, "that I don't want you to do it if you don't want to. I'm perfectly willing to go through with it if it means anything to you."

"Doesn't it mean anything to you? We could get along."

"Of course it does. But I don't want anybody but you. I don't want any one else. And I know it's perfectly simple."

"Yes, you know it's perfectly simple."

"It's all right for you to say that, but I do know it."

"Would you do something for me now?"

"I'd do anything for you."

"Would you please please please please please please please stop talking?"

He did not say anything but looked at the bags against the wall of the station. There were labels on them from all the hotels where they had spent nights.

"But I don't want you to," he said, "I don't care anything about it."

"I'll scream," the girl said.

The woman came out through the curtains with two glasses of beer and put them down on the damp felt pads. "The train comes in five minutes," she said.

"What did she say?" asked the girl.

"That the train is coming in five minutes."

The girl smiled brightly at the woman, to thank her.

"I'd better take the bags over to the other side of the station," the man said. She smiled at him.

"All right. Then come back and we'll finish the beer."

He picked up the two heavy bags and carried them around the station to the other tracks. He looked up the tracks but could not see the train. Coming back, he walked through the barroom, where people waiting for the train were drinking. He drank an Anis at the bar and looked at the people. They were all waiting reasonably for the train. He went out through the bead curtain. She was sitting at the table and smiled at him.

"Do you feel better?" he asked.

"I feel fine," she said. "There's nothing wrong with me. I feel fine."

ZORA NEALE HURSTON (1891–1960)

Sweat

It was eleven o'clock of a Spring night in Florida. It was Sunday. Any other night, Delia Jones would have been in bed for two hours by this time. But she was a washwoman, and Monday morning meant a great deal to her. So she collected the soiled clothes on Saturday when she returned the clean things. Sunday night after church, she sorted them and put the white things to soak. It saved her almost a half day's start. A great hamper in the bedroom held the clothes that she brought home. It was so much neater than a number of bundles lying around.

She squatted in the kitchen floor beside the great pile of clothes, sorting them into small heaps according to color, and humming a song in a mournful key, but wondering through it all where Sykes, her husband, had gone with her horse and buckboard.

Just then something long, round, limp and black fell upon her shoulders and slithered to the floor beside her. A great terror took hold of her. It softened her knees and dried her mouth so that it was a full minute before she could cry out or move. Then she saw that it was the big bull whip her husband liked to carry when he drove.

She lifted her eyes to the door and saw him standing there bent over with laughter at her fright. She screamed at him.

"Sykes, what you throw dat whip on me like dat? You know it would skeer me—looks just like a snake, an' you knows how skeered Ah is of snakes."

"Course Ah knowed it! That's how come Ah done it." He slapped his leg with his hand and almost rolled on the ground in his mirth. "If you such a big fool dat you got to have a fit over a earth worm or a string, Ah don't keer how bad Ah skeer you."

"You aint got no business doing it. Gawd knows it's a sin. Some day Ah'm gointuh drop dead from some of yo' foolishness. 'Nother thing, where you been wid mah rig? Ah feeds dat pony. He aint fuh you to be drivin' wid no bull whip."

"Yo sho is one aggravatin' nigger woman!" he declared and stepped into the room. She resumed her work and did not answer him at once. "Ah done tole you time and again to keep them white folks' clothes outa dis house."

He picked up the whip and glared down at her. Delia went on with her work. She went out into the yard and returned with a galvanized tub and set it on the washbench. She saw that Sykes had kicked all of the clothes together again, and now stood in her way truculently, his whole manner hoping, *praying*, for an argument. But she walked calmly around him and commenced to re-sort the things.

"Next time, Ah'm gointer to kick 'em outdoors," he threatened as he struck a match along the leg of his corduroy breeches.

Delia never looked up from her work, and her thin, stooped shoulders sagged further.

"Ah aint for no fuss t'night Sykes. Ah just come from taking sacrament at the church house."

He snorted scornfully. "Yeah, you just come from de church house on a Sunday night, but heah you is gone to work on them clothes. You ain't nothing but a hypocrite. One of them amen-corner Christians—sing, whoop, shout, then come home and wash white folks clothes on the Sabbath."

He stepped roughly upon the whitest pile of things, kicking them helter-skelter as he crossed the room. His wife gave a little scream of dismay, and quickly gathered them together again.

"Sykes, you quit grindin' dirt into these clothes! How can Ah git through by Sat'day if Ah don't start on Sunday?"

"Ah don't keer if you never git through. Anyhow, Ah done promised Gawd and a couple of other men, Ah aint gointer have it in mah house. Don't gimme no lip neither, else Ah'll throw 'em out and put mah fist up side yo' head to boot."

Delia's habitual meekness seemed to slip from her shoulders like a blown scarf. She was on her feet; her poor little body, her bare knuckly hands bravely defying the strapping hulk before her.

"Looka heah, Sykes, you done gone too fur. Ah been married to you fur fifteen years, and Ah been takin' in washin' for fifteen years. Sweat, sweat, sweat! Work and sweat, cry and sweat, pray and sweat!"

"What's that got to do with me?" he asked brutally.

"What's it got to do with you, Sykes? Mah tub of suds is filled yo' belly with vittles more times than yo' hands is filled it. Mah sweat is done paid for this house and Ah reckon Ah kin keep on sweatin' in it."

She seized the iron skillet from the stove and struck a defensive pose, which act surprised him greatly, coming from her. It cowed him and he did not strike her as he usually did.

"Naw you won't," she panted, "that ole snaggle-toothed black woman you runnin' with aint comin' heah to pile up on *mah* sweat and blood. You aint paid for nothin' on this place, and Ah'm gointer stay right heah till Ah'm toted out foot foremost."

"Well, you better quit gittin' me riled up, else they'll be totin' you out sooner than you expect. Ah'm so tired of you Ah don't know whut to do. Gawd! how Ah hates skinny wimmen!"

A little awed by this new Delia, he sidled out of the door and slammed the back gate after him. He did not say where he had gone, but she knew too well. She knew very well that he would not return until nearly daybreak also. Her work over, she went on to bed but not to sleep at once. Things had come to a pretty pass!

She lay awake, gazing upon the debris that cluttered their matrimonial trail. Not an image left standing along the way. Anything like flowers had long ago been drowned in the salty stream that had been pressed from her heart. Her tears, her sweat, her blood. She had brought love to the union and he had brought a longing for the flesh. Two months after the wedding, he had given her the first brutal beating. She had the memory of numerous trips to Orlando with all of his wages when he had returned to her penniless, even before the first year had passed. She was young and soft then, but now she thought of her knotty, muscled limbs, her harsh knuckly hands, and drew herself up into an unhappy little ball in the middle of the big feather bed. Too late now to hope for love, even if it were not Bertha it would be someone else. This case differed from the others only in that she was bolder than the others. Too late for everything except her little home. She had built it for her old days, and planted one by one the trees and flowers there. It was lovely to her, lovely.

Somehow before sleep came, she found herself saying aloud: "Oh well, whatever goes over the Devil's back, is got to come under his belly. Sometime or ruther, Sykes, like everybody else, is gointer reap his sowing." After that she was able to build a spiritual earthworks against her husband. His shells could no longer reach her. *Amen.* She went to sleep and slept until he announced his presence in bed by kicking her feet and rudely snatching the cover away.

"Gimme some kivah heah, an' git yo' damn foots over on yo' own side! Ah oughter mash you in yo' mouf fuh drawing dat skillet on me."

Delia went clear to the rail without answering him. A triumphant indifference to all that he was or did.

The week was as full of work for Delia as all other weeks, and Saturday found her behind her little pony, collecting and delivering clothes.

It was a hot, hot day near the end of July. The village men on Joe Clarke's porch even chewed cane listlessly. They did not hurl the cane-knots as usual. They let them dribble over the edge of the porch. Even conversation had collapsed under the heat.

"Heah comes Delia Jones," Jim Merchant said, as the shaggy pony came 'round the bend of the road toward them. The rusty buckboard was heaped with baskets of crisp, clean laundry.

"Yep," Joe Lindsay agreed. "Hot or col', rain or shine, jes ez reg'lar ez de weeks roll roun' Delia carries 'em an' fetches 'em on Sat'day."

"She better if she wanter eat," said Moss. "Syke Jones aint wuth de shot an' powder hit would tek tuh kill 'em. Not to *bub* he aint."

"He sho' aint," Walter Thomas chimed in. "It's too bad, too, cause she wuz a right pritty lil trick when he got huh. Ah'd uh mah'ied huh mahseff if he hadnter beat me to it."

Delia nodded briefly at the men as she drove past.

"Too much knockin' will ruin *any* 'oman. He done beat huh 'nough tuh kill three women, let 'lone change they looks," said Elijah Mosely. "How Syke kin stommuck dat big black greasy Mogul he's layin' roun' wid, gits me. Ah swear dat eight-rock couldn't kiss a sardine can Ah done thowed out de back do' 'way las' yeah."

"Aw, she's fat, thass how come. He's allus been crazy 'bout fat women," put in Merchant. "He'd a' been tied up wid one long time ago if he could a' found one tuh have him. Did Ah tell yuh 'bout him come sidlin' roun' *mah* wife—bringin' her a basket uh pee-cans outa his yard fuh a present? Yes-sir, mah wife! She tol' him tuh take 'em right straight back home, cause Delia works so hard ovah dat washtub she reckon everything en de place taste lak sweat an' soapsuds. Ah jus' wisht Ah'd a' caught 'im 'roun' dere! Ah'd a' made his hips ketch on fiah down dat shell road."

"Ah know he done it, too. Ah sees 'im grinnin' at every 'oman dat passes," Walter Thomas said. "But even so, he useter eat some mighty big hunks uh humble pie tuh git dat lil' 'oman he got. She wuz ez pritty ez a speckled pup! Dat wuz fifteen yeahs ago. He useter be so skeered uh losin' huh, she could make him do some parts of a husband's duty. Dey never wuz de same in de mind."

"There oughter be a law about him," said Lindsay. "He aint fit tuh carry guts tuh a bear."

Clarke spoke for the first time. "Taint no law on earth dat kin make a man be decent if it aint in 'im. There's plenty men dat takes a wife lak dey do a joint uh sugar-cane. It's round, juicy an' sweet when dey gits it. But dey squeeze an' grind, squeeze an' grind an' wring tell dey wring every drop uh pleasure dat's in 'em out. When dey's satisfied dat dey is wrung dry, dey treats 'em jes lak dey do a cane-chew. Dey thows 'em away. Dey knows whut dey is doin' while dey is at it, an' hates theirselves fuh it but they keeps on hangin' after huh tell she's empty. Den dey hates huh fuh bein' a cane-chew an' in de way."

"We oughter take Syke an' dat stray 'oman uh his'n down in Lake Howell swamp an' lay on de rawhide till they cain't say 'Lawd a' mussy.' He allus wuz uh ovahbearin' niggah, but since dat white 'oman from up north done teached 'im how to run a automobile, he done got too biggety to live—an' we oughter kill 'im," Old Man Anderson advised.

A grunt of approval went around the porch. But the heat was melting their civic virtue and Elijah Moseley began to bait Joe Clarke.

"Come on, Joe, git a melon outa dere an' slice it up for yo' customers. We'se all sufferin' wid de heat. De bear's done got *me!*"

"Thass right, Joe, a watermelon is jes' whut Ah needs tuh cure de eppizud-icks," Walter Thomas joined forces with Moseley. "Come on dere, Joe. We all is steady customers an' you aint set us up in a long time. Ah chooses dat long, bowlegged Floridy favorite."

"A god, an' be dough. You all gimme twenty cents and slice away," Clarke retorted. "Ah needs a col' slice m'self. Heah, everybody chip in. Ah'll lend y'll mah meat knife."

The money was quickly subscribed and the huge melon brought forth. At that moment, Sykes and Bertha arrived. A determined silence fell on the porch and the melon was put away again.

Merchant snapped down the blade of his jackknife and moved toward the store door.

"Come on in, Joe, an' gimme a slab uh sow belly an' uh pound uh coffee—almost fuhgot 'twas Sat'day. Got to git on home." Most of the men left also.

Just then Delia drove past on her way home, as Sykes was ordering magnifi-cently for Bertha. It pleased him for Delia to see.

"Git whutsoever yo' heart desires, Honey. Wait a minute, Joe. Give huh two botles uh strawberry soda-water, uh quart uh parched groundpeas, an' a block uh chewin' gum."

With all this they left the store, with Sykes reminding Bertha that this was his town and she could have it if she wanted it.

The men returned soon after they left, and held their watermelon feast. "Where did Syke Jones git dat 'oman from nohow?" Lindsay asked.

"Ovah Apopka. Guess dey musta been cleanin' out de town when she lef'. She don't look lak a thing but a hunk uh liver wid hair on it."

"Well, she sho' kin squall," Dave Carter contributed. "When she gits ready tuh laff, she jes' opens huh mouf an' latches it back tuh de las' notch. No ole grandpa alligator down in Lake Bell ain't got nothin' on huh."

Bertha had been in town three months now. Sykes was still paying her room rent at Della Lewis'—the only house in town that would have taken her in. Sykes took her frequently to Winter Park to "stomps." He still assured her that he was the swellest man in the state.

"Sho' you kin have dat lil' ole house soon's Ah kin git dat 'oman outa dere. Everything b'longs tuh me an' you sho' kin have it. Ah sho' 'bominates uh skinny 'oman. Lawdy, you sho' is got one portly shape on you! You kin git *anything* you wants. Dis is *mah* town an' you sho' kin have it."

Delia's work-worn knees crawled over the earth in Gethsemane and on the rocks of Calvary many, many times during these months. She avoided the villagers and meeting places in her efforts to be blind and deaf. But Bertha nullified this to a degree, by coming to Delia's house to call Sykes out to her at the gate.

Delia and Sykes fought all the time now with no peaceful interludes. They slept and ate in silence. Two or three times Delia had attempted a timid friendliness, but she was repulsed each time. It was plain that the breaches must remain agape.

The sun had burned July to August. The heat streamed down like a million hot arrows, smiting all things living upon the earth. Grass withered, leaves browned, snakes went blind in shedding and men and dogs went mad. Dog days!

Delia came home one day and found Sykes there before her. She wondered, but started to go on into the house without speaking, even though he was standing in the kitchen door and she must either stoop under his arm or ask him to move. He made no room for her. She noticed a soap box beside the steps, but paid no particular attention to it, knowing that he must have brought it there. As she was stooping to pass under his outstretched arm, he suddenly pushed her backward, laughingly.

"Look in de box dere Delia, Ah done brung yuh somethin'!"

She nearly fell upon the box in her stumbling, and when she saw what it held, she all but fainted outright.

"Syke! Syke, mah Gawd! You take dat rattlesnake 'way from heah! You *got-tuh*. Oh, Jesus, have mussy!"

"Ah aint gut tuh do nuthin' uh de kin'—fact is Ah aint got tuh do nothin' but die. Taint no use uh you puttin' on airs makin' out lak you sceered uh dat snake—he's gointer stay right heah tell he die. He wouldn't bite me cause Ah knows how tuh handle 'im. Nohow he wouldn't risk breakin' out his fangs 'gin yo' skinny laigs."

"Naw, now Syke, don't keep dat thing 'roun' heah tuh skeer me tuh death. You knows Ah'm even feared uh earth worms. Thass de biggest snake Ah evah did see. Kill 'im Syke, please."

"Doan ast me tuh do nothin' fuh yuh. Goin' 'roun' tryin' to be so damn asterperious. Naw, Ah aint' gonna kill it. Ah think uh damn sight mo' uh him dan you! Dat's a nice snake an' anybody doan lak 'im kin jes' hit de grit."

The village soon heard that Sykes had the snake, and came to see and ask questions.

"How de hen-fire did you ketch dat six-foot rattler, Syke?" Thomas asked.

"He's full uh frogs so he caint hardly move, thass how Ah eased up on 'm.

But Ah'm a snake charmer an' knows how tuh handle 'em. Shux, dat aint nothin'. Ah could ketch one eve'y day if Ah so wanted tuh."

"Whut he needs is a heavy hick'ry club leaned real heavy on his head. Dat's de bes' way tuh charm a rattlesnake."

"Naw, Walt, y'll jes' don't understand dese diamon' backs lak Ah do," said Sykes in a superior tone of voice.

The village agreed with Walter, but the snake stayed on. His box remained by the kitchen door with its screen wire covering. Two or three days later it had digested its meal of frogs and literally came to life. It rattled at every movement in the kitchen or the yard. One day as Delia came down the kitchen steps she saw his chalky-white fangs curved like scimitars hung in the wire meshes. This time she did not run away with averted eyes as usual. She stood for a long time in the doorway in a red fury that grew bloodier for every second that she regarded the creature that was her torment.

That night she broached the subject as soon as Sykes sat down to the table.

"Syke, Ah wants you tuh take dat snake 'way fum heah. You done starved me an' Ah put up widcher, you done beat me an Ah took dat, but you done kilt all mah insides bringin' dat varmint heah."

Sykes poured out a saucer full of coffee and drank it deliberately before he answered her.

"A whole lot Ah keer 'bout how you feels inside uh out. Dat snake aint goin' no damn wheah till Ah gits ready fuh 'im tuh go. So fur as beatin' is concerned, yuh aint took near all dat you gointer take ef yuh stay 'roun' *me*."

Delia pushed back her plate and got up from the table. "Ah hates you, Sykes," she said calmly. "Ah hates you tuh de same degree dat Ah useter love yuh. Ah done took an' took till mah belly is full up tuh mah neck. Dat's de reason Ah got mah letter fum de church an' moved mah membership tuh Woodbridge—so Ah don't haftuh take no sacrament wid yuh. Ah don't wantuh see yuh 'round' me atall. Lay 'roun' wid dat 'oman all yuh wants tuh, but gwan 'way fum me an' mah house. Ah hates yuh lak uh suck-egg dog."

Sykes almost let the huge wad of corn bread and collard greens he was chewing fall out of his mouth in amazement. He had a hard time whipping himself to the proper fury to try to answer Delia.

"Well, Ah'm glad you does hate me. Ah'm sho' tiahed uh you hangin' ontuh me. Ah don't want yuh. Look at yuh stringey ole neck! Yo' raw-bony laigs an' arms is enough tuh cut uh man tuh death. You looks jes' lak de devvul's doll-baby tuh *me*. You cain't hate me no worse dan Ah hates you. Ah been hatin' *you* fuh years."

"Yo' ole black hide don't look lak nothin' tuh me, but uh passle uh wrinkled up rubber, wid yo' big ole yeahs flappin' on each side lak up paih uh buzzard wings. Don't think Ah'm gointuh be run 'way fum mah house neither. Ah'm goin' tuh de white folks about *you*, mah young man, de very nex' time you lay yo' han's on me. Mah cup is done run ovah." Delia said this with no signs of fear and Sykes departed from the house, threatening her, but made not the slightest move to carry out any of them.

That night he did not return at all, and the next day being Sunday, Delia was glad that she did not have to quarrel before she hitched up her pony and drove the four miles to Woodbridge.

She stayed to the night service—"love feast"—which was very warm and full of spirit. In the emotional winds her domestic trials were borne far and wide so that she sang as she drove homeward,

> "Jurden water, black an' col'
> Chills de body, not de soul
> An' Ah wantah cross Jurden in uh calm time."

She came from the barn to the kitchen door and stopped.

"Whut's de mattah, ol' satan, you aint kickin' up yo' racket?" She addressed the snake's box. Complete silence. She went on into the house with a new hope in its birth struggles. Perhaps her threat to go to the white folks had frightened Sykes! Perhaps he was sorry! Fifteen years of misery and suppression had brought Delia to the place where she would hope *anything* that looked towards a way over or through her wall of inhibitions.

She felt in the match safe behind the stove at once for a match. There was only one there.

"Dat niggah wouldn't fetch nothin' heah tuh save his rotten neck, but he kin run thew whut Ah brings quick enough. Now he done toted off nigh on tuh haff uh box uh matches. He done had dat 'oman heah in mah house, too."

Nobody but a woman could tell how she knew this even before she struck the match. But she did and it put her into a new fury.

Presently she brought in the tubs to put the white things to soak. This time she decided she need not bring the hamper out of the bedroom; she would go in there and do the sorting. She picked up the pot-bellied lamp and went in. The room was small and the hamper stood hard by the foot of the white iron bed. She could sit and reach through the bedposts—resting as she worked.

"Ah wantah cross Jurden in uh calm time." She was singing again. The mood of the "love feast" had returned. She threw back the lid of the basket almost gaily. Then, moved by both horror and terror, she sprang back toward the door. *There lay the snake in the basket!* He moved sluggishly at first, but even as she turned round and round, jumped up and down in an insanity of fear, he began to stir vigorously. She saw him pouring his awful beauty from the basket upon the bed, then she seized the lamp and ran as fast as she could to the kitchen. The wind from the open door blew out the light and the darkness added to her terror. She sped to the darkness of the yard, slamming the door after her before she thought to set down the lamp. She did not feel safe even on the ground, so she climbed up in the hay barn.

There for an hour or more she lay sprawled upon the hay a gibbering wreck.

Finally she grew quiet, and after that, coherent thought. With this, stalked through her a cold, bloody rage. Hours of this. A period of introspection, a space of retrospection, then a mixture of both. Out of this an awful calm.

"Well, Ah done de bes' Ah could. If things aint right, Gawd knows taint mah fault."

She went to sleep—a twitchy sleep—and woke up to a faint gray sky. There was a loud hollow sound below. She peered out. Sykes was at the wood-pile, demolishing a wire-covered box.

He hurried to the kitchen door, but hung outside there some minutes before he entered, and stood some minutes more inside before he closed it after him.

The gray in the sky was spreading. Delia descended without fear now, and crouched beneath the low bedroom window. The drawn shade shut out the dawn, shut in the night. But the thin walls held back no sound.

"Dat ol' scratch is woke up now!" She mused at the tremendous whirr inside, which every woodsman knows, is one of the sound illusions. The rattler is a ventriloquist. His whirr sounds to the right, to the left, straight ahead, behind, close under foot—everywhere but where it is. Woe to him who guesses wrong unless he is prepared to hold up his end of the argument! Sometimes he strikes without rattling at all.

Inside, Sykes heard nothing until he knocked a pot lid off the stove while trying to reach the match safe in the dark. He had emptied his pockets at Bertha's.

The snake seemed to wake up under the stove and Sykes made a quick leap into the bedroom. In spite of the gin he had had, his head was clearing now.

"Mah Gawd!" he chattered, "ef Ah could on'y strack uh light!"

The rattling ceased for a moment as he stood paralyzed. He waited. It seemed that the snake waited also.

"Oh, fuh de light! Ah thought he'd be too sick"—Sykes was muttering to himself when the whirr began again, closer, right underfoot this time. Long before this, Sykes' ability to think had been flattened down to primitive instinct and he leaped—onto the bed.

Outside Delia heard a cry that might have come from a maddened chimpanzee, a stricken gorilla. All the terror, all the horror, all the rage that man possibly could express, without a recognizable human sound.

A tremendous stir inside there, another series of animal screams, the intermittent whirr of the reptile. The shade torn violently down from the window, letting in the red dawn, a huge brown hand seizing the window stick, great dull blows upon the wooden floor punctuating the gibberish of sound long after the rattle of the snake had abruptly subsided. All this Delia could see and hear from her place beneath the window, and it made her ill. She crept over to the four-o'clocks and stretched herself on the cool earth to recover.

She lay there. "Delia, Delia!" She could hear Sykes calling in a most despairing tone as one who expected no answer. The sun crept on up, and he called. Delia could not move—her legs were gone flabby. She never moved, he called, and the sun kept rising.

"Mah Gawd!" She heard him moan, "Mah Gawd fum Heben!" She heard him stumbling about and got up from her flower-bed. The sun was growing warm. As she approached the door she heard him call out hopefully, "Delia, is dat you Ah heah?"

She saw him on his hands and knees as soon as she reached the door. He crept an inch or two toward her—all that he was able, and she saw his horribly swollen neck and his one open eye shining with hope. A surge of pity too strong to support bore her away from that eye that must, could not, fail to see the tubs. He would see the lamp. Orlando with its doctors was too far. She could scarcely reach the Chinaberry tree, where she waited in the growing heat while inside she knew the cold river was creeping up and up to extinguish that eye which must know by now that she knew.

FRANZ KAFKA (1883–1924)

A Hunger Artist

During these last decades the interest in professional fasting has markedly diminished. It used to pay very well to stage such great performances under one's own management, but today that is quite impossible. We live in a different world now. At one time the whole town took a lively interest in the hunger artist; from day to day of his fast the excitement mounted; everybody wanted to see him at least once a day; there were people who bought season tickets for the last few days and sat from morning till night in front of his small barred cage; even in the nighttime there were visiting hours, when the whole effect was heightened by torch flares; on fine days the cage was set out in the open air, and then it was the children's special treat to see the hunger artist; for their elders he was often just a joke that happened to be in fashion, but the children stood open-mouthed, holding each other's hands for greater security, marvelling at him as he sat there pallid in black tights, with his ribs sticking out so prominently, not even on a seat but down among straw on the ground, sometimes giving a courteous nod, answering questions with a constrained smile, or perhaps stretching an arm through the bars so that one might feel how thin it was, and then again withdrawing deep into himself, paying no attention to anyone or anything, not even to the all-important striking of the clock that was the only piece of furniture in his cage, but merely staring into vacancy with half-shut eyes, now and then taking a sip from a tiny glass of water to moisten his lips.

Besides casual onlookers there were also relays of permanent watchers selected by the public, usually butchers, strangely enough, and it was their task to watch the hunger artist day and night, three of them at a time, in case he should have some secret recourse to nourishment. This was nothing but a formality, instituted to reassure the masses, for the initiates knew well enough that during his fast the artist would never in any circumstances, not even under forcible compulsion, swallow the smallest morsel of food; the honor of his profession forbade it. Not every watcher, of course, was capable of understanding this; there were often groups of night watchers who were very lax in carrying out their duties and deliberately huddled together in a retired corner to play cards with great absorption, obviously intending to give the hunger artist the chance of a little refreshment, which they supposed he could draw from some private hoard. Nothing annoyed the artist more than such watchers; they made him miserable; they made his fast seem unendurable; sometimes he mastered his feebleness sufficiently to sing during their watch for as long as he could keep going, to show them how unjust their suspicions were. But that was of little use; they only wondered at his cleverness in being able to fill his mouth even while singing. Much more to his taste were the watchers who sat close up to the bars, who were not content with the dim night lighting of the hall but focused him in the full glare of the electric pocket torch given them by the impresario. The harsh light did not trouble him at all, in any case he could never sleep properly, and he could always drowse a little, whatever the light, at any hour, even when the hall was thronged with noisy onlookers. He was quite happy at the prospect of spending a sleepless night with such watchers; he was ready to exchange jokes with them, to tell them stories out of his nomadic life, anything at all to keep them awake and demonstrate to them again that he had no eatables in his cage and that he was fasting as not one of them could fast. But his happiest moment was when the morning came and an enormous breakfast was brought them, at his expense, on which they flung themselves with the keen appetite of healthy men after a weary night of wakefulness. Of course there were people who argued that this breakfast was an unfair attempt to bribe the watchers, but that was going rather too far, and when they were invited to take on a night's vigil without a breakfast, merely for the sake of the cause, they made themselves scarce, although they stuck stubbornly to their suspicions.

Such suspicions, anyhow, were a necessary accompaniment to the profession of fasting. No one could possibly watch the hunger artist continuously, day and night, and so no one could produce first-hand evidence that the fast had really been rigorous and continuous; only the artist himself could know that; he was therefore bound to be the sole completely satisfied spectator of his own fast. Yet for other reasons he was never satisfied; it was not perhaps mere fasting that had brought him to such skeleton thinness that many people had regretfully to keep away from his exhibitions, because the sight of him was too much for them, perhaps it was dissatisfaction with himself that had worn him down. For he alone knew, what no other initiate knew, how easy it was to fast. It was the easiest thing in the world. He made no secret of this, yet people did not believe him, at the best they set him down as modest, most of them, however, thought he was out for publicity or else was some kind of cheat who found it easy to fast because he had discovered a way of making it easy, and then had the impudence to admit the fact, more or less. He had to put up with all that, and in the course of time had got used to it, but his inner dissatisfaction always rankled, and never yet, after any term of fasting—this must be granted to his credit—had he left the cage of his own free will. The longest period of fasting was fixed by his impresario at forty days, beyond that term he was not allowed to go, not even in great cities, and there was good reason for it, too. Experience had proved that for about forty days the interest of the public could be stimulated by a steadily increasing pressure of advertisement, but after that the town began to lose interest, sympathetic support began notably to fall off; there were of course local variations as between one town and another or one country and another, but as a general rule forty days marked the limit. So on the fortieth day the flower-bedecked cage was opened, enthusiastic spectators filled the hall, a military band played, two doctors entered the cage to measure the results of the fast, which were announced through a megaphone, and finally two young ladies appeared, blissful at having been selected for the honor, to help the hunger artist down the few steps leading to a small table on which was spread a carefully chosen invalid repast. And at this very moment the artist always turned stubborn. True, he would entrust his bony arms to the outstretched helping hands of the ladies bending over him, but stand up he would not. Why stop fasting at this particular moment, after forty days of it? He had held out for a long time, an illimitably long time; why stop now, when he was in his best fasting form, or rather, not yet quite in his best fasting form? Why should he be cheated of the fame he would get for fasting longer, for being not only the record hunger artist of all time, which presumably he was already, but for beating his own record by a performance beyond human imagination, since he felt that there were no limits to his capacity for fasting? His public pretended to admire him so much, why should it have so little patience with him; if he could endure fasting longer, why shouldn't the public endure it? Besides, he was tired, he was comfortable sitting in the straw, and now he was supposed to lift himself to his full height and go down to a meal the very thought of which gave him a nausea that only the presence of the ladies kept him from betraying, and even that with an effort. And he looked up into the eyes of the ladies who were apparently so friendly and in reality so cruel, and shook his head, which felt too heavy on its strengthless neck. But then there happened yet again what always happened. The impresario came forward, with-out a word—for the band made speech impossible—lifted his arms in the air above the artist, as if inviting Heaven to look down upon its creature here in the straw, this suffering martyr, which indeed he was, although in quite another sense; grasped him round the emaciated waist, with exaggerated caution, so that the frail condition he was in might be appreciated; and committed him to the care of the blenching[1] ladies, not without secretly giving him a shaking so that his legs and body tottered and swayed. The artist now submitted completely; his head lolled on his breast as if it had landed there by chance; his body was hollowed out; his legs in a spasm of self-preservation clung close to each other at the knees, yet scraped on the ground as if it were not really solid ground, as if they were only trying to find solid ground; and the whole weight of his body, a featherweight after all, relapsed onto one of the ladies, who, looking round for help and panting a little—this post of honor was not at all what she had expected it to be—first stretched her neck as far as she could to keep her face at least free from contact with the artist, then finding this impossible, and her more fortunate companion not coming to her aid but merely holding extended on her own trembling hand the little bunch of knucklebones that was the artist's, to the great delight of the spectators, burst into tears and had to be replaced by an attendant who had long been stationed in readiness. Then came the food, a

---

[1] Blenching is to turn away in cowardice, to flinch. It also suggests the pale color (the blanched color) that sometimes appears in the faces of frightened people.

little of which the impresario managed to get between the artist's lips, while he sat in a kind of half-fainting trance, to the accompaniment of cheerful patter designed to distract the public's attention from the artist's condition; after that, a toast was drunk to the public, supposedly prompted by a whisper from the artist in the impresario's ear; the band confirmed it with a mighty flourish, the spectators melted away, and no one had any cause to be dissatisfied with the proceedings, no one except the hunger artist himself, he only, as always.

So he lived for many years, with small regular intervals of recuperation, in visible glory, honored by the world, yet in spite of that troubled in spirit, and all the more troubled because no one would take his trouble seriously. What comfort could he possibly need? What more could he possibly wish for? And if some good-natured person, feeling sorry for him, tried to console him by pointing out that his melancholy was probably caused by fasting, it could happen, especially when he had been fasting for some time, that he reacted with an outburst of fury and to the general alarm began to shake the bars of his cage like a wild animal. Yet the impresario had a way of punishing these outbreaks which he rather enjoyed putting into operation. He would apologize publicly for the artist's behavior, which was only to be excused, he admitted, because of the irritability caused by fasting; a condition hardly to be understood by well-fed people; then by natural transition he went on to mention the artist's equally incomprehensible boast that he could fast for much longer than he was doing; he praised the high ambition, the good will, the great self-denial undoubtedly implicit in such a statement; and then quite simply countered it by bringing out photographs, which were also on sale to the public, showing the artist on the fortieth day of a fast lying in bed almost dead from exhaustion. This perversion of the truth, familiar to the artist though it was, always unnerved him afresh and proved too much for him. What was a consequence of the premature ending of his fast was here presented as the cause of it! To fight against this lack of understanding, against a whole world of non-understanding, was impossible. Time and again in good faith he stood by the bars listening to the impresario, but as soon as the photographs appeared he always let go and sank with a groan back on to his straw, and the reassured public could once more come close and gaze at him.

A few years later when the witnesses of such scenes called them to mind, they often failed to understand themselves at all. For meanwhile the aforementioned change in public interest had set in; it seemed to happen almost overnight; there may have been profound causes for it, but who was going to bother about that; at any rate the pampered hunger artist suddenly found himself deserted one fine day by the amusement seekers, who went streaming past him to other more favored attractions. For the last time the impresario hurried him over half Europe to discover whether the old interest might still survive here and there; all in vain; everywhere, as if by secret agreement, a positive revulsion from professional fasting was in evidence. Of course it could not really have sprung up so suddenly as all that, and many premonitory symptoms which had not been sufficiently remarked or suppressed during the rush and glitter of success now came retrospectively to mind, but it was now too late to take any countermeasures. Fasting would surely come into fashion again at some future date, yet that was no comfort for those living in the present. What, then, was the hunger artist to do? He had been applauded by thousands in his time and could hardly come down to showing himself in a street booth at village fairs, and as for adopting another profession, he was not only too old for that but too fanatically devoted to fasting. So he took leave of the impresario, his partner in an unparalleled career, and hired himself to a large circus; in order to spare his own feelings he avoided reading the conditions of his contract.

A large circus with its enormous traffic in replacing and recruiting men, animals and apparatus can always find a use for people at any time, even for a hunger artist, provided of course that he does not ask too much, and in this particular case anyhow it was not only the artist who was taken on but his famous and long-known name as well; indeed considering the peculiar nature of his performance, which was not impaired by advancing age, it could not be objected that here was an artist past his prime, no longer at the height of his professional skill, seeking a refuge in some quiet corner of a circus; on the contrary, the hunger artist averred that he could fast as well as ever, which was entirely credible; he even alleged that if he were allowed to fast as he liked, and this was at once promised him without more ado, he could astound the world by establishing a record never yet achieved, a statement which certainly provoked a smile among the other professionals, since it left out of account the change in public opinion, which the hunger artist in his zeal conveniently forgot.

He had not, however, actually lost his sense of the real situation and took it as a matter of course that he and his cage should be stationed, not in the middle of the ring as a main attraction, but outside, near the animal cages, on a site that was after all easily accessible. Large and gaily painted placards made a frame for the cage and announced what was to be seen inside it. When the public came thronging out in the intervals to see the animals, they could hardly avoid passing the hunger artist's cage and stopping there for a moment, perhaps they might even have stayed longer had not those pressing behind them in the narrow gangway, who did not understand why they should be held up on their way toward the excitements of the menagerie, made it impossible for anyone to stand gazing quietly for any length of time. And that was the reason why the hunger artist, who had of course been looking forward to these visiting hours as the main achievement of his life, began instead to shrink from them. At first he could hardly wait for the intervals; it was exhilarating to watch the crowds come streaming his way, until only too soon—not even the most obstinate self-deception, clung to almost consciously, could hold out against the fact—the conviction was borne in upon him that these people, most of them, to judge from their actions, again and again, without exception, were all on their way to the menagerie. And the first sight of them from the distance remained the best. For when they reached his cage he was at once deafened by the storm of shouting and abuse that arose from the two contending factions, which renewed themselves continuously, of those who wanted to stop and stare at him—he soon began to dislike them more than the others—not out of real interest but only out of obstinate self-assertiveness, and those who wanted to go straight on to the animals. When the first great rush was past, the stragglers came along, and these, whom nothing could have prevented from stopping to look at him as long as they had breath, raced past with long strides, hardly even glancing at him, in their haste to get to the menagerie in time. And all too rarely did it happen that he had a stroke of luck, when some father of a family fetched up before him with his children, pointed a finger at the hunger artist and explained at length what the phenomenon meant, telling stories of earlier years when he himself had watched similar but much more thrilling performances, and the children, still rather uncomprehending, since neither inside nor outside school had they been sufficiently prepared for this lesson—what did they care about fasting?—yet showed by the brightness of their intent eyes that new and better times might be coming. Perhaps, said the hunger artist to himself many a time, things would be a little better if his cage were set not quite so near the menagerie. That made it too easy for people to make their choice, to say nothing of what he suffered from the stench of the menagerie, the animals' restlessness by night, the carrying past of raw lumps of flesh for the beasts of prey, the roaring at feeding times, which depressed him continually. But he did not dare to lodge a complaint with the management; after all, he had the animals to thank for the troops of people who passed his cage, among whom there might always be one here and there to take an interest in him, and who could tell where they might seclude him if he called attention to his existence and thereby to the fact that, strictly speaking, he was only an impediment on the way to the menagerie.

A small impediment, to be sure, one that grew steadily less. People grew familiar with the strange idea that they could be expected, in times like these, to take an interest in a hunger artist, and with this familiarity the verdict went out against him. He might fast as much as he could, and he did so; but nothing could save him now, people passed him by. Just try to explain to anyone the art of fasting! Anyone who has no feeling for it cannot be made to understand it. The fine placards grew dirty and illegible, they were torn down; the little notice board telling the number of fast days achieved, which at first was changed carefully every day, had long stayed at the same figure, for after the first few weeks even this small task seemed pointless to the staff; and so the artist simply fasted on and on, as he had once dreamed of doing, and it was no trouble to him, just as he had always foretold, but no one counted the days, no one, not even the artist himself, knew what records he was already breaking, and his heart grew heavy. And when once in a time some leisurely passerby stopped, made merry over the old figure on the board and spoke of swindling, that was in its way the stupidest lie ever invented by indifference and inborn malice, since it was not the hunger artist who was cheating; he was working honestly, but the world was cheating him of his reward.

Many more days went by, however, and that too came to an end. An overseer's eye fell on the cage one day and he asked the attendants why this perfectly good cage should be left standing there unused with dirty straw inside it; nobody knew, until one man, helped out by the notice board, remembered about the hunger artist. They poked into the straw with sticks and found him in it. "Are you still fasting?" asked the overseer. "When on earth do you mean to stop?" "Forgive me, everybody," whispered the hunger artist; only the overseer, who had his ear to the bars, understood him. "Of course," said the overseer, and tapped his forehead with a finger to let the attendants know what state the man was in, "we forgive you." "I always wanted you to admire my fasting," said the hunger artist. "We do admire it," said the overseer, affably. "But you shouldn't admire it," said the hunger artist. "Well, then we don't admire it," said the overseer, "but why shouldn't we admire it?" "Because I have to fast, I can't help it," said the hunger artist. "What a fellow you are," said the overseer, "and why can't you help it?" "Because," said the hunger artist, lifting his head a little and speaking, with his lips pursed, as if for a kiss, right into the overseer's ear, so that no syllable might be lost, "because I couldn't find the food I liked. If I had found it, believe me, I should have made no fuss and stuffed myself like you or anyone else." These were his last words, but in his dimming eyes remained the firm though no longer proud persuasion that he was still continuing to fast.

"Well, clear this out now!" said the overseer, and they buried the hunger artist, straw and all. Into the cage they put a young panther. Even the most insensitive felt it refreshing to see this wild creature leaping around the cage that had so long been dreary. The panther was all right. The food he liked was brought him without hesitation by the attendants; he seemed not even to miss his freedom; his noble body, furnished almost to the bursting point with all that it needed, seemed to carry freedom around with it too; somewhere in his jaws it seemed to lurk; and the joy of life streamed with such ardent passion from his throat that for the onlookers it was not easy to stand the shock of it. but they braced themselves, crowded round the cage, and did not want ever to move away.

Translated by Willa and Edwin Mair

FLANNERY O'CONNOR (1925–1964)

Everything That Rises Must Converge

Her doctor had told Julian's mother that she must lose twenty pounds on account of her blood pressure, so on Wednesday nights Julian had to take her downtown on the bus for a reducing class at the Y. The reducing class was designed for working girls over fifty, who weighed from 165 to 200 pounds. His mother was one of the slimmer ones, but she said ladies did not tell their age or weight. She would not ride the buses by herself at night since they had been integrated, and because the reducing class was one of her few pleasures, necessary for her health, and *free*, she said Julian could at least put himself out to take her, considering all she did for him. Julian did not like to consider all she did for him, but every Wednesday night he braced himself and took her.

She was almost ready to go, standing before the hall mirror, putting on her hat, while he, his hands behind him, appeared pinned to the door frame, waiting like Saint Sebastian for the arrows to begin piercing him.[1] The hat was new and had cost her seven dollars and a half. She kept saying, "Maybe I shouldn't have paid that for it. No, I shouldn't have. I'll take it off and return it tomorrow. I shouldn't have bought it."

Julian raised his eyes to heaven. "Yes, you should have bought it," he said. "Put it on and let's go." It was a hideous hat. A purple velvet flap came down on one side of it and stood up on the other; the rest of it was green and looked like a cushion with the stuffing out. He decided it was less comical than jaunty and pathetic. Everything that gave her pleasure was small and depressed him.

She lifted the hat one more time and set it down slowly on top of her head. Two wings of gray hair protruded on either side of her florid face, but her eyes, sky-blue, were as innocent and untouched by experience as they must have been when she was ten. Were it not that she was a widow who had struggled fiercely to feed and clothe and put him through school and who was supporting him still, "until he got on his feet," she might have been a little girl that he had to take to town.

"It's all right, it's all right," he said. "Let's go." He opened the door himself and started down the walk to get her going. The sky was a dying violet and the houses stood out darkly against it, bulbous liver-colored monstrosities of a uniform ugliness though no two were alike. Since this had been a fashionable neighborhood forty years ago, his mother persisted in thinking they did well to have an apartment in it. Each house had a narrow collar of dirt around it in which sat, usually, a grubby child. Julian walked with his hands in his pockets, his head down and thrust forward and his eyes glazed with the determination to make himself completely numb during the time he would be sacrificed to her pleasure.

The door closed and he turned to find the dumpy figure, surmounted by the atrocious hat, coming toward him. "Well," she said, "you only live once and paying a little more for it, I at least won't meet myself coming and going."

"Some day I'll start making money." Julian said gloomily—he knew he never would—"and you can have one of those jokes whenever you take the fit." But first they would move. He visualized a place where the nearest neighbors would be three miles away on either side.

"I think you're doing fine," she said, drawing on her gloves. "You've only been out of school a year. Rome wasn't built in a day."

She was one of the few members of the Y reducing class who arrived in hat and gloves and who had a son who had been to college. "It takes time," she said, "and the world is in such a mess. This hat looked better on me than any of the others, though when she brought it out I said, 'Take that thing back. I wouldn't have it on my head,' and she said, 'Now wait till you see it on,' and when she put it on me, I said, 'we-ull,' and she said, 'If you ask me, that hat does something for you and you do something for that hat, and besides,' she said, 'with that hat, you won't meet yourself coming and going.'"

---

[1] St. Sebastian was an early Christian martyr. According to legend, Sebastian was an army officer condemned for his faith to be pierced with arrows shot by his fellow soldiers.

Julian thought he could have stood his lot better if she had been selfish, if she had been an old hag who drank and screamed at him. He walked along, saturated in depression, as if in the midst of his martyrdom he had lost his faith. Catching sight of his long, hopeless, irritated face, she stopped suddenly with a grief-stricken look, and pulled back on his arm. "Wait on me," she said. "I'm going back to the house and take this thing off and tomorrow I'm going to return it. I was out of my head. I can pay the gas bill with the seven-fifty."

He caught her arm in a vicious grip. "You are not going to take it back," he said. "I like it."

"Well," she said, "I don't think I ought . . ."

"Shut up and enjoy it," he muttered, more depressed than ever.

"With the world in the mess it's in," she said, "it's a wonder we can enjoy anything. I tell you, the bottom rail is on the top."

Julian sighed.

"Of course," she said, "if you know who you are, you can go anywhere." She said this every time he took her to the reducing class. "Most of them in it are not our kind of people," she said, "but I can be gracious to anybody. I know who I am."

"They don't give a damn for your graciousness," Julian said savagely. "Knowing who you are is good for one generation only. You haven't the foggiest idea where you stand now or who you are."

She stopped and allowed her eyes to flash at him. "I most certainly do know who I am," she said, "and if you don't know who you are, I'm ashamed of you."

"Oh hell," Julian said.

"Your great-grandfather was a former governor of this state," she said. "Your grandfather was a prosperous landowner. Your grandmother was a Godhigh."

"Will you look around you," he said tensely, "and see where you are now?" and he swept his arm jerkily out to indicate the neighborhood, which the growing darkness at least made less dingy.

"You remain what you are," she said. "Your great-grandfather had a plantation and two hundred slaves."

"There are no more slaves," he said irritably.

"They were better off when they were," she said. He groaned to see that she was off on that topic. She rolled onto it every few days like a train on an open track. He knew every stop, every junction, every swamp along the way, and knew the exact point at which her conclusion would roll majestically into the station: "It's ridiculous. It's simply not realistic. They should rise, yes, but on their own side of the fence."

"Let's skip it," Julian said.

"The ones I feel sorry for," she said, "are the ones that are half white. They're tragic."

"Will you skip it?"

"Suppose we were half white. We would certainly have mixed feelings."

"I have mixed feelings now," he groaned.

"Well let's talk about something pleasant," she said. "I remember going to

Grandpa's when I was a little girl. Then the house had double stairways that went up to what was really the second floor—all the cooking was done on the first. I used to like to stay down in the kitchen on account of the way the walls smelled. I would sit with my nose pressed against the plaster and take deep breaths. Actually the place belonged to the Godhighs but your grandfather Chestny paid the mortgage and saved it for them. They were in reduced circumstances," she said, "but reduced or not, they never forgot who they were."

"Doubtless that decayed mansion reminded them," Julian muttered. He never spoke of it without contempt or thought of it without longing. He had seen it once when he was a child before it had been sold. The double stairways had rotted and been torn down. Negroes were living in it. But it remained in his mind as his mother had known it. It appeared in his dreams regularly. He would stand on the wide porch, listening to the rustle of oak leaves, then wander through the high-ceilinged hall into the parlor that opened onto it and gaze at the worn rugs and faded draperies. It occurred to him that it was he, not she, who could have appreciated it. He preferred its threadbare elegance to anything he could name and it was because of it that all the neighborhoods they had lived in had been a torment to him—whereas she had hardly known the difference. She called her insensitivity "being adjustable."

"And I remember the old darky who was my nurse, Caroline. There was no better person in the world. I've always had a great respect for my colored friends," she said. "I'd do anything in the world for them and they'd . . ."

"Will you for God's sake get off that subject?" Julian said. When he got on a bus by himself, he made it a point to sit down beside a Negro, in reparation as it were for his mother's sins.

"You're mighty touchy tonight," she said. "Do you feel all right?"

"Yes I feel all right," he said. "Now lay off."

She pursed her lips. "Well, you certainly are in a vile humor," she observed. "I just won't speak to you at all."

They had reached the bus stop. There was no bus in sight and Julian, his hands still jammed in his pockets and his head thrust forward, scowled down the empty street. The frustration of having to wait on the bus as well as ride on it began to creep up his neck like a hot hand. The presence of his mother was borne in upon him as she gave a pained sigh. He looked at her bleakly. She was holding herself very erect under the preposterous hat, wearing it like a banner of her imaginary dignity. There was in him an evil urge to break her spirit. He suddenly unloosened his tie and pulled it off and put it in his pocket.

She stiffened. "Why must you look like *that* when you take me to town?" she said. "Why must you deliberately embarrass me?"

"If you'll never learn where you are," he said, "you can at least learn where I am."

"You look like a—thug," she said.

"Then I must be one," he murmured.

"I'll just go home," she said. "I will not bother you. If you can't do a little thing like that for me . . ."

Rolling his eyes upward, he put his tie back on. "Restored to my class," he muttered. He thrust his face toward her and hissed, "True culture is in the mind, the *mind*," he said, and tapped his head, "the mind."

"It's in the heart," she said, "and in how you do things and how you do things is because of who you *are*."

"Nobody in the damn bus cares who you are."

"I care who I am," she said icily.

The lighted bus appeared on top of the next hill and as it approached, they moved out into the street to meet it. He put his hand under her elbow and hoisted her up on the creaking step. She entered with a little smile, as if she were going into a drawing room where everyone had been waiting for her. While he put in the tokens, she sat down on one of the broad front seats for three which faced the aisle. A thin woman with protruding teeth and long yellow hair was sitting on the end of it. His mother moved up beside her and left room for Julian beside herself. He sat down and looked at the floor across the aisle where a pair of thin feet in red and white canvas sandals were planted.

His mother immediately began a general conversation meant to attract anyone who felt like talking. "Can it get any hotter?" she said and removed from her purse a folding fan, black with a Japanese scene on it, which she began to flutter before her.

"I reckon it might could,"[2] the woman with the protruding teeth said, "but I know for a fact my apartment couldn't get no hotter."

"It must get the afternoon sun," his mother said. She sat forward and looked up and down the bus. It was half filled. Everybody was white. "I see we have the bus to ourselves," she said. Julian cringed.

"For a change," said the woman across the aisle, the owner of the red and white canvas sandals. "I come on one the other day and they were thick as fleas—up front and all through."

"The world is in a mess everywhere," his mother said. "I don't know how we've let it get in this fix."

"What gets my goat is all those boys from good families stealing automobile tires," the woman with the protruding teeth said. "I told my boy, I said you may not be rich but you been raised right and if I ever catch you in any such mess, they can send you on to the reformatory. Be exactly where you belong."

"Training tells," his mother said. "Is your boy in high school?"

"Ninth grade," the woman said.

"My son just finished college last year. He wants to write but he's selling typewriters until he gets started," his mother said.

The woman leaned forward and peered at Julian. He threw her such a malevolent look that she subsided against the seat. On the floor across the aisle there was an abandoned newspaper. He got up and got it and opened it out in front of him. His mother discreetly continued the conversation in a lower tone

---

[2] "Might could" is a lower-class Southern expression meaning "perhaps" or "possibly."

but the woman across the aisle said in a loud voice, "Well that's nice. Selling typewriters is close to writing. He can go right from one to the other."

"I tell him," his mother said, "that Rome wasn't built in a day."

Behind the newspaper Julian was withdrawing into the inner compartment of his mind where he spent most of his time. This was a kind of mental bubble in which he established himself when he could not bear to be a part of what was going on around him. From it he could see out and judge but in it he was safe from any kind of penetration from without. It was the only place where he felt free of the general idiocy of his fellows. His mother had never entered it but from it he could see her with absolute clarity.

The old lady was clever enough and he thought that if she had started from any of the right premises, more might have been expected of her. She lived according to the laws of her own fantasy world, outside of which he had never seen her set foot. The law of it was to sacrifice herself for him after she had first created the necessity to do so by making a mess of things. If he had permitted her sacrifices, it was only because her lack of foresight had made them necessary. All of her life had been a struggle to act like a Chestny without the Chestny goods, and to give him everything she thought a Chestny ought to have; but since, said she, it was fun to struggle, why complain? And when you had won, as she had won, what fun to look back on the hard times! He could not forgive her that she had enjoyed the struggle and that she thought *she* had won.

What she meant when she said she had won was that she had brought him up successfully and had sent him to college and that he had turned out so well— good looking (her teeth had gone unfilled so that his could be straightened), intelligent (he realized he was too intelligent to be a success), and with a future ahead of him (there was of course no future ahead of him). She excused his gloominess on the grounds that he was still growing up and his radical ideas on his lack of practical experience. She said he didn't yet know a thing about "life," that he hadn't even entered the real world—when already he was as disenchanted with it as a man of fifty.

The further irony of all this was that in spite of her, he had turned out so well. In spite of going to only a third-rate college, he had, on his own initiative, come out with a first-rate education; in spite of growing up dominated by a small mind, he had ended up with a large one; in spite of all her foolish views, he was free of prejudice and unafraid to face facts. Most miraculous of all, instead of being blinded by love for her as she was for him, he had cut himself emotionally free of her and could see her with complete objectivity. He was not dominated by his mother.

The bus stopped with a sudden jerk and shook him from his meditation. A woman from the back lurched forward with little steps and barely escaped falling in his newspaper as she righted herself. She got off and a large Negro got on. Julian kept his paper lowered to watch. It gave him a certain satisfaction to see injustice in daily operation. It confirmed his view that with a few exceptions there was no one worth knowing within a radius of three hundred miles. The Negro was well dressed and carried a briefcase. He looked around and then sat down on the other end of the seat where the woman with the red and white canvas sandals was sitting. He immediately unfolded a newspaper and obscured himself behind it. Julian's mother's elbow at once prodded insistently into his ribs. "Now you see why I won't ride on these buses by myself," she whispered.

The woman with the red and white canvas sandals had risen at the same time the Negro sat down and had gone further back in the bus and taken the seat of the woman who had got off. His mother leaned forward and cast her an approving look.

Julian rose, crossed the aisle, and sat down in the place of the woman with the canvas sandals. From this position, he looked serenely across at his mother. Her face had turned an angry red. He stared at her, making his eyes the eyes of a stranger. He felt his tension suddenly lift as if he had openly declared war on her.

He would have liked to get in conversation with the Negro and to talk with him about art or politics or any subject that would be above the comprehension of those around them, but the man remained entrenched behind his paper. He was either ignoring the change of seating or had never noticed it. There was no way for Julian to convey his sympathy.

His mother kept her eyes fixed reproachfully on his face. The woman with the protruding teeth was looking at him avidly as if he were a type of monster new to her.

"Do you have a light?" he asked the Negro.

Without looking away from his paper, the man reached in his pocket and handed him a packet of matches.

"Thanks," Julian said. For a moment he held the matches foolishly. A NO SMOKING sign looked down upon him from over the door. This alone would not have deterred him; he had no cigarettes. He had quit smoking some months before because he could not afford it. "Sorry," he muttered and handed back the matches. The Negro lowered the paper and gave him an annoyed look. He took the matches and raised the paper again.

His mother continued to gaze at him but she did not take advantage of his momentary discomfort. Her eyes retained their battered look. Her face seemed to be unnaturally red, as if her blood pressure had risen. Julian allowed no glimmer of sympathy to show on his face. Having got the advantage, he wanted desperately to keep it and carry it through. He would have liked to teach her a lesson that would last her a while, but there seemed no way to continue the point. The Negro refused to come out from behind his paper.

Julian folded his arms and looked stolidly before him, facing her but as if he did not see her, as if he had ceased to recognize her existence. He visualized a scene in which, the bus having reached their stop, he would remain in his seat and when she said, "Aren't you going to get off?" he would look at her as at a stranger who had rashly addressed him. The corner they got off on was usually deserted, but it was well lighted and it would not hurt her to walk by herself the four blocks to the Y. He decided to wait until the time came and then decide whether or not he would let her get off by herself. He would have to be at the Y at ten to bring her back, but he could leave her wondering if he was going to show up. There was no reason for her to think she could always depend on him.

He retired again into the high-ceilinged room sparsely settled with large pieces of antique furniture. His soul expanded momentarily but then he became aware of his mother across from him and the vision shriveled. He studied her coldly. Her feet in little pumps dangled like a child's and did not quite reach the floor. She was training on him an exaggerated look of reproach. He felt completely detached from her. At that moment he could with pleasure have slapped her as he would have slapped a particularly obnoxious child in his charge.

He began to imagine various unlikely ways by which he could teach her a lesson. He might make friends with some distinguished Negro professor or lawyer and bring him home to spend the evening. He would be entirely justified but her blood pressure would rise to 300. He could not push her to the extent of making her have a stroke, and moreover, he had never been successful at making any Negro friends. He had tried to strike up an acquaintance on the bus with some of the better types, with ones that looked like professors or ministers or lawyers. One morning he had sat down next to a distinguished-looking dark brown man who had answered his questions with a sonorous solemnity but who had turned out to be an undertaker. Another day he had sat down beside a cigar-smoking Negro with a diamond ring on his finger, but after a few stilted pleasantries, the Negro had rung the buzzer and risen, slipping two lottery tickets into Julian's hand as he climbed over him to leave.

He imagined his mother lying desperately ill and his being able to secure only a Negro doctor for her. He toyed with that idea for a few minutes and then dropped it for a momentary vision of himself participating as a sympathizer in a sit-in demonstration.[3] This was possible but he did not linger with it. Instead, he approached the ultimate horror. He brought home a beautiful suspiciously Negroid woman. Prepare yourself, he said. There is nothing you can do about it. This is the woman I've chosen. She's intelligent, dignified, even good, and she's suffered and she hasn't thought it *fun*. Now persecute us, go ahead and persecute us. Drive her out of here, but remember, you're driving me too. His eyes were narrowed and through the indignation he had generated, he saw his mother across the aisle, purple-faced, shrunken to the dwarf-like proportions of her moral nature, sitting like a mummy beneath the ridiculous banner of her hat.

He was tilted out of his fantasy again as the bus stopped. The door opened with a sucking hiss and out of the dark a large, gaily dressed, sullen-looking colored woman got on with a little boy. The child, who might have been four, had on a short plaid suit and a Tyrolean hat with a blue feather in it. Julian hoped that he would sit down beside him and that the woman would push in beside his mother. He could think of no better arrangement.

As she waited for her tokens, the woman was surveying the seating possibilities—he hoped with the idea of sitting where she was least wanted. There was something familiar-looking about her but Julian could not place what it was.

---

[3] "Sit-in demonstrations" were a nonviolent technique used to change racist laws.

She was a giant of a woman. Her face was set not only to meet opposition but to seek it out. The downward tilt of her large lower lip was like a warning sign: DON'T TAMPER WITH ME. Her bulging figure was encased in a green crepe dress and her feet overflowed in red shoes. She had on a hideous hat. A purple velvet flap came down on one side of it and stood up on the other; the rest of it was green and looked like a cushion with the stuffing out. She carried a mammoth red pocketbook that bulged throughout as if it were stuffed with rocks.

To Julian's disappointment, the little boy climbed up on the empty seat beside his mother. His mother lumped all children, black and white, into the common category, "cute," and she thought little Negroes were on the whole cuter than little white children. She smiled at the little boy as he climbed on the seat.

Meanwhile the woman was bearing down upon the empty seat beside Julian. To his annoyance, she squeezed herself into it. He saw his mother's face change as the woman settled herself next to him and he realized with satisfaction that this was more objectionable to her than it was to him. Her face seemed almost gray and there was a look of dull recognition in her eyes, as if suddenly she had sickened at some awful confrontation. Julian saw that it was because she and the woman had, in a sense, swapped sons. Though his mother would not realize the symbolic significance of this, she would feel it. His amusement showed plainly on his face.

The woman next to him muttered something unintelligible to herself. He was conscious of a kind of bristling next to him, muted growling like that of an angry cat. He could not see anything but the red pocketbook upright on the bulging green thighs. He visualized the woman as she had stood waiting for her tokens— the ponderous figure, rising from the red shoes upward over the solid hips, the mammoth bosom, the haughty face, to the green and purple hat.

His eyes widened.

The vision of the two hats, identical, broke upon him with the radiance of a brilliant sunrise. His face was suddenly lit with joy. He could not believe that Fate had thrust upon his mother such a lesson. He gave a loud chuckle so that she would look at him and see that he saw. She turned her eyes on him slowly. The blue in them seemed to have turned a bruised purple. For a moment he had an uncomfortable sense of her innocence, but it lasted only a second before principle rescued him. Justice entitled him to laugh. His grin hardened until it said to her as plainly as if he were saying aloud: Your punishment exactly fits your pettiness. This should teach you a permanent lesson.

Her eyes shifted to the woman. She seemed unable to bear looking at him and to find the woman preferable. He became conscious again of the bristling presence at his side. The woman was rumbling like a volcano about to become active. His mother's mouth began to twitch slightly at one corner. With a sinking heart, he saw incipient signs of recovery on her face and realized that this was going to strike her suddenly as funny and was going to be no lesson at all. She kept her eyes on the woman and an amused smile came over her face as if the woman were a monkey that had stolen her hat. The little Negro was looking up at her with large fascinated eyes. He had been trying to attract her attention for some time.

"Carver!" the woman said suddenly. "Come heah!"

When he saw that the spotlight was on him at last, Carver drew his feet up and turned himself toward Julian's mother and giggled.

"Carver!" the woman said. "You heah me? Come heah!"

Carver slid down from the seat but remained squatting with his back against the base of it, his head turned slyly around toward Julian's mother, who was smiling at him. The woman reached a hand across the aisle and snatched him to her. He righted himself and hung backwards on her knees, grinning at Julian's mother. "Isn't he cute?" Julian's mother said to the woman with the protruding teeth.

"I reckon he is," the woman said without conviction.

The Negress yanked him upright but he eased out of her grip and shot across the aisle and scrambled, giggling wildly, onto the seat beside his love.

"I think he likes me," Julian's mother said, and smiled at the woman. It was the smile she used when she was being particularly gracious to an inferior. Julian saw everything lost. The lesson had rolled off her like rain on a roof.

The woman stood up and yanked the little boy off the seat as if she were snatching him from contagion. Julian could feel the rage in her at having no weapon like his mother's smile. She gave the child a sharp slap across his leg. He howled once and then thrust his head into her stomach and kicked his feet against her shins. "Behave," she said vehemently.

The bus stopped and the Negro who had been reading the newspaper got off. The woman moved over and set the little boy down with a thump between herself and Julian. She held him firmly by the knee. In a moment he put his hands in front of his face and peeped at Julian's mother through his fingers.

"I see yoooooooo!" she said and put her hand in front of her face and peeped at him.

The woman slapped his hand down. "Quit yo' foolishness," she said, "before I knock the living Jesus out of you!"

Julian was thankful that the next stop was theirs. He reached up and pulled the cord. The woman reached up and pulled it at the same time. Oh my God, he thought. He had the terrible intuition that when they got off the bus together, his mother would open her purse and give the little boy a nickel. The gesture would be as natural to her as breathing. The bus stopped and the woman got up and lunged to the front, dragging the child, who wished to stay on, after her. Julian and his mother got up and followed. As they neared the door, Julian tried to relieve her of her pocketbook.

"No," she murmured, "I want to give the little boy a nickel."

"No!" Julian hissed. "No!"

She smiled down at the child and opened her bag. The bus door opened and the woman picked him up by the arm and descended with him, hanging at her hip. Once in the street she set him down and shook him.

Julian's mother had to close her purse while she got down the bus step but as soon as her feet were on the ground, she opened it again and began to rummage inside. "I can't find but a penny," she whispered, "but it looks like a new one."

"Don't do it!" Julian said fiercely between his teeth. There was a streetlight on the corner and she hurried to get under it so that she could better see into her pocketbook. The woman was heading off rapidly down the street with the child still hanging backward on her hand.

"Oh little boy!" Julian's mother called and took a few quick steps and caught up with them just beyond the lamppost. "Here's a bright new penny for you," and she held out the coin, which shone bronze in the dim light.

The huge woman turned and for a moment stood, her shoulders lifted and her face frozen with frustrated rage, and stared at Julian's mother. Then all at once she seemed to explode like a piece of machinery that had been given one ounce of pressure too much. Julian saw the black fist swing out with the red pocketbook. He shut his eyes and cringed as he heard the woman shout, "He don't take nobody's pennies!" When he opened his eyes, the woman was disappearing down the street with the little boy staring wide-eyed over her shoulder. Julian's mother was sitting on the sidewalk.

"I told you not to do that," Julian said angrily. "I told you not to do that!"

He stood over her for a minute, gritting his teeth. Her legs were stretched out in front of her and her hat was on her lap. He squatted down and looked her in the face. It was totally expressionless. "You got exactly what you deserved," he said. "Now get up."

He picked up her pocketbook and put what had fallen out back in it. He picked the hat up off her lap. The penny caught his eye on the sidewalk and he picked that up and let it drop before her eyes into the purse. Then he stood up and leaned over and held his hands out to pull her up. She remained immobile. He sighed. Rising above them on either side were black apartment buildings, marked with irregular rectangles of light. At the end of the block a man came out of a door and walked off in the opposite direction. "All right," he said, "suppose somebody happens by and wants to know why you're sitting on the sidewalk?"

She took the hand and, breathing hard, pulled heavily up on it and then stood for a moment, swaying slightly as if the spots of light in the darkness were circling around her. Her eyes, shadowed and confused, finally settled on his face. He did not try to conceal his irritation. "I hope this teaches you a lesson," he said. She leaned forward and her eyes raked his face. She seemed trying to determine his identity. Then, as if she found nothing familiar about him, she started off with a headlong movement in the wrong direction.

"Aren't you going on to the Y?" he asked.

"Home," she muttered.

"Well, are we walking?"

For answer she kept going. Julian followed along, his hands behind him. He saw no reason to let the lesson she had had go without backing it up with an explanation of its meaning. She might as well be made to understand what had happened to her. "Don't think that was just an uppity Negro woman," he said. "That was the whole colored race which will no longer take your condescending pennies. That was your black double. She can wear the same hat as you, and to be sure," he added gratuitously (because he thought it was funny), "it looked better on her than it did on you. What all this means," he said, "is that the old world is gone. The old manners are obsolete and your graciousness is not worth a damn." He thought bitterly of the house that had been lost for him. "You aren't who you think you are," he said.

She continued to plow ahead, paying no attention to him. Her hair had come undone on one side. She dropped her pocketbook and took no notice. He stooped and picked it up and handed it to her but she did not take it.

"You needn't act as if the world had come to an end," he said, "because it hasn't. From now on you've got to live in a new world and face a few realities for a change. Buck up," he said, "it won't kill you."

She was breathing fast.

"Let's wait on the bus," he said.

"Home," she said thickly.

"I hate to see you behave like this," he said. "Just like a child. I should be able to expect more of you." He decided to stop where he was and make her stop and wait for a bus. "I'm not going any farther," he said, stopping. "We're going on the bus."

She continued to go on as if she had not heard him. He took a few steps and caught her arm and stopped her. He looked into her face and caught his breath. He was looking into a face he had never seen before. "Tell Grandpa to come get me," she said.

He stared, stricken.

"Tell Caroline to come get me," she said.

Stunned, he let her go and she lurched forward again, walking as if one leg were shorter than the other. A tide of darkness seemed to be sweeping her from him. "Mother!" he cried. "Darling, sweetheart, wait!" Crumpling, she fell to the pavement. He dashed forward and fell at her side, crying "Mamma, Mamma!" He turned her over. Her face was fiercely distorted. One eye, large and staring, moved slightly to the left as if it had become unmoored. The other remained fixed on him, raked his face again, found nothing and closed.

"Wait here, wait here!" he cried and jumped up and began to run for help toward a cluster of lights he saw in the distance ahead of him. "Help, help!" he shouted, but his voice was thin, scarcely a thread of sound. The lights drifted farther away the faster he ran and his feet moved numbly as if they carried him nowhere. The tide of darkness seemed to sweep him back to her, postponing from moment to moment his entry into the world of guilt and sorrow.

JOHN STEINBECK (1902–1968)

The Chrysanthemums

The high grey-flannel fog of winter closed off the Salinas Valley from the sky and from all the rest of the world. On every side it sat like a lid on the mountains and made of the great valley a closed pot. On the broad, level land floor the gang plows bit deep and left the black earth shining like metal where the shares had cut. On the foothill ranches across the Salinas River, the yellow stubble fields seemed to be bathed in pale cold sunshine, but there was no sunshine in the valley now in December. The thick willow scrub along the river flamed with sharp and positive yellow leaves.

It was a time of quiet and of waiting. The air was cold and tender. A light wind blew up from the southwest so that the farmers were mildly hopeful of a good rain before long; but fog and rain do not go together.

Across the river, on Henry Allen's foothill ranch there was a little work to be done, for the hay was cut and stored and the orchards were plowed up to receive the rain deeply when it should come. The cattle on the higher slopes were becoming shaggy and rough-coated.

Elisa Allen, working in her flower garden, looked down across the yard and saw Henry, her husband, talking to two men in business suits. The three of them stood by the tractor shed, each man with one foot on the side of the little Fordson. They smoked cigarettes and studied the machine as they talked.

Elisa watched them for a moment and then went back to her work. She was thirty-five. Her face was lean and strong and her eyes were as clear as water. Her figure looked blocked and heavy in her gardening costume, a man's black hat pulled low down over her eyes, clodhopper shoes, a figured print dress almost completely covered by a big corduroy apron with four big pockets to hold the snips, the trowel and scratcher, the seeds and the knife she worked with. She wore heavy leather gloves to protect her hands while she worked.

She was cutting down the old year's chrysanthemum stalks with a pair of short and powerful scissors. She looked down toward the men by the tractor shed now and then. Her face was eager and mature and handsome; even her work with the scissors was over-eager, over-powerful. The chrysanthemum stems seemed too small and easy for her energy.

She brushed a cloud of hair out of her eyes with the back of her glove, and left a smudge of earth on the cheek in doing it. Behind her stood the neat white farm house with red geraniums close-banked around it as high as the windows. It was a hard-swept looking little house, with hard-polished windows, and a clean mud-mat on the front steps.

Elisa cast another glance toward the tractor shed. The strangers were getting into their Ford coupe. She took off a glove and put her strong fingers down into the forest of new green chrysanthemum sprouts that were growing around the old roots. She spread the leaves and looked down among the close-growing stems. No aphids were there, no sowbugs or snails or cutworms. Her terrier fingers destroyed such pests before they could get started.

Elisa started at the sound of her husband's voice. He had come near quietly, and he leaned over the wire fence that protected her flower garden from cattle and dogs and chickens.

"At it again," he said. "You've got a strong new crop coming."

Elisa straightened her back and pulled on the gardening glove again. "Yes. They'll be strong this coming year." In her tone and on her face there was a little smugness.

"You've got a gift with things," Henry observed. "Some of those yellow chrysanthemums you had this year were ten inches across. I wish you'd work out in the orchard and raise some apples that big."

Her eyes sharpened. "Maybe I could do it, too. I've a gift with things, all right. My mother had it. She could stick anything in the ground and make it grow. She said it was having planters' hands that knew how to do it."

"Well, it sure works with flowers," he said.

"Henry, who were those men you were talking to?"

"Why, sure, that's what I came to tell you. They were from the Western Meat Company. I sold those thirty head of three-year-old steers. Got nearly my own price, too."

"Good," she said. "Good for you."

"And I thought," he continued, "I thought how it's Saturday afternoon, and we might go to Salinas for dinner at a restaurant, and then to a picture show— to celebrate, you see."

"Good," she repeated. "Oh, yes. That will be good."

Henry put on his joking tone. "There's fights tonight. How'd you like to go to the fights?"

"Oh, no," she said breathlessly. "No, I wouldn't like fights."

"Just fooling, Elisa. We'll go to a movie. Let's see. It's two now. I'm going to take Scotty and bring down those steers from the hill. It'll take us maybe two hours. We'll go in town about five and have dinner at the Cominos Hotel. Like that?"

"Of course I'll like it. It's good to eat away from home."

"All right, then. I'll go get up a couple of horses."

She said, "I'll have plenty of time to transplant some of these sets, I guess."

She heard her husband calling Scotty down by the barn. And a little later she saw the two men ride up the pale yellow hillside in search of the steers.

There was a little square sandy bed kept for rooting the chrysanthemums. With her trowel she turned the soil over and over, and smoothed it and patted it firm. Then she dug ten parallel trenches to receive the sets. Back at the chrysanthemum bed she pulled out the little crisp shoots, trimmed off the leaves of each one with her scissors and laid it on a small orderly pile.

A squeak of wheels and plod of hoofs came from the road. Elisa looked up. The country road ran along the dense bank of willows and cottonwoods that bordered the river, and up this road came a curious vehicle, curiously drawn. It was an old spring-wagon, with a round canvas top on it like the cover of a prairie schooner. It was drawn by an old bay horse and a little grey-and-white burro. A big stubble-bearded man sat between the cover flaps and drove the crawling team. Underneath the wagon, between the hind wheels, a lean and rangy mongrel dog walked sedately. Words were painted on the canvas in clumsy, crooked letters. "Pots, pans, knives, sisors, lawn mores. Fixed." Two rows of articles and the triumphantly definitive "Fixed" below. The black paint had run down in little sharp points beneath each letter.

Elisa, squatting on the ground, watched to see the crazy, loose-jointed wagon pass by. But it didn't pass. It turned into the farm road in front of her house, crooked old wheels skirling and squeaking. The rangy dog darted from between the wheels and ran ahead. Instantly the two ranch shepherds flew out at him. Then all three stopped, and with stiff and quivering tails, with taut straight legs, with ambassadorial dignity, they slowly circled, sniffing daintily. The caravan pulled up to Elisa's wire fence and stopped. Now the newcomer dog, feeling outnumbered, lowered his tail and retired under the wagon with raised hackles and bared teeth.

The man on the wagon seat called out. "That's a bad dog in a fight when he gets started."

Elisa laughed. "I see he is. How soon does he generally get started?"

The man caught up her laughter and echoed it heartily. "Sometimes not for weeks and weeks," he said. He climbed stiffly down, over the wheel. The horse and the donkey drooped like unwatered flowers.

Elisa saw that he was a very big man. Although his hair and beard were greying, he did not look old. His worn black suit was wrinkled and spotted with grease. The laughter had disappeared from his face and eyes the moment his laughing voice ceased. His eyes were dark and they were full of the brooding that gets in the eyes of teamsters and of sailors. The calloused hands he rested on the wire fence were cracked, and every crack was a black line. He took off his battered hat.

"I'm off my general road, ma'am," he said. "Does this dirt road cut over across the river to the Los Angeles highway?"

Elisa stood up and shoved the thick scissors in her apron pocket. "Well, yes, it does, but it winds around and then fords the river. I don't think your team could pull through the sand."

He replied with some asperity, "It might surprise you what them beasts can pull through."

"When they get started?" she asked.

He smiled for a second. "Yes. When they get started."

"Well," said Elisa, "I think you'll save time if you go back to the Salinas road and pick up the highway there."

He drew a big finger down the chicken wire and made it sing. "I ain't in any hurry, ma'am. I go from Seattle to San Diego and back every year. Takes all my time. About six months each way. I aim to follow nice weather."

Elisa took off her gloves and stuffed them in the apron pocket with the scissors. She touched the under edge of her man's hat, searching for fugitive hairs. "That sounds like a nice kind of a way to live," she said.

He leaned confidentially over the fence. "Maybe you noticed the writing on my wagon. I mend pots and sharpen knives and scissors. You got any of them things to do?"

"Oh, no," she said quickly. "Nothing like that." Her eyes hardened with resistance.

"Scissors is the worst thing," he explained. "Most people just ruin scissors trying to sharpen 'em, but I know how. I got a special tool. It's a little bobbit kind of thing, and patented. But it sure does the trick."

"No. My scissors are all sharp."

"All right, then. Take a pot," he continued earnestly, "a bent pot, or a pot with a hole. I can make it like new so you don't have to buy no new ones. That's a saving for you."

"No," she said shortly. "I tell you I have nothing like that for you to do."

His face fell to an exaggerated sadness. His voice took on a whining undertone. "I ain't had a thing to do today. Maybe I won't have no supper tonight. You see I'm off my regular road. I know folks on the highway clear from Seattle to San Diego. They save their things for me to sharpen up because they know I do it so good and save them money."

"I'm sorry," Elisa said irritably. "I haven't anything for you to do."

His eyes left her face and fell to searching the ground. They roamed about until they came to the chrysanthemum bed where she had been working. "What's them plants, ma'am?"

The irritation and resistance melted from Elisa's face. "Oh, those are chrysanthemums, giant whites and yellows. I raise them every year, bigger than anybody around here."

"Kind of a long-stemmed flower? Looks like a quick puff of colored smoke?" he asked.

"That's it. What a nice way to describe them."

"They smell kind of nasty till you get used to them," he said.

"It's a good bitter smell," she retorted, "not nasty at all."

He changed his tone quickly. "I like the smell myself."

"I had ten-inch blooms this year," she said.

The man leaned farther over the fence. "Look. I know a lady down the road a piece, has got the nicest garden you ever seen. Got nearly every kind of flower but no chrysanthemums. Last time I was mending a copper-bottom washtub for her (that's a hard job but I do it good), she said to me, 'If you ever run acrost some nice chrysanthemums I wish you'd try to get me a few seeds.' That's what she told me."

Elisa's eyes grew alert and eager. "She couldn't have known much about chrysanthemums. You can raise them from seed, but it's much easier to root the little sprouts you see there."

"Oh," he said. "I s'pose I can't take none to her, then."

"Why yes you can," Elisa cried. "I can put some in damp sand, and you can carry them right along with you. They'll take root in the pot if you keep them damp. And then she can transplant them."

"She'd sure like to have some, ma'am. You say they're nice ones?"

"Beautiful," she said. "Oh, beautiful." Her eyes shone. She tore off the battered hat and shook out her dark pretty hair. "I'll put them in a flower pot, and you can take them right with you. Come into the yard."

While the man came through the picket gate Elisa ran excitedly along the geranium-bordered path to the back of the house. And she returned carrying a big red flower pot. The gloves were forgotten now. She kneeled on the ground by the starting bed and dug up the sandy soil with her fingers and scooped it into the bright new flower pot. Then she picked up the little pile of shoots she had prepared. With her strong fingers she pressed them into the sand and tamped around them with her knuckles. The man stood over her. "I'll tell you what to do," she said. "You remember so you can tell the lady."

"Yes, I'll try to remember."

"Well, look. These will take root in about a month. Then she must set them out, about a foot apart in good rich earth like this, see?" She lifted a handful of dark soil for him to look at. "They'll grow fast and tall. Now remember this. In July tell her to cut them down, about eight inches from the ground."

"Before they bloom?" he asked.

"Yes, before they bloom." Her face was tight with eagerness. "They'll grow right up again. About the last of September the buds will start."

She stopped and seemed perplexed. "It's the budding that takes the most care," she said hesitantly. "I don't know how to tell you." She looked deep into his eyes, searchingly. Her mouth opened a little, and she seemed to be listening. "I'll try to tell you," she said. "Did you ever hear of planting hands?"

"Can't say I have, ma'am."

"Well, I can only tell you what it feels like. It's when you're picking off the buds you don't want. Everything goes right down into your fingertips. You watch your fingers work. They do it themselves. You can feel how it is. They pick and pick the buds. They never make a mistake. They're with the plant. Do you see? Your fingers and the plant. You can feel that, right up your arm. They know. They never make a mistake. You can feel it. When you're like that you can't do anything wrong. Do you see that? Can you understand that?"

She was kneeling on the ground looking up at him. Her breast swelled passionately.

The man's eyes narrowed. He looked away self-consciously. "Maybe I know," he said. "Sometimes in the night in the wagon there—"

Elisa's voice grew husky. She broke in on him. "I've never lived as you do, but I know what you mean. When the night is dark—why, the stars are sharp-pointed, and there's quiet. Why, you rise up and up! Every pointed star gets driven into your body. It's like that. Hot and sharp and—lovely."

Kneeling there, her hand went out toward his legs in the greasy black trousers. Her hesitant fingers almost touched the cloth. Then her hand dropped to the ground. She crouched low like a fawning dog.

He said, "It's nice, just like you say. Only when you don't have no dinner, it ain't."

She stood up then, very straight, and her face was ashamed. She held the flower pot out to him and placed it gently in his arms. "Here. Put it in your wagon, on the seat, where you can watch it. Maybe I can find something for you to do."

At the back of the house she dug in the can pile and found two old and battered aluminum saucepans. She carried them back and gave them to him. "Here, maybe you can fix these."

His manner changed. He became professional. "Good as new I can fix them." At the back of his wagon he set a little anvil, and out of an oily tool box dug a small machine hammer. Elisa came through the gate to watch him while he pounded out the dents in the kettles. His mouth grew sure and knowing. At a difficult part of the work he sucked his under-lip.

"You sleep right in the wagon?" Elisa asked.

"Right in the wagon, ma'am. Rain or shine I'm dry as a cow in there."

"It must be nice," she said. "It must be very nice. I wish women could do such things."

"It ain't the right kind of a life for a woman."

Her upper lip raised a little, showing her teeth. "How do you know? How can you tell?" she said.

"I don't know ma'am," he protested. "Of course I don't know. Now here's your kettles, done. You don't have to buy no new ones."

"How much?"

"Oh, fifty cents'll do. I keep my prices down and my work good. That's why I have all them satisfied customers up and down the highway."

Elisa brought him a fifty-cent piece from the house and dropped it in his hand. "You might be surprised to have a rival some time. I can sharpen scissors, too. And I can beat the dents out of little pots. I could show you what a woman might do."

He put his hammer back in the oily box and shoved the little anvil out of sight. "It would be a lonely life for a woman, ma'am, and a scarey life, too, with animals creeping under the wagon all night." He climbed over the single-tree, steadying himself with a hand on the burro's white rump. He settled himself in the seat, picked up the lines. "Thank you kindly, ma'am," he said. "I'll do like you told me; I'll go back and catch the Salinas road."

"Mind," she called, "if you're long in getting there, keep the sand damp."

"Sand, ma'am? . . . Sand? Oh, sure. You mean round the chrysanthemums. Sure I will." He clucked his tongue. The beasts leaned luxuriously into their collars. The mongrel dog took his place between the back wheels. The wagon turned and crawled out the entrance road and back the way it had come, along the river.

Elisa stood in front of her wire fence watching the slow progress of the caravan. Her shoulders were straight, her head thrown back, her eyes half-closed, so that the scene came vaguely into them. Her lips moved silently, forming the words "Good-bye—good-bye." Then she whispered, "That's a bright direction. There's a glowing there." The sound of her whisper startled her. She shook herself free and looked about to see whether anyone had been listening. Only the dogs had heard. They lifted their heads toward her from their sleeping in the dust, and then stretched out their chins and settled asleep again. Elisa turned and ran hurriedly into the house.

In the kitchen she reached behind the stove and felt the water tank. It was full of hot water from the noonday cooking. In the bathroom she tore off her soiled clothes and flung them into the corner. And then she scrubbed herself with a little block of pumice, legs and thighs, loins and chest and arms, until her skin was scratched and red. When she had dried herself she stood in front of a mirror in the bedroom and looked at her body. She tightened her stomach and threw out her chest. She turned and looked over her shoulder at her back.

After a while she began to dress, slowly. She put on her newest under-clothing and her nicest stockings and the dress which was the symbol of her prettiness. She worked carefully on her hair, pencilled her eyebrows and rouged her lips.

Before she was finished she heard the little thunder of hoofs and the shouts of Henry and his helper as they drove the red steers into the corral. She heard the gate bang shut and set herself for Henry's arrival.

His step sounded on the porch. He entered the house calling "Elisa, where are you?"

"In my room, dressing. I'm not ready. There's hot water for your bath. Hurry up. It's getting late."

When she heard him splashing in the tub, Elisa laid his dark suit on the bed, and shirt and socks and tie beside it. She stood his polished shoes on the floor beside the bed. Then she went to the porch and sat primly and stiffly down. She looked toward the river road where the willow-line was still yellow with frosted leaves so that under the high grey fog they seemed a thin band of sunshine. This was the only color in the grey afternoon. She sat unmoving for a long time. Her eyes blinked rarely.

Henry came banging out of the door, shoving his tie inside his vest as he came. Elisa stiffened and her face grew tight. Henry stopped short and looked at her. "Why—why, Elisa. You look so nice!"

"Nice? You think I look nice? What do you mean by 'nice?'"

Henry blundered on. "I don't know. I mean you look different, strong and happy."

"I am strong? Yes, strong. What do you mean 'strong?'"

He looked bewildered. "You're playing some kind of a game," he said helplessly. "It's a kind of a play. You look strong enough to break a calf over your knee, happy enough to eat it like watermelon."

For a second she lost her rigidity. "Henry! Don't talk like that. You didn't know what you said." She grew complete again. "I'm strong," she boasted. "I never knew before how strong."

Henry looked down toward the tractor shed, and when he brought his eyes back to her, they were his own again. "I'll get out the car. You can put on your coat while I'm starting."

Elisa went into the house. She heard him drive to the gate and idle down his motor, and then she took a long time to put on her hat. She pulled it here and pressed it there. When Henry turned the motor off she slipped into her coat and went out.

The little roadster bounced along on the dirt road by the river, raising the birds and driving the rabbits into the brush. Two cranes flapped heavily over the willow-line and dropped into the riverbed.

Far ahead on the road Elisa saw a dark speck. She knew.

She tried not to look as they passed it, but her eyes would not obey. She whispered to herself sadly. "He might have thrown them off the road. That wouldn't have been much trouble, not very much. But he kept the pot," she explained. "He had to keep the pot. That's why he couldn't get them off the road."

The roadster turned a bend and she saw the caravan ahead. She swung full around toward her husband so she could not see the little covered wagon and the mismatched team as the car passed them.

In a moment it was over. The thing was done. She did not look back. She said loudly, to be heard above the motor, "It will be good, tonight, a good dinner."

"Now you're changed again," Henry complained. He took one hand from the wheel and patted her knee. "I ought to take you in to dinner oftener. It would be good for both of us. We get so heavy out on the ranch."

"Henry," she asked, "could we have wine at dinner?"

"Sure we could. Say! That will be fine."

She was silent for a little while; then she said, "Henry, at those prize fights, do the men hurt each other very much?"

"Sometimes a little, not often. Why?"

"Well, I've read how they break noses, and blood runs down their chests. I've read how the fighting gloves get heavy and soggy with blood."

He looked around at her. "What's the matter, Elisa? I didn't know you read things like that." He brought the car to a stop, then turned to the right over the Salinas River bridge.

"Do any women ever go to the fights?" she asked.

"Oh, sure, some. What's the matter, Elisa? Do you want to go? I don't think you'd like it, but I'll take you if you really want to go."

She relaxed limply in the seat. "Oh, no. No. I don't want to go. I'm sure I don't." Her face was turned away from him. "It will be enough if we can have wine. It will be plenty." She turned up her coat collar so he could not see that she was crying weakly—like an old woman.

ROBERT STONE (1937–)

Helping

One gray November day, Elliot went to Boston for the afternoon. The wet streets seemed cold and lonely. He sensed a broken promise in the city's elegance and verve. Old hopes tormented him like phantom limbs, but he did not drink. He had joined Alcoholics Anonymous fifteen months before.

Christmas came, childless, a festival of regret. His wife went to Mass and cooked a turkey. Sober, Elliot walked in the woods.

In January, blizzards swept down from the Arctic until the weather became too cold for snow. The Shawmut Valley grew quiet and crystalline. In the white silences, Elliot could hear the boards of his house contract and feel a shrinking in his bones. Each dusk, starveling deer came out of the wooded swamp behind the house to graze his orchard for whatever raccoons had uncovered and left behind. At night he lay beside his sleeping wife listening to the baying of dog packs running them down in the deep moon-shadowed snow.

Day in, day out, he was sober. At times it was almost stimulating. But he could not shake off the sensations he had felt in Boston. In his mind's eye he could see dead leaves rattling along brick gutters and savor that day's desperation. The brief outing had undermined him.

Sober, however, he remained, until the day a man named Blankenship came into his office at the state hospital for counseling. Blankenship had red hair, a brutal face, and a sneaking manner. He was a sponger and petty thief whom Elliot had seen a number of times before.

"I been having this dream," Blankenship announced loudly. His voice was not pleasant. His skin was unwholesome. Every time he got arrested the court sent him to the psychiatrists and the psychiatrists, who spoke little English, sent him to Elliot.

Blankenship had joined the Army after his first burglary but had never served east of the Rhine. After a few months in Wiesbaden, he had been discharged for reasons of unsuitability, but he told everyone he was a veteran of the Vietnam War. He went about in a tiger suit. Elliot had had enough of him.

"Dreams are boring," Elliot told him.

Blankenship was outraged. "Whaddaya mean?" he demanded.

During counseling sessions Elliot usually moved his chair into the middle of the room in order to seem accessible to his clients. Now he stayed securely behind his desk. He did not care to seem accessible to Blankenship. "What I said, Mr. Blankenship. Other people's dreams are boring. Didn't you ever hear that?"

"Boring?" Blankenship frowned. He seemed unable to imagine a meaning for the word.

Elliot picked up a pencil and set its point quivering on his desk-top blotter. He gazed into his client's slack-jawed face. The Blankenship family made their way through life as strolling litigants, and young Blankenship's specialty was slipping on ice cubes. Hauled off the pavement, he would hassle the doctors in Emergency for pain pills and hurry to a law clinic. The Blankenships had threatened suit against half the property owners in the southern part of the state. What they could not extort at law they stole. But even the Blankenship family had abandoned Blankenship. His last visit to the hospital had been subsequent to an arrest for lifting a case of hot-dog rolls from Woolworth's. He lived in a Goodwill depository bin in Wyndham.

"Now I suppose you want to tell me your dream? Is that right, Mr. Blankenship?"

Blankenship looked left and right like a dog surrendering eye contact. "Don't you want to hear it?" he asked humbly.

Elliot was unmoved. "Tell me something, Blankenship. Was your dream about Vietnam?"

At the mention of the word "Vietnam," Blankenship customarily broke into a broad smile. Now he looked guilty and guarded. He shrugged. "Ya."

"How come you have dreams about that place, Blankenship? You were never there."

"Whaddaya mean?" Blankenship began to say, but Elliot cut him off.

"You were never there, my man. You never saw the goddamn place. You have no business dreaming about it! You better cut it out!"

He had raised his voice to the extent that the secretary outside his open door paused at her word processor.

"Lemme alone," Blankenship said fearfully. "Some doctor you are."

"It's all right," Elliot assured him. "I'm not a doctor."

"Everybody's on my case," Blankenship said. His moods were volatile. He began to weep.

Elliot watched the tears roll down Blankenship's chapped, pitted cheeks. He cleared his throat. "Look, fella . . ." he began. He felt at a loss. He felt like telling Blankenship that things were tough all over.

Blankenship sniffed and telescoped his neck and after a moment looked at Elliot. His look was disconcertingly trustful; he was used to being counseled.

"Really, you know, it's ridiculous for you to tell me your problems have to do with Nam. You were never over there. It was me over there, Blankenship. Not you."

Blankenship leaned forward and put his forehead on his knees.

"Your troubles have to do with here and now," Elliot told his client. "Fantasies aren't helpful."

His voice sounded overripe and hypocritical in his own ears. What a dreadful business, he thought. What an awful job this is. Anger was driving him crazy.

Blankenship straightened up and spoke through his tears. "This dream . . ." he said. "I'm scared."

Elliot felt ready to endure a great deal in order not to hear Blankenship's dream.

"I'm not the one you see about that," he said. In the end he knew his duty. He sighed. "O.K. All right. Tell me about it."

"Yeah?" Blankenship asked with leaden sarcasm. "Yeah? You think dreams are friggin' boring!"

"No, no," Elliot said. He offered Blankenship a tissue and Blankenship took one. "That was sort of off the top of my head. I didn't really mean it."

Blankenship fixed his eyes on dreaming distance. "There's a feeling that goes with it. With the dream." Then he shook his head in revulsion and looked at Elliot as though he had only just awakened. "So what do you think? You think it's boring?"

"Of course not," Elliot said. "A physical feeling?"

"Ya. It's like I'm floating in rubber."

He watched Elliot stealthily, aware of quickened attention. Elliot had caught dengue in Vietnam and during his weeks of delirium had felt vaguely as though he were floating in rubber.

"What are you seeing in this dream?"

Blankenship only shook his head. Elliot suffered a brief but intense attack of rage.

"Hey, Blankenship," he said equably, "here I am, man. You can see I'm listening."

"What I saw was black," Blankenship said. He spoke in an odd tremolo. His behavior was quite different from anything Elliot had come to expect from him.

"Black? What was it?"

"Smoke. The sky maybe."

"The sky?" Elliot asked.

"It was all black. I was scared."

In a waking dream of his own, Elliot felt the muscles on his neck distend. He was looking up at a sky that was black, filled with smoke-swollen clouds, lit with fires, damped with blood and rain.

"What were you scared of?" he asked Blankenship.

"I don't know," Blankenship said.

Elliot could not drive the black sky from his inward eye. It was as though Blankenship's dream had infected his own mind.

"You don't know? You don't know what you were scared of?"

Blankenship's posture was rigid. Elliot, who knew the aspect of true fear, recognized it there in front of him.

"The Nam," Blankenship said.

"You're not even old enough," Elliot told him.

Blankenship sat trembling with joined palms between his thighs. His face was flushed and not in the least ennobled by pain. He had trouble with alcohol and drugs. He had trouble with everything.

"So wherever your black sky is, it isn't Vietnam."

Things were so unfair, Elliot thought. It was unfair of Blankenship to appropriate the condition of a Vietnam veteran. The trauma inducing his post-traumatic stress had been nothing more serious than his own birth, a routine procedure. Now, in addition to the poverty, anxiety, and confusion that would always be his life's lot, he had been visited with irony. It was all arbitrary and some people simply got elected. Everyone knew that who had been where Blankenship had not.

"Because, I assure you, Mr. Blankenship, you were never there."

"Whaddaya mean?" Blankenship asked.

When Blankenship was gone Elliot leafed through his file and saw that the psychiatrists had passed him upstairs without recording a diagnosis. Disproportionately angry, he went out to the secretary's desk.

"Nobody wrote up that last patient," he said. "I'm not supposed to see people without a diagnosis. The shrinks are just passing the buck."

The secretary was a tall, solemn redhead with prominent front teeth and a slight speech disorder. "Dr. Sayyid will have kittens if he hears you call him a shrink, Chas. He's already complained. He hates being called a shrink."

"Then he came to the wrong country," Elliot said. "He can go back to his own."

The woman giggled. "He *is* the doctor, Chas."

"Hates being called a shrink!" He threw the file on the secretary's table and stormed back toward his office. "That fucking little zip couldn't give you a decent haircut. He's a prescription clerk."

The secretary looked about her guiltily and shook her head. She was used to him.

Elliot succeeded in calming himself down after a while, but the image of the black sky remained with him. At first he thought he would be able to simply shrug the whole thing off. After a few minutes, he picked up his phone and dialed Blankenship's probation officer.

"The Vietnam thing is all he has," the probation officer explained. "I guess he picked it up around."

"His descriptions are vivid," Elliot said.

"You mean they sound authentic?"

"I mean he had me going today. He was ringing my bells."

"Good for Blanky. Think he believes it himself?"

"Yes," Elliot said. "He believes it himself now."

Elliot told the probation officer about Blankenship's current arrest, which was for showering illegally at midnight in the Wyndham Regional High School. He asked what probation knew about Blankenship's present relationship with his family.

"You kiddin'?" the P.O. asked. "They're all locked down. The whole family's inside. The old man's in Bridgewater. Little Donny's in San Quentin or somewhere. Their dog's in the pound."

Elliot had lunch alone in the hospital staff cafeteria. On the far side of the double-glazed windows, the day was darkening as an expected snowstorm gathered. Along Route 7, ancient elms stood frozen against the gray sky. When he had finished his sandwich and coffee, he sat staring out at the winter afternoon. His anger had given way to an insistent anxiety.

On the way back to his office, he stopped at the hospital gift shop for a copy of *Sports Illustrated* and a candy bar. When he was inside again, he closed the door and put his feet up. It was Friday and he had no appointments for the remainder of the day, nothing to do but write a few letters and read the office mail.

Elliot's cubicle in the social services department was windowless and lined with bookshelves. When he found himself unable to concentrate on the magazine and without any heart for his paperwork, he ran his eye over the row of books beside his chair. There were volumes by Heinrich Muller and Carlos Casteneda, Jones's life of Freud, and *The Golden Bough*. The books aroused a revulsion in Elliot. Their present uselessness repelled him.

Over and over again, detail by detail, he tried to recall his conversation with Blankenship.

"You were never there," he heard himself explaining. He was trying to get the whole incident straightened out after the fact. Something was wrong. Dread crept over him like a paralysis. He ate his candy bar without tasting it. He knew that the craving for sweets was itself a bad sign.

Blankenship had misappropriated someone else's dream and made it his own. It made no difference whether you had been there, after all. The dreams had crossed the ocean. They were in the air.

He took his glasses off and put them on his desk and sat with his arms folded, looking into the well of light from his desk lamp. There seemed to be nothing but whirl inside him. Unwelcome things came and went in his mind's eye. His heart beat faster. He could not control the headlong promiscuity of his thoughts.

It was possible to imagine larval dreams traveling in suspended animation undetectable in a host brain. They could be divided and regenerate like flat-worms, hide in seams and bedding, in war stories, laughter, snapshots. They could rot your socks and turn your memory into a black-and-green blister. Green for the hills, black for the sky above. At daybreak they hung themselves up in rows like bats. At dusk they went out to look for dreamers.

Elliot put his jacket on and went into the outer office, where the secretary sat frowning into the measured sound and light of her machine. She must enjoy its sleekness and order, he thought. She was divorced. Four red-headed kids between ten and seventeen lived with her in an unpainted house across from Stop & Shop. Elliot liked her and had come to find her attractive. He managed a smile for her.

"Ethel, I think I'm going to pack it in," he declared. It seemed awkward to be leaving early without a reason.

"Jack wants to talk to you before you go, Chas."

Elliot looked at her blankly.

Then his colleague, Jack Sprague, having heard his voice, called from the adjoining cubicle. "Chas, what about Sunday's games? Shall I call you with the spread?"

"I don't know," Elliot said. "I'll phone you tomorrow."

"This is a big decision for him," Jack Sprague told the secretary. "He might lose twenty-five bucks."

At present, Elliot drew a slightly higher salary than Jack Sprague, although Jack had a Ph.D. and Elliot was simply an M.S.W. Different branches of the state government employed them.

"Twenty-five bucks," said the woman. "If you guys have no better use for twenty-five bucks, give it to me."

"Where are you off to, by the way?" Sprague asked.

Elliot began to answer, but for a moment no reply occurred to him. He shrugged. "I have to get back," he finally stammered. "I promised Grace."

"Was that Blankenship I saw leaving?"

Elliot nodded.

"It's February," Jack said. "How come he's not in Florida?"

"I don't know," Elliot said. He put on his coat and walked to the door. "I'll see you."

"Have a nice weekend," the secretary said. She and Sprague looked after him indulgently as he walked toward the main corridor.

"Are Chas and Grace going out on the town?" she said to Sprague. "What do you think?"

"That would be the day," Sprague said. "Tomorrow he'll come back over here and read all day. He spends every weekend holed up in this goddamn office while she does something or other at the church." He shook his head. "Every night he's at A.A. and she's home alone."

Ethel savored her overbite. "Jack," she said teasingly, "are you thinking what I think you're thinking? Shame on you."

"I'm thinking I'm glad I'm not him, that's what I'm thinking. That's as much as I'll say."

"Yeah, well, I don't care," Ethel said. "Two salaries and no kids, that's the way to go, boy."

Elliot went out through the automatic doors of the emergency bay and the cold closed over him. He walked across the hospital parking lot with his eyes on the pavement, his hands thrust deep in his overcoat pockets, skirting patches of shattered ice. There was no wind, but the motionless air stung; the metal frames of his glasses burned his skin. Curlicues of mud-brown ice coated the soiled snowbanks along the street. Although it was still afternoon, the street lights had come on.

The lock on his car door had frozen and he had to breathe on the keyhole to fit the key. When the engine turned over, Jussi Björling's recording of the Handel Largo filled the car interior. He snapped it off at once.

Halted at the first stoplight, he began to feel the want of a destination. The fear and impulse to flight that had got him out of the office faded, and he had no desire to go home. He was troubled by a peculiar impatience that might have been with time itself. It was as though he were waiting for something. The sensation made him feel anxious; it was unfamiliar but not altogether unpleasant. When the light changed he drove on, past the Gulf station and the firehouse and between the greens of Ilford Common. At the far end of the common he swung into the parking lot of the Packard Conway Library and stopped with the engine running. What he was experiencing, he thought, was the principle of possibility.

He turned off the engine and went out again into the cold. Behind the leaded library windows he could see the librarian pouring coffee in her tiny private office. The librarian was a Quaker of socialist principles named Candace Music, who was Elliot's cousin.

The Conway Library was all dark wood and etched mirrors, a Gothic saloon. Years before, out of work and booze-whipped, Elliot had gone to hide there. Because Candace was a classicist's widow and knew some Greek, she was one of the few people in the valley with whom Elliot had cared to speak in those days. Eventually, it had seemed to him that all their conversations tended toward Vietnam, so he had gone less and less often. Elliot was the only Vietnam veteran Candace knew well enough to chat with, and he had come to suspect that he was being probed for the edification of the East Ilford Friends Meeting. At that time he had still pretended to talk easily about his war and had prepared little discourses and picaresque anecdotes to recite on demand. Earnest seekers like Candace had caused him great secret distress.

Candace came out of her office to find him at the checkout desk. He watched her brow furrow with concern as she composed a smile. "Chas, what a surprise. You haven't been in for an age."

"Sure I have, Candace. I went to all the Wednesday films last fall. I work just across the road."

"I know, dear," Candace said. "I always seem to miss you."

A cozy fire burned in the hearth, an antique brass clock ticked along on the marble mantel above it. On a couch near the fireplace an old man sat upright, his mouth open, asleep among half a dozen soiled plastic bags. Two teenage girls whispered over their homework at a table under the largest window.

"Now that I'm here," he said, laughing, "I can't remember what I came to get."

"Stay and get warm," Candace told him. "Got a minute? Have a cup of coffee."

Elliot had nothing but time, but he quickly realized that he did not want to stay and pass it with Candace. He had no clear idea of why he had come to the library. Standing at the checkout desk, he accepted coffee. She attended him with an air of benign supervision, as though he were a Chinese peasant and she a medical missionary, like her father. Candace was tall and plain, more handsome in her middle sixties than she had ever been.

"Why don't we sit down?"

He allowed her to gentle him into a chair by the fire. They made a threesome with the sleeping old man.

"Have you given up translating, Chas? I hope not."

"Not at all," he said. Together they had once rendered a few fragments of Sophocles into verse. She was good at clever rhymes.

"You come in so rarely, Chas. Ted's books go to waste."

After her husband's death, Candace had donated his books to the Conway, where they reposed in a reading room inscribed to his memory, untouched among foreign-language volumes, local genealogies, and books in large type for the elderly.

"I have a study in the barn," he told Candace. "I work there. When I have time." The lie was absurd, but he felt the need of it.

"And you're working with Vietnam veterans," Candace declared.

"Supposedly," Elliot said. He was growing impatient with her nodding solicitude.

"Actually," he said, "I came in for the new Oxford *Classical World*. I thought you'd get it for the library and I could have a look before I spent my hard-earned cash."

Candace beamed. "You've come to the right place, Chas, I'm happy to say." He thought she looked disproportionately happy. "I have it."

"Good," Elliot said, standing. "I'll just take it, then. I can't really stay."

Candace took his cup and saucer and stood as he did. When the library telephone rang, she ignored it, reluctant to let him go. "How's Grace?" she asked.

"Fine," Elliot said. "Grace is well."

At the third ring she went to the desk. When her back was turned, he hesitated for a moment and then went outside.

The gray afternoon had softened into night, and it was snowing. The falling snow whirled like a furious mist in the headlight beams on Route 7 and settled implacably on Elliot's cheeks and eyelids. His heart, for no good reason, leaped up in childlike expectation. He had run away from a dream and encountered possibility. He felt in possession of a promise. He began to walk toward the roadside lights.

Only gradually did he begin to understand what had brought him there and what the happy anticipation was that fluttered in his breast. Drinking, he had started his evening from the Conway Library. He would arrive hung over in the early afternoon to browse and read. When the old pain rolled in with dusk, he would walk down to the Midway Tavern for a remedy. Standing in the snow outside the library, he realized that he had contrived to promise himself a drink.

Ahead, through the storm, he could see the beer signs in the Midway's window warm and welcoming. Snowflakes spun around his head like an excitement.

Outside the Midway's package store, he paused with his hand on the doorknob. There was an old man behind the counter whom Elliot remembered from his drinking days. When he was inside, he realized that the old man neither knew nor cared who he was. The package store was thick with dust; it was on the counter, the shelves, the bottles themselves. The old counterman looked dusty. Elliot bought a bottle of King William Scotch and put it in the inside pocket of his overcoat.

Passing the windows of the Midway Tavern, Elliot could see the ranks of bottles aglow behind the bar. The place was crowded with men leaving the afternoon shifts at the shoe and felt factories. No one turned to note him when he passed inside. There was a single stool vacant at the bar and he took it. His heart beat faster. Bruce Springsteen was on the jukebox.

The bartender was a club fighter from Pittsfield called Jackie G., with whom Elliot had often gossiped. Jackie G. greeted him as though he had been in the previous evening. "Say, babe?"

"How do," Elliot said.

A couple of men at the bar eyed his shirt and tie. Confronted with the bartender, he felt impelled to explain his presence. "Just thought I'd stop by," he told Jackie G. "Just thought I'd have one. Saw the light. The snow . . ." He chuckled expansively.

"Good move," the bartender said. "Scotch?"

"Double," Elliot said.

When he shoved two dollars forward along the bar, Jackie G. pushed one of the bills back to him. "Happy hour, babe."

"Ah," Elliot said. He watched Jackie pour the double. "Not a moment too soon."

• • •

For five minutes or so, Elliot sat in his car in the barn with the engine running and his Handel tape on full volume. He had driven over from East Ilford in a baroque ecstasy, swinging and swaying and singing along. When the tape ended, he turned off the engine and poured some Scotch into an apple juice container to store providentially beneath the car seat. Then he took the tape and the Scotch into the house with him. He was lying on the sofa in the dark living room, listening to the Largo, when he heard his wife's car in the driveway. By the time Grace had made her way up the icy back-porch steps, he was able to hide the Scotch and rinse his glass clean in the kitchen sink. The drinking life, he thought, was lived moment by moment.

Soon she was in the tiny cloakroom struggling off with her overcoat. In the process she knocked over a cross-country ski, which stood propped against the cloakroom wall. It had been more than a year since Elliot had used the skis.

She came into the kitchen and sat down at the table to take off her boots. Her lean, freckled face was flushed with the cold, but her eyes looked weary. "I wish you'd put those skis down in the barn," she told him. "You never use them."

"I always like to think," Elliot said, "that I'll start the morning off skiing."

"Well, you never do," she said. "How long have you been home?"

"Practically just walked in," he said. Her pointing out that he no longer skied in the morning enraged him. "I stopped at the Conway Library to get the new Oxford *Classical World*. Candace ordered it."

Her look grew troubled. She had caught something in his voice. With dread and bitter satisfaction, Elliot watched his wife detect the smell of whiskey.

"Oh God," she said. "I don't believe it."

Let's get it over with, he thought. Let's have the song and dance.

She sat up straight in her chair and looked at him in fear.

"Oh, Chas," she said, "how could you?"

For a moment he was tempted to try to explain it all.

"The fact is," Elliot told his wife, "I hate people who start the day cross-country skiing."

She shook her head in denial and leaned her forehead on her palm and cried.

He looked into the kitchen window and saw his own distorted image. "The fact is I think I'll start tomorrow morning by stringing head-high razor wire across Anderson's trail."

The Andersons were the Elliots' nearest neighbors. Loyall Anderson was a full professor of government at the state university, thirty miles away. Anderson and his wife were blond and both of them were over six feet tall. They had two blond children, who qualified for the gifted class in the local school but attended regular classes in token of the Andersons' opposition to elitism.

"Sure," Elliot said. "Stringing wire's good exercise. It's life-affirming in its own way."

The Andersons started each and every day with a brisk morning glide along a trail that they partly maintained. They skied well and presented a pleasing, wholesome sight. If, in the course of their adventure, they encountered a snowmobile, Darlene Anderson would affect to choke and cough, indicating her displeasure. If the snowmobile approached them from behind and the trail was narrow, the Andersons would decline to let it pass, asserting their statutory right-of-way.

"I don't want to hear your violent fantasies," Grace said.

Elliot was picturing razor wire, the Army kind. He was picturing the decapitated Andersons, their blood and jaunty ski caps bright on the white trail. He was picturing their severed heads, their earnest blue eyes and large white teeth reflecting the virginal morning snow. Although Elliot hated snowmobiles, he hated the Andersons far more.

He looked at his wife and saw that she had stopped crying. Her long, elegant face was rigid and lipless.

"Know what I mean? One string at Mommy and Daddy level for Loyall and Darlene. And a bitty wee string at kiddie level for Skippy and Samantha, those cunning little whizzes."

"Stop it," she said to him.

"Sorry," Elliot told her.

Stiff with shame, he went and took his bottle out of the cabinet into which he had thrust it and poured a drink. He was aware of her eyes on him. As he drank, a fragment from old Music's translation of *Medea* came into his mind. "Old friend, I have to weep. The gods and I went mad together and made things as they are." It was such a waste; eighteen months of struggle thrown away. But there was no way to get the stuff back in the bottle.

"I'm very sorry," he said. "You know I'm very sorry, don't you, Grace?"

The delectable Handel arias spun on in the next room.

"You must stop," she said. "You must make yourself stop before it takes over."

"It's out of my hands," Elliot said. He showed her his empty hands. "It's beyond me."

"You'll lose your job, Chas." She stood up at the table and leaned on it, staring wide-eyed at him. Drunk as he was, the panic in her voice frightened him. "You'll end up in jail again."

"One engages," Elliot said, "and then one sees."

"How can you have done it?" she demanded. "You promised me."

"First the promises," Elliot said, "and then the rest."

"Last time was supposed to be the last time," she said.

"Yes," he said, "I remember."

"I can't stand it," she said. "You reduce me to hysterics." She wrung her hands for him to see. "See? Here I am, I'm in hysterics."

"What can I say?" Elliot asked. He went to the bottle and refilled his glass. "Maybe you shouldn't watch."

"You want me to be forbearing, Chas? I'm not going to be."

"The last thing I want," Elliot said, "is an argument."

"I'll give you a fucking argument. You didn't have to drink. All you had to do was come home."

"That must have been the problem," he said.

Then he ducked, alert at the last possible second to the missile that came for him at hairline level. Covering up, he heard the shattering of glass, and a fine rain of crystals enveloped him. She had sailed the sugar bowl at him; it had smashed against the wall above his head and there was sugar and glass in his hair.

"You bastard!" she screamed. "You are undermining me!"

"You ought not to throw things at me," Elliot said. "I don't throw things at you."

He left her frozen into her follow-through and went into the living room to turn the music off. When he returned she was leaning back against the wall, rubbing her right elbow with her left hand. Her eyes were bright. She had picked up one of her boots from the middle of the kitchen floor and stood holding it.

"What the hell do you mean, that must have been the problem?"

He set his glass on the edge of the sink with an unsteady hand and turned to her. "What do I mean? I mean that most of the time I'm putting one foot in front of the other like a good soldier and I'm out of it from the neck up. But there are times when I don't think I will ever be dead enough—or dead long enough—to get the taste of this life off my teeth. That's what I mean!"

She looked at him dry-eyed. "Poor fella," she said.

"What you have to understand, Grace, is that this drink I'm having"—he raised the glass toward her in a gesture of salute—"is the only worthwhile thing I've done in the last year and a half. It's the only thing in my life that means jack shit, the closest thing to satisfaction I've had. Now how can you begrudge me that? It's the best I'm capable of."

"You'll go too far," she said to him. "You'll see."

"What's that, Grace? A threat to walk?" He was grinding his teeth. "Don't make me laugh. You, walk? You, the friend of the unfortunate?"

"Don't you hit me," she said when she looked at his face. "Don't you dare."

"You, the Christian Queen of Calvary, walk? Why, I don't believe that for a minute."

She ran a hand through her hair and bit her lip. "No, we stay," she said. Anger and distraction made her look young. Her cheeks blazed rosy against the general pallor of her skin. "In my family we stay until the fella dies. That's the tradition. We stay and pour it for them and they die."

He put his drink down and shook his head.

"I thought we'd come through," Grace said. "I was sure."

"No," Elliot said. "Not altogether."

They stood in silence for a minute. Elliot sat down at the oilcloth-covered table. Grace walked around it and poured herself a whiskey.

"You are undermining me, Chas. You are making things impossible for me and I just don't know." She drank and winced. "I'm not going to stay through another drunk. I'm telling you right now. I haven't got it in me. I'll die."

He did not want to look at her. He watched the flakes settle against the glass of the kitchen door. "Do what you feel the need of," he said.

"I just can't take it," she said. Her voice was not scolding but measured and reasonable. "It's February. And I went to court this morning and lost Vopotik."

Once again, he thought, my troubles are going to be obviated by those of the deserving poor. He said, "Which one was that?"

"Don't you remember them? The three-year-old with the broken fingers?"

He shrugged. Grace sipped her whiskey.

"I told you. I said I had a three-year-old with broken fingers, and you said, 'Maybe he owed somebody money.' "

"Yes," he said, "I remember now."

"You ought to see the Vopotiks, Chas. The woman is young and obese. She's so young that for a while I thought I could get to her as a juvenile. The guy is a biker. They believe the kid came from another planet to control their lives. They believe this literally, both of them."

"You shouldn't get involved that way," Elliot said. "You should leave it to the caseworkers."

"They scared their first caseworker all the way to California. They were following me to work."

"You didn't tell me."

"Are you kidding?" she asked. "Of course I didn't." To Elliot's surprise, his wife poured herself a second whiskey. "You know how they address the child? As 'dude.' She says to it, 'Hey, dude.' " Grace shuddered with loathing. "You can't imagine! The woman munching Twinkies. The kid smelling of shit. They're high morning, noon, and night, but you can't get anybody for that these days."

"People must really hate it," Elliot said, "when somebody tells them they're not treating their kids right."

"They definitely don't want to hear it," Grace said. "You're right." She sat stirring her drink, frowning into the glass. "The Vopotik child will die, I think."

"Surely not," Elliot said.

"This one I think will die," Grace said. She took a deep breath and puffed out her cheeks and looked at him forlornly. "The situation's extreme. Of course, sometimes you wonder whether it makes any difference. That's the big question, isn't it?"

"I would think," Elliot said, "that would be the one question you didn't ask."

"But you do," she said. "You wonder: Ought they to live at all? To continue the cycle?" She put a hand to her hair and shook her head as if in confusion. "Some of these folks, my God, the poor things cannot put Wednesday on top of Tuesday to save their lives."

"It's a trick," Elliot agreed, "a lot of them can't manage."

"And kids are small, they're handy and underfoot. They make noise. They can't hurt you back."

"I suppose child abuse is something people can do together," Elliot said.

"Some kids are obnoxious. No question about it."

"I wouldn't know," Elliot said.

"Maybe you should stop complaining. Maybe you're better off. Maybe your kids are better off unborn."

"Better off or not," Elliot said, "it looks like they'll stay that way."

"I mean our kids, of course," Grace said. "I'm not blaming you, understand? It's just that here we are with you drunk again and me losing Vopotik, so I thought why not get into the big unaskable questions." She got up and folded her arms and began to pace up and down the kitchen. "Oh," she said when her eye fell upon the bottle, "that's good stuff, Chas. You won't mind if I have another? I'll leave you enough to get loaded on."

Elliot watched her pour. So much pain, he thought; such anger and confusion. He was tired of pain, anger, and confusion; they were what had got him in trouble that very morning.

The liquor seemed to be giving him a perverse lucidity when all he now required was oblivion. His rage, especially, was intact in its salting of alcohol. Its contours were palpable and bleeding at the borders. Booze was good for rage. Booze could keep it burning through the darkest night.

"What happened in court?" he asked his wife.

She was leaning on one arm against the wall, her long, strong body flexed at the hip. Holding her glass, she stared angrily toward the invisible fields outside. "I lost the child," she said.

Elliot thought that a peculiar way of putting it. He said nothing.

"The court convened in an atmosphere of high hilarity. It may be Hate Month around here but it was buddy-buddy over at Ilford Courthouse. The room was full of bikers and bikers' lawyers. A colorful crowd. There was a lot of bonding." She drank and shivered. "They didn't think too well of me. They don't think too well of broads as lawyers. Neither does the judge. The judge has the common touch. He's one of the boys."

"Which judge?" Elliot asked.

"Buckley. A man of about sixty. Know him? Lots of veins on his nose?"

Elliot shrugged.

"I thought I had done my homework," Grace told him. "But suddenly I had nothing but paper. No witnesses. It was Margolis at Valley Hospital who spotted the radiator burns. He called us in the first place. Suddenly he's got to keep his reservation for a campsite in St. John. So Buckley threw his deposition out." She began to chew on a fingernail. "The caseworkers have vanished—one's in L.A., the other's in Nepal. I went in there and got run over. I lost the child."

"It happens all the time," Elliot said. "Doesn't it?"

"This one shouldn't have been lost, Chas. These people aren't simply confused. They're weird. They stink."

"You go messing into anybody's life," Elliot said, "that's what you'll find."

"If the child stays in that house," she said, "he's going to die."

"You did your best," he told his wife. "Forget it."

She pushed the bottle away. She was holding a water glass that was almost a third full of whiskey.

"That's what the commissioner said."

Elliot was thinking of how she must have looked in court to the cherry-faced judge and the bikers and their lawyers. Like the schoolteachers who had tormented their childhoods, earnest and tight-assed, humorless and self-righteous. It was not surprising that things had gone against her.

He walked over to the window and faced his reflection again. "Your optimism always surprises me."

"My optimism? Where I grew up our principal cultural expression was the funeral. Whatever keeps me going, it isn't optimism."

"No?" he asked. "What is it?"

"I forget," she said.

"Maybe it's your religious perspective. Your sense of the divine plan."

She sighed in exasperation. "Look, I don't think I want to fight anymore. I'm sorry I threw the sugar at you. I'm not your keeper. Pick on someone your own size."

"Sometimes," Elliot said, "I try to imagine what it's like to believe that the sky is full of care and concern."

"You want to take everything from me, do you?" She stood leaning against the back of her chair. "That you can't take. It's the only part of my life you can't mess up."

He was thinking that if it had not been for her he might not have survived. There could be no forgiveness for that. "Your life? You've got all this piety strung out between Monadnock and Central America. And look at yourself. Look at your life."

"Yes," she said, "look at it."

"You should have been a nun. You don't know how to live."

"I know that," she said. "That's why I stopped doing counseling. Because I'd rather talk the law than life." She turned to him. "You got everything I had, Chas. What's left I absolutely require."

"I swear I would rather be a drunk," Elliot said, "than force myself to believe such trivial horseshit."

"Well, you're going to have to do it without a straight man," she said, "because this time I'm not going to be here for you. Believe it or not."

"I don't believe it," Elliot said. "Not my Grace."

"You're really good at this," she told him. "You make me feel ashamed of my own name."

"I love your name," he said.

The telephone rang. They let it ring three times, and then Elliot went over and answered it.

"Hey, who's that?" a good-humored voice on the phone demanded.

Elliot recited their phone number.

"Hey, I want to talk to your woman, man. Put her on."

"I'll give her a message," Elliot said.

"You put your woman on, man. Run and get her."

Elliot looked at the receiver. He shook his head. "Mr. Vopotik?"

"Never you fuckin' mind, man. I don't want to talk to you. I want to talk to the skinny bitch."

Elliot hung up.

"Is it him?" she asked.

"I guess so."

They waited for the phone to ring again and it shortly did.

"I'll talk to him," Grace said. But Elliot already had the phone.

"Who are you, asshole?" the voice inquired. "What's your fuckin' name, man?"

"Elliot," Elliot said.

"Hey, don't hang up on me, Elliot. I won't put up with that. I told you go get that skinny bitch, man. You go do it."

There were sounds of festivity in the background on the other end of the line—a stereo and drunken voices.

"Hey," the voice declared. "Hey, don't keep me waiting, man."

"What do you want to say to her?" Elliot asked.

"That's none of your fucking business, fool. Do what I told you."

"My wife is resting," Elliot said. "I'm taking her calls."

He was answered by a shout of rage. He put the phone aside for a moment and finished his glass of whiskey. When he picked it up again the man on the line was screaming at him. "That bitch tried to break up my family, man! She almost got away with it. You know what kind of pain my wife went through?"

"What kind?" Elliot asked.

For a few seconds he heard only the noise of the party. "Hey, you're not drunk, are you, fella?"

"Certainly not," Elliot insisted.

"You tell that skinny bitch she's gonna pay for what she did to my family, man. You tell her she can run but she can't hide. I don't care where you go—California, anywhere—I'll get to you."

"Now that I have you on the phone," Elliot said, "I'd like to ask you a couple of questions. Promise you won't get mad?"

"Stop it!" Grace said to him. She tried to wrench the phone from his grasp, but he clutched it to his chest.

"Do you keep a journal?" Elliot asked the man on the phone. "What's your hat size?"

"Maybe you think I can't get to you," the man said. "But I can get to you, man. I don't care who you are, I'll get to you. The brothers will get to you."

"Well, there's no need to go to California. You know where we live."

"For God's sake," Grace said.

"Fuckin' right," the man on the telephone said. "Fuckin' right I know."

"Come on over," Elliot said.

"How's that?" the man on the phone asked.

"I said come on over. We'll talk about space travel. Comets and stuff. We'll talk astral projection. The moons of Jupiter."

"You're making a mistake, fucker."

"Come on over," Elliot insisted. "Bring your fat wife and your beat-up kid. Don't be embarrassed if your head's a little small."

The telephone was full of music and shouting. Elliot held it away from his ear.

"Good work," Grace said to him when he had replaced the receiver.

"I hope he comes," Elliot said. "I'll pop him."

He went carefully down the cellar stairs, switched on the overhead light, and began searching among the spiderwebbed shadows and fouled fishing line for his shotgun. It took him fifteen minutes to find it and his cleaning case. While he was still downstairs, he heard the telephone ring again and his wife answer it. He came upstairs and spread his shooting gear across the kitchen table. "Was that him?"

She nodded wearily. "He called back to play us the chain saw."

"I've heard that melody before," Elliot said.

He assembled his cleaning rod and swabbed out the shotgun barrel. Grace watched him, a hand to her forehead. "God," she said. "What have I done? I'm so drunk."

"Most of the time," Elliot said, sighting down the barrel, "I'm helpless in the face of human misery. Tonight I'm ready to reach out."

"I'm finished," Grace said. "I'm through, Chas. I mean it."

Elliot rammed three red shells into the shotgun and pumped one forward into the breech with a satisfying report. "Me, I'm ready for some radical problem solving. I'm going to spray that no-neck Slovak all over the yard."

"He isn't a Slovak," Grace said. She stood in the middle of the kitchen with her eyes closed. Her face was chalk white.

"What do you mean?" Elliot demanded. "Certainly he's a Slovak."

"No he's not," Grace said.

"Fuck him anyway. I don't care what he is. I'll grease his ass."

He took a handful of deer shells from the box and stuffed them in his jacket pockets.

"I'm not going to stay with you, Chas. Do you understand me?"

Elliot walked to the window and peered out at his driveway. "He won't be alone. They travel in packs."

"For God's sake!" Grace cried, and in the next instant bolted for the downstairs bathroom. Elliot went out, turned off the porch light and switched on a spotlight over the barn door. Back inside, he could hear Grace in the toilet being sick. He turned off the light in the kitchen.

He was still standing by the window when she came up behind him. It seemed strange and fateful to be standing in the dark near her, holding the shotgun. He felt ready for anything.

"I can't leave you alone down here drunk with a loaded shotgun," she said. "How can I?"

"Go upstairs," he said.

"If I went upstairs it would mean I didn't care what happened. Do you understand? If I go it means I don't care anymore. Understand?"

"Stop asking me if I understand," Elliot said. "I understand fine."

"I can't think," she said in a sick voice. "Maybe I don't care. I don't know. I'm going upstairs."

"Good," Elliot said.

When she was upstairs, Elliot took his shotgun and the whiskey into the dark living room and sat down in an armchair beside one of the lace-curtained windows. The powerful barn light illuminated the length of his driveway and the whole of the back yard. From the window at which he sat, he commanded a view of several miles in the direction of East Ilford. The two-lane blacktop road that ran there was the only one along which an enemy could pass.

He drank and watched the snow, toying with the safety of his 12-gauge Remington. He felt neither anxious nor angry now but only impatient to be done with whatever the night would bring. Drunkenness and the silent rhythm of the falling snow combined to make him feel outside of time and syntax.

Sitting in the dark room, he found himself confronting Blankenship's dream. He saw the bunkers and wire of some long-lost perimeter. The rank smell of night came back to him, the dread evening and quick dusk, the mysteries of outer darkness: fear, combat, and death. Enervated by liquor, he began to cry. Elliot was sympathetic with other people's tears but ashamed of his own. He thought of his own tears as childish and excremental. He stifled whatever it was that had started them.

Now his whiskey tasted thin as water. Beyond the lightly frosted glass, illuminated snowflakes spun and settled sleepily on weighted pine boughs. He had found a life beyond the war after all, but in it he was still sitting in darkness, armed, enraged, waiting.

His eyes grew heavy as the snow came down. He felt as though he could be drawn up into the storm and he began to imagine that. He imagined his life with all its artifacts and appetites easing up the spout into white oblivion, everything obviated and foreclosed. He thought maybe he could go for that.

When he awakened, his left hand had gone numb against the trigger guard of his shotgun. The living room was full of pale, delicate light. He looked outside and saw that the storm was done with and the sky radiant and cloudless. The sun was still below the horizon.

Slowly Elliot got to his feet. The throbbing poison in his limbs served to remind him of the state of things. He finished the glass of whiskey on the windowsill beside his easy chair. Then he went to the hall closet to get a ski jacket, shouldered his shotgun, and went outside.

There were two cleared acres behind his house; beyond them a trail descended into a hollow of pine forest and frozen swamp. Across the hollow, white pastures stretched to the ridge line, lambent under the lightening sky. A line of skeletal elms weighted with snow marked the course of frozen Shawmut Brook.

He found a pair of ski goggles in a jacket pocket and put them on and set out toward the tree line, gripping the shotgun, step by careful step in the knee-deep snow. Two raucous crows wheeled high overhead, their cries exploding the morning's silence. When the sun came over the ridge, he stood where he was and took in a deep breath. The risen sun warmed his face and he closed his eyes. It was windless and very cold.

Only after he had stood there for a while did he realize how tired he had become. The weight of the gun taxed him. It seemed infinitely wearying to contemplate another single step in the snow. He opened his eyes and closed them again. With sunup the world had gone blazing blue and white, and even with his tinted goggles its whiteness dazzled him and made his head ache. Behind his eyes, the hypnagogic patterns formed a monsoon-heavy tropical sky. He yawned. More than anything, he wanted to lie down in the soft, pure snow. If he could do that, he was certain he could go to sleep at once.

He stood in the middle of the field and listened to the crows. Fear, anger, and sleep were the three primary conditions of life. He had learned that over there. Once he had thought fear the worst, but he had learned that the worst was anger. Nothing could fix it; neither alcohol nor medicine. It was a worm. It left him no peace. Sleep was the best.

He opened his eyes and pushed on until he came to the brow that overlooked the swamp. Just below, gliding along among the frozen cattails and bare scrub maple, was a man on skis. Elliot stopped to watch the man approach.

The skier's face was concealed by a red-and-blue ski mask. He wore snow goggles, a blue jumpsuit, and a red woolen Norwegian hat. As he came, he leaned into the turns of the trail, moving silently and gracefully along. At the foot of the slope on which Elliot stood, the man looked up, saw him, and slid to a halt. The man stood staring at him for a moment and then began to herringbone up the slope. In no time at all the skier stood no more than ten feet away, removing his goggles, and inside the woolen mask Elliot recognized the clear blue eyes of his neighbor, Professor Loyall Anderson. The shotgun Elliot was carrying seemed to grow heavier. He yawned and shook his head, trying unsuccessfully to clear it. The sight of Anderson's eyes gave him a little thrill of revulsion.

"What are you after?" the young professor asked him, nodding toward the shotgun Elliot was cradling.

"Whatever there is," Elliot said.

Anderson took a quick look at the distant pasture behind him and then turned back to Elliot. The mouth hole of the professor's mask filled with teeth. Elliot thought that Anderson's teeth were quite as he had imagined them earlier. "Well, Polonski's cows are locked up," the professor said. "So they at least are safe."

Elliot realized that the professor had made a joke and was smiling. "Yes," he agreed.

Professor Anderson and his wife had been the moving force behind an initiative to outlaw the discharge of firearms within the boundaries of East Ilford Township. The initiative had been defeated, because East Ilford was not that kind of town.

"I think I'll go over by the river," Elliot said. He said it only to have something to say, to fill the silence before Anderson spoke again. He was afraid of what Anderson might say to him and of what might happen.

"You know," Anderson said, "that's all bird sanctuary over there now."

"Sure," Elliot agreed.

Outfitted as he was, the professor attracted Elliot's anger in an elemental manner. The mask made him appear a kind of doll, a kachina figure or a marionette. His eyes and mouth, all on their own, were disagreeable.

Elliot began to wonder if Anderson could smell the whiskey on his breath. He pushed the little red bull's-eye safety button on his gun to Off.

"Seriously," Anderson said, "I'm always having to run hunters out of there. Some people don't understand the word 'posted.' "

"I would never do that," Elliot said, "I would be afraid."

Anderson nodded his head. He seemed to be laughing. "Would you?" he asked Elliot merrily.

In imagination, Elliot rested the tip of his shotgun barrel against Anderson's smiling teeth. If he fired a load of deer shot into them, he thought, they might make a noise like broken china. "Yes," Elliot said. "I wouldn't know who they were or where they'd been. They might resent my being alive. Telling them where they could shoot and where not."

Anderson's teeth remained in place. "That's pretty strange," he said. "I mean, to talk about resenting someone for being alive."

"It's all relative," Elliot said. "They might think, 'Why should he be alive when some brother of mine isn't?' Or they might think, 'Why should he be alive when I'm not?' "

"Oh," Anderson said.

"You see?" Elliot said. Facing Anderson, he took a long step backward. "All relative."

"Yes," Anderson said.

"That's so often true, isn't it?" Elliot asked. "Values are often relative."

"Yes," Anderson said. Elliot was relieved to see that he had stopped smiling.

"I've hardly slept, you know," Elliot told Professor Anderson. "Hardly at all. All night. I've been drinking."

"Oh," Anderson said. He licked his lips in the mouth of the mask. "You should get some rest."

"You're right," Elliot said.

"Well," Anderson said, "got to go now."

Elliot thought he sounded a little thick in the tongue. A little slow in the jaw.

"It's a nice day," Elliot said, wanting now to be agreeable.

"It's great," Anderson said, shuffling on his skis.

"Have a nice day," Elliot said.

"Yes," Anderson said, and pushed off.

Elliot rested the shotgun across his shoulders and watched Anderson withdraw through the frozen swamp. It was in fact a nice day, but Elliot took no comfort in the weather. He missed night and the falling snow.

As he walked back toward his house, he realized that now there would be whole days to get through, running before the antic energy of whiskey. The whiskey would drive him until he dropped. He shook his head in regret. "It's a revolution," he said aloud. He imagined himself talking to his wife.

Getting drunk was an insurrection, a revolution—a bad one. There would be outsize bogus emotions. There would be petty moral blackmail and cheap remorse. He had said dreadful things to his wife. He had bullied Anderson with his violence and unhappiness, and Anderson would not forgive him. There would be damn little justice and no mercy.

Nearly to the house, he was startled by the desperate feathered drumming of a pheasant's rush. He froze, and out of instinct brought the gun up in the direction of the sound. When he saw the bird break from its cover and take wing, he tracked it, took a breath, and fired once. The bird was a little flash of opulent color against the bright-blue sky. Elliot felt himself flying for a moment. The shot missed.

Lowering the gun, he remembered the deer shells he had loaded. A hit with the concentrated shot would have pulverized the bird, and he was glad he had missed. He wished no harm to any creature. Then he thought of himself wishing no harm to any creature and began to feel fond and sorry for himself. As soon as he grew aware of the emotion he was indulging, he suppressed it. Pissing and moaning, mourning and weeping, that was the nature of the drug.

The shot echoed from the distant hills. Smoke hung in the air. He turned and looked behind him and saw, far away across the pasture, the tiny blue-and-red figure of Professor Anderson motionless against the snow. Then Elliot turned again toward his house and took a few labored steps and looked up to see his wife at the bedroom window. She stood perfectly still, and the morning sun lit her nakedness. He stopped where he was. She had heard the shot and run to the window. What had she thought to see? Burnt rags and blood on the snow. How relieved was she now? How disappointed?

Elliot thought he could feel his wife trembling at the window. She was hugging herself. Her hands clasped her shoulders. Elliot took his snow goggles off and shaded his eyes with his hand. He stood in the field staring.

The length of the gun was between them, he thought. Somehow she had got out in front of it, to the wrong side of the wire. If he looked long enough he would find everything out there. He would find himself down the sight.

How beautiful she is, he thought. The effect was striking. The window was so clear because he had washed it himself, with vinegar. At the best of times he was a difficult, fussy man.

Elliot began to hope for forgiveness. He leaned the shotgun on his forearm and raised his left hand and waved to her. Show a hand, he thought. Please just show a hand.

He was cold, but it had got light. He wanted no more than the gesture. It seemed to him that he could build another day on it. Another day was all you needed. He raised his hand higher and waited.

EUDORA WELTY (1909–)

A Worn Path

It was December—a bright frozen day in the early morning. Far out in the country there was an old Negro woman with her head tied in a red rag, coming along a path through the pinewoods. Her name was Phoenix Jackson. She was very old and small and she walked slowly in the dark pine shadows, moving a little from side to side in her steps, with the balanced heaviness and lightness of a pendulum in a grandfather clock. She carried a thin, small cane made from an umbrella, and with this she kept tapping the frozen earth in front of her. This made a grave and persistent noise in the still air, that seemed meditative like the chirping of a solitary little bird.

She wore a dark striped dress reaching down to her shoe tops, and an equally long apron of bleached sugar sacks, with a full pocket: all neat and tidy, but every time she took a step she might have fallen over her shoelaces, which dragged from her unlaced shoes. She looked straight ahead. Her eyes were blue with age. Her skin had a pattern all its own of numberless branching wrinkles and as though a whole little tree stood in the middle of her forehead, but a golden color ran underneath, and the two knobs of her cheeks were illumined by a yellow burning under the dark. Under the red rag her hair came down on her neck in the frailest of ringlets, still black, and with an odor like copper.

Now and then there was a quivering in the thicket. Old Phoenix said, "Out of my way, all you foxes, owls, beetles, jack rabbits, coons and wild animals! . . . Keep out from under these feet, little bobwhites. . . . Keep the big wild hogs out of my path. Don't let none of those come running my direction. I got a long way." Under her small black-freckled hand her cane, limber as a buggy whip, would switch at the brush as if to rouse up any hiding things.

On she went. The woods were deep and still. The sun made the pine needles almost too bright to look at, up where the wind rocked. The cones dropped as light as feathers. Down in the hollow was the mourning dove—it was not too late for him.

The path ran up a hill. "Seem like there is chains about my feet, time I get this far," she said, in the voice of argument old people keep to use with themselves. "Something always take a hold of me on this hill—pleads I should stay."

After she got to the top she turned and gave a full, severe look behind her where she had come. "Up through pines," she said at length. "Now down through oaks."

Her eyes opened their widest, and she started down gently. But before she got to the bottom of the hill a bush caught her dress.

Her fingers were busy and intent, but her skirts were full and long, so that before she could pull them free in one place they were caught in another. It was not possible to allow the dress to tear. "I in the thorny bush," she said. "Thorns, you doing your appointed work. Never want to let folks pass, no sir. Old eyes thought you was a pretty little *green* bush."

Finally, trembling all over, she stood free, and after a moment dared to stoop for her cane.

"Sun so high!" she cried, leaning back and looking, while the thick tears went over her eyes. "The time getting all gone here."

At the foot of this hill was a place where a log was laid across the creek.

"Now comes the trial," said Phoenix.

Putting her right foot out, she mounted the log and shut her eyes. Lifting her skirt, leveling her cane fiercely before her, like a festival figure in some parade, she began to march across. Then she opened her eyes and she was safe on the other side.

"I wasn't as old as I thought," she said.

But she sat down to rest. She spread her skirts on the bank around her and folded her hands over her knees. Up above her was a tree in a pearly cloud of mistletoe. She did not dare to close her eyes, and when a little boy brought her a plate with a slice of marble-cake on it she spoke to him. "That would be acceptable," she said. But when she went to take it there was just her own hand in the air.

So she left that tree, and had to go through a barbed-wire fence. There she had to creep and crawl, spreading her knees and stretching her fingers like a baby trying to climb the steps. But she talked loudly to herself: she could not let her dress be torn now, so late in the day, and she could not pay for having her arm or her leg sawed off if she got caught fast where she was.

At last she was safe through the fence and risen up out in the clearing. Big dead trees, like black men with one arm, were standing in the purple stalks of the withered cotton field. There sat a buzzard.

"Who you watching?"

In the furrow she made her way along.

"Glad this not the season for bulls," she said, looking sideways, "and the good Lord made his snakes to curl up and sleep in the winter. A pleasure I don't see no two-headed snake coming around that tree, where it come once. It took a while to get by him, back in the summer."

She passed through the old cotton and went into a field of dead corn. It whispered and shook and was taller than her head. "Through the maze now," she said, for there was no path.

Then there was something tall, black, and skinny there, moving before her.

At first she took it for a man. It could have been a man dancing in the field. But she stood still and listened, and it did not make a sound. It was as silent as a ghost.

"Ghost," she said sharply, "who be you the ghost of? For I have heard of nary death close by."

But there was no answer—only the ragged dancing in the wind.

She shut her eyes, reached out her hand, and touched a sleeve. She found a coat and inside that an emptiness, cold as ice.

"You scarecrow," she said. Her face lighted. "I ought to be shut up for good," she said with laughter. "My senses is gone. I too old. I the oldest people I ever know. Dance, old scarecrow," she said, "while I dancing with you."

She kicked her foot over the furrow, and with mouth drawn down, shook her head once or twice in a little strutting way. Some husks blew down and whirled in streamers about her skirts.

Then she went on, parting her way from side to side with the cane, through the whispering field. At last she came to the end, to a wagon track where the silver grass blew between the red ruts. The quail were walking around like pullets, seeming all dainty and unseen.

"Walk pretty," she said. "This the easy place. This the easy going."

She followed the track, swaying through the quiet bare fields, through the little strings of trees silver in their dead leaves, past cabins silver from weather, with the doors and windows boarded shut, all like old women under a spell sitting there. "I walking in their sleep," she said, nodding her head vigorously.

In a ravine she went where a spring was silently flowing through a hollow log. Old Phoenix bent and drank. "Sweet-gum makes the water sweet," she said, and drank more. "Nobody know who made this well, for it was here when I was born."

The track crossed a swampy part where the moss hung as white as lace from every limb. "Sleep on, alligators, and blow your bubbles." Then the track went into the road.

Deep, deep the road went down between the high green-colored banks. Overhead the live-oaks met, and it was as dark as a cave.

A black dog with a lolling tongue came up out of the weeds by the ditch. She was meditating, and not ready, and when he came at her she only hit him a little with her cane. Over she went in the ditch, like a little puff of milkweed.

Down there, her senses drifted away. A dream visited her, and she reached her hand up, but nothing reached down and gave her a pull. So she lay there and presently went to talking. "Old woman," she said to herself, "that black dog come up out of the weeds to stall you off, and now there he sitting on his fine tail, smiling at you."

A white man finally came along and found her—a hunter, a young man, with his dog on a chain.

"Well, Granny!" he laughed. "What are you doing there?"

"Lying on my back like a June-bug waiting to be turned over, mister," she said, reaching up her hand.

He lifted her up, gave her a swing in the air, and set her down. "Anything broken, Granny?"

"No sir, them old dead weeds is springy enough," said Phoenix, when she had got her breath. "I thank you for your trouble."

"Where do you live, Granny?" he asked, while the two dogs were growling at each other.

"Away back yonder, sir, behind the ridge. You can't even see it from here."

"On your way home?"

"No sir, I going to town."

"Why, that's too far! That's as far as I walk when I come out myself, and I get something for my trouble." He patted the stuffed bag he carried, and there hung down a little closed claw. It was one of the bob-whites, with its beak hooked bitterly to show it was dead. "Now you go on home, Granny!"

"I bound to go to town, mister," said Phoenix. "The time come around."

He gave another laugh, filling the whole landscape. "I know you old colored people! Wouldn't miss going to town to see Santa Claus!"

But something held old Phoenix very still. The deep lines in her face went into a fierce and different radiation. Without warning, she had seen with her own eyes a flashing nickel fall out of the man's pocket onto the ground.

"How old are you, Granny?" he was saying.

"There is no telling, mister," she said, "no telling."

Then she gave a little cry and clapped her hands and said, "Git on away from here, dog! Look! Look at that dog!" She laughed as if in admiration. "He ain't scared of nobody. He a big black dog." She whispered, "Sic him!"

"Watch me get rid of that cur," said the man. "Sic him, Pete! Sic him!"

Phoenix heard the dogs fighting, and heard the man running and throwing sticks. She even heard a gunshot. But she was slowly bending forward by that time, further and further forward, the lids stretched down over her eyes, as if she were doing this in her sleep. Her chin was lowered almost to her knees. The yellow palm of her hand came out from the fold of her apron. Her fingers slid down and along the ground under the piece of money with the grace and care they would have in lifting an egg from under a setting hen. Then she slowly straightened up, she stood erect, and the nickel was in her apron pocket. A bird flew by. Her lips moved. "God watching me the whole time. I come to stealing."

The man came back, and his own dog panted about them. "Well, I scared him off that time," he said, and then he laughed and lifted his gun and pointed it at Phoenix.

She stood straight and faced him.

"Doesn't the gun scare you?" he said, still pointing it.

"No, sir, I seen plenty go off closer by, in my day, and for less than what I done," she said, holding utterly still.

He smiled, and shouldered the gun. "Well, Granny," he said, "you must be a hundred years old, and scared of nothing. I'd give you a dime if I had any money with me. But you take my advice and stay home, and nothing will happen to you."

"I bound to go on my way, mister," said Phoenix. She inclined her head in the red rag. Then they went in different directions, but she could hear the gun shooting again and again over the hill.

She walked on. The shadows hung from the oak trees to the road like curtains. Then she smelled wood-smoke, and smelled the river, and she saw a steeple and the cabins on their steep steps. Dozens of little black children whirled around her. There ahead was Natchez shining. Bells were ringing. She walked on.

In the paved city it was Christmas time. There were red and green electric lights strung and crisscrossed everywhere, and all turned on in the daytime. Old Phoenix would have been lost if she had not distrusted her eyesight and depended on her feet to know where to take her.

She paused quietly on the sidewalk where people were passing by. A lady came along in the crowd, carrying an armful of red-, green- and silver-wrapped presents; she gave off perfume like the red roses in hot summer, and Phoenix stopped her.

"Please, missy, will you lace up my shoe?" She held up her foot.

"What do you want, Grandma?"

"See my shoe," said Phoenix. "Do all right for out in the country, but wouldn't look right to go in a big building."

"Stand still then, Grandma," said the lady. She put her packages down on the sidewalk beside her and laced and tied both shoes tightly.

"Can't lace 'em with a cane," said Phoenix. "Thank you, missy. I doesn't mind asking a nice lady to tie up my shoe, when I gets out on the street."

Moving slowly and from side to side, she went into the big building, and into a tower of steps, where she walked up and around and around until her feet knew to stop.

She entered a door, and there she saw nailed up on the wall the document that had been stamped with the gold seal and framed in the gold frame, which matched the dream that was hung up in her head.

"Here I be," she said. There was a fixed and ceremonial stiffness over her body.

"A charity case, I suppose," said an attendant who sat at the desk before her.

But Phoenix only looked above her head. There was sweat on her face, the wrinkles in her skin shone like a bright net.

"Speak up, Grandma," the woman said. "What's your name? We must have your history, you know. Have you been here before? What seems to be the trouble with you?"

Old Phoenix only gave a twitch to her face as if a fly were bothering her.

"Are you deaf?" cried the attendant.

But then the nurse came in.

"Oh, that's just old Aunt Phoenix," she said. "She doesn't come for herself— she has a little grandson. She makes these trips just as regular as clockwork. She lives away back off the Old Natchez Trace." She bent down. "Well, Aunt Phoenix, why don't you just take a seat? We won't keep you standing after your long trip." She pointed.

The old woman sat down, bolt upright in the chair.

"Now, how is the boy?" asked the nurse.

Old Phoenix did not speak.

"I said, how is the boy?"

But Phoenix only waited and stared straight ahead, her face very solemn and withdrawn into rigidity.

"Is his throat any better?" asked the nurse. "Aunt Phoenix, don't you hear me? Is your grandson's throat any better since the last time you came for the medicine?"

With her hands on her knees, the old woman waited, silent, erect and motionless, just as if she were in armor.

"You mustn't take up our time this way, Aunt Phoenix," the nurse said. "Tell us quickly about your grandson, and get it over. He isn't dead, is he?"

At last there came a flicker and then a flame of comprehension across her face, and she spoke.

"My grandson. It was my memory had left me. There I sat and forgot why I made my long trip."

"Forgot?" The nurse frowned. "After you came so far?"

Then Phoenix was like an old woman begging a dignified forgiveness for waking up frightened in the night. "I never did go to school, I was too old at the Surrender," she said in a soft voice. "I'm an old woman without an education. It was my memory fail me. My little grandson, he is just the same, and I forgot it in the coming."

"Throat never heals, does it?" said the nurse, speaking in a loud, sure voice to old Phoenix. By now she had a card with something written on it, a little list. "Yes. Swallowed lye. When was it?—January—two, three years ago—"

Phoenix spoke unasked now. "No, missy, he not dead, he just the same. Every little while his throat begin to close up again, and he not able to swallow. He not get his breath. He not able to help himself. So the time come around, and I go on another trip for the soothing medicine."

"All right. The doctor said as long as you came to get it, you could have it," said the nurse. "But it's an obstinate case."

"My little grandson, he sit up there in the house all wrapped up, waiting by himself," Phoenix went on. "We is the only two left in the world. He suffer and it don't seem to put him back at all. He got a sweet look. He going to last. He wear a little patch quilt and peep out holding his mouth open like a little bird. I remembers so plain now. I not going to forget him again, no, the whole enduring time. I could tell him from all the others in creation."

"All right." The nurse was trying to hush her now. She brought her a bottle of medicine. "Charity," she said, making a check mark in a book.

Old Phoenix held the bottle close to her eyes, and then carefully put it into her pocket.

"I thank you," she said.

"It's Christmas time, Grandma," said the attendant. "Could I give you a few pennies out of my purse?"

"Five pennies is a nickel," said Phoenix stiffly.

"Here's a nickel," said the attendant.

Phoenix rose carefully and held out her hand. She received the nickel and then fished the other nickel out of her pocket and laid it beside the new one. She stared at her palm closely, with her head on one side.

Then she gave a tap with her cane on the floor.

"This is what come to me to do," she said. "I going to the store and buy my child a little windmill they sells, made out of paper. He going to find it hard to believe there such a thing in the world. I'll march myself back where he waiting, holding it straight up in this hand."

She lifted her free hand, gave a little nod, turned around, and walked out of the doctor's office. Then her slow step began on the stairs, going down.

Poetry

1 🌿 The Definition of Poetry

Lovers of poetry have been searching for an accurate definition of it for at least two thousand years. The ideal definition would be short. It would enable us to know a real poem when we hear it, and help us understand the power and long life of great poetry. But the search for this definition has not yielded a single description or formula to satisfy all admirers of this various art. Like most things human, poetry will not be reduced, tagged, or made to sit in one corner for very long. And there are as many ways to account for its power as there are poets.

W. H. Auden's description of poetry as "memorable speech" applies to most poetry but also to many things that are not poetry, such as advertising jingles. Matthew Arnold called poetry a "criticism of life," a characterization that is certainly true of his own poetry and discounts advertising jingles, but that is not a useful description of limericks or of nonsense poems such as Lewis Carroll's "Jabberwocky." William Wordsworth believed that poetry was "the spontaneous overflow of powerful feelings," a dramatic but broad definition, and Robert Frost viewed it as that property of speech that is "untranslatable."

All these poets would agree, however, that poetry is markedly different from the prose of legal contracts, encyclopedias, or newspapers. Poetry is more intense than other writing—more intense with feeling, and more intense in its concentration of meaning. Poetry is the true language of emotion. We have all had the experience of joy, love, or sadness so great that no matter how urgently we need to express it, words fail us. The birth of a child, the return of a friend after long absence, the death of a parent: these events can leave us speechless. At such times we might wish we were poets. For poetry succeeds where ordinary speech fails to communicate those urgent and subtle feelings that are most essentially human. That is why poetry is the most enduring form of literature.

By saying that poetry is the language of emotion, we do not mean to suggest that poetry does not engage our thoughts and ideas. Poets may praise the theories of relativity and economics as well as the colors of the sunset. Like Hamlet, they may pose an abstract question: "To be, or not to be, that is the question." But if the writer does not communicate the emotion of discovering thought, we are not likely to find poetry in that writer's work.

Ezra Pound said that "literature is news that *stays* news." He must have had poetry in mind, for great poetry is eternally fresh. The poet writes what is most important in a given moment, and writes with such intensity and clarity that years later the verse can still seem important to a reader. How does a poet do this? Suiting the words and the rhythm of language perfectly to the experience, the poet says it so that we cannot imagine it being said any better.

Let us read a poem of joy and thoughtful discovery by a recent contemporary, James Wright.

JAMES WRIGHT (1927–1980)

A Blessing

Just off the highway to Rochester, Minnesota,
Twilight bounds softly forth on the grass.
And the eyes of those two Indian ponies
Darken with kindness.
5   They have come gladly out of the willows
To welcome my friend and me.
We step over the barbed wire into the pasture
Where they have been grazing all day, alone.
They ripple tensely, they can hardly contain their happiness
10   That we have come.
They bow shyly as wet swans. They love each other.
There is no loneliness like theirs.
At home once more,
They begin munching the young tufts of spring in the darkness.
15   I would like to hold the slenderer one in my arms,
For she has walked over to me
And nuzzled my left hand.
She is black and white,
Her mane falls wild on her forehead,
20   And the light breeze moves me to caress her long ear
That is delicate as the skin over a girl's wrist.
Suddenly I realize
That if I stepped out of my body I would break
Into blossom.

Our time for reading serious literature is limited. Therefore, we have every reason to ask our poets, What claim do you make on our attention? How has this poem arrived in front of us? And, now that it is here, what are we to make of it? You have noticed that poems usually have more white space around them than other literature, as if to say that they are somehow special, that they deserve extra attention. The great poems *are* special. They earn their space on the page and invite our attention.

In the case of James Wright's poem our opening questions are easily answered. How has the poem come to us? Wright and his friend turned "just off the highway" and encountered two ponies. Their beauty and affection for each other, and their delight in welcoming the two travelers, cause the poet to realize something important about himself. The poem comes to us because he wishes to share the experience and his discovery.

Is this an experience we wish to share? The title, "A Blessing," piques our curiosity, suggesting that something remarkable is about to happen. In the first lines Wright evokes a world rich with possibilities. Twilight is a charming hour, a time of day in which magic seems likely. When "twilight bounds softly forth" in the shape of two ponies, we find ourselves in a world that is both familiar and strange, and altogether enticing. The beauty of the horses, who "bow shyly as wet swans," and the warmth of their greeting add to the enchantment of the scene.

By the time Wright admits the impulse "to hold the slenderer one in my arms," we have identified with him and can share his love for these exquisite creatures. When he speaks of the pony's ear, "delicate as the skin over a girl's wrist," the comparison reveals that Wright sees the horses as nearly human in their capacity to inspire and receive love. At the same time we can understand that the skin that separates human from human, and person from animal, is a very thin one.

It is just one more stage in the poet's thought to realize that he himself is part of nature and that he might, in a single step out of his body, out of the slender confines of human life, break into blossom. Hence the great power and beauty of the last lines. It is an important revelation, perfectly expressed. Miracles are in short supply, and a poem that can provide one has earned our attention. It is indeed "A Blessing."

Not all poetry is so joyous. The next poem, Emily Dickinson's meditation on death, moves us in a quite different direction.

EMILY DICKINSON (1830–1886)

I Felt a Funeral in My Brain

I felt a Funeral, in my Brain,
And Mourners to and fro
Kept treading—treading—till it seemed
That Sense was breaking through—

5   And when they all were seated,
A Service, like a drum—
Kept beating—beating—till I thought
My Mind was going numb—

And then I heard them lift a Box
10 And creak across my Soul
With those same Boots of Lead, again,
Then Space—began to toll,

As all the heavens were a bell,
And being but an ear,
20   And I and silence some strange race
Wrecked solitary here.

And then a plank in reason broke,
And I dropped down and down
And hit a world at every plunge,
25   And finished knowing then.

Questions

1. Where is the action of the poem really taking place?
2. Whose funeral is it? The poet's? A friend's?
3. What is in the box?
4. Would the mourners actually wear "boots of lead"? If not, why does the poet describe them that way?
5. At the end of the poem, the poet says that she "hit a world at every plunge." What sorts of worlds do you imagine?

Emily Dickinson (*Amherst College Library*)

Everyone who has lived enough to value life has had a similar curiosity and fear about death. Emily Dickinson fashioned this poem out of the richness of those feelings, and we are moved to find them so similar to our own. Notice how the poet personalizes her fear by taking the funeral out of the real world and putting it into her own brain. Next she introduces ominous sounds and makes them more frightening through repetition: the footsteps of the mourners, the beating of the drum, the tolling of the bell. Try to imagine the horror of those sounds going on inside your own head. It is not at all surprising, then, when the poet tells us that "a plank in reason broke." No one's sanity could withstand such a racket. When her reason breaks, she feels herself falling through worlds and worlds until she finally arrives where there can be no knowing. Many of us are familiar with the fear of falling. The poet is telling us that death must be like falling through some plank of reason to a place where nothing is known. This is an exciting, if fearful, way of looking at death.

The two poems we have read so far represent the more thoughtful, serious side of the muse. The Muses, nine sister goddesses in Greek mythology, presided over the creative arts. From them we get the word *music* as well as the phrase *the muse*, which has come to designate the source of all poetic genius and inspiration. The muse has many different moods, as the multiplicity of the Greek goddesses suggests. Poetry is not always as mystical as Wright's "A Blessing" or as brooding as Dickinson's "I Felt a Funeral in My Brain." It can also be erotic or comical. In the following poem by Christopher Marlowe, we see the muse at its fun-loving best, as the speaker, a shepherd, tries to persuade his lady friend to be his love.

CHRISTOPHER MARLOWE (1564–1593)

The Passionate Shepherd to His Love

Come live with me and be my love,
And we will all the pleasures prove°   test, evaluate
That valleys, groves, hills, and fields,
Woods, or steepy mountain yields.

5   And we will sit upon the rocks,
Seeing the shepherds feed their flocks
By shallow rivers, to whose falls
Melodious birds sing madrigals.

And I will make thee beds of roses
10   And a thousand fragrant posies,
A cap of flowers and a kirtle°   gown
Embroidered all with leaves of myrtle;

A gown made of the finest wool
Which from our pretty lambs we pull;
15   Fair-lined slippers for the cold,
With buckles of the purest gold;

A belt of straw and ivy buds,
With coral clasps and amber studs.
And if these pleasures may thee move,
20 Come live with me and be my love.

The shepherds' swains shall dance and sing
For thy delight each May morning:
If these delights thy mind may move,
Then live with me and be my love.

Questions

1. Vocabulary: *posies* (10), *swains* (21).
2. What has moved the shepherd to speak? Is it the same emotion that has inspired Marlowe to write the poem?
3. Why does the shepherd take such care in describing the clothes he will make for his "love"?
4. Do you think that life with the shepherd would be as marvelous as he describes it?
5. Would the poem lend itself to music?
6. Do you think the shepherd's argument is persuasive?
7. Compare this poem with Sir Walter Raleigh's "The Nymph's Reply to the Shepherd" on pages 809–10.

The next poem, a whimsical children's story cast in rhyme, appeals to still another appetite in us, the love of nonsense and satire. The poem was written for children. But its portraiture of the ironic Bear and its gentle satire of the gushing Lady sustain reexamination by readers of all ages.

THEODORE ROETHKE (1908–1963)

The Lady and the Bear

A Lady came to a Bear by a Stream.
"O Why are you fishing that way?
Tell me, dear Bear there by the Stream,
Why are you fishing that way?"

5   "I am what is known as a Biddly Bear,—
That's why I'm fishing this way.
We Biddly's are Pee-culiar Bears,
And so,—I'm fishing this way.
"And besides, it seems there's a Law:
10 A most, most exactious Law
Says a Bear
Doesn't dare
Doesn't dare
Doesn't DARE
15 Use a Hook or a Line,
Or an old piece of Twine,

Not even the end of his Claw, Claw, Claw,
Not even the end of his Claw.
Yes, a Bear has to fish with his Paw, Paw, Paw.
20 A Bear has to fish with his Paw."

"O it's Wonderful how with a flick of your Wrist,
You can fish, out a fish, out a fish, out a fish.
If *I* were a fish I just couldn't resist
You, when you are fishing that way, that way,
25 When you are fishing that way."

And at that the Lady slipped from the Bank
And fell in the Stream still clutching a Plank,
But the Bear just sat there until she Sank;
As he went on fishing his way, his way,
30 As he went on fishing his way.

Questions

1. From the beginning of the poem, the Lady is quite complimentary to the Bear. From his comments in stanza 2, do you think that he appreciates her flattery, her presence?
2. When the Lady falls into the stream, why doesn't the Bear help her?

 Writers on Writing   *Emily Dickinson*

If I feel physically as if the top of my head were taken off, I know that is poetry.

2 🌿 Writing about Poetry: The In-Class Explication

Frank tried to remain calm. He had finished the short-answer part of the exam and had done, he thought, fairly well. But now he was facing the in-class essay about a poem and was particularly anxious about this part of the exam. In-class essays require working on very many levels—understanding the work's meaning, identifying the various metrical and linguistic figures, seeing how these figures and the theme of the poem interact, and then taking this analysis and forming it into coherent, well-organized prose that follows the rules of grammar and rhetoric. His comprehension and composition skills were always taxed by writing essays, but now they faced the additional strain of reading and writing under the pressure of time. The clock was ticking. He had to concentrate. But he knew that being anxious was not going to help him understand the poem or write better about it. To calm himself, he took a deep breath and let the air out slowly.

Read the Instructions

First Frank read the instructions carefully. His teacher often gave questions to help guide students through the thinking process. Long ago Frank came to understand that in order to do well you need to know what you are supposed to do. Frank underlined the parts of the directions that were especially important for reading the poem. His teacher had written:

> Directions: Discuss the following poem in a well-written, short essay. Be certain to explain the metaphor in lines seven and eight and the paradox in lines nine through twelve. Discuss the form of the poem in relation to the subject matter. How do line endings emphasize the meaning of the lines? How does the language embody Wilbur's thoughts on the changeability of the beautiful?

Frank underlined the words *metaphor, paradox, form, line endings*, and *language*. These obviously were aspects of the poem his professor was looking for him to discuss, and a good essay had better discuss them.

Reading the Poem

Next Frank began reading the poem. He read it very slowly to himself, trying to hear the poem in his head. As soon as he was finished, he read it over again, this time underlining and circling words, phrases, and even letters.

On his third reading, Frank began to jot down words and to place marks against the specific passages his professor had asked the class to comment on and those he thought he'd like to comment on. When he was finished, the poem looked like this:

THE BEAUTIFUL CHANGES

by Richard Wilbur

One wading a Fall meadow finds on all sides

The Queen Anne's Lace lying like lilies

On water; it glides

So from the walker, it <u>turns</u>

5   Dry grass to a lake, as the slightest shade of you

<u>Valleys</u> my mind in fabulous blue Lucernes.

The beautiful changes as a forest is changed

By a chameleon's tuning his skin to it;

As a mantis, arranged

10   On a green leaf grows

Into it, makes the leaf leafier, and proves

Any greenness is deeper than anyone knows.

Your hands hold roses always in a way that says

They are not only yours; the beautiful <u>changes</u>

15   In such <u>kind</u> ways,

Wishing ever to <u>sunder</u>

Things and things' selves for a second finding, to <u>lose</u>

For a moment all that it touches back to wonder.

His teacher's questions had alerted him to the three key aspects of this poem (but of course they were important in all poems)—he ought to pay attention to metaphor, paradox, and line endings (where he knew key concepts were often placed).

The metaphor in lines seven and eight compared the change in beauty to a chameleon's changing skin color. According to Wilbur, the chameleon changes his color to fit his background just as the beautiful changes to fit its context. One of the words that stood out for Frank was tuning. It is a musical term applied to color. Was this example of synesthesia—a figure of speech in which one sense turns into another—related to the ever-altering condition of beauty?

Frank then went to look at the paradox in lines nine through twelve. Where was the paradox? He saw two: how can a leaf become leafier? and how can a greenness "prove" to be deeper when no one knows about it? He tried to resolve the paradox. It seemed to him that what Wilbur meant was that by experiencing the changes within the beautiful, we become sensitive to an intensity we don't usually feel and of which we might not be fully aware. Now it struck Frank that the poem challenged the conventional notion that the beautiful was eternal and asserted, instead, that the beautiful constantly changed.

Frank then looked at the line endings. He noticed that almost all of the lines were enjambed, which gave the poem a kind of fluidity as it moved from one line to the next. The end words often referred to being enjambed: "glides," "turns," "grows," "sunder" all referred to movement.

Now it struck Frank what he found strange about the title when it appeared in the poem. At first he read "beautiful" as an adjective and "changes" as a noun. But in line seven "beautiful" is a noun and "changes" is a verb. Were there other such shifts in part of speech? He saw that "valleys" had become a verb, "finding" a noun, and "Fall" an adjective.

What other aspects of linguistic change could he find in the poem? The line lengths kept changing: each stanza began with two long lines, turned into two short lines and concluded with two long lines. Rhymes connected the long and short lines; some of the rhymes—for example, "says" and "ways"—were far from pure.

Does this poem fit any of the forms Frank knew about? He supposed one could call it a regular or Horatian ode. How would that form fit the subject? Horatian odes have to have lines of varying length, so one could say that change and variety were built into the form. However, unlike the irregular ode, the Horatian one repeats the same stanza pattern. One might say that the Horatian ode celebrates orderly, not chaotic change—variation within an overarching regularity.

The Short Outline

Frank then jotted down in the margin of the exam headings to help him order his paper.

Theme of change
Metaphors
Paradoxes
Line endings and line lengths
Other sound effects
Parts of speech

Frank didn't write anything more than these words and phrases because his outline was for his own use only—only he would have to understand what he meant. But it gave him a way of structuring his paper.

Writing in Class

Frank looked at his watch. He discovered he had only about thirty-five or forty minutes left. He had no time to waste on elaborate introductions or involved stylistic niceties. He had to get down what he understood as simply as he could.

Change and the Beautiful

[Frank always liked to give even in-class themes titles because they gave him focus as a writer.]

Richard Wilbur challenges the conventional notions of beauty in his poem "The Beautiful Changes."

[Frank had discovered that mentioning the author and title in the first sentence was an excellent way of forcing himself to get right to the subject. One important rule of in-class writing is to get straight to your point—don't beat about the bush. Frank also skipped every other line on the page so that he would have more room to make changes.]

Richard Wilbur challenges the conventional notions of beauty in his poem "The Beautiful Changes."

Unlike ~~other poets such as~~
Shakespeare, Wilbur does not try
to see the beautiful as eternal;
instead
, for him, the greatest beauty is
ever-changing, and those things
that make it change - or add
to our perception of change -
heighten beauty, instead of
detracting from it. Wilbur's
                    our sense of change
language underscores ~~the changeable-~~
~~ness~~ and consequently both expresses
the changeable beauty of nature
                              in itself
and becomes something beautiful.

[Frank read his opening paragraph over, and made some corrections in the style. He had done what he needed to do: (1) identify the poem he was going to write about and its author, (2) announce the theme of the poem, (3) and in the last sentence present a thesis. He went on to the next paragraph which would develop the theme *and* the thesis some more by looking at metaphors.]

metaphors by ~~thier~~ their very nature express change by turning one term into another. In stanza one, the dry grass and Queen Anne's lace change, in the poet's mind, the field into Lake Lucerne ~~in the poet's mind.~~ The walker, no less than the poet, has heightened the beauty of this scene by changing it. ~~making it change.~~ In the second stanza, Wilbur asserts ~~shows~~ that the beautiful like a forest is changed when someone blends into it, just as the chameleon by changing his skin heightens the beauty of the things around it, even as it disappears into the forest. The paradoxical image ~~paradox~~ in stanza two

Continues this idea of ~~by suggest~~
~~ing that those who imitate~~
ed by imitation.
beauty heighten, ~~it~~. ~~heightening~~
~~beauty by altering it through~~
~~imitation.~~ Wilbur introduces
the image of the mantis who
"arranged / On a green leaf .../
makes the leaf leafier." The
mantis's leaf-like appearance,
artificial
though ~~imitative~~, nevertheless
leafiness
heightens or increases the, ~~green~~
the   before it
of the leaf. Like, metaphors,,
es
the paradox, ~~expresses~~ change
its their
by ~~its~~, inherent instability.

[Frank was feeling good about the paper. He had established what he felt was the general theme of "The Beautiful Changes" fairly well, and he had shown how the metaphors in the first two stanzas both express and develop the basic idea. He had also shown how metaphors and paradoxes contribute to the theme. Now he took a deep breath, and plunged into the metrical technique of the poem.]

~~Wilbur uses a number of metrical techniques.~~

[Frank didn't like that beginning. He crossed it out and started the third paragraph over again, trying to link it more forcefully to the poem's theme and the paragraphs before it.]

Wilbur expresses the changes in the beautiful not only through metaphor and paradox, but through line length and ending. Twelve of the poem's eighteen lines are enjambed. So much enjambment ~~keeps~~ gives the poem ~~constantly flowing~~ fluidity. Furthermore, the words which end the enjambed lines — "glides," "turns," "sunder," and "lose" — ever so subtly I refer to the flow from line to line. In line ten, Wilbur ~~allows~~ suggests how the leaf "grows" not only by enjambing the line, but also by having the next line (into which it grows) be twice as long.

Even the rhymes in the poem suggest change. "Turns" and "Lucernes," although they don't look as if they'd rhyme, do in fact; while "says" and "ways," which are visual rhymes, sound very different. Wilbur plays other tricks with rhyme: "sides" in line one is unaccented, but "glides" is accented.

But perhaps the most dramatic way that Wilbur shows the constant change within what is beautiful is the surprising ways he uses words in unusual parts of speech. "Valleys," which is normally a noun, is here a verb. "Fall" and "finding," which are normally verbs, are made to serve as adjective and noun respectively. The title is perhaps the outstanding example of Wilbur's altering ~this alteration in~ parts of speech: "beautiful," which at first appears to be an adject ive, has changed into a noun in the text, and "changes," which originally seemed to be a noun, is used as a verb.

[Frank checked his watch. Only about seven minutes to go. He wrote hurriedly now, so he could get a chance to read over the entire paper.]

"The Beautiful Changes" celebrates
                stability
not the ~~eternity~~ of the Beautiful,
but it's constant flux. Through
metaphor and paradox, through
line ending and length, through
rhyme and syntax, Wilbur embodies
the changability of the beautiful
and makes his own poem a
thing of beauty.

[After the professor returned the exam to the class, Frank exchanged his paper with his friend Brooks. You might find it useful to compare Frank's essay to Brooks's.]

Brooks Headley

In-Class Explication of Wilbur's
"The Beautiful Changes"

Richard Wilbur's "The Beautiful Changes"
is a poem that actually changes in
front of the reader's eyes as it is
studied. There are several places in

the poem where change is mentioned, and change is an integral part of the poem's form. For example, line one ends with the phrase " on all sides," and the line actually creates a wall, or side, to the poem. Moreover, the fourth line ends in the word "turn" that makes a visual turn in the poem from that line to the next. Yet another place where meaning and form coincide directly are lines ten and eleven, in which Wilbur writes:

On a green leaf grows
Into it, makes the leaf leafier, and proves...

Wilbur makes the leaf grow with his words, and the words grow and stretch to become larger as well - with line eleven doubling the length of line ten.

Wilbur also makes use of figures of speech in the poem. Lines nine through twelve contain a paradox of a mantis and a leaf. The leaf is said to become bigger and greener with the mantis, but in reality this is contradictory because the leaf and mantis are separate and cannot truly grow together or turn color. Another figure of speech is the metaphor in lines seven and eight. It compares " the beautiful" and a chameleon, and says the beautiful changes as the chameleon's

Color changes.

Wilbur's word choices are very representative of the subject matter: they, too, change. The title of the poem can be read in two different ways. One may read it as the beautiful (adjective) changes (noun) or as the beautiful (noun) changes (verb). Like the chameleon words can change their color, and they are not less beautiful, but more wonderful, because they can change.

3 ❦ Listening in on the Poem

Distinguishing between eloquence and poetry, John Stuart Mill wrote that eloquence is heard, but poetry is overheard. This suggests a useful way to read poetry. Imagine that we have picked up a telephone to make a call. To our surprise, we hear someone talking on the other end. At first we do not understand what the person is saying, but because something in the speaker's voice interests us, we continue listening. By piecing together bits of information, we eventually come to understand the conversation. The same is true of many poems. At first we may be puzzled, but if we listen long and carefully enough, the good poets will tell us what we need to know to appreciate what they are saying.

Having the text of the poem gives us an advantage over the telephone eavesdropper. We can reread the poem in order to understand and appreciate the speaker fully. Also, the reader of a poem can look up unfamiliar words in the dictionary. Before tackling any poem, we should give ourselves time to reread it, and we should have a dictionary close at hand.

How then do we piece together the poet's conversation? One way to begin is by asking ourselves three basic questions:

1. Who is speaking?
2. To whom is he or she speaking?
3. What has prompted the speaker to talk?

Sometimes the answers to these questions will be obvious and unrevealing. But often they are necessary for understanding the poem. The following is a good example of an overheard poem.

WALTER SAVAGE LANDOR (1775–1864)

Mother, I Cannot Mind My Wheel

Mother, I cannot mind my wheel;
  My fingers ache, my lips are dry:

> Oh! if you felt the pain I feel!
> But oh, who ever felt as I?
>
> 5   No longer could I doubt him true;
>   All other men may use deceit:
> He always said my eyes were blue,
>   And often swore my lips were sweet.

The first word of this poem provides the answer to our second question: the poem is addressed to the speaker's mother. After reading the first line, we know that the daughter is speaking, trying to explain why she cannot sit quietly at the spinning wheel, a task that requires great patience. She tells her mother that her fingers ache and her lips are dry. But in the second stanza she reveals the true reason for her restlessness—her lover has abandoned her. His abandonment is especially painful for the speaker because she had trusted him. "All other men may use deceit," but her man, she thought, was honest. Moreover, he had flattered her by admiring her blue eyes and sweet lips.

We may also infer from the poem that the speaker—or *persona*, as the speaker is called—is young and naive. She asks her mother, "But oh, who ever felt as I?" as if no one else had ever known disappointed love. Her statement is not really a question, but an exclamation. For the moment, the woman feels utterly abandoned and heartsick.

What emerges from these eight short lines is a portrait of a young woman in the throes of her first disappointed love. Landor has given us a rich, vivid picture. No word is wasted.

Perhaps you have other questions. Is the girl ugly or pretty? Rich or poor? Was the man a neighbor or a stranger? Is the mother indifferent, angry, or sympathetic? These are all good questions, but we simply cannot answer them. The poet has not given us the necessary information. Instead of speculating, we will simply remain silent. The good reader will keep to the facts of the text and refrain from making unsupported guesses. We can do nothing more than read carefully. Where the poem is silent, we must be silent too.

The Persona and the Poet

In "Mother, I Cannot Mind My Wheel," the persona—or speaker—is obviously not Walter Savage Landor. But even in poems in which the speaker is not clearly distinguished from the author, it is often useful to think of the speaker as a fictional character. Here is a personal poem in which it is unimportant whether the speaker is the author or someone else.

LINDA PASTAN (1931–)

25th High School Reunion

> We come to hear the endings
> of all the stories

in our anthology
of false starts:
5   how the girl who seemed
as hard as nails
was hammered into shape;
how the athletes ran
out of races;
10   how under the skin
our skulls rise
to the surface
like rocks in the bed
of a drying stream.
15   Look! We have all
turned into
ourselves.

Questions

1. What does the speaker mean when he or she says, "We have all/turned into/ ourselves"?
2. To what might "our anthology/of false starts" refer?

The title of this poem is crucial to our understanding of it. (Titles are often important and should never be overlooked.) If we ask who the speaker is, we can say only that it is a high school graduate who has celebrated his or her twenty-fifth reunion and is, therefore, middle-aged. Linda Pastan may fit this description, but the poem does not require her to be the speaker. In fact, the speaker might be *any* middle-aged high school graduate.

The reunion has forced the speaker to reflect on how his or her classmates have changed. A tough student has been "hammered into shape." The athletes look worn out. Everyone appears to have dried up. The alumni's skulls are becoming prominent, signifying the approach of death.

The poem ends on a surprising note. The speaker turns directly to us, addressing us as fellow alumni and reminding us that we too will be middle-aged someday and will begin to show signs of approaching death.

✍️ Tips on Writing about Poetry

The speaker of poetry is usually prompted by one or more of the primary human emotions. These are love, hatred, happiness, sadness, fear, humor, anger, jealousy and pity. For instance, the speaker of "Mother, I Cannot Mind My Wheel" is prompted by love and sadness. The speaker of "25th High School Reunion" is prompted by awe, which is a subtler form of fear, and sadness. It is important when you are writing about poetry to recognize the emotion of the speaker, so that you may understand the true source of the poem's intense language.

Landscape with the Fall of Icarus, by Pieter Brueghel the Elder (*Royal Museums of Art and History, Brussels*)

The Importance of Context

Sometimes speakers do not refer to themselves at all in the poem; nevertheless, our appreciation of the poem may be enhanced by imagining a context for the speaker. In the following poem, "Musée des Beaux Arts" (which means "Fine Arts Museum" in French), we might find it useful to imagine the speaker as a tour guide pointing out one beautiful painting after another and commenting on the great artists—the Old Masters—who painted them.

For a moment we stop in front of Pieter Brueghel's painting *Landscape with the Fall of Icarus* in a museum in Brussels, Belgium, which Auden visited in 1939, just before he wrote this poem. Icarus was the son of Daedalus, whose name means literally "cunning worker." Father and son were imprisoned together in a tower, where Daedalus made wings out of wax and feathers so that they could escape. The device worked, but Icarus was so delighted with his wings that he flew toward the sun. The sun melted the wings, and Icarus fell to his death in the sea below. With that bit of information, you should be ready to begin to appreciate the poem.

W. H. AUDEN (1907–1973)

Musée des Beaux Arts

About suffering they were never wrong,
The Old Masters: how well they understood
Its human position; how it takes place
While someone else is eating or opening a window or just walking dully along;

5   How, when the aged are reverently, passionately waiting
     For the miraculous birth, there always must be
     Children who did not specially want it to happen, skating
     On a pond at the edge of the wood:
     They never forgot
10   That even the dreadful martyrdom must run its course
     Anyhow in a corner, some untidy spot
     Where the dogs go on with their doggy life and the torturer's horse
     Scratches its innocent behind on a tree.

     In Brueghel's *Icarus*, for instance: how everything turns away
15   Quite leisurely from the disaster; the ploughman may
     Have heard the splash, the forsaken cry,
     But for him it was not an important failure; the sun shone
     As it had to on the white legs disappearing into the green
     Water; and the expensive delicate ship that must have seen
20   Something amazing, a boy falling out of the sky,
     Had somewhere to get to and sailed calmly on.

Questions

1. Vocabulary: *martyrdom* (10).
2. What is the "human position" that suffering occupies?
3. How is suffering depicted in Brueghel's *Icarus*?
4. What political events of 1939 may have prompted Auden to write about suffering?
5. Does the speaker follow the Old Masters' examples for showing suffering?
6. Do you think the matter-of-fact tone is appropriate for this poem? Would the poem be more effective if the speaker were more emotional?
7. What sort of attitude should we adopt toward the poem? Toward suffering?

The Poet as Speaker

Finally, there are poems in which the speaker is unquestionably the poet. Biographical information may be useful for appreciating such poems, but they can move us even without such knowledge. Take Ben Jonson's poem on the death of his son:

BEN JONSON (1573?–1637)

On My First Son

Farewell, thou child of my right hand, and joy;
My sin was too much hope of thee, loved boy:
Seven years thou wert lent to me, and I thee pay,
Exacted by the fate, on the just day.[1]
5   O could I lose all father now! for why

---
[1] The boy was born in 1596 and died on his birthday in 1603.

Will man lament the state he should envy,
To have so soon 'scaped world's and flesh's rage,
And, if no other misery, yet age?
Rest in soft peace, and asked, say, "Here doth lie
10   Ben Jonson his best piece of poetry."
For whose sake henceforth all his vows be such
As what he loves may never like too much.

Questions

1. To whom is the poem addressed? Does this fact suggest something about Jonson's spiritual beliefs?
2. In what sense might a man "envy" the death of a young boy?
3. Would you call Jonson a proud father? Does Jonson feel there is any connection between his fatherly pride and his son's death?
4. What is the relationship between Jonson's son and poetry?
5. What relationship does Jonson hope to develop in the future between himself and those he loves?

This poem ably conveys the feeling of grief, whether or not we know anything about Ben Jonson. Additional information will, however, help us appreciate Jonson's sorrow. For example, Jonson's son was named Benjamin after his father. The first line of the poem contains the Hebrew meaning of the boy's name: "child of the right hand."

The poem contains one complicated line, "O could I lose all father now!" Jonson means that he wishes he could forget he possessed the attributes of fatherhood; then he might regard his son's death more philosophically. He could console himself with the knowledge that by dying young the boy has escaped many hardships.

The poet can have various relationships to the persona of a poem. Sometimes the speaker is not the poet, but a fictional character. At other times the speaker could be the poet but does not necessarily have to be. At still other times the speaker does not even appear as a character in the poem. Whatever relationship the poet adopts to the speaker, we should listen closely to the speaker's words and base our assumptions on the text of the poem and the context of the speaker.

 Writers on Writing   *Stephen Spender*

> *When you read and understand a poem, comprehending its rich and formal meanings, then you master chaos a little.*

4 ❧ Narrative Poetry

The Poet as Storyteller

We commonly think that stories, like laws, are best written in prose. Yet the ancient Greeks composed their laws in verse, and the earliest known poem, *The Epic of Gilgamesh*, composed in Sumer some five thousand years ago, is a long tale about the adventures of a king.

The first narrative or storytelling poems recounted the adventures of great heroes and their relations with gods and demons. Often these poems would record a nation's origins and history. They were also an early source of entertainment. Poet-reciters called *bards* regaled courts with these long heroic tales. Later, scribes committed the narrative poems to paper, and so they are preserved today. In England the scribes were often monks, who were scolded by their superiors for taking time away from religious studies to copy down pagan poems. In the nineteenth century, scholars like Francis Child roamed the countryside collecting the ballads and stories of illiterate peasants.

Formulae

How could an illiterate bard remember a poem that might take all evening to recite? First, the rhythms of the poem helped him to remember, just as we are more likely to remember a jingle than a flat piece of prose of equal length. Also, the bards had stock phrases, or *formulae*, that they used over and over again. Similarly, little formulae help parents tell bedtime stories. In "Goldilocks and the Three Bears," for example, there are constantly reworked phrases:
"Someone's been sitting in my chair."
"Someone's been eating my porridge."
"Someone's been sleeping in my bed."
These formulae help parents tell the story each night in roughly the same words. Like parents, bards did not remember their poems perfectly, and the

poems passed down through oral tradition usually appear in a number of different versions.

Let us look at a Scottish ballad, a poem composed orally and handed down from singer to singer. Like an epic, this ballad tells the story of a brave man, and it relies on the repetition of formulaic expressions. In the version that follows, most of the language has been modernized, but enough of the Scottish dialogue remains to give you a flavor of the original.

ANONYMOUS

Sir Patrick Spence

The king sits in Dumferling town
    Drinking the blood-red wine:
"O where will I get a good sailor,
    To sail this ship of mine?"

5   Up and spake an elder knight
    Sat at the king's right knee:
"Sir Patrick Spence is the best sailor,
    That sails upon the sea."

The king has written a broad letter
10   And signed it with his hand
And sent it to Sir Patrick Spence
    Was walking on the sand.

The first line that Sir Patrick read
    A loud lauch° lauched he;   *laugh*
15   The next line that Sir Patrick read
    The tear blinded his ee.°   *eye*

"O who is this has done this deed
    This ill deed done to me,
To send me out this time of the year,
20   To sail upon the sea!

"Make haste, make haste, my merry men all
    Our good ship sails the morn."
"O say not so, my master dear,
    For I fear a deadly storm.

25   "Late, late yestreen° I saw the new moon   *last evening*
    With the old moon in her arm
And I fear, I fear, my dear master
    That we will come to harm."

O our Scots nobles were richt laith°   *very loath*
30   To wet their cork-healed schoone;°   *shoes*
But long before the play was played
    Their hats they swam aboone.°   *above*

O long, long may their ladies sit,
    With their fans into their hand

35   Or e'er they see Sir Patrick Spence
          Come sailing to the land.

      O long, long may the ladies stand
          With their golden combs in their hair
      Waiting for their own dear lords
40   For they'll see them no mair.°   *more*

      Half o'er, half o'er to Aberdour,
          It's fifty fathoms deep,
      And there lies good Sir Patrick Spence,
          With the Scots lords at his feet.

"Sir Patrick Spence" is like a short story in many ways, but the differences are interesting and important. Like many short stories, it contains characters, a setting, conflict and dialogue, and a single significant action. But in "Sir Patrick Spence" these elements are more condensed. We never learn where Sir Patrick lived or how he achieved his fame. The poet tells us only that he was walking on the beach. Nor do we learn whether he is married or has children. These details would be important in a short story, but they are unimportant for the poetic narrator. Nevertheless, we do learn a good deal about Sir Patrick. He sees the foolish, vindictive, and thoughtless nature of the king's courtiers. But he is loyal and brave. He does not question his orders but immediately commands his sailors, despite their protests, to man the ship. His actions say more than words. Of course, the longer the narrative, the greater its detail. Book-length poems contain a rich supply of narrative detail.

Transitions in Narrative Poetry

"Sir Patrick Spence" illustrates another mark of the poetic narrative technique: rarely are there transitions from one scene to another. A narrative poem moves in much the same way as a film. Movie directors often shift instantaneously from one scene to another. Similarly, in "Sir Patrick Spence" we move from a scene in which Sir Patrick reads his orders to one in which he is on the deck encouraging his frightened sailors. Moreover, in a poetic narrative we do not necessarily begin at the beginning of the story. For example, Charles Dickens starts his novel *David Copperfield* with the sentence "I am born." But the poetic narrator begins, as critics have noted, *in medias res*—Latin for "in the middle of things." The shorter the poem, the more concentrated the action. In the most concentrated narrative poems, the climax alone is presented.

Still another feature of the narrative poem is omission of certain scenes. In "Sir Patrick Spence," for example, the scene of the shipwreck is entirely missing. The poet shows us only the hats floating above the sunken ship, markers signaling the disaster brought by vanity. The rhythm and music of the poem provide the continuity we would have missed if this were a prose account.

The ballad form provides an excellent mode for narration. A discussion of ballad form is provided in Chapter 13. Here it is enough to point out that the

Langston Hughes (*National Portrait Gallery*, Smithsonian Institution, Washington, D.C.)

four-line stanza, or *quatrain*, provides a handy short unit for developing a single scene. The second and fourth lines are shorter than the first and third. These shorter lines give the stanza its speed and propel the reader from stanza to stanza.

Ballads continue to be popular, especially with poets who wish to reach a wide audience. Here is a modern ballad.

LANGSTON HUGHES (1902–1967)

Sylvester's Dying Bed

I woke up this mornin'
'Bout half-past three.
All the womens in town
Was gathered round me.

5   Sweet gals was a-moanin',
"Sylvester's gonna die!"
And a hundred pretty mamas
Bowed their heads to cry.

I woke up a little later
10   'Bout half-past fo',
The doctor 'n' undertaker's
Both at ma do'.

Black gals was a-beggin',
"You can't leave us here!"
15 Brown-skins cryin', "Daddy!
Honey! Baby! Don't go, dear!"

But I felt ma time's a-comin',
And I know'd I's dyin' fast.
I seed the River Jerden
20 A-creepin' muddy past—
But I's still Sweet Papa 'Vester,
Yes, sir! Long as life do last!

So I hollers, "Com'ere, babies,
Fo' to love yo' daddy right!"
25 And I reaches up to hug 'em—
When the Lawd put out the light.

Then everything was darkness
In a great . . . big . . . night.

Questions

1. Is there anything heroic about Sylvester? How would you compare the way he approaches death with the way Sir Patrick Spence meets his fate?
2. Are there any repeated phrases or formulaic expressions in "Sylvester's Dying Bed"? How do they contribute to the story?
3. The four-line stanza pattern is broken twice in this poem. Why is stanza 5 longer than the others? Why is stanza 7 shorter?

Epic Poetry

The longest narratives are called *epics*. These poems do not simply recount a single action; they record a way of life. The Greek epics, the *Iliad* and the *Odyssey*, are among the greatest treasures of Western culture. These orally transmitted narratives are called *primary epics*. Later, poets consciously imitated these earlier works by writing epics of their own. Virgil's *Aeneid*, Dante's *Divine Comedy*, and John Milton's *Paradise Lost* are among the most famous secondary epics. Epics are too long for us to include a complete one in this book, but excerpts from the *Odyssey* and the *Divine Comedy* appear at the end of this chapter.

Personal History in Narrative Poems

Unlike the bards of ancient Greece or the minstrels of Scotland, contemporary poets are not responsible for recording national history, although some continue to narrate incidents of national importance. More often, however, today's poets tell personal or family histories that are more likely to be forgotten in the future. The following poem is one of several poems by Edward Field that recount his family's history.

EDWARD FIELD (1924–)

My Polish Grandmother

Grandma and the children left at night.
It was forbidden to go. In those days
the Czar and his cossacks rode through the town at whim
killing Jews and setting fire to straw roofs
5   while just down the road the local Poles
sat laughing as they drank liquor.

Grandpa had gone to America first
and earned the money for the rest of the family to come over.
So they left finally, the whole brood of them
10   with the hired agent running the show,
an impatient man, and there were so many kids
and the bundles kept falling apart
and poor grandma was frightened of him.

She gave the man all the money
15   but she couldn't round up the kids fast enough for him.
They were children after all and didn't understand
and she was so stupid and clumsy herself,
carrying food for all of them and their clothes
and could she leave behind her pots?
20   Her legs hurt already; they were always swollen
from the hard work, the childbearing, and the cold.

They caught the train and there was a terrible moment
when the conductor came by for the tickets:
The children mustn't speak or he would know they were Jewish,
25   they had no permits to travel—Jews weren't allowed.
But the agent knew how to handle it,
everybody got *shmeared*, that means money got you everywhere.

The border was the worst. They had to sneak across at night.
The children mustn't make a sound, not even the babies.
30   Momma was six and she didn't want to do anything wrong
but she wasn't sure what to do.
The man led them through the woods
and beyond they could hear dogs barking from the sentry hut,
and then they had to run all of them down the ravine to the other side,
35   grandma broken down from childbearing with her bundles
and bad legs and a baby in her arms,
they ran all the children across the border
or the guards might shoot them
and if the little ones cried, the agent said he would smother them.

40   They got to a port finally.
Grandpa had arranged for cabin passage, not steerage,
but the agent cheated and put them in the hold
so they were on the low deck looking up at the rich people.
My momma told me how grandma took care of all her children,
45   how Jake didn't move anymore he was so seasick, maybe even dead,

and if people thought he was dead
they would throw him overboard like garbage, so she hid him.
The rich tossed down oranges to the poor children—
my momma had never had one before.

50   They came to New York, to the tenements,
a fearful new place, a city, country people in the city.
My momma, who had been roly-poly in slow Poland,
got skinny and pimply in zippy New York.
Everybody grew up in a new way.
55   And now my grandma is dead and my momma is old
and we her children are all scattered over the earth
speaking a different language and forgetting
why it was so important
to go to a new country.

Questions

1. Vocabulary: *cossacks* (3), *ravine* (34), *steerage* (41).
2. Why does Field feel compelled to retell this story?
3. What is worth retelling about this story? Does your family have similar stories about coming to America?
4. How does the poem reflect political history?
5. In what way does this poem start *in medias res?*
6. Compare this poem to Gary Soto's "History" on pages 890–91.

Use of Language in Narrative Poetry

There is yet another difference between the traditional prose story and the poetic narrative. The prose writer, by and large, wants to make the scene so vivid that we look beyond the words and feel that we are actually present in the scene. The poet, however, at crucial moments draws our attention to the language. In fact, the poet would like to believe that the story is happening *in* the language. In the following poem we are asked to pay particularly close attention to the last line.

DANIEL MARK EPSTEIN (1948–)

Madonna (with Child Missing)[1]

Shouts from the street, spotlights crossfire
at a third story window. The woman
stares through smoked glass at a crowd
and firemen in glazed slickers—
5   flames climbing the stairs behind her two at a time.
She lifts up the window sash with one hand,
kisses the infant and rolls it out trusting the air,
the soft knock of skull on stone in her heart.

---

[1] *Madonna* is Italian for "my lady." It is often the name of works of art depicting the Virgin Mary.

Notice the last line. Would this be an acceptable ending in a prose story? If this were a prose account, wouldn't we demand to know whether the child was saved? In a poetic narrative these plot concerns are less important. For the mother, the child is both saved and injured. The sounds and rhythms of the last line imitate both the erratic beating of the mother's heart and the imagined disaster to the child. The story is secondary to the action of the language. It is this concern with language that makes a poetic narrative so memorable for both the original audience and the contemporary reader. In the poems that follow, you should try to attend not only to the engaging stories the poets write, but also to the language they use to enact the story.

Suggestions for Essayists

1. Retell in prose one of the narrative poems from this chapter. Discuss what you have gained in the translation and what you have lost.
2. Discuss how the ideas of loyalty and heroism have changed since the time of Sir Patrick Spence.
3. Narrate an episode of family history that you have either lived through or heard about and that is in danger of being forgotten.

Suggestions for Poets

1. Narrate an episode of family history that is in danger of being forgotten.
2. Find an episode in the newspaper and retell it in ballad form.

Poems for Further Study

DUDLEY RANDALL (1914–)

Ballad of Birmingham[2]

(On the bombing of a church in Birmingham, Alabama, 1963)

"Mother dear, may I go downtown
Instead of out to play,
And march the streets of Birmingham
In a Freedom March today?"

5   "No, baby, no, you may not go,
For the dogs are fierce and wild,
And clubs and hoses, guns and jails
Aren't good for a little child."

"But, mother, I won't be alone.
10   Other children will go with me,

---

[2] "Freedom marches" were parades organized to promote civil rights in the South during the 1950s and the 1960s.

And march the streets of Birmingham
To make our country free."

"No, baby, no, you may not go,
For I fear those guns will fire.
15 But you may go to church instead
And sing in the children's choir."

She has combed and brushed her night-dark hair,
And bathed rose petal sweet,
And drawn white gloves on her small brown hands,
20 And white shoes on her feet.

The mother smiled to know her child
Was in the sacred place,
But that smile was the last smile
To come upon her face.

25 For when she heard the explosion,
Her eyes grew wet and wild.
She raced through the streets of Birmingham
Calling for her child.

She clawed through bits of glass and brick,
30 Then lifted out a shoe.
"O, here's the shoe my baby wore,
But, baby, where are you?"

✍ Tips for Writing about Poetry

There is usually a moment of "crisis," a turning point in a narrative poem, as in a play or a story. All the action seems to lead towards the moment of crisis, and it determines the ending of the poem. For example, in Epstein's "Madonna (with Child Missing)," it is the moment the woman makes the decision to remove her baby from the burning house; in Frost's "Out, Out" it is the moment the saw meets the boy's hand. Look for the crisis of action in narrative poems—try to see the poem's structure in terms of images leading toward the turning point, and images or comments concerning the consequences of the crisis.

ROBERT FROST (1874–1963)

'Out, Out—'[3]

The buzz-saw snarled and rattled in the yard
And made dust and dropped stove-length sticks of wood,

---

[3] The title is an allusion to Shakespeare's *Macbeth*, Act V, Scene 5, in which Macbeth, hearing about his wife's death, says, "Out, out, brief candle! / Life's but a walking shadow, a poor player / That struts and frets his hour upon the stage / And then is heard no more."

Sweet-scented stuff when the breeze drew across it.
And from there those that lifted eyes could count
5   Five mountain ranges one behind the other
Under the sunset far into Vermont.
And the saw snarled and rattled, snarled and rattled,
As it ran light, or had to bear a load.
And nothing happened: day was all but done.
10   Call it a day, I wish they might have said
To please the boy by giving him the half hour
That a boy counts so much when saved from work.
His sister stood beside them in her apron
To tell them 'Supper.' At the word, the saw,
15   As if to prove saws knew what supper meant,
Leaped out at the boy's hand, or seemed to leap—
He must have given the hand. However it was,
Neither refused the meeting. But the hand!
The boy's first outcry was a rueful laugh,
20   As he swung toward them holding up the hand
Half in appeal, but half as if to keep
The life from spilling. Then the boy saw all—
Since he was old enough to know, big boy
Doing a man's work, though a child at heart—
25   He saw all spoiled. 'Don't let him cut my hand off—
The doctor, when he comes. Don't let him, sister!'

So. But the hand was gone already.
The doctor put him in the dark of ether.
He lay and puffed his lips out with his breath.
30   And then—the watcher at his pulse took fright.
No one believed. They listened at his heart.
Little—less—nothing!—and that ended it.
No more to build on there. And they, since they
Were not the one dead, turned to their affairs.

SHARON OLDS (1942–)

The Race

When I got to the airport I rushed up to the desk
and they told me the flight was cancelled. The doctors had
said my father would not live through the night
and the flight was cancelled. A young man with a
5   dark blond mustache told me
another airline had a non-stop
leaving in seven minutes—see that
elevator over there well go
down to the first floor, make a right you'll
10   see a yellow bus, get off at the
second Pan Am terminal—I
ran, I who have no sense of direction
raced exactly where he'd told me, like a fish

15 slipping upstream deftly against the
flow of the river. I jumped off that bus with my
heavy bags and ran, the bags
wagged me from side to side as if to
prove I was under the claims of the material, I
ran up to a man with a white flower on his breast,
20 I who always go to the end of the line, I said
Help me. He looked at my ticket, he said make a
left and then a right go up the moving stairs and then
run. I raced up the moving stairs
two at a time, at the top I saw the
25 long hollow corridor and
then I took a deep breath, I said
goodbye to my body, goodbye to comfort, I
used my legs and heart as if I would
gladly use them up for this, to
30 touch him again in this life. I ran and the
big heavy dark bags
banged me, wheeled and swam around me like
planets in wild orbits—I have seen
pictures of women running down roads with their
35 belongings tied in black scarves
grasped in their fists, running under serious
gray historical skies—I blessed my
long legs he gave me, my strong
heart I abandoned to its own purpose, I
40 ran to Gate 17 and they were
just lifting the thick white
lozenge of the door to fit it into the
socket of the plane. Like the man who is not
too rich, I turned to the side and
45 slipped through the needle's eye, and then I
walked down the aisle toward my father. The jet was
full and people's hair was shining, they were
smiling, the interior of the plane was filled with a
mist of gold endorphin° light,   *brain-produced anaesthetic*
50 I wept as people weep when they enter heaven,
in massive relief. We lifted up
gently from one tip of the continent and
did not stop until we set down lightly on the
other edge, I walked into his room and
55 watched his chest rise slowly and
sink again, all night
I watched him breathe.

EDGAR ALLAN POE (1809–1849)

The Raven

Once upon a midnight dreary, while I pondered, weak and weary,
Over many a quaint and curious volume of forgotten lore,—

While I nodded, nearly napping, suddenly there came a tapping,
As of some one gently rapping, rapping at my chamber door.
5   " 'T is some visitor," I muttered, "tapping at my chamber door:
                Only this and nothing more."

Ah, distinctly I remember it was in the bleak December,
And each separate dying ember wrought its ghost upon the floor.
Eagerly I wished the morrow;—vainly I had sought to borrow
10   From my books surcease of sorrow—sorrow for the lost Lenore,
For the rare and radiant maiden whom the angels name Lenore:
                Nameless here for evermore.

And the silken sad uncertain rustling of each purple curtain
Thrilled me—filled me with fantastic terrors never felt before;
15   So that now, to still the beating of my heart, I stood repeating
" 'T is some visitor entreating entrance at my chamber door,
Some late visitor entreating entrance at my chamber door:
                This it is and nothing more."

Presently my soul grew stronger; hesitating then no longer,
20   "Sir," said I, "or Madam, truly your forgiveness I implore;
But the fact is I was napping, and so gently you came rapping,
And so faintly you came tapping, tapping at my chamber door,
That I scarce was sure I heard you"—here I opened wide the door:—
                Darkness there and nothing more.

25   Deep into that darkness peering, long I stood there wondering, fearing,
Doubting, dreaming dreams no mortal ever dared to dream before;
But the silence was unbroken, and the stillness gave no token,
And the only word there spoken was the whispered word, "Lenore?"
This I whispered, and an echo murmured back the word, "Lenore:"
30   Merely this and nothing more.

Back into the chamber turning, all my soul within me burning,
Soon again I heard a tapping somewhat louder than before.
"Surely," said I, "surely that is something at my window lattice;
Let me see, then, what thereat is, and this mystery explore;
35   Let my heart be still a moment and this mystery explore:
                'T is the wind and nothing more."

Open here I flung the shutter, when, with many a flirt and flutter,
In there stepped a stately Raven of the saintly days of yore.
Not the least obeisance made he; not a minute stopped or stayed he;
40   But, with mien of lord or lady, perched above my chamber door,
Perched upon a bust of Pallas[4] just above my chamber door:
                Perched, and sat, and nothing more.

Then this ebony bird beguiling my sad fancy into smiling
By the grave and stern decorum of the countenance it wore,—
45   "Though thy crest be shorn and shaven, thou," I said, "art sure no craven,
Ghastly grim and ancient Raven wandering from the Nightly shore:

---

[4] *Pallas* is Greek for "maiden" and was the epithet used to refer to Athena, the goddess of war and wisdom.

Tell me what thy lordly name is on the Night's Plutonian⁵ shore!"
Quoth the Raven, "Nevermore."

Much I marvelled this ungainly fowl to hear discourse so plainly,
50 Though its answer little meaning—little relevancy bore;
For we cannot help agreeing that no living human being
Ever yet was blessed with seeing bird above his chamber door,
Bird or beast upon the sculptured bust above his chamber door,
With such name as "Nevermore."

55 But the Raven, sitting lonely on the placid bust, spoke only
That one word, as if his soul in that one word he did outpour.
Nothing further then he uttered, not a feather then he fluttered,
Till I scarcely more than muttered—"Other friends have flown before;
On the morrow *he* will leave me, as my Hopes have flown before."
60 Then the bird said, "Nevermore."

Startled at the stillness broken by reply so aptly spoken,
"Doubtless," said I, "what it utters is its only stock and store,
Caught from some unhappy master whom unmerciful Disaster
Followed fast and followed faster till his songs one burden bore:
65 Till the dirges of his Hope that melancholy burden bore
Of 'Never—nevermore.' "

But the Raven still beguiling all my fancy into smiling,
Straight I wheeled a cushioned seat in front of bird and bust and door;
Then, upon the velvet sinking, I betook myself to linking
70 Fancy unto fancy, thinking what this ominous bird of yore,
What this grim, ungainly, ghastly, gaunt, and ominous bird of yore
Meant in croaking "Nevermore."

This I sat engaged in guessing, but no syllable expressing
To the fowl whose fiery eyes now burned into my bosom's core;
75 This and more I sat divining, with my head at ease reclining
On the cushion's velvet lining that the lamp-light gloated o'er,
But whose velvet violet lining with the lamp-light gloating o'er
She shall press, ah, nevermore!

Then, methought, the air grew denser, perfumed from an unseen censer
80 Swung by seraphim whose foot-falls tinkled on the tufted floor.
"Wretch," I cried, "thy God hath lent thee—by these angels he hath sent thee
Respite—respite and nepenthe⁶ from thy memories of Lenore!
Quaff, oh quaff this kind nepenthe, and forget this lost Lenore!"
Quoth the Raven, "Nevermore."

85 "Prophet!" said I, "thing of evil! prophet still, if bird or devil!
Whether Tempter sent, or whether tempest tossed thee here ashore,
Desolate yet all undaunted, on this desert land enchanted—
On this home by Horror haunted—tell me truly, I implore:
Is there—*is* there balm in Gilead?⁷—tell me—tell me, I implore!"
90 Quoth the Raven, "Nevermore."

---

⁵ *Pluto* is the god of the underworld.
⁶ *Nepenthe* is a drug one uses to forget pain.
⁷ See Jeremiah 8:22.

"Prophet!" said I, "thing of evil—prophet still, if bird or devil!
By that Heaven that bends above us, by that God we both adore,
Tell this soul with sorrow laden if, within the distant Aidenn,[8]
It shall clasp a sainted maiden whom the angels name Lenore:
95   Clasp a rare and radiant maiden whom the angels name Lenore!"
                      Quoth the Raven, "Nevermore."

"Be that word our sign of parting, bird or fiend!" I shrieked, upstarting:
"Get thee back into the tempest and the Night's Plutonian shore!
Leave no black plume as a token of that lie thy soul hath spoken!
100 Leave my loneliness unbroken! quit the bust above my door!
Take thy beak from out my heart, and take thy form from off my door!"
                      Quoth the Raven, "Nevermore."

And the Raven, never flitting, still is sitting, *still* is sitting
On the pallid bust of Pallas just above my chamber door;
105 And his eyes have all the seeming of a demon's that is dreaming,
And the lamp-light o'er him streaming throws his shadow on the floor:
And my soul from out that shadow that lies floating on the floor
                Shall be lifted—nevermore!

 ### Writers on Writing   *Ezra Pound*

An epic is a poem including history.

HOMER (8th century B.C.)

From the Odyssey[9]

When the young Dawn with finger tips of rose
came in the east, I called my men together
and made a speech to them:
                      "Old shipmates, friends,
5   the rest of you stand by; I'll make the crossing
in my own ship, with my own company,
and find out what the mainland natives are—
for they may be wild savages, and lawless,
or hospitable and god fearing men."

10 At this I went aboard, and gave the word
to cast off by the stern. My oarsmen followed,

---

[8] *Aidenn* is a combination of Eden and Aden—thus, an exotic place of pleasure.

[9] The *Odyssey* narrates the adventures of Odysseus, or Ulysses (as he was called by the Romans). Odysseus wandered the world for ten years before returning to his kingdom, Ithaca. He was one of the Greek kings who defeated the Trojans. In this episode from Book IX of the *Odyssey*, Odysseus recounts his visit to the Kyklopês, or Cyclops, vicious one-eyed giants, and tells how he outsmarted them. The episode typifies many of Odysseus' exploits: he succeeds more by brains than brawn.

filing in to their benches by the rowlocks,
and all in line dipped oars in the grey sea.

As we rowed on, and nearer to the mainland,
15　at one end of the bay, we saw a cavern
yawning above the water, screened with laurel,
and many rams and goats about the place
inside a sheepfold—made from slabs of stone
earthfast between tall trunks of pine and rugged
20　towering oak trees.
　　　　　　　　　　　　　　　　A prodigious man
slept in this cave alone, and took his flocks
to graze afield—remote from all companions,
knowing none but savage ways, a brute
25　so huge, he seemed no man at all of those
who eat good wheaten bread; but he seemed rather
a shaggy mountain reared in solitude.
We beached there, and I told the crew
to stand by and keep watch over the ship;
30　as for myself I took my twelve best fighters
and went ahead. I had a goatskin full
of that sweet liquor that Euanthês' son,
Maron, had given me. He kept Apollo's
holy grove at Ísmaros; for kindness
35　we showed him there, and showed his wife and child,
he gave me seven shining golden talents°　　　　　　　　　　*gold medallions*
perfectly formed, a solid silver winebowl,
and then this liquor—twelve two-handled jars
of brandy, pure and fiery. Not a slave
40　in Maron's household knew this drink; only
he, his wife and the storeroom mistress knew;
and they would put one cupful—ruby-colored,
honey-smooth—in twenty more of water,
but still the sweet scent hovered like a fume
45　over the winebowl. No man turned away
when cups of this came round.
　　　　　　　　　　　　　　　　A wineskin full

I brought along, and victuals in a bag,
for in my bones I knew some towering brute
50　would be upon us soon—all outward power,
a wild man, ignorant of civility.

We climbed, then, briskly to the cave. But Kyklops
had gone afield, to pasture his fat sheep,
so we looked round at everything inside:
55　a drying rack that sagged with cheeses, pens
crowded with lambs and kids, each in its class:
firstlings apart from middlings, and the "dewdrops,"
or newborn lambkins, penned apart from both.
And vessels full of whey were brimming there—

60   bowls of earthenware and pails for milking.
      My men came pressing round me, pleading:

                                                    "Why not
      take these cheeses, get them stowed, come back,
      throw open all the pens, and make a run for it?
65   We'll drive the kids and lambs aboard. We say
      put out again on good salt water!"

                                                    Ah,

      how sound that was! Yet I refused. I wished
      to see the caveman, what he had to offer—
70   no pretty sight, it turned out, for my friends.
      We lit a fire, burnt an offering,
      and took some cheese to eat; then sat in silence
      around the embers, waiting. When he came
      he had a load of dry boughs on his shoulder
75   to stoke his fire at suppertime. He dumped it
      with a great crash into that hollow cave,
      and we all scattered fast to the far wall.
      Then over the broad cavern floor he ushered
      the ewes he meant to milk. He left his rams
80   and he-goats in the yard outside, and swung
      high overhead a slab of solid rock
      to close the cave. Two dozen four-wheeled wagons,
      with heaving wagon teams, could not have stirred
      the tonnage of that rock from where he wedged it
85   over the doorsill. Next he took his seat
      and milked his bleating ewes. A practiced job
      he made of it, giving each ewe her suckling;
      thickened his milk, then, into curds and whey,
      sieved out the curds to drip in withy° baskets,   *twig*
90   and poured the whey to stand in bowls
      cooling until he drank it for his supper.
      When all these chores were done, he poked the fire,
      heaping on brushwood. In the glare he saw us.
      "Strangers," he said, "who are you? And where from?
95   What brings you here by sea ways—a fair traffic?
      Or are you wandering rogues, who cast your lives
      like dice, and ravage other folk by sea?"

      We felt a pressure on our hearts, in dread
      of that deep rumble and that mighty man.
100   But all the same I spoke up in reply:
      "We are from Troy, Akhaians, blown off course
      by shifting gales on the Great South Sea;
      homeward bound, but taking routes and ways
      uncommon; so the will of Zeus would have it.
105   We served under Agamémnon, son of Atreus—
      the whole world knows what city
      he laid waste, what armies he destroyed.

It was our luck to come here; here we stand,
beholden for your help, or any gifts
110   you give—as custom is to honor strangers.
We would entreat you, great Sir, have a care
for the gods' courtesy; Zeus will avenge
the unoffending guest."

                                        He answered this
115   from his brute chest, unmoved:

                                        "You are a ninny,
or else you come from the other end of nowhere,
telling me, mind the gods! We Kyklopês
care not a whistle for your thundering Zeus
120   or all the gods in bliss; we have more force by far.
I would not let you go for fear of Zeus—
you or your friends—unless I had a whim to.
Tell me, where was it, now, you left your ship—
around the point, or down the shore, I wonder?"

125   He thought he'd find out, but I saw through this,
and answered with a ready lie:

                                        "My ship?
Poseidon Lord, who sets the earth a-tremble,
broke it up on the rocks at your land's end.
130   A wind from seaward served him, drove us there,
We are survivors, these good men and I."

Neither reply nor pity came from him,
but in one stride he clutched at my companions
and caught two in his hands like squirming puppies
135   to beat their brains out, spattering the floor.
Then he dismembered them and made his meal,
gaping and crunching like a mountain lion—
everything: innards, flesh, and marrow bones.
We cried aloud, lifting our hands to Zeus,
140   powerless, looking on at this, appalled;
but Kyklops went on filling up his belly
with manflesh and great gulps of whey,
then lay down like a mast among his sheep.
My heart beat high now at the chance of action,
145   and drawing the sharp sword from my hip I went
along his flank to stab him where the midriff
holds the liver. I had touched the spot
when sudden fear stayed me: if I killed him
we perished there as well, for we could never
150   move his ponderous doorway slab aside.
So we were left to groan and wait for morning.

When the young Dawn with finger tips of rose
lit up the world, the Kyklops built a fire

and milked his handsome ewes, all in due order,
155   putting the sucklings to the mothers. Then,
his chores being all dispatched, he caught
another brace of men to make his breakfast,
and whisked away his great door slab
to let his sheep go through—but he, behind,
160   reset the stone as one would cap a quiver.
There was a din of whistling as the Kyklops
rounded his flock to higher ground, then stillness.
And now I pondered how to hurt him worst,
if but Athena granted what I prayed for.
165   Here are the means I thought would serve my turn:

a club, or staff, lay there along the fold—
an olive tree, felled green and left to season
for Kyklops' hand. And it was like a mast
a lugger of twenty oars, broad in the beam—
170   a deep-sea-going craft—might carry:
so long, so big around, it seemed. Now I
chopped out a six foot section of this pole
and set it down before my men, who scraped it;
and when they had it smooth, I hewed again
175   to make a stake with pointed end. I held this
in the fire's heart and turned it, toughening it,
then hid it, well back in the cavern, under
one of the dung piles in profusion there.
Now came the time to toss for it: who ventured
180   along with me? whose hand could bear to thrust
and grind that spike in Kyklops' eye, when mild
sleep had mastered him? As luck would have it,
the men I would have chosen won the toss—
four strong men, and I made five as captain.

185   At evening came the shepherd with his flock,
his woolly flock. The rams as well, this time,
entered the cave: by some sheep-herding whim—
or a god's bidding—none were left outside.
He hefted his great boulder into place
190   and sat him down to milk the bleating ewes
in proper order, put the lambs to suck,
and swiftly ran through all his evening chores.
Then he caught two more men and feasted on them.
My moment was at hand, and I went forward
195   holding an ivy bowl of my dark drink,
looking up, saying:

                              "Kyklops, try some wine.
Here's liquor to wash down your scraps of men.
Taste it, and see the kind of drink we carried
200   under our planks. I meant it for an offering
if you would help us home. But you are mad,

unbearable, a bloody monster! After this,
will any other traveller come to see you?"

205 He seized and drained the bowl, and it went down
so fiery and smooth he called for more:

"Give me another, thank you kindly. Tell me,
how are you called? I'll make a gift will please you.
Even Kyklopês know the wine-grapes grow
out of grassland and loam in heaven's rain,
210 but here's a bit of nectar and ambrosia!"

Three bowls I brought him, and he poured them down.
I saw the fuddle and flush come over him,
then I sang out in cordial tones:

"Kyklops,
215 you ask my honorable name? Remember
the gift you promised me, and I shall tell you.
My name is Nohbdy: mother, father, and friends,
everyone calls me Nohbdy."

And he said:

220 "Nohbdy's my meat, then, after I eat his friends.
Others come first. There's a noble gift, now."

Even as he spoke, he reeled and tumbled backward,
his great head lolling to one side; and sleep
took him like any creature. Drunk, hiccuping,
225 he dribbled streams of liquor and bits of men.

Now, by the gods, I drove my big hand spike
deep in the embers, charring it again,
and cheered my men along with battle talk
to keep their courage up: no quitting now.
230 The pike of olive, green though it had been,
reddened and glowed as if about to catch.
I drew it from the coals and my four fellows
gave me a hand, lugging it near the Kyklops
as more than natural force nerved them; straight
235 forward they sprinted, lifted it, and rammed it
deep in his crater eye, and I leaned on it
turning it as a shipwright turns a drill
in planking, having men below to swing
the two-handled strap that spins it in the groove.
240 So with our brand we bored that great eye socket
while blood ran out around the red hot bar.
Eyelid and lash were seared; the pierced ball
hissed broiling, and the roots popped.

In a smithy
245 one sees a white-hot axehead or an adze°   *hatchet*
plunged and wrung in a cold tub, screeching steam—

the way they make soft iron hale and hard—:
just so that eyeball hissed around the spike.
The Kyklops bellowed and the rock roared round him,
250 and we fell back in fear. Clawing his face
he tugged the bloody spike out of his eye,
threw it away, and his wild hands went groping;
then he set up a howl for Kyklopês
who lived in caves on windy peaks nearby.
255 Some heard him; and they came by divers ways
to clump around outside and call:

                                "What ails you,
Polyphêmos? Why do you cry so sore
in the starry night? You will not let us sleep.
260 Sure no man's driving off your flock? No man
has tricked you, ruined you?"

                                Out of the cave
the mammoth Polyphêmos roared in answer:
"Nohbdy, Nohbdy's tricked me, Nohbdy's ruined me!"

265 To this rough shout they made a sage reply:

"Ah well, if nobody has played you foul
there in your lonely bed, we are no use in pain
given by great Zeus. Let it be your father,
Poseidon Lord, to whom you pray."

Translation by Robert Fitzgerald (1910–1989)

DANTE ALIGHIERI (1265–1321)

Ulysses' Speech *from* Inferno (Canto XXVI)

. . . "When I from Circe broke at last,
Who more than a year by Gaeta (before
Aeneas had so named it) held me fast,
Not sweet son, nor revered old father, nor
5   The long-due love which was to have made glad
    Penelope for all the pain she bore,
Could conquer the inward hunger that I had
    To master earth's experience, and to attain
    Knowledge of man's mind, both the good and bad.
10 But I put out on the deep, open main
    With one ship only, and with that little band
    Which chose not to desert me; far as Spain,
Far as Morocco, either shore I scanned.
    Sardinia's isle I coasted, steering true,
15   And the isles of which that water bathes the strand.
I and my crew were old and stiff of thew°   *muscle*
    When, at the narrow pass, we could discern
    The marks that Hercules set far in view

That none should dare beyond, or further learn.
20 Already I had Sevilla on the right,
And on the larboard Ceuta lay astern.
'Brothers,' I said, 'who manfully, despite
Ten thousand perils, have attained the West,
In the brief vigil that remains of light
25 To feel in, stoop not to renounce the quest
Of what may in the sun's path be essayed,
The world that never mankind hath possessed.
Think on the seed ye spring from! Ye were made
Not to live life of brute beasts of the field
30 But follow virtue and knowledge unafraid.'
With such few words their spirit so I steel'd,
That I thereafter scarce could have contained
My comrades from the voyage, had I willed.
And, our poop turned to where the Morning reigned,
35 We made, for the mad flight, wings of our oars,
And on the left continually we gained.
By now the Night beheld within her course
All stars of the other pole, and ours so low,
It was not lifted from the ocean-floors.
40 Five times beneath the moon rekindled slow
The light had been, and quenched as oft, since we
Broached the hard issue we were sworn to know,
When there arose a mountain in the sea,
Dimm'd by the distance: loftier than aught
45 That ever I beheld, it seemed to be.
Then we rejoiced; but soon to grief were brought.
A storm came out of the strange land, and found
The ship, and violently the forepart caught.
Three times it made her to spin round and round
50 With all the waves; and, as Another chose,
The fourth time, heaved the poop up, the prow drowned,
Till over us we heard the waters close."

Translation by Laurence Binyon (1869–1943)

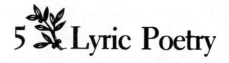

5 🌿 Lyric Poetry

The Solitary Singer

CATULLUS (84?–54 B.C.)

LXXXV

I hate and I love. Why? you might ask
but I can't tell. The feeling seizes me
and riddles me with pain.

Translation by Daniel Mark Epstein

Outside of literature we rarely have the opportunity to look into the hearts and minds of others. Many people are shy about themselves or feel that their language is inadequate for expressing what is most important to them. Great poets can open themselves to us in moments of crisis or discovery so that we can know their thoughts as intimately as we know our own.

The *lyric* is generally considered the most intense and personal form of poetry—indeed, of all literature. The word *lyric* comes from the Greek word for the lyre, a stringed instrument similar to a guitar and suitable for the accompaniment of a solitary singer. Like the concert of an impassioned singer, the lyric poem is a private, often visionary act of intelligence and emotion that becomes public through the music of language. Lyric poetry is also an artifact of language, capable of great beauty and excitement in its exploration of new perceptions. Language is a precious part of our heritage that is enriched by the vision and experience of each new generation of poets.

The Love Poem

Perhaps the form of lyric most familiar to us is the love poem.

WILLIAM BUTLER YEATS (1865–1939)

He Wishes for the Cloths of Heaven

Had I the heavens' embroidered cloths,
Enwrought with golden and silver light,

The blue and the dim and the dark cloths
Of night and light and the half-light,
5   I would spread the cloths under your feet:
But I, being poor, have only my dreams;
I have spread my dreams under your feet;
Tread softly because you tread on my dreams.

Question

1. Vocabulary: *enwrought* (2).

How does one express love? One common way is through gifts. We want the finest gift for the one we love, a gift that will be as beautiful and rare as what we feel. In this poem Yeats (or his persona) realizes that nothing he possesses would be adequate as a gift for his beloved. All he can do is wish for such a gift, the magnificent cloths he describes. If he had such cloths, he tells her, he would spread them before her as a path. But he is poor and cannot provide such a gift. Instead, he offers her his dreams. This, too, should be familiar to us. When we are in love, we want to share with those we love not only material things, but also our aspirations, our plans, our dreams. These are the finest gifts the lover can provide. When he has spread his dreams in her path, he asks her to "tread softly" because dreams are delicate, much more fragile than the cloths he described earlier.

Thus the first gift is the wish described in the poem's opening lines, and the second gift is the lover's dreams. But just as important as either of these is the gift of the poem itself.

William Butler Yeats (*Photograph by Howard Coster*)

We have considered the poem as a love lyric to a particular woman. But is it not also a gift to the reader? The "you" of the poem might be *any* reader, for as we read, we are admitted to the privacy of the poet's thoughts. We are in effect receiving a gift of his thoughts. We are being asked to read carefully, for we are treading on his dreams throughout the poem. It is as much a love poem to us as it is to a particular woman.

H. D. (HILDA DOOLITTLE) (1886–1961)

Never More Will the Wind

Never more will the wind
cherish you again,
never more will the rain.

Never more
5   shall we find you bright
in the snow and wind.

The snow is melted,
the snow is gone,
and you are flown:

10   Like a bird out of our hand,
like a light out of our heart,
you are gone.

Here is another kind of love lyric, one that expresses the anguish of loss. The poem is intensely private, for the poet is speaking to someone who is not there to listen. Maybe the one she loves has died, or perhaps he has gone to another country. The poem is not concerned with these questions. Rather, it shows us how the poet's world has changed in the absence of her beloved. Everything is emptier: the wind, the rain, the snow. Everywhere she looks, the landscape speaks of loneliness and absence. The poet clearly wishes to share this with us. She includes us in her world when she says "we" in the second stanza, and "our" in the final lines.

WILLIAM SHAKESPEARE (1564–1616)

When, in Disgrace with Fortune and Men's Eyes

When, in disgrace° with fortune and men's eyes,   *out of favor*
I all alone beweep my outcast state
And trouble deaf heaven with my bootless° cries   *useless*
And look upon myself and curse my fate,
5   Wishing me like to one more rich in hope,
Featured like him, like him with friends possess'd,
Desiring this man's art and that man's scope,°   *range of activity*
With what I most enjoy contented least;
Yet in these thoughts myself almost despising

10   Haply I think on thee, and then my state,
    Like to the lark at break of day arising
    From sullen earth, sings hymns at heaven's gate;
        For thy sweet love remember'd such wealth brings
        That then I scorn to change my state with kings.

Questions

1. Vocabulary: *beweep* (2), *sullen* (12).
2. Why is the speaker so upset in the first eight lines of the poem?
3. Why is he so happy in the last six lines?
4. What emotion has inspired the poem?

ANDREW MARVELL (1621–1678)

To His Coy Mistress

Had we but world enough, and time,
This coyness,° lady, were no crime.   *modesty, reluctance*
We would sit down and think which way
To walk, and pass our long love's day.
5   Thou by the Indian Ganges' side
Should'st rubies find; I by the tide
Of Humber[1] would complain.° I would   *sing sad songs*
Love you ten years before the Flood,
And you should, if you please, refuse
10   Till the conversion of the Jews.[2]
My vegetable° love should grow   *vegetative*
Vaster than empires, and more slow.
An hundred years should go to praise
Thine eyes, and on thy forehead gaze,
15   Two hundred to adore each breast,
But thirty thousand to the rest.
An age at least to every part,
And the last age should show your heart.
For, lady, you deserve this state,
20   Nor would I love at lower rate.
    But at my back I always hear
Time's winged chariot hurrying near;
And yonder all before us lie
Deserts of vast eternity.
25   Thy beauty shall no more be found,
Nor in thy marble vault shall sound
My echoing song; then worms shall try
That long preserved virginity,

---

[1] The Humber is a river that passed near Marvell's home.
[2] According to popular belief, the Jews would be converted just before the Last Judgment.

And your quaint honor turn to dust,
30   And into ashes all my lust.
The grave's a fine and private place,
But none, I think, do there embrace.
    Now therefore, while the youthful hue
Sits on thy skin like morning dew
35   And while thy willing soul transpires
At every pore with instant° fires,   *immediate*
Now let us sport us while we may;
And now, like am'rous birds of prey,
Rather at once our time devour,
40   Than languish in his slow-chapped° power,   *slowly chewing*
Let us roll all our strength, and all
Our sweetness, up into one ball;[3]
And tear our pleasures with rough strife
Thorough° the iron gates of life.   *through*
45   (Thus, though we cannot make our sun)
   (Stand still, yet we will make him run.)

Questions

1. Vocabulary: *conversion* (10), *vault* (26), *quaint* (29), *transpires* (35), *languish* (40).
2. Reading this poem is like overhearing a personal conversation or reading someone else's letter. What sort of lady is Marvell addressing?
3. What does he want?
4. Compare this poem with Marlowe's "The Passionate Shepherd to His Love" (pages 523–24). Which poet is more persuasive?
5. This poem is considered an eloquent statement of the *carpe diem* ("seize the day") philosophy, which urges us to live for the moment, without concern for the future. What are the advantages of *carpe diem*? The disadvantages?

Curses

Less familiar but no less human is the lyric poem that expresses hatred, or vengeance.

ARCHILOCHUS (7th century B.C.)

May He Lose His Way on the Cold Sea

May he lose his way on the cold sea
And swim to the heathen Salmydessos,
May the ungodly Thracians[4] with their hair
Done up in a fright on the top of their heads
5   Grab him, that he know what it is to be alone

---

[3] Falconers would roll fat and sinew into balls that would be thrown into the air for falcons to attack and eat.
[4] Inhabitants of Thrace, an ancient country that comprised what is now Bulgaria and parts of Greece and Turkey. The Athenians considered Thracians barbarians.

Without friend or family. May he eat slave's bread
And suffer the plague and freeze naked,
Laced about with the nasty trash of the sea.
May his teeth knock the top on the bottom
10   As he lies on his face, spitting brine,
At the edge of the cold sea, like a dog.
And all this it would be a privilege to watch,
Giving me great satisfaction as it would,
For he took back the word he gave in honor,
15   Over the salt and table at a friendly meal.

Translation by Guy Davenport (1927–)

The poem is a curse, written by a Greek poet in the seventh century B.C. But the sentiment is as fresh as if it had been written yesterday. Archilochos is angry at someone who has gone back on his word. The two of them were having a friendly meal, and the man made a promise. Did he promise to do a business favor, or to introduce Archilochos to a woman? We will have to live with our curiosity. The point is that the man lied, and the poet is enraged. How does he manage his rage? He imagines the most dreadful things that could befall his enemy, and then invites them to happen. More than two thousand years later we can read it with sympathy and some amusement.

Poems of Praise, Poems for the Dead

Two powerful and time-honored sources of lyric poetry are admiration of something or someone, and the impact of death. The first inspires the *encomium*, a poem of praise. The second inspires the *elegy*, or death song. One might argue that both of these are forms of love poetry.

Here is a poem of praise written to a woman that the poet hardly knows. Let us pretend for a moment that we are walking with the poet on a country road and that he has stopped us to listen to the reaper's singing.

WILLIAM WORDSWORTH (1770–1850)

The Solitary Reaper[5]

Behold her, single in the field,
Yon solitary Highland Lass!
Reaping and singing by herself:
Stop here, or gently pass!
5   Alone she cuts and binds the grain,
And sings a melancholy strain;
O listen! for the Vale° profound   *valley*
Is overflowing with the sound.

---

[5] The poem is based on a passage from Thomas Wilkinson's *Tour of Scotland*. Wilkinson describes seeing a young woman reaping in the field. She sings in Erse, the native Scottish language.

<pre>
        No Nightingale did ever chaunt°   *chant*
10   More welcome notes to weary bands
        Of travellers in some shady haunt,
        Among Arabian sands:
        A voice so thrilling ne'er was heard
        In spring-time from the Cuckoo-bird,
15   Breaking the silence of the seas
        Among the farthest Hebrides.⁶

        Will no one tell me what she sings?—
        Perhaps the plaintive numbers° flow   *verse rhythms*
        For old, unhappy, far-off things,
20   And battles long ago:
        Or is it some more humble lay,°   *song*
        Familiar matter of to-day?
        Some natural sorrow, loss, or pain,
        That has been, and may be again?

25   Whate'er the theme, the Maiden sang
        As if her song could have no ending;
        I saw her singing at her work,
        And o'er the sickle bending;—
        I listened, motionless and still;
30   And, as I mounted up the hill
        The music in my heart I bore,
        Long after it was heard no more.
</pre>

Questions

1. Vocabulary: *reap* (3), *haunt* (11), *plaintive* (18), *sickle* (28).
2. Why does the poet stop when he notices the "Highland Lass"?
3. Why does he admire her so? How does he express his admiration?
4. How is the woman's singing like poetry?
5. Is it possible that the poet is envious of the reaper?
6. In what way has Wordsworth imitated the singer in writing the poem?
7. Who is the reaper's audience? Who is Wordsworth's?

CLAUDE McKAY (1890–1948)

The Harlem Dancer

<pre>
        Applauding youths laughed with young prostitutes
        And watched her perfect, half-clothed body sway;
        Her voice was like the sound of blended flutes
        Blown by black players upon a picnic day.
5   She sang and danced on gracefully and calm,
</pre>

---

⁶ The Hebrides are islands off the west coast of Scotland.

The light gauze hanging loose about her form;
To me she seemed a proudly-swaying palm
Grown lovelier for passing through a storm.
Upon her swarthy neck black shiny curls
10   Luxuriant fell; and tossing coins in praise,
The wine-flushed, bold-eyes boys, and even the girls,
Devoured her shape with eager, passionate gaze;
But looking at her falsely-smiling face,
I knew her self was not in that strange place.

Questions

1. What do the applauding youths admire about the Harlem dancer?
2. What emotion does the speaker of the poem feel as he watches her? Does he feel the same as the others?
3. The word "self" in the last line of the poem is very important. What does the poet mean by it?

GERARD MANLEY HOPKINS (1844–1889)

Pied Beauty

Glory be to God for dappled things—
   For skies of couple-color as a brinded° cow;   *streaked*
      For rose-moles all in stipple upon trout that swim;
Fresh-firecoal chestnut-falls; finches' wings;
5   Landscape plotted and pieced—fold, fallow, and plow;
      And áll trádes, their gear and tackle and trim.°   *equipment*
All things counter, original, spare, strange;
   Whatever is fickle, freckled (who knows how?)
      With swift, slow; sweet, sour; adazzle, 'dim;
10   He fathers-forth whose beauty is past change:
                  Praise him.

Questions

1. Vocabulary: *pied*, *dappled* (1), *stipple* (3), *fallow* (5).
2. Hopkins prepares an extended list of items for which he is thankful. Are any of the items unexpected?
3. Is Hopkins thankful only for natural things?
4. How is God beautiful, according to Hopkins? How is His beauty different from that of the natural world?

Suggestion for Poets

Make a list of those special and peculiar things you are thankful for.

CHRISTOPHER SMART (1722–1771)

For I Will Consider My Cat Jeoffry, *From* Jubilate Agno

For I will consider my Cat Jeoffry.
For he is the servant of the Living God, duly and daily serving him.
For at the first glance of the glory of God in the East he worships in his way.
For is this done by wreathing his body seven times round with elegant quickness.
5 For then he leaps up to catch the musk,° which is the blessing of God upon his
    prayer.   *catnip*
For he rolls upon prank to work it in.
For having done duty and received blessing he begins to consider himself.
For this he performs in ten degrees.
For first he looks upon his fore-paws to see if they are clean.
10 For secondly he kicks up behind to clear away there.
For thirdly he works it upon stretch[7] with the fore-paws extended.
For fourthly he sharpens his paws by wood.
For fifthly he washes himself.
For sixthly he rolls upon wash.
15 For seventhly he fleas himself, that he may not be interrupted upon
    the beat.°   *patrol*
For eighthly he rubs himself against a post.
For ninthly he looks up for his instructions.
For tenthly he goes in quest of food.
For having considered God and himself he will consider his neighbor.
20 For if he meets another cat he will kiss her in kindness.
For when he takes his prey he plays with it to give it a chance.
For one mouse in seven escapes by his dallying.
For when his day's work is done his business more properly begins.
For he keeps the Lord's watch in the night against the Adversary.
25 For he counteracts the powers of darkness by his electrical skin and glaring eyes.
For he counteracts the Devil, who is death, by brisking about the life.
For in his morning orisons he loves the sun and the sun loves him.
For he is of the tribe of Tiger.
For the Cherub Cat is a term of the Angel Tiger.
30 For he has the subtlety and hissing of a serpent, which in goodness he suppresses.
For he will not do destruction if he is well-fed, neither will he spit without
    provocation.
For he purrs in thankfulness when God tells him he's a good Cat.
For he is an instrument for the children to learn benevolence upon.
For every house is incomplete without him, and a blessing is lacking in the spirit.

Question

1. The repetition of a word at the beginning of several lines of poetry is called anaphora.
   Do you find it agreeable in this poem? Musical? Wearying?

---

[7] "He works it upon stretch" means that he works his muscles, stretching.

Elegy

An elegy is a poem of lamentation that probably originated as the cry of mourning at ancient funerals. In classical Greece poets were engaged to inscribe elegiac lyrics on tombstones. The death song has evolved over the centuries into a highly sophisticated, diverse literary form, capable of expressing not only the grief of personal loss but also larger themes of the changes wrought by time. Here is a modern elegy, an exquisite personal statement of grief. Elegiac poets often describe the most vital qualities and scenes from the life of the deceased in order to emphasize their feelings of loss. Roethke also refers to the landscape, as did H. D. in her love poem, to show how the whole world shares in his sorrow.

THEODORE ROETHKE (1908–1963)

Elegy for Jane

My Student, Thrown by a Horse

I remember the neckcurls, limp and damp as tendrils;
And her quick look, a sidelong pickerel smile;
And how, once startled into talk, the light syllables leaped for her,
And she balanced in the delight of her thought,
5   A wren, happy tail into the wind,
Her song trembling the twigs and small branches.
The shade sang with her;
The leaves, their whispers turned to kissing;
And the mold sang in the bleached valleys under the rose.

10   Oh, when she was sad, she cast herself down into such a pure depth,
Even a father could not find her:
Scraping her cheek against straw;
Stirring the clearest water.

My sparrow, you are not here,
15   Waiting like a fern, making a spiny shadow.
The sides of wet stones cannot console me,
Nor the moss, wound with the last light.

If only I could nudge you from this sleep,
My maimed darling, my skittery pigeon.
20   Over this damp grave I speak the words of my love:
I, with no rights in this matter,
Neither father nor lover.

Questions

1. Vocabulary: *tendrils* (1), *pickerel* (2), *skittery* (19).
2. Who is the sparrow in the third section? The pigeon in the fourth?
3. T. S. Eliot says that appreciation of a poem should precede our understanding of it. Do you appreciate the emotion in the poem? Do you understand all of it?

4. In the last lines the poet says that he has no right to speak the words of his love. Do you agree?

MARGARET WALKER (1915–)

For Malcolm X

All you violated ones with gentle hearts;
You violent dreamers whose cries shout heartbreak;
Whose voices echo clamors of our cool capers,
And whose black faces have hollowed pits for eyes.
5   All you gambling sons and hooked children and bowery bums
Hating white devils and black bourgeoisie,
Thumbing your noses at your burning red suns,
Gather round this coffin and mourn your dying swan.

Snow-white moslem head-dress around a dead black face!
10   Beautiful were your sand-papering words against our skins!
Our blood and water pour from your flowing wounds.
You have cut open our breasts and dug scalpels in our brains.
When and Where will another come to take your holy place?
Old man mumbling in his dotage, or crying child, unborn?

ALFRED, LORD TENNYSON (1809–1892)

Dark House, by Which Once More I Stand[8]

Dark house, by which once more I stand
   Here in the long unlovely street,
   Doors, where my heart was used to beat
So quickly, waiting for a hand,

5   A hand that can be clasped no more—
   Behold me, for I cannot sleep,
   And like a guilty thing I creep
At earliest morning to the door.

He is not here; but far away
10   The noise of life begins again,
   And ghastly through the drizzling rain
On the bald street breaks the blank day.

Questions

1. In what ways is the house dark?
2. Why do you suppose Tennyson chose to describe the street as "unlovely" instead of "ugly"?

[8] This is a section of Tennyson's long poem *In Memoriam.*

3. What feeling do you get from the last line?
4. Why does Tennyson compare himself to "a guilty thing"? Of what offense is Tennyson guilty?

A. E. HOUSMAN (1859–1936)

To an Athlete Dying Young

The time you won your town the race
We chaired° you through the market-place;   *carried on a chair*
Man and boy stood cheering by,
And home we brought you shoulder-high.

5   Today, the road all runners come,
Shoulder-high we bring you home,
And set you at your threshold down,
Townsman of a stiller town.

Smart lad, to slip betimes away
10   From fields where glory does not stay,
And early though the laurel[9] grows
It withers quicker than the rose.

Eyes the shady night has shut
Cannot see the record cut,
15   And silence sounds no worse than cheers
After earth has stopped the ears.

Now you will not swell the rout
Of lads that wore their honors out,
Runners whom renown outran
20   And the name died before the man.

So set, before its echoes fade,
The fleet foot on the sill of shade,
And hold to the low lintel up
The still-defended challenge-cup.

25   And round that early-laureled head
Will flock to gaze the strengthless dead,
And find unwithered on its curls
The garland briefer than a girl's.

Question

1. Vocabulary: *betimes* (9), *rout* (17), *lintel* (23), *garland* (28).

---

[9] Laurel wreaths were awarded to the winners of competitions.

W. H. AUDEN (1907–1973)

In Memory of W. B. Yeats

(d. Jan. 1939)

I

He disappeared in the dead of winter:
The brooks were frozen, the airports almost deserted,
And snow disfigured the public statues;
The mercury sank in the mouth of the dying day.
5   What instruments we have agree
The day of his death was a dark cold day.

Far from his illness
The wolves ran on through the evergreen forests,
The peasant river was untempted by the fashionable quays;
10   By mourning tongues
The death of the poet was kept from his poems.

But for him it was his last afternoon as himself,
An afternoon of nurses and rumours;
The provinces of his body revolted,
15   The squares of his mind were empty,
Silence invaded the suburbs,
The current of his feeling failed; he became his admirers.

Now he is scattered among a hundred cities
And wholly given over to unfamiliar affections,
20   To find his happiness in another kind of wood[10]
And be punished under a foreign code of conscience.
The words of a dead man
Are modified in the guts of the living.

But in the importance and noise of to-morrow
25   When the brokers are roaring like beasts on the floor of the Bourse,[11]
And the poor have the sufferings to which they are fairly accustomed,
And each in the cell of himself is almost convinced of his freedom,
A few thousand will think of this day
As one thinks of a day when one did something slightly unusual.
30   What instruments we have agree
The day of his death was a dark cold day.

II

You were silly like us; your gift survived it all:
The parish of rich women, physical decay,
Yourself. Mad Ireland hurt you into poetry.

---

[10] An allusion to Dante's *Inferno,* in which he sees himself as being in a dark wood.
[11] The French stock exchange.

W. H. Auden (*Cecil Beaton Photograph/Courtesy of Sotheby's Belgravia*)

35   Now Ireland has her madness and her weather still,
For poetry makes nothing happen: it survives
In the valley of its making where executives
Would never want to tamper, flows on south
From ranches of isolation and busy griefs,
40   Raw towns that we believe and die in; it survives,
A way of happening, a mouth.

III

Earth, receive an honoured guest:
William Yeats is laid to rest.
Let the Irish vessel lie
45   Emptied of its poetry.

Time that is intolerant
Of the brave and innocent,
And indifferent in a week
To a beautiful physique,

50   Worships language and forgives
Everyone by whom it lives;
Pardons cowardice, conceit,
Lays its honours at their feet.

Time that with this strange excuse
55   Pardoned Kipling and his views,
And will pardon Paul Claudel,
Pardons him for writing well.

In the nightmare of the dark
All the dogs of Europe bark,[12]
60 And the living nations wait,
Each sequestered in its hate;

Intellectual disgrace
Stares from every human face,
And the seas of pity lie
65 Locked and frozen in each eye.

Follow, poet, follow right
To the bottom of the night,
With your unconstraining voice
Still persuade us to rejoice;

70 With the farming of a verse
Make a vineyard of the curse,
Sing of human unsuccess
In a rapture of distress;

In the deserts of the heart
75 Let the healing fountain start,
In the prison of his days
Teach the free man how to praise.

Question

1. Vocabulary: *quays* (9), *sequestered* (61), *unconstraining* (68).

 Writers on Writing   W. H. Auden

> As a poet, there is only one political duty, and that is to defend one's
> language from corruption.

The Meditative Poem

All the poetry we have read so far is thoughtful. Indeed, even the simplest
linguistic act, such as the naming of a flower, involves some thought. But there
is a kind of poetry in which thoughts, or ideas, are so much the center of
attention that it has been called *meditative* poetry. It seems to rise, as does
philosophy, out of a state of meditation, doubt, or curiosity. Unlike philosophers,
however, poets are not content to dwell with their doubts and curiosities exclu-

---

[12] Auden is alluding here to the imminent outbreak of World War II.

sively in the world of ideas. The ideas of poets are sparked by the real world and must return to the world of sense and emotion to find their music in language. One of the greatest meditative poets, Stéphane Mallarmé, expressed the relationship between poetry and ideas in conversation with the painter Edgar Degas; "One makes sonnets, Degas, not with ideas, but with words."

The excitement of meditative poetry lies in seeing the poet's mind in action, raising questions, and sometimes answering them, always on the threshold of new experience. We should read such work attentively in order to broaden our own experience.

OMAR KHAYYAM (A.D. 1050?–1123?)

XXVI and XXVII, the Rubaiyat

Oh, come with old Khayyam, and leave the Wise
To talk; one thing is certain, that life flies;
    One thing is certain, and the Rest is lies:
The Flower that once has blown forever dies.

5   Myself when young did eagerly frequent
Doctor and Saint, and heard great Argument
    About it and about: but evermore
Came out by the same Door as in I went.

Translation by Edward FitzGerald (1809–1883)

The Sufi poet Omar Khayyam spent a lifetime pursuing Truth and what one commentator refers to as "the Awakening of the Soul." In this concise, musical passage from his meditative poem the *Rubaiyat*, Omar Khayyam sums up years of education. In his youth he listened to the wisest discourse, of "Doctors," or those schooled in the world's wisdom, and of "Saints"—those well versed in the ways of God. What did Omar learn from them? "That life flies," and that "the Flower that once has blown forever dies." Is that all? You would have to read the rest of the *Rubaiyat* to get a better idea of what Omar learned. What is more important in this passage is what he did *not* learn. Look at the last line. No matter what he heard, the poet always left by the same door he entered! With wit and certainty Omar is saying that all the high conversation did not introduce him to a new door, a new path, or a new world. The *Rubaiyat* is a meditative journey that tells us something about the limits of meditation.

Meditative poets are usually testing the limits of their knowledge. Aristotle tells us that the desire to know is our fundamental nature. One way of reading meditative poetry is to join a poet in questioning, and then see how well the question is answered, for the poet and for us.

The poet John Milton became blind before his fiftieth year. In this meditation he considers the meaning of his blindness.

When I Consider How My Light Is Spent

When I consider how my light is spent,
   Ere half my days in this dark world and wide,
   And that one talent which is death to hide
   Lodged with me useless, though my soul more bent
5   To serve therewith my Maker, and present
   My true account, lest He returning chide;
   "Doth God exact day-labor, light denied?"
   I fondly° ask. But Patience, to prevent   *foolishly*
That murmur, soon replies, "God doth not need
10   Either man's work or His own gifts. Who best
   Bear His mild yoke, they serve Him best. His state
Is kingly: thousands at His bidding speed,
   And post o'er land and ocean without rest;
   They also serve who only stand and wait."

Questions

1. What is the question that Milton poses?
2. Who answers him?
3. Do you consider the answer satisfactory?

ROBERT FROST (1874–1963)

Fire and Ice

Some say the world will end in fire,
Some say in ice.
From what I've tasted of desire
I hold with those who favor fire.
5   But if it had to perish twice,
I think I know enough of hate
To say that for destruction ice
Is also great
And would suffice.

    In this epigram Frost considers the end of the world. The term *epigram* comes from a classical Greek word meaning to carve or inscribe, and an epigram is any terse, witty treatment of a single thought or question. Carving letters on stone or metal is difficult: we can understand why the epigram had to get right to the point. What is Frost's major question? He is asking how the world could end. He gives us a double answer: either fire or ice will do. But his reference to love and hate makes his answers much more subtle. Fire, he likens to desire, and we all know that uncontrolled desire leads to aggression and destruction. Ice, on the other hand, he compares to hatred, which could destroy the world as easily as desire.

Perhaps the greatest form of meditative lyric is the *ode*. Again the word comes to us from the ancients, from a Greek word for song, and the first great writer of odes, Pindar, was Greek. He wrote odes of praise to statesman and winners of the Olympian games. These odes were much admired because their flattering characterization and historical perspective raised their subjects to the level of mythic heroes. Full of epigrammatic wisdom or *gnomae*, of reflections on the poet's own grace or lack of grace, the Pindaric odes became a standard of lyric excellence in treating broad themes with intelligence and musicality. The Romantic poets Shelley, Keats, and Wordsworth used the form to great advantage, extending it to meditation on ideas and objects as well as people.

The following is among the most respected of these Romantic odes.

JOHN KEATS (1795–1821)

Ode on a Grecian Urn[13]

Thou still unravished bride of quietness,
    Thou foster-child of silence and slow time,
Sylvan historian, who canst thus express
    A flowery tale more sweetly than our rhyme:
5   What leaf-fringed legend haunts about thy shape
      Of deities or mortals, or of both,
        In Tempe or the dales of Arcady?[14]
    What men or gods are these? What maidens loth?
What mad pursuit? What struggle to escape?
10   What pipes and timbrels? What wild ecstasy?

Heard melodies are sweet, but those unheard
    Are sweeter; therefore, ye soft pipes, play on;
Not to the sensual° ear, but, more endeared,   *physical*
    Pipe to the spirit ditties of no tone:
15   Fair youth, beneath the trees, thou canst not leave
      Thy song, nor ever can those trees be bare;
        Bold Lover, never, never canst thou kiss,
Though winning near the goal—yet, do not grieve,
      She cannot fade, though thou hast not thy bliss,
20   For ever wilt thou love, and she be fair!

Ah, happy, happy boughs! that cannot shed
    Your leaves, nor ever bid the Spring adieu;
And, happy melodist, unwearièd,
    For ever piping songs for ever new;
25   More happy love! more happy, happy love!
      For ever warm and still to be enjoyed,
        For ever panting, and for ever young;

---

[13] The urn is decorated with a woodland, or sylvan, scene.
[14] Two valleys in Greece that represent the epitome of natural beauty.

Attic Red-Figured Urn, Four Women at
Bath *(Courtesy of the Museum of Fine
Arts, Boston, Catherine Page Perkins
Fund)*

    All breathing human passion far above,
       That leaves a heart high-sorrowful and cloyed,
30   A burning forehead, and a parching tongue.

    Who are these coming to the sacrifice?
       To what green altar, O mysterious priest,
    Lead'st thou that heifer lowing at the skies,
       And all her silken flanks with garlands drest?
35   What little town by river or sea shore,
       Or mountain-built with peaceful citadel,
         Is emptied of this folk, this pious morn?
    And, little town, thy streets for evermore
       Will silent be; and not a soul to tell
40   Why thou art desolate, can e'er return.

    O Attic shape![15] Fair attitude! with brede°   *design*
       Of marble men and maidens overwrought,
    With forest branches and the trodden weed;
       Thou, silent form, dost tease us out of thought
45   As doth Eternity: Cold Pastoral!
       When old age shall this generation waste,
       Thou shalt remain, in midst of other woe
    Than ours, a friend to man, to whom thou say'st,
    Beauty is truth, truth beauty,—that is all
50   Ye know on earth, and all ye need to know.

Questions

1. Vocabulary: *sylvan* (3), *loth* (8), *timbrels* (10), *melodist* (23), *cloyed* (29), *heifer* (33), *overwrought* (42).
2. It is clear from the first passages of the poem that Keats has observed the urn closely. Why does he want to know more?

---

[15] Attic shape—that is, possessing the Greek epitome of beauty.

3. Why does Keats admire the piper? Why the lover? Why does he so admire the leaves in the third section?
4. In .the fourth stanza, the townspeople have emptied the town in order to attend a sacrifice. They can never return, for the picture is locked in time. In what way are we too locked in time? Is their fate similar to ours?
5. Keats asks the urn many questions, and in the last lines the urn answers him. In fact, it answers a more important question than any he has asked so far. What is the question?

In the poem's opening lines the speaker is addressing the urn. Such a direct address, called an *apostrophe*, is a common poetic device. Poets have apostrophized clouds, skylarks, the moon and sun, roses, and so on. Another characteristic of this ode is that the urn, for Keats, plays a number of different roles. It is an "unravished bride of quietness," meaning, among other things, that its silence has remained unbroken and its surface unmarred. It is also a "sylvan historian," however, because it preserves the rural past. Both these phrases suggest that for Keats the urn is alive, not an ancient relic of a long-ago time.

As far as we know, Keats did not have any particular Grecian urn in mind when he wrote this poem. Rather, the urn he addresses is typical of most Grecian urns. Greek artists excelled in this form of painting, and they lavished time and craftsmanship on their urns, which depicted mythological scenes as well as scenes from daily life.

✍ Tips for Writing about Poetry

One of the delights of reading a meditative poem is in seeing a great mind at work musing upon questions of universal interest. When you have determined what questions are posed in a particular meditative poem, ask yourself these questions. Propose your own answer or answers. How is your answer conditioned by your environment, your religion and politics, the time in which you live? Is your opinion very different from the poet's? If it is, you should consider how the poet's answers are a response to his environment, religion, or other personal circumstances. This will require research.

❧ Poems for Further Study

E. E. CUMMINGS (1894–1962)

somewhere i have never travelled, gladly beyond

somewhere i have never travelled, gladly beyond
any experience, your eyes have their silence:
in your most frail gesture are things which enclose me,
or which i cannot touch because they are too near

your slightest look easily will unclose me
though i have closed myself as fingers,
you open always petal by petal myself as Spring opens
(touching skilfully, mysteriously) her first rose

or if your wish be to close me, i and
10   my life will shut very beautifully, suddenly,
as when the heart of this flower imagines
the snow carefully everywhere descending;

nothing which we are to perceive in this world equals
the power of your intense fragility: whose texture
15   compels me with the colour of its countries,
rendering death and forever with each breathing

(i do not know what it is about you that closes
and opens; only something in me understands
the voice of your eyes is deeper than all roses)
20   nobody, not even the rain, has such small hands

CESARE PAVESE (1908–1950)

Encounter

These hard hills which have made my body,
and whose many memories still shake me so, have revealed the miracle—
this *she* who does not know I live her and cannot understand her.

I encountered her one evening: a brighter presence
5   in the unsteady starlight, in the summer haze.
The smell of those hills was around me, everywhere,
a feeling deeper than shadow, and suddenly I heard,
as if it came from the hills, a voice at once purer
and harsher, a voice of vanished seasons.

10   Sometimes I see her, as she saw me, her presence
defined, unchangeable, like a memory.
I have never managed to hold her fast: always her reality
evades my grasp and carries me far away.
I do not know if she is beautiful. Among women she is very young:
15   when I think of her, I am surprised by a faint memory
of childhood lived among these hills,
she is so young. She is like morning. Her eyes suggest
all the distant skies of those faraway mornings.
And her eyes are firm with a purpose: the sharpest light
20   dawn has ever made upon these hills.

I created her from the ground of everything
I love the most, and I cannot understand her.

Translation by William Arrowsmith (1924–)

SYLVIA PLATH (1932–1963)

Daddy

You do not do, you do not do
Any more, black shoe
In which I have lived like a foot
For thirty years, poor and white,
5   Barely daring to breathe or Achoo.

Daddy, I have had to kill you.
You died before I had time—
Marble-heavy, a bag full of God,
Ghastly statue with one grey toe
10   Big as a Frisco seal

And a head in the freakish Atlantic
Where it pours bean green over blue
In the waters of beautiful Nauset.[16]
I used to pray to recover you.
15   Ach, du.

In the German tongue, in the Polish town
Scraped flat by the roller
Of wars, wars, wars.
But the name of the town is common.
20   My Polack friend

Says there are a dozen or two.
So I never could tell where you
Put your foot, your root,
I never could talk to you.
25   The tongue stuck in my jaw.

It stuck in a barb wire snare.
Ich, ich, ich, ich,[17]
I could hardly speak.
I thought every German was you.
30   And the language obscene

An engine, an engine
Chuffing me off like a Jew.
A Jew to Dachau, Auschwitz, Belsen.[18]
I began to talk like a Jew.
35   I think I may well be a Jew.

The snows of the Tyrol, the clear beer of Vienna
Are not very pure or true.
With my gypsy ancestress and my wierd luck

---

[16] Harbor on the east coast of Cape Cod, Massachusetts.
[17] *Ich* is German for "I."
[18] Sites of German concentration camps.

And my Taroc pack and my Taroc pack
40   I may be a bit of a Jew.

I have always been scared of *you*,
With your Luftwaffe,[19] your gobbledygoo.
And your neat moustache
And your Aryan eye, bright blue.
45   Panzer-man, panzer-man,[20] O You—

Not God but a swastika
So black no sky could squeak through.
Every woman adores a Fascist,
The boot in the face, the brute
50   Brute heart of a brute like you.

You stand at the blackboard, daddy,
In the picture I have of you.
A cleft in your chin instead of your foot
But no less a devil for that, no not
55   Any less the black man who

Bit my pretty red heart in two.
I was ten when they buried you.
At twenty I tried to die
And get back, back, back to you.
60   I thought even the bones would do

But they pulled me out of the sack,
And they stuck me together with glue.
And then I knew what to do.
I made a model of you,
65   A man in black with a Meinkampf look[21]

And a love of the rack and the screw.
And I said I do, I do.
So daddy, I'm finally through.
The black telephone's off at the root,
70   The voices just can't worm through.

If I've killed one man, I've killed two—
The vampire who said he was you
And drank my blood for a year,
Seven years, if you want to know.
75   Daddy, you can lie back now.

There's a stake in your fat black heart
And the villagers never liked you.
They are dancing and stamping on you.
They always *knew* it was you.
80   Daddy, daddy, you bastard, I'm through.

---

[19] The German air force.
[20] Tank driver in the German army.
[21] Adolf Hitler's *Mein Kampf* (two volumes, 1925–1927) stated Hitler's political views.

JOHN CROWE RANSOM (1888–1974)

Here Lies a Lady

Here lies a lady of beauty and high degree.
Of chills and fever she died, of fever and chills,
The delight of her husband, her aunt, an infant of three,
And of medicos marveling sweetly on her ills.

5   For either she burned, and her confident eyes would blaze,
And her fingers fly in a manner to puzzle their heads—
What was she making? Why, nothing; she sat in a maze
Of old scraps of laces, snipped into curious shreds—

Or this would pass, and the light of her fire decline
10   Till she lay discouraged and cold, like a thin stalk white and blown,
And would not open her eyes, to kisses, to wine;
The sixth of these states was her last; the cold settled down.

Sweet ladies, long may ye bloom, and toughly I hope ye may thole,°   *endure*
But was she not lucky? In flowers and lace and mourning,
15   In love and great honor we bade God rest her soul
After six little spaces of chill, and six of burning.

WILLIAM BLAKE (1757–1827)

To See a World in a Grain of Sand

To see a world in a grain of sand
And a heaven in a wild flower,
Hold infinity in the palm of your hand
And eternity in an hour.

IMAMU AMIRI BARAKA (LeROI JONES) (1934–)

Preface to a Twenty Volume Suicide Note

For Kellie Jones, Born 16 May 1959

Lately, I've become accustomed to the way
The ground opens up and envelopes me
Each time I go out to walk the dog.
Or the broad edged silly music the wind
5   Makes when I run for a bus . . .

Things have come to that.

And now, each night I count the stars,
And each night I get the same number.
And when they will not come to be counted,
10   I count the holes they leave.

Nobody sings anymore.

And then last night I tiptoed up
To my daughter's room and heard her
Talking to someone, and when I opened
15   The door, there was no one there . . .
Only she on her knees, peeking into

Her own clasped hands.

6 🌿 Dramatic Poetry

The Poet as Actor

How often have you wished to be someone else? Imagine leaving your body for a few hours and becoming a famous musician, a fashion model, a bank robber, or a senator. This is a common fantasy, the same one that prompts children to try on their parents' hats and shoes. One of the frustrations of being human is that we cannot escape who we are no matter how much we like or dislike ourselves. Certain poets, hypersensitive to the limits of personality, adopt someone else's voice in writing a poem. A young poet might speak in the voice of an old woman, or a rich poet in a beggar's voice. This adoption of another's voice, sometimes called a mask or persona, is the poet's effort to break out of his or her own consciousness and reach into the world of another. The result of that effort is *dramatic poetry*.

Dramatic poets are not merely ventriloquists with peculiar gifts for mimicry. They must identify with the persons they are portraying—a feat requiring a profound knowledge of character and an extraordinary degree of compassion. Dramatic poetry confirms certain constants in human nature that enable poets to understand people very different from themselves: the bishop, the queen, the murderer. For the reader, dramatic poetry provides an opportunity to hear the imagined thoughts of characters who lack the poet's gift or opportunity of expression.

The Soliloquy

The simplest form of dramatic poetry is the *soliloquy*, in which the speaker is merely overheard, talking to no one in particular.

WILLIAM CARLOS WILLIAMS (1883–1963)

The Widow's Lament in Springtime

Sorrow is my own yard
where the new grass

flames as it has flamed
often before but not
5   with the cold fire
that closes round me this year.
Thirtyfive years
I lived with my husband.
The plumtree is white today
10   with masses of flowers.
Masses of flowers
load the cherry branches
and color some bushes
yellow and some red
15   but the grief in my heart
is stronger than they
for though they were my joy
formerly, today I noticed them
and turned away forgetting.
20   Today my son told me
that in the meadows,
at the edge of the heavy woods
in the distance, he saw
trees of white flowers.
25   I feel that I would like
to go there
and fall into those flowers
and sink into the marsh near them.

If this had been written by a widow, we might consider it a simple lyric statement of sorrow. But Williams clearly is not a widow. Why do you suppose he contrived to write in a woman's voice? Perhaps the poem grew out of a conversation with a widow he knew. Or maybe some of the statements in the poem were overheard. Whether the widow is real or imagined, the poem certainly arose out of sympathy for a woman's grief, rendered here in a manner that some men might find embarrassing. Perhaps the man has found a freedom of expression in the widow's voice he might not have felt in his own—a chance to explore a more feminine side of his nature. Whatever his motivation, Williams has treated his theme with great intimacy by entering into the widow's thoughts and adopting her voice.

This form of poem, in which the poet speaks for a single character, is also called a *dramatic monologue*. Its use suggests a modern, relativistic attitude toward experience. That is, the world can look quite different to different people depending on their character and point of view. As writers became more concerned with human individuality in the nineteenth century, the dramatic monologue served to explore extreme psychological states and differing points of view. Robert Browning wrote a book-length poem, *The Ring and the Book*, in which a murder story is told ten times, once by each of the various participants in and witnesses to the crime. The resulting picture, as rich and complex as life itself, shows that the truth of a situation cannot be known by any single witness.

We must not take the statements of a persona at face value. The dramatic poet may be portraying a liar or a deranged person who is unable to report experiences clearly.

One of Browning's shorter dramatic monologues reveals how the poet speaks for a psychopathic killer. Like a playwright, the dramatic poet sets the scene: a rainy, windy night, a cottage by the lake, the lover who is waiting for the entrance of his Porphyria. Let's see what happens.

ROBERT BROWNING (1812–1889)

Porphyria's Lover

The rain set early in to-night,
    The sullen wind was soon awake,
It tore the elm-tops down for spite,
    And did its worst to vex the lake:
5   I listened with heart fit to break.
When glided in Porphyria; straight
    She shut the cold out and the storm,
And kneeled and made the cheerless grate
    Blaze up, and all the cottage warm;
10   Which done, she rose, and from her form
Withdrew the dripping cloak and shawl,
    And laid her soiled gloves by, untied
Her hat and let the damp hair fall,
    And, last, she sat down by my side
15   And called me. When no voice replied,
She put my arm about her waist,
    And made her smooth white shoulder bare,
And all her yellow hair displaced,
    And, stooping, made my cheek lie there,
20   And spread, o'er all, her yellow hair,
Murmuring how she loved me—she
    Too weak, for all her heart's endeavour,
To set its struggling passion free
    From pride, and vainer ties dissever,
25   And give herself to me for ever.
But passion sometimes would prevail,
    Nor could to-night's gay feast restrain
A sudden thought of one so pale
    For love of her, and all in vain:
30   So, she was come through wind and rain.
Be sure I looked up at her eyes
    Happy and proud; at last I knew
Porphyria worshipped me; surprise
    Made my heart swell, and still it grew
35   While I debated what to do.

That moment she was mine, mine, fair,
    Perfectly pure and good: I found
A thing to do, and all her hair
    In one long yellow string I wound
40   Three times her little throat around,
And strangled her. No pain felt she;
    I am quite sure she felt no pain.
As a shut bud that holds a bee,
    I warily oped her lids: again
45   Laughed the blue eyes without a stain.
And I untightened next the tress
    About her neck; her cheek once more
Blushed bright beneath my burning kiss:
    I propped her head up as before,
50   Only, this time my shoulder bore
Her head, which droops upon it still:
    The smiling rosy little head,
So glad it has its utmost will,
    That all it scorned at once is fled,
55   And I, its love, am gained instead!
Porphyria's love: she guessed not how
    Her darling one wish would be heard.
And thus we sit together now,
    And all night long we have not stirred,
60   And yet God has not said a word!

Questions

1. Vocabulary: *sullen* (2), *vex* (4), *dissever* (24).
2. What are the "vainer ties" the speaker refers to in line 24?
3. What was "Her darling one wish," mentioned in line 57?
4. How does your attitude toward the speaker change after line 30?
5. Why does he kill her? Do you believe she felt no pain?
6. Apart from the fact that he murders Porphyria, how can you tell the speaker is insane?
7. To whom is the speaker speaking? Is the poem a soliloquy?

    The most vivid dramatic monologues tell us not only the character of the persona, but also the character of an auditor, the person being addressed. The great vitality of such poetry owes much to the immediacy of the scene—it takes place before our very eyes, just like a movie or a play, or a scene glimpsed through a keyhole. To read such poems we must first identify the dramatic situation, answering the questions: Who is speaking? Who is being addressed? Where are they? What prompts the speech?

WILLIAM BLAKE (1757–1827)

The Little Vagabond

Dear mother, dear mother, the Church is cold,
But the Ale-house is healthy and pleasant and warm;

Besides I can tell where I am used well,
Such usage in Heaven will never do well.

5   But if at the Church they would give us some ale,
And a pleasant fire our souls to regale,
We'd sing and we'd pray all the livelong day,
Nor ever once wish from the Church to stray.

Then the Parson might preach, and drink, and sing,
10   And we'd be as happy as birds in the spring;
And modest Dame Lurch, who is always at church,
Would not have bandy children, nor fasting, nor birch.

And God, like a father, rejoicing to see
His children as pleasant and happy as He,
15   Would have no more quarrel with the Devil or the barrel,
But kiss him, and give him both drink and apparel.

Questions

1. Vocabulary: *regale* (6), *bandy* (12).
2. Who is the persona of the poem?
3. Who is the auditor?
4. What kind of scene is depicted?
5. Is the speaker persuasive?
6. Where do you think the speaker will end up—in church or at the ale-house?

ANNE SEXTON (1928–1974)

Unknown Girl in the Maternity Ward

Child, the current of your breath is six days long.
You lie, a small knuckle on my white bed;
lie, fisted like a snail, so small and strong
at my breast. Your lips are animals; you are fed
5   with love. At first hunger is not wrong.
The nurses nod their caps; you are shepherded
down starch halls with the other unnested throng
in wheeling baskets. You tip like a cup; your head
moving to my touch. You sense the way we belong.
10   But this is an institution bed.
You will not know me very long.

The doctors are enamel. They want to know
the facts. They guess about the man who left me,
some pendulum soul, going the way men go
15   and leave you full of child. But our case history
stays blank. All I did was let you grow.
Now we are here for all the ward to see.
They thought I was strange, although
I never spoke a word. I burst empty
20   of you, letting you learn how the air is so.

The doctors chart the riddle they ask of me
and I turn my head away. I do not know.

Yours is the only face I recognize.
Bone at my bone, you drink my answers in.
25   Six times a day I prize
your need, the animals of your lips, your skin
growing warm and plump. I see your eyes
lifting their tents. They are blue stones, they begin
to outgrow their moss. You blink in surprise
30   and I wonder what you can see, my funny kin,
as you trouble my silence. I am a shelter of lies.
Should I learn to speak again, or hopeless in
such sanity will I touch some face I recognize?

Down the hall the baskets start back. My arms
35   fit you like a sleeve, they hold
catkins of your willows, the wild bee farms
of your nerves, each muscle and fold
of your first days. Your old man's face disarms
the nurses. But the doctors return to scold
40   me. I speak. It is you my silence harms.
I should have known; I should have told
them something to write down. My voice alarms
my throat. "Name of father—none." I hold
you and name you bastard in my arms.

Anne Sexton (© *Thomas Victor*)

45   And now that's that. There is nothing more
    that I can say or lose.
    Others have traded life before
    and could not speak. I tighten to refuse
    your owling eyes, my fragile visitor.
50   I touch your cheeks, like flowers. You bruise
    against me. We unlearn. I am a shore
    rocking you off. You break from me. I choose
    your only way, my small inheritor
    and hand you off, trembling the selves we lose.
55   Go child, who is my sin and nothing more.

Questions

1. Vocabulary: *pendulum* (14), *catkins* (36), *disarms* (38).
2. The title and the first line of the poem introduce us to the dramatic situation. Why is the mother saying these things to an infant? For whose benefit is she speaking?
3. Why will the baby not know her long?
4. Why does she say, "The doctors are enamel" (line 12)? What does that suggest about their sympathy?
5. Why does she call herself "a shelter of lies" (line 30)?
6. Do you believe her in the last line when she says the child is "my sin and nothing more"?

    The reader of dramatic poems might wonder why these imagined speakers, who are not supposed to be poets, speak with the eloquence of poets. This is one of the central tensions of dramatic poetry—the tension between poetic, or heightened, speech and natural speech. Poets have resolved this tension in various ways, sometimes simplifying the language when a character could not be expected to speak poetry; at other times choosing a persona from a faraway time or exalted station, who seems quite comfortable with eloquence. In the following poem, Lord Tennyson's "Ulysses" comes to us from Homeric Greece, a heroic age when, it seems, anything was possible—even kings who spoke poetry.

ALFRED, LORD TENNYSON (1809–1892)

Ulysses

    It little profits that an idle king,
    By this still hearth, among these barren crags,
    Matched with an agèd wife, I mete and dole
    Unequal laws unto a savage race
5   That hoard, and sleep, and feed, and know not me.
    I cannot rest from travel; I will drink
    Life to the lees. All times I have enjoyed

Greatly, have suffered greatly, both with those
That loved me, and alone; on shore, and when
10   Through scudding drifts the rainy Hyades[1]
Vexed the dim sea. I am become a name;
For always roaming with a hungry heart
Much have I seen and known—cities of men
And manners, climates, councils, governments,
15   Myself not least, but honored of them all—
And drunk delight of battle with my peers,
Far on the ringing plains of windy Troy.
I am a part of all that I have met;
Yet all experience is an arch wherethrough
20   Gleams that untraveled world whose margin fades
Forever and forever when I move.
How dull it is to pause, to make an end,
To rust unburnished, not to shine in use!
As though to breathe were life! Life piled on life   *thirst for life*
25   Were all too little, and of one to me
Little remains; but every hour is saved
From that eternal silence, something more,
A bringer of new things; and vile it were
For some three suns to store and hoard myself,
30   And this grey spirit yearning in desire
To follow knowledge like a sinking star,
Beyond the utmost bound of human thought.
        This is my son, mine own Telemachus,
To whom I leave the scepter and the isle—
35   Well-loved of me, discerning to fulfill
This labor, by slow prudence to make mild
A rugged people, and through soft degrees
Subdue them to the useful and the good.
Most blameless is he, centered in the sphere
40   Of common duties, decent not to fail
In offices of tenderness, and pay
Meet adoration to my household gods,
When I am gone. He works his work, I mine.
        There lies the port; the vessel puffs her sail;
45   There gloom the dark, broad seas. My mariners,
Souls that have toiled, and wrought, and thought with me—
That ever with a frolic welcome took
The thunder and the sunshine, and opposed
Free hearts, free foreheads—you and I are old;
50   Old age hath yet his honor and his toil.
Death closes all; but something ere the end,
Some work of noble note, may yet be done,
Not unbecoming men that strove with Gods.

---

[1] The daughters of Atlas. They were transformed into a group of stars, and their rising is thought
to predict rain.

The lights begin to twinkle from the rocks;
55 The long day wanes; the slow moon climbs; the deep
Moans round with many voices. Come, my friends,
'Tis not too late to seek a newer world.
Push off, and sitting well in order smite
The sounding furrows; for my purpose holds
60 To sail beyond the sunset, and the baths
Of all the western stars, until I die.
It may be that the gulfs will wash us down;
It may be we shall touch the Happy Isles,
And see the great Achilles, whom we knew.
65 Though much is taken, much abides; and though
We are not now that strength which in old days
Moved earth and heaven, that which we are, we are—
One equal temper of heroic hearts,
Made weak by time and fate, but strong in will
70 To strive, to seek, to find, and not to yield.

Questions

1. Vocabulary: *mete* (3), *lees* (7), *burnished* (23), *prudence* (36), *smite* (58), *abides* (65).
2. *Ulysses* is the Latin name for Odysseus, hero of Homer's epic the *Odyssey*, a section of which is printed in Chapter 4. The scene here portrayed is recounted by Dante in the *Divine Comedy*. Ulysses was a great adventurer in his youth. At what stage of his life do we encounter him in this poem?
3. What is the scene? Whom is Ulysses addressing?
4. Ulysses has accomplished a great deal in his life. What does he want now? What does he intend to do?

✍ Tips on Writing about Dramatic Poetry

In writing about dramatic poetry, it is essential to determine why the poet has chosen to speak in someone else's voice. When you have determined why, for instance, Robert Browning has chosen to assume the role of a psychopathic murderer, a critical question of further concern is how well the poet has succeeded in "acting out" his role. Is it true to life? If it is not true to life this may be a flaw in the composition, or it may be a sign of irony. It is of interest to write about the tension between the poet's real voice and the voice of the persona, the tension between a real-life character and the artificial elegance of the poet.

The Epistolary Monologue

We all enjoy reading letters, whether addressed to ourselves or to other people. Abelard's love letters to Héloise and the impassioned notes of Dietrich Bonhoeffer from prison still make compelling reading, years after they were written. Dramatic poets, taking on the guise of imagined or historical correspondents, have made good use of the *epistolary*, or letter, form. In a significant way the epistolary monologue is more natural than the forms we have seen so far: the letter is *already* literature, whereas a monologue such as the preceding one is pretending to be spoken and then recorded.

The titles of epistolary poems usually indicate the letter writer as well as the addressee. The following letter is supposed to have been written by a young woman to her husband, a merchant who has been on the road for five months. The poem is prized for its autobiographical compression and the wife's dignity in controlling her emotion. She and her husband have been deeply in love since they were children, and she misses him, but she never utters a word of resentment or reproach.

RIHAKU (8th century A.D.)

The River Merchant's Wife, A Letter

While my hair was still cut straight across my forehead
I played about the front gate, pulling flowers.
You came by on bamboo stilts, playing horse,
You walked about my seat, playing with blue plums.
5   And we went on living in the village of Chokan:
Two small people, without dislike or suspicion.

At fourteen I married My Lord you.
I never laughed, being bashful.
Lowering my head, I looked at the wall.
10   Called to, a thousand times, I never looked back.

At fifteen I stopped scowling,
I desired my dust to be mingled with yours
Forever and forever and forever.
Why should I climb the look out?

15   At sixteen you departed,
You went into far Ku-to-yen, by the river of swirling eddies,
And you have been gone five months.
The monkeys make sorrowful noise overhead.

You dragged your feet when you went out.
20   By the gate now, the moss is grown, the different mosses,
Too deep to clear them away!
The leaves fall early this autumn, in wind.
The paired butterflies are already yellow with August
Over the grass in the West garden;
25   They hurt me. I grow older.
If you are coming down through the narrows of the river Kiang,

Please let me know beforehand,
And I will come out to meet you
                    As far as Cho-fu-Sa.

Translation from the Chinese by Ezra Pound (1885–1972)

EDWARD HIRSCH (1950–)

The River Merchant: A Letter Home

Sometimes the world seems so large,
You have no idea. Out here at dusk
The barges pull the heaviest cargo, sometimes
They drag whole ships to the sea. Imagine
5   The sound of geese shrieking everywhere,
More geese than you can imagine,
Clustered together and flapping like stars.
Sometimes there are two moons shining at
Once, one clouded in the treetops, one
10   Breaking into shadows on the river.
I don't know what this means.

But from the hill's brow I can see
The lights in every village flickering on,
One by one, but slowly, like this,
15   Until the whole world gleams
Like small coins. Believe me:
There are so many villages like ours,
So many lights all gleaming together
But all separate too, like those moons.
20   It is too much. I am older now.
I want to return to that fateful place
Where the river narrows toward home.

Poetic Dialogues

Do you remember the folk song that goes:

Where have you been, Billy Boy, Billy Boy
Oh, where have you been, charming Billy?

I have been to see my wife,
She's the darling of my life.
She's a young thing and cannot leave her mother.

This is a popular example of a dramatic lyric employing two speakers. Sometimes the words of the primary persona in a poem call for an answer. This need makes for the lively conversation in poetry known as *dramatic dialogue*. In "Billie Boy"

John Crowe Ransom *(Rollie McKenna)*

we overhear a dialogue between a mother and her son about his bride. The mother asks questions about the bride, and Billie delivers comic answers.

The dramatic dialogue is an effective form for exploring contrasts in personality and viewpoint. We often find conflict in poetic dialogues, just as we do in plays and movies. In the following dialogue between an old man and a young lady, John Crowe Ransom sketches a brief but vivid scene. It is a moonlit night in autumn. A beautiful young lady is standing on her piazza (front porch) waiting for her lover. We do not know all this at first; we must read this poem carefully twice in order to understand the dramatic situation. Without knowing the situation, we cannot appreciate the impact of the lover's first speech. The old man has been spying on the lady through a trellis. We can imagine her surprise when he whispers the first stanza to her.

JOHN CROWE RANSOM (1888–1974)

Piazza Piece

—I am a gentleman in a dustcoat trying
To make you hear. Your ears are soft and small
And listen to an old man not at all,
They want the young men's whispering and sighing.
5   But see the roses on your trellis dying
And hear the spectral° singing of the moon;   *ghostly*
For I must have my lovely lady soon,
I am a gentleman in a dustcoat trying.

<pre>
        —I am a lady young in beauty waiting
10   Until my truelove comes, and then we kiss.
        But what grey man among the vines is this
        Whose words are dry and faint as in a dream?
        Back from my trellis, Sir, before I scream!
        I am a lady young in beauty waiting.
</pre>

 ## Writers on Writing *Randall Jarrell*

> *His poems are full of an affection that cannot help itself, for an inno-*
> *cence that cannot help itself—for the stupid travellers lost in the maze of the*
> *world, for the clever travellers lost in the maze of the world.*

The old man wants the lovely lady, and soon. He does not have much time. The young lady, who has all the time in the world, has been waiting for her young lover. What does she get? A peeping old man. What does he get? A stern refusal.

This frustration of expectations is called *dramatic irony*, or the *irony of sit-uation*. "Piazza Piece" is a classic example, in which the irony underscores the desperation of the old man's desire and the young woman's vanity. You may wish to reread the other dramatic poems we have studied, especially "Porphyria's Lover" and "The Little Vagabond," and look for instances of dramatic irony.

The Posthumous Monologue

As suggested earlier, poets choose dramatic personae not only to reveal different sides of their own natures, but also to speak for those who cannot speak for themselves. This has given rise to one of the most dramatic forms of poetry, the *posthumous monologue*—the poem spoken by the dead. These poems have an aura of mystery and terror because we know nothing about death and because the act of dying seems so frightening, even though no one has ever been able to tell us about it.

The following poem comes to us from beyond the grave, spoken by a young man killed in air combat during World War II. The first sentence tells us he is young: he went from his mother to the state (or army) like a kitten, with his fur still wet. The ball turret is the armored position on the aircraft, from which the gunner can achieve a full circle of fire.

Ball turret of famous World War II B-17 bomber "Memphis Bell." *(The Granger Collection)*

RANDALL JARRELL (1914–1965)

The Death of the Ball Turret Gunner

From my mother's sleep I fell into the State,
And I hunched in its belly till my wet fur froze.
Six miles from earth, loosed from its dream of life,
I woke to black flak° and the nightmare fighters.   *shellfire*
5   When I died they washed me out of the turret with a hose.

Questions

1. What is the "dream of life" referred to in line 3?
2. The speaker mentions in line 2 that he hunched in the State's "belly" until his "wet
   fur froze." What does this suggest about his response to the military?

EDGAR LEE MASTERS (1869–1950)

Fiddler Jones

The earth keeps some vibration going
There in your heart, and that is you.
And if the people find you can fiddle,
Why, fiddle you must, for all your life.
5   What do you see, a harvest of clover?
Or a meadow to walk through to the river?
The wind's in the corn; you rub your hands
For beeves hereafter ready for market;
Or else you hear the rustle of skirts
10   Like the girls when dancing at Little Grove.

To Cooney Potter a pillar of dust
Or whirling leaves meant ruinous drouth;
They looked to me like Red-Head Sammy
Stepping it off, to "Toor-a-Loor."
15 How could I till my forty acres,
Not to speak of getting more,
With a medley of horns, bassoons and piccolos
Stirred in my brain by crows and robins
And the creak of a windmill—only these?
20 And I never started to plow in my life
That some one did not stop in the road
And take me away to a dance or picnic.
I ended up with forty acres;
I ended up with a broken fiddle—
25 And a broken laugh, and a thousand memories,
And not a single regret.

Questions

1. Vocabulary: *beeves* (8), *drouth* (12).
2. Why did Jones become a fiddler?
3. What did he gain from fiddling? What did he lose?
4. Do you think his was a happy life?

❧ Poems for Further Study

WILLIAM BUTLER YEATS (1865–1939)

An Irish Airman Foresees His Death

I know that I shall meet my fate
Somewhere among the clouds above;
Those that I fight I do not hate,
Those that I guard I do not love;
5 My country is Kiltartan Cross,
My countrymen Kiltartan's poor,
No likely end could bring them loss
Or leave them happier than before.
Nor law, nor duty bade me fight,
10 Nor public men, nor cheering crowds,
A lonely impulse of delight
Drove to this tumult in the clouds;
I balanced all, brought all to mind,
The years to come seemed waste of breath,
15 A waste of breath the years behind
In balance with this life, this death.

ROBERT BROWNING (1812–1889)

My Last Duchess[2]

That's my last Duchess painted on the wall,
Looking as if she were alive. I call
That piece a wonder, now: Frà Pandolf's hands
Worked busily a day, and there she stands.
5   Will 't please you sit and look at her? I said
"Frà Pandolf" by design, for never read
Strangers like you that pictured <u>countenance</u>,
The depth and passion of its earnest glance,
But to myself they turned (since none puts by
10   The curtain I have drawn for you, but I)
And seemed as they would ask me, if they durst,
How such a glance came there; so, not the first
Are you to turn as ask thus. Sir, 't was not
Her husband's presence only, called that spot
15   Of joy into the Duchess' cheek: perhaps
Frà Pandolf chanced to say "Her mantle laps
Over my lady's wrist too much," or "Paint
Must never hope to reproduce the faint
Half-flush that dies along her throat": such stuff
20   Was courtesy, she thought, and cause enough
For calling up that spot of joy. She had
A heart—how shall I say?—too soon made glad,
Too easily impressed; she liked whate'er
She looked on, and her looks went everywhere.
25   Sir, 't was all one! My favour at her breast,
The dropping of the daylight in the West,
The bough of cherries some officious fool
Broke in the orchard for her, the white mule
She rode with round the terrace—all and each
30   Would draw from her alike the approving speech,
Or blush, at least. She thanked men,—good! but thanked
Somehow—I know not how—as if she ranked
My gift of a nine-hundred-years-old name
With anybody's gift. Who'd stoop to blame
35   This sort of trifling? Even had you skill
In speech—(which I have not)—to make your will
Quite clear to such an one, and say, "Just this
Or that in you disgusts me; here you miss,
Or there exceed the mark"—and if she let
40   Herself be lessoned so, nor plainly set

---

[2] This famous monologue was inspired by Browning's first trip to Italy, in 1834. The Duke of Ferrara typifies the cruelty of the Renaissance beneath its superficial beauty. He is showing the portrait of his late wife, whom he has done away with, to a representative of the father of his intended bride.

Her wits to yours, forsooth, and made excuse,
—E'en then would be some stooping; and I choose
Never to stoop. Oh sir, she smiled, no doubt,
Whene'er I passed her; but who passed without
45　Much the same smile? This grew; I gave commands;
Then all smiles stopped together. There she stands
As if alive. Will 't please you rise? We'll meet
The company below, then. I repeat,
The Count your master's known munificence
50　Is ample warrant that no just pretence
Of mine for dowry will be disallowed;
Though his fair daughter's self, as I avowed
At starting, is my object. Nay, we'll go
Together down, sir! Notice Neptune, though,
55　Taming a sea-horse, thought a rarity,
Which Claus of Innsbruck cast in bronze for me!

MICHAEL HARPER (1938–)

A Mother Speaks:
The Algiers Motel Incident, Detroit[3]

It's too dark to see black
in the windows of Woodward
or Virginia Park.
The undertaker
5　pushed his body back
into place
with plastic and gum
but it wouldn't
hold water.
10　When I looked
for marks
or lineament
or fine stitching
I was led away
15　without seeing
this plastic
face they'd built
that was not my son's.
They tied the eye
20　torn out

---

[3] During the night of July 25–26, 1967, while rioting was going on, three policemen killed three unarmed black men. The incident is the subject of a book by John Hersey, *The Algiers Motel Incident.*

by shotgun
into place
and his shattered
arm cut away
25   with his buttocks
that remained.
My son's gone
by white hands
though he said
30   to his last word—
"Oh I'm so sorry,
officer, I broke your gun."

FRANK O'HARA (1926–1966)

A True Account of Talking to the Sun at Fire Island

The Sun woke me this morning loud
and clear, saying "Hey! I've been
trying to wake you up for fifteen
minutes. Don't be so rude, you are
5   only the second poet I've ever chosen
to speak to personally
               so why
aren't you more attentive? If I could
burn you through the window I would
10   to wake you up. I can't hang around
here all day."
              "Sorry, Sun, I stayed
up late last night talking to Hal."

"When I woke up Mayakovsky he was
15   a lot more prompt" the Sun said
petulantly. "Most people are up
already waiting to see if I'm going
to put in an appearance."
                 I tried
20   to apologize "I missed you yesterday."
"That's better" he said. "I didn't
know you'd come out." "You may be
wondering why I've come so close?"
"Yes" I said beginning to feel hot
25   wondering if maybe he wasn't burning me
anyway.
           "Frankly I wanted to tell you
I like your poetry. I see a lot
on my rounds and you're okay. You may
30   not be the greatest thing on earth, but
you're different. Now, I've heard some

say you're crazy, they being excessively
calm themselves to my mind, and other
crazy poets think that you're a boring
35   reactionary. Not me.
                   Just keep on
like I do and pay no attention. You'll
find that people always will complain
about the atmosphere, either too hot
40   or too cold too bright or too dark, days
too short or too long.
                  If you don't appear
at all one day they think you're lazy
or dead. Just keep right on, I like it.
45   And don't worry about your lineage
poetic or natural. The Sun shines on
the jungle, you know, on the tundra
the sea, the ghetto. Wherever you were
I knew it and saw you moving. I was waiting
50   for you to get to work.
                 And now that you
are making your own days, so to speak,
even if no one reads you but me
you won't be depressed. Not
55   everyone can look up, even at me. It
hurts their eyes."
              "Oh Sun, I'm so grateful to you!"

"Thanks and remember I'm watching. It's
easier for me to speak to you out
60   here. I don't have to slide down
between buildings to get your ear.
I know you love Manhattan, but
you ought to look up more often.
                    And
65   always embrace things, people earth
sky stars, as I do, freely and with
the appropriate sense of space. That
is your inclination, known in the heavens
and you should follow it to hell, if
70   necessary, which I doubt.
                Maybe we'll
speak again in Africa, of which I too
am specially fond. Go back to sleep now
Frank, and I may leave a tiny poem
75   in that brain of yours as my farewell."

"Sun, don't go!" I was awake
at last. "No, go I must, they're calling
me."
        "Who are they?"

80   Rising he said "Some
day you'll know. They're calling to you
too." Darkly he rose, and then I slept.

CHARLOTTE MEW (1869–1928)

The Farmer's Bride

Three Summers since I chose a maid,
Too young, may be—but more's to do
At harvest-time than bide and woo.
     When us was wed she turned afraid
5   Of love and me and all things human;
Like the shut of a winter's day
Her smile went out, and 'twadn't a woman—
     More like a little frightened fay.
         One night, in the Fall, she runned away.

10   'Out 'mong the sheep, her be,' they said,
'Should properly have been abed;
But sure enough she wasn't there
Lying awake with her wide brown stare.
So over seven-acre field and up-along across the down
15   We chased her, flying like a hare
Before our lanterns. To Church-Town
     All in a shiver and a scare
We caught her, fetched her home at last
     And turned the key upon her, fast.

20   She does the work about the house
As well as most, but like a mouse:
     Happy enough to chat and play
     With birds and rabbits and such as they,
     So long as men-folk keep away.
25   'Not near, not near!' her eyes beseech
When one of us comes within reach.
     The women say that beasts in stall
     Look round like children at her call.
     I've hardly heard her speak at all.

30   Shy as a leveret, swift as he,
Straight and slight as a young larch tree,
Sweet as the first wild violets, she,
To her wild self. But what to me?

The short days shorten and the oaks are brown,
35   The blue smoke rises to the low grey sky,
One leaf in the still air falls slowly down,
     A magpie's spotted feathers lie
On the black earth spread white with rime,
The berries redden up to Christmas-time.
40   What's Christmas-time without there be
     Some other in the house than we!

She sleeps up in the attic there
Alone, poor maid. 'Tis but a stair
Betwixt us. Oh! my God! the down,
45   The soft young down of her, the brown,
The brown of her—her eyes, her hair, her hair!

PETER KLAPPERT (1942–)

Mail at Your New Address

I

Did your car get you to Florida?
I know you don't like me
to say so but Mrs. Wilson says
the same thing. Please tell me
5   (collegt) if you are all
there. I hope you do not
sleep or do anything on the road.
In Georgia.
          Your father
10   should see all the leaves.
Walter has not raked
a girlfriend up the street and wont
rake anymore. Watch out or
theyll have the same thing Mrs. Wilson
15   says the friend stayed and look
what happened at Cornell?
                Even if you changed
college is no reason to come home.
But get a haircut. I know
20   the dean doesn't like you
to look like a gardener.

II

There have been so many deaths
due to carbon m. poisoning
that this is just
25   a note to suggest you leave
a little air come into your room. Also,

I hope you don't get involved
with young men or older
or made from popies (?) and Hippy's.
30   I hope you are not letting the drugs
get you. And don't get mixed up
with drugs. It might spoil your change
for getting the cert. you are working for.
Remember, it is costing quite a lot.

35   Don't scold. I am afraid of your
trips to and near Chicago.

LOUISE ERDRICH (1954–)

Windigo

For Angela

The Windigo is a flesh-eating, wintry demon with a man buried deep inside of it. In some Chippewa stories, a young girl vanquishes this monster by forcing boiling lard down its throat, thereby releasing the human at the core of ice.

You knew I was coming for you, little one,
when the kettle jumped into the fire.
Towels flapped on the hooks,
and the dog crept off, groaning,
5   to the deepest part of the woods.

In the hackles of dry brush a thin laughter started up.
Mother scolded the food warm and smooth in the pot
and called you to eat.
But I spoke in the cold trees:
10   *New one, I have come for you, child hide and lie still.*

The sumac pushed sour red cones through the air.
Copper burned in the raw wood.
You saw me drag toward you.
Oh touch me, I murmured, and licked the soles of your feet.
15   You dug your hands into my pale, melting fur.

I stole you off, a huge thing in my bristling armor.
Steam rolled from my wintry arms, each leaf shivered
from the bushes we passed
until they stood, naked, spread like the cleaned spines of fish.

20   Then your warm hands hummed over and shoveled themselves full
of the ice and the snow. I would darken and spill
all night running, until at last morning broke the cold earth
and I carried you home,
a river shaking in the sun.

LOUIS OMAR SALINAS (1937–)

In a Farmhouse

Fifteen miles
out of Robstown
with the Texas sun
fading in the distance
5   I sit in the bedroom
profoundly,
animated by the day's work
in the cottonfields.

I made two dollars and
10   thirty cents today

I am eight years old
and I wonder
how the rest of the Mestizos
do not go hungry
15   and if one were to die
of hunger
what an odd way
to leave for heaven.

7 🌿 Images

Seeing Is Feeling

Poets have traditionally admired the way pictures can "speak" to us without the use of language. In fact, many poets envy the painter's or photographer's ability to capture a moment in all its complexity, to freeze life in midcourse and render all its detail, texture, and color simultaneously.

Like painters, poets have their own images. An *image* is a group of words that records sense impressions directly. Images usually record what poets see, but they can also record sounds, tastes, and smells. For example, T. S. Eliot begins his poem "Preludes" by imagining a winter evening that "settles down/with smell of steaks in passageways." We are asked to recall the greasy, smoky cooking smells that hover in the hallways of apartment houses or in close tenement alleys. The odor is familiar and not entirely pleasant. If we concentrate, we can bring to mind the slightly bitter smell of burnt animal fat. Eliot wants us to remember that experience and all the fatigue, hunger, and unpleasantness that go along with it.

Poets use images not merely to give us sensory impressions of a person, place, or thing, but also to evoke emotions. The best poets choose images that suggest to the reader precisely the feelings they wish to convey. The best images evoke an almost magical reaction. A few words will suggest an entire picture to our minds, which in turn will elicit deep—often unexpected—feelings.

Images differ from description in subtle but important ways. A description tells us about an object; an image presents us with the object. A description gives us the information we should know; an image gives us an experience we should feel. Readers have difficulty with highly imagistic writing when they do not take time to let the image register on their imaginations and emotions. Try to picture what the poet presents, and focus on the image long enough to react to it emotionally.

614

Haiku

The Japanese have concentrated on the power that a single image can produce. The *haiku* often contain a single, simple event that suggests to the reader a variety of feelings and associations. Although poets can place many restrictions on themselves, the haiku generally has some distinct features. It usually contains a seasonal reference and is about seventeen syllables long (commonly with a first line of five syllables, a second of seven, and a third of five). Since the following are translations, the usual syllabic criteria have not been closely met.

> For the child who won't
> stop crying, she lights a lamp
> in the autumn dusk.
>> —*Kawahigashi Kekigodo (1873–1937)*

> To the sun's path
> The hollyhocks lean
> in the May rains.
>> —*Matsuo Basho (1644–1694)*

> At midnight
> a distant door is slid shut.
>
> At the dark bottom
> of a well I find my face.
>> —*Ozaki Hosai (1885–1926)*

The first of these poems shows a mother's efforts to comfort her child by lighting a lamp as the sky grows dark. The poet calls our attention not only to the mother's care, but also to her loneliness and the futility of her actions. In the second poem we sense the natural harmony of spring as the flowers bend toward the sun. In the third poem there is something final, perhaps even sinister, in the far-off sound of a closing door. In the last poem the poet registers both surprise and foreboding as he sees his reflection in the dark well water.

The Japanese have cultivated the limited image, but most Western writers feel the need to expand images or combine them with other images or commentary. The following is an example of an expanded image.

WILLIAM CARLOS WILLIAMS (1883–1963)

The Great Figure

> Among the rain
> and lights
> I saw the figure 5
> in gold
> 5   on a red
> firetruck

moving
tense
unheeded
10   to gong clangs
siren howls
and wheels rumbling
through the dark city.

Questions

1. Vocabulary: *unheeded* (9).
2. How many senses are employed in presenting this image?
3. Eliminate the lines that refer to senses other than sight. Is the poem enhanced? Weakened? Why?
4. Is there any progression in the sensations the poem presents?
5. What do you feel when you see a speeding fire truck? Did Williams capture the experience for you? If not, what did he leave out?

William Carlos Williams makes the poem a single sentence to underscore that he is presenting a single image. Yet this is an image in constant motion. The fire truck does not stay still long enough to allow a clearly focused picture. Were this a photograph, the fire truck would be blurred as it emerges out of "the rain/ and lights" and plunges back into "the dark city." Williams is careful to record the actual way we see a fast-moving object. We do not see it whole; we see bits and pieces of it. Williams's eye catches the gold number 5 painted on the truck before he notices the truck itself.

I Saw the Figure 5 in Gold, by Charles Demuth *(The Metropolitan Museum of Art, New York, The Alfred Stieglitz Collection, 1949)*

The following poem also controls the order in which the image is revealed. What governs the order of details in the poem?

THEODORE ROETHKE (1908–1963)

Child on Top of a Greenhouse

The wind billowing out the seat of my britches,
My feet crackling splinters of glass and dried putty,
The half-grown chrysanthemums staring up like accusers,
Up through the streaked glass, flashing with sunlight,
5   A few white clouds all rushing eastward,
A line of elms plunging and tossing like horses,
And everyone, everyone pointing up and shouting!

Questions

1. Who is the speaker in the poem? Through whose eyes do we see the event?
2. What does the child feel about being on top of the greenhouse? Is he frightened, delighted, surprised, guilty, fascinated? All of these?
3. Do the spectators share the child's feelings? If not, why not?
4. Why do you think the poem is in one sentence?

Combining Images

In both "The Great Figure" and "Child on Top of a Greenhouse," the authors expand the image by adding details to a central event. But poets also like to combine very different images. The result is often like a photograph in which one image is superimposed on another so that we see both images simultaneously. "In a Station of the Metro" is such a poem; it records Ezra Pound's impression of entering the Paris subway.

EZRA POUND (1885–1972)

In a Station of the Metro

The apparition of these faces in the crowd,
Petals on a wet, black bough.

This poem is both surprising and right. The pale faces of the people emerging from a subway *do* look like petals on a tree. Yet if we think about these two images, we find that they are very different. The word *apparition* suggests the deathly and supernatural. Petals, however, are natural—signs of renewed life. How can these two images so easily share the same poem? This mystery is part of the logic of poetry, the reasonings of the heart of which, according to Pascal, the mind knows nothing.

"In a Station of the Metro" is among the most famous examples of poems by *les Imagistes*, who, despite their French title, were mostly American poets, including at times Pound, Amy Lowell, Hilda Doolittle, and William Carlos Williams. They believed in the direct treatment of objects and feelings and in using "no word that doesn't contribute to the presentation." "In a Station of the Metro" started out as a poem sixty lines long. Pound spent months whittling the poem to these two intense lines.

Arthur Symons's "Pastel" contains an imagistic effect similar to the one in Pound's short poem.

ARTHUR SYMONS (1865–1948)

Pastel

The light of our cigarettes
    Went and came in the gloom:
    It was dark in the little room.

Dark, and then, in the dark,
5   Sudden, a flash, a glow,
    And a hand and a ring I know.

And then, through the dark, a flush
    Ruddy and vague, the grace—
    A rose—of her lyric face.

Questions

1. How does Symons prepare for the image of the rose?
2. The rose is a common image. How does Symons make it fresh? Is it expected?

The poems we have read so far have all used images to evoke visual sensations. But images can also suggest any kind of sensation: taste, smell, touch. In "Sound," Jim Harrison suggests the way sound moves away from its source.

JIM HARRISON (1937–)

Sound

At dawn I squat on the garage
with snuff under a lip
to sweeten the roofing nails—
my shoes and pant cuffs
5   are wet with dew.
In the orchard the peach trees
sway with the loud
weight of birds, green fruit, yellow haze.
And my hammer—the cold head taps,

10   then swings its first full arc;
      the sound echoes against the barn,
      muffled in the loft,
      and out the other side, then lost
      in the noise of the birds
15   as they burst from the trees.

Questions

1. What senses are referred to in lines 1–5? Why do you suppose there are no references to sound in the opening?
2. Does the noise dissipate after the speaker hammers, or does the sound increase?
3. Why do you suppose Harrison bothered to record this simple occurrence? Are there any seemingly trivial events that stick in your mind as noteworthy? What is memorable about them?

Synesthesia

In "Sound" Harrison writes that the trees "sway with the loud/weight of birds." These lines may strike you as odd. In what sense can a weight be loud? A weight usually is light or heavy, not loud or quiet. This manner of speaking of one sense in terms of another is called *synesthesia*, and it is really quite common. People speak of "hot pink," a "loud necktie," "cool music," or a "spicy story." Each of these expressions is synesthetic.

ANN STANFORD (1916–)

Listening to Color

      Now that blue has had its say
      has told its winds, wall, sick
      sky even, I can listen to white

      sweet poison flowers   hedge autumn
5   under a sky white at the edges
      like faded paper. My message keeps

      turning to yellow where few leaves
      set up first fires over branches
      tips of flames only, nothing here finished yet.

Questions

1. What are the synesthetic images in the poem?
2. In what ways do colors speak to us? Can you think of ways in which colors communicate? How do they speak to Stanford?
3. In what time of year is the poem set? How does nature communicate time?
4. Why does Stanford say in line 9 that nothing is finished? How does the word *yet* modify the sense of finality? How does it reinforce the sense of finality?

KIMIKO HAHN (1955–)

When You Leave

This sadness could only be a color
if we call it *momoiro*, Japanese

for *peach-color*, as in the first story
mother told us: It is the color of the hero's skin

5   when the barren woman discovered him
inside a peach floating down the river.

And of the banner and gloves she sewed
when he left her to battle the horsemen, then found himself

torn, like fruit off a tree. Even when he met a monkey,
10   dog and bird he could not release

the color he saw when he closed his eyes. In his boat
the lap of the waves against the hold

was too intimate as he leaned back to sleep. He wanted
to leave all thoughts of peach behind him—

15   the fruit that brought him to her
and she, the one who opened the color forever.

Questions

1. Who is the "You" the poet mentions in the title? What does the poet feel for him?
2. We often associate colors with emotions. Give some examples.
3. Do you think that the association of a color with an emotion is synesthesia, according to the definition we have been using?
4. The last line of this poem definitely uses synesthesia. Tell which senses are being used to inform each other.
5. Why has the poet told the involved story of the hero and his trials? How does it relate to the poem's title?

Images and Commentary

The most common way in which poets use images is in combination with commentary. The poet sees things and then meditates on their significance. In the following poem a sequence of images concludes in a line of commentary.

JAMES WRIGHT (1927–1980)

Lying in a Hammock at William Duffy's Farm in Pine Island, Minnesota

Over my head, I see the bronze butterfly,
Asleep on the black trunk,
Blowing like a leaf in green shadow.

Down the ravine behind the empty house,
5   The cowbells follow one another
Into the distances of the afternoon.
To my right,
In a field of sunlight between two pines,
The droppings of last year's horses
10   Blaze up into golden stones.
I lean back, as the evening darkens and comes on.
A chicken hawk floats over, looking for home.
I have wasted my life.

Questions

1. Is there any order to the observations? Or are they merely random?
2. Does Wright see anything unusual? If not, is that important to the poem?
3. Is the poem self-pitying? Do you feel sorry for Wright? Has he wasted his life?

Readers coming to this poem for the first time are often startled by the last line, which seems terribly out of place. At first it appears that Wright means that watching nature is a waste of time. On a closer reading, however, we realize that Wright means just the opposite: ignoring the beauties of nature is a waste. The poem records his sad recognition that he has not spent enough time lying in hammocks, looking at the world around him.

Wright's poem also illustrates two important ways poets make their work vivid: (1) by giving details rather than generalized pictures, and (2) by being specific about the details. For example, Wright gives us not a general picture of the landscape, but briefly worded details about particular things: the butterfly, the leaf, the cowbells. Because we see these small things so clearly, we have a sense of seeing the entire picture clearly. Second, Wright is specific about details. He writes not merely that a bird floats over, but, "A chicken hawk floats over, looking for home." By giving us the precise term, he makes the scene more vivid. Well-chosen, specific details are more powerful than general descriptions, both emotionally and imagistically.

There is a limit, however, to the amount of detail that is useful. If Wright had written, "I see a monarch butterfly with a wing span of three inches and a length of an inch and three quarters," he would certainly have been more specific, but he would not have been more vivid. We can easily imagine a bronze butterfly, but we cannot picture something as specific as one with a certain wing span. By giving too much information, a writer can make an image more difficult to imagine and thereby sacrifice the emotional impact of the scene. The great writers have an instinct for the appropriate detail to make a scene vivid.

The techniques Wright uses have been used by poets throughout the centuries. "The Soote Season" was written in the sixteenth century by Henry Howard, Earl of Surrey, the son of the wealthiest man in England. Like Wright's poem, it also concludes with a surprising last line.

HENRY HOWARD, EARL OF SURREY (1517–1547)

The Soote° Season

sweet

The soote season, that bud and bloom forth brings,
With green hath clad the hill and eke° the vale;   *also*
The nightingale with feathers new she sings;
The turtle° to her make° hath told her tale.   *turtle dove mate*
5   Summer is come, for every spray now springs;
The hart hath hung his old head on the pale;
The buck in brake his winter coat he flings,
The fishes float with new repairéd scale;
The adder all her slough away she slings,
10   The swift swallow pursueth the fliés small;
The busy bee her honey now she mings.°   *mingles*
Winter is worn, that was the flowers' bale.°   *harm*
And thus I see among these pleasant things,
Each care decays, and yet my sorrow springs.

Questions

1. Vocabulary: *vale* (2), *adder* (9).
2. Why do you suppose the speaker is sad?
3. Has summer arrived, as the poet proclaims in line 5? If not, why does he say so?
4. Are there any unexpected or unusual images in his catalogue? If so, how do they relate to the others?

Landscapes

Occasionally a friend or relative is so closely associated with a particular place or scene that, when we see the scene again, all our feelings and memories of the person revive. In "Neutral Tones" Thomas Hardy describes his former friend in terms of a landscape.

THOMAS HARDY (1840–1928)

Neutral Tones

We stood by a pond that winter day,
And the sun was white, as though chidden of God,
And a few leaves lay on the starving sod;
     —They had fallen from an ash, and were gray.

5   Your eyes on me were as eyes that rove
Over tedious riddles of years ago;
And some words played between us to and fro
     On which lost the more by our love.

The smile on your mouth was the deadest thing
10   Alive enough to have strength to die;

Thomas Hardy (*Dorset County Museum, Dorchester, England*)

And a grin of bitterness swept thereby
    Like an ominous bird a-wing. . . .

Since then, keen lessons that love deceives,
And wrings with wrong, have shaped to me
15   Your face, and the God-curst sun, and a tree,
    And a pond edged with grayish leaves.

Questions

1. Vocabulary: *chidden* (2), *rove* (5), *tedious* (6), *ominous* (12).
2. Whom is the poet addressing?
3. Why is he speaking to her? What has happened between them?
4. What is the speaker's feeling toward the woman? Does he express his feelings directly or indirectly?
5. How do you think the woman might respond?

    Poets have also used landscapes as a starting point for meditation. You may have had a similar experience while sitting beside a lake or ocean, or looking out across a valley or mountain range. At first you were attentive to the world around you, but soon you lost yourself in thought. Sometimes we meditate so deeply that we do not "return to reality" for a long time; and, when we do, reality seems to have changed. M. H. Abrams has called the kind of poem that records this process "the greater romantic lyric" because so many poets of the early nineteenth century wrote poems of this sort. Typically, these lyrics have three sections. The first section presents the landscape; the second section is the meditation; and the third section recreates the landscape in light of the poet's intervening insights. "Dover Beach" is a classic lyric of this sort. It records

Matthew Arnold's visit to Dover, a seaside resort and the point in England closest to France.

MATTHEW ARNOLD (1822–1888)

Dover Beach

The sea is calm tonight.
The tide is full, the moon lies fair
Upon the straits—on the French coast the light
Gleams and is gone; the cliffs of England stand,
5   Glimmering and vast, out in the tranquil bay.
Come to the window, sweet is the night air!
Only, from the long line of spray
Where the sea meets the moon-blanched land,
Listen! you hear the grating roar
10   Of pebbles which the waves draw back, and fling,
At their return, up the high strand,
Begin, and cease, and then again begin,
With tremulous cadence slow, and bring
The eternal note of sadness in.

15   Sophocles[1] long ago
Heard it on the Aegean,[2] and it brought
Into his mind the turbid ebb and flow
Of human misery;[3] we
Find also in the sound a thought,
20   Hearing it by this distant northern sea.

The Sea of Faith
Was once, too, at the full, and round earth's shore
Lay like the folds of a bright girdle° furled.   *sash*
But now I only hear
25   Its melancholy, long, withdrawing roar,
Retreating, to the breath
Of the night wind, down the vast edges drear
And naked shingles° of the world.   *beach pebbles*

Ah, love, let us be true
30   To one another! for the world, which seems
To lie before us like a land of dreams,
So various, so beautiful, so new,
Hath really neither joy, nor love, nor light,
Nor certitude, nor peace, nor help for pain;
35   And we are here as on a darkling plain
Swept with confused alarms of struggle and flight,
Where ignorant armies clash by night.

---

[1] Sophocles was a Greek playwright of the fifth century B.C.
[2] Aegean Sea, the waters between Greece and Asia Minor.
[3] See Sophocles' *Antigone*, lines 583 ff.

Questions

1. Vocabulary: *straits* (3), *blanched* (8), *tremulous* (13), *cadence* (13), *turbid* (17), *furled* (23), *certitude* (34).
2. Compare the opening description (lines 1–14) with the closing (lines 35–37). What accounts for the difference? Which images are most powerful?
3. Is the sadness Arnold feels a modern sadness or one that has always been with humankind?
4. According to Arnold, how can humanity avoid feelings of despair? Does he hold much hope for these methods?
5. Anthony Hecht has imagined, in his poem "The Dover Bitch" (page 857), how a woman might react to this poem if she received it. How would you respond?
6. Do you think conditions of life have changed since 1851, when Arnold wrote this poem?

✍ Tips on Writing about Poetry

The writers of imagistic poems uses techniques of composition similar to the methods of painting. The placement of images in positions of prominence, like the first and last lines, often indicates their thematic importance, as would a figure in the foreground of a painting. Thus the bronze butterfly at the beginning and the chicken hawk at the end of James Wright's poem hold a heightened interest for the reader. In writing about poems that consist largely of images, it is important to observe the "composition" of the picture, indicating which images are given the most prominence, and why.

Meanings of Words

Poets signal how we should respond to an image not only through commentary, but also by their choice of words. Most words have two messages: *denotative* and *connotative*. The denotative meaning is the dictionary meaning: what the word objectively signifies. But words also have connotations: associations with, for instance, social class, values, or historical periods.

We might call the same building a home, a residence, a mansion, or an estate. Each word carries a similar denotative meaning, but the words have various connotations. For example, *mansion* is a much more formal word than *home*. The word *home* evokes images of a family enjoying a television program or conversing in the kitchen, their car parked in the driveway. The word *mansion* suggests a book-lined study, quiet talks over sherry, a limousine in the garage.

Words also suggest attitudes or values. If we speak of someone's attitude as "devil-may-care," we might approve of it. If we call the same attitude "irresponsible," we appear to disapprove.

Exercise

The following are groups of roughly synonymous words. State how the connotations of the words differ, and use each word in a sentence that highlights its connotative meaning.

1. loaded with money, very rich, very wealthy
2. front door, entrance, portal
3. bushes, undergrowth, shrubbery
4. say yes, agree, state in the affirmative
5. ending, finishing, concluding
6. sailor, seaman, mariner
7. letter, correspondence, epistle
8. without sound, quiet, silent
9. wet, damp, moist
10. backside, rear end, behind

In the following poem we have italicized a number of key words whose connotative meaning directs our response to the images. Although the poem is mostly images—the overt commentary is confined to the first two lines—the poet's attitude is anything but neutral.

HENRY DAVID THOREAU (1817–1862)

Pray to What Earth Does This Sweet Cold Belong

Pray to what earth does this *sweet* cold belong,
Which asks no duties and no conscience?
The moon goes up by leaps her *cheerful* path
In some far summer stratum of the sky,
5   While stars with their *cold* shine *bedot* her way.
The fields *gleam mildly* back upon the sky,
And far and near upon the *leafless* shrubs
The snow dust still *emits* a *silver* light.
Under the hedge, where *drift* banks are their screen,
10   The titmice now pursue their *downy* dreams,
As often in the *sweltering* summer nights
The bee doth drop asleep in the flower cup,
When evening overtakes him with his load.
By the brooksides, in the *still genial* night,
15   The more *adventurous* wanderer may hear
The *crystals* shoot and form, and winter slow
Increase his rule by *gentlest* summer means.

Questions

1. What is Thoreau's attitude toward the winter?
2. Why is he surprised that an earthly winter is so sweet?
3. In what sense does the winter ask neither duties nor conscience?

4. Is there any order to these images? Why does the image of the moon precede the image of the frozen brook? Does this order condition our response to the scene?

An easy way to observe how the poet manipulates the reader's attitude is to eliminate or alter the key words of the poem. Consider how our attitude would change had Thoreau written:

> The fields *reflect* the sky,
> And far and near upon the *barren* shrubs
> The snow dust still *gives off* a *metallic* light.

Exercise

In the following poem, underline the key words whose connotative meaning directs the reader's attitude. Eliminate or alter them to suggest a different or opposite attitude.

GARY SNYDER (1930–)

Oil

soft rainsqualls on the swells
south of the Bonins,[4] late at night. Light
from the empty mess-hall
throws back bulky shadows
5   of winch and fairlead
over the slanting fantail where I stand.

but for men on watch in the engine room,
the man at the wheel, the lookout in the bow.
the crew sleeps in cots on deck
10   or narrow iron bunks down drumming
passageways below.

the ship burns with a furnace heart
steam veins and copper nerves
quivers and slightly twists and always goes—
15   easy roll of the hull and deep
vibration of the turbine underfoot

bearing what all these
crazed, hooked nations need:
steel plates and
20   long injections of pure oil.

Surrealistic Imagery

Sometimes the images a poet asks us to picture are not strictly those we see in the actual world. When Gary Snyder writes, "Light/from the empty mess-hall/

---

[4] Island group in the western Pacific.

throws back bulky shadows," we can easily imagine the actual scene. If someone were present, he or she might be able to photograph it. In Blake's "London," however, we are invited to picture things that could not be photographed, such as "mind-forg'd manacles."

WILLIAM BLAKE (1757–1827)

London

I wander thro' each charter'd⁵ street,
Near where the charter'd Thames does flow,
And mark in every face I meet
Marks of weakness, marks of woe.

5   In every cry of every Man,
In every Infant's cry of fear,
In every voice, in every ban,
The mind-forg'd manacles I hear.

How the Chimney-sweeper's cry
10   Every blackning Church appalls;
And the hapless Soldier's sigh
Runs in blood down Palace walls.

But most thro' midnight streets I hear
How the youthful Harlot's curse
15   Blasts the new-born Infant's tear,
And blights with plagues the Marriage hearse.

Questions

1. Vocabulary: *manacles* (8), *hapless* (11).
2. What does Blake mean in lines 1–2 when he calls the streets and river "charter'd"? What feelings do these details evoke?
3. What does Blake mean by "mind-forg'd manacles"? Can you think of any way in which you handcuff your own actions?
4. In what sense does the chimney sweeper's cry appall the church?
5. How does the harlot's curse blast the child's tear? Why does she curse?

Although Blake wrote "London" nearly two hundred years ago, he used a technique we think of as modern. In lines 11–12 he wrote:

And the hapless Soldier's sigh
Runs in blood down Palace walls.

The image is more complicated than the synesthetic images we have observed in other poems. He is speaking not of a watery sigh, but of a sigh that "runs in blood." The image contains the kind of concentration (and perhaps illogic) that

---

⁵ For a lengthy discussion of this word, see Part I, Chapter 3, page 40.

occurs in dreams. It is almost as if the soldier had been shot in front of the palace, but we do not see the execution. Rather, we hear the sigh and see the bloodstain, or, more precisely, we experience the two merged together. This dreamlike concentration of image, known as *surrealistic imagery*, is one of the techniques used in surrealistic poetry. Why do poets use such techniques? We might as well wonder why dream images are so condensed. In highly emotional states, fine distinctions become blurred; the sigh and the blood become one experience, not separated by time.

PIERRE REVERDY (1889–1960)

Departure

The horizon lowers
        The days lengthen
        Voyage
    A heart hops in a cage
5   A bird sings
        At the edge of death
Another door is about to open
        At the far end of the corridor
        Shines
10   One star
  A dark lady
      Lantern on a departing train

Translation by Michael Benedikt (1935–)

Questions

1. What dreamlike elements are present in this poem?
2. What sort of emotions does this poem evoke?
3. What is the significance of the door about to be opened in line 7?

Notice how this poem contains the type of confusion that occurs in dreams. It is not the *bird* that hops in a cage and the *heart* that is at the edge of death. They have exchanged places.

Poets use images for a number of purposes: to place us in a landscape or a dream, to present familiar people to us, to bring us to unknown lands. Images can be realistic, a mixture of sensory experiences, or dreamlike. But whatever the kinds of image, the poet always uses imagery to evoke emotions more fully and more powerfully than could mere statements of feelings.

Suggestions for Essayists

1. Discuss how images in popular culture (in magazines, films, and advertisements) control our emotions and ideas.

2. Describe a place where you have been and the meditations it evoked.

3. Compare Matthew Arnold's "Dover Beach" with Anthony Hecht's "The Dover Bitch" on page 857.

Suggestions for Poets

1. Select a series of different emotions. Then write one image for each emotion that will evoke the feeling for the reader.
2. Evoke a landscape in images.
3. Suggest your feelings toward a person by evoking the landscape that most typifies that person.

❧ Poems for Further Study

SAMUEL TAYLOR COLERIDGE (1772–1834)

Kubla Khan

In Xanadu did Kubla Khan
A stately pleasure dome decree:
Where Alph, the sacred river, ran
Through caverns measureless to man
5   Down to a sunless sea.
So twice five miles of fertile ground
With walls and towers were girdled round:
And there were gardens bright with sinuous rills,
Where blossomed many an incense-bearing tree;
10   And here were forests ancient as the hills,
Enfolding sunny spots of greenery.

But oh! that deep romantic chasm which slanted
Down the green hill athwart a cedarn cover!
A savage place! as holy and enchanted
15   As e'er beneath a waning moon was haunted
By woman wailing for her demon lover!
And from this chasm, with ceaseless turmoil seething,
As if this earth in fast thick pants were breathing,
A mighty fountain momently was forced:
20   Amid whose swift half-intermitted burst
Huge fragments vaulted like rebounding hail,
Or chaffy grain beneath the thresher's flail:
And 'mid these dancing rocks at once and ever
It flung up momently the sacred river.
25   Five miles meandering with a mazy motion
Through wood and dale the sacred river ran,
Then reached the caverns measureless to man,
And sank in tumult to a lifeless ocean:
And 'mid this tumult Kubla heard from far
30   Ancestral voices prophesying war!

The shadow of the dome of pleasure
Floated midway on the waves;
Where was heard the mingled measure
From the fountain and the caves.
35 It was a miracle of rare device,
A sunny pleasure dome with caves of ice!

A damsel with a dulcimer
In a vision once I saw:
It was an Abyssinian maid,
40 And on her dulcimer she played,
Singing of Mount Abora.
Could I revive within me
Her symphony and song,
To such a deep delight 'twould win me,
45 That with music loud and long,
I would build that dome in air,
That sunny dome! those caves of ice!
And all who heard should see them there,
And all should cry, Beware! Beware!
50 His flashing eyes, his floating hair!
Weave a circle round him thrice,
And close your eyes with holy dread,
For he on honeydew hath fed,
And drunk the milk of Paradise.

ALFRED, LORD TENNYSON (1809–1892)

The Eagle: A Fragment

He clasps the crag with crooked hands;
Close to the sun in lonely lands,
Ringed with the azure world, he stands.

The wrinkled sea beneath him crawls:
5 He watches from his mountain walls,
And like a thunderbolt he falls.

AMY LOWELL (1874–1925)

Chinoiseries°   *things Chinese*

Reflections
When I looked into your eyes,
I saw a garden
With peonies, and tinkling pagodas,
And round-arched bridges
5 Over still lakes.
A woman sat beside the water
In a rain-blue, silken garment.
She reached through the water

To pluck the crimson peonies
10 Beneath the surface,
But as she grasped the stems,
They jarred and broke into white-green ripples;
And as she drew out her hand,
The water-drops dripping from it
15 Stained her rain-blue dress like tears.

Falling Snow

The snow whispers about me,
And my wooden clogs
Leave holes behind me in the snow.
But no one will pass this way
20 Seeking my footsteps,
And when the temple bell rings again
They will be covered and gone.

Hoar-Frost

In the cloud-grey mornings
I heard the herons flying;
25 And when I came into my garden,
My silken outer-garment
Trailed over withered leaves.
A dried leaf crumbles at a touch,
But I have seen many Autumns
30 With herons blowing like smoke
Across the sky.

WILLIAM CARLOS WILLIAMS (1883–1963)

The Red Wheelbarrow

so much depends
upon

a red wheel
barrow

5 glazed with rain
water

beside the white
chickens.

ROBERT LOWELL (1917–1977)

Skunk Hour

(For Elizabeth Bishop)

Nautilus Island's hermit
heiress still lives through winter in her Spartan° cottage; *austere*

her sheep still graze above the sea.
Her son's a bishop. Her farmer
5   is first selectman in our village;
she's in her dotage.

Thirsting for
the hierarchic privacy
of Queen Victoria's century,
10   she buys up all
the eyesores facing her shore,
and lets them fall.

The season's ill—
we've lost our summer millionaire,
15   who seemed to leap from an L. L. Bean
catalogue. His nine-knot yawl
was auctioned off to lobstermen.
A red fox stain covers Blue Hill.

And now our fairy
20   decorator brightens his shop for fall;
his fishnet's filled with orange cork,
orange, his cobbler's bench and awl;
there is no money in his work,
he'd rather marry.

25   One dark night,
my Tudor Ford climbed the hill's skull;
I watched for love-cars. Lights turned down,
they lay together, hull to hull,
where the graveyard shelves on the town. . . .
30   My mind's not right.

A car radio bleats,
"Love, O careless Love. . . ." I hear
my ill-spirit sob in each blood cell,
as if my hand were at its throat. . . .
35   I myself am hell;
nobody's here—

only skunks, that search
in the moonlight for a bite to eat.
They march on their soles up Main Street:
40   white stripes, moonstruck eyes' red fire
under the chalk-dry and spar spire
of the Trinitarian Church.

I stand on top
of our back steps and breathe the rich air—
45   a mother skunk with her column of kittens swills the garbage pail.
She jabs her wedge-head in a cup
of sour cream, drops her ostrich tail,
and will not scare.

ETHERIDGE KNIGHT (1933–)

Haiku

1

Eastern guard tower
glints in sunset; convicts rest
like lizards on rocks.

2

The piano man
5   is sting at 3 am
his songs drop like plum.

3

Morning sun slants cell.
Drunks stagger like cripple flies
On Jailhouse floor.

4

10   To write a blues song
is to regiment riots
and pluck gems from graves.

5

A bare pecan tree
slips a pencil shadow down
15   a moonlit snow slope.

6

The falling snow flakes
Can not blunt the hard aches nor
Match the steel stillness.

7

Under moon shadows
20   A tall boy flashes knife and
Slices star bright ice.

8

In the August grass
Struck by the last rays of sun
The cracked teacup screams.

9

25   Making jazz swing in
Seventeen syllables AIN'T
No square° poet's job.   *straitlaced*

 Writers on Writing   *Robert Browning*

All poetry is putting the infinite with the finite.

8 ❧ The Dance of the Mind

Metaphor and Simile

Poetry must attempt extraordinary leaps of both association and logic to achieve its heights of emotion and its provocative thoughts. We can easily distinguish these verbal flights from ordinary speech, as when someone says, fearfully, "She is taking her life in her hands!"; or, in admiration, "He is a diamond in the rough." Although these expressions are quite worn with use, we continue to use them because they are truly poetic. If the speaker were not animated by emotion, such statements might be dismissed as lies. The abstraction "life" cannot be held in the hands, and a man obviously is not a diamond. These expressions are true to feelings rather than to facts. Emotion has set the mind of the speaker dancing and has inspired what is known as a *figure of speech*.

The Metaphor

CHARLES SIMIC (1938–)

Watermelons

Green Buddhas
On the fruit stand.
We eat the smile
And spit out the teeth.

What has happened to the watermelons? The poet has seen them displayed on a fruit stand in their round wholeness. He has seen them cut into edible wedges. To his mind the uncut watermelons become Buddhas, godlike as they rest peacefully on the fruit stand. The tasty wedges of fruit become smiles as he thinks of eating them. And the seeds, as he recalls spitting them out, become

635

teeth that he imagines in the red mouth of the smile. The watermelon, in short, has been transformed to express the poet's delight in all its shapes.

The transformation of one thing or idea into another is called *metaphor*. It is the most powerful figure of speech and very likely the most essential act of poetic intelligence. Metaphor is personal and visionary, requiring no allegiance to facts. A metaphor may seem quite sensible, as when someone says, "My house is a prison," or it may at first seem bizarre: "My house is a dark road." But the statements are equally metaphorical. Each is poetically true insofar as it conveys the mood of the speaker.

WALT WHITMAN (1819–1892)

From Leaves of Grass

A child said What is the grass? fetching it to me with full hands;
How could I answer the child? I do not know what it is anymore than he.

I guess it must be the flag of my disposition, out of hopeful green stuff woven.

Or I guess it is the handkerchief of the Lord,
5   A scented gift and remembrancer designedly dropt,
Bearing the owner's name someway in the corners, that we may see and remark, and say Whose?

Or I guess the grass is itself a child, the produced babe of the vegetation.

Or I guess it is a uniform hieroglyphic,
And it means, Sprouting alike in broad zones and narrow zones,

Walt Whitman *(National Portrait Gallery, Smithsonian Institution, Washington, D.C.)*

10   Growing among black folks as among white,
     Kanuck, Tuckahoe, Congressman, Cuff, I give them the same, I receive them the
        same.

     And now it seems to me the beautiful uncut hair of graves.

Metaphor is commonly thought of as a sort of comparison, but such a definition seriously limits our appreciation of this powerful figure of speech. A
metaphor *may* arise out of a comparison, as when, noticing that buttercups and
sunlight are both a certain shade of yellow, we call the sunlight a buttercup.
But when Walt Whitman says that the grass is "the beautiful uncut hair of
graves" or "the handkerchief of the Lord," his imagination has overwhelmed
any similarities between grass and hair or handkerchiefs. His delight has transformed the grass.

As easily as metaphor can turn one thing into another, it can transform an
idea into a thing. Here Emily Dickinson begins with the abstract noun *Hope*,
a complex idea without visual properties. Then she transforms hope into a bird
so that we can see, hear, and better appreciate it.

EMILY DICKINSON (1830–1886)

"Hope" is the thing with feathers

"Hope" is the thing with feathers—
That perches in the soul—
And sings the tune without the words—
And never stops—at all—

5   And sweetest—in the gale—is heard—
And sore must be the storm—
That could abash the little Bird
That kept so many warm—

I've heard it in the chillest land—
10   And on the strangest Sea—
Yet, never, in Extremity,
It asked a crumb—of Me.

Question

1. Vocabulary: *abash* (7), *extremity* (11).

In the first line, by mentioning feathers, Dickinson emphasizes the bird's
lightness. In line 4 she suggests that the creature's consoling music is constant.
She further characterizes Hope in the second stanza, when she tells us the
peculiar bird sings most sweetly during storms, warming us in adversity. As her
final compliment to the bird's nature, she tells us that Hope does its comforting
work free of charge. We need not offer it so much as a crumb in order to receive
its benefits.

Hilda Doolittle *(A/P Wide World Photos)*

H. D. (HILDA DOOLITTLE) (1886–1961)

Oread° mountain nymph

Whirl up, sea—
whirl your pointed pines,
splash your great pines
on our rocks,
5   hurl your green over us,
cover us with your pools of fir.

Questions

1. How does the poet transform the sea?
2. What emotion or mood is evoked by the metaphor?

HART CRANE (1899–1932)

My Grandmother's Love Letters

There are no stars to-night
But those of memory.
Yet how much room for memory there is
In the loose girdle° of soft rain.   sash

5   There is even room enough
For the letters of my mother's mother,

Hart Crane *(National Portrait Gallery, Smithsonian Institution, Washington, D.C.)*

Elizabeth,
That have been pressed so long
Into a corner of the roof
10   That they are brown and soft,
And liable to melt as snow.

Over the greatness of such space
Steps must be gentle.
It is all hung by an invisible white hair.
15   It trembles as birch limbs webbing the air.

And I ask myself:

"Are your fingers long enough to play
Old keys that are but echoes:
Is the silence strong enough
20   To carry back the music to its source
And back to you again
As though to her?"

Yet I would lead my grandmother by the hand
Through much of what she would not understand;
25   And so I stumble. And the rain continues on the roof
With such a sound of gently pitying laughter.

BILL KNOTT (1940–)

Hair Poem

Hair is heaven's water flowing eerily over us
Often a woman drifts off down her long hair and is lost

Questions

1. What mood or emotion do you suppose triggered the transformation of hair into "heaven's water"?
2. Is there a metaphor implied in line 2?

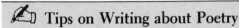

Tips on Writing about Poetry

Metaphor is considered by many writers to be the central act of poetic intelligence. Every metaphor, by virtue of transforming one thing into another, implies a judgment, sometimes extreme and sometimes ever so subtle: it either elevates the thing being transformed, or humbles it, like the touch of a sorcerer's wand that turns the frog into a prince, or the prince into a frog. As you write about metaphors, be aware of the judgments implied in them.

CHARLES HENRI FORD (1913–)

Somebody's Gone

There may be a basement to the Atlantic
but there's no top-storey
to my mountain of missing you.

I must say your deportment took a hunk
5   out of my peach of a heart.
I ain't insured against torpedoes!
My turpentine tears would fill a drugstore.

May I be blindfolded before you come my way again
if you're going to leave dry land like an amphibian;
10   I took you for some kind of ambrosial bird
with no thought of acoustics.

Maybe it's too late to blindfold me ever:
I'm just a blotter crisscrossed with the ink
of words that remind me of you.

15   Bareheaded aircastle,
you were as beautiful as a broom made of flesh and hair.

When you first disappeared
I couldn't keep up with my breakneck grief,
and now I know how grief can run away with the mind,
20   leaving the body desolate as a staircase.

Questions

1. Vocabulary: *deportment* (4), *amphibian* (9), *ambrosial* (10).
2. What do you suppose is the relationship of the poet to the "you" of the poem?

3. By suggesting there "may be a basement to the Atlantic," how is the poet transforming the ocean?
4. How does the poet express frustration in lines 13 and 14?
5. Why did Ford write this poem?

Exercise

You might try some metaphors of your own in order to discover the great power of this figure of speech. Look at the objects in your classroom, and transform them imaginatively. Write: *The desk is a desert. The blackboard is a door to night.* Transform a friend or an enemy: *John is a flagpole. Linda is a violin.* It does not take long to discover that every metaphor has emotional potential. In fact, it is difficult to make one that does not convey feeling as well as thought. Concentrate on a single object and transform it into as many other things as you can think of, trying for the greatest range of emotions.

The Simile

The simile is a more modest figure of speech. The common qualities of differing things may prompt a metaphor: "the sun is a buttercup," or "his ambition is a bubble." Having registered the similarity, however, a metaphor insists on total mental transformation of the one thing into the other. The simile, on the other hand, simply compares two different things on the basis of some shared quality.

> His head was as hairless as an egg.
> —*Anonymous*
>
> Her dress was as plain as an umbrella cover.
> —*Joseph Conrad*
>
> Thine eyes are like the deep, blue boundless heaven.
> —*William Shakespeare*

The charm of the simile comes from the observed likeness. Someone's eyes might be exactly the shade of the sky. The simile's force arises out of the differences between the things compared—by comparing someone's eyes to heaven, we attribute divine qualities to a mere mortal. But if we compare one person's eyes to another's or one tree to another, we are not making a figure of speech at all; we are simply writing prose.

Similes are easy to recognize, for they always declare their intentions by using the qualifiers *like* and *as:* "Debt is like a millstone about a person's neck" (Anon); "Childhood shows the man, as the morning shows the day" (John Milton). It is important to be able to recognize similes as we come upon them in our reading. It is even more important to appreciate the feelings and correspondences that inspire them. Let us examine a few similes with that in mind.

> A secret in his mouth is like
> a wild bird in a cage,
> whose door no sooner opens,
> than 'tis out.
> —*Ben Jonson*

The elements of the comparison are the "secret in his mouth" and the "wild bird in a cage." What is the similarity? Both the secret and the wild bird cannot resist the temptation to escape. What has inspired the figure of speech? Distrust. Ben Jonson is passing a harsh judgment on the man by means of his ingenious simile.

> Like to the moon am I, that cannot shine alone.
>
> —*Michelangelo*

Michelangelo, the great painter and sculptor, also wrote inspired poetry. What is the basis of comparison between the artist and the moon? He tells us that both require a light besides their own; they "cannot shine alone." The great force and emotion of this simile occur to us when we consider the great height and brilliance of the moon, the enormity of its loneliness when it cannot shine. The moon relies on the sun for its light; the artist needs love, the light of the world's approval, and inspiration. By comparing himself to the moon, Michelangelo is measuring himself on a grand scale indeed, suggesting the enormity of his needs and the grandeur of their satisfactions.

T. E. HULME (1883–1917)

Autumn

A touch of cold in the Autumn night—
I walked abroad,
And saw the ruddy moon lean over a hedge
Like a red-faced farmer.
5   I did not stop to speak, but nodded,
And round about were the wistful stars
With white faces like town children.

Questions

1. Vocabulary: *wistful* (6).
2. What does the moon have in common with the farmer? How does the idea of a moon with a farmer's face strike you? Is it frightening? Amusing?
3. What do the stars have in common with town children?
4. What mood is inspired by the last lines?

BILL KNOTT (1940–)

Death

Going to sleep, I cross my hands on my chest.
They will place my hands like this.
It will look as though I am flying into myself.

Questions

1. Who are "they" in line 2? Does the title give you a clue?
2. The final line is a striking image achieved through simile. What is being compared to what?

THOMAS MERTON (1915–1968)

The Regret

When cold November sits among the reeds like an unlucky fisher

And ducks drum up as sudden as the wind
Out of the rushy river,
We slowly come, robbed of our rod and gun,
5   Walking amid the stricken cages of the trees.

The stormy weeks have all gone home like drunken hunters,
Leaving the gates of the grey world open to December.

But now there is no speech of branches in these broken jails.
Acorns lie over the earth, no less neglected
10   Than our unrecognizable regret:

And here we stand as senseless as the oaks,
As dumb as elms.

And though we seem as grave as jailers, yet we did not come to wonder
Who picked the locks of the past days, and stole our summer.
15   (We are no longer listeners for curious saws, and secret keys!)

We are indifferent to seasons,
And stand like hills, deaf.
And never hear the last of the escaping year
Go ducking through the bended branches like a leaf.

Questions

1. This brooding meditation treats an old theme with a brilliant range of similes and metaphors. The theme is our neglect of nature, which is also a neglect of ourselves. Of all the similes, which one comes closest to summarizing that theme?
2. Why does Merton compare the stormy weeks to drunken hunters? What do they have in common?
3. Why does he compare the escaping year to a leaf in the last line?

The Conceit

A simile or metaphor that carries out a comparison in great detail is called a *conceit*.

Beauty, like the fair Hesperian[1] tree,
Laden with blooming gold, hath need the guard
Of dragon watch, with unenchanted eye,
To save her blossoms and defend her fruit
From the rash hand of bold incontinence°   *unchastity*
                    —*John Milton*

---

[1] In Greek literature Hesperus is a mythic treasure island.

This decorative figure of speech, which calls attention to the writer's ingenuity, was a popular mannerism of the Renaissance. Several seventeenth-century writers, sometimes called *metaphysical poets*, seem to try to outdo each other in the elaborateness of their figures. The following love poem elaborates a single comparison, between the loved one and a summer's day. Notice how the lover is flattered by the comparison and how wittily the poet takes credit for it in the last line.

WILLIAM SHAKESPEARE (1564–1616)

Shall I Compare Thee to a Summer's Day?

Shall I compare thee to a summer's day?
Thou art more lovely and more temperate.
Rough winds do shake the darling buds of May,
And summer's lease hath all too short a date.
5   Sometime too hot the eye of heaven shines,
And often is his gold complexion dimmed;
And every fair from fair sometime declines,
By chance, or nature's changing course, untrimmed.
But thy eternal summer shall not fade,
10   Nor lose possession of that fair thou ow'st;°   *possess*
Nor shall death brag thou wand'rest in his shade,
When in eternal lines to time thou grow'st.
So long as men can breathe or eyes can see,
So long lives this, and this gives life to thee.

Questions

1. Vocabulary: *temperate* (2).
2. What does the speaker emphasize about a summer's day? Could he find more flattering things to say about it?
3. What does the speaker's beloved have that the summer's day does not?

The following poem, a meditation on one of the Virgin's tears, is often cited for its overelaborate conceits. The poem survives despite the criticism, or perhaps because of it. We will leave it to the reader to judge the poem's effectiveness.

RICHARD CRASHAW (1613?–1649)

The Tear

What bright soft thing is this,
    Sweet Mary, thy fair eyes' expense?
A moist spark it is,

A wat'ry diamond; from whence
5   The very term, I think, was found,
The water of a diamond.

Oh! 'tis not a tear,
    'Tis a star about to drop
From thine eye, its sphere;
10   The Sun will stoop and take it up.
Proud will his sister be to wear
This thine eye's jewel in her ear.

Oh! 'tis a tear,
    Too true a tear; for no sad eyne,°   *plural for eyes*
15   How sad soe'er,
    Rain so true a tear as thine;
Each drop, leaving a place so dear,
Weeps for itself, is its own tear.

Such a pearl as this is,
20   (Slipped from Aurora's° dewy breast)   *dawn's*
The rose-bud's sweet lip kisses;
    And such the rose itself, when vexed
With ungentle flames, does shed,
Sweating in too warm a bed.

25   Such the maiden gem
    By the wanton Spring put on,
Peeps from her parent stem,
    And blushes on the manly Sun:
This wat'ry blossom of thy eyne,
30   Ripe, will make the richer wine.

Fair drop, why quak'st thou so?
    'Cause thou straight must lay thy head
In the dust? Oh no;
    The dust shall never be thy bed:
35   A pillow for thee will I bring,
Stuffed with down of angel's wing.

Thus carried up on high,
    (For to heaven thou must go)
Sweetly shalt thou lie,
40   And in soft slumbers bathe thy woe;
Till the singing orbs awake thee,
And one of their bright chorus make thee.

There thyself shalt be
    An eye, but not a weeping one;
45   Yet I doubt of thee,
    Whither th'hadst rather there have shone
An eye of Heaven; or still shine here
In th' Heaven of Mary's eye, a tear.

Questions

1. Vocabulary: *wanton* (26).
2. By what line of the poem has the tear become a distinct image?
3. By what line has the image of the tear become a metaphor? How many metaphors does Crashaw develop from the tear?
4. When do you sense that the figures have evolved into conceits?
5. Do the conceits become wearisome? Do they seem obsessive?

The Spanish philosopher José Ortega y Gasset refers to poetry as the "higher mathematics of literature." By that he means that poetry anticipates more popular movements in literature, and also that poetry is capable of great precision in expressing subtle states of the mind and heart. In those subtle areas no devices are more accurate in expression than metaphors and similes. If they cause us difficulty at first, we must be patient, for these figures produce some of the greatest riches in poetry. John Donne, in the following masterwork of similes and conceits, achieves extraordinary delicacy. He is treating a difficult subject: the different kinds of love, and how lovers are affected by separation. Donne composed this poem for his wife on the eve of his departure on a long trip. In the first two stanzas he urges her to help him take his leave with silence and dignity, like "virtuous men" at the hour of death. In the third stanza he compares the lovers to celestial bodies, "the spheres," which may move apart, or irregularly, without evil consequences. Pay close attention to the gold simile in stanza 6 and to the simile of the compass that concludes the poem.

JOHN DONNE (1572–1631)

A Valediction: Forbidding Mourning

As virtuous men pass mildly away,
    And whisper to their souls to go,
Whilst some of their sad friends do say
    The breath goes now, and some say no:

5   So let us melt, and make no noise,
    No tear-floods, nor sigh-tempests move;
'Twere profanation of our joys
    To tell the laity our love.

Moving of th' earth brings harms and fears;
10   Men reckon what it did and meant;
But trepidation of the spheres,[2]
    Though greater far, is innocent.

Dull sublunary lovers' love
    (Whose soul is sense) cannot admit

---

[2] Because of the movement of the earth, other planets appear to wobble or stand still. The odd movements were called the "trepidation of the spheres."

15   Absence, because it doth remove
        Those things which elemented it.

    But we, by a love so much refined
        That ourselves know not what it is,
    Inter-assurèd of the mind,
20   Care less, eyes, lips, and hands to miss.

    Our two souls, therefore, which are one,
        Though I must go, endure not yet
    A breach, but an expansion,
        Like gold to airy thinness beat.

25   If they be two, they are two so
        As stiff twin compasses are two:[3]
    Thy soul, the fixed foot, makes no show
        To move, but doth, if th' other do.

    And though it in the center sit,
30   Yet when the other far doth roam,
    It leans and harkens after it,
        And grows erect as that comes home.

    Such wilt thou be to me, who must,
        Like th' other foot, obliquely run;
35   Thy firmness makes my circle just,
        And makes me end where I begun.

Question

1. Vocabulary: *valediction*, *profanation* (7), *trepidation* (11), *sublunary* (13).

❧ Poems for Further Study

In reading the following poems, pay special attention to the metaphors and similes. Where you find a metaphor, determine what feelings have caused the transformation of images. Where you find a simile, look for the correspondences between the elements compared, and see how the elements complement each other by their differences.

FRAY ANGELICO CHAVEZ (1910–)

Rattlesnake

Line of beauty scrawled alive
by God's finger on the sand,

---

[3] Donne is referring to the compass used to draw circles.

diamond patterned inlaid band
scrolling inward like a hive—

5   Stay away,
crawl-created,
articulated
coil of cloisonné!

THOMAS MERTON (1915–1968)

Elegy for the Monastery Barn

As though an aged person were to wear
Too gay a dress
And walk about the neighborhood
Announcing the hour of her death,

5   So now, one summer day's end,
At suppertime, when wheels are still,
The long barn suddenly puts on the traitor, beauty,
And hails us with a dangerous cry,
For: "Look!" she calls to the country,
10   "Look how fast I dress myself in fire!"

Had we half guessed how long her spacious shadows
Harbored a woman's vanity
We would be less surprised to see her now
So loved, and so attended, and so feared.

15   She, in whose airless heart
We burst our veins to fill her full of hay,
Now stands apart.
She will not have us near her. Terribly,
Sweet Christ, how terribly her beauty burns us now!

20   And yet she has another legacy,°   *inheritance*
More delicate, to leave us, and more rare.

Who knew her solitude?
Who heard the peace downstairs
While flames ran whispering among the rafters?
25   Who felt the silence, there,
The long, hushed gallery
Clean and resigned and waiting for the fire?

Look! They have all come back to speak their summary:
Fifty invisible cattle, the past years
30   Assume their solemn places one by one.
This is the little minute of their destiny.
Here is their meaning found. Here is their end.

Laved° in the flame as in a Sacrament   *bathed*
The brilliant walls are holy
35   In their first-last hour of joy.

Fly from within the barn! Fly from the silence
Of this creature sanctified by fire!
Let no man stay inside to look upon the Lord!
Let no man wait within and see the Holy
40 One sitting in the presence of disaster
Thinking upon this barn His gentle doom!

N. SCOTT MOMADAY (1934–)

The Delight Song of Tsoai-Talee[4]

I am a feather on the bright sky
I am the blue horse that runs in the plain
I am the fish that rolls, shining, in the water
I am the shadow that follows a child
5 I am the evening light, the lustre of meadows
I am an eagle playing with the wind
I am a cluster of bright beads
I am the farthest star
I am the cold of the dawn
10 I am the roaring of the rain
I am the glitter on the crust of the snow
I am the long track of the moon in a lake
I am a flame of four colors
I am a deer standing away in the dusk
15 I am a field of sumac and the pomme blanche
I am an angle of geese in the winter sky
I am the hunger of a young wolf
I am the whole dream of these things

You see, I am alive, I am alive
20 I stand in good relation to the earth
I stand in good relation to the gods
I stand in good relation to all that is beautiful
I stand in good relation to the daughter of *Tsen-tainte*[5]
You see, I am alive, I am alive

Compare with W.E.B. DuBois's "The Song of the Smoke," page 832.

EZRA POUND (1885–1972)

The Bath Tub

As a bathtub lined with white porcelain,
When the hot water gives out or goes tepid,
So is the slow cooling of our chivalrous passion,
O my much praised but-not-altogether-satisfactory lady.

---

[4] N. Scott Momaday's Kiowa name, which means "Rock-Tree Boy."
[5] White Horse.

DYLAN THOMAS (1914–1953)

Fern Hill

Now as I was young and easy under the apple boughs
About the lilting house and happy as the grass was green,
    The night above the dingle[6] starry,
        Time let me hail and climb
5   Golden in the heydays of his eyes,
And honoured among wagons I was prince of the apple towns
And once below a time I lordly had the trees and leaves
        Trail with daisies and barley
    Down the rivers of the windfall light.

10 And as I was green and carefree, famous among the barns
About the happy yard and singing as the farm was home,
    In the sun that is young once only,
        Time let me play and be
    Golden in the mercy of his means,
15 And green and golden I was huntsman and herdsman, the calves
Sang to my horn, the foxes on the hills barked clear and cold,
        And the sabbath rang slowly
    In the pebbles of the holy streams.
All the sun long it was running, it was lovely, the hay
20 Fields high as the house, the tunes from the chimneys, it was air
    And playing, lovely and watery
        And fire green as grass.
    And nightly under the simple stars
As I rode to sleep the owls were bearing the farm away,
25 All the moon long I heard, blessed among stables, the nightjars
    Flying with the ricks, and the horses
        Flashing into the dark.

And then to awake, and the farm, like a wanderer white
With the dew, come back, the cock on his shoulder: it was all
30   Shining, it was Adam and maiden,
        The sky gathered again
    And the sun grew round that very day.
So it must have been after the birth of the simple light
In the first, spinning place, the spellbound horses walking warm
35   Out of the whinnying green stable
        On to the fields of praise.

And honoured among foxes and pheasants by the gay house
Under the new made clouds and happy as the heart was long,
    In the sun born over and over,
40   I ran my heedless ways,
     My wishes raced through the house high hay
And nothing I cared, at my sky blue trades, that time allows

---

[6] A *dingle* is a narrow wooded valley.

In all his tuneful turning so few and such morning songs
    Before the children green and golden
45   Follow him out of grace,

Nothing I cared, in the lamb white days, that time would take me
Up to the swallow thronged loft by the shadow of my hand,
    In the moon that is always rising,
        Nor that riding to sleep
50   I should hear him fly with the high fields
And wake to the farm forever fled from the childless land.
Oh as I was young and easy in the mercy of his means,
      Time held me green and dying
    Though I sang in my chains like the sea.

LOUISE GLÜCK (1943–)

The Pond

Night covers the pond with its wing.
Under the ringed moon I can make out
your face swimming among minnows and the small
echoing stars. In the night air
5   the surface of the pond is metal.

Within, your eyes are open. They contain
a memory I recognize, as though
we had been children together. Our ponies
grazed on the hill, they were gray
10   with white markings. Now they graze
with the dead who wait
like children under their granite breastplate
lucid and helpless:

The hills are far away. They rise up
15   blacker than childhood.
What do you think of, lying so quiet
by the water? When you look that way I want
to touch you, but do not, seeing
as in another life we were of the same blood.

WILLIAM SHAKESPEARE (1564–1616)

Let Me Not to the Marriage of True Minds

Let me not to the marriage of true minds
Admit impediments. Love is not love
Which alters when it alteration finds,
Or bends with the remover° to remove.   *faithless lover*
5   O, no! it is an ever-fixèd mark
That looks on tempests and is never shaken;
It is the star to every wand'ring bark,

Whose worth's unknown, although his height be taken.
Love's not Time's fool, though rosy lips and cheeks
10 Within his bending sickle's compass come;
Love alters not with his brief hours and weeks,
But bears it out even to the edge of doom.
  If this be error and upon me proved,
  I never writ, nor no man ever loved.

PERCY BYSSHE SHELLEY (1792–1822)

Fragment: Thoughts Come and Go in Solitude

My thoughts arise and fade in solitude,
  The verse that would invest them melts away
  Like moonlight in the heaven of spreading day:
How beautiful they were, how firm they stood,
5 Flecking the starry sky like woven pearl!

JOHN DONNE (1572–1631)

The Flea

Marke but this flea, and marke in this,
How little that which thou deny'st me is;
It suck'd me first, and now sucks thee,
And in this flea, our two bloods mingled bee;
5 Thou know'st that this cannot be said
A sinne, nor shame, nor losse of maidenhead,
  Yet this enjoyes before it wooe,
  And pamper'd swells with one blood made of two,
  And this, alas, is more than wee would doe.

10 Oh stay, three lives in one flea spare,
Where wee almost, yea more than maryed° are.   *married*
This flea is you and I, and this
Our mariage bed, and mariage temple is;
Though parents grudge, and you, w'are met,
15 And cloysterd in these living walls of Jet.   ╱ *flea*
  Though use make you apt to kill mee,
  Let not to that, selfe murder added bee,
  And sacrilege, three sinnes in killing three.

Cruell and sodaine,° hast thou since   *sudden*
20 Purpled thy naile, in blood of innocence?
Wherein could this flea guilty bee,
Except in that drop which it suckt from thee?
Yet thou triumph'st, and saist that thou
Find'st not thy selfe, nor mee the weaker now;
25   'Tis true, then learne how false, feares bee;
  Just so much honor, when thou yeeld'st to mee,
  Will wast,° as this flea's death tooke life from thee.   *be lost, wasted*

FEDERICO GARCÍA LORCA (1898–1936)

Half Moon

The moon goes over the water.
How tranquil the sky is!
She goes scything slowly
the old shimmer from the river;
5   meanwhile a young frog
takes her for a little mirror.

Translation by W. S. Merwin (1927–)

EMANUEL DI PASQUALE (1943–)

Rain

Like a drummer's brush,
the rain hushes the surface of tin porches.

 Writers on Writing   *Dylan Thomas*

> A good poem is a contribution to reality. The world is never the same once a good poem has been added to it. A good poem helps to change the shape and significance of the universe, helps to extend everyone's knowledge of himself and the world around him.

9 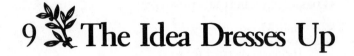 The Idea Dresses Up

Personification, Allegory, Symbol

Philosophers and mathematicians are generally more comfortable with abstractions than are poets. Mathematicians will talk about "infinite sets" or "imaginary numbers," and philosophers of "reason," "liberty," or "epistemes." Poets, however, feel more comfortable with what they can touch, see, hear, smell, or taste. Consequently, poets have developed a number of ways to make abstractions more concrete and familiar.

Personification

One of the simplest ways to make ideas concrete is *personification:* the granting of human attributes to things that are not human. Children's literature contains many examples of talking animals, trees, and stars. There are two primary reasons for the use of personification. First, we are better able to recognize attributes when they are given to an animal. An owl can be wiser, a cricket sillier, and a lion braver than a human could be. Second, we take a certain delight in such a transformation. On a basic, perhaps primitive level, we delight when unfamiliar experiences are made commonplace, and commonplace experiences are made unfamiliar.

Here, for example, is a short poem by the Greek poet Sappho. She wishes to convey the experience of being startled by the dawn. But "dawn" is a rather general condition. To gain the emotional intensity she desires, she has condensed the characteristics of daybreak into a personified figure.

SAPPHO (7th century B.C.)

Then

In gold sandals
dawn like a thief
fell upon me.

Translation by Willis Barnstone (1927–)

This poem is complicated by yet another factor. For the Greeks, Dawn is a goddess. Sappho is startled not only by the furtive sun, but also by a beautiful goddess who arrives on golden sandals. The scene, therefore, is doubly mysterious and awesome but also familiar and intimate.

Poets personify not only conditions and animals, but also abstract concepts like Freedom and Good Sense. In the following poem, Love, that often vague, abstract emotion, becomes a rich, generous, and distant patron.

MURIEL RUKEYSER (1913–1981)

Song: Love in Whose Rich Honor

Love
in whose rich honor
I stand looking from my window
over the starved trees of a dry September
5   Love
deep and so far forbidden
is bringing me
a gift
to claw at my skin
10   to break open my eyes
the gift longed for so long
The power
to write
out of the desperate ecstasy at last
15   death and madness

Questions

1. Where is the speaker of the poem? What is she looking at? What is the relationship between what the speaker sees and what she says?
2. Why should the gift claw at her skin and break open her eyes? Is Love's gift always gentle and kind, or is it sometimes cruel and painful?
3. What does the speaker mean by "desperate ecstasy" in line 14? To be in ecstasy means literally to be "beside oneself." In what sense is the speaker "beside herself"?
4. How has personifying Love made the poem more mysterious and intimate?

This poem concerns itself with a rather special question: can authors write with intensity on such subjects as death and madness from which others shy away? How can authors face those dreaded conditions not with philosophic detachment, but with joy? The persona of this poem answers that love gives her the power to write. But it is not merely an abstract love that enriches her. It is an almost godlike love, one that is "deep and so far forbidden." Rukeyser has taken a philosophical problem and turned it into a scene in which the mysterious figure of Love visits her with a gift of power.

Allegory

Emily Dickinson uses the personification of abstractions to explore the condition of death. Here again, the result is a poem that treats the subject with both familiarity and awe, mystery and intimacy.

EMILY DICKINSON (1830–1866)

Because I Could Not Stop for Death

Because I could not stop for Death—
He kindly stopped for me—
The Carriage held but just Ourselves—
And Immortality.

5   We slowly drove—He knew no haste
And I had put away
My labor and my leisure too,
For His Civility—

We passed the School, where Children strove
10   At Recess—in the Ring—
We passed the Fields of Gazing Grain—
We passed the Setting Sun—

Or rather—He passed Us—
The Dews drew quivering and chill—
15   For only Gossamer, my gown—
My Tippet—only Tulle—

We paused before a House that seemed
A Swelling of the Ground—
The Roof was scarcely visible—
20   The Cornice—in the Ground—

Since then—'tis Centuries—and yet
Feels shorter than the Day
I first surmised the Horses' Heads
Were toward Eternity—

Questions

1. Vocabulary: *civility* (8), *gossamer* (15), *tippet* (16), *tulle* (16), *cornice* (20).
2. What is the persona's attitude toward Death? Is he a fearsome creature or a politely stiff gentleman? How does the persona treat him?
3. What is the house they visit? What does it resemble?
4. Has the journey ended for the speaker? Has she arrived at Eternity? What can we say about the speaker's view of immortality?

Unlike Sappho or Rukeyser, Dickinson employs a number of abstractions in telling her story. Immortality is Death's traveling companion, and they are both headed toward Eternity. Dickinson has done something very complicated; she has made a small allegory. She has turned abstract ideas into people and places and then woven them into a story. Yet as complicated as this process sounds, the results are easy to understand. In fact, we often use allegory to explain complicated ideas to small children. Instead of trying to discuss in scientific terms the need for good oral hygiene, parents or dentists will tell children stories about Mr. Toothdecay, who enjoys drilling holes in new white teeth until Mr. Toothbrush comes to the rescue. The allegory is simpler, more immediate, and certainly more entertaining than a lecture. Finally, the allegory is more persuasive than charts, tables, and other means of convincing an audience.

George Herbert understood the value of allegory as a means of communicating complex notions in a lively, simple way. He left Cambridge University, where he had been elected public orator, to minister to a country parish. As public orator he had had to give flowery speeches in Latin to scholars at the university. But as a parish minister he had to persuade his poorly educated congregation to be better Christians. One of his allegorical poems follows.

GEORGE HERBERT (1593–1633)

The Pilgrimage

I traveled on, seeing the hill where lay
    My expectation.
A long it was and weary way.
The gloomy cave of desperation
5   I left on th'one, and on the other side
    The rock of pride.

And so I came to fancy's meadow, strowed
    With many a flower;
Fain would I here have made abode,
10   But I was quickened by my hour.
So to care's copse I came, and there got through
    With much ado.

That led me to the wild of passion, which
    Some call the wold°—   *treeless plain*
15   A wasted place but sometimes rich.
Here I was robbed of all my gold
Save one good angel,[1] which a friend had tied
    Close to my side.

At length I got unto the gladsome hill
20   Where lay my hope,
Where lay my heart; and, climbing still,
    When I had gained the brow and top,
A lake of brackish waters on the ground
    Was all I found.

---

[1] "Good angel" refers to a gold coin as well as to a guardian angel.

25   With that abashed, and struck with many a sting
                Of swarming fears,
        I fell, and cried, "Alas, my king!
          Can both the way and end be tears?"
    Yet taking heart I rose, and then perceived
30   I was deceived:

My hill was further; so I flung away,
            Yet heard a cry,
      Just as I went: *None goes that way*
    And lives: "If that be all," said I,
35   "After so foul a journey, death is fair,
            And but a chair."

Questions

1. Vocabulary: *copse* (11), *brackish* (23), *abashed* (25).
2. What is the significance of the "lake of brackish waters" in line 23 and the "good angel" in line 17?
3. What does the speaker feel in lines 25–30?
4. Does the speaker enjoy the pilgrimage? Is he supposed to?
5. What is the relationship between the life we live and our attitude toward death?
6. Is the pilgrim's life different from anyone else's?

Herbert's "pilgrimage" is another version of the "journey of life" on which we meet many difficulties. We must avoid the "cave of desperation" and "the rock of pride" and progress through "fancy's meadow," "care's copse," and "the wild of passion." The persona's destination is the "gladsome hill," which will be beautiful and refreshing, but as the voice informs him, *"None goes that way/ And lives."* Death is the only means of reaching the goal. But the speaker is not discouraged by the news. Dying seems a small price to pay for eternal happiness. Indeed, he is quite happy to die; he compares death to a sedan chair, like those on which the rich were comfortably carried about by servants.

Herbert's poem illustrates an important characteristic of allegory: the allegorical figures are not independent of one another. One understands the significance of the "rock of pride" in relation to the "gladsome hill" or the "cave of desperation." Moreover, the general pattern for life's journey illuminates all the allegorical figures. Each one helps us see the entire pattern, and it is the pattern that is most important in allegory.

Allegory often makes use of a dialogue in which the speaking is not colloquial. Here is such an allegorical scene.

AURELIAN TOWNSHEND (c. 1583–1643)

A Dialogue Betwixt Time and a Pilgrim

PILGRIM.   Aged man, that mows these fields.
TIME.   Pilgrim speak, what is thy will?

PILGRIM.	Whose soil is this that such sweet Pasture yields?
	Or who art thou whose Foot stands never still?
5	Or where am I? TIME. In love.
PILGRIM.	His Lordship lies above.
TIME.	Yes and below, and round about
	Where in all sorts of flow'rs are growing
	Which as the early Spring puts out,
10	Time falls as fast a mowing.
PILGRIM.	If thou art Time, these Flow'rs have Lives,
	And then I fear
	Under some Lily she I love
	May now be growing there.
15 TIME.	And in some Thistle or some spire of grass,
	My scythe thy stalk before hers come may pass.
PILGRIM.	Wilt thou provide it may? TIME. No.
PILGRIM.	Allege the cause.
TIME.	Because Time cannot alter but obey Fate's laws.
20 CHORUS.	Then happy those whom Fate, that is the stronger,
	Together twists their threads, and yet draws hers the longer.

Questions

1. Where does this meeting occur? How does the allegorical setting shape the dialogue?
2. How is Time portrayed? Is this a traditional view of Time?
3. Who is "His Lordship" in line 6? Why is he "below, and round about"?
4. What is the Chorus's moral?

Townshend, like Herbert, uses the figure of the pilgrim. We are all pilgrims on life's journey. He dramatizes a scene in which the pilgrim wanders into love even before he meets the object of his affection. Townshend uses the allegorical dialogue to explore the relationships among Love, Mortality, and Fate. The dialogue presents these ideas more simply and economically than could a lecture on the subject.

Fable

The fable, which is closely related to the allegory, is typically a story in which animals are given human attributes and represent certain moral qualities or philosophical positions. Most of the fables we know are derived from Aesop, a legendary Greek poet. The most famous, perhaps, is the story of the turtle and the rabbit who race one another. The moral or lesson of the story is: slow, steady work will triumph over impulsiveness.

Fables can be political as well. George Orwell's *Animal Farm* is a long prose allegorical fable about the rise of dictatorships. But Orwell was not the first author to write a political fable; he was participating in a long tradition, whose origins are buried in the distant past. "The Lion, the Fox, and Geese," a fable written by John Gay in the eighteenth century, still has relevance today.

JOHN GAY (1685–1732)

The Lion, the Fox, and Geese

A Lion, tired with state affairs,
Quite sick of pomp, and worn with cares,
Resolv'd (remote from noise and strife)
In peace to pass his latter life.
5   It was proclaim'd; the day was set;
Behold the gen'ral council met.
The Fox was Viceroy nam'd. The crowd
To the new Regent humbly bow'd
Wolves, bears, and mighty tygers bend,
10 And strive who most shall condescend.
He strait assumes a solemn grace,
Collects his wisdom in his face,
The crowd admire his wit, his sense:
Each word hath weight and consequence.
15 The flatt'rer all his art displays:
He who hath power, is sure of praise.
A Fox stept forth before the rest,
And thus the servile throng addrest.
      How vast his talents, born to rule,
20 And train'd in virtue's honest school!
What clemency his temper sways!
How uncorrupt are all his ways!
Beneath his conduct and command,
Rapine shall cease to waste the land.
25 His brain hath stratagem and art;
Prudence and mercy rule his heart;
What blessings must attend the nation
Under this good administration!
      He said. A Goose who distant stood,
30 Harangu'd apart the cackling brood.
      Whene'er I hear a knave commend,
He bids me shun his worthy friend.
What praise! what mighty commendation!
But 'twas a Fox who spoke th'oration.
35 Foxes this government might prize,
As gentle, plentiful, and wise;
If they enjoy the sweets, 'tis plain
We Geese must feel a tyrant reign.
What havock now shall thin our race,
40 When ev'ry petty clerk in place,
To prove his taste and seem polite,
Will feed on Geese both noon and night!

Questions

1. Vocabulary: *pomp* (2), *viceroy* (7), *Regent* (8), *servile* (18), *clemency* (21), *stratagem*
(25), *harangued* (30).

2. If the Lion represents "true kingship," what does the Fox represent?
3. Why is the Goose afraid of the Fox? Whom does the Goose represent? Are the Goose's fears justified?
4. Can you think of any political events to which this allegory might apply?

In Gay's time the Lion referred not just to any king but to King George I. The Fox was Sir Robert Walpole (1676–1745), whom historians generally consider the first prime minister in English history, a controversial figure who was greatly feared. The fables gave Gay an opportunity to make his political points and yet avoid imprisonment and the accusation of treason. Under tyranny, fables become a popular form of political expression.

Symbol

The term *symbol* refers to a large variety of literary practices, and it is important to distinguish among the various uses of the term. Allegory makes use of symbols. In Herbert's "Pilgrimage" the "gladsome hill" is a symbol for heaven; the "brackish lake" is a symbol of worldly difficulties. Indeed, we might define allegory as the narrative orchestration of a number of symbols into a coherent pattern.

In its broadest sense a symbol is any object or action that signifies more than itself. For example, the badge an officer wears is not merely a decorative silvery pin; it refers to, or symbolizes, legal authority. The candles on a birthday cake are not placed there primarily to light the room or to keep the cake warm. They symbolize the number of years the person has lived. The clothes you wear do not simply keep you comfortable and warm; they also communicate your values. You may have an embroidered alligator, Greek letters, or a numeral on your shirt or blouse. Each of these symbols has its social significance.

How are symbols formed? There are people who do nothing but design symbols intended to advertise products. But symbols appear to be a natural function of every mind. Psychiatrists tell us that our dreams are complicated allegories through which we work out our feelings. Our waking lives are no less involved with symbols. The following poem by D. H. Lawrence tells us about the formation of a symbol.

D. H. LAWRENCE (1885–1930)

Sorrow

Why does the thin grey strand
Floating up from the forgotten
Cigarette between my fingers,
Why does it trouble me?

5   Ah, you will understand;
When I carried my mother downstairs,
A few times only, at the beginning
Of her soft-foot malady,

I should find, for a reprimand
10   To my gaiety, a few long grey hairs
        On the breast of my coat; and one by one
        I watched them float up the dark chimney.

Questions

1. What specific words link the cigarette smoke to his mother's hair?
2. In what other senses are the hairs on his coat "a reprimand/To [his] gaiety"?
3. In line 12, what does the "dark chimney" symbolize?
4. Does the poem give you a logical explanation of why the smoke troubles the speaker? If not, why not?

Lawrence's poem shows how very different sensations become associated in our minds, especially during periods of emotional intensity. During his mother's final illness, the speaker had carried her about the house, and her hair had fallen on his clothing. Now the "thin grey strand" of cigarette smoke symbolizes the speaker's complex feelings about his mother's death.

One of the differences between the symbol of the cigarette smoke and that of the Lion in John Gay's fable is the number of associations the symbols have. The symbols in allegory and fable are relatively limited in reference. The Lion represents "natural leadership," "kingship," and—most specifically—King George I. These various references are closely related. But the cigarette smoke is associated with a complex and varied series of events, emotions, and ideas. It symbolizes the mother, her death, the speaker's continued existence. Symbols can also refer to other symbols. The cigarette smoke symbolizes the mother's hair, which in turn is "a reprimand/To [his] gaiety." The forgotten cigarette symbolizes the speaker's forgetfulness of his dying mother; it symbolizes his guilt.

One problem with symbols is that we sometimes recognize them without understanding their significance. Have you ever attended a religious ceremony of a different faith and been confused by the actions and symbols used in the ceremony, although you may have found them perfectly and even beautifully fitting? In "I Saw in Louisiana a Live-Oak Growing," Walt Whitman encounters a symbol that he finds difficult to comprehend.

WALT WHITMAN (1819–1892)

I Saw in Louisiana a Live-Oak Growing

    I saw in Louisiana a live-oak growing.
    All alone stood it and moss hung down from the branches.
    Without any companion it grew there uttering joyous leaves of dark green,
    And its look, rude, unbending, lusty, made me think of myself.
5   But I wonder'd how it could utter joyous leaves standing alone there without its
        friend near, for I knew I could not,
    And I broke off a twig with a certain number of leaves upon it, and twined around
        it a little moss

And brought it away, and I placed it in sight in my room,
It is not needed to remind me as of my own dear friends,
(For I believe lately I think of little else than them.)
10   Yet it remains to me a curious token, it makes me think of manly love;
For all that, and though the live-oak glistens there in Louisiana solitary in a wide
        flat space,
Uttering joyous leaves all its life without a friend a lover near,
I know very well I could not.

Questions

1. In what way does the tree symbolize Whitman? In what ways does it not?
2. Why does the tree make Whitman think of "manly love"?
3. Why does he break off a twig?
4. Do you ever collect things in your travels? Why do you do it? Do they ever come to symbolize something for you?

ROBERT FROST (1874–1963)

For Once, Then, Something

Others taunt me with having knelt at well-curbs
Always wrong to the light, so never seeing
Deeper down in the well than where the water
Gives me back in a shining surface picture
5   Me myself in the summer heaven, godlike,
Looking out of a wreath of fern and cloud puffs.

Robert Frost (*Rollie McKenna*)

Once, when trying with chin against a well-curb,
I discerned, as I thought, beyond the picture,
Through the picture, a something white, uncertain,
10   Something more of the depths—and then I lost it.
 Water came to rebuke the too clear water.
One drop fell from a fern, and lo, a ripple
Shook whatever it was lay there at bottom,
Blurred it, blotted it out. What was that whiteness?
15   Truth? A pebble of quartz? For once, then, something.

Questions

1. A Greek proverb says that "truth lies in the bottom of wells." How is this truth symbolized?
2. What does the "something" seen symbolize? Would the symbol be clearer if we were told what the speaker saw?
3. Does the whole action take on larger significance? Why does the speaker look into wells? What is peculiar about the way he does it?
4. At the poem's end, has the speaker lost the "godlike" feeling he had in line 5?

✒ *Writers on Writing* Robert Frost

> *A poem begins in delight and ends in wisdom.*

Traditional Symbols

The cigarette smoke, the live-oak, and the "whiteness" in the well are all unusual symbols, peculiar to the poets and to the poems in which they appear. Some symbols, however, are traditional. The cross symbolizes Christ's sacrifice; the unicorn is a symbol of purity; the apple represents forbidden knowledge. Poets often use traditional symbols in their work. The following song by Edmund Waller employs two traditional symbolic meanings of the rose: the rose is a symbol of love and of beauty's frailty.

EDMUND WALLER (1606–1687)

Go, Lovely Rose

Go, lovely Rose,
Tell her that wastes her Time and me,
   That now she knows,
When I resemble° her to thee,   *compare*
5   How sweet and fair she seems to be.

Tell her that's Young,
And shuns to have her Graces spy'd,
   That hadst thou sprung
In Desarts, where no Men abide,
10   Thou must have uncommended dy'd.

   Small is the Worth
Of Beauty from the Light retir'd;
   Bid her come forth,
Suffer her self to be desir'd,
15   And not blush so to be admir'd.

   Then die, that she
The common Fate of all Things rare
   May read in thee:
How small a Part of Time they share,
20   That are so wond'rous sweet and fair.

Questions

1. How is personification used in this poem?
2. Why does the speaker wish the rose to die?
3. If you were given a rose, how would you feel? How does the speaker wish his lady to feel?
4. Compare this poem to "To His Coy Mistress" on page 569.

Yeats was fond of the rose symbol. Notice how he relies on its traditional associations with love and beauty in this poem.

WILLIAM BUTLER YEATS (1865–1939)

The Rose of Peace

If Michael, leader of God's host,[2]
When Heaven and Hell are met,
Looked down on you from Heaven's door-post
He would his deeds forget.

5   Brooding no more upon God's wars
In his divine homestead,
He would go weave out of the stars
A chaplet° for your head.   *wreath*

And all folk seeing him bow down,
10   And white stars tell your praise,
Would come at last to God's great town,
Led on by gentle ways;

---

[2] The archangel Michael.

And God would bid His warfare cease,
Saying all things were well;
15 And softly make a rosy peace,
A peace of Heaven with Hell.

Questions

1. Why would Michael forget his deeds?
2. Is the rose a symbol of the woman to whom the poem is addressed or a symbol of her effect upon others?
3. How would this poem be different in feeling if it were about the "orchid of peace"? Is it important that the symbol be traditional?

Symbols are everywhere in poetry, as in the world around us, but one must be careful of them. Not everything is a symbol, though everything may contain the potential to become one. Before you interpret anything symbolically, you should try to find out if it is a traditional symbol or if the context in which it appears indicates its symbolic meaning. By being aware of context and tradition, you will become a seasoned reader able to distinguish well-chosen detail from symbol.

Suggestions for Essayists

1. With what sorts of symbols do you surround yourself? What message do you hope to convey about yourself?
2. Discuss the meanings of the symbols associated with a religious or secular holiday or ritual, such as Easter or Thanksgiving.
3. In the poems you have read, what sort of symbols have you found the most powerful? Why?

Suggestions for Poets

1. Carry on a discussion between two parts of your personality.
2. Speak to a traditional symbol, such as the rose. What do you want to tell it?
3. Retell a fable in your own words.

🌿 Poems for Further Study

THOMAS HARDY (1840–1928)

The Subalterns

I

"Poor wanderer," said the leaden sky,
   "I fain would lighten thee,

But there are laws in force on high
    Which say it must not be."

II

5   —"I would not freeze thee, shorn one," cried
    The North, "knew I but how
To warm my breath, to slack my stride;
    But I am ruled as thou."

III

—"To-morrow I attack thee, wight,"
10   Said Sickness. "Yet I swear
I bear thy little ark no spite,
    But am bid enter there."

IV

—"Come hither, Son," I heard Death say;
    "I did not will a grave
15 Should end thy pilgrimage to-day,
    But I, too, am a slave!"

V

We smiled upon each other then,
    And life to me had less
Of that fell look it wore ere when
20   They owned their passiveness.

MAY SARTON (1912–)

The Lady and the Unicorn

The Cluny Tapestries

I am the unicorn and bow my head
You are the lady woven into history
And here forever we are bound in mystery
Our wine, Imagination, and our bread,
5   And I the unicorn who bows his head.

You are all interwoven in my history
And you and I have been most strangely wed
I am the unicorn and bow my head
And lay my wildness down upon your knee
10 You are the lady woven into history.

And here forever we are sweetly wed
With flowers and rabbits in the tapestry
You are the lady woven into history
Imagination is our bridal bed:
15 We lie ghostly upon it, no word said.

Among the flowers of the tapestry
I am the unicorn and by your bed

Cluny Tapestry, *The Lady and the Unicorn (Editorial Photocolor Archives/Alinari)*

Come gently, gently to bow down my head,
Lay at your side this love, this mystery,
20   And call you lady of my tapestry.

I am the unicorn and bow my head
To one so sweetly lost, so strangely wed:

You sit forever under a small formal tree
Where I forever search your eyes to be

25   Rewarded with this shining tragedy
And know your beauty was not cast for me,

Know we are woven all in mystery,
The wound imagined where no one has bled,

My wild love chastened to this history
30   Where I before your eyes, bow down my head.

ROBINSON JEFFERS (1887–1962)

Rock and Hawk

Here is a symbol in which
Many high tragic thoughts
Watch their own eyes.

This gray rock, standing tall
5   On the headland, where the seawind
Lets no tree grow,

Earthquake-proved, and signatured
By ages of storms: on its peak
A falcon has perched.

10   I think, here is your emblem
To hang in the future sky;
Not the cross, not the hive,

But this; bright power, dark peace;
Fierce consciousness joined with final
15   Disinterestedness;

Life with calm death; the falcon's
Realist eyes and act
Married to the massive

Mysticism of stone,
20   Which failure cannot cast down
Nor success make proud.

DELMORE SCHWARTZ (1913–1966)

The Heavy Bear Who Goes with Me

"the withness of the body"
        —Whitehead[3]

The heavy bear who goes with me,
A manifold honey to smear his face,
Clumsy and lumbering here and there,
The central ton of every place,
5   The hungry beating brutish one
In love with candy, anger, and sleep,
Crazy factotum, dishevelling all,
Climbs the building, kicks the football,
Boxes his brother in the hate-ridden city.
10   Breathing at my side, that heavy animal,
That heavy bear who sleeps with me,
Howls in his sleep for a world of sugar,
A sweetness intimate as the water's clasp,
Howls in his sleep because the tight-rope
15   Trembles and shows the darkness beneath.
—The strutting show-off is terrified,
Dressed in his dress-suit, bulging his pants,
Trembles to think that his quivering meat
Must finally wince to nothing at all.

---

[3] Alfred North Whitehead (1861–1947), English mathematician and philosopher.

20   That inescapable animal walks with me,
       Has followed me since the black womb held,
       Moves where I move, distorting my gesture,
       A caricature, a swollen shadow,
       A stupid clown of the spirit's motive,
25   Perplexes and affronts with his own darkness,
       The secret life of belly and bone,
       Opaque, too near, my private, yet unknown,
       Stretches to embrace the very dear
       With whom I would walk without him near,
30   Touches her grossly, although a word
       Would bare my heart and make me clear,
       Stumbles, flounders, and strives to be fed
       Dragging me with him in his mouthing care,
       Amid the hundred million of his kind,
35   The scrimmage of appetite everywhere.

D. H. LAWRENCE (1885–1930)

Snake

A snake came to my water-trough
On a hot, hot day, and I in pyjamas for the heat,
To drink there.

In the deep, strange-scented shade of the great dark carob tree
5   I came down the steps with my pitcher
And must wait, must stand and wait, for there he was at the trough before me.

He reached down from a fissure in the earth-wall in the gloom
And trailed his yellow-brown slackness soft-bellied down, over the edge of the stone
      trough
And rested his throat upon the stone bottom,
10   And where the water had dripped from the tap, in a small clearness,
He sipped with his straight mouth,
Softly drank through his straight gums, into his slack long body,
Silently.

Someone was before me at my water-trough,
15   And I, like a second comer, waiting.

He lifted his head from his drinking, as cattle do,
And looked at me vaguely, as drinking cattle do,
And flickered his two-forked tongue from his lips, and mused a moment,
And stooped and drank a little more,
20   Being earth-brown, earth-golden from the burning bowels of the earth
On the day of Sicilian July, with Etna[4] smoking.

---

[4] Mt. Etna, a volcano in Sicily.

The voice of my education said to me
He must be killed,
For in Sicily the black, black snakes are innocent, the gold are venomous.

25 And voices in me said, If you were a man
You would take a stick and break him now, and finish him off.

But must I confess how I liked him,
How glad I was he had come like a guest in quiet, to drink at my water-trough
And depart peaceful, pacified, and thankless,
30 Into the burning bowels of this earth?

Was it cowardice, that I dared not kill him?
Was it perversity, that I longed to talk to him?
Was it humility, to feel so honoured?
I felt so honoured.

35 And yet those voices:
If you were not afraid, you would kill him!

And truly I was afraid, I was most afraid,
But even so, honoured still more
That he should seek my hospitality
40 From out the dark door of the secret earth.

He drank enough
And lifted his head, dreamily, as one who has drunken,
And flickered his tongue like a forked night on the air, so black,
Seeming to lick his lips,
45 And looked around like a god, unseeing, into the air,
And slowly turned his head,
And slowly, very slowly, as if thrice adream,
Proceeded to draw his slow length curving round
And climb again the broken bank of my wall-face.

50 And as he put his head into that dreadful hole,
And as he slowly drew up, snake-easing his shoulders, and entered farther,
A sort of horror, a sort of protest against his withdrawing into that horrid black
    hole,
Deliberately going into the blackness, and slowly drawing himself after,
Overcame me now his back was turned.

55 I looked around, I put down my pitcher,
I picked up a clumsy log
And threw it at the water-trough with a clatter.

I think I did not hit him,
But suddenly that part of him that was left behind convulsed in undignified haste,
60 Writhed like lightning, and was gone
Into the black hole, the earth-lipped fissure in the wall-front,
At which, in the intense still noon, I stared with fascination.

And immediately I regretted it.
I thought how paltry, how vulgar, what a mean act!
65 I despised myself and the voices of my accursed human education.

And I thought of the albatross,[5]
And I wished he would come back, my snake.

For he seemed to me again like a king,
Like a king in exile, uncrowned in the underworld,
70   Now due to be crowned again.

And so, I missed my chance with one of the lords
Of life.
And I have something to expiate;
A pettiness.

✏️ Tips on Writing about Poetry

When does an image become a symbol? It is helpful to remember that a symbol is always something concrete that stands for something that is abstract, as the rose is a symbol of beauty. If you are in doubt about whether an image in a poem is a symbol, consider first whether or not it is a *traditional* symbol, like the rose in Waller's and Yeats's poems, or the snake in Lawrence's poem. Then consider how much prominence the poet gives it in the poem. If the entire poem concentrates on a single image, and the image has an obvious abstract equivalent, like the live-oak in Whitman's poem, then you have found a "situational" symbol, one that the poem has created.

CHRISTOPHER SMART (1722–1771)

The Ant and the Caterpillar

As an ant, of his talents superiorly vain,
Was trotting with consequence over the plain,
A worm,° in his progress, remarkably slow,   *serpent*
Cry'd, "Bless your good worship, wherever you go?
5   "I hope your great mightiness won't take it ill,
"I pay my respects from an hearty good will."

With a look of contempt, and ineffable pride,
"Begone you vile reptile," his antship reply'd:
"But first—look at me—see—my limbs how complete:
10   "I guide all my motions with freedom and ease;
"I run back and forward, and turn when I please.
"Of nature (grown weary) thou shocking essay!°   *trial specimen*
"I spurn you thus from me;—crawl out of my way."

The reptile insulted, and vex'd to the soul,
15   Crept onwards, and hid himself close in his hole;

---

[5] In Coleridge's "Rime of the Ancient Mariner," the sailor brings a curse upon himself and his ship by senselessly killing an albatross.

But nature determin'd to end his distress,
Soon sent him abroad in a butterfly dress.

Ere long the proud ant was repassing the road,
(Fatigued from the harvest, and tugging his load)
20   The beau° on a violet bank he beheld,   *fop, dandy*
Whose vesture in glory, a monarch excell'd;
His plumage expanded!—'twas rare to behold
So lovely a mixture of purple and gold;
The ant, quite amaz'd at a figure so gay,
25   Bow'd low with respect, and was trudging away:
"Stop, friend," says the butterfly, "don't be surprised;
"I once was the reptile you spurn'd and despis'd;
"But now, I can mount—in the sun-beams I play,
"While you must, forever, drudge on in your way."

The Moral: *A wretch that to-day is o'erloaded with*
sorrow, May soar above those that oppressed him
tomorrow.

GEORGE HERBERT (1593–1633)

Love (III)

Love bade me welcome: yet my soul drew back,
    Guilty of dust and sin.
But quick-eyed Love, observing me grow slack
    From my first entrance in,
5   Drew nearer to me, sweetly questioning
    If I lacked anything.

"A guest," I answered, "worthy to be here":
    Love said, "You shall be he."
"I, the unkind, ungrateful? Ah, my dear,
10   I cannot look on thee."
Love took my hand, and smiling did reply,
    "Who made the eyes but I?"

"Truth, Lord; but I have marred them; let my shame
    Go where it doth deserve."
15   "And know you not," says Love, "who bore the blame?"
    "My dear, then I will serve."
"You must sit down," says Love, "and taste my meat."
    So I did sit and eat.

ROBERT SOUTHWELL (1561–1595)

The Burning Babe

As I in hoary winter's night stood shivering in the snow,
Surprised I was with sudden heat which made my heart to glow;
And lifting up a fearful eye to view what fire was near,

A pretty babe all burning bright did in the air appear;
5   Who, scorchéd with excessive heat, such floods of tears did shed
As though his floods should quench his flames which with his tears were fed.
"Alas," quoth he, "but newly born in fiery heats I fry,
Yet none approach to warm their hearts or feel my fire but I!
My faultless breast the furnace is, the fuel wounding thorns,
10   Love is the fire, and sighs the smoke, the ashes shame and scorns;
The fuel justice layeth on, and mercy blows the coals,
The metal in this furnace wrought are men's defiléd souls,
For which, as now on fire I am to work them to their good,
So will I melt into a bath to wash them in my blood."
15   With this he vanished out of sight and swiftly shrunk away,
And straight I calléd unto mind that it was Christmas day.

EDMUND SPENSER (1552–1599)

One Day As I Unwarily Did Gaze

One day as I unwarily did gaze
On those fayre eyes, my loves immortall light;
The whilest my stonisht hart stood in amaze,
Through sweet illusion of her lookes delight;
5   I mote perceive how, in her glauncing sight,
Legions of Loves with little wings did fly;
Darting their deadly arrows, fyry bright,
At every rash beholder passing by.
One of those archers closely I did spy,
10   Ayming his arrow at my very hart:
When suddenly, with twincle of her eye,
The Damzell broke his misintended dart.
       Had she not so doon, sure I had bene slayne;
       Yet as it was, I hardly scap't with paine.

MARGARET DANNER (1915–)

This Is an African Worm

This is an African worm
but then a worm in any land
is still a worm.

It will not stride, run, stand up
5   before the butterflies, who
have passed their worm-like state.

It must keep low, not lift its head.
I've had the dread experience, I know.
A worm can do no thing but crawl.

10   Crawl, and wait.

10 🌿 More Figures of Speech

Hyperbole

What do we do when we see something more beautiful than we have ever seen? So ugly we can hardly bear to look at it? How do we respond when we hear Pavarotti sing an aria more beautifully than we could have imagined, or see an outfielder make a seemingly impossible catch? Sportswriters, theater reviewers, and poets often respond with a figure of speech called *hyperbole*.

> The man was so fast he could kiss a bullet.
>
> He was so delicate he was knocked unconscious by a snowflake.
>
> The engine was as noisy as a living skeleton having a fit on a hardwood floor.

Hyperbole is an exaggeration, a statement that something has either much more or much less of a quality than it actually has. *Hyperbole*, from the Greek, literally means "to overshoot the mark." Since exaggeration is a principle of comedy, hyperbole is often comic:

> My belly is as cold as if I had swallowed
> snowballs for pills to cool the reins.
>
> —*William Shakespeare*

Although exaggeration is usually achieved through simile and metaphor, there are other forms of hyperbole. For example, we are familiar with hyperbole in the tall tale, a popular American entertainment from the time of the early settlers. Notice the narrative imagery of the following poem. The images are drawn to prove how extreme is the quality to be exaggerated: the hinges on the skyscraper "to let the moon go by" attest to its height. We can picture two or more "liars" sitting around a stove, each trying to come up with the most outlandish exaggerations.

CARL SANDBURG (1878–1967)

They Have Yarns

They have yarns
Of a skyscraper so tall they had to put hinges
On the two top stories so to let the moon go by,
Of one corn crop in Missouri when the roots
5   Went so deep and drew off so much water
The Mississippi riverbed that year was dry,
Of pancakes so thin they had only one side,
Of "a fog so thick we shingled the barn and six feet out on the fog,"
Of Pecos Pete straddling a cyclone in Texas and riding it to the west coast where
     "it rained out under him,"
10   Of the man who drove a swarm of bees across the Rocky Mountains and the Desert
     "and didn't lose a bee,"
Of a mountain railroad curve where the engineer in his cab can touch the caboose
     and spit in the conductor's eye,
Of the boy who climbed a cornstalk growing so fast he would have starved to death
     if they hadn't shot biscuits up to him,
Of the old man's whiskers: "When the wind was with him his whiskers arrived a
     day before he did,"
Of the hen laying a square egg and cackling, "Ouch!" and of hens laying eggs with
     the dates printed on them,
15   Of the ship captain's shadow: it froze to the deck one cold winter night,
Of mutineers on that same ship put to chipping rust with rubber hammers,
Of the sheep counter who was fast and accurate: "I just count their feet and divide
     by four,"
Of the man so tall he must climb a ladder to shave himself,
Of the runt so teeny-weeny it takes two men and a boy to see him,
20   Of mosquitoes: one can kill a dog, two of them a man,
Of a cyclone that sucked cookstoves out of the kitchen, up the chimney flue, and
     on to the next town,
Of the same cyclone picking up wagon-tracks in Nebraska and dropping them over
     in the Dakotas.

Questions

1. What characters of tall tales has Sandburg alluded to in this poem?
2. How has Sandburg exaggerated sizes and heights?
3. How have these exaggerations captured the vastness and vitality of the American spirit?
4. What sorts of exaggerations do you use when bragging to friends about your exploits?

CECCO ANGIOLIERI (c. 1260–c. 1312)

In Absence from Becchina

My heart's so heavy with a hundred things
    That I feel dead a hundred times a-day;
Yet death would be the least of sufferings,

For life's all suffering save what's slept away;
5   Though even in sleep there is no dream but brings
       From dream-land such dull torture as it may.
And yet one moment would pluck out these stings,
       If for one moment she were mine to-day
Who gives my heart the anguish that it has.
10   Each thought that seeks my heart for its abode
          Becomes a wan and sorrow-stricken guest:
Sorrow has brought me to so sad a pass
       That men look sad to meet me on the road;
          Nor any road is mine that leads to rest.

Translation by Dante Gabriel Rossetti (1828–1882)

Questions

1. Is it possible to "feel dead"? Is the poet exaggerating his pain in line 2?
2. What other hyperbole do you find in this poem?

RANDALL JARRELL (1914–1965)

The Mockingbird

Look one way and the sun is going down,
Look the other and the moon is rising.
The sparrow's shadow's longer than the lawn.
The bats squeak: "Night is here"; the birds cheep: "Day is gone."
5   On the willow's highest branch, monopolizing
Day and night, cheeping, squeaking, soaring,
The mockingbird is imitating life.

All day the mockingbird has owned the yard.
As light first woke the world, the sparrows trooped
10   Onto the seedy lawn: the mockingbird
Chased them off shrieking. Hour by hour, fighting hard
To make the world his own, he swooped
On thrushes, thrashers, jays, and chickadees—
At noon he drove away a big black cat.

15   Now, in the moonlight, he sits here and sings.
A thrush is singing, then a thrasher, then a jay—
Then, all at once, a cat begins meowing.
A mockingbird can sound like anything.
He imitates the world he drove away
20   So well that for a minute, in the moonlight,
Which one's the mockingbird? which one's the world?

Questions

1. Granted that shadows lengthen as the sun sets, is it possible that "the sparrow's shadow's longer than the lawn"? If not, why does the speaker exaggerate?
2. Does the mockingbird really "monopolize" day and night? Has he really "owned the

yard"? What does this hyperbole suggest about the importance of the bird to the speaker?

3. What other hyperbole do you find in the poem?
4. Does Jarrell exaggerate the significance of the mockingbird by suggesting he cannot distinguish it from the world?

Understatement

Understatement, or the deliberate avoidance of emphasis in description, is sometimes considered a figure of speech related to hyperbole. In the following excerpt from T. S. Eliot's poem "Aunt Helen" we find an amusing instance of understatement.

> Miss Helen Slingsby was my maiden aunt,
> And lived in a small house near a fashionable square
> Cared for by servants to the number of four.
> Now when she died there was silence in heaven
> And silence at her end of the street.
> The shutters were drawn and the undertaker wiped his feet—
> He was aware this sort of thing had occurred before.

Aware? The undertaker is not only "aware" of death, he is immersed in it, a veritable merchant of death. The delight of understatement is in the effect of verbal irony—we expect the writer to say something extreme, and he surprises us by saying something subtle. Thus understatement is not so much a figure of speech as a tone of voice. We will look at it again in our discussion of tone.

Synecdoche, Metonymy, Allusion, and Paradox

One of the things that distinguishes poetry from prose is the level of concentration of the language. Ezra Pound has written that "great literature is simply language charged with meaning to the utmost possible degree," and that poetry "is the most concentrated form of verbal expression."[1] In the effort to say more with less language, poets sometimes use a word or several words to suggest other words or some larger context of meaning.

Synecdoche

Synecdoche is a figure of speech in which part of a thing is mentioned to suggest the whole thing, or a larger concept is mentioned to suggest something specific. Either way there is a correspondence of information between part and whole that enriches our view of both. Everyday speech is full of synecdoche. When the car breaks down we may say we need "new wheels," although new wheels, without the rest of the car, would be useless. "New wheels" is a livelier expression than "car." When we refer to a sluggish person as "lazybones," we suggest the depth of his or her indolence. When the captain says, "All hands on deck," we know he wants the men as well as their hands, but the word "hands" tells us

---

[1] Ezra Pound, *The ABC of Reading* (New York: New Directions, 1934).

more about what he wants from them. And when, in despair over the loss of her mail, someone says, "My whole world is lost," she is not merely exaggerating; she is using synecdoche, expressing a specific misfortune in terms of a more general one. Robert Frost used to refer to himself as a "synecdochist," meaning that his own little *part* of life was valuable in relation to the *whole* of life.

In the following poem synecdoche is used both to specify poignant incidents and to broaden the implications of detail. The poem is addressed to an old man, presumably a close friend, who is leaving the speaker.

PO CHU-I (A.D. 772–846)

Seeing Hsia Chan Off by River

Because you are old and departing I have wetted my handkerchief,
You who are homeless at seventy, belonging to the wilderness.
Anxiously I watch the wind rising as the boat sails away,
A white-headed man amid white-headed waves.

Translation by Ching Ti

Questions

1. How does the speaker use synecdoche in line 1 to show that he wept?
2. In what way is the phrase "white-headed man" a synecdoche? Would "white-haired man" be synecdoche?
3. What is the emotional force of juxtaposing the white-headed man and the white-headed waves? Does the juxtaposition make the old man look strong? Vulnerable?

 Writers on Writing   *Gwendolyn Brooks*

Poetry is life distilled.

RALPH WALDO EMERSON (1803–1882)

Letters

Every day brings a ship,
Every ship brings a word;
Well for those who have no fear,
Looking seaward well assured
5   That the word the vessel brings
Is the word they wish to hear.

Question

1. How does this poem use synecdoche?

Ralph Waldo Emerson
(Harvard College Library)

Metonymy

Metonymy is a figure of speech in which the name of a person, place, or thing calls forth a more complex structure of things and ideas that the name signifies. Place names work that way. "Vermont" calls forth an image of gentle green hills, maple trees hung with sap buckets, and vivid foliage. When we talk of "New England weather," we may mean clear, cool summer nights, or snowy Januaries. "Texas" evokes flat, windy plains, ten-gallon hats, and oil wells. If you said that someone's manners were "pure Boston prep," people would have a good idea of what you meant. When the television commentator reports on the activities of "Washington," we know he is not merely telling us about the District of Columbia, but about the U.S. government. Likewise, "the Church" signifies the whole complex of organized religion, just as "the crown" signifies the entire government of a monarchy. These are all examples of metonymy, whereby a single name is used as shorthand, for its vividness or sound.

In the following ironic protest poem, practically every noun is used metonymically. We call the poem ironic because the speaker clearly hates what he is praising.

WILLIAM BUTLER YEATS (1865–1939)

The Great Day

Hurrah for revolution and more cannon-shot!
A beggar upon horseback lashes a beggar on foot.
Hurrah for revolution and cannon come again!
The beggars have changed places, but the lash goes on.

Questions

1. What complex of actions and emotions is suggested by the metonymy of "cannon-shot"?
2. What social position is signified by the "beggar upon horseback"? The "beggar on foot"?
3. Is the phrase "on foot" an instance of metonymy, synecdoche, or both?
4. What is the significance of the lash?

The following poem achieves great vividness and a warm intimacy with its subject through the skillful use of synecdoche and metonymy. The Ox Cart Man's life is filled with the sensual pleasures of his merchandise, and Hall uses figures of speech to communicate the richness of the man's experience.

DONALD HALL (1928–)

Ox Cart Man

In October of the year,
he counts potatoes dug from the brown field,
counting the seed, counting
the cellar's portion out,
5   and bags the rest on the cart's floor.

He packs wool sheared in April, honey
in combs, linen, leather
tanned from deerhide,
and vinegar in a barrel
10   hooped by hand at the forge's fire.

He walks by ox's head, ten days
to Portsmouth Market, and sells potatoes,
and the bag that carried potatoes,
flaxseed, birch brooms, maple sugar, goose
15   feathers, yarn.

When the cart is empty he sells the cart.
When the cart is sold he sells the ox,
harness and yoke, and walks
home, his pockets heavy
20   with the year's coin for salt and taxes,

and at home by fire's light in November cold
stitches new harness
for next year's ox in the barn,
and carves the yoke, and saws planks
25   building the cart again.

Questions

1. Locate a synecdoche in stanza 2.
2. Find a synecdoche in stanza 3.

3. Identify a metonymy in stanza 4.
4. Does the Ox Cart Man seem satisfied with his life? What statements in the poem suggest that he is?

JAMES DICKEY (1923–)

Buckdancer's Choice

So I would hear out those lungs,
The air split into nine levels,
Some gift of tongues of the whistler

In the invalid's bed: my mother,
5   Warbling all day to herself
The thousand variations of one song;

It is called Buckdancer's Choice.
For years, they have all been dying
Out, the classic buck-and-wing men

10   Of traveling minstrel shows;
With them also an old woman
Was dying of breathless angina,[2]

Yet still found breath enough
To whistle up in my head
15   A sight like a one-man band,

Freed black, with cymbals at heel,
An ex-slave who thrivingly danced
To the ring of his own clashing light

Through the thousand variations of one song
20   All day to my mother's prone music,
The invalid's warbler's note,

While I crept to the wall
Sock-footed, to hear the sounds alter,
Her tongue like a mockingbird's break

25   Through stratum after stratum of a tone
Proclaiming what choices there are
For the last dancers of their kind,

For ill women and for all slaves
Of death, and children enchanted at walls
30   With a brass-beating glow underfoot,

Not dancing but nearly risen
Through barnlike, theatrelike houses
On the wings of the buck and wing.

---

[2] A painful heart disease.

Questions

1. Vocabulary: *stratum* (25).
2. How many synecdoches can you find in the first stanza?
3. The buck-and-wing is a solo tap dance with a lot of angular arm movement and spring in the knees. The name itself tends to describe the dance. What figure of speech is it?
4. What other examples of synecdoche can you find? Do they make the poem more vivid?
5. Find two examples of metonymy.

Allusion

When American soldiers and sportsmen shout "Remember the Alamo," they are using a form of verbal economy called *allusion*. The Alamo was a mission in Texas that Americans defended with unparalleled valor and persistence during a war with Mexico. Most of us have learned about this in school. Think how awkward it would be for soldiers, in the heat of combat, to cry out, "Remember the mission in Texas that Americans defended with unparalleled valor and persistence. . . ." The allusion conserves energy.

By now we have seen several instances of allusion among our examples of synecdoche and metonymy, for in the general sense an allusion is any reference by word or phrase to something other than the literal meaning. For example, "the lash" is an allusion to tyranny. John Dickey's poem "Buckdancer's Choice" is rich in atmospheric allusion owing to his skillful use of synecdoche. But the term *allusion* is most commonly used in connection with literary references and references to special or technical knowledge. Appropriate allusion deepens the background of a poem—as long as the reader understands the allusion. A poet might add a level of meaning to his poem by introducing it with a fragment from Dante's *Inferno*. But if we have not read the *Inferno*, the poet's scholarship may be lost on us. Poets can educate us if we let them, and it is often worth our while to research their allusions.

ALEXANDER POPE (1688–1744)

Intended for Sir Isaac Newton

Nature and Nature's laws lay hid in night:
God said, "Let Newton be!" and all was light.

This short poem turns on two important allusions. First, there is the allusion to the "laws" of Sir Isaac Newton, the eighteenth-century mathematician who invented calculus and formulated laws of motion that served scientists until the twentieth century. During Pope's time Newton commanded as much awe as Einstein inspires today. Second, there is the allusion to the book of Genesis: "God said, let there be light, and there was light." If you fail to recognize these allusions, the poem's high praise and subtle irony are lost.

Poets do not use allusion simply to show off their special knowledge. Allusion is a way of achieving intimacy by referring the reader to the world from which the poem comes. In the following poem for blues singer Ray Charles, Bob Kaufman evokes the mood and history of Charles's music through allusions to songs and other blues singers. The reference to Kilimanjaro, a mountain in eastern Africa, is an allusion to the African roots of blues music. *I Got a Woman* is one of Ray Charles's most popular songs. "Bessie" is Bessie Smith, the great blues singer, who was killed in an auto accident. Line 6 is literally allusion, referring us to the birth of Athena from the skull of Zeus. The parenthetic " 'way cross town" is a phrase from *I Got a Woman*.

BOB KAUFMAN (1935–)

Blues Note

For Ray Charles's birthday
N.Y.C./1961

Ray Charles is the black wind of Kilimanjaro,
Screaming up-and-down blues,
Moaning happy on all the elevators of my time.

Smiling into the camera, with an African symphony
5   Hidden in his throat, and (*I Got a Woman*) wails, too.

He burst from Bessie's crushed black skull
One cold night outside of Nashville, shouting,
And grows bluer from memory, glowing bluer, still.

At certain times you can see the moon
10   Balanced on his head.

From his mouth he hurls chunks of raw soul.
He separated the sea of polluted sounds
And led the blues into the Promised Land.

Ray Charles is a dangerous man ('way cross town),
15   And I love him.

Questions

1. How does the poet use metaphor in line 1?
2. How does he use allusion in line 13?
3. Does the poet's use of allusion help you to understand his affection for Ray Charles?

Paradox

I may be blind
but I got my eye on you.

—*Paul Shapiro*

Paradox is a statement that at first seems self-contradictory or illogical, but that actually transcends logic to assert a greater truth. The idea of a blind man with his eye on you is bizarre and seems senseless until we consider that many sightless people are highly observant, and that the phrase "I got my eye on you" suggests something more important than literal vision.

> Twenty men crossing a bridge,
> Into a village
> Are twenty men crossing twenty bridges,
> Into twenty villages,
> Or one man
> Crossing a single bridge into a village.
>
> —*Wallace Stevens*

You may readily accept this sentence as a metaphor. But it is also a paradox, rich in philosophical implications. Literally, the sentence seems false. But if we think of it from the viewpoints of twenty men, each one crossing his own bridge, then the first part of the sentence begins to make sense. If each man sees the bridge, that makes twenty viewed bridges. If we think of the *common* vision of the twenty men, then the second part of the paradox begins to make sense—that they are "one man/Crossing a single bridge into a village." This is a sophisticated paradox that explores nothing less than the nature of consciousness, which is both shared and singular.

As an exercise of metaphysical wit, the paradox was very popular during the sixteenth and seventeenth centuries. The clown in Shakespeare's *As You Like It* strikes at the heart of human folly when he says, "The fool doth think he is wise, but the wise man knows himself to be a fool." The world is full of apparent contradictions; paradox is one figure of speech that resolves and delights in them.

GEORGE HERBERT (1593–1663)

Bitter-Sweet

> Ah, my dear angry Lord,
> Since Thou dost love, yet strike;
> Cast down, yet help afford;
> Sure I will do the like.
>
> 5   I will complain, yet praise;
> I will bewail, approve:
> And all my sour-sweet days
> I will lament, and love.

This poem resolves the paradoxes of fortune in religious terms, returning in prayer the mixture of love and wrath that the speaker finds in life. The second line appears illogical until we consider the writer's religious conviction—the Lord strikes him out of love, not to make him suffer but to chasten him. Life must be "bitter-sweet." The phrases "bitter-sweet" and "sour-sweet" are figures of speech called *oxymorons*. An oxymoron, which combines two seemingly contradictory elements, is a form of condensed paradox. Jaques, the great cynic in *As You Like It*, speaks of his "humorous sadness." Shakespeare's sonnets likewise are full of oxymorons; he speaks of "sightless view," the "profitless usurer," and "unseeing eyes." Let us look for paradoxes in one of the sonnets.

WILLIAM SHAKESPEARE (1564–1616)

When Most I Wink, Then Do Mine Eyes Best See

When most I wink, then do mine eyes best see,
For all the day they view things unrespected;°   *unregarded, unseen*
But when I sleep, in dreams they look on thee,
And darkly bright are bright in dark directed.
5   Then thou, whose shadow shadows doth make bright,
How would thy shadow's form form happy show
To the clear day with thy much clearer light,
When to unseeing eyes thy shade shines so!
How would, I say, mine eyes be blessed made
10   By looking on thee in the living day,
When in dead night thy fair imperfect shade
Through heavy sleep on sightless eyes doth stay!
     All days are nights to see till I see thee,
     And nights bright days when dreams do show thee me.

Questions

1. Does the first line appear to be true? How is the paradox made sensible in lines 2–4?
2. Can you find an oxymoron in line 8? How does it make sense?
3. What is the paradox in the final couplet? How does it seem false? What makes it true?

SIMONIDES (c. 556–c. 468 B.C.)

For the Spartan Dead at Plataia (479 B.C.)

These men clothed their land with incorruptible
Glory when they assumed death's misty cloak.
They are not dead in death; the memory
Lives with us, and their courage brings them back.

Translation by Peter Jay

Questions

1. Vocabulary: *incorruptible* (1).
2. Where do you find paradox in this elegy?
3. What other figures of speech can you find in the poem?

✍ Tips on Writing about Poetry

The paradox is one of the most effective tools that language can use to criticize itself, to demonstrate its limits. The most effective way to study a paradox is sometimes called "glossing" the paradox. First, you consider how the statement appears to be false. Then you consider how it transcends self-contradiction in order to assert a higher truth. As you "gloss" paradoxes in your reading and writing about poetry, consider how each paradox demonstrates the imprecision of words, and how the paradox draws extra power from that same "falseness" or ambiguity.

❧ Poems for Further Study

JAMES MERRILL (1926–)

Charles on Fire

Another evening we sprawled about discussing
Appearances. And it was the consensus
That while uncommon physical good looks
Continued to launch one, as before, in life
5   (Among its vaporous eddies and false calms),
Still, as one of us said into his beard,
"Without your intellectual and spiritual
Values, man, you are sunk." No one but squared
The shoulders of his own unloveliness.
10   Long-suffering Charles, having cooked and served the meal,
Now brought out little tumblers finely etched
He filled with amber liquor and then passed.
"Say," said the same young man, "in Paris, France,
They do it this way" — bounding to his feet
15   And touching a lit match to our host's full glass.
A blue flame, gentle, beautiful, came, went
Above the surface. In a hush that fell
We heard the vessel crack. The contents drained
As who should step down from a crystal coach.
20   Steward of spirits, Charles's glistening hand
All at once gloved itself in eeriness.
The moment passed. He made two quick sweeps and
Was flesh again. "It couldn't matter less,"
He said, but with a shocked, unconscious glance
25   Into the mirror. Finding nothing changed,
He filled a fresh glass and sank down among us.

Grief of a Girl's Heart

O Donal Oge, if you go across the sea,
Bring myself with you and do not forget it;
And you will have a sweetheart for fair days and market days,
And the daughter of the King of Greece beside you at night.

5   It is late last night the dog was speaking of you;
The snipe was speaking of you in her deep marsh.
It is you are the lonely bird through the woods;
And that you may be without a mate until you find me.

You promised me, and you said a lie to me,
10   That you would be before me where the sheep are flocked;
I gave a whistle and three hundred cries to you,
And I found nothing there but a bleating lamb.

You promised me a thing that was hard for you,
A ship of gold under a silver mast;
15   Twelve towns with a market in all of them,
And a fine white court by the side of the sea.

You promised me a thing that is not possible,
That you would give me gloves of the skin of a fish;
That you would give me shoes of the skin of a bird;
20   And a suit of the dearest silk in Ireland.

O Donal Oge, it is I would be better to you
Than a high, proud, spendthrift lady:
I would milk the cow; I would bring help to you;
And if you were hard pressed, I would strike a blow for you.

25   You have taken the east from me; you have taken the west from me,
You have taken what is before me and what is behind me;
You have taken the moon, you have taken the sun from me,
And my fear is great that you have taken God from me!

Translation from the Irish by Lady Augusta Gregory (1852–1932)

DYLAN THOMAS (1914–1953)

The Hand That Signed the Paper

The hand that signed the paper felled a city;
Five sovereign fingers taxed the breath,
Doubled the globe of dead and halved a country;
These five kings did a king to death.

5   The mighty hand leads to a sloping shoulder,
The finger joints are cramped with chalk;
A goose's quill has put an end to murder
That put an end to talk.

The hand that signed the treaty bred a fever,
10 And famine grew, and locusts came;
Great is the hand that holds dominion over
Man by a scribbled name.

The five kings count the dead but do not soften
The crusted wound nor stroke the brow;
15 A hand rules pity as a hand rules heaven;
Hands have no tears to flow.

JOHN CROWE RANSOM (1888–1974)

Winter Remembered

Two evils, monstrous either one apart,
Possessed me, and were long and loath at going:
A cry of Absence, Absence, in the heart,
And in the wood the furious winter blowing.

5 Think not, when fire was bright upon my bricks,
And past the tight boards hardly a wind could enter,
I glowed like them, the simple burning sticks,
Far from my cause, my proper heat and center.

Better to walk forth in the frozen air
10 And wash my wound in the snows; that would be healing;
Because my heart would throb less painful there,
Being caked with cold, and past the smart of feeling.

And where I walked, the murderous winter blast
Would have this body bowed, these eyeballs streaming,
15 And though I think this heart's blood froze not fast
It ran too small to spare one drop for dreaming.

Dear love, these fingers that had known your touch,
And tied our separate forces first together,
Were ten poor idiot fingers not worth much,
20 Ten frozen parsnips hanging in the weather.

WELDON KEES (1914–1955)

Aspects of Robinson

Robinson at cards at the Algonquin[3]; a thin
Blue light comes down once more outside the blinds.
Gray men in overcoats are ghosts blown past the door.
The taxis streak the avenues with yellow, orange, and red.
5 This is Grand Central,[4] Mr. Robinson.

---

[3] A hotel in mid-town Manhattan.
[4] Grand Central train station in New York City.

Robinson on a roof above the Heights; the boats
Mourn like the lost. Water is slate, far down.
Through sounds of ice cubes dropped in glass, an osteopath,
Dressed for the links, describes an old Intourist tour.
10   —Here's where old Gibbons jumped from, Robinson.

Robinson walking in the Park, admiring the elephant.
Robinson buying the *Tribune*, Robinson buying the *Times*, Robinson
Saying, "Hello. Yes, this is Robinson. Sunday
At five? I'd love to. Pretty well. And you?"
15   Robinson alone at Longchamps, staring at the wall.

Robinson afraid, drunk, sobbing Robinson
In bed with a Mrs. Morse. Robinson at home;
Decisions: Toynbee[5] or luminol? Where the sun
Shines, Robinson in flowered trunks, eyes toward
20   The breakers. Where the night ends, Robinson in East Side bars.

Robinson in Glen plaid jacket, Scotch-grain shoes,
Black four-in-hand° and oxford button-down,   *necktie*
The jeweled and silent watch that winds itself, the brief-
Case, covert topcoat, clothes for spring, all covering
25   His sad and usual heart, dry as a winter leaf.

SAMUEL TAYLOR COLERIDGE (1772–1834)

Pity

Sweet Mercy! how my very heart has bled
    To see thee, poor Old Man! and thy grey hairs
    Hoar with the snowy blast: while no one cares
To clothe thy shrivell'd limbs and palsied head.
5   My Father! throw away this tatter'd vest
    That mocks thy shivering! take my garment—use
    A young man's arm! I'll melt these frozen dews
That hang from thy white beard and numb thy breast.
My Sara too shall tend thee, like a child:
10   And thou shalt talk, in our fireside's recess,
    Of purple Pride, that scowls on Wretchedness.—
He did not so, the Galilaean mild,
Who met the Lazars° turn'd from rich men's doors   *lepers*
And call'd them Friends, and heal'd their noisome sores!

CHIDIOCK TICHBORNE (1558?—1586)

Elegy, Written with His Own Hand in the Tower Before His Execution

My prime of youth is but a frost of cares,
    My feast of joy is but a dish of pain,

---

5 Arnold Joseph Toynbee, a twentieth-century Catholic historian and educator.

My crop of corn is but a field of tares,°   *weeds*
    And all my good is but vain hope of gain:
5   The day is past, and yet I saw no sun,
    And now I live, and now my life is done.

My tale was heard, and yet it was not told,
    My fruit is fall'n, and yet my leaves are green,
My youth is spent; and yet I am not old,
10   I saw the world, and yet I was not seen:
My thread is cut, and yet it is not spun,
And now I live, and now my life is done.

I sought my death, and found it in my womb,
    I looked for life, and saw it was a shade,
15 I trod the earth, and knew it was my tomb,
        And now I die, and now I was but made:
My glass is full, and now my glass is run,
And now I live, and now my life is done.

JOHN ASHBERY (1927–)

Paradoxes and Oxymorons

This poem is concerned with language on a very plain level.
Look at it talking to you. You look out a window
Or pretend to fidget. You have it but you don't have it.
You miss it, it misses you. You miss each other.

5   The poem is sad because it wants to be yours, and cannot.
What's a plain level? It is that and other things,
Bringing a system of them into play. Play?
Well, actually, yes, but I consider play to be

A deeper outside thing, a dreamed role-pattern,
10 As in the division of grace these long August days
Without proof. Open-ended. And before you know
It gets lost in the steam and chatter of typewriters.

It has been played once more. I think you exist only
To tease me into doing it, on your level, and then you aren't there
15 Or have adopted a different attitude. And the poem
Has set me softly down beside you. The poem is you.

11 ❦ The Music of Poetry

Poetry is the rhythmical creation of beauty in words.

To the best of our knowledge, the earliest poetry was sung or chanted—by priestesses and priests in the temple, by bards in the court, and by actors on stage. In fact, the separation of poetry from music is a relatively recent phenomenon in the long history of literature. Surely poetry and melody arise from similar impulses. Ezra Pound has observed the historical interaction of these arts: "Music begins to atrophy when it departs too far from dance; poetry begins to atrophy when it gets too far from music."

All language is musical to some degree, from the vendor's street cry to the lawyer's plea to the orations of senators. All language has rhythm and pitch. But the rhythm and pitch of poetry is so intensified that it contributes an entire dimension of meaning to the language. The music of poetry can be so powerful and precise that some listeners can feel the basic emotion of a poem in a foreign language, even if they have no previous knowledge of that language.

Rhythm

The human voice is a musical instrument of great range and sensitivity. As we pronounce words and sentences, the voice rises and falls, growing louder and softer according to what is being communicated, and its urgency. In this the voice resembles all rhythmic movements in nature—the crests and hollows of waves, the rise and fall of daylight, the beating of the heart. The force gathers, exerts itself, and then subsides. In English poetry, rhythm comes from a certain regularity of stress on syllables. Notice how regularly the stresses occur in this memorable nursery rhyme.

> Péter, Péter, púmpkin éater,
> Hád a wífe and coúldn't kéep her.

For the sake of contrast let us read a sentence of editorial prose, marking the stresses.

As thís is wrítten, Wáll Stréet hás the jítters.
It máy be a pássing pháse and soón cúred.

Of course, most poetry is not as regular as a nursery rhyme, nor is all prose as haphazard in its rhythms as the editorial excerpt suggests. But it is apparent that in the more musical passage the stresses occur more regularly.

Accent and Emphasis

Two kinds of stress occur in speech: the stress of accents within a word, and the stress of emphasis on a word within a sentence. Thus in the nursery rhyme the stress on the first syllable of *Peter* is a stress of accent. The stress on the word *had* in the second line is due to emphasis on the word in the whole sentence.

As you listen to conversations, you will notice that usually the words and syllables that carry the most meaning are stressed, whereas the other syllables are relatively obscure. There is a good reason for this. The prominent syllable of a word is stressed because it usually contains the main idea. Thus: in-débt-ed-ness. Here the accented syllable, *debt*, is the root idea of the word. Our attention, though directed to this syllable, must also carry the other syllables that modify its meaning. This same principle applies to words in a sentence. Certain words are more important than others and are emphasized by the stress of voice, but we must not lose the meaning of the unstressed words.

Listening to the strong, important syllables and words and to the weak ones at the same time requires effort. This effort has its limits. For instance, it is difficult to hear more than two unaccented syllables attached to a stressed one, either before or after it. Poets are keenly aware of these limits, and a poet with a good ear places the stresses in his lines with great care for the listener's attention.

Scansion is the designation of stressed and unstressed syllables in a poem.

Ĭ stóod ĭn Vénicĕ, oń thĕ Brídge ŏf Síghs;
Ă pálăce ănd ă prísŏn oń eăch hánd:
Ĭ sáw frŏm oút thĕ wáve hĕr strúctŭres ríse
Aŭ frŏm thĕ stróke ŏf thĕ enchántĕr's wánd . . .

Scanning a poem is a way of determining what kind of rhythm the poem has. The stresses of accent are determined by the usage of the time, so we may look in the dictionary to find out which syllables to accent within a word. But the stress of emphasis on words depends on the voice of the poet and the reader. Not all of us will scan a particular poem in the same way. For instance, in the last line just scanned, we did not stress the word *the* preceding *enchanter's*. Another reader might have stressed it. When scanning a poem, it is helpful to read it aloud in your most natural voice, in order to hear where the stresses fall.

Exercise

Scan the following fragments of poetry, reading them aloud as you mark the stresses.

1. We sweetly curtsied each to each
   And deftly danced a saraband.

2. When the game began between them for a jest,
   He played king and she played queen to match the best;
   Laughter soft as tears, and tears that turned to laughter,
   These were things she sought for years and sorrowed after.

3. Simple and fresh and fair from winter's close emerging,
   As if no artifice of fashion, business, politics, had ever been,
   Forth from its sunny nook of sheltered grass—
        innocent, golden, calm as the dawn,
   The spring's first dandelion shows its trustful face.

Questions

1. Which of the foregoing passages has the most regular rhythm? The least?
2. In scanning the lines, you see that some have more stresses due to accent, whereas others have more stresses due to emphasis. Which passage depends more on accents for its rhythm? Which depends more on the emphasis on words?

Meter

When stresses occur with sufficient regularity in a poem, the result is called *meter*. Meter is the measuring of stresses in a line of verse, determining their number and placement.

The unit of meter is called a *foot*. A metrical foot usually consists of a stressed syllable and one or two unstressed syllables that precede or follow it. A line with a single foot is called *monometer*. A line with two feet is called *dimeter*; with three, *trimeter*; with four, *tetrameter*; with five, *pentameter*; with six, *hexameter*; with seven, *heptameter*; and with eight feet, *octometer*.

There are four principal kinds of feet in American and English verse. The most common is the *iambic* foot, where the stressed syllable is preceded by one unstressed, as in the word *surprise*.

But now | secure | the paint | ed ves | sel glides,

The sun | beams trem | bling on | the float | ing tides;

While melt | ing mu | sic steals | upon | the sky,

And soft | en'd sounds | along | the wat | ers die;

The foregoing verses by Pope are written in *iambic pentameter*, which has been called the staff of English verse. Unrhymed iambic pentameter is also called *blank verse*. Iambics are steady and natural, and a great deal of spoken and written English—prose as well as poetry—falls easily into iambic rhythm.

When the stress comes first, followed by an unaccented syllable, the foot is called a *trochee*:

Spláshĭng
Dáshĭng.

These two lines illustrate trochaic monometer. Here is an example of trochaic
tetrameter:

Hé wăs | próudĕr | thán thĕ | dévĭl:
Hŏw hĕ | múst hăve | cúrsĕd oŭr | révĕl!

The trochee is livelier than the iamb—the effect of putting the stressed syllable
first is sometimes described as *falling rhythm*, because one "falls" more quickly
from a point of stress to an unaccented syllable. It is slightly more of an effort
for the voice to move from unstressed to stressed syllables, which is why iambic
rhythm is called "rising rhythm."

The *anapest* is a foot with two unstressed syllables followed by a stressed one,
as in the word *intervéne*. The anapest is a rising rhythm, but it is more rapid
than the iamb because of the greater number of unstressed syllables. Here is a
sample of anapestic trimeter:

Frŏm thĕ cén | tĕr aĬl róund | tŏ thĕ séa
Ĭ ăm lórd | ŏf thĕ fówl | ănd thĕ brúte.

You may remember the galloping rhythms of Browning's poem "How We
Brought the Good News from Ghent to Aix," which depend on the anapest for
their speed and strength. The following is a description of the hero's horse:

Ănd hĭs lów | heăd ănd crést, | jŭst onĕ shárp | eăr bĕnt báck
Fŏr mў vóice, | ănd thĕ óth | ĕr prickĕd oút | ŏn hĭs tráck;
Ănd onĕ eўe's | bláck | intĕĬl | ĭgencĕ,—év | ĕr thăt gláncĕ
O'ĕr ĭts whíte | édge | ăt mé, | hĭs ówn măs | tĕr, askáncĕ!

The *dactyl* is a foot that begins with a stressed syllable, followed by two
unstressed syllables, as in the word *délĭcăte*, is a falling rhythm, the most rapid
and lively of English meters.

SONG
Heŕe's tŏ thĕ | máid ŏf | báshfŭl fíf | téen;
Heŕe's tŏ thĕ | wídŏw ŏf | fíftў;
Heŕe's tŏ thĕ | fláuntĭng éx | trávăgănt | quéen
Ănd heŕe's | tŏ thĕ hoúse | wĭfe thăt's | thríftў.

Notice that the poem is not all dactyls, but the dactylic foot is prominent and
gives the poem its momentum. The same is true for the following lines:

Cleárlў thĕ | blúe | rívĕr | chímes ĭn ĭts | flówĭng
Úndĕr mў | eўe;
Wármlў ănd | broádlў thĕ | sóuth wĭnds ăre | blówĭng
Ovĕr thĕ | ský.

In addition to the four principal feet—the iamb, the trochee, the anapest, and the dactyl—there are two other feet worth mentioning. The *spondee* is a unit of rhythm of double movement, in which both syllables are accented, as in the word ámén.

Roll ón | thóu deép | aňd dárk blúe | oćeaň, | róll.

The spondee is a rhythmic unit of great weight and solemnity.

Because of the frequency of particles in English grammar, the unit of rhythm occasionally loses its stress. When that happens, we get the *pyrrhic* foot.

Ĭ wór | shĭpped tȟe | iňvís | ĭbĭe | ălóne.

All this terminology is useful in describing poetic rhythm. But it is more important to understand a few principles of metrics that underlie centuries of versification. Since poetry is not a science, these generalizations have their exceptions; but they will be useful in comprehending why the different feet are used.

Generally, the more stresses in a metric line, the slower the line moves. That is why the spondee creates a mood of gravity.

Tȟe loňg | dáy waňes; | tȟe slów | móon clímbs; | tȟe deép
Moáns róund | wĭth mán | y̆ vói | cȇs.

That is a good rhythm for a stately meditation—but not for a wedding celebration. For a mirthful poem the poet will have fewer stresses per line, a faster rhythm with dactyls or anapests.

Riďe ă coȟck | hórse tŏ | Bánbŭry̆ | Cŕoss
Tŏ | śee aň oȟld | wómaň gȇt | úp oň her | horse.
Riňgs oň her | fíngȇrs, aňd | bélls oň her | tóes,
Shé shȧll hăve | músĭc wher | évȇr sȟe | goés.

Of course, most poetry is neither funereal nor merry. That explains the predominance of the iambic and trochaic lines, with their balance between stressed and unstressed syllables.

The so-called falling rhythms—trochaic and dactylic—are more rapid, respectively, than the rising rhythms—iambic and anapestic. As we have observed, this is the result of greater ease in moving from stressed to unstressed syllables.

Since we tend to pause at the end of a line of poetry, the shorter the lines, the slower the movement of the poem. All other things being equal, dimeter puts much more stress on individual words than does tetrameter, and pentameter slightly more than hexameter.

In the following lines, notice how Tennyson changes the line length and foot to vary rhythm. He poses the question of the first section with deliberate spondees and forceful dactyls. The dimeter of this section makes for a constrained opening, which breaks into lively trochaic and anapestic tetrameter in the second section.

ALFRED, LORD TENNYSON (1809–1892)

The Mermaid

I

Who would be
A mermaid fair,
Singing alone,
Combing her hair
Under the sea,
In a golden curl
With a comb of pearl,
On a throne?

II

I would be a mermaid fair;
I would sing to myself the whole of the day;
With a comb of pearl I would comb my hair;
And still as I comb'd I would sing and say,
"Who is it loves me? who loves not me?"
I would comb my hair till my ringlets would fall,
      Low adown, low adown,
From under my starry sea-bud crown
      Low adown and around
And I should look like a fountain of gold
      Springing alone
      With a shrill inner sound,
      Over the throne
      In the midst of the hall;
Till that great sea-snake under the sea
From his coiled sleeps in the central deeps
Would slowly trail himself sevenfold
Round the hall where I sate, and look in at the gate
With his large calm eyes for the love of me.
And all the mermen under the sea
Would feel their immortality
Die in their hearts for the love of me.

III

But at night I would wander away, away,
    I would fling on each side my low-flowing locks,
And lightly vault from the throne and play
    With the mermen in and out of the rocks;
We would run to and fro, and hide and seek,
    On the broad sea-wolds° in the crimson shells,   *sea-forests*
    Whose silvery spikes are nighest the sea.
But if any came near I would call, and shriek,
And adown the steep like a wave I would leap
    From the diamond-ledges that jut from the dells;
For I would not be kiss'd by all who would list,
Of the bold merry mermen under the sea;

They would sue° me, and woo me, and flatter me,   *pay suit to*
In the purple twilights under the sea;
45   But the king of them all would carry me,
Woo me, and win me, and marry me,
In the branching jaspers under the sea;
Then all the dry pied° things that be   *many-colored*
In the hueless mosses under the sea
50   Would curl round my silver feet silently,
All looking up for the love of me.
And if I should carol aloud, from aloft
All things that are forked, and horned, and soft
Would lean out from the hollow sphere of the sea,
55   All looking down for the love of me.

Samuel Taylor Coleridge composed the following lines as an aid to memory of the metrical units:

Trochee trips from long to short;°   *stressed to unstressed*
From long to long in solemn sort
Slow Spondee stalks, strong foot, yet ill able
Ever to come up with Dactyl trisyllable.
Iambics march from short to long;
With a leap and a bound the swift Anapests throng.

If you scan these lines you will see that each one illustrates the metrical unit it describes.

Students of meter should bear in mind that meter does not create the rhythms of poetry. The rhythms arise out of the poet's emotion, just as do images and figures of speech. Metrical scansion is the measuring of regular rhythms after they have occurred, and consciousness of meter is not a prerequisite for composition.

Exercise

Scan the following lines. Describe the line length as monometer, dimeter, trimeter, and so on. Then characterize the metrical units as iambic, trochaic, anapestic, dactylic, spondaic, and pyrrhic. Which lines are liveliest? Most forceful? Which lines seem most solemn? Which are the most sprightly? What other words can you use to describe the moods rhythm instills?

1. Come live with me and be my love
   And we will all the pleasures prove
   That valleys, groves, hills and fields
   Woods or steepy mountain yields.

2. Let us swear an oath and keep it with an equal mind.

3. Dear my friend and fellow student, I would lean my spirit o'er you.

4. If they rob us of name and pursue us with beagles,
   Give their roof to the flame and their flesh to the eagles.

5. And now the storm-blast came, and he
   Was tyrannous and strong;
   He struck with his o'ertaking wings
   And chased us south along.

6. Has any here an old gray Mare
   With three legs all her store,
   O put it to her Buttocks bare
   And straight she'll run on four.

7. Just for a handful of silver he left us,
   Just for a riband° to stick in his coat—   *ribbon of honor*
   Found the one gift of which fortune bereft us,
   Lost all the others she lets us devote . . .

8. Solomon Grundy
   Born on Monday,
   Christened on Tuesday,
   Married on Wednesday,
   Took ill on Thursday,
   Worse on Friday,
   Died on Saturday,
   Buried on Sunday.
   This is the end
   Of Solomon Grundy.

9. If I did take your kingdom from your sons,
   To make amends, I'll give it to your daughter.
   If I have killed the issue of your womb,
   To quicken your increase I will beget
   Mine issue of your blood upon your daughter:
   A grandam's name is little less in love
   Than in the doting title of a mother . . .

The Line and Line Endings

One of the more obvious features of poetry is that it is usually written in lines, or verses, and that each line functions as a rhythmic and sense unit. Charles Olson has suggested that the line length corresponds to the poet's breathing; thus Walt Whitman and Homer wrote long lines because they had prodigious energy and took deep breaths before uttering their epic verses. Whatever the case, the line certainly provides rhythmic opportunities unavailable in prose. We have already observed that shorter lines concentrate our attention on individual words and images.

> There is a spell, for instance
> in every sea-shell.
>   —H. D. (Hilda Doolittle)

We have also remarked that the way lines begin—with stressed or unstressed syllables—often determines the thrust of the line, as we naturally move more quickly from a stressed to an unstressed syllable.

The line ending is equally important in controlling the poem's rhythmic movement. Lines that end with a stressed word or syllable, sometimes called a *masculine ending*, come to a more resolute pause than those that end with an unstressed syllable or *feminine ending*. In the following verses, notice that the masculine endings seem to gather up the sense of the line, contain it, and pause before the poem moves on. The feminine endings leave us with a slight sense of irresolution that urges us on to the next line.

ALGERNON CHARLES SWINBURNE (1837–1909)

Rococo[1]

Take hand and part with laughter;
    Touch lips and part with tears;
Once more and no more after,
    Whatever comes with years.
5 We twain° shall not remeasure   *two*
    The ways that left us twain;
Nor crush the lees° of pleasure   *dregs*
    From sanguine grapes of pain.

We twain once well in sunder,°   *separated*
10   What will the mad gods do
For hate with me, I wonder,
    Or what for love with you?
Forget them till November,
    And dream there's April yet,
15 Forget that I remember,
    And dream that I forget.

Time found our tired love sleeping,
    And kissed away his breath;
But what should we do weeping,
20   Though light love sleep to death?
We have drained his lips at leisure,
    Till there's not left to drain
A single sob of pleasure,
    A single pulse of pain.

25 Dream that the lips once breathless
    Might quicken if they would;
Say that the soul is deathless;
    Dream that the gods are good;
Say March may wed September,
30   And time divorce regret;
But not that you remember,
    And not that I forget.

We have heard from hidden places
    What love scarce lives and hears:

---

[1] Elaborate design; works of art of the "mannerist" period or late baroque.

35   We have seen on fervent faces
         The pallor of strange tears:
     We have trod the wine-vats treasure,
         Whence ripe to steam and stain,
     Foams round the feet of pleasure
40   The blood-red must° of pain.   *juice*

     Remembrance may recover
         And time bring back to time
     The name of your first lover,
         The ring of my first rhyme;
45   But rose-leaves of December
         The frosts of June shall fret,
     The day that you remember,
         The day that I forget.

     The snake that hides and hisses
50   In heaven we twain have known;
     The grief of cruel kisses,
         The joy whose mouth makes moan;
     The pulses pause and measure,
         Where in one furtive vein
55   Throbs through the heart of pleasure
         The purpler blood of pain.

     We have done with tears and treasons
         And love for treason's sake;
     Room for the swift new seasons,
60   The years that burn and break,
     Dismantle and dismember
         Men's days and dreams, Juliette;
     For love may not remember,
         But time will not forget.

65   Life treads down love in flying,
         Time withers him at root;
     Bring all dead things and dying,
         Reaped sheaf and ruined fruit,
     Where, crushed by three days' pressure
70   Our three days' love lies slain;
     And earlier leaf of pleasure,
         And latter flower of pain.

     Breathe close upon the ashes,
         It may be flame will leap;
75   Unclose the soft close lashes,
         Lift up the lids and weep.
     Light love's extinguished ember,
         Let one tear leave it wet
     For one that you remember
80   And ten that you forget.

Swinburne is often praised for his mastery of classical meters and the lilting, songlike ease of his versification. This lies as much in his imaginative variations as in his adherence to the pattern. The line length is fairly strict trimeter. It is the fashioning of line openings and endings, the alternation of rising and falling rhythms, that give the poem its life. A poem with only masculine endings, or unrelieved trochaic trimeter, would be monotonous and slow by comparison.

Reading the poem aloud, you will notice that the lines usually end where the sense of the sentence requires a pause. If the poem were printed as prose, the reader would naturally pause in those places. Many of those pauses coincide with commas, semicolons, and periods. Any line that ends where the sentence calls for a grammatical pause is called an *end-stopped* line. The first four lines of "Rococo" are end-stopped:

> Take hand and part with laughter,
>   Touch lips and part with tears;
> Once more and no more after,
>   Whatever comes with years.

A line that ends before the sentence does, or before a pause is demanded by the sense, is called a *run-on* line. There is an example in lines 5 and 6 of "Rococo":

> We twain shall not remeasure
>   The ways that left us twain;

This running over of the sense unit from line to line is called *enjambment*. Again, this offers pleasant relief in a poem in which most of the lines are end-stopped.

When a poem is composed of long lines, there is sometimes a natural pause *within* the line.

> Gone—faded out of the story, | | the sea-faring friend I remember?
> Gone for a decade, they say: | | never a word or a sign.
> Gone with his hard red face | | that only his laughter could wrinkle,
> Down where men go to be still, | | by the old way of the sea.

Caesura is a grammatical or natural pause occurring within a line of poetry. The hexameters in the preceding poem might have been broken down into trimeters. But the poet, Edwin Arlington Robinson, has chosen the longer line with caesura to hasten the telling of his story.

EDNA ST. VINCENT MILLAY (1892–1950)

Recuerdo°   *I recall*

> We were very tired, we were very merry—
> We had gone back and forth all night on the ferry.
> It was bare and bright, and smelled like a stable—
> But we looked into a fire, we leaned across a table,

We lay on a hill-top underneath the moon;
     And the whistles kept blowing, and the dawn came soon.

     We were very tired, we were very merry—
     We had gone back and forth all night on the ferry;
     And you ate an apple, and I ate a pear,
10   From a dozen of each we had bought somewhere;
     And the sky went wan, and the wind came cold,
     And the sun rose dripping, a bucketful of gold.

     We were very tired, we were very merry,
     We had gone back and forth all night on the ferry.
15   We hailed, "Good morrow, mother!" to a shawl-covered head.
     And bought a morning paper, which neither of us read;
     And she wept, "God bless you!" for the apples and pears,
     And we gave her all our money but our subway fares.

Questions

1. Scan the poem, indicating the caesuras.
2. Which lines have masculine endings? Which have feminine endings? Do you see a pattern? If so, how does it contribute to the music of the poem?
3. What is the basic line length? Is it consistent?
4. From the number of caesuras, do you think one might cast the poem in shorter lines? How would that alter the rhythm?

Syllabic Verse

In an effort to break out of the strictures of traditional metrics without wholly abandoning predictable form, certain poets have adopted a metrical system called *syllabic verse*. Originating in Oriental and French poetry, syllabic verse counts syllables instead of accents in a line. From Chapter 7, you are familiar with the haiku, the Japanese syllabic form with seventeen syllables—five in the first line, seven in the second, and five again in the third.

> I must go begging
> for water . . . morning glories
> have captured my well.
> —From *Cricket Songs: Japanese Haiku*

By counting syllables, the poet gives shape to the poem without relying on strong rhythmic emphasis. The result is a quieter, more syncopated rhythm that still has a certain predictability of line length.

MARIANNE MOORE (1887–1972)

Nevertheless

> you've seen a strawberry
>   that's had a struggle; yet
>   was, where the fragments met,

Marianne Moore (*National Portrait Gallery, Smithsonian Institution, Washington, D.C.*)

a hedgehog or a star-
5   fish for the multitude
        of seeds. What better food

than apple-seeds—the fruit
        within the fruit—locked in
        like counter-curved twin

10 hazel-nuts? Frost that kills
        the little rubber-plant-
        leaves of *kok-saghyz*-stalks, can't

harm the roots; they still grow
        in frozen ground. Once where
15   there was a prickly-pear-

leaf clinging to barbed wire,
        a root shot down to grow
        in earth two feet below;

as carrots form mandrakes
20   or a ram's-horn root some-
        times. Victory won't come

to me unless I go
        to it; a grape-tendril
        ties a knot in knots till

25 knotted thirty times,—so
        the bound twig that's under-
        gone and over gone, can't stir.

The weak overcomes its
    meance, the strong over-
30   comes itself. What is there

like fortitude! What sap
    went through that little thread
    to make the cherry red!

Questions

1. Count the number of syllables in each line. What is the usual number of syllables per line?
2. Two lines of the poem break the pattern. One is slightly shorter, and one is slightly longer. Find those lines.
3. Where the poem breaks the pattern, do you see a justification in the meaning? Explain.

 ### Writers on Writing   Marianne Moore

In a poem the words should be as pleasing to the ear as the meaning is to the mind.

Rhyme

Many great poems do not use rhyme. Languages that are rich in rhyme words, such as French and Italian, use rhyme frequently; the classical Latin and Greek poets used it rarely, if at all. Verses that have little to offer *except* rhyme, such as greeting card sentiments and advertising jingles, are not dignified by the term poetry. We call them *doggerel*.

Poems that use rhyme depend on the rhyme words for structure, resolution, and tonal effects. The similarity of sounds is striking to the ear and serves as an aid to memory as well as an incitement of the reader's expectations.

ROBERT CREELEY (1926–)

If You

If you were going to get a pet
what kind of animal would you get.

A soft bodied dog, a hen—
feathers and fur to begin it again.

5   When the sun goes down and it gets dark
I saw an animal in a park.

Bring it home, to give it to you.
I have seen animals break in two.

You were hoping for something soft
10   and loyal and clean and wondrously careful—

a form of otherwise vicious habit
can have long ears and be called a rabbit.

Dead. Died. Will die. Want.
Morning, midnight. I asked you

15   if you were going to get a pet
what kind of animal would you get.

These intimate and deceptively simple verses by Robert Creeley have a remarkable appeal to readers of all ages. Much of this appeal can be attributed to the charm of rhyme. The first two lines rhyme at the end; this is called *end rhyme*. When a poem begins thus, with a rhymed couplet, the poem has created an expectation of rhyme. This expectation is satisfied in line 4, with the end rhyme of *again* with *hen*. By the time we get to line 5, a *rhyme scheme* has been established; the poem leads us on by our curiosity to discover the next rhyme word. This anticipation is not entirely conscious, for we are probably more concerned with the poem's sense. It is a musical anticipation, and the more effective because it works partly on an unconscious level.

    Creeley breaks the pattern in line 10. We are waiting for the rhyme to come in line 10, but it doesn't. Why not? Look at the sense of lines 9 and 10.

You were hoping for something soft,
and loyal and clean and wondrously careful—

He is talking about hope, and creating a mystery in these lines. The reader is waiting for an answer. What kind of animal are we hoping for? We are denied the resolution of rhyme because we are also being denied the answer to the question. This is a perfect adaptation of form to content. We get the rhyme when we get the answer.

a form of otherwise vicious habit
can have long ears and be called a rabbit.

When the rhyme at last comes, it is a more elaborate, outrageous rhyme than we have yet heard, and well worth the wait. All the other rhymes have been *masculine rhymes*, with the similarity of sounds falling on the last syllable. This last is a *feminine rhyme*, one where the similarity of sounds is in both of the last two syllables. Feminine rhyme is more noticeable than masculine rhyme and is often used to develop a comic tone (see Chapter 12 on tones of voice).

    Lines 13 and 14 challenge the rhyme scheme again, and again we see the connection of form and content. The tone of the poem has turned suddenly grave, from a discussion of pets to a meditation on death, and the lack of an immediate rhyme word suits the tone change. Also notice that line 14 has a rhyming antecedent in lines 7 and 8. The poet has not wholly abandoned rhyme, but he has attenuated its resolution in these lines. Thus the resolution is all the more satisfying when it comes in the closing couplet.

The best rhymes come naturally and seem inevitable without losing a certain freshness or surprise.

W. H. AUDEN (1907–1973)

Fleet Visit

The sailors come ashore
Out of their hollow ships,
Mild-looking middle class boys
Who read the comic strips;
5   One baseball game is more
To them than fifty Troys.

They look a bit lost, set down
In this unamerican place
Where natives pass with laws
10   And futures of their own;
They are not here because
But only just-in-case.

The whore and ne'er-do-well
Who pester them with junk
15   In their grubby ways at least
Are serving the Social Beast;
They neither make nor sell—
No wonder they get drunk.

But their ships on the vehement° blue   *powerful*
20   Of this harbour actually gain
From having nothing to do;
Without a human will
To tell them whom to kill
Their structures are humane

25   And, far from looking lost,
Look as if they were meant
To be pure abstract design
By some master of pattern and line,
Certainly worth every cent
30   Of the billions they must have cost.

The characterization of these young sailors, in the first stanza, is cast in rhymes as original and fresh as the context in which Auden sees them. Emerging from the "hollow ships" (an allusion to Greek vessels), the boys remind Auden of the great classical mariners. Yet they are still boys, readers of comic strips. Thus we hear the rhyming and concomitant association of *ships* and *strips*, *boys* and

Troys—fresh unpredictable rhymes that are nevertheless natural in the context, seemingly effortless.

Rhyme is reflexive. It joins not only words with similar sounds, but the things and ideas to which the words refer. Notice the witty closing of stanza 2 and how the rhyme words reinforce the meaning.

> They look a bit lost, set down
> In this unamerican place
> Where natives pass with laws
> And futures of their own;
> They are not here because
> But only just-in-case.

The natives have their own futures and *laws*. Yet the sailors are not here *because* of any specific destiny or lawful purpose. The navy does not belong in this *unamerican place*. They are here *just-in-case* they are needed. The rhymes— *laws* and *because*, *place* and *just-in-case*—are surprising ones that underscore the anomaly of the sailors' presence.

In "Fleet Visit" Auden employs both *exact rhyme* and *near rhyme*. Exact rhyme occurs when rhyme words have the same vowel sounds, and the consonant ending, if there is one, is identical. *Blue* and *do*, in stanza 4, are exact rhymes, as are *will* and *kill*, *gain* and *humane*. Near rhyme, also called *off rhyme* and *partial rhyme*, occurs when the vowel sound is different but the consonant is identical, as in *down* and *own*, *laws* and *because*. Near rhyme is not a defect, but a pleasant variation of rhyme.

Most rhyme comes at the end of lines and is called *end rhyme*. All the rhymes in "Fleet Visit" are end rhymes. When rhymes fall within the line, they are called *internal rhymes*.

> Come live within me, said the waterfall.
> There is a chamber of black stone
> High and dry behind my stunning life,
> Stay here a year or two, a year or ten,
> Until you've heard it all,
> The inside story deafening but true.
> —James Merrill

The internal rhyming of *high* and *dry* in line 3 and of *here* and *year* in line 4 helps to establish the resonance of the waterfall. Notice how smoothly Robert Frost uses end rhyme in the following poem.

ROBERT FROST (1874–1963)

The Road Not Taken

> Two roads diverged in a yellow wood,
> And sorry I could not travel both

And be one traveler, long I stood
And looked down one as far as I could
5   To where it bent in the undergrowth;

Then took the other, as just as fair,
And having perhaps the better claim,
Because it was grassy and wanted wear;
Though as for that the passing there
10   Had worn them really about the same,

And both that morning equally lay
In leaves no step had trodden black.
Oh, I kept the first for another day!
Yet knowing how way leads on to way,
15   I doubted if I should ever come back.

I shall be telling this with a sigh
Somewhere ages and ages hence:
Two roads diverged in a wood, and I—
I took the one less traveled by,
20   And that has made all the difference.

Questions

1. At what point in the poem do you notice that a rhyme scheme has developed?
2. Does the poem ever depart from the rhyme scheme?
3. Are the rhymes in the poem masculine or feminine?
4. Is there any near rhyme in the poem? Internal rhyme?
5. Suppose the poem were written in rhymed couplets. Would that be as suitable to the poem's theme? How does Frost's rhyme scheme relate to his subject?

✍️ Tips on Writing about Poetry

Rhyme is more than a musical ornamentation. The similarity of sounds frequently emphasizes a thematic connection between the words with similar sounds. As you discover rhyme schemes in poetry, and write about rhyme, be alert to the connections of *meaning* between the words that rhyme.

Alliteration and Assonance

By now you have noticed that repetition is a principle of music in language. It forges connections between words and phrases, creates expectations, and is pleasing in itself. We have seen the repetition of accent patterns in rhythm and of word endings in rhyme, and how both contribute to the mood and movement of the poem. *Alliteration* is the repetition of consonant sounds. Like rhyme, it binds together words with similar sounds. In the heat of emotion we have a tendency to use words with the same initial consonant: "You *dirty dog!*" Many proverbs are composed in this manner, for emphasis as well as memory: "*Time* and *tide* wait for no man." "When the *wine* is in, the *wit* is out." Judging from some current newspaper headlines, alliteration is as popular a mode of expression as ever.

Assonance is the repetition of vowel sounds.

> Be near me when my light is low,
>   When the blood creeps, and the nerves prick
>   And tingle and the heart is sick,
> And all the wheels of Being slow.
>   —*Alfred, Lord Tennyson*

The repetition of the ē sound in lines 1, 2, and 4 draws attention to the opening and helps to slow the phrase "wheels of Being." Assonance, like alliteration, attracts the reader to certain words and can create strong resonances.

MARGARET WALKER (1915–)

Lineage

My grandmothers were strong.
They followed plows and bent to toil.
They moved through fields sowing seed.
They touched earth and grain grew.
5   They were full of sturdiness and singing.
My grandmothers were strong.

My grandmothers are full of memories.
Smelling of soap and onions and wet clay
With veins rolling roughly over quick hands
10   They have many clean words to say.
My grandmothers were strong.
Why am I not as they?

Questions

1. Find an example of alliteration in stanza 1. Find an example of assonance. How do the techniques affect the meaning of the stanza?
2. What phrases in the second stanza stand out because of alliteration? Do those phrases deserve special attention? Why?

Alliteration and assonance sometimes imitate sounds of the things to which they refer. This is called *onomatopoeia* and is the purest relation of sound and meaning in poetry. The words *pop, sizzle,* and *crash* are onomatopoetic. Through the repetition of vowel or consonant sounds, an entire line may become onomatopoetic, as when Tennyson speaks of

The moan of doves in immemorial elms,
And murmuring of innumerable bees.

The repetition of the consonant *m* mimics the moaning and murmuring to
which the lines refer. Shakespeare, in *Venus and Adonis*, fills Venus's lines with
s's just as she is playing the serpent in tempting young Adonis.

Here come and sit, where never serpent hisses,
And being set, I'll smother thee with kisses . . .

One of the greatest studies in alliteration, assonance, and onomatopoeia in
American poetry is Edgar Allan Poe's "The Bells." Its effects are ingenious and
excessive; the poem has been praised, ridiculed, imitated, and parodied.

EDGAR ALLAN POE (1809–1849)

The Bells

I

Hear the sledges with the bells—
        Silver bells!
What a world of merriment their melody foretells!
        How they tinkle, tinkle, tinkle,
5   In the icy air of night!
        While the stars that oversprinkle
        All the heavens, seem to twinkle
            With a crystalline delight;
        Keeping time, time, time,
10   In a sort of runic rhyme,
To the tintinnabulation that so musically wells
        From the bells, bells, bells, bells,
            Bells, bells, bells—
From the jingling and the tinkling of the bells.

II

15   Hear the mellow wedding bells—
            Golden bells!
What a world of happiness their harmony foretells!
        Through the balmy air of night
        How they ring out their delight!—
20   From the molten-golden notes,
                And all in tune,
            What a liquid ditty floats
        To the turtledove that listens, while she gloats
                On the moon!
25   Oh, from out the sounding cells,
What a gush of euphony voluminously wells!
                How it swells!
                How it dwells

On the future!—how it tells

30   Of the rapture that impels
To the swinging and the ringing
         Of the bells, bells, bells—
Of the bells, bells, bells, bells,
         Bells, bells, bells—
35 To the rhyming and the chiming of the bells!

III

Hear the loud alarum bells—
         Brazen bells!
What a tale of terror, now, their turbulency tells!
         In the startled ear of night
40   How they scream out their affright!
         Too much horrified to speak,
         They can only shriek, shriek,
            Out of tune,
In a clamorous appealing to the mercy of the fire,
45 In a mad expostulation with the deaf and frantic fire,
            Leaping higher, higher, higher,
            With a desperate desire,
         And a resolute endeavor
         Now—now to sit, or never,
50   By the side of the pale-faced moon.
         Oh, the bells, bells, bells!
         What a tale their terror tells
            Of despair!
How they clang, and clash, and roar!
55   What a horror they outpour
On the bosom of the palpitating air!
         Yet the ear, it fully knows
            By the twanging
            And the clanging,
60   How the danger ebbs and flows;
Yet the ear distinctly tells,
            In the jangling
            And wrangling,
How the danger sinks and swells,
65 By the sinking or the swelling in the anger of the bells—
            Of the bells,—
Of the bells, bells, bells, bells,
         Bells, bells, bells—
In the clamor and the clangor of the bells!

IV

70   Hear the tolling of the bells—
         Iron bells!
What a world of solemn thought their monody compels!
         In the silence of the night,
         How we shiver with affright

75 At the melancholy menace of their tone!
　　For every sound that floats
　　From the rust within their throats
　　　　Is a groan.
　　And the people—ah, the people—
80 They that dwell up in the steeple,
　　　　All alone,
　　And who tolling, tolling, tolling,
　　　In that muffled monotone,
　　Feel a glory in so rolling
85 　　On the human heart a stone—
　　They are neither man nor woman—
　　They are neither brute nor human—
　　　　They are ghouls:—
　　　And their king it is who tolls:—
90 　　And he rolls, rolls, rolls,
　　　　Rolls
　　　A paean from the bells!
　　And his merry bosom swells
　　With the paean of the bells!
95 And he dances, and he yells;
　　Keeping time, time, time,
　　In a sort of runic rhyme,
　　　To the paean of the bells—
　　　　Of the bells—
100 Keeping time, time, time,
　　In a sort of runic rhyme,
　　　To the throbbing of the bells—
　　　Of the bells, bells, bells—
　　　To the sobbing of the bells;
105 Keeping time, time, time,
　　　As he knells, knells, knells,
　　In a happy runic rhyme,
　　　To the rolling of the bells—
　　　Of the bells, bells, bells:—
110 　　To the tolling of the bells—
　　Of the bells, bells, bells, bells,
　　　　Bells, bells, bells—
　To the moaning and the groaning of the bells.

Questions

1. Vocabulary: *euphony* (26), *voluminously* (26), *turbulency* (38), *monody* (72), *paean* (92), *runic* (97).
2. Underline or list all examples of alliteration, assonance, and onomatopoeia of words and phrases in stanza 1.
3. Find an example of interior rhyme in stanza 2.
4. What vowel sound is most frequent in lines 39–44? To what extent is that assonance onomatopoetic?

5. How does the poem's mood change from stanza 1 to stanza 4? How is that change reflected in the assonances of stanza 4?
6. It has been claimed that Poe's poetry has more ardent fans in France than in the United States. Perhaps one reason is that the musical effects we find excessive seem less prominent to a foreign ear. Do you find the great elaboration of sound effects pleasing? Exhilarating? Frightening?

Vowel Tones

English is rich in vowel sounds, from the wide and resonant *ah* sound to the piercing long *ē*. Our vowels are formed to reflect various emotional states and tensions through changes of pitch. The riders on a roller coaster scream the *ē* sound when the train takes a dive, and they sigh *ah* when the ride is over and the tension is released. Many words illustrate this connection between emotion and vowel tone. In "The Bells," notice that Poe's pleasant description of the bells in stanza 2 uses rich, open vowel sounds in words like "mellow," "golden," "harmony," and "molten-golden." But when he describes the "alarum bells" in stanza 3 he uses pinched, shrill vowels to express danger: "brazen," "scream," "affright," "shriek," and "leaping."

Generally the lower-register vowel sounds—the *aw* (awe), *oo* (doom), and *ō* (woe)—are effective in conveying horror, grief, solemnity, and great magnitude. The shorter vowel sounds—the *i* in little, the *e* in pet, the *a* in rattle—lend themselves to rapid movement, smallness, and gaiety. We have seen how, in the merry first stanza of "The Bells," Poe uses a preponderance of short vowels in words like "merriment," "tinkle," "crystalline," and "tintinnabulation"; and how in the horror of the last stanza he moves to the lower register, in words like "rolling," "tolling," "moaning," and "groaning." Listen to the short vowel sounds in Shakespeare's description of the tiny Queen Mab, from *Romeo and Juliet*, act 1, scene 4:

> She is the fairies' midwife and she comes
> In shape no bigger than an agate stone . . .
> Drawn with a team of little atomies . . .
> Her whip, of cricket's bone; the lash, of film . . .

There are vowel tones of lower register as well, but they are there to set off the diminutive sounds of "little atomies," "whips," and "cricket." Now listen to King Lear in the last act of Shakespeare's great tragedy, when he enters carrying his dead daughter.

> Howl, howl, howl, howl! O you are men of stones:
> Had I your tongues and eyes, I'd use them so
> That heaven's vault should crack. She's gone forever.
> I know when one is dead and when one lives . . .

The passage is dominated by the low vowel sounds *ō*, *ōō*, and *aw*, to render the magnitude of Lear's grief.

The metrics of the classical Greek and Latin poets depended on the duration of vowels, rather than accents, for its rhythm. Instead of accented and unaccented syllables, there were long and short syllables. This is called *quantitative meter*. Although our metrics is based primarily on accent, the duration of vowels also plays its part, as will be seen in the following selections.

Exercise

Explain the relation between vowel tones and meaning in the following lines.

1. You do not do, you do not do
   Any more, black shoe
   In which I have lived like a foot
   For thirty years, poor and white,
   Barely daring to breathe or Achoo.
   —*Sylvia Plath*

2. Roll on, thou deep and dark blue ocean, roll.
   —*George Gordon, Lord Byron*

3.   The brittle fleet
   Touch'd, clink'd, and clashed, and vanished.
   —*Alfred, Lord Tennyson*

4. The stoned dogs crawl back through the blood . . .
   —*Weldon Kees*

5. I dared not meet the daffodils
   For fear their yellow gown
   Would pierce me with a fashion
   So foreign to my own.
   —*Emily Dickinson*

6. He from forth the closet brought a heap
   Of candied apple, quince, and plum, and gourd;
   With jellies sooter° than the creamy curd   *sweeter*
   And lucent syrops, tinct° with cinnamon . . .   *flavored*
   —*John Keats*

7. A sudden little river crossed my path
   As unexpected as a serpent comes.
   —*Robert Browning*

Now that we have developed a working knowledge and a vocabulary of musical techniques, let us read some poems with ears attuned to rhythm, rhyme, and the relation of form and content. Read each poem aloud, exaggerating the rhythms, alliterations, and vowel tones.

MARY TALLMOUNTAIN (1918–)

Peeling Pippins

I sit down beside my brass lamp
To peel a pan of pippins.

How the spry sap springs, how
Quickly white flesh turns rust.
5   I muse on a green-skinned quarter.
The brass mirrors my fingers,
A brown cup holding a curve of green.
Pippin, created round: from pips
To plump dimples; inward to
10   Faint outline of its heart.
Taut little skins curl. The core
Falls abandoned to my sharp knife.
Saluting pippin's hardihood
I slice blizzard, thunder, deluge.
15   There will be jars of sauce.
Pippin shall feed bone and marrow;
Cells shall transmute,
Emerald be crimson; sap be blood
In pippin's winter odyssey:
20   Profusions of life, linked
In the continuum.

Questions

1. Vocabulary: *pippins, transmute* (17), *profusions* (20), *continuum* (21).
2. Underline all examples of alliteration and assonance in the poem.
3. What does the poet mean when she says, "Saluting pippin's hardihood/I slice blizzard, thunder, deluge"? What figure of speech is she using?
4. Is the poem's music pleasing to you?

WILLIAM BUTLER YEATS (1865–1939)

The Lake Isle of Innisfree

I will arise and go now, and go to Innisfree,
And a small cabin build there, of clay and
    wattles° made: *poles interwoven with branches*
Nine bean-rows will I have there, a hive for the honey-bee,
And live alone in the bee-loud glade.

5   And I shall have some peace there, for peace comes dropping slow,
Dropping from the veils of the morning to where the cricket sings;
There midnight's all a glimmer, and noon a purple glow,
And evening full of the linnet's wings.

I will arise and go now, for always night and day
10   I hear lake water lapping with low sounds by the shore;
While I stand on the roadway, or on the pavements gray,
I hear it in the deep heart's core.

Questions

1. At what line do you notice that a rhyme scheme has been established? Having established the scheme, does Yeats alter it?
2. Does the poem use internal rhyme? If so, what resonances are thereby created?
3. Scan the third stanza. Does it differ metrically from stanza 1? If so, does the meaning justify the difference?
4. Find an example of spondees in stanza 3. How does it affect our reading of the line in which it is found? Does it focus attention? Diffuse it?
5. Discuss the effect of short syllables on the movement of stanza 2.

Innisfree is a kind of Shangri-la for Yeats—a paradise of simplicity, peace, and solitude. The speaker is filled with longing and delight in contemplating this haven. The rhythm he has chosen in the first three lines is heptameter, with a caesura after the fourth foot. These lines have considerable momentum before the caesura and a peaceful resolution after it. The shorter fourth line achieves the most dramatic resolution, with its three stresses at the end. Notice that the basic movement of the lines in the stanza is rising rhythm, moving from unstressed to stressed syllables in an effective rhythmic expression of yearning. But see what happens in lines 5 and 6, when he imagines the dream attained:

And I | shall háve | sŏme peáce | thére, | fŏr peáce | cŏmes dróp | pĭng slów,
Dróppĭng | frŏm thĕ | veíls ŏf thĕ | mórnĭng | tŏ whére | thĕ críc | kĕt síngs;

The rhythm shifts radically from a rising to a falling rhythm, with a pyrrhic foot in line 6. This line is as light and ecstatic as his dream of peace.

WILLIAM CARLOS WILLIAMS (1883–1963)

The Dance

In Breughel's great picture, The Kermess,
the dancers go round, they go round and
around, the squeal and the blare and the
tweedle of bagpipes, a bugle and fiddles
5   tipping their bellies (round as the thick-
sided glasses whose wash they impound)
their hips and their bellies off balance
to turn them. Kicking and rolling about
the Fair Grounds, swinging their butts, those
10   shanks must be sound to bear up under such
rollicking measures, prance as they dance
in Breughel's great picture, The Kermess.

Peasants Dancing, by Pieter Brueghel the Elder (*Kunsthistorisches Museum, Vienna*)

Questions

1. Vocabulary: *impound* (6).
2. How many instances of onomatopoeia can you find in this poem?
3. Scan the poem. Are there more stressed syllables or unstressed ones? How does that affect the movement of the poem?
4. Which lines are end-stopped? Which lines are enjambed? How does enjambment contribute to the movement from line to line?
5. Does the rhythm of the poem remind you of any particular dance rhythm?

Songs

We began our discussion with the observation that poetry and songs have a common root in our emotions, and that literary, or unsung, poetry is a relatively new development in the history of literature. Since the Renaissance the distinction between song and literary poetry may be drawn along the following general lines. First, most songs demand greater adherence to regular rhythm and rhyme than does spoken poetry. We are accustomed to hearing rhyme and regular rhythm in our songs, and we are dissatisfied when it is lacking. Second, because songs are composed to be heard rather than studied, songwriters usually avoid the concentration of images and figures that strengthen literary poetry. They use them, but in less profusion, and in such a way that they may be grasped on first hearing. Songwriters have melodies to charge their lines with emotion, so their language can relax.

This is not to minimize the power of poetry in songwriting. The United States has been fortunate in its extraordinary poet-lyricists: the anonymous singers of ballads and spirituals, troubadours Woody Guthrie and Bob Dylan, urban song-writers Billie Holiday and Huddie Ledbetter, and the countless writers of Broad-way show tunes. These composers have created a tradition of lyric poetry of wit, beauty, and power.

Perhaps one of the true tests of a good song is that it loses its essential power when committed to cold type. If you have recordings of the following songs, you should listen to them before and after studying them as literature.

ANONYMOUS

Frankie and Albert

Frankie was a good girl,
As everybody knows.
She paid a hundred dollars
For Albert's suit of clothes.
5   He was her man and he done her wrong.

Frankie went down to the corner saloon,
Wasn't goin' to be there long.
Asked the bartender had he seen her Albert,
'Cause he done been home and gone.
10   He was her man and he done her wrong.

Well, the bartender he told Frankie,
Can't lie to you if I try.
Old Albert been here an hour ago
And gone home with Alice Fry.
15   He was her man and he done her wrong.

Frankie went down to Albert's house,
Only a couple of blocks away,
Peeped in the keyhole of his door,
Saw Albert lovin' Alice Fry.
20   He was her man and he done her wrong.

Frankie called out to Albert,
Albert said I don't hear.
If you don't come to the woman you love
Goin' to haul you out of here.
25   He was her man and he done her wrong.

Frankie she shot old Albert,
And she shot him three or four times.
Said I'll hang around a few minutes
And see if Albert's dyin'.
30   He was my man and he done me wrong.

An iron-tired wagon
With ribbons all hung in black
Took old Albert to the buryin' ground

And it didn't bring him back.
He was her man and he done her wrong.

Frankie told the sheriff
What goin' to happen to me?
Said looks like from the evidence
Goin' to be murder first degree.
He was your man and he done you wrong.

Judge heard Frankie's story,
Heard Albert's mother testify.
Judge said to Frankie,
You goin' to be justified.
He was your man and he done you wrong.

Dark was the night,
Cold was the ground,
The last words I heard Frankie say,
I done laid old Albert down.
He was my man and he done me wrong.

Last time I heard of Frankie
She was settin' in her cell,
Sayin' Albert done me wrong
And for that I sent him to hell.
He was my man and he done me wrong.

I aint goin' to tell no stories,
I aint goin' to tell no lies.
The woman who stole Frankie's Albert
Was the girl they call Alice Fry.
He was her man and he done her wrong.

Questions

1. If you were to classify "Frankie and Albert" as a genre of poetry, how would you classify it? As lyric? Dramatic? Narrative?
2. Is the imagery of the song denser than that of most lyric poems? Less dense? Do you find it at all difficult to follow?
3. Can you find many instances of near rhyme? Is it graceful, or is it awkward in print? Do you suppose these rhymes would be more pleasing if you heard them sung?

BILLIE HOLIDAY (1915–1959)

God Bless the Child

Them that's got shall get, Them that's not shall lose;
So the Bible said, and it still is news;
Moma may have, Papa may have, but,
God bless the child that's got his own; That's got his own.

Yes, the strong gets more, while the weak ones fade.
Empty pockets don't ever make the grade;

Moma may have, Papa may have, but
God bless the child that's got his own! That's got his own.

Money, you got lots o' friends, crowdin' 'round the door.
10   When you're gone, and spendin' ends, they don't come no more.
No. No. No.

Rich relations give, crust of bread and such.
You can help yourself, but don't take too much!
Moma may have, Papa may have, but
15   God bless the child that's got his own! That's got his own.

Questions

1. Find an example of allusion in stanza 1. How does it enrich the song?
2. Find an instance of synecdoche in stanza 2. Another in stanza 4.
3. The line repeated at the end of stanzas 1, 2, and 4 is the song's *refrain*. Why does she repeat it?

COLE PORTER (1893–1964)

My Heart Belongs to Daddy

I used to fall
In love with all
Those boys who maul
Refined ladies.
5   But now I tell
Each young gazelle
To go to hell—
I mean, hades,
For since I've come to care
10   For such a sweet millionaire.

While tearing off
A game of golf
I may make a play for the caddy.
But when I do
15   I don't follow through
'Cause my heart belongs to Daddy.

If I invite
A boy, some night,
To dine on my fine finnan haddie,°   *smoked haddock*
20   I just adore
His asking for more,
But my heart belongs to Daddy,
Yes, my heart belongs to Daddy.
So I simply couldn't be bad.
25   Yes, my heart belongs to Daddy,
Da-da, da-da-da, da-da-da, dad!
So I want to warn you, laddie,

Tho' I know you're perfectly swell,
That my heart belongs to Daddy
30 'Cause my Daddy, he treats me so well.
He treats it and treats it,
And then he repeats it,
Yes, Daddy, he treats it so well.

Saint Patrick's day,
35 Although I may
Be seen wearing green with a paddy,
I'm always sharp
When playing the harp,
'Cause my heart belongs to Daddy.
40 Though other dames
At football games
May long for a strong undergraddy,
I never dream
Of making the team
45 'Cause my heart belongs to Daddy.
Yes, my heart belongs to Daddy,
So I simply couldn't be bad.
Yes, my heart belongs to Daddy,
Da-da, da-da-da, da-da-da, dad!
50 So I want to warn you, laddie,
Tho' I simply hate to be frank,
That I can't be mean to Daddy
'Cause my Da-da-da-daddy might spank.
In matters artistic
55 He's not modernistic
So Da-da-da-daddy might spank.

12 🌿 Tones of Voice

There is more to speech than the literal meaning of words. We may mean what we say, or we may mean something quite different. In conversation our tone of voice indicates how we feel about what we are communicating. Even in privacy, we shout good news and whisper condolences. We sneer sarcasm. When your mother said, "Don't speak to me in that tone of voice," you may have been saying something quite agreeable in itself. You may have been saying, "Sure, I'll take out the garbage," but in such a bitter tone that it came out sounding like, "Sure, I'll take out the garbage (and spread it all over the lawn)."

Tone is the way writers or speakers indicate their attitudes and feelings toward the subject. Of course, it is difficult to capture on the printed page the qualities of the spoken voice. Through their rhythms, images, and word choices, poets can subtly suggest their underlying sentiments. How do we know when people are lying to us? The content of what they say may be perfectly believable, but something in the rhythm—perhaps it is too regular, too pat, too rehearsed—indicates that the speaker is insincere. Poets perfect their language, but they usually wish to achieve the spontaneity of a sincere expression. Most of the poems we have read are quite sincere, and you will notice in their music a sustained immediacy that is hard to fake.

The Range of Tones

Let us begin with a poem whose tone is subtle, almost neutral.

WILLIAM CARLOS WILLIAMS (1883–1963)

The Young Housewife

At ten A.M. the young housewife
moves about in negligee behind

William Carlos Williams *(Rollie McKenna)*

the wooden walls of her husband's house.
I pass solitary in my car.

5   Then again she comes to the curb
to call the ice-man,[1] fish-man, and stands
shy, uncorseted, tucking in
stray ends of hair, and I compare her
to a fallen leaf.

10   The noiseless wheels of my car
rush with a crackling sound over
dried leaves as I bow and pass smiling.

To determine the tone of a poem, first consider the poet's attitude toward the subject. How does Williams feel about the housewife? He seems so cool and unperturbed that we must scrutinize his *observations* for a clue. He mentions that she wears a negligee and is uncorseted. He notices her "tucking in/stray ends of hair." These observations suggest that Williams finds the woman attractive. But he does not say, "Look at the beautiful housewife!" He does not rhapsodize about her charms. In the only figure of speech he permits himself, he simply compares her to a fallen leaf. The tone of the poem is masterful in its restraint.

The following poem is equally masterful, in its lack of restraint. The subject is similar: a man is describing a woman. But Lawrence's admiration for this

---

[1] Before the advent of the home refrigerator, blocks of ice were delivered to homes by icemen.

woman is unembarrassed, and his enthusiasm drives the rhythms and figures of speech. The resulting tone is racy, ebullient.

D. H. LAWRENCE (1885–1930)

Gloire de Dijon[2]

When she rises in the morning
I linger to watch her;
She spreads the bath-cloth underneath the window
And the sunbeams catch her
5 Glistening white on the shoulders,
While down her sides the mellow
Golden shadow glows as
She stoops to the sponge, and her swung breasts
Sway like full-blown yellow
10 Gloire de Dijon roses.

She drips herself with water, and her shoulders
Glisten as silver, they crumple up
Like wet and falling roses, and I listen
For the sluicing of their rain-dishevelled petals.
15 In the window full of sunlight
Concentrates her golden shadow
Fold on fold, until it glows as
Mellow as the glory roses.

Here nothing is held back. The similes are sensual and fulsome. Notice how the lines tumble over one another in the excitement of long sentences, and how the speaker features the long ō vowel in "shadow glows" and "roses" at the ends of both stanzas. That ō sound is the sound of wonderment. The poem is an articulate "wow" from beginning to end. Since distinctive tone in poetry often results from rhythm and the arrangement of vowels, we will refer to the music of poetry again in our discussions of tone.

Irony

Although the tones of the foregoing poems differ in intensity, they share an important quality: they are both sincere. Nothing in the tone of either speaker would lead us to suspect that he does not mean what he says. When poets mean the opposite of what they say, they use the tone known as *irony*. This tone of voice is unmistakable in conversation. The compliment "That's a lovely hat" can become an ironic jibe if we overemphasize the word *lovely*. We often use irony to tease each other.

---

[2] *Gloire de Dijon* is French for "glory of Dijon." Dijon is a city in eastern France, also famous for its mustard.

Translating the ironic tone into literature is likewise done by overemphasis and understatement. Lacking the speaker's control of pitch and volume, the poet must rely on posturing, surprising diction, and excessive imagery to set the tone.

The following protest poem is a veritable test pattern of ironic tones. Whitman is describing a military parade. At first his irony is so subtle we might think he really admires "the show." But by the time he describes the phantom soldiers, "bandaged and bloodless," his repetition of "this is indeed a show" is downright bitter. The first time he calls the parade a "show," we think he means entertainment. He does not mean that at all: he hates it.

WALT WHITMAN (1819–1892)

A Boston Ballad

To get betimes in Boston town I rose this morning early,
Here's a good place at the corner, I must stand and see the show.

Clear the way there Jonathan!
Way for the President's marshal—way for the government cannon!
5   Way for the Federal foot and dragoons,
    (and the apparitions° copiously° tumbling.)   *phantoms plentifully*

I love to look on the Stars and Stripes,
    I hope the fifes will play Yankee Doodle.

How bright shine the cutlasses of the foremost troops!
10 Every man holds his revolver, marching stiff through Boston town.

A fog follows, antiques of the same come limping,
Some appear wooden-legged, and some appear bandaged and bloodless.

Why this is indeed a show—it has called the dead out of the earth!
The old graveyards of the hills have hurried to see!
15 Phantoms! phantoms countless by flank and rear!
Cock'd hats of mothy mould—crutches made of mist!
Arms in slings—old men leaning on young men's shoulders.

What troubles you Yankee phantoms? what is all this chattering
    of bare gums?
Does the ague° convulse your limbs? do you mistake your crutches   *fever*
    for firelocks and level them?

20 If you blind your eyes with tears you will not see the President's marshal,
If you groan such groans you might balk the government cannon.

For shame old maniacs—bring down those toss'd arms,
    and let your white hair be,
Here gape your great grandsons, their wives gaze at them from the windows,
25 See how well dress'd, see how orderly they conduct themselves.

Worse and worse—can't you stand it? are you retreating?
Is this hour with the living too dead for you?

Retreat then—pell-mell!
To your graves—back—back to the hills old limpers!
30 I do not think you belong here anyhow.

But there is one thing that belongs here—shall I tell you what it is,
    gentlemen of Boston?

I will whisper it to the Mayor, he shall send a committee to England,
They shall get a grant from the Parliament, go with a cart to the royal vault,
Dig out King George's coffin, unwrap him quick from the grave-clothes,
35   box up his bones for a journey,
Find a swift Yankee clipper—here is freight for you, black-bellied clipper,
Up with your anchor—shake out your sails—steer straight toward Boston bay.

Now call for the President's marshal again, bring out the government cannon,
Fetch home the roarers from Congress, make another procession,
40   guard it with foot and dragoons.
This centre-piece for them;
Look, all orderly citizens—look from the windows, women!

The committee open the box, set up the regal ribs, glue those that will not stay,
Clap the skull on top of the ribs, and clap a crown on top of the skull.

45 You have got your revenge, old buster—the crown is come to its own,
    and more than its own.

Stick your hands in your pockets, Jonathan—you are a made man from this day,
You are mighty cute—and here is one of your bargains.

The phantom veterans remind us of the deeper meaning of military shows. They
symbolize war and suffering. Whitman's description of the phantoms' maimed
decrepitude, their weeping and groaning in the presence of the orderly parade,
emphasizes the reality of war and the proud ignorance of the young dragoons.
When he finally dismisses the phantoms, saying, "I do not think you belong
here anyhow," the line resonates with bitterness and irony. It is classic
understatement.

    Then comes the most ironic image of all. What *does* belong in the midst of
this show of nationalism and militarism is the corpse of King George, whose
tyranny the phantom veterans died to depose. When Whitman says to Jonathan,
the gawking spectator, "here is one of your bargains," and "you are a made man
from this day," he cannot be taken literally. Whitman's vision of a militarized
United States is grim, and his tone is pure sarcasm. The drumbeat rhythms of
the poem underscore his sarcasm.

ALAN DUGAN (1923–)

Morning Song

Look, it's morning, and a little water gurgles in the tap.
I wake up waiting, because it's Sunday, and turn twice more
than usual in bed, before I rise to cereal and comic strips.

I have risen to the morning danger and feel proud,
5   and after shaving off the night's disguises, after searching
close to the bone for blood, and finding only a little,
I shall walk out bravely into the daily accident.

Questions

1. How does the speaker feel about the morning? Are the phrases "morning danger" and "the daily accident" accurate descriptions of the day, or are they excessive?
2. How does the speaker feel about his own response to the morning? Are the words "proud" and "bravely" sincere or excessive?
3. To what degree is the poem ironic in tone?

DENISE LEVERTOV (1923–)

To the Snake

Green Snake, when I hung you round my neck
and stroked your cold, pulsing throat
       as you hissed to me, glinting
arrowy gold scales, and I felt
5   the weight of you on my shoulders,
and the whispering silver of your dryness
       sounded close at my ears—

Green Snake—I swore to my companions that certainly
       you were harmless! But truly
10   I had no certainty, and no hope, only desiring
       to hold you, for that joy,
           which left
a long wake of pleasure, as the leaves moved
and you faded into the pattern
15   of grass and shadows, and I returned
smiling and haunted, to a dark morning.

Questions

1. What is the speaker's attitude toward the snake?
2. How does her description of the snake justify her attitude?
3. Is there any suggestion of irony in the poem?

Didactic Poetry

The Latin poet Horace, in a great didactic poem called "The Art of Poetry," said that the purpose of poetry is to teach or to delight. Sometimes it is both. Didactic poetry aims to teach; poems have been written to teach physics, beekeeping, even the art of love. The didactic tone is distinctive. The poet's attitude toward the subject is: I know about this, and now I'm going to let you in on it.

This is also the attitude of doctors, moralists, and a few teachers. The didactic tone can be charming, or it can be presumptuous. We are most familiar with it in little rhymes that help us remember important facts.

> Thirty days hath September,
> April, June and November . . .

> Red sky at night:
> Sailor's delight.
> Red sky at morning:
> Sailors take warning.

> Oysters into milk
> Go smooth as silk.

In all of literature no didactic speech has been more frequently quoted than the advice of Polonius to his son, from Shakespeare's *Hamlet*.

> And these few precepts in thy memory
> Look thou charácter. Give thy thoughts no tongue,
> Nor any unproportion'd thought his act.
> Be thou familiar, but by no means vulgar;
> Those friends thou hast, and their adoption tried,
> Grapple them unto thy soul with hoops of steel;
> But do not dull thy palm with entertainment
> Of each new-hatch'd, unfledg'd comráde. Beware
> Of entrance to a quarrel, but, being in,
> Bear 't that th' opposed may beware of thee.
> Give every man thy ear, but few thy voice;
> Take each man's censure, but reserve thy judgment.
> Costly thy habit as thy purse can buy,
> But not express'd in fancy; rich, not gaudy;
> For the apparel oft proclaims the man,
> And they in France of the best rank and station
> Are of a most select and generous clef° in that.   sort
> Neither a borrower, nor a lender be;
> For loan oft loses both itself and friend,
> And borrowing dulleth edge of husbandry.°   household management
> This above all: to thine own self be true,
> And it must follow, as the night the day,
> Thou canst not then be false to any man.
> Farewell; my blessing season this in thee!

Polonius, a professional advisor, has saved up the best advice for his son. He is a master of the didactic tone, and his instructions ring with confidence and conviction. They do not invite questions; they represent an end of questioning, the treasury of an old man's wisdom. In this certainty the didactic distinguishes itself from the meditative tone.

There is comedy in the tone as well. What begins as a "few precepts" runs on to twenty-four lines of moral disquisition, more than any young man could absorb or believe. Even the wisest advice is a little silly if there is too much of it.

At its best the didactic tone is both convincing and modest. Advice is easiest to hear when it seems hard won and is offered with humility.

EMILY DICKINSON (1830–1886)

Success is counted sweetest

Success is counted sweetest
By those who ne'er succeed.
To comprehend a nectar
Requires sorest need.

5   Not one of all the purple Host
Who took the Flag to-day
Can tell the definition
So clear of Victory

As he defeated—dying—
10   On whose forbidden ear
The distant strains of triumph
Burst agonized and clear!

The poem is organized like a simple lesson—a general proposition followed by a corollary and an illustration. Dickinson states the proposition so plainly that it seems incontestable. Should we be tempted to quibble, the example of the battle is so apt and moving that it disarms us. Unlike Polonius, Dickinson does not weary us with her wisdom.

English poets of the eighteenth century had greater confidence in reason and human perfectibility than those of any other period in history. To Alexander Pope any problem worth solving would yield to reason. Being supremely reasonable, Pope found the didactic tone natural. His verse is a model of clarity and balance, its tone even and assured, its rhythms highly regular. Such a tone is the mark of secure faith, a system that leaves little room for doubt.

ALEXANDER POPE (1688–1744)

From An Essay on Man (Epistle IV)

    Honour and shame from no condition rise;
Act well your part, there all the honour lies.
Fortune in men has some small diff'rence made,
One flaunts in rags, one flutters in brocade;
5   The cobbler aproned, and the parson gowned,
The friar hooded, and the monarch crowned.
"What differ more (you cry) than crown and cowl?"
I'll tell you, friend; a wise man and a fool.

You'll find, if once the monarch acts the monk,
10 Or, cobbler-like, the parson will be drunk,
Worth makes the man, and want of it, the fellow;
The rest is all but leather or prunella.°   *a woolen fabric*
    Stuck o'er with titles and hung round with strings,
That thou mayest be by kings, or whores of kings.
15 Boast the pure blood of an illustrious race,
In quiet flow from Lucrece° to Lucrece;   *a virtuous Roman woman*
But by your fathers' worth if yours you rate,
Count me those only who were good and great.

Questions

1. What is more important to the speaker—apparel or character?
2. Do you agree with the ideas expressed in lines 9–12?
3. What is the meter of the poem? Does it suit the didactic tone?

Toughness

Many readers tend to think of poets as soft-hearted creatures who bruise easily and have the most exquisite sympathy for all living things, but they are not. As evidence of this misconception, certain poets adopt a tone of toughness. There is a little of Mae West or Humphrey Bogart in all of us, an attitude that life is hard, kid, so you may as well brace up and plow through it. This poetry is not sighed or sung. It is spoken straight.

PHILIP LEVINE (1928–)

To a Child Trapped in a Barber Shop

You've gotten in through the transom
    and you can't get out
till Monday morning or, worse,
    till the cops come.

5 That six-year-old red face
    calling for mama
is yours; it won't help you
    because your case

is closed forever, hopeless.
10   So don't drink
the Lucky Tiger,° don't   *hair tonic*
    fill up on grease

because that makes it a lot worse,
    that makes it a crime
15 against property and the state
    and that costs time.

We've all been here before,
      we took our turn
under the electric storm
20   of the vibrator

and stiffened our wills to meet
      the close clippers
and heard the true blade mowing
      back and forth

25 on a strip of dead skin,
      and we stopped crying.
You think your life is over?
      It's just begun.

Questions

1. How serious is the child's predicament?
2. Does the speaker care about the child? What phrases suggest that he does?
3. The speaker is feeling both sympathy and distance from his side of the glass. How does the tone reveal these conflicting feelings?
4. Will the speaker try to rescue the child?

CHARLES BUKOWSKI (1920–)

Yellow

Seivers was one of the hardest running backs[3] since
Jimmy Brown, and lateral motion too,
like a chorus girl, really, until one day he got hit on
the blind side by Basil Skronski; we carried Seivers off the field
5 but Skronski had gotten one rib and cracked another.

the next year Seivers wasn't even good in practice, gun shy as a
squirrel in deer season; he stopped contact, fumbled, couldn't even
hold a look-in pass or a handoff—all that wasted and he could go the 100 in 9.7[4]

I'm 45 years old, out of shape, too much beer, but one of the best
10 assistant coaches in the pro game, and I can't stand to see a man
jaking° it. I got him in the locker room the other day when the whole   *shirking*
squad was in there. I told him, "Seivers, you used to be a player
but now you're chickenshit!"

"you can't talk that way to me, Manny!" he said, and I turned him
15 around, he was lacing on a shoe, and I right-cracked him
right on the chin. he fell against a locker
and then he began to cry—the greatest since Brown,
crying there against the locker, one shoe off, one on.

"come on, men, let's get outa here!" I told the gang, and we ran
20 on out, and when we got back he had cleared out, he was gone, his

---

[3] In football, a backfield ball carrier.
[4] The hundred-yard dash in 9.7 seconds.

gear was gone. we got some kid from Illinois running his spot now,
head down, knees high, he don't care where he's going.

guys like Seivers end up washing dishes for a buck an hour
and that's just what they deserve.

Questions

1. What is the speaker's attitude toward Seivers?
2. What figures of speech reveal this attitude in the first two stanzas?
3. Try to say the line "I can't stand to see a man/jaking it," in the speaker's voice. Do you hear the tone? What attitude does it express toward Seivers? Toward the game of football?
4. What does the speaker care more about—Seivers's feelings, or football?
5. Do you feel sorry for Seivers?
6. Would you like the speaker to be your coach? How would you like him to be your father?

 Tips on Writing about Poetry

Of all the qualities of poetry, the tone of a poem is most vulnerable to the subjective response of the reader. What one reader thinks is funny, another thinks is offensive; what one reader feels to be deeply moving, another reader may regard as grossly sentimental. When you are writing about the tonal qualities of a particular poem, it may be very useful to share the poem with a friend, or several friends, to see if your responses are similar. If they are different, consider how your background and beliefs may account for the difference.

The Comic Tone

When poets adopt a comic attitude toward a subject we sometimes can hear it in rollicking or off-beat rhythms, in clownish imagery and diction. The subject may or may not be funny—the tone is what makes us laugh.

ANONYMOUS

Miss Bailey's Ghost

A captain bold, in Halifax, who dwelt in country quarters,
Seduced a maid, who hang'd herself, one morning, in her garters,
His wicked conscience smited him, he lost his stomach daily,
He took to drinking ratafee,° and thought upon Miss Bailey.   *an almond liqueur*
5   Oh, Miss Bailey! unfortunate Miss Bailey.

One night betimes he went to rest, for he had caught a fever,
Says he, "I am a handsome man, but I'm a gay deceiver";

His candle just at twelve o'clock began to burn quite palely,
A ghost stepp'd up to his bedside, and said, "behold Miss Bailey."
10   Oh, Miss Bailey! unfortunate Miss Bailey.

"Avaunt, Miss Bailey," then he cried, "your face looks white and mealy,"
"Dear Captain Smith," the ghost replied, "you've used me ungenteely;
The Crowner's Quest goes hard with me, because I've acted frailly,
And parson Biggs won't bury me, though I am dead Miss Bailey."
15   Oh, Miss Bailey! unfortunate Miss Bailey.

"Dear Corpse," said he, "since you and I accounts must once for all close,
I've really got a one pound note in my regimental small clothes;
'Twill bribe the sexton for your grave."—The ghost then vanish'd gaily,
Crying "Bless you, wicked Captain Smith, remember poor Miss Bailey."
20   Oh, Miss Bailey! unfortunate Miss Bailey.

The situation itself is not very funny. Poe would have made a nightmare of it, Tennyson a dirge. But the rhyme of *quarters* and *garters* is so unexpected and silly that it quickly deflates the seriousness of the hanging. Likewise the captain's excessive stomach trouble and his vanity, as confessed in line 7. The dance-hall rhythm is so unsuited to the macabre events that its very inappropriateness is comic.

Max Beerbohm has observed that all humor is the result of exaggeration or incongruity. Comic poems usually make fun not only of their subjects but of poetry as well, either by exaggerating its techniques or misapplying them.

EDMUND CLERIHEW BENTLEY (1875–1956)

Lord Clive

What I like about Clive
Is that he is no longer alive.
There is a great deal to be said
For being dead.

Does poetry have to rhyme? All right then, says the comic poet, I'll make it rhyme to the most awkward rhythm. "Lord Clive" is not only a burlesque of rhythm and rhyme. It is a takeoff on the elegy, which is usually quite serious.

Verses that rhyme not only the last syllable, but the last two, are called feminine rhymes. Perhaps as a result of a sort of tonal overkill, the effect of feminine rhyme is often comic.

ANONYMOUS

There Was a King

There was a King and he had three daughters,
And they all lived in a basin of water;
    The basin bended,
    My story's ended.

5   If the basin had been stronger,
     My story would have been longer.

The comic charm of this poem depends on its tone, induced by eccentric rhythms and feminine rhymes. Its wit would be lost in prose.

Two popular tricks in the comic poet's repertoire are the *pun* and the *spoonerism*. The pun is a play on words with similar sounds or on a single word with different meanings: "I stuck my finger in the pie and meringue came off." That's a terrible pun. Here is a better one:

HILAIRE BELLOC (1870–1953)

On His Books

When I am dead, I hope it may be said
"His sins were scarlet, but his books were read."

Read: red. Get it? Roman audiences 2000 years ago acknowledged puns by groaning, and that response has not changed.

A spoonerism is a slip of the tongue that exchanges the parts of two words. Thus, "Let's sit by the fire and spin" becomes "Let's spit by the fire and sin." William Spooner once told one of his students: "You have hissed all of my mystery lessons and completely tasted two whole worms." (Translation: You have missed all of my history lessons and completely wasted two whole terms.)

Diction Levels

Some poets use unfamiliar words and complex literary sentences, whereas others never depart from plain speech. Customarily we refer to formal, literary language as *high diction* and to street language as *low diction*. We associate the former with pulpit, courtroom, and college, and the latter with racetrack and locker room. The poet's level of diction is an element of tone indicating both an attitude toward the subject and a regard for the reader. High diction suggests acuity, demands scholarship, and promises to reward it. Simple diction is humbler, more relaxed and inviting.

We have seen a range of diction levels, from the heights of "An Essay on Man" (pages 730–31) to the idiomatic force of Bukowski's "Yellow" (pages 732–33). Emily Dickinson's poem "Success Is Counted Sweetest" is neither as high toned as "An Essay on Man" nor as low as "Yellow." How would you rank the diction level if Dickinson's poem, in relation to Philip Levine's (pages 731–32)?

Ford Madox Ford, an English essayist, set a limit to the artificiality of diction. He said that a poet should not write anything that he could not, under the stress of some emotion, actually *say*. Modern poets have taken his advice to heart, but there is still a great range of diction levels, owing to our diverse educations and personalities. This makes for a lively variety of tones.

One of our more formal poets is Richard Wilbur.

RICHARD WILBUR (1921–)

The Death of a Toad

A toad the power mower caught,
Chewed and clipped of a leg, with a hobbling hop has got
   To the garden verge, and sanctuaried him
   Under the cineraria° leaves, in the shade   *exotic flowering plant*
5   Of the ashen heartshaped leaves, in a dim,
         Low, and a final glade.

The rare original heartsblood goes,
Spends on the earthen hide, in the folds and wizenings, flows
   In the gutters of the banked and staring eyes. He lies
10   As still as if he would return to stone,
      And soundlessly attending, dies
         Toward some deep monotone,

Toward misted and ebullient seas
And cooling shores, toward lost Amphibia's emperies.°   *empires*
15   Day dwindles, drowning, and at length is gone
   In the wide and antique eyes, which still appear
      To watch, across the castrate lawn,
         The haggard daylight steer.

Questions

1. Vocabulary: *sanctuaried* (3), *wizenings* (8), *ebullient* (13), *castrate* (17).
2. How would you describe the diction of the poem? Did it send you to the dictionary? How often?
3. Have you ever heard anyone talk like the speaker of this poem? Is there a single sentence or phrase that you could imagine someone saying?
4. What is Wilbur's attitude toward his subject? Serious? Frivolous?
5. Suppose the poet had used more natural speech. What subtleties might be lost? What music?

LANGSTON HUGHES (1902–1967)

Who but the Lord?

I looked and I saw
That man they call the Law.
He was coming
Down the street at me!
5 I had visions in my head
Of being laid out cold and dead,
Or else murdered
By the third degree.

I said, O, *Lord, if you can,*
10 *Save me from that man!*

Don't let him make a pulp out of me!
But the Lord he was not quick.
The Law raised up his stick
And beat the living hell
15   Out of me!

Now, I do not understand
Why God don't protect a man
From police brutality.
Being poor and black,
20   I've no weapon to strike back
So who but the Lord
Can protect me?

Questions

1. How would you describe the diction of this poem? Literary? Conversational?
2. The poet's attitude toward his subject is clearly serious. Why, then, has he chosen such common diction? What does this suggest about his attitude toward his reader? Intimacy? Distance?

Dialects

In many cultures the line between the literary tradition and the popular culture has been sharply drawn. There are some poems meant to be read by scholars and others that are meant for a popular audience. Where there is a significant difference between the written and the spoken language, some poets strive to capture the accents of the vernacular. Some of the most popular poets, such as Robert Burns, James Russell Lowell, and Paul Laurence Dunbar, have written in dialect. Unfortunately, the popularity of poetry in dialect is often as short-lived and local as the dialect itself.

ROBERT BURNS (1759–1796)

John Anderson My Jo

John Anderson my jo,° John,   *a term of endearment*
    When we were first acquent,
Your locks were like the raven,
    Your bonnie brow was brent;°   *smooth*
5   But now your brow is beld,° John,   *bald*
    Your locks are like the snow;
But blessings on your frosty pow,°   *head*
    John Anderson, my jo.

John Anderson my jo, John,
10   We clamb the hill thegither;
And mony a canty° day, John,   *cheerful*
    We've had wi' ane anither:

Now we maun° totter down, John,   must
    And hand in hand we'll go,
15 And sleep thegither at the foot,
    John Anderson, my jo.

Questions

1. What is the speaker's attitude toward John?
2. Would she be able to achieve such intimacy without her dialect?
3. Are you familiar with the Scots accent? If so, read the poem aloud, first with the Scots accent and then in your own. Which sounds better?

PAUL LAURENCE DUNBAR (1872–1906)

In the Morning

'Lias! 'Lias! Bless de Lawd!
Don' you know de day's erbroad?
Ef you don't git up, you scamp,
Dey'll be trouble· in dis camp.
5   T'ink I gwine to let you sleep
W'ile I meks yo' boa'd an' keep?
Dat's a putty howdy-do—
Don' you hyeah me, 'Lias—you?

Bet ef I come crost dis flo'
10 You won' fin' no time to sno'.
Daylight all a-shinin' in
W'ile you sleep—w'y hit's a sin!
Ain't de can'le-light enough
To bu'n out widout a snuff,
15 But you go de mo'nin' thoo
Bu'nin' up de daylight too?

'Lias, don' you hyeah me call?
No use tu'nin' to'ds de wall;
I kin hyeah dat mattuss° squeak;   mattress
20 Don' you hyeah me w'en I speak?
Dis hyeah clock done struck off six—
Ca'line, bring me dem ah sticks!
Oh, you down, suh; huh, you down—
Look hyeah, don' you daih to frown.

25 Ma'ch° yo'se'f an' wash yo' face,   march
Don' you splattah all de place;
I got somep'n else to do,
'Sides jes' cleanin' aftah you.
Tek dat comb an' fix yo' haid—
30 Looks jes' lak a feddah baid.°   feather bed

Paul Laurence Dunbar
(Ohio Historical Society)

Look hyeah, boy, I let you see
You sha'n't roll yo' eyes at me.

Come hyeah; bring me dat ah strap!
Boy, I'll whup you 'twell you drap;
35   You done felt yo'se'f too strong,
An' you sholy° got me wrong.   *surely*
Set down at dat table thaih;
Jes' you whimpah ef you daih!
Evah mo'nin' on dis place,
40   Seem lak I mus' lose my grace.
Fol' yo' han's an' bow yo' haid—
Wait ontwell de blessin' 's said;
"Lawd, have mussy on ouah souls—"
(Don' you daih to tech dem rolls—)
45   "Bless de food we gwine to eat—"
(You set still—I *see* yo' feet;
You jes' try dat trick again!)
"Gin us peace an' joy. Amen!"

Questions

1. This is one of the most popular poems ever written in America. It has been memorized and recited by thousands of schoolchildren. Can you explain its popularity?
2. Without the aid of the marginal glosses, could you have understood the poem?
3. Translate one of the stanzas into literary English, making as few changes as possible. What does the poem lose in translation? How much of the tone survives?

Writers on Writing Adrienne Rich

> But I do believe that words can *help us move or keep us paralyzed, and that our choices of language and verbal tone have something—a great deal—to do with how we live our lives.* . . .

13 ❧ The Poem's Shape

The everyday words we use become literature when they are given expressive shape. No literature is without shape. A playwright, for example, cannot merely tape-record a lively conversation and call it a play. A dialogue must be molded so that the conversation has a beginning and an end. Even interviewers shape a conversation by asking prepared questions and by carefully editing the transcript after the interview is over.

Why is shape necessary? Shape gives a work of literature unity and complete-ness. By *unity* we mean that everything in the poem belongs in it and is connected to everything else. In conversation, all sorts of extraneous and unconnected statements arise. In literature, the writer limits him- or herself to what contributes to the overall meaning and effectiveness of the work. By *completeness* we mean that everything needed by the poem is present, in its proper place. In conversation we often forget what we intended to say or later think of what we ought to have said. A good poem, however, contains everything it needs to be effective, and nothing extra. Its shape both highlights and determines the poem's unity and completeness.

We speak of shape in poetry in two general ways: form and structure. By *form* critics usually mean the outward container that shapes the work. By *structure* they mean the inner framework around which the work amasses. It might help to think of the shape of our bodies. The flesh gives the body outward form; bones give it inner structure. Of course, form and structure are not separate. In a poem, as in the body, form and structure work toward the same end—expressive efficiency.

The Structure of Free Verse

We generally think of a poem's shape in terms of rhyme schemes, yet the earliest English poetry did not rhyme. In fact, rhyme is an unusually late device imported to England from France and Italy, whose languages are much richer in rhyme words than is English. Some of the greatest poetry, not only in English but also in other languages, does not rhyme at all. The Psalms, for example, are un- rhymed but are organized through meaning. Each line has two parts, which are in parallel structure either to each other or to the line that follows. In this brief psalm watch for the ways in which ideas are repeated or mirrored.

Psalm 121: A Song of Degrees

I will lift up mine eyes unto the hills: from whence cometh my help.
My help cometh from the Lord: which made heaven and earth.
He will not suffer thy foot to be moved: he that keepeth thee will not slumber.
Behold, he that keepeth Israel; shall neither slumber nor sleep.
5   The Lord is thy keeper: the Lord is thy shade, upon thy right hand.
The sun shall not smite thee by day; nor the moon by night.
The Lord shall preserve thee from all evil; he shall preserve thy soul.
The Lord shall preserve thy going out, and thy coming in: from this time forth
    and even for evermore.

Line 1 has two ideas: hills and the coming of help. Line 2 speaks of the coming of help and of heaven and earth, a mirroring of the opening lines. Lines 3 and 4 mirror each other even more clearly. The two parts of line 7 repeat the same idea. Moreover, there is an overall structure to the poem. It begins by looking for help, and it ends by finding it.

Questions

1. What is the parallel concept in lines 5, 6, and 8? How is line 8 more complex than the others?
2. Are the lines linked together in other ways? What connections exist between lines 2 and 3 and lines 4 and 5?

Free verse is poetry that is unrhymed and lacks a regular metrical unity. Free verse is not free of shape, however. Indeed, one may say it dispenses with outward formal devices to give full range to internal structures.

DENISE LEVERTOV (1923–)

The Ache of Marriage

The ache of marriage:

thigh and tongue, beloved,
are heavy with it,
it throbs in the teeth

5   We look for communion
and are turned away, beloved,
each and each

It is leviathan° and we   *Biblical sea beast*
in its belly
10   looking for joy, some joy
not to be known outside it

two by two in the ark of
the ache of it.

Questions

1. How are the first and last lines related? Do you have a sense of completeness? How do they correspond to the self-enclosed feeling of marriage?
2. How are the allusions to "leviathan" and "the ark" related?
3. How is the belly image in stanza 4 related to the images in stanza 2?
4. Are there any words or images that seem out of place in the poem? Do all the words seem closely connected?

Notice that "The Ache of Marriage" is divided into units, or what are called *stanzas*. A stanza is any group of lines that make up a division of the poem, but it can sometimes be a single line. In "The Ache of Marriage" these units are of irregular length, both in meter and in number of lines. Frequently, the stanzas in a poem are determined by length, meter, or rhyme scheme.

The stanzas work like paragraphs by bringing together similar ideas or images. Levertov uses a period only at the end of the poem, but stanzas 2, 3, and 4 approximate sentences.

Because structure is internal, it is often less noticeable than rhyme as a shaping device. But a free verse poem is not free of shape, and a reader should pay strict attention to what joins the parts of the poem and gives them a sense of unity. Although the rest of this chapter will be concerned with verse forms, we wish to emphasize the fundamental nature of structure. Poets may dispense with rhyme; they may dispense with a clear metrical unity, with imagery and other devices. But poets can never give up internal structure. Without structure, there is no poem.

 Writers on Writing   *Denise Levertov*

> *Corresponding images are a kind of non-aural rhyme.*

Some Traditional English Forms
The Ballad

One of the most popular literary forms is the *ballad*. The ballad is built from four-line stanzas, or *quatrains*, in which the second and fourth lines must rhyme.

Usually the first and third lines have four feet, and the other two lines have three feet; but there are variant scansions. The ballad is an excellent form for narrative poetry because the shortened second and fourth lines give the stanza an unusual sense of propulsion (see the discussion in Chapter 4). "Incident" is an example of a short "literary" ballad; unlike traditional ballads, it has a known author.

COUNTEE CULLEN (1903–1946)

Incident

(For Eric Walrond)

Once riding in old Baltimore,
    Heart-filled, head-filled with glee,
I saw a Baltimorean
    Keep looking straight at me.

5   Now I was eight and very small,
    And he was no whit bigger,
And so I smiled, but he poked out
    His tongue, and called me, "Nigger."

I saw the whole of Baltimore
10   From May until December;
Of all the things that happened there
    That's all that I remember.

Questions

1. Does the poem have a sense of completeness? What gives the poem unity?
2. Why is the information in line 2 important for the poem? How does it set the stage for what follows?
3. Why would Cullen remember only this incident? What feeling do you take away from the poem?

The Couplet

A *couplet* is any two consecutive lines, usually ones that rhyme and have the same meter. Couplets appear in many different languages. In English, however, the couplet has had enormous influence, especially a specialized form of couplet, the *heroic couplet*, which dominated the poetry of the eighteenth century. A heroic couplet is in iambic pentameter, and the second line is end-stopped; thus each couplet is not only a metrical unit but a grammatical unit as well. Consequently, couplets on the same subject can be gathered into *verse paragraphs*, long poetic passages that function like prose paragraphs by grouping couplets that discuss the same topic. Occasionally three successive rhymed lines, called a *triplet*, were permitted in the verse paragraphs to give the passage variety.

    John Dryden was an early champion of the heroic couplet. In the following poem, he mourns a fellow poet who had died young.

JOHN DRYDEN (1631–1700)

To the Memory of Mr. Oldham

Farewell, too little, and too lately known,
Whom I began to think and call my own;
For sure our souls were near allied, and thine
Cast in the same poetic mold with mine.
5   One common note on either lyre did strike,
And knaves and fools we both abhorred alike.
To the same goal did both our studies drive;
The last set out the soonest did arrive.
Thus Nisus[1] fell upon the slippery place,
10   While his young friend performed and won the race.
O early ripe! to thy abundant store
What could advancing age have added more?
It might (what nature never gives the young)
Have taught the numbers° of thy native tongue.   *metrics*
15   But satire needs not those, and wit will shine
Through the harsh cadence of a rugged line:[2]
A noble error, and but seldom made,
When poets are by too much force betrayed.
Thy generous fruits, though gathered ere their prime,
20   Still showed a quickness; and maturing time
But mellows what we write to the dull sweets of rhyme.
Once more, hail and farewell; farewell, thou young,
But ah too short, Marcellus[3] of our tongue;
Thy brows with ivy, and with laurels[4] bound;
25   But fate and gloomy night encompass thee around.

Questions

1. Vocabulary: *knaves* (6), *abhorred* (6), *cadence* (16), *encompass* (25).
2. How does the reference to ivy and laurel relate to the opening lines? Is it an appropriate allusion? Does it give the poem a sense of unity?
3. Does the metaphor of fruit (lines 11–21) fit the poem?
4. Is the alexandrine (the long, six stress line) in line 21 fitting?
5. Is there a sense that the poem has concluded? How does Dryden achieve that sense of completeness?

The poets of the eighteenth century felt the heroic couplet possessed the grace, dignity, and flexibility they admired in the classical meters of Virgil and Homer. The heroic couplet is still used today. In "Moly" it suggests the "heroic" and classical origins of Gunn's subject.

---

[1] In Virgil's *Aeneid* (Book 5, lines 315–339) Nisus slipped in a pool of blood during a footrace.
[2] Dryden believed, as did Renaissance theorists, that satire should be in rough meter.
[3] Marcellus was heir to the Roman Empire when he died at the age of twenty.
[4] The traditional crown for poets.

THOM GUNN (1929–)

Moly[5]

Nightmare of beasthood, snorting, how to wake.
I woke. What beasthood skin she made me take?

Leathery toad that ruts for days on end,
Or cringing dribbling dog, man's servile friend,

5   Or cat that prettily pounces on its meat,
Tortures it hours, then does not care to eat:

Parrot, moth, shark, wolf, crocodile, ass, flea.
What germs, what jostling mobs there were in me.

    These seem like bristles, and the hide is tough.
10 No claw or web here: each foot ends in hoof.

Into what bulk has method disappeared?
Like ham, streaked. I am gross—grey, gross, flap-eared.

The pale-lashed eyes my only human feature.
My teeth tear, tear. I am the snouted creature

15 That bites through anything, root, wire, or can.
If I was not afraid I'd eat a man.

Oh a man's flesh already is in mine.
Hand and foot poised for risk. Buried in swine.

    I root and root, you think that it is greed,
20 It is, but I seek out a plant I need.

Direct me, gods, whose changes are all holy,
To where it flickers deep in grass, the moly:

Cool flesh of magic in each leaf and shoot,
From milky flower to the black forked root.

25 From this fat dungeon I could rise to skin
And human title, putting pig within.

I push my big grey wet snout through the green,
Dreaming the flower I have never seen.

Questions

1. Vocabulary: *servile* (4), *jostling* (8).
2. How does the dream in the final line contrast with the nightmare of the opening?
3. How does the persona contrast the human with the bestial?
4. How do the verse paragraphs emphasize the progress of the poem?
5. To what extent are we all part human and part beast? Can we ever become completely human, according to the persona?
6. Does this poem have a sense of completeness? What more would you say if you were the persona?

---

[5] *Moly* was a magic herb given by Hermes to Odysseus, whose men had been turned into swine by the enchantress Circe.

Italian Forms

The Sonnet

No other form has had the nearly universal appeal of the sonnet. Originating in Sicily, it took root on the Italian mainland, from which it spread as far as Russia to the east and the United States to the west. Since its arrival in England in the sixteenth century, the sonnet has found consistent favor.

The *Italian* or *Petrarchan* sonnet is a fourteen-line poem divided between an opening *octave* (eight lines) and a concluding *sestet* (six lines). It is rhymed *abba abba cdc cdc*. [6] The form is demanding, since it requires three endings to rhyme four times each. In Italian, where almost every word ends in a vowel, rhymes are plentiful. In English, however, the form is usually slightly altered to give the poet some freedom.

JOHN KEATS (1795–1821)

On First Looking into Chapman's Homer

Much have I traveled in the realms of gold,
    And many goodly states and kingdoms seen;
    Round many western islands have I been
Which bards in fealty° to Apollo[7] hold.   *allegiance*
5 Oft of one wide expanse had I been told
    That deep-browed Homer ruled as his demesne;
    Yet did I never breathe its pure serene°   *atmosphere*
Till I heard Chapman[8] speak out loud and bold:
Then felt I like some watcher of the skies
10   When a new planet swims into his ken;
Or like stout Cortez[9] when with eagle eyes
    He stared at the Pacific—and all his men
Looked at each other with a wild surmise—
    Silent, upon a peak in Darien.

Questions

1. Vocabulary: *fealty* (4), *desmesne* (6), *ken* (10).
2. Has Keats altered the rhyme scheme?
3. Has he preserved the distinction between octave and sestet? What sort of change occurs between the parts?

---

[6] Throughout this chapter and the next, we will refer to rhymed forms in a schematic way. Each rhyme ending is designated by a letter, starting with *a*. These schemes do not refer to the length of the lines.

[7] Apollo is the god of poetry.

[8] George Chapman (1559?–1634), English poet and translator of Homer.

[9] Hernando Cortez (1485–1534), Spanish conqueror of Mexico. Keats is historically inaccurate, however. The first European to see the Pacific was Vasco de Balboa, who viewed it from Darien, Panama.

4. Keats wrote this poem after his discovery of Chapman's translation, which revealed the splendor of Homer to him for the first time. Have you ever experienced a joyous discovery? How did you feel? Does Keats capture a similar experience?

The sonnet has maintained its popularity for a number of reasons. First, like all performers, poets enjoy doing the difficult with apparent ease. Sonnets are poets' high-wire acts, their perfect figure-eights. Second, the sonnet's length is attractive. It is long enough to tackle serious subjects but still short enough to require all of the poet's economy, exactitude, and grace.

In English the sonnet has been dominated by Shakespeare and the rhyme scheme he employed. Shakespeare divided the sonnet into three quatrains and a couplet. The *Shakespearean* or *English* sonnet is rhymed *abab cdcd efef gg*.

WILLIAM SHAKESPEARE (1564–1616)

That Time of Year Thou Mayst in Me Behold

[handwritten: getting older]

That time of year thou mayst in me behold
When yellow leaves, or none, or few, do hang
Upon those boughs which shake against the cold, *[handwritten: Autumn]*
Bare ruined choirs, where late the sweet birds sang.
5 In me thou see'st the twilight of such day
As after sunset fadeth in the west;
Which by and by black night doth take away, *[handwritten: twilight]*
Death's second self that seals up all in rest.
In me thou see'st the glowing of such fire,
10 That on the ashes of his youth doth lie,
As the deathbed whereon it must expire,
Consumed with that which it was nourished by.
This thou perceiv'st, which makes thy love more strong, *[handwritten: Fire symbol of his life]*
To love that well which thou must leave ere long.

Questions

1. What is the relationship among the three quatrains? What unites them? How are they individually organized?
2. What is the relationship between the quatrains and the final couplet?
3. Does the couplet give the poem a sense of completeness? Is there anything more that needs to be said?
4. Why does Shakespeare order line 2 as he does? What can you tell about the speaker from line 2?
5. If you were addressed in such a way, how would you feel about the speaker? About yourself?

Love and mortality are traditional themes of the sonnet. The following is a modern sonnet about a circumstance similar to Shakespeare's.

Pity Me Not Because the Light of Day

Pity me not because the light of day
At close of day no longer walks the sky;
Pity me not for beauties passed away
From field and thicket as the year goes by;
5   Pity me not the waning of the moon,
Nor that the ebbing tide goes out to sea,
Nor that a man's desire is hushed so soon,
And you no longer look with love on me.
This have I known always: Love is no more
10   Than the wide blossom which the wind assails,
Than the great tide that treads the shifting shore,
Strewing fresh wreckage gathered in the gales:
Pity me that the heart is slow to learn
What the swift mind beholds at every turn.

Questions

1. What is the relationship between the first two quatrains and the third? Is the internal structure more typical of the Shakespearean or the Italian sonnet?
2. What is the relationship between the quatrains and the couplet?
3. Does the couplet give the poem a sense of completion? Does anything more need to be said?
4. What is the difference between Shakespeare's attitude toward old age and Millay's attitude?
5. How would you describe the tone of the speaker in the sonnets of Shakespeare and Millay?

Although poets traditionally have used the sonnet as a love poem, they have also found it appropriate for theological meditation and political denunciation. Indeed, the brevity of the form makes it particularly useful for passionate cries of any kind. In 1919 Claude McKay, a Jamaican who had settled in Harlem, wrote "If We Must Die" in response to riots and the suppression of black intellectuals after World War I.

CLAUDE McKAY (1890–1948)

If We Must Die

If we must die, let it not be like hogs
Hunted and penned in an inglorious spot,
While round us bark the mad and hungry dogs,
Making their mock at our accursed lot.
5   If we must die, O let us nobly die,

So that our precious blood may not be shed
In vain; then even the monsters we defy
Shall be constrained to honor us though dead!
O kinsmen! we must meet the common foe!
10   Though far outnumbered let us show us brave,
And for their thousand blows deal one deathblow!
What though before us lies the open grave?
Like men we'll face the murderous, cowardly pack,
Pressed to the wall, dying, but fighting back!

Questions

1. Vocabulary: *constrained* (8).
2. What kind of sonnet is "If We Must Die"? Has McKay retained the internal structure of the sonnet?
3. Is McKay's poem optimistic? Does he believe his people will prevail?
4. Winston Churchill used this poem to rally the British against Nazi Germany in World War II. Can you identify any quality in this poem that would make it a powerful rallying cry?

Like most popular forms, the sonnet has been adapted to the uses of many writers. Shakespeare, Sidney, and Spenser collected them into sonnet series or sequences. One of the great masterpieces of Russian literature, *Eugene Onegin* by Alexander Pushkin, is a verse novel in sonnets. George Meredith, in his sonnet series *Modern Love*, employed a sixteen-line sonnet of his own creation. Although longer than the traditional sonnet, it deserves the name because it deals with the same material and has the same economy and force.

GEORGE MEREDITH (1828–1909)

In Our Old Shipwrecked Days There Was an Hour

In our old shipwrecked days there was an hour,
When in the firelight steadily aglow,
Joined slackly, we beheld the red chasm grow
Among the clicking coals. Our library-bower
5   That eve was left to us: and hushed we sat
As lovers to whom Time is whispering.
From sudden-opened doors we heard them sing:
The nodding elders mixed good wine with chat.
Well knew we that Life's greatest treasure lay
10   With us, and of it was our talk. "Ah, yes!
Love dies!" I said: I never thought it less.
She yearned to me that sentence to unsay.
Then when the fire domed blackening, I found
Her cheek was salt against my kiss, and swift

15   Up the sharp scale of sobs her breast did lift:—
     Now am I haunted by that taste! that sound!

Questions

1. Vocabulary: *chasm* (3), *bower* (4).
2. Do you see any similarity between the rhyme scheme of Meredith's poem and the traditional sonnet?
3. Where does the scene take place? Is the setting significant?
4. What is the significance of the burning coal?
5. What is the speaker's attitude toward the incident? Toward his life?

Exercise

Many literary forms have their own traditions—a history, manner, and identity developed over a period of time. A tradition develops in part when writers try to determine how to use a form by looking back at those poets who have used it in the past. One of the longest traditions is the sonnet tradition. The sonnets of Edna St. Vincent Millay look back toward the sonnets of Shakespeare and Spenser. Dante Gabriel Rossetti, who wrote sonnets of his own, also translated the sonnets of the Italian Renaissance, one of which, Cecco Angiolieri's "In Absence from Becchina," is reprinted on pages 676–77. There are many sonnets or sonnetlike poems in this book.

The following is a list of sonnets other than the ones printed in this chapter. Read these sonnets and try to formulate for yourself what sort of tradition these poems create. Then read the sonnetlike poems, and try to determine what they have borrowed from the tradition and how they have deviated from it. Remember, however, that traditions are not laws; traditions change and develop, and each writer contributes to the tradition by affirming, altering, or adding to it.

Sonnets

Cecco Angiolieri, "In Absence from Becchina," p. 676
Elizabeth Barrett Browning, "How Do I Love Thee," p. 823
Samuel Taylor Coleridge, "Pity," p. 690
John Donne, "Death Be Not Proud," p. 811
Robert Frost, "The Silken Tent," p. 836
Henry Howard, Earl of Surrey, "The Soote Season," p. 622
John Keats, "When I Have Fears," p. 819
John Milton, "When I Consider How My Light Is Spent," p. 582
Wilfred Owen, "Anthem for Doomed Youth," p. 838
Christina Rossetti, "After Death," p. 828
William Shakespeare, "Let Me Not to the Marriage of True Minds," p. 651
William Shakespeare, "My Mistress' Eyes Are Nothing Like the Sun," p. 778
William Shakespeare, "Shall I Compare Thee to a Summer's Day," p. 644
William Shakespeare, "When in Disgrace with Fortune and Men's Eyes," p. 568
William Shakespeare, "When Most I Wink, Then Do Mine Eyes Best See," p. 686

Percy Bysshe Shelley, "Ozymandias," p. 819
Edmund Spenser, "One Day as I Unwarily Did Gaze," p. 674
William Wordsworth, "The World Is Too Much with Us," p. 818

Sonnetlike Poems

E. E. Cummings, "the Cambridge ladies who live in furnished souls," p. 840
Seamus Heaney, "The Forge," p. 875
Daryl Hine, "The Survivors," p. 872
Gerard Manley Hopkins, "The Windhover," p. 829
John Crowe Ranson, "Piazza Piece," p. 602
Dave Smith, "Picking Cherries," p. 877

Terza Rima

Although Italy's most successful export to English poetry has been the sonnet, that country has contributed other verse forms as well. One of the most attractive and demanding is the *terza rima*, the verse form Dante used in *The Divine Comedy*. Terza rima is made up of three-line stanzas or *tercets* interlocked by rhymes so that the inner rhyme of one tercet becomes the outer rhyme of the subsequent tercet. In schematic terms, terza rima is rhymed *aba bcb cdc*. . . . Because terza rima requires triple rhymes for each ending, most English practitioners use occasional near rhymes and assonance instead of true rhymes. One aspect that draws poets to terza rima is the possibility of an unbroken chain of language. A poem in terza rima can continue indefinitely, without being forced to a close by the rhyme scheme.

Perhaps the most famous example of terza rima in English is Percy Bysshe Shelley's "Ode to the West Wind." Shelley, however, chose to break the terza rima periodically with a couplet. The result is five fourteen-line sections that resemble sonnets. In a sense, Shelley's ode is a combination of terza rima and sonnet sequence.

PERCY BYSSHE SHELLEY (1792–1822)

Ode to the West Wind

I

O wild West Wind, thou breath of Autumn's being,
Thou, from whose unseen presence the leaves dead
Are driven, like ghosts from an enchanter fleeing,

Yellow, and black, and pale, and hectic red,
5   Pestilence-stricken multitudes: O Thou,
Who chariotest to their dark wintry bed

The winged seeds, where they lie cold and low,
Each like a corpse within its grave, until
Thine azure sister of the Spring shall blow

10   Her clarion o'er the dreaming earth, and fill
      (Driving sweet buds like flocks to feed in air)
      With living hues and odours plain and hill:

      Wild Spirit, which art moving everyhere;
      Destroyer and Preserver; hear, O hear!

II

15   Thou on whose stream, 'mid the steep sky's commotion,
      Loose clouds like Earth's decaying leaves are shed,
      Shook from the tangled boughs of Heaven and Ocean,

      Angels of rain and lightning: there are spread
      On the blue surface of thine aery surge,
20   Like the bright hair uplifted from the head

      Of some fierce Mænad,[10] even from the dim verge
      Of the horizon to the zenith's height,
      The locks of the approaching storm. Thou Dirge

      Of the dying year, to which this closing night
25   Will be the dome of a vast sepulchre,
      Vaulted with all thy congregated might

      Of vapours, from whose solid atmosphere
      Black rain and fire and hail will burst: O hear!

III

      Thou who didst waken from his summer dreams
30   The blue Mediterranean, where he lay,
      Lulled by the coil of his chrystalline streams,

      Beside a pumice isle in Baiæ's bay,[11]
      And saw in sleep old palaces and towers
      Quivering within the wave's intenser day,

35   All overgrown with azure moss and flowers
      So sweet, the sense faints picturing them! Thou
      For whose path the Atlantic's level powers

      Cleave themselves into chasms, while far below
      The sea-blooms and the oozy woods which wear
40   The sapless foliage of the ocean, know

      Thy voice, and suddenly grow grey with fear,
      And tremble and despoil themselves: O hear!

IV

      If I were a dead leaf thou mightest bear;
      If I were a swift cloud to fly with thee;
45   A wave to pant beneath thy power, and share

---

[10] A nymph attendant on the god Dionysus.
[11] A bay in Naples around which kings built castles.

The impulse of thy strength, only less free
Than thou, O Uncontrollable! If even
I were as in my boyhood, and could be

The comrade of thy wanderings over Heaven,
50   As then, when to outstrip thy skiey speed
Scarce seemed a vision; I would ne'er have striven

As thus with thee in prayer in my sore need.
Oh! lift me as a wave, a leaf, a cloud!
I fall upon the thorns of life! I bleed!

55   A heavy weight of hours has chained and bowed
One too like thee: tameless, and swift, and proud.

V

Make me thy lyre,[12] even as the forest is:
What if my leaves are falling like its own!
The tumult of thy mighty harmonies

60   Will take from both a deep, autumnal tone,
Sweet though in sadness. Be thou, Spirit fierce,
My spirit! Be thou me, impetuous one!

Drive my dead thoughts over the universe
Like withered leaves to quicken a new birth!
65   And, by the incantation of this verse,

Scatter, as from an unextinguished hearth
Ashes and sparks, my words among mankind!
Be through my lips to unawakened Earth

The trumpet of a prophecy! O Wind,
70   If Winter comes, can Spring be far behind?

Questions

1. Vocabulary: *pestilence* (5), *multitudes* (5), *azure* (9), *clarion* (10), *zenith* (23), *sepulchre* (26), *pumice* (34), *chasms* (40), *harmonies* (59).
2. How does stanza 4 unify the three stanzas that precede it?
3. Why does Shelley want to be lifted by the wind? How does he feel about his adult experiences?
4. What does Shelley wish the wind to do to him in stanza 5?
5. In what sense is the poem optimistic? How does the concluding line recollect the opening one?
6. Does this poem have unity? Does it stand as a whole?

French Forms

Perhaps the greatest inventors of forms were the *troubadour* poets of southern France, who lived between the eleventh and thirteenth centuries. A troubadour

---

[12] The Aeolian harp, or wind harp.

could be a king—Richard the Lion-hearted was one—or a traveling adventurer. Usually the poets attached themselves to a court or noble family who acted as patrons of their art. The troubadours delighted in elaborate poetic forms and the skillful employment of complicated word games. Occasionally they were accompanied by an apprentice, called a *jongleur*, who might set their poems to music.

Villanelle

A form that has attracted much more attention in English is the *villanelle*, which contains five tercets and a concluding quatrain. What makes the villanelle special is that the first and third lines become the closing refrain of alternate tercets and reappear as the concluding two lines of the poem. Thus the form has remarkable unity of structure. The echoing and reechoing of the refrains give the villanelle a plaintive, delicate beauty that some poets find irresistible.

However, the villanelle is not without its difficulties. Since it has only two rhyme endings, the poem can easily become monotonous. The risk of monotony is increased by the incessant appearance of the refrains that constitute eight of the poem's <u>nineteen lines</u>—nearly half of the poem. The skilled author of the villanelle, thus, is careful to achieve the maximum tonal range and to fit the refrain lines as naturally as possible into the logic of the poem. Despite these difficulties, there are a number of excellent villanelles.

DYLAN THOMAS (1914–1953)

Do Not Go Gentle into That Good Night

Do not go gentle into that good night,
Old age should burn and rave at close of day;
Rage, rage against the dying of the light.

Though wise men at their end know dark is right,
5 Because their words had forked no lightning they
Do not go gentle into that good night.

Good men, the last wave by, crying how bright
Their frail deeds might have danced in a green bay,
Rage, rage against the dying of the light.

10 Wild men who caught and sang the sun in flight,
And learn, too late, they grieved it on its way,
Do not go gentle into that good night.

Grave men, near death, who see with <u>blinding sight</u>
Blind eyes could blaze like meteors and be gay,
15 Rage, rage against the dying of the light.

And you, my father, there on the sad height,
Curse, bless, me now with your fierce tears, I pray.
Do not go gentle into that good night.
Rage, rage against the dying of the light.

[Handwritten annotations: "Death is right", "Did not do what they wanted to", "live life to the fullest", "paradox", "paradox", "wants something from father"]

Dylan Thomas
(Rollie McKenna)

Questions

1. How are the middle stanzas of the poem organized? Is the relationship between them and the rest of the poem clear?
2. How has Thomas sought rhythmic variety? How has he integrated the refrains into the flow of the poem?
3. In line 8, what does Thomas mean by saying the deeds "might have danced in a green bay"?
4. What does he mean by "sang the sun in flight" (line 10)?

ELIZABETH BISHOP (1911–1979)

One Art

The art of losing isn't hard to master;
so many things seem filled with the intent
to be lost that their loss is no disaster.

Lose something every day. Accept the fluster
5   of lost door keys, the hour badly spent.
The art of losing isn't hard to master.

Then practice losing farther, losing faster:
places, and names, and where it was you meant
to travel. None of these will bring disaster.

10   I lost my mother's watch. And look! my last, or
next-to-last, of three loved houses went.
The art of losing isn't hard to master.

I lost two cities, lovely ones. And, vaster,
some realms I owned, two rivers, a continent.
15 I miss them, but it wasn't a disaster.

—Even losing you (the joking voice, a gesture
I love) I shan't have lied. It's evident
the art of losing's not too hard to master
though it may look like (*Write it!*) like disaster.

🖎 Tips on Writing about Poetry

The poet in writing his or her poem can choose from a number of different forms. It is challenging and useful to consider why the poet has chosen the sonnet form instead of the freer form of unrhymed pentameter; why the poet has chosen the villanelle instead of the terza rima, or the sestina instead of the ballad. Each form has its advantages and disadvantages. A thorough study of the content of the poem will reveal to you why the poet has made his choice of a particular form. As the poet Robert Creeley has written: "Form is never more than an extension of content."

Classic Forms

The French and the Italians did not exhaust the formal resources of poetry. Poets, restless for novelty, have sought elsewhere for means of shaping their feelings and expressions. Poets have borrowed forms from many countries and cultures.

The Ode

Because ancient Greece is the seat of Western culture, poets periodically return to it for poetic inspiration and guidance. Poets use Greek forms out of respect for the long Greek tradition and sometimes in the belief that these forms are unmatched vehicles of artistic perfection. Among the most popular forms is the ode. The word *ode* is used broadly in English to refer to any public expression of praise. However, there are three forms to which it more particularly refers: the *Pindaric*, the *Horatian*, and the *irregular* ode.

The oldest of these forms is the Pindaric or regular ode. Pindar lived in the fifth century B.C. and wrote odes celebrating athletic and political victories, often retelling myths in the process. The short ode that follows celebrates the victory of Hagesidamos, son of Archestratos, a boy from western Lokroi who won the laurel in boxing in 476 B.C.

PINDAR (5th century B.C.)

Olympian 11

<table>
<tr><td>Turn</td><td>Sometimes men need the winds most,</td></tr>
<tr><td></td><td>at other times</td></tr>
<tr><td></td><td>waters from the sky,</td></tr>
<tr><td></td><td>rainy descendants of the cloud.</td></tr>
<tr><td>5</td><td>And when a man has triumphed</td></tr>
<tr><td></td><td>and put his toil behind,</td></tr>
<tr><td></td><td>it is time for melodious song</td></tr>
<tr><td></td><td>to arise, laying</td></tr>
<tr><td></td><td>the foundation of future glory,</td></tr>
<tr><td>10</td><td>a sworn pledge securing proud success.</td></tr>
<tr><td>Counterturn</td><td>For Olympian victors, such acclaim</td></tr>
<tr><td></td><td>is laid in store</td></tr>
<tr><td></td><td>without limit, and I</td></tr>
<tr><td></td><td>am eager to tend it with my song.</td></tr>
<tr><td>15</td><td>For a man flourishes</td></tr>
<tr><td></td><td>in wise understanding,</td></tr>
<tr><td></td><td>as in all things,</td></tr>
<tr><td></td><td>through a god's favor.</td></tr>
<tr><td></td><td>Know now, son of Archestratos,</td></tr>
<tr><td>20</td><td>Hagesidamos, because of your boxing victory</td></tr>
<tr><td>Stand</td><td>I will sing, and my song will be</td></tr>
<tr><td></td><td>an added adornment</td></tr>
<tr><td></td><td>to your gold olive crown,</td></tr>
<tr><td></td><td>shining with love for Western Lokroi.</td></tr>
<tr><td>25</td><td>Go there</td></tr>
<tr><td></td><td>and join the revels, Muses.</td></tr>
<tr><td></td><td>By my bond,</td></tr>
<tr><td></td><td>you will not find a people indifferent to strangers</td></tr>
<tr><td></td><td>or blind to beauty, but men of keenest discernment</td></tr>
<tr><td>30</td><td>and courage in war.</td></tr>
<tr><td></td><td>For the crimson fox</td></tr>
<tr><td></td><td>and thunderous lion cannot change their inborn ways.</td></tr>
</table>

Translation by Frank J. Nisetich (1942–)

Questions

1. What is the purpose of poetry, according to Pindar?
2. How does the celebration of Hagesidamos's victory become a celebration of western Lokroi?
3. Have the politics of the Olympics changed since Hagesidamos's time?
4. Compare this poem to Housman's "To an Athlete Dying Young" in Chapter 5. What is the relationship between both athletes and their birthplaces?

As you can see, the Pindaric ode is divided into three parts: turn (or *strophe*), counterturn (or *antistrophe*), and stand (or *epode*). Poets can shape the turn however they like. But once the poet has chosen a shape, all the turns and counterturns must share the same stanza form. The stand (or epode) is shaped differently from the turn. However, in longer odes that contain more than one stand, the stands are identically shaped. The Pindaric ode gives poets freedom initially but then holds them to their chosen stanza patterns.

The Latin poet Horace wrote poems that have also become known as odes. The Horatian or stanzaic ode does away with the epode. Instead, the poet is free to create a stanza form that is repeated throughout the poem. The forms usually employ intricate rhyme and contain lines of varying length. Keats's "Ode to a Nightingale" is a Horatian ode.

JOHN KEATS (1795–1821)

Ode to a Nightingale

I

My heart aches, and a drowsy numbness pains
    My sense, as though of hemlock° I had drunk,   *a poison*
Or emptied some dull opiate to the drains
    One minute past, and Lethe-wards[13] had sunk:
5 'Tis not through envy of thy happy lot,
    But being too happy in thine happiness,—
        That thou, light-winged Dryad° of the trees,   *a tree spirit*
           In some melodious plot
    Of beechen green and shadows numberless,
10   Singest of summer in full-throated ease.

II

O, for a draught of vintage! that hath been
    Cool'd a long age in the deep-delved earth,
Tasting of Flora° and the country green,   *goddess of flowers*
    Dance, and Provençal song, and sunburnt mirth!
15 O for a beaker full of the warm South,
    Full of the true, the blushful Hippocrene,[14]
        With beaded bubbles winking at the brim,
           And purple-stained mouth;
That I might drink, and leave the world unseen,
20   And with thee fade away into the forest dim:

III

Fade far away, dissolve, and quite forget
    What thou among the leaves hast never known,
The weariness, the fever, and the fret
    Here, where men sit and hear each other groan;
25 Where palsy shakes a few, sad, last gray hairs,
    Where youth grows pale, and spectre-thin, and dies;
        Where but to think is to be full of sorrow
           And leaden-eyed despairs,

---

[13] Lethe is the river that separates the upper world and the underworld. Its waters bring forgetfulness.
[14] Hippocrene is a mythological spring whose waters inspired poetry.

Where Beauty cannot keep her lustrous eyes,
30   Or new Love pine at them beyond to-morrow.

IV

Away! away! for I will fly to thee,
    Not charioted by Bacchus° and his pards,°   *the god of wine   leopards*
But on the viewless wings of Poesy,
    Though the dull brain perplexes and retards:
35   Already with thee! tender is the night,
        And haply the Queen-Moon is on her throne,
            Cluster'd around by all her starry Fays;°   *fairies, elves*
            But here there is no light,
Save what from heaven is with the breezes blown
40   Through verdurous glooms and winding mossy ways.

V

I cannot see what flowers are at my feet,
    Nor what soft incense hangs upon the boughs,
But, in embalmed darkness, guess each sweet
    Wherewith the seasonable month endows
45   The grass, the thicket, and the fruit-tree wild;
        White hawthorn, and the pastoral eglantine;
            Fast fading violets cover'd up in leaves;
            And mid-May's eldest child,
The coming musk-rose, full of dewy wine,
50   The murmurous haunt of flies on summer eves.

VI

Darkling I listen; and, for many a time
    I have been half in love with easeful Death,
Call'd him soft names in many a mused rhyme,
    To take into the air my quiet breath;
55   Now more than ever seems it rich to die,
        To cease upon the midnight with no pain,
            While thou art pouring forth thy soul abroad
            In such an ecstasy!
    Still wouldst thou sing, and I have ears in vain—
60   To thy high requiem become a sod.

VII

Thou wast not born for death, immortal Bird!
    No hungry generations tread thee down;
The voice I hear this passing night was heard
    In ancient days by emperor and clown:
65   Perhaps the self-same song that found a path
        Through the sad heart of Ruth,[15] when, sick for home,
            She stood in tears amid the alien corn;
            The same that oft-times hath
    Charm'd magic casements, opening on the foam
70   Of perilous seas, in faery lands forlorn.

---

[15] In the Bible, Ruth was a Moabite who left her people to stay with her husband, Boaz, and her mother-in-law, Naomi.

VIII

Forlorn! the very word is like a bell
   To toll me back from thee to my sole self!
Adieu! the fancy cannot cheat so well
   As she is fam'd to do, deceiving elf.
75   Adieu! adieu! thy plaintive anthem fades
     Past the near meadows, over the still stream,
       Up the hill-side; and now 'tis buried deep
        In the next valley-glades:
     Was it a vision, or a waking dream?
80   Fled is that music:—Do I wake or sleep?

Questions

1. Vocabulary: *Dryad* (7), *spectre* (26), *verdurous* (40), *eglantine* (46), *requiem* (60), *plaintive* (75).
2. What is the stanza form of Keats's ode?
3. What does the nightingale represent for Keats?
4. Why does he wish to join the nightingale? How does he hope to join him?
5. What is Keats's attitude toward death?
6. Is there anything heroic about this poem?

Many poets no longer call their poems odes, not wishing to force comparison of their poems with those of Keats, Wordsworth, or Shelley. Nevertheless, their basic structure is that of a Horatian or stanzaic ode.

RICHARD WILBUR (1921–)

The Beautiful Changes

One wading a Fall meadow finds on all sides
The Queen Anne's Lace lying like lilies
On water; it glides
So from the walker, it turns
5   Dry grass to a lake, as the slightest shade of you
Valleys my mind in fabulous blue Lucernes.°   *a Swiss lake*

The beautiful changes as a forest is changed
By a chameleon's tuning his skin to it;
As a mantis, arranged
10   On a green leaf, grows
Into it, makes the leaf leafier, and proves
Any greenness is deeper than anyone knows.

Your hands hold roses always in a way that says
They are not only yours; the beautiful changes
15   In such kind ways,
Wishing ever to sunder
Things and things' selves for a second finding, to lose
For a moment all that it touches back to wonder.

Questions

1. Vocabulary: *sunder* (16).
2. What is the stanza pattern of the poem? Is the shape of the poem appropriate to the subject?
3. To whom is the poem addressed? What is the speaker's attitude toward the listener?
4. Odes celebrate momentous occasions—being victorious at the Olympian Games or first hearing the song of a nightingale. Is a great achievement celebrated in this poem? In what way is the listener heroic?
5. How does the beautiful change?

Asian Forms

Asian forms have been popular with Western writers since the turn of the century. Poets have admired the economy and clarity of the *haiku* and the *tanka*, two closely related forms. Both the tanka and the haiku are organized by the numbers of syllables per line rather than by rhyme. A haiku is a three-line poem, the lines having five, seven, and five syllables, respectively. The tanka is longer; its first and third lines have five syllables, and the rest contain seven syllables— thirty-one syllables in all. However, since Asian languages are so different from English, poets writing in English have freely adapted the forms. Because each syllable in Chinese represents a word, some poets prefer to think of the poems as containing seventeen or thirty-one words. Few poets try to translate these forms by preserving the syllable count. In their native language the haiku and tanka have other rules. Each haiku must contain a seasonal reference. In Japanese, the caesuras must be placed in specific places in the line. See Chapter 7 for more on the haiku.

MATSUO BASHO (1644–1694)

Nine Haiku

The beginning of art—
The depths of the country
And a rice-planting song.

Ailing on my travels,
Yet my dream wandering
Over withered moors.

Spring:
A hill without a name
Veiled in morning mist.

The beginning of autumn:
Sea and emerald paddy
Both the same green.

Silent and still: then
Even sinking into the rocks,
The cicada's screech.

Soon it will die,
Yet no trace of this
In the cicada's screech.

The winds of autumn
Blow: yet still green
The chestnut husks.

You say one word
And lips are chilled
By autumn's wind.

A flash of lightning:
Into the gloom
Goes the heron's cry.

Translation by Geoffrey Bownas and Anthony Thwaite (1930–)

Questions

1. Vocabulary: *cicada* (fifth haiku).
2. Is there a seasonal reference in each haiku? Is the reference always obvious?
3. What emotions do the haiku generate? Are they merely objective?
4. With what does art begin, according to Basho? In what way do the poems exemplify his idea of art?

Lady Kasa lived in the eighth century, but little else is known about her. These tanka have been translated into four-line stanzas.

LADY KASA (8th century)

Six Tanka

Like the pearl of dew
On the grass in my garden
In the evening shadows,
I shall be no more.

Even the grains of sand
On a beach eight hundred days wide
Would not be more than my love,
Watchman of the island coast.

The breakers of the Ise Sea
Roar like thunder on the shore.

As fierce as they, as proud as they,
Is he who pounds my heart.

I dreamt of a great sword
Girded to my side.
What does it signify?
That I shall meet you?

The bell has rung, the sign
For all to go to sleep.
Yet thinking of my love
How can I ever sleep?

To love a man without return
Is to offer a prayer
To a devil's back
In a huge temple.[16]

Translation by Geoffrey Bownas and Anthony Thwaite (1930–)

Questions

1. In what way do these tanka trace the relationship between lovers? What is the "plot" of the story?
2. How does the brevity of these poems make them poignant?
3. What is the overall feeling of these tanka? How does each tanka contribute to the feeling?

The influence of Asian poetry can be observed even in poems that do not strictly obey the forms of either the haiku or the tanka. These poems have small, self-contained units; an emphasis on the direct presentation of sensory experience; and an understated tone.

WALLACE STEVENS (1879–1955)

Thirteen Ways of Looking at a Blackbird

I

Among twenty snowy mountains,
The only moving thing
Was the eye of the blackbird.

II

I was of three minds,
5   Like a tree
In which there are three blackbirds.

---

[16] Devils were depicted in the back of Japanese temples to warn people that it was pointless to be bad and greedy.

III

The blackbird whirled in the autumn winds.
It was a small part of the pantomime.

IV

A man and a woman
10   Are one.
A man and a woman and a blackbird
Are one.

V

I do not know which to prefer,
The beauty of inflections,
15   Or the beauty of innuendoes,
The blackbird whistling
Or just after.

VI

Icicles filled the long window
With barbaric glass.
20   The shadow of the blackbird
Crossed it, to and fro.
The mood
Traced in the shadow
An indecipherable cause.

VII

25   O thin men of Haddam,[17]
Why do you imagine golden birds?
Do you not see how the blackbird
Walks around the feet
Of the women about you?

VIII

30   I know noble accents
And lucid, inescapable rhythms;
But I know, too,
That the blackbird is involved
In what I know.

IX

35   When the blackbird flew out of sight,
It marked the edge
Of one of many circles.

X

At the sight of blackbirds
Flying in a green light,
40   Even the bawds of euphony
Would cry out sharply.

---

[17] Haddam is a town in Connecticut. According to Stevens, he chose this town because he liked the sound of its name.

He rode over Connecticut
In a glass coach.
Once, a fear pierced him,
45   In that he mistook
The shadow of his equipage
For blackbirds.

XII

The river is moving.
The blackbird must be flying.

XIII

50   It was evening all afternoon.
It was snowing
And it was going to snow.
The blackbird sat
In the cedar-limbs.

Questions

1. Vocabulary: *inflections* (14), *innuendoes* (15), *bawds* (40), *euphony* (40), *equipage* (46).
2. Stevens wrote that he meant the poem to be a collection of "sensations" rather than "of epigrams or ideas." What various sensations do you get from the poem?
3. Seasonal references abound in the poem. How are they introduced? How do they function?
4. The poem reinforces what sorts of feelings toward blackbirds? Are they beautiful, common, sexy, ominous, deadly, delicate, wise?
5. In what ways are a "man and a woman and a blackbird/ . . . one"?
6. How is the first section related to the last?

Exercise

Take a common object (like a table) and use it as a focus of attention in a variety of circumstances and perspectives. Follow a tree, a swimming pool, a saltshaker through the course of a year or a day or even an hour.

Comic Forms

Comedy is rarely as freewheeling as it appears. In fact, of all types of expression, comedy is the most formulaic. The punch line must come at the very end, preceded by just the right number of interchanges. Poetry, because of its formal nature, is an excellent medium for comic expression. Poets have developed a number of forms exclusively suited to comedy.

Limericks

Limericks were popularized by Edward Lear (1812–1888) after Lear discovered this anonymous example:

> There was an old man of Tobago
> Who lived on rice, gruel, and sago
> Till, much to his bliss
> His physician said this
> To a leg, sir, of mutton you must go.

We can see several important components of the limerick in this example. The first line usually ends in a place or a proper name that has a comic sound, and there is often a dialogue involved. Here are two modern masters of the form.

OGDEN NASH (1902–1971)

Gervaise

> There was a young belle of old Natchez
> Whose garments were always in patchez.
> When comment arose
> On the state of her clothes,
> 5   She drawled, When Ah itchez, Ah scratchez!

Edouard

> A bugler named Dougal MacDougal
> Found ingenious ways to be frugal.
> He learned how to sneeze
> In various keys,
> 5   Thus saving the price of a bugle.

EDWARD GOREY (1925–)

There Was a Young Woman Named Plunnery

> There was a young woman named Plunnery
> Who rejoiced in the practice of gunnery,
>   Till one day unobservant,
>   She blew up a servant,
> 5   And was forced to retire to a nunnery.

Shaped Verses and Concrete Poetry
Shaped Verses

Poetry began as a purely oral mode of communication. But as soon as the first scribes began to copy down the poems they heard, poets became interested in the visual component of language. Poets usually write in lines; the line ending is a visual means of indicating rhythm, meaning, and form. It would be improper, therefore, to distinguish between texts that are visually oriented and those that are orally oriented. Once printed, all poems are visual to some degree. However, some poets make greater use of poetry's visual resources.

The simplest way to use the visual component of poetry is to arrange the lines or words in such a way that the poem looks like an object. There is a long tradition of such shaped verses. Perhaps the most famous in English is George Herbert's "Easter Wings."

GEORGE HERBERT (1593–1633)

Easter Wings[18]

Lord, who createdst man in wealth and store,
    Though foolishly he lost the same,
        Decaying   more   and   more
            Till   he   became
5   Most   poor.
                  With   thee
              O   let   me   rise
        As   larks,   harmoniously,
    And   sing   this   day   thy   victories:
10   Then   shall   the   fall   further   the   flight   in   me.

My   tender   age   in   sorrow   did   begin:
    And   still   with   sicknesses   and   shame
        Thou   didst   so   punish   sin,
            That   I   became
15   Most   thin.
                  With   thee
              Let me combine,
        And feel this day thy victory;
      For, if I imp° my wing on thine,   *graft*
20   Affliction   shall   advance   the   flight   in   me.

Questions

1. How does the rhyme of the poem reinforce its shape? Is the shape merely super-imposed on the poem?
2. Does the shape of the poem refer only to the Easter wings of the title? Why else do the lines contract and then expand?
3. How does the poem exemplify the concept of the *felix culpa*—the "fortunate fall" from Eden?

---

[18] Early editions of Herbert's "Easter Wings" are printed with the lines vertical.

Shaped verses are capable of remarkable delicacy and clarity.

MAY SWENSON (1919–)

Unconscious Came a Beauty

> Unconscious
> came a beauty to my
> wrist
> and stopped my pencil,
> merged its shadow profile with
> my hand's ghost
> on the page:
> Red Spotted Purple or else Mourning
> Cloak,
> paired thin-as-paper wings, near black,
> were edged on the seam side poppy orange,
> as were its spots.

UNCONSCIOUS

CAME A BEAUTY

> I sat arrested, for its soot-haired
> body's worm
> shone in the sun.
> It bent its tongue long as
> a leg
> black on my skin
> and clung without my
> feeling,
> while its tomb-stained
> duplicate parts of
> a window opened.
> And then I
> moved.

Questions

1. How does the poem reenact its subject?
2. How has Swenson made use of the title?
3. How does the shape of the poem enhance the music of the verse?
4. How does the poem end? How does its shape reinforce that sense of ending?

Shaped poems can become very intricate, especially as poets place restrictions on themselves. John Hollander's shaped verses are composed on a typewriter, and he uses the grid of the typewriter as an instrument of measure. In his shaped poems words are never broken, and he does not add extra spaces between words unless they are on the boundary of the picture.

JOHN HOLLANDER (1929–)

Swan and Shadow

```
                        Dusk
                     Above the
                 water hang the
                        loud
                        flies
                        Here
                        O so
                        gray
                        then
                 What              A pale signal will appear
                 When           Soon before its shadow fades
                 Where        Here in this pool of opened eye
                 In us    No Upon us As at the very edges
                   of where we take shape in the dark air
                     this object bares its image awakening
                       ripples of recognition that will
                          brush darkness up into light
       even after this bird this hour both drift by atop the perfect sad instant now
                          already passing out of sight
                         toward yet-untroubled reflection
                       this image bears its object darkening
                     into memorial shades Scattered bits of
                 Light      No of water Or something across
                 water         Breaking up No Being regathered
                 Soon           Yet by then a swan will have
                 gone                Yes Out of mind into what
                        vast
                        pale
                        hush
                        of a
                        place
                        past
                 sudden dark as
                    if a swan
                        sang
```

Questions

1. In what way does the shape of the poem reflect the concepts expressed in the poem?
2. Why does the poem begin by speaking of the flies?
3. Swans are supposed to sing before they die. Why is this reference appropriate to this poem? What other deaths occur in the poem?

A good test of a shaped verse is to write out the poem in the traditional way, lining up the lines along the left-hand margin. If the meaning is compromised or diminished, then the poem is strong. There should be an intimate connection between the shape and the content of the poem.

Concrete Poems

Modern poets have experimented with a more radical use of the visual properties of poetry. Shaped verses arrange lines of verse to form a picture; Herbert's poem even rhymes. Concrete poets, however, often will use only a few words. The placement of the letters gives the poem meaning.

MARY ELLEN SOLT (1920—)

Forsythia

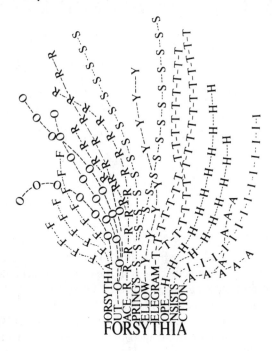

FORSYTHIA

Questions

1. How does a forsythia "telegraph" spring's message?
2. In what ways is all poetry telegraphic? How is this poem telegraphic?
3. Why is spring's message "Hope insists [on] action"? Is this message appropriate for spring?

Suggestions for Essayists

1. Compare two poems in the same form. How have the poets used the form? Have they treated it differently or in the same way?
2. Some people argue that instead of creating social forms that best express our desires, we are shaped by social forms. For example, some educators believe that schools are not formed around students' needs, but rather that students are shaped by what schools demand. Choose some social event—a dance, a wedding, a lecture—and discuss whether you shape it or it shapes you.

Suggestions for Poets

1. Take an idea and try to write it in two different forms. Observe the changes that happen to the idea as it is given shape.
2. Invent a form of your own and write three poems in it. Do you find that the possibilities of the form are exhausted?

14 ❧ The Well-Made Poem

Judging a work of art is difficult and often frustrating. Many people avoid the practice or argue that it is useless. "Since beauty is in the eye of the beholder," they reason, "any object I find pleasing must be good." Others refuse to form any opinions at all: "Who am I to judge a work of art?" they modestly ask.

There are important reasons for developing a critical faculty, however. One of the chief aims of education is to help people recognize excellence so that they may cultivate what is excellent in themselves. Sloppy, fuzzy writing breeds sloppy, fuzzy thinking. Mawkish, sentimental literature breeds vague, undifferentiated feeling. Good literature puts us into better contact with our thoughts and feelings and helps us distinguish the genuine and appropriate from the false and ill-fitting.

Part of the problem in developing critical skills is that poems are a lot like people: one has difficulty recognizing the truly worthwhile. Placed among strangers, we often gravitate to whoever seems at first the friendliest, kindest person. Often our first impressions are wrong. Later we may discover that bright spot to be merely a flash; the person we thought so interesting, clever, and kind may really be dull, slow, and mean. At the same time we may discover that someone we overlooked, a quiet person who spoke softly and with few words, really has the qualities we seek in a lasting friend.

Literary judgments, like personal ones, are best made over a period of time. Clearly, people who have been reading poems for a while have an advantage over the beginner: they have had time to test their first impressions. Similarly, older poems of merit are more easily recognized than contemporary works because they have had time to show their power. The best way to become a seasoned critic is to start reading now and take the suggestions of your teachers.

One must also be careful not to confuse *taste* with *excellence*. For example, we may like animals and enjoy having pictures of animals around us. Our taste for animal pictures may cloud our appreciation of nonanimal pictures, or it may cause us to overpraise a badly executed animal drawing. Similarly, people have moral or religious beliefs that may color their appreciation of certain works. Experienced readers will be able to recognize excellence even in works they do not particularly like, just as we can recognize that an unpleasant person may be an excellent athlete.

Taste and excellence can be confused in another way. Imagine eating a meal of some exotic cuisine for the first time. You are served course after course of foods you do not recognize, whose names you cannot even pronounce. Nevertheless, you find the food delicious. Can you say the food was well prepared? Not with any authority. To make such a judgment, you would have to have eaten several different versions of each dish. All you can honestly say is that you liked what you ate. People who are beginning to read poetry should acknowledge what they like and explore the experiences that please them. But it will take time to develop the knowledge of what is truly well prepared. What seems innovative may in fact be well worn. What appears dull may actually be subtle. Works we like may not necessarily be those of lasting excellence.

Overall Effectiveness

How then does one evaluate a poem? The principal test is whether each part of the poem contributes to its overall effectiveness. A poem is like a superbly integrated organism whose every feature contributes to the health and success of the body as a whole. The limbs of such a creature are neither too large nor too small. It does not carry an ounce more or less of weight than it needs. It is able to respond appropriately to circumstances, and its every action is animated by liveliness and a keen sense of intelligence. The healthy organism knows how and when to enjoy itself but can be tough and efficient when necessary.

No poem, as no person, is ever perfect. Paul Valéry, the great French poet, remarked that a poem is never completed, only abandoned. Thus the responsible judge balances a work's strengths against its weaknesses. A poem can contain many faults and still be good. Another work may contain no glaring errors, yet seem generally lifeless and unsatisfactory. Critics often disagree not about a poem's faults, but about the impact of those faults on the work's overall effectiveness.

Although the components of a good poem are all interrelated, it is easier to evaluate poems by looking at their various aspects separately. These aspects or areas of judgment will overlap, but for now it is useful to consider them as isolated.

Economy

The best poetry is noted for its concentration of expression and feeling. Poets try to use as few words as possible to gain their end. Thus each word must bear its part of the load and serve as many functions as possible. Bad poetry is marked by (1) looseness of expression, (2) redundancy, and (3) padding for rhyme or meter. The following quatrain exhibits all three weaknesses.

The Frog

The frog he sits upon the bank
   And catches bugs and flies
And after he gets tired of that
   He just jumps in and dives.

               —*James K. Elmore*

The first line should read simply "The frog sits upon the bank." The superfluous "he" is added to pad the rhythm. Lines 2 and 4 contain redundant expressions. "Jumps in" and "dives" are synonymous, and flies are a kind of bug, not a different type of creature. Line 3 is wordy: "gets tired" means the same as "tires." "The Frog" suffers more than most poems from uneconomical language. Indeed, it is an example of the worst sort of poetry, *doggerel*. Doggerel is language that has rhyme and meter but contains neither feeling nor thought nor music.

Here is a poem for your evaluation.

CLAUDE MacKAY (1814–1889)

Only a Thought

'Twas only a passing thought, my love,
   Only a passing thought,
That came o'er my mind like a ray of the sun
   In the ripples of waters caught;
5   And it seemed to me, and I say to thee,
   That sorrow and shame and sin
Might disappear from our happy sphere,
   If we knew but to begin;
If we knew but how to profit
10   By wisdom dearly bought:
'Twas only a passing thought, my love,
   Only a passing thought.

Questions

1. Is the "passing thought" original or clear enough to warrant the refrain of lines 1–2 and lines 11–12?
2. Is the "passing thought" buried in all the language used to introduce it?
3. Are there any redundant expressions in the poem? Does a thought pass anywhere but "o'er my mind"?
4. Do you find any padding in the poem? Is line 5 necessary to the poem?
5. Is it clear what we are to "begin" in line 8?
6. How would you evaluate this poem?

Coherence and Consistency

Another test of a poem is whether it is consistent. Careless poets make one statement at the outset and contradict themselves later on. More often, poets may express incompatible attitudes, seeming to approve and disapprove of the same object or person.

But before we accuse a poet of being contradictory, we must be careful. Often, a poet is tracing the evolution of feelings. Matthew Arnold's "Dover Beach," for instance, begins with a quiet, beautiful description of the English Channel but ends with the recognition that the world "Hath really neither joy, nor love, nor light, / Nor certitude, nor peace." The inconsistency is not a poetic fault; rather, it is the most direct and effective means of showing Arnold's evolving realizations. (For a longer discussion of "Dover Beach," see Chapter 7.) The contradictions in the following poem, however, cannot be justified in the same manner.

CHARLES KINGSLEY (1819–1875)

I Once Had a Sweet Little Doll, Dears

I once had a sweet little doll, dears,
    The prettiest doll in the world;
Her cheeks were so red and so white, dears,
    And her hair was so charmingly curled.
5 But I lost my poor little doll, dears,
    As I played in the heath one day;
And I cried for her more than a week, dears,
    But I never could find where she lay.

I found my poor little doll, dears,
10   As I played in the heath one day.
Folks say she is terribly changed, dears,
    For her paint is all washed away,
And her arm trodden off by the cows, dears,
    And her hair not the least bit curled:
15 Yet for old sakes' sake she is still, dears,
    The prettiest doll in the world.

Questions

1. Vocabulary: *heath* (10), *trodden* (13).
2. Is there any redundancy?
3. Are the repeated lines effective in creating unity, or are they merely repetitious?
4. Do you find that the "dears" that end alternate lines are well integrated in the poem? Do they add to the poem's overall effectiveness?
5. Do you believe that the doll is the prettiest one in the world?

This poem contains one glaring contradiction. In line 8 the speaker claims she *never* could find the doll; line 9 says that she found it. Are we to believe that the two stanzas are divided by time? If so, there is nothing to indicate that stanza 1 was written while the doll was still lost and stanza 2 after its recovery. This contradiction may not be enough to spoil this poem, but it is certainly a blemish.

A more difficult aesthetic problem than consistency is *coherence*. Because poetry is so condensed, often a poem will remain unclear after a first, second, or even third reading. Moreover, as discussed in Chapter 13, some poems are intentionally nonsensical or are organized as verbal collages. These poems do not yield their meanings in a conventional way. Third, there are poems whose worlds are drawn from dreams and fantasies. Things occur in them that could not happen in the normal world. Wise readers do not blame a poem for not doing what it never intended to do or for lacking what it never was meant to possess; they do not have rigid expectations of what a poem ought to be. Poems do not need to rhyme, but there are still people who consider a poem defective that doesn't. Conversely, there are those who regard with suspicion a poem that *does* rhyme. A good reader must decide whether a work is coherent within its own rules of composition.

Erasmus Darwin, the author of "Eliza," was a physician, inventor, and poet, and the grandfather of Charles Darwin, whose theory of evolution so revolutionized scientific thinking. "Eliza" is no fantasy; it is meant to be a somewhat romanticized and stylized account of an actual woman killed while impatiently watching for her husband's safety in battle. It should be noted that in the eighteenth century wives would follow their husbands to campsites close to the battlefields.

ERASMUS DARWIN (1731–1802)

Eliza

Now stood Eliza on the wood-crown'd height
O'er Minden's plains spectatress of the fight;
Sought with bold eye amid the bloody strife
Her dearer self, the partner of her life;
5   From hill to hill the rushing host pursued,
And view'd his banner, or believed she view'd.
Pleased with the distant roar, with quicker tread,
Fast by his hand one lisping boy she led;
And one fair girl, amid the loud alarm,
10   Slept on her kerchief, cradled on her arm:
While round her brows bright beams of honour dart,
And love's warm eddies circle round her heart.
—Near and more near th'intrepid beauty press'd,
Saw through the driving smoke his dancing crest,
15   Heard the exulting shout—"They run!—they run!"
"He's safe!" she cried, "he's safe! the battle's won!"
—A ball now hisses through the airy tides
(Some Fury wings it, and some Demon guides),
Parts the fine locks her graceful head that deck,

20   Wounds her fair ear, and sinks into her neck;
      The red stream issuing from her azure veins
      Dyes her white veil, her ivory bosom stains.
      —"Ah me!" she cried, and sinking on the ground,
      Kiss'd her dear babes, regardless of the wound:
25   "Oh, cease not yet to beat, thou vital urn,
      Wait, gushing life, oh! wait my love's return!"—
      Hoarse barks the wolf, the vulture screams from far,
      The angel, Pity, shuns the walks of war;—
      "Oh spare, ye war-hounds, spare their tender age!
30   On me, on me," she cried, "exhaust your rage!"
      Then with weak arms, her weeping babes caress'd,
      And sighing, hid them in her blood-stain'd vest.

            From tent to tent th'impatient warrior flies,
      Fear in his heart, and frenzy in his eyes:
35   Eliza's name along the camp he calls,
      Eliza echoes through the canvas walls;
      Quick through the murmuring gloom his footsteps tread,
      O'er groaning heaps, the dying and the dead,
      Vault o'er the plain,—and in the tangled wood,—
40   Lo! dead Eliza—weltering in her blood!
      Soon hears his listening son the welcome sounds,
      With open arms and sparkling eyes he bounds:
      "Speak low," he cries, and gives his little hand,
      "Mamma's asleep upon the dew-cold sand;
45   Alas! we both with cold and hunger quake—
      Why do you weep? Mamma will soon awake."
      —"She'll wake no more!" the hopeless mourner cried,
      Upturn'd his eyes, and clasp'd his hands, and sigh'd;
      Stretch'd on the ground, awhile entranced he lay,
50   And press'd warm kisses on the lifeless clay:
      And then upsprung with wild convulsive start,
      And all the father kindled in his heart:
      "Oh Heaven!" he cried, "my first rash vow forgive!
      These bind to earth, for these I pray to live."
55   Round his chill babes he wrapp'd his crimson vest,
      And clasp'd them sobbing, to his aching breast.

Questions

1. Vocabulary: *spectatress* (2), *eddies* (12), *intrepid* (13), *convulsive* (51).
2. Does it seem reasonable or possible that a bullet could part her hair, wound her ear, and sink into her neck? From what direction would such a bullet have to come? Does this seem probable since Eliza is in a "tangled wood"?
3. How far away is Eliza from the battlefield? She is close enough to see "through the driving smoke [her husband's] dancing crest"—how is she then in a "tangled wood"?
4. What is the "first rash vow" mentioned in line 53?
5. Who does the listening in line 41? Who does the bounding in line 42?

6. Is it consistent for the son to cry for his father to "Speak low"?
7. Is it logical that a mother anxious for her husband's safety would risk the lives of her children by taking them to a battle?
8. Is the language economical? Do you find any redundancy, padding, or ambiguous pronouns?
9. How would you evaluate this poem overall?

Naturalness

Poetry does not merely transcribe the speech of ordinary people. The language of poetry is shaped, altered, concentrated, and often heightened. Yet the language of a poem should usually be natural—that is, obey the laws of common word order and diction, and avoid rhythms and sounds that are difficult or ugly to pronounce. Of course, poets often create odd or unnatural effects in their poetry for specific expressive purposes. Each case of unnatural language must be judged on its own merits. One must determine whether a passage is justified by expressive power, economy, or variety, or whether it is merely the result of incompetence, haste, or insensitivity.

The following is one of Shakespeare's sonnets. Notice that the opening quatrain is in very plain, natural English. The word order is simple and ordinary. Indeed, the tone of the opening is blunt.

WILLIAM SHAKESPEARE (1564–1616)

My Mistress' Eyes Are Nothing like the Sun

My Mistress' eyes are nothing like the Sun,
Coral is far more red, than her lips red,
If snow be white, why then her breasts are dun:
If hairs be wires, black wires grow on her head:
5   I have seen Roses damasked, red and white,
But no such Roses see I in her cheeks,
And in some perfumes is there more delight,
Then in the breath that from my Mistress reeks.
I love to hear her speak; yet well I know,
10   That Music hath a far more pleasing sound:
I grant I never saw a goddess go,
My Mistress when she walks treads on the ground.
    And yet by heaven I think my love as rare,
    As any she belied with false compare.

Questions

1. Vocabulary: *damasked* (5), *belied* (14).
2. Besides "reeks," are there any other comic words used for rhymes?
3. Shakespeare calls the woman "my love"; yet he lists her defects. Does he resolve this contradiction? Is the poem contradictory?
4. Are any lines padded for rhythm?

5. Is there any redundancy, vague pronoun usage, or verbal looseness?
6. How would you evaluate the poem overall?

Despite the straightforward opening, lines 5 and 6 are in a slightly unusual order. Normally one would say, "I have seen Roses damasked, red and white,/But I see no such Roses in her cheeks." Shakespeare did not order this line for the sake of rhyme or meter, since the more natural line both rhymes and scans. Why, then, did Shakespeare order the words as he did?

First we must recognize that the line is a *chiasmus*, which means "crossing." In a chiasmus the word order of one phrase or clause is inverted in the next. For example, Samuel Johnson wrote, "For we that live to please, must please to live." We can see how these terms cross in this diagram.

> We that live to please
>
> must please to live

In Shakespeare's line there is a similar crossing or chiasmus.

> I have seen Roses . . .
>
> But no such Roses see I . . .

The chiasmus is an elegant but not too unusual variation that gives art to the poem. More important, it shows that the speaker is not being crude in the opening lines out of ignorance. Clearly, he can construct a line with elegance. He is blunt because he wishes to be brutally honest.

Lines 7 and 8 are also unusually ordered. One normally would say, "The breath that reeks from my mistress is not as delightful as some perfumes." However, such a sentence loses all the humor. "Reeks" is the harshest, most insulting word in the poem. Shakespeare wishes to delay it and emphasize it by locating it not only at the end of the line but also at the conclusion of the quatrain.

We now see that whenever Shakespeare deviates from normal word order in this poem, he does so deliberately, for expressive purposes. Moreover, none of these lines is so oddly ordered that it becomes incomprehensible.

The following poem is filled with lines having odd or unnatural word order. Locate each unusual line and try to reword it in a more standard manner. Compare your version with Empson's. Examine what has been lost and gained in the process. See whether Empson's word order is justifiable or unskilled. Are any of the rhymes forced?

WILLIAM EMPSON (1906–)

Villanelle

It is the pain, it is the pain, endures.
Your chemic beauty burned my muscles through.
Poise of my hands reminded me of yours.

What later purge from this deep toxin cures?
5   What kindness now could the old salve renew?
It is the pain, it is the pain, endures.

The infection slept (custom or change inures)
And when pain's secondary phase was due
Poise of my hands reminded me of yours.

10   How safe I felt, whom memory assures,
Rich that your grace safely by heart I knew.
It is the pain, it is the pain, endures.

My stare drank deep beauty that still allures.
My heart pumps yet the poison draught of you.
15   Poise of my hands reminded me of yours.

You are still kind whom the same shape immures.
Kind and beyond adieu. We miss our cue.
It is the pain, it is the pain, endures.
Poise of my hands reminded me of yours.

Questions

1. Vocabulary: *chemic* (2), *inures* (7).
2. Are any of the words difficult to pronounce? Are any of the sounds ineffective or ugly?
3. Are the repeated lines well integrated into the poem, or do they become mechanical and repetitious?
4. Is there any padding for rhythm?
5. Is the poem always comprehensible? If there are muddy places, is there an expressive justification for the muddiness?
6. Are there any ambiguous pronouns?
7. From what branch of knowledge is most of the language drawn? Is the theatrical term "cue" in line 17 out of place?
8. What is your overall evaluation of the poem?

Rhyme is not the only cause of forced, odd, or inexpressive word order. Metrical regularity can produce ineffective or simply bad uses of language. The following is a wholly commonplace observation about the industrious and muscular ant. But the passage is laughable because of its terrible sense of rhythm and awkward word order.

CORNELIUS WHUR (1782–1853)

From Village Musings

The poet questions the ant

Why did you, feeble as you were, attempt
A task so perfectly herculean?
Could it be to rear your tender offspring?

Did your concern touching their welfare
5   So impel? Was aught like conference held
Ere you began to calculate success? . . .
                    Man, physically
Your superior, could not with equal tools
The work have done. He, comparatively,
10   Might as soon this ponderous earth divide.

Questions

1. Vocabulary: *herculean* (2), *ponderous* (10).
2. Which lines are awkwardly ordered? Is there any expressive justification for the order?
3. What is the meaning of "comparatively" in line 9? Is this a standard use of the word?
4. Is there any padding, redundancy, or looseness of language?
5. What is your overall estimation of the passage?

Tone: Sentimentality and Coldness

Poetry, as we have said, is the language of emotion. A good poem effectively conveys emotion to the reader. Readers do not merely understand the emotion the poet wishes to convey, but feel the emotion themselves. A good elegy, for example, does not merely tell us about grief, but puts us through the process of grieving. Readers who set themselves against a poem will never be able to experience it; thus a poem is a partnership between the skilled writer and the responsive reader. As Walt Whitman said, in order to have great poetry there must be great audiences.

We should not, however, judge a poem simply by the intensity with which it conveys emotion. Of greater importance are subtlety, honesty, and depth of feeling. As any seasoned moviegoer knows, horror and suspense are more easily and intensely conveyed than is the confusion of grief or the disenchantment of youth. We may be thrilled as the latest monster destroys downtown Tokyo, but we are often more profoundly touched by some less spectacular event.

Most readers have a sense of what is an appropriate response to a situation and will reject a feeling that seems unsuitable. Most readers will sympathize with a poet who expresses annoyance at ruining a new coat. They will empathize with a poet depressed over having ruined a car. They will be moved by a poet desperate over the loss of a loved one. But readers will be amused or disgusted by the poet wailing over a ruined coat. "What a crybaby," they will complain— and rightly. Such emotional overreaction is called *sentimentality*. Sentimentality occurs when a poet attempts to bestow on an experience more emotion than it can reasonably sustain.

Sentimentality is any excessive emotion, but it usually takes the form of excessive tenderness. A good test of sentimentality is whether the poem accurately depicts the object or experience. Sentimental people are usually blind to the true nature of their love object. They see the world through "rose-colored glasses."

For example, we may cling to objects long after their usefulness, beauty, and worth are exhausted. The following poem is an example of such a sentimental attachment.

ELIZA COOK (1818–1889)

The Old Arm Chair

I love it! I love it! And who shall dare
To chide me for loving that old arm-chair?
I've treasured it long as a sainted prize;
I've bedewed it with tears, and embalmed it with sighs.
5   'Tis bound by a thousand bands to my heart;
Not a tie will break, not a link will start.
Would ye learn the spell?—a mother sat there;
And a sacred thing is that old arm-chair.

In childhood's hour I lingered near
10   The hallowed seat with list'ning ear;
And gentle words that mother would give,
To fit me to die, and teach me to live.
She told me shame would never betide
With truth for my creed, and God for my guide;
15   She taught me to lisp my earliest prayer,
As I knelt beside that old arm-chair.

I sat and watched her many a day,
When her eyes grew dim, and her locks were grey;
And I almost worshipped her when she smiled,
20   And turned from her Bible to bless her child.
Years rolled on; but the last one sped—
My idol was shattered; my earth-star fled.
I learnt how much the heart can bear,
When I saw her die in that old arm-chair.

25   'Tis past! 'tis past! But I gaze on it now
With quivering breath and sobbing brow:
'Twas there she nursed me; 'twas there she died:
And memory flows with lava tide.
Say it is folly, and deem me weak,
30   While the scalding drops start down my cheek;
But I love it! I love it! and cannot tear
My soul from a mother's old arm-chair.

Questions

1. Do we ever get to see the armchair? What does it look like? Is it in good condition?
2. Does the speaker really value the armchair for itself? Why is it valuable?
3. In what sense is the poem an example of metonymy?

4. Cook calls the chair "a sainted prize," "a sacred thing," and a "hallowed seat." Is this sort of idolatry suitable to an old armchair? Is it consistent with the religious sentiments she was supposed to have learned?
5. The speaker says she "embalmed" the chair with sighs. Does the word convey the emotion she wishes to convey? She also says her "memory flows with lava tide." Is the violence and destructiveness of lava an appropriate image here? Does it convey the feelings Cook wishes to convey? Do you see any other inappropriate expressions?
6. Does the situation warrant the hyperbole Cook employs?
7. What do we usually mean by a "shattered" idol? How does Cook use the idea in line 22? Is it appropriate?
8. How would you evaluate this poem overall?

Some people believe that certain situations are inherently sentimental. Although it is true that some situations lend themselves to sentimental treatment, a good poet can render a potentially sentimental situation with depth, perception, and toughness. The two poems that follow portray poor old women who have fallen on hard times. The subject lends itself to a sentimental treatment, but it can also be handled with conviction.

THOMAS ASHE (1836–1889)

Old Jane

I love old women best, I think:
    She knows a friend in me,—
Old Jane, who totters on the brink
    Of God's Eternity;
5   Whose limbs are stiff, whose cheek is lean,
    Whose eyes look up, afraid;
Though you may gather she has been
    A little laughing maid.

Once had she with her doll what times,
10   And with her skipping-rope!
Her head was full of lovers' rhymes,
    Once, and her heart of hope;
Who, now, with eyes as sad as sweet—
    I love to look on her,—
15   At corner of the gusty street,
    Asks, "Buy a pencil, Sir?"

Her smile is as the litten West,
    Nigh-while the sun is gone;
She is more fain to be at rest
20   Than here to linger on:
Beneath her lids the pictures flit
    Of memories far-away:
Her look has not a hint in it
    Of what she sees to-day.

Questions

1. Vocabulary: *litten* (17).
2. Are there any phrases or sentences whose meaning is obscure?
3. Do the last two lines contradict anything in the poem? Is there really no hint of old Jane's present condition?
4. Are any lines forced? Do the rhymes come naturally? Whose eyes are "as sad as sweet"?
5. Does Ashe provide any clues to how old Jane came to sell pencils on street corners? Do the memories of her past seem an accurate picture of the complexities of youth? Has Jane always been poor? Has she slipped from a better economic condition?
6. Is it reasonable to think that Jane thinks only about dolls, jump rope, and lovers' rhymes?
7. What is Ashe's attitude toward Jane? Can one reasonably share his attitude given the facts he has supplied?
8. Is this poem sentimental? Why?

ROBERT FROST (1874–1963)

Provide, Provide

The witch that came (the withered hag)
To wash the steps with pail and rag,
Was once the beauty Abishag,[1]

The picture pride of Hollywood.
5 Too many fall from great and good
For you to doubt the likelihood.

Die early and avoid the fate.
Or if predestined to die late,
Make up your mind to die in state.

10 Make the whole stock exchange your own!
If need be occupy a throne,
Where nobody can call *you* crone.

Some have relied on what they knew;
Others on being simply true.
15 What worked for them might work for you.

No memory of having starred
Atones for later disregard
Or keeps the end from being hard.

Better to go down dignified
20 With boughten friendship at your side.
Than none at all. Provide, provide!

---

[1] Abishag was a beautiful young woman who nursed King David in his old age.

Questions

1. Vocabulary: *atones* (17).
2. Do you understand the meaning of each phrase? Does the poem contain any contradictions? Is there any padding or redundancy? If so, is there any reason for it?
3. Do the lines seem forced? Are the rhymes natural? If any seem comic, is that intended or the result of artistic miscalculation?
4. Does Frost provide enough background on the scrubwoman to make her seem realistic? Is all the information good?
5. What is Frost's attitude toward the old woman? Can you reasonably share his attitude?
6. Is this poem sentimental?

Exercise

The foregoing two poems develop their subject in very different ways. One tries to be coldhearted; the other is extremely sentimental. The next two poems take as their subject women who are struggling to survive. Try to place them on the scale between indifference and sentimentality. Then try to determine whether the poems are successful and finely crafted.

WILLIAM BUTLER YEATS (1865–1939)

Crazy Jane Talks with the Bishop

I met the Bishop on the road
And much said he and I.
"Those breasts are flat and fallen now,
Those veins must soon be dry;
5   Live in a heavenly mansion,
Not in some foul sty."

"Fair and foul are near of kin,
And fair needs foul," I cried.
"My friends are gone, but that's a truth
10   Nor grave nor bed denied,
Learned in bodily lowliness
And in the heart's pride.

"A woman can be proud and stiff
When on love intent;
15   But Love has pitched his mansion in
The place of excrement;
For nothing can be sole or whole
That has not been rent."

PATRICK KAVANAGH (1904–1967)

Tinker's Wife

I saw her amid the dunghill debris
Looking for things

Such as an old pair of shoes or gaiters.
She was a young woman,
5   A tinker's wife.
Her face had streaks of care
Like wires across it,
But she was supple
As a young goat
10   On a windy hill.
She searched on the dunghill debris,
Tripping gingerly
Over tin canisters
And sharp-broken
15   Dinner plates.

GREGORY CORSO (1930–)

The Vestal Lady on Brattle

Within a delicate grey ruin
the vestal lady on Brattle°   *street in Cambridge, Mass.*
is up at dawn, as is her custom,
with the raise of a shade.

5   Swan-boned slippers revamp her aging feet;
she glides within an outer room . . .
pours old milk for an old cat.

Full-bodied and randomly young she clings,
peers down; hovers over a wine-filled vat,
10   and with outstretched arms like wings,
revels in the forming image of child below.

Despaired, she ripples a sunless finger
across the liquid eyes; in darkness
the child spirals down; drowns.
15   Pain leans her forward—face absorbing all—
mouth upon broken mouth, she drinks . . .

Within a delicate grey ruin
the vestal lady on Brattle
is up and about, as is her custom,
20   drunk with child.

    Sentimentality is a form of emotional exaggeration. In the best poems each element is in proportion to the others. Thus sentimentality can distort a poem that is in other respects well made. In judging a poem, one should examine each element of the poem to see how and why it is functioning. Only then can one decide whether each element best serves the poem as a whole or whether it is a defect in the poem's overall design.

    Coldness is a problem closely related to sentimentality. Instead of overreacting emotionally, a poet may underreact. This coldness often appears in official or public poetry. Poets may be asked to write for a specific occasion that may not engage them emotionally. Or, sometimes, poets will moralize on a public event that they have failed to grasp emotionally. In the following poem Robert Service used the occasion of Dylan Thomas's death from alcoholism to moralize about the evils of drink. Dylan Thomas was a poet, and several of his poems are included in this book. Service seems less moved by the human and poetic loss of Thomas than by the opportunity to sermonize.

ROBERT SERVICE (1876–1958)

Dylan

And is it not a gesture grand
    To drink oneself to death?
Oh sure 'tis I can understand,
    Being of sober breath.
5   And so I do not sing success,
    But dirge the damned who fall,
And who contempt for life express
    Through alcohol.

Of Stephen Foster and of Poe,
10   Of Burns and Wilde[2] I think;
And weary men who dared to go
    The wanton way of drink.
Strange mortals blind to bitter blame,
    And deaf to loud delight,
15   Who from the shades of sin and shame
    Enstar our night.

Among those dupes of destiny
    Add D.T.[3] to my list,
Although his verse you may agree
20   Leaves one in mental mist . . .
Oh ye mad poets, loth of life,
    Who peace in death divine,
Pass not by pistol, poison, knife,—
    Drown, drown in wine!

Questions

1. Vocabulary: *dirge* (6), *wanton* (12), *dupes* (17).
2. Service may have shortened the last line to suggest the way Thomas's life had been unnaturally shortened. However, does this feeling come across? Do the rhythm and sound of line 8 suggest the seriousness of the subject?

---

[2] Stephen Foster, Edgar Allan Poe, Robert Burns, and Oscar Wilde all suffered from alcoholic tendencies.
[3] The Welsh poet Dylan Thomas (1914–1953).

3. "D.T." in line 18 refers to Dylan Thomas but also suggests *delirium tremens*, commonly known as the D.T.'s, the horrifying hallucinations of alcoholics. Is such a pun appropriate in a serious elegy?
4. Is "although" in line 19 the proper connective? Is "sober breath" (line 4) a logical or natural expression? Does it mean anything other than sober?
5. What is the tone of lines 21–24? Is it consistent with the rest of the poem?
6. Do you sense that Service is deeply saddened by Thomas's death? Is he more concerned about Thomas or about the evils of alcohol?

The following is a poem that Dr. Sprat, bishop of Rochester, wrote on the death of a lady friend. Although he expresses the extremes of grief, try to determine, as you are reading, how sincere those expressions are.

THOMAS SPRAT (1635–1713)

On His Mistress Drowned

Sweet stream, that dost with equal pace
Both thyself fly, and thyself chase,
    Forbear awhile to flow,
    And listen to my woe.
5   Then go, and tell the sea that all its brine
      Is fresh, compar'd to mine;
Inform it that the gentle dame,
Who was the lite of all my flame,
    In th' glory of her bud
10   Has pass'd the fatal flood.

Death by this only stroke triumphs above
      The greatest power of love:
    Alas, alas! I must give o'er,
    My sighs will let me add no more.

15   Go on, sweet stream, and henceforth rest
    No more than does my troubled breast;
And if my sad complaints have made thee stay,
    These tears, these tears shall mend thy way.

Questions

1. Does the speaker want the stream to flow? Is there any contradiction in his attitude?
2. What evidence does the speaker give that "the gentle dame . . . was the life of all [his] flame"?
3. Does he give you a picture of the woman? Was she young, old, rich, poor, well educated, innocent, a relative?
4. How has death triumphed over love in lines 11–12? Do we know? Did the speaker do anything to save his mistress?

Sentimentality may be laughable, but such cold-bloodedness seems far more offensive.

Completeness

Like any organism, a poem must be complete in order for it to function at maximum effectiveness. We must come to understand what motivates speakers to talk as they do, and what is the significance of their words. Without this knowledge, the poem will seem incomplete. The poet is not obliged to tell us everything; some details are insignificant, and readers should be prepared to make important inferences on their own. If essentials are left out, however, readers will be unable to respond emotionally or intellectually to the poem.

In the following poem the author has failed to give important information that would help us empathize with the speaker's plight. The general outlines are clear, however. A parent—we do not know whether it is a mother or father—grieves over the death of a child—we cannot tell whether it is a son or daughter. The child had apparently been a good one, who had not wished to worry the parent. Yet it is difficult to understand the speaker's guilt and self-mockery. When the speaker says, "It is not true that Love will do no wrong," he or she is apparently referring to some bad act mistakenly committed out of love. But what is the action? Who perpetrated it? Did this action lead to the child's death? We do not and can never know; and without this knowledge, we readers will remain distanced from the speaker and cut off from the poem's potential power.

COVENTRY PATMORE (1823–1896)

If I Were Dead

"If I were dead, you'd sometimes say, Poor Child!"
The dear lips quiver'd as they spake,
And the tears brake
From eyes which, not to grieve me, brightly smiled.
5   Poor Child, poor Child!
I seem to hear your laugh, your talk, your song.
It is not true that Love will do no wrong.
Poor Child!
And did you think, when you so cried and smiled,
10   How I, in lonely nights, should lie awake,
And of those words your full avengers make?
Poor Child, poor Child!
And now unless it be
That sweet amends thrice told are come to thee,
15   O God, have Thou *no* mercy upon me!
Poor Child!

Questions

1. Is it clear why the child says, "If I were dead, you'd sometimes say, Poor Child!"? What did the child mean? Was the child angry, frightened, spiteful, or tender in saying this line?
2. How old is the child? Of what does the child die?
3. What evidence is there in the poem that God has shown the speaker "*no* mercy"?

4. Does the rhyme contribute to the overall effectiveness of the poem?
5. Is the poem sentimental?
6. Is the language natural? Are there any ambiguities without purpose?
7. How would you rate this poem?

The purpose of criticism is to increase a reader's awareness of excellence and the variety of his or her responses to literature. Mature critical judgments are never simple or clear. As we have seen, they are based on a number of different criteria whose relative importance must constantly be reevaluated. Good critics understand the limitations of their views and are prepared to consider alternatives, to reexamine their judgments, to be more open and varied. W. H. Auden, the great poet and critic, once wrote:

> As readers, we remain in the nursery stage so long as we cannot distinguish between taste and judgments, so long, that is, as the only possible verdicts we can pass on a book are two: this I like; this I don't like.
>
> For an adult reader, the possible verdicts are five: I can see this is good and I like it; I can see this is good but I don't like it; I can see this is good and, though at present I don't like it, I believe that with perseverance I shall come to like it; I can see that this is trash but I like it; I can see that this is trash and I don't like it.

Mature critics, rather than limiting their response to literature, have learned to increase their responses and appreciations.

The Good and the Great

A poem is considered great not because it is better made than other poems but for a variety of other reasons. Usually great poems have greater scope or emotional intensity than other poems. As we all know, some subjects and conditions are more easily articulated than others. Great poems explore the most difficult areas of human experience or express concerns in the subtlest, most original ways.

Poems can also become great for other reasons. Some are considered great because they are the first of their kind; they break new artistic ground. Other works articulate the spirit of their age so clearly and succinctly that they become a touchstone for their time. Byron's *Childe Harold's Pilgrimage* is an example of a poem whose fame may well be greater than its craftsmanship. It was the most widely read work of its time.

Works can also become especially valued because they represent a pivotal period in the artistic output of a great poet. As Shakespeare wrote, "Some are born great, some achieve greatness, and some have greatness thrust upon them." Likewise, greatness is something that comes mysteriously to a work. It is a quality so elusive, so special to each great work, that no criteria can be formulated to describe how it works. We may be able to analyze why a work is excellent, but we can do no more than recognize when a work is truly great.

We have chosen five poems that are almost universally regarded as great works. They come from different periods and nations; there are one by an American, one by an Irishman, two by Englishmen, and one by an American who became a British citizen. These poems are somewhat longer than most of the poems in the book. Great poems often have wider scope and more ambitious subject matter. Take your time with them as you would with all the other poems in this book. These poems continue to pose emotional and intellectual challenges even to the most sophisticated reader.

 ## Writers on Writing   *Ezra Pound*

A classic is classic not because it conforms to certain structural rules, or fits certain definitions (of which its author had quite probably never heard). It is classic because of a certain eternal and irrepressible freshness.

JOHN MILTON (1608–1674)

Lycidas

In this monody[4] the author bewails a learned friend, unfortunately drowned in his passage from Chester on the Irish seas, 1637. And by occasion foretells the ruin of our corrupted clergy, then in their height.

	Yet once more, O ye laurels, and once more	
	Yet myrtles brown, with ivy never sere,[5]	
	I come to pluck your berries harsh and crude,°	*unripe*
	And with forced fingers rude,	
5	Shatter your leaves before the mellowing year.	
	Bitter constraint, and sad occasion dear,	
	Compels me to disturb your season due;	
	For Lycidas is dead, dead ere his prime,	
	Young Lycidas, and hath not left his peer.	
10	Who would not sing for Lycidas? He knew	
	Himself to sing, and build the lofty rhyme.	
	He must not float upon his watery bier	
	Unwept, and welter to the parching wind,	
	Without the meed° of some melodious tear.	*reward*
15	Begin then, sisters of the sacred well[6]	

---

[4] A solo song in Greek drama.

[5] Laurel, myrtle, and ivy are plants associated with poetic inspiration. Laurel is given by Apollo, the god of poetry; myrtle by Venus, the goddess of love; and ivy is associated with Bacchus, the god of wine.

[6] The muses inspire the arts.

That from beneath the seat of Jove doth spring,
Begin, and somewhat loudly sweep the string.
Hence with denial vain, and coy excuse;
So may some gentle Muse
20   With lucky words favor my destined urn,
And as he passes turn,
And bid fair peace be to my sable shroud.
For we were nursed upon the selfsame hill,
Fed the same flock, by fountain, shade, and rill.
25   Together both, ere the high lawns appeared
Under the opening eyelids of the morn,
We drove afield, and both together heard
What time the grayfly winds her sultry horn.[7]
Battening° our flocks with the fresh dews of night,   *feeding*
30   Oft till the star that rose at evening bright
Toward Heaven's descent had sloped his westering wheel.
Meanwhile the rural ditties were not mute,
Tempered to th' oaten flute,
Rough satyrs danced, and fauns with cloven heel
35   From the glad sound would not be absent long,
And old Damoetas[8] loved to hear our song.
      But O the heavy change, now thou art gone,
Now thou art gone, and never must return!
Thee, shepherd, thee the woods and desert caves,
40   With wild thyme and the gadding° vine o'ergrown,   *straggling*
And all their echoes mourn.
The willows and the hazel copses green
Shall now no more be seen,
Fanning their joyous leaves to thy soft lays.
45   As killing as the canker° to the rose,   *cankerworm*
Or taint-worm to the weanling° herds that graze,   *newly weaned*
Or frost to flowers that their gay wardrobe wear,
When first the white thorn blows,°   *blossoms*
Such, Lycidas, thy loss to shepherd's ear.
50   Where were ye, nymphs, when the remorseless deep
Closed o'er the head of your loved Lycidas?
For neither were ye playing on the steep,
Where your old Bards, the famous Druids[9] lie,
Nor on the shaggy top of Mona high,
55   Nor yet where Deva spreads her wizard stream:[10]
Ay me! I fondly° dream—   *foolishly*
Had ye been there—for what could that have done?
What could the Muse herself that Orpheus bore,

---

[7] That is, buzzes.
[8] A typical shepherd's name.
[9] Druids were the ancient priests of Britain.
[10] "Mona" is the island of Anglesey, a center of Druid activity. "Deva" is the river Dee in Cheshire.

The Muse herself, for her inchanting[11] son
60 Whom universal Nature did lament,
When by the rout° that made the hideous roar,   *mob*
His gory visage down the stream was sent,
Down the swift Hebrus to the Lesbian shore?
    Alas! What boots° it with incessant care   *profits*
65 To tend the homely slighted shepherd's trade,
And strictly meditate the thankless Muse?
Were it not better done as others use,
To sport with Amaryllis in the shade,
Or with the tangles of Neaera's hair?[12]
70 Fame is the spur that the clear spirit doth raise
(That last infirmity of noble mind)
To scorn delights, and live laborious days;
But the fair guerdon° when we hope to find,   *reward*
And think to burst out into sudden blaze,
75 Comes the blind Fury with th' abhorréd shears,[13]
And slits the thin spun life. "But not the praise,"
Phoebus[14] replied, and touched my trembling ears;
"Fame is no plant that grows on mortal soil,
Not in the glistering foil[15]
80 Set off to th' world, nor in broad rumor lies,
But lives and spreads aloft by those pure eyes,
And perfect witness of all-judging Jove;
As he pronounces lastly on each deed,
Of so much fame in Heaven expect thy meed."
85   O fountain Arethuse, and thou honored flood,
Smooth-sliding Mincius, crowned with vocal reeds,[16]
That strain I heard was of a higher mood.
But now my oat° proceeds,   *flute song*
And listens to the herald of the sea
90 That came in Neptune's[17] plea.
He asked the waves, and asked the felon° winds,   *whipping*
"What hard mishap hath doomed this gentle swain?"
And questioned every gust of rugged wings
That blows from off each beakéd promontory;
95 They knew not of his story,
And sage Hippotades[18] their answer brings,
That not a blast was from his dungeon strayed,
The air was calm, and on the level brine,

---

[11] Orpheus, the great poet-singer of Greek mythology, was torn to pieces by Thracian women, who threw his head into the river Hebrus.
[12] Amaryllis and Neaera were typical names for nymphs.
[13] A fury is an avenging spirit.
[14] Phoebus Apollo, the god of poetic inspiration.
[15] A glistering foil was a thin metal backing used to give sparkle to glass gems.
[16] Arethusa was a fountain in Sicily; Mincius, a river in Lombardy.
[17] Neptune is the Roman god of the sea.
[18] Hippotades is the god of winds.

Sleek Panope[19] with all her sisters played.
100 It was that fatal and perfidious bark
Built in th' eclipse, and rigged with curses dark,
That sunk so low that sacred head of thine.
        Next Camus,[20] reverend sire, went footing slow,
His mantle hairy, and his bonnet sedge,
105 Inwrought with figures dim, and on the edge
Like to that sanguine flower° inscribed with woe.   *hyacinth*
"Ah! who hath reft," quoth he, "my dearest pledge?"
Last came and last did go
The pilot of the Galilean lake,°   *St. Peter*
110 Two massy keys he bore of metals twain
(The golden opes, the iron shuts amain).
He shook his mitered locks, and stern bespake:
"How well could I have spared for thee, young swain,
Enow° of such as for their bellie's sake,   *enough*
115 Creep and intrude, and climb into the fold!
Of other care they little reckoning make,
Than how to scramble at the shearers' feast,
And shove away the worthy bidden guest.
Blind mouths! That scarce themselves know how to hold
120 A sheep-hook, or have learned aught else the least
That to the faithful herdsman's art belongs!
What recks it° them? What need they? They are sped;   *does it matter to*
And when they list,° their lean and flashy songs   *choose*
Grate on their scrannel° pipes of wretched straw.   *harsh, meager*
125 The hungry sheep look up, and are not fed,
But swoln with wind, and the rank mist they draw,
Rot inwardly, and foul contagion spread,
Besides what the grim wolf with privy paw
Daily devours apace, and nothing said.
130 But that two-handed engine at the door
Stands ready to smite once, and smite no more."
        Return, Alpheus, the dread voice is past,
That shrunk thy streams; return, Sicilian muse,
And call the vales, and bid them hither cast
135 Their bells and flowerets of a thousand hues.
Ye valleys low where the mild whispers use,
Of shades and wanton winds, and gushing brooks,
On whose fresh lap the swart star[21] sparely looks,
Throw hither all your quaint enameled° eyes,   *adorned*
140 That on the green turf suck the honeyed showers,
And purple all the ground with vernal flowers.
Bring the rathe° primrose that foresaken dies.   *early*
The tufted crow-toe, and pale jessamine,

---

[19] The most important sea nymph, or nereid.
[20] The god of the river Cam.
[21] The Dog Star, Sirius.

The white pink, and the pansy freaked° with jet,   *flecked*
145   The glowing violet,
       The musk-rose, and the well attired woodbine.
       With cowslips wan that hang the pensive head,
       And every flower that sad embroidery wears:
       Bid amaranthus[22] all his beauty shed,
150   And daffadillies fill their cups with tears,
       To strew the laureate hearse where Lycid lies.
       For so to interpose a little ease,
       Let our frail thoughts dally with false surmise.
       Ay me! Whilst thee the shores and sounding seas
155   Wash far away, where'er thy bones are hurled,
       Whether beyond the stormy Hebrides,[23]
       Where thou perhaps under the whelming tide
       Visit'st the bottom of the monstrous world;
       Or whether thou, to our moist vows denied,
160   Sleep'st by the fable of Bellerus old,[24]
       Where the great vision of the guarded mount
       Looks toward Namancos and Bayona's hold:[25]
       Look homeward angel now, and melt with ruth:°   *grief and pity*
       And, O ye dolphins, waft the hapless youth.
165   Weep no more, woeful shepherds, weep no more,
       For Lycidas your sorrow is not dead,
       Sunk though he be beneath the watery floor,
       So sinks the day-star in the ocean bed,
       And yet anon repairs his drooping head,
170   And tricks° his beams, and with new-spangled ore,   *dresses, adorns*
       Flames in the forehead of the morning sky:
       So Lycidas sunk low, but mounted high,
       Through the dear might of him that walked the waves,
       Where other groves, and other streams along,
175   With nectar pure his oozy locks he laves,
       And hears the unexpressive nuptial song,
       In the blest kingdoms meek of joy and love.
       There entertain him all the saints above,
       In solemn troops and sweet societies
180   That sing, and singing in their glory move,
       And wipe the tears forever from his eyes.
       Now, Lycidas, the shepherds weep no more;
       Henceforth thou art the genius of the shore,
       In thy large recompense, and shalt be good
185   To all that wander in that perilous flood.
           Thus sang the uncouth swain to th' oaks and rills,
       While the still morn went out with sandals gray;

---

[22] Amaranth is a mythical flower that never fades.
[23] Islands off the coast of Scotland.
[24] A giant who, according to fable, is buried in Cornwall.
[25] Bayona and Namancos are places in northern Spain.

He touched the tender stops of various quills,
With eager thought warbling his Doric lay:
190   And now the sun had stretched out all the hills,
And now was dropped into the western bay;
At last he rose, and twitched his mantle blue:
Tomorrow to fresh woods, and pastures new.

WILLIAM WORDSWORTH (1770–1850)

Lines

*Composed a Few Miles above Tintern Abbey on Revisiting
the Banks of the Wye during a Tour. July 13, 1798*

Five years have passed; five summers, with the length
Of five long winters! and again I hear
These waters, rolling from their mountain-springs
With a soft inland murmur. Once again
5   Do I behold these steep and lofty cliffs,
That on a wild secluded scene impress
Thoughts of more deep seclusion; and connect
The landscape with the quiet of the sky.
The day is come when I again repose
10   Here, under this dark sycamore, and view
These plots of cottage ground, these orchard tufts,
Which at this season, with their unripe fruits,
Are clad in one green hue, and lose themselves
'Mid groves and copses. Once again I see
15   These hedgerows, hardly hedgerows, little lines
Of sportive wood run wild; these pastoral farms,
Green to the very door; and wreaths of smoke
Sent up, in silence, from among the trees!
With some uncertain notice, as might seem
20   Of vagrant dwellers in the houseless woods,
Or of some Hermit's cave, where by his fire
The Hermit sits alone.

                              These beauteous forms,
Through a long absence, have not been to me
As is a landscape to a blind man's eye;
25   But oft, in lonely rooms, and 'mid the din
Of towns and cities, I have owed to them,
In hours of weariness, sensations sweet,
Felt in the blood, and felt along the heart;
And passing even into my purer mind,
30   With tranquil restoration—feelings too
Of unremembered pleasure; such, perhaps,
As have no slight or trivial influence
On that best portion of a good man's life,
His little, nameless, unremembered, acts

35 Of kindness and of love. Nor less, I trust,
    To them I may have owed another gift,
    Of aspect more sublime; that blessed mood,
    In which the burthen of the mystery,
    In which the heavy and the weary weight
40 Of all this unintelligible world,
    Is lightened—that serene and blesséd mood,
    In which the affections gently lead us on—
    Until, the breath of this corporeal frame
    And even the motion of our human blood
45 Almost suspended, we are laid asleep
    In body, and become a living soul;
    While with an eye made quiet by the power
    Of harmony, and the deep power of joy,
    We see into the life of things.
                                    If this
50 Be but a vain belief, yet, oh! how oft—
    In darkness and amid the many shapes
    Of joyless daylight; when the fretful stir
    Unprofitable, and the fever of the world,
    Have hung upon the beatings of my heart—
55 How oft, in spirit, have I turned to thee,
    O sylvan Wye! thou wanderer through the woods,
    How often has my spirit turned to thee!

    And now, with gleams of half-extinguished thought
    With many recognitions dim and faint,
60 And somewhat of a sad perplexity,
    The picture of the mind revives again;
    While here I stand, not only with the sense
    Of present pleasure, but with pleasing thoughts
    That in this moment there is life and food
65 For future years. And so I dare to hope,
    Though changed, no doubt, from what I was when first
    I came among these hills; when like a roe
    I bounded o'er the mountains, by the sides
    Of the deep rivers, and the lonely streams,
70 Wherever nature led—more like a man
    Flying from something that he dreads than one
    Who sought the thing he loved. For nature then
    (The coarser pleasures of my boyish days,
    And their glad animal movements all gone by)
75 To me was all in all.—I cannot paint
    What then I was. The sounding cataract
    Haunted me like a passion; the tall rock,
    The mountain, and the deep and gloomy wood,
    Their colors and their forms, were then to me
80 An appetite; a feeling and a love,
    That had no need of a remoter charm,
    By thought supplied, nor any interest

Unborrowed from the eye.—That time is past,
And all its aching joys are now no more,
85 And all its dizzy raptures. Not for this
Faint° I, nor mourn nor murmur; other gifts   *lose heart*
Have followed; for such loss, I would believe,
Abundant recompense. For I have learned
To look on nature, not as in the hour
90 Of thoughtless youth; but hearing oftentimes
The still, sad music of humanity,
Nor harsh nor grating, though of ample power
To chasten and subdue. And I have felt
A presence that disturbs me with the joy
95 Of elevated thoughts; a sense sublime
Of something far more deeply interfused,
Whose dwelling is the light of setting suns,
And the round ocean and the living air,
And the blue sky, and in the mind of man:
100 A motion and a spirit, that impels
All thinking things, all objects of all thought,
And rolls through all things. Therefore am I still
A lover of the meadows and the woods,
And mountains; and of all that we behold
105 From this green earth; of all the mighty world
Of eye, and ear—both what they half create,
And what perceive; well pleased to recognize
In nature and the language of the sense
The anchor of my purest thoughts, the nurse,
110 The guide, the guardian of my heart, and soul
Of all my moral being.
                                    Nor perchance,
If I were not thus taught, should I the more
Suffer my genial spirits[26] to decay:
For thou art with me here upon the banks
115 Of this fair river; thou my dearest Friend,[27]
My dear, dear Friend; and in thy voice I catch
The language of my former heart, and read
My former pleasures in the shooting lights
Of thy wild eyes. Oh! yet a little while
120 May I behold in thee what I was once,
My dear, dear Sister! and this prayer I make,
Knowing that Nature never did betray
The heart that loved her; 'tis her privilege,
Through all the years of this our life, to lead
125 From joy to joy: for she can so inform
The mind that is within us, so impress
With quietness and beauty, and so feed

---

[26] Genius, a spirit that watches over a place or person.
[27] Wordsworth's sister, Dorothy.

With lofty thoughts, that neither evil tongues,
Rash judgments, nor the sneers of selfish men,
130   Nor greetings where no kindness is, nor all
The dreary intercourse of daily life,
Shall e'er prevail against us, or disturb
Our cheerful faith, that all which we behold
Is full of blessings. Therefore let the moon
135   Shine on thee in thy solitary walk;
And let the misty mountain winds be free
To blow against thee: and, in after years,
When these wild ecstasies shall be matured
Into a sober pleasure; when thy mind
140   Shall be a mansion for all lovely forms,
Thy memory be as a dwelling place
For all sweet sounds and harmonies; oh! then,
If solitude, or fear, or pain, or grief
Should be thy portion, with what healing thoughts
145   Of tender joy wilt thou remember me,
And these my exhortations! Nor, perchance—
If I should be where I no more can hear
Thy voice, nor catch from thy wild eyes these gleams
Of past existence—wilt thou then forget
150   That on the banks of this delightful stream
We stood together; and that I, so long
A worshiper of Nature, hither came
Unwearied in that service; rather say
With warmer love—oh! with far deeper zeal
155   Of holier love. Nor wilt thou then forget,
That after many wanderings, many years
Of absence, these steep woods and lofty cliffs,
And this green pastoral landscape, were to me
More dear, both for themselves and for thy sake!

MARIANNE MOORE (1887–1972)

The Steeple-Jack

(Revised, 1961)

Dürer[28] would have seen a reason for living
    in a town like this, with eight stranded whales
to look at; with the sweet air coming into your house
on a fine day, from water etched
5   with waves as formal as the scales
    on a fish.

---

[28] Albrecht Dürer (1471–1528), German artist famed for the perfection of his drawings.

One by one in two's and three's, the seagulls keep
    flying back and forth over the town clock,
or sailing around the lighthouse without moving their wings—
10   rising steadily with a slight
        quiver of the body—or flock
mewing where

a sea the purple of the peacock's neck is
    paled to greenish azure as Dürer changed
15   the pine green of the Tyrol to peacock blue and guinea
gray. You can see a twenty-five-
        pound lobster; and fishnets arranged
to dry. The

whirlwind fife-and-drum of the storm bends the salt
20   marsh grass, disturbs stars in the sky and the
star on the steeple; it is a privilege to see so
much confusion. Disguised by what
    might seem the opposite, the sea-
side flowers and

25   trees are favored by the fog so that you have
    the tropics at first hand: the trumpet-vine,
fox-glove, giant snap-dragon, a salpiglossis that has
spots and stripes; morning-glories, gourds,
    or moon-vines trained on fishing-twine
30   at the back

door; cat-tails, flags, blueberries and spiderwort,
    stripped grass, lichens, sunflowers, asters, daisies—
yellow and crab-claw ragged sailors with green bracts—toad-plant,
petunias, ferns; pink lilies, blue
35   ones, tigers; poppies; black sweet-peas.
The climate

is not right for the banyan, frangipani, or
    jack-fruit trees; or an exotic serpent
life. Ring lizard and snake-skin for the foot, if you see fit;
40   but here they've cats, not cobras, to
    keep down the rats. The diffident
little newt

with white pin-dots on black horizontal spaced
    out bands lives here; yet there is nothing that
45   ambition can buy or take away. The college student
named Ambrose sits on the hillside
    with his not-native books and hat
and sees boats

at sea progress white and rigid as if in
50   a groove. Liking an elegance of which
the source is not bravado, he knows by heart the antique
sugar-bowl shaped summer-house of

interlacing slats, and the pitch
of the church

55 spire, not true, from which a man in scarlet lets
  down a rope as a spider spins a thread;
he might be part of a novel, but on the sidewalk a
sign says C. J. Poole, Steeple Jack,
  in black and white; and one in red
60 and white says

Danger. The church portico has four fluted
  columns, each a single piece of stone, made
modester by white-wash. This would be a fit haven for
waifs, children, animals, prisoners,
65   and presidents who have repaid
sin-driven

senators by not thinking about them. The
  place has a school-house, a post-office in a
store, fish-houses, hen-houses, a three-masted
70   schooner on
the stocks. The hero, the student,
  the steeple-jack, each in his way,
is at home.

It could not be dangerous to be living
75   in a town like this, of simple people,
who have a steeple-jack placing danger-signs by the church
while he is gilding the solid-
  pointed star, which on a steeple
stands for hope.

WILLIAM BUTLER YEATS (1865–1939)

Sailing to Byzantium[29]

I

That is no country for old men. The young
In one another's arms, birds in the trees
—Those dying generations—at their song,
The salmon-falls, the mackerel-crowded seas,
5 Fish, flesh, or fowl, commend all summer long
Whatever is begotten, born, and dies.
Caught in that sensual music all neglect
Monuments of unageing intellect.

---

[29] The ancient name for Istanbul. Yeats viewed the civilization of Byzantium as the height of art
and artifice.

II

An aged man is but a paltry thing,
10 A tattered coat upon a stick, unless
Soul clap its hands and sing, and louder sing
For every tatter in its mortal dress,
Nor is there singing school but studying
Monuments of its own magnificence;
15 And therefore I have sailed the seas and come
To the holy city of Byzantium.

III

O sages standing in God's holy fire
As in the gold mosaic of a wall,
Come from the holy fire, perne in a gyre,[30]
20 And be the singing-masters of my soul.
Consume my heart away; sick with desire
And fastened to a dying animal
It knows not what it is; and gather me
Into the artifice of eternity.

IV

25 Once out of nature I shall never take
My bodily form from any natural thing,
But such a form as Grecian goldsmiths make
Of hammered gold and gold enamelling
To keep a drowsy Emperor awake;
30 Or set upon a golden bough to sing
To lords and ladies of Byzantium
Of what is past, or passing, or to come.

T. S. ELIOT (1888–1965)

The Love Song of J. Alfred Prufrock

S'io credesse che mia risposta fosse
a persona che mai tornasse al mondo,
questa fiamma staria senza più scosse.
Ma perciòcche giammai di questo fondo
*   non tornò vivo alcun, s'i'odo il vero,*
senza tema d'infamia ti rispondo.[31]

Let us go then, you and I,
When the evening is spread out against the sky
Like a patient etherised upon a table;

---

[30] The gyre symbolizes for Yeats the spinning of the soul.
[31] From Dante's *Inferno*, XXVII, 61–66. These lines are the words of Guido da Montefeltro, a distinguished Florentine who gave bad counsel. They mean:

> If I believe that my reply were made
> To one who would revisit earth, the flame
> Would be at rest, and its commotion laid.
> But seeing that alive none ever came
> Back from this deep, if it be truth I hear,
> I answer without dread of injured fame.

Let us go, through certain half-deserted streets,
5 The muttering retreats
Of restless nights in one-night cheap hotels
And sawdust restaurants with oyster-shells:
Streets that follow like a tedious argument
Of insidious intent
10 To lead you to an overwhelming question. . .
Oh, do not ask, "What is it?"
Let us go and make our visit.

In the room the women come and go
Talking of Michelangelo.[32]

15 The yellow fog that rubs its back upon the window-panes,
The yellow smoke that rubs its muzzle on the window-panes,
Licked its tongue into the corners of the evening,
Lingered upon the pools that stand in drains,
Let fall upon its back the soot that falls from chimneys,
20 Slipped by the terrace, made a sudden leap,
And seeing that it was a soft October night,
Curled once about the house, and fell asleep.

And indeed there will be time
For the yellow smoke that slides along the street
25 Rubbing its back upon the window-panes;
There will be time, there will be time
To prepare a face to meet the faces that you meet;
There will be time to murder and create,
And time for all the works and days of hands
30 That lift and drop a question on your plate;
Time for you and time for me,
And time yet for a hundred indecisions,
And for a hundred visions and revisions,
Before the taking of a toast and tea.

35 In the room the women come and go
Talking of Michelangelo.

And indeed there will be time
To wonder, "Do I dare?" and, "Do I dare?"
Time to turn back and descend the stair,
40 With a bald spot in the middle of my hair—
(They will say: "How his hair is growing thin!")
My morning coat, my collar mounting firmly to the chin,
My necktie rich and modest, but asserted by a simple pin—
(They will say: "But how his arms and legs are thin!")
45 Do I dare
Disturb the universe?
In a minute there is time
For decisions and revisions which a minute will reverse.

---

[32] Michelangelo (1475–1564) was one of the greatest painters of the Italian Renaissance, as well as
a poet. He never married and had no children.

For I have known them all already, known them all—
50 Have known the evenings, mornings, afternoons,
I have measured out my life with coffee spoons;
I know the voices dying with a dying fall
Beneath the music from a farther room.
    So how should I presume?

55 And I have known the eyes already, known them all—
The eyes that fix you in a formulated phrase,
And when I am formulated, sprawling on a pin,
When I am pinned and wriggling on the wall,
Then how should I begin
60 To spit out all the butt-ends of my days and ways?
    And how should I presume?

And I have known the arms already, known them all—
Arms that are braceleted and white and bare
(But in the lamplight, downed with light brown hair!)
65 Is it perfume from a dress
That makes me so digress?
Arms that lie along a table, or wrap about a shawl.
    And should I then presume?
    And how should I begin?
        *   *   *   *   *

70 Shall I say, I have gone at dusk through narrow streets
And watched the smoke that rises from the pipes
Of lonely men in shirt-sleeves, leaning out of windows? . . .

T. S. Eliot (*National Portrait Gallery, Smithsonian
Institution, Washington, D.C.*)

I should have been a pair of ragged claws
Scuttling across the floors of silent seas.[33]

    *   *   *   *   *

75   And the afternoon, the evening, sleeps so peacefully!
Smoothed by long fingers,
Asleep . . . tired . . . or it malingers,
Stretched on the floor, here beside you and me.
Should I, after tea and cakes and ices,
80   Have the strength to force the moment to its crisis?
But though I have wept and fasted, wept and prayed,
Though I have seen my head (grown slightly bald) brought in upon a platter,[34]
I am no prophet—and here's no great matter;
I have seen the moment of my greatness flicker,
85   And I have seen the eternal Footman hold my coat, and snicker,
And in short, I was afraid.

And would it have been worth it, after all,
After the cups, the marmalade, the tea,
Among the porcelain, among some talk of you and me,
90   Would it have been worth while,
To have bitten off the matter with a smile,
To have squeezed the universe into a ball
To roll it towards some overwhelming question,
To say: "I am Lazarus, come from the dead,[35]
95   come back to tell you all, I shall tell you all"—
If one, settling a pillow by her head,
        Should say: "That is not what I meant at all.
        That is not it, at all."

And would it have been worth it, after all,
100   Would it have been worth while,
After the sunsets and the dooryards and the sprinkled streets,
After the novels, after the teacups, after the skirts that trail along the floor—
and this, and so much more?—
It is impossible to say just what I mean!
105   But as if a magic lantern threw the nerves in patterns on a screen:
Would it have been worth while
If one, settling a pillow or throwing off a shawl,
And turning toward the window, should say:
        "That is not it at all,
110   That is not what I meant, at all."

    *   *   *   *   *

No! I am not Prince Hamlet, nor was meant to be;
Am an attendant lord, one that will do
To swell a progress, start a scene or two,
Advise the prince; no doubt, an easy tool,

---

[33] The crab travels backward. Eliot is alluding to Hamlet's words (Act II, Scene 2, line 195), "for you . . . shall grow old as I am, if like a crab you could go backward."
[34] Salome, the daughter of King Herod, had John the Baptist's head brought to her on a platter.
[35] Jesus raised Lazarus from the dead.

115   Deferential, glad to be of use,
         Politic, cautious, and meticulous;
         Full of high sentence, but a bit obtuse;
         At times, indeed, almost ridiculous—
         Almost, at times, the Fool.

120   I grow old . . . I grow old . . .
         I shall wear the bottoms of my trousers rolled.

         Shall I part my hair behind? Do I dare to eat a peach?
         I shall wear white flannel trousers, and walk upon the beach.
         I have heard the mermaids singing, each to each.

125   I do not think that they will sing to me.

         I have seen them riding seaward on the waves
         Combing the white hair of the waves blown back
         When the wind blows the water white and black.

         We have lingered in the chambers of the sea
130   By sea-girls wreathed with seaweed red and brown
         Till human voices wake us, and we drown.

Checklist of Questions for Evaluating Poetry

A list of questions follows that should help you evaluate poetry. Because each poem is different, no list can be complete, and you will need to supplement this list with other questions. Moreover, many great poems defy simple explanation. A poem may break many norms and yet remain a compelling and coherent expression.

Economy

1. Are there any repeated expressions or words? Is this repetition necessary or effective?
2. If the poem has a refrain, is the refrain well integrated, or is it mechanical?
3. Is any line padded to keep the rhythm regular?

Coherence and Consistency

1. Are all the ideas and attitudes consistent? If they are paradoxical, do they reflect a more subtle philosophical or psychological position? Are any inconsistencies part of the poetic development?
2. Are any expressions vague? Can the vagueness be justified by the context of the poem?
3. Are the images comprehensible? Is any oddness the result of dreamlike concentration, or is it the result of thoughtlessness?
4. If the poem seems nonsensical, is it the case that it is not supposed to be comprehensible in a traditional way?

Naturalness

1. Is the order of the language unnatural? Where it is unnatural, has the language been altered for expressive purposes?
2. Are the rhymes forced?
3. Is the diction natural? Where the word choice seems odd, is there some special reason?

4. Can the poem be read easily? Do the sounds fit the subject?
5. Do the rhythms seem appropriate to the subject and mood? Are they boring and mechanical?

Tone

1. Does the tone seem appropriate to the poem's subject and the speaker's attitude?
2. Is the poem sentimental?
3. Is the poem unfeeling?
4. Does the tone vary naturally, or is it mechanical and constant?

Completeness

1. Has the poet provided all the details necessary for the reader's full emotional and intellectual response? If not, is there a good reason?
2. Does the poem conclude or does it merely end?
3. Has the poet satisfied your expectations? If not, has the poet made an acceptable substitute?

Suggestions for Essayists

1. Compare two poems on a similar subject.
2. Select any object (e.g., a car, a house) and describe the criteria by which you decide whether it is good or bad.
3. Discuss the necessity of making critical evaluations.

Suggestions for Poets

1. Find a poem that you think is especially poor and rewrite it.
2. Take a poem you think is especially good and, by using redundancy, inconsistency, and rhythmic alterations, make it bad.

GEOFFREY CHAUCER (1340?–1400)

The Complaint of Chaucer to His Purse

To yow, my purse, and to noon other wight°	person
Complayne I, for ye be my lady dere!	
I am so sory, now that ye been lyght;	
For certes,° but° ye make me hevy chere,	surely unless
5 Me were as leef° be layd upon my bere;	I would like to be
For which unto your mercy thus I crye:	
Beth hevy ageyn, or elles moote° I dye!	must
Now voucheth sauf° this day, or° yt be nyght,	vouchsafe before
That I of yow the blisful soun° may here,	sound
10 Or see your colour lyk the sonne bryght,	
That of yelownesse hadde never pere.	
Ye be my lyf, ye be myn hertes stere,°	guide
Quene of comfort and of good companye:	
Beth hevy ageyn, or elles moote I dye!	
15 Now purse, that ben to me my lyves lyght	
And saveour, as° doun in this world here,	while
Out of this toune helpe me thurgh your myght,	
Syn that ye wole nat ben my tresorere;	
For I am shave as nye° as any frere.°	close friar
20 But yet I pray unto your curtesye:	
Beth hevy ageyn, or elles moote I dye!	

Lenvoy de Chaucer:

O conquerour of Brutes° Albyon,°	Brutus's England
Which that by lyne and free eleccion[1]	

---

[1] Henry IV, though a usurper, claimed the throne because he was the grandson of Edward II and thus was in the line of succession, and also because he had been placed on the throne by an act of Parliament—therefore, by "free eleccion."

Been verray° kyng, this song to yow I sende;   *true*
25 And ye, that mowen° alle our harmes amende,   *can*
Have mynde upon my supplicacion!

SIR THOMAS WYATT (1503–1542)

They Flee from Me[2]

They flee from me, that sometime did me seek,
With naked foot stalking in my chamber.
I have seen them, gentle, tame, and meek,
That now are wild, and do not remember
5 That sometime they put themselves in danger
To take bread at my hand; and now they range,
Busily seeking with a continual change.

Thankèd be fortune it hath been otherwise.
Twenty times better; but once in special,
10 In thin array, after a pleasant guise,
When her loose gown from her shoulders did fall,
And she me caught in her arms long and small,°   *thin*
Therewithall sweetly did me kiss
And softly said, "Dear heart, how like you this?"

15 It was no dream, I lay broad waking.
But all is turned, thorough my gentleness,
Into a strange fashion of forsaking;
And I have leave to go, of her goodness,
And she also to use newfangleness[3]
20 But since that I so kindely am servèd.
I fain would know what she hath deservéd.

SIR WALTER RALEIGH (1552–1618)

The Nymph's Reply to the Shepherd

If all the world and love were young,
And truth in every shepherd's tongue,
These pretty pleasures might me move
To live with thee and be thy love.

5 Time drives the flocks from field to fold
When rivers rage and rocks grow cold,
And Philomel° becometh dumb;   *the nightingale*
The rest complains of cares to come.

The flowers do fade, and wanton fields
10 To wayward winter reckoning yields;
A honey tongue, a heart of gall,
Is fancy's spring, but sorrow's fall.

---

[2] This poem is discussed at length in Part I, Chapter 4, pages 56–57.
[3] "To use newfangleness" means to explore new things—that is, to be fickle.

Thy gowns, thy shoes, thy beds of roses,
Thy cap, thy kirtle°, and thy posies   *dress*
15   Soon break, soon wither, soon forgotten—
In folly ripe, in reason rotten.

Thy belt of straw and ivy buds,
Thy coral clasps and amber studs,
All these in me no means can move
20   To come to thee and be thy love.

But could youth last and love still breed,
Had joys no date° nor age no need,   *conclusion*
Then these delights my mind might move
To live with thee and be thy love.

Compare "The Nymph's reply to the Shepherd" with Christopher Marlowe's "The Passionate Shepherd to His Love," on pages 523–24.

SIR PHILIP SIDNEY (1554–1586)

From Astrophel and Stella,[4] Sonnet #71

Who will in fairest book of Nature know
How virtue may best lodged in beauty be,
Let him but learn of love to read in thee,
Stella, those fair lines which true goodness show.
5   There shall he find all vices' overthrow,
Not by rude force, but sweetest sovereignty
Of reason, from whose light those night birds fly,
That inward sun in thine eyes shineth so.
And, not content to be perfection's heir
10   Thyself, dost strive all minds that way to move,
Who mark in thee what is in thee most fair.
So while thy beauty draws the heart to love,
As fast thy virtue bends that love to good.
"But ah," Desire still cries, "give me some food."

Compare Sonnet #71 to Herbert's "Love (III)" on page 673, and Shakespeare's "My Mistress' Eyes Are Nothing Like the Sun," on page 778.

THOMAS CAMPION (1567–1620)

There Is a Garden in Her Face

There is a garden in her face
Where roses and white lilies grow;
A heav'nly paradise is that place

---

[4] Astrophel and Stella are the names of the two characters in Sidney's sonnet series. Their names literally mean "star-lover" and "star."

Wherein all pleasant fruits do flow.
5   There cherries grow which none may buy
     Till "Cherry-ripe" themselves do cry.[5]

Those cherries fairly do enclose
Of orient pearl a double row,
Which when her lovely laughter shows,
10 They look like rose-buds filled with snow;
     Yet them nor peer nor prince can buy,
     Till "Cherry-ripe" themselves do cry.

Her eyes like angels watch them still;
Her brows like bended bows do stand,
15   Threat'ning with piercing frowns to kill
All that attempt, with eye or hand
     Those sacred cherries to come nigh
     Till "Cherry-ripe" themselves do cry.

Consider "There Is a Garden in Her Face" as an example of metaphor or allegory.

JOHN DONNE (1572–1631)

Death Be Not Proud

Death, be not proud, though some have callèd thee
Mighty and dreadful, for thou art not so;
For those whom thou think'st thou dost overthrow
Die not, poor Death, nor yet canst thou kill me.
5 From rest and sleep, which but thy pictures be,
Much pleasure; then from thee much more must flow,
And soonest our best men with thee do go,
Rest of their bones, and soul's delivery.
Thou art slave to fate, chance, kings, and desperate men,
10 And dost with poison, war, and sickness dwell,
And poppy[6] or charms can make us sleep as well
And better than thy stroke; why swell'st thou then?
One short sleep past, we wake eternally
And death shall be no more; Death, thou shalt die.

Consider "Death Be Not Proud" as an example of personification.

ROBERT HERRICK (1591–1674)

Delight in Disorder

A sweet disorder in the dress
Kindles in clothes a wantonness.

---

[5] "Cherry-ripe" was the cry of a London fruit seller.
[6] Poppies are the raw ingredient for opium, which can produce sleep and ease pain as well as cause death.

A lawn° about the shoulders thrown   *fine shawl*
Into a fine distractión;
5   An erring° lace, which here and there   *wandering*
Enthralls the crimson stomacher;°   *bodice*
A cuff neglectful, and thereby
Ribbons to flow confusedly;
A winning wave, deserving note,
10 In the tempestuous petticoat;
A careless shoestring, in whose tie
I see a wild civility;
Do more bewitch me than when art
Is too precise in every part.

ROBERT HERRICK (1591–1674)

Upon Julia's Clothes

Whenas in silks my Julia goes,
Then, then, methinks, how sweetly flows
That liquefaction[7] of her clothes.

Next, when I cast mine eyes, and see
5   That brave vibration, each way free,
O, how that glittering taketh me!

ANNE BRADSTREET (1612?–1672)

To My Dear and Loving Husband

If ever two were one, then surely we.
If ever man were lov'd by wife, then thee;
If ever wife was happy in a man,
Compare with me ye women if you can.
5   I prize thy love more than whole Mines of gold,
Or all the riches that the East doth hold.
My love is such that Rivers cannot quench,
Nor ought but love from thee, give recompence.
Thy love is such I can no way repay,
10 The heavens reward thee manifold I pray.
Then while we live, in love lets so persever,
That when we live no more, we may live ever.

APHRA BEHN (1640–1689)

A Thousand Martyrs I Have Made

A thousand martyrs I have made,
   All sacrific'd to my desire;

---

[7] *Liquefaction* is the act of making a liquid, especially from a solid.

A thousand beauties have betray'd,
    That languish in resistless fire.
5   The untam'd heart to hand I brought,
    And fixed the wild and wandering thought.

I never vow'd nor sigh'd in vain,
    But both, tho' false, were well receiv'd.
The fair are pleas'd to give us pain,
10   And what they wish is soon believ'd.
And tho' I talk'd of wounds and smart,
Love's pleasures only touched my heart.

Alone the glory and the spoil
    I always laughing bore away;
15 The triumphs, without pain or toil,
    Without the hell, the heav'n of joy.
And while I thus at random rove
Despis'd the fools that whine for love.

EDWARD TAYLOR (1645?–1729)

Upon a Spider Catching a Fly

Thou sorrow, venom Elfe:
    Is this thy play,
To spin a web out of thyselfe
    To Catch a Fly?
5   For Why?

I saw a pettish° wasp   *peevish*
    Fall foule therein.
Whom yet thy Whorle[8] pins not clasp
    Lest he should fling
10   His sting.

But as affraid, remote
    Didst stand hereat
And with thy little fingers stroke
    And gently tap
15   His back.

Thus gently him didst treate
    Lest he should pet,
And in a froppish,° waspish heate   *fretful*
    Should greatly fret
20   Thy net.

Whereas the silly Fly,
    Caught by its leg
Thou by the throate tookst hastily
    And 'hinde the head
25   Bite Dead.

---

[8] A "whorle" is the flywheel of a spindle.

This goes to pot, that not
    Nature doth call.
Strive not above what strength hath got
    Lest in the brawle
30   Thou fall.

This Frey° seems thus to us.   *fray, fight*
    Hells Spider gets
His intrails spun to whip Cords thus
    And wove to nets
35   And sets.

To tangle Adams race
    In's stratigems
To their Destructions, spoil'd, made base
    By venom things
40   Damn'd Sins.

But mighty, Gracious Lord
    Communicate
Thy Grace to breake the Cord, afford
    Us Glorys Gate
45   And State.

We'l Nightingaile sing like
    When pearcht on high
In Glories Cage, thy glory, bright,
    And thankfully,
50   For joy.

Compare "Upon a Spider Catching a Fly" with Walt Whitman's "A Noiseless Patient Spider" on pages 825–26.

JONATHAN SWIFT (1667–1745)

A Description of the Morning

Now hardly here and there a hackney-coach
Appearing showed the ruddy morn's approach.
Now Betty from her master's bed had flown,
And softly stole to discompose her own;
5   The slipshod 'prentice from his master's door
Had pared the dirt and sprinkled around the floor.
Now Moll had whirled her mop with dexterous airs,
Prepared to scrub the entry and the stairs.
The youth with broomy stumps began to trace
10   The kennel-edge,° where wheels had worn the place.   *gutter*
The small-coal man was heard with cadence deep,
Till drowned in shriller notes of chimney-sweep:

Duns[9] at his lordship's gate began to meet;
And brickdust Moll had screamed through half the street.
15   The turnkey° now his flock returning sees,   *prison guard*
Duly let out a-nights to steal for fees:
The watchful bailiffs take their silent stands,
And schoolboys lag with satchels in their hands.

THOMAS GRAY (1716–1771)

Ode on the Death of a Favorite Cat[10]

Drowned in a tub of goldfishes

'Twas on a lofty vase's side,
Where China's gayest art had dyed
   The azure flowers that blow;
Demurest of the tabby kind,
5   The pensive Selima reclined,
   Gazed on the lake below.

Her conscious tail her joy declared;
The fair round face, the snowy beard,
   The velvet of her paws,
10   Her coat, that with the tortoise vies,
Her ears of jet,° and emerald eyes,   *black*
   She saw; and purred applause.

Still had she gazed; but 'midst the tide
Two angel forms were seen to glide,
15   The genii[11] of the stream:
Their scaly armor's Tyrian° hue   *purple*
Through richest purple to the view
   Betrayed a golden gleam.

The hapless nymph with wonder saw:
20   A whisker first and then a claw,
   With many an ardent wish,
She stretched in vain to reach the prize.
What female heart can gold despise?
   What cat's averse to fish?

25   Presumptuous maid! with looks intent
Again she stretched, again she bent,
   Nor knew the gulf between.
(Malignant Fate sat by and smiled)

---

[9] "Duns" are people requesting money.
[10] Gray wrote this elegy at the request of Horace Walpole (1717–1797), the author. Walpole's cat, Selima, died by drowning in a cistern.
[11] Genii, the plural of genius. They are the protecting spirits of a place or person.

The slippery verge her feet beguiled,
30   She tumbled headlong in.

Eight times emerging from the flood
She mewed to every watery god,
      Some speedy aid to send.
No dolphin came,[12] no nereid° stirred: *sea nymph*
35   Nor cruel Tom, nor Susan heard.
      A favorite has no friend!

From hence, ye beauties, undeceived,
Know, one false step is ne'er retrieved,
      And be with caution bold.
40   Not all that tempts your wandering eyes
And heedless hearts is lawful prize;
      Nor all that glisters gold.

WILLIAM BLAKE (1757–1827)

The Tyger

Tyger! Tyger! burning bright,
In the forests of the night;
What immortal hand or eye,
Could frame thy fearful symmetry?

5   In what distant deeps or skies
Burnt the fire of thine eyes!
On what wings dare he aspire?
What the hand, dare seize the fire?

And what shoulder, & what art,
10   Could twist the sinews of thy heart?
And when thy heart began to beat,
What dread hand? & what dread feet?

What the hammer? what the chain,
In what furnace was thy brain?
15   What the anvil? what dread grasp,
Dare its deadly terrors clasp?

When the stars threw down their spears
And water'd heaven with their tears:
Did he smile his work to see?
20   Did he who made the Lamb make thee?

Tyger! Tyger! burning bright,
In the forests of the night:
What immortal hand or eye,
Dare frame thy fearful symmetry?

---

[12] Dolphins have the reputation for saving people in distress. Tom and Susan are typical names for servants.

ROBERT BURNS (1759–1796)

A Red, Red Rose

O My Luve's like a red, red rose,
    That's newly sprung in June;
O My Luve's like the melodie
    That's sweetly played in tune.

5   As fair art thou, my bonnie lass,
    So deep in luve am I;
And I will luve thee still, my dear,
    Till a' the seas gang° dry.   *go*

Till a' the seas gang dry, my dear,
10   And the rocks melt wi' the sun:
O I will love thee still, my dear,
    While the sands o' life shall run.

And fare thee weel, my only luve,
    And fare thee weel awhile!
15   And I will come again, my luve,
    Though it were ten thousand mile.

WILLIAM WORDSWORTH (1770–1850)

I Wandered Lonely as a Cloud

I wandered lonely as a cloud
    That floats on high o'er vales and hills,
When all at once I saw a crowd,
    A host, of golden daffodils,
5   Beside the lake, beneath the trees,
Fluttering and dancing in the breeze.

Continuous as the stars that shine
    And twinkle on the milky way,
They stretched in never-ending line
10   Along the margin of a bay:
Ten thousand saw I at a glance,
Tossing their heads in sprightly dance.

The waves beside them danced; but they
    Out-did the sparkling waves in glee;
15   A poet could not but be gay,
    In such a jocund company;
I gazed—and gazed—but little thought
What wealth the show to me had brought:

For oft, when on my couch I lie
20   In vacant or in pensive mood,
They flash upon that inward eye
    Which is the bliss of solitude;
And then my heart with pleasure fills,
And dances with the daffodils.

WILLIAM WORDSWORTH (1770–1850)

The World Is Too Much with Us

The world is too much with us; late and soon,
Getting and spending, we lay waste our powers: —
Little we see in Nature that is ours;
We have given our hearts away, a sordid boon![13]
5   This Sea that bares her bosom to the moon,
The winds that will be howling at all hours,
And are up-gathered now like sleeping flowers,
For this, for everything, we are out of tune; —
It moves us not.—Great God! I'd rather be
10   A Pagan suckled in a creed outworn;
So might I, standing on this pleasant lea,
Have glimpses that would make me less forlorn;
Have sight of Proteus[14] rising from the sea;
Or hear old Triton° blow his wreathèd horn.   *a sea god*

[handwritten margin notes: love our feeling & senses for simple things; be in harmony with Nature]

WALTER SAVAGE LANDOR (1775–1864)

On His Seventy-fifth Birthday[15]

I strove with none; for none was worth my strife,[16]
    Nature I loved, and next to Nature, Art;
I warmed both hands before the fire of life,
    It sinks, and I am ready to depart.

Discuss "On His Seventy-fifth Birthday" as an epigram.

GEORGE GORDON, LORD BYRON (1788–1824)

She Walks in Beauty[17]

1

She walks in beauty, like the night
    Of cloudless climes and starry skies;
And all that's best of dark and bright
    Meet in her aspect and her eyes:
5   Thus mellowed to that tender light
    Which heaven to gaudy day denies.

---

[13] We have given our hearts away to the sordid gift of "getting and spending"—that is, commercial enterprise.

[14] The old man of the sea, sometimes described as the son of Poseidon.

[15] Landor lived into his ninetieth year.

[16] Landor was constantly in litigation and was forced into exile because of court battles.

[17] This poem was written for Mrs. Robert John Wilmot, Byron's cousin. When Byron first met her, she was wearing a black dress with spangles because she was in mourning.

2

One shade the more, one ray the less,
    Had half impaired the nameless grace
Which waves in every raven tress,
10   Or softly lightens o'er her face;
Where thoughts serenely sweet express
    How pure, how dear their dwelling place.

And on that cheek, and o'er that brow,
    So soft, so calm, yet eloquent,
15 The smiles that win, the tints that glow,
    But tell of days in goodness spent,
A mind at peace with all below,
    A heart whose love is innocent!

PERCY BYSSHE SHELLEY (1792–1822)

Ozymandias[18]

I met a traveler from an antique° land   *ancient*
Who said: Two vast and trunkless legs of stone
Stand in the desert. Near them, on the sand,
Half sunk, a shattered visage lies, whose frown,
5   And wrinkled lip, and sneer of cold command,
Tell that its sculptor well those passions read
Which yet survive, stamped on these lifeless things,
The hand that mocked° them and the heart that fed;   *carved and ridiculed*
And on the pedestal these words appear:
10 "My name is Ozymandias, king of kings:
Look on my works, ye Mighty, and despair!"
Nothing beside remains. Round the decay
Of that colossal wreck, boundless and bare
The lone and level sands stretch far away.

JOHN KEATS (1795–1821)

When I Have Fears

When I have fears that I may cease to be
    Before my pen has gleaned my teeming brain,
Before high-pilèd books, in charact'ry,°   *print*
    Hold like rich garners the full-ripened grain;
5   When I behold, upon the night's starred face,
    Huge cloudy symbols of a high romance,
And think that I may never live to trace
    Their shadows, with the magic hand of chance;
And when I feel, fair creature of an hour,

---

[18] Ozymandias, or Ramses II, was pharaoh of Egypt in the thirteenth century B.C.

10   That I shall never look upon thee more,
        Never have relish in the faery power
            Of unreflecting love!—then on the shore
        Of the wide world I stand alone, and think
        Till Love and Fame to nothingness do sink.

JOHN KEATS (1795–1821)

To Autumn

1

Season of mists and mellow fruitfulness,
    Close bosom-friend of the maturing sun;
Conspiring with him how to load and bless
    With fruit the vines that round the thatch-eaves run;
5   To bend with apples the mossed cottage-trees,
        And fill all fruit with ripeness to the core;
            To swell the gourd, and plump the hazel shells
        With a sweet kernel; to set budding more,
    And still more, later flowers for the bees,
10 Until they think warm days will never cease,
            For Summer has o'er-brimmed their clammy cells.

2

Who hath not seen thee oft amid thy store?
    Sometimes whoever seeks abroad may find
Thee sitting careless on a granary floor,
15   Thy hair soft-lifted by the winnowing[19] wind;
    Or on a half-reaped furrow sound asleep,
        Drowsed with the fume of poppies, while thy hook°   *scythe*
            Spares the next swath and all its twinèd flowers:
And sometimes like a gleaner[20] thou dost keep
20   Steady thy laden head across a brook;
        Or by a cider-press, with patient look,
            Thou watchest the last oozings hours by hours.

3

Where are the songs of Spring? Aye, where are they?
    Think not of them, thou hast thy music too—
25 While barred clouds bloom the soft-dying day,
        And touch the stubble-plains with rosy hue;
    Then in a wailful choir the small gnats mourn
        Among the river sallows,° borne aloft   *willows*
            Or sinking as the light wind lives or dies;
30 And full-grown lambs loud bleat from hilly bourn;°   *region*

---

[19] The process by which the chaff or husk is separated from the grain, usually by the wind.
[20] One who gathers the remains of a crop after it has been harvested.

Hedge crickets sing; and now with treble soft
The redbreast whistles from a garden croft;[21]
And gathering swallows twitter in the skies.

Discuss "To Autumn" as an example of personification.

THOMAS LOVELL BEDDOES (1803–1849)

Song: How Many Times Do I Love Thee, Dear?

How many times do I love thee, dear?
    Tell me how many thoughts there be
        In the atmosphere
        Of a new-fall'n year,
5 Whose white and sable hours appear
    The latest flake of Eternity—
So many times do I love thee, dear.

How many times do I love again?
    Tell me how many beads there are
10   In a silver chain
        Of evening rain,
Unraveled from the tumbling main,
    And threading the eye of a yellow star—
So many times do I love again.

Compare Beddoes's "Song" with Elizabeth Barrett Browning's "How Do I Love Thee"
on page 823.

HENRY WADSWORTH LONGFELLOW (1807–1882)

The Jewish Cemetery at Newport[22]

How strange it seems! These Hebrews in their graves,
    Close by the street of this fair seaport town,
Silent beside the never-silent waves,
    At rest in all this moving up and down!

5 The trees are white with dust, that o'er their sleep
    Wave their broad curtains in the south-wind's breath,
While underneath these leafy tents they keep
    The long, mysterious Exodus of Death[23]

And these sepulchral stones, so old and brown,
10   That pave with level flags their burial-place,

---

[21] An enclosed farm plot.
[22] The oldest Jewish synagogue in the United States is located in Newport, Rhode Island.
[23] Exodus, the second book of the Old Testatment, records the expulsion of the Jews from Egypt
and their subsequent wanderings. During their travels they made their homes in tents.

Seem like the tablets of the Law, thrown down
    And broken by Moses at the mountain's base.[24]

The very names recorded here are strange,
    Of foreign accent, and of different climes;
15   Alvares and Rivera interchange
    With Abraham and Jacob of old times.[25]

"Blessed be God, for he created Death!"
    The mourners said, "and Death is rest and peace;"
Then added, in the certainty of faith,
20   "And giveth Life that nevermore shall cease."

Closed are the portals of their Synagogue,
    No Psalms of David now the silence break,
No Rabbi reads the ancient Decalogue°   *the Ten Commandments*
    In the grand dialect the Prophets spake.

25   Gone are the living, but the dead remain,
    And not neglected; for a hand unseen,
Scattering its bounty, like a summer rain,
    Still keeps their graves and their remembrance green.

How came they here? What burst of Christian hate,
30   What persecution, merciless and blind,
Drove o'er the sea—that desert desolate—
    These Ishmaels and Hagars of mankind?[26]

They lived in narrow streets and lanes obscure,
    Ghetto and Judenstrass,[27] in mirk and mire;
35   Taught in the school of patience to endure
    The life of anguish and the death of fire.

All their lives long, with the unleavened bread
    And bitter herbs of exile and its fears,
The wasting famine of the heart they fed,
40   And slaked its thirst with marah of their tears.[28]

Anathema marantha![29] was the cry
    That rang from town to town, from street to street;
At every gate the accursed Mordecai[30]
    Was mocked and jeered, and spurned by Christian feet.

45   Pride and humiliation hand in hand
    Walked with them through the world where'er they went;
Trampled and beaten were they as the sand,
    And yet unshaken as the continent.

---

[24] The incident is recorded in Exodus 32:19.

[25] The Jews of Newport were of mostly Spanish and Portuguese descent.

[26] Two exiles whose stories are told in the Bible.

[27] In German, literally "Jew Street."

[28] *Marah* means bitterness in Hebrew. During Passover, the Jewish celebration of the Exodus, Jews eat unleavened bread (matzoh) and bitter herbs in commemoration of that bitter time.

[29] St. Paul's epithet for those who did not believe in Christ; it became a phrase applied only to Jews.

[30] Mordecai was a famous Persian Jew. Here the word is used as a synonym for "Jew."

Compare "The Sun Has Set" with James Joyce's "All Day I Hear the Noise of Waters" on page 837.

Compare "The Sun Has Set" with James Joyce's "All Day I Hear the Noise of Waters" on page 837.

HERMAN MELVILLE (1819–1891)

On the Photograph of a Corps Commander

Ay, man is manly. Here you see
    The warrior-carriage of the head,
And brave dilation of the frame;
    And lighting all, the soul that led
5   In Spottsylvania's[32] charge to victory,
    Which justifies his fame.

A cheering picture. It is good
    To look upon a Chief like this,
In whom the spirit moulds the form.
10   Here favoring Nature, oft remiss,
With eagle mien expressive has endued
    A man to kindle strains that warm.

Trace back his lineage, and his sires,
    Yeoman or noble, you shall find
15   Enrolled with men of Agincourt,[33]
    Heroes who shared great Harry's mind.
Down to us come the knightly Norman fires,
    And front the Templars bore.[34]

Nothing can lift the heart of man
20   Like manhood in a fellow-man.
The thought of heaven's great King afar
But humbles us—too weak to scan;
But manly greatness men can span,
    And feel the bonds that draw.

WALT WHITMAN (1819–1892)

A Noiseless Patient Spider

A noiseless patient spider,
I mark'd where on a little promontory it stood isolated,
Mark'd how to explore the vacant vast surrounding,
It launch'd forth filament, filament, filament, out of itself,
5   Ever unreeling them, ever tirelessly speeding them.

And you O my soul where you stand,
Surrounded, detached, in measureless oceans of space,

---

[32] A Civil War battleground where the Confederate army inflicted severe losses on the Union forces.
[33] The scene of Henry V's victory over the French in 1415. King Henry was also called Harry.
[34] The Templars are one of the three great orders of knighthood founded at the time of the Crusades.

Ceaselessly musing, venturing, throwing, seeking the spheres to connect them,
Till the bridge you will need be form'd, till the ductile anchor hold,
10   Till the gossamer thread you fling catch somewhere, O my soul.

Compare "A Noiseless Patient Spider" with Edward Taylor's "Upon a Spider Catching a Fly" on pages 813–14.

FRANCES E. W. HARPER (1825–1911)

(The Slave Auction)

The sale began—young girls were there,
    Defenceless in their wretchedness,
Whose stifled sobs of deep despair
    Revealed their anguish and distress.

5   And mothers stood with streaming eyes,
        And saw their dearest children sold;
Unheeded rose their bitter cries,
        While tyrants bartered them for gold.

And woman, with her love and truth—
10   For these in sable° forms may dwell—   *black*
Gaz'd on the husband of her youth,
        With anguish none may paint or tell.   Color

And men, whose sole crime was their hue,
    The impress of their Maker's hand,
15   And frail and shrinking children, too,
        Were gathered in that mournful band.

Ye who have laid your love to rest,
    And wept above their lifeless clay,
Know not the anguish of that breast,
20   Whose lov'd are rudely torn away.

Ye may not know how desolate
    Are bosoms rudely forced to part,
And how a dull and heavy weight
        Will press the life-drops from the heart.

EMILY DICKINSON (1830–1886)

My Life had stood, a Loaded Gun

My Life had stood—a Loaded Gun—
In Corners—till a Day
The Owner passed—identified—
And carried Me away—

5   And now We roam in Sovereign Woods—
    And now We hunt the Doe—

And every time I speak for Him—
The Mountains straight reply—

And do I smile, such cordial light
10   Upon the Valley glow—
It is as a Vesuvian face[35]
Had let its pleasure through—

And when at Night—Our good Day done—
I guard My Master's Head—
15   'Tis better than the Eider-Duck's[36]
Deep Pillow—to have shared—

To foe of His—I'm deadly foe—
None stir the second time—
On whom I lay a Yellow Eye—
20   Or an emphatic Thumb—

Though I than He— may longer live
He longer must—than I—
For I have but the power to kill,
Without—the power to die—

Discuss "My Life Had Stood, a Loaded Gun" as an example of metaphor.

EMILY DICKINSON (1830–1886)

Apparently with No Surprise

Apparently with no surprise
To any happy flower,
The frost beheads it at its play
In accidental power.

5   The blond assassin passes on,
The sun proceeds unmoved
To measure off another day
For an approving God.

Discuss "Apparently with No Surprise" as an example of personification.

EMILY DICKINSON (1830–1886)

I Heard a Fly Buzz—When I Died

I heard a Fly buzz—when I died—
The Stillness in the Room

---

[35] Vesuvius is an active volcano in Italy, overlooking the Bay of Naples.
[36] The down of the eider is particularly suited for stuffing pillows and quilts.

Was like the Stillness in the Air—
Between the Heaves of Storm—

5   The Eyes around—had wrung them dry—
And Breaths were gathering firm
For that last Onset—when the King
Be witnessed—in the Room—

I willed my Keepsakes—Signed away
10   What portion of me be
Assignable—and then it was
There interposed a Fly—

With Blue—uncertain stumbling Buzz—
Between the light—and me—
15   And then the Windows failed—and then
I could not see to see—

EMILY DICKINSON (1830–1886)

After Great Pain, a Formal Feeling Comes

After great pain, a formal feeling comes—
The Nerves sit ceremonious, like Tombs—
The stiff Heart questions was it He, that bore,
And Yesterday, or Centuries before?

5   The Feet, mechanical, go round—
Of Ground, or Air, or Ought—
A Wooden way
Regardless grown,
A Quartz contentment, like a stone—

10   This is the Hour of Lead—
Remembered, if outlived,
As Freezing persons, recollect the Snow—
First—Chill—then Stupor—then the letting go—

CHRISTINA ROSSETTI (1830–1894)

After Death

The curtains were half drawn; the floor was swept
    And strewn with rushes; rosemary and may
    Lay thick upon the bed on which I lay,
Where, through the lattice, ivy-shadows crept.
5   He leaned above me, thinking that I slept
    And could not hear him; but I heard him say,
    "Poor child, poor child"; and as he turned away
Came a deep silence, and I knew he wept.
He did not touch the shroud, or raise the fold
10   That hid my face, or take my hand in his,

Or ruffle the smooth pillows for my head.
He did not love me living: but once dead
He pitied me; and very sweet it is
To know he still is warm though I am cold.

Compare "After Death" with Coventry Patmore's "If I Were Dead" on page 789.

GERARD MANLEY HOPKINS (1844–1889)

Spring and Fall

To a young child

Márgarét, are you gríeving
Over Goldengrove unleaving?
Leáves, líke the things of man, you
With your fresh thoughts care for, can you?
5   Áh! ás the heart grows older
It will come to such sights colder
By and by, nor spare a sigh
Through worlds of wanwood leafmeal[37] lie;
And yet you wíll weep and know why.
10   Now no matter, child, the name:
Sórrow's spríngs áre the same.
Nor mouth had, no nor mind, expressed
What heart heard of, ghost° guessed: spirit
It ís the blight man was born for,
15   It is Margaret you mourn for.

GERARD MANLEY HOPKINS (1844–1889)

The Windhover[38]

To Christ Our Lord

I caught this morning morning's minion,° king-   darling
    dom of daylight's dauphin,° dapple-dawn-drawn Falcon, in his riding   prince
    Of the rolling level underneath him steady air, and striding
High there, how he rung upon the rein of a wimpling° wing   rippling as a veil
5   In his ecstasy! then off, off forth on swing,
    As a skate's heel sweeps smooth on a bow-bend: the hurl and gliding
    Rebuffed the big wind. My heart in hiding
Stirred for a bird,—the achieve of, the mastery of the thing!

Brute beauty and valour and act, oh, air, pride, plume, here
10   Buckle! AND the fire that breaks from thee then, a billion
    Times told lovelier, more dangerous, O my chevalier!°   knight

---

[37] *Wanwood* and *leafmeal* are two *portmanteau words*. Wan + wood is meant to suggest bloodless
limbs, and leaf + (piece) meal suggests the random pattern of the fallen leaves.
[38] The windhover is the common name for the kestrel, a European falcon that flies with its head
into the wind.

No wonder of it: shéer plód makes plough down sillion[39]
Shine, and blue-bleak embers, ah my dear,
 Fall, gall themselves, and gash gold-vermilion.

ALICE MEYNELL (1847–1922)

The Threshing-Machine

No "fan[40] is in his hand" for these
Young villagers beneath the trees,
 Watching the wheels. But I recall
 The rhythm of rods° that rise and fall,   *flails*
5 Purging the harvest, over-seas.

No fan, no flail, no threshing-floor!
And all their symbols evermore
 Forgone in England now—the sign,
 The visible pledge, the threat divine.
10 The chaff° dispersed, the wheat in store.   *husk*

The unbreathing engine marks no tune,
Steady at sunrise, steady at noon.
 Inhuman, perfect, saving time,
 And saving measure, and saving rhyme.
15 And did our Ruskin speak too soon?[41]

"No noble strength on earth" he sees
"Save Hercules' arm"[42] His grave decrees
 Curse wheel and steam. As the wheels ran
 I saw the other strength of man.
20 I knew the brain of Hercules.

OSCAR WILDE (1856–1900)

The Harlot's House

We caught the tread of dancing feet,
We loitered down the moonlit street,
And stopped beneath the harlot's house.

Inside, above the din and fray,
5 We heard the loud musicians play
The "Treues Liebes Herz" of Strauss.[43]

Like strange mechanical grotesques,
Making fantastic arabesques,
The shadows raced across the blind.

---

[39] The ridge between two plowed furrows.
[40] A *fan* is a basket used to winnow grain.
[41] John Ruskin (1819–1900) was an English essayist and critic who believed that by following agricultural pursuits, people could avoid the horrors of industrialism.
[42] Hercules was a mythical strong man.
[43] In German, "love's true heart."

10 We watched the ghostly dancers spin
To sound of horn and violin,
Like black leaves wheeling in the wind.

Like wire-pulled automatons,
Slim silhouetted skeletons
15 Went sidling through the slow quadrille.

They took each other by the hand,
And danced a stately saraband;
Their laughter echoed thin and shrill.

Sometimes a clockwork puppet pressed
20 A phantom lover to her breast,
Sometimes they seemed to try to sing.

Sometimes a horrible marionette
Came out, and smoked its cigarette
Upon the steps like a live thing.

25 Then, turning to my love, I said,
"The dead are dancing with the dead,
The dust is whirling with the dust."

But she—she heard the violin,
And left my side, and entered in:
30 Love passed into the house of lust.

Then suddenly the tune went false,
The dancers wearied of the waltz,
The shadows ceased to wheel and whirl.

And down the long and silent street,
35 The dawn, with silver-sandaled feet,
Crept like a frightened girl.

A. E. HOUSMAN (1859–1936)

Loveliest of Trees

Loveliest of trees, the cherry now
Is hung with bloom along the bough,
And stands about the woodland ride
Wearing white for Eastertide.

5 Now, of my threescore years and ten,
Twenty will not come again,
And take from seventy springs a score,
It only leaves me fifty more.

And since to look at things in bloom
10 Fifty springs are little room,
About the woodlands I will go
To see the cherry hung with snow.

A. E. HOUSMAN (1859–1936)

When I Was One-and-Twenty

When I was one-and-twenty
    I heard a wise man say,
"Give crowns and pounds and guineas
    But not your heart away;
5 Give pearls away and rubies
    But keep your fancy free."
But I was one-and-twenty,
    No use to talk to me.

When I was one-and-twenty
10   I heard him say again,
"The heart out of the bosom
    Was never given in vain:
'Tis paid with sighs a plenty
    And sold for endless rue."
15 And I am two-and-twenty,
    And oh, 'tis true, 'tis true.

Compare "When I Was One-and-Twenty" with John Crowe Ransom's "Piazza Piece" on pages 602–3.

W. E. B. DuBOIS (1868–1963)

The Song of the Smoke

I am the smoke king,
I am black.
I am swinging in the sky,
I am ringing worlds on high:
5 I am the thought of the throbbing mills,
I am the soul toil kills,
I am the ripple of trading rills.

Up I'm curling from the sod,
I am whirling home to God.
10 I am the smoke king,
I am black.

I am the smoke king,
I am black.
I am wreathing broken hearts,
15 I am sheathing devils' darts;
Dark inspiration of iron times,
Wedding the toil of toiling climes
Shedding the blood of bloodless crimes.

Down I lower in the blue,
20 Up I tower toward the true,

I am the smoke king,
I am black.

I am the smoke king,
I am black.

25 I am darkening with song,
I am hearkening to wrong;
I will be black as blackness can,
The blacker the mantle the mightier the man,
My purpl'ing midnights no day dawn may ban.

30 I am carving God in night,
I am painting hell in white.
I am the smoke king,
I am black.

Compare "The Song of the Smoke" with N. Scott Momaday's "The Delight Song of Tsoai-Talee" on page 649.

EDWIN ARLINGTON ROBINSON (1869–1935)

Mr. Flood's Party

Old Eben Flood, climbing alone one night
Over the hill between the town below
And the forsaken upland hermitage
That held as much as he should ever know
5   On earth again of home, paused warily.
The road was his with not a native near;
And Eben, having leisure, said aloud,
For no man else in Tilbury Town to hear:

"Well, Mr. Flood, we have the harvest moon
10   Again, and we may not have many more;
The bird is on the wing, the poet says,
And you and I have said it here before.
Drink to the bird."[44] He raised up to the light
The jug that he had gone so far to fill,
15   And answered huskily: "Well, Mr. Flood,
Since you propose it, I believe I will."

Alone, as if enduring to the end
A valiant armor of scarred hopes outworn,
He stood there in the middle of the road
20   Like Roland's ghost winding° a silent horn.[45]   blowing
Below him, in the town among the trees,
Where friends of other days had honored him,

[44] From the *Rubaiyat of Omar Khayyam*. The bird referred to is the bird of time.
[45] Roland was a knight who delayed calling for help with his horn at the Battle of Roncesvalles (A.D. 778) until the situation was hopeless.

A phantom salutation of the dead
Rang thinly till old Eben's eyes were dim.

25 Then, as a mother lays her sleeping child
Down tenderly, fearing it may awake,
He set the jug down slowly at his feet
With trembling care, knowing that most things break;
And only when assured that on firm earth
30 It stood, as the uncertain lives of men
Assuredly did not, he paced away,
And with his hand extended paused again:

"Well, Mr. Flood, we have not met like this
In a long time; and many a change has come
35 To both of us, I fear, since last it was
We had a drop together. Welcome home!"
Convivially returning with himself,
Again he raised the jug up to the light;
And with an acquiescent quaver said:
40 "Well, Mr. Flood, if you insist, I might.

"Only a very little, Mr. Flood—
For auld lang syne.[46] No more, sir; that will do."
So, for the time, apparently it did,
And Eben evidently thought so too;
45 For soon amid the silver loneliness
Of night he lifted up his voice and sang,
Secure, with only two moons listening,
Until the whole harmonious landscape rang—

"For auld lang syne." The weary throat gave out,
50 The last word wavered; and the song being done,
He raised again the jug regretfully
And shook his head, and was again alone.
There was not much that was ahead of him,
And there was nothing in the town below—
55 Where strangers would have shut the many doors
That many friends had opened long ago.

STEPHEN CRANE (1871–1900)

A Man Adrift on a Slim Spar

A man adrift on a slim spar
A horizon smaller than the rim of a bottle
Tented waves rearing lashy dark points
The near whine of froth in circles.
5   God is cold.

The incessant raise and swing of the sea
And growl after growl of crest

---

[46] The good old times.

The sinkings, green, seething, endless
The upheaval half-completed.
10   God is cold.

The seas are in the hollow of The Hand;
Oceans may be turned to a spray
Raining down through the stars
Because of a gesture of pity toward a babe.
15   Oceans may become grey ashes,
Die with a long moan and a roar
Amid the tumult of the fishes
And the cries of the ships,
Because The Hand beckons the mice.

20   A horizon smaller than a doomed assassin's cap,
Inky, surging tumults
A reeling, drunken sky and no sky
A pale hand sliding from a polished spar.
                                      God is cold.

25   The puff of a coat imprisoning air:
A face kissing the water-death
A weary slow sway of a lost hand
And the sea, the moving sea, the sea.
                                      God is cold.

PAUL LAURENCE DUNBAR (1872–1906)

Compensation

Because I had loved so deeply,
    Because I had loved so long,
God in His great compassion
    Gave me the gift of song.

5   Because I have loved so vainly,
    And sung with such faltering breath,
The Master in infinite mercy
    Offers the boon of Death.

ROBERT FROST (1874–1963)

After Apple-Picking

My long two-pointed ladder's sticking through a tree
Toward heaven still,
And there's a barrel that I didn't fill
Beside it, and there may be two or three
5   Apples I didn't pick upon some bough.
But I am done with apple-picking now.
Essence of winter sleep is on the night,
The scent of apples: I am drowsing off.
I cannot rub the strangeness from my sight

10 I got from looking through a pane of glass
 I skimmed this morning from the drinking trough
 And held against the world of hoary grass.
 It melted, and I let it fall and break.
 But I was well
15 Upon my way to sleep before it fell,
 And I could tell
 What form my dreaming was about to take.
 Magnified apples appear and disappear,
 Stem end and blossom end,
20 And every fleck of russet showing clear.
 My instep arch not only keeps the ache,
 It keeps the pressure of a ladder-round.
 I feel the ladder sway as the boughs bend.
 And I keep hearing from the cellar bin
25 The rumbling sound
 Of load on load of apples coming in.
 For I have had too much
 Of apple-picking: I am overtired
 Of the great harvest I myself desired.
30 There were ten thousand thousand fruit to touch,
 Cherish in hand, lift down, and not let fall.
 For all
 That struck the earth,
 No matter if not bruised or spiked with stubble,
35 Went surely to the cider-apple heap
 As of no worth.
 One can see what will trouble
 This sleep of mine, whatever sleep it is.
 Were he not gone,
40 The woodchuck could say whether it's like his
 Long sleep, as I describe its coming on,
 Or just some human sleep.

Compare "After Apple-Picking" with Dave Smith's "Picking Cherries" on page 877.

ROBERT FROST (1874–1963)

The Silken Tent

 She is as in a field a silken tent
 At midday when a sunny summer breeze
 Has dried the dew and all its ropes relent,
 So that in guys° it gently sways at ease,   *ropes*
5 And its supporting central cedar pole,
 That is its pinnacle to heavenward
 And signifies the sureness of the soul,
 Seems to owe naught to any single cord,

But strictly held by none, is loosely bound
10   By countless silken ties of love and thought
To everything on earth the compass round,
And only by one's going slightly taut
In the capriciousness of summer air
Is of the slightest bondage made aware.

Show how "The Silken Tent" is an allegory.

JAMES JOYCE (1880–1941)

All Day I Hear the Noise of Waters

All day I hear the noise of waters
        Making moan,
Sad as the sea-bird is, when going
        Forth alone,
5   He hears the winds cry to the waters'
        Monotone.

The grey winds, the cold winds are blowing
        Where I go.
I hear the noise of many waters
10   Far below.
All day, all night, I hear them flowing
        To and fro.

Compare "All Day I Hear the Noise of Waters" with Emily Brontë's "The Sun Has Set" on page 824.

ARCHIBALD MacLEISH (1892–1982)

Ars Poetica[47]

A poem should be palpable and mute
As a globed fruit,

Dumb
As old medallions to the thumb,

5   Silent as the sleeve-worn stone
Of casement ledges where the moss has grown—

A poem should be wordless
As the flight of birds.

A poem should be motionless in time
10   As the moon climbs,

---

[47] Latin for "the art of poetry."

Leaving, as the moon releases
Twig by twig the night-entangled trees,

Leaving, as the moon behind the winter leaves,
Memory by memory the mind—

15   A poem should be motionless in time
As the moon climbs.

A poem should be equal to:
Not true.

For all the history of grief
20   An empty doorway and a maple leaf.

For love
The leaning grasses and two lights above the sea—

A poem should not mean
But be.

ELINOR WYLIE (1885–1928)

Prophecy

I shall lie hidden in a hut
   In the middle of an alder wood,
With the back door blind and bolted shut,
   And the front door locked for good.

5   I shall lie folded like a saint,
   Lapped in a scented linen sheet,
On a bedstead striped with bright-blue paint,
   Narrow and cold and neat.

The midnight will be glassy black
10   Behind the panes, with wind about
To set his mouth against a crack
   And blow the candle out.

WILFRED OWEN (1893–1918)

Anthem for Doomed Youth

What passing-bells for these who die as cattle?
Only the monstrous anger of the guns.
Only the stuttering rifles' rapid rattle
Can patter out their hasty orisons.
5   No mockeries for them from prayers or bells,
Nor any voice of mourning save the choirs—
The shrill, demented choirs of wailing shells;
And bugles calling for them from sad shires.

What candles may be held to speed them all?
10 Not in the hands of boys, but in their eyes
Shall shine the holy glimmers of good-byes.
The pallor of girls' brows shall be their pall;
Their flowers the tenderness of patient minds,
And each slow dusk a drawing-down of blinds.

Compare "Anthem for Doomed Youth" with A. E. Housman's "To an Athlete Dying Young" on page 577 and Randall Jarrell's "The Death of the Ball Turret Gunner" on page 604.

E. E. CUMMINGS (1894–1962)

in Just-

in Just-
spring   when the world is mud-
luscious the little
lame balloonman

5   whistles   far   and wee

and eddieandbill come
running from marbles and
piracies and it's
spring

10 when the world is puddle-wonderful

the queer
old balloonman whistles
far   and   wee
and bettyandisbel come dancing

15 from hop-scotch and jump-rope and

it's
spring
and
    the
20 goat-footed[48]

balloonMan   whistles
far
and
wee

---

[48] The word *goat-footed* suggests that the "balloonman" resembles Pan, the Greek god of flocks and pastures, who is depicted as having the ears and hooves of a goat.

E. E. CUMMINGS (1894–1962)

the Cambridge[49] ladies who live in furnished souls

the Cambridge ladies who live in furnished souls
are unbeautiful and have comfortable minds
(also, with the church's protestant blessings
daughters, unscented shapeless spirited)
5   they believe in Christ and Longfellow,[50] both dead,
are invariably interested in so many things—
at the present writing one still finds
delighted fingers knitting for the is it Poles?
perhaps. While permanent faces coyly bandy
10   scandal of Mrs. N and Professor D
. . . . the Cambridge ladies do not care, above
Cambridge if sometimes in its box of
sky lavender and cornerless, the
moon rattles like a fragment of angry candy

Compare "the Cambridge ladies who live in furnished souls" with Gwendolyn Brooks's "Sadie and Maud" on page 850 and the excerpt from T. S. Eliot's "Aunt Helen" on page 678.

LOUISE BOGAN (1897–1970)

Night

The cold remote islands
And the blue estuaries
Where what breathes, breathes
The restless wind of the inlets,
5   And what drinks, drinks
The incoming tide;

Where shell and weed
Wait upon the salt of the sea,
And the clear nights of stars
10   Swing their lights westward
To set behind the land;

Where the pulse clinging to the rocks
Renews itself forever;
Where, again on cloudless nights,
15   The water reflects
The firmament's partial setting;

---

[49] Cambridge, Massachusetts, is the home of Harvard University, where Cummings's father taught and where Cummings himself was educated.
[50] Henry Wadsworth Longfellow, the American poet, made his home in Cambridge. One of Longfellow's poems may be found on pages 821–23.

—O remember
In your narrowing dark hours
That more things move
20   Than blood in the heart.

Compare "Night" with Emily Brontë's "The Sun Has Set" on page 824 and James Joyce's "All Day I Hear the Noise of Waters" on page 837.

ARNA BONTEMPS (1902–)

Southern Mansion

Poplars are standing there still as death
And ghosts of dead men
Meet their ladies walking
Two by two beneath the shade
5   And standing on the marble steps.

There is a sound of music echoing
Through the open door
And in the field there is
Another sound tinkling in the cotton:
10   Chains of bondmen dragging on the ground.

The years go back with an iron clank,
A hand is on the gate,
A dry leaf trembles on the wall.
Ghosts are walking.
15   They have broken roses down
And poplars stand there still as death.

W. H. AUDEN (1907–1973)

Lay Your Sleeping Head, My Love

Lay your sleeping head, my love,
Human on my faithless arm;
Time and fevers burn away
Individual beauty from
5   Thoughtful children, and the grave
Proves the child ephemeral:
But in my arms till break of day
Let the living creature lie,
Mortal, guilty, but to me
10   The entirely beautiful.

Soul and body have no bounds:
To lovers as they lie upon
Her tolerant enchanted slope
In their ordinary swoon,

15   Grave the vision Venus[51] sends
       Of supernatural sympathy,
       Universal love and hope;
       While an abstract insight wakes
       Among the glaciers and the rocks
20   The hermit's sensual ecstasy.

       Certainty, fidelity
       On the stroke of midnight pass
       Like vibrations of a bell,
       And fashionable madmen raise
25   Their pedantic boring cry:
       Every farthing° of the cost,   *quarter of a penny*
       All the dreaded cards foretell,
       Shall be paid, but from this night
       Not a whisper, not a thought,
30   Not a kiss nor look be lost.

       Beauty, midnight, vision dies:
       Let the winds of dawn that blow
       Softly round your dreaming head
       Such a day of sweetness show
35   Eye and knocking heart may bless,
       Find the mortal world enough;
       Noons of dryness see you fed
       By the involuntary powers,
       Nights of insult let you pass
40   Watched by every human love.

W. H. AUDEN (1907–1973)

As I Walked Out One Evening

       As I walked out one evening,
         Walking down Bristol Street,
       The crowds upon the pavement
         Were fields of harvest wheat.

5   And down by the brimming river
         I heard a lover sing
       Under an arch of the railway:
         "Love has no ending.

       "I'll love you, dear, I'll love you
10   Till China and Africa meet,
       And the river jumps over the mountain
         And the salmon sing in the street,

---

[51] Venus is the goddess of love.

"I'll love you till the ocean
  Is folded and hung up to dry
15 And the seven stars go squawking
  Like geese about the sky.

"The years shall run like rabbits,
  For in my arms I hold
The Flower of the Ages,
20 And the first love of the world."

But all the clocks in the city
  Began to whirr and chime:
"O let not Time deceive you,
  You cannot conquer Time.

25 "In the burrows of the Nightmare
  Where Justice naked is,
Time watches from the shadow
  And coughs when you would kiss.

"In headaches and in worry
30 Vaguely life leaks away,
And Time will have his fancy
  Tomorrow or today.

"Into many a green valley
  Drifts the appalling snow;
35 Time breaks the threaded dances
  And the diver's brilliant bow.

"O plunge your hands in water,
  Plunge them in up to the wrist;
Stare, stare in the basin
40 And wonder what you've missed.

"The glacier knocks in the cupboard,
  The desert sighs in the bed,
And the crack in the teacup opens
  A lane to the land of the dead.

45 "Where the beggars raffle the banknotes
  And the Giant is enchanting to Jack,
And the Lily-white Boy is a Roarer,°   *noisy reveler*
  And Jill goes down on her back.

"O look, look in the mirror,
50 O look in your distress;
Life remains a blessing
  Although you cannot bless.

"O stand, stand at the window
  As the tears scald and start;
55 You shall love your crooked neighbor
  With your crooked heart."

It was late, late in the evening,
   The lovers they were gone;
The clocks had ceased their chiming,
60   And the deep river ran on.

Discuss "As I Walked Out One Evening" as an example of a ballad.

THEODORE ROETHKE (1908–1963)

My Papa's Waltz

The whiskey on your breath
Could make a small boy dizzy;
But I hung on like death:
Such waltzing was not easy.

5   We romped until the pans
Slid from the kitchen shelf;
My mother's countenance
Could not unfrown itself.

The hand that held my wrist
10   Was battered on one knuckle;
At every step you missed
My right ear scraped a buckle.

You beat time on my head
With a palm caked hard by dirt,
15   Then waltzed me off to bed
Still clinging to your shirt.

Compare "My Papa's Waltz" with Lucille Clifton's "Good Times" on pages 871–72.

THEODORE ROETHKE (1908–1963)

I Knew a Woman

I knew a woman, lovely in her bones,
When small birds sighed, she would sigh back at them;
Ah, when she moved, she moved more ways than one:
The shapes a bright container can contain!
5   Of her choice virtues only gods should speak,
Or English poets who grew up on Greek
(I'd have them sing in chorus, cheek to cheek).

How well her wishes went! She stroked my chin,
She taught me Turn, and Counter-turn, and Stand,
10   She taught me Touch, that undulant white skin;
I nibbled meekly from her proffered hand;
She was the sickle; I, poor I, the rake,

Coming behind her for her pretty sake
(But what prodigious mowing we did make).

15 Love likes a gander, and adores a goose:
Her full lips pursed, the errant note to seize;
She played it quick, she played it light and loose;
My eyes, they dazzled at her flowing knees;
Her several parts could keep a pure repose,
20 Or one hip quiver with a mobile nose
(She moved in circles, and those circles moved).

Let seed be grass, and grass turn into hay:
I'm martyr to a motion not my own;
What's freedom for? To know eternity.
25 I swear she cast a shadow white as stone.
But who would count eternity in days?
These old bones live to learn her wanton ways:
(I measure time by how a body sways).

RICHARD WRIGHT (1908–1960)

Four Haiku

A balmy spring wind
Reminding me of something
I cannot recall.

The green cockleburrs
Caught in the thick wooly hair
Of the black boy's head.

Standing in the field,
I hear the whispering of
Snowflake to snowflake.

It is September
The month in which I was born,
And I have no thoughts.

IRVING LAYTON (1912–)

Cain[52]

Taking the air rifle from my son's hand
I measured back five paces, the Hebrew
In me, narcissist, father of children
Laid to rest. From there I took aim and fired.
5 The silent ball hit the frog's back an inch

---

[52] In the Bible, Cain is the son of Adam and the brother of Abel, whom Cain kills. Thus Cain is the prototypical murderer.

Below the head. He jumped at the surprise
Of it, suddenly tickled or startled
(He must have thought) and leaped from the wet sand
Into the surrounding brown water. But
10 The ball had done its mischief. His next spring
Was a miserable flop, the thrust all gone
Out of his legs. He tried—like Bruce—again,
Throwing out his sensitive pianist's
Hands as a dwarf might or a helpless child.
15 His splash disturbed the quiet pondwater
And one old frog behind his weedy moat
Blinking, looking self-complacently on.
The lin's° surface at once became closing   pond
Eyelids and bubbles like notes of music
20 Liquid, luminous, dropping from the page
White, white-bearded, a rapid crescendo[53]
Of inaudible sounds and a crones' whispering
Backstage among the reeds and bullrushes
As for an expiring Lear or Oedipus.[54]

25 But Death makes us all look ridiculous.
Consider this frog (dog, hog, what you will)
Sprawling, his absurd corpse rocked by the tides
That his last vain spring had set in movement.
Like a retired oldster, I couldn't help sneer,
30 Living off the last of his insurance:
Billows—now crumbling—the premiums paid.
Absurd, how absurd. I wanted to kill
At the mockery of it. Kill and kill
Again—the self-infatuate frog, dog, hog,
35 Anything with the stir of life in it,
Seeing that dead leaper, Chaplin-footed,[55]
Rocked and cradled in this afternoon
Of tranquil water, reeds, and blazing sun,
The hole in his back clearly visible
40 And the torn skin a blob of shadow
Moving when the quiet poolwater moved.
O Egypt, marbled Greece, resplendent Rome,
Did you also finally perish from a small bore
In your back you could not scratch? And would
45 Your mouths open ghostily, gasping out
Among the murky reeds, the hidden frogs,
We climb with crushed spines toward the heavens?
When the next morning I came the same way
The frog was on his back, one delicate

---

[53] *Crescendo* is the musical term for increasing volume.
[54] Oedipus and Lear are both tragic heroes—the former in Sophocles' *Oedipus Rex*, the latter in Shakespeare's *King Lear*.
[55] Charlie Chaplin, the silent screen comic actor, had a distinctive waddling walk.

50 Hand on his belly, and his white shirt front
    Spotless. He looked as if he might have been
    A comic; tap dancer apologizing
    For a fall, or an Emcee, his wide grin
    Coaxing a laugh from us for an aside
55 Or perhaps a joke we didn't quite hear.

Compare "Cain" with Richard Wilbur's "The Death of a Toad" on page 736.

MAY SARTON (1912–)

Lady with a Falcon

Flemish tapestry, fifteenth century

Gentleness and starvation tame
The falcon to this lady's wrist,
Natural flight hooded from blame
By what ironic fate or twist?

5   For now the hunched bird's contained flight
    Pounces upon her inward air,
    To plunder that mysterious night
    Of poems blooded as the hare.

    Heavy becomes the lady's hand,
10 And heavy bends the gentle head
    Over her hunched and brooding bird
    Until it is she who seems hooded.

    Lady, your falcon is a peril,
    Is starved, is mastered, but not kind.
15 The bird who sits your hand so gentle,
    The captured hunter hunts your mind.

    Better to starve the senseless wind
    Than wrist a falcon's stop and start:
    The bolt of flight you thought to bend
20 Plummets into your inmost heart.

Compare "Lady with a Falcon" with Robert Duncan's "My Mother Would Be a Falconress" on pages 851–52 and Ted Hughes's "Hawk Roosting" on pages 863–64.

ROBERT HAYDEN (1913–1980)

Those Winter Sundays

Sundays too my father got up early
and put his clothes on in the blueblack cold,
then with cracked hands that ached
from labor in the weekday weather made
5   banked fires blaze. No one ever thanked him.

I'd wake and hear the cold splintering, breaking.
When the rooms were warm, he'd call,
and slowly I would rise and dress,
fearing the chronic angers of that house.

10 Speaking indifferently to him,
who had driven out the cold
and polished my good shoes as well.
What did I know, what did I know
of love's austere and lonely offices?

RANDALL JARRELL (1914–1965)

The Woman at the Washington Zoo

The saris go by me from the embassies.

Cloth from the moon. Cloth from another planet.
They look back at the leopard like the leopard.

And I. . . .
5   this print of mine, that has kept its color
Alive through so many cleanings; this dull null
Navy I wear to work, and wear from work, and so
To my bed, so to my grave, with no
Complaints, no comment: neither from my chief,
10 The Deputy Chief Assistant, nor his chief—
Only I complain. . . . this serviceable
Body that no sunlight dyes, no hand suffuses
But, dome-shadowed, withering among columns,
Wavy beneath fountains—small, far-off, shining
15 In the eyes of animals, these beings trapped
As I am trapped but not, themselves, the trap,
Aging, but without knowledge of their age,
Kept safe here, knowing not of death, for death—
Oh, bars of my own body, open, open!
20 The world goes by my cage and never sees me.
And there come not to me, as come to these,
The wild beast, sparrows pecking the llamas' grain,
Pigeons settling on the bears' bread, buzzards
Tearing the meat the flies have clouded. . . .
25   Vulture,
When you come for the white rat that the foxes left,
Take off the red helmet of your head, the black
Wings that have shadowed me, and step to me as man:
The wild brother at whose feet the white wolves fawn,
30 To whose hand of power the great lioness
Stalks, purring. . . .
          You know what I was,
You see what I am: change me, change me!

Naming of Parts

Today we have naming of parts. Yesterday,
We had daily cleaning. And tomorrow morning,
We shall have what to do after firing. But today,
Today we have naming of parts. Japonica
5   Glistens like coral in all of the neighboring gardens,
      And today we have naming of parts.

This is the lower sling swivel. And this
Is the upper sling swivel, whose use you will see,
When you are given your slings. And this is the piling swivel,
10   Which in your case you have not got. The branches
Hold in the gardens their silent, eloquent gestures,
      Which in our case we have not got.

This is the safety-catch, which is always released
With an easy flick of the thumb. And please do not let me
15   See anyone using his finger. You can do it quite easy
If you have any strength in your thumb. The blossoms
Are fragile and motionless, never letting anyone see
      Any of them using their finger.

And this you can see is the bolt. The purpose of this
20   Is to open the breech, as you see. We can slide it
Rapidly backwards and forwards: we call this
Easing the spring. And rapidly backwards and forwards
The early bees are assaulting and fumbling the flowers:
      They call it easing the Spring.

25   They call it easing the Spring: it is perfectly easy
If you have any strength in your thumb: like the bolt,
And the breech, and the cocking-piece, and the point of balance,
Which in our case we have not got; and the almond-blossom

Silent in all of the gardens and the bees going backwards and forwards,
30   For today we have naming of parts.

Traveling Through the Dark

Traveling through the dark I found a deer
dead on the edge of the Wilson River road.
It is usually best to roll them into the canyon:
that road is narrow; to swerve might make more dead.

5   By glow of the tail-light I stumbled back of the car
and stood by the heap, a doe, a recent killing;
she had stiffened already, almost cold.
I dragged her off; she was large in the belly.

My fingers touching her side brought me the reason—
10   her side was warm; her fawn lay there waiting,
alive, still, never to be born.
Beside that mountain road I hesitated.

The car aimed ahead its lowered parking lights;
under the hood purred the steady engine.
15   I stood in the glare of the warm exhaust turning red;
around our group I could hear the wilderness listen.

I thought hard for us all—my only swerving—
then pushed her over the edge into the river.

GWENDOLYN BROOKS (1917–)

Sadie and Maud

Maud went to college.
Sadie stayed at home.
Sadie scraped life
With a fine-tooth comb.

5   She didn't leave a tangle in.
Her comb found every strand.
Sadie was one of the livingest chits°   *young girls*
In all the land.

Sadie bore two babies
10   Under her maiden name.
Maud and Ma and Papa
Nearly died of shame.

When Sadie said her last so-long
Her girls struck out from home.
15   (Sadie had left as heritage
Her fine-tooth comb.)

Maud, who went to college,
Is a thin brown mouse.
She is living all alone
20   In this old house.

Compare "Sadie and Maud" with the excerpt from T. S. Eliot's "Aunt Helen" on page 678.

ROBERT LOWELL (1917–1977)

Robert Frost

Robert Frost at midnight, the audience gone
to vapor, the great act laid on the shelf in mothballs,
his voice musical, raw and raw—he writes in the flyleaf:

"Robert Lowell from Robert Frost, his friend in the art."
5   "Sometimes I feel too full of myself," I say.
And he, misunderstanding, "When I am low,
I stray away. My son wasn't your kind. The night
we told him Merrill Moore[56] would come to treat him,
he said, 'I'll kill him first.' One of my daughters thought things,
10 knew every male she met was out to make her;
the way she dresses, she couldn't make a whorehouse."
And I, "Sometimes I'm so happy I can't stand myself."
And he, "When I am too full of joy, I think
how little good my health did anyone near me."

ROBERT DUNCAN (1919–)

My Mother Would Be a Falconress

My mother would be a falconress,
And I, her gay falcon treading her wrist,
would fly to bring back
from the blue of the sky to her, bleeding, a prize,
5   where I dream in my little hood with many bells
jangling when I'd turn my head.

My mother would be a falconress,
and she sends me as far as her will goes.
She lets me ride to the end of her curb
10 where I fall back in anguish.
I dread that she will cast me away,
for I fall, I mis-take, I fail in her mission.

She would bring down the little birds.
And I would bring down the little birds.
15 When will she let me bring down the little birds,
pierced from their flight with their necks broken,
their heads like flowers limp from the stem?

I tread my mother's wrist and would draw blood.
Behind the little hood my eyes are hooded.
20 I have gone back into my hooded silence,
talking to myself and dropping off to sleep.

For she has muffled my dreams in the hood she has made me,
sewn round with bells, jangling when I move.
She rides with her little falcon upon her wrist.
25 She uses a barb that brings me to cower.
She sends me abroad to try my wings
and I come back to her. I would bring down
the little birds to her
I may not tear into, I must bring back perfectly.

---

[56] Merrill Moore (1903–1957) was a poet and psychoanalyst and Frost's friend. Frost's son committed
suicide.

30   I tear at her wrist with my beak to draw blood,
    and her eye holds me, anguisht, terrifying.
    She draws a limit to my flight.
    Never beyond my sight, she says.
    She trains me to fetch and to limit myself in fetching.
35   She rewards me with meat for my dinner.
    But I must never eat what she sends me to bring her.

    Yet it would have been beautiful, if she would have carried me,
    always, in a little hood with the bells ringing,
    at her wrist, and her riding
40   to the great falcon hunt, and me
    flying up to the curb of my heart from her heart
    to bring down the skylark from the blue to her feet,
    straining, and then released for the flight.

    My mother would be a falconress,
45   and I her gerfalcon,° raised at her will,   *large Arctic falcon*
    from her wrist sent flying, as if I were her own
    pride, as if her pride
    knew no limits, as if her mind
    sought in me flight beyond the horizon.

50   Ah, but high, high in the air I flew.
    And far, far beyond the curb of her will,
    were the blue hills where the falcons nest.
    And then I saw west to the dying sun—
    it seemed my human soul went down in flames.

55   I tore at her wrist, at the hold she had for me,
    until the blood ran hot and I heard her cry out,
    far, far beyond the curb of her will   •

    to horizons of stars beyond the ringing hills of the world where the falcons nest
    I saw, and I tore at her wrist with my savage beak.
60   I flew, as if sight flew from the anguish in her eye beyond her sight,
    sent from my striking loose, from the cruel strike at her wrist,
    striking out from the blood to be free of her.

    My mother would be a falconress,
    and even now, years after this,
65   when the wounds I left her had surely heald,
    and the woman is dead,
    her fierce eyes closed, and if her heart
    were broken, it is stilld   •

    I would be a falcon and go free.
70   I tread her wrist and wear the hood,
    talking to myself, and would draw blood.

Compare "My Mother Would Be a Falconress" with May Sarton's "Lady with a Falcon"
on page 847 and Ted Hughes's "Hawk Roosting" on pages 863–64.

With or Without Reason, from the *Disasters of War*, by Francisco Goya
(Courtesy of the Museum of Fine Arts, Boston, William A. Sargent Bequest)

LAWRENCE FERLINGHETTI (1919–)

[In Goya's Greatest Scenes We Seem to See]

In Goya's greatest scenes[57] we seem to see

        the people of the world

   exactly at the moment when

    they first attained the title of

5   "suffering humanity"

    They writhe upon the page

      in a veritable rage

        of adversity

  Heaped up

10   groaning with babies and bayonets

        under cement skies

   in an abstract landscape of blasted trees

    bent statues bats wings and beaks

     slippery gibbets°   *gallows*

15   cadavers and carnivorous cocks

   and all the final hollering monsters

    of the

      "imagination of disaster"

---

[57] Francisco Goya (1746–1828) was a Spanish painter and etcher. His *Disasters of War* series of etchings depicted the horrors of warfare.

                    they are so bloody real
20   it is as if they really still existed
         And they do

              Only the landscape is changed

         They still are ranged along the roads
                plagued by legionaires
25   false windmills and demented roosters

         They are the same people
                          only further from home
              on freeways fifty lanes wide
                      on a concrete continent
30   spaced with bland billboards
                    illustrating imbecile illusions of happiness

Compare "[In Goya's Greatest Scenes We Seem to See]" with W. H. Auden's "Musée des Beaux Arts" on pages 542–43.

MONA VAN DUYN (1921–)

Open Letter from a Constant Reader

     To all who carve their love on a picnic table
     or scratch it on smoked glass panes of a public toilet,
     I send my thanks for each plain and perfect fable
     of how the three pains of the body, surfeit,

5   hunger, and chill (or loneliness), create
     a furniture and art of their own easing.
     And I bless two public sites and, like Yeats,[58]
     two private sites where the body receives its blessing.

     Nothing is banal or lowly that tells us how well
10   the world, whose highways proffer table and toilet
     as signs and occasions of comfort for belly and bowel,
     can comfort the heart too, somewhere in secret.

     Where so much constant news of good has been put,
     both fleeting and lasting lines compel belief.
15   Not by talent or riches or beauty, but
     by the world's grace, people have found relief

     from the worst pain of the body, loneliness,
     and say so with a simple heart as they sit
     being relieved of one of the others. I bless
20   all knowledge of love, all ways of publishing it.

Compare Van Duyn's poem to Yeats's "Crazy Jane Talks with the Bishop" on page 785.

---

[58] W. B. Yeats (1865–1939) was among the greatest poets in English. Several of his poems appear throughout this book.

RICHARD WILBUR (1921–)

Love Calls Us to the Things of This World[59]

The eyes open to a cry of pulleys,
And spirited from sleep, the astounded soul
Hangs for a moment bodiless and simple
As false dawn.
                    Outside the open window
5   The morning air is all awash with angels.

Some are in bed-sheets, some are in blouses,
Some are in smocks: but truly there they are.
Now they are rising together in calm swells
Of halcyon feeling, filling whatever they wear
10 With the deep joy of their impersonal breathing;

Now they are flying in place, conveying
The terrible speed of their omnipresence, moving
And staying like white water; and now of a sudden
They swoon down into so rapt a quiet
That nobody seems to be there.
15   The soul shrinks

From all that it is about to remember,
From the punctual rape of every blessèd day,
And cries,
                "Oh, let there be nothing on earth but laundry,
Nothing but rosy hands in the rising steam
20 And clear dances done in the sight of heaven."

Yet, as the sun acknowledges
With a warm look the world's hunks and colors,
The soul descends once more in bitter love
To accept the waking body, saying now
25 In a changed voice as the man yawns and rises,

"Bring them down from their ruddy gallows;
Let there be clean linen for the backs of thieves;
Let lovers go fresh and sweet to be undone,
And the heaviest nuns walk in a pure floating
Of dark habits,
30   keeping their difficult balance."

PHILIP LARKIN (1922–1984)

Faith Healing

Slowly the women file to where he stands
Upright in rimless glasses, silver hair,
Dark suit, white collar. Stewards tirelessly
Persuade them onwards to his voice and hands,

---

[59] The title is taken from the words of St. Augustine.

5   Within whose warm spring rain of loving care
Each dwells some twenty seconds. *Now, dear child,*
What's wrong, the deep American voice demands,
And, scarcely pausing, goes into a prayer
Directing God about this eye, that knee.
10   Their heads are clasped abruptly; then, exiled

Like losing thoughts, they go in silence; some
Sheepishly stray, not back into their lives
Just yet; but some stay stiff, twitching and loud
With deep hoarse tears, as if a kind of dumb
15   And idiot child within them still survives
To re-awake at kindness, thinking a voice
At last calls them alone, that hands have come
To lift and lighten; and such joy arrives
Their thick tongues blort, their eyes squeeze grief, a crowd
20   Of huge unheard answers jam and rejoice—

What's wrong! Moustached in flowered frocks they shake:
By now, all's wrong. In everyone there sleeps
A sense of life lived according to love.
To some it means the difference they could make
25   By loving others, but across most it sweeps
As all they might have done had they been loved.
That nothing cures. An immense slackening ache,
As when, thawing, the rigid landscape weeps,
Spreads slowly through them—that, and the voice above
30   Saying *Dear child,* and all time has disproved.

AMY CLAMPITT (1920–)

The Sun Underfoot Among the Sundews

An ingenuity too astonishing
to be quite fortuitous is
this bog full of sundews, sphagnum-
lined and shaped like a teacup.
5   A step
down and you're into it; a
wilderness swallows you up:
ankle-, then knee-, then midriff-
to-shoulder-deep in wetfooted
10   understory, an overhead
spruce-tamarack horizon hinting
you'll never get out of here.
                       But the sun
among the sundews, down there,
15   is so bright, an underfoot
webwork of carnivorous rubies,
a star-swarm thick as the gnats
they're set to catch, delectable

double-faced cockleburs, each
20   hair-tip a sticky mirror
afire with sunlight, a million
of them and again a million,
each mirror a trap set to
unhand unbelieving,
25   that either
a First Cause[60] said once, "Let there
be sundews," and there were, or they've
made their way here unaided
other than by that backhand, round-
30   about refusal to assume responsibility
known as Natural Selection.[61]
                              But the sun

underfoot is so dazzling
down there among the sundews,
35   there is so much light
in the cup that, looking,
you start to fall upward.

ANTHONY HECHT (1923–)

The Dover Bitch, A Criticism of Life

For Andrews Wanning

So there stood Matthew Arnold and this girl
With the cliffs of England crumbling away behind them,
And he said to her, "Try to be true to me,
And I'll do the same for you, for things are bad
5   All over, etc., etc."
Well now, I knew this girl. It's true she had read
Sophocles in a fairly good translation
And caught that bitter allusion to the sea,
But all the time he was talking she had in mind
10   The notion of what his whiskers would feel like
On the back of her neck. She told me later on
That after a while she got to looking out
At the lights across the channel, and really felt sad,
Thinking of all the wine and enormous beds
15   And blandishments in French and the perfumes.
And then she got really angry. To have been brought
All the way down from London, and then be addressed
As a sort of mournful cosmic last resort
Is really tough on a girl, and she was pretty.
20   Anyway, she watched him pace the room
And finger his watch-chain and seem to sweat a bit,

---

[60] God is referred to by some philosophers as The First Cause.
[61] Natural Selection is the process, according to Charles Darwin, by which species evolved.

And then she said one or two unprintable things.
But you mustn't judge her by that. What I mean to say is,
She's really all right. I still see her once in a while
25 And she always treats me right. We have a drink
And I give her a good time, and perhaps it's a year
Before I see her again, but there she is,
Running to fat, but dependable as they come.
And sometimes I bring her a bottle of *Nuit d'Amour*.[62]

Compare "The Dover Bitch" with Matthew Arnold's "Dover Beach" on page 624.

RICHARD HUGO (1923–1982)

Driving Montana

The day is a woman who loves you. Open.
Deer drink close to the road and magpies
spray from your car. Miles from any town
your radio comes in strong, unlikely
5 Mozart from Belgrade, rock and roll
from Butte. Whatever the next number,
you want to hear it. Never has your Buick
found this forward a gear. Even
the tuna salad in Reedpoint is good.

10 Towns arrive ahead of imagined schedule.
Absorakee at one. Or arrive so late—
Silesia at nine—you recreate the day.
Where did you stop along the road
and have fun? Was there a runaway horse?
15 Did you park at that house, the one
alone in a void of grain, white with green
trim and red fence, where you know you lived
once? You remembered the ringing creek,
the soft brown forms of far off bison.
20 You must have stayed hours, then drove on.
In the motel you know you'd never seen it before.

Tomorrow will open again, the sky wide
as the mouth of a wild girl, friable
clouds you lose yourself to. You are lost
25 in miles of land without people, without
one fear of being found, in the dash
of rabbits, soar of antelope, swirl
merge and clatter of streams.

---

[62] *Nuit d'Amour* is French for "night of love."

A. R. AMMONS (1926–)

The Visit

It is not far to my place:
you can come smallboat,
pausing under shade in the eddies
    or going ashore
5   to rest, regard the leaves

or talk with birds and
shore weeds: hire a full-grown man not
late in years to oar you
    and choose a canoe-like thin ship;
10   (a dumb man is better and no

costlier; he will attract
the reflections and silences under leaves:)
travel light: a single book, some twine:
    the river is muscled at rapids with trout
15   and a laurel limb

will make a suitable spit: if you
leave in the forenoon, you will arrive
with plenty of light
    the afternoon of the third day: I will
20   come down to the landing

(tell your man to look for it,
the dumb have clear sight and are free of
visions) to greet you with some made
    wine and a special verse:
25   or you can come by shore:

choose the right: there the rocks
cascade less frequently, the grade more gradual:
treat yourself gently: the ascent thins both
    mind and blood and you must
30   keep still a dense reserve

of silence we can poise against
conversation: there is little news:
I found last month a root with shape and
    have heard a new sound among
35   the insects: come.

ALLEN GINSBERG (1926–)

A Supermarket in California

What thoughts I have of you tonight, Walt Whitman, for
I walked down the sidestreets under the trees with a headache
self-conscious looking at the full moon.
    In my hungry fatigue, and shopping for images, I went

5   into the neon fruit supermarket, dreaming of your enumerations!
       What peaches and what penumbras! Whole families shopping
at night! Aisles full of husbands! Wives in the avocados,
babies in the tomatoes!—and you, Garcia Lorca,[63] what were you
doing down by the watermelons?

10   I saw you, Walt Whitman, childless, lonely old grubber,
poking among the meats in the refrigerator and eyeing the
grocery boys.
       I heard you asking questions of each: Who killed the
pork chops? What price bananas? Are you my Angel?

15   I wandered in and out of the brilliant stacks of cans
following you, and followed in my imagination by the store
detective.
       We strode down the open corridors together in our
solitary fancy tasting artichokes, possessing every frozen

20   delicacy, and never passing the cashier.

       Where are we going, Walt Whitman? The doors close in
an hour. Which way does your beard point tonight?
       (I touch your book and dream of our odyssey in the
supermarket and feel absurd.)

25   Will we walk all night through solitary streets? The trees
add shade to shade, lights out in the houses, we'll both be
lonely.
       Will we stroll dreaming of the lost America of love past
blue automobiles in driveways, home to our silent cottage?

30   Ah, dear father, graybeard, lonely old courage-teacher,
what America did you have when Charon[64] quit poling his ferry
and you got out on a smoking bank and stood watching the
boat disappear on the black waters of Lethe?

ANNE SEXTON (1928–1974)

Pain for a Daughter

Blind with love, my daughter
has cried nightly for horses,
those long-necked marchers and churners
that she has mastered, any and all,
5   reigning them in like a circus hand—
the excitable muscles and the ripe neck;
tending this summer, a pony and a foal.
She who is too squeamish to pull
a thorn from the dog's paw,
10   watched her pony blossom with distemper,
the underside of the jaw swelling
like an enormous grape.

---

[63] García Lorca (1899–1936) was a Spanish poet and playwright noted for his haunting imagery.
[64] In Greek mythology Charon ferried dead souls across the river Lethe to the underworld.

Gritting her teeth with love,
she drained the boil and scoured it
15 with hydrogen peroxide until pus
ran like milk on the barn floor.

Blind with loss all winter,
in dungarees, a ski jacket and a hard hat,
she visits the neighbors' stable,
20 our acreage not zoned for barns;
they who own the flaming horses
and the swan-whipped thoroughbred
that she tugs at and cajoles,
thinking it will burn like a furnace
25 under her small-hipped English seat.[65]

Blind with pain she limps home.
The thoroughbred has stood on her foot.
He rested there like a building.
He grew into her foot until they were one.
30 The marks of the horseshoe printed
into her flesh, the tips of her toes
ripped off like pieces of leather,
three toenails swirled like shells
and left to float in blood in her riding boot.

35 Blind with fear, she sits on the toilet,
her foot balanced over the washbasin,
her father, hydrogen peroxide in hand,
performing the rites of the cleansing.
She bites on a towel, sucked in breath,
40 sucked in and arched against the pain,
her eyes glancing off me where
I stand at the door, eyes locked
on the ceiling, eyes of a stranger,
and then she cries . . .
45 *Oh my God, help me!*
Where a child would have cried *Mama!*
Where a child would have believed *Mama!*
she bit the towel and called on God
and I saw her life stretch out . . .
50 I saw her torn in childbirth,
and I saw her, at that moment,
in her own death and I knew that she
knew.

Compare "Pain for a Daughter" with Maxine Kumin's "For a Shetland Pony Brood Mare Who Died in Her Barren Year" on page 882.

---

[65] An English seat is a type of riding saddle.

The Last Judgment by Fra Angelico. (Scala / Art Resource)

RICHARD HOWARD (1929–)

Giovanni da Fiesole on the Sublime, or Fra Angelico's Last Judgement[66]

For Adrienne Rich[67]

How to behold what cannot be held?
Start from the center and from all that
lies or flies or merely rises left
of center. You may have noticed how
5   Hell, in these affairs, is on the right
invariably (though for an inside Judge,
of course, that would be the left. And we
are not inside.) I have no doctrine
intricate enough for Hell, which I leave
10   in its own right, where it will be left.

Right down the center, then, in two rows,
run nineteen black holes, their square lids off;
also one sarcophagus, up front.
Out of these has come the world; out of
15   that coffin, I guess, the Judge above
the world. Nor is my doctrine liable
to smooth itself out for the blue ease
of Heaven outlining one low hill

---

[66] Giovanni da Fiesole, also known as Fra Angelico, was born as Guido di Pietro (c. 1400–1455). He was one of the greatest painters of the Italian Renaissance. This poem describes his painting *The Last Judgment* in the Convento degli Angioli, Florence.

[67] Adrienne Rich is an American poet. A poem by Adrienne Rich appears on pages 883–84.

20 against the sky at the graveyard's end
like a woman's body—a hill like Eve.

Some of us stand, still, at the margin
of this cemetery, marvelling
that no more than a mortared pavement can
separate us from the Other Side
25 which numbers as many nuns and priests
(even Popes and Empresses!) as ours.
The rest, though, stirring to a music
that our startled blood remembers now,
embrace each other or the Angels
30 of this green place: the dancing begins.

We dance in a circle of bushes,
red and yellow roses, round a pool
of green water. There is one lily,
gold as a lantern in the dark grass,
35 and all the trees accompany us
with gestures of fruition. We stop!
The ring of bodies opens where a last
Angel, in scarlet, hands us on. Now
we go, we are leaving this garden
40 of colors and gowns. We walk into

a light falling upon us, falling
out of the great rose gate upon us,
light so thick we cannot trust our eyes
to walk into it so. We lift up
45 our hands then and walk into the light.

How to behold what cannot be held?
Make believe you hold it, no longer
lighting but light, and walk into that
gold success. The world must be its own
50 *witness, we judge ourselves, raise your hands.*

Compare "Giovanni da Fiesole" with W. H. Auden's "Musée des Beaux Arts" on pages 542–43.

TED HUGHES (1930–)

Hawk Roosting

I sit in the top of the wood, my eyes closed.
Inaction, no falsifying dream
Between my hooked head and hooked feet:
Or in sleep rehearse perfect kills and eat.

5 The convenience of the high trees!
The air's buoyancy and the sun's ray

Are of advantage to me;
And the earth's face upward for my inspection.

My feet are locked upon the rough bark.
10 It took the whole of Creation
To produce my foot, my each feather:
Now I hold Creation in my foot

Or fly up, and revolve it all slowly—
I kill where I please because it is all mine.
15 There is no sophistry in my body:
My manners are tearing off heads—

The allotment of death.
For the one path of my flight is direct
Through the bones of the living.
20 No arguments assert my right:

The sun is behind me.
Nothing has changed since I began.
My eye has permitted no change.
I am going to keep things like this.

Compare "Hawk Roosting" with Robert Duncan's "My Mother Would Be a Falconress"
on pages 851–52 and May Sarton's "Lady with a Falcon" on page 847.

DEREK WALCOTT (1930–)

Sea Grapes

That sail in cloudless light
which tires of islands,
a schooner beating up the Caribbean

for home, could be Odysseus[68]
5 home-bound through the Aegean,
just as that husband's

sorrow under the sea-grapes, repeats
the adulterer's hearing Nausicaa's name
in every gull's outcry.

10 But whom does this bring peace? The classic war
between a passion and responsibility
is never finished, and has been the same

to the sea-wanderer and the one on shore,
now wriggling on his sandals to walk home,
15 since Troy sighed its last flame,

---

[68] Odysseus, or Ulysses, is the hero of Homer's *Odyssey*, a section of which may be found on
pages 558–64.

and the blind giant's boulder heaved the trough[69]
from which The Odyssey's hexameters come[70]
to finish up as Caribbean surf.

The classics can console. But not enough.

COLETTE INEZ (1931–)

Spanish Heaven

My heaven is Hispanic ladies in satin tube dresses,
their hair like a chocolate sundae melts into waves.
They are giving me transparent nightgowns
and kisses on my face.
5   Lotteria tickets bulging in my purse.
They are saying *qué bonita*[71] in the house
of their throats
and we all eat mangoes and fritos d'amor
selling Avon products to each other forever.

10   And damning Fidel, Trujillo,[72] what bums.
But Evita,[73] what heart and Elizabeth Taylor
there in her shrine,
Monacos of pleasure as Grace takes our hand.[74]
Eyepads of freedom, Avons of love.

15   Mascara of angels, hairspray of God,
they are teasing my hair like a heavenly cloud
while the acid of husbands eating alone
rumbles Dolores, *putas*[75] and rape
in the hell of machismo.

SYLVIA PLATH (1932–1963)

Lady Lazarus[76]

I have done it again.[77]
One year in every ten
I manage it—

---

[69] An allusion to Odysseus' fight with the Cyclops (see pages 563–64).

[70] The *Odyssey* is in dactylic hexameter.

[71] *Qué bonita* is Spanish for "how beautiful."

[72] Fidel Castro and Rafael Trujillo Molina, two Caribbean dictators, Castro in Cuba and Trujillo in the Dominican Republic until his assassination in 1961.

[73] Eva (Evita) Perón, wife of Juan Perón. Both were dictators of Argentina. Evita Perón was known for her great beauty, among other things.

[74] Elizabeth Taylor and Grace Kelly, American screen actresses. Grace Kelly later became Princess Grace of Monaco.

[75] *Putas* is the Spanish word for prostitutes.

[76] Jesus raised Lazarus from the dead (John 11:44).

[77] Plath repeatedly attempted suicide and finally died by her own hand in 1963.

Sylvia Plath *(Rollie McKenna)*

A sort of walking miracle, my skin
5   Bright as a Nazi lampshade,[78]
My right foot

A paperweight,
My face a featureless, fine
Jew linen.

10   Peel off the napkin
O my enemy.
Do I terrify?—

The nose, the eye pits, the full set of teeth?
The sour breath
15   Will vanish in a day.

Soon, soon the flesh
The grave cave ate will be
At home on me

And I a smiling woman.
20   I am only thirty.
And like the cat I have nine times to die.

This is Number Three.
What a trash
To annihilate each decade.

---

[78] The Nazis sometimes used the skins of Jews they had killed in the concentration camps for lamp shades.

25   What a million filaments.
      The peanut-crunching crowd
      Shoves in to see

      Them unwrap me hand and foot—
      The big strip tease.
30   Gentleman, ladies,

      These are my hands,
      My knees.
      I may be skin and bone,

      Nevertheless, I am the same, identical woman.
35   The first time it happened I was ten.
      It was an accident.

      The second time I meant
      To last it out and not come back at all.
      I rocked shut

40   As a seashell.
      They had to call and call
      And pick the worms off me like sticky pearls.

      Dying
      Is an art, like everything else.
45   I do it exceptionally well.

      I do it so it feels like hell.
      I do it so it feels real.
      I guess you could say I've a call.

      It's easy enough to do it in a cell.
50   It's easy enough to do it and stay put.
      It's the theatrical

      Comeback in broad day
      To the same place, the same face, the same brute
      Amused shout:

55   "A miracle!"
      That knocks me out.
      There is a charge

      For the eyeing of my scars, there is a charge
      For the hearing of my heart—
60   It really goes.

      And there is a charge, a very large charge
      For a word or a touch
      Or a bit of blood

      Or a piece of my hair or my clothes.
65   So, so, Herr Doktor.
      So, Herr Enemy.

I am your opus,°   work, composition
I am your valuable,
The pure gold baby

70   That melts to a shriek.
I turn and burn.
Do not think I underestimate your great concern.

Ash, ash—
You poke and stir.
75   Flesh, bone, there is nothing there—

A cake of soap,
A wedding ring,
A gold filling.

Herr God, Herr Lucifer,
80   Beware
Beware.

Out of the ash
I rise with my red hair
And I eat men like air.

WENDELL BERRY (1934–)

The Old Elm Tree by the River

Shrugging in the flight of its leaves,
it is dying. Death is slowly
standing up in its trunk and branches
like a camouflaged hunter. In the night
5   I am wakened by one of its branches
crashing down, heavy as a wall, and then
lie sleepless, the world changed.
That is a life I know the country by.
Mine is a life I know the country by.
10   Willing to live and die, we stand here,
timely and at home, neighborly as two men.
Our place is changing in us as we stand,
and we hold up the weight that will bring us down.
In us the land enacts its history.
15   When we stood it was beneath us, and was
the strength by which we held to it
and stood, the daylight over it
a mighty blessing we cannot bear for long.

Compare "The Old Elm Tree by the River" with James Wright's "A Blessing" on page 520.

JIM BARNES (1933–)

A Season of Loss

We left the horses in the draw
and climbed the painted ledge to see
the blue and distance home but saw
an autumn sun set fire to trees

5   on ridges we had yet to pass:
gnarled trees that burned and stood
more than a shifting phoenix, cast
in colors other than mild moods.

Our blood was now too thin to know
10   the half-moon brother, our skin too pale;
yet we, hands out, tried again to sow
our spirit in the stars. A frail

effort: our father's blood pulsed slow.
At our back a glyph grew perfect:
15   hard in stone a hand drew back to throw,
a sun stood still, a moon arced, sticks

grew into bones. Only human,
we touched thoughts, hands, eyes,
assured ourselves of the moment,
20   and leaned together hard against the sky.

AUDRE LORDE (1934–)

Now That I Am Forever with Child

How the days went
while you were blooming within me
I remember each upon each—
the swelling changed planes of my body
5   and how you first fluttered, then jumped
and I thought it was my heart.

How the days wound down
and the turning of winter
I recall, with you growing heavy
10 against the wind. I thought
now her hands
are formed, and her hair
has started to curl
now her teeth are done
15 now she sneezes.
Then the seed opened
I bore you one morning just before spring
My head rang like a fiery piston

my legs were towers between which
20   A new world was passing.

Since then
I can only distinguish
one thread within running hours
You, flowing through selves
25   toward You.

Compare "Now That I Am Forever with Child" with Erica Jong's "How You Get Born" on page 876.

N. SCOTT MOMADAY (1934–)

Earth and I Gave You Turquoise

Earth and I gave you turquoise
    when you walked singing
We lived laughing in my house
    and told old stories
5   You grew ill when the owl cried
We will meet on Black Mountain

I will bring you corn for planting
    and we will make fire
Children will come to your breast
10   You will heal my heart
I speak your name many times
The wild cane remembers you

My young brother's house is filled
    I go there to sing
15   We have not spoken of you
        but our songs are sad
When the Moon Woman goes to you
I will follow her white way

Tonight they dance near Chinle
20   by the seven elms
There your loom whispered beauty
        They will eat mutton
and drink coffee till morning
You and I will not be there

25   I saw a crow by Red Rock
        standing on one leg
It was the black of your hair
        The years are heavy
I will ride the swiftest horse
30   You will hear the drumming of hooves

SONIA SANCHEZ (1935–)

summer words of a sistuh addict

the first day i shot dope
was on a sunday.
                    i had just come
home from church
5   got mad at my motha
cuz she got mad at me.   u dig?
                   went out.   shot up
behind a feelen gainst her.
                      it felt good.
10   gooder than dooing it.   yeah.
                      it was nice.
i did it. uh. huh.   i did it.   uh. huh.
i want to do it again.   it felt so gooooood.
             and as the sistuh
15   sits in her silent/
             remembered/high
             someone leans for
             ward gently asks her:
             sistuh.
20   did u
             finally
         learn how to hold yo/mother?
and the music of the day
               drifts in the room
25   to mingle with the sistuh's young tears.
             and we all sing.

Compare "summer words of a sistuh addict" with Adrienne Rich's "A Woman Mourned by Daughters" on pages 883–84.

LUCILLE CLIFTON (1936–)

Good Times

My Daddy has paid the rent
and the insurance man is gone
and the lights is back on
and my uncle Brud has hit
5   for one dollar straight
and they is good times
good times
good times

My Mama has made bread
10 and Grampaw has come

and everybody is drunk
and dancing in the kitchen
and singing in the kitchen
oh these is good times
15   good times
good times

oh children think about the
good times

DARYL HINE (1936–)

The Survivors

Nowadays the mess is everywhere
And getting worse. Earth after all
Is a battlefield. Through the static
We used to call the music of the spheres

5   Someone, a survivor, sends this message:
"When it happened I was reading Homer.

Sing—will nobody sing?—the wrath,
Rats and tanks and radioactive rain."

That was before rationing was enforced
10   On words, of course. Particles went first,
Then substantives. Now only verbs abide
The law, and the odd anarchistic scrawl

How above the crumbling horizon
Brightly shine our neighbours, Venus, Mars.

JUNE JORDAN (1936–)

My Sadness Sits Around Me

My sadness sits around me
    not on haunches not in any
    placement near a move
and the tired roll-on
5   of a boredom without grief

If there were war
I would watch the hunting
I would chase the dogs
and blow the horn
10   *because blood is commonplace*

As I walk in peace
    unencountered unmolested
    unimpinging unbelieving unrevealing
    undesired under every O
15   My sadness sits around me

Compare "My Sadness Sits Around Me" with Delmore Schwartz's "The Heavy Bear Who Goes with Me" on pages 669–70.

DIANE WAKOSKI (1937–)

Backing Up, Or Tearing Up the Garden Next to the Driveway

Does it mean anything
that I just can't back up?
My eyes take me forward,
my body not wanting
5   to be part
                of what is behind
me.
The driveway,
like a scar in life,
10   the paving left there from former acts,
                        actions,
and I not wanting to retrace
the days, hours, minutes, that made it,
not wanting to go back over
15   old ground.

ISHMAEL REED (1938–)

beware   :   do not read this poem

tonite, thriller was
abt an ol woman, so vain she
surrounded herself w /
        many mirrors

5   it got so bad that finally she
locked herself indoors & her
whole life became the
        mirrors

one day the villagers broke
10   into her house , but she was too
swift for them . she disappeared
        into a mirror
each tenant who bought the house
after that , lost a loved one to

15   the ol woman in the mirror :
first a little girl
then a young woman
then the young woman/s husband

the hunger of this poem is legendary
20   it has taken in many victims
back off from this poem

it has drawn in yr feet
back off from this poem
it has drawn in yr legs

25 back off from this poem
it is a greedy mirror
you are into this poem . from
    the waist down
nobody can hear you can they ?
30 this poem has had you up to here
    belch
this poem aint got no manners
you cant call out frm this poem
relax now & go w / this poem

35 move & roll on to this poem
do not resist this poem
this poem has yr eyes
this poem has his head
this poem has his arms
40 this poem has his fingers
this poem has his fingertips

this poem is the reader & the
reader this poem

statistic : the us bureau of missing persons re-
45   ports that in 1968 over 100,000 people
        disappeared leaving no solid clues
            nor trace   only
    a space   in the lives of their friends

MARGARET ATWOOD (1939–)

You Are Happy

The water turns
a long way down over the raw stone,
ice crusts around it.

We walk separately
5 along the hill to the open
beach, unused
picnic tables, wind
shoving the brown waves, erosion, gravel
rasping on gravel.

10 In the ditch a deer
carcass, no head. Bird
running across the glaring
road against the low pink sun.

When you are this
15   cold you can think about
nothing but the cold, the images

hitting into your eyes
like needles, crystals, you are happy.

Compare "You Are Happy" with William Stafford's "Traveling Through the Dark" on
pages 849–50.

SEAMUS HEANEY (1939–)

The Forge

All I know is a door into the dark.
Outside, old axles and iron hoops rusting;
Inside, the hammered anvil's short-pitched ring,
The unpredictable fantail of sparks
5   Or hiss when a new shoe toughens in water.
The anvil must be somewhere in the centre,
Horned as a unicorn, at one end square,
Set there immovable: an altar
Where he expends himself in shape and music.
10   Sometimes, leather-aproned, hairs in his nose,
He leans out on the jamb, recalls a clatter
Of hoofs where traffic is flashing in rows;
Then grunts and goes in, with a slam and flick
To beat real iron out, to work the bellows.

MARILYN HACKER (1942–)

Villanelle

For D.G.B.

Every day our bodies separate,
exploded torn and dazed.
Not understanding what we celebrate

we grope through languages and hesitate
5   and touch each other, speechless and amazed;
and every day our bodies separate

us farther from our planned, deliberate
ironic lives. I am afraid, disphased,
not understanding what we celebrate

10   when our fused limbs and lips communicate
the unlettered power we have raised.
Every day our bodies' separate

routines are harder to perpetuate.
In wordless darkness we learn wordless praise,
15   not understanding what we celebrate;

wake to ourselves, exhausted, in the late
morning as the wind tears off the haze,
not understanding how we celebrate
our bodies. Every day we separate.

ERICA JONG (1942–)

How You Get Born

One night, your mother is listening to the walls.
The clock whirrs like insect wings.
The ticking says lonely lonely lonely.

In the living room, the black couch swallows her.
5   She trusts it more than men,
but no one will ever love her
enough.

She doesn't yet know you
so how can she love you?
10   She loves you like God or Shakespeare.
She loves you like Mozart.

You are trembling in the walls like music.
You cross the ceiling in a phantom car of light.

Meanwhile unborn,
15   You wait in a heavy rainsoaked cloud
for your father's thunderbolt.
Your mother lies in the living room dreaming your hands.
Your mother lies in the living room dreaming your eyes.

She awakens & a shudder shakes her teeth.
20   The world is beginning again after the flood.

She slides into bed beside that gray-faced man,
your father.
She opens her legs to your coming.

Compare "How You Get Born" with Audre Lorde's "Now That I Am Forever with Child"
on pages 869–70.

JAMES WELCH (1940–)

The Man from Washington

The end came easy for most of us.
Packed away in our crude beginnings
in some far corner of a flat world,
we didn't expect much more
5   than firewood and buffalo robes
to keep us warm. The man came down

a slouching dwarf with rainwater eyes,
and spoke to us. He promised
that life would go on as usual,
10   that treaties would be signed, and everyone—
man, woman, and child—would be inoculated
against a world in which we had no part,
a world of money, promise and disease.

DAVE SMITH (1942–)

Picking Cherries

The ladder quakes and sways under me, old wood
I put too much faith in, like ancestors strained.
You circle me, cradling the baby, sun guttering
in your face, parading through the leaves, glad.
5   If I looked down I would see your calm fear, see
in your narrowed eyes my bones chipped, useless.
The bucket hangs from my belt, pulling obscenely
at my pants, but the cherries drop in and grow
one by one. I keep reaching higher than I need
10   because I want the one that tickles your tongue.
When I come down we will both be older, slower,
but what of that? Haven't we loved this climbing?
If the ladder gives way I still believe I can
catch one branch, drop the bucket and ease down.

Compare "Picking Cherries" with Robert Frost's "After Apple-Picking" on pages 835–36.

ALFRED CORN (1943–)

Fifty-Seventh Street and Fifth[79]

Hard-edged buildings; cloudless blue enamel;
Lapidary hours—and that numerous woman,
Put-together, in many a smashing
Suit or dress is somehow what it's, well,
5   All about. A city designed by *Halston:*[80]
Clean lines, tans, grays, expense; no sentiment.
Off the mirrored boxes the afternoon
Glare fires an instant in her sunglasses
And reflects some of the armored ambition
10   Controlling deed here; plus the byword
That "only the best really counts." Awful
And awe-inspiring. How hard the task,

---

[79] Cross streets of New York City's famed retail district.
[80] Roy Halston Frowick (1932–), the well-known fashion designer who goes by the name of Halston.

Keeping up to the mark: opinions, output,
Presentation—strong on every front. So?
15   Life is strife, the city says, a theory
That tastes of iron and demands assent.

A big lump of iron that's been magnetized.
All the faces I see are—Believers,
Pilgrims immigrated from fifty states
20   To discover, to surrender, themselves.
Success. Money. Fame. Insular dreams all,
Begotten of the dream of Manhattan, island
Of the possessed. When a man's tired of New York,
He's tired of life? Or just of possession?
25   A whirlpool animates the terrific
Streets, violence of our praise, blockbuster
Miracles down every vista, scored by
Accords and discords intrinsic to this air.
Concerted mind performs as the genius
30   Of place: competition, a trust in facts
And expense. Who loves or works here assumes,
For better or worse, the ground rules. A fate.

NIKKI GIOVANNI (1943–)

Nikki-Rosa

childhood remembrances are always a drag
if you're Black
you always remember things like living in Woodlawn[81]
with no inside toilet
5   and if you become famous or something
they never talk about how happy you were to have your mother
all to yourself and
how good the water felt when you got your bath from one of those
big tubs that folk in chicago barbecue in
10   and somehow when you talk about home
it never gets across how much you
understood their feelings
as the whole family attended meetings about Hollydale
and even though you remember
15   your biographers never understand
your father's pain as he sells his stock
and another dream goes
and though you're poor it isn't poverty that
concerns you
20   and though they fought a lot
it isn't your father's drinking that makes any difference
but only that everybody is together and you
and your sister have happy birthdays and very good christmasses

---

[81] Woodlawn is a suburb of Cincinnati.

and I really hope no white person ever has cause to write about me
25 because they never understand Black love is Black wealth and they'll
probably talk about my hard childhood and never understand that
all the while I was quite happy

TOM WAYMAN (1945–)

Unemployment

The chrome lid of the coffee pot
twists off, and the glass knob rinsed.
Lift out the assembly, dump
the grounds out. Wash the pot and
5 fill with water, put everything back with
fresh grounds and snap the top down.
Plug in again and wait.

Unemployment is also
a great snow deep around the house
10 choking the street, and the City.
Nothing moves. Newspaper photographs
show the traffic backed up for miles.
Going out to shovel the walk
I think how in a few days the sun will clear this.
15 No one will know I worked here.

This is like whatever I do.
How strange that so magnificent a thing as a body
with its twinges, its aches
should have all that chemistry, that bulk
20 the intricate electrical brain
subjected to something as tiny
as buying a postage stamp.
Or selling it.

Or waiting.

GREGORY ORR (1947–)

All Morning

All morning the dream lingers.
I am like thick grass
in a meadow, still
soaked with dew at noon.

MOLLY PEACOCK (1947–)

Petting and Being a Pet

Dogs, lambs, chickens, women—pets of all nations!
Fur or feathers under the kneading fingers
of those who long to have pets, relations

of softness to fleshiness, how a hand lingers
5   on a head or on the ear of a head, thus the sound
of petting and being a pet, a sounding horn:
needing met by kneading of bone which is found
through flesh. Have you ever felt forlorn
looking at a cat on someone else's lap, wishing
10   the cat was you? Look how an animal is passed
from lap to lap in a room, so many wishing
to hold it. We wish to be in the vast
caress, both animal and hand. Like eyes make sense
of seeing, touch makes being make sense.

LESLIE MARMON SILKO (1948–)

Love Poem

Rain smell comes with the wind
                     out of the southwest.
Smell of the sand dunes
           tall grass glistening
5   in the rain.
Warm raindrops that fall easy
               (this woman)
The summer is born.
Smell of her breathing new life
10   small gray toads on damp sand.
(this woman)
        whispering to dark wide leaves
        white moon blossoms dripping
                   tracks in the sand.
15   Rain smell
       I am full of hunger
       deep and longing to touch
wet tall grass, green and strong beneath.
This woman loved a man
20   and she breathed to him
            her damp earth song.
I am haunted by this story
I remember it in cottonwood leaves
             their fragrance in the shade.
25   I remember it in the wide blue sky
when the rain smell comes with the wind.

JOHN YAU (1950–)

For Alexander Pope's Garden[82]

In a garden every plant and flower
Memorizes the proper manner

---

[82] Alexander Pope (1688–1744) was a great English poet who established a large and famous garden
on his estate at Twickenham.

In which to behave, or else they are discarded.
The lessons are simple; the growth must be retarded
5   Until they stand like dragoons in an orderly row,
Keep their thoughts private, and occasionally bow.

Poems about Death

STEVIE SMITH (1902–1971)

Not Waving but Drowning

Nobody heard him, the dead man,
But still he lay moaning:
I was much further out than you thought
And not waving but drowning.

5   Poor chap, he always loved larking
And now he's dead
It must have been too cold for him his heart gave way.
They said.

Oh, no no no, it was too cold always
10   (Still the dead one lay moaning)
I was much too far out all my life
And not waving but drowning.

STANLEY KUNITZ (1905–)

The Portrait

My mother never forgave my father
for killing himself,
especially at such an awkward time
and in a public park,
5   that spring
when I was waiting to be born.
She locked his name
in her deepest cabinet
and would not let him out,
10 though I could hear him thumping.
When I came down from the attic
with the pastel portrait in my hand
of a long-lipped stranger
with a brave moustache
15 and deep brown level eyes,
she ripped it into shreds
without a single word
and slapped me hard.
In my sixty-fourth year
20 I can feel my cheek
still burning.

MAXINE KUMIN (1925–)

For a Shetland Pony Brood Mare[83]
Who Died in Her Barren Year

After bringing forth eighteen
foals in as many Mays
you might, old Trinket girl,
have let yourself be lulled
5   this spring into the green days
of pasture and first curl
of timothy.° Instead,   *a kind of grass*
your milk bag swelled again,
an obstinate machine.

10   Your long pale tongue
waggled in every feed box.
You slicked your ears back
to scatter other mares
from the salt lick.[84]
15   You were full of winter burdocks
and false pregnancy.

By midsummer all the foals
had breached, except the ghost
you carried. In the bog
20   where you came down each noon
to ease your deer-thin hoofs in mud,
a jack-in-the-pulpit cocked
his overhang like a question mark.
We saw some autumn soon
25   that botflies would take your skin
and bloodworms settle
inside the cords and bands
that laced your belly,
your church of folded hands.

30   But all in good time, Trinket!
Was it something you understood?
Full of false pride
you lay down and died
in the sun,
35   all silken on one side,
all mud on the other one.

Compare "For a Shetland Pony Brood Mare" with Anne Sexton's "Pain for a Daughter" on pages 860–61.

---

[83] A brood mare is a female horse kept for breeding purposes.
[84] A salt lick is a block of salt set out for animals to lick.

W. S. MERWIN (1927–)

For the Anniversary of My Death

Every year without knowing it I have passed the day
When the last fires will wave to me
And the silence will set out
Tireless traveller
5   Like the beam of a lightless star

Then I will no longer
Find myself in life as in a strange garment
Surprised at the earth
And the love of one woman
10   And then shamelessness of men
As today writing after three days of rain
Hearing the wren sing and the falling cease
And bowing not knowing to what

ADRIENNE RICH (1929–)

A Woman Mourned by Daughters

Now, not a tear begun,
we sit here in your kitchen,
spent, you see, already.
You are swollen till you strain
5   this house and the whole sky.
You, whom we so often
succeeded in ignoring!
You are puffed up in death
like a corpse pulled from the sea;
10   we groan beneath your weight.
And yet you were a leaf,
a straw blown on the bed,
you had long since become
crisp as a dead insect.
15   What is it, if not you,
that settles on us now
like satin you pulled down
over our bridal heads?
What rises in our throats
20   like food you prodded in?
Nothing could be enough.
You breathe upon us now
through solid assertions
of yourself: teaspoons, goblets,
25   seas of carpet, a forest
of old plants to be watered,
an old man in an adjoining
room to be touched and fed.

And all this universe
30   dares us to lay a finger
anywhere, save exactly
as you would wish it done.

Compare "A Woman Mourned by Daughters" with Sonia Sanchez's "summer words of a sistuh addict" on page 871.

Poems about Families

JIM MITSUI (1940–)

When Father Came Home for Lunch

I listen to my parent's language,
watch my father eat his separate meal,
the railroad motor car
cooling off and waiting
5   on the siding by the section house.
He sits with his back to the burning
woodstove in a captain's chair
and eats the family left-overs,
a bowl of rice balanced in his hand,
10   chopsticks flicking
around to the bowls & dishes
arranged in front of him.

Mother adds fried onions, a fried egg
and potatoes to his main bowl.
15   He adds catsup, shoyu
and mixes it with the white radish,
egg plant and cold chicken.
He works around to the mustard caked bowl
before each mouth of rice,
20   sauce hanging from his mustache.
Hot coffee, heavy with sugar & cream,
steams from a china mug.
Half-an-hour of noisy manners
and he's gone, back to work
25   in oily bib overalls.
I can still smell sweat
soaking his long-sleeved workshirt.

ALBERTO RÍOS (1952–)

Nani°

nani *means granny*

Sitting at her table, she serves
the sopa de arroz° to me   *rice soup*
instinctively, and I watch her,
the absolute *mamá,* and eat words

Alberto Ríos (*Hal Martin Fogel*)

5   I might have had to say more
       out of embarrassment. To speak,
       now foreign words I used to speak,
       too, dribble down her mouth as she serves
       me albóndigas.° No more   *spiced meatballs*
10   than a third are easy to me.
       By the stove she does something with words
       and looks at me only with her
       back. I am full. I tell her
       I taste the mint, and watch her speak
15   smiles at the stove. All my words
       make her smile. Nani never serves
       herself, she only watches me
       with her skin, her hair. I ask for more.

       I watch the *mamá* warming more
20   tortillas for me. I watch her
       fingers in the flame for me.
       Near her mouth, I see a wrinkle speak
       of a man whose body serves
       the ants like she serves me, then more words
25   from more wrinkles about children, words
       about this and that, flowing more
       easily from these other mouths. Each serves
       as a tremendous string around her,

holding her together. They speak
30 nani was this and that to me
and I wonder just how much of me
will die with her, what were the words
I could have been, was. Her insides speak
through a hundred wrinkles, now, more
35 than she can bear, steel around her,
shouting then, What is this thing she serves?

She asks me if I want more.
I own no words to stop her.
Even before I speak, she serves.

LISEL MUELLER (1924–)

After Whistler

There are girls who should have been swans.
At birth their feathers are burned;
their human skins never fit.
When the other children
5   line up on the side of the sun,
they will choose the moon,
that precious aberration.
They are the daughters mothers
worry about. All summer,
10 dressed in gauze, they flicker
inside the shaded house,
drawn to the mirror, where their eyes,
blue, languid moths, hang dreaming.
It's winter they wait for, the first snowfall
15 with the steady interior hum
only they can hear;
they stretch their arms, as if they were wounded,
toward the bandages of snow.
Briefly, the world is theirs
20 in its perfect frailty.

CATHY SONG (1955–)

Lucky

The baby brought us luck
from the day we brought him home.
White curtains lifted
to let in the pale lemon light.

5   We hung his hat on the doorknob
and raised a flag
in the shape of a fish.

The man selling corn,
the woman folding sheets,

Cathy Song (*Andrea Gelber*)

10   smiled and waved their approval.
      The nurse left a poem in the mailbox.

      Those who visited tiptoed around
      the light that had landed in our living room.
      The drunk declined his usual drink.
15   The lady with the many bracelets
      stopped her jangling in mid-gesture.
      It was as if they were entering a church.

      We succumbed to sleep,
      the three of us and slept
20   through the long mornings cool
      with magnolias opening beneath our window.

      His small hand curled around my thumb.
      When I opened his rosebud fist, I found,
      already etched, a complex map of his future.

25   My breasts were sweet for days.
      The smell of milk
      enticed a trail of black ants
      to migrate out of the Boston fern.
      Like a moving signature
30   weaving across the carpet,
      it was his first alphabet.

GAIL N. HARADA (1953–)

New Year

      This is the old way,
      the whole clan gathered,

the rice steaming over the charcoal,
the women in the room, talking,
5   a layer of potato starch on the table.

This is the old way,
the father watching his son lift the mallet,
pound the rice, pound mochi,
the children watching or playing,
10   the run of the dough to the women,
the rolling of the round cakes.

This is the old way,
eating ozoni, new year's soup:
mochi for longevity,
15   daikon, long white radish
rooted firmly like families;
eating burdock, also deeply rooted,
fish for general good luck,
and lotus root, wheel of life.

20   This is the old way,
setting off firecrackers
to drive away evil spirits,
leaving the driveways red for good fortune.

The new year arrives,
25   deaf, smelling of gunpowder.

ALICE WALKER (1944–)

My Daughter Is Coming!

My daughter is coming!
I have bought her a bed
and a chair
a mirror, a lamp
5   and a desk.
Her room is all ready
except that the curtains
are torn.
Do I have time to buy shoji panels[85]
10   for the window?
I do not.

First I must WRITE A SPEECH
see the doctor about my tonsils
which are dying ahead of schedule
15   see the barber and do a wash
cross the country
cross Brooklyn and Manhattan

---

[85] Shoji panels are the translucent panels found in traditional Japanese homes.

MAKE A SPEECH
READ A POEM
20   liberate my daughter
from her father and Washington, D.C.
recross the country
and present her to her room.

My daughter is coming!
25   Will she like her bed,
her chair, her mirror
desk and lamp

Or will she see only
the torn curtains?

Compare "My Daughter Is Coming" to Adrienne Rich's "A Woman Mourned by Daughters" on pages 883–84 and Anne Sexton's "Pain for a Daughter" on pages 860–61.

GARRETT HONGO (1951–)

The Hongo Store
29 Miles Volcano
Hilo, Hawaii

From a Photograph

My parents felt those rumblings
Coming deep from the earth's belly,
Thudding like the bell of the Buddhist Church.
Tremors in the ground swayed the bathinette
5   Where I lay squalling in soapy water.

My mother carried me around the house,
Back through the orchids, ferns, and plumeria
Of that greenhouse world behind the store,
And jumped between gas pumps into the car.

10   My father gave it the gun
And said, "Be quiet," as he searched
The frequencies, flipping for the right station
(The radio squealing more loudly than I could cry).

And then even the echoes stopped—
15   The only sound the Edsel's grinding
And the bark and crackle of radio news
Saying stay home or go to church.

"Dees time she no blow!"
My father said, driving back
20   Over the red ash covering the road.
"I worried she went go for broke already!"

So in this print the size of a matchbook,
The dark skinny man, shirtless and grinning,

A toothpick in the corner of his smile,
25 Lifts a naked baby above his head—
Behind him the plate glass of the store only cracked.

Compare "The Hongo Store" to the next poem, Gary Soto's "History," and to Edward
Field's "My Polish Grandmother" on pages 550–51.

GARY SOTO (1952–)

History

Grandma lit the stove.
Morning sunlight
Lengthened in spears
Across the linoleum floor.
5   Wrapped in a shawl,
Her eyes small
With sleep,
She sliced papas,
Pounded chiles
10 With a stone
Brought from Guadalajara.[86]

                                        After

Grandpa left for work,
She hosed down
15 The walk her sons paved
And in the shade
Of a chinaberry,
Unearthed her
Secret cigar box
20 Of bright coins
And bills, counted them
In English,
Then in Spanish,
And buried them elsewhere.
25 Later, back
From the market,
Where no one saw her,
She pulled out
Pepper and beet, spines
30 Of asparagus
From her blouse,
Tiny chocolates
From under a paisley bandana,
And smiled.
35 That was the '50s,
And Grandma in her '50s,

---

[86] Guadalajara is a city in west-central Mexico.

A face streaked
From cutting grapes
And boxing plums.
40   I remember her insides
Were washed of tapeworm,
Her arms swelled into knobs
Of small growths—
Her second son
45   Dropped from a ladder
And was dust.
And yet I do not know
The sorrows
That sent her praying
50   In the dark of a closet,
The tear that fell
At night
When she touched
Loose skin
55   Of belly and breasts.
I do not know why
Her face shines
Or what goes beyond this shine,
Only the stories
60   That pulled her
From Taxco[87] to San Joaquin,
Delano to Westside,[88]
The places
In which we all begin.

Compare "History" with Edward Field's "My Polish Grandmother" on pages 550–51, and with Garrett Hongo's "The Hongo Store," the poem preceding this one.

LORNA DEE CERVANTES (1954–)

Para un Revolucionario

You speak of art
and your soul is like snow,
a soft powder raining from your
mouth,
5   covering my breasts and hair.
You speak of your love of mountains,
freedom,
and your love for a sun
whose warmth is like *una liberación*
10   pouring down upon brown bodies.

---

[87] Taxco is a city of Mexico.
[88] Places in California.

Your books are of the souls of men,
carnales° with a spirit   *flesh*
that no army, pig or *ciudad*
could ever conquer.
15   You speak of a new way,
a new life.

When you speak like this
I could listen forever.

Pero° your voice is lost to me, *carnal,*   *brother*
20   in the wail of *tus hijos,*
in the clatter of dishes
and the pucker of beans upon the stove.
Your conversations come to me
de la sala where you sit,
25   spreading your dream to brothers,
where you spread that dream like damp clover
for them to trod upon,
when I stand here reaching
para ti con manos bronces° that spring   *bronze hands*
30   from *mi espíritu*
(for I too am *Raza°*).   *clan or family*

Pero, it seems I can only touch you
with my body.
You lie with me
35   and my body *es la hamaca*
that spans the void between us.
Hermano Raza,°   *blood brother*
I am afraid that you will lie with me
and awaken too late
40   to find that you have fallen
and my hands will be left groping
for you and your dream
in the midst of *la revolución.*

Drama

1 ❧ Literature Onstage

A great drama is in many ways the liveliest vehicle for literature. No author is so admired and applauded as the playwright Shakespeare, while his gifted contemporary Spenser, a narrative poet, is treasured in respectful silence. No hero of fiction has excited as much laughter as Rostand's theatrical Cyrano, or as many sighs and tears as Romeo and Juliet. The stage amplifies character and emotion. Plays of Sophocles and Aristophanes, performed twenty-five hundred years ago, are still terrifying and delighting audiences the world over, while the lyric poetry of Periclean Athens lives on in the studies of only a few earnest readers.

The fact is, drama is more popular than fiction and poetry. It nearly always has been, in every culture with a viable theater. Drama, which has come to include the movies and television, is more accessible to more people. In order to enjoy poetry and fiction, one needs not only the ability to read, but also the leisure and attention to read carefully, thoughtfully. But, with little or no education and the price of admission, anyone can enjoy a stageplay.

So, in drama we are dealing with an art form that is not wholly literature. It is a "performance art," which may be greatly enhanced and enriched by literature, which uses literature for its blueprint and its record. A drama may be an *occasion* for eloquent language, but many plays do quite well without it. Marcel Marceau, the French mime, can act out a play in utter silence, and the story he is playing will be appreciated as much by the Chinese as the French. Technically, drama does not require language. We must remember this lest we disregard the greatest gift of the playwright—the planning of dramatic action on the stage.

Dramatic Action

For the purposes of our study we will consider a dramatic action to be any action by characters on stage that will hold the attention of the audience. Clowns and tightrope walkers have at least this in common with the cast of *Hamlet*: all are

895

able to hold the attention of a crowd. These performers are interesting because they present us with startling images of ourselves. The clown with his painted smile and oversized shoes mirrors our folly. The tightrope walker reflects our terror, courage, and desire for virtuosity. Hamlet and his fellow actors play several compelling stories—a love affair, a son seeking revenge for his father's murder, a friend's betrayal—situations that interest us because they are familiar. The dramatic actors of the play *Hamlet* have a special attraction. Though their predicaments are movingly familiar, they are not real. They invite us to share emotions while relieving us of responsibility for the outcome. We may weep briefly for the slain Hamlet, but when the curtain is down, we need not mourn him.

A play is a sympathetic human spectacle, like clowning and tight-rope walking, requiring performers and audience. But unlike tight-rope walking, a play is not real. It is a fiction acted out. In his unsurpassed analysis of drama, *The Poetics*, the Greek philosopher Aristotle (384–322 B.C.) defines drama as "an imitation of an action." The play arouses in us lifelike emotions without the usual responsibility for them. The theater permits us a peculiar and exhilarating freedom, providing what Aristotle calls a "catharsis," a sort of refreshening of our emotional channels. We will explore the much-disputed idea of catharsis in our discussion of tragedy; for the moment let it suffice to say that there is a certain relief that comes when we witness a dreaded disaster on the stage, just as there is relief when we witness a happy ending. We need to laugh and cry for characters invented primarily for that purpose, who ask no more of us than this intense, fleeting affection. This need is so old and so persistent that the stock characters of ancient Greek drama appear, slightly revised, in our television comedies and soap operas: the jealous husband, the sighing lover, the braggart, the villain, and many others.

Of course, a good play presents characters richer than these, and may make a more lasting impression on us. But we should remember that a great dramatic character shares with those stock characters an immediate appeal to the whole audience. Not to just a few of them. For a play, unlike a poem or novel, is a public phenomenon requiring the collaboration of actors and a live audience. No audience, no play. The idea of performing *Hamlet* for a house of three or four special people is unthinkable. Actors in such a predicament would strain, grow dispirited, and finally lifeless. They need the nourishment of the crowd's laughter, tears, and applause.

The Audience

Let us consider the character of an audience at a play. The spectator in the theater is in a very different state of mind than the individual who sits alone reading a story. He is at once inhibited and stimulated by the company. He is aware that he is a member of the audience, and that his response is public. If he does not hiss the villain and cry for the heroine, his neighbor might think

Audience, from Steichen's *Family of Man* (*Photograph by Arthur Witmann. Courtesy the St. Louis Post-Dispatch*)

him unfeeling, inhuman. Or he may not feel free to laugh while his neighbor is silent. He may be more likely to cry if his neighbor does.

This socialization of audience response makes the theater a natural incubator for morals and politics during revolutionary times; during ordinary times, though, the playwright is bound to uphold the prevailing morals. While the audience may be stimulated by villainy, they will rarely tolerate a stage play in which evil triumphs.

The Playwright as Collaborator

Playwrights receive full credit for the final scripts of their plays. But witnesses of the rehearsal process know that most scripts represent a collaboration between the writer and an artistic staff including actors, directors, producers, and designers of scenery, costumes, props, and lighting. A playwright working year in and year out with the same company of actors learns to trust their instincts and respond to their suggestions. We know Shakespeare admired the actor William Burbage, who was first to play Hamlet. Perhaps Burbage suggested a line or two of dialogue. This occurs in contemporary theater and there is no reason to think it could not happen in Elizabethan times. Elia Kazan, who first directed several of Tennessee Williams's scripts, ordered a number of changes in them, from specific lines to entire scenes. We must acknowledge him as a significant contributor to the final scripts.

Of course the playwright's role is central. The playwright usually conceives the story and scenes and writes most of the dialogue. Since it is primarily these things that are preserved as "literature," we will be concerned mainly with the playwright's work. But before we move on to the literary side of drama, let us give some attention to the "artistic staff" that so richly contributes to the literature.

First comes the producer. Producers choose a script they wish to bring before a specific audience. They select and secure a theater. Then they assemble an artistic staff, choosing a director first, who helps select the others. The producer publicizes the play and raises whatever funds are necessary to bring the play to the audience.

The director casts the play, with the playwright's approval if the playwright is living. Sometimes, as in the case of certain plays of Shakespeare and Molière, the play is "pre-cast," which means it was written with specific actors in mind. In rehearsals, the director strives to create an atmosphere in which the actors can work freely and effectively in developing their roles. Where necessary, he offers interpretation of the script. The director also supervises the work of the various designers—of sets, costumes, and lighting—and orchestrates them into a unified and tasteful production.

The actor's job is to interpret his or her lines and stage directions, creating from those signs a role that expresses the playwright's intentions and the actor's own special gift and inspiration. There are many ways to portray St. Joan, and quite a few might satisfy the playwright. Sometimes an actor or actress is so effective in "creating" a role that it is hard to imagine another actor reviving the role.

There are usually independent designers of stage scenery, costumes, and lighting. The stage designer, in consultation with the director, plans the layout, architecture, and colors of the stage scenery, and often selects the furniture. The costume designer creates or appropriates whatever the actors wear in the play, striving, like the stage designer, to fulfill the playwright's vision. The lighting designer creates illusions of daylight or nightlight, and through changes in color and intensity contributes to the mood of the play.

The designer's efforts in the first production of a drama are often described in the published script as if they were the playwright's own work. Modern playwrights usually credit the first designers, as well as the creators of the roles, in the preface to the published script. But it is still difficult to know how much of that which is described in scenic notes is the playwright's work, and how much is the designer's.

There are countless other contributors to the living play which ends up in our book as a finished script: stage managers, ushers, fencing coaches, and make-up artists. But let us turn to the script, for this is what is left us as literature.

2 🌿 The Script—How to Read a Play

The script is both the blueprint and record of a play. It has the same relation to a play as a sheet of musical notation has to the performance of a symphony. By the time we settle into our seats in the theater, the actors and their director have done valuable reading and interpreting of the characters and the story. We have only to listen attentively, and respond. But when we read a script we must do the imaginative work of the actors and their director. This requires somewhat more effort than theater-going.

On the other hand, reading drama offers certain pleasures and advantages that sitting in the audience does not. For instance, when a speech delights us we may reread it. If we miss the point of a particular scene, we may go back to the beginning. Most important, we do not have to suffer the misinterpretations and imperfections of the live performance. The play becomes ours to cast as we like, with our favorite actors, or with the characters the story suggests to our imaginations. We may go at our own pace, and make our own decisions about the playwright's intentions.

When you read a script, your head becomes the theater. You are the designer of the sets, the lighting, and the costumes. You are the actors and the director. Only when you have accomplished some of the work of these interpreters can you fully enjoy your role as the audience in reading a play.

Genre and Length

Until modern times the script often indicated a play's genre—comedy, tragedy, farce, melodrama, and so forth—and then the number of acts. In reading an unfamiliar play, it is helpful to have a hint as to its dramatic tone. Since most dialogue in scripts is presented without tonal comment such as "he said, gravely," it is extremely useful to know the play's genre from the beginning so that we know how to take the characters' speeches, and what tone to imagine for them.

John Millington Synge (*Culver Pictures, Inc.*)

One could waste a great deal of time misunderstanding *Hamlet* if one believed it to be a comedy.

In modern times, with the emergence of mixed genres, it has become more common simply to call the play "A Play in One Act" or "A Play in Three Acts," leaving it to the reader to discover whether the play is a tragedy, comedy, melodrama, or farce. At the opening of our first script, John Millington Synge tells us we are about to read *Riders to the Sea*, "A Play in One Act," so he is not preparing us for the genre or tone. He tells us it is a "One Act" play, which means that if we were in the theater the play would be performed without intermission. We should try to read it at one sitting.

Technically, a "One Act" play is any play comfortably performed without intermission, but it differs from the so-called full-length play in particulars other than its brevity. Generally the "One Act" play has fewer characters, takes place in a single setting, and tells a single story, whereas a full-length drama may have any number of characters and scene-changes, and tell several related stories over the course of two or three hours. The one-act play may be more impressionistic, less conclusive than a full-length play; more of a "slice-of-life," to borrow a phrase from the study of the short story. In any case, the "one act" is a good place to begin our reading of dramatic literature because it has all the elements of grander plays without their complications.

The Characters

The next information the playwright gives us is a list of characters that will appear in the play. These are sometimes listed under the title *Dramatis Personae*, which is Latin for "the persons in the play." Sometimes the playwright will credit the actors who performed in the first production of the play, in which case he will also include the date and theater of the first performance, or *première*, as well as the names of those actors who first created the roles. This was the case with our first play, *Riders to the Sea*.

On the left are the characters of the drama; on the right are the real-life actors who performed at the Molesworth Hall in Dublin. If you were a theatergoer in 1904 and happened to miss the performance at Molesworth Hall, your knowledge of the famous Honor Lavelle and W. G. Fay would help you, in reading the script, to envision the kind of *an old woman* Maurya is, and what Bartley (*her son*) looks like. Since we have no firsthand knowledge of those actors, we must do our best to describe the characters to ourselves, with the help of the descriptive aids on the "characters" page and in the text.

Many playwrights, particularly the moderns, take great pains to describe their characters in detail, as an aid to the director in casting and as a stimulus to the imagination of the reader. Playwrights in former times did not do so. Synge's descriptions on the "characters" page, and upon the first appearance of each character, are minimal but essential. We should not read a line of dialogue until we have studied his descriptions and done what we can to envision the characters.

Thus, we learn that Maurya is an old woman. The phrase "old woman" may bring to your mind a particular old woman, or maybe a favorite elderly actress. If so, use her image until something in the dialogue contradicts it. We don't know yet whether Synge's Maurya is good-natured and soft-spoken or shrewish and shrill, but it is better to begin with an image that may later be revised than to try to imagine her speeches coming out of the empty air. We also know that she is the mother of three, and this may help us to envision her.

Her daughters are shadowy figures until the play begins. We learn from the "characters" page that Cathleen is the elder, perhaps ten years older than Nora, whom Synge describes as a "young girl." You may know sisters of the ages of Cathleen and Nora, and it is likely they share characteristics common to most older and younger sisters. The older may be more responsible and domineering, the younger more dependent. Again, these images are only a starting point, but such models are useful until the dialogue defines a more specific personality. About Bartley we know almost nothing from Synge's description. But the information that he is Maurya's son and the girls' brother is essential for the reader when Bartley makes his entrance.

The *Men and Women* mentioned last are not so much characters as extras of no particular age or number. They will provide a choral background and support for the principal actors at the end of the play. We will have more to say about the function of the dramatic chorus in our discussion of *Oedipus Rex* in Chapter 3.

Envisioning characters in a play is like developing a photograph. The image becomes sharper with every speech. But at the beginning we have only the shadowy figures provided by the descriptions on the "characters" page and at the entrance of each actor. We must pay close attention to this descriptive material no matter how minimal it is.

The Scene

One of the things that distinguishes theater from movies and television is that a stageplay must occur within a more strictly confined setting. Movies can range from an open meadow to the inside of a car for their scenes, as quickly as the camera can shift its angle. But the theater must rebuild the entire scene—that, or leave it up to the actors to *pretend* that they have moved to a different place, as the actors do in Shakespeare's plays.

From the audience we can see only one part of the world in which the drama takes place: that is "the set" or "playing area." Beyond what we see on the stage is the rest of the imaginary world from which the characters enter and into which they exit. Important action may take place "offstage." In order fully to appreciate the play, we must be able to imagine not only the playing area but what exists beyond it. These locales constitute the "scene."

At the beginning of any play the script provides a description of the scene which, in more or less detail, tells us what is within the playing area, "onstage," and what lies beyond it, "offstage." Our scene description at the beginning of *Riders to the Sea* tells us that the playing area is a "cottage kitchen" and that beyond the cottage is "an island off the West of Ireland." So, if one goes out the door of the kitchen, the sea is not far off. Since a cottage cannot have many rooms, we may assume that if there are two entrances, one at the right and one at the left of the kitchen, one leads to the outdoors and the other leads to the living quarters. The following diagram is an aerial view of the scene as it might look on a proscenium stage. The proscenium arch is the framed space at the front of the auditorium across which a stage curtain is drawn in most theaters. A "proscenium" stage is the sort provided in the typical school auditorium, where the audience sits in front of the proscenium and the play goes on behind it.

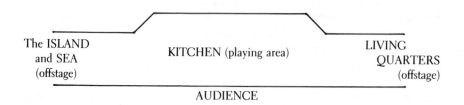

| The ISLAND and SEA (offstage) | KITCHEN (playing area) | LIVING QUARTERS (offstage) |

AUDIENCE

We should not overlook the other stage props: the nets, oil-skins, and the like, tell us that this is not the summer residence of wealthy city-dwellers, but rather a humble fishing cottage.

Now we are ready to read the play.

The Action

The action proper begins with Cathleen. When the curtain goes up she is finishing her baking and beginning her weaving. Whatever we might have thought of her before, now we must certainly think of her as industrious, no idler.

> "*Cathleen, a girl of about twenty, finishes kneading cake, and puts it down in the pot-oven by the fire.*"

This is the first *stage direction* of *Riders to the Sea*. A stage direction is any description of the actor's behavior that is not indicated by the dialogue. Stage directions are usually italicized and often appear in parentheses. Playwrights always try to keep such directions to a minimum, for the speeches themselves are usually the best indicators of the action. Shakespeare's plays are nearly free of stage directions.

As Cathleen is spinning, Nora "puts her head in at the door." This is another stage direction rich in implications. She does not stride in, or skip in, singing; she "puts her head in at the door" and speaks "in a low voice." This is not a bold or carefree entrance into her own home. We may assume that Nora, at an enthusiastic age, is either unusually shy, or is entering a situation that requires delicacy, maybe caution, and that Nora is capable of such delicacy. Her question and Cathleen's answer confirm that the house is not in a festive mood. Someone is lying down in the other room who needs not only sleep, but God's help.

Thus, with minimal stage directions and linguistic concentration worthy of a poet, J. M. Synge sets up a dramatic situation within two lines of dialogue. Already the audience is in some suspense, curious to know the plight of the mysterious woman in the next room. We suspect from our study of the *dramatis personae* that the woman offstage must be Maurya, the mother of these sisters. What is troubling her? Let us read on.

"*Nora comes in softly, and takes a bundle from under her shawl.*" Another stage direction, as dramatic an action as the theater can provide. If the art of drama could be captured in a single image, it might be just such a wrapped bundle, of unknown, significant contents. The playwright presents his bundle as the magician his unpredictable hat, and the audience is helpless with curiosity. What's in the bundle? Nora tells her sister it is clothing "got off a drowned man in Donegal," and that they are to determine whether or not the clothing belongs to Michael. We have only to read a little further to discover that Michael is the girls' brother and Maurya's son. They fear Michael has drowned; if the clothing is his, there can be no further doubt. So that they might break the news to her gently, the girls must wait until Maurya is "down looking by the sea" before they inspect the contents of the bundle. The audience must share their suspense.

By the time we are nine lines into the script we are aware not only of a dramatic situation, but of the *problem* of the play. Someone has drowned, and it may be Michael. The girls could find out by opening the bundle, but they cannot while Maurya is in the house, because the old woman is frail and might be overwhelmed by the sight of Michael's clothes. Most plays begin with such a dilemma and part of the dramatic interest lies in how the characters resolve their problem.

A secondary problem of the dramatic situation of *Riders to the Sea* involves the second son, Bartley. If Michael is indeed drowned, then Bartley is Maurya's only remaining son. And he is planning to cross the sea to Galway in perilous weather. Will he leave, against his mother's wishes? And if he departs for Galway, will he too be drowned, leaving Maurya "with no son living"? These are the questions the play poses. But, enough suspense. Let us read on, and see what happens.

 Writers on Writing   J. M. Synge

> In a good play, every speech should be as fully flavoured as a nut or apple. . . . In countries where the imagination of the people, and the language they use, is rich and living, it is possible for a writer to be rich and copious in his words, and at the same time to give the reality, which is the root of all poetry, in a comprehensive and natural form.

JOHN MILLINGTON SYNGE (1871–1909)

Riders to the Sea
A Play in One Act

CHARACTERS

MAURYA, an old woman	NORA, a younger daughter
BARTLEY, her son	MEN *and* WOMEN
CATHLEEN, her daughter	

SCENE. *An Island off the West of Ireland.*

Cottage kitchen, with nets, oil-skins, spinning-wheel, some new boards standing by the wall, etc. Cathleen, a girl of about twenty, finishes kneading cake, and puts it down in the pot-oven by the fire; then wipes her hands, and begins to spin at the wheel. Nora, a young girl, puts her head in at the door.

NORA *(in a low voice)* Where is she?
CATHLEEN She's lying down, God help her, and may be sleeping, if she's able.

Nora comes in softly, and takes a bundle from under her shawl.

A performance of *Riders to the Sea* (Holloway Collection, National Library of Ireland)

CATHLEEN (*spinning the wheel rapidly*) What is it you have?

NORA The young priest is after bringing them. It's a shirt and a plain stocking were got off a drowned man in Donegal.

Cathleen stops her wheel with a sudden movement, and leans out to listen.

NORA We're to find out if it's Michael's they are, some time herself will be down looking by the sea.

CATHLEEN How would they be Michael's, Nora? How would he go the length of that way to the far north?

NORA The young priest says he's known the like of it. "If it's Michael's they are," says he, "you can tell herself he's got a clean burial by the grace of God, and if they're not his, let no one say a word about them, for she'll be getting her death," says he, "with crying and lamenting."

The door which Nora half-closed is blown open by a gust of wind.

CATHLEEN (*looking out anxiously*) Did you ask him would he stop Bartley going this day with the horses to the Galway fair?

NORA "I won't stop him," says he, "but let you not be afraid. Herself does be saying prayers half through the night, and the Almighty God won't leave her destitute," says he, "with no son living."

CATHLEEN Is the sea bad by the white rocks, Nora?

NORA Middling bad, God help us. There's a great roaring in the west, and it's worse it'll be getting when the tide's turned to the wind.

She goes over to the table with the bundle.

Shall I open it now?

CATHLEEN Maybe she'd wake up on us, and come in before we'd done. (*Coming to the table.*) It's a long time we'll be, and the two of us crying.

NORA (*goes to the inner door and listens*) She's moving about on the bed. She'll be coming in a minute.

CATHLEEN Give me the ladder, and I'll put them up in the turf-loft, the way she won't know of them at all, and maybe when the tide turns she'll be going down to see would he be floating from the east.

They put the ladder against the gable of the chimney; Cathleen goes up a few steps and hides the bundle in the turf-loft. Maurya comes from the inner room.

MAURYA (*looking up at Cathleen and speaking querulously*) Isn't it turf enough you have for this day and evening?

CATHLEEN There's a cake baking at the fire for a short space (*throwing down the turf*) and Bartley will want it when the tide turns if he goes to Connemara.

Nora picks up the turf and puts it round the pot-oven.

MAURYA (*sitting down on a stool at the fire*) He won't go this day with the wind rising from the south and west. He won't go this day, for the young priest will stop him surely.

NORA He'll not stop him, mother, and I heard Eamon Simon and Stephen Pheety and Colum Shawn saying he would go.

MAURYA Where is he itself?

NORA He went down to see would there be another boat sailing in the week, and I'm thinking it won't be long till he's here now, for the tide's turning at the green head, and the hooker's[1] tacking from the east.

CATHLEEN I hear some one passing the big stones.

NORA (*looking out*) He's coming now, and he in a hurry.

BARTLEY (*comes in and looks round the room. Speaking sadly and quietly*) Where is the bit of new rope, Cathleen, was bought in Connemara?

CATHLEEN (*coming down*) Give it to him, Nora; it's on a nail by the white boards. I hung it up this morning, for the pig with the black feet was eating it.

NORA (*giving him a rope*) Is that it, Bartley?

MAURYA You'd do right to leave that rope, Bartley, hanging by the boards. (*Bartley takes the rope.*) It will be wanting in this place, I'm telling you, if Michael is washed up to-morrow morning, or the next morning, or any morning in the week, for it's a deep grave we'll make him by the grace of God.

BARTLEY (*beginning to work with the rope*) I've no halter the way I can ride down on the mare, and I must go now quickly. This is the one boat going for two weeks or beyond it, and the fair will be a good fair for horses I heard them saying below.

MAURYA It's a hard thing they'll be saying below if the body is washed up and there's no man in it to make the coffin, and I after giving a big price for the finest white boards you'd find in Connemara.

She looks round at the boards.

---

[1] *hooker:* a single-masted fishing boat.

BARTLEY How would it be washed up, and we after looking each day for nine days, and a strong wind blowing a while back from the west and south?

MAURYA If it wasn't found itself, that wind is raising the sea, and there was a star up against the moon, and it rising in the night. If it was a hundred horses, or a thousand horses you had itself, what is the price of a thousand horses against a son where there is one son only?

BARTLEY (working at the halter, to Cathleen) Let you go down each day, and see the sheep aren't jumping in on the rye, and if the jobber comes you can sell the pig with the black feet if there is a good price going.

MAURYA How would the like of her get a good price for a pig?

BARTLEY (to Cathleen) If the west wind holds with the last bit of the moon let you and Nora get up weed enough for another cock for the kelp.[2] It's hard set we'll be from this day with no one in it but one man to work.

MAURYA It's hard set we'll be surely the day you're drownd'd with the rest. What way will I live and the girls with me, and I an old woman looking for the grave?

Bartley lays down the halter, takes off his old coat, and puts on a newer one of the same flannel.

BARTLEY (to Nora) Is she coming to the pier?

Nora (looking out) She's passing the green head and letting fall her sails.

BARTLEY (getting his purse and tobacco) I'll have half an hour to go down, and you'll see me coming again in two days, or in three days, or maybe in four days if the wind is bad.

MAURYA (turning round to the fire, and putting her shawl over her head) Isn't it a hard and cruel man won't hear a word from an old woman, and she holding him from the sea?

CATHLEEN It's the life of a young man to be going on the sea, and who would listen to an old woman with one thing and she saying it over?

BARTLEY (taking the halter) I must go now quickly. I'll ride down on the red mare, and the gray pony'll run behind me. . . . The blessing of God on you.

He goes out.

MAURYA (crying out as he is in the door) He's gone now, God spare us, and we'll not see him again. He's gone now, and when the black night is falling I'll have no son left me in the world.

CATHLEEN Why wouldn't you give him your blessing and he looking round in the door? Isn't it sorrow enough is on every one in this house without your sending him out with an unlucky word behind him, and a hard word in his ear?

Maurya takes up the tongs and begins raking the fire aimlessly without looking round.

NORA (turning towards her) You're taking away the turf from the cake.

CATHLEEN (crying out) The Son of God forgive us, Nora, we're after forgetting his bit of bread.

She comes over to the fire.

---

[2] *kelp*: seaweed (used for fertilizer).

NORA And it's destroyed he'll be going till dark night, and he after eating nothing since the sun went up.

CATHLEEN (*turning the cake out of the oven*) It's destroyed he'll be, surely. There's no sense left on any person in a house where an old woman will be talking for ever.

Maurya sways herself on her stool.

CATHLEEN (*cutting off some of the bread and rolling it in a cloth; to Maurya*) Let you go down now to the spring well and give him this and he passing. You'll see him then and the dark word will be broken, and you can say "God speed you," the way he'll be easy in his mind.

MAURYA (*taking the bread*) Will I be in it as soon as himself?

CATHLEEN If you go now quickly.

MAURYA (*standing up unsteadily*) It's hard set I am to walk.

CATHLEEN (*looking at her anxiously*) Give her the stick, Nora, or maybe she'll slip on the big stones.

NORA What stick?

CATHLEEN The stick Michael brought from Connemara.

MAURYA (*taking a stick Nora gives her*) In the big world the old people do be leaving things after them for their sons and children, but in this place it is the young men do be leaving things behind for them that do be old.

She goes out slowly. Nora goes over to the ladder.

CATHLEEN Wait, Nora, maybe she'd turn back quickly. She's that sorry, God help her, you wouldn't know the thing she'd do.

NORA Is she gone around by the bush?

CATHLEEN (*looking out*) She's gone now. Throw it down quickly, for the Lord knows when she'll be out of it again.

NORA (*getting the bundle from the loft*) The young priest said he'd be passing to-morrow, and we might go down and speak to him below if it's Michael's they are surely.

CATHLEEN (*taking the bundle*) Did he say what way they were found?

NORA (*coming down*) "There were two men," says he, "and they rowing round with poteen[3] before the cocks crowed, and the oar of one of them caught the body, and they passing the black cliffs of the north."

CATHLEEN (*trying to open the bundle*) Give me a knife, Nora, the string's perished with the salt water, and there's a black knot on it you wouldn't loosen in a week.

NORA (*giving her a knife*) I've heard tell it was a long way to Donegal.

CATHLEEN (*cutting the string*) It is surely. There was a man in here a while ago—the man sold us that knife—and he said if you set off walking from the rock beyond, it would be seven days you'd be in Donegal.

NORA And what time would a man take, and he floating?

Cathleen opens the bundle and takes out a bit of a stocking. They look at them eagerly.

CATHLEEN (*in a low voice*) The Lord spare us, Nora! isn't it a queer hard thing to say if it's his they are surely?

NORA I'll get his shirt off the hook the way we can put the one flannel on the other.

---

[3] *poteen:* illegal whiskey.

(*She looks through some clothes hanging in the corner.*) It's not with them, Cathleen, and where will it be?

CATHLEEN I'm thinking Bartley put it on him in the morning, for his own shirt was heavy with the salt in it. (*Pointing to the corner.*) There's a bit of a sleeve was of the same stuff. Give me that and it will do.

Nora brings it to her and they compare the flannel.

CATHLEEN It's the same stuff, Nora; but if it is itself aren't there great rolls of it in the shops of Galway, and isn't it many another man may have a shirt of it as well as Michael himself?

NORA (*who has taken up the stocking and counted the stitches, crying out*) It's Michael, Cathleen, it's Michael; God spare his soul, and what will herself say when she hears this story, and Bartley on the sea?

CATHLEEN (*taking the stocking*) It's a plain stocking.

NORA It's the second one of the third pair I knitted, and I put up three score stiches, and I dropped four of them.

CATHLEEN (*counts the stitches*) It's that number is in it. (*Crying out.*) Ah, Nora, isn't it a bitter thing to think of him floating that way to the far north, and no one to keen[4] him but the black hags that do be flying on the sea?

NORA (*swinging herself round, and throwing out her arms on the clothes*) And isn't it a pitiful thing when there is nothing left of a man who was a great rower and fisher, but a bit of an old shirt and a plain stocking?

CATHLEEN (*after an instant*) Tell me is herself coming, Nora? I hear a little sound on the path.

NORA (*looking out*) She is, Cathleen. She's coming up to the door.

CATHLEEN Put these things away before she'll come in. Maybe it's easier she'll be after giving her blessing to Bartley, and we won't let on we've heard anything the time he's on the sea.

NORA (*helping Cathleen to close the bundle*) We'll put them here in the corner.

They put them into a hole in the chimney corner. Cathleen goes back to the spinning-wheel.

NORA Will she see it was crying I was?

CATHLEEN Keep your back to the door the way the light'll not be on you.

Nora sits down at the chimney corner, with her back to the door. Maurya comes in very slowly, without looking at the girls, and goes over to her stool at the other side of the fire. The cloth with the bread is still in her hand. The girls look at each other, and Nora points to the bundle of bread.

CATHLEEN (*after spinning for a moment*) You didn't give him his bit of bread?

Maurya begins to keen softly, without turning round.

CATHLEEN Did you see him riding down?

Maurya goes on keening.

---

[4] *keen*: lament.

CATHLEEN (*a little impatiently*) God forgive you; isn't it a better thing to raise your voice and tell what you seen, than to be making lamentation for a thing that's done? Did you see Bartley, I'm saying to you.

MAURYA (*with a weak voice*) My heart's broken from this day.

CATHLEEN (*as before*) Did you see Bartley?

MAURYA I seen the fearfulest thing.

CATHLEEN (*leaves her wheel and looks out*) God forgive you; he's riding the mare now over the green head, and the gray pony behind him.

MAURYA (*starts, so that her shawl falls back from her head and shows her white tossed hair. With a frightened voice*) The gray pony behind him.

CATHLEEN (*coming to the fire*) What is it ails you, at all?

MAURYA (*speaking very slowly*) I've seen the fearfulest thing any person has seen, since the day Bride Dara seen the dead man with the child in his arms.

CATHLEEN AND NORA Uah.

They crouch down in front of the old woman at the fire.

NORA Tell us what it is you seen.

MAURYA I went down to the spring well, and I stood there saying a prayer to myself. Then Bartley came along, and he riding on the red mare with the gray pony behind him. (*She puts up her hands, as if to hide something from her eyes.*) The Son of God spare us, Nora!

CATHLEEN What is it you seen?

MAURYA I seen Michael himself.

CATHLEEN (*speaking softly*) You did not, mother; it wasn't Michael you seen, for his body is after being found in the far north, and he's got a clean burial by the grace of God.

MAURYA (*a little defiantly*) I'm after seeing him this day, and he riding and galloping. Bartley came first on the red mare; and I tried to say "God speed you," but something choked the words in my throat. He went by quickly; and "the blessing of God on you," says he, and I could say nothing. I looked up then, and I crying, at the gray pony, and there was Michael upon it—with fine clothes on him, and new shoes on his feet.

CATHLEEN (*begins to keen*) It's destroyed we are from this day. It's destroyed, surely.

NORA Didn't the young priest say the Almighty God wouldn't leave her destitute with no son living?

MAURYA (*in a low voice, but clearly*) It's little the like of him knows of the sea. . . . Bartley will be lost now, and let you call in Eamon and make me a good coffin out of the white boards, for I won't live after them. I've had a husband, and a husband's father, and six sons in this house—six fine men, though it was a hard birth I had with every one of them and they coming to the world—and some of them were found and some of them were not found, but they're gone now the lot of them. . . . There were Stephen, and Shawn, were lost in the great wind, and found after in the Bay of Gregory of the Golden Mouth, and carried up the two of them, on the one plank, and in by that door.

She pauses for a moment, the girls start as if they heard something through the door that is half open behind them.

NORA (*in a whisper*) Did you hear that, Cathleen? Did you hear a noise in the north-east?

CATHLEEN (*in a whisper*) There's some one after crying out by the seashore.

MAURYA *(continues without hearing anything)* There was Sheamus and his father, and his own father again, were lost in a dark night, and not a stick or sign was seen of them when the sun went up. There was Patch after was drowned out of a curagh[5] that turned over. I was sitting here with Bartley, and he a baby, lying on my two knees, and I seen two women, and three women, and four women coming in, and they crossing themselves, and not saying a word. I looked out then, and there were men coming after them, and they holding a thing in the half of a red sail, and water dripping out of it—it was a dry day, Nora—and leaving a track to the door.

She pauses again with her hand stretched out towards the door. It opens softly and old women begin to come in, crossing themselves on the threshold, and kneeling down in front of the stage with red petticoats over their heads.

MAURYA *(half in a dream, to Cathleen)* Is it Patch, or Michael, or what is it at all?

CATHLEEN Michael is after being found in the far north, and when he is found there how could he be here in this place?

MAURYA There does be a power of young men floating round in the sea, and what way would they know if it was Michael they had, or another man like him, for when a man is nine days in the sea, and the wind blowing, it's hard set his own mother would be to say what man was it.

CATHLEEN It's Michael, God spare him, for they're after sending us a bit of his clothes from the far north.

She reaches out and hands Maurya the clothes that belonged to Michael. Maurya stands up slowly and takes them in her hand. Nora looks out.

NORA They're carrying a thing among them and there's water dripping out of it and leaving a track by the big stones.

CATHLEEN *(in a whisper to the women who have come in)* Is it Bartley it is?

ONE OF THE WOMEN. It is surely, God rest his soul.

Two younger women come in and pull out the table. Then men carry in the body of Bartley, laid on a plank, with a bit of sail over it, and lay it on the table.

CATHLEEN *(to the women, as they are doing so)* What way was he drowned?

ONE OF THE WOMEN. The gray pony knocked him into the sea, and he was washed out where there is a great surf on the white rocks.

Maurya has gone over and knelt down at the head of the table. The women are keening softly and swaying themselves with a slow movement. Cathleen and Nora kneel at the other end of the table. The men kneel near the door.

MAURYA *(raising her head and speaking as if she did not see the people around her)* They're all gone now, and there isn't anything more the sea can do to me. . . . I'll have no call now to be up crying and praying when the wind breaks from the south, and you can hear the surf is in the east, and the surf is in the west, making a great stir with the two noises, and they hitting one on the other. I'll have no call now to be going down and getting Holy Water in the dark nights after Samhain,[6] and I won't care what

---

[5] *curagh:* unstable vessel of tarred canvas on a wood frame; canoe.
[6] *Samhain:* November 1, All Saints' Day.

way the sea is when the other women will be keening. (*To Nora.*) Give me the Holy Water, Nora, there's a small sup still on the dresser.

Nora gives it to her.

MAURYA (*drops Michael's clothes across Bartley's feet, and sprinkles the Holy Water over him*) It isn't that I haven't prayed for you, Bartley, to the Almighty God. It isn't that I haven't said prayers in the dark night till you wouldn't know what I'ld be saying; but it's a great rest I'll have now, and it's time surely. It's a great rest I'll have now, and great sleeping in the long nights after Samhain, if it's only a bit of wet flour we do have to eat, and maybe a fish that would be stinking.

She kneels down again, crossing herself, and saying prayers under her breath.

CATHLEEN (*to an old man*) Maybe yourself and Eamon would make a coffin when the sun rises. We have fine white boards herself bought, God help her, thinking Michael would be found, and I have a new cake you can eat while you'll be working.
THE OLD MAN (*looking at the boards*) Are there nails with them?
CATHLEEN There are not, Colum; we didn't think of the nails.
ANOTHER MAN It's a great wonder she wouldn't think of the nails, and all the coffins she's seen made already.
CATHLEEN It's getting old she is, and broken.

Maurya stands up again very slowly and spreads out the pieces of Michael's clothes beside the body, sprinkling them with the last of the Holy Water.

NORA (*in a whisper to Cathleen*) She's quiet now and easy; but the day Michael was drowned you could hear her crying out from this to the spring well. It's fonder she was of Michael, and would any one have thought that?
CATHLEEN (*slowly and clearly*) An old woman will be soon tired with anything she will do, and isn't it nine days herself is after crying and keening, and making great sorrow in the house?
MAURYA (*puts the empty cup mouth downwards on the table, and lays her hands together on Bartley's feet*) They're all together this time, and the end is come. May the Almighty God have mercy on Bartley's soul, and on Michael's soul, and on the souls of Sheamus and Patch, and Stephen and Shawn (*bending her head*); and may He have mercy on my soul, Nora, and on the soul of every one is left living in the world.

She pauses, and the keen rises a little more loudly from the women, then sinks away.

MAURYA (*continuing*) Michael has a clean burial in the far north, by the grace of the Almighty God. Bartley will have a fine coffin out of the white boards, and a deep grave surely. What more can we want than that? No man at all can be living for ever, and we must be satisfied.

She kneels down again and the curtain falls slowly.

Questions

1. When Maurya enters, Cathleen is on the ladder hiding the bundle of clothes in the turf-loft. How does Cathleen's action add to the dramatic interest of Maurya's entrance? How does Cathleen allay her mother's suspicion?

2. What is Maurya's chief concern?
3. What do you know about Bartley before his entrance on page 906? What do the stage directions and his first speech tell you about his character? Is he more concerned about his mother, or about his own business?
4. Do you think Bartley is cruel, or do you sympathize with Cathleen's defense of him on page 907?
5. When Bartley exits Maurya says, "we'll not see him again," and "when the black night is falling I'll have no son left in the world." In view of the play's outcome these statements are prophetic—instances of what is called dramatic "foreshadowing." What do these remarks tell you about Maurya's state of mind?
6. Cathleen and Nora send their mother after Bartley with "his bit of bread." They want Maurya to give Bartley her blessing. For what other reason do they send her out of the house?
7. What finally convinces the sisters that Michael is dead? How does Synge develop suspense during this scene of discovery?
8. There is dramatic tension in the kitchen when Maurya enters on page 909. Why?
9. On page 910 Maurya says she has seen Michael. Cathleen tells her his body has been found. What has Maurya *really* seen? What is the significance of her vision?
10. After the old women enter on page 911, Cathleen announces that Michael's body is being carried to the house. Are you shocked when you discover it is Bartley's? Is this more moving than if it were in fact Michael's corpse? Why?
11. Is Maurya surprised that the body is Bartley's rather than Michael's? What is her response? Hysteria? Relief?
12. *Riders to the Sea* has been called "one of the finest tragedies ever written." A great tragic heroine learns from her suffering. What has Maurya learned? What is her state of mind and heart at the fall of the curtain? What can we learn from her?

Suggestions for Dramatists

Think of a familiar location, indoors or outdoors, that is frequented by interesting characters. Could it be reproduced in a theater and used as a scene for a stage play? Draw a floor plan of a possible set, marking exits and the location of stage props (furniture).

3 ❧ Writing about Drama: The Review

The lights go down. The curtains part. You have your first glimpse of the scene. Then an actor speaks, another answers, and before you know it, you are drawn into the action on stage. This is what drama is all about: the mysterious power of performance, the embodiment of words and actions which were once merely lines on a page, imaginings in a writer's brain.

Drama differs from other forms of literature because the script—the written text—is only a blueprint for a performance. A play is not drama until it is acted, until it is given life on a stage or on the screen. Consequently, many teachers ask students not just to write another paper on a literary subject, but to review a performance that may be on stage, screen, or video. But reviewing a performance requires different skills than explicating a poem or analyzing a story. The reviewer must take in not just the spoken words, but all the sights and sounds (and sometimes smells) that are part of the performance and bring these varied experiences to bear in the review.

Why Review

While only a few people read literary criticism, almost everyone has read in newspapers and magazines or heard on television a review of the latest film or concert. For better or worse, reviews are a part of our lives, and for a very simple reason: no one has the time to see or hear everything. Most of us have a limited amount to spend on tickets, rentals, tapes, and records. Reviews *help* us figure out how to spend our time and money. We emphasize *help* because no critic, no matter how widely experienced, well informed, or sound of judgment should be the sole arbiter of what you think or experience. Over the years, readers have sometimes learned to trust the judgment of particular critics, but no two people will agree entirely all the time.

If reviews are useful, they can also be enjoyable. Even if we don't go to see a particular peformance, a good writer can interest, inform, and amuse us. Some of our best writers have worked as reviewers. George Bernard Shaw was an important music and theater critic before he became a playwright. The novelist John Updike and the poet John Ashbery have worked extensively as art critics. Their reviews are worth reading long after the performances and exhibitions they wrote about have faded from memory. The sharpness of their prose, the liveliness of their observations, the skill of their presentation make their reviews valuable in their own right. The best critics know how to write well and interestingly even about events that are boring and badly executed.

Good reviewers never forget that they have a dual function: they must write fairly about the quality of the performance they have seen, and they must write well enough to satisfy readers who may never see the performance under review. Reviewers must treat their subject fairly and with the proper respect, but reviewers must also treat readers to lively and interesting prose.

Reviewers sometimes find it very hard being fair to the performance and interesting to readers. It's easier to write lively prose when performances are extremely bad or good. A truly excellent performance energizes the reviewer, who wants to make others aware of this wonderful event. Similarly, reviewers can have a find old time describing a disastrous performance. But most performances are neither superb nor dismal. Usually they fall somewhere in between, and a reviewer must carefully structure the review to express the proper balance between the performance's strengths and weaknesses. Such a balancing act is more difficult to make good, interesting reading than either the rave review or the "pan." Yet the honest critic will struggle to find a way to be both fair and interesting. Stark Young's review (among those reprinted later in this chapter) is an example of the fact that even an excellent production can have its weaknesses, and Robert Brustein's review discusses a good example of a weak production that has some strong points.

Preparations

Although sometimes reviewers can't help but come to a performance without preparation, they try to be prepared when it is at all possible. Specifically, you should try to read the script before seeing it performed. With Shakespeare or other playwrights whose language is difficult, reading a play ahead of time will increase your comprehension and alert you to specific challenges actors, directors, and designers may face in performance. For example, any actor performing Hamlet must figure out how to give the famous soliloquies, such as "To be or not to be," in a way that is fresh, truthful, and consistent. Reading commentary on the play will also inform you about directorial problems. For example, much has been written about Hamlet's relationship to his mother. Directors, in collaboration with the actors, must decide how to perform the scenes between Hamlet and Gertrude, how close to make them, how much they should physically interact. Knowing something about the production history will also help you put the performance into perspective. *Hamlet* has been played in historical costumes, in modern dress, or in costumes that make no reference to time or place. Knowing what has been done may help you decide whether what you see is new, old-fashioned, or ordinary.

Good reviewers will come to a performance both informed and as open as if they knew nothing about the play. Such a paradoxical position is difficult to maintain, but provides the best basis for appreciation. Arriving at a performance with knowledge of the work and its history gives you a context in which to place the production. But such preconceptions can sometimes bias you. Many knowledgeable people carry around prejudices about how a work ought to be performed. They are unwilling to listen or to appreciate alternative approaches. Yet the most exciting things happen when a classic, like *Hamlet*, is given a new and valid interpretation, when an actor has brought out a part of the character you had never before considered, when a director has developed for the play a new and compelling perspective, or when the designers have found an original and effective manner of lighting, costuming, or setting the play. The fairest reviews are ones that present a production both on its own merits, and in relation to the work's and the performers' history. John Mason Brown's review of *Hamlet* places John Gielgud's performances in relation to John Barrymore's, while still evaluating Gielgud on his own merits. The best reviewers are people with a wide knowledge and experience of drama; nevertheless, they can approach any particular performance on its own terms and merits.

It is also important that you have reasonable expectations. An amateur or college production—even the best amateur and college production—may not be as good as a professional production. A local professional or touring company usually doesn't have the multimillion-dollar resources that film productions have. But just because a production is small-scale and staffed by amateurs does not mean it has to be poor drama. The intimacy of a small theatrical space and the energy and commitment of nonprofessional actors can result in truly memorable performances.

When we are reviewing a play, we get to the theater early to get used to the physical space and read the program if one is available. Programs are filled with useful information sometimes including the biographies of the actors and backstage designers and staff, and occasionally notes by or about the playwright and the play. Take the time to read the program. Note anything that strikes you as interesting or potentially helpful to you as a member of the audience.

Taking Notes

Taking notes during a performance of a play, movie, or some other dramatic performance can be very helpful to you while writing a review. If you are watching a video, you can always stop the action and rewind the tape in order to see a scene again and again. But in film and theater, the audience usually has only one chance to see a scene, unless it returns at another time, and you must find a way to help you recall specific details, lines, and observations.

But taking notes in a theater has two drawbacks. First, the lighting is usually so low that you may not be able to see, much less read, the notes during the performance. Second, you must not disturb the audience around you by taking notes. In a quiet theater, the sound of pen and paper can seem loud and very disturbing.

Professional journalists have developed various ways to take notes without disturbing the audience. They have found that ball-point pens write more quietly than either pencils or felt-tipped pens. Journalists bring a single sheet that is large enough to hold all their notes, or a small pad whose pages can be turned silently. Finally, journalists don't try to get whole sentences or phrases down. A single word can often prompt your memory of a complex idea or observation. A reviewer's notes are not a permanent record; they are just a series of jottings meant to jog your memory when you think about what you have seen in a performance. One reason for keeping your notes short is that you may not be able to see well enough to write more than a word or two. Second, you don't want to divert your attention from the stage or screen. (We've noticed in class that students lose valuable information because they can't listen and take notes simultaneously.) Try to keep your eyes up while you're writing something down.

What sorts of things should you note? Anything that strikes you as potentially interesting or useful to you. It's usually a good idea to mark down specific information such as dates, names, places, and amounts. Sometimes programs give only the characters' first names when the script gives you their full names. Sometimes the program leaves out the place and time of the action. Your review may need such specifics. Often characters will refer to figures who never appear on stage—a dead friend and absent spouse. Put these names in your notes. There's an old playwright's rule that anything important should be mentioned three times to make certain that the audience hears the information. When we hear repeated references to something or someone, we usually jot it down.

In the theater, it's a good thing to keep your eyes moving and not merely focus on whoever is speaking at the moment. Good actors are acting even when they are listening, even when they are standing silently in the background. In the movies directors can give the audience a "reaction shot," a picture of a character's response to a statement or an event. In the theater you can't give the audience a close-up, so as a member of the audience you will have to observe more attentively and actively for the telling gesture or response. And don't just look at the actors. Keep your eyes and ears alert for music, lighting, scenery, and costumes. All these are important in producing the complete dramatic event. No one can notice everything. But a good reviewer tries to take in as much as possible.

Beginning a Review

Like any good essay, a well-written review has a central thread or organizing principle. It is *never* a series of miscellaneous notes. Your opening paragraph should determine the central topic of the review and your attitude toward that topic. The topic, or central thread, or principle focus (you may conceive of it in any of these terms) may concern the play, the actors (or one particular actor), the director, the designers, the play's history, or its relevance to current events.

Choosing this focus is one of the hardest parts of writing a review. If you make the focus too narrow you may not get to discuss many of the things your reader needs to know to make an informed decision about whether to see the production. If you broaden the focus too much, you won't be able to talk about specifics. How broad a focus you should have in a review depends upon the play, your skill as a writer, and the needs of your reader. Time, practice, and feedback from your readers will help you figure out how narrowly you should focus your remarks.

The opening paragraph, indeed the opening sentence, should announce the subject of the review. Try to get the work's title and its author mentioned in the first paragraph. The first paragraph should also tell the reader in what direction you're taking the review. For example, the reader ought to know if the review is going to be about the quality of the performances, the symbolism of the set, the talent of the star, the relevance of the play, the quality of the writing, or the psychology of the characters. You should also give the reader a good sense of how you feel about the subject: whether you were pleased, interested, disappointed, offended, transported, amused, and so forth.

Examine these opening sentences from reviews that Eric Bentley wrote about productions in the 1950s and collected together in his study *What Is Theatre?*

> *The Ponder Heart*, adapted by Joseph Fields and Jerome Chodorov from the story by Eudora Welty, is about . . . to tell the truth, when I left the theatre, I was very unsure *what* it was about.

This review will be about the incoherence of the play's exposition and development.

> To my mind, Chekhov's supreme achievement is *The Three Sisters*, but the fact that *The Cherry Orchard* is more famous indicates that it has made easier contact with the public, which takes from an author what it craves and leaves the rest alone.

This review of *The Cherry Orchard* will be about how a production panders to the simplistic tastes of the public.

> To mention Orson Welles in any company, literary or theatrical, is to call forth tired jokes about his alleged decline and fall. Yet, to my mind, this man who bids fair to be only another of the disasters of the American theatre, could have been one of its chief glories.

This review of a production of Shakespeare's *Othello* will center on Orson Welles's failures as an actor.

The Middle and Conclusion of a Review

Having pointed the direction in which you are headed in the review, you may need to back up in your second or third paragraphs to give a synopsis of the action. Most readers get uncomfortable reading a review of a play or film whose basic story is unknown to them. Give a short summary. Usually you don't want to give away the ending, especially if you're reviewing a mystery or suspense drama. Depending upon your readers and their familiarity with the play, you may dispense with a summary. Robert Brustein wrote his review of *Hamlet* for *The New Republic*, which prides itself on having very literate readers. Brustein does not feel obliged to summarize this famous tragedy. But usually critics give at least a paragraph to sketching the outlines of the story, emphasizing as much as possible the elements that correspond to the major focus of the review. Notice how Stark Young summarizes *The Glass Menagerie* in a review written on the occasion of the play's New York premiere, and how a student, Robert Coldhill, reviews a revival of Lorraine Hansberry's *A Raisin in the Sun*.

After the summary, reviews develop their basic theme more directly. In Stark Young's review of *The Glass Menagerie*, he has a double focus: Laurette Taylor's triumphant return to the stage and Tennessee Williams's skill in providing a great role for her. Thus, after summarizing the action, Young returns first to Laurette Taylor's gifts as an actress and then to defending Williams's play from its detractors. In order to defend Williams, Young undertakes another of the reviewer's obligations—evaluating the performances of actors in the major roles. Young argues that the play isn't too slow; the problem is that Eddie Dowling gives a poor performance as Tom, so the play appears to drag. Young then defends Williams's language from the attacks of *The New York Times* critic, after which he praises the work of two other actors, the set designer, and the composer of the play's incidental music.

Concluding a review presents its own problems. Usually, when reviews are published in newspapers and magazines, the author has a fairly strict word limit. The standard review is 750 to 1,000 words. Thus journalists don't always have the space to put together a full, complete conclusion. Instead, their conclusion frequently refers to the focus of the review briefly and indirectly. Notice that Stark Young's review ends with the phrase "strangely beautiful and strangely right." Although this comment is specifically about Paul Bowles's music, it encapsulates his feelings about the entire play, echoing his belief in the "inexplicable rightness" of Laurette Taylor's performance as Amanda and the "almost unconscious freedom . . . of true realism" in Williams's writing. Thus, in a very condensed and oblique manner, the concluding words tie the entire review together.

Supporting Detail

It is not enough to say what you liked or disliked in a performance or whether you think the work bad or good. You need to support your opinions with specifics. You need to provide these specifics so that readers will have a better sense of what you mean and of what to look for should they see the production. Readers must feel that you have some basis for your opinions and are not merely speaking out of prejudice or ignorance. Of course, it is often impossible to pin down exactly what makes one performance come to life and leaves another performance boring and cold. The rule of thumb is that you need to be more specific when you disapprove of work than when you praise it.

Professional reviewers have an added obligation: to help the production get better. Often actors, directors and designers learn from what reviewers say and make changes to correct flaws in their performance or production. Read the reviews below, and notice the various ways that reviewers have bolstered their opinions by citing specifics. Take special note of how carefully these critics have attempted to be specific about things they disliked or which they felt weakened the overall performance.

JOHN MASON BROWN

John Gielgud's Hamlet

Not since John Barrymore made Elsinore his own, has a Hamlet of the interest of John Gielgud's been seen—and heard—in New York. If to some of us the Mr. Barrymore who was remains even now the Hamlet we shall continue to see in our mind's eye as the perfect embodiment of the Prince, it will be Mr. Gielgud's voice in the future we shall hear lending its color to many of the nobler speeches. Such a voice, such diction, and such a gift for maintaining the melody of Shakespeare's verse even while keeping it edged from speech to speech with dramatic significance, is a new experience to those of us who since the twilight days of Forbes-Robertson have seen a small army of actors try their wings, and sometimes our patience, as Hamlet.

Mr. Gielgud is young enough to be the part and old enough in Shakespearean experience to play it exceptionally. The verse offers him no difficulties. He is its master and gives abundant proof of his mastery. He is no mere reciter, but an illuminator of what he has to say. He turns the searchlight of his thinking and his feeling on sentence after sentence which gains a new force and meaning because of what he finds in it to reveal.

He is an actor who, though he lacks Mr. Barrymore's natural endowment as far as looks are concerned, is nonetheless possessed of a sensitive, clear-cut face. It is so molded that it can amplify every passing thought which takes possession of his mind. It equals his voice in flexibility.

Without tearing a passion to tatters or sawing the air too much, Mr. Gielgud can suggest the whirlwind of the frenzy which has overtaken him. He has an exciting personality. He moves with grace and is not afraid of taking full advantage of the many steps which Jo Mielziner has placed at his disposal for some of the full stage scenes in Mr. McClintic's visually arresting production at the Empire.

If, in spite of the frequent brilliance, occasional superiorities and steady interest of Mr. Gielgud's Hamlet, his Prince still plays second-best to Mr. Barrymore's, one reason is that Mr. Gielgud's Hamlet lacks the consistency Mr. Barrymore brought to the part. Many of the details of his Hamlet are fine. Some are magnificent. But they are not assembled into a characterization which is large enough to connect and explain them all. Their validity is for the scene in which they occur, rather than for the total impression.

Mr. Gielgud's Hamlet is frequently more mercurial than is good for it. He changes it to fit new speeches, and in the process often seems to be presenting us new Hamlets to whom he has not hitherto introduced us. The Mr. Gielgud, for example, who reads the speech to the players benevolently, with a professional's interest in its admonitions and no remembrance of the scheme to trap the King which underlies that interest, is an entirely different person from the Mr. Gielgud who delivers with tremendous austerity the seldom heard "How all occasions do inform against me" soliloquy.

Then the Mr. Gielgud who solemnly speaks his first bitter aside about "A little more than kin, and less than kind," wakes up slowly to the wit which he must later show in his encounters with Polonius, Ophelia, Rosencrantz and Guildenstern, the First Grave Digger and Osric. It takes almost two acts for Mr. Gielgud's Hamlet to become aware of the sharpness of his tongue. Mr. Barrymore's was caustic from the first. Furthermore, the Mr. Gielgud who swears his love for Ophelia at the grave gives no indication of having really loved her before that time, as Mr. Barrymore did in the unforgettable intensity of his "Get thee to a nunnery" scene.

Yet because of the excellence of its details and the thrilling revelation of some of its single readings, Mr. Gielgud's Hamlet is a performance which deserves the loud cheers that greeted it last night when the final curtain had fallen. Mr. Gielgud is strangely disappointing in the Closet scene, when he dispenses with the traditional properties for the "Look here, upon this picture, and on this"; and is weakest throughout in his irony. He is at his best—and a fiery and exciting best it is—in the play-within-a-play, in his first encounter with the Ghost, and in the blood-stained last scene. Again and again during the course of the evening he delivers his individual speeches with such beauty and intelligence, such insight and tension, that one gladly overlooks the lapses in his interpretation.

Mr. McClintic has brought to the patterning of his production the same sweep which made his direction of Miss Cornell's *Romeo and Juliet* notable. His staging is vivifying, pictorial and inventive, especially in the uses to which it puts the levels and steps of Mr. Mielziner's unit setting for the inner stage. But the performances of the well-known players Mr. McClintic has gathered about Mr. Gielgud are of varying merits.

Although completely negative until the mad scene, Lillian Gish's Ophelia then turns into the most effective, if untraditional, Ophelia we have yet witnessed. Judith Anderson's Queen is stately and captures the eye, but leaves much to be desired in the Closet scene. Malcolm Keen's Claudius is, especially at the beginning, a welcome relief from the red-bearded, ranting Claudiuses usually on hand. John Emery's Laertes has real verve and distinction. And Arthur Byron's Polonius is handsome enough, but a Polonius who is as slow to suggest his humorous garrulity as Mr. Gielgud is to suggest Hamlet's wit.

The Ghost, who is always a problem to a generation whose belief in the supernatural stops with ghost-writers, is now almost as adventurously dealt with as he was when Robert Edmond Jones turned him into Tinkerbell by suggesting him with a shaft of light. There are two or three Ghosts lurking around the stage of the Empire these nights, one of whom remains unseen and speaks the Ghost's speeches through an amplifier, which makes him seem just a little ahead of his times in Elsinore.

Mr. Mielziner's settings, like the Vandyke costumes in which he has dressed most of the characters, are interesting. But, next to Mr. Shakespeare's play, the most interesting feature of the evening is, as goes without saying, Mr. Gielgud. Although one may quarrel with this or that feature of his Hamlet, Mr. Gielgud is unquestionably a rare actor, possessed of the stuffs from which rare actors have always been made. He is decidedly worth seeing—and seeing again and again.

New York Evening Post
October 9, 1936

ROBERT BRUSTEIN

Shakespeare with a Few Tears

HAMLET *by William Shakespeare;* A COMEDY OF ERRORS *and* KING LEAR *by William Shakespeare: Royal Shakespeare Company*

In honor of Shakespeare's four hundredth, three candles were recently lighted on the birthday cake: Sir John Gielgud's production of *Hamlet*, with Richard Burton in the lead, and the Royal Shakespeare Company's versions of *A Comedy of Errors* and *King Lear*. Of these, the *Hamlet* flickers most feebly, partly because of an unfortunate directorial choice by Gielgud, who has designed the performance to look like a final runthrough. The stage is bare, except for some unfinished steps and platforms; sandbags hang from the flies; a canvas flat has been painted to simulate the brick back wall of a theatre; and the actors wear rehearsal outfits and street clothes. The purpose of all this ostentatious simplicity, I suppose, is to introduce some spontaneity into a familiar work, withdrawing the play from history and returning to the actors what has been expropriated by costumers and set designers. But the informality is too calculated, and it is ultimately self-defeating. When Gertrude appears with a mink draped over her shoulder, and Claudius sports a blazer, the action, instead of being left unlocated, is automatically transferred from Renaissance Denmark to twentieth-century Suburbia; and when the curtain rises on a rehearsal, one begins to suspect that this particular *Hamlet* is not yet ready to open.

This suspicion is confirmed as the evening proceeds. As often happens with pickup casts, the actors all seem very strange and well bred and uncomfortable with one another. Some of the performances are simply amateur; others are hamstrung by the obstacles of the production. Still, Hume Cronyn's Polonius is interesting to watch: a cranky, rheumatic, avuncular but forthright and sagacious counselor. Cronyn undoubtedly knows that this interpretation is wrong-headed—he is obviously unwilling to repeat the cliché of the "tedious old fool"—but although he thereby sacrifices Polonius' comic possibilities, it is a pleasure to observe him at work. Cronyn approaches a part like a textual scholar doing a critical gloss; every word is crisply interpreted and cleanly communicated. Since his vision is fresh, his technique certain, and his intelligence wide, he teaches us plenty about a role, even in the act of misplaying it.

Whereas Cronyn illuminates and clarifies, Burton darkens and shades. One performance is all line, the other is all color, like an Action painting. The resources of Burton are almost entirely emotional, with the result that his Hamlet is chancy and erratic—effective from moment to moment, but lacking a consistent design. Some of Burton's difficulties are technical; his voice, for example, is limited in range and squeezed and issues mostly through his nose. He sniffs, brays, and barks too much; and he is more dour and surly than truly melancholy. Burton, furthermore, is not of the natural nobility; his Hamlet is less a scholar-courtier than a virile peasant, poetic but slightly muscle-bound. Still, for all these limitations, he occasionally achieves some startling effects, primarily through abrupt changes in volume and rhythm, and he does not lack for daring. What he is best at is ironic self-hatred. He builds the soliloquy "Oh what a rogue and peasant slave" toward a hysterical climax in the manner of John Barrymore; but after turning his hand into a hideous claw on the word *vengeance*, he examines the gesture with wry amusement, then lets his hand fall with disgust. This shows thought, but too much of the performance is thoughtless, breathless, and febrile—less a Hamlet than a Hamlet Coloring Book. The colors are brighter than those he painted on the part in 1953 with the Old Vic; but they are still splashed. I should like to see him do it again in a few years with more competent support.

The New Republic, 1984

STARK YOUNG

The Glass Menagerie

Of all our actors, certainly of all those who have become known, Miss Laurette Taylor could not be called the most cultured, the most versatile in divers styles, the most gracious-minded, but few would deny that she is the most talented. She is the real and first talent of them all. She has been largely absent from the stage during so many years that her return is an event and everybody knows it. It turns out, in *The Glass Menagerie*, to be a triumph as well. So is the role she plays.

Miss Taylor's role in Mr. Williams' play is that of a frowsy, aging woman who lives with her son and daughter, in a flat off a St. Louis alley. It is a far cry from the Deep South, where her girlhood was spent and her memories dwell, and where she has refused the rich planters' sons because she lost her heart to a man who worked for the telephone company and whose smile misled everybody. The daughter is a cripple, too shy and hurt and vague ever to have got through school. She spends her time playing old phonograph records that her father had left behind when he abandoned her mother and went away for good, and collecting glass animals—hence the title of the play. The son is a failure, discontented with his job in the warehouse, vaguely itching to write poetry, and longing to roam the world. The mother worships, nags, scolds, and tries to do her best by her children. Finally, when she thinks it is time her daughter got married, she plagues the son into bringing a man home with him; he brings a friend from the warehouse. The visitor, impressed though he is with the daughter, turns out to be in love and engaged.

In the end the son follows his father's example and goes off to make his way over the world. The scheme of *The Glass Menagerie* includes a Narrator, who opens the play and appears between the scenes from time to time. This role is played by the actor who takes the part of the son. The story, as we see it on the stage, all happens in the son's mind long afterward, and in the last narration, a kind of epilogue, we are told in the midst of the years and in far, strange places, wherever he goes, the image of his sister there at home, he can never lose; all things bring her back to him.

What Miss Laurette Taylor does with these matters can be at least partially imagined if you know the quality of her special gift. This, even after seeing the play, is almost impossible to convey with anything like the full, wonderful truth. Hers is naturalistic acting of the most profound, spontaneous, unbroken continuity and moving life. There is an inexplicable rightness, moment by moment, phrase by phrase, endlessly varied in the transitions. Technique, which is always composed of skill and instinct working together, is in this case so overlaid with warmth, tenderness, and wit that any analysis is completely baffled. Only a trained theatre eye and ear can see what is happening, and then only at times.

But true as all this may be of Miss Taylor, we must not let that blind us to the case of the play itself and of the whole occasion. The play gives every one of the four characters that it presents a glowing, rich opportunity, genuine emotional motivations, a rhythm of situations that are alive, and speech that is fresh, living, abundant, and free of stale theatre diction. The author is not awed by the usual sterilities of our playwriting patterns. On the other hand he is too imaginative, genuine, or has too much good taste, to be coy about the free devices on which his play is built.

The Glass Menagerie appears to drag, or go slow, at times, though I am not sure about this and certainly found it less so than a number of people I have heard speak of it. These slow places occur in the Narrator portions and some-times in the scenes between mother and son. In my opinion this may be almost entirely due to the fact that Mr. Eddie Dowling does not let himself go enough to make you believe that he is the son of such a mother or such a father, that he longs to wander, to write poetry—I even forgot to remember what he was working at when he sat before the papers on the table, supposed, however, to be bent on a poem. He speaks his Narrator scenes plainly and serviceably, by which, I think, they are made to seem to be a mistake on the playwright's part, a mistake to include them at all; for they seem extraneous and tiresome in the midst of the play's emotional current. If these speeches were spoken with variety, impulse, and intensity, as if the son himself were speaking—which is the case, since the play is a dream within his memory—if they were spoken as if they were from a born wanderer and adventurer, a chip off the old block, wild-headed like his father—and like his mother for that matter, for she too had wandered far from home indeed—the whole thing would be another matter, truly a part of the story.

To say, as Mr. Nichols does in his review in *The New York Times* that there are such unconnected things with the story as "snatches of talk about the war, bits of psychology, occasional moments of rather florid writing" is mistaken indeed. The part Miss Taylor plays is, quite aside from her rendering of it, the best-written role that I have seen in a play for years. All the language and all the motifs are free and true; I recognized them inch by inch, and I should know, for I came from the same part of the country, the same locality and life, in fact, that Mr. Williams does. Such a response and attitude as that Mr. Nichols expresses is the kind of thing that helps to tie our threatre down. It is the application of Times Square practical knowledge, the kind of thing that makes the writing, the talk, in *The Late George Apley* so sterile and so little like the Boston it assumes to be. What we need in the theatre is a sense of language, a sense of texture in speech, vibration, and impulse in speech. Behind the Southern speech in the mother's part is the echo of great literature, or at least a respect for it. There is the sense in it of her having been born out of a tradition, not out of a box. It has echo and the music of it. The mother's characterization is both appalling and human, cold and loving. No role could be more realistically written than this, but it has the variety, suddenness, passion and freedom, almost unconscious freedom perhaps, of true realism.

Miss Julie Haydon gave one of her translucent performances of a dreaming, wounded, half-out-of-this-world young girl. Mr. Anthony Ross, as the visitor, for whom the author has written a long and excellent scene, original and tender, with the girl, played admirably.

Mr. Jo Mielziner did the complicated setting for *The Glass Menagerie*, streets at the side, a front room, a back room, a wall shutting them off when needed. The scene is effectively ingenious. But even though the story happens in a dream and vagueness may be called for, I see no reason why the color should be so dun. I could not make out whether the enlarged picture of the father that was often played up as a dramatic motif in the story, was made from Mr. Dowling's likeness or not. At any rate to do so would be an effective device, a way of commenting on both the son's and the father's running true to the same form.

In the Narrator's opening speech Mr. Williams has provided an excuse for music by saying that the play all happens in the memory and memory always seems to move in music. For *The Glass Menagerie*, therefore, Mr. Paul Bowles has written music that runs in and out of the scenes, sometimes for a long interval, sometimes less. It seems to be a special gift of his, this writing music for a play that becomes a part of the play, strangely beautiful and strangely right.

The New Republic
April 16, 1945

ROBERT COLDHILL
Professor Bergman
Writing About Literature
May 6, 1988

A Review Of *A Raisin in the Sun*

Next year will be the thirtieth anniversary of the Broadway opening of *A Raisin in the Sun*. The play has a central
role in the history of black theater. While still in her
twenties, Lorraine Hansberry had written one of the most
acclaimed plays of the year, a singular achievement for a
black playwright, and particularly a black woman playwright. Moreover, *A Raisin in the Sun* proved the vehicle
that advanced the careers of Sidney Poitier, Claudia
McNeil, Ruby Dee, and Louis Gossett among many other black
actors. This revival is a fitting recognition of the
play's importance and merits. One feels the tragedy of
Hansberry's early death five years later. She certainly
had the talent to create a significant body of work had she
lived beyond the age of 34.

   A Raisin in the Sun is a conservative work in theatrical
terms. The single set is the small tenement apartment in
which the Younger family has lived for decades. The central character is Lena Younger, the matriarch of the family, who is to receive ten thousand dollars, the premium on
her husband's life insurance policy. Everyone in the family recognizes the significance of the money—it is the
means by which the family can lift itself out of the jaws of
poverty and squalor.

   But a member of the family has a different idea of how to
use the money. Walter Lee, Lena's son, wants to use it to
buy a liquor store with some friends of his. Beneatha,
Lena's daughter, wants to go to medical school on the
money. Ruth, Walter Lee's wife, hopes the money will be
used to buy a home where there will be room for the baby she
is carrying. Lena wishes to make everyone happy.

   Although *A Raisin in the Sun* contains almost exclusively
black characters, it now seems more about class than about
race. The Younger family's problems appear to stem more
from poverty than from racial prejudice. Of course, racism
keeps them poor. Yet the wealthiest person we meet on stage
is not the white chairperson of a homeowner's association
that wishes to keep the Youngers out of their neighborhood, but George Murchison, Beneatha's boyfriend and
scion of a rich black family. It is Beneatha who pointedly
remarks, ''The only people more snobbish than rich white

people are rich colored people.'' The play's emphasis on class is, I suppose, one reason it was able to cross over racial lines and speak poignantly to white people.

Perhaps what marks *A Raisin in the Sun* most strongly as a black play is the family structure. The Younger family, despite Walter Lee's importance as ''the man in the family,'' is really controlled by Mama. Although her children are clearly adults, they must show obedience to her. She slaps Beneatha when she asserts her atheist beliefs, forcing her to recite ''In my mother's house, there is still God.'' She thinks nothing of contradicting her daughter-in-law's rearing of her grandson, and she beats Walter Lee when he loses the money. To be sure during the course of the play she learns that she must hide her tyranny, but the end of the play, which is meant to dramatize Walter Lee's ascension into manhood, really shows his final capitulation to his mother's will.

Perhaps because I am a white male, I was disturbed by how differently Walter Lee's and Beneatha's career plans are treated. Walter Lee is discouraged from leaving his job as a chauffeur to become a businessman. This is not the first time his family has dissuaded him from taking a better job. The family had already talked him out of becoming a partner in a successful dry cleaning store, and they are adamant that he not involve himself in the liquor business. ''We ain't no business people,'' Mama insists, ''We just plain working folk.'' The message he gets from all the women around him is that he should be content at his menial job. Beneatha, however, is encouraged in her desire to become a surgeon. When Walter Lee gets annoyed at her selfishness and suggests that she isn't pulling her financial weight, everyone gangs up on him. Beneatha is encouraged in her studies, allowed privileges afforded no one else. Mama heartily supports Beneatha's professional dreams. If Walter Lee acts foolishly and selfishly when he gets in control of the insurance money, it is in part because he has never before been allowed to have so much power and privilege and he doesn't know how to handle it.

The present production is finely acted. As Mama, Esther Rolle gives a deeply felt performance. Her voice has a deep sadness and weariness of the downtrodden, but her body the stiffness of someone used to wielding power. Starletta Du-Pois is excellent as the equally weary Ruth, who must bear not only her husband's abuse, but her mother-in-law's bossiness. Kim Yancey has the right brightness, self-assurance and ease as Beneatha. Robert Gossett was fine as

Walter Lee, and I particularly liked Joseph C. Phillips as the wealthy George Murchison. This is an excellent cast.

Indeed, my one complaint with the production is that it is far too long. By my count, it ran three hours and ten minutes. Harold Scott, the director, not only hasn't cut the original script, but has added scenes removed from the original production. The result is that this fine but limited play has been sadly overinflated. The plot and characters simply cannot bear the weight of a three-hour production. My criticism is not of Hansberry's artistry. Even *King Lear* can't afford to run so long.

I know that everyone in the company wishes to show that *A Raisin the Sun* is a great American play, worthy of being a permanent part of the American repertory, but the play is not enhanced and its virtues not properly exhibited in this slow, overinflated manner. The passionate, fierce, warm artistry of Lorraine Hansberry is better revealed by a more human-scale production, one that suggests the heroic achievements that might have been had her career not been cut short by her untimely death.

4  Action

The essence of a stage play is the action. Whereas the novelist may present a heroine in an armchair, and go on for pages relating her rich inner life, the playwright must put characters on their feet immediately, telling us who they are by showing us what they do. This requires an engaging dramatic situation and ingenious plotting of the action. Eugène Labiche, the nineteenth-century French playwright, compared the novel to a leisurely journey in a carriage. "You make stops, you spend a night at the inn, you get out to look at the country. . . . You are in no hurry." But a play is a different matter. "A play," says Labiche, "is a railway journey by an express train . . . and if the locomotive ceases rushing and hissing, you hiss." The rapid action of a play begins with the introduction of the dramatic situation, or *problem*, and does not end until the situation has been resolved.

The Dramatic Situation

The action of a great play arises from the dramatic situation. A character or group of characters is in some sort of distress. This has been described as a condition of *conflict*, but is perhaps more accurately defined as a dynamic relationship of a character to an objective and the obstacle that comes between them. That is, a *character* has some goal or *objective*, but some *obstacle* stands in the way. Romeo wants Juliet, but her family (and his) stands in the way. In *Riders to the Sea*, Maurya wants Bartley to stay home, but his horses (his sense of independence) stand in the way. This elemental structure underlies most dramatic situations. The action flows naturally from the dramatic situation as the characters pursue their various objectives, and either succeed or fail in overcoming the obstacles that come between them and happiness.

The Plot

The first systematic study of dramatic action was Aristotle's *Poetics*. Aristotle observes that a play must have a beginning, a middle, and an end—a rough analysis that has been considerably refined since Aristotle's time. We now recognize that most great plays have a five-part movement which corresponds roughly to the five-act structure of classical comedy and tragedy: Exposition, Rising Action, Climax, Falling Action, and Denouement or Catastrophe, depending upon whether the play has a happy or a sad ending. A stage play is perhaps the most conventional and restricted of all literary forms. It is an uncommon stage play that succeeds in violating this five-part structure, whether it be tragedy, comedy, melodrama, or farce. The five-part structure has its greatest analyst in the nineteenth-century critic Gustave Freytag, who originated the famous pyramid of the dramatic plot:

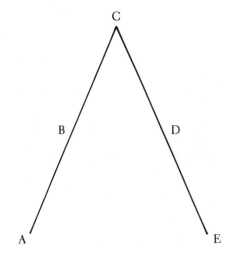

A) exposition
B) rising action
C) climax
D) falling action/return
E) catastrophe (denouement)

Freytag's Pyramid of Dramatic Structure

Exposition

The exposition is the play's introduction to the characters and the dramatic situation. Whatever history of the characters we need in order to understand their present predicament will be given as economically as possible in the exposition. In the Prologue to *Oedipus Rex*, the Priest tells us that the city of Thebes has been suffering from a plague. We learn that King Oedipus is a wise and capable ruler, for he once outwitted the wicked Sphinx to save Thebes from her fury. His people believe that only Oedipus can save them from the plague. We also learn that Oedipus, ever-vigilant, has sent his Queen's brother, Creon, to Delphi to ask advice of the oracle. In the next scene of exposition Creon comes to tell Oedipus what he learned from the oracle: Someone murdered the previous king, Laïos. The god Apollo will not lift the plague from Thebes until the people find the murderer and punish him.

All this is background, helping us to understand the dramatic situation. Classical plays, like epics, often begin *in medias res*, in the middle of the story, and the exposition is the play's main gesture toward the past. Though the play returns occasionally to exposition to fill in gaps in the audience's knowledge, most of the background information emerges in the first minutes of classical drama. After that, the dramatic interest is fixed squarely in the present. When we have learned the dramatic situation of *Oedipus Rex*, that Oedipus wants to save Thebes from the plague but cannot until he finds the murderer of Laïos, then the real action of the play can begin.

The Rising Action

When the chief characters of the drama begin pursuing their objectives in earnest, the play has begun its *rising action*. From the moment that Oedipus learns the cause of the plague and resolves "to avenge the city and the city's god," to find and punish the murderer, he is engaged in a series of actions and crises that lead inevitably to the play's climax and Oedipus's downfall. Oedipus makes his proclamation to hunt down the murderer. He summons the prophet Teiresias and asks him to name the guilty party. This brings on the first *crisis*, or *complication*, of the rising action. Teiresias shocks Oedipus by telling him "you are the murderer whom you seek," a fascinating complication, for we may suspect for the first time the true nature of Oedipus's dramatic situation. He is his own obstacle. Oedipus himself is standing in the way of his objective. At first he does not believe it, and he is enraged. He curses Teiresias and sends him away.

The rising action consists of all those scenes that lead to the major turning point or climax in the play's story. In a comedy as well as a tragedy, the rising action shows the hero struggling to solve the play's problem, though in a comedy the hero appears to be more vulnerable and threatened with failure. Defiance and pride characterize Oedipus's behavior in the rising action of *Oedipus Rex* as he fights the allegations of his own guilt. He threatens the good Creon with exile or death. Despite the assurances of Queen Iocastê and the townspeople that Creon is innocent, Oedipus continues to suspect him, arrogantly looking for the source of evil outside himself instead of within. His crisis with Creon leads to the play's climax, in which Iocastê, intending to reassure Oedipus, lends him information that points to his guilt.

The Climax

The *climax* of a stage play is sometimes hotly disputed. We will avoid unnecessary confusion if we recognize that this term has been used to describe two different moments in the theater. There is the climax of dramatic action, sometimes called the turning point of the play. Then there is the climax of emotion, that point in the drama that moves the audience most deeply.

In this chapter we are chiefly concerned with the climax of action. This is the exact point at which the hero's fortune turns—from better to worse in a tragedy, and from bad to good in a comedy. During the exposition and rising action of *Oedipus Rex* the hero ascends from strength to arrogance. But when Iocastê tells him Laïos was killed "where three highways meet," and Oedipus recalls murdering a man in that time and place, his position falters. Oedipus begins his descent into self-suspicion, self-loathing, and finally blindness and exile as his fate overwhelms him.

Anyone who has seen *Oedipus Rex* knows that the emotional climax of the play comes near the end, after the hero's guilt has been proven to everyone. But by the time the old shepherd delivers final proof of Oedipus's guilt, and the hero blinds himself, King Oedipus's fortunes have been declining for quite a few scenes. In the plotting of *Oedipus Rex* the emotional climax of the play occurs during the falling action and catastrophe.

Locating the climax of a play's action, or the "turning point," is one of the most challenging and rewarding pursuits in the study of drama, for it is at this point in the story that the hero's strengths and weaknesses are most visible. In some plays the climax is conspicuous, as it is in the powerful scene of *Othello* wherein the great Moor begins to suspect his wife of infidelity. In other plays the turning point is difficult to determine, as in *Oedipus Rex*, which has a lengthy falling action and violent catastrophe, but whose early climax may seem to some like one more crisis in the rising action.

We will be searching for the climax of the action in all of our plays. Whether or not we agree on where it occurs, the search for the climax we hope will produce lively discussion.

The Falling Action

Sometimes called the *declining action* or the *return*, the *falling action* in a tragedy includes those scenes that show the hero or heroine as falling from power and fate closing in on him or her. In a comedy it shows the villains or forces of adversity in decline, as the more sympathetic characters gain the upper hand.

At the climax of *Oedipus Rex*, the hero begins to suspect his guilt. After that, each scene of the *falling action* brings him closer to the awful truth about himself. First a messenger from Corinth, and then a shepherd, bring him evidence that proves beyond any doubt that Oedipus himself is the murderer he has been seeking. The falling action leads directly to the play's resolution.

Catastrophe and Denouement

Drama has been likened to the weaving of a net or the tying of a knot to catch the characters in a predicament, and to hold the audience in suspense about the fate of these characters they have come to admire. *Catastrophe* comes from the Greek and means literally "a downward turn," while the gentler term *denouement*, from the French, means "an untying." Though the terms have been used interchangeably, we usually call the outcome of a tragedy a catastrophe, and the outcome of a comedy its denouement.

These are the scenes of the play that answer our questions. In comedies, where there is a love interest and we may have been wondering if the heroine would live happily ever after with the hero, the denouement is usually a marriage, engagement, or other reconciliation. In tragedies, where we have been fearing the demise of the hero, the scenes of catastrophe are often violent and swift. There may be scenes of great tenderness and *pathos* at this point to soothe the agitated feelings of the audience. In any case, this moment of the play may not be prolonged, for once our questions have been answered and the knot untied, the action must end.

Greek Drama and *Oedipus Rex*

Legend says that Thespis, the father of Greek tragedy, was the first actor. Until the time of Thespis, who lived in the sixth century B.C., the most popular form of storytelling was a kind of choral speaking in which the verses of the story were chanted by a number of performers in unison. According to legend Thespis, in a great state of excitement about the story his chorus was chanting, stepped out of the ranks of the chorus and began addressing them in the voice of the story's hero. The immediate response of his fellow choristers is not recorded, but they must have been impressed, for this dialogue between the hero and the chorus became the backbone of Greek tragedy. The hero is the extraordinary man or woman who separates himself or herself from the group. This leads to disaster. The Greeks were probably no more moralistic than any civilized people, but the theater of Sophocles was rigid in its pieties. The chorus, a familiar holdover from the earlier form of narration, reflected the morals and sentiments of the Athenians. As a group onstage, the chorus mirrors the audience, and Sophocles uses the chorus to predict and explain the action as well as to lead the audience in their response.

In addition to the dialogues between the main characters of *Oedipus Rex*, there are five choral odes (songs) of great conviction and lyric beauty. They provide rest from the action as well as comment upon it. They help to explain why the myth of Oedipus had such an impact on the audience of Athens. They tell us that Oedipus has violated their deepest principles of piety, that

> Haughtiness and the high hand of disdain
> Tempt and outrage god's holy law;
> And any mortal who dares hold
> No immortal Power in awe
> Will be caught up in a net of pain.

Oedipus Rex was first performed about 430 B.C. on a feast day called the Great Dionysia in honor of Dionysus, the god of wine and fertility. This festival was held every spring, and wealthy citizens offered prizes for the best play presented.

Theater of Dionysus (*National Archeological Museum of Athens*)

The stage stood before a colonnade at the foot of a hillside amphitheater. A chorus of fifteen performed from an orchestra space in front of the playing area, and sometimes danced as well as sang the choral interludes. The actors, all men, wore masks that were highly stylized projections of their character's appearance,

Greek actors in 1963 staging of Aeschylus' *Prometheus Bound* (*National Theatre of Greece*)

and a special elevator shoe called a *cothurnus*. They must have looked very weird, but perhaps the stylization of their appearance lent them a special dramatic power beyond the possibilities of "realistic" play-acting.

Sophocles was probably the most admired of the three great Athenian tragedians. The comedian Aristophanes ridiculed the others, Euripides and Aeschylus, in his play *The Frogs*, but had only good to say about Sophocles. When Sophocles was twenty-seven years old he defeated Aeschylus, fifty-six, in the playwright's contest with his first tragedy. Before Sophocles, no more than two characters ever appeared in the same scene. He introduced the three-character scene and, according to some accounts, increased the size of the chorus. Sophocles is said to have written over one hundred plays, of which only seven tragedies survive. The best known are *Oedipus Rex* and two companion plays, *Oedipus at Colonus* and *Antigone*.

SOPHOCLES (496?–406 B.C.)

Oedipus Rex

An English Version by Dudley Fitts and Robert Fitzgerald

CHARACTERS

OEDIPUS	MESSENGER
A PRIEST	SHEPHERD OF LAÏOS
CREON	SECOND MESSENGER
TEIRESIAS	CHORUS OF THEBAN ELDERS
IOCASTÊ	

THE SCENE: *Before the palace of Oedipus, King of Thebes. A central door and two lateral doors open onto a platform which runs the length of the façade. On the platform, right and left, are altars; and three steps lead down into the "orchestra," or chorus-ground. At the beginning of the action these steps are crowded by Suppliants who have brought branches and chaplets of olive leaves and who lie in various attitudes of despair. Oedipus enters.*

PROLOGUE°

OEDIPUS: My children, generations of the living
    In the line of Kadmos°, nursed at his ancient hearth:
    Why have you strewn yourselves before these altars
    In supplication, with your boughs and garlands?
5   The breath of incense rises from the city
    With a sound of prayer and lamentation.
                    Children,
    I would not have you speak through messengers,
    And therefore I have come myself to hear you—

Prologue: the exposition.
² *line of Kadmos:* The city of Thebes, scene of the action, is said to have been founded by the hero Cadmus.

I, Oedipus, who bear the famous name.
10　*(To a Priest.)* You, there, since you are eldest in the company,
Speak for them all, tell me what preys upon you,
Whether you come in dread, or crave some blessing:
Tell me, and never doubt that I will help you
In every way I can; I should be heartless
15　Were I not moved to find you suppliant here.
PRIEST: Great Oedipus, O powerful King of Thebes!
You see how all the ages of our people
Cling to your altar steps: here are boys
Who can barely stand alone, and here are priests
20　By weight of age, as I am a priest of God,
And young men chosen from those yet unmarried;
As for the others, all that multitude,
They wait with olive chaplets in the squares,
At the two shrines of Pallas°, and where Apollo°
Speaks in the glowing embers.
25　　　　　　　　　　　　　Your own eyes
Must tell you: Thebes is in her extremity
And can not lift her head from the surge of death.
A rust consumes the buds and fruits of the earth;
The herds are sick; children die unborn,
30　And labor is vain. The god of plague and pyre
Raids like detestable lightning through the city,
And all the house of Kadmos is laid waste,
All emptied, and all darkened: Death alone
Battens upon the misery of Thebes.

35　You are not one of the immortal gods, we know;
Yet we have come to you to make our prayer
As to the man of all men best in adversity
And wisest in the ways of God. You saved us
From the Sphinx, that flinty singer, and the tribute
40　We paid to her so long; yet you were never
Better informed than we, nor could we teach you:
It was some god breathed in you to set us free.

Therefore, O mighty King, we turn to you:
Find us our safety, find us a remedy,
45　Whether by counsel of the gods or men.
A king of wisdom tested in the past
Can act in a time of troubles, and act well.
Noblest of men, restore
Life to your city! Think how all men call you
50　Liberator for your triumph long ago;
Ah, when your years of kingship are remembered,

---

²⁴ *Pallas:* Athena, goddess of wisdom.
²⁴ *Apollo:* a god associated with light, prophecy, and poetry. His priests used ashes to predict the future.

936　Action

Let them not say *We rose, but later fell*—
Keep the State from going down in the storm!
Once, years ago, with happy augury,
55 You brought us fortune; be the same again!
No man questions your power to rule the land:
But rule over men, not over a dead city!
Ships are only hulls, citadels are nothing,
When no life moves in the empty passageways.
60 OEDIPUS: Poor children! You may be sure I know
All that you longed for in your coming here.
I know that you are deathly sick; and yet,
Sick as you are, not one is as sick as I.
Each of you suffers in himself alone
65 His anguish, not another's; but my spirit
Groans for the city, for myself, for you.

I was not sleeping, you are not waking me.
No, I have been in tears for a long while
And in my restless thought walked many ways.
70 In all my search, I found one helpful course,
And that I have taken: I have sent Creon,
Son of Menoikeus, brother of the Queen,
To Delphi, Apollo's place of revelation,
To learn there, if he can,
75 What act or pledge of mine may save the city.
I have counted the days, and now, this very day,
I am troubled, for he has overstayed his time.
What is he doing? He has been gone too long.
Yet whenever he comes back, I should do ill
80 To scant whatever hint the god may give.
PRIEST: It is a timely promise. At this instant
They tell me Creon is here.
OEDIPUS: O Lord Apollo!
May his news be fair as his face is radiant!
PRIEST: It could not be otherwise: he is crowned with bay,
The chaplet is thick with berries.
85 OEDIPUS: We shall soon know;
He is near enough to hear us now.

Enter Creon.

                              O prince:
Brother: son of Menoikeus:
What answer do you bring us from the god?
CREON: It is favorable. I can tell you, great afflictions
90 Will turn out well, if they are taken well.
OEDIPUS: What was the oracle? These vague words
Leave me still hanging between hope and fear.
CREON: Is it your pleasure to hear me with all these
Gathered around us? I am prepared to speak,
But should we not go in?

95 OEDIPUS: Let them all hear it.
     It is for them I suffer, more than for myself.
     CREON: Then I will tell you what I heard at Delphi.

     In plain words
     The god commands us to expel from the land of Thebes
100 An old defilement that it seems we shelter.
     It is a deathly thing, beyond expiation.
     We must not let it feed upon us longer.
     OEDIPUS: What defilement? How shall we rid ourselves of it?
     CREON: By exile or death, blood for blood. It was
105 Murder that brought the plague-wind on the city.
     OEDIPUS: Murder of whom? Surely the god has named him?
     CREON: My lord: long ago Laïos was our king,
     Before you came to govern us.
     OEDIPUS: I know;
     I learned of him from others; I never saw him.
110 CREON: He was murdered; and Apollo commands us now
     To take revenge upon whoever killed him.
     OEDIPUS: Upon whom? Where are they? Where shall we find a clue
     To solve that crime, after so many years?
     CREON: Here in this land, he said.
                              If we make enquiry,
115 We may touch things that otherwise escape us.
     OEDIPUS: Tell me: Was Laïos murdered in his house,
     Or in the fields, or in some foreign country?
     CREON: He said he planned to make a pilgrimage.
     He did not come home again.
     OEDIPUS: And was there no one,
120 No witness, no companion, to tell what happened?
     CREON: They were all killed but one, and he got away
     So frightened that he could remember one thing only.
     OEDIPUS: What was that one thing? One may be the key
     To everything, if we resolve to use it.
125 CREON: He said that a band of highwaymen attacked them,
     Outnumbered them, and overwhelmed the King.
     OEDIPUS: Strange, that a highwayman should be so daring—
     Unless some faction here bribed him to do it.
130 CREON: We thought of that. But after Laïos' death
     New troubles arose and we had no avenger.
     OEDIPUS: What troubles could prevent your hunting down the killers?
     CREON: The riddling Sphinx's song
     Made us deaf to all mysteries but her own.
     OEDIPUS: Then once more I must bring what is dark to light.
135 It is most fitting that Apollo shows,
     As you do, this compunction for the dead.
     You shall see how I stand by you, as I should,
     To avenge the city and the city's god,
     And not as though it were for some distant friend,
140 But for my own sake, to be rid of evil.

     938   Action

Whoever killed King Laïos might—who knows?—
Decide at any moment to kill me as well.
By avenging the murdered king I protect myself.
Come, then, my children: leave the altar steps,
Lift up your olive boughs!
145   One of you go
And summon the people of Kadmos to gather here.
I will do all that I can; you may tell them that.

Exit a Page

So, with the help of God,
We shall be saved—or else indeed we are lost.
150 PRIEST: Let us rise, children. It was for this we came,
And now the King has promised it himself.
Phoibos° has sent us an oracle; may he descend
Himself to save us and drive out the plague.

Exeunt Oedipus and Creon into the palace by the central door. The Priest and the
Suppliants disperse right and left. After a short pause the Chorus enters the orchestra.

PARODOS°

Strophe 1

CHORUS: What is God singing in his profound
    Delphi of gold and shadow?
    What oracle for Thebes, the sunwhipped city?
    Fear unjoints me, the roots of my heart tremble.
5   Now I remember, O Healer, your power, and wonder;
    Will you send doom like a sudden cloud, or weave it
    Like nightfall of the past?
    Speak, speak to us, issue of holy sound:
    Dearest to our expectancy: be tender!

Antistrophe 1

10 Let me pray to Athenê, the immortal daughter of Zeus,
    And to Artemis her sister
    Who keeps her famous throne in the market ring,
    And to Apollo, bowman at the far butts of heaven—

    O gods, descend! Like three streams leap against
15 The fires of our grief, the fires of darkness;
    Be swift to bring us rest!

    As in the old time from the brilliant house
    Of air you stepped to save us, come again!

---

¹⁵² *Phoibos:* Apollo.
Parodos: ode sung upon the first entrance of the chorus. The *strophe* is said to have accompanied
their dance from right to left; the *antistrophe* their return from stage left to right.

Strophe 2

> Now our afflictions have no end,
> Now all our stricken host lies down
> And no man fights off death with his mind;
>
> The noble plowland bears no grain,
> And groaning mothers can not bear—
>
> See, how our lives like birds take wing,
> Like sparks that fly when a fire soars,
> To the shore of the god of evening.

Antistrophe 2

> The plague burns on, it is pitiless,
> Though pallid children laden with death
> Lie unwept in the stony ways,
>
> And old gray women by every path
> Flock to the strand about the altars
>
> There to strike their breasts and cry
> Worship of Phoibos in wailing prayers:
> Be kind, God's golden child!

Strophe 3

> There are no swords in this attack by fire,
> No shields, but we are ringed with cries.
> Send the besieger plunging from our homes
> Into the vast sea-room of the Atlantic
> Or into the waves that foam eastward of Thrace—
> For the day ravages what the night spares—
> Destroy our enemy, lord of the thunder!
> Let him be riven by lightning from heaven!

Antistrophe 3

> Phoibos Apollo, stretch the sun's bowstring,
> That golden cord, until it sing for us,
> Flashing arrows in heaven!
>   Artemis, Huntress,
> Race with flaring lights upon our mountains!
>
> O scarlet god, O golden-banded brow,
> O Theban Bacchos in a storm of Maenads°,

Enter Oedipus, center.

°⁴⁸*Bacchos . . . Maenads:* the wine god and attendant nymphs.

Whirl upon Death, that all the Undying hate!
50   Come with blinding cressets, come in joy!

SCENE I.

OEDIPUS: Is this your prayer? It may be answered. Come,
    Listen to me, act as the crisis demands,
    And you shall have relief from all these evils.

    Until now I was a stranger to this tale,
5   As I had been a stranger to the crime.
    Could I track down the murderer without a clue?
    But now, friends,
    As one who became a citizen after the murder,
    I make this proclamation to all Thebans:
10   If any man knows by whose hand Laïos, son of Labdakos,
    Met his death, I direct that man to tell me everything,
    No matter what he fears for having so long withheld it.
    Let it stand as promised that no further trouble
    Will come to him, but he may leave the land in safety.

15   Moreover: If anyone knows the murderer to be foreign,
    Let him not keep silent: he shall have his reward from me.
    However, if he does conceal it; if any man
    Fearing for his friend or for himself disobeys this edict,
    Hear what I propose to do:

20   I solemnly forbid the people of this country,
    Where power and throne are mine, ever to receive that man
    Or speak to him, no matter who he is, or let him
    Join in sacrifice, lustration, or in prayer.
    I decree that he be driven from every house,
25   Being, as he is, corruption itself to us: the Delphic
    Voice of Zeus has pronounced this revelation.
    Thus I associate myself with the oracle
    And take the side of the murdered king.

    As for the criminal, I pray to God—
30   Whether it be a lurking thief, or one of a number—
    I pray that that man's life be consumed in evil and wretchedness.
    And as for me, this curse applies no less
    If it should turn out that the culprit is my guest here,
    Sharing my hearth.
                 You have heard the penalty.
35   I lay it on you now to attend to this
    For my sake, for Apollo's, for the sick
    Sterile city that heaven has abandoned.
    Suppose the oracle had given you no command:
    Should this defilement go uncleansed for ever?
40   You should have found the murderer: your king,

A noble king, had been destroyed!
                                    Now I,
Having the power that he held before me,
Having his bed, begetting children there
Upon his wife, as he would have, had he lived—
45   Their son would have been my children's brother,
If Laïos had had luck in fatherhood!
(But surely ill luck rushed upon his reign)—
I say I take the son's part, just as though
I were his son, to press the fight for him
50   And see it won! I'll find the hand that brought
Death to Labdakos' and Polydoros' child,
Heir of Kadmos' and Agenor's line.
And as for those who fail me,
May the gods deny them the fruit of the earth,
55   Fruit of the womb, and may they rot utterly!
Let them be wretched as we are wretched, and worse!

For you, for loyal Thebans, and for all
Who find my actions right, I pray the favor
Of justice, and of all the immortal gods.
60   CHORAGOS°: Since I am under oath, my lord, I swear
I did not do the murder, I can not name
The murderer. Might not the oracle
That has ordained the search tell where to find him?
OEDIPUS: An honest question. But no man in the world
65   Can make the gods do more than the gods will.
CHORAGOS: There is one last expedient—
OEDIPUS: Tell me what it is.
Though it seem slight, you must not hold it back.
CHORAGOS: A lord clairvoyant to the lord Apollo,
As we all know, is the skilled Teiresias.
70   One might learn much about this from him, Oedipus.
OEDIPUS: I am not wasting time:
Creon spoke of this, and I have sent for him—
Twice, in fact; it is strange that he is not here.
CHORAGOS: The other matter—that old report—seems useless.
75   OEDIPUS: Tell me. I am interested in all reports.
CHORAGOS: The King was said to have been killed by highwaymen.
OEDIPUS: I know. but we have no witnesses to that.
CHORAGOS: If the killer can feel a particle of dread,
Your curse will bring him out of hiding!
OEDIPUS: No.
80   The man who dared that act will fear no curse.

Enter the blind seer Teiresias, led by a Page.

---

⁶⁰ *Choragos*: leader of the chorus.

CHORAGOS: But there is one man who may detect the criminal.
This is Teiresias, this is the holy prophet
In whom, alone of all men, truth was born.
OEDIPUS: Teiresias: seer: student of mysteries,
85   Of all that's taught and all that no man tells,
Secrets of Heaven and secrets of the earth:
Blind though you are, you know the city lies
Sick with plague; and from this plague, my lord,
We find that you alone can guard or save us.

90   Possibly you did not hear the messengers?
Apollo, when we sent to him,
Sent us back word that this great pestilence
Would lift, but only if we established clearly
The identity of those who murdered Laïos.
They must be killed or exiled.
95   Can you use
Birdflight or any art of divination
To purify yourself, and Thebes, and me
From this contagion? We are in your hands.
There is no fairer duty
100   Than that of helping others in distress.
TEIRESIAS: How dreadful knowledge of the truth can be
When there's no help in truth! I knew this well,
But did not act on it: else I should not have come.
OEDIPUS: What is troubling you? Why are your eyes so cold?
105 TEIRESIAS: Let me go home. Bear your own fate, and I'll
Bear mine. It is better so: trust what I say.
OEDIPUS: What you say is ungracious and unhelpful
To your native country. Do not refuse to speak.
TEIRESIAS: When it comes to speech, your own is neither temperate
110   Nor opportune. I wish to be more prudent.
OEDIPUS: In God's name, we all beg you—
TEIRESIAS: You are all ignorant.
No; I will never tell you what I know.
Now it is my misery; then, it would be yours.
OEDIPUS: What! You do know something, and will not tell us?
115   You would betray us all and wreck the State?
TEIRESIAS: I do not intend to torture myself, or you.
Why persist in asking? You will not persuade me.
OEDIPUS: What a wicked old man you are! You'd try a stone's
Patience! Out with it! Have you no feeling at all?
120 TEIRESIAS: You call me unfeeling. If you could only see
The nature of your own feelings . . .
OEDIPUS: Why,
Who would not feel as I do? Who could endure
Your arrogance toward the city?
TEIRESIAS: What does it matter!
Whether I speak or not, it is bound to come.
125 OEDIPUS: Then, if "it" is bound to come, you are bound to tell me.

The scene from Tyrone Guthrie's
version of the play in classic Greek
tradition: *(Above)* Oedipus surrounded
by members of the chorus, *(Below)*
Eleanor Stuart as Iocastê, Douglas
Campbell as Oedipus, and Robert
Goodier as Creon *(The Granger
Collection)*

TEIRESIAS: No, I will not go on. Rage as you please.
OEDIPUS: Rage? Why not!

              And I'll tell you what I think:
  You planned it, you had it done, you all but
  Killed him with your own hands: if you had eyes,
130 I'd say the crime was yours, and yours alone.
TEIRESIAS: So? I charge you, then,
  Abide by the proclamation you have made:
  From this day forth

Never speak again to these men or to me;
135   You yourself are the pollution of this country.
    OEDIPUS: You dare say that! Can you possibly think you have
        Some way of going free, after such insolence?
    TEIRESIAS: I have gone free. It is the truth sustains me.
    OEDIPUS: Who taught you shamelessness? It was not your craft.
140 TEIRESIAS: You did. You made me speak. I did not want to.
    OEDIPUS: Speak what? Let me hear it again more clearly.
    TEIRESIAS: Was it not clear before? Are you tempting me?
    OEDIPUS: I did not understand it. Say it again.
    TEIRESIAS: I say that you are the murderer whom you seek.
145 OEDIPUS: Now twice you have spat out infamy. You'll pay for it!
    TEIRESIAS: Would you care for more? Do you wish to be really angry?
    OEDIPUS: Say what you will. Whatever you say is worthless.
    TEIRESIAS: I say you live in hideous shame with those
        Most dear to you. You can not see the evil.
150 OEDIPUS: It seems you can go on mouthing like this for ever.
    TEIRESIAS: I can, if there is power in truth.
    OEDIPUS: There is:
    But not for you, not for you,
    You sightless, witless, senseless, mad old man!
    TEIRESIAS: You are the madman. There is no one here
155   Who will not curse you soon, as you curse me.
    OEDIPUS: You child of endless night! You can not hurt me
    Or any other man who sees the sun.
    TEIRESIAS: True: it is not from me your fate will come.
    That lies within Apollo's competence,
    As it is his concern.
160 OEDIPUS: Tell me:
    Are you speaking for Creon, or for yourself?
    TEIRESIAS: Creon is no threat. You weave your own doom.
    OEDIPUS: Wealth, power, craft of statesmanship!
    Kingly position, everywhere admired!
165   What savage envy is stored up against these,
    If Creon, whom I trusted, Creon my friend,
    For this great office which the city once
    Put in my hands unsought—if for this power
    Creon desires in secret to destroy me!

170   He has brought this decrepit fortune-teller, this
    Collector of dirty pennies, this prophet fraud—
    Why, he is no more clairvoyant than I am!
                           Tell us:
    Has your mystic mummery ever approached the truth?
    When that hellcat the Sphinx was performing here,
175   What help were you to these people?
    Her magic was not for the first man who came along:
    It demanded a real exorcist. Your birds—
    What good were they? or the gods, for the matter of that?

But I came by,
180 Oedipus, the simple man, who knows nothing—
I thought it out for myself, no birds helped me!
And this is the man you think you can destroy,
That you may be close to Creon when he's king!
Well, you and your friend Creon, it seems to me,
185 Will suffer most. If you were not an old man,
You would have paid already for your plot.
CHORAGOS: We can not see that his words or yours
Have been spoken except in anger, Oedipus,
And of anger we have no need. How can God's will
190 Be accomplished best? That is what most concerns us.
TEIRESIAS: You are a king. But where argument's concerned
I am your man, as much a king as you.
I am not your servant, but Apollo's.
I have no need of Creon to speak for me.

195 Listen to me. You mock my blindness, do you?
But I say that you, with both your eyes, are blind:
You can not see the wretchedness of your life,
Nor in whose house you live, no, nor with whom.
Who are your father and mother? Can you tell me?
200 You do not even know the blind wrongs
That you have done them, on earth and in the world below.
But the double lash of your parents' curse will whip you
Out of this land some day, with only night
Upon your precious eyes.
205 Your cries then—where will they not be heard?
What fastness of Kithairon will not echo them?
And that bridal-descant of yours—you'll know it then,
The song they sang when you came here to Thebes
And found your misguided berthing.
210 All this, and more, that you can not guess at now,
Will bring you to yourself among your children.

Be angry, then. Curse Creon. Curse my words.
I tell you, no man that walks upon the earth
Shall be rooted out more horribly than you.
215 OEDIPUS: Am I to bear this from him?—Damnation
Take you! Out of this place! Out of my sight!
TEIRESIAS: I would not have come at all if you had not asked me.
OEDIPUS: Could I have told that you'd talk nonsense, that
You'd come here to make a fool of yourself, and of me?
220 TEIRESIAS: A fool? Your parents thought me sane enough.
OEDIPUS: My parents again!—Wait: who were my parents?
TEIRESIAS: This day will give you a father, and break your heart.
OEDIPUS: Your infantile riddles! Your damned abracadabra!
TEIRESIAS: You were a great man once at solving riddles.
225 OEDIPUS: Mock me with that if you like; you will find it true.

TEIRESIAS: It was true enough. It brought about your ruin.

OEDIPUS: But if it saved this town?

TEIRESIAS *(to the Page)*: Boy, give me your hand.

OEDIPUS: Yes, boy; lead him away.

—While you are here
We can do nothing. Go; leave us in peace.

230 TEIRESIAS: I will go when I have said what I have to say.
How can you hurt me? And I tell you again:
The man you have been looking for all this time,
The damned man, the murderer of Laïos,
That man is in Thebes. To your mind he is foreignborn,
235 But it will soon be shown that he is a Theban,
A revelation that will fail to please.

A blind man,
Who has his eyes now; a penniless man, who is rich now;
And he will go tapping the strange earth with his staff;
To the children with whom he lives now he will be
240 Brother and father—the very same; to her
Who bore him, son and husband—the very same
Who came to his father's bed, wet with his father's blood.

Enough. Go think that over.
If later you find error in what I have said,
245 You may say that I have no skill in prophecy.

Exit Teiresias, led by his Page. Oedipus goes into the palace.

ODE I°

Strophe 1

CHORUS: The Delphic stone of prophecies
Remembers ancient regicide
And a still bloody hand.
That killer's hour of flight has come.
5 He must be stronger than riderless
Coursers of untiring wind,
For the son of Zeus° armed with his father's thunder
Leaps in lightning after him;
And the Furies° follow him, the sad Furies.

Antistrophe 1

10 Holy Parnassos' peak of snow
Flashes and blinds that secret man,
That all shall hunt him down:
Though he may roam the forest shade
Like a bull gone wild from pasture

Ode: a choral song.
⁷ *son of Zeus:* Apollo.
⁹ *Furies:* three terrible female spirits who pursue and torment evil-doers.

15   To rage through glooms of stone.
      Doom comes down on him; flight will not avail him;
      For the world's heart calls him desolate,
      And the immortal Furies follow, for ever follow.

Strophe 2

      But now a wilder thing is heard
20   From the old man skilled at hearing Fate in the wingbeat of a bird.
      Bewildered as a blown bird, my soul hovers and can not find
      Foothold in this debate, or any reason or rest of mind.
      But no man ever brought—none can bring
      Proof of strife between Thebes' royal house,
25   Labdakos' line,° and the son of Polybos°;
      And never until now has any man brought word
      Of Laïos' dark death staining Oedipus the King.

Antistrophe 2

      Divine Zeus and Apollo hold
      Perfect intelligence alone of all tales ever told;
30   And well though this diviner works, he works in his own night;
      No man can judge that rough unknown or trust in second sight,
      For wisdom changes hands among the wise.
      Shall I believe my great lord criminal
      At a raging word that a blind old man let fall?
35   I saw him, when the carrion woman faced him of old,
      Prove his heroic mind! These evil words are lies.

SCENE II.

CREON: Men of Thebes:
      I am told that heavy accusations
      Have been brought against me by King Oedipus.

      I am not the kind of man to bear this tamely.

5   If in these present difficulties
      He holds me accountable for any harm to him
      Through anything I have said or done—why, then,
      I do not value life in this dishonor.
      It is not as though this rumor touched upon
10   Some private indiscretion. The matter is grave.
      The fact is that I am being called disloyal
      To the State, to my fellow citizens, to my friends.
CHORAGOS: He may have spoken in anger, not from his mind.
CREON: But did you not hear him say I was the one
15   Who seduced the old prophet into lying?

---

[25] *Labdakos' line*: descendants of Labdakos. The chorus is unaware that Laïos is the true father of
      Oedipus.
[25] *Polybos*: king of Corinth, who adopted Oedipus as an infant.

CHORAGOS: The thing was said; I do not know how seriously.
CREON: But you were watching him! Were his eyes steady?
  Did he look like a man in his right mind?
CHORAGOS: I do not know.
  I can not judge the behavior of great men.
  But here is the King himself.

Enter Oedipus.

20 OEDIPUS: So you dared come back.
  Why? How brazen of you to come to my house,
  You murderer!
                      Do you think I do not know
  That you plotted to kill me, plotted to steal my throne?
  Tell me, in God's name: am I coward, a fool,
25 That you should dream you could accomplish this?
  A fool who could not see your slippery game?
  A coward, not to fight back when I saw it?
  You are the fool, Creon, are you not? hoping
  Without support or friends to get a throne?
30 Thrones may be won or bought: you could do neither.
CREON: Now listen to me. You have talked; let me talk, too.
  You can not judge unless you know the facts.
OEDIPUS: You speak well: there is one fact; but I find it hard
  To learn from the deadliest enemy I have.
35 CREON: That above all I must dispute with you.
OEDIPUS: That above all I will not hear you deny.
CREON: If you think there is anything good in being stubborn
  Against all reason, then I say you are wrong.
OEDIPUS: If you think a man can sin against his own kind
40 And not be punished for it, I say you are mad.
CREON: I agree. But tell me: what have I done to you?
OEDIPUS: You advised me to send for that wizard, did you not?
CREON: I did. I should do it again.
OEDIPUS: Very well. Now tell me:
  How long has it been since Laïos—
CREON: What of Laïos?
45 OEDIPUS: Since he vanished in that onset by the road?
CREON: It was long ago, a long time.
OEDIPUS: And this prophet,
  Was he practicing here then?
CREON: He was; and with honor, as now.
OEDIPUS: Did he speak of me at that time?
CREON: He never did;
  At least, not when I was present.
OEDIPUS: But . . . the enquiry?
  I suppose you held one?
50 CREON: We did, but we learned nothing.
OEDIPUS: Why did the prophet not speak against me then?

CREON: I do not know; and I am the kind of man
  Who holds his tongue when he has no facts to go on.
OEDIPUS: There's one fact that you know, and you could tell it.
55 CREON: What fact is that? If I know it, you shall have it.
OEDIPUS: If he were not involved with you, he could not say
  That it was I who murdered Laïos.
CREON: If he says that, you are the one that knows it!—
  But now it is my turn to question you.
60 OEDIPUS: Put your questions. I am no murderer.
CREON: First then: You married my sister?
OEDIPUS: I married your sister.
CREON: And you rule the kingdom equally with her?
OEDIPUS: Everything that she wants she has from me.
CREON: And I am the third, equal to both of you?
65 OEDIPUS: That is why I call you a bad friend.
CREON: No. Reason it out, as I have done.
  Think of this first. Would any sane man prefer
  Power, with all a king's anxieties,
  To that same power and the grace of sleep?
70 Certainly not I.
  I have never longed for the king's power—only his rights.
  Would any wise man differ from me in this?
  As matters stand, I have my way in everything
  With your consent, and no responsibilities.
75 If I were king, I should be a slave to policy.

  How could I desire a scepter more
  Than what is now mine—untroubled influence?
  No, I have not gone mad; I need no honors,
  Except those with the perquisites I have now.
80 I am welcome everywhere; every man salutes me,
  And those who want your favor seek my ear,
  Since I know how to manage what they ask.
  Should I exchange this ease for that anxiety?
  Besides, no sober mind is treasonable.
85 I hate anarchy
  And never would deal with any man who likes it.

  Test what I have said. Go to the priestess
  At Delphi, ask if I quoted her correctly.
  And as for this other thing: if I am found
90 Guilty of treason with Teiresias,
  Then sentence me to death! You have my word
  It is a sentence I should cast my vote for—
  But not without evidence!
                              You do wrong
  When you take good men for bad, bad men for good.
95 A true friend thrown aside—why, life itself
  Is not more precious!

> In time you will know this well:
> For time, and time alone, will show the just man,
> Though scoundrels are discovered in a day.

CHORAGOS: This is well said, and a prudent man would ponder it.
100 Judgments too quickly formed are dangerous.

OEDIPUS: But is he not quick in his duplicity?
And shall I not be quick to parry him?
Would you have me stand still, hold my peace, and let
This man win everything, through my inaction?

105 CREON: And you want—what is it, then? To banish me?

OEDIPUS: No, not exile. It is your death I want,
So that all the world may see what treason means.

CREON: You will persist, then? You will not believe me?

OEDIPUS: How can I believe you?

CREON: Then you are a fool.

OEDIPUS: To save myself?

110 CREON: In justice, think of me.

OEDIPUS: You are evil incarnate.

CREON: But suppose that you are wrong?

OEDIPUS: Still I must rule.

CREON: But not if you rule badly.

OEDIPUS: O city, city!

CREON: It is my city, too!

CHORAGOS: Now, my lords, be still. I see the Queen,
115 Iocastê, coming from her palace chambers;
And it is time she came, for the sake of you both.
This dreadful quarrel can be resolved through her.

Enter Iocastê.

IOCASTÊ: Poor foolish men, what wicked din is this?
With Thebes sick to death, is it not shameful
120 That you should rake some private quarrel up?
(To Oedipus.) Come into the house.
                          —And you, Creon, go now:
Let us have no more of this tumult over nothing.

CREON: Nothing? No, sister: what your husband plans for me
Is one of two great evils: exile or death.

OEDIPUS: He is right.
125   Why, woman, I have caught him squarely
Plotting against my life.

CREON: No! Let me die
Accurst if ever I have wished you harm!

IOCASTÊ: Ah, believe it, Oedipus!
In the name of the gods, respect this oath of his
130 For my sake, for the sake of these people here!

Strophe 1

CHORAGOS: Open your mind to her, my lord. Be ruled by her, I beg
you!

OEDIPUS: What would you have me do?

CHORAGOS: Respect Creon's word. He has never spoken like a fool,
And now he has sworn an oath.

OEDIPUS: You know what you ask?

CHORAGOS: I do.

OEDIPUS: Speak on, then.

135 CHORAGOS: A friend so sworn should not be baited so,
In blind malice, and without final proof.

OEDIPUS: You are aware, I hope, that what you say
Means death for me, or exile at the least.

Strophe 2

CHORAGOS: No, I swear by Helios, first in Heaven!
140   May I die friendless and accurst,
The worst of deaths, if ever I meant that!
    It is the withering fields
        That hurt my sick heart:
        Must we bear all these ills,
145   And now your bad blood as well?

OEDIPUS: Then let him go. And let me die, if I must,
Or be driven by him in shame from the land of Thebes.
It is your unhappiness, and not his talk,
That touches me.
                As for him—
150   Wherever he is, I will hate him as long as I live.

CREON: Ugly in yielding, as you were ugly in rage!
Natures like yours chiefly torment themselves.

OEDIPUS: Can you not go? Can you not leave me?

CREON: I can.
You do not know me; but the city knows me,
155   And in its eyes I am just, if not in yours.

Exit Creon.

Antistrophe 1

CHORAGOS: Lady Iocastê, did you not ask the King to go to his chambers?

IOCASTÊ: First tell me what has happened.

CHORAGOS: There was suspicion without evidence; yet it rankled
As even false charges will.

IOCASTÊ: On both sides?

CHORAGOS: On both.

IOCASTÊ: But what was said?

160 CHORAGOS: Oh let it rest, let it be done with!
Have we not suffered enough?

OEDIPUS: You see to what your decency has brought you:
You have made difficulties where my heart saw none.

Antistrophe 2

CHORAGOS: Oedipus, it is not once only I have told you—
165   You must know I should count myself unwise
To the point of madness, should I now forsake you—
        You, under whose hand,
            In the storm of another time,
        Our dear land sailed out free.
170   But now stand fast at the helm!
IOCASTÉ: In God's name, Oedipus, inform your wife as well:
Why are you so set in this hard anger?
OEDIPUS: I will tell you, for none of these men deserves
My confidence as you do. It is Creon's work,
175   His treachery, his plotting against me.
IOCASTÉ: Go on, if you can make this clear to me.
OEDIPUS: He charges me with the murder of Laïos.
IOCASTÉ: Has he some knowledge? Or does he speak from hearsay?
OEDIPUS: He would not commit himself to such a charge,
180   But he has brought in that damnable soothsayer
To tell his story.
IOCASTÉ: Set your mind at rest.
If it is a question of soothsayers, I tell you
That you will find no man whose craft gives knowledge
Of the unknowable.
                        Here is my proof:

185   An oracle was reported to Laïos once
(I will not say from Phoibos himself, but from
His appointed ministers, at any rate)
That his doom would be death at the hands of his own son—
His son, born of his flesh and of mine!

190   Now, you remember the story: Laïos was killed
By marauding strangers where three highways meet;
But his child had not been three days in this world
Before the King had pierced the baby's ankles
And left him to die on a lonely mountainside.

195   Thus, Apollo never caused that child
To kill his father, and it was not Laïos' fate
To die at the hands of his son, as he had feared.
This is what prophets and prophecies are worth!
Have no dread of them.
                        It is God himself
200   Who can show us what he wills, in his own way.
OEDIPUS: How strange a shadowy memory crossed my mind,
Just now while you were speaking; it chilled my heart.
IOCASTÉ: What do you mean? What memory do you speak of?
OEDIPUS: If I understand you, Laïos was killed
At a place where three roads meet.

205 IOCASTÊ: So it was said;
We have no later story.
OEDIPUS: Where did it happen?
IOCASTÊ: Phokis, it is called: at a place where the Theban Way
Divides into the roads toward Delphi and Daulia.
OEDIPUS: When?
IOCASTÊ: We had the news not long before you came
210   And proved the right to your succession here.
OEDIPUS: Ah, what net has God been weaving for me?
IOCASTÊ: Oedipus! Why does this trouble you?
OEDIPUS: Do not ask me yet.
First, tell me how Laïos looked, and tell me
How old he was.
IOCASTÊ: He was tall, his hair just touched
215   With white; his form was not unlike your own.
OEDIPUS: I think that I myself may be accurst
By my own ignorant edict.
IOCASTÊ: You speak strangely.
It makes me tremble to look at you, my King.
OEDIPUS: I am not sure that the blind man can not see.
220   But I should know better if you were to tell me—
IOCASTÊ: Anything—though I dread to hear you ask it.
OEDIPUS: Was the King lightly escorted, or did he ride
With a large company, as a ruler should?
IOCASTÊ: There were five men with him in all: one was a herald;
225   And a single chariot, which he was driving.
OEDIPUS: Alas, that makes it plain enough!
                                    But who—
Who told you how it happened?
IOCASTÊ: A household servant,
The only one to escape.
OEDIPUS: And is he still
A servant of ours?
IOCASTÊ: No; for when he came back at last
230   And found you enthroned in the place of the dead king,
He came to me, touched my hand with his, and begged
That I would send him away to the frontier district
Where only the shepherds go—
As far away from the city as I could send him.
235   I granted his prayer; for although the man was a slave,
He had earned more than this favor at my hands.
OEDIPUS: Can he be called back quickly?
IOCASTÊ: Easily.
But why?
OEDIPUS: I have taken too much upon myself
Without enquiry; therefore I wish to consult him.
IOCASTÊ: Then he shall come.
240   But am I not one also
To whom you might confide these fears of yours?

OEDIPUS: That is your right; it will not be denied you,
    Now least of all; for I have reached a pitch
    Of wild foreboding. Is there anyone
245   To whom I should sooner speak?
    Polybos of Corinth is my father.
    My mother is a Dorian: Meropê.
    I grew up chief among the men of Corinth
    Until a strange thing happened—
250   Not worth my passion, it may be, but strange.
    At a feast, a drunken man maundering in his cups
    Cries out that I am not my father's son!

    I contained myself that night, though I felt anger
    And a sinking heart. The next day I visited
255   My father and mother, and questioned them. They stormed,
    Calling it all the slanderous rant of a fool;
    And this relieved me. Yet the suspicion
    Remained always aching in my mind;
    I knew there was talk; I could not rest;
260   And finally, saying nothing to my parents,
    I went to the shrine at Delphi.
    The god dismissed my question without reply;
    He spoke of other things.
                 Some were clear,
    Full of wretchedness, dreadful, unbearable:
265   As, that I should lie with my own mother, breed
    Children from whom all men would turn their eyes;
    And that I should be my father's murderer.

    I heard all this, and fled. And from that day
    Corinth to me was only in the stars
270   Descending in that quarter of the sky,
    As I wandered farther and farther on my way
    To a land where I should never see the evil
    Sung by the oracle. And I came to this country
    Where, so you say, King Laïos was killed.

275   I will tell you all that happened there, my lady.

    There were three highways
    Coming together at a place I passed;
    And there a herald came towards me, and a chariot
    Drawn by horses, with a man such as you describe
280   Seated in it. The groom leading the horses
    Forced me off the road at his lord's command;
    But as this charioteer lurched over towards me
    I struck him in my rage. The old man saw me
    And brought his double goad down upon my head

As I came abreast.
He was paid back, and more!

285 Swinging my club in this right hand I knocked him
Out of his car, and he rolled on the ground.

I killed him.

I killed them all.
Now if that stranger and Laïos were—kin,
290 Where is a man more miserable than I?
More hated by the gods? Citizen and alien alike
Must never shelter me or speak to me—
I must be shunned by all.

And I myself

Pronounced this malediction upon myself!

295 Think of it: I have touched you with these hands,
These hands that killed your husband. What defilement!

Am I all evil, then? It must be so,
Since I must flee from Thebes, yet never again
See my own countrymen, my own country,
300 For fear of joining my mother in marriage
And killing Polybos, my father.

Ah,

If I was created so, born to this fate,
Who could deny the savagery of God?

O holy majesty of heavenly powers!
305 May I never see that day! Never!
Rather let me vanish from the race of men
Than know the abomination destined me!

CHORAGOS: We too, my lord, have felt dismay at this.
But there is hope: you have yet to hear the shepherd.
310 OEDIPUS: Indeed, I fear no other hope is left me.
IOCASTÊ: What do you hope from him when he comes?
OEDIPUS: This much:
If his account of the murder tallies with yours,
Then I am cleared.
IOCASTÊ: What was it that I said
Of such importance?
OEDIPUS: Why, "marauders," you said,
315 Killed the King, according to this man's story.
If he maintains that still, if there were several,
Clearly the guilt is not mine: I was alone.
But if he says one man, singlehanded, did it,
Then the evidence all points to me.
320 IOCASTÊ: You may be sure that he said there were several;
And can he call back that story now? He can not.

The whole city heard it as plainly as I.
But suppose he alters some detail of it:
He can not ever show that Laïos' death
325   Fulfilled the oracle: for Apollo said
My child was doomed to kill him; and my child—
Poor baby!—it was my child that died first.

No. From now on, where oracles are concerned,
I would not waste a second thought on any.
OEDIPUS: You may be right.
330   But come: let someone go
For the shepherd at once. This matter must be settled.
IOCASTÊ: I will send for him.
I would not wish to cross you in anything,
And surely not in this.—Let us go in.

Exeunt into the palace.

ODE II
Strophe 1

CHORUS: Let me be reverent in the ways of right,
Lowly the paths I journey on;
Let all my words and actions keep
The laws of the pure universe
5   From highest Heaven handed down.
For Heaven is their bright nurse,
Those generations of the realms of light;
Ah, never of mortal kind were they begot,
Nor are they slaves of memory, lost in sleep:
10   Their Father is greater than Time, and ages not.

Antistrophe 1

The tyrant is a child of Pride
Who drinks from his great sickening cup
Recklessness and vanity,
Until from his high crest headlong
15   He plummets to the dust of hope.
That strong man is not strong.
But let no fair ambition be denied;
May God protect the wrestler for the State
In government, in comely policy,
20   Who will fear God, and on His ordinance wait.

Strophe 2

Haughtiness and the high hand of disdain
Tempt and outrage God's holy law;
And any mortal who dares hold
No immortal Power in awe
25   Will be caught up in a net of pain:

The price for which his levity is sold.
Let each man take due earnings, then,
And keep his hands from holy things,
And from blasphemy stand apart—
30   Else the crackling blast of heaven
Blows on his head, and on his desperate heart;
Though fools will honor impious men,
In their cities no tragic poet sings.

Antistrophe 2

Shall we lose faith in Delphi's obscurities,
35   We who have heard the world's core
Discredited, and the sacred wood
Of Zeus at Elis praised no more?
The deeds and the strange prophecies
Must make a pattern yet to be understood.
40   Zeus, if indeed you are lord of all,
Throned in light over night and day,
Mirror this in your endless mind:
Our masters call the oracle
Words on the wind, and the Delphic vision blind!
45   Their hearts no longer know Apollo,
And reverence for the gods has died away.

SCENE III.

Enter Iocastê.

IOCASTÊ: Princes of Thebes, it has occurred to me
To visit the altars of the gods, bearing
These branches as a suppliant, and this incense.
Our King is not himself: his noble soul
5   Is overwrought with fantasies of dread,
Else he would consider
The new prophecies in the light of the old.
He will listen to any voice that speaks disaster,
And my advice goes for nothing.

She approaches the altar, right.

To you, then, Apollo,
10   Lycean lord, since you are nearest, I turn in prayer.
Receive these offerings, and grant us deliverance
From defilement. Our hearts are heavy with fear
When we see our leader distracted, as helpless sailors
Are terrified by the confusion of their helmsman.

Enter Messenger.

15   MESSENGER: Friends, no doubt you can direct me:
Where shall I find the house of Oedipus,
Or, better still, where is the King himself?

CHORAGOS: It is this very place, stranger; he is inside.
This is his wife and mother of his children.

20 MESSENGER: I wish her happiness in a happy house,
Blest in all the fulfillment of her marriage.

IOCASTÊ: I wish as much for you: your courtesy
Deserves a like good fortune. But now, tell me:
Why have you come? What have you to say to us?

25 MESSENGER: Good news, my lady, for your house and your husband.

IOCASTÊ: What news? Who sent you here?

MESSENGER: I am from Corinth.
The news I bring ought to mean joy for you,
Though it may be you will find some grief in it.

IOCASTÊ: What is it? How can it touch us in both ways?

30 MESSENGER: The people of Corinth, they say,
Intend to call Oedipus to be their king.

IOCASTÊ: But old Polybos—is he not reigning still?

MESSENGER: No. Death holds him in his sepulchre.

IOCASTÊ: What are you saying? Polybos is dead?

35 MESSENGER: If I am not telling the truth, may I die myself.

IOCASTÊ (to a Maidservant): Go in, go quickly; tell this to your master.

O riddlers of God's will, where are you now!
This was the man whom Oedipus, long ago,
Feared so, fled so, in dread of destroying him—
40 But it was another fate by which he died.

Enter Oedipus, center.

OEDIPUS: Dearest Iocastê, why have you sent for me?

IOCASTÊ: Listen to what this man says, and then tell me
What has become of the solemn prophecies.

OEDIPUS: Who is this man? What is his news for me?

45 IOCASTÊ: He has come from Corinth to announce your father's death!

OEDIPUS: Is it true, stranger? Tell me in your own words.

MESSENGER: I can not say it more clearly: the King is dead.

OEDIPUS: Was it by treason? Or by an attack or illness?

MESSENGER: A little thing brings old men to their rest.

OEDIPUS: It was sickness, then?

50 MESSENGER: Yes, and his many years.

OEDIPUS: Ah!
Why should a man respect the Pythian hearth°, or
Give heed to the birds that jangle above his head?
They prophesied that I should kill Polybos,
55 Kill my own father; but he is dead and buried,
And I am here—I never touched him, never,
Unless he died of grief for my departure,

---

⁵² *Pythian hearth:* the oracle at Delphi; its priestess was famous for her profound and sometimes enigmatic prophecies.

And thus, in a sense, through me. No. Polybos
Has packed the oracles off with him underground.
They are empty words.

60 IOCASTÊ: Had I not told you so?

OEDIPUS: You had; it was my faint heart that betrayed me.

IOCASTÊ: From now on never think of those things again.

OEDIPUS: And yet—must I not fear my mother's bed?

IOCASTÊ: Why should anyone in this world be afraid,

65   Since Fate rules us and nothing can be foreseen?
A man should live only for the present day.

Have no more fear of sleeping with your mother:
How many men, in dreams, have lain with their mothers!
No reasonable man is troubled by such things.

70 OEDIPUS: That is true; only—
If only my mother were not still alive!
But she is alive. I can not help my dread.

IOCASTÊ: Yet this news of your father's death is wonderful.

OEDIPUS: Wonderful. But I fear the living woman.

75 MESSENGER: Tell me, who is this woman that you fear?

OEDIPUS: It is Meropê, man; the wife of King Polybos.

MESSENGER: Meropê? Why should you be afraid of her?

OEDIPUS: An oracle of the gods, a dreadful saying.

MESSENGER: Can you tell me about it or are you sworn to silence?

80 OEDIPUS: I can tell you, and I will.
Apollo said through his prophet that I was the man
Who should marry his own mother, shed his father's blood
With his own hands. And so, for all these years
I have kept clear of Corinth, and no harm has come—

85   Though it would be have been sweet to see my parents again.

MESSENGER: And is this the fear that drove you out of Corinth?

OEDIPUS: Would you have me kill my father?

MESSENGER: As for that
You must be reassured by the news I gave you.

OEDIPUS: If you could reassure me, I would reward you.

90 MESSENGER: I had that in mind, I will confess: I thought
I could count on you when you returned to Corinth.

OEDIPUS: No: I will never go near my parents again.

MESSENGER: Ah, son, you still do not know what you are doing—

OEDIPUS: What do you mean? In the name of God tell me!

95 MESSENGER: —If these are your reasons for not going home.

OEDIPUS: I tell you, I fear the oracle may come true.

MESSENGER: And guilt may come upon you through your parents?

OEDIPUS: That is the dread that is always in my heart.

MESSENGER: Can you not see that all your fears are groundless?

100 OEDIPUS: How can you say that? They are my parents, surely?

MESSENGER: Polybos was not your father.

OEDIPUS: Not my father?

MESSENGER: No more your father than the man speaking to you.

OEDIPUS: But you are nothing to me!

MESSENGER: Neither was he.

OEDIPUS: Then why did he call me son?

MESSENGER: I will tell you:

105   Long ago he had you from my hands, as a gift.

OEDIPUS: Then how could he love me so, if I was not his?

MESSENGER: He had no children, and his heart turned to you.

OEDIPUS: What of you? Did you buy me? Did you find me by chance?

MESSENGER: I came upon you in the crooked pass of Kithairon.

OEDIPUS: And what were you doing there?

110   MESSENGER: Tending my flocks.

OEDIPUS: A wandering shepherd?

MESSENGER: But your savior, son, that day.

OEDIPUS: From what did you save me?

MESSENGER: Your ankles should tell you that.

OEDIPUS: Ah, stranger, why do you speak of that childhood pain?

MESSENGER: I cut the bonds that tied your ankles together.

115   OEDIPUS: I have had the mark as long as I can remember.

MESSENGER: That was why you were given the name you bear.

OEDIPUS: God! Was it my father or my mother who did it?
       Tell me!

MESSENGER: I do not know. The man who gave you to me
       Can tell you better than I.

120   OEDIPUS: It was not you that found me, but another?

MESSENGER: It was another shepherd gave you to me.

OEDIPUS: Who was he? Can you tell me who he was?

MESSENGER: I think he was said to be one of Laïos' people.

OEDIPUS: You mean the Laïos who was king here years ago?

125   MESSENGER: Yes; King Laïos; and the man was one of his herdsmen.

OEDIPUS: Is he still alive? Can I see him?

MESSENGER: These men here
       Know best about such things.

OEDIPUS: Does anyone here
       Know this shepherd that he is talking about?
       Have you seen him in the fields, or in the town?

130   If you have, tell me. It is time things were made plain.

CHORAGOS: I think the man he means is that same shepherd
       You have already asked to see. Iocastê perhaps
       Could tell you something.

OEDIPUS: Do you know anything
       About him, Lady? Is he the man we have summoned?
       Is that the man this shepherd means?

135   IOCASTÊ: Why think of him?
       Forget this herdsman. Forget it all.
       This talk is a waste of time.

OEDIPUS: How can you say that,
       When the clues to my true birth are in my hands?

IOCASTÊ: For God's love, let us have no more questioning!

140   Is your life nothing to you?

My own is pain enough for me to bear.
OEDIPUS: You need not worry. Suppose my mother a slave,
And born of slaves: no baseness can touch you.
IOCASTÊ: Listen to me, I beg you: do not do this thing!
145 OEDIPUS: I will not listen; the truth must be made known.
IOCASTÊ: Everything that I say is for your own good!
OEDIPUS: My own good
Snaps my patience, then; I want none of it.
IOCASTÊ: You are fatally wrong! May you never learn who you are!
OEDIPUS: Go, one of you, and bring the shepherd here.
150 Let us leave this woman to brag of her royal name.
IOCASTÊ: Ah, miserable!
That is the only word I have for you now.
That is the only word I can ever have.

Exit into the palace.

CHORAGOS: Why has she left us, Oedipus? Why has she gone
155 In such a passion of sorrow? I fear this silence:
Something dreadful may come of it.
OEDIPUS: Let it come!
However base my birth, I must know about it.
The Queen, like a woman, is perhaps ashamed
To think of my low origin. But I
160 Am a child of Luck; I can not be dishonored.
Luck is my mother; the passing months, my brothers,
Have seen me rich and poor.
                              If this is so,
How could I wish that I were someone else?
How could I not be glad to know my birth?

ODE III
Strophe

CHORUS: If ever the coming time were known
To my heart's pondering,
Kithairon, now by Heaven I see the torches
At the festival of the next full moon,
5 And see the dance, and hear the choir sing
A grace to your gentle shade:
Mountain where Oedipus was found,
O mountain guard of a noble race!
May the god who heals us lend his aid,
10 And let that glory come to pass
For our king's cradling-ground.

Antistrophe

Of the nymphs that flower beyond the years,
Who bore you, royal child,
To Pan of the hills or the timberline Apollo,
15 Cold in delight where the upland clears,

Or Hermês for whom Kyllenê's° heights are piled?
Or flushed as evening cloud,
Great Dionysos, roamer of mountains,
He—was it he who found you there,
20 And caught you up in his own proud
Arms from the sweet god-ravisher
Who laughed by the Muses' fountains?

SCENE IV.

OEDIPUS: Sirs: though I do not know the man,
   I think I see him coming, this shepherd we want:
   He is old, like our friend here, and the men
   Bringing him seem to be servants of my house.
5   But you can tell, if you have ever seen him.

Enter Shepherd escorted by servants.

CHORAGOS: I know him, he was Laïos' man. You can trust him.
OEDIPUS: Tell me first, you from Corinth: is this the shepherd
   We were discussing?
MESSENGER: This is the very man.
OEDIPUS *(to Shepherd)*: Come here. No, look at me. You must answer
10   Everything I ask—You belonged to Laïos?
SHEPHERD: Yes: born his slave, brought up in his house.
OEDIPUS: Tell me: what kind of work did you do for him?
SHEPHERD: I was a shepherd of his, most of my life.
OEDIPUS: Where mainly did you go for pasturage?
15 SHEPHERD: Sometimes Kithairon, sometimes the hills near-by.
OEDIPUS: Do you remember ever seeing this man out there?
SHEPHERD: What would he be doing there? This man?
OEDIPUS: This man standing here. Have you ever seen him before?
SHEPHERD: No. At least, not to my recollection.
20 MESSENGER: And that is not strange, my lord. But I'll refresh
   His memory: he must remember when we two
   Spent three whole seasons together, March to September,
   On Kithairon or thereabouts. He had two flocks;
   I had one. Each autumn I'd drive mine home
25   And he would go back with his to Laïos' sheepfold.—
   Is this not true, just as I have described it?
SHEPHERD: True, yes; but it was all so long ago.
MESSENGER: Well, then: do you remember, back in those days
   That you gave me a baby boy to bring up as my own?
30 SHEPHERD: What if I did? What are you trying to say?
MESSENGER: King Oedipus was once that little child.
SHEPHERD: Damn you, hold your tongue!

---

16 *Kyllenê*: birthplace of Hermês, the deities' messenger. The chorus assumes that this holy mountain
   was created in order to afford Hermês birth.

OEDIPUS: No more of that!
It is your tongue needs watching, not this man's.
SHEPHERD: My King, my Master, what is it I have done wrong?
35 OEDIPUS: You have not answered his question about the boy.
SHEPHERD: He does not know . . . He is only making trouble . . .
OEDIPUS: Come, speak plainly, or it will go hard with you.
SHEPHERD: In God's name, do not torture an old man!
OEDIPUS: Come here, one of you; bind his arms behind him.
40 SHEPHERD: Unhappy king! What more do you wish to learn?
OEDIPUS: Did you give this man the child he speaks of?
SHEPHERD: I did.
And I would to God I had died that very day.
OEDIPUS: You will die now unless you speak the truth.
SHEPHERD: Yet if I speak the truth, I am worse than dead.
45 OEDIPUS: Very well; since you insist upon delaying—
SHEPHERD: No! I have told you already that I gave him the boy.
OEDIPUS: Where did you get him? From your house? From somewhere
   else?
SHEPHERD: Not from mine, no. A man gave him to me.
OEDIPUS: Is that man here? Do you know whose slave he was?
50 SHEPHERD: For God's love, my King, do not ask me any more!
OEDIPUS: You are a dead man if I have to ask you again.
SHEPHERD: Then . . . Then the child was from the palace of Laïos.
OEDIPUS: A slave child? or a child of his own line?
SHEPHERD: Ah, I am on the brink of dreadful speech!
55 OEDIPUS: And I of dreadful hearing. Yet I must hear.
SHEPHERD: If you must be told, then . . .
                          They said it was Laïos' child,
But it is your wife who can tell you about that.
OEDIPUS: My wife!—Did she give it to you?
SHEPHERD: My lord, she did.
OEDIPUS: Do you know why?
SHEPHERD: I was told to get rid of it.
OEDIPUS: An unspeakable mother!
60 SHEPHERD: There had been prophecies . . .
OEDIPUS: Tell me.
SHEPHERD: It was said that the boy would kill his own father.
OEDIPUS: Then why did you give him over to this old man?
SHEPHERD: I pitied the baby, my King,
And I thought that this man would take him far away
To his own country.
65   He saved him—but for what a fate!
For if you are what this man says you are,
No man living is more wretched than Oedipus.
OEDIPUS: Ah God!
It was true!
          All the prophecies!
                          —Now,
70 O Light, may I look on you for the last time!

I, Oedipus,
Oedipus, damned in his birth, in his marriage damned,
Damned in the blood he shed with his own hand!

He rushes into the palace.

ODE IV
Strophe 1

CHORUS: Alas for the seed of men.

What measure shall I give these generations
That breathe on the void and are void
And exist and do not exist?

5   Who bears more weight of joy
Than mass of sunlight shifting in images,
Or who shall make his thought stay on
That down time drifts away?

Your splendor is all fallen.

10   O naked brow of wrath and tears,
O change of Oedipus!
I who saw your days call no man blest—
Your great days like ghósts góne.

Antistrophe 1

That mind was a strong bow.
15   Deep, how deep you drew it then, hard archer,
At a dim fearful range,
And brought dear glory down!

You overcame the stranger—
The virgin with her hooking lion claws—
20   And though death sang, stood like a tower
To make pale Thebes take heart.

Fortress against our sorrow!

Divine king, giver of laws,
Majestic Oedipus!
25   No prince in Thebes had ever such renown,
No prince won such grace of power.

Strophe 2

And now of all men ever known
Most pitiful is this man's story:
His fortunes are most changed, his state
30   Fallen to a low slave's
Ground under bitter fate.

O Oedipus, most royal one!
The great door that expelled you to the light
Gave at night—ah, gave night to your glory:
35   As to the father, to the fathering son.

All understood too late.

How could that queen whom Laïos won,
The garden that he harrowed at his height,
Be silent when that act was done?

Antistrophe 2

40   But all eyes fail before time's eye,
All actions come to justice there.
Though never willed, though far down the deep past,
Your bed, your dread sirings,
Are brought to book at last.
45   Child by Laïos doomed to die,
Then doomed to lose that fortunate little death,
Would God you never took breath in this air
That with my wailing lips I take to cry:

For I weep the world's outcast.

50   I was blind, and now I can tell why:
Asleep, for you had given ease of breath
To Thebes, while the false years went by.

EXODOS°

Enter, from the palace, Second Messenger.

SECOND MESSENGER: Elders of Thebes, most honored in this land,
What horrors are yours to see and hear, what weight
Of sorrow to be endured, if, true to your birth,
You venerate the line of Labdakos!
5   I think neither Istros nor Phasis, those great rivers,
Could purify this place of the corruption
It shelters now, or soon must bring to light—
Evil not done unconsciously, but willed.

The greatest griefs are those we cause ourselves.

10 CHORAGOS: Surely, friend, we have grief enough already;
What new sorrow do you mean?
SECOND MESSENGER: The Queen is dead.
CHORAGOS: Iocastê? Dead? But at whose hand?

Exodos: the resolution.

SECOND MESSENGER: Her own.
The full horror of what happened, you can not know,
For you did not see it; but I, who did, will tell you

15 As clearly as I can how she met her death.

When she had left us,
In passionate silence, passing through the court,
She ran to her apartment in the house,
Her hair clutched by the fingers of both hands.

20 She closed the doors behind her; then, by that bed
Where long ago the fatal son was conceived—
That son who should bring about his father's death—
We heard her call upon Laïos, dead so many years,
And heard her wail for the double fruit of her marriage,

25 A husband by her husband, children by her child.

Exactly how she died I do not know:
For Oedipus burst in moaning and would not let us
Keep vigil to the end: it was by him
As he stormed about the room that our eyes were caught.

30 From one to another of us he went, begging a sword,
Cursing the wife who was not his wife, the mother
Whose womb had carried his own children and himself.
I do not know: it was none of us aided him,
But surely one of the gods was in control!

35 For with a dreadful cry
He hurled his weight, as though wrenched out of himself,
At the twin doors: the bolts gave, and he rushed in.
And there we saw her hanging, her body swaying
From the cruel cord she had noosed about her neck.

40 A great sob broke from him, heartbreaking to hear,
As he loosed the rope and lowered her to the ground.

I would blot out from my mind what happened next!
For the King ripped from her gown the golden brooches
That were her ornament, and raised them, and plunged them down

45 Straight into his own eyeballs, crying, "No more,
No more shall you look on the misery about me,
The horrors of my own doing! Too long you have known
The faces of those whom I should never have seen,
Too long been blind to those for whom I was searching!

50 From this hour, go in darkness!" And as he spoke
He struck at his eyes—not once, but many times;
And the blood spattered his beard,
Bursting from his ruined sockets like red hail.
So from the unhappiness of two this evil has sprung,

55 A curse on the man and woman alike. The old
Happiness of the house of Labdakos
Was happiness enough: where is it today?

It is all wailing and ruin, disgrace, death—all
The misery of mankind that has a name—
60   And it is wholly and for ever theirs.
CHORAGOS: Is he in agony still? Is there no rest for him?
SECOND MESSENGER: He is calling for someone to lead him to the gates
So that all the children of Kadmos may look upon
His father's murderer, his mother's—no,
I can not say it!
65   And then he will leave Thebes,
Self-exiled, in order that the curse
Which he himself pronounced may depart from the house.
He is weak, and there is none to lead him,
So terrible is his suffering.
                              But you will see:
70   Look, the doors are opening; in a moment
You will see a thing that would crush a heart of stone.

The central door is opened; Oedipus, blinded, is led in.

CHORAGOS: Dreadful indeed for men to see.
Never have my own eyes
Looked on a sight so full of fear.

75   Oedipus!
What madness came upon you, what daemon
Leaped on your life with heavier
Punishment than a mortal man can bear?
No: I can not even
80   Look at you, poor ruined one.
And I would speak, question, ponder,
If I were able. No.
You make me shudder.
OEDIPUS: God. God.
85   Is there a sorrow greater?
Where shall I find harbor in this world?
My voice is hurled far on a dark wind.
What has God done to me?
CHORAGOS: Too terrible to think of, or to see.

Strophe 1

90   OEDIPUS: O cloud of night,
Never to be turned away: night coming on,
I can not tell how: night like a shroud!

My fair winds brought me here.
                              Oh God. Again
The pain of the spikes where I had sight,
95   The flooding pain
Of memory, never to be gouged out.

CHORAGOS: This is not strange.
    You suffer it all twice over, remorse in pain,
    Pain in remorse.

Antistrophe 1

100 OEDIPUS: Ah dear friend
    Are you faithful even yet, you alone?
    Are you still standing near me, will you stay here,
    Patient, to care for the blind?
                    The blind man!
    Yet even blind I know who it is attends me,
105   By the voice's tone—
    Though my new darkness hide the comforter.
    CHORAGOS: Oh fearful act!
    What god was it drove you to rake black
    Night across your eyes?

Strophe 2

110 OEDIPUS: Apollo. Apollo. Dear
    Children, the god was Apollo.
    He brought my sick, sick fate upon me.
    But the blinding hand was my own!
    How could I bear to see
115   When all my sight was horror everywhere?
    CHORAGOS: Everywhere; that is true.
    OEDIPUS: And now what is left?
    Images? Love? A greeting even,
    Sweet to the senses? Is there anything?
120   Ah, no, friends: lead me away.
    Lead me away from Thebes.
                    Lead the great wreck
    And hell of Oedipus, whom the gods hate.
    CHORAGOS: Your fate is clear, you are not blind to that.
    Would God you had never found it out!

Antistrophe 2

125 OEDIPUS: Death take the man who unbound
    My feet on that hillside
    And delivered me from death to life! What life?
    If only I had died,
    This weight of monstrous doom
130   Could not have dragged me and my darlings down.
    CHORAGOS: I would have wished the same.
    OEDIPUS: Oh never to have come here
    With my father's blood upon me! Never
    To have been the man they call his mother's husband!
135   Oh accurst! Oh child of evil,
    To have entered that wretched bed—
                    the selfsame one!

More primal than sin itself, this fell to me.

CHORAGOS: I do not know how I can answer you.
You were better dead than alive and blind.

140 OEDIPUS: Do not counsel me any more. This punishment
That I have laid upon myself is just.
If I had eyes,
I do not know how I could bear the sight
Of my father, when I came to the house of Death,
145 Or my mother: for I have sinned against them both
So vilely that I could not make my peace
By strangling my own life.

       Or do you think my children,
Born as they were born, would be sweet to my eyes?
Ah never, never! Nor this town with its high walls,
Nor the holy images of the gods.
150   For I,
Thrice miserable!—Oedipus, noblest of all the line
Of Kadmos, have condemned myself to enjoy
These things no more, by my own malediction
Expelling that man whom the gods declared
155 To be a defilement in the house of Laïos.
After exposing the rankness of my own guilt,
How could I look men frankly in the eyes?
No, I swear it,
If I could have stifled my hearing at its source,
160 I would have done it and made all this body
A tight cell of misery, blank to light and sound:
So I should have been safe in a dark agony
Beyond all recollection.

       Ah Kithairon!
Why did you shelter me? When I was cast upon you,
165 Why did I not die? Then I should never
Have shown the world my execrable birth.

Ah Polybos! Corinth, city that I believed
The ancient seat of my ancestors: how fair
I seemed, your child! And all the while this evil
Was cancerous within me!
170   For I am sick
In my daily life, sick in my origin.

O three roads, dark ravine, woodland and way
Where three roads met: you, drinking my father's blood,
My own blood, spilled by my own hand: can you remember
175 The unspeakable things I did there, and the things
I went on from there to do?

       O marriage, marriage!
The act that engendered me, and again the act
Performed by the son in the same bed—

                                                            Ah, the net
        Of incest, mingling fathers, brothers, sons,
180   With brides, wives, mothers: the last evil
        That can be known by men: no tongue can say
        How evil!
                        No. For the love of God, conceal me
        Somewhere far from Thebes; or kill me; or hurl me
        Into the sea, away from men's eyes for ever.

185   Come, lead me. You need not fear to touch me.
        Of all men, I alone can bear this guilt.

        Enter Creon.

        CHORAGOS: We are not the ones to decide; but Creon here
            May fitly judge of what you ask. He only
            Is left to protect the city in your place.
190   OEDIPUS: Alas, how can I speak to him? What right have I
            To beg his courtesy whom I have deeply wronged?
        CREON: I have not come to mock you, Oedipus,
            Or to reproach you, either.
            (To Attendants.)   —You, standing there:
            If you have lost all respect for man's dignity,
195   At least respect the flame of Lord Helios:
            Do not allow this pollution to show itself
            Openly here, an affront to the earth
            And Heaven's rain and the light of day. No, take him
            Into the house as quickly as you can.
200   For it is proper
            That only the close kindred see his grief.
        OEDIPUS: I pray you in God's name, since your courtesy
            Ignores my dark expectation, visiting
            With mercy this man of all men most execrable:
205   Give me what I ask—for your good, not for mine.
        CREON: And what is it that you would have me do?
        OEDIPUS: Drive me out of this country as quickly as may be
            To a place where no human voice can ever greet me.
        CREON: I should have done that before now—only,
210   God's will had not been wholly revealed to me.
        OEDIPUS: But his command is plain: the parricide
            Must be destroyed. I am that evil man.
        CREON: That is the sense of it, yes; but as things are,
            We had best discover clearly what is to be done.
215   OEDIPUS: You would learn more about a man like me?
        CREON: You are ready now to listen to the god.
        OEDIPUS: I will listen. But it is to you
            That I must turn for help. I beg you, hear me.

        The woman in there—
220   Give her whatever funeral you think proper:

She is your sister.
                              —But let me go, Creon!
Let me purge my father's Thebes of the pollution
Of my living here, and go out to the wild hills,
To Kithairon, that has won such fame with me,
225   The tomb my mother and father appointed for me,
And let me die there, as they willed I should.
And yet I know
Death will not ever come to me through sickness
Or in any natural way: I have been preserved
230   For some unthinkable fate. But let that be.
As for my sons, you need not care for them.
They are men, they will find some way to live.
But my poor daughters, who have shared my table,
Who never before have been parted from their father—
235   Take care of them, Creon; do this for me.
And will you let me touch them with my hands
A last time, and let us weep together?
Be kind, my lord,
Great prince, be kind!
                              Could I but touch them,
240   They would be mine again, as when I had my eyes.

Enter Antigone and Ismene, attended.

Ah, God!
Is it my dearest children I hear weeping?
Has Creon pitied me and sent my daughters?
CREON: Yes, Oedipus: I knew that they were dear to you
245   In the old days, and you know you must love them still.
OEDIPUS: May God bless you for this—and be a friendlier
Guardian to you than he has been to me!

Children, where are you?
Come quickly to my hands: they are your brother's—
250   Hands that have brought your father's once clear eyes
To this way of seeing—
                              Ah dearest ones,
I had neither sight nor knowledge then, your father
By the woman who was the source of his own life!
And I weep for you—having no strength to see you—
255   I weep for you when I think of the bitterness
That men will visit upon you all your lives.
What homes, what festivals can you attend
Without being forced to depart again in tears?
And when you come to marriageable age,
260   Where is the man, my daughters, who would dare
Risk the bane that lies on all my children?
Is there any evil wanting? Your father killed

His father; sowed the womb of her who bore him;
Engendered you at the fount of his own existence!
That is what they will say of you.

265
                                Then, whom
Can you ever marry? There are no bridegrooms for you,
And your lives must wither away in sterile dreaming.
O Creon, son of Menoikeus!
You are the only father my daughters have,
270
Since we, their parents, are both of us gone for ever.
They are your own blood: you will not let them
Fall into beggary and loneliness;
You will keep them from the miseries that are mine!
Take pity on them; see, they are only children,
275
Friendless except for you. Promise me this,
Great Prince, and give me your hand in token of it.

Creon clasps his right hand.

Children:
I could say much, if you could understand me,
But as it is, I have only this prayer for you:
280
Live where you can, be as happy as you can—
Happier, please God, than God has made your father!
CREON: Enough. You have wept enough. Now go within.
OEDIPUS: I must; but it is hard.
CREON: Time eases all things.
OEDIPUS: But you must promise—
CREON: Say what you desire.
OEDIPUS: Send me from Thebes!
285 CREON: God grant that I may!
OEDIPUS: But since God hates me . . .
CREON: No, he will grant your wish.
OEDIPUS: You promise?
CREON: I can not speak beyond my knowledge.
OEDIPUS: Then lead me in.
CREON: Come now, and leave your children.
OEDIPUS: No! Do not take them from me!
CREON: Think no longer
290
That you are in command here, but rather think
How, when you were, you served your own destruction.

Exeunt into the house all but the Chorus; the Choragos chants directly to the audience.

CHORAGOS: Men of Thebes: look upon Oedipus.

This is the king who solved the famous riddle
And towered up, most powerful of men.
295
No mortal eyes but looked on him with envy,
Yet in the end ruin swept over him.
Let every man in mankind's frailty

Consider his last day; and let none
Presume on his good fortune until he find
300   Life, at his death, a memory without pain.

Questions

1. What does the exposition tell us about Oedipus's virtues as a ruler?
2. What does Creon tell us about the murder of Laïos? How does this help to define the dramatic situation?
3. Why doesn't Teiresias answer Oedipus immediately? Does his delay add to the suspense of the rising action?
4. Why does Oedipus suspect Creon (p. 945)? Is this suspicion justified, or rash? What defects of character does Oedipus reveal in this scene with Teiresias? In the rest of the rising action?
5. What is Iocastê's approach to the quarrel between Oedipus and Creon? What does this tell you about her character?
6. In his scene with Iocastê (page 953), Oedipus's mood changes radically from rage to terror. Can you pinpoint the speech where this change occurs? What causes the change?
7. Oedipus returns briefly to exposition as he recalls his youth and the murder to the strangers at the crossroads (pp. 955–56). This speech, in light of other evidence, points to his guilt. Only one piece of the puzzle is missing. What is it? Who can provide the missing piece?
8. How does the chorus judge Oedipus in Ode II? How do they respond to the action thereafter?
9. What are the two major scenes of the falling action? Tell how each brings Oedipus closer to catastrophe.
10. The messenger is bringing news he believes will cheer Oedipus, but it has the opposite effect. This is an instance of dramatic irony, wherein a character's actions have unforseen results. Can you find other examples of dramatic irony in Oedipus Rex?
11. Oedipus's recognition of his guilt completes the falling action and begins the final movement of the plot, the catastrophe. Pinpoint the "recognition" speech.
12. Of the major events of the catastrophe, some occur onstage and some offstage. What are the major events of the catastrophe? Which is the most terrifying? Which is the most pathetic? How do these scenes answer the dramatic questions posed in the exposition?
13. What is Oedipus's tragic flaw, his frailty of character? To what extent is this flaw responsible for his downfall?
14. Could Oedipus have avoided his fate? How?

Suggestions for Dramatists

1. Read the front page of your daily newspaper looking for stories in which a character is faced with a definite dramatic situation. Describe that situation in terms of the character, his or her objective, and the obstacle.
2. Do you have friends or relatives, middle-aged or older, whose fortunes have changed considerably, from good to bad, or from bad to good? Was the change owing to their own actions, or to circumstances beyond their control? Select a familiar character who

has had some control over his or her own destiny. What was this character's ambition? Were there significant obstacles? Did he or she overcome them?

Try to think of a particular incident that was the turning point in this character's career. Describe it. Was there a single moment at which this character faced a decision that sealed his or her fate? Describe it. Now, considering this as the climax of your drama, describe the scenes that led up to it, and the scenes that resulted from it.

3. Which of the stories in the Fiction section of this book would lend itself to the theater? Which ones would be impossible to stage? Remember that there can be few changes of scene, and a limited number of characters. Choose a story you believe would be stageworthy, and write a scenario for it, describing the five-act structure, and the entrances and exits of characters. Then begin writing the dialogue.

 Writers on Writing   *Arthur Miller on Oedipus Rex*

> *Tragedy, called a more exalted kind of consciousness, is so called because it makes us aware of what a man might have been. But to say or strongly imply what a man might have been requires of the author a soundly based, completely believed vision of man's great possibilities. . . . Tragedy, therefore, is inseparable from a certain modest hope regarding the human animal. And it is the glimpse of this brighter possibility that raises sadness out of the pathetic toward the tragic. . . .*

 Tips for Writing about Action

1. We are familiar with the old saying, "Actions speak louder than words." But sometimes the words in a play are so full of impact that they amount to an action, as when Maurya in *Riders to the Sea* "curses" her son by refusing to confer her blessing upon him. As you write about the action of a play, never forget that strong words can have the effect of an action.

2. It is helpful, in reconstructing the action of a play, to write down its most vivid scenes in the order in which you remember them. Then figure out where the vivid scenes belong in Freytag's pyramid of action, if at all. There are fine plays that do not fit the classic mold, though most do.

3. Usually the climax of emotion in a play is not the climax of the action. It is easier to determine what scene of a play most moves the audience. When you have determined the climax of emotion (which is always toward the end of the play, in the catastrophe or denouement) look for the climax of action prior to it, where the hero or heroine makes the critical decision that leads to disaster (in tragedy) or success (in comedy).

5 ❧ Heroes and Heroines— Dramatic Character

When talking about someone's virtues we often say that he or she is someone of "character," meaning good character rather than bad, for the word when used in that way is always complimentary. When we refer to a person in a play as a *character* we get closer to the general and intrinsic meaning of the word. For character is really personality, that special combination of good and bad qualities that makes a person different from all others.

Character shapes our fate. A man born with great speed, eyesight, and determination might become a rich and famous baseball player, while his brother, possessing all those virtues except determination, becomes a pickpocket. The shy child may learn in solitude the art of making great paintings, while her outgoing sister becomes a senator. Cyrano de Bergerac, cursed with a monstrous nose, becomes a valiant fighter in defense of it. Likewise, the actions of a play arise from its major characters. *Oedipus Rex* is very much the play of Oedipus's character, the proud man who must live out a terrible prophecy. His character is his fate, and it would be hard to imagine the events of that play befalling anyone else.

What makes a great dramatic character? What kinds of characters lend themselves to presentation in a stage play? As we suggested in our introduction, any character who can sustain the interest of a live audience has dramatic potential. To understand what makes a great dramatic character, it is helpful to reconsider the dynamics of the dramatic situation. A *character* has an *objective*, but some *obstacle* stands in the way. That is, the character wants something. The great heroes and heroines of dramatic literature may have nothing else in common; they may vary enormously in wisdom, beauty, pride, and power, but they all share one characteristic. They have enormous desires. It is desire that creates the dramatic situation, and desire that drives the rising action. In *Riders to the Sea*, Maurya desperately wants Bartley to stay home. Bartley's desire to sail to

Connemara is equally desperate. If either of them were half-hearted, the play would not work. Oedipus's desire to find and punish the murderer of Laïos is absolute, larger than life. We have the feeling that he would move heaven and earth to solve the crime.

It is this, chiefly, that distinguishes a great dramatic character from his counterpart in fiction: this strong desire, and a disposition inclined to act upon one's desires rather than deliberate upon them. Some great heroes and heroines of fiction—Don Quixote, Carmen, Huck Finn—have dramatic desires, and when they do they usually find their way to the stage. Others, beset by boredom or paralyzed by conflicting desires, like the heroes of Dostoyevski's *Notes From The Underground* and Salinger's *Catcher In The Rye*, are impossible to depict on the stage because their characters manifest themselves in thought rather than action. One of the fascinations of Hamlet is that he is an intensely meditative character whose desire forces him to act. It has been suggested that the play would make a good novel.

Virtues and Flaws

Aristotle says that the hero of a tragedy should be good. Clearly, if the character is not "good" in some way, we will not care what happens to him or her, and the play will not hold our interest. Oedipus is arrogant and overbearing, yet his motivation is moral: he wants the best for his people. In the play you are about to read, the central character, Amanda Wingfield, has some unappealing qualities, but we sympathize with her because she is striving to do the best for her children. Characters with dramatic desires are not likely to be perfect. Yet if they do not have some virtue they are neither believable nor appealing. Even Richard III, Shakespeare's desperate villain who kills every man, woman, and child who stands between him and the throne, charms us with his wit, his courage, and his self-honesty.

The great characters of tragedy and comedy have admirable strengths, but they also have some *flaw* that gets them into trouble. The sooner we, as readers, recognize the flaw, the sooner we can appreciate the dramatic character. Since the flaw of the central character is frequently the cause of the play's *problem*, we may look for it in the exposition. Amanda Wingfield, who has such admirable energy and intentions, has a dreadful character flaw, evident in the first scenes of *The Glass Menagerie*. She wants to live her children's lives for them, and believes she can.

Heroes, Heroines, Villains, and Others

The central character in a drama is called the *protagonist*. Most classical plays have a single protagonist from whom the play takes its name, and from whose character the plot takes its course. Other plays, like *Romeo and Juliet*, may have two or three characters who share the spotlight and the sympathies of the audience, and it is fair to call these actors protagonists. Plays without obvious protagonists, where the interest is diffused among several characters, as in Chekhov's *The Cherry Orchard,* are called plays of *atmosphere.*

We use the terms *hero* and *heroine* somewhat loosely and romantically to refer to protagonists who win our admiration or affection. The word *hero* has a military origin; strictly speaking, it ought to be reserved for those protagonists who display the virtues of courage and fortitude in the face of physical danger. Likewise with the term *heroine.* However, there are so many dramas that do not place their protagonists in such peril that a strict respect of word origins would deprive us of two handy terms.

The *antagonist* of a drama, sometimes called the *villain,* is the character who opposes the protagonist. When we hear the word "villain" we think of a sly man in black hat and cape, sneering and twirling his mustache. This image comes from *melodrama,* a sensational form of nineteenth-century drama where organ music accompanied the action, where the hero was handsome and fearless, the heroine beautiful and helpless, and the villain evil incarnate. The villain of a stage play, however, need not be rotten through and through. Villains tend to be more interesting when they have understandable human motives, like Hamlet's uncle, King Claudius, who opposes Hamlet in order to preserve his kingdom and the peace. In order to appreciate the villains of drama, we must consider carefully their motives.

Villainy as a principle of drama does not always reside in a single character. Many plays have no villains as such. *Riders to the Sea* and *Oedipus Rex* are cases in which we must search for the principle of evil, or villainy, in the protagonists. We have seen how Oedipus stands in the way of his own efforts to rid Thebes of the plague. He is the villain of his own drama. In *The Glass Menagerie,* Amanda, the protagonist in the major action, causes her children more grief than the Gentleman Caller who foils her plans for happiness.

Dramatic characters, like real people, are a fascinating mixture of good and bad qualities. We must not be hasty to label them as heroes or villains. As serious readers, we do the greatest justice to characters by carefully examining their motives, their strengths, and their weaknesses.

In most plays there are characters whose fate is incidental to the major action. These are the *minor* or *supporting characters.* The sisters in *Riders to the Sea,* Creon and Teiresias in *Oedipus Rex,* and the choruses of both plays, are all supporting characters. They help to forward the action, but they are neither the cause nor the major victims of it. One could imagine the story being told without them. Playwrights use minor characters for contrast, enrichment, and comic relief.

Stock characters, more frequent in comedy and melodrama, are those whose qualities are so exaggerated and common that they represent a *type* of human nature. The bragging soldier, the stingy old man, the shrewish housewife, and the lovesick adolescent have lasting and universal appeal. Such characters begin to appear in the comedies of Menander in the fourth century B.C. The commedia dell'arte, an Italian theatrical genre dating from the mid-sixteenth century, dramatized hundreds of different comedies with the same stock characters. These characters reappear in movies and television, and sometimes as supporting figures in serious drama.

Actions and Words

In the theater actions speak louder than words. As readers we may be greatly impressed with a character's speeches. But we must carefully consider the character's words in the light of what he is doing, his actions in the particular scene. This is one of the keys to reading dramatic character. Oedipus *says* that he will find the murderer of Laïos. But as soon as the prophet tells Oedipus he himself is the murderer, Oedipus begins avoiding the issue, accusing Creon of treason. Here the contradiction between word and deed points to Oedipus's flaw, his pride. In the first scene of *The Glass Menagerie*, Amanda may sound as though she is giving her son good advice, and her daughter kind attention. Actually, she is spoiling her son's dinner and hurting her daughter's feelings. This contrast between words and actions indicates a flaw in Amanda's character, her self-absorption and insensitivity to her children's feelings. Her cruelty probably is not intentional.

But sometimes dramatic characters are intentionally deceitful, and we can tell because their actions betray their words. Rosencrantz and Guildenstern appear to be warm and charming friends of Prince Hamlet. They flatter him and offer to serve him. But, remember, these charming fellows have been paid by the King to spy on their old friend. They are contemptible scoundrels. On the other hand, we have Hamlet's true friend Horatio, perhaps the play's most virtuous character, whose words and deeds are always of a piece.

Dramatic irony is often the result of the discrepancy between speech and action, as in the scene between Oedipus and the Messenger. All of the information the Messenger relates to relieve Oedipus brings him more grief. In *The Glass Menagerie* the misguided Gentleman Caller, who says he is being sincere and trying to build up poor Laura's confidence, is actually dealing her a dreadful blow. We have all been in situations where our noblest intentions and plans backfire.

Dramatic Diction and Character

In drama, as in life, a character's language is very revealing. Well-educated people are likely to be more eloquent than those from less-privileged backgrounds, and use longer words and more complex sentences. Businessmen and military officers, whose success depends upon maximum efficiency, tend toward clipped, direct language without ornamentation, while imaginative people use more figures of speech. Craftsmen and laborers employ the special jargon of their trades. Often we can tell someone's place of origin by his or her accent.

Playwrights know the relation of speech to character. Whether they write in formal verse or realistic prose, their diction suits the characters and can tell us a great deal about them. Oedipus speaks in long and stately sentences. His rhythms and words befit a king. Teiresias speaks poetically, in mysterious, unfinished sentences, the perfect style for a prophet. The Messenger and the Shepherd speak in the simple words of peasants.

Each time you are introduced to new dramatic characters, see how much you can find out about them from their manner of speech.

A Drama of Character: *The Glass Menagerie*

We praise some dramas for their ingenuity of plot, others for their rich and appealing characters. The plot of *Oedipus Rex*, with its classic rise and fall, its complications and its catastrophe worked out with watchlike precision, is considered one of the greatest plots of all time. The play you are about to read, like many twentieth-century dramas, is admired more for its characters than its plot, though the plot is quite serviceable and will hold up under classic analysis.

Tennessee Williams's play *The Glass Menagerie* has three major characters and one minor character, minor only in the sense that he has fewer lines and a smaller part in the action. All four of the characters—Amanda Wingfield, the mother; Tom and Laura, her children; and the Gentleman Caller who briefly enters their lives—are fully drawn, credible, and sympathetic figures, with the strengths and weaknesses we have come to look for in dramatic characters. We call Amanda the protagonist because she is responsible for the major action of the plot, the pursuit of the Gentleman Caller. But our sympathies lie at least as much with Tom, the young poet who works long hours in a factory to support the family, and with the frail Laura, who is the victim of her mother's ambitions.

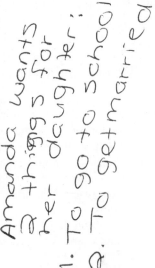

Laurette Taylor as Amanda in *The Glass Menagerie* (*Culver Pictures, Inc.*)

Amanda wants things for her daughter:
1. To go to school
2. To get married

By the end of the play we have come to care so much about all three of these characters that all of their fates concern us equally.

The Glass Menagerie, first performed in 1944, is a relatively recent addition to the dramatic literature that includes *Oedipus Rex.* One of many great intervening developments was the Moscow Art Theatre, a naturalistic repertory group that produced the plays of Anton Chekhov (1860–1904). His plays de-emphasized the fate of the protagonist, dividing the dramatic interest among several compelling, realistic characters. Williams's play shows the influence of Chekhov.

Tennessee Williams is considered by many to be America's most important playwright of the post-World War II era. *The Glass Menagerie* won the New York Drama Critic's Circle Award. Two other plays, *A Streetcar Named Desire* (1947) and *Cat On A Hot Tin Roof* (1955), won Pulitzer prizes; these and several other of his dramas have been made into movies starring such actors and actresses as Marlon Brando, Elizabeth Taylor, and Paul Newman.

TENNESSEE WILLIAMS (1911–1983)

The Glass Menagerie

CHARACTERS

AMANDA WINGFIELD, *the mother.*

A little woman of great but confused vitality clinging frantically to another time and place. Her characterization must be carefully created, not copied from type. She is not paranoiac, but her life is paranoia. There is much to admire in AMANDA, and as much to love and pity as there is to laugh at. Certainly she has endurance and a kind of heroism, and though her foolishness makes her unwittingly cruel at times, there is tenderness in her slight person.

LAURA WINGFIELD, *her daughter.*

AMANDA, having failed to establish contact with reality, continues to live vitally in her illusions, but LAURA's situation is even graver. A childhood illness has left her crippled, one leg slightly shorter than the other, and held in a brace. This defect need not be more than suggested on the stage. Stemming from this, LAURA's separation increases till she is like a piece of her own glass collection, too exquisitely fragile to move from the shelf.

TOM WINGFIELD, *her son, and the narrator of the play.*

A poet with a job in a warehouse. His nature is not remorseless, but to escape from a trap he has to act without pity.

JIM O'CONNOR, *the gentleman caller.*

A nice, ordinary, young man.

SCENE. *An alley in St. Louis.*
Part I: *Preparation for a Gentleman Caller.*
Part II: *The Gentleman Calls.*
Time: *Now and the Past.*

SCENE I.

The Wingfield apartment is in the rear of the building, one of those vast hive-like conglomerations of cellular living-units that flower as warty growths in overcrowded urban centers of lower middle-class population and are symptomatic of the impulse of this largest and fundamentally enslaved section of American society to avoid fluidity and differentiation and to exist and function as one interfused mass of automatism.

The apartment faces an alley and is entered by a fire-escape, a structure whose name is a touch of accidental poetic truth, for all of these huge buildings are always burning with the slow and implacable fires of human desperation. The fire-escape is included in the set—that is, the landing of it and steps descending from it.

The scene is memory and is therefore nonrealistic. Memory takes a lot of poetic license. It omits some details; others are exaggerated, according to the emotional value of the articles it touches, for memory is seated predominantly in the heart. The interior is therefore rather dim and poetic.

At the rise of the curtain, the audience is faced with the dark, grim rear wall of the Wingfield tenement. This building, which runs parallel to the footlights, is flanked on both sides by dark, narrow alleys which run into murky canyons of tangled clotheslines, garbage cans and the sinister latticework of neighboring fire-escapes. It is up and down these side alleys that exterior entrances and exits are made, during the play. At the end of TOM's *opening commentary, the dark tenement wall slowly reveals (by means of a transparency) the interior of the ground floor Wingfield apartment.*

Downstage is the living room, which also serves as a sleeping room for LAURA, *the sofa unfolding to make her bed. Upstage, center, and divided by a wide arch or second pro-scenium with transparent faded portieres (or second curtain), is the dining room. In an old-fashioned what-not in the living room are seen scores of transparent glass animals. A blown-up photograph of the father hangs on the wall of the living room, facing the audience, to the left of the archway. It is the face of a very handsome young man in a doughboy's First World War cap. He is gallantly smiling, ineluctably smiling, as if to say, "I will be smiling forever."*

The audience hears and sees the opening scene in the dining room through both the transparent fourth wall of the building and the transparent gauze portieres of the dining-room arch. It is during this revealing scene that the fourth wall slowly ascends, out of sight. This transparent exterior wall is not brought down again until the very end of the play, during TOM's *final speech.*

The narrator is an undisguised convention of the play. He takes whatever license with dramatic convention as is convenient to his purposes.

TOM *enters dressed as a merchant sailor from alley, stage left, and strolls across the front of the stage to the fire-escape. There he stops and lights a cigarette. He addresses the audience.*

TOM   Yes, I have tricks in my pocket, I have things up my sleeve. But I am the opposite of a stage magician. He gives you illusion that has the appearance of truth. I give you truth in the pleasant disguise of illusion. To begin with, I turn back time. I reverse it to that quaint period, the thirties, when the huge middle class of America was matriculating in a school for the blind. Their eyes had failed them, or they had failed their eyes, and so they were having their fingers pressed forcibly down on the fiery Braille alphabet of a dissolving economy. In Spain there was revolution. Here there was only shouting and confusion. In Spain there was Guernica.[1] Here there were disturbances of labor, sometimes pretty violent, in otherwise peaceful cities such as Chicago, Cleveland, Saint Louis. . . . This is the social background of the play.

(MUSIC.)

---

[1] Basque town infamously bombed by German planes supporting the rebels during the Spanish Civil War.

The play is memory. Being a memory play, it is dimly lighted, it is sentimental, it is not realistic. In memory everything seems to happen to music. That explains the fiddle in the wings. I am the narrator of the play, and also a character in it. The other characters are my mother, Amanda, my sister, Laura, and a gentleman caller who appears in the final scenes. He is the most realistic character in the play, being an emissary from a world of reality that we were somehow set apart from. But since I have a poet's weakness for symbols, I am using this character also as a symbol; he is the long delayed but always expected something that we live for. There is a fifth character in the play who doesn't appear except in this larger-than-life photograph over the mantel. This is our father who left us a long time ago. He was a telephone man who fell in love with long distances; he gave up his job with the telephone company and skipped the light fantastic out of town. . . . The last we heard of him was a picture post-card from Mazatlan, on the Pacific coast of Mexico, containing a message of two words—"Hello—Good-bye!" and an address. I think the rest of the play will explain itself. . . .

AMANDA's *voice becomes audible through the portieres.*

(LEGEND ON SCREEN: "OÙ SONT LES NEIGES."[2])

He divides the portieres and enters the upstage area.

AMANDA *and* LAURA *are seated at a drop-leaf table. Eating is indicated by gestures without food or utensils.* AMANDA *faces the audience.* TOM *and* LAURA *are seated in profile.*

The interior has lit up softly and through the scrim we see AMANDA *and* LAURA *seated at the table in the upstage area.*

AMANDA *(calling)* Tom?

TOM Yes, Mother.

AMANDA We can't say grace until you come to the table!

TOM Coming, Mother. *(He bows slightly and withdraws, reappearing a few moments later in his place at the table.)*

AMANDA *(to her son)* Honey, don't *push* with your *fingers.* If you have to push with something, the thing to push with is a crust of bread. And chew—chew! Animals have sections in their stomachs which enable them to digest food without mastication, but human beings are supposed to chew their food before they swallow it down. Eat food leisurely, son, and really enjoy it. A well-cooked meal has lots of delicate flavors that have to be held in the mouth for appreciation. So chew your food and give your salivary glands a chance to function!

TOM *deliberately lays his imaginary fork down and pushes his chair back from the table.*

TOM I haven't enjoyed one bite of this dinner because of your constant directions on how to eat it. It's you that makes me rush through meals with your hawk-like attention to every bite I take. Sickening—spoils my appetite—all this discussion of animals' secretion—salivary glands—mastication!

AMANDA *(lightly)* Temperament like a Metropolitan star! *(He rises and crosses downstage.)* You're not excused from the table.

TOM I am getting a cigarette.

---

[2] *Où sont les neiges:* line from a poem by François Villon, "Where are the snows of yesteryear," concerning the yearning for past glory.

AMANDA You smoke too much.

LAURA *rises.*

LAURA I'll bring in the blancmange.

He remains standing with his cigarette by the portieres during the following.

AMANDA *(rising)* No, sister, no, sister—you be the lady this time and I'll be the darky.
LAURA I'm already up.
AMANDA Resume your seat, little sister—I want you to stay fresh and pretty—for gentlemen callers!
LAURA I'm not expecting any gentlemen callers.
AMANDA *(crossing out to kitchenette. Airily)* Sometimes they come when they are least expected! Why, I remember one Sunday afternoon in Blue Mountain—*(Enters kitchenette.)*
TOM I know what's coming!
LAURA Yes. But let her tell it.
TOM Again?
LAURA She loves to tell it.

AMANDA *returns with bowl of dessert.*

AMANDA One Sunday afternoon in Blue Mountain—your mother received—*seventeen!*—gentlemen callers! Why, sometimes there weren't chairs enough to accommodate them all. We had to send the nigger over to bring in folding chairs from the parish house.
TOM *(remaining at portieres)* How did you entertain those gentlemen callers?
AMANDA I understood the art of conversation!
TOM I bet you could talk.
AMANDA Girls in those days *knew* how to talk, I can tell you.
TOM Yes?

(IMAGE: AMANDA AS A GIRL ON A PORCH GREETING CALLERS.)

AMANDA They knew how to entertain their gentlemen callers. It wasn't enough for a girl to be possessed of a pretty face and a graceful figure—although I wasn't slighted in either respect. She also needed to have a nimble wit and a tongue to meet all occasions.
TOM What did you talk about?
AMANDA Things of importance going on in the world! Never anything coarse or common or vulgar. *(She addresses* TOM *as though he were seated in the vacant chair at the table though he remains by portieres. He plays this scene as though he held the book.*[3]*)* My callers were gentlemen—all! Among my callers were some of the most prominent young planters of the Mississippi Delta—planters and sons of planters!

TOM *motions for music and a spot of light on* AMANDA.
Her eyes lift, her face glows, her voice becomes rich and elegiac.

(SCREEN LEGEND: "OÙ SONT LES NEIGES.")

There was young Champ Laughlin who later became vice-president of the Delta Planters Bank. Hadley Stevenson who was drowned in Moon Lake and left his widow

---

[3] Prompt-book, script.

one hundred and fifty thousand in Government bonds. There were the Cutrere brothers, Wesley and Bates. Bates was one of my bright particular beaux! He got in a quarrel with that wild Wainright boy. They shot it out on the floor of Moon Lake Casino. Bates was shot through the stomach. Died in the ambulance on his way to Memphis. His widow was also well-provided for, came into eight or ten thousand acres, that's all. She married him on the rebound—never loved her—carried my picture on him the night he died! And there was that boy that every girl in the Delta had set her cap for! That beautiful, brilliant young Fitzhugh boy from Green County!

TOM What did he leave his widow?

AMANDA He never married! Gracious, you talk as though all of my old admirers had turned up their toes to the daisies!

TOM Isn't this the first you mentioned that still survives?

AMANDA That Fitzhugh boy went North and made a fortune—came to be known as the Wolf of Wall Street! He had the Midas touch, whatever he touched turned to gold! And I could have been Mrs. Duncan J. Fitzhugh, mind you! But—I picked your *father!*

LAURA *(rising)* Mother, let me clear the table.

AMANDA No, dear, you go in front and study your typewriter chart. Or practice your shorthand a little. Stay fresh and pretty—It's almost time for our gentlemen callers to start arriving. *(She flounces girlishly toward the kitchenette.)* How many do you suppose we're going to entertain this afternoon?

TOM *throws down the paper and jumps up with a groan.*

LAURA *(alone in the dining room)* I don't believe we're going to receive any, Mother.

AMANDA *(reappearing, airily)* What? No one—not one? You must be joking! (LAURA *nervously echoes her laugh. She slips in a fugitive manner through the half-open portieres and draws them gently behind her. A shaft of very clear light is thrown on her face against the faded tapestry of the curtains.* MUSIC: "THE GLASS MENAGERIE" UNDER FAINTLY. *Lightly.)* Not one gentleman caller? It can't be true! There must be a flood, there must have been a tornado!

LAURA It isn't a flood, it's not a tornado, Mother. I'm just not popular like you were in Blue Mountain. . . . *(*TOM *utters another groan.* LAURA *glances at him with a faint, apologetic smile. Her voice catching a little.)* Mother's afraid I'm going to be an old maid.

(THE SCENE DIMS OUT WITH "GLASS MENAGERIE" MUSIC.)

SCENE II. *"Laura, Haven't You Ever Liked Some Boy?"*

On the dark stage the screen is lighted with the image of blue roses.
    Gradually LAURA's *figure becomes apparent and the screen goes out.*
    The music subsides.
    LAURA *is seated in the delicate ivory chair at the small claw-foot table.*
    She wears a dress of soft violet material for a kimono—her hair tied back from her forehead with a ribbon.
    She is washing and polishing her collection of glass.
    AMANDA *appears on the fire-escape steps. At the sound of her ascent,* LAURA *catches her breath, thrusts the bowl of ornaments away and seats herself stiffly before the diagram of the typewriter keyboard as though it held her spellbound. Something has happened to* AMANDA. *It is written in her face as she climbs to the landing: a look that is grim and hopeless and a little absurd.*

She has on one of those cheap or imitation velvety-looking cloth coats with imitation fur collar. Her hat is five or six years old, one of those dreadful cloche hats that were worn in the late twenties and she is clasping an enormous black patent-leather pocketbook with nickel clasp and initials. This is her full-dress outfit, the one she usually wears to the D.A.R.[4]

Before entering she looks through the door.

She purses her lips, opens her eyes wide, rolls them upward, and shakes her head.

Then she slowly lets herself in the door. Seeing her mother's expression LAURA *touches her lips with a nervous gesture.*

LAURA Hello, Mother, I was—(*She makes a nervous gesture toward the chart on the wall.* AMANDA *leans against the shut door and stares at* LAURA *with a martyred look.*)

AMANDA Deception? Deception? (*She slowly removes her hat and gloves, continuing the swift suffering stare. She lets the hat and gloves fall on the floor—a bit of acting.*)

LAURA (*shakily*) How was the D.A.R. meeting? (AMANDA *slowly opens her purse and removes a dainty white handkerchief which she shakes out delicately and delicately touches to her lips and nostrils.*) Didn't you go to the D.A.R. meeting, Mother?

AMANDA (*faintly, almost inaudibly*) —No.—No. (*Then more forcibly.*) I did not have the strength—to go to the D.A.R. In fact, I did not have the courage! I wanted to find a hole in the ground and hide myself in it forever! (*She crosses slowly to the wall and removes the diagram of the typewriter keyboard. She holds it in front of her for a second, staring at it sweetly and sorrowfully—then bites her lips and tears it in two pieces.*)

LAURA (*faintly*) Why did you do that, Mother? (AMANDA *repeats the same procedure with the chart of the Gregg Alphabet.[5]*) Why are you—

AMANDA Why? Why? How old are you, Laura?

LAURA Mother, you know my age.

AMANDA I thought that you were an adult; it seems that I was mistaken. (*She crosses slowly to the sofa and sinks down and stares at* LAURA).

LAURA Please don't stare at me, Mother.

AMANDA *closes her eyes and lowers her head. Count ten.[6]*

AMANDA What are we going to do, what is going to become of us, what is the future?

Count ten.

LAURA Has something happened, Mother? (AMANDA *draws a long breath and takes out the handkerchief again. Dabbing process.*) Mother, has—something happened?

AMANDA I'll be all right in a minute. I'm just bewildered—(*Count five.*)—by life. . . .

LAURA Mother, I wish that you would tell me what's happened.

AMANDA As you know, I was supposed to be inducted into my office at the D.A.R. this afternoon. (IMAGE: A SWARM OF TYPEWRITERS.) But I stopped off at Rubicam's Business College to speak to your teachers about your having a cold and ask them what progress they thought you were making down there.

LAURA Oh. . . .

AMANDA I went to the typing instructor and introduced myself as your mother. She didn't know who you were. Wingfield, she said. We don't have any such student enrolled at the school! I assured her she did, that you had been going to classes since

---

[4] Daughters of the American Revolution, a conservative women's club.

[5] Gregg shorthand system.

[6] Instruction to the actor to pause for ten seconds.

early in January. "I wonder," she said, "if you could be talking about that terribly shy little girl who dropped out of school after only a few days' attendance?" "No," I said, "Laura, my daughter, has been going to school every day for the past six weeks!" "Excuse me," she said. She took the attendance book out and there was your name, unmistakably printed, and all the dates you were absent until they decided that you had dropped out of school. I still said, "No, there must have been some mistake! There must have been some mix-up in the records!" And she said, "No—I remember her perfectly now. Her hand shook so that she couldn't hit the right keys! The first time we gave a speed-test, she broke down completely—was sick at the stomach and almost had to be carried into the wash-room! After that morning she never showed up any more. We phoned the house but never got any answer"—while I was working at Famous and Barr, I suppose, demonstrating those—Oh! I felt so weak I could barely keep on my feet! I had to sit down while they got me a glass of water! Fifty dollars' tuition, all of our plans—my hopes and ambitions for you—just gone up the spout, just gone up the spout like that. (LAURA *draws a long breath and gets awkwardly to her feet. She crosses to the victrola and winds it up.*) What are you doing?

LAURA Oh! (*She releases the handle and returns to her seat.*)

AMANDA Laura, where have you been going when you've gone out pretending that you were going to business college?

LAURA I've just been going out walking.

AMANDA That's not true.

LAURA It is. I just went walking.

AMANDA Walking? Walking? In winter? Deliberately courting pneumonia in that light coat? Where did you walk to, Laura?

LAURA All sorts of places—mostly in the park.

AMANDA Even after you'd started catching that cold?

LAURA It was the lesser of two evils, Mother. (IMAGE: WINTER SCENE IN PARK.) I couldn't go back up. I—threw up—on the floor!

AMANDA From half past seven till after five every day you mean to tell me you walked around in the park, because you wanted to make me think that you were still going to Rubicam's Business College?

LAURA It wasn't as bad as it sounds. I went inside places to get warmed up.

AMANDA Inside where?

LAURA I went in the art museum and the bird-houses at the Zoo. I visited the penguins every day! Sometimes I did without lunch and went to the movies. Lately I've been spending most of my afternoons in the Jewel-box, that big glass house where they raise the tropical flowers.

AMANDA You did all this to deceive me, just for the deception? (LAURA *looks down.*) Why?

LAURA Mother, when you're disappointed, you get that awful suffering look on your face, like the picture of Jesus' mother in the museum!

AMANDA Hush!

LAURA I couldn't face it.

Pause. A whisper of strings.

(LEGEND: "THE CRUST OF HUMILITY.")

AMANDA (*hopelessly fingering the huge pocketbook*) So what are we going to do the rest of our lives? Stay home and watch the parades go by? Amuse ourselves with the glass menagerie, darling? Eternally play those worn-out phonograph records your father left as a painful reminder of him? We won't have a business career—we've given that up because it gave us nervous indigestion! *(Laughs wearily.)* What is there left but dependency all our lives? I know so well what becomes of unmarried women who aren't prepared to occupy a position. I've seen such pitiful cases in the South—barely tolerated spinsters living upon the grudging patronage of sister's husband or brother's wife!—stuck away in some little mouse-trap of a room—encouraged by one in-law to visit another—little birdlike women without any nest—eating the crust of humility all their life! Is that the future that we've mapped out for ourselves? I swear it's the only alternative I can think of! It isn't a very pleasant alternative, is it? Of course—some girls *do marry.* *(*Laura *twists her hands nervously.)* Haven't you ever liked some boy?

LAURA Yes. I liked one once. *(Rises.)* I came across his picture a while ago.

AMANDA *(with some interest)* He gave you his picture?

LAURA No, it's in the year-book.

AMANDA *(disappointed)* Oh—a high-school boy.

(SCREEN IMAGE: JIM AS A HIGH-SCHOOL HERO BEARING A SILVER CUP.)

LAURA Yes. His name was Jim. *(*Laura *lifts the heavy annual from the claw-foot table.)* Here he is in *The Pirates of Penzance.*

AMANDA *(absently)* The what?

LAURA The operetta the senior class put on. He had a wonderful voice and we sat across the aisle from each other Mondays, Wednesdays and Fridays in the Aud. Here he is with the silver cup for debating! See his grin?

AMANDA *(absently)* He must have had a jolly disposition.

LAURA He used to call me—Blue Roses.

(IMAGE: BLUE ROSES.)

AMANDA Why did he call you such a name as that?

LAURA When I had that attack of pleurosis—he asked me what was the matter when I came back. I said pleurosis—he thought that I said Blue Roses! So that's what he always called me after that. Whenever he saw me, he'd holler, "Hello, Blue Roses!" I didn't care for the girl that he went out with. Emily Meisenbach. Emily was the best-dressed girl at Soldan. She never struck me, though, as being sincere. . . . It says in the Personal Section—they're engaged. That's—six years ago! They must be married by now.

AMANDA Girls that aren't cut out for business careers usually wind up married to some nice man. *(Gets up with a spark of revival.)* Sister, that's what you'll do.

LAURA *utters a startled, doubtful laugh. She reaches quickly for a piece of glass.*

LAURA But, Mother—

AMANDA Yes? *(Crossing to photograph.)*

LAURA *(in a tone of frightened apology)* I'm—crippled!

(IMAGE: SCREEN.)

AMANDA Nonsense! Laura, I've told you never, never to use that word. Why, you're not crippled, you just have a little defect—hardly noticeable, even! When people have some slight disadvantage like that, they cultivate other things to make up for it—develop charm—and vivacity—and—*charm!* That's all you have to do! *(She turns again to the photograph.)* One thing your father had *plenty* of—was *charm!*

TOM *motions to the fiddle in the wings.*

(THE SCENE FADES OUT WITH MUSIC.)

SCENE III.

(LEGEND ON SCREEN: "AFTER THE FIASCO—")

TOM *speaks from the fire-escape landing.*

TOM After the fiasco at Rubicam's Business College, the idea of getting a gentleman caller for Laura began to play a more important part in Mother's calculations. It became an obsession. Like some archetype of the universal unconscious, the image of the gentleman caller haunted our small apartment. . . . (IMAGE: YOUNG MAN AT DOOR WITH FLOWERS.) An evening at home rarely passed without some allusion to this image, this spectre, this hope. . . . Even when he wasn't mentioned, his presence hung in Mother's preoccupied look and in my sister's frightened, apologetic manner— hung like a sentence passed upon the Wingfields! Mother was a woman of action as well as words. She began to take logical steps in the planned direction. Late that winter and in the early spring—realizing that extra money would be needed to properly feather the nest and plume the bird—she conducted a vigorous campaign on the telephone, roping in subscribers to one of those magazines for matrons called *The Home-maker's Companion,* the type of journal that features the serialized sublimations of ladies of letters who think in terms of delicate cup-like breasts, slim, tapering waists, rich, creamy thighs, eyes like wood-smoke in autumn, fingers that soothe and caress like strains of music, bodies as powerful as Etruscan sculpture.

(SCREEN IMAGE: GLAMOR MAGAZINE COVER.)

AMANDA *enters with phone on long extension cord. She is spotted in the dim stage.*

AMANDA Ida Scott? This is Amanda Wingfield! We *missed* you at the D.A.R. last Monday! I said to myself: She's probably suffering with that sinus condition! How is that sinus condition? Horrors! Heaven have mercy!—You're a Christian martyr, yes, that's what you are, a Christian martyr! Well, I just now happened to notice that your subscription to the *Companion's* about to expire! Yes, it expires with the next issue, honey!—just when that wonderful new serial by Bessie Mae Hopper is getting off to such an exciting start. Oh, honey, it's something that you can't miss! You remember how *Gone With the Wind* took everybody by storm? You simply couldn't go out if you hadn't read it. All everybody *talked* was Scarlett O'Hara. Well, this is a book that critics already compare to *Gone With the Wind.* It's the *Gone With the Wind* of the post–World War generation!—What?—Burning?—Oh, honey, don't let them burn, go take a look in the oven and I'll hold the wire! Heavens—I think she's hung up!

(DIM OUT.)

(LEGEND ON SCREEN: "YOU THINK I'M IN LOVE WITH CONTINENTAL SHOEMAKERS?")

Before the stage is lighted, the violent voices of TOM *and* AMANDA *are heard.*
    They are quarreling behind the portieres. In front of them stands LAURA *with clenched hands and panicky expression.*
    A clear pool of light on her figure throughout this scene.

TOM What in Christ's name am I—

AMANDA *(shrilly)* Don't you use that—

TOM Supposed to do!

AMANDA Expression! Not in my—

TOM Ohhh!

AMANDA Presence! Have you gone out of your senses?

TOM I have, that's true, *driven* out!

AMANDA What is the matter with you, you—big—big—IDIOT!

TOM Look—I've got *no thing*, no single thing—

AMANDA Lower your voice!

TOM In my life here that I can call my OWN! Everything is—

AMANDA Stop that shouting!

TOM Yesterday you confiscated my books! You had the nerve to—

AMANDA I took that horrible novel back to the library—yes! That hideous book by that insane Mr. Lawrence. (TOM *laughs wildly.*) I cannot control the output of diseased minds or people who cater to them— (TOM *laughs still more wildly.*) BUT I WON'T ALLOW SUCH FILTH BROUGHT INTO MY HOUSE! No, no, no, no, no!

TOM House, house! Who pays rent on it, who makes a slave of himself to—

AMANDA *(fairly screeching)* Don't you DARE to—

TOM No, no, I mustn't say things! I've got to just—

AMANDA Let me tell you—

TOM I don't want to hear any more! *(He tears the portieres open. The upstage area is lit with a turgid smoky red glow.)*

AMANDA's *hair is in metal curlers and she wears a very old bathrobe, much too large for her slight figure, a relic of the faithless Mr. Wingfield.*

An upright typewriter and a wild disarray of manuscripts is on the drop-leaf table. The quarrel was probably precipitated by AMANDA's *interruption of his creative labor. A chair lying overthrown on the floor.*

Their gesticulating shadows are cast on the ceiling by the fiery glow.

AMANDA You *will* hear more, you—

TOM No, I won't hear more, I'm going out!

AMANDA You come right back in—

TOM Out, out, out! Because I'm—

AMANDA Come back here, Tom Wingfield! I'm not through talking to you!

TOM Oh, go—

LAURA *(desperately)* —Tom!

AMANDA You're going to listen, and no more insolence from you! I'm at the end of my patience! *(He comes back toward her.)*

TOM What do you think I'm at? Aren't I supposed to have any patience to reach the end of, Mother? I know, I know. It seems unimportant to you, what I'm *doing*—what I *want* to do—having a little *difference* between them! You don't think that—

AMANDA I think you've been doing things that you're ashamed of. That's why you act like this. I don't believe that you go every night to the movies. Nobody goes to the movies night after night. Nobody in their right minds goes to the movies as often as you pretend to. People don't go to the movies at nearly midnight, and movies don't let out at two A.M. Come in stumbling. Muttering to yourself like a maniac! You get three hours sleep and then go to work. Oh, I can picture the way you're doing down there. Moping, doping, because you're in no condition!

TOM (*wildly*) No, I'm in no condition!

AMANDA What right have you got to jeopardize your job? Jeopardize the security of us all? How do you think we'd manage if you were—

TOM Listen! You think I'm crazy *about* the *warehouse*? (*He bends fiercely toward her slight figure.*) You think I'm in love with the Continental Shoemakers? You think I want to spend fifty-five *years* down there in that—*celotex interior!* with—*fluorescent— tubes!* Look! I'd rather somebody picked up a crowbar and battered out my brains— than go back mornings! I *go!* Every time you come in yelling that God damn "*Rise and Shine!*" "*Rise and Shine!*" I say to myself "How *lucky dead* people are!" But I get up. I *go!* For sixty-five dollars a month I give up all that I dream of doing and being *ever!* And you say self—*self's* all I ever think of. Why, listen, if self is what I thought of, Mother, I'd be where he is—GONE! (*Pointing to father's picture.*) As far as the system of transportation reaches! (*He starts past her. She grabs his arm.*) Don't grab me, Mother!

AMANDA Where are you going?

TOM I'm going to the *movies!*

AMANDA I don't believe that lie!

TOM (*crouching toward her, overtowering her tiny figure. She backs away, gasping*) I'm going to opium dens! Yes, opium dens, dens of vice and criminals' hang-outs, Mother. I've joined the Hogan gang, I'm a hired assassin, I carry a tommy-gun in a violin case! I run a string of cat-houses in the Valley! They call me Killer, Killer Wingfield, I'm leading a double-life, a simple, honest warehouse worker by day, by night, a dynamic *the devil* czar of the *underworld, Mother.* I go to gambling casinos, I spin away fortunes on the roulette table! I wear a patch over one eye and a false mustache, sometimes I put on green whiskers. On those occasions they call me—*El Diablo!* Oh, I could tell you things to make you sleepless! My enemies plan to dynamite this place. They're going to blow us all sky-high some night! I'll be glad, very happy, and so will you! You'll go up, up on a broomstick, over Blue Mountain with seventeen gentlemen callers! You ugly—babbling old—*witch.* . . . (*He goes through a series of violent, clumsy movements, seizing his overcoat, lunging to the door, pulling it fiercely open. The women watch him, aghast. His arm catches in the sleeve of the coat as he struggles to pull it on. For a moment he is pinioned by the bulky garment. With an outraged groan he tears the coat off again, splitting the shoulders of it, and hurls it across the room. It strikes against the shelf of* LAURA's *glass collection, there is a tinkle of shattering glass.* LAURA *cries out as if wounded.*)

(MUSIC LEGEND: "THE GLASS MENAGERIE.")

LAURA (*shrilly*) My glass!—menagerie. . . . (*She covers her face and turns away.*)

But AMANDA *is still stunned and stupefied by the "ugly witch" so that she barely notices this occurrence. Now she recovers her speech.*

AMANDA (*in an awful voice*) I won't speak to you—until you apologize! (*She crosses through portieres and draws them together behind her.* TOM *is left with* LAURA. LAURA *clings weakly to the mantel with her face averted.* TOM *stares at her stupidly for a moment. Then he crosses to shelf. Drops awkwardly to his knees to collect the fallen glass, glancing at* LAURA *as if he would speak but couldn't.*)

"The Glass Menagerie" *steals in as the scene dims out.*

SCENE IV.

The interior is dark. Faint light in the alley.

A deep-voiced bell in a church is tolling the hour of five as the scene commences.

Tom *appears at the top of the alley. After each solemn boom of the bell in the tower, he shakes a little noise-maker or rattle as if to express the tiny spasm of man in contrast to the sustained power and dignity of the Almighty. This and the unsteadiness of his advance make it evident that he has been drinking.*

As he climbs the few steps to the fire-escape landing light steals up inside. Laura *appears in night-dress, observing* Tom's *empty bed in the front room.*

Tom *fishes in his pockets for the door-key, removing a motley assortment of articles in the search, including a perfect shower of movie-ticket stubs and an empty bottle. At last he finds the key, but just as he is about to insert it, it slips from his fingers. He strikes a match and crouches below the door.*

TOM *(bitterly)* One crack—and it falls through!

Laura *opens the door.*

LAURA Tom! Tom, what are you doing?

TOM Looking for a door-key.

LAURA Where have you been all this time?

TOM I have been to the movies.

LAURA All this time at the movies?

TOM There was a very long program. There was a Garbo picture and a Mickey Mouse and a travelogue and a newsreel and a preview of coming attractions. And there was an organ solo and a collection for the milk-fund—simultaneously—which ended up in a terrible fight between a fat lady and an usher!

LAURA *(innocently)* Did you have to stay through everything?

TOM Of course! And, oh, I forgot! There was a big stage show! The headliner on this stage show was Malvolio the Magician. He performed wonderful tricks, many of them, such as pouring water back and forth between pitchers. First it turned to wine and then it turned to beer and then it turned to whiskey. I know it was whiskey it finally turned into because he needed somebody to come up out of the audience to help him, and I came up—both shows! It was Kentucky Straight Bourbon. A very generous fellow, he gave souvenirs. *(He pulls from his back pocket a shimmering rainbow-colored scarf.)* He gave me this. This is his magic scarf. You can have it, Laura. You wave it over a canary cage and you get a bowl of gold-fish. You wave it over the gold-fish bowl and they fly away canaries. . . .But the wonderfullest trick of all was the coffin trick. We nailed him into a coffin and he got out of the coffin without removing one nail. *(He has come inside.)* There is a trick that would come in handy for me—get me out of this 2 by 4 situation! *(Flops onto bed and starts removing shoes.)*

LAURA Tom—Shhh!

TOM What you shushing me for?

LAURA You'll wake up Mother.

TOM Goody, goody! Pay 'er back for all those "Rise an' Shines." *(Lies down, groaning.)* You know it don't take much intelligence to get yourself into a nailed-up coffin, Laura. But who in hell ever got himself out of one without removing one nail?

As if in answer, the father's grinning photograph lights up.

(SCENE DIMS OUT.)

Immediately following: The church bell is heard striking six. At the sixth stroke the alarm clock goes off in AMANDA's *room, and after a few moments we hear her calling: "Rise and Shine! Rise and Shine! Laura, go tell your brother to rise and shine!"*

TOM (*sitting up slowly*) I'll rise—but I won't shine.

The light increases.

AMANDA Laura, tell your brother his coffee is ready.

LAURA *slips into front room.*

LAURA Tom! it's nearly seven. Don't make Mother nervous. (*He stares at her stupidly. Beseechingly.*) Tom, speak to Mother this morning. Make up with her, apologize, speak to her!

TOM She won't to me. It's her that started not speaking.

LAURA If you just say you're sorry she'll start speaking.

TOM Her not speaking—is that such a tragedy?

LAURA Please—please!

AMANDA (*calling from kitchenette*) Laura, are you going to do what I asked you to do, or do I have to get dressed and go out myself?

LAURA Going, going—soon as I get on my coat! (*She pulls on a shapeless felt hat with nervous, jerky movement, pleadingly glancing at* TOM. *Rushes awkwardly for coat. The coat is one of* AMANDA's, *inaccurately made-over, the sleeves too short for* LAURA.) Butter and what else?

AMANDA (*entering upstage*) Just butter. Tell them to charge it.

LAURA Mother, they make such faces when I do that.

AMANDA Sticks and stones may break my bones, but the expression on Mr. Garfinkel's face won't harm us! Tell your brother his coffee is getting cold.

LAURA (*at door*) Do what I asked you, will you, will you, Tom?

He looks sullenly away.

AMANDA Laura, go now or just don't go at all!

LAURA (*rushing out*) Going—going! (*A second later she cries out.* TOM *springs up and crosses to the door.* AMANDA *rushes anxiously in.* TOM *opens the door.*)

TOM Laura?

LAURA I'm all right. I slipped, but I'm all right.

AMANDA (*peering anxiously after her*) If anyone breaks a leg on those fire-escape steps, the landlord ought to be sued for every cent he possesses! (*She shuts door. Remembers she isn't speaking and returns to other room.*)

As TOM *enters listlessly for his coffee, she turns her back to him and stands rigidly facing the window on the gloomy gray vault of the areaway. Its light on her face with its aged but childish features is cruelly sharp, satirical as a Daumier print.*

(MUSIC UNDER: "AVE MARIA.")

TOM *glances sheepishly but sullenly at her averted figure and slumps at the table. The coffee is scalding hot; he sips it and gasps and spits it back in the cup. At his gasp,* AMANDA *catches her breath and half turns. Then catches herself and turns back to window.*

   TOM *blows on his coffee, glancing sidewise at his mother. She clears her throat.* TOM *clears his. He starts to rise. Sinks back down again, scratches his head, clears his throat again.* AMANDA *coughs.* TOM *raises his cup in both hands to blow on it, his eyes staring over the rim of it at his mother for several moments. Then he slowly sets the cup down and awkwardly and hesitantly rises from the chair.*

TOM (*hoarsely*) Mother. I—I apologize. Mother. (AMANDA *draws a quick, shuddering breath. Her face works grotesquely. She breaks into childlike tears.*) I'm sorry for what I said, for everything that I said, I didn't mean it.

AMANDA (*sobbingly*) My devotion has made me a witch and so I make myself hateful to my children!

TOM No, you *don't*.

AMANDA I worry so much, don't sleep, it makes me nervous!

TOM (*gently*) I understand that.

AMANDA I've had to put up a solitary battle all these years. But you're my right-hand bower! Don't fall down, don't fail!

TOM (*gently*) I try, Mother.

AMANDA (*with great enthusiasm*) Try and you will SUCCEED! (*The notion makes her breathless.*) Why, you—you're just *full* of natural endowments! Both of my children— they're *unusual* children! Don't you think I know it? I'm so—*proud*! Happy and—feel I've—so much to be thankful for but—Promise me one thing, son!

TOM What, Mother?

AMANDA Promise, son, you'll—never be a drunkard!

TOM (*turns to her grinning*) I will never be a drunkard, Mother.

AMANDA That's what frightened me so, that you'd be drinking! Eat a bowl of Purina!

TOM Just coffee, Mother.

AMANDA Shredded wheat biscuit?

TOM No. No, Mother, just coffee.

AMANDA You can't put in a day's work on an empty stomach. You've got ten minutes— don't gulp! Drinking too-hot liquids makes cancer of the stomach. . . . Put cream in.

TOM No, thank you.

AMANDA To cool it.

TOM No! No, thank you, I want it black.

AMANDA I know, but it's not good for you. We have to do all that we can to build ourselves up. In these trying times we live in, all that we have to cling to is—each other. . . . That's why it's so important to—Tom, I—I sent out your sister so I could discuss something with you. If you hadn't spoken I would have spoken to you. (*Sits down.*)

TOM (*gently*) What is it, Mother, that you want to discuss?

AMANDA Laura!

TOM *puts his cup down slowly.*

(LEGEND ON SCREEN: "LAURA.")

(MUSIC: "THE GLASS MENAGERIE.")

TOM —Oh.—Laura . . .

AMANDA (*touching his sleeve*) You know how Laura is. So quiet but—still water runs deep! She notices things and I think she—broods about them. (TOM *looks up.*) A few days ago I came in and she was crying.

TOM What about?

AMANDA You.

TOM Me?

AMANDA She has an idea that you're not happy here.

TOM What gave her that idea?

AMANDA What gives her any idea? However, you do act strangely. I—I'm not criticizing, understand *that!* I know your ambitions do not lie in the warehouse, that like everybody in the whole wide world—you've had to—make sacrifices, but—Tom—Tom—life's not easy, it calls for—Spartan endurance! There's so many things in my heart that I cannot describe to you! I've never told you but I—*loved* your father. . . .

TOM (*gently*) I know that, Mother.

AMANDA And you—when I see you taking after his ways! Staying out late—and—well, you *had* been drinking the night you were in that—terrifying condition! Laura says that you hate the apartment and that you go out nights to get away from it! Is that true, Tom?

TOM No. You say there's 'so much in your heart that you can't describe to me. That's true of me, too. There's so much in my heart that I can't describe to *you!* So let's respect each other's—

AMANDA But, why—*why*, Tom—are you always so *restless?* Where do you go to, nights?

TOM I—go to the movies.

AMANDA Why do you go to the movies so much, Tom?

TOM I go to the movies because—I like adventure. Adventure is something I don't have much of at work, so I go to the movies.

AMANDA But, Tom, you go to the movies *entirely* too *much!*

TOM I like a lot of adventure.

AMANDA *looks baffled, then hurt. As the familiar inquisition resumes he becomes hard and impatient again.* AMANDA *slips back into her querulous attitude toward him.*

(IMAGE ON SCREEN: SAILING VESSEL WITH JOLLY ROGER.)

AMANDA Most young men find adventure in their careers.

TOM Then most young men are not employed in a warehouse.

AMANDA The world is full of young men employed in warehouses and offices and factories.

TOM Do all of them find adventure in their careers?

AMANDA They do or they do without it! Not everybody has a craze for adventure.

TOM Man is by instinct a lover, a hunter, a fighter, and none of those instincts are given much play at the warehouse!

AMANDA Man is by instinct! Don't quote instinct to me! Instinct is something that people have got away from! It belongs to animals! Christian adults don't want it!

TOM What do Christian adults want, then, Mother?

AMANDA Superior things! Things of the mind and the spirit! Only animals have to satisfy instincts! Surely your aims are somewhat higher than theirs! Than monkeys—pigs—

TOM I reckon they're not.

AMANDA You're joking. However, that isn't what I wanted to discuss.

TOM (*rising*) I haven't much time.

AMANDA (*pushing his shoulders*) Sit down.

TOM You want me to punch in red at the warehouse, Mother?

AMANDA You have five minutes. I want to talk about Laura.

TOM All right! What about Laura?

AMANDA We have to be making plans and provisions for her. She's older than you, two years, and nothing has happened. She just drifts along doing nothing. It frightens me terribly how she just drifts along.

TOM I guess she's the type that people call home-girls.

AMANDA There's no such type, and if there is, it's a pity! That is unless the home is hers, with a husband!

TOM What?

AMANDA Oh, I can see the handwriting on the wall as plain as I see the nose in front of my face! It's terrifying! More and more you remind me of your father! He was out all hours without explanation—Then *left! Goodbye!* And me with a bag to hold. I saw that letter you got from the Merchant Marine. I know what you're dreaming of. I'm not standing here blindfolded. Very well, then. Then *do* it! But not till there's somebody to take your place.

TOM What do you mean?

AMANDA I mean that as soon as Laura has got somebody to take care of her, married, a home of her own, independent—why, then you'll be free to go wherever you please, on land, on sea, whichever way the wind blows! But until that time you've got to look out for your sister. I don't say me because I'm old and don't matter! I say for your sister because she's young and dependent. I put her in business college—a dismal failure! Frightened her so it made her sick to her stomach. I took her over to the Young People's League at the church. Another fiasco. She spoke to nobody, nobody spoke to her. Now all she does is fool with those pieces of glass and play those worn-out records. What kind of a life is that for a girl to lead?

TOM What can I do about it?

AMANDA Overcome selfishness! Self, self, self is all that you ever think of! (TOM *springs up and crosses to get his coat. It is ugly and bulky. He pulls on a cap with earmuffs.*) Where is your muffler? Put your wool muffler on! (*He snatches it angrily from the closet and tosses it around his neck and pulls both ends tight.*) Tom! I haven't said what I had in mind to ask you.

TOM I'm too late to—

AMANDA (*catching his arm—very importunately. Then shyly.*) Down at the warehouse, aren't there some—nice young men?

TOM No!

AMANDA There *must* be—*some* . . .

TOM Mother—

Gesture.

AMANDA Find out one that's clean-living—doesn't drink and—ask him out for sister!

TOM What?

AMANDA For *sister!* To *meet!* Get *acquainted!*

TOM (*stamping to door*) Oh, my go-osh!

AMANDA Will you? (*He opens door. Imploringly.*) Will you? (*He starts down.*) Will you? *Will* you, dear?

TOM (*calling back*) YES!

AMANDA *closes the door hesitantly and with a troubled but faintly hopeful expression.*

(SCREEN IMAGE: GLAMOR MAGAZINE COVER.)

Spot AMANDA *at phone.*

AMANDA Ella Cartwright? This is Amanda Wingfield! How are you, honey? How is that kidney condition? *(Count five.) Horrors! (Count five.)* You're a Christian martyr, yes, honey, that's what you are, a Christian martyr! Well, I just happened to notice in my little red book that your subscription to the *Companion* has just run out! I knew that you wouldn't want to miss out on the wonderful serial starting in this new issue. It's by Bessie Mae Hopper, the first thing she's written since *Honeymoon for Three*. Wasn't that a strange and interesting story? Well, this one is even lovelier, I believe. It has a sophisticated society background. It's all about the horsey set on Long Island!

(FADE OUT.)

SCENE V.

(LEGEND ON SCREEN: "ANNUNCIATION.")

Fade with music.
    It is early dusk of a spring evening. Supper has just been finished in the Wingfield apartment. AMANDA *and* LAURA *in light colored dresses are removing dishes from the table, in the upstage area, which is shadowy, their movements formalized almost as a dance or ritual, their moving forms as pale and silent as moths.*
    TOM, *in white shirt and trousers, rises from the table and crosses toward the fire-escape.*

AMANDA *(as he passes her)* Son, will you do me a favor?
TOM What?
AMANDA Comb your hair! You look so pretty when your hair is combed! *(*TOM *slouches on sofa with evening paper. Enormous caption "Franco Triumphs."*)* There is only one respect in which I would like you to emulate your father.
TOM What respect is that?
AMANDA The care he always took of his appearance. He never allowed himself to look untidy. *(He throws down the paper and crosses to fire-escape.)* Where are you going?
TOM I'm going out to smoke.
AMANDA You smoke too much. A pack a day at fifteen cents a pack. How much would that amount to in a month? Thirty times fifteen is how much, Tom? Figure it out and you will be astounded at what you could save. Enough to give you a night-school course in accounting at Washington U! Just think what a wonderful thing that would be for you, son!

TOM *is unmoved by the thought.*

TOM I'd rather smoke. *(He steps out on landing, letting the screen door slam.)*
AMANDA *(sharply)* I know! That's the tragedy of it. . . . *(Alone, she turns to look at her husband's picture.)*

(DANCE MUSIC: "ALL THE WORLD IS WAITING FOR THE SUNRISE!")

TOM *(to the audience)* Across the alley from us was the Paradise Dance Hall. On evenings in spring the windows and doors were open and the music came outdoors. Sometimes the lights were turned out except for a large glass sphere that hung from the ceiling. It would turn slowly about and filter the dusk with delicate rainbow colors. Then the orchestra played a waltz or a tango, something that had a slow and sensuous rhythm. Couples would come outside, to the relative privacy of the alley. You could see them kissing behind ash-pits and telephone poles. This was the compensation for lives that passed like mine, without any change or adventure. Adventure and change were imminent in this year. They were waiting around the corner for all these kids. Suspended in the mist over Berchtesgaden, caught in the folds of Chamberlain's umbrella[7]— In Spain there was Guernica! But here there was only hot swing music and liquor, dance halls, bars, and movies, and sex that hung in the gloom like a chandelier and flooded the world with brief, deceptive rainbows. . . . All the world was waiting for bombardments!

AMANDA *turns from the picture and comes outside.*

AMANDA *(sighing)* A fire-escape landing's a poor excuse for a porch. *(She spreads a newspaper on a step and sits down, gracefully and demurely as if she were settling into a swing on a Mississippi veranda.)* What are you looking at?

TOM The moon.

AMANDA Is there a moon this evening?

TOM It's rising over Garfinkel's Delicatessen.

AMANDA So it is! A little silver slipper of a moon. Have you made a wish on it yet?

TOM Um-hum.

AMANDA What did you wish for?

TOM That's a secret.

AMANDA A secret, huh? Well, I won't tell mine either. I will be just as mysterious as you.

TOM I bet I can guess what yours is.

AMANDA Is my head so transparent?

TOM You're not a sphinx.

AMANDA No, I don't have secrets. I'll tell you what I wished for on the moon. Success and happiness for my precious children! I wish for that whenever there's a moon, and when there isn't a moon, I wish for it, too.

TOM I thought perhaps you wished for a gentleman caller.

AMANDA Why do you say that?

TOM Don't you remember asking me to fetch one?

AMANDA I remember suggesting that it would be nice for your sister if you brought home some nice young man from the warehouse. I think I've made that suggestion more than once.

TOM Yes, you have made it repeatedly.

AMANDA Well?

TOM We are going to have one.

AMANDA *What?*

TOM A gentleman caller!

(THE ANNUNCIATION IS CELEBRATED WITH MUSIC.)

AMANDA *rises.*

(IMAGE ON SCREEN: CALLER WITH BOUQUET.)

---

[7] British Prime Minister Neville Chamberlain met with Adolf Hitler at Berchtesgaden, Hitler's private mountain retreat, in 1938.

AMANDA You mean you have asked some nice young man to come over?

TOM Yep. I've asked him to dinner.

AMANDA You really did?

TOM I did!

AMANDA You did, and did he—*accept?*

TOM He did!

AMANDA Well, well—well, well! That's—lovely!

TOM I thought that you would be pleased.

AMANDA It's definite, then?

TOM Very definite.

AMANDA Soon?

TOM Very soon.

AMANDA For heaven's sake, stop putting on and tell me some things, will you?

TOM What things do you want me to tell you?

AMANDA *Naturally* I would like to know when he's *coming!*

TOM He's coming tomorrow.

AMANDA *Tomorrow?*

TOM Yep. Tomorrow.

AMANDA But, Tom!

TOM Yes, Mother?

AMANDA Tomorrow gives me no time!

TOM Time for what?

AMANDA Preparations! Why didn't you phone me at once, as soon as you asked him, the minute that he accepted? Then, don't you see, I could have been getting ready!

TOM You don't have to make any fuss.

AMANDA Oh, Tom, Tom, Tom, of course I have to make a fuss! I want things nice, not sloppy! Not thrown together. I'll certainly have to do some fast thinking, won't I?

TOM I don't see why you have to think at all.

AMANDA You just don't know. We can't have a gentleman caller in a pig-sty! All my wedding silver has to be polished, the monogrammed table linen ought to be laundered! The windows have to be washed and fresh curtains put up. And how about clothes? We have to *wear* something, don't we?

TOM Mother, this boy is no one to make a fuss over!

AMANDA Do you realize he's the first young man we've introduced to your sister? It's terrible, dreadful, disgraceful that poor little sister has never received a single gentleman caller! Tom, come inside! *(She opens the screen door.)*

TOM What for?

AMANDA I want to ask you some things.

TOM If you're going to make such a fuss, I'll call it off, I'll tell him not to come.

AMANDA You certainly won't do anything of the kind. Nothing offends people worse than broken engagements. It simply means I'll have to work like a Turk! We won't be brilliant, but we'll pass inspection. Come on inside. *(*TOM *follows, groaning.)* Sit down.

TOM Any particular place you would like me to sit?

AMANDA Thank heavens I've got that new sofa! I'm also making payments on a floor lamp I'll have sent out! And put the chintz covers on, they'll brighten things up! Of course I'd hoped to have these walls re-papered. . . . What is the young man's name?

TOM His name is O'Connor.

AMANDA That, of course, means fish—tomorrow is Friday! I'll have that salmon loaf— with Durkee's dressing! What does he do? He works at the warehouse?

TOM Of course! How else would I—

AMANDA Tom, he—doesn't drink?

TOM Why do you ask me that?

AMANDA Your father *did!*

TOM Don't get started on that!

AMANDA He *does* drink, then?

TOM Not that I know of!

AMANDA Make sure, be certain! The last thing I want for my daughter's a boy who drinks!

TOM Aren't you being a little premature? Mr. O'Connor has not yet appeared on the scene!

AMANDA But will tomorrow. To meet your sister, and what do I know about his character? Nothing! Old maids are better off than wives of drunkards!

TOM Oh, my God!

AMANDA Be still!

TOM *(leaning forward to whisper)* Lots of fellows meet girls whom they don't marry!

AMANDA Oh, talk sensibly, Tom—and don't be sarcastic! *(She has gotten a hairbrush.)*

TOM What are you doing?

AMANDA I'm brushing that cow-lick down! What is this young man's position at the warehouse?

TOM *(submitting grimly to the brush and the interrogation)* This young man's position is that of a shipping clerk, Mother.

AMANDA Sounds to me like a fairly responsible job, the sort of a job *you* would be in if you just had more *get-up.* What is his salary? Have you got any idea?

TOM I would judge it to be approximately eighty-five dollars a month.

AMANDA Well—not princely, but—

TOM Twenty more than I make.

AMANDA Yes, how well I know! But for a family man, eighty-five dollars a month is not much more than you can just get by on. . . .

TOM Yes, but Mr. O'Connor is not a family man.

AMANDA He might be, mightn't he? Some time in the future?

TOM I see. Plans and provisions.

AMANDA You are the only young man that I know of who ignores the fact that the future becomes the present, the present the past, and the past turns into everlasting regret if you don't plan for it!

TOM I will think that over and see what I can make of it.

AMANDA Don't be supercilious with your mother! Tell me some more about this—what do you call him?

TOM James D. O'Connor. The D. is for Delaney.

AMANDA Irish on *both* sides! *Gracious!* And doesn't drink?

TOM Shall I call him up and ask him right this minute?

AMANDA The only way to find out about those things is to make discreet inquiries at the proper moment. When I was a girl in Blue Mountain and it was suspected that a young man drank, the girl whose attentions he had been receiving, if any girl *was,* would sometimes speak to the minister of his church, or rather her father would if her father was living, and sort of feel him out on the young man's character. That is the way such things are discreetly handled to keep a young woman from making a tragic mistake!

TOM Then how did you happen to make a tragic mistake?

AMANDA That innocent look of your father's had everyone fooled! He *smiled*—the world was *enchanted!* No girl can do worse than put herself at the mercy of a handsome appearance! I hope that Mr. O'Connor is not too good-looking.

TOM No, he's not too good-looking. He's covered with freckles and hasn't too much of a nose.

AMANDA He's not right-down homely, though?

TOM Not right-down homely. Just medium homely. I'd say.

AMANDA Character's what to look for in a man.

TOM That's what I've always said, Mother.

AMANDA You've never said anything of the kind and I suspect you would never give it a thought.

TOM Don't be suspicious of me.

AMANDA At least I hope he's the type that's up and coming.

TOM I think he really goes in for self-improvement.

AMANDA What reason have you to think so?

TOM He goes to night school.

AMANDA *(beaming)* Splendid! What does he do, I mean study?

TOM Radio engineering and public speaking!

AMANDA Then he has visions of being advanced in the world! Any young man who studies public speaking is aiming to have an executive job some day! And radio engineering? A thing for the future! Both of these facts are very illuminating. Those are the sort of things that a mother should know concerning any young man who comes to call on her daughter. Seriously or—not.

TOM One little warning. He doesn't know about Laura. I didn't let on that we had dark ulterior motives. I just said, why don't you come have dinner with us? He said okay and that was the whole conversation.

AMANDA I bet it was! You're eloquent as an oyster. However, he'll know about Laura when he gets here. When he sees how lovely and sweet and pretty she is, he'll thank his lucky stars he was asked to dinner.

TOM Mother, you mustn't expect too much of Laura.

AMANDA What do you mean?

TOM Laura seems all those things to you and me because she's ours and we love her. We don't even notice she's crippled any more.

AMANDA Don't say crippled! You know that I never allow that word to be used!

TOM But face facts, Mother. She is and—that's not all—

AMANDA What do you mean "not all"?

TOM Laura is very different from other girls.

AMANDA I think the difference is all to her advantage.

TOM Not quite all—in the eyes of others—strangers—she's terribly shy and lives in a world of her own and those things make her seem a little peculiar to people outside the house.

AMANDA Don't say peculiar.

TOM Face the facts. She is.

(THE DANCE-HALL MUSIC CHANGES TO A TANGO THAT HAS A MINOR AND SOMEWHAT OMINOUS TONE.)

AMANDA In what way is she peculiar—may I ask?

TOM *(gently)* She lives in a world of her own—a world of—little glass ornaments, Mother. . . . *(Gets up.* AMANDA *remains holding brush, looking at him, troubled.)* She plays old phonograph records and—that's about all—*(He glances at himself in the mirror and crosses to door.)*

AMANDA *(sharply)* Where are you going?

TOM I'm going to the movies. *(Out screen door.)*

AMANDA Not to the movies, every night to the movies! *(Follows quickly to screen door.)* I don't believe you always go to the movies! *(He is gone. AMANDA looks worriedly after him for a moment. Then vitality and optimism return and she turns from the door. Crossing to portieres.)* Laura! Laura! *(LAURA answers from kitchenette.)*

LAURA Yes, Mother.

AMANDA Let those dishes go and come in front! *(LAURA appears with dish towel. Gaily)* Laura, come here and make a wish on the moon!

LAURA *(entering)* Moon—moon?

AMANDA A little silver slipper of a moon. Look over your left shoulder, Laura, and make a wish! *(LAURA looks faintly puzzled as if called out of sleep. AMANDA seizes her shoulders and turns her at an angle by the door.)* No! Now, darling, *wish!*

LAURA What shall I wish for, Mother?

AMANDA *(her voice trembling and her eyes suddenly filling with tears)* Happiness! Good Fortune!

The violin rises and the stage dims out.

SCENE VI.

(IMAGE: HIGH-SCHOOL HERO.)

TOM And so the following evening I brought Jim home to dinner. I had known Jim slightly in high school. In high school Jim was a hero. He had tremendous Irish good nature and vitality with the scrubbed and polished look of white chinaware. He seemed to move in a continual spotlight. He was a star in basketball, captain of the debating club, president of the senior class and the glee club and he sang the male lead in the annual light operas. He was always running or bounding, never just walking. He seemed always at the point of defeating the law of gravity. He was shooting with such velocity through his adolescence that you would logically expect him to arrive at nothing short of the White House by the time he was thirty. But Jim apparently ran into more interference after his graduation from Soldan. His speed had definitely slowed. Six years after he left high school he was holding a job that wasn't much better than mine.

(IMAGE: CLERK.)

He was the only one at the warehouse with whom I was on friendly terms. I was valuable to him as someone who could remember his former glory, who had seen him win basketball games and the silver cup in debating. He knew of my secret practice of retiring to a cabinet of the washroom to work on poems when business was slack in the warehouse. He called me Shakespeare. And while the other boys in the warehouse regarded me with suspicious hostility, Jim took a humorous attitude toward me. Gradually his attitude affected the others, their hostility wore off and they also began to smile at me as people smile at an oddly fashioned dog who trots across their path at some distance.

I knew that Jim and Laura had known each other at Soldan, and I had heard Laura speak admiringly of his voice. I didn't know if Jim remembered her or not. In high school Laura had been as unobtrusive as Jim had been astonishing. If he did remember Laura, it was not as my sister, for when I asked him to dinner, he grinned and said, "You know, Shakespeare, I never thought of you as having folks!"

He was about to discover that I did. . . .

(LIGHT UP STAGE.)

(LEGEND ON SCREEN: "THE ACCENT OF A COMING FOOT.")

Friday evening. It is about five o'clock of a late spring evening which comes "scattering poems in the sky."

A delicate lemony light is in the Wingfield apartment.

AMANDA *has worked like a Turk in preparation for the gentleman caller. The results are astonishing. The new floor lamp with its rose-silk shade is in place, a colored paper lantern conceals the broken light fixture in the ceiling, new billowing white curtains are at the windows, chintz covers are on chairs and sofa, a pair of new sofa pillows make their initial appearance.*

Open boxes and tissue paper are scattered on the floor.

LAURA *stands in the middle with lifted arms while* AMANDA *crouches before her, adjusting the hem of the new dress, devout and ritualistic. The dress is colored and designed by memory. The arrangement of* LAURA's *hair is changed; it is softer and more becoming. A fragile, unearthly prettiness has come out in* LAURA: *she is like a piece of translucent glass touched by light, given a momentary radiance, not actual, not lasting.*

AMANDA *(impatiently)* Why are you trembling?

LAURA Mother, you've made me so nervous!

AMANDA How have I made you nervous?

LAURA By all this fuss! You make it seem so important!

AMANDA I don't understand you, Laura. You couldn't be satisfied with just sitting home, and yet whenever I try to arrange something for you, you seem to resist it. *(She gets up.)* Now take a look at yourself. No, wait! Wait just a moment—I have an idea!

LAURA What is it now?

AMANDA *produces two powder puffs which she wraps in handkerchiefs and stuffs in* LAURA's *bosom.*

LAURA Mother, what are you doing?

AMANDA They call them "Gay Deceivers"!

LAURA I won't wear them!

AMANDA You will!

LAURA Why should I?

AMANDA Because, to be painfully honest, your chest is flat.

LAURA You make it seem like we were setting a trap.

AMANDA All pretty girls are a trap, a pretty trap, and men expect them to be. (LEGEND: "A PRETTY TRAP.") Now look at yourself, young lady. This is the prettiest you will ever be! I've got to fix myself now! You're going to be surprised by your mother's appearance! *(She crosses through portieres, humming gaily.)*

LAURA *moves slowly to the long mirror and stares solemnly at herself.*

A wind blows the white curtains inward in a slow, graceful motion and with a faint, sorrowful sighing.

AMANDA *(off stage)* It isn't dark enough yet. *(She turns slowly before the mirror with a troubled look.)*

(LEGEND ON SCREEN: "THIS IS MY SISTER: CELEBRATE HER WITH STRINGS!" MUSIC.)

AMANDA *(laughing, off)* I'm going to show you something. I'm going to make a spectacular appearance!

LAURA What is it, mother?

AMANDA Possess your soul in patience—you will see! Something I've resurrected from that old trunk! Styles haven't changed so terribly much after all. . . . *(She parts the portieres.)* Now just look at your mother! *(She wears a girlish frock of yellowed voile with a blue silk sash. She carries a bunch of jonquils—the legend of her youth is nearly revived. Feverishly.)* This is the dress in which I led the cotillion. Won the cakewalk twice at Sunset Hill, wore one spring to the Governor's ball in Jackson! See how I sashayed around the ballroom, Laura? *(She raises her skirt and does a mincing step around the room.)* I wore it on Sundays for my gentlemen callers! I had it on the day I met your father—I had malaria fever all that spring. The change of climate from East Tennessee to the Delta—weakened resistance—I had a little temperature all the time—not enough to be serious—just enough to make me restless and giddy! Invitations poured in—parties all over the Delta!—"Stay in bed," said Mother, "you have fever!"— but I just wouldn't.—I took quinine but kept on going, going!—Evenings, dances!— Afternoons, long, long rides! Picnics—lovely!—So lovely, that country in May.—All lacy with dogwood, literally flooded with jonquils!—That was the spring I had the craze for jonquils. Jonquils became an absolute obsession. Mother said, "Honey, there's no more room for jonquils." And still I kept bringing in more jonquils. Whenever, wherever I saw them, I'd say, "Stop! Stop! I see jonquils!" I made the young men help me gather the jonquils! It was a joke, Amanda and her jonquils! Finally there were no more vases to hold them, every available space was filled with jonquils. No vases to hold them? All right, I'll hold them myself! And then I—*(She stops in front of the picture. MUSIC.)* met your father! Malaria fever and jonquils and then—this—boy. . . . *(She switches on the rose-colored lamp.)* I hope they get here before it starts to rain. *(She crosses upstage and places the jonquils in bowl on table.)* I gave your brother a little extra change so he and Mr. O'Connor could take the service car[8] home.

LAURA *(with altered look)* What did you say his name was?

AMANDA O'Connor.

LAURA What is his first name?

AMANDA I don't remember. Oh, yes, I do. It was—Jim!

LAURA *sways slightly and catches hold of a chair.*

(LEGEND ON SCREEN: "NOT JIM!")

LAURA *(faintly)* Not—Jim!

AMANDA Yes, that was it, it was Jim! I've never known a Jim that wasn't nice!

(MUSIC: OMINOUS.)

LAURA Are you sure his name is Jim O'Connor?

AMANDA Yes. Why?

LAURA Is he the one that Tom used to know in high school?

AMANDA He didn't say so. I think he just got to know him at the warehouse.

LAURA There was a Jim O'Connor we both knew in high school—*(Then, with effort.)* If that is the one that Tom is bringing to dinner—you'll have to excuse me, I won't come to the table.

---

[8] Streetcar.

AMANDA What sort of nonsense is this?

LAURA You asked me once if I'd ever liked a boy. Don't you remember I showed you this boy's picture?

AMANDA You mean the boy you showed me in the year-book?

LAURA Yes, that boy.

AMANDA Laura, Laura, were you in love with that boy?

LAURA I don't know, Mother. All I know is I couldn't sit at the table if it was him!

AMANDA It won't be him! It isn't the least bit likely. But whether it is or not, you will come to the table. You will not be excused.

LAURA I'll have to be, Mother.

AMANDA I don't intend to humor your silliness, Laura. I've had too much from you and your brother, both! So just sit down and compose yourself till they come. Tom has forgotten his key so you'll have to let them in, when they arrive.

LAURA (panicky) Oh, Mother—you answer the door!

AMANDA (lightly) I'll be in the kitchen—busy!

LAURA Oh, Mother, please answer the door, don't make me do it!

AMANDA (crossing into kitchenette) I've got to fix the dressing for the salmon. Fuss, fuss—silliness!—over a gentleman caller!

Door swings shut. LAURA is left alone.

(LEGEND: "TERROR!")

She utters a low moan and turns off the lamp—sits stiffly on the edge of the sofa, knotting her fingers together.

(LEGEND ON SCREEN: "THE OPENING OF A DOOR!")

TOM *and* JIM *appear on the fire-escape steps and climb to landing. Hearing their approach,* LAURA *rises with a panicky gesture. She retreats to the portieres.*
  The doorbell. LAURA *catches her breath and touches her throat. Low drums.*

AMANDA (calling) Laura, sweetheart! The door!

LAURA *stares at it without moving.*

JIM I think we just beat the rain.

TOM Uh-huh. (*He rings again, nervously,* JIM *whistles and fishes for a cigarette.*)

AMANDA (very, very gaily) Laura, that is your brother and Mr. O'Connor! Will you let them in, darling?

LAURA *crosses toward kitchenette door.*

LAURA (breathlessly) Mother—you go to the door!

AMANDA *steps out of kitchenette and stares furiously at* LAURA. *She points imperiously at the door.*

LAURA Please, please!

AMANDA (in a fierce whisper) What is the matter with you, you silly thing?

LAURA (desperately) Please, you answer it, please!

AMANDA I told you I wasn't going to humor you, Laura. Why have you chosen this moment to lose your mind?

LAURA Please, please, please, you go!

AMANDA You'll have to go to the door because I can't!

LAURA *(despairingly)* I can't either!

AMANDA Why?

LAURA I'm *sick!*

AMANDA I'm sick, too—of your nonsense! Why can't you and your brother be normal people? Fantastic whims and behavior! *(*TOM *gives a long ring.)* Preposterous goings on! Can you give me one reason—*(Calls out lyrically.)* COMING! JUST ONE SECOND!— why should you be afraid to open a door? Now you answer it, Laura!

LAURA Oh, oh, oh . . . *(She returns through the portieres. Darts to the victrola and winds it frantically and turns it on.)*

AMANDA Laura Wingfield, you march right to that door!

LAURA Yes—yes, Mother!

A faraway, scratchy rendition of "Dardanella" softens the air and gives her strength to move through it. She slips to the door and draws it cautiously open.

TOM *enters with the caller,* JIM O'CONNOR.

TOM Laura, this is Jim. Jim, this is my sister, Laura.

JIM *(stepping inside)* I didn't know that Shakespeare had a sister!

LAURA *(retreating stiff and trembling from the door)* How—how do you do?

JIM *(heartily extending his hand)* Okay!

LAURA *touches it hesitantly with hers.*

JIM Your hand's *cold,* Laura!

LAURA Yes, well—I've been playing the victrola. . . .

JIM Must have been playing classical music on it! You ought to play a little hot swing music to warm you up!

LAURA Excuse me—I haven't finished playing the victrola. . . .

She turns awkwardly and hurries into the front room. She pauses a second by the victrola. Then catches her breath and darts through the portieres like a frightened deer.

JIM *(grinning)* What was the matter?

TOM Oh—with Laura? Laura is—terribly shy.

JIM Shy, huh? It's unusual to meet a shy girl nowadays. I don't believe you ever mentioned you had a sister.

TOM Well, now you know. I have one. Here is the *Post Dispatch.* You want a piece of it?

JIM Uh-huh.

TOM What piece? The comics?

JIM Sports! *(Glances at it.)* Ole Dizzy Dean is on his bad behavior.

TOM *(disinterest)* Yeah? *(Lights cigarette and crosses back to fire-escape door.)*

JIM Where are *you* going?

TOM I'm going out on the terrace.

JIM *(goes after him)* You know, Shakespeare—I'm going to sell you a bill of goods!

TOM What goods?

JIM A course I'm taking.

TOM Huh?

JIM In public speaking! You and me, we're not the warehouse type.

TOM Thanks—that's good news. But what has public speaking got to do with it?

JIM It fits you for—executive positions!

TOM Awww.

JIM I tell you it's done a helluva lot for me.

(IMAGE: EXECUTIVE AT DESK.)

TOM In what respect?

JIM In every! Ask yourself what is the difference between you an' me and men in the office down front? Brains?—No!—Ability?—No! Then what? Just one little thing—

TOM What is that one little thing?

JIM Primarily it amounts to—social poise! Being able to square up to people and hold your own on any social level!

AMANDA (off stage) Tom?

TOM Yes, Mother?

AMANDA Is that you and Mr. O'Connor?

TOM Yes, Mother.

AMANDA Well, you just make yourselves comfortable in there.

TOM Yes, Mother.

AMANDA Ask Mr. O'Connor if he would like to wash his hands.

JIM Aw—no—no—thank you—I took care of that at the warehouse. Tom—

TOM Yes?

JIM Mr. Mendoza was speaking to me about you.

TOM Favorably?

JIM What do you think?

TOM Well—

JIM You're going to be out of a job if you don't wake up.

TOM I am waking up—

JIM You show no signs.

TOM The signs are interior.

(IMAGE ON SCREEN: THE SAILING VESSEL WITH JOLLY ROGER AGAIN.)

TOM I'm planning to change. (He leans over the rail speaking with quiet exhilaration. The incandescent marquees and signs of the first-run movie houses light his face from across the alley. He looks like a voyager.) I'm right at the point of committing myself to a future that doesn't include the warehouse and Mr. Mendoza or even a night-school course in public speaking.

JIM What are you gassing about?

TOM I'm tired of the movies.

JIM Movies!

TOM Yes, movies! Look at them—(A wave toward the marvels of Grand Avenue.) All of those glamorous people—having adventures—hogging it all, gobbling the whole thing up! You know what happens? People go to the movies instead of moving! Hollywood characters are supposed to have all the adventures for everybody in America, while everybody in America sits in a dark room and watches them have them! Yes, until there's a war. That's when adventure becomes available to the masses! Everyone's dish, not only Gable's! Then the people in the dark room come out of the dark room to have some adventures themselves—Goody, goody!—It's our turn now, to go to the South Sea Island—to make a safari—to be exotic, far-off!—But I'm not patient. I don't want to wait till then. I'm tired of the movies and I am about to move!

JIM *(incredulously)* Move?

TOM Yes.

JIM When?

TOM Soon!

JIM Where? Where?

(THEME THREE MUSIC SEEMS TO ANSWER THE QUESTION, WHILE TOM THINKS IT OVER. HE SEARCHES AMONG HIS POCKETS.)

TOM I'm starting to boil inside. I know I seem dreamy, but inside—well, I'm boiling! Whenever I pick up a shoe, I shudder a little thinking how short life is and what I am doing!—Whatever that means. I know it doesn't mean shoes—except as something to wear on a traveler's feet! *(Finds paper.)* Look—

JIM What?

TOM I'm a member.

JIM *(reading)* The Union of Merchant Seamen.

TOM I paid my dues this month, instead of the light bill.

JIM You will regret it when they turn the lights off.

TOM I won't be here.

JIM How about your mother?

TOM I'm like my father. The bastard son of a bastard! See how he grins? And he's been absent going on sixteen years!

JIM You're just talking, you drip. How does your mother feel about it?

TOM Shhh!—Here comes Mother! Mother is not acquainted with my plans!

AMANDA *(enters portieres)* Where are you all?

TOM On the terrace, Mother.

They start inside. She advances to them. TOM *is distinctly shocked at her appearance. Even* JIM *blinks a little. He is making his first contact with girlish Southern vivacity and in spite of the night-school course in public speaking is somewhat thrown off the beam by the unexpected outlay of social charm.*

Certain responses are attempted by JIM *but are swept aside by* AMANDA's *gay laughter and chatter.* TOM *is embarrassed but after the first shock* JIM *reacts very warmly. Grins and chuckles, is altogether won over.*

(IMAGE: AMANDA AS A GIRL.)

AMANDA *(coyly smiling, shaking her girlish ringlets)* Well, well, well, so this is Mr. O'Connor. Introductions entirely unnecessary. I've heard so much about you from my boy. I finally said to him, Tom—good gracious!—why don't you bring this paragon to supper? I'd like to meet this nice young man at the warehouse!—Instead of just hearing him sing your praises so much! I don't know why my son is so stand-offish—that's not Southern behavior! Let's sit down and—I think we could stand a little more air in here! Tom, leave the door open. I felt a nice fresh breeze a moment ago. Where has it gone? Mmm, so warm already! And not quite summer, even. We're going to burn up when summer really gets started. However, we're having—we're having a very light supper. I think light things are better fo' this time of year. The same as light clothes are. Light clothes an' light food are what warm weather calls fo'. You know our blood gets so thick during th' winter—it takes a while fo' us to *adjust* ou'selves!—when the season changes. . . . It's come so quick this year. I wasn't prepared. All of a sudden—heavens! Already summer!—I ran to the trunk an' pulled out this light dress—Terribly old! Historical almost! But feels so good—so good an' co-ol, y'know. . . .

TOM Mother—

AMANDA Yes, honey?

TOM How about—supper?

AMANDA Honey, you go ask Sister if supper is ready! You know that Sister is in full charge of supper! Tell her you hungry boys are waiting for it. *(To* JIM.) Have you met Laura?

JIM She—

AMANDA Let you in? Oh, good, you've met already! It's rare for a girl as sweet an' pretty as Laura to be domestic! But Laura is, thank heavens, not only pretty but also very domestic. I'm not at all. I never was a bit. I never could make a thing but angel-food cake. Well, in the South we had so many servants. Gone, gone, gone. All vestige of gracious living! Gone completely! I wasn't prepared for what the future brought me. All of my gentlemen callers were sons of planters and so of course I assumed that I would be married to one and raise my family on a large piece of land with plenty of servants. But man proposes—and woman accepts the proposal!—To vary that old, old saying a little bit—I married no planter! I married a man who worked for the telephone company!—That gallantly smiling gentleman over there! *(Points to the picture.)* A telephone man who—fell in love with long-distance!—Now he travels and I don't even know where!—But what am I going on for about my—tribulations? Tell me yours— I hope you don't have any! Tom?

TOM *(returning)* Yes, Mother?

AMANDA Is supper nearly ready?

TOM It looks to me like supper is on the table.

AMANDA Let me look—*(She rises prettily and looks through portieres.)* Oh, lovely!—But where is Sister?

TOM Laura is not feeling well and she says that she thinks she'd better not come to the table.

AMANDA What?—Nonsense!—Laura? Oh, Laura!

LAURA *(off stage, faintly)* Yes, Mother.

AMANDA You really must come to the table. We won't be seated until you come to the table! Come in, Mr. O'Connor. You sit over there and I'll—Laura? Laura Wingfield! You're keeping us waiting, honey! We can't say grace until you come to the table!

The back door is pushed weakly open and LAURA *comes in. She is obviously quite faint, her lips trembling, her eyes wide and staring. She moves unsteadily toward the table.*

(LEGEND: "TERROR!")

Outside a summer storm is coming abruptly. The white curtains billow inward at the windows and there is a sorrowful murmur and deep blue dusk.
    LAURA *suddenly stumbles—she catches at a chair with a faint moan.*

TOM Laura!

AMANDA Laura! *(There is a clap of thunder.)* (LEGEND: "AH!") *(Despairingly)* Why, Laura, you *are* sick, darling! Tom, help your sister into the living room, dear! Sit in the living room, Laura—rest on the sofa. Well! *(To the gentleman caller.)* Standing over the hot stove made her ill!—I told her that it was just too warm this evening, but—(TOM *comes back in.* LAURA *is on the sofa.)* Is Laura all right now?

TOM Yes.

AMANDA What *is* that? Rain? A nice cool rain has come up! *(She gives the gentleman caller a frightened look.*) I think we may—have grace—now. . . . (TOM *looks at her stupidly.*) Tom, honey—you say grace!

TOM   Oh. . . . "For these and all thy mercies—" *(They bow their heads, AMANDA stealing a nervous glance at JIM. In the living room LAURA, stretched on the sofa, clenches her hand to her lips, to hold back a shuddering sob.)* God's Holy Name be praised—

(THE SCENE DIMS OUT.)

SCENE VII.

(LEGEND: "A SOUVENIR.")

Half an hour later. Dinner is just being finished in the upstage area which is concealed by the drawn portieres.

As the curtain rises LAURA is still huddled upon the sofa, her feet drawn under her, her head resting on a pale blue pillow, her eyes wide and mysteriously watchful. The new floor lamp with its shade of rose-colored silk gives a soft, becoming light to her face, bringing out the fragile, unearthly prettiness which usually escapes attention. There is a steady murmur of rain, but it is slackening and stops soon after the scene begins; the air outside becomes pale and luminous as the moon breaks out.

A moment after the curtain rises, the lights in both rooms flicker and go out.

JIM   Hey, there, Mr. Light Bulb!

AMANDA *laughs nervously.*

(LEGEND: "SUSPENSION OF A PUBLIC SERVICE.")

AMANDA   Where was Moses when the lights went out? Ha-ha. Do you know the answer to that one, Mr. O'Connor?

JIM   No, Ma'am, what's the answer?

AMANDA   In the dark! (JIM *laughs appreciatively.*) Everybody sit still. I'll light the candles. Isn't it lucky we have them on the table? Where's a match? Which of you gentlemen can provide a match?

JIM   Here.

AMANDA   Thank you, sir.

JIM   Not at all, Ma'am!

AMANDA   I guess the fuse has burnt out. Mr. O'Connor, can you tell a burnt-out fuse? I know I can't and Tom is a total loss when it comes to mechanics. (SOUND: GETTING UP: VOICES RECEDE A LITTLE TO KITCHENETTE.) Oh, be careful you don't bump into something. We don't want our gentleman caller to break his neck. Now wouldn't that be a fine howdy-do?

JIM   Ha-ha! Where is the fuse-box?

AMANDA   Right here next to the stove. Can you see anything?

JIM   Just a minute.

AMANDA   Isn't electricity a mysterious thing? Wasn't it Benjamin Franklin who tied a key to a kite? We live in such a mysterious universe, don't we? Some people say that science clears up all the mysteries for us. In my opinion it only creates more! Have you found it yet?

JIM   No, Ma'am. All these fuses look okay to me.

AMANDA   Tom!

TOM Yes, Mother?

AMANDA That light bill I gave you several days ago. The one I told you we got the notices about?

TOM Oh.—Yeah.

(LEGEND: "HA!")

AMANDA You didn't neglect to pay it by any chance?

TOM Why, I—

AMANDA Didn't! I might have known it!

JIM Shakespeare probably wrote a poem on that light bill, Mrs. Wingfield.

AMANDA I might have known better than to trust him with it! There's such a high price for negligence in the world!

JIM Maybe the poem will win a ten-dollar prize.

AMANDA We'll just have to spend the remainder of the evening in the nineteenth century, before Mr. Edison made the Mazda lamp!

JIM Candlelight is my favorite kind of light.

AMANDA That shows you're romantic! But that's no excuse for Tom. Well, we got through dinner. Very considerate of them to let us get through dinner before they plunged us into everlasting darkness, wasn't it, Mr. O'Connor?

JIM Ha-ha!

AMANDA Tom, as a penalty for your carelessness you can help me with the dishes.

JIM Let me give you a hand.

AMANDA Indeed you will not!

JIM I ought to be good for something.

AMANDA Good for something? (*Her tone is rhapsodic.*) You? Why, Mr. O'Connor, nobody, *nobody's* given me this much entertainment in years—as you have!

JIM Aw, now, Mrs. Wingfield!

AMANDA I'm not exaggerating, not one bit! But Sister is all by her lonesome. You go keep her company in the parlor! I'll give you this lovely old candelabrum that used to be on the altar at the church of the Heavenly Rest. It was melted a little out of shape when the church burnt down. Lightning struck it one spring. Gypsy Jones was holding a revival at the time and he intimated that the church was destroyed because the Episcopalians gave card parties.

JIM Ha-ha.

AMANDA And how about coaxing Sister to drink a little wine? I think it would be good for her! Can you carry both at once?

JIM Sure. I'm Superman!

AMANDA Now, Thomas, get into this apron!

The door of kitchenette swings closed on AMANDA's *gay laughter; the flickering light approaches the portieres.*

LAURA *sits up nervously as he enters. Her speech at first is low and breathless from the almost intolerable strain of being alone with a stranger.*

(THE LEGEND: "I DON'T SUPPOSE YOU REMEMBER ME AT ALL!")

In her first speeches in this scene, before JIM's *warmth overcomes her paralyzing shyness,* LAURA's *voice is thin and breathless as though she has just run up a steep flight of stairs.*

JIM's *attitude is gently humorous. In playing this scene it should be stressed that while the incident is apparently unimportant, it is to* LAURA *the climax of her secret life.*

JIM Hello there, Laura.

LAURA *(faintly)* Hello. *(She clears her throat.)*

JIM How are you feeling now? Better?

LAURA Yes. Yes, thank you.

JIM This is for you. A little dandelion wine. *(He extends it toward her with extravagant gallantry.)*

LAURA Thank you.

JIM Drink it—but don't get drunk! *(He laughts heartily.* LAURA *takes the glass uncertainly; laughs shyly.)* Where shall I set the candles?

LAURA Oh—oh, anywhere . . .

JIM How about here on the floor? Any objections?

LAURA No.

JIM I'll spread a newspaper under to catch the drippings. I like to sit on the floor. Mind if I do?

LAURA Oh, no.

JIM Give me a pillow?

LAURA What?

JIM A pillow!

LAURA Oh . . . *(Hands him one quickly.)*

JIM How about you? Don't you like to sit on the floor?

LAURA Oh—yes.

JIM Why don't you, then?

LAURA I—will.

JIM Take a pillow! *(*LAURA *does. Sits on the other side of the candelabrum.* JIM *crosses his legs and smiles engagingly at her.)* I can't hardly see you sitting way over there.

LAURA I can—see you.

JIM I know, but that's not fair, I'm in the limelight. *(*LAURA *moves her pillow closer.)* Good! Now I can see you! Comfortable?

LAURA Yes.

JIM So am I. Comfortable as a cow. Will you have some gum?

LAURA No, thank you.

JIM I think that I will indulge, with your permission. *(Musingly unwraps it and holds it up.)* Think of the fortune made by the guy that invented the first piece of chewing gum. Amazing, huh? The Wrigley Building is one of the sights in Chicago.—I saw it summer before last when I went up to the Century of Progress. Did you take in the Century of Progress?

LAURA No, I didn't.

JIM Well, it was quite a wonderful exposition. What impressed me most was the Hall of Science. Gives you an idea of what the future will be in America, even more wonderful than the present time is! *(Pause. Smiling at her.)* Your brother tells me you're shy. Is that right, Laura?

LAURA I—don't know.

JIM I judge you to be an old-fashioned type of girl. Well, I think that's a pretty good type to be. Hope you don't think I'm being too personal—do you?

LAURA *(hastily, out of embarrassment)* I believe I *will* take a piece of gum, if you—don't mind. *(Clearing her throat.)* Mr. O'Connor, have you—kept up with your singing?

JIM Singing? Me?

LAURA Yes. I remember what a beautiful voice you had.

JIM When did you hear me sing?

(VOICE OFF STAGE IN THE PAUSE.)

VOICE (*off stage*)

> O blow, ye winds, heigh-ho,
> A-roving I will go!
> I'm off to my love
> With a boxing glove—
> Ten thousand miles away!

JIM You say you've heard me sing?

LAURA Oh, yes! Yes, very often. . . . I—don't suppose you remember me—at all?

JIM (*smiling doubtfully*) You know I have an idea I've seen you before. I had that idea as soon as you opened the door. It seemed almost like I was about to remember your name. But the name that I started to call you—wasn't a name! And so I stopped myself before I said it.

LAURA Wasn't it—Blue Roses?

JIM (*springs up, grinning*) Blue Roses! My gosh, yes—Blue Roses! That's what I had on my tongue when you opened the door! Isn't it funny what tricks your memory plays? I didn't connect you with the high school somehow or other. But that's where it was; it was high school. I didn't even know you were Shakespeare's sister! Gosh, I'm sorry.

LAURA I didn't expect you to. You—barely knew me!

JIM But we did have a speaking acquaintance, huh?

LAURA Yes, we—spoke to each other.

JIM When did you recognize me?

LAURA Oh, right away!

JIM Soon as I came in the door?

LAURA When I heard your name I thought it was probably you. I knew that Tom used to know you a little in high school. So when you came in the door—Well, then I was—sure.

JIM Why didn't you *say* something, then?

LAURA (*breathlessly*) I didn't know what to say, I was—too surprised!

JIM For goodness' sakes! You know, this sure is funny!

LAURA Yes! Yes, isn't it, though . . .

JIM Didn't we have a class in something together?

LAURA Yes, we did.

JIM What class was that?

LAURA It was—singing—Chorus!

JIM Aw!

LAURA I sat across the aisle from you in the Aud.

JIM Aw.

LAURA Mondays, Wednesdays and Fridays.

JIM Now I remember—you always came in late.

LAURA Yes, it was so hard for me, getting upstairs. I had that brace on my leg—it clumped so loud!

JIM I never heard any clumping.

LAURA (*wincing at the recollection*) To me it sounded like—thunder!

JIM Well, well, well. I never even noticed.

LAURA And everybody was seated before I came in. I had to walk in front of all those people. My seat was in the back row. I had to go clumping all the way up the aisle with everyone watching!

JIM You shouldn't have been self-conscious.

LAURA I know, but I was. It was always such a relief when the singing started.

JIM Aw, yes. I've placed you now! I used to call you Blue Roses. How was it that I got started calling you that?

LAURA I was out of school a little while with pleurosis. When I came back you asked me what was the matter. I said I had pleurosis—you thought I said Blue Roses. That's what you always called me after that!

JIM I hope you didn't mind.

LAURA Oh, no—I liked it. You see, I wasn't acquainted with many—people. . . .

JIM As I remember you sort of stuck by yourself.

LAURA I—I—never had much luck at—making friends.

JIM I don't see why you wouldn't.

LAURA Well, I—started out badly.

JIM You mean being—

LAURA Yes, it sort of—stood between me—

JIM You shouldn't have let it!

LAURA I know, but it did, and—

JIM You were shy with people!

LAURA I tried not to be but never could—

JIM Overcome it?

LAURA No, I—I never could!

JIM I guess being shy is something you have to work out of kind of gradually.

LAURA (*sorrowfully*) Yes—I guess it—

JIM Takes time!

LAURA Yes—

JIM People are not so dreadful when you know them. That's what you have to remember! And everybody has problems, not just you, but practically everybody has got some problems. You think of yourself as having the only problems, as being the only one who is disappointed. But just look around you and you will see lots of people as disappointed as you are. For instance, I hoped when I was going to high school that I would be further along at this time, six years later, than I am now—You remember that wonderful write-up I had in *The Torch?*

LAURA Yes! (*She rises and crosses to table.*)

JIM It said I was bound to succeed in anything I went into! (LAURA *returns with the annual.*) Holy Jeez! *The Torch!* (*He accepts it reverently. They smile across it with mutual wonder.* LAURA *crouches beside him and they begin to turn through it.* LAURA's *shyness is dissolving in his warmth.*)

LAURA Here you are in *Pirates of Penzance!*

JIM (*wistfully*) I sang the baritone lead in that operetta.

LAURA (*rapidly*) So—*beautifully!*

JIM (*protesting*) Aw—

LAURA Yes, yes—beautifully—beautifully!

JIM You heard me?

LAURA All three times!

JIM No!

LAURA Yes!

JIM All three performances?

LAURA (*looking down*) Yes.

JIM Why?

LAURA I—wanted to ask you to—autograph my program.

JIM Why didn't you ask me to.

LAURA You were always surrounded by your own friends so much that I never had a chance to.

JIM You should have just—

LAURA Well, I—thought you might think I was—

JIM Thought I might think you was—what?

LAURA Oh—

JIM (*with reflective relish*) I was beleaguered by females in those days.

LAURA You were terribly popular!

JIM Yeah—

LAURA You had such a—friendly way—

JIM I was spoiled in high school.

LAURA Everybody—liked you!

JIM Including you?

LAURA I—yes, I—I did, too—(*She gently closes the book in her lap.*)

JIM Well, well, well!—Give me that program, Laura. (*She hands it to him. He signs it with a flourish.*) There you are—better late than never!

LAURA Oh, I—what a—surprise!

JIM My signature isn't worth very much right now. But some day—maybe—it will increase in value! Being disappointed is one thing and being discouraged is something else. I am disappointed but I am not discouraged. I'm twenty-three years old. How old are you?

LAURA I'll be twenty-four in June.

JIM That's not old age!

LAURA No, but—

JIM You finished high school?

LAURA (*with difficulty*) I didn't go back.

JIM You mean you dropped out?

LAURA I made bad grades in my final examinations. (*She rises and replaces the book and the program. Her voice strained.*) How is—Emily Meisenbach getting along?

JIM Oh, that kraut-head!

LAURA Why do you call her that?

JIM That's what she was.

LAURA You're not still—going with her?

JIM I never see her.

LAURA It said in the Personal Section that you were—engaged!

JIM I know, but I wasn't impressed by that—propaganda!

LAURA It wasn't—the truth?

JIM Only in Emily's optimistic opinion!

LAURA Oh—

(LEGEND: "WHAT HAVE YOU DONE SINCE HIGH SCHOOL?")

JIM *lights a cigarette and leans indolently back on his elbows smiling at* LAURA *with a warmth and charm which lights her inwardly with altar candles. She remains by the table and turns in her hands a piece of glass to cover her tumult.*

JIM (*after several reflective puffs on a cigarette*) What have you done since high school? (*She seems not to hear him.*) Huh? (LAURA *looks up.*) I said what have you done since high school, Laura?
LAURA Nothing much.
JIM You must have been doing something in these six long years.
LAURA Yes.
JIM Well, then, such as what?
LAURA I took a business course at business college—
JIM How did that work out?
LAURA Well, not very—well—I had to drop out, it gave me—indigestion—

JIM *laughs gently.*

JIM What are you doing now?
LAURA I don't do anything—much. Oh, please don't think I sit around doing nothing! My glass collection takes up a good deal of my time. Glass is something you have to take good care of.
JIM What did you say—about glass?
LAURA Collection I said—I have one—(*She clears her throat and turns away again, acutely shy.*)
JIM (*abruptly*) You know what I judge to be the trouble with you? Inferiority complex! Know what that is? That's what they call it when someone low-rates himself! I understand it because I had it, too. Although my case was not so aggravated as yours seems to be. I had it until I took up public speaking, developed my voice, and learned that I had an aptitude for science. Before that time I never thought of myself as being outstanding in any way whatsoever! Now I've never made a regular study of it, but I have a friend who says I can analyze people better than doctors that make a profession of it. I don't claim that to be necessarily true, but I can sure guess a person's psychology, Laura! (*Takes out his gum.*) Excuse me, Laura. I always take it out when the flavor is gone. I'll use this scrap of paper to wrap it in. I know how it is to get it stuck on a shoe. Yep—that's what I judge to be your principal trouble. A lack of confidence in yourself as a person. You don't have the proper amount of faith in yourself. I'm basing that fact on a number of your remarks and also on certain observations I've made. For instance that clumping you thought was so awful in high school. You say that you even dreaded to walk into class. You see what you did? You dropped out of school, you gave up an education because of a clump, which as far as I know was practically non-existent! A little physical defect is what you have. Hardly noticeable even! Magnified thousands of times by imagination! You know what my strong advice to you is? Think of yourself as *superior* in some way!
LAURA In what way would I think?
JIM Why, man alive, Laura! Just look about you a little. What do you see? A world full of common people! All of 'em born and all of 'em going to die! Which of them has one-tenth of your good points! Or mine! Or anyone else's, as far as that goes—Gosh! Everybody excels in some one thing. Some in many! (*Unconsciously glances at himself in the mirror.*) All you've got to do is discover in *what!* Take me, for instance. (*He*

adjusts his tie at the mirror.) My interest happens to lie in electro-dynamics. I'm taking a course in radio engineering at night school, Laura, on top of a fairly responsible job at the warehouse. I'm taking that course and studying public speaking.

LAURA Ohhhh.

JIM Because I believe in the future of television! (*Turning back to her.*) I wish to be ready to go up right along with it. Therefore I'm planning to get in on the ground floor. In fact, I've already made the right connections and all that remains is for the industry itself to get under way! Full steam—(*His eyes are starry.*) Knowledge—Zzzzzp! Money—Zzzzzzp!—Power! That's the cycle democracy is built on! (*His attitude is convincingly dynamic.* LAURA *stares at him, even her shyness eclipsed in her absolute wonder. He suddenly grins.*) I guess you think I think a lot of myself!

LAURA No—o-o-o, I—

JIM Now how about you? Isn't there something you take more interest in than anything else?

LAURA Well, I do—as I said—have my—glass collection—

A peal of girlish laughter from the kitchen.

JIM I'm not right sure I know what you're talking about. What kind of glass is it?

LAURA Little articles of it, they're ornaments mostly! Most of them are little animals made out of glass, the tiniest little animals in the world. Mother calls them a glass menagerie! Here's an example of one, if you'd like to see it! This one is one of the oldest. It's nearly thirteen. (*He stretches out his hand.*) (MUSIC: "THE GLASS MENAGERIE.") Oh, be careful—if you breathe, it breaks!

JIM I'd better not take it. I'm pretty clumsy with things.

LAURA Go on, I trust you with him! (*Places it in his palm.*) There now—you're holding him gently! Hold him over the light, he loves the light! You see how the light shines through him?

JIM It sure does shine!

LAURA I shouldn't be partial, but he is my favorite one.

JIM What kind of a thing is this one supposed to be?

LAURA Haven't you noticed the single horn on his forehead?

JIM A unicorn, huh?

LAURA Mmm-hmmm!

JIM Unicorns, aren't they extinct in the modern world?

LAURA I know!

JIM Poor little fellow, he must feel sort of lonesome.

LAURA (*smiling*) Well, if he does he doesn't complain about it. He stays on a shelf with some horses that don't have horns and all of them seem to get along nicely together.

JIM How do you know?

LAURA (*lightly*) I haven't heard any arguments among them!

JIM (*grinning*) No arguments, huh? Well, that's a pretty good sign! Where shall I set him?

LAURA Put him on the table. They all like a change of scenery once in a while!

JIM (*stretching*) Well, well, well, well—Look how big my shadow is when I stretch!

LAURA Oh, oh, yes—it stretches across the ceiling!

JIM (*crossing to door*) I think it's stopped raining. (*Opens fire-escape door.*) Where does the music come from?

LAURA From the Paradise Dance Hall across the alley.

JIM How about cutting the rug a little, Miss Wingfield?

LAURA Oh, I—

JIM Or is your program filled up? Let me have a look at it. (*Grasps imaginary card.*) Why, every dance is taken! I'll just have to scratch some out. (WALTZ MUSIC: "LA GOLONDRINA.") Ahhh, a waltz! (*He executes some sweeping turns by himself, then holds his arms toward* LAURA.)

LAURA (*breathlessly*) I—can't dance!

JIM There you go, that inferiority stuff!

LAURA I've never danced in my life!

JIM Come on, try!

LAURA Oh, but I'd step on you!

JIM I'm not made out of glass.

LAURA How—how—how do we start?

JIM Just leave it to me. You hold your arms out a little.

LAURA Like this?

JIM A little bit higher. Right. Now don't tighten up, that's the main thing about it—relax.

LAURA (*laughing breathlessly*) It's hard not to.

JIM Okay.

LAURA I'm afraid you can't budge me.

JIM What do you bet I can't? (*He swings her into motion.*)

LAURA Goodness, yes, you can!

JIM Let yourself go, now, Laura, just let yourself go.

LAURA I'm—

JIM Come on!

LAURA Trying!

JIM Not so stiff—Easy does it!

LAURA I know but I'm—

JIM Loosen th' backbone! There now, that's a lot better.

LAURA Am I?

JIM Lots, lots better! (*He moves her about the room in a clumsy waltz.*)

LAURA Oh, my!

JIM Ha-ha!

LAURA Oh, my goodness!

JIM Ha-ha-ha! (*They suddenly bump into the table.* JIM *stops.*) What did we hit on?

LAURA Table.

JIM Did something fall off it? I think—

LAURA Yes.

JIM I hope that it wasn't the little glass horse with the horn!

LAURA Yes.

JIM Aw, aw, aw. Is it broken?

LAURA Now it is just like all the other horses.

JIM It's lost its—

LAURA Horn! It doesn't matter. Maybe it's a blessing in disguise.

JIM You'll never forgive me. I bet that that was your favorite piece of glass.

LAURA I don't have favorites much. It's no tragedy, Freckles. Glass breaks so easily. No matter how careful you are. The traffic jars the shelves and things fall off them.

JIM Still I'm awfully sorry that I was the cause.

LAURA (*smiling*) I'll just imagine he had an operation. The horn was removed to make him feel less—freakish! (*They both laugh.*) Now he will feel more at home with the other horses, the ones that don't have horns. . . .

JIM Ha-ha, that's very funny! (*Suddenly serious.*) I'm glad to see that you have a sense of humor. You know—you're—well—very different! Surprisingly different from anyone else I know! (*His voice becomes soft and hesitant with a genuine feeling.*) Do you mind me telling you that? (LAURA *is abashed beyond speech.*) You make me feel sort of—I don't know how to put it! I'm usually pretty good at expressing things, but— This is something that I don't know how to say! (LAURA *touches her throat and clears it—turns the broken unicorn in her hands.*) (*Even softer.*) Has anyone ever told you that you were pretty? (PAUSE: MUSIC.) (LAURA *looks up slowly, with wonder, and shakes her head.*) Well, you are! In a very different way from anyone else. And all the nicer because of the difference, too. (*His voice becomes low and husky.* LAURA *turns away, nearly faint with the novelty of her emotions.*) I wish that you were my sister. I'd teach you to have some confidence in yourself. The different people are not like other people, but being different is nothing to be ashamed of. Because other people are not such wonderful people. They're one hundred times one thousand. You're one times one! They walk all over the earth. You just stay here. They're common as—weeds, but— you—well, you're—*Blue Roses!*

(IMAGE ON SCREEN: BLUE ROSES.)

(MUSIC CHANGES.)

LAURA But blue is wrong for—roses . . .

JIM It's right for you—You're—pretty!

LAURA In what respect am I pretty?

JIM In all respects—believe me! Your eyes—your hair—are pretty! Your hands are pretty! (*He catches hold of her hand.*) You think I'm making this up because I'm invited to dinner and have to be nice. Oh, I could do that! I could put on an act for you, Laura, and say lots of things without being very sincere. But this time I am. I'm talking to you sincerely. I happened to notice you had this inferiority complex that keeps you from feeling comfortable with people. Somebody needs to build your confidence up and make you proud instead of shy and turning away and—blushing—Somebody ought to—Ought to—*kiss* you, Laura! (*His hand slips slowly up her arm to her shoulder.*) (MUSIC SWELLS TUMULTUOUSLY.) (*He suddenly turns her about and kisses her on the lips. When he releases her* LAURA *sinks on the sofa with a bright, dazed look.* JIM *backs away and fishes in his pocket for a cigarette.*) (LEGEND ON SCREEN: "SOUVENIR.") Stumble-john! (*He lights the cigarette, avoiding her look. There is a peal of girlish laughter from* AMANDA *in the kitchen.* LAURA *slowly raises and opens her hand. It still contains the little broken glass animal. She looks at it with a tender, bewildered expression.*) Stumble-john! I shouldn't have done that—That was way off the beam. You don't smoke, do you? (*She looks up, smiling, not hearing the question. He sits beside her a little gingerly. She looks at him speechlessly—waiting. He coughs decorously and moves a little farther aside as he considers the situation and senses her feelings, dimly, with perturbation. Gently*) Would you—care for a—mint? (*She doesn't seem to hear him but her look grows brighter even.*) Peppermint—Life Saver? My pocket's a regular drug store—wherever I go . . . (*He pops a mint in his mouth. Then gulps and decides to make a clean breast of it. He speaks slowly and gingerly.*) Laura, you know, if I had a sister like you, I'd do the same thing as Tom. I'd bring out fellows—introduce her to them. The right type of boys of a type to—appreciate her. Only—well—he made a mistake about me. Maybe I've got no call to be saying this. That may not have been the idea in having me over. But what if it was? There's nothing wrong about that. The only trouble is that in my case—I'm not in a situation to—do the right thing. I can't take down your number and say I'll phone. I can't call up next week and—ask for a date. I thought I had better explain the situation in case you misunderstood it and—hurt your feelings. . . . (*Pause. Slowly, very slowly,* LAURA's *look changes, her eyes returning slowly from his to the ornament in her palm.*)

AMANDA *utters another gay laugh in the kitchen.*

LAURA (*faintly*) You—won't—call again?

JIM No, Laura, I can't. (*He rises from the sofa.*) As I was just explaining, I've—got strings on me, Laura, I've—been going steady! I go out all the time with a girl named Betty. She's a home-girl like you, and Catholic, and Irish, and in a great many ways we—get along fine. I met her last summer on a moonlight boat trip up the river to Alton, on the *Majestic.* Well—right away from the start it was—love! (LEGEND: "LOVE!") (LAURA *sways slightly forward and grips the arm of the sofa. He fails to notice, now enrapt in his own comfortable being.*) Being in love has made a new man of me! (*Leaning stiffly forward, clutching the arm of the sofa,* LAURA *struggles visibly with her storm. But* JIM *is oblivious, she is a long way off.*) The power of love is really pretty tremendous! Love is something that—changes the whole world, Laura! (*The storm abates a little and* LAURA *leans back. He notices her again.* It happened that Betty's aunt took sick, she got a wire and had to go to Centralia. So Tom—when he asked me to dinner—I naturally just accepted the invitation, not knowing that you—that he—that I—(*He stops awkwardly.*) Huh—I'm a stumble-john! (*He flops back on the sofa. The holy candles in the altar of* LAURA's *face have been snuffed out! There is a look of almost infinite desolation.* JIM *glances at her uneasily.*) I wish that you would—say something. (*She bites her lip which was trembling and then bravely smiles. She opens her hand again on the broken glass ornament. Then she gently takes his hand and raises it level with her own. She carefully places the unicorn in the palm of his hand, then pushes his fingers closed upon it.*) What are you—doing that for? You want me to have him?—Laura? (*She nods.*) What for?

LAURA A—souvenir . . .

She rises unsteadily and crouches beside the victrola to wind it up.

(LEGEND ON SCREEN: "THINGS HAVE A WAY OF TURNING OUT SO BADLY.")

(OR IMAGE: GENTLEMAN CALLER WAVING GOOD-BYE!—GAILY.)

At this moment AMANDA *rushes brightly back in the front room. She bears a pitcher of fruit punch in an old-fashioned cut-glass pitcher and a plate of macaroons. The plate has a gold border and poppies painted on it.*

AMANDA Well, well, well! Isn't the air delightful after the shower? I've made you children a little liquid refreshment. (*Turns gaily to the gentleman caller.*) Jim, do you know that song about lemonade?

> "Lemonade, lemonade
> Made in the shade and stirred with a spade—
> Good enough for any old maid!"

JIM (*uneasily*) Ha-ha! No—I never heard it.

AMANDA Why, Laura! You look so serious!

JIM We were having a serious conversation.

AMANDA Good! Now you're better acquainted!

JIM (*uncertainly*) Ha-ha! Yes.

AMANDA You modern young people are much more serious-minded than my generation.
I was so gay as a girl!

JIM You haven't changed, Mrs. Wingfield.

AMANDA Tonight I'm rejuvenated! The gaiety of the occasion, Mr. O'Connor! (*She tosses
her head with a peal of laughter. Spills lemonade.*) Oooo! I'm baptizing myself!

JIM Here—let me—

AMANDA (*setting the pitcher down*) There now. I discovered we had some maraschino
cherries. I dumped them in, juice and all!

JIM You shouldn't have gone to that trouble, Mrs. Wingfield.

AMANDA Trouble, trouble? Why it was loads of fun! Didn't you hear me cutting up in
the kitchen? I bet your ears were burning! I told Tom how outdone with him I was
for keeping you to himself so long a time! He should have brought you over much,
much sooner! Well, now that you've found your way, I want you to be a very frequent
caller! Not just occasional but all the time. Oh, we're going to have a lot of gay times
together! I see them coming! Mmm, just breathe that air! So fresh, and the moon's
so pretty! I'll skip back out—I know where my place is when young folks are having
a—serious conversation!

JIM Oh, don't go out, Mrs. Wingfield. The fact of the matter is I've got to be going.

AMANDA Going now? You're joking! Why, it's only the shank of the evening, Mr.
O'Connor!

JIM Well, you know how it is.

AMANDA You mean you're a young workingman and have to keep workingmen's hours.
We'll let you off early tonight. But only on the condition that next time you stay later.
What's the best night for you? Isn't Saturday night the best night for you workingmen?

JIM I have a couple of time-clocks to punch, Mrs. Wingfield. One at morning, another
one at night!

AMANDA My, but you *are* ambitious! You work at night, too?

JIM No, Ma'am, not work but—Betty! (*He crosses deliberately to pick up his hat. The
band at the Paradise Dance Hall goes into a tender waltz.*)

AMANDA Betty? Betty? Who's—Betty! (*There is an ominous cracking sound in the sky.*)

JIM Oh, just a girl. The girl I go steady with! (*He smiles charmingly. The sky falls.*)

(LEGEND: "THE SKY FALLS.")

AMANDA (*a long-drawn exhalation*) Ohhhh . . . Is it a serious romance, Mr. O'Connor?

JIM We're going to be married the second Sunday in June.

AMANDA Ohhhh—how nice! Tom didn't mention that you were engaged to be married.

JIM The cat's not out of the bag at the warehouse yet. You know how they are. They
call you Romeo and stuff like that. (*He stops at the oval mirror to put on his hat. He
carefully shapes the brim and the crown to give a discreetly dashing effect.*) It's been a
wonderful evening, Mrs. Wingfield. I guess this is what they mean by Southern
hospitality.

AMANDA It really wasn't anything at all.

JIM I hope it don't seem like I'm rushing off. But I promised Betty I'd pick her up at the Wabash depot, an' by the time I get my jalopy down there her train'll be in. Some women are pretty upset if you keep 'em waiting.

AMANDA Yes, I know—The tyranny of women! (*Extends her hand.*) Good-bye, Mr. O'Connor. I wish you luck—and happiness—and success! All three of them, and so does Laura!—Don't you, Laura?

LAURA Yes!

JIM (*taking her hand*) Good-bye, Laura. I'm certainly going to treasure that souvenir. And don't you forget the good advice I gave you. (*Raises his voice to a cheery shout.*) So long, Shakespeare! Thanks again, ladies—Good night!

He grins and ducks jauntily out.

Still bravely grimacing, AMANDA *closes the door on the gentleman caller. Then she turns back to the room with a puzzled expression. She and* LAURA *don't dare to face each other.* LAURA *crouches beside the victrola to wind it.*

AMANDA (*faintly*) Things have a way of turning out so badly. I don't believe that I would play the victrola. Well, well—well—Our gentleman caller was engaged to be married! Tom!

TOM (*from back*) Yes, Mother?

AMANDA Come in here a minute. I want to tell you something awfully funny.

TOM (*enters with a macaroon and a glass of the lemonade*) Has the gentleman caller gotten away already?

AMANDA The gentleman caller has made an early departure. What a wonderful joke you played on us!

TOM How do you mean?

AMANDA You didn't mention that he was engaged to be married.

TOM Jim? Engaged?

AMANDA That's what he just informed us.

TOM I'll be jiggered! I didn't know about that.

AMANDA That seems very peculiar.

TOM What's peculiar about it?

AMANDA Didn't you call him your best friend down at the warehouse?

TOM He is, but how did I know?

AMANDA It seems extremely peculiar that you wouldn't know your best friend was going to be married!

TOM The warehouse is where I work, not where I know things about people!

AMANDA You don't know things anywhere! You live in a dream; you manufacture illusions! (*He crosses to door.*) Where are you going?

TOM I'm going to the movies.

AMANDA That's right, now that you've had us make such fools of ourselves. The effort, the preparations, all the expense! The new floor lamp, the rug, the clothes for Laura! All for what? To entertain some other girl's fiancé! Go to the movies, go! Don't think about us, a mother deserted, an unmarried sister who's crippled and has no job! Don't let anything interfere with your selfish pleasure! Just go, go, go—to the movies!

TOM All right, I will! The more you shout about my selfishness to me the quicker I'll go, and I won't go to the movies!

AMANDA Go, then! Then go to the moon—you selfish dreamer!

TOM *smashes his glass on the floor. He plunges out on the fire-escape, slamming the door,* LAURA *screams—cut off by the door.*

Dance-hall music up. TOM *goes to the rail and grips it desperately, lifting his face in the chill white moonlight penetrating the narrow abyss of the alley.*

(LEGEND ON SCREEN: "AND SO GOOD-BYE . . .")

TOM's *closing speech is timed with the interior pantomime. The interior scene is played as though viewed through soundproof glass.* AMANDA *appears to be making a comforting speech to* LAURA *who is huddled upon the sofa. Now that we cannot hear the mother's speech, her silliness is gone and she has dignity and tragic beauty.* LAURA's *dark hair hides her face until at the end of the speech she lifts it to smile at her mother.* AMANDA's *gestures are slow and graceful, almost dancelike, as she comforts the daughter. At the end of her speech she glances a moment at the father's picture—then withdraws through the portieres. At close of* TOM's *speech,* LAURA *blows out the candles, ending the play.*

TOM I didn't go to the moon, I went much further—for time is the longest distance between two places—Not long after that I was fired for writing a poem on the lid of a shoe-box. I left Saint Louis. I descended the steps of this fire-escape for a last time and followed, from then on, in my father's footsteps, attempting to find in motion what was lost in space—I traveled around a great deal. The cities swept about me like dead leaves, leaves that were brightly colored but torn away from the branches. I would have stopped, but I was pursued by something. It always came upon me unawares, taking me altogether by surprise. Perhaps it was a familiar bit of music. Perhaps it was only a piece of transparent glass—Perhaps I am walking along a street at night, in some strange city, before I have found companions. I pass the lighted window of a shop where perfume is sold. The window is filled with pieces of colored glass, tiny transparent bottles in delicate colors, like bits of a shattered rainbow. Then all at once my sister touches my shoulder. I turn around and look into her eyes. . . . Oh, Laura, Laura, I tried to leave you behind me, but I am more faithful than I intended to be! I reach for a cigarette, I cross the street, I run into the movies or a bar, I buy a drink, I speak to the nearest stranger—anything that can blow your candles out! (LAURA *bends over the candles.*) —for nowadays the world is lit by lightning! Blow out your candles, Laura—and so good-bye. . . .

She blows the candles out.

(THE SCENE DISSOLVES.)

Questions

1. Assuming that Amanda is the protagonist, state the dramatic situation. What is her objective? What is standing in her way?
2. Suppose we consider the story from Tom's point of view. What is his objective? What are his obstacles? Does his disagreement with his mother make him a villain?
3. Laura initiates very little action in the play. Does she interest you? Why? How is her character symbolized by the image of the glass animals?

4. Several times Tom tells his mother he is going to the movies. Do you think that is where he always goes? If he does not, then where does he go? What strengths and/or weaknesses of character are revealed by this discrepancy between words and actions?
5. The rising action of the play concerns the pursuit of the Gentleman Caller. What are some of the complications and crises that threaten Amanda before Jim O'Connor arrives? What virtues does Amanda reveal in handling these crises? What flaws?
6. What is the climax of the play? Can you pin it down to a specific scene? A single action or speech?
7. What are Jim's virtues? What is his flaw? Do you consider him a villain?
8. How does Amanda handle the news that Jim is engaged? Do you feel sorry for her?
9. After Jim leaves, Laura has no more lines. What do you suppose she is feeling? What do you feel for her?
10. Tom leaves his home, never to return. What strength of character does that action reveal? What flaw?
11. There is one flaw shared by every character in *The Glass Menagerie*. What is it?

Suggestions for Dramatists

1. What do you want more than anything in the world? Money? Fame? Be as specific as you can in defining your goal. What is keeping you from getting it? Think of yourself as the protagonist of a drama, in which you are called upon to take risks or make sacrifices to achieve your goal. Imagine scenes of challenge, scenes of temptation. How do you respond? Are you courageous and imaginative in the pursuit of your goal, or timid and dull?
2. What makes you different from your friends? List as many qualities of your character as you can. Would any of these be particularly interesting in a play?
3. Do you know someone whom you consider a villain? Describe a particular instance of that individual's villainy. Now try to describe the motive behind it. Does the person seem less a villain once you have explained his or her motive?

 Writers on Writing   *Tennessee Williams*

> *Whether he likes it or not, a writer for the stage must face the fact that the making of a play is, finally, a collaborative venture, and plays have rarely achieved a full-scale success without being in some manner raised above their manuscript level by the brilliant gifts of actors, directors, designers, and frequently even the seasoned theatrical instincts of their producers. I often wonder, for personal instance, if* The Glass Menagerie *might not have been a mere succès d'estime, snobbishly remembered by a small coterie, if Laurette Taylor had not poured into it her startling light and power. . . .*

✍ Tips for Writing about Dramatic Character

1. There is an important difference between a great stage character and a character in a short story or novel. The great character onstage displays extraordinary desire in pursuit of an obvious goal. A novelist may interest us in the thoughts of a languid character sitting in an armchair. The playwright cannot. The great stage hero or heroine manifests his or her character in *action*, pursuing a goal.
2. In order to determine the most important characters in a play, look for the figures with the greatest desires.
3. Determine exactly what is the goal of the character.
4. What is he or she willing to risk in order to get it?
5. The great stage character always has an obvious flaw. Figure out what it is. Evaluate the playwright's success in terms of how this flaw brings joy or sadness to the world of the play.
6. The great stage character is always attractive to us because of certain virtues. Define them. Evaluate the playwright's success in delineating character in terms of his ability to balance the hero's virtues and flaws.

6 🌿 Tragedy

"A perfect Tragedy," said the English essayist Joseph Addison, "is the noblest production of human nature." It may come as no surprise that what is noblest in us is also rare and difficult to produce; nevertheless, the evidence is astonishing. Since the birth of tragedy in the sixth century B.C., fewer than two dozen playwrights have made enduring contributions to the form. There are cultures that have not produced a single great tragedian. Others, like England, that can boast of several, have seen generations pass between them.

What is a tragedy? What is it about this dramatic form that a culture values so highly? And why does this form make such demands upon the playwright? No comment on these issues is more helpful than Aristotle's: A tragedy portrays "incidents arousing pity and fear." It is important that the cross-section of culture represented by a theater audience should share pity and fear for the same hero. People who cannot agree on a tax structure, a political candidate, or a dinner menu, can all weep for Oedipus and Hamlet. Tragedy brings people together. Ancient Greeks and medieval Christians understood this religious principle of drama. As a forum for ultimate human concerns, tragic theater still has this power. American theatergoers, who may agree on little else, will all agree that Abbie Putnam, heroine of *Desire Under the Elms*, is a liar and a ruthless manipulator of men; yet life has dealt with her more cruelly than she deserved. It is painfully difficult to create such a character and to devise an action that will capture the tragic sympathies of a diverse public.

The scholar Bernard Knox observes: "It sometimes happens that a great poet [dramatist] creates a character in whom the essence of an age is distilled, a representative figure who in his action and suffering presents to his own time the image of its victory and defeat. . . . The poet who created him has penetrated so deeply into the permanent elements of the human situation that his creation transcends time. One such figure is Hamlet, Prince of Denmark, and such another is Oedipus, King of Thebes." It is possible that Abbie Putnam, mistress of the Cabot farmhouse of New England, is another such figure.

Fear and Pity

As we noted in Chapter 4, a tragedy is a play that shows the change in the protagonist's fortunes from good to bad. The incidents must inspire *fear* and *pity*. Let us consider these emotions. We *fear* most deeply for characters who are like ourselves, when they are in danger. What threatens them may threaten us: sickness, old age, betrayal, fire. No one, apart from their families, could be more fearful for the firefighters climbing into a burning house than their fellow firefighters. Likewise, a dramatic character, to inspire fear in the spectators, must be like them in some important way. We have all known to some degree the pride of Oedipus, the bitterness and confusion of Hamlet, the intemperate passion of Abbie Putnam. Otherwise we would not care enough for these characters to fear for them.

It is particularly fearful to watch someone fall from a position of high rank or power. The heroes of classical tragedy are always members of the nobility. Their fates are terrifying to us, for we sense that if these great, privileged figures are vulnerable, then none of us is safe.

Pity is the final proof of tragic drama. In order to feel pity, we must believe that the protagonist's suffering is undeserved, the punishment greater than the crime. Yet tragic heroes must not be totally guiltless. If they were, their fall would not inspire fear and pity in us. It would inspire anger and disgust, as does news of the slaughter of baby seals. Tragic heroes must not be outright victims. A flaw must contribute to their undoing if we are to feel pity as well as fear.

Recognition and Reversal

In our discussion of *Riders to the Sea* we mentioned that Maurya's suffering leads her to a new and deeper understanding of life. This is the ultimate recognition for the tragic character. But such understanding does not come at once. It usually results from several scenes of *recognition* that occur from climax to catastrophe of a tragedy. The Greeks used the word *anagnorisis* (recognition) to refer to any change from ignorance to knowledge. In scenes of recognition the protagonist may learn the true nature of his predicament, or he may learn what weakness of his character has caused it. He may learn both at once. When Oedipus discovers that Laïos was murdered "where three highways meet," he recognizes that he may have killed his father. At the same time he realizes his arrogance as he says, "I may be accurst by my own ignorant edict." Of course, the most dramatic discovery of *Oedipus Rex*, the beginning of the catastrophe, is his recognition that the prophecy has come true, that he has killed his father and married his mother. This discovery is accompanied by a violent reversal of Oedipus's fortunes.

In the broadest sense the action of any play is a *reversal*, from bad to good fortune in a comedy, and from good to bad fortune in a tragedy. But in most plays there are one or more points in the action when the reversal of fortune is particularly conspicuous or violent. The Greeks called these *peripeteia*. The *peripeteia* is especially moving when the characters' actions have an effect opposite to that which they intended. This is *tragic irony*. The climax and catastrophe of *Oedipus Rex* described above are both examples of *peripateia* with *tragic irony*. Iocastê wishes to reassure Oedipus but fires his suspicions; the Messenger and Shepherd are called to prove Oedipus's innocence; instead they confirm his guilt.

Recognition sometimes brings on a reversal of fortunes, and sometimes a reversal, or *peripeteia*, brings about an important recognition on the part of the protagonist. It is most dramatic when these events happen at the same time.

Catharsis

All the events of a tragedy have been leading us to fear the worst for our hero. When the catastrophe comes at last, we are not surprised. We feel sorry for the hero and may weep, caught up in a mixture of sadness for him and for ourselves, and a bittersweet feeling of relief. After all that dread, the thing we most feared has happened. Yet we are still alive and somehow better off for what we have witnessed. Leaving the theater, we may feel the comfort of one who has awakened from a nightmare, or walked away from an automobile accident unharmed. We have witnessed suffering, known terror, and yet life goes on. These feelings and thoughts that follow tragedy Aristotle calls *catharsis*.

In ancient Greek, catharsis was originally a medical term that meant "cleansing." Aristotle probably intended to use the concept of catharsis as a defense against philosophers like Plato, who believed that drama incited dishonorable emotions and bad behavior. Aristotle suggests that tragedy is good for us because it cleanses us of violent and mean emotions in a controlled environment. The debate still rages between censors who believe drama is dangerous, and the advocates of free expression who believe the emotional adventures of drama are healthy.

Aristotle's contemporaries may have understood precisely what he meant by "cleansing emotions." He may have meant something as simple as: "We all feel better after a good cry." Unfortunately the philosopher did not elaborate. The concept remains vague and provokes considerable debate among scholars. Each critic and culture tends to interpret catharsis according to its own experience of tragic drama. We have described catharsis as a kind of relief. Your experience of tragedy in the theater may cause you to describe catharsis in a different way.

The Tragic Hero

In our discussion of *Oedipus Rex* in Chapter 4, we remarked that the hero of Greek tragedy is an extraordinary man or woman who separates himself or herself from others. This separation is central to all tragedies. Oedipus begins his play in a position somewhat isolated by his own power as a king. Then in his obsessive search for the killer of Laïos he increases his isolation by alienating Teiresias, his brother-in-law Creon, and his queen Iocastê. Once the old shepherd proves Oedipus's guilt, the king cuts himself off from humankind by putting out his eyes. Then the movement toward isolation culminates in Oedipus's exile from Thebes.

In the *Anatomy of Criticism*, Northrop Frye examines the causes and implications of the tragic hero's isolation. "The tragic hero is typically on top of the wheel of fortune, half-way between human society on the ground and the something greater in the sky. . . . Tragic heroes are so much the highest points in their human landscapes that they seem the inevitable conductors of the power about them, great trees more likely to be struck by lightning than a clump of grass . . . tragic heroes are wrapped in the mystery of their communion with that something beyond which we can see only through them, and which is the source of their strength and their fate alike."[1] That "something beyond" may be called God, or nature, or society, but in all cases it reveals some sort of eternal law, of the way things are or must be. Tragedy gives us an image of the hero struggling against that law, alone. Further struggle leads the hero into further isolation.

In reading *Hamlet, Desire Under the Elms*, and other tragedies, we should mark the characteristics of the protagonist that set him or her apart from their fellows. We should also try to determine the religious or moral law against which the protagonist is struggling in his or her movement toward isolation.

Shakespeare and the Elizabethan Theater

Shakespeare's *Hamlet* is one of the decisive masterpieces of the Elizabethan stage. From the defeat of the Spanish Armada in 1588 until the closing of the theaters in 1642 because of the Civil War, the English theater experienced a flowering of genius unparalleled in history. Christopher Marlowe (1564–1593) developed the "mighty line" of blank verse that became the rhythmic heart of dramatic diction in such plays as *Tamburlaine* and *Dr. Faustus*. Ben Jonson wrote comedies of satiric wit, such as *Volpone* and *The Alchemist*. Thomas Dekker, John Webster, and others wrote plays that were not only popular but intelligent, proving that it was a culture of thoughtful audiences as well as gifted dramatists.

The most gifted of them all was William Shakespeare. As a poet, deviser of plots, and creator of character, Shakespeare was outstanding in a generation of extraordinary talents. He is one of the few who wrote comedies as well as tragedies and histories. His friend Ben Jonson said of him, "He was not of an age, but for all time!" John Dryden wrote that Shakespeare "had an Universal mind."

For someone who was so brilliant and made such an impact on the popular culture, Shakespeare has left remarkably few biographical traces. We know that he was baptized in Stratford-on-Avon on April 26, 1564, and that his father was a glover. We know he married Anne Hathaway when he was eighteen, and they had a daughter a few months later, the first of three children. He was a member

---

[1] Northrop Frye, *The Anatomy of Criticism: Four Essays* (Princeton, NJ: Princeton University Press, 1957), pp. 207–208.

Model depicting a theatre of Shakespeare's time (*Richard Southern Accession, University of Bristol Theatre Collection*)

of the Lord Chamberlain's company of actors in 1594. In 1599 he joined a syndicate that built and managed the Globe Theatre, one of the most successful theaters of the time. In 1597 he bought one of the largest houses in Stratford. On April 23, 1616, he died and a few days later was buried at Stratford Church. That is nearly all we know about him. The thousands of pages of biography written about Shakespeare are mostly guesswork based on the plays and the history of the period. His personality remains as mysterious as his genius. Many cranks and some serious scholars have argued that Shakespeare did not write the masterpieces bearing his name. They say it is impossible that a man of such humble origins and rudimentary education could have created those thirty-odd dramas. And why aren't there more records, contemporary accounts of this famous man? No one really knows. We do know that the personal lives of dramatists did not stir up as much interest then as they do now. Playwrights were not considered serious "literary men" during Elizabethan times. We know as much about Shakespeare as about any other dramatist of his age except Ben Jonson, who had a literary reputation in addition to his theatrical fame. Whoever Shakespeare was, we are satisfied that he wrote *Hamlet* and the other great dramas assigned to him.

    Hamlet was registered for printing in 1602; we believe it was first performed a year or two before that by the renowned actor Richard Burbage. It was probably among the first plays produced in the newly built Globe Theatre. No pictures have survived, and though there is some controversy over the arrangement of the Globe, we assume that it was a typical theater of the period.

Elizabethan theaters were much more intimate than the Greek amphitheaters. The entire Globe would have fit into the orchestra of the Theater of Dionysus. The Globe was an outdoor theater surrounded by covered galleries. The stage was a raised platform thrusting into the audience area. To the rear there was a curtained area that might have been used for a bedroom, an entrance hall, or other intimate scenes. Above this space was the balcony, famous for the love scene in *Romeo and Juliet*. It could also be used as the top of a wall for a battle scene, a prison room, or the upper deck of a ship. There was a trap door in the stage for the entrance of demons from the underworld, which would serve as the grave in the cemetery scenes from *Hamlet*. Ghosts and angels sometimes descended on ropes from the canopy extending over the stage.

There was no curtain between the main playing area and the audience to ease the transition between scenes. There were probably no painted sets, and few stage props. Much of the "scene-painting" is done with poetry. Shakespeare's characters verbally create the scene, and the audience must imagine it. The plays we have read thus far take place in a single, stationary setting. *Hamlet* is much more cinematic, its action moving from chamber to chamber within Elsinore Castle, then to the ramparts outside, or to a churchyard. There may be little more to indicate the change in scene than a rearrangement of chairs, or the opening of the trap door as a makeshift grave for the churchyard. The rest is done with words. Thus, at the opening of Act I, Scene 4, Hamlet says

Detail of Visscher's map of London c. 1616 showing the Globe Theatre (*Folger Shakespeare Library*)

to Horatio: "The air bites shrewdly; it is very cold," and Horatio answers: "It is a nipping and an eager air." Such poetic reporting of the weather is worth any number of wind-machines, particularly to the reader.

Although the stage props were minimal, the costuming was elaborate and beautiful. As in the Greek theater, all the actors were men. Apprentices, whose voices had not changed, played the roles of women.

Before the theaters were built, players performed in taverns and inns, and the atmosphere of the Elizabethan theater preserved much of its rowdy origin. The inns had an inner courtyard and rooms overlooking the yard where the actors set up their temporary stage. So the poor folks, or *groundlings*, watched the play from the yard, and the ladies and gentlemen who could afford rooms lounged on their balconies. The Globe was built with two or three tiers of covered balconies around the stage, and an open yard in front where the poorer spectators sat, stood, or rolled drunkenly. The atomosphere of the Elizabethan theater was a blend of the prize fight, the revival meeting, and a session of parliament— with musicians, pickpockets, and prostitutes moving through the crowd, and a good deal of conversation and spontaneous applause. This accounts for the oratory of some scenes and the slapstick humor of others in Shakespeare. It was no mean feat to hold the attention of such a varied and lively audience.

The story of *Hamlet* is an old one out of the *Historica Danica* (c. 1200; printed 1514) by the Danish chronicler Saxo Grammaticus. Shakespeare was not the first to dramatize it. He often took his plots from history, old legends, Italian novels, and other plays.

The text you will read is the product of nearly four hundred years of editing, scholarship, and controversy. Shakespeare wrote the dialogue. He did not divide the plays into acts and scenes, for the action in his theater was continuous. These divisions, as well as the scenic notes and stage directions, were done by John Heming and Henry Condell, two of Shakespeare's former colleagues who prepared the First Folio of his plays in 1623. They printed the Folio from playhouse scripts which probably were not all written in verses. Therefore, even the pentameter lines may be, to some extent, the result of editing.

WILLIAM SHAKESPEARE (1564–1616)

The Tragedy of Hamlet, Prince of Denmark

DRAMATIS PERSONAE

CLAUDIUS, *King of Denmark*	VOLTEMAND ⎫
HAMLET, *son to the late King Hamlet, and*	CORNELIUS ⎪
nephew to the present King	ROSENCRANTZ ⎬ *courtiers*
POLONIUS, *Lord Chamberlain*	GUILDENSTERN ⎪
HORATIO, *friend to Hamlet*	OSRIC ⎪
LAERTES, *son to Polonius*	GENTLEMAN ⎭

Tradgety of a man who could not make up his mind.

MARCELLUS } *officers*	ENGLISH AMBASSADORS
BARNARDO }	
FRANCISCO, *a soldier*	GERTRUDE, *Queen of Denmark, and mother to*
REYNALDO, *servant to Polonius*	*Hamlet*
FORTINBRAS, *Prince of Norway*	OPHELIA, *daughter to Polonius*
NORWEGIAN CAPTAIN	
DOCTOR OF DIVINITY	GHOST *of Hamlet's Father*
PLAYERS	
Two CLOWNS, *grave-diggers*	LORDS, LADIES, OFFICERS, SOLDIERS,
SCENE. *Denmark*	SAILORS, MESSENGERS, *and* ATTENDANTS

ACT I

SCENE I.

Enter BARNARDO *and* FRANCISCO, *two sentinels,* [*meeting*].

BAR. Who's there?
FRAN. Nay, answer me. Stand and unfold yourself.
BAR. Long live the King!
FRAN. Barnardo.
5 BAR. He.
FRAN. You come most carefully upon your hour.
BAR. 'Tis now strook twelf. Get thee to bed, Francisco.
FRAN. For this relief much thanks. 'Tis bitter cold,
  And I am sick at heart.
BAR. Have you had quiet guard?
10 FRAN.   Not a mouse stirring.
BAR. Well, good night.
  If you do meet Horatio and Marcellus,
  The rivals of my watch, bid them make haste.

Enter HORATIO *and* MARCELLUS.

FRAN. I think I hear them. Stand ho! Who is there?
HOR. Friends to this ground.
15 MAR.   And liegemen to the Dane.
FRAN. Give you good night.
MAR.   O, farewell, honest [soldier].
  Who hath reliev'd you?

Words and passages enclosed in square brackets in the text above are either emendations of the copy-text or additions to it.

I.i. Location: Elsinore. A guard-platform of the castle.
2 **answer me:** i.e. *you* answer *me.* Francisco is on watch; Barnardo has come to relieve him. **unfold yourself:** make known who you are.
3 **Long . . . King.** Perhaps a password, perhaps simply an utterance to allow the voice to be recognized.
7 **strook twelf:** struck twelve.
9 **sick at heart:** in low spirits.
13 **rivals:** partners.
15 **liegemen . . . Dane:** loyal subjects to the King of Denmark.
16 **Give:** God give.

FRAN.   Barnardo hath my place.
  Give you good night.

Exit FRANCISCO.

MAR.   Holla, Barnardo!
BAR.   Say—
  What, is Horatio there?
HOR.   A piece of him.
20 BAR. Welcome, Horatio, welcome, good Marcellus.
HOR. What, has this thing appear'd again to-night?
BAR. I have seen nothing.
MAR. Horatio says 'tis but our fantasy,
  And will not let belief take hold of him
25   Touching this dreaded sight twice seen of us;
  Therefore I have entreated him along,
  With us to watch the minutes of this night,
  That if again this apparition come,
  He may approve our eyes and speak to it.
HOR. Tush, tush, 'twill not appear.
30 BAR.   Sit down a while,
  And let us once again assail your ears,
  That are so fortified against our story,
  What we have two nights seen.
HOR.   Well, sit we down,
  And let us hear Barnardo speak of this.
35 BAR. Last night of all,
  When yond same star that's westward from the pole
  Had made his course t' illume that part of heaven
  Where now it burns, Marcellus and myself,
  The bell then beating one—

Enter GHOST.

40 MAR. Peace, break thee off! Look where it comes again!
BAR. In the same figure like the King that's dead.
MAR. Thou art a scholar, speak to it, Horatio.
BAR. Looks 'a not like the King? Mark it, Horatio.
HOR. Most like; it [harrows] me with fear and wonder.
BAR. It would be spoke to.
45 MAR.   Speak to it, Horatio.
HOR. What art thou that usurp'st this time of night,

---

[23] **fantasy:** imagination.

[29] **approve:** corroborate.

[36] **pole:** pole star.

[37] **his:** its (the commonest form of the neuter possessive singular in Shakespeare's day).

[41] **like:** in the likeness of.

[42] **a scholar:** i.e. one who knows how best to address it.

[43] **'a:** he.

[45] **It . . . to.** A ghost had to be spoken to before it could speak.

[46] **usurp'st.** The ghost, a supernatural being, has invaded the realm of nature.

Together with that fair and warlike form
In which the majesty of buried Denmark
Did sometimes march? By heaven I charge thee speak!
MAR. It is offended.
50 BAR.   See, it stalks away!
HOR. Stay! Speak, speak, I charge thee speak!

Exit GHOST.

MAR. 'Tis gone, and will not answer.
BAR. How now, Horatio? you tremble and look pale.
Is not this something more than fantasy?
55   What think you on't?
HOR. Before my God, I might not this believe
Without the sensible and true avouch
Of mine own eyes.
MAR.   Is it not like the King?
HOR. As thou art to thyself.
60   Such was the very armor he had on
When he the ambitious Norway combated.
So frown'd he once when in an angry parle
He smote the sledded [Polacks] on the ice.
'Tis strange.
65 MAR. Thus twice before, and jump at this dead hour,
With martial stalk hath he gone by our watch.
HOR. In what particular thought to work I know not,
But in the gross and scope of mine opinion,
This bodes some strange eruption to our state.
70 MAR. Good now, sit down, and tell me, he that knows,
Why this same strict and most observant watch
So nightly toils the subject of the land,
And [why] such daily [cast] of brazen cannon,
And foreign mart for implements of war,
75   Why such impress of shipwrights, whose sore task
Does not divide the Sunday from the week,
What might be toward, that this sweaty haste

---

48 **majesty . . . Denmark:** late King of Denmark.
49 **sometimes:** formerly.
57 **sensible:** relating to the senses.   **avouch:** guarantee.
61 **Norway:** King of Norway.
62 **parle:** parley.
63 **sledded:** using sleds or sledges.   **Polacks:** Poles.
65 **jump:** precisely.
67–68 **In . . . opinion:** while I have no precise theory about it, my general feeling is that. *Gross* = wholeness, totality; *scope* = range.
69 **eruption:** upheaval.
72 **toils:** causes to work.   **subject:** subjects.
74 **foreign mart:** dealing with foreign markets.
75 **impress:** forced service.
77 **toward:** in preparation.

Doth make the night joint-laborer with the day:
Who is't that can inform me?

HOR.   That can I,
80   At least the whisper goes so: our last king,
Whose image even but now appear'd to us,
Was, as you know, by Fortinbras of Norway,
Thereto prick'd on by a most emulate pride,
Dar'd to the combat; in which our valiant Hamlet
85   (For so this side of our known world esteem'd him)
Did slay this Fortinbras, who, by a seal'd compact
Well ratified by law and heraldy,
Did forfeit (with his life) all [those] his lands
Which he stood seiz'd of, to the conqueror;
90   Against the which a moi'ty competent
Was gaged by our king, which had [return'd]
To the inheritance of Fortinbras,
Had he been vanquisher; as by the same comart
And carriage of the article [design'd],
95   His fell to Hamlet. Now, sir, young Fortinbras,
Of unimproved mettle hot and full,
Hath in the skirts of Norway here and there
Shark'd up a list of lawless resolutes
For food and diet to some enterprise
100   That hath a stomach in't, which is no other,
As it doth well appear unto our state,
But to recover of us, by strong hand
And terms compulsatory, those foresaid lands
So by his father lost; and this, I take it,
105   Is the main motive of our preparations,
The source of this our watch, and the chief head
Of this post-haste and romage in the land.

BAR. I think it be no other but e'en so.
Well may it sort that this portentous figure
110   Comes armed through our watch so like the King
That was and is the question of these wars.

---

83 **emulate:** emulous, proceeding from rivalry.
87 **law and heraldy:** heraldic law (governing combat). *Heraldy* is a variant of *heraldry*.
89 **seiz'd of:** possessed of.
90 **moi'ty:** portion.   **competent:** adequate, i.e. equivalent.
91 **gaged:** pledged.   **had:** would have.
92 **inheritance:** possession.
93 **comart:** bargain.
94 **carriage:** tenor.   **design'd:** drawn up.
96 **unimproved:** untried (?) or not directed to any useful end (?).
97 **skirts:** outlying territories.
98 **Shark'd up:** gathered up hastily and indiscriminately.
100 **stomach:** relish of danger (?) or demand for courage (?).
106 **head:** source.
107 **romage:** rummage, bustling activity.
109 **sort:** fit.   **portentous:** ominous.

HOR. A mote it is to trouble the mind's eye.
    In the most high and palmy state of Rome,
    A little ere the mightiest Julius fell,
115   The graves stood [tenantless] and the sheeted dead
    Did squeak and gibber in the Roman streets.
    As stars with trains of fire, and dews of blood,
    Disasters in the sun; and the moist star
    Upon whose influence Neptune's empire stands
120   Was sick almost to doomsday with eclipse.
    And even the like precurse of [fear'd] events,
    As harbingers preceding still the fates
    And prologue to the omen coming on,
    Have heaven and earth together demonstrated
125   Unto our climatures and countrymen.

Enter GHOST.

    But soft, behold! lo where it comes again!

It spreads his arms.

    I'll cross it though it blast me. Stay, illusion!
    If thou hast any sound or use of voice,
    Speak to me.
130   If there be any good thing to be done
    That may to thee do ease, and grace to me,
    Speak to me.
    If thou art privy to thy country's fate,
    Which happily foreknowing may avoid,
135   O speak!
    Or if thou hast uphoarded in thy life
    Extorted treasure in the womb of earth,
    For which, they say, your spirits oft walk in death,
    Speak of it, stay and speak! (*The cock crows.*) Stop it, Marcellus.
140 MAR. Shall I strike it with my partisan?
    HOR. Do, if it will not stand.
    BAR.   'Tis here!

---

116 One or more lines may have been lost between this line and the next.
118 **Disasters:** ominous signs. **moist star:** moon.
119 **Neptune's empire stands:** the seas are dependent.
120 **sick . . . doomsday:** i.e. almost totally darkened. When the Day of Judgment is imminent, says
    Matthew 24:29, "the moon shall not give her light." **eclipse.** There were a solar and two total
    lunar eclipses visible in England in 1598; they caused gloomy speculation.
121 **precurse:** foreshadowing.
122 **harbingers:** advance messengers. **still:** always.
123 **omen:** i.e. the events portended.
125 **climatures:** regions.
126 s.d. **his:** its.
127 **cross it:** cross its path, confront it directly. **blast:** wither (by supernatural means).
134 **happily:** haply, perhaps.
138 **your.** Colloquial and impersonal; cf. I.v.167, IV.iii.20–21. Most editors adopt *you* from F1.
140 **partisan:** long-handled spear.

HOR.   'Tis here!
MAR. 'Tis gone!

[Exit GHOST.]

　　　We do it wrong, being so majestical,
　　　　To offer it the show of violence,
145　　For it is as the air, invulnerable,
　　　　And our vain blows malicious mockery.
　　BAR. It was about to speak when the cock crew.
　　HOR. And then it started like a guilty thing
　　　　Upon a fearful summons. I have heard
150　　The cock, that is the trumpet to the morn,
　　　　Doth with his lofty and shrill-sounding throat
　　　　Awake the god of day, and at his warning,
　　　　Whether in sea or fire, in earth or air,
　　　　Th' extravagant and erring spirit hies
155　　To his confine; and of the truth herein
　　　　This present object made probation.
　　MAR. It faded on the crowing of the cock.
　　　　Some say that ever 'gainst that season comes
　　　　Wherein our Saviour's birth is celebrated,
160　　This bird of dawning singeth all night long,
　　　　And then they say no spirit dare stir abroad,
　　　　The nights are wholesome, then no planets strike,
　　　　No fairy takes, nor witch hath power to charm,
　　　　So hallowed, and so gracious, is that time.
165 HOR. So have I heard and do in part believe it.
　　　　But look, the morn in russet mantle clad
　　　　Walks o'er the dew of yon high eastward hill.
　　　　Break we our watch up, and by my advice
　　　　Let us impart what we have seen to-night
170　　Unto young Hamlet, for, upon my life,
　　　　This spirit, dumb to us, will speak to him.
　　　　Do you consent we shall acquaint him with it,
　　　　As needful in our loves, fitting our duty?
　　MAR. Let's do't, I pray, and I this morning know
175　　Where we shall find him most convenient.

Exeunt.

────────────

146 **malicious mockery:** mockery of malice, i.e. empty pretenses of harming it.
150 **trumpet:** trumpeter.
154 **extravagant:** wandering outside its proper bounds. **erring:** wandering abroad. **hies:** hastens.
156 **object:** sight. **probation:** proof.
158 **'gainst:** just before.
162 **strike:** exert malevolent influence.
163 **takes:** bewitches, charms.
164 **gracious:** blessed.
166 **russet:** coarse greyish-brown cloth.

SCENE II.

Flourish. Enter CLAUDIUS, KING OF DENMARK, GERTRUDE THE QUEEN; COUNCIL: *as* POLONIUS; *and his son* LAERTES, HAMLET, *cum aliis [including* VOLTEMAND *and* CORNELIUS].

KING Though yet of Hamlet our dear brother's death
 The memory be green, and that it us befitted
 To bear our hearts in grief, and our whole kingdom
 To be contracted in one brow of woe,
5 Yet so far hath discretion fought with nature
 That we with wisest sorrow think on him
 Together with remembrance of ourselves.
 Therefore our sometime sister, now our queen,
 Th' imperial jointress to this warlike state,
10 Have we, as 'twere with a defeated joy,
 With an auspicious, and a dropping eye,
 With mirth in funeral, and with dirge in marriage,
 In equal scale weighing delight and dole,
 Taken to wife; nor have we herein barr'd
15 Your better wisdoms, which have freely gone
 With this affair along. For all, our thanks.
 Now follows that you know young Fortinbras,
 Holding a weak supposal of our worth,
 Or thinking by our late dear brother's death
20 Our state to be disjoint and out of frame,
 Co-leagued with this dream of his advantage,
 He hath not fail'd to pester us with message
 Importing the surrender of those lands
 Lost by his father, with all bands of law,
25 To our most valiant brother. So much for him.
 Now for ourself, and for this time of meeting,
 Thus much the business is: we have here writ
 To Norway, uncle of young Fortinbras—
 Who, impotent and bedred, scarcely hears
30 Of this his nephew's purpose—to suppress

I.ii. Location: The castle.
o.s.d. **Flourish:** trumpet fanfare. **cum aliis:** with others.
2 **befitted:** would befit.
4 **contracted in:** (1) reduced to; (2) knit or wrinkled in. **brow of woe:** mournful brow.
9 **jointress:** joint holder.
10 **defeated:** impaired.
11 **auspicious . . . dropping:** cheerful . . . weeping.
15 **freely:** fully, without reservation.
17 **know:** be informed, learn.
18 **supposal:** conjecture, estimate.
21 **Co-leagued:** joined.
22 **pester . . . message:** trouble me with persistent messages (the original sense of *pester* is "overcrowd").
23 **Importing:** having as import.
24 **bands:** bonds, binding terms.
29 **impotent and bedred:** feeble and bedridden.

His further gait herein, in that the levies,
The lists, and full proportions are all made
Out of his subject; and we here dispatch
You, good Cornelius, and you, Voltemand,
35   For bearers of this greeting to old Norway,
Giving to you no further personal power
To business with the King, more than the scope
Of these delated articles allow.

[Giving a paper.]

Farewell, and let your haste commend your duty.
40   COR., VOL. In that, and all things, will we show our duty.
KING We doubt it nothing; heartily farewell.

[Exeunt VOLTEMAND *and* CORNELIUS.]

And now, Laertes, what's the news with you?
You told us of some suit, what is't, Laertes?
You cannot speak of reason to the Dane
45   And lose your voice. What wouldst thou beg, Laertes,
That shall not be my offer, not thy asking?
The head is not more native to the heart,
The hand more instrumental to the mouth,
Than is the throne of Denmark to thy father.
What wouldst thou have, Laertes?
50   LAER.   My dread lord,
Your leave and favor to return to France,
From whence though willingly I came to Denmark
To show my duty in your coronation,
Yet now I must confess, that duty done,
55   My thoughts and wishes bend again toward France,
And bow them to your gracious leave and pardon.
KING Have you your father's leave? What says Polonius?
POL. H'ath, my lord, wrung from me my slow leave
By laborsome petition, and at last
60   Upon his will I seal'd my hard consent.
I do beseech you give him leave to go.

---

31 **gait**: proceeding.
31–33 **in . . . subject**: since the troops are all drawn from his subjects.
38 **delated**: extended, detailed (a variant of *dilated*).
41 **nothing**: not at all.
45 **lose**: waste.
47 **native**: closely related.
48 **instrumental**: serviceable.
51 **leave and favor**: gracious permission.
56 **pardon**: permission to depart.
58 **H'ath**: he hath.
60 **hard**: reluctant.

KING Take thy fair hour, Laertes, time be thine,
    And thy best graces spend it at thy will!
    But now, my cousin Hamlet, and my son—
65 HAM. *[Aside.]* A little more than kin, and less than kind.
    KING How is it that the clouds still hang on you?
    HAM. Not so, my lord, I am too much in the sun.
    QUEEN Good Hamlet, cast thy nighted color off,
    And let thine eye look like a friend on Denmark.
70   Do not for ever with thy vailed lids
    Seek for thy noble father in the dust.
    Thou know'st 'tis common, all that lives must die,
    Passing through nature to eternity.
    HAM. Ay, madam, it is common.
    QUEEN   If it be,
75   Why seems it so particular with thee?
    HAM. Seems, madam? nay, it is, I know not "seems."
    'Tis not alone my inky cloak, [good] mother,
    Nor customary suits of solemn black,
    Nor windy suspiration of forc'd breath,
80   No, nor the fruitful river in the eye,
    Nor the dejected havior of the visage,
    Together with all forms, moods, [shapes] of grief,
    That can [denote] me truly. These indeed seem,
    For they are actions that a man might play,
85   But I have that within which passes show,
    These but the trappings and the suits of woe.
    KING 'Tis sweet and commendable in your nature, Hamlet,
    To give these mourning duties to your father.
    But you must know your father lost a father,
90   That father lost, lost his, and the survivor bound
    In filial obligation for some term
    To do obsequious sorrow. But to persever
    In obstinate condolement is a course
    Of impious stubbornness, 'tis unmanly grief,
95   It shows a will most incorrect to heaven,
    A heart unfortified, or mind impatient,
    An understanding simple and unschool'd:

---

64 **cousin:** kinsman (used in familiar address to any collateral relative more distant than a brother
    or sister; here to a nephew).
65 **A little . . . kind:** closer than a nephew, since you are my mother's husband; yet more distant
    than a son, too (and not well disposed to you).
67 **sun.** With obvious quibble on *son.*
70 **vailed:** downcast.
72 **common:** general, universal.
75 **particular:** individual, personal.
80 **fruitful:** copious.
92 **obsequious:** proper to obsequies.
93 **condolement:** grief.
95 **incorrect:** unsubmissive.

For what we know must be, and is as common
As any the most vulgar thing to sense,
100 Why should we in our peevish opposition
Take it to heart? Fie, 'tis a fault to heaven,
A fault against the dead, a fault to nature,
To reason most absurd, whose common theme
Is death of fathers, and who still hath cried,
105 From the first corse till he that died to-day,
"This must be so." We pray you throw to earth
This unprevailing woe, and think of us
As of a father, for let the world take note
You are the most immediate to our throne,
110 And with no less nobility of love
Than that which dearest father bears his son
Do I impart toward you. For your intent
In going back to school in Wittenberg,
It is most retrograde to our desire,
115 And we beseech you bend you to remain
Here in the cheer and comfort of our eye,
Our chiefest courtier, cousin, and our son.
QUEEN Let not thy mother lose her prayers, Hamlet,
I pray thee stay with us, go not to Wittenberg.
120 HAM. I shall in all my best obey you, madam.
KING Why, 'tis a loving and a fair reply.
Be as ourself in Denmark. Madam, come.
This gentle and unforc'd accord of Hamlet
Sits smiling to my heart, in grace whereof,
125 No jocund health that Denmark drinks to-day,
But the great cannon to the clouds shall tell,
And the King's rouse the heaven shall bruit again,
Respeaking earthly thunder. Come away.

Flourish. Exeunt all but HAMLET.

HAM. O that this too too sallied flesh would melt,
130 Thaw, and resolve itself into a dew!
Or that the Everlasting had not fix'd
His canon 'gainst [self-]slaughter! O God, God,
How [weary], stale, flat, and unprofitable

---

99 **any . . . sense:** what is perceived to be commonest.
101 **to:** against.
103 **absurd:** contrary.
107 **unprevailing:** unavailing.
111 **dearest:** most loving.
112 **impart:** i.e. impart love.
127 **rouse:** bumper, drink. **bruit:** loudly declare.
129 **sallied:** sullied. Many editors prefer the F1 reading, *solid.*
132 **canon:** law.

John Barrymore as Hamlet (*Harvard Theatre Collection*)

Seem to me all the uses of this world!
135 Fie on't, ah fie! 'tis an unweeded garden
That grows to seed, things rank and gross in nature
Possess it merely. That it should come [to this]!
But two months dead, nay, not so much, not two.
So excellent a king, that was to this
140 Hyperion to a satyr, so loving to my mother
That he might not beteem the winds of heaven
Visit her face too roughly. Heaven and earth,
Must I remember? Why, she should hang on him
As if increase of appetite had grown
145 By what it fed on, and yet, within a month—
Let me not think on't! Frailty, thy name is woman!—
A little month, or ere those shoes were old
With which she followed my poor father's body,
Like Niobe, all tears—why, she, [even she]—
150 O God, a beast that wants discourse of reason
Would have mourn'd longer—married with my uncle,
My father's brother, but no more like my father
Than I to Hercules. Within a month,

---

134 **uses:** customs.
137 **merely:** utterly.
139 **to:** in comparison with.
140 **Hyperion:** the sun-god.
141 **beteem:** allow.
147 **or ere:** before.
149 **Niobe.** She wept endlessly for her children, whom Apollo and Artemis had killed.
150 **wants . . . reason:** lacks the power of reason (which distinguishes men from beasts).

Ere yet the salt of most unrighteous tears
155   ⌐Had left the flushing in her galled eyes,
–She married—O most wicked speed: to post
⌐With such dexterity to incestious sheets,
⌐It is not, nor it cannot come to good,
—But break my heart, for I must hold my tongue.

Enter HORATIO, MARCELLUS, *and* BARNARDO.

HOR. Hail to your lordship!
160 HAM.   I am glad to see you well.
    Horatio—or do I forget myself.
HOR. The same, my lord, and your poor servant ever.
HAM. Sir, my good friend—I'll change that name with you.
    And what make you from Wittenberg, Horatio?
165   Marcellus.
MAR. My good lord.
HAM. I am very glad to see you. *[To* BARNARDO.*]* Good even, sir.—
    But what, in faith, make you from Wittenberg?
HOR. A truant disposition, good my lord.
170 HAM. I would not hear your enemy say so,
    Nor shall you do my ear that violence
    To make it truster of your own report
    Against yourself. I know you are no truant.
    But what is your affair in Elsinore?
175   We'll teach you to drink [deep] ere you depart.
HOR. My lord, I came to see your father's funeral.
HAM. I prithee do not mock me, fellow studient,
    I think it was to [see] my mother's wedding.
HOR. Indeed, my lord, it followed hard upon.
180 HAM. Thrift, thrift, Horatio, the funeral bak'd-meats
    Did coldly furnish forth the marriage tables.
    Would I had met my dearest foe in heaven
    Or ever I had seen that day, Horatio!
    My father—methinks I see my father.
HOR. Where, my lord?
185 HAM.   In my mind's eye, Horatio.
HOR. I saw him once, 'a was a goodly king.
HAM. 'A was a man, take him for all in all,
    I shall not look upon his like again.

---

154 **unrighteous:** i.e. hypocritical.
155 **flushing:** redness. **galled:** inflamed.
157 **incestious:** incestuous. The marriage of a man to his brother's widow was so regarded until long after Shakespeare's day.
163 **change:** exchange.
164 **what . . . from:** what are you doing away from.
169 **truant disposition:** inclination to play truant.
177 **studient:** student.
181 **coldly:** when cold.
182 **dearest:** most intensely hated.
183 **Or:** ere, before.

HOR. My lord, I think I saw him yesternight.
190 HAM. Saw, who?
HOR. My lord, the King your father.
HAM. The King my father?
HOR. Season your admiration for a while
With an attent ear, till I may deliver,
Upon the witness of these gentlemen,
This marvel to you.
195 HAM. For God's love let me hear!
HOR. Two nights together had these gentlemen,
Marcellus and Barnardo, on their watch,
In the dead waste and middle of the night,
Been thus encount'red: a figure like your father,
200 Armed at point exactly, cap-a-pe,
Appears before them, and with solemn march
Goes slow and stately by them; thrice he walk'd
By their oppress'd and fear-surprised eyes
Within his truncheon's length, whilst they, distill'd
205 Almost to jelly with the act of fear,
Stand dumb and speak not to him. This to me
In dreadful secrecy impart they did,
And I with them the third night kept the watch,
Where, as they had delivered, both in time,
210 Form of the thing, each word made true and good,
The apparition comes. I knew your father,
These hands are not more like.
HAM. But where was this?
MAR. My lord, upon the platform where we watch.
HAM. Did you not speak to it?
HOR. My lord, I did,
215 But answer made it none. Yet once methought
It lifted up it head and did address
Itself to motion like as it would speak;
But even then the morning cock crew loud,
And at the sound it shrunk in haste away
And vanish'd from our sight.
220 HAM. 'Tis very strange.
HOR. As I do live, my honor'd lord, 'tis true,
And we did think it writ down in our duty
To let you know of it.

---

192 **Season:** temper. **admiration:** wonder.
193 **deliver:** report.
198 **waste:** empty expanse.
200 **at point exactly:** in every particular. **cap-a-pe:** from head to foot.
203 **fear-surprised:** overwhelmed by fear.
204 **truncheon:** short staff carried as a symbol of military command.
205 **act:** action, operation.
207 **dreadful:** held in awe, i.e. solemnly sworn.
212 **are . . . like:** i.e. do not resemble each other more closely than the apparition resembled him.
216 **it:** its.
216–17 **address . . . motion:** begin to make a gesture.

HAM. Indeed, [indeed,] sirs. But this troubles me.
  Hold you the watch to-night?

225 [MAR., BAR.]   We do, my lord.
HAM. Arm'd, say you?
[MAR., BAR.] Arm'd, my lord.
HAM. From top to toe?
[MAR., BAR.]   My lord, from head to foot.
HAM. Then saw you not his face.

230 HOR. O yes, my lord, he wore his beaver up.
HAM. What, look'd he frowningly?
HOR.   A countenance more
  In sorrow than in anger.
HAM.   Pale, or red?
HOR. Nay, very pale.
HAM.   And fix'd his eyes upon you?
HOR. Most constantly.
HAM.   I would I had been there.

235 HOR. It would have much amaz'd you.
HAM. Very like, [very like]. Stay'd it long?
HOR. While one with moderate haste might tell a hundreth.
BOTH [MAR., BAR.] Longer, longer.
HOR. Not when I saw't.
HAM.   His beard was grisl'd, no?

240 HOR. It was, as I have seen it in his life,
  A sable silver'd.
HAM.   I will watch to-night,
  Perchance 'twill walk again.
HOR.   I warr'nt it will.
HAM. If it assume my noble father's person,
  I'll speak to it though hell itself should gape

245 And bid me hold my peace. I pray you all,
  If you have hitherto conceal'd this sight,
  Let it be tenable in your silence still,
  And whatsomever else shall hap to-night,
  Give it an understanding but no tongue.

250 I will requite your loves. So fare you well.
  Upon the platform 'twixt aleven and twelf
  I'll visit you.
ALL   Our duty to your honor.
HAM. Your loves, as mine to you; farewell.

Exeunt [all but HAMLET].

  My father's spirit—in arms! All is not well,
255 I doubt some foul play. Would the night were come!

---

230 **beaver:** visor.
237 **tell a hundreth:** count a hundred.
239 **grisl'd:** grizzled, mixed with grey.
247 **tenable:** held close.
251 **aleven:** eleven.
255 **doubt:** suspect.

Till then sit still, my soul. [Foul] deeds will rise,
Though all the earth o'erwhelm them, to men's eyes.

Exit.

SCENE III.

Enter LAERTES *and* OPHELIA, *his sister.*

LAER. My necessaries are inbark'd. Farewell.
   And, sister, as the winds give benefit
   And convey [is] assistant, do not sleep,
   But let me hear from you.
OPH.   Do you doubt that?
5 LAER. For Hamlet, and the trifling of his favor,
   Hold it a fashion and a toy in blood,
   A violet in the youth of primy nature,
   Forward, not permanent, sweet, not lasting,
   The perfume and suppliance of a minute—
   No more.
OPH.   No more but so?
10 LAER.   Think it no more:
   For nature crescent does not grow alone
   In thews and [bulk], but as this temple waxes,
   The inward service of the mind and soul
   Grows wide withal. Perhaps he loves you now,
15   And now no soil nor cautel doth besmirch
   The virtue of his will, but you must fear,
   His greatness weigh'd, his will is not his own,
   [For he himself is subject to his birth:]
   He may not, as unvalued persons do,
20   Carve for himself, for on his choice depends
   The safety and health of this whole state,
   And therefore must his choice be circumscrib'd
   Unto the voice and yielding of that body
   Whereof he is the head. Then if he says he loves you,

I.iii. Location: Polonius' quarters in the castle.
[1] **inbark'd:** embarked, abroad.
[3] **convey is assistant:** means of transport is available.
[6] **a fashion:** i.e. standard behavior for a young man.   **toy in blood:** idle fancy of youthful passion.
[7] **primy:** springlike.
[8] **Forward:** early of growth.
[9] **suppliance:** pastime.
[11] **crescent:** growing, increasing.
[12] **thews:** muscles, sinews.
[12-14] **as . . . withal:** as the body develops, the powers of mind and spirit grow along with it.
[15] **soil:** stain.   **cautel:** deceit.
[16] **will:** desire.
[17] **His greatness weigh'd:** considering his princely status.
[19] **unvalued:** of low rank.
[20] **Carve for himself:** indulge his own wishes.
[23] **voice:** vote, approval.   **yielding:** consent.   **that body:** i.e. the state.

25 It fits your wisdom so far to believe it
As he in his particular act and place
May give his saying deed, which is no further
Than the main voice of Denmark goes withal.
Then weigh what loss your honor may sustain
30 If with too credent ear you list his songs,
Or lose your heart, or your chaste treasure open
To his unmast'red importunity.
Fear it, Ophelia, fear it, my dear sister,
And keep you in the rear of your affection,
35 Out of the shot and danger of desire.
The chariest maid is prodigal enough
If she unmask her beauty to the moon.
Virtue itself scapes not calumnious strokes.
The canker galls the infants of the spring
40 Too oft before their buttons be disclos'd,
And in the morn and liquid dew of youth
Contagious blastments are most imminent.
Be wary then, best safety lies in fear:
Youth to itself rebels, though none else near.
45 OPH. I shall the effect of this good lesson keep
As watchman to my heart. But, good my brother,
Do not, as some ungracious pastors do,
Show me the steep and thorny way to heaven,
Whiles, [like] a puff'd and reckless libertine,
50 Himself the primrose path of dalliance treads,
And reaks not his own rede.
LAER.   O, fear me not.

Enter POLONIUS.

I stay too long—but here my father comes.
A double blessing is a double grace,
Occasion smiles upon a second leave.
55 POL. Yet here, Laertes? Aboard, aboard, for shame!
The wind sits in the shoulder of your sail,
And you are stay'd for. There—*[laying his hand on* LAERTES' *head]* my blessing with
    thee!

---

26 **in . . . place:** i.e. acting as he must act in the position he occupies.
28 **main:** general.   **goes withal:** accord with.
30 **credent:** credulous.
35 **shot:** range.
39 **canker:** canker-worm.
40 **buttons:** buds.   **disclos'd:** opened.
42 **blastments:** withering blights.
44 **to:** of.
47 **ungracious:** graceless.
49 **puff'd:** bloated.
51 **reaks:** recks, heeds.   **rede:** advice.   **fear me not:** don't worry about me.
54 **Occasion:** opportunity (here personified, as often).   **smiles upon:** i.e. graciously bestows.

And these few precepts in thy memory
Look thou character. Give thy thoughts no tongue,
60   Nor any unproportion'd thought his act.
Be thou familiar, but by no means vulgar:
Those friends thou hast, and their adoption tried,
Grapple them unto thy soul with hoops of steel,
But do not dull thy palm with entertainment
65   Of each new-hatch'd, unfledg'd courage. Beware
Of entrance to a quarrel, but being in,
Bear't that th' opposed may beware of thee.
Give every man thy ear, but few thy voice,
Take each man's censure, but reserve thy judgment.
70   Costly thy habit as thy purse can buy,
But not express'd in fancy, rich, not gaudy,
For the apparel oft proclaims the man,
And they in France of the best rank and station
[Are] of a most select and generous chief in that.
75   Neither a borrower nor a lender [be],
For [loan] oft loses both itself and friend,
And borrowing dulleth [th'] edge of husbandry.
This above all: to thine own self be true,
And it must follow, as the night the day,
80   Thou canst not then be false to any man.
Farewell, my blessing season this in thee!
LAER. Most humbly do I take my leave, my lord.
POL. The time invests you, go, your servants tend.
LAER. Farewell, Ophelia, and remember well
What I have said to you.
85   OPH.   'Tis in my memory lock'd,
And you yourself shall keep the key of it.
LAER. Farewell.

Exit LAERTES.

POL. What is't, Ophelia, he hath said to you?
OPH. So please you, something touching the Lord Hamlet.
90   POL. Marry, well bethought.
'Tis told me, he hath very oft of late

---

⁵⁹ **character**: inscribe.
⁶⁰ **unproportion'd**: unfitting.
⁶¹ **familiar**: affable, sociable.   **vulgar**: friendly with everybody.
⁶² **their adoption tried**: their association with you tested and proved.
⁶⁵ **courage**: spirited, young blood.
⁶⁷ **Bear't that**: manage it in such a way that.
⁶⁹ **Take**: listen to.   **censure**: opinion.
⁷⁴ **generous**: noble.   **chief**: eminence (?). But the line is probably corrupt. Perhaps *of a* is intrusive, in which case *chief* = chiefly.
⁷⁷ **husbandry**: thrift.
⁸¹ **season**: preserve (?) or ripen, make fruitful (?).
⁸³ **invests**: besieges.   **tend**: wait.
⁹⁰ **Marry**: indeed (originally the name of the Virgin Mary used as an oath).

Given private time to you, and you yourself
Have of your audience been most free and bounteous.
If it be so—as so 'tis put on me,
95 And that in way of caution—I must tell you,
You do not understand yourself so clearly
As it behooves my daughter and your honor.
What is between you? Give me up the truth.
OPH. He hath, my lord, of late made many tenders
100 Of his affection to me.
POL. Affection, puh! You speak like a green girl,
Unsifted in such perilous circumstance.
Do you believe his tenders, as you call them?
OPH. I do not know, my lord, what I should think.
105 POL. Marry, I will teach you: think yourself a baby
That you have ta'en these tenders for true pay,
Which are not sterling. Tender yourself more dearly,
Or (not to crack the wind of the poor phrase,
[Wringing] it thus) you'll tender me a fool.
110 OPH. My lord, he hath importun'd me with love
In honorable fashion.
POL. Ay, fashion you may call it. Go to, go to.
OPH. And hath given countenance to his speech, my lord,
With almost all the holy vows of heaven.
115 POL. Ay, springes to catch woodcocks. I do know,
When the blood burns, how prodigal the soul
Lends the tongue vows. These blazes, daughter,
Giving more light than heat, extinct in both
Even in their promise, as it is a-making,
120 You must not take for fire. From this time
Be something scanter of your maiden presence,
Set your entreatments at a higher rate
Than a command to parle. For Lord Hamlet,
Believe so much in him, that he is young,
125 And with a larger teder may he walk
Than may be given you. In few, Ophelia,

---

94 **put on:** told to.
99 **tenders:** offers.
102 **Unsifted:** untried.
106 **tenders.** With play on the sense "money offered in payment" (as in *legal tender*).
107 **Tender:** hold, value.
109 **Wringing:** straining, forcing to the limit.   **tender . . . fool:** (1) show me that you are a fool; (2) make me look like a fool; (3) present me with a (bastard) grandchild.
112 **fashion.** See note on line 6.
113 **countenance:** authority.
115 **springes:** snares.   **woodcocks.** Proverbially gullible birds.
122-23 **Set . . . parle:** place a higher value on your favors; do not grant interviews simply because he asks for them. Polonius uses a military figure: *entreatments* = negotiations for surrender; *parle* = parley, discuss terms.
124 **so . . . him:** no more than this with respect to him.
125 **larger teder:** longer tether.

Do not believe his vows, for they are brokers,
Not of that dye which their investments show,
But mere [implorators] of unholy suits,
130   Breathing like sanctified and pious bonds,
The better to [beguile]. This is for all:
I would not, in plain terms, from this time forth
Have you so slander any moment leisure
As to give words or talk with the Lord Hamlet.
135   Look to't, I charge you. Come your ways.
OPH. I shall obey, my lord.

Exeunt.

SCENE IV.

Enter HAMLET, HORATIO, *and* MARCELLUS.

HAM. The air bites shrowdly, it is very cold.
HOR. It is [a] nipping and an eager air.
HAM. What hour now?
HOR.   I think it lacks of twelf.
MAR. No, it is strook.
5   HOR. Indeed? I heard it not. It then draws near the season
Wherein the spirit held his wont to walk.

A flourish of trumpets, and two pieces goes off [within].

What does this mean, my lord?
HAM. The King doth wake to-night and takes his rouse,
Keeps wassail, and the swagg'ring up-spring reels;
10   And as he drains his draughts of Rhenish down,
The kettle-drum and trumpet thus bray out
The triumph of his pledge.
HOR.   Is it a custom?
HAM. Ay, marry, is't,
But to my mind, though I am native here

---

127 **brokers:** procurers.
128 **Not . . . show:** not of the color of their garments (*investments*) exhibit, i.e. not what they seem.
129 **mere:** out-and-out.
130 **bonds:** (lover's) vows or assurances. Many editors follow Theobald in reading *bawds*.
133 **slander:** disgrace. **moment:** momentary.
135 **Come your ways:** come along.

I.iv. Location: The guard-platform of the castle.
1 **shrowdly:** shrewdly, wickedly.
2 **eager:** sharp.
6 s.d. **pieces:** cannon.
8 **doth . . . rouse:** i.e. holds revels far into the night.
9 **wassail:** carousal. **up-spring:** wild dance.
10 **Rhenish:** Rhine wine.
12 **triumph . . . pledge:** accomplishment of his toast (by draining his cup at a single draft).

15   And to the manner born, it is a custom
      More honor'd in the breach than the observance.
      This heavy-headed revel east and west
      Makes us traduc'd and tax'd of other nations.
      They clip us drunkards, and with swinish phrase
20   Soil our addition, and indeed it takes
      From our achievements, though perform'd at height,
      The pith and marrow of our attribute.
      So, oft it chances in particular men,
      That for some vicious mole of nature in them,
25   As in their birth, wherein they are not guilty
      (Since nature cannot choose his origin),
      By their o'ergrowth of some complexion
      Oft breaking down the pales and forts of reason,
      Or by some habit, that too much o'er-leavens
30   The form of plausive manners—that these men,
      Carrying, I say, the stamp of one defect,
      Being nature's livery, or fortune's star,
      His virtues else, be they as pure as grace,
      As infinite as man may undergo,
35   Shall in the general censure take corruption
      From that particular fault: the dram of [ev'l]
      Doth all the noble substance of a doubt
      To his own scandal.

Enter GHOST.

HOR.   Look, my lord, it comes!
HAM. Angels and ministers of grace defend us!
40   Be thou a spirit of health, or goblin damn'd,

---

[15] **manner:** custom (of carousing).
[16] **More . . . observance:** which it is more honorable to break than to observe.
[18] **tax'd of:** censured by.
[19] **clip:** clepe, call.
[20] **addition:** titles of honor.
[21] **at height:** most excellently.
[22] **attribute:** reputation.
[23] **particular:** individual.
[24] **vicious . . . nature:** small natural blemish.
[26] **his:** its.
[27] **By . . . complexion:** by the excess of some one of the humors (which were thought to govern the disposition).
[28] **pales:** fences.
[29] **o'er-leavens:** makes itself felt throughout (as leaven works in the whole mass of dough).
[30] **plausive:** pleasing.
[32] **Being . . . star:** i.e. whether they were born with it, or got it by misfortune. *Star* means "blemish."
[34] **undergo:** carry the weight of, sustain.
[35] **general censure:** popular opinion.
[36] **dram:** minute amount. **ev'l:** evil, with a pun on *eale*, "yeast" (cf. *o'er-leavens* in line 29).
[37] **of a doubt.** A famous crux, for which many emendations have been suggested, the most widely accepted being Steevens' *often dout* (i.e. extinguish).
[38] **To . . . scandal:** i.e. so that it all shares in the disgrace.
[40] **of health:** wholesome, good.

Bring with thee airs from heaven, or blasts from hell,
Be thy intents wicked, or charitable,
Thou com'st in such a questionable shape
That I will speak to thee. I'll call thee Hamlet,
45   King, father, royal Dane. O, answer me!
Let me not burst in ignorance, but tell
Why thy canoniz'd bones, hearsed in death,
Have burst their cerements; why the sepulchre,
Wherein we saw thee quietly interr'd,
50   Hath op'd his ponderous and marble jaws
To cast thee up again. What may this mean,
That thou, dead corse, again in complete steel
Revisits thus the glimpses of the moon,
Making night hideous, and we fools of nature
55   So horridly to shake our disposition
With thoughts beyond the reaches of our souls?
Say why is this? wherefore? what should we do?

[GHOST] *beckons* [HAMLET].

HOR. It beckons you to go away with it,
As if it some impartment did desire
To you alone.
60 MAR.   Look with what courteous action
It waves you to a more removed ground,
But do not go with it.
HOR.   No, by no means.
HAM. It will not speak, then I will follow it.
HOR. Do not, my lord.
HAM.   Why, what should be the fear?
65   I do not set my life at a pin's fee,
And for my soul, what can it do to that,
Being a thing immortal as itself?
It waves me forth again, I'll follow it.
HOR. What if it tempt you toward the flood, my lord,
70   Or to the dreadful summit of the cliff
That beetles o'er his base into the sea,
And there assume some other horrible form
Which might deprive your sovereignty of reason,
And draw you into madness? Think of it.

---

⁴³ **questionable:** inviting talk.
⁴⁷ **canoniz'd:** buried with the prescribed rites.
⁴⁸ **cerements:** grave clothes.
⁵² **complete steel:** full armor.
⁵³ **Revisits.** The *-s* ending in the second person singular is common.
⁵⁴ **fools of nature:** the children (or the dupes) of a purely natural order, baffled by the supernatural.
⁵⁵ **disposition:** nature.
⁵⁹ **impartment:** communication.
⁶⁵ **fee:** worth.
⁷³ **deprive . . . reason:** unseat reason from the rule of your mind.

75 The very place puts toys of desperation,
Without more motive, into every brain
That looks so many fadoms to the sea
And hears it roar beneath.
HAM. It waves me still.—
Go on, I'll follow thee.
MAR. You shall not go, my lord.
80 HAM. Hold off your hands.
HOR. Be rul'd, you shall not go.
HAM. My fate cries out,
And makes each petty artere in this body
As hardy as the Nemean lion's nerve.
Still am I call'd. Unhand me, gentlemen.
85 By heaven, I'll make a ghost of him that lets me!
I say away!—Go on, I'll follow thee.

Exeunt GHOST *and* HAMLET.

HOR. He waxes desperate with [imagination].
MAR. Let's follow. 'Tis not fit thus to obey him.
HOR. Have after. To what issue will this come?
90 MAR. Something is rotten in the state of Denmark.
HOR. Heaven will direct it.
MAR. Nay, let's follow him.

Exeunt.

SCENE V.

Enter GHOST *and* HAMLET.

HAM. Whither wilt thou lead me? Speak, I'll go no further.
GHOST Mark me.
HAM. I will.
GHOST My hour is almost come
When I to sulph'rous and tormenting flames
Must render up myself.
HAM. Alas, poor ghost!
5 GHOST Pity me not, but lend thy serious hearing
To what I shall unfold.
HAM. Speak, I am bound to hear.
GHOST So art thou to revenge, when thou shalt hear.

---

⁷⁵ **toys of desperation:** fancies of desperate action, i.e. inclinations to jump off.
⁷⁷ **fadoms:** fathoms.
⁸² **artere:** variant spelling of *artery*; here, ligament, sinew.
⁸³ **Nemean lion.** Slain by Hercules as one of his twelve labors.   **nerve:** sinew.
⁸⁵ **lets:** hinders.
⁹¹ **it:** i.e. the issue.

I.v. Location: On the battlements of the castle.

HAM. What?

GHOST I am thy father's spirit,

10   Doom'd for a certain term to walk the night,
    And for the day confin'd to fast in fires,
    Till the foul crimes done in my days of nature
    Are burnt and purg'd away. But that I am forbid
    To tell the secrets of my prison-house,

15   I could a tale unfold whose lightest word
    Would harrow up thy soul, freeze thy young blood,
    Make thy two eyes like stars start from their spheres,
    Thy knotted and combined locks to part,
    And each particular hair to stand an end,

20   Like quills upon the fearful porpentine.
    But this eternal blazon must not be
    To ears of flesh and blood. List, list, O, list!
    If thou didst ever thy dear father love—

HAM. O God!

25 GHOST Revenge his foul and most unnatural murther.

HAM. Murther!

GHOST Murther most foul, as in the best it is,
    But this most foul, strange, and unnatural.

HAM. Haste me to know't, that I with wings as swift

30   As meditation, or the thoughts of love,
    May sweep to my revenge.

GHOST   I find thee apt,
    And duller shouldst thou be than the fat weed
    That roots itself in ease on Lethe wharf,
    Wouldst thou not stir in this. Now, Hamlet, hear:

35   'Tis given out that, sleeping in my orchard,
    A serpent stung me, so the whole ear of Denmark
    Is by a forged process of my death
    Rankly abus'd; but know, thou noble youth,
    The serpent that did sting thy father's life
    Now wears his crown.

40 HAM.   O my prophetic soul!
    My uncle?

---

[11] **fast:** do penance.

[12] **crimes:** sins.

[17] **spheres:** eye sockets; with allusion to the revolving spheres in which, according to the Ptolemaic astronomy, the stars were fixed.

[19] **an end:** on end.

[20] **fearful porpentine:** frightened porcupine.

[21] **eternal blazon:** revelation of eternal things.

[30] **meditation:** thought.

[33] **Lethe:** river of Hades, the water of which made the drinker forget the past.   **wharf:** bank.

[35] **orchard:** garden.

[37] **forged process:** false account.

[38] **abus'd:** deceived.

GHOST Ay, that incestuous, that adulterate beast,
With witchcraft of his wits, with traitorous gifts—
O wicked wit and gifts that have the power
45 So to seduce!—won to his shameful lust
The will of my most seeming virtuous queen.
O Hamlet, what [a] falling-off was there
From me, whose love was of that dignity
That it went hand in hand even with the vow
50 I made to her in marriage, and to decline
Upon a wretch whose natural gifts were poor
To those of mine!
But virtue, as it never will be moved,
Though lewdness court it in a shape of heaven,
55 So [lust], though to a radiant angel link'd,
Will [sate] itself in a celestial bed
And prey on garbage.
But soft, methinks I scent the morning air,
Brief let me be. Sleeping within my orchard,
60 My custom always of the afternoon,
Upon my secure hour thy uncle stole,
With juice of cursed hebona in a vial,
And in the porches of my ears did pour
The leprous distillment, whose effect
65 Holds such an enmity with blood of man
That swift as quicksilver it courses through
The natural gates and alleys of the body,
And with a sudden vigor it doth [posset]
And curd, like eager droppings into milk,
70 The thin and wholesome blood. So did it mine,
And a most instant tetter bark'd about,
Most lazar-like, with vile and loathsome crust
All my smooth body.
Thus was I, sleeping, by a brother's hand
75 Of life, of crown, of queen, at once dispatch'd,
Cut off even in the blossoms of my sin,
Unhous'led, disappointed, unanel'd,
No reck'ning made, but sent to my account
With all my imperfections on my head.

---

42 **adulterate:** adulterous.
54 **shape of heaven:** angelic form.
61 **secure:** carefree.
62 **hebona:** ebony (which Shakespeare, following a literary tradition, and perhaps also associating the word with *henbane*, thought the name of a poison).
68 **posset:** curdle.
69 **eager:** sour.
71 **tetter:** scabby eruption. **bark'd:** formed a hard covering, like bark on a tree.
72 **lazar-like:** leperlike.
75 **at once:** all at the same time. **dispatch'd:** deprived.
77 **Unhous'led:** without the Eucharist. **disappointed:** without (spiritual) preparation. **unanel'd:** unanointed, without extreme unction.

80   O, horrible, O, horrible, most horrible!
      If thou hast nature in thee, bear it not,
      Let not the royal bed of Denmark be
      A couch for luxury and damned incest.
      But howsomever thou pursues this act,
85   Taint not thy mind, nor let thy soul contrive
      Against thy mother aught. Leave her to heaven,
      And to those thorns that in her bosom lodge
      To prick and sting her. Fare thee well at once!
      The glow-worm shows the matin to be near,
90   And gins to pale his uneffectual fire.
      Adieu, adieu, adieu! remember me.

     [Exit.]

    HAM. O all you host of heaven! O earth! What else?
      And shall I couple hell? O fie, hold, hold, my heart,
      And you, my sinows, grow not instant old,
95   But bear me [stiffly] up. Remember thee!
      Ay, thou poor ghost, whiles memory holds a seat
      In this distracted globe. Remember thee!
      Yea, from the table of my memory
      I'll wipe away all trivial fond records,
100   All saws of books, all forms, all pressures past
      That youth and observation copied there,
      And thy commandement all alone shall live
      Within the book and volume of my brain,
      Unmix'd with baser matter. Yes, by heaven!
105   O most pernicious woman!
      O villain, villain, smiling, damned villain!
      My tables—meet it is I set it down
      That one may smile, and smile, and be a villain!
      At least I am sure it may be so in Denmark.

     [He writes.]

110   So, uncle, there you are. Now to my word:
      It is "Adieu, adieu! remember me."
      I have sworn't.
    HOR. *[Within.]* My lord, my lord!
    MAR. *[Within.]*   Lord Hamlet!

---

81 **nature:** natural feeling.
83 **luxury:** lust.
89 **matin:** morning.
90 **gins:** begins.
94 **sinows:** sinews.
97 **globe:** head.
98 **table:** writing tablet.
99 **fond:** foolish.
100 **saws:** wise sayings. **forms:** shapes, images. **pressures:** impressions.
110 **word:** i.e. word of command from the Ghost.

Enter HORATIO *and* MARCELLUS.

HOR.   Heavens secure him!

HAM. So be it!

115 MAR. Illo, ho, ho, my lord!

HAM. Hillo, ho, ho, boy! come, [bird,] come.

MAR. How is't, my noble lord?

HOR.   What news, my lord?

HAM. O, wonderful!

HOR. Good my lord, tell it.

HAM.   No, you will reveal it.

HOR. Not I, my lord, by heaven.

120 MAR.   Nor I, my lord.

HAM. How say you then, would heart of man once think it?—
      But you'll be secret?

BOTH [HOR., MAR.]   Ay, by heaven, [my lord].

HAM. There's never a villain dwelling in all Denmark
      But he's an arrant knave.

125 HOR. There needs no ghost, my lord, come from the grave
      To tell us this.

HAM.   Why, right, you are in the right,
      And so, without more circumstance at all,
      I hold it fit that we shake hands and part,
      You, as your business and desire shall point you,

130   For every man hath business and desire,
      Such as it is, and for my own poor part,
      I will go pray.

HOR. These are but wild and whirling words, my lord.

HAM. I am sorry they offend you, heartily,
      Yes, faith, heartily.

135 HOR.   There's no offense, my lord.

HAM. Yes, by Saint Patrick, but there is, Horatio,
      And much offense too. Touching this vision here,
      It is an honest ghost, that let me tell you.
      For your desire to know what is between us,

140   O'ermaster't as you may. And now, good friends,
      As you are friends, scholars, and soldiers,
      Give me one poor request.

HOR. What is't, my lord, we will.

HAM. Never make known what you have seen tonight.

BOTH [HOR., MAR.] My lord, we will not.

HAM.   Nay, but swear't.

145 HOR.   In faith.
      My lord, not I.

MAR.   Nor I, my lord, in faith.

---

116 **Hillo . . . come.** Hamlet answers Marcellus' halloo with a falconer's cry.
127 **circumstance:** ceremony.
138 **honest:** true, genuine.
143 **What is't:** whatever it is.

HAM. Upon my sword.
MAR.   We have sworn, my lord, already.
HAM. Indeed, upon my sword, indeed.

GHOST *cries under the stage.*

GHOST Swear.
150 HAM. Ha, ha, boy, say'st thou so? Art thou there, truepenny?
        Come on, you hear this fellow in the cellarage,
        Consent to swear.
     HOR.   Propose the oath, my lord.
     HAM. Never to speak of this that you have seen,
        Swear by my sword.
155 GHOST *[Beneath.]* Swear.
     HAM. *Hic et ubique?* Then we'll shift our ground.
        Come hither, gentlemen,
        And lay your hands again upon my sword.
        Swear by my sword
160   Never to speak of this that you have heard.
     GHOST *[Beneath.]* Swear by his sword.
     HAM. Well said, old mole, canst work i' th' earth so fast?
        A worthy pioner! Once more remove, good friends.
     HOR. O day and night, but this is wondrous strange!
165 HAM. And therefore as a stranger give it welcome.
        There are more things in heaven and earth, Horatio,
        Than are dreamt of in your philosophy.
        But come—
        Here, as before, never, so help you mercy,
170   How strange or odd some'er I bear myself—
        As I perchance hereafter shall think meet
        To put an antic disposition on—
        That you, at such times seeing me, never shall,
        With arms encumb'red thus, or this headshake,
175   Or by pronouncing of some doubtful phrase,
        As "Well, well, we know," or "We could, and if we would,"
        Or "If we list to speak," or "There be, and if they might,"
        Or such ambiguous giving out, to note
        That you know aught of me—this do swear,
180   So grace and mercy at your most need help you.

---

147 **Upon my sword:** i.e. on the cross formed by the hilt.
150 **truepenny:** trusty fellow.
156 **Hic et ubique:** here and everywhere.
163 **pioner:** digger, miner (variant of *pioneer*).
165 **as . . . welcome:** give it the welcome due in courtesy to strangers.
167 **your.** See note on I.i.138.   **philosophy:** i.e. natural philosophy, science.
172 **put . . . on:** behave in some fantastic manner, act like a madman.
174 **encumb'red:** folded.
176 **and if:** if.
177 **list:** cared, had a mind.
178 **note:** indicate.

GHOST *[Beneath.]* Swear.

[They swear.]

HAM. Rest, rest, perturbed spirit! So, gentlemen,
 With all my love I do commend me to you,
 And what so poor a man as Hamlet is
185 May do t' express his love and friending to you,
 God willing, shall not lack. Let us go in together,
 And still your fingers on your lips, I pray.
 The time is out of joint—O cursed spite,
 That ever I was born to set it right!
190 Nay, come, let's go together.

Exeunt.

ACT II

SCENE I.

Enter old POLONIUS *with his man* [REYNALDO].

POL. Give him this money and these notes, Reynaldo.
REY. I will, my lord.
POL. You shall do marvell's wisely, good Reynaldo,
 Before you visit him, to make inquire
 Of his behavior.
5 REY.   My lord, I did intend it.
POL. Marry, well said, very well said. Look you, sir,
 Inquire me first what Danskers are in Paris,
 And how, and who, what means, and where they keep,
 What company, at what expense; and finding
10 By this encompassment and drift of question
 That they do know my son, come you more nearer
 Than your particular demands will touch it.
 Take you as 'twere some distant knowledge of him,
 As thus, "I know his father and his friends,
15 And in part him." Do you mark this, Reynaldo?
REY. Ay, very well, my lord.
POL. "And in part him—but," you may say, "not well.
 But if't be he I mean, he's very wild,
 Addicted so and so," and there put on him

---

187 **still:** always.
190 **Nay . . . together.** They are holding back to let him go first.

II.i. Location: Polonius' quarters in the castle.
3 **marvell's:** marvelous(ly).
7 **Danskers:** Danes.
8 **keep:** lodge.
10 **encompassment:** circuitousness. **drift of question:** directing of the conversation.
12 **particular demands:** direct questions.

20   What forgeries you please: marry, none so rank
      As may dishonor him, take heed of that,
      But, sir, such wanton, wild, and usual slips
      As are companions noted and most known
      To youth and liberty.
   REY.   As gaming, my lord.
25 POL. Ay, or drinking, fencing, swearing, quarrelling,
      Drabbing—you may go so far.
   REY. My lord, that would dishonor him.
   POL. Faith, as you may season it in the charge:
      You must not put another scandal on him,
30   That he is open to incontinency—
      That's not my meaning. But breathe his faults so quaintly
      That they may seem the taints of liberty,
      The flash and outbreak of a fiery mind,
      A savageness in unreclaimed blood,
      Of general assault.
35 REY.   But, my good lord—
   POL. Wherefore should you do this?
   REY.   Ay, my lord,
      I would know that.
   POL.   Marry, sir, here's my drift,
      And I believe it is a fetch of wit:
      You laying these slight sallies on my son,
40   As 'twere a thing a little soil'd [wi' th'] working,
      Mark you,
      Your party in converse, him you would sound,
      Having ever seen in the prenominate crimes
      The youth you breathe of guilty, be assur'd
45   He closes with you in this consequence:
      "Good sir," or so, or "friend," or "gentleman,"
      According to the phrase or the addition
      Of man and country.
   REY.   Very good, my lord.

---

20 **forgeries:** invented charges.
22 **wanton:** sportive.
26 **Drabbing:** whoring.
28 **Faith.** Most editors read *Faith, no,* following F1; this makes easier sense.   **season:** qualify, temper.
30 **open to incontinency:** habitually profligate.
31 **quaintly:** artfully.
34 **unreclaimed:** untamed.
35 **Of general assault:** i.e. to which young men are generally subject.
38 **fetch of wit:** ingenious device.
39 **sallies:** sullies, blemishes.
40 **soil'd . . . working:** i.e. shopworn.
43 **Having:** if he has.   **prenominate crimes:** aforementioned faults.
45 **closes:** falls in.   **in this consequence:** as follows.
47 **addition:** style of address.

POL. And then, sir, does 'a this—'a does—what was I about to say?
50   By the mass, I was about to say something.
    Where did I leave?
REY.   At "closes in the consequence."
POL. At "closes in the consequence," ay, marry.
    He closes thus: "I know the gentleman.
    I saw him yesterday, or th' other day,
55   Or then, or then, with such or such, and as you say,
    There was 'a gaming, there o'ertook in 's rouse,
    There falling out at tennis"; or, perchance,
    "I saw him enter such a house of sale,"
    Videlicet, a brothel, or so forth. See you now,
60   Your bait of falsehood take this carp of truth,
    And thus do we of wisdom and of reach,
    With windlasses and with assays of bias,
    By indirections find directions out;
    So by my former lecture and advice
65   Shall you my son. You have me, have you not?
REY. My lord, I have.
POL.   God buy ye, fare ye well.
REY. Good my lord.
POL. Observe his inclination in yourself.
REY. I shall, my lord.
POL. And let him ply his music.
70 REY.   Well, my lord.
POL. Farewell.

Exit REYNALDO.

Enter OPHELIA.

          How now, Ophelia, what's the matter?
OPH. O my lord, my lord, I have been so affrighted!
POL. With what, i' th' name of God?
OPH. My lord, as I was sewing in my closet,
75   Lord Hamlet, with his doublet all unbrac'd,
    No hat upon his head, his stockins fouled,

---

⁵⁶ **o'ertook in 's rouse:** overcome by drink.
⁶¹ **reach:** capacity, understanding.
⁶² **windlasses:** roundabout methods.   **assays of bias:** indirect attempts (a figure from the game of bowls, in which the player must make allowance for the curving course his bowl will take toward its mark).
⁶³ **directions:** the way things are going.
⁶⁵ **have me:** understand me.
⁶⁶ **God buy ye:** good-bye (a contraction of *God be with you*).
⁶⁸ **in:** by. Polonius asks him to observe Laertes directly, as well as making inquiries.
⁷⁰ **let him ply:** see that he goes on with.
⁷⁴ **closet:** private room.
⁷⁵ **unbrac'd:** unlaced.
⁷⁶ **stockins fouled:** stockings dirty.

Ungart'red, and down-gyved to his ankle,
Pale as his shirt, his knees knocking each other,
And with a look so piteous in purport
80   As if he had been loosed out of hell
To speak of horrors—he comes before me.
POL. Mad for thy love?
OPH.   My lord, I do not know,
But truly I do fear it.
POL.   What said he?
OPH. He took me by the wrist, and held me hard,
85   Then goes he to the length of all his arm,
And with his other hand thus o'er his brow,
He falls to such perusal of my face
As 'a would draw it. Long stay'd he so.
At last, a little shaking of mine arm,
90   And thrice his head thus waving up and down,
He rais'd a sigh so piteous and profound
As it did seem to shatter all his bulk
And end his being. That done, he lets me go,
And with his head over his shoulder turn'd,
95   He seem'd to find his way without his eyes,
For out a' doors he went without their helps,
And to the last bended their light on me.
POL. Come, go with me. I will go seek the King.
This is the very ecstasy of love,
100   Whose violent property fordoes itself,
And leads the will to desperate undertakings
As oft as any passions under heaven
That does afflict our natures. I am sorry—
What, have you given him any hard words of late?
105 OPH. No, my good lord, but as you did command
I did repel his letters, and denied
His access to me.
POL.   That hath made him mad.
I am sorry that with better heed and judgment
I had not coted him. I fear'd he did but trifle
110   And meant to wrack thee, but beshrow my jealousy!
By heaven, it is as proper to our age
To cast beyond ourselves in our opinions,
As it is common for the younger sort

---

77 **down-gyved:** hanging down like fetters on a prisoner's legs.
92 **bulk:** body.
99 **ecstasy:** madness.
100 **property:** quality.   **fordoes:** destroys.
109 **coted:** observed.
110 **beshrow:** beshrew, plague take.   **jealousy:** suspicious mind.
111 **proper . . . age:** characteristic of men of my age.
112 **cast beyond ourselves:** overshoot, go too far (by way of caution).

To lack discretion. Come, go we to the King.
115 This must be known, which, being kept close, might move
More grief to hide, than hate to utter love.
Come.

Exeunt.

SCENE II.

Flourish. Enter KING *and* QUEEN, ROSENCRANTZ *and* GUILDENSTERN *[cum aliis].*

KING Welcome, dear Rosencrantz and Guildenstern!
Moreover that we much did long to see you,
The need we have to use you did provoke
Our hasty sending. Something have you heard
5 Of Hamlet's transformation; so call it,
Sith nor th' exterior nor the inward man
Resembles that it was. What it should be,
More than his father's death, that thus hath put him
So much from th' understanding of himself,
10 I cannot dream of. I entreat you both
That, being of so young days brought up with him,
And sith so neighbored to his youth and havior,
That you voutsafe your rest here in our court
Some little time, so by your companies
15 To draw him on to pleasures, and to gather
So much as from occasion you may glean,
Whether aught to us unknown afflicts him thus,
That, open'd, lies within our remedy.
QUEEN Good gentlemen, he hath much talk'd of you,
20 And sure I am two men there is not living
To whom he more adheres. If it will please you
To show us so much gentry and good will
As to expend your time with us a while
For the supply and profit of our hope,
25 Your visitation shall receive such thanks
As fits a king's remembrance.
ROS.   Both your Majesties
Might, by the sovereign power you have of us,

---

¹¹⁵ **close:** secret.
^{115–16} **move . . . love:** cause more grievous consequences by its concealment than we shall incur
displeasure by making it known.

II.ii. Location: The castle.
² **Moreover . . . you:** besides the fact that we wanted to see you for your own sakes.
⁶ **Sith:** since.
¹¹ **of:** from.
¹³ **voutsafe your rest:** vouchsafe to remain.
²¹ **more adheres:** is more attached.
²² **gentry:** courtesy.
²⁴ **supply and profit:** support and advancement.

Put your dread pleasures more into command
Than to entreaty.
GUIL.   But we both obey,
30   And here give up ourselves, in the full bent,
To lay our service freely at your feet,
To be commanded.
KING Thanks, Rosencrantz and gentle Guildenstern.
QUEEN Thanks, Guildenstern and gentle Rosencrantz.
35   And I beseech you instantly to visit
My too much changed son. Go some of you
And bring these gentlemen where Hamlet is.
GUIL. Heavens make our presence and our practices
Pleasant and helpful to him!
QUEEN   Ay, amen!

Exeunt ROSENCRANTZ *and* GUILDENSTERN *[with some* ATTENDANTS].

Enter POLONIUS.

40 POL. Th' embassadors from Norway, my good lord,
Are joyfully return'd.
KING Thou still hast been the father of good news.
POL. Have I, my lord? I assure my good liege
I hold my duty as I hold my soul,
45   Both to my God and to my gracious king;
And I do think, or else this brain of mine
Hunts not the trail of policy so sure
As it hath us'd to do, that I have found
The very cause of Hamlet's lunacy.
50 KING O, speak of that, that do I long to hear.
POL. Give first admittance to th' embassadors;
My news shall be the fruit to that great feast.
KING Thyself do grace to them, and bring them in.

[Exit POLONIUS.]

He tells me, my dear Gertrude, he hath found
55   The head and source of all your son's distemper.
QUEEN I doubt it is no other but the main,
His father's death and our [o'erhasty] marriage.

*Enter [*POLONIUS *with* VOLTEMAND *and* CORNELIUS, THE] EMBASSADORS.

---

30 **in . . . bent:** to our utmost.
40 **embassadors:** ambassadors.
42 **still:** always.
43 **liege:** sovereign.
47 **policy:** statecraft.
52 **fruit:** dessert.
55 **head.** Synonymous with *source.* **distemper:** (mental) illness.
56 **doubt:** suspect. **main:** main cause.

KING Well, we shall sift him.—Welcome, my good friends!
Say, Voltemand, what from our brother Norway?

60 VOL. Most fair return of greetings and desires.
Upon our first, he sent out to suppress
His nephew's levies, which to him appear'd
To be a preparation 'gainst the Polack;
But better look'd into, he truly found

65 It was against your Highness. Whereat griev'd,
That so his sickness, age, and impotence
Was falsely borne in hand, sends out arrests
On Fortinbras, which he, in brief, obeys,
Receives rebuke from Norway, and in fine,

70 Makes vow before his uncle never more
To give th' assay of arms against your Majesty.
Whereon old Norway, overcome with joy,
Gives him threescore thousand crowns in annual fee,
And his commission to employ those soldiers,

75 So levied, as before, against the Polack,
With an entreaty, herein further shown,

[Giving a paper.]

That it might please you to give quiet pass
Through your dominions for this enterprise,
On such regards of safety and allowance
As therein are set down.

80 KING   It likes us well,
And at our more considered time we'll read,
Answer, and think upon this business.
Mean time, we thank you for your well-took labor.
Go to your rest, at night we'll feast together.
Most welcome home!

Exeunt EMBASSADORS *[and* ATTENDANTS].

85 POL.   This business is well ended.
My liege, and madam, to expostulate
What majesty should be, what duty is,
Why day is day, night night, and time is time,
Were nothing but to waste night, day, and time;

---

61 **Upon our first:** at our first representation.
65 **griev'd:** aggrieved, offended.
67 **borne in hand:** taken advantage of.
69 **in fine:** in the end.
71 **assay:** trial.
79 **On . . . allowance:** with such safeguards and provisos.
80 **likes:** pleases.
81 **consider'd:** suitable for consideration.
86 **expostulate:** expound.

90   Therefore, [since] brevity is the soul of wit,
     And tediousness the limbs and outward flourishes,
     I will be brief. Your noble son is mad:
     Mad call I it, for to define true madness,
     What is't but to be nothing else but mad?
     But let that go.
95   QUEEN   More matter with less art.
     POL. Madam, I swear I use no art at all.
     That he's mad, 'tis true, 'tis true 'tis pity,
     And pity 'tis 'tis true—a foolish figure,
     But farewell it, for I will use no art.
100 Mad let us grant him then, and now remains
     That we find out the cause of this effect,
     Or rather say, the cause of this defect,
     For this effect defective comes by cause:
     Thus it remains, and the remainder thus.
105 Perpend.
     I have a daughter—have while she is mine—
     Who in her duty and obedience, mark,
     Hath given me this. Now gather, and surmise.

[Reads the salutation of the letter.]

     "To the celestial and my soul's idol, the most beautified Ophelia"—
110 That's an ill phrase, a vile phrase, "beautified" is a vile phrase. But you shall hear.
     Thus:
     "In her excellent white bosom, these, etc."
     QUEEN Came this from Hamlet to her?
     POL. Good madam, stay awhile. I will be faithful.

[Reads the] letter.

115 "Doubt thou the stars are fire,
     Doubt that the sun doth move,
     Doubt truth to be a liar,
     But never doubt I love.
     O dear Ophelia, I am ill at these numbers. I have not art to reckon my groans, but
120 that I love thee best, O most best, believe it. Adieu.
     Thine evermore, most dear lady,
          whilst this machine is to him, Hamlet."

---

90 **wit**: understanding, wisdom.
95 **art**: i.e. rhetorical art.
98 **figure**: figure of speech.
103 **For . . . cause**: for this effect (which shows as a defect in Hamlet's reason) is not merely accidental, and has a cause we may trace.
105 **Perpend**: consider.
110 **beautified**: beautiful (not an uncommon usage).
117 **Doubt**: suspect.
119 **ill . . . numbers**: bad at versifying.   **reckon**: count (with a quibble on *numbers*).
122 **machine**: body.

This in obedience hath my daughter shown me,
And more [above], hath his solicitings,
125 As they fell out by time, by means, and place,
All given to mine ear.
KING   But how hath she
Receiv'd his love?
POL.   What do you think of me?
KING As of a man faithful and honorable.
POL. I would fain prove so. But what might you think,
130 When I had seen this hot love on the wing—
As I perceiv'd it (I must tell you that)
Before my daughter told me—what might you,
Or my dear Majesty your queen here, think,
If I had play'd the desk or table-book,
135 Or given my heart a [winking,] mute and dumb,
Or look'd upon this love with idle sight,
What might you think? No, I went round to work,
And my young mistress thus I did bespeak:
"Lord Hamlet is a prince out of thy star;
140 This must not be"; and then I prescripts gave her,
That she should lock herself from [his] resort,
Admit no messengers, receive no tokens.
Which done, she took the fruits of my advice;
And he repell'd, a short tale to make,
145 Fell into a sadness, then into a fast,
Thence to a watch, thence into a weakness,
Then to [a] lightness, and by this declension,
Into the madness wherein now he raves,
And all we mourn for.
KING   Do you think ['tis] this?
150 QUEEN It may be, very like.
POL. Hath there been such a time—I would fain know that—
That I have positively said, "'Tis so,"
When it prov'd otherwise?
KING   Not that I know.
POL. [Points to his head and shoulder.] Take this from this, if this be otherwise.

---

124 **more above:** furthermore.
129 **fain:** willingly, gladly.
134 **play'd . . . table-book:** i.e. noted the matter secretly.
135 **winking:** closing of the eyes.
136 **idle sight:** uncomprehending eyes.
137 **round:** straightforwardly.
138 **bespeak:** address.
139 **star:** i.e. sphere, lot in life.
143 **took . . . of:** profited by, i.e. carried out.
144 **repell'd:** repulsed.
146 **watch:** sleeplessness.
147 **lightness:** lightheadedness.

155   If circumstances lead me, I will find
    Where truth is hid, though it were hid indeed
    Within the centre.
    KING   How may we try it further?
    POL. You know sometimes he walks four hours together
    Here in the lobby.
    QUEEN   So he does indeed.
160 POL. At such a time I'll loose my daughter to him.
    Be you and I behind an arras then,
    Mark the encounter: if he love her not,
    And be not from his reason fall'n thereon,
    Let me be no assistant for a state,
    But keep a farm and carters.
165 KING   We will try it.

Enter HAMLET *[reading on a book].*

QUEEN But look where sadly the poor wretch comes reading.
POL. Away, I do beseech you, both away.
    I'll board him presently.

Exeunt KING *and* QUEEN.

                        O, give me leave,
    How does my good Lord Hamlet?
170 HAM. Well, God-a-mercy.
    POL. Do you know me, my lord?
    HAM. Excellent well, you are a fishmonger.
    POL. Not I, my lord.
    HAM. Then I would you were so honest a man.
175 POL. Honest, my lord?
    HAM. Ay, sir, to be honest, as this world goes, is to be one man pick'd out of ten thousand.
    POL. That's very true, my lord.
    HAM. For if the sun breed maggots in a dead dog, being a good kissing carrion—Have you a daughter?
180 POL. I have, my lord.
    HAM. Let her not walk i' th' sun. Conception is a blessing, but as your daughter may conceive, friend, look to't.
    POL. *[Aside.]* How say you by that? still harping on my daughter. Yet he knew me not at first, 'a said I was a fishmonger. 'A is far gone. And truly in my youth I suff'red

---

[157] **centre:** i.e. of the earth (which in the Ptolemaic system is also the center of the universe).
[161] **arras:** hanging tapestry.
[163] **thereon:** because of that.
[168] **board:** accost.   **presently:** at once.
[170] **God-a-mercy:** thank you.
[172] **fishmonger.** Usually explained as slang for "bawd," but no evidence has been produced for such a usage in Shakespeare's day.
[178] **good kissing carrion:** flesh good enough for the sun to kiss.
[181] **Conception:** understanding (with following play on the sense "conceiving a child").

185   much extremity for love—very near this. I'll speak to him again.—What do you read,
      my lord?

HAM. Words, words, words.

POL. What is the matter, my lord?

HAM. Between who?

190 POL. I mean, the matter that you read, my lord.

HAM. Slanders, sir; for the satirical rogue says here that old men have grey beards, that
      their faces are wrinkled, their eyes purging thick amber and plum-tree gum, and that
      they have a plentiful lack of wit, together with most weak hams; all which, sir, though
      I most powerfully and potently believe, yet I hold it not honesty to have it thus set

195   down, for yourself, sir, shall grow old as I am, if like a crab you could go backward.

POL. [Aside.] Though this be madness, yet there is method in't.—Will you walk out of
      the air, my lord?

HAM. Into my grave.

POL. Indeed that's out of the air. [Aside.] How pregnant sometimes his replies are! a

200   happiness that often madness hits on, which reason and [sanity] could not so prosper-
      ously be deliver'd of. I will leave him, [and suddenly contrive the means of meeting
      between him] and my daughter.—My lord, I will take my leave of you.

HAM. You cannot take from me any thing that I will not more willingly part withal—
      except my life, except my life, except my life.

205 POL. Fare you well, my lord.

HAM. These tedious old fools!

Enter GUILDENSTERN *and* ROSENCRANTZ.

POL. You go to seek the Lord Hamlet, there he is.

ROS. [*To* POLONIUS.] God save you, sir!

[*Exit* POLONIUS.]

GUIL. My honor'd lord!

210 ROS. My most dear lord!

HAM. My [excellent] good friends! How dost thou, Guildenstern? Ah, Rosencrantz! Good
      lads, how do you both?

ROS. As the indifferent children of the earth.

GUIL. Happy, in that we are not [over-]happy, on Fortune's [cap] we are not the very

215   button.

HAM. Nor the soles of her shoe?

ROS. Neither, my lord.

HAM. Then you live about her waist, or in the middle of her favors?

GUIL. Faith, her privates we.

---

188 **matter:** subject; but Hamlet replies as if he had understood Polonius to mean "cause for a
    quarrel."

194 **honesty:** a fitting thing.

196 **method:** orderly arrangement, sequence of ideas.

196–97 **out . . . air:** Outdoor air was thought to be bad for invalids.

199 **pregnant:** apt.

201 **suddenly:** at once.

213 **indifferent:** average.

219 **privates:** (1) intimate friends; (2) genitalia.

220 HAM. In the secret parts of Fortune? O, most true, she is a strumpet. What news?

ROS. None, my lord, but the world's grown honest.

HAM. Then is doomsday near. But your news is not true. [Let me question more in particular. What have you, my good friends, deserv'd at the hands of Fortune, that she sends you to prison hither?

225 GUIL. Prison, my lord?

HAM. Denmark's a prison.

ROS. Then is the world one.

HAM. A goodly one, in which there are many confines, wards, and dungeons, Denmark being one o' th' worst.

230 ROS. We think not so, my lord.

HAM. Why then 'tis none to you; for there is nothing either good or bad, but thinking makes it so. To me it is a prison.

ROS. Why then your ambition makes it one. 'Tis too narrow for your mind.

HAM. O God, I could be bounded in a nutshell, and count myself a king of infinite
235 space—were it not that I have bad dreams.

GUIL. Which dreams indeed are ambition, for the very substance of the ambitious is merely the shadow of a dream.

HAM. A dream itself is but a shadow.

ROS. Truly, and I hold ambition of so airy and light a quality that it is but a shadow's
240 shadow.

HAM. Then are our beggars bodies, and our monarchs and outstretch'd heroes the beggars' shadows. Shall we to th' court? for, by my fay, I cannot reason.

BOTH [ROS., GUIL.] We'll wait upon you.

HAM. No such matter. I will not sort you with the rest of my servants; for to speak to
245 you like an honest man, I am most dreadfully attended.] But in the beaten way of friendship, what make you at Elsinore?

ROS. To visit you, my lord, no other occasion.

HAM. Beggar that I am, I am [even] poor in thanks—but I thank you, and sure, dear friends, my thanks are too dear a halfpenny. Were you not sent for? is it your own
250 inclining? is it a free visitation? Come, come, deal justly with me. Come, come— nay, speak.

GUIL. What should we say, my lord?

HAM. Any thing but to th' purpose. You were sent for, and there is a kind of confession in your looks, which your modesties have not craft enough to color. I know the good
255 King and Queen have sent for you.

---

220 **strumpet.** A common epithet for Fortune, because she grants favors to all men.

228 **wards:** cells.

241 **bodies:** i.e. not shadows (since they lack ambition). **outstretch'd:** i.e. with their ambition extended to the utmost (and hence producing stretched-out or elongated shadows).

242 **fay:** faith.

243 **wait upon you:** attend you thither.

244 **sort:** associate.

245 **dreadfully:** execrably.

249 **too . . . halfpenny:** too expensive priced at a halfpenny, i.e. not worth much.

250 **justly:** honestly.

253 **but.** Ordinarily punctuated with a comma preceding, to give the sense "provided that it is"; but Q2 has no comma, and Hamlet may intend, or include, the sense "except."

254 **modesties:** sense of shame.

ROS. To what end, my lord?

HAM. That you must teach me. But let me conjure you, by the rights of our fellowship, by the consonancy of our youth, by the obligation of our ever-preserv'd love, and by what more dear a better proposer can charge you withal, be even and direct with me, whether you were sent for or no!

260

ROS. [Aside to GUILDENSTERN.] What say you?

HAM. [Aside.] Nay then I have an eye of you!—If you love me, hold not off.

GUIL. My lord, we were sent for.

HAM. I will tell you why, so shall my anticipation prevent your discovery, and your secrecy to the King and Queen moult no feather. I have of late—but wherefore I know not —lost all my mirth, forgone all custom of exercises; and indeed it goes so heavily with my disposition, that this goodly frame, the earth, seems to me a sterile promontory; this most excellent canopy, the air, look you, this brave o'erhanging firmament, this majestical roof fretted with golden fire, why, it appeareth nothing to me but a foul and pestilent congregation of vapors. What [a] piece of work is a man, how noble in reason, how infinite in faculties, in form and moving, how express and admirable in action, how like an angel in apprehension, how like a god! the beauty of the world; the paragon of animals; and yet to me what is this quintessence of dust? Man delights not me—nor women neither, though by your smiling you seem to say so.

265

270

275

ROS. My lord, there was no such stuff in my thoughts.

HAM. Why did ye laugh then, when I said, "Man delights not me"?

ROS. To think, my lord, if you delight not in man, what lenten entertainment the players shall receive from you. We coted them on the way, and hither are they coming to offer you service.

280

HAM. He that plays the king shall be welcome—his Majesty shall have tribute on me, the adventerous knight shall use his foil and target, the lover shall not sigh gratis, the humorous man shall end his part in peace, [the clown shall make those laugh whose lungs are [tickle] a' th' sere,] and the lady shall say her mind freely, or the [blank] verse shall halt for't. What players are they?

285

ROS. Even those you were wont to take such delight in, the tragedians of the city.

---

258 **consonancy . . . youth:** similarity of our ages.

259 **charge:** urge, adjure. **even:** frank, honest (cf. modern "level with me").

262 **of:** on.

264 **prevent your discovery:** forestall your disclosure (of what the King and Queen have said to you in confidence).

265 **moult no feather:** not be impaired in the least.

266 **custom of exercises:** my usual athletic activities.

268 **brave:** splendid.

269 **fretted:** ornamented as with fretwork.

270 **piece of work:** masterpiece.

272 **express:** exact.

274 **quintessence:** finest and purest extract.

278 **lenten entertainment:** meager reception.

279 **coted:** outstripped.

281 **on:** of, from.

282 **adventerous:** adventurous, i.e. wandering in search of adventure. **foil and target:** light fencing sword and small shield. **gratis:** without reward.

283 **humorous:** dominated by some eccentric trait (like the melancholy Jaques in *As You Like It*).

284 **tickle . . . sere:** i.e. easily made to laugh (literally, describing a gun that goes off easily; *sere* = a catch in the gunlock; *tickle* = easily affected, highly sensitive to stimulus).

285 **halt:** limp, come off lamely (the verse will not scan if she omits indecent words).

HAM. How chances it they travel? Their residence, both in reputation and profit, was better both ways.

ROS. I think their inhibition comes by the means of the late innovation.

290 HAM. Do they hold the same estimation they did when I was in the city? Are they so follow'd?

ROS. No indeed are they not.

[HAM. How comes it? do they grow rusty?

ROS. Nay, their endeavor keeps in the wonted pace; but there is, sir, an aery of children,
295 little eyases, that cry out on the top of question, and are most tyrannically clapp'd for't. These are now the fashion, and so [berattle] the common stages—so they call them— that many wearing rapiers are afraid of goose-quills and dare scarce come thither.

HAM. What, are they children? Who maintains 'em? How are they escoted? Will they pursue the quality no longer than they can sing? Will they not say afterwards, if they
300 should grow themselves to common players (as it is [most like], if their means are [no] better), their writers do them wrong, to make them exclaim against their own succession?

ROS. Faith, there has been much to do on both sides, and the nation holds it no sin to tarre them to controversy. There was for a while no money bid for argument, unless
305 the poet and the player went to cuffs in the question.

HAM. Is't possible?

GUIL. O, there has been much throwing about of brains.

HAM. Do the boys carry it away?

ROS. Ay, that they do, my lord—Hercules and his load too.]

---

289 **inhibition:** hindrance (to playing in the city). The word could be used of an official prohibition. See next note. **innovation.** Shakespeare elsewhere uses this word of a political uprising or revolt, and line 289 is often explained as meaning that the company had been forbidden to play in the city as the result of some disturbance. It is commonly conjectured that the allusion is to the Essex rebellion of 1601, but it is known that Shakespeare's company, though to some extent involved on account of the special performance of *Richard II* it was commissioned to give on the eve of the rising, was not in fact punished by inhibition. A second interpretation explains *innovation* as referring to the new theatrical vogue described in lines 294 ff., and conjectures that *inhibition* may allude to a Privy Council order of 1600 restricting the number of London playhouses to two and the number of performances to two a week.

293–309 **How . . . too.** This passage refers topically to the "War of the Theatres" between the child actors and their poet Jonson on the one side, and on the other the adults, with Dekker, Marston, and possibly Shakespeare as spokesmen, in 1600–1601.

294 **aery:** nest.

295 **eyases:** unfledged hawks. **cry . . . question:** cry shrilly above others in controversy. **tyrannically:** outrageously.

296 **berattle:** cry down, satirize. **common stages:** public theaters (the children played at the Blackfriars, a private theater).

297 **goose-quills:** pens (of satirical playwrights).

298 **escoted:** supported.

299 **quality:** profession (of acting). **no . . . sing:** i.e. only until their voices change.

302 **succession:** future.

303 **to do:** ado.

304 **tarre:** incite. **argument:** plot of a play.

305 **in the question:** i.e. as part of the script.

308 **carry it away:** win.

309 **Hercules . . . too.** Hercules in the course of one of his twelve labors supported the world for Atlas; the children do better, for they carry away the world and Hercules as well. There is an allusion to the Globe playhouse, which reportedly had for its sign the figure of Hercules upholding the world.

310   HAM. It is not very strange, for my uncle is King of Denmark, and those that would make
mouths at him while my father liv'd, give twenty, forty, fifty, a hundred ducats a-
piece for his picture in little. 'Sblood, there is something in this more than natural,
if philosophy could find it out.

A flourish [for the PLAYERS].

  GUIL. There are the players.
315   HAM. Gentlemen, you are welcome to Elsinore. Your hands, come then: th' appurte-
nance of welcome is fashion and ceremony. Let me comply with you in this garb,
[lest my] extent to the players, which, I tell you, must show fairly outwards, should
more appear like entertainment than yours. You are welcome; but my uncle-father
and aunt-mother are deceiv'd.
320   GUIL. In what, my dear lord?
  HAM. I am but mad north-north-west. When the wind is southerly I know a hawk from
a hand-saw.

Enter POLONIUS.

  POL. Well be with you, gentlemen!
  HAM. *[Aside to them.]* Hark you, Guildenstern, and you too—at each ear a hearer—
325   that great baby you see there is not yet out of his swaddling-clouts.
  ROS. Happily he is the second time come to them, for they say an old man is twice a
child.
  HAM. I will prophesy, he comes to tell me of the players, mark it. *[Aloud.]* You say
right, sir, a' Monday morning, 'twas then indeed.
330   POL. My lord, I have news to tell you.
  HAM. My lord, I have news to tell you. When Roscius was an actor in Rome—
  POL. The actors are come hither, my lord.
  HAM. Buzz, buzz!
  POL. Upon my honor—
335   HAM. "Then came each actor on his ass"—
  POL. The best actors in the world, either for tragedy, comedy, history, pastoral, pastoral-
comical, historical-pastoral, [tragical-historical, tragical-comical-historical-pastoral,]
scene individable, or poem unlimited; Seneca cannot be too heavy, nor Plautus
too light, for the law of writ and the liberty: these are the only men.

---

311 **mouths:** derisive faces.
312 **'Sblood:** by God's (Christ's) blood.
316 **comply:** observe the formalities.   **garb:** fashion, manner.
317 **my extent:** i.e. the degree of courtesy I show.
318 **more . . . yours:** seem to be a warmer reception than I have given you.
321–22 **hawk, hand-saw.** Both cutting tools; but also both birds, if *hand-saw* quibbles on *hernshaw*,
"heron," a bird preyed upon by the hawk.
325 **swaddling-clouts:** swaddling clothes.
326 **Happily:** haply, perhaps.   **twice:** i.e. for the second time.
331 **Roscius:** the most famous of Roman actors (died 62 B.C.). News about him would be stale news
indeed.
333 **Buzz:** exclamation of impatience at someone who tells news already known.
338 **scene individable:** play observing the unity of place.   **poem unlimited:** play ignoring rules such
as the three unities.   **Seneca:** Roman writer of tragedies.   **Plautus:** Roman writer of comedies.
339 **for . . . liberty:** for strict observance of the rules, or for freedom from them (with possible allusion

340 HAM. O Jephthah, judge of Israel, what a treasure hadst thou!
POL. What a treasure had he, my lord?

HAM. Why—

> "One fair daughter, and no more,
> The which he loved passing well."

345 POL. *[Aside.]* Still on my daughter.
HAM. Am I not i' th' right, old Jephthah?
POL. If you call me Jephthah, my lord, I have a daughter that I love passing well.
HAM. Nay, that follows not.
POL. What follows then, my lord?
350 HAM. Why—

> "As by lot, God wot,"

and then, you know,

> "It came to pass, as most like it was"—

the first row of the pious chanson will show you more, for look where my abridgment
355 comes.

Enter the PLAYERS, *[four or five].*

You are welcome, masters, welcome all. I am glad to see thee well. Welcome, good
friends. O, old friend! why, thy face is valanc'd since I saw thee last; com'st thou to
beard me in Denmark? What, my young lady and mistress! by' lady, your ladyship is
nearer to heaven than when I saw you last, by the altitude of a chopine. Pray God
360 your voice, like a piece of uncurrent gold, be not crack'd within the ring. Masters,
you are all welcome. We'll e'en to't like [French] falc'ners—fly at any thing we see;
we'll have a speech straight. Come give us a taste of your quality, come, a passionate
speech.
[1] PLAY. What speech, my good lord?
365 HAM. I heard thee speak me a speech once, but it was never acted, or if it was, not above
once; for the play, I remember, pleas'd not the million, 'twas caviary to the general,
but it was—as I receiv'd it, and others, whose judgments in such matters cried in the
top of mine—an excellent play, well digested in the scenes, set down with as much
modesty as cunning. I remember one said there were no sallets in the lines to make

---

to the location of playhouses, which were not built in properties under city jurisdiction, but in
the "liberties"—land once monastic and now outside the jurisdiction of the city authorities).
only: very best (a frequent use).
340 **Jephthah . . . Israel:** title of a ballad, from which Hamlet goes on to quote. For the story of
Jephthah and his daughter, see Judges 11.
354 **row:** stanza. **chanson:** song, ballad. **abridgment:** (1) interruption; (2) pastime.
357 **valanc'd:** fringed, i.e. bearded.
358 **beard:** confront boldly (with obvious pun). **by' lady:** by Our Lady.
359 **chopine:** thick-soled shoe.
360 **crack'd . . . ring:** i.e. broken to the point where you can no longer play female roles. A coin
with a crack extending far enough in from the edge to cross the circle surrounding the stamp of
the sovereign's head was unacceptable in exchange (*uncurrent*).
362 **straight:** straightway. **quality:** professional skill.
366 **caviary . . . general:** caviar to the common people, i.e. too choice for the multitude.
367–68 **cried . . . of:** were louder than, i.e. carried more authority than.
369 **sallets:** salads, i.e. spicy jokes.

370　　the matter savory, nor no matter in the phrase that might indict the author of
　　　affection, but call'd it an honest method, as wholesome as sweet, and by very much
　　　more handsome than fine. One speech in't I chiefly lov'd, 'twas Aeneas' [tale] to Dido,
　　　and thereabout of it especially when he speaks of Priam's slaughter. If it live in your
　　　memory, begin at this line—let me see, let me see:
375　　"The rugged Pyrrhus, like th' Hyrcanian beast—"
　　　'Tis not so, it begins with Pyrrhus:
　　　"The rugged Pyrrhus, he whose sable arms,
　　　Black as his purpose, did the night resemble
　　　When he lay couched in th' ominous horse,
380　　Hath now this dread and black complexion smear'd
　　　With heraldy more dismal: head to foot
　　　Now is he total gules, horridly trick'd
　　　With blood of fathers, mothers, daughters, sons,
　　　Bak'd and impasted with the parching streets,
385　　That lend a tyrannous and a damned light
　　　To their lord's murther. Roasted in wrath and fire,
　　　And thus o'er-sized with coagulate gore,
　　　With eyes like carbuncles, the hellish Pyrrhus
　　　Old grandsire Priam seeks."
390　　So proceed you.
　　　POL. 'Fore God, my lord, well spoken, with good accent and good discretion.
　　　[1] PLAY. "Anon he finds him
　　　Striking too short at Greeks. His antique sword,
　　　Rebellious to his arm, lies where it falls,
395　　Repugnant to command. Unequal match'd,
　　　Pyrrhus at Priam drives, in rage strikes wide,
　　　But with the whiff and wind of his fell sword
　　　Th' unnerved father falls. [Then senseless Ilium,]
　　　Seeming to feel this blow, with flaming top
400　　Stoops to his base, and with a hideous crash
　　　Takes prisoner Pyrrhus' ear; for lo his sword,
　　　Which was declining on the milky head
　　　Of reverent Priam, seem'd i' th' air to stick.

---

370 **savory:** zesty.
371 **affection:** affectation.
372 **fine:** showily dressed (in language).
373 **Priam's slaughter:** the slaying of Priam (at the fall of Troy).
375 **Pyrrhus:** another name for Neoptolemus, Achilles' son. **Hyrcanian beast.** Hyrcania in the
　　Caucasus was notorious for its tigers.
377 **sable arms.** The Greeks within the Trojan horse had blackened their skin so as to be inconspicuous
　　when they emerged at night.
381 **heraldy:** heraldry. **dismal:** ill-boding.
382 **gules:** red (heraldic term). **trick'd:** adorned.
384 **Bak'd:** caked. **impasted:** crusted. **with . . . streets:** i.e. by the heat from the burning streets.
387 **o'er-sized:** covered over as with a coat of sizing.
388 **carbuncles:** jewels believed to shine in the dark.
395 **Repugnant:** resistant, hostile.
397 **fell:** cruel.
398 **unnerved:** drained of strength. **senseless:** insensible. **Ilium:** the citadel of Troy.
403 **reverent:** reverend, aged.

So as a painted tyrant Pyrrhus stood
405 [And,] like a neutral to his will and matter,
Did nothing.
But as we often see, against some storm,
A silence in the heavens, the rack stand still,
The bold winds speechless, and the orb below
410 As hush as death, anon the dreadful thunder
Doth rend the region; so after Pyrrhus' pause,
A roused vengeance sets him new a-work,
And never did the Cyclops' hammers fall
On Mars's armor forg'd for proof eterne
415 With less remorse than Pyrrhus' bleeding sword
Now falls on Priam.
Out, out, thou strumpet Fortune! All you gods,
In general synod take away her power!
Break all the spokes and [fellies] from her wheel,
420 And bowl the round nave down the hill of heaven
As low as to the fiends!"
POL. This is too long.
HAM. It shall to the barber's with your beard. Prithee say on, he's for a jig or a tale of
bawdry, or he sleeps. Say on, come to Hecuba.
425 [1] PLAY. "But who, ah woe, had seen the mobled queen"—
HAM. "The mobled queen"?
POL. That's good, ["[mobled] queen" is good].
[1] PLAY. "Run barefoot up and down, threat'ning the flames
With bisson rheum, a clout upon that head
430 Where late the diadem stood, and for a robe,
About her lank and all o'er-teemed loins,
A blanket, in the alarm of fear caught up—
Who this had seen, with tongue in venom steep'd,
'Gainst Fortune's state would treason have pronounc'd.
435 But if the gods themselves did see her then,
When she saw Pyrrhus make malicious sport
In mincing with his sword her [husband's] limbs,
The instant burst of clamor that she made,
Unless things mortal move them not at all,

---

405 **like . . . matter:** i.e. poised midway between intention and performance.
407 **against:** just before.
408 **rack:** cloud mass.
411 **region:** i.e. air.
413 **Cyclops:** giants who worked in Vulcan's smithy, where armor was made for the gods.
414 **proof eterne:** eternal endurance.
415 **remorse:** pity.
419 **fellies:** rims.
420 **nave:** hub.
423 **jig:** song-and-dance entertainment performed after the main play.
425 **mobled:** muffled.
429 **bisson rheum:** blinding tears. **clout:** cloth.
431 **o'er-teemed:** worn out by childbearing.
434 **state:** rule, government.

440   Would have made milch the burning eyes of heaven,
       And passion in the gods."
    POL. Look whe'er he has not turn'd his color and has tears in 's eyes. Prithee no more.
    HAM. 'Tis well, I'll have thee speak out the rest of this soon. Good my lord, will you see
       the players well bestow'd? Do you hear, let them be well us'd, for they are the abstract
445   and brief chronicles of the time. After your death you were better have a bad epitaph
       than their ill report while you live.
    POL. My lord, I will use them according to their desert.
    HAM. God's bodkin, man, much better: use every man after his desert, and who shall
       scape whipping? Use them after your own honor and dignity—the less they deserve,
450   the more merit is in your bounty. Take them in.
    POL. Come, sirs.

[Exit.]

    HAM. Follow him, friends, we'll hear a play tomorrow.

[Exeunt all the PLAYERS *but the* FIRST.]

    Dost thou hear me, old friend? Can you play "The Murther of Gonzago"?
    [1] PLAY. Ay, my lord.
455   HAM. We'll ha't to-morrow night. You could for need study a speech of some dozen
       lines, or sixteen lines, which I would set down and insert in't, could you not?
    [1] PLAY. Ay, my lord.
    HAM. Very well. Follow that lord, and look you mock him not. *[Exit* FIRST PLAYER.]
    My good friends, I'll leave you [till] night. You are welcome to Elsinore.
460   ROS. Good my lord!
    HAM. Ay so, God buy to you.

Exeunt [ROSENCRANTZ *and* GUILDENSTERN].

                  Now I am alone.
    O, what a rogue and peasant slave am I!
    It is not monstrous that this player here,
    But in a fiction, in a dream of passion,
465   Could force his soul so to his own conceit
    That from her working all the visage wann'd,
    Tears in his eyes, distraction in his aspect,
    A broken voice, an' his whole function suiting
    With forms to his conceit? And all for nothing,
470   For Hecuba!
    What's Hecuba to him, or he to [Hecuba],
    That he should weep for her? What would he do

---

440 **milch:** moist (literally, milky).
441 **passion:** grief.
442 **Look . . . not:** i.e. note how he has.
444 **bestow'd:** lodged. **us'd:** treated.
448 **God's bodkin:** by God's (Christ's) little body.
455 **for need:** if necessary.
465 **conceit:** imaginative conception.
468 **his whole function:** the operation of his whole body.
469 **forms:** actions, expressions.

Had he the motive and [the cue] for passion
That I have? He would drown the stage with tears,
475 And cleave the general ear with horrid speech,
Make mad the guilty, and appall the free,
Confound the ignorant, and amaze indeed
The very faculties of eyes and ears. Yet I,
A dull and muddy-mettled rascal, peak
480 Like John-a-dreams, unpregnant of my cause,
And can say nothing; no, not for a king,
Upon whose property and most dear life
A damn'd defeat was made. Am I a coward?
Who calls me villain, breaks my pate across,
485 Plucks off my beard and blows it in my face,
Tweaks me by the nose, gives me the lie i' th' throat
As deep as to the lungs? Who does me this?
Hah, 'swounds, I should take it; for it cannot be
But I am pigeon-liver'd, and lack gall
490 To make oppression bitter, or ere this
I should 'a' fatted all the region kites
With this slave's offal. Bloody, bawdy villain!
Remorseless, treacherous, lecherous, kindless villain!
Why, what an ass am I! This is most brave,
495 That I, the son of a dear [father] murthered,
Prompted to my revenge by heaven and hell,
Must like a whore unpack my heart with words,
And fall a-cursing like a very drab,
A stallion. Fie upon't, foh!
500 About, my brains! Hum—I have heard
That guilty creatures sitting at a play
Have by the very cunning of the scene
Been strook so to the soul, that presently
They have proclaim'd their malefactions:
505 For murther, though it have no tongue, will speak
With most miraculous organ. I'll have these players
Play something like the murther of my father

---

476 **free:** innocent.
477 **amaze:** confound.
479 **muddy-mettled:** dull-spirited. **peak:** mope.
480 **John-a-dreams:** a sleepy fellow. **unpregnant of:** unquickened by.
483 **defeat:** destruction.
486–87 **gives . . . lungs:** calls me a liar in the extremest degree.
488 **'swounds:** by God's (Christ's) wounds. **should:** would certainly.
489 **am . . . gall:** i.e. am constitutionally incapable of resentment. That doves were mild because they had no gall was a popular belief.
491 **region kites:** kites of the air.
492 **offal:** entrails.
493 **kindless:** unnatural.
499 **stallion:** male whore. Most editors adopt the F1 reading *scullion*, "kitchen menial."
500 **About:** to work.
503 **presently:** at once, then and there.

Before mine uncle. I'll observe his looks,
I'll tent him to the quick. If 'a do blench,
510 I know my course. The spirit that I have seen
May be a [dev'l], and the [dev'l] hath power
T' assume a pleasing shape, yea, and perhaps,
Out of my weakness and my melancholy,
As he is very potent with such spirits,
515 Abuses me to damn me. I'll have grounds
More relative than this—the play's the thing
Wherein I'll catch the conscience of the King.

Exit.

ACT III

SCENE I.

Enter KING, QUEEN, POLONIUS, OPHELIA, ROSENCRANTZ, GUILDENSTERN, LORDS.

KING An' can you by no drift of conference
Get from him why he puts on this confusion,
Grating so harshly all his days of quiet
With turbulent and dangerous lunacy?
5 ROS. He does confess he feels himself distracted,
But from what cause 'a will by no means speak.
GUIL. Nor do we find him forward to be sounded,
But with a crafty madness keeps aloof
When we would bring him on to some confession
Of his true state.
10 QUEEN   Did he receive you well?
ROS. Most like a gentleman.
GUIL. But with much forcing of his disposition.
ROS. Niggard of question, but of our demands
Most free in his reply.
QUEEN   Did you assay him
15 To any pastime?
ROS. Madam, it so fell out that certain players
We o'erraught on the way; of these we told him,

---

509 **tent:** probe. **blench:** flinch.
514 **spirits:** states of temperament.
515 **Abuses:** deludes.
516 **relative:** closely related (to fact), i.e. conclusive.

III.i. Location: The castle.
1 **An':** and. **drift of conference:** leading on of conversation.
7 **forward:** readily willing. **sounded:** plumbed, probed.
8 **crafty madness:** i.e. mad craftiness, the shrewdness that mad people sometimes exhibit.
12 **disposition:** inclination.
13 **question:** conversation. **demands:** questions.
14 **assay:** attempt to win.
17 **o'erraught:** passed (literally, overreached).

And there did seem in him a kind of joy
To hear of it. They are here about the court,
20 And as I think, they have already order
This night to play before him.
POL.   'Tis most true,
And he beseech'd me to entreat your Majesties
To hear and see the matter.
KING With all my heart, and it doth much content me
25 To hear him so inclin'd.
Good gentlemen, give him a further edge,
And drive his purpose into these delights.
ROS. We shall, my lord.

Exeunt ROSENCRANTZ *and* GUILDENSTERN.

KING   Sweet Gertrude, leave us two,
For we have closely sent for Hamlet hither,
30 That he, as 'twere by accident, may here
Affront Ophelia. Her father and myself,
We'll so bestow ourselves that, seeing unseen,
We may of their encounter frankly judge,
And gather by him, as he is behav'd,
35 If't be th' affliction of his love or no
That thus he suffers for.
QUEEN   I shall obey you.
And for your part, Ophelia, I do wish
That your good beauties be the happy cause
Of Hamlet's wildness. So shall I hope your virtues
40 Will bring him to his wonted way again,
To both your honors.
OPH.   Madam, I wish it may.

[Exit QUEEN.*]*

POL. Ophelia, walk you here.—Gracious, so please you,
We will bestow ourselves. *[To* OPHELIA.*]* Read on this book,
That show of such an exercise may color
45 Your [loneliness]. We are oft to blame in this—
'Tis too much prov'd—that with devotion's visage
And pious action we do sugar o'er
The devil himself.

---

[26] **edge:** stimulus.
[27] **into:** on to.
[29] **closely:** privately.
[31] **Affront:** meet.
[33] **frankly:** freely.
[44] **exercise:** i.e. religious exercise (as the next sentence makes clear).
[44-45] **color Your loneliness:** make your solitude seem natural.
[46] **too much prov'd:** too often proved true.
[47] **action:** demeanor.

KING   [*Aside.*] O, 'tis too true!
       How smart a lash that speech doth give my conscience!
50   The harlot's cheek, beautied with plast'ring art,
       Is not more ugly to the thing that helps it
       Than is my deed to my most painted word.
       O heavy burthen!
POL.   I hear him coming. Withdraw, my lord.

[*Exeunt* KING *and* POLONIUS.]

Enter HAMLET.

55 HAM. To be, or not to be, that is the question:
          Whether 'tis nobler in the mind to suffer
          The slings and arrows of outrageous fortune,
          Or to take arms against a sea of troubles,
          And by opposing, end them. To die, to sleep—
60   No more, and by a sleep to say we end
          The heart-ache and the thousand natural shocks
          That flesh is heir to; 'tis a consummation
          Devoutly to be wish'd. To die, to sleep—
          To sleep, perchance to dream—ay, there's the rub,
65   For in that sleep of death what dreams may come,
          When we have shuffled off this mortal coil,
          Must give us pause; there's the respect
          That makes calamity of so long life:
          For who would bear the whips and scorns of time,
70   Th' oppressor's wrong, the proud man's contumely,
          The pangs of despis'd love, the law's delay,
          The insolence of office, and the spurns
          That patient merit of th' unworthy takes,
          When he himself might his quietus make
75   With a bare bodkin; who would fardels bear,
          To grunt and sweat under a weary life,
          But that the dread of something after death,
          The undiscover'd country, from whose bourn
          No traveller returns, puzzles the will,
80   And makes us rather bear those ills we have,

---

51 **to . . . it**: in comparison with the paint that makes it look beautiful.
56 **suffer**: submit to, endure patiently.
62 **consummation**: completion, end.
64 **rub**: obstacle (a term from the game of bowls).
66 **shuffled off**: freed ourselves from.   **this mortal coil**: the turmoil of this mortal life.
67 **respect**: consideration.
68 **of . . . life**: so long-lived.
69 **time**: the world.
74 **his quietus make**: write paid to his account.
75 **bare bodkin**: mere dagger.   **fardels**: burdens.
78 **undiscover'd**: not disclosed to knowledge; about which men have no information.   **bourn**: boundary, i.e. region.
79 **puzzles**: paralyzes.

Than fly to others that we know not of?
Thus conscience does make cowards [of us all],
And thus the native hue of resolution
Is sicklied o'er with the pale cast of thought,
85 And enterprises of great pitch and moment
With this regard their currents turn awry,
And lose the name of action.—Soft you now,
The fair Ophelia. Nymph, in thy orisons
Be all my sins rememb'red.

OPH.   Good my lord,
90 How does your honor for this many a day?

HAM. I humbly thank you, well, [well, well].

OPH. My lord, I have remembrances of yours
That I have longed long to redeliver.
I pray you now receive them.

HAM.   No, not I,
95 I never gave you aught.

OPH. My honor'd lord, you know right well you did,
And with them words of so sweet breath compos'd
As made these things more rich. Their perfume lost,
Take these again, for to the noble mind
100 Rich gifts wax poor when givers prove unkind.
There, my lord.

HAM. Ha, ha! are you honest?

OPH. My lord?

HAM. Are you fair?

105 OPH. What means your lordship?

HAM. That if you be honest and fair, [your honesty] should admit no discourse to your
beauty.

OPH. Could beauty, my lord, have better commerce than with honesty?

HAM. Ay, truly, for the power of beauty will sooner transform honesty from what it is
110 to a bawd than the force of honesty can translate beauty into his likeness. This was
sometime a paradox, but now the time gives it proof. I did love you once.

OPH. Indeed, my lord, you made me believe so.

HAM. You should not have believ'd me, for virtue cannot so [inoculate] our old stock
but we shall relish of it. I lov'd you not.

115 OPH. I was the more deceiv'd.

HAM. Get thee [to] a nunn'ry, why wouldst thou be a breeder of sinners? I am myself
indifferent honest, but yet I could accuse me of such things that it were better my

---

82 **conscience:** reflection (but with some of the modern sense, too).

83 **native hue:** natural (ruddy) complexion.

84 **pale cast:** pallor.   **thought:** i.e. melancholy thought, brooding.

85 **pitch:** loftiness (a term from falconry, signifying the highest point of a hawk's flight).

88 **orisons:** prayers.

102 **honest:** chaste.

111 **sometime:** formerly.   **paradox:** tenet contrary to accepted belief.

113-14 **virtue . . . it:** virtue, engrafted on our old stock (of viciousness), cannot so change the nature
of the plant that no trace of the original will remain.

117 **indifferent honest:** tolerably virtuous.

mother had not borne me: I am very proud, revengeful, ambitious, with more offenses at my beck than I have thoughts to put them in, imagination to give them shape, or
120 time to act them in. What should such fellows as I do crawling between earth and heaven? We are arrant knaves, believe none of us. Go thy ways to a nunn'ry. Where's your father?

OPH. At home, my lord.

HAM. Let the doors be shut upon him, that he may play the fool no where but in 's own
125 house. Farewell.

OPH. O, help him, you sweet heavens!

HAM. If thou dost marry, I'll give thee this plague for thy dowry: be thou as chaste as ice, as pure as snow, thou shalt not escape calumny. Get thee to a nunn'ry, fare-well. Or if thou wilt needs marry, marry a fool, for wise men know well enough what
130 monsters you make of them. To a nunn'ry, go, and quickly too. Farewell.

OPH. Heavenly powers, restore him!

HAM. I have heard of your paintings, well enough. God hath given you one face, and you make yourselves another. You jig and amble, and you [lisp,] you nickname God's creatures and make your wantonness [your] ignorance. Go to, I'll no more on't, it
135 hath made me mad. I say we will have no moe marriage. Those that are married already (all but one) shall live, the rest shall keep as they are. To a nunn'ry, go.

Exit.

OPH. O, what a noble mind is here o'erthrown!
       The courtier's, soldier's, scholar's, eye, tongue, sword,
       Th' expectation and rose of the fair state,
140   The glass of fashion and the mould of form,
       Th' observ'd of all observers, quite, quite down!
       And I, of ladies most deject and wretched,
       That suck'd the honey of his [music] vows,
       Now see [that] noble and most sovereign reason
145   Like sweet bells jangled out of time, and harsh;
       That unmatch'd form and stature of blown youth
       Blasted with ecstasy. O, woe is me
       T' have seen what I have seen, see what I see!

[OPHELIA *withdraws.*]

Enter KING *and* POLONIUS.

---

130 **monsters.** Alluding to the notion that the husbands of unfaithful wives grew horns.   **you:** you women.
133–34 **You . . . creatures:** i.e. you walk and talk affectedly.
134 **make . . . ignorance:** excuse your affectation as ignorance.
135 **moe:** more.
139 **expectation:** hope.   **rose:** ornament.   **fair.** Probably proleptic: "(the kingdom) made fair by his presence."
140 **glass:** mirror.   **mould of form:** pattern of (courtly) behavior.
141 **observ'd . . . observers.** Shakespeare uses *observe* to mean not only "behold, mark attentively" but also "pay honor to."
146 **blown:** in full bloom.
147 **Blasted:** withered.   **ecstasy:** madness.

KING Love? his affections do not that way tend,
150   Nor what he spake, though it lack'd form a little,
      Was not like madness. There's something in his soul
      O'er which his melancholy sits on brood,
      And I do doubt the hatch and the disclose
      Will be some danger; which for to prevent,
155   I have in quick determination
      Thus set it down: he shall with speed to England
      For the demand of our neglected tribute.
      Haply the seas, and countries different,
      With variable objects, shall expel
160   This something-settled matter in his heart,
      Whereon his brains still beating puts him thus
      From fashion of himself. What think you on't?
POL. It shall do well; but yet do I believe
      The origin and commencement of his grief
165   Sprung from neglected love. [OPHELIA *comes forward.*] How now, Ophelia?
      You need not tell us what Lord Hamlet said,
      We heard it all. My lord, do as you please,
      But if you hold it fit, after the play
      Let his queen-mother all alone entreat him
170   To show his grief. Let her be round with him,
      And I'll be plac'd (so please you) in the ear
      Of all their conference. If she find him not,
      To England send him, or confine him where
      Your wisdom best shall think.
KING   It shall be so.
175   Madness in great ones must not [unwatch'd] go.

Exeunt.

SCENE II.

Enter HAMLET *and three of the* PLAYERS.

HAM. Speak the speech, I pray you, as I pronounc'd it to you, trippingly on the tongue,
      but if you mouth it, as many of our players do, I had as live the town-crier spoke my
      lines. Nor do not saw the air too much with your hand, thus, but use all gently, for
      in the very torrent, tempest, and, as I may say, whirlwind of your passion, you must
5   acquire and beget a temperance that may give it smoothness. O, it offends me to the
      soul to hear a robustious periwig-pated fellow tear a passion to totters, to very rags, to

---

149 **affections:** inclinations, feelings.
153 **doubt:** fear. **disclose.** Synonymous with *hatch*; see also V.i.231.
165 **neglected:** unrequited.
170 **his grief:** what is troubling him. **round:** blunt, outspoken.
172 **find him:** learn the truth about him.

III.ii. Location: The castle.
2 **mouth:** pronounce with exaggerated distinctness or declamatory effect. **live:** lief, willingly.
6 **totters:** tatters.

spleet the ears of the groundlings, who for the most part are capable of nothing but inexplicable dumb shows and noise. I would have such a fellow whipt for o'erdoing Termagant, it out-Herods Herod, pray you avoid it.

10 [1] PLAY. I warrant your honor.

HAM. Be not too tame neither, but let your own discretion be your tutor. Suit the action to the word, the word to the action, with this special observance, that you o'erstep not the modesty of nature: for any thing so o'erdone is from the purpose of playing, whose end, both at the first and now, was and is, to hold as 'twere the mirror up to
15 nature: to show virtue her feature, scorn her own image, and the very age and body of the time his form and pressure. Now this overdone, or come tardy off, though it makes the unskillful laugh, cannot but make the judicious grieve; the censure of which one must in your allowance o'erweigh a whole theatre of others. O, there be players that I have seen play—and heard others [praise], and that highly—not to speak
20 it profanely, that, neither having th' accent of Christians nor the gait of Christian, pagan, nor man, have so strutted and bellow'd that I have thought some of Nature's journeymen had made men, and not made them well, they imitated humanity so abominably.

[1] PLAY. I hope we have reform'd that indifferently with us, [sir].

25 HAM. O, reform it altogether. And let those that play your clowns speak no more than is set down for them, for there be of them that will themselves laugh to set on some quantity of barren spectators to laugh too, though in the mean time some necessary question of the play be then to be consider'd. That's villainous, and shows a most pitiful ambition in the fool that uses it. Go make you ready.

[Exeunt PLAYERS.]

Enter POLONIUS, GUILDENSTERN, and ROSENCRANTZ.

30 How now, my lord? Will the King hear this piece of work?

POL. And the Queen too, and that presently.

HAM. Bid the players make haste.

[Exit POLONIUS.]

Will you two help to hasten them?

ROS. Ay, my lord.

---

7 **spleet:** split.   **groundlings:** those who paid the lowest admission price and stood on the ground in the "yard" or pit of the theater.   **capable of:** able to take in.
9 **Termagant:** a supposed god of the Saracens, whose role in medieval drama, like that of Herod, was noisy and violent.
13 **modesty:** moderation.   **from:** contrary to.
15 **scorn:** i.e. that which is worthy of scorn.
16 **pressure:** impression (as of a seal), exact image.   **tardy:** inadequately.
17 **censure:** judgment.
18 **which one:** (even) one of whom.   **allowance:** estimation.
20 **profanely:** irreverently.
21–23 **some . . . abominably:** i.e. they were so unlike men that it seemed Nature had not made them herself, but had delegated the task to mediocre assistants.
24 **indifferently:** pretty well.
26 **of them:** some of them.
29 **fool:** (1) stupid person; (2) actor playing a fool's role.
30 **piece of work:** masterpiece (said jocularly).
31 **presently:** at once.

Exeunt they two.

35 HAM. What ho, Horatio!

Enter HORATIO.

HOR. Here, sweet lord, at your service.
HAM. Horatio, thou art e'en as just a man
    As e'er my conversation cop'd withal.
HOR. O my dear lord—
HAM.   Nay, do not think I flatter,
40   For what advancement may I hope from thee
    That no revenue hast but thy good spirits
    To feed and clothe thee? Why should the poor be flatter'd?
    No, let the candied tongue lick absurd pomp,
    And crook the pregnant hinges of the knee
45   Where thrift may follow fawning. Dost thou hear?
    Since my dear soul was mistress of her choice
    And could of men distinguish her election,
    Sh' hath seal'd thee for herself, for thou hast been
    As one in suff'ring all that suffers nothing,
50   A man that Fortune's buffets and rewards
    Hast ta'en with equal thanks; and blest are those
    Whose blood and judgment are so well co-meddled,
    That they are not a pipe for Fortune's finger
    To sound what stop she please. Give me that man
55   That is not passion's slave, and I will wear him
    In my heart's core, ay, in my heart of heart,
    As I do thee. Something too much of this.
    There is a play to-night before the King,
    One scene of it comes near the circumstance
60   Which I have told thee of my father's death.
    I prithee, when thou seest that act afoot,
    Even with the very comment of thy soul
    Observe my uncle. If his occulted guilt
    Do not itself unkennel in one speech,
65   It is a damned ghost that we have seen,
    And my imaginations are as foul

---

[37] **thou . . . man:** i.e. you come as close to being what a man should be (*just* = exact, precise).
[38] **my . . . withal:** my association with people has brought me into contact with.
[43] **candied:** sugared, i.e. flattering.   **absurd:** tasteless (Latin sense).
[44] **pregnant:** moving readily.
[45] **thrift:** thriving, profit.
[52] **blood:** passions.   **co-meddled:** mixed, blended.
[56] **my heart of heart:** the heart of my heart.
[62] **very . . . soul:** your most intense critical observation.
[63] **occulted:** hidden.
[64] **unkennel:** bring into the open.
[65] **damned ghost:** evil spirit, devil.

As Vulcan's stithy. Give him heedful note,
For I mine eyes will rivet to his face,
And after we will both our judgments join
In censure of his seeming.
70 HOR.   Well, my lord.
If 'a steal aught the whilst this play is playing,
And scape [detecting], I will pay the theft.

[Sound a flourish. Danish march.] Enter Trumpets and Kettle-drums, KING, QUEEN,
POLONIUS, OPHELIA, [ROSENCRANTZ, GUILDENSTERN, *and other* LORDS *attendant, with
his* GUARD *carrying torches]*.

HAM. They are coming to the play. I must be idle;
     Get you a place.
75 KING How fares our cousin Hamlet?
HAM. Excellent, i' faith, of the chameleon's dish: I eat the air, promise-cramm'd—you
     cannot feed capons so.
KING I have nothing with this answer, Hamlet, these words are not mine.
HAM. No, nor mine now. *[To* POLONIUS.] My lord, you play'd once i' th' university,
80   you say?
POL. That did I, my lord, and was accounted a good actor.
HAM. What did you enact?
POL. I did enact Julius Caesar. I was kill'd i' th' Capitol; Brutus kill'd me.
HAM. It was a brute part of him to kill so capital a calf there. Be the players ready?
85 ROS. Ay, my lord, they stay upon your patience.
QUEEN Come hither, my dear Hamlet, sit by me.
HAM. No, good mother, here's metal more attractive.

[Lying down at OPHELIA's *feet.]*

POL. *[To the* KING.] O ho, do you mark that?
HAM. Lady, shall I lie in your lap?
90 OPH. No, my lord
[HAM. I mean, my head upon your lap?
OPH. Ay, my lord.]
HAM. Do you think I meant country matters?
OPH. I think nothing, my lord.
95 HAM. That's a fair thought to lie between maids' legs.
OPH. What is, my lord?
HAM. Nothing.
OPH. You are merry, my lord.

---

67 **stithy:** forge.
70 **censure . . . seeming:** reaching a verdict on his behavior.
73 **be idle:** act foolish, pretend to be crazy.
75 **fares.** Hamlet takes up this word in another sense.
76 **chameleon's dish.** Chameleons were thought to feed on air. Hamlet says that he subsists on an
   equally nourishing diet, the promise of succession. There is probably a pun on *air/heir.*
78 **have nothing with:** do not understand.   **mine:** i.e. an answer to my question.
84 **part:** action.
93 **country matters:** indecency.

HAM. Who, I?

100 OPH. Ay, my lord.

HAM. O God, your only jig-maker. What should a man do but be merry, for look you how cheerfully my mother looks, and my father died within 's two hours.

OPH. Nay, 'tis twice two months, my lord.

HAM. So long? Nay then let the dev'l wear black, for I'll have a suit of sables. O heavens,

105 die two months ago, and not forgotten yet? Then there's hope a great man's memory may outlive his life half a year, but, by'r lady, 'a must build churches then, or else shall 'a suffer not thinking on, with the hobby-horse, whose epitaph is, "For O, for O, the hobby-horse is forgot."

The trumpets sound. Dumb show follows.

Enter a King and a Queen [very lovingly], the Queen embracing him and he her. [She kneels and makes show of protestation unto him.] He takes her up and declines his head upon her neck. He lies him down upon a bank of flowers. She, seeing him asleep, leaves him. Anon come in another man, takes off his crown, kisses it, pours poison in the sleeper's ears, and leaves him. The Queen returns, finds the King dead, makes passionate action. The pois'ner with some three or four [mutes] come in again, seem to condole with her. The dead body is carried away. The pois'ner woos the Queen with gifts; she seems harsh [and unwilling] awhile, but in the end accepts love.

[Exeunt.]

OPH. What means this, my lord?

110 HAM. Marry, this' [miching] mallecho, it means mischief

OPH. Belike this show imports the argument of the play.

Enter PROLOGUE.

HAM. We shall know by this fellow. The players cannot keep [counsel], they'll tell all.

OPH. Will 'a tell us what this show meant?

HAM. Ay, or any show that you will show him. Be not you asham'd to show, he'll

115 not shame to tell you what it means.

OPH. You are naught, you are naught. I'll mark the play.

PRO. For us, and for our tragedy,

Here stooping to your clemency,

We beg your hearing patiently.

[Exit.]

---

101 **only:** very best. **jig-maker:** one who composed or played in the farcical song-and-dance entertainments that followed plays.

102 **'s:** this.

104 **let . . . sables:** i.e. to the devil with my garments; after so long a time I am ready for the old man's garb of sables (fine fur).

107 **not thinking on:** not being thought of, i.e. being forgotten.

107–08 **For . . . forgot:** line from a popular ballad lamenting puritanical suppression of such country sports as the May-games, in which the hobby-horse, a character costumed to resemble a horse, traditionally appeared.

110 **this' miching mallecho:** this is sneaking mischief.

111 **argument:** subject, plot.

112 **counsel:** secrets.

114 **Be not you:** if you are not.

116 **naught:** wicked.

120 HAM. Is this a prologue, or the posy of a ring?
OPH. 'Tis brief, my lord.
HAM. As woman's love.

Enter [two PLAYERS,] KING *and* QUEEN.

[P.] KING Full thirty times hath Phoebus' cart gone round
Neptune's salt wash and Tellus' orbed ground,
125 And thirty dozen moons with borrowed sheen
About the world have times twelve thirties been,
Since love our hearts and Hymen did our hands
Unite comutual in most sacred bands.
[P.] QUEEN So many journeys may the sun and moon
130 Make us again count o'er ere love be done!
But woe is me, you are so sick of late,
So far from cheer and from [your] former state,
That I distrust you. Yet though I distrust,
Discomfort you, my lord, it nothing must,
135 [For] women's fear and love hold quantity
In neither aught, or in extremity.
Now what my [love] is, proof hath made you know,
And as my love is siz'd, my fear is so.
Where love is great, the littlest doubts are fear;
140 Where little fears grow great, great love grows there.
[P.] KING Faith, I must leave thee, love, and shortly too;
My operant powers their functions leave to do,
And thou shalt live in this fair world behind,
Honor'd, belov'd, and haply one as kind
For husband shalt thou—
145 [P.] QUEEN   O, confound the rest!
Such love must needs be treason in my breast.
In second husband let me be accurs'd!
None wed the second but who kill'd the first.
HAM. *[Aside.]* That's wormwood!
150 [P.] QUEEN The instances that second marriage move
Are base respects of thrift, but none of love.
A second time I kill my husband dead,
When second husband kisses me in bed.

---

120 **posy . . . ring:** verse motto inscribed in a ring (necessarily short).
123 **Phoebus' cart:** the sun-god's chariot.
124 **Tellus:** goddess of the earth.
127 **Hymen:** god of marriage.
128 **bands:** bonds.
133 **distrust:** fear for.
135 **hold quantity:** are related in direct proportion.
137 **proof:** experience.
142 **operant:** active, vital.   **leave to do:** cease to perform.
145 **confound the rest:** may destruction befall what you are about to speak of—a second marriage on my part.
150 **instances:** motives.   **move:** give rise to.
151 **respects of thrift:** considerations of advantage.

[P.] KING I do believe you think what now you speak,
155 But what we do determine, oft we break.
Purpose is but the slave to memory,
Of violent birth, put poor validity,
Which now, the fruit unripe, sticks on the tree,
But fall unshaken when they mellow be.
160 Most necessary 'tis that we forget
To pay ourselves what ourselves is debt.
What to ourselves in passion we propose,
The passion ending, doth the purpose lose.
The violence of either grief or joy
165 Their own enactures with themselves destroy.
Where joy most reveals, grief doth most lament;
Grief [joys], joy grieves, on slender accident.
This world is not for aye, nor 'tis not strange
That even our loves should with our fortunes change:
170 For 'tis a question left us yet to prove,
Whether love lead fortune, or else fortune love.
The great man down, you mark his favorite flies,
The poor advanc'd makes friends of enemies.
And hitherto doth love on fortune tend,
175 For who not needs shall never lack a friend,
And who in want a hollow friend doth try,
Directly seasons him his enemy.
But orderly to end where I begun,
Our wills and fates do so contrary run
180 That our devices still are overthrown,
Our thoughts are ours, their ends none of our own:
So think thou wilt no second husband wed,
But die thy thoughts when thy first lord is dead.
[P.] QUEEN Nor earth to me give food, nor heaven light,
185 Sport and repose lock from me day and night,
To desperation turn my trust and hope,
[An] anchor's cheer in prison be my scope!
Each opposite that blanks the face of joy
Meet what I would have well and it destroy!
190 Both here and hence pursue me lasting strife,
If once I be a widow, ever I be a wife!

---

157 **validity:** strength, power to last.
160–61 **Most . . . debt:** i.e. such resolutions are debts we owe to ourselves, and it would be foolish
 to pay such debts.
162 **passion:** violent emotion.
164–65 **The violence . . . destroy:** i.e. both violent grief and violent joy fail of their intended acts
 because they destroy themselves by their very violence.
167 **slender accident:** slight occasion.
177 **seasons:** ripens, converts into.
180 **devices:** devisings, intentions. **still:** always.
187 **anchor's cheer:** hermit's fare. **my scope:** the extent of my comforts.
188 **blanks:** blanches, makes pale (a symptom of grief).

HAM. If she should break it now!

[P.] KING 'Tis deeply sworn. Sweet, leave me here a while,
My spirits grow dull, and fain I would beguile
The tedious day with sleep.

[Sleeps.]

195 [P.] QUEEN   Sleep rock thy brain,
And never come mischance between us twain!

Exit.

HAM. Madam, how like you this play?

QUEEN The lady doth protest too much, methinks.

HAM. O but she'll keep her word.

200 KING Have you heard the argument? is there no offense in't?   200

HAM. No, no, they do but jest, poison in jest—no offense i' th' world.

KING What do you call the play?

HAM. "The Mouse-trap." Marry, how? tropically: this play is the image of a murther
done in Vienna; Gonzago is the duke's name, his wife, Baptista. You shall see anon.

205   'Tis a knavish piece of work, but what of that? Your Majesty, and we that have free
souls, it touches us not. Let the gall'd jade winch, our withers are unwrung.

Enter LUCIANUS.

This is one Lucianus, nephew to the king.

OPH. You are as good as a chorus, my lord.

HAM. I could interpret between you and your love, if I could see the puppets dallying.

210 OPH. You are keen, my lord, you are keen.   210

HAM. It would cost you a groaning to take off mine edge.

OPH. Still better, and worse.

HAM. So you mistake your husbands. Begin, murtherer, leave thy damnable faces and
begin. Come, the croaking raven doth bellow for revenge.

215 LUC. Thoughts black, hands apt, drugs fit, and time agreeing,   215
    [Confederate] season, else no creature seeing,
    Thou mixture rank, of midnight weeds collected,

---

200 **offense:** offensive matter (but Hamlet quibbles on the sense "crime").

201 **jest:** i.e. pretend.

203 **tropically:** figuratively (with play on *tropically*—which is the reading of Q1—and probably with
allusion to the children's saying *marry trap*, meaning "now you're caught").   **image:** representation.

205–06 **free souls:** clear consciences.

206 **gall'd jade:** chafed horse.   **winch:** wince.   **withers:** ridge between a horse's shoulders.   **unwrung:** not rubbed sore.

208 **chorus:** i.e. one who explains the forthcoming action.

209 **I . . . dallying:** I could speak the dialogue between you and your lover like a puppet-master (with
an indecent jest).

210 **keen:** bitter, sharp.

212 **better, and worse:** i.e. more pointed and less decent.

213 **So:** i.e. "for better, for worse," in the words of the marriage service.   **mistake:** i.e. mis-take,
take wrongfully. Their vows, Hamlet suggests, prove false.   **faces:** facial expressions.

214 **the croaking . . . revenge.** Misquoted from an old play, *The True Tragedy of Richard III.*

216 **Confederate season:** the time being my ally.

With Hecat's ban thrice blasted, thrice [infected],
Thy natural magic and dire property
220 On wholesome life usurps immediately.

[Pours the poison in his ears.]

HAM. 'A poisons him i' th' garden for his estate. His name's Gonzago, the story is extant, and written in very choice Italian. You shall see anon how the murtherer gets the love of Gonzago's wife.
OPH. The King rises.
225 [HAM. What, frighted with false fire?]
QUEEN How fares my lord?
POL. Give o'er the play.
KING Give me some light. Away!
POL. Lights, lights, lights!

Exeunt all but HAMLET *and* HORATIO.

230 HAM.   "Why, let the strooken deer go weep,
                       The hart ungalled play,
                 For some must watch while some must sleep,
                     Thus runs the world away."

Would not this, sir, and a forest of feathers—if the rest of my fortunes turn Turk with
235 me—with [two] Provincial roses on my raz'd shoes, get me a fellowship in a cry of players?
HOR. Half a share.
HAM. A whole one, I.

               "For thou dost know, O Damon dear,
240   This realm dismantled was
               Of Jove himself, and now reigns here
                  A very, very"—pajock.

HOR. You might have rhym'd.
HAM. O good Horatio, I'll take the ghost's word for a thousand pound. Didst perceive?
245 HOR. Very well, my lord.
HAM. Upon the talk of the pois'ning?
HOR. I did very well note him.
HAM. Ah, ha! Come, some music! Come, the recorders!
   For if the King like not the comedy,

---

218 **Hecat's ban:** the curse of Hecate, goddess of witchcraft.
225 **false fire:** i.e. a blank cartridge.
230 **strooken:** struck, i.e. wounded.
231 **ungalled:** unwounded.
232 **watch:** stay awake.
234 **feathers:** the plumes worn by tragic actors. **turn Turk:** i.e. go to the bad.
235 **Provincial roses:** rosettes designed to look like a variety of French rose. **raz'd:** with decorating slashing. **fellowship:** partnership. **cry:** company.
240 **dismantled:** divested, deprived.
242 **pajock:** peacock (substituting for the rhyme-word *ass*). The natural history of the time attributed many vicious qualities to the peacock.

250   Why then belike he likes it not, perdy.
          Come, some music!

Enter ROSENCRANTZ *and* GUILDENSTERN.

GUIL. Good my lord, voutsafe me a word with you.
HAM. Sir, a whole history.
GUIL. The King, sir—
255 HAM. Ay, sir, what of him?
GUIL. Is in his retirement marvellous distemp'red.
HAM. With drink, sir?
GUIL. No, my lord, with choler.
HAM. Your wisdom should show itself more richer to signify this to the doctor, for for
260   me to put him to his purgation would perhaps plunge him into more choler.
GUIL. Good my lord, put your discourse into some frame, and [start] not so wildly from
     my affair.
HAM. I am tame, sir. Pronounce.
GUIL. The Queen, your mother, in most great affliction of spirit, hath sent me to you.
265 HAM. You are welcome.
GUIL. Nay, good my lord, this courtesy is not of the right breed. If it shall please you
     to make me a wholesome answer, I will do your mother's commandement; if not,
     your pardon and my return shall be the end of [my] business.
HAM. Sir, I cannot.
270 ROS. What, my lord?
HAM. Make you a wholesome answer—my wit's diseas'd. But, sir, such answer as I can
     make, you shall command, or rather, as you say, my mother. Therefore no more, but
     to the matter: my mother, you say—
ROS. Then thus she says: your behavior hath strook her into amazement and admiration.
275 HAM. O wonderful son, that can so stonish a mother! But is there no sequel at the heels
     of this mother's admiration? Impart.
ROS. She desires to speak with you in her closet ere you go to bed.
HAM. We shall obey, were she ten times our mother. Have you any further trade with
     us?
280 ROS. My lord, you once did love me.
HAM. And do still, by these pickers and stealers.
ROS. Good my lord, what is your cause of distemper? You do surely bar the door upon
     your own liberty if you deny your griefs to your friend.
HAM. Sir, I lack advancement.

---

250 **perdy:** assuredly (French *pardieu,* "by God").
258 **choler:** anger (but Hamlet willfully takes up the word in the sense "biliousness").
260 **put . . . purgation:** i.e. prescribe for what's wrong with him.
261 **frame:** logical structure.
267 **wholesome:** sensible, rational.
268 **pardon:** permission for departure.
274 **amazement and admiration:** bewilderment and wonder.
275 **stonish:** astound.
277 **closet:** private room.
281 **pickers and stealers:** hands; which, as the Catechism says, we must keep "from picking and stealing."

285 ROS. How can that be, when you have the voice of the King himself for your succession in Denmark?

HAM. Ay, sir, but "While the grass grows"—the proverb is something musty.

Enter the PLAYERS *with recorders.*

O, the recorders! Let me see one.—To withdraw with you—why do you go about to recover the wind of me, as if you would drive me into a toil?

290 GUIL. O my lord, if my duty be too bold, my love is too unmannerly.

HAM. I do not well understand that. Will you play upon this pipe?

GUIL. My lord, I cannot.

HAM. I pray you.

GUIL. Believe me, I cannot.

295 HAM. I do beseech you.

GUIL. I know no touch of it, my lord.

HAM. It is as easy as lying. Govern these ventages with your fingers and [thumbs], give it breath with your mouth, and it will discourse most eloquent music. Look you, these are the stops.

300 GUIL. But these cannot I command to any utt'rance of harmony. I have not the skill.

HAM. Why, look you now, how unworthy a thing you make of me! You would play upon me, you would seem to know my stops, you would pluck out the heart of my mystery, you would sound me from my lowest note to [the top of] my compass; and there is much music, excellent voice, in this little organ, yet cannot you make it speak.

305 'Sblood, do you think I am easier to be play'd on than a pipe? Call me what instrument you will, though you fret me, [yet] you cannot play upon me.

Enter POLONIUS.

God bless you, sir.

POL. My lord, the Queen would speak with you, and presently.

HAM. Do you see yonder cloud that's almost in shape of a camel?

310 POL. By th' mass and 'tis, like a camel indeed.

HAM. Methinks it is like a weasel.

POL. It is back'd like a weasel.

HAM. Or like a whale.

POL. Very like a whale.

315 HAM. Then I will come to my mother by and by. *[Aside.]* They fool me to the top of my bent.—I will come by and by.

[POL.] I will say so.

[Exit.]

---

287 **proverb:** i.e. "While the grass grows, the steed starves." **something musty:** somewhat stale.
289 **recover the wind:** get to windward. **toil:** snare.
297 **ventages:** stops.
304 **organ:** instrument.
306 **fret:** (1) finger (an instrument); (2) vex.
308 **presently:** at once.
315–16 **They . . . bent:** they make me play the fool to the limit of my ability.
316 **by and by:** at once.

HAM. "By and by" is easily said. Leave me, friends.

[Exeunt all but HAMLET.*]*

'Tis now the very witching time of night,
320   When churchyards yawn and hell itself [breathes] out
Contagion to this world. Now could I drink hot blood,
And do such [bitter business as the] day
Would quake to look on. Soft, now to my mother.
O heart, lose not thy nature! let not ever
325   The soul of Nero enter this firm bosom,
Let me be cruel, not unnatural;
I will speak [daggers] to her, but use none.
My tongue and soul in this be hypocrites—
How in my words somever she be shent,
330   To give them seals never my soul consent!

Exit.

SCENE III.

Enter KING, ROSENCRANTZ, *and* GUILDENSTERN.

KING I like him not, nor stands it safe with us
To let his madness range. Therefore prepare you.
I your commission will forthwith dispatch,
And he to England shall along with you.
5   The terms of our estate may not endure
Hazard so near 's as doth hourly grow
Out of his brows.
GUIL.   We will ourselves provide.
Most holy and religious fear it is
To keep those many many bodies safe
10   That live and feed upon your Majesty.
ROS. The single and peculiar life is bound
With all the strength and armor of the mind
To keep itself from noyance, but much more
That spirit upon whose weal depends and rests

---

319 **witching:** i.e. when the powers of evil are at large.
324 **nature:** natural affection, filial feeling.
325 **Nero.** Murderer of his mother.
329 **shent:** rebuked.
330 **give them seals:** confirm them by deeds.

III.iii. Location: The castle.
1 **him:** i.e. his state of mind, his behavior.
3 **dispatch:** have drawn up.
5 **terms:** conditions, nature. **our estate:** my position (as king).
7 **his brows:** the madness visible in his face (?).
8 **fear:** concern.
11 **single and peculiar:** individual and private.
13 **noyance:** injury.

15 The lives of many. The cess of majesty
   Dies not alone, but like a gulf doth draw
   What's near it with it. Or it is a massy wheel
   Fix'd on the summit of the highest mount,
   To whose [huge] spokes ten thousand lesser things
20 Are mortis'd and adjoin'd, which when it falls,
   Each small annexment, petty consequence,
   Attends the boist'rous [ruin]. Never alone
   Did the King sigh, but [with] a general groan.
   KING Arm you, I pray you, to this speedy viage,
25 For we will fetters put about this fear,
   Which now goes too free-footed.
   ROS.   We will haste us.

Exeunt GENTLEMEN [ROSENCRANTZ *and* GUILDENSTERN].

Enter POLONIUS.

   POL. My lord, he's going to his mother's closet.
   Behind the arras I'll convey myself
   To hear the process. I'll warrant she'll tax him home,
30 And as you said, and wisely was it said,
   'Tis meet that some more audience than a mother,
   Since nature makes them partial; should o'erhear
   The speech, of vantage. Fare you well, my liege,
   I'll call upon you ere you go to bed,
35 And tell you what I know.
   KING   Thanks, dear my lord.

Exit [POLONIUS].

   O, my offense is rank, it smells to heaven,
   It hath the primal eldest curse upon't,
   A brother's murther. Pray can I not,
   Though inclination be as sharp as will.
40 My stronger guilt defeats my strong intent,
   And, like a man to double business bound,
   I stand in pause where I shall first begin,
   And both neglect. What if this cursed hand
   Were thicker than itself with brother's blood,

---

15 **cess:** cessation, death.
16 **gulf:** whirlpool.
20 **mortis'd:** fixed.
22 **Attends:** accompanies.   **ruin:** fall.
24 **Arm:** prepare.   **viage:** voyage.
25 **fear:** object of fear.
29 **process:** course of the talk.   **tax him home:** take him severely to task.
33 **of vantage:** from an advantageous position (?) or in addition (?).
37 **primal eldest curse:** i.e. God's curse on Cain, who also slew his brother.
39 **Though . . . will:** though my desire is as strong as my resolve to do so.
41 **bound:** committed.
43 **neglect:** omit.

45   Is there not rain enough in the sweet heavens
       To wash it white as snow? Whereto serves mercy
       But to confront the visage of offense?
       And what's in prayer but this twofold force,
       To be forestalled ere we come to fall,
50   Or [pardon'd] being down? then I'll look up.
       My fault is past, but, O, what form of prayer
       Can serve my turn? "Forgive me my foul murther"?
       That cannot be, since I am still possess'd
       Of those effects for which I did the murther:
55   My crown, mine own ambition, and my queen.
       May one be pardon'd and retain th' offense?
       In the corrupted currents of this world
       Offense's gilded hand may [shove] by justice,
       And oft 'tis seen the wicked prize itself
60   Buys out the law, but 'tis not so above:
       There is no shuffling, there the action lies
       In his true nature, and we ourselves compell'd,
       Even to the teeth and forehead of our faults,
       To give in evidence. What then? What rests?
65   Try what repentance can. What can it not?
       Yet what can it, when one can not repent?
       O wretched state! O bosom black as death!
       O limed soul, that struggling to be free
       Art more engag'd! Help, angels! Make assay,
70   Bow, stubborn knees, and heart, with strings of steel,
       Be soft as sinews of the new-born babe!
       All may be well.

[He kneels.]

Enter HAMLET.

HAM. Now might I do it [pat], now 'a is a-praying;
       And now I'll do't—and so 'a goes to heaven,
75   And so am I [reveng'd]. That would be scann'd:
       A villain kills my father, and for that
       I, his sole son, do this same villain send
       To heaven.
       Why, this is [hire and salary], not revenge.

46–47 **Whereto . . . offense:** i.e. what function has mercy except when there has been sin.
56 **th' offense:** i.e. the "effects" or fruits of the offense.
57 **currents:** courses.
58 **gilded:** i.e. bribing.
59 **wicked prize:** rewards of vice.
61 **shuffling:** evasion.   **the action lies:** the charge comes for legal consideration.
63 **Even . . . forehead:** i.e. fully recognizing their features, extenuating nothing.
64 **rests:** remains.
68 **limed:** caught (as in birdlime, a sticky substance used for catching birds).
69 **engag'd:** entangled.
75 **would be scann'd:** must be carefully considered.

80 'A took my father grossly, full of bread,
With all his crimes broad blown, as flush as May,
And how his audit stands who knows save heaven?
But in our circumstance and course of thought
'Tis heavy with him. And am I then revenged,
85 To take him in the purging of his soul,
When he is fit and season'd for his passage?
No!
Up, sword, and know thou a more horrid hent:
When he is drunk asleep, or in his rage,
90 Or in th' incestious pleasure of his bed,
At game a-swearing, or about some act
That has no relish of salvation in't—
Then trip him, that his heels may kick at heaven,
And that his soul may be as damn'd and black
95 As hell, whereto it goes. My mother stays,
This physic but prolongs thy sickly days.

Exit.

KING *[Rising.]* My words fly up, my thoughts remain below:
Words without thoughts never to heaven go.

Exit.

SCENE IV.

Enter [QUEEN] GERTRUDE *and* POLONIUS.

POL. 'A will come straight. Look you lay home to him.
Tell him his pranks have been too broad to bear with,
And that your Grace hath screen'd and stood between
Much heat and him. I'll silence me even here;
5 Pray you be round [with him].
QUEEN I'll [warr'nt] you, fear me not. Withdraw,
I hear him coming.

[POLONIUS *hides behind the arras.*]

Enter HAMLET.

---

⁸⁰ **grossly:** in a gross state; not spiritually prepared.
⁸¹ **crimes:** sins. **broad blown:** in full bloom. **flush:** lusty, vigorous.
⁸² **audit:** account.
⁸³ **in . . . thought:** i.e. to the best of our knowledge and belief.
⁸⁸ **Up:** into the sheath. **know . . . hent:** be grasped at a more dreadful time.
⁹² **relish:** trace.
⁹⁶ **physic:** (attempted) remedy, i.e. prayer.

III.iv. Location: The Queen's closet in the castle.
¹ **lay . . . him:** reprove him severely.
² **broad:** unrestrained.
⁵ **round:** plain-spoken.
⁶ **fear me not:** have no fears about my handling of the situation.

HAM. Now, mother, what's the matter?

QUEEN Hamlet, thou hast thy father much offended.

10 HAM. Mother, you have my father much offended.

QUEEN Come, come, you answer with an idle tongue.

HAM. Go, go, you question with a wicked tongue.

QUEEN Why, how now, Hamlet?

HAM.   What's the matter now?

QUEEN Have you forgot me?

HAM.   No, by the rood, not so:

15 You are the Queen, your husband's brother's wife,

And would it were not so, you are my mother.

QUEEN Nay, then I'll set those to you that can speak.

HAM. Come, come, and sit you down, you shall not boudge;

You go not till I set you up a glass

20 Where you may see the [inmost] part of you.

QUEEN What wilt thou do? Thou wilt not murther me?

Help ho!

POL. *[Behind.]* What ho, help!

HAM. *[Drawing.]* How now? A rat? Dead, for a ducat, dead!

[Kills POLONIUS *through the arras.]*

POL. *[Behind.]* O, I am slain.

25 QUEEN   O me, what hast thou done?

HAM. Nay, I know not, is it the King?

QUEEN O, what a rash and bloody deed is this!

HAM. A bloody deed! almost as bad, good mother,

As kill a king, and marry with his brother.

QUEEN As kill a king!

30 HAM.   Ay, lady, it was my word.

[Parts the arras and discovers POLONIUS.*]*

Thou wretched, rash, intruding fool, farewell!

I took thee for thy better. Take thy fortune;

Thou find'st to be too busy is some danger.—

Leave wringing of your hands. Peace, sit you down,

35 And let me wring your heart, for so I shall

If it be made of penetrable stuff,

If damned custom have not brass'd it so

That it be proof and bulwark against sense.

QUEEN What have I done, that thou dar'st wag thy tongue

40 In noise so rude against me?

---

11 **idle:** foolish.

14 **rood:** cross.

18 **boudge:** budge.

24 **for a ducat:** I'll wager a ducat.

33 **busy:** officious, meddlesome.

37 **damned custom:** i.e. the habit of ill-doing.   **brass'd:** hardened, literally, plated with brass.

38 **proof:** armor.   **sense:** feeling.

HAM.   Such an act
       That blurs the grace and blush of modesty,
       Calls virtue hypocrite, takes off the rose
       From the fair forehead of an innocent love
       And sets a blister there, makes marriage vows
45   As false as dicers' oaths, O, such a deed
       As from the body of contraction plucks
       The very soul, and sweet religion makes
       A rhapsody of words. Heaven's face does glow
       O'er this solidity and compound mass
50   With heated visage, as against the doom;
       Is thought-sick at the act.
       QUEEN   Ay me, what act,
       That roars so loud and thunders in the index?
HAM.   Look here upon this picture, and on this,
       The counterfeit presentment of two brothers.
55   See what a grace was seated on this brow:
       Hyperion's curls, the front of Jove himself,
       An eye like Mars, to threaten and command,
       A station like the herald Mercury
       New lighted on a [heaven-]kissing hill,
60   A combination and a form indeed,
       Where every god did seem to set his seal
       To give the world assurance of a man.
       This was your husband. Look you now what follows:
       Here is your husband, like a mildewed ear,
65   Blasting his wholesome brother. Have you eyes?
       Could you on this fair mountain leave to feed,
       And batten on this moor? ha, have you eyes?
       You cannot call it love, for at your age
       The heyday in the blood is tame, it's humble,
70   And waits upon the judgment, and what judgment
       Would step from this to this? Sense sure you have,
       Else could you not have motion, but sure that sense

---

44 **blister:** brand of shame.
46 **contraction:** the making of contracts, i.e. the assuming of solemn obligation.
47 **religion:** i.e. sacred vows.
48 **rhapsody:** miscellaneous collection, jumble.   **glow:** i.e. with anger.
49 **this . . . mass:** i.e. the earth. *Compound* = compounded of the four elements.
50 **as . . . doom:** as if for Judgment Day.
52 **index:** i.e. table of contents. The index was formerly placed at the beginning of a book.
54 **counterfeit presentment:** painted likenesses.
56 **Hyperion's:** the sun-god's.   **front:** forehead.
58 **station:** bearing.
64 **ear:** i.e. of grain.
67 **batten:** gorge.
69 **heyday:** excitement.
71 **Sense:** sense perception, the five senses.

Is apoplex'd, for madness would not err,
Nor sense to ecstasy was ne'er so thrall'd
75 But it reserv'd some quantity of choice
To serve in such a difference. What devil was't
That thus hath cozen'd you at hoodman-blind?
Eyes without feeling, feeling without sight,
Ears without hands or eyes, smelling sans all,
80 Or but a sickly part of one true sense
Could not so mope. O shame, where is thy blush?
Rebellious hell,
If thou canst mutine in a matron's bones,
To flaming youth let virtue be as wax
85 And melt in her own fire. Proclaim no shame
When the compulsive ardure gives the charge,
Since frost itself as actively doth burn,
And reason [panders] will.
QUEEN   O Hamlet, speak no more!
Thou turn'st my [eyes into my very] soul,
90 And there I see such black and [grained] spots
As will [not] leave their tinct.
HAM.   Nay, but to live
In the rank sweat of an enseamed bed,
Stew'd in corruption, honeying and making love
Over the nasty sty!
QUEEN   O, speak to me no more!
95 These words like daggers enter in my ears.
No more, sweet Hamlet!
HAM.   A murtherer and a villain!
A slave that is not twentith part the [tithe]
Of your precedent lord, a Vice of kings,
A cutpurse of the empire and the rule,
100 That from a shelf the precious diadem stole,
And put it in his pocket—
QUEEN   No more!

---

73 **apoplex'd**: paralyzed.
73–76 **madness . . . difference**: i.e. madness itself could not go so far astray, nor were the senses ever
   so enslaved by lunacy that they did not retain the power to make so obvious a distinction.
77 **cozen'd**: cheated.   **hoodman-blind**: blindman's bluff.
79 **sans**: without.
81 **mope**: be dazed.
83 **mutine**: rebel.
85–88 **Proclaim . . . will**: do not call it sin when the hot blood of youth is responsible for lechery,
   since here we see people of calmer age on fire for it; and reason acts as procurer for desire,
   instead of restraining it. *Ardure* = ardor.
90 **grained**: fast-dyed, indelible.
91 **leave their tinct**: lose their color.
92 **enseamed**: greasy.
97 **twentith**: twentieth.
98 **precedent**: former.   **Vice**: buffoon (like the Vice of the morality plays).

Enter GHOST *[in his night-gown].*

HAM. A king of shreds and patches—
    Save me, and hover o'er me with your wings,
    You heavenly guards! What would your gracious figure!
105 QUEEN Alas, he's mad!
HAM. Do you not come your tardy son to chide,
    That, laps'd in time and passion, lets go by
    Th' important acting of your dread command?
    O, say!
110 GHOST Do not forget! This visitation
    Is but to whet thy almost blunted purpose.
    But look, amazement on thy mother sits,
    O, step between her and her fighting soul.
    Conceit in weakest bodies strongest works,
115   Speak to her, Hamlet.
HAM.   How is it with you, lady?
QUEEN Alas, how is't with you,
    That you do bend your eye on vacancy,
    And with th' incorporal air do hold discourse?
    Forth at your eyes your spirits wildly peep,
120   And as the sleeping soldiers in th' alarm,
    Your bedded hair, like life in excrements,
    Start up and stand an end. O gentle son,
    Upon the heat and flame of thy distemper
    Sprinkle cool patience. Whereon do you look?
125 HAM. On him, on him! look you how pale he glares!
    His form and cause conjoin'd, preaching to stones,
    Would make them capable.—Do not look upon me,
    Lest with this piteous action you convert
    My stern effects, then what I have to do
130   Will want true color—tears perchance for blood.
QUEEN To whom do you speak this?
HAM.   Do you see nothing there?
QUEEN Nothing at all, yet all that is I see.

---

101 s.d. **night-gown:** dressing gown.
102 **of . . . patches:** clownish (alluding to the motley worn by jesters) (?) or patched up, beggarly (?).
107 **laps'd . . . passion:** "having suffered time to slip and passion to cool" (Johnson).
108 **important:** urgent.
112 **amazement:** utter bewilderment.
114 **Conceit:** imagination.
120 **in th' alarm:** when the call to arms is sounded.
121 **excrements:** outgrowths; here, hair (also used of nails).
122 **an end:** on end.
124 **patience:** self-control.
126 **His . . . cause:** his appearance and what he has to say.
127 **capable:** sensitive, receptive.
128 **convert:** alter.
129 **effects:** (purposed) actions.
130 **want true color:** lack its proper appearance.

HAM. Nor did you nothing hear?
QUEEN   No, nothing but ourselves.
HAM. Why, look you there, look how it steals away!
135   My father, in his habit as he lived!
       Look where he goes, even now, out at the portal!

Exit GHOST.

QUEEN This is the very coinage of your brain,
       This bodiless creation ecstasy
       Is very cunning in.
HAM.   [Ecstasy?]
140   My pulse as yours doth temperately keep time,
       And makes as healthful music. It is not madness
       That I have utt'red. Bring me to the test,
       And [I] the matter will reword, which madness
       Would gambol from. Mother, for love of grace,
145   Lay not that flattering unction to your soul,
       That not your trespass but my madness speaks;
       It will but skin and film the ulcerous place,
       Whiles rank corruption, mining all within,
       Infects unseen. Confess yourself to heaven,
150   Repent what's past, avoid what is to come,
       And do not spread the compost on the weeds
       To make them ranker. Forgive me this my virtue,
       For in the fatness of these pursy times
       Virtue itself of vice must pardon beg,
155   Yea, curb and woo for leave to do him good.
QUEEN O Hamlet, thou hast cleft my heart in twain.
HAM. O, throw away the worser part of it,
       And [live] the purer with the other half.
       Good night, but go not to my uncle's bed—
160   Assume a virtue, if you have it not.
       That monster custom, who all sense doth eat,
       Of habits devil, is angel yet in this,
       That to the use of actions fair and good
       He likewise gives a frock or livery
165   That aptly is put on. Refrain [to-]night,
       And that shall lend a kind of easiness

---

¹³⁵ **habit:** dress.
¹³⁸ **ecstasy:** madness.
¹⁴⁴ **gambol:** start, jerk away.
¹⁴⁵ **flattering unction:** soothing ointment.
¹⁵¹ **compost:** manure.
¹⁵³ **pursy:** puffy, out of condition.
¹⁵⁵ **curb and woo:** bow and entreat.
¹⁶¹ **all . . . eat:** wears away all natural feeling.
¹⁶² **Of habits devil:** i.e. though it acts like a devil in establishing bad habits. Most editors read (in lines 161–62) *eat / Of habits evil*, following Theobald.
¹⁶⁴⁻⁶⁵ **frock . . . on:** i.e. a "habit" or customary garment, readily put on without need of any decision.

To the next abstinence, the next more easy;
For use almost can change the stamp of nature,
And either [. . . .] the devil or throw him out
170 With wondrous potency. Once more good night,
And when you are desirous to be blest,
I'll blessing beg of you. For this same lord,

[*Pointing to* POLONIUS.]

I do repent; but heaven hath pleas'd it so
To punish me with this, and this with me,
175 That I must be their scourge and minister.
I will bestow him, and will answer well
The death I gave him. So again good night.
I must be cruel only to be kind.
This bad begins and worse remains behind.
One word more, good lady.
180 QUEEN   What shall I do?
HAM. Not this, by no means, that I bid you do:
Let the bloat king tempt you again to bed,
Pinch wanton on your cheek, call you his mouse,
And let him, for a pair of reechy kisses,
185 Or paddling in your neck with his damn'd fingers,
Make you to ravel all this matter out,
That I essentially am not in madness,
But mad in craft. 'Twere good you let him know,
For who that's but a queen, fair, sober, wise,
190 Would from a paddock, from a bar, a gib,
Such dear concernings hide? Who would do so?
No, in despite of sense and secrecy,
Unpeg the basket on the house's top,
Let the birds fly, and like the famous ape,
195 To try conclusions in the basket creep,
And break your own neck down.
QUEEN Be thou assur'd, if words be made of breath,
And breath of life, I have no life to breathe
What thou hast said to me.

---

168 **use:** habit.
169 A word seems to be wanting after *either.*
171 **desirous . . . blest:** i.e. repentant.
175 **scourge and minister:** the agent of heavenly justice against human crime. *Scourge* suggests a
permissive cruelty (Tamburlaine was the "scourge of God"), but "woe to him by whom the
offense cometh"; the scourge must suffer for the evil it performs.
176 **bestow:** dispose of. **answer:** answer for.
179 **behind:** to come.
184 **reechy:** filthy.
190 **paddock:** toad. **gib:** tomcat.
191 **dear concernings:** matters of intense concern.
193 **Unpeg the basket:** open the door of the cage.
194 **famous ape.** The actual story has been lost.
195 **conclusions:** experiments (to see whether he too can fly if he enters the cage and then leaps out).
196 **down:** by the fall.

HAM. I must to England, you know that?

200 QUEEN   Alack,
　　　I had forgot. 'Tis so concluded on.
　　HAM. There's letters seal'd, and my two schoolfellows,
　　　Whom I will trust as I will adders fang'd,
　　　They bear the mandate, they must sweep my way
205　And marshal me to knavery. Let it work,
　　　For 'tis the sport to have the enginer
　　　Hoist with his own petar, an't shall go hard
　　　But I will delve one yard below their mines,
　　　And blow them at the moon. O, 'tis most sweet
210　When in one line two crafts directly meet.
　　　This man shall set me packing;
　　　I'll lug the guts into the neighbor room.
　　　Mother, good night indeed. This counsellor
　　　Is now most still, most secret, and most grave,
215　Who was in life a foolish prating knave.
　　　Come, sir, to draw toward an end with you.
　　　Good night, mother.

Exeunt [severally, HAMLET *tugging in* POLONIUS].

ACT IV

SCENE I.

Enter KING *and* QUEEN *with* ROSENCRANTZ *and* GUILDENSTERN.

KING There's matter in these sighs, these profound heaves—
　　　You must translate, 'tis fit we understand them.
　　　Where is your son?
QUEEN Bestow this place on us a little while.

[*Exeunt* ROSENCRANTZ *and* GUILDENSTERN.]

5　　Ah, mine own lord, what have I seen to-night!
KING What, Gertrude? How does Hamlet?
QUEEN Mad as the sea and wind when both contend
　　　Which is the mightier. In his lawless fit,
　　　Behind the arras hearing something stir,
10　Whips out his rapier, cries, "A rat, a rat!"
　　　And in this brainish apprehension kills
　　　The unseen good old man.

---

²⁰⁵ **knavery**: some knavish scheme against me.
²⁰⁶ **enginer**: deviser of military "engines" or contrivances.
²⁰⁷ **Hoist with**: blown up by.　**petar**: petard, bomb.
²¹⁰ **crafts**: plots.
²¹¹ **packing**: (1) taking on a load; (2) leaving in a hurry.
²¹⁶ **draw . . . end**: finish my conversation.

IV.i. Location: The castle.
¹¹ **brainish apprehension**: crazy notion.

KING   O heavy deed!
          It had been so with us had we been there.
          His liberty is full of threats to all,
15   To you yourself, to us, to every one.
          Alas, how shall this bloody deed be answer'd?
          It will be laid to us, whose providence
          Should have kept short, restrain'd, and out of haunt
          This mad young man; but so much was our love,
20   We would not understand what was most fit,
          But like the owner of a foul disease,
          To keep it from divulging, let it feed
          Even on the pith of life. Where is he gone?
QUEEN To draw apart the body he hath kill'd,
25   O'er whom his very madness, like some ore
          Among a mineral of metals base,
          Shows itself pure: 'a weeps for what is done.
KING O Gertrude, come away!
          The sun no sooner shall the mountains touch,
30   But we will ship him hence, and this vile deed
          We must with all our majesty and skill
          Both countenance and excuse. Ho, Guildenstern!

Enter ROSENCRANTZ *and* GUILDENSTERN.

          Friends both, go join you with some further aid:
          Hamlet in madness hath Polonius slain,
35   And from his mother's closet hath he dragg'd him.
          Go seek him out, speak fair, and bring the body
          Into the chapel. I pray you haste in this.

[Exeunt ROSENCRANTZ *and* GUILDENSTERN.*]*

          Come, Gertrude, we'll call up our wisest friends
          And let them know both what we mean to do
40   And what's untimely done, [. . . .]
          Whose whisper o'er the world's diameter,
          As level as the cannon to his blank,
          Transports his pois'ned shot, may miss our name,
          And hit the woundless air. O, come away!
45   My soul is full of discord and dismay.

Exeunt.

---

16 **answer'd:** i.e. satisfactorily accounted for to the public.
17 **providence:** foresight.
18 **short:** on a short leash.   **out of haunt:** away from other people.
22 **divulging:** being revealed.
25 **ore:** vein of gold.
26 **mineral:** mine.
40 Some words are wanting at the end of the line. Capell's conjecture, *so, haply, slander,* probably
  indicates the intended sense of the passage.
42 **As level:** with aim as good.   **blank:** target.
44 **woundless:** incapable of being hurt.

SCENE II.

Enter HAMLET.

HAM. Safely stow'd.
[GENTLEMEN (*Within.*) Hamlet! Lord Hamlet!]
[HAM.] But soft, what noise? Who calls on Hamlet?
   O, here they come.

Enter ROSENCRANTZ *and* [GUILDENSTERN].

5 ROS. What have you done, my lord, with the dead body?
HAM. [Compounded] it with dust, whereto 'tis kin.
ROS. Tell us where 'tis, that we may take it thence,
   And bear it to the chapel.
HAM. Do not believe it.
10 ROS. Believe what?
HAM. That I can keep your counsel and not mine own. Besides, to be demanded of a
   spunge, what replication should be made by the son of a king?
ROS. Take you me for a spunge, my lord?
HAM. Ay, sir, that soaks up the King's countenance, his rewards, his authorities. But such
15   officers do the King best service in the end: he keeps them, like [an ape] an apple, in
   the corner of his jaw, first mouth'd, to be last swallow'd. When he needs what you
   have glean'd, it is but squeezing you, and, spunge, you shall be dry again.
ROS. I understand you not, my lord.
HAM. I am glad of it, a knavish speech sleeps in a foolish ear.
20 ROS. My lord, you must tell us where the body is, and go with us to the King.
HAM. The body is with the King, but the King is not with the body. The King is a thing—
GUIL. A thing, my lord?
HAM. Of nothing, bring me to him. [Hide fox, and all after.]

Exeunt.

SCENE III.

Enter KING *and two or three.*

KING I have sent to seek him, and to find the body.
   How dangerous is it that this man goes loose!
   Yet must not we put the strong law on him.
   He's lov'd of the distracted multitude,

IV.ii. Location: The castle.
[11] **demanded of:** questioned by.
[12] **spunge:** sponge.   **replication:** reply.
[14] **countenance:** favor.
[19] **sleeps:** is meaningless.
[21] **The body . . . the body.** Possibly alluding to the legal fiction that the king's dignity is separate from his mortal body.
[23] **Of nothing:** of no account. Cf. "Man is like a thing of nought, his time passeth away like a shadow" (Psalm 144:4 in the Prayer Book version). "Hamlet at once insults the King and hints that his days are numbered" (Dover Wilson). **Hide . . . after.** Probably a cry in some game resembling hide-and-seek.

IV.iii. Location: The castle.
[4] **distracted:** unstable.

5   Who like not in their judgment, but their eyes,
       And where 'tis so, th' offender's scourge is weigh'd,
       But never the offense. To bear all smooth and even,
       This sudden sending him away must seem
       Deliberate pause. Diseases desperate grown
10   By desperate appliance are reliev'd,
       Or not at all.

Enter ROSENCRANTZ.

               How now, what hath befall'n?
ROS. Where the dead body is bestow'd, my lord,
   We cannot get from him.
KING   But where is he?
ROS. Without, my lord, guarded, to know your pleasure.
15 KING Bring him before us.
ROS.   Ho, bring in the Lord.

They [HAMLET *and* GUILDENSTERN] *enter.*

KING Now, Hamlet, where's Polonius?
HAM. At supper.
KING At supper? where?
HAM. Not where he eats, but where 'a is eaten; a certain convocation of politic worms
20   are e'en at him. Your worm is your only emperor for diet: we fat all creatures else to
   fat us, and we fat ourselves for maggots; your fat king and your lean beggar is but
   variable service, two dishes, but to one table—that's the end.
KING Alas, alas!
HAM. A man may fish with the worm that hath eat of a king, and eat of the fish that
25   hath fed of that worm.
KING What dost thou mean by this?
HAM. Nothing but to show you how a king may go a progress through the guts of a
   beggar.
KING Where is Polonius?
30 HAM. In heaven, send thither to see; if your messenger find him not there, seek him i'
   th' other place yourself. But if indeed you find him not within this month, you shall
   nose him as you go up the stairs into the lobby.
KING *[To* ATTENDANTS.] Go seek him there.
HAM. 'A will stay till you come.

[Exeunt ATTENDANTS.]

35 KING Hamlet, this deed, for thine especial safety—
   Which we do tender, as we dearly grieve

---

[6] **scourge:** i.e. punishment.
[7] **bear:** manage.
[8-9] **must . . . pause:** i.e. must be represented as a maturely considered decision.
[19] **politic:** crafty, prying; "such worms as might breed in a politician's corpse" (Dowden).
[20] **e'en:** even now.   **for diet:** with respect to what it eats.
[22] **variable service:** different courses of a meal.
[27] **progress:** royal journey of state.
[36] **tender:** regard with tenderness, hold dear.   **dearly:** with intense feeling.

For that which thou hast done—must send thee hence
[With fiery quickness]; therefore prepare thyself,
The bark is ready, and the wind at help,
40   Th' associates tend, and every thing is bent
For England.

HAM.   For England.

KING   Ay, Hamlet.

HAM.   Good.

KING So is it, if thou knew'st our purposes.

HAM. I see a cherub that sees them. But come, for England! Farewell, dear mother.

KING Thy loving father, Hamlet.

45   HAM. My mother: father and mother is man and wife, man and wife is one flesh—so, my mother. Come, for England!

Exit.

KING Follow him at foot, tempt him with speed aboard.
Delay it not, I'll have him hence to-night.
Away, for every thing is seal'd and done
50   That else leans on th' affair. Pray you make haste.

[*Exeunt* ROSENCRANTZ *and* GUILDENSTERN.]

And, England, if my love thou hold'st at aught—
As my great power thereof may give thee sense,
Since yet thy cicatrice looks raw and red
After the Danish sword, and thy free awe
55   Pays homage to us—thou mayst not coldly set
Our sovereign process, which imports at full,
By letters congruing to that effect,
The present death of Hamlet. Do it, England,
For like the hectic in my blood he rages,
60   And thou must cure me. Till I know 'tis done,
How e'er my haps, my joys [were] ne'er [begun].

Exit.

---

³⁹ **at help:** favorable.
⁴⁰ **Th':** thy.   **tend:** await.   **bent:** made ready.
⁴³ **I . . . them:** i.e. heaven sees them.
⁴⁷ **at foot:** at his heels, close behind.
⁵⁰ **leans on:** relates to.
⁵¹ **England:** King of England.
⁵³ **cicatrice:** scar.
⁵⁴⁻⁵⁵ **thy . . . Pays:** your fear makes you pay voluntarily.
⁵⁵ **coldly set:** undervalue, disregard.
⁵⁶ **process:** command.
⁵⁷ **congruing to:** in accord with.
⁵⁸ **present:** immediate.
⁵⁹ **hectic:** continuous fever.
⁶¹ **haps:** fortunes.

SCENE IV.

Enter FORTINBRAS *with his army over the stage.*

FORT. Go, captain, from me greet the Danish king.
　　Tell him that by his license Fortinbras
　　Craves the conveyance of a promis'd march
　　Over his kingdom. You know the rendezvous.
5　　If that his Majesty would aught with us,
　　We shall express our duty in his eye,
　　And let him know so.
CAP. 　　　　　　　　　I will do't, my lord.
FORT. Go softly on.

[Exeunt all but the CAPTAIN.*]*

Enter HAMLET, ROSENCRANTZ, [GUILDENSTERN,] *etc.*

HAM. Good sir, whose powers are these?
10　CAP. They are of Norway, sir.
HAM. How purpos'd, sir, I pray you?
CAP. Against some part of Poland.
HAM. Who commands them, sir?
CAP. The nephew to old Norway, Fortinbras.
15　HAM. Goes it against the main of Poland, sir,
　　Or for some frontier?
CAP. Truly to speak, and with no addition,
　　We go to gain a little patch of ground
　　That hath in it no profit but the name.
20　To pay five ducats, five, I would not farm it;
　　Nor will it yield to Norway or the Pole
　　A ranker rate, should it be sold in fee.
HAM. Why then the Polack never will defend it.
CAP. Yes, it is already garrison'd.
25　HAM. Two thousand souls and twenty thousand ducats
　　Will not debate the question of this straw.
　　This is th' imposthume of much wealth and peace,
　　That inward breaks, and shows no cause without
　　Why the man dies. I humbly thank you, sir.
CAP. God buy you, sir.

[Exit.]

IV.iv. Location: The Danish coast, near the castle.
³ **conveyance of:** escort for.
⁶ **eye:** presence.
⁸ **softly:** slowly.
⁹ **powers:** forces.
¹⁵ **main:** main territory.
²⁰ **To pay:** i.e. for an annual rent of. 　**farm:** lease.
²² **ranker:** higher. 　**in fee:** outright.
²⁶ **Will not debate:** i.e. will scarcely be enough to fight out.
²⁷ **imposthume:** abscess.

30 ROS.   Will't please you go, my lord?
HAM. I'll be with you straight—go a little before.

[Exeunt all but HAMLET.]

How all occasions do inform against me,
And spur my dull revenge! What is a man,
If his chief good and market of his time
35   Be but to sleep and feed? a beast, no more.
Sure He that made us with such large discourse,
Looking before and after, gave us not
That capability and godlike reason
To fust in us unus'd. Now whether it be
40   Bestial oblivion, or some craven scruple
Of thinking too precisely on th' event—
A thought which quarter'd hath but one part wisdom
And ever three parts coward—I do not know
Why yet I live to say, "This thing's to do,"
45   Sith I have cause, and will, and strength, and means
To do't. Examples gross as earth exhort me:
Witness this army of such mass and charge,
Led by a delicate and tender prince,
Whose spirit with divine ambition puff'd
50   Makes mouths at the invisible event,
Exposing what is mortal and unsure
To all that fortune, death, and danger dare,
Even for an egg-shell. Rightly to be great
Is not to stir without great argument,
55   But greatly to find quarrel in a straw
When honor's at the stake. How stand I then,
That have a father kill'd, a mother stain'd,
Excitements of my reason and my blood,
And let all sleep, while to my shame I see
60   The imminent death of twenty thousand men,
That for a fantasy and trick of fame
Go to their graves like beds, fight for a plot
Whereon the numbers cannot try the cause,

---

³² **inform against:** denounce, accuse.
³⁴ **market:** purchase, profit.
³⁶ **discourse:** reasoning power.
³⁹ **fust:** grow mouldy.
⁴⁰ **oblivion:** forgetfulness.
⁴¹ **event:** outcome.
⁴⁶ **gross:** large, obvious.
⁴⁷ **mass and charge:** size and expense.
⁵⁰ **Makes mouths at:** treats scornfully.   **invisible:** i.e. unforeseeable.
⁵⁴ **Is not to:** i.e. is *not* not to.   **argument:** cause.
⁵⁵ **greatly:** nobly.
⁵⁸ **Excitements of:** urgings by.
⁶¹ **fantasy:** caprice.   **trick:** trifle.
⁶³ **Whereon . . . cause:** which isn't large enough to let the opposing armies engage upon it.

Which is not tomb enough and continent
65   To hide the slain? O, from this time forth,
My thoughts be bloody, or be nothing worth!

Exit.

SCENE V.

Enter HORATIO, [QUEEN] GERTRUDE, *and a* GENTLEMAN.

QUEEN I will not speak with her.
GENT. She is importunate, indeed distract.
Her mood will needs be pitied.
QUEEN   What would she have?
GENT. She speaks much of her father, says she hears
5   There's tricks i' th' world, and hems, and beats her heart,
Spurns enviously at straws, speaks things in doubt
That carry but half sense. Her speech is nothing,
Yet the unshaped use of it doth move
The hearers to collection; they yawn at it,
10   And botch the words up fit to their own thoughts,
Which as her winks and nods and gestures yield them,
Indeed would make one think there might be thought,
Though nothing sure, yet much unhappily.
HOR. 'Twere good she were spoken with, for she may strew
15   Dangerous conjectures in ill-breeding minds.
[QUEEN] Let her come in.

[Exit GENTLEMAN.]

[Aside.] To my sick soul, as sin's true nature is,
Each toy seems prologue to some great amiss,
So full of artless jealousy is guilt,
20   It spills itself in fearing to be spilt.

Enter OPHELIA *[distracted, with her hair down, playing on a lute].*

OPH. Where is the beauteous majesty of Denmark?
QUEEN How now, Ophelia?

---

64 **continent:** container.

IV.v. Location: The castle.
6 **Spurns . . . straws:** spitefully takes offense at trifles.   **in doubt:** obscurely.
7 **Her speech:** what she says.
8 **unshaped use:** distracted manner.
9 **collection:** attempts to gather the meaning.   **yawn at:** strive, as if openmouthed, to grasp (?). Most
editors adopt the F1 reading *aim at.*
10 **botch:** patch.
11 **Which:** i.e. the words.
12 **thought:** inferred, conjectured.
15 **ill-breeding:** conceiving ill thoughts, prone to think the worst.
18 **toy:** trifle.   **amiss:** calamity.
19 **artless jealousy:** uncontrolled suspicion.
20 **spills:** destroys.

OPH. (*She sings*)

> "How should I your true-love know
>   From another one?
> By his cockle hat and staff,
>   And his sandal shoon."

QUEEN Alas, sweet lady, what imports this song?

OPH. Say you? Nay, pray you mark.

Song.

> "He is dead and gone, lady,
>   He is dead and gone,
> At his head a grass-green turf,
>   At his heels a stone."

O ho!

QUEEN Nay, but, Ophelia—

OPH. Pray you mark.

[Sings.]

> "White his shroud as the mountain snow"—

Enter KING.

QUEEN Alas, look here, my lord.

OPH.

Song.

> "Larded all with sweet flowers,
> Which bewept to the ground did not go
>   With true-love showers."

KING How do you, pretty lady?

OPH. Well, God dild you! They say the owl was a baker's daughter. Lord, we know what we are, but know not what we may be. God be at your table!

KING Conceit upon her father.

OPH. Pray let's have no words of this, but when they ask you what it means, say you this:

25

30

35

40

45

23-24 These lines resemble a passage in an earlier ballad beginning "As you came from the holy land / Of Walsingham." Probably all the song fragments sung by Ophelia were familiar to the Globe audience, but only one other line (177) is from a ballad still extant.

25 **cockle hat**: hat bearing a cockle shell, the badge of a pilgrim to the shrine of St. James of Compostela in Spain.   **staff**. Another mark of a pilgrim.

26 **shoon**: shoes (already an archaic form in Shakespeare's day).

38 **Larded**: adorned.

39 **not**. Contrary to the expected sense, and unmetrical; explained as Ophelia's alteration of the line to accord with the facts of Polonius' burial (see line 80).

42 **dild**: yield, reward.   **owl**. Alluding to the legend of a baker's daughter whom Jesus turned into an owl because she did not respond generously to his request for bread.

44 **Conceit**: fanciful brooding.

Song.

> "To-morrow is Saint Valentine's day
> All in the morning betime,
> And I a maid at your window,
> To be your Valentine.

50
> "Then up he rose and donn'd his clo'es,
> And dupp'd the chamber-door,
> Let in the maid, that out a maid
> Never departed more."

KING Pretty Ophelia!

55 OPH. Indeed without an oath I'll make an end on't.

[Sings.]

> "By Gis, and by Saint Charity,
> Alack, and fie for shame!
> Young men will do't if they come to't,
> By Cock, they are to blame.

60
> "Quoth she, 'Before you tumbled me,
> You promis'd me to wed.'"

(He answers.)

> " 'So would I 'a' done, by yonder sun,
> And thou hadst not come to my bed.'"

65 KING How long hath she been thus?

OPH. I hope all will be well. We must be patient, but I cannot choose but weep to think they would lay him i' th' cold ground. My brother shall know of it, and so I thank you for your good counsel. Come, my coach! Good night, ladies, good night. Sweet ladies, good night, good night.

[Exit.]

70 KING Follow her close, give her good watch, I pray you.

[Exit HORATIO.*]*

> O, this is the poison of deep grief, it springs
> All from her father's death—and now behold!
> O Gertrude, Gertrude,
> When sorrows come, they come not single spies,
75
> But in battalions: first, her father slain;
> Next, your son gone, and he most violent author

---

⁵¹ **dupp'd:** opened.
⁵⁶ **Gis:** contraction of *Jesus.*
⁵⁹ **Cock:** corruption of *God.*
⁶⁴ **And:** if.
⁷⁴ **spies:** i.e. soldiers sent ahead of the main force to reconnoiter, scouts.

Of his own just remove; the people muddied,
Thick and unwholesome in [their] thoughts and whispers
For good Polonius' death; and we have done but greenly
80   In hugger-mugger to inter him; poor Ophelia
Divided from herself and her fair judgment,
Without the which we are pictures, or mere beasts;
Last, and as much containing as all these,
Her brother is in secret come from France,
85   Feeds on this wonder, keeps himself in clouds,
And wants not buzzers to infect his ear
With pestilent speeches of his father's death,
Wherein necessity, of matter beggar'd,
Will nothing stick our person to arraign
90   In ear and ear. O my dear Gertrude, this,
Like to a murd'ring-piece, in many places
Gives me superfluous death.

A noise within.

[QUEEN   Alack, what noise is this?]
KING Attend!
   Where is my Swissers? Let them guard the door.

Enter a MESSENGER.

   What is the matter?
95   MESS.   Save yourself, my lord!
The ocean, overpeering of his list,
Eats not the flats with more impiteous haste
Than young Laertes, in a riotous head,
O'erbears your officers. The rabble call him lord,
100 And as the world were now but to begin,
Antiquity forgot, custom not known,
The ratifiers and props of every word,
[They] cry, "Choose we, Laertes shall be king!"
Caps, hands, and tongues applaud it to the clouds,
105 "Laertes shall be king, Laertes king!"

A noise within.

---

[77] **muddied:** confused.
[79] **greenly:** unwisely.
[80] **In hugger-mugger:** secretly and hastily.
[85] **in clouds:** i.e. in cloudy surmise and suspicion (rather than the light of fact).
[86] **wants:** lacks.   **buzzers:** whispering informers.
[88] **of matter beggar'd:** destitute of facts.
[89] **nothing . . . arraign:** scruple not at all to charge me with the crime.
[91] **murd'ring-piece:** cannon firing a scattering charge.
[94] **Swissers:** Swiss guards.
[96] **overpeering . . . list:** rising higher than its shores.
[98] **in . . . head:** with a rebellious force.
[100] **as:** as if.
[102] **word:** pledge, promise.

QUEEN How cheerfully on the false trail they cry!
O, this is counter, you false Danish dogs!

Enter LAERTES *with others.*

KING The doors are broke.
LAER. Where is this king? Sirs, stand you all without.
ALL No, let's come in.
110 LAER.   I pray you give me leave.
ALL We will, we will.
LAER. I thank you, keep the door. *[Exeunt* LAERTES' *followers.]* O thou vile king,
Give me my father!
QUEEN   Calmly, good Laertes.
LAER. That drop of blood that's calm proclaims me bastard,
115 Cries cuckold to my father, brands the harlot
Even here between the chaste unsmirched brow
Of my true mother.
KING   What is the cause, Laertes,
That thy rebellion looks so giant-like?
Let him go, Gertrude, do not fear our person:
120 There's such divinity doth hedge a king
That treason can but peep to what it would,
Acts little of his will. Tell me, Laertes,
Why thou art thus incens'd. Let him go, Gertrude.
Speak, man.
LAER. Where is my father?
KING   Dead.
125 QUEEN   But not by him.
KING Let him demand his fill.
LAER. How came he dead? I'll not be juggled with.
To hell, allegiance! vows, to the blackest devil!
Conscience and grace, to the profoundest pit!
130 I dare damnation. To this point I stand,
That both the worlds I give to negligence,
Let come what comes, only I'll be reveng'd
Most throughly for my father.
KING   Who shall stay you?
LAER. My will, not all the world's:
135 And for my means, I'll husband them so well,
They shall go far with little.
KING   Good Laertes,
If you desire to know the certainty
Of your dear father, is't writ in your revenge

---

107 **counter:** on the wrong scent (literally, following the scent backward).
119 **fear:** fear for.
121 **would:** i.e. would like to do.
131 **both . . . negligence:** i.e. I don't care what the consequences are in this world or in the next.
133 **throughly:** thoroughly.
134 **world's:** i.e. world's will.

That, swoopstake, you will draw both friend and foe,
140   Winner and loser?
    LAER. None but his enemies.
    KING   Will you know them then?
    LAER. To his good friends thus wide I'll ope my arms,
        And like the kind life-rend'ring pelican,
        Repast them with my blood.
    KING   Why, now you speak
145   Like a good child and a true gentleman.
        That I am guiltless of your father's death,
        And am most sensibly in grief for it,
        It shall as level to your judgment 'pear
        As day does to your eye.

A noise within.

                      "Let her come in!"
150 LAER. How now, what noise is that?

Enter OPHELIA.

    O heat, dry up my brains! tears seven times salt
    Burn out the sense and virtue of mine eye!
    By heaven, thy madness shall be paid with weight
    [Till] our scale turn the beam. O rose of May!
155   Dear maid, kind sister, sweet Ophelia!
    O heavens, is't possible a young maid's wits
    Should be as mortal as [an old] man's life?
    [Nature is fine in love, and where 'tis fine,
    It sends some precious instance of itself
160   After the thing it loves.]
    OPH.

Song.

              "They bore him barefac'd on the bier,
              [Hey non nonny, nonny, hey nonny,]
              And in his grave rain'd many a tear"—

    Fare you well, my dove!
165 LAER. Hadst thou thy wits and didst persuade revenge,
        It could not move thus.

---

139 **swoopstake**: sweeping up everything without discrimination (modern *sweepstake*).
143 **pelican.** The female pelican was believed to draw blood from her own breast to nourish her young.
145 **good child**: faithful son.
147 **sensibly**: feelingly.
148 **level**: plain.
152 **virtue**: faculty.
158 **fine in**: refined or spiritualized by.
159 **instance**: proof, token. So delicate is Ophelia's love for her father that her sanity has pursued him into the grave.
165 **persuade**: argue logically for.

OPH. You must sing, "A-down, a-down," and you call him a-down-a. O how the wheel becomes it! It is the false steward, that stole his master's daughter.

LAER. This nothing's more than matter.

170 OPH. There's rosemary, that's for remembrance; pray you, love, remember. And there is pansies, that's for thoughts.

LAER. A document in madness, thoughts and remembrance fitted.

OPH. [To CLAUDIUS.] There's fennel for you, and columbines. [To GERTRUDE.] There's rue for you, and here's some for me; we may call it herb of grace a' Sundays. You 175 may wear your rue with a difference. There's a daisy. I would give you some violets, but they wither'd all when my father died. They say 'a made a good end—

[Sings.]

"For bonny sweet Robin is all my joy."

LAER. Thought and afflictions, passion, hell itself,
She turns to favor and to prettiness.

OPH.

Song.

180   "And will 'a not come again?
            And will 'a not come again?
               No, no, he is dead,
               Go to thy death-bed,
            He never will come again.

185   "His beard was as white as snow,
            [All] flaxen was his pole,
               He is gone, he is gone,
               And we cast away moan,
            God 'a' mercy on his soul!"

190   And of all Christians' souls, [I pray God]. God buy you.

[Exit.]

LAER. Do you [see] this, O God?

KING Laertes, I must commune with your grief,
   Or you deny me right. Go but apart,
   Make choice of whom your wisest friends you will,

---

167 **and . . . a-down-a:** "if he indeed agrees that Polonius is 'a-down,' i.e. fallen low" (Dover Wilson). **wheel:** refrain (?) or spinning wheel, at which women sang ballads (?).
169 **matter:** lucid speech.
172 **A document in madness:** a lesson contained in mad talk.
173 **fennel, columbines.** Symbols respectively of flattery and ingratitude.
174 **rue.** Symbolic of sorrow and repentance.
175 **with a difference:** i.e. to represent a different cause of sorrow. *Difference* is a term from heraldry, meaning a variation in a coat of arms made to distinguish different members of a family. **daisy, violets.** Symbolic respectively of dissembling and faithfulness. It is not clear who are the recipients of these.
178 **Thought:** melancholy.
179 **favor:** grace, charm.
186 **flaxen:** white. **pole:** poll, head.

195　And they shall hear and judge 'twixt you and me.
　　　If by direct or by collateral hand
　　　They find us touch'd, we will our kingdom give,
　　　Our crown, our life, and all that we call ours,
　　　To you in satisfaction; but if not,
200　Be you content to lend your patience to us,
　　　And we shall jointly labor with your soul
　　　To give it due content.
　　LAER.　　　　　　　　　Let this be so.
　　　His means of death, his obscure funeral—
　　　No trophy, sword, nor hatchment o'er his bones,
205　No noble rite nor formal ostentation—
　　　Cry to be heard, as 'twere from heaven to earth,
　　　That I must call't in question.
　　KING　　　　　　　　　So you shall,
　　　And where th' offense is, let the great axe fall.
　　　I pray you go with me.

Exeunt.

SCENE VI.

Enter HORATIO *and others.*

HOR. What are they that would speak with me?
GENTLEMAN Sea-faring men, sir. They say they have letters for you.
HOR. Let them come in.

[Exit GENTLEMAN.*]*

　　　I do not know from what part of the world
5　　I should be greeted, if not from Lord Hamlet.

Enter SAILORS.

[1] SAIL. God bless you, sir.
HOR. Let him bless thee too.
[1] SAIL. 'A shall, sir, and ['t] please him. There's a letter for you, sir—it came from th'
　　embassador that was bound for England—if your name be Horatio, as I am let to know
10　it is.
HOR. *[Reads.]* "Horatio, when thou shalt have overlook'd this, give these fellows some
　　means to the King, they have letters for him. Ere we were two days old at sea, a pirate
　　of very warlike appointment gave us chase. Finding ourselves too slow of sail, we put
　　on a compell'd valor, and in the grapple I boarded them. On the instant they got clear
15　of our ship, so I alone became their prisoner. They have dealt with me like thieves of
　　mercy, but they knew what they did: I am to do a [good] turn for them. Let the King

---

196 **collateral:** i.e. indirect.
197 **touch'd:** guilty
204 **trophy:** memorial.　**hatchment:** heraldic memorial tablet.
205 **formal ostentation:** fitting and customary ceremony.
207 **That:** so that.

IV.vi. Location: The castle.
15–16 **thieves of mercy:** merciful thieves.

have the letters I have sent, and repair thou to me with as much speed as thou wouldest
fly death. I have words to speak in thine ear will make thee dumb, yet are they much
too light for the [bore] of the matter. These good fellows will bring thee where I am.
20   Rosencrantz and Guildenstern hold their course for England, of them I have much
to tell thee. Farewell.

> [He] that thou knowest thine,
>
>   Hamlet."

Come, I will [give] you way for these your letters,
25   And do't the speedier that you may direct me
To him from whom you brought them.

Exeunt.

SCENE VII.

Enter KING *and* LAERTES.

KING Now must your conscience my acquittance seal,
    And you must put me in your heart for friend,
    Sith you have heard, and with a knowing ear,
    That he which hath your noble father slain
    Pursued my life.
5   LAER.   It well appears. But tell me
    Why you [proceeded] not against these feats
    So criminal and so capital in nature,
    As by your safety, greatness, wisdom, all things else
    You mainly were stirr'd up.
    KING   O, for two special reasons,
10   Which may to you perhaps seem much unsinow'd,
    But yet to me th' are strong. The Queen his mother
    Lives almost by his looks, and for myself—
    My virtue or my plague, be it either which—
    She is so [conjunctive] to my life and soul,
15   That, as the star moves not but in his sphere,
    I could not but by her. The other motive,
    Why to a public count I might not go,
    Is the great love the general gender bear him,
    Who, dipping all his faults in their affection,
20   Work like the spring that turneth wood to stone,

---

¹⁹ **bore:** caliber, size (gunnery term).

IV.vii. Location: The castle.
¹ **my acquittance seal:** ratify my acquittal, i.e. acknowledge my innocence in Polonius' death.
⁶ **feats:** acts.
⁸ **safety:** i.e. regard for your own safety.
⁹ **mainly:** powerfully.
¹⁰ **unsinow'd:** unsinewed, i.e. weak.
¹³ **either which:** one or the other.
¹⁴ **conjunctive:** closely joined.
¹⁵ **in his sphere:** by the movement of the sphere in which it is fixed (as the Ptolemaic astronomy taught).
¹⁷ **count:** reckoning.
¹⁸ **the general gender:** everybody.

Convert his gyves to graces, so that my arrows,
Too slightly timber'd for so [loud a wind],
Would have reverted to my bow again,
But not where I have aim'd them.
25 LAER. And so have I a noble father lost,
A sister driven into desp'rate terms,
Whose worth, if praises may go back again,
Stood challenger on mount of all the age
For her perfections—but my revenge will come.
30 KING Break not your sleeps for that. You must not think
That we are made of stuff so flat and dull
That we can let our beard be shook with danger
And think it pastime. You shortly shall hear more.
I lov'd your father, and we love ourself,
35 And that, I hope, will teach you to imagine—

Enter a MESSENGER *with letters.*

[How now? What news?
MESS.   Letters, my lord, from Hamlet:]
These to your Majesty, this to the Queen.
KING From Hamlet? Who brought them?
MESS. Sailors, my lord, they say, I saw them not.
40 They were given me by Claudio. He receiv'd them
Of him that brought them.
KING   Laertes, you shall hear them.
—Leave us.

[Exit MESSENGER.*]*

[Reads.]

"High and mighty, You shall know I am set naked on your kingdom. To-morrow shall
I beg leave to see your kingly eyes, when I shall, first asking you pardon thereunto,
45 recount the occasion of my sudden [and more strange] return.
          [Hamlet.]"
What should this mean? Are all the rest come back?
Or is it some abuse, and no such thing?
LAER. Know you the hand?

---

21 **gyves:** fetters.
26 **terms:** condition.
27 **go back again:** i.e. refer to what she was before she went mad.
28 **on mount:** preeminent.
30 **for that:** i.e. for fear of losing your revenge.
31 **flat:** spiritless.
32 **let . . . shook.** To ruffle or tweak a man's beard was an act of insolent defiance that he could
not disregard without loss of honor. Cf. II.ii. 485.   **with:** by.
43 **naked:** destitute.
44 **pardon thereunto:** permission to do so.
48 **abuse:** deceit.

KING   'Tis Hamlet's character. "Naked"!

50   And in a postscript here he says "alone."
        Can you devise me?

        LAER. I am lost in it, my lord. But let him come,
        It warms the very sickness in my heart
        That I [shall] live and tell him to his teeth,
        "Thus didst thou."

55   KING   If it be so, Laertes—
        As how should it be so? how otherwise?—
        Will you be rul'd by me?

        LAER.   Ay, my lord,
        So you will not o'errule me to a peace.

        KING To thine own peace. If he be now returned
60   As [checking] at his voyage, and that he means
        No more to undertake it, I will work him
        To an exploit, now ripe in my device,
        Under the which he shall not choose but fall;
        And for his death no wind of blame shall breathe,
65   But even his mother shall uncharge the practice,
        And call it accident.

        LAER.   My lord, I will be rul'd,
        The rather if you could devise it so
        That I might be the organ.

        KING   It falls right.
        You have been talk'd of since your travel much,
70   And that in Hamlet's hearing, for a quality
        Wherein they say you shine. Your sum of parts
        Did not together pluck such envy from him
        As did that one, and that, in my regard,
        Of the unworthiest siege.

        LAER.   What part is that, my lord?

75   KING A very riband in the cap of youth,
        Yet needful too, for youth no less becomes
        The light and careless livery that it wears
        Than settled age his sables and his weeds,
        Importing health and graveness. Two months since
80   Here was a gentleman of Normandy:

---

49 **character:** handwriting.
51 **devise me:** explain it to me.
56 **As . . . otherwise:** How can he have come back? Yet he obviously has.
58 **So:** provided that.
60 **checking at:** turning from (like a falcon diverted from its quarry by other prey).
65 **uncharge the practice:** adjudge the plot no plot, i.e. fail to see the plot.
68 **organ:** instrument, agent.
70 **quality:** skill.
71 **Your . . . parts:** all your (other) accomplishments put together.
74 **unworthiest:** i.e. least important (with no implication of unsuitableness).   **siege:** status, position.
78 **weeds:** (characteristic) garb.
79 **Importing . . . graveness:** signifying prosperity and dignity.

I have seen myself, and serv'd against, the French,
And they can well on horseback, but this gallant
Had witchcraft in't, he grew unto his seat,
And to such wondrous doing brought his horse,
85   As had he been incorps'd and demi-natur'd
With the brave beast. So far he topp'd [my] thought,
That I in forgery of shapes and tricks
Come short of what he did.
LAER.   A Norman was't?
KING A Norman.
LAER. Upon my life, Lamord.
90   KING   The very same.
LAER. I know him well. He is the brooch indeed
   And gem of all the nation.
KING He made confession of you,
And gave you such a masterly report
95   For art and exercise in your defense,
And for your rapier most especial,
That he cried out 'twould be a sight indeed
If one could match you. The scrimers of their nation
He swore had neither motion, guard, nor eye,
100   If you oppos'd them. Sir, this report of his
Did Hamlet so envenom with his envy
That he could nothing do but wish and beg
Your sudden coming o'er to play with you.
Now, out of this—
LAER.   What out of this, my lord?
105 KING Laertes, was your father dear to you?
Or are you like the painting of a sorrow,
A face without a heart?
LAER.   Why ask you this?
KING Not that I think you did not love your father,
But that I know love is begun by time,
110   And that I see, in passages of proof,
Time qualifies the spark and fire of it.
There lives within the very flame of love
A kind of week or snuff that will abate it,
And nothing is at a like goodness still,

---

82 **can . . . horseback:** are excellent riders.
85 **incorps'd:** made one body.   **demi-natur'd:** i.e. become half of a composite animal.
87 **forgery:** mere imagining.
91 **brooch:** ornament (worn in the hat).
93 **made . . . you:** acknowledged your excellence.
98 **scrimers:** fencers.
103 **sudden:** speedy.
109 **time:** i.e. a particular set of circumstances.
110 **in . . . proof:** i.e. by the test of experience, by actual examples.
111 **qualifies:** moderates.
113 **week:** wick.
114 **nothing . . . still:** nothing remains forever at the same pitch of perfection.

115   For goodness, growing to a plurisy,
         Dies in his own too much. That we would do,
         We should do when we would; for this "would" changes,
         And hath abatements and delays as many
         As there are tongues, are hands, are accidents,
120   And then this "should" is like a spendthrift's sigh,
         That hurts by easing. But to the quick of th' ulcer:
         Hamlet comes back. What would you undertake
         To show yourself indeed your father's son
         More than in words?
      LAER.   To cut his throat i' th' church.
125   KING No place indeed should murther sanctuarize,
         Revenge should have no bounds. But, good Laertes,
         Will you do this, keep close within your chamber.
         Hamlet return'd shall know you are come home.
         We'll put on those shall praise your excellence,
130   And set a double varnish on the fame
         The Frenchman gave you, bring you in fine together,
         And wager o'er your heads. He, being remiss,
         Most generous, and free from all contriving,
         Will not peruse the foils, so that with ease,
135   Or with a little shuffling, you may choose
         A sword unbated, and in a [pass] of practice
         Requite him for your father.
      LAER.   I will do't,
         And for [that] purpose I'll anoint my sword.
         I bought an unction of a mountebank,
140   So mortal that, but dip a knife in it,
         Where it draws blood, no cataplasm so rare,
         Collected from all simples that have virtue
         Under the moon, can save the thing from death

---

115 **plurisy:** plethora (a variant spelling of *pleurisy*, which was erroneously related to *plus*, stem *plur-*, "more, overmuch."

116 **too much:** excess.

120 **spendthrift's sigh.** A sigh was supposed to draw blood from the heart.

121 **hurts by easing:** injures us at the same time that it gives us relief.

125 **sanctuarize:** offer asylum to.

127 **Will . . . this:** if you want to undertake this.

129 **put on those:** incite those who.

130 **double varnish:** second coat of varnish.

131 **in fine:** finally.

132 **remiss:** careless, overtrustful.

133 **generous:** noble-minded.   **free . . . contriving:** innocent of sharp practices.

134 **peruse:** examine.

135 **shuffling:** cunning exchange.

136 **unbated:** not blunted.   **pass of practice:** tricky thrust.

139 **unction:** ointment.   **mountebank:** traveling quack-doctor.

140 **mortal:** deadly.

141 **cataplasm:** poultice.

142 **simples:** medicinal herbs.   **virtue:** curative power.

That is but scratch'd withal. I'll touch my point
145 With this contagion, that if I gall him slightly,
It may be death.
KING   Let's further think of this,
Weigh what convenience both of time and means
May fit us to our shape. If this should fail,
And that our drift look through our bad performance,
150 'Twere better not assay'd; therefore this project
Should have a back or second, that might hold
If this did blast in proof. Soft, let me see.
We'll make a solemn wager on your cunnings—
I ha't!
155 When in your motion you are hot and dry—
As make your bouts more violent to that end—
And that he calls for drink, I'll have preferr'd him
A chalice for the nonce, whereon but sipping,
If he by chance escape your venom'd stuck,
160 Our purpose may hold there. But stay, what noise?

Enter QUEEN.

QUEEN One woe doth tread upon another's heel,
So fast they follow. Your sister's drown'd, Laertes.
LAER. Drown'd! O, where?
QUEEN There is a willow grows askaunt the brook,
165 That shows his hoary leaves in the glassy stream,
Therewith fantastic garlands did she make
Of crow-flowers, nettles, daisies, and long purples
That liberal shepherds give a grosser name,
But our cull-cold maids do dead men's fingers call them.
170 There on the pendant boughs her crownet weeds
Clamb'ring to hang, an envious sliver broke,
When down her weedy trophies and herself
Fell in the weeping brook. Her clothes spread wide,

---

145 **gall:** graze.
148 **fit . . . shape:** i.e. suit our purposes best.
149 **drift:** purpose. **look through:** become visible, be detected.
151 **back or second:** i.e. a second plot in reserve for emergency.
152 **blast in proof:** blow up while being tried (an image from gunnery).
156 **As:** i.e. and you should.
157 **preferr'd:** offered to. Most editors adopt the F1 reading *prepar'd*.
158 **nonce:** occasion.
159 **stuck:** thrust (from *stoccado*, a fencing term).
164 **askaunt:** sideways over.
165 **hoary:** grey-white.
166 **Therewith:** i.e. with willow branches.
167 **long purples:** wild orchids.
168 **liberal:** free-spoken.
169 **cull-cold:** chaste.
170 **crownet:** made into coronets.
171 **envious sliver:** malicious branch.

And mermaid-like awhile they bore her up,
175 Which time she chaunted snatches of old lauds,
As one incapable of her own distress,
Or like a creature native and indued
Unto that element. But long it could not be
Till that her garments, heavy with their drink,
180 Pull'd the poor wretch from her melodious lay
To muddy death.
LAER.   Alas, then she is drown'd?
QUEEN Drown'd, drown'd.
LAER. Too much of water hast thou, poor Ophelia,
And therefore I forbid my tears; but yet
185 It is our trick, Nature her custom holds,
Let shame say what it will; when these are gone,
The woman will be out. Adieu, my lord,
I have a speech a' fire that fain would blaze,
But that this folly drowns it.

Exit.

KING   Let's follow, Gertrude.
190 How much I had to do to calm his rage!
Now fear I this will give it start again,
Therefore let's follow.

Exeunt.

ACT V

SCENE I.

Enter two CLOWNS *[with spades and mattocks].*

1 CLO. Is she to be buried in Christian burial when she willfully seeks her own salvation?
2 CLO. I tell thee she is, therefore make her grave straight. The crowner hath sate on her, and finds it Christian burial.
1 CLO. How can that be, unless she drown'd herself in her own defense?
5 2 CLO. Why, 'tis found so.
1 CLO. It must be [*se offendendo*], it cannot be else. For here lies the point: if I drown myself wittingly, it argues an act, and an act hath three branches—it is to act, to do, to perform; [argal], she drown'd herself wittingly.

---

175 **lauds:** hymns.
176 **incapable:** insensible.
177 **indued:** habituated.
185 **It:** i.e. weeping.   **trick:** natural way.
186 **these:** these tears.
187 **The woman . . . out:** my womanish traits will be gone for good.

V.i. Location: A churchyard.
o.s.d. **Clowns:** rustics.
2 **straight:** immediately.   **crowner:** coroner.
6 **se offendendo:** blunder for *se defendendo,* "in self-defense."
8 **argal:** blunder for *ergo,* "therefore."

2 CLO. Nay, but hear you, goodman delver—

10 1 CLO. Give me leave. Here lies the water; good. Here stands the man; good. If the man go to this water and drown himself, it is, will he, nill he, he goes, mark you that. But if the water come to him and drown him, he drowns not himself; argal, he that is not guilty of his own death shortens not his own life.

2 CLO. But is this law?

15 1 CLO. Ay, marry, is't—crowner's quest law.

2 CLO. Will you ha' the truth an't? If this had not been a gentlewoman, she should have been buried out a' Christian burial.

1 CLO. Why, there thou say'st, and the more pity that great folk should have count'nance in this world to drown or hang themselves, more than their even-Christen. Come, my

20 spade. There is no ancient gentlemen but gard'ners, ditchers, and grave-makers; they hold up Adam's profession.

2 CLO. Was he a gentleman?

1 CLO. 'A was the first that ever bore arms.

[2 CLO. Why, he had none.

25 1 CLO. What, art a heathen? How dost thou understand the Scripture? The Scripture says Adam digg'd; could he dig without arms?] I'll put another question to thee. If thou answerest me not to the purpose, confess thyself—

2 CLO. Go to.

1 CLO. What is he that builds stronger than either the mason, the shipwright, or the

30 carpenter?

2 CLO. The gallows-maker, for that outlives a thousand tenants.

1 CLO. I like thy wit well, in good faith. The gallows does well; but how does it well? It does well to those that do ill. Now thou dost ill to say the gallows is built stronger than the church; argal, the gallows may do well to thee. To't again, come.

35 2 CLO. Who builds stronger than a mason, a shipwright, or a carpenter?

1 CLO. Ay, tell me that, and unyoke.

2 CLO. Marry, now I can tell.

1 CLO. To't.

2 CLO. Mass, I cannot tell.

Enter HAMLET *and* HORATIO *[afar off]*.

40 1 CLO. Cudgel thy brains no more about it, for your dull ass will not mend his pace with beating, and when you are ask'd this question next, say "a grave-maker": the houses he makes lasts till doomsday. Go get thee in, and fetch me a sup of liquor.

[Exit SECOND CLOWN. FIRST CLOWN *digs.]*

10–13 **Here . . . life.** Alluding to a very famous suicide case, that of Sir James Hales, a judge who drowned himself in 1554; it was long cited in the courts. The clown gives a garbled account of the defense summing-up and the verdict.

11 **nill he:** he will not.

15 **quest:** inquest.

19 **even-Christen:** fellow Christians.

24 **none:** i.e. no coat of arms.

36 **unyoke:** i.e. cease to labor, call it a day.

39 **Mass:** by the mass.

"In youth when I did love, did love,
  Methought it was very sweet,
45   To contract—O—the time for—a—my behove,
  O, methought there—a—was nothing—a—meet."

HAM. Has this fellow no feeling of his business? 'a sings in grave-making.
HOR. Custom hath made it in him a property of easiness.
HAM. 'Tis e'en so, the hand of little employment hath the daintier sense.
1 CLO.

Song.

50   "But age with his stealing steps
  Hath clawed me in his clutch,
  And hath shipped me into the land,
  As if I had never been such."

[Throws up a shovelful of earth with a skull in it.]

HAM. That skull had a tongue in it, and could sing once. How the knave jowls it to the
55   ground, as if 'twere Cain's jaw-bone, that did the first murder! This might be the pate
  of a politician, which this ass now o'erreaches, one that would circumvent God, might
  it not?
HOR. It might, my lord.
HAM. Or of a courtier, which could say, "Good morrow, sweet lord! How dost thou,
60   sweet lord?" This might be my Lord Such-a-one, that prais'd my Lord Such-a-one's
  horse when 'a [meant] to beg it, might it not?
HOR. Ay, my lord.
HAM. Why, e'en so, and now my Lady Worm's, chopless, and knock'd about the [mazzard]
  with a sexton's spade. Here's fine revolution, and we had the trick to see't. Did these
65   bones cost no more the breeding, but to play at loggats with them? Mine ache to
  think on't.
1 CLO.

Song.

"A pickaxe and a spade, a spade,
  For and a shrouding sheet:

---

⁴⁵ **contract . . . behove:** shorten, i.e. spend agreeably . . . advantage. The song, punctuated by the
grunts of the clown as he digs, is a garbled version of a poem by Thomas Lord Vaux, entitled
"The Aged Lover Renounceth Love."
⁴⁸ **Custom:** habit.   **a property of easiness:** i.e. a thing he can do with complete ease of mind.
⁴⁹ **daintier sense:** more delicate sensitivity.
⁵⁴ **jowls:** dashes.
⁵⁶ **politician:** schemer, intriguer.   **o'erreaches:** gets the better of (with play on the literal sense).
circumvent God: bypass God's law.
⁶³ **chopless:** lacking the lower jaw.   **mazzard:** head.
⁶⁴ **revolution:** change.   **and:** if.   **trick:** knack, ability.
⁶⁴⁻⁶⁵ **Did . . . cost:** were . . . worth.
⁶⁵ **loggats:** a game in which blocks of wood were thrown at a stake.

O, a pit of clay for to be made
For such a guest is meet."

[Throws up another skull.]

HAM. There's another. Why may not that be the skull of a lawyer? Where be his quiddities now, his quillities, his cases, his tenures, and his tricks? Why does he suffer this mad knave now to knock him about the sconce with a dirty shovel, and will not tell him of his action of battery? Hum! This fellow might be in 's time a great buyer of land, with his statutes, his recognizances, his fines, his double vouchers, his recoveries. [Is this the fine of his fines, and the recovery of his recoveries,] to have his fine pate full of fine dirt? Will [his] vouchers vouch him no more of his purchases, and [double ones too], than the length and breadth of a pair of indentures? The very conveyances of his lands will scarcely lie in this box, and must th' inheritor himself have no more, ha?

HOR. Not a jot more, my lord.

HAM. Is not parchment made of sheep-skins?

HOR. Ay, my lord, and of calves'-skins too.

HAM. They are sheep and calves which seek out assurance in that. I will speak to this fellow. Whose grave's this, sirrah?

1 CLO. Mine, sir.

[Sings.]

"[O], a pit of clay for to be made
[For such a guest is meet]."

HAM. I think it be thine indeed, for thou liest in't.

1 CLO. You lie out on't, sir, and therefore 'tis not yours; for my part, I do not lie in't, yet it is mine.

HAM. Thou dost lie in't, to be in't and say it is thine. 'Tis for the dead, not for the quick; therefore thou liest.

1 CLO. 'Tis a quick lie, sir, 'twill away again from me to you.

HAM. What man dost thou dig it for?

1 CLO. For no man, sir.

HAM. What woman then?

1 CLO. For none neither.

HAM. Who is to be buried in't?

1 CLO. One that was a woman, sir, but, rest her soul, she's dead.

---

71 **quiddities**: subtleties, quibbles.

72 **quillities**: fine distinctions.   **tenures**: titles to real estate.

73 **sconce**: head.

75 **statutes, recognizances**: bonds securing debts by attaching land and property.   **fines, recoveries**: procedures for converting an entailed estate to freehold.   **double vouchers**: documents guaranteeing title to real estate, signed by two persons.

76 **fine**: end.

78 **pair of indentures**: legal document cut into two parts that fit together on a serrated edge. Perhaps Hamlet thus refers to the two rows of teeth in the skull, or to the bone sutures.   **conveyances**: documents relating to transfer of property.

79 **this box**: i.e. the skull itself.   **inheritor**: owner.

85 **sirrah**: term of address to inferiors.

HAM. How absolute the knave is! we must speak by the card, or equivocation will undo us. By the Lord, Horatio, this three years I have took note of it: the age is grown so pick'd that the toe of the peasant comes so near the heel of the courtier, he galls his kibe. How long hast thou been grave-maker?

105 1 CLO. Of [all] the days i' th' year, I came to't that day that our last king Hamlet overcame Fortinbras.

HAM. How long is that since?

1 CLO. Cannot you tell that? Every fool can tell that. It was that very day that young Hamlet was born—he that is mad, and sent into England.

110 HAM. Ay, marry, why was he sent into England?

1 CLO. Why, because 'a was mad. 'A shall recover his wits there, or if 'a do not, 'tis no great matter there.

HAM. Why?

1 CLO. 'Twill not be seen in him there, there the men are as mad as he.

115 HAM. How came he mad?

1 CLO. Very strangely, they say.

HAM. How strangely?

1 CLO. Faith, e'en with losing his wits.

HAM. Upon what ground?

120 1 CLO. Why, here in Denmark. I have been sexton here, man and boy, thirty years.

HAM. How long will a man lie i' th' earth ere he rot?

1 CLO. Faith, if 'a be not rotten before 'a die—as we have many pocky corses, that will scarce hold the laying in—'a will last you some eight year or nine year. A tanner will last you nine year.

125 HAM. Why he more than another?

1 CLO. Why, sir, his hide is so tann'd with his trade that 'a will keep out water a great while, and your water is a sore decayer of your whoreson dead body. Here's a skull now hath lien you i' th' earth three and twenty years.

HAM. Whose was it?

130 1 CLO. A whoreson mad fellow's it was. Whose do you think it was?

HAM. Nay, I know not.

1 CLO. A pestilence on him for a mad rogue! 'a pour'd a flagon of Rhenish on my head once. This same skull, sir, was, sir, Yorick's skull, the King's jester.

HAM. This?

[Takes the skull.]

135 1 CLO. E'en that.

HAM. Alas, poor Yorick! I knew him, Horatio, a fellow of infinite jest, of most excellent fancy. He hath bore me on his back a thousand times, and now how abhorr'd in my imagination it is! my gorge rises at it. Here hung those lips that I have kiss'd I know not how oft. Where be your gibes now, your gambols, your songs, your flashes of

140 merriment, that were wont to set the table on a roar? Not one now to mock your own

---

101 **absolute:** positive. **by the card:** by the compass, i.e. punctiliously. **equivocation:** ambiguity.

103 **pick'd:** refined.

103–04 **galls his kibe:** rubs the courtier's chilblain.

122 **pocky:** rotten with venereal disease.

123 **hold . . . in:** last out the burial.

grinning—quite chop-fall'n. Now get you to my lady's [chamber], and tell her, let her paint an inch thick, to this favor she must come; make her laugh at that. Prithee, Horatio, tell me one thing.

HOR. What's that, my lord?

145   HAM. Dost thou think Alexander look'd a' this fashion i' th' earth?

HOR. E'en so.

HAM. And smelt so? pah!

[Puts down the skull.]

HOR. E'en so, my lord.

150   HAM. To what base uses we may return, Horatio! Why may not imagination trace the noble dust of Alexander, till 'a find it stopping a bunghole?

HOR. 'Twere to consider too curiously, to consider so.

HAM. No, faith, not a jot, but to follow him thither with modesty enough and likelihood to lead it: Alexander died, Alexander was buried, Alexander returneth to dust, the dust is earth, of earth we make loam, and why of that loam whereto he was converted

155   might they not stop a beer-barrel?

Imperious Caesar, dead and turn'd to clay,

Might stop a hole to keep the wind away.

O that that earth which kept the world in awe

Should patch a wall t' expel the [winter's] flaw!

160   But soft, but soft awhile, here comes the King,

Enter KING, QUEEN, LAERTES, *and [a* DOCTOR OF DIVINITY, *following] the corse, [with* LORDS *attendant].*

The Queen, the courtiers. Who is this they follow?

And with such maimed rites? This doth betoken

The corse they follow did with desp'rate hand

Foredo it own life. 'Twas of some estate.

165   Couch we a while and mark.

[Retiring with HORATIO.*]*

LAER. What ceremony else?

HAM. That is Laertes, a very noble youth. Mark.

LAER. What ceremony else?

DOCTOR Her obsequies have been as far enlarg'd

170   As we have warranty. Her death was doubtful,

And but that great command o'ersways the order,

---

141 **chop-fall'n:** (1) lacking the lower jaw; (2) downcast.

142 **favor:** appearance.

151 **curiously:** closely, minutely.

152 **modesty:** moderation.

154 **loam:** a mixture of moistened clay with sand, straw, etc.

156 **Imperious:** imperial.

159 **flaw:** gust.

162 **maimed rites:** lack of customary ceremony.

164 **Foredo:** fordo, destroy. **it:** its.   **estate:** rank.

165 **Couch we:** let us conceal ourselves.

170 **doubtful:** i.e. the subject of an "open verdict."

171 **order:** customary procedure.

She should in ground unsanctified been lodg'd
Till the last trumpet; for charitable prayers,
[Shards,] flints, and pebbles should be thrown on her.
175   Yet here she is allow'd her virgin crants,
Her maiden strewments, and the bringing home
Of bell and burial.
LAER. Must there no more be done?
DOCTOR   No more be done:
We should profane the service of the dead
180   To sing a requiem and such rest to her
As to peace-parted souls.
LAER.   Lay her i' th' earth,
And from her fair and unpolluted flesh
May violets spring! I tell thee, churlish priest,
A minist'ring angel shall my sister be
When thou liest howling.
185 HAM.   What, the fair Ophelia!
QUEEN *[Scattering flowers.]* Sweets to the sweet, farewell!
I hop'd thou shouldst have been my Hamlet's wife.
I thought thy bride-bed to have deck'd, sweet maid,
And not have strew'd thy grave.
LAER.   O, treble woe
190   Fall ten times [treble] on that cursed head
Whose wicked deed thy most ingenious sense
Depriv'd thee of! Hold off the earth a while,
Till I have caught her once more in mine arms.

[Leaps in the grave.]

Now pile your dust upon the quick and dead,
195   Till of this flat a mountain you have made
T' o'ertop old Pelion, or the skyish head
Of blue Olympus.
HAM. *[Coming forward.]* What is he whose grief
Bears such an emphasis, whose phrase of sorrow
200   Conjures the wand'ring stars and makes them stand
Like wonder-wounded hearers? This is I,
Hamlet the Dane!

---

172 **should:** would certainly.
173 **for:** instead of.
175 **crants:** garland.
176 **maiden strewments:** flowers scattered on the grave of an unmarried girl.
176-77 **bringing . . . burial:** i.e. burial in consecrated ground, with the bell tolling.
180 **requiem:** dirge.
186 **Sweets:** flowers.
191 **ingenious:** intelligent.
196, 197 **Pelion, Olympus:** mountains in northeastern Greece.
199 **emphasis, phrase.** Rhetorical terms, here used in disparaging reference to Laertes' inflated language.
200 **Conjures:** puts a spell upon. **wand'ring stars:** planets.
202 **the Dane.** This title normally signifies the King.

[HAMLET *leaps in after* LAERTES.]

LAER. The devil take thy soul!

[*Grappling with him.*]

HAM.   Thou pray'st not well.
    I prithee take thy fingers from my throat.
205   For though I am not splenitive [and] rash,
    Yet have I in me something dangerous,
    Which let thy wisdom fear. Hold off thy hand!
KING Pluck them asunder.
QUEEN   Hamlet, Hamlet!
ALL   Gentlemen!
HOR. Good my lord, be quiet.

[*The* ATTENDANTS *part them, and they come out of the grave.*]

210 HAM. Why, I will fight with him upon this theme
    Until my eyelids will no longer wag.
QUEEN O my son, what theme?
HAM. I lov'd Ophelia. Forty thousand brothers
    Could not with all their quantity of love
215   Make up my sum. What wilt thou do for her?
KING O, he is mad, Laertes.
QUEEN For love of God, forbear him.
HAM. 'Swounds, show me what thou't do.
    Woo't weep, woo't fight, woo't fast, woo't tear thyself?
220   Woo't drink up eisel, eat a crocadile?
    I'll do't. Dost [thou] come here to whine?
    To outface me with leaping in her grave?
    Be buried quick with her, and so will I.
    And if thou prate of mountains, let them throw
225   Millions of acres on us, till our ground,
    Singeing his pate against the burning zone,
    Make Ossa like a wart! Nay, and thou'lt mouth,
    I'll rant as well as thou.
QUEEN   This is mere madness,
    And [thus] a while the fit will work on him;
230   Anon, as patient as the female dove,

---

205 **splenitive:** impetuous.
218 **thou't:** thou wilt.
219 **Woo't:** wilt thou.
220 **eisel:** vinegar. **crocadile:** crocodile.
224 **if . . . mountains.** Referring to lines 194–97.
226 **burning zone:** sphere of the sun.
227 **Ossa:** another mountain in Greece, near Pelion and Olympus. **mouth:** talk bombast (synonymous with *rant* in the next line).
228 **mere:** utter.
230 **patient:** calm.

When that her golden couplets are disclosed,
His silence will sit drooping.
HAM.   Hear you, sir,
What is the reason that you use me thus?
I lov'd you ever. But it is no matter.
235 Let Hercules himself do what he may,
The cat will mew, and dog will have his day.

Exit HAMLET.

KING I pray thee, good Horatio, wait upon him.

[Exit] HORATIO.

[To LAERTES.]   Strengthen your patience in our last night's speech,
We'll put the matter to the present push.—
240 Good Gertrude, set some watch over your son.
This grave shall have a living monument.
An hour of quiet [shortly] shall we see,
Till then in patience our proceeding be.

Exeunt.

SCENE II.

Enter HAMLET *and* HORATIO.

HAM. So much for this, sir, now shall you see the other—
You do remember all the circumstance?
HOR. Remember it, my lord!
5 HAM. Sir, in my heart there was a kind of fighting
That would not let me sleep. [Methought] I lay
Worse than the mutines in the [bilboes]. Rashly—
And prais'd be rashness for it—let us know
Our indiscretion sometime serves us well
10 When our deep plots do pall, and that should learn us
There's a divinity that shapes our ends,
Rough-hew them how we will—

---

231 **golden couplets:** pair of baby birds, covered with yellow down.   **disclosed:** hatched.
235-36 **Let . . . day:** i.e. nobody can prevent another from making the scenes he feels he has
   a right to.
238 **in:** i.e. by recalling.
239 **present push:** immediate test.
241 **living:** enduring (?) or in the form of a lifelike effigy (?).

V.ii. Location: The castle.
1 **see the other:** i.e. hear the other news I have to tell you (hinted at in the letter to Horatio,
   IV.vi.18).
6 **mutines:** mutineers (but the term *mutiny* was in Shakespeare's day used of almost any act of
   rebellion against authority).   **bilboes:** fetters attached to a heavy iron bar.   **Rashly:** on impulse.
7 **know:** recognize, acknowledge.
9 **pall:** lose force, come to nothing.   **learn:** teach.
10 **shapes our ends:** gives final shape to our designs.
11 **Rough-hew them:** block them out in initial form.

HOR.   That is most certain.
HAM. Up from my cabin,
    My sea-gown scarf'd about me, in the dark
    Grop'd I to find out them, had my desire,
15 Finger'd their packet, and in fine withdrew
    To mine own room again, making so bold,
    My fears forgetting manners, to [unseal]
    Their grand commission; where I found, Horatio—
    Ah, royal knavery!—an exact command,
20 Larded with many several sorts of reasons,
    Importing Denmark's health and England's too,
    With, ho, such bugs and goblins in my life,
    That, on the supervise, no leisure bated,
    No, not to stay the grinding of the axe,
    My head should be strook off.
25 HOR.   Is't possible?
HAM. Here's the commission, read it at more leisure.
    But wilt thou hear now how I did proceed?
HOR. I beseech you.
HAM. Being thus benetted round with [villainies],
30 Or I could make a prologue to my brains,
    They had begun the play. I sat me down,
    Devis'd a new commission, wrote it fair.
    I once did hold it, as our statists do,
    A baseness to write fair, and labor'd much
35 How to forget that learning, but, sir, now
    It did me yeman's service. Wilt thou know
    Th' effect of what I wrote?
HOR.   Ay, good my lord.
HAM. An earnest conjuration from the King,
    As England was his faithful tributary,
40 As love between them like the palm might flourish,
    As peace should still her wheaten garland wear
    And stand a comma 'tween their amities,
    And many such-like [as's] of great charge,

---

¹⁵ **Finger'd:** filched, "pinched."
²⁰ **Larded:** garnished.
²¹ **Importing:** relating to.
²² **bugs . . . life:** terrifying things in prospect if I were permitted to remain alive. *Bugs* = bugaboos.
²³ **supervise:** perusal.   **bated:** deducted (from the stipulated speediness).
²⁴ **stay:** wait for.
³⁰ **Or:** before.
³² **fair:** i.e. in a beautiful hand (such as a professional scribe would use).
³³ **statists:** statesmen, public officials.
³⁴ **A baseness:** i.e. a skill befitting men of low rank.
³⁶ **yeman's:** yeoman's, i.e. solid, substantial.
³⁷ **effect:** purport, gist.
⁴² **comma:** connective, link.
⁴³ **as's . . . charge:** (1) weighty clauses beginning with *as*; (2) asses with heavy loads.

That on the view and knowing of these contents,
45 Without debatement further, more or less,
He should those bearers put to sudden death,
Not shriving time allow'd.
HOR.   How was this seal'd?
HAM. Why, even in that was heaven ordinant.
I had my father's signet in my purse,
50 Which was the model of that Danish seal;
Folded the writ up in the form of th' other,
[Subscrib'd] it, gave't th' impression, plac'd it safely,
The changeling never known. Now the next day
Was our sea-fight, and what to this was sequent
55 Thou knowest already.
HOR. So Guildenstern and Rosencrantz go to't.
HAM. [Why, man, they did make love to this employment,]
They are not near my conscience. Their defeat
Does by their own insinuation grow.
60 'Tis dangerous when the baser nature comes
Between the pass and fell incensed points
Of mighty opposites.
HOR.   Why, what a king is this!
HAM. Does it not, think thee, stand me now upon—
He that hath kill'd my king and whor'd my mother,
65 Popp'd in between th' election and my hopes,
Thrown out his angle for my proper life,
And with such coz'nage—is't not perfect conscience
[To quit him with this arm? And is't not to be damn'd,
To let this canker of our nature come
70 In further evil?
HOR. It must be shortly known to him from England
What is the issue of the business there.

---

47 **shriving time:** time for confession and absolution.
48 **ordinant:** in charge, guiding.
50 **model:** small copy.
52 **Subscrib'd:** signed.
53 **changeling:** i.e. Hamlet's letter, substituted secretly for the genuine letter, as fairies substituted their children for human children.   **never known:** never recognized as a substitution (unlike the fairies' changelings).
56 **go to't:** i.e. are going to their death.
58 **defeat:** ruin, overthrow.
59 **insinuation:** winding their way into the affair.
60 **baser:** inferior.
61 **pass:** thrust.   **fell:** fierce.
63 **stand . . . upon:** i.e. rest upon me as a duty.
65 **election:** i.e. as King of Denmark.
66 **angle:** hook and line.   **proper:** very.
67 **coz'nage:** trickery.
68 **quit him:** pay him back.
69 **canker:** cancerous sore.
69–70 **come In:** grow into.

HAM. It will be short; the interim's mine,
And a man's life's no more than to say "one."
75 But I am very sorry, good Horatio,
That to Laertes I forgot myself,
For by the image of my cause I see
The portraiture of his. I'll [court] his favors.
But sure the bravery of his grief did put me
Into a tow'ring passion.
80 HOR.   Peace, who comes here?]

Enter [young OSRIC,] a courtier.

OSR. Your lordship is right welcome back to Denmark.
HAM. I humbly thank you, sir.—Dost know this water-fly?
HOR. No, my good lord.
HAM. Thy state is the more gracious, for 'tis a vice to know him. He hath much land,
85 and fertile; let a beast be lord of beasts, and his crib shall stand at the King's mess.
'Tis a chough, but, as I say, spacious in the possession of dirt.
OSR. Sweet lord, if your lordship were at leisure, I should impart a thing to you from
his Majesty.
HAM. I will receive it, sir, with all diligence of spirit. [Put] your bonnet to his right use,
90 'tis for the head.
OSR. I thank your lordship, it is very hot.
HAM. No, believe me, 'tis very cold, the wind is northerly.
OSR. It is indifferent cold, my lord, indeed.
HAM. But yet methinks it is very [sultry] and hot [for] my complexion.
95 OSR. Exceedingly, my lord, it is very sultry—as 'twere—I cannot tell how. My lord, his
Majesty bade me signify to you that 'a has laid a great wager on your head. Sir, this
is the matter—
HAM. I beseech you remember.

[HAMLET moves him to put on his hat.]

OSR. Nay, good my lord, for my ease, in good faith. Sir, here is newly come to court
100 Laertes, believe me, an absolute [gentleman], full of most excellent differences, of very

---

74 **a man's . . . more:** i.e. to kill a man takes no more time.   **say "one."** Perhaps this is equivalent
   to "deliver one sword thrust"; see line 237 below, where Hamlet says "One" as he makes the first
   hit.
77 **image:** likeness.
79 **bravery:** ostentatious expression.
82 **water-fly:** i.e. tiny, vainly agitated creature.
84 **gracious:** virtuous.
85 **let . . . mess:** i.e. if a beast owned as many cattle as Osric, he could feast with the King.
86 **chough:** jackdaw, a bird that could be taught to speak.
89 **bonnet:** hat.
93 **indifferent:** somewhat.
94 **complexion:** temperament.
99 **for my ease:** i.e. I am really more comfortable with my hat off (a polite insistence on maintaining
   ceremony).
100 **absolute:** complete, possessing every quality a gentleman should have.   **differences:** distinguishing characteristics, personal qualities.

soft society, and great showing; indeed, to speak sellingly of him, he is the card or calendar of gentry; for you shall find in him the continent of what part a gentleman would see.

105 HAM. Sir, his definement suffers no perdition in you, though I know to divide him inventorially would dozy th' arithmetic of memory, and yet but yaw neither in respect of his quick sail; but in the verity of extolment, I take him to be a soul of great article, and his infusion of such dearth and rareness as, to make true diction of him, his semblable is his mirror, and who else would trace him, his umbrage, nothing more.

OSR. Your lordship speaks most infallibly of him.

110 HAM. The concernancy, sir? Why do we wrap the gentleman in our more rawer breath?

OSR. Sir?

HOR. Is't not possible to understand in another tongue? You will to't, sir, really.

HAM. What imports the nomination of this gentleman?

OSR. Of Laertes?

115 HOR. His purse is empty already: all 's golden words are spent.

HAM. Of him, sir.

OSR. I know you are not ignorant—

HAM. I would you did, sir, yet, in faith, if you did, it would not much approve me. Well, sir?

120 OSR. You are not ignorant of what excellence Laertes is—

HAM. I dare not confess that, lest I should compare with him in excellence, but to know a man well were to know himself.

OSR. I mean, sir, for [his] weapon, but in the imputation laid on him by them, in his meed he's unfellow'd.

125 HAM. What's his weapon?

OSR. Rapier and dagger.

HAM. That's two of his weapons—but well.

---

101 **soft:** agreeable.   **great showing:** splendid appearance.   **sellingly:** i.e. like a seller to a prospective buyer; in a fashion to do full justice. Most editors follow Q3 in reading *feelingly* = with exactitude, as he deserves.

101–02 **card or calendar:** chart or register, i.e. compendious guide.

102 **gentry:** gentlemanly behavior.   **the continent . . . part:** one who contains every quality.

104 **perdition:** loss.

105 **dozy:** make dizzy.   **yaw:** keep deviating erratically from its course (said of a ship).   **neither:** for all that.

105–06 **in respect of:** compared with.

106 **in . . . extolment:** to praise him truly.   **article:** scope (?) or importance (?).

107 **infusion:** essence, quality.   **dearth:** scarceness.   **make true diction:** speak truly.

107–08 **his semblable:** his only likeness or equal.

108 **who . . . him:** anyone else who tries to follow him.   **umbrage:** shadow.

110 **concernancy:** relevance.   **more rawer breath:** i.e. words too crude to describe him properly.

112 **in another tongue:** i.e. when someone else is the speaker.   **You . . . really:** i.e. you can do it if you try.

113 **nomination:** naming, mention.

118 **approve:** commend.

121 **compare . . . excellence:** i.e. seem to claim the same degree of excellence for myself.   **but.** The sense seems to require *for*.

122 **himself:** i.e. oneself.

123 **in . . . them:** i.e. in popular estimation.

124 **meed:** merit.

OSR. The King, sir, hath wager'd with him six Barbary horses, against the which he has
impawn'd, as I take it, six French rapiers and poniards, with their assigns, as girdle,
130 [hangers], and so. Three of the carriages, in faith, are very dear to fancy, very responsive
to the hilts, most delicate carriages, and of very liberal conceit.

HAM. What call you the carriages?

HOR. I knew you must be edified by the margent ere you had done.

OSR. The [carriages], sir, are the hangers.

135 HAM. The phrase would be more germane to the matter if we could carry a cannon by
our sides; I would it [might be] hangers till then. But on: six Barb'ry horses against six
French swords, their assigns, and three liberal-conceited carriages; that's the French
bet against the Danish. Why is this all [impawn'd, as] you call it?

OSR. The King, sir, hath laid, sir, that in a dozen passes between yourself and him, he
140 shall not exceed you three hits; he hath laid on twelve for nine; and it would come to
immediate trial, if your lordship would vouchsafe the answer.

HAM. How if I answer no?

OSR. I mean, my lord, the opposition of your person in trial.

HAM. Sir, I will walk here in the hall. If it please his Majesty, it is the breathing time
145 of day with me. Let the foils be brought, the gentleman willing, and the King hold his
purpose, I will win for him and I can; if not, I will gain nothing but my shame and
the odd hits.

OSR. Shall I deliver you so?

HAM. To this effect, sir—after what flourish your nature will.

150 OSR. I commend my duty to your lordship.

HAM. Yours. *[Exit Osric.]* ['A] does well to commend it himself, there are no tongues
else for 's turn.

HOR. This lapwing runs away with the shell on his head.

HAM. 'A did [comply], sir, with his dug before 'a suck'd it. Thus has he, and many more
155 of the same breed that I know the drossy age dotes on, only got the tune of the time,
and out of an habit of encounter, a kind of [yesty] collection, which carries them

---

129 **impawn'd:** staked.   **assigns:** appurtenances.

130 **hangers:** straps on which the swords hang from the girdle.   **carriages:** properly, gun carriages;
here used affectedly in place of *hangers*.   **fancy:** taste.

130–31 **very responsive to:** matching well.

131 **liberal conceit:** elegant design.

133 **must . . . margent:** would require enlightenment from a marginal note.

139 **laid:** wagered.

139–40 **he . . . hits.** Laertes must win by at least eight to four (if none of the "passes" or bouts are
draws), since at seven to five he would be only two up.

140 **he . . . nine.** Not satisfactorily explained despite much discussion. One suggestion is that Laertes
has raised the odds against himself by wagering that out of twelve bouts he will win nine.

141 **answer:** encounter (as Hamlet's following quibble forces Osric to explain in his next speech).

144–45 **breathing . . . me:** my usual hour for exercise.

149 **after what flourish:** with whatever embellishment of language.

150 **commend my duty:** offer my dutiful respects (but Hamlet picks up the phrase in the sense "praise
my manner of bowing").

153 **lapwing:** a foolish bird that upon hatching was supposed to run with part of the eggshell still
over its head. (Osric has put his hat on at last.)

154 **comply . . . dug:** bow politely to his mother's nipple.

155 **drossy:** i.e. worthless.   **tune . . . time:** i.e. fashionable ways of talk.

156 **habit of encounter:** mode of social intercourse.   **yesty:** yeasty, frothy.   **collection:** i.e. anthology
of fine phrases.

through and through the most [profound] and [winnow'd] opinions, and do but blow them to their trial, the bubbles are out.

Enter a LORD.

LORD My lord, his Majesty commended him to you by young Osric, who brings back
160   to him that you attend him in the hall. He sends to know if your pleasure hold to play with Laertes, or that you will take longer time.

HAM. I am constant to my purposes, they follow the King's pleasure. If his fitness speaks, mine is ready; now or whensoever, provided I be so able as now.

LORD The King and Queen and all are coming down.
165 HAM. In happy time.

LORD The Queen desires you to use some gentle entertainment to Laertes before you fall to play.

HAM. She well instructs me.

[Exit LORD.]

HOR. You will lose, my lord.
170 HAM. I do not think so; since he went into France I have been in continual practice. I shall win at the odds. Thou wouldst not think how ill all's here about my heart—but it is no matter.

HOR. Nay, good my lord—

HAM. It is but foolery, but it is such a kind of [gain-]giving, as would perhaps trouble a
175   woman.

HOR. If your mind dislike any thing, obey it. I will forestall their repair hither, and say you are not fit.

HAM. Not a whit, we defy augury. There is special providence in the fall of a sparrow. If it be [now], 'tis not to come; if it be not to come, it will be now; if it be not now,
180   yet it [will] come—the readiness is all. Since no man, of aught he leaves, knows what is't to leave betimes, let be.

A table prepar'd, [and flagons of wine on it. Enter] Trumpets, Drums, and OFFICERS *with cushions, foils, daggers;* KING, QUEEN, LAERTES, [OSRIC,] *and all the State.*

KING Come, Hamlet, come, and take this hand from me.

[The KING *puts* LAERTES' *hand into* HAMLET'*s.]*

HAM. Give me your pardon, sir. I have done you wrong,
But pardon't as you are a gentleman.

---

157 **winnow'd:** sifted, choice.   **opinions:** judgments.
157–58 **blow . . . trial:** test them by blowing on them, i.e. make even the least demanding trial of them.
158 **out:** blown away (?) or at an end, done for (?).
162–63 **If . . . ready:** i.e. if this is a good moment for him, it is for me also.
166 **gentle entertainment:** courteous greeting.
174 **gain-giving:** misgiving.
178 **special . . . sparrow.** See Matthew 10:29.
180 **of aught:** i.e. whatever.
180–81 **knows . . . betimes:** knows what is the best time to leave it.
181 s.d. **State:** nobles.

185   This presence knows,
      And you must needs have heard, how I am punish'd
      With a sore distraction. What I have done
      That might your nature, honor, and exception
      Roughly awake, I here proclaim was madness.
190   Was't Hamlet wrong'd Laertes? Never Hamlet!
      If Hamlet from himself be ta'en away,
      And when he's not himself does wrong Laertes,
      Then Hamlet does it not, Hamlet denies it.
      Who does it then? His madness. If 't be so,
195   Hamlet is of the faction that is wronged,
      His madness is poor Hamlet's enemy.
      [Sir, in this audience,]
      Let my disclaiming from a purpos'd evil
      Free me so far in your most generous thoughts,
200   That I have shot my arrow o'er the house
      And hurt my brother.
      LAER.   I am satisfied in nature,
      Whose motive in this case should stir me most
      To my revenge, but in my terms of honor
      I stand aloof, and will no reconcilement
205   Till by some elder masters of known honor
      I have a voice and president of peace
      To [keep] my name ungor'd. But [till] that time
      I do receive your offer'd love like love,
      And will not wrong it.
      HAM.   I embrace it freely,
210   And will this brothers' wager frankly play.
      Give us the foils. [Come on.]
      LAER.   Come, one for me.
      HAM. I'll be your foil, Laertes; in mine ignorance
      Your skill shall like a star i' th' darkest night
      Stick fiery off indeed.
      LAER.   You mock me, sir.
215   HAM. No, by this hand.
      KING Give them the foils, young Osric. Cousin Hamlet,
      You know the wager?

---

185 **presence**: assembled court.
186 **punish'd**: afflicted.
188 **exception**: objection.
198 **my . . . evil**: my declaration that I intended no harm.
199 **Free**: absolve.
201 **in nature**: so far as my personal feelings are concerned.
203 **in . . . honor**: i.e. as a man governed by an established code of honor.
206–07 **have . . . ungor'd**: can secure an opinion backed by precedent that I can make peace with
     you without injury to my reputation.
210 **brothers'**: i.e. amicable, as if between brothers.   **frankly**: freely, without constraint.
212 **foil**: thin sheet of metal placed behind a jewel to set it off.
214 **Stick . . . off**: blaze out in contrast.

HAM.   Very well, my lord.
 Your Grace has laid the odds a' th' weaker side.
KING I do not fear it, I have seen you both;
220 But since he is [better'd], we have therefore odds.
 LAER. This is too heavy; let me see another.
 HAM. This likes me well. These foils have all a length?

[Prepare to play.]

OSR. Ay, my good lord.
KING Set me the stoups of wine upon that table.
225 If Hamlet give the first or second hit,
 Or quit in answer of the third exchange,
 Let all the battlements their ord'nance fire.
 The King shall drink to Hamlet's better breath,
 And in the cup an [union] shall he throw,
230 Richer than that which four successive kings
 In Denmark's crown have worn. Give me the cups,
 And let the kettle to the trumpet speak,
 The trumpet to the cannoneer without,
 The cannons to the heavens, the heaven to earth,
235 "Now the King drinks to Hamlet." Come begin;

Trumpets the while.

 And you, the judges, bear a wary eye.
HAM. Come on, sir.
LAER.   Come, my lord.

[They play and HAMLET *scores a hit.]*

HAM.   One.
LAER.   No.
HAM.   Judgment.

OSR. A hit, a very palpable hit.
LAER.   Well, again.
240 KING Stay, give me drink. Hamlet, this pearl is thine,
 Here's to thy health! Give him the cup.

Drum, trumpets [sound] flourish. A piece goes off [within].

HAM. I'll play this bout first, set it by a while.
 Come. *[They play again.]* Another hit; what say you?
LAER. [A touch, a touch,] I do confess't.

---

218 **laid the odds:** i.e. wagered a higher stake (horses to rapiers).
220 **is better'd:** has perfected his skill. **odds:** i.e. the arrangement that Laertes must take more bouts than Hamlet to win.
222 **likes:** pleases. **a length:** the same length.
224 **stoups:** tankards.
226 **quit . . . exchange:** pays back wins by Laertes in the first and second bouts by taking the third.
229 **union:** an especially fine pearl.
232 **kettle:** kettledrum.

KING Our son shall win.

QUEEN   He's fat, and scant of breath.

245   Here, Hamlet, take my napkin, rub thy brows.

    The Queen carouses to thy fortune, Hamlet.

HAM. Good madam!

KING   Gertrude, do not drink.

QUEEN I will, my lord, I pray you pardon me.

KING *[Aside.]* It is the pois'ned cup, it is too late.

250 HAM. I dare not drink yet, madam; by and by.

QUEEN Come, let me wipe thy face.

LAER. My lord, I'll hit him now.

KING   I do not think't.

LAER. *[Aside.]* And yet it is almost against my conscience.

HAM. Come, for the third, Laertes, you do but dally.

255   I pray you pass with your best violence;

    I am sure you make a wanton of me.

LAER. Say you so? Come on.

[They play.]

OSR. Nothing, neither way.

LAER. Have at you now!

*[*LAERTES *wounds* HAMLET; *then, in scuffling, they change rapiers.]*

KING   Part them, they are incens'd.

HAM. Nay, come again.

*[*HAMLET *wounds* LAERTES. *The* QUEEN *falls.]*

260 OSR.   Look to the Queen there ho!

HOR. They bleed on both sides. How is it, my lord?

OSR. How is't, Laertes?

LAER. Why, as a woodcock to mine own springe, Osric:

    I am justly kill'd with mine own treachery.

HAM. How does the Queen?

265 KING   She sounds to see them bleed.

QUEEN No, no, the drink, the drink—O my dear Hamlet—

    The drink, the drink! I am pois'ned.

[Dies.]

HAM. O villainy! Ho, let the door be lock'd!

    Treachery! Seek it out.

---

244 **fat:** sweaty.

246 **carouses:** drinks a toast.

256 **make . . . me:** i.e. are holding back in order to let me win, as one does with a spoiled child (*wanton*).

263 **springe:** snare.

265 **sounds:** swoons.

270 LAER. It is here, Hamlet. [Hamlet,] thou art slain.
No med'cine in the world can do thee good;
In thee there is not half an hour's life.
The treacherous instrument is in [thy] hand,
Unbated and envenom'd. The foul practice
275 Hath turn'd itself on me. Lo here I lie,
Never to rise again. Thy mother's pois'ned.
I can no more—the King, the King's to blame.
HAM. The point envenom'd too!
Then, venom, to thy work.

[Hurts the KING.]

280 ALL Treason! treason!
KING O, yet defend me, friends, I am but hurt.
HAM. Here, thou incestious, [murd'rous], damned Dane,
Drink [off] this potion! Is [thy union] here?
Follow my mother!

[KING dies.]

LAER.   He is justly served,
285 It is a poison temper'd by himself.
Exchange forgiveness with me, noble Hamlet.
Mine and my father's death come not upon thee,
Nor thine on me!

[Dies.]

HAM. Heaven make thee free of it! I follow thee.
290 I am dead, Horatio. Wretched queen, adieu!
You that look pale, and tremble at this chance,
That are but mutes or audience to this act,
Had I but time—as this fell sergeant, Death,
Is strict in his arrest—O, I could tell you—
295 But let it be. Horatio, I am dead,
Thou livest. Report me and my cause aright
To the unsatisfied.
HOR.   Never believe it;
I am more an antique Roman than a Dane.
Here's yet some liquor left.
HAM.   As th' art a man,
300 Give me the cup. Let go! By heaven, I'll ha't!
O God, Horatio, what a wounded name,
Things standing thus unknown, shall I leave behind me!

---

274 **Unbated:** not blunted.   **foul practice:** vile plot.
279s.d. **Hurts:** wounds.
285 **temper'd:** mixed.
289 **make thee free:** absolve you.
292 **mutes or audience:** silent spectators.
293 **fell:** cruel.   **sergeant:** sheriff 's officer.
298 **antique Roman:** i.e. one who will commit suicide on such an occasion.

If thou didst ever hold me in thy heart,
Absent thee from felicity a while,
305 And in this harsh world draw thy breath in pain
To tell my story.

A march afar off [and a shot within].

What warlike noise is this?

[OSRIC *goes to the door and returns.*]

OSR. Young Fortinbras, with conquest come from Poland,
To th' embassadors of England gives
This warlike volley.
HAM.   O, I die, Horatio,
310 The potent poison quite o'er-crows my spirit.
I cannot live to hear the news from England,
But I do prophesy th' election lights
On Fortinbras, he has my dying voice.
So tell him, with th' occurrents more and less
315 Which have solicited—the rest is silence.

[Dies.]

HOR. Now cracks a noble heart. Good night, sweet prince,
And flights of angels sing thee to thy rest!

[March within.]

Why does the drum come hither?

Enter FORTINBRAS *with the* [ENGLISH] EMBASSADORS, *[with Drum, Colors, and* ATTENDANTS].

FORT. Where is this sight?
HOR.   What is it you would see?
320 If aught of woe or wonder, cease your search.
FORT. This quarry cries on havoc. O proud death,
What feast is toward in thine eternal cell,
That thou so many princes at a shot
So bloodily hast strook?
[1] EMB.   The sight is dismal,
325 And our affairs from England come too late.
The ears are senseless that should give us hearing,
To tell him his commandement is fulfill'd,
That Rosencrantz and Guildenstern are dead.
Where should we have our thanks?

---

310 **o'er-crows**: triumphs over (a term derived from cockfighting).   **spirit**: vital energy.
313 **voice**: vote.
314 **occurrents**: occurrences.
315 **solicited**: instigated.
321 **This . . . havoc**: this heap of corpses proclaims a massacre.
322 **toward**: in preparation.

HOR.   Not from his mouth,
330   Had it th' ability of life to thank you.
        He never gave commandement for their death.
        But since so jump upon this bloody question,
        You from the Polack wars, and you from England,
        Are here arrived, give order that these bodies
335   High on a stage be placed to the view,
        And let me speak to [th'] yet unknowing world
        How these things came about. So shall you hear
        Of carnal, bloody, and unnatural acts,
        Of accidental judgments, casual slaughters,
340   Of deaths put on by cunning and [forc'd] cause,
        And in this upshot, purposes mistook
        Fall'n on th' inventors' heads: all this can I
        Truly deliver.
FORT.   Let us haste to hear it,
        And call the noblest to the audience.
345   For me, with sorrow I embrace my fortune.
        I have some rights, of memory in this kingdom,
        Which now to claim my vantage doth invite me.
HOR.   Of that I shall have also cause to speak,
        And from his mouth whose voice will draw [on] more.
350   But let this same be presently perform'd
        Even while men's minds are wild, lest more mischance
        On plots and errors happen.
FORT.   Let four captains
        Bear Hamlet like a soldier to the stage,
        For he was likely, had he been put on,
355   To have prov'd most royal; and for his passage,
        The soldiers' music and the rite of war
        Speak loudly for him.
        Take up the bodies. Such a sight as this
        Becomes the field, but here shows much amiss.
360   Go bid the soldiers shoot.

        Exeunt [marching; after the which a peal of ordinance are shot off].

---

329 **his:** i.e. the King's.
332 **jump:** precisely, pat.   **question:** matter.
335 **stage:** platform.
339 **judgments:** retributions.   **casual:** happening by chance.
340 **put on:** instigated.
346 **of memory:** unforgotten.
347 **my vantage:** i.e. my opportune presence at a moment when the throne is empty.
349 **his . . . more:** the mouth of one (Hamlet) whose vote will induce others to support your claim.
350 **presently:** at once.
351 **wild:** distraught.
354 **put on:** put to the test (by becoming king).
355 **passage:** death.
359 **Becomes . . . amiss:** befits the battlefield, but appears very much out of place here.

Desire Under the Elms—An American Tragedy

Oedipus and Hamlet are members of the aristocracy. They have the dignity that ancient Greeks and Tudor Englishmen associated with high social position. Their fates concern not only themselves and their loved ones, but entire nations. Watching aristocrats fall from power is especially moving, because aristocrats have farther to fall and because they will take more people down with them than, say, the corner grocer, should he suffer a similar fate. Some critics, Aristotle among them, have suggested that the tragic hero or heroine must be of noble stature. It is a difficult question. Obviously, if a character is already in a state of ruin or squalor, it is not tragic to see him or her ruined further. On the other hand, if the hero is to be considered noble, the audience must agree on what is noble. This was easier two hundred years ago when class structure was clearly defined and everyone knew a member of the nobility by his or her title.

Desire Under the Elms presents three characters with tragic potential: Ephraim Cabot, domineering father of Eben Cabot; the sensitive son Eben, who is plotting to claim title to his deceased mother's property; and the young woman who comes between them, Abbie Putnam. The old man is so powerful he seems more a force of nature than a real person worthy of our sympathies. His son, on the other hand, is too weak for us ever to hope that he might prevail.

So, of the three characters, Abbie comes closest to suffering the fate of heroes and heroines in classic tragedy. Through her own shrewdness and determination she has achieved considerable power in a world that offers little opportunity to an independent woman. She has married the wealthy old widower Ephraim, thus laying claim to his valuable farm and livestock. She is lady and mistress of the house, with considerable power over the men in it. She is not a queen or a duchess, but then there are no titled nobles in America. While Abbie is not the richest woman, or the most highly bred, she has enough to lose so that we know it will hurt her to lose it. If she had more power, American audiences might be glad to see her destroyed, and then there would be no tragedy either. In short, Abbie Putnam is a shrewdly selected figure for our tragic sympathies.

Oedipus Rex and *Hamlet*, whose noble protagonists inspire not only compassion but religious or philosophical awe, are often called "high tragedies." Society having changed so drastically since Shakespeare's time, some critics believe that high tragedy is no longer possible. Northrop Frye, whose comments on the loftiness of tragic heroes were quoted earlier, has this to say about tragedy's place in the history of civilization: "Tragedy belongs chiefly to the two indigenous developments of tragic drama in fifth century Athens and seventeenth century Europe from Shakespeare to Racine. Both belong to a period of social history in which an aristocracy is fast losing its effective power but still retains a good deal of ideological prestige."

The protagonist of *Desire Under the Elms* has never stood at the top of the wheel of fortune, at least not in the glorious manner that those aristocrats, Oedipus and Hamlet, have stood "halfway between human society and something greater in the sky." Abbie Putnam remains a common woman; therefore her struggle and her suffering hold greater human than religious significance. Because she resembles us more closely than do Oedipus and Hamlet, she inspires more pathos, more immediate compassion. We might refer to her story as a domestic tragedy rather than a high tragedy. To create "high tragedy" in the tradition of Sophocles or Shakespeare, a playwright would have to portray a hero more exalted than Abbie Putnam, a character standing somewhere between heaven and earth. Whether or not this remains possible in a civilization wherein aristocracy has lost both prestige and power is still a subject for debate.

Eugene O'Neill—The First American Tragedian

Theater was second nature to Eugene O'Neill. He was born in New York City in 1888, son of the famous actor James O'Neill, who made his fortune playing the hero in *The Count of Monte Cristo*. In his mid-twenties Eugene O'Neill began writing plays and entered the playwriting workshop at Harvard University. There he studied with the great drama theorist George Pierce Baker. Baker was teaching his budding playwrights to create "realistic" stageplays with classic proportions. Young O'Neill came to Harvard with a firm grounding in the work of the ancient playwrights and a deep sympathy with the more pessimistic voices of European philosophy, the violent ethics of Nietzsche and the social Darwinism of Herbert Spencer.

The result of all this, and Baker's workshop, was a very original sort of American stageplay. O'Neill was heralded as the first American realist after his plays *Beyond the Horizon* (1920) and *Anna Christie* (1921) won Pulitzer Prizes. But in fact his greatest works before 1950, including *Desire Under the Elms* (1924), may more accurately be described as "expressionist." That is, the characters are a little larger than life, the dramatic situations extreme, though the skillful playwright mostly keeps them from degenerating into melodrama. Ephraim Cabot is a perfect example of an "expressionist" character: he can out-work, out-dance, out-talk, and outlive any other man in New England. Abbie Putnam, as well, challenges the laws of dramatic probability: her passion for Ephraim's son Eben leads her to commit an act so unnatural we can only accept it within the expressionistic world O'Neill has established.

This play is, of course, just as realistic as any number of classical tragedies from *Oedipus Rex* to the *Hippolytus* of Euripides. The plot for *Desire Under the Elms* actually comes from the *Hippolytus*, in which Theseus's wife Phaedra falls in love with Theseus's son. Eugene O'Neill was determined to create an American tragedy along classic lines. In 1931 he produced a play based upon Aeschelus's *Oresteia* called *Mourning Becomes Electra*.

Now O'Neill is remembered chiefly for his two masterpieces *Long Day's Journey Into Night* and *Moon for the Misbegotten*, autobiographical dramas, heartbreaking and purely realistic. He would not permit them to be performed until after his death in 1953.

EUGENE O'NEILL (1888–1953)

Desire Under the Elms

CHARACTERS

EPHRAIM CABOT

SIMEON
PETER } *his sons*
EBEN

ABBIE PUTNAM

YOUNG GIRL, TWO FARMERS, THE FIDDLER, THE SHERIFF, OTHER FOLK *from the neighboring farms*

The action of the entire play takes place in, and immediately outside of, the CABOT *farmhouse in New England, in the year 1850. The south end of the house faces front to a stone wall with a wooden gate at center opening on a country road. The house is in good condition but in need of paint. Its walls are a sickly grayish, the green of the shutters faded. Two enormous elms are on each side of the house. They bend their trailing branches down over the roof. They appear to protect and at the same time subdue. There is a sinister maternity in their aspect, a crushing, jealous absorption. They have developed from their intimate contact with the life of man in the house an appalling humaneness. They brood oppressively over the house. They are like exhausted women resting their sagging breasts and hands and hair on its roof, and when it rains their tears trickle down monotonously and rot on the shingles.*

There is a path running from the gate around the right corner of the house to the front door. A narrow porch is on this side. The end wall facing us has two windows in its upper story, two larger ones on the floor below. The two upper are those of the father's bedroom and that of the brothers. On the left, ground floor, is the kitchen—on the right, the parlor, the shades of which are always drawn down.

PART I

SCENE 1.

Exterior of the farmhouse. It is sunset of a day at the beginning of summer in the year 1850. There is no wind and everything is still. The sky above the roof is suffused with deep colors, the green of the elms glows, but the house is in shadow, seeming pale and washed out by contrast.

A door opens and EBEN CABOT *comes to the end of the porch and stands looking down the road to the right. He has a large bell in his hand and this he swings mechanically, awakening a deafening clangor. Then he puts his hands on his hips and stares up at the sky. He sighs with a puzzled awe and blurts out with halting appreciation.*

EBEN God! Purty! (*His eyes fall and he stares about him frowningly. He is twenty-five, tall and sinewy. His face is well-formed, good-looking, but its expression is resentful and defensive. His defiant, dark eyes remind one of a wild animal's in captivity. Each day is a cage in which he finds himself trapped but inwardly unsubdued. There is a fierce repressed vitality about him. He has black hair, mustache, a thin curly trace of beard. He is dressed in rough farm clothes.*

He spits on the ground with intense disgust, turns and goes back into the house.

SIMEON *and* PETER *come in from their work in the fields. They are tall men, much older than their half-brother [*SIMEON *is thirty-nine and* PETER *thirty-seven], built on a squarer, simpler model, fleshier in body, more bovine and homelier in face, shrewder* *and more practical. Their shoulders stoop a bit from years of farm work. They clump heavily along in their clumsy thick-soled boots caked with earth. Their clothes, their faces, hands, bare arms and throats are earth-stained. They smell of earth. They stand together for a moment in front of the house and, as if with the one impulse, stare dumbly up at the sky, leaning on their hoes. Their faces have a compressed, unresigned expression. As they look upward, this softens.)*

SIMEON (*grudgingly*) Purty.

PETER Ay-eh.

SIMEON (*suddenly*) Eighteen year ago.

PETER What?

SIMEON Jenn. My woman. She died.

PETER I'd fergot.

SIMEON I rec'lect—now an' agin. Makes it lonesome. She'd hair long's a hoss' tail—an' yaller like gold!

PETER Waal—she's gone. (*This with indifferent finality—then after a pause*) They's gold in the West, Sim.

SIMEON (*still under the influence of sunset—vaguely*) In the sky?

PETER Waal—in a manner o' speakin'—thar's the promise. (*growing excited*) Gold in the sky—in the West—Golden Gate—Californi-a!—Goldest West!—fields o' gold!

SIMEON (*excited in his turn*) Fortunes layin' just atop o' the ground waitin' t' be picked! Solomon's mines, they says! (*For a moment they continue looking up at the sky—then their eyes drop.*)

PETER (*with sardonic bitterness*) Here's—it's stones atop o' the ground—stones atop o' stones—makin' stone walls—year atop o' year—him 'n' yew 'n' me 'n' then Eben—makin' stone walls fur him to fence us in!

SIMEON We've wuked. Give our strength. Give our years. Plowed 'em under in the ground—(*he stamps rebelliously*)—rottin'—makin' soil for his crops! (*a pause*) Waal—the farm pays good for hereabouts.

PETER If we plowed in Californi-a, they'd be lumps o' gold in the furrow!

SIMEON Californi-a's t'other side o' earth, a'most. We got t' calc'late—

PETER (*after a pause*) 'Twould be hard fur me, too, to give up what we've 'arned here by our sweat. (*A pause, EBEN sticks his head out of the dining-room window, listening.*)

SIMEON Ay-eh. (*a pause*) Mebbe—he'll die soon.

PETER (*doubtfully*) Mebbe.

SIMEON Mebbe—fur all we knows—he's dead now.

PETER Ye'd need proof.

SIMEON He's been gone two months—with no word.

PETER Left us in the fields an' evenin' like this. Hitched up an' druv off into the West. That's plum onnateral. He hain't never been off this farm 'ceptin' t' the village in thirty year or more, not since he married Eben's maw. (*A pause. Shrewdly*) I calc'late we might git him declared crazy by the court.

SIMEON He skinnned 'em too slick. He got the best o' all on 'em. They'd never b'lieve him crazy. (*a pause*) We got t' wait—till he's under ground.

EBEN (*with a sardonic chuckle*) Honor thy father! (*They turn, startled, and stare at him. He grins, then scowls.*) I pray he's died. (*They stare at him. He continues matter-of-factly*) Supper's ready.

SIMEON *and* PETER (*together*) Ay-eh.

EBEN (*gazing up at the sky*) Sun's downin' purty.

SIMEON *and* PETER (*together*) Ay'eh. They's gold in the West.

EBEN Ay-eh. (*pointing*) Yonder atop o' the hill pasture, ye mean?

SIMEON *and* PETER (together) In Californi-a!

EBEN Hunh? (*Stares at them indifferently for a second, then drawls*) Waal—supper's gittin' cold. (*He turns back into kitchen.*)

SIMEON (*startled—smacks his lips*) I air hungry!

PETER (*sniffing*) I smells bacon!

SIMEON (*with hungry appreciation*) Bacon's good!

PETER (*in same tone*) Bacon's bacon! (*They turn, shouldering each other, their bodies bumping and rubbing together as they hurry clumsily to their food, like two friendly oxen toward their evening meal. They disappear around the right corner of house and can be heard entering the door.*)

SCENE 2.

The color fades from the sky. Twilight begins. The interior of the kitchen is now visible. A pine table is at center, a cookstove in the right rear corner, four rough wooden chairs, a tallow candle on the table. In the middle of the rear wall is fastened a big advertising poster with a ship in full sail and the word "California" in big letters. Kitchen utensils hang from nails. Everything is neat and in order but the atmosphere is of a men's camp kitchen rather than that of a home.

Places for three are laid. EBEN *takes boiled potatoes and bacon from the stove and puts them on the table, also a loaf of bread and a crock of water.* SIMEON *and* PETER *shoulder in, slump down in their chairs without a word.* EBEN *joins them. The three eat in silence for a moment, the two elder as naturally unrestrained as beasts of the field,* EBEN *picking at his food without appetite, glancing at them with a tolerant dislike.*

SIMEON (*suddenly turns to* EBEN) Looky here! Ye'd oughtn't t' said that, Eben.

PETER 'Twa'n't righteous.

EBEN What?

SIMEON Ye prayed he'd died.

EBEN Waal—don't yew pray it? (*a pause*)

PETER He's our Paw.

EBEN (*violently*) Not mine!

SIMEON (*dryly*) Ye'd not let no one else say that about yer Maw! Ha! (*He gives one abrupt sardonic guffaw.* PETER *grins.*)

EBEN (*very pale*) I meant—I hain't his'n—I hain't like him—he hain't me!

PETER (*dryly*) Wait till ye've growed his age!

EBEN (*intensely*) I'm Maw—every drop o' blood! (*A pause. They stare at him with indifferent curiosity.*)

PETER (*reminiscently*) She was good t' Sim 'n' me. A good stepmaw's scurse.

SIMEON She was good t' everyone.

EBEN (*greatly moved, gets to his feet and makes an awkward bow to each of them—stammering*) I be thankful t' ye. I'm her—her heir. (*He sits down in confusion.*)

PETER (*after a pause—judicially*) She was good even t' him.

EBEN (*fiercely*) An' fur thanks he killed her!

SIMEON (*after a pause*) No one never kills nobody. It's allus somethin'. That's the murderer.

EBEN Didn't he slave Maw t' death?

PETER He's slaved himself t' death. He's slaved Sim 'n' me 'n' yew t' death—on'y none o' us hain't died—yit.

SIMEON It's somethin'—drivin' him—t' drive us!

EBEN (*vengefully*) Waal—I hold him t' jedgment! (*then scornfully*) Somethin'! What's somethin'?

SIMEON Dunno.

EBEN (*sardonically*) What's drivin' yew to Californi-a, mebbe? (*They look at him in surprise.*) Oh, I've heerd ye! (*then, after a pause*) But ye'll never go t' the gold fields!

PETER (*assertively*) Mebbe!

EBEN Whar'll ye git the money?

PETER We kin walk. It's an a'mighty ways—Californi-a—but if yew was t' put all the steps we've walked on this farm end t' end we'd be in the moon!

EBEN The Injuns'll skulp ye on the plains.

SIMEON (*with grim humor*) We'll mebbe make 'em pay a hair fur a hair!

EBEN (*decisively*) But t'ain't that. Ye won't never go because ye'll wait here fur yer share o' the farm, thinkin' allus he'll die soon.

SIMEON (*after a pause*) We've a right.

PETER Two-thirds belongs t' us.

EBEN (*jumping to his feet*) Ye've no right! She wa'n't yewr Maw! It was her farm! Didn't he steal it from her? She's dead. It's my farm.

SIMEON (*sardonically*) Tell that t' Paw—when he comes! I'll bet ye a dollar he'll laugh—fur once in his life. Ha! (*He laughs himself in one single mirthless bark.*)

PETER (*amused in turn, echoes his brother*) Ha!

SIMEON (*after a pause*) What've ye got held agin us, Eben? Year arter year it's skulked in yer eye—somethin'.

PETER Ay-eh.

EBEN Ay-eh. They's somethin'. (*suddenly exploding*) Why didn't ye never stand between him 'n' my maw when he was slavin' her to her grave—t' pay her back fur the kindness she done t' yew? (*There is a long pause. They stare at him in surprise.*)

SIMEON Waal—the stock'd got t' be watered.

PETER 'R they was woodin' t' do.

SIMEON 'R plowin'.

PETER 'R hayin'.

SIMEON 'R spreadin' manure.

PETER 'R weedin'.

SIMEON 'R prunin'.

PETER 'R milkin'.

EBEN (*breaking in harshly*) An' makin' walls—stone atop o' stone—makin' walls till yer heart's a stone ye heft up out o' the way o' growth onto a stone wall t' wall in yer heart!

SIMEON (*matter-of-factly*) We never had no time t' meddle.

PETER (*to* EBEN) Yew was fifteen afore yer Maw died—an' big fur yer age. Why didn't ye never do nothin'?

EBEN (*harshly*) They was chores t' do, wa'n't they? (*a pause—then slowly*) It was on'y arter she died I come to think o' it. Me cookin'—doin' her work—that made me know her, suffer her sufferin'—she'd come back t' help—come back t' bile potatoes—come back t' fry bacon—come back t' bake biscuits—come back all cramped up t' shake the fire, an' carry ashes, her eyes weepin' an' bloody with smoke an' cinders same's they used t' be. She still comes back—stands by the stove thar in the evenin'—she can't find it nateral sleepin' an' restin' in peace. She can't git used t' bein' free—even in her grave.

SIMEON She never complained none.

EBEN She'd got too tired. She'd got too used t' bein' too tired. That was what he done.

(*with vengeful passion*) An' sooner'r later, I'll meddle. I'll say the thin's I didn't say then t' him! I'll yell 'em at the top o' my lungs. I'll see t' it my Maw gits some rest an' sleep in her grave! (*He sits down again, relapsing into a brooding silence. They look at him with a queer indifferent curiosity.*)

PETER (*after a pause*) Whar in tarnation d'ye s'pose he went, Sim?

SIMEON Dunno. He druv off in the buggy, all spick an' span, with the mare all breshed an' shiny, druv off clackin' his tongue an' wavin' his whip. I remember it right well. I was finishin' plowin', it was spring an' May an' sunset, an' gold in the West, an' he druv off into it. I yells "Whar ye goin', Paw?" an' he hauls up by the stone wall a jiffy. His old snake's eyes was glitterin' in the sun like he'd been drinkin' a jugful an' he says with a mule's grin: "Don't ye run away till I come back!"

PETER Wonder if he knowed we was wantin' fur Californi-a?

SIMEON Mebbe. I didn't say nothin' and he says, lookin' kinder queer an' sick: "I been hearin' the hens cluckin' an' the roosters crowin' all the durn day. I been listenin' t' the cows lowin' an' everythin' else kickin' up till I can't stand it no more. It's spring an' I'm feelin' damned," he says. "Damned like an old bare hickory tree fit on'y fur burnin'," he says. An' then I calc'late I must've looked a mite hopeful, fur he adds real spry and vicious: "But don't git no fool idee I'm dead. I've sworn t' live a hundred an' I'll do it, if on'y t' spite yer sinful greed! An' now I'm ridin' out t' learn God's message t' me in the spring, like the prophets done. An' yew git back t' yer plowin'," he says. An' he druv off singin' a hymn. I thought he was drunk—'r I'd stopped him goin'.

EBEN (*scornfully*) No, ye wouldn't! Ye're scared o' him. He's stronger—inside—than both o' ye put together!

PETER (*sardonically*) An' yew—be yew Samson?

EBEN I'm gittin' stronger. I kin feel it growin' in me—growin' an' growin'—till it'll bust out—! (*He gets up and puts on his coat and a hat. They watch him, gradually breaking into grins. EBEN avoids their eyes sheepishly.*) I'm goin' out fur a spell—up the road.

PETER T' the village?

SIMEON T' see Minnie?

EBEN (*defiantly*) Ay-eh!

PETER (*jeeringly*) The Scarlet Woman!

SIMEON Lust—that's what's growin' in ye!

EBEN Waal—she's purty!

PETER She's been purty fur twenty year!

SIMEON A new coat o' paint'll make a heifer out of forty.

EBEN She hain't forty!

PETER If she hain't, she's teeterin' on the edge.

EBEN (*desperately*) What d'yew know—

PETER All they is . . . Sim knew her—an' then me arter—

SIMEON An' Paw kin tell yew somethin' too! He was fust!

EBEN D'ye mean t' say he . . . ?

SIMEON (*with a grin*) Ay-eh! We air his heirs in everythin'!

EBEN (*intensely*) That's more to it! That grows on it! It'll bust soon! (*then violently*) I'll go smash my fist in her face! (*He pulls open the door in rear violently.*)

SIMEON (*with a wink at* PETER—*drawlingly*) Mebbe—but the night's wa'm—purty—by the time ye git thar mebbe ye'll kiss her instead!

PETER Sart'n he will! (*They both roar with coarse laughter. EBEN rushes out and slams the door—then the outside front door—comes around the corner of the house and stands still by the gate, staring up at the sky.*)

SIMEON (*looking after him*) Like his Paw.

PETER Dead spit an' image!

SIMEON Dog'll eat dog!

PETER Ay-eh. (*Pause. With yearning*) Mebbe a year from now we'll be in Californi-a.

SIMEON Ay-eh. (*A pause. Both yawn.*) Let's git t' bed. (*He blows out the candle. They go out door in rear.* EBEN *stretches his arms up to the sky—rebelliously.*)

EBEN Waal—thar's a star, an' somewhar's they's him, an' here's me, an' thar's Min up the road—in the same night. What if I does kiss her? She's like t'night, she's soft 'n' wa'm, her eyes kin wink like a star, her mouth's wa'm, her arms're wa'm, she smells like a wa'm plowed field, she's purty . . . Ay-eh! By God A'mighty she's purty, an' I don't give a damn how many sins she's sinned afore mine or who she's sinned 'em with, my sin's as purty as any one on 'em! (*He strides off down the road to the left.*)

SCENE 3.

It is the pitch darkness just before dawn. EBEN *comes in from the left and goes around to the porch, feeling his way, chuckling bitterly and cursing half-aloud to himself.*

EBEN The cussed old miser! (*He can be heard going in the front door. There is a pause as he goes upstairs, then a loud knock on the bedroom door of the brothers.*) Wake up!

SIMEON (*startedly*) Who's thar?

EBEN (*pushing open the door and coming in, a lighted candle in his hand. The bedroom of the brothers is revealed. Its ceiling is the sloping roof. They can stand upright only close to the center dividing wall of the upstairs.* SIMEON *and* PETER *are in a double bed, front.* EBEN'S *cot is to the rear.* EBEN *has a mixture of silly grin and vicious scowl on his face*) I be!

PETER (*angrily*) What in hell's-fire . . . ?

EBEN I got news fur ye! Ha! (*He gives one abrupt sardonic guffaw.*)

SIMEON (*angrily*) Couldn't ye hold it 'til we'd got our sleep?

EBEN It's nigh sunup. (*then explosively*) He's gone an' married agen!

SIMEON *and* PETER (*explosively*) Paw?

EBEN Got himself hitched to a female 'bout thirty-five—an' purty, they says . . .

SIMEON (*aghast*) It's a durn lie!

PETER Who says?

SIMEON They been stringin' ye!

EBEN Think I'm a dunce, do ye? The hull village says. The preacher from New Dover, he brung the news—told it t' our preacher—New Dover, that's whar the old loon got himself hitched—that's whar the woman lived—

PETER (*no longer doubting—stunned*) Waal . . . !

SIMEON (*the same*) Waal . . . !

EBEN (*sitting down on a bed—with vicious hatred*) Ain't he a devil out o' hell? It's jest t' spite us—the damned old mule!

PETER (*after a pause*) Everythin'll go t' her now.

SIMEON Ay-eh. (*A pause—dully*) Waal—if it's done—

PETER It's done us. (*pause—then persuasively*) They's gold in the fields o' Californi-a, Sim. No good a-stayin' here now.

SIMEON Jest what I was a-thinkin'. (*then with decision*) S'well fust's last! Let's light out and git this mornin'.

PETER Suits me.

EBEN Ye must like walkin'.

SIMEON (*sardonically*) If ye'd grow wings on us we'd fly thar!

EBEN Ye'd like ridin' better—on a boat, wouldn't ye? (*Fumbles in his pocket and takes out a crumpled sheet of foolscap.*) Waal, if ye sign this ye kin ride on a boat. I've had it writ out an' 'ready in case ye'd ever go. It says fur three hundred dollars t' each ye agree yewr shares o' the farm is sold t' me. (*They look suspiciously at the paper. A pause.*)

SIMEON (*wonderingly*) But if he's hitched agen—

PETER An' whar'd yew git that sum o' money, anyways?

EBEN (*cunningly*) I know whar it's hid. I been waitin'—Maw told me. She knew whar it lay fur years, but she was waitin' . . . It's her'n—the money he hoarded from her farm an' hid from Maw. It's my money by rights now.

PETER Whar's it hid?

EBEN (*cunningly*) Whar yew won't never find it without me. Maw spied on him—'r she'd never knowed. (*A pause. They look at him suspiciously, and he at them.*) Waal, is it fa'r trade?

SIMEON Dunno.

PETER Dunno.

SIMEON (*looking at window*) Sky's grayin'.

PETER Ye better start the fire, Eben.

SIMEON An' fix some vittles.

EBEN Ay-eh. (*Then with a forced jocular heartiness*) I'll git ye a good one. If ye're startin' t' hoof it t' Californi-a ye'll need somethin' that'll stick t' yer ribs. (*He turns to the door, adding meaningly*) But ye kin ride on a boat if ye'll swap. (*He stops at the door and pauses. They stare at him.*)

SIMEON (*suspiciously*) Whar was ye all night?

EBEN (*defiantly*) Up t' Min's. (*then slowly*) Walkin' thar, fust I felt 's if I'd kiss her; then I got a-thinkin' o' what ye'd said o' him an' her an' I says, I'll bust her nose fur that! Then I got t' the village an' heerd the news an' I got madder'n hell an' run all the way t' Min's not knowin' what I'd do—(*He pauses—then sheepishly but more defiantly*) Waal—when I seen her, I didn't hit her—nor I didn't kiss her nuther—I begun t' beller like a calf an' cuss at the same time, I was so durn mad—an' she got scared—an' I jest grabbed holt an' tuk her! (*Proudly*) Yes, sirree! I tuk her. She may've been his'n—an' your'n, too—but she's mine now!

SIMEON (*dryly*) In love, air yew?

EBEN (*with lofty scorn*) Love! I don't take no stock in sech slop!

PETER (*winking at* SIMEON) Mebbe Eben's aimin' t' marry, too.

SIMEON Min'd make a true faithful he'pmeet! (*They snicker.*)

EBEN What do I care fur her—'ceptin' she's round an' wa'm? The p'int is she was his'n—an' now she belongs t' me! (*He goes to the door—then turns—rebelliously.*) An' Min hain't sech a bad un. They's worse'n Min in the world, I'll bet ye! Wait'll we see this cow the Old Man's hitched t'! She'll beat Min, I got a notion! (*He starts to go out.*)

SIMEON (*suddenly*) Mebbe ye'll try t' make her your'n, too?

PETER Ha! (*He gives a sardonic laugh of relish at this idea.*)

EBEN (*spitting with disgust*) Her—here—sleepin' with him—stealin' my Maw's farm! I'd as soon pet a skunk 'r kiss a snake! (*He goes out. The two stare after him suspiciously. A pause. They listen to his steps receding.*)

PETER He's startin' the fire.

SIMEON I'd like t' ride t' Californi-a—but—

PETER Min might o' put some scheme in his head.

SIMEON Mebbe it's all a lie 'bout Paw marryin'. We'd best wait an' see the bride.

PETER An' don't sign nothin' till we does!

SIMEON Nor till we've tested it's good money! (*then with a grin*) But if Paw's hitched we'd be sellin' Eben somethin' we'd never git nohow!

PETER We'll wait an' see. (*then with sudden vindictive anger*) An' till he comes, let's yew 'n' me not wuk a lick, let Eben tend to thin's if he's a mind t', let's us jest sleep an' eat an' drink likker, an' let the hull damned farm go t' blazes!

SIMEON (*excitedly*) By God, we've 'arned a rest! We'll play rich fur a change. I hain't a-going to stir outa bed till breakfast's ready.

PETER An' on the table!

SIMEON (*after a pause—thoughtfully*) What d'ye calc'late she'll be like—our new Maw? Like Eben thinks?

PETER More'n likely.

SIMEON (*vindictively*) Waal—I hope she's a she-devil that'll make him wish he was dead an' livin' in the pit o' hell fur comfort!

PETER (*fervently*) Amen!

SIMEON (*imitating his father's voice*) "I'm ridin' out t' learn God's message t' me in the spring like the prophets done," he says. I'll bet right then an' thar he knew plumb well he was goin' whorin', the stinkin' old hypocrite!

SCENE 4.

Same as SCENE 2—*shows the interior of the kitchen with a lighted candle on table. It is gray dawn outside.* SIMEON *and* PETER *are just finishing their breakfast.* EBEN *sits before his plate of untouched food, brooding frowningly.*

PETER (*glancing at him rather irritably*) Lookin' glum don't help none.

SIMEON (*sarcastically*) Sorrowin' over his lust o' the flesh!

PETER (*with a grin*) Was she yer fust?

EBEN (*angrily*) None o' yer business. (*a pause*) I was thinkin' o' him. I got a notion he's gittin' near—I kin feel him comin' on like yew kin feel malaria chill afore it takes ye.

PETER It's too early yet.

SIMEON Dunno. He'd like t' catch us nappin'—jest t' have somethin' t' hoss us 'round over.

PETER (*mechanically gets to his feet.* SIMEON *does the same*) Waal—let's git t' wuk. (*They both plod mechanically toward the door before they realize. Then they stop short.*)

SIMEON (*grinning*) Ye're a cussed fool, Pete—and I be wuss! Let him see we hain't wukin'! We don't give a durn!

PETER (*as they go back to the table*) Not a damned durn! It'll serve t' show him we're done with him. (*They sit down again.* EBEN *stares from one to the other with surprise.*)

SIMEON (*grins at him*) We're aimin' t' start bein' lilies o' the field.

PETER Nary a toil 'r spin 'r lick o' wuk do we put in!

SIMEON Ye're sole owner—till he comes—that's what ye wanted. Waal, ye got t' be sole hand, too.

PETER The cows air bellerin'. Ye better hustle at the milkin'.

EBEN (*with excited joy*) Ye mean ye'll sign the paper?

SIMEON (*dryly*) Mebbe.

PETER Mebbe.

SIMEON We're considerin'. (*peremptorily*) Ye better git t' wuk.

EBEN (*with queer excitement*) It's Maw's farm agen! It's my farm! Them's my cows! I'll milk my durn fingers off fur cows o' mine! (*He goes out door in rear, they stare after him indifferently.*)

SIMEON Like his Paw.

PETER Dead spit 'n' image!

SIMEON Waal—let dog eat dog! (EBEN *comes out of front door and around the corner of the house. The sky is beginning to grow flushed with sunrise.* EBEN *stops by the gate and stares around him with glowing, possessive eyes. He takes in the whole farm with his embracing glance of desire.*)

EBEN It's purty! It's damned purty! It's mine! (*He suddenly throws his head back boldly and glares with hard, defiant eyes at the sky.*) Mine, d'ye hear? Mine! (*He turns and walks quickly off left, rear, toward the barn. The two brothers light their pipes.*)

SIMEON (*putting his muddy boots up on the table, tilting back his chair, and puffing defiantly*) Waal—this air solid comfort—fur once.

PETER Ay-eh. (*He follows suit. A pause. Unconsciously they both sigh.*)

SIMEON (*suddenly*) He never was much o' a hand at milkin', Eben wa'n't.

PETER (*with a snort*) His hands air like hoofs! (*a pause*)

SIMEON Reach down the jug thar! Let's take a swaller. I'm feelin' kind o' low.

PETER Good idee! (*He does so—gets two glasses—they pour out drinks of whisky.*) Here's t' the gold in Californi-a!

SIMEON An' luck t' find it! (*They drink—puff resolutely—sigh—take their feet down from the table.*)

PETER Likker don't pear t' sot right.

SIMEON We hain't used t' it this early. (*A pause. They become very restless.*)

PETER Gittin' close in this kitchen.

SIMEON (*with immense relief*) Let's git a breath o' air. (*They arise briskly and go out rear—appear around house and stop by the gate. They stare up at the sky with a numbed appreciation.*)

PETER Purty!

SIMEON Ay-eh. Gold's t' the East now.

PETER Sun's startin' with us fur the Golden West.

SIMEON (*staring around the farm, his compressed face tightened, unable to conceal his emotion*) Waal—it's our last mornin'—mebbe.

PETER (*the same*) Ay-eh.

SIMEON (*stamps his foot on the earth and addresses it desperately*) Waal—ye've thirty year o' me buried in ye—spread out over ye—blood an' bone an' sweat—rotted away—fertilizin' ye—richin' yer soul—prime manure, by God, that's what I been t' ye!

PETER Ay-eh! An' me!

SIMEON An' yew, Peter. (*He sighs—then spits.*) Waal—no use'n cryin' over spilt milk.

PETER They's gold in the West—an' freedom, mebbe. We been slaves t' stone walls here.

SIMEON (*defiantly*) We hain't nobody's slaves from this out—nor nothin's slaves nuther. (*a pause—restlessly*) Speakin' o' milk, wonder how Eben's managin'?

PETER I s'pose he's managin'.

SIMEON Mebbe we'd ought t' help—this once.

PETER Mebbe. The cows knows us.

SIMEON An' likes us. They don't know him much.

PETER An' the hosses, an' pigs, an' chickens. They don't know him much.

SIMEON They knows us like brothers—an' likes us! (*proudly*) Hain't we raised 'em t' be fust-rate, number one prize stock?

PETER We hain't—not no more.

SIMEON (*dully*) I was fergittin'. (*then resignedly*) Waal, let's go help Eben a spell an' git waked up.

PETER Suits me. (*They are starting off down left, rear, for the barn when* EBEN *appears from there hurrying toward them, his face excited.*)

EBEN (*breathlessly*) Waal—har they be! The old mule an' the bride! I seen 'em from the barn down below at the turnin'.

PETER How could ye tell that far?

EBEN Hain't I as far-sight as he's near-sight? Don't I know the mare 'n' buggy, an' two people settin' in it? Who else . . . ? An' I tell ye I kin feel 'em a'comin', too! (*He squirms as if he had the itch.*)

PETER (*beginning to be angry*) Waal—let him do his own unhitchin'!

SIMEON (*angry in his turn*) Let's hustle in an' git our bundles an be a-goin' as he's a-comin'. I don't want never t' step inside the door agen arter he's back. (*They both start back around the corner of the house.* EBEN *follows them.*)

EBEN (*anxiously*) Will ye sign it afore ye go?

PETER Let's see the color o' the old skinflint's money an' we'll sign. (*They disappear left. The two brothers clump upstairs to get their bundles.* EBEN *appears in the kitchen, runs to the window, peers out, comes back and pulls up a strip of flooring in under stove, takes out a canvas bag and puts it on table, then sets the floorboard back in place. The two brothers appear a moment after. They carry old carpet bags.*)

EBEN (*puts his hand on bag guardingly*) Have ye signed?

SIMEON (*shows paper in his hand*) Ay-eh. (*greedily*) Be that the money?

EBEN (*opens bag and pours out pile of twenty-dollar gold pieces*) Twenty-dollar pieces—thirty on 'em. Count 'em. (PETER *does so, arranging them in stacks of five, biting one or two to test them.*)

PETER Six hundred. (*He puts them in bag and puts it inside his shirt carefully.*)

SIMEON (*handing paper to* EBEN) Har ye be.

EBEN (*after a glance, folds it carefully and hides it under his shirt—gratefully*) Thank yew.

PETER Thank yew fur the ride.

SIMEON We'll send ye a lump o' gold fur Christmas. (*A pause.* EBEN *stares at them and they at him.*)

PETER (*awkwardly*) Waal—we're a-goin'.

SIMEON Comin' out t' the yard?

EBEN No. I'm waiting' in here a spell. (*Another silence. The brothers edge awkwardly to door in rear—then turn and stand.*)

SIMEON Waal—good-by.

PETER Good-by.

EBEN Good-by. (*They go out. He sits down at the table, faces the stove and pulls out the paper. He looks from it to the stove. His face, lighted up by the shaft of sunlight from the window, has an expression of trance. His lips move. The two brothers come out to the gate.*)

PETER (*looking off toward barn*) Thar he be—unhitchin'.

SIMEON (*with a chuckle*) I'll bet ye he's riled!

PETER An' thar she be.

SIMEON Let's wait 'n' see what our new Maw looks like.

PETER (*with a grin*) An' give him our partin' cuss!

SIMEON (*grinning*) I feel like raisin' fun. I feel light in my head an' feet.

PETER Me, too. I feel like laffin' till I'd split up the middle.

SIMEON Reckon it's the likker?

PETER No. My feet feel itchin' t' walk an' walk—an' jump high over thin's—an' . . . .

SIMEON Dance? (*a pause*)

PETER (*puzzled*) It's plumb onnateral.

SIMEON (*a light coming over his face*) I calc'late it's 'cause school's out. It's holiday. Fur once we're free!

PETER (*dazedly*) Free?

SIMEON The halter's broke—the harness is busted—the fence bars is down—the stone walls air crumblin' an' tumblin'! We'll be kickin' up an' tearin' away down the road!

PETER (*drawing a deep breath—oratorically*) Anybody that wants this stinkin' old rock-pile of a farm kin hev it. 'Tain't our'n, no sirree!

SIMEON (*takes the gate off its hinges and puts it under his arm*) We harby 'bolishes shet gates an' open gates, an' all gates, by thunder!

PETER We'll take it with us fur luck an' let 'er sail free down some river.

SIMEON (*as a sound of voices comes from left, rear*) Har they comes! (*The two brothers congeal into two stiff, grim-visaged statues. EPHRAIM CABOT and ABBIE PUTNAM come in. CABOT is seventy-five, tall and gaunt, with great, wiry, concentrated power, but stoop-shouldered from toil. His face is as hard as if it were hewn out of a boulder, yet there is a weakness in it, a pretty pride in its own narrow strength. His eyes are small, close together, and extremely near-sighted, blinking continually in the effort to focus on objects, their stare having a straining, ingrowing quality. He is dressed in his dismal black Sunday suit. ABBIE is thirty-five, buxom, full of vitality. Her round face is pretty but marred by its rather gross sensuality. There is strength and obstinacy in her jaw, a hard determination in her eyes, and about her whole personality the same unsettled, untamed, desperate quality which is so apparent in EBEN.*)

CABOT (*as they enter—a queer strangled emotion in his dry cracking voice*) Har we be t' hum, Abbie.

ABBIE (*with lust for the word*) Hum! (*Her eyes gloating on the house without seeming to see the two stiff figures at the gate.*) It's purty—purty! I can't b'lieve it's r'ally mine.

CABOT (*sharply*) Yewr'n? Mine! (*He stares at her penetratingly. She stares back. He adds relentingly.*) Our'n—mebbe! It was lonesome too long. I was growin' old in the spring. A hum's got t' hev a woman.

ABBIE (*her voice taking possession*) A woman's got t' hev a hum!

CABOT (*nodding uncertainly*) Ay-eh. (*then irritably*) Whar be they? Ain't thar nobody about—'r wukin'—'r nothin'?

ABBIE (*sees the brothers. She returns their stare of cold appraising contempt with interest—slowly*) Thar's two men loafin' at the gate an' starin' at me like a couple o' strayed hogs.

CABOT (*straining his eyes*) I kin see 'em—but I can't make out. . . .

SIMEON It's Simeon.

PETER It's Peter.

CABOT (*exploding*) Why hain't ye wukin'?

SIMEON (*dryly*) We're waitin' t' welcome ye hum—yew an' the bride!

CABOT (*confusedly*) Huh? Waal—this be yer new Maw, boys. (*She stares at them and they at her.*)

SIMEON (*turns away and spits contemptuously*) I see her!

PETER (*spits also*) An' I see her!

ABBIE (*with the conqueror's conscious superiority*) I'll go in an' look at *my* house. (*She goes slowly around to porch.*)

SIMEON (*with a snort*) Her house!

PETER (*calls after her*) Ye'll find Eben inside. Ye better not tell him it's *yewr* house.

ABBIE (*mouthing the name*) Eben. (*then quietly*) I'll tell Eben.

CABOT (*with a contemptuous sneer*) Ye needn't heed Eben. Eben's a dumb fool—like his Maw—soft an' simple!

SIMEON (*with his sardonic burst of laughter*) Ha! Eben's a chip o' yew—spit 'n' image— hard 'n' bitter's a hickory tree! Dog'll eat dog. He'll eat ye yet, old man!

CABOT (*commandingly*) Ye git t' wuk!

SIMEON (*as* ABBIE *disappears in house—winks at* PETER *and says tauntingly*) So that thar's our new Maw, be it? Whar in hell did ye dig her up? (*He and* PETER *laugh.*)

PETER Ha! Ye'd better turn her in the pen with the other sows. (*They laugh uproariously, slapping their thighs.*)

CABOT (*so amazed at their effrontery that he stutters in confusion*) Simeon! Peter! What's come over ye? Air ye drunk?

SIMEON We're free, old man—free o' yew an' the hull damned farm! (*They grow more and more hilarious and excited.*)

PETER An' we're startin' out fur the gold fields o' Californi-a!

SIMEON Ye kin take this place an' burn it!

PETER An' bury it—fur all we cares!

SIMEON We're free, old man! (*He cuts a caper.*)

PETER Free! (*He gives a kick in the air.*)

SIMEON (*in a frenzy*) Whoop!

PETER Whoop! (*They do an absurd Indian war dance about the old man who is petrified between rage and the fear that they are insane.*)

SIMEON We're free as Injuns! Lucky we don't sculp ye!

PETER An' burn yer barn an' kill the stock!

SIMEON An' rape yer new woman! Whoop! (*He and* PETER *stop their dance, holding their sides, rocking with wild laughter.*)

CABOT (*edging away*) Lust fur gold—fur the sinful, easy gold o' Californi-a! It's made ye mad!

SIMEON (*tauntingly*) Wouldn't ye like us to send ye back some sinful gold, ye old sinner?

PETER They's gold besides what's in Californi-a! (*He retreats back beyond the vision of the old man and takes the bag of money and flaunts it in the air above his head, laughing.*)

SIMEON And sinfuller, too!

PETER We'll be voyagin' on the sea! Whoop! (*He leaps up and down.*)

SIMEON Livin' free! Whoop! (*He leaps in turn.*)

CABOT (*suddenly roaring with rage*) My cuss on ye!

SIMEON Take our'n in trade fur it! Whoop!

CABOT I'll hev ye both chained up in the asylum!

PETER Ye old skinflint! Good-by!

SIMEON Ye old blood sucker! Good-by!

CABOT Go afore I . . . !

PETER Whoop! (*He picks a stone from the road.* SIMEON *does the same.*)

SIMEON Maw'll be in the parlor.

PETER Ay-eh! One! Two!

CABOT (*frightened*) What air ye . . . ?

PETER Three! (*They both throw, the stones hitting the parlor window with a crash of glass, tearing the shade.*)

SIMEON Whoop!

PETER Whoop!

CABOT (*in a fury now, rushing toward them*) If I kin lay hands on ye—I'll break yer bones fur ye! (*But they beat a capering retreat before him, SIMEON with the gate still under his arm. CABOT comes back, panting with impotent rage. Their voices as they go off take up the song of the gold-seekers to the old tune of "Oh, Susannah!"*)

> "I jumped aboard the Liza ship,
> And traveled on the sea,
> And every time I thought of home
> I wished it wasn't me!
> Oh! Californi-a,
> That's the land fur me!
> I'm off to Californi-a!
> With my wash bowl on my knee."

(*In the meantime, the window of the upper bedroom on right is raised and ABBIE sticks her head out. She looks down at CABOT—with a sigh of relief.*)

ABBIE Waal—that's the last o' them two, hain't it? (*He doesn't answer. Then in possessive tones*) This here's a nice bedroom, Ephraim. It's a r'al nice bed. Is it my room, Ephraim?

CABOT (*grimly—without looking up*) Our'n! (*She cannot control a grimace of aversion and pulls back her head slowly and shuts the window. A sudden horrible thought seems to enter CABOT's head.*) They been up to somethin'! Mebbe—mebbe they've pizened the stock—'r somethin'! (*He almost runs off down toward the barn. A moment later the kitchen door is slowly pushed open and ABBIE enters. For a moment she stands looking at EBEN. He does not notice her at first. Her eyes take him in penetratingly with a calculating appraisal of his strength as against hers. But under this her desire is dimly awakened by his youth and good looks. Suddenly he becomes conscious of her presence and looks up. Their eyes meet. He leaps to his feet, glowering at her speechlessly.*)

ABBIE (*in her most seductive tones which she uses all through this scene*) Be you—Eben? I'm Abbie—(*She laughs.*) I mean, I'm yer new Maw.

EBEN (*viciously*) No, damn ye!

ABBIE (*as if she hadn't heard—with a queer smile*) Yer Paw's spoke a lot o' yew. . . .

EBEN Ha!

ABBIE Ye mustn't mind him. He's an old man. (*A long pause. They stare at each other.*) I don't want t' pretend playin' Maw t' ye, Eben. (*admiringly*) Ye're too big an' too strong fur that. I want t' be frens with ye. Mebbe with me fur a fren ye'd find ye'd like livin' here better. I kin made it easy fur ye with him, mebbe. (*with a scornful sense of power*) I calc'late I kin git him t' do most anythin' fur me.

EBEN (*with bitter scorn*) Ha! (*They stare again, EBEN obscurely moved, physically attracted to her—in forced stilted tones*) Yew kin go t' the devil!

ABBIE (*calmly*) If cussin' me does ye good, cuss all ye've a mind t'. I'm all prepared t' have ye agin me—at fust. I don't blame ye nuther. I'd feel the same at any stranger comin' t' take my Maw's place. (*He shudders. She is watching him carefully.*) Yew must've cared a lot fur yewr Maw, didn't ye? My Maw died afore I'd growed. I don't remember her none. (*A pause.*) But yew won't hate me long, Eben. I'm not the wust in the world—an' yew an' me've got a lot in common. I kin tell that by lookin' at ye. Waal—I've had a hard life, too—oceans o' trouble an' nuthin' but wuk fur reward. I was a orphan early an' had t' wuk fur others in other folks' hums. Then I married an' he turned out a drunken spreer an' so he had to wuk fur others an' me too agen in other folks' hums, an' the baby died, an' my husband got sick an' died too, an' I was glad sayin' now I'm free fur once, on'y I diskivered right away all I was free fur was t' wuk agen in other folks' hums, doin' other folks' wuk till I'd most give up hope o' ever doin' my own wuk in my own hum, an' then your Paw come. . . . (CABOT *appears returning from the barn. He comes to the gate and looks down the road the brothers have gone. A faint strain of their retreating voices is heard: "Oh, Californi-a! That's the place for me." He stands glowering, his fist clenched, his face grim with rage.*)

EBEN (*fighting against his growing attraction and sympathy—harshly*) An' bought yew— like a harlot! (*She is stung and flushes angrily. She has been sincerely moved by the recital of her troubles. He adds furiously*) An' the price he's payin' ye—this farm—was my Maw's, damn ye!—an' mine now!

ABBIE (*with a cool laugh of confidence*) Yewr'n? We'll see 'bout that! (*then strongly*) Waal—what if I did need a hum? What else'd I marry an old man like him fur?

EBEN (*maliciously*) I'll tell him ye said that!

ABBIE (*smiling*) I'll say ye're lyin' a-purpose—an' he'll drive ye off the place!

EBEN Ye devil!

ABBIE (*defying him*) This be my farm—this be my hum—this be my kitchen—!

EBEN (*furiously, as if he were going to attack her*) Shut up, damn ye!

ABBIE (*walks up to him—a queer coarse expression of desire in her face and body— slowly*) An' upstairs—that be my bedroom—an' my bed! (*He stares into her eyes, terribly confused and torn. She adds softly*) I hain't bad nor mean—'ceptin' fur an enemy—but I got t' fight fur what's due me out o' life, if I ever 'spect t' git it. (*Then putting her hand on his arm—seductively*) Let's yew 'n' me be frens, Eben.

EBEN (*stupidly—as if hypnotized*) Ay-eh. (*Then furiously flinging off her arm*) No, ye durned old witch! I hate ye! (*He rushes out the door.*)

ABBIE (*looks after him smiling satisfiedly—then half to herself, mouthing the word*) Eben's nice. (*She looks at the table, proudly.*) I'll wash up my dishes now. (EBEN *appears outside, slamming the door behind him. He comes around corner, stops on seeing his father, and stands staring at him with hate.*)

CABOT (*raising his arms to heaven in the fury he can no longer control*) Lord God o' Hosts, smite the undutiful sons with Thy wust cuss!

EBEN (*breaking in violently*) Yew 'n' yewr God! Allus cussin' folks—allus naggin' 'em!

CABOT (*oblivious to him—summoningly*) God o' the old! God o' the lonesome!

EBEN (*mockingly*) Naggin' His sheep t' sin! T' hell with yewr God! (*Cabot turns. He and* EBEN *glower at each other.*)

CABOT (*harshly*) So it's yew. I might've knowed it. (*shaking his finger threateningly at him*) Blasphemin' fool! (*then quickly*) Why hain't ye t' wuk?

EBEN Why hain't yew? They've went. I can't wuk it all alone.

CABOT (*contemptuously*) Nor noways! I'm wuth ten o' ye yit, old's I be! Ye'll never be more'n half a man! (*then, matter-of-factly*) Waal—let's git t' the barn. (*They go. A last faint note of the "Californi-a" song is heard from the distance.* ABBIE *is washing her dishes.*)

PART II

SCENE 1.

The exterior of the farmhouse, as in PART I—*a hot Sunday afternoon two months later.* ABBIE, *dressed in her best, is discovered sitting in a rocker at the end of the porch. She rocks listlessly, enervated by the heat, staring in front of her with bored, half-closed eyes.*

EBEN *sticks his head out of his bedroom window. He looks around furtively and tries to see—or hear—if anyone is on the porch, but although he has been careful to make no noise,* ABBIE *has sensed his movement. She stops rocking, her face grows animated and eager, she waits attentively.* EBEN *seems to feel her presence, he scowls back his thoughts of her and spits with exaggerated disdain—then withdraws back into the room.* ABBIE *waits, holding her breath as she listens with passionate eagerness for every sound within the house.*

EBEN *comes out. Their eyes meet. His falter, he is confused, he turns away and slams the door resentfully. At this gesture,* ABBIE *laughs tantalizingly, amused but at the same time piqued and irritated. He scowls, strides off the porch to the path and starts to walk past her to the road with a grand swagger of ignoring her existence. He is dressed in his store suit, spruced up, his face shines from soap and water.* ABBIE *leans forward on her chair, her eyes hard and angry now, and, as he passes her, gives a sneering, taunting chuckle.*

EBEN (*stung—turns on her furiously*) What air yew cacklin' 'bout?

ABBIE (*triumphant*) Yew!

EBEN What about me?

ABBIE Ye look all slicked up like a prize bull.

EBEN (*with a sneer*) Waal—ye hain't so durned purty yerself, be ye? (*They stare into each other's eyes, his held by hers in spite of himself, hers glowingly possessive. Their physical attraction becomes a palpable force quivering in the hot air.*)

ABBIE (*softly*) Ye don't mean that, Eben. Ye may think ye mean it, mebbe, but ye don't. Ye can't. It's agin nature, Eben. Ye been fightin' yer nature ever since the day I come—tryin' t' tell yerself I hain't purty t'ye. (*She laughs a low humid laugh without taking her eyes from his. A pause—her body squirms desirously—she murmurs languorously.*) Hain't the sun strong an' hot? Ye kin feel it burnin' into the earth—Nature—makin' thin's grow—bigger 'n' bigger—burnin' inside ye—makin' ye want t' grow—into somethin' else—till ye're jined with it—an' it's your'n—but it owns ye, too—an' makes ye grow bigger—like a tree—like them elums— (*She laughs again softly, holding his eyes. He takes a step toward her, compelled against his will.*) Nature'll beat ye, Eben. Ye might's well own up t' it fust 's last.

EBEN (*trying to break from her spell—confusedly*) If Paw'd hear ye goin' on. . . . (*resentfully*) But ye've made such a damned idjit out o' the old devil . . . ! (ABBIE *laughs.*)

ABBIE Waal—hain't it easier fur yew with him changed softer?

EBEN (*defiantly*) No. I'm fightin' him—fightin' yew—fightin' fur Maw's right t' her hum! (*This breaks her spell for him. He glowers at her.*) An' I'm onto ye. Ye hain't foolin' me a mite. Ye're aimin' t' swaller up everythin' an' make it your'n. Waal, you'll find I'm a heap sight bigger hunk nor yew kin chew! (*He turns from her with a sneer.*)

ABBIE (*trying to regain her ascendancy—seductively*) Eben!

EBEN Leave me be! (*He starts to walk away.*)

ABBIE (*more commandingly*) Eben!

EBEN (*stops—resentfully*) What d'ye want?

ABBIE (*trying to conceal a growing excitement*) Whar air ye goin'?

EBEN (*with malicious nonchalance*) Oh—up the road a spell.

ABBIE T' the village?

EBEN (*airily*) Mebbe.

ABBIE (*excitedly*) T' see that Min, I s'pose?

EBEN Mebbe.

ABBIE (*weakly*) What d'ye want t' waste time on her fur?

EBEN (*revenging himself now—grinning at her*) Ye can't beat Nature, didn't ye say? (*He laughs and again starts to walk away.*)

ABBIE (*bursting out*) An ugly old hake!

EBEN (*with a tantalizing sneer*) She's purtier'n yew be!

ABBIE That every wuthless drunk in the country has. . . .

EBEN (*tauntingly*) Mebbe—but she's better'n yew. She owns up fa'r 'n' squar' t' her doin's.

ABBIE (*furiously*) Don't ye dare compare. . . .

EBEN She don't go sneakin' an' stealin'—what's mine.

ABBIE (*savagely seizing on his weak point*) Your'n? Yew mean—my farm?

EBEN I mean the farm yew sold yerself fur like any other old whore—my farm!

ABBIE (*stung—fiercely*) Ye'll never live t' see the day when even a stinkin' weed on it 'll belong t' ye! (*then in a scream*) Git out o' my sight! Go on t' yer slut—disgracin' yer Paw 'n' me! I'll git yer Paw t' horsewhip ye off the place if I want t'! Ye're only livin' here 'cause I tolerate ye! Git along! I hate the sight o' ye! (*She stops, panting and glaring at him.*)

EBEN (*returning her glance in kind*) An' I hate the sight o' yew! (*He turns and strides off up the road. She follows his retreating figure with concentrated hate. Old CABOT appears coming up from the barn. The hard, grim expression of his face has changed. He seems in some queer way softened, mellowed. His eyes have taken on a strange, incongruous dreamy quality. Yet there is no hint of physical weakness about him—rather he looks more robust and younger. ABBIE sees him and turns away quickly with unconcealed aversion. He comes slowly up to her.*)

CABOT (*mildly*) War yew an' Eben quarrelin' agen?

ABBIE (*shortly*) No.

CABOT Ye was talkin' a'mighty loud. (*He sits down on the edge of porch.*)

ABBIE (*snappishly*) If ye heerd us they hain't no need askin' questions.

CABOT I didn't hear what ye said.

ABBIE (*relieved*) Waal—it wa'n't nothin' t' speak on.

CABOT (*after a pause*) Eben's queer.

ABBIE (*bitterly*) He's the dead spit 'n' image o' yew!

CABOT (*queerly interested*) D'ye think so, Abbie? (*After a pause, ruminatingly*) Me 'n' Eben's allus fit 'n' fit. I never could b'ar him noways. He's so thunderin' soft—like his Maw.

ABBIE (*scornfully*) Ay-eh! 'Bout as soft as yew be!

CABOT (*as if he hadn't heard*) Mebbe I been too hard on him.

ABBIE (*jeeringly*) Waal—ye're gittin' soft now—soft as slop! That's what Eben was sayin'.

CABOT (*his face instantly grim and ominous*) Eben was sayin'? Waal, he'd best not do nothin' t' try me 'r he'll soon diskiver. . . . (*A pause. She keeps her face turned away. His gradually softens. He stares up at the sky.*) Purty, hain't it?

ABBIE (*crossly*) I don't see nothin' purty.

CABOT The sky. Feels like a wa'm field up thar.

ABBIE (*sarcastically*) Air yew aimin' t' buy up over the farm too? (*She snickers contemptuously.*)

CABOT (*strangely*) I'd like t' own my place up thar. (*a pause*) I'm gittin' old, Abbie. I'm gittin' ripe on the bough. (*A pause. She stares at him mystified. He goes on.*) It's allus lonesome cold in the house—even when it's bilin' hot outside. Hain't yew noticed?

ABBIE No.

CABOT It's wa'm down t' the barn—nice smellin' an' warm—with the cows. (*a pause*) Cows is queer.

ABBIE Like yew?

CABOT Like Eben. (*a pause*) I'm gittin' t' feel resigned t' Eben—jest as I got t' feel 'bout his Maw. I'm gittin' t' learn to b'ar his softness—jest like her'n. I calc'late I c'd a'most take t' him—if he wa'n't sech a dumb fool! (*a pause*) I s'pose it's old age a-creepin' in my bones.

ABBIE (*indifferently*) Waal—ye hain't dead yet.

CABOT (*roused*) No, I hain't, yew bet—not by a hell of a sight—I'm sound 'n' tough as hickory! (*then moodily*) But arter three score and ten the Lord warns ye t' prepare. (*a pause*) That's why Eben's come in my head. Now that his cussed sinful brothers is gone their path t' hell, they's no one left but Eben.

ABBIE (*resentfully*) They's me, hain't they? (*Agitatedly*) What's all this sudden likin' ye tuk to Eben? Why don't ye say nothin' 'bout me? Hain't I yer lawful wife?

CABOT (*simply*) Ay-eh. Ye be. (*A pause—he stares at her desirously—his eyes grow avid—then with a sudden movement he seizes her hands and squeezes them, declaiming in a queer camp meeting preacher's tempo*) Yew air my Rose o' Sharon! Behold, yew air fair; yer eyes air doves; yer lips air like scarlet; yer two breasts air like two fawns; yer navel be like a round goblet; yer belly be like a heap o' wheat. . . . (*He covers her hand with kisses. She does not seem to notice. She stares before her with hard angry eyes.*)

ABBIE (*jerking her hands away—harshly*) So ye're plannin' t' leave the farm t' Eben, air ye?

CABOT (*dazedly*) Leave . . . ? (*then with resentful obstinacy*) I hain't a-givin' it t' no one!

ABBIE (*remorselessly*) Ye can't take it with ye.

CABOT (*thinks a moment—then reluctantly*) No, I calc'late not. (*after a pause—with a strange passion*) But if I could, I would, by the Etarnal! 'R if I could, in my dyin' hour, I'd set it afire an' watch it burn—this house an' every ear o' corn an' every tree down t' the last blade o' hay! I'd sit an' know it was all a-dying with me an' no one else'd ever own what was mine, what I'd made out o' nothin' with my own sweat 'n' blood! (*a pause—then he adds with a queer affection*) 'Ceptin' the cows. Them I'd turn free.

ABBIE (*harshly*) An' me?

CABOT (*with a queer smile*) Ye'd be turned free, too.

ABBIE (*furiously*) So that's the thanks I git fur marryin' ye—t' have ye change kind to Eben who hates ye, an' talk o' turnin' me out in the road.

CABOT (*hastily*) Abbie! Ye know I wa'n't. . . .

ABBIE (*vengefully*) Just let me tell ye a thing or two 'bout Eben! Whar's he gone? T' see that harlot, Min! I tried fur t' stop him. Disgracin' yew an' me—on the Sabbath, too!

CABOT (*rather guiltily*) He's a sinner—nateral-born. It's lust eatin' his heart.

ABBIE (*enraged beyond endurance—wildly vindictive*) An' his lust fur me! Kin ye find excuses fur that?

CABOT (*stares at her—after a dead pause*) Lust—fur yew?

ABBIE (*defiantly*) He was tryin' t' make love t' me—when ye heerd us quarrelin'.

CABOT (*stares at her—then a terrible expression of rage comes over his face—he springs to his feet shaking all over*) By the A'mighty God—I'll end him!

ABBIE (*frightened now for* EBEN) No! Don't ye!

CABOT (*violently*) I'll git the shotgun an' blow his soft brains t' the top o' them elums!

ABBIE (*throwing her arms around him*) No, Ephraim!

CABOT (*pushing her away violently*) I will, by God!

ABBIE (*in a quieting tone*) Listen, Ephraim. 'Twa'n't nothin' bad—on'y a boy's foolin'—'twa'n't meant serious—jest jokin' an' teasin'. . . .

CABOT Then why did ye say—lust?

ABBIE It must hev sounded wusser'n I meant. An' I was mad at thinkin'—ye'd leave him the farm.

CABOT (*quieter but still grim and cruel*) Waal then, I'll horsewhip him off the place if that much'll content ye.

ABBIE (*reaching out and taking his hand*) No. Don't think o' me! Ye mustn't drive him off. 'Tain't sensible. Who'll ye get to help ye on the farm? They's no one hereabouts.

CABOT (*considers this—then nodding his appreciation*) Ye got a head on ye. (*then irritably*) Waal, let them stay. (*He sits down on the edge of the porch. She sits beside him. He murmurs contemptuously*) I oughtn't t' git riled so—at that 'ere fool calf. (*a pause*) But har's the p'int. What son o' mine'll keep on here t' the farm—when the Lord does call me? Simeon an' Peter air gone t' hell—an' Eben's follerin' 'em.

ABBIE They's me.

CABOT Ye're on'y a woman.

ABBIE I'm yewr wife.

CABOT That hain't me. A son is me—my blood—mine. Mine ought t' git mine. An' then it's still mine—even though I be six foot under. D'ye see?

ABBIE (*giving him a look of hatred*) Ay-eh. I see. (*She becomes very thoughtful, her face growing shrewd, her eyes studying* CABOT *craftily.*)

CABOT I'm gittin' old—ripe on the bough. (*then with a sudden forced reassurance*) Not but what I hain't a hard nut t' crack even yet—an' fur many a year t' come! By the Etarnal, I kin break most o' the young fellers' backs at any kind o' work any day o' the year!

ABBIE (*suddenly*) Mebbe the Lord'll give *us* a son.

CABOT (*turns and stares at her eagerly*) Ye mean—a son—t' me 'n' yew?

ABBIE (*with a cajoling smile*) Ye're a strong man yet, hain't ye? 'Tain't noways impossible, be it? We know that. Why d'ye stare so? Hain't ye never thought o' that afore? I been thinkin' o' it all along. Ay-eh—an' I been prayin' it'd happen, too.

CABOT (*his face growing full of joyous pride and a sort of religious ecstasy*) Ye been prayin', Abbie?—fur a son?—t' us?

ABBIE Ay-eh. (*with a grim resolution*) I want a son now.

CABOT (*excitedly clutching both of her hands in his*) It'd be the blessin' o' God, Abbie—the blessin' o' God A'mighty on me—in my old age—in my lonesomeness! They hain't nothin' I wouldn't do fur ye then, Abbie. Ye'd hev on'y ask it—anythin' ye'd a mind t'!

ABBIE (*interrupting*) Would ye will the farm t' me then—t' me an' it . . . ?

CABOT (*vehemently*) I'd do anythin' ye axed, I tell ye! I swar it! May I be everlastin' damned t' hell if I wouldn't! (*He sinks to his knees pulling her down with him. He trembles all over with the fervor of his hopes.*) Pray t' the Lord agen, Abbie. It's the Sabbath! I'll jine ye! Two prayers air better nor one. "An' God hearkened unto Rachel"!

An' God hearkened unto Abbie! Pray, Abbie! Pray fur him to hearken! (*He bows his head, mumbling. She pretends to do likewise but gives him a side glance of scorn and triumph.*)

SCENE 2.

About eight in the evening. The interior of the two bedrooms on the top floor is shown— EBEN *is sitting on the side of his bed in the room on the left. On account of the heat he has taken off everything but his undershirt and pants. His feet are bare. He faces front, brooding moodily, his chin propped on his hands, a desperate expression on his face.*

In the other room CABOT *and* ABBIE *are sitting side by side on the edge of their bed, an old four-poster with feather mattress. He is in his night shirt, she in her nightdress. He is still in the queer, excited mood into which the notion of a son has thrown him. Both rooms are lighted dimly and flickeringly by tallow candles.*

CABOT The farm needs a son.

ABBIE I need a son.

CABOT Ay-eh. Sometimes ye air the farm an' sometimes the farm be yew. That's why I clove t' ye in my lonesomeness. (*A pause. He pounds his knee with his fist.*) Me an' the farm has got t' beget a son!

ABBIE Ye'd best go t' sleep. Ye're gittin' thin's all mixed.

CABOT (*with an impatient gesture*) No, I hain't. My mind's clear's a bell. Ye don't know me, that's it. (*He stares hopelessly at the floor.*)

ABBIE (*indifferently*) Mebbe. (*In the next room* EBEN *gets up and paces up and down distractedly.* ABBIE *hears him. Her eyes fasten on the intervening wall with concentrated attention.* EBEN *stops and stares. Their hot glances seem to meet through the wall. Unconsciously he stretches out his arms for her and she half rises. Then aware, he mutters a curse at himself and flings himself face downward on the bed, his clenched fists above his head, his face buried in the pillow.* ABBIE *relaxes with a faint sigh but her eyes remain fixed on the wall; she listens with all her attention for some movement from* EBEN.)

CABOT (*suddenly raises his head and looks at her—scornfully*) Will ye ever know me—'r will any man 'r woman? (*Shaking his head*) No. I calc'late wa'n't t' be. (*He turns away.* ABBIE *looks at the wall. Then, evidently unable to keep silent about his thoughts, without looking at his wife, he puts out his hand and clutches her knee. She starts violently, looks at him, sees he is not watching her, concentrates again on the wall and pays no attention to what he says.*) Listen, Abbie. When I come here fifty odd year ago—I was jest twenty an' the strongest an' hardest ye ever seen—ten times as strong an' fifty times as hard as Eben. Waal—this place was nothin' but fields o' stones. Folks laughed when I tuk it. They couldn't know what I knowed. When he kin make corn sprout out o' stones, God's livin' in yew! They wa'n't strong enuf fur that! They reckoned God was easy. They laughed. They don't laugh no more. Some died here-abouts. Some went West an' died. They're all under ground—fur follerin' arter an easy God. God hain't easy. (*He shakes his head slowly.*) An' I growed hard. Folks kept allus sayin' he's a hard man like 'twas sinful t' be hard, so's at last I said back at 'em: Waal then, by thunder, ye'll git me hard an' see how ye like it! (*Then suddenly*) But I give in t' weakness once. 'Twas arter I'd been here two year. I got weak—despairful— they was so many stones. They was a party leavin', givin' up, goin' West. I jined 'em. We tracked on 'n on. We come t' broad medders, plains, whar the soil was black an' rich as gold. Nary a stone. Easy. Ye'd on'y to plow an' sow an' then set an' smoke yer pipe an' watch thin's grow. I could o' been a rich man—but somethin' in me fit me an' fit me—the voice o' God sayin': "This hain't wuth nothin' t' Me. Get ye back t' hum!" I got afeerd o' that voice an' I lit out back t' hum here, leavin' my claim an' crops t' whoever'd a mind t' take 'em. Ay-eh. I actoolly give up what was rightful mine! God's hard, not easy! God's in the stones! Build my church on a rock—out o' stones an' I'll be in them! That's what He meant t' Peter! (*He sighs heavily—a pause*) Stones. I picked 'em up an' piled 'em into walls. Ye kin read the years o' my life in them walls, every day a hefted stone, climbin' over the hills up and down, fencin' in the fields that was mine, whar I'd made thin's grow out o' nothin'—like the will o' God, like the servant o' His hand. It wa'n't easy. It was hard an' He made me hard fur it. (*He pauses.*) All the time I kept gittin' lonesomer. I tuk a wife. She bore Simeon an' Peter. She was a good woman. She wuked hard. We was married twenty year. She never knowed me. She helped but she never knowed what she was helpin'. I was allus lonesome. She died. After that it wa'n't so lonesome for a spell. (*a pause*) I lost count o' the years. I had no time t' fool away countin' 'em. Sim an' Peter helped. The farm growed. It was all mine! When I thought o' that I didn't feel lonesome. (*a pause*) But ye can't hitch yer mind t' one thin' day an' night. I tuk another wife—Eben's Maw. Her folks was contestin' me at law over my deeds t' the farm—my farm! That's why Eben keeps a'talkin' his fool talk o' this bein' his Maw's farm. She bore Eben. She was purty—but soft. She tried t' be hard. She couldn't. She never knowed me nor nothin'. It was lonesomer 'n hell with her. After a matter o' sixteen odd years, she died. (*a pause*) I lived with the boys. They hated me 'cause I was hard. I hated them 'cause they was soft. They coveted the farm without knowin' what it meant. It made me bitter 'n wormwood. It aged me—them covetin' what I'd made fur mine. Then this spring the call come—the voice o' God cryin' in my wilderness, in my lonesomeness—t' go out an' seek an' find! (*Turning to her with strange passion*) I sought ye an' I found ye! Yew air my Rose o' Sharon! Yer eyes air like. . . . (*She has turned a blank face, resentful eyes to his. He stares at her for a moment—then harshly*) Air ye any the wiser fur all I've told ye?

ABBIE (*confusedly*) Mebbe.

CABOT (*pushing her away from him—angrily*) Ye don't know nothin'—nor never will. If ye don't hev a son t' redeem ye . . . (*this in a tone of cold threat*)

ABBIE (*resentfully*) I've prayed, hain't I?

CABOT (*bitterly*) Pray agen—fur understandin'!

ABBIE (*a veiled threat in her tone*) Ye'll have a son out o' me, I promise ye.

CABOT How kin ye promise?

ABBIE I got second-sight mebbe. I kin foretell. (*She gives a queer smile.*)

CABOT I believe ye have. Ye give me the chills sometimes. (*He shivers.*) It's cold in this house. It's oneasy. They's thin's pokin' about in the dark—in the corners. (*He pulls on his trousers, tucking in his night shirt, and pulls on his boots.*)

ABBIE (*surprised*) Whar air ye goin'?

CABOT (*queerly*) Down whar it's restful—whar it's warm—down t' the barn. (*bitterly*) I kin talk t' the cows. They know. They know the farm an' me. They'll give me peace. (*He turns to go out the door.*)

ABBIE (*a bit frightenedly*) Air ye ailin' tonight, Ephraim?

CABOT Growin'. Growin' ripe on the bough. (*He turns and goes, his boots clumping down the stairs. EBEN sits up with a start, listening. ABBIE is conscious of his movement and stares at the wall. CABOT comes out of the house around the corner and stands by the gate, blinking at the sky. He stretches up his hands in a tortured gesture*) God

A'mighty, call from the dark! (*He listens as if expecting an answer. Then his arms drop, he shakes his head and plods off toward the barn.* EBEN *and* ABBIE *stare at each other through the wall.* EBEN *sighs heavily and* ABBIE *echoes it. Both become terribly nervous, uneasy. Finally* ABBIE *gets up and listens, her ear to the wall. He acts as if he saw every move she was making, he becomes resolutely still. She seems driven into a decision—goes out the door in rear determinedly. His eyes follow her. Then as the door of his room is opened softly, he turns away, waits in an attitude of strained fixity.* ABBIE *stands for a second staring at him, her eyes burning with desire. Then with a little cry she runs over and throws her arms about his neck, she pulls his head back and covers his mouth with kisses. At first, he submits dumbly; then he puts his arms about her neck and returns her kisses, but finally, suddenly aware of his hatred, he hurls her away from him, springing to his feet. They stand speechless and breathless, panting like two animals.*)

ABBIE (*at last—painfully*) Ye shouldn't, Eben—ye shouldn't—I'd make ye happy!

EBEN (*harshly*) I don't want t' be happy—from yew!

ABBIE (*helplessly*) Ye do, Eben! Ye do! Why d'ye lie?

EBEN (*viciously*) I don't take t'ye, I tell ye! I hate the sight o' ye!

ABBIE (*with an uncertain troubled laugh*) Waal, I kissed ye anyways—an' ye kissed back—yer lips was burnin'—ye can't lie 'bout that! (*intensely*) If ye don't care, why did ye kiss me back—why was yer lips burnin'?

EBEN (*wiping his mouth*) It was like pizen on 'em (*then tauntingly*) When I kissed ye back, mebbe I thought 'twas someone else.

ABBIE (*wildly*) Min?

EBEN Mebbe.

ABBIE (*torturedly*) Did ye go t' see her? Did ye r'ally go? I thought ye mightn't. Is that why ye throwed me off jest now?

EBEN (*sneeringly*) What if it be?

ABBIE (*raging*) Then ye're a dog, Eben Cabot!

EBEN (*threateningly*) Ye can't talk that way t' me!

ABBIE (*with a shrill laugh*) Can't I? Did ye think I was in love with ye—a weak thin' like yew? Not much! I on'y wanted ye fur a purpose o' my own—an' I'll hev ye fur it yet 'cause I'm stronger'n yew be!

EBEN (*resentfully*) I knowed well it was on'y part o' yer plan t' swaller everythin'!

ABBIE (*tauntingly*) Mebbe!

EBEN (*furious*) Git out o' my room!

ABBIE This air my room an' ye're on'y hired help!

EBEN (*threateningly*) Git out afore I murder ye!

ABBIE (*quite confident now*) I hain't a mite afeerd. Ye want me, don't ye? Yes, ye do! An' yer Paw's son'll never kill what he wants! Look at yer eyes! They's lust fur me in 'em, burnin' 'em up! Look at yer lips now! They're tremblin' an' longin' t' kiss me, an' yer teeth t' bite! (*He is watching her now with a horrible fascination. She laughs a crazy triumphant laugh.*) I'm a-goin' t' make all o' this hum my hum! They's one room hain't mine yet, but it's a-goin' t' be tonight. I'm a-goin' down now an' light up! (*She makes him a mocking bow.*) Won't ye come courtin' me in the best parlor, Mister Cabot?

EBEN (*staring at her—horribly confused—dully*) Don't ye dare! It hain't been opened since Maw died an' was laid out thar! Don't ye . . . ! (*But her eyes are fixed on his so burningly that his will seems to wither before hers. He stands swaying toward her helplessly.*)

ABBIE (*holding his eyes and putting all her will into her words as she backs out the door*) I'll expect ye afore long, Eben.

EBEN (*stares after her for a while, walking toward the door. A light appears in the parlor window. He murmurs*) In the parlor? (*This seems to arouse connotations for he comes back and puts on his white shirt, collar, half ties the tie mechanically, puts on coat, takes his hat, stands barefooted looking about him in bewilderment, mutters wonderingly*) Maw! Whar air yew? (*Then goes slowly toward the door in rear.*)

SCENE 3.

A few minutes later. The interior of the parlor is shown. A grim, repressed room like a tomb in which the family has been interred alive. ABBIE *sits on the edge of the horsehair sofa. She has lighted all the candles and the room is revealed in all its preserved ugliness. A change has come over the woman. She looks awed and frightened now, ready to run away.*

The door is opened and EBEN *appears. His face wears an expression of obsessed confusion. He stands staring at her, his arms hanging disjointedly from his shoulders, his feet bare, his hat in his hand.*

ABBIE (*after a pause—with a nervous, formal politeness*) Won't ye set?

EBEN (*dully*) Ay-eh. (*Mechanically he places his hat carefully on the floor near the door and sits stiffly beside her on the edge of the sofa. A pause. They both remain rigid, looking straight ahead with eyes full of fear.*)

ABBIE When I fust came in—in the dark—they seemed somethin' here.

EBEN (*simply*) Maw.

ABBIE I kin still feel—somethin'. . . .

EBEN It's Maw.

ABBIE At fust I was feered o' it. I wanted t' yell an' run. Now—since yew come—seems like it's growin' soft an' kind t' me. (*Addressing the air—queerly*) Thank yew.

EBEN Maw allus loved me.

ABBIE Mebbe it knows I love yew too. Mebbe that makes it kind t' me.

EBEN (*dully*) I dunno. I should think she'd hate ye.

ABBIE (*with certainty*) No. I kin feel it don't—not no more.

EBEN Hate yer fur stealin' her place—here in her hum—settin' in her parlor whar she was laid— (*He suddenly stops, staring stupidly before him.*)

ABBIE What is it, Eben?

EBEN (*in a whisper*) Seems like Maw didn't want me t' remind ye.

ABBIE (*excitedly*) I knowed, Eben! It's kind t' me! It don't b'ar me no grudges fur what I never knowed an' couldn't help!

EBEN Maw b'ars him a grudge.

ABBIE Waal, so does all o' us.

EBEN Ay-eh. (*with passion*) I does, by God!

ABBIE (*taking one of his hands in hers and patting it*) Thar! Don't git riled thinkin' o' him. Think o' yer Maw who's kind t' us. Tell me about yer Maw, Eben.

EBEN They hain't nothin' much. She was kind. She was good.

ABBIE (*putting one arm over his shoulder. He does not seem to notice—passionately*) I'll be kind an' good t' ye!

EBEN Sometimes she used t' sing fur me.

ABBIE I'll sing fur ye!

EBEN This was her hum. This was her farm.

ABBIE This is my hum! This is my farm!

EBEN He married her t' steal 'em. She was soft an' easy. He couldn't 'preciate her.

ABBIE He can't 'preciate me!

EBEN He murdered her with his hardness.

ABBIE He's murderin' me!

EBEN She died. (*a pause*) Sometimes she used to sing fur me. (*He bursts into a fit of sobbing.*)

ABBIE (*both arms around him—with wild passion*) I'll sing fur ye! I'll die fur ye! (*In spite of her overwhelming desire for him, there is a sincere maternal love in her manner and voice—a horribly frank mixture of lust and mother love.*) Don't cry, Eben! I'll take yer Maw's place! I'll be everythin' she was t' ye! Let me kiss ye, Eben! (*She pulls his head around. He makes a bewildered pretense of resistance. She is tender.*) Don't be afeered! I'll kiss ye pure, Eben—same 's if I was a Maw t' ye—an' ye kin kiss me back 's if yew was my son—my boy—sayin' goodnight t' me! Kiss me, Eben. (*They kiss in restrained fashion. Then suddenly wild passion overcomes her. She kisses him lustfully again and again and he flings his arms about her and returns her kisses. Suddenly, as in the bedroom, he frees himself from her violently and springs to his feet. He is trembling all over, in a strange state of terror. ABBIE strains her arms toward him with fierce pleading.*) Don't ye leave me, Eben! Can't ye see it hain't enuf—lovin' ye like a Maw—can't ye see it's got t' be that an' more—much more—a hundred times more—fur me t' be happy—fur yew t' be happy?

EBEN (*to the presence he feels in the room*) Maw! Maw! What d'ye want? What air ye tellin' me?

ABBIE She's tellin' ye t' love me. She knows I love ye an' I'll be good t' ye. Can't ye feel it? Don't ye know? She's tellin' ye t' love me, Eben!

EBEN Ay-eh. I feel—mebbe she—but—I can't figger out—why—when ye've stole her place—here in her hum—in the parlor whar she was—

ABBIE (*fiercely*) She knows I love ye!

EBEN (*his face suddenly lighting up with a fierce triumphant grin*) I see it! I sees why. It's her vengeance on him—so's she kin rest quiet in her grave!

ABBIE (*wildly*) Vengeance o' God on the hull o' us! What d'we give a durn? I love ye, Eben! God knows I love ye! (*She stretches out her arms for him.*)

EBEN (*throws himself on his knees beside the sofa and grabs her in his arms—releasing all his pent-up passion*) An' I love yew, Abbie!—now I kin say it! I been dyin' fur want o' ye—every hour since ye come! I love ye! (*Their lips meet in a fierce, bruising kiss.*)

SCENE 4.

Exterior of the farmhouse. It is just dawn. The front door at right is opened.

EBEN *comes out and walks around to the gate. He is dressed in his working clothes. He seems changed. His face wears a bold and confident expression, he is grinning to himself with evident satisfaction. As he gets near the gate, the window of the parlor is heard opening and the shutters are flung back and* ABBIE *sticks her head out. Her hair tumbles over her shoulders in disarray, her face is flushed, she looks at* EBEN *with tender, languorous eyes and calls softly.*

ABBIE Eben. (*As he turns—playfully*) Jest one more kiss afore ye go. I'm goin' to miss ye fearful all day.

EBEN An' me yew, ye kin bet! (*He goes to her. They kiss several times. He draws away, laughingly.*) Thar. That's enuf, hain't it? Ye won't hev none left fur next time.

ABBIE I got a million o' 'em left fur yew! (*then a bit anxiously*) D'ye r'ally love me, Eben?

EBEN (*emphatically*) I like ye better'n any gal I ever knowed! That's gospel!

ABBIE Likin' hain't lovin'.

EBEN Waal then—I love ye. Now air yew satisfied?

ABBIE Ay-eh, I be. (*She smiles at him adoringly.*)

EBEN I better git t' the barn. The old critter's liable t' suspicion an' come sneakin' up.

ABBIE (*with a confident laugh*) Let him! I kin allus pull the wool over his eyes. I'm goin' t' leave the shutters open and let in the sun 'n' air. This room's been dead long enuf. Now it's going' t' be my room!

EBEN (*frowning*) Ay-eh.

ABBIE We made it our'n last night, didn't we? We give it life—our lovin' did. (*a pause*)

EBEN (*with a strange look*) Maw's gone back t' her grave. She kin sleep now.

ABBIE May she rest in peace! (*then tenderly rebuking*) Ye oughtn't t' talk o' sad thin's—this mornin'.

EBEN It jest come up in my mind o' itself.

ABBIE Don't let it. (*He doesn't answer. She yawns.*) Waal, I'm a-goin' t' steal a wink o' sleep. I'll tell the Old Man I hain't feelin' pert. Let him git his own vittles.

EBEN I see him comin' from the barn. Ye better look smart an' git upstairs.

ABBIE Ay-eh. Good-by. Don't fergit me. (*She throws him a kiss. He grins—then squares his shoulders and awaits his father confidently.* CABOT *walks slowly up from the left, staring up at the sky with a vague face.*)

EBEN (*jovially*) Mornin', Paw. Star-gazin' in daylight?

CABOT Purty, hain't it?

EBEN (*looking around him possessively*) It's a durned purty farm.

CABOT I mean the sky.

EBEN (*grinning*) How d'ye know? Them eyes o' your'n can't see that fur. (*This tickles his humor and he slaps his thigh and laughs.*) Ho-Ho! That's a good un!

CABOT (*grimly sarcastic*) Ye're feelin' right chipper, hain't ye? Whar'd ye steal the likker?

EBEN (*good-naturedly*) 'Taint likker. Jest life. (*Suddenly holding out his hand—soberly*) Yew 'n' me is quits. Let's shake hands.

CABOT (*suspiciously*) What's come over ye?

EBEN Then don't. Mebbe it's jest as well. (*a moment's pause*) What's come over me? (*queerly*) Didn't ye feel her passin'—going' back t' her grave?

CABOT (*dully*) Who?

EBEN Maw. She kin rest now an' sleep content. She's quit with ye.

CABOT (*confusedly*) I rested. I slept good—down with the cows. They know how t' sleep. They're teachin' me.

EBEN (*suddenly jovial again*) Good fur the cows! Waal—ye better git t' work.

CABOT (*grimly amused*) Air yew bossin' me, ye calf?

EBEN (*beginning to laugh*) Ay-eh! I'm bossin' yew! Ha-ha-ha! see how ye like it! Ha-ha-ha! I'm the prize rooster o' this roost. Ha-ha-ha! (*He goes off toward the barn laughing.*)

CABOT (*looks after him with scornful pity*) Soft-headed. Like his Maw. Dead spit 'n' image. No hope in him! (*He spits with contemptuous disgust.*) A born fool! (*Then matter-of-factly*) Waal—I'm gittin' peckish. (*He goes toward door.*)

PART III

SCENE 1.

A night in late spring the following year. The kitchen and the two bedrooms upstairs are shown. The two bedrooms are dimly lighted by a tallow candle in each. EBEN is sitting on the side of the bed in his room, his chin propped on his fists, his face a study of the struggle he is making to understand his conflicting emotions. The noisy laughter and music from below where a kitchen dance is in progress annoy and distract him. He scowls at the floor. In the next room a cradle stands beside the double bed.

In the kitchen all is festivity. The stove has been taken down to give more room to the dancers. The chairs, with wooden benches added, have been pushed back against the walls. On these are seated, squeezed in tight against one another, farmers and their wives and their young folks of both sexes from the neighboring farms. They are all chattering and laughing loudly. They evidently have some secret joke in common. There is no end of winking, of nudging, of meaning nods of the head toward CABOT who, in a state of extreme hilarious excitement increased by the amount he has drunk, is standing near the rear door where there is a small keg of whisky and serving drinks to all the men. In the left corner, front, dividing the attention with her husband, ABBIE is sitting in a rocking chair, a shawl wrapped about her shoulders. She is very pale, her face is thin and drawn, her eyes are fixed anxiously on the open door in rear as if waiting for someone.

The MUSICIAN is tuning up his fiddle, seated in the far right corner. He is a lanky young fellow with a long, weak face. His pale eyes blink incessantly and he grins about him slyly with a greedy malice.

ABBIE (*suddenly turning to a young girl on her right*) Whar's Eben?

YOUNG GIRL (*eying her scornfully*) I dunno, Mrs. Cabot. I hain't seen Eben in ages. (*meaningly*) Seems like he's spent most o' his time t' hum since yew come.

ABBIE (*vaguely*) I tuk his Maw's place.

YOUNG GIRL Ay-eh. So I've heerd. (*She turns away to retail this bit of gossip to her mother sitting next to her. ABBIE turns to her left to a big stoutish middle-aged man whose flushed face and staring eyes show the amount of "likker" he has consumed.*)

ABBIE Ye hain't seen Eben, hev ye?

MAN No, I hain't. (*then he adds with a wink*) If yew hain't, who would?

ABBIE He's the best dancer in the county. He'd ought t' come an' dance.

MAN (*with a wink*) Mebbe he's doin' the dutiful an' walkin' the kid t' sleep. It's a boy, hain't it?

ABBIE (*nodding vaguely*) Ay-eh—born two weeks back—purty's a picter.

MAN They all is—t' their Maws. (*then in a whisper, with a nudge and a leer*) Listen, Abbie—if ye ever git tired o' Eben, remember me! Don't fergit now! (*He looks at her uncomprehending face for a second—then grunts disgustedly.*) Waal—guess I'll likker agin. (*He goes over and joins CABOT who is arguing noisily with an old farmer over cows. They all drink.*)

ABBIE (*this time appealing to nobody in particular*) Wonder what Eben's a-doin'? (*Her remark is repeated down the line with many a guffaw and titter until it reaches the fiddler. He fastens his blinking eyes on ABBIE.*)

FIDDLER (*raising his voice*) Bet I kin tell ye, Abbie, what Eben's doin'! He's down t' the church offerin' up prayers o' thanksgivin'. (*They all titter expectantly.*)

MAN What fur? (*Another titter.*)

FIDDLER 'Cause unto him a—(*He hesitates just long enough.*)—brother is born! (*A roar of laughter. They all look from* ABBIE *to* CABOT. *She is oblivious, staring at the door.* CABOT, *although he hasn't heard the words, is irritated by the laughter and steps forward, glaring about him. There is an immediate silence.*)

CABOT What're ye all bleatin' about—like a flock o' goats? Why don't ye dance, damn ye? I axed ye here t' dance—t' eat, drink an' be merry—an' thar ye set cacklin' like a lot o' wet hens with the pip! Ye've swilled my likker an' guzzled my vittles like hogs, hain't ye? Then dance fur me, can't ye? That's fa'r an' squar', hain't it? (*A grumble of resentment goes around but they are all evidently in too much awe of him to express it openly.*)

FIDDLER (*slyly*) We're waitin' fur Eben. (*a suppressed laugh*)

CABOT (*with a fierce exultation*) T'hell with Eben! Eben's done fur now! I got a new son! (*his mood switching with drunken suddenness*) But ye needn't t' laugh at Eben, none o' ye! He's my blood, if he be a dumb fool. He's better nor any o' yew! He kin do a day's work a'most up t' what I kin—an' that'd put any o' yew pore critters t' shame!

FIDDLER An' he kin do a good night's work, too! (*a roar of laughter*)

CABOT Laugh, ye damn fools! Ye're right jist the same, Fiddler. He kin work day an' night too, like I kin, if need be!

OLD FARMER (*from behind the keg where he is weaving drunkenly back and forth—with great simplicity*) They hain't many t' touch ye, Ephraim—a son at seventy-six. That's a hard man fur ye! I be on'y sixty-eight an' I couldn't do it. (*a roar of laughter in which* CABOT *joins uproariously*)

CABOT (*slapping him on the back*) I'm sorry fur ye, Hi. I'd never suspicion sech weakness from a boy like yew!

OLD FARMER An' I never reckoned yew had it in ye nuther, Ephraim. (*There is another laugh.*)

CABOT (*suddenly grim*) I got a lot in me—a hell of a lot—folks don't know on. (*turning to the* FIDDLER) Fiddle 'er up, durn ye! Give 'em somethin' t' dance t'! What air ye, an ornament? Hain't this a celebration? Then grease yer elbow an' go it!

FIDDLER (*seizes a drink which the* OLD FARMER *holds out to him and downs it*) Here goes! (*He starts to fiddle "Lady of the Lake." Four young fellows and four girls form in two lines and dance a square dance. The* FIDDLER *shouts directions for the different movements, keeping his words in the rhythm of the music and interspersing them with jocular personal remarks to the dancers themselves. The people seated along the walls stamp their feet and clap their hands in unison.* CABOT *is especially active in this respect. Only* ABBIE *remains apathetic, staring at the door as if she were alone in a silent room.*)

FIDDLER Swing your partner t' the right! That's it, Jim! Give her a b'ar hug! Her Maw hain't lookin'. (*laughter*) Change partners! That suits ye, don't it, Essie, now ye got Reub afore ye? Look at her redden up, will ye! Waal, life is short an' so's love, as the feller says. (*laughter*)

CABOT (*excitedly, stamping his foot*) Go it, boys! Go it, gals!

FIDDLER (*with a wink at the others*) Ye're the spryest seventy-six ever I sees, Ephraim! Now if ye'd on'y good eye-sight . . . ! (*Suppressed laughter. He gives* CABOT *no chance to retort but roars*) Promenade! Ye're walkin' like a bride down the aisle, Sarah! Waal, while they's life they's allus hope, I've heerd tell. Swing your partner to the left! Gosh A'mighty, look at Johnny Cook high-steppin'! They hain't goin' t' be much strength left fur howin' in the corn lot t'morrow. (*laughter*)

CABOT Go it! Go it! (*Then suddenly, unable to restrain himself any longer, he prances into the midst of the dancers, scattering them, waving his arms about wildly.*) Ye're all hoofs! Git out o' my road! Give me room! I'll show ye dancin'. Ye're all too soft! (*He pushes them roughly away. They crowd back toward the walls, muttering, looking at him resentfully.*)

FIDDLER (*jeeringly*) Go it, Ephraim! Go it! (*He starts "Pop Goes the Weasel," increasing the tempo with every verse until at the end he is fiddling crazily as fast as he can go.*)

CABOT (*starts to dance, which he does very well and with tremendous vigor. Then he begins to improvise, cuts incredibly grotesque capers, leaping up and cracking his heels together, prancing around in a circle with body bent in an Indian war dance, then suddenly straightening up and kicking as high as he can with both legs. He is like a monkey on a string. And all the while he intersperses his antics with shouts and derisive comments*) Whoop! Here's dancin' fur ye! Whoop! See that! Seventy-six, if I'm a day! Hard as iron yet! Beatin' the young 'uns like I allus done! Look at me! I'd invite ye t' dance on my hundredth birthday on'y ye'll all be dead by then. Ye're a sickly generation! Yer hearts air pink, not red! Yer veins is full o' mud an' water! I be the on'y man in the county! Whoop! See that! I'm a Injun! I've killed Injuns in the West afore ye was born—an' skulped 'em too! They's a arrer wound on my backside I c'd show ye! The hull tribe chased me. I outrun 'em all—with the arrer stuck in me! An' I tuk vengeance on 'em. Ten eyes fur an eye, that was my motter! Whoop! Look at me! I kin kick the ceilin' off the room! Whoop!

FIDDLER (*stops playing—exhaustedly*) God A'mighty, I got enuf. Ye got the devil's strength in ye.

CABOT (*delightedly*) Did I beat yew, too? Wa'al, ye played smart. Hev a swig. (*He pours whisky for himself and* FIDDLER. *They drink. The others watch* CABOT *silently with cold, hostile eyes. There is a dead pause. The* FIDDLER *rests.* CABOT *leans against the keg, panting, glaring around him confusedly. In the room above,* EBEN *gets to his feet and tiptoes out the door in rear, appearing a moment later in the other bedroom. He moves silently, even frightenedly, toward the cradle and stands there looking down at the baby. His face is as vague as his reactions are confused, but there is a trace of tenderness, of interested discovery. At the same moment that he reaches the cradle,* ABBIE *seems to sense something. She gets up weakly and goes to* CABOT.)

ABBIE I'm goin' up t' the baby.

CABOT (*with real solicitude*) Air ye able fur the stairs? D'ye want me t' help ye, Abbie?

ABBIE No. I'm able. I'll be down agen soon.

CABOT Don't ye git wore out! He needs ye, remember—our son does! (*He grins affectionately, patting her on the back. She shrinks from his touch.*)

ABBIE (*dully*) Don't—tech me. I'm goin'—up. (*She goes.* CABOT *looks after her. A whisper goes around the room.* CABOT *turns. It ceases. He wipes his forehead streaming with sweat. He is breathing pantingly.*)

CABOT I'm a-goin' out t' git fresh air. I'm feelin' a mite dizzy. Fiddle up thar! Dance, all o' ye! Here's likker fur them as wants it. Enjoy yerselves. I'll be back. (*He goes, closing the door behind him.*)

FIDDLER (*sarcastically*) Don't hurry none on our account! (*A suppressed laugh. He imitates* ABBIE.) Whar's Eben? (*more laughter*)

A WOMAN (*loudly*) What's happened in this house is plain as the nose on yer face! (ABBIE *appears in the doorway upstairs and stands looking in surprise and adoration at* EBEN *who does not see her.*)

A MAN Ssshh! He's li'ble t' be listenin' at the door. That'd be like him. (*Their voices die to an intensive whispering. Their faces are concentrated on this gossip. A noise as of dead leaves in the wind comes from the room.* CABOT *has come out from the porch and stands by the gate, leaning on it, staring at the sky blinkingly.* ABBIE *comes across the room silently.* EBEN *does not notice her until quite near.*)

EBEN (*starting*) Abbie!

ABBIE Ssshh! (*She throws her arms around him. They kiss—then bend over the cradle together.*) Ain't he purty?—dead spit 'n' image o' yew!

EBEN (*pleased*) Air he? I can't tell none.

ABBIE E-zactly like!

EBEN (*frowningly*) I don't like this. I don't like lettin' on what's mine's his'n. I been doin' that all my life. I'm gittin' t' the end o' b'arin' it!

ABBIE (*putting her finger on his lips*) We're doin' the best we kin. We got t' wait. Somethin's bound t' happen. (*She puts her arms around him.*) I got t' go back.

EBEN I'm goin' out. I can't b'ar it with the fiddle playin' an' the laughin'.

ABBIE Don't git feelin' low. I love ye, Eben. Kiss me. (*He kisses her. They remain in each other's arms.*)

CABOT (*at the gate, confusedly*) Even the music can't drive it out—somethin'. Ye kin feel it droppin' off the elums, climbin' up the roof, sneakin' down the chimney, pokin' in the corners! They's no peace in houses, they's no rest livin' with folks. Somethin's always livin' with ye. (*with a deep sigh*) I'll go t' the barn an' rest a spell. (*He goes wearily toward the barn.*)

FIDDLER (*tuning up*) Let's celebrate the old skunk gittin' fooled! We kin have some fun now he's went. (*He starts to fiddle "Turkey in the Straw." There is real merriment now. The young folks get up to dance.*)

SCENE 2.

A half hour later—exterior.

EBEN *is standing by the gate looking up at the sky, an expression of dumb pain bewildered by itself on his face.* CABOT *appears, returning from the barn, walking wearily, his eyes on the ground. He sees* EBEN *and his whole mood immediately changes. He becomes excited, a cruel, triumphant grin comes to his lips, he strides up and slaps* EBEN *on the back. From within comes the whining of the fiddle and the noise of stamping feet and laughing voices.*

CABOT So har ye be!

EBEN (*startled, stares at him with hatred for a moment—then dully*) Ay-eh.

CABOT (*surveying him jeeringly*) Why hain't ye been in t' dance? They was all axin' fur ye.

EBEN Let 'em ax!

CABOT They's a hull pasel o' purty gals.

EBEN T' hell with 'em!

CABOT Ye'd ought t' be marryin' one o' 'em soon.

EBEN I hain't marryin' no one.

CABOT Ye might 'arn a share o' a farm that way.

EBEN (*with a sneer*) Like yew did, ye mean? I hain't that kind.

CABOT (*stung*) Ye lie! 'Twas yer Maw's folks aimed t' steal my farm from me.

EBEN Other folks don't say so. (*after a pause—defiantly*) An' I got a farm, anyways!

CABOT (*derisively*) Whar?

EBEN (*stamps a foot on the ground*) Har!

CABOT (*throws his head back and laughs coarsely*) Ho-ho! Ye hev, hev ye? Waal, that's a good un!

EBEN (*controlling himself—grimly*) Ye'll see!

CABOT (*stares at him suspiciously, trying to make him out—a pause—then with scornful confidence*) Ay-eh. I'll see. So'll ye. It's ye that's blind—blind as a mole underground. (EBEN *suddenly laughs, one short sardonic bark: "Ha." A pause.* CABOT *peers at him with renewed suspicion.*) Whar air ye hawin' 'bout? (EBEN *turns away without answering.* CABOT *grows angry.*) God A'mighty, yew air a dumb dunce! They's nothin' in that thick skull o' your'n but noise—like a empty keg it be! (EBEN *doesn't seem to hear*—CABOT's *rage grows.*) Yewr farm! God A'mighty! If we wa'n't a born donkey ye'd know ye'll never own stick nor stone on it, specially now arter him bein' born. It's his'n, I tell ye—his'n arter I die—but I'll live a hundred jest t' fool ye all—an' he'll be growed then—yewr age a'most! (EBEN *laughs again his sardonic "Ha." This drives* CABOT *into a fury.*) Ha? Ye think ye kin git 'round that someways, do ye? Waal, it'll be her'n, too—Abbie's—ye won't git 'round her—she knows yer tricks—she'll be too much fur ye—she wants the farm her'n—she was afeerd o' ye—she told me ye was sneakin' 'round tryin' t' make love t' her t' git her on yer side . . . ye . . . ye mad fool, ye! (*He raises his clenched fists threateningly.*)

EBEN (*is confronting him choking with rage*) Ye lie, ye old skunk! Abbie never said no sech thing!

CABOT (*suddenly triumphant when he sees how shaken* EBEN *is*) She did. An' I says, I'll blow his brains t' the top o' them elums—an' she says no, that hain't sense, who'll ye git t'help ye on the farm in his place—an' then she says yew'n me ought t' have a son—I know we kin, she says—an' I says, if we do, ye kin have anythin' I've got ye've a mind t'. An' she says, I wants Eben cut off so's this farm'll be mine when ye die! (*with terrible gloating*) An' that's what's happened, hain't it? An' the farm's her'n! An' the dust o' the road—that's you'rn! Ha! Now who's hawin'?

EBEN (*has been listening, petrified with grief and rage—suddenly laughs wildly and brokenly*) Ha-ha-ha! So that's her sneakin' game—all along!—like I suspicioned at fust—t' swaller it all—an' me, too . . . ! (*madly*) I'll murder her! (*He springs toward the porch but* CABOT *is quicker and gets in between.*)

CABOT No, ye don't!

EBEN Git out o' my road! (*He tries to throw* CABOT *aside. They grapple in what becomes immediately a murderous struggle. The old man's concentrated strength is too much for* EBEN. CABOT *gets one hand on his throat and presses him back across the stone wall. At the same moment,* ABBIE *comes out on the porch. With a stifled cry she runs toward them.*)

ABBIE Eben! Ephraim! (*She tugs at the hand on* EBEN'S *throat.*) Let go, Ephraim! Ye're chokin' him!

CABOT (*removes his hand and flings* EBEN *sideways full length on the grass, gasping and choking. With a cry,* ABBIE *kneels beside him, trying to take his head on her lap, but he pushes her away.* CABOT *stands looking down with fierce triumph*) Ye needn't t've fret, Abbie, I wa'n't aimin' t' kill him. He hain't wuth hangin' fur—not by a hell of a sight! (*more and more triumphantly*) Seventy-six an' him not thirty yit—an' look whar he be fur thinkin' his Paw was easy! No, by God, I hain't easy! An' him upstairs, I'll raise him t' be like me! (*He turns to leave them.*) I'm goin' in an' dance!—sing an' celebrate! (*He walks to the porch—then turns with a great grin.*) I don't calc'late it's left in him, but if he gits pesky, Abbie, ye jest sing out. I'll come a-runnin' an' by the Etarnal, I'll put him across my knee an' birch him! Ha-ha-ha! (*He goes into the house laughing. A moment later his loud "whoop" is heard.*)

ABBIE (*tenderly*) Eben. Air ye hurt? (*She tries to kiss him but he pushes her violently away and struggles to a sitting position.*)

EBEN (*gaspingly*) T'hell—with ye!

ABBIE (*not believing her ears*) It's me, Eben—Abbie—don't ye know me?

EBEN (*glowering at her with hatred*) Ay-eh—I know ye—now! (*He suddenly breaks down, sobbing weakly.*)

ABIE (*fearfully*) Eben—what's happened t' ye—why did ye look at me 's if ye hated me?

EBEN (*violently, between sobs and gasps*) I do hate ye! Ye're a whore—a damn trickin' whore!

ABBIE (*shrinking back horrified*) Eben! Ye don't know what ye're sayin'!

EBEN (*scrambling to his feet and following her—accusingly*) Ye're nothin' but a stinkin' passel o' lies! Ye've been lyin' t' me every word ye spoke, day an' night, since we fust—done it. Ye've kept sayin' ye loved me. . . .

ABBIE (*frantically*) I do love ye! (*She takes his hand but he flings hers away.*)

EBEN (*unheeding*) Ye've made a fool o' me—a sick, dumb fool—a-purpose! Ye've been on'y playin' yer sneakin', stealin' game all along—gittin' me t' lie with ye so's ye'd hev a son he'd think was his'n, an' makin' him promise he'd give ye the farm and let me eat dust, if ye did git him a son! (*staring at her with anguished, bewildered eyes*) They must be a devil livin' in ye! 'Tain't human t' be as bad as that be!

ABBIE (*stunned—dully*) He told yew . . . ?

EBEN Hain't it true? It hain't no good in yew lyin'.

ABBIE (*pleadingly*) Eben, listen—ye must listen—it was long ago—afore we done nothin'—yew was scornin' me—goin' t' see Min—when I was lovin' ye—an' I said it t' him t' git vengeance on ye!

EBEN (*unheedingly. With tortured passion*) I wish ye was dead! I wish I was dead along with ye afore this come! (*ragingly*) But I'll git my vengeance too! I'll pray Maw t' come back t' help me—t' put her cuss on yew an' him!

ABBIE (*brokenly*) Don't ye, Eben! Don't ye! (*She throws herself on her knees before him, weeping.*) I didn't mean t' do bad t'ye! Fergive me, won't ye?

EBEN (*not seeming to hear her—fiercely*) I'll git squar' with the old skunk—an' yew! I'll tell him the truth 'bout the son he's so proud o'! Then I'll leave ye here t' pizen each other—with Maw comin' out o' her grave at nights—an' I'll go t' the gold fields o' Californi-a whar Sim an' Peter be!

ABBIE (*terrified*) Ye won't—leave me? Ye can't!

EBEN (*with fierce determination*) I'm a-goin', I tell ye! I'll git rich thar an' come back an' fight him fur the farm he stole—an' I'll kick ye both out in the road—t' beg an' sleep in the woods—an' yer son along with ye—t' starve an' die! (*He is hysterical at the end.*)

ABBIE (*with a shudder—humbly*) He's yewr son, too, Eben.

EBEN (*torturedly*) I wish he never was born! I wish he'd die this minit! I wish I'd never sot eyes on him! It's him—yew havin' him—a-purpose t' steal—that's changed everythin'!

ABBIE (*gently*) Did ye believe I loved ye—afore he come?

EBEN Ay-eh—like a dumb ox!

ABBIE An' ye don't believe no more?

EBEN B'lieve a lyin' thief! Ha!

ABBIE (*shudders—then humbly*) An did ye r'ally love me afore?

EBEN (*brokenly*) Ay-eh—an' ye was trickin' me!

ABBIE An' ye don't love me now!

EBEN (*violently*) I hate ye, I tell ye!

ABBIE An' ye're truly goin' West—goin' t' leave me—all account o' him being born?

EBEN I'm a-goin' in the mornin'—or may God strike me t' hell!

ABBIE (*after a pause—with a dreadful cold intensity—slowly*) If that's what his comin's done t' me—killin' yewr love—takin' yew away—my on'y joy—the on'y joy I've ever knowed—like heaven t' me—purtier'n heaven—then I hate him, too, even if I be his Maw!

EBEN (*bitterly*) Lies! Ye love him! He'll steal the farm fur ye! (*brokenly*) But 'tain't the farm so much—not no more—it's yew foolin' me—gittin' me t' love ye—lyin' yew loved me—jest t' git a son t' steal!

ABBIE (*distractedly*) He won't steal! I'd kill him fust! I do love ye! I'll prove t' ye . . . !

EBEN (*harshly*) 'Tain't no use lyin' no more. I'm deaf t' ye! (*He turns away.*) I hain't seein' ye agen. Good-by!

ABBIE (*pale with anguish*) Hain't ye even goin' t' kiss me—not once—arter all we loved?

EBEN (*in a hard voice*) I hain't wantin' t' kiss ye never agen! I'm wantin' t' forgit I ever sot eyes on ye!

ABBIE Eben!—ye mustn't—wait a spell—I want t' tell ye. . . .

EBEN I'm a-goin' in t' git drunk. I'm a-goin' t' dance.

ABBIE (*clinging to his arm—with passionate earnestness*) If I could make it—'s if he'd never come up between us—if I could prove t' ye I wa'n't schemin' t' steal from ye—so's everythin' could be jest the same with us, lovin' each other jest the same, kissin' an' happy the same's we've been happy afore he come—if I could do it— ye'd love me agen, wouldn't ye? Ye'd kiss me agen? You wouldn't never leave me, would ye?

EBEN (*moved*) I calc'late not. (*Then shaking her hand off his arm—with a bitter smile*) But ye hain't God, be ye?

ABBIE (*exultantly*) Remember ye've promised! (*Then with strange intensity*) Mebbe I kin take back one thin' God does!

EBEN (*peering at her*) Ye're gittin' cracked, hain't ye? (*Then going towards door*) I'm a-goin' t' dance.

ABBIE (*calls after him intensely*) I'll prove t' ye! I'll prove I love ye better'n. . . . (*He goes in the door, not seeming to hear. She remains standing where she is, looking after him—then she finishes desperately*) Better'n everythin' else in the world!

SCENE 3.

Just before dawn in the morning—shows the kitchen and CABOT's *bedroom.*

In the kitchen, by the light of a tallow candle on the table, EBEN *is sitting, his chin propped on his hands, his drawn face blank and expressionless. His carpetbag is on the floor beside him. In the bedroom, dimly lighted by a small whale-oil lamp,* CABOT *lies asleep.* ABBIE *is bending over the cradle, listening, her face full of terror yet with an undercurrent of desperate triumph. Suddenly, she breaks down and sobs, appears about to throw herself on her knees beside the cradle; but the old man turns restlessly, groaning in his sleep, and she controls herself, and shrinking away from the cradle with a gesture of horror, backs swiftly toward the door in rear and goes out. A moment later she comes into the kitchen and, running to* EBEN, *flings her arms about his neck and kisses him wildly. He hardens himself, he remains unmoved and cold, he keeps his eyes straight ahead.*

ABBIE (*hysterically*) I done it, Eben! I told ye I'd do it! I've proved I love ye—better'n everythin'—so's ye can't never doubt me no more!

EBEN (*dully*) Whatever ye done, it hain't no good now.

ABBIE (*wildly*) Don't ye say that! Kiss me, Eben, won't ye? I need ye t' kiss me arter what I done! I need ye t' say ye love me!

EBEN (*kisses her without emotion—dully*) That's fur good-by. I'm a-goin' soon.

ABBIE No! No! Ye won't go—not now!

EBEN (*going on with his own thoughts*) I been a-thinkin'—an' I hain't goin' t' tell Paw nothin'. I'll leave Maw t' take vengeance on ye. If I told him, the old skunk'd jest be stinkin' mean enuf to take it out on that baby. (*His voice showing emotion in spite of him*) An' I don't want nothin' bad t' happen t' him. He hain't t' blame fur yew. (*He adds with a certain queer pride*) An' he looks like me! An' by God, he's mine! An' some day I'll be a-comin' back an' . . . !

ABBIE (*too absorbed in her own thoughts to listen to him—pleadingly*) They's no cause fur ye t' go now—they's no sense—it's all the same's it was—they's nothin' come b'tween us now—arter what I done!

EBEN (*something in her voice arouses him. He stares at her a bit frightenedly*) Ye look mad, Abbie. What did ye do?

ABBIE I—I killed him, Eben.

EBEN (*amazed*) Ye killed him?

ABBIE (*dully*) Ay-eh.

EBEN (*recovering from his astonishment—savagely*) An' serves him right! But we got t' do somethin' quick t' make it look s'if the old skunk'd killed himself when he was drunk. We kin prove by 'em all how drunk he got.

ABBIE (*wildly*) No! No! Not him! (*Laughing distractedly*) But that's what I ought t' done, hain't it? I oughter killed him instead! Why didn't ye tell me?

EBEN (*appalled*) Instead? What d'ye mean?

ABBIE Not him.

EBEN (*his face grown ghastly*) Not—not that baby!

ABBIE (*dully*) Ay-eh!

EBEN (*falls to his knees as if he'd been struck—his voice trembling with horror*) Oh, God A'mighty! A'mighty God! Maw, whar was ye, why didn't ye stop her?

ABBIE (*simply*) She went back t' her grave that night we fust done it, remember? I hain't felt her about since. (*A pause.* EBEN *hides his head in his hands, trembling all over as if he had the ague. She goes on dully*) I left the piller over his little face. Then he killed himself. He stopped breathin'. (*She begins to weep softly.*)

EBEN (*rage beginning to mingle with grief*) He looked like me. He was mine, damn ye!

ABBIE (*slowly and brokenly*) I didn't want t' do it. I hated myself fur doin' it. I loved him. He was so purty—dead spit 'n' image o' yew. But I loved yew more—an' yew was goin' away—far off whar I'd never see ye agen, never kiss ye, never feel ye pressed agin me agen—an' ye said ye hated me fur havin' him—ye said ye hated him an' wished he was dead—ye said if it hadn't been fur him comin' it'd be the same's afore between us.

EBEN (*unable to endure this, springs to his feet in a fury, threatening her, his twitching fingers seeming to reach out for her throat*) Ye lie! I never said—I never dreamed ye'd—I'd cut off my head afore I'd hurt his finger!

ABBIE (*piteously, sinking on her knees*) Eben, don't ye look at me like that—hatin' me—not after what I done fur ye—fur us—so's we could be happy agen—

EBEN (*furiously now*) Shut up, or I'll kill ye! I see yer game now—the same old sneakin' trick—ye're aimin' t' blame me fur the murder ye done!

ABBIE (*moaning—putting her hands over her ears*) Don't ye, Eben! Don't ye! (*She grasps his legs.*)

EBEN (*his mood suddenly changing to horror, shrinks away from her*) Don't ye tech me! Ye're pizen! How could ye—t' murder a pore little critter—Ye must've swapped yer soul t' hell! (*suddenly raging*) Ha! I kin see why ye done it! Not the lies ye jest told—but 'cause ye wanted t' steal agen—steal the last thin' ye'd left me—my part o' him—no, the hull o' him—ye saw he looked like me—ye knowed he was all mine—an' ye couldn't b'ar it—I know ye! Ye killed him fur bein' mine! (*All this has driven him almost insane. He makes a rush past her for the door—then turns—shaking both fists at her, violently.*) But I'll take vengeance now! I'll git the Sheriff! I'll tell him everythin'! Then I'll sing "I'm off to Californi-a!" an' go—gold—Golden Gate—gold sun—fields o' gold in the West! (*This last he half shouts, half croons incoherently, suddenly breaking off passionately.*) I'm a-goin' fur the Sheriff t' come an' git ye! I want ye tuk away, locked up from me! I can't stand t' luk at ye! Murderer an' thief 'r not, ye still tempt me! I'll give ye up t' the Sheriff! (*He turns and runs out, around the corner of house, panting and sobbing, and breaks into a swerving sprint down the road.*)

ABBIE (*struggling to her feet, runs to the door, calling after him*) I love ye, Eben! I love ye! (*She stops at the door weakly, swaying, about to fall.*) I don't care what ye do—if ye'll on'y love me agen—(*She falls limply to the floor in a faint.*)

SCENE 4.

About an hour later. Same as SCENE 3. *Shows the kitchen and* CABOT's *bedroom. It is after dawn. The sky is brilliant with the sunrise.*

In the kitchen, ABBIE *sits at the table, her body limp and exhausted, her head bowed down over her arms, her face hidden. Upstairs,* CABOT *is still asleep but awakens with a start. He looks toward the window and gives a snort of surprise and irritation—throws back the covers and begins hurriedly pulling on his clothes. Without looking behind him, he begins talking to* ABBIE *whom he supposes beside him.*

CABOT Thunder 'n' lightnin', Abbie! I hain't slept this late in fifty year! Looks 's if the sun was full riz a'most. Must've been the dancin' an' likker. Must be gittin' old. I hope Eben's t' wuk. Ye might've tuk the trouble t' rouse me, Abbie. (*He turns—sees no one there—surprised.*) Waal—whar air she? Gittin' vittles, I calc'late. (*He tiptoes to the cradle and peers down—proudly*) Mornin', sonny. Purty's a picter! Sleepin' sound. He don't beller all night like most o' 'em. (*He goes quietly out the door in rear—a few moments later enters kitchen—sees* ABBIE—*with satisfaction*) So thar ye be. Ye got any vittles cooked?

ABBIE (*without moving*) No.

CABOT (*coming to her, almost sympathetically*) Ye feelin' sick?

ABBIE No.

CABOT (*pats her on shoulder. She shudders*) Ye'd best lie down a spell. (*half jocularly*) Yer son'll be needin' ye soon. He'd ought t' wake up with a gnashin' appetite, the sound way he's sleepin'.

ABBIE (*shudders—then in a dead voice*) He ain't never goin' to wake up.

CABOT (*jokingly*) Takes after me this mornin'. I ain't slept so late in . . .

ABBIE He's dead.

CABOT (*stares at her—bewilderedly*) What . . .

ABBIE I killed him.

CABOT (*stepping back from her—aghast*) Air ye drunk—'r crazy—'r . . . !

ABBIE (*suddenly lifts her head and turns on him—wildly*) I killed him, I tell ye! I smothered him. Go up an' see if ye don't b'lieve me! (CABOT *stares at her a second, then bolts out the rear door, can be heard bounding up the stairs, and rushes into the bedroom and over to the cradle.* ABBIE *has sunk back lifelessly into her former position.* CABOT *puts his hand down on the body in the crib. An expression of fear and horror comes over his face.*)

CABOT (*shrinking away—tremblingly*) God A'mighty! God A'mighty. (*He stumbles out the door—in a short while returns to the kitchen—comes to* ABBIE, *the stunned expression still on his face—hoarsely*) Why did ye do it? Why? (*As she doesn't answer, he grabs her violently by the shoulder and shakes her.*) I ax ye why ye done it! Ye'd better tell me 'r . . . !

ABBIE (*gives him a furious push which sends him staggering back and springs to her feet—with wild rage and hatred*) Don't ye dare tech me! What right hev ye t' question me 'bout him? He wa'n't yewr son! Think I'd have a son by yew? I'd die fust! I hate the sight o' ye an' allus did! It's yew I should've murdered, if I'd had good sense! I hate ye! I love Eben. I did from the fust. An' he was Eben's son—mine an' Eben's—not your'n!

CABOT (*stands looking at her dazedly—a pause—finding his words with an effort—dully*) That was it—what I felt—pokin' round the corners—while ye lied—holdin' herself from me—sayin' ye'd a'ready conceived—(*He lapses into crushed silence—then with a strange emotion*) He's dead, sart'n. I felt his heart. Pore little critter! (*He blinks back one tear, wiping his sleeve across his nose.*)

ABBIE (*hysterically*) Don't ye! Don't ye! (*She sobs unrestrainedly.*)

CABOT (*with a concentrated effort that stiffens his body into a rigid line and hardens his face into a stony mask—through his teeth to himself*) I got t' be—like a stone—a rock o' jedgment! (*A pause. He gets complete control over himself—harshly*) If he was Eben's, I be glad he air gone! An' mebbe I suspicioned it all along. I felt they was somethin' onnateral—somewhars—the house got so lonesome—an' cold—drivin' me down t' the barn—t' the beasts o' the field. . . . Ay-eh. I must've suspicioned—somethin'. Ye didn't fool me—not altogether, leastways—I'm too old a bird—growin' ripe on the bough. . . . (*He becomes aware he is wandering, straightens again, looks at* ABBIE *with a cruel grin.*) So ye'd liked t' hev murdered me 'stead o' him, would ye? Waal, I'll live to a hundred! I'll live t' see ye hung! I'll deliver ye up t' the jedgment o' God an' the law! I'll git the Sheriff now. (*Starts for the door.*)

ABBIE (*dully*) Ye needn't. Eben's gone fur him.

CABOT (*amazed*) Eben—gone fur the Sheriff?

ABBIE Ay-eh.

CABOT T' inform agen ye?

ABBIE Ay-eh.

CABOT (*considers this—a pause—then in a hard voice*) Waal, I'm thankful fur him savin' me the trouble. I'll git t' wuk. (*He goes to the door—then turns—in a voice full of strange emotion*) He'd ought t' been my son, Abbie. Ye'd ought t' loved me. I'm a man. If ye'd loved me, I'd never told no Sheriff on ye no matter what ye did, if they was t' brile me alive!

ABBIE (*defensively*) They's more to it nor yew know, makes him tell.

CABOT (*dryly*) Fur yewr sake, I hope they be. (*He goes out—comes around to the gate—stares up at the sky. His control relaxes. For a moment he is old and weary. He murmurs despairingly*) God A'mighty, I be lonesomer'n ever! (*He hears running footsteps from the left, immediately is himself again.* EBEN *runs in, panting exhaustedly, wild-eyed and mad looking. He lurches through the gate.* CABOT *grabs him by the shoulder.* EBEN *stares at him dumbly.*) Did ye tell the Sheriff?

EBEN (*nodding stupidly*) Ay-eh.

CABOT (*gives him a push away that sends him sprawling—laughing with withering contempt*) Good fur ye! A prime chip o' yer Maw ye be! (*He goes toward the barn, laughing harshly.* EBEN *scrambles to his feet. Suddenly* CABOT *turns—grimly threatening*) Git off this farm when the Sheriff takes her—or, by God, he'll have t' come back an' git me fur murder, too! (*He stalks off.* EBEN *does not appear to have heard him. He runs to the door and comes into the kitchen.* ABBIE *looks up with a cry of anguished joy.* EBEN *stumbles over and throws himself on his knees beside her—sobbing brokenly.*)

EBEN Fergive me!

ABBIE (*happily*) Eben! (*She kisses him and pulls his head over against her breast.*)

EBEN I love ye! Fergive me!

ABBIE (*ecstatically*) I'd fergive ye all the sins in hell fur sayin' that! (*She kisses his head, pressing it to her with a fierce passion of possession.*)

EBEN (*brokenly*) But I told the Sheriff. He's comin' fur ye!

ABBIE I kin b'ar what happens t' me—now!

EBEN I woke him up. I told him. He says, wait 'til I git dressed. I was waiting. I got to thinkin' o' yew. I got to thinkin' how I'd loved ye. It hurt like somethin' was bustin' in my chest an' head. I got t' cryin'. I knowed sudden I loved ye yet, an' allus would love ye!

ABBIE (*caressing his hair—tenderly*) My boy, hain't ye?

EBEN I begun t' run back. I cut across the fields an' through the woods. I thought ye might have time t' run away—with me—an' . . .

ABBIE (*shaking her head*) I got t' take my punishment—t' pay fur my sin.

EBEN Then I want t' share it with ye.

ABBIE Ye didn't do nothin'.

EBEN I put it in yer head. I wisht he was dead! I as much as urged ye t' do it!

ABBIE No. It was me alone!

EBEN I'm as guilty as yew be! He was the child o' our sin.

ABBIE (*lifting her head as if defying God*) I don't repent that sin! I hain't askin' God t' fergive that!

EBEN Nor me—but it led up t' the other—an' the murder ye did, ye did 'count o' me—an' it's my murder, too, I'll tell the Sheriff—an' if ye deny it, I'll say we planned it t'gether—an' they'll all b'lieve me, fur they suspicion everythin' we've done, an' it'll seem likely an' true to 'em. An' it is true—way down. I did help ye—somehow.

ABBIE (*laying her head on his—sobbing*) No! I don't want ye t' suffer!

EBEN I got t' pay fur my part o' the sin! An' I'd suffer wuss leavin' ye, goin' West, thinkin' o' ye day an' night, bein' out when yew was in—(*lowering his voice*)—'r bein' alive when yew was dead. (*a pause*) I want t' share with ye, Abbie—prison 'r death 'r hell 'r anythin'! (*He looks into her eyes and forces a trembling smile.*) If I'm sharin' with ye, I won't feel lonesome, leastways.

ABBIE (*weakly*) Eben! I won't let ye! I can't let ye!

EBEN (*kissing her—tenderly*) Ye can't he'p yerself. I got ye beat fur once!

ABBIE (*forcing a smile—adoringly*) I hain't beat—s'long's I got ye!

EBEN (*hears the sound of feet outside*) Ssshh! Listen! They've come t' take us!

ABBIE No, it's him. Don't give him no chance to fight ye, Eben. Don't say nothin'—no matter what he says. An' I won't neither. (*It is* CABOT. *He comes up from the barn in a great state of excitement and strides into the house and then into the kitchen.* EBEN *is kneeling beside* ABBIE, *his arm around her, hers around him. They stare straight ahead.*)

CABOT (*stares at them, his face hard. A long pause—vindictively*) Ye make a slick pair o' murderin' turtle doves! Ye'd ought t' be both hung on the same limb an' left thar t' swing in the breeze an' rot—a warnin' t' old fools like me t' b'ar their lonesomeness alone—an' fur young fools like ye t' hobble their lust. (*A pause. The excitement returns to his face, his eyes snap, he looks a bit crazy.*) I couldn't work today. I couldn't take no interest. T' hell with the farm! I'm leavin' it! I've turned the cows an' other stock loose! I've druv 'em into the woods whar they kin be free! By freein' 'em, I'm freein' myself! I'm quittin' here today! I'll set fire t' house an' barn an' watch 'em burn, an' I'll leave yer Maw t' haunt the ashes, an' I'll will the fields back t' God, so that nothin' human kin never touch 'em! I'll be a-goin' to Californi-a—t' jine Simeon an' Peter—true sons o' mine if they be dumb fools—an' the Cabots'll find Solomon's Mines t'gether! (*He suddenly cuts a mad caper.*) Whoop! What was the song they sung? "Oh, Californi-a! That's the land fur me." (*He sings this—then gets on his knees by the floorboard under which the money was hid.*) An' I'll sail thar on one o' the finest clippers I kin find! I've got the money! Pity ye didn't know whar this was hidden so's ye could steal . . . (*He has pulled up the board. He stares—feels—stares again. A pause of dead silence. He slowly turns, slumping into a sitting position on the floor, his eyes like those of a dead fish, his face the sickly green of an attack of nausea. He swallows painfully several times—forces a weak smile at last.*) So—ye did steal it!

EBEN (*emotionlessly*) I swapped it t' Sim an' Peter fur their share o' the farm—t' pay their passage t' Californi-a.

CABOT (*with one sardonic*) Ha! (*He begins to recover. Gets slowly to his feet—strangely*) I calc'late God give it to 'em—not yew! God's hard, not easy! Mebbe they's easy gold in the West but it hain't God's gold. It hain't fur me. I kin hear His voice warnin' me agen t' be hard an' stay on my farm. I kin see his hand usin' Eben t' steal t' keep me from weakness. I kin feel I be in the palm o' His hand, His fingers guidin' me. (*A pause—then he mutters sadly*) It's a-goin' t' be lonesomer now than ever it war afore—an' I'm gittin' old, Lord—ripe on the bough. . . . (*Then stiffening*) Waal—what d'ye want? God's lonesome, hain't He? God's hard an' lonesome! (*A pause. The SHERIFF with two men comes up the road from the left. They move cautiously to the door. The SHERIFF knocks on it with the butt of his pistol.*)

SHERIFF Open in the name o' the law! (*They start.*)

CABOT They've come fur ye. (*He goes to the rear door.*) Come in, Jim! (*The three men enter. CABOT meets them in doorway.*) Jest a minit, Jim. I got 'em safe here. (*The SHERIFF nods. He and his companions remain in the doorway.*)

EBEN (*suddenly calls*) I lied this mornin', Jim. I helped her to do it. Ye kin take me, too.

ABBIE (*brokenly*) No!

CABOT Take 'em both. (*He comes forward—stares at EBEN with a trace of grudging admiration*) Purty good—fur yew! Waal, I got t' round up the stock. Good-by.

EBEN Good-by.

ABBIE Good-by. (*CABOT turns and strides past the men—comes out and around the corner of the house, his shoulders squared, his face stony, and stalks grimly toward the barn. In the meantime the SHERIFF and men have come into the room.*)

SHERIFF (*embarrassedly*) Waal—we'd best start.

ABBIE Wait. (*Turns to EBEN*) I love ye, Eben.

EBEN I love ye, Abbie. (*They kiss. The three men grin and shuffle embarrassedly. EBEN takes ABBIE'S hand. They go out the door in rear, the men following, and come from the house, walking hand in hand to the gate. EBEN stops there and points to the sunrise sky.*) Sun's a-rizin'. Purty, hain't it?

ABBIE Ay-eh. (*They both stand for a moment looking up raptly in attitudes strangely aloof and devout.*)

SHERIFF (*looking around at the farm enviously—to his companion*) It's a jim-dandy farm, no denyin'. Wished I owned it!

Questions

1. In many ways the most interesting character at the beginning of this play is Eben Cabot. How is he different from his brothers? How is he like his father? How is he different from his father?
2. What does Eben want? How does he intend to get it?
3. Ephraim Cabot is by far the most powerful figure in this drama. What are his strengths? Might he be considered the hero of this tragedy? Explain your answer.
4. Abbie Putnam creates the greatest changes in the world of the Cabots. What does she want? How does she intend to get it?
5. Aristotle says that the hero or heroine of tragedy always has an obvious "tragic flaw" of character. What is Abbie's tragic flaw?
6. What do you admire about Abbie Putnam?
7. Do you think that Eben and Abbie are truly in love at first, or is their affair motivated by ignoble intentions?
8. After the fight between Ephraim and Eben, Eben accuses Abbie of not really loving him. Do you think he is justified?
9. How does Abbie intend to prove her love to Eben? Discuss how Abbie's crime is the result of a misunderstanding of his desire.
10. In this play there are two classic examples of recognition and reversal: the first involves Abbie's recognition that she had wrongly interpreted Eben's desire "to have everything as it was before . . ."; the second involves Ephraim's recognition that the baby is not his. Which is the most tragic?
11. To what extent does the play succeed in inspiring fear and pity? Which character do you most fear for? Which character do you most pity?
12. How does the plot of this play resemble *Oedipus Rex?* How is it like *Hamlet?*

✍ Tips for Writing about Tragedy

1. In a tragedy, the protagonist always goes from a position of strength to one of weakness. Describe the movement of the drama in terms of decline and fall.
2. In many tragedies, there are moments of "reversal," where the hero or heroine suffers a very dramatic decline in fortune, finding suddenly that the opposite of what was expected occurs. This is called *dramatic irony.* Locate these moments in the play.
3. It has been said that the tragic hero is always brought down partly by his character flaws or poor judgment and partly by forces of society or the cosmos. Frequently the theme of the play is the conflict between the desire of the hero and the opposing requirements of society. When you have defined this conflict, you may evaluate the play's success in terms of its logical resolution of the conflict, in support of the individual or of the social order.
4. In a true tragedy, we always feel that the tragic hero might knowingly have avoided his fate. He or she is to some extent responsible. Otherwise what we are witnessing is pathetic rather than tragic. Discuss the balance of pathos and tragedy in any play under consideration.

7  Comedy

Veterans of the stage often remark that audiences come to the theater to laugh, cry, or be frightened out of their wits. Notice that they mention laughter first. For every successful tragedy, there are ten comedies that usually have longer commercial runs and play to larger audiences. Tragedy produces *catharsis*, the relief of tension that comes when we have witnessed what we most dreaded. Comedy provides a purer delight—laughter in the face of danger, and serenity as we find that everything we hoped for comes true. The villain gets trapped and punished. The boy gets the girl, gold is found in a flowerpot, and everyone lives happily ever after.

But comedy is much more than an entertainment that makes us laugh, much more than an exciting story with a happy ending. Comedy originates from a source as deep and complex as the origin of tragedy. The novelist Thackeray said that "humor is the mistress of tears," and indeed great comedies often make us laugh at human situations that, if they happened to us, we would consider very serious. The subjects of comedy are frequently tragic, as you will soon discover in reading *Los Vendidos*, which concerns racial prejudice in America. The genius of the comic dramatist encourages us to view difficulties of life with a sense of humor.

Let us consider the difference between the tragic vision and the comic. Tragedy, with its noble heroes, concerns us with the moral government of the universe, and all that is godlike in our efforts to live in it. Comedy, with its clowns and lovesick youths, has always mocked at any attempt of humans to behave like gods. You may have seen Charlie Chaplin aping the imperious scowls of Hitler, or Groucho Marx in a professor's robes and mortarboard doing a jig at a mock commencement. Comedy looks at the individual from the outside, viewing the folly, injustice, and misery of humans with critical detachment. From a distance the worst troubles and heartaches seem smaller, lighter. We are relieved that they are not ours. As the American cowboy humorist Will Rogers once said: "Everything is funny as long as it is happening to someone else."

The historical origins of comedy are dim. The word *comedy* comes from the Greek *Komos*, meaning "revel," and we believe that comic drama began with the festivities to celebrate spring and Dionysus, the god of fertility and wine. Mating rituals and drunkenness have always been rich sources of humor. In the ancient satyr plays of Euripides and others, the chorus consists of goatlike, horsetailed satyrs who leap and cavort drunkenly on the stage. Such plays provided comic relief after a series of tragedies at the festival of Dionysus. Later the satyr plays developed into the sophisticated Old Comedy, as practiced by Aristophanes.

High and Low Comedy

When the cook puts a foot in the soap-bucket and then slides into the ashbin, that is low comedy. It appeals to our lowest sense of humor, the impulse to laugh when someone else suffers a temporary physical discomfort or indignity.

High comedy appeals to the intellect. When Algernon in *The Importance of Being Earnest* gains entrance to his friend Jack's house under the guise of being Jack's imaginary brother, Ernest, that is high comedy. There is high comedy in mistaken identity, in excessive or mechanical behavior, and in frustrated expectations. High comedy onstage often relies heavily on displays of verbal wit. Shakespeare's verbal humor shines throughout *Twelfth Night*. When Olivia agrees to be questioned by the Clown he catches her in his net of wit:

CLOWN Good madonna, why mourn'st thou?
OLIVIA Good fool, for my brother's death.
CLOWN I think his soul is in hell, madonna.
OLIVIA I know his soul is in heaven, fool.
CLOWN The more fool, madonna, to mourn for your brother's soul being in heaven.
   Take away the fool, gentlemen.

High and *low* comedy, as the words suggest, are relative terms; most comic plays are a blend of both. Although *The Importance of Being Earnest* turns upon the high comic predicament of mistaken identity, there are elements of low humor in the circumstances: the central character John Worthing was orphaned at birth, having been mistaken for a three-volume novel and left in a hand-bag in Victoria Station.

Farce is the genre of dramatic comedy that relies most heavily upon clowning, slapstick, and low humor. Originating in medieval France, the farce reached its full expressions in the romantic plays of Georges Feydeau (1862–1921). The characters of farce are less realistic and complex than those of high comedy, and the situations are less probable. In these particulars the farce resembles Italian commedia dell'arte, with its stock characters Lucinda (the beautiful young lady), Scaramuccia (the braggart captain), and Pantalone (the rich, foolish father), and its fantastic turns of plot.

High comedy reaches its zenith in the English *comedy of manners*, a form developed during the Restoration, after 1660, when Charles II opened the theaters that the Puritan Cromwell had closed. The subtle wit and ingenious dramatic situations of these comedies deflate the pretensions of the most civilized behavior. Many critics consider the comic playwright William Congreve (1670–1729) to be the greatest dramatist of the Restoration period. He wrote *The Way of the World, Love for Love* and other great comedies of manners. Richard Brinsley Sheridan (1751–1816), who wrote *The School for Scandal*, and Oscar Wilde (1854–1900), who wrote *The Importance of Being Earnest*, have made enduring contributions to the form.

Romantic Comedy

The fantastical satires of the Greek Old Comedy gave way to the New Comedy in the third century B.C. The New Comedy, as practiced by Menander (342–292 B.C.), portrays ordinary domestic situations and contemporary manners and usually involves a love affair which begins in trouble and ends in happiness. Menander's romantic plays served as models for the Roman playwrights Plautus (254–184 B.C.) and Terence (185–159 B.C.), who wrote romantic comedies that were both amusing and moral. In a typical plot the young gentleman falls in love with the servant girl. He schemes to buy her, but in the course of the play discovers she is the lost child of noble parents. Through all her trials she has preserved her chastity, in keeping with traditional morals, so they can be married. Many of the stock characters of Roman comedy entered into the Renaissance Italian commedia dell'arte and into Elizabethan and classical French comedy. The plots of Shakespeare's *Comedy of Errors* as well as Molière's *The Miser* come from Plautus, who probably got them from Menander.

Romantic comedies culminate in marriage as surely as tragedies end in isolation and death for their protagonists. Since Menander, the lovers in classical comedy have struggled to be together in the face of societies that frown upon their love. Again and again the lovers overcome the objections of society, either by altering it or by changing themselves, and achieve an integration—of themselves into society, and of the conflicting social forces that kept the lovers apart. The success of the lovers in romantic comedy is an affirmation of life. Comedy, which had its origins in a fertility ritual, celebrates humanity and the future through love and marriage.

The Importance of Being Earnest

Oscar Wilde's *The Importance of Being Earnest* is a delightful blend of romantic comedy and social satire. In the ancient tradition of romantic comedy, two pairs of lovers struggle to overcome conventions that threaten their happiness. But, in the zany society of Wilde's theater, those conventions—parental consent and legitimate courtship—are rendered utterly ridiculous. Lady Bracknell, who alone can give consent to the marriage between her daughter Gwendolen and Jack Worthy, interviews the prospective bridegroom as follows:

> LADY BRACKNELL I have always been of the opinion that a man who desires to get married should know either everything or nothing. Which do you know?
> JACK (*after some hesitation*) I know nothing, Lady Bracknell.
> LADY BRACKNELL I am pleased to hear it. I do not approve of anything that tampers with natural ignorance. Ignorance is like a delicate exotic fruit; touch it and the bloom is gone.

With such epigrammatic humor Wilde reduces the conventions of courtship to absurdity. And the lovers themselves are in a predicament worthy of a farce. Each heroine has fallen in love with a man she believes to be named Ernest, and both profess as much love for the name as for the man. The discovery that neither man is named Ernest presents a major obstacle to the two marriages.

Oscar Wilde was the most extravagantly gifted all-around man of letters of the late nineteenth century, one of the few writers ever to have created masterpieces in the novel, drama, and verse. Born in Ireland in 1854, Wilde studied at Oxford, where he came under the influence of the critic Walter Pater. Wilde led an aesthetic movement that advocated "Art for Art's sake," the doctrine that the aim of art should be the perfection of expression rather than any moral or political effect. *The Importance of Being Earnest* (1895) is his greatest work for the stage. He is also known for his short novel *The Picture of Dorian Gray* (1891) and *The Ballad of Reading Gaol*, a poem.

OSCAR WILDE (1854–1900)

The Importance of Being Earnest

CHARACTERS

JOHN WORTHING, J.P.	LADY BRACKNELL
ALGERNON MONCRIEFF	HON. GWENDOLEN FAIRFAX
REV. CANON CHASUBLE, D.D.	CECILY CARDEW
MERRIMAN, *butler*	MISS PRISM, *governess*
LANE, *manservant*	

THE SCENES OF THE PLAY

ACT I. *Algernon Moncrieff's Flat in Half-Moon Street, W.*
ACT II. *The Garden at the Manor House, Woolton.*
ACT III. *Drawing-Room of the Manor House, Woolton.*

TIME—*The Present.*
PLACE—*London.*

Oscar Wilde (*Bettman Archive*)

ACT I

SCENE. *Morning-room in* ALGERNON'S *flat in Half-Moon Street. The room is luxuriously and artistically furnished. The sound of a piano is heard in the adjoining room.*

(LANE *is arranging afternoon tea on the table, and after the music has ceased,* ALGERNON *enters.*)

ALGERNON. Did you hear what I was playing, Lane?

LANE. I didn't think it polite to listen, sir.

ALGERNON. I'm sorry for that, for your sake. I don't play accurately—any one can play accurately—but I play with wonderful expression. As far as the piano is concerned, sentiment is my forte. I keep science for Life.

LANE. Yes, sir.

ALGERNON. And, speaking of the science of Life, have you got the cucumber sandwiches cut for Lady Bracknell?

LANE. Yes, sir. (*Hands them on a salver.*)

ALGERNON (*inspects them, takes two, and sits down on the sofa*) Oh! . . . by the way, Lane, I see from your book that on Thursday night, when Lord Shoreman and Mr. Worthing were dining with me, eight bottles of champagne are entered as having been consumed.

LANE Yes, sir; eight bottles and a pint.

ALGERNON Why is it that at a bachelor's establishment the servants invariably drink the champagne? I ask merely for information.

LANE I attribute it to the superior quality of the wine, sir. I have often observed that in married households the champagne is rarely of a first-rate brand.

ALGERNON Good Heavens! Is marriage so demoralizing as that?

LANE I believe it *is* a very pleasant state, sir. I have had very little experience of it myself up to the present. I have only been married once. That was in consequence of a misunderstanding between myself and a young woman.

ALGERNON (*languidly*) I don't know that I am much interested in your family life, Lane.

LANE No, sir; it is not a very interesting subject. I never think of it myself.

ALGERNON Very natural, I am sure. That will do, Lane, thank you.

LANE Thank you, sir.(LANE *goes out.*)

ALGERNON Lane's views on marriage seem somewhat lax. Really, if the lower orders don't set us a good example, what on earth is the use of them? They seem, as a class, to have absolutely no sense of moral responsibility.

Enter LANE.

LANE Mr. Ernest Worthing.

Enter JACK. LANE *goes out.*

ALGERNON How are you, my dear Ernest? What brings you up to town?

JACK Oh, pleasure, pleasure! What else should bring one anywhere? Eating as usual, I see, Algy!

ALGERNON (*stiffly*) I believe it is customary in good society to take some slight refreshment at five o'clock. Where have you been since last Thursday?

JACK (*sitting down on the sofa*) In the country.

ALGERNON What on earth do you do there?

JACK (*pulling off his gloves*) When one is in town one amuses oneself. When one is in the country one amuses other people. It is excessively boring.

ALGERNON And who are the people you amuse?

JACK (*airily*) Oh, neighbors, neighbors.

ALGERNON Got nice neighbors in your part of Shropshire?

JACK Perfectly horrid! Never speak to one of them.

ALGERNON How immensely you must amuse them! (*Goes over and takes sandwich.*) By the way, Shropshire is your county, is it not?

JACK Eh? Shropshire? Yes, of course. Hallo! Why all these cups? Why cucumber sandwiches? Why such reckless extravagance in one so young? Who is coming to tea?

ALGERNON Oh! merely Aunt Augusta and Gwendolen.

JACK How perfectly delightful!

ALGERNON Yes, that is all very well; but I am afraid Aunt Augusta won't quite approve of your being here.

JACK May I ask why?

ALGERNON My dear fellow, the way you flirt with Gwendolen is perfectly disgraceful. It is almost as bad as the way Gwendolen flirts with you.

JACK I am in love with Gwendolen. I have come up to town expressly to propose to her.

ALGERNON I thought you had come up for pleasure? . . . I call that business.

JACK How utterly unromantic you are!

ALGERNON I really don't see anything romantic in proposing. It is very romantic to be in love. But there is nothing romantic about a definite proposal. Why, one may be accepted. One usually is, I believe. Then the excitement is all over. The very essence of romance is uncertainty. If ever I get married, I'll certainly try to forget the fact.

JACK I have no doubt about that, dear Algy. The Divorce Court was specially invented for people whose memories are so curiously constituted.

ALGERNON Oh! there is no use speculating on that subject. Divorces are made in

Heaven—(JACK *puts out his hand to take a sandwich.* ALGERNON *at once interferes.*) Please don't touch the cucumber sandwiches. They are ordered specially for Aunt Augusta. (*Takes one and eats it.*)

JACK Well, you have been eating them all the time.

ALGERNON That is quite a different matter. She is my aunt. (*Takes plate from below.*) Have some bread and butter. The bread and butter is for Gwendolen. Gwendolen is devoted to bread and butter.

JACK (*advancing to table and helping himself*) And very good bread and butter it is, too.

ALGERNON Well, my dear fellow, you need not eat as if you were going to eat it all. You behave as if you were married to her already. You are not married to her already, and I don't think you ever will be.

JACK Why on earth do you say that?

ALGERNON Well, in the first place girls never marry the men they flirt with. Girls don't think it right.

JACK Oh, that is nonsense!

ALGERNON It isn't. It is a great truth. It accounts for the extraordinary number of bachelors that one sees all over the place. In the second place, I don't give my consent.

JACK Your consent!

ALGERNON My dear fellow, Gwendolen is my first cousin. And before I allow you to marry her, you will have to clear up the whole question of Cecily. (*Rings bell.*)

JACK Cecily! What on earth do you mean? What do you mean, Algy, by Cecily? I don't know any one of the name of Cecily.

Enter LANE.

ALGERNON Bring me that cigarette case Mr. Worthing left in the smoking-room the last time he dined here.

LANE Yes, sir. (LANE *goes out.*)

JACK Do you mean to say you have had my cigarette case all this time? I wish to goodness you had let me know. I have been writing frantic letters to Scotland Yard about it. I was very nearly offering a large reward.

ALGERNON Well, I wish you would offer one. I happen to be more than usually hard up.

JACK There is no good offering a large reward now that the thing is found.

Enter LANE *with the cigarette case on a salver.* ALGERNON *takes it at once.* LANE *goes out.*

ALGERNON I think that is rather mean of you, Ernest, I must say. (*Opens case and examines it.*) However, it makes no matter, for, now that I look at the inscription, I find that the thing isn't yours after all.

JACK Of course it's mine. (*Moving to him.*) You have seen me with it a hundred times, and you have no right whatsoever to read what is written inside. It is a very ungentlemanly thing to read a private cigarette case.

ALGERNON Oh! it is absurd to have a hard-and-fast rule about what one should read and what one shouldn't. More than half of modern culture depends on what one shouldn't read.

JACK I am quite aware of the fact, and I don't propose to discuss modern culture. It isn't the sort of thing one should talk of in private. I simply want my cigarette case back.

ALGERNON Yes; but this isn't your cigarette case. This cigarette case is a present from some one of the name of Cecily, and you said you didn't know any one of that name.

JACK Well, if you want to know, Cecily happens to be my aunt.

ALGERNON Your aunt!

JACK Yes. Charming old lady she is, too. Lives at Tunbridge Wells. Just give it back to me, Algy.

ALGERNON (*retreating to back of sofa*) But why does she call herself little Cecily if she is your aunt and lives at Tunbridge Wells? (*Reading.*) "From little Cecily with her fondest love."

JACK (*moving to sofa and kneeling upon it*) My dear fellow, what on earth is there in that? Some aunts are tall, some aunts are not tall. That is a matter that surely an aunt may be allowed to decide for herself. You seem to think that every aunt should be exactly like your aunt! That is absurd! For Heaven's sake give me back my cigarette case. (*Follows* ALGERNON *round the room.*)

ALGERNON Yes. But why does your aunt call you her uncle? "From little Cecily, with her fondest love to her dear Uncle Jack." There is no objection, I admit, to an aunt being a small aunt, but why an aunt, no matter what her size may be, should call her own nephew her uncle, I can't quite make out. Besides, your name isn't Jack at all; it is Ernest.

JACK It isn't Ernest; it's Jack.

ALGERNON You have always told me it was Ernest. I have introduced you to every one as Ernest. You answer to the name of Ernest. You look as if your name was Ernest. You are the most earnest looking person I ever saw in my life. It is perfectly absurd your saying that your name isn't Ernest. It's on your cards. Here is one of them. (*Taking it from case.*) "Mr. Ernest Worthing, B 4, The Albany." I'll keep this as a proof your name is Ernest if ever you attempt to deny it to me, or to Gwendolen, or to any one else. (*Puts the card in his pocket.*)

JACK Well, my name is Ernest in town and Jack in the country, and the cigarette case was given to me in the country.

ALGERNON Yes, but that does not account for the fact that your small Aunt Cecily, who lives at Tunbridge Wells, calls you her dear uncle. Come, old boy, you had much better have the thing out at once.

JACK My dear Algy, you talk exactly as if you were a dentist. It is very vulgar to talk like a dentist when one isn't a dentist. It produces a false impression.

ALGERNON Well, that is exactly what dentists always do. Now, go on! Tell me the whole thing. I may mention that I have always suspected you of being a confirmed and secret Bunburyist; and I am quite sure of it now.

JACK Bunburyist? What on earth do you mean by a Bunburyist?

ALGERNON I'll reveal to you the meaning of that incomparable expression as soon as you are kind enough to inform me why you are Ernest in town and Jack in the country.

JACK Well, produce my cigarette case first.

ALGERNON Here it is. (*Hands cigarette case.*) Now produce your explanation, and pray make it improbable. (*Sits on sofa.*)

JACK My dear fellow, there is nothing improbable about my explanation at all. In fact it's perfectly ordinary. Old Mr. Thomas Cardew, who adopted me when I was a little boy, made me in his will guardian to his grand-daughter, Miss Cecily Cardew. Cecily, who addresses me as her uncle from motives of respect that you could not possibly appreciate, lives at my place in the country under the charge of her admirable governess, Miss Prism.

ALGERNON Where is that place in the country, by the way?

JACK That is nothing to you, dear boy. You are not going to be invited. . . . I may tell you candidly that the place is not in Shropshire.

ALGERNON I suspected that, my dear fellow! I have Bunburyed all over Shropshire on two separate occasions. Now, go on. Why are you Ernest in town and Jack in the country?

JACK My dear Algy, I don't know whether you will be able to understand my real motives. You are hardly serious enough. When one is placed in the position of guardian, one has to adopt a very high moral tone on all subjects. It's one's duty to do so. And as a high moral tone can hardly be said to conduce very much to either one's health or one's happiness, in order to get up to town I have always pretended to have a younger brother of the name of Ernest, who lives in the Albany, and gets into the most dreadful scrapes. That, my dear Algy, is the whole truth pure and simple.

ALGERNON The truth is rarely pure and never simple. Modern life would be very tedious if it were either, and modern literature a complete impossibility!

JACK That wouldn't be at all a bad thing.

ALGERNON Literary criticism is not your forte, my dear fellow. Don't try it. You should leave that to people who haven't been at a University. They do it so well in the daily papers. What you really are is a Bunburyist. I was quite right in saying you were a Bunburyist. You are one of the most advanced Bunburyists I know.

JACK What on earth do you mean?

ALGERNON You have invented a very useful younger brother called Ernest, in order that you may be able to come up to town as often as you like. I have invented an invaluable permanent invalid called Bunbury, in order that I may be able to go down into the country whenever I choose. Bunbury is perfectly invaluable. If it wasn't for Bunbury's extraordinary bad health, for instance, I wouldn't be able to dine with you at Willis's to-night, for I have been really engaged[1] to Aunt Augusta for more than a week.

JACK I haven't asked you to dine with me anywhere tonight.

ALGERNON I know. You are absolutely careless about sending out invitations. It is very foolish of you. Nothing annoys people so much as not receiving invitations.

JACK You had much better dine with your Aunt Augusta.

ALGERNON I haven't the smallest intention of doing anything of the kind. To begin with, I dined there on Monday, and once a week is quite enough to dine with one's own relatives. In the second place, whenever I do dine there I am always treated as a member of the family, and sent down with[2] either no woman at all, or two. In the third place, I know perfectly well whom she will place me next to, tonight. She will place me next Mary Farquhar, who always flirts with her own husband across the dinner-table. That is not very pleasant. Indeed, it is not even decent . . . and that sort of thing is enormously on the increase. The amount of women in London who flirt with their own husbands is perfectly scandalous. It looks so bad. It is simply washing one's clean linen in public. Besides, now that I know you to be a confirmed Bunburyist I naturally want to talk to you about Bunburying. I want to tell you the rules.

JACK I'm not a Bunburyist at all. If Gwendolen accepts me, I am going to kill my brother, indeed I think I'll kill him in any case. Cecily is a little too much interested in him. It is rather a bore. So I am going to get rid of Ernest. And I strongly advise you to do the same with Mr. ———— with your invalid friend who has the absurd name.

ALGERNON Nothing will induce me to part with Bunbury, and if you ever get married, which seems to me extremely problematic, you will be very glad to know Bunbury. A man who marries without knowing Bunbury has a very tedious time of it.

---

[1] *engaged:* committed.
[2] *sent down with:* seated.

JACK That is nonsense. If I marry a charming girl like Gwendolen, and she is the only girl I ever saw in my life that I would marry, I certainly won't want to know Bunbury.

ALGERNON Then your wife will. You don't seem to realize, that in married life three is company and two is none.

JACK (*sententiously*) That, my dear young friend, is the theory that the corrupt French Drama has been propounding for the last fifty years.

ALGERNON Yes; and that the happy English home has proved in half the time.

JACK For heaven's sake, don't try to be cynical. It's perfectly easy to be cynical.

ALGERNON My dear fellow, it isn't easy to be anything now-a-days. There's such a lot of beastly competition about. (*The sound of an electric bell is heard.*) Ah! that must be Aunt Augusta. Only relatives, or creditors, ever ring in that Wagnerian manner. Now, if I get her out of the way for ten minutes, so that you can have an opportunity for proposing to Gwendolen, may I dine with you to-night at Willis's?

JACK I suppose so, if you want to.

ALGERNON Yes, but you must be serious about it. I have people who are not serious about meals. It is so shallow of them.

Enter LANE.

LANE Lady Bracknell and Miss Fairfax. (ALGERNON *goes forward to meet them. Enter* LADY BRACKNELL *and* GWENDOLEN.)

LADY BRACKNELL Good afternoon, dear Algernon, I hope you are behaving very well.

ALGERNON I'm feeling very well, Aunt Augusta.

LADY BRACKNELL That's not quite the same thing. In fact the two things rarely go together. (*Sees* JACK *and bows to him with icy coldness.*)

ALGERNON (*to* GWENDOLEN) Dear me, you are smart!

GWENDOLEN I am always smart! Aren't I, Mr. Worthing?

JACK You're quite perfect, Miss Fairfax.

GWENDOLEN Oh! I hope I am not that. It would leave no room for developments, and I intend to develop in *many directions*. (GWENDOLEN *and* JACK *sit down together in the corner.*)

LADY BRACKNELL I'm sorry if we are a little late, Algernon, but I was obliged to call on dear Lady Harbury. Hadn't been there since her poor husband's death. I never saw a woman so altered; she looks quite twenty years younger. And now I'll have a cup of tea, and one of those nice cucumber sandwiches you promised me.

ALGERNON Certainly, Aunt Augusta. (*Goes over to tea-table.*)

LADY BRACKNELL Won't you come and sit here, Gwendolen?

GWENDOLEN Thanks, mamma, I'm quite comfortable where I am.

ALGERNON (*picking up empty plate in horror*) Good heavens! Lane! Why are there no cucumber sandwiches? I ordered them specially.

LANE (*gravely*) There were no cucumbers in the market this morning, sir. I went down twice.

ALGERNON No cucumbers!

LANE No, sir. Not even for ready money.

ALGERNON That will do, Lane, thank you.

LANE Thank you, sir. (*Goes out.*)

ALGERNON I am greatly distressed, Aunt Augusta, about there being no cucumbers, not even for ready money.

LADY BRACKNELL It really makes no matter, Algernon. I had some crumpets with Lady Harbury, who seems to me to be living entirely for pleasure now.

ALGERNON I hear her hair has turned quite gold from grief.

LADY BRACKNELL It certainly has changed its color. From what cause I, of course, cannot say. (ALGERNON *crosses and hands tea.*) Thank you. I've quite a treat for you to-night, Algernon. I am going to send you down with Mary Farquhar. She is such a nice woman, and so attentive to her husband. It's delightful to watch them.

ALGERNON I am afraid, Aunt Augusta, I shall have to give up the pleasure of dining with you to-night after all.

LADY BRACKNELL (*frowning*) I hope not, Algernon. It would put my table completely out. Your uncle would have to dine upstairs. Fortunately he is accustomed to that.

ALGERNON It is a great bore, and, I need hardly say, a terrible disappointment to me, but the fact is I have just had a telegram to say that my poor friend Bunbury is very ill again. (*Exchanges glances with* JACK.) They seem to think I should be with him.

LADY BRACKNELL It is very strange. This Mr. Bunbury seems to suffer from curiously bad health.

ALGERNON Yes; poor Bunbury is a dreadful invalid.

LADY BRACKNELL Well, I must say, Algernon, that I think it is high time that Mr. Bunbury made up his mind whether he was going to live or to die. This shilly-shallying with the question is absurd. Nor do I in any way approve of the modern sympathy with invalids. I consider it morbid. Illness of any kind is hardly a thing to be encouraged in others. Health is the primary duty of life. I am always telling that to your poor uncle, but he never seems to take much notice . . . as far as any improvement in his ailments goes. I should be much obliged if you would ask Mr. Bunbury, from me, to be kind enough not to have a relapse on Saturday, for I rely on you to arrange my music for me. It is my last reception and one wants something that will encourage conversation, particularly at the end of the season when every one has practically said whatever they had to say, which, in most cases, was probably not much.

ALGERNON I'll speak to Bunbury, Aunt Augusta, if he is still conscious, and I think I can promise you he'll be all right by Saturday. You see, if one plays good music, people don't listen, and if one plays bad music people don't talk. But I'll run over the program I've drawn out, if you will kindly come into the next room for a moment.

LADY BRACKNELL Thank you, Algernon. It is very thoughtful of you. (*Rising, and following* ALGERNON.) I'm sure the program will be delightful, after a few expurgations. French songs I cannot possibly allow. People always seem to think that they are improper, and either look shocked, which is vulgar, or laugh, which is worse. But German sounds a thoroughly respectable language, and indeed, I believe is so. Gwendolen, you will accompany me.

GWENDOLEN Certainly, mamma. (LADY BRACKNELL AND ALGERNON *go into the music-room,* GWENDOLEN *remains behind.*)

JACK Charming day it has been, Miss Fairfax.

GWENDOLEN Pray don't talk to me about the weather, Mr. Worthing. Whenever people talk to me about the weather, I always feel quite certain that they mean something else. And that makes me so nervous.

JACK I do mean something else.

GWENDOLEN I thought so. In fact, I am never wrong.

JACK And I would like to be allowed to take advantage of Lady Bracknell's temporary absence . . .

GWENDOLEN I would certainly advise you to do so. Mamma has a way of coming back suddenly into a room that I have often had to speak to her about.

JACK (*nervously*) Miss Fairfax, ever since I met you I have admired you more than any girl . . . I have ever met since . . . I met you.

GWENDOLEN Yes, I am quite aware of the fact. And I often wish that in public, at any rate, you had been more demonstrative. For me you have always had an irresistible fascination. Even before I met you I was far from indifferent to you. (JACK *looks at her in amazement.*) We live, as I hope you know, Mr. Worthing, in an age of ideals. The fact is constantly mentioned in the more expensive monthly magazines, and has reached the provincial pulpits I am told: and my ideal has always been to love some one of the name of Ernest. There is something in that name that inspires absolute confidence. The moment Algernon first mentioned to me that he had a friend called Ernest, I knew I was destined to love you.

JACK You really love me, Gwendolen?

GWENDOLEN Passionately!

JACK Darling! You don't know how happy you've made me.

GWENDOLEN My own Ernest!

JACK But you don't really mean to say that you couldn't love me if my name wasn't Ernest?

GWENDOLEN But your name is Ernest.

JACK Yes, I know it is. But supposing it was something else? Do you mean to say you couldn't love me then?

GWENDOLEN (*glibly*) Ah! that is clearly a metaphysical speculation, and like most metaphysical speculations has very little reference at all to the actual facts of real life, as we know them.

JACK Personally, darling, to speak quite candidly, I don't much care about the name of Ernest . . . I don't think that name suits me at all.

GWENDOLEN It suits you perfectly. It is a divine name. It has a music of its own. It produces vibrations.

JACK Well, really, Gwendolen, I must say that I think there are lots of other much nicer names. I think, Jack, for instance, a charming name.

GWENDOLEN Jack? . . . No, there is very little music in the name Jack, if any at all, indeed. It does not thrill. It produces absolutely no vibrations. . . . I have known several Jacks, and they all, without exception, were more than usually plain. Besides, Jack is a notorious domesticity for John! And I pity any woman who is married to a man called John. She would probably never be allowed to know the entrancing pleasure of a single moment's solitude. The only really safe name is Ernest.

JACK Gwendolen, I must get christened at once—I mean we must get married at once. There is no time to be lost.

GWENDOLEN Married, Mr. Worthing?

JACK (*astounded*) Well . . . surely. You know that I love you, and you led me to believe, Miss Fairfax, that you were not absolutely indifferent to me.

GWENDOLEN I adore you. But you haven't proposed to me yet. Nothing has been said at all about marriage. The subject has not even been touched on.

JACK Well . . . may I propose to you now?

GWENDOLEN I think it would be an admirable opportunity. And to spare you any possible disappointment, Mr. Worthing, I think it only fair to tell you quite frankly beforehand that I am fully determined to accept you.

JACK Gwendolen!

GWENDOLEN Yes, Mr. Worthing, what have you got to say to me?

JACK You know what I have got to say to you.

GWENDOLEN Yes, but you don't say it.

JACK Gwendolen, will you marry me? (*Goes on his knees.*)

GWENDOLEN Of course I will, darling. How long you have been about it! I am afraid you have had very little experience in how to propose.

JACK My own one, I have never loved any one in the world but you.

GWENDOLEN Yes, but men often propose for practice. I know my brother Gerald does. All my girl-friends tell me so. What wonderfully blue eyes you have, Ernest! They are quite, quite blue. I hope you will always look at me just like that, especially when there are other people present.

Enter LADY BRACKNELL.

LADY BRACKNELL Mr. Worthing! Rise, sir, from this semi-recumbent posture. It is most indecorous.

GWENDOLEN Mamma! (*He tries to rise; she restrains him.*) I must beg you to retire. This is no place for you. Besides, Mr. Worthing has not quite finished yet.

LADY BRACKNELL Finished what, may I ask?

GWENDOLEN I am engaged to Mr. Worthing, mamma. (*They rise together.*)

LADY BRACKNELL Pardon me, you are not engaged to any one. When you do become engaged to some one, I, or your father, should his health permit him, will inform you of the fact. An engagement should come on a young girl as a surprise, pleasant or unpleasant, as the case may be. It is hardly a matter that she could be allowed to arrange for herself. . . . And now I have a few questions to put to you, Mr. Worthing. While I am making these inquiries, you, Gwendolen, will wait for me below in the carriage.

GWENDOLEN (*reproachfully*) Mamma!

LADY BRACKNELL In the carriage, Gwendolen! (GWENDOLEN *goes to the door. She and* JACK *blow kisses to each other behind* LADY BRACKNELL'S *back.* LADY BRACKNELL *looks vaguely about as if she could not understand what the noise was. Finally turns round.*) Gwendolen, the carriage!

GWENDOLEN Yes, mamma. (*Goes out, looking back at* JACK.)

LADY BRACKNELL (*sitting down*) You can take a seat, Mr. Worthing. (*Looks in her pocket for note-book and pencil.*)

JACK Thank you, Lady Bracknell, I prefer standing.

LADY BRACKNELL (*pencil and note-book in hand*) I feel bound to tell you that you are not down on my list of eligible young men, although I have the same list as the dear Duchess of Bolton has. We work together, in fact. However, I am quite ready to enter your name, should your answers be what a really affectionate mother requires. Do you smoke?

JACK Well, yes, I must admit I smoke.

LADY BRACKNELL I am glad to hear it. A man should always have an occupation of some kind. There are far too many idle men in London as it is. How old are you?

JACK Twenty-nine.

LADY BRACKNELL A very good age to be married at. I have always been of opinion that a man who desires to get married should know either everything or nothing. Which do you know?

JACK (*after some hesitation*) I know nothing, Lady Bracknell.

LADY BRACKNELL I am pleased to hear it. I do not approve of anything that tampers with natural ignorance. Ignorance is like a delicate exotic fruit; touch it and the bloom is gone. The whole theory of modern education is radically unsound. Fortunately in England, at any rate, education produces no effect whatsoever. If it did, it would prove a serious danger to the upper classes, and probably lead to acts of violence in Grosvenor Square. What is your income?

JACK Between seven and eight thousand a year.

LADY BRACKNELL (*makes a note in her book*) In land, or in investments?

JACK In investments, chiefly.

LADY BRACKNELL That is satisfactory. What between the duties expected of one during one's life-time, and the duties exacted from one after one's death, land has ceased to be either a profit or a pleasure. It gives one position, and prevents one from keeping it up. That's all that can be said about land.

JACK I have a country house with some land, of course, attached to it, about fifteen hundred acres, I believe; but I don't depend on that for my real income. In fact, as far as I can make out, the poachers are the only people who make anything out of it.

LADY BRACKNELL A country house! How many bedrooms? Well, that point can be cleared up afterwards. You have a town house, I hope? A girl with a simple, unspoiled nature, like Gwendolen, could hardly be expected to reside in the country.

JACK Well, I own a house in Belgrave Square, but it is let by the year to Lady Bloxham. Of course, I can get it back whenever I like, at six months' notice.

LADY BRACKNELL Lady Bloxham? I don't know her.

JACK Oh, she goes about very little. She is a lady considerably advanced in years.

LADY BRACKNELL Ah, now-a-days that is no guarantee of respectability of character. What number in Belgrave Square?

JACK 149.

LADY BRACKNELL (*shaking her head*) The unfashionable side. I thought there was something. However, that could easily be altered.

JACK Do you mean the fashion, or the side?

LADY BRACKNELL (*sternly*) Both, if necessary, I presume. What are your politics?

JACK Well, I am afraid I really have none. I am a Liberal Unionist.

LADY BRACKNELL Oh, they count as Tories. They dine with us. Or come in the evening, at any rate. Now to minor matters. Are your parents living?

JACK I have lost both my parents.

LADY BRACKNELL Both? . . . That seems like carelessness. Who was your father? He was evidently a man of some wealth. Was he born in what the Radical papers call the purple of commerce, or did he rise from the ranks of the aristocracy?

JACK I am afraid I really don't know. The fact is, Lady Bracknell, I said I had lost my parents. It would be nearer the truth to say that my parents seem to have lost me . . . I don't actually know who I am by birth. I was . . . well, I was found.

LADY BRACKNELL Found!

JACK The late Mr. Thomas Cardew, an old gentleman of a very charitable and kindly disposition, found me, and gave me the name of Worthing, because he happened to have a first-class ticket for Worthing in his pocket at the time. Worthing is a place in Sussex. It is a seaside resort.

LADY BRACKNELL Where did the charitable gentleman who had a first-class ticket for this seaside resort find you?

JACK (*gravely*) In a hand-bag.

LADY BRACKNELL A hand-bag?

JACK (*very seriously*) Yes, Lady Bracknell. I was in a hand-bag—a somewhat large, black leather hand-bag, with handles to it—an ordinary hand-bag in fact.

LADY BRACKNELL In what locality did this Mr. James, or Thomas, Cardew come across this ordinary hand-bag?

JACK In the cloak-room at Victoria Station. It was given to him in mistake for his own.

LADY BRACKNELL The cloak-room at Victoria Station?

JACK Yes. The Brighton line.

LADY BRACKNELL The line is immaterial. Mr. Worthing, I confess I feel somewhat bewildered by what you have just told me. To be born, or at any rate bred, in a hand-bag, whether it had handles or not, seems to me to display a contempt for the ordinary decencies of family life that remind one of the worst excesses of the French Revolution. And I presume you know what that unfortunate movement led to? As for the particular locality in which the hand-bag was found, a cloak-room at a railway station might serve to conceal a social indiscretion—has probably, indeed, been used for that purpose before now—but it could hardly be regarded as an assured basis for a recognized position in good society.

JACK May I ask you then what you would advise me to do? I need hardly say I would do anything in the world to ensure Gwendolen's happiness.

LADY BRACKNELL I would strongly advise you, Mr. Worthing, to try and acquire some relations as soon as possible, and to make a definite effort to produce at any rate one parent, of either sex, before the season is quite over.

JACK Well, I don't see how I could possibly manage to do that. I can produce the hand-bag at any moment. It is in my dressing-room at home. I really think that should satisfy you, Lady Bracknell.

LADY BRACKNELL Me, sir! What has it to do with me? You can hardly imagine that I and Lord Bracknell would dream of allowing our only daughter—a girl brought up with the utmost care—to marry into a cloak-room, and form an alliance with a parcel? Good morning, Mr. Worthing! (LADY BRACKNELL sweeps out in majestic indignation.)

JACK Good morning! (ALGERNON, from the other room, strikes up the Wedding March. JACK looks perfectly furious, and goes to the door.) For goodness' sake don't play that ghastly tune, Algy! How idiotic you are! (The music stops, and ALGERNON enters cheerily.)

ALGERNON Didn't it go off all right, old boy? You don't mean to say Gwendolen refused you? I know it is a way she has. She is always refusing people. I think it is most ill-natured of her.

JACK Oh, Gwendolen is as right as a trivet. As far as she is concerned, we are engaged. Her mother is perfectly unbearable. Never met such a Gorgon . . . I don't really know what a Gorgon is like, but I am quite sure that Lady Bracknell is one. In any case, she is a monster, without being a myth, which is rather unfair. . . . I beg your pardon, Algy, I suppose I shouldn't talk about your own aunt in that way before you.

ALGERNON My dear boy, I love hearing my relations abused. It is the only thing that makes me put up with them at all. Relations are simply a tedious pack of people, who haven't got the remotest knowledge of how to live, nor the smallest instinct about when to die.

JACK Oh, that is nonsense!

ALGERNON It isn't!

JACK Well, I won't argue about the matter. You always want to argue about things.

ALGERNON That is exactly what things were originally made for.

JACK Upon my word, if I thought that, I'd shoot myself . . . (A pause.) You don't think there is any chance of Gwendolen becoming like her mother in about a hundred and fifty years, do you, Algy?

ALGERNON All women become like their mothers. That is their tragedy. No man does. That's his.

JACK Is that clever?

ALGERNON It is perfectly phrased! and quite as true as any observation in civilized life should be.

JACK I am sick to death of cleverness. Everybody is clever now-a-days. You can't go anywhere without meeting clever people. The thing has become an absolute public nuisance. I wish to goodness we had a few fools left.

ALGERNON We have.

JACK I should extremely like to meet them. What do they talk about?

ALGERNON The fools? Oh! about the clever people, of course.

JACK What fools!

ALGERNON By the way, did you tell Gwendolen the truth about your being Ernest in town, and Jack in the country?

JACK (*in a very patronizing manner*) My dear fellow, the truth isn't quite the sort of thing one tells to a nice, sweet, refined girl. What extraordinary ideas you have about the way to behave to a woman!

ALGERNON The only way to behave to a woman is to make love to her, if she is pretty, and to some one else if she is plain.

JACK Oh, that is nonsense.

ALGERNON What about your brother? What about the profligate Ernest?

JACK Oh, before the end of the week I shall have got rid of him. I'll say he died in Paris of apoplexy. Lots of people die of apoplexy, quite suddenly, don't they?

ALGERNON Yes, but it's hereditary, my dear fellow. It's a sort of thing that runs in families. You had much better say a severe chill.

JACK You are sure a severe chill isn't hereditary, or anything of that kind?

ALGERNON Of course it isn't!

JACK Very well, then. My poor brother Ernest is carried off suddenly in Paris, by a severe chill. That gets rid of him.

ALGERNON But I thought you said that . . . Miss Cardew was a little too much interested in your poor brother Ernest? Won't she feel his loss a good deal?

JACK Oh, that is all right. Cecily is not a silly, romantic girl, I am glad to say. She has got a capital appetite, goes for long walks, and pays no attention at all to her lessons.

ALGERNON I would rather like to see Cecily.

JACK I will take very good care you never do. She is excessively pretty, and she is only just eighteen.

ALGERNON Have you told Gwendolen yet that you have an excessively pretty ward who is only just eighteen?

JACK Oh, one doesn't blurt these things out to people. Cecily and Gwendolen are perfectly certain to be extremely great friends. I'll bet you anything you like that half an hour after they have met, they will be calling each other sister.

ALGERNON Women only do that when they have called each other a lot of other things first. Now, my dear boy, if we want to get a good table at Willis's, we really must go and dress. Do you know it is nearly seven?

JACK (*irritably*) Oh! it always is nearly seven.

ALGERNON Well, I'm hungry.

JACK I never knew you when you weren't. . . .

ALGERNON What shall we do after dinner? Go to a theater?

JACK Oh, no! I loathe listening.

ALGERNON Well, let us go to the Club?

JACK Oh, no! I hate talking.

ALGERNON Well, we might trot round to the Empire at ten?

JACK Oh, no! I can't bear looking at things. It is so silly.

ALGERNON Well, what shall we do?

JACK Nothing!

ALGERNON It is awfully hard work doing nothing. However, I don't mind hard work where there is no definite object of any kind.

Enter LANE.

LANE Miss Fairfax.

Enter GWENDOLEN. LANE *goes out.*

ALGERNON Gwendolen, upon my word!

GWENDOLEN Algy, kindly turn your back. I have something very particular to say to Mr. Worthing.

ALGERNON Really, Gwendolen, I don't think I can allow this at all.

GWENDOLEN Algy, you always adopt a strictly immoral attitude towards life. You are not quite old enough to do that. (ALGERNON *retires to the fireplace.*)

JACK My own darling!

GWENDOLEN Ernest, we may never be married. From the expression on mamma's face I fear we never shall. Few parents now-a-days pay any regard to what their children say to them. The old-fashioned respect for the young is fast dying out. Whatever influence I ever had over mamma, I lost at the age of three. But although she may prevent us from becoming man and wife, and I may marry some one else, and marry often, nothing that she can possibly do can alter my eternal devotion to you.

JACK Dear Gwendolen.

GWENDOLEN The story of your romantic origin, as related to me by mamma, with unpleasing comments, has naturally stirred the deeper fibers of my nature. Your Christian name has an irresistible fascination. The simplicity of your character makes you exquisitely incomprehensible to me. Your town address at the Albany I have. What is your address in the country?

JACK The Manor House, Woolton, Hertfordshire. (ALGERNON, *who has been carefully listening, smiles to himself, and writes the address on his shirt-cuff. Then picks up the Railway Guide.*)

GWENDOLEN There is a good postal service, I suppose? It may be necessary to do something desperate. That, of course, will require serious consideration. I will communicate with you daily.

JACK My own one!

GWENDOLEN How long do you remain in town?

JACK Till Monday.

GWENDOLEN Good! Algy, you may turn round now.

ALGERNON Thanks, I've turned round already.

GWENDOLEN You may also ring the bell.

JACK You will let me see you to your carriage, my own darling?

GWENDOLEN Certainly.

JACK (*to* LANE, *who now enters*) I will see Miss Fairfax out.

LANE Yes, sir. (JACK *and* GWENDOLEN *go off.* LANE *presents several letters on a salver to* ALGERNON. *It is to be surmised that they are bills, as* ALGERNON, *after looking at the envelopes, tears them up.*)

ALGERNON A glass of sherry, Lane.

LANE Yes, sir.

ALGERNON To-morrow, Lane, I'm going Bunburying.

LANE Yes, sir.

ALGERNON I shall probably not be back till Monday. You can put up my dress clothes, my smoking jacket, and all the Bunbury suits . . .

LANE Yes, sir. (*Handing sherry.*)

ALGERNON I hope to-morrow will be a fine day, Lane.

LANE It never is, sir.

ALGERNON Lane, you're a perfect pessimist.

LANE I do my best to give satisfaction, sir.

Enter JACK. LANE *goes off.*

JACK There's a sensible, intellectual girl! the only girl I ever cared for in my life. (AL-GERNON *is laughing immoderately.*) What on earth are you so amused at?

ALGERNON Oh, I'm a little anxious about poor Bunbury, that's all.

JACK If you don't take care, your friend Bunbury will get you into a serious scrape some day.

ALGERNON I love scrapes. They are the only things that are never serious.

JACK Oh, that's nonsense, Algy. You never talk anything but nonsense.

ALGERNON Nobody ever does. (JACK *looks indignantly at him, and leaves the room.* ALGERNON *lights a cigarette, reads his shirt-cuff and smiles.*)

CURTAIN

ACT II

SCENE *Garden at the Manor House. A flight of gray stone steps leads up to the house. The garden, an old-fashioned one, full of roses. Time of year, July. Basket chairs, and a table covered with books, are set under a large yew tree.*

(MISS PRISM *discovered seated at the table.* CECILY *is at the back watering flowers.*)

MISS PRISM (*calling*) Cecily, Cecily! Surely such a utilitarian occupation as the watering of flowers is rather Moulton's duty than yours? Especially at a moment when intellectual pleasures await you. Your German grammar is on the table. Pray open it at page fifteen. We will repeat yesterday's lesson.

CECILY (*coming over very slowly*) But I don't like German. It isn't at all a becoming language. I know perfectly well that I look quite plain after my German lesson.

MISS PRISM Child, you know how anxious your guardian is that you should improve yourself in every way. He laid particular stress on your German, as he was leaving for town yesterday. Indeed, he always lays stress on your German when he is leaving for town.

CECILY Dear Uncle Jack is so very serious! Sometimes he is so serious that I think he cannot be quite well.

MISS PRISM (*drawing herself up*) Your guardian enjoys the best of health, and his gravity of demeanor is especially to be commended in one so comparatively young as he is. I know no one who has a higher sense of duty and responsibility.

CECILY I suppose that is why he often looks a little bored when we three are together.

MISS PRISM Cecily! I am surprised at you. Mr. Worthing has many troubles in his life. Idle merriment and triviality would be out of place in his conversation. You must remember his constant anxiety about that unfortunate young man, his brother.

CECILY I wish Uncle Jack would allow that unfortunate young man, his brother, to come down here sometimes. We might have a good influence over him, Miss Prism. I am sure you certainly would. You know German, and geology, and things of that kind influence a man very much. (CECILY begins to write in her diary.)

MISS PRISM (*shaking her head*) I do not think that even I could produce any effect on a character that, according to his own brother's admission, is irretrievably weak and vacillating. Indeed, I am not sure that I would desire to reclaim him. I am not in favor of this modern mania for turning bad people into good people at a moment's notice. As a man sows so let him reap. You must put away your diary, Cecily. I really don't see why you should keep a diary at all.

CECILY I keep a diary in order to enter the wonderful secrets of my life. If I didn't write them down I should probably forget all about them.

MISS PRISM Memory, my dear Cecily, is the diary that we all carry about with us.

CECILY Yes, but it usually chronicles the things that have never happened, and couldn't possibly have happened. I believe that Memory is responsible for nearly all the three-volume novels that Mudie[3] sends us.

MISS PRISM Do not speak slightingly of the three-volume novel, Cecily. I wrote one myself in earlier days.

CECILY Did you really, Miss Prism? How wonderfully clever you are! I hope it did not end happily? I don't like novels that end happily. They depress me so much.

MISS PRISM The good ended happily, and the bad unhappily. That is what Fiction means.

CECILY I suppose so. But it seems very unfair. And was your novel ever published?

MISS PRISM Alas! no. The manuscript unfortunately was abandoned. I use the word in the sense of lost or mislaid. To your work, child, these speculations are profitless.

CECILY (*smiling*) But I see dear Dr. Chasuble coming up through the garden.

MISS PRISM (*rising and advancing*) Dr. Chasuble! This is indeed a pleasure.

Enter CANON CHASUBLE.

CHASUBLE And how are we this morning? Miss Prism, you are, I trust, well?

CECILY Miss Prism has just been complaining of a slight headache. I think it would do her so much good to have a short stroll with you in the park, Dr. Chasuble.

MISS PRISM Cecily, I have not mentioned anything about a headache.

CECILY No, dear Miss Prism, I know that, but I felt instinctively that you had a headache. Indeed I was thinking about that, and not about my German lesson, when the Rector came in.

CHASUBLE I hope, Cecily, you are not inattentive.

CECILY Oh, I am afraid I am.

CHASUBLE That is strange. Were I fortunate enough to be Miss Prism's pupil, I would hang upon her lips. (Miss Prism *glares*.) I spoke metaphorically.—My metaphor was drawn from bees. Ahem! Mr. Worthing, I suppose, has not returned from town yet?

MISS PRISM We do not expect him till Monday afternoon.

CHASUBLE Ah, yes, he usually likes to spend his Sunday in London. He is not one of those whose sole aim is enjoyment, as, by all accounts, that unfortunate young man, his brother, seems to be. But I must not disturb Egeria and her pupil any longer.

MISS PRISM Egeria? My name is Laetitia, Doctor.

---

[3] A popular lending-library service.

CHASUBLE (*bowing*) A classical allusion merely, drawn from the Pagan authors. I shall see you both no doubt at Evensong.

MISS PRISM I think, dear Doctor, I will have a stroll with you. I find I have a headache after all, and a walk might do it good.

CHASUBLE With pleasure, Miss Prism, with pleasure. We might go as far as the schools and back.

MISS PRISM That would be delightful. Cecily, you will read your Political Economy in my absence. The chapter on the Fall of the Rupee you may omit. It is somewhat too sensational. Even these metallic problems have their melodramatic side. (*Goes down the garden with* DR. CHASUBLE.)

CECILY (*picks up books and throws them back on table*) Horrid Political Economy! Horrid Geography! Horrid, horrid German!

Enter MERRIMAN *with a card on a salver.*

MERRIMAN Mr. Ernest Worthing has just driven over from the station. He has brought his luggage with him.

CECILY (*takes the card and reads it*) "Mr. Ernest Worthing, B 4, The Albany, W." Uncle Jack's brother! Did you tell him Mr. Worthing was in town?

MERRIMAN Yes, Miss. He seemed very much disappointed. I mentioned that you and Miss Prism were in the garden. He said he was anxious to speak to you privately for a moment.

CECILY Ask Mr. Ernest Worthing to come here. I suppose you had better talk to the housekeeper about a room for him.

MERRIMAN Yes, Miss. (MERRIMAN *goes off.*)

CECILY I have never met any really wicked person before. I feel rather frightened. I am so afraid he will look just like every one else.

Enter ALGERNON, *very gay and debonair.*

He does!

ALGERNON (*raising his hat*) You are my little cousin Cecily, I'm sure.

CECILY You are under some strange mistake. I am not little. In fact, I am more than usually tall for my age. (ALGERNON *is rather taken aback.*) But I am your cousin Cecily. You, I see from your card, are Uncle Jack's brother, my cousin Ernest, my wicked cousin Ernest.

ALGERNON Oh! I am not really wicked at all, cousin Cecily. You mustn't think that I am wicked.

CECILY If you are not, then you have certainly been deceiving us all in a very inexcusable manner. I hope you have not been leading a double life, pretending to be wicked and being really good all the time. That would be hypocrisy.

ALGERNON (*looks at her in amazement*) Oh! of course I have been rather reckless.

CECILY I am glad to hear it.

ALGERNON In fact, now you mention the subject, I have been very bad in my own small way.

CECILY I don't think you should be so proud of that, though I am sure it must have been very pleasant.

ALGERNON It is much pleasanter being here with you.

CECILY I can't understand how you are here at all. Uncle Jack won't be back till Monday afternoon.

ALGERNON That is a great disappointment. I am obliged to go up by the first train on Monday morning. I have a business appointment that I am anxious . . . to miss.

CECILY Couldn't you miss it anywhere but in London?

ALGERNON No; the appointment is in London.

CECILY Well, I know, of course, how important it is not to keep a business engagement, if one wants to retain any sense of the beauty of life, but still I think you had better wait till Uncle Jack arrives. I know he wants to speak to you about your emigrating.

ALGERNON About my what?

CECILY Your emigrating. He has gone up to buy your outfit.

ALGERNON I certainly wouldn't let Jack buy my outfit. He has no taste in neckties at all.

CECILY I don't think you will require neckties. Uncle Jack is sending you to Australia.

ALGERNON Australia! I'd sooner die.

CECILY Well, he said at dinner on Wednesday night, that you would have to choose between this world, the next world, and Australia.

ALGERNON Oh, well! The accounts I have received of Australia and the next world, are not particularly encouraging. This world is good enough for me, cousin Cecily.

CECILY Yes, but are you good enough for it?

ALGERNON I'm afraid I'm not that. That is why I want you to reform me. You might make that your mission, if you don't mind, cousin Cecily.

CECILY I'm afraid I've not time, this afternoon.

ALGERNON Well, would you mind my reforming myself this afternoon?

CECILY That is rather Quixotic of you. But I think you should try.

ALGERNON I will. I feel better already.

CECILY You are looking a little worse.

ALGERNON That is because I am hungry.

CECILY How thoughtless of me. I should have remembered that when one is going to lead an entirely new life, one requires regular and wholesome meals. Won't you come in?

ALGERNON Thank you. Might I have a button-hole first? I never have any appetite unless I have a button-hole first.

CECILY A Maréchal Niel? (*Picks up scissors.*)

ALGERNON No, I'd sooner have a pink rose.

CECILY Why? (*Cuts a flower.*)

ALGERNON Because you are like a pink rose, cousin Cecily.

CECILY I don't think it can be right for you to talk to me like that. Miss Prism never says such things to me.

ALGERNON Then Miss Prism is a short-sighted old lady. (CECILY *puts the rose in his button-hole.*) You are the prettiest girl I ever saw.

CECILY Miss Prism says that all good looks are a snare.

ALGERNON They are a snare that every sensible man would like to be caught in.

CECILY Oh! I don't think I would care to catch a sensible man. I shouldn't know what to talk to him about. (*They pass into the house.* MISS PRISM *and* DR. CHASUBLE *return*)

MISS PRISM You are too much alone, dear Dr. Chasuble. You should get married. A misanthrope I can understand—a womanthrope, never!

CHASUBLE (*with a scholar's shudder*) Believe me, I do not deserve so neologistic a phrase. The precept as well as the practice of the Primitive Church was distinctly against matrimony.

MISS PRISM (*sententiously*) That is obviously the reason why the Primitive Church has not lasted up to the present day. And you do not seem to realize, dear Doctor, that by persistently remaining single, a man converts himself into a permanent public temptation. Men should be careful; this very celibacy leads weaker vessels astray.

CHASUBLE But is a man not equally attractive when married?

MISS PRISM No married man is ever attractive except to his wife.

CHASUBLE And often, I've been told, not even to her.

MISS PRISM That depends on the intellectual sympathies of the woman. Maturity can always be depended on. Ripeness can be trusted. Young women are green. (DR. CHASUBLE *starts*.) I spoke horticulturally. My metaphor was drawn from fruits. But where is Cecily?

CHASUBLE Perhaps she followed us to the schools.

Enter JACK *slowly from the back of the garden. He is dressed in the deepest mourning, with crape hatband and black gloves.*

MISS PRISM Mr. Worthing!

CHASUBLE Mr. Worthing?

MISS PRISM This is indeed a surprise. We did not look for you till Monday afternoon.

JACK (*shakes* MISS PRISM'S *hand in a tragic manner*) I have returned sooner than I expected. Dr. Chasuble, I hope you are well?

CHASUBLE Dear Mr. Worthing, I trust this garb of woe does not betoken some terrible calamity?

JACK My brother.

MISS PRISM More shameful debts and extravagance?

CHASUBLE Still leading his life of pleasure?

JACK (*shaking his head*) Dead!

CHASUBLE Your brother Ernest dead?

JACK Quite dead.

MISS PRISM What a lesson for him! I trust he will profit by it.

CHASUBLE Mr. Worthing, I offer you my sincere condolence. You have at least the consolation of knowing that you were always the most generous and forgiving of brothers.

JACK Poor Ernest! He had many faults, but it is a sad, sad blow.

CHASUBLE Very sad indeed. Were you with him at the end?

JACK No. He died abroad; in Paris, in fact. I had a telegram last night from the manager of the Grand Hotel.

CHASUBLE Was the cause of death mentioned?

JACK A severe chill, it seems.

MISS PRISM As a man sows, so shall he reap.

CHASUBLE (*raising his hand*) Charity, dear Miss Prism, charity! None of us are perfect. I myself am peculiarly susceptible to draughts. Will the interment take place here?

JACK No. He seems to have expressed a desire to be buried in Paris.

CHASUBLE In Paris! (*Shakes his head.*) I fear that hardly points to any very serious state of mind at the last. You would no doubt wish me to make some slight allusion to this tragic domestic affliction next Sunday. (JACK *presses his hand convulsively.*) My sermon on the meaning of the manna in the wilderness can be adapted to almost any occasion, joyful, or, as in the present case, distressing. (*All sigh.*) I have preached it at harvest celebrations, christenings, confirmations, on days of humiliation and festal days. The last time I delivered it was in the Cathedral, as a charity sermon on behalf of the Society for the Prevention of Discontentment among the Upper Orders. The Bishop, who was present, was much struck by some of the analogies I drew.

JACK Ah, that reminds me, you mentioned christenings I think, Dr. Chasuble? I suppose you know how to christen all right? (DR. CHASUBLE *looks astounded.*) I mean, of course, you are continually christening, aren't you?

MISS PRISM It is, I regret to say, one of the Rector's most constant duties in this parish. I have often spoken to the poorer classes on the subject. But they don't seem to know what thrift is.

CHASUBLE But is there any particular infant in whom you are interested, Mr. Worthing? Your brother was, I believe, unmarried, was he not?

JACK Oh, yes.

MISS PRISM (*bitterly*) People who live entirely for pleasure usually are.

JACK But it is not for any child, dear Doctor. I am very fond of children. No! the fact is, I would like to be christened myself, this afternoon, if you have nothing better to do.

CHASUBLE But surely, Mr. Worthing, you have been christened already?

JACK I don't remember anything about it.

CHASUBLE But have you any grave doubts on the subject?

JACK I certainly intend to have. Of course, I don't know if the thing would bother you in any way, or if you think I am a little too old now.

CHASUBLE Not at all. The sprinkling, and, indeed, the immersion of adults is a perfectly canonical practice.

JACK Immersion!

CHASUBLE You need have no apprehensions. Sprinkling is all that is necessary, or indeed I think advisable. Our weather is so changeable. At what hour would you wish the ceremony performed?

JACK Oh, I might trot around about five if that would suit you.

CHASUBLE Perfectly, perfectly! In fact I have two similar ceremonies to perform at that time. A case of twins that occurred recently in one of the outlying cottages on your own estate. Poor Jenkins the carter, a most hard-working man.

JACK Oh! I don't see much fun in being christened along with other babies. It would be childish. Would half-past five do?

CHASUBLE Admirably! Admirably! (*Takes out watch.*) And now, dear Mr. Worthing, I will not intrude any longer into a house of sorrow. I would merely beg you not to be too much bowed down by grief. What seem to us bitter trials at the moment are often blessings in disguise.

MISS PRISM This seems to me a blessing of an extremely obvious kind.

Enter CECILY *from the house.*

CECILY Uncle Jack! Oh, I am pleased to see you back. But what horrid clothes you have on! Do go and change them.

MISS PRISM Cecily!

CHASUBLE My child! my child! (CECILY *goes towards* JACK; *he kisses her brow in a melancholy manner.*)

CECILY What is the matter, Uncle Jack? Do look happy! You look as if you had a toothache and I have such a surprise for you. Who do you think is in the dining-room? Your brother!

JACK Who?

CECILY Your brother Ernest. He arrived about half an hour ago.

JACK What nonsense! I haven't got a brother.

CECILY Oh, don't say that. However badly he may have behaved to you in the past he is still your brother. You couldn't be so heartless as to disown him. I'll tell him to come out. And you will shake hands with him, won't you, Uncle Jack? (*Runs back into the house.*)

CHASUBLE These are very joyful tidings.

MISS PRISM After we had all been resigned to his loss, his sudden return seems to me peculiarly distressing.

JACK My brother is in the dining-room? I don't know what it all means. I think it is perfectly absurd.

Enter ALGERNON *and* CECILY *hand in hand. They come slowly up to* JACK.

JACK Good heavens! (*Motions* ALGERNON *away.*)

ALGERNON Brother John, I have come down from town to tell you that I am very sorry for all the trouble I have given you, and that I intend to lead a better life in the future. (JACK *glares at him and does not take his hand.*)

CECILY Uncle Jack, you are not going to refuse your own brother's hand?

JACK Nothing will induce me to take his hand. I think his coming down here disgraceful. He knows perfectly well why.

CECILY Uncle Jack, do be nice. There is some good in every one. Ernest has just been telling me about his poor invalid friend, Mr. Bunbury, whom he goes to visit so often. And surely there must be much good in one who is kind to an invalid, and leaves the pleasures of London to sit by a bed of pain.

JACK Oh, he has been talking about Bunbury, has he?

CECILY Yes, he has told me all about poor Mr. Bunbury, and his terrible state of health.

JACK Bunbury! Well, I won't have him talk to you about Bunbury or about anything else. It is enough to drive one perfectly frantic.

ALGERNON Of course I admit that the faults were all on my side. But I must say that I think that Brother John's coldness to me is peculiarly painful. I expected a more enthusiastic welcome, especially considering it is the first time I have come here.

CECILY Uncle Jack, if you don't shake hands with Ernest I will never forgive you.

JACK Never forgive me?

CECILY Never, never, never!

JACK Well, this is the last time I shall ever do it. (*Shakes hands with* ALGERNON *and glares.*)

CHASUBLE It's pleasant, is it not, to see so perfect a reconciliation? I think we might leave the two brothers together.

MISS PRISM Cecily, you will come with us.

CECILY Certainly, Miss Prism. My little task of reconciliation is over.

CHASUBLE You have done a beautiful action to-day, dear child.

MISS PRISM We must not be premature in our judgments.

CECILY I feel very happy. (*They all go off.*)

JACK You young scoundrel, Algy, you must get out of this place as soon as possible. I don't allow any Bunburying here.

Enter MERRIMAN.

MERRIMAN I have put Mr. Ernest's things in the room next to yours, sir. I suppose that is all right?

JACK What?

MERRIMAN Mr. Ernest's luggage, sir. I have unpacked it and put it in the room next to your own.

JACK His luggage?

MERRIMAN Yes, sir. Three portmanteaus, a dressing-case, two hat-boxes, and a large luncheon-basket.

ALGERNON I am afraid I can't stay more than a week this time.

JACK Merriman, order the dog-cart at once. Mr. Ernest has been suddenly called back to town.

MERRIMAN Yes, sir. (*Goes back into the house.*)

ALGERNON What a fearful liar you are, Jack. I have not been called back to town at all.

JACK Yes, you have.

ALGERNON I haven't heard any one call me.

JACK Your duty as a gentleman calls you back.

ALGERNON My duty as a gentleman has never interfered with my pleasures in the smallest degree.

JACK I can quite understand that.

ALGERNON Well, Cecily is a darling.

JACK You are not to talk of Miss Cardew like that. I don't like it.

ALGERNON Well, I don't like your clothes. You look perfectly ridiculous in them. Why on earth don't you go up and change? It is perfectly childish to be in deep mourning for a man who is actually staying for a whole week with you in your house as a guest. I call it grotesque.

JACK You are certainly not staying with me for a whole week as a guest or anything else. You have got to leave . . . by the four-five train.

ALGERNON I certainly won't leave you so long as you are in mourning. It would be most unfriendly. If I were in mourning you would stay with me, I suppose. I should think it very unkind if you didn't.

JACK Well, will you go if I change my clothes?

ALGERNON Yes, if you are not too long. I never saw anybody take so long to dress, and with such little result.

JACK Well, at any rate, that is better than being always over-dressed as you are.

ALGERNON If I am occasionally a little over-dressed, I make up for it by being always immensely over-educated.

JACK Your vanity is ridiculous, your conduct an outrage, and your presence in my garden utterly absurd. However, you have got to catch the four-five, and I hope you will have a pleasant journey back to town. This Bunburying, as you call it, has not been a great success for you. (*Goes into the house.*)

ALGERNON I think it has been a great success. I'm in love with Cecily, and that is everything. (*Enter* CECILY *at the back of the garden. She picks up the can and begins to water the flowers.*) But I must see her before I go, and make arrangements for another Bunbury. Ah, there she is.

CECILY Oh, I merely came back to water the roses. I thought you were with Uncle Jack.

ALGERNON He's gone to order the dog-cart for me.

CECILY Oh, is he going to take you for a nice drive?

ALGERNON He's going to send me away.

CECILY Then have we got to part?

ALGERNON I am afraid so. It's a very painful parting.

CECILY It is always painful to part from people whom one has known for a very brief space of time. The absence of old friends one can endure with equanimity. But even a momentary separation from any one to whom one has just been introduced is almost unbearable.

ALGERNON Thank you.

Enter MERRIMAN.

MERRIMAN The dog-cart is at the door, sir. (ALGERNON *looks appealingly at* CECILY.)
CECILY It can wait, Merriman . . . for . . . five minutes.
MERRIMAN Yes, miss.

Exit MERRIMAN.

ALGERNON I hope, Cecily, I shall not offend you if I state quite frankly and openly that
you seem to me to be in every way the visible personification of absolute perfection.
CECILY I think your frankness does you great credit, Ernest. If you will allow me I will
copy your remarks into my diary. (*Goes over to table and begins writing in diary.*)
ALGERNON Do you really keep a diary? I'd give anything to look at it. May I?
CECILY Oh, no. (*Puts her hand over it.*) You see it is simply a very young girl's record
of her own thoughts and impressions, and consequently meant for publication. When
it appears in volume form I hope you will order a copy. But pray, Ernest, don't stop.
I delight in taking down from dictation. I have reached "absolute perfection." You
can go on. I am quite ready for more.
ALGERNON (*somewhat taken aback*) Ahem! Ahem!
CECILY Oh, don't cough, Ernest. When one is dictating one should speak fluently and
not cough. Besides, I don't know how to spell a cough. (*Writes as* ALGERNON *speaks.*)
ALGERNON (*speaking very rapidly*) Cecily, ever since I first looked upon your wonderful
and incomparable beauty, I have dared to love you wildly, passionately, devotedly,
hopelessly.
CECILY I don't think that you should tell me that you love me wildly, passionately,
devotedly, hopelessly. Hopelessly doesn't seem to make much sense, does it?
ALGERNON Cecily!

Enter MERRIMAN.

MERRIMAN The dog-cart is waiting, sir.
ALGERNON Tell it to come round next week, at the same hour.
MERRIMAN (*looks at* CECILY, *who makes no sign*) Yes, sir.

MERRIMAN *retires.*

CECILY Uncle Jack would be very much annoyed if he knew you were staying on till
next week, at the same hour.
ALGERNON Oh, I don't care about Jack. I don't care for anybody in the whole world but
you. I love you, Cecily. You will marry me, won't you?
CECILY You silly you! Of course. Why, we have been engaged for the last three months.
ALGERNON For the last three months?
CECILY Yes, it will be exactly three months on Thursday.
ALGERNON But how did we become engaged?
CECILY Well, ever since dear Uncle Jack first confessed to us that he had a younger
brother who was very wicked and bad, you of course have formed the chief topic of
conversation between myself and Miss Prism. And of course a man who is much talked
about is always very attractive. One feels there must be something in him after all. I
daresay it was foolish of me, but I fell in love with you, Ernest.
ALGERNON Darling! And when was the engagement actually settled?
CECILY On the 4th of February last. Worn out by your entire ignorance of my existence,
I determined to end the matter one way or the other, and after a long struggle with

myself I accepted you under this dear old tree here. The next day I bought this little ring in your name, and this is the little bangle with the true lovers' knot I promised you always to wear.

ALGERNON Did I give you this? It's very pretty, isn't it?

CECILY Yes, you've wonderfully good taste, Ernest. It's the excuse I've always given for your leading such a bad life. And this is the box in which I keep all your dear letters. (*Kneels at table, opens box, and produces letters tied up with blue ribbon.*)

ALGERNON My letters! But my own sweet Cecily, I have never written you any letters.

CECILY You need hardly remind me of that, Ernest. I remember only too well that I was forced to write your letters for you. I wrote always three times a week, and sometimes oftener.

ALGERNON Oh, do let me read them, Cecily?

CECILY Oh, I couldn't possibly. They would make you far too conceited. (*Replaces box.*) The three you wrote me after I had broken off the engagement are so beautiful, and so badly spelled, that even now I can hardly read them without crying a little.

ALGERNON But was our engagement ever broken off?

CECILY Of course it was. On the 22nd of last March. You can see the entry if you like. (*Shows diary.*) "To-day I broke off my engagement with Ernest. I feel it is better to do so. The weather still continues charming."

ALGERNON But why on earth did you break it off? What had I done? I had done nothing at all. Cecily, I am very much hurt indeed to hear you broke it off. Particularly when the weather was so charming.

CECILY It would hardly have been a really serious engagement if it hadn't been broken off at least once. But I forgave you before the week was out.

ALGERNON (*crossing to her, and kneeling*). What a perfect angel you are, Cecily.

CECILY You dear romantic boy. (*He kisses her, she puts her fingers through his hair.*) I hope your hair curls naturally, does it?

ALGERNON Yes, darling, with a little help from others.

CECILY I am so glad.

ALGERNON You'll never break off our engagement again, Cecily?

CECILY I don't think I could break it off now that I have actually met you. Besides, of course, there is the question of your name.

ALGERNON Yes, of course. (*Nervously.*)

CECILY You must not laugh at me, darling, but it had always been a girlish dream of mine to love some one whose name was Ernest. (ALGERNON *rises,* CECILY *also.*) There is something in that name that seems to inspire absolute confidence. I pity any poor married woman whose husband is not called Ernest.

ALGERNON But, my dear child, do you mean to say you could not love me if I had some other name?

CECILY But what name?

ALGERNON Oh, any name you like—Algernon, for instance. . . .

CECILY But I don't like the name of Algernon.

ALGERNON Well, my own dear, sweet, loving little darling, I really can't see why you should object to the name of Algernon. It is not at all a bad name. In fact, it is rather an aristocratic name. Half of the chaps who get into the Bankruptcy Court are called Algernon. But seriously, Cecily . . . (*moving to her*) . . . if my name was Algy, couldn't you love me?

CECILY (*rising*) I might respect you, Ernest, I might admire your character, but I fear that I should not be able to give you my undivided attention.

ALGERNON Ahem! Cecily! (*Picking up hat.*) Your Rector here is, I suppose, thoroughly experienced in the practice of all the rites and ceremonials of the church?

CECILY Oh, yes. Dr. Chasuble is a most learned man. He has never written a single book, so you can imagine how much he knows.

ALGERNON I must see him at once on a most important christening—I mean on most important business.

CECILY Oh!

ALGERNON I sha'n't be away more than half an hour.

CECILY Considering that we have been engaged since February the 14th, and that I only met you to-day for the first time, I think it is rather hard that you should leave me for so long a period as half an hour. Couldn't you make it twenty minutes?

ALGERNON I'll be back in no time (*Kisses her and rushes down the garden.*)

CECILY What an impetuous boy he is. I like his hair so much. I must enter his proposal in my diary.

Enter MERRIMAN.

MERRIMAN A Miss Fairfax has just called to see Mr. Worthing. On very important business, Miss Fairfax states.

CECILY Isn't Mr. Worthing in his library?

MERRIMAN Mr. Worthing went over in the direction of the Rectory some time ago.

CECILY Pray ask the lady to come out here; Mr. Worthing is sure to be back soon. And you can bring tea.

MERRIMAN Yes, miss. (*Goes out.*)

CECILY Miss Fairfax! I suppose one of the many good elderly women who are associated with Uncle Jack in some of his philanthropic work in London. I don't quite like women who are interested in philanthropic work. I think it is so forward of them.

Enter MERRIMAN.

MERRIMAN Miss Fairfax.

Enter GWENDOLEN. *Exit* MERRIMAN.

CECILY (*advancing to meet her*) Pray let me introduce myself to you. My name is Cecily Cardew.

GWENDOLEN Cecily Cardew? (*Moving to her and shaking hands.*) What a very sweet name! Something tells me that we are going to be great friends. I like you already more than I can say. My first impressions of people are never wrong.

CECILY How nice of you to like me so much after we have known each other such a comparatively short time. Pray sit down.

GWENDOLEN (*still standing up*) I may call you Cecily, may I not?

CECILY With pleasure!

GWENDOLEN And you will always call me Gwendolen, won't you?

CECILY If you wish.

GWENDOLEN Then that is all quite settled, is it not?

CECILY I hope so. (*A pause. they both sit down together.*)

GWENDOLEN Perhaps this might be a favorable opportunity for my mentioning who I am. My father is Lord Bracknell. You have never heard of papa, I suppose?

CECILY I don't think so.

GWENDOLEN Outside the family circle, papa, I am glad to say, is entirely unknown. I think that is quite as it should be. The home seems to me to be the proper sphere for the man. And certainly once a man begins to neglect his domestic duties he becomes painfully effeminate, does he not? And I don't like that. It makes men so very attractive. Cecily, mamma, whose views on education are remarkably strict, has brought me up to be extremely short-sighted; it is part of her system; so do you mind my looking at you through my glasses?

CECILY Oh, not at all, Gwendolen. I am very fond of being looked at.

GWENDOLEN (*after examining* CECILY *carefully through a lorgnette*) You are here on a short visit, I suppose.

CECILY Oh, no, I live here.

GWENDOLEN (*severely*) Really? Your mother, no doubt, or some female relative of advanced years, resides here also?

CECILY Oh, no. I have no mother, nor, in fact, any relations.

GWENDOLEN Indeed?

CECILY My dear guardian, with the assistance of Miss Prism, has the arduous task of looking after me.

GWENDOLEN Your guardian?

CECILY Yes, I am Mr. Worthing's ward.

GWENDOLEN Oh! It is strange he never mentioned to me that he had a ward. How secretive of him! He grows more interesting hourly. I am not sure, however, that the news inspires me with feelings of unmixed delight (*Rising and going to her.*) I am very fond of you, Cecily; I have liked you ever since I met you. But I am bound to state that now that I know that you are Mr. Worthing's ward, I cannot help expressing a wish you were—well, just a little older than you seem to be—and not quite so very alluring in appearance. In fact, if I may speak candidly—

CECILY Pray do! I think that whenever one has anything unpleasant to say, one should always be quite candid.

GWENDOLEN Well, to speak with perfect candor, Cecily, I wish that you were fully forty-two, and more than usually plain for your age. Ernest has a strong upright nature. He is the very soul of truth and honor. Disloyalty would be as impossible to him as deception. But even men of the noblest possible moral character are extremely susceptible to the influence of the physical charms of others. Modern, no less than Ancient History, supplies us with many most painful examples of what I refer to. If it were not so, indeed, History would be quite unreadable.

CECILY I beg your pardon, Gwendolen, did you say Ernest?

GWENDOLEN Yes.

CECILY Oh, but it is not Mr. Ernest Worthing who is my guardian. It is his brother—his elder brother.

GWENDOLEN (*sitting down again*) Ernest never mentioned to me that he had a brother.

CECILY I am sorry to say they have not been on good terms for a long time.

GWENDOLEN Ah! that accounts for it. And now that I think of it I have never heard any man mention his brother. The subject seems distasteful to most men. Cecily, you have lifted a load from my mind. I was growing almost anxious. It would have been terrible if any cloud had come across a friendship like ours, would it not? Of course you are quite, quite sure that it is not Mr. Ernest Worthing who is your guardian?

CECILY Quite sure (*A pause.*) In fact, I am going to be his.

GWENDOLEN (*enquiringly*) I beg your pardon?

CECILY (*rather shy and confidingly*) Dearest Gwendolen, there is no reason why I should make a secret of it to you. Our little county newspaper is sure to chronicle the fact next week. Mr. Ernest Worthing and I are engaged to be married.

GWENDOLEN (*quite politely, rising*) My darling Cecily, I think there must be some slight error. Mr. Ernest Worthing is engaged to me. The announcement will appear in the *Morning Post* on Saturday at the latest.

CECILY (*very politely, rising*) I am afraid you must be under some misconception. Ernest proposed to me exactly ten minutes ago. (*Shows diary.*)

GWENDOLEN (*examines diary through her lorgnette carefully*) It is certainly very curious, for he asked me to be his wife yesterday afternoon at 5:30. If you would care to verify the incident, pray do so. (*Produces diary of her own.*) I never travel without my diary. One should always have something sensational to read in the train. I am so sorry, dear Cecily, if it is any disappointment to you, but I'm afraid I have the prior claim.

CECILY It would distress me more than I can tell you, dear Gwendolen, if it caused you any mental or physical anguish, but I feel bound to point out that since Ernest proposed to you he clearly has changed his mind.

GWENDOLEN (*meditatively*) If the poor fellow has been entrapped into any foolish promise I shall consider it my duty to rescue him at once, and with a firm hand.

CECILY (*thoughtfully and sadly*) Whatever unfortunate entanglement my dear boy may have got into, I will never reproach him with it after we are married.

GWENDOLEN Do you allude to me, Miss Cardew, as an entanglement? You are presumptuous. On an occasion of this kind it becomes more than a moral duty to speak one's mind. It becomes a pleasure.

CECILY Do you suggest, Miss Fairfax, that I entrapped Ernest into an engagement? How dare you? This is no time for wearing the shallow mask of manners. When I see a spade I call it a spade.

GWENDOLEN (*satirically*) I am glad to say that I have never seen a spade. It is obvious that our social spheres have been widely different.

Enter MERRIMAN, *followed by the footman. He carries a salver, tablecloth, and plate-stand.* CECILY *is about to retort. The presence of the servants exercises a restraining influence, under which both girls chafe.*

MERRIMAN Shall I lay tea here as usual, miss?

CECILY (*sternly, in a calm voice*) Yes, as usual. (MERRIMAN *begins to clear and lay cloth. A long pause.* CECILY *and* GWENDOLEN *glare at each other.*)

GWENDOLEN Are there many interesting walks in the vicinity, Miss Cardew?

CECILY Oh, yes, a great many. From the top of one of the hills quite close one can see five counties.

GWENDOLEN Five counties! I don't think I should like that. I hate crowds.

CECILY (*sweetly*) I suppose that is why you live in town? (GWENDOLEN *bites her lip, and beats her foot nervously with her parasol.*)

GWENDOLEN (*looking round*) Quite a well-kept garden this is, Miss Cardew.

CECILY So glad you like it, Miss Fairfax.

GWENDOLEN I had no idea there were any flowers in the country.

CECILY Oh, flowers are as common here, Miss Fairfax, as people are in London.

GWENDOLEN Personally I cannot understand how anybody manages to exist in the country, if anybody who is anybody does. The country always bores me to death.

CECILY Ah! This is what the newspapers call agricultural depression, is it not? I believe the aristocracy are suffering very much from it just at present. It is almost an epidemic amongst them, I have been told. May I offer you some tea, Miss Fairfax?

GWENDOLEN (*with elaborate politeness*) Thank you. (*Aside.*) Detestable girl! But I require tea!

CECILY (*sweetly*) Sugar?

GWENDOLEN (*superciliously*) No, thank you. Sugar is not fashionable any more. (CECILY *looks angrily at her, takes up the tongs and puts four lumps of sugar into the cup.*)

CECILY (*severely*) Cake or bread and butter?

GWENDOLEN (*in a bored manner*) Bread and butter, please. Cake is rarely seen at the best houses now-a-days.

CECILY (*cuts a very large slice of cake, and puts it on the tray*). Hand that to Miss Fairfax. (MERRIMAN *does so, and goes out with footman.* GWENDOLEN *drinks the tea and makes a grimace. Puts down cup at once, reaches out her hand to the bread and butter, looks at it, and finds it is cake. Rises in indignation.*)

GWENDOLEN You have filled my tea with lumps of sugar, and though I asked most distinctly for bread and butter, you have given me cake. I am known for the gentleness of my disposition, and the extraordinary sweetness of my nature, but I warn you, Miss Cardew, you may go too far.

CECILY (*rising*) To save my poor, innocent, trusting boy from the machinations of any other girl there are no lengths to which I would not go.

GWENDOLEN From the moment I saw you I distrusted you. I felt that you were false and deceitful. I am never deceived in such matters. My first impressions of people are invariably right.

CECILY It seems to me, Miss Fairfax, that I am trespassing on your valuable time. No doubt you have many other calls of a similar character to make in the neighborhood.

Enter JACK.

GWENDOLEN (*catching sight of him*) Ernest! My own Ernest!

JACK Gwendolen! Darling! (*Offers to kiss her.*)

GWENDOLEN (*drawing back*) A moment! May I ask if you are engaged to be married to this young lady? (*Points to* CECILY.)

JACK (*laughing*) To dear little Cecily! Of course not! What could have put such an idea into your pretty little head?

GWENDOLEN Thank you. You may. (*Offers her cheek.*)

CECILY (*very sweetly*) I knew there must be some misunderstanding, Miss Fairfax. The gentleman whose arm is at present around your waist is my dear guardian, Mr. John Worthing.

GWENDOLEN I beg your pardon?

CECILY This is Uncle Jack.

GWENDOLEN (*receding*) Jack! Oh!

Enter ALGERNON.

CECILY Here is Ernest.

ALGERNON (*goes straight over to* CECILY *without noticing any one else*). My own love! (*Offers to kiss her.*)

CECILY (*drawing back*) A moment, Ernest! May I ask you—are you engaged to be married to this young lady?

ALGERNON (*looking round*) To what young lady? Good heavens! Gwendolen!

CECILY Yes, to good heavens, Gwendolen, I mean to Gwendolen.

ALGERNON (*laughing*) Of course not! What could have put such an idea into your pretty little head?

CECILY Thank you. (*Presenting her cheek to be kissed.*) You may. (ALGERNON *kisses her.*)

GWENDOLEN I felt there was some slight error, Miss Cardew. The gentleman who is now embracing you is my cousin, Mr. Algernon Moncrieff.

CECILY (*breaking away from* ALGERNON) Algernon Moncrieff! Oh! (*The two girls move towards each other and put their arms round each other's waists as if for protection.*)

CECILY Are you called Algernon?

ALGERNON I cannot deny it.

CECILY Oh!

GWENDOLEN Is your name really John?

JACK (*standing rather proudly*) I could deny it if I liked. I could deny anything if I liked. But my name certainly is John. It has been John for years.

CECILY (*to* GWENDOLEN) A gross deception has been practiced on both of us.

GWENDOLEN My poor wounded Cecily!

CECILY My sweet, wronged Gwendolen!

GWENDOLEN (*slowly and seriously*) You will call me sister, will you not? (*They embrace. JACK and* ALGERNON *groan and walk up and down.*)

CECILY (*rather brightly*) There is just one question I would like to be allowed to ask my guardian.

GWENDOLEN An admirable idea! Mr. Worthing, there is just one question I would like to be permitted to put to you. Where is your brother Ernest? We are both engaged to be married to your brother Ernest, so it is a matter of some importance to us to know where your brother Ernest is at present.

JACK (*slowly and hesitatingly*) Gwendolen—Cecily—it is very painful for me to be forced to speak the truth. It is the first time in my life that I have ever been reduced to such a painful position, and I am really quite inexperienced in doing anything of the kind. However I will tell you quite frankly that I have no brother Ernest. I have no brother at all. I never had a brother in my life, and I certainly have not the smallest intention of ever having one in the future.

CECILY (*surprised*) No brother at all?

JACK (*cheerily*) None!

GWENDOLEN (*severely*) Had you never a brother of any kind?

JACK (*pleasantly*) Never. Not even of any kind.

GWENDOLEN I am afraid it is quite clear, Cecily, that neither of us is engaged to be married to any one.

CECILY It is not a very pleasant position for a young girl suddenly to find herself in. Is it?

GWENDOLEN Let us go into the house. They will hardly venture to come after us there.

CECILY No, men are so cowardly, aren't they? (*They retire into the house with scornful looks.*)

JACK This ghastly state of things is what you call Bunburying, I suppose?

ALGERNON Yes, and a perfectly wonderful Bunbury it is. The most wonderful Bunbury I have ever had in my life.

JACK Well, you've no right whatsoever to Bunbury here.

ALGERNON That is absurd. One has a right to Bunbury anywhere one chooses. Every serious Bunburyist knows that.

JACK Serious Bunburyist! Good heavens!

ALGERNON Well, one must be serious about something, if one wants to have any amusement in life. I happen to be serious about Bunburying. What on earth you are serious about I haven't got the remotest idea. About everything, I should fancy. You have such an absolutely trivial nature.

JACK Well, the only small satisfaction I have in the whole of this wretched business is that your friend Bunbury is quite exploded. You won't be able to run down to the country quite so often as you used to do, dear Algy. And a very good thing, too.

ALGERNON Your brother is a little off color, isn't he, dear Jack? You won't be able to disappear to London quite so frequently as your wicked custom was. And not a bad thing, either.

JACK As for your conduct towards Miss Cardew, I must say that your taking in a sweet, simple, innocent girl like that is quite inexcusable. To say nothing of the fact that she is my ward.

ALGERNON I can see no possible defense at all for your deceiving a brillant, clever, thoroughly experienced young lady like Miss Fairfax. To say nothing of the fact that she is my cousin.

JACK I wanted to be engaged to Gwendolen, that is all. I love her.

ALGERNON Well, I simply wanted to be engaged to Cecily. I adore her.

JACK There is certainly no chance of your marrying Miss Cardew.

ALGERNON I don't think there is much likelihood, Jack, of you and Miss Fairfax being united.

JACK Well, that is no business of yours.

ALGERNON If it was my business, I wouldn't talk about it. (*Begins to eat muffins.*) It is very vulgar to talk about one's business. Only people like stock-brokers do that, and then merely at dinner parties.

JACK How you can sit there, calmly eating muffins, when we are in this horrible trouble, I can't make out. You seem to me to be perfectly heartless.

ALGERON Well, I can't eat muffins in an agitated manner. The butter would probably get on my cuffs. One should always eat muffins quite calmly. It is the only way to eat them.

JACK I say it's perfectly heartless your eating muffins at all, under the circumstances.

ALGERNON When I am in trouble, eating is the only thing that consoles me. Indeed, when I am in really great trouble, as any one who knows me intimately will tell you, I refuse everything except food and drink. At the present moment I am eating muffins because I am unhappy. Besides, I am particularly fond of muffins. (*Rising.*)

JACK (*rising*) Well, that is no reason why you should eat them all in that greedy way. (*Takes muffins from* ALGERNON.)

ALGERNON (*offering tea-cake*) I wish you would have tea-cake instead. I don't like tea-cake.

JACK Good heavens! I suppose a man may eat his own muffins in his own garden.

ALGERNON But you have just said it was perfectly heartless to eat muffins.

JACK I said it was perfectly heartless of you, under the circumstances. That is a very different thing.

ALGERNON That may be. But the muffins are the same. (*He seizes the muffin-dish from* JACK.)

JACK Algy, I wish to goodness you would go.

ALGERNON You can't possibly ask me to go without having some dinner. It's absurd. I never go without my dinner. No one ever does, except vegetarians and people like that. Besides I have just made arrangements with Dr. Chasuble to be christened at a quarter to six under the name of Ernest.

JACK My dear fellow, the sooner you give up that nonsense the better. I made arrangements this morning with Dr. Chasuble to be christened myself at 5.30, and I naturally will take the name of Ernest. Gwendolen would wish it. We can't both be christened Ernest. It's absurd. Besides, I have a perfect right to be christened if I like. There is no evidence at all that I ever have been christened by anybody. I should think it extremely probable I never was, and so does Dr. Chasuble. It is entirely different in your case. You have been christened already.

ALGERNON Yes, but I have not been christened for years.

JACK Yes, but you have been christened. That is the important thing.

ALGERNON Quite so. So I know my constitution can stand it. If you are not quite sure about your ever having been christened, I must say I think it rather dangerous your venturing on it now. It might make you very unwell. You can hardly have forgotten that some one very closely connected with you was very nearly carried off this week in Paris by a severe chill.

JACK Yes, but you said yourself that a severe chill was not hereditary.

ALGERNON It usedn't to be, I know—but I daresay it is now. Science is always making wonderful improvements in things.

JACK (*picking up the muffin-dish*) Oh, that is nonsense; you are always talking nonsense.

ALGERNON Jack, you are at the muffins again! I wish you wouldn't. There are only two left. (*Takes them.*) I told you I was particularly fond of muffins.

JACK But I hate tea-cake.

ALGERNON Why on earth then do you allow tea-cake to be served up for your guests? What ideas you have of hospitality!

JACK Algernon! I have already told you to go. I don't want you here. Why don't you go?

ALGERNON I haven't quite finished my tea yet, and there is still one muffin left. (JACK *groans, and sinks into a chair.* ALGERNON *still continues eating.*)

CURTAIN

ACT III

SCENE *Morning-room at the Manor House.* GWENDOLEN *and* CECILY *are at the window, looking out into the garden.*

GWENDOLEN The fact that they did not follow us at once into the house, as any one else would have done, seems to me to show that they have some sense of shame left.

CECILY They have been eating muffins. That looks like repentance.

GWENDOLEN (*after a pause*) They don't seem to notice us at all. Couldn't you cough?

GWENDOLEN They're looking at us. What effrontery!

CECILY They're approaching. That's very forward of them.

GWENDOLEN Let us preserve a dignified silence.

CECILY Certainly. It's the only thing to do now.

Enter JACK, *followed by* ALGERNON. *They whistle some dreadful popular air from a British opera.*

GWENDOLEN This dignified silence seems to produce an unpleasant effect.

CECILY A most distasteful one.

GWENDOLEN But we will not be the first to speak.

CECILY Certainly not.

GWENDOLEN Mr. Worthing, I have something very particular to ask you. Much depends on your reply.

CECILY Gwendolen, your common sense is invaluable. Mr. Moncrieff, kindly answer me the following question. Why did you pretend to be my guardian's brother?

ALGERNON In order that I might have an opportunity of meeting you.

CECILY (*to* GWENDOLEN) That certainly seems a satisfactory explanation, does it not?

GWENDOLEN Yes, dear, if you can believe him.

CECILY I don't. But that does not affect the wonderful beauty of his answer.

GWENDOLEN True. In matters of grave importance, style, not sincerity, is the vital thing. Mr. Worthing, what explanation can you offer to me for pretending to have a brother? Was it in order that you might have an opportunity of coming up to town to see me as often as possible?

JACK Can you doubt it, Miss Fairfax?

GWENDOLEN I have the gravest doubts upon the subject. But I intend to crush them. This is not the moment for German skepticism. (*Moving to* CECILY.) Their explanations appear to be quite satisfactory, especially Mr. Worthing's. That seems to me to have the stamp of truth upon it.

CECILY I am more than content with what Mr. Moncrieff said. His voice alone inspires one with absolute credulity.

GWENDOLEN Then you think we should forgive them?

CECILY Yes. I mean no.

GWENDOLEN True! I had forgotten. There are principles at stake that one cannot surrender. Which of us should tell them? The task is not a pleasant one.

CECILY Could we not both speak at the same time?

GWENDOLEN An excellent idea! I nearly always speak at the same time as other people. Will you take the time from me?

CECILY Certainly. (GWENDOLEN *beats time with uplifted finger.*)

GWENDOLEN and CECILY (*speaking together*) Your Christian names are still an insuperable barrrier. That is all!

JACK and ALGERNON (*speaking together*) Our Christian names! Is that all? But we are going to be christened this afternoon.

GWENDOLEN (*to* JACK) For my sake you are prepared to do this terrible thing?

JACK I am.

CECILY (*to* ALGERNON) To please me you are ready to face this fearful ordeal?

ALGERNON I am!

GWENDOLEN How absurd to talk of the equality of the sexes! Where questions of self-sacrifice are concerned, men are infinitely beyond us.

JACK We are. (*Clasps hands with* ALGERNON.)

CECILY They have moments of physical courage of which we women know absolutely nothing.

GWENDOLEN (*to* JACK) Darling!

ALGERNON (*to* CECILY) Darling! (*They fall into each other's arms.*)

Enter MERRIMAN. *When he enters he coughs loudly, seeing the situation.*

MERRIMAN Ahem! Ahem! Lady Bracknell!

JACK Good heavens!

Enter LADY BRACKNELL. *The couples separate in alarm. Exit* MERRIMAN.

LADY BRACKNELL Gwendolen! What does this mean?

GWENDOLEN Merely that I am engaged to be married to Mr. Worthing, Mamma.

LADY BRACKNELL Come here. Sit down. Sit down immediately. Hesitation of any kind is a sign of mental decay in the young, of physical weakness in the old. (*Turns to* JACK.) Apprised, sir, of my daughter's sudden flight by her trusty maid, whose confidence I purchased by means of a small coin, I followed her at once by a luggage train. Her unhappy father is, I am glad to say, under the impression that she is attending a more than usually lengthy lecture by the University Extension Scheme on the Influence of a Permanent Income on Thought. I do not propose to undeceive him. Indeed I have never undeceived him on any question. I would consider it wrong. But of course you will clearly understand that all communication between yourself and my daughter must cease immediately from this moment. On this point, as indeed on all points, I am firm.

JACK I am engaged to be married to Gwendolen, Lady Bracknell!

LADY BRACKNELL You are nothing of the kind, sir. And now, as regards Algernon! . . . Algernon!

ALGERNON Yes, Aunt Augusta.

LADY BRACKNELL May I ask if it is in this house that your invalid friend Mr. Bunbury resides?

ALGERNON (*stammering*) Oh, no! Bunbury doesn't live here. Bunbury is somewhere else at present. In fact, Bunbury is dead.

LADY BRACKNELL Dead! When did Mr. Bunburry die? His death must have been extremely sudden.

ALGERNON (*airily*) Oh, I killed Bunbury this afternoon. I mean poor Bunbury died this afternoon.

LADY BRACKNELL What did he die of?

ALGERNON Bunbury? Oh, he was quite exploded.

LADY BRACKNELL Exploded! Was he the victim of a revolutionary outrage? I was not aware that Mr. Bunbury was interested in social legislation. If so, he is well punished for his morbidity.

ALGERNON My dear Aunt Augusta, I mean he was found out! The doctors found out that Bunbury could not live, that is what I mean—so Bunbury died.

LADY BRACKNELL He seems to have had great confidence in the opinion of his physicians. I am glad, however, that he made up his mind at the last to some definite course of action, and acted under proper medical advice. And now that we have finally got rid of this Mr. Bunbury, may I ask, Mr. Worthing, who is that young person whose hand my nephew Algernon is now holding in what seems to me a peculiarly unnecessary manner?

JACK That lady is Miss Cecily Cardew, my ward. (LADY BRACKNELL *bows coldy to* CECILY.)

ALGERNON I am engaged to be married to Cecily, Aunt Augusta.

LADY BRACKNELL I beg your pardon?

CECILY Mr. Moncrieff and I are engaged to be married, Lady Bracknell.

LADY BRACKNELL (*with a shiver, crossing to the sofa and sitting down*) I do not know whether there is anything peculiarly exciting in the air of this particular part of Hertfordshire, but the number of engagements that go on seems to me considerably above the proper average that statistics have laid down for our guidance. I think some preliminary enquiry on my part would not be out of place. Mr. Worthing, is Miss Cardew at all connected with any of the larger railway stations in London? I merely desire information. Until yesterday I had no idea that there were any families or persons whose origin was a Terminus. (JACK *looks perfectly furious, but restrains himself.*)

JACK (*in a clear, cold voice*) Miss Cardew is the granddaughter of the late Mr. Thomas Cardew of 149, Belgrave Square, S.W.; Gervase Park, Dorking, Surrey; and the Sporran, Fifeshire, N.B.

LADY BRACKNELL That sounds not unsatisfactory. Three addresses always inspire confidence, even in tradesmen. But what proof have I of their authenticity?

JACK I have carefully preserved the Court Guide of the period. They are open to your inspection, Lady Bracknell.

LADY BRACKNELL (*grimly*) I have known strange errors in that publication.

JACK Miss Cardew's family solicitors are Messrs. Markby, Markby, and Markby.

LADY BRACKNELL Markby, Markby, and Markby? A firm of the very highest position in their profession. Indeed I am told that one of the Mr. Markbys is occasionally to be seen at dinner parties. So far I am satisfied.

JACK (*very irritably*) How extremely kind of you, Lady Bracknell! I have also in my possession, you will be pleased to hear, certificates of Miss Cardew's birth, baptism, whooping cough, registration, vaccination, confirmation, and the measles; both the German and the English variety.

LADY BRACKNELL Ah! A life crowded with incident, I see; though perhaps somewhat too exciting for a young girl. I am not myself in favor of premature experiences. (*Rises, looks at her watch.*) Gwendolen! the time approaches for our departure. We have not a moment to lose. As a matter of form, Mr. Worthing, I had better ask you if Miss Cardew has any little fortune?

JACK Oh, about a hundred and thirty thousand pounds in the Funds. That is all. Goodby, Lady Bracknell. So pleased to have seen you.

LADY BRACKNELL (*sitting down again*) A moment, Mr. Worthing. A hundred and thirty thousand pounds! And in the Funds! Miss Cardew seems to me a most attractive young lady, now that I look at her. Few girls of the present day have any really solid qualities, any of the qualities that last, and improve with time. We live, I regret to say, in an age of surfaces. (*To* CECILY.) Come over here, dear. (CECILY *goes across.*) Pretty child! your dress is sadly simple, and your hair seems almost as Nature might have left it. But we can soon alter all that. A thoroughly experienced French maid produces a really marvelous result in a very brief space of time. I remember recommending one to young Lady Lancing, and after three months her own husband did not know her.

JACK (*aside*) And after six months nobody knew her.

LADY BRACKNELL (*glares at* JACK *for a few moments, then bends, with a practiced smile, to* CECILY) Kindly turn round, sweet child. (CECILY *turns completely round.*) No, the side view is what I want. (CECILY *presents her profile.*) Yes, quite as I expected. There are distinct social possibilities in your profile. The two weak points in our age are its want of principle and its want of profile. The chin a little higher, dear. Style largely depends on the way the chin is worn. They are worn very high, just at present, Algernon!

ALGERNON Yes, Aunt Augusta!

LADY BRACKNELL There are distinct social possibilities in Miss Cardew's profile.

ALGERNON Cecily is the sweetest, dearest, prettiest girl in the whole world. And I don't care twopence about social possibilities.

LADY BRACKNELL Never speak disrespectfully of society, Algernon. Only people who can't get into it do that. (*To* CECILY.) Dear child, of course you know that Algernon has nothing but his debts to depend upon. But I do not approve of mercenary marriages. When I married Lord Bracknell I had no fortune of any kind. But I never dreamed for a moment of allowing that to stand in my way. Well, I suppose I must give my consent.

ALGERNON Thank you, Aunt Augusta.

LADY BRACKNELL Cecily, you may kiss me!

CECILY (*kisses her*) Thank you, Lady Bracknell.

LADY BRACKNELL You may also address me as Aunt Augusta for the future.

CECILY Thank you, Aunt Augusta.

LADY BRACKNELL The marriage, I think, had better take place quite soon.

ALGERNON Thank you, Aunt Augusta.

CECILY Thank you, Aunt Augusta.

LADY BRACKNELL To speak frankly, I am not in favor of long engagements. They give people the opportunity of finding out each other's character before marriage, which I think is never advisable.

JACK I beg your pardon for interrupting you, Lady Bracknell, but this engagement is quite out of the question. I am Miss Cardew's guardian, and she cannot marry without my consent until she comes of age. That consent I absolutely decline to give.

LADY BRACKNELL Upon what grounds, may I ask? Algernon is an extremely, I may almost say an ostentatiously, eligible young man. He has nothing, but he looks everything. What more can one desire?

JACK It pains me very much to have to speak frankly to you, Lady Bracknell, about your nephew, but the fact is that I do not approve at all of his moral character. I suspect him of being untruthful. (ALGERNON *and* CECILY *look at him in indignant amazement.*)

LADY BRACKNELL Untruthful! My nephew Algernon? Impossible! He is an Oxonian.

JACK I fear there can be no possible doubt about the matter. This afternoon, during my temporary absence in London on an important question of romance, he obtained admission to my house by means of the false pretense of being my brother. Under an assumed name he drank, I've just been informed by my butler, an entire pint bottle of my Perrier-Jouet, Brut, '89; a wine I was specially reserving for myself. Continuing his disgraceful deception, he succeeded in the course of the afternoon in alienating the affections of my only ward. He subsequently stayed to tea, and devoured every single muffin. And what makes his conduct all the more heartless is, that he was perfectly well aware from the first that I have no brother, that I never had a brother, and that I don't intend to have a brother, not even of any kind. I distinctly told him so myself yesterday afternoon.

LADY BRACKNELL Ahem! Mr. Worthing, after careful consideration I have decided entirely to overlook my nephew's conduct to you.

JACK That is very generous of you, Lady Bracknell. My own decision, however, is unalterable. I decline to give my consent.

LADY BRACKNELL (*to* CECILY) Come here, sweet child. (CECILY *goes over.*) How old are you, dear?

CECILY Well, I am really only eighteen, but I always admit to twenty when I go to evening parties.

LADY BRACKNELL You are perfectly right in making some slight alteration. Indeed, no woman should ever be quite accurate about her age. It looks so calculating. . . . (*In meditative manner.*) Eighteen, but admitting to twenty at evening parties. Well, it will not be very long before you are of age and free from the restraints of tutelage. So I don't think your guardian's consent is, after all, a matter of any importance.

JACK Pray excuse me, Lady Bracknell, for interrupting you again, but it is only fair to tell you that according to the terms of her grandfather's will Miss Cardew does not come legally of age till she is thirty-five.

LADY BRACKNELL That does not seem to me to be a grave objection. Thirty-five is a very attractive age. London society is full of women of the very highest birth who have, of their own free choice, remained thirty-five for years. Lady Dumbleton is an instance in point. To my own knowledge she has been thirty-five ever since she arrived at the age of forty, which was many years ago now. I see no reason why our dear Cecily should not be even still more attractive at the age you mention than she is at present. There will be a large accumulation of property.

CECILY Algy, could you wait for me till I was thirty-five?

ALGERNON Of course I could, Cecily. You know I could.

CECILY Yes, I felt it instinctively, but I couldn't wait all that time. I hate waiting even five minutes for anybody. It always makes me rather cross. I am not punctual myself, I know, but I do like punctuality in others, and waiting, even to be married, is quite out of the question.

ALGERNON Then what is to be done, Cecily?

CECILY I don't know, Mr. Moncrieff.

LADY BRACKNELL My dear Mr. Worthing, as Miss Cardew states positively that she cannot wait till she is thirty-five—a remark which I am bound to say seems to me to show a somewhat impatient nature—I would beg of you to reconsider your decision.

JACK But, my dear Lady Bracknell, the matter is entirely in your own hands. The moment you consent to my marriage with Gwendolen, I will most gladly allow your nephew to form an alliance with my ward.

LADY BRACKNELL (*rising and drawing herself up*) You must be quite aware that what you propose is out of the question.

JACK Then a passionate celibacy is all that any of us can look forward to.

LADY BRACKNELL That is not the destiny I propose for Gwendolen. Algernon, of course, can choose for himself. (*Pulls out her watch.*) Come, dear (GWENDOLEN *rises*), we have already missed five, if not six, trains. To miss any more might expose us to comment on the platform.

Enter DR. CHASUBLE.

CHASUBLE Everything is quite ready for the christenings.

LADY BRACKNELL The christenings, sir! Is not that somewhat premature?

CHASUBLE (*looking rather puzzled, and pointing to* JACK *and* ALGERNON) Both these gentlemen have expressed a desire for immediate baptism.

LADY BRACKNELL At their age? The idea is grotesque and irreligious! Algernon, I forbid you to be baptized. I will not hear of such excesses. Lord Bracknell would be highly displeased if he learned that that was the way in which you wasted your time and money.

CHASUBLE Am I to understand then that there are to be no christenings at all this afternoon?

JACK I don't think that, as things are now, it would be of much practical value to either of us, Dr. Chasuble.

CHASUBLE I am grieved to hear such sentiments from you, Mr. Worthing. They savor of the heretical views of the Anabaptists, views that I have completely refuted in four of my unpublished sermons. However, as your present mood seems to be one peculiarly secular, I will return to the church at once. Indeed, I have just been informed by the pewopener that for the last hour and a half Miss Prism has been waiting for me in the vestry.

LADY BRACKNELL (*starting*) Miss Prism! Did I hear you mention a Miss Prism?

CHASUBLE Yes, Lady Bracknell. I am on my way to join her.

LADY BRACKNELL Pray allow me to detain you for a moment. This matter may prove to be one of vital importance to Lord Bracknell and myself. Is this Miss Prism a female of repellent aspect, remotely connected with education?

CHASUBLE (*somewhat indignantly*) She is the most cultivated of ladies, and the very picture of respectability.

LADY BRACKNELL It is obviously the same person. May I ask what position she holds in your household?

CHASUBLE (*severely*) I am a celibate, madam.

JACK (*interposing*) Miss Prism, Lady Bracknell, has been for the last three years Miss Cardew's esteemed governess and valued companion.

LADY BRACKNELL In spite of what I hear of her, I must see her at once. Let her be sent for.

CHASUBLE (*looking off*) She approaches; she is nigh.

Enter MISS PRISM *hurriedly.*

MISS PRISM I was told you expected me in the vestry, dear Canon. I have been waiting for you there for an hour and three-quarters. (*Catches sight of* LADY BRACKNELL, *who has fixed her with a stony glare.* MISS PRISM *grows pale and quails. She looks anxiously round as if desirous to escape.*)

LADY BRACKNELL (*in a severe, judicial voice*) Prism! (MISS PRISM *bows her head in shame.*) Come here, Prism! (MISS PRISM *approaches in a humble manner.*) Prism! Where is that' baby? (*General consternation. The Canon starts back in horror.* ALGERNON *and* JACK *pretend to be anxious to shield* CECILY *and* GWENDOLEN *from hearing the details of a terrible public scandal.*) Twenty-eight years ago, Prism, you left Lord Bracknell's house, Number 104, Upper Grosvenor Street, in charge of a perambulator that contained a baby, of the male sex. You never returned. A few weeks later, through the elaborate investigations of the Metropolitan police, the perambulator was discovered at midnight, standing by itself in a remote corner of Bayswater. It contained the manuscript of a three-volume novel of more than usually revolting sentimentality. (MISS PRISM *starts in involuntary indignation.*) But the baby was not there! (*Every one looks at* MISS PRISM.) Prism, where is that baby? (*A pause.*)

MISS PRISM Lady Bracknell, I admit with shame that I do not know. I only wish I did. The plain facts of the case are these. On the morning of the day you mention, a day that is forever branded on my memory, I prepared as usual to take the baby out in its perambulator. I had also with me a somewhat old but capacious hand-bag in which I had intended to place the manuscript of a work of fiction that I had written during my few unoccupied hours. In a moment of mental abstraction, for which I never can forgive myself, I deposited the manuscript in the bassinet, and placed the baby in the hand-bag.

JACK (*who has been listening attentively*) But where did you deposit the hand-bag?

MISS PRISM Do not ask me, Mr. Worthing.

JACK Miss Prism, this is a matter of no small importance to me. I insist on knowing where you deposited the hand-bag that contained that infant.

MISS PRISM I left it in the cloak-room of one of the larger railway stations in London.

JACK What railway station?

MISS PRISM (*quite crushed*) Victoria. The Brighton line. (*Sinks into a chair.*)

JACK I must retire to my room for a moment. Gwendolen, wait here for me.

GWENDOLEN If you are not too long, I will wait here for you all my life.

Exit JACK *in great excitement.*

CHASUBLE What do you think this means, Lady Bracknell?

LADY BRACKNELL I dare not even suspect, Dr. Chasuble. I need hardly tell you that in families of high position strange coincidences are not supposed to occur. They are hardly considered the thing. (*Noises heard overhead as if some one was throwing trunks about. Everybody looks up.*)

CECILY Uncle Jack seems strangely agitated.

CHASUBLE Your guardian has a very emotional nature.

LADY BRACKNELL This noise is extremely unpleasant. It sounds as if he was having an argument. I dislike arguments of any kind. They are always vulgar, and often convincing.

CHASUBLE (*looking up*) It has stopped now. (*The noise is redoubled.*)

LADY BRACKNELL I wish he would arrive at some conclusion.

GWENDOLEN This suspense is terrible. I hope it will last.

Enter JACK *with a hand-bag of black leather in his hand.*

JACK (*rushing over to* MISS PRISM) Is this the hand-bag, Miss Prism? Examine it carefully before you speak. The happiness of more than one life depends on your answer.

MISS PRISM (*calmly*) It seems to be mine. Yes, here is the injury it received through the upsetting of a Gower Street omnibus in younger and happier days. Here is the stain on the lining caused by the explosion of a temperance beverage, an incident that occurred at Leamington. And here, on the lock, are my initials. I had forgotten that in an extravagant mood I had had them placed there. The bag is undoubtedly mine. I am delighted to have it so unexpectedly restored to me. It has been a great inconvenience being without it all these years.

JACK (*in a pathetic voice*) Miss Prism, more is restored to you than this hand-bag. I was the baby you placed in it.

MISS PRISM (*amazed*) You?

JACK (*embracing her*) Yes . . . mother!

MISS PRISM (*recoiling in indignant astonishment*) Mr. Worthing! I am unmarried!

JACK Unmarried! I do not deny that is a serious blow. But after all, who has the right to cast a stone against one who has suffered? Cannot repentance wipe out an act of folly? Why should there be one law for men and another for women? Mother, I forgive you. (*Tries to embrace her again.*)

MISS PRISM (*still more indignant*) Mr. Worthing, there is some error. (*Pointing to* LADY BRACKNELL.) There is the lady who can tell you who you really are.

JACK (*after a pause*) Lady Bracknell, I hate to seem inquisitive, but would you kindly inform me who I am?

LADY BRACKNELL I am afraid that the news I have to give you will not altogether please you. You are the son of my poor sister, Mrs. Moncrieff, and consequently Algernon's elder brother.

JACK Algy's elder brother! Then I have a brother after all. I knew I had a brother! I always said I had a brother! Cecily,—how could you have ever doubted that I had a brother? (*Seizes hold of* ALGERNON.) Dr. Chasuble, my unfortunate brother. Miss Prism, my unfortunate brother. Gwendolen, my unfortunate brother. Algy, you young scoundrel, you will have to treat me with more respect in the future. You have never behaved to me like a brother in all your life.

ALGERNON Well, not till to-day, old boy, I admit. I did my best, however, though I was out of practice. (*Shakes hands.*)

GWENDOLEN (*to* JACK) My own! but what own are you? What is your Christian name, now that you have become some one else?

JACK Good heavens! . . . I had quite forgotten that point. Your decision on the subject of my name is irrevocable, I suppose?

GWENDOLEN I never change, except in my affections.

CECILY What a noble nature you have, Gwendolen!

JACK Then the question had better be cleared up at once. Aunt Augusta, a moment. At the time when Miss Prism left me in the hand-bag, had I been christened already?

LADY BRACKNELL Every luxury that money could buy, including christening, had been lavished on you by your fond and doting parents.

JACK Then I was christened! That is settled. Now, what name was I given? Let me know the worst.

LADY BRACKNELL Being the eldest son you were naturally christened after your father.

JACK (*irritably*) Yes, but what was my father's Christian name?

LADY BRACKNELL (*meditatively*) I cannot at the present moment recall what the General's Christian name was. But I have no doubt he had one. He was eccentric, I admit. But only in later years. And that was the result of the Indian climate, and marriage, and indigestion, and other things of that kind.

JACK Algy! Can't you recollect what our father's Christian name was?

ALGERNON My dear boy, we were never even on speaking terms. He died before I was a year old.

JACK His name would appear in the Army Lists of the period, I suppose, Aunt Augusta?

LADY BRACKNELL The General was essentially a man of peace, except in his domestic life. But I have no doubt his name would appear in any military directory.

JACK The Army Lists of the last forty years are here. These delightful records should have been my constant study. (*Rushes to bookcase and tears the books out.*) M. Generals . . . Mallam, Maxbohm, Magley, what ghastly names they have—Markby, Migsby, Mobbs, Moncrieff! Lieutenant 1840, Captain, Lieutenant-Colonel, Colonel, General 1869, Christian names, Ernest John. (*Puts book very quietly down and speaks quite calmly.*) I always told you, Gwendolen, my name was Ernest, didn't I? Well, it is Ernest after all. I mean it naturally is Ernest.

LADY BRACKNELL Yes, I remember that the General was called Ernest. I knew I had some particular reason for disliking the name.

GWENDOLEN Ernest! My own Ernest! I felt from the first that you could have no other name!

JACK Gwendolen, it is a terrible thing for a man to find out suddenly that all his life he has been speaking nothing but the truth. Can you forgive me?

GWENDOLEN I can. For I feel that you are sure to change.

JACK My own one!

CHASUBLE (*to* MISS PRISM) Laetitia! (*Embraces her.*)

MISS PRISM (*enthusiastically*) Frederick! At last!

ALGERNON Cecily! (*Embraces her.*) At last!

JACK Gwendolen! (*Embraces her.*) At last!

LADY BRACKNELL My nephew, you seem to be displaying signs of triviality.

JACK On the contrary, Aunt Augusta, I've now realized for the first time in my life the vital Importance of Being Earnest.

TABLEAU

CURTAIN

Questions

1. The tone of the first conversation between Algernon and Jack (pp. 1192–93) alerts us that this is not a serious drama, but a comedy. Identify specific instances of humorous irony.

2. Oscar Wilde—and his characters—delight in word-play and the invention of neologisms (new words). "Bunburyist" and "Bunburying" are instances of neologisms. Define "Bunburying" in your own words, and explain how "Bunburying" contributes to the dramatic situation of this play.

3. How much of what Lady Bracknell says can be taken seriously? How do her attitudes satirize the English upper class?

4. *The Importance of Being Earnest* burlesques not only the manners of society but also the clichés of nineteenth-century melodrama. Discuss the love-scene between Jack and Gwendolen (pp. 1197–99) and how it burlesques a conventional, sentimental love-scene.

5. Foreshadowing, in the theater, is a clue or suggestion that some important event will transpire or that some secret will be revealed. Is there any foreshadowing early in the play of the fact that Miss Prism left Jack in the hand-bag at Victoria Station?

6. To what extent do the opinions and behavior of Canon Chasuble satirize the Church of England?

7. A common form of comic irony occurs when a character suffers embarrassment because he does not immediately understand his predicament. How is Jack an object of comic irony in Act II (pp. 1209–10)?

8. In ancient Greek drama, threatened characters were sometimes rescued by a *deus ex machina*, or god from the machine, who would swoop down on the stage to carry them out of harm's way. The term has come to refer to any last-minute action or revelation that improves a character's fortune. Explain how Jack benefits from the *deus ex machina* effect in Act III.

Satire

One of the most important social functions of comedy is *satire*. Satire is the ridiculing of any human vice or folly. But it is particularly useful in ridiculing people and institutions whose esteem exceeds their true value. Satire deflates the overblown and pompous, cuts them down to size. The oldest comedies extant, called the Greek Old Comedy, attacked the political and cultural institutions of Athens with a savage wit. These comedies of Aristophanes (477–380 B.C.) were performed in the same Theater of Dionysus as the tragedies of Sophocles. In his hilarious *Lysistrata* (411 B.C.) Aristophanes portrays a group of Greek wives who sexually blackmail their warrior husbands into declaring peace. The play is a relentless satire of the Peloponnesian War, the Athenian magistrate, and the whole masculine political establishment. In one of the scenes Lysistrata and her disciples transform the obnoxious magistrate into a woman. Comedy can be subtle or gentle when it deals with humble or romantic subjects. But satire, when it chooses vicious and powerful subjects, can be brutally cruel.

Most comedies depend upon a certain element of satire. Satire requires an object of attack, and we can always depend upon the villain to display some mean quality worthy of ridicule, even in romantic comedies, where the heroes are admirable. In some comedies such as Molière's *The Misanthrope, The Miser,* and *Tartuffe,* the protagonist becomes the main object of ridicule. Many critics prefer to call these dramas satires or tragicomedies, reserving the term comedy for romantic plays with virtuous heroes.

Luis M. Valdez (*Writers & Artists Agency, Los Angeles, California*)

Los Vendidos (English title, "The Salesmen")

Los Vendidos (literally, "The Sold") is a miniature masterpiece of satire. It is arguably the most powerful play ever to depict the tragicomic nature of the Chicano struggle for survival in American culture.

The author of *Los Vendidos*, Luis M. Valdez, was born in 1940. Writer, actor, and director, he has also served on the United Farmworkers organizing committee in Delano, California, and worked as a union organizer. "The most persistent, undying cause in my life," he once said, "is the struggle of the United Farm Workers of America." He has taught Chicano history and theater at the University of California at Santa Cruz and at Berkeley.

Luis Valdez founded the *Teatro Campesino*, which has toured and performed throughout the United States. In 1969 and 1972 his theater company was invited to perform in the World Theater Festival in Nancy, France. In 1971 Valdez received the Drama Critics Circle Award for his play *Corridos*.

Los Vendidos displays the playwright's mastery of both classical and contemporary theatrical technique, as well as mime and "guerrilla" (intensely political) drama.

You will notice immediately in reading this play that it is not realistic: the premise of a "Used Mexican Lot," where human beings are sold like used cars, insists upon interpretation. The people being offered for sale represent stereotypes of Mexicans in the American mind. The actors will exaggerate their roles comically in order to satirize those stereotypes.

A secretary has come from the Governor's Office (Ronald Reagan was governor of California in the nineteen sixties) in order to purchase a Mexican for display purposes in the administration, as a "token" Spanish-speaking American.

The underlying horror of the secretary's mission is relieved by the antics of the "mechanical" Mexicans. And the way they defeat her purpose in the end is pure theatrical magic.

LUIS M. VALDEZ (1940–)

Los Vendidos

CHARACTERS

HONEST SANCHO	JOHNNY
SECRETARY	REVOLUCIONARIO
FARM WORKER	MEXICAN-AMERICAN

(*Scene: Honest Sancho's Used Mexican Lot and Mexican Curio Shop. Three models are on display in* HONEST SANCHO'S *shop: to the right, there is a* REVOLUCIONARIO, *complete with* sombrero, carrilleras, *and* carabina .30–.30. *At center, on the floor, there is the* FARM WORKER, *under a broad straw* sombrero. *At stage left is the* PACHUCO, filero *in hand.*)
(HONEST SANCHO *is moving among his models, dusting them off and preparing for another day of business.*)

SANCHO *Bueno, bueno, mis monos, vamos a ver a quien vendemos ahora, ¿no?* (*To audience.*) *¡Quihubo!* I'm Honest Sancho and this is my shop. *Antes fuí contratista pero ahora logré tener mi negocito.* All I need now is a customer. (*A bell rings offstage.*) Ay, a customer!

SECRETARY (*Entering*) Good morning, I'm Miss Jiménez from—

SANCHO *¡Ah, una chicana!* Welcome, welcome *Señorita* Jiménez.

SECRETARY (*Anglo pronunciation*) JIM-enez.

SANCHO *¿Qué?*

SECRETARY My name is Miss JIM-enez. Don't you speak English? What's wrong with you?

SANCHO Oh, nothing, Señorita JIM-enez. I'm here to help you.

SECRETARY That's better. As I was starting to say, I'm a secretary from Governor Reagan's office, and we're looking for a Mexican type for the administration.

SANCHO Well, you come to the right place, lady. This is Honest Sancho's Used Mexican lot, and we got all types here. Any particular type you want?

SECRETARY Yes, we were looking for somebody suave—

SANCHO Suave.

SECRETARY Debonair.

SANCHO *De buen aire.*

SECRETARY Dark.

SANCHO *Prieto.*

SECRETARY But of course not too dark.

SANCHO *No muy prieto.*

SECRETARY Perhaps, beige.

SANCHO Beige, just the tone. *Así como cafecito con leche, ¿no?*

SECRETARY One more thing. He must be hard-working.

SANCHO That could only be one model. Stop right over here to the center of the shop, lady. (*They cross to the* FARM WORKER.) This is our standard farm worker model. As you can see, in the words of our beloved Senator George Murphy, he is "built close to the ground." Also take special notice of his four-ply Goodyear *huaraches*, made from the rain tire. This wide-brimmed sombrero is an extra added feature—keeps off the sun, rain, and dust.

SECRETARY Yes, it does look durable.

SANCHO And our farm worker model is friendly. *Muy amable.* Watch. (*Snaps his fingers.*)

FARM WORKER (*Lifts up head*) *Buenos días, señorita.* (*His head drops.*)

SECRETARY My, he's friendly.

SANCHO Didn't I tell you? Loves his *patrones!* But his most attractive feature is that he's hard working. Let me show you. (*Snaps fingers.* FARM WORKER *stands.*)

FARM WORKER *¡El jale!* (*He begins to work.*)

SANCHO As you can see, he is cutting grapes.

SECRETARY Oh, I wouldn't know.

SANCHO He also picks cotton. (*Snap.* FARM WORKER *begins to pick cotton.*)

SECRETARY Versatile isn't he?

SANCHO He also picks melons. (*Snap.* FARM WORKER *picks melons.*) That's his slow speed for late in the season. Here's his fast speed. (*Snap.* FARM WORKER *picks faster.*)

SECRETARY *¡Chihuahua!* . . . I mean, goodness, he sure is a hard worker.

SANCHO (*Pulls the* FARM WORKER *to his feet*) And that isn't the half of it. Do you see these little holes on his arms that appear to be pores? During those hot sluggish days in the field, when the vines or the branches get so entangled, it's almost impossible to move; these holes emit a certain grease that allow our model to slip and slide right through the crop with no trouble at all.

SECRETARY Wonderful. But is he economical?

SANCHO Economical? *Señorita,* you are looking at the Volkswagen of Mexicans. Pennies a day is all it takes. One plate of beans and tortillas will keep him going all day. That, and chile. Plenty of chile. *Chile jalapenos, chile verde, chile colorado.* But, of course, if you do give him chile (*Snap.* FARM WORKER *turns left face. Snap.* FARM WORKER *bends over.*) then you have to change his oil filter once a week.

SECRETARY What about storage?

SANCHO No problem. You know these new farm labor camps our Honorable Governor Reagan has built out by Parlier or Raisin City? They were designed with our model in mind. Five, six, seven, even ten in one of those shacks will give you no trouble at all. You can also put him in old barns, old cars, river banks. You can even leave him out in the field overnight with no worry!

SECRETARY Remarkable.

SANCHO And here's an added feature: Every year at the end of the season, this model goes back to Mexico and doesn't return, automatically, until next Spring.

SECRETARY How about that. But tell me: does he speak English?

SANCHO Another outstanding feature is that last year this model was programmed to go out on STRIKE! (*Snap.*)

FARM WORKER: *¡HUELGA! ¡HUELGA! Hermanos, sálganse de esos files.* (*Snap. He stops.*)

SECRETARY No! Oh no, we can't strike in the State Capitol.

SANCHO Well, he also scabs. (*Snap.*)

FARM WORKER *Me vendo barato, ¿y qué?* (*Snap.*)

SECRETARY That's much better, but you didn't answer my question. Does he speak English?

SANCHO *Bueno* . . . no, *pero* he has other—

SECRETARY No.

SANCHO Other features.

SECRETARY NO! He just won't do!

SANCHO Okay, okay *pues.* We have other models.

SECRETARY I hope so. What we need is something a little more sophisticated.

SANCHO Sophisti—*¿qué?*

SECRETARY An urban model.

SANCHO Ah, from the city! Step right back. Over here in this corner of the shop is exactly what you're looking for. Introducing our new 1969 JOHNNY PACHUCO model! This is our fast-back model. Streamlined. Built for speed, low-riding, city life. Take a look at some of these features. Mag shoes, dual exhausts, green chartreuse paint-job, dark-tint windshield, a little poof on top. Let me just turn him on. (*Snap.* JOHNNY *walks to stage center with a* pachuco *bounce.*)

SECRETARY What was that?

SANCHO That, *señorita*, was the Chicano shuffle.

SECRETARY Okay, what does he do?

SANCHO Anything and everything necessary for city life. For instance, survival: He knife fights. (*Snap.* JOHNNY *pulls out switch blade and swings at* SECRETARY.)

(SECRETARY *screams.*)

SANCHO He dances. (*Snap.*)

JOHNNY (*Singing*) "Angel Baby, my Angel Baby . . ." (*Snap.*)

SANCHO And here's a feature no city model can be without. He gets arrested, but not without resisting, of course. (*Snap.*)

JOHNNY *¡En la madre, la placa!* I didn't do it! I didn't do it! (JOHNNY *turns and stands up against an imaginary wall, legs spread out, arms behind his back.*)

SECRETARY Oh no, we can't have arrests! We must maintain law and order.

SANCHO But he's bilingual!

SECRETARY Bilingual?

SANCHO *Simón que* yes. He speaks English! Johnny, give us some English. (*Snap.*)

JOHNNY (*Comes downstage*) Fuck-you!

SECRETARY (*Gasps*) Oh! I've never been so insulted in my whole life!

SANCHO Well, he learned it in your school.

SECRETARY I don't care where he learned it.

SANCHO But he's economical!

SECRETARY Economical?

SANCHO Nickels and dimes. You can keep Johnny running on hamburgers, Taco Bell tacos, Lucky Lager beer, Thunderbird wine, *yesca*—

SECRETARY *Yesca?*

SANCHO *Mota.*

SECRETARY *Mota?*

SANCHO *Leños . . . Marijuana.* (*Snap.* JOHNNY *inhales on an imaginary joint.*)

SECRETARY That's against the law!

JOHNNY (*Big smile, holding his breath*) Yeah.

SANCHO He also sniffs glue. (*Snap.* JOHNNY *inhales glue, big smile.*)

JOHNNY Tha's too much man, *ése.*

SECRETARY No, Mr. Sancho, I don't think this—

SANCHO Wait a minute, he has other qualities I know you'll love. For example, an inferiority complex. (*Snap.*)

JOHNNY (*To* SANCHO) You think you're better than me, huh *ése?* (*Swings switch blade.*)

SANCHO He can also be beaten and he bruises, cut him and he bleeds; kick him and he—(*He beats, bruises and kicks* PACHUCO.) would you like to try it?

SECRETARY Oh, I couldn't.

SANCHO Be my guest. He's a great scape goat.

SECRETARY No, really.

SANCHO Please.

SECRETARY Well, all right. Just once. (*She kicks* PACHUCO.) Oh, he's so soft.

SANCHO Wasn't that good? Try again.

SECRETARY (*Kicks* PACHUCO) Oh, he's so wonderful! (*She kicks him again.*)

SANCHO Okay, that's enough, lady. You ruin the merchandise. Yes, our JOHNNY PA-CHUCO model can give you many hours of pleasure. Why, the L.A.P.D. just bought twenty of these to train their rookie cops on. And talk about maintenance. *Señorita,* you are looking at an entirely self-supporting machine. You're never going to find our JOHNNY PACHUCO model on the relief rolls. No, sir, this model knows how to liberate.

SECRETARY Liberate?

SANCHO He steals. (*Snap.* JOHNNY *rushes the* SECRETARY *and steals her purse.*)

JOHNNY *¡Dame esa bolsa, vieja!* (*He grabs the purse and runs. Snap by* SANCHO. *He stops.*)

(SECRETARY *runs after* JOHNNY *and grabs purse away from him, kicking him as she goes.*)

SECRETARY No, no, no! We can't have any *more* thieves in the State Administration. Put him back.

SANCHO Okay, we still got other models. Come on, Johnny, we'll sell you to some old lady. (SANCHO *takes* JOHNNY *back to his place.*)

SECRETARY Mr. Sancho, I don't think you quite understand what we need. What we need is something that will attract the women voters. Something more traditional, more romantic.

SANCHO Ah, a lover. (*He smiles meaningfully.*) Step right over here, *señorita.* Introducing our standard Revolucionario and/or Early California Bandit type. As you can see he is well-built, sturdy, durable. This is the International Harvester of Mexicans.

SECRETARY What does he do?

SANCHO You name it, he does it. He rides horses, stays in the mountains, crosses deserts, plains, rivers, leads revolutions, follows revolutions, kills, can be killed, serves as a martyr, hero, movie star—did I say movie star? Did you ever see *Viva Zapata? Viva Villa? Villa Rides? Pancho Villa Returns? Pancho Villa Goes Back? Pancho Villa Meets Abbott and Costello*—

SECRETARY I've never seen any of those.

SANCHO Well, he was in all of them. Listen to this. (*Snap.*)

REVOLUCIONARIO (*Scream*) ¡VIVA VILLAAAAA!

SECRETARY That's awfully loud.

SANCHO He has a volume control. (*He adjusts volume. Snap.*)

REVOLUCIONARIO (*Mousey voice*) ¡Viva Villa!

SECRETARY That's better.

SANCHO And even if you didn't see him in the movies, perhaps you saw him on TV. He makes commercials. (*Snap.*)

REVOLUCIONARIO Is there a Frito Bandito in your house?

SECRETARY Oh yes, I've seen that one!

SANCHO Another feature about this one is that he is economical. He runs on raw horsemeat and tequila!

SECRETARY Isn't that rather savage?

SANCHO *Al contrario*, it makes him a lover. (*Snap.*)

REVOLUCIONARIO (*To* SECRETARY) ¡Ay, *mamasota, cochota, ven pa'ca!* (*He grabs* SECRETARY *and folds her back—Latin-Lover style.*)

SANCHO (*Snap.* REVOLUCIONARIO *goes back upright.*) Now wasn't that nice?

SECRETARY Well, it was rather nice.

SANCHO And finally, there is one outstanding feature about this model I KNOW the ladies are going to love: He's a GENUINE antique! He was made in Mexico in 1910!

SECRETARY Made in Mexico?

SANCHO That's right. Once in Tijuana, twice in Guadalajara, three times in Cuernavaca.

SECRETARY Mr. Sancho, I thought he was an American product.

SANCHO No, but—

SECRETARY No, I'm sorry. We can't buy anything but American-made products. He just won't do.

SANCHO But he's an antique!

SECRETARY I don't care. You still don't understand what we need. It's true we need Mexican models such as these, but it's more important that he be *American.*

SANCHO American?

SECRETARY That's right, and judging from what you've shown me, I don't think you have what we want. Well, my lunch hour's almost over, I better

SANCHO Wait a minute! Mexican but American?

SECRETARY That's correct.

SANCHO Mexican but . . . (*A sudden flash.*) AMERICAN! Yeah, I think we've got exactly what you want. He just came in today! Give me a minute. (*He exits. Talks from backstage.*) Here he is in the shop. Let me just get some papers off. There. Introducing our new 1970 Mexican-American! Ta-ra-ra-ra-ra-ra-RA-RAAA!

(SANCHO *brings out the* MEXICAN-AMERICAN *model, a clean-shaven middle-class type in a business suit, with glasses.*)

SECRETARY (*Impressed*) Where have you been hiding this one?

SANCHO He just came in this morning. Ain't he a beauty? Feast your eyes on him! Sturdy US STEEL frame, streamlined, modern. As a matter of fact, he is built exactly like our Anglo models except that he comes in a variety of darker shades: naugahyde, leather, or leatherette.

SECRETARY Naugahyde.

SANCHO Well, we'll just write that down. Yes, *señorita,* this model represents the apex of American engineering! He is bilingual, college educated, ambitious! Say the word "acculturate" and he accelerates. He is intelligent, well-mannered, clean—did I say clean? (*Snap.* MEXICAN-AMERICAN *raises his arm.*) Smell.

SECRETARY (*Smells*) Old Sobaco, my favorite.

SANCHO (*Snap.* MEXICAN-AMERICAN *turns toward* SANCHO) Eric! (*To* SECRETARY.) We call him Eric García. (*To* ERIC.) I want you to meet Miss JIM-enez, Eric.

MEXICAN-AMERICAN Miss JIM-enez, I am delighted to make your acquaintance. (*He kisses her hand.*)

SECRETARY Oh, my, how charming!

SANCHO Did you feel the suction? He has seven especially engineered suction cups right behind his lips. He's a charmer all right!

SECRETARY How about boards? Does he function on boards?

SANCHO You name them, he is on them. Parole boards, draft boards, school boards, taco quality control boards, surf boards, two-by-fours.

SECRETARY Does he function in politics?

SANCHO *Señorita,* you are looking at a political MACHINE. Have you ever heard of the OEO, EOC, COD, WAR ON POVERTY? That's our model! Not only that, he makes political speeches.

SECRETARY May I hear one?

SANCHO With pleasure. (*Snap.*) Eric, give us a speech.

MEXICAN-AMERICAN Mr. Congressman, Mr. Chairman, members of the board, honored guests, ladies and gentlemen. (SANCHO *and* SECRETARY *applaud.*) Please, please. I come before you as a Mexican-American to tell you about the problems of the Mexican. The problems of the Mexican stem from one thing and one thing alone: He's stupid. He's uneducated. He needs to stay in school. He needs to be ambitious, forward-looking, harder-working. He needs to think American, American, American, AMERICAN, AMERICAN, AMERICAN. GOD BLESS AMERICA! GOD BLESS AMERICA! GOD BLESS AMERICA!! (*He goes out of control.*)

(SANCHO *snaps frantically and the* MEXICAN-AMERICAN *finally slumps forward, bending at the waist.*)

SECRETARY Oh my, he's patriotic too!

SANCHO *Sí, señorita,* he loves his country. Let me just make a little adjustment here. (*Stands* MEXICAN-AMERICAN *up.*)

SECRETARY What about upkeep? Is he economical?

SANCHO Well, no, I won't lie to you. The Mexican-American costs a little bit more, but you get what you pay for. He's worth every extra cent. You can keep him running on dry Martinis, Langendorf bread.

SECRETARY Apple pie?

SANCHO Only Mom's. Of course, he's also programmed to eat Mexican food on ceremonial functions, but I must warn you: an overdose of beans will plug up his exhaust.

SECRETARY: Fine! There's just one more question: HOW MUCH DO YOU WANT FOR HIM?

SANCHO Well, I tell you what I'm gonna do. Today and today only, because you've been so sweet, I'm gonna let you steal this model from me! I'm gonna let you drive him off the lot for the simple price of—let's see taxes and license included—$15,000.

SECRETARY Fifteen thousand DOLLARS? For a MEXICAN!

SANCHO Mexican? What are you talking, lady? This is a Mexican-AMERICAN! We had to melt down two *pachucos,* a farm worker and three *gabachos* to make this model! You want quality, but you gotta pay for it! This is no cheap run-about. He's got class!

SECRETARY Okay, I'll take him.

SANCHO You will?

SECRETARY Here's your money.

SANCHO You mind if I count it?

SECRETARY Go right ahead.

SANCHO Well, you'll get your pink slip in the mail. Oh, do you want me to wrap him up for you? We have a box in the back.

SECRETARY No, thank you. The Governor is having a luncheon this afternoon, and we need a brown face in the crowd. How do I drive him?

SANCHO Just snap your fingers. He'll do anything you want.

(SECRETARY snaps. MEXICAN-AMERICAN steps forward.)

MEXICAN-AMERICAN RAZA QUERIDA, ¡VAMOS LEVANTANDO ARMAS PARA LIBERARNOS DE ESTOS DESGRACIADOS GABACHOS QUE NOS EXPLO-TAN! VAMOS.

SECRETARY What did he say?

SANCHO Something about lifting arms, killing white people, etc.

SECRETARY But he's not suppose to say that!

SANCHO Look, lady, don't blame me for bugs from the factory. He's your Mexican-American; you bought him, now drive him off the lot!

SECRETARY But he's broken!

SANCHO Try snapping another finger.

(SECRETARY snaps. MEXICAN-AMERICAN comes to life again.)

MEXICAN-AMERICAN ¡ESTA GRAN HUMANIDAD HA DICHO BASTA! Y SE HA PUESTO EN MARCHA! ¡BASTA! ¡BASTA! ¡VIVA LA RAZA! ¡VIVA LA CAUSA! ¡VIVA LA HUELGA! ¡VIVAN LOS BROWN BERETS! ¡VIVAN LOS ESTUDI-ANTES! ¡CHICANO POWER!

(The MEXICAN-AMERICAN turns toward the SECRETARY, who gasps and backs up. He keeps turning toward the PACHUCO, FARM WORKER, and REVOLUCIONARIO, snapping his fingers and turning each of them on, one by one.)

PACHUCO (Snap. To SECRETARY) I'm going to get you, baby! ¡Viva La Raza!

FARM WORKER (Snap. To SECRETARY) ¡Viva la huelga! ¡Viva la Huelga! ¡VIVA LA HUELGA!

REVOLUCIONARIO (Snap. To SECRETARY) ¡Viva la revolución! ¡VIVA LA REVO-LUCION!

(The three models join together and advance toward the SECRETARY who backs up and runs out of the shop screaming. SANCHO is at the other end of the shop holding his money in his hand. All freeze. After a few seconds of silence, the PACHUCO moves and stretches, shaking his arms and loosening up. The FARM WORKER and REVOLUCIONARIO do the same. SANCHO stays where he is, frozen to his spot.)

JOHNNY Man, that was a long one, ése. (Others agree with him.)

FARM WORKER How did we do?

JOHNNY Perty good, look all that lana, man! (He goes over to SANCHO and removes the money from his hand. SANCHO stays where he is.)

REVOLUCIONARIO En la madre, look at all the money.

JOHNNY We keep this up, we're going to be rich.

FARM WORKER They think we're machines.

REVOLUCIONARIO *Burros.*

JOHNNY Puppets.

MEXICAN-AMERICAN The only thing I don't like is—how come I always got to play the godamn Mexican-American?

JOHNNY That's what you get for finishing high school.

FARM WORKER How about our wages, *ése?*

JOHNNY Here it comes right now. $3,000 for you, $3,000 for you, $3,000 for you, and $3,000 for me. The rest we put back into the business.

MEXICAN-AMERICAN Too much, man. Heh, where you *vatos* going tonight?

FARM WORKER I'm going over to Concha's. There's a party.

JOHNNY Wait a minute, vatos. What about our salesman? I think he needs an oil job.

REVOLUCIONARIO Leave him to me.

(*The* PACHUCO, FARM WORKER, *and* MEXICAN-AMERICAN *exit, talking loudly about their plans for the night. The* REVOLUCIONARIO *goes over to* SANCHO, *removes his derby hat and cigar, lifts him up and throws him over his shoulder.* SANCHO *hangs loose, lifeless.*)

REVOLUCIONARIO (*To audience*) He's the best model we got! *¡Ajua!* (*Exit.*) (*End.*)

Questions

1. In his first speech of the play, Sancho introduces himself as "Honest Sancho." In light of all that follows, how is this ironic?
2. Why does the Secretary insist upon the Anglo pronunciation of her name? What does this tell you about her character?
3. Why does the Secretary reject the farm worker model? The Johnny Pachuco model? The Revolucionario?
4. Clearly the Secretary loves the Mexican-American model. Why is she so taken with him?
5. The playwright Valdez invests Sancho's descriptions of his Mexican-American model with a strong satiric humor. What exactly is he satirizing? Do you find it humorous? Explain.
6. Describe how the "models" have swindled the Secretary.
7. What is the moral significance of Sancho's transformation at the end?

 Writers on Writing Luis Valdez

> I believe that Chicano contributions to American culture, coming as they do from the soon-to-be largest minority in the country, are vital and necessary to a true perception of our national reality.
>
> I view art as a human necessity and as a social right. Participation in any democratic society requires open and free expression, and art is the quintessence of human communication. Through the years I have endeavored in my personal and public life to make the tools of the performing arts accessible to

Tragicomedy

The dramas of Aeschylus and Sophocles are tragic throughout, and the comedies of Aristophanes maintain their comic tone even in scenes that reveal an underlying seriousness. Such consistency in the playwright's attitude toward his characters and story is called consistency of tone. Most classical drama and some modern plays have such consistency. *The Importance of Being Earnest* is so thoroughly funny that we do not doubt for a moment that the play we are reading is a comedy.

Not all plays maintain such evenness of tone. Starting with Euripides, the classical consistency of tone begins to dissolve, giving rise to tragicomedy. In a tragicomedy serious scenes alternate with comic scenes, providing comic relief and a richly ironic blend of emotions. Euripides' first play, *Alcestis* (434 B.C.), dramatizes the story of a king's wife who voluntarily descends into Hades in place of her doomed husband. Heracles goes to rescue her. His drunken, wise-cracking character lends comic relief to a play that is otherwise quite serious. We find it difficult to call *Alcestis* a tragedy or a comedy, so we call it a tragicomedy. The Elizabethan playwrights were great masters of tragicomedy, particularly Shakespeare in *Measure for Measure, A Winter's Tale,* and *Troilus and Cressida.* Some critics consider *Hamlet,* with its amusing graveyard scene and the protagonist's antics, to be a tragicomedy. *King Lear,* with its hilarious Fool, and *Macbeth,* with its drunken Porter, also mingle serious and comic scenes. Yet these plays remain fundamentally tragic because they compel sympathy for their ill-fated protagonists.

Twelfth Night

Strictly speaking, *Twelfth Night* is a romantic comedy. Yet its tone is not so uniformly funny as Oscar Wilde's tone in *The Importance of Being Earnest.* The great love poetry of this play arises from ideal passions struggling for harmonious expression in an imperfect world.

Twelfth Night is enlivened by the dark intrigues of Malvolio, who illustrates the persistence of evil in the social order. Eventually he makes himself ridiculous because of his own vanity, losing his influence. But at first he seems a real threat to the thoroughly virtuous heroine. The lovesickness of the Duke, who speaks the famous opening speech, is genuine and profound. And the sadness of Viola and Sebastian, the brother and sister separated by shipwreck, each mourning the other's loss, is a tragic note played again and again until the final scenes of the play.

WILLIAM SHAKESPEARE (1564–1616)

Twelfth Night; or, What You Will

ACT I

SCENE I. [*The* DUKE'*s Palace.*]

Enter ORSINO (*Duke of Illyria*), CURIO, *and other* LORDS; [*with* MUSICIANS].

DUKE If music be the food of love, play on,
    Give me excess of it, that, surfeiting,
    The appetite may sicken, and so die.
    That strain again! It had a dying fall;
5   O, it came o'er my ear like the sweet sound
    That breathes upon a bank of violets,
    Stealing and giving odour! Enough, no more!
    'Tis not so sweet now as it was before.
    O spirit of love, how quick and fresh art thou!
10   That, notwithstanding thy capacity
    Receiveth as the sea, naught enters there,
    Of what validity and pitch soe'er,
    But falls into abatement and low price
    Even in a minute! So full of shapes is fancy
15   That it alone is high fantastical.

---

[1] **If music . . . play on,** etc.: If music is food for love, play on, until love's appetite for music is fully satisfied.

[4] **fall:** cadence.

[5-7] **it came . . . odour!:** It charmed my ear with a sound as soothing as the pleasant murmur of the wind that brings with it the sweetness of the violets growing upon some bank upon which it has breathed and from which it has stolen the perfume it brings.

[9] **how quick and fresh:** how keenly alive to new thoughts and notions.

[10] **That:** in that; inasmuch as. **capacity:** receptive power. Used in a more active sense than in modern English.

[11-14] **naught enters there . . . minute:** every new idea that enters the lover's mind—however highly he regards it at first—loses its value in a minute. The grammatical antecedent of *there* is *capacity*.

[12] **Of what validity and pitch soe'er:** of whatsoever value; however valuable and highly esteemed. *Validity* and *pitch* are synonymous. *Pitch* is the regular term for the height reached by a soaring falcon. It is often used metaphorically.

[13] **abatement:** reduction in value.

[14-15] **So full of shapes is fancy . . . fantastical:** Fancy (i.e., love, the lover's brain) is so 'full of shapes' (figures of the imagination) that—though limitless in its capacity (its ability to take them in)—it soon tires of each and every one of them.

CUR. Will you go hunt, my lord?

DUKE   What, Curio?

CUR. The hart.

DUKE Why, so I do, the noblest that I have.

20   O, when mine eyes did see Olivia first,
Methought she purg'd the air of pestilence!
That instant was I turn'd into a hart,
And my desires, like fell and cruel hounds,
E'er since pursue me.

Enter VALENTINE.

25   How now? What news from her?

VAL. So please my lord, I might not be admitted.
But from her handmaid do return this answer:
The element itself, till seven years' heat,
Shall not behold her face at ample view;

30   But like a cloistress she will veiled walk,
And water once a day her chamber round
With eye-offending brine: all this to season
A brother's dead love, which she would keep fresh
And lasting in her sad remembrance.

35 DUKE O, she that hath a heart of that fine frame
To pay this debt of love but to a brother,
How will she love when the rich golden shaft
Hath kill'd the flock of all affections else
That live in her; when liver, brain, and heart,

40   These sovereign thrones, are all supplied and fill'd,
Her sweet perfections, with one self king!
Away before me to sweet beds of flow'rs!
Love-thoughts lie rich when canopied with bow'rs.

---

[22] **a hart:** The story of Actæon, transformed by Diana to a stag because he had seen her bathing (Ovid, *Metamorphoses*, iii, 138 ff.), was familiar to every reader. Actæon 'represents a man who, indulging his eyes, or his imagination, with the view of a woman that he cannot gain, has his heart torn with incessant longing' (Johnson).

[23] **fell:** fierce.

[26] **So please my lord:** Literally, 'so may it please'; but used like *if you please* (i.e., if it be pleasing to you) as a courteous formula of submission or apology.

[28] **The element:** the sky; the heavens. **heat:** course.

[30] **like a cloistress:** as if her chamber were a cloister and she a nun.

[32] **eye-offending brine:** That tears are salt, that they irritate the eyes, and that salt is a preservative, are facts which Shakespeare kept vividly in mind.

[32-33] **to season A brother's dead love:** to preserve her love for a dead brother.

[34] **remembrance:** Quadrisyllabic—*rememberance*.

[37] **golden shaft:** Cupid has two arrows: one (tipped with gold) causes love; the other (tipped with lead) causes indifference or aversion.

[38] **all affections else:** all other thoughts, emotions, and feelings.

[39-41] **when liver . . . king!:** when her liver (the seat of the passion of love), her brain (the organ of thought), and her heart (the organ of emotion)—these thrones which sway her nature are all three filled (to the exclusion of every other thought or feeling) with passionate love for one and the same person.

[40] **supplied and fill'd:** Synonymous.

[41] **Her sweet perfections:** In apposition with 'liver, brain, and heart.'

[43] **rich:** as if in a chamber adorned with splendid tapestry hangings.

Exeunt.

SCENE II. [*The seacoast.*]

Enter VIOLA, *a* CAPTAIN, *and* SAILORS.

VIO. What country, friends, is this?
CAPT. This is Illyria, lady.
VIO. And what should I do in Illyria?
    My brother he is in Elysium.
5   Perchance he is not drown'd. What think you, sailors?
CAPT. It is perchance that you yourself were sav'd.
VIO. O my poor brother! and so perchance may he be.
CAPT. True, madam; and, to comfort you with chance,
    Assure yourself, after our ship did split,
10   When you, and those poor number sav'd with you,
    Hung on our driving boat, I saw your brother,
    Most provident in peril, bind himself
    (Courage and hope both teaching him the practice)
    To a strong mast that liv'd upon the sea;
15   Where, like Arion on the dolphin's back,
    I saw him hold acquaintance with the waves
    So long as I could see.
VIO. For saying so, there's gold.
    Mine own escape unfoldeth to my hope,
20   Whereto thy speech serves for authority,
    The like of him. Know'st thou this country?
CAPT. Ay, madam, well, for I was bred and born
    Not three hours' travel from this very place.
VIO. Who governs here?
25 CAPT. A noble duke, in nature as in name.
VIO. What is his name?
CAPT. Orsino.
VIO. Orsino! I have heard my father name him.
    He was a bachelor then.
30 CAPT. And so is now, or was so very late;
    For but a month ago I went from hence,

---

[4] **Elysium:** heaven. The selection of a word that resembles *Illyria* is manifestly intentional.

[6] **perchance:** Spoken with emphasis on *-chance:* 'It is by mere *chance.*'

[11] **driving:** drifting; driving before the wind.

[13] **the practice:** the plan; the method of procedure.

[14] **liv'd:** floated unsubmerged.

[15] **like Arion:** According to the ancient story the bard Arion, on a voyage from Sicily to Corinth, sprang overboard to escape from the sailors, who were about to murder him for his treasures. He was rescued by a dolphin, which had been enchanted by his music. Riding on the dolphin's back, he sang and played on his lyre. The waves grew calm at the sound, and Arion was carried ashore in safety.

[16] **hold acquaintance with the waves:** i.e., rise and fall with them without being overwhelmed.

[19] **unfoldeth:** reveals.

[20] **Whereto . . . authority:** which what you have just said suffices to justify.

[21] **country:** Trisyllabic.

[22] **bred:** begotten.

And then 'twas fresh in murmur (as you know
What great ones do, the less will prattle of)
That he did seek the love of fair Olivia.

35 VIO. What's she?

CAPT. A virtuous maid, the daughter of a count
That died some twelvemonth since; then leaving her
In the protection of his son, her brother,
Who shortly also died; for whose dear love,
40 They say, she hath abjur'd the company
And sight of men.

VIO.   O that I serv'd that lady,
And might not be delivered to the world,
Till I had made mine own occasion mellow,
45 What my estate is!

CAPT.   That were hard to compass,
Because she will admit no kind of suit;
No, not the Duke's.

VIO. There is a fair behaviour in thee, Captain;
50 And though that nature with a beauteous wall
Doth oft close in pollution, yet of thee
I will believe thou hast a mind that suits
With this thy fair and outward character.
I prithee (and I'll pay thee bounteously)
55 Conceal me what I am, and be my aid
For such disguise as haply shall become
The form of my intent. I'll serve this duke,
Thou shalt present me as an eunuch to him;
It may be worth thy pains. For I can sing,
60 And speak to him in many sorts of music
That will allow me very worth his service.
What else may hap, to time I will commit;
Only shape thou thy silence to my wit.

CAPT. Be you his eunuch, and your mute I'll be.

---

32 **as:** as [it naturally would be, for]. This use of *as* in ellipsis is an old idiom.

40 **abjur'd.** Used in the full sense of the word—'renounced by a solemn vow.'

43 **delivered:** reported, revealed.

44 **Till . . . mellow:** 'till I had myself provided a fit occasion' (Child).

45 **estate:** rank; station in life.

46 **to compass:** to bring about; to effect.

48 **not:** not even.

50 **though that:** Particles and relative adverbs are often reinforced by the addition of *that: if that, though that, since that, lest that, when that,* etc.

53 **character:** appearance.

56 **haply shall become:** perchance will suit.

58 **eunuch:** This particular feature of Viola's plan seems to have been dropped. It is never referred to again.

61 **allow me . . . service:** cause me to be approved by him as very worthy to be taken into his service.

62 **What:** whatever.

63 **Only . . . wit:** All I ask of you is to consent to my plan and then to keep silence, leaving it to my skill to carry it out successfully. **to:** in accordance with.

64 **mute:** dumb attendant; silent accomplice.

65   When my tongue blabs, then let mine eyes not see.

VIO. I thank thee. Lead me on.

Exeunt.

SCENE III. [OLIVIA's *house.*]

Enter SIR TOBY *and* MARIA.

TO. What a plague means my niece to take the death of her brother thus? I am sure care's an enemy to life.

MAR. By my troth, Sir Toby, you must come in earlier o' nights. Your cousin, my lady, takes great exceptions to your ill hours.

5 TO. Why, let her except before excepted!

MAR. Ay, but you must confine yourself within the modest limits of order.

TO. Confine? I'll confine myself no finer than I am. These clothes are good enough to drink in, and so be these boots too. An they be not, let them hang themselves in their own straps.

10 MAR. That quaffing and drinking will undo you. I heard my lady talk of it yesterday; and of a foolish knight that you brought in one night here to be her wooer.

TO. Who? Sir Andrew Aguecheek?

MAR. Ay, he.

TO. He's as tall a man as any's in Illyria.

15 MAR. What's that to th' purpose?

TO. Why, he has three thousand ducats a year.

MAR. Ay, but he'll have but a year in all these ducats. He's a very fool and a prodigal.

TO. Fie that you'll say so! He plays o' th' viol-de-gamboys, and speaks three or four languages word for word without book, and hath all the good gifts of nature.

20 MAR. He hath, indeed, almost natural! for, besides that he's a fool, he's a great quarreller; and but that he hath the gift of a coward to allay the gust he hath in quarrelling, 'tis thought among the prudent he would quickly have the gift of a grave.

---

⁶⁵ **When my tongue . . . see:** If I prove a blabber, let my eyes be smitten with blindness!

³ **By my troth:** literally, 'by my pledged faith.' **cousin:** niece. *Cousin* was a word of varied application—cousin, uncle or aunt, nephew or niece.

⁵ **except before excepted!:** A law phrase providing for exceptions in a lease or other grant: 'the matters previously excepted being excepted,' 'except for the exceptions already made,' 'with all necessary exceptions,' 'exceptis excipiendis.' Sir Toby echoes Maria's word *exceptions* (i.e., objections) and applies the law phrase in a new sense: 'Let her take exception to my conduct as much as she likes! What do I care?'

⁶ **modest:** moderate. **order:** orderly conduct; good behaviour.

⁷ **confine myself:** clothe myself.

⁸ **be.** A good old plural. **An:** if.

¹⁰ **will undo you:** will be your ruin.

¹⁴ **tall:** sturdy and valiant. Thus the audience is led to expect a very different figure from the spindle-shanked Sir Andrew who enters later.

¹⁷ **ducats:** The ducat was an Italian coin worth, in Shakespeare's time, about four or five shillings.

¹⁸ **viol-de-gamboys:** a kind of bass viol—Italian *viola da gamba* ('viol for the leg'), so called 'because men hold it betweene or vpon their legges.'

¹⁹ **word . . . book:** The suggestion is that Sir Andrew had learned a number of phrases by heart and can speak them off glibly without referring to the phrase-book. He uses a little French, but does not know what *pourquoi* means.

²⁰ **almost natural:** almost like a natural—i.e., a born fool, an idiot.

²¹ **the gust . . . in:** his taste for; his fondness for.

²³ **the prudent:** the foreseeing; those who have the gift of foresight.

TO. By this hand, they are scoundrels and substractors that say so of him. Who are they?

MAR. They that add, moreover, he's drunk nightly in your company.

25 TO. With drinking healths to my niece. I'll drink to her as long as there is a passage in my throat and drink in Illyria. He's a coward and a coystrill that will not drink to my niece till his brains turn o' th' toe like a parish top. What, wench! Castiliano vulgo! for here comes Sir Andrew Agueface.

Enter SIR ANDREW.

AND. Sir Toby Belch! How now, Sir Toby Belch?

30 TO. Sweet Sir Andrew!

AND. Bless you, fair shrew.

MAR. And you too, sir.

TO. Accost, Sir Andrew, accost.

AND. What's that?

35 TO. My niece's chambermaid.

AND. Good Mistress Accost, I desire better acquaintance.

MAR. My name is Mary, sir.

AND. Good Mistress Mary Accost—

TO. You mistake, knight. 'Accost' is front her, board her, woo her, assail her.

40 AND. By my troth, I would not undertake her in this company. Is that the meaning of 'accost'?

MAR. Fare you well, gentlemen.

TO. An thou let part so, Sir Andrew, would thou mightst never draw sword again!

---

23 **substractors:** for *subtractors*—i.e., persons who maliciously *take away* one's actual merits; slanderers.

26 **coystrill:** base fellow. A coystrill is, literally, a groom who takes care of a knight's horses.

27 **a parish top:** 'A large top was formerly kept in every village, to be whipped in frosty weather, that the peasants might be kept warm by exercise, and out of mischief, while they could not work' (Steevens). **wench:** girl—merely a familiar term, with no special significance. **Castiliano vulgo.** The exact sense is beyond reasonable conjecture. Obviously Sir Toby means to exhort Maria to receive Sir Andrew with decorum and not to make open fun of him as she might be tempted to do. The Castilians (Spaniards) were proverbially grave and ceremonious. Warburton and Hanmer emend to 'Castiliano volto'—i.e., 'a Castilian countenance.'

28 **Agueface.** Sir Andrew, as his name Aguecheek implies, is pale and 'thin-faced' like a man who suffers from 'fever and ague'—malarial fever—an ailment very common in England in Shakespeare's time on account of the undrained marshes.

29 **How now?:** Merely a greeting: 'How d'ye do?'

30 **Sweet:** Very common as a synonym for 'dear.' Not so saccharine as in modern usage.

31 **shrew:** Sir Andrew makes an attempt at lively humour.

32 **And you too:** And God bless you also! Maria uses the regular formula in answering Sir Andrew's 'bless you.'

34 **What's that?:** What does that word *accost* mean? Sir Toby perversely takes 'that' to refer to Maria.

35 **chambermaid:** Perhaps Sir Toby uses the word in the sense of 'confidential lady-in-waiting' or the like; perhaps he is joking—and mystifying Sir Andrew. The audience, at all events, could not possibly take Maria for a chambermaid in the ordinary sense. She is obviously a 'gentlewoman,' and, from the outset, she is flirting with Sir Toby, who marries her just before the end of the play.

36 **I desire better acquaintance:** An old formula of politeness: 'I am glad to meet you and hope to know you better in the future.'

39 **board her:** To *board* (French *aborder*) in the sense of 'accost' is common, but the word also suggests the figure of *boarding* a ship.

43 **An thou let part so:** If you allow her to go without further ceremony. **never draw sword again:** for such conduct would be unworthy of a knight. Sir Andrew repeats the phrase mechanically, as if it were the proper thing to say.

AND. An you part so, mistress, I would I might never draw sword again! Fair lady, do
45 you think you have fools in hand?

MAR. Sir, I have not you by th' hand.

AND. Marry, but you shall have! and here's my hand.

MAR. Now, sir, thought is free. I pray you, bring your hand to th' butt'ry bar and let it
drink.

50 AND. Wherefore, sweetheart? What's your metaphor?

MAR. It's dry, sir.

AND. Why, I think so. I am not such an ass but I can keep my hand dry. But what's
your jest?

MAR. A dry jest, sir.

55 AND. Are you full of them?

MAR. Ay, sir, I have them at my fingers' ends. Marry, now I let go your hand, I am
barren.

Exit.

TO. O knight, thou lack'st a cup of canary!
When did I see thee so put down?

60 AND. Never in your life, I think, unless you see canary put me down. Methinks sometimes I have no more wit than a Christian or an ordinary man has. But I am a great
eater of beef, and I believe that does harm to my wit.

TO. No question.

AND. An I thought that, I'd forswear it. I'll ride home tomorrow, Sir Toby.

65 TO. Pourquoi, my dear knight?

AND. What is 'pourquoi'? Do, or not do? I would I had bestowed that time in the tongues
that I have in fencing, dancing, and bear-baiting. O, had I but followed the arts!

TO. Then hadst thou had an excellent head of hair.

AND. Why, would that have mended my hair?

70 TO. Past question, for thou seest it will not curl by nature.

AND. But it becomes me well enough, does't not?

---

⁴⁴⁻⁴⁵ **do you think you have fools in hand?** Do you think you have fools to deal with?

⁴⁷ **Marry:** sure enough; to be sure; true. *Marry* (originally an oath by the Virgin Mary) is used as a
mere interjection.

⁴⁸ **thought is free.** A proverb, meaning 'No matter what I may or may not feel at liberty to speak,
I can think what I like.' **th' butt'ry bar:** the bar where drinks are served. The buttery was the
storeroom for the *butts* or casks of liquor.

⁵¹ **dry.** A dry hand was regarded as an indication of debility. Maria puns on *dry* in the sense of
'thirsty.'

⁵⁴⁻⁵⁶ **a dry jest . . . fingers' ends:** Maria puns on *dry* in the sense of 'sharply witty' and in the literal
sense of 'dry,' as applied to Sir Andrew's hand. When he fails to understand her, she dwells on
the jest in her next remark. The pun in 'at my fingers' ends' is obvious.

⁵⁷ **barren:** destitute of all jesting material.

⁵⁸ **canary:** A favourite sweet wine in Elizabethan times. It came from the Canary Islands.

⁶¹ **wit:** intelligence.

⁶⁷ **the arts:** polite learning. Compare the titles 'Bachelor' and 'Master of Arts.' Sir Toby's pun on
arts is inevitable, *art* and *nature* being antonyms. But we are not obliged to accept the suggestion
that he also puns on *tongues* and *tongs.* For 'curl by' the Folio reads 'coole my.' The emendation
is Theobald's. **bear-baiting.** See iii, 1, 97, note.

⁶⁹ **mended:** improved.

TO. Excellent. It hangs like flax on a distaff; and I hope to see a housewife take thee between her legs and spin it off.

AND. Faith, I'll home to-morrow, Sir Toby. Your niece will not be seen; or if she be,
75 it's four to one she'll none of me. The Count himself here hard by wooes her.

TO. She'll none o' th' Count. She'll not match above her degree, neither in estate, years, nor wit; I have heard her swear't. Tut, there's life in't, man.

AND. I'll stay a month longer. I am a fellow o' th' strangest mind i' th' world. I delight in masques and revels sometimes altogether.

80 TO. Art thou good at these kickshawses, knight?

AND. As any man in Illyria, whatsoever he be, under the degree of my betters; and yet I will not compare with an old man.

TO. What is thy excellence in a galliard, knight?

AND. Faith, I can cut a caper.

85 TO. And I can cut the mutton to't.

AND. And I think I have the back-trick simply as strong as any man in Illyria.

TO. Wherefore are these things hid? Wherefore have these gifts a curtain before 'em? Are they like to take dust, like Mistress Mall's picture? Why dost thou not go to church in a galliard and come home in a coranto? My very walk should be a jig. I would not
90 so much as make water but in a sink-a-pace. What dost thou mean? Is it a world to hide virtues in? I did think, by the excellent constitution of thy leg, it was form'd under the star of a galliard.

AND. Ay, 'tis strong, and it does indifferent well in a flame-colour'd stock. Shall we set about some revels?

---

72 **like flax:** i.e., in long straight strands. **a distaff:** a staff used in spinning.

75 **she'll none of me:** she'll never accept me.

76 **estate:** rank.

77 **there's life in't:** your suit promises to be successful. Cf. the proverb 'While there is life there is hope.'

80 **kickshawses:** elegant trifles. The old form of the singular is *kickshaws* (French *quelque chose*, 'something').

81 **under the degree of my betters.** Sir Andrew means: 'unless he is of higher rank in society than I am.' He uses a customary phrase of modesty, but in so doing he makes himself doubly ridiculous; for he implies that skill in sports depends, somehow, on social position, and he also seems to say that he's as skilful as anybody who is not more skilful than he!

82 **I will not compare with an old man.** *Old* is emphatic: 'I do not wish to compare myself with an elderly expert—a veteran.' Another modest disclaimer, expressed in a deliciously absurd fashion.

83 **a galliard:** A very lively and active dance.

85 **the mutton:** In Ford and Dekker, *The Sun's Darling* (Pearson ed., IV, 308), a French dancer is described as 'one that loves mutton so well, he alwaies carries capers about him.'

86 **the back-trick:** a backward step in the galliard, accompanied by an elaborate 'caper' of some kind.

87 **curtain:** For curtains before portraits see i, 5, 163.

88 **Are they like:** Are they likely. **like Mistress Mall's picture:** like a lady's portrait. *Mistress Mall* (i.e., Moll) is merely a general term. No particular Moll is designated.

89 **coranto:** a rapid-moving dance, as its name ('running') signifies.

90 **sink-a-pace:** cinque-pace—a kind of galliard.

91 **virtues:** accomplishments.

93 **indifferent well:** well enough; pretty well. **flame-colour'd.** Rowe's emendation for the Folio reading 'dam'd colour'd.' See Textual Notes. Nicholson (5 *Notes and Queries*, XI [1879], 124) thinks *dam'd colour'd* may mean 'black' or 'dark-coloured,' and Furnivall (*New Shakspere Society Transactions*, 1880–85, Part II, p. 69*) quotes Cotgrave's *Dictionarie*, 1611: 'Couleur d'enfer. . . . Noir-brun enfumé,' and 'Couleur d'enfer. A darke, and smoakie browne.' **stock:** stocking.

95 TO. What shall we do else? Were we not born under Taurus?

AND. Taurus? That's sides and heart.

TO. No, sir; it is legs and thighs. Let me see thee caper, [SIR ANDREW *dances.*] Ha, higher! Ha, ha, excellent!

Exeunt.

SCENE IV. [*The* DUKE'*s Palace.*]

Enter VALENTINE, *and* VIOLA *in man's attire.*

VAL. If the Duke continue these favours towards you, Cesario, you are like to be much advanc'd. He hath known you but three days, and already you are no stranger.

VIO. You either fear his humour or my negligence, that you call in question the continuance of his love. Is he inconstant, sir, in his favours?

5 VAL. No, believe me.

Enter DUKE, CURIO, *and* ATTENDANTS.

VIO. I thank you. Here comes the Count.

DUKE Who saw Cesario, ho?

VIO. On your attendance, my lord, here.

DUKE Stand you awhile aloof.—Cesario,

10 Thou know'st no less but all. I have unclasp'd
    To thee the book even of my secret soul.
    Therefore, good youth, address thy gait unto her;
    Be not denied access, stand at her doors,
    And tell them there thy fixed foot shall grow

15 Till thou have audience.

VIO.   Sure, my noble lord,
    If she be so abandon'd to her sorrow
    As it is spoke, she never will admit me.

DUKE. Be clamorous and leap all civil bounds

20 Rather than make unprofited return.

VIO. Say I do speak with her, my lord, what then?

DUKE O, then unfold the passion of my love;

---

95 **born under Taurus?**: etc. The Twelve Signs of the Zodiac were supposed to govern or influence different parts of the body. Old almanacs contain a picture of a man—the *Homo Signorum*—encircled by the symbols of the Twelve Signs, each symbol connected by a line with some part of the man's body. Such a figure was used in determining the time of year when a particular prescription would be most efficacious. The sign Leo, not Taurus, governs sides and heart. Taurus, according to some old authorities, governs neck and throat, but others of equal validity agree with Sir Toby.

3 **his humour or my negligence**: capriciousness on his part or negligent service on mine. **that**: in that; inasmuch as.

8 **On your attendance, my lord, here**: Here, my lord, awaiting your orders! *Your* is the objective genitive: 'attending upon you,' 'at your service.'

9 **Stand you aloof**: Addressed to Valentine and all the rest except Viola.

10 **no less but all**: no less than everything.

12 **address thy gait**: direct thy steps.

13 **accéss**. Note the accent.

20 **unprofited**: unsuccessful.

Surprise her with discourse of my dear faith!
It shall become thee well to act my woes.
25   She will attend it better in thy youth
Than in a nuncio's of more grave aspect.
VIO. I think not so, my lord.
DUKE   Dear lad, believe it;
For they shall yet belie thy happy years
30   That say thou art a man. Diana's lip
Is not more smooth and rubious; thy small pipe
Is as the maiden's organ, shrill and sound,
And all is semblative a woman's part.
I know thy constellation is right apt
35   For this affair. Some four or five attend him—
All, if you will; for I myself am best
When least in company. Prosper well in this,
And thou shalt live as freely as thy lord
To call his fortunes thine.
40   VIO.   I'll do my best
To woo your lady. [Aside] yet a barful strife!
Whoe'er I woo, myself would be his wife.

Exeunt.

SCENE V. [OLIVIA's *house.*]

Enter MARIA *and* CLOWN.

MAR. Nay, either tell me where thou hast been, or I will not open my lips so wide as a
bristle may enter in way of thy excuse. My lady will hang thee for thy absence.
CLOWN Let her hang me! He that is well hang'd in this world needs to fear no colours.
MAR. Make that good.
5   CLOWN He shall see none to fear.
MAR. A good lenten answer. I can tell thee where that saying was born, of 'I fear no
colours.'
CLOWN Where, good Mistress Mary?

MAR. In the wars; and that may you be bold to say in your foolery.

10 CLOWN Well, God give them wisdom that have it; and those that are fools, let them use their talents.

MAR. Yet you will be hang'd for being so long absent, or to be turn'd away—is not that as good as a hanging to you?

CLOWN Many a good hanging prevents a bad marriage; and for turning away, let summer 15 bear it out.

MAR. You are resolute then?

CLOWN Not so, neither; but I am resolv'd on two points.

MAR. That if one break, the other will hold; or if both break, your gaskins fall.

CLOWN Apt, in good faith; very apt. Well, go thy way! If Sir Toby would leave drinking, 20 thou wert as witty a piece of Eve's flesh as any in Illyria.

MAR. Peace, you rogue; no more o' that. Here comes my lady. Make your excuse wisely, you were best. [*Exit.*]

Enter LADY OLIVIA *with* MALVOLIO.

CLOWN Wit, an't be thy will, put me into good fooling! Those wits that think they have thee do very oft prove fools; and I that am sure I lack thee may pass for a wise man. 25 For what says Quinapalus? 'Better a witty fool than a foolish wit.'—God bless thee, lady!

OLI. Take the fool away.

CLOWN Do you not hear, fellows? Take away the lady.

OLI. Go to, y'are a dry fool! I'll no more of you. Besides, you grow dishonest.

30 CLOWN Two faults, madonna, that drink and good counsel will amend. For give the dry fool drink, then is the fool not dry. Bid the dishonest man mend himself: if he mend, he is no longer dishonest; if he cannot, let the botcher mend him. Anything that's mended is but patch'd; virtue that transgresses is but patch'd with sin, and sin that amends is but patch'd with virtue. If that this simple syllogism will serve, so; if it will

---

⁹ **that . . . foolery:** you may confidently use that answer to the conundrum in your jesting talk.

¹⁰⁻¹¹ **God . . . have it . . . talents:** May God enable those who (like you) have the full possession of their wits to use their wits wisely; and let fools make what use they can of their small stock of intellect. Feste suggests that he must rely on his skill as a jester to induce his mistress to overlook his truancy. The dialogue in ll. 25 ff. shows that his confidence is not misplaced.

¹⁴ **for:** as for.

¹⁵ **bear it out:** make it endurable.

¹⁸ **if one break:** Maria puns on *points*—tagged laces that attached the breeches to the doublet (jacket). **gaskins:** galligaskins, loose breeches.

¹⁹ **Apt:** to the point; clever.

²⁰ **thou wert . . . Eve's flesh:** you would make as clever a wife for him.

²² **you were best:** it would be best for you.

²³ **wits:** sane and clever persons.

²⁵ **Quinapalus:** Feste invents the name of the philosopher he pretends to quote.

²⁹ **Go to:** A phrase of rejection or contempt. It means, literally, 'go away!' like our colloquial 'go way' (which is an old idiom). It may be used in expostulation, reproof, impatience, or incredulity. Sometimes it merely closes or shuts off discourse, like 'very well!' or 'enough said!' **dry:** stupid. **you grow dishonest:** you are becoming untrustworthy. *Dishonest* is a vague term for any infraction of honourable principles or conduct. Here Olivia applies it to the fault for which Maria has just threatened Feste with punishment: that is, playing truant—'being so long absent.'

³⁰ **madonna:** my lady. **dry:** thirsty.

³¹ **mend himself:** reform.

³² **botcher:** The regular old term for a tailor who mends clothing.

³²⁻³³ **Anything . . . virtue, etc.:** Feste parodies the formal style of the logicians. He undertakes to prove that no human being is either all bad or all good.

³⁴ **will serve:** will answer—i.e., will satisfy you as an excuse for my fault. **so:** well and good!

35   not, what remedy? As there is no true cuckold but calamity, so beauty's a flower. The
    lady bade take away the fool; therefore, I say again, take her away.

    OLI. Sir, I bade them take away you.

    CLOWN Misprision in the highest degree! Lady, cucullus non facit monachum. That's
    as much to say as, I wear not motley in my brain. Good madonna, give me leave to
40   prove you a fool.

    OLI. Can you do it?

    CLOWN Dexteriously, good madonna.

    OLI. Make your proof.

    CLOWN I must catechize you for it, madonna. Good my mouse of virtue, answer me.

45   OLI. Well, sir, for want of other idleness, I'll bide your proof.

    CLOWN Good madonna, why mourn'st thou?

    OLI. Good fool, for my brother's death.

    CLOWN I think his soul is in hell, madonna.

    OLI. I know his soul is in heaven, fool.

50   CLOWN The more fool, madonna, to mourn for your brother's soul, being in heaven.
    Take away the fool, gentlemen.

    OLI. What think you of this fool, Malvolio? Doth he not mend?

    MAL. Yes, and shall do till the pangs of death shake him. Infirmity, that decays the wise,
    doth ever make the better fool.

55   CLOWN God send you, sir, a speedy infirmity, for the better increasing your folly! Sir
    Toby will be sworn that I am no fox; but he will not pass his word for twopence that
    you are no fool.

    OLI. How say you to that, Malvolio?

    MAL. I marvel your ladyship takes delight in such a barren rascal. I saw him put down
60   the other day with an ordinary fool that has no more brain than a stone. Look you
    now, he's out of his guard already. Unless you laugh and minister occasion to him,
    he is gagg'd. I protest I take these wise men that crow so at these set kind of fools no
    better than the fools' zanies.

---

[35] **what remedy?** There's no help for it—I must submit to misfortune. Then Feste solemnly adds
two maxims—one original, the other trite. Taken together, they remind Olivia that, as every man
must yield to the inevitable, so must every woman, for beauty is a flower that fades.   **there is no
true cuckold but calamity:** Every man is wedded to fortune; hence, when one's fortune is unfaithful, one may in very truth be called a cuckold—the husband of an unfaithful wife.

[35-36] **The lady . . . away:** Feste turns aside from Olivia and addresses Malvolio.

[38] **Misprision in the highest degree!:** An error of the worst kind! You meant *me*, but should have
meant *yourself*; for *you* are the fool, not *I*.   **cucullus non facit monachum:** A cowl doesn't make
a monk. So, Feste argues, his motley (particoloured) uniform does not prove him a fool.

[42] **Dexteriously:** An old by-form of *dexterously*—not a verbal trick of Feste's.

[44] **Good my mouse of virtue:** My good little virtuous mouse. *Mouse* was often used as a term of
playful affection.

[45] **idleness:** trivial occupation to pass away the time.   **I'll bide your proof:** I'll wait patiently for you
to prove your statement.

[52] **mend:** improve.

[53] **Yes:** Malvolio, who does not enjoy Feste's jesting talk, means that he grows more and more
foolish the longer he lives.

[59] **barren:** stupid.

[60] **with:** by.

[61] **out of his guard:** defenceless.   **minister occasion:** afford opportunity.

[62] **crow:** i.e., with laughter.   **these set kind of fools:** fools of this artificial sort.

[63] **zanies:** subordinate buffoons who attend upon professional jesters, imitate them, and serve as
butts for their jokes.

OLI. O, you are sick of self-love, Malvolio, and taste with a distemper'd appetite. To be
65   generous, guiltless, and of free disposition, is to take those things for birdbolts that you
deem cannon bullets. There is no slander in an allow'd fool, though he do nothing
but rail; nor no railing in a known discreet man, though he do nothing but reprove.
CLOWN Now Mercury indue thee with leasing, for thou speak'st well of fools!

Enter MARIA.

MAR. Madam, there is at the gate a young gentleman much desires to speak with you.
70   OLI. From the Count Orsino, is it?
MAR. I know not, madam. 'Tis a fair young man, and well attended.
OLI. Who of my people hold him in delay?
MAR. Sir Toby, madam, your kinsman.
OLI. Fetch him off, I pray you. He speaks nothing but madman. Fie on him! [*Exit*
75   MARIA.] Go you, Malvolio. If it be a suit from the Count, I am sick, or not at home.
What you will, to dismiss it. [*Exit* MALVOLIO.] Now you see, sir, how your fooling
grows old, and people dislike it.
CLOWN Thou hast spoke for us, madonna, as if thy eldest son should be a fool; whose
skull Jove cram with brains!

Enter SIR TOBY.

80   for—here he comes—one of thy kin has a most weak pia mater.
OLI. By mine honour, half drunk! What is he at the gate, cousin?
CLOWN Good Sir Toby!
TO. A gentleman.
OLI. A gentleman? What gentleman?
85   TO. 'Tis a gentleman here. A plague o' these pickle-herring! How now, sot?
OLI. Cousin, cousin, how have you come so early by this lethargy?
TO. Lechery? I defy lechery. There's one at the gate.
OLI. Ay, marry, what is he?
TO. Let him be the devil an he will, I care not! Give me faith, say I. Well, it's all one.

[*Exit*]

---

64 **of:** because of; with.   **distemper'd:** diseased, unhealthy.
65 **generous:** high-minded.   **birdbolts:** blunt arrows used for shooting birds.
66 **an allow'd fool:** a privileged fool—one who has, as it were, a license to practise his profession.
68 **Now Mercury . . . fools!** Now may Mercury endow thee with the art of lying! Mercury was the
god of craftiness and trickery. His help, Feste suggests, will be necessary if Olivia is to continue
her defence of fools and foolery.
77 **old:** outworn, trite.
78 **should be:** were destined to be.
80 **pia mater:** brain—literally, the inner membrane enclosing the brain. Cf. Nashe, *Strange Newes*,
1593 (ed. Grosart, II, 272): 'Thou turmoilst thy *pia mater* to proue base births better than the
offspring of many discents.'
85 **A plague o' these pickle-herring!** Sir Toby's announcement has been followed by a hiccough,
which he apologetically ascribes to herring rather than to drink.   **How now, sot?** How d'ye do,
fool! *Sot* is not here used in the sense of 'drunkard.'
86 **Cousin:** uncle.
88 **Ay, marry:** Yes, to be sure.
89 **faith:** to enable me to resist the devil.   **it's all one:** no matter about that!

90 OLI. What's a drunken man like, fool?

CLOWN Like a drown'd man, a fool, and a madman. One draught above heat makes him a fool, the second mads him, and a third drowns him.

OLI. Go thou and seek the crowner, and let him sit o' my coz; for he's in the third degree of drink—he's drown'd. Go look after him.

95 CLOWN He is but mad yet, madonna, and the fool shall look to the madman. [*Exit.*]

Enter MALVOLIO.

MAL. Madam, yond young fellow swears he will speak with you. I told him you were sick: he takes on him to understand so much, and therefore comes to speak with you. I told him you were asleep: he seems to have a foreknowledge of that too, and therefore comes to speak with you. What is to be said to him, lady? He's fortified against any 100 denial.

OLI. Tell him he shall not speak with me.

MAL. Has been told so; and he says he'll stand at your door like a sheriff's post, and be the supporter to a bench, but he'll speak with you.

OLI. What kind o' man is he?

105 MAL. Why, of mankind.

OLI. What manner of man?

MAL. Of very ill manner. He'll speak with you, will you or no.

OLI. Of what personage and years is he?

MAL. Not yet old enough for a man nor young enough for a boy; as a squash is before 110 'tis a peascod, or a codling when 'tis almost an apple. 'Tis with him in standing water, between boy and man. He is very well-favour'd and he speaks very shrewishly. One would think his mother's milk were scarce out of him.

OLI. Let him approach. Call in my gentlewoman.

MAL. Gentlewoman, my lady calls. *Exit.*

Enter MARIA.

115 OLI. Give me my veil; come, throw it o'er my face. We'll once more hear Orsino's embassy.

Enter VIOLA.

VIO. The honourable lady of the house, which is she?

OLI. Speak to me; I shall answer for her. Your will?

VIO. Most radiant, exquisite, and unmatchable beauty—I pray you tell me if this be the

---

[91] **above heat:** 'above the state of being warm in a proper degree' (Steevens).

[93] **crowner:** coroner. **sit o':** hold an inquest on.

[97] **takes on him:** takes upon himself; presumes.

[102] **Has:** he has. **a sheriff's post:** 'The houses of mayors and sheriffs of towns were distinguished by large posts set up before the doors. These posts were often elaborately carved' (Halliwell).

[105] **Why, of mankind:** Why, just like the general run of human beings.

[109] **a squash:** an unripe peascod (pea pod).

[110] **codling:** an unripe apple—what we call a 'green apple.' **in standing water:** like the tide in the interval between ebb and flood, when it moves neither way.

[111-112] **well-favour'd:** handsome. *Favour* is common in the sense of one's 'features.' **One would think . . . him:** To judge by his fretful tone and manner, one would think him only just weaned. The expression was proverbial.

[113] **my gentlewoman:** my lady-in-waiting.

120   lady of the house, for I never saw her. I would be loath to cast away my speech; for,
besides that it is excellently well penn'd, I have taken great pains to con it. Good
beauties, let me sustain no scorn. I am very comptible, even to the least sinister usage.

OLI. Whence came you, sir?

VIO. I can say little more than I have studied, and that question's out of my part. Good
125   gentle one, give me modest assurance if you be the lady of the house, that I may
proceed in my speech.

OLI. Are you a comedian?

VIO. No, my profound heart; and yet (by the very fangs of malice I swear) I am not that
I play. Are you the lady of the house?

130 OLI. If I do not usurp myself, I am.

VIO. Most certain, if you are she, you do usurp yourself; for what is yours to bestow is
not yours to reserve. But this is from my commission. I will on with my speech in
your praise and then show you the heart of my message.

OLI. Come to what is important in't. I forgive you the praise.

135 VIO. Alas, I took great pains to study it, and 'tis poetical.

OLI. It is the more like to be feigned; I pray you keep it in. I heard you were saucy at
my gates; and allow'd your approach rather to wonder at you than to hear you. If you
be not mad, be gone; if you have reason, be brief. 'Tis not that time of moon with
me to make one in so skipping a dialogue.

140 MAR. Will you hoist sail, sir? Here lies your way.

VIO. No, good swabber; I am to hull here a little longer. Some mollification for your
giant, sweet lady!

OLI. Tell me your mind.

VIO. I am a messenger.

---

[121] **con:** study, learn.

[122] **let me sustain no scorn:** do not subject me to any scornful treatment. **comptible:** sensitive. **sinister:** uncivil.

[125] **modest:** moderate, reasonable.

[127] **comedian:** In the general sense of 'actor.'

[128] **my profound heart:** my excellent deep-thinking lady. *Heart* (or *hearts*) is often used as a vocative in familiar or lightly affectionate address.

[128-129] **and yet . . . play:** and yet I challenge my bitterest enemy to deny that I am playing a part. This remark is understood by the audience but not by Olivia.

[130] **If I do not usurp myself:** if I am not in wrongful possession of my own personality; if I am really what I am.

[131-132] **you do usurp yourself; . . . reserve:** Viola catches up Olivia's word *usurp* and applies it in a different sense: 'You *do* make a wrong use of yourself; for it is your duty as a woman to give yourself to a husband.' **this is from my commission:** this is not the message with which I am entrusted. *From* is emphatic: 'away from,' 'foreign to.' Viola pretends that she has committed her message to memory and that all this talk interrupts its delivery. **I will on:** I will proceed.

[134] **forgive you:** excuse you from repeating.

[138-139] **'Tis not that time of moon . . . dialogue:** I am not just now so subject to the moon's influence as to take part in such a fantastic dialogue. Olivia alludes to the moon's supposed influence in causing lunacy. *Skipping* suggests also the inconstancy of which the ever-changing moon is a symbol. Olivia implies that Viola's talk is not quite coherent.

[140] **Here lies your way:** With a gesture of dismissal.

[141-142] **swabber:** A petty officer whose duty was 'to make and keep the ship clean, and that as well in the great cabin as everywhere betwixt the decks.' **to hull:** to lie adrift with all sails furled. **Some mollification for your giant:** 'Ladies, in romance, are guarded by giants, who repel all improper or troublesome advances. Viola, seeing [Maria] so eager to oppose her message, intreats Olivia to pacify her giant' (Johnson).

145 OLI. Sure you have some hideous matter to deliver, when the courtesy of it is so fearful. Speak your office.

VIO. It alone concerns your ear. I bring no overture of war, no taxation of homage. I hold the olive in my hand. My words are as full of peace as matter.

OLI. Yet you began rudely. What are you? What would you?

150 VIO. The rudeness that hath appear'd in me have I learn'd from my entertainment. What I am, and what I would, are as secret as maidenhead: to your ears, divinity; to any other's, profanation.

OLI. Give us the place alone; we will hear this divinity. [*Exit* MARIA.] Now, sir, what is your text?

155 VIO. Most sweet lady—

OLI. A comfortable doctrine, and much may be said of it. Where lies your text?

VIO. In Orsino's bosom.

OLI. In his bosom? In what chapter of his bosom?

VIO. To answer by the method, in the first of his heart.

160 OLI. O, I have read it! it is heresy. Have you no more to say?

VIO. Good madam, let me see your face.

OLI. Have you any commission from your lord to negotiate with my face? You are now out of your text. But we will draw the curtain and show you the picture. [*Unveils.*] Look you, sir, such a one I was this present. Is't not well done?

165 VIO. Excellently done, if God did all.

OLI. 'Tis in grain, sir; 'twill endure wind and weather.

VIO. 'Tis beauty truly blent, whose red and white
Nature's own sweet and cunning hand laid on.
Lady, you are the cruell'st she alive

170 If you will lead these graces to the grave,
And leave the world no copy.

OLI. O, sir, I will not be so hard-hearted. I will give out divers schedules of my beauty. It shall be inventoried, and every particle and utensil labell'd to my will:—as, item,

---

145 **deliver:** report. **when the courtesy of it is so fearful:** when, instead of polite manners, you assume so defiant an air.

146 **your office:** your business.

147 **overture:** declaration. **no taxation of homage:** no demand for surrender and submission.

148 **the olive:** The symbol of peace. **matter:** subject matter, substance.

150 **my entertainment:** the manner in which I have been received.

151 **maidenhead:** maidenhood. **divinity:** sacred discourse.

152 **profanation:** the impious disclosure of a sacred message.

159 **by the method:** in accordance with the preaching style that you have adopted.

163 **out of your text:** for you are now speaking of *faces*, not of *hearts*.

164 **such . . . present:** This is the kind of person I was just a moment ago—i.e., this is the picture that you wished to see. *This present* is adverbial—'just now.'

165 **if God did all:** The Elizabethan dramatists never tire of satirical remarks about artificial aids to beauty.

166 **in grain:** dyed in fast colours.

168 **cunning:** skilful.

169 **she:** Often used as a noun.

170 **graces:** beauties.

171 **no copy.** In the speech that follows Olivia refuses to take Viola's words in the sense intended and interprets *copy* literally.

173 **utensil:** a furnishing—a detail which helps to furnish me with the beauty you speak of. **labell'd to my will:** entered in a slip of parchment attached to my last will and testament. **item:** literally, 'also.' Used originally with all the articles in a list or inventory except the first.

two lips, indifferent red; item, two grey eyes, with lids to them; item, one neck, one
175 chin, and so forth. Were you sent hither to praise me?
VIO. I see you what you are—you are too proud;
But if you were the devil, you are fair.
My lord and master loves you. O, such love
Could be but recompens'd though you were crown'd
180 The nonpareil of beauty!
OLI.   How does he love me?
VIO. With adorations, with fertile tears,
With groans that thunder love, with sighs of fire.
OLI. Your lord does know my mind; I cannot love him.
185 Yet I suppose him virtuous, know him noble,
Of great estate, of fresh and stainless youth;
In voices well divulg'd, free, learn'd, and valiant,
And in dimension and the shape of nature
A gracious person. But yet I cannot love him.
190 He might have took his answer long ago.
VIO. If I did love you in my master's flame,
With such a suff'ring, such a deadly life,
In your denial I would find no sense;
I would not understand it.
195 OLI.   Why, what would you?
VIO. Make me a willow cabin at your gate
And call upon my soul within the house;
Write loyal cantons of contemned love
And sing them loud even in the dead of night;
200 Halloa your name to the reverberate hills
And make the babbling gossip of the air
Cry out 'Olivia!' O, you should not rest
Between the elements of air and earth
But you should pity me!

---

174 **indifferent**: more or less; rather.
175 **to praise me**: to appraise me; to make an inventory of my qualities.
177 **if**: even if.   **the devil**: whose pride is supreme in degree. Compare the proverbial phrase 'as proud as Lucifer.'
182 **fertile**: plenteous, abundant.
187 **In voices well divulg'd, free**, etc.: well reputed by public testimony as of noble nature, etc.
188 **dimension**: Synonymous with *the shape of nature* (i.e., his natural form). This phrase is added as an explanation of *dimension*.
189 **gracious**: full of grace—i.e., of beauty.
192 **such . . . life**: with such intensity that his life is merely one long pang of death. *Suffering* is (like *deadly*) an adjective modifying *life*.
196 **a willow cabin**: a tent of willow boughs. The weeping willow was the symbol of disconsolate love.
197 **my soul**: i.e., you, Olivia.
198 **cantons**: songs.
200 **reverberate**: reverberating, reëchoing.
201 **the babbling gossip of the air**: echo.
204 **But**: but that.

205 OLI. You might do much. What is your parentage?
VIO. Above my fortunes, yet my state is well.
    I am a gentleman.
OLI.   Get you to your lord.
    I cannot love him. Let him send no more,
210   Unless, perchance, you come to me again
    To tell me how he takes it. Fare you well.
    I thank you for your pains. Spend this for me.
VIO. I am no fee'd post, lady; keep your purse;
    My master, not myself, lacks recompense.
215   Love make his heart of flint that you shall love;
    And let your fervour, like my master's, be
    Plac'd in contempt! Farewell, fair cruelty.   *Exit.*
OLI. 'What is your parentage?'
    'Above my fortunes, yet my state is well.
220   I am a gentleman.' I'll be sworn thou art.
    Thy tongue, thy face, thy limbs, actions, and spirit
    Do give thee fivefold blazon. Not too fast! soft, soft!
    Unless the master were the man. How now?
    Even so quickly may one catch the plague?
225   Methinks I feel this youth's perfections
    With an invisible and subtle stealth
    To creep in at mine eyes. Well, let it be.
    What ho, Malvolio!

Enter MALVOLIO.

MAL.   Here, madam, at your service.
230 OLI. Run after that same peevish messenger,
    The County's man. He left this ring behind him,
    Would I or not. Tell him I'll none of it.
    Desire him not to flatter with his lord
    Nor hold him up with hopes. I am not for him.

---

206 **my state:** my condition in life.

213 **fee'd post:** hired messenger.

215 **that:** The antecedent is implied in *his* (= *of him*).

217 **Plac'd in contempt:** held in contempt; despised.

220 **thou art:** Olivia, in conversing with Viola, has used the formal pronoun *you*. Now, in soliloquy (that is, to all intents and purposes, in thought), she changes to the familiar and affectionate *thou*.

222 **blazon:** heraldic warrant of gentility. *Blazon* is, literally, the description of a coat of arms in the proper heraldic terms. **soft!:** slowly! Used as an interjection to warn against haste.

223 **Unless the master were the man:** Olivia implies that she might well accept Orsino if he were as irresistibly attractive as this servant of his.

225 **perfections:** Cf. i, 1, 41.

227 **To creep in at mine eyes:** and thus take possession of my mind and heart. **let it be!** Thus Olivia yields to fate.

230 **peevish:** childishly ill-tempered. Olivia is thinking of Viola's parting words (ll. 213–217).

231 **County's:** Count's. *Count* in this play is loosely used as a synonym for *Duke*.

232 **I'll none of it:** I'll have nothing to do with it; I've no use for it.

233 **to flatter with his lord:** to give his master any false encouragement.

235   If that the youth will come this way to-morrow,
       I'll give him reasons for't. Hie thee, Malvolio.
    MAL. Madam, I will.   *Exit.*
    OLI. I do know not what, and fear to find
       Mine eye too great a flatterer for my mind.
240   Fate, show thy force! Ourselves we do not owe.
       What is decreed must be—and be this so!   *[Exit.]*

ACT II

SCENE I. [*The seacoast.*]

Enter ANTONIO *and* SEBASTIAN.

ANT. Will you stay no longer? nor will you not that I go with you?

SEB. By your patience, no. My stars shine darkly over me; the malignancy of my fate might perhaps distemper yours. Therefore I shall crave of you your leave, that I may bear my evils alone. It were a bad recompense for your love to lay any of them on
5   you.

ANT. Let me yet know of you whither you are bound.

SEB. No, sooth, sir. My determinate voyage is mere extravagancy. But I perceive in you so excellent a touch of modesty that you will not extort from me what I am willing to keep in; therefore it charges me in manners the rather to express myself. You must
10 know of me then, Antonio, my name is Sebastian, which I call'd Roderigo. My father was that Sebastian of Messaline whom I know you have heard of. He left behind him myself and a sister, both born in an hour. If the heavens had been pleas'd, would we had so ended! But you sir, alter'd that, for some hour before you took me from the breach of the sea was my sister drown'd.

15 ANT. Alas the day!

SEB. A lady, sir, though it was said she much resembled me, was yet of many accounted beautiful. But though I could not with such estimable wonder overfar believe that, yet thus far I will boldly publish her: she bore a mind that envy could not but call

---

fair. She is drown'd already, sir, with salt water, though I seem to drown her remem-
20 brance again with more.

ANT. Pardon me, sir, your bad entertainment.

SEB. O good Antonio, forgive me your trouble!

ANT. If you will not murther me for my love, let me be your servant.

SEB. If you will not undo what you have done, that is, kill him whom you have recover'd,
25 desire it not. Fare ye well at once. My bosom is full of kindness; and I am yet so near
the manners of my mother that, upon the least occasion more, mine eyes will tell
tales of me. I am bound to the Count Orsino's court. Farewell.   *Exit.*

ANT. The gentleness of all the gods go with thee!
I have many enemies in Orsino's court,
30 Else would I very shortly see thee there.
But come what may, I do adore thee so
That danger shall seem sport, and I will go.   *Exit.*

SCENE II. [*A street.*]*

Enter VIOLA *and* MALVOLIO *at several doors.*

MAL. Were not you ev'n now with the Countess Olivia?

VIO. Even now, sir. On a moderate pace I have since arriv'd but hither.

MAL. She returns this ring to you, sir. You might have saved me my pains, to have taken
it away yourself. She adds, moreover, that you should put your lord into a desperate
5 assurance she will none of him. And one thing more, that you be never so hardy to
come again in his affairs, unless it be to report your lord's taking of this. Receive it
so.

VIO. She took the ring of me. I'll none of it.

MAL. Come, sir, you peevishly threw it to her; and her will is, it should be so return'd.
10 If it be worth stooping for, there it lies, in your eye; if not, be it his that finds it.

Exit.

VIO. I left no ring with her. What means this lady?
Fortune forbid my outside have not charm'd her!

---

21 **your bad entertainment:** the poorness of the rough hospitality that I have afforded you.

23 **murther me:** i.e., by forcing me to part company with you.   **for:** in return for.

26-27 **the manners of my mother:** my mother's temperament.   **tell tales of me:** reveal how unmanly
I am.

28 **gentleness:** love and favour.

* This scene takes place in the street and at a short distance from Olivia's mansion. 'At several
doors' in the stage direction means 'each at one of the two doors at the back of the stage.' Only
time enough has elapsed since Malvolio's exit at the end of Act I to allow for the first scene of
Act II.

3 **to have taken:** by taking.

4-5 **a desperate assurance:** a certainty that leaves him no hope of any change of mind on her
part.   **will none of him.** Cf. i, 5, 232.

5-6 **to come:** as to come.   **in his affairs:** on his business.   **your lord's taking of this:** that your lord
has accepted this message of rejection and will trouble her no more.

6-7 **Receive it so:** Take the ring back on these terms—with this understanding.

8 **She took the ring of me:** Viola (who has not failed to understand Olivia's words and manner in
their recent interview) perceives that this ring is a love token from Olivia. But she must not reveal
the facts of the case to Malvolio; and so she falls in with Olivia's fiction—that the ring had been
sent by the Duke.

12 **not:** This repeats and emphasizes the negative idea of *forbid*.

She made good view of me; indeed, so much
That, as methought, her eyes had lost her tongue,
15 For she did speak in starts distractedly.
She loves me sure; the cunning of her passion
Invites me in this churlish messenger.
None of my lord's ring? Why, he sent her none!
I am the man. If it be so—as 'tis—
20 Poor lady, she were better love a dream!
Disguise, I see thou art a wickedness
Wherein the pregnant enemy does much.
How easy is it for the proper false
In women's waxen hearts to set their forms!
25 Alas, our frailty is the cause, not we!
For such as we are made of, such we be.
How will this fadge? My master loves her dearly;
And I (poor monster) fond as much on him;
And she (mistaken) seems to dote on me.
30 What will become of this? As I am man,
My state is desperate for my master's love.
As I am woman (now alas the day!),
What thriftless sighs shall poor Olivia breathe!
O Time, thou must untangle this, not I;
35 It is too hard a knot for me t' untie!   [*Exit.*]

SCENE III. [OLIVIA'*s house.*]

Enter SIR TOBY *and* SIR ANDREW.

TO. Approach, Sir Andrew. Not to be abed after midnight is to be up betimes; and
'diluculo surgere,' thou know'st—

---

¹⁴ **her eyes had lost her tongue:** the intensity of her gaze had deprived her of the power of coherent
speech. *Lost* is causative: 'made her lose.'
¹⁶ **cunning:** craftiness.
¹⁷ **in:** in the person of.
¹⁹ **I am the man:** the man of her choice.
²⁰ **she were better.** In the idiom *you were better, you* was originally a dative. It was felt as a
nominative, however, and '*I* (*thou, he, she*) were better' was used instead of *me* (*thee, him, her*).
²¹⁻²² **Disguise . . . much:** Since disguise is a form of deceit, the father of lies, the devil—that artful
enemy of mankind—takes advantage of my using such trickery to carry out plans of his own.
²³ **the proper false:** men who are handsome but deceitful.
²⁶ **such as we are made of, such we be:** we are composed of frail material, and therefore we are
frail.
²⁷ **How will this fadge?:** How will this fit? How can this state of things adjust itself to any reasonable
outcome?
²⁸ **monster:** because both man and woman. **fond:** dote.
³¹ **My state is desperate for my master's love:** I cannot hope to win my master's love, since he does
not know I am a woman. **state:** condition.
³³ **thriftless:** unprofitable, unavailing.
¹ **Not . . . betimes,** etc. The Elizabethans amused themselves and sharpened their wits by devising
paradoxes and arguing logically to prove them. Sir Toby plays this game. His demonstration (in
ll. 4–6) depends on the ambiguity of 'early'; for late at night may be early in the morning. **betimes:** in good season.
² **diluculo surgere.** An old maxim once familiar to every schoolboy, from Lily's Latin Grammar:
'Diluculo surgere saluberrimum est'—'to rise at dawn is very good for the health.'

AND. Nay, by my troth, I know not; but I know to be up late is to be up late.

TO. A false conclusion! I hate it as an unfill'd can. To be up after midnight, and to go
5   to bed then, is early; so that to go to bed after midnight is to go to bed betimes. Does
not our life consist of the four elements?

AND. Faith, so they say; but I think it rather consists of eating and drinking.

TO. Th'art a scholar! Let us therefore eat and drink. Marian I say! a stoup of wine!

Enter CLOWN.

AND. Here comes the fool, i' faith.
10 CLOWN How now, my hearts? Did you never see the picture of We Three?

TO. Welcome, ass. Now let's have a catch.

AND. By my troth, the fool has an excellent breast. I had rather than forty shillings I
had such a leg, and so sweet a breath to sing, as the fool has. In sooth, thou wast in
very gracious fooling last night, when thou spok'st of Pigrogromitus, of the Vapians
15   passing the equinoctial of Queubus. 'Twas very good, i' faith. I sent thee sixpence for
thy leman. Hadst it?

CLOWN I did impeticos thy gratillity; for Malvolio's nose is no whipstock. My lady has a
white hand, and the Myrmidons are no bottle-ale houses.

AND. Excellent! Why, this is the best fooling, when all is done. Now a song!
20 TO. Come on! there is sixpence for you. Let's have a song.

AND. There's a testril of me too. If one knight give a—

CLOWN Would you have a love song, or a song of good life?

TO. A love song, a love song.

AND. Ay, ay! I care not for good life.

CLOWN *sings.*

25   O mistress mine, where are you roaming?
            O, stay and hear! your true-love's coming,
                That can sing both high and low.
            Trip no further, pretty sweeting;
            Journeys end in lovers meeting,
30   Every wise man's son doth know.

---

[3] **by my troth:** An oath by one's plighted (pledged) faith.

[5-6] **Does not . . . elements?:** According to ancient science, every living creature owes life and health
to the harmonious blend of the four elements (fire, air, earth, and water) in his system.

[8] **Th'art a scholar!:** You are right! I accept your doctrine, and we will follow it in practice. Let us
eat and drink. **stoup:** a large cup or goblet.

[10] **my hearts:** my fine fellows, a term of friendship or *camaraderie.* **the picture of We Three?** A
picture (sometimes an inn sign) of two idiotic heads—the person who looks at it being of course
the third fool.

[11] **a catch:** a round.

[12] **breast:** voice. *Breath* in 1. 13 is a synonym.

[14-15] **gracious:** pleasing, delightful. **Pigrogromitus . . . Queubus:** Mere high-sounding nonsense—
the kind of fooling that jesters practised when true wit and humour were not needed.

[16] **leman:** sweetheart.

[17-18] **I did impeticos thy gratillity:** I pocketed your little gratuity. **impeticos:** literally, put it in my
petticoat—i.e., the pocket of my gown. **for Malvolio's nose . . . bottle-ale houses:** Pure
nonsense again—to please Sir Andrew. **the Myrmidons:** the troop of Achilles.

[19] **when all is done:** after all—a phrase emphasizing the superlative.

[21] **testril:** a tester; a sixpence. The word appears to be a diminutive—like Feste's 'gratillity.' **of:**
from.

[22] **a song of good life:** a song that teaches one how to live righteously; a moral ditty.

[29] **in lovers meeting:** when lovers meet.

AND. Excellent good, i' faith!

TO. Good, good!

CLOWN [*sings*].
What is love? 'Tis not hereafter;
Present mirth hath present laughter;
35   What's to come is still unsure:
In delay there lies no plenty;
Then come kiss me, sweet and twenty!
    Youth's a stuff will not endure.

AND. A mellifluous voice, as I am true knight.

40 TO. A contagious breath.

AND. Very sweet and contagious, i' faith.

TO. To hear by the nose, it is dulcet in contagion. But shall we make the welkin dance indeed? Shall we rouse the night owl in a catch that will draw three souls out of one weaver? Shall we do that?

45 AND. An you love me, let's do't! I am dog at a catch.

CLOWN By'r Lady, sir, and some dogs will catch well.

AND. Most certain. Let our catch be 'Thou knave.'

CLOWN 'Hold thy peace, thou knave,' knight? I shall be constrain'd in't to call thee knave, knight.

50 AND. 'Tis not the first time I have constrained one to call me knave. Begin, fool. It begins, 'Hold thy peace.'

CLOWN I shall never begin if I hold my peace.

AND. Good, i' faith! Come, begin.

Catch sung. Enter MARIA.

MAR. What a caterwauling do you keep here! If my lady have not call'd up her steward
55 Malvolio and bid him turn you out of doors, never trust me.

TO. My lady's a Catayan, we are politicians, Malvolio's a Peg-a-Ramsey, and [*sings*] 'Three merry men be we.' Am not I consanguineous? Am I not of her blood? Tilly-vally, lady! [*sings*] 'There dwelt a man in Babylon, lady, lady!'

---

³⁵ **still:** always.

³⁷ **sweet and twenty!:** sweet, and twenty times sweet! sweet in the twentieth degree!

⁴⁰ **contagious breath:** a 'catchy' voice—with a pun on *breath* and on *contagious*.

⁴² **To hear by the nose . . . contagion:** If we may use our noses for hearing as well as for smelling, we may say that the Fool's breath is sweet to hear but malodorous. **make the welkin dance:** sing a song that shall be loud and merry enough to make the stars in the sky dance to our tune.

⁴³⁻⁴⁴ **draw three souls out of one weaver?:** Weavers were noted for singing.

⁴⁵ **An:** if. **I am dog:** I am very skilful; I'm a regular adept.

⁴⁶ **By'r Lady:** Originally an oath by 'our Lady'—the Virgin Mary.

⁴⁷ **'Thou knave.':** The words of this catch are 'Hold thy peace, thou knave; and I prithee hold thy peace.'

⁵⁰ **'Tis not the first time I have constrained one:** Sir Andrew means that he has often shown his valour by provoking a quarrel.

⁵⁶ **a Catayan:** a native of Cathay (China). It was a slang term for a 'cheat,' a 'humbug.' **politicians:** statesmen. 'We are occupied with an important matter of statesmanship.' **a Peg-a-Ramsey.** Peg of Ramsey or Peggie Ramsey is the sportive heroine of an old song and dance tune. Sir Toby merely expresses extreme contempt: 'Malvolio's a light-headed fellow of no account.'

⁵⁷⁻⁵⁸ **'Three merry men be we.'** An old song. **consanguineous:** or, as Sir Toby translates—'of her blood.' **Tilly-vally:** An interjection of contempt: 'fiddle-faddle'; 'fiddlesticks.'

CLOWN Beshrew me, the knight's in admirable fooling.
60 AND. Ay, he does well enough if he be dispos'd, and so do I too. He does it with a better
grace, but I do it more natural.
TO. [sings] 'O' the twelf day of December'—
MAR. For the love o' God, peace!

Enter MALVOLIO.

MAL. My masters, are you mad? or what are you? Have you no wit, manners, nor
65 honesty, but to gabble like tinkers at this time of night? Do ye make an alehouse of
my lady's house, that ye squeak out your coziers' catches without any mitigation or
remorse of voice? Is there no respect of place, persons, nor time in you?
TO. We did keep time, sir, in our catches. Sneck up!
MAL. Sir Toby, I must be round with you. My lady bade me tell you that, though she
70 harbours you as her kinsman, she's nothing allied to your disorders. If you can separate
yourself and your misdemeanours, you are welcome to the house. If not, and it would
please you to take leave of her, she is very willing to bid you farewell.
TO. [sings] 'Farewell, dear heart since I must needs be gone.'
MAR. Nay, good Sir Toby!
75 CLOWN. [sings] 'His eyes do show his days are almost done.'
MAL. Is't even so?
TO. 'But I will never die.'
CLOWN Sir Toby, there you lie.
MAL. This is much credit to you!
80 TO. 'Shall I bid him go?'
CLOWN 'What an if you do?'
TO. 'Shall I bid him go, and spare not?'
CLOWN 'O, no, no, no, no, you dare not!'
TO. Out o' tune, sir? Ye lie. Art any more than a steward? Dost thou think, because
85 thou art virtuous, there shall be no more cakes and ale?
CLOWN Yes, by Saint Anne! and ginger shall be hot i' th' mouth too.

---

[59] **Beshrew:** literally, 'curse'; but regularly used in a light sense.
[60] **dispos'd:** inclined to make merry.
[62] **twelf:** An old form of *twelfth*.
[64] **My masters:** Gentlemen.   **wit:** common sense.
[65] **honesty:** regard for honourable conduct; decency.   **tinkers:** proverbially given to talkative drunkenness.
[66-67] **coziers':** cobblers'.   **catches:** Cf. 1. 11.   **mitigation or remorse:** Synonymous: 'softening.' Malvolio affects a dignified and elegant style. *Remorse* is often used for 'compassion.'   **respect of:** consideration for.
[68] **Sneck up!:** Be hanged!
[69] **round:** outspoken.
[70] **disorders:** disorderly conduct.
[73] **'Farewell . . . be gone.'** The beginning of the old song 'Corydon's Farewell to Phyllis.'
[74] **Nay:** Merely a term of expostulation. 'Is't even so?' is likewise expostulatory: 'Is *this* the kind of conduct we have to put up with?'
[78] **there you lie:** 'In *that* point, at all events, you're a liar! for you certainly are not immortal.'
[81] **an if:** if.
[82] **spare not?:** refrain not? not shrink from so decisive an action?
[86] **ginger:** A favourite spice for ale in old times. It was thought to reduce the intoxicating effect.

TO. Th'art i' th' right.—Go, sir, rub your chain with crumbs. A stoup of wine, Maria!

MAL. Mistress Mary, if you priz'd my lady's favour at anything more than contempt, you would not give means for this uncivil rule. She shall know of it, by this hand. *Exit.*

90 MAR. Go shake your ears!

AND. 'Twere as good a deed as to drink when a man's ahungry, to challenge him the field, and then to break promise with him and make a fool of him.

TO. Do't, knight. I'll write thee a challenge; or I'll deliver thy indignation to him by word of mouth.

95 MAR. Sweet Sir Toby, be patient for to-night. Since the youth of the Count's was to-day with my lady, she is much out of quiet. For Monsieur Malvolio, let me alone with him. If I do not gull him into a nayword, and make him a common recreation, do not think I have wit enough to lie straight in my bed. I know I can do it.

TO. Possess us, possess us! Tell us something of him.

100 MAR. Marry, sir, sometimes he is a kind of Puritan.

AND. O, if I thought that, I'd beat him like a dog!

TO. What, for being a Puritan? Thy exquisite reason, dear knight?

AND. I have no exquisite reason for't, but I have reason good enough.

MAR. The devil a Puritan that he is, or anything constantly but a time-pleaser; an
105 affection'd ass, that cons state without book and utters it by great swarths; the best persuaded of himself; so cramm'd, as he thinks, with excellencies that it is his grounds of faith that all that look on him love him; and on that vice in him will my revenge find notable cause to work.

TO. What wilt thou do?

110 MAR. I will drop in his way some obscure epistles of love, wherein by the colour of his beard, the shape of his leg, the manner of his gait, the expressure of his eye, forehead, and complexion, he shall find himself most feelingly personated. I can write very like my lady your niece; on a forgotten matter we can hardly make distinction of our hands.

TO. Excellent! I smell a device.

115 AND. I have't in my nose too.

TO. He shall think by the letters that thou wilt drop that they come from my niece, and that she's in love with him.

MAR. My purpose is indeed a horse of that colour.

AND. And your horse now would make him an ass.

120 MAR. Ass, I doubt not.

AND. O, 'twill be admirable!

MAR. Sport royal, I warrant you. I know my physic will work with him. I will plant you two, and let the fool make a third, where he shall find the letter. Observe his construction of it. For this night, to bed, and dream on the event. Farewell.   *Exit.*

125 TO. Good night, Penthesilea.

AND. Before me, she's a good wench.

TO. She's a beagle true-bred, and one that adores me. What o' that?

AND. I was ador'd once too.

TO. Let's to bed, knight. Thou hadst need send for more money.

130 AND. If I cannot recover your niece, I am a foul way out.

TO. Send for money, knight. If thou hast her not i' th' end, call me Cut.

AND. If I do not, never trust me, take it how you will.

TO. Come, come; I'll go burn some sack. 'Tis too late to go to bed now. Come, knight; come, knight.

Exeunt.

SCENE IV. [*The* DUKE's *Palace.*]

Enter DUKE, VIOLA, CURIO, *and others.*

DUKE Give me some music. Now good morrow, friends.
　　Now, good Cesario, but that piece of song,
　　That old and antique song we heard last night.
　　Methought it did relieve my passion much,
5　　More than light airs and recollected terms
　　Of these most brisk and giddy-paced times.
　　Come, but one verse.

CUR. He is not here, so please your lordship, that should sing it.

DUKE Who was it?

---

[120] **Ass:** The standard pun on *ass* and *as*.

[123-124] **let the fool make the third:** When Maria's plot is carried out, Fabian—not Feste—'makes the third' (ii, 5). **construction:** interpretation. **the event:** the outcome; the result; the upshot.

[125] **Penthesilea:** Queen of the Amazons. In humorous laudation of the rather diminutive Maria.

[126] **Before me:** A light oath. As *before God!* means 'I swear, taking God to witness,' so *before me!* or *afore me!* means 'I swear, taking myself to witness.'

[127] **a beagle:** a very small dog noted for its keenness as a hunter.—**one that adores me:** See v, 1, 347.

[130] **recover:** win. **a foul way out:** out of pocket in a very unpleasant fashion—to a very disagreeable extent.

[131] **call me Cut:** a dock-tailed horse. The horse often serves as an emblem of stupidity.

[1] **morrow:** morning.

[3] **ántique:** old-fashioned, quaint.

[4] **passion:** love pangs.

[5] **recollected:** 'studied' (Warburton)—in contrast with the 'plain' style of the old-fashioned song (l. 45).

10 CUR. Feste the jester, my lord, a fool that the Lady Olivia's father took much delight
   in. He is about the house.
   DUKE Seek him out. [*Exit* CURIO.] And play the tune the while.   *Music plays.*
   Come hither, boy. If ever thou shalt love,
   In the sweet pangs of it remember me;
15 For such as I am all true lovers are,
   Unstaid and skittish in all motions else
   Save in the constant image of the creature
   That is belov'd. How dost thou like this tune?
   VIO. It gives a very echo to the seat
20 Where Love is thron'd.
   DUKE   Thou dost speak masterly.
   My life upon't, young though thou art, thine eye
   Hath stay'd upon some favour that it loves.
   Hath it not, boy?
25 VIO.   A little, by your favour.
   DUKE What kind of woman is't?
   VIO.   Of your complexion.
   DUKE She is not worth thee then. What years, i' faith?
   VIO. About your years, my lord.
30 DUKE Too old, by heaven! Let still the woman take
   An elder than herself: so wears she to him,
   So sways she level in her husband's heart;
   For, boy, however we do praise ourselves,
   Our fancies are more giddy and unfirm,
35 More longing, wavering, sooner lost and won,
   Than women's are.
   VIO.   I think it well, my lord.
   DUKE Then let thy love be younger than thyself,
   Or thy affection cannot hold the bent;
40 For women are as roses, whose fair flow'r,
   Being once display'd, doth fall that very hour.
   VIO. And so they are; alas, that they are so!
   To die, even when they to perfection grow!

---

10 **father:** The fact that Olivia's father has taken delight in Feste's foolery explains the privileged
   position the jester enjoys in her household.
16 **Unstaid and skittish:** Synonymous. To explain or emphasize a word by adding a synonym is a
   favourite rhetorical device.
19-20 **the seat Where Love is thron'd:** the heart. It gives the loving heart a voice that expresses truly
   what the heart feels.
23 **stay'd:** lingered. **favour:** features, face.
25 **by your favour:** Viola catches up Orsino's word and plays with it. Orsino naturally takes 'by your
   favour' in its ordinary sense, as a courteous formula—'if you please.'
30 **still:** always.
31 **so wears she to him:** thus she adapts herself to him instinctively.
32 **So sways she level:** thus she maintains an equipoise in the love that her husband bears her.
34 **Our fancies are:** the love that we men feel is. *Fancy* is very common in this sense.
39 **hold the bent:** maintain its intensity—literally, its tension. The figure comes from bending a
   bow.
41 **display'd:** full blown.

Enter CURIO *and* CLOWN.

DUKE O, fellow, come, the song we had last night.
45 Mark it, Cesario; it is old and plain.
The spinsters and the knitters in the sun,
And the free maids that weave their thread with bones,
Do use to chant it. It is silly sooth,
And dallies with the innocence of love,
50 Like the old age.
CLOWN Are you ready, sir?
DUKE Ay; prithee sing.

Music.

The [*Clown's*] Song.
Come away, come away, death,
    And in sad cypress let me be laid.
55 Fly away, fly away, breath;
    I am slain by a fair cruel maid.
My shroud of white, stuck all with yew,
    O, prepare it!
My part of death, no one so true
60   Did share it.

Not a flower, not a flower sweet,
    On my black coffin let there be strown;
Not a friend, not a friend greet
    My poor corpse, where my bones shall be thrown.
65 A thousand thousand sighs to save,
    Lay me, O, where
Sad true lover never find my grave,
    To weep there!

DUKE There's for thy pains.
70 CLOWN No pains, sir. I take pleasure in singing, sir.
DUKE I'll pay thy pleasure then.
CLOWN Truly, sir, and pleasure will be paid one time or another.
DUKE Give me now leave to leave thee.

---

[46] **spinsters:** spinners.
[47] **free:** care-free. **weave their thread with bones:** weave thread on bone bobbins to make 'bone lace.'
[48] **silly sooth:** 'plain, simple truth' (Johnson).
[49-50] **dallies with the innocence of love Like the old age:** expresses a true lover's feelings in such figures as were used in the good old days of childlike sincerity. To *dally* is to 'play' or 'sport.'
[53] **Come away:** Come hither—literally, Come away from where you are.
[54] **cypress:** a coffin of cypress wood.
[59-60] **My part . . . share it:** 'Though *Death* is a *part* in which every one acts his *share*, yet of all these actors no one is *so true* as I' (Johnson).
[69] **There's:** Emphatic: 'There is payment.'
[72] **pleasure will be paid:** we always have to pay for any indulgence in pleasure. *Will be paid* means 'insists on being paid': *will* is emphatic.

CLOWN Now the melancholy god protect thee, and the tailor make thy doublet of change-
75   able taffeta, for thy mind is a very opal! I would have men of such constancy put to
      sea, that their business might be everything, and their intent everywhere; for that's it
      that always makes a good voyage of nothing. Farewell.

Exit.

DUKE Let all the rest give place.

[*Exeunt* CURIO *and* ATTENDANTS.]

                              Once more, Cesario,
80   Get thee to yond same sovereign cruelty.
      Tell her, my love, more noble than the world,
      Prizes not quantity of dirty lands.
      The parts that fortune hath bestow'd upon her,
      Tell her I hold as giddily as fortune;
85   But 'tis that miracle and queen of gems
      That nature pranks her in, attracts my soul.
VIO. But if she cannot love you, sir—
DUKE I cannot be so answer'd.
VIO.   Sooth, but you must.
90   Say that some lady, as perhaps there is,
      Hath for your love as great a pang of heart
      As you have for Olivia. You cannot love her.
      You tell her so. Must she not then be answer'd?
DUKE There is no woman's sides
95   Can bide the beating of so strong a passion
      As love doth give my heart; no woman's heart
      So big to hold so much; they lack retention.
      Alas, their love may be call'd appetite—
      No motion of the liver, but the palate—

74-75 **doublet:** jacket. **changeable taffeta:** a kind of thin silk woven of threads of different colours
      so as to give an opalescent effect.
76-77 **intent:** destination. **that's it that always makes a good voyage of nothing:** That is the character
      that is very successful in bringing home a fine cargo of nothing as the result of its voyaging.
78 **give place:** withdraw, depart.
80 **sovereign:** supreme, transcendant. **cruelty:** An abstract noun is often used to designate a person.
83 **The parts . . . her:** the qualities and endowments that she owes to fortune—i.e., her rank and
   riches.
84 **I hold as giddily as fortune:** I value as slightly as fortune does. Fickle Fortune may at any moment
   take them away from her, but that would make no difference to *me.*
85-86 **that miracle . . . pranks her in:** her own miraculously beautiful self, as Nature has created
   her—as distinguished from Fortune's gifts. *Nature* is emphatic, as opposed to *Fortune.* **pranks
   her in:** adorns her with. She herself is her own adornment, being, as she is, a 'miracle' of
   beauty.
89 **Sooth:** But in very truth.
93 **she:** Emphatic: 'that lady.' **be answer'd:** accept your answer.
95 **bide:** endure. **passion:** Cf. 1. 4.
97 **to hold:** as to contain. **retention:** 'the power of retaining' (Wright).
98 **may be call'd appetite:** 'as being soon satisfied' (Child).
99 **No motion of the liver, but the palate:** not a genuine passion but a mere casual liking. The liver
   was anciently regarded as the seat of the passion of love. *Motion* for 'impulse,' 'emotion,' 'passion'
   is common.

100 That suffers surfeit, cloyment, and revolt;
But mine is all as hungry as the sea
And can digest as much. Make no compare
Between that love a woman can bear me
And that I owe Olivia.
105 VIO.   Ay, but I know—
DUKE What dost thou know?
VIO. Too well what love women to men may owe.
In faith, they are as true of heart as we.
My father had a daughter lov'd a man
110 As it might be perhaps, were I a woman,
I should your lordship.
DUKE   And what's her history?
VIO. A blank, my lord. She never told her love,
But let concealment, like a worm i' th' bud,
115 Feed on her damask cheek. She pin'd in thought;
And, with a green and yellow melancholy,
She sat like Patience on a monument,
Smiling at grief. Was not this love indeed?
We men may say more, swear more; but indeed
120 Our shows are more than will; for still we prove
Much in our vows but little in our love.
DUKE But died thy sister of her love, my boy?
VIO. I am all the daughters of my father's house,
And all the brothers too—and yet I know not.
125 Sir, shall I to this lady?
DUKE   Ay, that's the theme.
To her in haste! Give her this jewel: Say
My love can give no place, bide no denay.

Exeunt.

SCENE V. [OLIVIA's *orchard.*]

Enter SIR TOBY, SIR ANDREW, *and* FABIAN.

---

100 **suffers:** experiences. **surfeit:** overeating. **cloyment:** satiety. **revolt:** revulsion—the change
from appetite or desire to distaste or rejection.
102 **compare:** comparison.
114 **a worm i' th' bud:** a rose canker—the worm that eats out the inside of the bud and kills the
rose.
115 **damask:** of mingled red and white, like a damask rose.   **in thought:** in melancholy brooding.
116 **green and yellow:** pale and sallow (in complexion).
117 **like Patience on a monument:** like a monumental figure of calmness and fortitude.
118 **Smiling at grief:** bearing her grief with a smile of resignation. This goes with *she,* not with
Patience.
120 **Our shows are more than will:** What we *show* in our love-making is greater than the passion
that we actually *feel.*   **still:** ever, always.
124 **I know not:** Viola still hopes that her brother Sebastian has not been drowned.
128 **can give no place:** cannot give way; must hold its course.   **bide no denay:** submit to no denial
(refusal).

TO. Come thy ways, Signior Fabian.

FAB. Nay, I'll come. If I lose a scruple of this sport, let me be boil'd to death with melancholy.

TO. Wouldst thou not be glad to have the niggardly rascally sheep-biter come by some notable shame?

FAB. I would exult, man. You know he brought me out o' favour with my lady about a bear-baiting here.

TO. To anger him we'll have the bear again; and we will fool him black and blue. Shall we not, Sir Andrew?

AND. An we do not, it is pity of our lives.

Enter MARIA.

TO. Here comes the little villain. How now, my metal of India?

MAR. Get ye all three into the box tree. Malvolio's coming down this walk. He has been yonder i' the sun practising behaviour to his own shadow this half hour. Observe him, for the love of mockery; for I know this letter will make a contemplative idiot of him. Close, in the name of jesting! [*The others hide.*] Lie thou there [*Throws down a letter*]; for here comes the trout that must be caught with tickling. *Exit.*

Enter MALVOLIO.

MAL. 'Tis but fortune; all is fortune. Maria once told me she did affect me; and I have heard herself come thus near, that, should she fancy, it should be one of my complexion. Besides, she uses me with a more exalted respect than any one else that follows her. What should I think on't?

TO. Here's an overweening rogue!

FAB. O, peace! Contemplation makes a rare turkey cock of him. How he jets under his advanc'd plumes!

---

[1] **Come thy ways:** Come on; come along. *Ways* is, literally, 'on your way.' It is an adverbial genitive.   **Fabian:** a gentleman in the service of Olivia.

[2] **a scruple:** the least bit—literally, a third of a dram (in apothecary's weight).   **this sport:** Sir Toby has just explained the proposed trick.   **boil'd to death:** an old method of execution for the crime of poisoning.

[4] **sheep-biter:** sneak—literally, a dog that bites sheep.

[8] **black and blue:** thoroughly—within an inch of his life.

[10] **it is pity of our lives:** As we might say now-a-days, 'life won't be worth living.' Literally the phrase means 'it would be a pity about our lives'—i.e., 'our lives would be in danger.'

[11] **little villain.** Cf. i, 5, 141; ii, 3, 125; iii, 2, 44.   **my metal of India:** my golden girl. *India* means 'the East Indies.'

[14] **make a contemplative idiot of him:** fill his mind with idiotic meditation.

[15] **Close:** keep in hiding.

[16] **trout . . . tickling.** For this method of catching trout Steevens quotes Cogan, *The Haven of Health*, 1589, p. 143: 'This fishe of nature loueth flatterie; for being in the water it will suffer it selfe to bee rubbed and clawed, and so to be taken.'

[17] **she:** i.e., Olivia.   **did affect me:** was fond of me; loved me.

[18-19] **should she fancy . . . complexion:** if she were ever to fall in love, it would certainly be with a man of my temperament—a staid, sober, dignified person. One's *complexion* (in the old sense) was thought to be the result of the compounding of the four humours in the system—blood, phlegm, bile, and melancholy (i.e., black bile—an imaginary substance).

[19-20] **follows her:** is in her service.

[22-23] **jets under his advanc'd plumes:** struts like a turkey cock that elevates his feathers when he is showing off. *Advance* often means 'raise.'

AND. 'Slight, I could so beat the rogue!

25 FAB. Peace, I say.

MAL. To be Count Malvolio!

TO. Ah, rogue!

AND. Pistol him, pistol him!

FAB. Peace, peace!

30 MAL. There is example for't. The Lady of the Strachy married the yeoman of the wardrobe.

AND. Fie on him, Jezebel!

FAB. O, peace! Now he's deeply in. Look how imagination blows him.

MAL. Having been three months married to her, sitting in my state—

35 TO. O for a stone-bow, to hit him in the eye!

MAL. Calling my officers about me, in my branch'd velvet gown; having come from a day-bed, where I have left Olivia sleeping—

TO. Fire and brimstone!

FAB. O, peace, peace!

40 MAL. And then to have the humour of state; and after a demure travel of regard—telling them I know my place, as I would they should do theirs—to ask for my kinsman Toby—

TO. Bolts and shackles!

FAB. O, peace, peace, peace! Now, now.

45 MAL. Seven of my people, with an obedient start, make out for him. I frown the while, and perchance wind up my watch, or play with my—some rich jewel. Toby approaches; curtsies there to me—

TO. Shall this fellow live?

FAB. Though our silence be drawn from us by th' ears, yet peace!

50 MAL. I extend my hand to him thus, quenching my familiar smile with an austere regard of control—

TO. And does not Toby take you a blow o' the lips then?

---

²⁴ 'Slight. An oath 'by God's light!' See *Genesis*, i, 3.

³⁰⁻³¹ the Lady of the Strachy: An otherwise unheard of personage. Some old romantic story is in Malvolio's mind. the yeoman of the wardrobe: one of a staff of servants in charge of the wardrobe of a noble family.

³² Fie on him!: A much stronger curse than in modern usage. Jezebel: The cruel and haughty wife of Ahab, King of Israel. 'Pride will have a fall!'

³³ blows him: makes him swell; puffs him up with pride.

³⁴ my state: my chair of state: 'a chair with a canopy over it' (Steevens). The word also suggests 'stateliness.'

³⁵ a stone-bow: 'a cross-bow, a bow which shoots stones' (Johnson).

³⁶ branch'd: embroidered with figures of branches, leaves, etc.

³⁷ a day-bed: a sofa.

⁴⁰ to have the humour of state: to express in speech and demeanour a majestic disposition. after a demure travel of regard: after surveying the assembled household with a grave and dignified air.

⁴⁵ make out: make their way out; leave the room.

⁴⁶ play . . . jewel. Malvolio is about to say 'with my chain,' when he remembers that he will no longer be a steward or major-domo, and so 'he stops short . . . and alters his phrase to "some rich jewel" '(Nicholson).

⁴⁹ Though . . . by th' ears: though to keep silence may be a mighty effort.

⁵⁰⁻⁵¹ with an austere regard of control: with a stern look of authority.

⁵² take you a blow: give you a blow.

MAL. Saying, 'Cousin Toby, my fortunes having cast me on your niece, give me this
prerogative of speech.'
55 TO. What, what?
MAL. 'You must amend your drunkenness.'
TO. Out, scab!
FAB. Nay, patience, or we break the sinews of our plot.
MAL. 'Besides, you waste the treasure of your time with a foolish knight'—
60 AND. That's me, I warrant you.
MAL. 'One Sir Andrew'—
AND. I knew 'twas I, for many do call me fool.
MAL. What employment have we here? [*Takes up the letter.*]
FAB. Now is the woodcock near the gin.
65 TO. O, peace! and the spirit of humours intimate reading aloud to him!
MAL. By my life, this is my lady's hand! These be her very C's, her U's, and her T's;
and thus makes she her great P's. It is, in contempt of question, her hand.
AND. Her C's, her U's, and her T's? Why that?
MAL. [*reads*] 'To the unknown belov'd, this, and my good wishes.' Her very phrases! By
70 your leave, wax. Soft! and the impressure her Lucrece, with which she uses to seal!
'Tis my lady. To whom should this be?
FAB. This wins him, liver and all.
MAL. [*reads*]

'Jove knows I love—
75 But who?
Lips, do not move;
No man must know.'

'No man must know.' What follows? The numbers alter'd!
'No man must know.' If this should be thee, Malvolio?
80 TO. Marry, hang thee, brock!
MAL. [*reads*]

---

[57] **Out**: a common interjection of scorn or anger: 'away with you!' The modern slang phrase 'get
out!' is a direct descendant.   **scab!**: vile fellow!

[58] **patience**: be calm; control yourself.

[63] **employment**: business. 'What's going on here?' 'What does this mean?'

[64] **woodcock . . . gin**: Cf. iv, 2, 40. The woodcock (though in fact an intelligent bird) was a
proverbial symbol of credulous foolishness. It was even thought to fumble with the gin (the snare)
in stupid curiosity and thus to achieve its own capture.

[65] **the spirit of humours . . . to him!**: May the impulse that governs one's whims suggest to him
the idea of reading it aloud!

[66] **her very C's**, etc.: If anybody in the audience is minutely observant, he may note that there is
neither a C nor a P in the address of the letter.

[67] **in contempt of question**: so manifestly that it would be absurd to doubt the fact.

[69-70] **By your leave, wax**: Malvolio addresses the seal, with an apology for breaking it. The phrase
was conventional.   **Soft!**: An interjection of pausing: 'Wait a moment!'   **Lucrece**: The chaste
Lucretia, 'attired in mourning garment,' would be a good emblem of Olivia's vow.   **uses**: is
accustomed.

[72] **This wins him, liver and all**: This makes a complete conquest of him; is enough to make him
passionately in love.

[78] **The numbers alter'd!**: More verses, but in a different metre!

[80] **Marry**: See i, 3, 47, note.   **brock!**: badger. Used as a term of contempt, the badger being a
malodorous beast.

1272   Comedy

'I may command where I adore;
   But silence, like a Lucrece knife,
With bloodless stroke my heart doth gore.
85   M. O. A. I. doth sway my life.'

FAB. A fustian riddle!

TO. Excellent wench, say I.

MAL. 'M. O. A. I. doth sway my life.' Nay, but first, let me see, let me see, let me
    see.

90 FAB. What dish o' poison has she dress'd him!

TO. And with what wing the staniel checks at it!

MAL. 'I may command where I adore.' Why, she may command me: I serve her; she is
    my lady. Why, this is evident to any formal capacity. There is no obstruction in this.
    And the end—what should that alphabetical position portend? If I could make that
95   resemble something in me! Softly! M. O. A. I.

TO. O, ay, make up that! He is now at a cold scent.

FAB. Sowter will cry upon't for all this, though it be as rank as a fox.

MAL. M.—Malvolio. M.—Why, that begins my name!

FAB. Did not I say he would work it out? The cur is excellent at faults.

100 MAL. M.—But then there is no consonancy in the sequel. That suffers under probation.
    A should follow, but O does.

FAB. And O shall end, I hope.

TO. Ay, or I'll cudgel him, and make him cry O!

MAL. And then I comes behind.

105 FAB. Ay, an you had any eye behind you, you might see more detraction at your heels
    than fortunes before you.

---

[86] **fustian:** nonsensical. Fustian is a kind of coarse cotton cloth.

[87] **wench:** girl. Sir Toby is admiring Maria's cleverness.

[90] **What dish:** What a dish! **dress'd:** prepared.

[91] **staniel:** kestrel—an inferior species of hawk. **checks at it:** A falcon is said to *check* 'when she forsakes her proper game, and follows some other of inferior kind that crossed her in her flight.' Sir Toby means: 'How readily the silly fellow is attracted by this nonsense and led astray from the truth in his attempt to interpret it!"

[93] **to any formal capacity:** to any normal understanding; to anybody who has a normal mind. **no obstruction in this:** no difficulty about the meaning of this.

[95] **Softly!** Cf. 1. 70.

[96] **make up that:** fit *that* together; make sense out of *that*. **He is now at a cold scent:** He is now attempting to follow the hare when the scent is cold—i.e., to solve a riddle which is too hard for him.

[97] **Sowter . . . fox:** The dog will have a try at it, nevertheless, though the deceit is as obvious as the smell of a fox. *Sowter* is the name of a hound. It means, literally, 'cobbler,' and may or may not be intended to suggest clumsiness or stupidity. To *cry upon't* is, literally, to 'give tongue' like a hound that discovers the scent of the animal he is hunting.

[99] **excellent at faults:** A *fault* is a 'break in the scent.' Fabian is punning. He appears to praise Malvolio for skill in following the game, even when the scent is cold; but he implies that, in fact, Malvolio is a first-rate follower-up of false trails.

[100] **there is . . . sequel . . . probation:** there is no consistency in what follows. That breaks down when one tests it.

[102] **O:** lamentation.

[105] **any eye behind you.** Fabian alludes (with a phantom pun) to the symbolic figure of *Prudence*, which has three eyes—one in the back of the head. **more detraction at your heels:** more defamatory speech in pursuit of you.

MAL. M, O, A, I. This simulation is not as the former; and yet, to crush this a little, it would bow to me, for every one of these letters are in my name. Soft! here follows prose.

110   [*Reads*] 'If this fall into thy hand, revolve. In my stars I am above thee; but be not afraid of greatness. Some are born great, some achieve greatness, and some have greatness thrust upon 'em. Thy Fates open their hands; let thy blood and spirit embrace them; and to inure thyself to what thou art like to be, cast thy humble slough and appear fresh. Be opposite with a kinsman, surly with servants. Let thy tongue tang
115   arguments of state; put thyself into the trick of singularity. She thus advises thee that sighs for thee. Remember who commended thy yellow stockings and wish'd to see thee ever cross-garter'd. I say, remember. Go to, thou art made, if thou desir'st to be so. If not, let me see thee a steward still, the fellow of servants, and not worthy to touch Fortune's fingers. Farewell. She that would alter services with thee,
120   'THE FORTUNATE UNHAPPY.'

Daylight and champian discovers not more. This is open. I will be proud, I will read politic authors, I will baffle Sir Toby, I will wash off gross acquaintance, I will be point-devise, the very man. I do not now fool myself, to let imagination jade me; for every reason excites to this, that my lady loves me. She did commend my yellow
125   stockings of late, she did praise my leg being cross-garter'd; and in this she manifests herself to my love, and with a kind of injunction drives me to these habits of her liking. I thank my stars, I am happy. I will be strange, stout, in yellow stockings, and cross-garter'd, even with the swiftness of putting on. Jove and my stars be praised! Here is yet a postscript.

130   'Thou canst not choose but know who I am. If thou entertain'st my love, let it appear in thy smiling. Thy smiles become thee well. Therefore in my presence still smile, dear my sweet, I prithee.'

[107-108] **This simulation:** this expression of a hidden meaning. **the former:** i.e., 'I command where I adore'—which was very easy to understand. **to crush this a little, it would bow to me:** if I should use a little force with this 'M, O, A, I,' it would yield and come into agreement with *me*—would signify *me*, Malvolio. **Soft!** See i, 5, 222, note.

[110] **revolve:** consider. **my stars:** my lot in life; my rank and fortunes.

[112-113] **open their hands:** offer bounteous gifts. So *open-handed* means 'generous.' **let thy blood . . . them:** accept their offers with the whole strength of thy nature. **inure:** accustom. **like:** likely. **cast thy humble slough:** throw off thy garb of lowliness as a snake casts his old skin.

[114-115] **tang . . . state:** sound forth matters of public policy (statecraft) in thy talk. To fulfil this injunction Malvolio determines to 'read politic authors' (l. 122). **singularity:** peculiarity—almost equivalent to 'eccentricity.'

[117] **cross-garter'd:** with 'hose garters going acrosse, or ouerthwart, both aboue and beneath the knee' (Junius, *Nomenclator*, English edition, 1585, quoted by Douce). Such garters would be particularly conspicuous. **Go to.** A common interjection of impatience or protest.

[119] **alter services with thee:** make thee her master and become thy servant.

[121] **champian:** champaign; open country. **discovers:** discloses, reveals—'This is as plain as day.'

[122] **politic authors:** writers on statecraft and political subjects, from whose works I can learn 'arguments of state.' **baffle:** treat contemptuously; put down. To *baffle* was, literally, to 'degrade one from knighthood.' **gross:** low, vulgar.

[123] **point-devise:** exactly what the letter advises—to a T. *The very man* repeats this idea. **to let imagination jade me:** by letting my imagination trick me. *Jade* is a contemptuous term for a worthless or tricky horse.

[124] **excites to this:** prompts me to this conclusion.

[125-127] **in this . . . liking:** in this letter she reveals herself as wishing to be loved by me and, as it were, imposes on me the duty of adopting this costume that she likes. **happy:** fortunate. **strange:** haughty. *Stout* is practically synonymous.

[130] **canst not choose but know:** cannot help knowing. **entertain'st:** acceptest.

Jove, I thank thee. I will smile; I will do everything that thou wilt have me.

Exit.

FAB. I will not give my part of this sport for a pension of thousands to be paid from the
135   Sophy.

TO. I could marry this wench for this device—

AND. So could I too.

TO. And ask no other dowry with her but such another jest.

Enter MARIA.

AND. Nor I neither.

140 FAB. Here comes my noble gull-catcher.

TO. Wilt thou set thy foot o' my neck?

AND. Or o' mine either?

TO. Shall I play my freedom at tray-trip and become thy bondslave?

AND. I' faith, or I either?

145 TO. Why, thou hast put him in such a dream that, when the image of it leaves him,
    he must run mad.

MAR. Nay, but say true, does it work upon him?

TO. Like aqua-vitæ with a midwife.

MAR. If you will, then, see the fruits of the sport, mark his first approach before my lady.
150   He will come to her in yellow stockings, and 'tis a colour she abhors, and cross-garter'd,
    a fashion she detests; and he will smile upon her, which will now be so unsuitable to
    her disposition, being addicted to a melancholy as she is, that it cannot but turn him
    into a notable contempt. If you will see it, follow me.

TO. To the gates of Tartar, thou most excellent devil of wit!

155 AND. I'll make one too.

Exeunt.

ACT III

SCENE I. [OLIVIA's *orchard.*]

Enter VIOLA, *and* CLOWN [*with a tabor and pipe*].

VIO. Save thee, friend, and thy music! Dost thou live by thy tabor?

CLOWN No, sir, I live by the church.

VIO. Art thou a churchman?

---

¹³⁴⁻¹³⁵ **the Sophy:** the Shah of Persia.
¹⁴⁰ **gull-catcher:** A *gull* is a young bird, a nestling; then, figuratively, a person easily cheated, a
dupe.
¹⁴³ **play:** stake—and lose. **tray-trip:** an old gambling game, played with dice.
¹⁴⁵ **when the image of it leaves him:** when he awakes and the vision fades away.
¹⁴⁸ **aqua-vitæ:** distilled liquor; brandy or whiskey. The word *whiskey* is a clipped form of the Irish
phrase *uisce baugh,* 'water of life.'
¹⁵⁴ **Tartar:** Tartarus; hell.
¹⁵⁵ **I'll make one too:** I'll accompany you.
¹ **Save thee:** God save thee. **live by:** get thy living by. **tabor:** a small drum. Tabor and pipe were
the regular musical equipment of a jester.
³ **a churchman:** an ecclesiastic; a clergyman. Viola plays up to the jester, giving him a chance to
explain his joke.

CLOWN No such matter, sir. I do live by the church; for I do live at my house, and my
5 house doth stand by the church.

VIO. So thou mayst say, the king lies by a beggar, if a beggar dwell near him; or, the
church stands by thy tabor, if thy tabor stand by the church.

CLOWN You have said, sir. To see this age! A sentence is but a chev'ril glove to a good
wit. How quickly the wrong side may be turn'd outward!

10 VIO. Nay, that's certain. They that dally nicely with words may quickly make them
wanton.

CLOWN I would therefore my sister had had no name, sir.

VIO. Why, man?

CLOWN Why, sir her name's a word, and to dally with that word might make my sister
15 wanton. But indeed words are very rascals since bonds disgrac'd them.

VIO. Thy reason, man?

CLOWN Troth, sir, I can yield you none without words, and words are grown so false I
am loath to prove reason with them.

VIO. I warrant thou art a merry fellow and car'st for nothing.

20 CLOWN Not so, sir; I do care for something; but in my conscience, sir, I do not care for
you. If that be to care for nothing, sir, I would it would make you invisible.

VIO. Art not thou the Lady Olivia's fool?

CLOWN No, indeed, sir. The Lady Olivia has no folly. She will keep no fool, sir, till she
be married; and fools are as like husbands as pilchers are to herrings—the husband's
25 the bigger. I am indeed not her fool, but her corrupter of words.

VIO. I saw thee late at the Count Orsino's.

CLOWN Foolery, sir, does walk about the orb like the sun; it shines everywhere. I would
be sorry, sir, but the fool should be as oft with your master as with my mistress. I
think I saw your wisdom there.

---

[4] **No such matter:** nothing of the kind; not at all; by no means.

[6] **lies by:** lodges or dwells near—with an obvious pun.

[8] **You have said:** You have made your point. **A sentence:** any expression of a fact or opinion.
a chev'ril glove: Cheveril was a kind of light and flexible kid.

[10-11] **They that dally nicely with words . . . wanton:** Those who play subtly with words (making
fine distinctions) can soon make the words ambiguous. *Dally* often means to 'toy amorously'
and *wanton* often means 'unchaste.' Viola, then, is suggesting a pun, and Feste picks up the
suggestion and goes on 'dallying with words.'

[15] **bonds disgrac'd them:** because now we have to make a man give his bond if we are to feel sure
that he will keep his promise. A man's 'word' is no longer 'as good as his bond.'

[17] **Troth:** literally, 'by my pledged faith.' **yield:** give. **words.** Feste continues his pun on *word* in
the sense of 'promise.'

[18] **to prove reason with them:** to test the reasonableness of any proposition by means of words.

[19] **car'st for nothing:** feelest no anxiety about anything; dost never worry.

[20] **in my conscience:** to tell you precisely my inmost thoughts; to confess the truth to you.

[21] **you.** Emphatic. **to care for nothing:** to care for something is the same as not to care for nothing;
then perhaps the fact that I do not care for *you* makes you equivalent to *nothing*; and, in that
case, I wish you might be actually nothing, and so—invisible.

[23-24] **till she be married.** The regular joke—that husbands are always befooled by their wives. **pilchers:** pilchards—a kind of small fish.

[25] **corrupter of words.** A witty definition of the kind of foolery that has so far occupied Feste and
Viola in this scene.

[27-28] **the orb:** this round earth. **I would be sorry.** *Would* for *should* is common in Elizabethan
English. **but:** but that.

[29] **your wisdom.** A title imitated from 'your honour,' 'your lordship,' etc. Thus Feste ironically
suggests that Viola is as big a fool as *he* is.

30 VIO. Nay, an thou pass upon me, I'll no more with thee. Hold, there's expenses for
thee. [*Gives a piece of money.*]

CLOWN Now Jove, in his next commodity of hair, send thee a beard!

VIO. By my troth, I'll tell thee, I am almost sick for one, though I would not have it
grow on my chin. Is thy lady within?

35 CLOWN Would not a pair of these have bred, sir?

VIO. Yes, being kept together and put to use.

CLOWN I would play Lord Pandarus of Phrygia, sir, to bring a Cressida to this Troilus.

VIO. I understand you, sir. 'Tis well begg'd. [*Gives another piece.*]

CLOWN The matter, I hope, is not great, sir, begging but a beggar: Cressida was a beg-
40 gar. My lady is within, sir. I will conster to them whence you come. Who you are and
what you would are out of my welkin—I might say 'element,' but the word is over-
worn. *Exit.*

VIO. This fellow is wise enough to play the fool,
And to do that well craves a kind of wit.
45 He must observe their mood on whom he jests,
The quality of persons, and the time;
Not, like the haggard, check at every feather
That comes before his eye. This is a practice
As full of labour as a wise man's art;
50 For folly that he wisely shows, is fit;
But wise men, folly-fall'n, quite taint their wit.

Enter SIR TOBY *and* [SIR] ANDREW.

TO. Save you, gentleman!

VIO. And you, sir.

---

30 **an thou pass upon me,** etc.: if you mean to make thrusts at me (with your witticisms), I'll have
no more talk with you. **expenses:** spending money.

32 **commodity:** lot.

33 **sick for one:** lovesick for a certain man.

35 **a pair of these.** Thus Feste suggests that he should like to have another coin to match that which
Viola has given him.

36 **put to use:** put out at interest.

37 **Pandarus:** Cressida's uncle, who brought Troilus and Cressida together.

38 **well:** skilfully, adroitly.

39 **The matter . . . is not great:** It is not a great piece of begging.

40 **conster:** construe, interpret, explain.

41 **welkin.** *Welkin* means 'the sky,' and *element* often had the same meaning. Hence Feste's elegant
pun, which modern English cannot reproduce. He means 'beyond my comprehension.'

43 **wise enough to play the fool:** This speech is enough to show that Feste is not a 'natural'—a born
fool—as most of the jesters were in old times, but (like Touchstone) a clever fellow who has taken
up folly as a profession.

44 **wit:** mental agility; cleverness.

45 **observe:** adapt himself to.

46 **quality:** This word suggests 'rank' as well as 'quality in general.'

47 **the haggard:** a wild or untrained hawk. **check at every feather:** fly off heedlessly at every bird
he sees—i.e., make personal jests without discrimination. For *check at* see ii, 5, 91, note.

48 **a practice:** a piece of professional skill.

50 **fit:** fitting, proper.

51 **folly-fall'n:** when they fall into folly—foolish speech and conduct. **taint their wit:** disgrace their
natural wisdom.

AND. Dieu vous garde, monsieur.

55 VIO. Et vous aussi; vostre serviteur.

AND. I hope, sir, you are, and I am yours.

TO. Will you encounter the house? My niece is desirous you should enter, if your trade be to her.

VIO. I am bound to your niece, sir. I mean, she is the list of my voyage.

60 TO. Taste your legs, sir; put them to motion.

VIO. My legs do better understand me, sir, than I understand what you mean by bidding me taste my legs.

TO. I mean, to go, sir, to enter.

VIO. I will answer you with gait and entrance. But we are prevented.

Enter OLIVIA *and* GENTLEWOMAN, [MARIA].

65 Most excellent accomplish'd lady, the heavens rain odours on you!

AND. [*aside*] That youth's a rare courtier. 'Rain odours'—well!

VIO. My matter hath no voice, lady, but to your own most pregnant and vouchsafed ear.

AND. [*aside*] 'Odours,' 'pregnant,' and 'vouchsafed'—I'll get 'em all three all ready.

70 OLI. Let the garden door be shut, and leave me to my hearing. [*Exeunt* SIR TOBY, SIR ANDREW, *and* MARIA.] Give me your hand, sir.

VIO. My duty, madam, and most humble service.

OLI. What is your name?

VIO. Cesario is your servant's name, fair princess.

75 OLI. My servant, sir? 'Twas never merry world
Since lowly feigning was call'd compliment.
Y'are servant to the Count Orsino, youth.

VIO. And he is yours, and his must needs be yours.
Your servant's servant is your servant, madam.

80 OLI. For him, I think not on him; for his thoughts,
Would they were blanks, rather than fill'd with me!

VIO. Madam, I come to whet your gentle thoughts
  On his behalf.
OLI.   O, by your leave, I pray you!
85 I bade you never speak again of him;
  But, would you undertake another suit,
  I had rather hear you to solicit that
  Than music from the spheres.
VIO.   Dear lady—
90 OLI. Give me leave, beseech you. I did send,
  After the last enchantment you did here,
  A ring in chase of you. So did I abuse
  Myself, my servant, and, I fear me, you.
  Under your hard construction must I sit,
95 To force that on you in a shameful cunning
  Which you knew none of yours. What might you think?
  Have you not set mine honour at the stake
  And baited it with all th' unmuzzled thoughts
  That tyrannous heart can think? To one of your receiving
100 Enough is shown; a cypress, not a bosom,
  Hides my heart. So, let me hear you speak.
VIO. I pity you.
OLI.   That's a degree to love.
VIO. No, not a grize; for 'tis a vulgar proof
105 That very oft we pity enemies.
OLI. Why, then, methinks 'tis time to smile again.
  O world, how apt the poor are to be proud!
  If one should be a prey, how much the better
  To fall before the lion than the wolf!

---

[84] **by your leave:** allow me. A courteous phrase of interruption: 'Pray let me speak.'
[85] **I bade you never speak again of him.** See i, 5, 209: 'I cannot love him. Let him send no more.'
[88] **music from the spheres:** The stars were supposed, in their revolution about the earth, to give utterance to a superb harmony, which mortals cannot hear.
[90] **beseech:** I beseech.
[91] **enchantment:** Cf. i, 5, 225–227. Viola uses the same figure (ii, 2, 12): 'Fortune forbid my outside have not charm'd her!'
[92] **abuse:** deceive.
[93] **you:** Emphatic. Olivia fears that Cesario may have misinterpreted her character.
[94] **Under . . . sit:** I must, I fear, have subjected myself to very harsh judgment on your part. *Construction* is, literally, 'interpretation.'
[95] **To force:** by forcing. **in a shameful cunning:** by a trick that was disgraceful.
[96] **none of yours:** not yours at all. **might:** could.
[97] **at the stake:** The figure comes from bear-baiting. The bear was tied to a stake and the dogs were set on to attack him. To *bait* means, literally, to 'cause [the dogs] to bite [the bear].'
[99] **tyrannous:** cruel, savage. **To one of your receiving:** to one as quick of apprehension as you.
[100] **cypress:** a veil of black crape—almost transparent.
[103-104] **degree, grize:** Synonymous: 'step.'
[104] **a vulgar proof:** a thing of ordinary experience.
[106] **'tis time to smile again:** it is time for me to dismiss these love-pangs from my mind—if he is my enemy. Olivia is talking to herself rather than to Viola.
[107] **apt:** ready.
[108-109] **If one should be a prey . . . wolf:** If I had to be a prey to love, would it not have been better to fall in love with my noble suitor Orsino than with this hard-hearted youngster?

Clock strikes.

110 The clock upbraids me with the waste of time.
Be not afraid, good youth, I will not have you;
And yet, when wit and youth is come to harvest,
Your wife is like to reap a proper man.
There lies your way, due west.
115 VIO.   Then westward ho!
Grace and good disposition attend your ladyship!
You'll nothing, madam, to my lord by me?
OLI. Stay.
I prithee tell me what thou think'st of me.
120 VIO. That you do think you are not what you are.
OLI. If I think so, I think the same of you.
VIO. Then think you right. I am not what I am.
OLI. I would you were as I would have you be!
VIO. Would it be better, madam, than I am?
125 I wish it might; for now I am your fool.
OLI. O, what a deal of scorn looks beautiful
In the contempt and anger of his lip!
A murd'rous guilt shows not itself more soon
Than love that would seem hid: love's night is noon.
130 Cesario, by the roses of the spring,
By maidhood, honour, truth, and everything,
I love thee so that, maugre all thy pride,
Nor wit nor reason can my passion hide.
Do not extort thy reasons from this clause,
135 For that I woo, thou therefore hast no cause;
But rather reason thus with reason fetter:
Love sought is good, but given unsought is better.
VIO. By innocence I swear, and by my youth,
I have one heart, one bosom, and one truth,
140 And that no woman has; nor never none
Shall mistress be of it, save I alone.

---

[112] **when . . . harvest:** when you are mature in age and wisdom. Olivia implies that Cesario is too young to know what is good for himself.

[113] **proper:** handsome.

[114] **due west:** toward the setting sun—with a suggestion that she is dismissing him from her favourable thoughts.

[116] **Grace:** the favour of heaven.   **good disposition:** a happy frame of mind.

[117] **You'll nothing?:** You do not wish to send any reply?

[120] **That you do think you are not what you are:** that you think you are in love *with a man*, not with a woman.

[125] **I am your fool:** you are making a fool of me. Viola pretends to think that Olivia is not in earnest; but she really means that she herself is put in a ridiculous position by Olivia's wooing.

[129] **love's night is noon:** All attempts to conceal one's love make it only the more evident.

[132] **maugre all thy pride:** in spite of the scorn you show.

[134-136] **Do not extort . . . better:** Do not draw forced arguments for your action in this case from the proposition that, because I offer my love unsought, you have no reason to accept it; but, on the contrary, attach firmly one proposition to another, and so conclude that 'love sought is good, but given unsought is better.'

[140] **nor never none:** nor ever any one.

And so adieu, good madam. Never more
Will I my master's tears to you deplore.

OLI. Yet come again; for thou perhaps mayst move

145   That heart which now abhors to like his love.

Exeunt.

SCENE II. [OLIVIA's *house.*]

Enter SIR TOBY, SIR ANDREW, *and* FABIAN.

AND. No, faith, I'll not stay a jot longer.

TO. Thy reason, dear venom; give thy reason.

FAB. You must needs yield your reason, Sir Andrew.

AND. Marry, I saw your niece do more favours to the Count's servingman than ever she

5   bestow'd upon me. I saw't i' th' orchard.

TO. Did she see thee the while, old boy? Tell me that.

AND. As plain as I see you now.

FAB. This was a great argument of love in her toward you.

AND. 'Slight! will you make an ass o' me?

10   FAB. I will prove it legitimate, sir, upon the oaths of judgment and reason.

TO. And they have been grand-jurymen since before Noah was a sailor.

FAB. She did show favour to the youth in your sight only to exasperate you, to awake
your dormouse valour, to put fire in your heart and brimstone in your liver. You
should then have accosted her; and with some excellent jests, fire-new from the mint,

15   you should have bang'd the youth into dumbness. This was look'd for at your hand,
and this was balk'd. The double gilt of this opportunity you let time wash off, and you
are now sail'd into the North of my lady's opinion, where you will hang like an icicle
on a Dutchman's beard unless you do redeem it by some laudable attempt either of
valour or policy.

20   AND. An't be any way, it must be with valour; for policy I hate. I had as lief be a Brownist
as a politician.

---

3 **yield:** give.
4 **Marry:** See i, 3, 47, note.
5 **orchard:** garden—not limited, as in modern usage, to a plantation of fruit trees.
8 **argument of love in her:** evidence to prove love on her part.
9 **'Slight:** See ii, 5, 24, note.
10 **legitimate:** legitimately—i.e., as it were, legally, by the sworn testimony of judgment and logical
reasoning.
11 **grand-jurymen:** and therefore good judges of evidence.
13 **dormouse:** sleepy, dormant.   **valour:** courage as a suitor.   **brimstone in your liver:** i.e., to heat
it. The liver was regarded as the seat of the passion of love.
14 **fire-new:** brand-new.
16 **this was balk'd:** this opportunity was missed.
17-18 **an icicle on a Dutchman's beard:** Barentz, a Dutchman, had made a voyage to the Arctic
regions which was famous when TWELFTH NIGHT was written.
19 **policy:** strategy.
20 **Brownist:** a member of the religious denomination founded by Robert Browne (b. *ca.* 1550, d.
ca. 1633). They were opposed both to the Episcopal and the Presbyterian form of church government and adopted that form now called Congregational. Sir Andrew, who was hostile to the
Puritan party, was of course even more horrified by Brownist principles.
21 **politician:** Sir Andrew has taken *policy* in the sense of 'political trickery.'

TO. Why then, build me thy fortunes upon the basis of valour. Challenge me the Count's youth to fight with him; hurt him in eleven places. My niece shall take note of it; and assure thyself there is no love-broker in the world can more prevail in man's commendation with woman than report of valour.

FAB. There is no way but this, Sir Andrew.

AND. Will either of you bear me a challenge to him?

TO. Go, write it in a martial hand. Be curst and brief; it is no matter how witty, so it be eloquent and full of invention. Taunt him with the license of ink. If thou thou'st him some thrice, it shall not be amiss; and as many lies as will lie in thy sheet of paper, although the sheet were big enough for the bed of Ware of England, set 'em down. Go, about it! Let there be gall enough in thy ink, though thou write with a goose-pen, no matter. About it!

AND. Where shall I find you?

TO. We'll call thee at the cubiculo. Go.

Exit SIR ANDREW.

FAB. This is a dear manikin to you, Sir Toby.

TO. I have been dear to him, lad—some two thousand strong, or so.

FAB. We shall have a rare letter from him—but you'll not deliver 't?

TO. Never trust me then; and by all means stir on the youth to an answer. I think oxen and wainropes cannot hale them together. For Andrew, if he were open'd, and you find so much blood in his liver as will clog the foot of a flea, I'll eat the rest of th' anatomy.

FAB. And his opposite, the youth, bears in his visage no great presage of cruelty.

Enter MARIA.

TO. Look where the youngest wren of nine comes.

MAR. If you desire the spleen, and will laugh yourselves into stitches, follow me. Yond

---

[23] **to fight with him:** i.e., offering to fight with him.

[24] **love-broker:** agent in love matters; go-between.   **can:** that can.

[28] **curst:** ill-tempered, cross.   **so:** provided that; if only.

[29-30] **with the license of ink:** with all the freedom in language that written speech allows.   **If thou thou'st him:** if you use *thou* instead of *you* in your letter. *Thou* was the pronoun of familiar address and was therefore common in insulting language.

[31] **the bed of Ware:** a famous bedstead—one of the sights of Shakespeare's time.

[32-33] **gall:** Oak galls were used in ink-making. The pun on *gall*, 'bitterness,' is obvious.   **with a goose-pen:** a goose quill, such as was regularly used for a pen. Sir Toby implies that Sir Andrew will write in a foolish style.

[35] **cubiculo:** cubicle; the chamber or private room where you are to write the letter.

[36] **a dear manikin to you:** a little man that you like to play with as if he were a puppet. Sir Toby catches up the word *dear* and applies it in the sense of 'costly,' 'expensive.'

[37] **some two thousand.** Cf. ii, 3, 130, 131.

[40] **wainropes:** wagon ropes.   **hale:** haul.   **For:** as for.

[41-42] **blood in his liver.** Fear was supposed to be caused by lack of blood in the liver. Hence *white-livered* for 'cowardly.'   **th' anatomy:** his dissected body. Since *anatomy* sometimes means 'skeleton,' Sir Toby may be alluding to Sir Andrew's thin frame.

[43] **opposite:** opponent.

[44] **nine:** 'The Wren is remarkable for laying many eggs at a time, nine or ten and sometimes more: and as she is the smallest of birds, the last of so large a brood may be supposed to be little indeed, which is the image here intended to be given of Maria' (Hanmer).

[45] **If you desire the spleen:** Laughter was supposed to be caused by the action of the spleen.

gull Malvolio is turned heathen, a very renegado; for there is no Christian that means
to be saved by believing rightly can ever believe such impossible passages of grossness.
He's in yellow stockings!

TO. And cross-garter'd?

50 MAR. Most villanously; like a pedant that keeps a school i' th' church. I have dogg'd him
like his murtherer. He does obey every point of the letter that I dropp'd to betray him.
He does smile his face into more lines than is in the new map with the augmentation
of the Indies. You have not seen such a thing as 'tis. I can hardly forbear hurling
things at him. I know my lady will strike him. If she do, he'll smile, and take't for a

55 great favour.

TO. Come bring us, bring us where he is!

Exeunt omnes.

SCENE III. [*A street.*]

Enter SEBASTIAN *and* ANTONIO.

SEB. I would not by my will have troubled you;
But since you make your pleasure of your pains,
I will no further chide you.

ANT.   I could not stay behind you. My desire,
5   More sharp than filed steel, did spur me forth;
And not all love to see you (though so much
As might have drawn one to a longer voyage)
But jealousy what might befall your travel,
Being skilless in these parts; which to a stranger,
10   Unguided and unfriended, often prove
Rough and unhospitable. My willing love,
The rather by these arguments of fear,
Set forth in your pursuit.

SEB.   My kind Antonio,
15   I can no other answer make but thanks,
And thanks, and ever thanks; and oft good turns
Are shuffled off with such uncurrent pay.

---

[46] **gull:** dupe.   **renegado:** renegade, apostate—one who 'turns traitor.'

[47] **such impossible passages of grossness:** such grossly (obviously) impossible statements (as those in
the letter). *Gross* is, literally, 'big'; then, 'manifest,' 'obvious.' *Passages* often means 'facts'—and
so, here, 'alleged facts,' which are really impossibilities.

[50] **pedant:** pedagogue.

[52-53] **the new map . . . Indies:** a map prepared by Edward Wright and others which shows the East
Indies as well as North America in an augmented form—that is, in a fuller delineation than
in any previous map.

[57] **by my will:** willingly.

[6] **And not all love to see you,** etc.: and it was not merely my fondness for your company that
'spurred me forth'—though that was great enough to induce me to make a longer journey—but
also anxiety about what might befall you in your wanderings.

[9] **skilless:** unacquainted.

[12] **The rather . . . fear:** made all the more willing by these considerations urged by fear.

[17] **shuffled off:** put aside; rewarded inadequately.   **uncurrent pay:** payment in coin that does not
pass current—for thanks are mere *words*, not *deeds*.

But, were my worth as is my conscience firm,
You should find better dealing. What's to do?
20   Shall we go see the relics of this town?
  ANT. To-morrow, sir; best first go see your lodging.
  SEB. I am not weary, and 'tis long to night.
      I pray you let us satisfy our eyes
      With the memorials and the things of fame
25   That do renown this city.
  ANT.   Would you'ld pardon me.
      I do not without danger walk these streets.
      Once in a sea-fight 'gainst the Count his galleys
      I did some service; of such note indeed
30   That, were I ta'en here, it would scarce be answer'd.
  SEB. Belike you slew great number of his people?
  ANT. Th' offence is not of such a bloody nature,
      Albeit the quality of the time and quarrel
      Might well have given us bloody argument.
35   It might have since been answer'd in repaying
      What we took from them, which for traffic's sake
      Most of our city did. Only myself stood out;
      For which, if I be lapsed in this place,
      I shall pay dear.
40 SEB.   Do not then walk too open.
  ANT. It doth not fit me. Hold, sir, here's my purse.
      In the south suburbs at the Elephant
      Is best to lodge. I will bespeak our diet,
      Whiles you beguile the time and feed your knowledge
45   With viewing of the town. There shall you have me.
  SEB. Why I your purse?
  ANT. Haply your eye shall light upon some toy
      You have desire to purchase; and your store
      I think is not for idle markets, sir.
50 SEB. I'll be your purse-bearer, and leave you for
      An hour.

---

[18] **my worth:** my wealth. **my conscience:** my consciousness of my indebtedness to you.
[19] **dealing:** payment.
[26] **pardon me:** excuse me (from going with you to see the sights).
[28] **the Count his galleys:** the Count's ships of war.
[30] **it would scarce be answer'd:** I should find it hard to justify myself in his eyes.
[31] **Belike:** Perhaps; very likely.
[33] **Albeit:** although.
[34] **bloody argument:** cause for bloodshed.
[35] **answer'd:** settled.
[36] **for traffic's sake:** in order to resume trade relations with the city.
[38] **lapsed:** taken when off my guard; surprised. A *lapse* is a 'slip,' a 'heedless mistake': cf. 'a lapse of memory'; to 'slip up.'
[42] **the Elephant:** A well-known inn sign in Shakespeare's day.
[44] **Whiles:** while.
[45] **have me:** find me whenever you wish.
[47] **toy:** trifle.
[48-49] **your store . . . markets:** your supply of money is not large enough for unnecessary spending.

ANT. To th' Elephant.

SEB.   I do remember.

Exeunt.

SCENE IV. [OLIVIA's *orchard.*]

Enter OLIVIA *and* MARIA.

OLI. I have sent after him; he says he'll come.
How shall I feast him? what bestow of him?
For youth is bought more oft than begg'd or borrow'd.
I speak too loud.
5   Where is Malvolio? He is sad and civil,
And suits well for a servant with my fortunes.
Where is Malvolio?

MAR. He's coming, madam; but in very strange manner.
He is sure possess'd, madam.

10 OLI. Why, what's the matter? Does he rave?

MAR. No, madam, he does nothing but smile. Your ladyship were best to have some
guard about you if he come, for sure the man is tainted in 's wits.

OLI. Go call him hither. [*Exit* MARIA.] I am as mad as he, if sad and merry madness
equal be.

Enter [MARIA, *with*] MALVOLIO.

15   How now, Malvolio?

MAL. Sweet lady, ho, ho!

OLI. Smil'st thou?
I sent for thee upon a sad occasion.

MAL. Sad, lady? I could be sad. This does make some obstruction in the blood, this
20   cross-gartering; but what of that? If it please the eye of one, it is with me as the very
true sonnet is, 'Please one, and please all.'

OLI. Why, how dost thou, man? What is the matter with thee?

MAL. Not black in my mind, though yellow in my legs. It did come to his hands, and
commands shall be executed. I think we do know the sweet Roman hand.

25 OLI. Wilt thou go to bed, Malvolio?

MAL. To bed? Ay, sweetheart; and I'll come to thee.

OLI. God comfort thee! Why dost thou smile so, and kiss thy hand so oft?

MAR. How do you, Malvolio?

---

[1] **him**: Cesario. **he says he'll come**: suppose he consents to come.

[2] **of him**: on him.

[5] **sad and civil**: serious-minded and sedate.

[9] **possess'd**: i.e., with a devil; distracted.

[18] **sad**: serious. Malvolio picks up the word and echoes it in the sense of 'gloomy in expression.'

[21] **sonnet**: often used for any form of short lyric. **'Please one, and please all'**: If I can please *one*
(the one that I love), that is enough for me—I am satisfied.

[24] **Roman hand**: An Italian style of handwriting, much like modern script. It was fashionable,
especially with ladies, when *Twelfth Night* was written.

[27] **God comfort thee!**: God sustain thee!—i.e., support thy crazed wits, restore thee to sanity.

MAL. At your request? Yes, nightingales answer daws!

30 MAR. Why appear you with this ridiculous boldness before my lady?

MAL. 'Be not afraid of greatness.' 'Twas well writ.

OLI. What mean'st thou by that, Malvolio?

MAL. 'Some are born great'—

OLI. Ha?

35 MAL. 'Some achieve greatness'—

OLI. What say'st thou?

MAL. 'And some have greatness thrust upon them.'

OLI. Heaven restore thee!

MAL. 'Remember who commended thy yellow stockings'—

40 OLI. My yellow stockings?

MAL. 'And wish'd to see thee cross-garter'd.'

OLI. Cross-garter'd?

MAL. 'Go to, thou art made, if thou desir'st to be so'—

OLI. Am I made?

45 MAL. 'If not, let me see thee a servant still.'

OLI. Why, this is very midsummer madness.

Enter SERVANT.

SER. Madam, the young gentleman of the Count Orsino's is return'd. I could hardly entreat him back. He attends your ladyship's pleasure.

OLI. I'll come to him. [*Exit* SERVANT.] Good Maria, let this fellow be look'd to. Where's
50 my cousin Toby? Let some of my people have a special care of him. I would not have him miscarry for the half of my dowry.

Exit [OLIVIA; *then* MARIA].

MAL. O ho! do you come near me now? No worse man than Sir Toby to look to me! This concurs directly with the letter. She sends him on purpose, that I may appear stubborn to him; for she incites me to that in the letter. 'Cast thy humble slough,'
55 says she; 'be opposite with a kinsman, surly with servants; let thy tongue tang with arguments of state; put thyself into the trick of singularity';—and consequently sets down the manner how: as, a sad face, a reverend carriage, a slow tongue, in the habit of some sir of note, and so forth. I have lim'd her; but it is Jove's doing, and Jove make me thankful! And when she went away now, 'Let this fellow be look'd to.'

---

[29] **At your request? . . . daws!:** Am I to give an account of my health at the request of a servant like you? 'Yes, indeed,' he adds, ironically, 'for that would be as reasonable as for a nightingale to reply to the call of a jackdaw!'

[34] **Ha?:** The ordinary interrogative—'huh?'

[46] **midsummer madness:** Midsummer was traditionally a mad season.

[51] **miscarry:** come to harm.

[52] **do you come near me now?:** do you get some idea who I am?—what an important person?

[54] **stubborn:** The best explanation of this word is given by Malvolio's treatment of Sir Toby in l. 69.

[55] **tang:** sound.

[57] **sad:** serious. **habit:** attire.

[58] **some sir of note:** some distinguished personage. **lim'd:** caught.

60 'Fellow!' not 'Malvolio,' nor after my degree, but 'fellow.' Why, everything adheres together, that no dram of a scruple, no scruple of a scruple, no obstacle, no incredulous or unsafe circumstance—What can be said? Nothing that can be can come between me and the full prospect of my hopes. Well, Jove, not I, is the doer of this, and he is to be thanked.

Enter [SIR] TOBY, FABIAN, *and* MARIA.

65 TO. Which way is he, in the name of sanctity? If all the devils of hell be drawn in little, and Legion himself possess'd him, yet I'll speak to him.

FAB. Here he is, here he is! How is't with you, sir?

TO. How is't with you, man?

MAL. Go off; I discard you. Let me enjoy my private. Go off.

70 MAR. Lo, how hollow the fiend speaks within him! Did not I tell you? Sir Toby, my lady prays you to have a care of him.

MAL. Aha! does she so?

TO. Go to, go to; peace, peace! We must deal gently with him. Let me alone. How do you, Malvolio? How is't with you? What, man! defy the devil! Consider, he's an
75 enemy to mankind.

MAL. Do you know what you say?

MAR. La you, an you speak ill of the devil, how he takes it at heart! Pray God he be not bewitch'd!

FAB. Carry his water to th' wise woman.

80 MAR. Marry, and it shall be done to-morrow morning if I live. My lady would not lose him for more than I'll say.

MAL. How now, mistress?

MAR. O Lord!

TO. Prithee hold thy peace. This is not the way. Do you not see you move him? Let
85 me alone with him.

FAB. No way but gentleness; gently, gently. The fiend is rough and will not be roughly us'd.

TO. Why, how now, my bawcock? How dost thou, chuck?

60-61 **after my degree:** according to my rank.   **fellow:** Malvolio takes this word in the sense of 'companion' or 'associate.'   **adheres together:** coheres; is consistent.   **no dram of a scruple,** etc.: Malvolio begins by using *dram* in the general sense of 'little bit' and *scruple* in the sense of 'doubt'; but the words suggest to him the terms of apothecaries' weight, and so he adds (in emphasis) 'not even a *scruple* of a scruple'—'no scruple, however scrupulous.'   **incredulous:** incredible.

62 **unsafe:** risky (as evidence); dubious; doubtful.

65 **be drawn in little:** should be portrayed in miniature—i.e., were brought together in possessing this one man.

66 **Legion:** An allusion to the demoniac in *Mark*, v. 8, 9: 'He [Jesus] said unto him, Come out of the man, thou unclean spirit. And he asked him, What is thy name? And he answered, saying, My name is Legion: for we are many.'

69 **discard you:** cast you off; refuse to associate with you.   **private:** privacy.

73 **Let me alone:** Leave him to me; don't interfere! Sir Toby proceeds to 'deal gently with him,' and speaks in a comically coaxing tone.

74 **defy:** renounce.

77 **La you:** 'Lo!' 'Just see!'

79 **Carry . . . woman:** i.e., for medical diagnosis.

84-85 **move:** excite.   **Let me alone with him:** Leave him to me to manage.

88 **bawcock, chuck:** Familiar terms of affection. *Bawcock* (*beau coq*) is masculine, *chuck* ('chick') usually feminine.

MAL. Sir!

90 TO. Ay, biddy, come with me. What, man! 'tis not for gravity to play at cherry-pit with Satan. Hang him, foul collier!

MAR. Get him to say his prayers. Good Sir Toby, get him to pray.

MAL. My prayers, minx?

MAR. No, I warrant you, he will not hear of godliness.

95 MAL. Go hang yourselves all! You are idle shallow things; I am not of your element. You shall know more hereafter. *Exit.*

TO. Is't possible?

FAB. If this were play'd upon a stage now, I could condemn it as an improbable fiction.

TO. His very genius hath taken the infection of the device, man.

100 MAR. Nay, pursue him now, lest the device take air and taint.

FAB. Why, we shall make him mad indeed.

MAR. The house will be the quieter.

TO. Come, we'll have him in a dark room and bound. My niece is already in the belief that he's mad. We may carry it thus, for our pleasure and his penance, till our very
105 pastime, tired out of breath, prompt us to have mercy on him; at which time we will bring the device to the bar and crown thee for a finder of madmen. But see, but see!

Enter SIR ANDREW.

FAB. More matter for a May morning.

AND. Here's the challenge; read it. I warrant there's vinegar and pepper in't.

FAB. Is't so saucy?

110 AND. Ay, is't, I warrant him. Do but read.

TO. Give me. [*Reads*] 'Youth, whatsoever thou art, thou art but a scurvy fellow.'

FAB. Good, and valiant.

TO. [*reads*] 'Wonder not nor admire not in thy mind why I do call thee so, for I will show thee no reason for't.'

115 FAB. A good note! That keeps you from the blow of the law.

TO. [*reads*] 'Thou com'st to the Lady Olivia, and in my sight she uses thee kindly. But thou liest in thy throat; that is not the matter I challenge thee for.'

FAB. Very brief, and to exceeding good sense—less.

TO. [*reads*] 'I will waylay thee going home; where if it be thy chance to kill me'—

[90-91] **Ay, biddy, come with me:** Still in Sir Toby's comical parody of a gentle, coaxing style. *Biddy* is still common as a childish name for a hen or chicken. **'tis not . . . Satan:** It is not proper for a dignified person like you to take Satan for a playfellow. *Cherry-pit* was a child's game in which the players pitched cherry stones into a little hole.

[95] **idle:** foolish. **I am not of your element:** I belong to a higher sphere than you.

[99] **His very genius:** The *genius*, in Elizabethan usage, commonly means a guardian spirit, inseparable from the man himself and sharing his fortunes. Here, however, 'his genius' is practically equivalent to 'his ego,' 'his ruling personality.'

[100] **take air and taint:** be exposed to the air (revealed) and so spoiled.

[103] **in a dark room and bound.** The regular expert treatment for insanity in old times.

[104] **carry it:** manage it; carry out the plot.

[106] **to the bar:** i.e., to be judged. **a finder:** a finder out; a detector.

[107] **More matter for a May morning:** Here is more subject matter for a comic May-day drama.

[109] **saucy?:** With a pun on the literal meaning of the word—'highly spiced.'

[110] **Ay, is't, I warrant him:** Yes indeed it is, I can assure him (Cesario).

[113] **admire:** A synonym for *wonder.*

[115] **A good note!** A good point! **That keeps you . . . law:** since you bring no definite charge against him, you cannot be accused of defamation of character, *scurvy* being a mere vague epithet.

120   FAB. Good.

TO. [*reads*] 'Thou kill'st me like a rogue and a villain.'

FAB. Still you keep o' th' windy side of the law. Good.

TO. [*reads*] 'Fare thee well, and God have mercy upon one of our souls! He may have mercy upon mine, but my hope is better; and so look to thyself. Thy friend, as thou
125   usest him, and thy sworn enemy,

'ANDREW AGUECHEEK.'

If this letter move him not, his legs cannot. I'll give't him.

MAR. You may have very fit occasion for't. He is now in some commerce with my lady and will by-and-by depart.

130   TO. Go, Sir Andrew! Scout me for him at the corner of the orchard like a bum-baily. So soon as ever thou seest him, draw; and as thou draw'st, swear horrible; for it comes to pass oft that a terrible oath, with a swaggering accent sharply twang'd off, gives manhood more approbation than ever proof itself would have earn'd him. Away!

AND. Nay, let me alone for swearing.   *Exit.*

135   TO. Now will not I deliver his letter; for the behaviour of the young gentleman gives him out to be of good capacity and breeding; his employment between his lord and my niece confirms no less. Therefore this letter, being so excellently ignorant, will breed no terror in the youth. He will find it comes from a clodpoll. But, sir, I will deliver his challenge by word of mouth, set upon Aguecheek a notable report of valour,
140   and drive the gentleman (as I know his youth will aptly receive it) into a most hideous opinion of his rage, skill, fury, and impetuosity. This will so fright them both that they will kill one another by the look, like cockatrices.

Enter OLIVIA *and* VIOLA.

FAB. Here he comes with your niece. Give them way till he take leave, and presently after him.

145   TO. I will meditate the while upon some horrid message for a challenge.

[*Exeunt* SIR TOBY, FABIAN, *and* MARIA.]

OLI. I have said too much unto a heart of stone
And laid mine honour too unchary out.

---

[122] **o' th' windy side of the law:** to the windward of the law and therefore not exposed to its blasts.

[124] **my hope is better:** Thus Sir Andrew ludicrously expresses the hope that he shall not be killed in the duel.   **as:** according as—i.e., thy friend insofar as thou treatest me in friendly fashion.

[128] **occasion:** opportunity.   **in some commerce:** in conversation about some business or other.

[129] **by-and-by:** very soon.

[130] **orchard:** garden.   **like a bum-baily:** as if you were a bailiff (sheriff's officer) lurking there to arrest him as soon as he should leave the premises.

[132-133] **gives manhood . . . him:** gives a man more reputation for courage than any actual test of his valour would have won for him.

[134] **let me alone:** don't worry about me on that point—you may trust me for swearing!

[138] **a clodpoll:** a dunce; a stupid fellow—literally, one who has a clod of earth for a head.

[140] **as . . . receive it:** as [well I may, for] I am sure the gentleman's youth and inexperience will make him ready to accept my report as the truth.

[142] **cockatrices:** basilisks. A fabulous serpent with a cock's head; it killed by the venomous glance of its eye.

[143-144] **Give them way:** Let them go on without interference.   **presently after him:** then follow him immediately.

[147] **laid mine . . . out:** made too lavish an expenditure of my honour in trying to win your love. Olivia feels that her outspoken wooing of Cesario has been out of accord with womanly modesty. *Out* is Theobald's correction of the Folio reading ('on't').

There's something in me that reproves my fault;
But such a headstrong potent fault it is
150   That it but mocks reproof.
    VIO. With the same haviour that your passion bears
    Goes on my master's grief.
    OLI. Here, wear this jewel for me; 'tis my picture.
    Refuse it not; it hath no tongue to vex you.
155   And I beseech you come again to-morrow.
    What shall you ask of me that I'll deny,
    That honour, sav'd, may upon asking give?
    VIO. Nothing but this—your true love for my master.
    OLI. How with mine honour may I give him that
160   Which I have given to you?
    VIO.   I will acquit you.
    OLI. Well, come again to-morrow. Fare thee well.
    A fiend like thee might bear my soul to hell.   [*Exit.*]

Enter [SIR] TOBY *and* FABIAN.

    TO. Gentleman, God save thee!
165   VIO. And you, sir.
    TO. That defence thou hast, betake thee to't. Of what nature the wrongs are thou hast
    done him, I know not; but thy intercepter, full of despite, bloody as the hunter, attends
    thee at the orchard end. Dismount thy tuck, be yare in thy preparation; for thy assailant
    is quick, skilful, and deadly.
170   VIO. You mistake, sir. I am sure no man hath any quarrel to me. My remembrance is
    very free and clear from any image of offence done to any man.
    TO. You'll find it otherwise, I assure you. Therefore, if you hold your life at any price,
    betake you to your guard; for your opposite hath in him what youth, strength, skill,
    and wrath can furnish man withal.
175   VIO. I pray you, sir, what is he?
    TO. He is knight, dubb'd with unhatch'd rapier and on carpet consideration; but he is a
    devil in private brawl. Souls and bodies hath he divorc'd three; and his incensement

---

[149] **potent:** powerful.
[151] **haviour:** behaviour.
[156] **deny:** refuse.
[157] **That . . . give:** that honour can grant at your request without being infringed.
[158] **Nothing but this:** I will ask nothing of you except *this*.
[161] **acquit you:** release you from your offer of love.
[163] **like thee:** in thy shape.
[166] **defence:** skill in fencing.
[167] **despite:** angry defiance.   **bloody:** bloodthirsty.   **the hunter:** a hunting dog; a hound on the trail.
[168] **Dismount thy tuck:** unsheathe thy rapier. Sir Toby uses grandiloquent language—as if the rapier were a cannon.   **yare:** ready; on the alert.
[170] **quarrel to me:** cause of quarrel with me.
[173] **opposite:** opponent.   **what:** whatsoever.
[174] **withal:** with. Very common in this sense at the end of a clause.
[176] **with unhatch'd rapier and on carpet consideration:** not for military service but for reasons connected with the affairs of peace. *Unhatch'd* is, literally, 'unhacked.' *Carpet* is opposed to battlefield. *Consideration* suggests that Sir Andrew's service was a gift of money to some influential person.
[177] **incensement:** anger.

at this moment is so implacable that satisfaction can be none but by pangs of death and sepulchre. 'Hob, nob' is his word; 'give't or take't.'

180 VIO. I will return again into the house and desire some conduct of the lady. I am no fighter. I have heard of some kind of men that put quarrels purposely on others to taste their valour. Belike this is a man of that quirk.

TO. Sir, no. His indignation derives itself out of a very competent injury; therefore get you on and give him his desire. Back you shall not to the house, unless you undertake

185 that with me which with as much safety you might answer him. Therefore on! or strip your sword stark naked; for meddle you must, that's certain, or forswear to wear iron about you.

VIO. This is as uncivil as strange. I beseech you do me this courteous office, as to know of the knight what my offence to him is. It is something of my negligence, nothing

190 of my purpose.

TO. I will do so. Signior Fabian, stay you by this gentleman till my return.

Exit.

VIO. Pray you, sir, do you know of this matter?

FAB. I know the knight is incens'd against you, even to a mortal arbitrement; but nothing of the circumstance more.

195 VIO. I beseech you, what manner of man is he?

FAB. Nothing of that wonderful promise, to read him by his form, as you are like to find him in the proof of his valour. He is indeed, sir, the most skilful, bloody, and fatal opposite that you could possibly have found in any part of Illyria. Will you walk towards him? I will make your peace with him if I can.

200 VIO. I shall be much bound to you for't. I am one that had rather go with sir priest than sir knight. I care not who knows so much of my mettle.

Exeunt.

Enter [SIR] TOBY *and* [SIR] ANDREW [*at the orchard end*].

---

[179] **Hob, nob.** The original meaning seems to have been 'Have it, or have it not!' This accords with Sir Toby's translation: 'Give it, or take it!' Other forms are *hab, nab* and *hab or nab*. The implication is that Sir Andrew's only terms are an immediate contest—hand to hand.   **word:** watchword, motto.

[180] **conduct:** escort.   **of:** from.

[182] **taste:** test.   **Belike:** probably.   **quirk:** peculiar habit; eccentric fashion.

[183] **competent:** sufficient, adequate.

[184-185] **undertake that:** i.e., a duel.   **answer him:** undertake in accepting *his* challenge. *Me* and *him* are emphatic.

[186-187] **meddle:** engage in the affair; fight.   **forswear . . . about you:** renounce your claim to wear a sword; admit that you are a coward and no fit associate for gentlemen.

[188-189] **uncivil:** discourteous.   **this courteous office, as to know of the knight:** so courteous a service as to learn from the knight.   **something of my negligence:** some oversight on my part; something unintentional.

[193] **even to a mortal arbitrement:** to such an extent that only death can settle the matter.

[194] **circumstance:** circumstances.

[196] **to read:** to interpret, to judge.

[197] **proof:** test, experience.

[198] **opposite:** opponent.

[200] **go with:** associate with.   **sir priest:** *Sir* (i.e., *Dominus*) was a priest's title. See iv, 2, 2: 'Sir Topas the curate.'

[201] **my mettle:** my constitution.

TO. Why, man, he's a very devil; I have not seen such a firago. I had a pass with him, rapier, scabbard, and all, and he gives me the stuck-in with such a mortal motion that it is inevitable; and on the answer he pays you as surely as your feet hit the ground
205　they step on. They say he has been fencer to the Sophy.

AND. Pox on't, I'll not meddle with him.

TO. Ay, but he will not now be pacified. Fabian can scarce hold him yonder.

AND. Plague on't, an I thought he had been valiant, and so cunning in fence, I'd have seen him damn'd ere I'd have challeng'd him. Let him let the matter slip, and I'll
210　give him my horse, grey Capilet.

TO. I'll make the motion. Stand here; make a good show on't. This shall end without the perdition of souls. [*Aside*] Marry, I'll ride your horse as well as I ride you.

Enter FABIAN *and* VIOLA.

I have his horse to take up the quarrel. I have persuaded him the youth's a devil.

FAB. He is as horribly conceited of him; and pants and looks pale, as if a bear were at
215　his heels.

TO. There's no remedy, sir; he will fight with you for 's oath sake. Marry, he hath better bethought him of his quarrel, and he finds that now scarce to be worth talking of. Therefore draw for the supportance of his vow. He protests he will not hurt you.

VIO. [*aside*] Pray God defend me! A little thing would make me tell them how much I
220　lack of a man.

FAB. Give ground if you see him furious.

TO. Come, Sir Andrew, there's no remedy. The gentleman will for his honour's sake have one bout with you; he cannot by the duello avoid it; but he has promised me, as he is a gentleman and a soldier, he will not hurt you. Come on, to't!

225　AND. Pray God he keep his oath!　　　　　　　　　　　　　　　　　　[*Draws.*]

Enter ANTONIO.

VIO. I do assure you 'tis against my will.　　　　　　　　　　　　　　[*Draws.*]

ANT. Put up your sword. If this young gentleman
Have done offence, I take the fault on me;
If you offend him, I for him defy you.

202　**firago**: virago. Sir Toby applies this feminine term, for comic effect, to one whom he supposes to be a man; but the audience, aware that Cesario is a woman, enjoys both the joke and the mistake.　**a pass**: a bout—literally, a thrust.

203　**the stuck-in**: the stoccado or stoccata; the thrust.

204　**on the answer**: at the return; when he parries a thrust he gives you a thrust in return.

205　**the Sophy**: the Shah of Persia.

206　**Pox on't**: A common curse: 'plague take it!'　**meddle with him**: have anything to do with him.

208　**cunning**: skilful, expert.

210　**Capilet**. *Capil* or *capul* is an old term for 'horse' and *Capilet* (as Wright suggests) seems to be a diminutive of this word.

211　**the motion**: the proposal; the offer.

212　**the perdition of souls**: Merely Sir Toby's high style for 'loss of life.'

213　**take up**: settle (without a duel).

214　**is as horribly conceited**: has as horrible an idea.

216　**for 's oath sake**: for the sake of his oath. *Oath* instead of *oath's*—the two *s's* coalescing, as often.

217　**his quarrel**: his cause of offence.

218　**draw . . . vow**: draw your sword to enable him to keep his oath.

223　**one bout**: one exchange of thrust and parry.　**by the duello**: in accordance with the rules of honour that gentlemen must observe in the matter of duels.

229　**If you offend him**: if it is *you* that have given him cause of offence.

230 TO. You sir? Why, what are you?

ANT. [*draws*] One, sir, that for his love dares yet do more

Than you have heard him brag to you he will.

TO. Nay, if you be an undertaker, I am for you. [*Draws.*]

Enter OFFICERS.

FAB. O good Sir Toby, hold! Here come the officers.

235 TO. [*to* ANTONIO] I'll be with you anon.

VIO. [*to* SIR ANDREW] Pray, sir, put your sword up, if you please.

AND. Marry, will I, sir; and for that I promis'd you, I'll be as good as my word. He will

bear you easily, and reins well.

1. OFF. This is the man; do thy office.

240 2. OFF. Antonio, I arrest thee at the suit

Of Count Orsino.

ANT. You do mistake me, sir.

1. OFF. No, sir, no jot. I know your favour well,

Though now you have no sea-cap on your head.

245 Take him away. He knows I know him well.

ANT. I must obey. [*To* VIOLA] This comes with seeking you.

But there's no remedy; I shall answer it.

What will you do, now my necessity

Makes me to ask you for my purse? It grieves me

250 Much more for what I cannot do for you

Than what befalls myself. You stand amaz'd,

But be of comfort.

2. OFF. Come, sir, away.

ANT. I must entreat of you some of that money.

255 VIO. What money, sir?

For the fair kindness you have show'd me here,

And part being prompted by your present trouble,

Out of my lean and low ability

I'll lend you something. My having is not much.

260 I'll make division of my present with you.

Hold, there's half my coffer.

ANT. Will you deny me now?

Is't possible that my deserts to you

---

233 **if you be an undertaker:** if you wish to take up the matter—to undertake responsibility in this
affair.

235 **I'll be with you anon:** Sir Toby sheathes his sword but promises Antonio to fight with him at
the first opportunity.

237 **for that I promis'd you:** as for my promise to give you my horse.

238 **reins:** minds the rein.

239 **do thy office:** perform thy function (as an officer).

243 **favour:** features, face.

247 **I shall answer it:** i.e., make what defence I can to the charge the Duke brings against me and
submit to my sentence.

251 **amaz'd:** in a maze; bewildered.

257 **part:** partly.

259 **My having:** what I have.

260 **my present:** my cash in hand.

261 **my coffer:** my store of money.

Can lack persuasion? Do not tempt my misery,
265   Lest that it make me so unsound a man
       As to upbraid you with those kindnesses
       That I have done for you.
vio.   I know of none,
       Nor know I you by voice or any feature.
270   I hate ingratitude more in a man
       Than lying, vainness, babbling, drunkenness,
       Or any taint of vice whose strong corruption
       Inhabits our frail blood.
ANT.   O heavens themselves!
275 2. off. Come, sir, I pray you go.
ANT. Let me speak a little. This youth that you see here
       I snatch'd one half out of the jaws of death;
       Reliev'd him with such sanctity of love,
       And to his image, which methought did promise
280   Most venerable worth, did I devotion.
1. off. What's that to us? The time goes by. Away!
ANT. But, O, how vile an idol proves this god!
       Thou hast, Sebastian, done good feature shame.
       In nature there's no blemish but the mind;
285   None can be call'd deform'd but the unkind.
       Virtue is beauty; but the beauteous evil
       Are empty trunks, o'erflourish'd by the devil.
1. off. The man grows mad. Away with him! Come, come, sir.
ANT. Lead me on.   *Exit [with* OFFICERS.]
290 vio. Methinks his words do from such passion fly
       That he believes himself; so do not I.
       Prove true, imagination, O, prove true,
       That I, dear brother, be now ta'en for you!
to. Come hither, knight; come hither, Fabian. We'll whisper o'er a couplet or two of
295   most sage saws.

---

264 **persuasion:** 'persuasive efficacy' (Child).   **tempt:** put too hard a test upon; try too severely.
265 **Lest that:** lest.   **so unsound a man:** so lacking in manly dignity and self-control; so unmanly.
271 **vainness:** untrustworthiness—not, vanity.   **babbling:** lack of the power to hold one's tongue in
       confidential matters—not, mere talkativeness.
272 **vice:** in the general sense of 'fault.'
273 **blood:** human nature.
278 **such.** This merely emphasizes the meaning of *sanctity.*
279 **to his image:** 'to what he appeared to me to be' (Child).
280 **Most venerable worth:** worthiness of devout reverence.
283 **feature:** form and features.
284-285 **In nature . . . unkind:** No natural blemish in a man's *body* can be called a blemish. The
       word can be applied only to one's *mind* or *disposition;* for unkindness is the only real deformity.
       Antonio is thinking especially of ingratitude.
287 **empty trunks . . . the devil.** Chests for clothing, etc., ornamented with carving or painting,
       were features of old-fashioned house-furnishing.   **empty:** because they have no good qualities
       of heart or mind. Their beauty is all external; it is given them by Satan as a delusion and a
       snare.
291 **he believes himself; so do not I:** This man believes his own assertion—i.e., that I am my brother
       Sebastian; but I cannot yet trust the hope that his words give me that Sebastian is alive.
295 **sage saws:** wise moral maxims—like those which this stranger has been uttering.

VIO. He nam'd Sebastian. I my brother know
　　Yet living in my glass. Even such and so
　　In favour was my brother, and he went
　　Still in this fashion, colour, ornament,
300　For him I imitate. O, if it prove,
　　Tempests are kind, and salt waves fresh in love!　　　　　[Exit.]
TO. A very dishonest paltry boy, and more a coward than a hare. His dishonesty appears
　　in leaving his friend here in necessity and denying him; and for his cowardship, ask
　　Fabian.
305　FAB. A coward, a most devout coward; religious in it.
　　AND. 'Slid, I'll after him again and beat him!
　　TO. Do; cuff him soundly, but never draw thy sword.
　　AND. An I do not—　　　　　　　　　　　　　　　　　　[Exit.]
　　FAB. Come, let's see the event.
310　TO. I dare lay any money 'twill be nothing yet.

Exeunt.

ACT IV

SCENE I. [*Before* OLIVIA's *house.*]

Enter SEBASTIAN *and* CLOWN.

CLOWN Will you make me believe that I am not sent for you?
SEB. Go to, go to, thou art a foolish fellow. Let me be clear of thee.
CLOWN Well held out, i' faith! No, I do not know you; nor I am not sent to you by my
　　lady, to bid you come speak with her; nor your name is not Master Cesario; nor this
5　is not my nose neither. Nothing that is so is so.
SEB. I prithee vent thy folly somewhere else. Thou know'st not me.
CLOWN Vent my folly! He has heard that word of some great man, and now applies it
　　to a fool. Vent my folly! I am afraid this great lubber, the world, will prove a cockney.
　　I prithee now, ungird thy strangeness, and tell me what I shall vent to my lady. Shall
10　I vent to her that thou art coming?

---

²⁹⁷ **living in my glass:** whenever I look in my mirror, I see my brother's image to the life.
²⁹⁸ **favour:** features.
²⁹⁹ **Still:** always.
³⁰⁰ **prove:** if my hope prove true.
³⁰² **dishonest:** dishonourable.
³⁰⁵ **religious in it:** as if he had taken a vow to devote himself to cowardice.
³⁰⁶ **'Slid:** literally, 'by God's eyelid.' Many such grotesque oaths were in use.
³⁰⁹ **the event:** the outcome; the upshot of the affair.
³¹⁰ **lay:** bet, wager.　**yet:** after all.
² **Go to!** An interjection of protest.
³ **Well held out!:** Well maintained! Feste declares ironically that Sebastian shows excellent persever-
　　ance in refusing to admit that he is Cesario.
⁴⁻⁵ **nor this is not my nose neither;** 'It is as plain that you are Master Cesario as that this [*points to
　　his nose*] is the nose on my face'
⁶ **vent thy folly:** utter thy foolish talk.
⁷ **of:** with reference to.
⁸ **I am afraid . . . a cockney:** I fear the whole stupid world will turn out to be as silly as may be.
　　Since you talk so foolishly, I despair of finding common sense anywhere in creation.
⁹ **ungird thy strangeness:** Feste is imitating the elaborate style that he pretends to have detected in
　　Sebastian's 'vent.' He means, 'Let thyself loose from thy pretence of not being Cesario and not
　　understanding my message.'

Shakespeare: Act IV　1295

SEB. I prithee, foolish Greek, depart from me.
There's money for thee. If you tarry longer,
I shall give worse payment.

CLOWN By my troth, thou hast an open hand. These wise men that give fools money
15   get themselves a good report—after fourteen years' purchase.

Enter [SIR] ANDREW, [SIR] TOBY, *and* FABIAN.

AND. Now, sir, have I met you again? There's for you!

[*Strikes* SEBASTIAN.]

SEB. Why, there's for thee, and there, and there!

[*Strikes* SIR ANDREW.]

Are all the people mad?
TO. Hold, sir, or I'll throw your dagger o'er the house.

[*Seizes* SEBASTIAN.]

20   CLOWN This will I tell my lady straight. I would not be in some of your coats for
two-pence.   [*Exit.*]
TO. Come on, sir; hold!
AND. Nay, let him alone. I'll go another way to work with him. I'll have an action of
battery against him, if there be any law in Illyria. Though I stroke him first, yet it's
25   no matter for that.
SEB. Let go thy hand.
TO. Come, sir, I will not let you go. Come, my young soldier, put up your iron. You
are well flesh'd. Come on.
SEB. I will be free from thee. [*Disengages himself.*] What wouldst thou now?
30   If thou dar'st tempt me further, draw thy sword. [*Draws.*]
TO. What, what? Nay then, I must have an ounce or two of this malapert blood from
you.   [*Draws.*]

Enter OLIVIA.

---

¹¹ **Greek**: nonsensical talker—because what you say is Greek to me. *Greek* for 'unintelligible language' is common enough.
¹⁵ **report**: reputation (as reported by the fools). **after fourteen years' purchase**: but it is a long time
before they get that reputation from the fools. To buy land at the price of 'fourteen years' purchase'
is to pay in cash what the rent of the land (its annual return) will amount to in fourteen years.
This was a high price for land and it would certainly be a long delay for a good reputation!
¹⁹ **I'll throw your dagger o'er the house**: This indicates that Sebastian has drawn his dagger and
used it to beat Sir Toby—not, manifestly, to stab him.
²⁰⁻²¹ **straight**: straightway, immediately.
²² **Come on, sir; hold!**: Addressed to Sebastian, who is struggling to free himself from Sir Toby.
Come on means 'Come along'—away from Sir Andrew.
²³⁻²⁴ **I'll have . . . battery**: I'll bring him to trial for assault and battery.
²⁷⁻²⁸ **Come, sir, . . . Come on**: All this is manifestly addressed to Sebastian, who is struggling in Sir
Toby's grasp. **put up your iron**: sheathe your dagger. **You are well flesh'd**: You have had a
good taste of fighting. To *flesh* means to give a dog a taste of raw meat in order to make him
fierce. **Come on**: Come along with me—away from Sir Andrew.
³⁰ **tempt me**: make trial of me; try my mettle.
³¹ **malapert**: saucy.

OLI. Hold, Toby! On thy life I charge thee hold!
TO. Madam!
35 OLI. Will it be ever thus? Ungracious wretch,
Fit for the mountains and the barbarous caves,
Where manners ne'er were preach'd! Out of my sight!
Be not offended, dear Cesario.
Rudesby, be gone!

[*Exeunt* SIR TOBY, SIR ANDREW, *and* FABIAN.]

40   I prithee, gentle friend,
Let thy fair wisdom, not thy passion, sway
In this uncivil and unjust extent
Against thy peace. Go with me to my house,
And hear thou there how many fruitless pranks
45 This ruffian hath botch'd up, that thou thereby
Mayst smile at this. Thou shalt not choose but go;
Do not deny. Beshrew his soul for me!
He started one poor heart of mine, in thee.
SEB. What relish is in this? How runs the stream?
50 Or I am mad, or else this is a dream.
Let fancy still my sense in Lethe steep;
If it be thus to dream, still let me sleep!
OLI. Nay, come, I prithee. Would thou'dst be rul'd by me!
SEB. Madam, I will.
55 OLI.   O, say so, and so be!

Exeunt.

SCENE II [OLIVIA's *house.*]

Enter MARIA *and* CLOWN.

MAR. Nay, I prithee put on this gown and this beard; make him believe thou art Sir
Topas the curate; do it quickly. I'll call Sir Toby the whilst.   [*Exit.*]
CLOWN. Well, I'll put it on, and I will dissemble myself in't, and I would I were the

---

³⁵ **Ungracious:** graceless.
³⁹ **Rudesby:** quarrelsome fellow; ruffian.
⁴¹ **fair:** i.e., using fair judgment. **sway:** rule.
⁴² **uncivil:** Much stronger than in modern usage—almost equivalent to 'barbarous,' 'outrageous.' **extent:** exhibition (of violence), display.
⁴⁵ **botch'd up:** clumsily contrived and managed.
⁴⁶ **Thou shalt not choose but go:** I insist on your going with me.
⁴⁷ **deny:** refuse. **Beshrew:** literally 'curse,' but in common use a mild and ladylike term. **for me!:** on my account.
⁴⁸ **heart:** With an allusion to *hart.* Cf. i, 1, 18 ff.
⁴⁹ **What relish is in this?:** 'How does this taste? What judgment am I to make of it?' (Johnson).
⁵⁰ **Or . . . or:** either . . . or.
⁵¹ **fancy:** imagination. **still:** ever, always.
¹⁻² **Sir:** See iii, 4, 200, note. *Sir Topas* (i.e., Topaz), the burlesque parish priest, seems to take his name from Chaucer's burlesque knight Sir Thopas. **the whilst:** in the meantime.
³ **dissemble myself:** disguise myself. Feste chooses the word for the sake of the pun on *dissemble*—'hide one's true character'; 'conceal the truth about one's self.'

first that ever dissembled in such a gown. I am not tall enough to become the function

5 well, nor lean enough to be thought a good student; but to be said an honest man and a good housekeeper goes as fairly as to say a careful man and a great scholar. The competitors enter.

Enter [SIR] TOBY [*and* MARIA].

TO. Jove bless thee, Master Parson.

CLOWN Bonos dies, Sir Toby; for, as the old hermit of Prague, that never saw pen and

10 ink, very wittily said to a niece of King Gorboduc, 'That that is is'; so I, being Master Parson, am Master Parson; for what is 'that' but that, and 'is' but is?

TO. To him, Sir Topas.

CLOWN What ho, I say. Peace in this prison!

TO. The knave counterfeits well; a good knave.

MALVOLIO *within*.

15 MAL. Who calls there?

CLOWN Sir Topas the curate, who comes to visit Malvolio the lunatic.

MAL. Sir Topas, Sir Topas, good Sir Topas, go to my lady.

CLOWN Out, hyperbolical fiend! How vexest thou this man! Talkest thou nothing but of ladies?

20 TO: Well said, Master Parson.

MAL. Sir Topas, never was man thus wronged. Good Sir Topas, do not think I am mad. They have laid me here in hideous darkness.

CLOWN Fie, thou dishonest Satan! I call thee by the most modest terms; for I am one of those gentle ones that will use the devil himself with courtesy. Say'st thou that house

25 is dark?

MAL. As hell, Sir Topas.

CLOWN Why, it hath bay windows transparent as barricadoes, and the clerestories toward the south north are as lustrous as ebony; and yet complainest thou of obstruction?

MAL. I am not mad, Sir Topas. I say to you this house is dark.

30 CLOWN Madman, thou errest. I say there is no darkness but ignorance, in which thou art more puzzled than the Egyptians in their fog.

MAL. I say this house is as dark as ignorance, though ignorance were as dark as hell; and I say there was never man thus abus'd. I am no more mad than you are. Make the trial of it in any constant question.

---

⁴ **the function:** the priestly office.

⁵ **student:** a common old by-form of *student*. **said:** called, styled.

⁶⁻⁷ **goes as fairly:** sounds as well; is quite as respectable. **careful:** studious, as befits a clergy-man. **The competitors:** my associates in this plot.

¹⁰ **King Gorboduc:** a famous king of ancient British legend.

¹⁴ **knave:** fellow—literally, boy (cf. German *knabe*).

¹⁸ **hyperbolical:** A technical term in rhetoric ('exaggerated in style'), used by Feste as an elegant word for 'raging,' 'turbulent.'

²³ **dishonest:** dishonourable. **modest:** moderate, mild. *Dishonest* is a milder term than the outspoken word *liar*. Satan is 'the father of lies.'

²⁷ **barricadoes:** barricades. **clerestories:** the windows in the upper part of the wall.

²⁹ **house:** 'A darkened room was sometimes called a dark house' (Halliwell).

³¹ **the Egyptians in their fog:** See *Exodus*, x, 21–23.

³⁴ **in any constant question:** on any consistent subject—any subject that calls for rational speech on my part.

35 CLOWN What is the opinion of Pythagoras concerning wild fowl?
MAL. That the soul of our grandam might happily inhabit a bird.
CLOWN What think'st thou of his opinion?
MAL. I think nobly of the soul and no way approve his opinion.
CLOWN Fare thee well. Remain thou still in darkness. Thou shalt hold th' opinion of
40   Pythagoras ere I will allow of thy wits, and fear to kill a woodcock, lest thou dispossess
the soul of thy grandam. Fare thee well.
MAL. Sir Topas, Sir Topas!
TO. My most exquisite Sir Topas!
CLOWN Nay, I am for all waters.
45 MAR. Thou mightst have done this without thy beard and gown. He sees thee not.
TO. To him in thine own voice, and bring me word how thou find'st him.—[To MARIA]
I would we were well rid of this knavery. If he may be conveniently deliver'd, I would
he were; for I am now so far in offence with my niece that I cannot pursue with any
safety this sport to the upshot.—[To the CLOWN] Come by-and-by to my chamber.

Exit [with MARIA].

50 CLOWN [*sings*] 'Hey, Robin, jolly Robin,
                Tell me how thy lady does.'
MAL. Fool!
CLOWN 'My lady is unkind, perdie!'
MAL. Fool!
55 CLOWN 'Alas, why is she so?'
MAL. Fool, I say!
CLOWN 'She loves another'—Who calls, ha?
MAL. Good fool, as ever thou wilt deserve well at my hand, help me to a candle, and
pen, ink, and paper. As I am a gentleman, I will live to be thankful to thee for't.
60 CLOWN Master Malvolio?
MAL. Ay, good fool.
CLOWN Alas, sir, how fell you besides your five wits?
MAL. Fool, there was never man so notoriously abus'd. I am as well in my wits, fool,
as thou art.
65 CLOWN But as well? Then you are mad indeed, if you be no better in your wits than a
fool.
MAL. They have here propertied me; keep me in darkness, send ministers to me, asses,
and do all they can to face me out of my wits.

---

35 **Pythagoras:** the Greek philosopher who was regarded as having originated or taught the doctrine of the transmigration of souls.

36 **happily:** haply, perchance.

40 **allow of thy wits:** approve thy intellect as sound. **a woodcock.** Reputed to be a silly bird.

44 **Nay:** Merely an interjection, like 'Why.' **I am for all waters:** 'I can turn my hand to anything' (Malone). The origin of the phrase is obscure; perhaps it meant, 'I am ready for any voyage.'

47 **deliver'd:** released.

49 **to the upshot:** to its conclusion; to the last detail. *Upshot* is, literally, 'the final shot' in archery.

53 **perdie!:** assuredly. An oath (*par dieu*), but always lightly used.

57 **ha?:** The interrogative interjection—'huh?'

62 **how fell you besides your five wits?:** How did you happen to lose your mind? **besides:** out of. We still use 'beside one's self' for 'out of one's head,' 'distracted.'

63 **notoriously abus'd:** notably ill used.

67 **propertied me:** made me a mere thing or utensil—a mere tool, as opposed to 'a person.'

CLOWN Advise you what you say. The minister is here.—Malvolio, Malvolio, thy wits
70   the heavens restore! Endeavour thyself to sleep and leave thy vain bibble babble.
MAL. Sir Topas!
CLOWN Maintain no words with him, good fellow.—Who, I, sir? Not I, sir. God b' wi'
   you, good Sir Topas!—Marry, amen.—I will, sir, I will.
MAL. Fool, fool, fool, I say!
75 CLOWN Alas, sir, be patient. What say you, sir? I am shent for speaking to you.
MAL. Good fool, help me to some light and some paper. I tell thee, I am as well in my
   wits as any man in Illyria.
CLOWN Well-a-day that you were, sir!
MAL. By this hand, I am. Good fool, some ink, paper, and light; and convey what I will
80   set down to my lady. It shall advantage thee more than ever the bearing of letter did.
CLOWN I will help you to't. But tell me true, are you not mad indeed? or do you but
   counterfeit?
MAL. Believe me, I am not. I tell thee true.
CLOWN Nay, I'll ne'er believe a madman till I see his brains. I will fetch you light and
85   paper and ink.
MAL. Fool, I'll requite it in the highest degree. I prithee be gone.
CLOWN [sings]

        I am gone, sir;
        And anon, sir,
        I'll be with you again,
90   In a trice,
           Like to the old Vice,
        Your need to sustain;
        Who, with dagger of lath,
        In his rage and his wrath,
95   Cries 'aha!' to the devil.
        Like a mad lad,
        'Pare thy nails, dad.'
        Adieu, goodman devil.   *Exit.*

---

[69] **Advise you:** Consider with yourself; be careful. **Malvolio:** Here Feste resumes the part of Sir Topas.

[70] **vain bibble babble:** senseless babbling; foolish chatter.

[72-73] **Maintain . . . I will:** Feste plays both parts—Sir Topas's and his own. **God b' wi' you:** Good-bye. **Marry, amen:** Sir Topas's conclusion of his prayer 'Thy wits the heavens restore!' (l. 69–70). *Marry* is here used with some sense of its original meaning. **I will, sir, I will:** In assent to some order that he pretends Sir Topas has given him.

[75] **patient:** calm. **shent:** scolded, rebuked (by Sir Topas).

[78] **Well-a-day that you were, sir!:** Alas, sir, I wish you were!

[81-82] **do you but counterfeit?** are you only pretending?

[91] **the old Vice:** the comic character in the old morality plays—impersonating Iniquity in general or some particular sin.

[92] **Your need to sustain:** i.e., to lend you my assistance in your contest with the devil that possesses you.

[93] **dagger of lath:** the Vice (like the fool in real life) was sometimes armed with a wooden dagger.

[97] **Pare thy nails:** The Vice shows his dagger to Satan and offers to pare his nails.

[98] **Adieu, goodman devil:** Thus Feste bids good-bye to the devil that possesses Malvolio, and so to Malvolio himself. **Goodman:** A title appropriate for a person below the rank of gentleman. It was an insult to the devil.

SCENE III. [OLIVIA's *orchard*.]

Enter SEBASTIAN.

SEB. This is the air; that is the glorious sun;
    This pearl she gave me, I do feel't and see't;
    And though 'tis wonder that enwraps me thus,
    Yet 'tis not madness. Where's Antonio then?
5   I could not find him at the Elephant;
    Yet there he was; and there I found this credit,
    That he did range the town to seek me out.
    His counsel now might do me golden service;
    For though my soul disputes well with my sense
10   That this may be some error, but no madness,
    Yet doth this accident and flood of fortune
    So far exceed all instance, all discourse,
    That I am ready to distrust mine eyes
    And wrangle with my reason, that persuades me
15   To any other trust but that I am mad,
    Or else the lady's mad. Yet, if 'twere so,
    She could not sway her house, command her followers,
    Take and give back affairs and their dispatch
    With such a smooth, discreet, and stable bearing
20   As I perceive she does. There's something in't
    That is deceivable. But here the lady comes.

Enter OLIVIA *and* PRIEST.

OLI. Blame not this haste of mine. If you mean well,
    Now go with me and with this holy man
    Into the chantry by. There, before him,
25   And underneath that consecrated roof,
    Plight me the full assurance of your faith,
    That my most jealous and too doubtful soul
    May live at peace. He shall conceal it
    Whiles you are willing it shall come to note,

6-7 **was**: Emphatic: 'had been.' **there I found this credit . . . out**: there I found that this was what
    they believed—that he was roaming about the town in search of me.
9-15 **though my soul disputes . . . I am mad**: though my reason agrees with my senses in arguing
    that my present experiences are real, even if they are the result of some error on the lady's part,
    yet this good fortune is so unexampled, so far beyond all reason, that I am ready to disagree
    with my reason when it tries to make me believe that I am not insane.
12 **instance**: example. **discourse**: reason.
18 **Take and give back affairs and their dispatch**: take affairs and give back their dispatch—i.e.,
    receive reports on matters of business and give directions for their management.
19 **stable**: settled, steady.
21 **deceivable**: deceptive, misleading.
24 **the chantry by**: the chapel that is near by.
26 **Plight . . . faith**: give me full assurance of your fidelity by the ceremony of betrothal.
27 **jealous**: a common form of *jealous*—a synonym for *doubtful*.
29 **Whiles . . . note**: until you consent that our betrothal shall be made public.

30   What time we will our celebration keep
        According to my birth. What do you say?
    SEB. I'll follow this good man and go with you
        And having sworn truth, ever will be true.
    OLI. Then lead the way, good father; and heavens so shine
35   That they may fairly note this act of mine!

Exeunt.

ACT V

SCENE I. [*Before* OLIVIA's *house.*]

Enter CLOWN *and* FABIAN.

FAB. Now as thou lov'st me, let me see his letter.
CLOWN Good Master Fabian, grant me another request.
FAB. Anything.
CLOWN Do not desire to see this letter.
5   FAB. This is to give a dog, and in recompense desire my dog again.

Enter DUKE, VIOLA, CURIO, *and* LORDS.

DUKE Belong you to the Lady Olivia, friends?
CLOWN Ay, sir, we are some of her trappings.
DUKE I know thee well. How dost thou, my good fellow?
CLOWN Truly, sir, the better for my foes, and the worse for my friends.
10 DUKE Just the contrary: the better for thy friends.
CLOWN No, sir, the worse.
DUKE How can that be?
CLOWN Marry, sir, they praise me and make an ass of me. Now my foes tell me plainly
    I am an ass; so that by my foes, sir, I profit in the knowledge of myself, and by my
15 friends I am abused; so that, conclusions to be as kisses, if your four negatives make
    your two affirmatives, why then, the worse for my friends and the better for my foes.
DUKE Why, this is excellent.
CLOWN By my troth, sir, no; though it please you to be one of my friends.
DUKE Thou shalt not be the worse for me. There's gold.
20 CLOWN But that it would be double-dealing, sir, I would you could make it another.
DUKE O, you give me ill counsel.
CLOWN Put your grace in your pocket, sir, for this once, and let your flesh and blood
    obey it.

---

³⁰ **What time:** when—i.e., and at that time; and then.   **our celebration:** the public ceremony of
    our marriage.
³¹ **According to my birth:** with such splendour as befits my high birth.
³⁵ **fairly note:** mark with their favour; show that they approve. Olivia's prayer is prompted by a
    scruple of conscience. She hopes that the Lord will forgive her for breaking her vow (i, 1, 28–34).
¹³ **and make an ass of me:** fool me by making me think well of myself.
¹⁵ **abused:** deceived, deluded.
¹⁸ **By my troth.** See ii, 3, 3, note.
²⁰ **But that:** but for the fact that.   **double-dealing:** The pun on *deal* in the sense of 'give' is manifest.
    The ordinary meaning of *double-dealing* is 'duplicity,' 'trickery,' 'cheating.'
²²⁻²³ **Put your grace in your pocket . . . obey it:** Never mind if I *am* giving you evil counsel! Pocket
    up (lay aside, repress) your virtue for once in your life and let your human nature follow my
    advice.

DUKE Well, I will be so much a sinner to be a double-dealer. There's another.

25 CLOWN Primo, secundo, tertio is a good play; and the old saying is 'The third pays for all.' The triplex, sir, is a good tripping measure; or the bells of Saint Bennet, sir, may put you in mind—one, two, three.

DUKE You can fool no more money out of me at this throw. If you will let your lady know I am here to speak with her, and bring her along with you, it may awake my 30 bounty further.

CLOWN Marry, sir, lullaby to your bounty till I come again! I go, sir; but I would not have you to think that my desire of having is the sin of covetousness. But, as you say, let your bounty take a nap; I will awake it anon. *Exit.*

Enter ANTONIO *and* OFFICERS.

VIO. Here comes the man, sir, that did rescue me.

35 DUKE That face of his I do remember well;
Yet when I saw it last, it was besmear'd
As black as Vulcan in the smoke of war.
A baubling vessel was he captain of,
For shallow draught and bulk unprizable,
40 With which such scathful grapple did he make
With the most noble bottom of our fleet
That very envy and the tongue of loss
Cried fame and honour on him. What's the matter?

1. OFF. Orsino, this is that Antonio
45 That took the Phœnix and her fraught from Candy;
And this is he that did the Tiger board
When your young nephew Titus lost his leg.
Here in the streets, desperate of shame and state,
In private brabble did we apprehend him.

50 VIO. He did me kindness, sir; drew on my side;
But in conclusion put strange speech upon me.
I know not what 'twas but distraction.

25-26 **Primo, secundo, tertio:** This appears to be an allusion to a childish game. **The third pays for all:** An old maxim equivalent to 'The third time never fails.' **triplex:** triple time in music. **Saint Bennet:** Saint Benedict. Some think that Shakespeare was referring to Saint Bennet's Church at Paul's Wharf, near the Globe Theatre; but we are at liberty to imagine a church in Illyria dedicated to this same saint.

28 **fool:** get by your arts as a jester—with a pun on *fool* in the sense of 'cheat.' **at this throw:** at this throw of the dice; at this stage of the game. The Duke has lost money on the first two 'throws' and he declines to follow the gambler's superstition that the third throw will make up for everything.

38 **A baubling vessel:** a mere plaything in the way of a ship. *Bauble* for 'toy' or 'trifle' is common. *Bauble* (or *bable*) *boat* was a term for a vessel of slight tonnage.

39 **For shallow draught . . . unprizable:** of little account because of its slight draught and small size.

40 **scathful:** destructive.

41 **bottom:** ship.

42 **very envy:** even enmity; even we, his enemies. **loss:** us, the losers in the battle.

45 **fraught:** cargo. **from:** on her voyage from. **Candy:** Candia—Crete.

48 **desperate of shame and state:** in utter disregard both of such shameful conduct as to engage in a street brawl and of his dangerous situation as a public enemy. Compare Antonio's own words: 'I do not without danger walk these streets' (iii, 3, 27).

49 **brabble:** a brawl. **apprehend:** arrest.

51 **put strange speech upon me:** addressed me in extraordinary language.

DUKE Notable pirate, thou salt-water thief!
What foolish boldness brought thee to their mercies
55 Whom thou in terms so bloody and so dear
Hast made thine enemies?

ANT.   Orsino, noble sir,
Be pleas'd that I shake off these names you give me.
Antonio never yet was thief or pirate,
60 Though I confess, on base and ground enough,
Orsino's enemy. A witchcraft drew me hither.
That most ingrateful boy there by your side
From the rude sea's enrag'd and foamy mouth
Did I redeem. A wrack past hope he was.
65 His life I gave him, and did thereto add
My love without retention or restraint,
All his in dedication. For his sake
Did I expose myself (pure for his love)
Into the danger of this adverse town;
70 Drew to defend him when he was beset;
Where being apprehended, his false cunning
(Not meaning to partake with me in danger)
Taught him to face me out of his acquaintance,
And grew a twenty years removed thing
75 While one would wink; denied me mine own purse,
Which I had recommended to his use
Not half an hour before.

VIO.   How can this be?

DUKE When came he to this town?

80 ANT. To-day, my lord; and for three months before,
No int'rim, not a minute's vacancy,
Both day and night did we keep company.

Enter OLIVIA *and* ATTENDANTS.

DUKE Here comes the Countess; now heaven walks on earth.
But for thee, fellow—fellow, thy words are madness.
85 Three months this youth hath tended upon me;
But more of that anon. Take him aside.

---

⁵³ **Notable:** notorious.   **thief:** robber. A much stronger word than in modern usage.
⁵⁵ **Whom:** The antecedent is implied in *their* (= *of those*).   **in terms so bloody and so dear:** by conduct involving such bloodshed and such intense hostility. *Dear* is very common as an emphasizing adjective.
⁶⁰ **base and ground:** Synonymous.
⁶⁶ **retention:** holding back.
⁶⁷ **All . . . dedication:** devoted all-in-all to him.
⁶⁸ **pure:** purely, solely.
⁶⁹ **adverse:** hostile.
⁷³ **to face me out of his acquaintance:** to deny, with shameless effrontery, that he knew me.
⁷⁶ **had recommended to his use:** had handed over to him to use as his own.
⁸⁴ **for thee:** as for thee.

OLI. What would my lord, but that he may not have,
    Wherein Olivia may seem serviceable?
    Cesario, you do not keep promise with me.
90 VIO. Madam!
    DUKE Gracious Olivia—
    OLI. What do you say, Cesario?—Good my lord—
    VIO. My lord would speak; my duty hushes me.
    OLI. If it be aught to the old tune, my lord,
95   It is as fat and fulsome to mine ear
    As howling after music.
    DUKE   Still so cruel?
    OLI. Still so constant, lord.
    DUKE What, to perverseness? You uncivil lady,
100   To whose ingrate and unauspicious altars
    My soul the faithfull'st off'rings hath breath'd out
    That e'er devotion tender'd! What shall I do?
    OLI. Even what it please my lord, that shall become him.
    DUKE Why should I not, had I the heart to do it,
105   Like to th' Egyptian thief at point of death,
    Kill what I love?—a savage jealousy
    That sometime savours nobly. But hear me this:
    Since you to non-regardance cast my faith,
    And that I partly know the instrument
110   That screws me from my true place in your favour,
    Live you the marble-breasted tyrant still.
    But this your minion, whom I know you love,
    And whom, by heaven I swear, I tender dearly,
    Him will I tear out of that cruel eye
115   Where he sits crowned in his master's spite.
    Come, boy, with me. My thoughts are ripe in mischief.
    I'll sacrifice the lamb that I do love
    To spite a raven's heart within a dove.   [*Going.*]
    VIO. And I, most jocund, apt, and willingly,
120   To do you rest a thousand deaths would die.   [*Following.*]
    OLI. Where goes Cesario?
    VIO.   After him I love

---

[87] **but that he may not have:** except what I cannot grant him—i.e., my love.

[95] **fat and fulsome:** Synonyms: 'nauseous.'

[99] **uncivil:** A much stronger word than in modern usage—almost equivalent to 'cruel' or 'barbarous.'

[100] **ingrate:** ungrateful, thankless.   **unauspicious:** refusing all favour; obstinately unpropitious.

[105] **th' Egyptian thief:** A reference (as Theobald noted) to the story of *Theagenes and Chariclea* in the *Æthiopica* (i, 30, 31; ii, 5, 6, 14), a Greek novel by Heliodorus. Thyamis, an Egyptian robber chieftain, in love with his captive, Chariclea, is in danger of death or capture, and, fearing she may be taken from him, kills a Grecian woman whom he mistakes for her in the darkness of the cave where she was imprisoned.

[109] **that:** since that; since.

[110] **screws:** forces.

[112] **minion:** darling.

[113] **I tender dearly:** I hold dear.

[115] **in his master's spite:** as if in despiteful defiance of his master.

[119] **apt:** readily. One -*ly* does duty for three adverbs.

More than I love these eyes, more than my life,
More, by all mores, than e'er I shall love wife.
125 If I do feign, you witnesses above
Punish my life for tainting of my love!
OLI. Ay me detested! how am I beguil'd!
VIO. Who does beguile you? Who does do you wrong?
OLI. Hast thou forgot thyself? Is it so long?
130 Call forth the holy father.   [*Exit an* ATTENDANT.]
DUKE   [*to* VIOLA] Come, away!
OLI. Whither, my lord? Cesario, husband, stay.
DUKE Husband?
OLI.   Ay, husband. Can he that deny?
135 DUKE Her husband, sirrah?
VIO.   No, my lord, not I.
OLI. Alas, it is the baseness of thy fear
That makes thee strangle thy propriety.
Fear not, Cesario; take thy fortunes up;
140 Be that thou know'st thou art, and then thou art
As great as that thou fear'st.

Enter PRIEST.

                      O, welcome, father!
Father, I charge thee by thy reverence
Here to unfold—though lately we intended
145 To keep in darkness what occasion now
Reveals before 'tis ripe—what thou dost know
Hath newly pass'd between this youth and me.
PRIEST A contract of eternal bond of love,
Confirm'd by mutual joinder of your hands,
150 Attested by the holy close of lips,
Strength'ned by interchangement of your rings;
And all the ceremony of this compact
Seal'd in my function, by my testimony;
Since when, my watch hath told me, toward my grave
155 I have travell'd but two hours.
DUKE O thou dissembling cub! What wilt thou be

---

124 **by all mores**: by all possible standards of comparison.
125 **you witnesses above**: you heavenly powers.
126 **for tainting of my love**: for hypocrisy in my protestations of love.
127 **Ay me detested!**: Alas for me—cast off with a curse! Cesario has rejected her as a wife by the
oath that he has just taken (ll. 122–126).
129 **forgot thyself?**: forgotten who thou art? forgotten that thou art my husband?
135 **sirrah**: A form of *sir*: used in familiar address, sometimes in speaking to a servant or an inferior,
sometimes in contempt or reproof, sometimes (as to children) in more or less jocose affection.
138 **strangle thy propriety**: choke thine own identity by denying that thou art thyself—my husband.
141 **As great as that thou fear'st**: as high in rank as the Duke.
145 **To keep in darkness**: See iv, 3, 28–31.
152 **compáct**: Regularly so accented in Shakespeare.
153 **in my function**: in the regular exercise of my priestly office.
156 **dissembling**: Cf. iv, 2, 3, note.

When time hath sow'd a grizzle on thy case?
Or will not else thy craft so quickly grow
That thine own trip shall be thine overthrow?
160 Farewell, and take her; but direct thy feet
Where thou and I, henceforth, may never meet.
VIO. My lord, I do protest—
OLI.   O, do not swear!
Hold little faith, though thou hast too much fear.

Enter SIR ANDREW.

165 AND. For the love of God, a surgeon! Send one presently to Sir Toby.
OLI. What's the matter?
AND. Has broke my head across, and has given Sir Toby a bloody coxcomb too. For the
love of God, your help! I had rather than forty pound I were at home.
OLI. Who has done this, Sir Andrew?
170 AND. The Count's gentleman, one Cesario. We took him for a coward, but he's the very
devil incardinate.
DUKE My gentleman Cesario?
AND. Od's lifelings, here he is! You broke my head for nothing; and that that I did, I
was set on to do't by Sir Toby.
175 VIO. Why do you speak to me? I never hurt you.
You drew your sword upon me without cause,
But I bespake you fair and hurt you not.

Enter [SIR] TOBY *and* CLOWN.

AND. If a bloody coxcomb be a hurt, you have hurt me. I think you set nothing by a
bloody coxcomb. Here comes Sir Toby halting—you shall hear more. But if he had
180 not been in drink, he would have tickled you othergates than he did.
DUKE How now, gentleman? How is't with you?
TO. That's all one! Has hurt me, and there's th' end on't.—Sot, didst see Dick Surgeon,
sot?
CLOWN O, he's drunk, Sir Toby, an hour agone. His eyes were set at eight i' th' morning.

---

[157] **a grizzle on thy case:** mingled dark and grey hair on thy skin. *Case* was the regular term for the
skin of a fox.
[158-159] **Or . . . overthrow?:** or else will not your craftiness develop so rapidly that, while you are still
a beardless boy, you will destroy yourself in some attempt at trickery?—literally, your attempt
to trip up somebody (in wrestling) shall cause you to be thrown yourself?
[164] **little:** a little, some little.
[165] **presently:** immediately.
[167] **Has:** he has. **broke my head:** broken the skin of my head—drawn blood. **coxcomb:** pate.
[170] **gentleman:** gentleman in waiting, attendant.
[171] **incardinate:** for *incarnate*—'in the flesh,' 'in human shape.'
[173] **lifelings:** a diminutive of *life*, reducing the sonorous oath 'by God's life' to a ladylike asseveration.
[177] **bespake you fair:** addressed you courteously.
[178] **set nothing by:** think nothing of.
[179] **halting:** limping.
[180] **othergates:** otherwise.
[182] **That's all one!:** That makes no difference! Never mind about that! **there's th' end on't:** that's
the whole story. **sot:** fool.
[184] **agone:** ago.

185 TO. Then he's a rogue and a passy measures pavin. I hate a drunken rogue.

OLI. Away with him! Who hath made this havoc with them?

AND. I'll help you, Sir Toby, because we'll be dress'd together.

TO. Will you help—an ass-head and a coxcomb and a knave—a thin-fac'd knave, a gull?

190 OLI. Get him to bed, and let his hurt be look'd to.

[*Exeunt* CLOWN, FABIAN, SIR TOBY, *and* SIR ANDREW.]

Enter SEBASTIAN.

SEB. I am sorry, madam, I have hurt your kinsman;
But had it been the brother of my blood,
I must have done no less with wit and safety.
You throw a strange regard upon me, and by that
195 I do perceive it hath offended you.
Pardon me, sweet one, even for the vows
We made each other but so late ago.

DUKE One face, one voice, one habit, and two persons!
A natural perspective, that is and is not!

200 SEB. Antonio! O my dear Antonio!
How have the hours rack'd and tortur'd me
Since I have lost thee!

ANT. Sebastian are you?

SEB.   Fear'st thou that, Antonio?

205 ANT. How have you made division of yourself?
An apple cleft in two is not more twin
Than these two creatures. Which is Sebastian?

OLI. Most wonderful!

SEB. Do I stand there? I never had a brother;
210 Nor can there be that deity in my nature
Of here and everywhere. I had a sister,
Whom the blind waves and surges have devour'd.
Of charity, what kin are you to me?
What countryman? what name? what parentage?

---

[185] **a passy measures pavin:** The *pavin* was a stately dance. *Passy measures* is Sir Toby's form for *passamezzo*, a slow tune. He means to call the surgeon 'a grave and solemn humbug.'

[187] **be dress'd:** have our wounds dressed.

[188-189] **you:** Scornfully emphasized. **coxcomb:** fool. **knave:** fellow. **thin-fac'd:** See i, 3, 28, note.

[189] **gull:** dupe.

[193] **with wit and safety:** with a sensible regard for my own safety. Hendiadys.

[194] **a strange regard:** an estranged (offended) look.

[198] **habit:** costume.

[199] **A natural perspective, that is and is not!:** Perspective glasses were optical toys which distorted the shapes of objects or otherwise misrepresented them. Orsino means that, in the present instance, nature not art gives the effect of an optical illusion—makes us see something that we cannot believe to exist.

[201] **rack'd and tortur'd:** Synonymous.

[204] **Fear'st thou that?** Why are you actually shocked to recognize me? The question is prompted by Antonio's air of amazement.

[210-211] **that deity . . . Of here and everywhere:** that quality of omnipresence, which belongs to God alone.

[213] **Of charity:** I pray you to be so kind as to tell me. Literally, *of charity* means 'out of kindness.'

215　VIO. Of Messaline; Sebastian was my father—
　　　　Such a Sebastian was my brother too;
　　　　So went he suited to his watery tomb.
　　　　If spirits can assume both form and suit,
　　　　You come to fright us.
220　SEB.　　　　　　　　　A spirit I am indeed,
　　　　But am in that dimension grossly clad
　　　　Which from the womb I did participate.
　　　　Were you a woman, as the rest goes even,
　　　　I should my tears let fall upon your cheek
225　　　And say, 'Thrice welcome, drowned Viola!'
　　　VIO. My father had a mole upon his brow—
　　　SEB. And so had mine.
　　　VIO. And died that day when Viola from her birth
　　　　Had numb'red thirteen years.
230　SEB. O, that record is lively in my soul!
　　　　He finished indeed his mortal act
　　　　That day that made my sister thirteen years.
　　　VIO. If nothing lets to make us happy both
　　　　But this my masculine usurp'd attire,
235　　　Do not embrace me till each circumstance
　　　　Of place, time, fortune do cohere and jump
　　　　That I am Viola; which to confirm,
　　　　I'll bring you to a captain in this town,
　　　　Where lie my maiden weeds; by whose gentle help
240　　　I was preserv'd to serve this noble Count.
　　　　All the occurrence of my fortune since
　　　　Hath been between this lady and this lord.
　　　SEB. [to OLIVIA] So comes it, lady, you have been mistook.
　　　　But nature to her bias drew in that.
245　　　You would have been contracted to a maid;
　　　　Nor are you therein, by my life, deceiv'd:
　　　　You are betroth'd both to a maid and man.
　　　DUKE Be not amaz'd; right noble is his blood.
　　　　If this be so, as yet the glass seems true,
250　　　I shall have share in this most happy wrack.

---

217 **suited:** clad, clothed.

218 **suit:** costume.

221 **in that dimension grossly clad:** clothed in that bodily form of material substance.

222 **participate:** derive, inherit.

223 **as the rest goes even:** as [may well be the case, for] all the other circumstances accord with your being my sister.

230 **recórd:** recollection, memory.

233 **lets:** hinders.

236 **cohere and jump:** Synonymous: 'coincide,' 'agree.'

239 **weeds:** garments.

244 **nature to her bias drew:** your nature followed its inborn tendency. A figure from bowling. The *bias* is the 'curve' which the bowl takes.　**in that:** in your mistake in taking a maid for a man.

248 **amaz'd:** in a daze.

249 **as . . . true:** as [so it appears to be, for] the perspective glass still seems to be showing reality—not a deceptive appearance.

250 **wrack:** the wreck mentioned in ll. 211–217.

[*To* VIOLA] Boy, thou hast said to me a thousand times
Thou never shouldst love woman like to me.
VIO. And all those sayings will I over swear,
And all those swearings keep as true in soul
255   As doth that orbed continent the fire
That severs day from night.
DUKE   Give me thy hand,
And let me see thee in thy woman's weeds.
VIO. The captain that did bring me first on shore
260   Hath my maid's garments. He upon some action
Is now in durance, at Malvolio's suit,
A gentleman, and follower of my lady's.
OLI. He shall enlarge him. Fetch Malvolio hither.
And yet alas! now I remember me,
265   They say, poor gentleman, he's much distract.

Enter CLOWN *with a letter, and* FABIAN.

A most extracting frenzy of mine own
From my remembrance clearly banish'd his.
How does he, sirrah?
CLOWN Truly, madam, he holds Belzebub at the stave's end as well as a man in his case
270   may do. Has here writ a letter to you; I should have given't you to-day morning.
[*Offers the letter.*] But as a madman's epistles are no gospels, so it skills not much
when they are deliver'd.
OLI. Open't and read it.
CLOWN Look then to be well edified, when the fool delivers the madman. [*Reads in a*
275   *loud voice*] 'By the Lord, madam'—
OLI. How now? Art thou mad?
CLOWN No, madam, I do but read madness. An your ladyship will have it as it ought
to be, you must allow vox.
OLI. Prithee read i' thy right wits.
280   CLOWN So I do, madonna; but to read his right wits is to read thus. Therefore perpend,
my princess, and give ear.

---

252 **like to me**: as much as you loved me.
253 **over**: over again; in repetition.
255 **that orbed continent**: the sun. Literally, 'that spherical container (of fire).' *Fire* is the object of
the verb 'doth [keep].'
260 **upon some action**: in consequence of some law business.
261 **in durance**: imprisoned; under arrest.
263 **enlarge**: release.
266-267 **A most extracting frenzy . . . his**: A madness of my own, which violently drew me out of my
wits, completely banished *his* attack of madness from my memory.
269 **he holds Belzebub at the stave's end**: He makes the fiend keep his distance; defends himself
from the attacks of the demon. The figure comes from a duel with staffs—long heavy
sticks. **case**: condition.
271 **it skills not much**: it doesn't make much difference.
274 **delivers**: reads the message of.
278 **allow vox**: permit the use of a loud voice—of vociferation.
280 **to read his right wits . . . thus**: to read in such a way as to express his state of mind correctly is
to read as I have already done—with crazy emphasis. **perpend**: give careful attention.

OLI. [*to* FABIAN] Read it you, sirrah.

FAB. (*reads*) 'By the Lord, madam, you wrong me, and the world shall know it. Though you have put me into darkness, and given your drunken cousin rule over me, yet have
285   I the benefit of my senses as well as your ladyship. I have your own letter that induced me to the semblance I put on; with the which I doubt not but to do myself much right, or you much shame. Think of me as you please. I leave my duty a little unthought of, and speak out of my injury.

'THE MADLY US'D MALVOLIO.'

290   OLI. Did he write this?

CLOWN Ay, madam.

DUKE This savours not much of distraction.

OLI. See him deliver'd, Fabian; bring him hither.

[*Exit* FABIAN.]

    My lord, so please you, these things further thought on,
295   To think me as well a sister as a wife,
    One day shall crown th' alliance on't, so please you,
    Here at my house and at my proper cost.

DUKE Madam, I am most apt t' embrace your offer.
    [*To* VIOLA] Your master quits you; and for your service done him,
300   So much against the mettle of your sex,
    So far beneath your soft and tender breeding,
    And since you call'd me master, for so long,
    Here is my hand: you shall from this time be
    Your master's mistress.
305   OLI.   A sister! you are she.

Enter [FABIAN, *with*] MALVOLIO.

DUKE Is this the madman?

OLI.   Ay, my lord, this same.
    How now, Malvolio?

MAL.   Madam, you have done me wrong,
310   Notorious wrong.

OLI.   Have I, Malvolio? No.

MAL. Lady, you have. Pray you peruse that letter.
    You must not now deny it is your hand.

---

286 **with the which:** i.e., by producing your letter.

287-288 **I leave . . . injury:** In thus expressing myself I somewhat disregard the respect that is due you and speak as the injury you have done me prompts.

294-295 **so please you . . . on't:** If you are willing, after further consideration of what we have just learned, to accept me as a sister-in-law instead of as a wife, the two weddings that shall make me your sister-in-law shall be celebrated on the same day.

297 **proper:** own.

298 **apt:** ready.

299 **quits you:** releases you from his service.

300 **mettle:** nature, disposition.

310 **Notorious:** notable, egregious.

Write from it if you can, in hand or phrase,
315   Or say 'tis not your seal, not your invention.
You can say none of this. Well, grant it then,
And tell me, in the modesty of honour,
Why you have given me such clear lights of favour,
Bade me come smiling and cross-garter'd to you,
320   To put on yellow stockings, and to frown
Upon Sir Toby and the lighter people;
And, acting this in an obedient hope,
Why have you suffer'd me to be imprison'd,
Kept in a dark house, visited by the priest,
325   And made the most notorious geck and gull
That e'er invention play'd on? Tell me why.
OLI.   Alas, Malvolio, this is not my writing,
Though I confess much like the character;
But, out of question, 'tis Maria's hand.
330   And now I do bethink me, it was she
First told me thou wast mad. Thou cam'st in smiling,
And in such forms which here were presuppos'd
Upon thee in the letter. Prithee be content.
This practice hath most shrewdly pass'd upon thee;
335   But when we know the grounds and authors of it,
Thou shalt be both the plaintiff and the judge
Of thine own cause.
FAB.   Good madam, hear me speak,
And let no quarrel, nor no brawl to come,
340   Taint the condition of this present hour,
Which I have wond'red at. In hope it shall not,
Most freely I confess myself and Toby
Set this device against Malvolio here,
Upon some stubborn and uncourteous parts
345   We had conceiv'd against him. Maria writ
The letter, at Sir Toby's great importance,

---

[314] **from it:** *From* is emphatic: 'Write, if you can, in a hand or a style that shall be different from the hand and style shown in this letter.' For *hand* cf. ii, 3, 112, 113. For a similar use of *from* cf. i, 5, 132.

[317] **in the modesty of honour:** with some little regard for your own honour.

[321] **the lighter people:** 'people of less dignity or importance' (Johnson).

[322] **acting . . . hope:** when I acted this part in obedience to your orders and in hope to receive your favour.

[325] **geck and gull:** dupe. The words are synonymous.

[326] **play'd on:** made sport with; victimized.

[328] **the character:** my handwriting.

[329] **out of question:** unquestionably.

[332-333] **presuppos'd Upon thee:** suggested for thy adoption.

[334] **This practice . . . upon thee:** This plot has succeeded in working upon thee (in making thee its victim) to the very limit. *Shrewdly* means 'cursedly,' 'confoundedly.'

[339] **nor no:** Such double negatives are common. **to come:** in the future.

[340] **the condition:** the (happy) nature.

[334-335] **Upon . . . against him:** because of some rude and discourteous acts on his part which had prompted us to feel offended with him.

[336] **importance:** importunity; urgent request.

In recompense whereof he hath married her.
How with a sportful malice it was follow'd
May rather pluck on laughter than revenge,
350 If that the injuries be justly weigh'd
That have on both sides pass'd.
OLI. Alas poor fool, how have they baffled thee!
CLOWN Why, 'some are born great, some achieve greatness, and some have greatness
thrown upon them.' I was one, sir, in this interlude—one Sir Topas, sir; but that's
355 all one. 'By the Lord, fool, I am not mad!' But do you remember—'Madam, why
laugh you at such a barren rascal? An you smile not, he's gagg'd'? And thus the
whirligig of time brings in his revenges.
MAL. I'll be reveng'd on the whole pack of you!   [*Exit.*]
OLI. He hath been most notoriously abus'd.
360 DUKE Pursue him and entreat him to a peace.
He hath not told us of the captain yet.
When that is known, and golden time convents,
A solemn combination shall be made
Of our dear souls. Meantime, sweet sister,
365 We will not part from hence. Cesario, come—
For so you shall be while you are a man;
But when in other habits you are seen,
Orsino's mistress and his fancy's queen.

Exeunt [all but the CLOWN].

CLOWN *sings.*
When that I was and a little tiny boy,
370   With hey, ho, the wind and the rain,
A foolish thing was but a toy,
          For the rain it raineth every day.

But when I came to man's estate,
          With hey, ho, the wind and the rain,
375 'Gainst knaves and thieves men shut their gate,
          For the rain it raineth every day.

But when I came, alas! to wive,
          With hey, ho, the wind and the rain,

---

[348] **it was follow'd**: the plan was carried out.

[349] **pluck on**: prompt, induce.

[350] **If that**: if.

[352] **fool**: dupe. **baffled thee!**: put thee to shame.

[354-357] **interlude**: farce. **that's all one**: that's of no consequence; never mind that. **Madam, why . . . gagg'd**. See i, 5, 59 ff. **Thus the whirligig of time brings in his revenges**: Thus time in its whirling course brings with it its appropriate repayments for injuries. That time revolves in a circle is an ancient idea.

[359] **notoriously abus'd**: notably (egregiously) ill used.

[361] **the captain**. See ll. 259–262.

[362] **convents**: agrees; is convenient.

[367] **habits**: attire.

[368] **mistress**: lady love. **fancy's**: love's.

[369] **and a**: This means merely *a*. *And* is used to carry a note.

[371] **a toy**: a trifle.

                  By swaggering could I never thrive,
380   For the rain it raineth every day.

                  But when I came unto my beds,
                      With hey, ho, the wind and the rain,
                  With tosspots still had drunken heads,
                      For the rain it raineth every day.

385   A great while ago the world begun,
                      With hey, ho, the wind and the rain;
                  But that's all one, our play is done,
                      And we'll strive to please you every day.

                  [*Exit.*]

Questions

1. Clearly the Duke is in love with Olivia. Why doesn't she return his affection?
2. Why does Viola disguise herself in order to become the Duke's servant?
3. What is Viola's real feeling for the Duke?
4. The name Malvolio comes from the Latin words for "ill will." His story presents a dark moral dilemma within the framework of a gentle comedy. What is the major flaw in the man's character?
5. Describe the plot to ruin Malvolio. How does it prey upon his fatal flaw?
6. Viola's mission to Olivia at the Duke's command results in several scenes of high comedy. Explain.
7. Why is Antonio not welcome in Illyria?
8. By the end of Act IV, all the potential love relationships in the play are tied in knots of mistaken identity. In Act V the plot of *Twelfth Night* undergoes a classic "denouement," which is a French word for unknotting. Describe the problems and then describe Shakespeare's denouement.
9. *Hamlet* is a tragedy with comic elements; *Twelfth Night* is a comedy with tragic elements. What slight changes in the plot of *Twelfth Night* would turn the play into a tragedy?

381-383 **But . . . heads:** If this stanza is taken as continuous in sense with the preceding stanza, the meaning may well be: 'I was such a swaggering reveller that I could never prosper, but, whenever I went to bed I always had a drunken head, like other tosspots [i.e., revellers].' As to *had* for 'I had' cf. *has* for 'he has' (i, 5, 102; v, 1, 167, 182, 270). The plurals, *beds* and *heads*, seem to signify the different occasions on which he went to bed drunk.

387 **But that's all one:** But never mind about that.

388 **And we'll strive to please you every day:** Such promises from the actors were the regular thing in epilogues.

✍ Tips for Writing about Comedy

1. In writing about any comedy, there are fascinating genre distinctions to be considered, depending upon the degree to which the characters and situations are lifelike. Determine whether the play under consideration is a farce, a satire, a poetic romance, or a "realistic" comic drama. Discuss whether or not it might be considered a tragicomedy.

2. A true comedy is more than a string of jokes. It always concerns one or more protagonists in the pursuit of a goal. The goal appears early in the play; immediately problems arise, which the protagonists then overcome. Summarize the plot in your review in terms of this convention.

3. Comedies, influenced by the Renaissance tradition of *commedia dell'arte*, frequently have "stock" characters: the bully, the lovesick teenager, the skinflint, the braggart. Evaluate the play's success in bringing new life to these old roles.

4. Tragedies end in catastrophe, and comedies usually end in the denouement, or "unknotting" of the problem. You may wish to consider how gracefully the playwright "unknots" the problems he has created for his characters earlier in the play. Does he or she "force" the issue by unnatural means? Is this good, or bad?

5. Frequently the theme of a play arises from the conflict between the protagonist's desire and the larger will of the society in which he or she lives. When the protagonist prevails, he or she has a definite influence upon the social order. Consider the political implications of any comedy under consideration.

8 ❧ The Rise of Realism

In art and literature, realism is the accurate representation of the real world and human nature. In drama, realism avoids all that is improbable in events and characters, and all that is visionary in theatrical presentation. We have grown so accustomed to realism in modern theater and film, we may forget that most drama before the twentieth century, and a good deal of drama since, is not at all realistic. Consider the plays we have read. The plot of *Oedipus Rex*, as well as the character of Teiresias, is highly improbable. So is the acting and chanting of the chorus. The events of *Hamlet* are quite probable, but the appearance of the ghost in Act I is not. Nor is the manner of speech probable. No one ever spoke as beautifully as the characters in *Hamlet*. Then there are Hamlet's asides, his stage whispers only the audience can hear, and soliloquies where he speaks at length to himself and the audience. Have you ever heard of anybody speaking so long and eloquently to himself? Of course not. You accept these things because the theater is a world of illusion, and these are accepted conventions within that world of illusion.

Realism is just such a convention. It has roots in the Greek New Comedy that portrayed ordinary people and domestic situations, instead of demigods struggling against fate. These comedies and their European successors, with their stock characters and happy endings, may be more probable than the tragedies of Sophocles and Marlowe. Yet they are not truly realistic. Realism as we know it is largely the invention of a nineteenth-century Norwegian, Henrik Ibsen.

In the early nineteenth century the spirit of Romanticism swept through the arts in Europe and England. Romanticism emphasizes the emotions and imagination above reason and intellect. The plays of Lord Byron, Victor Hugo, and Heinrich von Kleist dramatized historical and sentimental subjects in a grand style that often verged on melodrama. Ibsen's realism was partly a reaction to romantic excess. In his most influential plays, both the characters and the situations seem highly probable, and the language is natural prose. There are no choruses, soliloquies, ghosts, nor other "stagey" trappings—just real people with serious personal and social problems. This approach was totally shocking to the audiences of the time. They went to the theater expecting a show, and what they found was embarrassingly lifelike.

Ibsen's achievement is all the more stunning when you recall that before the nineteenth century only comic playwrights dared to be realistic, and in that case only to make people laugh at human folly. Ibsen's plays are not funny. They show the frailties of real people and society in a tragic light.

Social Realism

We have mentioned the effectiveness of theater as an incubator of manners and morals during revolutionary times. Ibsen's plays of the late nineteenth century correspond with a cultural revolution. Society had changed enormously since the Renaissance, but theater had not kept pace with the change. The Napoleonic Wars, the Industrial Revolution, and the rise of the middle class had bred a new audience that longed for serious criticism of outmoded social institutions. They wanted exploration of their psychology. Henrik Ibsen, contemporary of Marx and Freud, was able to provide both. He created a new kind of hero. The tragic heroes of Sophocles and Shakespeare struggle with their fates and against the gods. They are exalted, universal figures. Ibsen's characters are middle-class, flesh-and-blood, struggling against social and economic systems, and with psychological problems clearly provoked by those systems. Drama that portrays such characters and situations has been called *social realism*.

A Doll's House

A Doll's House (1879) was one of the first and most controversial plays of social realism. In Norway, as in much of Europe at the time, women's rights was a hot topic. The heroine of Ibsen's play, Nora, has been petted, spoiled, and humiliated by her father and her husband. Millions of middle-class women saw themselves in Nora Helmer. Nora's slamming of the door on her husband and their outmoded ideal of marriage echoed around the world. The play was damned and praised in journals, in pamphlets and books, and at public meetings. Preachers denounced it from the pulpit. *A Doll's House* was a scandalous success; by the end of the eighties, it had been staged in nearly every civilized country. In England the play was first performed privately in a Bloomsbury lodging house, with Karl Marx's daughter as Nora, and Krogstad played by Bernard Shaw. The latter was a great fan and advocate of Ibsen, and obviously learned a good deal from him.

Henrik Ibsen was born in Skien, Norway, in 1828, the son of a businessman whose reversals of fortune kept the family in financial straits. Ibsen worked as a pharmacist's assistant and later studied medicine in Oslo. He was not a good student. Though he managed to write his first play, *Catilina*, during those years

(1848–1850) he failed to matriculate at the University. In 1851 Ibsen accepted a position as producer of the National Theater in Bergen. Later he was invited to write a play yearly for the theater's anniversary. In 1857 he became the manager of the Norwegian Theater at Christiania. In 1858 the playwright married Suzannah Thoresen.

Ibsen's early works are not realistic. *The Vikings of Helgoland* (1858) and *The Pretenders* (1864) are romantic histories characteristic of the period. *Brand* (1865) and *Peer Gynt* (1867) are symbolic and mock-heroic. Although *The League of Youth* has elements of the prose drama, his first decisive play of social realism is *Pillars of Society*, about the double-dealings of a successful, hypocritical businessman. It established his fame in Europe and was followed by *A Doll's House* in 1879.

Shortly after the failure of the Norwegian Theater in 1862, Ibsen left Norway for Rome. He lived abroad for the next twenty-seven years—mostly in Rome, Dresden, and Munich—and like the novelists James Joyce and Henry James, did his greatest work in exile, including *Ghosts*, *Hedda Gabler*, *The Master Builder*, *The Wild Duck*, *Lady from the Sea*, and *When We Dead Awaken*.

In 1891 Ibsen returned to Norway and took up residence in Christiania. By then he was world famous. In 1901 he suffered a stroke that left him helpless. He wrote no more, and died in Christiania in 1906.

The Drama of Catastrophe

Ibsen's mastery of psychological portraiture resulted partly from the innovative plotting of his plays. During his years at Bergen, Ibsen became quite familiar with classic plot structure through the works of Eugène Scribe (1791–1861). More than half of the hundred and forty-five plays Ibsen produced were French, and were influenced by Scribe's *well-made-play*, a kind of comedy full of suspense and reversals, based on the classic five-part plot. Restless action, constant play and counterplay, expressed the changing attitudes of Scribe's shallow characters. Ibsen adopted the dynamic movement of Scribe's drama, but internalized the changes in his characters, making them mental rather than physical. To achieve this end, he had to re-order the narrative and create what is called the *catastrophic* plot.

Classic drama shows us the protagonist moving toward the central action of his story. We see Hamlet working to prove his uncle's guilt. We watch Oedipus search for the murderer of Laios. Then we see the central action, which makes the play's turning point: Hamlet fails to murder Claudius at his prayers; Oedipus begins to suspect he, himself, is the murderer. After the climax we get the catastrophe, or dénouement.

Ibsen's plot is quite different. The central event of *A Doll's House*, Nora's forging of a contract, occurs eight years before the curtain goes up. In the classical sense the whole play is catastrophe, or dénouement. There is little action, but a great deal of reflection, a marvelous opportunity to see how the characters

Liv Ullman with Sam Waterston in *A Doll's House* (*Photograph by Friedman-Abeles from Performing Arts Research Center, The New York Public Library*)

have been spiritually affected by the past action. The emotional climax of *A Doll's House* comes, at last, with the *discovery* of the central action rather than the dramatization of it.

A *Doll's House* is considered the first great drama of catastrophe. Eugene O'Neill's *Long Day's Journey into Night* is another highly regarded drama of catastrophe.

HENRIK IBSEN (1828–1906)

A Doll's House

Newly translated from the Norwegian by Michael Meyer

CHARACTERS

TORVALD HELMER, *a lawyer*	THE HELMERS' THREE SMALL CHILDREN
NORA, *his wife*	ANNE-MARIE, *their nurse*
DR. RANK	HELEN, *the maid*
MRS. LINDE	A PORTER
NILS KROGSTAD, *also a lawyer*	

The action takes place in the Helmers' apartment.

This translation of A DOLL'S HOUSE *was first performed on 16 October 1964 at the Oxford Playhouse with the following cast:*

TORVALD HELMER	Richard Gale
NORA	Barbara Young
DR. RANK	James Cairncross
MRS. LINDE	Pamela Lane
KROGSTAD	John Warner
ANNE-MARIE	Gabrielle Hamilton
HELEN	Yvette Byrne

Directed by Robert Chetwyn

ACT I

A comfortably and tastefully, but not expensively furnished room. Backstage right a door leads out to the hall; backstage left, another door to HELMER's study. Between these two doors stands a piano. In the middle of the left-hand wall is a door, with a window downstage of it. Near the window, a round table with armchairs and a small sofa. In the right-hand wall, slightly upstage, is a door; downstage of this, against the same wall, a stove lined with porcelain tiles, with a couple of armchairs and a rocking-chair in front of it. Between the stove and the side door is a small table. Engravings on the wall. A what-not with china and other bric-a-brac; a small bookcase with leather-bound books. A carpet on the floor; a fire in the stove. A winter day.

A bell rings in the hall outside. After a moment, we hear the front door being opened. NORA enters the room, humming contentedly to herself. She is wearing outdoor clothes and carrying a lot of parcels, which she puts down on the table right. She leaves the door to the hall open; through it, we can see a PORTER carrying a Christmas tree and a basket. He gives these to the MAID, who has opened the door for them.

NORA Hide that Christmas tree away, Helen. The children mustn't see it before I've decorated it this evening. (*To the* PORTER, *taking out her purse.*) How much—?
PORTER A shilling.
NORA Here's half a crown. No, keep it.

The PORTER *touches his cap and goes.* NORA *closes the door. She continues to laugh happily to herself as she removes her coat, etc. She takes from her pocket a bag containing macaroons and eats a couple. Then she tiptoes across and listens at her husband's door.*

NORA Yes, he's here. (*Starts humming again as she goes over to the table, right.*)
HELMER (*from his room*) Is that my skylark twittering out there?
NORA (*opening some of the parcels*) It is!
HELMER Is that my squirrel rustling?
NORA Yes!
HELMER When did my squirrel come home?
NORA Just now. (*Pops the bag of macaroons in her pocket and wipes her mouth.*) Come out here, Torvald, and see what I've bought.
HELMER You mustn't disturb me! (*Short pause; then he opens the door and looks in, his pen in his hand.*) Bought, did you say? All that? Has my little squanderbird been overspending again?
NORA Oh, Torvald, surely we can let ourselves go a little this year! It's the first Christmas we don't have to scrape.
HELMER Well, you know, we can't afford to be extravagant.
NORA Oh yes, Torvald, we can be a little extravagant now. Can't we? Just a tiny bit? You've got a big salary now, and you're going to make lots and lots of money.
HELMER Next year, yes. But my new salary doesn't start till April.

NORA Pooh; we can borrow till then.

HELMER Nora! (*Goes over to her and takes her playfully by the ear.*) What a little spend-thrift you are! Suppose I were to borrow fifty pounds today, and you spent it all over Christmas, and then on New Year's Eve a tile fell off a roof on to my head—

NORA (*puts her hand over his mouth*) Oh, Torvald! Don't say such dreadful things!

HELMER Yes, but suppose something like that did happen? What then?

NORA If anything as frightful as that happened, it wouldn't make much difference whether I was in debt or not.

HELMER But what about the people I'd borrowed from?

NORA Them? Who cares about them? They're strangers.

HELMER Oh, Nora, Nora, how like a woman! No, but seriously, Nora, you know how I feel about this. No debts! Never borrow! A home that is founded on debts can never be a place of freedom and beauty. We two have stuck it out bravely up to now; and we shall continue to do so for the short time we still have to.

NORA (*goes over towards the stove*) Very well, Torvald. As you say.

HELMER (*follows her*) Now, now! My little songbird mustn't droop her wings. What's this? Is little squirrel sulking? (*Takes out his purse.*) Nora; guess what I've got here!

NORA (*turns quickly*) Money!

HELMER Look. (*Hands her some banknotes.*) I know how these small expenses crop up at Christmas.

NORA (*counts them*) One—two—three—four. Oh, thank you, Torvald, thank you! I should be able to manage with this.

HELMER You'll have to.

NORA Yes, yes, of course I will. But come over here, I want to show you everything I've bought. And so cheaply! Look, here are new clothes for Ivar—and a sword. And a horse and a trumpet for Bob. And a doll and a cradle for Emmy—they're nothing much, but she'll pull them apart in a few days. And some bits of material and handkerchiefs for the maids. Old Anne-Marie ought to have had something better, really.

HELMER And what's in that parcel?

NORA (*cries*) No, Torvald, you mustn't see that before this evening!

HELMER Very well. But now, tell me, you little spendthrift, what do you want for Christmas?

NORA Me? Oh, pooh, I don't want anything.

HELMER Oh, yes, you do. Now tell me, what, within reason, would you most like?

NORA No, I really don't know. Oh, yes—Torvald—!

HELMER Well?

NORA (*plays with his coat-buttons; not looking at him*) If you really want to give me something, you could—you could—

HELMER Come on, out with it.

NORA (*quickly*) You could give me money, Torvald. Only as much as you feel you can afford; then later I'll buy something with it.

HELMER But, Nora—

NORA Oh yes, Torvald dear, please! Please! Then I'll wrap up the notes in pretty gold paper and hang them on the Christmas tree. Wouldn't that be fun?

HELMER What's the name of that little bird that can never keep any money?

NORA Yes, yes, squanderbird; I know. But let's do as I say, Torvald; then I'll have time to think about what I need most. Isn't that the best way? Mm?

HELMER (*smiles*) To be sure it would be, if you could keep what I give you and really buy yourself something with it. But you'll spend it on all sorts of useless things for the house, and then I'll have to put my hand in my pocket again.

NORA Oh, but Torvald—

HELMER You can't deny it, Nora dear. (*Puts his arm round her waist.*) The squanderbird's a pretty little creature, but she gets through an awful lot of money. It's incredible what an expensive pet she is for a man to keep.

NORA For shame! How can you say such a thing? I save every penny I can.

HELMER (*laughs*) That's quite true. Every penny you can. But you can't.

NORA (*hums and smiles, quietly gleeful*) Hm. If you only knew how many expenses we larks and squirrels have, Torvald.

HELMER You're a funny little creature. Just like your father used to be. Always on the look-out for some way to get money, but as soon as you have any it just runs through your fingers, and you never know where it's gone. Well, I suppose I must take you as you are. It's in your blood. Yes, yes, yes, these things are hereditary, Nora.

NORA Oh, I wish I'd inherited more of Papa's qualities.

HELMER And I wouldn't wish my darling little songbird to be any different from what she is. By the way, that reminds me. You look awfully—how shall I put it?—awfully guilty today.

NORA Do I?

HELMER Yes, you do. Look me in the eyes.

NORA (*looks at him*) Well?

HELMER (*wags his finger*) Has my little sweet-tooth been indulging herself in town today, by any chance?

NORA No, how can you think such a thing?

HELMER Not a tiny little digression into a pastry shop?

NORA No, Torvald, I promise—

HELMER Not just a wee jam tart?

NORA Certainly not.

HELMER Not a little nibble at a macaroon?

NORA No, Torvald—I promise you, honestly—

HELMER There, there. I was only joking.

NORA (*goes over to the table, right*) You know I could never act against your wishes.

HELMER Of course not. And you've given me your word— (*Goes over to her.*) Well, my beloved Nora, you keep your little Christmas secrets to yourself. They'll be revealed this evening, I've no doubt, once the Christmas tree has been lit.

NORA Have you remembered to invite Dr. Rank?

HELMER No. But there's no need; he knows he'll be dining with us. Anyway, I'll ask him when he comes this morning. I've ordered some good wine. Oh, Nora, you can't imagine how I'm looking forward to this evening.

NORA So am I. And, Torvald, how the children will love it!

HELMER Yes, it's a wonderful thing to know that one's position is assured and that one has an ample income. Don't you agree? It's good to know that, isn't it?

NORA Yes, it's almost like a miracle.

HELMER Do you remember last Christmas? For three whole weeks you shut yourself away every evening to make flowers for the Christmas tree, and all those other things you were going to surprise us with. Ugh, it was the most boring time I've ever had in my life.

NORA I didn't find it boring.

HELMER (*smiles*) But it all came to nothing in the end, didn't it?

NORA Oh, are you going to bring that up again? How could I help the cat getting in and tearing everything to bits?

HELMER No, my poor little Nora, of course you couldn't. You simply wanted to make us happy, and that's all that matters. But it's good that those hard times are past.

NORA Yes, it's wonderful.

HELMER I don't have to sit by myself and be bored. And you don't have to tire your pretty eyes and your delicate little hands—

NORA (claps her hands) No, Torvald, that's true, isn't it—I don't have to any longer? Oh, it's really all just like a miracle. (Takes his arm.) Now, I'm going to tell you what I thought we might do, Torvald. As soon as Christmas is over— (A bell rings in the hall.) Oh, there's the doorbell. (Tidies up one or two things in the room.) Someone's coming. What a bore.

HELMER I'm not at home to any visitors. Remember!

MAID (in the doorway) A lady's called, madam. A stranger.

NORA Well, ask her to come in.

MAID And the doctor's here too, sir.

HELMER Has he gone to my room?

MAID Yes, sir.

HELMER goes into his room. The MAID shows in MRS. LINDE, who is dressed in travelling clothes, and closes the door.

MRS. LINDE (shyly and a little hesitantly) Good evening, Nora.

NORA (uncertainly) Good evening—

MRS. LINDE I don't suppose you recognize me.

NORA No, I'm afraid I— Yes, wait a minute—surely— (Exclaims.) Why, Christine! Is it really you?

MRS. LINDE Yes, it's me.

NORA Christine! And I didn't recognize you! But how could I—? (More quietly.) How you've changed, Christine!

MRS. LINDE Yes, I know. It's been nine years—nearly ten—

NORA Is it so long? Yes, it must be. Oh, these last eight years have been such a happy time for me! So you've come to town? All that way in winter! How brave of you!

MRS. LINDE I arrived by the steamer this morning.

NORA Yes, of course—to enjoy yourself over Christmas. Oh, how splendid! We'll have to celebrate! But take off your coat. You're not cold, are you? (Helps her off with it.) There! Now let's sit down here by the stove and be comfortable. No, you take the armchair. I'll sit here in the rocking-chair. (Clasps MRS. LINDE's hands.) Yes, now you look like your old self. It was just at first that—you've got a little paler, though, Christine. And perhaps a bit thinner.

MRS. LINDE And older, Nora. Much, much older.

NORA Yes, perhaps a little older. Just a tiny bit. Not much. (Checks herself suddenly and says earnestly.) Oh, but how thoughtless of me to sit here and chatter away like this! Dear, sweet Christine, can you forgive me?

MRS. LINDE What do you mean, Nora?

NORA (quietly) Poor Christine, you've become a widow.

MRS. LINDE Yes. Three years ago.

NORA I know, I know—I read it in the papers. Oh, Christine, I meant to write to you so often, honestly. But I always put it off, and something else always cropped up.

MRS. LINDE I understand, Nora dear.

NORA No, Christine, it was beastly of me. Oh, my poor darling, what you've gone through! And he didn't leave you anything?

MRS. LINDE No.

NORA No children, either?

MRS. LINDE No.

NORA Nothing at all, then?

MRS. LINDE Not even a feeling of loss or sorrow.

NORA (*looks incredulously at her*) But, Christine, how is that possible?

MRS. LINDE (*smiles sadly and strokes* NORA's *hair*) Oh, these things happen, Nora.

NORA All alone. How dreadful that must be for you. I've three lovely children. I'm afraid you can't see them now, because they're out with nanny. But you must tell me everything—

MRS. LINDE No, no, no. I want to hear about you.

NORA No, you start. I'm not going to be selfish today, I'm just going to think about you. Oh, but there's one thing I *must* tell you. Have you heard of the wonderful luck we've just had?

MRS. LINDE No. What?

NORA Would you believe it—my husband's just been made manager of the bank!

MRS. LINDE Your husband? Oh, how lucky—!

NORA Yes, isn't it? Being a lawyer is so uncertain, you know, especially if one isn't prepared to touch any case that isn't—well—quite nice. And of course Torvald's been very firm about that—and I'm absolutely with him. Oh, you can imagine how happy we are! He's joining the bank in the New Year, and he'll be getting a big salary, and lots of percentages too. From now on we'll be able to live quite differently—we'll be able to do whatever we want. Oh, Christine, it's such a relief! I feel so happy! Well, I mean, it's lovely to have heaps of money and not to have to worry about anything. Don't you think?

MRS. LINDE It must be lovely to have enough to cover one's needs, anyway.

NORA Not just our needs! We're going to have heaps and heaps of money!

MRS. LINDE (*smiles*) Nora, Nora, haven't you grown up yet? When we were at school you were a terrible little spendthrift.

NORA (*laughs quietly*) Yes, Torvald still says that. (*Wags her finger.*) But "Nora, Nora" isn't as silly as you think. Oh, we've been in no position for me to waste money. We've both had to work.

MRS. LINDE You too?

NORA Yes, little things—fancy work, crocheting, embroidery and so forth. (*Casually.*) And other things too. I suppose you know Torvald left the Ministry when we got married? There were no prospects of promotion in his department, and of course he needed more money. But the first year he overworked himself quite dreadfully. He had to take on all sorts of extra jobs, and worked day and night. But it was too much for him, and he became frightfully ill. The doctors said he'd have to go to a warmer climate.

MRS. LINDE Yes, you spent a whole year in Italy, didn't you?

NORA Yes. It wasn't easy for me to get away, you know. I'd just had Ivar. But of course we had to do it. Oh, it was a marvellous trip! And it saved Torvald's life. But it cost an awful lot of money, Christine.

MRS. LINDE I can imagine.

NORA Two hundred and fifty pounds. That's a lot of money, you know.

MRS. LINDE How lucky you had it.

NORA Well, actually, we got it from my father.

MRS. LINDE Oh, I see. Didn't he die just about that time?

NORA Yes, Christine, just about then. Wasn't it dreadful, I couldn't go and look after him. I was expecting little Ivar any day. And then I had my poor Torvald to care for— we really didn't think he'd live. Dear, kind Papa! I never saw him again, Christine. Oh, it's the saddest thing that's happened to me since I got married.

MRS. LINDE I know you were very fond of him. But you went to Italy—?

NORA Yes. Well, we had the money, you see, and the doctors said we mustn't delay. So we went the month after Papa died.

MRS. LINDE And your husband came back completely cured?

NORA Fit as a fiddle!

MRS. LINDE But—the doctor?

NORA How do you mean?

MRS. LINDE I thought the maid said that the gentleman who arrived with me was the doctor.

NORA Oh yes, that's Doctor Rank, but he doesn't come because anyone's ill. He's our best friend, and he looks us up at least once every day. No, Torvald hasn't had a moment's illness since we went away. And the children are fit and healthy and so am I. (*Jumps up and claps her hands.*) Oh God, oh God, Christine, isn't it a wonderful thing to be alive and happy! Oh, but how beastly of me! I'm only talking about myself. (*Sits on a footstool and rests her arms on* MRS. LINDE's *knee.*) Oh, please don't be angry with me! Tell me, is it really true you didn't love your husband? Why did you marry him, then?

MRS. LINDE Well, my mother was still alive; and she was helpless and bedridden. And I had my two little brothers to take care of. I didn't feel I could say no.

NORA Yes, well, perhaps you're right. He was rich then, was he?

MRS. LINDE Quite comfortably off, I believe. But his business was unsound, you see, Nora. When he died it went bankrupt, and there was nothing left.

NORA What did you do?

MRS. LINDE Well, I had to try to make ends meet somehow, so I started a little shop, and a little school, and anything else I could turn my hand to. These last three years have been just one endless slog for me, without a moment's rest. But now it's over, Nora. My poor dear mother doesn't need me any more; she's passed away. And the boys don't need me either; they've got jobs now and can look after themselves.

NORA How relieved you must feel—

MRS. LINDE No, Nora. Just unspeakably empty. No one to live for any more. (*Gets up restlessly.*) That's why I couldn't bear to stay out there any longer, cut off from the world. I thought it'd be easier to find some work here that will exercise and occupy my mind. If only I could get a regular job—office work of some kind—

NORA Oh but, Christine, that's dreadfully exhausting; and you look practically finished already. It'd be much better for you if you could go away somewhere.

MRS. LINDE (*goes over to the window*) I have no Papa to pay for my holidays, Nora.

NORA (*gets up*) Oh, please don't be angry with me.

MRS. LINDE My dear Nora, it's I who should ask you not to be angry. That's the worst thing about this kind of situation—it makes one so bitter. One has no one to work for; and yet one has to be continually sponging for jobs. One has to live; and so one becomes completely egocentric. When you told me about this luck you've just had with Torvald's new job—can you imagine?—I was happy not so much on your account, as on my own.

NORA How do you mean? Oh, I understand. You mean Torvald might be able to do something for you?

MRS. LINDE Yes, I was thinking that.

NORA He will too, Christine. Just you leave it to me. I'll lead up to it so delicately, so delicately; I'll get him in the right mood. Oh, Christine, I do so want to help you.

MRS. LINDE It's sweet of you to bother so much about me, Nora. Especially since you know so little of the worries and hardships of life.

NORA I? You say I know little of—?

MRS. LINDE (smiles) Well, good heavens—those bits of fancy work of yours—well, really—! You're a child, Nora.

NORA (tosses her head and walks across the room) You shouldn't say that so patronisingly.

MRS. LINDE Oh?

NORA You're like the rest. You all think I'm incapable of getting down to anything serious—

MRS. LINDE My dear—

NORA You think I've never had any worries like the rest of you.

MRS. LINDE Nora dear, you've just told me about all your difficulties—

NORA Pooh—that! (Quietly.) I haven't told you about the big thing.

MRS. LINDE What big thing? What do you mean?

NORA You patronise me, Christine; but you shouldn't. You're proud that you've worked so long and so hard for your mother.

MRS. LINDE I don't patronise anyone, Nora. But you're right—I am both proud and happy that I was able to make my mother's last months on earth comparatively easy.

NORA And you're also proud of what you've done for your brothers.

MRS. LINDE I think I have a right to be.

NORA I think so too. But let me tell you something, Christine. I too have done something to be proud and happy about.

MRS. LINDE I don't doubt it. But—how do you mean?

NORA Speak quietly! Suppose Torvald should hear! He mustn't, at any price—no one must know, Christine—no one but you.

MRS. LINDE But what is this?

NORA Come over here. (Pulls her down on to the sofa beside her.) Yes, Christine—I too have done something to be happy and proud about. It was I who saved Torvald's life.

MRS. LINDE Saved his—? How did you save it?

NORA I told you about our trip to Italy. Torvald couldn't have lived if he hadn't managed to get down there—

MRS. LINDE Yes, well—your father provided the money—

NORA (smiles) So Torvald and everyone else thinks. But—

MRS. LINDE Yes?

NORA Papa didn't give us a penny. It was I who found the money.

MRS. LINDE You? All of it?

NORA Two hundred and fifty pounds. What do you say to that?

MRS. LINDE But Nora, how could you? Did you win a lottery or something?

NORA (scornfully) Lottery? (Sniffs.) What would there be to be proud of in that?

MRS. LINDE But where did you get it from, then?

NORA (hums and smiles secretively) Hm; tra-la-la-la!

MRS. LINDE You couldn't have borrowed it.

NORA Oh? Why not?

MRS. LINDE Well, a wife can't borrow money without her husband's consent.[1]

---

[1] According to Norwegian law at the time the play takes place.

NORA (*tosses her head*) Ah, but when a wife has a little business sense, and knows how to be clever—

MRS. LINDE But Nora, I simply don't understand—

NORA You don't have to. No one has said I borrowed the money. I could have got it in some other way. (*Throws herself back on the sofa.*) I could have got it from an admirer. When a girl's as pretty as I am—

MRS. LINDE Nora, you're crazy!

NORA You're dying of curiosity now, aren't you, Christine?

MRS. LINDE Nora dear, you haven't done anything foolish?

NORA (*sits up again*) Is it foolish to save one's husband's life?

MRS. LINDE I think it's foolish if without his knowledge you—

NORA But the whole point was that he mustn't know! Great heavens, don't you see? He hadn't to know how dangerously ill he was. I was the one they told that his life was in danger and that only going to a warm climate could save him. Do you suppose I didn't try to think of other ways of getting him down there? I told him how wonderful it would be for me to go abroad like other young wives; I cried and prayed; I asked him to remember my condition, and said he ought to be nice and tender to me; and then I suggested he might quite easily borrow the money. But then he got almost angry with me, Christine. He said I was frivolous, and that it was his duty as a husband not to pander to my moods and caprices—I think that's what he called them. Well, well, I thought, you've got to be saved somehow. And then I thought of a way—

MRS. LINDE But didn't your husband find out from your father that the money hadn't come from him?

NORA No, never. Papa died just then. I'd thought of letting him into the plot and asking him not to tell. But since he was so ill—! And as things turned out, it didn't become necessary.

MRS. LINDE And you've never told your husband about this?

NORA For heaven's sake, no! What an idea! He's frightfully strict about such matters. And besides—he's so proud of being a *man*—it'd be so painful and humiliating for him to know that he owed anything to me. It'd completely wreck our relationship. This life we have built together would no longer exist.

MRS. LINDE Will you never tell him?

NORA (*thoughtfully, half-smiling*) Yes—some time, perhaps. Years from now, when I'm no longer pretty. You mustn't laugh! I mean of course, when Torvald no longer loves me as he does now; when it no longer amuses him to see me dance and dress up and play the fool for him. Then it might be useful to have something up my sleeve. (*Breaks off.*) Stupid, stupid, stupid! That time will never come. Well, what do you think of my big secret, Christine? I'm not completely useless, am I? Mind you, all this has caused me a frightful lot of worry. It hasn't been easy for me to meet my obligations punctually. In case you don't know, in the world of business there are things called quarterly instalments and interest, and they're a terrible problem to cope with. So I've had to scrape a little here and save a little there as best I can. I haven't been able to save much on the housekeeping money, because Torvald likes to live well; and I couldn't let the children go short of clothes—I couldn't take anything out of what he gives me for them. The poor little angels!

MRS. LINDE So you've had to stint yourself, my poor Nora?

NORA Of course. Well, after all, it was my problem. Whenever Torvald gave me money to buy myself new clothes, I never used more than half of it; and I always bought what was cheapest and plainest. Thank heaven anything suits me, so that Torvald's never noticed. But it made me a bit sad sometimes, because it's lovely to wear pretty clothes. Don't you think?

MRS. LINDE Indeed it is.

NORA And then I've found one or two other sources of income. Last winter I managed to get a lot of copying to do. So I shut myself away and wrote every evening, late into the night. Oh, I often got so tired, so tired. But it was great fun, though, sitting there working and earning money. It was almost like being a man.

MRS. LINDE But how much have you managed to pay off like this?

NORA Well, I can't say exactly. It's awfully difficult to keep an exact check on these kind of transactions. I only know I've paid everything I've managed to scrape together. Sometimes I really didn't know where to turn. (*Smiles.*) Then I'd sit here and imagine some rich old gentleman had fallen in love with me—

MRS. LINDE What! What gentleman?

NORA Silly! And that now he'd died and when they opened his will it said in big letters: "Everything I possess is to be paid forthwith to my beloved Mrs. Nora Helmer in cash."

MRS. LINDE But, Nora dear, who was this gentleman?

NORA Great heavens, don't you understand? There wasn't any old gentleman; he was just something I used to dream up as I sat here evening after evening wondering how on earth I could raise some money. But what does it matter? The old bore can stay imaginary as far as I'm concerned, because now I don't have to worry any longer! (*Jumps up.*) Oh, Christine, isn't it wonderful? I don't have to worry any more! No more troubles! I can play all day with the children, I can fill the house with pretty things, just the way Torvald likes. And, Christine, it'll soon be spring, and the air'll be fresh and the skies blue,—and then perhaps we'll be able to take a little trip somewhere. I shall be able to see the sea again. Oh, yes, yes, it's a wonderful thing to be alive and happy!

The bell rings in the hall.

MRS. LINDE (*gets up*) You've a visitor. Perhaps I'd better go.

NORA No, stay. It won't be for me. It's someone for Torvald—

MAID (*in the doorway*) Excuse me, madam, a gentleman's called who says he wants to speak to the master. But I didn't know—seeing as the doctor's with him—

NORA Who is this gentleman?

KROGSTAD (*in the doorway*) It's me, Mrs. Helmer.

MRS. LINDE *starts, composes herself and turns away to the window.*

NORA (*takes a step towards him and whispers tensely*) You? What is it? What do you want to talk to my husband about?

KROGSTAD Business—you might call it. I hold a minor post in the bank, and I hear your husband is to become our new chief—

NORA Oh—then it isn't—?

KROGSTAD Pure business, Mrs. Helmer. Nothing more.

NORA Well, you'll find him in his study.

Nods indifferently as she closes the hall door behind him. Then she walks across the room and sees to the stove.

MRS. LINDE Nora, who was that man?

NORA A lawyer called Krogstad.

MRS. LINDE It was him, then.

NORA Do you know that man?

MRS. LINDE I used to know him—some years ago. He was a solicitor's clerk in our town, for a while.

NORA Yes, of course, so he was.

MRS. LINDE How he's changed!

NORA He was very unhappily married, I believe.

MRS. LINDE Is he a widower now?

NORA Yes, with a lot of children. Ah, now it's alight.

She closes the door of the stove and moves the rocking-chair a little to one side.

MRS. LINDE He does—various things now, I hear?

NORA Does he? It's quite possible—I really don't know. But don't let's talk about business. It's so boring.

DR. RANK *enters from* HELMER's *study.*

RANK (*still in the doorway*) No, no, my dear chap, don't see me out. I'll go and have a word with your wife. (*Closes the door and notices* MRS. LINDE.) Oh, I beg your pardon. I seem to be *de trop*[2] here too.

NORA Not in the least. (*Introduces them.*) Dr. Rank. Mrs. Linde.

RANK Ah! A name I have often heard in this house. I believe I passed you on the stairs as I came up.

MRS. LINDE Yes. Stairs tire me; I have to take them slowly.

RANK Oh, have you hurt yourself?

MRS. LINDE No, I'm just a little run down.

RANK Ah, is that all? Then I take it you've come to town to cure yourself by a round of parties?

MRS. LINDE I have come here to find work.

RANK Is that an approved remedy for being run down?

MRS. LINDE One has to live, Doctor.

RANK Yes, people do seem to regard it as a necessity.

NORA Oh, really, Dr. Rank. I bet you want to stay alive.

RANK You bet I do. However miserable I sometimes feel, I still want to go on being tortured for as long as possible. It's the same with all my patients; and with people who are morally sick, too. There's a moral cripple in with Helmer at this very moment—

MRS. LINDE (*softly*) Oh!

NORA Whom do you mean?

RANK Oh, a lawyer fellow called Krogstad—you wouldn't know him. He's crippled all right; morally twisted. But even he started off by announcing, as though it were a matter of enormous importance, that he had to live.

NORA Oh? What did he want to talk to Torvald about?

RANK I haven't the faintest idea. All I heard was something about the bank.

NORA I didn't know that Krog—that this man Krogstad had any connection with the bank.

RANK Yes, he's got some kind of job down there. (*To* MRS. LINDE.) I wonder if in your part of the world you too have a species of human being that spends its time fussing around trying to smell out moral corruption? And when they find a case they give him some nice, comfortable position so that they can keep a good watch on him. The healthy ones just have to lump it.

MRS. LINDE But surely it's the sick who need care most?

---

[2] French meaning "too much," in this case, a fifth wheel.

RANK (*shrugs his shoulders*) Well, there we have it. It's that attitude that's turning human society into a hospital.

NORA, *lost in her own thoughts, laughs half to herself and claps her hands.*

RANK Why are you laughing? Do you really know what society is?

NORA What do I care about society? I think it's a bore. I was laughing at something else—something frightfully funny. Tell me, Dr. Rank—will everyone who works at the bank come under Torvald now?

RANK Do you find that particularly funny?

NORA (*smiles and hums*) Never you mind! Never you mind! (*Walks around the room.*) Yes, I find it very amusing to think that we—I mean, Torvald—has obtained so much influence over so many people. (*Takes the paper bag from her pocket.*) Dr. Rank, would you like a small macaroon?

RANK Macaroons! I say! I thought they were forbidden here.

NORA Yes, well, these are some Christine gave me.

MRS. LINDE What? I—?

NORA All right, all right, don't get frightened. You weren't to know Torvald had forbidden them. He's afraid they'll ruin my teeth. But, dash it—for once—! Don't you agree, Dr. Rank? Here! (*Pops a macaroon into his mouth.*) You too, Christine. And I'll have one too. Just a little one. Two at the most. (*Begins to walk round again.*) Yes, now I feel really, really happy. Now there's just one thing in the world I'd really love to do.

RANK Oh? And what is that?

NORA Just something I'd love to say to Torvald.

RANK Well, why don't you say it?

NORA No, I daren't. It's too dreadful.

MRS. LINDE Dreadful?

RANK Well, then, you'd better not. But you can say it to us. What is it you'd so love to say to Torvald?

NORA I've the most extraordinary longing to say: "Bloody hell!"

RANK Are you mad?

MRS. LINDE My dear Nora—!

RANK Say it. Here he is

NORA (*hiding the bag of macaroons*). Ssh! Ssh!

HELMER, *with his overcoat on his arm and his hat in his hand, enters from his study.*

NORA (*goes to meet him*) Well, Torvald dear, did you get rid of him?

HELMER Yes, he's just gone.

NORA May I introduce you—? This is Christine. She's just arrived in town.

HELMER Christine—? Forgive me, but I don't think—

NORA Mrs. Linde, Torvald dear. Christine Linde.

HELMER Ah. A childhood friend of my wife's, I presume?

MRS. LINDE Yes, we knew each other in earlier days.

NORA And imagine, now she's travelled all this way to talk to you.

HELMER Oh?

MRS. LINDE Well, I didn't really—

NORA You see, Christine's frightfully good at office work, and she's mad to come under some really clever man who can teach her even more than she knows already—

HELMER Very sensible, madam.

NORA So when she heard you'd become head of the bank—it was in her local paper—
she came here as quickly as she could and—Torvald, you will, won't you? Do a little
something to help Christine? For my sake?

HELMER Well, that shouldn't be impossible. You are a widow, I take it, Mrs. Linde?

MRS. LINDE Yes.

HELMER And you have experience of office work?

MRS. LINDE Yes, quite a bit.

HELMER Well then, it's quite likely I may be able to find some job for you—

NORA (claps her hands) You see, you see!

HELMER You've come at a lucky moment, Mrs. Linde.

MRS. LINDE Oh, how can I ever thank you—?

HELMER There's absolutely no need. (Puts on his overcoat.) But now I'm afraid I must
ask you to excuse me—

RANK Wait. I'll come with you.

He gets his fur coat from the hall and warms it at the stove.

NORA Don't be long, Torvald dear.

HELMER I'll only be an hour.

NORA Are you going too, Christine?

MRS. LINDE (puts on her outdoor clothes) Yes, I must start to look round for a room.

HELMER Then perhaps we can walk part of the way together.

NORA (helps her) It's such a nuisance we're so cramped here—I'm afraid we can't offer
to—

MRS. LINDE Oh, I wouldn't dream of it. Goodbye, Nora dear, and thanks for everything.

NORA Au revoir. You'll be coming back this evening, of course. And you too, Dr. Rank.
What? If you're well enough? Of course you'll be well enough. Wrap up warmly,
though.

They go out, talking, into the hall. CHILDREN's *voices are heard from the stairs.*

NORA Here they are! Here they are!

She runs out and opens the door. ANNE-MARIE, *the* NURSE, *enters with the* CHILDREN.

NORA Come in, come in! (Stoops down and kisses them.) Oh, my sweet darlings—! Look
at them, Christine! Aren't they beautiful?

RANK Don't stand here chattering in this draught!

HELMER Come, Mrs. Linde. This is for mothers only.

DR. RANK, HELMER *and* MRS. LINDE *go down the stairs. The* NURSE *brings the* CHILDREN
into the room. NORA *follows, and closes the door to the hall.*

NORA Now well you look! What red cheeks you've got! Like apples and roses! (The
CHILDREN answer her inaudibly as she talks to them.) Have you had fun? That's
splendid. You gave Emmy and Bob a ride on the sledge? What, both together? I say!
What a clever boy you are, Ivar! Oh, let me hold her for a moment, Anne-Marie!
My sweet little baby doll! (Takes the smallest child from the NURSE and dances with
her.) Yes, yes, Mummy will dance with Bob too. What? Have you been throwing
snowballs? Oh, I wish I'd been there! No, don't—I'll undress them myself, Anne-
Marie. No, please let me; it's such fun. Go inside and warm yourself; you look frozen.

There's some hot coffee on the stove. (*The* NURSE *goes into the room on the left.* NORA *takes off the* CHILDREN'S *outdoor clothes and throws them anywhere while they all chatter simultaneously.*) What? A big dog ran after you? But he didn't bite you? No, dogs don't bite lovely little baby dolls. Leave those parcels alone, Ivar. What's in them? Ah, wouldn't you like to know! No, no; it's nothing nice. Come on, let's play a game. What shall we play? Hide and seek. Yes, let's play hide and seek. Bob shall hide first. You want me to? All right, let me hide first.

NORA *and the* CHILDREN *play around the room, and in the adjacent room to the left, laughing and shouting. At length* NORA *hides under the table. The* CHILDREN *rush in, look, but cannot find her. Then they hear her half-stifled laughter, run to the table, lift up the cloth and see her. Great excitement. She crawls out as though to frighten them. Further excitement. Meanwhile, there has been a knock on the door leading from the hall, but no one has noticed it. Now the door is half-opened and* KROGSTAD *enters. He waits for a moment; the game continues.*

KROGSTAD Excuse me, Mrs. Helmer—

NORA (*turns with a stifled cry and half jumps up*) Oh! What do you want?

KROGSTAD I beg your pardon; the front door was ajar. Someone must have forgotten to close it.

NORA (*gets up*) My husband is not at home, Mr. Krogstad.

KROGSTAD I know.

NORA Well, what do want here, then?

KROGSTAD A word with you.

NORA With—? (*To the* CHILDREN, *quietly.*) Go inside to Anne-Marie. What? No, the strange gentleman won't do anything to hurt Mummy. When he's gone we'll start playing again.

She takes the CHILDREN *into the room on the left and closes the door behind them.*

NORA (*uneasy, tense*) You want to speak to me?

KROGSTAD Yes.

NORA Today? But it's not the first of the month yet.

KROGSTAD No, it is Christmas Eve. Whether or not you have a merry Christmas depends on you.

NORA What do you want? I can't give you anything today—

KROGSTAD We won't talk about that for the present. There's something else. You have a moment to spare?

NORA Oh, yes. Yes, I suppose so; though—

KROGSTAD Good. I was sitting in the café down below and I saw your husband cross the street—

NORA Yes.

KROGSTAD With a lady.

NORA Well?

KROGSTAD Might I be so bold as to ask: was not that lady a Mrs. Linde?

NORA Yes.

KROGSTAD Recently arrived in town?

NORA Yes, today.

KROGSTAD She is a good friend of yours, is she not?

NORA Yes, she is. But I don't see—

KROGSTAD I used to know her too once.

NORA I know.

KROGSTAD Oh? You've discovered that. Yes, I thought you would. Well then, may I ask you a straight question: is Mrs. Linde to be employed at the bank?

NORA How dare you presume to cross-examine me, Mr. Krogstad? You, one of my husband's employees? But since you ask, you shall have an answer. Yes, Mrs. Linde is to be employed by the bank. And I arranged it, Mr. Krogstad. Now you know.

KROGSTAD I guessed right, then.

NORA (*walks up and down the room*) Oh, one has a little influence, you know. Just because one's a woman it doesn't necessarily mean that— When one is in a humble position, Mr. Krogstad, one should think twice before offending someone who—hm—

KROGSTAD —who has influence?

NORA Precisely.

KROGSTAD (*changes his tone*) Mrs. Helmer, will you have the kindness to use your influence on my behalf?

NORA What? What do you mean?

KROGSTAD Will you be so good as to see that I keep my humble position at the bank?

NORA What do you mean? Who is thinking of removing you from your position?

KROGSTAD Oh, you don't need to play innocent with me. I realize it can't be very pleasant for your friend to risk bumping into me; and now I also realize whom I have to thank for being hounded out like this.

NORA But I assure you—

KROGSTAD Look, let's not beat about the bush. There's still time, and I'd advise you to use your influence to stop it.

NORA But, Mr. Krogstad, I have no influence!

KROGSTAD Oh? I thought you just said—

NORA But I didn't mean it like that! I? How on earth could you imagine that I would have any influence over my husband?

KROGSTAD Oh, I've known your husband since we were students together. I imagine he has his weaknesses like other married men.

NORA If you speak impertinently of my husband, I shall show you the door.

KROGSTAD You're a bold woman, Mrs. Helmer.

NORA I'm not afraid of you any longer. Once the New Year is in, I'll soon be rid of you.

KROGSTAD (*more controlled*) Now listen to me, Mrs. Helmer. If I'm forced to, I shall fight for my little job at the bank as I would fight for my life.

NORA So it sounds.

KROGSTAD It isn't just the money; that's the last thing I care about. There's something else—well, you might as well know. It's like this, you see. You know of course, as everyone else does, that some years ago I committed an indiscretion.

NORA I think I did hear something—

KROGSTAD It never came into court; but from that day, every opening was barred to me. So I turned my hand to the kind of business you know about. I had to do something; and I don't think I was one of the worst. But now I want to give up all that. My sons are growing up; for their sake, I must try to regain what respectability I can. This job in the bank was the first step on the ladder. And now your husband wants to kick me off that ladder back into the dirt.

NORA But my dear Mr. Krogstad, it simply isn't in my power to help you.

KROGSTAD You say that because you don't want to help me. But I have the means to make you.

NORA You don't mean you'd tell my husband that I owe you money?

KROGSTAD And if I did?

NORA That'd be a filthy trick! (*Almost in tears.*) This secret that is my pride and my joy—that he should hear about it in such a filthy, beastly way—hear about it from you! It'd involve me in the most dreadful unpleasantness—

KROGSTAD Only—unpleasantness?

NORA (*vehemently*) All right, do it! You'll be the one who'll suffer. It'll show my husband the kind of man you are, and then you'll never keep your job.

KROGSTAD I asked you whether it was merely domestic unpleasantness you were afraid of.

NORA If my husband hears about it, he will of course immediately pay you whatever is owing. And then we shall have nothing more to do with you.

KROGSTAD (*takes a step closer*) Listen, Mrs. Helmer. Either you've a bad memory or else you know very little about financial transactions. I had better enlighten you.

NORA What do you mean?

KROGSTAD When your husband was ill, you came to me to borrow two hundred and fifty pounds.

NORA I didn't know anyone else.

KROGSTAD I promised to find that sum for you—

NORA And you did find it.

KROGSTAD I promised to find that sum for you on certain conditions. You were so worried about your husband's illness and so keen to get the money to take him abroad that I don't think you bothered much about the details. So it won't be out of place if I refresh your memory. Well—I promised to get you the money in exchange for an I.O.U., which I drew up.

NORA Yes, and which I signed.

KROGSTAD Exactly. But then I added a few lines naming your father as security for the debt. This paragraph was to be signed by your father.

NORA Was to be? He did sign it.

KROGSTAD I left the date blank for your father to fill in when he signed this paper. You remember, Mrs. Helmer?

NORA Yes, I think so—

KROGSTAD Then I gave you back this I.O.U. for you to post to your father. Is that not correct?

NORA Yes.

KROGSTAD And of course you posted it at once; for within five or six days you brought it along to me with your father's signature on it. Whereupon I handed you the money.

NORA Yes, well. Haven't I repaid the instalments as agreed?

KROGSTAD Mm—yes, more or less. But to return to what we were speaking about—that was a difficult time for you just then, wasn't it, Mrs. Helmer?

NORA Yes, it was.

KROGSTAD And your father was very ill, if I am not mistaken.

NORA He was dying.

KROGSTAD He did in fact die shortly afterwards?

NORA Yes.

KROGSTAD Tell me, Mrs. Helmer, do you by any chance remember the date of your father's death? The day of the month, I mean.

NORA Papa died on the twenty-ninth of September.

KROGSTAD Quite correct; I took the trouble to confirm it. And that leaves me with a curious little problem— (*Takes out a paper.*) —which I simply cannot solve.

NORA Problem? I don't see—

KROGSTAD The problem, Mrs. Helmer, is that your father signed this paper three days after his death.

NORA What? I don't understand—

KROGSTAD Your father died on the twenty-ninth of September. But look at this. Here your father has dated his signature the second of October. Isn't that a curious little problem, Mrs. Helmer? (NORA *is silent.*) Can you suggest any explanation? (*She remains silent.*) And there's another curious thing. The words "second of October" and the year are written in a hand which is not your father's, but which I seem to know. Well, there's a simple explanation to that. Your father could have forgotten to write in the date when he signed, and someone else could have added it before the news came of his death. There's nothing criminal about that. It's the signature itself I'm wondering about. It *is* genuine, I suppose, Mrs. Helmer? It was your father who wrote his name here?

NORA (*after a short silence, throws back her head and looks defiantly at him*) No, it was not. It was I who wrote Papa's name there.

KROGSTAD Look, Mrs. Helmer, do you realize this is a dangerous admission?

NORA Why? You'll get your money.

KROGSTAD May I ask you a question? Why didn't you send this paper to your father?

NORA I couldn't. Papa was very ill. If I'd asked him to sign this, I'd have had to tell him what the money was for. But I couldn't have told him in his condition that my husband's life was in danger. I couldn't have done that!

KROGSTAD Then you would have been wiser to have given up your idea of a holiday.

NORA But I couldn't! It was to save my husband's life. I couldn't put it off.

KROGSTAD But didn't it occur to you that you were being dishonest towards me?

NORA I couldn't bother about that. I didn't care about you. I hated you because of all the beastly difficulties you'd put in my way when you knew how dangerously ill my husband was.

KROGSTAD Mrs. Helmer, you evidently don't appreciate exactly what you have done. But I can assure you that it is no bigger nor worse a crime than the one I once committed, and thereby ruined my whole social position.

NORA You? Do you expect me to believe that you would have taken a risk like that to save your wife's life?

KROGSTAD The law does not concern itself with motives.

NORA Then the law must be very stupid.

KROGSTAD Stupid or not, if I show this paper to the police, you will be judged according to it.

NORA I don't believe that. Hasn't a daughter the right to shield her father from worry and anxiety when he's old and dying? Hasn't a wife the right to save her husband's life? I don't know much about the law, but there must be something somewhere that says that such things are allowed. You ought to know about that, you're meant to be a lawyer, aren't you? You can't be a very good lawyer, Mr. Krogstad.

KROGSTAD Possibly not. But business, the kind of business we two have been transacting—I think you'll admit I understand something about that? Good. Do as you please. But I tell you this. If I get thrown into the gutter for a second time, I shall take you with me.

He bows and goes out through the hall.

NORA (*stands for a moment in thought, then tosses her head*) What nonsense! He's trying to frighten me! I'm not that stupid. (*Busies herself gathering together the* CHILDREN's *clothes; then she suddenly stops.*) But—? No, it's impossible. I did it for love, didn't I?

CHILDREN (*in the doorway, left*) Mummy, the strange gentleman's gone out into the street.

NORA Yes, yes, I know. But don't talk to anyone about the strange gentleman. You hear? Not even to Daddy.

CHILDREN No, Mummy. Will you play with us again now?

NORA No, no. Not now.

CHILDREN Oh but, Mummy, you promised!

NORA I know, but I can't just now. Go back to the nursery. I've a lot to do. Go away, my darlings, go away. (*She pushes them gently into the other room, and closes the door behind them. She sits on the sofa, takes up her embroidery, stitches for a few moments, but soon stops.*) No! (*Throws the embroidery aside, gets up, goes to the door leading to the hall and calls.*) Helen! Bring in the Christmas tree! (*She goes to the table on the left and opens the drawer in it; then pauses again.*) No, but it's utterly impossible!

MAID (*enters with the tree*) Where shall I put it, madam?

NORA There, in the middle of the room.

MAID Will you be wanting anything else?

NORA No, thank you. I have everything I need.

The MAID *puts down the tree and goes out.*

NORA (*busy decorating the tree*) Now—candles here—and flowers here. That loathsome man! Nonsense, nonsense, there's nothing to be frightened about. The Christmas tree must be beautiful. I'll do everything that you like, Torvald. I'll sing for you, dance for you—

HELMER, *with a bundle of papers under his arm, enters.*

NORA Oh—are you back already?

HELMER Yes. Has anyone been here?

NORA Here? No.

HELMER That's strange. I saw Krogstad come out of the front door.

NORA Did you? Oh yes, that's quite right—Krogstad was here for a few minutes.

HELMER Nora, I can tell from your face, he's been here and asked you to put in a good word for him.

NORA Yes.

HELMER And you were to pretend you were doing it of your own accord? You weren't going to tell me he'd been here? He asked you to do that too, didn't he?

NORA Yes, Torvald. But—

HELMER Nora, Nora! And you were ready to enter into such a conspiracy? Talking to a man like that, and making him promises—and then, on top of it all, to tell me an untruth!

NORA An untruth?

HELMER Didn't you say no one had been here? (*Wags his finger.*) My little songbird must never do that again. A songbird must have a clean beak to sing with; otherwise she'll start twittering out of tune. (*Puts his arm round her waist*). Isn't that the way we want things? Yes, of course it is. (*Lets go of her.*) So let's hear no more about that. (*Sits down in front of the stove.*) Ah, how cosy and peaceful it is here. (*Glances for a few moments at his papers.*)

NORA (*busy with the tree; after a short silence*) Torvald.

HELMER Yes.

NORA I'm terribly looking forward to that fancy dress ball at the Stenborgs on Boxing Day.

HELMER And I'm terribly curious to see what you're going to surprise me with.

NORA Oh, it's so maddening.

HELMER What is?

NORA I can't think of anything to wear. It all seems so stupid and meaningless.

HELMER So my little Nora's come to that conclusion, has she?

NORA (*behind his chair, resting her arms on its back*) Are you very busy, Torvald?

HELMER Oh—

NORA What are those papers?

HELMER Just something to do with the bank.

NORA Already?

HELMER I persuaded the trustees to give me authority to make certain immediate changes in the staff and organization. I want to have everything straight by the New Year.

NORA Then that's why this poor man Krogstad—

HELMER Hm.

NORA (*still leaning over his chair, slowly strokes the back of his head*) If you hadn't been so busy, I was going to ask you an enormous favour, Torvald.

HELMER Well, tell me. What was it to be?

NORA You know I trust your taste more than anyone's. I'm so anxious to look really beautiful at the fancy dress ball. Torvald, couldn' you help me to decide what I shall go as, and what kind of costume I ought to wear?

HELMER Aha! So little Miss Independent's in trouble and needs a man to rescue her, does she?

NORA Yes, Torvald. I can't get anywhere without your help.

HELMER Well, well, I'll give the matter thought. We'll find something.

NORA Oh, how kind of you! (*Goes back to the tree. Pause.*) How pretty these red flowers look! But, tell me, is it so dreadful, this thing that Krogstad's done?

HELMER He forged someone else's name. Have you any idea what that means?

NORA Mightn't he have been forced to do it by some emergency?

HELMER He probably just didn't think—that's what usually happens. I'm not so heartless as to condemn a man for an isolated action.

NORA No, Torvald, of course not!

HELMER Men often succeed in re-establishing themselves if they admit their crime and take their punishment.

NORA Punishment?

HELMER But Krogstad didn't do that. He chose to try and trick his way out of it; and that's what has morally destroyed him.

NORA You think that would—?

HELMER Just think how a man with that load on his conscience must always be lying and cheating and dissembling; how he must wear a mask even in the presence of those who are dearest to him, even his own wife and children! Yes, the children. That's the worst danger, Nora.

NORA Why?

HELMER Because an atmosphere of lies contaminates and poisons every corner of the home. Every breath that the children draw in such a house contains the germs of evil.

NORA (*comes closer behind him*) Do you really believe that?

HELMER Oh, my dear, I've come across it so often in my work at the bar. Nearly all young criminals are the children of mothers who are constitutional liars.

NORA Why do you say mothers?

HELMER It's usually the mother; though of course the father can have the same influence. Every lawyer knows that only too well. And yet this fellow Krogstad has been sitting at home all these years poisoning his children with his lies and pretences. That's why I say that, morally speaking, he is dead. (*Stretches out his hands towards her.*) So my pretty little Nora must promise me not to plead his case. Your hand on it. Come, come, what's this? Give me your hand. There. That's settled, now. I assure you it'd be quite impossible for me to work in the same building as him. I literally feel physically ill in the presence of a man like that.

NORA (*draws her hand from his and goes over to the other side of the Christmas tree*) How hot it is in here! And I've so much to do.

HELMER (*gets up and gathers his papers*) Yes, and I must try to get some of this read before dinner. I'll think about your costume too. And I may even have something up my sleeve to hang in gold paper on the Christmas tree. (*Lays his hand on her head.*) My precious little songbird!

He goes into his study and closes the door.

NORA (*softly, after a pause*) It's nonsense. It must be. It's impossible. It *must* be impossible!

NURSE (*in the doorway, left*) The children are asking if they can come in to Mummy.

NORA No, no, no; don't let them in! You stay with them, Anne-Marie.

NURSE Very good, madam. (*Closes the door.*)

NORA (*pale with fear*) Corrupt my little children—! Poison my home! (*Short pause. She throws back her head.*) It isn't true! It *couldn't* be true!

ACT II

The same room. In the corner by the piano the Christmas tree stands, stripped and dishevelled, its candles burned to their sockets. NORA's outdoor clothes lie on the sofa. She is alone in the room, walking restlessly to and fro. At length she stops by the sofa and picks up her coat.

NORA (*drops the coat again*) There's someone coming! (*Goes to the door and listens.*) No, it's no one. Of course—no one'll come today, it's Christmas Day. Nor tomorrow. But perhaps—! (*Opens the door and looks out.*) No. Nothing in the letter-box. Quite empty. (*Walks across the room.*) Silly, silly. Of course he won't do anything. It couldn't happen. It isn't possible. Why, I've three small children.

The NURSE, carrying a large cardboard box, enters from the room on the left.

NURSE I found those fancy dress clothes at last, madam.

NORA Thank you. Put them on the table.

NURSE (*does so*) They're all rumpled up.

NORA Oh, I wish I could tear them into a million pieces!

NURSE Why, madam! They'll be all right. Just a little patience.

NORA Yes, of course. I'll go and get Mrs. Linde to help me.

NURSE What, out again? In this dreadful weather? You'll catch a chill, madam.

NORA Well, that wouldn't be the worst. How are the children?

NURSE Playing with their Christmas presents, poor little dears. But—

NORA Are they still asking to see me?

NURSE They're so used to having their Mummy with them.

NORA Yes, but, Anne-Marie, from now on I shan't be able to spend so much time with them.

NURSE Well, children get used to anything in time.

NORA Do you think so? Do you think they'd forget their mother if she went away from them—for ever?

NURSE Mercy's sake, madam! For ever!

NORA Tell me, Anne-Marie—I've so often wondered. How could you bear to give your child away—to strangers?

NURSE But I had to when I came to nurse my little Miss Nora.

NORA Do you mean you wanted to?

NURSE When I had the chance of such a good job? A poor girl what's got into trouble can't afford to pick and choose. That good-for-nothing didn't lift a finger.

NORA But your daughter must have completely forgotten you.

NURSE Oh no, indeed she hasn't. She's written to me twice, once when she got confirmed and then again when she got married.

NORA (hugs her) Dear old Anne-Marie, you were a good mother to me.

NURSE Poor little Miss Nora, you never had any mother but me.

NORA And if my little ones had no one else, I know you would—no, silly, silly, silly! (Opens the cardboard box.) Go back to them, Anne-Marie. Now I must— Tomorrow you'll see how pretty I shall look.

NURSE Why, there'll be no one at the ball as beautiful as my Miss Nora.

She goes into the room, left.

NORA (begins to unpack the clothes from the box, but soon throws them down again) Oh, if only I dared to go out! If I could be sure no one would come, and nothing would happen while I was away! Stupid, stupid! No one will come. I just mustn't think about it. Brush this muff. Pretty gloves, pretty gloves! Don't think about it, don't think about it! One, two, three, four, five, six— (Cries.) Ah—they're coming—!

She begins to run towards the door, but stops uncertainly. MRS. LINDE *enters from the hall, where she has been taking off her outdoor clothes.*

NORA Oh, it's you, Christine. There's no one else out there, is there? Oh, I'm so glad you've come.

MRS. LINDE I hear you were at my room asking for me.

NORA Yes, I just happened to be passing. I want to ask you to help me with something. Let's sit down here on the sofa. Look at this. There's going to be a fancy dress ball tomorrow night upstairs at Consul Stenborg's, and Torvald wants me to go as a Neapolitan fisher-girl and dance the tarantella. I learned it on Capri.

MRS. LINDE I say, are you going to give a performance?

NORA Yes, Torvald says I should. Look, here's the dress. Torvald had it made for me in Italy; but now it's all so torn, I don't know—

MRS. LINDE Oh, we'll soon put that right; the stitching's just come away. Needle and thread? Ah, here we are.

NORA You're being awfully sweet.

MRS. LINDE (*sews*) So you're going to dress up tomorrow, Nora? I must pop over for a moment to see how you look. Oh, but I've completely forgotten to thank you for that nice evening yesterday.

NORA (*gets up and walks across the room*) Oh, I didn't think it was as nice as usual. You ought to have come to town a little earlier, Christine. . . . Yes, Torvald understands how to make a home look attractive.

MRS. LINDE I'm sure you do, too. You're not your father's daughter for nothing. But, tell me. Is Dr. Rank always in such low spirits as he was yesterday?

NORA No, last night it was very noticeable. But he's got a terrible disease; he's got spinal tuberculosis, poor man. His father was a frightful creature who kept mistresses and so on. As a result Dr. Rank has been sickly ever since he was a child—you understand—

MRS. LINDE (*puts down her sewing*) But, my dear Nora, how on earth did you get to know about such things?

NORA (*walks about the room*) Oh, don't be silly, Christine—when one has three children, one comes into contact with women who—well, who know about medical matters, and they tell one a thing or two.

MRS. LINDE (*sews again; a short silence*) Does Dr. Rank visit you every day?

NORA Yes, every day. He's Torvald's oldest friend, and a good friend to me too. Dr. Rank's almost one of the family.

MRS. LINDE But, tell me—is he quite sincere? I mean, doesn't he rather say the sort of thing he thinks people want to hear?

NORA No, quite the contrary. What gave you that idea?

MRS. LINDE When you introduced me to him yesterday, he said he'd often heard my name mentioned here. But later I noticed your husband had no idea who I was. So how could Dr. Rank—?

NORA Yes, that's quite right, Christine. You see, Torvald's so hopelessly in love with me that he wants to have me all to himself—those were his very words. When we were first married, he got quite jealous if I as much as mentioned any of my old friends back home. So naturally, I stopped talking about them. But I often chat with Dr. Rank about that kind of thing. He enjoys it, you see.

MRS. LINDE Now listen, Nora. In many ways you're still a child; I'm a bit older than you and have a little more experience of the world. There's something I want to say to you. You ought to give up this business with Dr. Rank.

NORA What business?

MRS. LINDE Well, everything. Last night you were speaking about this rich admirer of yours who was going to give you money—

NORA Yes, and who doesn't exist—unfortunately. But what's that got to do with—?

MRS. LINDE Is Dr. Rank rich?

NORA Yes.

MRS. LINDE And he has no dependants?

NORA No, no one. But—

MRS. LINDE And he comes here to see you every day?

NORA Yes, I've told you.

MRS. LINDE But how dare a man of his education be so forward?

NORA What on earth are you talking about?

MRS. LINDE Oh, stop pretending, Nora. Do you think I haven't guessed who it was who lent you that two hundred pounds?

NORA Are you out of your mind? How could you imagine such a thing? A friend, someone who comes here every day! Why, that'd be an impossible situation!

MRS. LINDE Then it really wasn't him?

NORA No, of course not. I've never for a moment dreamed of—anyway, he hadn't any money to lend then. He didn't come into that till later.

MRS. LINDE Well, I think that was a lucky thing for you, Nora dear.

NORA No, I could never have dreamed of asking Dr. Rank—Though I'm sure that if I ever did ask him—

MRS. LINDE But of course you won't.

NORA Of course not. I can't imagine that it should ever become necessary. But I'm perfectly sure that if I did speak to Dr. Rank—

MRS. LINDE Behind your husband's back?

NORA I've got to get out of this other business; and *that's* been going on behind his back. I've *got* to get out of it.

MRS. LINDE Yes, well, that's what I told you yesterday. But—

NORA (*walking up and down*) It's much easier for a man to arrange these things than a woman—

MRS. LINDE One's own husband, yes.

NORA Oh, bosh. (*Stops walking.*) When you've completely repaid a debt, you get your I.O.U. back, don't you?

MRS. LINDE Yes, of course.

NORA And you can tear it into a thousand pieces and burn the filthy, beastly thing!

MRS. LINDE (*looks hard at her, puts down her sewing and gets up slowly*) Nora, you're hiding something from me.

NORA Can you see that?

MRS. LINDE Something has happened since yesterday morning. Nora, what is it?

NORA (*goes towards her*) Christine! (*Listens.*) Ssh! There's Torvald. Would you mind going into the nursery for a few minutes? Torvald can't bear to see sewing around. Anne-Marie'll help you.

MRS. LINDE (*gathers some of her things together*) Very well. But I shan't leave this house until we've talked this matter out.

She goes into the nursery, left. As she does so, HELMER *enters from the hall.*

NORA (*runs to meet him*) Oh, Torvald dear, I've been so longing for you to come back!

HELMER Was that the dressmaker?

NORA No, it was Christine. She's helping me mend my costume. I'm going to look rather splendid in that.

HELMER Yes, that was quite a bright idea of mine, wasn't it?

NORA Wonderful! But wasn't it nice of me to give in to you?

HELMER (*takes her chin in his hand*) Nice—to give in to your husband? All right, little silly, I know you didn't mean it like that. But I won't disturb you. I expect you'll be wanting to try it on.

NORA Are you going to work now?

HELMER Yes. (*Shows her a bundle of papers.*) Look at these. I've been down to the bank— (*Turns to go into his study.*)

NORA Torvald.

HELMER (*stops*) Yes.

NORA If little squirrel asked you really prettily to grant her a wish—

HELMER Well?

NORA Would you grant it to her?

HELMER First I should naturally have to know what it was.

NORA Squirrel would do lots of pretty tricks for you if you granted her wish.

HELMER Out with it, then.

NORA Your little skylark would sing in every room—

HELMER My little skylark does that already.

NORA I'd turn myself into a little fairy and dance for you in the moonlight, Torvald.

HELMER Nora, it isn't that business you were talking about this morning?

NORA (comes closer) Yes, Torvald—oh, please! I beg of you!

HELMER Have you really the nerve to bring that up again?

NORA Yes, Torvald, yes, you must do as I ask! You must let Krogstad keep his place at the bank!

HELMER My dear Nora, his is the job I'm giving to Mrs. Linde.

NORA Yes, that's terribly sweet of you. But you can get rid of one of the other clerks instead of Krogstad.

HELMER Really, you're being incredibly obstinate. Just because you thoughtlessly promised to put in a word for him, you expect me to—

NORA No, it isn't that, Helmer. It's for your own sake. That man writes for the most beastly newspapers—you said so yourself. He could do you tremendous harm. I'm so dreadfully frightened of him—

HELMER Oh, I understand. Memories of the past. That's what's frightening you.

NORA What do you mean?

HELMER You're thinking of your father, aren't you?

NORA Yes, yes. Of course. Just think what those dreadful men wrote in the papers about Papa! The most frightful slanders. I really believe it would have lost him his job if the Ministry hadn't sent you down to investigate, and you hadn't been so kind and helpful to him.

HELMER But my dear little Nora, there's a considerable difference between your father and me. Your father was not a man of unassailable reputation. But I am; and I hope to remain so all my life.

NORA But no one knows what spiteful people may not dig up. We could be so peaceful and happy now, Torvald—we could be free from every worry—you and I and the children. Oh, please, Torvald, please—!

HELMER The very fact of your pleading his cause makes it impossible for me to keep him. Everyone at the bank already knows that I intend to dismiss Krogstad. If the rumour got about that the new manager had allowed his wife to persuade him to change his mind—

NORA Well, what then?

HELMER Oh, nothing, nothing. As long as my little Miss Obstinate gets her way—! Do you expect me to make a laughing-stock of myself before my entire staff—give people the idea that I am open to outside influence? Believe me, I'd soon feel the consequences! Besides—there's something else that makes it impossible for Krogstad to remain in the bank while I am its manager.

NORA What is that?

HELMER I might conceivably have allowed myself to ignore his moral obloquies—

NORA Yes, Torvald, surely?

HELMER And I hear he's quite efficient at his job. But we—well, we were schoolfriends. It was one of those friendships that one enters into over-hastily and so often comes to regret later in life. I might as well confess the truth. We—well, we're on Christian name terms. And the tactless idiot makes no attempt to conceal it when other people are present. On the contrary, he thinks it gives him the right to be familiar with me. He shows off the whole time, with "Torvald this," and "Torvald that." I can tell you, I find it damned annoying. If he stayed, he'd make my position intolerable.

NORA Torvald, you can't mean this seriously.

HELMER Oh? And why not?

NORA But it's so petty.

HELMER What did you say? Petty? You think I am petty?

NORA No, Torvald dear, of course you're not. That's just why—

HELMER Don't quibble! You call my motives petty. Then I must be petty too. Petty! I see. Well, I've had enough of this. (*Goes to the door and calls into the hall.*) Helen!

NORA What are you going to do?

HELMER (*searching among his papers*) I'm going to settle this matter once and for all. (*The* MAID *enters.*) Take this letter downstairs at once. Find a messenger and see that he delivers it. Immediately! The address is on the envelope. Here's the money.

MAID Very good, sir. (*Goes out with the letter.*)

HELMER (*putting his papers in order*) There now, little Miss Obstinate.

NORA (*tensely*) Torvald—what was in that letter?

HELMER Krogstad's dismissal.

NORA Call her back, Torvald! There's still time. Oh, Torvald, call her back! Do it for my sake—for your own sake—for the children! Do you hear me, Torvald? Please do it! You don't realize what this may do to us all!

HELMER Too late.

NORA Yes. Too late.

HELMER My dear Nora, I forgive you this anxiety. Though it is a bit of an insult to me. Oh, but it is! Isn't it an insult to imply that I should be frightened by the vindictiveness of a depraved hack journalist? But I forgive you, because it so charmingly testifies to the love you bear me. (*Takes her in his arms.*) Which is as it should be, my own dearest Nora. Let what will happen, happen. When the real crisis comes, you will not find me lacking in strength or courage. I am man enough to bear the burden for us both.

NORA (*fearfully*) What do you mean?

HELMER The whole burden, I say—

NORA (*calmly*) I shall never let you do that.

HELMER Very well. We shall share it, Nora—as man and wife. And that is as it should be. (*Caresses her.*) Are you happy now? There, there, there; don't look at me with those frightened little eyes. You're simply imagining things. You go ahead now and do your tarantella, and get some practice on that tambourine. I'll sit in my study and close the door. Then I won't hear anything, and you can make all the noise you want. (*Turns in the doorway.*) When Dr. Rank comes, tell him where to find me. (*He nods to her, goes into his room with his papers and closes the door.*)

NORA (*desperate with anxiety, stands as though transfixed, and whispers*) He said he'd do it. He will do it. He will do it, and nothing'll stop him. No, never that. I'd rather anything. There must be some escape—! Some way out—! (*The bell rings in the hall.*) Dr. Rank—! Anything but that! Anything, I don't care—!

She passes her hand across her face, composes herself, walks across and opens the door to the hall. DR. RANK *is standing there, hanging up his fur coat. During the following scene it begins to grow dark.*

NORA Good evening, Dr. Rank. I recognized your ring. But you mustn't go in to Torvald yet. I think he's busy.

RANK And—you?

NORA (*as he enters the room and she closes the door behind him*) Oh, you know very well I've always time to talk to you.

RANK Thank you. I shall avail myself of that privilege as long as I can.

NORA What do you mean by that? As long as you *can?*

RANK Yes. Does that frighten you?

NORA Well, it's rather a curious expression. Is something going to happen?

RANK Something I've been expecting to happen for a long time. But I didn't think it would happen quite so soon.

NORA (*seizes his arm*) What is it? Dr. Rank, you must tell me!

RANK (*sits down by the stove*) I'm on the way out. And there's nothing to be done about it.

NORA (*sighs with relief*) Oh, it's you—?

RANK Who else? No, it's no good lying to oneself. I am the most wretched of all my patients, Mrs. Helmer. These last few days I've been going through the books of this poor body of mine, and I find I am bankrupt. Within a month I may be rotting up there in the churchyard.

NORA Ugh, what a nasty way to talk!

RANK The facts aren't exactly nice. But the worst is that there's so much else that's nasty to come first. I've only one more test to make. When that's done I'll have a pretty accurate idea of when the final disintegration is likely to begin. I want to ask you a favour. Helmer's a sensitive chap, and I know how he hates anything ugly. I don't want him to visit me when I'm in hospital—

NORA Oh but, Dr. Rank—

RANK I don't want him there. On any pretext. I shan't have him allowed in. As soon as I know the worst, I'll send you my visiting card with a black cross on it, and then you'll know that the final filthy process has begun.

NORA Really, you're being quite impossible this evening. And I did hope you'd be in a good mood.

RANK With death on my hands? And all this to atone for someone else's sin? Is there justice in that? And in every single family, in one way or another, the same merciless law of retribution is at work—

NORA (*holds her hands to her ears*) Nonsense! Cheer up! Laugh!

RANK Yes, you're right. Laughter's all the damned thing's fit for. My poor innocent spine must pay for the fun my father had as a gay young lieutenant.

NORA (*at the table, left*) You mean he was too fond of asparagus and *foie gras?*

RANK Yes; and truffles too.

NORA Yes, of course, truffles, yes. And oysters too, I suppose?

RANK Yes, oysters, oysters. Of course.

NORA And all that port and champagne to wash them down. It's too sad that all those lovely things should affect one's spine.

RANK Especially a poor spine that never got any pleasure out of them.

NORA Oh yes, that's the saddest thing of all.

RANK (*looks searchingly at her*) Hm—

NORA (*after a moment*) Why did you smile?

RANK No, it was you who laughed.

NORA No, it was you who smiled, Dr. Rank!

RANK (*gets up*) You're a worse little rogue than I thought.

NORA Oh, I'm full of stupid tricks today.

RANK So it seems.

NORA (*puts both her hands on his shoulders*) Dear, dear Dr. Rank, you mustn't die and leave Torvald and me.

RANK Oh, you'll soon get over it. Once one is gone, one is soon forgotten.

NORA (*looks at him anxiously*) Do you believe that?

RANK One finds replacements, and then—

NORA Who will find a replacement?

RANK You and Helmer both will, when I am gone. You seem to have made a start already, haven't you? What was this Mrs. Linde doing here yesterday evening?

NORA Aha! But surely you can't be jealous of poor Christine?

RANK Indeed I am. She will be my successor in this house. When I have moved on, this lady will—

NORA Ssh—don't speak so loud! She's in there!

RANK Today again? You see!

NORA She's only come to mend my dress. Good heavens, how unreasonable you are! (*Sits on the sofa.*) Be nice now, Dr. Rank. Tomorrow you'll see how beautifully I shall dance; and you must imagine that I'm doing it just for you. And for Torvald, of course; obviously. (*Takes some things out of the box.*) Dr. Rank, sit down here and I'll show you something.

RANK (*sits*) What's this?

NORA Look here! Look!

RANK Silk stockings!

NORA Flesh-coloured. Aren't they beautiful? It's very dark in here now, of course, but tomorrow—! No, no, no; only the soles. Oh well, I suppose you can look a bit higher if you want to.

RANK Hm—

NORA Why are you looking so critical? Don't you think they'll fit me?

RANK I can't really give you a qualified opinion on that.

NORA (*looks at him for a moment*) Shame on you! (*Flicks him on the ear with the stockings.*) Take that. (*Puts them back in the box.*)

RANK What other wonders are to be revealed to me?

NORA I shan't show you anything else. You're being naughty.

She hums a little and looks among the things in the box.

RANK (*after a short silence*) When I sit here like this being so intimate with you, I can't think—I cannot imagine what would have become of me if I had never entered this house.

NORA (*smiles*) Yes, I think you enjoy being with us, don't you?

RANK (*more quietly, looking into the middle distance*) And now to have to leave it all—

NORA Nonsense. You're not leaving us.

RANK (*as before*) And not to be able to leave even the most wretched token of gratitude behind; hardly even a passing sense of loss; only an empty place, to be filled by the next comer.

NORA Suppose I were to ask you to—? No—

RANK To do what?

NORA To give me proof of your friendship—

RANK Yes, yes?

NORA No, I mean—to do me a very great service—

RANK Would you really for once grant me that happiness?

NORA But you've no idea what it is.

RANK Very well, tell me, then.

NORA No, but, Dr. Rank, I can't. It's far too much—I want your help and advice, and I want you to do something for me.

RANK The more the better. I've no idea what it can be. But tell me. You do trust me, don't you?

NORA Oh, yes, more than anyone. You're my best and truest friend. Otherwise I couldn't tell you. Well then, Dr. Rank—there's something you must help me to prevent. You know how much Torvald loves me—he'd never hesitate for an instant to lay down his life for me—

RANK (*leans over towards her*) Nora—do you think he is the only one—?

NORA (*with a slight start*) What do you mean?

RANK Who would gladly lay down his life for you?

NORA (*sadly*) Oh, I see.

RANK I swore to myself I would let you know that before I go. I shall never have a better opportunity. . . . Well, Nora, now you know that. And now you also know that you can trust me as you can trust nobody else.

NORA (*rises; calmly and quietly*) Let me pass, please.

RANK (*makes room for her but remains seated*) Nora—

NORA (*in the doorway to the hall*) Helen, bring the lamp. (*Goes over to the stove.*) Oh, dear Dr. Rank, this was really horrid of you.

RANK (*gets up*) That I have loved you as deeply as anyone else has? Was that horrid of me?

NORA No—but that you should go and tell me. That was quite unnecessary—

RANK What do you mean? Did you know, then—?

The MAID *enters with the lamp, puts it on the table and goes out.*

RANK Nora—Mrs. Helmer—I am asking you, did you know this?

NORA Oh, what do I know, what did I know, what didn't I know—I really can't say. How could you be so stupid, Dr. Rank? Everything was so nice.

RANK Well, at any rate now you know that I am ready to serve you, body and soul. So—please continue.

NORA (*looks at him*) After this?

RANK Please tell me what it is.

NORA I can't possibly tell you now.

RANK Yes, yes! You mustn't punish me like this. Let me be allowed to do what I can for you.

NORA You can't do anything for me now. Anyway, I don't need any help. It was only my imagination—you'll see. Yes, really. Honestly. (*Sits in the rocking-chair, looks at him and smiles.*) Well, upon my word you *are* a fine gentleman, Dr. Rank. Aren't you ashamed of yourself, now that the lamp's been lit?

RANK Frankly, no. But perhaps I ought to say—*adieu?*

NORA Of course not. You will naturally continue to visit us as before. You know quite well how Torvald depends on your company.

RANK Yes, but you?

NORA Oh, I always think it's enormous fun having you here.

RANK That was what misled me. You're a riddle to me, you know. I'd often felt you'd just as soon be with me as with Helmer.

NORA Well, you see, there are some people whom one loves, and others whom it's almost more fun to be with.

RANK Oh yes, there's some truth in that.

NORA When I was at home, of course I loved Papa best. But I always used to think it was terribly amusing to go down and talk to the servants; because they never told me what I ought to do; and they were such fun to listen to.

RANK I see. So I've taken their place?

NORA (jumps up and runs over to him) Oh, dear, sweet Dr. Rank, I didn't mean that at all. But I'm sure you understand—I feel the same about Torvald as I did about Papa.

MAID (enters from the hall) Excuse me, madam. (Whispers to her and hands her a visiting card.)

NORA (glances at the card) Oh! (Puts it quickly in her pocket.)

RANK Anything wrong?

NORA No, no, nothing at all. It's just something that—it's my new dress.

RANK What? But your costume is lying over there.

NORA Oh—that, yes—but there's another—I ordered it specially—Torvald mustn't know—

RANK Ah, so that's your big secret?

NORA Yes, yes. Go in and talk to him—he's in his study—keep him talking for a bit—

RANK Don't worry. He won't get away from me. (Goes into HELMER's study.)

NORA (to the MAID) Is he waiting in the kitchen?

MAID Yes, madam, he came up the back way—

NORA But didn't you tell him I had a visitor?

MAID Yes, but he wouldn't go.

NORA Wouldn't go?

MAID No, madam, not until he'd spoken with you.

NORA Very well, show him in; but quietly. Helen, you mustn't tell anyone about this. It's a surprise for my husband.

MAID Very good, madam. I understand. (Goes.)

NORA It's happening. It's happening after all. No, no, no, it can't happen, it mustn't happen.

She walks across and bolts the door of HELMER's study. The MAID opens the door from the hall to admit KROGSTAD, and closes it behind him. He is wearing an overcoat, heavy boots and a fur cap.

NORA (goes towards him) Speak quietly. My husband's at home.

KROGSTAD Let him hear.

NORA What do you want from me?

KROGSTAD Information.

NORA Hurry up, then. What is it?

KROGSTAD I suppose you know I've been given the sack.

NORA I couldn't stop it, Mr. Krogstad. I did my best for you, but it didn't help.

KROGSTAD Does your husband love you so little? He knows what I can do to you, and yet he dares to—

NORA Surely you don't imagine I told him?

KROGSTAD No, I didn't really think you had. It wouldn't have been like my old friend Torvald Helmer to show that much courage—

NORA Mr. Krogstad, I'll trouble you to speak respectfully of my husband.

KROGSTAD Don't worry, I'll show him all the respect he deserves. But since you're so anxious to keep this matter hushed up, I presume you're better informed than you were yesterday of the gravity of what you've done?

NORA I've learned more than you could ever teach me.

KROGSTAD Yes, a bad lawyer like me—

NORA What do you want from me?

KROGSTAD I just wanted to see how things were with you, Mrs. Helmer. I've been thinking about you all day. Even duns and hack journalists have hearts, you know.

NORA Show some heart, then. Think of my little children.

KROGSTAD Have you and your husband thought of mine? Well, let's forget that. I just wanted to tell you, you don't need to take this business too seriously. I'm not going to take any action, for the present.

NORA Oh, no—you won't, will you? I knew it.

KROGSTAD It can all be settled quite amicably. There's no need for it to become public. We'll keep it among the three of us.

NORA My husband must never know about this.

KROGSTAD How can you stop him? Can you pay the balance of what you owe me?

NORA Not immediately.

KROGSTAD Have you any means of raising the money during the next few days?

NORA None that I would care to use.

KROGSTAD Well, it wouldn't have helped anyway. However much money you offered me now I wouldn't give you back that paper.

NORA What are you going to do with it?

KROGSTAD Just keep it. No one else need ever hear about it. So in case you were thinking of doing anything desperate—

NORA I am.

KROGSTAD Such as running away—

NORA I am.

KROGSTAD Or anything more desperate—

NORA How did you know?

KROGSTAD —just give up the idea.

NORA How did you know?

KROGSTAD Most of us think of that at first. I did. But I hadn't the courage—

NORA (*dully*) Neither have I.

KROGSTAD (*relieved*) It's true, isn't it? You haven't the courage either?

NORA No. I haven't. I haven't.

KROGSTAD It'd be a stupid thing to do anyway. Once the first little domestic explosion is over. . . . I've got a letter in my pocket here addressed to your husband—

NORA Telling him everything?

KROGSTAD As delicately as possible.

NORA (*quickly*) He must never see that letter. Tear it up. I'll find the money somehow—

KROGSTAD I'm sorry, Mrs. Helmer, I thought I'd explained—

NORA Oh, I don't mean the money I owe you. Let me know how much you want from my husband, and I'll find it for you.

KROGSTAD I'm not asking your husband for money.

NORA What do you want, then?

KROGSTAD I'll tell you. I want to get on my feet again, Mrs. Helmer. I want to get to the top. And your husband's going to help me. For eighteen months now my record's been clean. I've been in hard straits all that time; I was content to fight my way back inch by inch. Now I've been chucked back into the mud, and I'm not going to be satisfied with just getting back my job. I'm going to get to the top, I tell you. I'm going to get back into the bank, and it's going to be higher up. Your husband's going to create a new job for me—

NORA He'll never do that!

KROGSTAD Oh, yes he will. I know him. He won't dare to risk a scandal. And once I'm in there with him, you'll see! Within a year I'll be his right-hand man. It'll be Nils Krogstad who'll be running that bank, not Torvald Helmer!

NORA That will never happen.

KROGSTAD Are you thinking of—?

NORA Now I *have* the courage.

KROGSTAD Oh, you can't frighten me. A pampered little pretty like you—

NORA You'll see! You'll see!

KROGSTAD Under the ice? Down in the cold, black water? And then, in the spring, to float up again, ugly, unrecognizable, hairless—?

NORA You can't frighten me.

KROGSTAD And you can't frighten me. People don't do such things, Mrs. Helmer. And anyway, what'd be the use? I've got him in my pocket.

NORA But afterwards? When I'm no longer—?

KROGSTAD Have you forgotten that then your reputation will be in my hands? (*She looks at him speechlessly.*) Well, I've warned you. Don't do anything silly. When Helmer's read my letter, he'll get in touch with me. And remember, it's your husband who's forced me to act like this. And for that I'll never forgive him. Goodbye, Mrs. Helmer. (*He goes out through the hall*).

NORA (*runs to the hall door, opens it a few inches and listens*) He's going. He's not going to give him the letter. Oh, no, no, it couldn't possibly happen. (*Opens the door a little wider.*) What's he doing? Standing outside the front door. He's not going downstairs. Is he changing his mind? Yes, he—!

A letter falls into the letter-box. KROGSTAD's *footsteps die away down the stairs.*

NORA (*with a stifled cry, runs across the room towards the table by the sofa. A pause*) In the letter-box. (*Steals timidly over towards the hall door.*) There it is! Oh, Torvald, Torvald! Now we're lost!

MRS. LINDE (*enters from the nursery with* NORA's *costume*) Well, I've done the best I can. Shall we see how it looks—?

NORA (*whispers hoarsely*) Christine, come here.

MRS. LINDE (*throws the dress on the sofa*) What's wrong with you? You look as though you'd seen a ghost!

NORA Come here. Do you see that letter? There—look—through the glass of the letter-box.

MRS. LINDE Yes, yes, I see it.

NORA That letter's from Krogstad—

MRS. LINDE Nora! It was Krogstad who lent you the money!

NORA Yes. And now Torvald's going to discover everything.

MRS. LINDE Oh, believe me, Nora, it'll be best for you both.

NORA You don't know what's happened. I've committed a forgery—

MRS. LINDE But, for heaven's sake—!

NORA Christine, all I want is for you to be my witness.

MRS. LINDE What do you mean? Witness what?

NORA If I should go out of my mind—and it might easily happen—

MRS. LINDE Nora!

NORA Or if anything else should happen to me—so that I wasn't here any longer—

MRS. LINDE Nora, Nora, you don't know what you're saying!

NORA If anyone should try to take the blame, and say it was all his fault—you understand—?

MRS. LINDE Yes, yes—but how can you think—?

NORA Then you must testify that it isn't true, Christine. I'm not mad—I know exactly what I'm saying—and I'm telling you, no one else knows anything about this. I did it entirely on my own. Remember that.

MRS. LINDE All right. But I simply don't understand—

NORA Oh, how could you understand? A—miracle—is about to happen.

MRS. LINDE Miracle?

NORA Yes. A miracle. But it's so frightening, Christine. It *mustn't* happen, not for anything in the world.

MRS. LINDE I'll go over and talk to Krogstad.

NORA Don't go near him. He'll only do something to hurt you.

MRS. LINDE Once upon a time he'd have done anything for my sake.

NORA He?

MRS. LINDE Where does he live?

NORA Oh, how should I know—? Oh, yes, wait a moment—! (*Feels in her pocket.*) Here's his card. But the letter, the letter—!

HELMER (*from his study, knocks on the door*) Nora!

NORA (*cries in alarm*) What is it?

HELMER Now, now, don't get alarmed. We're not coming in; you've closed the door. Are you trying on your costume?

NORA Yes, yes—I'm trying on my costume. I'm going to look so pretty for you, Torvald.

MRS. LINDE (*who has been reading the card*) Why, he lives just around the corner.

NORA Yes; but it's no use. There's nothing to be done now. The letter's lying there in the box.

MRS. LINDE And your husband has the key?

NORA Yes, he always keeps it.

MRS. LINDE Krogstad must ask him to send the letter back unread. He must find some excuse—

NORA But Torvald always opens the box at just about this time—

MRS. LINDE You must stop him. Go in and keep him talking. I'll be back as quickly as I can.

She hurries out through the hall.

NORA (*goes over to* HELMER's *door, opens it and peeps in*) Torvald!

HELMER (*offstage*) Well, may a man enter his own drawing-room again? Come on, Rank, now we'll see what— (*In the doorway.*) But what's this?

NORA What, Torvald dear?

HELMER Rank's been preparing me for some great transformation scene.

RANK (*in the doorway*) So I understood. But I seem to have been mistaken.

NORA Yes, no one's to be allowed to see me before tomorrow night.

HELMER But, my dear Nora, you look quite worn out. Have you been practising too hard?

NORA No, I haven't practised at all yet.

HELMER Well, you must.

NORA Yes, Torvald, I must, I know. But I can't get anywhere without your help. I've completely forgotten everything.

HELMER Oh, we'll soon put that to rights.

NORA Yes, help me, Torvald. Promise me you will? Oh, I'm so nervous. All those people—! You must forget everything except me this evening. You mustn't think of business—I won't even let you touch a pen. Promise me, Torvald?

HELMER I promise. This evening I shall think of nothing but you—my poor, helpless little darling. Oh, there's just one thing I must see to—(*Goes towards the hall door.*)

NORA What do you want out there?

HELMER I'm only going to see if any letters have come.

NORA No, Torvald, no!

HELMER Why, what's the matter?

NORA Torvald, I beg you. There's nothing there.

HELMER Well, I'll just make sure.

He moves towards the door. NORA *runs to the piano and plays the first bars of the tarantella.*

HELMER (*at the door, turns*) Aha!

NORA I can't dance tomorrow if I don't practise with you now.

HELMER (*goes over to her*) Are you really so frightened, Nora dear?

NORA Yes, terribly frightened. Let me start practising now, at once—we've still time before dinner. Oh, do sit down and play for me, Torvald dear. Correct me, lead me, the way you always do.

HELMER Very well, my dear, if you wish it.

He sits down at the piano. NORA *seizes the tambourine and a long multi-coloured shawl from the cardboard box, wraps the latter hastily around her, then takes a quick leap into the centre of the room.*

NORA Play for me! I want to dance!

HELMER *plays and* NORA *dances.* DR. RANK *stands behind* HELMER *at the piano and watches her.*

HELMER (*as he plays*) Slower, slower!

NORA I can't!

HELMER Not so violently, Nora.

NORA I must!

HELMER (*stops playing*) No, no, this won't do at all.

NORA (*laughs and swings her tambourine*) Isn't that what I told you?

RANK Let me play for her.

HELMER (*gets up*) Yes, would you? Then it'll be easier for me to show her.

RANK *sits down at the piano and plays.* NORA *dances more and more wildly.* HELMER *has stationed himself by the stove and tries repeatedly to correct her, but she seems not to hear him. Her hair works loose and falls over her shoulders; she ignores it and continues to dance.* MRS. LINDE *enters.*

MRS. LINDE (*stands in the doorway as though tongue-tied*) Ah—!

NORA (*as she dances*) Oh, Christine, we're having such fun!

HELMER But, Nora darling, you're dancing as if your life depended on it.

NORA It does.

HELMER Rank, stop it! This is sheer lunacy. Stop it, I say!

RANK *ceases playing.* NORA *suddenly stops dancing.*

HELMER (*goes over to her*) I'd never have believed it. You've forgotten everything I taught you.

NORA (*throws away the tambourine*) You see!

HELMER I'll have to show you every step.

NORA You see how much I need you! You must show me every step of the way. Right to the end of the dance. Promise me you will, Torvald?

HELMER Never fear. I will.

NORA You mustn't think about anything but me—today or tomorrow. Don't open any letters—don't even open the letter-box—

HELMER Aha, you're still worried about that fellow—

NORA Oh, yes, yes, him too.

HELMER Nora, I can tell from the way you're behaving, there's a letter from him already lying there.

NORA I don't know. I think so. But you mustn't read it now. I don't want anything ugly to come between us till it's all over.

RANK (*quietly, to* HELMER) Better give her her way.

HELMER (*puts his arm round her*) My child shall have her way. But tomorrow night, when your dance is over—

NORA Then you will be free.

MAID (*appears in the doorway, right*) Dinner is served, madam.

NORA Put out some champagne, Helen.

MAID Very good, madam. (*Goes.*)

HELMER I say! What's this, a banquet?

NORA We'll drink champagne until dawn! (*Calls.*) And, Helen! Put out some macaroons! Lots of macaroons—for once!

HELMER (*takes her hands in his*) Now, now, now. Don't get so excited. Where's my little songbird, the one I know?

NORA All right. Go and sit down—and you too, Dr. Rank. I'll be with you in a minute. Christine, you must help me put my hair up.

RANK (*quietly, as they go*) There's nothing wrong, is there? I mean, she isn't—er—expecting—?

HELMER Good heavens no, my dear chap. She just gets scared like a child sometimes—I told you before—

They go out right.

NORA Well?

MRS. LINDE He's left town.

NORA I saw it from your face.

MRS. LINDE He'll be back tomorrow evening. I left a note for him.

NORA You needn't have bothered. You can't stop anything now. Anyway, it's wonderful really, in a way—sitting here and waiting for the miracle to happen.

MRS. LINDE Waiting for what?

NORA Oh, you wouldn't understand. Go in and join them. I'll be with you in a moment.

MRS. LINDE *goes into the dining-room.*

NORA (*stands for a moment as though collecting herself. Then she looks at her watch*) Five o'clock. Seven hours till midnight. Then another twenty-four hours till midnight tomorrow. And then the tarantella will be finished. Twenty-four and seven? Thirty-one hours to live.

HELMER (*appears in the doorway, right*) What's happened to my little songbird?

NORA (*runs to him with her arms wide*) Your songbird is here!

ACT III

The same room. The table which was formerly by the sofa has been moved into the centre of the room; the chairs surround it as before. The door to the hall stands open. Dance music can be heard from the floor above. MRS. LINDE is seated at the table, absent-mindedly glancing through a book. She is trying to read, but seems unable to keep her mind on it. More than once she turns and listens anxiously towards the front door.

MRS. LINDE (*looks at her watch*) Not here yet. There's not much time left. Please God he hasn't—! (*Listens again.*) Ah, here he is. (*Goes out into the hall and cautiously opens the front door. Footsteps can be heard softly ascending the stairs. She whispers.*) Come in. There's no one here.

KROGSTAD (*in the doorway*) I found a note from you at my lodgings. What does this mean?

MRS. LINDE I must speak with you.

KROGSTAD Oh? And must our conversation take place in this house?

MRS. LINDE We couldn't meet at my place; my room has no separate entrance. Come in. We're quite alone. The maid's asleep, and the Helmers are at the dance upstairs.

KROGSTAD (*comes into the room*) Well, well! So the Helmers are dancing this evening? Are they indeed?

MRS. LINDE Yes, why not?

KROGSTAD True enough. Why not?

MRS. LINDE Well, Krogstad. You and I must have a talk together.

KROGSTAD Have we two anything further to discuss?

MRS. LINDE We have a great deal to discuss.

KROGSTAD I wasn't aware of it.

MRS. LINDE That's because you've never really understood me.

KROGSTAD Was there anything to understand? It's the old story, isn't it—a woman chucking a man because something better turns up?

MRS. LINDE Do you really think I'm so utterly heartless? You think it was easy for me to give you up?

KROGSTAD Wasn't it?

MRS. LINDE Oh, Nils, did you really believe that?

KROGSTAD Then why did you write to me the way you did?

MRS. LINDE I had to. Since I had to break with you, I thought it my duty to destroy all the feelings you had for me.

KROGSTAD (*clenches his fists*) So that was it. And you did this for money!

MRS. LINDE You mustn't forget I had a helpless mother to take care of, and two little brothers. We couldn't wait for you, Nils. It would have been so long before you'd had enough to support us.

KROGSTAD Maybe. But you had no right to cast me off for someone else.

MRS. LINDE Perhaps not. I've often asked myself that.

KROGSTAD (*more quietly*) When I lost you, it was just as though all solid ground had been swept from under my feet. Look at me. Now I am a shipwrecked man, clinging to a spar.

MRS. LINDE Help may be near at hand.

KROGSTAD It was near. But then you came, and stood between it and me.

MRS. LINDE I didn't know, Nils. No one told me till today that this job I'd found was yours.

KROGSTAD I believe you, since you say so. But now you know, won't you give it up?

MRS. LINDE No—because it wouldn't help you even if I did.

KROGSTAD Wouldn't it? I'd do it all the same.

MRS. LINDE I've learned to look at things practically. Life and poverty have taught me that.

KROGSTAD And life has taught me to distrust fine words.

MRS. LINDE Then it's taught you a useful lesson. But surely you still believe in actions?

KROGSTAD What do you mean?

MRS. LINDE You said you were like a shipwrecked man clinging to a spar.

KROGSTAD I have good reason to say it.

MRS. LINDE I'm in the same position as you. No one to care about, no one to care for.

KROGSTAD You made your own choice.

MRS. LINDE I had no choice—then.

KROGSTAD Well?

MRS. LINDE Nils, suppose we two shipwrecked souls could join hands?

KROGSTAD What are you saying?

MRS. LINDE Castaways have a better chance of survival together than on their own.

KROGSTAD Christine!

MRS. LINDE Why do you suppose I came to this town?

KROGSTAD You mean—you came because of me?

MRS. LINDE I must work if I'm to find life worth living. I've always worked, for as long as I can remember; it's been the greatest joy of my life—my only joy. But now I'm alone in the world, and I feel so dreadfully lost and empty. There's no joy in working just for oneself. Oh, Nils, give me something—someone—to work for.

KROGSTAD I don't believe all that. You're just being hysterical and romantic. You want to find an excuse for self-sacrifice.

MRS. LINDE Have you ever known me to be hysterical?

KROGSTAD You mean you really—? Is it possible? Tell me—you know all about my past?

MRS. LINDE Yes.

KROGSTAD And you know what people think of me here?

MRS. LINDE You said just now that with me you might have become a different person.

KROGSTAD I know I could have.

MRS. LINDE Couldn't it still happen?

KROGSTAD Christine—do you really mean this? Yes—you do—I see it in your face. Have you really the courage—?

MRS. LINDE I need someone to be a mother to; and your children need a mother. And you and I need each other. I believe in you, Nils. I am afraid of nothing—with you.

KROGSTAD (*clasps her hands*) Thank you, Christine—thank you! Now I shall make the world believe in me as you do! Oh—but I'd forgotten—

MRS. LINDE (*listens*) Ssh! The tarantella! Go quickly, go!

KROGSTAD Why? What is it?

MRS. LINDE You hear that dance? As soon as it's finished, they'll be coming down.

KROGSTAD All right, I'll go. It's no good, Christine. I'd forgotten—you don't know what I've just done to the Helmers.

MRS. LINDE Yes, Nils. I know.

KROGSTAD And yet you'd still have the courage to—?

MRS. LINDE I know what despair can drive a man like you to.

KROGSTAD Oh, if only I could undo this!

MRS. LINDE You can. Your letter is still lying in the box.

KROGSTAD Are you sure?

MRS. LINDE Quite sure. But—

KROGSTAD (*looks searchingly at her*) Is that why you're doing this? You want to save your friend at any price? Tell me the truth. Is that the reason?

MRS. LINDE Nils, a woman who has sold herself once for the sake of others doesn't make the same mistake again.

KROGSTAD I shall demand my letter back.

MRS. LINDE No, no.

KROGSTAD Of course I shall. I shall stay here till Helmer comes down. I'll tell him he must give me back my letter—I'll say it was only to do with my dismissal, and that I don't want him to read it—

MRS. LINDE No, Nils, you mustn't ask for that letter back.

KROGSTAD But—tell me—wasn't that the real reason you asked me to come here?

MRS. LINDE Yes—at first, when I was frightened. But a day has passed since then, and in that time I've seen incredible things happen in this house. Helmer must know the truth. This unhappy secret of Nora's must be revealed. They must come to a full understanding; there must be an end of all these shiftings and evasions.

KROGSTAD Very well. If you're prepared to risk it. But one thing I can do—and at once—

MRS. LINDE (*listens*) Hurry! Go, go! The dance is over. We aren't safe here another moment.

KROGSTAD I'll wait for you downstairs.

MRS. LINDE Yes, do. You can see me home.

KROGSTAD I've never been so happy in my life before!

He goes out through the front door. The door leading from the room into the hall remains open.

MRS. LINDE (*tidies the room a little and gets her hat and coat*) What a change! Oh, what a change! Someone to work for—to live for! A home to bring joy into! I won't let this chance of happiness slip through my fingers. Oh, why don't they come? (*Listens.*) Ah, here they are. I must get my coat on.

She takes her hat and coat. HELMER's *and* NORA's *voices become audible outside. A key is turned in the lock and* HELMER *leads* NORA *almost forcibly into the hall. She is dressed in an Italian costume with a large black shawl. He is in evening dress, with a black cloak.*

NORA (*still in the doorway, resisting him*) No, no, no—not in here! I want to go back upstairs. I don't want to leave so early.

HELMER But my dearest Nora—

NORA Oh, please, Torvald, please! Just another hour!

HELMER Not another minute, Nora, my sweet. You know what we agreed. Come along, now. Into the drawing-room. You'll catch cold if you stay out here.

He leads her, despite her efforts to resist him, gently into the room.

MRS. LINDE Good evening.

NORA Christine!

HELMER Oh, hullo, Mrs. Linde. You still here?

MRS. LINDE Please forgive me. I did so want to see Nora in her costume.

NORA Have you been sitting here waiting for me?

MRS. LINDE Yes. I got here too late, I'm afraid. You'd already gone up. And I felt I really couldn't go back home without seeing you.

HELMER (*takes off* NORA's *shawl*) Well, take a good look at her. She's worth looking at, don't you think? Isn't she beautiful, Mrs. Linde?

MRS. LINDE Oh, yes, indeed—

HELMER Isn't she unbelievably beautiful? Everyone at the party said so. But dreadfully stubborn she is, bless her pretty little heart. What's to be done about that? Would you believe it, I practically had to use force to get her away!

NORA Oh, Torvald, you're going to regret not letting me stay—just half an hour longer.

HELMER Hear that, Mrs. Linde? She dances her tarantella—makes a roaring success— and very well deserved—though possibly a trifle too realistic—more so than was aesthetically necessary, strictly speaking. But never mind that. Main thing is—she had a success—roaring success. Was I going to let her stay on after that and spoil the impression? No, thank you. I took my beautiful little Capri signorina—my capricious little Capricienne, what?—under my arm—a swift round of the ballroom, a curtsey to the company, and, as they say in novels, the beautiful apparition disappeared! An exit should always be dramatic, Mrs. Linde. But unfortunately that's just what I can't get Nora to realize. I say, it's hot in here. (*Throws his cloak on a chair and opens the door to his study.*) What's this? It's dark in here. Ah, yes, of course—excuse me. (*Goes in and lights a couple of candles.*)

NORA (*whispers swiftly, breathlessly*) Well?

MRS. LINDE (*quietly*) I've spoken to him.

NORA Yes?

MRS. LINDE Nora—you must tell your husband everything.

NORA (*dully*) I knew it.

MRS. LINDE You've nothing to fear from Krogstad. But you must tell him.

NORA I shan't tell him anything.

MRS. LINDE Then the letter will.

NORA Thank you, Christine. Now I know what I must do. Ssh!

HELMER (*returns*) Well, Mrs. Linde, finished admiring her?

MRS. LINDE Yes. Now I must say good night.

HELMER Oh, already? Does this knitting belong to you?

MRS. LINDE (*takes it*) Thank you, yes. I nearly forgot it.

HELMER You knit, then?

MRS. LINDE Why, yes.

HELMER Know what? You ought to take up embroidery.

MRS. LINDE Oh? Why?

HELMER It's much prettier. Watch me, now. You hold the embroidery in your left hand, like this, and then you take the needle in your right hand and go in and out in a slow, easy movement—like this. I am right, aren't I?

MRS. LINDE Yes, I'm sure—

HELMER But knitting, now—that's an ugly business—can't help it. Look—arms all huddled up—great clumsy needles going up and down—makes you look like a damned Chinaman. I say, that really was a magnificent champagne they served us.

MRS. LINDE Well, good night, Nora. And stop being stubborn. Remember!

HELMER Quite right, Mrs. Linde!

MRS. LINDE Good night, Mr. Helmer.

HELMER (accompanies her to the door) Good night, good night! I hope you'll manage to get home all right? I'd gladly—but you haven't far to go, have you? Good night, good night. (She goes. He closes the door behind her and returns.) Well, we've got rid of her at last. Dreadful bore that woman is!

NORA Aren't you very tired, Torvald?

HELMER No, not in the least.

NORA Aren't you sleepy?

HELMER Not a bit. On the contrary, I feel extraordinarily exhilarated. But what about you? Yes, you look very sleepy and tired.

NORA Yes, I am very tired. Soon I shall sleep.

HELMER You see, you see! How right I was not to let you stay longer!

NORA Oh, you're always right, whatever you do.

HELMER (kisses her on the forehead) Now my little songbird's talking just like a real big human being. I say, did you notice how cheerful Rank was this evening?

NORA Oh? Was he? I didn't have a chance to speak with him.

HELMER I hardly did. But I haven't seen him in such a jolly mood for ages. (Looks at her for a moment, then comes closer.) I say, it's nice to get back to one's home again, and be all alone with you. Upon my word, you're a distractingly beautiful young woman.

NORA Don't look at me like that, Torvald!

HELMER What, not look at my most treasured possession? At all this wonderful beauty that's mine, mine alone, all mine.

NORA (goes round to the other side of the table) You mustn't talk to me like that tonight.

HELMER (follows her) You've still the tarantella in your blood, I see. And that makes you even more desirable. Listen! Now the other guests are beginning to go. (More quietly.) Nora—soon the whole house will be absolutely quiet.

NORA Yes, I hope so.

HELMER Yes, my beloved Nora, of course you do! Do you know—when I'm out with you among other people like we were tonight, do you know why I say so little to you, why I keep so aloof from you, and just throw you an occasional glance? Do you know why I do that? It's because I pretend to myself that you're my secret mistress, my clandestine little sweetheart, and that nobody knows there's anything at all between us.

NORA Oh, yes, yes, yes—I know you never think of anything but me.

HELMER And then when we're about to go, and I wrap the shawl round your lovely young shoulders, over this wonderful curve of your neck—then I pretend to myself that you are my young bride, that we've just come from the wedding, that I'm taking you to my house for the first time—that, for the first time, I am alone with you— quite alone with you, as you stand there young and trembling and beautiful. All evening I've had no eyes for anyone but you. When I saw you dance the tarantella, like a huntress, a temptress, my blood grew hot, I couldn't stand it any longer! That was why I seized you and dragged you down here with me—

NORA Leave me, Torvald! Get away from me! I don't want all this.

HELMER What? Now, Nora, you're joking with me. Don't want, don't want—? Aren't I your husband—?

There is a knock on the front door.

NORA (*starts*) What was that?

HELMER (*goes towards the hall*) Who is it?

RANK (*outside*) It's me. May I come in for a moment?

HELMER (*quietly, annoyed*) Oh, what does he want now? (*Calls.*) Wait a moment. (*Walks over and opens the door.*) Well! Nice of you not to go by without looking in.

RANK I thought I heard your voice, so I felt I had to say goodbye. (*His eyes travel swiftly around the room.*) Ah, yes—these dear rooms, how well I know them. What a happy, peaceful home you two have.

HELMER You seemed to be having a pretty happy time yourself upstairs.

RANK Indeed I did. Why not? Why shouldn't one make the most of this world? As much as one can, and for as long as one can. The wine was excellent—

HELMER Especially the champagne.

RANK You noticed that too? It's almost incredible how much I managed to get down.

NORA Torvald drank a lot of champagne too, this evening.

RANK Oh?

NORA Yes. It always makes him merry afterwards.

RANK Well, why shouldn't a man have a merry evening after a well-spent day?

HELMER Well-spent? Oh, I don't know that I can claim that.

RANK (*slaps him across the back*) I can, though, my dear fellow!

NORA Yes, of course, Dr. Rank—you've been carrying out a scientific experiment today, haven't you?

RANK Exactly.

HELMER Scientific experiment! Those are big words for my little Nora to use!

NORA And may I congratulate you on the finding?

RANK You may indeed.

NORA It was good, then?

RANK The best possible finding—both for the doctor and the patient. Certainty.

NORA (*quickly*) Certainty?

RANK Absolute certainty. So aren't I entitled to have a merry evening after that?

NORA Yes, Dr. Rank. You were quite right to.

HELMER I agree. Provided you don't have to regret it tomorrow.

RANK Well, you never get anything in this life without paying for it.

NORA Dr. Rank—you like masquerades, don't you?

RANK Yes, if the disguises are sufficiently amusing.

NORA Tell me. What shall we two wear at the next masquerade?

HELMER You little gadabout! Are you thinking about the next one already?

RANK We two? Yes, I'll tell you. You must go as the Spirit of Happiness—

HELMER You try to think of a costume that'll convey that.

RANK Your wife need only appear as her normal, everyday self—

HELMER Quite right! Well said! But what are you going to be? Have you decided that?

RANK Yes, my dear friend. I have decided that.

HELMER Well?

RANK At the next masquerade, I shall be invisible.

HELMER Well, that's a funny idea.

RANK There's a big, black hat—haven't you heard of the invisible hat? Once it's over your head, no one can see you any more.

HELMER (*represses a smile*) Ah yes, of course.

RANK But I'm forgetting what I came for. Helmer, give me a cigar. One of your black Havanas.

HELMER With the greatest pleasure. (*Offers him the box.*)

RANK (*takes one and cuts off the tip*) Thank you.

NORA (*strikes a match*) Let me give you a light.

RANK Thank you. (*She holds out the match for him. He lights his cigar.*) And now—goodbye.

HELMER Goodbye, my dear chap, goodbye.

NORA Sleep well, Dr. Rank.

RANK Thank you for that kind wish.

NORA Wish me the same.

RANK You? Very well—since you ask. Sleep well. And thank you for the light. (*He nods to them both and goes.*)

HELMER (*quietly*) He's been drinking too much.

NORA (*abstractedly*) Perhaps.

HELMER *takes his bunch of keys from his pocket and goes out into the hall.*

NORA Torvald, what do you want out there?

HELMER I must empty the letter-box. It's absolutely full. There'll be no room for the newspapers in the morning.

NORA Are you going to work tonight?

HELMER You know very well I'm not. Hullo, what's this? Someone's been at the lock.

NORA At the lock—?

HELMER Yes, I'm sure of it. Who on earth—? Surely not one of the maids? Here's a broken hairpin. Nora, it's yours—

NORA (*quickly*) Then it must have been the children.

HELMER Well, you'll have to break them of that habit. Hm, hm. Ah, that's done it. (*Takes out the contents of the box and calls into the kitchen.*) Helen! Put out the light on the staircase. (*Comes back into the drawing-room with the letters in his hand and closes the door to the hall.*) Look at this! You see how they've piled up? (*Glances through them.*) What on earth's this?

NORA (*at the window*) The letter! Oh, no, Torvald, no!

HELMER Two visiting cards—from Rank.

NORA From Dr. Rank?

HELMER (*looks at them*) Peter Rank, M.D. They were on top. He must have dropped them in as he left.

NORA Has he written anything on them?

HELMER There's a black cross above his name. Look. Rather gruesome, isn't it? It looks just as though he was announcing his death.

NORA He is.

HELMER What? Do you know something? Has he told you anything?

NORA Yes. When these cards come, it means he's said goodbye to us. He wants to shut himself up in his house and die.

HELMER Ah, poor fellow. I knew I wouldn't be seeing him for much longer. But so soon—! And now he's going to slink away and hide like a wounded beast.

NORA When the time comes, it's best to go silently. Don't you think so, Torvald?

HELMER (*walks up and down*) He was so much a part of our life. I can't realize that he's gone. His suffering and loneliness seemed to provide a kind of dark background to the happy sunlight of our marriage. Well, perhaps it's best this way. For him, anyway. (*Stops walking.*) And perhaps for us too, Nora. Now we have only each other. (*Embraces her.*) Oh, my beloved wife—I feel as though I could never hold you close enough. Do you know, Nora, often I wish some terrible danger might threaten you, so that I could offer my life and my blood, everything, for your sake.

NORA (*tears herself loose and says in a clear, firm voice*) Read your letters now, Torvald.

HELMER No, no. Not tonight. Tonight I want to be with you, my darling wife—

NORA When your friend is about to die—?

HELMER You're right. This news has upset us both. An ugliness has come between us; thoughts of death and dissolution. We must try to forget them. Until then—you go to your room; I shall go to mine.

NORA (*throws her arms round his neck*) Good night, Torvald! Good night!

HELMER (*kisses her on the forehead*) Good night, my darling little songbird. Sleep well, Nora. I'll go and read my letters.

He goes into the study with the letters in his hand, and closes the door.

NORA (*wild-eyed, fumbles around, seizes* HELMER's *cloak, throws it round herself and whispers quickly, hoarsely*) Never see him again. Never. Never. Never. (*Throws the shawl over her head.*) Never see the children again. Them too. Never. Never. Oh— the icy black water! Oh—that bottomless—that—! Oh, if only it were all over! Now he's got it—he's reading it. Oh, no, no! Not yet! Goodbye, Torvald! Goodbye, my darlings!

She turns to run into the hall. As she does so, HELMER *throws open his door and stands there with an open letter in his hand.*

HELMER Nora!

NORA (*shrieks*) Ah—!

HELMER What is this? Do you know what is in this letter?

NORA Yes, I know. Let me go! Let me go!

HELMER (*holds her back*) Go? Where?

NORA (*tries to tear herself loose*) You mustn't try to save me, Torvald!

HELMER (*staggers back*) Is it true? Is it true, what he writes? Oh, my God! No, no—it's impossible, it can't be true!

NORA It *is* true. I've loved you more than anything else in the world.

HELMER Oh, don't try to make silly excuses.

NORA (*takes a step towards him*) Torvald—

HELMER Wretched woman! What have you done?

NORA Let me go! You're not going to suffer for my sake. I won't let you!

HELMER Stop being theatrical. (*Locks the front door.*) You're going to stay here and explain yourself. Do you understand what you've done? Answer me! Do you understand?

NORA (*looks unflinchingly at him and, her expression growing colder, says*) Yes. Now I am beginning to understand.

HELMER (*walking round the room*) Oh, what a dreadful awakening! For eight whole years—she who was my joy and my pride—a hypocrite, a liar—worse, worse—a criminal! Oh, the hideousness of it! Shame on you, shame!

NORA *is silent and stares unblinkingly at him.*

HELMER (*stops in front of her*) I ought to have guessed that something of this sort would happen. I should have foreseen it. All your father's recklessness and instability—be quiet!—I repeat, all your father's recklessness and instability he has handed on to you. No religion, no morals, no sense of duty! Oh, how I have been punished for closing my eyes to his faults! I did it for your sake. And now you reward me like this.

NORA Yes. Like this.

HELMER Now you have destroyed all my happiness. You have ruined my whole future. Oh, it's too dreadful to contemplate! I am in the power of a man who is completely without scruples. He can do what he likes with me, demand what he pleases, order me to do anything—I dare not disobey him. I am condemned to humiliation and ruin simply for the weakness of a woman.

NORA When I am gone from this world, you will be free.

HELMER Oh, don't be melodramatic. Your father was always ready with that kind of remark. How would it help me if you were "gone from this world," as you put it? It wouldn't assist me in the slightest. He can still make all the facts public; and if he does, I may quite easily be suspected of having been an accomplice in your crime. People may think that I was behind it—that it was I who encouraged you! And for all this I have to thank you, you whom I have carried on my hands through all the years of our marriage! Now do you realize what you've done to me?

NORA (*coldly calm*) Yes.

HELMER It's so unbelievable I can hardly credit it. But we must try to find some way out. Take off that shawl. Take it off, I say! I must try to buy him off somehow. This thing must be hushed up at any price. As regards our relationship—we must appear to be living together just as before. Only *appear*, of course. You will therefore continue to reside here. That is understood. But the children shall be taken out of your hands. I dare no longer entrust them to you. Oh, to have to say this to the woman I once loved so dearly—and whom I still—! Well, all that must be finished. Henceforth there can be no question of happiness; we must merely strive to save what shreds and tatters—(*The front door bell rings.* HELMER *starts.*) What can that be? At this hour? Surely not—? He wouldn't—? Hide yourself, Nora. Say you're ill.

NORA *does not move.* HELMER *goes to the door of the room and opens it. The* MAID *is standing half-dressed in the hall.*

MAID A letter for madam.

HELMER Give it to me. (*Seizes the letter and shuts the door.*) Yes, it's from him. You're not having it. I'll read this myself.

NORA Read it.

HELMER (*by the lamp*) I hardly dare to. This may mean the end for us both. No I must know. (*Tears open the letter hastily; reads a few lines; looks at a piece of paper which is enclosed with it; utters a cry of joy.*) Nora! (*She looks at him questioningly.*) Nora! No—I must read it once more. Yes, yes, it's true! I am saved! Nora, I am saved!

NORA What about me?

HELMER You too, of course. We're both saved, you and I. Look! He's returning your I.O.U. He writes that he is sorry for what has happened—a happy accident has changed his life—oh, what does it matter what he writes? We are saved, Nora! No one can harm you now. Oh, Nora, Nora—no, first let me destroy this filthy thing. Let me see—! (*Glances at the I.O.U.*) No, I don't want to look at it. I shall merely regard the whole business as a dream. (*He tears the I.O.U. and both letters into pieces, throws them into the stove and watches them burn.*) There. Now they're destroyed. He wrote that ever since Christmas Eve you've been—oh, these must have been three dreadful days for you, Nora.

NORA Yes. It's been a hard fight.

HELMER It must have been terrible—seeing no way out except—no, we'll forget the whole sordid business. We'll just be happy and go on telling ourselves over and over again: "It's over! It's over!" Listen to me, Nora. You don't seem to realize. It's over! Why are you looking so pale? Ah, my poor little Nora, I understand. You can't believe that I have forgiven you. But I have, Nora. I swear it to you. I have forgiven you everything. I know that what you did you did for your love of me.

NORA That is true.

HELMER You have loved me as a wife should love her husband. It was simply that in your inexperience you chose the wrong means. But do you think I love you any the less because you don't know how to act on your own initiative? No, no. Just lean on me. I shall counsel you. I shall guide you. I would not be a true man if your feminine helplessness did not make you doubly attractive in my eyes. You mustn't mind the hard words I said to you in those first dreadful moments when my whole world seemed to be tumbling about my ears. I have forgiven you, Nora. I swear it to you; I have forgiven you.

NORA Thank you for your forgiveness.

She goes out through the door, right.

HELMER No, don't go—(*Looks in.*) What are you doing there?

NORA (*offstage*) Taking off my fancy dress.

HELMER (*by the open door*) Yes, do that. Try to calm yourself and get your balance again, my frightened little songbird. Don't be afraid. I have broad wings to shield you. (*Begins to walk around near the door.*) How lovely and peaceful this little home of ours is, Nora. You are safe here; I shall watch over you like a hunted dove which I have snatched unharmed from the claws of the falcon. Your wildly beating little heart shall find peace with me. It will happen, Nora; it will take time, but it will happen, believe me. Tomorrow all this will seem quite different. Soon everything will be as it was before. I shall no longer need to remind you that I have forgiven you; your own heart will tell you that it is true. Do you really think I could ever bring myself to disown you, or even to reproach you? Ah, Nora, you don't understand what goes on in a husband's heart. There is something indescribably wonderful and satisfying for a husband in knowing that he has forgiven his wife—forgiven her unreservedly, from the bottom of his heart. It means that she has become his property in a double sense; he has, as it were, brought her into the world anew; she is now not only his wife but also his child. From now on that is what you shall be to me, my poor, helpless, bewildered little creature. Never be frightened of anything again, Nora. Just open your heart to me. I shall be both your will and your conscience. What's this? Not in bed? Have you changed?

NORA (*in her everyday dress*) Yes, Torvald. I've changed.

HELMER But why now—so late—?

NORA I shall not sleep tonight.

HELMER But, my dear Nora—

NORA (*looks at her watch*) It isn't that late. Sit down here, Torvald. You and I have a lot to talk about.

She sits down on one side of the table.

HELMER Nora, what does this mean? You look quite drawn—

NORA Sit down. It's going to take a long time. I've a lot to say to you.

HELMER (*sits down on the other side of the table*) You alarm me, Nora. I don't understand you.

NORA No, that's just it. You don't understand me. And I've never understood you— until this evening. No, don't interrupt me. Just listen to what I have to say. You and I have got to face facts, Torvald.

HELMER What do you mean by that?

NORA (*after a short silence*) Doesn't anything strike you about the way we're sitting here?

HELMER What?

NORA We've been married for eight years. Does it occur to you that this is the first time that we two, you and I, man and wife, have ever had a serious talk together?

HELMER Serious? What do you mean, serious?

NORA In eight whole years—no, longer—ever since we first met—we have never exchanged a serious word on a serious subject.

HELMER Did you expect me to drag you into all my worries—worries you couldn't possibly have helped me with?

NORA I'm not talking about worries. I'm simply saying that we have never sat down seriously to try to get to the bottom of anything.

HELMER But, my dear Nora, what on earth has that got to do with you?

NORA That's just the point. You have never understood me. A great wrong has been done to me, Torvald. First by Papa, and then by you.

HELMER What? But we two have loved you more than anyone in the world!

NORA (*shakes her head*) You have never loved me. You just thought it was fun to be in love with me.

HELMER Nora, what kind of a way is this to talk?

NORA It's the truth, Torvald. When I lived with Papa, he used to tell me what he thought about everything, so that I never had any opinions but his. And if I did have any of my own, I kept them quiet, because he wouldn't have liked them. He called me his little doll, and he played with me just the way I played with my dolls. Then I came here to live in your house—

HELMER What kind of a way is that to describe our marriage?

NORA (*undisturbed*) I mean, then I passed from Papa's hands into yours. You arranged everything the way you wanted it, so that I simply took over your taste in everything— or pretended I did—I don't really know—I think it was a little of both—first one and then the other. Now I look back on it, it's as if I've been living here like a pauper, from hand to mouth. I performed tricks for you, and you gave me food and drink. But that was how you wanted it. You and Papa have done me a great wrong. It's your fault that I have done nothing with my life.

HELMER Nora, how can you be so unreasonable and ungrateful? Haven't you been happy here?

NORA No; never. I used to think I was; but I haven't ever been happy.

HELMER Not—not happy?

NORA No. I've just had fun. You've always been very kind to me. But our home has never been anything but a playroom. I've been your doll-wife, just as I used to be Papa's doll-child. And the children have been my dolls. I used to think it was fun when you came in and played with me, just as they think it's fun when I go in and play games with them. That's all our marriage has been, Torvald.

HELMER There may be a little truth in what you say, though you exaggerate and romanticize. But from now on it'll be different. Playtime is over. Now the time has come for education.

NORA Whose education? Mine or the children's?

HELMER Both yours and the children's, my dearest Nora.

NORA Oh, Torvald, you're not the man to educate me into being the right wife for you.

HELMER How can you say that?

NORA And what about me? Am I fit to educate the children?

HELMER Nora!

NORA Didn't you say yourself a few minutes ago that you dare not leave them in my charge?

HELMER In a moment of excitement. Surely you don't think I meant it seriously?

NORA Yes. You were perfectly right. I'm not fitted to educate them. There's something else I must do first. I must educate myself. And you can't help me with that. It's something I must do by myself. That's why I'm leaving you.

HELMER (*jumps up*) What did you say?

NORA I must stand on my own feet if I am to find out the truth about myself and about life. So I can't go on living here with you any longer.

HELMER Nora, Nora!

NORA I'm leaving you now, at once. Christine will put me up for tonight—

HELMER You're out of your mind! You can't do this! I forbid you!

NORA It's no use your trying to forbid me any more. I shall take with me nothing but what is mine. I don't want anything from you, now or ever.

HELMER What kind of madness is this?

NORA Tomorrow I shall go home—I mean, to where I was born. It'll be easiest for me to find some kind of a job there.

HELMER But you're blind! You've no experience of the world—

NORA I must try to get some, Torvald.

HELMER But to leave your home, your husband, your children! Have you thought what people will say?

NORA I can't help that. I only know that I must do this.

HELMER But this is monstrous! Can you neglect your most sacred duties?

NORA What do you call my most sacred duties?

HELMER Do I have to tell you? Your duties towards your husband, and your children.

NORA I have another duty which is equally sacred.

HELMER You have not. What on earth could that be?

NORA My duty towards myself.

HELMER First and foremost you are a wife and a mother.

NORA I don't believe that any longer. I believe that I am first and foremost a human being, like you—or anyway, that I must try to become one. I know most people think as you do, Torvald, and I know there's something of the sort to be found in books. But I'm no longer prepared to accept what people say and what's written in books. I must think things out for myself, and try to find my own answer.

HELMER Do you need to ask where your duty lies in your own home? Haven't you an infallible guide in such matters—your religion?

NORA Oh, Torvald, I don't really know what religion means.

HELMER What are you saying?

NORA I only know what Pastor Hansen told me when I went to confirmation. He explained that religion meant this and that. When I get away from all this and can think things out on my own, that's one of the questions I want to look into. I want to find out whether what Pastor Hansen said was right—or anyway, whether it is right for me.

HELMER But it's unheard of for so young a woman to behave like this! If religion cannot guide you, let me at least appeal to your conscience. I presume you have some moral feelings left? Or—perhaps you haven't? Well, answer me.

NORA Oh, Torvald, that isn't an easy question to answer. I simply don't know. I don't know where I am in these matters. I only know that these things mean something quite different to me from what they do to you. I've learned now that certain laws are different from what I'd imagined them to be; but I can't accept that such laws can be right. Has a woman really not the right to spare her dying father pain, or save her husband's life? I can't believe that.

HELMER You're talking like a child. You don't understand how society works.

NORA No, I don't. But now I intend to learn. I must try to satisfy myself which is right, society or I.

HELMER Nora, you're ill; you're feverish. I almost believe you're out of your mind.

NORA I've never felt so sane and sure in my life.

HELMER You feel sure that it is right to leave your husband and your children?

NORA Yes. I do.

HELMER Then there is only one possible explanation.

NORA What?

HELMER That you don't love me any longer.

NORA No, that's exactly it.

HELMER Nora! How can you say this to me?

NORA Oh, Torvald, it hurts me terribly to have to say it, because you've always been so kind to me. But I can't help it. I don't love you any longer.

HELMER (*controlling his emotions with difficulty*) And you feel quite sure about this too?

NORA Yes, absolutely sure. That's why I can't go on living here any longer.

HELMER Can you also explain why I have lost your love?

NORA Yes, I can. It happened this evening, when the miracle failed to happen. It was then that I realized you weren't the man I'd thought you to be.

HELMER Explain more clearly. I don't understand you.

NORA I've waited so patiently, for eight whole years—well, good heavens, I'm not such a fool as to suppose that miracles occur every day. Then this dreadful thing happened to me, and then I *knew*: "Now the miracle will take place!" When Krogstad's letter was lying out there, it never occurred to me for a moment that you would let that man trample over you. I *knew* that you would say to him: "Publish the facts to the world." And when he had done this—

HELMER Yes, what then? When I'd exposed my wife's name to shame and scandal—

NORA Then I was certain that you would step forward and take all the blame on yourself, and say: "I am the one who is guilty!"

HELMER Nora!

NORA You're thinking I wouldn't have accepted such a sacrifice from you? No, of course I wouldn't! But what would my word have counted for against yours? That was the miracle I was hoping for, and dreading. And it was to prevent it happening that I wanted to end my life.

HELMER Nora, I would gladly work for you night and day, and endure sorrow and hardship for your sake. But no man can be expected to sacrifice his honour, even for the person he loves.

NORA Millions of women have done it.

HELMER Oh, you think and talk like a stupid child.

NORA That may be. But you neither think nor talk like the man I could share my life with. Once you'd got over your fright—and you weren't frightened of what might threaten me, but only of what threatened you—once the danger was past, then as far as you were concerned it was exactly as though nothing had happened. I was your little songbird just as before—your doll whom henceforth you would take particular care to protect from the world because she was so weak and fragile. (*Gets up.*) Torvald, in that moment I realized that for eight years I had been living here with a complete stranger, and had borne him three children—! Oh, I can't bear to think of it! I could tear myself to pieces!

HELMER (*sadly*) I see it, I see it. A gulf has indeed opened between us. Oh, but Nora—couldn't it be bridged?

NORA As I am now, I am no wife for you.

HELMER I have the strength to change.

NORA Perhaps—if your doll is taken from you.

HELMER But to be parted—to be parted from you! No, no, Nora, I can't conceive of it happening!

NORA (*goes into the room, right*) All the more necessary that it should happen.

She comes back with her outdoor things and a small travelling-bag, which she puts down on a chair by the table.

HELMER Nora, Nora, not now! Wait till tomorrow!

NORA (*puts on her coat*) I can't spend the night in a strange man's house.

HELMER But can't we live here as brother and sister, then—?

NORA (*fastens her hat*) You know quite well it wouldn't last. (*Puts on her shawl.*) Goodbye, Torvald. I don't want to see the children. I know they're in better hands than mine. As I am now, I can be nothing to them.

HELMER But some time, Nora—some time—?

NORA How can I tell? I've no idea what will happen to me.

HELMER But you are my wife, both as you are and as you will be.

NORA Listen, Torvald. When a wife leaves her husband's house, as I'm doing now, I'm told that according to the law he is freed of any obligations towards her. In any case, I release you from any such obligations. You mustn't feel bound to me in any way, however small, just as I shall not feel bound to you. We must both be quite free. Here is your ring back. Give me mine.

HELMER That too?

NORA That too.

HELMER Here it is.

NORA Good. Well, now it's over. I'll leave the keys here. The servants know about everything to do with the house—much better than I do. Tomorrow, when I have left town, Christine will come to pack the things I brought here from home. I'll have them sent on after me.

HELMER This is the end then! Nora, will you never think of me any more?

NORA Yes, of course. I shall often think of you and the children and this house.

HELMER May I write to you, Nora?

NORA No. Never. You mustn't do that.

HELMER But at least you must let me send you—

NORA Nothing. Nothing.

HELMER But if you should need help?—

NORA I tell you, no. I don't accept things from strangers.

HELMER Nora—can I never be anything but a stranger to you?

NORA (*picks up her bag*) Oh, Torvald! Then the miracle of miracles would have to happen.

HELMER The miracle of miracles?

NORA You and I would both have to change so much that—oh, Torvald, I don't believe in miracles any longer.

HELMER But I want to believe in them. Tell me. We should have to change so much that—?

NORA That life together between us two could become a marriage. Goodbye.

She goes out through the hall.

HELMER (*sinks down on a chair by the door and buries his face in his hands*) Nora! Nora! (*Looks round and gets up.*) Empty! She's gone! (*A hope strikes him.*) The miracle of miracles—?

The street door is slammed shut downstairs.

Questions

1. What do you think of the way Helmer addresses Nora? How much are his pet names for her an expression of affection, and how much do they express condescension?
2. What is Nora's attitude toward money? Is it realistic? Does her attitude toward money point to a significant flaw in her character?
3. What is the dramatic situation? Describe it in terms of Nora as protagonist, her objective, and obstacles
4. Nora wants to help Mrs. Linde, and yet in certain ways she is unable to comprehend Mrs. Linde's plight. Cite instances of Nora's naiveté in her first scene with Mrs. Linde.
5. Describe the differences in character between Dr. Rank and Helmer. Why do you suppose Ibsen included Dr. Rank in the story?
6. With the dialogue between Nora and Krogstad at the end of Act I we become aware of the play's problem. What is it? Why did Nora forget the I.O.U.? Would you have done the same?
7. Is Krogstad a villain? Explain his change of heart in Act III. Does it seem realistic?
8. In Act II (p. 1343) Helmer tells Nora "Let what will happen, happen. When the real crisis comes, you will not find me lacking in strength or courage. I am man enough to bear the burden for us both." How do these words contradict his actions in Act III? What does this contradiction tell you about Helmer's character?
9. Discuss the irony of Helmer's response to Krogstad's first letter. Discuss the irony of his response to the second letter.
10. What is the "miracle" Nora was hoping for?
11. The most famous dialogue in A *Doll's House* comes near the end of Act III:

> NORA What do you call my most sacred duties?
> HELMER Do I have to tell you? Your duties towards your husband, and your children.
> NORA I have another duty which is equally sacred.

HELMER You have not. What on earth could that be?
NORA My duty towards myself.

Do you think Nora is right in leaving her husband and children?
12. Discuss the symbolic significance of the play's title.

 Writers on Writing   Henrik Ibsen

> *Environment has a great influence upon the forms in which the imagination creates.*

Realism in America

Before 1900, drama in this country was the least sophisticated of the arts. Melodramas, sentimental comedies, and revivals of Shakespeare were about all the commercial theater had to offer. But then young Americans traveling abroad saw the plays of Ibsen, Shaw, and Chekhov. They returned to establish the Little Theater Movement—small theaters, far from the pressures of the commercial stage, where they could experiment with techniques discovered in Europe. This movement, spawning groups like the Washington Square Players and The Provincetown Players, began to attract talented actors, professional producers, and playwrights such as Eugene O'Neill.

At the same time, the popular critic H. L. Mencken was championing the realistic works of Ibsen and Shaw in America. By the early twenties one could see their influence on Eugene O'Neill in his plays *Anna Christie* (1922) and *Desire under the Elms* (1924). O'Neill's psychological dramas benefited most from Ibsen's sensitive portraiture and the "catastrophic" plot. Other playwrights, such as Clifford Odets, followed in Ibsen's footsteps as social realists, as critics of ideas and morals. Realism became the dominant mode of drama in twentieth-century America. The plays of Tennessee Williams are a kind of poetic realism, their characters and situations generally probable, their language occasionally elevated and figurative.

One of the most successful realistic dramas of our time is Lorraine Hansberry's *A Raisin in the Sun*. The first effort of a twenty-nine-year old black playwright, the play opened on Broadway in 1959 and was a spectacular hit. *Raisin* ran for 530 performances. It made a star of Sidney Poitier in the role of Walter Lee Younger, and thrust Lorraine Hansberry into the national spotlight. Not only was she the youngest American ever to win the Drama Critic's Circle Award, she also was the first black woman to have her work produced on Broadway. Hansberry became an advocate of human rights during a decade of racial strife, a role for which she was well prepared.

Born in Chicago in 1930, she was the daughter of Carl Augustus Hansberry, who sued to break the covenants that barred blacks from living in certain neighborhoods. He argued the case before the Supreme Court in 1940 and won. When Lorraine was a child, she received verbal and physical threats as a result of her father's courage. In the early fifties she took a job in New York as a reporter for her friend Paul Robeson's radical magazine *Freedom*. Later, while she was developing her skills as a playwright, she studied history with W. E. B. Du Bois.

Hansberry wrote other plays, including *Les Blancs* and *The Sign in Sidney Brustein's Window*, and continued her political activities into the mid-sixties in spite of fatigue and failing health. Her death from cancer on January 12, 1965, was a tragic loss to the theater in America.

LORRAINE HANSBERRY (1930–1965)

A Raisin in the Sun

To Mama: in gratitude for the dream

CHARACTERS

RUTH YOUNGER	JOSEPH ASAGAI
TRAVIS YOUNGER	GEORGE MURCHISON
WALTER LEE YOUNGER (*Brother*)	KARL LINDNER
BENEATHA YOUNGER	BOBO
LENA YOUNGER (*Mama*)	MOVING MEN

The action of the play is set in Chicago's Southside, sometime between World War II and the present.

ACT I
SCENE I. *Friday morning*
SCENE II. *The following morning*

ACT II
SCENE I. *Later, the same day*
SCENE II. *Friday night, a few weeks later*
SCENE III. *Saturday, moving day, one week later*

ACT III
An hour later

> What happens to a dream deferred?
> Does it dry up
> Like a raisin in the sun?
> Or fester like a sore—
>
> And then run?
> Does it stink like rotten meat?
> Or crust and sugar over—
> Like a syrupy sweet?

Sidney Poitier and Claudia McNeil in *A Raisin in the Sun* (*Photograph by Friedman-Abeles from Performing Arts Research Center, The New York Public Library*)

Maybe it just sags
Like a heavy load.

Or does it explode?

Langston Hughes[1]

ACT I

SCENE I.

The Younger living room would be a comfortable and well-ordered room if it were not for a number of indestructible contradictions to this state of being. Its furnishings are typical and undistinguished and their primary feature now is that they have clearly had to accommodate the living of too many people for too many years—and they are tired. Still, we can see that at some time, a time probably no longer remembered by the family (except perhaps for MAMA*), the furnishings of this room were actually selected with care and love and even hope—and brought to this apartment and arranged with taste and pride.*

That was a long time ago. Now the once loved pattern of the couch upholstery has to fight to show itself from under acres of crocheted doilies and couch covers which have themselves finally come to be more important than the upholstery. And here a table or a chair has been moved to disguise the worn places in the carpet; but the carpet has fought back by showing its weariness, with depressing uniformity, elsewhere on its surface.

[1] From "Dream Deferred." Copyright 1951 by Langston Hughes. Reprinted from *The Panther and the Lash* by Langston Hughes, by permission of Alfred A. Knopf, Inc.

Weariness has, in fact, won in this room. Everything has been polished, washed, sat on, used, scrubbed too often. All pretenses but living itself have long since vanished from the very atmosphere of this room.

Moreover, a section of this room, for it is not really a room unto itself, though the landlord's lease would make it seem so, slopes backward to provide a small kitchen area, where the family prepares the meals that are eaten in the living room proper, which must also serve as dining room. The single window that has been provided for these "two" rooms is located in this kitchen area. The sole natural light the family may enjoy in the course of a day is only that which fights its way through this little window.

At left, a door leads to a bedroom which is shared by MAMA *and her daughter,* BENEATHA. *At right, opposite, is a second room (which in the beginning of the life of this apartment was probably a breakfast room), which serves as a bedroom for* WALTER *and his wife,* RUTH.

Time: Sometime between World War II and the present.

Place: Chicago's Southside.

At rise: It is morning dark in the living room. TRAVIS *is asleep on the make-down bed at center. An alarm clock sounds from within the bedroom at right, and presently* RUTH *enters from that room and closes the door behind her. She crosses sleepily toward the window. As she passes her sleeping son she reaches down and shakes him a little. At the window she raises the shade and a dusky Southside morning light comes in feebly. She fills a pot with water and puts it on to boil. She calls to the boy, between yawns, in a slightly muffled voice.*

RUTH *is about thirty. We can see that she was a pretty girl, even exceptionally so, but now it is apparent that life has been little that she expected, and disappointment has already begun to hang in her face. In a few years, before thirty-five even, she will be known among her people as a "settled woman."*

She crosses to her son and gives him a good, final, rousing shake.

RUTH Come on now, boy, it's seven thirty! (*Her son sits up at last, in a stupor of sleepiness.*) I say hurry up, Travis! You ain't the only person in the world got to use a bathroom! (*The child, a sturdy, handsome little boy of ten or eleven, drags himself out of the bed and almost blindly takes his towels and "today's clothes" from drawers and a closet and goes out to the bathroom, which is in an outside hall and which is shared by another family or families on the same floor.* RUTH *crosses to the bedroom door at right and opens it and calls in to her husband.*) Walter Lee! . . . It's after seven thirty! Lemme see you do some waking up in there now! (*She waits.*) You better get up from there, man! It's after seven thirty I tell you. (*She waits again.*) All right, you just go ahead and lay there and next thing you know Travis be finished and Mr. Johnson'll be in there and you'll be fussing and cussing round here like a mad man! And be late too! (*She waits, at the end of patience.*) Walter Lee—it's time for you to get up!

She waits another second and then starts to go into the bedroom, but is apparently satisfied that her husband has begun to get up. She stops, pulls the door to, and returns to the kitchen area. She wipes her face with a moist cloth and runs her fingers through her sleep-disheveled hair in a vain effort and ties an apron around her housecoat. The bedroom door at right opens and her husband stands in the doorway in his pajamas, which are rumpled and mismated. He is a lean, intense young man in his middle thirties, inclined to quick nervous movements and erratic speech habits—and always in his voice there is a quality of indictment.

WALTER Is he out yet?

RUTH What you mean *out*? He ain't hardly got in there good yet.

WALTER (*wandering in, still more oriented to sleep than to a new day*) Well, what was you doing all that yelling for if I can't even get in there yet? (*Stopping and thinking*) Check coming today?

RUTH They *said* Saturday and this is just Friday and I hopes to God you ain't going to get up here first thing this morning and start talking to me 'bout no money—'cause I 'bout don't want to hear it.

WALTER Something the matter with you this morning?

RUTH No—I'm just sleepy as the devil. What kind of eggs you want?

WALTER Not scrambled. (RUTH *starts to scramble eggs.*) Paper come? (RUTH *points impatiently to the rolled up* Tribune *on the table, and he gets it and spreads it out and vaguely reads the front page.*) Set off another bomb yesterday.

RUTH (*maximum indifference*) Did they?

WALTER (*looking up*) What's the matter with you?

RUTH Ain't nothing the matter with me. And don't keep asking me that this morning.

WALTER Ain't nobody bothering you. (*Reading the news of the day absently again*) Say Colonel McCormick is sick.

RUTH (*affecting tea-party interest*) Is he now? Poor thing.

WALTER (*sighing and looking at his watch*) Oh, me. (*He waits.*) Now what is that boy doing in that bathroom all this time? He just going to have to start getting up earlier. I can't be being late to work on account of him fooling around in there.

RUTH (*turning on him*) Oh, no he ain't going to be getting up no earlier no such thing! It ain't his fault that he can't get to bed no earlier nights 'cause he got a bunch of crazy good-for-nothing clowns sitting up running their mouths in what is supposed to be his bedroom after ten o'clock at night. . . .

WALTER That's what you mad about, ain't it? The things I want to talk about with my friends just couldn't be important in your mind, could they?

He rises and finds a cigarette in her handbag on the table and crosses to the little window and looks out, smoking and deeply enjoying this first one.

RUTH (*almost matter of factly, a complaint too automatic to deserve emphasis*) Why you always got to smoke before you eat in the morning?

WALTER (*at the window*) Just look at 'em down there. . . . Running and racing to work . . . (*He turns and faces his wife and watches her a moment at the stove, and then, suddenly*) You look young this morning, baby.

RUTH (*indifferently*) Yeah?

WALTER Just for a second—stirring them eggs. It's gone now—just for a second it was— you looked real young again. (*Then, drily*) It's gone now—you look like yourself again.

RUTH Man, if you don't shut up and leave me alone.

WALTER (*looking out to the street again*) First thing a man ought to learn in life is not to make love to no colored woman first thing in the morning. You all some evil people at eight o'clock in the morning.

TRAVIS *appears in the hall doorway, almost fully dressed and quite wide awake now, his towels and pajamas across his shoulders. He opens the door and signals for his father to make the bathroom in a hurry.*

TRAVIS (*watching the bathroom*) Daddy, come on!

WALTER *gets his bathroom utensils and flies out to the bathroom.*

RUTH Sit down and have your breakfast, Travis.

TRAVIS Mama, this is Friday. (*Gleefully*) Check coming tomorrow, huh?

RUTH You get your mind off money and eat your breakfast.

TRAVIS (*eating*) This is the morning we supposed to bring the fifty cents to school.

RUTH Well, I ain't got no fifty cents this morning.

TRAVIS Teacher say we have to.

RUTH I don't care what teacher say. I ain't got it. Eat your breakfast, Travis.

TRAVIS I *am* eating.

RUTH Hush up now and just eat!

The boy gives her an exasperated look for her lack of understanding, and eats grudgingly.

TRAVIS You think Grandmama would have it?

RUTH No! And I want you to stop asking your grandmother for money, you hear me?

TRAVIS (*outraged*) Gaaaleee! I don't ask her, she just gimme it sometimes!

RUTH Travis Willard Younger—I got too much on me this morning to be—

TRAVIS Maybe Daddy—

RUTH *Travis!*

The boy hushes abruptly. They are both quiet and tense for several seconds.

TRAVIS (*presently*) Could I maybe go carry some groceries in front of the supermarket for a little while after school then?

RUTH Just hush, I said. (TRAVIS *jabs his spoon into his cereal bowl viciously, and rests his head in anger upon his fists.*) If you through eating, you can get over there and make up your bed.

The boy obeys stiffly and crosses the room, almost mechanically, to the bed and more or less carefully folds the covering. He carries the bedding into his mother's room and returns with his books and cap.

TRAVIS (*sulking and standing apart from her unnaturally*) I'm gone.

RUTH (*looking up from the stove to inspect him automatically*) Come here. (*He crosses to her and she studies his head.*) If you don't take this comb and fix this here head, you better! (TRAVIS *puts down his books with a great sigh of oppression, and crosses to the mirror. His mother mutters under her breath about his "slubbornness."*) 'Bout to march out of here with that head looking just like chickens slept in it! I just don't know where you get your slubborn ways. . . . And get your jacket, too. Looks chilly out this morning.

TRAVIS (*with conspicuously brushed hair and jacket*) I'm gone.

RUTH Get carfare and milk money—(*waving one finger*)—and not a single penny for no caps, you hear me?

TRAVIS (*with sullen politeness*) Yes'm.

He turns in outrage to leave. His mother watches after him as in his frustration he approaches the door almost comically. When she speaks to him, her voice has become a very gentle tease.

RUTH (*mocking; as she thinks he would say it*) Oh, Mama makes me so mad sometimes, I don't know what to do! (*She waits and continues to his back as he stands stock-still in front of the door.*) I wouldn't kiss that woman good-bye for nothing in this world this morning! (*The boy finally turns around and rolls his eyes at her, knowing the mood has changed and he is vindicated; he does not, however, move toward her yet.*) Not for nothing in this world! (*She finally laughs aloud at him and holds out her arms to him and we see that it is a way between them, very old and practiced. He crosses to her and allows her to embrace him warmly but keeps his face fixed with masculine rigidity. She holds him back from her presently and looks at him and runs her fingers over the features of his face. With utter gentleness—*) Now—whose little old angry man are you?

TRAVIS (*the masculinity and gruffness start to fade at last*) Aw gaalee—Mama . . .

RUTH (*mimicking*) Aw—gaaaaalleeeee, Mama! (*She pushes him, with rough playfulness and finality, toward the door.*) Get on out of here or you going to be late.

TRAVIS (*in the face of love, new aggressiveness*) Mama, could I *please* go carry groceries?

RUTH Honey, it's starting to get so cold evenings.

WALTER (*coming in from the bathroom and drawing a make-believe gun from a make-believe holster and shooting at his son*) What is it he wants to do?

RUTH Go carry groceries after school at the supermarket.

WALTER Well, let him go . . .

TRAVIS (*quickly, to the ally*) I *have* to—she won't gimme the fifty cents. . . .

WALTER (*to his wife only*) Why not?

RUTH (*simply, and with flavor*) 'Cause we don't have it.

WALTER (*to* RUTH *only*) What you tell the boy things like that for? (*Reaching down into his pants with a rather important gesture*) Here, son—

He hands the boy the coin, but his eyes are directed to his wife's. TRAVIS *takes the money happily.*

TRAVIS Thanks, Daddy.

He starts out. RUTH *watches both of them with murder in her eyes.* WALTER *stands and stares back at her with defiance, and suddenly reaches into his pocket again on an afterthought.*

WALTER (*without even looking at his son, still staring hard at his wife*) In fact, here's another fifty cents. . . . Buy yourself some fruit today—or take a taxicab to school or something!

TRAVIS Whoopee—

He leaps up and clasps his father around the middle with his legs, and they face each other in mutual appreciation; slowly WALTER LEE *peeks around the boy to catch the violent rays from his wife's eyes and draws his head back as if shot.*

WALTER You better get down now—and get to school, man.

TRAVIS (*at the door*) O.K. Good-bye. (*He exits.*)

WALTER (*after him, pointing with pride*) That's my boy. (*She looks at him in disgust and turns back to her work.*) You know what I was thinking 'bout in the bathroom this morning?

RUTH No.

WALTER How come you always try to be so pleasant!

RUTH What is there to be pleasant 'bout!

WALTER You want to know what I was thinking 'bout in the bathroom or not!

RUTH I know what you thinking 'bout.

WALTER (*ignoring her*) 'Bout what me and Willy Harris was talking about last night.

RUTH (*immediately—a refrain*) Willy Harris is a good-for-nothing loud mouth.

WALTER Anybody who talks to me has got to be a good-for-nothing loud mouth, ain't he? And what you know about who is just a good-for-nothing loud mouth? Charlie Atkins was just a "good-for-nothing loud mouth" too, wasn't he! When he wanted me to go in the dry-cleaning business with him. And now—he's grossing a hundred thousand a year. A hundred thousand dollars a year! You still call *him* a loud mouth!

RUTH (*bitterly*) Oh, Walter Lee. . . . (*She folds her head on her arms over the table.*)

WALTER (*rising and coming to her and standing over her*) You tired, ain't you? Tired of everything. Me, the boy, the way we live—this beat-up hole—everything. Ain't you? (*She doesn't look up, doesn't answer.*) So tired—moaning and groaning all the time, but you wouldn't do nothing to help, would you? You couldn't be on my side that long for nothing, could you?

RUTH Walter, please leave me alone.

WALTER A man needs for a woman to back him up. . . .

RUTH Walter—

WALTER Mama would listen to you. You know she listen to you more than she do me and Bennie. She think more of you. All you have to do is just sit down with her when you drinking your coffee one morning and talking 'bout things like you do and—(*he sits down beside her and demonstrates graphically what he thinks her methods and tone should be*)—you just sip your coffee, see, and say easy like that you been thinking 'bout that deal Walter Lee is so interested in, 'bout the store and all, and sip some more coffee, like what you saying ain't really that important to you—And the next thing you know, she be listening good and asking you questions and when I come home—I can tell her the details. This ain't no fly-by-night proposition, baby. I mean we figured it out, me and Willy and Bobo.

RUTH (*with a frown*) Bobo?

WALTER Yeah. You see, this little liquor store we got in mind cost seventy-five thousand and we figured the initial investment on the place be 'bout thirty thousand, see. That be ten thousand each. Course, there's a couple of hundred you got to pay so's you don't spend your life just waiting for them clowns to let your license get approved—

RUTH You mean graft?

WALTER (*frowning impatiently*) Don't call it that. See there, that just goes to show you what women understand about the world. Baby, don't *nothing* happen for you in this world 'less you pay *somebody* off!

RUTH Walter, leave me alone! (*She raises her head and stares at him vigorously—then says, more quietly*) Eat your eggs, they gonna be cold.

WALTER (*straightening up from her and looking off*) That's it. There you are. Man say to his woman: I got me a dream. His woman say: Eat your eggs. (*Sadly, but gaining in power*) Man say: I got to take hold of this here world, baby! And a woman will say: Eat your eggs and go to work. (*Passionately now*) Man say: I got to change my life, I'm choking to death, baby! And his woman say—(*in utter anguish as he brings his fists down on his thighs*)—Your eggs is getting cold!

RUTH (*softly*) Walter, that ain't none of our money.

WALTER (*not listening at all or even looking at her*) This morning, I was lookin' in the mirror and thinking about it. . . . I'm thirty-five years old; I been married eleven years and I got a boy who sleeps in the living room—(*very, very quietly*)—and all I got to give him is stories about how rich white people live. . . .

RUTH Eat your eggs, Walter.

WALTER *Damn my eggs . . . damn all the eggs that ever was!*

RUTH Then go to work.

WALTER (*looking up at her*) See— I'm trying to talk to you 'bout myself—(*shaking his head with the repetition*)—and all you can say is eat them eggs and go to work.

RUTH (*wearily*) Honey, you never say nothing new. I listen to you every day, every night and every morning, and you never say nothing new. (*Shrugging*) So you would rather *be* Mr. Arnold than be his chauffeur. So—I would *rather* be living in Buckingham Palace.

WALTER That is just what is wrong with the colored woman in this world. . . . Don't understand about building their men up and making 'em feel like they somebody. Like they can do something.

RUTH (*drily, but to hurt*) There *are* colored men who do things.

WALTER No thanks to the colored woman.

RUTH Well, being a colored woman, I guess I can't help myself none.

She rises and gets the ironing board and sets it up and attacks a huge pile of rough-dried clothes, sprinkling them in preparation for the ironing and then rolling them into tight fat balls.

WALTER (*mumbling*) We one group of men tied to a race of women with small minds.

His sister BENEATHA enters. She is about twenty, as slim and intense as her brother. She is not as pretty as her sister-in-law, but her lean, almost intellectual face has a handsomeness of its own. She wears a bright-red flannel nightie, and her thick hair stands wildly about her head. Her speech is a mixture of many things; it is different from the rest of the family's insofar as education has permeated her sense of English—and perhaps the Midwest rather than the South has finally—at last—won out in her inflection; but not altogether, because over all of it is a soft slurring and transformed use of vowels which is the decided influence of the Southside. She passes through the room without looking at either RUTH or WALTER and goes to the outside door and looks, a little blindly, out to the bathroom. She sees that it has been lost to the Johnsons. She closes the door with a sleepy vengeance and crosses to the table and sits down a little defeated.

BENEATHA I am going to start timing those people.

WALTER You should get up earlier.

BENEATHA (*her face in her hands. She is still fighting the urge to go back to bed*) Really— would you suggest dawn? Where's the paper?

WALTER (*pushing the paper across the table to her as he studies her almost clinically, as though he has never seen her before*) You a horrible-looking chick at this hour.

BENEATHA (*drily*) Good morning, everybody.

WALTER (*senselessly*) How is school coming?

BENEATHA (*in the same spirit*) Lovely. Lovely. And you know, biology is the greatest. (*Looking up at him*) I dissected something that looked just like you yesterday.

WALTER I just wondered if you've made up your mind and everything.

BENEATHA (*gaining in sharpness and impatience*) And what did I answer yesterday morning—and the day before that?

RUTH (*from the ironing board, like someone disinterested and old*) Don't be so nasty, Bennie.

BENEATHA (*still to her brother*) And the day before that and the day before that!

WALTER (*defensively*) I'm interested in you. Something wrong with that? Ain't many girls who decide—

WALTER AND BENEATHA (*in unison*) —"to be a doctor."

Silence.

WALTER Have we figured out yet just exactly how much medical school is going to cost?

RUTH Walter Lee, why don't you leave that girl alone and get out of here to work?

BENEATHA (*exits to the bathroom and bangs on the door*) Come on out of there, please! (*She comes back into the room.*)

WALTER (*looking at his sister intently*) You know the check is coming tomorrow.

BENEATHA (*turning on him with a sharpness all her own*) That money belongs to Mama, Walter, and it's for her to decide how she wants to use it. I don't care if she wants to buy a house or a rocket ship or just nail it up somewhere and look at it. It's hers. Not ours—*hers.*

WALTER (*bitterly*) Now ain't that fine! You just got your mother's interest at heart, ain't you, girl? You such a nice girl—but if Mama got that money she can always take a few thousand and help you through school too—can't she?

BENEATHA I have never asked anyone around here to do anything for me!

WALTER No! And the line between asking and just accepting when the time comes is big and wide—ain't it!

BENEATHA (*with fury*) What do you want from me, Brother—that I quit school or just drop dead, which!

WALTER I don't want nothing but for you to stop acting holy 'round here. Me and Ruth done made some sacrifices for you—why can't you do something for the family?

RUTH Walter, don't be dragging me in it.

WALTER You are in it—Don't you get up and go work in somebody's kitchen for the last three years to help put clothes on her back?

RUTH Oh, Walter—that's not fair. . . .

WALTER It ain't that nobody expects you to get on your knees and say thank you, Brother; thank you, Ruth; thank you, Mama—and thank you, Travis, for wearing the same pair of shoes for two semesters—

BENEATHA (*dropping to her knees*) Well—I *do*—all right?—thank everybody . . . and forgive me for ever wanting to be anything at all . . . forgive me, forgive me!

RUTH Please stop it! Your mama'll hear you.

WALTER Who the hell told you you had to be a doctor? If you so crazy 'bout messing 'round with sick people—then go be a nurse like other women—or just get married and be quiet. . . .

BENEATHA Well—you finally got it said. . . . It took you three years but you finally got it said. Walter, give up; leave me alone—it's Mama's money.

WALTER *He was my father, too!*

BENEATHA So what? He was mine, too—and Travis' grandfather—but the insurance money belongs to Mama. Picking on me is not going to make her give it to you to invest in any liquor stores—(*underbreath, dropping into a chair*)—and I for one say, God bless Mama for that!

WALTER (*to* RUTH) See—did you hear? Did you hear!

RUTH Honey, please go to work.

WALTER Nobody in this house is ever going to understand me.

BENEATHA Because you're a nut.

WALTER Who's a nut?

BENEATHA You—you are a nut. Thee is mad, boy.

WALTER (*looking at his wife and his sister from the door, very sadly*) The world's most backward race of people, and that's a fact.

BENEATHA (*turning slowly in her chair*) And then there are all those prophets who would lead us out of the wilderness—(WALTER *slams out of the house.*)—into the swamps!

RUTH Bennie, why you always gotta be pickin' on your brother? Can't you be a little sweeter sometimes? (*Door opens.* WALTER *walks in.*)

WALTER (*to* RUTH) I need some money for carfare.

RUTH (*looks at him, then warms; teasing, but tenderly*) Fifty cents? (*She goes to her bag and gets money.*) Here, take a taxi.

WALTER *exits.* MAMA *enters. She is a woman in her early sixties, full-bodied and strong. She is one of those women of a certain grace and beauty who wears it so unobtrusively that it takes a while to notice. Her dark-brown face is surrounded by the total whiteness of her hair, and, being a woman who has adjusted to many things in life and overcome many more, her face is full of strength. She has, we can see, wit and faith of a kind that keep her eyes lit and full of interest and expectancy. She is, in a word, a beautiful woman. Her bearing is perhaps most like the noble bearing of the women of the Hereros of Southwest Africa—rather as if she imagines that as she walks she still bears a basket or a vessel upon her head. Her speech, on the other hand, is as careless as her carriage is precise—she is inclined to slur everything—but her voice is perhaps not so much quiet as simply soft.*

MAMA Who that 'round here slamming doors at this hour?

She crosses through the room, goes to the window, opens it, and brings in a feeble little plant growing doggedly in a small pot on the window sill. She feels the dirt and puts it back out.

RUTH That was Walter Lee. He and Bennie was at it again.

MAMA My children and they tempers. Lord, if this little old plant don't get more sun than it's been getting it ain't never going to see spring again. (*She turns from the window.*) What's the matter with you this morning, Ruth? You looks right peaked. You aiming to iron all them things? Leave some for me. I'll get to 'em this afternoon. Bennie honey, it's too drafty for you to be sitting 'round half dressed. Where's your robe?

BENEATHA In the cleaners.

MAMA Well, go get mine and put it on.

BENEATHA I'm not cold, Mama, honest.

MAMA I know—but you so thin. . . .

BENEATHA (*irritably*) Mama, I'm not cold.

MAMA (*seeing the make-down bed as* TRAVIS *has left it*) Lord have mercy, look at that poor bed. Bless his heart—he tries, don't he? (*She moves to the bed* TRAVIS *has sloppily made up.*)

RUTH No—he don't half try at all 'cause he knows you going to come along behind him and fix everything. That's just how come he don't know how to do nothing right now— you done spoiled that boy so.

MAMA Well—he's a little boy. Ain't supposed to know 'bout housekeeping. My baby, that's what he is. What you fix for his breakfast this morning?

RUTH (*angrily*) I feed my son, Lena!

MAMA I ain't meddling—(*underbreath; busy-bodyish*) *I just noticed all last week he had cold cereal, and when it starts getting this chilly in the fall a child ought to have some hot grits or something when he goes out in the cold—*

RUTH (*furious*) I gave him hot oats—is that all right!

MAMA I ain't meddling. (*Pause*) Put a lot of nice butter on it? (RUTH *shoots her an angry look and does not reply.*) He likes lots of butter.

RUTH (*exasperated*) Lena—

MAMA (*to* BENEATHA. MAMA *is inclined to wander conversationally sometimes*) What was you and your brother fussing 'bout this morning?

BENEATHA It's not important, Mama.

She gets up and goes to look out at the bathroom, which is apparently free, and she picks up her towels and rushes out.

MAMA What was they fighting about?

RUTH Now you know as well as I do.

MAMA (*shaking her head*) Brother still worrying his self sick about that money?

RUTH You know he is.

MAMA You had breakfast?

RUTH Some coffee.

MAMA Girl, you better start eating and looking after yourself better. You almost thin as Travis.

RUTH Lena—

MAMA Un-hunh?

RUTH What are you going to do with it?

MAMA Now don't you start, child. It's too early in the morning to be talking about money. It ain't Christian.

RUTH It's just that he got his heart set on that store—

MAMA You mean that liquor store that Willy Harris want him to invest in?

RUTH Yes—

MAMA We ain't no business people, Ruth. We just plain working folks.

RUTH Ain't nobody business people till they go into business. Walter Lee say colored people ain't never going to start getting ahead till they start gambling on some different kinds of things in the world—investments and things.

MAMA What done got into you, girl? Walter Lee done finally sold you on investing.

RUTH No. Mama, something is happening between Walter and me. I don't know what it is—but he needs something—something I can't give him any more. He needs this chance, Lena.

MAMA (*frowning deeply*) But liquor, honey—

RUTH Well—like Walter say—I spec people going to always be drinking themselves some liquor.

MAMA Well—whether they drinks it or not ain't none of my business. But whether I go into business selling it to 'em *is*, and I don't want that on my ledger this late in life. (*Stopping suddenly and studying her daughter-in-law*) Ruth Younger, what's the matter with you today? You look like you could fall over right there.

RUTH I'm tired.

MAMA Then you better stay home from work today.

RUTH I can't stay home. She'd be calling up the agency and screaming at them, "My girl didn't come in today—send me somebody! My girl didn't come in!" Oh, she just have a fit. . . .

MAMA Well, let her have it. I'll just call her up and say you got the flu—

RUTH (*laughing*) Why the flu?

MAMA 'Cause it sounds respectable to 'em. Something white people get, too. They know 'bout the flu. Otherwise they think you been cut up or something when you tell 'em you sick.

RUTH I got to go in. We need the money.

MAMA Somebody would of thought my children done all but starved to death the way they talk about money here late. Child, we got a great big old check coming tomorrow.

RUTH (*sincerely, but also self-righteously*) Now that's your money. It ain't got nothing to do with me. We all feel like that—Walter and Bennie and me—even Travis.

MAMA (*thoughtfully, and suddenly very far away*) Ten thousand dollars—

RUTH Sure is wonderful.

MAMA Ten thousand dollars.

RUTH You know what you should do, Miss Lena? You should take yourself a trip somewhere. To Europe or South America or someplace—

MAMA (*throwing up her hands at the thought*) Oh, child!

RUTH I'm serious. Just pack up and leave! Go on away and enjoy yourself some. Forget about the family and have yourself a ball for once in your life—

MAMA (*drily*) You sound like I'm just about ready to die. Who'd go with me? What I look like wandering 'round Europe by myself?

RUTH Shoot—these here rich white women do it all the time. They don't think nothing of packing up they suitcases and piling on one of them big steamships and—swoosh!—they gone, child.

MAMA Something always told me I wasn't no rich white woman.

RUTH Well—what are you going to do with it then?

MAMA I ain't rightly decided. (*Thinking. She speaks now with emphasis.*) Some of it got to be put away for Beneatha and her schoolin'—and ain't nothing going to touch that part of it. Nothing. (*She waits several seconds, trying to make up her mind about something, and looks at* RUTH *a little tentatively before going on.*) Been thinking that we maybe could meet the notes on a little old two-story somewhere, with a yard where Travis could play in the summertime, if we use part of the insurance for a down payment and everybody kind of pitch in. I could maybe take on a little day work again, few days a week—

RUTH (*studying her mother-in-law furtively and concentrating on her ironing, anxious to encourage without seeming to*) Well, Lord knows, we've put enough rent into this here rat trap to pay for four houses by now. . . .

MAMA (*looking up at the words "rat trap" and then looking around and leaning back and sighing—in a suddenly reflective mood—*) "Rat trap"—yes, that's all it is. (*Smiling*) I remember just as well the day me and Big Walter moved in here. Hadn't been married but two weeks and wasn't planning on living here no more than a year. (*She shakes her head at the dissolved dream.*) We was going to set away, little by little, don't you know, and buy a little place out in Morgan Park. We had even picked out the house. (*Chuckling a little*) Looks right dumpy today. But Lord, child, you should know all the dreams I had 'bout buying that house and fixing it up and making me a little garden in the back— (*She waits and stops smiling.*) And didn't none of it happen. (*Dropping her hands in a futile gesture*)

RUTH (*keeps her head down, ironing*) Yes, life can be a barrel of disappointments, sometimes.

MAMA Honey, Big Walter would come in here some nights back then and slump down on that couch there and just look at the rug, and look at me and look at the rug and then back at me—and I'd know he was down then . . . really down. (*After a second very long and thoughtful pause; she is seeing back to times that only she can see.*) And then, Lord, when I lost that baby—little Claude—I almost thought I was going to lose Big Walter too. Oh, that man grieved hisself! He was one man to love his children.

RUTH Ain't nothin' can tear at you like losin' your baby.

MAMA I guess that's how come that man finally worked hisself to death like he done. Like he was fighting his own war with this here world that took his baby from him.

RUTH He sure was a fine man, all right. I always liked Mr. Younger.

MAMA Crazy 'bout his children! God knows there was plenty wrong with Walter Younger—hard-headed, mean, kind of wild with women—plenty wrong with him. But he sure loved his children. Always wanted them to have something—be something. That's where Brother gets all these notions, I reckon. Big Walter used to say, he'd get right wet in the eyes sometimes, lean his head back with the water standing in his eyes and say, "Seem like God didn't see fit to give the black man nothing but dreams—but He did give us children to make them dreams seem worth while." (*She smiles.*) He could talk like that, don't you know.

RUTH Yes, he sure could. He was a good man, Mr. Younger.

MAMA Yes, a fine man—just couldn't never catch up with his dreams, that's all.

BENEATHA *comes in, brushing her hair and looking up to the ceiling, where the sound of a vacuum cleaner has started up.*

BENEATHA What could be so dirty on that woman's rugs that she has to vacuum them every single day?

RUTH I wish certain young women 'round here who I could name would take inspiration about certain rugs in a certain apartment I could also mention.

BENEATHA (*shrugging*) How much cleaning can a house need, for Christ's sakes.

MAMA (*not liking the Lord's name used thus*) Bennie!

RUTH Just listen to her—just listen!

BENEATHA Oh, God!

MAMA If you use the Lord's name just one more time—

BENEATHA (*a bit of a whine*) Oh, Mama—

RUTH Fresh—just fresh as salt, this girl!

BENEATHA (*drily*) Well—if the salt loses its savor—

MAMA Now that will do. I just ain't going to have you 'round here reciting the scriptures in vain—you hear me?

BENEATHA How did I manage to get on everybody's wrong side by just walking into a room?

RUTH If you weren't so fresh—

BENEATHA Ruth, I'm twenty years old.

MAMA What time you be home from school today?

BENEATHA Kind of late. (*With enthusiasm*) Madeline is going to start my guitar lessons today.

MAMA *and* RUTH *look up with the same expression.*

MAMA Your *what* kind of lessons?

BENEATHA Guitar.

RUTH Oh, Father!

MAMA How come you done taken it in your mind to learn to play the guitar?

BENEATHA I just want to, that's all.

MAMA (*smiling*) Lord, child, don't you know what to do with yourself? How long it going to be before you get tired of this now—like you got tired of that little play-acting group you joined last year? (*Looking at* RUTH) And what was it the year before that?

RUTH The horseback-riding club for which she bought that fifty-five-dollar riding habit that's been hanging in the closet ever since!

MAMA (to BENEATHA) Why you got to flit so from one thing to another, baby?

BENEATHA (sharply) I just want to learn to play the guitar. Is there anything wrong with that?

MAMA Ain't nobody trying to stop you. I just wonders sometimes why you has to flit so from one thing to another all the time. You ain't never done nothing with all that camera equipment you brought home—

BENEATHA I don't flit! I—I experiment with different forms of expression—

RUTH Like riding a horse?

BENEATHA —People have to express themselves one way or another.

MAMA What is it you want to express?

BENEATHA (angrily) Me! (MAMA and RUTH look at each other and burst into raucous laughter.) Don't worry—I don't expect you to understand.

MAMA (to change the subject) Who you going out with tomorrow night?

BENEATHA (with displeasure) George Murchison again.

MAMA (pleased) Oh—you getting a little sweet on him?

RUTH You ask me, this child ain't sweet on nobody but herself— (Underbreath) Express herself!

They laugh.

BENEATHA Oh—I like George all right, Mama. I mean I like him enough to go out with him and stuff, but—

RUTH (for devilment) What does and stuff mean?

BENEATHA Mind your own business.

MAMA Stop picking at her now, Ruth. (A thoughtful pause, and then a suspicious sudden look at her daughter as she turns in her chair for emphasis) What does it mean?

BENEATHA (wearily) Oh, I just mean I couldn't ever really be serious about George. He's—he's so shallow.

RUTH Shallow—what do you mean he's shallow? He's rich!

MAMA Hush, Ruth.

BENEATHA I know he's rich. He knows he's rich, too.

RUTH Well—what other qualities a man got to have to satisfy you, little girl?

BENEATHA You wouldn't even begin to understand. Anybody who married Walter could not possibly understand.

MAMA (outraged) What kind of way is that to talk about your brother?

BENEATHA Brother is a flip—let's face it.

MAMA (to RUTH, helplessly) What's a flip?

RUTH (glad to add kindling) She's saying he's crazy.

BENEATHA Not crazy. Brother isn't really crazy yet—he—he's an elaborate neurotic.

MAMA Hush your mouth!

BENEATHA As for George. Well. George looks good—he's got a beautiful car and he takes me to nice places and, as my sister-in-law says, he is probably the richest boy I will ever get to know and I even like him sometimes—but if the Youngers are sitting around waiting to see if their little Bennie is going to tie up the family with the Murchisons, they are wasting their time.

RUTH You mean you wouldn't marry George Murchison if he asked you someday? That pretty, rich thing? Honey, I knew you was odd—

BENEATHA No I would not marry him if all I felt for him was what I feel now. Besides, George's family wouldn't really like it.

MAMA Why not?

BENEATHA Oh, Mama—The Murchisons are honest-to-God-real-*live*-rich colored people, and the only people in the world who are more snobbish than rich white people are rich colored people. I thought everybody knew that. I've met Mrs. Murchison. She's a scene!

MAMA You must not dislike people 'cause they well off, honey.

BENEATHA Why not? It makes just as much sense as disliking people 'cause they are poor, and lots of people do that.

RUTH (*a wisdom-of-the-ages manner. To* MAMA) Well, she'll get over some of this—

BENEATHA Get over it? What are you talking about, Ruth? Listen, I'm going to be a doctor. I'm not worried about who I'm going to marry yet—if I ever get married.

MAMA AND RUTH *If!*

MAMA Now, Bennie—

BENEATHA Oh, I probably will . . . but first I'm going to be a doctor, and George, for one, still thinks that's pretty funny. I couldn't be bothered with that, I am going to be a doctor and everybody around here better understand that!

MAMA (*kindly*) 'Course you going to be a doctor, honey, God willing.

BENEATHA (*drily*) God hasn't got a thing to do with it.

MAMA Beneatha—that just wasn't necessary.

BENEATHA Well—neither is God. I get sick of hearing about God.

MAMA Beneatha!

BENEATHA I mean it! I'm just tired of hearing about God all the time. What has He got to do with anything? Does He pay tuition?

MAMA You 'bout to get your fresh little jaw slapped!

RUTH That's just what she needs, all right!

BENEATHA Why? Why can't I say what I want to around here, like everybody else?

MAMA It don't sound nice for a young girl to say things like that—you wasn't brought up that way. Me and your father went to trouble to get you and Brother to church every Sunday.

BENEATHA Mama, you don't understand. It's all a matter of ideas, and God is just one idea I don't accept. It's not important. I am not going out and be immoral or commit crimes because I don't believe in God. I don't even think about it. It's just that I get tired of Him getting credit for all the things the human race achieves through its own stubborn effort. There simply is no blasted God—there is only man and it is he who makes miracles!

MAMA *absorbs this speech, studies her daughter and rises slowly and crosses to* BENEATHA *and slaps her powerfully across the face. After, there is only silence and the daughter drops her eyes from her mother's face, and* MAMA *is very tall before her.*

MAMA Now—you say after me, in my mother's house there is still God. (*There is a long pause and* BENEATHA *stares at the floor wordlessly.* MAMA *repeats the phrase with precision and cool emotion.*) In my mother's house there is still God.

BENEATHA In my mother's house there is still God.

A long pause.

MAMA (*walking away from* BENEATHA, *too disturbed for triumphant posture. Stopping and turning back to her daughter*) There are some ideas we ain't going to have in this house. Not long as I am at the head of this family.

BENEATHA Yes, ma'am.

MAMA *walks out of the room.*

RUTH (*almost gently, with profound understanding*) You think you a woman, Bennie—but you still a little girl. What you did was childish—so you got treated like a child.

BENEATHA I see. (*Quietly*) I also see that everybody thinks it's all right for Mama to be a tyrant. But all the tyranny in the world will never put a God in the heavens! (*She picks up her books and goes out.*)

RUTH (*goes to* MAMA's *door*) She said she was sorry.

MAMA (*coming out, going to her plant*) They frightens me, Ruth. My children.

RUTH You got good children, Lena. They just a little off sometimes—but they're good.

MAMA No—there's something come down between me and them that don't let us understand each other and I don't know what it is. One done almost lost his mind thinking 'bout money all the time and the other done commence to talk about things I can't seem to understand in no form or fashion. What is it that's changing, Ruth?

RUTH (*soothingly, older than her years*) Now . . . you taking it all too seriously. You just got strong-willed children and it takes a strong woman like you to keep 'em in hand.

MAMA (*looking at her plant and sprinkling a little water on it*) They spirited all right, my children. Got to admit they got spirit—Bennie and Walter. Like this little old plant that ain't never had enough sunshine or nothing—and look at it. . . .

She has her back to RUTH, *who has had to stop ironing and lean against something and put the back of her hand to her forehead.*

RUTH (*trying to keep* MAMA *from noticing*) You . . . sure . . . loves that little old thing, don't you? . . .

MAMA Well, I always wanted me a garden like I used to see sometimes at the back of the houses down home. This plant is close as I ever got to having one. (*She looks out of the window as she replaces the plant.*) Lord, ain't nothing as dreary as the view from this window on a dreary day, is there? Why ain't you singing this morning, Ruth? Sing that "No Ways Tired." That song always lifts me up so—(*She turns at last to see that* RUTH *has slipped quietly into a chair, in a state of semiconsciousness.*) Ruth! Ruth honey—what's the matter with you . . . Ruth!

Curtain

SCENE II.

It is the following morning; a Saturday morning, and house cleaning is in progress at the Youngers. Furniture has been shoved hither and yon and MAMA *is giving the kitchen-area walls a washing down.* BENEATHA, *in dungarees, with a handkerchief tied around her face, is spraying insecticide into the cracks in the walls. As they work, the radio is on and a Southside disc-jockey program is inappropriately filling the house with a rather exotic saxophone blues.* TRAVIS, *the sole idle one, is leaning on his arms, looking out of the window.*

TRAVIS Grandmama, that stuff Bennie is using smells awful. Can I go downstairs, please?

MAMA Did you get all them chores done already? I ain't see you doing much.

TRAVIS Yes'm—finished early. Where did mama go this morning?

MAMA (*looking at* BENEATHA) She had to go on a little errand.

TRAVIS Where?

MAMA To tend to her business.

TRAVIS Can I go outside then?

MAMA Oh, I guess so. You better stay right in front of the house, though . . . and keep a good lookout for the postman.

TRAVIS Yes'm. (*He starts out and decides to give his* AUNT BENEATHA *a good swat on the legs as he passes her.*) Leave them poor little old cockroaches alone, they ain't bothering you none.

He runs as she swings the spray gun at him both viciously and playfully. WALTER *enters from the bedroom and goes to the phone.*

MAMA Look out there, girl, before you be spilling some of that stuff on that child!

TRAVIS (*teasing*) That's right—look out now! (*He exits.*)

BENEATHA (*drily*) I can't imagine that it would hurt him—it has never hurt the roaches.

MAMA Well, little boys' hides ain't as tough as Southside roaches.

WALTER (*into phone*) Hello—Let me talk to Willy Harris.

MAMA You better get over there behind the bureau. I seen one marching out of there like Napoleon yesterday.

WALTER Hello. Willy? It ain't come yet. It'll be here in a few minutes. Did the lawyer give you the papers?

BENEATHA There's really only one way to get rid of them, Mama—

MAMA How?

BENEATHA Set fire to this building.

WALTER Good. Good. I'll be right over.

BENEATHA Where did Ruth go, Walter?

WALTER I don't know. (*He exits abruptly.*)

BENEATHA Mama, where did Ruth go?

MAMA (*looking at her with meaning*) To the doctor, I think.

BENEATHA The doctor? What's the matter? (*They exchange glances.*) You don't think—

MAMA (*with her sense of drama*) Now I ain't saying what I think. But I ain't never been wrong 'bout a woman neither.

The phone rings.

BENEATHA (*at the phone*) Hay-lo . . . (*Pause, and a moment of recognition*) Well—when did you get back! . . . And how was it? . . . Of course I've missed you—in my way . . . This morning? No . . . house cleaning and all that and Mama hates it if I let people come over when the house is like this . . . You *have?* Well, that's different. . . . What is it—Oh, what the hell, come on over . . . Right, see you then. (*She hangs up.*)

MAMA Who?

BENEATHA Asagai—Joseph Asagai. He's an African boy I met on campus. He's been studying in Canada all summer.

MAMA What's his name?

BENEATHA Asagai, Joseph. Ah-sah-guy . . . He's from Nigeria.

MAMA Oh, that's the little country that was founded by slaves way back . . .

BENEATHA No, Mama—that's Liberia.

MAMA I don't think I never met no African before.

BENEATHA Well, do me a favor and don't ask him a whole lot of ignorant questions about Africans. I mean, do they wear clothes and all that—

MAMA Well, now, I guess if you think we so ignorant 'round here maybe you shouldn't bring your friends here—

BENEATHA It's just that people ask such crazy things. All anyone seems to know about when it comes to Africa is Tarzan—

MAMA (*indignantly*) Why should I know anything about Africa?

BENEATHA Why do you give money at church for the missionary work?

MAMA Well, that's to help save people.

BENEATHA You mean to save them from *heathenism*—

MAMA (*innocently*) Yes.

BENEATHA I'm afraid they need more salvation from the British and the French.

RUTH *comes in forlornly and pulls off her coat with dejection. They both turn to look at her.*

RUTH (*dispiritedly*) Well, I guess from all the happy faces—everybody knows.

BENEATHA You pregnant?

MAMA Lord have mercy, I sure hope it's a little old girl. Travis ought to have a sister.

BENEATHA *and* RUTH *give her a hopeless look for this grandmotherly enthusiasm.*

BENEATHA How far along are you?

RUTH Two months.

BENEATHA Did you mean to? I mean did you plan it or was it an accident?

MAMA What do you know about planning or not planning?

BENEATHA Oh, Mama.

RUTH (*wearily*) She's twenty years old, Lena.

BENEATHA Did you plan it, Ruth?

RUTH Mind your own business.

BENEATHA It is my business—where is he going to live, on the roof? (*There is silence following the remark as the three women react to the sense of it.*) Gee—I didn't mean that, Ruth, honest. Gee, I don't feel like that at all. I—I think it is wonderful.

RUTH (*dully*) Wonderful.

BENEATHA Yes—really.

MAMA (*looking at* RUTH, *worried*) Doctor say everything going to be all right?

RUTH (*far away*) Yes—she says everything is going to be fine. . . .

MAMA (*immediately suspicious*) "She"—What doctor you went to?

RUTH *folds over, near hysteria.*

MAMA (*worriedly hovering over* RUTH) Ruth honey—what's the matter with you—you sick?

RUTH *has her fists clenched on her thighs and is fighting hard to suppress a scream that seems to be rising in her.*

BENEATHA What's the matter with her, Mama?

MAMA (*working her fingers in* RUTH's *shoulder to relax her*) She be all right. Women gets right depressed sometimes when they get her way. (*Speaking softly, expertly, rapidly*) Now you just relax. That's right . . . just lean back, don't think 'bout nothing at all . . . nothing at all—

RUTH I'm all right. . . .

The glassy-eyed look melts and then she collapses into a fit of heavy sobbing. The bell rings.

BENEATHA Oh, my God—that must be Asagai.

MAMA (*to* RUTH) Come on now, honey. You need to lie down and rest awhile . . . then have some nice hot food.

They exit, RUTH's *weight on her mother-in-law.* BENEATHA, *herself profoundly disturbed, opens the door to admit a rather dramatic-looking young man with a large package.*

ASAGAI *Hello, Alaiyo—*

BENEATHA (*holding the door open and regarding him with pleasure*) Hello . . . (*Long pause*) Well—come in. And please excuse everything. My mother was very upset about my letting anyone come here with the place like this.

ASAGAI (*coming into the room*) You look disturbèd too. . . . Is something wrong?

BENEATHA (*still at the door, absently*) Yes . . . we've all got acute ghetto-itus. (*She smiles and comes toward him, finding a cigarette and sitting.*) So—sit down! How was Canada?

ASAGAI (*a sophisticate*) Canadian.

BENEATHA (*looking at him*) I'm very glad you are back.

ASAGAI (*looking back at her in turn*) Are you really?

BENEATHA Yes—very.

ASAGAI Why—you were quite glad when I went away. What happened?

BENEATHA You went away.

ASAGAI Ahhhhhhhh.

BENEATHA Before—you wanted to be so serious before there was time.

ASAGAI How much time must there be before one knows what one feels?

BENEATHA (*stalling this particular conversation. Her hands pressed together, in a deliberately childish gesture*) What did you bring me?

ASAGAI (*handing her the package*) Open it and see.

BENEATHA (*eagerly opening the package and drawing out some records and the colorful robes of a Nigerian woman*) Oh, Asagai! . . . You got them for me! . . . How beautiful . . . and the records too! (*She lifts out the robes and runs to the mirror with them and holds the drapery up in front of herself.*)

ASAGAI (*coming to her at the mirror*) I shall have to teach you how to drape it properly. (*He flings the material about her for the moment and stands back to look at her.*) Ah— Oh-pay-gay-day, oh-gbah-mu-shay. (*A Yoruba exclamation for admiration*) You wear it well . . . very well . . . mutilated hair and all.

BENEATHA (*turning suddenly*) My hair—what's wrong with my hair?

ASAGAI (*shrugging*) Were you born with it like that?

BENEATHA (*reaching up to touch it*) No . . . of course not. (*She looks back to the mirror, disturbed.*)

ASAGAI (*smiling*) How then?

BENEATHA You know perfectly well how . . . as crinkly as yours . . . that's how.

ASAGAI And it is ugly to you that way?

BENEATHA (*quickly*) Oh, no—not ugly . . . (*More slowly, apologetically*) But it's so hard to manage when it's, well—raw.

ASAGAI And so to accommodate that—you mutilate it every week?

BENEATHA It's not mutilation!

ASAGAI (*laughing aloud at her seriousness*) Oh . . . please! I am only teasing you because you are so very serious about these things. (*He stands back from her and folds his arms across his chest as he watches her pulling at her hair and frowning in the mirror.*) Do you remember the first time you met me at school? . . . (*He laughs.*) You came up to me and you said—and I thought you were the most serious little thing I had ever seen—you said: (*He imitates her.*) "Mr. Asagai—I want very much to talk with you. About Africa. You see, Mr. Asagai, I am looking for my *identity!*" (*He laughs.*)

BENEATHA (*turning to him, not laughing*) Yes—(*Her face is quizzical, profoundly disturbed.*)

ASAGAI (*still teasing and reaching out and taking her face in his hands and turning her profile to him*) Well . . . it is true that this is not so much a profile of a Hollywood queen as perhaps a queen of the Nile—(*A mock dismissal of the importance of the question*) But what does it matter? Assimilationism is so popular in your country.

BENEATHA (*wheeling, passionately, sharply*) I am not an assimilationist!

ASAGAI (*the protest hangs in the room for a moment and* ASAGAI *studies her, his laughter fading*) Such a serious one. (*There is a pause.*) So—you like the robes? You must take excellent care of them—they are from my sister's personal wardrobe.

BENEATHA (*with incredulity*) You—you sent all the way home—for me?

ASAGAI (*with charm*) For you—I would do much more. . . . Well, that is what I came for. I must go.

BENEATHA Will you call me Monday?

ASAGAI Yes . . . We have a great deal to talk about. I mean about identity and time and all that.

BENEATHA Time?

ASAGAI Yes. About how much time one needs to know what one feels.

BENEATHA You never understood that there is more than one kind of feeling which can exist between a man and a woman—or, at least, there should be.

ASAGAI (*shaking his head negatively but gently*) No. Between a man and a woman there need be only one kind of feeling. I have that for you. . . . Now even . . . right this moment. . . .

BENEATHA I know—and by itself—it won't do. I can find that anywhere.

ASAGAI For a woman it should be enough.

BENEATHA I know—because that's what it says in all the novels that men write. But it isn't. Go ahead and laugh—but I'm not interested in being someone's little episode in America or—(*with feminine vengeance*)—one of them! (ASAGAI *has burst into laughter again.*) That's funny as hell, huh!

ASAGAI It's just that every American girl I have known has said that to me. White— black—in this you are all the same. And the same speech, too!

BENEATHA (*angrily*) Yuk, yuk, yuk!

ASAGAI It's how you can be sure that the world's most liberated women are not liberated at all. You all talk about it too much!

MAMA *enters and is immediately all social charm because of the presence of a guest.*

BENEATHA Oh—Mama—this is Mr. Asagai.

MAMA How do you do?

ASAGAI (*total politeness to an elder*) How do you do, Mrs. Younger. Please forgive me for coming at such an outrageous hour on a Saturday.

MAMA Well, you are quite welcome. I just hope you understand that our house don't always look like this. (*Chatterish*) You must come again. I would love to hear all about—(*not sure of the name*)—your country. I think it's so sad the way our American Negroes don't know nothing about Africa 'cept Tarzan and all that. And all that money they pour into these churches when they ought to be helping you people over there drive out them French and Englishmen done taken away your land.

The mother flashes a slightly superior look at her daughter upon completion of the recitation.

ASAGAI (*taken aback by this sudden and acutely unrelated expression of sympathy*) Yes
. . . yes. . . .

MAMA (*smiling at him suddenly and relaxing and looking him over*) How many miles is
it from here to where you come from?

ASAGAI Many thousands.

MAMA (*looking at him as she would* WALTER) I bet you don't half look after yourself,
being away from your mama either. I spec you better come 'round here from time to
time and get yourself some decent home-cooked meals. . . .

ASAGAI (*moved*) Thank you. Thank you very much. (*They are all quiet, then—*) Well
. . . I must go. I will call you Monday, Alaiyo.

MAMA What's that he call you?

ASAGAI Oh—"Alaiyo." I hope you don't mind. Is it what you would call a nickname,
I think. It is a Yoruba word. I am a Yoruba.

MAMA (*looking at* BENEATHA) I—I thought he was from—

ASAGAI (*understanding*) Nigeria is my country. Yoruba is my tribal origin—

BENEATHA You didn't tell us what Alaiyo means . . . for all I know, you might be calling
me Little Idiot or something. . . .

ASAGAI Well . . . let me see . . . I do not know how just to explain it. . . . The sense
of a thing can be so different when it changes languages.

BENEATHA You're evading.

ASAGAI No—really it is difficult. . . . (*Thinking*) It means . . . it means One for Whom
Bread—Food—Is Not Enough. (*He looks at her.*) Is that all right?

BENEATHA (*understanding, softly*) Thank you.

MAMA (*looking from one to the other and not understanding any of it*) Well . . . that's
nice. . . . You must come see us again—Mr.—

ASAGAI Ah-sah-guy . . .

MAMA Yes . . . Do come again.

ASAGAI Good-bye. (*He exits.*)

MAMA (*after him*) Lord, that's a pretty thing just went out here! (*Insinuatingly, to her
daughter*) Yes, I guess I see why we done commence to get so interested in Africa
'round here. Missionaries my aunt Jenny! (*She exits.*)

BENEATHA Oh, Mama! . . .

*She picks up the Nigerian dress and holds it up to her in front of the mirror again. She
sets the headdress on haphazardly and then notices her hair again and clutches at it and
then replaces the headdress and frowns at herself. Then she starts to wriggle in front of
the mirror as she thinks a Nigerian woman might.* TRAVIS *enters and regards her.*

TRAVIS You cracking up?

BENEATHA Shut up.

*She pulls the headdress off and looks at herself in the mirror and clutches at her hair
again and squinches her eyes as if trying to imagine something. Then, suddenly, she gets
her raincoat and kerchief and hurriedly prepares for going out.*

MAMA (*coming back into the room*) She's resting now. Travis, baby, run next door and
ask Miss Johnson to please let me have a little kitchen cleanser. This here can is empty
as Jacob's kettle.

TRAVIS I just come in.

MAMA Do as you told. (*He exits and she looks at her daughter.*) Where you going?

BENEATHA (*halting at the door*) To become a queen of the Nile!

She exits in a breathless blaze of glory. RUTH *appears in the bedroom doorway.*

MAMA Who told you to get up?

RUTH Ain't nothing wrong with me to be lying in no bed for. Where did Bennie go?

MAMA (*drumming her fingers*) Far as I could make out—to Egypt. (RUTH *just looks at her.*) What time is it getting to?

RUTH Ten twenty. And the mailman going to ring that bell this morning just like he done every morning for the last umpteen years.

TRAVIS *comes in with the cleanser can.*

TRAVIS She say to tell you that she don't have much.

MAMA (*angrily*) Lord, some people I could name sure is tight-fisted! (*Directing her grandson*) Mark two cans of cleanser down on the list there. If she that hard up for kitchen cleanser, I sure don't want to forget to get her none!

RUTH Lena—maybe the woman is just short on cleanser—

MAMA (*not listening*) —Much baking powder as she done borrowed from me all these years, she could of done gone into the baking business!

The bell sounds suddenly and sharply and all three are stunned—serious and silent— mid-speech. In spite of all the other conversations and distractions of the morning, this is what they have been waiting for, even TRAVIS, *who looks helplessly from his mother to his grandmother.* RUTH *is the first to come to life again.*

RUTH (*to* TRAVIS) Get down them steps, boy!

TRAVIS *snaps to life and flies out to get the mail.*

MAMA (*her eyes wide, her hand to her breast*) You mean it done really come?

RUTH (*excitedly*) Oh, Miss Lena!

MAMA (*collecting herself*) Well . . . I don't know what we all so excited about 'round here for. We known it was coming for months.

RUTH That's a whole lot different from having it come and being able to hold it in your hands . . . a piece of paper worth ten thousand dollars. . . . (TRAVIS *bursts back into the room. He holds the envelope high above his head, like a little dancer, his face is radiant and he is breathless. He moves to his grandmother with sudden slow ceremony and puts the envelope into her hands. She accepts it, and then merely holds it and looks at it.*) Come on! Open it . . . Lord have mercy, I wish Walter Lee was here!

TRAVIS Open it, Grandmama!

MAMA (*staring at it*) Now you all be quiet. It's just a check.

RUTH Open it. . . .

MAMA (*still staring at it*) Now don't act silly. . . . We ain't never been no people to act silly 'bout no money—

RUTH (*swiftly*) We ain't never had none before—open it!

MAMA *finally makes a good strong tear and pulls out the thin blue slice of paper and inspects it closely. The boy and his mother study it raptly over* MAMA's *shoulders.*

MAMA Travis! (*She is counting off with doubt.*) Is that the right number of zeros.

TRAVIS Yes'm . . . ten thousand dollars. Gaalee, Grandmama, you rich.

MAMA (*she holds the check away from her, still looking at it. Slowly her face sobers into a mask of unhappiness*) Ten thousand dollars. (*She hands it to* RUTH.) Put it away somewhere, Ruth. (*She does not look at* RUTH; *her eyes seem to be seeing something somewhere very far off.*) Ten thousand dollars they give you. Ten thousand dollars.

TRAVIS (*to his mother, sincerely*) What's the matter with Grandmama—don't she want to be rich?

RUTH (*distractedly*) You go on out and play now, baby. (TRAVIS *exits.* MAMA *starts wiping dishes absently, humming intently to herself.* RUTH *turns to her, with kind exasperation.*) You're gone and got yourself upset.

MAMA (*not looking at her*) I spec if it wasn't for you all . . . I would just put that money away or give it to the church or something.

RUTH Now what kind of talk is that. Mr. Younger would just be plain mad if he could hear you talking foolish like that.

MAMA (*stopping and staring off*) Yes . . . he sure would. (*Sighing*) We got enough to do with that money, all right. (*She halts then, and turns and looks at her daughter-in-law hard;* RUTH *avoids her eyes and* MAMA *wipes her hands with finality and starts to speak firmly to* RUTH.) Where did you go today, girl?

RUTH To the doctor.

MAMA (*impatiently*) Now, Ruth . . . you know better than that. Old Doctor Jones is strange enough in his way but there ain't nothing 'bout him make somebody slip and call him "she"—like you done this morning.

RUTH Well, that's what happened—my tongue slipped.

MAMA You went to see that woman, didn't you?

RUTH (*defensively, giving herself away*) What woman you talking about?

MAMA (*angrily*) That woman who—

WALTER *enters in great excitement.*

WALTER Did it come?

MAMA (*quietly*) Can't you give people a Christian greeting before you start asking about money?

WALTER (*to* RUTH) Did it come? (RUTH *unfolds the check and lays it quietly before him, watching him intently with thoughts of her own.* WALTER *sits down and grasps it close and counts off the zeros.*) Ten thousand dollars—(*He turns suddenly, frantically to his mother and draws some papers out of his breast pocket.*) Mama—look. Old Willy Harris put everything on paper—

MAMA Son—I think you ought to talk to your wife. . . . I'll go on out and leave you alone if you want—

WALTER I can talk to her later—Mama, look—

MAMA Son—

WALTER WILL SOMEBODY PLEASE LISTEN TO ME TODAY!

MAMA (*quietly*) I don't 'low no yellin' in this house, Walter Lee, and you know it— (WALTER *stares at them in frustration and starts to speak several times.*) And there ain't going to be no investing in no liquor stores. I don't aim to have to speak on that again.

A long pause.

WALTER Oh—so you don't aim to have to speak on that again? So *you* have decided. . . . (*Crumpling his papers*) Well, *you* tell that to my boy tonight when you put him to sleep on the living-room couch. . . . (*Turning to* MAMA *and speaking directly to her*) Yeah—and tell it to my wife, Mama, tomorrow when she has to go out of here to look after somebody else's kids. And tell it to *me*, Mama, every time we need a new pair of curtains and I have to watch *you* go out and work in somebody's kitchen. Yeah, you tell me then!

WALTER *starts out.*

RUTH Where you going?
WALTER I'm going out!
RUTH Where?
WALTER Just out of this house somewhere—
RUTH (*getting her coat*) I'll come too.
WALTER I don't want you to come!
RUTH I got something to talk to you about, Walter.
WALTER That's too bad.
MAMA (*still quietly*) Walter Lee— (*She waits and he finally turns and looks at her.*) Sit down.
WALTER I'm a grown man, Mama.
MAMA Ain't nobody said you wasn't grown. But you still in my house and my presence. And as long as you are—you'll talk to your wife civil. Now sit down.
RUTH (*suddenly*) Oh, let him go on out and drink himself to death! He makes me sick to my stomach! (*She flings her coat against him.*)
WALTER (*violently*) And you turn mine too, baby! (RUTH *goes into their bedroom and slams the door behind her.*) That was my greatest mistake—
MAMA (*still quietly*) Walter, what is the matter with you?
WALTER Matter with me? Ain't nothing the matter with *me*!
MAMA Yes there is. Something eating you up like a crazy man. Something more than me not giving you this money. The past few years I been watching it happen to you. You get all nervous acting and kind of wild in the eyes— (WALTER *jumps up impatiently at her words.*) I said sit there now, I'm talking to you!
WALTER Mama—I don't need no nagging at me today.
MAMA Seem like you getting to a place where you always tied up in some kind of knot about something. But if anybody ask you 'bout it you just yell at 'em and bust out the house and go out and drink somewheres. Walter Lee, people can't live with that. Ruth's a good, patient girl in her way—but you getting to be too much. Boy, don't make the mistake of driving that girl away from you.
WALTER Why—what she do for me?
MAMA She loves you.
WALTER Mama—I'm going out. I want to go off somewhere and be by myself for a while.
MAMA I'm sorry 'bout your liquor store, son. It just wasn't the thing for us to do. That's what I want to tell you about—
WALTER I got to go out, Mama— (*He rises.*)
MAMA It's dangerous, son.
WALTER What's dangerous?
MAMA When a man goes outside his home to look for peace.
WALTER (*beseechingly*) Then why can't there never be no peace in this house then?
MAMA You done found it in some other house?

WALTER No—there ain't no woman! Why do women always think there's a woman somewhere when a man gets restless. (*Coming to her*) Mama—Mama—I want so many things. . . .

MAMA Yes, son—

WALTER I want so many things that they are driving me kind of crazy. . . . Mama—look at me.

MAMA I'm looking at you. You a good-looking boy. You got a job, a nice wife, a fine boy and—

WALTER A job. (*Looks at her*) Mama, a job? I open and close car doors all day long. I drive a man around in his limousine and I say, "Yes, sir; no, sir; very good, sir; shall I take the Drive, sir?" Mama, that ain't no kind of job . . . that ain't nothing at all. (*Very quietly*) Mama, I don't know if I can make you understand.

MAMA Understand what, baby?

WALTER (*quietly*) Sometimes it's like I can see the future stretched out in front of me—just plain as day. The future, Mama. Hanging over there at the edge of my days. Just waiting for me—a big, looming blank space—full of *nothing*. Just waiting for *me*. (*Pause*) Mama—sometimes when I'm downtown and I pass them cool, quiet-looking restaurants where them white boys are sitting back and talking 'bout things . . . sitting there turning deals worth millions of dollars . . . sometimes I see guys don't look much older than me—

MAMA Son—how come you talk so much 'bout money?

WALTER (*with immense passion*) Because it is life, Mama!

MAMA (*quietly*) Oh— (*Very quietly*) So now it's life. Money is life. Once upon a time freedom used to be life—now it's money. I guess the world really do change. . . .

WALTER No—it was always money, Mama. We just didn't know about it.

MAMA No . . . something has changed. (*She looks at him.*) You something new, boy. In my time we was worried about not being lynched and getting to the North if we could and how to stay alive and still have a pinch of dignity too. . . . Now here come you and Beneatha—talking 'bout things we ain't never even thought about hardly, me and your daddy. You ain't satisfied or proud of nothing we done. I mean that you had a home; that we kept you out of trouble till you was grown; that you don't have to ride to work on the back of nobody's streetcar—You my children—but how different we done become.

WALTER You just don't understand, Mama, you just don't understand.

MAMA Son—do you know your wife is expecting another baby? (WALTER *stands, stunned, and absorbs what his mother has said.*) That's what she wanted to talk to you about. (WALTER *sinks down into a chair.*) This ain't for me to be telling—but you ought to know. (*She waits.*) I think Ruth is thinking 'bout getting rid of that child.

WALTER (*slowly understanding*) No—no—Ruth wouldn't do that.

MAMA When the world gets ugly enough—a woman will do anything for her family. *The part that's already living.*

WALTER You don't know Ruth, Mama, if you think she would do that.

RUTH *opens the bedroom door and stands there a little limp.*

RUTH (*beaten*) Yes I would too, Walter. (*Pause*) I gave her a five-dollar down payment.

There is total silence as the man stares at his wife and the mother stares at her son.

MAMA (*presently*) Well— (*Tightly*) Well—son, I'm waiting to hear you say something.

. . . I'm waiting to hear how you be your father's son. Be the man he was. . . . (*Pause*) Your wife say she going to destroy your child. And I'm waiting to hear you talk like him and say we a people who give children life, not who destroys them— (*She rises.*) I'm waiting to see you stand up and look like your daddy and say we done give up one baby to poverty and that we ain't going to give up nary another one. . . . I'm waiting.

WALTER Ruth—

MAMA If you a son of mine, tell her! (WALTER *turns, looks at her and can say nothing. She continues, bitterly.*) You . . . you are a disgrace to your father's memory. Somebody get me my hat.

Curtain

ACT II

SCENE I.

Time: Later the same day.

At rise: RUTH *is ironing again. She has the radio going. Presently* BENEATHA'S *bedroom door opens and* RUTH'S *mouth falls and she puts down the iron in fascination.*

RUTH What have we got on tonight!

BENEATHA (*emerging grandly from the doorway so that we can see her thoroughly robed in the costume* ASAGAI *brought*) You are looking at what a well-dressed Nigerian woman wears— (*She parades for* RUTH, *her hair completely hidden by the headdress; she is coquettishly fanning herself with an ornate oriental fan, mistakenly more like Butterfly than any Nigerian that ever was.*) Isn't it beautiful? (*She promenades to the radio and, with an arrogant flourish, turns off the good loud blues that is playing.*) Enough of this assimilationist junk! (RUTH *follows her with her eyes as she goes to the phonograph and puts on a record and turns and waits ceremoniously for the music to come up. Then, with a shout—*) OCOMOGOSIAY!

RUTH *jumps. The music comes up, a lovely Nigerian melody.* BENEATHA *listens, enraptured, her eyes far away—"back to the past." She begins to dance.* RUTH *is dumbfounded.*

RUTH What kind of dance is that?

BENEATHA A folk dance.

RUTH (*Pearl Bailey*) What kind of folks do that, honey?

BENEATHA It's from Nigeria. It's a dance of welcome.

RUTH Who you welcoming?

BENEATHA The men back to the village.

RUTH Where they been?

BENEATHA How should I know—out hunting or something. Anyway, they are coming back now. . . .

RUTH Well, that's good.

BENEATHA (*with the record*)

> Alundi, alundi
> Alundi alunya
> Jop pu a jeepua
> Ang gu soooooooooo
>
> Ai yai yae . . .
> Ayehaye—alundi . . .

WALTER *comes in during this performance; he has obviously been drinking. He leans against the door heavily and watches his sister, at first with distaste. Then his eyes look off—"back to the past"—as he lifts both his fists to the roof, screaming.*

WALTER YEAH . . . AND ETHIOPIA STRETCH FORTH HER HANDS AGAIN!. . .

RUTH *(drily, looking at him)* Yes—and Africa sure is claiming her own tonight. *(She gives them both up and starts ironing again.)*

WALTER *(all in a drunken, dramatic shout)* Shut up! . . . . I'm digging them drums . . . them drums move me! . . . *(He makes his weaving way to his wife's face and leans in close to her.)* In my heart of hearts—*(he thumps his chest)*—I am much warrior!

RUTH *(without even looking up)* In your heart of hearts you are much drunkard.

WALTER *(coming away from her and starting to wander around the room, shouting)* Me and Jomo . . . *(Intently, in his sister's face. She has stopped dancing to watch him in this unknown mood.)* That's my man, Kenyatta. *(Shouting and thumping his chest)* FLAMING SPEAR! HOT DAMN! *(He is suddenly in possession of an imaginary spear and actively spearing enemies all over the room.)* OCOMOGOSIAY . . . THE LION IS WAKING . . . OWIMOWEH! *(He pulls his shirt open and leaps up on a table and gestures with his spear. The bell rings. RUTH goes to answer.)*

BENEATHA *(to encourage WALTER, thoroughly caught up with this side of him)* OCOMOGOSIAY, FLAMING SPEAR!

WALTER *(on the table, very far gone, his eyes pure glass sheets. He sees what we cannot, that he is a leader of his people, a great chief, a descendant of Chaka, and that the hour to march has come)* Listen, my black broth—ers—

BENEATHA OCOMOGOSIAY!

WALTER —Do you hear the waters rushing against the shores of the coastlands—

BENEATHA OCOMOGOSIAY!

WALTER —Do you hear the screeching of the cocks in yonder hills beyond where the chiefs meet in council for the coming of the mighty war—

BENEATHA OCOMOGOSIAY!

WALTER —Do you hear the beating of the wings of the birds flying low over the mountains and the low places of our land—

RUTH *opens the door.* GEORGE MURCHISON *enters.*

BENEATHA OCOMOGOSIAY!

WALTER —Do you hear the singing of the women, singing the war songs of our fathers to the babies in the great houses . . . singing the sweet war songs? OH, DO YOU HEAR, MY BLACK BROTHERS!

BENEATHA *(completely gone)* We hear you, Flaming Spear—

WALTER Telling us to prepare for the greatness of the time— *(To GEORGE)* Black Brother! *(He extends his hand for the fraternal clasp.)*

GEORGE Black Brother, hell!

RUTH *(having had enough, and embarrassed for the family)* Beneatha, you got company— what's the matter with you? Walter Lee Younger, get down off that table and stop acting like a fool. . . .

WALTER *comes down off the table suddenly and makes a quick exit to the bathroom.*

RUTH He's had a little to drink. . . . I don't know what her excuse is.

GEORGE (*to* BENEATHA) Look honey, we're going *to* the theater—we're not going to be *in* it . . . so go change, huh?

RUTH You expect this boy to go out with you looking like that?

BENEATHA (*looking at* GEORGE) That's up to George. If he's ashamed of his heritage—

GEORGE Oh, don't be so proud of yourself, Bennie—just because you look eccentric.

BENEATHA How can something that's natural be eccentric?

GEORGE That's what being eccentric means—being natural. Get dressed.

BENEATHA I don't like that, George.

RUTH Why must you and your brother make an argument out of everything people say?

BENEATHA Because I hate assimilationist Negroes!

RUTH Will somebody please tell me what assimila-whoever means!

GEORGE Oh, it's just a college girl's way of calling people Uncle Toms—but that isn't what it means at all.

RUTH Well, what does it mean?

BENEATHA (*cutting* GEORGE *off and staring at him as she replies to* RUTH) It means someone who is willing to give up his own culture and submerge himself completely in the dominant, and in this case, *oppressive* culture!

GEORGE Oh, dear, dear, dear! Here we go! A lecture on the African past! On our Great West African Heritage! In one second we will hear all about the great Ashanti empires; the great Songhay civilizations; and the great sculpture of Bénin—and then some poetry in the Bantu—and the whole monologue will end with the word *heritage*! (*Nastily*) Let's face it, baby, your heritage is nothing but a bunch of raggedy-assed spirituals and some grass huts!

BENEATHA *Grass huts!* (RUTH *crosses to her and forcibly pushes her toward the bedroom.*) See there . . . you are standing there in your splendid ignorance talking about people who were the first to smelt iron on the face of the earth! (RUTH *is pushing her through the door.*) The Ashanti were performing surgical operations when the English—(RUTH *pulls the door to, with* BENEATHA *on the other side, and smiles graciously at* GEORGE. BENEATHA *opens the door and shouts the end of the sentence defiantly at* GEORGE)— were still tattooing themselves with blue dragons. . . . (*She goes back inside.*)

RUTH Have a seat, George. (*They both sit.* RUTH *folds her hands rather primly on her lap, determined to demonstrate the civilization of the family.*) Warm, ain't it? I mean for September. (*Pause*) Just like they always say about Chicago weather: If it's too hot or cold for you, just wait a minute and it'll change. (*She smiles happily at this cliché of clichés.*) Everybody say it's got to do with them bombs and things they keep setting off. (*Pause*) Would you like a nice cold beer?

GEORGE No, thank you. I don't care for beer. (*He looks at his watch*). I hope she hurries up.

RUTH What time is the show?

GEORGE It's an eight-thirty curtain. That's just Chicago, though. In New York standard curtain time is eight forty. (*He is rather proud of this knowledge.*)

RUTH (*properly appreciating it*) You get to New York a lot?

GEORGE (*offhand*) Few times a year.

RUTH Oh—that's nice. I've never been to New York.

WALTER *enters. We feel he has relieved himself, but the edge of unreality is still with him.*

WALTER New York ain't got nothing Chicago ain't. Just a bunch of hustling people all squeezed up together—being "Eastern." (*He turns his face into a screw of displeasure.*)

GEORGE Oh—you've been?

WALTER *Plenty* of times.

RUTH (*shocked at the lie*) Walter Lee Younger!

WALTER (*staring her down*) Plenty! (*Pause*) What we got to drink in this house? Why don't you offer this man some refreshment? (*To* GEORGE) They don't know how to entertain people in this house, man.

GEORGE Thank you—I don't really care for anything.

WALTER (*feeling his head; sobriety coming*) Where's Mama?

RUTH She ain't come back yet.

WALTER (*looking* MURCHISON *over from head to toe, scrutinizing his carefully casual tweed sports jacket over cashmere V-neck sweater over soft eyelet shirt and tie, and soft slacks, finished off with white buckskin shoes*) Why all you college boys wear them fairyish-looking white shoes?

RUTH Walter Lee!

GEORGE MURCHISON *ignores the remark.*

WALTER (*to* RUTH) Well, they look crazy as hell—white shoes, cold as it is.

RUTH (*crushed*) You have to excuse him—

WALTER No he don't! Excuse me for what? What you always excusing me for! I'll excuse myself when I needs to be excused! (*A pause*) They look as funny as them black knee socks Beneatha wears out of here all the time.

RUTH It's the college *style*, Walter.

WALTER Style, hell. She looks like she got burnt legs or something!

RUTH Oh, Walter—

WALTER (*an irritable mimic*) Oh, Walter! Oh, Walter! (*To* MURCHISON) How's your old man making out? I understand you all going to buy that big hotel on the Drive? (*He finds a beer in the refrigerator, wanders over to* MURCHISON, *sipping and wiping his lips with the back of his hand, and straddling a chair backwards to talk to the other man.*) Shrewd move. Your old man is all right, man. (*Tapping his head and half winking for emphasis*) I mean he knows how to operate. I mean he thinks *big*, you know what I mean, I mean for a *home*, you know? But I think he's kind of running out of ideas now. I'd like to talk to him. Listen, man, I got some plans that could turn this city upside down. I mean I think like he does. *Big.* Invest big, gamble big, hell, lose *big* if you have to, you know what I mean. It's hard to find a man on this whole Southside who understands my kind of thinking—you dig? (*He scrutinizes* MURCHISON *again, drinks his beer, squints his eyes and leans in close, confidential, man to man.*) Me and you ought to sit down and talk sometimes, man. Man, I got me some ideas. . . .

GEORGE (*with boredom*) Yeah—sometimes we'll have to do that, Walter.

WALTER (*understanding the indifference, and offended*) Yeah—well, when you get the time, man. I know you a busy little boy.

RUTH Walter, please—

WALTER (*bitterly, hurt*) I know ain't nothing in this world as busy as you colored college boys with your fraternity pins and white shoes. . . .

RUTH (*covering her face with humiliation*) Oh, Walter Lee—

WALTER I see you all all the time—with the books tucked under your arms—going to your (*British A—a mimic*) "clahsses." And for what! What the hell you learning over there? Filling up your heads—(*counting off on his fingers*)—with the sociology and the psychology—but they teaching you how to be a man? How to take over and run the world? They teaching you how to run a rubber plantation or a steel mill? Naw—just to talk proper and read books and wear white shoes. . . .

GEORGE (*looking at him with distaste, a little above it all*) You're all wacked up with bitterness, man.

WALTER (*intently, almost quietly, between the teeth, glaring at the boy*) And you—ain't you bitter, man? Ain't you just about had it yet? Don't you see no stars gleaming that you can't reach out and grab? You happy?—You contented son-of-a-bitch—you happy? You got it made? Bitter? Man, I'm a volcano. Bitter? Here I am a giant—surrounded by ants! Ants who can't even understand what it is the giant is talking about.

RUTH (*passionately and suddenly*) Oh, Walter—ain't you with nobody!

WALTER (*violently*) No! 'Cause ain't nobody with me! Not even my own mother!

RUTH Walter, that's a terrible thing to say!

BENEATHA *enters, dressed for the evening in a cocktail dress and earrings.*

GEORGE Well—hey, you look great.

BENEATHA Let's go, George. See you all later.

RUTH Have a nice time.

GEORGE Thanks. Good night. (*To* WALTER, *sarcastically*) Good night, *Prometheus.* (BENEATHA *and* GEORGE *exit.*)

WALTER (*to* RUTH) Who is Prometheus?

RUTH I don't know. Don't worry about it.

WALTER (*in fury, pointing after* GEORGE) See there—they get to a point where they can't insult you man to man—they got to go talk about something ain't nobody never heard of!

RUTH How do you know it was an insult? (*To humor him*) Maybe Prometheus is a nice fellow.

WALTER Prometheus! I bet there ain't even no such thing! I bet that simple-minded clown—

RUTH Walter— (*She stops what she is doing and looks at him.*)

WALTER (*yelling*) Don't start!

RUTH Start what?

WALTER Your nagging! Where was I? Who was I with? How much money did I spend?

RUTH (*plaintively*) Walter Lee—why don't we just try to talk about it. . . .

WALTER (*not listening*) I been out talking with people who understand me. People who care about the things I got on my mind.

RUTH (*wearily*) I guess that means people like Willy Harris.

WALTER Yes, people like Willy Harris.

RUTH (*with a sudden flash of impatience*) Why don't you all just hurry up and go into the banking business and stop talking about it!

WALTER Why? You want to know why? 'Cause we all tied up in a race of people that don't know how to do nothing but moan, pray and have babies!

The line is too bitter even for him and he looks at her and sits down.

RUTH Oh, Walter . . . (*Softly*) Honey, why can't you stop fighting me?

WALTER (*without thinking*) Who's fighting you? Who even cares about you?

This line begins the retardation of his mood.

RUTH Well— (*She waits a long time, and then with resignation starts to put away her things.*) I guess I might as well go on to bed. . . . (*More or less to herself*) I don't know where we lost it . . . but we have. . . . (*Then, to him*) I—I'm sorry about this new baby, Walter. I guess maybe I better go on and do what I started . . . I guess I just didn't realize how bad things was with us . . . I guess I just didn't really realize— (*She starts out to the bedroom and stops.*) You want some hot milk?

WALTER Hot milk?

RUTH Yes—hot milk.

WALTER Why hot milk?

RUTH 'Cause after all that liquor you come home with you ought to have something hot in your stomach.

WALTER I don't want no milk.

RUTH You want some coffee then?

WALTER No, I don't want no coffee. I don't want nothing hot to drink. (*Almost plaintively*) Why you always trying to give me something to eat?

RUTH (*standing and looking at him helplessly*) What else can I give you, Walter Lee Younger?

She stands and looks at him and presently turns to go out again. He lifts his head and watches her going away from him in a new mood which began to emerge when he asked her "Who cares about you?"

WALTER It's been rough, ain't it, baby? (*She hears and stops but does not turn around and he continues to her back.*) I guess between two people there ain't never as much understood as folks generally thinks there is. I mean like between me and you— (*She turns to face him.*) How we gets to the place where we scared to talk softness to each other. (*He waits, thinking hard himself.*) Why you think it got to be like that? (*He is thoughtful, almost as a child would be.*) Ruth, what is it gets into people ought to be close?

RUTH I don't know, honey. I think about it a lot.

WALTER On account of you and me, you mean? The way things are with us. The way something done come down between us.

RUTH There ain't so much between us, Walter. . . . Not when you come to me and try to talk to me. Try to be with me . . . a little even.

WALTER (*total honesty*) Sometimes . . . sometimes . . . I don't even know how to try.

RUTH Walter—

WALTER Yes?

RUTH (*coming to him, gently and with misgiving, but coming to him*) Honey . . . life don't have to be like this. I mean sometimes people can do things so that things are better. . . . You remember how we used to talk when Travis was born . . . about the way we were going to live . . . the kind of house . . . (*She is stroking his head.*) Well, it's all starting to slip away from us. . . .

MAMA *enters, and* WALTER *jumps up and shouts at her.*

WALTER Mama, where have you been?

MAMA My—them steps is longer than they used to be. Whew! (*She sits down and ignores him.*) How you feeling this evening, Ruth?

RUTH *shrugs, disturbed some at having been prematurely interrupted and watching her husband knowingly.*

WALTER Mama, where have you been all day?

MAMA (*still ignoring him and leaning on the table and changing to more comfortable shoes*) Where's Travis?

RUTH I let him go out earlier and he ain't come back yet. Boy, is he going to get it!

WALTER Mama!

MAMA (*as if she has heard him for the first time*) Yes, son?

WALTER Where did you go this afternoon?

MAMA I went downtown to tend to some business that I had to tend to.

WALTER What kind of business?

MAMA You know better than to question me like a child, Brother.

WALTER (*rising and bending over the table*) Where were you, Mama? (*Bringing his fists down and shouting*) Mama, you didn't go do something with that insurance money, something crazy?

The front door opens slowly, interrupting him, and TRAVIS *peeks his head in, less than hopefully.*

TRAVIS (*to his mother*) Mama, I—

RUTH "Mama I" nothing! You're going to get, it boy! Get on in that bedroom and get yourself ready!

TRAVIS But I—

MAMA Why don't you all never let the child explain hisself.

RUTH Keep out of it now, Lena.

MAMA *clamps her lips together, and* RUTH *advances toward her son menacingly.*

RUTH A thousand times I have told you not to go off like that—

MAMA (*holding out her arms to her grandson*) Well—at least let me tell him something. I want him to be the first one to hear. . . . Come here, Travis. (*The boy obeys, gladly.*) Travis—(*she takes him by the shoulder and looks into his face*)—you know that money we got in the mail this morning?

TRAVIS Yes'm—

MAMA Well—what you think your grandmama gone and done with that money?

TRAVIS I don't know, Grandmama.

MAMA (*putting her finger on his nose for emphasis*) She went out and she bought you a house! (*The explosion comes from* WALTER *at the end of the revelation and he jumps up and turns away from all of them in a fury.* MAMA *continues, to* TRAVIS) You glad about the house? It's going to be yours when you get to be a man.

TRAVIS Yeah—I always wanted to live in a house.

MAMA All right, gimme some sugar then— (TRAVIS *puts his arms around her neck as she watches her son over the boy's shoulder. Then to* TRAVIS, *after the embrace*) Now when you say your prayers tonight, you thank God and your grandfather—'cause it was him who give you the house—in his way.

RUTH (*taking the boy from* MAMA *and pushing him toward the bedroom*) Now you get out of here and get ready for your beating.

TRAVIS Aw, Mama—

RUTH Get on in there— (*Closing the door behind him and turning radiantly to her mother-in-law*) So you went and did it!

MAMA (*quietly, looking at her son with pain*) Yes, I did.

RUTH (*raising both arms classically*) Praise God! (*Looks at* WALTER *a moment, who says nothing. She crosses rapidly to her husband.*) Please honey—let me be glad . . . you be glad too. (*She has laid her hands on his shoulders, but he shakes himself free of her roughly, without turning to face her.*) Oh, Walter . . . a home . . . a home. (*She comes back to* MAMA.) Well—where is it? How big is it? How much it going to cost?

MAMA Well—

RUTH When we moving?

MAMA (*smiling at her*) First of the month.

RUTH (*throwing back her head with jubilance*) Praise God!

MAMA (*tentatively, still looking at her son's back turned against her and* RUTH) It's—it's a nice house too. . . . (*She cannot help speaking directly to him. An imploring quality in her voice, her manner, makes her almost like a girl now.*) Three bedrooms—nice big one for you Ruth. . . . Me and Beneatha still have to share our room, but Travis have one of his own—and (*with difficulty*) I figure if the—new baby—is a boy, we could get one of them double-decker outfits. . . . And there's a yard with a little patch of dirt where I could maybe get to grow me a few flowers. . . . And a nice big basement. . . .

RUTH Walter honey, be glad—

MAMA (*still to his back, fingering things on the table*) 'Course I don't want to make it sound fancier than it is. . . . It's just a plain little old house—but it's made good and solid—and it will be *ours*. Walter Lee—it makes a difference in a man when he can walk on the floors that belong to *him*. . . .

RUTH Where is it?

MAMA (*frightened at this telling*) Well—well—it's out there in Clybourne Park—

RUTH's *radiance fades abruptly, and* WALTER *finally turns slowly to face his mother with incredulity and hostility.*

RUTH Where?

MAMA (*matter-of-factly*) Four o six Clybourne Street, Clybourne Park.

RUTH Clybourne Park? Mama, there ain't no colored people living in Clybourne Park.

MAMA (*almost idiotically*) Well, I guess there's going to be some now.

WALTER (*bitterly*) So that's the peace and comfort you went out and bought for us today!

MAMA (*raising her eyes to meet his finally*) Son—I just tried to find the nicest place for the least amount of money for my family.

RUTH (*trying to recover from the shock*) Well—well—'course I ain't one never been 'fraid of no crackers, mind you—but—well, wasn't there no other houses nowhere?

MAMA Them houses they put up for colored in them areas way out all seem to cost twice as much as other houses. I did the best I could.

RUTH (*struck senseless with the news, in its various degrees of goodness and trouble, she sits a moment, her fists propping her chin in thought, and then she starts to rise, bringing her fists down with vigor, the radiance spreading from cheek to cheek again*) Well—well!—All I can say is—if this is my time in life—*my time*—to say good-bye—(*and she builds with momentum as she starts to circle the room with an exuberant, almost tearfully happy release*)—to these Goddamned cracking walls!—(*she pounds the walls*)—and these marching roaches!—(*she wipes at an imaginary army of marching roaches*)—and this cramped little closet which ain't now or never was no kitchen! . . . then I say it loud and good, Hallelujah! and good-bye misery. . . . I don't never want to see your ugly face again! (*She laughs joyously, having practically destroyed the apartment, and flings her arms up and lets them come down happily, slowly, reflectively, over her abdomen, aware for the first time perhaps that the life therein pulses with happiness and not despair.*) Lena?

MAMA moved, watching her happiness) Yes, honey?

RUTH (*looking off*) Is there—is there a whole lot of sunlight?

MAMA (*understanding*) Yes, child, there's a whole lot of sunlight.

Long pause.

RUTH (*collecting herself and going to the door of the room* TRAVIS *is in*) Well—I guess I better see 'bout Travis. (*To* MAMA) Lord, I sure don't feel like whipping nobody today! (*She exits.*)

MAMA (*the mother and son are left alone now and the mother waits a long time, considering deeply, before she speaks*) Son—you—you understand what I done, don't you? (WALTER *is silent and sullen.*) I—I just seen my family falling apart today . . . just falling to pieces in front of my eyes. . . . We couldn't of gone on like we was today. We was going backwards 'stead of forwards—talking 'bout killing babies and wishing each other was dead. . . . When it gets like that in life—you just got to do something different, push on out and do something bigger. . . . (*She waits.*) I wish you say something, son . . . I wish you'd say how deep inside you you think I done the right thing—

WALTER (*crossing slowly to his bedroom door and finally turning there and speaking measuredly*) What you need me to say you done right for? You the head of this family. You run our lives like you want to. It was your money and you did what you wanted with it. So what you need for me to say it was all right for? (*Bitterly, to hurt her as deeply as he knows is possible*) So you butchered up a dream of mine—you—who always talking 'bout your children's dreams. . . .

MAMA Walter Lee—

He just closes the door behind him. MAMA *sits alone, thinking heavily.*

Curtain

SCENE II.

Time: Friday night, a few weeks later.
    At rise: Packing crates mark the intention of the family to move. BENEATHA *and* GEORGE *come in, presumably from an evening out again.*

GEORGE O.K. . . . O.K., whatever you say. . . . (*They both sit on the couch. He tries to kiss her. She moves away.*) Look, we've had a nice evening; let's not spoil it, huh? . . .

He again turns her head and tries to nuzzle in and she turns away from him, not with distaste but with momentary lack of interest; in a mood to pursue what they were talking about.

BENEATHA I'm *trying* to talk to you.

GEORGE We always talk.

BENEATHA Yes—and I love to talk.

GEORGE (*exasperated; rising*) I know it and I don't mind it sometimes . . . I want you to cut it out, see—The moody stuff, I mean. I don't like it. You're a nice-looking girl . . . all over. That's all you need, honey, forget the atmosphere. Guys aren't going to go for the atmosphere—they're going to go for what they see. Be glad for that. Drop the Garbo routine. It doesn't go with you. As for myself, I want a nice—(*groping*)—simple (*thoughtfully*)—sophisticated girl . . . not a poet—O.K.?

She rebuffs him again and he starts to leave.

BENEATHA Why are you angry?

GEORGE Because this is stupid! I don't go out with you to discuss the nature of "quiet desperation" or to hear all about your thoughts—because the world will go on thinking what it thinks regardless—

BENEATHA Then why read books? Why go to school?

GEORGE (*with artificial patience, counting on his fingers*) It's simple. You read books— to learn facts—to get grades—to pass the course—to get a degree. That's all—it has nothing to do with thoughts.

A long pause.

BENEATHA I see. (*A longer pause as she looks at him*) Good night, George.

GEORGE *looks at her a little oddly, and starts to exit. He meets* MAMA *coming in.*

GEORGE Oh—hello, Mrs. Younger.

MAMA Hello, George, how you feeling?

GEORGE Fine—fine, how are you?

MAMA Oh, a little tired. You know them steps can get you after a day's work. You all have a nice time tonight?

GEORGE Yes—a fine time. Well, good night.

MAMA Good night. (*He exits.* MAMA *closes the door behind her.*) Hello, honey. What you sitting like that for?

BENEATHA I'm just sitting.

MAMA Didn't you have a nice time?

BENEATHA No.

MAMA No? What's the matter?

BENEATHA Mama, George is a fool—honest. (*She rises.*)

MAMA (*hustling around unloading the packages she has entered with. She stops*) Is he, baby?

BENEATHA Yes.

BENEATHA *makes up* TRAVIS' *bed as she talks.*

MAMA You sure?

BENEATHA Yes.

MAMA Well—I guess you better not waste your time with no fools.

BENEATHA *looks up at her mother, watching her put groceries in the refrigerator. Finally she gathers up her things and starts into the bedroom. At the door she stops and looks back at her mother.*

BENEATHA Mama—

MAMA Yes, baby—

BENEATHA Thank you.

MAMA For what?

BENEATHA For understanding me this time.

She exits quickly and the mother stands, smiling a little, looking at the place where BENEATHA *just stood.* RUTH *enters.*

RUTH Now don't you fool with any of this stuff, Lena—

MAMA Oh, I just thought I'd sort a few things out.

The phone rings. RUTH *answers.*

RUTH (*at the phone*) Hello—Just a minute. (*Goes to the door*) Walter, it's Mrs. Arnold. (*Waits. Goes back to the phone. Tense*) Hello. Yes, this is his wife speaking . . . He's lying down now. Yes . . . well, he'll be in tomorrow. He's been very sick. Yes—I know we should have called, but we were so sure he'd be able to come in today. Yes— yes, I'm very sorry. Yes . . . Thank you very much. (*She hangs up.* WALTER *is standing in the doorway of the bedroom behind her.*) That was Mrs. Arnold.

WALTER (*indifferently*) Was it?

RUTH She said if you don't come in tomorrow that they are getting a new man. . . .

WALTER Ain't that sad—ain't that crying sad.

RUTH She said Mr. Arnold has had to take a cab for three days. . . . Walter, you ain't been to work for three days! (*This is a revelation to her.*) Where you been, Walter Lee Younger? (WALTER *looks at her and starts to laugh.*) You're going to lose your job.

WALTER That's right . . .

RUTH Oh, Walter, and with your mother working like a dog every day—

WALTER That's sad too—Everything is sad.

MAMA What you been doing for these three days, son?

WALTER Mama—you don't know all the things a man what got leisure can find to do in this city. . . . What's this—Friday night? Well—Wednesday I borrowed Willy Harris' car and I went for a drive . . . just me and myself and I drove and drove . . . Way out . . . way past South Chicago, and I parked the car and I sat and looked at the steel mills all day long. I just sat in the car and looked at them big black chimneys for hours. Then I drove back and I went to the Green Hat. (*Pause*) And Thursday— Thursday I borrowed the car again and I got in it and I pointed it the other way and I drove the other way—for hours—way, way up to Wisconsin, and I looked at the farms. I just drove and looked at the farms. Then I drove back and I went to the Green Hat. (*Pause*) And today—today I didn't get the car. Today I just walked. All over the South side. And I looked at the Negroes and they looked at me and finally I just sat down on the curb at Thirty-ninth and South Parkway and I just sat there and watched the Negroes go by. And then I went to the Green Hat. You all sad? You all depressed? And you know where I am going right now—

RUTH *goes out quietly.*

MAMA Oh, Big Walter, is this the harvest of our days?

WALTER You know what I like about the Green Hat? (*He turns the radio on and a steamy, deep blues pours into the room.*) I like this little cat they got there who blows a sax. . . . He blows. He talks to me. He ain't but 'bout five feet tall and he's got a conked head and his eyes is always closed and he's all music—

MAMA (*rising and getting some papers out of her handbag*) Walter—

WALTER And there's this other guy who plays the piano . . . and they got a sound. I mean they can work on some music. . . . They got the best little combo in the world in the Green Hat. . . . You can just sit there and drink and listen to them three men play and you realize that don't nothing matter worth a damn, but just being there—

MAMA I've helped do it to you, haven't I, son? Walter, I been wrong.

WALTER Naw—you ain't never been wrong about nothing, Mama.

MAMA Listen to me, now. I say I been wrong, son. That I been doing to you what the rest of the world been doing to you. (*She stops and he looks up slowly at her and she meets his eyes pleadingly.*) Walter—what you ain't never understood is that I ain't got nothing, don't own nothing, ain't never really wanted nothing that wasn't for you. There ain't nothing as precious to me. . . . There ain't nothing worth holding on to, money, dreams, nothing else—if it means—if it means it's going to destroy my boy. (*She puts her papers in front of him and he watches her without speaking or moving.*) I paid the man thirty-five hundred dollars down on the house. That leaves sixty-five hundred dollars. Monday morning I want you to take this money and take three thousand dollars and put it in a savings account for Beneatha's medical schooling. The rest you put in a checking account—with your name on it. And from now on any penny that come out of it or that go in it is for you to look after. For you to decide. (*She drops her hands a little helplessly.*) It ain't much, but it's all I got in the world and I'm putting it in your hands. I'm telling you to be the head of this family from now on like you supposed to be.

WALTER (*stares at the money*) You trust me like that, Mama?

MAMA I ain't never stop trusting you. Like I ain't never stop loving you.

She goes out, and WALTER *sits looking at the money on the table as the music continues in its idiom, pulsing in the room. Finally, in a decisive gesture, he gets up, and, in mingled joy and desperation, picks up the money. At the same moment,* TRAVIS *enters for bed.*

TRAVIS What's the matter, Daddy? You drunk?

WALTER (*sweetly, more sweetly than we have ever known him*) No, Daddy ain't drunk. Daddy ain't going to never be drunk again. . . .

TRAVIS Well, good night, Daddy.

The father has come from behind the couch and leans over, embracing his son.

WALTER Son, I feel like talking to you tonight.

TRAVIS About what?

WALTER Oh, about a lot of things. About you and what kind of man you going to be when you grow up. . . . Son—son, what do you want to be when you grow up?

TRAVIS A bus driver.

WALTER (*laughing a little*) A what? Man, that ain't nothing to want to be!

TRAVIS Why not?

WALTER 'Cause, man—it ain't big enough—you know what I mean.

TRAVIS I don't know then. I can't make up my mind. Sometimes Mama asks me that too. And sometimes when I tell her I just want to be like you—she says she don't want me to be like that and sometimes she says she does. . . .

WALTER (*gathering him up in his arms*) You know what, Travis? In seven years you going to be seventeen years old. And things is going to be very different with us in seven years, Travis. . . . One day when you are seventeen I'll come home—home from my office downtown somewhere—

TRAVIS You don't work in no office, Daddy.

WALTER No—but after tonight. After what your daddy gonna do tonight, there's going to be offices—a whole lot of offices. . . .

TRAVIS What you gonna do tonight, Daddy?

WALTER You wouldn't understand yet, son, but your daddy's gonna make a transaction . . . a business transaction that's going to change our lives. . . . That's how come one day when you 'bout seventeen years old I'll come home and I'll be pretty tired, you know what I mean, after a day of conferences and secretaries getting things wrong the way they do . . . 'cause an executive's life is hell, man— (*The more he talks, the farther away he gets.*) And I'll pull the car up on the driveway . . . just a plain black Chrysler, I think, with white walls—no—black tires. More elegant. Rich people don't have to be flashy . . . though I'll have to get something a little sportier for Ruth—maybe a Cadillac convertible to do her shopping in. . . . And I'll come up the steps to the house and the gardener will be clipping away at the hedges and he'll say, "Good evening, Mr. Younger." And I'll say, "Hello, Jefferson, how are you this evening?" And I'll go inside and Ruth will come downstairs and meet me at the door and we'll kiss each other and she'll take my arm and we'll go up to your room to see you sitting on the floor with the catalogues of all the great schools in America around you. . . . All the great schools in the world! And—and I'll say, all right son—it's your seventeenth birthday, what is it you've decided? . . . Just tell me where you want to go to school and you'll *go*. Just tell me, what it is you want to be—and you'll *be* it. . . . Whatever you want to be—Yessir! (*He holds his arms open for* TRAVIS.) You just name it, son . . . (TRAVIS *leaps into them.*) and I hand you the world!

WALTER's *voice has risen in pitch and hysterical promise and on the last line he lifts* TRAVIS *high.*

Blackout

SCENE III.

Time: Saturday, moving day, one week later.

Before the curtain rises, RUTH's *voice, a strident, dramatic church alto cuts through the silence.*

It is, in the darkness a triumphant surge, a penetrating statement of expectation: "Oh, Lord, I don't feel no ways tired! Children, oh, glory hallelujah!"

As the curtain rises we see that RUTH *is alone in the living room, finishing up the family's packing. It is moving day. She is nailing crates and tying cartons.* BENEATHA *enters, carrying a guitar case, and watches her exuberant sister-in-law.*

RUTH Hey!
BENEATHA (*putting away the case*) Hi.
RUTH (*pointing at a package*) Honey—look in that package there and see what I found on sale this morning at the South Center. (RUTH *gets up and moves to the package and draws out some curtains.*) Lookahere—hand-turned hems!
BENEATHA How do you know the window size out there?
RUTH (*who hadn't thought of that*) Oh—Well, they bound to fit something in the whole house. Anyhow, they was too good a bargain to pass up. (RUTH *slaps her head, suddenly remembering something.*) Oh, Bennie—I meant to put a special note on that carton over there. That's your mamma's good china and she wants 'em to be very careful with it.
BENEATHA I'll do it.

BENEATHA *finds a piece of paper and starts to draw large letters on it.*

RUTH You know what I'm going to do soon as I get in that new house?
BENEATHA What?
RUTH Honey—I'm going to run me a tub of water up to here. . . . (*With her fingers practically up to her nostrils*) And I'm going to get in it—and I am going to sit . . . and sit in that hot water and the first person who knocks to tell *me* to hurry up and come out—

BENEATHA Gets shot at sunrise.

RUTH (*laughing happily*) You said it, sister! (*Noticing how large* BENEATHA *is absent-mindedly making the note*) Honey, they ain't going to read that from no airplane.

BENEATHA (*laughing herself*) I guess I always think things have more emphasis if they are big, somehow.

RUTH (*looking up at her and smiling*) You and your brother seem to have that as a philosophy of life. Lord, that man—done changed so 'round here. You know—you know what we did last night? Me and Walter Lee?

BENEATHA What?

RUTH (*smiling to herself*) We went to the movies. (*Looking at* BENEATHA *to see if she understands*) We went to the movies. You know the last time me and Walter went to the movies together?

BENEATHA No.

RUTH Me neither. That's how long it been. (*Smiling again*) But we went last night. The picture wasn't much good, but that didn't seem to matter. We went—and we held hands.

BENEATHA Oh, Lord!

RUTH We held hands—and you know what?

BENEATHA What?

RUTH When we come out of the show it was late and dark and all the stores and things was closed up . . . and it was kind of chilly and there wasn't many people on the streets . . . and we was still holding hands, me and Walter.

BENEATHA You're killing me.

WALTER *enters with a large package. His happiness is deep in him; he cannot keep still with his new-found exuberance. He is singing and wiggling and snapping his fingers. He puts his package in a corner and puts a phonograph record, which he has brought in with him, on the record player. As the music comes up he dances over to* RUTH *and tries to get her to dance with him. She gives in at last to his raunchiness and in a fit of giggling allows herself to be drawn into his mood and together they deliberately burlesque an old social dance of their youth.*

BENEATHA (*regarding them a long time as they dance, then drawing in her breath for a deeply exaggerated comment which she does not particularly mean*) Talk about—oldddddddddd-fashionedddddddd—Negroes!

WALTER (*stopping momentarily*) What kind of Negroes?

He says this in fun. He is not angry with her today, nor with anyone. He starts to dance with his wife again.

BENEATHA Old-fashioned.

WALTER (*as he dances with* RUTH) You know, when these *New Negroes* have their convention—(*pointing at his sister*)—that is going to be the chairman of the Committee on Unending Agitation. (*He goes on dancing, then stops.*) Race, race, race! . . . Girl, I do believe you are the first person in the history of the entire human race to successfully brainwash yourself. (BENEATHA *breaks up and he goes on dancing. He stops again, enjoying his tease.*) Damn, even the N double A C P takes a holiday sometimes! (BENEATHA *and* RUTH *laugh. He dances with* RUTH *some more and starts to laugh and stops and pantomimes someone over an operating table.*) I can just see that chick someday looking down at some poor cat on an operating table before she starts to slice him, saying . . . (*pulling his sleeves back maliciously*) "By the way, what are your views on civil rights down there? . . ."

He laughs at her again and starts to dance happily. The bell sounds.

BENEATHA Sticks and stones may break my bones but . . . words will never hurt me!

BENEATHA *goes to the door and opens it as* WALTER *and* RUTH *go on with the clowning.* BENEATHA *is somewhat surprised to see a quiet-looking middle-aged white man in a business suit holding his hat and a briefcase in his hand and consulting a small piece of paper.*

MAN Uh—how do you do, miss. I am looking for a Mrs.— (*he looks at the slip of paper*) Mrs. Lena Younger?

BENEATHA (*smoothing her hair with slight embarrassment*) Oh—yes, that's my mother. Excuse me. (*She closes the door and turns to quiet the other two.*) Ruth! Brother! Somebody's here. (*Then she opens the door. The man casts a curious quick glance at all of them.*) Uh—come in please.

MAN (*coming in*) Thank you.

BENEATHA My mother isn't here just now. Is it business?

MAN Yes . . . well, of a sort.

WALTER (*freely, the Man of the House*) Have a seat. I'm Mrs. Younger's son. I look after most of her business matters.

RUTH *and* BENEATHA *exchange amused glances.*

MAN (*regarding* WALTER, *and sitting*) Well—My name is Karl Lindner . . .

WALTER (*stretching out his hand*) Walter Younger. This is my wife—(RUTH *nods politely*)—and my sister.

LINDNER How do you do.

WALTER (*amiably, as he sits himself easily on a chair, leaning with interest forward on his knees and looking expectantly into the newcomer's face*) What can we do for you, Mr. Lindner!

LINDNER (*some minor shuffling of the hat and briefcase on his knees*) Well—I am a representative of the Clybourne Park Improvement Association—

WALTER (*pointing*) Why don't you sit your things on the floor?

LINDNER Oh—yes. Thank you. (*He slides the briefcase and hat under the chair.*) And as I was saying—I am from the Clybourne Park Improvement Association and we have had it brought to our attention at the last meeting that you people—or at least your mother—has bought a piece of residential property at—(*he digs for the slip of paper again*)—four o six Clybourne Street. . . .

WALTER That's right. Care for something to drink? Ruth, get Mr. Lindner a beer.

LINDNER (*upset for some reason*) Oh—no, really. I mean thank you very much, but no thank you.

RUTH (*innocently*) Some coffee?

LINDNER Thank you, nothing at all.

BENEATHA *is watching the man carefully.*

LINDNER Well, I don't know how much you folks know about our organization. (*He is a gentle man; thoughtful and somewhat labored in his manner.*) It is one of those community organizations set up to look after—oh, you know, things like block upkeep and special projects and we also have what we call our New Neighbors Orientation Committee. . . .

BENEATHA (*drily*) Yes—and what do they do?

LINDNER (*turning a little to her and then returning the main force to* WALTER) Well— it's what you might call a sort of welcoming committee, I guess. I mean they, we, I'm the chairman of the committee—go around and see the new people who move into the neighborhood and sort of give them the lowdown on the way we do things out in Clybourne Park.

BENEATHA (*with appreciation of the two meanings, which escape* RUTH *and* WALTER) Un-huh.

LINDNER And we also have the category of what the association calls—(*he looks else-where*)—uh—special community problems. . . .

BENEATHA Yes—and what are some of those?

WALTER Girl, let the man talk.

LINDNER (*with understated relief*) Thank you. I would like to explain this thing in my own way. I mean I want to explain to you in a certain way.

WALTER Go ahead.

LINDNER Yes. Well. I'm going to try to get right to the point. I'm sure we'll all appreciate that in the long run.

BENEATHA Yes.

LINDNER Well—

WALTER Be still now!

LINDNER Well—

RUTH (*still innocently*) Would you like another chair—you don't look comfortable.

LINDNER (*more frustrated than annoyed*) No, thank you very much. Please. Well—to get right to the point I—(*a great breath, and he is off at last*) I am sure you people must be aware of some of the incidents which have happened in various parts of the city when colored people have moved into certain areas— (BENEATHA *exhales heavily and starts tossing a piece of fruit up and down in the air.*) Well—because we have what I think is going to be a unique type of organization in American community life—not only do we deplore that kind of thing—but we are trying to do something about it. (BENEATHA *stops tossing and turns with a new and quizzical interest to the man.*) We feel—(*gaining confidence in his mission because of the interest in the faces of the people he is talking to*)—we feel that most of the trouble in this world, when you come right down to it—(*he hits his knee for emphasis*)—most of the trouble exists because people just don't sit down and talk to each other.

RUTH (*nodding as she might in church, pleased with the remark*) You can say that again, mister.

LINDNER (*more encouraged by such affirmation*) That we don't try hard enough in this world to understand the other fellow's problem. The other guy's point of view.

RUTH Now that's right.

BENEATHA *and* WALTER *merely watch and listen with genuine interest.*

LINDNER Yes—that's the way we feel out in Clybourne Park. And that's why I was elected to come here this afternoon and talk to you people. Friendly like, you know, the way people should talk to each other and see if we couldn't find some way to work this thing out. As I say, the whole business is a matter of *caring* about the other fellow. Anybody can see that you are a nice family of folks, hard-working and honest I'm sure. (BENEATHA *frowns slightly, quizzically, her head tilted regarding him.*) Today everybody knows what it means to be on the outside of *something*. And of course, there is always somebody who is out to take the advantage of people who don't always understand.

WALTER What do you mean?

LINDNER Well—you see our community is made up of people who've worked hard as the dickens for years to build up that little community. They're not rich and fancy people; just hard-working, honest people who don't really have much but those little homes and a dream of the kind of community they want to raise their children in. Now, I don't say we are perfect and there is a lot wrong in some of the things they want. But you've got to admit that a man, right or wrong, has the right to want to have the neighborhood he lives in a certain kind of way. And at the moment the overwhelming majority of our people out there feel that people get along better, take more of a common interest in the life of the community, when they share a common background. I want you to believe me when I tell you that race prejudice simply doesn't enter into it. It is a matter of the people of Clybourne Park believing, rightly or wrongly, as I say, that for the happiness of all concerned that our Negro families are happier when they live in their *own* communities.

BENEATHA (*with a grand and bitter gesture*) This, friends, is the Welcoming Committee!

WALTER (*dumbfounded, looking at* LINDER) Is this what you came marching all the way over here to tell us?

LINDNER Well, now we've been having a fine conversation. I hope you'll hear me all the way through.

WALTER (*tightly*) Go ahead, man.

LINDNER You see—in the face of all the things I have said, we are prepared to make your family a very generous offer. . . .

BENEATHA Thirty pieces and not a coin less!

WALTER Yeah?

LINDNER (*putting on his glasses and drawing a form out of the briefcase*) Our association is prepared, through the collective effort of our people, to buy the house from you at a financial gain to your family.

RUTH Lord have mercy, ain't this the living gall!

WALTER All right, you through?

LINDNER Well, I want to give you the exact terms of the financial arrangement—

WALTER We don't want to hear no exact terms of no arrangements. I want to know if you got any more to tell us 'bout getting together?

LINDNER (*taking off his glasses*) Well—I don't suppose that you feel. . . .

WALTER Never mind how I feel—you got any more to say 'bout how people ought to sit down and talk to each other? . . . Get out of my house, man. (*He turns his back and walks to the door.*)

LINDNER (*looking around at the hostile faces and reaching and assembling his hat and briefcase*) Well—I don't understand why you people are reacting this way. What do you think you are going to gain by moving into a neighborhood where you just aren't wanted and where some elements—well—people can get awful worked up when they feel that their whole way of life and everything they've ever worked for is threatened.

WALTER Get out.

LINDNER (*at the door, holding a small card*) Well—I'm sorry it went like this.

WALTER Get out.

LINDNER (*almost sadly, regarding* WALTER) You just can't force people to change their hearts, son.

He turns and puts his card on the table and exits. WALTER *pushes the door to with stinging hatred, and stands looking at it.* RUTH *just sits and* BENEATHA *just stands. They say nothing.* MAMA *and* TRAVIS *enter.*

MAMA Well—this all the packing got done since I left out of here this morning. I testify before God that my children got all the energy of the dead. What time the moving men due?

BENEATHA Four o'clock. You had a caller, Mama. (*She is smiling, teasingly.*)

MAMA Sure enough—who?

BENEATHA (*her arms folded saucily*) The Welcoming Committee.

WALTER *and* RUTH *giggle.*

MAMA (*innocently*) Who?

BENEATHA The Welcoming Committee. They said they're sure going to be glad to see you when you get there.

WALTER (*devilishly*) Yeah, they said they can't hardly wait to see your face.

Laughter.

MAMA (*sensing their facetiousness*) What's the matter with you all?

WALTER Ain't nothing the matter with us. We just telling you 'bout the gentleman who came to see you this afternoon. From the Clybourne Park Improvement Association.

MAMA What he want?

RUTH (*in the same mood as* BENEATHA *and* WALTER) To welcome you, honey.

WALTER He said they can't hardly wait. He said the one thing they don't have, that they just *dying* to have out there is a fine family of colored people! (*To* RUTH *and* BENEATHA) Ain't that right!

RUTH AND BENEATHA (*mockingly*) Yeah! He left his card in case—

They indicate the card, and MAMA *picks it up and throws it on the floor—understanding and looking off as she draws her chair up to the table on which she has put her plant and some sticks and some cord.*

MAMA Father, give us strength. (*Knowingly—and without fun*) Did he threaten us?

BENEATHA Oh—Mama—they don't do it like that any more. He talked Brotherhood. He said everybody ought to learn how to sit down and hate each other with good Christian fellowship.

She and WALTER *shake hands to ridicule the remark.*

MAMA (*sadly*) Lord, protect us. . . .

RUTH You should hear the money those folks raised to buy the house from us. All we paid and then some.

BENEATHA What they think we going to do—eat 'em?

RUTH No, honey, marry 'em.

MAMA (*shaking her head*) Lord, Lord, Lord. . . .

RUTH Well—that's the way the crackers crumble. Joke.

BENEATHA (*laughingly noticing what her mother is doing*) Mama, what are you doing?

MAMA Fixing my plant so it won't get hurt none on the way. . . .

BENEATHA Mama, you going to take *that* to the new house?

MAMA Un-huh—

BENEATHA That raggedy-looking old thing?

MAMA (*stopping and looking at her*) It expresses *me*.

RUTH (*with delight, to* BENEATHA) So there, Miss Thing!

WALTER *comes to* MAMA *suddenly and bends down behind her and squeezes her in his arms with all his strength. She is overwhelmed by the suddenness of it and, though delighted, her manner is like that of* RUTH *with* TRAVIS.

MAMA Look out now, boy! You make me mess up my thing here!

WALTER (*his face lit, he slips down on his knees beside her, his arms still about her*) Mama . . . you know what it means to climb up in the chariot?

MAMA (*gruffly, very happy*) Get on away from me now. . . .

RUTH (*near the gift-wrapped package, trying to catch* WALTER's *eye*) Psst—

WALTER What the old song say, Mama. . . .

RUTH Walter—Now? (*She is pointing at the package.*)

WALTER (*speaking the lines, sweetly, playfully, in his mother's face*)

> I got wings . . . you got wings . . .
> All God's children got wings . . .

MAMA Boy—get out of my face and do some work. . . .

WALTER

> When I get to heaven gonna put on my wings.
> Gonna fly all over God's heaven . . .

BENEATHA (*teasingly, from across the room*) Everybody talking 'bout heaven ain't going there!

WALTER (*to* RUTH, *who is carrying the box across to them*) I don't know, you think we ought to give her that. . . . Seems to me she ain't been very appreciative around here.

MAMA (*eyeing the box, which is obviously a gift*) What is that?

WALTER (*taking it from* RUTH *and putting it on the table in front of* MAMA) Well— what you all think? Should we give it to her?

RUTH Oh—she was pretty good today.

MAMA I'll good you— (*She turns her eyes to the box again.*)

BENEATHA Open it, Mama.

She stands up, looks at it, turns and looks at all of them, and then presses her hands together and does not open the package.

WALTER (*sweetly*) Open it, Mama. It's for you. (MAMA *looks in his eyes. It is the first present in her life without its being Christmas. Slowly she opens her package and lifts out, one by one, a brand-new sparkling set of gardening tools.* WALTER *continues, prodding*) Ruth made up the note—read it . . .

MAMA (*picking up the card and adjusting her glasses*) "To our own Mrs. Miniver—Love from Brother, Ruth and Beneatha." Ain't that lovely. . . .

TRAVIS (*tugging at his father's sleeve*) Daddy, can I give her mine now?

WALTER All right, son. (TRAVIS *flies to get his gift.*) Travis didn't want to go in with the rest of us, Mama. He got his own. (*Somewhat amused*) We don't know what it is. . . .

TRAVIS (*racing back in the room with a large hatbox and putting it in front of his grandmother*) Here!

MAMA Lord have mercy, baby. You done gone and bought your grandmother a hat?
TRAVIS (*very proud*) Open it!

She does and lifts out an elaborate, but very elaborate, wide gardening hat, and all the adults break up at the sight of it.

RUTH Travis, honey, what is that?
TRAVIS (*who thinks it is beautiful and appropriate*) It's a gardening hat! Like the ladies always have on in the magazines when they work in their gardens.
BENEATHA (*giggling fiercely*) Travis—we were trying to make Mama Mrs. Miniver—not Scarlett O'Hara!
MAMA (*indignantly*) What's the matter with you all! This here is a beautiful hat! (*Absurdly*) I always wanted me one just like it!

She pops it on her head to prove it to her grandson, and the hat is ludicrous and considerably oversized.

RUTH Hot dog! Go, Mama!
WALTER (*doubled over with laughter*) I'm sorry, Mama—but you look like you ready to go out and chop you some cotton sure enough!

They all laugh except MAMA, *out of deference to* TRAVIS' *feelings.*

MAMA (*gathering the boy up to her*) Bless your heart—this is the prettiest hat I ever owned— (WALTER, RUTH, *and* BENEATHA *chime in noisily, festively and insincerely congratulating* TRAVIS *on his gift.*) What are we all standing around here for? We ain't finished packin' yet. Bennie, you ain't packed one book.

The bell rings.

BENEATHA That couldn't be the movers . . . it's not hardly two good yet—

BENEATHA *goes into her room.* MAMA *starts for door.*

WALTER (*turning, stiffening*) Wait—wait—I'll get it. (*He stands and looks at the door.*)
MAMA You expecting company, son?
WALTER (*just looking at the door*) Yeah—yeah. . . .

MAMA *looks at* RUTH, *and they exchange innocent and unfrightened glances.*

MAMA (*not understanding*) Well, let them in, son.
BENEATHA (*from her room*) We need some more string.
MAMA Travis—you run to the hardware and get me some string cord.

MAMA *goes out and* WALTER *turns and looks at* RUTH. TRAVIS *goes to a dish for money.*

RUTH Why don't you answer the door, man?
WALTER (*suddenly bounding across the floor to her*) 'Cause sometimes it hard to let the future begin! (*Stooping down in her face*)

> I got wings! You got wings!
> All God's children got wings!

(*He crosses to the door and throws it open. Standing there is a very slight little man in a not too prosperous business suit and with haunted frightened eyes and a hat pulled down tightly, brim up, around his forehead.* TRAVIS *passes between the men and exits.* WALTER *leans deep in the man's face, still in his jubilance.*)

> When I get to heaven gonna put on my wings.
> Gonna fly all over God's heaven . . .
>
> (*The little man just stares at him.*)
>
> Heaven—

(*Suddenly he stops and looks past the little man into the empty hallway.*) Where's Willy, man?

BOBO He ain't with me.

WALTER (*not disturbed*) Oh—come on in. You know my wife.

BOBO (*dumbly, taking off his hat*) Yes—h'you, Miss Ruth.

RUTH (*quietly, a mood apart from her husband already, seeing* BOBO) Hello, Bobo.

WALTER You right on time today. . . . Right on time. That's the way! (*He slaps* BOBO *on his back.*) Sit down . . . lemme hear.

RUTH *stands stiffly and quietly in back of them, as though somehow she senses death, her eyes fixed on her husband.*

BOBO (*his frightened eyes on the floor, his hat in his hands*) Could I please get a drink of water, before I tell you about it, Walter Lee?

WALTER *does not take his eyes off the man.* RUTH *goes blindly to the tap and gets a glass of water and brings it to* BOBO.

WALTER There ain't nothing wrong, is there?

BOBO Lemme tell you—

WALTER Man—didn't nothing go wrong?

BOBO Lemme tell you—Walter Lee. (*Looking at* RUTH *and talking to her more than to* WALTER) You know how it was. I got to tell you how it was. I mean first I got to tell you how it was all the way . . . I mean about the money I put in, Walter Lee. . . .

WALTER (*with taut agitation now*) What about the money you put in?

BOBO Well—it wasn't much as we told you—me and Willy— (*He stops.*) I'm sorry, Walter. I got a bad feeling about it. I got a real bad feeling about it. . . .

WALTER Man, what you telling me about all this for? . . . Tell me what happened in Springfield. . . .

BOBO Springfield.

RUTH (*like a dead woman*) What was supposed to happen in Springfield?

BOBO (*to her*) This deal that me and Walter went into with Willy—Me and Willy was going to go down to Springfield and spread some money 'round so's we wouldn't have to wait so long for the liquor license. . . . That's what we were going to do. Everybody said that was the way you had to do, you understand, Miss Ruth?

WALTER Man—what happened down there?

BOBO (*a pitiful man, near tears*) I'm trying to tell you, Walter.

WALTER (*screaming at him suddenly*) THEN TELL ME, GODDAMMIT . . . WHAT'S THE MATTER WITH YOU?

BOBO Man . . . I didn't go to no Springfield, yesterday.

WALTER (*halted, life hanging in the moment*) Why not?

BOBO (*the long way, the hard way to tell*) 'Cause I didn't have no reasons to. . . .

WALTER Man, what are you talking about!

BOBO I'm talking about the fact that when I got to the train station yesterday morning—eight o'clock like we planned . . . Man—*Willy didn't never show up.*

WALTER Why . . . where was he . . . where is he?

BOBO That's what I'm trying to tell you . . . I don't know . . . I waited six hours . . . I called his house . . . and I waited . . . six hours . . . I waited in that train station six hours . . . (*Breaking into tears*) That was all the extra money I had in the world. . . . (*Looking up at* WALTER *with the tears running down his face*) Man, *Willy is gone.*

WALTER Gone, what you mean Willy is gone? Gone where? You mean he went by himself. You mean he went off to Springfield by himself—to take care of getting the license— (*Turns and looks anxiously at* RUTH) You mean maybe he didn't want too many people in on the business down there? (*Looks to* RUTH *again, as before*) You know Willy got his own ways. (*Looks back to* BOBO) Maybe you was late yesterday and he just went on down there without you. Maybe—maybe—he's been callin' you at home tryin' to tell you what happened or something. Maybe—maybe—he just got sick. He's somewhere—he's got to be somewhere. We just got to find him—me and you got to find him. (*Grabs* BOBO *senselessly by the collar and starts to shake him*) We got to!

BOBO (*in sudden angry, frightened agony*) What's the matter with you, Walter! *When a cat take off with your money he don't leave you no maps!*

WALTER (*turning madly, as though he is looking for* WILLY *in the very room*) Willy! . . . Willy . . . don't do it. . . . Please don't do it. . . . Man, not with that money . . . Man, please, not with that money . . . Oh, God . . . Don't let it be true. . . . (*He is wandering around, crying out for* WILLY *and looking for him or perhaps for help from God.*) Man . . . I trusted you . . . Man, I put my life in your hands. . . . (*He starts to crumple down on the floor as* RUTH *just covers her face in horror.* MAMA *opens the door and comes into the room, with* BENEATHA *behind her.*) Man . . . (*He starts to pound the floor with his fists, sobbing wildly.*) That money is made out of my father's flesh. . . .

BOBO (*standing over him helplessly*) I'm sorry, Walter. . . . (*Only* WALTER's *sobs reply.* BOBO *puts on his hat.*) I had my life staked on this deal, too. . . . (*He exits.*)

MAMA (*to* WALTER) Son— (*She goes to him, bends down to him, talks to his bent head.*) Son . . . Is it gone? Son, I gave you sixty-five hundred dollars. Is it gone? All of it? Beneatha's money too?

WALTER (*lifting his head slowly*) Mama . . . I never . . . went to the bank at all. . . .

MAMA (*not wanting to believe him*) You mean . . . your sister's school money . . . you used that too . . . Walter? . . .

WALTER Yessss! . . . All of it. . . . It's all gone. . . .

There is total silence. RUTH *stands with her face covered with her hands;* BENEATHA *leans forlornly against a wall, fingering a piece of red ribbon from the mother's gift.* MAMA *stops and looks at her son without recognition and then, quite without thinking about it, starts to beat him senselessly in the face.* BENEATHA *goes to them and stops it.*

BENEATHA Mama!

MAMA *stops and looks at both of her children and rises slowly and wanders vaguely, aimlessly away from them.*

MAMA I seen . . . him . . . night after night . . . come in . . . and look at that rug . . . and then look at me . . . the red showing in his eyes . . . the veins moving in his head. . . . I seen him grow thin and old before he was forty . . . working and working and working like somebody's old horse . . . killing himself . . . and you—you give it all away in a day. . . .

BENEATHA Mama—

MAMA Oh, God . . . (*She looks up to Him.*) Look down here—and show me the strength.

BENEATHA Mama—

MAMA (*folding over*) Strength . . .

BENEATHA (*plaintively*) Mama . . .

MAMA Strength!

Curtain

ACT III

An hour later.

At curtain, there is a sullen light of gloom in the living room, gray light not unlike that which began the first scene of Act I. At left we can see WALTER *within his room, alone with himself. He is stretched out on the bed, his shirt out and open, his arms under his head. He does not smoke, he does not cry out, he merely lies there, looking up at the ceiling, much as if he were alone in the world.*

In the living room BENEATHA *sits at the table, still surrounded by the now almost ominous packing crates. She sits looking off. We feel that this is a mood struck perhaps an hour before, and it lingers now, full of the empty sound of profound disappointment. We see on a line from her brother's bedroom the sameness of their attitudes. Presently the bell rings and* BENEATHA *rises without ambition or interest in answering. It is* ASAGAI, *smiling broadly, striding into the room with energy and happy expectation and conversation.*

ASAGAI I came over . . . I had some free time. I thought I might help with the packing. Ah, I like the look of packing crates! A household in preparation for a journey! It depresses some people . . . but for me . . . it is another feeling. Something full of the flow of life, do you understand? Movement, progress . . . It makes me think of Africa.

BENEATHA Africa!

ASAGAI What kind of a mood is this? Have I told you how deeply you move me?

BENEATHA He gave away the money, Asagai. . . .

ASAGAI Who gave away what money?

BENEATHA The insurance money. My brother gave it away.

ASAGAI Gave it away?

BENEATHA He made an investment! With a man even Travis wouldn't have trusted.

ASAGAI And it's gone?

BENEATHA Gone!

ASAGAI I'm very sorry. . . . And you, now?

BENEATHA Me? . . . Me? . . . Me I'm nothing. . . . Me. When I was very small . . . we used to take our sleds out in the wintertime and the only hills we had were the ice-covered stone steps of some houses down the street. And we used to fill them in with snow and make them smooth and slide down them all day . . . and it was very dangerous you know . . . far too steep . . . and sure enough one day a kid named Rufus came down too fast and hit the sidewalk . . . and we saw his face just split open right there in front of us. . . . And I remember standing there looking at his bloody open face thinking that was the end of Rufus. But the ambulance came and they took him to the hospital and they fixed the broken bones and they sewed it all up . . . and the next time I saw Rufus he just had a little line down the middle of his face. . . . I never got over that. . . .

WALTER *sits up, listening on the bed. Throughout this scene it is important that we feel his reaction at all times, that he visibly respond to the words of his sister and* ASAGAI.

ASAGAI What?

BENEATHA That was what one person could do for another, fix him up—sew up the problem, make him all right again. That was the most marvelous thing in the world. . . . I wanted to do that. I always thought it was the one concrete thing in the world that a human being could do. Fix up the sick, you know—and make them whole again. This was truly being God. . . .

ASAGAI You wanted to be God?

BENEATHA No—I wanted to cure. It used to be so important to me. I wanted to cure. It used to matter. I used to care. I mean about people and how their bodies hurt. . . .

ASAGAI And you've stopped caring?

BENEATHA Yes—I think so.

ASAGAI Why?

WALTER *rises, goes to the door of his room and is about to open it, then stops and stands listening, leaning on the door jamb.*

BENEATHA Because it doesn't seem deep enough, close enough to what ails mankind— I mean this thing of sewing up bodies or administering drugs. Don't you understand? It was a child's reaction to the world. I thought that doctors had the secret to all the hurts. . . . That's the way a child sees things—or an idealist.

ASAGAI Children see things very well sometimes—and idealists even better.

BENEATHA I know that's what you think. Because you are still where I left off—you still care. This is what you see for the world, for Africa. You with the dreams of the future will patch up all Africa—you are going to cure the Great Sore of colonialism with Independence—

ASAGAI Yes!

BENEATHA Yes—and you think that one word is the penicillin of the human spirit: "Independence!" But then what?

ASAGAI That will be the problem for another time. First we must get there.

BENEATHA And where does it end?

ASAGAI End? Who even spoke of an end? To life? To living?

BENEATHA An end to misery!

ASAGAI (*smiling*) You sound like a French intellectual.

BENEATHA No! I sound like a human being who just had her future taken right out of her hands! While I was sleeping in my bed in there, things were happening in this world that directly concerned me—and nobody asked me, consulted me—they just went out and did things—and changed my life. Don't you see there isn't any real progress, Asagai, there is only one large circle that we march in, around and around, each of us with our own little picture—in front of us—our own little mirage that we think is the future.

ASAGAI That is the mistake.

BENEATHA What?

ASAGAI What you just said—about the circle. It isn't a circle—it is simply a long line— as in geometry, you know, one that reaches into infinity. And because we cannot see the end—we also cannot see how it changes. And it is very odd but those who see the changes are called "idealists"—and those who cannot, or refuse to think, they are the "realists." It is very strange, and amusing too, I think.

BENEATHA You—you are almost religious.

ASAGAI Yes . . . I think I have the religion of doing what is necessary in the world—and of worshipping man—because he is so marvelous, you see.

BENEATHA Man is foul! And the human race deserves its misery!

ASAGAI You see: *you* have become the religious one in the old sense. Already, and after such a small defeat, you are worshipping despair.

BENEATHA From now on, I worship the truth—and the truth is that people are puny, small and selfish. . . .

ASAGAI Truth? Why is it that you despairing ones always think that only you have the truth? I never thought to see *you* like that. You! Your brother made a stupid, childish mistake—and you are grateful to him. So that now you can give up the ailing human race on account of it. You talk about what good is struggle; what good is anything? Where are we all going? And why are we bothering?

BENEATHA *And you cannot answer it!* All your talk and dreams about Africa and Independence. Independence and then what? What about all the crooks and petty thieves and just plain idiots who will come into power to steal and plunder the same as before—only now they will be black and do it in the name of the new Independence— You cannot answer that.

ASAGAI (*shouting over her*) *I live the answer!* (*Pause*) In my village at home it is the exceptional man who can even read a newspaper . . . or who ever *sees* a book at all. I will go home and much of what I will have to say will seem strange to the people of my village. . . . But I will teach and work and things will happen, slowly and swiftly. At times it will seem that nothing changes at all . . . and then again . . . the sudden dramatic events which make history leap into the future. And then quiet again. Retrogression even. Guns, murder, revolution. And I even will have moments when I wonder if the quiet was not better than all that death and hatred. But I will look about my village at the illiteracy and disease and ignorance and I will not wonder long. And perhaps . . . perhaps I will be a great man. . . . I mean perhaps I will hold on to the substance of truth and find my way always with the right course . . . and perhaps for it I will be butchered in my bed some night by the servants of the empire. . . .

BENEATHA *The martyr!*

ASAGAI . . . or perhaps I shall live to be a very old man, respected and esteemed in my new nation. . . . And perhaps I shall hold office and this is what I'm trying to tell you, Alaiyo; perhaps the things I believe now for my country will be wrong and outmoded, and I will not understand and do terrible things to have things my way or merely to keep my power. Don't you see that there will be young men and women, not British soldiers then, but my own black countrymen . . . to step out of the shadows some evening and slit my then useless throat? Don't you see they have always been there . . . that they always will be. And that such a thing as my own death will be an advance? They who might kill me even . . . actually replenish me!

BENEATHA Oh, Asagai, I know all that.

ASAGAI Good! Then stop moaning and groaning and tell me what you plan to do.

BENEATHA Do?

ASAGAI I have a bit of a suggestion.

BENEATHA What?

ASAGAI (*rather quietly for him*) That when it is all over—that you come home with me—

BENEATHA (*slapping herself on the forehead with exasperation born of misunderstanding*) Oh—Asagai—at this moment you decide to be romantic!

ASAGAI (*quickly understanding the misunderstanding*) My dear, young creature of the

New World—I do not mean across the city—I mean across the ocean; home—to Africa.

BENEATHA (*slowly understanding and turning to him with murmured amazement*) To—to Nigeria?

ASAGAI Yes! . . . (*Smiling and lifting his arms playfully*) Three hundred years later the African Prince rose up out of the seas and swept the maiden back across the middle passage over which her ancestors had come—

BENEATHA (*unable to play*) Nigeria?

ASAGAI Nigeria. Home. (*Coming to her with genuine romantic flippancy*) I will show you our mountains and our stars; and give you cool drinks from gourds and teach you the old songs and the ways of our people—and, in time, we will pretend that—(*very softly*)—you have only been away for a day—

She turns her back to him, thinking. He swings her around and takes her full in his arms in a long embrace which proceeds to passion.

BENEATHA (*pulling away*) You're getting me all mixed up—

ASAGAI Why?

BENEATHA Too many things—too many things have happened today. I must sit down and think. I don't know what I feel about anything right this minute. (*She promptly sits down and props her chin on her fist.*)

ASAGAI (*charmed*) All right, I shall leave you. No—don't get up. (*Touching her, gently, sweetly*) Just sit awhile and think. . . . Never be afraid to sit awhile and think. (*He goes to door and looks at her.*) How often I have looked at you and said, "Ah—so this is what the New World hath finally wrought. . . ."

He exits. BENEATHA sits on alone. Presently WALTER enters from his room and starts to rummage through things, feverishly looking for something. She looks up and turns in her seat.

BENEATHA (*hissingly*) Yes—just look at what the New World hath wrought! . . . Just look! (*She gestures with bitter disgust.*) There he is! *Monsieur le petit bourgeois noir*[2]— himself! There he is—Symbol of a Rising Class! Entrepreneur! Titan of the system! (*WALTER ignores her completely and continues frantically and destructively looking for something and hurling things to floor and tearing things out of their place in his search. BENEATHA ignores the eccentricity of his actions and goes on with the monologue of insult.*) Did you dream of yachts on Lake Michigan, Brother? Did you see yourself on that Great Day sitting down at the Conference Table, surrounded by all the mighty bald-headed men in America? All halted, waiting, breathless, waiting for your pronouncements on industry? Waiting for you—Chairman of the Board? (*WALTER finds what he is looking for—a small piece of white paper—and pushes it in his pocket and puts on his coat and rushes out without ever having looked at her. She shouts after him.*) I look at you and I see the final triumph of stupidity in the world!

The door slams and she returns to just sitting again. RUTH comes quickly out of MAMA's room.

RUTH Who was that?

BENEATHA Your husband.

RUTH Where did he go?

---

[2] "Little Mr. Black Bourgeois."

BENEATHA Who knows—maybe he has an appointment at U.S. Steel.

RUTH (*anxiously, with frightened eyes*) You didn't say nothing bad to him, did you?

BENEATHA Bad? Say anything bad to him? No—I told him he was a sweet boy and full of dreams and everything is strictly peachy keen, as the ofay kids say!

MAMA *enters from her bedroom. She is lost, vague, trying to catch hold, to make some sense of her former command of the world, but it still eludes her. A sense of waste overwhelms her gait; a measure of apology rides on her shoulders. She goes to her plant, which has remained on the table, looks at it, picks it up and takes it to the window sill and sits it outside, and she stands and looks at it a long moment. Then she closes the window, straightens her body with effort and turns around to her children.*

MAMA Well—ain't it a mess in here, though? (*A false cheerfulness, a beginning of something*) I guess we all better stop moping around and get some work done. All this unpacking and everything we got to do. (RUTH *raises her head slowly in response to the sense of the line; and* BENEATHA *in similar manner turns very slowly to look at her mother.*) One of you all better call the moving people and tell 'em not to come.

RUTH Tell 'em not to come?

MAMA Of course, baby. Ain't no need in 'em coming all the way here and having to go back. They charges for that too. (*She sits down, fingers to her brow, thinking.*) Lord, ever since I was a little girl, I always remembers people saying, "Lena—Lena Eggleston, you aims too high all the time. You needs to slow down and see life a little more like it is. Just slow down some." That's what they always used to say down home—"Lord, that Lena Eggleston is a high-minded thing. She'll get her due one day!"

RUTH No, Lena. . . .

MAMA Me and Big Walter just didn't never learn right.

RUTH Lena, no! We gotta go. Bennie—tell her. . . . (*She rises and crosses to* BENEATHA *with her arms outstretched.* BENEATHA *doesn't respond.*) Tell her we can still move . . . the notes ain't but a hundred and twenty-five a month. We got four grown people in this house—we can work. . . .

MAMA (*to herself*) Just aimed too high all the time—

RUTH (*turning and going to* MAMA *fast—the words pouring out with urgency and desperation*) Lena—I'll work. . . . I'll work twenty hours a day in all the kitchens in Chicago. . . . I'll strap my baby on my back if I have to and scrub all the floors in America and wash all the sheets in America if I have to—but we got to move. . . . We got to get out of here. . . .

MAMA *reaches out absently and pats* RUTH's *hand.*

MAMA No—I see things differently now. Been thinking 'bout some of the things we could do to fix this place up some. I seen a second-hand bureau over on Maxwell Street just the other day that could fit right there. (*She points to where the new furniture might go.* RUTH *wanders away from her.*) Would need some new handles on it and then a little varnish and then it look like something brand-new. And—we can put up them new curtains in the kitchen. . . . Why this place be looking fine. Cheer us all up so that we forget trouble ever came. . . . (*To* RUTH) And you could get some nice screens to put up in your room round the baby's bassinet. . . . (*She looks at both of them, pleadingly.*) Sometimes you just got to know when to give up some things . . . and hold on to what you got.

WALTER *enters from the outside, looking spent and leaning against the door, his coat hanging from him.*

MAMA Where you been, son?

WALTER (*breathing hard*) Made a call.

MAMA To who, son?

WALTER To The Man.

MAMA What man, baby?

WALTER The Man, Mama. Don't you know who The Man is?

RUTH Walter Lee?

WALTER *The Man.* Like the guys in the streets say—The Man. Captain Boss—Mistuh Charley . . . Old Captain Please Mr. Bossman . . .

BENEATHA (*suddenly*) Lindner!

WALTER That's right! That's good. I told him to come right over.

BENEATHA (*fiercely, understanding*) For what? What do you want to see him for!

WALTER (*looking at his sister*) We going to do business with him.

MAMA What you talking 'bout, son?

WALTER Talking 'bout life, Mama. You all always telling me to see life like it is. Well— I laid in there on my back today . . . and I figured it out. Life just like it is. Who gets and who don't get. (*He sits down with his coat on and laughs.*) Mama, you know it's all divided up. Life is. Sure enough. Between the takers and the "tooken." (*He laughs.*) I've figured it out finally. (*He looks around at them.*) Yeah. Some of us always getting "tooken." (*He laughs.*) People like Willy Harris, they don't never get "tooken." And you know why the rest of us do? 'Cause we all mixed up. Mixed up bad. We get to looking 'round for the right and the wrong; and we worry about it and cry about it and stay up nights trying to figure out 'bout the wrong and the right of things all the time. . . . And all the time, man, them takers is out there operating, just taking and taking. Willy Harris? Shoot—Willy Harris don't even count. He don't even count in the big scheme of things. But I'll say one thing for old Willy Harris . . . he's taught me something. He's taught me to keep my eye on what counts in this world. Yeah— (*shouting out a little*) Thanks, Willy!

RUTH What did you call that man for, Walter Lee?

WALTER Called him to tell him to come on over to the show. Gonna put on a show for the man. Just what he wants to see. You see, Mama, the man came here today and he told us that them people out there where you want us to move—well they so upset they willing to pay us not to move out there. (*He laughs again.*) And—and oh, Mama— you would of been proud of the way me and Ruth and Bennie acted. We told him to get out . . . Lord have mercy! We told the man to get out. Oh, we was some proud folks this afternoon, yeah. (*He lights a cigarette.*) We were still full of that old-time stuff. . . .

RUTH (*coming toward him slowly*) You talking 'bout taking them people's money to keep us from moving in that house?

WALTER I ain't just talking 'bout it, baby—I'm telling you that's what's going to happen.

BENEATHA Oh, God! Where is the bottom! Where is the real honest-to-God bottom so he can't go any farther!

WALTER See—that's old stuff. You and that boy that was here today. You all want everybody to carry a flag and a spear and sing some marching songs, huh? You wanna spend your life looking into things and trying to find the right and the wrong part, huh? Yeah. You know what's going to happen to that boy someday—he'll find himself sitting in a dungeon, locked in forever—and the takers will have the key! Forget it, baby! There ain't no causes—there ain't nothing but taking in this world, and he who takes most is smartest—and it don't make a damn bit of difference *how.*

MAMA You making something inside me cry, son. Some awful pain inside me.

WALTER Don't cry, Mama. Understand. That white man is going to walk in that door able to write checks for more money than we ever had. It's important to him and I'm going to help him . . . I'm going to put on the show, Mama.

MAMA Son—I come from five generations of people who was slaves and sharecroppers—but ain't nobody in my family never let nobody pay 'em no money that was a way of telling us we wasn't fit to walk the earth. We ain't never been that poor. (*Raising her eyes and looking at him*) We ain't never been that dead inside.

BENEATHA Well—we are dead now. All the talk about dreams and sunlight that goes on in this house. All dead.

WALTER What's the matter with you all! I didn't make this world! It was give to me this way! Hell, yes, I want me some yachts someday! Yes, I want to hang some real pearls 'round my wife's neck. Ain't she supposed to wear no pearls? Somebody tell me—tell me, who decides which women is suppose to wear pearls in this world. I tell you I am a *man*—and I think my wife should wear some pearls in this world!

This last line hangs a good while and WALTER *begins to move about the room. The word "man" has penetrated his consciousness; he mumbles it to himself repeatedly between strange agitated pauses as he moves about.*

MAMA Baby, how you going to feel on the inside?

WALTER Fine! . . . Going to feel fine . . . a man. . . .

MAMA You won't have nothing left then, Walter Lee.

WALTER (*coming to her*) I'm going to feel fine, Mama. I'm going to look that son-of-a-bitch in the eyes and say—(*he falters*)—and say, "All right, Mr. Lindner—(*he falters even more*)—that's your neighborhood out there. You got the right to keep it like you want. You got the right to have it like you want. Just write the check and—the house is yours." And, and I am going to say— (*His voice almost breaks.*) And you—you people just put the money in my hand and you won't have to live next to this bunch of stinking niggers! . . . (*He straightens up and moves away from his mother, walking around the room.*) Maybe—maybe I'll just get down on my black knees. . . . (*He does so;* RUTH *and* BENNIE *and* MAMA *watch him in frozen horror.*) Captain, Mistuh, Bossman. (*He starts crying.*) A-hee-hee-hee! (*Wringing his hands in profoundly anguished imitation*) Yasssssuh! Great White Father, just gi' ussen de money, fo' God's sake, and we's ain't gwine come out deh and dirty up yo' white folks neighborhood. . . .

He breaks down completely, then gets up and goes into the bedroom.

BENEATHA That is not a man. That is nothing but a toothless rat.

MAMA Yes—death done come in this here house. (*She is nodding, slowly, reflectively.*) Done come walking in my house. On the lips of my children. You what supposed to be my beginning again. You—what supposed to be my harvest. (*To* BENEATHA) You—you mourning your brother?

BENEATHA He's no brother of mine.

MAMA What you say?

BENEATHA I said that that individual in that room is no brother of mine.

MAMA That's what I thought you said. You feeling like you better than he is today? (BENEATHA *does not answer.*) Yes? What you tell him a minute ago? That he wasn't a man? Yes? You give him up for me? You done wrote his epitaph too—like the rest of the world? Well, who give you the privilege?

BENEATHA Be on my side for once! You saw what he just did, Mama! You saw him— down on his knees. Wasn't it you who taught me—to despise any man who would do that. Do what he's going to do.

MAMA Yes—I taught you that. Me and your daddy. But I thought I taught you something else too . . . I thought I taught you to love him.

BENEATHA Love him? There is nothing left to love.

MAMA There is always something left to love. And if you ain't learned that, you ain't learned nothing. (*Looking at her*) Have you cried for that boy today? I don't mean for yourself and for the family 'cause we lost the money. I mean for him; what he been through and what it done to him. Child, when do you think is the time to love somebody the most; when they done good and made things easy for everybody? Well then, you ain't through learning—because that ain't the time at all. It's when he's at his lowest and can't believe in hisself 'cause the world done whipped him so. When you starts measuring somebody, measure him right, child, measure him right. Make sure you done taken into account what hills and valleys he come through before he got to wherever he is.

TRAVIS *bursts into the room at the end of the speech, leaving the door open.*

TRAVIS Grandmama—the moving men are downstairs! The truck just pulled up.

MAMA (*turning and looking at him*) Are they, baby? They downstairs?

She sighs and sits. LINDNER *appears in the doorway. He peers in and knocks lightly, to gain attention, and comes in. All turn to look at him.*

LINDNER (*hat and briefcase in hand*) Uh—hello . . .

RUTH *crosses mechanically to the bedroom door and opens it and lets it swing open freely and slowly as the lights come up on* WALTER *within, still in his coat, sitting at the far corner of the room. He looks up and out through the room to* LINDNER.

RUTH He's here.

A long minute passes and WALTER *slowly gets up.*

LINDNER (*coming to the table with efficiency, putting his briefcase on the table and starting to unfold papers and unscrew fountain pens*) Well, I certainly was glad to hear from you people. (WALTER *has begun the trek out of the room, slowly and awkwardly, rather like a small boy, passing the back of his sleeve across his mouth from time to time.*) Life can really be so much simpler than people let it be most of the time. Well—with whom do I negotiate? You, Mrs. Younger, or your son here? (MAMA *sits with her hands folded on her lap and her eyes closed as* WALTER *advances.* TRAVIS *goes close to* LINDNER *and looks at the papers curiously.*) Just some official papers, sonny.

RUTH Travis, you go downstairs.

MAMA (*opening her eyes and looking into* WALTER's) No. Travis, you stay right here. And you make him understand what you doing, Walter Lee. You teach him good. Like Willy Harris taught you. You show where our five generations done come to. Go ahead, son—

WALTER (*looks down into his boy's eyes.* TRAVIS *grins at him merrily and* WALTER *draws him beside him with his arm lightly around his shoulders*) Well, Mr. Lindner. (BE-NEATHA *turns away.*) We called you—(*there is a profound, simple groping quality in his speech*)—because, well, me and my family— (*He looks around and shifts from one foot to the other.*) Well—we are very plain people. . . .

LINDNER Yes—

WALTER I mean—I have worked as a chauffeur most of my life—and my wife here, she does domestic work in people's kitchens. So does my mother. I mean—we are plain people. . . .

LINDNER Yes, Mr. Younger—

WALTER (*really like a small boy, looking down at his shoes and then up at the man*) And— uh—well, my father, well, he was a laborer most of his life.

LINDNER (*absolutely confused*) Uh, yes—

WALTER (*looking down at his toes once again*) My father almost beat a man to death once because this man called him a bad name or something, you know what I mean?

LINDNER No, I'm afraid I don't.

WALTER (*finally straightening up*) Well, what I mean is that we come from people who had a lot of pride. I mean—we are very proud people. And that's my sister over there and she's going to be a doctor—and we are very proud—

LINDNER Well—I am sure that is very nice, but—

WALTER (*starting to cry and facing the man eye to eye*) What I am telling you is that we called you over here to tell you that we are very proud and that this is—this is my son, who makes the sixth generation of our family in this country, and that we have all thought about your offer and we have decided to move into our house because my father—my father—he earned it. (MAMA *has her eyes closed and is rocking back and forth as though she were in church, with her head nodding the amen yes.*) We don't want to make no trouble for nobody or fight no causes—but we will try to be good neighbors. That's all we got to say. (*He looks the man absolutely in the eyes.*) We don't want your money. (*He turns and walks away from the man.*)

LINDNER (*looking around at all of them*) I take it then that you have decided to occupy.

BENEATHA That's what the man said.

LINDNER (*to* MAMA *in her reverie*) Then I would like to appeal to you, Mrs. Younger. You are older and wiser and understand things better I am sure. . . .

MAMA (*rising*) I am afraid you don't understand. My son said we was going to move and there ain't nothing left for me to say. (*Shaking her head with double meaning*) You know how these young folks is nowadays, mister. Can't do a thing with 'em. Goodbye.

LINDNER (*folding up his materials*) Well—if you are that final about it. . . . There is nothing left for me to say. (*He finishes. He is almost ignored by the family, who are concentrating on* WALTER LEE. *At the door* LINDNER *halts and looks around.*) I sure hope you people know what you're doing. (*He shakes his head and exits.*)

RUTH (*looking around and coming to life*) Well, for God's sake—if the moving men are here—LET'S GET THE HELL OUT OF HERE!

MAMA (*into action*) Ain't it the truth! Look at all this here mess. Ruth, put Travis' good jacket on him. . . . Walter Lee, fix your tie and tuck your shirt in, you look just like somebody's hoodlum. Lord have mercy, where is my plant? (*She flies to get it amid the general bustling of the family, who are deliberately trying to ignore the nobility of the past moment.*) You all start on down. . . . Travis child, don't go empty-handed. . . . Ruth, where did I put that box with my skillets in it? I want to be in charge of it myself. . . . I'm going to make us the biggest dinner we ever ate tonight. . . . Beneatha, what's the matter with them stockings? Pull them things up, girl. . . .

The family starts to file out as two moving men appear and begin to carry out the heavier pieces of furniture, bumping into the family as they move about.

BENEATHA Mama, Asagai—asked me to marry him today and go to Africa—

MAMA (*in the middle of her getting-ready activity*) He did? You ain't old enough to marry nobody— (*Seeing the moving men lifting one of her chairs precariously*) Darling, that ain't no bale of cotton, please handle it so we can sit in it again. I had that chair twenty-five years. . . .

The movers sigh with exasperation and go on with their work.

BENEATHA (*girlishly and unreasonably trying to pursue the conversation*) To go to Africa, Mama—be a doctor in Africa. . . .

MAMA (*distracted*) Yes, baby—

WALTER Africa! What he want you to go to Africa for?

BENEATHA To practice there. . . .

WALTER Girl, if you don't get all them silly ideas out your head! You better marry yourself a man with some loot. . . .

BENEATHA (*angrily, precisely as in the first scene of the play*) What have you got to do with who I marry!

WALTER Plenty. Now I think George Murchison—

He and BENEATHA *go out yelling at each other vigorously;* BENEATHA *is heard saying that she would not marry* GEORGE MURCHISON *if he were Adam and she were Eve, etc. The anger is loud and real till their voices diminish.* RUTH *stands at the door and turns to* MAMA *and smiles knowingly.*

MAMA (*fixing her hat at last*) Yeah—they something all right, my children. . . .

RUTH Yeah—they're something. Let's go, Lena.

MAMA (*stalling, starting to look around at the house*) Yes—I'm coming. Ruth—

RUTH Yes?

MAMA (*quietly, woman to woman*) He finally come into his manhood today, didn't he? Kind of like a rainbow after the rain. . . .

RUTH (*biting her lip lest her own pride explode in front of* MAMA) Yes, Lena.

WALTER'S *voice calls for them raucously.*

MAMA (*waving* RUTH *out vaguely*) All right, honey—go on down. I be down directly.

RUTH *hesitates, then exits.* MAMA *stands, at last alone in the living room, her plant on the table before her as the lights start to come down. She looks around at all the walls and ceilings and suddenly, despite herself, while the children call below, a great heaving thing rises in her and she puts her fist to her mouth, takes a final desperate look, pulls her coat about her, pats her hat and goes out. The lights dim down. The door opens and she comes back in, grabs her plant, and goes out for the last time.*

Curtain

Questions

1. Who is the protagonist of the play? Does it have a single protagonist or is it a play of "atmosphere"?

2. Which character do you most admire? Why?

3. Consider the dramatic situation with Mama as protagonist, stating her objective and the obstacles that stand in her way. Then consider the dramatic situation with Walter Lee as protagonist. What does he want? What is standing in his way?

4. What is Mama's major flaw? What is Walter's?

5. Compare Beneatha's sense of values with Walter Lee's. What does each value most in the world? Whose sense of values is most like your own?

6. One of the most powerful scenes in the play comes when Mama slaps Beneatha in Act I. Do you think Beneatha deserves it? Why is Mama so furious?

7. Do you think it was wrong for Walter Lee to invest Beneatha's school money in the liquor store? How does this action show the weaknesses and/or strengths of his character?

8. What is the play's climax?

9. Mama's triumph in A Raisin in the Sun is that she has managed to instill in her children certain virtues that enable them to survive as a family. What lessons has she strived to teach them?

10. Is the play a comedy, a tragedy, or a tragicomedy?

✍ Tips for Writing about "Realism" in Drama

1. Drama has always been considered the most social of literary forms, because it requires a sizable audience. Live audiences are extremely sensitive to the political meanings of stage action, which unite or divide spectators according to the prevailing morals. Playwrights like Ibsen know the political implications of their stories, and how they might challenge the opinions of a live audience. Look for social and political themes, along with psychological themes, in realistic drama. Often there is one character that represents the established morals and another who rebels against tradition.

2. The writers of "realistic" literature draw upon their own experience for their story-lines. The writer's social background usually has an enormous influence upon political themes in his or her work. Familiarize yourself with the background of the playwright, wherever possible, by reading a biography, or at least the information available in an encyclopedia. Sometimes a realistic drama actually has a character based upon the playwright.

9 🌿 New Directions

In adopting the conventions of realism, twentieth-century theater was giving up certain traditional sources of dramatic power. For instance poetry, which had been the most effective medium of communication on the stage for centuries, lost favor because "people don't talk like that." Popular theater audiences grew accustomed to lifelike behavior and probable events in new plays. Bizarre happenings like the ghost's appearance in *Hamlet* were discouraged because they destroyed the illusion of realism. It was as if playwrights and audiences had forgotten that what matters most in the theater is the illusion itself, not the fashionable convention of realism. What happens on the stage need not be probable in order to move us to tears or laughter.

Several modern dramatists were well aware of this. Their plays reflect a reaction to realism, as well as a development of ancient techniques of communication and illusion in the theater.

Symbolist Drama

We are familiar with symbolism as a technique of poetry and fiction. A symbol is an object or concrete word that stands for something abstract, an idea or concept. Thus the rose stands for the eternal beauty of womanhood, and the cross represents suffering and deliverance. In a symbolist drama the actions as well as the characters, props, and setting, refer to eternal ideas and states of being in a "higher" world. Thus, a person walking down a road in a symbolist play might represent Humankind's progress through Time. If that character should trip over a corpse, the corpse might symbolize the obstacles that Ancestors leave in Humankind's way.

If we work at it, we can interpret almost any dramatic action in symbolic terms. But we should not. Most plays are not so intended, preferring to focus our attention on the immediate event. There are symbols in *Oedipus Rex* and

Desire Under the Elms, but the world to which they refer is not nearly as important to us as the play's setting. A thoroughgoing symbolist drama shows a dreamlike indifference to the particulars of the present scene. Characters often have figurative names—Mr. Cactus or Mrs. Ablebody—and there is a liberal use of traditional poetic symbols.

The Sound of a Voice

The play you are about to read, David Hwang's *The Sound of a Voice*, declares its nonrealistic intentions in its title, in the characters' names (Man and Woman), in the sometimes poetic dialogue, and in the symbolic meaning of the playing space and the props.

The encounter between the man and the woman in her forest dwelling seems to happen in an enchanted dimension removed from ordinary time and place. He asks her at the beginning of the play how long it has been since she last received a visitor. And the woman replies: "Perhaps five months ago, perhaps ten years, perhaps yesterday. I don't consider time when there is no voice in the air. It's pointless. Time begins with the entrance of a visitor, and ends with his exit."

So we are invited to read *The Sound of a Voice* as a symbolic play, or allegory. On the surface, it is a simple drama, based upon folk legend, about a man who goes to kill the famous witch in the woods. Generations of young men have gone into the woods on that mission, but none has returned, so the legend goes, because they fall in love with her. On this level we can appreciate the drama as a passionate love story. We watch the man and woman fall in love, the man against his will, and the woman in dread of the pain of loneliness she may feel when he is gone.

On the symbolic level this play means much more. The man represents all men, in their fear of losing themselves in love. The woman represents all women, in their fear of loneliness. Even beyond the sex roles, the play has valuable symbolic resonance. The two characters are acting out the drama of *any* human relationship, with its risks and rewards.

Stylistically, *The Sound of a Voice* owes a debt to the Kabuki theater, the Japanese Noh plays, and the poetic folk dramas of the Irish dramatists W. B. Yeats and J. M. Synge.

David Hwang is the son of first-generation Chinese-Americans. He grew up in San Gabriel, California, where he went to high school and distinguished himself as a debater. Hwang went to Stanford University, where in his senior year, 1979, he directed the first production of his play *FOB* in a dormitory lounge. Like all of Hwang's plays, *FOB* concerns the confrontation of two diametrically opposed characters. *M. Butterfly*, which had an enormous success on Broadway in 1988, winning the Pulitzer Prize for drama, concerns the relationship between a French diplomat and a Chinese actor with whom he falls in love. Other plays include *The Dance and the Railroad* and *Family Devotions*.

David Henry Hwang (*Writers & Artists Agency, New York, New York*)

DAVID HWANG (1957–)

The Sound of a Voice

SCENE I. WOMAN *pours tea for* MAN. MAN *rubs himself, trying to get warm.*

MAN You're very kind to take me in.

WOMAN This is a remote corner of the world. Guests are rare.

MAN The tea—you pour it well.

WOMAN No.

MAN The sound it makes—in the cup—very soothing.

WOMAN That is the tea's skill, not mine. (*She hands the cup to him.*) May I get you something else? Rice, perhaps?

MAN No.

WOMAN And some vegetables?

MAN No, thank you.

WOMAN Fish? (*Pause.*) It is at least two days walk to the nearest village. I saw no horse. You must be very hungry. You would do a great honor to dine with me. Guests are rare.

MAN Thank you.

WOMAN (WOMAN *gets up, leaves.* MAN *holds the cup in his hands, using it to warm himself. He gets up, walks around the room. It is sparsely furnished, drab, except for one shelf on which stands a vase of brightly colored flowers. The flowers stand out in sharp contrast to the starkness of the room. Slowly, he reaches out towards them. He touches them. Quickly, he takes one of the flowers from the vase, hides it in his clothes. He returns to where he had sat previously. He waits. WOMAN re-enters. She carries a tray with food.)* Please. Eat. It will give me great pleasure.

MAN This—this is magnificent.

WOMAN Eat.

MAN Thank you. (*He motions for WOMAN to join him.*)

WOMAN No, thank you.

MAN This is wonderful. The best I've tasted.

WOMAN You are reckless in your flattery. But anything you say, I will enjoy hearing. It's not even the words. It's the sound of a voice, the way it moves through the air.

MAN How long has it been since you last had a visitor? (*Pause.*)

WOMAN I don't know.

MAN Oh?

WOMAN I lose track. Perhaps five months ago, perhaps ten years, perhaps yesterday. I don't consider time when there is no voice in the air. It's pointless. Time begins with the entrance of a visitor, and ends with his exit.

MAN And in between? You don't keep track of the days? You can't help but notice—

WOMAN Of course I notice.

MAN Oh.

WOMAN I notice, but I don't keep track. (*Pause.*) May I bring out more?

MAN More? No. No. This was wonderful.

WOMAN I have more.

MAN Really—the best I've had.

WOMAN You must be tired. Did you sleep in the forest last night?

MAN Yes.

WOMAN Or did you not sleep at all?

MAN I slept.

WOMAN Where?

MAN By a waterfall. The sound of the water put me to sleep. It rumbled like the sounds of a city. You see, I can't sleep in too much silence. It scares me. It makes me feel that I have no control over what is about to happen.

WOMAN I feel the same way.

MAN But you live here—alone?

WOMAN Yes.

MAN It's so quiet here. How can you sleep?

WOMAN Tonight, I'll sleep. I'll lie down in the next room, and hear your breathing through the wall, and fall asleep shamelessly. There will be no silence.

MAN You're very kind to let me stay here.

WOMAN This is yours. (*She unrolls a mat; there is a beautiful design of a flower on the mat. The flower looks exactly like the flowers in the vase.*)

MAN Did you make it yourself?

WOMAN Yes. There is a place to wash outside.

MAN Thank you.

WOMAN Goodnight.

MAN Goodnight. (*MAN starts to leave.*)

WOMAN May I know your name?

MAN No. I mean, I would rather not say. If I gave you a name, it would only be made-up. Why should I deceive you? You are too kind for that.

WOMAN Then what should I call you? Perhaps—"Man Who Fears Silence?"

MAN How about, "Man Who Fears Women?"

WOMAN That name is much too common.

MAN And you?

WOMAN Yokiko.

MAN That's your name?

WOMAN It's what you may call me.

MAN Goodnight, Yokiko. You are very kind.

WOMAN You are very smart. Goodnight. (MAN *exits.* HANAKO[1] *goes to the mat. She tidies it, brushes it off. She goes to the vase. She picks up the flowers, studies them. She carries them out of the room with her.* MAN *re-enters. He takes off his outer clothing. He glimpses the spot where the vase used to sit. He reaches into his clothing, pulls out the stolen flower. He studies it. He puts it underneath his head as lies down to sleep, like a pillow. He starts to fall asleep. Suddenly, a start. He picks up his head. He listens.*)

SCENE II. *Dawn.* MAN *is getting dressed.* WOMAN *enters with food.*

WOMAN Good morning.

MAN Good morning, Yokiko.

WOMAN You weren't planning to leave?

MAN I have quite a distance to travel today.

WOMAN Please. (*She offers him food.*)

MAN Thank you.

WOMAN May I ask where you're travelling to?

MAN It's far.

WOMAN I know this region well.

MAN Oh? Do you leave the house often?

WOMAN I used to. I used to travel a great deal. I know the region from those days.

MAN You probably wouldn't know the place I'm headed.

WOMAN Why not?

MAN It's new. A new village. It didn't exist in "those days." (*Pause.*)

WOMAN I thought you said you wouldn't deceive me.

MAN I didn't. You don't believe me, do you?

WOMAN No.

MAN Then I didn't deceive you. I'm travelling. That much is true.

WOMAN Are you in such a hurry?

MAN Travelling is a matter of timing. Catching the light. (WOMAN *exits;* MAN *finishes eating, puts down his bowl.* WOMAN *re-enters with the vase of flowers.*) Where did you find those? They don't grow native around these parts, do they?

WOMAN No; they've all been brought in. They were brought in by visitors. Such as yourself. They were left here. In my custody.

MAN But—they look so fresh, so alive.

WOMAN I take care of them. They remind me of the people and places outside this house.

MAN May I touch them?

WOMAN Certainly.

MAN These have just blossomed.

---

[1] The woman.

WOMAN No; they were in bloom yesterday. If you'd noticed them before, you would know that.

MAN You must have received these very recently. I would guess—within five days.

WOMAN I don't know. But I wouldn't trust your estimate. It's all in the amount of care you show to them. I create a world which is outside the realm of what you know.

MAN What do you do?

WOMAN I can't explain. Words are too inefficient. It takes hundreds of words to describe a single act of caring. With hundreds of acts, words become irrelevant. (*Pause.*) But perhaps you can stay.

MAN How long?

WOMAN As long as you'd like.

MAN Why?

WOMAN To see how I care for them.

MAN I *am* tired.

WOMAN Rest.

MAN The light?

WOMAN It will return.

SCENE III. MAN *is carrying chopped wood. He is stripped to the waist.* WOMAN *enters.*

WOMAN You're very kind to do that for me.

MAN I enjoy it, you know. Chopping wood. It's clean. No questions. You take your axe, you stand up the log, you aim—pow!—you either hit it or you don't. Success or failure.

WOMAN You seem to have been very successful today.

MAN Why shouldn't I be? It's a beautiful day. I can see to those hills. The trees are cool. The sun is gentle. Ideal. If a man can't be successful on a day like this, he might as well kick the dust up into his own face. (MAN *notices* WOMAN *staring at him.* MAN *pats his belly, looks at her.*) Protection from falls.

WOMAN What? (MAN *pinches his belly, showing some fat.*) Oh. Don't be silly. (MAN *begins slapping the fat on his belly to a rhythm.*)

MAN Listen—I can make music—see?—that wasn't always possible. But now—that I've developed this—whenever I need entertainment.

WOMAN You shouldn't make fun of your body.

MAN Why not? I saw you. You were staring.

WOMAN I wasn't making fun. (MAN *inflates his cheeks.*) I was just—stop that!

MAN Then why were you staring?

WOMAN I was—

MAN Laughing?

WOMAN No.

MAN Well?

WOMAN I was—Your body. It's . . . strong. (*Pause.*)

MAN People say that. But they don't know. I've heard that age brings wisdom. That's a laugh. The years don't accumulate here. They accumulate here. (*Pause; he pinches his belly.*) But today is a day to be happy, right? The woods. The sun. Blue. It's a happy day. I'm going to chop wood.

WOMAN There's nothing left to chop. Look.

MAN Oh. I guess . . . that's it.

WOMAN Sit. Here.

MAN But—

WOMAN There's nothing left. (MAN *sits;* WOMAN *stares at his belly.*) Learn to love it.

MAN Don't be ridiculous.

WOMAN Touch it.

MAN It's flabby.

WOMAN It's strong.

MAN It's weak.

WOMAN And smooth.

MAN Do you mind if I put on my shirt?

WOMAN Of course not. Shall I get it for you?

MAN No. No. Just sit there. (MAN *starts to put on his shirt. He pauses, studies his body.*) You think it's cute, huh?

WOMAN I think you should learn to love it. (MAN *pats his belly, talks to it.*)

MAN (*To belly:*) You're okay, sir. You hang onto my body like a great horseman.

WOMAN Not like that.

MAN (*Ibid.*) You're also faithful. You'll never leave me for another man.

WOMAN No.

MAN What do you want me to say? (WOMAN *walks over to* MAN. *She touches his belly with her hand. They look at each other.*)

SCENE IV. *Night.* MAN *is alone. Flowers are gone from stand. Mat is unrolled.* MAN *lies on it, sleeping. Suddenly, he starts. He lifts up his head. He listens. Silence. He goes back to sleep. Another start. He lifts up his head, strains to hear. Slowly, we begin to make out the strains of a single* shakuhachi[2] *playing a haunting line. It is very soft. He strains to hear it. The instrument slowly fades out. He waits for it to return, but it does not. He takes out the stolen flower. He stares into it.*

SCENE V. *Day.* WOMAN *is cleaning, while* MAN *relaxes. She is on her hands and knees, scrubbing. She is dressed in a simple outfit, for working. Her hair is tied back.* MAN *is sweating. He has not, however, removed his shirt.*

MAN I heard your playing last night.

WOMAN My playing?

MAN *Shakuhachi.*

WOMAN Oh.

MAN You played very softly. I had to strain to hear it. Next time, don't be afraid. Play out. Fully. Clear. It must've been very beautiful, if only I could've heard it clearly. Why don't you play for me sometime?

WOMAN I'm very shy about it.

MAN Why?

WOMAN I play for my own satisfaction. That's all. It's something I developed on my own. I don't know if it's at all acceptable by outside standards.

MAN Play for me. I'll tell you.

WOMAN No; I'm sure you're too knowledgeable in the arts.

MAN Who? Me?

WOMAN You being from the city and all.

MAN I'm ignorant, believe me.

WOMAN I'd play, and you'd probably bite your cheek.

---

[2] A Japanese end-blown bamboo flute.

MAN Ask me a question about music. Any question. I'll answer incorrectly. I guarantee it.

WOMAN Look at this.

MAN What?

WOMAN A stain.

MAN Where?

WOMAN Here? See? I can't get it out.

MAN Oh. I hadn't noticed it before.

WOMAN I notice it every time I clean.

MAN Here. Let me try.

WOMAN Thank you.

MAN Ugh. It's tough.

WOMAN I know.

MAN How did it get here?

WOMAN It's been there as long as I've lived here.

MAN I hardly stand a chance. (*Pause.*) But I'll try. Uh—one—two—three—four! One—two—three—four! See, you set up . . . gotta set up . . . a rhythm—two—three—four. Like fighting! Like battle! One—two—three—four! Used to practice with a rhythm . . . beat . . . battle! Yes! (*The stain starts to fade away.*) Look—it's—yes!—whoo!—there it goes—got the sides—the edges—yes!—fading quick—fading away—ooo—here we come—towards the center—to the heart—two—three—four—slow—slow death—tough—dead! (MAN *rolls over in triumphant laughter.*)

WOMAN Dead.

MAN I got it! I got it! Whoo! A little rhythm! All it took! Four! Four!

WOMAN Thank you.

MAN I didn't think I could do it—but there—it's gone—I did it!

WOMAN Yes. You did.

MAN And you—you were great.

WOMAN No—I was carried away.

MAN We were a team! You and me!

WOMAN I only provided encouragement.

MAN You were great! You were! (MAN *grabs* WOMAN. *Pause.*)

WOMAN It's gone. Thank you. Would you like to hear me play *shakuhachi?*

MAN Yes I would.

WOMAN I don't usually play for visitors. It's so . . . I'm not sure. I developed it—all by myself—in times when I was alone. I heard nothing—no human voice. So I learned to play *shakuhachi.* I tried to make these sounds resemble the human voice. The *shakuhachi* became my weapon. To ward off the air. It kept me from choking on many a silent evening.

MAN I'm here. You can hear my voice.

WOMAN Speak again.

MAN I will.

SCENE VI. *Night.* MAN *is sleeping. Suddenly, a start. He lifts his head up. He listens. Silence. He strains to hear. The* shakuhachi *melody rises up once more. This time, however, it becomes louder and more clear than before. He gets up. He cannot tell from what direction the music is coming. He walks around the room, putting his ear to different places in the wall, but he cannot locate the sound. It seems to come from all directions at once, as omnipresent as the air. Slowly, he moves towards the wall with the sliding panel through which the* WOMAN *enters and exits. He puts his ear against it, thinking the music may be coming from there. Slowly, he slides the door open just a crack, ever so carefully. He peeks through the crack. As he peeks through, the Upstage wall of the set becomes transparent, and through the scrim, we are able to see what he sees.* WOMAN *is Upstage of the scrim. She is tending a room filled with potted and vased flowers of all variety. The lushness and beauty of the room Upstage of the scrim stands out in stark contrast to the barrenness of the main set. She is also transformed. She is a young woman. She is beautiful. She wears a brightly colored kimono.* MAN *observes this scene for a long time. He then slides the door shut. The scrim returns to opaque. The music continues. He returns to his mat. He picks up the stolen flower. It is brown and wilted, dead. He looks at it. The music slowly fades out.*

SCENE VII. *Morning.* MAN *is half-dressed. He is practicing sword maneuvers. He practices with the feel of a man whose spirit is willing, but the flesh is inept. He tries to execute deft movements, but is dissatisfied with his efforts. He curses himself, and returns to basic exercises. Suddenly, he feels something buzzing around his neck—a mosquito. He slaps his neck, but misses it. He sees it flying near him. He swipes at it with his sword. He keeps missing. Finally, he thinks he's hit it. He runs over, kneels down to recover the fallen insect. He picks up two halves of a mosquito on two different fingers.* WOMAN *enters the room. She looks as she normally does. She is carrying a vase of flowers, which she places on its shelf.*

MAN Look.
WOMAN I'm sorry?
MAN Look.
WOMAN What? (*He brings over the two halves of mosquito to show her.*)
MAN See?
WOMAN Oh.
MAN I hit it—chop!
WOMAN These are new forms of target practice?
MAN Huh? Well—yes—in a way.
WOMAN You seem to do well at it.
MAN Thank you. For last night. I heard your *shakuhachi*. It was very loud, strong—good tone.
WOMAN Did you enjoy it? I wanted you to enjoy it. If you wish, I'll play it for you every night.
MAN Every night!
WOMAN If you wish.
MAN No—I don't—I don't want you to treat me like a baby.
WOMAN What? I'm not.
MAN Oh, yes. Like a baby. Who you must feed in the middle of the night or he cries. Waaah! Waaah!
WOMAN Stop that!
MAN You need your sleep.
WOMAN I don't mind getting up for you. (*Pause.*) I would enjoy playing for you. Every night. While you sleep. It will make me feel—like I'm shaping your dreams. I go through long stretches when there is no one in my dreams. It's terrible. During those times, I avoid my bed as much as possible. I paint. I weave. I play *shakuhachi*. I sit

on mats and rub powder into my face. Anything to keep from facing a bed with no dreams. It is like sleeping on ice.

MAN What do you dream of now?

WOMAN Last night—I dreamt of you. I don't remember what happened. But you were very funny. Not in a mocking way. I wasn't laughing at you. But you made me laugh. And you were very warm. I remember that. (*Pause.*) What do you remember about last night?

MAN Just your playing. That's all. I got up, listened to it, and went back to sleep. (MAN *gets up, resumes practicing with his sword.*)

WOMAN Another mosquito bothering you?

MAN Just practicing. Ah! Weak! Too weak! I tell you, it wasn't always like this. I'm telling you, there were days when I could chop the fruit from a tree without ever taking my eyes off the ground. (*He continues practicing.*) You ever use one of these?

WOMAN I've had to pick one up, yes.

MAN Oh?

WOMAN You forget—I live alone—out here—there is . . . not much to sustain me but what I manage to learn myself. It wasn't really a matter of choice.

MAN I used to be very good, you know. Perhaps I can give you some pointers.

WOMAN I'd really rather not.

MAN C'mon—a woman like you—you're absolutely right. You need to know how to defend yourself.

WOMAN As you wish.

MAN Do you have something to practice with?

WOMAN Yes. Excuse me. (*She exits. He practices more. She re-enters with two wooden sticks. He takes one of them.*) Will these do?

MAN Nice. Now, show me what you can do.

WOMAN I'm sorry?

MAN Run up and hit me.

WOMAN Please.

MAN Go on—I'll block it.

WOMAN I feel so . . . undignified.

MAN Go on. (*She hits him playfully with stick.*) Not like that!

WOMAN I'll try to be gentle.

MAN What?

WOMAN I don't want to hurt you.

MAN You won't—Hit me! (WOMAN *charges at* MAN, *quickly, deftly. She scores a hit.*) Oh!

WOMAN Did I hurt you?

MAN No—you were—let's try that again. (*They square off again.* WOMAN *rushes forward. She appears to attempt a strike. He blocks that apparent strike, which turns out to be a feint. She scores.*) Huh?

WOMAN Did I hurt you? I'm sorry.

MAN No.

WOMAN I hurt you.

MAN No.

WOMAN Do you wish to hit me?

MAN No.

WOMAN Do you want me to try again?

MAN No.

WOMAN Thank you.

MAN Just practice there—by yourself—let me see you run through some maneuvers.

WOMAN Must I?

MAN Yes! Go! (*She goes to an open area.*) My greatest strength was always as a teacher. (WOMAN *executes a series of deft movements. Her whole manner is transformed.* MAN *watches with increasing amazement. Her movements end. She regains her submissive manner.*)

WOMAN I'm so embarrassed. My skills—they're so—inappropriate. I look like a man.

MAN Where did you learn that?

WOMAN There is much time to practice here.

MAN But you—the techniques.

WOMAN I don't know what's fashionable in the outside world. (*Pause.*) Are you unhappy?

MAN No.

WOMAN Really?

MAN I'm just . . . surprised.

WOMAN You think it's unbecoming for a woman.

MAN No, no. Not at all.

WOMAN You want to leave.

MAN No!

WOMAN All visitors do. I know. I've met many. They say they'll stay. And they do. For a while. Until they see too much. Or they learn something new. There are boundaries outside of which visitors do not want to see me step. Only who knows what those boundaries are? Not I. They change with every visitor. You have to be careful not to cross them, but you never know where they are. And one day, inevitably, you step outside the lines. The visitor knows. You don't. You didn't know that you'd done anything different. You thought it was just another part of you. The visitor sneaks away. The next day, you learn that you had stepped outside his heart. I'm afraid you've seen too much.

MAN There are stories.

WOMAN What?

MAN People talk.

WOMAN Where? We're two days from the nearest village.

MAN Word travels.

WOMAN What are you talking about?

MAN There are stories about you. I heard them. They say that your visitors never leave this house.

WOMAN That's what you heard?

MAN They say you imprison them.

WOMAN Then you were a fool to come here.

MAN Listen.

WOMAN Me? Listen? You. Look! Where are these prisoners? Have you seen any?

MAN They told me you were very beautiful.

WOMAN Then they are blind as well as ignorant.

MAN You are.

WOMAN What?

MAN Beautiful.

WOMAN Stop that! My skin feels like seaweed.

MAN I didn't realize it at first. I must confess—I didn't. But over these few days—your face has changed for me. The shape of it. The feel of it. The color. All changed. I look at you now, and I'm no longer sure you are the same woman who had poured tea for me just a week ago. And because of that I remembered—how little I know about a face that changes in the night. (*Pause.*) Have you heard those stories?

WOMAN I don't listen to old wives' tales.

MAN But have you heard them?

WOMAN Yes. I've heard them. From other visitors—young—hotblooded—or old—who came here because they were told great glory was to be had by killing the witch in the woods.

MAN I was told that no man could spend time in this house without falling in love.

WOMAN Oh? So why did you come? Did you wager gold that you could come out untouched? The outside world is so flattering to me. And you—are you like the rest? Passion passing through your heart so powerfully that you can't hold onto it?

MAN No! I'm afraid!

WOMAN Of what?

MAN Sometimes—when I look into the flowers, I think I hear a voice—from inside—a voice beneath the petals. A human voice.

WOMAN What does it say? "Let me out?"

MAN No. Listen. It hums. It hums with the peacefulness of one who is completely imprisoned.

WOMAN I understand that if you listen closely enough, you can hear the ocean.

MAN No. Wait. Look at it. See the layers? Each petal—hiding the next. Try and see where they end. You can't. Follow them down, further down, around—and as you come down—faster and faster—the breeze picks up. The breeze becomes a wail. And in that rush of air—in the silent midst of it—you can hear a voice. (WOMAN *grabs flower from* MAN.)

WOMAN So, you believe I water and prune my lovers? How can you be so foolish? (*She snaps the flower in half, at the stem. She throws it to the ground.*) Do you come only to leave again? To take a chunk of my heart, then leave with your booty on your belt, like a prize? You say that I imprison hearts in these flowers? Well, bits of my heart are trapped with travellers across this land. I can't even keep track. So kill me. If you came here to destroy a witch, kill me now. I can't stand to have it happen again.

MAN I won't leave you.

WOMAN I believe you. (*She looks at the flower that she has broken, bends to pick it up. He touches her. They embrace.*)

SCENE VIII. *Day.* WOMAN *wears a simple undergarment, over which she is donning a brightly colored kimono, the same one we saw her wearing Upstage of the scrim.* MAN *stands apart.*

WOMAN I can't cry. I don't have the capacity. Right from birth, I didn't cry. My mother and father were shocked. They thought they'd given birth to a ghost, a demon. Sometimes I've thought myself that. When great sadness has welled up inside me, I've prayed for a means to release the pain from my body. But my prayers went unanswered. The grief remained inside me. It would sit like water, still. (*Pause; she models her kimono.*) Do you like it?

MAN Yes, it's beautiful.

WOMAN I wanted to wear something special today.

MAN It's beautiful. Excuse me. I must practice.

WOMAN Shall I get you something?

MAN No.

WOMAN Some tea, maybe?

MAN No. (MAN *resumes swordplay.*)

WOMAN Perhaps later today—perhaps we can go out—just around here. We can look for flowers.

MAN All right.

WOMAN We don't have to.

MAN No. Let's.

WOMAN I just thought if—

MAN Fine. Where do you want to go?

WOMAN There are very few recreational activities around here, I know.

MAN All right. We'll go this afternoon. (*Pause.*)

WOMAN Can I get you something?

MAN (*Turning around.*) What?

WOMAN You might be—

MAN I'm not hungry or thirsty or cold or hot.

WOMAN Then what are you?

MAN Practicing. (MAN *resumes practicing;* WOMAN *exits. As soon as she exits, he rests. He sits down. He examines his sword. He runs his finger along the edge of it. He takes the tip, runs it against the soft skin under his chin. He places the sword on the ground with the tip pointed directly upwards. He keeps it from falling by placing the tip under his chin. He experiments with different degrees of pressure.* WOMAN *re-enters. She sees him in this precarious position. She jerks his head upward; the sword falls.*)

WOMAN Don't do that!

MAN What?

WOMAN You can hurt yourself!

MAN I was practicing!

WOMAN You were playing!

MAN I was practicing!

WOMAN It's dangerous.

MAN What do you take me for—a child?

WOMAN Sometimes wise men do childish things.

MAN I knew what I was doing!

WOMAN It scares me.

MAN Don't be ridiculous. (*He reaches for the sword again.*)

WOMAN Don't! Don't do that!

MAN Get back! (*He places the sword back in its previous position, suspended between the floor and his chin, upright.*)

WOMAN But—

MAN Sssssh!

WOMAN I wish—

MAN Listen to me! The slightest shock, you know—the slightest shock—surprise—it might make me jerk or—something—and then . . . So you must be perfectly still and quiet.

WOMAN But I—

MAN Sssssh! (*Silence.*) I learned this exercise from a friend—I can't even remember his name—good swordsman—many years ago. He called it his meditation position. He said, like this, he could feel the line between this world and the others because he rested on it. If he saw something in another world that he liked better, all he would have to do is let his head drop, and he'd be there. Simple. No fuss. One day, they found him with the tip of his sword run clean out the back of his neck. He was smiling. I guess he saw something he liked. Or else he'd fallen asleep.

WOMAN Stop that.

MAN Stop what?

WOMAN Tormenting me.

MAN I'm not.

WOMAN Take it away!

MAN You don't have to watch, you know.

WOMAN Do you want to die that way—an accident?

MAN I was doing this before you came in.

WOMAN If you do, all you need to do is tell me.

MAN What?

WOMAN I can walk right over. Lean on the back of your head.

MAN Don't try to threaten—

WOMAN Or jerk your sword up.

MAN Or scare me. You can't threaten—

WOMAN I'm not. But if that's what you want.

MAN You can't threaten me. You wouldn't do it.

WOMAN Oh?

MAN Then I'd be gone. You wouldn't let me leave that easily.

WOMAN Yes, I would.

MAN You'd be alone.

WOMAN No. I'd follow you. Forever. (*Pause.*) Now, let's stop this nonsense.

MAN No! I can do what I want! Don't come any closer!

WOMAN Then release your sword.

MAN Come any closer and I'll drop my head.

WOMAN (WOMAN *slowly approaches* MAN. *She grabs the hilt of the sword. She looks into his eyes. She pulls it out from under his chin.*) There will be no more of this. (*She exits with the sword. He starts to follow her, then stops. He touches under his chin. On his finger, he finds a drop of blood.*)

SCENE IX. *Night.* MAN *is leaving the house. He is just about out, when he hears a* shakuhachi *playing. He looks around, trying to locate the sound.* WOMAN *appears in the doorway to the outside.* Shakuhachi *slowly fades out.*

WOMAN It's time for you to go?

MAN Yes. I'm sorry.

WOMAN You're just going to sneak out? A thief in the night? A frightened child?

MAN I care about you.

WOMAN You express it strangely.

MAN I leave in shame because it is proper. (*Pause.*) I came seeking glory.

WOMAN To kill me? You can say it. You'll be surprised at how little I blanche. As if you'd said, "I came for a bowl of rice," or "I came seeking love" or "I came to kill you."

MAN Weakness. All weakness. Too weak to kill you. Too weak to kill myself. Too weak to do anything but sneak away in shame. (WOMAN *brings out* MAN's *sword.*)

WOMAN Were you even planning to leave without this? (*He takes sword.*) Why not stay here?

MAN I can't live with someone who's defeated me.

WOMAN I never thought of defeating you. I only wanted to take care of you. To make you happy. Because that made me happy and I was no longer alone.

MAN You defeated me.

WOMAN Why do you think that way?

MAN I came here with a purpose. The world was clear. You changed the shape of your face, the shape of my heart—rearranged everything—created a world where I could do nothing.

WOMAN I only tried to care for you.

MAN I guess that was all it took. (*Pause.*)

WOMAN You still think I'm a witch. Just because old women gossip. You are so cruel. Once you arrived, there were only two possibilities: I would die or you would leave. (*Pause.*) If you believe I'm a witch, then kill me. Rid the province of one more evil.

MAN I can't—

WOMAN Why not? If you believe that about me, then it's the right thing to do.

MAN You know I can't.

WOMAN Then stay.

MAN Don't try and force me.

WOMAN I won't force you to do anything. (*Pause.*) All I wanted was an escape—for both of us. The sound of a human voice—the simplest thing to find, and the hardest to hold onto. This house—my loneliness is etched into the walls. Kill me, but don't leave. Even in death, my spirit would rest here and be comforted by your presence.

MAN Force me to stay.

WOMAN I won't. (MAN *starts to leave.*) Beware.

MAN What?

WOMAN The ground on which you walk is weak. It could give way at any moment. The crevice beneath is dark.

MAN Are you talking about death? I'm ready to die.

WOMAN Fear for what is worse than death.

MAN What?

WOMAN Falling. Falling through the darkness. Waiting to hit the ground. Picking up speed. Waiting for the ground. Falling faster. Falling alone. Waiting. Falling. Waiting. Falling.

(WOMAN *wails and runs out through the door to her room.* MAN *stands, confused, not knowing what to do. He starts to follow her, then hesitates, and rushes out the door to the outside. Silence. Slowly, he re-enters from the outside. He looks for her in the main room. He goes slowly towards the panel to her room. He throws down his sword. He opens the panel. He goes inside. He comes out. He unrolls his mat. He sits on it, cross-legged. He looks out into space. He notices near him a shakuhachi. He picks it up. He begins to blow into it. He tries to make sounds. He continues trying through the end of the play. The Upstage scrim lights up. Upstage, we see the* WOMAN. *She is young. She is hanging from a rope suspended from the roof. She has hung herself. Around her, are scores of vases with flowers in them whose blossoms have been blown off. Only the stems remain in the vases. Around her swirl the thousands of petals from the flowers. They fill the Upstage scrim area like a blizzard of color.* MAN *continues to attempt to play. Lights fade to black.*)

Questions

1. You will recall from our discussion of symbolism in poetry that a symbol is something concrete which stands for something abstract. For instance, a cross symbolizes human suffering. In a symbolic drama like *The Sound of a Voice* that is so sparse in its details

the stage props become very rich in meaning. Consider the flowers. What do they stand for? Discuss how the playwright uses the symbol of the flowers throughout his play.

2. How does the woman persuade the man to stay?
3. In a symbolic drama not only the objects and characters on the stage have meaning beyond the physical, but so do the actions. The man takes great pleasure in chopping wood. What does this tell you about him? What does this tell you about men in general?
4. As the play develops, we discover that the woman has certain qualities usually considered "male"; the man has certain qualities we might consider feminine. Explain.
5. The most striking theatrical image in this short play appears in Scene Eight, where the man places the butt of his sword on the ground with the point pressed under his chin. A sensational physical action, it is rich in conveying the conflicts of the man's emotional state. Explain the symbolic meaning of this image.
6. This play ends in an extraordinary swirl of symbolic images and actions, whose meaning is as complex as the human relationships that have been recounted. What does the ending mean to you. Is it tragic?

 Writers on Writing   David Hwang

> *It always seemed to me, intellectually, that a blend of Asian and Western theatre would be interesting. I didn't know how to go about it and I managed to find people to help me figure it out. It's not like I'm the first Asian-American writer to come along, there have been lots of others before me. But they had been trying to create some sort of Asian-American synthesis in terms of the ideas advanced—political notions, or even polemics. I thought it was much more interesting to deal with that question in terms of form. It seemed to me if you took forms and merged them, you'd be making your political statement in a much more theatrical fashion.*
>
> * * *
>
> *With almost all the plays there's been a period of substantial rewrites before rehearsals. But some more than others. I'm always open to rewriting during rehearsal, too, and sometimes have rewritten great chunks. But that's tricky. On the one hand, although the theatrical experience comes from the text, once you start seeing the play on its feet, the text doesn't actually take precedence over the experience. If the text looks good but the experience isn't working, you fiddle with the direction, but if it still doesn't work, it's really the responsibility of the words. On the other hand, in some ways rehearsal is the worst time to rewrite because you're under a lot of time pressure. If you've spent a year with the play, there's something absurd about rewriting the whole thing in four weeks.*

A Quarreling Pair

As children we have all enjoyed puppet shows at a fair or carnival. But great modern puppeteers, like Jim Henson and Robert Anton, among others, have proven that puppets interest adults as well. The puppet show, with its tiny stage, miniature characters, and its tradition of satirizing humanity, has evolved over centuries into a dramatic art capable of great focus and subtlety. Several sophisticated modern writers have written plays for puppets, and Greek tragedies have been adapted for marionettes.

The puppet stage is well suited for symbolism. The puppets are more obviously fictional than living actors, so anything they do immediately rules out any literal interpretation. In A Quarreling Pair Jane Bowles uses the puppet theatre in order to dramatize certain tensions that exist between sisters who live together. As in many relationships, one is dominant and tough, while the other is submissive and more sensitive. But the characteristics of the puppets, aggressive Harriet and sentimental Rhoda, are exaggerated for dramatic, and symbolic, effect.

Jane Bowles (1917–1973) lived in New York City until 1947, then spent most of her life abroad in Paris, Ceylon, and Tangiers. She was married to the writer and composer Paul Bowles. She is known for her novel *Two Serious Ladies* and her great short stories.

Truman Capote wrote of Jane Bowles: "Though the tragic view is central to her vision, Jane Bowles is a very funny writer, a humorist of sorts—but *not*, by the way, of the Black School. Black Comedy, as its perpetrators label it, is, when successful, all lovely artifice and lacking any hint of compassion." Certainly this is not true of Jane Bowles, whose ironic artifice always accompanies great human tenderness. Let us bear Capote's comments in mind as we read A *Quarreling Pair* and then Beth Henley's *Crimes of the Heart*, which has been called a black comedy.

JANE BOWLES (1917–1973)

A Quarreling Pair

The two puppets are sisters in their early fifties. The puppet stage should have a rod or string dividing it down the middle to indicate two rooms. One puppet is seated on each side of the dividing line. If it is not possible to seat them they will have to stand. HARRIET, *the older puppet, is stronger-looking and wears brighter colors.*

HARRIET (*The stronger puppet*) I hope you are beginning to think about our milk.

RHODA (*After a pause*) Well, I'm not.

HARRIET Now what's the matter with you? You're not going to have a visitation from our dead, are you?

RHODA I don't have visitations this winter because I'm too tired to love even our dead. Anyway, I'm disgusted with the world.

HARRIET Just mind your business. I mind mine and I *am* thinking about our milk.

RHODA I'm so tired of being sad. I'd like to change.

HARRIET You don't get enough enjoyment out of your room. Why don't you?

RHODA Oh, because the world and its sufferers are always on my mind.

HARRIET That's not normal. You're not smart enough to be of any use to the outside, anyway.

RHODA If I were young I'd succor the sick. I wouldn't care about culture, even, if I were young.

HARRIET You don't have any knack for making a home. There's blessed satisfaction in that, at any rate.

RHODA My heart's too big to make a home.

HARRIET No. It's because you have no self-sufficiency.. If I wasn't around, you wouldn't have the leisure to worry. You're a lost soul, when I'm not around. You don't even have the pep to worry about the outside when I'm not around. Not that the outside loses by that! (*She sniffs with scorn.*)

RHODA You're right. But I swear that my heart is big.

HARRIET I've come to believe that what is inside of people is not so very interesting. You can breed considerable discontent around you with a big heart, and considerable harmony with a small one. Compare your living quarters to mine. And my heart is small like Papa's was.

RHODA You chill me to the marrow when you tell me that your heart is small. You do love me, though, don't you?

HARRIET You're my sister, aren't you?

RHODA Sisterly love is one of the few boons in this life.

HARRIET Now, that's enough exaggerating. I could enumerate other things.

RHODA I suppose it's wicked to squeeze love from a small heart. I suppose it's a sin. I suppose God meant for small hearts to be busy with other things.

HARRIET Possibly. Let's have our milk in my room. It's so much more agreeable to sit in here. Partly because I'm a neater woman than you are.

RHODA Even though you have a small heart, I wish there were no one but you and me in the world. Then I would never feel that I had to go among the others.

HARRIET Well, I wish I could hand you my gift for contentment in a box. It would be so lovely if you were like me. Then we could have our milk in *either* room. One day in your room and the next day in mine.

RHODA I'm sure that's the sort of thing that never happens.

HARRIET It happens in a million homes, seven days a week. I'm the type that's in the majority.

RHODA Never, never, never . . .

HARRIET (*Very firmly*) It happens in a million homes.

RHODA *Never, never, never!*

HARRIET (*Rising*) Are you going to listen to me when I tell you that it happens in a million homes, or must I lose my temper?

RHODA You have already lost it. (HARRIET *exits rapidly in a rage.* RHODA *goes to the chimes and sings*)

> My horse was frozen like a stone
> A long, long time ago.
> Frozen near the flower bed
> In the wintry sun.
> Or maybe in the night time
> Or maybe not at all.

My horse runs across the fields
On many afternoons.
Black as dirt and filled with blood
I glimpse him fleeing toward the woods
And then not at all.

HARRIET (*Offstage*) I'm coming with your milk, and I hope the excitement is over for today. (*Enters, carrying two small white glasses*) Oh, why do I bring milk to a person who is dead-set on making my life a real hell?

RHODA (*Clasping her hands with feeling*) Yes, Why? Why? Why? Why? Oh, what a hideous riddle!

HARRIET You love to pretend that everything is a riddle. You think that's the way to be intellectual. There is no riddle. I am simply keeping up my end of the bargain.

RHODA Oh, bargains, bargains, bargains!

HARRIET Will you let me finish, you excitable thing? I'm trying to explain that I'm behaving the way I was molded to behave. I happen to be appreciative of the mold I was cast in, and neither heaven, nor earth is going to make me damage it. Your high-strung emotions are not going to affect me. Here's your milk.

(*She enters* RHODA's *side of the stage and hands her the milk, but* RHODA *punches the bottom of the glass with her closed fist and sends it flying out of* HARRIET's *hand.* HARRIET *deals* RHODA *a terrific blow on the face and scurries back to her own room. There is silence for a moment. Then* HARRIET *buries her face in her hands and weeps.* RHODA *exits and* HARRIET *goes to the chimes and sings.*)

HARRIET (*Singing*)

I dreamed I climbed upon a cliff,
My sister's hand in mine.
Then searched the valley for my house
But only sunny fields could see
And the church spire shining.
I searched until my heart was cold
But only sunny fields could see
And the church spire shining.
A girl ran down the mountainside
With bluebells in her hat.
I asked the valley for her name
But only wind and rain could hear
And the church bell tolling.
I asked until my lips were cold
But wakened not yet knowing
If the name she bore was my sister's name
Or if it was my own.

HARRIET Rhoda?

RHODA What do you want?

HARRIET Go away if you like.

RHODA The moment hasn't come yet, and it won't come today because the day is finished and the evening is here. Thank God!

HARRIET I know I should get some terrible disease and die if I thought I did not live in the right. It would break my heart.

RHODA You do live in the right, sweetie, so don't think about it. (*Pause*) I'll go and get your milk.

HARRIET I'll go too. But let's drink it in here because it really *is* much pleasanter in here, isn't it? (*They rise*) Oh, I'm so glad the evening has come! I'm nervously exhausted. (*They exit*)

Questions

1. So much is made of the milk, in the quarrel between the two sisters. It is clearly a symbol, a concrete image that stands for something more abstract. How do you interpret it?
2. In the most obvious ways, Harriet dominates the relationship. Yet Rhoda has her own power. Discuss the balance of power in the relationship between the sisters.
3. Rhoda says: "I suppose it's wicked to squeeze love from a small heart. I suppose it's a sin. I suppose God meant for small hearts to be busy with other things." Do you agree? What does this comment tell you about Harriet's personality?
4. Discuss the two poems. How does each express the deepest yearnings of the two women?

American Gothic—*Crimes of the Heart*

We have remarked that realism avoids all that is improbable in events and characters and all that is visionary in theatrical presentation. The symbolic plays you have just read, *The Sound of a Voice* and *A Quarreling Pair* are clearly unrealistic. A more common and subtle reaction to the realism in modern drama may be seen in Beth Henley's *Crimes of the Heart*. The central character, Babe Botrelle, has shot her husband because she "didn't like his looks." Her sister Lenny's pet horse has just been struck dead by lightning. A young lawyer, Barnette Lloyd, has taken on Babe's defense, despite its hopelessness, because he fell in love with her years ago when she sold him pound cake at a bazaar. These situations are more and less probable when we consider each one singly; considered together they make an altogether bizarre and improbable picture. In the manner of Eudora Welty, Beth Henley is working in a great tradition of Gothic American storytelling, in which characters and situations are exaggerated up to the point of incredibility. She also shares with many contemporary playwrights a penchant for black humor, the comic treatment of subjects that are not in themselves very funny. In fact, Babe's shooting of her husband, which sets the play in motion, is hardly taken seriously. The more the characters refer to the assault in their flippant manner, the more humorous it seems. What rescues the play from silliness, or plain bad taste, is the characters' innocence— the sisters seem utterly unaware of their own shortcomings and have a true affection for one another that we, as readers, are invited to share.

Beth Henley, born in Mississippi in 1952, studied at Southern Methodist University and the University of Illinois. In 1979 her *Crimes of the Heart* was the co-winner of the Great American Play Contest, Actors Theatre of Louisville; a year later it opened Off-Broadway at the Manhattan Theatre Club. It won the

Pulitzer Prize and New York Drama Critics Circle Award before its successful run on Broadway.

BETH HENLEY (1952–)

Crimes of the Heart

"For Len, C.C., and Kayo."

THE CAST

LENNY MAGRATH, 30, *the oldest sister*   MEG MAGRATH, 27, *the middle sister*
CHICK BOYLE, 29, *the sisters' first cousin*   BABE BOTRELLE, 24, *the youngest sister*
DOC PORTER, 30, *Meg's old boyfriend*   BARNETTE LLOYD, 26, *Babe's lawyer*

THE SETTING

The setting of the entire play is the kitchen in the Magrath sisters' house in Hazlehurst, Mississippi, a small southern town. The oldfashioned kitchen is unusually spacious, but there is a lived-in, cluttered look about it. There are four different entrances and exits to the kitchen: the back door; the door leading to the dining room and the front of the house; a door leading to the downstairs bedroom; and a staircase leading to the upstairs room. There is a table near the center of the room, and a cot has been set up in one of the corners.

THE TIME

In the fall; five years after Hurricane Camille

ACT I

The lights go up on the empty kitchen. It is late afternoon. LENNY MAGRATH, *a thirty-year-old woman with a round figure and face, enters from the back door carrying a white suitcase, a saxophone case, and a brown paper sack. She sets the suitcase and the sax case down and takes the brown sack to the kitchen table. After glancing quickly at the door, she gets the cookie jar from the kitchen counter, a box of matches from the stove and then brings both objects back down to the kitchen table. Excitedly, she reaches into the brown sack and pulls out a package of birthday candles. She quickly opens the package and removes a candle. She tries to stick the candle into a cookie—it falls off. She sticks the candle in again but the cookie is too hard and it crumbles. Frantically, she gets a second cookie from the jar. She strikes a match, lights the candle and begins dripping wax onto the cookie. Just as she is beginning to smile we hear* CHICK'S *voice from Offstage.*

CHICK'S VOICE Lenny! Oh, Lenny! (LENNY *quickly blows out the candle and stuffs the cookie and candle into her dress pocket.* CHICK, 29, *enters from the back door. She is a brightly dressed matron with yellow hair and shiny, red lips.*)
CHICK Hi! I saw your car pull up.
LENNY Hi.
CHICK Well, did you see today's paper? (LENNY *nods.*) It's just too awful! It's just way too awful! How I'm gonna continue holding my head up high in this community, I do not know. Did you remember to pick up those pantyhose for me?
LENNY They're in the sack.
CHICK Well, thank goodness, at least I'm not gonna have to go into town wearing holes in my stockings. (CHICK *gets the package, tears it open and proceeds to take off one*

*pair of stockings and put on another, throughout the following scene. There should be
something slightly grotesque about this woman changing her stockings in the kitchen.)*

LENNY Did Uncle Watson call?

CHICK Yes, Daddy has called me twice already. He said Babe's ready to come home.
We've got to get right over and pick her up before they change their simple minds.

LENNY *(hesitantly)* Oh, I know, of course, it's just—

CHICK What?

LENNY Well, I was hoping Meg would call.

CHICK Meg?

LENNY Yes, I sent her a telegram: about Babe, and—

CHICK A telegram?! Couldn't you just phone her up?

LENNY Well, no, 'cause her phone's . . . out of order.

CHICK Out of order?

LENNY Disconnected. I don't know what.

CHICK Well, that sounds like Meg. My, these are snug. Are your sure you bought my
right size?

LENNY *(looking at the box)* Size extra petite.

CHICK Well, they're skimping on the nylon material. *(Struggling to pull up the stockings.)*
That's all there is to it. Skimping on the nylon. *(She finishes on one leg and starts on
the other.)* Now, just what all did you say in this "telegram" to Meg?

LENNY I don't recall exactly. I, well, I just told her to come on home.

CHICK To come on home! Why, Lenora Josephine, have you lost your only brain, or
what?

LENNY *(nervously, as she begins to pick up the mess of dirty stockings and plastic wrap-
pings)* But Babe wants Meg home. She asked me to call her.

CHICK I'm not talking about what Babe wants.

LENNY Well, what then?

CHICK Listen, Lenora, I think it's pretty accurate to assume that after this morning's
paper, Babe's gonna be incurring some mighty negative publicity around this town.
And Meg's appearance isn't gonna help out a bit.

LENNY What's wrong with Meg?

CHICK She had a loose reputation in high school.

LENNY *(weakly)* She was popular.

CHICK She was known all over Copiah County as cheap Christmas trash, and that was
the least of it. There was that whole sordid affair with Doc Porter, leaving him a
cripple.

LENNY A cripple—he's got a limp. Just, kind of, barely a limp.

CHICK Well, his mother was going to keep *me* out of the Ladies' Social League because
of it.

LENNY What?

CHICK That's right. I never told you, but I had to go plead with that mean, old woman
and convince her that I was just as appalled and upset with what Meg had done as
she was, and that I was only a first cousin anyway and I could hardly be blamed for
all the skeletons in the Magraths' closet. It was humiliating. I tell you, she even brought
up your mother's death. And that poor cat.

LENNY Oh! Oh! Oh, please, Chick! I'm sorry. But you're in the Ladies' League now.

CHICK Yes. That's true, I am. But frankly, if Mrs. Porter hadn't developed that tumor
in her bladder, I wouldn't be in the club today, much less a committee head. *(As she
brushes her hair.)* Anyway, you be a sweet potato and wait right here for Meg to call,

so's you can convince her not to come back home. It would make things a whole lot easier on everybody. Don't you think it really would?

LENNY Probably.

CHICK Good, then suit yourself. How's my hair?

LENNY Fine.

CHICK Not pooching out in the back, is it?

LENNY No.

CHICK (*cleaning the hair from her brush*) All right then, I'm on my way. I've got Annie May over there keeping an eye on Peekay and Buck Jr., but I don't trust her with them for long periods of time. (*Dropping the ball of hair onto the floor.*) Her mind is like a loose sieve. Honestly it is. (*She puts the brush back into her purse.*) Oh! Oh! Oh! I almost forgot. Here's a present for you. Happy Birthday to Lenny, from the Buck Boyles! (CHICK *takes a wrapped package from her bag and hands it to* LENNY.)

LENNY Why, thank you, Chick. It's so nice to have you remember my birthday every year like you do.

CHICK (*modestly*) Oh well, now, that's just the way I am, I suppose. That's just the way I was brought up to be. Well, why don't you go on and open up the present?

LENNY All right. (*She starts to unwrap the gift.*)

CHICK It's a box of candy—assorted cremes.

LENNY Candy—that's always a nice gift.

CHICK And you have a sweet tooth, don't you?

LENNY I guess.

CHICK Well, I'm glad you like it.

LENNY I do.

CHICK Oh, speaking of which, remember that little polka dot dress you got Peekay for her fifth birthday last month?

LENNY The red and white one?

CHICK Yes; well, the first time I put it in the washing machine, I mean the very first time, it fell all to pieces. Those little polka dots just dropped right off in the water.

LENNY (*crushed*) Oh, no. Well, I'll get something else for her then—a little toy.

CHICK Oh, no, no, no, no, no! We wouldn't hear of it! I just wanted to let you know so you wouldn't go and waste any more of your hard-earned money on that make of dress. Those inexpensive brands just don't hold up. I'm sorry but not in these modern washing machines.

DOC PORTER'S VOICE Hello! Hello, Lenny!

CHICK (*taking over*) Oh, look, it's Doc Porter! Come on in, Doc! Please come right on in! (DOC PORTER *enters through the back door. He is carrying a large sack of pecans. Doc is an attractively worn man with a slight limp that adds rather than detracts from his quiet seductive quality. He is 30 years old, but appears slightly older.*) Well, how are you doing? How in the world are you doing?

DOC Just fine, Chick.

CHICK And how are you liking it now that you're back in Hazlehurst?

DOC Oh, I'm finding it somewhat enjoyable.

CHICK Somewhat! Only somewhat! Will you listen to him! What a silly, silly, silly man! Well, I'm on my way. I've got some people waiting on me. (*Whispering to* DOC.) It's Babe. I'm on my way to pick her up.

DOC Oh.

CHICK Well, goodbye! Farewell and goodbye!

LENNY Bye. (CHICK *exits.*)

DOC Hello.

LENNY Hi. I guess you heard about the thing with Babe.

DOC Yeah.

LENNY It was in the newspaper.

DOC Uh huh.

LENNY What a mess.

DOC Yeah.

LENNY Well, come on and sit down. I'll heat us up some coffee.

DOC That's okay. I can only stay a minute. I have to pick up Scott; he's at the dentist's.

LENNY Oh; well, I'll heat some up for myself. I'm kinda thirsty for a cup of hot coffee.
(LENNY *puts the coffeepot on the burner.*)

DOC Lenny—

LENNY What?

DOC (*not able to go on*) Ah . . .

LENNY Yes?

DOC Here, some pecans for you (*He hands her the sack.*)

LENNY Why, thank you, Doc. I love pecans.

DOC My wife and Scott picked them up around the yard.

LENNY Well, I can use them to make a pie. A pecan pie.

DOC Yeah. Look, Lenny, I've got some bad news for you.

LENNY What?

DOC Well, you know, you've been keeping Billy Boy out on our farm; he's been grazing
out there.

LENNY Yes—

DOC Well, last night, Billy Boy died.

LENNY He died?

DOC Yeah. I'm sorry to tell you when you've got all this on you; but I thought you'd
want to know.

LENNY Well, yeah. I do. He died?

DOC Uh huh. He was struck by lightning.

LENNY Struck by lightning? In that storm yesterday?

DOC That's what we think.

LENNY Gosh, struck by lightning. I've had Billy Boy so long. You know. Ever since I
was ten years old.

DOC Yeah. He was a mighty old horse.

LENNY (*stung*) Mighty old.

DOC Almost twenty years old.

LENNY That's right, twenty years. 'Cause; ah; I'm thirty years old today. Did you know
that?

DOC No, Lenny, I didn't know. Happy Birthday.

LENNY Thanks. (*She begins to cry.*)

DOC Oh, come on now, Lenny. Come on. Hey, hey, now. You know I can't stand it
when you Magrath women start to cry. You know it just gets me.

LENNY Oh-ho! Sure! You mean when Meg cries! Meg's the one you could never stand
to watch cry! Not me! I could fill up a pig's trough!

DOC Now, Lenny . . . stop it. Come on. Jesus!

LENNY Okay! Okay! I don't know what's wrong with me. I don't mean to make a scene.
I've been on this crying jag. (*She blows her nose.*) All this stuff with Babe and old
Granddaddy's gotten worse in the hospital and I can't get in touch with Meg.

DOC You tried calling Meggy?

LENNY Yes.

DOC Is she coming home?

LENNY Who knows. She hasn't called me. That's what I'm waiting here for—hoping she'll call.

DOC She still living in California?

LENNY Yes; in Hollywood.

DOC Well, give me a call if she gets in. I'd like to see her.

LENNY Oh, you would, huh?

DOC Yeah, Lenny, sad to say, but I would.

LENNY It is sad. It's very sad indeed. (*They stare at each other, then look away. There is a moment of tense silence.*)

DOC Hey, Jello Face, your coffee's boiling.

LENNY (*going to check*) Oh, it is? Thanks. (*After she checks the pot.*) Look, you'd better go on and pick Scott up. You don't want him to have to wait for you.

DOC Yeah, you're right. Poor kid. It's his first time at the dentist.

LENNY Poor thing.

DOC Well, 'bye. I'm sorry to have to tell you about your horse.

LENNY Oh, I know. Tell Joan thanks for picking up the pecans.

DOC I will. (*He starts to leave.*)

LENNY Oh, how's the baby?

DOC She's fine. Real pretty. She, ah, holds your finger in her hand; like this.

LENNY Oh, that's cute.

DOC Yeah. 'Bye, Lenny.

LENNY 'Bye. (DOC *exits.* LENNY *stares after him for a moment, then goes and sits back down at the kitchen table. She reaches into her pocket and pulls out a somewhat crumbled cookie and a wax candle. She lights the candle again, lets the wax drip onto the cookie, then sticks the candle on top of the cookie. She begins to sing the "Happy Birthday Song" to herself. At the end of the song she pauses, silently makes a wish, and blows out the candle. She waits a moment, then re-lights the candle, and repeats her actions, only this time making a different wish at the end of the song. She starts to repeat the procedure for the third time, as the phone begins to ring. She goes to answer it.*) Hello . . . oh, hello, Lucille, how's Zackery? . . . Oh, no! . . . Oh, I'm so sorry. Of course, it must be grueling for you . . . Yes, I understand. Your only brother . . . no, she's not here yet. Chick just went to pick her up . . . oh, now, Lucille, she's still his wife, I'm sure she'll be interested . . . Well, you can just tell me the information and I'll relate it all to her . . . Uh-hum, his liver's saved. Oh, that's good news! . . . Well, of course, when you look at it like that . . . Breathing stabilized . . . Damage to the spinal column, not yet determined . . . Okay . . . Yes, Lucille, I've got it all down . . . Uh-huh, I'll give her that message. 'Bye, 'bye. (LENNY *drops the pencil and paper down. She sighs deeply, wipes her cheeks with the back of her hand, and goes to the stove to pour herself a cup of coffee. After a few moments, the front door is heard slamming.* LENNY *starts. A whistle is heard, then* MEG'S *voice.*)

MEG'S VOICE I'm home! (*She whistles the family whistle.*) Anybody home?!!

LENNY Meg? Meg! (MEG, 27, *enters from the dining room. She has sad, magic eyes and wears a hat. She carries a worn-out suitcase.*)

MEG (*dropping her suitcase, running to hug* LENNY) Lenny—

LENNY Well, Meg! Why, Meg! Oh, Meggy! Why didn't you call? Did you fly in? You didn't take a cab, did you? Why didn't you give us a call?

MEG (*overlapping*) Oh, Lenny! Why, Lenny! Dear, Lenny! (*Then she looks at* LENNY'S *face.*) My God, we're getting so old! Oh, I called for heaven's sake. Of course, I called!

LENNY Well, I never talked to you—

MEG Well, I know! I let the phone ring right off the hook!

LENNY Well, as a matter of fact, I was out most of the morning seeing to Babe—!

MEG Now just what's all this business about Babe? How could you send me such a telegram about Babe? And Zackery! You say somebody's shot Zackery?!

LENNY Yes; they have.

MEG Well, good Lord! Is he dead?

LENNY No. But he's in the hospital. He was shot in his stomach.

MEG In his stomach! How awful! Do they know who shot him? (LENNY *nods*.) Well, who? Who was it? Who? Who?

LENNY Babe! They're all saying Babe shot him! They took her to jail! And they're saying she shot him! They're all saying it! It's horrible! It's awful!

MEG (*overlapping*) Jail! Good Lord, jail! Well, who? Who's saying it? Who?!!

LENNY Everyone!! The policemen, the sheriff, Zackery, even Babe's saying it! Even Babe herself!!

MEG Well, for God's sake. For God's sake.

LENNY (*overlapping as she falls apart*) It's horrible! It's horrible! It's just horrible!!!

MEG Now calm down, Lenny. Just calm down. Would you like a Coke? Here, I'll get you some Coke. (MEG *gets a Coke from the refrigerator. She opens it and downs a large swig.*) Why? Why would she shoot him? Why? (MEG *hands the Coke bottle to* LENNY.)

LENNY I talked to her this morning and I asked her that very question. I said, "Babe, why would you shoot Zackery? He was your own husband. Why would you shoot him?" And do you know what she said? (MEG *shakes her head*.) She said, " 'Cause I didn't like his looks. I just didn't like his looks."

MEG (*after a pause*) Well, I don't like his looks.

LENNY But you didn't shoot him! You wouldn't shoot a person 'cause you didn't like their looks! You wouldn't do that! Oh, I hate to say this—I do hate to say this—but I believe Babe is ill. I mean in-her-head-ill.

MEG Oh, now, Lenny, don't you say that! There're plenty of good sane reasons to shoot another person and I'm sure that Babe had one. Now what we've got to do is get her the best lawyer in town. Do you have any ideas on who's the best lawyer in town?

LENNY Well, Zackery is, of course; but he's been shot!

MEG Well, count him out! Just count him and his whole firm out!

LENNY Anyway, you don't have to worry, she's already got her lawyer.

MEG She does? Who?

LENNY Barnette Lloyd. Annie Lloyd's boy. He just opened his office here in town. And Uncle Watson said we'd be doing Annie a favor by hiring him up.

MEG Doing Annie a favor? Doing Annie a favor?! Well, what about Babe? Have you thought about Babe? Do we want to do her a favor of thirty or forty years in jail?! Have you thought about that?

LENNY Now, don't snap at me! Just don't snap at me! I try to do what's right! All this responsibility keeps falling on my shoulders, and I try to do what's right!

MEG Well, boo hoo, hoo, hoo! And how in the hell could you send me such a telegram about Babe!

LENNY Well, if you had a phone, or if you didn't live way out there in Hollywood and not even come home for Christmas maybe I wouldn't have to pay all that money to send you a telegram!!!

MEG (*overlapping*) 'Babe's in terrible trouble—Stop! Zackery's been shot—Stop! Come home immediately—Stop! Stop! Stop!'

LENNY And what was that you said about how old we're getting? When you looked at my face, you said, "My God, we're getting so old!" But you didn't mean we—you meant me! Didn't you? I'm thirty years old today and my face is getting all pinched up and my hair is falling out in the comb.

MEG Why, Lenny! It's your birthday, October 23rd. How could I forget. Happy Birthday!

LENNY Well, it's not. I'm thirty years old and Billy Boy died last night. He was struck by lightning. He was struck dead.

MEG (*reaching for a cigarette*) Struck dead. Oh, what a mess. What a mess. Are you really thirty? Then I must be twenty-seven and Babe is twenty-four. My God, we're getting so old. (*They are silent for several moments as* MEG *drags off her cigarette and* LENNY *drinks her Coke.*) What's the cot doing in the kitchen?

LENNY Well, I rolled it out when Old Granddaddy got sick. So I could be close and hear him at night if he needed something.

MEG (*glancing toward the door leading to the downstairs bedroom*) Is Old Granddaddy here?

LENNY Why, no. Old Granddaddy's at the hospital.

MEG Again?

LENNY Meg!

MEG What?

LENNY I wrote you all about it. He's been in the hospital over three months straight.

MEG He has?

LENNY Don't you remember? I wrote you about all those blood vessels popping in his brain?

MEG Popping—

LENNY And how he was so anxious to hear from you and to find out about your singing career. I wrote it all to you. How they have to feed him through those tubes now. Didn't you get my letters?

MEG Oh, I don't know, Lenny. I guess I did. To tell you the truth, sometimes I kinda don't read your letters.

LENNY What?

MEG I'm sorry. I used to read them. It's just since Christmas reading them gives me these slicing pains right here in my chest.

LENNY I see. I see. Is that why you didn't use that money Old Granddaddy sent you to come home Christmas; because you hate us so much? We never did all that much to make you hate us. We didn't!

MEG Oh, Lenny! Do you think I'd be getting slicing pains in my chest, if I didn't care about you? If I hated you? Honestly, now, do you think I would?

LENNY No.

MEG Okay, then. Let's drop it. I'm sorry I didn't read your letters. Okay?

LENNY Okay.

MEG Anyway, we've got this whole thing with Babe to deal with. The first thing is to get her a good lawyer and get her out of jail.

LENNY Well, she's out of jail.

MEG She is?

LENNY That young lawyer, he's gotten her out.

MEG Oh, he has?

LENNY Yes, on bail. Uncle Watson's put it up. Chick's bringing her back right now— she's driving her home.

MEG Oh; well, that's a relief.

LENNY Yes, and they're due home any minute now; so we can just wait right here for 'em.

MEG Well, good. That's good. (*As she leans against the counter.*) So, Babe shot Zackery Botrelle, the richest and most powerful man in all of Hazlehurst, slap in the gut. It's hard to believe.

LENNY It certainly is. Little Babe—shooting off a gun.

MEG Little Babe.

LENNY She was always the prettiest and most perfect of the three of us. Old Granddaddy used to call her his Dancing Sugar Plum. Why, remember how proud and happy he was the day she married Zackery.

MEG Yes, I remember. It was his finest hour.

LENNY He remarked how Babe was gonna skyrocket right to the heights of Hazlehurst society. And how Zackery was just the right man for her whether she knew it now or not.

MEG Oh, Lordy, Lordy. And what does Old Granddaddy say now?

LENNY Well, I haven't had the courage to tell him all about this as yet. I thought maybe tonight we could go to visit him at the hospital and you could talk to him and . . .

MEG Yeah, well, we'll see. We'll see. Do we have anything to drink around here—to the tune of straight bourbon?

LENNY No. There's no liquor.

MEG Hell. (MEG *gets a Coke from the refrigerator and opens it.*)

LENNY Then you will go with me to see Old Granddaddy at the hospital tonight?

MEG Of course. (MEG *goes to her purse and gets out a bottle of Empirin Compound. She takes out a tablet and puts it on her tongue.*) Brother, I know he's gonna go on about my singing career. Just like he always does.

LENNY Well, how is your career going?

MEG It's not.

LENNY Why, aren't you still singing at the club down on Malibu beach?

MEG No. Not since Christmas.

LENNY Well, then, are you singing some place new?

MEG No, I'm not singing. I'm not singing at all.

LENNY Oh. Well, what do you do then?

MEG What I do is I pay cold storage bills for a dog food company. That's what I do.

LENNY (*trying to be helpful*) Gosh, don't you think it'd be a good idea to stay in the show business field?

MEG Oh, maybe.

LENNY Like Old Granddaddy says, "With your talent all you need is exposure. Then you can make your own breaks!" Did you hear his suggestion about getting your foot put in one of those blocks of cement they've got out here? He thinks that's real important.

MEG Yeh. I think I've heard that. And I'll probably hear it again when I go to visit him at the hospital tonight; so let's just drop it. Okay? (*She noticed the sack of pecans.*) What's this? Pecans? Great, I love pecans! (MEG *takes out two pecans and tries to open them by cracking them together.*) Come on . . . Crack, you demons! Crack!

LENNY We have a nutcracker!

MEG (*trying with her teeth*) Ah, where's the sport in a nutcracker? Where's the challenge?

LENNY (*getting up to get the nutcracker*) It's over here in the utensil drawer. (As LENNY *gets the nutcracker,* MEG *opens the pecan by stepping on it with her shoe.*)

MEG There! Open! (MEG *picks up the crumbled pecan and eats it.*) Mmmm, delicious. Delicious. Where'd you get the fresh pecans?

LENNY Oh . . . I don't know.

MEG They sure are tasty.

LENNY Doc Porter brought them over.

MEG Doc. What's Doc doing here in town?

LENNY Well, his father died a couple of months ago. Now he's back home seeing to his property.

MEG Gosh, the last I heard of Doc, he was up in the East painting the walls of houses to earn a living. (*Amused.*) Heard he was living with some Yankee woman who made clay pots.

LENNY Joan.

MEG What?

LENNY Her name's Joan. She came down here with him. That's one of her pots. Doc's married to her.

MEG Married—

LENNY Uh huh.

MEG Doc married a Yankee?

LENNY That's right; and they've got two kids.

MEG Kids—

LENNY A boy and a girl.

MEG God. Then his kids must be half-Yankee.

LENNY I suppose.

MEG God. That really gets me. I don't know why, but somehow that really gets me.

LENNY I don't know why it should.

MEG And what a stupid-looking pot! Who'd buy it anyway?

LENNY Wait—I think that's them. Yeah, that's Chick's car! Oh, there's Babe! Hello, Babe! They're home, Meg! They're home. (MEG *hides.*)

BABES VOICE Lenny! I'm home! I'm free! (BABE, 24, *enters exuberantly. She has an angelic face and fierce, volatile eyes. She carries a pink pocketbook.*) I'm home! (MEG *jumps out of hiding.*) Oh, Meg—Look it's Meg! (*Running to hug her.*) Meg! When did you get home?

MEG Just now!

BABE Well, it's so good to see you! I'm so glad you're home! I'm so relieved. (CHICK *enters.*)

MEG Why, Chick; hello.

CHICK Hello, Cousin Margaret. What brings you back to Hazlehurst?

MEG Oh, I came on home . . . (*turning to* BABE) I came on home to see about Babe.

BABE (*running to hug* MEG) Oh, Meg—

MEG How are things with you, Babe?

CHICK Well, they are dismal, if you want my opinion. She is refusing to cooperate with her lawyer, that nice-looking young Lloyd boy. She won't tell any of us why she committed this heinous crime, except to say that she didn't like Zackery's looks—

BABE Oh, look, Lenny brought my suitcase from home! And my saxophone! Thank you! (BABE *runs over to the cot and gets out her saxophone.*)

CHICK Now that young lawyer is coming over here this afternoon, and when he gets here he expects to get some concrete answers! That's what he expects! No more of this nonsense and stubborness from you, Rebecca Magrath, or they'll put you in jail and throw away the key!

BABE Meg, come look at my new saxophone. I went to Jackson and bought it used. Feel it. I'ts so heavy.

MEG It's beautiful. (*The room goes silent.*)

CHICK Isn't that right, won't they throw away the key?

LENNY Well, honestly, I don't know about that—

CHICK They will! And leave you there to rot. So, Rebecca, what are you going to tell Mr. Lloyd about shooting Zackery when he gets here? What are your reasons going to be?

BABE (*glaring*) That I didn't like his looks! I just didn't like his stinking looks! And I don't like yours much either, Chick-the-Stick! So, just leave me alone! I mean it! Leave me alone! Oooh! (BABE *exits up the stairs. There is a long moment of silence.*)

CHICK Well, I was only trying to warn her that she's going to have to help herself. It's just that she doesn't understand how serious the situation is. Does she? She doesn't have the vaguest idea. Does she now?

LENNY Well, it's true, she does seem a little confused.

CHICK And that's putting it mildly, Lenny honey. That's putting it mighty mild. So, Margaret, how's your singing career going? We keep looking for your picture in the movie magazines. (MEG *moves to light a cigarette.*) You know, you shouldn't smoke. It causes cancer. Cancer of the lungs. They say each cigarette is just a little stick of cancer. A little death stick.

MEG That's what I like about it, Chick—taking a drag off of death. (MEG *takes a long, deep drag.*) Mmm! Gives me a sense of controlling my own destiny. What power! What exhilaration! Want a drag?

LENNY (*trying to break the tension*) Ah, Zackery's liver's been saved! His sister called up and said his liver was saved. Isn't that good news?

MEG Well, yes, that's fine news. Mighty fine news. Why I've been told that the liver's a powerful important bodily organ. I believe it's used to absorb all our excess bile.

LENNY Yes—well—it's been saved. (*The phone rings.* LENNY *gets it.*)

MEG So! Did you hear all that good news about the liver, Litttle Chicken?

CHICK I heard it. And don't you call me Chicken! (MEG *clucks like a chicken.*) I've told you a hundred times if I've told you once not to call me Chicken. You cannot call me Chicken.

LENNY . . . Oh, no! . . . Of course, we'll be right over! Bye! (*She hangs up the phone.*) That was Annie May—Peekay and Buck Jr. have eaten paints!

CHICK Oh, no! Are they all right? They're not sick? They're not sick, are they?

LENNY I don't know. I don't know. Come on. We've got to run on next door.

CHICK (*overlapping.*) Oh, God! Oh, please! Please let them be all right! Don't let them die!! Please, don't let them die!!

CHICK *runs Off howling with* LENNY *following after.* MEG *sits alone, finishing her cigarette. After a moment,* BABE'S *voice is heard.*

BABE'S VOICE Pst—Psst!

MEG *looks around. Babe comes tiptoeing down the stairs.*

BABE Has she gone?

MEG She's gone. Peekay and Buck Jr. just ate their paints.

BABE What idiots.

MEG Yeah.

BABE You know, Chick's hated us ever since we had to move here from Vicksburg to live with Old Grandmama and Old Granddaddy.

MEG She's an idiot.

BABE Yeah. Do you know what she told me this morning while I was still behind bars and couldn't get away?

MEG What?

BABE She told me how embarrassing it was for her all those years ago, you know, when mama—

MEG Yeah, down in the cellar.

BABE She said our mama had shamed the entire family, and we were known notoriously all through Hazelhurst. (*About to cry.*) Then she went on to say how I would now be getting just as much bad publicity and humiliating her and the family all over again.

MEG Ah, forget it, Babe. Just forget it.

BABE I told her, "Mama got national coverage! National!" And if Zackery wasn't a senator from Copiah County, I probably wouldn't even be getting state-wide.

MEG Of course you wouldn't.

BABE (*after a pause.*) Gosh, sometimes I wonder . . .

MEG What?

BABE Why she did it. Why mama hung herself.

MEG I don't know. She had a bad day. A real bad day. You know how it feels on a real bad day.

BABE And that old yellow cat. It was sad about that old cat.

MEG Yeah.

BABE I bet if Daddy hadn't of left us, they'd still be alive.

MEG Oh, I don't know.

BABE 'Cause it was after he left that she started spending whole days just sitting there and smoking on the back porch steps. She'd sling her ashes down onto the different bugs and ants that'd be passing by.

MEG Yeah. Well, I'm glad he left.

BABE That old yellow cat'd stay back there with her.

MEG God, he was a bastard.

BABE I thought if she felt something for anyone it would a been that old cat. Guess I musta been mistaken.

MEG Really, with his white teeth, Daddy was such a bastard.

BABE Was he? I don't remember. (MEG *blows out a mouthful of smoke. After a moment, uneasily.*) I think I'm gonna make some lemonade. You want some?

MEG Sure. (BABE *cuts lemons, dumps sugar, stirs ice cubes, etc. throughout the following exchange.*) Babe. Why won't you talk? Why won't you tell anyone about shooting Zackery?

BABE Oooh—

MEG Why not? You must have had a good reason. Didn't you?

BABE I guess I did.

MEG Well, what was it?

BABE I . . . I can't say.

MEG Why not? (*Pause.*) Babe, why not? You can tell me.

BABE 'Cause . . . I'm sort of . . . protecting someone.

MEG Protecting someone? Oh, Babe, then you really didn't shoot him?! I knew you couldn't have done it!! I knew it!!!

BABE No, I shot him. I shot him all right. I meant to kill him. I was aiming for his heart, but I guess my hands were shaking and I—just got him in the stomach.

MEG (*collapsing*) I see.

BABE (*stirring the lemonade*) So I'm guilty. And I'm just gonna have to take my punishment and go on to jail.

MEG Oh, Babe—

BABE Don't worry, Meg, jail's gonna be a relief to me. I can learn to play my new saxophone. I won't have to live with Zackery anymore. And I won't have his snoopy old sister, Lucille, coming over and pushing me around. Jail will be a relief. Here's your lemonade.

MEG Thanks.

BABE It taste okay?

MEG Perfect.

BABE I like a lot of sugar in mine. I'm gonna add some more sugar. (BABE *goes to add more sugar to her lemonade, as* LENNY *bursts through the back door in a state of excitement and confusion.*)

LENNY Well, it looks like the paint is primarily on their arms and faces; but Chick wants me to drive them all over to Doctor Winn's just to make sure. (LENNY *grabs her car keys off of the counter and as she does so, she notices the mess of lemons and sugar.*) Oh, now, Babe, try not to make a mess here; and be careful with this sharp knife. Honestly, all that sugar's gonna get you sick. Well, 'bye, 'bye. I'll be back as soon as I can.

MEG Bye, Lenny.

BABE 'Bye. (LENNY *exits.*) Boy, I don't know what's happening to Lenny.

MEG What do you mean?

BABE "Don't make a mess; don't make yourself sick; don't cut yourself with that sharp knife." She's turning into Old Grandmama.

MEG You think so?

BABE More and more. Do you know she's taken to wearing Old Grandmama's torn sunhat and her green garden gloves?

MEG Those old lime green ones?

BABE Yeah; she works out in the garden wearing the lime green gloves of a dead woman. Imagine wearing those gloves on your hands.

MEG Poor Lenny. She needs some love in her life. All she does is work out at that brick yard and take care of Old Granddaddy.

BABE Yeah. But she's so shy with men.

MEG (*biting into an apple*) Probably because of that *shrunken* ovary she has.

BABE (*slinging ice cubes*) Yeah, that *deformed* ovary.

MEG Old Granddaddy's the one who's made her feel self-conconscious about it. It's his fault. The old fool.

BABE It's so sad.

MEG God—you know what?

BABE What?

MEG I bet Lenny's never even slept with a man. Just think, thirty years old and never even had it once.

BABE (*slyly*) Oh; I don't know. Maybe she's . . . had it once?

MEG She has?

BABE Maybe. I think so.

MEG When? When?

BABE Well . . . maybe I shouldn't say—

MEG Babe!

BABE (*rapidly telling the story*) All right then; it was after Old Granddaddy went back to the hospital this second time. Lenny was really in a state of deep depression. I could tell that she was. Then one day she calls me up and asks me to come over and to bring along my polaroid camera. Well, when I arrive she's waiting for me out there in the sun parlour wearing her powder blue Sunday dress and this old curled up wig.

She confided that she was gonna try sending in her picture to one of those lonely hearts clubs.

MEG Oh, my God.

BABE Lonely Hearts of the South. She'd seen their ad in a magazine.

MEG Jesus.

BABE Anyway, I take some snapshots and she sends them on in to the club, and about two weeks later she receives in the mail this whole load of pictures of available men, most of 'em fairly odd looking. But of course she doesn't call any of 'em up 'cause she's real shy. But one of 'em, this Charlie Hill from Memphis, Tennessee, he calls her.

MEG He does?

BABE Yeah. And time goes on and she says he's real funny on the phone; so they decide to get together to meet.

MEG Yeah?!

BABE Well, he drives down here to Hazlehurst 'bout three or four different times and has supper with her, then one weekend she goes up to Memphis to visit him; and I think that is where it happened.

MEG What makes you think so?

BABE Well, when I went to pick her up from the bus depot, she ran off the bus and threw her arms around me and started crying and sobbing as though she'd like to never stop. I asked her, I said, "Lenny, what's the matter?" And she said, "I've done it, Babe! Honey, I've done it!"

MEG (whispering) And you think she meant that she'd done it?

BABE (whispering back, slyly) I think so.

MEG Well, goddamn! (They laugh with glee.)

BABE But she didn't say anything else about it. She just went on to tell me about the boot factory where Charlie worked and what a nice city Memphis was.

MEG So, what happened to this Charlie?

BABE Well, he came to Hazlehurst just one more time. Lenny took him over to meet Old Granddaddy at the hospital and after that they broke it off.

MEG 'Cause of Old Granddaddy?

BABE Well, she said it was on account of her missing ovary. That Charlie didn't want to marry her on account of it.

MEG Ah, how mean. How hateful.

BABE Oh, it was. He seemed like such a nice man, too—kinda chubby with red hair and freckles, always telling these funny jokes.

MEG Hmmm, that just doesn't seem right. Something about that doesn't seem exactly right. (MEG paces about the kitchen and comes across the box of candy LENNY got for her birthday.) Oh, God. "Happy Birthday to Lenny from the Buck Boyles."

BABE Oh, no! Today's Lenny's birthday!

MEG That's right.

BABE I forgot all about it!

MEG I know. I did too.

BABE Gosh, we'll have to order up a big cake for her. She always loves to make those wishes on her birthday cake.

MEG Yeah, let's get her a big cake! A huge one! (Suddenly noticing the plastic wrapper on the candy box.) Oh, God, that Chick's so cheap!

BABE What do you mean?

MEG This plastic has poinsettias on it!

BABE (running to see) Oh, let me see—(She looks at the package with disgust.) Boy, oh, boy! I'm calling that bakery and ordering the very largest size cake they have! That Jumbo Deluxe!

MEG Good!

BABE Why, I imagine they can make one up to be about—*this* big. (*She demonstrates.*)

MEG Oh, at least; at least that big. Why, maybe, it'll even be *this* big. (*She makes a very, very, very, large size cake.*)

BABE You think it could be *that* big?

MEG Sure!

BABE (*after a moment, getting the idea*) Or, or what if it were *this* big? (*She maps out a cake that covers the room.*) What if we get the cake and it's *this* big?!! (*She gulps down a fistful of cake.*) Gulp! Gulp! Gulp! Tasty treat!

MEG Hmmm—I'll have me some more! Give me some more of that birthday cake!

Suddenly there is a loud knock at the door.

BARNETTE'S VOICE Hello . . . hello! May I come in?

BABE (*to Meg, in a whisper, as she takes cover*) Who's that?

MEG I don't know.

BARNETTE'S VOICE (*still knocking*) Hello! Hello, Mrs. Botrelle!

BABE Oh, shoot! It's that lawyer. I don't want to see him.

MEG Oh, Babe, come on. You've got to see him sometime.

BABE No, I don't! (*She starts up the stairs.*) Just tell him I died—I'm going upstairs.

MEG Oh, Babe! Will you come back here!

BABE (*as she exits*) You talk to him, please, Meg. Please! I just don't want to see him—

MEG Babe—Babe! Oh, shit . . . ah, come on in! Door's open!

BARNETTE LLOYD, 26, *enters carrying a briefcase. He is a slender, intelligent young man with an almost fanatical intensity that he subdues by sheer will.*

BARNETTE How do you do? I'm Barnette Lloyd.

MEG Pleased to meet you. I'm Meg Magrath, Babe's older sister.

BARNETTE Yes, I know. You're the singer.

MEG Well, yes . . .

BARNETTE I came to hear you five different times when you were singing at the club in Biloxi. Greeny's I believe was the name of it.

MEG Yes, Greeny's.

BARNETTE You were very good. There was something sad and moving about how you sang those songs. It was like you had some sort of vision. Some special sort of vision.

MEG Well, thank you. You're very kind. Now . . . about Babe's case—

BARNETTE Yes?

MEG We've just got to win it.

BARNETTE I intend to.

MEG Of course. But, ah . . . (*She looks at him.*) Ah, you know, you're very young.

BARNETTE Yes. I am. I'm young.

MEG It's just, I'm concerned, Mr. Lloyd—

BARNETTE Barnette. Please.

MEG Barnette; that, ah, just maybe we need someone with, well, with more experience. Someone totally familiar with all the ins and outs and the this and thats of the legal dealings and such. As that.

BARNETTE Ah, you have reservations.

MEG (*relieved*) Reservations. Yes, I have . . . reservations.

BARNETTE Well, possibly it would help you to know that I graduated first in my class from Ole Miss Law School. I also spent three different summers taking advanced courses in criminal law at Harvard Law School. I made A's in all the given courses. I was fascinated!

MEG I'm sure.

BARNETTE And even now, I've just completed one year working with Jackson's top criminal law firm, Manchester and Wayne. I was invaluable to them. Indispensable. They offered to double my percentage, if I'd stay on; but I refused. I wanted to return to Hazlehurst and open my own office. The reason being, and this is a key point, that I have a personal vendetta to settle with one Zackery F. Botrelle.

MEG A personal vendetta?

BARNETTE Yes, ma'am. You are correct. Indeed, I do.

MEG Hmmm. A personal vendetta . . . I think I like that. So you have some sort of a personal vendetta to settle with Zackery?

BARNETTE Precisely. Just between the two of us, I not only intend to keep that sorry S.O.B. from ever being re-elected to the state senate by exposing his shady, criminal dealings; but I also intend to decimate his personal credibility by exposing him as a bully, a brute, and a red-neck thug!

MEG Well; I can see that you're—fanatical about this.

BARNETTE Yes; I am. I'm sorry, if I seem outspoken. But, for some reason, I feel I can talk to you . . . those songs you sang. Excuse me; I feel like a jackass.

MEG It's all right. Relax. Relax, Barnette. Let me think this out a minute. (*She takes out a cigarette. He lights it for her.*) Now just exactly how do you intend to get Babe off? You know, keep her out of jail.

BARNETTE It seems to me that we can get her off with a plea of self-defense, or possibly we could go with innocent by reason of temporary insanity. But basically, I intend to prove that Zackery Botrelle brutalized and tormented this poor woman to such an extent that she had no recourse but to defend herself in the only way she knew how!

MEG I like that!

BARNETTE Then, of course, I'm hoping this will break the ice and we'll be able to go on to prove that the man's a total criminal, as well as an abusive bully and contemptible slob!

MEG That sounds good! To me that sounds very good!

BARNETTE It's just our basic game plan.

MEG But, now, how are you going to prove all this about Babe being brutalized? We don't want anyone perjured. I mean to commit perjury.

BARNETTE Perjury? According to my sources, the'll be no need for perjury.

MEG You mean it's the truth?

BARNETTE This is a small town, Miss Magrath. The word gets out.

MEG It's really the truth?

BARNETTE (*opening his briefcase*) Just look at this. It's a photostatic copy of Mrs. Botrelle's medical chart over the past four years. Take a good look at it, if you want your blood to boil!

MEG (*looking over the chart*) What! What! This is maddening. This is madness! Did he do this to her? I'll kill him; I will—I'll fry his blood!! Did he do this?

BARNETTE (*alarmed*) To tell you the truth, I can't say for certain what was accidental and what was not. That's why I need to talk with Mrs. Botrelle. That's why it's very important that I see her!

MEG (*her eyes are wild, as she shoves him toward the door*) Well, look, I've got to see her first. I've got to talk to her first. What I'll do is I'll give you a call. Maybe you can come back over later on—

BARNETTE Well, then, here's my card—

MEG Okay. Goodbye.

BARNETTE 'Bye!

MEG Oh, wait! Wait! There's one problem with you.

BARNETTE What?

MEG What if you get so fanatically obsessed with this vendetta thing that you forget about Babe? You forget about her and sell her down the river just to get at Zackery. What about that?

BARNETTE I—wouldn't do that.

MEG You wouldn't?

BARNETTE No.

MEG Why not?

BARNETTE Because, I'm—I'm fond of her.

MEG What do you mean you're fond of her?

BARNETTE Well, she . . . she sold me a pound cake at a bazaar once. And I'm fond of her.

MEG All right; I believe you. Goodbye.

BARNETTE Goodbye. (BARNETTE *exits.*)

MEG Babe! Babe, come down here! Babe!

BABE *comes hurrying down the stairs.*

BABE What? What is it? I called about the cake—

MEG What did Zackery do to you?

BABE They can't have it for today.

MEG Did he hurt you? Did he? Did he do that?

BABE Oh, Meg, please—

MEG Did he? Goddamnit, Babe—

BABE Yes, he did.

MEG Why? Why?

BABE I don't know! He started hating me, 'cause I couldn't laugh at his jokes. I just started finding it impossible to laugh at his jokes the way I used to. And then the sound of his voice got to where it tired me out awful bad to hear it. I'd fall asleep just listening to him at the dinner table. He'd say, "Hand me some of that gravy!" Or, "This roast beef is too damn bloody." And suddenly I'd be out cold like a light.

MEG Oh, Babe. BABE, this is very important. I want you to sit down here and tell me what all happened right before you shot Zackery. That's right, just sit down and tell me.

BABE (*after a pause*) I told you I can't tell you on account of I'm protecting someone.

MEG But Babe, you've just got to talk to someone about all this. You just do.

BABE Why?

MEG Because it's a human need. To talk about our lives. It's an important human need.

BABE Oh. Well, I do feel like I want to talk to someone. I do.

MEG Then talk to me; please.

BABE (*a decision*) All right. (*After thinking a minute.*) I don't know where to start.

MEG Just start at the beginning. Just there at the beginning.

BABE (*after a moment*) Well, do you remember Willie Jay? (MEG *shakes her head.*) Cora's youngest boy?

MEG Oh, yeah, that little kid we used to pay a nickel to, to run down to the drugstore and bring us back a cherry Coke.

BABE Right. Well, Cora irons at my place on Wednesdays now, and she just happened to mention that Willie Jay'd picked up this old stray dog and that he'd gotten real fond of him. But now they couldn't afford to feed him anymore, so she was gonna have to tell Willie Jay to set him loose in the woods.

MEG (*trying to be patient*) Uh huh.

BABE Well, I said I liked dogs and if he wanted to bring the dog over here, I'd take care of him. You see, I was alone by myself most of the time 'cause the senate was in session, and Zackery was up in Jackson.

MEG Uh huh. (MEG *reaches for* LENNY'S *box of birthday candy. She takes little nibbles out of each piece, throughout the rest of the scene.*)

BABE So the next day, Willie Jay brings over this skinny, old dog with these little crossed-eyes. Well, I asked Willie Jay what his name was, and he said they called him Dog. Well, I liked the name; so I thought I'd keep it.

MEG (*getting up*) Uh huh. I'm listening. I'm just gonna get me a glass of cold water; do you want one?

BABE Okay.

MEG So you kept the name—Dog.

BABE Yeah. Anyway, when Willie Jay was leaving he gave Dog a hug and said, "Goodbye, Dog. You're a fine ole dog." Well, I felt something for him, so I told Willie Jay he could come back and visit with Dog any time he wanted, and his face just kinda lit right up.

MEG (*offering the candy*) Candy—

BABE No thanks. Anyhow, time goes on and Willie Jay keeps coming over and over. And we talk about Dog and how fat he's getting and then, well, you know, things start up.

MEG No, I don't know. What things start up?

BABE Well, things start up. Like sex. Like that.

MEG Babe, wait a minute—Willie Jay's a boy. A small boy, about this tall. He's about this tall!

BABE No! Oh, no! He's taller now! He's fifteen now. When you knew him he was only about seven or eight.

MEG But, even so—fifteen. And he's a black boy; a colored boy; a Negro.

BABE (*flustered*) Well, I realize that, Meg. Why do you think I'm so worried about his getting public exposure? I don't want to ruin his reputation!

MEG I'm amazed, Babe. I'm really, completely amazed. I didn't even know you were a liberal.

BABE Well, I'm not! I'm not a liberal! I'm a democratic! I was just lonely! I was so lonely. And he was good. Oh, he was so, so good. I'd never had it that good. We'd always go out into the garage and—

MEG It's okay. I've got the picture; I've got the picture! Now, let's just get back to the story. To yesterday, when you shot Zackery.

BABE All right, then. Let's see . . . Willie Jay was over. And it was after we'd—

MEG Yeah! Yeah.

BABE And we were just standing around on the back porch playing with Dog. Well, suddenly, Zackery comes from around the side of the house. And he startled me 'cause he's supposed to be away at the office, and there he is coming from 'round the side of the house. Anyway, he says to Willie Jay, "Hey, boy, what are you doing back here?" And I said, "He's not doing anything. You just go on home, Willie Jay! You just run right on home." Well, before he can move, Zackery comes up and knocks him once right across the face and then shoves him down the porch steps, causing him to skin up his elbow real bad on that hard concrete. Then he says, "Don't you ever come around here again, or I'll have them cut out your gizzard!" Well, Willie Jay starts crying, these tears come streaming down his face, then he gets up real quick and runs away with Dog following off after him. After that, I don't remember much too clearly; let's see . . . I went on into the living room, and I went right up to the davenport and opened the drawer where we keep the burglar gun . . . I took it out. Then I—I brought it up to my ear. That's right. I put it right inside my ear. Why, I was gonna shoot off my own head! That's what I was gonna do. Then I heard the back door slamming and suddenly, for some reason, I thought about mama . . . how she'd hung herself. And here I was about ready to shoot myself. Then I realized—that's right I realized how I didn't want to kill myself! And she—she probably didn't want to kill herself. She wanted to kill him, and I wanted to kill him, too. I wanted to kill Zackery, not myself 'Cause I—I wanted to live! So I waited for him to come on into the living room. Then I held out the gun, and I pulled the trigger. aiming for his heart, but getting him in the stomach. (*After a pause.*) It's funny that I really did that.

MEG It's a good thing that you did. It's a damn good thing that you did.

BABE It was.

MEG Please, Babe, talk to Barnette Lloyd. Just talk to him and see if he can help.

BABE But how about Willie Jay?

MEG (*starting towards the phone*) Oh, he'll be all right. You just talk to that lawyer like you did to me. (*Looking at the number on the card, she begins dialing.*) See, 'cause he's gonna be on your side.

BABE No! Stop, Meg, stop! Don't call him up! Please don't call him up! You can't! It's too awful. (*She runs over and jerks the bottom half of the phone away from* MEG. MEG *stands, holding the receiver.*)

MEG Babe! (BABE *slams her half of the phone into the refrigerator.*)

BABE I just can't tell some stranger all about my personal life. I just can't.

MEG Well, hell, Babe; you're the one who said you wanted to live.

BABE That's right. I did. (*She takes the phone out of the refrigerator and hands it to* MEG.) Here's the other part of the phone. (BABE *moves to sit at the kitchen table.* MEG *takes the phone back to the counter. Babe, as she fishes a lemon out of her glass and begins sucking on it.*) Meg.

MEG What?

BABE I called the bakery. They're gonna have Lenny's cake ready first thing tomorrow morning. That's the earliest they can get it.

MEG All right.

BABE I told them to write on it, "Happy Birthday Lenny—A Day Late." That sound okay?

MEG (*at the phone*) It sounds nice.

BABE I ordered up the very largest size cake they have. I told them chocolate cake with white icing and red trim. Think she'll like that?

MEG (*dialing on the phone*) Yeah, I'm sure she will. She'll like it.

BABE I'm hoping.

BLACKOUT

END OF ACT I

ACT II

The lights go up on the kitchen. It is later that evening on the same day. MEG's *suitcase has been moved upstairs.* BABE's *saxophone has been taken out of the case and put together.*

BABE *and* BARNETTE *are sitting at the kitchen table.* BARNETTE *is writing and re-checking notes with explosive intensity.* BABE, *who has changed into a casual shift, sits eating a bowl of oatmeal, slowly.*

BARNETTE (*to himself*) Mmm-huh! Yes! I see, I see! Well, we can work on that! And of course, this is mere conjecture! Difficult, if not impossible, to prove. Ha! Yes. Yes, indeed. Indeed—

BABE Sure you don't want any oatmeal?

BARNETTE What? Oh, no. No, thank you. Let's see, ah, where were we?

BABE I just shot Zackery.

BARNETTE (*looking at his notes*) Right. Correct. You've just pulled the trigger.

BABE Tell me, do you think Willie Jay can stay out of all this?

BARNETTE Believe me, it is in our interest to keep him as far out of this as possible.

BABE Good.

BARNETTE (*throughout the following,* BARNETTE *stays glued to* BABE'S *every word*) All right, you've just shot one Zackery Botrelle, as a result of his continual physical and mental abuse—what happens now?

BABE Well, after I shot him, I put the gun down on the piano bench and then I went out into the kitchen and made up a pitcher of lemonade.

BARNETTE Lemonade?

BABE Yes, I was dying of thirst. My mouth was just as dry as a bone.

BARNETTE So in order to quench this raging thirst that was choking you dry and preventing any possibility of you uttering intelligible sounds or phrases, you went out to the kitchen and made up a pitcher of lemonade?

BABE Right. I made it just the way I like it with lots of sugar and lots of lemon—about ten lemons in all. Then I added two trays of ice and stirred it up with my wooden stirring spoon.

BARNETTE Then what?

BABE Then I drank three glasses, one right after the other. They were large glasses, about this tall. Then suddenly, my stomach kind of swoll all up. I guess what caused it was all that sour lemon.

BARNETTE Could be.

BABE Then what I did was . . . I wiped my mouth off with the back of my hand, like this . . . (*She demonstrates.*)

BARNETTE Hmmm.

BABE I did it to clear off all those little beads of water that had settled there.

BARNETTE I see.

BABE Then I called out to Zackery. I said, "Zackery, I've made some lemonade. Can you use a glass?"

BARNETTE Did he answer? Did you hear an answer?

BABE No. He didn't answer.

BARNETTE So, what'd you do?

BABE I poured him a glass anyway and took it out to him.

BARNETTE You took it out to the living room?

BABE I did. And there he was; lying on the rug. He was looking up at me trying to speak words. I said, "What? . . . Lemonade? . . . You don't want it? Would you like a Coke instead?" Then I got the idea, he was telling me to call on the phone for medical help. So I got on the phone and called up the hospital. I gave my name and address and I told them my husband was shot and he was lying on the rug and there was plenty of blood. (BABE *pauses a minute, as* BARNETTE *works frantically on his notes.*) I guess that's gonna look kinda bad.

BARNETTE What?

BABE Me fixing that lemonade, before I called the hospital.

BARNETTE Well, not . . . necessarily.

BABE I tell you, I think the reason I made up the lemonade, I mean besides the fact that my mouth was bone dry, was that I was afraid to call the authorities. I was afraid. I— I really think I was afraid they would see that I had tried to shoot Zackery, in fact, that I had shot him, and they would accuse me of possible murder and send me away to jail.

BARNETTE Well, that's understandable.

BABE I think so. I mean, in fact, that's what did happen. That's what is happening— 'cause here I am just about ready to go right off to the Parchment Prison Farm. Yes, here I am just practically on the brink of utter doom. Why, I feel so all alone.

BARNETTE Now, now, look—Why, there's no reason for you to get yourself so all upset and worried. Please, don't. Please. (*They look at each other for a moment.*) You just keep filling in as much detailed information as you can about those incidents on the medical reports. That's all you need to think about. Don't you worry, Mrs. Botrelle, we're going to have a solid defense.

BABE Please, don't call me Mrs. Botrelle.

BARNETTE All right.

BABE My name's Becky. People in the family call me Babe; but my real name's Becky.

BARNETTE All right, Becky. (BARNETTE *and* BABE *stare at each other for a long moment.*)

BABE Are you sure you didn't go to Hazlehurst High?

BARNETTE No, I went away to a boarding school.

BABE Gosh, you sure do look familiar. You sure do.

BARNETTE Well, I—I doubt you'll remember, but I did meet you once.

BABE You did? When?

BARNETTE At the Christmas bazaar, year before last. You were selling cakes and cookies and . . . candy.

BABE Oh, yes! You bought the orange pound cake!

BARNETTE Right.

BABE Of course, and then we talked for a while. We talked about the Christmas angel.

BARNETTE You do remember.

BABE I remember it very well. You were even thinner then than you are now.

BARNETTE Well, I'm surprised. I'm certainly . . . surprised. (*The phone begins to ring.*)

BABE (*as she goes to answer the phone*) This is quite a coincidence! Don't you think it is? Why, it's almost a fluke. (*She answers the phone.*) Hello . . . Oh, hello, Lucille . . . Oh, he is? . . . Oh, he does? . . . Okay. Oh, Lucille, wait! Has Dog come back to the house? . . . Oh, I see . . . Okay. Okay. (*After a brief pause.*) Hello, Zackery? How are you doing? . . . Uh huh . . . uh huh . . . oh, I'm sorry . . . Please, don't scream . . . uh huh . . . uh huh . . . You want what? . . . No, I can't come up there now . . . Well, for one thing, I don't even have the car. Lenny and Meg are up at the hospital right now, visiting with Old Granddaddy . . . What? . . . Oh, really? . . . Oh, really? . . . Well, I've got me a lawyer that's over here right now, and he's building me up a solid defense! . . . Wait just a minute, I'll see. (*To* BARNETTE.) He wants to talk to you. He says he's got some blackening evidence that's gonna convict me of attempting to murder him on the first degree!

BARNETTE (*disgustedly*) Oh, bluff! He's bluffing! Here, hand me the phone. (*He takes the phone and becomes suddenly cool and suave.*) Hello, this is Mr. Barnette Lloyd speaking. I'm Mrs. . . . ah, Becky's attorney . . . Why, certainly, Mr. Botrelle, I'd be more than glad to check out any pertinent information that you may have . . . Fine, then I'll be right over. Goodbye. (*He hangs up the phone.*)

BABE What did he say?

BARNETTE He wants me to come to see him at the hospital this evening. Says he's got some sort of evidence. Sounds highly suspect to me.

BABE Oooh! Didn't you just hate his voice? Doesn't he have the most awful voice! I just hate it! I can't bear to hear it!

BARNETTE Well, now—now, wait. Wait just a minute.

BABE What?

BARNETTE I have a solution. From now on I'll handle all communications between you two. You can simply refuse to speak with him.

BABE All right—I will. I'll do that.

BARNETTE (*starting to pack his briefcase*) Well, I'd better get over there and see just what he's got up his sleeve.

BABE (*after a pause*) Barnette.

BARNETTE Yes?

BABE What's the personal vendetta about? You know, the one you have to settle with Zackery.

BARNETTE Oh, it's—it's complicated. It's a very complicated matter.

BABE I see.

BARNETTE The major thing he did was to ruin my father's life. He took away his job, his home, his health, his respectability. I don't like to talk about it.

BABE I'm sorry. I just wanted to say—I hope you win it. I hope you win your vendetta.

BARNETTE Thank you.

BABE I think it's an important thing that a person could win a life long vendetta.

BARNETTE Yes. Well, I'd better be going.

BABE All right. Let me know what happens.

BARNETTE I will. I'll get back to you right away.

BABE Thanks.

BARNETTE Goodbye, Becky.

BABE Goodbye, Barnette. (BARNETTE *exits.* BABE *looks around the room for a moment, then goes over to her white suitcase and opens it up. She takes out her pink hair curlers and a brush. She begins brushing her hair.*) Goodbye, Becky. Goodbye, Barnette. Goodbye Becky. Oooh. (LENNY *enters. She is fuming.* BABE *is rolling her hair throughout most of the following scene.*) Lenny, hi!

LENNY Hi.

BABE Where's Meg?

LENNY Oh, she had to go by the store and pick some things up. I don't know what.

BABE Well, how's Old Granddaddy?

LENNY (*as she picks up Babe's bowl of oatmeal*) He's fine. Wonderful! Never been better!

BABE Lenny, what's wrong? What's the matter?

LENNY It's Meg! I could just wring her neck! I could just wring it!

BABE Why? Wha'd she do?

LENNY She lied! She sat in that hospital room and shamelessly lied to Old Granddaddy. She went on and on telling such untrue stories and lies.

BABE Well, what? What did she say?

LENNY Well, for one thing she said she was gonna have a RCA record coming out with her picture on the cover, eating pineapples under a palm tree.

BABE Well, gosh, Lenny, maybe she is! Don't you think she really is?

LENNY Babe, she sat here this very afternoon and told me how all that she's done this whole year is work as a clerk for a dog food company.

BABE Oh, shoot. I'm disappointed.

LENNY And then she goes on to say that she'll be appearing on the "Johnny Carson Show" in two weeks' time. Two weeks' time! Why, Old Granddaddy's got a TV set right in his room. Imagine what a letdown it's gonna be.

BABE Why, mercy me.

LENNY (*slamming the coffeepot on*) Oh, and she told him the reason she didn't use the money he sent her to come home Christmas was that she was right in the middle of making a huge multi-million-dollar motion picture and was just under too much pressure.

BABE My word!

LENNY The movie's coming out this spring. It's called, "Singing in a Shoe Factory." But she only has a small leading role—not a large leading role.

BABE (*laughing*) For heaven's sake—

LENNY I'm sizzling. Oh, I just can't help it! I'm sizzling!

BABE Sometimes Meg does such strange things.

LENNY (*slowly, as she picks up the opened box of birthday candy*) Who ate this candy?

BABE (*hesitantly*) Meg.

LENNY My one birthday present, and look what she does! Why, she's taken one little bite out of each piece and then just put it back in! Ooh! That's just like her! That is just like her!

BABE Lenny, please—

LENNY I can't help it! It gets me mad! It gets me upset! Why, Meg's always run wild— she started smoking and drinking when she was fourteen years old, she never made good grades—never made her own bed! But somehow she always seemed to get what she wanted. She's the one who got singing and dancing lessons; and a store-bought dress to wear to her senior prom. Why do you remember how Meg always got to wear twelve jingle bells on her petticoats, while we were only allowed to wear three apiece? Why?! Why should Old Grandmama let her sew twelve golden jingle bells on her petticoats and us only three!!!

BABE (*who has heard all this before*) I don't know!! Maybe she didn't jingle them as much!

LENNY I can't help it! It gets me mad! I resent it. I do.

BABE Oh, don't resent Meg. Things have been hard for Meg. After all, she was the one who found Mama.

LENNY Oh, I know; she's the one who found Mama. But that's always been the excuse.

BABE But, I tell you, Lenny, after it happened, Meg started doing all sorts of these strange things.

LENNY She did? Like what?

BABE Like things I never wanted to tell you about.

LENNY What sort of things?

BABE Well, for instance, back when we used to go over to the library, Meg would spend all her time reading and looking through this old, black book called *Diseases of the Skin*. It was full of the most sickening pictures you'd ever seen. Things like rotting- away noses and eyeballs drooping off down the sides of people's faces and scabs and sores and eaten-away places all over *all* parts of people's bodies.

LENNY (*trying to pour her coffee*) Babe, please! That's enough.

BABE Anyway, she'd spend hours and hours just forcing herself to look through this book. Why, it was the same way she'd force herself to look at the poster of crippled children stuck up in the window at Dixieland Drugs. You know, that one where they want you to give a dime. Meg would stand there and stare at their eyes and look at the braces on their little crippled-up legs—then she'd purposely go and spend her dime on a double scoop ice cream cone and eat it all down. She'd say to me, "See, I can stand it. I can stand it. Just look how I'm gonna be able to stand it."

LENNY That's awful.

BABE She said she was afraid of being a weak person. I guess 'cause she cried in bed every night for such a long time.

LENNY Goodness mercy. (*After a pause.*) Well, I suppose you'd have to be a pretty hard person to be able to do what she did to Doc Porter.

BABE (*exasperated*) Oh, shoot! It wasn't Meg's fault that hurricane wiped Biloxi away. I never understood why people were blaming all that on Meg—just because that roof fell in and crunched Doc's leg. It wasn't her fault.

LENNY Well, it was Meg who refused to evacuate. Jim Craig and some of Doc's other friends were all down there and they kept trying to get everyone to evacuate. But Meg refused. She wanted to stay on because she thought a hurricane would be—oh, I don't know—a lot of fun. Then everyone says she baited Doc into staying with her. She said she'd marry him if he'd stay.

BABE (*taken aback by this new information*) Well, he has a mind of his own. He could have gone.

LENNY But he didn't. 'Cause . . . 'cause he loved her. And then after the roof caved, and they got Doc to the high school gym, Meg just left. She just left him there to leave for California—'cause of her career, she says. I think it was a shameful thing to do. It took almost a year for his leg to heal and after that he gave up his medical career altogether. He said he was tired of hospitals. It's such a sad thing. Everyone always knew he was gonna be a doctor. We've called him Doc for years.

BABE I don't know. I guess, I don't have any room to talk; 'cause I just don't know. (*Pause.*) Gosh, you look so tired.

LENNY I feel tired.

BABE They say women need a lot of iron . . . so they won't feel tired.

LENNY What's got iron in it? Liver?

BABE Yeah, liver's got it. And vitamin pills.

After a moment, MEG *enters. She carries a bottle of bourbon that is already minus a few slugs and a newspaper. She is wearing black boots, a dark dress, and a hat. The room goes silent.*

MEG Hello.

BABE (*fooling with her hair*) Hi, Meg. (LENNY *quietly sips her coffee.*)

MEG (*handing the newspaper to* BABE) Here's your paper.

BABE Thanks. (*She opens it.*) Oh, here it is, right on the front page. (MEG *lights a cigarette.*) Where's the scissors, Lenny?

LENNY Look in there in the ribbon drawer.

BABE Okay. (BABE *gets the scissors and glue out of the drawer and slowly begins cutting out the newspaper article.*)

MEG (*after a few moments, filled only with the snipping of scissors*) All right—I lied! I lied! I couldn't help it . . . these stories just came pouring out of my mouth! When I saw how tired and sick Old Granddaddy'd gotten—they just flew out! All I wanted was to see him smiling and happy. I just wasn't going to sit there and look at him all miserable and sick and sad! I just wasn't!

BABE Oh, Meg, he is sick, isn't he—

MEG Why, he's gotten all white and milky—he's almost evaporated!

LENNY (*gasping and turning to* MEG) But still you shouldn't have lied! It just was wrong for you to tell such lies—

MEG Well, I know that! Don't you think I know that? I hate myself when I lie for that old man. I do. I feel so weak. And then I have to go and do at least three or four things that I know he'd despise just to get even with that miserable, old, bossy man!

LENNY Oh, Meg, please, don't talk so about Old Granddaddy! It sounds so ungrateful. Why, he went out of his way to make a home for us; to treat us like we were his very own children. All he ever wanted was the best for us. That's all he ever wanted.

MEG Well, I guess it was; but sometimes I wonder what we wanted.

BABE (*taking the newspaper article and glue over to her suitcase*) Well, one thing I wanted was a team of white horses to ride Mama's coffin to her grave. That's one thing I wanted. (LENNY *and* MEG *exchange looks*.) Lenny, did you remember to pack my photo album?

LENNY It's down there at the bottom, under all that night stuff.

BABE Oh, I found it.

LENNY Really, Babe, I don't understand why you have to put in the articles that are about the unhappy things in your life. Why would you want to remember them?

BABE (*pasting the article in*) I don't know. I just like to keep an accurate record, I suppose. There. (*She begins flipping through the book.*) Look, here's a picture of me when I got married.

MEG Let's see.

BABE *brings the photo album over to the table. They all look at it.*

LENNY My word, you look about twelve years old.

BABE I was just eighteen.

MEG You're smiling, Babe. Were you happy then?

BABE (*laughing*) Well, I was drunk on champagne punch. I remember that! (*They turn the page.*)

LENNY Oh, there's Meg singing at Greeny's!

BABE Oooh, I wish you were still singing at Greeny's! I wish you were!

LENNY You're so beautiful!

BABE Yes, you are. You're beautiful.

MEG Oh, stop! I'm not—

LENNY Look, Meg's starting to cry.

BABE Oh, Meg—

MEG I'm not—

BABE Quick, better turn the page; we don't want Meg crying—(*She flips the pages.*)

LENNY Why, it's Daddy.

MEG Where'd you get that picture, Babe? I thought she burned them all.

BABE Ah, I just found it around.

LENNY What does it say here? What's that inscription?

BABE It says "Jimmy—clowning at the beach—1952."

LENNY Well, will you look at that smile.

MEG Jesus, those white teeth—turn the page, will you; we can't do any worse than this! (*They turn the page. The room goes silent.*)

BABE It's Mama and the cat.

LENNY Oh, turn the page—

BABE That old yellow cat. You know, I bet if she hadn't of hung that old cat along with her, she wouldn't have gotten all that national coverage.

MEG (*after a moment, hopelessly*) Why are we talking about this?

LENNY Meg's right. It was so sad. It was awfully sad. I remember how we all three just sat up on that bed the day of the service all dressed up in our black velveteen suits crying the whole morning long.

BABE We used up one whole big box of Kleenexes.

MEG And then Old Granddaddy came in and said he was gonna take us out to breakfast. Remember, he told us not to cry anymore 'cause he was gonna take us out to get banana splits for breakfast.

BABE That's right—banana splits for breakfast!

MEG Why, Lenny was fourteen years old and he thought that would make it all better—

BABE Oh, I remember he said for us to eat all we wanted. I think I ate about five! He kept shoving them down us!

MEG God, we were so sick!

LENNY Oh, we were!

MEG (*laughing*) Lenny's face turned green—

LENNY I was just as sick as a dog!

BABE Old Grandmama was furious!

LENNY Oh, she was!

MEG The thing about Old Granddaddy is he keeps trying to make us happy and we end up getting stomach aches and turning green and throwing up in the flower arrangements.

BABE Oh, that was me! I threw up in the flowers! Oh, no! How embarrassing!

LENNY (*laughing*) Oh, Babe—

BABE (*hugging her sisters*) Oh, Lenny! Oh, Meg!

MEG Oh, Babe! Oh, Lenny! It's so good to be home!

LENNY Hey, I have an idea—

BABE What?

LENNY Let's play cards!!

BABE Oh, let's do!

MEG All right!

LENNY Oh, good! It'll be just like when we used to sit around the table playing hearts all night long.

BABE I know! (*getting up*) I'll fix us up some popcorn and hot chocolate—

MEG (*getting up*) Here, let me get out that old black popcorn pot.

LENNY (*getting up*) Oh, yes! Now, let's see, I think I have a deck of cards around here somewhere.

BABE Gosh, I hope I remember all the rules—Are hearts good or bad?

MEG Bad, I think. Aren't they, Lenny?

LENNY That's right. Hearts are bad, but the Black Sister is the worst of all—

MEG Oh, that's right! And the Black Sister is the Queen of Spades.

BABE (*figuring it out*) And spades are the black cards that aren't the puppy dog feet?

MEG (*thinking a moment*) Right. And she counts a lot of points.

BABE And points are bad?

MEG Right. Here, I'll get some paper so we can keep score.

The phone begins to ring.

LENNY Oh, here they are!

MEG I'll get it—

LENNY Why, look at these cards! They're years old!

BABE Oh, let me see!

MEG Hello . . . No, this is Meg Magrath . . . Doc. How are you? . . . Well, good . . .
You're where? . . . Well, sure. Come on over . . . Sure, I'm sure. Yeah, come right
on over . . . All right. Bye. (*She hangs up.*) That was Doc Porter. He's down the street
at Al's Grill. He's gonna come on over.

LENNY He is?

MEG He said he wanted to come see me.

LENNY Oh. (*after a pause*) Well, do you still want to play?

MEG No, I don't think so.

LENNY All right. (LENNY *starts to shuffle the cards, as* MEG *brushes her hair.*) You know,
it's really not much fun playing hearts with only two people.

MEG I'm sorry; maybe after Doc leaves, I'll join you.

LENNY I know; maybe Doc'll want to play, then we can have a game of bridge.

MEG I don't think so. Doc never liked cards. Maybe we'll just go out somewhere.

LENNY (*putting down the cards;* BABE *picks them up*) Meg—

MEG What?

LENNY Well, Doc's married now.

MEG I know. You told me.

LENNY Oh. Well, as long as you know that. (*Pause*) As long as you know that.

MEG (*still primping*) Yes, I know. She made the pot.

BABE How many cards do I deal out?

LENNY (*leaving the table*) Excuse me.

BABE All of 'em, or what?

LENNY Ah, Meg? Could I—could I ask you something? (BABE *proceeds to deal out all
the cards.*)

MEG What?

LENNY I just wanted to ask you—

MEG What?

Unable to go on with what she really wants to say, LENNY *runs up and picks up the box
of candy.*

LENNY Well, just why did you take one little bite out of each piece of candy in this box
and then just put it back in?

MEG Oh. Well, I was looking for the ones with nuts.

LENNY The ones with nuts.

MEG Yeah.

LENNY But there are none with nuts. It's a box of assorted cremes—all it has in it are
cremes!

MEG Oh.

LENNY Why couldn't you just read the box? It says right here, "Assorted Cremes," not
nuts! Besides this was a birthday present to me! My one and only birthday present; my
only one!

MEG I'm sorry. I'll get you another box.

LENNY I don't want another box. That's not the point!

MEG What is the point?

LENNY I don't know; it's—it's—You have no respect for other people's property! You
just take whatever you want. You just take it! Why, remember how you had layers
and layers of jingle bells sewed onto your petticoats while Babe and I only had three
apiece?!

MEG Oh, God! She's starting up about those stupid jingle bells!

LENNY Well, it's an example! A specific example of how you always got what you wanted!

MEG Oh, come on, Lenny, you're just upset because Doc called.

LENNY Who said anything about Doc? Do you think I'm upset about Doc? Why, I've long since given up worrying about you and all your men.

MEG (*turning in anger*) Look, I know I've had too many men. Believe me, I've had way too many men. But it's not my fault you haven't had any—or maybe just that one from Memphis.

LENNY (*stopping*) What one from Memphis?

MEG (*slowly*) The one Babe told me about. From the—club.

LENNY Babe!!!

BABE Meg!!!

LENNY How could you?!! I asked you not to tell anyone! I'm so ashamed! How could you?! Who else have you told? Did you tell anyone else?

BABE (*overlapping, to* MEG) Why'd you have to open your big mouth?!

MEG (*overlapping*) How am I supposed to know? You never said not to tell!

BABE Can't you use your head just for once?!! (*Then to* LENNY.) No, I never told anyone else. Somehow it just slipped out to Meg. Really, it just flew out of my mouth—

LENNY What do you two have—wings on your tongues?

BABE I'm sorry, Lenny. Really sorry.

LENNY I'll just never, never, never be able to trust you again—

MEG (*furiously, coming to* BABE's *defense*) Oh, for heaven's sake, Lenny, we were just worried about you! We wanted to find a way to make you happy!

LENNY Happy! Happy! I'll never be happy!

MEG Well, not if you keep living your life as Old Granddaddy's nursemaid—

BABE Meg, shut up!

MEG I can't help it! I just know that the reason you stopped seeing this man from Memphis was because of Old Granddaddy.

LENNY What—Babe didn't tell you the rest of the story—

MEG Oh, she said it was something about your shrunken ovary.

BABE Meg!!

LENNY Babe!!

BABE I just mentioned it!

MEG But I don't believe a word of that story!

LENNY Oh, I don't care what you believe! It's so easy for you—you always have men falling in love with you! But I have this underdeveloped ovary and I can't have children and my hair is falling out in the comb—so what man can love me?! What man's gonna love me?

MEG A lot of men!

BABE Yeah, a lot! A whole lot!

MEG Old Granddaddy's the only one who seems to think otherwise.

LENNY 'Cause he doesn't want to see me hurt! He doesn't want to see me rejected and humiliated.

MEG Oh, come on now, Lenny, don't be so pathetic! God, you make me angry when you just stand there looking so pathetic! Just tell me, did you really ask the man from Memphis? Did you actually ask that man from Memphis all about it?

LENNY (*breaking apart*) No; I didn't. I didn't. Because I just didn't want him not to want me—

MEG Lenny—

LENNY (*furious*) Don't talk to me anymore! Don't talk to me! I think I'm gonna vomit—
I just hope all this doesn't cause me to vomit! (LENNY *exits up the stairs sobbing.*)

MEG See! See! She didn't even ask him about her stupid ovary! She just broke it all off
'cause of Old Granddaddy! What a jackass fool!

BABE Oh, Meg, shut up! Why do you have to make Lenny cry? I just hate it when you
make Lenny cry! (BABE *runs up the stairs.*) Lenny! Oh, Lenny—(MEG *takes a long
sigh and goes to get a cigarette and a drink.*)

MEG I feel like hell. (MEG *sits in despair—smoking and drinking bourbon. There is a
knock at the back door.* MEG *starts. She brushes her hair out of her face and goes to
answer the door. It is* DOC.)

DOC Hello, Meggy.

MEG Well, Doc. Well, it's Doc.

DOC (*after a pause*) You're home, Meggy.

MEG Yeah; I've come home. I've come on home to see about Babe.

DOC And how's Babe?

MEG Oh, fine. Well, fair. She's fair. (DOC *nods.*) Hey, do you want a drink?

DOC Whatcha got?

MEG Bourbon.

DOC Oh, don't tell me Lenny's stocking bourbon.

MEG Well, no. I've been to the store. (MEG *gets him a glass and pours them each a
drink. They click glasses.*) So, how's your wife?

DOC She's fine.

MEG I hear ya got two kids.

DOC Yeah. Yeah, I got two kids.

MEG A boy and a girl.

DOC That's right, Meggy, a boy and a girl.

MEG That's what you always said you wanted, wasn't it? A boy and a girl.

DOC Is that what I said?

MEG I don't know. I thought it's what you said. (*They finish their drinks in silence.*)

DOC Whose cot?

MEG Lenny's. She's taken to sleeping in the kitchen.

DOC Ah. Where is Lenny?

MEG She's in the upstairs room. I made her cry. Babe's up there seeing to her.

DOC How'd you make her cry?

MEG I don't know. Eating her birthday candy; talking on about her boyfriend from
Memphis. I don't know. I'm upset about it. She's got a lot on her. Why can't I keep
my mouth shut?

DOC I don't know, Meggy. Maybe it's because you don't want to.

MEG Maybe. (*They smile at each other.* MEG *pours each of them another drink.*)

DOC Well, it's been a long time.

MEG It has been a long time.

DOC Let's see—when was the last time we saw each other?

MEG I can't quite recall.

DOC Wasn't it in Biloxi?

MEG Ah, Biloxi. I believe so.

DOC And wasn't there a—a hurricane going on at the time?

MEG Was there?

DOC Yes, there was, one hell of a hurricane. Camille, I believe they called it. Hurricane
Camille.

MEG Yes, now I remember. It was a beautiful hurricane.

DOC We had a time down there. We had quite a time. Drinking vodka, eating oysters on the half shell, dancing all night long. And the wind was blowing.

MEG Oh, God, was it blowing.

DOC Goddamn, was it blowing.

MEG There never has been such a wind blowing.

DOC Oh, God, Meggy. Oh, God.

MEG I know, Doc. It was my fault to leave you. I was crazy. I thought I was choking. I felt choked!

DOC I felt like a fool.

MEG No.

DOC I just kept on wondering why.

MEG I don't know why . . . 'Cause I didn't want to care. I don't know. I did care though. I did.

DOC (after a pause) Ah, hell—(He pours them both another drink.) Are you still singing those sad songs?

MEG No.

DOC Why not?

MEG I don't know, Doc. Things got worse for me. After a while, I just couldn't sing anymore. I tell you, I had one hell of a time over Christmas.

DOC What do you mean?

MEG I went nuts. I went insane. Ended up in L.A. County Hospital. Psychiatric ward.

DOC Hell. Ah, hell, Meggy. What happened?

MEG I don't really know. I couldn't sing anymore; so I lost my job. And I had a bad toothache. I had this incredibly painful toothache. For days I had it, but I wouldn't do anything about it. I just stayed inside my apartment. All I could do was sit around in chairs, chewing on my fingers. Then one afternoon I ran screaming out of the apartment with all my money and jewelry and valuables and tried to stuff it all into one of those March of Dimes collection boxes. That was when they nabbed me. Sad story. Meg goes mad. (DOC stares at her for a long moment. He pours them both another drink.)

DOC (after quite a pause) There's a moon out.

MEG Is there?

DOC Wanna go take a ride in my truck and look out at the moon?

MEG I don't know, Doc. I don't wanna start up. It'll be too hard, if we start up.

DOC Who says we're gonna start up? We're just gonna look at the moon. For one night just you and me are gonna go for a ride in the country and look out at the moon.

MEG One night?

DOC Right.

MEG Look out at the moon?

DOC You got it.

MEG Well . . . all right. (She gets up.)

DOC Better take your coat. (He helps her into her coat.) And the bottle—(He takes the bottle. Meg picks up the glasses.) Forget the glasses—

MEG (laughing) Yeah—forget the glasses. Forget the goddamn glasses.

MEG shuts off the kitchen lights, leaving the kitchen lit by only a dim light over the kitchen sink. MEG and DOC leave. After a moment, BABE comes down the stairs in her slip.

BABE Meg—Meg?

She stands for a moment in the moonlight wearing only a slip. She sees her saxophone then moves to pick it up. She plays a few shrieking notes. There is a loud knock on the back door.

BARNETTE'S VOICE Becky! Becky, is that you? (BABE *puts down the saxophone.*)

BABE Just a minute. I'm coming. (*She puts a raincoat on over her slip and goes to answer the door. It is* BARNETTE.) Hello, Barnette. Come on in. (BARNETTE *comes in. He is troubled but is making a great effort to hide the fact.*)

BARNETTE Thank you.

BABE What is it?

BARNETTE I've, ah, I've just come from seeing Zackery at the hospital.

BABE Oh?

BARNETTE It seems . . . Well, it seems his sister, Lucille, was somewhat suspicious.

BABE Suspicious?

BARNETTE About you?

BABE Me?

BARNETTE She hired a private detective, he took these pictures. (*He hands* BABE *a small envelope containing several photographs.* BABE *opens the envelope and begins looking at the pictures in stunned silence.*) They were taken about two weeks ago. It seems, she wasn't going to show them to Botrelle straight away. She, ah, wanted to wait till the time was right. (*The phone rings one and a half times.* BARNETTE *glances uneasily towards the phone.*) Becky? (*The phone stops ringing.*)

BABE (*looking up at* BARNETTE, *slowly*) These are pictures of Willie Jay and me . . . out in the garage.

BARNETTE (*looking away*) I know.

BABE You looked at these pictures?

BARNETTE Yes—I—well . . . professionally, I looked at them.

BABE Oh, mercy. Oh, mercy! We can burn them, can't we? Quick, we can burn them—

BARNETTE It won't do any good. They have the negatives.

BABE (*holding the pictures, as she bangs herself hopelessly into the stove, table, cabinets, etc.*) Oh, no; oh, no; oh, no! Oh, no—

BARNETTE There—there, now—there—

LENNY'S VOICE Babe? Are you all right? Babe—

BABE (*hiding the pictures*) What? I'm all right. Go on back to bed. (LENNY *comes down the stairs. She is wearing a coat and wiping white night cream off of her face with a wash rag.*)

LENNY What's the matter? What's going on down here?

BABE Nothin! (*Then as she begins dancing ballet style around the room.*) We're—we're just dancing. We were just dancing around down here. (*Signaling to* BARNETTE *to dance.*)

LENNY Well, you'd better get your shoes on, 'cause we've got—

BABE All right, I will! That's a good idea! (*As she goes to get her shoes, she hides the pictures.*) Now, you go on back to bed. It's pretty late and—

LENNY Babe, will you listen a minute—

BABE (*holding up her shoes*) I'm putting 'em on—

LENNY That was the hospital that just called. We've got to get over there. Old Grand-daddy's had himself another stroke.

BABE Oh. All right. My shoes are on. (*She stands. They all look at each other as the lights black out.*)

END OF ACT II

ACT III

The lights go up on the empty kitchen. It is the following morning. After a few moments, BABE *enters from the back door. She is carrying her hair curlers in her hands. She goes and lies down on the cot. A few moments later,* LENNY *enters. She is tired and weary.* CHICK'S *voice is heard.*

CHICK'S VOICE Lenny! Oh, Lenny! (LENNY *turns to the door.* CHICK *enters energetically.*) Well . . . how is he?

LENNY He's stabilized; they say for now his functions are all stabilized.

CHICK Well, is he still in the coma?

LENNY Uh huh.

CHICK Hmmm. So do they think he's gonna be . . . passing on?

LENNY He may be. He doesn't look so good. They said they'd phone us if there were any sudden changes.

CHICK Well, it seems to me we'd better get busy phoning on the phone ourselves. (*Removing a list from her pocket.*) Now I've made out this list of all the people we need to notify about Old Granddaddy's predicament. I'll phone half if you'll phone half.

LENNY But—what would we say?

CHICK Just tell them the facts; that Old Granddaddy's got himself in a coma, and it could be, he doesn't have long for this world.

LENNY I—I don't know. I don't feel like phoning.

CHICK Why, Lenora, I'm surprised, how can you be this way? I went to all the trouble of making up the list. And I offered to phone half of the people on it, even though I'm only one-fourth of the granddaughters. I mean, I just get tired of doing more than my fair share, when people like Meg can suddenly just disappear to where they can't even be reached in case of emergency!

LENNY All right; give me the list. I'll phone half.

CHICK Well, don't do it just to suit me.

LENNY (*she wearily tears the list into two halves*) I'll phone these here.

CHICK (*taking her half of the list*) Fine then. Suit yourself. Oh, wait—let me call Sally Bell. I need to talk to her anyway.

LENNY All right.

CHICK So you add Great Uncle Spark Dude to your list.

LENNY Okay.

CHICK Fine. Well, I've got to get on back home and see to the kids. It is gonna be an uphill struggle till I can find someone to replace that good-for-nothing Annie May Jenkins. Well, you let me know if you hear anymore.

LENNY All right.

CHICK Goodbye, Rebecca. I said goodbye. (BABE *blows her sax.* CHICK *starts to exit in a flurry then pauses to add:*) And you really ought to try to get that phoning done before twelve noon. (CHICK *exits.*)

LENNY (*after a long pause*) Babe; I feel bad. I feel real bad.

BABE Why, Lenny?

LENNY Because yesterday I—I wished it.

BABE You wished what?

LENNY I wished that Old Granddaddy would be put out of his pain. I wished on one of my birthday candles. I did. And now he's in this coma, and they say he's feeling no pain.

BABE Well, when did you have a cake yesterday? I don't remember you having any cake.

LENNY Well, I didn't . . . have a cake. But I just blew out the candles anyway.

BABE Oh. Well, those birthday wishes don't count unless you have a cake.

LENNY They don't?

BABE No. A lot of times they don't even count when you do have a cake. It just depends.

LENNY Depends on what?

BABE On how deep your wish is, I suppose.

LENNY Still, I just wish I hadn't of wished it. Gosh, I wonder when Meg's coming home.

BABE Should be soon.

LENNY I just wish we wouldn't fight all the time. I don't like it when we do.

BABE Me, neither.

LENNY I guess it hurts my feelings, a little, the way Old Granddaddy's always put so much stock in Meg and all her singing talent. I think I've been, well, envious of her 'cause I can't seem to do too much.

BABE Why, sure you can.

LENNY I can?

BABE Sure. You just have to put your mind to it; that's all. It's like how I went out and bought that saxophone, just hoping I'd be able to attend music school and start up my own career. I just went out and did it. Just on hope. Of course, now it looks like . . . Well, it just doesn't look like things are gonna work out for me. But I know they would for you.

LENNY Well, they'll work out for you, too.

BABE I doubt it.

LENNY Listen, I heard up at the hospital that Zackery's already in fair condition. They say soon he'll probably be able to walk and everything.

BABE Yeah. And life sure can be miserable.

LENNY Well, I know, 'cause—day before yesterday, Billy Boy was struck down by lightning.

BABE He was?

LENNY (*nearing sobs*) Yeah. He was struck dead.

BABE (*crushed*) Life sure can be miserable.

(*They sit together for several moments in morbid silence.* MEG *is heard singing a loud happy song. She suddenly enters through the dining room door. She is exuberant! Her hair is a mess and the heel of one shoe has broken off. She is laughing radiantly and limping as she sings into the broken heel.*)

MEG (*spotting her sisters*) Good morning! Good morning! Oh, it's a wonderful morning! I tell you, I am surprised I feel this good. I should feel like hell. By all accounts, I should feel like utter hell! (*She is looking for the glue.*) Where's that glue? This damn heel has broken off my shoe. La, la, la, la, la! Ah, here it is! Now let me just get these shoes off. Zip, zip, zip, zip, zip! Well, what's wrong with you two? My God, you look like doom! (BABE *and* LENNY *stare helplessly at* MEG.) Oh, I know, you're mad at me 'cause I stayed out all night long. Well; I did.

LENNY No, we're—we're not mad at you. We're just . . . depressed. (*She starts to sob.*)

MEG Oh, Lenny, listen to me, now, everything's all right with Doc. I mean nothing happened. Well, actually a lot did happen, but it didn't come to anything. Not because of me, I'm afraid. (*Smearing glue on her heel.*) I mean, I was out there thinking, "What will I say when he begs me to run away with him? Will I have pity on his wife and those two half-Yankee children? I mean, can I sacrifice their happiness for mine? Yes!

Oh, yes! Yes, I can!" But . . . he didn't ask me. He didn't even want to ask me. I could tell by this certain look in his eyes that he didn't even want to ask me. Why aren't I miserable! Why aren't I morbid! I should be humiliated! Devastated! Maybe these feelings are coming—I don't know. But for now it was . . . just such fun. I'm happy. I realized I could care about someone. I could want someone. And I sang! I sang all night long! I sang right up into the trees! But not for Old Granddaddy. None of it was to please Old Granddaddy! (LENNY *and* BABE *look at each other.*)

BABE Ah, Meg—

MEG What—

BABE Well, it's just—It's . . .

LENNY It's about Old Granddaddy—

MEG Oh, I know; I know. I told him all those stupid lies. Well, I'm gonna go right over there this morning and tell him the truth. I mean every horrible thing. I don't care if he wants to hear it or not. He's just gonna have to take me like I am. And if he can't take it, if it sends him into a coma, that's just too damn bad!

BABE *and* LENNY *look at each other;* BABE *cracks a smile.* LENNY *cracks a smile.*

BABE You're too late—Ha, ha, ha! (*They both break up laughing.*)

LENNY Oh, stop! Please! Ha, ha, ha!

MEG What is it? What' so funny?

BABE (*still laughing*) It's not—It's not funny!

LENNY (*still laughing*) No, it's not! It's not a bit funny!

MEG Well, what is it then? What?

BABE (*trying to calm down*) Well, it's just—it's just—

MEG What?

BABE Well, Old Granddaddy—he—he's in a coma! (BABE *and* LENNY *break up laughing.*)

MEG He's what?

BABE (*shrieking*) In a coma!

MEG My God! That's not funny!

BABE (*calming down*) I know. I know. For some reason it just struck us as funny.

LENNY I'm sorry. It's—it's not funny. It's sad. It's very sad. We've been up all night long.

BABE We're really tired.

MEG Well, my God. How is he? Is he gonna live?

(BABE *and* LENNY *look at each other.*)

BABE They don't think so! (*They both break up again*)

LENNY Oh, I don't know why we're laughing like this. We're just sick! We're just awful!

BABE We are—we're awful!

LENNY (*as she collects herself*) Oh, good; now I feel bad. Now, I feel like crying. I do; I feel like crying.

BABE Me, too. Me, too.

MEG Well, you've gotten me depressed!

LENNY I'm sorry. I'm sorry. It, ah happened last night. He had another stroke. (*They laugh again.*)

MEG I see.

LENNY But he's stabilized now. (*She chokes up once more.*)

MEG That's good. You two okay? (BABE *and* LENNY *nod.*) You look like you need some rest. (BABE *and* LENNY *nod again.* MEG *goes on, about her heel.*) I hope that'll stay. (MEG *puts the top on the glue. A realization*—) Oh, of course, now I won't be able to tell him the truth about all those lies I told. I mean, finally, I get my wits about me, and he conks out. It's just like him. Babe, can I wear your slippers till this glue dries?

BABE Sure.

LENNY (*after a pause*) Things sure are gonna be different around here . . . when Old Granddaddy dies. Well, not for you two really, but for me.

BABE (*depressed*) Yeah. It'll work out.

LENNY I hope so. I'm afraid of being here all by myself. All alone.

MEG Well, you don't have to be alone. Maybe Babe'll move back in here.

(LENNY *looks at* BABE *hopefully.*)

BABE No; I don't think I'll be living here.

MEG (*realizing her mistake*) Well, anyway, you're your own woman. Invite some people over. Have some parties. Go out with strange men.

LENNY I don't know any strange men.

MEG Well you know that Charlie.

LENNY (*shaking her head*) Not anymore.

MEG Why not?

LENNY (*breaking down*) I told him we should never see each other again.

MEG Well; if you told him, you can just untell him.

LENNY Oh, no I couldn't. I'd feel like a fool.

MEG Oh, that's not a good enough reason! All people in love feel like fools. Don't they, Babe?

BABE Sure.

MEG Look, why don't you give him a call right now? See how things stand?

LENNY Oh, no! I'd be too scared—

MEG But what harm could it possibly do? I mean, it's not gonna make things any worse than this never seeing him again, at all, forever.

LENNY I suppose that's true.

MEG Of course it is; so call him up! Take a chance, will you? Just take some sort of chance!

LENNY You think I should?

MEG Of course! You've got to try—You do! (LENNY *looks over at* BABE.)

BABE You do, Lenny—I think you do.

LENNY Really? Really, really?

MEG Yes! Yes!

BABE You should!

LENNY All right. I will! I will!

MEG Oh, good!

BABE Good!

LENNY I'll call him right now, while I've got my confidence up!

MEG Have you got the number?

LENNY Uh huh. But, ah, I think I wanna call him upstairs. It'll be more private.

MEG Ah, good idea.

LENNY I'm just gonna go on; and call him up; and see what happens—(*She has started up the stairs.*) Wish me good luck!

MEG Good luck!

BABE Good luck, Lenny!

LENNY Thanks.

(LENNY *gets almost out of sight, when the phone begins to ring. She stops,* MEG *picks up the phone.*)

MEG Hello? (*Then in a whisper.*) Oh, thank you very much . . . Yes, I will. 'Bye, 'bye.

LENNY Who was it?

MEG Wrong number. They wanted Weed's Body Shop.

LENNY Oh. Well, I'll be right back down in a minute. (LENNY *exits.*)

MEG (*after a moment, whispering to* BABE) That was the bakery; Lenny's cake is ready!

BABE (*who has become increasingly depressed*) Oh.

MEG I think I'll sneak on down to the corner and pick it up. (*She starts to leave.*)

BABE Meg—

MEG What?

BABE Nothing.

MEG You okay? (BABE *shakes her head.*) What is it?

BABE It's just—

MEG What?

(BABE *gets up and goes to her suitcase. She opens it and removes the envelope containing the photographs.*)

BABE Here. Take a look.

MEG (*taking the envelope*) What is it?

BABE It's some evidence Zackery's collected against me. Looks like my goose is cooked. (MEG *opens the envelope and looks at the photographs.*)

MEG My God, it's—it's you and . . . is *that* Willie Jay?

BABE Yeh.

MEG Well, he certainly *has* grown. You were right about that. My, oh, my.

BABE Please don't tell Lenny. She'd hate me.

MEG I won't. I won't tell Lenny. (*Putting the pictures back into the envelope.*) What are you gonna do?

BABE What can I do? (*There is a knock on the door.* BABE *grabs the envelope and hides it.*)

MEG Who is it?

BARNETTE'S VOICE It's Barnette Lloyd.

MEG Oh. Come on in, Barnette.

(BARNETTE *enters. His eyes are ablaze with excitement.*)

BARNETTE (*as he paces around the room*) Well; good morning! (*Shaking* MEG'S *hand.*) Good morning, Miss Magrath. (*Touching* BABE *on the shoulder.*) Becky. (*Moving away.*) What I meant to say is . . . how are you doing this morning?

MEG Ah—fine. Fine.

BARNETTE Good. Good. I—I just had time to drop by for a minute.

MEG Oh.

BARNETTE So, ah, how's your Granddad doing?

MEG Well, not very, ah—ah, he's in this coma. (*She breaks up laughing.*)

BARNETTE I see . . . I see. (*To* BABE.) Actually, the primary reason I came by was to pick up that—envelope. I left it here last night in all the confusion. (*Pause.*) You, ah, still do have it? (BABE *hands him the envelope.*) Yes. (*Taking the envelope.*) That's the one. I'm sure it'll be much better off in my office safe. (*He puts the envelope into his coat pocket.*)

MEG I'm sure it will.

BARNETTE Beg your pardon?

BABE It's all right. I showed her the pictures.

BARNETTE Ah; I see.

MEG So what's going to happen now, Barnette? What are those pictures gonna mean?

BARNETTE (*after pacing a moment*) Hmmm. May I speak frankly and openly?

BABE Uh huh.

MEG Please do—

BARNETTE Well, I tell you now, at first glance, I admit those pictures had me considerably perturbed and upset. Perturbed to the point that I spent most of last night going over certain suspect papers and reports that had fallen into my hands—rather recklessly.

BABE What papers do you mean?

BARNETTE Papers that pending word from three varied and unbiased experts, could prove graft, fraud, forgery, as well as a history of unethical behavior.

MEG You mean about Zackery?

BARNETTE Exactly. You see, I now intend to make this matter just as sticky and gritty for one Z. Botrelle as it is for us. Why, with the amount of scandal I'll dig up, Botrelle will be forced to settle this affair on our own terms!

MEG Oh, Babe! Did you hear that?!

BABE Yes! Oh, yes! So you've won it! You've won your lifelong vendetta!

BARNETTE Well . . . well, now of course it's problematic in that, well, in that we won't be able to expose him openly in the courts. That was the original game plan.

BABE But why not? Why?

BARNETTE Well, it's only that if, well, if a jury were to—to get, say, a glance at these, ah, photographs, well . . . well possibly . . .

BABE We could be sunk.

BARNETTE In a sense. But! On the other hand, if a newspaper were to get a hold of our little item, Mr. Zackery Botrelle could find himself boiling in some awfully hot water. So what I'm looking for very simply, is—a deal.

BABE A deal?

MEG Thank you, Barnette. It's a sunny day, Babe. (*Realizing she is in the way.*) Ooh, where's that broken shoe? (*She grabs her boots and runs upstairs.*)

BABE So, you're having to give up your vendetta?

BARNETTE Well, in a way. For the time. It, ah, seems to me you shouldn't always let your life be ruled by such things as, ah, personal vendettas. (*Looking at BABE with meaning.*) Other things can be important.

BABE I don't know, I don't exactly know. How 'bout Willie Jay? Will he be all right?

BARNETTE Yes, it's all been taken care of. He'll be leaving incognito on the midnight bus—heading north.

BABE North.

BARNETTE I'm sorry, it seemed the only . . . way. (BARNETTE *moves to her—She moves away.*)

BABE Look, you'd better be getting on back to your work.

BARNETTE (*awkwardly*) Right—'cause I—I've got those important calls out. (*Full of hope for her.*) They'll be pouring in directly. (*He starts to leave, then says to her with love.*) We'll talk.

MEG (*reappearing in her boots*) Oh, Barnette—

BARNETTE Yes?

MEG Could you give me a ride just down to the corner? I need to stop at Helen's Bakery.

BARNETTE Be glad to.

MEG Thanks. Listen, Babe, I'll be right back with the cake. We're gonna have the best celebration! Now, ah, if Lenny asks where I've gone, just say I'm . . . just say, I've gone out back to, ah, pick up some paw paws! Okay?

BABE Okay.

MEG Fine; I'll be back in a bit. Goodbye.

BABE 'Bye.

BARNETTE Goodbye, Becky.

BABE Goodbye, Barnette. Take care. (MEG *and* BARNETTE *exit.* BABE *sits staring ahead, in a state of deep despair.*) Goodbye, Becky. Goodbye, Barnette. Goodbye, Becky. (*She stops when* LENNY *comes down the stairs in a fluster.*)

LENNY Oh! Oh! Oh! I'm so ashamed! I'm such a coward! I'm such a yellow-bellied chicken! I'm so ashamed! Where's Meg?

BABE (*suddenly bright*) She's, ah—gone out back—to pick up some paw paws.

LENNY Oh. Well, at least I don't have to face her! I just couldn't do it! I couldn't make the call!! My heart was pounding like a hammer. Pound! Pound! Pound! Why, I looked down and I could actually see my blouse moving back and forth! Oh, Babe, you look so disappointed. Are you?

BABE (*despondently*) Uh huh.

LENNY Oh, no! I've disappointed Babe! I can't stand it! I've gone and disappointed my little sister, Babe! Oh, no! I feel like howling like a dog!

CHICK'S VOICE Oooh, Lenny! (CHICK *enters dramatically; dripping with sympathy.*) Well, I just don't know what to say! I'm so sorry! I am so sorry for you! And for Little Babe, here, too. I mean to have such a sister as that!

LENNY What do you mean?

CHICK Oh, you don't need to pretend with me. I saw it all from over there in my own backyard; I saw Meg stumbling out of Doc Porter's pickup truck, not 15 minutes ago. And her looking such a disgusting mess. You must be so ashamed! You must just want to die! Why, I always said that girl was nothing but cheap Christmas trash!

LENNY Don't talk that way about Meg.

CHICK Oh, come on now. Lenny, honey, I know exacly how you feel about Meg. Why, Meg's a low-class tramp and you need not have one more blessed thing to do with her and her disgusting behavior.

LENNY I said don't you ever talk that way about my sister Meg again.

CHICK Well, my goodness gracious, Lenora, don't be such a noodle—it's the truth!

LENNY I don't care if it's the Ten Commandments. I don't want to hear it in my home. Not ever again.

CHICK In your home?! Why, I never in all my life—This is my Grandfather's home! And you're just living here on his charity; so don't you get high-falutin' with me, Miss Lenora Josephine Magrath!

LENNY Get out of here—

CHICK Don't you tell me to get out! What makes you think you can order me around? Why, I've had just about my fill of you trashy Magraths and your trashy ways; hanging your selves in cellars; carrying on with married men; shooting your own husbands!

LENNY Get out!

CHICK (*to* BABE) And don't think she's not gonna end up at the state prison farm or in some—mental institution. Why it's a clear-cut case of manslaughter with intent to kill!

LENNY Out! Get out!

CHICK (*running on*) That's what everyone's saying, deliberate intent to kill! And you'll pay for that! Do you hear me? You'll pay!

LENNY (*she picks up a broom and threatens* CHICK *with it*) And I'm telling you to get out!

CHICK You—you put that down this minute—are you a raving lunatic?

LENNY (*beating* CHICK *with the broom*) I said for you to get out! That means out! And never, never, never come back!

CHICK (*overlapping, as she runs around the room*) Oh! Oh! Oh! You're crazy! You're crazy!

LENNY (*chasing* CHICK *out the door*) Do you hear me, Chick the Stick! This is my home! This is my house! Get out! Out!

CHICK (*overlapping*) Oh! Oh! Police! Police! You're crazy! Help! Help! (LENNY *chases* CHICK *out of the house. They are both screaming. The phone rings.* BABE *goes and picks it up.*)

BABE Hello? . . . Oh, hello, Zackery! . . . Yes, he showed them to me! . . . You're what! . . . What do you mean? . . . What! . . . You can't put me out to Whitfield . . . 'Cause I'm not crazy . . . I'm not! I'm not! . . . She wasn't crazy either . . . Don't you call my mother crazy! . . . No, you're not! You're not gonna. You're not! (*She slams the phone down and stares wildly ahead.*) He's not. He's not. (*As she walks over to the ribbon drawer.*) I'll do it. I will. And he won't . . . (*She opens the drawer; pulls out the rope; becomes terrified; throws the rope back in the drawer and slams it shut.* LENNY *enters from the back door swinging the broom and laughing.*)

LENNY Oh, my! Oh, my! You should have seen us! Why, I chased Chick the Stick right up the mimosa tree. I did! I left her right up there screaming in the tree!

BABE (*laughing; she is insanely delighted*) Oh, you did!

LENNY Yes, I did! And I feel so good! I do! I feel good! I feel good!

BABE (*overlapping*) Good! Good, Lenny! Good for you! (*They dance around the kitchen.*)

LENNY (*stopping*) You know what—

BABE What?

LENNY I'm gonna call Charlie!!! I'm gonna call him right now!

BABE You are?

LENNY Yeah, I feel like I can really do it!

BABE You do?

LENNY My courage is up; my heart's in it; the time is right! No more beating around the bush! Let's strike while the iron is hot!

BABE Right! Right! No more beating around the bush! Strike while the iron is hot! (LENNY *goes to the phone.* BABE *rushes over to the ribbon drawer. She begins tearing through it.*)

LENNY (*with the receiver in her hand*) I'm calling him up, Babe—I'm really gonna do it!

BABE (*still tearing through the drawer*) Good! Do it! Good!

LENNY (*as she dials*) Look. My hands aren't even shaking.

BABE (*pulling out a red cord of rope*) Don't we have any stronger rope than this?

LENNY I guess not. All the rope we've got's in that drawer. (*About her hands.*) Now they're shaking a little. (BABE *takes the rope and goes up the stairs.* LENNY *finishes dialing the number. She waits for an answer.*) Hello? . . . Hello, Charlie. This is Lenny Magrath . . . Well, I'm fine. I'm just fine. (*An awkward pause.*) I was, ah, just calling to see—how you're getting on . . . Well, good. Good . . . Yes, I know I said that. Now I wish I didn't say it . . . Well, the reason I said that before, about not seeing each other again, was 'cause of me, not you . . . Well, it's just I—can't have any children. I—have this ovary problem . . . Why, Charlie, what a thing to say! . . . Well, they're not all little snot-nosed pigs! . . . You think they are! . . . Oh, Charlie, stop, stop! You're making me laugh . . . Yes, I guess I was. I can see now that I was . . . You are? . . . Well, I'm dying to see you, too . . . Well, I don't know when, Charlie . . . soon. How about, well, how about tonight? . . . You will? . . . Oh, you will! . . . All right, I'll be here. I'll be right here . . . Goodbye, then, Charlie. Goodbye for now. (*She hangs up the phone in a daze.*) Babe. Oh, Babe! He's coming. He's coming! Babe! Oh, Babe, where are you? Meg! Oh . . . out back—picking up paw paws. (*As she exits through the back door.*) And those paw paws are just ripe for picking up!

(*There is a moment of silence, then a loud, horrible thud is heard coming from upstairs. The telephone begins ringing immediately. It rings five times before* BABE *comes hurrying down the stairs with a broken piece of rope hanging around her neck. The phone continues to ring.*)

BABE (*to the phone*) Will you shut up! (*She is jerking the rope from around her neck. She grabs a knife to cut it off.*) Cheap! Miserable! I hate you! I hate you! (*She throws the rope violently around the room. The phone stops ringing.*) Thank God. (*She looks at the stove, goes over to it, and turns the gas on. The sound of gas escaping is heard.* BABE *sniffs at it.*) Come on. Come on . . . Hurry up . . . I beg of you—hurry up! (*Finally,* BABE *feels the oven is ready; she takes a deep breath and opens the oven door to stick her head into it. She spots the rack and furiously jerks it out. Taking another breath, she sticks her head into the oven. She stands for several moments tapping her fingers furiously on top of the stove. She speaks from inside the oven . . .*) Oh, please. Please. (*After a few moments, she reaches for the box of matches with her head still in the oven. She tries to strike a match. It doesn't catch.*) Oh, Mama, please! (*She throws the match away and is getting a second one.*) Mama . . . Mama . . . So that's why you done it!

(*In her excitement she starts to get up, bangs her head and falls back in the stove.* MEG *enters from the back door, carrying a birthday cake in a pink box.*)

MEG Babe! (MEG *throws the box down and runs to pull* BABE'S *head out of the oven.*) Oh, my God! What are you doing? What the hell are you doing?

BABE (*dizzily*) Nothing. I don't know. Nothing. (MEG *turns off the gas and moves* BABE *to a chair near the open door.*)

MEG Sit down. Sit down! Will you sit down!

BABE I'm okay. I'm okay.

MEG Put your head between your knees and breathe deep!

BABE Meg—

MEG Just do it! I'll get you some water. (MEG *gets some water for* BABE.) Here.

BABE Thanks.

MEG Are you okay?

BABE Uh-huh.

MEG Are you sure?

BABE Yeah, I'm sure. I'm okay.

MEG (*getting a damp rag and putting it over her own face*) Well good. That's good.

BABE Meg—

MEG Yes?

BABE I know why she did it.

MEG What? Why who did what?

BABE (*with joy*) Mama. I know why she hung that cat along with her.

MEG You do?

BABE (*with enlightenment*) It's 'cause she was afraid of dying all alone.

MEG Was she?

BABE She felt so unsure, you know, as to what was coming. It seems the best thing coming up would be a lot of angels and all of them singing. But I imagine they have high, scary voices and little gold pointed fingers that are as sharp as blades and you don't want to meet 'em all alone. You'd be afraid to meet 'em all alone. So it wasn't like what people were saying about her hating that cat. Fact is, she loved that cat. She needed him with her 'cause she felt so all alone.

MEG Oh, Babe . . . Babe. Why, Babe? Why?

BABE Why what?

MEG Why did you stick your head into the oven?!

BABE I don't know, Meg. I'm having a bad day. It's been a real bad day; those pictures; and Barnette giving up his vendetta; then Willie Jay, heading north; and—Zackery called me up. (*Trembling with terror.*) He says he's gonna have me classified insane and send me on out to the Whitfield asylum.

MEG What! Why, he could never do that!

BABE Why not?

MEG 'Cause you're not insane.

BABE I'm not?

MEG No! He's trying to bluff you. Don't you see it? Barnette's got him running scared.

BABE Really?

MEG Sure. He's scared to death—calling you insane. Ha! Why, you're just as perfectly sane as anyone walking the streets of Hazlehurst, Mississippi.

BABE I am?

MEG More so! A lot more so!

BABE Good!

MEG But, Babe, we've just got to learn how to get through these real bad days here. I mean, it's getting to be a thing in our family. (*Slight pause as she looks at* BABE.) Come on now. Look, we've got Lenny's cake right here. I mean don't you wanna be around to give her her cake; watch her blow out the candles?

BABE (*realizing how much she wants to be here*) Yeah, I do, I do. Cause she always loves to make her birthday wishes on those candles.

MEG Well, then we'll give her her cake and maybe you won't be so miserable.

BABE Okay.

MEG Good. Go on and take it out of the box.

BABE Okay. (*She takes the cake out of the box. It is a magical moment.*) Gosh, it's a pretty cake.

MEG (*handing her some matches*) Here now. You can go on and light up the candles.

BABE All right. (*She starts to light the candles.*) I love to light up candles. And there are so many here. Thirty pink ones in all plus one green one to grow on.

MEG (*watching her light the candles*) They're pretty.

BABE They are. (*She stops lighting the candles.*) And I'm not like Mama. I'm not so all alone.

MEG You're not.

BABE (*as she goes back to lighting candles*) Well, you'd better keep an eye out for Lenny. She's supposed to be surprised.

MEG All right. Do you know where she's gone?

BABE Well, she's not here inside—so she must have gone on outside.

MEG Oh, well, then I'd better run and find her.

BABE Okay 'cause these candles are gonna melt down. (MEG *starts out the door.*)

MEG Wait—there she is coming. Lenny! Oh, Lenny! Come on! Hurry up!

BABE (*overlapping and improvising as she finishes lighting candles*) Oh, no! No! Well, yes—yes! No, wait! Wait! Okay! (LENNY *enters.* MEG *covers* LENNY's *eyes with her hands.*)

LENNY (*terrified*) What?! What is it?!! What?!!

MEG & BABE Surprise! Happy Birthday! Happy Birthday to Lenny!!

LENNY Oh, no! Oh me!!! What a surprise! I could just cry! Oh, look, "Happy Birthday to Lenny—A Day Late!" How cute! My! Will you look at all those candles—it's absolutely frightening.

BABE (*spontaneous thought*) Oh, no, Lenny, it's good! 'Cause—'cause the more candles you have on your cake, the stronger your wish is.

LENNY Really?

BABE Sure!

LENNY Mercy. (*They start the song.* LENNY, *interrupting the song.*) Oh, but wait! I—I can't think of my wish! My body's gone all nervous inside.

MEG For God's sake, Lenny—come on!

BABE The wax is all melting!

LENNY My mind is just a blank, a total blank!

MEG Will you please just—

BABE (*overlapping*) Lenny, hurry! Come on!

LENNY Okay! Okay! Just go!! (MEG *and* BABE *burst into the* "Happy Birthday Song." *As it ends* LENNY *blows out all of the candles on the cake.* MEG *and* BABE *applaud loudly.*)

MEG Oh, you made it!

BABE Hurray!

LENNY Oh, me! Oh, me! I hope that wish comes true! I hope it does!

BABE Why? What did you wish for?

LENNY (*as she removes the candles from the cake*) Why. I can't tell you that.

BABE Oh, sure you can—

LENNY Oh, no! Then it won't come true.

BABE Why, that's just superstition! Of course it will, if you made it deep enough.

MEG Really? I didn't know that.

LENNY Well, Babe's the regular expert on birthday wishes.

BABE It's just I get these feelings. Now come on and tell us. What was it you wished for?

MEG Yes, tell us. What was it?

LENNY Well, I guess, it wasn't really a specific wish. This—this vision just sort of came into my mind.

BABE A vision? What was it of?

LENNY I don't know exactly. It was something about the three of us smiling and laughing together.

BABE Well, when was it? Was it far away or near?

LENNY I'm not sure, but it wasn't forever; it wasn't for every minute. Just this one moment and we were all laughing.

BABE What were we laughing about?

LENNY I don't know. Just nothing I guess.

MEG Well, that's a nice wish to make. *(LENNY and MEG look at each other a moment.)* Here, now, I'll get a knife so we can go ahead and cut the cake in celebration of Lenny being born!

BABE Oh, yes! And give each one of us a rose. A whole rose apiece!

LENNY *(cutting the cake nervously)* Well, I'll try—I'll try!

MEG *(licking the icing off a candle)* Mmmm—this icing is delicious! Here, try some!

BABE Mmmm! It's wonderful! Here, Lenny!

LENNY *(laughing joyously as she licks icing from her fingers and cuts huge pieces of cake that her sisters bite into ravenously)* Oh, how I do love having birthday cake for breakfast! How I do! *(The sisters freeze for a moment laughing and eating cake; the lights change and frame them in a magical, golden, sparkling glimmer; saxophone music is heard. The lights dim to blackout, and the saxophone continues to play.)*

END OF PLAY

Questions

1. What is the relationship between Chick and Lenny? Why does Chick look down on the Magraths?
2. Why do you suppose Babe shot Zackery?
3. What is particularly comic about Babe's entrance on p. 1455 and the several lines of dialogue following?
4. What is Meg's chief character flaw? Do you like her in spite of it?
5. Explain the relationship between Meg and Doc.
6. The Magraths have inherited a capacity for suffering. How does their family history relate to their present misfortunes?
7. How does Lenny change over the course of the drama?
8. *The New York Times* drama critic wrote that "*Crimes of the Heart* is finally the story of how its young characters escape the past to seize the future." Do you agree or not? Explain.

New Directions in Staging: *A Son, Come Home*

The story that Ed Bullins is telling in his poignant one-act play, *A Son, Come Home*, is thoroughly realistic. The young man who comes home to visit his mother in Philadelphia finds it difficult to relate to her. They have both changed. He has become a writer, and she has joined a group of charismatic Christians. Yet they yearn to make some connection, particularly to understand their past together. Their tragedy is that, though they obviously love each other, the mother and child cannot reconcile their differences or forgive each other for their past disagreements.

While the story is realistic, the theatrical technique is quite innovative and rather bizarre, especially as it appears on the page. In live performance it would

Ed Bullins *(Woodward
Associates & BMT Productions,
San Francisco, CA)*

not be so confusing. The main part of the play is acted out in the present
between the Mother and Son, who maintain their characters throughout. But
there are two other actors onstage dramatizing the story: the Boy and the Girl.
These are *not* a boy and a girl at all, they are full-grown actors dressed in tights,
who play a number of different roles, mostly from the Mother's and Son's past.
For instance, at first the "Boy" is playing the Son as he tries to find his mother
in her apartment, and the "Girl" is playing a neighbor in the same building.

Then the Girl actress plays the Son's Aunt Sophie in California, as the
Boy actor plays the Son, in several important scenes that dramatize his recent
misfortunes in California. Several times the Boy and the Girl are simply playing
the Son and Mother in scenes from their past.

It may be helpful to clear a space in front of the classroom, set up the two
chairs and "act out" this short play during your class time.

Poet, short-story writer, novelist, and the author of more than fifty plays, Ed
Bullins is one of the most gifted dramatists to emerge from the black arts movement of the late 1960s.

He was born in 1935 and raised in North Philadelphia. After high school he
went into the navy. In 1958 he went to Los Angeles where he enrolled at Los
Angeles City College and began writing short stories and poetry. In 1964 he went
to San Francisco State College and began writing plays, under the influence of

Ionesco and other playwrights of the "theater of the absurd." His first play realistically depicting street people and tenement dwellers was *Clara's Old Man*. This was the first play in a trilogy that would include *A Son, Come Home* and win Bullins the Vernon Rice Drama Desk award when it was produced in New York in 1968.

Between 1968 and 1980 more than 25 of his plays were produced in New York, ten of them at the New Lafayette Theatre in Harlem, and 15 at such theaters as La Mama, The Public Theater, and Lincoln Center. His honors include the 1975 New York Drama Critic's Circle Award, two Guggenheim Fellowships, three Rockefeller Grants, and an honorary doctorate of letters from Columbia College in Chicago.

ED BULLINS (1935–)

A Son, Come Home

A Son, Come Home was first produced at the American Place Theatre on March 26th, 1968. It was directed by Robert MacBeth, with scenery by John Jay Moore and lighting by Roger Morgan. The cast was as follows:

MOTHER, early 50's	Estelle Evans
SON, 30 years old	Wayne Grice
THE GIRL	Kelly-Marie Berry
THE BOY	Gary Bolling

Music for the production was composed by Gordon Watkins.

The BOY *and the* GIRL *wear black tights and shirts. They move the action of the play and express the* MOTHER'S *and the* SON'S *moods and tensions. They become various embodiments recalled from memory and history: they enact a number of personalities and move from mood to mood.*

The players are Black.

At rise: Scene: Bare stage but for two chairs positioned so as not to interfere with the actions of the BOY *and the* GIRL.

The MOTHER *enters, sits in chair and begins to use imaginary iron and board. She hums a spiritual as she works.*

MOTHER You came three times . . . Michael? It took you three times to find me at home?

(*The* GIRL *enters, turns and peers through the cracked, imaginary door*)

SON'S VOICE (*Offstage*) Is Mrs. Brown home?
GIRL (*An old woman*) What?
MOTHER It shouldn't have taken you three times. I told you that I would be here by two and you should wait, Michael.

(*The* SON *enters, passes the* GIRL *and takes his seat upon the other chair.*

The BOY *enters, stops on other side of the imaginary door and looks through at the* GIRL)

BOY Is Mrs. Brown in?

GIRL Miss Brown ain't come in yet. Come back later . . . She'll be in before dark.

MOTHER It shouldn't have taken you three times . . . You should listen to me, Michael. Standin' all that time in the cold.

SON It wasn't cold, Mother.

MOTHER I told you that I would be here by two and you should wait, Michael.

BOY Please tell Mrs. Brown that her son's in town to visit her.

GIRL You little Miss Brown's son? Well, bless the Lord. (*Calls over her shoulder*) Hey, Mandy, do you hear that? Little Miss Brown upstairs got a son . . . a great big boy . . . He's come to visit her.

BOY You'll tell her, won't you?

GIRL Sure, I'll tell her. (*Grins and shows gums*) I'll tell her soon as she gets in.

MOTHER Did you get cold, Michael?

SON No, Mother. I walked around some . . . sightseeing.

BOY I walked up Twenty-third Street toward South. I had phoned that I was coming.

MOTHER Sightseeing? But this is your home, Michael . . . always has been.

BOY Just before I left New York I phoned that I was taking the bus. Two hours by bus, that's all. That's all it takes. Two hours.

SON This town seems so strange. Different than how I remember it.

MOTHER Yes, you have been away for a good while . . . How long has it been, Michael?

BOY Two hours down the Jersey Turnpike, the trip beginning at the New York Port Authority Terminal . . .

SON . . . and then straight down through New Jersey to Philadelphia . . .

GIRL . . . and home . . . Just imagine . . . little Miss Brown's got a son who's come home.

SON Yes, home . . . an anachronism.

MOTHER What did you say, Michael?

BOY He said . . .

GIRL (*Late teens*) What's an anachronism, Mike?

SON Anachronism: 1: an error in chronology; *esp*: a chronological misplacing of persons, events, objects, or customs in regard to each other 2: a person or a thing that is chronologically out of place—anachronistic/ *also* anachronic/ *or* anachronous— anachronistically/ *also* anachronously.

MOTHER I was so glad to hear you were going to school in California.

BOY College.

GIRL Yes, I understand.

MOTHER How long have you been gone, Michael?

SON Nine years.

BOY Nine years it's been. I wonder if she'll know me . . .

MOTHER You've put on so much weight, son. You know that's not healthy.

GIRL (*20 years old*) And that silly beard . . . how . . .

SON Oh . . . I'll take it off. I'm going on a diet tomorrow.

BOY I wonder if I'll know her.

SON You've put on some yourself, Mother.

MOTHER Yes, the years pass. Thank the Lord.

BOY I wonder if we've changed much.

GIRL Yes, thank the Lord.

SON The streets here seem so small.

MOTHER Yes, it seems like that when you spend a little time in Los Angeles.

GIRL I spent eighteen months there with your aunt when she was sick. She had nobody else to help her . . . she was so lonely. And you were in the service . . . away. You've always been away.

BOY In Los Angeles the boulevards, the avenues, the streets . . .

SON . . . are wide. Yes, they have some wide ones out West. Here, they're so small and narrow. I wonder how cars get through on both sides.

MOTHER Why, you know how . . . we lived on Derby Street for over ten years, didn't we?

SON Yeah, that was almost an alley.

MOTHER Did you see much of your aunt before you left Los Angeles?

SON What?

GIRL (*Middle-aged woman*) (*To* BOY) Have you found a job yet, Michael?

MOTHER Your aunt. My sister.

BOY Nawh, not yet . . . Today I just walked downtown . . . quite a ways . . . this place is plenty big, ain't it?

SON I don't see too much of Aunt Sophie.

MOTHER But you're so much alike.

GIRL Well, your bags are packed and are sitting outside the door.

BOY My bags?

MOTHER You shouldn't be that way, Michael. You shouldn't get too far away from your family.

SON Yes, Mother.

BOY But I don't have any money. I had to walk downtown today. That's how much money I have. I've only been here a week.

GIRL I packed your bags, Michael.

MOTHER You never can tell when you'll need or want your family, Michael.

SON That's right, Mother.

MOTHER You and she are so much alike.

BOY Well, goodbye, Aunt Sophie.

GIRL (*Silence*)

MOTHER All that time in California and you hardly saw your aunt. My baby sister.

BOY Tsk tsk tsk.

SON I'm sorry, Mother.

MOTHER In the letters I'd get from both of you there'd be no mention of the other. All these years. Did you see her again?

SON Yes.

GIRL (*On telephone*) Michael? Michael who? . . . Ohhh . . . Bernice's boy.

MOTHER You didn't tell me about this, did you?

SON No, I didn't.

BOY Hello, Aunt Sophie. How are you?

GIRL I'm fine, Michael. How are you? You're looking well.

BOY I'm getting on okay.

MOTHER I prayed for you.

SON Thank you.

MOTHER Thank the Lord, Michael.

BOY Got me a job working for the city.

GIRL You did now.

BOY Yes, I've brought you something.

GIRL What's this, Michael . . . ohhh . . . it's money.

BOY It's for the week I stayed with you.

GIRL Fifty dollars. But, Michael, you didn't have to.

MOTHER Are you still writing that radical stuff, Michael?

SON Radical?

MOTHER Yes . . . that stuff you write and send me all the time in those little books.

SON My poetry, Mother?

MOTHER Yes, that's what I'm talking about.

SON No.

MOTHER Praise the Lord, son. Praise the Lord. Didn't seem like anything I had read in school.

BOY (*On telephone*) Aunt Sophie? . . . Aunt Sophie? . . . It's me, Michael . . .

GIRL Michael?

BOY Yes . . . Michael . . .

GIRL Oh . . . Michael . . . yes . . .

BOY I'm in jail, Aunt Sophie . . . I got picked up for drunk driving.

GIRL You did . . . how awful . . .

MOTHER When you going to get your hair cut, Michael?

BOY Aunt Sophie . . . will you please come down and sign my bail. I've got the money . . . I just got paid yesterday . . . They're holding more than enough for me . . . but the law says that someone has to sign for it.

MOTHER You look almost like a hoodlum, Michael.

BOY All you need to do is come down and sign . . . and I can get out.

MOTHER What you tryin' to be . . . a savage or something? Are you keeping out of trouble, Michael?

GIRL Ohhh . . . Michael . . . I'm sorry but I can't do nothin' like that . . .

BOY But all you have to do is sign . . . I've got the money and everything . . .

GIRL I'm sorry . . . I can't stick my neck out.

BOY But, Aunt Sophie . . . if I don't get back to work I'll lose my job and everything . . . please . . .

GIRL I'm sorry, Michael . . . I can't stick my neck out . . . I have to go now . . . Is there anyone I can call?

BOY No.

GIRL I could call your mother. She wouldn't mind if I reversed the charges on her, would she? I don't like to run my bills up.

BOY No, thanks.

MOTHER You and your aunt are so much alike.

SON Yes, Mother. Our birthdays are in the same month.

MOTHER Yes, that year was so hot . . . so hot and I was carrying you . . .

(*As the* MOTHER *speaks the* BOY *comes over and takes her by the hand and leads her from the chair, and they stroll around the stage, arm in arm.*

The GIRL *accompanies them and she and the* BOY *enact scenes from the* MOTHER's *mind*)

. . . carrying you, Michael . . . and you were such a big baby . . . kicked all the time. But I was happy. Happy that I was having a baby of my own . . . I worked as long as I could and bought you everything you might need . . . diapers . . . and bottles . . . and your own spoon . . . and even toys . . . and even books . . . And it was so hot in Philadelphia that year . . . Your Aunt Sophie used to come over and we'd go for walks . . . sometimes up on the avenue . . . I was living in West Philly then . . . in that old terrible section they called "The Bottom." That's where I met your father.

GIRL You're such a fool, Bernice. No nigger . . . man or boy's . . . ever going to do a thing to me like that.

MOTHER Everything's going to be all right, Sophia.

GIRL But what is he going to do? How are you going to take care of a baby by yourself?

MOTHER Everything's going to be all right, Sophia. I'll manage.

GIRL You'll manage? How? Have you talked about marriage?

MOTHER Oh, please, Sophia!

GIRL What do you mean "please"? Have you?

MOTHER I just can't. He might think . . .

GIRL Think! That dirty nigger better think. He better think before he really messes up. And you better too. You got this baby comin' on. What are you going to do?

MOTHER I don't know . . . I don't know what I can do.

GIRL Is he still tellin' you those lies about . . .

MOTHER They're not lies.

GIRL Haaaa . . .

MOTHER They're not.

GIRL Some smooth-talkin' nigger comes up from Georgia and tell you he escaped from the chain gang and had to change his name so he can't get married 'cause they might find out . . . What kinda shit is that, Bernice?

MOTHER Please, Sophia. Try and understand. He loves me. I can't hurt him.

GIRL Loves you . . . and puts you through this?

MOTHER Please . . . I'll talk to him . . . Give me a chance.

GIRL It's just a good thing you got a family, Bernice. It's just a good thing. You know that, don't cha?

MOTHER Yes . . . yes, I do . . . but please don't say anything to him.

SON I've only seen my father about a half dozen times that I remember, Mother. What was he like?

MOTHER Down in The Bottom . . . that's where I met your father. I was young and hinkty then. Had big pretty brown legs and a small waist. Everybody used to call me Bernie . . . and me and my sister would go to Atlantic City on the weekends and work as waitresses in the evenings and sit all afternoon on the black part of the beach at Boardwalk and Atlantic . . . getting blacker . . . and having the times of our lives. Your father probably still lives down in The Bottom . . . perched over some bar down there . . . drunk to the world . . . I can see him now . . . He had good white teeth then . . . not how they turned later when he started in drinkin' that wine and wouldn't stop . . . he was so nice then.

BOY Awwww, listen, kid. I got my problems too.

GIRL But Andy . . . I'm six months gone . . . and you ain't done nothin'.

BOY Well, what can I do?

GIRL Don't talk like that . . . What can you do? . . . You know what you can do.

BOY You mean marry you? Now lissen, sweetheart . . .

GIRL But what about our baby?

BOY Your baby.

GIRL Don't talk like that! It took more than me to get him.

BOY Well . . . look . . . I'll talk to you later, kid. I got to go to work now.

GIRL That's what I got to talk to you about too, Andy. I need some money.

BOY Money! Is somethin' wrong with your head, woman? I ain't got no money.

GIRL But I can't work much longer, Andy. You got to give me some money. Andy . . . you just gotta.

BOY Woman . . . all I got to *ever* do is die and go to hell.

GIRL Well, you gonna do that, Andy. You sho are . . . you know that, don't you? . . . You know that.

MOTHER . . . Yes, you are, man. Praise the Lord. We all are . . . All of us . . . even though he ain't come for you yet to make you pay. Maybe he's waitin' for us to go together so I can be a witness to the retribution that's handed down. A witness to all that He'll bestow upon your sinner's head . . . A witness! . . . That's what I am, Andy! Do you hear me? . . . A witness!

SON Mother . . . what's wrong? What's the matter?

MOTHER Thank the Lord that I am not blinded and will see the fulfillment of divine . . .

SON Mother!

MOTHER Oh . . . is something wrong, Michael?

SON You're shouting and walking around . . .

MOTHER Oh . . . it's nothing, son. I'm just feeling the power of the Lord.

SON Oh . . . is there anything I can get you, Mother?

MOTHER No, nothing at all. (*She sits again and irons*)

SON Where's your kitchen? . . . I'll get you some coffee . . . the way you like it. I bet I still remember how to fix it.

MOTHER Michael . . . I don't drink anything like that no more.

SON No?

MOTHER Not since I joined the service of the Lord.

SON Yeah? . . . Well, do you mind if I get myself a cup?

MOTHER Why, I don't have a kitchen. All my meals are prepared for me.

SON Oh . . . I thought I was having dinner with you.

MOTHER No. There's nothing like that here.

SON Well, could I take you out to a restaurant? . . . Remember how we used to go out all the time and eat? I've never lost my habit of liking to eat out. Remember . . . we used to come down to this part of town and go to restaurants. They used to call it home cooking then . . . now, at least where I been out West and up in Harlem . . . we call it soul food. I bet we could find a nice little restaurant not four blocks from here, Mother. Remember that old man's place we used to go to on Nineteenth and South? I bet he's dead now . . . but . . .

MOTHER I don't even eat out no more, Michael.

SON No?

MOTHER Sometimes I take a piece of holy bread to work . . . or some fruit . . . if it's been blessed by my Spiritual Mother.

SON I see.

MOTHER Besides . . . we have a prayer meeting tonight.

SON On Friday?

MOTHER Every night. You'll have to be going soon.

SON Oh.

MOTHER You're looking well.

SON Thank you.

MOTHER But you look tired.

SON Do I?

MOTHER Yes, those rings around your eyes might never leave. Your father had them.

SON Did he?

MOTHER Yes . . . and cowlicks . . . deep cowlicks on each side of his head.

SON Yes . . . I remember.

MOTHER Do you?

(*The* BOY *and the* GIRL *take crouching positions behind and in front of them. They are in a streetcar. The* BOY *behind the* MOTHER *and* SON, *the* GIRL *across the aisle, a passenger*)

MOTHER (*Young woman*) (*To the* BOY) Keep your damn hands off him, Andy!

BOY (*Chuckles*) Awww, c'mon . . . Bernie. I ain't seen him since he was in the crib.

MOTHER And you wouldn't have seen neither of us . . . if I had anything to do with it . . . Ohhh . . . why did I get on this trolley?

BOY C'mon . . . Bernie . . . don't be so stuckup.

MOTHER Don't even talk to us . . . and stop reaching after him.

BOY Awww . . . c'mon . . . Bernie. Let me look at him.

MOTHER Leave us alone. Look . . . people are looking at us.

(*The* GIRL *across the aisle has been peeking at the trio but looks toward front at the mention of herself*)

BOY Hey, big boy . . . do you know who I am?

MOTHER Stop it, Andy! Stop it, I say . . . Mikie . . . don't pay any attention to him . . . you hear?

BOY Hey, big boy . . . know who I am? . . . I'm your daddy. Hey, there . . .

MOTHER Shut up . . . shut up, Andy . . . you nothin' to us.

BOY Where you livin' at . . . Bernie? Let me come on by and see the little guy, huh?

MOTHER No! You're not comin' near us . . . ever . . . you hear?

BOY But I'm his father . . . look . . . Bernie . . . I've been an ass the way I've acted but . . .

MOTHER He ain't got no father.

BOY Oh, come off that nonsense, woman.

MOTHER Mikie ain't got no father . . . his father's dead . . . you hear?

BOY Dead?

MOTHER Yes, dead. My son's father's dead.

BOY What you talkin' about? . . . He's the spittin' image of me.

MOTHER Go away . . . leave us alone, Andrew.

BOY See there . . . he's got the same name as me. His first name is Michael after your father . . . and Andrew after me.

MOTHER No, stop that, you hear?

BOY Michael Andrew . . .

MOTHER You never gave him no name . . . his name is Brown . . . Brown. The same as mine . . . and my sister's . . . and my daddy . . . You never gave him nothin' . . . and you're dead . . . go away and get buried.

BOY You know that trouble I'm in . . . I got a wife down there, Bernie. I don't care about her . . . what could I do?

MOTHER (*Rises, pulling up the* SON) We're leavin' . . . don't you try and follow us . . . you hear, Andy? C'mon . . . Mikie . . . watch your step now.

BOY Well . . . bring him around my job . . . you know where I work. That's all . . . bring him around on payday.

MOTHER (*Leaving*) We don't need anything from you . . . I'm working . . . just leave us alone.

(*The* BOY *turns to the* GIRL)

BOY (*Shrugs*) That's the way it goes . . . I guess. Ships passing on the trolley car . . . Hey . . . don't I know you from up around 40th and Market?

(*The* GIRL *turns away*)

SON Yeah . . . I remember him. He always had liquor on his breath.

MOTHER Yes . . . he did. I'm glad that stuff ain't got me no more . . . Thank the Lord.

GIRL (35 years old) You want to pour me another drink, Michael?

BOY (15 years old) You drink too much, Mother.

GIRL Not as much as some other people I know.

BOY Well, me and the guys just get short snorts, Mother. But you really hide some port.

GIRL Don't forget you talkin' to your mother. You gettin' more like your father every day.

BOY Is that why you like me so much?

GIRL (Grins drunkenly) Oh, hush up now, boy . . . and pour me a drink.

BOY There's enough here for me too.

GIRL That's okay . . . when Will comes in he'll bring something.

SON How is Will, Mother?

MOTHER I don't know . . . haven't seen Will in years.

SON Mother.

MOTHER Yes, Michael.

SON Why you and Will never got married? . . . You stayed together for over ten years.

MOTHER Oh, don't ask me questions like that, Michael.

SON But why not?

MOTHER It's just none of your business.

SON But you could be married now . . . not alone in this room . . .

MOTHER Will had a wife and child in Chester . . . you know that.

SON He could have gotten a divorce, Mother . . . Why . . .

MOTHER Because he just didn't . . . that's why.

SON You never hear from him?

MOTHER Last I heard . . . Will had cancer.

SON Oh, he did.

MOTHER Yes.

SON Why didn't you tell me? . . . You could have written.

MOTHER Why?

SON So I could have known.

MOTHER So you could have known? Why?

SON Because Will was like a father to me . . . the only one I've really known.

MOTHER A father? And you chased him away as soon as you got big enough.

SON Don't say that, Mother.

MOTHER You made me choose between you and Will.

SON Mother.

MOTHER The quarrels you had with him . . . the mean tricks you used to play . . . the lies you told to your friends about Will . . . He wasn't much . . . when I thought I had a sense of humor I us'ta call him just plain Will. But we was his family.

SON Mother, listen.

MOTHER And you drove him away . . . and he didn't lift a hand to stop you.

SON Listen, Mother.

MOTHER As soon as you were big enough you did all that you could to get me and Will separated.

SON Listen.

MOTHER All right, Michael . . . I'm listening.

(Pause)

SON Nothing. (*Pause. Lifts an imaginary object*) Is this your tambourine?

MOTHER Yes.

SON Do you play it?

MOTHER Yes.

SON Well?

MOTHER Everything I do in the service of the Lord I do as well as He allows.

SON You play it at your meetings.

MOTHER Yes, I do. We celebrate the life He has bestowed upon us.

SON I guess that's where I get it from.

MOTHER Did you say something, Michael?

SON Yes. My musical ability.

MOTHER Oh . . . you've begun taking your piano lessons again?

SON No . . . I was never any good at that.

MOTHER Yes, three different teachers and you never got past the tenth lesson.

SON You have a good memory, Mother.

MOTHER Sometimes, son. Sometimes.

SON I play an electric guitar in a combo.

MOTHER You do? That's nice.

SON That's why I'm in New York. We got a good break and came East.

MOTHER That's nice, Michael.

SON I was thinking that Sunday I could rent a car and come down to get you and drive you up to see our show. You'll get back in plenty of time to rest for work Monday.

MOTHER No, I'm sorry. I can't do that.

SON But you would like it, Mother. We could have dinner up in Harlem, then go down and . . .

MOTHER I don't do anything like that any more, Michael.

SON You mean you wouldn't come to see me play even if I were appearing here in Philly?

MOTHER That's right, Michael. I wouldn't come. I'm past all that.

SON Oh, I see.

MOTHER Yes, thank the Lord.

SON But it's my life, Mother.

MOTHER Good . . . then you have something to live for.

SON Yes.

MOTHER Well, you're a man now, Michael . . . I can no longer live it for you. Do the best with what you have.

SON Yes . . . Yes, I will, Mother.

GIRL'S VOICE (*Offstage*) Sister Brown . . . Sister Brown . . . hello.

MOTHER (*Uneasy; peers at watch*) Oh . . . it's Mother Ellen . . . I didn't know it was so late.

GIRL (*Enters*) Sister Brown . . . how are you this evening?

MOTHER Oh, just fine, Mother.

GIRL Good. It's nearly time for dinner.

MOTHER Oh, yes, I know.

GIRL We don't want to keep the others waiting at meeting . . . do we?

MOTHER No, we don't.

GIRL (*Self-assured*) Hello, son.

SON Hello.

MOTHER Oh, Mother . . . Mother . .

GIRL Yes, Sister Brown, what is it?

MOTHER Mother . . . Mother . . . this is . . . this is . . . (*Pause*) . . . this is . . .

SON Hello, I'm Michael. How are you?

MOTHER (*Relieved*) Yes, Mother . . . This is Michael . . . my son.

GIRL Why, hello, Michael. I've heard so much about you from your mother. She prays
for you daily.

SON (*Embarrassed*) Oh . . . good.

GIRL (*Briskly*) Well . . . I have to be off to see about the others.

MOTHER Yes, Mother Ellen.

GIRL (*As she exits; chuckles*) Have to tell everyone that you won't be keeping us waiting,
Bernice.

(*Silence*)

SON Well, I guess I better be going, Mother.

MOTHER Yes.

SON I'll write.

MOTHER Please do.

SON I will.

MOTHER You're looking well . . . Thank the Lord.

SON Thank you, so are you, Mother. (*He moves toward her and hesitates*)

MOTHER You're so much like your aunt. Give her my best . . . won't you?

SON Yes, I will, Mother.

MOTHER Take care of yourself, son.

SON Yes, Mother. I will.

(*The SON exits. The MOTHER stands looking after him as the lights go slowly down to . . .*)

BLACKNESS

Questions

1. It is clear from the first lines of the play that Michael had some reluctance to enter
   and wait for his mother in the apartment where she was expecting him. Why?
2. Describe the relationship between Michael's Aunt Sophie and Michael. Is she supportive of her nephew?
3. On p. 1496 a scene from the past takes place on a bus. What roles are the different
   actors playing? What do we discover about Michael's father in this scene?
4. Michael's mother believes that he discouraged her relationship with Will. What do
   you think?
5. How does Michael feel about his mother's religion?
6. At the end of the play Michael's mother says to him: "You're so much like your
   aunt." Do you agree? What does this quote tell you about the Mother of this play?

Glossary of Literary Terms

Action. In a drama, the behavior of characters and succession of events that tell the story. 895–96, 929–35

Allegory. A literary or dramatic device in which the events of a narrative or an implied narrative obviously and continuously refer to another simultaneous structure of events or ideas, whether historical events, moral or philosophical ideas, or natural phenomena. 656–59

Alliteration. The repetition of an initial consonant sound in two or more words of a line (or line group), to produce a noticeable artistic effect, as in "The sails did sigh like sedge" (Coleridge). 709–14

Allusion. Tactic reference to another literary work, to another art, to history, to contemporary figures, and the like. 683–84

Amphitheater. An outdoor theater with tiers of seats rising gradually outward from the central playing area. 934

Amplificatio. The Latin term in classical rhetoric for amplification of style or the expansion of detail and elaboration of effects. 350

Anagnorisis. See *Recognition.*

Anapest. A metrical unit of three syllables, of which the first two are unstressed and the last is stressed. 695

Anaphora. Repetition of the initial word in several successive lines of poetry. 574

Antagonist. A character who forms an obstacle to the protagonist's completion of his goal. See *Villain.* 234

Antistrophe. See *Pindaric ode.*

Note: Page numbers following definitions refer to discussion in the text.

Aside. See *Stage whisper.*

Assonance. As distinguished from rhyme, the repetition of vowel sounds preceded by unlike consonants, as in "Be near me when my light is low." 709–14

Ballad. Usually a narrative poem in quatrains in which the second and fourth lines rhyme. In a ballad, the first and third lines are typically four feet long, and the second and fourth lines three feet long. 547–48, 743–44

Ballade. A form that consists of three eight-line stanzas and an envoi.

Bard. A poet-reciter in a preliterate or semiliterate society; more loosely, a poet or poet-singer. 545, 549

Blank verse. Unrhymed iambic pentameter lines. 694

Brevitas. The Latin term in classical rhetoric for brevity—for concise, to-the-point writing. 350

Caesura. A rhetorical pause within a poetic line, usually in the middle. 702

Carpe diem. A theme in many love poems, in which a lover is implored not to be hesitant in affection (Latin for "seize the day"). 570 live for the moment.

Casting. The selection of actors for a drama.

Catastrophe. The outcome of a tragedy; from the Greek, meaning "a downward turn." 932–33

Catastrophic plot. A drama where the action begins *after* the climactic event, and the emotional climax comes in the discovery of that event.

Catharsis. From Greek "cleansing." The relief that comes after witnessing the catastrophe of a tragedy. 1028

A character. The performer of a fictional action. 228, 976

The Character. A literary form in which a character type is described. The form was originated by the Greek writer Theophrastus. 229

Chiasmus. A rhetorical device in which words initially presented are restated in reverse order. An example is the sentence, "For we that live to please, must please to live." 779

Chorus. In ancient Greek drama, a group of actors who sang and danced in unison, predicting and commenting upon the actions of the main characters. 933

Climax. The point in the story at which protagonists have definitely achieved or failed to achieve their central goal. 172

Climax of dramatic action (turning point). The point at which the hero's fortune turns from good to bad in a tragedy, and from bad to good in a comedy. 931–32

Climax of emotion. The point in a drama that moves the audience most deeply.

Comedy. From the Greek *komos*, meaning revel. A drama that shows the change in the protagonist's fortune from bad to good.

Comedy of ideas. Comedies that support philosophical or political dialogue.

Comedy of manners. High comedy developed during the Restoration, characterized by subtle wit and ingenious dramatic situations that satirize prevailing manners and morals. 1189

Comic relief. In a tragedy, a scene of light humor that provides relief for the spectator after a violent or pathetic scene.

Complication. The introduction of an obstacle to the goal of the protagonist of a drama.

Conceit. An intricate, extended, or far-fetched metaphor or simile that arouses a feeling of surprise, shock, or amusement. 643–47

Concrete poem. A poem in which the visual arrangement of the letters and words suggests the meaning. 767–71

Conflict. The obstacles which prevent the protagonist from achieving his or her goal. In drama, the disagreement between characters or within a character that precipitates the play's action. 171

Connotative meaning. See *Denotative meaning.*

Consistency of character. A convention in which a character's actions are consistent with his or her behavioral traits. 232–33

Corpus. A Latin term used to refer to an author's entire "body" of work. 303

Costume designer. The member of the artistic staff of a dramatic production who creates or appropriates whatever the actors wear in the play. 898

Cothurnus. An elevator shoe used by actors in ancient Greek drama. 935

Couplet. A two-line stanza, usually rhymed. 744–46

Crisis. In drama, the most intense moment of any scene. 931

Cross-purposes. A technique of comic irony, in which two characters think they are discussing the same thing, but are not.

Dactyl. A metrical unit of three syllables, of which the first is stressed and the second two are not. 695

Denotative meaning. Literal meaning; the dictionary meaning as opposed to connotative meaning, which is the associations (historical, evaluative, and economic) the word conveys. For example, *car* and *automobile* refer to the same object, but *automobile* is more formal and old-fashioned than *car.* 625

Denouement. French for "untying." In fiction, the end of the story in which the fate of the characters is clearly set out. In drama, the part of a play that answers our questions. In a comedy, the solving of the problems of the protagonists. 172, 932–33

Deus ex machina. Latin for "the god from the machine." In ancient drama, a god who descended upon the stage to rescue the protagonist from doom. Hence, any unexpected or unlikely event that changes the outcome of a drama.

Developing characters. Characters whose personality traits alter in the course of a story, usually as a result of events narrated in the story. 234

Diction. The writer's choice of words. 735–37

Didactic poetry. Poetry whose purpose is to teach. 728–31

Dimeter. A metrical line with two feet. 694

Director. The head of the artistic staff of a dramatic production. It is the director's responsibility to see that all aspects of production—casting, scenery, lighting, etc.—express the playwrights' intention. 898

Doggerel. Rough, poorly constructed verse, characterized by strong and monotonous rhyme and rhythm, cheap sentiment, triviality, and lack of dignity. 705–7, 774

Double dactyl. A complicated comic form of eight lines, the fourth and eighth of which rhyme.

Drama of character. A drama in which the development of character is more important than the plotting or progress of action.

✓ *Dramatic irony* (also called *irony of situation*). A situation in which the author and the audience share knowledge by which they can recognize the characters' actions as wholly inappropriate, or the characters' words as possessing a significance unknown to the characters themselves. 664, 979.

✓ *Dramatic monologue.* A poem in which the poet adopts a fictive or historical voice, or persona, and from which an entire dramatic scene may be inferred. 592–93

Dramatic situation. The dynamic relation of a character to an objective and its intervening obstacles. 903–4, 929

Dramatis personae. Latin for "the persons in the play." 900–902

Elegy. A lyric, usually formal in tone and diction, suggested either by the death of an actual person or by the poet's contemplation of tragic aspects of life. 575–80

Encomium. A song praising not a god but a hero, sung at the *komos*, the jubilant procession or revels that celebrated the victor in the Olympic games. 571–74

End rhyme. Rhymes at the ends of lines of poetry. 706

End-stopped line. A line that ends where the syntactic unit ends, at a clear pause, or at the end of a sentence. 702

English or Shakespearean sonnet. A fourteen-line poem rhyming *abab cdcd efef gg*. It consists of three quatrains and a closing couplet. 748–49

✓ *Enjambment.* The employment of run-on lines that carry the sense of statement from one line to another without rhetorical or syntactic pause at the end of the line. 702

Envoi. A short concluding section of a poem that bids the poem farewell or contains concluding remarks.

Epic. A long narrative poem. Primary epics are passed down orally and have a legendary author (for example, the *Iliad* and the *Odyssey*, which are traditionally ascribed to Homer). A secondary epic is one written by a known author. 549

Epigram. A poem with the qualities of an inscription, and thus short, pointed, and often with a witty or surprising turn of thought. 582

Epistolary poem. A letter in verse. 599–601

Epode. See *Pindaric ode.* 758–59

Exposition. In fiction, those narrative passages that establish the basic details of the story, such as the setting, time, and characters. In drama, the scenes that introduce the characters and the dramatic situation. 171–72, 930–31, 1030–31

Expressionism. In theater, the dramatization of a character's emotion or thought at the expense of realism. Characters of expressionist dramas tend to be types, the scenes roughly or mysteriously defined.

Extras. Minor characters in a drama who have neither specific names nor significant roles in the progress of the action. 901–2

Fable. A story in which animals are given human attributes and represent moral, philosophic, psychological, or political positions. Fables typically have morals as their conclusions. 659–61

Falling action (also called *declining action,* or *the return*). The scenes of a tragedy that show the hero or heroine as they fall from power. In a comedy, those scenes that show the villains or forces of adversity in decline. 932

Farce. Dramatic comedy relying heavily upon clowning, slap-stick, and improbable romantic situations. 1188–89

Feminine ending. An unstressed syllable at the end of a line. 700

Feminine rhyme. A rhyme in which the similarity of sound is in both of the last two syllables—for example, *dreary/weary.* 706

Figurative language. Language that uses figures of speech and that cannot be taken literally. 635

First-person narrative. A story told in the voice of one of the characters who participates in the action. 116–18

Flat character. A character with a single behavioral trait or a stereotyped group of behaviors. 229

Foils - 2 characters who are opposite that high light each other

Foot. A measurable, patterned unit of poetic rhythm usually consisting of one stressed syllable and one or more unstressed syllables. 694

Formulae. Stock phrases used by poets in reciting oral poems. 545–47

Framed story. A story in which another story is told, frequently by one of the characters. In Chaucer's *Canterbury Tales,* a band of pilgrims journeying to Canterbury Cathedral amuse each other on the way with short tales. The framed story is made up of two parts: (1) the frame, and (2) the tale-within-a-tale. 172–73

Free verse. Poetry that is both unrhymed and without a regular meter, although it may be more or less rhythmical. 741–43

Freytag's pyramid. A diagram of the five-part movement of plot in classic drama. 930

Genre. A term used to describe various types of literature. For example, prose can be divided into fiction, autobiography, biography, history, essays, letters, etc. These genres can be further divided into smaller genres or *sub-genres.* 899–900

Greek Old Comedy. The fantastical satires of Aristophanes (447–380 B.C.). 1188

Groundlings. The spectators who sat or stood on the ground at performances of Elizabethan plays. 1032.

Haiku. An Oriental lyric form of seventeen syllables in three lines of five, seven, and five syllables, respectively. The haiku must state or imply a season and, except for modern innovations, is almost wholly restricted to natural images. 615–16, 703, 762–66

Heptameter. A metrical line with seven feet. 694

Hero. In Greek literature, a noble warrior. The principal male character in a story, poem, or play. 234, 976, 1028–29

Heroic couplet. A rhymed couplet in iambic pentameter whose second line is end-stopped. 744–45

Heroine. The principal female character in a story, poem, or play. 863, 914–15, 976, 1028–29

Hexameter. A metrical line with six feet. 694

High comedy. Comedy appealing to the intellect, depending upon ingenuity of plot and verbal wit. 1188

High diction. Formal literary language. 735–37

High tragedy. Tragedy concerning the fall of noble heroes or heroines. 1027

Horatian ode. An ode that repeats the same irregular stanza pattern throughout. It is personal rather than public, general rather than occasional, tranquil rather than intense, and is intended for the reader in privacy rather than for the spectator in the theater. 757, 759–61

Hyperbole. An exaggeration; a statement that something has either much more or much less of a quality than it truly has. 559–562, 675–78

Iamb. A metrical unit of two syllables in which the second is stressed. 694

✓ *Image.* A direct presentation of sensory experience. 497–504, 614–22

In medias res. Literally, "in the middle of things"—the way in which epics traditionally start. Classical plays, like epics, frequently begin in the middle of a story, *in medias res.* 547

Internal rhyme. Rhyme that occurs in the middle of a line. 708

Invective. See *Satire*

Irony of situation. See *Dramatic irony.*

Irregular ode. An ode in which each stanza has a different irregular shape. 757

Italian or petrarchan sonnet. A poem fourteen lines long and divided between an opening octet and a closing sestet. The rhyme scheme is *abba abba/cdc cdc.* 747–50

Lighting. The illumination of the acting area for purposes of clarity and artistic effect. 898

Lighting designer. The member of the artistic staff of a dramatic production who creates illusions of daylight or nightlight, who specifies changes in light color and intensity contributing to the mood of the play. 898

Limerick. A five-line comic form rhyming *aabba*, of which the first, second, and fifth lines are trimeter and the third and fourth dimeter. 767

Limited third-person narrative. A story told by a voice which is outside the action, but which limits itself to the thoughts and perceptions of one of the characters. 120

Literary ballad. A ballad intended to be read rather than sung. 743–44

Low comedy. Comedy that plays upon the audience's lowest sense of humor, the impulse to laugh when someone else suffers physical discomfort or indignity. 1188

Low diction. Street language; simple or vulgar words. 735–37

Lyric. A highly concentrated poem of direct personal emotion, most often written in the first person. Lyric poetry is generally considered the most intense genre of poetry, the form that most honors its musical origins. The love poem, the elegy, and the meditation are all forms of lyric poetry. 566–71

Main plot. The principal sequence of actions of a narrative or drama. 351

Masculine ending. A stressed syllable at the end of a line. 700

Masculine rhyme. A rhyme in which the similarity of sounds is in the final syllables of the words involved. 706

Melodrama. A sensational form of nineteenth-century drama, in which organ music often accompanied the action. Thus, any sensational and romantic drama, usually with a happy ending. 978

Metaphor. A figure of speech in which a person, an object, or an idea is imaginatively transformed, as in "The grass is itself a child, the produced babe of the vegetation" (Whitman). A metaphor may be suggested by comparison, but it need not be. 635–41, 685

Meter. The measure of stressed and unstressed syllables in lines of poetry. When stresses occur at regular intervals, the poetry is said to have regular meter. 694–99

Metonymy. A figure of speech in which a single name of a person, place, or thing comes to stand for a more complex situation or experience with which the name is associated—for example, *Washington* for the U.S. government, *the press* for the enterprise of journalism. 680–83

Microcosm. Means "a small world." In fiction it refers to a model which, in miniature, depicts events and processes going on in the larger world. For example, a family squabble might be a microcosm of a disagreement between nations. 350

Mimesis - imitation

Monometer. A metrical line of one foot. 694

Motivation. The reason a character performs an action. 231–32

Narrative. The recounting of actions in prose or poetic form. 116–21, 145–47, 171–72

Narrative focus. Occurs when less important narrative events are subordinated to the more important ones. 169

Narrator. The voice that tells the story. See *First-person narrative, Limited third-person narrative,* and *Omniscient third-person narrative.*

Near rhyme. Two words or syllables that have approximate sounds, such as "lids" and "lads." 708

The New Comedy. Ancient Greek comedy as first practiced by Menander (342–292 B.C.), portraying domestic situations and contemporary manners, and usually involving a love affair. 1189

Novel. A lengthy work of prose fiction depicting a number of characters in various settings covering a relatively long period of time. 349

Novella. A combination of the short story and novel. It usually develops one aspect as completely as does a novel, but compresses other aspects, as in a short story. 349–52

Objective. In drama, the goal that motivates a character's actions. 976

Obstacle. In a dramatic situation, a person or circumstance that comes between the protagonist and his or her objective. 976

Octave. An eight-line stanza or section; often, the first eight lines of an Italian or Petrarchan sonnet. 747

Octometer. A metrical line with eight feet, rare in English. 694

Ode. The name of the most formal, ceremonious, and complexly organized form of lyric poetry, usually of considerable length. The ode is often used as a poem of praise for a formal occasion such as a marriage, a funeral, or a state ceremonial. 583–85, 757–62

Off rhyme. See *Near rhyme.*

Offstage. The area beyond that which the audience sees on stage—the rest of the imaginary world from which the characters enter and into which they exit. 902

Omniscient third-person narrative. A story told by the voice of a person outside the action who can read the thoughts of the characters and is aware of everything that takes place. 117

One act play. A play performed without intermission, with a few characters, a single setting and (usually) a single story. 900

Onomatopoeia. A word whose sound imitates the actual sound to which it refers, such as *pop*, *sizzle* and *crash*. 710–14

Onstage. The acting or playing area of a theater. 902

Orchestra. In the ancient Greek theater, the playing area, located between the scene proper and the audience, where the chorus performed. 934

Oxymoron. A phrase that combines two seemingly contradictory elements, such as *icy heat, loud silence, painful ease*. 685–86

✓ *Paradox.* A seemingly contradictory statement. 684–87

Partial rhyme. See *Near rhyme.*

Pastoral. An artistic work that contains an urban nostalgia for the simplicity of the shepherd's life and of country conventions, and which thus depicts rural living in a highly idealized and stylized manner; a classical dialogue between shepherds.

Pathos. Feelings of tender sympathy often evoked by the closing scenes of a drama. 933

Pentameter. A metrical line with five feet. 694

Peripeteia. See *Reversal.*

✓ *Persona.* The speaker of the poem, who may or may not be the same as the poet. 540–44

Personification. The granting of human attributes to things that are not human. 654–55

Petrarchan sonnet. See *Italian sonnet.*

Pindaric ode. An ode of three parts—strophe, antistrophe, and epode. The strophe and antistrophe are the same irregularly shaped form, invented by the poet for each ode. The epode contrasts in shape. 583, 757–59

Play of atmosphere. A drama which has several equally important characters, instead of an obvious protagonist. 977–78

Playwright. The writer of the play script, the composer of the dialogue and action of a play. 897–98

Plot. The choice and arrangement of events within a story, the order of scenes in a drama. In classical drama, the articulation of a story in scenes of exposition, rising action, climax, falling action, and catastrophe or denouement. 167–74, 930

Popular ballad. A ballad passed on orally, with no known author. 546–47

Posthumous monologue. A poem spoken by the dead. 604

Premiere. The first performance of a drama.

Primary epic. See *Epic*.

Producer. The individual responsible for bringing a play to an audience. The producer selects the script, hires the artistic staff, and provides the performance space for the play. 898

Production. All the elements contributing to the presentation of a drama to an audience.

Proscenium. The part of the stage in front of the curtain. The proscenium arch is the structure separating the playing area from the audience. The "proscenium" stage is the sort in most school auditoriums. 902

Prose poem. A form that uses imagery and figurative language but forfeits the effects of versification, meter, and line endings.

Protagonist. The central character of a drama or other literary work. See *Hero*. 172, 977

Psalm. A sacred song or hymn, such as any of the sacred songs collected in the Old Testament Book of Psalms. Psalms are organized through a complex series of parallel and opposed ideas. 742

Psychomachia. Literally, "conflict of the soul"; a work in which parts of the personality or mind are in conflict with one another, sometimes depicted as an inner debate or quarrel.

Pun. A play on words with similar sounds or on a single word with different meanings. 735

Pyrrhic. A metrical unit of two unaccented syllables. 696

Quantitative meter. Meter determined by the duration of syllables rather than by their accents. 715

Quatrain. A stanza of four lines, rhymed or unrhymed. 548, 743

Realism. A quality in fiction and drama in which the events depicted correspond to events that might occur in real life. Realistic art avoids supernatural occurrences or improbable coincidences. In drama, realism is a 19th and 20th century theatrical convention. Dramatic realism avoids all that is improbable in events and characters, and all that is fantastic in presentation. 78–79, 1316, 1368

Recognition. A scene in which a dramatic character becomes aware of the nature of his predicament, or the weakness of character that has caused it. 1027–28

Reversal. A change from bad to good fortune in a comedy, from good to bad in a tragedy. 1027–28

Rhyme. The occurrence of the same stressed vowel sounds in two words, such as in *spring–sing, dies–eyes, day–gray.* This is known as perfect rhyme and assumes that the accented vowel sounds involved are preceded by different consonant sounds. For variations, see *Feminine rhyme, Internal rhyme, Near rhyme,* and *Masculine rhyme.* 705–9

Rhyme scheme. A pattern of rhyme throughout a stanza or poem. 706–7

Rising action. The scenes in which the chief characters of a drama begin pursuing their objectives in earnest. 931

Romantic comedy. A comic drama in which there is a love interest. 1189

Round characters. Characters who have a variety of personality traits and seem to have a life that extends beyond the story. 231

Satire. The ridiculing of any human vice or folly, frequently by means of exaggeration. When such attacks lose their humor, they become *invective.* 1229

Scansion. The system of describing more or less conventional poetic rhythms by visual symbols for purposes of metrical analysis and study. 693–94

Scene. A unit of dramatic action which tells one part of the play's story. An action that takes place in a specific time and place. See *Set.* 902–3

Script. The dialogue and stage directions of a play. The blueprint and record of a play, the printed text of dialogue and stage directions. 899–904

Secondary epic. See *Epic.*

Sestet. A six-line unit that can stand alone as a stanza or as the concluding six lines of an Italian or Petrarchan sonnet. 747

Sestina. A verse form that consists of six six-line stanzas and a concluding tercet. The end words of each line of the first stanza are repeated in subsequent stanzas.

Set. The acting or playing area of the theater; the props and scenery for a particular scene or act of a drama. 902

Setting. The place, time, or circumstance in which the action of a story takes place. 141–45, 250–55

Shakespearean sonnet. See *English sonnet.*

Shaped form. A poem whose lines, taken together, form a visual representation of its subject. 767–71

Short story. A work of prose fiction which generally involves a small number of characters in a limited number of settings, and is condensed into a short span of time.

Simile. A comparison of one thing with another, explicitly announced by the word *like* or *as.* 641–43

Skit. An informal dramatic exercise that has neither the depth nor completeness of a play.

Social realism. In drama, a play that portrays characters struggling with social and economic problems. 1317

Soliloquy. A speech to oneself. 591–99

Sonnet. A fourteen-line poem in iambic pentameter whose rhyme scheme has, in practice, been widely varied. Sonnets concern themselves with love, death, politics,
and other topics that evoke intense personal feelings. 747–52

Spondee. A metrical unit of two accented syllables. 696

Stage designer. The member of the artistic staff of a dramatic production who plans the
layout, architecture, and colors of the stage scenery. 898

Stage direction. Any description in a script of an actor's behavior that is not indicated
by dialogue. 903

Stage props. Furniture and other movable effects that make up the scene of a play. 903

Stage whisper. Words spoken by an actor which, by dramatic convention, are supposed
not to be heard by the other actors onstage.

Stanza. A sequence of lines that form a metrical, tonal, or intellectual unit. 547, 568,
743–44

Static characters. Characters that do not change during the course of a narrative. 233

Stock characters. Characters, usually found in comedy and melodrama, whose qualities
are so exaggerated and common that they represent a type of human nature. 978

Stream-of-consciousness. A narrative technique which gives the reader the impression of
listening to a character's innermost thoughts. 233

Stress. Emphasis given to a word or syllable. There are two forms of stress: stress of
accent and stress of emphasis. Stress of accent occurs in polysyllabic words. Thus
we say beaúty rather than beautý. Stress of emphasis is the stress we give to
particular words in a sentence. In the sentence, "I have a bad headache," the
word *bad* is stressed. 693–94

Strophe. See *Pindaric ode.*

Sub-plot. One or more sequences of action subordinated to the main plot. 351

Supporting character. In drama, a character who helps to forward the action but is
neither the cause nor the major victim of it. 978

Surprise. An aspect of plot construction in which events are sprung upon the unsuspecting reader. Surprise is frequently a function of point-of-view. 169–70

Suspense. The feeling of pleasurable tension experienced by the reader or spectator in
anticipation of learning the outcome of a narrative situation. 170

Syllabic verse. A poem whose line lengths are calculated by the number of syllables in
each line rather than the number of feet per line. 703–5

Symbol. An object, person, action, or situation that signifies more than itself and thus
may be read both literally and metaphorically. 282–85, 661–66

Symbolist drama. Plays in which actions as well as characters, props, and setting refer
to eternal ideas and states of being in a "higher" world. 1427–28

Synecdoche. A figure of speech wherein part of a thing is employed to suggest the whole,
or a larger concept is used to suggest something specific. *Example:* "All hands
were on deck." 678–79

Synesthesia. The manner of speaking about one sense in terms of another. "He wore a *screaming* yellow necktie" is an example of synesthesia because *yellow* is described as if it were a sound. 619

Tale-within-a-tale. See *Framed story.*

Talon. The last word of the line of a sestina.

Tanka. A Japanese lyric form of thirty-one syllables, in lines of five, seven, five, seven, seven. Historically, its diction has been traditional and elevated, and its subjects most often include love, lament, felicitations, travel, and nature. 762–66

Tercet. A three-line stanza. 752

Terza rima. A form of interconnected three-line stanzas that rhyme *aba bcb cdc ded efe.* . . . 752–54

Tetrameter. A metrical line with four feet. 694

Theater of the absurd. A twentieth-century school of drama concerned with human alienation, the death of God, and the futility of language.

Theme – main idea of a story or meaning

Third-person narrative. A story told by a voice outside the action. See also *Omniscient third-person narrative* and *Limited third-person narrative.* 117

Tone. The writer's attitude toward a subject as exhibited through rhythms, sounds, and the selection of words. 723–40

Tragedy. A stage play that shows the change in the protagonist's fortune from good to bad, inspiring fear and pity. 1026–29

Tragic flaw. In drama, the flaw in the character of the protagonist that leads to his or her downfall. 977

Tragic irony. In drama, a misfortune contrary to the expectations of the protagonist. 914

Tragicomedy. A drama that alternates comic and serious scenes, producing a richly ironic blend of emotions. 1239

Trimeter. A metrical line with three feet. 694

Triplet. A verse unit of three lines, usually containing rhyme, employed as a stanzaic form, as a variation on the couplet, or occasionally as a complete poem in itself. 744

Trochee. A metrical unit of two syllables in which the first is stressed. 694

Turning point. See *Climax of action.*

Twist ending. The surprise conclusion of a narrative, often the result of an odd or unexpected turn of events. 172

Unreliable narrator. A narrator whose account of events is recognized by the reader as being faulty, distorted, or untrustworthy. 145–47

Villain. An antagonist who is deliberately evil. 234, 978

Villanelle. A poem made up of five tercets, all rhyming *aba*, and a concluding quatrain, rhyming *abaa*. Lines 6, 12, and 18 repreat line 1; lines 9, 15, and 19 repeat line 3. 755–57

Acknowledgments

FICTION

Margaret Atwood. "Giving Birth" from *Dancing Girls and Other Stories* by Margaret Atwood. Copyright © 1977, 1982 by O. W. Toad, Ltd. Reprinted by permission of Simon & Schuster, Inc.

Isaac Babel. "My First Goose." Reprinted by permission of S. G. Phillips, Inc. from *The Collected Stories of Isaac Babel.* Copyright © 1955 by S. G. Philips, Inc.

James Baldwin. "Sonny's Blues" from *Going to Meet the Man* by James Baldwin. Copyright © 1957 by James Baldwin. Used by permission of Doubleday, a division of Bantam Doubleday Dell Publishing Group, Inc.

Toni Cade Bambara. "My Man Bovanne" from *Gorilla, My Love* by Toni Cade Bambara. Copyright © 1971 by Toni Cade Bambara. Reprinted by permission of Random House Inc.

Anne Beattie. "Janus" by Ann Beattie, Copyright © 1986 by Irony and Pity, Inc. Reprinted by permission of Linden Press, a division of Simon & Schuster, Inc.

Giovanni Boccaccio. "A Dinner of Hens" from *The Decameron* by Giovanni Boccaccio, trans. by Richard Aldington © Catherine Guillaume. Reprinted by permission of Rosica Colin Ltd.

Italo Calvino. "The Canary Prince" from *Italian Folktales* by Italo Calvino, copyright © 1956 by Giulio Einaudi editore s.p.a., English translation copyright © 1980 by Harcourt Brace Jovanovich, Inc., reprinted by permission of Harcourt Brace Jovanovich, Inc.

Elias Canetti. "Earwitness" from *Earwitness: Fifty Characters* by Elias Canetti. English translation copyright © 1979 by The Seabury Press, Inc. Used by permission of The Continuum Publishing Company.

Ethan Canin. "Emperor of the Air" from *Emperor of the Air* by Ethan Canin, Copyright © 1988 by Ethan Canin. Reprinted by permission of Houghton Mifflin Company.

Anton Chekov. "Lady with Lapdog" from *Lady with Lapdog and Other Stories* translated by David Magarshack (Penguin Classics, 1964). Copyright 1964 by David Magarshack. Reprinted by permission of Penguin Books, Ltd.

Julio Cortázar. "Continuity of Parks" from *End of the Game and Other Stories* by Julio Cortázar and translated by Paul Blackburn. Copyright © 1963, 1967 by Random House Inc. Reprinted by permission of Pantheon Books, a division of Random House, Inc.

Louise Erdrich. "The Red Convertible" from *Love Medicine* by Louise Erdrich. Copyright © 1984 by Louise Erdrich. Reprinted by permission of Henry Holt and Company, Inc.

William Faulkner. "A Rose for Emily" from *Collected Stories of William Faulkner* by William Faulkner. Copyright 1930 and renewed 1958 by William Faulkner. Reprinted by permission of Random House Inc.

Gabriel García Márquez. "The Very Old Man with Enormous Wings" from *Collected Stories* by Gabriel García Márquez. Copyright © 1984 by Gabriel García Márquez. Reprinted by permission of HarperCollins Publishers.

Ernest Hemingway. "Hills Like White Elephants." Reprinted with permission of Charles Scribner's Sons, an imprint of Macmillan Publishing Company from *Men Without Women* by Ernest Hemingway. Copyright 1927 by Charles Scribner's Sons; copyright renewed 1955 by Ernest Hemingway.

James Joyce. "Araby" from *Dubliners* by James Joyce. Copyright 1916 by B. W. Heubsch. Definitive text Copyright © 1967 by the Estate of James Joyce. Used by permission of Viking Penguin, a division of Penguin Books USA Inc.

Franz Kafka. "The Penal Colony" from *The Metamorphosis, The Penal Colony, and Other Stories* by Franz Kafka, trans. by Willa & Edwin Muir. Copyright 1948 by Schocken Books, Inc. Copyright renewed 1975 by Schocken Books, Inc. Reprinted by permission of Schocken Books, published by Pantheon Books, a division of Random House, Inc.

Maxine Hong Kingston. "On Mortality" from *China Men* by Maxine Hong Kingston. Copyright © 1977, 1978, 1979, 1980 by Maxine Hong Kingston. Reprinted by permission of Alfred A. Knopf, Inc.

D. H. Lawrence. "The Horse Dealer's Daughter," from *Complete Short Stories of D.H. Lawrence* by D. H. Lawrence. Copyright 1922 by Thomas B. Seltzer, Inc., renewed 1950 by Frieda Lawrence. Used by permission of Viking Penguin, a division of Penguin Books USA Inc.

Doris Lessing. "Homage to Isaac Babel" by Doris Lessing, Copyright © 1958, 1962, 1963 by Doris Lessing. Reprinted by permission of Simon & Schuster, Inc.

Sinclair Lewis. "Virga Vay and Allan Cedar" from *Cass Timberlane* by Sinclair Lewis. Copyright 1945 by Sinclair Lewis. Reprinted by permission of Random House Inc.

Bernard Malamud. "The Jewbird" from *Idiots First* by Bernard Malamud. Copyright © 1963. Reprinted by permission of Farrar, Straus & Giroux, Inc.

Bobbie Anne Mason. "Shiloh" from *Shiloh and Other Stories* by Bobbie Anne Mason. Copyright © 1982 by Bobbie Anne Mason. Reprinted by permission of HarperCollins Publishers.

V. S. Naipaul. "The Night Watchman's Occurrence Book" from *A Flag on the Island* by V. S. Naipaul. Reprinted by permission of Gillon Aitken, Ltd.

Flannery O'Connor. "Everything That Rises Must Converge" from *The Complete Stories* by Flannery O'Connor. Copyright © 1961, 1965 by the Estate of Mary Flannery O'Connor. Reprinted by permission of Farrar, Straus & Giroux, Inc.

Grace Paley. "A Conversation with My Father" from *Enormous Changes at the Last Minute* by Grace Paley. Copyright © 1972, 1974 by Grace Paley. Reprinted by permission of Farrar, Straus & Giroux, Inc.

Katherine Anne Porter. "The Jilting of Granny Weatherall" from *Flowering Judas and Other Stories*, copyright 1930 and renewed 1958 by Katherine Anne Porter, reprinted by permission of Harcourt Brace Jovanovich, Inc.

Raymond Queneau. "The Subjective Side," "Another Subjectivity," and "Narrative" from *Exercises in Style.* Copyright © 1957 by Editions Gallimard. Reprinted by permission of New Directions Publishing Corporation.

Jean Rhys. "I Used to Live Here Once" by Jean Rhys from *Jean Rhys: The Collected Short Stories*, published by W. W. Norton & Co. (1987) Copyright © 1976 by Jean Rhys. Reprinted by permission of the Wallace Literary Agency, Inc.

John Steinbeck. "Chrysanthemums," from *The Long Valley* by John Steinbeck. Copyright 1937, renewed © 1965 by John Steinbeck. Used by permission of Viking Penguin, a division of Penguin Books USA Inc.

Robert Stone. "Helping" by Robert Stone, Copyright 1987 by Robert Stone. First appeared in *The New Yorker.* Reprinted by permission of Donadio & Ashworth, Inc.

POETRY AND ESSAYS

H. D. (Hilda Doolittle). "Never More Will the Wind," "Oread" from *H. D.: Selected Poems of H. D.* Copyright © 1957 by Normal Holmes Pearson. Reprinted by permission of New Directions Publishing Corporation.

Alan Dugan. "Morning Song" from *New and Collected Poems: 1961–1983* by Alan Dugan. Copyright © 1961, 1962, 1968, 1972, 1974, 1983 by Alan Dugan. First published by the Ecco Press in 1983. Reprinted by permission.

Paul Laurence Dunbar. "In the Morning" from *The Complete Poems of Paul Laurence Dunbar* (1970). Reprinted by permission of Dodd, Mead & Company, Inc.

Robert Duncan. "My Mother Would be a Falconress" from *Bending the Bow*. Copyright © 1968 by Robert Duncan. Reprinted by permission of New Directions Publishing Corporation.

T. S. Eliot. "The Love Song of J. Alfred Prufrock" from *Collected Poems 1909–1962*, copyright 1936 by Harcourt Brace Jovanovich, Inc., copyright © 1964, 1963 by T. S. Eliot, reprinted by permission of the publisher.

William Empson. "Villanelle" from *Collected Poems of William Empson*, copyright 1949 and renewed 1977 by William Empson, reprinted by permission of Harcourt Brace Jovanovich, Inc.

Daniel Mark Epstein. "Madonna (with Child Missing)" reprinted from *No Vacancies in Hell*, Poems by Daniel Mark Epstein, by permission of Liveright Publishing Corporation. Copyright © 1973, 1972, 1971 by Daniel Mark Epstein.

Louise Erdrich. "Windigo" from *Jacklight* poems by Louise Erdrich. Copyright © 1984 by Louise Erdrich. Reprinted by permission of Henry Holt and Company, Inc.

Lawrence Ferlinghetti. "In Goya's Greatest Scenes We Seem to See" from *Coney Island of the Mind* by Lawrence Ferlinghetti. Copyright © 1958 by Lawrence Ferlinghetti. Reprinted by permission of New Directions Publishing Corporation.

Edward Field. "My Polish Grandmother" reprinted by permission of Edward Field.

Charles Henri Ford. "Somebody's Gone" from *Overturned Lake* by Charles Henri Ford, published by New Directions Publishing Corporation. Reprinted by permission of Charles Henri Ford.

Robert Frost. "Out, Out," "Fire and Ice," "For Once, Then, Something," "The Road Not Taken," "Provide, Provide," "After Apple-Picking," "The Silken Tent" from *The Poetry of Robert Frost* edited by Edward Connery Lathem. Copyright 1919, 1923, 1930, 1939, © 1969 by Holt, Rinehart and Winston. Copyright 1936, 1942, 1944, 1951, © 1958 by Robert Frost. Copyright © 1964, 1967, 1970, by Lesley Frost Ballantine. Reprinted by permission of Henry Holt and Company, Inc.

Federico García Lorca. "Half Moon" from *The Selected Poems of Federico García Lorca*. Copyright © 1955 by New Directions Publishing Corporation. Reprinted by permission of New Directions Publishing Corporation.

Allen Ginsberg. "A Supermarket in California" from *Collected Poems 1947–1980*. Copyright © 1955, 1984 by Allen Ginsberg. Reprinted by permission of Harper & Row, Publishers, Inc.

Nikki Giovanni. "Nikki-Rosa" from *Black Feeling, Black Talk, Black Judgement*. Copyright © 1968, 1970 by Nikki Giovanni. By permission of William Morrow & Company.

Louise Glück. "The Pond" from *The House on Marshland* by Louise Glück. Copyright © 1971, 1972, 1973, 1974, 1975 by Louise Glück. First published by the Ecco Press in 1975. Reprinted by permission.

Edward Gorey. "There Was a Young Woman Named Plunnery" from *Listing Attic*, 1954, by Duell, Sloane and Pearce. From *Oxford Anthology of Light Verse*, edited by William Harmon. Reprinted by permission of Edward Gorey.

Thom Gunn. "Moly" from *Moly and My Sad Captains* by Thom Gunn. Copyright © 1961, 1971, 1973 by Thom Gunn. Reprinted by permission of Farrar, Straus and Giroux, Inc.

Marilyn Hacker. "Villanelle" from *Presentation Piece* by Marilyn Hacker. Copyright © 1974 by Marilyn Hacker. Reprinted by permission of Frances Collin, Literary Agent.

Donald Hall. "Ox-Cart Man" from *Ox-Cart Man* by Donald Hall. Copyright © 1977 by Donald Hall.

Gail N. Harada. "New Year" by Gail N. Harada, reprinted by permission of the poet.

Michael S. Harper. "A Mother Speaks: The Algiers Motel Incident, Detroit" from *Dear John, Dear Coltrane* by Michael S. Harper. Copyright 1970 by the University of Illinois Press. Reprinted by permission of the University of Illinois Press.

Jim Harrison. "Sound" from *Outlyers and Ghazals* by Jim Harrison, published by Liveright Publishing Corporation. Copyright © 1969, 1971 by Jim Harrison. Reprinted by permission of Jim Harrison.

Seamus Heaney. "The Forge" from *Poems 1965–1975* by Seamus Heaney. Copyright © 1969 by Seamus Heaney. Reprinted by permission of Farrar, Straus and Giroux, Inc.

Anthony Hecht. "The Dover Bitch" from *Collected Earlier Poems* by Anthony Hecht. Copyright © 1990 by Anthony E. Hecht. Reprinted by permission of Alfred A. Knopf, Inc.

Daryl Hine. "The Survivors" from *Minutes* by Daryl Hine. Reprinted with permission of Atheneum Publishers, an imprint of Macmillan Publishing Company. Copyright © 1965, 1966, 1967, 1968 by Daryl Hine.

Edward Hirsch. "A Letter" from *For the Sleepwalkers* by Edward Hirsch. Copyright © 1981 by Edward Hirsch. Reprinted by permission of Alfred A. Knopf, Inc.

Billie Holiday, Arthur Herzog, Jr. "God Bless the Child." Copyright © 1941 by Edward B. Marks Music Co. Copyright renewed. Used by permission. All rights reserved.

John Hollander. "Swan and Shadow" from *Types of Shape* by John Hollander. Copyright © 1969 by John Hollander. Reprinted by permission.

Homer. From *The Odyssey* by Homer, translated by R. Fitzgerald. Copyright © 1961, 1963 by Robert Fitzgerald and renewed 1989 by Benedict R. C. Fitzgerald. Reprinted by permission of Vintage Books, a Division of Random House, Inc.

Garrett Hongo. "The Hongo Store" © 1982 by Garrett Hongo, reprinted from *Yellow Light* by permission of Wesleyan University Press and University Press of New England.

A. E. Housman. "To An Athlete Dying Young," "Loveliest of Trees, the Cherry Now," "When I Was One and Twenty" from "A Shropshire Lad" -authorised edition- from *The Collected Poems of A. E. Housman*. Copyright 1939, 1940, © 1965 by Holt, Rinehart and Winston. Copyright © 1967, 1968 by Robert E. Symons. Reprinted by permission of Henry Holt and Company.

Richard Howard. "Giovanni Da Fiesole on the Sublime or Fra Angelico's Last Judgement" from *Findings* by Richard Howard. Copyright © 1971 by Richard Howard (New York: Atheneum, 1971). Reprinted by permission of the author.

Langston Hughes. "Sylvester's Dying Bed" from *Selected Poems of Langston Hughes* by Langston Hughes. Copyright 1942 by Alfred A. Knopf, Inc. "Who but the Lord?" from *Selected Poems of Langston Hughes* by Langston Hughes. Both are reprinted by permission of Alfred A. Knopf, Inc.

Ted Hughes. "Hawk Roosting" from *Selected Poems* by Ted Hughes. Copyright © 1959 by Ted Hughes. Reprinted by permission of Harper & Row, Publishers, Inc.

Richard Hugo. "Driving Montana" reprinted from *The Lady in Kicking Horse Reservoir* by Richard Hugo, by permission of W. W. Norton & Company, Inc. Copyright © 1973 by Richard Hugo.

T. E. Hulme. "Autumn" from *Personae* by Ezra Pound. Copyright 1926 by Ezra Pound. Reprinted by permission of New Directions Publishing Corporation.

Colette Inez. "Spanish Heaven" from *Alive and Taking Names* by Colette Inez (Athens, Ohio: Ohio University Press, 1977). "Spanish Heaven" was first published by Salt Creek Reader. Reprinted by permission of Windflower Press.

Randall Jarrell. "The Death of the Ball Turret Gunner" from *The Complete Poems* by Randall Jarrell. Copyright © 1945, 1972 by Mrs. Randall Jarrell. Reprinted by permission of Farrar, Straus & Giroux, Inc. "The Mockingbird" from *The Bat-Poet* by Randall Jarrell. Reprinted with permission of Macmillan Publishing Co., Inc. Copyright © Macmillan Publishing Company 1963, 1964. Originally appeared in *The New Yorker*. "The Woman at the Washington Zoo" by Randall Jarrell. Permission granted by Ms. Mary Jarrell.

Robinson Jeffers. "Rock and Hawk" from *The Selected Poetry of Robinson Jeffers* by Robinson Jeffers. Copyright 1934 and renewed 1962 by Donnan Jeffers and Garth Jeffers. Reprinted by permission of Random House Inc.

Erica Jong. "How You Get Born" from *Half Lives* by Erica Mann Jong. Reprinted by permission of Henry Holt and Company, Inc.

James Joyce. "Chamber Music XXXV: All Day I hear the Noise . . .", from *Collected Poems* by James Joyce. Copyright 1918 by B. W. Huebsch, Inc., 1927, 1936 by James Joyce, 1946 by Nora Joyce. Used by permission of Viking Penguin, a division of Penguin Books USA Inc.

Lady Kasa. "Six Tanka" from *The Penguin Book of Japanese Verse*, translated by Geoffrey Bownas and Anthony Thwaite (The Penguin Poets, 1964). Copyright © 1964 by Geoffrey Bownas and Anthony Thwaite. Reprinted by permission of Penguin Books Ltd.

Bob Kaufman. "Blues Note" from *Solitudes Crowded with Loneliness*. Copyright © 1965 by Bob Kaufman. Reprinted by permission of New Directions Publishing Corporation.

Patrick Kavanagh. "Tinker's Wife" Copyright © 1946 by Patrick Kavanaugh. Reprinted by permission of Devin-Adair Co., Old Greenwich, CT.

Weldon Kees. "Aspects of Robinson." Reprinted from *The Collected Poems of Weldon Kees*, edited by Donald Justice, by permission of University of Nebraska Press. Copyright © 1975 by the University of Nebraska Press.

Peter Klappert. "Mail at Your New Address" from *Lugging Vegetables to Nantucket* by Peter Klappert. (Yale University: 1971). All rights held by Peter Klappert.

Ethridge Knight. "Haiku" from *Poems from Prison* by Ethridge Knight. Reprinted by permission of the author.

Bill Knott. "The Hair Poem" and "Death" Reprinted from *Poems 1963–1988*, by Bill Knott. © Bill Knott.

Maxine Kumin. "For a Shetland Pony Brood Mare Who Died in Her Barren Year," from *Our Ground Time Here Will Be Brief* by Maxine Kumin. Copyright © 1969 by Maxine Kumin. Used by permission of Viking Penguin, a division of Penguin Books USA Inc.

Stanley Kunitz. "The Portrait" from *The Poems of Stanley Kunitz, 1928–1978* by Stanley Kunitz. Copyright © 1971 by Stanley Kunitz. By permission of Little, Brown and Company.

Philip Larkin. "Faith Healing" from *The Witsun Weddings* by Philip Larkin. Reprinted by permission of Faber & Faber Ltd.

D. H. Lawrence. "Sorrow," "Snake," "Gloire de Dijon" from *The Complete Poems of D. H. Lawrence* by D. H. Lawrence Eds. de Sola Pinto & Roberts. Copyright © 1964, 1971 by Angelo Ravagli and C. M. Weekley, Executors of the Estate of Frieda Lawrence Ravagli. Used by permission of Viking Penguin, a division of Penguin Books USA Inc.

Irving Layton. "Cain" from *The Collected Poems of Irving Layton* by Irving Layton. Used by permission of the Canadian Publishers, McClelland & Stewart, Toronto.

Denise Levertov. "To the Snake" from *Collected Earlier Poems 1940–1960*. Copyright 1958 by Denise Levertov Goodman. First printed in *Poetry*. "The Ache of Marriage" from *Poems 1960–1967* Copyright © 1964 by Denise Levertov Goodman. Reprinted by permission of New Directions Publishing Corporation.

Philip Levine. "To a Child Trapped in a Barber Shop" © 1968 by Philip Levine, reprinted from *Not This Pig* by permission of Wesleyan University Press and University Press of New England.

Audre Lorde. "Now That I am Forever with Child" reprinted from *Coal*, poems by Audre Lorde, by permission of W. W. Norton & Company, Inc. Copyright © 1968, 1970, 1976 by Audre Lorde.

Amy Lowell. "Chinoiseries" from *The Complete Poetical Works of Amy Lowell* by Amy Lowell. Copyright © 1955 by Houghton Mifflin Co. Copyright © 1953 by Houghton Mifflin Co., Brinton P. Roberts, and G. D'Andelot Belin, Esquire. Reprinted by permission of Houghton Mifflin Company.

Robert Lowell. "Skunk Hour" from *Life Studies* by Robert Lowell. Copyright © 1956, 1959 by Robert Lowell. Renewal copyright © 1981, 1986, 1987 by Harriet W. Lowell. Caroline Lowell and Sheridan Lowell. "Robert Frost" from *History* by Robert Lowell. Copyright © 1973 by Robert Lowell. Both are reprinted by permission of Farrar, Straus & Giroux, Inc.

Archibald MacLeish. "Ars Poetica" from *New and Collected Poems 1917–1982* by Archibald MacLeish. Copyright © 1985 by the Estate of Archibald MacLeish. Reprinted by permission of Houghton Mifflin Company.

Claude McKay. "The Harlem Dancer," "If We Must Die" from *Selected Poems of Claude McKay* by Claude McKay. Copyright 1953. Reprinted with the permission of Twayne Publishers, a division of G. K. Hall & Co., Boston.

James Merrill. "Charles on Fire" and "Maisie" from *Nights and Days* by James Merrill, 1967. Copyright by James Merrill, reprinted with his permission.

Thomas Merton. "The Regret," "Elegy for the Monastery Barn" from *Collected Poems of Thomas Merton*. Copyright 1944, 1957 by Our Lady of Gethsemani Monastery, Inc. Reprinted by permission of New Directions Publishing Corporation.

W. S. Merwin. "For the Anniversary of My Death" from *The Lice* by W. S. Merwin. Copyright © 1967 by W. S. Merwin. Reprinted by permission of Georges Borchardt Inc., for the author.

Edna St. Vincent Millay. "Recuerdo" and "Pity Me Not Because the Light of Day" by Edna St. Vincent Millay. From *Collected Poems*, Harper & Row. Copyright 1922, 1923, 1950, 1951 by Edna St. Vincent Millay and Norma Millay Ellis. Reprinted by permission of Elizabeth Barnett, Literary Executor.

N. Scott Momaday. "The Delight Song of Tsoai-talee," "Earth and I gave You Turquoise" from *The Gourd Dancer* by N. Scott Momaday. Copyright © 1975 by N. Scott Momaday. Reprinted by permission.

Marianne Moore. "Nevertheless" by Marianne Moore. From *Collected Poems* by Marianne Moore. Copyright 1944, and renewed 1972, by Marianne Moore. "The Steeple-Jack" from *Collected Poems* by Marianne Moore. Copyright 1951 by Marianne Moore, renewed 1979 by Lawrence E. Brinn and Louise Crane. Both reprinted with permission of Macmillan Publishing Company.

Mary Tall Mountain. "Peeling Pippins" by Mary Tall Mountain. Reprinted with permission of the poet.

Lisel Mueller. "After Whistler" from *Second Language* by Lisel Mueller. Copyright © 1986 by Lisel Mueller. Reprinted by permission of Louisiana State University Press.

Ogden Nash. "Requiem" (Formerly titled "Gervaise"), "Edouard" from *Verses from 1929 On* by Ogden Nash. Copyright 1938 and 1940 by Ogden Nash. By permission of Little, Brown and Company.

Sharon Olds. "The Race" by Sharon Olds. Reprinted by permission; © 1985 Sharon Olds. Originally in *The New Yorker*.

Gregory Orr. "All Morning" from *Gathering the Bones Together* by Gregory Orr. Reprinted by permission of the poet.

Wilfred Owen. "Anthem from Doomed Youth" from *The Collected Poems of Wilfred Owen*. Copyright © 1963 by Chatto & Windus, Ltd. Reprinted by permission of New Directions Publishing Corporation.

Linda Pastan. "25th High School Reunion" reprinted from *The Five Stages of Grief*, Poems by Linda Pastan by permission of W. W. Norton & Company, Inc. Copyright © 1978 by Linda Pastan.

Cesare Pavese. "Encounter" from *Hard Labor* by Cesare Pavese. Copyright 1943 by Einaudi editore, Torino. English translation copyright © 1976 by Willima Arrowsmith. Reprinted by permission of Viking Penguin, Inc.

Molly Peacock. "Petting and Being a Pet" from *Raw Heaven* by Molly Peacock. Copyright 1984 by Molly Peacock. Reprinted by permission of Random House, Inc.

Sylvia Plath. "Daddy" and "Lady Lazarus" from *Ariel* by Sylvia Plath edited by Ted Hughes. Copyright © 1963 by Sylvia Plath. Reprinted by permission of HarperCollins Publishers.

Cole Porter. "My Heart Belongs to Daddy" by Cole Porter. © 1938 (renewed) Chappell & Co. All rights reserved. Used by permission.

Ezra Pound. "In a Station of the Metro," "The Bath Tub," and "The River Merchant's Wife" by T. E. Hulme from *Personae* by Ezra Pound. Copyright 1926 by Ezra Pound. Reprinted by permission of New Directions Publishing Corporation.

Dudley Randall. "Ballad of Birmingham" from *Poems, Counterpoems* by Dudley Randall. Published by Broadside Press. Reprinted by permission of Dudley Randall.

John Crowe Ransom. "Here Lies a Lady," "Winter Remembered" from *Selected Poems of John Crowe Ransom*. Copyright 1924 by Alfred A. Knopf, Inc. and renewed 1952 by John Crowe Ransom. "Piazza Piece" from *Selected Poems of John Crowe Ransom*. Copyright 1927 by Alfred A. Knopf, Inc. and renewed 1955 by John Crowe Ransom. Reprinted by permission of Alfred A. Knopf, Inc.

Henry Reed. "Naming of Parts" from *A Map of Verona* by Henry Reed, Copyright Henry Reed, reproduced by permission of Curtis Brown Ltd., London.

Ishmael Reed. "beware, do not read this poem" *Catechism of a Neo-American* (too-doo Church). Copyright © 1969. Reprinted by permission of International Publishers, Inc., NY.

Pierre Reverdy. "Departure" by Pierre Reverdy. Reprinted by permission of Flammarion et Cie, France.

Adrienne Rich. "A Woman Mourned by Daughters" reprinted from *Poems, Selected and New, 1950–1974*, by Adrienne Rich, by permission of W. W. Norton & Company, Inc. Copyright © 1975, 1973, 1971, 1969, 1966, by W. W. Norton & Company, Inc. Copyright © 1967, 1963, 1962, 1961, 1960, 1959, 1958, 1957, 1956, 1955, 1954, 1953, 1952, 1951 by Adrienne Rich.

Alberto Ríos. "Nani" by Alberto Ríos, Copyright © 1982 by Alberto Ríos. Reprinted by permission of the author.

Theodore Roethke. "The Lady and the Bear" from *The Collected Poems of Theodore Roethke*. Copyright 1951 by Theodore Roethke. "Elegy for Jane," "My Papa's Waltz," and "I Knew A Woman" from *The Collected Poems of Theodore Roethke*. Copyright 1950, 1954 by Theodore Roethke. Copyright 1946 by Editorial Publications, Inc. Used by permission of Doubleday, a division of Bantam Doubleday Dell Publishing Group, Inc.

Muriel Rukeyser. "Song: Love in Whose Rich Honor" from *The Speed of Darkness* by Muriel Rukeyser. Copyright © 1968 by Muriel Rukeyser. Reprinted by permission of International Creative Management.

Louis Omar Salinas. "In a Farmhouse" from *From the Barrio* by Louis Omar Salinas and Lillian Faderman. Copyright © 1973 by Louis Omar Salinas and Lillian Faderman. Reprinted by permission of HarperCollins Publishers.

Sonia Sanchez. "summer words of a sistuh addict" by Sonia Sanchez. Reprinted by permission of the poet.

Carl Sandburg. "They Have Yarns" from *The People, Yes*, copyright 1936 by Harcourt Brace Jovanovich, Inc. and renewed 1964 by Carl Sandburg, reprinted by permission of the publisher.

Sappho. "Then" from *Greek Lyric Poetry* by Willis Barnstone. Copyright © 1962, 1967 by Willis Barnstone. Reprinted by permission of Schocken Books, published by Pantheon Books, a division of Random House Inc.

May Sarton. "The Lady and the Unicorn" and "Lady with a Falcon." Reprinted from *Selected Poems of May Sarton*, Edited by Serena Sue Hilsinger and Lois Brynes, by permission of W. W. Norton & Company, Inc. Copyright © 1978 by May Sarton.

Delmore Schwartz. "The Heavy Bear Who Goes With Me" by Delmore Schwartz from *Selected Poems: Summer Knowledge*. Copyright 1938 by New Directions Publishing Corporation. Reprinted by permission of New Directions Publishing Corporation.

Robert Service. "Dylan" from *Later Collected Verse* by Robert Service. Copyright © 1954, 1956, 1965 by Dodd, Mead & Company. Copyright © 1960 by Germaine Service. Reprinted by permission of Dodd, Mead & Company, Inc.

Anne Sexton. "Unknown Girl in the Maternity Ward" from *To Bedlam and Part Way Back* by Anne Sexton. Copyright © 1960 by Anne Sexton. "Pain for a Daughter" from *Live or Die* by Anne Sexton. Copyright © 1966 by Anne Sexton. Reprinted by permission of Houghton Mifflin Co.

Index of First Lines

A balmy spring wind, 845

About suffering they were never wrong, 542

A bugler named Dougal MacDougal, 767

A captain bold, in Halifax, who dwelt in country quarters, 733

A child said What is the grass? fetching it to me with full hands; 636

After bringing forth eighteen, 882

After great pain, a formal feeling comes— 828

Aged man, that mows these fields. 658

Ah, my dear angry Lord, 685

A Lady came to a Bear by a Stream. 524

A Lion, tired with state affairs, 660

All day I hear the noise of waters, 837

All I know is a door into the dark. 875

All morning the dream lingers. 879

All you violated ones with gentle hearts, 576

A man adrift on a slim spar, 834

Among the rain, 615

Among twenty snowy mountains, 764

And is it not a gesture grand, 787

An ingenuity too astonishing, 856

A noiseless patient spider, 825

Another evening we sprawled about discussing, 687

A poem should be palpable and mute, 837

Apparently with no surprise, 827

Applauding youths laughed with young prostitutes, 572

As a bathtub lined with white porcelain, 649

As an ant, of his talents superiorly vain, 672
As I in hoary winter's night stood shivering in the snow, 673
As I walked out one evening, 842
A snake came to my water-trough, 670
As though an aged person were to wear, 648
As virtuous men pass mildly away, 646
A sweet disorder in the dress, 811
At dawn I squat on the garage, 618
A thousand martyrs I have made, 812
At midnight, 615
A toad the power mower caught, 736
At the dark bottom, 615
A touch of cold in the Autumn night— 642
At ten A.M. the young housewife, 723
Ay, man is manly. Here you see, 825

Because I could not stop for Death— 656
Because I had loved so deeply, 835
Because you are old and departing I have wetted my handkerchief, 679
Behold her, single in the field, 571
Blind with love, my daughter, 860

Child, the current of your breath is six days long, 594
childhood remembrances are always a drag, 878
Come live with me and be my love, 523

Dark house, by which once more I stand, 576
Dear mother, dear mother, the Church is cold, 594
Death, be not proud, though some have called thee, 811
Did your car get you to Florida? 611
Does it mean anything, 873
Dogs, lambs, chickens, women—pets of all nations! 879
Do not go gentle into that good night, 755
Dürer would have seen a reason for living, 799
Dusk, 770

Earth and I gave you turquoise, 870
Eastern guard tower, 634
Every day brings a ship, 679
Every day our bodies separate, 875

Farewell, thou child of my right hand, and joy; 543
Farewell, too little, and too lately known, 745
Fifteen miles, 612
Five years have passed; five summers, with the length, 796

For I will consider my Cat Jeoffry. 574
forsythia, 771
Frankie was good girl, 719
From my mother's sleep I fell into the State, 604

Gentleness and starvation tame, 847
Glory be to God for dappled things— 573
Going to sleep, I cross my hands on my chest. 642
Go, lovely Rose, 664
Grandma and the children left at night. 550
Grandma lit the stove. 890
Green Buddhas, 635
Green snake, when I hung you round my neck, 728

Had I the heavens' embroidered cloths, 566
Had we but world enough, and time, 569
Hair is heaven's water flowing eerily over us, 639
Hard-edged buildings; cloudless blue enamel; 877
Hear the sledges with the bells— 711
He clasps the crag with crooked hands; 631
He disappeared in the dead of winter: 578
Here is a symbol in which, 668
Here lies a lady of beauty and high degree. 589
Honour and shame from no condition rise; 730
Hope is the thing with feathers, 637
How do I love thee? Let me count the ways. 823
How the days went, 869
How many times do I love thee, dear? 821
How strange it seems! These Hebrews in their graves, 821
How to behold what cannot be held? 862
Hurrah for revolution and more cannon-shot! 680

I am a feather on the bright sky, 649
—I am a gentleman in a dustcoat trying, 602
I am the smoke king, 832
I am the unicorn and bow my head, 667
I caught this morning morning's minion, king- 829
If all the world and love were young, 809
I felt a funeral in my brain, 521
If ever two were one, then surely we. 812
"If I were dead, you'd sometimes say, Poor Child!" 789
If Michael, leader of God's host, 665
If we must die, let it not be like hogs, 749
If you were going to get a pet, 705
I hate and I love. Why? you might ask, 566

I have done it again. 865
I heard a Fly buzz—when I died— 827
I knew a woman, lovely in her bones, 844
I know that I shall meet my fate, 605
I listen to my parent's language, 884
I looked and I saw, 736
I love it! I love it! And who shall dare, 782
I love old women best, I think: 783
I met a traveler from an antique land, 819
I met the Bishop on the road, 785
In a garden every plant and flower, 880
In Breughel's great picture, The Kermess, 717
In gold sandals, 654
In Goya's greatest scenes we seem to see, 853
in Just- 839
In October of the year, 681
In our old shipwrecked days there was an hour, 750
In Xanadu did Kubla Khan, 630
I once had a sweet little doll, dears, 775
I remember the neckcurls, limp and damp as tendrils; 575
I saw her amid the dunghill debris, 785
I saw in Louisiana a live-oak growing. 662
I shall be hidden in a hut, 838
I sit down beside my brass lamp, 715
I sit in the top of the wood, my eyes closed, 863
I strove with none; for none was worth my strife, 818
It is not far to my place: 859
It is the pain, it is the pain, endures. 779
It little profits that an idle king, 597
I traveled on, seeing the hill where lay, 657
It's too dark to see black, 607
I used to fall, 721
I wandered lonely as a cloud, 817
I wander thro' each charter'd street, 628
I will arise and go now, and go to Innisfree, 716
I will lift up mine eyes unto the hills: from whence cometh my help. 742
I woke up this mornin', 548

John Anderson my jo, John, 737
Just off the highway to Rochester, Minnesota, 520

Lately, I've become accustomed to the way, 589
Lay your sleeping head, my love, 841
Let me not to the marriage of true minds, 651
Let us go then, you and I, 802

'Lias! 'Lias! Bless de Lawd! 738
Like a drummer's brush, 653
Like the pearl of dew, 763
Line of beauty scrawled alive, 647
Look, it's morning, and a little water gurgles in the tap. 727
Look one way and the sun is going down, 677
Lord, who createdst man in wealth and store, 768
Love, 655
Love bade me welcome: yet my soul drew back, 673
Loveliest of trees, the cherry now, 831

Márgarét, are you grievíng, 829
Marke but this flea, and marke in this, 656
Maud went to college, 850
May he lose his way on the cold sea, 570
Mother, I cannot mind my wheel; 539
"Mother dear, may I go downtown, 552
Much have I traveled in the realms of gold, 747
My Daddy has paid the rent, 871
My daughter is coming! 888
My grandmothers were strong, 710
My heart aches, and a drowsy numbness pains, 759
My heart's so heavy with a hundred things, 676
My heaven is Hispanic ladies in satin tube dresses, 865
My life had stood, a loaded gun, 826
My long two-pointed ladder's sticking through a tree, 835
My Mistress' eyes are nothing like the Sun, 778
My mother never forgave my father, 881
My mother would be a falconress, 851
My parents felt those rumblings, 889
My prime of youth is but a frost of cares, 690
My sadness sits around me, 872
My thoughts arise and fade in solitude, 652

Nature and Nature's laws lay hid in night: 683
Nautilus Island's hermit, 632
Never more will the wind, 568
Night covers the pond with its wing. 651
Nightmare of beasthood, snorting, how to wake. 746
Nobody heard him, the dead man, 881
No "fan is in his hand" for these, 830
Nowadays the mess is everywhere, 872
Now as I was young and easy under the apple boughs, 650
Now hardly here and there a hackney-coach, 814
Now, not a tear begun, 883

Now stood Eliza on the wood-crown'd height, 776
Now that blue has had its say, 619

O Donal Oge, if you go across the sea, 688
Oh, come with old Khayyam, and leave the Wise, 581
Old Eben Flood, climbing alone one night, 833
O My Luve's like a red, red rose, 817
Once riding in old Baltimore, 744
Once upon a midnight dreary, while I pondered, weak and weary, 555
One day as I unwarily did gaze, 674
One night, your mother is listening to the walls. 876
One wading a Fall meadow finds on all sides, 761
Others taunt me with having knelt at well-curbs, 663
Over my head, I see the bronze butterfly, 620
O wild West Wind, thou breath of Autumn's being, 752

Pity me not because the light of day, 749
"Poor wanderer," said the leaden sky, 666
Poplars are standing there still as death, 841
Pray to what earth does this *sweet* cold belong, 626

Rain smell comes with the wind, 880
Ray Charles is the black wind of Kilimanjaro, 684
Robert Frost at midnight, the audience gone, 850
Robinson at Cards at the Algonquin; a thin, 689
Round the cape of a sudden came the sea, 823

Season of mists and mellow fruitfulness, 819
Seivers was one of the hardest running backs since, 732
Shall I compare thee to a summer's day? 644
She is as in a field a silken tent, 836
She walks in beauty, like the night, 818
Shouts from the street, spotlights crossfire, 551
Shrugging in the flight of its leaves, 868
Sitting at her table, she serves, 884
Slowly the women file to where he stands, 855
soft rainsqualls on the swells, 627
So I would hear out those lungs, 682
Some say the world will end in fire, 582
Sometimes men need the winds most, 758
Sometimes the world seems so large, 601
somewhere i have never travelled, gladly beyond, 585
so much depends, 632
Sorrow is my own yard, 591
So there stood Matthew Arnold and this girl, 857

Success is counted sweetest, 730
Sundays too my father got up early, 847
Sweet Mercy! how my very heart has bled, 690
Sweet stream, that dost with equal pace,788

Take hand and part with laughter; 700
Taking the air rifle from my son's hand, 845
That is no country for old men. The young, 801
That sail in cloudless light, 864
That's my last Duchess painted on the wall, 606
That time of year thou mayst in me behold, 748
The ache of marriage: 742
The apparition of these faces in the crowd, 617
The art of losing isn't hard to master, 756
The baby brought us luck, 886
The beginning of art— 762
The buzz-saw snarled and rattled in the yard, 553
the Cambridge ladies who live in furnished souls, 840
The chrome lid of the coffee pot, 879
The cold remote islands, 840
The curtains were half drawn; the floor was swept, 828
The day is a woman who loves you. Open. 858
The earth keeps some vibration going, 604
The end came easy for most of us. 876
The eyes open to a cry of pulleys, 855
the first day i shot dope, 871
The frog he sits upon the bank, 774
The gray sea and the long black land; 823
The hand that signed the paper felled a city; 688
The heavy bear who goes with me, 669
The horizon lowers, 629
The king sits in Dumferling town, 546
The ladder quakes and sways under me, old wood, 877
The light of our cigarettes, 618
The moon goes over the water. 653
Them that's got shall get, Them that's not shall lose; 720
The rain set early in to-night, 593
There are girls who should have been swans, 886
There are no stars to-night, 638
There is a garden in her face, 810
There may be a basement to the Atlantic, 640
There was a King and he had three daughters, 734
There was an old man of Tobago, 767
There was a young belle of old Natchez, 767
There was a young woman named Plunnery, 767

The sailors come ashore, 707
The sale began—young girls were there, 826
The saris go by me from the embassies. 848
The sea is calm tonight. 624
These hard hills which have made my body, 586
These men clothed their land with incorruptible, 686
The soote season, that bud and bloom forth brings, 622
The sun has set, and the long grass now, 824
The Sun woke me this morning loud, 608
The time you won your town the race, 577
The water turns, 874
The whiskey on your breath, 844
The wind billowing out the seat of my britches, 617
The witch that came (the withered hag), 784
The world is too much with us; late and soon, 818
They flee from me, that sometime did me seek, 809
They have yarns, 676
This is an African worm, 674
This poem is concerned with language on a very plain level. 691
This is the old way, 887
This sadness could only be a color, 620
Thou sorrow, venom Elfe: 813
Thou still unravished bride of quietness, 583
Three Summers since I chose a maid, 610
To all who carve their love on a picnic table, 854
Today we have naming of parts. Yesterday, 849
To get betimes in Boston town I rose this morning early, 726
tonite, thriller was, 873
To see a world in a grain of sand, 589
To yow, my purse, and to noon other wight, 808
Traveling through the dark I found a deer, 849
'Twas on a lofty vase's side, 815
'Twas only a passing thought, my love, 774
Two evils, monstrous either one apart, 689
Two roads diverged in a yellow wood, 708
Tyger! Tyger! burning bright, 816

Unconscious, 769

We caught the tread of dancing feet, 830
We come to hear the endings, 540
We left the horses in the draw, 869
We stood by a pond that winter day, 622
We were very tired, we were very merry— 702
What bright soft thing is this, 644

What I like about Clive, 734
What passing-bells for these who die as cattle? 838
What thoughts I have of you tonight, Walt Whitman, for, 859
Whenas in silks my Julia goes, 812
When cold November sits among the reeds like an unlucky fisher, 643
When I am dead, I hope it may be said, 735
When I consider how my light is spent, 582
"When I from Circe broke at last, 564
When I got to the airport I rushed up to the desk 554
When I have fears that I may cease to be, 819
When I looked into your eyes, 631
When, in disgrace with fortune and men's eyes, 568
When I was one-and-twenty, 832
When most I wink, then do mine eyes best see, 686
When she rises in the morning, 725
When the young Dawn with finger tips of rose, 558
While my hair was still cut straight across my forehead, 600
Whirl up, sea— 638
Who will in fairest book of Nature know, 810
Who would be, 697
Why did you, feeble as you were, attempt, 780
Why does the thin grey strand, 661
Within a delicate grey ruin, 786

Yet once more, O ye laurels, and once more, 791
You do not do, you do not do, 587
You knew I was coming for you, little one, 612
You speak of art, 891
You've gotten in through the transom, 731
You've seen a strawberry, 703

Index of Authors and Titles

Ache of Marriage, The, 742
Adventure of the Speckled Band, The, 175
After Apple-Picking, 835
After Death, 828
After Great Pain, a Formal Feeling Comes, 828
After Whistler, 886
ALIGHIERI, DANTE
  Ulysses' Speech from *Inferno* (Canto XXVI), 564
All Day I Hear the Noise of Waters, 837
All Morning, 879
AMMONS, A.R.
  Visit, The, 859
ANGIOLIERE, CECCO
  In Absence from Becchina, 676
ANONYMOUS
  Frankie and Albert, 719
  Grief of a Girl's Heart, 688
  Miss Bailey's Ghost, 733
  Psalm 121: A Song of Degrees, 742
  Sir Patrick Spence, 546
  There Was a King, 734
  There Was an Old Man of Tobago, 767
Ant and the Caterpillar, The, 672
Anthem for Doomed Youth, 838
Apparently with No Surprise, 827
Araby, 267
ARCHILOCHUS
  May He lose His Way on the Cold Sea, 570

ARNOLD, MATTHEW
  Dover Beach, 624
Ars Poetica, 837
Artificial Family, The, 334
ASHBERY, JOHN
  Paradoxes and Oxymorons, 691
ASHE, THOMAS
  Old Jane, 783
As I Walked Out One Evening, 842
Aspects of Robinson, 689
Astrophel and Stella, Sonnet #71 (excerpt), 810
ATOOD, MARGARET
  Giving Birth, 126
  You Are Happy, 874
AUDEN, W.H.
  As I Walked Out One Evening, 842
  Fleet Visit, 707
  In Memory of W.B. Yeats, 578
  Lay Your Sleeping Head, My Love, 841
  Musée des Beaux Arts, 542
Autumn, 642

BABEL, ISAAC
  My First Goose, 328
Backing Up, or Tearing Up the Garden Next to the Driveway, 873
BALDWIN, JAMES
  Sonny's Blues, 405
Ballad of Birmingham, 552

BAMBARA, TONI CADE
My Man Bovanne, 121
BARAKA, IMAMU AMIRI (LEROI JONES)
Preface to a Twenty Volume Suicide Note, 589
BARNES, JIM
A Season of Loss, 869
Bartleby the Scrivener, 353
BASHO, MATSUO
Haiku, 615
Nine Haiku, 762
Bath Tub, The, 649
BEATTIE, ANNE
Janus, 299
Beautiful Changes, The, 761
Because I Could Not Stop for Death, 656
BEDDOES, THOMAS LOVELL
Song: How Many Times Do I Love Thee, Dear?, 821
BEHN, APHRA
A Thousand Martyrs I Have Made, 812
BELLOC, HILLAIRE
On His Books, 735
Bells, The, 711
BENTLEY, EDMUND CLERIHEW
Lord Clive, 734
BERRY, WENDELL
The Old Elm Tree by the River, 868
beware: do not read this poem, 873
BISHOP, ELIZABETH
One Art, 756
Bitter-Sweet, 685
BLAKE, WILLIAM
The Little Vagabond, 594
London, 628
To See a World in a Grain of Sand, 589
The Tyger, 816
Blessing, A, 520
Blues Note, 684
BOCCACCIO, GIOVANNI
A Dinner of Hens (from The Decameron), 86
BOGAN, LOUISE
Night, 840
BONTEMPS, ARNA
Southern Mansion, 841
Boston Ballad, A, 726
BOWLES, JANE
A Quarreling Pair, 1443
BRADSTREET, ANNE
To My Dear and Loving Husband, 812
Bride Comes to Yellow Sky, The, 429

BRONTE, EMILY
The Sun Has Set, 824
BROOKS, GWENDOLYN
Sadie and Maud, 850
BROWNING, ELIZABETH BARRETT
How Do I Love Thee?, 823
BROWNING, ROBERT
Meeting at Night, 823
My Last Duchess, 606
Parting at Morning, 824
Porphyria's Lover, 593
Buckdancer's Choice, 682
BUKOWSKI, CHARLES
Yellow, 732
BULLINS, ED
A Son, Come Home, 1490
Burning Babe, The, 673
Burning, The, 243
BURNS, ROBERT
John Anderson My Jo, 737
A Red, Red Rose, 817
BYRON, GEORGE GORDON, LORD
She Walks in Beauty, 818

Cain, 845
CALVINO, ITALO
The Canary Prince, 81
Cambridge ladies who live in furnished souls, the, 840
CAMPION, THOMAS
There Is a Garden in Her Face, 810
Canary Prince, The, 81
CANETTI, ELIAS
The Earwitness, 230
CANIN, ETHAN
Emperor of the Air, 272
Cask of Amontillado, The, 160
CATULLUS
LXXXV, 566
CERVANTES, LORNA DEE
Para un Revolucionario, 891
Charles on Fire, 687
CHAUCER, GEOFFREY
The Complaint of Chaucer to His Purse, 808
CHAVEZ, FRAY ANGELICO
Rattlesnake, 647
CHEKHOV, ANTON
Lady with Lapdog, 392
Child on Top of a Greenhouse, 617
Chinoiseries, 631
Chrysanthemums, The, 481

CLAMPITT, AMY
  The Sun Underfoot Among the Sundews, 856
CLIFTON, LUCILLE
  Good Times, 871
COLERIDGE, SAMUEL TAYLOR
  Kubla Khan, 630
  Pity, 690
Compensation, 835
Complaint of Chaucer to His Purse, The, 808
Continuity of Parks, 91
Conversation with My Father, A, 215
COOK, ELIZA
  The Old Arm Chair, 782
CORN, ALFRED
  Fifty-Seventh Street and Fifth, 877
CORSO, GREGORY
  The Vestal Lady on Brattle, 786
CORTÁZAR, JULIO
  Continuity of Parks, 91
CRANE, HART
  My Grandmother's Love Letters, 638
CRANE, STEPHEN
  A Man Adrift on a Slim Spar, 834
  The Bride Comes to Yellow Sky, 429
CRASHAW, RICHARD
  The Tear, 644
Crazy Jane Talks with the Bishop, 785
CREELEY, ROBERT
  If You, 705
Crimes of the Heart, 1447
CULLEN, COUNTEE
  Incident, 744
CUMMINGS, E. E.
  the Cambridge ladies who live in furnished souls, 743, 840
  in Just-, 839
  somewhere i have never travelled, gladly beyond, 585

Daddy, 587
Dance, The, 717
DANNER, MARGARET
  This Is an African Worm, 674
DANTE (see ALIGHIERI)
Dark House, by Which Once More I Stand, 576
DARWIN, ERASMUS
  Eliza, 776
Death, 642
Death Be Not Proud, 811

Death of a Toad, The, 736
Death of the Ball Turret Gunner, The, 604
Delight in Disorder, 811
Delight Song of Tsoai-Talee, The, 649
Departure, 629
Description of the Morning, A, 814
Desire Under the Elms, 1150
Dialogue Betwixt Time and a Pilgrim, A, 658
DICKEY, JAMES
  Buckdancer's Choice, 682
DICKINSON, EMILY
  After Great Pain, a Formal Feeling Comes, 828
  Apparently with No Surprise, 827
  Because I Could Not Stop for Death, 656
  Hope Is the Thing with Feathers, 637
  I Felt a Funeral in My Brain, 521
  I Heard a Fly Buzz—When I Died, 827
  My Life Had Stood, a Loaded Gun, 826
  Success Is Counted Sweetest, 730
Dinner of Hens, A, 86
DI PASQUALE, EMANUEL
  Rain, 653
Doll's House, A, 1319
DONNE, JOHN
  Death Be Not Proud, 811
  The Flea, 652
  A Valediction: Forbidding Mourning, 646
Do Not Go Gentle into That Good Night, 755
DOOLITTLE, HILDA (see H.D.)
Dover Beach, 624
Dover Bitch, The, A Criticism of Life, 857
DOYLE, ARTHUR CONAN
  The Adventure of the Speckled Band, 175
Driving Montana, 858
DRYDEN, JOHN
  To the Memory of Mr. Oldham, 745
DUBOIS, W.E.B.
  The Song of the Smoke, 832
DUGAN, ALAN
  Morning Song, 727
DUNBAR, PAUL LAWRENCE
  Compensation, 835
  In the Morning, 738
DUNCAN, ROBERT
  My Mother Would Be a Falconress, 851
Dylan, 787

Eagle, The: A Fragment, 631
Earth and I Gave You Turquoise, 870
Earwitness, The, 230
Easter Wings, 768
Edouard, 767
Elegy, Written with His Own Hand in the Tower Before His Execution, 690
Elegy for Jane, 575
Elegy for the Monastery Barn, 648
ELIOT, T.S.
    The Love Song of J. Alfred Prufrock, 802
Eliza, 776
ELMORE, JAMES K.
    The Frog, 774
EMERSON, RALPH WALDO
    Letters, 679
Emperor of the Air, 272
EMPSON, WILLIAM
    Villanelle, 779
Encounter, 586
EPSTEIN, DANIEL MARK
Madonna (with Child Missing), 551
ERDRICH, LOUISE
    Windigo, 612
    The Red Convertible, 437
Essay on Man, An (Epistle IV) (excerpt), 730
Everyday Use, 219
Everything that Rises Must Converge, 470
Exercises in Style, 118

Faith Healing, 855
Farmer's Bride, The, 610
FAULKNER, WILLIAM
    A Rose for Emily, 445
FERLINGHETTI, LAWRENCE
    [In Goya's Greatest Scenes We Seem to See], 853
Fern Hill, 650
Fiddler Jones, 604
FIELD, EDWARD
    My Polish Grandmother, 550
Fifty-Seventh Street and Fifth, 877
Fire and Ice, 582
Flea, The, 652
Fleet Visit, 707
For Alexander Pope's Garden, 880
For a Shetland Pony Brood Mare Who Died in Her Barren Year, 882
FORD, CHARLES HENRI
    Somebody's Gone, 640
Forge, The, 875

For I Will Consider My Cat Jeoffrey, 574
For Once, Then, Something, 663
Forsythia, 771
For Malcolm X, 576
For the Anniversary of My Death, 883
For the Spartan Dead at Plataia (479 B.C.), 686
Four Haiku (WRIGHT), 845
Fragment: Thoughts Come and Go in Solitude, 652
Frankie and Albert, 719
Frog, The, 774
FROST, ROBERT
    After Apple-Picking, 835
    Fire and Ice, 582
    For Once, Then, Something, 663
    'Out, Out—,' 553
    Provide, Provide, 784
    The Road Not Taken, 708
    The Silken Tent, 836

GARCÍA LORCA, FEDERICO
    Half Moon, 653
GARCÍA MÁRQUEZ, GABRIEL
    A Very Old Man with Enormous Wings, 293
GAY, JOHN
    The Lion, the Fox, and Geese, 660
Gervaise, 767
GILMAN, CHARLOTTE PERKINS
    The Yellow Wall-Paper, 148
GINSBURG, ALLEN
    A Supermarket in California, 859
GIOVANNI, NIKKI
    Nikki-Rosa, 878
Giovanni de Fiesole on the Sublime, or Fra Angelico's Last Judgment, 862
Giving Birth, 126
Glass Menagerie, The, 981
Gloire de Dijon, 725
GLÜCK, LOUISE
    The Pond, 651
God Bless the Child, 720
Go, Lovely Rose, 664
Good Times, 871
GORDON, GEORGE, LORD BYRON
    She Walks in Beauty, 818
GOREY, EDWARD
    There Was a Young Woman Named Plunnery, 767
GRAY, THOMAS
    Ode on the Death of a Favorite Cat, 815
Great Day, The, 680

Great Figure, The, 615
Grief of a Girl's Heart, 688
GUNN, THOM
  Moly, 746

HACKER, MARILYN
  Villanelle, 875
HAHN, KIMIKO
  When You Leave, 620
Haiku (KEKIGODO, BASHO, HOSAI),
  615
Haiku (KNIGHT), 634
Hair Poem, 639
Half Moon, 653
HALL, DONALD
  Ox Cart Man, 681
Hamlet, Prince of Denmark, The Tragedy
  of, 1032
Hand That Signed the Paper, The, 688
HANSBERRY, LORRAINE
  A Raisin in the Sun, 1369
HARADA, GAIL
  New Year, 887
HARDY, THOMAS
  Neutral Tones, 622
  The Subalterns, 666
Harlem Dancer, The, 572
Harlot's House, The, 830
HARPER, FRANCES E.W.
  The Slave Auction, 826
HARPER, MICHAEL
  A Mother Speaks: The Algiers Motel In-
    cident, Detroit, 607
HARRISON, JIM
  Sound, 618
Hawk Roosting, 863
HAWTHORNE, NATHANIEL
  The Minister's Black Veil, 308
  Young Goodman Brown, 318
HAYDEN, ROBERT
  Those Winter Sundays, 847
H.D. (HILDA DOOLITTLE)
  Never More Will the Wind, 568
  Oread, 638
HEANEY, SEAMUS
  The Forge, 875
Heavy Bear Who Goes with Me, The, 669
HECHT, ANTHONY
  The Dover Bitch, A Criticism of Life,
    857
Helping, 489
HEMINGWAY, ERNEST
  Hills Like White Elephants, 472

HENLEY, BETH
  Crimes of the Heart, 1447
HERBERT, GEORGE
  Bitter-Sweet, 685
  Easter Wings, 768
  Love (III), 673
  The Pilgrimage, 657
Here Lies a Lady, 589
HERRICK, ROBERT
  Delight in Disorder, 811
  Upon Julia's Clothes, 812
He Wishes for the Cloths of Heaven, 566
Hills Like White Elephants, 452
HINE, DARYL
  The Survivors, 872
HIRSCH, EDWARD
  The River Merchant: A Letter Home,
    601
History, 890
HOLIDAY, BILLIE
  God Bless the Child, 720
HOLLANDER, JOHN
  Swan and Shadow, 770
Homage for Isaac Babel, 331
HOMER
  The Odyssey (excerpt), 558
HONGO, GARRETT
  The Hongo Store, 889
"Hope" Is the Thing with Feathers, 637
HOPKINS, GERARD MANLEY
  Pied Beauty, 573
  Spring and Fall, 829
  The Windhover, 829
Horse Dealer's Daughter, The, 203
HOSAI, OZAKI
  Haiku, 615
HOUSMAN, A.E.
  Loveliest of Trees, 831
  To an Athlete Dying Young, 577
  When I Was One-and-Twenty, 832
HOWARD, HENRY, EARL OF SUR-
  REY
  The Soote Season, 622
HOWARD, RICHARD
  Giovanni de Fiesole on the Sublime, or
    Fra Angelico's Last Judgment, 862
How Do I Love Thee?, 823
How You Get Born, 876
HUGHES, LANGSTON
  Sylvester's Dying Bed, 548
  Who but the Lord?, 736
HUGHES, TED
  Hawk Roosting, 863

HUGO, RICHARD
  Driving Montana, 858
HULME, T.E.
  Autumn, 642
Hunger Artist, A, 464
HURSTON, ZORA NEALE
  Sweat, 455
HWANG, DAVID
  The Sound of a Voice, 1429

I Am a Little World Made Cunningly, 710
IBSEN, HENRIK
  A Doll's House, 1319
I Felt A Funeral in My Brain, 521
If I Were Dead, 789
If We Must Die, 749
If You, 705
I Heard a Fly Buzz—When I Died, 827
I Knew a Woman, 844
Importance of Being Earnest, The, 1190
In Absence from Becchina, 676
In a Farmhouse, 612
In a Station of the Metro, 617
Incident, 744
INEZ, COLETTE
  Spanish Heaven, 865
Inferno (excerpt), 564
[In Goya's Greatest Scenes We Seem to
  See], 853
in Just-, 839
In Memory of W.B. Yeats, 578
In Our Old Shipwrecked Days There Was
  an Hour, 750
Intended for Sir Isaac Newton, 683
In the Morning, 738
I Once Had a Sweet Little Doll, Dears,
  775
Irish Airman Foresees His Death, An, 605
I Saw in Louisiana a Live-Oak Growing,
  662
I Used to Live Here Once, 87
I Wandered Lonely as a Cloud, 817

Janus, 299
JARRELL, RANDALL
  The Death of the Ball Turret Gunner,
  604
  Mockingbird, 677
  The Woman at the Washington Zoo,
  848
JEFFERS, ROBINSON
  Rock and Hawk, 668
Jewbird, The, 286
Jewish Cemetery at Newport, The, 821

Jilting of Granny Weatherall, The, 235
John Anderson My Jo, 737
JONES, LEROI (see BARAKA, IMAMU
  AMIRI)
JONG, ERICA
  How You Get Born, 876
JONSON, BEN
  On My First Son, 543
JORDAN, JUNE
  My Sadness Sits Around Me, 872
JOYCE, JAMES
  All Day I Hear the Noise of Waters, 837
  Araby, 267

KAFKA, FRANZ
  A Hunger Artist, 464
KASA, LADY
  Six Tanka, 763
KAUFMAN, BOB
  Blues Note, 684
KAVANAGH, PATRICK
  Tinker's Wife, 785
KEATS, JOHN
  Ode on a Grecian Urn, 583
  Ode to a Nightingale, 759
  On First Looking into Chapman's
  Homer, 747
  To Autumn, 819
  When I Have Fears, 819
KEES, WELDON
  Aspects of Robinson, 689
KEKIGODO, KAWAHIGASHI
  Haiku, 615
KHAYYAM, OMAR
  The Rubaiyat, XXVI and XXVII, 581
KINGSLEY, CHARLES
  I Once Had a Sweet Little Doll, Dears,
  775
KINGSTON, MAXINE HONG
  On Mortality, 88
KLAPPERT, PETER
  Mail at Your New Address, 611
KNIGHT, ETHERIDGE
  Haiku, 634
KNOTT, BILL
  Death, 642
  Hair Poem, 639
Kubla Khan, 630
KUMIN, MAXINE
  For a Shetland Pony Brood Mare Who
  Died in Her Barren Year, 882
KUNITZ, STANLEY
  The Portrait, 881

Lady and the Bear, The, 524
Lady and the Unicorn, The, 667
Lady Lazarus, 865
Lady with a Falcon, 847
Lady with Lapdog, 392
Lake Isle of Innisfree, The, 716
LANDOR, WALTER SAVAGE
  Mother, I Cannot Mind My Wheel, 539
  On His Seventy-Fifth Birthday, 818
LARKIN, PHILIP
  Faith Healing, 855
LAWRENCE, D.H.
  Gloire de Dijon, 725
  The Horse Dealer's Daughter, 203
  Snake, 670
  Sorrow, 661
LAYTON, IRVING
  Cain, 845
Lay Your Sleeping Head, My Love, 841
Leaves of Grass (excerpt), 636
LESSING, DORIS
  Homage for Isaac Babel, 331
Let Me Not to the Marriage of True
  Minds, 651
Letters, 679
LEVERTOV, DENISE
  The Ache of Marriage, 742
  To the Snake, 728
LEVINE, PHILIP
  To a Child Trapped in a Barber Shop,
  731
LEWIS, SINCLAIR
  Virga Vay and Allan Cedar, 386
Lineage, 710
Lines Composed a Few Miles above Tin-
  tern Abbey, 796
Lion, the Fox, and Geese, The, 660
Listening to Color, 619
Little Vagabond, The, 594
London, 628
LONGFELLOW, HENRY
  WADSWORTH
  The Jewish Cemetery at Newport, 821
Lord Clive, 734
LORDE, AUDRE
  Now That I Am Forever with Child, 869
Lover (III), 673
Love Calls Us to the Things of This
  World, 855
Loveliest of Trees, 831
Love Poem, 880
Love Song of J. Alfred Prufrock, The,
  802

LOWELL, AMY
  Chinoiseries, 631
LOWELL, ROBERT
  Robert Frost, 850
  Skunk Hour, 632
Lucky, 886
LXXXV (Catullus), 566
Lycidas, 791
Lying in a Hammock at William Duffy's
  Farm in Pine Island, Minnesota, 620

MacKAY, CLAUDE
  Only a Thought, 774
MacLEISH, ARCHIBALD
  Ars Poetica, 837
Madonna (with Child Missing), 551
Mail at Your New Address, 611
MALAMUD, BERNARD
  The Jewbird, 286
Man Adrift on a Slim Spar, A, 834
Man from Washington, The, 876
MARLOWE, CHRISTOPHER
  The Passionate Shepherd to His Love,
  523
MARVELL, ANDREW
  To His Coy Mistress, 569
MASON, BOBBIE ANNE
  Shiloh, 255
MASTERS, EDGAR LEE
  Fiddler Jones, 664
May He Lose His Way on the Cold Sea,
  570
McKay, Claude
  The Harlem Dancer, 572
  If We Must Die, 749
Meeting at Night, 823
MELVILLE, HERMAN
  Bartleby the Scrivener, 353
  On the Photograph of a Corps Com-
  mander, 825
MEREDITH, GEORGE
  In Our Old Shipwrecked Days There
  Was an Hour, 750
Mermaid, The, 697
MERRILL, JAMES
  Charles on Fire, 687
MERTON, THOMAS
  Elegy for the Monastery Barn, 648
  The Regret, 643
MERWIN, W.S.
  For the Anniversary of My Death, 883
MEYNELL, ALICE
  The Threshing-Machine, 830

MEW, CHARLOTTE
  The Farmer's Bride, 610
MILLAY, EDNA ST. VINCENT
  Pity Me Not Because the Light of Day,
    749
  Recuerdo, 702
MILTON, JOHN
  Lycidas, 791
  When I Consider How My Light Is
    Spent, 582
Minister's Black Veil, The, 308
Miss Bailey's Ghost, 733
MITSUI, JIM
  When Father Came Home for Lunch,
    884
Mockingbird, The, 677
Moly, 746
MOMADAY, N. SCOTT
  The Delight Song of Tsoai-Talee, 649
  Earth and I Gave You Turquoise, 870
MOORE, MARIANNE
  Nevertheless, 703
  The Steeple-Jack, 799
Morning Song, 727
Mother, I Cannot Mind My Wheel, 539
Mother Speaks, A: The Algiers Motel Inci-
    dent, Detroit, 607
Mr. Flood's Party, 833
MUELLER, LISEL
  After Whistler, 886
Musée des Beaux Arts, 542
My Daughter Is Coming, 888
My First Goose, 328
My Grandmother's Love Letters, 638
My Heart Belongs to Daddy, 721
My Last Duchess, 606
My Life Had Stood, a Loaded Gun, 826
My Man Bovanne, 121
My Mistress' Eyes Are Nothing like the
    Sun, 778
My Mother Would Be a Falconress, 851
My Papa's Waltz, 844
My Polish Grandmother, 550
My Sadness Sits Around Me, 872

NAIPAUL, V.S.
  The Night Watchman's Occurrence
    Book, 137
Naming of Parts, 849
Nani, 884
NASH, OGDEN
  Edouard, 767
  Gervaise, 767
Neutral Tones, 622

Never More Will the Wind, 568
Nevertheless, 703
New Year, 887
Night, 840
Night Watchman's Occurrence Book,
    The, 137
Nikki-Rosa, 878
Nine Haiku, 762
Noiseless Patient Spider, A, 825
Not Waving but Drowning, 881
Now That I Am Forever with Child, 869
Nymph's Reply to the Shepherd, The, 809

O'CONNOR, FLANNERY
  Everything that Rises Must Converge,
    470
Ode on a Grecian Urn, 583
Ode on the Death of a Favorite Cat, 815
Ode to a Nightingale, 759
Ode to the West Wind, 752
Odyssey, The (excerpt), 558
Oedipus Rex, 935
O'HARA, FRANK
  A True Account of Talking to the Sun
    at Fire Island, 608
Oil, 627
Old Arm Chair, The, 782
Old Elm Tree by the River, The, 868
Old Jane, 783
OLDS, SHARON
  The Race, 554
Olympian 11, 758
One Art, 756
One Day as I Unwarily Did Gaze, 674
O'NEILL, EUGENE
  Desire Under the Elms, 1150
On First Looking into Chapman's Homer,
    747
On His Books, 735
On His Mistress Drowned, 788
On His Seventy-fifth Birthday, 818
Only a Thought, 774
On Mortality, 88
On My First Son, 543
On the Photograph of a Corps Com-
    mander, 825
Open Letter from a Constant Reader,
    854
Oread, 638
ORR, GREGORY
  All Morning, 879
'Out, Out—,' 553
OWEN, WILFRED
  Anthem for Doomed Youth, 838

Ox Cart Man, 681
Ozymandias, 819

Pain for a Daughter, 860
PALEY, GRACE
  A Conversation with My Father, 215
Paradoxes and Oxymorons, 691
Para un Revolucionario, 891
Parting at Morning, 824
Passionate Shepherd to His Love, The,
  523
PASTAN, LINDA
  25th High School Reunion, 540
Pastel, 618
PATMORE, COVENTRY
  If I Were Dead, 789
PAVESE, CESARE
  Encounter, 586
PEACOCK, MOLLY
  Petting and Being a Pet, 879
Peeling Pippins, 715
Petting and Being a Pet, 879
Piazza Piece, 602
Picking Cherries, 877
Pied Beauty, 573
Pilgrimage, The, 657
PINDAR
  Olympian 11, 758
Pity, 690
Pity Me Not Because the Light of Day,
  749
PLATH, SYLVIA
  Daddy, 587
  Lady Lazarus, 865
PO CHU-I
  Seeing Hsia Chan Off by River, 679
POE, EDGAR ALLEN
  The Bells, 711
  The Cask of Amontillado, 160
  The Raven, 555
Pond, The, 651
POPE, ALEXANDER
  An Essay on Man (Epistle IV) (excerpt),
    730
  Intended for Sir Isaac Newton, 683
Porphyria's Lover, 593
PORTER, COLE
  My Heart Belongs to Daddy, 721
PORTER, KATHERINE ANNE
  The Jilting of Granny Weatherall,
    235
Portrait, The, 881
POUND, EZRA
  The Bath Tub, 649

The River Merchant's Wife: A Letter,
  600
In a Station of the Metro, 617
Pray to What Earth Does This Sweet Cold
  Belong, 626
Preface to a Twenty Volume Suicide Note,
  589
Prophecy, 838
Provide, Provide, 784
Psalm 121: A Song of Degrees, 742

Quarreling Pair, A, 1443
QUENEAU, RAYMOND
  Exercises in Style, 118

Race, The, 554
Rain, 653
Raisin in the Sun, A, 1369
RALEIGH, SIR WALTER
  Nymph's Reply to the Shepherd, The,
    809
RANDALL, DUDLEY
  Ballad of Birmingham, 552
RANSOM, JOHN CROWE
  Here Lies a Lady, 589
  Piazza Piece, 602
  Winter Remembered, 689
Rattlesnake, 647
Raven, The, 555
Recuerdo, 702
Red Convertible, The, 437
Red, Red Rose, A, 817
Red Wheelbarrow, The, 632
REED, HENRY
  Naming of Parts, 849
REED, ISHMAEL
  beware: do not read this poem, 873
Regret, The, 643
REVERDY, PIERRE
  Departure, 629
RHYS, JEAN
  I Used to Live Here Once, 87
RICH, ADRIENNE
  A Woman Mourned by Daughters, 883
Riders to the Sea, 904
RIHAKU (POUND)
  The River Merchant's Wife: A Letter,
    600
RÍOS, ALBERTO
  Nani, 884
River Merchant, The: A Letter Home, 601
River Merchant's Wife, The: A Letter, 600
Road Not Taken, The, 708

Robert Frost, 850
ROBINSON, EDWIN ARLINGTON
  Mr. Flood's Party, 833
Rock and Hawk, 668
Rococo, 700
ROETHKE, THEODORE
  Child on Top of a Greenhouse, 617
  Elegy for Jane, 575
  I Knew a Woman, 844
  The Lady and the Bear, 524
  My Papa's Waltz, 844
Rose for Emily, A, 445
Rose of Peace, The, 665
ROSSETTI, CHRISTINA
  After Death, 828
Rubaiyat of Omar Khayyam, The (ex-
  cerpt), 581
RUKEYSER, MURIEL
  Song: Love in Whose Rich Honor, 655

Sadie and Maud, 850
Sailing to Byzantium, 801
SALINAS, LOUIS OMAR
  In a Farmhouse, 612
SANCHEZ, SONIA
  summer words of a sistuh addict, 871
SANDBURG, CARL
  They Have Yarns, 676
SAPPHO
  Then, 654
SARTON, MAY
  The Lady and the Unicorn, 667
  Lady with a Falcon, 847
SCHWARTZ, DELMORE
  The Heavy Bear Who Goes with Me,
  669
Sea Grapes, 864
Season of Loss, A, 869
Seeing Hsia Chan Off by River, 679
Separating, 340
SERVICE, ROBERT
  Dylan, 787
Seventeen Syllables, 193
SEXTON, ANNE
  Pain for a Daughter, 860
  Unknown Girl in the Maternity Ward,
  595
SHAKESPEARE, WILLIAM
  Hamlet, Prince of Denmark, the Tragedy
  of, 1032
  Let Me Not to the Marriage of True
  Minds, 651
  My Mistress' Eyes Are Nothing like the
  Sun, 778

Shall I Compare Thee to a Summer's
  Day?, 644
That Time of Year Thou Mayst in Me
  Behold, 748
Twelfth Night, 1240
When, in Disgrace with Fortune and
  Men's Eyes, 568
When Most I Wink, Then Do Mine
  Eyes Best See, 686
Shall I Compare Thee to a Summer's
  Day?, 644
SHELLY, PERCY BYSSHE
  Fragment: Thoughts Come and Go in
  Solitude, 652
  Ode to the West Wind, 752
  Ozymandias, 819
She Walks in Beauty, 818
Shiloh, 255
SIDNEY, SIR PHILIP
  Astrophel and Stella, Sonnet #71 (ex-
  cerpt), 810
Silken Tent, The, 836
SILKO, LESLIE MARMON
  Love Poem, 880
SIMIC, CHARLES
  Watermelons, 635
SIMONIDES
  For the Spartan Dead at Plataia (479
  B.C.), 686
Sir Patrick Spence, 546
Six Tanka, 763
Skunk Hour, 632
Slave Auction, The, 826
SMART, CHRISTOPHER
  The Ant and the Caterpillar, 672
  For I Will Consider My Cat Jeoffry, 574
SMITH, DAVE
  Picking Cherries, 877
SMITH, STEVIE
  Not Waving but Drowning, 881
Snake, 670
SNYDER, GARY
  Oil, 627
Solitary Reaper, The, 571
SOLT, MARY ELLEN
  Forsythia, 771
Somebody's Gone, 640
somewhere i have never travelled, gladly
  beyond, 585
Son, Come Home, A, 1490
SONG, CATHY
  Lucky, 886
Song: How Many Times Do I Love Thee,
  Dear?, 821

Song: Love in Whose Rich Honor, 655
Song of the Smoke, The, 832
Sonny's Blues, 405
Soote Season, The, 622
SOPOCLES
  Oedipus Rex, 935
SOTO, GARY
  History, 890
Sorrow, 661
Sound, 618
Sound of a Voice, 1429
Southern Mansion, 841
SOUTHWELL, ROBERT
  The Burning Babe, 673
Spanish Heaven, 865
SPENSER, EDMUND
  One Day as I Unwarily Did Gaze, 674
SPRAT, THOMAS
  On His Mistress Drowned, 788
Spring and Fall, 829
STAFFORD, WILLIAM
  Traveling Through the Dark, 849
STANFORD, ANN
  Listening to Color, 619
Steeple-Jack, The, 799
STEINBECK, JOHN
  The Chrysanthemums, 481
STEVENS, WALLACE
  Thirteen Ways of Looking at a Blackbird, 764
STONE, ROBERT
  Helping, 489
Subalterns, The, 666
Success Is Counted Sweetest, 730
summer words of a sistuh addict, 871
Sun Has Set, The, 824
Sun Underfoot Among the Sundews, The, 856
Supermarket in California, A, 859
Survivors, The, 872
Swan and Shadow, 770
Sweat, 455
SWENSON, MAY
  Unconscious Came a Beauty, 769
SWIFT, JONATHAN
  A Description of the Morning, 814
SWINBURNE, ALGERNON CHARLES
  Rococo, 700
Sylvester's Dying Bed, 548
SYMONS, ARTHUR
  Pastel, 618
SYNGE, JOHN MILLINGTON
  Riders to the Sea, 904

TALLMOUNTAIN, MARY
  Peeling Pippins, 715
TAYLOR, EDWARD
  Upon a Spider Catching a Fly, 813
Tear, The, 644
TENNYSON, ALFRED, LORD
  Dark House, by Which Once More I Stand, 576
  The Eagle: A Fragment, 631
  The Mermaid, 697
  Ulysses, 597
That Time of Year Thou Mayst in Me Behold, 748
Then, 654
There Is a Garden in Her Face, 810
There Was a King, 734
There Was an Old Man of Tobago, 767
There Was a Young Woman Named Plunnery, 767
They Flee from Me, 809
They Have Yarns, 676
Thirteen Ways of Looking at a Blackbird, 764
This Is an African Worm, 674
THOMAS, DYLAN
  Do Not Go Gentle into That Good Night, 755
  Fern Hill, 650
  The Hand That Signed the Paper, 688
THOREAU, HENRY DAVID
  Pray to What Earth Does This *Sweet Cold* Belong, 626
Those Winter Sundays, 847
Thousand Martyrs I Have Made, A, 812
Threshing-Machine, The, 830
TICHBORNE, CHIDIOCK
  Elegy, Written with His Own Hand in the Tower Before His Execution, 690
Tinker's Wife, 785
To a Child Trapped in a Barber Shop, 731
To an Athlete Dying Young, 577
To Autumn, 819
To His Coy Mistress, 569
To My Dear and Loving Husband, 812
To See a World in a Grain of Sand, 589
To the Memory of Mr. Oldham, 745
To the Snake, 728
TOWNSHEND, AURELIAN
  A Dialogue Betwixt Time and a Pilgrim, 658
TRAMBLEY, ESTELA PORTILLO
  The Burning, 243
Traveling Through the Dark, 849

True Account of Talking to the Sun at Fire Island, A, 608
Twelfth Night, 1240
25th High School Reunion, 540
Tyger, The, 816
TYLER, ANNE
  The Artificial Family, 334

Ulysses, 597
Ulysses' Speech (from *Inferno*, Canto XXVI), 564
Unconscious Came a Beauty, 769
Unemployment, 879
Unknown Girl in the Maternity Ward, 595
UPDIKE, JOHN
  Separating, 340
Upon a Spider Catching a Fly, 813
Upon Julia's Clothes, 812

Valediction, A: Forbidding Mourning, 646
VALDEZ, LUIS M.
  Los Vendidos, 1231
VAN DUYN, MONA
  Open letter from a Constant Reader, 854
Vendidos, Los, 1231
Very Old Man with Enormous Wings, A, 293
Vestal Lady on Brattle, 786
Village Musings (excerpt), 780
Villanelle (EMPSON), 779
Villanelle (HACKER), 875
Virga Vay and Allan Cedar, 386
Visit, 859

WAKOWSKI, DIANE
  Backing Up, or Tearing Up the Garden Next to the Driveway, 873
WALCOTT, DEREK
  Sea Grapes, 864
WALKER, ALICE
  Everyday Use, 219
  My Daughter Is Coming, 888
WALKER, MARGARET
  For Malcolm X, 576
  Lineage, 710
WALLER, EDMUND
  Go, Lovely Rose, 664
Watermelons, 635
WAYMAN, TOM
  Unemployment, 879
WELCH, JAMES
  The Man from Washington, 876

WELTY, EUDORA
  A Worn Path, 510
When Father Came Home for Lunch, 884
When I Consider How My Light Is Spent, 582
When I Have Fears, 819
When, in Disgrace with Fortune and Men's Eyes, 568
When I Was One-and-Twenty, 832
When Most I Wink, Then Do Mine Eyes Best See, 686
When You Leave, 620
WHITMAN, WALT
  A Boston Ballad, 726
  I Saw in Louisiana a Live-Oak Growing, 662
  Leaves of Grass (excerpt), 636
  A Noiseless Patient Spider, 825
Who but the Lord?, 736
WHUR, CORNELIUS
  Village Musings (excerpt), 780
Widow's Lament in Springtime, The, 591
WILBUR, RICHARD
  The Beautiful Changes, 761
  The Death of a Toad, 736
  Love Calls Us to the Things of This World, 855
WILDE, OSCAR
  The Harlot's House, 830
  The Importance of Being Earnest, 1190
WILLIAMS, TENNESSEE
  The Glass Menagerie, 981
WILLIAMS, WILLIAM CARLOS
  The Dance, 717
  The Great Figure, 615
  The Red Wheelbarrow, 632
  The Widow's Lament in Springtime, 591
  The Young Housewife, 723
Windhover, The, 829
Windigo, 612
Winter Remembered, 689
Woman at the Washington Zoo, The, 848
Woman Mourned by Daughters, A, 883
WORDSWORTH, WILLIAM
  I Wandered Lonely as a Cloud, 817
  Lines Composed a Few Miles above Tintern Abbey, 796
  The Solitary Reaper, 571
  The World Is Too Much with Us, 818
World Is Too Much with Us, The, 818
Worn Path, A, 510

WRIGHT, JAMES
  A Blessing, 520
  Lying in a Hammock at William Duffy's
    Farm in Pine Island, Minnesota, 620
WRIGHT, RICHARD
  Four Haiku, 845
WYATT, SIR THOMAS
  They Flee from Me, 809
WYLIE, ELINOR
  Prophecy, 838

YAMAMOTO, HISAYE
  Seventeen Syllables, 193
YAU, JOHN
  For Alexander Pope's Garden, 880

YEATS, WILLIAM BUTLER
  Crazy Jane Talks with the Bishop, 785
  The Great Day, 680
  He Wishes for the Cloths of Heaven,
    566
  An Irish Airman Foresees His Death,
    605
  The Lake Isle of Innisfree, 716
  The Rose of Peace, 665
  Sailing to Byzantium, 801
Yellow, 732
Yellow Wall-Paper, The, 148
You Are Happy, 874
Young Goodman Brown, 318
Young Housewife, The, 721